Illustrative Student Writing

PARAGRAPHS

A Paragraph Assignment: What do the Loisels do to overcome their indebtedness? What do Mathilde's efforts say about her character?, 37

A Paraphrase of Hardy's "The Man He Killed," 562

Wordsworth's Use of Overstatement in "London, 1802," 673

CRITICAL APPROACH PARAGRAPHS

The Probable Harm Caused by Religious Belief in Hawthorne's "Young Goodman Brown," 1568

Moral Issues in Stafford's "Traveling Through the Dark," 156

The Effect of Overzealousness on Family Life in "Young Goodman Brown," 1570

The Impersonality of War in Jarrell's "The Death of the Ball Turret Gunner," 1570

Young Goodman Brown's Personal Failure, 1572

The Tight Structure of Robinson's "Richard Cory," 1572

The Passivity of Young Goodman Brown, 1574

Shirley Jackson's Dramatic Point of View in "The Lottery," 1575

Goodman Brown's Literal and Figurative Neglect of Faith, 1576

The Suppression of the Humanity of Women in Chopin's "The Story of an Hour," 1577

The Economic Implications of "Young Goodman Brown," 1578

The Issue of Economic Disparity in Bambara's "The Lesson," 1579

The Destructiveness Caused by Guilt in "Young Goodman Brown," 1581

The Egocentric and Cruel Duke in Browning's "My Last Duchess," 1581

Goodman Brown's Disturbed Standard of Judgment, 1583

Frost's Symbolism in "Birches," 1583

The Misuse of Conscience in "Young Goodman Brown," 1585

Misunderstanding the Suffering of Others as described in Auden's "Musée des Beaux Arts," 1585

Good Intentions and Harmful Results in "Young Goodman Brown," 1587

The Speaker's Complex Attitude toward his Father in Roethke's "My Papa's Waltz," 1587

ESSAY EXAM RESPONSES

The Setting of Bierce's "An Occurrence at Owl Creek Bridge" (Answer B), 1620

The Discovery of the Dead Canary in Glaspell's Trifles, 1626

LITERARY ANALYSIS ESSAYS

Plot in Faulkner's "A Rose for Emily," 115

Shirley Jackson's Dramatic Point of View in "The Lottery," 170

The Character of Minnie Wright in Glaspell's "A Jury of Her Peers," 232

The Interaction of Story and Setting in James Joyce's "Araby," 259

The Structure of Eudora Welty's "A Worn Path," 295

Frank O'Connor's Control of Tone and Style in "First Confession," 327

Symbols of Light and Darkness in Porter's "The Jilting of Granny Weatherall," 368

The Allegory of Hawthorne's "Young Goodman Brown," 372

D. H. Lawrence's "The Horse Dealer's Daughter" as an Expression of the Idea that Loving Commitment Is Essential in Life, 408

Diction and Character in Robinson's "Richard Cory," 598

The Images of Masefield's "Cargoes," 634

A Study of Shakespeare's Metaphors in Sonnet 30: "When to the Sessions of Sweet Silent Thought," 674

The Speaker's Attitudes in Sharon Olds' "The Planned Child," 716

How Setting in "The Necklace" Is Related to the Character of Mathilde, 38

Form and Meaning in George Herbert's "Virtue," 757

Symbolism in Oliver's "Wild Geese," 796

Eugene O'Neill's Use of Negative Descriptions and Stage Directions in Before Breakfast as a Means of Revealing Character, 1016

The Problem of Hamlet's Apparent Delay, 1250

Setting as Symbol and Comic Structure in A Midsummer Night's Dream, 1339

Realism and Nonrealism in Tom's Triple Role in The Glass Menagerie, 1478

EXPLICATION ESSAYS

An Explication of Thomas Hardy's "The Man He Killed," 565

(continued)

Illustrative Student Writing (*continued*)

COMPARISON/CONTRAST ESSAYS

The Treatment of Responses to War in Amy Lowell's "Patterns" and Wilfred Owen's "Anthem for Doomed Youth," 1589

Literary Treatments of the Conflicts Between Private and Public Life, 1600

READER-RESPONSE ESSAY

Opposite Personal Responses to W. H. Auden's "Musée des Beaux Arts," 1608

LITERARY ARGUMENT

Sammy's Decision to Become an Adult, 1615

RESEARCH ESSAYS

The Structure of Katherine Mansfield's "Miss Brill," 524

"Beat! Beat! Drums!" and "I Hear America Singing": Two Whitman Poems Spanning the Civil War, 952

The Ghost in *Hamlet*, 1552

Research Coverage

Bibliography—Setting Up a Working Bibliography, 502

Creative and Original Research, 515

Databases—Gaining Access to Books and Articles Through Databases, 507

Documenting Your Work, 517

Drama: Research Essay, 1550

Endnotes, 520

Fiction: Research Essay, 500

Footnotes, 520

Library—Searching Library Resources, 505

Internet—Searching Internet, 503

Outlining: Strategies for Organizing Ideas in Your Research Essay, 522

MLA Documentation—Appendix II: MLA, 1641

Paraphrasing, 509

Plagiarism, 511

Poetry: Research Essay, 951

Sources—Evaluating Sources, 503

Sources—Locating Sources, 502

Taking Notes, 509

Topic—Selecting a Topic, 501

Using Sources Effectively, *see below*

Using Sources Effectively

Using Sources Effectively, 52

Using Sources Effectively: Quoting an Author's Work, 119

Using Sources Effectively: Summary, 174

Using Sources Effectively: Paraphrasing to Avoid Plagiarism, 531

Using Sources Effectively: Paraphrasing to Set the Stage for Analysis, 568

Using Sources Effectively: Summarizing to Provide Necessary Background, 602

Using Sources Effectively: Quoting Texts to Illustrate Point, 957

Using Sources Effectively: Paraphrasing to Make Readers Understand the Work

Using Sources Effectively: Quoting Texts to Illustrate your Key Point, 1254

Using Sources Effectively: Summarizing Sources Lend Authority to Your Argument, 1563

Literature

An Introduction to Reading and Writing

COMPACT EDITION

SIXTH EDITION

Edgar V. Roberts

Lehman College, The City University of New York

Robert Zweig

Borough of Manhattan Community College

PEARSON

Boston   Columbus   Indianapolis   New York   San Francisco   Upper Saddle River   Amsterdam   Cape Town
Dubai   London   Madrid   Milan   Munich   Paris   Montréal   Toronto   Delhi   Mexico City
São Paulo   Sydney   Hong Kong   Seoul   Singapore   Taipei   Tokyo

Vice President & Editor in Chief: Joseph Terry
Development Editor: Paul A. Smith
Editorial Assistant: Nicole DeSantis Wade
Executive Marketing Manager: Joyce Nilsen
Senior Supplements Editor: Donna Campion
Executive Digital Producer: Stefanie A. Snajder
Digital Media Editor: Sara Gordus
Content Specialist: Erin Jenkins
Project Manager: Savoula Amanatidis
Project Coordination, Text Design, and Electronic Page Makeup: Cenveo® Publisher Services
Cover Designer/Manager: Wendy Ann Fredericks
Cover Image: © WDG Photo/Shutterstock
Photo Researcher: Integra–New York
Senior Manufacturing Buyer: Dennis J. Para
Printer and Binder: LSC Communications–Crawfordsville
Cover Printer: Lehigh-Phoenix Color Corporation–Hagerstown

Cataloging-in-Publication Data on file at the Library of Congress

---

15 2020

Print Edition
ISBN-10: 0-321-94478-X
ISBN-13: 978-0-321-94478-8

Digital Edition
ISBN-10: 0-321-97491-3
ISBN-13: 978-0-321-97491-4

www.pearsonhighered.com

Brief Contents

Detailed Contents   vii
Topical and Thematic Contents   xli
Preface   liii

PART I   **The Process of Reading, Responding to, and Writing About Literature**   1

PART II   **Reading and Writing About Fiction**   **59**

1   FICTION: AN OVERVIEW   60

2   POINT OF VIEW: THE POSITION OR STANCE OF THE WORK'S NARRATOR OR SPEAKER   121

3   CHARACTERS: THE PEOPLE IN FICTION   176

4   SETTING: THE BACKGROUND OF PLACE, OBJECTS, AND CULTURE IN STORIES   238

5   STRUCTURE: THE ORGANIZATION OF STORIES   265

6   TONE AND STYLE: THE WORDS THAT CONVEY ATTITUDES IN FICTION   300

7   SYMBOLISM AND ALLEGORY: KEYS TO EXTENDED MEANING   332

8   IDEA OR THEME: THE MEANING AND THE MESSAGE IN FICTION   379

9   A CASEBOOK OF FOUR STORIES BY EDGAR ALLAN POE WITH CRITICAL READINGS FOR RESEARCH   414

10   COLLECTION OF STORIES FOR ADDITIONAL ENJOYMENT AND STUDY   462

10A   WRITING A RESEARCH ESSAY ON FICTION   500

PART III   **Reading and Writing About Poetry**   **533**

11   MEETING POETRY: AN OVERVIEW   534

12   WORDS: THE BUILDING BLOCKS OF POETRY   571

13   IMAGERY: THE POEM'S LINK TO THE SENSES   604

14   FIGURES OF SPEECH, OR METAPHORICAL LANGUAGE: A SOURCE OF DEPTH AND RANGE IN POETRY   639

15 TONE: THE CREATION OF ATTITUDE IN POETRY   678

16 FORM: THE SHAPE OF POEMS   721

17 SYMBOLISM AND ALLUSION: WINDOWS TO WIDE EXPANSES
OF MEANING   763

18 FOUR MAJOR AMERICAN POETS: EMILY DICKINSON,
ROBERT FROST, LANGSTON HUGHES, AND SYLVIA PLATH   801

19 COLLECTION OF POEMS FOR ADDITIONAL ENJOYMENT AND STUDY   880

19A WRITING A RESEARCH ESSAY ON POETRY   951

PART IV   Reading and Writing About Drama   959

20 THE DRAMATIC VISION: AN OVERVIEW   960

21 THE TRAGIC VISION: AFFIRMATION THROUGH LOSS   1022

22 THE COMIC VISION: RESTORING THE BALANCE   1257

23 VISIONS OF DRAMATIC REALITY AND NONREALITY:
VARYING THE IDEA OF DRAMA AS IMITATION   1344

24 HENRIK IBSEN AND THE REALISTIC PROBLEM PLAY: *A DOLLHOUSE*   1484

24A WRITING A RESEARCH ESSAY ON DRAMA   1550

PART V   Special Writing Topics About Literature   1565

25 CRITICAL APPROACHES IMPORTANT TO THE STUDY OF LITERATURE   1566

26 THREE TYPES OF WRITING ABOUT LITERATURE   1589

27 TAKING EXAMINATIONS ON LITERATURE   1619

APPENDIXES

I.   DRAMATIC VISION ON FILM: FROM THE SILVER SCREEN
TO THE WORLD OF DIGITAL FANTASY   1630

II. MLA RECOMMENDATIONS FOR DOCUMENTING SOURCES   1641

A GLOSSARY OF IMPORTANT LITERARY TERMS   1652
CREDITS   1672
INDEX OF AUTHORS, TITLES, AND FIRST LINES   1682

Detailed Contents

Topical and Thematic Contents   xli

Preface   liii

PART I   **The Process of Reading, Responding to, and Writing About Literature**   1

WHAT IS LITERATURE, AND WHY DO WE STUDY IT?   3

     Types of Literature: The Genres   4

     Reading Literature and Responding to It Actively   5

     GUY DE MAUPASSANT *The Necklace*   7

     To go to a ball, Mathilde Loisel borrows a necklace from a rich friend, but the evening of her dreams has unforeseen consequences.

     Reading and Responding in a Computer File or Notebook   13

     Sample Notebook Entries on Maupassant's "The Necklace"   15

MAJOR STAGES IN THINKING AND WRITING ABOUT LITERARY TOPICS: DISCOVERING IDEAS, PREPARING TO WRITE, MAKING AN INITIAL DRAFT OF YOUR ESSAY, AND COMPLETING THE ESSAY   19

     Writing Does Not Come Easily—for Anyone   19   •   *The Goal of Writing: To Show a Process of Thought*   19

     Discovering Ideas ("Brainstorming")   21

     Study the Characters in the Work   22   •   *Determine the Work's Historical Period and Background*   24   •   *Analyze the Work's Economic and Social Conditions*   24   •   *Explain the Work's Major Ideas*   25   •   *Describe the Work's Artistic Qualities*   25   •   *Explain Any Other Approaches That Seem Important*   25

     Preparing to Write   26

     Build Ideas from Your Original Notes   26   •   *Trace Patterns of Action and Thought*   27   •   *Raise and Answer Your Own Questions*   27

The Need for the Actual Physical Process of Writing   28

Put Ideas Together Using a Plus-Minus, Pro-Con, or Either-Or Method   29
Originate and Develop Your Thoughts Through Writing   29
Making an Initial Draft of Your Essay   30

Base Your Essay on a Central Idea, Argument, or Statement   30

The Need for a Sound Argument in Essays About
Literature   31

Create a Thesis Sentence as Your Guide to Organization   32   •   *Begin*
Each Paragraph with a Topic Sentence   33   •   *Select Only One Topic—*
No More—for Each Paragraph   33   •   *Use Your Topic Sentences as the*
Arguments for Your Paragraph Development   33

Referring to the Names of Authors   34

Develop an Outline as the Means of Organizing Your Essay   34

The Use of Verb Tenses in the Discussion of Literary Works   35

Basic Writing Types: Paragraphs and Essays   36

A Paragraph Assignment   37   •   *Commentary on the Paragraph*   38

Illustrative Student Essay (First Draft) How Setting in "The Necklace" Is
Related to the Character of Mathilde   38

Completing the Essay: Developing and Strengthening Your Essay Through
Revision   40

Make Your Own Arrangement of Details and Ideas   40   •   *Use Literary*
Material as Evidence to Support Your Argument   41   •   *Always Keep to*
Your Point; Stick to It Tenaciously   42   •   *Check Your Development and*
Organization   44   •   *Try to Be Original*   44   •   *Write with Specific*
Readers as Your Intended Audience   45   •   *Use Exact, Comprehensive,*
and Forceful Language   45

Illustrative Student Essay (Improved Draft)   47

Commentary on the Essay   50   •   *Essay Commentaries*   51

A Summary of Guidelines   51

Writing Topics About the Writing Process   51

Using Sources Effectively   52

**A SHORT GUIDE TO THE USE OF REFERENCES AND
QUOTATIONS IN ESSAYS ABOUT LITERATURE**   **53**

Integrate Passages and Ideas into Your Essay   53

Distinguish Your Thoughts from Those of Your Author   53

Integrate Material by Using Quotation Marks   54

Blend Quotations into Your Own Sentences   54

Indent Long Quotations and Set Them in Block Format   55

Use an Ellipsis to Show Omissions   56

Use Square Brackets to Enclose Words That You Add Within Quotations   56

Be Careful Not to Overquote   56

Preserve the Spellings in Your Source   57

PART II   Reading and Writing About Fiction   59

1   FICTION: AN OVERVIEW   60

Modern Fiction   61

The Short Story   62

Elements of Fiction I: Verisimilitude and Donnée   63

Elements of Fiction II: Character, Plot, Structure, and Idea or Theme   64

Elements of Fiction III: The Writer's Tools   67

Visualizing Fiction Cartoons, Graphic Narratives, and Graphic Novels   67

Dan Piraro, Cartoon From Bizarro   •   *Art Spiegelman, Excerpt From*
Maus   69

STORIES FOR STUDY   80

NEW   INÉS CAMELO ARREDONDO   *The Shunammite   81*
A young woman agrees to nurse her dying uncle but then must face a more
difficult decision.

AMBROSE BIERCE   *An Occurrence at Owl Creek Bridge   88*
A condemned man dreams of escape, freedom, and family.

SANDRA CISNEROS   *Mericans   93*
As a group of Mexican American children play together, they develop an
understanding of both their personal and national identities.

WILLIAM FAULKNER   *A Rose for Emily   96*
Even seemingly ordinary people hide deep and bizarre mysteries.

TIM O'BRIEN   *The Things They Carried   101*
During the Vietnam War, American soldiers carry not only their weighty
equipment but many memories.

Plot: The Motivation and Causality of Fiction   **112**

Writing About the Plot of a Story   **114**   •   📄 *Illustrative Student Essay: Plot in Faulkner's "A Rose for Emily"*   **115**

Commentary on the Essay   **118**

Using Sources Effectively: Quoting an Author's Work   **119**

Writing Topics About Plot in Fiction   **120**

2   POINT OF VIEW: THE POSITION OR STANCE OF THE WORK'S NARRATOR OR SPEAKER   121

An Exercise in Point of View: Reporting an Accident   **122**

Conditions That Affect Point of View   **124**

Point of View and Opinions   **124**

Determining a Work's Point of View   **125**

Mingling Points of View   **128**

Point of View and Verb Tense   **128**

Summary: Guidelines for Point of View   **129**

STORIES FOR STUDY   **130**

🍂 **RAYMOND CARVER** *Cathedral* **131**
A husband and wife receive a blind visitor who affects the husband's way of seeing things.

🍂 **SHIRLEY JACKSON** *The Lottery* **139**
What would it be like if the prize at a community-sponsored lottery were not the cash that people ordinarily hope to win?

🍂 **JOYCE CAROL OATES** *Where Are You Going, Where Have You Been?* **145**
A teenage girl is visited by an aggressive stranger who does not take "no" for an answer.

🍂 **ZZ PACKER** *Brownies* **155**
What happens at Camp Crescendo after the girls in Laurel's Brownie Troop decide to attack the girls in Brownie Troop 909?

Writing About Point of View   **167**   •   📄 *Illustrative Student Essay: Shirley Jackson's Dramatic Point of View in "The Lottery"*   **170**

Commentary on the Essay   **173**

Using Sources Effectively: Summary   174

Writing Topics About Point of View   175

3   CHARACTERS: THE PEOPLE IN FICTION   **176**

Character Traits   177

How Authors Disclose Character in Literature   178

Types of Characters: Round and Flat   180

Reality and Probability: Verisimilitude   182

STORIES FOR STUDY   183

NEW   **ERNEST J. GAINES *The Sky Is Gray* 184**
On a trip with his mother, a boy learns about the harshness of life and what it takes to survive.

SUSAN GLASPELL *A Jury of Her Peers* 202
In a small farmhouse kitchen early in the twentieth century, the wives of men investigating a murder discover significant evidence that forces them to make an urgent decision.

NEW   **ZORA NEALE HURSTON *Spunk* 215**
What is the definition of a "brave" man, and does that mean he commands fear or respect?

KATHERINE MANSFIELD *Miss Brill* 219
Miss Brill goes to the park for a pleasant afternoon, but she does not find what she was expecting.

AMY TAN *Two Kinds* 222
Jing-Mei leads her own kind of life despite the wishes and hopes of her mother.

Writing About Character   229   •   📄 *Illustrative Student Essay: The Character of Minnie Wright in Glaspell's "A Jury of Her Peers"*   232

Commentary on the Essay   235

Writing Topics About Character   236

4   SETTING: THE BACKGROUND OF PLACE, OBJECTS, AND CULTURE IN STORIES   **238**

What Is Setting?   238

The Literary Uses of Setting   239

STORIES FOR STUDY   242

JAMES JOYCE *Araby   242*
An introspective boy learns much about himself when he tries to keep a promise.

CYNTHIA OZICK *The Shawl   246*
Can a mother in a Nazi concentration camp save her starving and crying baby?

EDGAR ALLAN POE *The Cask of Amontillado   250*
A vengeful courtier tempts an enemy with a bottle of fine wine.

NEW   **LESLIE MARMON SILKO** *The Man to Send Rain Clouds   254*
When a Native American dies, his friends must juxtapose their respect for ancient tribal beliefs with the conventions of contemporary religion.

Writing About Setting   257   •   Illustrative Student Essay: The Interaction of Story and Setting in James Joyce's "Araby"   259

Commentary on the Essay   263

Writing Topics About Setting   263

5   STRUCTURE: THE ORGANIZATION OF STORIES   265

Formal Categories of Structure   265

Formal and Actual Structure   266

STORIES FOR STUDY   267

RALPH ELLISON *Battle Royal   268*
An intelligent black student, filled with hopes and dreams, is treated with monstrous indignity.

NEW   **GERI LIPSCHULTZ** *Slow Dance of the Heart   277*
Mei Ling Teng's long life leading from Hong Kong to the United States has been filled with the deprivation, agony, and insult of war, but she has also known love.

DANIEL OROZCO *Orientation   284*
A new employee is introduced to the rather unusual and surprising situations in the office.

EUDORA WELTY *A Worn Path* **288**

Phoenix Jackson, a devoted grandmother, walks a worn path on a mission of great love.

Writing About Structure in a Story **294** • *Illustrative Student Essay: The Structure of Eudora Welty's "A Worn Path"* **295**

Commentary on the Essay **297**

Writing Topics About Structure **298**

6 TONE AND STYLE: THE WORDS THAT CONVEY ATTITUDES IN FICTION   **300**

Diction: The Writer's Choice and Control of Words **301**

Tone, Irony, and Style **304**

Tone, Humor, and Style **305**

STORIES FOR STUDY **306**

KATE CHOPIN *The Story of an Hour* **307**

Louise Mallard is shocked and grieved by news that her husband has been killed, but she is in for an even greater shock.

DAGOBERTO GILB *Love in L.A.* **309**

In Los Angeles, people often meet each other under the most unusual and improbable circumstances.

ERNEST HEMINGWAY *Hills Like White Elephants* **311**

While waiting for a train, a man and woman reluctantly discuss an urgent situation.

FRANK O'CONNOR *First Confession* **315**

Jackie as a young man tells about his first childhood experience with confession.

JOHN UPDIKE *A & P* **320**

As a checkout clerk at the A & P near the local beaches, Sammy experiences the consequences of a difficult choice.

Writing About Tone and Style **324** • *Illustrative Student Essay: Frank O'Connor's Control of Tone and Style in "First Confession"* **327**

Commentary on the Essay **330**

Writing Topics About Tone and Style **330**

7 SYMBOLISM AND ALLEGORY: KEYS TO EXTENDED MEANING 332

Symbolism 332

Allegory 334

Fable, Parable, and Myth 335

Allusion in Symbolism and Allegory 336

STORIES FOR STUDY 337

AESOP The Fox and the Grapes 337
What do people think about things that they can't have?

ANONYMOUS (ANCIENT WRITER) The Myth of Atalanta 338
In ancient times, how could a superior woman maintain power?

NEW **ANITA SCOTT COLEMAN Unfinished Masterpieces 339**
How do we judge whether people have lived up to their fullest potential, and what affects the way they develop over their lives?

NATHANIEL HAWTHORNE Young Goodman Brown 342
In colonial Salem, Goodman Brown has a bewildering experience that changes his outlook on life.

LUKE The Parable of the Prodigal Son 350
Is there any limit to what a person can do to make divine forgiveness impossible?

KATHERINE ANNE PORTER The Jilting of Granny Weatherall 352
As the end nears, Granny Weatherall has her memories and is surrounded by her loving adult children.

JOHN STEINBECK The Chrysanthemums 358
As a housewife on a small ranch, Elisa Allen experiences changes to her sense of self-worth.

Writing About Symbolism and Allegory 364 • ▤ Illustrative Student Essay (Symbolism): Symbols of Light and Darkness in Porter's "The Jilting of Granny Weatherall" 368

Commentary on the Essay About Symbolism 371

▤ Second Illustrative Student Essay (Allegory): The Allegory of Hawthorne's "Young Goodman Brown" 372

Commentary on the Essay About Allegory 376

Writing Topics About Symbolism and Allegory 377

8 IDEA OR THEME: THE MEANING AND THE MESSAGE IN FICTION   **379**

    Ideas and Assertions   *379*

    Ideas and Issues   *380*

    Ideas and Values   *380*

    The Place of Ideas in Literature   *381*

    How to Find Ideas   *382*

  STORIES FOR STUDY   **384**

NEW   **MARGARET ATWOOD *Happy Endings* 385**
    How accurately does the word "happy" fit any of these endings, and why?

TONI CADE BAMBARA *The Lesson* 387
    When a group of children visits a toy store for the wealthy, some of them draw conclusions about society and themselves.

D. H. LAWRENCE *The Horse Dealer's Daughter* 392
    Dr. Jack Fergusson and Mabel Pervin find, in each other's love, a new reason for being.

AMÉRICO PAREDES *The Hammon and the Beans* 403
    Is American liberty restricted to people of only one group, or is it for everyone?

    Writing About a Major Idea in Fiction   406   •   Illustrative Student Essay: D. H. Lawrence's "The Horse Dealer's Daughter" as an Expression of the Idea That Loving Commitment Is Essential in Life   408

    Commentary on the Essay   412

    Writing Topics About Ideas   412

9 A CASEBOOK OF FOUR STORIES BY EDGAR ALLAN POE WITH CRITICAL READINGS FOR RESEARCH   **414**

  POE'S LIFE AND CAREER (1809–1849)   *414*

    Poe's Work as a Journalist and Writer of Fiction   416

    Poe's Reputation   417

    Bibliographic Sources   418

    Writing Topics About Poe   419

FOUR STORIES BY EDGAR ALLAN POE (CHRONOLOGICALLY
ARRANGED)   420

The Fall of the House of Usher (1839)   420

The Masque of the Red Death (1842)   431

The Black Cat (1843)   435

NEW   The Tell-Tale Heart (1843/1845)   440

Edited Selections from Criticism of Poe's Stories   443
   1. Poe's Irony   443   •   2. The Narrators of "The Cask of Amontillado"
(Chapter 4) and "The Fall of the House of Usher"   444
3. "The Fall of the House of Usher"   445   •   4. "The Black Cat"
and "The Tell-Tale Heart"   446   •   5. "The Masque of the Red
Death"   446   •   6. Symbolism in "The Masque of the Red Death"   447
7. "The Masque of the Red Death" as Representative of a "Diseased
Age"   447   •   8. Sources and Analogues of "The Cask of Amontillado"   448
9. Poe's Idea of Unity and "The Fall of the House of Usher"   455
10. The Narrators of "The Cask of Amontillado" (Chapter 4) and "The
Black Cat"   456   •   11. Poe, Women, and "The Fall of the House of
Usher"   459   •   12. The Deceptive Narrator of "The Black Cat"   460

10   COLLECTION OF STORIES FOR ADDITIONAL ENJOYMENT
     AND STUDY   462

WILLIAM FAULKNER Barn Burning 462
A young country boy grows in awareness, conscience, and individuality
despite his hostile father.

CHARLOTTE PERKINS GILMAN The Yellow
Wallpaper 473
Who is the woman who is trying to emerge from behind the yellow
wallpaper?

NEW   JAMAICA KINCAID Girl 483
Despite the "generation gap," a mother tries to teach her daughter how to
behave properly.

FLANNERY O'CONNOR A Good Man Is Hard
to Find 484
"The grandmother didn't want to go to Florida. She wanted to visit some of
her connections in east Tennessee. . . ."

ALICE WALKER *Everyday Use 494*
Mrs. Johnson, with her daughter Maggie, is visited by her citified daughter
Dee, whose return home is accompanied by surprises.

10A Writing a Research Essay on Fiction   500

Selecting a Topic 501

Setting Up a Working Bibliography 502

Locating Sources 502 • Searching the Internet 503

Evaluating Sources 503

Searching Library Resources 505

Important Considerations About Computer-Aided Research 506

Reviewing the Bibliographies in Major Critical Studies on Your
Topic 506 • Consulting Bibliographical Guides 506
Gaining Access to Books and Articles Through Databases 507

Taking Notes and Paraphrasing Material 509

Taking Complete and Accurate Notes 509

Plagiarism: An Embarrassing but Vital Subject—and a Danger
to Be Overcome 511

Being Creative and Original While Doing Research 515

Documenting Your Work 517

Include All the Works You Have Used in a List of Works Cited
(Bibliography) 517 • Refer to Works Parenthetically as You
Draw Details from Them 519

Integrating and Attributing Your Sources 519

Use Footnotes and Endnotes—Formal and Traditional Reference
Formats 520 • Sample Footnotes 521 • Follow the Requirements
for Documentation Set by Other Academic Disciplines 522 • When in
Doubt, Consult Your Instructor 522

Strategies for Organizing Ideas in Your Research Essay 522

Illustrative Student Essay Using Research: The Structure of Katherine
Mansfield's "Miss Brill" 523

Commentary on the Essay 530

Using Sources Effectively: Paraphrasing to Avoid
Plagiarism 531

Writing Topics About How to Undertake a Research Essay 532

PART III   **Reading and Writing About Poetry**   533

11   MEETING POETRY: AN OVERVIEW   534

The Nature of Poetry   534

BILLY COLLINS *Schoolsville* 534

LISEL MUELLER *Hope* 536

ROBERT HERRICK *Here a Pretty Baby Lies* 537

Poetry of the English Language   539

How to Read a Poem   540

Studying Poetry   541

ANONYMOUS *Sir Patrick Spens* 541

POEMS FOR STUDY   544

GWENDOLYN BROOKS *The Mother* 544

EMILY DICKINSON *Because I Could Not Stop for Death* 545

RITA DOVE *The House Slave* 546

ROBERT FRANCIS *Catch* 547

ROBERT FROST *Stopping by Woods on a Snowy Evening* 548

THOMAS HARDY *The Man He Killed* 548

JOY HARJO *Eagle Poem* 549

RANDALL JARRELL *The Death of the Ball Turret Gunner*   550

BEN JONSON *On My First Daughter* 550

NEW   KENNETH KOCH from *Variations on a Theme by William Carlos Williams* 551

LOUIS MACNEICE *Snow* 552

NEW   MAGUS MAGNUS *An Old Soldier Cleans His Rifle for the Last Time* 552

JIM NORTHRUP *Ogichidag* 553

NAOMI SHIHAB NYE *Where Children Live* 554

NEW   LOUIS SIMPSON *American Poetry* 555

WILLIAM SHAKESPEARE *Sonnet 55: Not Marble, Nor the Gilded Monuments* 555

ELAINE TERRANOVA *Rush Hour* 556

NEW **WILLIAM CARLOS WILLIAMS** *This Is Just to Say* 557

WILLIAM WORDSWORTH *Lines Composed a Few Miles Above Tintern Abbey* 557

Writing a Paraphrase of a Poem (Paragraph Length) 561

Illustrative Student Paraphrase: A Paraphrase of Thomas Hardy's "The Man He Killed" 562

Commentary on the Paraphrase 562

Writing an Explication of a Poem (Essay Length) 563

Illustrative Student Essay: An Explication of Thomas Hardy's "The Man He Killed" 565

Commentary on the Essay 567

Using Sources Effectively: Paraphrasing to Set the Stage for Analysis 568

Writing Topics About the Nature of Poetry 569

12 **WORDS: THE BUILDING BLOCKS OF POETRY** **571**

Choice of Diction: Specific and Concrete, General and Abstract 571

Levels of Diction 572

Special Types of Diction 573

Syntax 574

Decorum: The Matching of Subject and Word 575

Denotation and Connotation 576

ROBERT GRAVES *The Naked and the Nude* 578

POEMS FOR STUDY 579

NEW **JOHN ASHBERY** *The Cathedral Is* 580

CHARLES BAUDELAIRE *Exotic Perfume* 580

WILLIAM BLAKE *The Lamb* 581

LEWIS CARROLL *Jabberwocky* 581

HAYDEN CARRUTH *An Apology for Using the Word "Heart" in Too Many Poems* 582

ROBERT CREELEY *I Know a Man* 583

E. E. CUMMINGS *next to of course god america i* 584

JOHN DONNE *Holy Sonnet 14: Batter My Heart, Three-Personed God* 585

NEW   A. E. HOUSMAN *To an Athlete Dying Young* 585

CAROLYN KIZER *Night Sounds* 586

DENISE LEVERTOV *Of Being* 587

NEW   GERI LIPSCHULTZ *In the Beginning of the End* 588

JUDITH ORTIZ COFER *Latin Women Pray* 589

EDWIN ARLINGTON ROBINSON *Richard Cory* 590

THEODORE ROETHKE *Dolor* 591

KAY RYAN *Crib* 591

STEPHEN SPENDER *I Think Continually of Those Who Were Truly Great* 592

WALLACE STEVENS *Disillusionment of Ten O'Clock* 593

MARK STRAND *Eating Poetry* 593

NEW   NATASHA TRETHEWEY *White Lies* 594

WILLIAM WORDSWORTH *Daffodils (I Wandered Lonely as a Cloud)* 595

PAUL ZIMMER *The Day Zimmer Lost Religion* 596

Writing About Diction and Syntax in Poetry   596

Illustrative Student Essay: Diction and Character in Robinson's "Richard Cory"   598

Commentary on the Essay   601

Using Sources Effectively: Summarizing to Provide Necessary Background   602

Writing Topics About the Words of Poetry   603

13 IMAGERY: THE POEM'S LINK TO THE SENSES   **604**

Responses and the Poet's Use of Detail   604

The Relationship of Imagery to Ideas and Attitudes   605

Types of Imagery   605

JOHN MASEFIELD *Cargoes 606*

WILFRED OWEN *Anthem for Doomed Youth 607*

ELIZABETH BISHOP *The Fish 608*

POEMS FOR STUDY 610

ELIZABETH BARRETT BROWNING *Sonnets from the Portuguese, Number 14: If Thou Must Love Me 611*

SAMUEL TAYLOR COLERIDGE *Kubla Khan 612*

T. S. ELIOT *Preludes 613*

LOUISE ERDRICH *Indian Boarding School: The Runaways 615*

SUSAN GRIFFIN *Love Should Grow Up Like a Wild Iris in the Fields 616*

THOMAS HARDY *Channel Firing 617*

NEW H. D. (HILDA DOOLITTLE) *Heat 618*

GEORGE HERBERT *The Pulley 619*

GERARD MANLEY HOPKINS *Spring 620*

NEW ROBINSON JEFFERS *Hurt Hawks 620*

DENISE LEVERTOV *A Time Past 621*

NEW AMY LOWELL *The Taxi 622*

THOMAS LUX *The Voice You Hear When You Read Silently 623*

MARIANNE MOORE *The Fish 624*

PABLO NERUDA *Every Day You Play 625*

NEW EDGAR ALLAN POE *To Helen 626*

EZRA POUND *In a Station of the Metro 627*

NEW BENJAMIN ALIRE SÁENZ *To the Desert 628*

WILLIAM SHAKESPEARE *Sonnet 130: My Mistress' Eyes Are Nothing Like the Sun 628*

NEW CHARLES SIMIC *Fork 629*

JAMES TATE *Dream On 629*

DAVID WOJAHN *"It's Only Rock and Roll, but I Like It":* *The Fall of Saigon* **631**

Writing About Imagery 632

📄 *Illustrative Student Essay: Imagery in Masefield's "Cargoes"* 634

Commentary on the Essay 636

Writing Topics About Imagery in Poetry 637

14 **FIGURES OF SPEECH, OR METAPHORICAL LANGUAGE:**
A SOURCE OF DEPTH AND RANGE IN POETRY   **639**

Metaphors and Similes: The Major Figures of Speech 639

Characteristics of Metaphorical Language 641

JOHN KEATS *On First Looking into Chapman's Homer* **641**

Vehicle and Tenor 642

Other Figures of Speech 643

JOHN KEATS *Bright Star* **644**

JOHN GAY *Let Us Take the Road* **645**

POEMS FOR STUDY **647**

WILLIAM BLAKE *The Tyger* **647**

ROBERT BURNS *A Red, Red Rose* **648**

JOHN DONNE *A Valediction: Forbidding Mourning* **649**

NEW **ALAN DUGAN** *Untitled Poem* **651**

NEW **FEDERICO GARCÍA LORCA** *Sonnet of the Sweet Complaint* **651**

THOMAS HARDY *The Convergence of the Twain* **652**

JOY HARJO *Remember* **653**

JOHN KEATS *To Autumn* **654**

JANE KENYON *Let Evening Come* **655**

JUDITH MINTY *Conjoined* **656**

NEW **OGDEN NASH** *Exit, Pursued by a Bear* **657**

PABLO NERUDA *If You Forget Me* **658**

MARY OLIVER *Showing the Birds* **660**

MARGE PIERCY *A Work of Artifice* **660**

NEW   MARGUERITE RIVAS *Pilgrimage 661*

MURIEL RUKEYSER *Looking at Each Other 662*

WILLIAM SHAKESPEARE *Sonnet 18: Shall I Compare Thee to a Summer's Day? 663*

WILLIAM SHAKESPEARE *Sonnet 30: When to the Sessions of Sweet Silent Thought 663*

NEW   ALFRED, LORD TENNYSON *Break, Break, Break 664*

ELIZABETH TUDOR, QUEEN ELIZABETH I *On Monsieur's Departure 665*

MONA VAN DUYN *Earth Tremors Felt in Missouri 666*

NEW   DIANE WAKOSKI *Inside Out 666*

WALT WHITMAN *Facing West from California's Shores 667*

WILLIAM WORDSWORTH *London, 1802 668*

SIR THOMAS WYATT *I Find No Peace 669*

Writing Topics About Figures of Speech 670

Illustrative Student Paragraph: Wordsworth's Use of Overstatement in "London, 1802" 673

Commentary on the Paragraph 673

Illustrative Student Essay: A Study of Shakespeare's Metaphors in Sonnet 30: "When to the Sessions of Sweet Silent Thought" 674

Commentary on the Essay 676

Writing Topics About Figures of Speech in Poetry 676

15   TONE: THE CREATION OF ATTITUDE IN POETRY   678

Tone, Choice, and Response 678

CORNELIUS WHUR *The First-Rate Wife 679*

Tone and the Need for Control 680

WILFRED OWEN *Dulce et Decorum Est 680*

Tone and Common Grounds of Assent 681

Tone in Conversation and Poetry 682

Tone and Irony 682

THOMAS HARDY *The Workbox 683*

Tone and Satire 685

ALEXANDER POPE *Epigram from the French*   685

ALEXANDER POPE *Epigram, Engraved on the Collar of a Dog Which I Gave to His Royal Highness*   686

POEMS FOR STUDY   686

W. H. AUDEN *The Unknown Citizen*   687

WILLIAM BLAKE *On Another's Sorrow*   688

JIMMY CARTER *I Wanted to Share My Father's World*   689

LUCILLE CLIFTON *homage to my hips*   690

BILLY COLLINS *The Names*   691

NEW   COUNTEE CULLEN *Yet Do I Marvel*   692

E. E. CUMMINGS *she being Brand / -new*   693

MARTÍN ESPADA *Bully*   694

MARI EVANS *I Am a Black Woman*   695

SEAMUS HEANEY *Mid-Term Break*   697

WILLIAM ERNEST HENLEY *When You Are Old*   697

NEW   DAVID IGNATOW *The Bagel*   698

NEW   YUSEF KOMUNYAKAA *Facing It*   699

ABRAHAM LINCOLN *My Childhood's Home*   700

NEW   CHRISTOPHER OKIGBO *Bright*   701

SHARON OLDS *The Planned Child*   702

ARTHUR O'SHAUGHNESSY *A Love Symphony*   702

ROBERT PINSKY *Dying*   703

SALVATORE QUASÍMODO *Auschwitz*   704

THEODORE ROETHKE *My Papa's Waltz*   706

WILLIAM SHAKESPEARE *Fear No More the Heat o' th' Sun*   707

CATHY SONG *Lost Sister*   708

C. K. WILLIAMS *Dimensions*   709

WILLIAM WORDSWORTH *The Solitary Reaper*   710

NEW   JAMES WRIGHT *Autumn Begins in Martin's Ferry, Ohio*   711

NEW   JAMES WRIGHT *Two Hangovers* *712*

WILLIAM BUTLER YEATS *When You Are Old* *713*

Writing About Tone in Poetry *714*

📄 *Illustrative Student Essay: The Speaker's Attitudes in Sharon Olds's "The Planned Child"* *716*

Commentary on the Essay *719*

Writing Topics About Tone in Poetry *719*

16 FORM: THE SHAPE OF POEMS   721

Closed-Form Poetry *721*

ALFRED, LORD TENNYSON *The Eagle* *723*

ANONYMOUS *Spun in High, Dark Clouds* *727*

WILLIAM SHAKESPEARE *Sonnet 116: Let Me Not to the Marriage of True Minds* *728*

Open-Form Poetry *729*

NEW   WALT WHITMAN *When I Heard the Learn'd Astronomer* *730*

Visualizing Poetry: Poetry and Artistic Expression. Visual Poetry, Concrete Poetry, and Prose Poems *730*

E. E. CUMMINGS *Buffalo Bill's Defunct* *731*

WILLIAM HEYEN *Mantle* *732*

MAY SWENSON *Women* *733*

CAROLYN FORCHÉ *The Colonel* *734*

POEMS FOR STUDY *735*

NEW   JOHN BERRYMAN *Dream Song 14* *736*

ELIZABETH BISHOP *One Art* *736*

NEW   ELIZABETH BISHOP *Sestina* *737*

BILLY COLLINS *Sonnet* *738*

JOHN DRYDEN *To the Memory of Mr. Oldham* *739*

NEW   LAWRENCE FERLINGHETTI *Constantly Risking Absurdity* *740*

ROBERT FROST *Desert Places* *741*

ALLEN GINSBERG *A Supermarket in California* 742

GEORGE HERBERT *Virtue* 743

NEW BEN JONSON *To Celia* 744

JOHN KEATS *Ode to a Nightingale* 745

YUSEF KOMUNYAKAA *Grenade* 747

CLAUDE MCKAY *In Bondage* 748

JOHN MILTON *On His Blindness (When I Consider How My Light Is Spent)* 749

DUDLEY RANDALL *Ballad of Birmingham* 749

THEODORE ROETHKE *The Waking* 751

PERCY BYSSHE SHELLEY *Ozymandias* 751

DYLAN THOMAS *Do Not Go Gentle into That Good Night* 752

JEAN TOOMER *Reapers* 753

PHYLLIS WEBB *Poetics Against the Angel of Death* 753

WALT WHITMAN *Reconciliation* 754

NEW WILLIAM CARLOS WILLIAMS *The Dance* 754

Writing About Form in Poetry 755

Illustrative Student Essay: Form and Meaning in George Herbert's "Virtue" 757

Commentary on the Essay 760

Writing Topics About Poetic Form 761

17 SYMBOLISM AND ALLUSION: WINDOWS TO WIDE EXPANSES OF MEANING **763**

Symbolism and Meanings 763

VIRGINIA SCOTT *Snow* 764

The Function of Symbolism in Poetry 766

Allusions and Meaning 767

Studying for Symbols and Allusions 769

POEMS FOR STUDY   770

NEW   AMIRI BARAKA *Legacy*   770

EMILY BRONTË *No Coward Soul Is Mine*   771

NEW   MARILYN CHIN *Autumn Leaves*   772

NEW   LUCILLE CLIFTON *cutting greens*   772

ARTHUR HUGH CLOUGH *Say Not the Struggle Nought Availeth*   773

JOHN DONNE *The Canonization*   774

STEPHEN DUNN *Hawk*   776

ISABELLA GARDNER *Collage of Echoes*   777

DAN GEORGAKAS *Hiroshima Crewman*   777

THOMAS HARDY *In Time of "The Breaking of Nations"*   778

GEORGE HERBERT *The Collar*   778

ROBINSON JEFFERS *The Purse-Seine*   780

JOHN KEATS *La Belle Dame Sans Merci: A Ballad*   781

X. J. KENNEDY *Old Men Pitching Horseshoes*   783

ANDREW MARVELL *To His Coy Mistress*   784

NEW   CAROL MUSKE-DUKES *Real Estate*   785

MARY OLIVER *Wild Geese*   786

KAY RYAN *We're Building the Ship as We Sail It*   787

GARY SNYDER *Milton by Firelight*   788

JUDITH VIORST *A Wedding Sonnet for the Next Generation*   789

WALT WHITMAN *A Noiseless Patient Spider*   790

RICHARD WILBUR *Year's End*   790

WILLIAM BUTLER YEATS *The Second Coming*   792

Writing About Symbolism and Allusion in Poetry   793

Illustrative Student Essay: Symbolism in Oliver's "Wild Geese"   796

Commentary on the Essay   798

Writing Topics About Symbolism and Allusion in Poetry   799

18 FOUR MAJOR AMERICAN POETS: EMILY DICKINSON, ROBERT FROST, LANGSTON HUGHES, AND SYLVIA PLATH   801

EMILY DICKINSON'S LIFE AND WORK   801

Topics for Writing About the Poetry of Emily Dickinson   806

POEMS BY EMILY DICKINSON (ALPHABETICALLY ARRANGED)   806

NEW   A Narrow Fellow in the Grass (J986, F1096)   807

After Great Pain, a Formal Feeling Comes (J341, F372)   808

Because I Could Not Stop for Death (J712, F479)   545, 808

The Bustle in a House (J1078, F1108)   808

NEW   "Faith" Is a Fine Invention (J185, F202)   809

I Cannot Live with You (J640, F706)   809

I Died for Beauty – but Was Scarce (J449, F448)   810

I Dwell in Possibility (F466, J657)   810

I Felt a Funeral in My Brain (J280, F340)   811

I Heard a Fly Buzz – When I Died (J465, F591)   811

I Like to See It Lap the Miles (J585, F383)   812

I'm Nobody! Who Are You? (J288, F260)   812

I Never Lost as Much but Twice (J49, F39)   812

I Taste a Liquor Never Brewed (J214, F207)   813

Much Madness Is Divinest Sense (J435, F620)   813

My Life Closed Twice Before Its Close (J1732, F1773)   813

One Need Not Be a Chamber – To Be Haunted (J670, F407)   814

Safe in Their Alabaster Chambers (J216, F124)   814

Some Keep the Sabbath Going to Church (J324, F236)   814

The Soul Selects Her Own Society (J303, F409)   815

Success Is Counted Sweetest (J67, F112)   815

Tell All the Truth but Tell It Slant (J1129, F1263)   816

NEW   There Is No Frigate Like a Book (J1263, F1286)   816

There's a Certain Slant of Light (J258, F320)   816

Triumph May Be of Several Kinds (J455, F680)   817

Wild Nights – Wild Nights! (J249, F269)   817

Edited Selections from Criticism of Dickinson's Poems   817
    1. From "Orthodox Modernisms"   818   •   2. From "The Landscape of the
    Spirit"   823   •   3. From "The American Plain Style"   827
    •   4. From "The Histrionic Imagination"   830   •   5. From "The Gothic
    Mode: 'Tis so appalling – it exhilarates –'"   832

ROBERT FROST'S LIFE AND WORK   837

    Writing Topics About the Poetry of Robert Frost   841

POEMS BY ROBERT FROST (CHRONOLOGICALLY ARRANGED)   842

NEW   In White (An Early Version of "Design," p. 848) (1912)   842

Mending Wall (1914)   842

NEW   After Apple-Picking (1915)   843

Birches (1915)   844

The Road Not Taken (1915)   845

"Out, Out—" (1916)   846

The Oven Bird (1916)   847

Fire and Ice (1920)   847

Nothing Gold Can Stay (1923)   847

Acquainted with the Night (1928)   848

Design (1936)   848

The Silken Tent (1936)   848

The Gift Outright (1941)   849

LANGSTON HUGHES'S LIFE AND WORK   849

Writing Topics About the Poetry of Langston Hughes   852

POEMS BY LANGSTON HUGHES (ALPHABETICALLY ARRANGED)   853

NEW   Bad Man   853

Ballad of the Landlord   853

Dead in There   854

NEW   Dream Boogie   855

Dream Variations   855

Harlem   856

NEW   I, Too   856

Let America Be America Again   857

Negro   859

The Negro Speaks of Rivers   859

125th Street   860

Po' Boy Blues   860

Subway Rush Hour   860

Theme for English B   861

The Weary Blues   862

SYLVIA PLATH'S LIFE AND WORK   863

Writing Topics About the Poetry of Sylvia Plath   866

POEMS BY SYLVIA PLATH (ALPHABETICALLY ARRANGED)   867

Ariel   867

The Colossus   868

Cut   869

Daddy   870

Edge   872

The Hanging Man   873

Lady Lazarus   873

     Last Words   876

     Metaphors   876

     Mirror   877

     The Rival   877

     Song for a Summer's Day   878

     Tulips   878

19   COLLECTION OF POEMS FOR ADDITIONAL ENJOYMENT AND STUDY   **880**

     AI (FLORENCE ANTHONY) *Conversation*   882

     ANNA AKHMATOVA *Willow*   883

     SHERMAN ALEXIE *On the Amtrak from Boston to New York City*   883

NEW   AGHA SHAHID ALI *Postcard from Kashmir*   883

NEW   JULIA ALVAREZ *Woman's Work*   884

     MAYA ANGELOU *Still I Rise*   885

     ANONYMOUS (NAVAJO) *Healing Prayer from the Beautyway Chant (traditional nineteenth century)*   886

     MATTHEW ARNOLD *Dover Beach*   887

NEW   MARGARET ATWOOD *You fit into me*   888

     W. H. AUDEN *Musée des Beaux Arts*   888

     LOUISE BOGAN *Women*   888

     JORGE LUIS BORGES *The Art of Poetry*   889

NEW   ANNE BRADSTREET *The Author to Her Book*   890

     ANNE BRADSTREET *To My Dear and Loving Husband*   890

     EMILY BRONTË *Love and Friendship*   891

     GWENDOLYN BROOKS *We Real Cool*   891

     ELIZABETH BARRETT BROWNING *Sonnets from the Portuguese: Number 43, How Do I Love Thee?*   892

     ROBERT BROWNING *My Last Duchess*   892

GEORGE GORDON, LORD BYRON *She Walks in Beauty* 893

BILLY COLLINS *Days* 894

STEPHEN CRANE *Do Not Weep, Maiden, for War Is Kind* 895

NEW   E. E. CUMMINGS *anyone lived in a pretty how town* 895

E. E. CUMMINGS *if there are any heavens* 896

JOHN DONNE *Holy Sonnet 10: Death Be Not Proud* 897

RITA DOVE *Daystar* 897

NEW   SIR EDWARD DYER *My Mind to Me a Kingdom Is* 898

NEW   BOB DYLAN *The Times They Are a-Changin'* 899

T. S. ELIOT *The Love Song of J. Alfred Prufrock* 900

NEW   MARTÍIN ESPADA *Latin Night at the Pawnshop* 904

NEW   RHINA ESPAILLAT *Bilingual/Bilingue* 904

CHIEF DAN GEORGE *The Beauty of the Trees* 905

NIKKI GIOVANNI *Poetry* 905

DANIEL HALPERN *Snapshot of Hué* 906

THOMAS HARDY *The Ruined Maid* 907

FRANCES E. W. HARPER *She's Free!* 908

ROBERT HASS *Spring Rain* 908

ROBERT HAYDEN *Those Winter Sundays* 909

NEW   ROBERT HERRICK *Corinna's Going A-Maying* 909

NEW   JANET HOLMES *Cinquains for Rocky* 911

A. D. HOPE *Advice to Young Ladies* 911

GERARD MANLEY HOPKINS *Pied Beauty* 912

NEW   A. E. HOUSMAN *When I was one-and-twenty* 913

ROBINSON JEFFERS *The Answer* 913

NEW   DONALD JUSTICE *On the Death of Friends in Childhood* 914

DONALD JUSTICE *Order in the Streets* 914

JOHN KEATS *Ode on a Grecian Urn* 914

GALWAY KINNELL *After Making Love We Hear Footsteps* 917

YAHIA LABABIDI *What Do Animals Dream?* 917

PHILIP LARKIN *Talking in Bed* 918

LI-YOUNG LEE *A Final Thing* 919

NEW   AUDRE LORDE *Now That I Am Forever with Child* 920

AMY LOWELL *Patterns* 921

NEW   MAGUS MAGNUS *Antaeus / Anchises* 923

NEW   EDNA ST. VINCENT MILLAY *Travel* 924

EDNA ST. VINCENT MILLAY *What Lips My Lips Have Kissed, and Where, and Why* 924

N. SCOTT MOMADAY *The Bear* 924

HOWARD NEMEROV *Life Cycle of Common Man* 925

JIM NORTHRUP *wahbegan* 926

NEW   SHARON OLDS *The Moment the Two Worlds Meet* 927

SIMON ORTIZ *A Story of How a Wall Stands* 927

NEW   DOROTHY PARKER *Afternoon* 928

DOROTHY PARKER *Résumé* 929

LINDA PASTAN *Marks* 929

MARGE PIERCY *The Secretary Chant* 929

EDGAR ALLAN POE *Annabel Lee* 930

EDGAR ALLAN POE *The Raven* 931

NEW   EZRA POUND *A Girl* 933

NEW   ADRIENNE RICH *Aunt Jennifer's Tigers* 934

NEW   ADRIENNE RICH *Living in Sin* 934

ALBERTO RÍOS *The Vietnam Wall* 935

LUIS OMAR SALINAS *In a Farmhouse* 936

CARL SANDBURG *Chicago* 936

SIEGFRIED SASSOON *Dreamers* 937

BRENDA SEROTTE *My Mother's Face* 938

NEW ANNE SEXTON *Cinderella* 938

WILLIAM SHAKESPEARE *Sonnet 29: When in Disgrace with Fortune and Men's Eyes* 941

KARL SHAPIRO *Auto Wreck* 941

STEVIE SMITH *Not Waving but Drowning* 942

NEW GARY SOTO *Mexicans Begin Jogging* 942

GARY SOTO *Oranges* 943

WILLIAM STAFFORD *Traveling Through the Dark* 944

WALLACE STEVENS *The Emperor of Ice-Cream* 945

MAY SWENSON *Question* 945

DYLAN THOMAS *A Refusal to Mourn the Death, by Fire, of a Child in London* 945

JOHN UPDIKE *Perfection Wasted* 947

ALICE WALKER *Revolutionary Petunias* 947

PHILLIS WHEATLEY *On Being Brought from Africa to America* 948

WALT WHITMAN *Beat! Beat! Drums!* 948

WALT WHITMAN *Full of Life Now* 949

WALT WHITMAN *I Hear America Singing* 949

RICHARD WILBUR *Love Calls Us to the Things of This World* 949

WILLIAM CARLOS WILLIAMS *The Red Wheelbarrow* 950

19A WRITING A RESEARCH ESSAY ON POETRY   **951**

Topics to Discover in Research 951

Illustrative Student Essay Written with the Aid of Research: "Beat! Beat! Drums!" and "I Hear America Singing": Two Whitman Poems Spanning the Civil War 952

Commentary on the Essay 956

Using Sources Effectively: Quoting Texts to Illustrate Your Point 957

PART IV   **Reading and Writing About Drama**   **959**

20   **THE DRAMATIC VISION: AN OVERVIEW**   **960**

Drama as Literature   *960*

Performance: The Unique Aspect of Drama   *967*

Drama from Ancient Times to Our Own: Tragedy, Comedy, and Additional
Forms   *971*

ANONYMOUS *The Visit to the Sepulcher (Visitatio
Sepulchri)* **973**

Visualizing Plays: Imagining Dramatic Scenes and Actions   *977*

PLAYS FOR STUDY **982**

SUSAN GLASPELL *Trifles* **983**
*In a small farmhouse kitchen early in the twentieth century, the wives
of men investigating a murder discover significant evidence that forces
them to make an urgent decision.*

NEW **DAVID HENRY HWANG** *Trying to Find
Chinatown* **994**
*Two young men meet in New York City and engage in a surprising dialogue
about racial identity.*

JANE MARTIN *Beauty* **1000**
As Carla and Bethany talk together, they go through a transformational experience.

EUGENE O'NEILL *Before Breakfast* **1006**
*What happens to people facing disappointment, anger, alienation,
and lost hope?*

Writing About the Elements of Drama   *1012*

Referring to Plays and Parts of Plays   *1015*

Illustrative Student Essay: Eugene O'Neill's Use of Negative
Descriptions and Stage Directions in **Before Breakfast** as a Means
of Revealing Character   *1016*

Commentary on the Essay   *1019*

Using Sources Effectively: Paraphrasing to Make Sure Readers
Understand the Work   *1019*

Writing Topics About the Elements of Drama   *1021*

21 THE TRAGIC VISION: AFFIRMATION THROUGH LOSS   1022

The Origins of Tragedy   1023

The Origin of Tragedy in Brief   1025

The Ancient Athenian Competitions in Tragedy   1025

Aristotle and the Nature of Tragedy   1027

Aristotle's View of Tragedy in Brief   1031

Irony in Tragedy   1032

The Ancient Athenian Audience and Theater   1033

Ancient Greek Tragic Actors and Their Costumes   1035

Performance and the Formal Organization of Greek Tragedy   1036

PLAYS FOR STUDY   1038

SOPHOCLES *Oedipus the King*   1039
A king discovers how his past actions have doomed him.

Renaissance Drama and Shakespeare's Theater   1075

WILLIAM SHAKESPEARE *The Tragedy of Hamlet, Prince of Denmark*   1080
A prince grapples with his conscience in seeking to avenge his murdered father.

Tragedy from Shakespeare to Arthur Miller   1179

Death of a Salesman: *Tragedy, Symbolism, and Broken Dreams*   1180

ARTHUR MILLER *Death of a Salesman*   1182
With all his hopes unfulfilled, Willy Loman still clings to his dreams.

Writing About Tragedy   1246

Illustrative Student Essay: *The Problem of Hamlet's Apparent Delay*   1250

Commentary on the Essay   1253

Using Sources Effectively: *Quoting Texts to Illustrate Your Key Point*   1254

Writing Topics About Tragedy   1255

22 THE COMIC VISION: RESTORING THE BALANCE   1257

The Origins of Comedy   1257

Comedy from Roman Times to the Renaissance   1260

The Patterns, Characters, and Language of Comedy   1261

Types of Comedy   1263

PLAYS FOR STUDY 1265

WILLIAM SHAKESPEARE *A Midsummer Night's Dream* *1267*

Comedy Since Shakespeare 1320

ANTON CHEKHOV *The Bear, A Joke in One Act* *1323*
A bachelor and a widow meet and immediately berate each other, but their lives are about to undergo great change.

NEW **PAUL DOOLEY AND WINNIE HOLZMAN** *Post-its (Notes on a Marriage)* *1331*
A married couple enjoy a comic but cryptic mode of communication.

NEW **EDWIN SÁNCHEZ** *POPS* *1335*
A young Hispanic man finds a sweet, humorous way to memorialize his lost father.

Writing About Comedy 1336

Illustrative Student Essay: Setting as Symbol and Comic Structure in Shakespeare's A Midsummer Night's Dream *1339*

Commentary on the Essay 1342

Writing Topics About Comedy 1342

23 VISIONS OF DRAMATIC REALITY AND NONREALITY: VARYING THE IDEA OF DRAMA AS IMITATION **1344**

Realism and Nonrealism in Drama 1344

Elements of Realistic and Nonrealistic Drama 1347

PLAYS FOR STUDY 1349

Hughes and the African American Theater After 1350

Hughes's Career as a Dramatist 1350

Mulatto *and the Reality of the Southern Black Experience 1351*

LANGSTON HUGHES *Mulatto* *1352*
On a Southern plantation in the 1930s, a young man tries to assert his rights, but there are those who will not grant him any rights at all.

NEW **EDWARD BOK LEE** *El Santo Americano* *1374*
A professional wrestler tries to forge a better life for himself and his family.

TENNESSEE WILLIAMS *The Glass Menagerie* *1379*
Tom would like to escape the memory of his home life, in which he finds only confusion and entrapment.

The Background of Fences   *1428*

🖈 **AUGUST WILSON *Fences* *1430***
Troy Maxson, who as a young athlete could knock baseballs over fences, has led a life enclosed by other fences.

Writing About Realistic and Nonrealistic Drama   1476

📄 *Illustrative Student Essay: Realism and Nonrealism in Tom's Triple Role in* The Glass Menagerie   *1478*

Commentary on the Essay   1481

Writing Topics About Dramatic Reality and Nonreality   1481

24   HENRIK IBSEN AND THE REALISTIC PROBLEM PLAY: *A DOLLHOUSE*   **1484**

Ibsen's Life and Early Work   1484

Ibsen's Major Prose Plays   1485

A Dollhouse: *Ibsen's Best-Known Problem Play   1486*

Ibsen's Symbolism in A Dollhouse   *1486*

A Dollhouse *as a "Well-Made Play"   1487*

The Timeliness and Dramatic Power of A Dollhouse   *1487*

Bibliographic Studies   1487

🖈 **HENRIK IBSEN *A Dollhouse (Et Dukkehjem)* *1488***
In their seemingly perfect household, Nora and Torvald discover the severe differences between them.

Edited Selections from Criticism of Ibsen's A Dollhouse *and Other Plays   1536*

1. *Freedom, Truth, and Society—Rhetoric and Reality   1537*
2. *Ibsen's Feminist Characters   1542* • 3. *A Marxist Approach to* A Doll House   *1547*

24A WRITING A RESEARCH ESSAY ON DRAMA   **1550**

Topics to Discover in Research   1550

📄 *Illustrative Student Essay Written with the Aid of Research: The Ghost in Hamlet   1552*

Commentary on the Essay   1562

Using Sources Effectively: Summarizing Sources Lends Authority to Your Argument   1563

PART V   Special Writing Topics About Literature   1565

25   Critical Approaches Important in the Study of Literature   1566

    Moral/Intellectual   1567

    Topical/Historical   1569

    New Critical/Formalist   1571

    Structuralist   1573

    Feminist Criticism/Gender Studies/Queer Theory   1575

    Economic Determinist/Marxist   1578

    Psychological/Psychoanalytic   1580

    Archetypal/Symbolic/Mythic   1582

    Deconstructionist   1584

    Reader-Response   1586

26   Three Types of Writing About Literature   1589

1. Comparison-Contrast and Extended Comparison-Contrast   1589

    Guidelines for the Comparison-Contrast Method   1590

    The Extended Comparison-Contrast Essay   1593

    Citing References in a Longer Comparison-Contrast Essay   1594

    Writing a Comparison-Contrast Essay   1594

    Illustrative Student Essay (Two Works): The Treatment of Responses to War in Amy Lowell's "Patterns" and Wilfred Owen's "Anthem for Doomed Youth"   1596

    Commentary on the Essay   1599

    Illustrative Student Essay (Extended Comparison-Contrast): Literary Treatments of the Conflicts Between Private and Public Life   1600

    Commentary on the Essay   1604

    Writing Topics for Comparison and Contrast   1605

2. Reader-Response: How a Reader's Reactions Lead Toward Interpretation   1606

    Important Elements of a Reader-Response Essay   1606

    Illustrative Student Essay (Reader-Response): Opposite Personal Responses to W. H. Auden's "Musée des Beaux Arts"   1608

Commentary on the Essay 1612

Writing Topics for Reader-Response 1612

3. Argument: The Use of Persuasive Reasoning 1613

Defining an Argument Essay 1613

Important Elements of a Reader-Response Essay 1613

Arrive at a Claim for a Thesis Statement 1614

📄 *Illustrative Student Essay (Argument): Sammy's Decision to Become an Adult* 1615

Commentary on the Essay 1618

Writing Topics for Literary Argument 1618

27 TAKING EXAMINATIONS ON LITERATURE   1619

Answer the Questions That Are Asked 1619

Systematic Preparation 1621

Two Basic Types of Questions About Literature 1624

Appendixes

**I. DRAMATIC VISION ON FILM: FROM THE SILVER SCREEN TO THE
WORLD OF DIGITAL FANTASY**   **1630**
II. MLA RECOMMENDATIONS FOR DOCUMENTING SOURCES   **1641**

A GLOSSARY OF IMPORTANT LITERARY TERMS   **1652**
CREDITS   **1672**
INDEX OF AUTHORS, TITLES, AND FIRST LINES   **1682**

Topical and Thematic Contents

For analytical purposes, the following lists of topical and thematic contents group the selections into twenty-seven categories. The idea is that the topical categories will facilitate a thematic and focused study and comparison of a number of works (see Chapter 26). Obviously each of the works brings out many other issues than are suggested by the topics. For comparison, however, the topics invite analyses based on specific issues. Thus, the category "Women" suggests that the listed works may profitably be examined for what they have to say about the lives and problems specifically of women, just as the category "Men" suggests a concentration on the lives and problems specifically of men. The topical headings are suggestive only; they are by no means intended to mandate interpretations or approaches. For emphasis, we will repeat this, and also we will italicize, underline, and boldface it: ***<u>The topical headings are suggestive only; they are by no means intended to mandate interpretations or approaches</u>***. We have accordingly assigned a number of works to two and sometimes even more categories. Ibsen's *A Dollhouse*, for example, is not easily classified within a single category.

Because entries for the topical and thematic contents are to be as brief as possible, we use only the last names of authors. In listing works we shorten a number of longer titles. Thus we refer to *Let America* (Hughes) rather than *Let America Be America Again*, and to *Not Marble* (Shakespeare) rather than *Not Marble, Nor the Gilded Monuments*, and so on, using such recognizable short titles rather than the full titles that appear in the regular table of contents, in the text itself, and in the index. Of course, some titles are already brief, such as *Reconciliation* (Whitman), *Eating Poetry* (Strand), *Edge* (Plath), and *A Worn Path* (Welty). Obviously, such titles are included in their entirety.

AMERICA IN PEACE, WAR, AND TRIBULATION

Stories

Bierce, An Occurrence   88
Cisneros, Mericans   93
O'Brien, The Things They Carried   101
Packer, Brownies   155
Paredes, The Hammon and the
  Beans   403
Updike, A & P   320
Welty, A Worn Path   288

Poems

Alexie, On the Amtrak   883
Anonymous, Healing Prayer   886
Collins, The Names   691
Dickinson, I Like to See It Lap   812
Dove, The House Slave   540
Dunn, Hawk   776
Dylan, The Times They Are
  a-Changin'   899
Erdrich, Indian Boarding School   615
Espada, Bully   694
Frost, The Gift Outright   849
George, The Beauty of the Trees   905
Harjo, Remember   653
Hass, Spring Rain   908
Hughes, I, Too   856
Hughes, Let America   857
Hughes, 125th Street   860
Komunyakaa, Facing It   699
Lincoln, My Childhood's Home   700
Magnus, An Old Soldier Cleans   552
Momaday, The Bear   924
Terranova, Rush Hour   556
Walker, Revolutionary Petunias   947
Whitman, Facing West   667
Whitman, I Hear America Singing   949

Plays

Glaspell, Trifles   973
Miller, Death of a Salesman   1182
Wilson, Fences   1430

ART, LANGUAGE, AND IMAGINATION

Stories

Bierce, An Occurrence   88
Carver, Cathedral   131
Porter, Jilting of Granny
  Weatherall   352

Poems

Ashbery, The Cathedral Is   580
Auden, Musée des Beaux Arts   888
Berryman, Dream Song   736
Bishop, Sestina   737
Bradstreet, The Author to Her
  Book   890
Baudelaire, Exotic Perfume   580
Carroll, Jabberwocky   581
Carruth, An Apology   582
Collins, Sonnet   738
Creeley, I Know a Man   583
Cummings, Anyone lived in a pretty how
  town   895
Dickinson, I Taste a Liquor   813
Dickinson, There Is No Frigate   816
Dickinson, Triumph May Be of Several
  Kinds   817
Dugan, Untitled Poem II   651
Ferlinghetti, Constantly Risking
  Absurdity   740
Francis, Catch   547
Giovanni, Poetry   905
Graves, Naked and the Nude   578
Keats, Ode on a Grecian Urn   914
Keats, Ode to a Nightingale   745
Koch, Variations on a Theme   551
Lux, The Voice You Hear   623
Magnus, Antaeus / Anchises   923
Nash, Exit, Pursued by a Bear   657
Okigbo, Bright   701
Pope, Epigram from the French   685
Simpson, American Poetry   555
Shakespeare, Not Marble   555
Simic, Fork   629
Spender, I Think Continually   592
Stevens, Emperor of Ice Cream   945
Strand, Eating Poetry   593
Webb, Poetics   753
Williams, The Dance   754
Williams, This Is Just to Say   557
Wordsworth, London, 1802   668

COMEDY AND HUMOR

Stories

Orozco, Orientation   384

Poems

Collins, Schoolsville   534
Collins, Sonnet   738
Cummings, Buffalo Bill's Defunct   731
Dickinson, I Like to See It Lap   812
Hardy, The Ruined Maid   907

Ignatow, **The Bagel** 698
Koch, **Variations on a Theme** 551
Lipschultz, **In the Beginning of the End** 588
Nash, **Exit, Pursued by a Bear** 657
Ortiz Cofer, **Latin Women Pray** 589
Pope **Epigram, Engraved on the Collar** 686
Pope, **Epigram from the French** 685
Simic, **Fork** 629
Strand, **Eating Poetry** 593
Zimmer, **The Day Zimmer Lost Religion** 596

Plays

Chekhov, **The Bear** 1323
Dooley and Holzman, **Post-its** 1331
Martin, **Beauty** 1000
Shakespeare, **Midsummer Night's Dream** 1267

CONFORMITY AND REBELLION

Stories

Atwood, **Happy Endings** 385
Chopin, **Story of an Hour** 307
Gilman, **The Yellow Wallpaper** 473
O'Connor, **First Confession** 315
Tan, **Two Kinds** 222

Poems

Berryman, **Dream Song** 736
Cummings, **next to of course god** 584
Dickinson, **Some Keep the Sabbath** 814
Dickinson, **Triumph May Be of Several Kinds** 817
Dylan, **The Times They are a-Changin'** 899
Erdrich, **Indian Boarding School** 615
Nemerov, **Life Cycle** 925
Pound, **In a Station** 627
Song, **Lost Sister** 708
Stevens, **Disillusionment** 593
Walker, **Revolutionary Petunias** 947

Plays

Hwang, **Trying to Find Chinatown** 994
Ibsen, **A Dollhouse** 1448
Wilson, **Fences** 1430

DEATH

Stories

Bierce, **An Occurrence** 88
Chopin, **Story of an Hour** 307
Faulkner, **A Rose for Emily** 96

Hurston, **Spunk** 215
Jackson, **The Lottery** 139
O'Brien, **The Things They Carried** 101
O'Connor, **A Good Man Is** 484
Ozick, **The Shawl** 246
Poe, **The Black Cat** 435
Poe, **House of Usher** 420
Porter, **Jilting of Granny Weatherall** 352
Silko, **The Man to Send Rain Clouds** 254

Poems

Anonymous, **Sir Patrick Spens** 541
Cummings, **Buffalo Bill's Defunct** 731
Dickinson, **Alabaster Chambers** 814
Dickinson, **Because I Could Not Stop** 808
Dickinson, **The Bustle in a House** 808
Dickinson, **I Heard a Fly Buzz** 811
Donne, **Death Be Not Proud** 897
Dryden, **Memory of Mr. Oldham** 739
Frost, **"Out, Out—"** 846
Hardy, **Convergence of the Twain** 652
Heaney, **Mid-Term Break** 697
Herrick, **Here a Pretty Baby** 537
Housman, **To an Athlete Dying Young** 585
Jarrell, **Ball Turret Gunner** 550
Jeffers, **The Purse-Seine** 780
Jonson, **On My First Daughter** 550
Kenyon, **Let Evening Come** 655
Komunyakaa, **Grenade** 747
Lowell, **Patterns** 921
Northrup, **wahbegan** 926
Oliver, **Showing the Birds** 660
Pinsky, **Dying** 703
Plath, **Edge** 876
Plath, **Last Words** 876
Robinson, **Richard Cory** 590
Shapiro, **Auto Wreck** 941
Thomas, **Do Not Go Gentle** 752
Webb, **Poetics** 753

Plays

Miller, **Death of a Salesman** 1182
O'Neill, **Before Breakfast** 1006
Sánchez, **Pops** 1335
Shakespeare, **Hamlet** 1080

ENDINGS AND BEGINNINGS

Stories

Bierce, **An Occurrence** 88
Coleman, **Unfinished Masterpieces** 339
Gilman, **The Yellow Wallpaper** 473
Hemingway, **Hills Like White Elephants** 311
Lawrence, **Horse Dealer's Daughter** 392
Orozco, **Orientation** 284

Poems

Bishop, **One Art** 736
Brooks, **The Mother** 544
Dickinson, **I Never Lost as Much** 812
Herrick, **Here a Pretty Baby Lies** 537
Levertov, **A Time Past** 621
Millay, **Travel** 924
Parker, **Résumé** 929
Plath, **Ariel** 867
Wright, **Autumn Begins in Martins Ferry, Ohio** 711
Rivas, **Pilgrimage** 661
Ryan, **Crib** 591
Soto, **Mexicans Begin Jogging** 942
Updike, **Perfection Wasted** 947
Webb, **Poetics** 753
Whitman, **Facing West** 667
Whitman, **Full of Life Now** 949

Plays

Bok Lee, **El Santo Americano** 1374
Ibsen, **A Dollhouse** 1488
O'Neill, **Before Breakfast** 1006

FAITH AND DOUBT

Stories

Hawthorne, **Young Goodman Brown** 342
Luke, **The Prodigal Son** 350
O'Connor, **First Confession** 315
Porter, **Jilting of Granny Weatherall** 352
Silko, **The Man to Send Rain Clouds** 254
Tan, **Two Kinds** 222

Poems

Anonymous, **Healing Prayer** 886
Arnold, **Dover Beach** 887
Brontë, **No Coward Soul Is Mine** 771
Dickinson, **"Faith" Is a Fine Invention** 809
Dickinson, **My Life Closed Twice** 813
Dickinson, **Some Keep the Sabbath** 814
Dickinson, **Certain Slant of Light** 816
Donne, **Death Be Not Proud** 897
Herbert, **The Collar** 778
Housman, **To an Athlete Dying Young** 585
Kizer, **Night Sounds** 586
Lababidi, **What Do Animals Dream?** 917
Ryan, **Crib** 591
Shakespeare, **When to the Sessions** 663
Tennyson, **Break, Break, Break** 664
Whitman, **Noiseless Patient Spider** 790

Williams, **Dimensions** 709
Zimmer, **The Day Zimmer Lost Religion** 596

Plays

Shakespeare, **Hamlet** 1080
Sophocles, **Oedipus the King** 1039
Wilson, **Fences** 1430

FIDELITY AND LOYALTY

Stories

Bierce, **An Occurrence** 88
Luke, **The Prodigal Son** 350
O'Brien, **The Things They Carried** 101
Porter, **Jilting of Granny Weatherall** 352

Poems

Akhmatova, **Willow** 883
Brontë, **Love and Friendship** 891
Cummings, **if there are any heavens** 896
Cummings, **next to of course god** 584
Hardy, **The Man He Killed** 548
Hayden, **Those Winter Sundays** 909
Jarrell, **Ball Turret Gunner** 550
Komunyakaa, **Facing It** 699
Lincoln, **My Childhood's Home** 700
García Lorca, **Sonnet of the Sweet Complaint** 651
Minty, **Conjoined** 656
Neruda, **If You Forget Me** 658
Owen, **Anthem for Doomed Youth** 607
Poe, **Annabel Lee** 930
Sassoon, **Dreamers** 937
Viorst, **A Wedding Sonnet** 789

Plays

Ibsen, **A Dollhouse** 1488
Shakespeare, **Midsummer Night's Dream** 1267

GOD, INSPIRATION, AND HUMANITY

Stories

Luke, **The Prodigal Son** 350
O'Connor, **First Confession** 315
Packer, **Brownies** 155
Porter, **Jilting of Granny Weatherall** 352

Poems

Arnold, **Dover Beach**   887
Blake, **The Tyger**   647
Brontë, **Love and Friendship**   891
Cullen, **Yet Do I Marvel**   692
Dickinson, **"Faith" Is a Fine
   Invention**   809
Dickinson, **I Dwell in Possibility**   810
Frost, **After Apple-Picking**   843
Harjo, **Eagle Poem**   549
Harjo, **Remember**   653
Herbert, **The Collar**   778
Herbert, **The Pulley**   619
Herbert, **Virtue**   743
Housman, **To an Athlete Dying
   Young**   585
Levertov, **Of Being**   587
Ortiz Cofer, **Latin Women Pray**   589
Ryan, **Crib**   591
Wordsworth, **The Solitary Reaper**   710

Play

Wilson, **Fences**   1430

HOPE AND RENEWAL

Stories

Coleman, **Unfinished Masterpieces**   339
Lawrence, **Horse Dealer's
   Daughter**   392
Welty, **A Worn Path**   288

Poems

Angelou, **Still I Rise**   885
Baraka, **Legacy**   770
Clough, **Say Not the Struggle**   773
Collins, **Days**   894
Collins, **The Names**   691
Cullen, **Yet Do I Marvel**   692
Dickinson, **Triumph May Be of Several
   Kinds**   817
Donne, **Death Be Not Proud**   897
García Lorca, **Sonnet of the Sweet
   Complaint**   651
George, **Beauty of the Trees**   905
Hughes, **125th Street**   860
Ignatow, **The Bagel**   698
Levertov, **Of Being**   587
Millay, **Travel**   924
Mueller, **Hope**   536
Neruda, **Every Day You Play**   625
Rivas, **Pilgrimage**   661
Scott, **Snow**   764

Whitman, **Full of Life Now**   949
Wilbur, **Year's End**   790
Wright, **Two Hangovers**   712

Plays

Anonymous, **Visit to the Sepulcher**   973
Bok Lee, **El Santo Americano**   1374
Shakespeare, **Midsummer Night's
   Dream**   1267

HUSBANDS AND WIVES

Stories

Arredondo, **The Shunammite**   81
Atwood, **Happy Endings**   385
Carver, **Cathedral**   131
Chopin, **Story of an Hour**   307
Gilman, **The Yellow Wallpaper**   473
Glaspell, **A Jury of Her Peers**   202
Hawthorne, **Young Goodman
   Brown**   342
Hurston, **Spunk**   215
Poe, **The Black Cat**   435
Steinbeck, **The Chrysanthemums**   358

Poems

Bradstreet, **To My . . . Husband**   890
E. Browning, **How Do I Love Thee**   892
E. Browning, **If Thou Must**   611
R. Browning, **My Last Duchess**   892
Frost, **The Silken Tent**   848
Hardy, **The Workbox**   683
Kinnell, **After Making Love**   917
Pastan, **Marks**   929
Poe, **Annabel Lee**   930
Rich, **Aunt Jennifer's Tigers**   934
Viorst, **A Wedding Sonnet**   789
Whur, **First-Rate Wife**   679

Plays

Dooley and Holzman, **Post-its**   1331
Glaspell, **Trifles**   983
Ibsen, **A Dollhouse**   1488
O'Neill, **Before Breakfast**   1006

THE INDIVIDUAL AND SOCIETY

Stories

Bambara, **The Lesson**   387
Cisneros, **Mericans**   93
Hemingway, **Hills Like White
   Elephants**   311

Oates, **Where Are You Going**   145
O'Connor, **A Good Man Is**   484
Welty, **A Worn Path**   288

Poems

Auden, **The Unknown Citizen**   687
Baraka, **Legacy**   770
Auden, **Musée des Beaux Arts**   888
Blake, **On Another's Sorrow**   688
Dickinson, **Much Madness**   813
Dickinson, **The Soul Selects**   815
Dove, **The House Slave**   546
Dylan, **The Times They Are a-Changin'**   899
Hope, **Advice**   911
Hughes, **Ballad of the Landlord**   853
Hughes, **Theme for English B**   861
Komunyakaa, **Facing It**   699
Milton, **On His Blindness**   749
Nemerov, **Life Cycle**   925
Pope, **Epigram, Engraved on the Collar**   686
Sandburg, **Chicago**   936
Spender, **I Think Continually**   592
Whitman, **Full of Life Now**   949
Williams, **The Dance**   754

Plays

Hwang, **Trying to Find Chinatown**   994
Hughes, **Mulatto**   1352
Wilson, **Fences**   1430

INNOCENCE AND EXPERIENCE

Stories

Bambara, **The Lesson**   387
Coleman, **Unfinished Masterpieces**   339
Joyce, **Araby**   242
Lipschultz, **Slow Dance of the Heart**   277
Packer, **Brownies**   155
Tan, **Two Kinds**   222

Poems

Bishop, **Sestina**   737
Blake, **The Lamb**   581
Blake, **On Another's Sorrow**   688
Blake, **The Tyger**   647
Carter, **My Father's World**   689
Cummings, **she being Brand**   693
Eliot, **Preludes**   613
Frost, **Acquainted with the Night**   848
Frost, **Desert Places**   741
Griffin, **Love Should Grow Up**   616
Housman, **When I was one-and-twenty**   913
Lincoln, **My Childhood's Home**   700
Roethke, **Dolor**   591

Plays

Hwang, **Trying to Find Chinatown**   994
Shakespeare, **Hamlet**   1080
Sophocles, **Oedipus**   1039

LIFE'S VALUES, CONDUCT, AND MEANING

Stories

Aesop, **Fox and the Grapes**   337
Chopin, **Story of an Hour**   307
Gaines, **The Sky Is Gray**   184
Hemingway, **Hills Like White Elephants**   311
Luke, **The Prodigal Son**   350
Maupassant, **The Necklace**   7
O'Connor, **First Confession**   315

Poems

Akhmatova, **Willow**   883
Auden, **Musée des Beaux Arts**   888
Brontë, **Love and Friendship**   891
Dickinson, **After Great Pain**   808
Dickinson, **I Dwell in Possibility**   810
Dove, **Daystar**   897
Espada, **Latin Night at the Pawnshop**   904
Frost, **Birches**   844
Frost, **Fire and Ice**   847
Frost, **Mending Wall**   842
Frost, **The Road Not Taken**   845
Frost, **Stopping by Woods**   548
Halpern, **Snapshot of Hué**   906
Hardy, **The Man He Killed**   648
Jeffers, **The Answer**   913
Jeffers, **Hurt Hawks**   620
Keats, **Bright Star**   644
Levertov, **A Time Past**   621
Oliver, **Wild Geese**   786
Shakespeare, **When in Disgrace**   941
Shelley, **Ozymandias**   751
Spender, **I Think Continually**   592
Swenson, **Question**   945
Trethewey, **White Lies**   594
Updike, **Perfection Wasted**   947
Whitman, **Facing West**   667
Williams, **Dimensions**   709

Plays

Ibsen, **A Dollhouse**   1488
Miller, **Death of a Salesman**   1182
Sánchez, **Pops**   1335
Shakespeare, **Hamlet**   1080

LOVE AND COURTSHIP

Stories

Arredondo, **The Shunammite** 81
Atwood, **Happy Endings** 385
Faulkner, **A Rose for Emily** 96
Joyce, **Araby** 242
Kincaid, **Girl** 483
Lawrence, **Horse Dealer's
  Daughter** 392

Poems

Atwood, **You fit into me** 888
Baudelaire, **Exotic Perfume** 580
E. Browning, **How Do I Love Thee** 892
Burns, **A Red, Red Rose** 648
Cummings, **she being Brand** 693
Frost, **The Silken Tent** 848
Housman, **When I was one-and-twenty** 913
Johnson, **To Celia** 714
García Lorca, **Sonnet of the Sweet
  Complaint** 651
Larkin, **Talking in Bed** 918
Lowell, **The Taxi** 622
Marvell, **To His Coy Mistress** 784
Neruda, **Every Day You Play** 625
Neruda, **If You Forget Me** 658
O'Shaughnessy, **A Love Symphony** 702
Plath, **Song for a Summer's Day** 868
Poe, **Annabel Lee** 930
Rich, **Living in Sin** 934
Queen Elizabeth I, **Departure** 665
Rukeyser, **Looking at Each Other** 662
Sáenz, **To the Desert** 628
Shakespeare, **Let Me Not** 728
Shakespeare, **Shall I Compare Thee** 663
Wakoski, **Inside Out** 666
Wyatt, **I Find No Peace** 669

Plays

Chekhov, **The Bear** 1323
Shakespeare, **Midsummer Night's
  Dream** 1267

MEN

Stories

Bierce, **An Occurrence** 88
Chopin, **Story of an Hour** 307
Ellison, **Battle Royal** 268
Hemingway, **Hills Like White
  Elephants** 311
Hurston, **Spunk** 215

Lawrence, **Horse Dealer's
  Daughter** 392
Luke, **The Prodigal Son** 350
Steinbeck, **The Chrysanthemums** 358

Poems

Anonymous, **Sir Patrick Spens** 541
Auden, **The Unknown Citizen** 687
Cummings, **Buffalo Bill's Defunct** 731
Frost, **Birches** 843
Holmes, **Cinquains for Rocky** 911
Hughes, **Bad Man** 853
Jarrell, **Ball Turret Gunner** 550
Magnus, **Antaeus / Anchises** 923
Robinson, **Richard Cory** 590
Spender, **I Think Continually** 592

Plays

Chekhov, **The Bear** 1323
Glaspell, **Trifles** 983
Ibsen, **A Dollhouse** 1488
Sánchez, **Pops** 1335
Wilson, **Fences** 1430

NATURE AND HUMANITY

Stories

Silko, **The Man to Send Rain
  Clouds** 254
Steinbeck, **The Chrysanthemums** 358
Welty, **A Worn Path** 288

Poems

Akhmatova, **Willow** 883
Bishop, **The Fish** 608
Clifton, **Cutting Greens** 772
Cummings, **Anyone lived in a pretty how
  town** 895
Dickinson, **A Narrow Fellow in the
  Grass** 807
Frost, **After Apple-Picking** 843
Frost, **In White** 842
Hass, **Spring Rain** 908
H. D., **Heat** 618
Herrick, **Corinna's Going
  A-Maying** 909
Hopkins, **Spring** 620
Jeffers, **Hurt Hawks** 620
Keats, **To Autumn** 654
Momaday, **The Bear** 924
Moore, **The Fish** 624
Oliver, **Wild Geese** 786

Plath, **Song for a Summer's Day**   868
Stafford, **Traveling**   944
Tennyson, **The Eagle**   723
Whitman, **Noiseless Patient Spider**   790
Whitman, **When I Heard the Learn'd Astronomer**   730
Wordsworth, **Daffodils**   595
Wordsworth, **Solitary Reaper**   710

Play

Bok Lee, *El Santo Americano*   1374

PARENTS AND CHILDREN

Stories

Gaines, **The Sky Is Gray**   184
Luke, **The Prodigal Son**   350
Ozick, **The Shawl**   246
Porter, **Jilting of Granny Weatherall**   352
Tan, **Two Kinds**   222

Poems

Bishop, **Sestina**   737
Brooks, **The Mother**   554
Carter, **I Wanted to Share**   689
Cummings, **if there are any heavens**   896
Dove, **Daystar**   897
Dylan, **The Times They Are a-Changin'**   899
Espaillat, **Bilingual/Bilingüe**   904
Hayden, **Those Winter Sundays**   909
Hughes, **Dream Boogie**   855
Jonson, **On My First Daughter**   550
Lorde, **Now That I Am Forever with Child**   920
Nye, **Where Children Live**   554
Olds, **The Moment the Two Worlds Meet**   927
Olds, **The Planned Child**   702
Pastan, **Marks**   929
Plath, **Daddy**   870
Roethke, **My Papa's Waltz**   706
Serotte, **My Mother's Face**   938

Plays

Miller, **Death of a Salesman**   1182
Sánchez, **Pops**   1335
Wilson, **Fences**   1430

PAST AND PRESENT

Stories

Coleman, **Unfinished Masterpieces**   339
Faulkner, **A Rose for Emily**   96

Jackson, **The Lottery**   139
Lipschultz, **Slow Dance of the Heart**   277
Porter, **Jilting of Granny Weatherall**   352

Poems

Espada, **Bully**   694
Frost, **Nothing Gold Can Stay**   847
Housman, **When I was one-and-twenty**   913
Keats, **Ode on a Grecian Urn**   914
Levertov, **A Time Past**   621
Parker, **Afternoon**   928
Shakespeare, **Shall I Compare Thee**   663
Shakespeare, **When to the Sessions**   663
Whitman, **Full of Life Now**   949

Plays

Hughes, **Mulatto**   1352
Sánchez, **Pops**   1335
Sophocles, **Oedipus the King**   1039

RACE, ETHNICITY, AND NATIONALITY

Stories

Bambara, **The Lesson**   387
Cisneros, **Mericans**   93
Ellison, **Battle Royal**   268
Gaines, **The Sky Is Gray**   184
Kincaid, **Girl**   483
Ozick, **The Shawl**   246
Packer, **Brownies**   155
Paredes, **The Hammon and the Beans**   403

Poems

Alexie, **On the Amtrak**   883
Baraka, **Legacy**   770
Chin, **Autumn Leaves**   772
Dove, **The House Slave**   546
Erdrich, **Indian Boarding School**   615
Espada, **Latin Night at the Pawnshop**   904
Espaillat, **Bilingual/Bilingüe**   904
Evans, **I Am a Black Woman**   695
Harper, **She's Free!**   908
Hughes, **Ballad of the Landlord**   853
Hughes, **Dream Boogie**   855
Hughes, **Harlem**   856
Hughes, **I, Too**   856
Hughes, **125th Street**   860
Hughes, **The Negro Speaks**   859

Hughes, **Theme for English B** 861
McKay, **In Bondage** 748
Randall, **Ballad of Birmingham** 749
Rivas, **Pilgrimage** 661
Salinas, **In a Farmhouse** 936
Soto, **Mexicans Begin Jogging** 941
Toomer, **Reapers** 753
Trethewey, **White Lies** 594

Plays

Hughes, **Mulatto** 1352
Hwang, **Trying to Find
   Chinatown** 994
Sánchez, **Pops** 1335
Wilson, **Fences** 1430

REALITY AND UNREALITY

Stories

Atwood, **Happy Endings** 385
Bierce, **An Occurrence** 88
Carver, **Cathedral** 131
Gilman, **The Yellow Wallpaper** 473
Hawthorne, **Young Goodman
   Brown** 342
Jackson, **The Lottery** 139
Maupassant, **The Necklace** 7
Oates, **Where Are You Going** 145
Orozco, **Orientation** 284
Poe, **Masque of the Red Death** 431
Poe, **The Tell-Tale Heart** 440

Poems

Collins, **Schoolsville** 534
Cummings, **next to of course god** 584
Dickinson, **I Felt a Funeral** 811
Hardy, **Convergence of the Twain** 652
Ignatow, **The Bagel** 698
Lababidi, **What Do Animals
   Dream?** 917
Okigbo, **Bright** 701
Parker, **Résumé** 929
Plath, **Mirror** 877
Poe, **Annabel Lee** 930
Smith, **Not Waving** 942
Stevens, **Disillusionment** 593
Strand, **Eating Poetry** 593
Van Duyn, **Earth Tremors** 666

Plays

Martin, **Beauty** 1000
Miller, **Death of a Salesman** 1182

RECONCILIATION AND UNDER-STANDING

Stories

Gaines, **The Sky Is Gray** 184
Luke, **The Prodigal Son** 350
Maupassant, **The Necklace** 7
Paredes, **The Hammon and the Beans** 403
Porter, **Jilting of Granny Weatherall** 352
Tan, **Two Kinds** 222

Poems

Blake, **On Another's Sorrow** 688
Cummings, **if there are any heavens** 896
Dickinson, **I Dwell in Possibility** 810
Larkin, **Talking in Bed** 918
Henley, **When You Are Old** 697
Kenyon, **Let Evening Come** 655
Plath, **Edge** 872
Tate, **Dream On** 629
Whitman, **Reconciliation** 754
Williams, **This Is Just to Say** 557
Wilbur, **Love Calls Us** 949

Plays

Sophocles, **Oedipus the King** 1039
Williams, **The Glass Menagerie** 1379

SALVATION AND DAMNATION

Stories

Hawthorne, **Young Goodman Brown** 342
Hurston, **Spunk** 215
Luke, **The Prodigal Son** 350
O'Connor, **A Good Man Is** 484
O'Connor, **First Confession** 315
Parédes, **The Hammon and the
   Beans** 403
Poe, **Masque of the Red Death** 431
Silko, **The Man to Send Rain Clouds** 254

Poems

Brontë, **No Coward Soul Is Mine** 771
Dickinson, **I Heard a Fly Buzz** 811
Dickinson, **Some Keep the Sabbath** 814
Dickinson, **Triumph May Be of Several
   Kinds** 817
Donne, **Batter My Heart** 585
Donne, **Death Be Not Proud** 897
Frost, **Fire and Ice** 847
Frost, **Desert Places** 848
Masefield, **Cargoes** 606

Plath, **Last Words** 876
Ryan, **Crib** 591
Tate, **Dream On** 629
Webb, **Poetics** 753

Play

Dooley and Holzman, **Post-its** 1331

WAR AND VIOLENCE

Stories

Bierce, **An Occurrence** 88
O'Brien, **The Things They Carried** 101
Ozick, **The Shawl** 246

Poems

Crane, **Do Not Weep, Maiden** 895
Gay, **Let Us Take the Road** 645
Georgakas, **Hiroshima Crewman** 777
Hardy, **Breaking of Nations** 778
Hardy, **Channel Firing** 617
Hardy, **The Man He Killed** 518
Jarrell, **Ball Turret Gunner** 550
Komunyakaa, **Grenade** 747
Northrup, **Ogichidag** 553
Northrup, **wahbegan** 926
Owen, **Doomed Youth** 607
Owen, **Dulce et Decorum Est** 680
Quasimodo, **Auschwitz** 704
Randall, **Ballad of Birmingham** 749
Sassoon, **Dreamers** 937
Terranova, **Rush Hour** 556
Thomas, **Refusal to Mourn** 945
Whitman, **Beat! Beat! Drums!** 948
Whitman, **Reconciliation** 754
Yeats, **The Second Coming** 792

Play

Hughes, **Mulatto** 1352

WOMEN

Stories

Chopin, **Story of an Hour** 307
Hemingway, **Hills Like White
    Elephants** 311
Lipschultz, **Slow Dance of the
    Heart** 277
Maupassant, **The Necklace** 7
Porter, **Jilting of Granny Weatherall** 352
Steinbeck, **The Chrysanthemums** 358
Walker, **Everyday Use** 494

Poems

Bogan, **Women** 888
R. Browning, **My Last Duchess** 892
Clifton, **homage to my hips** 690
Herrick, **Corinna's Going A-Maying** 909
Hope, **Advice to Young Ladies** 911
Lorde, **Now That I Am Forever with
    Child** 920
Lowell, **Patterns** 921
Minty, **Conjoined** 656
Piercy, **Secretary Chant** 929
Piercy, **A Work of Artifice** 660
Plath, **Lady Lazarus** 873
Plath, **Metaphors** 876
Pound, **A Girl** 933
Queen Elizabeth I, **Departure** 665
Sexton, **Cinderella** 938
Song, **Lost Sister** 708
Terranova, **Rush Hour** 556
Whur, **First-Rate Wife** 679

Plays

Ibsen, **A Dollhouse** 1488
Glaspell, **Trifles** 983
Martin, **Beauty** 1000

WOMEN AND MEN

Stories

Arredondo, **The Shunammite** 81
Atwood, **Happy Endings** 385
Chopin, **Story of an Hour** 307
Gilman, **The Yellow Wallpaper** 473
Hemingway, **Hills Like White
    Elephants** 311
Hurston, **Spunk** 215
Lawrence, **Horse Dealer's
    Daughter** 392
Oates, **Where Are You Going** 145
Steinbeck, **The Chrysanthemums** 358

Poems

Atwood, **You fit into me** 888
E. Browning, **How Do I Love** 892
R. Browning, **My Last Duchess** 892
Dickinson, **I Cannot Live with You** 809
Dickinson, **Wild Nights** 817
Donne, **The Canonization** 774
Donne, **Valediction** 649
Frost, **The Silken Tent** 848
Griffin, **Love Should Grow** 616
Henley, **When You Are Old** 697
Justice, **Order in the Streets** 914
Keats, **La Belle Dame** 781

Minty, **Conjoined** 656
Neruda, **If You Forget Me** 658
Pastan, **Marks** 929
Plath, **Song for a Summer's Day** 878
Rich, **Aunt Jennifer's Tigers** 934
Rich, **Living in Sin** 934
Sexton, **Cinderella** 938
Swenson, **Women** 945
Terranova, **Rush Hour** 556
Viorst, **A Wedding Sonnet** 789
Whur, **First-Rate Wife** 679
Yeats, **When You Are Old** 713

Plays

Shakespeare, **Midsummer Night's Dream** 1267
Wilson, **Fences** 1430

YOUTH AND AGE

Stories

Coleman, **Unfinished Masterpieces** 339
Ellison, **Battle Royal** 268
Faulkner, **Barn Burning** 462
Gaines, **The Sky Is Gray** 184
Joyce, **Araby** 242

Kincaid, **Girl** 483
O'Connor, **First Confession** 315
Packer, **Brownies** 155
Paredes, **The Hammon and the Beans** 403
Porter, **Jilting of Granny Weatherall** 352

Poems

Bishop, **Sestina** 737
Brooks, **The Mother** 544
Collins, **Schoolsville** 534
Frost, **Birches** 844
Frost, **Nothing Gold Can Stay** 847
Henley, **When You Are Old** 697
Herrick, **Corinna's Going A-Maying** 909
Heyen, **Mantle** 732
Housman, **When I was one-and-twenty** 813
Muske-Dukes, **Real Estate** 785
Parker, **Afternoon** 928
Plath, **Mirror** 877
Plath, **Song for a Summer's Day** 878
Whitman, **Full of Life** 949
Yeats, **When You Are Old** 713

Plays

Miller, **Death of a Salesman** 1182
Sánchez, **Pops** 1335

Preface

In an age when many people question whether courses in the humanities, especially literature courses, are relevant or practical, we should be reminded of William Carlos Williams's argument for the importance of poetry:

> It is difficult
> to get the news from poems
> yet men die every day
> for lack
> of what is found
> there.

The statement is applicable to the more than 400 separate works contained in this anthology—works that present ideas that matter in ways that should engage, challenge, and move readers. Equally important, students will encounter these works in a course that requires them not only to read the works carefully and critically, but also to write reasoned, documented academic arguments and analyses. We believe that writing is essential in the study of literature, or of any other discipline. It is the finished product of reading and thinking, and it is a skill that will serve students in virtually all walks of twenty-first century life. *Literature: An Introduction to Reading and Writing*, Compact Sixth Edition, is dedicated to this idea.

New to This Edition

Revising a successful textbook requires careful evaluation of what has worked in past classrooms, what might be improved upon, and what new things might make the experience even more valuable for teachers and students. Here is an overview of the improvements and enhancements we have made to this new edition:

- **NEW**—In consultation with our colleagues at colleges across the country, we have actively sought to include both well-known works of lasting artistic and historical significance as well as more contemporary works that allow us to examine emerging voices, cultures, communities, and situations that we might encounter in going about our everyday lives. We have carefully refreshed our rich existing collection of more than 400 literary selections and are very proud of our choices:

- 48 stories (9 new), allowing for masters of the form such as Ernest Hemingway and Raymond Carver to be taught alongside fresh and unique voices such as those of Leslie Marmon Silko and Jamaica Kincaid;
- 346 poems (73 new), juxtaposing canonical figures—Keats, Milton, and Whitman—with important contemporary figures, including Rita Dove, Sharon Olds, Gary Soto, and singer-songwriter Bob Dylan;
- 17 plays (4 new), where seminal tragedies such as Shakespeare's *Hamlet* and Arthur Miller's *Death of a Salesman* provide a provocative background from which to consider experimental modern short plays such as those by David Henry Hwang and Edward Bok Lee.

- **NEW**—In our teaching experience, we have found that one of the hardest things for student writers to master is using sources correctly and strategically, allowing them to write papers that conform to the conventions of the field and to argue their positions convincingly and authoritatively. We have added a new boxed feature, *Using Sources Effectively*, in selected chapters throughout the text to provide in-depth illustration and analysis of how critical writers make purposeful choices in quoting, paraphrasing, and summarizing their sources to make their essays stronger and more compelling.
- **NEW**—Many students come to literature with no relevant background for understanding specific works that may date from the seventeenth century or describe an unfamiliar culture. It is our position that everyone brings valuable personal experience and insight to any text he or she might encounter and that "reader response" theory provides students a valuable and confidence-building way into any work upon first reading. To that end, many of the question sets following primary works throughout the text get students started by asking them to consider the work in light of their own history, culture, or personal feelings. We think this type of question demystifies the notion of literary criticism and motivates students to engage personally with each work.
- **NEW**—In our digital age, many students prefer to get their reading and course materials digitally for the sake of convenience or economy, and we are proud to make this book available as an easily accessed, reasonably priced e-text, available within MyLiteratureLab.

NEW—Technology/Multimedia for Literature

MyLiteratureLab (www.myliteraturelab.com)

To engage students in the study of literature and to help professors address their teaching challenges, we developed MyLiteratureLab. This online learning program offers rich multimedia resources as part of a personalized learning experience that aims to help students think critically and improve their literary research and writing skills.

MyLiteratureLab provides a wealth of resources for literary studies that are designed to engage students:

- **Lessons** (formerly called "Longman Lectures") help students interpret and write about key works.

- **Interactive Readings** provide students with annotated texts and questions to guide analysis.

- **Writers on Writing** uses videos to give students insight into the creative process of well-known poets and fiction writers and provides inspiration for aspiring students.

- **Feature-length films** help students interpret the works of Shakespeare and Sophocles.

MyLiteratureLab helps students to improve their results through a personalized learning experience with diagnostic tests, adaptive learning, and individualized feedback. If desired, instructors can administer writing assignments using rubrics of their choice, customizing the preloaded rubrics provided or creating their own.

Students stay focused in the course by taking a macro-level pre-assessment that generates a Learning Path—a personalized module that enables students to better understand fiction, poetry, drama, and writing about literature. Each module contains a pre-test and post-test, along with the following resources:

- **Overview:** a text-based introduction to the topic.

- **Animation:** a video-based lesson that expands on the overview.

- **Recall Quiz:** a multiple-choice quiz that tests students on their comprehension of the lesson taught in the Overview and Animation.

- **Application Quizzes:** a multiple-choice quiz that challenges students to apply the lesson taught in the Overview and Animation to a literary text.

- **Writing Prompts:** a series of prompts that challenge students to apply the type of analysis being explored to a reading assigned by the instructor.

All work is tracked in a powerful grade book, which also enables instructors to create outcomes-based reports for administrators. Our hope is that these features will offer support for student learning while also saving instructors' time by—relieving some of the burden of "data crunching" and freeing up time for more meaningful student-centered activities.

Text Features

- Part I: The Process of Reading, Responding to, and Writing About Literature includes Guy de Maupassant's much-beloved classic short story, "The Necklace," which serves as a focal point to illustrate techniques of active reading and writing.

- Paragraph-length writing assignments receive particular attention throughout the entire text to recognize that much of the writing students do in courses is not formal, extended essays.

- Chapter 26: Three Types of Writing About Literature focuses on comparison-contrast essays, reader-response essays, and literary arguments, providing hands-on instruction for employing these three common strategies for writing about literature.

- Writing Topic prompts appear throughout the book, divided into four categories—Paragraph-length Assignments, Essay-length Assignments, Library Assignments, and Creative Writing Assignments—helping instructors see at a glance the suggested assignments.
- Thorough yet accessible guidelines show students how to perform academic research and use proper MLA documentation style for print, digital, and other sources consulted.

The Integration of Writing and Reading

Because writing reinforces reading so strongly, the sixth edition presents more than thirty illustrative writing examples embodying the strategies and methods described in the various chapters and appendixes. These essays and paragraphs are intended as specimens to illustrate what students might do with a particular topic. The goal of these essays is to show that the creation of thought does not take place until writers are able to fuse their reading responses with particular topics and issues (e.g., the symbolism in a poem, the theme in a story, the use of stage directions in a play).

The illustrative essays are comparatively short and not as long as some instructors might assign, on the grounds that when responding to longer assignments about literature, many students inflate their papers with needless summary. It is clear that without a guiding, argumentative point, we do not have thought, and that without thought we cannot have a good essay. A simple summary of a work does not qualify as good writing.

In the major chapters, following each of the illustrative essays there are analytical discussions (titled "Commentary on the Essay") that point out how the topics have served as the basis of the writer's thought. Graphically, the format of underlining thesis and topic sentences in the illustrative essays is a way of emphasizing the connections, and the format is thus a complementary way of fulfilling an essential aim of the book.

A logical extension (and a major hope) of this combined approach is that the techniques students acquire in studying literature as both a reading and a writing undertaking will help them in every course they may ever take and in whatever professions or occupations they may follow. Students will always read—if not the authors contained here, then other authors, and certainly newspapers, letters, legal documents, memoranda, directions, instructions, magazine articles, technical and nontechnical reports, business proposals, Internet communications, and much more. Although as students advance into their working years they may never again need to write about topics such as setting, imagery, or symbolism, they will certainly always find a future need to write.

The sixth edition includes a total of 411 separate works. Each work is suitable for discussion either alone or in conjunction with other works. For purposes of analytical comparison, we include here the works in two genres by a number of writers—specifically Atwood, Glaspell, Hughes, Poe, Shakespeare, and Updike. In addition, there are two plays by Shakespeare—*Hamlet* and *A Midsummer Night's Dream*—and there are two or more poems by a number of poets. For more intensive study, we offer Chapter 9, "A Casebook of Four Stories by Edgar Allan Poe"; Chapter 18, "Four Major American Poets, " containing a rich selection of poems by Emily Dickinson, Robert Frost, Langston Hughes, and Sylvia Plath; and Chapter 24, "Henrik Ibsen and the Realistic Problem Play: *A Dollhouse*." Each of these chapters supplements the primary works with biographical and critical materials.

Reading and Writing Now and in the Future

The more effectively students write about literature when taking their literature courses, the better they will be able to write later on—no matter what the topic. It is axiomatic that the power to analyze problems and make convincing written and oral presentations is a major characteristic of leadership and success in all fields. To acquire the skills of disciplined reading and strong writing is therefore the best possible preparation that students can make for the future, whatever it may hold.

While we stress the value of the sixth edition as a teaching tool, we also emphasize that literature is to be enjoyed and loved. Sometimes we neglect the truth that study and delight are complementary and that intellectual stimulation and emotional enjoyment develop not only from the immediate responses of pleasure, involvement, and sympathy but also from the understanding, contemplation, and confidence generated by knowledge and developing skill. We therefore hope that the selections in the compact sixth edition of *Literature: An Introduction to Reading and Writing* will teach students about humanity; about their own perceptions, feelings, and lives; and about the timeless patterns of human existence. We hope they will take delight in such discoveries and become engaged as they make them. We see the book as a stepping-stone to lifelong understanding, future achievement, and never-ending joy in great literature.

Instructor's Manual

This comprehensive Instructor's Manual helps teachers prepare to teach any of the works contained in the text and also offers numerous suggestions for assignments and pedagogically useful comparisons of individual works with other works. Each of the chapters in the manual begins with introductory remarks and interpretive comments about the works (stories, poems, plays) within the chapters of the book. These are followed by detailed suggestions for discussing every study question accompanying the works. The manual also contains detailed discussions of videos and DVD performances of a number of stories in the book and references to available audio clips of poetry selections. Additional Writing Assignments and Workshops with sample guidelines for student editors provide even more guidance for students learning to write about literature effectively.

Acknowledgments

As this book goes into its sixth edition, we wish to acknowledge the many people who at various times have offered helpful advice, information, and suggestions. They are Professors Belinda Adams, Chris Allen, Eileen Allman, Marty Ambrose, Rebecca Andrews, David Bady, Allison Boldt, Andrew Brilliant, Kristi Brock, Rex Butt, Pamela A. Clark, Stanley Coberly, Peggy Cole, Robert E. Cummings, Betty

L. Dixon, Elizabeth Keats Flores, Matthew Gainous, Kristin Gardner, Alice Griffin, Loren C. Gruber, Catherine Hadley, Robert Halli, Leslie Healey, Catherine Heath, Rebecca Heintz, Karen Holt, Claudia Johnson, Joselle Laguerre, Matthew Marino, Edward Martin, Evan Matthews, Victoria McClure, Pearl McHaney, Daniel McNamarra, Ruth Milberg-Kaye, Nancy K. Miller, JoAnna Stephens Mink, Ervin Nieves, Dean Glen T. Nygreen, Michael Paull, Norman Prinsky, Jonathan Purkiss, Bonnie Ronson, Dan Rubey, Margaret Ellen Sherwood, Mary Simpson, Beverly J. Slaughter, Jean Sorensen, Terry Tiernan, Donald Tuthill, Mardi Valgemae, Keith Walters, Chloe Warner, Carol Warren, Scott Westrem, Matthew Winston, and Ruth Zerner. We also thank Christel Bell, Linda Bridgers, Gary Brown, Catherine Davis, Diane Foster, Jim Freund, Edward Hoeppner, Anna F. Jacobs, Brooke Mitchell, April Roberts, David Roberts, Eleanor Tubbs, Braden Welborn, and Eve Zarin. We give special recognition and thanks to Ann Marie Radaskiewicz. The skilled assistance of Jonathan Roberts has been essential and invaluable at every stage of all the editions.

A number of other people have provided sterling guidance for the preparation of the sixth edition. They are Professors Kenet Adamson, Southwestern Community College; Deborah Albritton, Jefferson Davis Community College; Robert T. Canipe, Catawba Valley Community College; Edward Coursey, Hillsborough Community College; Howard Cox, Angelina College; Loretta Crosson, Georgia Piedmont Technical College; Gary Grassinger, Community College of Allegheny County; Kay Heck, Walters State Community College; Christina Heckman, Augusta State University; Fredrick Holloman, Georgia Piedmont Technical College; Kristel Minnock, Ventura College; Lesley J. Pullen, El Paso Community College; Todd Ramsey, Bevill State Community College; Paula Rash, Caldwell Community College and Technical Institute; Douglas Robillard, University of Arkansas Pine Bluff; Kevin Lynn Sanders, University of Arkansas Pine Bluff; Barbara Urban, Central Piedmont Community College; Heather Weiss, Technical College of the Lowcountry; Matt Williams, Caldwell Community College & Technical Institute; David A. Willis, Jefferson Davis Community College; Robert Womack, Catawba Valley Community College.

We wish especially to thank the Pearson English editorial staff for helping in the preparation of this revision. It has been a team effort throughout the process, and we hope all are pleased with the result.

—EDGAR V. ROBERTS AND ROBERT ZWEIG

PART I

The Process of Reading, Responding to, and Writing About Literature

The chapters that follow introduce a number of analytical approaches important in the study of literature, along with guidance for writing informative and well-focused essays based on these approaches. The chapters will help you fulfill two goals of composition and English courses: (1) to write good essays and (2) to understand and assimilate great works of literature.

The premise of this book is that no educational process is complete until you can apply what you study. That is, you have not learned something—really *learned* it—*until you talk or write about it*. This does not mean that you retell a story, state an undeveloped opinion, or describe an author's life, but rather that you deal directly with intellectual and artistic issues about individual works. The need to write requires you to strengthen your understanding and knowledge through the recognition of where your original study might have fallen short. Thus, it is easy for you to read the chapter on point of view (Chapter 2), and it is also easy to read Shirley Jackson's story "The Lottery." Your grasp of point of view as a concept will not be complete, however, nor will your appreciation of the technical artistry of this story be complete, until you have prepared yourself to write about the technique. As you do so, you will need to reread parts of the work, study your notes, and apply your knowledge to the problem at hand; you must check facts, grasp relationships, develop insights, and try to express yourself with as much exactness and certainty as possible.

Primarily, then, this book aims to help you improve your writing skills through the use of literature as subject matter. After you have finished a number of essays derived from the chapters ahead, you will be able to approach just about any literary work with the confidence that you can understand it and write about it.

What Is Literature, and Why Do We Study It?

AFTER STUDYING THIS MATERIAL, YOU SHOULD BE ABLE TO DO THE FOLLOWING:
- Identify the different genres of literature
- Respond actively and knowledgeably to literary works
- Understand the major stages of thinking and writing about literature
- Use quotations and references effectively in essays about literature

We use the word **literature,** in a broad sense, to mean compositions that tell stories, dramatize situations, express emotions, and analyze and advocate ideas. Before the invention of writing thousands of years ago, literary works were necessarily spoken or sung, and they were retained only as long as living people continued to repeat them. In some societies, the oral tradition of literature still exists, with many poems and stories designed exclusively for spoken delivery. Even in our modern age of writing, printing, and electronic communication, much literature is still heard aloud rather than read silently. Parents delight their children with stories and poems read aloud; poets and storywriters read their works directly before live audiences; plays and scripts are interpreted on stages and before movie and television cameras for the benefit of a vast public.

No matter how we assimilate literature, we gain much from it. In truth, readers often cannot explain why they enjoy reading, for goals and ideals are not easily articulated. There are, however, areas of general agreement about the value of systematic and extensive reading.

Literature helps us grow, both personally and intellectually. It opens doors for us. It stretches our minds. It develops our imagination, increases our understanding, and enlarges our power of sympathy. It helps us see beauty in the world around us. It links us with the cultural, philosophical, and religious world of which we are a part. It enables us to recognize human dreams and struggles in different places and times. It helps us develop mature sensibility and compassion for all living beings. It nurtures our ability to appreciate the beauty of order and arrangement—gifts that are also bestowed by a well-structured song, a beautifully painted canvas, or a skillfully chiseled statue. It enables us to see worthiness in the aims of all people. It exercises our emotions through interest, concern, sympathy, tension, excitement, regret, fear, laughter, and hope. It encourages us to assist creative and talented people who need recognition and support. Through our cumulative experience in reading, literature shapes our goals and values by clarifying our own identities—both positively, through acceptance of the admirable in human beings, and negatively, through rejection of the sinister. It enables us to develop perspectives on events occurring locally and globally, and thereby it gives us understanding and control. It is one of the shaping influences of life. It makes us human.

Types of Literature: The Genres

Literature may be classified into four categories or *genres:* (1) prose fiction, (2) poetry, (3) drama, and (4) nonfiction prose. Usually the first three are classified as **imaginative literature.**

The genres of imaginative literature have much in common, but they also have distinguishing characteristics. **Prose fiction,** or **narrative fiction,** includes **myths, parables, romances, novels,** and **short stories.** Originally, *fiction* meant anything made up, crafted, or shaped, but today the word refers to prose stories based in the imaginations of authors. The essence of fiction is **narration,** the relating or recounting of a sequence of events or actions. Fictional works usually focus on one or a few major characters who change and grow (in their ability to make decisions, their awareness or insight, their intellect, their attitude toward others, their sensitivity, and their moral capacity) as a result of how they deal with other characters and how they attempt to solve their problems. Although fiction, like all imaginative literature, can introduce true historical details, it is not real history, for its main purpose is to interest, stimulate, instruct, and divert, not to create a precise historical record.

If prose is expansive, **poetry** tends toward brevity. It offers us high points of emotion, reflection, thought, and feeling in what the English poet Wordsworth called "narrow room[s]." Yet in this context, it expresses the most powerful and deeply felt experiences of human beings, often awakening deep responses of welcome recognition: "Yes, I know what that's like. I would feel the same way. That's exactly right." Poems make us think, make us reflect, and generally instruct us. They can also stimulate us, surprise us, make us laugh or cry, inspire us, exalt us. Many poems become our lifelong friends, and we visit them again and again for insight, understanding, laughter, or the quiet reflection of joy or sorrow.

Poetry's power lies not only in its words and thoughts, but also in its music, using rhyme and a variety of rhythms to intensify its emotional impact. Although poems themselves vary widely in length, individual lines are often short because poets distill the greatest meaning and imaginative power from their words through rhetorical devices such as **imagery** and **metaphor.** Though poetry often requires many formal and metrical restrictions, it is paradoxically the very restrictiveness of poetry that provides poets with great freedom. Traditionally important poetic forms include the fourteen-line **sonnet,** as well as **ballads, blank verse, couplets, elegies, epigrams, hymns, limericks, odes, quatrains, songs** or **lyrics, tercets** or **triplets, villanelles,** and the increasingly popular **haiku.** Many songs or lyrics have been set to music, and some were written expressly for that purpose. Some poems are long and discursive, like many poems by the American poet Walt Whitman. **Epic poems,** such as those by Homer and Milton, contain thousands of lines. Since the time of Whitman, many poets have abandoned rhymes and regular rhythms in favor of **free verse,** a far-ranging type of poetry growing out of content and the natural rhythms of spoken language.

Drama is literature designed for stage or film presentation by people—**actors**—for the benefit and delight of other people—an **audience.** The essence of drama is the development of **character** and **situation** through **speech** and **action.** Like fiction, drama may focus on a single character or a small number of characters, and it enacts fictional (and sometimes historical) events as if they were happening right before our eyes. The audience therefore is a direct witness to the ways in which characters are influenced and changed by events and by other characters. Although most modern plays use prose **dialogue** (the conversation of two or more characters), on the principle that the language of drama should resemble the language of ordinary people as much as possible, many plays from the past, such as those of ancient Greece and Renaissance England, are in poetic form.

Nonfiction prose consists of news reports, feature articles, essays, editorials, textbooks, historical and biographical works, and the like, all of which describe or interpret facts and present judgments and opinions. The goal of nonfiction prose is to present truths and conclusions about the factual world. Imaginative literature, although also grounded in facts, is less concerned with the factual record than with the revelation of truths about life and human nature. Recently another genre has been emphasized within the category of nonfiction prose. This is **creative non-fiction,** a type of literature that is technically nonfiction, such as essays, articles, diaries, and journals, but that nevertheless introduces carefully structured form, vivid examples, relevant quotations, and highly creative and imaginative insights.

Reading Literature and Responding to It Actively

Sometimes we find it difficult, after we have finished reading a work, to express thoughts about it and to answer pointed questions about it. But more active and thoughtful reading gives us the understanding to develop well-considered answers. Obviously, we need to follow the work and to understand its details, but just as importantly, we need to respond to the words, get at the ideas, and understand the implications of what is happening. We rely on our own fund of knowledge and experience to verify the accuracy and truth of situations and incidents, and we try to articulate our own emotional responses to the characters and their problems.

Proceeding through all the chapters of this text, you will acquire new awareness of how writers employ literary elements and strategies (point of view, symbolism, etc.) to try to create certain effects on readers. However, even before readers bring the knowledge of such strategies to bear on a work, they approach the work with certain personal expectations, interests, and beliefs based on life experiences, prior reading, and an initial notion of what the work may be about. These are valuable and valid tools to bring to any literary work for an initial reading. Age, family background, political beliefs, nationality, cultural background, and other experiences will all influence the way readers approach a text. This means that they will always be in certain ways "entitled" to their own interpretation of any work. Readers have a particular view of the world, and they impose it on what they may read. After having encountered a work, their worldview might then change—a reason why literature has such great value to people. The "meaning" of a work may well change for a given reader as that reader gains more experience. Someone who has never been in love will respond to and interpret a romantic story much differently from a reader—perhaps the same person in later years—who reads the story after having his or her heart broken in a relationship. The reader's response to the work can notably change or evolve over time, even though the words on the page will remain the same.

To acknowledge the value of responsive reading, we have included occasional questions throughout this text about specific selections that ask you to think about a work in light of your own experiences and your own personal reactions to it. Then, as you gain expertise in recognizing and writing about the writer's technical use of literary elements, you can also apply what you know about these to help you craft more thorough and critical responses to the works and to offer a richer analytical interpretation grounded in your understanding of the world and the work itself, your familiarity with writers' techniques, and critical responses and observations of other readers.

To illustrate such active responding, we will examine "The Necklace" (1884), by the French writer Guy de Maupassant. "The Necklace" is one of the best known of all stories, and it is included here with marginal notes like those that any reader might make during original and follow-up readings. Many notes, particularly at the beginning, are *assimilative*; that is, they record details about the action. But as the story progresses, the marginal comments are more concerned with conclusions about the story's meaning. Toward the end, the comments are full rather than minimal; they result not only from first responses but also from considered thought. Here, then, is Maupassant's "The Necklace."

GUY DE MAUPASSANT (1850–1893)

Henri-René-Albert-Guy de Maupassant (1850–1893) is considered one of the major nineteenth-century French naturalist writers. Scion of an aristocratic Norman family, he received his baccalaureate degree from a lycée at Le Havre, after which he began studying law. When the Franco–Prussian War broke out, he served in the French army, including battlefield duty. After leaving the military he became a minor bureaucrat, first in the Ministry of Marine and then in the Ministry of Education (also the workplace of Loisel, the husband of "The Necklace").

As a youth Maupassant was an energetic oarsman, swimmer, and boatman—a power that he also devoted to his career as a writer. During the 1870s in Paris, he had regularly submitted his literary efforts to the novelist Gustave Flaubert (1821–1880), a family friend who regarded him as a son and whose criticism both improved and encouraged him. In Maupassant's thirties, after the death of his mentor Flaubert, his career flourished. His first published volume was a collection of poems (Des Vers, 1880), which he had to withdraw after it created a scandal and a lawsuit because of its sexual openness. After this time, until his death in 1893, he produced thirty volumes—novels, poems, articles, travel books, and three hundred short stories. In addition to "The Necklace," a few of his better-known stories are "The Ball of Fat," "Mademoiselle Fifi," and "A Piece of String."

Maupassant was a meticulous writer, devoting much attention to the reality of everyday existence (hence his status as a naturalist writer). A number of his stories are about events occurring during the Franco–Prussian War. Some are about life among bureaucrats, some about peasant life in Normandy, and a large number, including "The Necklace," about Parisian life. His major stories are characterized by strong irony; human beings are influenced by forces they cannot control, and their wishes are often frustrated by their own defects. Under such circumstances, Maupassant's characters exhibit varying degrees of weakness, hypocrisy, vanity, insensitivity, callousness, and even cruelty, but those who are victimized are viewed with understanding and sympathy.

🍂 The Necklace (1884)

Translated by Edgar V. Roberts

She was one of those pretty and charming women, born, as if by an error of destiny, into a family of clerks and copyists. She had no dowry, no prospects, no way of getting known, courted, loved, married by a rich and distinguished man. She finally settled for a marriage with a minor clerk in the Ministry of Education.

She was a simple person, without the money to dress well, but she was as unhappy as if she had gone through bankruptcy, for women have neither rank nor race. In place of high birth or important family connections, they can rely only on their beauty, their grace, and their charm. Their inborn finesse, their elegant taste, their engaging personalities, which are their only power, make working-class women the equals of the grandest ladies.

She suffered constantly, feeling herself destined for all delicacies and luxuries. She suffered because of her grim apartment with its drab walls, threadbare furniture, ugly curtains. All such things, which most other women in her situation would not even have noticed, tortured her and filled her with despair. The sight of the young country girl who did her simple housework awakened in her only a sense of desolation and lost hopes. She daydreamed of large, silent anterooms, decorated with oriental tapestries and lighted by high bronze floor lamps, with two elegant valets in short culottes dozing in large armchairs under the effects of forced-air heaters. She imagined large drawing rooms draped in the most expensive silks, with fine end tables on which were placed knickknacks of inestimable value. She dreamed of the perfume of dainty private rooms, which were designed only for intimate tête-à-têtes with the closest friends, who because of their achievements and fame would make her the envy of all other women.

When she sat down to dinner at her round little table covered with a cloth that had not been washed for three days, in front of her husband who opened the kettle while declaring ecstatically, "Ah, good old beef stew! I don't know anything better," she dreamed of expensive banquets with shining place settings, and wall hangings portraying ancient heroes and exotic birds in an enchanted forest. She imagined a gourmet-prepared main course carried on the most exquisite trays and served on the most beautiful dishes, with whispered gallantries which she would hear with a sphinxlike smile as she dined on the pink meat of a trout or the delicate wing of a quail.

She had no decent dresses, no jewels, nothing. And she loved nothing but these; she believed herself born only for these. She burned with the desire to please, to be envied, to be attractive and sought after.

She had a rich friend, a comrade from convent days, whom she did not want to see anymore because she suffered so much when she returned home. She would weep for the entire day afterward with sorrow, regret, despair, and misery.

Margin notes:

"She" is pretty but poor, and has no chance in life unless she marries. Without connections, she has no entry into high society and marries an insignificant clerk.

She is unhappy.

A view of women who have no chance for an independent life and a career. In 1884, women had nothing more than this. Sad.

She suffers because of her cheap belongings, wanting expensive things. She dreams of wealth and of how other women would envy her if she could display finery. But such luxuries are unrealistic and unattainable for her.

Her husband's taste is for plain things, while she dreams of expensive gourmet food. He has adjusted to his status. She has not.

She lives for her unrealistic dreams, and these increase her frustration.

She even thinks of giving up a rich friend because she is so depressed after visiting her.

5

Well, one evening, her husband came home glowing and carrying a large envelope.

"Here," he said, "this is something for you."

She quickly tore open the envelope and took out a card engraved with these words:

> The CHANCELLOR OF EDUCATION and
> MRS. GEORGE RAMPONNEAU
> *request that*
> MR. AND MRS. LOISEL
> *do them the honor of coming to dinner*
> *at the Ministry of Education*
> *on the evening of January 8.*

10   Instead of being delighted, as her husband had hoped, she threw the invitation spitefully on the table, muttering:

"What do you expect me to do with this?"

"But honey, I thought you'd be glad. You never get to go out, and this is a special occasion! I had a lot of trouble getting the invitation. Everyone wants one. The demand is high and not many clerks get invited. Everyone important will be there."

She looked at him angrily and stated impatiently:

"What do you want me to wear to go there?"

15   He had not thought of that. He stammered:

"But your theater dress. That seems nice to me . . ."

He stopped, amazed and bewildered, as his wife began to cry. Large tears fell slowly from the corners of her eyes to her mouth. He said falteringly:

"What's wrong? What's the matter?"

But with a strong effort she had recovered, and she answered calmly as she wiped her damp cheeks:

20   "Nothing, except that I have nothing to wear and therefore can't go to the party. Give your invitation to someone else at the office whose wife will have nicer clothes than mine."

Distressed, he responded:

"Well, all right, Mathilde. How much would a new dress cost, something you could use at other times, but not anything fancy?"

She thought for a few moments, adding things up and thinking also of an amount that she could ask without getting an immediate refusal and a frightened outcry from the frugal clerk.

Finally she responded tentatively:

25   "I don't know exactly, but it seems to me that I could get by on four hundred francs."

He blanched slightly at this, because he had set aside just that amount to buy a shotgun for Sunday lark-hunts the next summer with a few friends in the Plain of Nanterre.

However, he said:

"All right, you've got four hundred francs, but make it a pretty dress."

As the day of the party drew near, Mrs. Loisel seemed sad, uneasy, anxious, even though her gown was all ready. One evening her husband said to her:

Marginal annotations:

A new section in the story.

An invitation to dinner at the Ministry of Education. A big plum.

It only upsets her.

Loisel really doesn't understand her. He can't sympathize with her unhappiness.

She declares that she hasn't anything to wear.
He tries to persuade her that her theater dress might do for the occasion.

Her name is Mathilde.
He volunteers to pay for a new dress.

She is manipulating him.

The dress will cost him his next summer's vacation. (He doesn't seem to have included her in his plans.)

A new section, the third in the story. The day of the party is near. Tension is mounting.

"What's the matter? You've been acting funny for several days."

She answered:

"It's awful, but I don't have any jewels to wear, not a single gem, nothing to dress up my outfit. I'll look like a beggar. I'd almost rather not go to the party."

He responded:

"You can wear a corsage of cut flowers. This year it's all the rage. For only ten francs you can get two or three gorgeous roses."

She was not convinced.

"No . . . there's nothing more humiliating than looking shabby in the company of rich women."

But her husband exclaimed:

"God, but you're silly! Go to your friend Mrs. Forrestier, and ask her to lend you some jewelry. You know her well enough to do that."

She uttered a cry of joy:

"That's right. I hadn't thought of that."

The next day she went to her friend's house and described her problem.

Mrs. Forrestier went to her mirrored wardrobe, took out a large jewel box, opened it, and said to Mrs. Loisel:

"Choose, my dear."

She saw bracelets, then a pearl necklace, then a Venetian cross of finely worked gold and gems. She tried on the jewelry in front of a mirror, and hesitated, unable to make up her mind about each one. She kept asking:

"Do you have anything else?"

"Certainly. Look to your heart's content. I don't know what you'd like best."

Suddenly she found a superb diamond necklace in a black satin box, and her heart throbbed with desire for it. Her hands shook as she picked it up. She fastened it around her neck, watched it gleam at her throat, and looked at herself ecstatically.

Then she asked, haltingly and anxiously:

"Could you lend me this, nothing but this?"

"Why yes, certainly."

She jumped up, hugged her friend joyfully, then hurried away with her treasure.

The day of the party came. Mrs. Loisel was a success. She was prettier than anyone else, stylish, graceful, smiling and wild with joy. All the men saw her, asked her name, sought to be introduced. All the important administrators stood in line to waltz with her. The Chancellor himself eyed her.

She danced joyfully, passionately, intoxicated with pleasure, thinking of nothing but the moment, in the triumph of her beauty, in the glory of her success, on cloud nine with happiness made up of all the admiration, of all the aroused desire, of this victory so complete and so sweet to the heart of any woman.

Margin annotations:

30

Now she complains that she doesn't have any nice jewelry. She is manipulating him again.

35

She has a good point, but there seems to be no way out.

He proposes a solution: Borrow jewelry from Mrs. Forrestier, who is apparently the rich friend mentioned earlier.

40

Mathilde has her choice of her friend's jewels.

45

A "superb" diamond necklace. This is what the story has been building up to.

This is what she wants, just this.

50

She leaves with the "treasure." Things might be looking up for her.

A new section.

The party. Mathilde is a huge success.

Another judgment about women. Does the author mean that only women want to be admired? Don't men want admiration, too?

She did not leave until four o'clock in the morning. Her husband, since midnight, had been sleeping in a little empty room with three other men whose wives had also been enjoying themselves.

55   He threw, over her shoulders, the shawl that he had brought for the trip home—a modest everyday wrap, the poverty of which contrasted sharply with the elegance of her evening gown. She felt it and hurried away to avoid being noticed by the other women who luxuriated in rich furs.

Loisel tried to hold her back:

"Wait a minute. You'll catch cold outdoors. I'll call a cab."

But she paid no attention and hurried down the stairs. When they reached the street they found no carriages. They began to look for one, shouting at cabmen passing by at a distance.

They walked toward the Seine, desperate, shivering. Finally, on a quay, they found one of those old night-going buggies that are seen in Paris only after dark, as if they were ashamed of their wretched appearance in daylight.

60   It took them to their door, on the Street of Martyrs, and they sadly climbed the stairs to their flat. For her, it was finished. As for him, he could think only that he had to begin work at the Ministry of Education at ten o'clock.

She took the shawl off her shoulders, in front of the mirror, to see herself once more in her glory. But suddenly she cried out. The necklace was no longer around her neck!

Her husband, already half undressed, asked:

"What's wrong?"

She turned toward him frantically:

65   "I . . . I . . . I no longer have Mrs. Forrestier's necklace."

He stood up, bewildered:

"What! . . . How! . . . It's not possible!"

And they looked in the folds of the gown, in the folds of the shawl, in the pockets, everywhere. They found nothing.

He asked:

70   "You're sure you still had it when you left the party?"

"Yes. I checked it in the vestibule of the Ministry."

"But if you'd lost it in the street, we would've heard it fall. It must be in the cab."

"Yes, probably. Did you notice the number?"

"No. Did you see it?"

75   "No."

Overwhelmed, they looked at each other. Finally, Loisel got dressed again:

"I'm going out to retrace all our steps," he said, "to see if I can find the necklace that way."

And he went out. She stayed in her evening dress, without the energy to get ready for bed, stretched out in a chair, drained of strength and thought.

Her husband came back at about seven o'clock. He had found nothing.

Marginal notes (right column):

Loisel, with other husbands, is bored, while the wives are literally having a ball.

Ashamed of her shabby everyday shawl, she rushes away to avoid being seen. She is forced back into the reality of her true situation. Her glamour is gone.

A comedown after the nice evening. They take a wretched-looking buggy home.

"Street of Martyrs" — Is this name significant?

Loisel is down-to-earth.

SHE HAS LOST THE NECKLACE!

They can't locate it. It seems to be lost. What a horrible feeling. What a comedown.

He goes out to search for the necklace.

But is unsuccessful.

He went to Police Headquarters and to the newspapers to announce a reward. He went to the small cab companies, and finally he followed up even the slightest hopeful lead.

She waited the entire day, in the same enervated state, in the face of this frightful disaster.

Loisel came back in the evening, his face pale and haggard. He had found nothing.

"You'll have to write to your friend," he said, "that you broke a clasp on her necklace and that you're having it fixed. That'll give us time to look around."

She wrote as he dictated.

By the end of the week they had lost all hope.

And Loisel, looking five years older, declared:

"We'll have to see about replacing the jewels."

The next day they took the case which had contained the necklace and went to the jeweler whose name was inside. He looked at his books:

"I wasn't the one, Madam, who sold the necklace. I only made the case."

Then they went from jeweler to jeweler, searching for a necklace like the other one, racking their memories, both of them sick with worry and anguish.

In a shop in the Palais-Royal, they found a necklace of diamonds that seemed to them exactly like the one they were looking for. It was priced at forty thousand francs. They could buy it for thirty-six thousand.

They got the jeweler to promise not to sell it for three days. And they made an agreement that he would buy it back for thirty-four thousand francs if the original was recovered before the end of February.

Loisel had saved eighteen thousand francs that his father had left him. He would have to borrow the rest.

He borrowed, asking a thousand francs from one, five hundred from another, five louis° here, three louis there. He wrote promissory notes, undertook ruinous obligations, did business with finance companies and the whole tribe of loan sharks. He compromised himself for the remainder of his days, risked his signature without knowing whether he would be able to honor it; and, terrified by anguish over the future, by the black misery that was about to descend on him, by the prospect of all kinds of physical deprivations and moral tortures, he went to get the new necklace, and put down thirty-six thousand francs on the jeweler's counter.

Mrs. Loisel took the necklace back to Mrs. Forrestier, who said with an offended tone:

°*louis:* a gold coin worth twenty francs.

He really tries. He's doing his best.   80

Loisel's plan to explain delaying the return. He takes charge, is resourceful.

Things are hopeless.   85

Note that Loisel does not even suggest that they explain things to Mrs. Forrestier.

They hunt for a replacement.

90

A new diamond necklace will cost 36,000 francs, a monumental amount.

They make a deal with the jeweler. (Is Maupassant hinting that things might work out for them?)

It will take all of Loisel's inheritance . . .

. . . plus another 18,000 francs that must be borrowed at enormous rates of interest.

Mrs. Forrestier is offended and complains about Mathilde's delay.   95

"You should have brought it back sooner; I might have needed it."

She did not open the case, as her friend feared she might. If she had noticed the substitution, what would she have thought? What would she have said? Would she not have taken her for a thief?

Is this enough justification for not telling the truth? It seems to be for the Loisels.

Mrs. Loisel soon discovered the horrible life of the needy. She did her share, however, completely, heroically. That horrifying debt had to be paid. She would pay. They dismissed the maid; they changed their address; they rented an attic flat.

A new section, the fifth.

She learned to do the heavy housework, dirty kitchen jobs. She washed the dishes, wearing away her manicured fingernails on greasy pots and encrusted baking dishes. She handwashed dirty linen, shirts, and dish towels that she hung out on the line to dry. Each morning, she took the garbage down to the street, and she carried up water, stopping at each floor to catch her breath. And, dressed in cheap house dresses, she went to the fruit dealer, the grocer, the butcher's, with her basket under her arms, haggling, insulting, defending her measly cash penny by penny.

They suffer to repay their debts. Mathilde accepts a cheap attic flat, and does all the heavy housework herself to save on domestic help.

She pinches pennies and haggles with the local merchants.

100   They had to make installment payments every month, and, to buy more time, to refinance loans.

They struggle to meet payments.

The husband worked evenings to make fair copies of tradesmen's accounts, and late into the night he made copies at five cents a page.

Mr. Loisel moonlights to make extra money.

And this life lasted ten years.

At the end of ten years, they had paid back everything—everything—including the extra charges imposed by loan sharks and the accumulation of compound interest.

For ten years they struggle, but they endure.

Mrs. Loisel looked old now. She had become the strong, hard, and rude woman of poor households. Her hair unkempt, with uneven skirts and rough, red hands, she spoke loudly, washed floors with large buckets of water. But sometimes, when her husband was at work, she sat down near the window, and she dreamed of that evening so long ago, of that party, where she had been so beautiful and so admired.

Another new section, the sixth of the story.

The Loisels have successfully paid back the loans. They have been quite virtuous.

105   What would life have been like if she had not lost that necklace? Who knows? Who knows? Life is so peculiar, so uncertain. How little a thing it takes to destroy you or to save you!

Mrs. Loisel (why does the narrator not say "Mathilde"?) is roughened and aged by the work. But she has behaved "heroically" (paragraph 98) and has shown her mettle.

Well, one Sunday, when she had gone for a stroll along the Champs-Elysées to relax from the cares of the week, she suddenly noticed a woman walking with a child. It was Mrs. Forrestier, still youthful, still beautiful, still attractive.

Mrs. Loisel felt moved. Would she speak to her? Yes, certainly. And now that she had paid, she could tell all. Why not?

She walked closer.

"Hello, Jeanne."

The seventh part of the story, a scene on the Champs-Elysées. Mathilde sees Jeanne Forrestier for the first time in the previous ten years.

110   The other gave no sign of recognition and was astonished to be addressed so familiarly by this working-class woman. She stammered:

"But . . . Madam! . . . I don't know. . . . You must have made a mistake."

"No. I'm Mathilde Loisel."

Her friend cried out:

"Oh! . . . My poor Mathilde, you've changed so much."

Jeanne notes Mathilde's changed appearance. 115

"Yes. I've had some tough times since I saw you last; in fact hardships . . . and all because of you! . . ."

"Of me . . . how so?"

"You remember the diamond necklace that you lent me to go to the party at the Ministry of Education?"

"Yes. What then?"

"Well, I lost it."

"How, since you gave it back to me?"

Mathilde tells Jeanne everything. 120

"I returned another exactly like it. And for ten years we've been paying for it. You understand this wasn't easy for us, who have nothing. . . . Finally it's over, and I'm damned glad."

Mrs. Forrestier stopped her.

"You say that you bought a diamond necklace to replace mine?"

"Yes, you didn't notice it, eh? It was exactly like yours."

And she smiled with proud and childish joy.

Mrs. Forrestier, deeply moved, took both her hands.

"Oh, my poor Mathilde! But mine was only costume jewelry. At most, it was worth only five hundred francs! . . ."

SURPRISE! The lost necklace was not made of real diamonds, and the Loisels have slaved for no reason at all. But hard work and sacrifice probably brought out better qualities in Mathilde than she otherwise might have shown. Is this the point of the story? Look again at paragraph 105. 125

Reading and Responding in a Computer File or Notebook

The marginal comments printed with "The Necklace" demonstrate the active reading-responding process you should apply to everything you read. Use the margins in your text similarly to record your comments and questions, but plan also to record your more lengthy responses in a notebook, on note cards, on separate sheets of paper, or in a computer file. Be careful not to lose anything; keep all your notes. As you progress from work to work, you will find that your written or saved comments will be immensely important to you as your record, or journal, of your first impressions together with your more carefully considered and expanded thoughts.

In keeping your notebook, your objective should be to learn assigned works inside and out and then to say perceptive things about them. To achieve this goal, you need to read the work more than once. Develop a good note-taking system so that as you read, you will create a "memory bank" of your own knowledge. You can make withdrawals from this fund of ideas when you begin to write. As an aid in developing your own procedures for reading and "depositing" your ideas, you may wish to begin with the following guidelines for reading. Of course, you will want to modify these suggestions and add to them as you become a more experienced and disciplined reader.

GUIDELINES FOR READING

1. **Observations for basic understanding**
   a. Explain words, situations, and concepts. Write down words that are new or not immediately clear. Use your dictionary, and record the relevant meanings in your notebook. Write down special difficulties so that you can ask your instructor about them.
   b. Determine what is happening in the work. For a story or play, where do the actions take place? What do they show? Who is involved? Who is the major figure? Why is he or she major? What relationships do the characters have with one another? What concerns do the characters have? What do they do? Who says what to whom? How do the speeches advance the action and reveal the characters? For a poem, what is the situation? Who is talking, and to whom? What does the speaker say about the situation? Why does the poem end as it does and where it does?

2. **Notes on first impressions**
   a. Make a record of your reactions and responses. What did you think was memorable, noteworthy, funny, or otherwise striking? Did you worry, get scared, laugh, smile, feel a thrill, learn a great deal, feel proud, find a lot to think about?
   b. Describe interesting characterizations, events, techniques, and ideas. If you like a character or an idea, explain what you like, and do the same for characters and ideas you don't like. Is there anything else in the work that you especially like or dislike? Are parts easy or difficult to understand? Why? Are there any surprises? What was your reaction to them? Be sure to use your own words when writing your explanations.

3. **Development of ideas and enlargement of responses**
   a. Trace developing patterns. Make an outline or a scheme: What conflicts appear? Do these conflicts exist between people, groups, or ideas? How are the conflicts resolved? Is one force, idea, or side the winner? How do you respond to the winner or to the loser?
   b. Write expanded notes about characters, situations, and actions. What explanations need to be made about the characters? What is the nature of the situations (e.g., young people discover a damaged boat, and themselves, in the spring; a prisoner tries to hide her baby from cruel guards, and so on)? What is the nature of the actions (e.g., a mother and daughter go shopping, a series of strangers intrude upon the celebration of a christening, a woman is told that her husband has been killed in a train wreck, a group of children are taken to a fashionable toy store, and so on)? What are the people like, and what are their habits and customs? What sort of language do they use?
   c. Memorize important, interesting, and well-written passages. Copy them in full on note cards, and keep these in your pocket or purse. When walking to class, riding public transportation, or otherwise not occupying your time, learn them by heart. Please take memorization seriously.
   d. Always write down questions that come up during your reading. You may raise these in class, and trying to write out your own answers will also aid your own study.

Sample Notebook Entries on Maupassant's "The Necklace"

The following entries demonstrate how you can use the foregoing guidelines in your first thoughts about a work. You should try to develop enough observations and responses to be useful later, both for additional study and for developing essays. Notice that the entries are not only comments but also questions.

Early in the story, Mathilde seems to be spoiled. She and her husband are not well off, but she is unable to face her own situation.

She is a dreamer but seems harmless. Her daydreams about a fancy home, with all the expensive belongings, are not unusual. It would be unusual to find people who do not have such dreams.

She is embarrassed by her husband's taste for plain food. The storyteller contrasts her taste for trout and quail with Loisel's cheaper favorites.

When the Loisels get the invitation to the ball, Mathilde becomes difficult. Her wish for an expensive dress (the cost of Loisel's shotgun) creates a problem, and she creates another problem by wanting to wear fine jewelry.

Her change in character can be related to the places in the story: the Street of Martyrs, the dinner party scene, the attic flat. Also she fills the places she daydreams about with the most expensive things she can imagine.

Her success at the party shows that she has the charm the storyteller talks about in paragraph 2. She seems never to have had any other chance to exert her power.

The worst part of her personality is shown in rushing away from the party because she is ashamed of her ordinary and shabby shawl, which she had worn because the time of the story is January. It is Mathilde's unhappiness and unwillingness to adjust to her modest means that cause the financial downfall of the Loisels. This disaster is her fault.

Borrowing the money to replace the necklace shows that both Loisel and Mathilde have a strong sense of honor. Making up the loss is good, even if it destroys them financially.

There are some nice touches, like Loisel's seeming to be five years older (paragraph 86) and his staying with the other husbands of women enjoying themselves (paragraph 54). These are well done.

It's too bad that Loisel and Mathilde don't confess to Jeanne that the jewels are lost. Their pride or their honor stops them — or perhaps their fear of being accused of theft.

Their ten years of slavish work (paragraphs 98–102) show how they have come down in life. Mathilde does all her work by hand, so she really does pitch in and is, as the narrator says, heroic.

The attic flat is important. Mathilde becomes loud and frumpy when living there (paragraph 99), but she also develops strength. She does what she has to. The earlier apartment and the elegance of her imaginary rooms had brought out her limitations.

The setting of the Champs-Élysées also reflects her character, for she feels free there to tell Jeanne about the disastrous loss and the ten years of sacrifice (paragraph 121), producing the surprise ending. A curious point: Is it likely that Mathilde would not have had any contact with Mrs. Forrestier during that ten-year period?

The narrator's statement "How little a thing it takes to destroy you or to save you!" (paragraph 105) is full of thought. The necklace is little, and it makes a gigantic problem. This creates the story's irony.

Questions: Is this story more about the surprise ending or about the character of Mathilde? Is she to be condemned or admired? Does the outcome stem from the little things that make us or break us, as

the narrator suggests, or from the difficulty of rising above one's

economic class, which seems true, or both? What do the speaker's

remarks about women's status mean? (Remember, the story was

published in 1884.) This probably isn't relevant, but wouldn't

Jeanne, after hearing about the substitution, give the full value of the

necklace to the Loisels (or at least return the necklace to them), and

wouldn't they then be pretty well off?

These are reasonable—and also fairly full—remarks and observations about "The Necklace." Use your notebook or journal similarly for all reading assignments. If your assignment is simply to learn about a work, general notes like these should be enough. If you are preparing for a test, you might write pointed observations more in line with what is happening in your class, and also write and answer your own questions (see Chapter 27, "Taking Examinations on Literature"). If you have a writing assignment, observations like these can help you focus more closely on your topic—such as character, idea, or setting. Whatever your purpose, always take good notes, and put in as many details and responses as you can. The notes will be invaluable to you as a mind refresher and as a wellspring of thought.

Major Stages in Thinking and Writing About Literary Topics: Discovering Ideas, Preparing to Write, Making an Initial Draft of Your Essay, and Completing the Essay

Finished writing is the sharpened, focused expression of thought and study. It begins with the search for something to say—an idea. Not all ideas are equal; some are better than others, and getting good ideas is an ability that you will develop the more you think and write. As you discover ideas and explain them in words, you will also improve your perceptions and increase your critical faculties.

In addition, because literature itself contains the subject material (though not in a systematic way) of philosophy, religion, psychology, sociology, and politics, learning to analyze literature and to write about it will also improve your capacity to deal with these and other disciplines.

Writing Does Not Come Easily—for Anyone

A major purpose of your being in college, of which your composition and literature course is a vital part, is to develop your capacity to think and to express your thoughts clearly and fully. However, the process of creating a successfully argued essay—the actual process itself of writing—is not automatic. Writing begins in uncertainty and hesitation, and it becomes certain and confident—accomplished—only as a result of great care, applied thought, a certain amount of experimentation, the passage of time, and much effort. When you read complete, polished, well-formed pieces of writing, you might assume, as many of us do, that the writers wrote their successful versions the first time they tried and never needed to make any changes and improvements at all. In an ideal world, perhaps, something like this could happen, but not in this one.

If you could see the early drafts of writing you admire, you would be surprised and startled—and also encouraged—to see that good writers are also human and that what they first write is often uncertain, vague, tangential, tentative, incomplete, and messy. Good writers do not always like their first drafts; nevertheless, they work with their efforts and build upon them. They reconsider their ideas and try to restate them, discard some details, add others, chop paragraphs in half and reassemble the parts elsewhere, throw out much (and then maybe recover some of it), revise or completely rewrite sentences, change words, correct misspellings, sharpen expressions, and add new material to tie all the parts together in a smooth, natural flow.

The Goal of Writing: To Show a Process of Thought

As you approach the task of writing, you should constantly realize that your goal should always be to *explain* the work you are analyzing. You should never be satisfied simply to restate the events in the work. Too often students fall easily into a pattern of retelling a story or play, or of summarizing the details of a poem. But nothing could be further from what is expected from good writing. *Good writing should be the embodiment of your thought; it should show your thought in action.* Thinking is an active process that does not happen accidentally. Thinking requires that you develop ideas, draw conclusions, exemplify them and support them with details, and connect everything in a coherent manner. Your goal should constantly be to explain the results of your thinking—your ideas, your play of mind over the materials of a work, your insights, your conclusions.

Approach each writing assignment in light of the following objectives: You should consider your reader as a person who has read the work, just as you have done. This person knows what is in the work, and therefore does not need you to restate what she or he already knows. Instead, your reader wants to learn from you what to think about it. Therefore, always, your task as a writer is to explain something about the work, to describe the thoughts that you can develop about it. Let us consider again Maupassant's "The Necklace." We have recognized that the main character, Mathilde Loisel, is a young Parisian house-wife who is married to a minor clerk in the Ministry of Education. We know this, but if we are reading an essay about the story we will want to learn more. Let us then suppose that a first goal of one of your paragraphs is to explain the deep dissatisfaction Mathilde feels in the early part of the story. Your paragraph might go as follows:

> In the early part of the story Maupassant establishes that Mathilde is deeply dissatisfied with her life. Her threadbare furniture and drab walls are a cause of her unhappiness. Under these circumstances her daydreams of beautiful rooms staffed by "elegant valets," together with a number of rooms for intimate conversations with friends, multiply her dissatisfaction. The meager meals that she shares with her husband make her imagine sumptuous banquets that she feels are rightfully hers by birth but that are denied her because of her circumstances. The emphasis in these early scenes of the story is always on Mathilde's discontentment and frustration.

Notice that this paragraph does not simply go over the story's events, but rather refers to the events in order to explain to us, as readers, the causes for Mathilde's unhappiness. The paragraph illustrates your process of thought. Here is another way in which you might use a thought to connect the same materials:

> In the early part of the story Maupassant emphasizes the economic difficulty of Mathilde's life. The threadbare furniture and ugly curtains, for example, highlight that there is no money to purchase better things. The same sparseness of existence is shown by the meager meals that she shares with her husband. With the capacity to appreciate better things, Mathilde is forced by circumstances to make do with worse. Her dreams of sumptuous banquets are therefore natural, given her level of frustration with the life around her. In short, her unhappiness is an understandable consequence of her aver-sion to her plain and drab apartment and the tightness of money.

Here the details are substantially the same as in the first paragraph, but they are unified by a different idea—namely, the economic constraints of Mathilde's life. What is important is that neither paragraph tells only the details. Instead the paragraphs illustrate the goal of writing with a purpose. Whenever you write, you should always be trying, as in these examples, to use a dominating thought or thoughts to shape the details in the work you are analyzing.

For both practiced and beginning writers alike, there are four stages of thinking and writing, and in each of these there are characteristic activities. In the beginning stage, writers try to find the details and thoughts that seem to be right for eventual inclusion in what they are hoping to write. The next (or middle) stage is characterized by written drafts, or sketches—ideas, sentences, paragraphs. An advanced stage of writing is the forming and ordering of what has previously been done— the creation and determination of a final essay. Although these stages occur in a natural order, they are not separate and distinct, but merge with each other and in effect are fused together. However, when you think you are close to finishing your essay, you may find that you are not as close as you might have thought. You are now in the finishing or completing stage, when you need to include something else, something more, something different, and something to make things complete. At this point you can easily re-create an earlier stage to discover new details and ideas. You might say that your work is always tentative until you regard it as finished or until you need to turn it in.

Discovering Ideas ("Brainstorming")

With the foregoing general goal in mind, let us assume that you have read the work about which you are to write and have made notes and observations on which you are planning to base your thought. You are now ready to consider and plan what to include in your essay. This earliest stage of writing is unpredictable and somewhat frustrating because you are on a search. You do not know quite what you want, for you are reaching out for ideas and you are not yet sure what they are and what you might say about them. This process of searching and discovery, sometimes also called **brainstorming,** requires you to examine any and every subject that your mind can produce.

Just as you are trying to reach for ideas, however, you also should try to introduce purpose and resolution into your thought. You have to zero in on something specific, and develop your ideas through this process. Although what you first write may seem indefinite, the best way to help your thinking is to put your mind, figuratively, into specific channels or grooves, and then to confine your thoughts within these boundaries. What matters is to get your mind going on a particular topic and to get your thoughts down on paper or onto a computer screen. Once you can see your thoughts in front of you, you can work with them and develop them. The drawing on the next page can be helpful to you as an illustration of the various facets of a literary work, or ways of talking about it.

Consider the work you have read—story, poem, play—as the central circle, from which a number of points, like the rays of a star, shine out, some of them prominently, others less so. These points, or rays, are the various subjects, or topics, that you might decide to select in exploration, discovery, and discussion. Because some elements in a work may be more significant than others, the points are not all equal in size. Notice also that the points grow larger as they get nearer to the work, suggesting that once you select a point of discussion you may amplify that point with details and your own observations about the work.

You can consider literary works in many ways, but for now, as a way of getting started, you might choose to explore (1) the work's characters, (2) its historical period and background, (3) the social and economic conditions it depicts, (4) its major ideas, (5) any of its artistic qualities, or (6) any additional ideas that seem important to you.[1] These topics, of course, have many subtopics, but any one of them can help you in the concentration you will need for beginning your essay (and also for classroom discussion). All you need is one topic, just one; don't try everything at the same time. Let us see how our illustration can be revised to account for these topics. In the drawing on the next page the number of points is reduced to illustrate the points or approaches we have just raised (with an additional and unnamed point to represent all the other approaches that might be used for other studies). These points represent your ways of discovering ideas about the work.

Study the Characters in the Work

You do not need to be a professional psychologist to discuss the persons or characters that you find in a work (see also Chapter 3). You need to raise only issues about the characters and what they do and what they represent. What are the characters like at the beginning of the work? What happens to them? Do they do anything that causes them to change, and how are they changed? Are the changes for good or for bad? Why do the characters do the things they do? What do they do correctly? What do they do incorrectly? Why? For example, Mathilde is wrong not to tell Jeanne about the lost necklace. Such an immediate admission of truth would save her and her husband ten years of hardship and deprivation. But Mathilde

---

Together with additional topics, these critical approaches are discussed in more detail in Chapter 25.

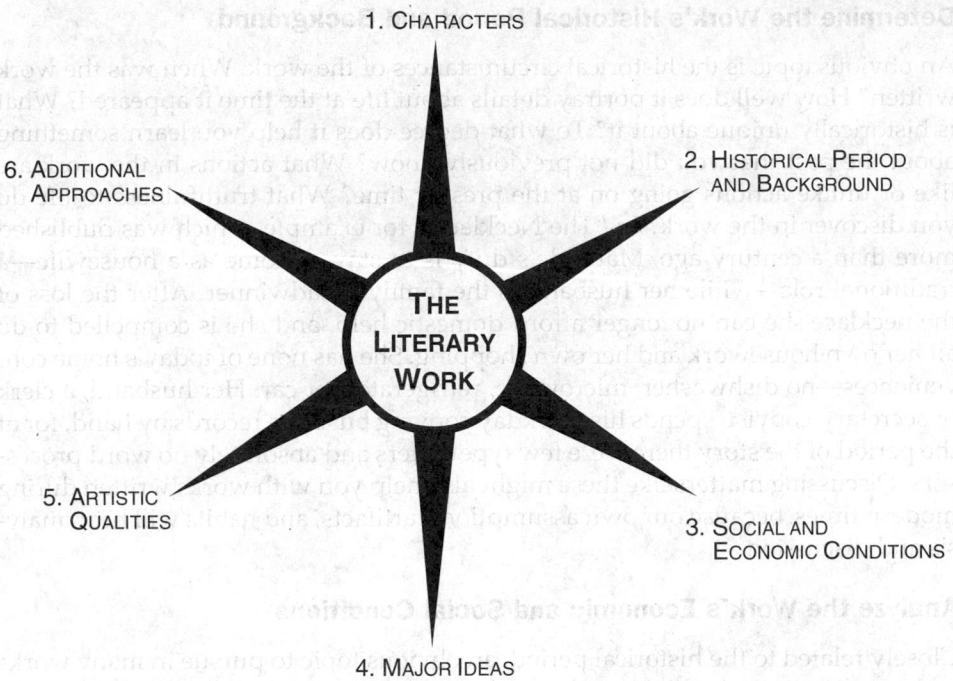

1. CHARACTERS

6. ADDITIONAL
APPROACHES

2. HISTORICAL PERIOD
AND BACKGROUND

THE
LITERARY
WORK

5. ARTISTIC
QUALITIES

3. SOCIAL AND
ECONOMIC CONDITIONS

4. MAJOR IDEAS

does not tell the truth. Why not? What do we learn about her character because she avoids or ignores this admission? Is her avoidance understandable? Why?

In discussing character, you might also wish to raise the issue of whether the characters in the work do or do not do what might normally be expected from people in their circumstances. Do they correspond to type? The idea here is that certain attitudes and behaviors are typical of people at particular stages of life (e.g., children behaving like children, lovers dealing with their relationship, a young couple coping with difficult finances). Thus we might ask questions about whether the usual circumstances experienced by the characters affect them, either by limiting them in some way or by freeing them. What attitudes seem typical of the characters? How do these attitudes govern what the characters do, or do not do? For example, one of the most typical circumstances of life is marriage. According to the positive and ideal type of marriage, a husband and wife should be forthcoming with each other; they should tell each other things and should not conceal what is on their minds. If they have problems, they should discuss them and try to solve them together. In "The Necklace" we see that Mathilde and Loisel do not show these desired qualities, and their absence of communication can be seen as an element in their financial catastrophe. However, during their long years of trouble they work together; they eventually exhibit the quality of honesty, and in this respect they fulfill their role, or type, as a married couple.

An analysis of typical attitudes themselves can also furnish you with material for discussion. For example, Mathilde, who is a member of the lower commercial class, has attitudes that are more appropriate to the upper or leisure class. She cannot bridge this gap, and her frustration causes her to nag her husband to give her enough money to live out her dream, if only for a moment.

Determine the Work's Historical Period and Background

An obvious topic is the historical circumstances of the work. When was the work written? How well does it portray details about life at the time it appeared? What is historically unique about it? To what degree does it help you learn something about the past that you did not previously know? What actions in the work are like or unlike actions going on at the present time? What truthfulness to life do you discover in the work? In "The Necklace," for example, which was published more than a century ago, Mathilde's duty is to stay at home as a housewife—a traditional role—while her husband is the family breadwinner. After the loss of the necklace she can no longer afford domestic help, and she is compelled to do all her own housework and her own shopping. She has none of today's home conveniences—no dishwasher, microwave, refrigerator, or car. Her husband, a clerk or secretary-copyist, spends his workday copying business records by hand, for at the period of the story there were few typewriters and absolutely no word processors. Discussing matters like these might also help you with works written during modern times, because our own assumptions, artifacts, and habits will bear analysis and discussion.

Analyze the Work's Economic and Social Conditions

Closely related to the historical period, an obvious topic to pursue in many works is the economic and social condition of the characters. To what level of life, economically, do the characters belong? How are events in the work related to their condition? How does their money, or lack of it, limit what they do? How do their economic circumstances either restrict or liberate their imaginations? How do their jobs and their apparent income determine their way of life? If we ask some of these questions about "The Necklace," as we have seen, we find that Mathilde and her husband are greatly burdened by their lack of money, and also that their obligation to repay their huge loan drives them into economic want and sacrifice.

An important part of the economic and social analysis of literature is the consideration of female characters and what it means to be a woman. This is the feminist analysis of literature, which asks questions like these: What role is Mathilde compelled to take as a result of her sex and family background? How does Jeanne's way of life contrast with that of Mathilde? What can Mathilde do with her life? To what degree is she limited by her role as a housewife? Does she have any chance of an occupation outside the home? How does her economic condition cause her to yearn for better things? What causes her to borrow the necklace? What is her contribution, as a woman, to the repayment of the loans? Should Mathilde's limited life in "The Necklace" be considered as a political argument for greater freedom for women? Once you start asking questions like these, you will find that your thinking is developing along with your ideas for writing.

The feminist approach to the interpretation of literature has been well established, and it will usually provide you with a way to discuss a work. It is also possible, of course, to analyze what a work says about the condition of being a man, or being a child. Depending on the work, many of the questions important in a feminist approach are not dissimilar to those you might use if you are dealing with childhood or male adulthood.

One of the most important social and economic topics is that of race and ethnicity. What happens in the work that seems to occur mainly because of the race of the characters? Is the author pointing out any deprivations, any absence of opportunity, any oppression? What do the characters do under such circumstances? Do they succeed or not? Are they negative? Are they angry? Are they resolute and determined? Your aim in an inquiry of this type should be to concentrate on actions and ideas in the work that are clearly related to race.

Explain the Work's Major Ideas

One of the major ways of focusing on a work is to zero in on various ideas and values or issues to be discovered there. What ideas might we gain from the story of the lengthy but needless sacrifice and drudgery experienced by Mathilde and her husband? An obvious and acceptable idea is presented by the speaker—namely, that even the smallest, most accidental incident can cause immense consequences. This is an idea that we might expand and illustrate in an entire essay. Here are some other ideas that we might also pursue, all of them based on the story's actions:

- Many actions have unforeseeable and uncontrollable consequences.
- Lack of communication is a major cause of hardship.
- Adversity brings out a character's good qualities.
- Mutual effort enables people to overcome difficulties.

These ideas are all to be found in Maupassant's story. In other works, of course, we may find comparable ideas, in addition to other major ideas and issues.

Describe the Work's Artistic Qualities

A work's artistic qualities provide many possible topics for studying, but basically here you may consider matters such as the work's plan or organization and the author's narrative method, writing style, or poetic techniques. In "The Necklace," we thus observe that almost the entire story develops with Mathilde at the center (narrative method; see also Chapter 2, on point of view). At first, the story brings us close to Mathilde, for we are told of her dissatisfaction and impatience with her surroundings. As the story progresses, the storyteller/speaker presents her person and actions more objectively and also more distantly. Another artistic approach would be to determine the story's pattern of development—how, chronologically, the loss of the necklace brings financial misfortune to the Loisels. We might also look for the author's inclusion of symbols in the story, such as the name of the street where the Loisels originally live, their move to an attic flat, or the roughness of Mathilde's hands as a result of her constant housework. There are many other ways to consider the formal aspects of a literary work.

Explain Any Other Approaches That Seem Important

Additional ways of looking at a work such as "The Necklace" might occur to you beyond those just described. One reader might raise the issue that the story's speaker seems to exhibit a particularly patronizing attitude toward women. He draws attention to Mathilde's joy because of the party, and generalizes about how her "victory" was so "sweet to the heart of any woman" (paragraph 53). A writer might want to make more of this attitude. Another aspect of the story might be the way in which Mathilde's physical appearance undergoes change as a result of her dismissing the maid and taking on the household chores herself. Still another aspect is the attitude of Loisel and his relationship with Mathilde, which seems rather distant. The story tells nothing about his reactions to the misfortune beyond how he pitches in to restore the borrowed money, almost to the point of enslaving himself to the task. Would he never have uttered any reproachful words toward his wife? The point here is that additional ideas may suggest themselves to you, and that you should keep yourself open to explore and discuss any of these other ways of seeing and thinking.

Preparing to Write

By this time you will already have been focusing on your topic and will have assembled much that you can put into your essay. You should now aim to develop paragraphs and sketches of what you will eventually include. You should think constantly of the point or argument you want to develop, but invariably digressions will occur, together with other difficulties—false starts, dead ends, total cessation of thought, digressions, despair, hopelessness, and general frustration. Remember, however, that it is important just to start. Jump right in and start writing anything at all—no matter how unacceptable your first efforts may seem— and force yourself to deal with the materials. The writing down of ideas does not commit you. You should not think that these first ideas are untouchable and holy just because you have written them on paper or on your computer screen. You can throw them out in favor of new ideas, you can make cross-outs and changes, and you can move paragraphs or even sections around as you wish. However, if you do not start writing, your first thoughts will remain locked in your mind and you will have nothing to work with. You must learn to accept the uncertainties in the writing process and make them work *for* you rather than *against* you.

Build Ideas from Your Original Notes

You need to get your mind going by mining your notebook or computer file for useful things you have already written. Thus, let us use an observation in our original set of notes—"The attic flat is important"—in reference to the poorer rooms where Mathilde and her husband live while they are paying back their creditors. With such a note as a start, you might develop a number of ideas to support an argument about Mathilde's character, as in the following:

> The attic flat is important. Early in the story, in her apartment, Mathilde is dreamy and impractical. She seems delicate, but after losing the necklace, she is delicate no longer. She becomes a worker after they move to the flat. She does a lot more when living there.
>
> In the flat, Mathilde has to sacrifice. She gives up her servant, washes greasy pots, climbs stairs carrying buckets of water, sloshes water around to clean floors, and does all the clothes washing by hand.
>
> When living in the flat she gets stronger, but she also becomes loud and common. She argues with shopkeepers to get the lowest prices. She stops caring for herself. There is a reversal here, from incapable and well groomed to capable but coarse.

In this way, even in an assertion as basic as "The attic flat is important," the process of putting together details is a form of concentrated thought that leads you creatively forward. You can express thoughts and conclusions that you could not express at the beginning. Such an exercise in stretching your mind leads you to put elements of the work together in ways that create ideas for good essays.

Trace Patterns of Action and Thought

You can also discover ideas by making a list or scheme for the story or main idea. What conflicts appear? Do these conflicts exist between people, groups, or ideas? How does the author resolve them? Is one force, idea, or side the winner? Why? How do you respond to the winner or to the loser? Using this method, you might make a list similar to this one:

At the beginning, Mathilde is a fish out of water. She dreams of wealth, but her life is drab and her husband is dull.

Fantasies make her even more dissatisfied; she punishes herself by thinking of a wealthy life.

When the Loisels get the dinner invitation Mathilde pouts and whines. Her husband feels discomfort when she manipulates him into buying her an expensive party dress.

Her world of daydreams hurts her real life when her desire for wealth causes her to borrow the necklace. Losing the necklace is just plain bad luck.

These arguments all focus on Mathilde's character, but you may wish to trace other patterns you find in the story. If you start planning an essay about another pattern, be sure to account for all the actions and scenes that relate to your topic. Otherwise, you may miss a piece of evidence that could lead you to new conclusions.

Raise and Answer Your Own Questions

A habit you should always cultivate is to raise your own questions, and try to answer them yourself as you consider your reading. The guidelines for reading (p. 14) will help you formulate questions, but you can raise additional questions like these:

- What is happening as the work unfolds? How does an action at the beginning of the work bring about later actions and speeches?
- Who are the main characters? What seems unusual or different about what they do in the work?
- What conclusions can you draw about the work's actions, scenes, and situations? Explain these conclusions.
- What are the characters and speakers like? What do they do and say about themselves, their goals, the people around them, their families, their friends, their work, and the general circumstances of their lives?

- What kinds of words do the characters use: formal or informal words, slang or profanity?
- What literary conventions and devices have you discovered, and how do these affect the work? (When an author addresses readers directly, for example, that is a convention; when a comparison is used, that is a device, which might be either a metaphor or a simile.)

Of course, you can raise other questions as you reread the piece, or you can be left with one or two major questions that you decide to pursue.

THE NEED FOR THE ACTUAL PHYSICAL PROCESS OF WRITING

Thinking and writing are interdependent processes. If you don't get your thoughts into words that are visible to you on a paper or computer screen, your thinking will be impeded. It is therefore vital for you to use the writing process as the most significant means of developing your ideas. If you are doing an assignment in class—tests, or impromptu essays—write your initial responses on a single side of your paper. This strategy will enable you to spread your materials out to get an actual physical overview of them when you begin writing. Everything will be open to you; none of your ideas will be hidden on the other side of the paper.

Outside of class, however, when you are at home or otherwise able to use a computer, your machine is an indispensable tool for your writing. It will help you develop ideas, for it quickly enables you to eliminate unworkable thoughts and to replace them with others. You can move sentences and paragraphs into new contexts, test how they look, and move them somewhere else if you choose.

In addition, the ability to print initial and tentative stages of writing makes rewriting easier. Using the printed draft, you can make additional notes, corrections, and suggestions for further development. With the marked-up draft as a guide, you can go back to the word processor and fill in your changes and improvements, repeating this procedure as often as you can. You can also make edits directly to your draft and track changes to see your edits versus your original draft. This facility makes the machine an incentive for improvement, right up to your final draft.

Word processing also helps you in the final preparation of your essays. Studies have shown that errors and awkward sentences are frequently found at the bottoms of handwritten pages. The reason is that writers hesitate to make improvements when they get near the end of a page because they shun the dreariness of starting the page over. Word processors eliminate this difficulty completely. Changes can be made anywhere in the draft, at any time, without any ill effect on the final appearance of your essay.

Regardless of your writing method, you should always remember that unwritten thought is incomplete thought. You cannot lay everything out at once on the word processor's screen. You can see only a small part of what you are writing. Therefore, somewhere in your writing process, you need to prepare a complete draft of what you have written. A clean, readable draft permits you to gather everything together and to make even more improvements through revision.

Put Ideas Together Using a Plus-Minus, Pro-Con, or Either-Or Method

A common and very helpful method of discovering ideas is to develop a set of contrasts: plus-minus, pro-con, either-or. Let us suppose a plus-minus method of considering the following question about Mathilde: Should she be "admired" (plus) or "condemned" (minus)?

PLUS: ADMIRED?	MINUS: CONDEMNED?
After she cries when they get the invitation, she recovers with a "strong effort"—maybe she doesn't want her husband to feel bad.	She wants to be envied and admired only for being attractive and intriguing, not for more important qualities. She seems spoiled and selfish.
She scores a great victory at the dance. She really does have the power to charm and captivate.	She wastes her time in daydreaming about things she can't have, and she whines because she is unhappy.
Once she loses the necklace, she and her husband become poor and deprived. But she does "her share . . . completely, heroically" (paragraph 98) to make up for the loss.	Even though the Loisels live poorly, Mathilde manipulates her husband into giving her more money than they can afford for a party dress.
Even when she is poor, she dreams about that marvelous, shining moment at the great ball. This is pathetic, because Mathilde gets worse than she deserves.	She assumes that her friend Jeanne would think her a thief if she admitted losing the necklace. Shouldn't she have had more confidence in Jeanne?
At the end, after everything is paid back, and her reputation is secure, Mathilde confesses the loss to Jeanne.	She becomes loud and coarse, and haggles about pennies, thus undergoing a cheapening of her person and manner.

By putting contrasting observations side by side in this way, you will find that ideas will start to come naturally and will be helpful to you when you begin writing, regardless of how you finally organize your essay. It is possible, for example, that you might develop either column as the argumentative basis of an essay, or you might use your notes to support the idea that Mathilde is too complex to be either wholly admired or wholly condemned. You might also want to introduce an entirely new topic of development—for example, that Mathilde should be pitied rather than condemned or admired. In short, arranging materials in the plus-minus pattern is a powerful way to discover ideas—a truly helpful habit of promoting thought—that can lead to ways of development that you do not at first realize.

Originate and Develop Your Thoughts Through Writing

You should always write down what you are thinking for, as a principle, *unwritten thought is incomplete thought.* Make a practice of writing your observations about the work, in addition to any questions that occur to you. This is an exciting step in preliminary writing because it can be useful when you write later drafts. You will discover that looking at what you have written can not only enable you to correct and improve the writing you have done but also lead you to recognize that you need more. The process goes just about like this: "Something needs to be added here—important details that my reader will not have noticed, new support for my argument, a new idea that has just occurred to me, a significant connection to link my thoughts." If you follow such a process, you will be using your own written ideas to create new ideas. You will be advancing your own abilities as a thinker and writer.

The processes just described of searching for ideas, or brainstorming, are useful for you at any stage of composition. Even when you are fairly close to finishing your essay, you might suddenly recognize that you need to add something more (or subtract something you don't like). When that happens, you may return to the discovery or brainstorming process to initiate and develop new ideas and new arguments.

Making an Initial Draft of Your Essay

As you use the brainstorming and focusing techniques, you are also in fact beginning your essay. You will need to revise your ideas as connections among them become clearer and as you reexamine the work to discover details to support the argument you are making. By this stage, however, you already have many of the raw materials you need for developing your topic.

Base Your Essay on a Central Idea, Argument, or Statement

By definition, an essay *is an organized, connected, and fully developed set of paragraphs that expand on a* **central idea, central argument,** or **central statement.** All parts of an essay should contribute to the reader's understanding of the idea. To achieve unity and completeness, each paragraph refers to the argument and demonstrates how selected details from the work relate to it and support it. The central idea helps you control and shape your essay, just as it also provides guidance for your reader.

A successful essay about literature is a brief but thorough (not exhaustive) examination of a literary work in light of topics like those we have already raised—from character, background, and economic conditions to circumstances of gender, major ideas, artistic qualities, and any additional topic such as point of view and symbolism. Central ideas or arguments might be (1) that a character is strong and tenacious, or (2) that the story shows the unpredictability of action, or (3) that the point of view makes the action seem "distant and objective," or (4) that a major symbol governs the actions and thoughts of the major characters. In essays on these topics, all materials must be tied to such central ideas or arguments. Thus, it is a fact that Mathilde in "The Necklace" endures ten years of slavish work and sacrifice as she and her husband accumulate enough money to repay their monumental debt. This we know, but it is not relevant to an essay on her character unless you connect it by a central argument showing how it demonstrates one of her major traits—her growing strength and perseverance.

Look through all of your ideas for one or two that catch your eye for development. In all the early stages of preliminary writing, the chances are that you have already discovered at least a few ideas that are more thought provoking, or more important, than the others.

Once you choose an idea you think you can work with, write it as a complete sentence that is essential to the argument of your essay. A simple phrase such as "setting and character" does not focus thought the way a sentence does. The following sentence moves the topic toward new exploration and discovery because it combines a topic with an outcome: "The setting of 'The Necklace' reflects Mathilde's character." You can choose to be even more specific: "Mathilde's strengths and weaknesses are reflected in the real and imaginary places in 'The Necklace.'"

Now that you have phrased a single, central idea or argument for your essay, you have also established a guide by which you can accept, reject, rearrange, and change the ideas you have been planning to develop. You can now draft a few paragraphs (which you may base on some of the sketches you have already made; always use as much as you can of your early observations) to see whether your idea seems valid, or you can decide that it would be more helpful to make an outline or a list before you do more writing. In either case, you should use your notes for evidence to connect to your central idea. If you need to bolster your argument with more supporting details and ideas, go once again to the techniques of discovery and brainstorming.

⚜ THE NEED FOR A SOUND ARGUMENT IN ESSAYS ABOUT LITERATURE

As you write about literature, you should always try to connect your explanations to a specific argument; that is, you are writing about a specific work, but you are trying to prove—or argue—or demonstrate—a point or idea about it. This book provides you with a number of separate subjects relating to the study of literature. As you select one of these and begin writing, however, you are not to explain just that such-and-such a story has a character who changes and grows, or that such-and-such a poem contains the thought that nature creates great beauty. Rather, you should assert the importance of your topic to the work as a whole in relation to a specific point or argument. One example of an argument might be that a story's first-person point of view permits readers to draw their own conclusions about the speaker's character. Another argument might be that the poet's thought is shown in a poem's details about the bustling sounds and sights of animals in springtime.

Let us therefore repeat and stress that your writing *should always have an argumentative edge*—a goal of demonstrating the truth of your conclusions and clarifying and illuminating your idea about the topic and also about the work. It is here that the accuracy of your choices of details from the work, the soundness of your conclusions, and the cumulative weight of your evidence are essential. You cannot allow your main ideas to rest on one detail alone, but must support your conclusions by showing that the bulk of material leads to them and that they are linked in a reasonable chain of fact and logic. It is such clarification that is the goal of argumentation.

Using the central idea that the changes in the story's settings reflect Mathilde's character might produce a paragraph like the following, which presents an argument about her negative qualities:

> The original apartment in the Street of Martyrs and the dream world of wealthy places both show negative sides of Mathilde's character. The real-life apartment, though livable, is shabby. The furnishings all bring out her discontent. The shabbiness makes her think only of luxuriousness, and having one servant girl causes her to dream of having many servants. The luxury of her dream life heightens her unhappiness with what she actually has.

In such a preliminary draft, in which the purpose is to connect details and thoughts to the major idea, many details from the story are used in support. In the final draft, this kind of support is essential.

Create a Thesis Sentence as Your Guide to Organization

With your central idea or argument as your focus, you can decide which of the earlier observations and ideas can be developed further. Your goal is to establish a number of major topics to support your argument and to express them in a **thesis sentence** or **thesis statement**—an organizing sentence that contains the major topics you plan to treat in your essay. Suppose you choose three ideas from your discovery stage of development. If you put the central idea at the left and the list of topics at the right, you have the shape of the thesis sentence. Note that the first two topics below are taken from the discovery paragraph.

CENTRAL IDEA	TOPICS
The setting of "The Necklace" reflects Mathilde's character.	1. First apartment
	2. Dream-life mansion rooms
	3. Attic flat

This arrangement leads to the following thesis statement or thesis sentence.

> Mathilde's character growth is connected to her first apartment, her dream-life mansion rooms, and her attic flat.

You can revise the thesis sentence at any stage of the writing process if you find that you do not have enough evidence from the work to support it. Perhaps a new topic will occur to you, and you can include it, appropriately, as a part of your thesis sentence.

As we have seen, the central idea or central argument is the *glue* of the essay. The thesis sentence lists the parts to be fastened together—that is, the topics in which the central idea is to be demonstrated and argued. To alert your readers to your essay's structure, the thesis sentence is usually placed at the end of the introductory paragraph, just before the body of the essay.

As you write your first draft, you need to support the points of your thesis sentence with your notes and discovery materials. You can alter, reject, and rearrange ideas and details as you wish, as long as you change your thesis sentence to account for the changes (a major reason why many writers write their introductions last). The thesis sentence just shown contains three topics (it could be two, or four, or more) to be used in forming the body of the essay.

Begin Each Paragraph with a Topic Sentence

Just as the organization of the *entire essay* is based on the thesis, the form of each *paragraph* is based on its **topic sentence**—an assertion about how a topic from the predicate of the thesis statement supports the argument contained or implied in the central idea. The first topic in our example is the relationship of Mathilde's character to her first apartment, and the resulting paragraph should emphasize this relationship. If your topic is the coarsening of her character during the ten-year travail, you can then form a topic sentence by connecting the trait with the location, as follows:

The attic flat reflects the coarsening of Mathilde's character.

Beginning with this sentence, the paragraph will present details that argue how Mathilde's rough, heavy housework changes her behavior, appearance, and general outlook.

Select Only One Topic—No More—for Each Paragraph

You should treat each separate topic in a single paragraph—one topic, one paragraph. However, if a topic seems especially difficult, long, and heavily detailed, you can divide it into two or more subtopics, each receiving a separate paragraph of its own—two or more subtopics, two or more separate paragraphs. Should you make this division, your topic then is really a section, and each paragraph in the section should have its own topic sentence.

Use Your Topic Sentences as the Arguments for Your Paragraph Development

Once you create a topic sentence, you can use it to focus your observations and conclusions. Let us see how our topic about the attic flat can be developed in a paragraph of argument:

The attic flat reflects the coarsening of Mathilde's character. Maupassant emphasizes the burdens Mathilde endures to save money, such as mopping floors, cleaning greasy and encrusted pots and pans, taking out the garbage, and washing clothes and dishes by hand. This work makes her rough and coarse, an effect also shown by her giving up care of her hair and hands, wearing the cheapest dresses possible, haggling with the local shopkeepers, and becoming loud and penny-pinching. If at the beginning she is delicate and attractive, at the end she is unpleasant and coarse.

REFERRING TO THE NAMES OF AUTHORS

As a general principle, for both men and women writers, you should regularly include the author's *full name* in the *first sentence* of your essay. Here are model first sentences.

> Shirley Jackson's "The Lottery" is a story featuring both suspense and horror.

> "The Lottery," by Shirley Jackson, is a story featuring both suspense and horror.

For all later references, use only last names, such as *Jackson, Maupassant, Lawrence,* or *Porter.* However, for the "giants" of literature, you should use the last names exclusively. In referring to writers like Shakespeare and Dickinson, for example, there is no need to include *William* or *Emily.*

In spite of today's informal standards, never use an author's first name alone, as in "*Shirley* skillfully creates suspense and horror in 'The Lottery.'" Also, do not use a courtesy title before the names of dead authors, such as "*Ms.* Jackson's 'The Lottery' is a suspenseful horror story," or "*Mr.* Shakespeare's idea is that information is uncertain." Use the last names alone.

As with all conventions, of course, there are exceptions. If you are referring to a childhood work of a writer, the first name might be appropriate, but be sure to shift to the last name when referring to the writer's mature works. If your writer has a professional or a noble title, such as "*Lord* Byron" or "*Queen* Elizabeth," it is not improper to use the title. Even then, however, the titles are commonly omitted for males, so that most references to Lord Byron and Alfred, Lord Tennyson, should be simply to "Byron" and "Tennyson."

Referring to living authors is somewhat problematical. Some journals and newspapers often use the courtesy titles *Mr.* and *Ms.* in their reviews. However, scholarly journals, which are likely to remain on library shelves and website for many decades, follow the general principle of beginning with the entire name and then using only the last name for later references.

Here, details from the story are introduced to provide support for the topic sentence. All the subjects—the hard work, the lack of personal care, the wearing of cheap dresses, and the haggling with the shopkeepers—are introduced not to retell the story but rather to exemplify the argument the writer is making about Mathilde's character.

Develop an Outline as the Means of Organizing Your Essay

So far we have been creating a de facto **outline**—that is, a skeletal plan of organization. Some writers never use any outline but prefer informal lists of ideas; others always rely on outlines; still others insist that they cannot make an outline until they have finished writing. And then there are those writers who simply hate outlines. Regardless of your preference, your final essay should have a tight structure. Therefore, you should use a guiding outline to develop and shape your essay.

THE USE OF VERB TENSES IN THE DISCUSSION OF LITERARY WORKS

Literary works spring into life with each and every reading. You may thus assume that everything happening takes place in the present, and when writing about literature you should use the *present tense of verbs*. It is correct to say, "Mathilde and her husband *work* and *economize* [not *worked* and *economized*] for ten years to pay off the 18,000-franc loan they *take out* [not *took out*] to pay for the lost necklace."

When you consider an author's ideas, the present tense is also proper, on the principle that the words of an author are just as alive and current today (and tomorrow) as they were at the moment of writing, even if this same author might have been dead for hundreds or even thousands of years.

Because it is incorrect to shift tenses inappropriately, you may encounter a problem when you refer to actions that have occurred prior to the time of the main action. An instance is Bierce's "An Occurrence at Owl Creek Bridge" (Chapter 1), in which the main character, a Southern gentleman during the Civil War, is about to be hanged by Union soldiers because he tried to sabotage a strategically important bridge. The story emphasizes the relationship between cause (the attempted sabotage, occurring in the past) and effect (the punishment, occurring in the present). In discussing such a narrative it is important to keep details in order, and thus you can introduce the past tense as long as you make the relationship clear between past and present, as in this example: "Farquhar *is actually hanged* [present tense] by the Union soldiers. But his perceptions *turn him* [present tense] toward the past, and his final thoughts *dwell* [present tense] on the life and happiness he *knew* [past tense] at his own home with his dearest wife." This intermingling of past and present tenses is correct because it corresponds to the pattern of time brought out in the story.

A problem also arises when you introduce historical or biographical details about a work or author. It is appropriate to use the *past tense* for such details if they genuinely do belong to the past. Thus it is correct to state, "Shakespeare *lived* from 1564 to 1616," or that "Shakespeare *wrote* his tragedy *Hamlet* in about 1600–1601." It is also permissible to mix past and present tenses when you are treating historical facts about a literary work and are also considering it as a living text. Of prime importance is to keep things straight. Here is an example showing how past tenses (in bold) and present tenses (in italic) may be used when appropriate:

Because *Hamlet* **was** first **performed** in about 1601, Shakespeare most probably **wrote** it shortly before this time. In the play, a tragedy, Shakespeare *treats* an act of vengeance, but more importantly he *demonstrates* the difficulty of ever learning the exact truth. The hero, Prince Hamlet, *is* the focus of this difficulty, for the task of revenge *is assigned* to him by the Ghost of his father. Though the Ghost *claims* that his brother, Claudius, *is* his murderer, Hamlet *is* not able to verify this claim.

Here, the historical details are in the past tense, while all details about the play *Hamlet*, including Shakespeare as the creating author whose ideas and words are still alive, are in the present.

As a general principle, you will be right most of the time if you use the present tense exclusively for literary details and the past tense for historical details. When in doubt, however, *consult your instructor*.

The outline we focus on here is the **analytical sentence outline.** This type is easier to create than it sounds. It consists of (1) an introduction, including the central idea and the thesis sentence, together with (2) topic sentences that are to be used in each paragraph of the body, followed by (3) a conclusion. When applied to the subject we have been developing, such an outline looks like this:

TITLE: *How Setting in "The Necklace" Is Connected to Mathilde's Character*

1. **Introduction:**
   a. *Central idea*: Maupassant uses setting to show Mathilde's character.
   b. *Thesis statement*: Her character growth is brought out by her first apartment, her daydreams about elegant rooms in a mansion, and her attic flat.

2. **Body:** *Topic sentences*: a, b, and c (and d, e, and f, if necessary)
   a. Details about her first apartment explain her dissatisfaction and depression.
   b. Her daydreams about mansion rooms are like the apartment because they too make her unhappy.
   c. The attic flat reflects the coarsening of her character.

3. **Conclusion:** *Topic sentence*: All details in the story, particularly the setting, are focused on the character of Mathilde.

The *conclusion* may be a summary of the body; it may evaluate the main idea; it may briefly suggest further points of discussion; or it may be a reflection on the details of the body.

The illustrative essays included throughout this book are organized according to the principles of the analytical sentence outline. To emphasize the shaping effect of these outlines, all central ideas, thesis sentences, and topic sentences are underlined. In your own writing, you can underline or italicize these "skeletal" sentences as a check on your organization. Unless your instructor requires such markings, however, remove them in your final drafts.

Basic Writing Types: Paragraphs and Essays

Depending on the available time for both out-of-class and in-class writing (including the writing of tests), your instructors may wish to have you write either full-scale essays or single paragraphs for your assignments—probably some of each. Writing a single paragraph assignment helps you build up your preparation for essays. Accordingly, the writing of paragraphs will help you control topic sentences and immediately related topical development, meaning that you include details that illustrate the ideas you have stated at the beginnings of your paragraphs. You should constantly be practicing this habit of mind as you develop your analytical skills for all your courses, not just for those in reading and writing about literature. Throughout this book, therefore, each of the writing sections will be directed toward possible assignments for either single paragraphs or full-scale essays. The successful writing of paragraphs leads naturally toward the buildup of paragraphs in full essays, just as the successful writing of essays depends on the proper development and ordering of individual paragraphs.

A Paragraph Assignment

What do the Loisels do to overcome their indebtedness? What do Mathilde's efforts say about her character?

Mathilde, a woman who despises her simple life and longs for wealth, [1]
luxury and admiration, positions herself and her husband in extensive
debt when she loses and must replace a wealthy friend's diamond necklace
which she borrowed to impress others at a party. Despite the unfortunate [2]
circumstance, Mathilde's determination to overcome indebtedness
highlights an admirable work ethic that was initially absent in Mathilde's
character. Mathilde's character is easy to condemn because she initially [3]
appears superficial, ungrateful and obsessed with luxury. These obsessions [4]
prevent her from acknowledging or appreciating any positive qualities or
opportunities in her own life and drive her to attempt to live outside her
means at great cost. Both she and her husband are forced to accept a lower [5]
quality of living, discovering "the horrible life of the needy," in order to
pay back the debt they have incurred. To repay the loan, they move into [6]
a small attic apartment, Mathilde's husband works two jobs late into
the evening, and Mathilde is forced to release their maid, do the heavy
housework and haggle at the markets, "defending her measly cash penny
by penny." After ten years the Loisels are able to pay back the debt but at [7]
great cost to their physical and financial well-being. Mathilde's greatest [8]
pride was her beauty and charm which is stripped from her after the years
of hardship, and she becomes "the strong, hard, and rude woman of poor
households." In contrast to the selfish and superficial traits initially present [9]
in Mathilde's character, the author explains that faced with repayment of
the debt Mathilde "did her share, however, completely, heroically" and
with determination. She even confronts her wealthy friend years later when [10]
she sees her along the Champs-Elysées, admitting to the lost necklace and
its replacement with a sense of pride in the hardship required to pay off the
debt. Maupassant's story highlights the importance of practicality, living [11]
within one's means, and finding satisfaction rather than discontent in
your life.

Commentary on the Paragraph

Sentence 1, the topic sentence, briefly summarizes the story and outlines the central problem faced by the Loisels. Sentence 2 announces the central thesis that is the student's response to the assignment prompt above. Sentences 3 and 4 offer contrasting evidence of the character's initial shallowness—traits that will change over the course of the story. The actions taken by the Loisels to repay the debt are related in sentences 5 and 6, providing specific examples and short quotes to vividly illustrate their plight. By also including the consequences of their actions (7, 8) the student writer nicely sets up the conclusion, including specific examples with both a quote and a summary (9, 10) as evidence of Mathilde's changed character. The final sentence (11) then ties it all together by connecting this argument to the central themes of the story—a successful strategy for showing that the student understood the significance of the questions being asked.

Illustrative Student Essay (First Draft)

The following illustrative essay is a first draft of the subject we have been developing. It follows our outline, and it includes details from the story in support of the various topics. It is by no means, however, as good a piece of writing as it could be. The draft omits a topic, some additional details, and some new insights that are included in the second draft, which follows later (pp. 48–50). It therefore reveals the need to make improvements through additional brainstorming and discovering-prewriting techniques. The handwritten comments are like those that an instructor might make to help in the improvement of the essay.

Although underlined sentences are not recommended by MLA style, they are used in this illustrative essay as teaching tools to emphasize the central idea, thesis sentence, and topic sentences.

Deal 1

James Deal

Professor Smith

English 102

16 April 2014

How Setting in "The Necklace" Is Related

to the Character of Mathilde°

[1] In "The Necklace" Guy de Maupassant does not give much detail

Explain what setting is used for? about the setting. He does not even describe the necklace itself, which is the

°This story appears on pages 7–13.

Deal 2

central object in his plot, but he says only that it is "superb" (paragraph 47). *Does Mathilde's character grow or change?*

Rather, he uses the setting to reflect the character of the central figure, <u>Mathilde Loisel.</u>* All his details are presented to bring out her traits. <u>Her character growth is related to her first apartment, her dream-life mansion rooms, and her attic flat.</u>† *More specific word needed*

[2]

<u>Details about her first apartment explain her dissatisfaction and depression.</u> The walls are "drab," the furniture "threadbare," and the curtains "ugly" (paragraph 3). There is only a simple country girl to do the housework. The tablecloth is not changed daily, and the best dinner dish is beef stew. Mathilde has no evening clothes, only a theater dress that she does not like. These details show her dissatisfaction about her life with her low-salaried husband. *Explain her reaction to this*

Dissatisfaction is with husband or her life?

[3]

<u>Her dream-life images of wealth are like the apartment because they too make her unhappy.</u> In her daydreams about life in a mansion, the rooms are large, filled with expensive furniture and bric-a-brac, and draped in silk. She imagines private rooms for intimate talks, and big dinners with delicacies like trout and quail. With dreams of such a rich home, she feels even more despair about her modest apartment on the Street of Martyrs in Paris. *Be more specific about her dream world*

Quote from story?

[4]

<u>The attic flat reflects the coarsening of Mathilde's character.</u> Maupassant emphasizes the burdens she endures to save money, such as mopping floors, cleaning greasy and encrusted pots and pans, taking out the garbage, and washing clothes and dishes by hand. This work makes her rough and coarse, a fact also shown by her giving up care of her hair and hands, wearing the cheapest dresses possible, haggling with local shopkeepers, and becoming loud and penny-pinching. If at the beginning she is delicate and attractive, at the end she is unpleasant and coarse. *Perhaps a paragraph about her walk on the Champs-Elysées*

What else does the attic flat indicate about Mathilde? (Her work ethic?)

[5]

<u>Maupassant focuses everything in the story, including the setting, on the character of Mathilde.</u> He does not add anything extra. Thus he says little about the big party scene, but emphasizes the necessary detail that *Any other details that highlight Mathilde's character?*

*Central idea
†Thesis sentence

Good first draft. Work on more specific topic sentences and more details in body paragraphs. Make sure details in body paragraphs are related to topic sentences. You may wish to include another paragraph about the walk on the Champs-Élysées.

Mathilde was a great "success" (paragraph 52). It is this detail that brings out some of her early attractiveness and charm, despite her more usual frustration and unhappiness. Thus in "The Necklace," Maupassant uses setting as a means to his end—the story of Mathilde and her unnecessary sacrifice.

Deal 3

Work Cited

Maupassant, Guy de. "The Necklace." *Literature: An Introduction to Reading and Writing, Compact Edition.* Ed. Edgar V. Roberts and Robert Zweig. 6th ed. New York: Pearson, 2015. 7–13. Print.

Completing the Essay: Developing and Strengthening Your Essay Through Revision

After finishing your first draft, like this one, you may wonder what more you can do. Things may seem to be complete as they are, and that's it. You have read the work several times, have used discovering and brainstorming techniques to establish ideas to write about, have made an outline of your ideas, and have written a full draft. How can you do better?

The best way to begin is to observe that a major mistake writers make when writing about literature is to do no more than retell a story or summarize an idea. Retelling a story shows only that you have read it, not that you have thought about it. Writing a good essay requires you to arrange a pattern of argument and thought.

Make Your Own Arrangement of Details and Ideas

One way to escape the trap of summarizing stories and to set up a pattern of development is to stress your own order when referring to parts of a work. Rearrange details to suit your own central idea or argument. It is often important to write first about the conclusion or middle. Should you find that you have followed the chronological order of the work instead of stressing your own order, you can use one of the preliminary writing techniques to figure out new ways to connect your materials. The principle is that you should introduce details about the work *only* to support the points you wish to make. Details for the sake of detail are unnecessary.

Use Literary Material as Evidence to Support Your Argument

When you write, you are like a detective using clues as evidence for building a case, or a lawyer citing evidence to support an argument. Your goal is to convince your readers of your knowledge and the reasonableness of your conclusions. It is vital to use evidence convincingly so that your readers can follow your ideas. Let us look briefly at two drafts of a new example to see how writing can be improved by the pointed use of details. These are from drafts of an essay on the character of Mathilde.

PARAGRAPH 1

The major flaw of Mathilde's character is that she seems to be isolated, locked away from other people. She and her husband do not talk to each other much, except about external things. He speaks about his liking for beef stew, and she states that she cannot accept the big invitation because she has no nice dresses. Once she gets the dress, she complains because she has no jewelry. Even when borrowing the necklace from Jeanne Forrestier, she does not say much. When she and her husband discover that the necklace is lost, they simply go over the details, and Loisel dictates a letter of explanation, which Mathilde writes in her own hand. Even when she meets Jeanne on the Champs-Elysées, Mathilde does not say a great deal about her life but only goes through enough details about the loss and replacement of the necklace to make Jeanne exclaim about the need-lessness of the ten-year sacrifice.

PARAGRAPH 2

The major flaw of Mathilde's character is that she is withdrawn and uncommunicative, apparently unwilling or unable to form an intimate relationship. For example, she and her husband do not talk to each other much, except about external things such as his taste for beef stew and her lack of a party dress and jewelry. With such an uncommunicative marriage, one might suppose that she would be more open with her close friend, Jeanne Forrestier, but Mathilde does not say much even to her. This flaw hurts her greatly, because if she were more open she might have explained the loss and avoided the horrible sacrifice. This lack of openness, along with her self-indulgent dreaminess, is her biggest defect.

A comparison of these paragraphs shows that the first has more words than the second (157 compared to 120) but that it is more appropriate for a rough than a final draft because the writer does little more than retell the story. Paragraph 1 is cluttered with details that do not support any conclusions. If you try to find what it says about Maupassant's actual use of Mathilde's solitary traits in "The Necklace," you will get little help. The writer needs to revise the paragraph by eliminating details that do not support the central idea.

On the other hand, the details in paragraph 2 actually do support the declared topic. Phrases such as "for example," "with such," and "this lack" show that the writer of paragraph 2 has assumed that the audience knows the story and now wants to read an argument in support of a particular interpretation. Paragraph 2 therefore guides readers by connecting the details to the topic. It uses these details as evidence, *not* as a retelling of actions. By contrast, paragraph 1 recounts a number of relevant actions *but does not connect them to the topic*. More details, of course, could have been added to the second paragraph, but they are unnecessary because the paragraph develops the argument with the details used. Good writing has many qualities, but one of the most important is shown in a comparison of the two paragraphs: *In good writing, no details are included unless they are used as supporting evidence in a pattern of thought and argument.*

Always Keep to Your Point; Stick to It Tenaciously

To show another distinction between first- and second-draft writing, let us consider a third example. The following unrevised paragraph, in which the writer assumes an audience that is interested in the relationship of economics to literature, is drawn from an essay about the idea of economic determinism in Maupassant's "The Necklace." In this paragraph the writer is trying to argue the point that economic circumstances underlie a number of incidents in the story. The idea is to assert that Mathilde's difficulties result not from her character traits but rather from her financial restrictions.

> More important than chance in governing life is the idea that people are controlled by economic circumstances. Mathilde, as is shown at the story's opening, is born poor. Therefore she doesn't get the right doors opened for her, and she settles down to marriage with a minor clerk, Loisel. With a vivid imagination and a burning desire for luxury, seeming to be born only for a life of ease and wealth, she finds that her poor home brings out her daydreams of expensive surroundings. She taunts her husband when he brings the big invitation, because she does not have a suitable (that is, "expensive") dress. Once she gets the dress it is jewelry she lacks, and she borrows that and loses it. The loss of the necklace means great trouble because it forces the Loisels to borrow heavily and to struggle financially for ten years.

This paragraph begins with an effective topic sentence, indicating that the writer has a good plan. The remaining part, however, shows how easily writers can be diverted from their objective. The flaw is that the material of the paragraph, while accurate, is not clearly connected to the topic. Once the second sentence is under way, the paragraph gets lost in a retelling of events, and the promising topic sentence is forgotten. The paragraph therefore shows that the use of detail alone will not support an intended meaning or argument. *As a writer, you must do the connecting yourself, and make sure that all relationships are explicitly clear.* This point cannot be overstressed.

Let us see how the problem can be treated. If the ideal paragraph can be schematized with line drawings, we might say that the paragraph's topic should be a straight line, moving toward and reaching a specific goal (the topic or argument of the paragraph), with an exemplifying line moving away from the straight line briefly to bring in evidence but returning to the line to demonstrate the relevance of each new fact. Thus, the ideal scheme looks like this, with a straight line touched a number of times by an undulating line:

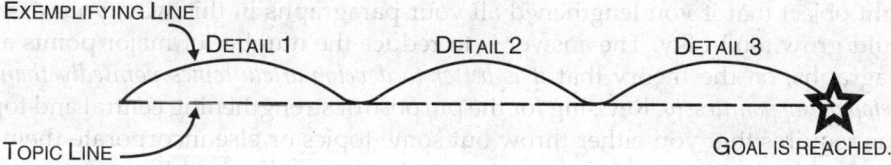

Notice that the exemplifying line, fluctuating to illustrate how documentation or exemplification is to be used, always returns to the topic line. A visual scheme for the faulty paragraph on "The Necklace," however, looks like this, with the line never returning but flying out into space.

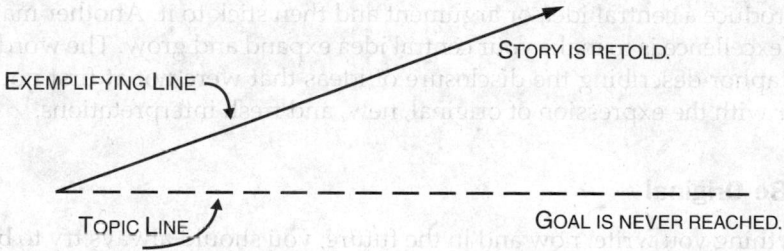

How might the faulty paragraph be improved? The best way is to remind the reader again and again of the topic and to use examples from the text in support.

As our model wavy-line diagram indicates, each time a topic is mentioned, the undulating line merges with the straight, or central-idea line. This relationship of argument to illustrative examples should prevail no matter what subject you write about, and you have to be tenacious in forming these connecting relationships. If you are analyzing *point of view*, for example, you should keep connecting your material to the speaker, or narrator, and the same applies to topics such as character, idea, or setting. According to this principle, we might revise the paragraph on economic determinism in "The Necklace" as follows. (Parts of sentences stressing the relationship of the examples to the topic sentence are underlined.)

> *More important than chance in governing life is the idea that people are controlled by economic circumstances.* As illustration, the speaker begins by emphasizing that Mathilde, the main character, is born poor. Therefore she doesn't get the right doors opened for her, and she settles down to marriage with a minor clerk, Loisel. In keeping with the idea, her vivid imagination and burning desire for luxury feed on her weakness of character as she feels deep unhappiness and depression because of the contrast between her daydreams of expensive surroundings and the poor home she actually has. These straitened economic circumstances inhibit her relationship with her husband, and she taunts him when he brings the big invitation because she does not have a suitable (that is, "expensive") dress. As a merging of her unrealistic dream life with actual reality, her borrowing of the necklace suggests the impossibility of overcoming economic restrictions. In the context of the idea, the ten-year sacrifice to pay for the lost necklace demonstrates that being poor keeps people down, destroying their dreams and their hopes for a better life.

The paragraph now successfully develops the argument promised by the topic sentence. While it has also been lengthened, the length has been caused not by inessential detail but by phrases and sentences that give form and direction. You might object that if you lengthened all your paragraphs in this way, your essays would grow too bulky. The answer is to reduce the number of major points and paragraphs, on the theory that *it is better to develop a few topics pointedly than to develop many pointlessly*. Revising for the purpose of strengthening central and topic ideas requires that you either throw out some topics or else incorporate them as subpoints in the topics you keep. To control your writing in this way can result only in improvement.

Check Your Development and Organization

It bears repeating over and over again that the first requirement of a good essay is to introduce a central idea or argument and then stick to it. Another major step toward excellence is to make your central idea expand and grow. The word *growth* is a metaphor describing the disclosure of ideas that were not at first noticeable, together with the expression of original, new, and fresh interpretations.

Try to Be Original

In everything you write, now and in the future, you should always try to be original. You might claim that originality is impossible because you are writing about someone else's work. "The author has said everything," might be the argument, "and therefore I can do little more than follow the story." This claim rests on the mistaken assumption that you have no choice in selecting material and no opportunity to have individual thoughts and make original contributions.

But you do have choices and opportunities to be original. You really do. One obvious area of originality is the development and formulation of your central idea. For example, a natural first response to "The Necklace" is "The story is about a woman who loses a borrowed necklace and endures hardship to help pay for it." But this response does not promise an argument because it refers only to events in the story and not to any idea. You can point the sentence toward an argument, however, if you call the hardship "needless." Just this word alone demands that you explain the differences between needed and unneeded hardships, and your application of these differences to the heroine's plight would produce an original essay. Even better and more original insights could result if the topic of the budding essay were to connect the dreamy, withdrawn traits of the main character to her misfortunes. A resulting central idea might be "People themselves create their own difficulties." Such an argument would require you to define not only the personal but also the representative nature of Mathilde's experiences, an avenue of exploration that could produce much in the way of a fresh, original essay about "The Necklace."

You can also develop your ability to treat your subject originally if you plan the body of the essay to build up to what you think is your most important and incisive idea. As examples of such planning, the following brief outline suggests how a central idea can be widened and expanded:

ARGUMENT: *Mathilde Grows as a Character in "The Necklace"*

1. She has normal daydreams about a better life.
2. In trying to make her daydreams seem real, she takes a risk but then loses.
3. She develops by facing her mistake and working hard to correct it.

The list shows how you can enlarge a subject if you treat your exemplifying details in an increasing order of importance. In this case, the order moves from Mathilde's habit of daydreaming to her growing strength of character. The pattern shows how you can meet two primary standards of excellence in writing—organization and growth.

Clearly, you should always try to develop your central idea or argument. Constantly adhere to your topic, and constantly develop it. Nurture it and make it grow. Admittedly, in a short essay you will be able to move only a short distance with an idea or argument, but you should never be satisfied to leave the idea exactly where you found it. To the degree that you can learn to develop your ideas, you will receive recognition for increasingly original writing.

Write with Specific Readers as Your Intended Audience

Whenever you write, you must decide how much detail to discuss. Usually you base this decision on your judgment of your readers. For example, if you assume that they have not read the work, you will need to include a short summary as background. Otherwise, they may not understand your argument.

Consider, too, whether your readers have any special interests or concerns. If they are particularly interested in politics, sociology, religion, or psychology, for example, you may need to select and develop your materials along one of these lines.

Your instructor will let you know who your audience is. Usually, it will be your instructor or your fellow students. They will be familiar with the work and will not expect you to retell a story or summarize an argument. Rather, they will want you to explain and interpret the work in the light of your main assertions about it. Thus, you can omit details that do not exemplify and support your argument, even if these details are important parts of the work. What you write should always be based on your developing idea together with your assessment of your readers.

Use Exact, Comprehensive, and Forceful Language

In addition to being original, organized, and well-developed, the best writing is exact, comprehensive, and forceful. At any stage of the composition process, you should try to correct and improve your earliest sentences and paragraphs, which usually need to be rethought, reworded, and rearranged.

Try to make your sentences meaningful. First, ask yourself whether your sentences mean what you really intend, or whether you can make them more exact and therefore stronger. For example, consider these two sentences from essays about "The Necklace":

1. It seems as though the main character's dreams of luxury cause her to respond as she does in the story.
2. This incident, although it may seem trivial or unimportant, has substantial significance in the creation of the story; by this I mean the incident that occurred is essentially what the story is all about.

These sentences are inexact and vague and therefore are unhelpful. Neither of them goes anywhere. Sentence 1 is satisfactory up to the verb *cause*, but then it falls apart because the writer has lost sight of an argumentative or thematic purpose. It would be better to describe what the response *is* rather than to say nothing more than that some kind of response *exists*. To make the sentence more exact, we might try the following revision.

> Mathilde's dreams of luxury make her dissatisfied with her own possessions, and therefore she goes beyond her financial means to attend the big party.

With this revision, the writer could readily go on to consider the relationship of the early part of the story to the later parts. Without the revision, it is not clear where the writer might go.

Sentence 2 is vague because the writer has lost all contact with the main thread of argument. If we adopt the principle of trying to be exact, however, we can create more meaning and more promise:

> The accidental loss of the necklace, which is trivial though costly, supports the narrator's claim that major turns in life are produced not by earthshaking events but rather by minor ones.

In addition to working for exactness, try to make sentences—all sentences, but particularly thesis and topic sentences—complete and comprehensive. Consider the following sentence:

> The idea in "The Necklace" is that Mathilde and her husband work hard to pay for the lost necklace.

Although this sentence promises to describe an idea, it does no more than state the story's major action. It needs additional rethinking and rephrasing to make it more comprehensive, as in these two revisions:

1. In "The Necklace" Maupassant brings out the importance of overcoming mistakes through hard work and responsibility.
2. Maupassant's surprise ending in "The Necklace" symbolizes the need for always being truthful.

Both new sentences are connected to the action described by the original phrasing, "Mathilde and her husband work hard to pay for the lost necklace," although they point toward differing treatments. The first sentence concerns the virtue shown by the Loisels in their sacrifice. Because the second sentence includes the word *symbolizes*, an essay stemming from it would stress the Loisels' mistake in not confessing the loss. In dealing with the symbolic meaning of their failure, an essay developed along the lines of the second sentence would focus on the negative sides of their characters, and an essay developed from the first sentence would stress their positive sides. Both of the revised sentences, therefore, are more comprehensive than the original sentence and thus would help a writer get on the track toward a thoughtful and analytical essay.

Of course, creating fine sentences is never easy, but as a mode of improvement, you might use some self-testing mechanisms:

- *For story materials.* Always relate the materials to a point or argument. Do not say simply, "Mathilde works constantly for ten years to help pay off the debt." Instead, blend the material into a point, like this: "Mathilde's ten-year effort shows her resolution to overcome the horror of indebtedness," or "Mathilde's ten-year effort brings out her strength of character."
- *For responses and impressions.* Do not say simply, "The story's ending left me with a definite impression." What are you giving your readers with a sentence like this? They want to know what your impression is, and therefore you need to describe it, as in the following: "The story's ending surprised me and also made me sympathetic to the major character," or "The story's ending struck me with the idea that life is unpredictable and unfair."
- *For ideas.* Make the idea clear and direct. Do not say, "Mathilde lives in a poor household," but rather refer to the story to bring out an idea, as follows: "Mathilde's story shows that economic deprivation hurts a person's quality of life."
- *For critical commentary.* Do not be satisfied with a statement such as "I found 'The Necklace' interesting." All right, the story is interesting, but what does that tell us? Instead, try to describe *what* was interesting and *why* it was interesting, as in this sentence: "I found 'The Necklace' interesting because it shows how chance and bad luck may disrupt or even destroy people's lives."

Good writing begins with attempts, like these, to rephrase sentences to make them really say something. If you always name and pin down descriptions, responses, and judgments, no matter how difficult the task seems, your sentences can be strong and forceful because you will be making them exact and comprehensive.

Illustrative Student Essay (Improved Draft)

If you refer again to the first draft of the essay about Maupassant's use of setting to illustrate Mathilde's character (pp. 38–40), you might notice that several parts of the draft need extensive reworking and revising. For example, paragraph 2 contains a series of short, unconnected comments; and the last sentence of that paragraph implies that Mathilde's dissatisfaction relates mainly to her husband rather than to her general circumstances. Paragraph 4 focuses too much on Mathilde's coarseness and not enough on her sacrifice and cooperation. The first draft also ignores the fact that the story ends in another location—the fashionable Parisian street the Champs-Elysées, where Maupassant continues to demonstrate the nature of Mathilde's character. Finally, there is not enough support in this draft for the contention (in paragraph 5) that everything in the story is related to the character of Mathilde.

To discover how these issues can be more fully considered, the following revision of the earlier draft creates more introductory detail, includes an additional paragraph, and reshapes each of the paragraphs to stress the relationship of the central idea or argument to the topics of the various paragraphs. Within the limits of a short assignment, the essay illustrates all the principles of organization and unity that we have been discussing here.

Although underlined sentences are not recommended by MLA style, they are used in this illustrative essay as teaching tools to emphasize the central idea, thesis sentence, and topic sentences.

Deal 1

James Deal

Professor Smith

English 102

16 April 2014

How Maupassant Uses Setting in "The Necklace" to Show the

Character of Mathilde

[1]   <u>In "The Necklace" Guy de Maupassant uses setting to reflect the</u> <u>character and development of the main character, Mathilde Loisel.</u>* As a result, his setting is not particularly vivid or detailed. He does not even describe the ill-fated necklace—the central object in the story—but states only that it is "superb" (paragraph 47). In fact he includes descriptions of setting only if they illuminate qualities about Mathilde. <u>Her changing</u> <u>character can be connected to the first apartment, the dream-life mansion</u> <u>rooms, the attic flat, and a fashionable public street.</u>†

[2]   <u>Details about the modest apartment of the Loisels on the Street of</u> <u>Martyrs indicate Mathilde's peevish lack of adjustment to life.</u> Though everything is serviceable, she is unhappy with the "drab" walls, "threadbare" furniture, and "ugly" curtains (paragraph 3). She has domestic help, but she wants more servants than the simple country girl who does the household chores in the apartment. Her embarrassment and dissatisfaction are shown by details of her irregularly cleaned tablecloth and the plain and inelegant beef stew that her husband adores. Even her best theater dress, which is appropriate for apartment life but which is inappropriate for more wealthy surroundings, makes her unhappy. All these details of the apartment establish that Mathilde's major trait at the story's beginning is maladjustment. She therefore seems unpleasant and unsympathetic.

*Central idea.
†Thesis sentence.

Deal 2

Like the real-life apartment, the impossibly wealthy setting of her [3]
daydreams about owning a mansion strengthens her unhappiness and her
avoidance of reality. All the rooms of her fantasies are large and expensive,
draped in silk and filled with nothing but the best furniture and bric-a-
brac. Maupassant gives us the following description of her dream world:

> She imagined a gourmet-prepared main course carried on the most
> exquisite trays and served on the most beautiful dishes, with whispered
> gallantries that she would hear with a sphinxlike smile as she dined on
> the pink meat of a trout or the delicate wing of a quail. (paragraph 4)

With such impossible dreams, her despair is complete. Ironically, this
despair, together with her inability to live with reality, brings about her
undoing. It makes her agree to borrow the necklace (which is just as unreal
as her daydreams of wealth), and losing the necklace drives her into the
reality of giving up her apartment and moving into the attic flat.

Also ironically, the attic flat is related to the coarsening of her [4]
character while at the same time it brings out her best qualities of hard
work and honesty. Maupassant emphasizes the drudgery of the work
Mathilde endures to maintain the flat, such as walking up many stairs,
washing floors with large buckets of water, cleaning greasy and encrusted
pots and pans, taking out the garbage, washing clothes by hand, and
haggling loudly with local shopkeepers. All this reflects her coarsening and
loss of sensibility, also shown by her giving up hair and hand care and by
wearing cheap dresses. The work she performs, however, makes her heroic
(paragraph 98). As she cooperates to help her husband pay back the loans,
her dreams of a mansion fade, and all she has left is the memory of her
triumphant appearance at the Minister of Education's party. Thus the attic
flat brings out her physical change for the worse at the same time that it
also brings out her psychological change for the better.

Her walk on the Champs-Elysées illustrates another combination of [5]
traits—self-indulgence and frankness. The Champs-Elysées is the most
fashionable street in Paris, and her walk to it is similar to her earlier

Deal 3

indulgences in her daydreams of upper-class wealth. But it is on this street where she meets Jeanne, and it is her frankness in confessing to Jeanne that makes her completely honest. While the walk thus serves as the occasion for the story's concluding surprise and irony, Mathilde's being on the Champs-Elysées is totally in character, in keeping with her earlier reveries about luxury.

[6]   Other details in the story also have a similar bearing on Mathilde's character. For example, the story presents little detail about the party scene beyond the statement that Mathilde is a great "success" (paragraph 52)—a judgment that shows her ability to shine if given the chance. After she and Loisel accept the fact that the necklace cannot be found, Maupassant includes details about the Parisian streets, about the visits to loan sharks, and about the jewelry shops in order to bring out Mathilde's sense of honesty and pride as she "heroically" prepares to live her new life of poverty. Thus, in "The Necklace," Maupassant uses setting to highlight Mathilde's maladjustment, her needless misfortune, her loss of youth and beauty, and finally her growth as a responsible human being.

Deal 4

Work Cited

Maupassant, Guy de. "The Necklace." *Literature: An Introduction to Reading and Writing, Compact Edition.* Ed. Edgar V. Roberts and Robert Zweig. 6th ed. New York: Pearson, 2015. 7–13. Print.

Commentary on the Essay

Several improvements to the first draft are seen here. The language of paragraph 2 has been revised to show more clearly the inappropriateness of Mathilde's dissatisfaction. In paragraph 3, the irony of the story is brought out, and the writer has connected the details to the central idea in a richer pattern of ideas, showing the effects of Mathilde's despair. Paragraph 5—new in the improved draft—includes additional details about how Mathilde's walk on the Champs-Elysées is related to her character. In paragraph 6, the fact that Mathilde is able "to shine" at the dinner party is interpreted according to the central idea. Finally, the conclusion is now much more specific, summarizing the change in Mathilde's character rather than saying simply that the setting reveals "her needless misfortune." In short, the second draft reflects the complexity of "The Necklace" better than the first draft. Because the writer has revised the first-draft ideas about the story, the final essay is tightly structured, insightful, and forceful.

Essay Commentaries

Throughout this book, the illustrative essays are followed by short commentaries that show how the essays embody the chapter instructions and guidelines. For each essay that has a number of possible approaches, the commentary points out which one is used; and when an essay uses two or more approaches, the commentary makes this fact clear. In addition, each commentary singles out one of the paragraphs for more detailed analysis of its argument and use of detail. The commentaries will hence help you develop the insights necessary to use the essays as aids in your own study and writing.

A Summary of Guidelines

To sum up, follow these guidelines whenever you write about a story or any kind of literature:

- Do not simply retell the story or summarize the work. Bring in story materials only when you can use them as support for your central idea or argument.
- Throughout your essay, keep reminding your reader of your central idea.
- Within each paragraph, make sure that you stress your topic idea.
- Develop your subject. Make it bigger than it was when you began.
- Always make your statements exact, comprehensive, and forceful.
- And this bears repeating: Do not simply retell the story or summarize the work.

Writing Topics About the Writing Process

1. Write a brainstorming paragraph on the topic of anything in a literary work that you find especially good or interesting. Write as the thoughts occur to you; do not slow yourself down in an effort to make your writing seem perfect. You can make corrections and improvements later.

2. Using marginal and notebook notations, together with any additional thoughts, describe the way in which the author of a particular work has expressed important ideas and difficulties.

3. Create a plus-minus table to list your responses about a character or ideas in a work.

4. Raise questions about the actions of characters in a story or play in order to determine the various customs and manners of the society out of which the work is derived.

5. Analyze and explain the way in which the conflicts in a story or play are developed. What pattern or patterns do you find? Determine the relationship of the conflicts to the work's development, and fashion your idea of this relationship as an argument for a potential essay.

6. Basing your ideas on your marginal and notebook notations, select an idea and develop a thesis sentence from it, using your idea and a list of possible topics for an argument or central idea for an essay.

7. Using the thesis sentence you write for exercise 6, develop a brief analytical sentence outline that could help you in writing a full essay.

USING SOURCES EFFECTIVELY

After selected student essays in each genre covered in the text, we will include a feature called "Using Sources Effectively," in which we will analyze the student writers' practices in quoting, summarizing, and paraphrasing both primary and secondary sources to make their writing more authoritative, more compelling, and more scholarly.

Writing about literature requires that you read the primary work carefully, think critically about what it means to the author and to yourself, and employ writing strategies and academic conventions that will most convincingly make your case about the work's content, techniques, effectiveness, and importance. In order to demonstrate that you are grounding your analysis firmly in the work itself, you will want to judiciously quote from or refer directly to the work itself and, in some papers, from critical works of others, often described as "secondary sources." To do this properly, you need to consider the following questions:

1. Do the words and passages you are quoting, summarizing, or paraphrasing truly and articulately help to advance your argument? (See "A Short Guide to the Use of References and Quotations in Essays About Literature" on p. 53.)

2. Are you using the proper conventions for punctuation and citation required by the field? (See "Recommendations for MLA Documentation" in Appendix II.)

3. Are you writing an honest, original interpretation or analysis of the work, even if you may also be incorporating or reacting to ideas from other critics? (See the discussion of plagiarism in Chapter 10A, p. 500.)

A Short Guide to the Use of References and Quotations in Essays About Literature

In establishing evidence for the points you make in your essays and essay examinations, you constantly need to refer to various parts of stories, plays, and poems. You also need to include shorter and longer quotations and to keep the time sequences straight within the works you are writing about. In addition, you may need to refer to biographical and historical details that have a bearing on the work or works you are studying. So that your own writing may flow as accurately and naturally as possible, you must be able to integrate these references and distinctions of time clearly and easily.

Integrate Passages and Ideas into Your Essay

Your essays should reflect your own thought as you study and analyze the characteristics, ideas, and qualities of an author's work. In a typical discussion of literature, you constantly need to introduce brief summaries, quotations, general interpretations, observations, and independent applications of everything you are discussing. It is not easy to keep these various elements integrated and to keep confusion from arising.

Distinguish Your Thoughts from Those of Your Author

Often a major problem is that it is hard for your reader to figure out when *your* ideas have stopped and your *author's* have begun. You must therefore arrange your sentences to make the distinctions clear, but you must also blend your materials so that your reader may follow you easily. Let us see an example of how such problems may be handled. Here, the writer being discussed is the Victorian poet Matthew Arnold (1822–1888). The passage moves from reference to Arnold's ideas to the essay writer's independent application of the ideas.

[1] In his poem "Dover Beach," Arnold states that in past times religious faith was accepted as absolute truth. [2] To symbolize this idea he refers to the ocean, which surrounds all land, and the surf, which constantly rushes onto the earth's shores. [3] According to this symbolism, religious ideas are as vast as the ocean and as regular as the surf, and these ideas at one time constantly and irresistibly replenished people's lives. [4] Arnold's symbol of the flowing ocean changes, however, to a symbol of the ebbing ocean, thus illustrating his idea that belief and religious certainty were falling away. [5] It is this personal sense of spiritual emptiness that Arnold is associating with his own times, because what he describes, in keeping with the symbolism, is that in the present time the "drear" shoreline has been left vacant by the "melancholy long withdrawing roar" of retreat and reduction (lines 25–27).

This specimen paragraph combines but also separates paraphrase, interpretation, and quotation, and it thereby eliminates any possible confusion about the origin of the ideas and also about who is saying what. In the first three sentences the writer uses the phrases "Arnold states," "To symbolize this idea," and "According to this symbolism" to show clearly that interpretation is to follow. Although the fourth sentence marks a new direction of Arnold's ideas, it continues to separate restatement from interpretation. The fifth sentence indicates, through the phrase "in keeping with the symbolism," what seems to the writer to be the major idea of "Dover Beach."

Integrate Material by Using Quotation Marks

It is often necessary, and also interesting, to use short quotations from your author to illustrate and reinforce your ideas and interpretations. Here the problem of separating your thoughts from the author's is solved by quotation marks. In such an internal quotation, you may treat prose and poetry in the same way. If a poetic quotation extends from the end of one line to the beginning of another, however, indicate the line break with a virgule (/), and use a capital letter to begin the next line, as in the following:

> In "Lines Written in Early Spring" Wordsworth describes a condition in which his speaker is united with the surrounding natural world. Nature is a combination of the "thousand blended notes" of joyful birds (line 1) and the sights of "budding twigs" (line 17) and the "periwinkle" (line 10). In the exact words of the speaker, these "fair works" directly "link / The human soul that through me ran" (lines 5 and 6).

Blend Quotations into Your Own Sentences

The use of internal quotations still creates the problem of blending materials, however, for quotations should never be brought in unless you prepare your reader for them in some way. *Do not*, for example, use quotations in the following manner:

> Wordsworth states that his woodland grove is filled with the sounds of birds, the sights of flowers, and the feeling of the light wind, making for the thought that creatures of the natural world take pleasure in life. "The birds around me hopped and played."

This abrupt quotation throws the reader off balance because it is not blended into the previous sentence. It is necessary to prepare the reader to move from your discussion to the quotation, as in the following revision:

> Wordsworth claims that his woodland scene is made joyful by the surrounding flowers and the gentle breeze, causing his speaker, who states that "The birds around me hopped and played," to conclude that the natural world has resulted from a "holy plan" created by Nature.

Here the quotation is made an actual part of the sentence. This sort of blending is satisfactory, provided that the quotation is brief.

Indent Long Quotations and Set Them in Block Format

You can follow a general rule for incorporating quotations in your writing: Do not quote within a sentence any passage longer than twenty or twenty-five words (but consult your instructor, for the allowable number of words may vary). Quotations of greater length demand so much separate attention that they interfere with your own sentence. It is possible but not desirable to conclude one of your sentences with a quotation, but you should never make an extensive quotation in the *middle* of a sentence. By the time you finish such an unwieldy sentence, your reader will have lost sight of how it began. When your quotation is long, you should make a point of introducing it and setting it off separately as a block.

The physical layout of block quotations should be this: Double-space the quotation (like the rest of your essay), and indent it ten spaces from your left margin to distinguish it from your own writing. You might use fewer spaces for longer lines of poetry, but the standard should always be to create a balanced, neat page. After the quotation, resume your own discourse at the left margin or with a new paragraph. Do not leave extra lines of space above or below the quotation. Here is a specimen, from an essay about Wordsworth's "Lines Written in Early Spring":

> In "Lines Written in Early Spring" Wordsworth develops an idea that the world of nature is linked directly to the moral human consciousness. He speaks of no religious systems or books of moral values. Instead, he derives his ideas directly from his experience, assuming that the world was made for the joy of the living creatures in it, including human beings ("man"), and that anyone disturbing that power of joy is violating "Nature's holy plan" itself. Wordsworth's moral criticism, in other words, is derived from his faith in the integrity of creation:
>
>> If this belief from heaven be sent,
>> If such be Nature's holy plan,
>> Have I not reason to lament
>> What man has made of man?
>>   (lines 21–24)
>
> The concept that morality and life are joined is the most interesting and engaging aspect of the poem. It seems to encourage a live-and-let-live attitude toward others, however, not an active program of direct outreach and help.

When quoting lines of poetry, always remember to quote them *as lines.* Do not run them together as though they were continuous prose. When you create such block quotations, as in the preceding example, you do *not* need quotation marks.

Today, computer usage is the established means of preparing papers, and therefore computer styling has become prominent in the handling of the matters discussed here. If you have style features in your menu, such as "Poem Text" or "Quotation," each of which sets block quotations apart from "Normal" text, you may certainly make use of the features. Be sure to explain to your instructor what you are doing, however, to make sure that your computer's features correspond to the styles that are required for your class.

Use an Ellipsis to Show Omissions

Whether your quotation is long or short, you will often need to change some of the material in it to conform to your own sentence requirements. You might wish to omit something from the quotation that is not essential to your point or to the flow of your sentence. Indicate such omissions with an ellipsis (three spaced periods), as follows (from an essay about Bierce's "An Occurrence at Owl Creek Bridge"):

> Under the immediate threat of death, Farquhar's perceptions are sharpened and heightened. In actuality there is "swirling water . . . racing madly beneath his feet," but it is his mind that is racing swiftly, and he accordingly perceives that a "piece of dancing driftwood . . . down the current" moves so slowly that he believes the stream is "sluggish."

If your quotation is very brief, however, do not use ellipses as they might be more distracting than helpful. For example, do not use them in a quotation like this:

> Keats asserts that ". . . a thing of beauty . . ." always gives joy.

Instead, make your quotation without the ellipses:

> Keats asserts that "a thing of beauty" always gives joy.

Use Square Brackets to Enclose Words
That You Add Within Quotations

If you add words of your own to integrate the quotation into your own train of discourse or to explain words that may seem obscure, put square brackets around these words, as in the following passage:

> In "Lines Written in Early Spring," Wordsworth refers to a past experience of extreme happiness, in which Nature seemed to "link/The human soul that through . . . [him] ran." He is describing a state of mystical awareness in which "pleasant thoughts / Bring [him] sad thoughts," and make him "lament" moral and political cruelty (lines 2–8).

Be Careful Not to Overquote

A word of caution: *Do not use too many quotations.* You will be judged on your own thought and on the continuity and development of your own essay. It is tempting to include many quotations on the theory that you need to use examples from the text to illustrate and support your ideas. Naturally, it is important to introduce examples, but you should understand that too many quotations can disturb the flow of your own thought. If your essay consists of many illustrations linked together by no more than your introductory sentences, how much thinking have you actually shown? Try, therefore, to create your own discussion, using appropriate examples to connect your thought to the text or texts you are analyzing.

Preserve the Spellings in Your Source

Always reproduce your source exactly. Sometimes the works of British authors may include words like *tyre, defence, honour,* and *labour*. Duplicate these as you find them. Although most anthologies, such as this one, modernize the spelling of older writers, you may often encounter "old-spelling" editions in which all words— such as *entring, Shew, beautie, ore* (for "over"), *witte* (for "wit"), *specifick, 'twas, guaranty* (for "guarantee"), or *determin'd*—are spelled and capitalized exactly as they were centuries ago. Your principle should be *to duplicate everything exactly as you find it*, even if this means spelling words like *achieve* as *atchieve, music* as *Musick,* or *joke* as *joak*. A student once changed the word *an* to "and" in the construction "an I were" in a Shakespeare play. The result was misleading, because in introductory clauses *an* really meant *if* (or *and if*) and not *and*. Difficulties like this one are rare, but you can avoid them if you reproduce the text as you find it. Should you think that something is either misspelled or confusing as it stands, you may do one of two things:

1. Clarify or correct the confusing word or phrase within brackets, as in the following:

   In 1714, fencing was considered a "Gentlemany [i.e., gentlemanly] subject."

2. Use the word *sic* (Latin for *thus*, meaning "It is this way in the text") in brackets immediately after the problematic word or obvious mistake:

   He was just "finning [sic] his way back to health" when the next disaster struck.

PART II

Reading and Writing
About Fiction

Chapter 1
Fiction: An Overview

AFTER STUDYING THIS MATERIAL, YOU SHOULD BE ABLE TO DO THE FOLLOWING:

- Understand the broad history of fiction
- Define the specific characteristics of the short story
- Identify the elements of fiction: character, plot, structure, and theme
- Evaluate an author's use of narrative tools: style, point of view, tone, and symbolism

Fiction originally meant anything *made up* or *shaped*. As we understand the word today, it refers to *short or long prose stories*—and it has retained this meaning since 1599, the first year for which we have a record for it in print. Fiction is distinguished from the works it imitates, such as *historical accounts, reports, biographies, autobiographies, letters,* and *personal memoirs* and *meditations*. Although fiction often resembles these forms, it has a separate identity because it originates not in historical facts but in the imaginative and creative powers of the author. Writers of fiction may include historically accurate details, but their overriding goal is to tell a story and say something significant about life.

The essence of fiction, as opposed to drama, is **narration,** the recounting or telling of a sequence of events or actions. The earliest works of fiction relied almost exclusively on narration, with speeches or dialogue being reported rather than quoted directly. Much recent fiction includes extended passages of dialogue, thereby becoming more *dramatic* even though narration is still the primary mode.

Fiction is rooted in ancient legends and **myths.** Local priests told stories about their gods and heroes, as shown in some of the narratives of ancient Egypt. In the course of history, traveling storytellers would appear in a court or village to entertain listeners with tales of adventure in faraway countries. Although many of these were fictionalized accounts of events and people who may not ever have existed, they were largely accepted as fact or history. An especially long tale, an **epic,** was recited during a period of days. To aid their memories and to impress and entertain their listeners, the storytellers chanted their tales in poetry, often accompanying themselves on a stringed instrument.

Legends and epics also reinforced the local religions and power structures. Myths of gods like Zeus and Athena (Greece), Jupiter and Minerva (Rome), and Baal and Ishtar (Mesopotamia) abounded, together with stories of famous men and women like Achilles, Aeneas, Atalanta, David, Helen of Troy, Hercules, Joseph, Odysseus, Oedipus, Penelope, Ruth, Romulus and Remus, and Utu-Napishtim. The ancient Macedonian king and general Alexander the Great (356–323 BCE) developed many of his ideas about nobility and valor from *The Iliad,* Homer's epic about the Trojan War—and, we might add, from discussing the epic with his tutor, the philosopher Aristotle.

Perhaps nowhere is the moral-instructive aspect of ancient storytelling better illustrated than in the **fables** of Aesop, a Greek who probably wrote in the sixth century BCE, and in the **parables** of Jesus as told in the Gospels of the New Testament (see Chapter 7). In these works, a short narrative provides an illustration of a religious, philosophic, or psychological conclusion.

Starting about eight hundred years ago, storytelling in Western civilization was developed to a fine art by writers such as Marie de France, a Frenchwoman who wrote in England near the end of the twelfth century, Giovanni Boccaccio (Italian, 1313–1375), and Geoffrey Chaucer (English, c. 1340–1400). William Shakespeare (1564–1616) drew heavily on history and legend for the stories and characters in his plays.

Modern Fiction

Fiction as we understand the word today did not begin to spread until the seventeenth and eighteenth centuries, when changes in the idea of human nature began to develop. For many centuries the belief prevailed that human beings were in a fallen moral state—a state of "total depravity"—and that by themselves they needed the controlling hands of church and monarchy to keep them moral, peaceful, and pious. During the Renaissance, however, thinkers began to claim that humanity should be viewed within a perspective of greater and broader latitude. Some people were fallen, yes, but many others were not; and they could become moral through their own efforts without the control of political and moral authorities. It was this analysis that provided the foundation for the development of the democratic theory of government that has been accepted in much of modern society.

In literature, it thus became possible to view human beings of all social positions and ways of life as important literary topics. As one writer put it in 1709, human nature is by no means simple, for it is governed by many complex motives such as "passion, humor, caprice, zeal, faction, and a thousand other springs."[1] Observations such as this were the basis of the individual and psychological concerns that characterize fiction today. Indeed, fiction is strong because it is so real and personal. Characters have both first and last names; the countries and cities in which they live are visualized as real places, with real influences on the inhabitants; and their actions and interactions are like those that readers themselves have experienced, could experience, or could readily imagine themselves experiencing.

Along with attention to character, fiction is also concerned with the significance of place or environment on the lives of people. In the simplest sense, location is a backdrop or setting within which characters speak, move, and act. But more broadly, environment comprises the social, economic, and political conditions that affect the outcomes of people's lives. Fiction is primarily about the interactions among people, but it also involves these larger interactions—either directly or indirectly. Indeed, a typical work of fiction includes many forces, both small and large, that influence the ways in which characters meet and deal with their problems.

Anthony Ashley Cooper, Third Earl of Shaftesbury, "Sensus Communis," III, 3.

The first true works of fiction in Europe, however, were less concerned with society or politics than adventure. These were the lengthy Spanish and French **romances** of the sixteenth and seventeenth centuries. In English the word **novel** was borrowed from French and Italian to describe these works and to distinguish them from medieval and classical romances as something that was *new* (the meaning of *novel*). In England the word *story* was used along with *novel* in reference to the new literary form.

The increased levels of education and literacy in the eighteenth century encouraged the development of fiction. During the times of Shakespeare (1564–1616) and John Dryden (1631–1700), the only way a writer could make a living from writing was either to be a member of the nobility or have an allowance from a member of the nobility, or else to have a play accepted at a theater and then receive either a direct payment or the proceeds of an "author's benefit." The paying audiences, however, were limited to people who lived within a short distance of the theater or who had the money and free time to stay in town and attend the plays during the theater season.

Once great numbers of people could read for themselves, the paying audience for literature expanded. A writer could write a novel and receive money for it from a publisher, who would then profit from a wide sale. Readers could start reading the book when they wished, and they would finish it when it was convenient to do so. Reading a novel could even be a social event, for people would gather together and read to each other as a means of sharing the reading experience. Quite often, as tastes for fiction developed, the writers would publish monthly installments of their novels. When the mail brought these new episodes and chapters, the principal activity would quickly focus on circles of listeners, who would listen eagerly while a fluent and spirited reader would bring the stories to life. Often these episodes would extend for many months, and the fiction-consuming public would discuss the latest experiences and try to guess what would happen next. With this wider audience of people whom authors would never see or know, it became possible for writers to develop a profitable career out of their trade. Lengthy fictional stories had arrived as a major genre of literature.

The Short Story

Because novels were long, they took a long time to read—hours, days, even weeks. The early nineteenth-century American writer Edgar Allan Poe (1809–1849) addressed this problem and developed a theory of the **short story,** which he described in a review of Nathaniel Hawthorne's *Twice-Told Tales*. Poe was convinced that "worldly interests" prevented people from gaining the "totality" of comprehension and response that he believed reading should provide. A short, concentrated story (he called it "a brief prose tale" that could be read at a single sitting) was ideal for producing such a strong impression.

In the wake of the taste for short fiction after Poe, many writers have worked in the form. Today, stories are printed in many magazines, such as *Harper's Magazine, The Atlantic*, and *Zoetrope*, and in many collections, such as *American Short Story Masterpieces*. Some of the better-established writers—William Faulkner, Ernest Hemingway, Shirley Jackson, Flannery O'Connor, Joyce Carol Oates, John Updike, Alice Walker, and Eudora Welty, to name only a small number—were able to publish their stories in separate volumes.

Elements of Fiction I: Verisimilitude and *Donnée*

Fiction, along with drama, has a basis in **realism** or **verisimilitude.** That is, the situations or characters, although they are the invention of writers, are similar to those that many human beings experience, know, or think. Even fantasy, the creation of events that are dreamlike or fantastic, is based in the real world, however remotely. This connection of art and life has led some critics to label fiction, and also drama, as an art of imitation. Shakespeare's Hamlet states that an actor attempts to portray real human beings in realistic situations (to "hold a mirror up to Nature").

The same may also be said about writers of fiction, with the clarification that reality is not easily defined and that authors can follow many paths in imitating it. What matters in fiction is the way in which authors establish the ground rules for their works, whether with realistic or nonrealistic characters, places, actions, and physical and chemical laws. The assumption that authors make about the nature of their story material is called a *postulate* or a *premise*—what the American novelist Henry James called a *donnée* (something given). The *donnée* of some stories is to resemble the everyday world as much as possible. Eudora Welty's "A Worn Path" (Chapter 5) is such a story. In it we follow the difficult walk of an elderly woman as she goes from home to a medical office in Natchez, Mississippi, and we also learn of the virtual hopelessness of her mission. The events of the story are not uncommon; they could happen in life just as Welty presents them.

Once a *donnée* is established, it governs the directions in which the story moves. Jackson's "The Lottery" (Chapter 2), for example, contains a premise or *donnée* that may be phrased like this: "Suppose that a small, ordinary town held a lottery in which the prize was not something good but instead was something bad." Everything in Jackson's story follows from this premise. At first we seem to be reading about innocent actions in a rural American community. By the end, however, in accord with the premise, the story enters the realm of nightmare.

Before going too far into this realm, however, it would be appropriate to consider that most stories are devoted to less shocking and bizarre levels of narration. The essential ingredients of stories are events in sequence, leading to a conclusion that may be interesting, elevating, serious, or comic. The perceptive reader will discover the *why* of particular actions, along with the *what*, the *where*, and the *when*. There may be a romance in a story, or an attempt to solve a particularly difficult problem or issue. If the topic is romantic, the principal characters will be devoted to making their difficulties disappear as they try to create a happy outcome with the anticipation of future and lifelong happiness. If the story should end on such a note, we may conclude that all is, and will be, well. But some stories ask us to examine the life of the characters after the events of the story, as in Inés Arredondo's "The Shunammite" (p.81). In this work, we see how a young woman's feeling about herself in the world, especially in her relations with men, is not only changed by the story's events, but she is left with a far different view of what her life will be in the future. In short, the action described in the story affects her immediately but also initiates a change in her perspective that will follow her through time that the reader must consider.

In such ways authors may lead us into remote, fanciful, and symbolic levels of reality, as in Gilman's "The Yellow Wallpaper" (Chapter 10), in which we readers become drawn in to the disoriented world of a narrator who has totally lost her grip on the reality of the situations around her. In Poe's "The Masque of the Red Death" (Chapter 9), the supernatural *donnée* is that Death may assume a human but sinister shape. Literally nothing is out of bounds as long as the author makes clear the premise for the action.

Scenes and actions such as these, which are not realistic in our ordinary sense of the word, are normal in stories *as long as they follow the author's own stated or implied ground rules*. You may always judge a work by the standard of whether it is consistent with the premise, or the *donnée*, created by the writer.

In addition to referring to various levels of reality, the word *donnée* may also be taken more broadly. In *futuristic* and *science fiction*, for example, there is an assumption or *donnée* of certain situations and technological developments (e.g., interstellar space travel) that are not presently in existence. In a *love story*, the *donnée* is that two people meet and overcome an obstacle of some sort (usually not a serious one) on the way to fulfilling their love. Interesting variations of the love story are James Joyce's "Araby" (Chapter 4) and D. H. Lawrence's "The Horse Dealer's Daughter" (Chapter 8).

There are, of course, other types. A *growth* or *apprenticeship story*, for example, is about the development of a major character, such as Jackie in Frank O'Connor's "First Confession" (Chapter 6). In the *detective story*, a mysterious event is presented, and then an individual draws conclusions from the available evidence, as in Susan Glaspell's "A Jury of Her Peers" (Chapter 3), in which the correct detective work is done by two women, not by the legally authorized police investigators.

In addition to setting levels of reality and fictional types, authors may use other controls or springboards as their *donnée*. Sometimes an initial situation may be the springboard of the narrative, such as the at-first unidentified man standing "upon a railroad bridge in northern Alabama" in Bierce's "An Occurrence at Owl Creek Bridge" (p. 87). Or the key may be a pattern of behavior, such as the boy's reactions to the people around him in O'Connor's "First Confession," or the solution of a mystery about a community icon, as in Faulkner's "A Rose for Emily." A shaping force, or *donnée*, always guides the actions, and often a number of such controls operate at the same time.

Elements of Fiction II: Character, Plot, Structure, and Idea or Theme

Works of fiction share a number of common elements. For reference here, the more significant ones are *character, plot, structure*, and *idea* or *theme*.

Character Brings Fiction to Life

Stories, like plays, are about characters, who are *not* real people but who are nevertheless *like* real people. A **character** may be defined as a reasonable representation of a human being, with all the good and bad traits of being human. Most stories are concerned with characters who are facing a major problem that develops from misunderstanding, misinformation, unfocused ideals and goals, difficult situations, troubled relationships, and generally challenging situations. The characters may win, lose, or tie. They may learn and be the better for the experience or may miss the point and be unchanged.

As we have stated, modern fiction has accompanied the development of a psychological interest in human beings. Psychology itself has grown out of the philosophical and religious idea that people have many inborn qualities—some of them good and others bad. People encounter many problems in their lives, and they make many mistakes; they expend much effort in coping and adjusting. But they nevertheless are important and interesting and are therefore worth writing about, whether male or female; young or old; white, black, tan, or yellow; rich or poor; worker or industrialist; traveler or resident; doctor, librarian, mother, daughter, homemaker, prince, ship captain, bartender, or army lieutenant.

The range of fictional characters is vast: A married couple struggling to repay an enormous debt, a young man learning about the nature of his desires, a woman recalling many conflicts with her mother, two close relatives considering the loss of their past, a woman surrounded by her insensitive and self-seeking brothers, a man making triumphs out of his blunders, an unmarried couple dealing with the serious issue of what to do about the possibility of future childbirth, a woman feverishly recollecting her long experience without a man whom she had loved—all these, and more, may be found in fiction just as they may also be found in all levels and conditions of life. Because we all share the same capacities for concern, involvement, sympathy, happiness, sorrow, exhilaration, and disappointment, we are able to find endless interest in such characters and their ways of coping with their circumstances.

Plot Is the Plan of Fiction

Fictional characters, who are drawn from life, go through a series of lifelike actions or incidents, which make up the story. In a well-done story, all the actions or incidents, speeches, thoughts, and observations are linked together to make up an entirety, sometimes called an **organic unity**. The essence of this unity is the development and resolution of a **conflict**—or conflicts—in which the **protagonist**, or central character, is engaged. The interactions of causes and effects as they develop sequentially or chronologically make up the story's **plot**. (See the section on writing on pp. 114–18.) That is, a story's actions follow one another in time as the protagonist meets and tries to overcome opposing forces. Sometimes plot has been compared to a story's *map, scheme,* or *blueprint.*

Often the protagonist's struggle is directed against another character—an **antagonist.** Just as often, however, the struggle may occur between the protagonist and opposing groups, forces, ideas, and choices—all of which make up a collective antagonist. The conflict may be carried out wherever human beings spend their lives, such as a kitchen, a hotel, a railway station bar, a restaurant, a town square, a schoolroom, an ordinary living room, a church, an exclusive store, a vacation resort, a café, or a battlefield. The conflict may also take place internally, within the mind of the protagonist.

Structure Is the Knitting Together of Fiction

Structure refers to the way a story is put together according to some sort of plan. Chronologically, all stories are similar because they move from beginning to end in accord with the time needed for *causes* to produce *effects*. But authors choose many different ways to put their stories together. Some stories are told in straightforward sequential order, and a description of the plot of such stories is identical to a description of the structure. Other stories, however, may get pieced together through out-of-sequence and widely separated episodes, speeches, secondhand reports, vague recollections, accidental discoveries, dreams, nightmares, periods of insanity, fragments of letters, overheard conversations, and the like. In such stories, the plot and the structure diverge widely. Therefore, in dealing with the structure of stories, we emphasize not chronological order but the actual *arrangement* and *development* of the stories as they unfold, part by part. Usually we study an entire story, but we may also direct our attention toward the structure of a smaller aspect of arrangement such as an episode or passage of dialogue.

Idea or Theme Is the Life-Giving Thought of Fiction

The word **idea** refers to the result or results of general and abstract thinking. A **theme** is an exploration of an idea—an idea in movement that persists throughout the story. Often the two words are used interchangeably. Either directly or indirectly, fiction embodies ideas and **themes** that underlie and give life to stories and novels. Writers do not need to state their ideas in specific words, but the strength of their works depends on the power with which they exemplify ideas and make them clear. Thus, writers of comic works are committed to the idea that human difficulties can be treated with humor. More serious works often show characters confronting difficult and sometimes agonizing moral choices—the idea being that in a losing situation the only winners are those who maintain honor and self-respect. Mystery and suspense stories develop from the idea that problems have solutions, although the solutions at first may seem remote or impossible. Even stories written for entertainment alone, some of which may at first seem devoid of ideas, stem out of an idea or position that the work itself makes clear. Writers may deal with the triumphs and defeats of life, the admirable and the despicable, the humorous and the pathetic; but whatever their goal, they are always expressing ideas about human experience. We may therefore raise questions such as these as we look for ideas in fiction:

- What does this mean?
- Why does the author include it?
- What idea or ideas does it show?
- Why is it significant?

Many works can be discussed in terms of the *issues* that they raise. An **issue** (which today has become a broad and perhaps overused word) may involve a work's characters in direct or indirect argument or opposition, and it may also bring out vitally important moments of decision about matters of private or public concern. In addition to the issues that the characters face, the works themselves may be considered for their more general issues.

Fictional ideas can also be considered as major themes that tie individual works together. Often an author makes the theme obvious, as in the Aesop fable in which a man uses an ax to kill a fly on another man's forehead. The theme of this fable might loosely be expressed in the sentence "The cure should not be worse than the disease." A major theme in Maupassant's "The Necklace" (Part I) is that people may be destroyed or saved by the most minor of unforeseeable and or even unlucky events. The accidental loss of the borrowed necklace is just such an event, for this misfortune ruins the lives of both Mathilde and her husband.

The process of determining and describing the themes or ideas in stories is never complete; there is always another theme that we can discuss, another idea that may be explored. Thus in "The Necklace," we might note the additional themes that adversity brings out worth, that telling the truth is better than concealing it, that envy often produces ill fortune, that people may build their lives on incorrect assumptions, and that good fortune is never recognized until it is gone. Indeed, one of the ways in which we judge stories is to determine the degree to which they explore a number of valid and important ideas.

Elements of Fiction III: The Writer's Tools

Narration Creates the Sequence and Logic of Fiction

Writers have a number of modes of presentation, or "tools," that they use in their stories. The principal tool (and the heart of fiction) is **narration,** the reporting of actions in sequential order. The object of narration is to *render* the story, to make it clear and to bring it alive to the reader's imagination through the movement of sentences through time.

VISUALIZING FICTION

Cartoons, Graphic Narratives, Graphic Novels

A modern popular development of art is the single line-drawn cartoon together with a caption, brought to perfection by the many cartoonists who provided comic panels for *The New Yorker* and also the innumerable other publications that continue to flourish today. The point about most of the cartoons is that they are based in narrative, as are the history and genre painting traditions. In no more than a single picture drawing, clever cartoonists supply the graphic means by which viewers are able to infer how a situation has developed, and how it will conclude.

Whereas the painting traditions featured realistic or semirealistic visions of humanity, the cartoonists developed caricatures in their portrayal of their human and animal subjects. One of the many cartoons done for *The New Yorker* by Charles Addams (1912–1988) shows the Addams family, in their characteristically ghoulish garb and appearance, high on a terraced area of their ghostly house, preparing to pour boiling oil down on a group of Christmas carolers. One may easily imagine both the history and future of this event. The Addams cartoons, in this eerily weird vein, were so popular that a series of films and TV programs were successfully developed that dramatized various actions of the family. One of the most popular of modern cartoonists has been Gary Larson

(b. 1950), who created thousands of panels for *The Far Side,* the title of the syndicated cartoons he drew to popular acclaim from 1980 to 1995. Many of Larson's devoted followers expressed great regret when he gave up these cartoons. As his narrative technique, Larson created a situation that is easily followed because of the situations and also the apparent actions of his characters, many of whom are not just caricatures of doughy and distorted human beings, but also of alien travelers, cows, ducks, dogs, snakes, spiders, ocean monsters, bears, deer, rhinoceroses, and comparable creatures. Even though there is no more than just a single picture in the typical Larson cartoon, Larson skillfully supplies comic captions and quotations, together with artistic narrative details from which readers may easily infer both the beginning and the ending.

Closely connected to the single-panel cartoon, another major popular mode of narrative presentation is the comic strip, which became a part of regular daily newspapers in the twentieth century. Indeed, very often people buy the papers and then spend more time reading the comics than the news. Usually the comics are printed in three or four panels during each day of the week, and then on Sundays there is a color strip, usually containing half a dozen or more narrative cartoon panels. Often there is a continuous story in these strips that holds the interest of readers for a number of months. From 1933 until 1987, for example, a strip featuring "Brick Bradford" continued regularly. The story, mainly science fiction, was played out on both a global and universal scale. One interesting adventure in the late 1930s involved Brick and company taking a trip in a uniquely compressing and expanding spaceship, which reduced them to such an infinitely tiny degree that they could engage in an adventure on one of the atoms within the eye of a Lincoln-head penny. (Remember, this was science fiction.) Other extremely popular comics featured Dick Tracy, a famous detective concerned with solving crimes and capturing criminals (still regularly published), and *Terry and the Pirates* (1934–1973), a strip that was set amid those wars in Asia that led up to and included American involvement in the Pacific Theater of operations during World War II. So popular were these comic strips that quarterly publications were soon issued, in which crime fighters like Superman, Batman, and The Specter would be the heroes of as many as four separate and complete adventure narratives.

Following World War II, many writers, teaming up with cartoonists, went beyond the traditional comic book limitations and started to adapt the comic book format for more serious and systematic novels. Well-known literary works first reached many readers through this medium, and many readers became so interested that they actually went on to read and appreciate the originals. In addition, many writers and cartoonists worked to create new graphically based works, often called "graphic novels." Perhaps the most famous of these is *Maus,* by Art Spiegelman, the winner of a Special Pulitzer Prize award in 1992. *Maus* is a work in the comic/graphic format that describes the horror and brutality of the German concentration camps, as witnessed by his father, during World War II (see pp. 69–75). The form has gained popularity, and has reached the level of its own narrative/dramatic type. A number of separate "Sin City yarns" by Frank Miller (b. 1957), for example, has been used as the basis for popular films. In 2007, a graphic novel originally by Miller, with Lynn Varley, was *300,* which was made into a film dramatizing the story of the ancient battle between Greeks and Persians at Thermopylae in 480 BCE.

DAN PIRARO (b. 1958) Cartoon From *Bizarro*

Dan Piraro is a multitalented and prize-winning cartoonist, who was born in the latter twen-tieth century and educated in Oklahoma. He was especially artistic, and when working in the advertising department at Neiman-Marcus he would sketch out unique cartoons that fascinated and entertained his co-workers. With such material, he successfully began syndicating his work in 1985, just five years after Gary Larson first syndicated The Far Side. *Piraro named his car-toons* Bizarro *because of the closeness in sound to his own name, and also because of the obvious closeness to the Italian word* bizzarro *and our own word* bizarre. *His devoted followers, who look forward eagerly to his daily* Bizarro *cartoons which appear in many newspapers through-out the country, have termed his work as "surreal," "ascerbic," "oddball," and "off the wall." In addition to being a cartoonist, Piraro has also developed his skills as a speaker and a showman. He continues to do fine art, and to date has published fifteen separate books, two of which are the recent* The Three Little Pigs Buy the White House *(2004) and* Bizarro and Other Strange Manifestations of the Art of Dan Piraro *(2006). He produces his own "Bizarroblog," which is regularly available on the Internet.*

BIZARRO (NEW) © 2007 DAN PIRARO. KING FEATURES SYNDICATE.

QUESTIONS

1. How does Piraro establish the narrative situation of this cartoon? On what very famous work of art by what famous artist does the drawing depend? What is the narrative in the original work? What is the narrative in Piraro's cartoon? How is the cartoon narrative particularly modern?

2. Why would the cartoon not be as funny as it is if we did not recognize the original from which the cartoon is derived?

3. On the basis of the contrast between the story in the cartoon and the story in the origi-nal to which it alludes, what principles of humor can you develop and describe?

ART SPIEGELMAN (b. 1948) Excerpt From *Maus*

Art Spiegelman was born in Sweden and came to the United States with his parents. When in high school, he became fascinated with the art of cartooning and made that his profession. For more than twenty years he worked at designing popular products, including such things as candy wrappers. He also spent a number of years teaching at the School for Visual Arts in New York, and he founded a comic magazine, Raw. *His most accomplished work is his graphic novel* Maus, *an episode of which is included here as an illustration of his subject and technique. Another of Spiegelman's honors was a Guggenheim Fellowship.*

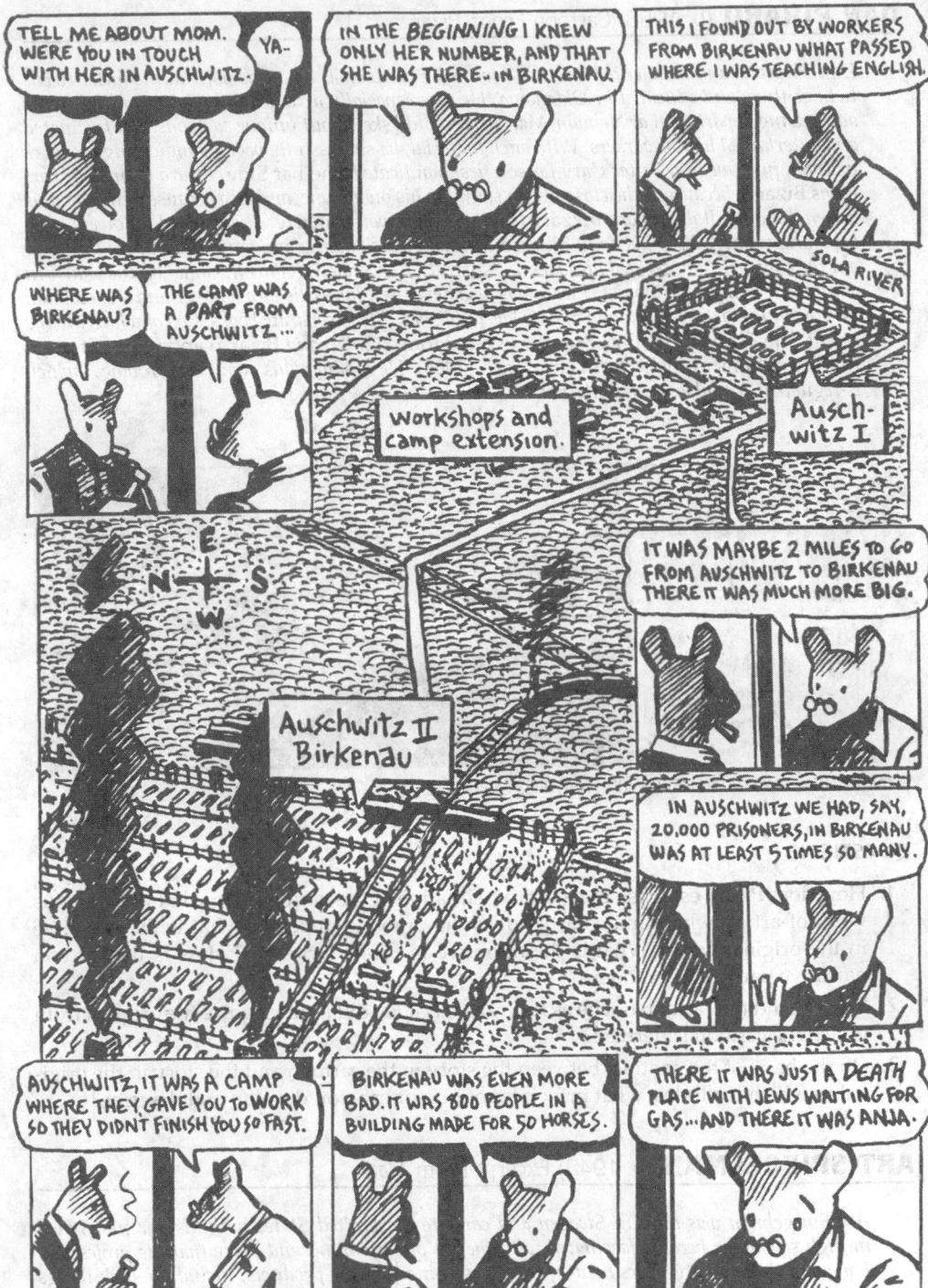

COME...IT'S TIME NOW WE'LL HURRY FOR LUNCH HOME TO THE BUNGALOW.

SO YOU WERE ACTUALLY IN TOUCH WITH ANJA IN BIRKENAU?

YAH. FROM MANCIE I HAD A REAL CONTACT WITH MOTHER, UNTIL LATER I COULD BRING ANJA TO—

WAIT! WHO'S MANCIE?

SHE WAS A HUNGARIAN, MANCIE, WHO WORKED SOMETIMES THERE. BEAUTIFUL. A TALL BLONDE GIRL. AND CLEVER.

(PSST, MISS—UP HERE! I SEE HOW KIND YOU ARE. HELP ME. PLEASE!)

HUH? (WHAT DO YOU WANT?)

REST BEHIND THAT STACK OF WOOD. I'LL WARN YOU IF A GUARD COMES CLOSE.

SHE HAD A LOVER, I HEARD LATER AN S.S. MAN. HE GOT FOR HER A GOOD POSITION OVER 10 OR 12 OTHER GIRLS FROM BIRKENAU.

(NOTHING FOR ME, BUT I'M AFRAID FOR MY WIFE IN BIRKENAU. CAN YOU FIND OUT IF SHE'S STILL ALIVE?)

I TOLD TO HER ANJA'S NAME AND NUMBER.

(I'VE SAVED SOME FOOD. I CAN PAY FOR YOUR HELP.)

(KEEP YOUR FOOD. WE'LL BE WORKING HERE AGAIN IN A FEW DAYS. I'LL SEE WHAT I CAN FIND OUT.)

EACH DAY I LOOKED. FOUR DAYS AFTER, I SAW HER.

I MET A WOMAN NAMED ANJA FROM SOSNOWIEC. SHE'S VERY FRAIL...

SHE SPOKE OVER TO ONE OF HER WORKERS; I SPOKE ONLY TO MY TIN SO NOBODY WILL NOTICE.

SOMEONE TOLD HER THAT HER HUSBAND IS STILL ALIVE AND SHE STARTED SOBBING WITH JOY.

I HEARD THIS, AND I STARTED ALSO CRYING A LITTLE. AND MANCIE, SHE TOO STARTED CRYING.

A FEW DAYS AFTER, MANCIE AGAIN CAME THERE.

I PUT SOME "GARBAGE" UNDER A ROCK NEAR THE DOORWAY.

SHE BROUGHT TO ME A LETTER— A REAL LETTER!—FROM ANJA.

"I MISS YOU," SHE WROTE TO ME. "EACH DAY I THINK TO RUN INTO THE ELECTRIC WIRES AND FINISH EVERYTHING. BUT TO KNOW YOU ARE ALIVE IT GIVES ME STILL TO HOPE..."

SHE TOLD ME HER KAPO WAS VERY MEAN ON HER AND GAVE WORK ANJA REALLY COULDN'T DO.

LIKE TO RUN FROM THE KITCH- EN WITH THE BIG CANS OF SOUP.

EVEN FOR ME SUCH CANS WERE HEAVY, AND FOR ANJA—SHE WAS SO SMALL—IT WAS IMPOSSIBLE.

SHE COULDN'T HOLD WELL HER END. ALWAYS SHE SPILLED.

THE KAPO BEAT ANJA VERY HARD BUT KEPT HER TO THIS JOB.

AND IF ANJA SPILLED OVER ALL FROM THE SOUP, THEN NOBODY GOT WHAT TO EAT, ESPECIALLY ANJA.

I WROTE TO HER: "I THINK OF YOU ALWAYS," AND SENT WITH MANCIE TWO PIECES OF BREAD.

IF THE S.S. WOULD SEE SHE IS TAKING FOOD INTO THE CAMP, RIGHT AWAY THEY WILL KILL HER. BUT ALWAYS SHE TOOK.

SO SHE SAID. "IF A COUPLE IS LOVING EACH OTHER SO MUCH, I MUST HELP HOWEVER I CAN."

EACH DAY I MARCHED TO WORK AND HOPED AGAIN I'LL SEE MANCIE...

SHE COULD HAVE MORE NEWS OF ANJA.

I JUST READ ABOUT THE CAMP ORCHESTRA THAT PLAYED AS YOU MARCHED OUT THE GATE...

AN ORCHESTRA?..

NO. I REMEMBER ONLY *MARCHING*, NOT ANY ORCHESTRAS...

FROM THE GATE GUARDS TOOK US OVER TO THE WORK-SHOP. HOW COULD IT BE THERE AN ORCHESTRA?

I DUNNO, BUT IT'S VERY WELL DOCUMENTED...

NO. AT THE GATE I HEARD ONLY GUARDS SHOUTING.

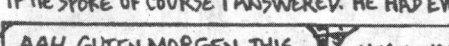

IF HE SPOKE OF COURSE I ANSWERED. HE HAD EVEN A LITTLE HEART.

DID YOU EVER *TALK* WITH ANY OF THE GUARDS?

ACH! WE WERE BELOW THEIR DIGNITY. WE WERE NOT EVEN MEN. BUT IT WAS ONE GUY...

AAH. GUTEN MORGEN. THIS SPRING AIR REMINDS ME OF HOME... OF NUREMBURG...

YES. I WAS THERE ONCE. IT'S A BEAUTIFUL CITY.

AND IF HE LIKED ME, MAYBE SOMEDAY HE WON'T SHOOT ME

ONE TIME HE WAS MISSING A FEW DAYS...

YOU LOOK PALE. WERE YOU SICK HERR SOLDAT?

NO...I WAS... WORKING... IN BIRKENAU.

YES...I'VE HEARD ABOUT WHAT GOES ON THERE....

SHUT UP!

AND HE WAS *AFRAID* ANYMORE TO SPEAK.

QUESTIONS

1. On the first sheet of the selection, what is the purpose of the overhead view of the grounds of Auschwitz I and Auschwitz II, and, on the fifth sheet, the drawing of the railroad cars entering the camp, together with the smoke from the chimneys?

2. What animals represent the faces of the Jewish characters in *Maus*? For what reason or reasons do you think the author chose this animal? How are men and women distinguished in the drawings? What animal represents the German guards? What benefits do these representations give to the narrative and the drama of *Maus*?

3. Who tells the story in *Maus*? To whom does he tell the story? For the most part, how is the narrative developed? How does this method of narrative development give au thoritative realism to the story?

4. Describe the language used by Vladek Spiegelman, the father. Why does the author, Art Spiegelman, use this type of language throughout for the father's speeches?

5. Who is Mancie? Why can Vladek and Mancie speak to each other only from a distance? What kindness does Mancie do for Vladek and Anja?

6. Describe the terror experienced by the characters in the story. What is the principal reason for which characters are fearful? Is it only the prisoners who are afraid? Who else seems afraid in the story? What happens to Anja for spilling the soup? For what infractions might characters in the Death Camp suffer physical punishment? How are both Vladek and Anja able to survive the experience of the Death Camp?

Style Is the Author's Skill in Bringing Language to Life

The medium of fiction and of all literature is language, and the manipulation of language—the style—is a primary skill of the writer. A mark of a good style is the use of active verbs and nouns that are specific and concrete. Even with the most active and graphic diction possible, writers can never render their incidents and scenes exactly, but they may be judged on how vividly they tell their stories.

Point of View Guides What We See and Understand in Fiction

One of the most important ways in which writers knit their stories together, and also an important way in which they try to interest and engage readers, is through the careful control of **point of view**—the *voice* of the story, the speaker who does the narrating. It is the way the story establishes authenticity, either in reality or unreality. It may be regarded as the story's *focus*, the *angle of vision* from which things are not only seen and reported but also judged.

Basically, there are three kinds of point of view, and there are many variations, sometimes obvious and sometimes subtle. In the **first-person point of view,** a fictitious observer tells us what he or she saw, heard, concluded, and thought. This viewpoint is characterized by the use of the pronoun *I*, as the speaker refers to his or her position as an observer or commentator. The **speaker** or **narrator**—terms that are interchangeable—may sometimes seem to be the author speaking directly using an authorial voice. More often, however, the speaker is an independent character—a persona with characteristics that separate her or him from the author.

In common with all narrators, the first-person narrator establishes a clearly defined relationship to the story's events. Some narrators are deeply engaged in the action and are major movers; others are only minor participants or observers; still others have had nothing to do with the action but are passing on the reports of others who were more fully involved. Sometimes the narrator uses the *we* pronoun if he or she is or has been part of a group that has witnessed the action or participated in it. Often, too, the narrator might use *we* when referring to ideas and interpretations shared with the reader or listener—the idea being to draw readers into the story as much as possible.

The **second-person point of view** can be recognized by the use of "you" throughout, as though the speaker is telling a listener about things that the listener knows or has done. There are a number of variants in how the second-person point of view can be used, but essentially, this type of narration is similar to ordinary, conversational speech, as a way of making the listener feel almost like a participant in the story. Obviously the listener has not done the things being told about, but psychologically, the use of the "you" point of view—common as it is in ordinary speech, and rare as it is in literature—is a special means of creating interest in the narration.[2]

The **third-person point of view** uses third-person pronouns (*she, he, it, they, her, him, them,* etc.). The third-person point of view may be (1) **limited,** with the focus being on one particular character and what he or she does, says, hears, thinks, and otherwise experiences; (2) **omniscient,** with the possibility that the activities and thoughts of all the characters are open and fully known by the speaker; or (3) **dramatic,** or **objective,** in which the story is confined *only* to the reporting of actions and speeches, with no commentary and no revelation of the thoughts of any of the characters unless the characters themselves express their thoughts dramatically.

Understanding point of view usually requires subtlety of perception—indeed, it may be one of the most difficult of all concepts in the study of fiction. In fuller perspective, therefore, we may think of it as the *total position* from which things are viewed, understood, and communicated. The position might be simply physical: *Where was the speaker located when the events occurred? Does the speaker give us a close or distant view of the events?* The position might also be personal or philosophical: *Do the events illustrate any personal opinions* (Maupassant's "The Necklace" [Part I]), *embody a philosophical judgment* (Hawthorne's "Young Goodman Brown" [Chapter 7, p. 342]), or *argue a theological principle* (St. Luke's "The Parable of the Prodigal Son" [Chapter 7, p. 350])?

Point of view is one of the major ways by which authors make fiction come to life. By controlling point of view, an author helps us make reasonable inferences about the story's actions. Authors use point of view to raise some of the same questions in fiction that confuse us in life. We need to evaluate what fictional narrators as well as real people tell us, for what they say is affected by their limitations, attitudes, opinions, and degree of openness. The first-person narrator of James Joyce's "Araby" (Chapter 4) describes a series of boyhood incidents

---

The second-person narrative method is more fully discussed in Chapter 2, page 126.

leading up to his memory that he had deceived himself with foolish desires. In other words, he emphasizes what he considers to be his own weaknesses. But we might also realize that this narrator is unknowingly showing that it was not he who was at fault, but rather the religious and moral structure of which he was a part. For readers, the perception of a fictional point of view can be as complex as life itself, and it may be as difficult—in fiction as in life—to evaluate our sources of information.

Description Creates the World of Fiction

Together with narration, an essential aspect of fiction is **description**—those words that cause readers to imagine or re-create the scenes and actions of a story. Description can be both physical (places and persons) and psychological (an emotion or set of emotions). Because excessive description sometimes interrupts or postpones a story's actions, many writers include only as much as is necessary to provide locations for what is happening in the story.

Mood and atmosphere are important aspects of descriptive writing, and to the degree that descriptions are thought provoking, they may reach the level of **metaphor** and **symbolism.** These characteristics of fiction are a property of all literature, and you will also encounter them whenever you read poems and plays.

Dialogue Creates Interactions Among Fictional Characters

Another major tool of the writer of fiction is **dialogue.** By definition, dialogue is the conversation of two people, but more than two characters may also participate. It is of course the major tool of the playwright, and it is one of the means by which fiction writers bring vividness and dramatic tension to their stories. Straight narration and description can do no more than make a secondhand assertion ("hearsay") that a character's thoughts and responses exist, but dialogue makes everything firsthand and real.

Dialogue is hence a means of *showing* or *actualizing* rather than *reporting*. If characters feel pain or declare love, their own words may be taken as the expression of what is on their minds. Some dialogue may be terse and minimal. Other dialogue may be expanded, depending on the situation, the personalities of the characters, and the author's intent. Dialogue may concern any topic, including everyday and practical matters, personal feelings, reactions to the past, future plans, changing thoughts, sudden realizations, and ideas—be they political, social, philosophical, or religious.

The language of dialogue indicates the intelligence, articulateness, educational levels, or emotional states of the speakers. Hence the author might use *grammatical mistakes, faulty pronunciation,* or *slang* to show a character of limited or disadvantaged background or a character who is trying to be seen in that light. *Dialect* shows the region from which the speaker comes, just as *accent* indicates a place of national origin. *Jargon* and *cliché* suggest self-inflation or intellectual limitations—usually reasons for laughter. The use of *private or intimate expressions* clearly shows people who are close to each other emotionally. Speech that is interrupted by *voiced pauses* (for example, "er," "ah," "um," "y'know") or speech characterized by *inappropriate words* might show a character who is unsure or not in control. There are many possibilities in dialogue, but no matter what qualities you find, writers include dialogue to enable you to know their characters better.

Tone and Irony Guide Our Perceptions of Fictional Works

In every story we may consider **tone**—the ways in which authors convey attitudes toward readers and also toward the work's subjects. One of the major components of tone—**irony**—refers to language and situations that seem to reverse normal expectations. *Word choice* is the characteristic of **verbal irony,** in which what is meant is usually the opposite of what is said, as when we *mean* that people are doing badly even though we *say* that they are doing well. Broader forms of irony are situational and dramatic. **Situational irony** refers to circumstances in which bad things happen to good people, or in which rewards are not earned because forces beyond human comprehension seem to be in total control, making the world seem arbitrary and often absurd. In **dramatic irony** characters have only a nonexistent, partial, incorrect, or misguided understanding of what is happening to them, while both readers and other characters understand the situation more fully. Readers hence become concerned about the characters and hope that the characters will develop understanding quickly enough to avoid the problems troubling them and the pitfalls endangering them.

Symbolism and Allegory Relate Fiction to the Larger World

In literature, even seemingly ordinary things may be seen as symbols. That is, many objects may signify not only our ordinary level of meaning but go beyond that to express and probe meaning that reaches depths that exceed our common understanding. Symbols stretch our minds into levels that ordinarily we might never have thought about, to unfold for us new levels of insight. Symbolism is therefore continually new, and it is expansive. Based in the description of things that are ordinary, it expands our understanding in ways that are both unexpected and also expansive. Literature relies on seemingly ordinary and functional objects, characters, and circumstances to lead us into byways of understanding through the use of symbols. Some widely recognized objects are often considered as cultural or universal symbols. Water, flowers, jewels, the sun, certain stars or constellations, flags, altars, and minarets are just a few examples of such symbols. Other symbols are contextual—that is, they take on symbolic meaning in their individual works, as happens in Maupassant's "The Necklace" when Mathilde and her husband move into an attic flat, which may be taken as representative or symbolic of the downward spiral of their economic and social status.

When a complete story, in addition to its own narrative integrity, can be applied point by point to a parallel set of situations, we might often consider it as an allegory. Many stories are not complete allegories, however, even though they may contain sections having allegorical parallels. For instance, the Loisels' ten-year struggles in Maupassant's "The Necklace" is similar to the lives and activities of many people who perform tasks for mistaken or meaningless reasons. "The Necklace" therefore has allegorical overtones even though it is not, in totality, an allegory.

Commentary Provides Us with an Author's Thoughts

Writers may also include **commentary**, analysis, or interpretation, in the expectation that readers need insight into the characters and their actions. When fiction was new, authors often expressed such commentary directly. Henry Fielding (1707–1754) divided his novels into "books" and included a chapter of personal and philosophical commentary at the beginning of each of these. In the next century, George Eliot (1819–1880) included many extensive passages of commentary in her novels.

Later writers have kept commentary at a minimum, preferring instead to concentrate on direct action and dialogue, thereby allowing readers to draw their own conclusions about meaning. In first-person narrations, however, we may expect the narrators to make their own personal comments. Such observations may be accepted at face value, but we should recognize that anything the speakers say is also a mode of character disclosure and therefore just as much a part of the total story as the narrative incidents.

The Elements Together Are Present in Works of Fiction

These, then, are the major tools of fiction, which authors generally use simultaneously in their works. Thus the story may be told by a character who is a witness, and thus it has a *first-person point of view*. The major *character*, the *protagonist*, goes through a series of actions as a result of a carefully arranged *plot*. Because of this plot, together with the author's chosen method of *narration*, the story will follow a certain kind of arrangement, or *structure*, such as a straightforward sequence or a disjointed series of episodes. The action may demonstrate the story's *theme* or central *idea*. The writer's *style* may be revealed in ironic expressions. The description of the character's actions may show *irony of situation*, while at the same time this situation is made vivid through *dialogue* in which the character is a participant. Because the situation of the character is like the plight of many persons in the world, this character may be considered as a *symbol*, and the various actions of his story may be considered as an *allegory*.

Throughout each story we read, no matter what characteristics we are considering, it is most important to realize that a work of fiction is an entirety, a unity. Any reading of a story should be undertaken not to break things down into parts but to understand and take in the work *as a whole*. The separate analysis of various topics is thus a *means* to that end, *not* the end itself. The study of fiction, like the study of all literature, is designed to encourage our growth and to increase our understanding of the human condition.

Stories for Study

Inés Arredondo . . . . The Shunammite, 81
Ambrose Bierce . . . . An Occurrence at Owl Creek Bridge, 87
Sandra Cisneros . . . . Mericans, 93
William Faulkner . . . . A Rose for Emily, 95
Tim O'Brien . . . . The Things They Carried, 101

INÉS CAMELO ARREDONDO (1928–1989)

In her difficult and relatively brief lifetime, Inés Camelo Arredondo experienced both ill health and financial uncertainty, relying on her writing to meet her ongoing obligations and to resolve some of her personal difficulties. She also taught at a number of universities in her native Mexico and in the United States. Originally published in Arredondo's Underground River and Other Stories *(1965). "The Shunammite" was one of her particularly noteworthy efforts, which she was also able to develop into a film in 1965. She based the story on the concluding years of the biblical King David's life, when he was under the personal care of Abishag, who in this modernized story is named Luisa.*

The Shunammite (1965)

Translated by Alberto Manguel

So they sought for a fair damsel throughout all the coasts of Israel, and found Abishag, a Shunammite, and brought her to the king. And the damsel was very fair, and cherished the king, and ministered to him; but the king knew her not.

—1 Kings 1:3–4

The summer had been a fiery furnace. The last summer of my youth.

Tense, concentrated in the arrogance that precedes combustion, the city shone in a dry and dazzling light. I stood in the very midst of the light, dressed in mourning, proud, feeding the flames with my blonde hair, alone. Men's sly glances slid over my body without soiling it, and my haughty modesty forced them to barely nod at me, full of respect. I was certain of having the power to dominate passions, to purify anything in the scorching air that surrounded but did not singe me.

Nothing changed when I received the telegram; the sadness it brought me did not affect in the least my feelings towards the world. My uncle Apolonio was dying at the age of seventy odd years and wanted to see me. I had lived as a daughter in his house for many years and I sincerely felt pain at the thought of his inevitable death. All this was perfectly normal, and not a single omen, not a single shiver made me suspect anything. Quickly I made arrangements for the journey, in the very same untouchable midst of the motionless summer.

I arrived at the village during the hour of siesta.

Walking down the empty streets with my small suitcase, I fell to daydreaming, in that   5
dusky zone between reality and time, born of the excessive heat. I was not remembering; I was almost reliving things as they had been. "Look, Licha, the *amapas*° are blooming again." The clear voice, almost childish. "I want you to get yourself a dress like that of Margarita Ibarra to wear on the sixteenth." I could hear her, feel her walking by my side, her shoulders bent a little forwards, light in spite of her plumpness, happy and old. I carried on walking in the company of my aunt Panchita, my mother's sister. "Well, my dear, if you *really* don't like Pepe . . . but he's such a *nice* boy." Yes, she had used those exact words, here, in front of Tichi Valenzuela's window, with her gay smile, innocent and impish. I walked a little further, where the paving stones seemed to fade away in the haze, and when the bells rang, heavy and real, ending the siesta and announcing the Rosary, I opened my eyes and gave the village a good, long look: it was not the same. The *amapas* had not bloomed and I was crying, in my mourning dress, at the door of my uncle's house.

The front gate was open, as always, and at the end of the courtyard rose the bougainvillea. As always: but not the same. I dried my tears, and felt that I was not arriving: I was leaving. Everything looked motionless, pinioned in my memory, and the heat and the silence seemed to wither it all. My footsteps echoed with a new sound, and María came out to greet me.

°*amapas:* a small tree with colorful blossoms.

"Why didn't you let us know? We'd have sent . . ."

We went straight into the sick man's room. As I entered, I felt cold. Silence and gloom preceded death.

"Luisa, is that you?"

10 The dear voice was dying out and would soon be silent forever.

"I'm here, uncle."

"God be praised! I won't die alone."

"Don't say that; you'll soon be much better."

He smiled sadly; he knew I was lying but he did not want to make me cry.

15 "Yes, my daughter. Yes. Now have a rest, make yourself at home and then come and keep me company. I'll try to sleep a little."

Shriveled, wizened, toothless, lost in the immense bed and floating senselessly in whatever was left of his life, he was painful to be with, like something superfluous, out of place, like so many others at the point of death. Stepping out of the overheated passageway, one would take a deep breath, instinctively, hungry for light and air.

I began to nurse him and I felt happy doing it. This house was *my* house, and in the morning, while tidying up, I would sing long-forgotten songs. The peace that surrounded me came perhaps from the fact that my uncle no longer awaited death as something imminent and terrible, but instead let himself be carried by the passing days towards a more or less distant or nearby future, with the unconscious tenderness of a child. He would go over his past life with great pleasure and enjoy imagining that he was bequeathing me his images, as grandparents do with their children.

"Bring me that small chest, there, in the large wardrobe. Yes, that one. The key is underneath the mat, next to Saint Anthony. Bring the key as well."

And his sunken eyes would shine once again at the sight of all his treasures.

20 "Look: this necklace—I gave it to your aunt for our tenth wedding anniversary. I bought it in Mazatlán from a Polish jeweler who told me God-knows-what story about an Austrian princess, and asked an impossible price for it. I brought it back hidden in my pistol-holder and didn't sleep a wink in the stagecoach—I was so afraid someone would steal it!"

The light of dusk made the young, living stones glitter in his calloused hands.

"This ring, so old, belonged to my mother; look carefully at the miniature in the other room and you'll see her wearing it. Cousin Begoña would mutter behind her back that a sweetheart of hers . . . "

The ladies in the portraits would move their lips and speak, once again, would breathe again—all these ladies he had seen, he had touched. I would picture them in my mind and understand the meaning of these jewels.

"Have I told you about the time we traveled to Europe, in 1908, before the Revolution?° You had to take a ship to Colima. And in Venice your aunt Panchita fell in love with a certain pair of earrings. They were much too expensive, and I told her so. 'They are fit for a queen.' Next day I bought them for her. You just can't imagine what it was like because all this took place long, long before you were born, in 1908, in Venice, when your aunt was so young, so . . . "

25 "Uncle, you're getting tired, you should rest."

"You're right, I'm tired. Leave me a while and take the small chest to your room. It's yours."

"But, uncle . . . "

"It's all yours, that's all! I trust I can give away whatever I want!"

His voice broke into a sob: the illusion was vanishing and he found himself again on the point of dying, of saying goodbye to the things he had loved. He turned to the wall and I left with the box in my hands, not knowing what to do.

30 On other occasions he would tell me about "the year of the famine," or "the year of the yellow corn," or "the year of the plague," and very old tales of murderers and ghosts. Once

---

°*the Revolution*: the Mexican Revolution, which began in 1910.

he even tried to sing a *corrido*° from his youth, but it shattered in his jagged voice. He was leaving me his life, and he was happy.

The doctor said that yes, he could see some recovery, but that we were not to raise our hopes, there was no cure, it was merely a matter of a few days more or less.

One afternoon of menacing dark clouds, when I was bringing in the clothes hanging out to dry in the courtyard, I heard María cry out. I stood still, listening to her cry as if it were a peal of thunder, the first of the storm to come. Then silence, and I was left alone in the court-yard, motionless. A bee buzzed by and the rain did not fall. No one knows as well as I do how awful a foreboding can be, a premonition hanging above a head turned towards the sky.

"Lichita, he's dying! He's gasping for air!"

"Go get the doctor . . . No! I'll go. But call doña Clara to stay with you till I'm back."

"And the priest, fetch the priest."   35

I ran, I ran away from that unbearable moment, blunt and asphyxiating. I ran, hurried back, entered the house, made coffee; I greeted the relatives who began to arrive dressed in half-mourning; I ordered candles; I asked for a few holy relics; I kept on feverishly trying to fulfill my only obligation at the time, to be with my uncle. I asked the doctor: he had given him an injection, so as not to leave anything untried, but he knew it was useless. I saw the priest arrive with the Eucharist, even then I lacked the courage to enter. I knew I would regret it afterwards. "Thank God, now I won't die alone"—but I couldn't. I covered my face with my hands and prayed.

The priest came and touched my shoulder. I thought that all was over and I shivered.

"He's calling you. Come in."

I don't know how I reached the door. Night had fallen and the room, lit by a bedside lamp, seemed enormous. The furniture, larger than life, looked black, and a strange clogging atmo-sphere hung about the bed. Trembling, I felt I was inhaling death.

"Stand next to him," said the priest.   40

I obeyed, moving towards the foot of the bed, unable to look even at the sheets.

"Your uncle's wish, unless you say otherwise, is to marry you *in articulo mortis*,° so that you may inherit his possessions. Do you accept?"

I stifled a cry of horror. I opened my eyes wide enough to let in the whole terrible room. "Why does he want to drag me into his grave?" I felt death touching my skin.

"Luisa . . . ."

It was uncle Apolonio. Now I had to look at him. He could barely mouth the words, his   45
jaw seemed slack and he spoke moving his face like that of a ventriloquist's doll.

"Please."

And he fell silent with exhaustion.

I could take no more. I left the room. That was not my uncle, it did not even look like him. Leave everything to me, yes, but not only his possessions, his stories, his life. I didn't want it, his life, his death. I didn't want it. When I opened my eyes I was standing once again in the courtyard and the sky was still overcast. I breathed in deeply, painfully.

"Already?" the relatives drew near to ask, seeing me so distraught.

I shook my head. Behind me, the priest explained.   50

"Don Apolonio wants to marry her with his last breath, so that she may inherit him."

"And you won't?" the old servant asked anxiously. "Don't be silly, no one deserves it more than you. You were a daughter to them, and you have worked very hard looking

---

°*corrido*: Although a *corrido* sometimes might take a political turn, it was more appropriately romantic because it was, in truth, romantic by definition.

°*in articulo mortis*: at the verge of death; a marriage made when either the bride or the groom is mortally ill and near death. Such marriages are nevertheless legal, and therefore still binding. Don Apolonio is aware of this right that marriage gives him as a husband, and he takes advantage of it.

after him. If you don't marry him, the cousins in Mexico City will leave you without a cent. Don't be silly!"

"It's a fine gesture on his part."

"And afterwards you'll be left a rich widow, as untouched as you are now." A young cousin laughed nervously.

55 "It's a considerable fortune, and I, as your uncle several times removed, would advise you to . . ."

"If you think about it, not accepting shows a lack of both charity and humility."

"That's true, that's absolutely true."

I did not want to give an old man his last pleasure, a pleasure I should, after all, be thankful for, because my youthful body, of which I felt so proud, had not dwelt in any of the regions of death. I was overcome by nausea. That was my last clear thought that night. I woke from a kind of hypnotic slumber as they forced me to hold his hand covered in cold sweat. I felt nauseous again, but said "yes."

I remember vaguely that they hovered over me all the time, talking all at once, taking me over there, bringing me over here, making me sign, making me answer. The taste of that night—a taste that has stayed with me for the rest of my life—was that of an evil ring-around-the-rosies turning vertiginously around me, while everyone laughed and sang grotesquely

> This is the way the widow is wed,
> The widow is wed, the widow is wed

while I stood, a slave, in the middle. Something inside me hurt, and I could not lift my eyes.

60 When I came to my senses, all was over, and on my hand shone the braided ring which I had seen so many times on my aunt Panchita's finger: there had been no time for anything else.

The guests began to leave.

"If you need me, don't hesitate to call. In the meantime give him these drops every six hours."

"May God bless you and give you strength."

"Happy honeymoon," whispered the young cousin in my ear, with a nasty laugh.

65 I returned to the sickbed. "Nothing has changed, nothing has changed." My fear certainly had not changed. I convinced María to stay and help me look after uncle Apolonio. I only calmed down once I saw dawn was breaking. It had started to rain, but without thunder or lightning, very still.

It kept on drizzling that day and the next, and the day after. Four days of anguish. Nobody came to visit, nobody other than the doctor and the priest. On days like these no one goes out, everyone stays indoors and waits for life to start again. These are the days of the spirit, sacred days.

If at least the sick man had needed plenty of attention my hours would have seemed shorter, but there was little that could be done for him.

On the fourth night María went to bed in a room close by, and I stayed alone with the dying man. I was listening to the monotonous rain and praying unconsciously, half asleep and unafraid, waiting. My fingers stopped turning the rosary, and as I held the beads I could feel through my fingertips a peculiar warmth, a warmth both alien and intimate, the warmth we leave in things and which is returned to us transformed, a comrade, a brother foreshadowing the warmth of others, a warmth both unknown and recollected, never quite grasped and yet inhabiting the core of my bones. Softly, deliciously, my nerves relaxed, my fingers felt light, I fell asleep.

I must have slept many hours: it was dawn when I woke up. I knew because the lights had been switched off and the electric plant stops working at two in the morning. The room, barely lit by an oil lamp at the feet of the Holy Virgin on the chest of drawers, made me think of the wedding night, my wedding night. It was so long ago, an empty eternity.

From the depth of the gloomy darkness don Apolonio's broken and tired breathing   70 reached me. There he still was, not the man himself, simply the persistent and incomprehensible shred that hangs on, with no goal, with no apparent motive. Death is frightening, but life mingled with death, soaked in death, is horrible in a way that owes little to either life or death. Silence, corruption of the flesh, the stench, the monstrous transformation, the final vanishing act, all this is painful, but it reaches a climax and then gives way, dissolves into the earth, into memory, into history. But not this: this arrangement worked out between life and death—echoed in the useless exhaling and inhaling—could carry on forever. I would hear him trying to clear his anaesthetized throat and it occurred to me that air was not entering that body, or rather, that it was not a human body breathing the air: it was a machine, puffing and panting, stopping in a curious game, a game to kill time without end. That thing was no human being: it was somebody playing with huffs and snores. And the horror of it all won me over: I began to breathe to the rhythm of his panting; to inhale, stop suddenly, choke, breathe, choke again, unable to control myself, until I realized I had been deceived by what I thought was the sense of the game. What I really felt was the pain and shortness of breath of an animal in pain. But I kept on, on, until there was one single breathing, one single inhuman breath, one single agony. I felt calmer, terrified but calmer: I had lifted the barrier, I could let myself go and simply wait for the common end. It seemed to me that by abandoning myself, by giving myself up unconditionally, the end would happen quickly, would not be allowed to continue. It would have fulfilled its purpose and its persistent search in the world.

Not a hint of farewell, not a glimmer of pity towards me. I carried on the mortal game for a long, long while, from someplace where time had ceased to matter.

The shared breathing became less agitated, more peaceful, but also weaker. I seemed to be drifting back. I felt so tired I could barely move, exhaustion nestling in forever inside my body. I opened my eyes. Nothing had changed.

No: far away, in the shadows, is a rose. Alone, unique, alive. There it is, cut out against the darkness, clear as day, with its fleshy, luminous petals, shining. I look at it and my hand moves and I remember its touch and the simple act of putting it in a vase. I looked at it then, but I only understand it now. I stir, I blink, and the rose is still there, in full bloom, identical to itself.

I breathe freely, with my own breath. I pray, I remember, I doze off, and the untouched rose mounts guard over the dawning light and my secret. Death and hope suffer change.

And now day begins to break and in the clean sky I see that at last the days of rain are   75 over. I stay at the window a long time, watching everything change in the sun. A strong ray enters and the suffering seems a lie. Unjustified bliss fills my lungs and unwittingly I smile. I turn to the rose as if to an accomplice but I can't find it: the sun has withered it.

Clear days came again, and maddening heat. The people went to work, and sang, but don Apolonio would not die; in fact he seemed to get better. I kept on looking after him, but no longer in a cheerful mood—my eyes downcast, I turned the guilt I felt into hard work. My wish, now clearly, was that it all end, that he die. The fear, the horror I felt looking at him, at his touch, his voice, were unjustified because the link between us was not real, could never be real, and yet he felt like a dead weight upon me. Through politeness and shame I wanted to get rid of it.

Yes, don Apolonio was visibly improving. Even the doctor was surprised and offered no explanation.

On the very first morning I sat him up among the pillows, I noticed that certain look in my uncle's eyes. The heat was stifling and I had to lift him all by myself. Once I had propped him up I noticed: the old man was staring as if dazed at my heaving chest, his face

distorted and his trembling hands unconsciously moving towards me. I drew back instinctively and turned my head away.

"Please close the blinds, it's too hot."

80   His almost dead body was growing warm.

"Come here, Luisa, sit by my side. Come."

"Yes, uncle." I sat, my knees drawn up, at the foot of the bed, without looking at him.

"Polo, you must call me Polo, after all we are closer relatives now." There was mockery
in the tone of his voice.

"Yes, uncle."

85   "Polo, Polo." His voice was again sweet and soft. "You'll have a lot to forgive me. I'm old
and sick, and a man in my condition is like a child."

"Yes."

"Let's see. Try saying, 'Yes, Polo.'"

"Yes, Polo."

The name on my lips seemed to me an aberration, made me nauseated.

90   Polo got better, but became fussy and irritable. I realized he was fighting to be the man he
once had been, and yet the resurrected self was not the same, but another.

"Luisa, bring me . . . Luisa, give me . . . Luisa, plump up my pillows . . . pour me some
water . . . prop up my leg . . . . "

He wanted me to be there all day long, always by his side, seeing to his needs, touching
him. And the fixed look and distorted face kept coming back, more and more frequently,
growing over his features like a mask.

"Pick up my book. It fell underneath the bed, on this side."

I kneeled and stuck my head and almost half my body underneath the bed, and had
to stretch my arm as far as it would go, to reach it. At first I thought it had been my own
movements, or maybe the bedclothes, but once I had the book in my hand and was shuffling to get out, I froze, stunned by what I had long foreseen, even expected: the outburst,
the scream, the thunder. A rage never before felt raced through me when the realization of
what was happening reached my consciousness, when his shaking hand, taking advantage
of my amazement, became surer and heavier, and enjoyed itself, adventuring with no restraints, feeling and exploring my thighs—a fleshless hand glued to my skin, fingering my
body with delight, a dead hand searching impatiently between my legs, a bodyless hand.

95   I rose as quickly as I could, my face burning with shame and determination, but when I
saw him I forgot myself and entered like an automaton into the nightmare. Polo was laughing softly through his toothless mouth. And then, suddenly serious, with a coolness that
terrified me, he said:

"What? Aren't you my wife before God and men? Come here, I'm cold, heat my bed. But
first take off your dress, you don't want to get it creased."

What followed, I know, is my story, my life, but I can barely remember it; like a disgusting dream I can't even tell whether it was long or short. Only one thought kept me sane during the early days: "This can't go on, it can't go on." I imagined that God would not allow it,
would prevent it in some way or another. He, personally, God, would interfere. Death, once
dreaded, seemed my only hope. Not Apolonio's—he was a demon of death—but mine, the
just and necessary death for my corrupted flesh. But nothing happened. Everything stayed
on, suspended in time, without future. Then, one morning, taking nothing with me, I left.

It was useless. Three days later they let me know that my husband was dying, and they
called me back. I went to see the father confessor and told him my story.

"What keeps him alive is lust, the most horrible of all sins. This isn't life, Father, it's
death. Let him die!"

100   "He would die in despair. I can't allow it."

"And I?"

"I understand, but if you don't go to him, it would be like murder. Try not to arouse him, pray to the Blessed Virgin, and keep your mind on your duties."

I went back. And lust drew him out of the grave once more.

Fighting, endlessly fighting, I managed, after several years, to overcome my hatred, and finally, at the very end, I even conquered the beast: Apolonio died in peace, sweetly, his old self again.

But I was not able to go back to who I was. Now wickedness, malice, shine in the eyes of   105
the men who look at me, and I feel I have become an occasion of sin for all, I, the vilest of harlots. Alone, a sinner, totally engulfed by the never-ending flames of this cruel summer which surrounds us all, like an army of ants.

QUESTIONS

1. In light of the fact that Luisa had lived in don Apolonio's house when she was a child, what does his interest in having her close to him during his dying days say about his interest in her during the time when she was a dependent and he was her guardian? To what extent might this story be seen as a critique of male domination over women? What power does Luisa have to say "no" once her Uncle Apolonio has asked that she come to him before he dies?

2. Explain the attitude underlying the cousin's wish that Luisa have a "happy honey-moon" after the wedding.

3. To what degree does it seem that there are strong hints of suspicion about Luisa that dramatically pervade this story, an attitude shared even by Luisa herself? After don Apolonio's death, why does she say "I was not able to go back to who I was"?

4. To what extent may this story be understood as a critique of the biblical King David story? What are some of the elements of this critique?

AMBROSE BIERCE (1842 1914?)

Ambrose Bierce was a native of Ohio, the youngest of nine children in the highly religious family of a poor farmer. When the Civil War began in 1861, he enlisted in the Union army as a drummer boy and rose to the rank of major by the war's end. After the war he went to San Francisco to begin a career in journalism. At various times he reported, edited, and wrote reviews for papers such as the San Francisco Examiner *and the* San Francisco News-Letter. *After he married, he and his wife spent five years in England, but eventually she left him and their two children died—events that left him embittered. In 1913 he traveled to Mexico, and nothing further is known about him after that; he is presumed to have died in revolutionary fighting there in 1914. Bierce published his first story in 1871 and later published two volumes of stories:* In the Midst of Life *(1892, originally published in 1891 as* Tales of Soldiers and Civilians, *which included "An Occurrence at Owl Creek Bridge"), and* Can Such Things Be? *(1893). He is perhaps best known for his cynical work* The Devil's Dictionary *(1911). He favored the short story as a form over the novel on much the same grounds as Poe—namely, that a story could be designed to produce a single effect. He believed that fiction should be realistic and should build to concluding twists and surprises—goals that are seen in "An Occurrence at Owl Creek Bridge." His complete works, which he edited himself, appeared in twelve volumes from 1909 to 1912.*

An Occurrence at Owl Creek Bridge (1891)

I

A man stood upon a railroad bridge in northern Alabama, looking down into the swift water twenty feet below. The man's hands were behind his back, the wrists bound with a cord. A rope closely encircled his neck. It was attached to a stout cross-timber above his head and the slack fell to the level of his knees. Some loose boards laid upon the sleepers supporting the metals of the railway supplied a footing for him and his executioners—two private soldiers of the Federal army, directed by a sergeant who in civil life may have been a deputy sheriff. At a short remove upon the same temporary platform was an officer in the uniform of his rank, armed. He was a captain. A sentinel at each end of the bridge stood with his rifle in the position known as "support," that is to say, vertical in front of the left shoulder, the hammer resting on the forearm thrown straight across the chest—a formal and unnatural position, enforcing an erect carriage of the body. It did not appear to be the duty of these two men to know what was occurring at the center of the bridge; they merely blockaded the two ends of the foot planking that traversed it.

Beyond one of the sentinels nobody was in sight; the railroad ran straight away into a forest for a hundred yards, then, curving, was lost to view. Doubtless there was an outpost farther along. The other bank of the stream was open ground—a gentle acclivity topped with a stockade of vertical tree trunks, loopholed for rifles, with a single embrasure through which protruded the muzzle of a brass cannon commanding the bridge. Midway of the slope between the bridge and fort were the spectators—a single company of infantry in line, at "parade rest," the butts of the rifles on the ground, the barrels inclining slightly backward against the right shoulder, the hands crossed upon the stock. A lieutenant stood at the right of the line, the point of his sword upon the ground, his left hand resting upon his right. Excepting the group of four at the center of the bridge, not a man moved. The company faced the bridge, staring stonily, motionless. The sentinels, facing the banks of the stream, might have been statues to adorn the bridge. The captain stood with folded arms, silent, observing the work of his subordinates, but making no sign. Death is a dignitary who when he comes announced is to be received with formal manifestations of respect, even by those most familiar with him. In the code of military etiquette silence and fixity are forms of deference.

The man who was engaged in being hanged was apparently about thirty-five years of age. He was a civilian, if one might judge from his habit, which was that of a planter. His features were good—a straight nose, firm mouth, broad forehead, from which his long, dark hair was combed straight back, falling behind his ears to the collar of his well-fitting frock coat. He wore a mustache and pointed beard, but no whiskers; his eyes were large and dark gray, and had a kindly expression which one would hardly have expected in one whose neck was in the hemp. Evidently this was no vulgar assassin. The liberal military code makes provision for hanging many kinds of persons, and gentlemen are not excluded.

The preparations being complete, the two private soldiers stepped aside and each drew away the plank upon which he had been standing. The sergeant turned to the captain, saluted and placed himself immediately behind that officer, who in turn moved apart one pace. These movements left the condemned man and the sergeant standing on the two ends of the same plank, which spanned three of the cross-ties of the bridge. The end upon which the civilian stood almost, but not quite, reached a fourth. This plank had been held in place by the weight of the captain; it was now held by that of the sergeant. At a signal from the former the latter would step aside, the plank would tilt and the condemned man go down between two ties. The arrangement commended itself to his judgment as simple and effective. His face had not been covered nor his eyes bandaged. He looked a moment at his "unsteadfast footing," then let his gaze wander to the swirling water of the stream racing madly beneath his feet. A piece of dancing driftwood caught his attention and his eyes followed it down the current. How slowly it appeared to move! What a sluggish stream!

He closed his eyes in order to fix his last thoughts upon his wife and children. The water, touched to gold by the early sun, the brooding mists under the banks at some distance down the stream, the fort, the soldiers, the piece of driftwood—all had distracted him. And now he became conscious of a new disturbance. Striking through the thought of his dear ones was a sound which he could neither ignore nor understand, a sharp, distinct, metallic percussion like the stroke of a blacksmith's hammer upon the anvil; it had the same ringing quality. He wondered what it was, and whether immeasurably distant or near by—it seemed both. Its recurrence was regular, but as slow as the tolling of a death knell. He awaited each stroke with impatience and—he knew not why—apprehension. The intervals of silence grew progressively longer; the delays became maddening. With their greater infrequency the sounds increased in strength and sharpness. They hurt his ear like the thrust of a knife; he feared he would shriek. What he heard was the ticking of his watch.

He unclosed his eyes and saw again the water below him. "If I could free my hands," he thought, "I might throw off the noose and spring into the stream. By diving I could evade the bullets and, swimming vigorously, reach the bank, take to the woods and get away home. My home, thank God, is as yet outside their lines; my wife and little ones are still beyond the invader's farthest advance."

As these thoughts, which have here to be set down in words, were flashed into the doomed man's brain rather than evolved from it the captain nodded to the sergeant. The sergeant stepped aside.

II

Peyton Farquhar was a well-to-do planter, of an old and highly respected Alabama family. Being a slave owner and like other slave owners a politician he was naturally an original secessionist and ardently devoted to the Southern cause. Circumstances of an imperious nature, which it is unnecessary to relate here, had prevented him from taking service with the gallant army that had fought the disastrous campaigns ending with the fall of Corinth,° and he chafed under the inglorious restraint, longing for the release of his energies, the larger life of the soldier, the opportunity for distinction. That opportunity, he felt, would come, as it comes to all in war time. Meanwhile he did what he could. No service was too humble for him to perform in aid of the South, no adventure too perilous for him to undertake if consistent with the character of a civilian who was at heart a soldier, and who in good faith and without too much qualification assented to at least a part of the frankly villainous dictum that all is fair in love and war.

One evening while Farquhar and his wife were sitting on a rustic bench near the entrance to his grounds, a gray-clad soldier rode up to the gate and asked for a drink of water. Mrs. Farquhar was only too happy to serve him with her own white hands. While she was fetching the water her husband approached the dusty horseman and inquired eagerly for news from the front.

"The Yanks are repairing the railroads," said the man, "and are getting ready for another advance. They have reached the Owl Creek bridge, put it in order and built a stockade on the north bank. The commandant has issued an order, which is posted everywhere, declaring that any civilian caught interfering with the railroad, its bridges, tunnels or trains will be summarily hanged. I saw the order."

"How far is it to the Owl Creek bridge?" Farquhar asked.

"About thirty miles."

°*Corinth:* In the northeast corner of Mississippi, near the Alabama state line, Corinth was the site of a battle in 1862 won by the Union army.

"Is there no force on this side of the creek?"

"Only a picket post half a mile out, on the railroad, and a single sentinel at this end of the bridge."

15 "Suppose a man—a civilian and student of hanging—should elude the picket post and perhaps get the better of the sentinel," said Farquhar, smiling, "what could he accomplish?"

The soldier reflected. "I was there a month ago," he replied, "I observed that the flood of last winter had lodged a great quantity of driftwood against the wooden pier at this end of the bridge. It is now dry and would burn like tow."

The lady had now brought the water, which the soldier drank. He thanked her ceremoniously, bowed to her husband and rode away. An hour later, after nightfall, he repassed the plantation, going northward in the direction from which he had come. He was a Federal scout.

III

As Peyton Farquhar fell straight downward through the bridge he lost consciousness and was as one already dead. From this state he was awakened—ages later, it seemed to him—by the pain of a sharp pressure upon his throat, followed by a sense of suffocation. Keen, poignant agonies seemed to shoot from his neck downward through every fiber of his body and limbs. These pains appeared to flash along well-defined lines of ramification and to beat with an inconceivably rapid periodicity. They seemed like streams of pulsating fire heating him to an intolerable temperature. As to his head, he was conscious of nothing but a feeling of fulness—of congestion. These sensations were unaccompanied by thought. The intellectual part of his nature was already effaced; he had power only to feel, and feeling was torment. He was conscious of motion. Encompassed in a luminous cloud, of which he was now merely the fiery heart, without material substance, he swung through unthinkable arcs of oscillation, like a vast pendulum. Then all at once, with terrible suddenness, the light about him shot upward with the noise of a loud plash; a frightful roaring was in his ears, and all was cold and dark. The power of thought was restored; he knew that the rope had broken and he had fallen into the stream. There was no additional strangulation; the noose about his neck was already suffocating him and kept the water from his lungs. To die of hanging at the bottom of a river!—the idea seemed to him ludicrous. He opened his eyes in the darkness and saw above him a gleam of light, but how distant, how inaccessible! He was still sinking, for the light became fainter and fainter until it was a mere glimmer. Then it began to grow and brighten, and he knew that he was rising toward the surface—knew it with reluctance, for he was now very comfortable. "To be hanged and drowned," he thought, "that is not so bad; but I do not wish to be shot. No; I will not be shot; that is not fair."

He was not conscious of an effort, but a sharp pain in his wrist apprised him that he was trying to free his hands. He gave the struggle his attention, as an idler might observe the feat of a juggler, without interest in the outcome. What splendid effort—what magnificent, what superhuman strength! Ah, that was a fine endeavor! Bravo! The cord fell away; his arms parted and floated upward; the hands dimly seen on each side in the growing light. He watched them with a new interest as first one and then the other pounced upon the noose at his neck. They tore it away and thrust it fiercely aside, its undulations resembling those of a water snake. "Put it back, put it back!" He thought he shouted these words to his hands, for the undoing of the noose had been succeeded by the direst pang that he had yet experienced. His neck ached horribly; his brain was on fire; his heart, which had been fluttering faintly, gave a great leap, trying to force itself out at his mouth. His whole body was racked and wrenched with an insupportable anguish! But his disobedient hands gave no heed to the command. They beat the water vigorously with quick, downward strokes, forcing him to the surface. He felt his head emerge; his eyes were blinded by the sunlight; his chest expanded convulsively, and with a supreme and crowning agony his lungs engulfed a great draught of air, which instantly he expelled in a shriek!

He was now in full possession of his physical senses. They were indeed, preternaturally
keen and alert. Something in the awful disturbance of his organic system had so exalted
and refined them that they made record of things never before perceived. He felt the ripples
upon his face and heard their separate sounds as they struck. He looked at the forest on the
bank of the stream, saw the individual trees, the leaves and the veining of each leaf—saw
the very insects upon them: the locusts, the brilliant-bodied flies, the gray spiders stretching
their webs from twig to twig. He noted the prismatic colors in all the dewdrops upon a million blades of grass. The humming of the gnats that danced above the eddies of the stream,
the beating of the dragon flies' wings, the strokes of the water-spiders' legs, like oars which
had lifted their boat—all these made audible music. A fish slid along beneath his eyes and
he heard the rush of its body parting the water.

He had come to the surface facing down the stream; in a moment the visible world
seemed to wheel slowly round, himself the pivotal point, and he saw the bridge, the fort,
the soldiers upon the bridge, the captain, the sergeant, the two privates, his executioners.
They were in silhouette against the blue sky. They shouted and gesticulated, pointing at
him. The captain had drawn his pistol, but did not fire; the others were unarmed. Their
movements were grotesque and horrible, their forms gigantic.

Suddenly he heard a sharp report and something struck the water smartly within a few
inches of his head, spattering his face with spray. He heard a second report, and saw one
of the sentinels with his rifle at his shoulder, a light cloud of blue smoke rising from the
muzzle. The man in the water saw the eye of the man on the bridge gazing into his own
through the sights of the rifle. He observed that it was a gray eye and remembered having
read that gray eyes were keenest, and that all famous marksmen had them. Nevertheless,
this one had missed.

A counter-swirl had caught Farquhar and turned him half round; he was again looking
into the forest on the bank opposite the fort. The sound of a clear, high voice in a monotonous singsong now rang out behind him and came across the water with a distinctness that
pierced and subdued all other sounds, even the beating of the ripples in his ears. Although no
soldier, he had frequented camps enough to know the dread significance of that deliberate,
drawling, aspirated chant; the lieutenant on shore was taking a part in the morning's work.
How coldly and pitilessly—with what an even, calm intonation, presaging, and enforcing
tranquility in the men—with what accurately measured intervals fell those cruel words:

"Attention, company! . . . Shoulder arms! . . . Ready! . . . Aim! . . . Fire!"

Farquhar dived—dived as deeply as he could. The water roared in his ears like the voice
of Niagara, yet he heard the dulled thunder of the volley and, rising again toward the surface, met shining bits of metal, singularly flattened, oscillating slowly downward. Some
of them touched him on the face and hands, then fell away, continuing their descent. One
lodged between his collar and neck; it was uncomfortably warm and he snatched it out.

As he rose to the surface, gasping for breath, he saw that he had been a long time under water; he was perceptibly farther down stream—nearer to safety. The soldiers had almost finished reloading; the metal ramrods flashed all at once in the sunshine as they were
drawn from the barrels, turned in the air, and thrust into their sockets. The two sentinels
fired again, independently and ineffectually.

The hunted man saw all this over his shoulder; he was now swimming vigorously with
the current. His brain was as energetic as his arms and legs; he thought with the rapidity
of lightning.

"The officer," he reasoned, "will not make that martinet's error a second time. It is as
easy to dodge a volley as a single shot. He has probably already given the command to fire
at will. God help me, I cannot dodge them all!"

An appalling plash within two yards of him was followed by a loud, rushing sound,
diminuendo, which seemed to travel back through the air to the fort and died in an explosion

which stirred the very river to its deeps! A rising sheet of water curved over him, fell down upon him, blinded him, strangled him! The cannon had taken a hand in the game. As he shook his head free from the commotion of the smitten water he heard the deflected shot humming through the air ahead, and in an instant it was cracking and smashing the branches in the forest beyond.

30   "They will not do that again," he thought; "the next time they will use a charge of grape. I must keep my eye upon the gun; the smoke will apprise me—the report arrives too late; it lags behind the missile. That is a good gun."

Suddenly he felt himself whirled round and round—spinning like a top. The water, the banks, the forests, the now distant bridge, fort and men—all were commingled and blurred. Objects were represented by their colors only; circular horizontal streaks of color—that was all he saw. He had been caught in a vortex and was being whirled on with a velocity of advance and gyration that made him giddy and sick. In a few moments he was flung upon the gravel at the foot of the left bank of the stream—the southern bank—and behind a projecting point which concealed him from his enemies. The sudden arrest of his motion, the abrasion of one of his hands on the gravel, restored him, and he wept with delight. He dug his fingers into the sand, threw it over himself in handfuls and audibly blessed it. It looked like diamonds, rubies, emeralds; he could think of nothing beautiful which it did not resemble. The trees upon the bank were giant garden plants; he noted a definite order in their arrangement, inhaled the fragrance of their blooms. A strange, roseate light shone through the spaces among their trunks and the wind made in their branches the music of æolian harps. He had no wish to perfect his escape—was content to remain in that enchanting spot until retaken.

A whiz and rattle of grapeshot among the branches high above his head roused him from his dream. The baffled cannoneer had fired him a random farewell. He sprang to his feet, rushed up the sloping bank, and plunged into the forest.

All that day he traveled, laying his course by the rounding sun. The forest seemed interminable; nowhere did he discover a break in it, not even a woodman's road. He had not known that he lived in so wild a region. There was something uncanny in the revelation.

By nightfall he was fatigued, footsore, famishing. The thought of his wife and children urged him on. At last he found a road which led him in what he knew to be the right direction. It was as wide and straight as a city street, yet it seem untraveled. No fields bordered it, no dwelling anywhere. Not so much as the barking of a dog suggested human habitation. The black bodies of the trees formed a straight wall on both sides, terminating on the horizon in a point, like a diagram in a lesson in perspective. Overhead, as he looked up through this rift in the wood, shone great golden stars looking unfamiliar and grouped in strange constellations. He was sure they were arranged in some order which had a secret and malign significance. The wood on either side was full of singular noises, among which—once, twice, and again—he distinctly heard whispers in an unknown tongue.

35   His neck was in pain and lifting his hand to it found it horribly swollen. He knew that it had a circle of black where the rope had bruised it. His eyes felt congested; he could no longer close them. His tongue was swollen with thirst; he relieved its fever by thrusting it forward from between his teeth into the cold air. How softly the turf had carpeted the untraveled avenue—he could no longer feel the roadway beneath his feet!

Doubtless, despite his suffering, he had fallen asleep while walking, for now he sees another scene—perhaps he has merely recovered from a delirium. He stands at the gate of his own home. All is as he left it, and all bright and beautiful in the morning sunshine. He must have traveled the entire night. As he pushes open the gate and passes up the wide white walk, he sees a flutter of female garments; his wife, looking fresh and cool and sweet, steps down from the veranda to meet him. At the bottom of the steps she stands waiting, with a smile of ineffable joy, an attitude of matchless grace and dignity. Ah, how beautiful she is! He springs forward with extended arms. As he is about to clasp her he feels a stunning blow upon the back of the neck; a blinding white light blazes all about him with a sound like the shock of a cannon—then all is darkness and silence!

Peyton Farquhar was dead; his body, with a broken neck, swung gently from side to side beneath the timbers of the Owl Creek bridge.

QUESTIONS

1. What is the situation in the story? What did Farquhar do to deserve his execution?
2. Describe the various shifts in the story's point of view, particularly as indicated in paragraphs 5 and 37. How does Bierce make you aware of Farquhar's heightened consciousness?
3. According to Farquhar's perception of time, how long does it take him to get home after his escape (see paragraphs 33 and 36)?
4. What evidence can you find to indicate that Farquhar is experiencing great pain, despite his feelings that he is escaping?
5. What is the effect of the shift into the present tense in paragraph 36?

SANDRA CISNEROS (b. 1954)

Sandra Cisneros, a Mexican American, was born in Illinois and was educated there. Her higher education was at Loyola University and the University of Iowa Writers' Workshop. She has been a "poet in the schools" in addition to teaching and also working as a college recruiter. She has held two NEA fellowships, and in 2005 she received a prestigious MacArthur Foundation Fellowship. The House on Mango Street, the first of her books, published in 1983 and reissued in 1991, has made her one of the widest selling and best known Hispanic authors in the United States. Her Woman Hollering Creek and Other Stories, from which "Mericans" is taken, was published in 1991, and her poetry volume Loose Woman: Poems appeared in 1991. She published Hairs/Pelitos, a book for small children, in 1997. In 2002 she published her second novel, Caramelo, which is based on the immigrant lives of her father and other members of her family.

Mericans (1991)

We're waiting for the awful grandmother who is inside dropping pesos into *la ofrenda*° box before the altar to *La Divina Providencia*. Lighting votive candles and genuflecting. Blessing herself and kissing her thumb. Running a crystal rosary between her fingers. Mumbling, mumbling, mumbling.

There are so many prayers and promises and thanks-be-to-God to be given in the name of the husband and the sons and the only daughter who never attend mass. It doesn't matter. Like La Virgen de Guadalupe, the awful grandmother intercedes on their behalf. For the grandfather who hasn't believed in anything since the first PRI4 elections. For my father, El Periquin,° so skinny he needs his sleep. For Auntie Light-skin, who only a few hours before

---

°*la ofrenda:* offering box.
°*El Periquin:* the tiny parakeet.

was breakfasting on brain and goat tacos after dancing all night in the pink zone.° For Uncle Fat-face, the blackest of the black sheep—*Always remember your Uncle Fat-face in your prayers.* And Uncle Baby—*You go for me, Mamá—God listens to you.*

The awful grandmother has been gone a long time. She disappeared behind the heavy leather outer curtain and the dusty velvet inner. We must stay near the church entrance. We must not wander over to the balloon and punch-ball vendors. We cannot spend our allowance on fried cookies or Familia Burron comic books° or those clear cone-shaped suckers that make everything look like a rainbow when you look through them. We cannot run off and have our picture taken on the wooden ponies. We must not climb the steps up the hill behind the church and chase each other through the cemetery. We have promised to stay right where the awful grandmother left us until she returns.

There are those walking to church on their knees. Some with fat rags tied around their legs and others with pillows, one to kneel on, and one to flop ahead. There are women with black shawls crossing and uncrossing themselves.

5   There are armies of penitents carrying banners and flowered arches while musicians play tinny trumpets and tinny drums.

La Virgen de Guadalupe is waiting inside behind a plate of thick glass. There's also a gold crucifix bent crooked as a mesquite tree when someone once threw a bomb. La Virgen de Guadalupe is on the main altar because she's a big miracle, the crooked crucifix on a side altar because that's a little miracle.

But we're outside in the sun. My big brother Junior hunkered against the wall with his eyes shut. My little brother Keeks running around in circles.

Maybe and most probably my little brother is imagining he's a flying feather dancer, like the ones we saw swinging high up from a pole on the Virgin's birthday. I want to be a flying feather dancer too, but when he circles past me he shouts, "I'm a B-Fifty-two bomber, you're a German," and shoots me with an invisible machine gun. I'd rather play flying feather dancers, but if I tell my brother this, he might not play with me at all.

"Girl. We can't play with a girl." *Girl.* It's my brothers' favorite insult now instead of "sissy." "You *girl*," they yell at each other. "You throw that ball like a *girl.*"

10   I've already made up my mind to be a German when Keeks swoops past again, this time yelling, "I'm Flash Gordon. You're Ming the Merciless and the Mud People." I don't mind being Ming the Merciless, but I don't like being the Mud People. Something wants to come out of the corners of my eyes, but I don't let it. Crying is what *girls* do.

I leave Keeks running around in circles—"I'm the Lone Ranger, you're Tonto." I leave Junior squatting on his ankles and go look for the awful grandmother.

Why do churches smell like the inside of an ear? Like incense and the dark and candles in blue glass? And why does holy water smell of tears? The awful grandmother makes me kneel and fold my hands. The ceiling high and everyone's prayers bumping up there like balloons.

If I stare at the eyes of the saints long enough, they move and wink at me, which makes me a sort of saint too. When I get tired of winking saints, I count the awful grandmother's mustache hairs while she prays for Uncle Old, sick from the worm,° and Auntie Cuca, suffering from a life of troubles that left half her face crooked and the other half sad.

There must be a long, long list of relatives who haven't gone to church. The awful grandmother knits the names of the dead and the living into one long prayer fringed with the grandchildren born in that barbaric country with its barbarian ways.

°*pink zone:* a district of popular entertainment in Mexico City.
°*Familia Burron comic books:* a popular Mexican comic strip series.
°*the worm:* an intestinal parasite.

I put my weight on one knee, then the other, and when they both grow fat as a mattress of pins, I slap them each awake. *Micaela, you may wait outside with Alfredito and Enrique.* The awful grandmother says it all in Spanish, which I understand when I'm paying attention. "What?" I say, though it's neither proper nor polite. "What?" which the awful grandmother hears as "*¿Güat?*" But she only gives me a look and shoves me toward the door. 15

After all that dust and dark, the light from the plaza makes me squinch my ~~eyes like~~ if I just came out of the movies. My brother Keeks is drawing squiggly lines on the concrete with a wedge of glass and the heel of his shoe. My brother Junior squatting against the entrance, talking to a lady and man. They're not from here. Ladies don't come to church dressed in pants. And everybody knows men aren't supposed to wear shorts.

"*¿Quieres chicle?*"° the lady asks in a Spanish too big for her mouth.

"*Gracias,*" The lady gives him a whole handful of gum for free, little cellophane cubes of Chiclets, cinnamon and aqua and the white ones that don't taste like anything but are good for pretend buck teeth.

"*Por favor,*" says the lady. "*¿Un foto?*" pointing to her camera.

"*Sí.*" 20

She's so busy taking Junior's picture, she doesn't notice me and Keeks.

"Hey, Michele, Keeks. You guys want gum?"

"But you speak English!"

"Yeah," my brother says, "we're Mericans."

We're Mericans, we're Mericans, and inside the awful grandmother prays. 25

°*¿Quieres chicle?:* Would you like chewing-gum?

QUESTIONS

1. Who is telling this story? What is her name? What is the significance of her name being spelled and pronounced in two different ways?

2. Describe the story's basic theme, as represented by what the children say about their own concerns. Why does Michelle describe her grandmother as "awful"? What does she think of her grandmother's religion? How do the games being played by the boys illustrate the differences between the Hispanic and the American influences acting upon the children?

3. What is the importance of the attitude of the brothers toward girls? How does Michelle react to this attitude?

4. Explain why the issue of being "Mericans" is not brought up until the story's end.

WILLIAM FAULKNER (1897–1962)

William Faulkner spent his childhood in Mississippi and became one of the foremost American novelists of the twentieth century. He twice received the Pulitzer Prize for Fiction (in 1955 and 1963), and he also received the Nobel Prize in Literature (in 1949). Throughout his extensive fiction about the special world that he named "Yoknapatawpha County," which is modeled on his own home area in Oxford, Mississippi, he treats life in the Southern United States as a symbol of humankind generally, emphasizing the decline of civilization and culture in the decades after the Civil War. Emily Grierson in "A Rose for Emily" is representative of this decline, for she maintains the appearances of status long after the substance is past. It is not unusual to find degraded, sullen, disturbed, and degenerate characters in Faulkner's fiction.

A Rose for Emily (1931)

I

When Miss Emily Grierson died, our whole town went to her funeral; the men through a sort of respectful affection for a fallen monument, the women mostly out of curiosity to see the inside of her house, which no one save an old manservant—a combined gardener and cook—had seen in at least ten years.

It was a big, squarish frame house that had once been white, decorated with cupolas and spires and scrolled balconies in the heavily lightsome style of the seventies, set on what had once been our most select street. But garages and cotton gins had encroached and obliterated even the august names of that neighborhood; only Miss Emily's house was left, lifting its stubborn and coquettish decay above the cotton wagons and the gasoline pumps—an eyesore among eyesores. And now Miss Emily had gone to join the representatives of those august names where they lay in the cedar-bemused cemetery among the ranked and anonymous graves of Union and Confederate soldiers who fell at the battle of Jefferson.

Alive, Miss Emily had been a tradition, a duty, and a care; a sort of hereditary obligation upon the town, dating from that day in 1894 when Colonel Sartoris, the mayor—he who fathered the edict that no Negro woman should appear on the streets without an apron—remitted her taxes, the dispensation dating from the death of her father on into perpetuity. Not that Miss Emily would have accepted charity. Colonel Sartoris invented an involved tale to the effect that Miss Emily's father had loaned money to the town, which the town, as a matter of business, preferred this way of repaying. Only a man of Colonel Sartoris' generation and thought could have invented it, and only a woman could have believed it.

When the next generation, with its more modern ideas, became mayors and aldermen, this arrangement created some little dissatisfaction. On the first of the year they mailed her a tax notice. February came, and there was no reply. They wrote her a formal letter, asking her to call at the sheriff's office at her convenience. A week later the mayor wrote her himself, offering to call or to send his car for her, and received in reply a note on paper of an archaic shape, in a thin, flowing calligraphy in faded ink, to the effect that she no longer went out at all. The tax notice was also enclosed, without comment.

5 They called a special meeting of the Board of Aldermen. A deputation waited upon her, knocked at the door through which no visitor had passed since she ceased giving china-painting lessons eight or ten years earlier. They were admitted by the old Negro into a dim hall from which a stairway mounted into still more shadow. It smelled of dust and disuse—a close, dank smell. The Negro led them into the parlor. It was furnished in heavy, leather-covered furniture. When the Negro opened the blinds of one window, they could see that the leather was cracked; and when they sat down, a faint dust rose sluggishly about their thighs, spinning with slow motes in the single sun-ray. On a tarnished gilt easel before the fireplace stood a crayon portrait of Miss Emily's father.

They rose when she entered—a small, fat woman in black, with a thin gold chain descending to her waist and vanishing into her belt, leaning on an ebony cane with a tarnished gold head. Her skeleton was small and spare; perhaps that was why what would have been merely plumpness in another was obesity in her. She looked bloated, like a body long submerged in motionless water, and of that pallid hue. Her eyes, lost in the fatty ridges of her face, looked like two small pieces of coal pressed into a lump of dough as they moved from one face to another while the visitors stated their errand.

She did not ask them to sit. She just stood in the door and listened quietly until the spokesman came to a stumbling halt. Then they could hear the invisible watch ticking at the end of the gold chain.

Her voice was dry and cold. "I have no taxes in Jefferson. Colonel Sartoris explained it to me. Perhaps one of you can gain access to the city records and satisfy yourselves."

"But we have. We are the city authorities, Miss Emily. Didn't you get a notice from the sheriff, signed by him?"

"I received a paper, yes," Miss Emily said. "Perhaps he considers himself the sheriff . . .   10
I have no taxes in Jefferson."

"But there is nothing on the books to show that, you see. We must go by the—"

"See Colonel Sartoris. I have no taxes in Jefferson."

"But, Miss Emily—"

"See Colonel Sartoris." (Colonel Sartoris had been dead almost ten years.) "I have no taxes in Jefferson. Tobe!" The Negro appeared. "Show these gentlemen out."

II

So she vanquished them, horse and foot, just as she had vanquished their fathers thirty years   15
before about the smell. That was two years after her father's death and a short time after
her sweetheart—the one we believed would marry her—had deserted her. After her father's
death she went out very little; after her sweetheart went away, people hardly saw her at all. A
few of the ladies had the temerity to call, but were not received, and the only sign of life about
the place was the Negro man—a young man then—going in and out with a market basket.

"Just as if a man—any man—could keep a kitchen properly," the ladies said; so they
were not surprised when the smell developed. It was another link between the gross, teeming world and the high and mighty Griersons.

A neighbor, a woman, complained to the mayor, Judge Stevens, eighty years old.

"But what will you have me do about it, madam?" he said.

"Why, send her word to stop it," the woman said. "Isn't there a law?"

"I'm sure that won't be necessary," Judge Stevens said. "It's probably just a snake or a   20
rat that nigger of hers killed in the yard. I'll speak to him about it."

The next day he received two more complaints, one from a man who came in diffident
deprecation. "We really must do something about it, Judge. I'd be the last one in the world
to bother Miss Emily, but we've got to do something." That night the Board of Aldermen
met—three graybeards and one younger man, a member of the rising generation.

"It's simple enough," he said. "Send her word to have her place cleaned up. Give her a
certain time to do it in, and if she don't . . . "

"Dammit, sir," Judge Stevens said, "will you accuse a lady to her face of smelling bad?"

So the next night, after midnight, four men crossed Miss Emily's lawn and slunk about
the house like burglars, sniffing along the base of the brickwork and at the cellar openings
while one of them performed a regular sowing motion with his hand out of a sack slung
from his shoulder. They broke open the cellar door and sprinkled lime there, and in all the
outbuildings. As they recrossed the lawn, a window that had been dark was lighted and
Miss Emily sat in it, the light behind her, and her upright torso motionless as that of an idol.
They crept quietly across the lawn and into the shadow of the locusts that lined the street.
After a week or two the smell went away.

That was when people had begun to feel really sorry for her. People in our town, remem-   25
bering how old lady Wyatt, her great-aunt, had gone completely crazy at last, believed that
the Griersons held themselves a little too high for what they really were. None of the young
men were quite good enough for Miss Emily and such. We had long thought of them as
a tableau, Miss Emily a slender figure in white in the background, her father a spraddled
silhouette in the foreground, his back to her and clutching a horsewhip, the two of them
framed by the back flung front door. So when she got to be thirty and was still single, we
were not pleased exactly, but vindicated; even with insanity in the family she wouldn't
have turned down all of her chances if they had really materialized.

When her father died, it got about that the house was all that was left to her; and in a
way, people were glad. At last they could pity Miss Emily. Being left alone, and a pauper,

she had become humanized. Now she too would know the old thrill and the old despair of a penny more or less.

The day after his death all the ladies prepared to call at the house and offer condolence and aid, as is our custom. Miss Emily met them at the door, dressed as usual and with no trace of grief on her face. She told them that her father was not dead. She did that for three days, with the ministers calling on her, and the doctors, trying to persuade her to let them dispose of the body. Just as they were about to resort to law and force, she broke down, and they buried her father quickly.

We did not say she was crazy then. We believed she had to do that. We remembered all the young men her father had driven away, and we knew that with nothing left, she would have to cling to that which had robbed her, as people will.

III

She was sick for a long time. When we saw her again, her hair was cut short, making her look like a girl, with a vague resemblance to those angels in colored church windows—sort of tragic and serene.

30   The town had just let the contracts for paving the sidewalks, and in the summer after her father's death they began the work. The construction company came with niggers and mules and machinery, and a foreman named Homer Barron, a Yankee—a big, dark, ready man, with a big voice and eyes lighter than his face. The little boys would follow in groups to hear him cuss the niggers, and the niggers singing in time to the rise and fall of picks. Pretty soon he knew everybody in town. Whenever you heard a lot of laughing anywhere about the square, Homer Barron would be in the center of the group. Presently we began to see him and Miss Emily on Sunday afternoons driving in the yellow-wheeled buggy and the matched team of bays from the livery stable.

At first we were glad that Miss Emily would have an interest, because the ladies all said, "Of course a Grierson would not think seriously of a Northerner, a day laborer." But there were still others, older people, who said that even grief could not cause a real lady to forget *noblesse oblige* without calling it *noblesse oblige*. They just said, "Poor Emily. Her kinsfolk should come to her." She had some kin in Alabama; but years ago her father had fallen out with them over the estate of old lady Wyatt, the crazy woman, and there was no communication between the two families. They had not even been represented at the funeral.

And as soon as the old people said, "Poor Emily," the whispering began. "Do you suppose it's really so?" they said to one another. "Of course it is. What else could . . . ." This behind their hands; rustling of craned silk and satin behind jalousies closed upon the sun of Sunday afternoon as the thin, swift clop-clop-clop of the matched team passed: "Poor Emily."

She carried her head high enough—even when we believed that she was fallen. It was as if she demanded more than ever the recognition of her dignity as the last Grierson; as if it had wanted that touch of earthiness to reaffirm her imperviousness. Like when she bought the rat poison, the arsenic. That was over a year after they had begun to say "Poor Emily," and while the two female cousins were visiting her.

"I want some poison," she said to the druggist. She was over thirty then, still a slight woman, though thinner than usual, with cold, haughty black eyes in a face the flesh of which was strained across the temples and about the eyesockets as you imagine a light-house-keeper's face ought to look. "I want some poison," she said.

35   "Yes, Miss Emily. What kind? For rats and such? I'd recom—"

"I want the best you have. I don't care what kind."

The druggist named several. "They'll kill anything up to an elephant. But what you want is—"

"Arsenic," Miss Emily said. "Is that a good one?"

"Is . . . arsenic? Yes, ma'am. But what you want—"

"I want arsenic."   40

The druggist looked down at her. She looked back at him, erect, her face like a strained flag. "Why, of course," the druggist said. "If that's what you want. But the law requires you to tell what you are going to use it for."

Miss Emily just stared at him, her head tilted back in order to look him eye for eye, until he looked away and went and got the arsenic and wrapped it up. The Negro delivery boy brought her the package; the druggist didn't come back. When she opened the package at home there was written on the box, under the skull and bones: "For rats."

IV

So the next day we all said, "She will kill herself"; and we said it would be the best thing. When she had first begun to be seen with Homer Barron, we had said, "She will marry him." Then we said, "She will persuade him yet," because Homer himself had remarked—he liked men, and it was known that he drank with the younger men in the Elks' Club—that he was not a marrying man. Later we said, "Poor Emily" behind the jalousies as they passed on Sunday afternoon in the glittering buggy, Miss Emily with her head high and Homer Barron with his hat cocked and a cigar in his teeth, reins and whip in a yellow glove.

Then some of the ladies began to say that it was a disgrace to the town and a bad example to the young people. The men did not want to interfere, but at last the ladies forced the Baptist minister—Miss Emily's people were Episcopal—to call upon her. He would never divulge what happened during that interview, but he refused to go back again. The next Sunday they again drove about the streets, and the following day the minister's wife wrote to Miss Emily's relations in Alabama.

So she had blood-kin under her roof again and we sat back to watch developments. At   45
first nothing happened. Then we were sure that they were to be married. We learned that Miss Emily had been to the jeweler's and ordered a man's toilet set in silver, with the letters H. B. on each piece. Two days later we learned that she had bought a complete outfit of men's clothing, including a nightshirt, and we said, "They are married." We were really glad. We were glad because the two female cousins were even more Grierson than Miss Emily had ever been.

So we were not surprised when Homer Barron—the streets had been finished some time since—was gone. We were a little disappointed that there was not a public blowing-off, but we believed that he had gone on to prepare for Miss Emily's coming, or to give her a chance to get rid of the cousins. (By that time it was a cabal, and we were all Miss Emily's allies to help circumvent the cousins.) Sure enough, after another week they departed. And, as we had expected all along, within three days Homer Barron was back in town. A neighbor saw the Negro man admit him at the kitchen door at dusk one evening.

And that was the last we saw of Homer Barron. And of Miss Emily for some time. The Negro man went in and out with the market basket, but the front door remained closed. Now and then we would see her at a window for a moment, as the men did that night when they sprinkled the lime, but for almost six months she did not appear on the streets. Then we knew that this was to be expected too; as if that quality of her father which had thwarted her woman's life so many times had been too virulent and too furious to die.

When we next saw Miss Emily, she had grown fat and her hair was turning gray. During the next few years it grew grayer and grayer until it attained an even pepper-and-salt iron gray, when it ceased turning. Up to the day of her death at seventy-four it was still that vigorous iron-gray, like the hair of an active man.

From that time on her front door remained closed, save for a period of six or seven years, when she was about forty, during which she gave lessons in china-painting. She fitted up a studio in one of the downstairs rooms, where the daughters and granddaughters of Colonel Sartoris' contemporaries were sent to her with the same regularity and in the same spirit that they were sent to church on Sundays with a twenty-five-cent piece for the collection plate. Meanwhile her taxes had been remitted.

50   Then the newer generation became the backbone and the spirit of the town, and the painting pupils grew up and fell away and did not send their children to her with boxes of color and tedious brushes and pictures cut from the ladies' magazines. The front door closed upon the last one and remained closed for good. When the town got free postal delivery, Miss Emily alone refused to let them fasten the metal numbers above her door and attach a mailbox to it. She would not listen to them.

Daily, monthly, yearly we watched the Negro grow grayer and more stooped, going in and out with the market basket. Each December we sent her a tax notice, which would be returned by the post office a week later, unclaimed. Now and then we would see her in one of the downstairs windows—she had evidently shut up the top floor of the house—like the carven torso of an idol in a niche, looking or not looking at us, we could never tell which. Thus she passed from generation to generation—dear, inescapable, impervious, tranquil, and perverse.

And so she died. Fell ill in the house filled with dust and shadows, with only a doddering Negro man to wait on her. We did not even know she was sick; we had long since given up trying to get any information from the Negro. He talked to no one, probably not even to her, for his voice had grown harsh and rusty, as if from disuse.

She died in one of the downstairs rooms, in a heavy walnut bed with a curtain, her gray head propped on a pillow yellow and moldy with age and lack of sunlight.

V

The Negro met the first of the ladies at the front door and let them in, with their hushed, sibilant voices and their quick, curious glances, and then he disappeared. He walked right through the house and out the back and was not seen again.

55   The two female cousins came at once. They held the funeral on the second day, with the town coming to look at Miss Emily beneath a mass of bought flowers, with the crayon face of her father musing profoundly above the bier and the ladies sibilant and macabre; and the very old men—some in their brushed Confederate uniforms—on the porch and the lawn, talking of Miss Emily as if she had been a contemporary of theirs, believing that they had danced with her and courted her perhaps, confusing time with its mathematical progression, as the old do, to whom all the past is not a diminishing road but, instead, a huge meadow which no winter ever quite touches, divided from them now by the narrow bottle-neck of the most recent decade of years.

Already we knew that there was one room in that region above stairs which no one had seen in forty years, and which would have to be forced. They waited until Miss Emily was decently in the ground before they opened it.

The violence of breaking down the door seemed to fill this room with pervading dust. A thin, acrid pall as of the tomb seemed to lie everywhere upon this room decked and furnished as for a bridal: upon the valance curtains of faded rose color, upon the rose-shaded lights, upon the dressing table, upon the delicate array of crystal and the man's toilet things backed with tarnished silver, silver so tarnished that the monogram was obscured. Among them lay a collar and tie, as if they had just been removed, which, lifted, left upon the surface a pale crescent in the dust. Upon a chair hung the suit, carefully folded; beneath it the two mute shoes and the discarded socks.

The man himself lay in the bed.

For a long while we just stood there, looking down at the profound and fleshless grin. The body had apparently once lain in the attitude of an embrace, but now the long sleep that outlasts love, that conquers even the grimace of love, had cuckolded him. What was left of him, rotted beneath what was left of the nightshirt, had become inextricable from the bed in which he lay; and upon him and upon the pillow beside him lay that even coating of the patient and biding dust.

Then we noticed that in the second pillow was the indentation of a head. One of us lifted 60
something from it, and leaning forward, that faint and invisible dust dry and acrid in the
nostrils, we saw a long strand of iron-gray hair.

QUESTIONS

1. Who is Emily Grierson? What was the former position of her family in the town? What
   has happened to Emily after her father died? What are her economic circumstances?
   How does the deputation of aldermen from the town of Jefferson treat her?

2. How do we learn about Emily? How do reports and rumors about her create the narrative of her life?

3. What has happened between Emily and Homer Barron? What is the significance, if
   any, of the fact that Homer is from the North?

4. Describe the plot of "A Rose for Emily." What contrasts and oppositions are developed
   in the story?

5. How does Faulkner shape the story's events to make Emily mysterious or enigmatic?
   In what ways does the ending come as a surprise?

TIM O'BRIEN (b. 1946)

*William Timothy O'Brien was born in Minnesota and attended
Macalester College in St. Paul. He saw duty in Vietnam during
some of the more controversial times of that conflict, and after returning home he did graduate study, worked as a reporter, and became a writer. Among the works he has regularly published since
the 1970s are* If I Die in a Combat Zone, Box Me Up and Ship
Me Home *(1973);* Northern Lights *(1974);* Going After Cacciato
(1978); The Things They Carried *(1990);* Tomcat in Love *(1998);
and* July, July *(2002). In his stories, which interweave fiction and
autobiography, he realistically treats both the horrors of the Vietnam War and the ways in
which returning veterans and their loved ones adjust to life after returning home. Because
he portrays the lives and feelings of combat soldiers so well, he has been called one of the best
American writers about war.*

The Things They Carried (1990)

First Lieutenant Jimmy Cross carried letters from a girl named Martha, a junior at Mount
Sebastian College in New Jersey. They were not love letters, but Lieutenant Cross was
hoping, so he kept them folded in plastic at the bottom of his rucksack. In the late afternoon, after a day's march, he would dig his foxhole, wash his hands under a canteen,
unwrap the letters, hold them with the tips of his fingers, and spend the last hour of
light pretending. He would imagine romantic camping trips into the White Mountains in
New Hampshire. He would sometimes taste the envelope flaps, knowing her tongue had
been there. More than anything, he wanted Martha to love him as he loved her, but the
letters were mostly chatty, elusive on the matter of love. She was a virgin, he was almost
sure. She was an English major at Mount Sebastian, and she wrote beautifully about her
professors and roommates and midterm exams, about her respect for Chaucer and her
great affection for Virginia Woolf. She often quoted lines of poetry; she never mentioned
the war, except to say, Jimmy, take care of yourself. The letters weighed 10 ounces. They
were signed Love, Martha, but Lieutenant Cross understood that Love was only a way
of signing and did not mean what he sometimes pretended it meant. At dusk, he would

carefully return the letters to his rucksack. Slowly, a bit distracted, he would get up and move among his men, checking the perimeter, then at full dark he would return to his hole and watch the night and wonder if Martha was a virgin.

The things they carried were largely determined by necessity. Among the necessities or near-necessities were P-38 can openers, pocket knives, heat tabs, wristwatches, dog tags, mosquito repellent, chewing gum, candy, cigarettes, salt tablets, packets of Kool-Aid, lighters, matches, sewing kits, Military Payment Certificates, C rations, and two or three canteens of water. Together, these items weighed between 15 and 20 pounds, depending upon a man's habits or rate of metabolism. Henry Dobbins, who was a big man, carried extra rations; he was especially fond of canned peaches in heavy syrup over pound cake. Dave Jensen, who practiced field hygiene, carried a toothbrush, dental floss, and several hotel-sized bars of soap he'd stolen on R&R in Sydney, Australia. Ted Lavender, who was scared, carried tranquilizers until he was shot in the head outside the village of Than Khe in mid-April. By necessity, and because it was SOP, they all carried steel helmets that weighed 5 pounds including the liner and camouflage cover. They carried the standard fatigue jackets and trousers. Very few carried underwear. On their feet they carried jungle boots—2.1 pounds—and Dave Jensen carried three pairs of socks and a can of Dr. Scholl's foot powder as a precaution against trench foot. Until he was shot, Ted Lavender carried six or seven ounces of premium dope, which for him was a necessity. Mitchell Sanders, the RTO, carried condoms. Norman Bowker carried a diary. Rat Kiley carried comic books. Kiowa, a devout Baptist, carried an illustrated New Testament that had been presented to him by his father, who taught Sunday school in Oklahoma City, Oklahoma. As a hedge against bad times, however, Kiowa also carried his grandmother's distrust of the white man, his grandfather's old hunting hatchet. Necessity dictated. Because the land was mined and booby-trapped, it was SOP for each man to carry a steel-centered, nylon-covered flak jacket, which weighed 6.7 pounds, but which on hot days seemed much heavier. Because you could die so quickly, each man carried at least one large compress bandage, usually in the helmet band for easy access. Because the nights were cold, and because the monsoons were wet, each carried a green plastic poncho that could be used as a raincoat or groundsheet or makeshift tent. With its quilted liner, the poncho weighed almost two pounds, but it was worth every ounce. In April, for instance, when Ted Lavender was shot, they used his poncho to wrap him up, then to carry him across the paddy, then to lift him into the chopper that took him away.

They were called legs or grunts.

To carry something was to hump it, as when Lieutenant Jimmy Cross humped his love for Martha up the hills and through the swamps. In its intransitive form, to hump meant to walk, or to march, but it implied burdens far beyond the intransitive.

5   Almost everyone humped photographs. In his wallet, Lieutenant Cross carried two photographs of Martha. The first was a Kodacolor snapshot signed Love, though he knew better. She stood against a brick wall. Her eyes were gray and neutral, her lips slightly open as she stared straight-on at the camera. At night, sometimes, Lieutenant Cross wondered who had taken the picture, because he knew she had boyfriends, because he loved her so much, and because he could see the shadow of the picture-taker spreading out against the brick wall. The second photograph had been clipped from the 1968 Mount Sebastian yearbook. It was an action shot—women's volleyball—and Martha was bent horizontal to the floor, reaching, the palms of her hands in sharp focus, the tongue taut, the expression frank and competitive. There was no visible sweat. She wore white gym shorts. Her legs, he thought, were almost certainly the legs of a virgin, dry and without hair, the left knee cocked and carrying her entire weight, which was just over one hundred pounds. Lieutenant Cross remembered touching that left knee. A dark theater, he remembered, and the movie was *Bonnie and Clyde*, and Martha wore a tweed skirt, and during the final scene,

when he touched her knee, she turned and looked at him in a sad, sober way that made him pull his hand back, but he would always remember the feel of the tweed skirt and the knee beneath it and the sound of the gunfire that killed Bonnie and Clyde, how embarrassing it was, how slow and oppressive. He remembered kissing her good night at the dorm door. Right then, he thought, he should've done something brave. He should've carried her up the stairs to her room and tied her to the bed and touched that left knee all night long. He should've risked it. Whenever he looked at the photographs, he thought of new things he should've done.

What they carried was partly a function of rank, partly of field specialty.

As a first lieutenant and platoon leader, Jimmy Cross carried a compass, maps, code books, binoculars, and a .45-caliber pistol that weighed 2.9 pounds fully loaded. He carried a strobe light and the responsibility for the lives of his men.

As an RTO, Mitchell Sanders carried the PRC-25 radio, a killer, 26 pounds with its battery.

As a medic, Rat Kiley carried a canvas satchel filled with morphine and plasma and malaria tablets and surgical tape and comic books and all the things a medic must carry, including M&M's for especially bad wounds, for a total weight of nearly 20 pounds.

As a big man, therefore a machine gunner, Henry Dobbins carried the M-60, which weighed 23 pounds unloaded, but which was almost always loaded. In addition, Dobbins carried between 10 and 15 pounds of ammunition draped in belts across his chest and shoulders.

As PFCs or Spec 4s, most of them were common grunts and carried the standard M-16 gas-operated assault rifle. The weapon weighed 7.5 pounds unloaded, 8.2 pounds with its full 20-round magazine. Depending on numerous factors, such as topography and psychology, the riflemen carried anywhere from 12 to 20 magazines, usually in cloth bandoliers, adding on another 8.4 pounds at minimum, 14 pounds at maximum. When it was available, they also carried M-16 maintenance gear—rods and steel brushes and swabs and tubes of LSA oil—all of which weighed about a pound. Among the grunts, some carried the M-79 grenade launcher, 5.9 pounds unloaded, a reasonably light weapon except for the ammunition, which was heavy. A single round weighed 10 ounces. The typical load was 25 rounds. But Ted Lavender, who was scared, carried 34 rounds when he was shot and killed outside Than Khe, and he went down under an exceptional burden, more than 20 pounds of ammunition, plus the flak jacket and helmet and rations and water and toilet paper and tranquilizers and all the rest, plus the unweighed fear. He was dead weight. There was no twitching or flopping. Kiowa, who saw it happen, said it was like watching a rock fall, or a big sandbag or something—just boom, then down—not like the movies where the dead guy rolls around and does fancy spins and goes ass over teakettle—not like that, Kiowa said, the poor bastard just flat-fuck fell. Boom. Down. Nothing else. It was a bright morning in mid-April. Lieutenant Cross felt the pain. He blamed himself. They stripped off Lavender's canteens and ammo, all the heavy things, and Rat Kiley said the obvious, the guy's dead, and Mitchell Sanders used his radio to report one U.S. KIA and to request a chopper. Then they wrapped Lavender in his poncho. They carried him out to a dry paddy, established security, and sat smoking the dead man's dope until the chopper came. Lieutenant Cross kept to himself. He pictured Martha's smooth young face, thinking he loved her more than anything, more than his men, and now Ted Lavender was dead because he loved her so much and could not stop thinking about her. When the dustoff arrived, they carried Lavender aboard. Afterward they burned Than Khe. They marched until dusk, then dug their holes, and that night Kiowa kept explaining how you had to be there, how fast it was, how the poor guy just dropped like so much concrete. Boom-down, he said. Like cement.

10

In addition to the three standard weapons—the M-60, M-16, and M-79—they carried whatever presented itself, or whatever seemed appropriate as a means of killing or staying alive. They carried catch-as-catch-can. At various times, in various situations, they carried M-14s and CAR-15s and Swedish Ks and grease guns and captured AK-47s and Chi-Coms and RPGs and Simonov carbines and black market Uzis and .38-caliber Smith & Wesson handguns and 66 mm LAWs and shotguns and silencers and blackjacks and bayonets and C-4 plastic explosives. Lee Strunk carried a slingshot; a weapon of last resort, he called it. Mitchell Sanders carried brass knuckles. Kiowa carried his grandfather's feathered hatchet. Every third or fourth man carried a Claymore antipersonnel mine—3.5 pounds with its firing device. They all carried fragmentation grenades—14 ounces each. They all carried at least one M-18 colored smoke grenade—24 ounces. Some carried CS or tear gas grenades. Some carried white phosphorus grenades. They carried all they could bear, and then some, including a silent awe for the terrible power of the things they carried.

• • •

In the first week of April, before Lavender died, Lieutenant Jimmy Cross received a good-luck charm from Martha. It was a simple pebble, an ounce at most. Smooth to the touch, it was a milky white color with flecks of orange and violet, oval-shaped, like a miniature egg. In the accompanying letter, Martha wrote that she had found the pebble on the Jersey shoreline, precisely where the land touched water at high tide, where things came together but also separated. It was this separate-but-together quality, she wrote, that had inspired her to pick up the pebble and to carry it in her breast pocket for several days, where it seemed weightless, and then to send it through the mail, by air, as a token of her truest feelings for him. Lieutenant Cross found this romantic. But he wondered what her truest feelings were, exactly, and what she meant by separate-but-together. He wondered how the tides and waves had come into play on that afternoon along the Jersey shoreline when Martha saw the pebble and bent down to rescue it from geology. He imagined bare feet. Martha was a poet, with the poet's sensibilities, and her feet would be brown and bare, the toenails unpainted, the eyes chilly and somber like the ocean in March, and though it was painful, he wondered who had been with her that afternoon. He imagined a pair of shadows moving along the strip of sand where things came together but also separated. It was phantom jealousy, he knew, but he couldn't help himself. He loved her so much. On the march, through the hot days of early April, he carried the pebble in his mouth, turning it with his tongue, tasting sea salt and moisture. His mind wandered. He had difficulty keeping his attention on the war. On occasion he would yell at his men to spread out the column, to keep their eyes open, but then he would slip away into day-dreams, just pretending, walking barefoot along the Jersey shore, with Martha, carrying nothing. He would feel himself rising. Sun and waves and gentle winds, all love and lightness.

What they carried varied by mission.

When a mission took them to the mountains, they carried mosquito netting, machetes, canvas tarps, and extra bug juice.

If a mission seemed especially hazardous, or if it involved a place they knew to be bad, they carried everything they could. In certain heavily mined AOs, where the land was dense with Toe Poppers and Bouncing Betties, they took turns humping a 28-pound mine detector. With its headphones and big sensing plate, the equipment was a stress on the lower back and shoulders, awkward to handle, often useless because of the shrapnel in the earth, but they carried it anyway, partly for safety, partly for the illusion of safety.

On ambush, or other night missions, they carried peculiar little odds and ends. Kiowa always took along his New Testament and a pair of moccasins for silence. Dave

Jensen carried night-sight vitamins high in carotene. Lee Strunk carried his slingshot; ammo, he claimed, would never be a problem. Rat Kiley carried brandy and M&M's candy. Until he was shot, Ted Lavender carried the starlight scope, which weighed 6.3 pounds with its aluminum carrying case. Henry Dobbins carried his girlfriend's pantyhose wrapped around his neck as a comforter. They all carried ghosts. When dark came, they would move out single file across the meadows and paddies to their ambush coordinates, where they would quietly set up the Claymores and lie down and spend the night waiting.

Other missions were more complicated and required special equipment. In mid-April, it was their mission to search out and destroy the elaborate tunnel complexes in the Than Khe area south of Chu Lai. To blow the tunnels, they carried one-pound blocks of pentrite high explosives, four blocks to a man, 68 pounds in all. They carried wiring, detonators, and battery-powered clackers. Dave Jensen carried earplugs. Most often, before blowing the tunnels, they were ordered by higher command to search them, which was considered bad news, but by and large they just shrugged and carried out orders. Because he was a big man, Henry Dobbins was excused from tunnel duty. The others would draw numbers. Before Lavender died there were 17 men in the platoon, and whoever drew the number 17 would strip off his gear and crawl in headfirst with a flashlight and Lieutenant Cross's .45-caliber pistol. The rest of them would fan out as security. They would sit down or kneel, not facing the hole, listening to the ground beneath them, imagining cobwebs and ghosts, whatever was down there—the tunnel walls squeezing in—how the flashlight seemed impossibly heavy in the hand and how it was tunnel vision in the very strictest sense, compression in all ways, even time, and how you had to wiggle in—ass and elbows— a swallowed-up feeling—and how you found yourself worrying about odd things: Will your flashlight go dead? Do rats carry rabies? If you screamed, how far would the sound carry? Would your buddies hear it? Would they have the courage to drag you out? In some respects, though not many, the waiting was worse than the tunnel itself. Imagination was a killer.

On April 16, when Lee Strunk drew the number 17, he laughed and muttered something and went down quickly. The morning was hot and very still. Not good, Kiowa said. He looked at the tunnel opening, then out across a dry paddy toward the village of Than Khe. Nothing moved. No clouds or birds or people. As they waited, the men smoked and drank Kool-Aid, not talking much, feeling sympathy for Lee Strunk but also feeling the luck of the draw. You win some, you lose some, said Mitchell Sanders, and sometimes you settle for a rain check. It was a tired line and no one laughed.

Henry Dobbins ate a tropical chocolate bar. Ted Lavender popped a tranquilizer and   20
went off to pee.

After five minutes, Lieutenant Jimmy Cross moved to the tunnel, leaned down, and examined the darkness. Trouble, he thought—a cave-in maybe. And then suddenly, without willing it, he was thinking about Martha. The stresses and fractures, the quick collapse, the two of them buried alive under all that weight. Dense, crushing love. Kneeling, watching the hole, he tried to concentrate on Lee Strunk and the war, all the dangers, but his love was too much for him, he felt paralyzed, he wanted to sleep inside her lungs and breathe her blood and be smothered. He wanted her to be a virgin and not a virgin, all at once. He wanted to know her. Intimate secrets: Why poetry? Why so sad? Why that grayness in her eyes? Why so alone? Not lonely, just alone—riding her bike across campus or sitting off by herself in the cafeteria—even dancing, she danced alone—and it was the aloneness that filled him with love. He remembered telling her that one evening. How she nodded and looked away. And how, later, when he kissed her, she received the kiss without returning it, her eyes wide open, not afraid, not a virgin's eyes, just flat and uninvolved.

Lieutenant Cross gazed at the tunnel. But he was not there. He was buried with Martha under the white sand at the Jersey shore. They were pressed together, and the pebble in his mouth was her tongue. He was smiling. Vaguely, he was aware of how quiet the day was, the sullen paddies, yet he could not bring himself to worry about matters of security. He was beyond that. He was just a kid at war, in love. He was twenty-four years old. He couldn't help it.

A few moments later Lee Strunk crawled out of the tunnel. He came up grinning, filthy but alive. Lieutenant Cross nodded and closed his eyes while the others clapped Strunk on the back and made jokes about rising from the dead.

Worms, Rat Kiley said. Right out of the grave. Fuckin' zombie.

25   The men laughed. They all felt great relief.

Spook city, said Mitchell Sanders.

Lee Strunk made a funny ghost sound, a kind of moaning, yet very happy, and right then, when Strunk made that high happy moaning sound, when he went *Ahhooooo*, right then Ted Lavender was shot in the head on his way back from peeing. He lay with his mouth open. The teeth were broken. There was a swollen black bruise under his left eye. The cheekbone was gone. Oh shit, Rat Kiley said, the guy's dead. The guy's dead, he kept saying, which seemed profound—the guy's dead. I mean really.

•   •

The things they carried were determined to some extent by superstition. Lieutenant Cross carried his good-luck pebble. Dave Jensen carried a rabbit's foot. Norman Bowker, otherwise a very gentle person, carried a thumb that had been presented to him as a gift by Mitchell Sanders. The thumb was dark brown, rubbery to the touch, and weighed four ounces at most. It had been cut from a VC corpse, a boy of fifteen or sixteen. They'd found him at the bottom of an irrigation ditch, badly burned, flies in his mouth and eyes. The boy wore black shorts and sandals. At the time of his death he had been carrying a pouch of rice, a rifle and three magazines of ammunition.

You want my opinion, Mitchell Sanders said, there's a definite moral here.

30   He put his hand on the dead boy's wrist. He was quiet for a time, as if counting a pulse, then he patted the stomach, almost affectionately, and used Kiowa's hunting hatchet to remove the thumb.

Henry Dobbins asked what the moral was.

Moral?

You know. *Moral*.

Sanders wrapped the thumb in toilet paper and handed it across to Norman Bowker. There was no blood. Smiling, he kicked the boy's head, watched the flies scatter, and said, It's like with that old TV show—Paladin. Have gun, will travel.

35   Henry Dobbins thought about it.

Yeah, well, he finally said. I don't see no moral.

There it *is*, man.

Fuck off.

They carried USO stationery and pencils and pens. They carried Sterno, safety pins, trip flares, signal flares, spools of wire, razor blades, chewing tobacco, liberated joss sticks and statuettes of the smiling Buddha, candles, grease pencils, *The Stars and Stripes*, fingernail clippers, Psy Ops leaflets, bush hats, bolos, and much more. Twice a week, when the resupply choppers came in, they carried hot chow in green mermite cans and large canvas bags filled with iced beer and soda pop. They carried plastic water containers, each with a two-gallon capacity. Mitchell Sanders carried a set of starched tiger fatigues for special occasions. Henry Dobbins carried Black Flag insecticide. Dave Jensen carried empty sandbags that could be filled at night for added protection. Lee Strunk carried tanning lotion. Some things they carried in common. Taking turns, they carried the big PRC-77 scrambler radio, which weighed 30 pounds with its battery. They shared the weight of memory. They took up what others could no longer bear. Often, they carried each other, the wounded or weak. They carried infections. They carried chess sets, basketballs, Vietnamese-English dictionaries, insignia of rank, Bronze Stars and Purple Hearts, plastic cards imprinted with the Code of Conduct. They carried diseases, among them malaria and dysentery. They carried lice and ringworm and leeches and paddy algae and various rots and molds. They carried the land itself—Vietnam, the place, the soil—a powdery orange-red dust that covered their boots and fatigues and faces. They carried the sky. The whole atmosphere, they carried it, the humidity, the monsoons, the stink of fungus and decay, all of it, they carried gravity. They moved like mules. By daylight they took sniper fire, at night they were mortared, but it was not battle, it was just the endless march, village to village, without purpose, nothing won or lost. They marched for the sake of the march. They plodded along slowly, dumbly, leaning forward against the heat, unthinking, all blood and bone, simple grunts, soldiering with their legs, toiling up the hills and down into the paddies and across the rivers and up again and down, just humping, one step and then the next and then another, but no volition, no will, because it was automatic, it was anatomy, and the war was entirely a matter of posture and carriage, the hump was everything, a kind of inertia, a kind of emptiness, a dullness of desire and intellect and conscience and hope and human sensibility. Their principles were in their feet. Their calculations were biological. They had no sense of strategy or mission. They searched the villages without knowing what to look for, not caring, kicking over jars of rice, frisking children and old men, blowing tunnels, sometimes setting fires and sometimes not, then forming up and moving on to the next village, then other villages, where it would always be the same. They carried their own lives. The pressures were enormous. In the heat of early afternoon, they would remove their helmets and flak jackets, walking bare, which was dangerous but which helped ease the strain. They would often discard things along the route of march. Purely for comfort, they would throw away rations, blow their Claymores and grenades, no matter, because by nightfall the resupply choppers would arrive with more of the same, then a day or two later still more, fresh watermelons and crates of ammunition and sunglasses and woolen sweaters—the resources were stunning—sparklers for the Fourth of July, colored eggs for Easter—it was the great American war chest—the fruits of science, the smokestacks, the canneries, the arsenals at Hartford, the Minnesota forests, the machine shops, the vast fields of corn and wheat—they carried like freight trains; they carried it on their backs and shoulders—and for all the ambiguities of Vietnam, all the mysteries and unknowns, there was at least the single abiding certainty that they would never be at a loss for things to carry.

After the chopper took Lavender away, Lieutenant Jimmy Cross led his men into the 40 village of Than Khe. They burned everything. They shot chickens and dogs, they trashed the village well, they called in artillery and watched the wreckage, then they marched for several hours through the hot afternoon, and then at dusk, while Kiowa explained how Lavender died, Lieutenant Cross found himself trembling.

He tried not to cry. With his entrenching tool, which weighed five pounds, he began digging a hole in the earth.

He felt shame. He hated himself. He had loved Martha more than his men, and as a consequence Lavender was now dead, and this was something he would have to carry like a stone in his stomach for the rest of the war.

All he could do was dig. He used his entrenching tool like an ax, slashing, feeling both love and hate, and then later, when it was full dark, he sat at the bottom of his foxhole and wept. It went on for a long while. In part, he was grieving for Ted Lavender, but mostly it was for Martha, and for himself, because she belonged to another world, which was not quite real, and because she was a junior at Mount Sebastian College in New Jersey, a poet and a virgin and uninvolved, and because he realized she did not love him and never would.

Like cement, Kiowa whispered in the dark. I swear to God—boom, down. Not a word.

45   I've heard this, said Norman Bowker.

A pisser, you know? Still zipping himself up. Zapped while zipping.

All right, fine. That's enough.

Yeah, but you had to see it, the guy just—

I *heard*, man. Cement. So why not shut the fuck *up*?

50   Kiowa shook his head sadly and glanced over at the hole where Lieutenant Jimmy Cross sat watching the night. The air was thick and wet. A warm dense fog had settled over the paddies and there was the stillness that precedes rain.

After a time Kiowa sighed.

One thing for sure, he said. The lieutenant's in some deep hurt. I mean that crying jag— the way he was carrying on—it wasn't fake or anything, it was real heavy-duty hurt. The man cares.

Sure, Norman Bowker said.

Say what you want, the man does care.

55   We all got problems.

Not Lavender.

No, I guess not, Bowker said. Do me a favor, though.

Shut up?

That's a smart Indian. Shut up.

60   Shrugging, Kiowa pulled off his boots. He wanted to say more, just to lighten up his sleep, but instead he opened his New Testament and arranged it beneath his head as a pillow. The fog made things seem hollow and unattached. He tried not to think about Ted Lavender, but then he was thinking how fast it was, no drama, down and dead, and how it was hard to feel anything except surprise. It seemed unchristian. He wished he could find some great sadness, or even anger, but the emotion wasn't there and he couldn't make it happen. Mostly he felt pleased to be alive. He liked the smell of the New Testament under his cheek, the leather and ink and paper and glue, whatever the chemicals were. He liked hearing the sounds of night. Even his fatigue, it felt fine, the stiff muscles and the prickly awareness of his own body, a floating feeling. He enjoyed not being dead. Lying there, Kiowa admired Lieutenant Jimmy Cross's capacity for grief. He wanted to share the man's pain, he wanted to care as Jimmy Cross cared. And yet when he closed his eyes, all he could think was Boom-down, and all he could feel was the pleasure of having his boots off and the fog curling in around him and the damp soil and the Bible smells and the plush comfort of night.

After a moment Norman Bowker sat up in the dark.

What the hell, he said. You want to talk, *talk*. Tell it to me.

Forget it.

No, man, go on. One thing I hate, it's a silent Indian.

65   For the most part they carried themselves with poise, a kind of dignity. Now and then, however, there were times of panic, when they squealed or wanted to squeal but couldn't, when they twitched and made moaning sounds and covered their heads and

said Dear Jesus and flopped around on the earth and fired their weapons blindly and cringed and sobbed and begged for the noise to stop and went wild and made stupid promises to themselves and to God and to their mothers and fathers, hoping not to die. In different ways, it happened to all of them. Afterward, when the firing ended, they would blink and peek up. They would touch their bodies, feeling shame, then quickly hiding it. They would force themselves to stand. As if in slow motion, frame by frame, the world would take on the old logic—absolute silence, then the wind, then sunlight, then voices. It was the burden of being alive. Awkwardly, the men would reassemble themselves, first in private, then in groups, becoming soldiers again. They would repair the leaks in their eyes. They would check for casualties, call in dust-offs, light cigarettes, try to smile, clear their throats and spit and begin cleaning their weapons. After a time someone would shake his head and say, No lie. I almost shit my pants, and someone else would laugh, which meant it was bad, yes, but the guy had obviously not shit his pants, it wasn't that bad, and in any case nobody would ever do such a thing and then go ahead and talk about it. They would squint into the dense, oppressive sunlight. For a few moments, perhaps, they would fall silent, lighting a joint and tracking its passage from man to man, inhaling, holding in the humiliation. Scary stuff, one of them might say. But then someone else would grin or flick his eyebrows and say, Roger-dodger, almost cut me a new asshole, *almost*.

There were numerous such poses. Some carried themselves with a sort of wistful resignation, others with pride or stiff soldierly discipline or good humor or macho zeal. They were afraid of dying but they were even more afraid to show it.

They found jokes to tell.

They used a hard vocabulary to contain the terrible softness. *Greased* they'd say. *Offed, lit up, zapped while zipping*. It wasn't cruelty, just stage presence. They were actors. When someone died, it wasn't quite dying, because in a curious way it seemed scripted, and because they had their lines mostly memorized, irony mixed with tragedy, and because they called it by other names, as if to encyst and destroy the reality of death itself. They kicked corpses. They cut off thumbs. They talked grunt lingo. They told stories about Ted Lavender's supply of tranquilizers, how the poor guy didn't feel a thing, how incredibly tranquil he was.

There's a moral here, said Mitchell Sanders.

They were waiting for Lavender's chopper, smoking the dead man's dope.   70

The moral's pretty obvious, Sanders said, and winked. Stay away from drugs. No joke, they'll ruin your day every time.

Cute, said Henry Dobbins.

Mind blower, get it? Talk about wiggy. Nothing left, just blood and brains.

They made themselves laugh.

There it is, they'd say. Over and over—there it is, my friend, there it is—as if the repeti-   75
tion itself were an act of poise, a balance between crazy and almost crazy, knowing without going, there it is, which meant be cool, let it ride, because Oh yeah, man, you can't change what can't be changed, there it is, there it absolutely and positively and fucking well *is*.

They were tough.

They carried all the emotional baggage of men who might die. Grief, terror, love, longing—these were intangibles, but the intangibles had their own mass and specific gravity, they had tangible weight. They carried shameful memories. They carried the common secret of cowardice barely restrained, the instinct to run or freeze or hide, and in many respects this was the heaviest burden of all, for it could never be put down, it required perfect balance and perfect posture. They carried their reputations. They carried the soldier's greatest fear, which was the fear of blushing. Men killed, and died, because they were embarrassed not to. It was what had brought them to the war in the first place, nothing positive, no dreams of glory or honor, just to avoid the blush of dishonor. They died so as not to die of embarrassment. They crawled into tunnels and walked point and advanced under fire. Each morning, despite the unknowns, they made their legs move. They endured. They kept humping. They did not submit to the obvious alternative, which was simply to close the eyes and fall. So easy, really. Go limp and tumble to the ground and let the muscles unwind and not speak and not budge until your buddies picked you up and lifted you into the chopper that would roar and dip its nose and carry you off to the world. A mere matter of falling, yet no one ever fell. It was not courage, exactly; the object was not valor. Rather, they were too frightened to be cowards.

By and large they carried these things inside, maintaining the masks of composure. They sneered at sick call. They spoke bitterly about guys who had found release by shooting off their own toes or fingers. Pussies, they'd say. Candy-asses. It was fierce, mocking talk, with only a trace of envy or awe, but even so the image played itself out behind their eyes.

They imagined the muzzle against flesh. So easy: squeeze the trigger and blow away a toe. They imagined it. They imagined the quick, sweet pain, then the evacuation to Japan, then a hospital with warm beds and cute geisha nurses.

80   And they dreamed of freedom birds.

At night, on guard, staring into the dark, they were carried away by jumbo jets. They felt the rush of takeoff. *Gone!* they yelled. And then velocity—wings and engines—a smiling stewardess—but it was more than a plane, it was a real bird, a big sleek silver bird with feathers and talons and high screeching. They were flying. The weights fell off; there was nothing to bear. They laughed and held on tight, feeling the cold slap of wind and altitude, soaring, thinking *It's over, I'm gone!*—they were naked, they were light and free—it was all lightness, bright and fast and buoyant, light as light, a helium buzz in the brain, a giddy bubbling in the lungs as they were taken up over the clouds and the war, beyond duty, beyond gravity and mortification and global entanglements—*Sin loi!* they yelled. *I'm sorry, motherfuckers, but I'm out of it, I'm goofed, I'm on a space cruise, I'm gone!*—and it was a restful, unencumbered sensation, just riding the light waves, sailing that big silver freedom bird over the mountains and oceans, over America, over the farms and great sleeping cities and cemeteries and highways and the golden arches of McDonald's, it was flight, a kind of fleeing, a kind of falling, falling higher and higher, spinning off the edge of the earth and beyond the sun and through the vast, silent vacuum where there were no burdens and where everything weighed exactly nothing—*Gone!* they screamed. *I'm sorry but I'm gone!*—and so at night, not quite dreaming, they gave themselves over to lightness, they were carried, they were purely borne.

On the morning after Ted Lavender died, First Lieutenant Jimmy Cross crouched at the bottom of his foxhole and burned Martha's letters. Then he burned the two photographs. There was a steady rain falling, which made it difficult, but he used heat tabs and Sterno to build a small fire, screening it with his body, holding the photographs over the tight blue flame with the tips of his fingers.

He realized it was only a gesture. Stupid, he thought. Sentimental, too, but mostly just stupid.

Lavender was dead. You couldn't burn the blame.

85   Besides, the letters were in his head. And even now, without photographs, Lieutenant Cross could see Martha playing volleyball in her white gym shorts and yellow T-shirt. He could see her moving in the rain.

When the fire died out, Lieutenant Cross pulled his poncho over his shoulders and ate breakfast from a can.

There was no great mystery, he decided.

In those burned letters Martha had never mentioned the war, except to say, Jimmy, take care of yourself. She wasn't involved. She signed the letters Love, but it wasn't love, and all the fine lines and technicalities did not matter. Virginity was no longer an issue. He hated her. Yes, he did. He hated her. Love, too, but it was a hard, hating kind of love.

The morning came up wet and blurry. Everything seemed part of everything else, the fog and Martha and the deepening rain.

He was a soldier, after all.

Half smiling, Lieutenant Jimmy Cross took out his maps. He shook his head hard, as if to clear it, then bent forward and began planning the day's march. In ten minutes, or maybe twenty, he would rouse the men and they would pack up and head west, where the maps showed the country to be green and inviting. They would do what they had always done. The rain might add some weight, but otherwise it would be one more day layered upon all the other days.

He was realistic about it. There was that new hardness in his stomach. He loved her but he hated her.

No more fantasies, he told himself.

Henceforth, when he thought about Martha, it would be only to think that she belonged elsewhere. He would shut down the daydreams. This was not Mount Sebastian, it was another world, where there were no pretty poems or midterm exams, a place where men died because of carelessness and gross stupidity. Kiowa was right. Boom-down, and you were dead, never partly dead.

Briefly, in the rain, Lieutenant Cross saw Martha's gray eyes gazing back at him.

He understood.

It was very sad, he thought. The things men carried inside. The things men did or felt they had to do.

He almost nodded at her, but didn't.

Instead he went back to his maps. He was now determined to perform his duties firmly and without negligence. It wouldn't help Lavender, he knew that, but from this point on he would comport himself as an officer. He would dispose of his good-luck pebble. Swallow it, maybe, or use Lee Strunk's slingshot, or just drop it along the trail. On the march he would impose strict field discipline. He would be careful to send out flank security, to prevent straggling or bunching up, to keep his troops moving at the proper pace and at the proper interval. He would insist on clean weapons. He would confiscate the remainder of Lavender's dope. Later in the day, perhaps, he would call the men together and speak to them plainly. He would accept the blame for what had happened to Ted Lavender. He would be a man about it. He would look them in the eyes, keeping his chin level, and he would issue the new SOPs in a calm, impersonal tone of voice, a lieutenant's voice, leaving no room for argument or discussion. Commencing immediately, he'd tell them, they would no longer abandon equipment along the route of march. They would police up their acts. They would get their shit together, and keep it together, and maintain it neatly and in good working order.

He would not tolerate laxity. He would show strength, distancing himself.

Among the men there would be grumbling, of course, and maybe worse, because their days would seem longer and their loads heavier, but Lieutenant Jimmy Cross reminded himself that his obligation was not to be loved but to lead. He would dispense with love; it was not now a factor. And if anyone quarreled or complained, he would simply tighten his lips and arrange his shoulders in the correct command posture. He might give a curt little nod. Or he might not. He might just shrug and say, Carry on, then they would saddle up and form into a column and move out toward the villages west of Than Khe.

QUESTIONS

1. What do we learn about Lieutenant Jimmy Cross? How do we learn about him? Why does he blame himself for Lavender's death? How does Kiowa misinterpret his emotions? How do his concerns unify the story? What other unifying elements does the story contain?

2. What is the effect of the repetitions in the story (the constant descriptions of how much things weigh, the regular need to carry things, the way in which Lavender died)?

3. Why is Mitchell Sanders unable to put into words the moral of the dead man's thumb? How would you describe the moral?

4. Analyze paragraph 39. Discuss the various burdens the men of the platoon must carry. What bearing does this paragraph have upon other parts of the story?

Plot: The Motivation and Causality of Fiction

Stories are made up mostly of actions or incidents that follow one another in chronological order. The same is also true of life, but there is a major difference. Fiction must make sense even though life itself does not always seem to make sense at all. Finding a sequential or narrative order is therefore only a first step in our consideration of fiction. What we depend on for the sense or meaning of fiction is plot—the elements governing the unfolding of the actions.

The English novelist E. M. Forster, in *Aspects of the Novel*, presents a memorable illustration of plot. To illustrate a bare set of actions, he proposes the following: "The king died, and then the queen died." Forster points out, however, that this sequence does not form a plot because it lacks *motivation* and *causation*; it is too much like life itself to be fictional. Thus he introduces motivation and causation in his next example: "The king died, and then the queen died of grief." The phrase "of grief" shows that one thing (grief) controls or overcomes another (the normal desire to live), and motivation and causation enter the sequence to form a plot. In a well-plotted story or play, one thing precedes or follows another not simply because time ticks away, but more importantly because *effects* follow *causes.* In a good work of fiction, nothing is irrelevant or accidental; everything is related and causative.

Determining the Conflicts in a Story

The controlling impulse in a connected pattern of causes and effects is **conflict,** which refers to people or circumstances that a character must face and try to overcome. Conflicts bring out extremes of human energy, causing characters to engage in the decisions, actions, responses, and interactions that make up fictional literature.

In its most elemental form, a conflict is the opposition of two people. Their conflict may take the shape of anger, hatred, envy, argument, avoidance, political or moral opposition, gossip, lies, fighting, and many other actions and attitudes. Conflicts may also exist between groups, although conflicts between individuals are more identifiable and therefore more suitable for stories. Conflicts may also be abstract—for example, when an individual opposes larger forces such as natural objects, ideas, modes of behavior, or public opinion. A difficult or even impossible *choice*—a **dilemma**—is a natural conflict for an individual person. A conflict may also be brought out in ideas and opinions that clash. In short, conflict shows itself in many ways.

DIRECTLY RELATING CONFLICT TO DOUBT, TENSION, AND INTEREST. Conflict is the major element of plot because opposing forces arouse *curiosity*, cause *doubt*, create *tension*, and produce *interest*. The same responses are the lifeblood of athletic competition. Consider which kind of athletic event is more interesting: (1) One team gets so far ahead that the outcome is no longer in doubt, or (2) both teams are so evenly matched that the outcome is uncertain until the final seconds. Obviously, games are uninteresting—as games—unless they develop as contests between teams of comparable strength. The same principle applies to conflicts in stories and dramas. There should be uncertainty about a protagonist's success or failure. Unless there is doubt, there is no tension, and without tension there is no interest.

FINDING THE CONFLICTS TO DETERMINE THE PLOT. To see a plot in operation, let us build on Forster's description. Here is a simple plot for a story of our own: "John and Jane meet, fall in love, and get married." This sentence contains a plot because it shows cause and effect (they get married *because* they fall in love), but with no conflict, the plot is not interesting. However, let us introduce conflicting elements into this common "boy meets girl" story:

John and Jane meet in college and fall in love. They go together for a number of years and plan to marry, but a problem arises. Jane first wants to establish herself in a career, and after marriage she wants to be an equal contributor to the family. John understands Jane's wishes for equality, but he wants to get married first and let her finish her studies and have her career after they have children. Jane believes that John's plan is unacceptable because she thinks of it as a trap from which she might not escape. As they discuss their options they find themselves increasingly more irritated and unhappy with each other. Finally they bring their plans to an end, and they part in both anger and sorrow. Their love is not dead, however, but both go on to marry someone else and build separate lives and careers. In their new lives, neither is totally happy even though they like and respect their spouses. The years pass, and, after children and grandchildren, Jane and John meet again. He is now divorced and she is a widow. Because their earlier conflict is no longer a barrier, they rekindle their love, marry, and try to make up for the past. Even their new happiness, however, is tinged with regret and reproach because of their earlier conflicts, their unhappy decision to part, their lost years, and their increasing age.

Here we find a true plot because our original "boy meets girl" topic now contains a major conflict from which a number of related complications develop. These complications embody disagreements, choices, arguments, and ill feelings that produce tension, uncertainty, rupture, and regret. When we learn that John and Jane finally join together at the end we might still find the story painful to contemplate because it does not give us a "happily ever after" ending. Nevertheless, the story makes sense—as a story—because its plot brings out the plausible consequences of the understandable aims and hopes of John and Jane during their long relationship. It is the imposition of necessary causes and effects upon a series of events in time that creates the story's plot.

Writing About the Plot of a Story

An essay about plot is an analysis of the story's conflict and its developments. The organization of your essay should not be modeled on sequential sections and principal events, however, because these invite only a retelling of the story. Instead, the organization is to be developed from the important elements of conflict. As you look for ideas about plot, try to answer the questions below.

QUESTIONS FOR DISCOVERING IDEAS

1. Who are the major and minor characters, and how do their characteristics put them in conflict? How can you describe the conflict or conflicts?
2. How does the story's action grow out of the major conflict?
3. If the conflict stems from contrasting ideas or values, what are these, and how are they brought out?
4. What problems do the major characters face? How do the characters deal with these problems?
5. How do the major characters achieve (or not achieve) their major goal(s)? What obstacles do they overcome? What obstacles overcome them or alter them?
6. At the end, are the characters successful or unsuccessful, happy or unhappy, satisfied or dissatisfied, changed or unchanged, enlightened or ignorant? How has the resolution of the major conflict produced these results?

Strategies for Organizing Ideas

To keep your essay brief, you need to be selective. Rather than detailing everything a character does, for example, stress the major elements in his or her conflict. Such an essay on Eudora Welty's "A Worn Path"(p. 288) might emphasize Phoenix as she encounters the various obstacles both in the woods and in town. When there is a conflict between two major characters, the obvious approach is to focus equally on both. For brevity, however, emphasis might be placed on just one. Thus, an essay on the plot of "A Rose for Emily" might stress the details about Emily's life that make her the central participant in the story's conflict.

In addition, the plot may be analyzed more broadly in terms of impulses, goals, values, issues, and historical perspectives. Thus, you might emphasize the elements of chance working against Mathilde in Maupassant's "The Necklace" (Part I) as a contrast to her dreams about wealth. A discussion of the plot of Poe's "The Masque of the Red Death" (Chapter 9) might stress the haughtiness of Prospero, the major character, because the plot could not develop without his egotism.

The conclusion may contain a brief summary of the points you have made. It is also a fitting location for a brief consideration of the effect or impact produced by the conflict. Additional ideas might focus on whether the author has arranged actions and dialogue to direct your favor toward one side or the other, or whether the plot is possible or impossible, serious or comic, fair or unfair, powerful or indifferent, and so on.

Illustrative Student Essay

Although underlined sentences are not recommended by MLA style, they are used in this illustrative essay as teaching tools to emphasize the central idea, thesis sentence, and topic sentences.

Getty 1

Beth Getty

Professor Farmer

English 214

12 March 2014

Plot in Faulkner's "A Rose for Emily"°

William Faulkner's "A Rose for Emily" may seem at first to be about   [1]
a murder in a small southern town, but even a first reading of the story
reveals that the conflict does not arise from the search for a killer. It can't,
because no one knows that a murder has even occurred until the murderess
herself has died and been respectfully honored at her own funeral. Instead,
incidents in the story indicate that the conflict is actually between those
who are capable of change and those who are not, as well as those who
want it and those who don't.* Both the major and minor events in the
story's plot develop the idea that in the progress from an aristocratic
but romanticized past to a more egalitarian present and future, there are
unhealthy consequences for those who persist in clinging to the past.†

Faulkner begins to develop this conflict by relating several incidents   [2]
that establish the story's main character, Emily Grierson, to be one
of those older Southerners who are incapable of changing with the
times. When Emily's father dies, for example, she refuses to accept
his death. Some of the ladies of the town come to her home to offer
their condolences, and "she told them her father was not dead. She
did that for three days, with the minister calling on her, and the doctors,
trying to persuade her to let them dispose of the body. Just as they

°This story appears on pages 95–101.
*Central idea.
†Thesis sentence.

were about to resort to law and force, she broke down, and they buried her father quickly" (99). This incident reveals that Emily cannot cope with big changes. Yet another incident—Emily's refusal to have a mailbox affixed to her house when the town gets free postal delivery (100)—reveals that she cannot cope with smaller changes either. The event that most clearly reveals the unhealthy—and even disastrous— consequences of Emily's denial of change is her murder of her lover, who had apparently tried to end his relationship with her. The reader must piece the details together to understand what happened, but Faulkner provides enough information to indicate that Emily poisoned Homer Barron, who had said that "he was not a marrying man" (99), and then kept his decomposing corpse in her bed, continuing to sleep beside it after she had become an old woman with gray hair. Emily does not want to progress, and she refuses all change—both good and bad—with all of her might. As a result, she resorts to murder to prevent change from occurring at all.

[3]   The past has an unhealthy grip on others, too, as brought out by two major plot incidents which show that Emily is not the only Jefferson resident who struggles with change. The first is the disagreement between Emily and the town's Board of Aldermen over the issue of her taxes. Emily claims that she owes no taxes because of an arrangement she made in 1894 with the town's former mayor Colonel Sartoris. Her dispensation is overlooked until "the next generation, with its more modern ideas, became mayors and aldermen." These younger residents respond to her arrangement with "dissatisfaction" (96), for in the egalitarian spirit of modern times, they believe that everyone in the town should be obliged to share the tax burden. True to form, Emily resists the idea that she should change. She repeats the statement, "I have no taxes in Jefferson" four different times before finally ending the alderman's visit to her home (97). In this case, the younger and more modern townspeople try to force their newer and fairer standards upon Emily.

Getty 3

Although their request is valid, Faulkner's narrator tells us that "she vanquished them" (97). So even those who advocate needed change end up deferring to a relic from their past, and the unhealthy consequence is the continuation of inequality in Jefferson.

The second major incident that develops the clash between stagnation [4] and progress is the townspeople's response to the awful smell that comes from Emily's house. When neighbors complain to the Board of Aldermen, the issue pits the older residents against the younger ones, for the board is composed of "three graybeards, and one younger man, a member of the rising generation." This younger man proposes to deal with the problem as though Emily is no one special: " 'It's simple enough,' he said. 'Send her word to have her place cleaned up. Give her a certain time to do it in, and if she don't . . . '" (97). His suggestion reflects a newer democratic spirit, one that does not defer to people on the basis of status or position. Eighty-year-old Judge Stevens, however, speaks for the other older aldermen when he reacts with horror to this suggestion: " 'Dammit, sir,' Judge Stevens said, 'will you accuse a lady to her face of smelling bad?'" (97). These older officials adhere to more old-fashioned, romantic notions of deference to ladies and to members of the old aristocracy. Once again, in the struggle between the past and the present, the status quo and progress, tradition is the winner. Emily (along with the past she represents) easily vanquishes the objections of the younger residents, for the aldermen agree only to sprinkle lime around her house secretly, under cover of darkness (97). The result, however, is injustice, for an investigation into the smell that would have revealed its source to be a murdered corpse never takes place.

Without a doubt, in "A Rose for Emily" the characters who resist [5] progress prevail over the ones who advocate it. And yet, two terrible consequences are the result of this opposition to change: a man is murdered and the killer escapes justice, all because the residents of the town, by consensus, defer to out-dated and romantic notions from the past. Emily Grierson is not held—not by herself nor by others—to the standards

Getty 4

and rules that apply to everyone else in a democratic society. As a result, she ends up getting away with murder. Even so, Faulkner suggests that for those who *cannot* change, some pity may be in order, for the South's transformation completely overwhelms former aristocrats such as Emily. Faulkner is less sympathetic toward those like the older townspeople, however, who will not change, for as they seek to preserve the gentility of their heritage, they also perpetuate its flaws.

Getty 5

Work Cited

Faulkner, William. "A Rose for Emily." *Literature: An Introduction to Reading and Writing, Compact Edition.* Ed. Edgar V. Roberts and Robert Zweig. 6th ed. New York: Pearson, 2015. 95–101. Print.

Commentary on the Essay

Because the subject is plot, this essay emphasizes the conflicting elements in Faulkner's "A Rose for Emily"—change and resistance to change—in the town of Jefferson. The first paragraph demonstrates how this conflict emerges only slowly in the story, inasmuch as the most lurid detail is not brought out until the story's end. Throughout the body of the essay, the conflict between change and nonchange is stressed as the major element of Faulkner's plot.

Note that the essay assumes that readers know the story already. Hence the essay is not a plot summary but is instead an analysis of a number of the elements making up the plot. Whatever summary is included is presented as evidence to support points about the plot of the story. As with any essay, it is important to realize that thematic thrust is the overriding need in the shaping of the essay.

Paragraph 2 of the body deals with three major plot incidents revealing how Emily is part of the old aristocracy and serves to crystallize resistance to change in Jefferson. Paragraph 3 demonstrates that many of the Jefferson townspeople are also resistant to change. This paragraph also asserts one of Faulkner's major ideas—namely, that this resistance to change has ill consequences. Paragraph 4 considers the issue of how the townspeople react to the terrible smell at the

USING SOURCES EFFECTIVELY

QUOTING AN AUTHOR'S WORK

When writing about literature, including direct quotations from the work you are writing about will make your essay more persuasive by grounding it firmly and authoritatively in the author's own words and the work's events and details. Be selective about which passages you choose to quote, and do not quote too often. Your instructor is most interested in your ideas about the work: the passages you use should only be the *most* elegant or *most* pertinent to the main points you wish to make about the work. When done correctly, they will not only support your argument but will also infuse your writing with some memorable lines and passages.

In her essay, "Plot in Faulkner's 'A Rose for Emily,'" Beth Getty refers directly back to the story in her second paragraph as she relates key incidents that show how Emily has difficulty changing with the times. She writes:

> **Transition from Getty's writing to the quoted passage forms a complete sentence.**
>
> When Emily's father dies, for example, she refuses to accept his death. Some of the ladies of the town come to her home to offer their condolences, and "she told them her father was not dead. She did that for three days, with the minister calling on her, and the doctors, trying to persuade her to let them dispose of the body. Just as they were about to resort to law and force, she broke down, and they buried her father quickly."
>
> **Getty not only sets off the passage with quotation marks but also includes the page number where the specific passage can be found in parentheses.**
>
> (98) This incident reveals that Emily cannot cope with big changes. Yet another incident—Emily's refusal to have a mailbox affixed to her house when the town gets free postal delivery (100)—reveals that she cannot cope with smaller changes either.
>
> **This passage is both particularly moving and serves to illustrate Getty's point, which she clarifies in the very next sentence.**

Note how Getty embeds the quotation from page 98 into her own sentence structure in order to help her argument flow smoothly. Quotation marks and the page reference clearly show where she moves from her language to Faulkner's. This way, she gives her essay authority, and documents exactly where the passage can be found so a reader can refer back to it, if necessary.

Getty provides a second example of Emily's resistance to change by paraphrasing how she refused to get a mailbox when the town modernized its postal service. However, rather than use another long, extended quotation, she instead paraphrases this incident to present her second "smaller" piece of evidence. Even so, she again provides the page citation in parentheses to show that she is grounding her thesis solidly in the actual text. (For more information on using paraphrase when writing about fiction, see p. 511.)

Grierson household, and thus Emily and her circumstances are a focal point for the town's evasion of the issue.

Paragraph 5 summarizes the conflicts of the plot and concludes with a modification of the central idea—that those resisting change are victors over those wanting change, and that the murder of Homer Barron is, symbolically, a negative comment on the town's way of dealing with the past.

Writing Topics About Plot in Fiction

Writing Paragraphs

1. Write contrasting paragraphs about a character (whom you know or about whom you have read). In the first, try to make your reader like the character. In the second, try to create a hostile response to the character. Write an additional paragraph explaining the ways in which you tried to create these opposite responses. How fair would it be for a reader to dislike your negative paragraph even though your hostile portrait is successful?

2. Consider the illustrative essay on the plot of Faulkner's "A Rose for Emily." In a paragraph discuss how well the essay organizes the details about the story's plot? Do you accept the arguments in the essay? What other details and arguments can you think of that might explain Faulkner's plot more fully?

Writing Essays

1. Suppose that someone has told you that "The Things They Carried" is too detailed and realistic to be considered a story. In an essay argue that the assertion should be considered wrong. What elements of narrative, character, plot, point of view, idea, and description justify calling "The Things They Carried" a story?

2. In an essay discuss how the separate sections of "An Occurrence at Owl Creek Bridge" affect the development of the story's plot? Why is the second section a "flashback" of events that occurred before the actual story is taking place? Why is this flashback necessary to your understanding of the plot?

3. In an essay consider the various conflicts that develop in "Mericans," by Sandra Cisneros. You might consider this issue in terms of Michelle and the comic-book interests of her brothers, Michelle and her "awful grandmother," the prohibitions about the behavior of the children, the need for Michelle to pay attention before she can understand Spanish, and the surprise of the tourist couple when they discover that the boys speak English.

Creative Writing Assignment

1. Write a brief episode or story that takes place in a historical period you believe you know well, being as factually accurate as you can. Introduce your own fictional characters as important "movers and shakers," and deal with their public or personal affairs or both. You may model your characters and episodes on historical persons, but you are free to exercise your imagination completely and construct your own characters.

Chapter 2
Point of View: The Position or Stance of the Work's Narrator or Speaker

AFTER STUDYING THIS MATERIAL, YOU SHOULD BE ABLE TO DO THE FOLLOWING:

- Distinguish the speaker of a story from the actual author
- Determine the "authority" of the story's events
- Recognize that the speaker is not the same as the author
- Understand how various fictional speakers tell their stories

The term **point of view** refers to the **speaker, narrator, persona,** or **voice** created by authors to tell stories, make observations, present arguments, and express personal attitudes and judgments. Literally, point of view deals with how action and dialogue have been seen and heard. How does the speaker learn about the situation? Is the speaker a participant in the events, or no more than a witness, either close or distant? How close to the action is she or he? How much does the speaker know? How accurate and complete are his or her reports? Is the speaker also involved in what happened? How thoroughly? Did he or she see everything, miss anything? How much did she or he understand? Point of view involves not only the speaker's actual position as an observer and recorder but also the ways in which the speaker's social, political, and mental circumstances affect the narrative. For this reason, point of view is one of the most complex and subtle aspects of literary study.

The underlying issue of point of view is wrapped up in the nature of human knowledge: How do we acquire information? How can we verify its authenticity? How can we trust those who explain the world to us? What is their authority? Are they partial or impartial? What is their interest in telling us things? How reliable are their explanations? What physical and psychological positions might affect, or even distort, what they are saying? Do they have anything to hide? When they speak, are they trying to justify themselves to any degree?

Bear in mind that authors try not only to make their works vital and interesting but also to bring their presentations alive. The presentation is similar to a dramatic performance: In a play, the actors are always themselves, but as they perform their roles they impersonate and temporarily become the characters they act. In fictional works, not only do authors impersonate or pretend to be characters who do the talking, but they also create these characters. One such character is Jackie, the narrator of Frank O'Connor's "First Confession" (Chapter 6), who is telling about events that occurred when he was a child. Because he is the subject as well as the narrator, he has firsthand knowledge of the actions, even though he also says things indicating that he, as an adult, has not fully understood his childhood experience. Similarly, the husband narrating Raymond Carver's "Cathedral" (this chapter) can give us a very detailed rendition of the events and of the story and some insight into his married life while grappling with his much more vague understanding of these events' significance. The husband is the one we read about and hear, but Carver is the one supplying the words because the husband is a literary creation. In Poe's "The Masque of the Red Death" (Chapter 9), we constantly hear the speaker's voice and are influenced not only by his narration but also by his attitudes.

Because of the implications of creating a narrative voice, point of view may also be considered as the centralizing or guiding intelligence in a work—the mind that filters the fictional experience and presents only the most important details to create the maximum impact. Point of view fashioned by the author of a literary work determines how we read, respond, and understand.

An Exercise in Point of View: Reporting an Accident

As an exercise to show that point of view is based on lifelike situations, let us imagine that there has been an auto accident. Two cars, driven by Alice and Bill, have collided, and the after-crash scene is represented in the drawing on the following page. How might this accident be described? What would Alice say? What would Bill say?

Now assume that Frank, who is Bill's best friend, and Mary, who knows neither Bill nor Alice, were witnesses. What might Frank say about who was responsible? What might Mary say? Additionally, assume that you are a reporter for a local newspaper and are sent to report on the accident. You know none of the people involved. How will your report differ from the other reports? Finally, to what degree are all the statements designed to persuade listeners and readers that the details and claims made in the respective reports are true?

The likely differences in the various reports may be explained by reference to point of view. Obviously, because both Alice and Bill are deeply involved—each of them is a major participant or what may be called a **major mover**—they will likely arrange their words to make themselves seem blameless. Frank, because he is Bill's best friend, will report things in Bill's favor. Mary will favor neither Alice nor Bill, but let us assume that she did not look up to see the colliding cars until she heard the crash. Thus, she did not see the accident happening but saw only the immediate aftereffects. Amid all this mixture of partial and impartial views of the action, to whom should we attribute the greatest reliability?

Each person's report will have the "hidden agenda" of making herself or himself seem honest, objective, intelligent, impartial, and thorough. Thus, although both Alice and Bill may be truthful to the best of their abilities, their reports will not be reliable because they both have something to gain from avoiding responsibility for the accident. Also, Frank may be questionable as a witness because he is Bill's friend and may report things to Bill's advantage. Mary could be reliable, but she did not see everything; therefore she is unreliable not because of motivation but rather because of her location as a

Independent Reporters

Frank

Alice

Bill

Mary

witness. Most likely, your account as an impartial reporter will be the most reliable and objective of all, because your major interest is to learn all the details and to report the truth accurately, with no concern about the personal interests of either Alice or Bill.

As you can see, the consequences of describing actions are far-reaching, and the consideration of the various interests and situations is subtle. Indeed, of all the aspects of literature, point of view is the most complex because it is so much like life itself. On the one hand, point of view is tangled with the many interests and wishes of humanity at large; on the other, it is linked to the enormous difficulty of uncovering and determining truth.

Conditions That Affect Point of View

As this exercise in observation and expression demonstrates, point of view depends on two major factors. The first factor, as we have seen, is the physical situation of the narrator, or speaker, as an observer. How do the speaker's characteristics emerge from the narration? What are his or her qualifications or limitations as an observer? The second factor is the speaker's intellectual and emotional position. How might the speaker gain or lose from what takes place in the story? Are the speaker's observations and words colored by these interests? Does he or she have any persuasive purpose beyond being a straightforward recorder or observer? What values does the speaker impose upon the action?

In a story, as in many poems using narrative, authors take into account all these subtleties. For example, O'Connor's narrator, Jackie, in "First Confession" (Chapter 6) tells about boyhood family problems and his first experience with the sacrament of confession, but he has not yet fully separated himself from some of his youthful troubles. The speaker in Poe's "The Tell-Tale Heart" (Chapter 9) describes in detail the scene he is directly involved in, but his manner causes us to question his objectivity. These narrators show their own involvement and concern about the events they describe. The speaker in Jackson's "The Lottery," however, does not seem personally involved in the actions. This narrator listens, sees, and reports, but does not express deep involvement in the events of the story's country village. As readers, we need to develop our understanding of how such differing modes of presentation create the effects of these and all other stories and narrative poems.

For our purposes in this chapter, however, a discussion of point of view should emphasize how the narration and dramatic situation of a work create and shape the work. If ideas seem to be particularly important in a story, your objective should be not to analyze and discuss the ideas as ideas, but rather to consider whether and how these ideas affect what the narrator concludes and says about the story's actions and situations.

Point of View and Opinions

Because point of view is often popularly understood to mean ideas, opinions, or beliefs, it must be stressed that the term is not exactly the same as any of these. Point of view refers to a work's mode of narration—comprising narrator, language, audience, and perceptions of events and characters—whereas opinions and beliefs are thoughts and ideas that may or may not have anything to do with a narration. One may grant, however, that the position from which people see and understand things (e.g., established positions of political party, religion, social philosophy, and morality) has a most definite bearing on how they think and therefore on their opinions and beliefs. Opinions also affect how people view reality, and opinions affect, if not control, what they say about their perceptions of the world around them. Therefore, opinions stem out of point of view and at the same time have an influence on point of view. A four-star general and a buck private will have different things to say about what happens on a wartime battlefield.

Determining a Work's Point of View

In your reading you will encounter a wide variety of points of view. To begin your analysis, first determine the work's grammatical voice (i.e., first, second, or third person). Then study the ways in which the subject, characterization, dialogue, and form interact with the point of view.

In the First-Person Point of View, the Narrator Tells About Events He or She Has Personally Witnessed

If the voice of the work is an "I," the author is using the **first-person point of view**—the impersonation of a fictional narrator or speaker who may be named or unnamed. In our hypothetical accident reports, both Alice and Bill are first-person speakers who are named. Similarly, the narrator of O'Connor's "First Confession" (Chapter 6), Jackie, is named and identified. By contrast, the narrator of Poe's "The Masque of the Red Death" (Chapter 9) is an unnamed speaker.

First-person speakers report events as though they have acquired their knowledge in a number of ways:

- What they themselves have done, said, heard, and thought (firsthand experience).
- What they have observed others doing and saying (firsthand witness).
- What others have said to them or otherwise communicated to them (second-hand testimony and hearsay).
- What they are able to figure out from the information they have discovered (inferential information).
- What conclusions they are able to draw, or what guesses they are able to make about how a character or characters might think and act, given their knowledge of a situation (conjectural, imaginative, or intuitive information).

FIRST-PERSON SPEAKERS COME IN MANY VARIETIES.   Of all the points of view, the first person is the most independent of the author, because the first-person speaker may have a unique identity, with name, job, and economic and social position—a life separate totally from that of the author. Often, however, the author creates a more anonymous but still independent first-person speaker, as with the unnamed speaker-narrator of Poe's "The Masque of the Red Death" (Chapter 9). There are also situations in which an "I" speaker is pluralized by "we" when the first person includes other characters. Such a first-person plural point of view lends reliability to the narrative, as in Ellison's "Battle Royal" (Chapter 5), because the characters included as "we," even if they are sometimes unidentified by the speaker, may be considered additional witnesses.

SOME FIRST-PERSON SPEAKERS ARE RELIABLE, AND OTHERS ARE UNRELIABLE.   When you encounter a first-person narrative (whether a story or narrative poem), determine the narrator's position and ability, prejudices or self-interest, and judgment of his or her readers or listeners. Most first-person speakers describing their own experiences are to be accepted as **reliable** and authoritative. But sometimes first-person speakers are **unreliable** because they may have interests or limitations that lead them to mislead, distort, or even lie. There is reason, for example, to question Jackie's reliability as the speaker of O'Connor's "First Confession" (Chapter 6). As an adult he is describing the events within his family and his after-school preparation sessions prior to his attending his first confession; but he is giving us his childhood memories, and he is not including the potential views of those in his family about the ways in which things happened. Whether first-person speakers are reliable or unreliable, however, they are one of the means by which authors confer an authentic, lifelike quality to their works.

In the Second-Person Point of View, the Narrator Is Speaking to Someone Else Who Is Addressed as "You"

The **second-person point of view,** the least common of the points of view, and the most difficult for authors to manage, offers two major possibilities. In the first, a narrator (almost necessarily a first-person speaker) tells a listener what he or she has done and said at a past time. The actions might be a simple retelling of events, as when a parent tells a child about something the child did during infancy, or when a doctor tells a patient with amnesia about past events. Also, the actions might be subject to dispute and interpretation, as when a prosecuting attorney describes a crime for which a defendant is on trial or when a spouse lists complaints about an alienated spouse in a custody or divorce case. Still another situation of the second-person point of view might occur when an angry person accuses the listener of a betrayal or some other wrong. In such instances, it is worth bearing in mind that the point of view may possibly be considered first person rather than second, for the speaker is likely to be speaking subjectively about his or her own perception or analysis of the listener's actions. It is also worth bearing in mind that the second-person point of view in such instances may be totally wrong, and possibly also totally wrongheaded.

The second possibility is equally complex. Some narrators are obviously addressing a "you" but are instead referring mainly to themselves—and to listeners only secondarily—in preference to an "I." In addition, some narrators follow the usage—not uncommon in everyday, informal speech—of the indefinite "you." In this point of view, the "you" refers not only to a specific listener, who may or may not be present, but also to anyone at all, or maybe, and above all, to the speaker himself/herself. In this way the writer avoids the more formal use of such words as *one, a person*, or *people*. (Incidentally, the selection of *you* is non–gender-specific because it eliminates the need for the pronouns *he, she; she/he; he/she;* or *he or she*.) Anita Scott Coleman movingly employs the second-person point of view in "Unfinished Masterpieces" (Chapter 7), having the narrator use "you" and "your" frequently to describe the her life experiences, hopes, and dreams in a way that avoids self-pity or bitterness about what has come to pass.

In the Third-Person Point of View, the Speaker Emphasizes the Actions and Speeches of Others

If events in the work are described in the third person (*he, she, it, they*), the author is using the **third-person point of view.** It is not always easy to characterize the voice in this point of view. Sometimes the speaker uses an "I," as in Poe's "The Masque of the Red Death" (Chapter 9), and this "I" may seemingly be identical with the author, but at other times the author creates a distinct **authorial voice** that may be included at times within the voice of the narrator, as in Hawthorne's "Young Goodman Brown" (Chapter 7). There are three variants of the third-person point of view: (1) *dramatic or objective,* (2) *omniscient,* and (3) *limited omniscient.*

THE DRAMATIC OR OBJECTIVE POINT OF VIEW IS THE BASIC METHOD OF NARRATION. The most direct presentation of action and dialogue is the **dramatic or objective point of view** (also called *third-person objective*). It is the basic method of rendering action and speech that all the points of view share. The narrator of the dramatic point of view is an unidentified speaker who reports things in a way that is similar to a hovering or tracking video camera or to what some critics have called "a fly on the wall (or tree)." Somehow, the narrator is always on the spot—in rooms, forests, village squares, moving vehicles, or even in outer space—to tell us what is happening and what is being said.

The dramatic presentation is limited only to what is said and what happens. The writer does not overtly draw conclusions or make interpretations, because the premise of the dramatic point of view is that readers, like a jury, can form their own interpretations if they are shown the right evidence. Jackson's "The Lottery"—a powerful example of the dramatic point of view—is an objective story about a bizarre public occasion in a small town. We, the readers, draw many conclusions about the story (such as that the people are tradition bound, insensitive, cruel, and so on), but because of the dramatic point of view Jackson does not state any of these conclusions for us.

THE NARRATOR OF THE OMNISCIENT POINT OF VIEW CAN SEE ALL, KNOW ALL, AND POTENTIALLY DISCLOSE ALL. The third-person point of view is **omniscient** (all-knowing) when the speaker not only presents action and dialogue but also, at times, reports the thoughts and reactions of the characters. In our everyday real world, we never know, nor can we ever know, what other people are thinking. For practical purposes, their minds are closed to us. However, we always make assumptions about the thoughts of others, and these assumptions are the basis of the omniscient point of view. Authors use it freely but carefully to explain responses, thoughts, feelings, and plans—an additional dimension that aids in the development of character. For example, in Maupassant's "The Necklace" (Part I), the speaker takes an omniscient stance to explain the responses and thoughts of the major character and also, though in just a short passage, of her husband. Even in an omniscient point-of-view story, however, relatively little description is actually devoted to the thoughts of the characters, for most of the narration must necessarily be taken up with dramatic third-person descriptions.

THE NARRATOR OR SPEAKER IN THE LIMITED OR LIMITED-OMNISCIENT POINT OF VIEW FOCUSES ON THOUGHTS AND DEEDS OF A MAJOR CHARACTER.   More common than the omniscient and dramatic points of view is the **limited third person** or **limited omniscient third person,** in which the author concentrates on or limits the narration to the actions and thoughts of a major character. In our accident case (p. 122), Frank, being Bill's friend, would be sympathetic to Bill. Thus Frank's report of the collision would likely be third-person limited, with Bill as the center of interest. Depending on whether a narration focuses on action or motivation, the limited third-person narrator may explore the mentality of the major character either lightly or in depth. The name given to the central figure on whom the third-person omniscient point of view is focused is the **point-of-view character.** Thus, Peyton Farquhar in "An Occurrence at Owl Creek Bridge" (Chapter 1) and Miss Brill in Mansfield's "Miss Brill" (Chapter 3) are both point-of-view characters. Almost everything in these stories is there because the point-of-view characters see it, hear it, respond to it, think about it, imagine it entirely, do it or share in it, try to control it, or are controlled by it.

Mingling Points of View

In some works, authors mingle points of view in order to imitate reality. For example, many first-person narrators use various types of the third-person point of view during much of their narration. Authors also vary points of view to sustain interest, create suspense, or put the burden of response entirely upon readers. For example, in "An Occurrence at Owl Creek Bridge" (Chapter 1) Bierce keeps our attention focused on the reactions of the major character, Peyton Farquhar, until the last paragraph of the story, when there is a shift to a dramatic point of view as Farquhar is hanging from the bridge. This shift in point of view is an almost brutal declaration that none of Farquhar's hopes could ever have come true. A comparable but contrasting change in point of view occurs at the end of Hawthorne's "Young Goodman Brown" (Chapter 7), where the narrator objectively summarizes Brown's loveless and bleak life after his nightmare about evil.

Point of View and Verb Tense

As discussed in this chapter, point of view refers to the ways narrators and speakers perceive and report actions and speeches. In the broadest sense, however, point of view may be considered as a total way of rendering truth, and for this reason the tense chosen by the narrators is important. Most narratives rely on the past tense: The actions happened in the past, and they are now over.

The introduction of dialogue, however, even in a past-tense narration, dramatically brings the story into the present. Such dramatic rendering is accomplished by the dialogue contained in Jackson's "The Lottery," for example, where the past tense is mixed with the conversations and opinions of the people of the nameless town who have come together to carry on their grisly game of chance.

The narrator of a past-tense narrative may also introduce present-tense commentary during the narration—a strong means of signifying the importance of past events. Examples can be seen in O'Connor's "First Confession" (Chapter 6), in which the narrator Jackie makes personal comments about the events he is describing. In addition, as noted in Chapter 7, the narrators of parables and fables use past-tense narratives as vehicles for teaching current lessons in philosophy and religion.

In recent years a number of writers have used the present tense as their principal time reference. With the present tense, the narrative story or poem is rendered as a virtual drama that is unfolded moment by moment, as in "A & P" (Chapter 6) when Updike uses the present tense to show the main character beginning to learn about the difficult world as he makes decisions about his life.

Some writers intermingle tenses to show how time itself can be blended within the human mind, because our consciousness never exists only in the present but instead is a composite made up of past memories cresting upon a never-ending wave carrying us into the future. Thus at the end of Bierce's "An Occurrence at Owl Creek Bridge," the past-tense narration shifts into the present tense to demonstrate the vividness of the main character's perceptions just before his death.

Summary: Guidelines for Point of View

The following guidelines summarize and further classify the types of points of view. Use them to distinguish differences and shades of variation in stories and poems.

1. **First Person (*I, my, mine, me,* and sometimes *we, our,* and *us*).** First-person speakers are involved to at least some degree in the actions of the work. Such narrators may have (1) complete understanding, (2) partial or incorrect understanding, (3) no understanding at all, or (4) complete understanding with the motive to mislead or lie. Although the first three of these narrators probably tell the truth and are therefore **reliable,** they may also sometimes be **unreliable.** The only way to determine their reliability is to study the story closely. Obviously, the narrator of the fourth type—the one who misleads or lies—is by nature unreliable, but nevertheless the mode might possibly be accepted (although critically) on matters of detail. The three types of first-person speakers are these:
   a. *A Major Participant*
      i. Who tells his or her own story and thoughts as a major mover.
      ii. Who tells a story about others and also about herself or himself as one of the major movers.
      iii. Who tells a story mainly about others, and about himself or herself only incidentally.
   b. *A Minor Participant,* who tells a story about events experienced and witnessed.
   c. *A Nonparticipating but Identifiable Speaker,* who learns about events in other ways (e.g., listening to participants through direct conversation, overhearing conversation, examining documents, hearing news reports, and also rumors, imagining what might have occurred). The narrative of such a speaker is a combination of fact and conjectural reconstruction.

2. **Second Person (*you,* or possibly but rarely *thou*).** This is a point of view that authors use often enough to justify our knowing about it. Its premise is that the speaker knows more about the actions of a character (the "you") than the character himself or herself. It is used when the speaker (e.g., lawyer, spouse, friend, sports umpire, psychologist, parent, angry person) talks directly to

the other person and explains this other person's past actions and statements. More generally, and in an everyday and informal style, the speaker may also use "you" to mean himself or herself, the reader, or anyone at all.

3. **Third Person** (*she, he, it, they*). The speaker is outside the action and is mainly a reporter of actions and speeches. Some speakers may have unique and distinguishing traits even though no separate identity is claimed for them ("the unnamed third-person narrator"). Other third-person speakers who are not separately identified may represent the words and views of the authors themselves ("the authorial voice").

   a. *A Dramatic or Third-Person Objective Narrator.* The objective narrator reports only what can be seen and heard. The thoughts of characters are included only if they are spoken or written (dialogue, reported or overheard conversation, letters, reports, etc.).

   b. *An Omniscient Narrator.* The omniscient speaker sees all, knows all, and can report all. When necessary, the omniscient narrator can reveal the inner workings of the minds of any or all of a story's characters. Even an omniscient speaker, however, makes a mostly dramatic third-person presentation.

   c. *A Limited, or Limited Omniscient Narrator.* This narrator focuses on the actions, responses, thoughts, and feelings of a single major character. Although the resulting narration may concentrate on the major character's actions, it may also probe deeply within the mind of this character.

Stories for Study

Raymond Carver .... Cathedral, 130
Shirley Jackson .... The Lottery, 139
Joyce Carol Oates ...... Where Are You Going, Where Have You Been?, 144
ZZ Packer .... Brownies, 155

RAYMOND CARVER (1938–1988)

Originally from Oregon, Raymond Carver lived in Washington and spent much of his adult life as a Californian. He studied at Chico State in California and then at the Iowa Writers' Workshop. After doing blue-collar jobs for a time, he worked as an editor but, finally, as a teacher. His collections include Will You Please Be Quiet, Please? *(1976) and* Cathedral *(1983). *Where I'm Calling From *(1988) collects earlier stories and adds a number of new ones. In the film* Short Cuts *(1993) director Robert Altman wove together ten of Carver's stories. Carver is considered a master of minimalism—that is, fiction that stresses only the essentials of action and description. Generally, his writing is economical, stripped to the bone. Many of his characters seem unusual if not odd or even cruel. For example, one of his brief stories, "Popular Mechanics," takes little more than a single page to depict how a couple breaking up is also about to break up (literally) their child.*

Cathedral (1983)

This blind man, an old friend of my wife's, he was on his way to spend the night. His wife had died. So he was visiting the dead wife's relatives in Connecticut. He called my wife from his in-laws'. Arrangements were made. He would come by train, a five-hour trip, and my wife would meet him at the station. She hadn't seen him since she worked for him one summer in Seattle ten years ago. But she and the blind man had kept in touch. They made tapes and mailed them back and forth. I wasn't enthusiastic about his visit. He was no one I knew. And his being blind bothered me. My idea of blindness came from the movies. In the movies, the blind moved slowly and never laughed. Sometimes they were led by seeing-eye dogs. A blind man in my house was not something I looked forward to.

That summer in Seattle she had needed a job. She didn't have any money. The man she was going to marry at the end of the summer was in officers' training school. He didn't have any money, either. But she was in love with the guy, and he was in love with her, etc. She'd seen something in the paper: HELP WANTED—*Reading to Blind Man*, and a telephone number. She phoned and went over, was hired on the spot. She'd worked with this blind man all summer. She read stuff to him, case studies, reports, that sort of thing. She helped him organize his little office in the county social-service department. They'd become good friends, my wife and the blind man. How do I know these things? She told me. And she told me something else. On her last day in the office, the blind man asked if he could touch her face. She agreed to this. She told me he touched his fingers to every part of her face, her nose—even her neck! She never forgot it. She even tried to write a poem about it. She was always trying to write a poem. She wrote a poem or two every year, usually after something really important had happened to her.

When we first started going out together, she showed me the poem. In the poem, she recalled his fingers and the way they had moved around over her face. In the poem, she talked about what she had felt at the time, about what went through her mind when the blind man touched her nose and lips. I can remember I didn't think much of the poem. Of course, I didn't tell her that. Maybe I just don't understand poetry. I admit it's not the first thing I reach for when I pick up something to read.

Anyway, this man who'd first enjoyed her favors, the officer-to-be, he'd been her childhood sweetheart. So okay. I'm saying that at the end of the summer she let the blind man run his hands over her face, said good-bye to him, married her childhood etc., who was now a commissioned officer, and she moved away from Seattle. But they'd kept in touch, she and the blind man. She made the first contact after a year or so. She called him up one night from an Air Force base in Alabama. She wanted to talk. They talked. He asked her to send a tape and tell him about her life. She did this. She sent the tape. On the tape, she told the blind man about her husband and about their life together in the military. She told the blind man she loved her husband but she didn't like it where they lived and she didn't like it that he was part of the military-industrial thing. She told the blind man she'd written a poem and he was in it. She told him that she was writing a poem about what it was like to be an Air Force officer's wife. The poem wasn't finished yet. She was still writing it. The blind man made a tape. He sent her the tape. She made a tape. This went on for years. My wife's officer was posted to one base and then another. She sent tapes from Moody AFB, McGuire, McConnell, and finally Travis, near Sacramento, where one night she got to feeling lonely and cut off from people she kept losing in that moving-around life. She got to feeling she couldn't go it another step. She went in and swallowed all the pills and capsules in the medicine chest and washed them down with a bottle of gin. Then she got into a hot bath and passed out.

But instead of dying, she got sick. She threw up. Her officer—why should he have a name? he was the childhood sweetheart, and what more does he want?—came home from somewhere, found her, and called the ambulance. In time, she put it all on a tape and sent the tape to the blind man. Over the years, she put all kinds of stuff on tapes and sent the tapes off

5

lickety-split. Next to writing a poem every year, I think it was her chief means of recreation. On one tape, she told the blind man she'd decided to live away from her officer for a time. On another tape, she told him about her divorce. She and I began going out, and of course she told her blind man about it. She told him everything, or so it seemed to me. Once she asked me if I'd like to hear the latest tape from the blind man. This was a year ago. I was on the tape, she said. So I said okay, I'd listen to it. I got us drinks and we settled down in the living room. We made ready to listen. First she inserted the tape into the player and adjusted a couple of dials. Then she pushed a lever. The tape squeaked and someone began to talk in this loud voice. She lowered the volume. After a few minutes of harmless chitchat, I heard my own name in the mouth of this stranger, this blind man I didn't even know! And then this: "From all you've said about him, I can only conclude—" But we were interrupted, a knock at the door, something, and we didn't ever get back to the tape. Maybe it was just as well. I'd heard all I wanted to.

Now this same blind man was coming to sleep in my house.

"Maybe I could take him bowling," I said to my wife. She was at the draining board doing scalloped potatoes. She put down the knife she was using and turned around.

"If you love me," she said, "you can do this for me. If you don't love me, okay. But if you had a friend, any friend, and the friend came to visit, I'd make him feel comfortable." She wiped her hands with the dish towel.

"I don't have any blind friends," I said.

10   "You don't have any friends," she said. "Period. Besides," she said, "goddamn it, his wife's just died! Don't you understand that? The man's lost his wife!"

I didn't answer. She'd told me a little about the blind man's wife. Her name was Beulah. Beulah! That's a name for a colored woman.

"Was his wife a Negro?" I asked.

"Are you crazy?" my wife said. "Have you just flipped or something?" She picked up a potato. I saw it hit the floor, then roll under the stove. "What's wrong with you?" she said. "Are you drunk?"

"I'm just asking," I said.

15   Right then my wife filled me in with more detail than I cared to know. I made a drink and sat at the kitchen table to listen. Pieces of the story began to fall into place.

Beulah had gone to work for the blind man the summer after my wife had stopped working for him. Pretty soon Beulah and the blind man had themselves a church wedding. It was a little wedding—who'd want to go to such a wedding in the first place?—just the two of them, plus the minister and the minister's wife. But it was a church wedding just the same. It was what Beulah had wanted, he'd said. But even then Beulah must have been carrying the cancer in her glands. After they had been inseparable for eight years—my wife's word, inseparable—Beulah's health went into a rapid decline. She died in a Seattle hospital room, the blind man sitting beside the bed and holding on to her hand. They'd married, lived and worked together, slept together—had sex, sure—and then the blind man had to bury her. All this without his having ever seen what the goddamned woman looked like. It was beyond my understanding. Hearing this, I felt sorry for the blind man for a little bit. And then I found myself thinking what a pitiful life this woman must have led. Imagine a woman who could never see herself as she was seen in the eyes of her loved one. A woman who could go on day after day and never receive the smallest compliment from her beloved. A woman whose husband could never read the expression on her face, be it misery or something better. Someone who could wear makeup or not—what difference to him? She could, if she wanted, wear green eye-shadow around one eye, a straight pin in her nostril, yellow slacks, and purple shoes, no matter. And then to slip off into death, the blind man's hand on her hand, his blind eyes streaming tears—I'm imagining now—her last thought maybe this: that he never even knew what she looked like, and she on an express to the grave. Robert was left with a small insurance policy and a half of a twenty-peso Mexican coin. The other half of the coin went into the box with her. Pathetic.

So when the time rolled around, my wife went to the depot to pick him up. With nothing to do but wait—sure, I blamed him for that—I was having a drink and watching the TV when I heard the car pull into the drive. I got up from the sofa with my drink and went to the window to have a look.

I saw my wife laughing as she parked the car. I saw her get out of the car and shut the door. She was still wearing a smile. Just amazing. She went around to the other side of the car to where the blind man was already starting to get out. This blind man, feature this, he was wearing a full beard! A beard on a blind man! Too much, I say. The blind man reached into the backseat and dragged out a suitcase. My wife took his arm, shut the car door, and, talking all the way, moved him down the drive and then up the steps to the front porch. I turned off the TV. I finished my drink, rinsed the glass, dried my hands. Then I went to the door.

My wife said, "I want you to meet Robert. Robert, this is my husband. I've told you all about him." She was beaming. She had this blind man by his coat sleeve.

The blind man let go of his suitcase and up came his hand.   20

I took it. He squeezed hard, held my hand, and then he let it go.

"I feel like we've already met," he boomed.

"Likewise," I said. I didn't know what else to say. Then I said, "Welcome. I've heard a lot about you." We began to move then, a little group, from the porch into the living room, my wife guiding him by the arm. The blind man was carrying his suitcase in his other hand. My wife said things like, "To your left here, Robert. That's right. Now watch it, there's a chair. That's it. Sit down right here. This is the sofa. We just bought this sofa two weeks ago."

I started to say something about the old sofa. I'd liked that old sofa. But I didn't say anything. Then I wanted to say something else, small-talk, about the scenic ride along the Hudson. How going to New York, you should sit on the right-hand side of the train, and coming *from* New York, the left-hand side.

"Did you have a good train ride?" I said. "Which side of the train did you sit on, by the way?"   25

"What a question, which side!" my wife said. "What's it matter which side?" she said.

"I just asked," I said.

"Right side," the blind man said. "I hadn't been on a train in nearly forty years. Not since I was a kid. With my folks. That's been a long time. I'd nearly forgotten the sensation. I have winter in my beard now," he said. "So I've been told, anyway. Do I look distinguished, my dear?" the blind man said to my wife.

"You look distinguished, Robert," she said. "Robert," she said. "Robert, it's just so good to see you."

My wife finally took her eyes off the blind man and looked at me. I had the feeling she   30
didn't like what she saw. I shrugged.

I've never met, or personally known, anyone who was blind. This blind man was late forties, a heavy-set, balding man with stooped shoulders, as if he carried a great weight there. He wore brown slacks, brown shoes, a light-brown shirt, a tie, a sports coat. Spiffy. He also had this full beard. But he didn't use a cane and he didn't wear dark glasses. I'd always thought dark glasses were a must for the blind. Fact was, I wished he had a pair. At first glance, his eyes looked like anyone else's eyes. But if you looked close, there was something different about them. Too much white in the iris, for one thing, and the pupils seemed to move around in the sockets without his knowing it or being able to stop it. Creepy. As I stared at his face, I saw the left pupil turn in toward his nose while the other made an effort to keep in one place. But it was only an effort, for that eye was on the roam without his knowing it or wanting it to be.

I said, "Let me get you a drink. What's your pleasure? We have a little of everything. It's one of our pastimes."

"Bub, I'm a Scotch man myself," he said fast enough in this big voice.

"Right," I said. Bub! "Sure you are. I knew it."

He let his fingers touch his suitcase, which was sitting alongside the sofa. He was taking   35
his bearings. I didn't blame him for that.

"I'll move that up to your room," my wife said.

"No, that's fine," the blind man said loudly. "It can go up when I go up."

"A little water with the Scotch?" I said.

"Very little," he said.

40   "I knew it," I said.

He said, "Just a tad. The Irish actor, Barry Fitzgerald? I'm like that fellow. When I drink water, Fitzgerald said, I drink water. When I drink whiskey, I drink whiskey." My wife laughed. The blind man brought his hand up under his beard. He lifted his beard slowly and let it drop.

I did the drinks, three big glasses of Scotch with a splash of water in each. Then we made ourselves comfortable and talked about Robert's travels. First the long flight from the West Coast to Connecticut, we covered that. Then from Connecticut up here by train. We had another drink concerning that leg of the trip.

I remembered having read somewhere that the blind didn't smoke because, as speculation had it, they couldn't see the smoke they exhaled. I thought I knew that much and that much only about blind people. But this blind man smoked his cigarette down to the nubbin and then lit another one. This blind man filled his ashtray and my wife emptied it.

When we sat down at the table for dinner, we had another drink. My wife heaped Robert's plate with cube steak, scalloped potatoes, green beans. I buttered him up two slices of bread. I said, "Here's bread and butter for you." I swallowed some of my drink. "Now let us pray," I said, and the blind man lowered his head. My wife looked at me, her mouth agape. "Pray the phone won't ring and the food doesn't get cold," I said.

45   We dug in. We ate everything there was to eat on the table. We ate like there was no tomorrow. We didn't talk. We ate. We scarfed. We grazed that table. We were into serious eating. The blind man had right away located his foods, he knew just where everything was on his plate. I watched with admiration as he used his knife and fork on the meat. He'd cut two pieces of meat, fork the meat into his mouth, and then go all out for the scalloped potatoes, the beans next, and then he'd tear off a hunk of buttered bread and eat that. He'd follow this up with a big drink of milk. It didn't seem to bother him to use his fingers once in a while, either.

We finished everything, including half a strawberry pie. For a few moments, we sat as if stunned. Sweat beaded on our faces. Finally, we got up from the table and left the dirty plates. We didn't look back. We took ourselves into the living room and sank into our places again. Robert and my wife sat on the sofa. I took the big chair. We had us two or three more drinks while they talked about the major things that had come to pass for them in the past ten years. For the most part, I just listened. Now and then I joined in. I didn't want him to think I'd left the room, and I didn't want her to think I was feeling left out. They talked of things that had happened to them—to them!—these past ten years. I waited in vain to hear my name on my wife's sweet lips: "And then my dear husband came into my life"—something like that. But I heard nothing of the sort. More talk of Robert. Robert had done a little of everything, it seemed, a regular blind jack-of-all-trades. But most recently he and his wife had had an Amway distributorship, from which, I gathered, they'd earned their living, such as it was. The blind man was also a ham radio operator. He talked in his loud voice about conversations he'd had with fellow operators in Guam, in the Philippines, in Alaska, and even in Tahiti. He said he'd have a lot of friends there if he ever wanted to go visit those places. From time to time, he'd turn his blind face toward me, put his hand under his beard, ask me something. How long had I been in my present position? (Three years.) Did I like my work? (I didn't.) Was I going to stay with it? (What were the options?) Finally, when I thought he was beginning to run down, I got up and turned on the TV.

My wife looked at me with irritation. She was heading toward a boil. Then she looked at the blind man and said, "Robert, do you have a TV?"

The blind man said, "My dear, I have two TVs. I have a color set and a black-and-white thing, an old relic. It's funny, but if I turn the TV on, and I'm always turning it on, I turn on the color set. It's funny, don't you think?"

I didn't know what to say to that. I had absolutely nothing to say to that. No opinion. So I watched the news program and tried to listen to what the announcer was saying.

"This is a color TV," the blind man said. "Don't ask me how, but I can tell."   50
"We traded up a while ago," I said.

The blind man had another taste of this drink. He lifted his beard, sniffed it, and let it fall. He leaned forward on the sofa. He positioned his ashtray on the coffee table, then put the lighter to his cigarette. He leaned back on the sofa and crossed his legs at the ankles.

My wife covered her mouth, and then she yawned. She stretched. She said, "I think I'll go upstairs and put on my robe. I think I'll change into something else. Robert, you make yourself comfortable," she said.

"I'm comfortable," the blind man said.
"I want you to feel comfortable in this house," she said.   55
"I am comfortable," the blind man said.

After she'd left the room, he and I listened to the weather report and then to the sports roundup. By that time, she'd been gone so long I didn't know if she was going to come back. I thought she might have gone to bed. I wished she'd come back downstairs. I didn't want to be left alone with a blind man. I asked him if he wanted another drink, and he said sure. Then I asked if he wanted to smoke some dope with me. I said I'd just rolled a number. I hadn't, but I planned to do so in about two shakes.

"I'll try some with you," he said.
"Damn right," I said. "That's the stuff."

"I got our drinks and sat down on the sofa with him. Then I rolled us two fat numbers. I   60
lit one and passed it. I brought it to his fingers. He took it and inhaled.

"Hold it as long as you can," I said. I could tell he didn't know the first thing.
My wife came back downstairs wearing her pink robe and her pink slippers.
"What do I smell?" she said.
"We thought we'd have us some cannabis," I said.

My wife gave me a savage look. Then she looked at the blind man and said, "Robert, I   65
didn't know you smoked."

He said, "I do now, my dear. There's a first time for everything. But I don't feel anything yet."
"This stuff is pretty mellow," I said. "This stuff is mild. It's dope you can reason with," I said. "It doesn't mess you up."
"Not much it doesn't, bub," he said, and laughed.

My wife sat on the sofa between the blind man and me. I passed her the number. She took it and toked and then passed it back to me. "Which way is this going?" she said. Then she said, "I shouldn't be smoking this. I can hardly keep my eyes open as it is. That dinner did me in. I shouldn't have eaten so much."

"It was the strawberry pie," the blind man said. "That's what did it," he said, and he   70
laughed his big laugh. Then he shook his head.

"There's more strawberry pie," I said.
"Do you want some more, Robert?" my wife said.
"Maybe in a little while," he said.

We gave our attention to the TV. My wife yawned again. She said, "Your bed is made up when you feel like going to bed, Robert. I know you must have had a long day. When you're ready to go to bed, say so." She pulled his arm. "Robert?"

He came to and said, "I've had a real nice time. This beats tapes, doesn't it?"   75

I said, "Coming at you," and I put the number between his fingers. He inhaled, held the smoke, and then let it go. It was like he'd been doing it since he was nine years old.

"Thanks, bub," he said. "But I think this is all for me. I think I'm beginning to feel it," he said. He held the burning roach out for my wife.

"Same here," she said. "Ditto. Me, too." She took the roach and passed it to me. "I may just sit here for a while between you two guys with my eyes closed. But don't let me bother you, okay?

Either one of you. If it bothers you, say so. Otherwise, I may just sit here with my eyes closed until you're ready to go to bed," she said. "Your bed's made up, Robert, when you're ready. It's right next to our room at the top of the stairs. We'll show you up when you're ready. You wake me up now, you guys, if I fall asleep." She said that and then she closed her eyes and went to sleep.

The news program ended. I got up and changed the channel. I sat back down on the sofa. I wished my wife hadn't pooped out. Her head lay across the back of the sofa, her mouth open. She'd turned so that her robe slipped away from her legs, exposing a juicy thigh. I reached to draw her robe back over her, and it was then that I glanced at the blind man. What the hell! I flipped the robe open again.

80 "You say when you want some strawberry pie," I said.

"I will," he said.

I said, "Are you tired? Do you want me to take you up to your bed? Are you ready to hit the hay?"

"Not yet," he said. "No, I'll stay up with you, bub. If that's all right. I'll stay up until you're ready to turn in. We haven't had a chance to talk. Know what I mean? I feel like me and her monopolized the evening." He lifted his beard and he let it fall. He picked up his cigarettes and his lighter.

"That's all right," I said. Then I said, "I'm glad for the company."

85 And I guess I was. Every night I smoked dope and stayed up as long as I could before I fell asleep. My wife and I hardly ever went to bed at the same time. When I did go to sleep, I had these dreams. Sometimes I'd wake up from one of them, my heart going crazy.

Something about the church and the Middle Ages was on the TV. Not your run-of-the-mill TV fare. I wanted to watch something else. I turned to the other channels. But there was nothing on them, either. So I turned back to the first channel and apologized.

"Bub, it's all right," the blind man said. "It's fine with me. Whatever you want to watch is okay. I'm always learning something. Learning never ends. It won't hurt me to learn something tonight. I got ears," he said.

We didn't say anything for a time. He was leaning forward with his head turned at me, his right ear aimed in the direction of the set. Very disconcerting. Now and then his eyelids drooped and then they snapped open again. Now and then he put his fingers into his beard and tugged, like he was thinking about something he was hearing on the television.

On the screen, a group of men wearing cowls was being set upon and tormented by men dressed in skeleton costumes and men dressed as devils. The men dressed as devils wore devil masks, horns, and long tails. This pageant was part of a procession. The Englishman who was narrating the thing said it took place in Spain once a year. I tried to explain to the blind man what was happening.

"Skeletons," he said. "I know about skeletons," he said, and he nodded.

90 The TV showed this one cathedral. Then there was a long, slow look at another one. Finally, the picture switched to the famous one in Paris, with its flying buttresses and its spires reaching up to the clouds. The camera pulled away to show the whole of the cathedral rising above the skyline.

There were times when the Englishman who was telling the thing would shut up, would simply let the camera move around the cathedrals. Or else the camera would tour the countryside, men in fields walking behind oxen. I waited as long as I could. Then I felt I had to say something. I said, "They're showing the outside of this cathedral now. Gargoyles. Little statues carved to look like monsters. Now I guess they're in Italy. Yeah, they're in Italy. There's paintings on the walls of this one church."

"Are those fresco paintings, bub?" he asked, and he sipped from his drink.

I reached for my glass. But it was empty. I tried to remember what I could remember. "You're asking me are those frescoes?" I said. "That's a good question. I don't know."

95 The camera moved to a cathedral outside Lisbon. The differences in the Portuguese cathedral compared with the French and Italian were not that great. But they were there.

Mostly the interior stuff. Then something occurred to me, and I said, "Something has occurred to me. Do you have any idea what a cathedral is? What they look like, that is? Do you follow me? If somebody says cathedral to you, do you have any notion what they're talking about? Do you know the difference between that and a Baptist church, say?"

He let the smoke dribble from his mouth. "I know they took hundreds of workers fifty or a hundred years to build," he said. "I just heard the man say that, of course. I know generations of the same families worked on a cathedral. I heard him say that, too. The men who began their life's work on them, they never lived to see the completion of their work. In that wise, bub, they're no different from the rest of us, right?" He laughed. Then his eyelids drooped again. His head nodded. He seemed to be snoozing. Maybe he was imagining himself in Portugal. The TV was showing another cathedral now. This one was in Germany. The Englishman's voice droned on. "Cathedrals," the blind man said. He sat up and rolled his head back and forth. "If you want the truth, bub, that's about all I know. What I just said. What I heard him say. But maybe you could describe one to me? I wish you'd do it. I'd like that. If you want to know, I really don't have a good idea."

I stared hard at the shot of the cathedral on the TV. How could I even begin to describe it? But say my life depended on it. Say my life was being threatened by an insane guy who said I had to do it or else.

I stared some more at the cathedral before the picture flipped off into the countryside. There was no use. I turned to the blind man and said, "To begin with, they're very tall." I was looking around the room for clues. "They reach way up. Up and up. Toward the sky. They're so big, some of them, they have to have these supports. To help hold them up, so to speak. These supports are called buttresses. They remind me of viaducts, for some reason. But maybe you don't know viaducts, either? Sometimes the cathedrals have devils and such carved into the front. Sometimes lords and ladies. Don't ask me why this is," I said.

He was nodding. The whole upper part of his body seemed to be moving back and forth.

"I'm not doing so good, am I?" I said.

100

He stopped nodding and leaned forward on the edge of the sofa. As he listened to me, he was running his fingers through his beard. I wasn't getting through to him, I could see that. But he waited for me to go on just the same. He nodded, like he was trying to encourage me. I tried to think what else to say. "They're really big," I said. "They're massive. They're built of stone. Marble, too, sometimes. In those olden days, when they built cathedrals, men wanted to be close to God. In those olden days, God was an important part of everyone's life. You could tell this from their cathedral-building. I'm sorry," I said, "but it looks like that's the best I can do for you. I'm just no good at it."

"That's all right, bub," the blind man said. "Hey, listen. I hope you don't mind my asking you. Can I ask you something? Let me ask you a simple question, yes or no. I'm just curious and there's no offense. You're my host. But let me ask if you are in any way religious? You don't mind my asking?"

I shook my head. He couldn't see that, though. A wink is the same as a nod to a blind man. "I guess I don't believe in it. In anything. Sometimes it's hard. You know what I'm saying?"

"Sure, I do," he said.

"Right," I said.

105

The Englishman was still holding forth. My wife sighed in her sleep. She drew a long breath and went on with her sleeping.

"You'll have to forgive me," I said. "But I can't tell you what a cathedral looks like. It just isn't in me to do it. I can't do any more than I've done."

The blind man sat very still, his head down, as he listened to me.

I said, "The truth is, cathedrals don't mean anything special to me. Nothing. Cathedrals. They're something to look at on late-night TV. That's all they are."

It was then that the blind man cleared his throat. He brought something up. He took a handkerchief from his back pocket. Then he said, "I get it, bub. It's okay. It happens. Don't

110

worry about it," he said. "Hey, listen to me. Will you do me a favor? I got an idea. Why don't you find us some heavy paper? And a pen. We'll do something. We'll draw one together. Get us a pen and some heavy paper. Go on, bub, get the stuff," he said.

So I went upstairs. My legs felt like they didn't have any strength in them. They felt like they did after I'd done some running. In my wife's room I looked around. I found some ballpoints in a little basket on her table. And then I tried to think where to look for the kind of paper he was talking about.

Downstairs, in the kitchen, I found a shopping bag with onion skins in the bottom of the bag. I emptied the bag and shook it. I brought it into the living room and sat down with it near his legs. I moved some things, smoothed the wrinkles from the bag, spread it out on the coffee table.

The blind man got down from the sofa and sat next to me on the carpet.

He ran his fingers over the paper. He went up and down the sides of the paper. The edges, even the edges. He fingered the corners.

115   "All right," he said. "All right, let's do her."

He found my hand, the hand with the pen. He closed his hand over my hand. "Go ahead, bub, draw," he said. "Draw. You'll see. I'll follow along with you. It'll be okay. Just begin now like I'm telling you. You'll see. Draw," the blind man said.

So I began. First I drew a box that looked like a house. It could have been the house I lived in. Then I put a roof on it. At either end of the roof, I drew spires. Crazy.

"Swell," he said. "Terrific. You're doing fine," he said. "Never thought anything like this could happen in your lifetime, did you, bub? Well, it's a strange life, we all know that. Go on now. Keep it up."

I put in windows with arches. I drew flying buttresses. I hung great doors. I couldn't stop. The TV station went off the air. I put down the pen and closed and opened my fingers. The blind man felt around over the paper. He moved the tips of his fingers over the paper, all over what I had drawn, and he nodded.

120   "Doing fine," the blind man said.

I took up the pen again, and he found my hand. I kept at it. I'm no artist. But I kept drawing just the same.

My wife opened up her eyes and gazed at us. She sat up on the sofa, her robe hanging open. She said, "What are you doing? Tell me, I want to know."

I didn't answer her.

The blind man said, "We're drawing a cathedral. Me and him are working on it. Press hard," he said to me. "That's right. That's good," he said. "Sure. You got it, bub, I can tell. You didn't think you could. But you can, can't you? You're cooking with gas now. You know what I'm saying? We're going to really have us something here in a minute. How's the old arm?" he said. "Put some people in there now. What's a cathedral without people?"

125   My wife said, "What's going on? Robert, what are you doing? What's going on?"

"It's all right," he said to her. "Close your eyes now," the blind man said to me.

I did it. I closed them just like he said.

"Are they closed?" he said. "Don't fudge."

"They're closed," I said.

130   "Keep them that way," he said. He said, "Don't stop now. Draw."

So we kept on with it. His fingers rode my fingers as my hand went over the paper. It was like nothing else in my life up to now.

Then he said, "I think that's it. I think you got it," he said. "Take a look. What do you think?"

But I had my eyes closed. I thought I'd keep them that way for a little longer. I thought it was something I ought to do.

"Well?" he said. "Are you looking?"

135   My eyes were still closed. I was in my house. I knew that. But I didn't feel like I was inside anything.

"It's really something," I said.

QUESTIONS

1. Who is the speaker/narrator of "Cathedral"? How much do we learn about his character? What kind of person is he? Would you describe the home life of the speaker and his wife as interesting or dull, and why? What is his attitude toward his wife's former employer, Robert, who is visiting his home? How does Robert first seem when he first appears? What is the speaker's response to being called "Bub"?

2. Why does the speaker continually refer to Robert as the "blind man," rather than by name? What change is detectable in the speaker's attitudes toward Robert at the end of the story? Why does the speaker keep his eyes closed at the very end? In what ways is the speaker different at the story's end from the way he is at the beginning?

3. Describe the character of the speaker's wife. What connection does she have with Robert? How does Robert's visit affect her attitude toward the speaker, her husband?

4. What connection can you perceive between the story's title and the principal action? Why does the speaker describe the various cathedrals of Europe that are shown and discussed on the TV program?

SHIRLEY JACKSON (1919–1965)

Shirley Jackson was a native of California. She graduated from Syracuse University in New York and lived for many years in Vermont. Although her life was short, she was a successful writer of novels, short stories, biographies, and children's fiction. Her stories often depict unusual, unreal, or bizarre events in common settings, of which "The Lottery" is a major example. She wrote the story in only two hours and submitted it to The New Yorker without major revisions. When it was published, many readers raised questions about how to interpret the conclusion. Jackson steadfastly refused to explain, leaving readers to decide for themselves.

The Lottery (1948)

The morning of June 27th was clear and sunny, with the fresh warmth of a full summer day; the flowers were blossoming profusely and the grass was richly green. The people of the village began to gather in the square, between the post office and the bank, around ten o'clock; in some towns there were so many people that the lottery took two days and had to be started on June 26th, but in this village, where there were only about three hundred people, the whole lottery took less than two hours, so it could begin at ten o'clock in the morning and still be through in time to allow the villagers to get home for noon dinner.

The children assembled first, of course. School was recently over for the summer, and the feeling of liberty sat uneasily on most of them; they tended to gather together quietly for a while before they broke into boisterous play, and their talk was still of the classroom and the teacher, of books and reprimands. Bobby Martin had already stuffed his pockets full of stones, and the other boys soon followed his example, selecting the smoothest and roundest stones; Bobby and Harry Jones and Dickie Delacroix—the villagers pronounced this name "Dellacroy"—eventually made a great pile of stones in one corner of the square and guarded it against the raids of the other boys. The girls stood aside, talking among themselves, looking over their shoulders at the boys, and the very small children rolled in the dust or clung to the hands of their older brothers or sisters.

Soon the men began to gather, surveying their own children, speaking of planting and rain, tractors and taxes. They stood together, away from the pile of stones in the corner, and their jokes were quiet and they smiled rather than laughed. The women, wearing faded house dresses and sweaters, came shortly after their menfolk. They greeted one another and exchanged bits of gossip as they went to join their husbands. Soon the women, standing by their husbands, began to call to their children, and the children came reluctantly, having to be called four or five times. Bobby Martin ducked under his mother's grasping hand and ran, laughing, back to the pile of stones. His father spoke up sharply, and Bobby came quickly and took his place between his father and his oldest brother.

The lottery was conducted—as were the square dances, the teen-age club, the Halloween program—by Mr. Summers, who had time and energy to devote to civic activities. He was a round-faced, jovial man and he ran the coal business, and people were sorry for him, because he had no children and his wife was a scold. When he arrived in the square, carrying the black wooden box, there was a murmur of conversation among the villagers, and he waved and called, "Little late today, folks." The postmaster, Mr. Graves, followed him, carrying a three-legged stool, and the stool was put in the center of the square and Mr. Summers set the black box down on it. The villagers kept their distance, leaving a space between themselves and the stool, and when Mr. Summers said, "Some of you fellows want to give me a hand?" there was a hesitation before two men, Mr. Martin and his oldest son, Baxter, came forward to hold the box steady on the stool while Mr. Summers stirred up the papers inside it.

5   The original paraphernalia for the lottery had been lost long ago, and the black box now resting on the stool had been put into use even before Old Man Warner, the oldest man in town, was born. Mr. Summers spoke frequently to the villagers about making a new box, but no one liked to upset even as much tradition as was represented by the black box. There was a story that the present box had been made with some pieces of the box that had preceded it, the one that had been constructed when the first people settled down to make a village here. Every year, after the lottery, Mr. Summers began talking again about a new box, but every year the subject was allowed to fade off without anything's being done. The black box grew shabbier each year; by now it was no longer completely black but splintered badly along one side to show the original wood color, and in some places faded or stained.

Mr. Martin and his oldest son, Baxter, held the black box securely on the stool until Mr. Summers had stirred the papers thoroughly with his hand. Because so much of the ritual had been forgotten or discarded, Mr. Summers had been successful in having slips of paper substituted for the chips of wood that had been used for generations. Chips of wood, Mr. Summers had argued, had been all very well when the village was tiny, but now that the population was more than three hundred and likely to keep on growing, it was necessary to use something that would fit more easily into the black box. The night before the lottery, Mr. Summers and Mr. Graves made up the slips of paper and put them in the box, and it was then taken to the safe of Mr. Summers's coal company and locked up until Mr. Summers was ready to take it to the square next morning. The rest of the year, the box was put away, sometimes one place, sometimes another; it had spent one year in Mr. Graves's barn and another year underfoot in the post office, and sometimes it was set on a shelf in the Martin grocery and left there.

There was a great deal of fussing to be done before Mr. Summers declared the lottery open. There were the lists to make up—of heads of families, heads of households in each family, members of each household in each family. There was the proper swearing-in of Mr. Summers by the postmaster, as the official of the lottery; at one time, some people remembered, there had been a recital of some sort, performed by the official of the lottery, a perfunctory, tuneless chant that had been rattled off duly each year; some people believed that the official of the lottery used to stand just so when he said or sang it, others believed that he was supposed to walk among the people, but years and years ago this part of the ritual had been allowed to lapse. There had been, also, a ritual salute, which the official of the lottery had had to use in addressing each person who came up to draw from the box, but this also had changed with time, until now it was felt necessary only for the official to speak to each person approaching. Mr. Summers was very good at all this; in his clean white shirt and blue jeans, with one hand resting carelessly on the black box, he seemed very proper and important as he talked interminably to Mr. Graves and the Martins.

Just as Mr. Summers finally left off talking and turned to the assembled villagers, Mrs. Hutchinson came hurriedly along the path to the square, her sweater thrown over her shoulders, and slid into place in the back of the crowd. "Clean forgot what day it was," she said to Mrs. Delacroix, who stood next to her, and they both laughed softly. "Thought my old man was out back stacking wood," Mrs. Hutchinson went on, "and then I looked out the window and the kids was gone, and then I remembered it was the twenty-seventh and came a-running." She dried her hands on her apron, and Mrs. Delacroix said, "You're in time, though. They're still talking away up there."

Mrs. Hutchinson craned her neck to see through the crowd and found her husband and children standing near the front. She tapped Mrs. Delacroix on the arm as a farewell and began to make her way through the crowd. The people separated good-humoredly to let her through; two or three people said, in voices just loud enough to be heard across the crowd, "Here comes your Missus, Hutchinson," and "Bill, she made it after all." Mrs. Hutchinson reached her husband, and Mr. Summers, who had been waiting, said cheerfully, "Thought we were going to have to get on without you, Tessie." Mrs. Hutchinson said, grinning, "Wouldn't have me leave m'dishes in the sink, now, would you, Joe?," and soft laughter ran through the crowd as the people stirred back into position after Mrs. Hutchinson's arrival.

"Well, now," Mr. Summers said soberly, "guess we better get started, get this over with, so's we can go back to work. Anybody ain't here?" 10

"Dunbar," several people said. "Dunbar, Dunbar."

Mr. Summers consulted his list. "Clyde Dunbar," he said. "That's right. He's broke his leg, hasn't he? Who's drawing for him?"

"Me, I guess," a woman said, and Mr. Summers turned to look at her. "Wife draws for her husband," Mr. Summers said. "Don't you have a grown boy to do it for you, Janey?" Although Mr. Summers and everyone else in the village knew the answer perfectly well, it was the business of the official of the lottery to ask such questions formally. Mr. Summers waited with an expression of polite interest while Mrs. Dunbar answered.

"Horace's not but sixteen yet," Mrs. Dunbar said regretfully. "Guess I gotta fill in for the old man this year."

"Right," Mr. Summers said. He made a note on the list he was holding. Then he asked, 15 "Watson boy drawing this year?"

A tall boy in the crowd raised his hand. "Here," he said. "I'm drawing for m'mother and me." He blinked his eyes nervously and ducked his head as several voices in the crowd said things like "Good fellow, Jack," and "Glad to see your mother's got a man to do it."

"Well," Mr. Summers said, "guess that's everyone. Old Man Warner make it?"

"Here," a voice said, and Mr. Summers nodded.

A sudden hush fell on the crowd as Mr. Summers cleared his throat and looked at the list. "All ready?" he called. "Now, I'll read the names—heads of families first—and the men come up and take a paper out of the box. Keep the paper folded in your hand without looking at it until everyone has had a turn. Everything clear?"

The people had done it so many times that they only half listened to the directions; 20 most of them were quiet, wetting their lips, not looking around. Then Mr. Summers raised one hand high and said, "Adams." A man disengaged himself from the crowd and came forward. "Hi, Steve," Mr. Summers said, and Mr. Adams said, "Hi, Joe." They grinned at one another humorlessly and nervously. Then Mr. Adams reached into the black box and took out a folded paper. He held it firmly by one corner as he turned and went hastily back to his place in the crowd, where he stood a little apart from his family, not looking down at his hand.

"Allen," Mr. Summers said. "Anderson . . . . Bentham."

"Seems like there's no time at all between lotteries any more," Mrs. Delacroix said to Mrs. Graves in the back row. "Seems like we got through with the last one only last week."

"Time sure goes fast," Mrs. Graves said.

"Clark . . . Delacroix."

25   "There goes my old man," Mrs. Delacroix said. She held her breath while her husband went forward.

"Dunbar," Mr. Summers said, and Mrs. Dunbar went steadily to the box while one of the women said, "Go on, Janey," and another said, "There she goes."

"We're next," Mrs. Graves said. She watched while Mr. Graves came around from the side of the box, greeted Mr. Summers gravely, and selected a slip of paper from the box. By now, all through the crowd there were men holding the small folded papers in their large hands, turning them over and over nervously. Mrs. Dunbar and her two sons stood together, Mrs. Dunbar holding the slip of paper.

"Harburt . . . . Hutchinson."

"Get up there, Bill," Mrs. Hutchinson said, and the people near her laughed.

30   "Jones."

"They do say," Mr. Adams said to Old Man Warner, who stood next to him, "that over in the north village they're talking of giving up the lottery."

Old Man Warner snorted. "Pack of crazy fools," he said. "Listening to the young folks, nothing's good enough for *them*. Next thing you know, they'll be wanting to go back to living in caves, nobody work any more, live *that* way for a while. Used to be a saying about 'Lottery in June, corn be heavy soon.' First thing you know, we'd all be eating stewed chickweed and acorns. There's *always* been a lottery," he added petulantly. "Bad enough to see young Joe Summers up there joking with everybody."

"Some places have already quit lotteries," Mrs. Adams said.

"Nothing but trouble in *that*," Old Man Warner said stoutly. "Pack of young fools."

35   "Martin." And Bobby Martin watched his father go forward. "Overdyke. . . . Percy."

"I wish they'd hurry," Mrs. Dunbar said to her older son. "I wish they'd hurry."

"They're almost through," her son said.

"You get ready to run tell Dad," Mrs. Dunbar said.

Mr. Summers called his own name and then stepped forward precisely and selected a slip from the box. Then he called, "Warner."

40   "Seventy-seventh year I been in the lottery," Old Man Warner said as he went through the crowd. "Seventy-seventh time."

"Watson." The tall boy came awkwardly through the crowd. Someone said, "Don't be nervous, Jack," and Mr. Summers said, "Take your time, son."

"Zanini."

After that, there was a long pause, a breathless pause, until Mr. Summers, holding his slip of paper in the air, said, "All right, fellows." For a minute, no one moved, and then all the slips of paper were opened. Suddenly, all the women began to speak at once, saying, "Who is it?" "Who's got it?" "Is it the Dunbars?" "Is it the Watsons?" Then the voices began to say, "It's Hutchinson. It's Bill." "Bill Hutchinson's got it."

"Go tell your father," Mrs. Dunbar said to her older son.

45   People began to look around to see the Hutchinsons. Bill Hutchinson was standing quiet, staring down at the paper in his hand. Suddenly, Tessie Hutchinson shouted to Mr. Summers, "You didn't give him time enough to take any paper he wanted. I saw you. It wasn't fair!"

"Be a good sport, Tessie," Mrs. Delacroix called, and Mrs. Graves said, "All of us took the same chance."

"Shut up, Tessie," Bill Hutchinson said.

"Well, everyone," Mr. Summers said, "that was done pretty fast, and now we've got to be hurrying a little more to get done in time." He consulted his next list. "Bill," he said, "you draw for the Hutchinson family. You got any other households in the Hutchinsons?"

"There's Don and Eva," Mrs. Hutchinson yelled. "Make *them* take their chance!"

"Daughters draw with their husbands' families, Tessie," Mr. Summers said gently. "You know that as well as anyone else." 50

"It wasn't *fair*," Tessie said.

"I guess not, Joe," Bill Hutchinson said regretfully. "My daughter draws with her husband's family, that's only fair. And I've got no other family except the kids."

"Then, as far as drawing for families is concerned, it's you," Mr. Summers said in explanation, "and as far as drawing for households is concerned, that's you, too. Right?"

"Right," Bill Hutchinson said.

"How many kids, Bill?" Mr. Summers asked formally. 55

"Three," Bill Hutchinson said. "There's Bill, Jr., and Nancy, and little Dave. And Tessie and me."

"All right, then," Mr. Summers said. "Harry, you got their tickets back?"

Mr. Graves nodded and held up the slips of paper. "Put them in the box, then," Mr. Summers directed. "Take Bill's and put it in."

"I think we ought to start over," Mrs. Hutchinson said, as quietly as she could. "I tell you it wasn't *fair*. You didn't give him time enough to choose. *Every*body saw that."

Mr. Graves had selected the five slips and put them in the box, and he dropped all the 60 papers but those onto the ground, where the breeze caught them and lifted them off.

"Listen, everybody," Mrs. Hutchinson was saying to the people around her.

"Ready, Bill?" Mr. Summers asked, and Bill Hutchinson, with one quick glance around at his wife and children, nodded.

"Remember," Mr. Summers said, "take the slips and keep them folded until each person has taken one. Harry, you help little Dave." Mr. Graves took the hand of the little boy, who came willingly with him up to the box. "Take a paper out of the box, Davy," Mr. Summers said. Davy put his hand into the box and laughed. "Take just *one* paper," Mr. Summers said. "Harry, you hold it for him." Mr. Graves took the child's hand and removed the folded paper from the tight fist and held it while little Dave stood next to him and looked up at him wonderingly.

"Nancy next," Mr. Summers said. Nancy was twelve, and her school friends breathed heavily as she went forward, switching her skirt, and took a slip daintily from the box. "Bill, Jr.," Mr. Summers said, and Billy, his face red and his feet over-large, nearly knocked the box over as he got a paper out. "Tessie," Mr. Summers said. She hesitated for a minute, looking around defiantly, and then set her lips and went up to the box. She snatched a paper out and held it behind her.

"Bill," Mr. Summers said, and Bill Hutchinson reached into the box and felt around, 65 bringing his hand out at last with the slip of paper in it.

The crowd was quiet. A girl whispered, "I hope it's not Nancy," and the sound of the whisper reached the edges of the crowd.

"It's not the way it used to be," Old Man Warner said clearly. "People ain't the way they used to be."

"All right," Mr. Summers said. "Open the papers. Harry, you open little Dave's."

Mr. Graves opened the slip of paper and there was a general sigh through the crowd as he held it up and everyone could see that it was blank. Nancy and Bill, Jr., opened theirs at the same time, and both beamed and laughed, turning around to the crowd and holding their slips of paper above their heads.

"Tessie," Mr. Summers said. There was a pause, and then Mr. Summers looked at Bill 70 Hutchinson, and Bill unfolded his paper and showed it. It was blank.

"It's Tessie," Mr. Summers said, and his voice was hushed. "Show us her paper, Bill."

Bill Hutchinson went over to his wife and forced the slip of paper out of her hand. It had a black spot on it, the black spot Mr. Summers had made the night before with the heavy pencil in the coal-company office. Bill Hutchinson held it up, and there was a stir in the crowd.

"All right, folks," Mr. Summers said. "Let's finish quickly."

Although the villagers had forgotten the ritual and lost the original black box, they still remembered to use stones. The pile of stones the boys had made earlier was ready; there were stones on the ground with the blowing scraps of paper that had come out of the box. Mrs. Delacroix selected a stone so large she had to pick it up with both hands and turned to Mrs. Dunbar. "Come on," she said. "Hurry up."

75   Mrs. Dunbar had small stones in both hands, and she said, gasping for breath, "I can't run at all. You'll have to go ahead and I'll catch up with you."

The children had stones already, and someone gave little Davy Hutchinson a few pebbles.

Tessie Hutchinson was in the center of a cleared space by now, and she held her hands out desperately as the villagers moved in on her. "It isn't fair," she said. A stone hit her on the side of the head.

Old Man Warner was saying, "Come on, come on, everyone." Steve Adams was in the front of the crowd of villagers with Mrs. Graves beside him.

"It isn't fair, it isn't right," Mrs. Hutchinson screamed, and then they were upon her.

QUESTIONS

1. Describe the point of view of the story. What seems to be the position from which the narrator sees and describes the events? How much extra information does the narrator provide?

2. What would the story be like if it were done with an omniscient point of view? With the first person? Could the story be as suspenseful as it is? In what other ways might the story be different with another point of view?

3. Does the conclusion of "The Lottery" seem to come as a surprise? In retrospect, what hints earlier in the story tell about what is to come?

4. A scapegoat, in the ritual of purification described in the Old Testament, was an actual goat that was released into the wilderness after having been ceremonially heaped with the "iniquities" of the people (Leviticus 16:22). What traces of such a ritual are suggested in "The Lottery"? Can you think of any other kinds of rituals that are retained today even though their purpose is now remote or even nonexistent?

5. Is "The Lottery" a horror story or a surprise story, or neither or both? Explain.

JOYCE CAROL OATES (b. 1938)

A superabundantly productive and richly acclaimed author of more than thirty novels—some under pseudonyms—and many collections of stories, books of poems, and collections of criticism, Joyce Carol Oates attended a one-room school as a child, and went on to receive her higher education at Syracuse University and the University of Wisconsin. She began her teaching career at the University of Detroit and currently, in addition to various guest positions, is Distinguished Professor in the Humanities at Princeton University. Just a few of her many novels are With Shuddering Fall *(1964),* Angel of Light *(1981),* Solstice *(1985),* Foxfire *(1993),* Middle Age: A Romance *(2001),* Missing Mom *(2005), and* Black Girl/White Girl *(2006). Recent story collections are* Faithless: Tales of Transgression *(2001),* I Am No One You Know *(2004), and* High Lonesome: Selected Stories, 1966–2006 *(2006). Among her many awards and distinctions are a Guggenheim Fellowship, the Continuing Achievement Award of the O. Henry Award Prize Stories series, a National Book Award, and the Chicago Tribune Literary Prize, not to mention three nominations for the Pulitzer Prize.*

Where Are You Going, Where Have You Been? (1970)

For Bob Dylan

Her name was Connie. She was fifteen and she had a quick nervous giggling habit of craning her neck to glance into mirrors, or checking other people's faces to make sure her own was all right. Her mother, who noticed everything and knew everything and who hadn't much reason any longer to look at her own face, always scolded Connie about it. "Stop gawking at yourself, who are you? You think you're so pretty?" she would say. Connie would raise her eyebrows at these familiar complaints and look right through her mother, into a shadowy vision of herself as she was right at that moment: she knew she was pretty and that was everything. Her mother had been pretty once too, if you could believe those old snapshots in the album, but now her looks were gone and that was why she was always after Connie.

"Why don't you keep your room clean like your sister? How've you got your hair fixed—what the hell stinks? Hair spray? You don't see your sister using that junk."

Her sister June was twenty-four and still lived at home. She was a secretary in the high school Connie attended, and if that wasn't bad enough—with her in the same building—she was so plain and chunky and steady that Connie had to hear her praised all the time by her mother and her mother's sisters. June did this, June did that, she saved money and helped clean the house and cooked and Connie couldn't do a thing, her mind was all filled with trashy daydreams. Their father was away at work most of the time and when he came home he wanted supper and he read the newspaper at supper and after supper he went to bed. He didn't bother talking much to them, but around his bent head Connie's mother kept picking at her until Connie wished her mother was dead and she herself was dead and it was all over. "She makes me want to throw up sometimes," she complained to her friends. She had a high, breathless, amused voice which made everything she said sound a little forced, whether it was sincere or not.

There was one good thing: June went places with girl friends of hers, girls who were just as plain and steady as she, and so when Connie wanted to do that her mother had no objections. The father of Connie's best girl friend drove the girls the three miles to town and left them off at a shopping plaza, so that they could walk through the stores or go to a movie, and when he came to pick them up again at eleven he never bothered to ask what they had done.

They must have been familiar sights, walking around that shopping plaza in their shorts   5
and flat ballerina slippers that always scuffed the sidewalk, with charm bracelets jingling on their thin wrists; they would lean together to whisper and laugh secretly if someone passed by who amused or interested them. Connie had long dark blond hair that drew anyone's eye to it, and she wore part of it pulled up on her head and puffed out and the rest of it she let fall down her back. She wore a pull-over jersey blouse that looked one way when she was at home and another way when she was away from home. Everything about her had two sides to it, one for home and one for anywhere that was not home: her walk that could be childlike and bobbing, or languid enough to make anyone think she was hearing music in her head, her mouth which was pale and smirking most of the time, but bright and pink on these evenings out, her laugh which was cynical and drawling at home—"Ha, ha, very funny"—but high-pitched and nervous anywhere else, like the jingling of the charms on her bracelet.

Sometimes they did go shopping or to a movie, but sometimes they went across the highway, ducking fast across the busy road, to a drive-in restaurant where older kids hung out. The restaurant was shaped like a big bottle, though squatter than a real bottle, and on its cap was a revolving figure of a grinning boy who held a hamburger aloft. One night in mid-summer they ran across, breathless with daring, and right away someone leaned out a car window and invited them over, but it was just a boy from high school they didn't like. It made them feel good to be able to ignore him. They went up through the maze of parked and cruising cars to the bright-lit, fly-infested restaurant, their faces pleased and expectant as if they were entering a sacred building that loomed out of the night to give them what haven and what blessing they yearned for. They sat at the counter and crossed their legs at the ankles, their thin shoulders rigid with excitement, and listened to the music that made everything so good: the music was always in the background like music at a church service, it was something to depend upon.

A boy named Eddie came in to talk with them. He sat backwards on his stool, turning himself jerkily around in semi-circles and then stopping and turning again, and after a while he asked Connie if she would like something to eat. She said she did and so she tapped her friend's arm on her way out—her friend pulled her face up into a brave droll look—and Connie said she would meet her at eleven, across the way. "I just hate to leave her like that," Connie said earnestly, but the boy said that she wouldn't be alone for long. So they went out to his car and on the way Connie couldn't help but let her eyes wander over the windshields and faces all around her, her face gleaming with a joy that had nothing to do with Eddie or even this place; it might have been the music. She drew her shoulders up and sucked in her breath with the pure pleasure of being alive, and just at that moment she happened to glance at a face just a few feet from hers. It was a boy with shaggy black hair, in a convertible jalopy painted gold. He stared at her and then his lips widened into a grin. Connie slit her eyes at him and turned away, but she couldn't help glancing back and there he was still watching her. He wagged a finger and laughed and said, "Gonna get you, baby," and Connie turned away again without Eddie noticing anything.

She spent three hours with him, at the restaurant where they ate hamburgers and drank Cokes in wax cups that were always sweating, and then down an alley a mile or so away, and when he left her off at five to eleven only the movie house was still open at the plaza. Her girl friend was there, talking with a boy. When Connie came up the two girls smiled at each other and Connie said, "How was the movie?" and the girl said, "*You* should know." They rode off with the girl's father, sleepy and pleased, and Connie couldn't help but look at the darkened shopping plaza with its big empty parking lot and its signs that were faded and ghostly now, and over at the drive-in restaurant where cars were still circling tirelessly. She couldn't hear the music at this distance.

Next morning June asked her how the movie was and Connie said, "So-so."

10   She and that girl and occasionally another girl went out several times a week that way, and the rest of the time Connie spent around the house—it was summer vacation—getting in her mother's way and thinking, dreaming, about the boys she met. But all the boys fell back and dissolved into a single face that was not even a face, but an idea, a feeling, mixed up with the urgent insistent pounding of the music and the humid night air of July. Connie's mother kept dragging her back to the daylight by finding things for her to do or saying, suddenly, "What's this about the Pettinger girl?"

And Connie would say nervously, "Oh, her. That dope." She always drew thick clear lines between herself and such girls, and her mother was simple and kindly enough to believe her. Her mother was so simple, Connie thought, that it was maybe cruel to fool her so much. Her mother went scuffling around the house in old bedroom slippers and complained over the telephone to one sister about the other, then the other called up and the two of them complained about the third one. If June's name was mentioned her mother's tone was approving, and if Connie's name was mentioned it was disapproving. This did not really mean she disliked Connie and actually Connie thought that her mother preferred her to June because she was prettier, but the two of them kept up a pretense of exasperation, a sense that they were tugging and struggling over something of little value to either of them. Sometimes, over coffee, they were almost friends, but something would come up—some vexation that was like a fly buzzing suddenly around their heads—and their faces went hard with contempt.

One Sunday Connie got up at eleven—none of them bothered with church—and washed her hair so that it could dry all day long, in the sun. Her parents and sister were going to a barbecue at an aunt's house and Connie said no, she wasn't interested, rolling her eyes to let her mother know just what she thought of it. "Stay home alone then," her mother said sharply. Connie sat out back in a lawn chair and watched them drive away, her father quiet and bald, hunched around so that he could back the car out, her mother with a look that was still angry and not at all softened through the windshield, and in the back seat poor old June all dressed up as if she didn't know what a barbecue was, with all the running yelling kids and the flies. Connie sat with her eyes closed in the sun, dreaming and dazed with the warmth about her as if this were a kind of love, the caresses of love, and her mind slipped over onto thoughts of the boy she had been with the night before and how nice he had been, how sweet it always was, not the way someone like June would suppose but sweet, gentle, the way it was in movies and promised in songs; and when she opened her eyes she hardly knew where she was, the back yard ran off into weeds and a fence-line of trees and behind it the sky was perfectly blue and still. The asbestos "ranch house" that was now three years old startled her—it looked small. She shook her head as if to get awake.

It was too hot. She went inside the house and turned on the radio to drown out the quiet. She sat on the edge of her bed, barefoot, and listened for an hour and a half to a program called XYZ Sunday Jamboree, record after record of hard, fast, shrieking songs she sang along with, interspersed by exclamations from "Bobby King": "An' look here you girls at Napoleon's—Son and Charley want you to pay real close attention to this song coming up!"

And Connie paid close attention herself, bathed in a glow of slow-pulsed joy that seemed to rise mysteriously out of the music itself and lay languidly about the airless little room, breathed in and breathed out with each gentle rise and fall of her chest.

After a while she heard a car coming up the drive. She sat up at once, startled, because it   15
couldn't be her father so soon. The gravel kept crunching all the way in from the road—the driveway was long—and Connie ran to the window. It was a car she didn't know. It was an open jalopy, painted a bright gold that caught the sunlight opaquely. Her heart began to pound and her fingers snatched at her hair, checking it, and she whispered "Christ, Christ," wondering how bad she looked. The car came to a stop at the side door and the horn sounded four short taps as if this were a signal Connie knew.

She went into the kitchen and approached the door slowly, then hung out the screen door, her bare toes curling down off the step. There were two boys in the car and now she recognized the driver: he had shaggy, shabby black hair that looked crazy as a wig and he was grinning at her.

"I ain't late, am I?" he said.

"Who the hell do you think you are?" Connie said.

"Toldja I'd be out, didn't I?"

"I don't even know who you are."   20

She spoke sullenly, careful to show no interest or pleasure, and he spoke in a fast bright monotone. Connie looked past him to the other boy, taking her time. He had fair brown hair, with a lock that fell onto his forehead. His sideburns gave him a fierce, embarrassed look, but so far he hadn't even bothered to glance at her. Both boys wore sunglasses. The driver's glasses were metallic and mirrored everything in miniature.

"You wanta come for a ride?" he said.

Connie smirked and let her hair fall loose over one shoulder.

"Don'tcha like my car? New paint job," he said. "Hey."

"What?"   25

"You're cute."

She pretended to fidget, chasing flies away from the door.

"Don'tcha believe me, or what?" he said.

"Look, I don't even know who you are," Connie said in disgust.

"Hey, Ellie's got a radio, see. Mine's broke down." He lifted his friend's arm and showed   30
her the little transistor the boy was holding, and now Connie began to hear the music. It was the same program that was playing inside the house.

"Bobby King?" she said.

"I listen to him all the time. I think he's great."

"He's kind of great," Connie said reluctantly.

"Listen, that guy's great. He knows where the action is."

35   Connie blushed a little, because the glasses made it impossible for her to see just what this boy was looking at. She couldn't decide if she liked him or if he was just a jerk, and so she dawdled in the doorway and wouldn't come down or go back inside. She said, "What's all that stuff painted on your car?"

"Can'tcha read it?" He opened the door very carefully, as if he was afraid it might fall off. He slid out just as carefully, planting his feet firmly on the ground, the tiny metallic world in his glasses slowing down like gelatine hardening and in the midst of it Connie's bright green blouse. "This here is my name, to begin with," he said. ARNOLD FRIEND was written in tarlike black letters on the side, with a drawing of a round grinning face that reminded Connie of a pumpkin, except it wore sunglasses. "I wanta introduce myself, I'm Arnold Friend and that's my real name and I'm gonna be your friend, honey, and inside the car's Ellie Oscar, he's kinda shy." Ellie brought his transistor radio up to his shoulder and balanced it there. "Now these numbers are a secret code, honey," Arnold Friend explained. He read off the numbers 33, 19, 17 and raised his eyebrows at her to see what she thought of that, but she didn't think much of it. The left rear fender had been smashed and around it was written, on the gleaming gold background: DONE BY CRAZY WOMAN DRIVER. Connie had to laugh at that. Arnold Friend was pleased at her laughter and looked up at her. "Around the other side's a lot more—you wanta come and see them?"

"No."

"Why not?"

"Why should I?"

40   "Don'tcha wanta see what's on the car? Don'tcha wanta go for a ride?"

"I don't know."

"Why not?"

"I got things to do."

"Like what?"

45   "Things."

He laughed as if she had said something funny. He slapped his thighs. He was standing in a strange way, leaning back against the car as if he were balancing himself. He wasn't tall, only an inch or so taller than she would be if she came down to him. Connie liked the way he was dressed, which was the way all of them dressed: tight faded jeans stuffed into black, scuffed boots, a belt that pulled his waist in and showed how lean he was, and a white pull-over shirt that was a little soiled and showed the hard small muscles of his arms and shoulders. He looked as if he probably did hard work, lifting and carrying things. Even his neck looked muscular. And his face was a familiar face, somehow: the jaw and chin and cheeks slightly darkened, because he hadn't shaved for a day or two, and the nose long and hawk-like, sniffing as if she were a treat he was going to gobble up and it was all a joke.

"Connie, you ain't telling the truth. This is your day set aside for a ride with me and you know it," he said, still laughing. The way he straightened and recovered from his fit of laughing showed that it had been all fake.

"How do you know what my name is?" she said suspiciously.

"It's Connie."

50   "Maybe and maybe not."

"I know my Connie," he said, wagging his finger. Now she remembered him even better, back at the restaurant, and her cheeks warmed at the thought of how she sucked in her breath just at the moment she passed him—how she must have looked to him. And he had remembered her. "Ellie and I come out here especially for you," he said. "Ellie can sit in back. How about it?"

"Where?"

"Where what?"

"Where're we going?"

He looked at her. He took off the sunglasses and she saw how pale the skin around his   55
eyes was, like holes that were not in shadow but instead in light. His eyes were chips of
broken glass that catch the light in an amiable way. He smiled. It was as if the idea of going
for a ride somewhere, to some place, was a new idea to him.

"Just for a ride, Connie sweetheart."

"I never said my name was Connie," she said.

"But I know what it is. I know your name and all about you, lots of things," Arnold Friend
said. He had not moved yet but stood still leaning back against the side of his jalopy. "I took a
special interest in you, such a pretty girl, and found out all about you like I know your parents
and sister are gone somewheres and I know where and how long they're going to be gone,
and I know who you were with last night, and your best girl friend's name is Betty. Right?"

He spoke in a simple lilting voice, exactly as if he were reciting the words to a song. His
smile assured her that everything was fine. In the car Ellie turned up the volume on his
radio and did not bother to look around at them.

"Ellie can sit in the back seat," Arnold Friend said. He indicated his friend with a casual   60
jerk of his chin, as if Ellie did not count and she should not bother with him.

"How'd you find out all that stuff?" Connie said.

"Listen: Betty Schultz and Tony Fitch and Jimmy Pettinger and Nancy Pettinger," he
said, in a chant. "Raymond Stanley and Bob Hutter—"

"Do you know all those kids?"

"I know everybody."

"Look, you're kidding. You're not from around here."   65

"Sure."

"But—how come we never saw you before?"

"Sure you saw me before," he said. He looked down at his boots, as if he were a little
offended. "You just don't remember."

"I guess I'd remember you," Connie said.

"Yeah?" He looked up at this, beaming. He was pleased. He began to mark time with the   70
music from Ellie's radio, tapping his fists lightly together. Connie looked away from his smile
to the car, which was painted so bright it almost hurt her eyes to look at it. She looked at that
name, ARNOLD FRIEND. And up at the front fender was an expression that was familiar—MAN
THE FLYING SAUCERS. It was an expression kids had used the year before, but didn't use this year.
She looked at it for a while as if the words meant something to her that she did not yet know.

"What're you thinking about? Huh?" Arnold Friend demanded. "Not worried about
your hair blowing around in the car, are you?"

"No."

"Think I maybe can't drive good?"

"How do I know?"

"You're a hard girl to handle. How come?" he said. "Don't you know I'm your friend?   75
Didn't you see me put my sign in the air when you walked by?"

"What sign?"

"My sign." And he drew an X in the air, leaning out toward her. They were maybe ten
feet apart. After his hand fell back to his side the X was still in the air, almost visible. Connie
let the screen door close and stood perfectly still inside it, listening to the music from her
radio and the boy's blend together. She stared at Arnold Friend. He stood there so stiffly
relaxed, pretending to be relaxed, with one hand idly on the door handle as if he were keeping himself up that way and had no intention of ever moving again. She recognized most
things about him, the tight jeans that showed his thighs and buttocks and the greasy leather
boots and the tight shirt, and even that slippery friendly smile of his, that sleepy dreamy

smile that all the boys used to get across ideas they didn't want to put into words. She recognized all this and also the singsong way he talked, slightly mocking, kidding, but serious and a little melancholy, and she recognized the way he tapped one fist against the other in homage to the perpetual music behind him. But all these things did not come together.

She said suddenly, "Hey, how old are you?"

His smile faded. She could see then that he wasn't a kid, he was much older—thirty, maybe more. At this knowledge her heart began to pound faster.

80   "That's a crazy thing to ask. Can'tcha see I'm your own age?"

"Like hell you are."

"Or maybe a coupla years older, I'm eighteen."

"Eighteen?" she said doubtfully.

He grinned to reassure her and lines appeared at the corners of his mouth. His teeth were big and white. He grinned so broadly his eyes became slits and she saw how thick the lashes were, thick and black as if painted with a black tarlike material. Then he seemed to become embarrassed, abruptly, and looked over his shoulder at Ellie. "*Him,* he's crazy," he said. "Ain't he a riot, he's a nut, a real character." Ellie was still listening to the music. His sunglasses told nothing about what he was thinking. He wore a bright orange shirt unbuttoned halfway to show his chest, which was a pale, bluish chest and not muscular like Arnold Friend's. His shirt collar was turned up all around and the very tips of the collar pointed out past his chin as if they were protecting him. He was pressing the transistor radio up against his ear and sat there in a kind of daze, right in the sun.

85   "He's kinda strange," Connie said.

"Hey, she says you're kinda strange! Kinda strange!" Arnold Friend cried. He pounded on the car to get Ellie's attention. Ellie turned for the first time and Connie saw with shock that he wasn't a kid either—he had a fair, hairless face, cheeks reddened slightly as if the veins grew too close to the surface of his skin, the face of a forty-year-old baby. Connie felt a wave of dizziness rise in her at this sight and she stared at him as if waiting for something to change the shock of the moment, make it all right again. Ellie's lips kept shaping words, mumbling along, with the words blasting in his ear.

"Maybe you two better go away," Connie said faintly.

"What? How come?" Arnold Friend cried. "We come out here to take you for a ride. It's Sunday." He had the voice of the man on the radio now. It was the same voice, Connie thought. "Don'tcha know it's Sunday all day and honey, no matter who you were with last night today you're with Arnold Friend and don't you forget it!—Maybe you better step out here," he said, and this last was in a different voice. It was a little flatter, as if the heat was finally getting to him.

"No. I got things to do."

90   "Hey."

"You two better leave."

"We ain't leaving until you come with us."

"Like hell I am—"

"Connie, don't fool around with me. I mean, I mean, don't fool *around,*" he said, shaking his head. He laughed incredulously. He placed his sunglasses on top of his head, carefully, as if he were indeed wearing a wig, and brought the stems down behind his ears. Connie stared at him, another wave of dizziness and fear rising in her so that for a moment he wasn't even in focus but was just a blur, standing there against his gold car, and she had the idea that he had driven up the driveway all right but had come from nowhere before that and belonged nowhere and that everything about him and even about the music that was so familiar to her was only half real.

95   "If my father comes and sees you—"

"He ain't coming. He's at the barbecue."

"How do you know that?"

"Aunt Tillie's. Right now they're—uh—they're drinking. Sitting around," he said vaguely, squinting as if he were staring all the way to town and over to Aunt Tillie's backyard. Then the vision seemed to get clear and he nodded energetically. "Yeah. Sitting around. There's your sister in a blue dress, huh? And high heels, the poor sad bitch—nothing like you, sweetheart! And your mother's helping some fat woman with the corn, they're cleaning the corn—husking the corn—"

"What fat woman?" Connie cried.

"How do I know what fat woman. I don't know every goddam fat woman in the world!" 100
Arnold Friend laughed.

"Oh, that's Mrs. Hornby. . . . Who invited her?" Connie said. She felt a little light-headed. Her breath was coming quickly.

"She's too fat. I don't like them fat. I like them the way you are, honey," he said, smiling sleepily at her. They stared at each other for a while, through the screen door. He said softly, "Now what you're going to do is this: you're going to come out that door. You're going to sit up front with me and Ellie's going to sit in the back, the hell with Ellie, right? This isn't Ellie's date. You're my date. I'm your lover, honey."

"What? You're crazy—"

"Yes, I'm your lover. You don't know what that is but you will," he said. "I know that too. I know all about you. But look: it's real nice and you couldn't ask for nobody better than me, or more polite. I always keep my word. I'll tell you how it is, I'm always nice at first, the first time. I'll hold you so tight you won't think you have to try to get away or pretend anything because you'll know you can't. And I'll come inside you where it's all secret and you'll give in to me and you'll love me—"

"Shut up! You're crazy!" Connie said. She backed away from the door. She put her 105
hands against her ears as if she'd heard something terrible, something not meant for her. "People don't talk like that, you're crazy," she muttered. Her heart was almost too big now for her chest and its pumping made sweat break out all over her. She looked out to see Arnold Friend pause and then take a step toward the porch lurching. He almost fell. But, like a clever drunken man, he managed to catch his balance. He wobbled in his high boots and grabbed hold of one of the porch posts.

"Honey?" he said. "You still listening?"

"Get the hell out of here!"

"Be nice, honey. Listen."

"I'm going to call the police—"

He wobbled again and out of the side of his mouth came a fast spat curse, an aside not 110
meant for her to hear. But even this "Christ!" sounded forced. Then he began to smile again. She watched this smile come, awkward as if he were smiling from inside a mask. His whole face was a mask, she thought wildly, tanned down onto his throat but then running out as if he had plastered makeup on his face but had forgotten about his throat.

"Honey—? Listen, here's how it is. I always tell the truth and I promise you this: I ain't coming in that house after you."

"You better not! I'm going to call the police if you—if you don't—"

"Honey," he said, talking right through her voice, "honey, I'm not coming in there but you are coming out here. You know why?"

She was panting. The kitchen looked like a place she had never seen before, some room she had run inside but which wasn't good enough, wasn't going to help her. The kitchen window had never had a curtain, after three years, and there were dishes in the sink for her to do—probably—and if you ran your hand across the table you'd probably feel something sticky there.

"You listening, honey? Hey?" 115

"—going to call the police—"

"Soon as you touch the phone I don't need to keep my promise and can come inside. You won't want that."

She rushed forward and tried to lock the door. Her fingers were shaking. "But why lock it," Arnold Friend said gently, talking right into her face. "It's just a screen door. It's just nothing." One of his boots was at a strange angle, as if his foot wasn't in it. It pointed out to the left, bent at the ankle. "I mean, anybody can break through a screen door and glass and wood and iron or anything else if he needs to, anybody at all and specially Arnold Friend. If the place got lit up with a fire honey you'd come running out into my arms, right into my arms and safe at home—like you knew I was your lover and'd stopped fooling around. I don't mind a nice shy girl but I don't like no fooling around." Part of those words were spoken with a slight rhythmic lilt, and Connie somehow recognized them—the echo of a song from last year, about a girl rushing into her boyfriend's arms and coming home again—

Connie stood barefoot on the linoleum floor, staring at him. "What do you want?" she whispered.

120 "I want you," he said.

"What?"

"Seen you that night and thought, that's the one, yes sir. I never needed to look any more."

"But my father's coming back. He's coming to get me. I had to wash my hair first—" She spoke in a dry, rapid voice, hardly raising it for him to hear.

"No, your daddy is not coming and yes, you had to wash your hair and you washed it for me. It's nice and shining and all for me, I thank you, sweetheart," he said, with a mock bow, but again he almost lost his balance. He had to bend and adjust his boots. Evidently his feet did not go all the way down; the boots must have been stuffed with something so that he would seem taller. Connie stared out at him and behind him Ellie in the car, who seemed to be looking off toward Connie's right, into nothing. This Ellie said, pulling the words out of the air one after another as if he were just discovering them, "You want me to pull out the phone?"

125 "Shut your mouth and keep it shut," Arnold Friend said, his face red from bending over or maybe from embarrassment because Connie had seen his boots. "This ain't none of your business."

"What—what are you doing? What do you want?" Connie said. "If I call the police they'll get you, they'll arrest you—"

"Promise was not to come in unless you touch that phone, and I'll keep that promise," he said. He resumed his erect position and tried to force his shoulders back. He sounded like a hero in a movie, declaring something important. He spoke too loudly and it was as if he were speaking to someone behind Connie. "I ain't made plans for coming in that house where I don't belong but just for you to come out to me, the way you should. Don't you know who I am?"

"You're crazy," she whispered. She backed away from the door but did not want to go into another part of the house, as if this would give him permission to come through the door. "What do you . . . You're crazy, you . . ."

"Huh? What're you saying, honey?"

130 Her eyes darted everywhere in the kitchen. She could not remember what it was, this room.

"This is how it is, honey: you come out and we'll drive away, have a nice ride. But if you don't come out we're gonna wait till your people come home and then they're all going to get it."

"You want that telephone pulled out?" Ellie said. He held the radio away from his ear and grimaced, as if without the radio the air was too much for him.

"I toldja shut up, Ellie," Arnold Friend said, "you're deaf, get a hearing aid, right? Fix yourself up. This little girl's no trouble and's gonna be nice to me, so Ellie keep to yourself, this ain't your date—right? Don't hem in on me. Don't hog. Don't crush. Don't bird dog.

Don't trail me," he said in a rapid meaningless voice, as if he were running through all the expressions he'd learned but was no longer sure which one of them was in style, then rushing on to new ones, making them up with his eyes closed, "Don't crawl under my fence, don't squeeze in my chipmunk hole, don't sniff my glue, suck my popsicle, keep your own greasy fingers on yourself!" He shaded his eyes and peered in at Connie, who was backed against the kitchen table. "Don't mind him honey he's just a creep. He's a dope. Right? I'm the boy for you and like I said you come out here nice like a lady and give me your hand, and nobody else gets hurt, I mean, your nice old bald-headed daddy and your mummy and your sister in her high heels. Because listen: why bring them in this?"

"Leave me alone," Connie whispered.

"Hey, you know that old woman down the road, the one with the chickens and stuff—   135
you know her?"

"She's dead!"

"Dead? What? You know her?" Arnold Friend said.

"She's dead—"

"Don't you like her?"

"She's dead—she's—she isn't here any more—"   140

"But don't you like her, I mean, you got something against her? Some grudge or something?" Then his voice dipped as if he were conscious of a rudeness. He touched the sunglasses perched on top of his head as if to make sure they were still there. "Now you be a good girl."

"What are you going to do?"

"Just two things, or maybe three," Arnold Friend said. "But I promise it won't last long and you'll like me that way you get to like people you're close to. You will. It's all over for you here, so come on out. You don't want your people in any trouble, do you?"

She turned and bumped against a chair or something, hurting her leg, but she ran into the back room and picked up the telephone. Something roared in her ear, a tiny roaring, and she was so sick with fear that she could do nothing but listen to it—the telephone was clammy and very heavy and her fingers groped down to the dial but were too weak to touch it. She began to scream into the phone, into the roaring. She cried out, she cried for her mother, she felt her breath start jerking back and forth in her lungs as if it were something Arnold Friend were stabbing her with again and again with no tenderness. A noisy sorrowful wailing rose all about her and she was locked inside it the way she was locked inside the house.

After a while she could hear again. She was sitting on the floor with her wet back against   145
the wall.

Arnold Friend was saying from the door, "That's a good girl. Put the phone back."

She kicked the phone away from her.

"No, honey. Pick it up. Put it back right."

She picked it up and put it back. The dial tone stopped.

"That's a good girl. Now come outside."   150

She was hollow with what had been fear, but what was now just an emptiness. All that screaming had blasted it out of her. She sat, one leg cramped under her, and deep inside her brain was something like a pinpoint of light that kept going and would not let her relax. She thought, I'm not going to see my mother again. She thought, I'm not going to sleep in my bed again. Her bright green blouse was all wet.

Arnold Friend said, in a gentle-loud voice that was like a stage voice, "The place where you came from ain't there any more, and where you had in mind to go is cancelled out. This place you are now—inside your daddy's house—is nothing but a cardboard box I can knock down any time. You know that and always did know it. You hear me?"

She thought, I have got to think. I have to know what to do.

"We'll go out to a nice field, out in the country here where it smells so nice and it's sunny," Arnold Friend said. "I'll have my arms around you so you won't need to try to get away and I'll show you what love is like, what it does. The hell with this house! It looks solid all right," he said. He ran a fingernail down the screen and the noise did not make Connie shiver, as it would have the day before. "Now put your hand on your heart, honey. Feel that? That feels solid too but we know better, be nice to me, be sweet like you can be—cause what else is there for a girl like you but to be sweet and pretty and give in?—and get away before her people come back?"

155   She felt her pounding heart. Her hand seemed to enclose it. She thought for the first time in her life that it was nothing that was hers, that belonged to her, but just a pounding, living thing inside this body that wasn't really hers either.

"You don't want them to get hurt," Arnold Friend went on. "Now get up, honey. Get up all by yourself."

She stood up.

"Now turn this way. That's right. Come over here to me—Ellie, put that away, didn't I tell you? You dope. You miserable creepy dope," Arnold Friend said. His words were not angry but only part of an incantation. The incantation was kindly. "Now come out through the kitchen to me honey and let's see a smile, try it, you're a brave sweet little girl and now they're eating corn and hotdogs cooked to bursting over an outdoor fire, and they don't know one thing about you and never did and honey you're better than them because not a one of them would have done this for you."

Connie felt the linoleum under her feet; it was cool. She brushed her hair back out of her eyes. Arnold Friend let go of the post tentatively and opened his arms for her, his elbows pointing in toward each other and his wrists limp, to show that this was an embarrassed embrace and a little mocking, he didn't want to make her self-conscious.

160   She put out her hand against the screen. She watched herself push the door slowly open as if she were safe back somewhere in the other doorway, watching this body and this head of long hair moving out into the sunlight where Arnold Friend waited.

"My sweet little blue-eyed girl," he said, in a half-sung sigh that had nothing to do with her brown eyes but was taken up just the same by the vast sunlit reaches of the land behind him and on all sides of him, so much land that Connie had never seen before and did not recognize except to know that she was going to it.

QUESTIONS

1. Is this story realistic or fantastic, or a combination of the two? How much fantasy is apparent in the ostensibly realistic level of the story, and how much realism is apparent when the story becomes more and more of a fantasy? At what point does the story shift from everyday realism to the unusual? How does the latter part of the story become less and less realistic? How should this part be described? Is there any way, at the story's beginning, to anticipate what is going to be happening at the end? Explain.

2. Describe the characteristics of Arnold Friend. Why does Oates connect him with the blackness of tar and tarlike substance? What do you make out of his apparent ability to know about Connie's family, and about people at the party with the family? What do you make of his wobbling in his boots (paragraphs 105, 124), and his seeming to speak to someone, unseen, behind Connie?

3. Describe Connie. Is she unusual at all? What happens to her perceptions of her situation as she stands within the kitchen and Arnold Friend stands outside? Why does she leave the house with Arnold at the end?

4. Why does Arnold Friend speak so coarsely and angrily to his companion, Ellie? What does Ellie represent? How can Arnold Friend be construed not as realistic but demonic? If he is symbolic, what does he symbolize?

ZZ PACKER (b. 1973)

Born in Chicago, ZZ Packer (Zuwena Packer) received a master's degree from Johns Hopkins and an MFA from the University of Iowa Writers' Workshop. She has published stories and essays in The New Yorker, Harper's, Story, Ploughshares, Zoetrope, *and the essay collection* Why I'm Still Married *(2006). "Brownies" was first published in* Harper's *in 1999, and was included in Packer's collection* Drinking Coffee Elsewhere *in 2003. This book has been separately published in the United Kingdom and Australia, and has been published in French, Spanish, Dutch, Italian, and Polish. She has received a number of honors, including a Guggenheim Fellowship. She lives in San Francisco.*

🖋 Brownies (1999)

By our second day at Camp Crescendo, the girls in my Brownie troop had decided to kick the asses of each and every girl in Brownie Troop 909. Troop 909 was doomed from the first day of camp; they were white girls, their complexions a blend of ice cream: strawberry, vanilla. They turtled out from their bus in pairs, their rolled-up sleeping bags chromatized with Disney characters: Sleeping Beauty, Snow White, Mickey Mouse; or the generic ones cheap parents bought: washed-out rainbows, unicorns, curly-eyelashed frogs. Some clutched Igloo coolers and still others held on to stuffed toys like pacifiers, looking all around them like tourists determined to be dazzled.

Our troop was wending its way past their bus, past the ranger station, past the colorful trail guide drawn like a treasure map, locked behind glass.

"Man, did you smell them?" Arnetta said, giving the girls a slow once-over, "They smell like Chihuahuas. *Wet* Chihuahuas." Their troop was still at the entrance, and though we had passed them by yards, Arnetta raised her nose in the air and grimaced.

Arnetta said this from the very rear of the line, far away from Mrs. Margolin, who always strung our troop behind her like a brood of obedient ducklings. Mrs. Margolin even looked like a mother duck—she had hair cropped close to a small ball of a head, almost no neck, and huge, miraculous breasts. She wore enormous belts that looked like the kind that weightlifters wear, except hers would be cheap metallic gold or rabbit fur or covered with gigantic fake sunflowers, and often these belts would become nature lessons in and of themselves. "See," Mrs. Margolin once said to us, pointing to her belt, "this one's made entirely from the feathers of baby pigeons."

The belt layered with feathers was uncanny enough, but I was more disturbed by the realization that I had never actually *seen* a baby pigeon. I searched weeks for one, in vain—scampering after pigeons whenever I was downtown with my father.   5

But nature lessons were not Mrs. Margolin's top priority. She saw the position of troop leader as an evangelical post. Back at the A.M.E. church° where our Brownie meetings were held, Mrs. Margolin was especially fond of imparting religious aphorisms by means of acrostics—"Satan" was the "Serpent Always Tempting and Noisome"; she'd refer to the "Bible" as "Basic Instructions Before Leaving Earth." Whenever she quizzed us on these, expecting to hear the acrostics parroted back to her, only Arnetta's correct replies soared over our vague mumblings. "Jesus?" Mrs. Margolin might ask expectantly, and Arnetta alone would dutifully answer, "Jehovah's Example, Saving Us Sinners."

Arnetta always made a point of listening to Mrs. Margolin's religious talk and giving her what she wanted to hear. Because of this, Arnetta could have blared through a megaphone

---

A.M.E. *church:* American Methodist Episcopal Church.

that the white girls of Troop 909 were "wet Chihuahuas" without so much as a blink from Mrs. Margolin. Once, Arnetta killed the troop goldfish by feeding it a french fry covered in ketchup, and when Mrs. Margolin demanded that she explain what had happened, claimed the goldfish had been eyeing her meal for *hours,* then the fish—giving in to temptation— had leapt up and snatched a whole golden fry from her fingertips.

"*Serious* Chihuahua," Octavia added, and though neither Arnetta nor Octavia could *spell* "Chihuahua," had ever *seen* a Chihuahua, trisyllabic words had gained a sort of exoticism within our fourth-grade set at Woodrow Wilson Elementary. Arnetta and Octavia would flip through the dictionary, determined to work the vulgar-sounding ones like "Djibouti" and "asinine" into conversation.

"*Caucasian* Chihuahuas," Arnetta said.

10   That did it. The girls in my troop turned elastic: Drema and Elise doubled up on one another like inextricably entwined kites; Octavia slapped her belly; Janice jumped straight up in the air, then did it again, as if to slam-dunk her own head. They could not stop laughing. No one had laughed so hard since a boy named Martez had stuck a pencil in the electric socket and spent the whole day with a strange grin on his face.

"Girls, girls," said our parent helper, Mrs. Hedy. Mrs. Hedy was Octavia's mother, and she wagged her index finger perfunctorily, like a windshield wiper. "Stop it, now. Be good." She said this loud enough to be heard, but lazily, bereft of any feeling or indication that she meant to be obeyed, as though she could say these words again at the exact same pitch if a button somewhere on her were pressed.

But the rest of the girls didn't stop; they only laughed louder. It was the word "Caucasian" that got them all going. One day at school, about a month before the Brownie camping trip, Arnetta turned to a boy wearing impossibly high-ankled floodwater jeans and said, "What are you? *Caucasian?*" The word took off from there, and soon everything was Caucasian. If you ate too fast you ate like a Caucasian, if you ate too slow you ate like a Caucasian. The biggest feat anyone at Woodrow Wilson could do was to jump off the swing in midair, at the highest point in its arc, and if you fell (as I had, more than once) instead of landing on your feet, knees bent Olympic gymnast-style, Arnetta and Octavia were prepared to comment. They'd look at each other with the silence of passengers who'd narrowly escaped an accident, then nod their heads, whispering with solemn horror, "*Caucasian.*"

Even the only white kid in our school, Dennis, got in on the Caucasian act. That time when Martez stuck a pencil in the socket, Dennis had pointed and yelled, "That was *so* Caucasian!"

When you lived in the south suburbs of Atlanta, it was easy to forget about whites. Whites were like those baby pigeons: real and existing, but rarely seen or thought about. Everyone had been to Rich's° to go clothes shopping, everyone had seen white girls and their mothers coo-cooing over dresses; everyone had gone to the downtown library and seen white businessmen swish by importantly, wrists flexed in front of them to check the time as though they would change from Clark Kent into Superman at any second. But those images were as fleeting as cards shuffled in a deck, whereas the ten white girls behind us—*invaders,* Arnetta would later call them—were instantly real and memorable, with their long, shampoo-commercial hair, straight as spaghetti from the box. This alone was reason for envy and hatred. The only black girl most of us had ever seen with hair that long was Octavia, whose hair hung past her butt like a Hawaiian hula dancer's. The sight of Octavia's mane prompted other girls to listen to her reverentially, as though whatever she had to say would somehow activate their own follicles. For example, when, on the first day of camp, Octavia made as if to speak, and everyone fell silent. "Nobody," Octavia said, "calls us niggers."

15   At the end of that first day, when half of our troop made their way back to the cabin after tag-team restroom visits, Arnetta said she'd heard one of the Troop 909 girls call Daphne a

---

Rich's: a large retail chain based in Atlanta from 1867 to 2005.

nigger. The other half of the girls and I were helping Mrs. Margolin clean up the pots and pans from the campfire ravioli dinner. When we made our way to the restrooms to wash up and brush our teeth, we met up with Arnetta midway.

"Man, I completely heard the girl," Arnetta reported. "Right, Daphne?"

Daphne hardly ever spoke, but when she did, her voice was petite and tinkly, the voice one might expect from a shiny new earring. She'd written a poem once, for Langston Hughes Day, a poem brimming with all the teacher-winning ingredients—trees and oceans, sunsets and moons—but what cinched the poem for the grown-ups, snatching the win from Octavia's musical ode to Grandmaster Flash and the Furious Five, were Daphne's last lines:

> You are my father, the veteran
> When you cry in the dark
> It rains and rains and rains in my heart

She'd always worn clean, though faded, jumpers and dresses when Chic jeans were the fashion, but when she went up to the dais to receive her prize journal, pages trimmed in gold, she wore a new dress with a velveteen bodice and a taffeta skirt as wide as an umbrella. All the kids clapped, though none of them understood the poem. I'd read encyclopedias the way others read comics, and I didn't get it. But those last lines pricked me, they were so eerie, and as my father and I ate cereal, I'd whisper over my Froot Loops, like a mantra, *"You are my father, the veteran. You are my father, the veteran, the veteran, the veteran,"* until my father, who acted in plays as Caliban and Othello and was not a veteran, marched me up to my teacher one morning and said, "Can you tell me what's wrong with this kid?"

I thought Daphne and I might become friends, but I think she grew spooked by me whispering those lines to her, begging her to tell me what they meant, and I soon understood that two quiet people like us were better off quiet alone.

"Daphne? Didn't you hear them call you a nigger?" Arnetta asked, giving Daphne a nudge.   20

The sun was setting behind the trees, and their leafy tops formed a canopy of black lace for the flame of the sun to pass through. Daphne shrugged her shoulders at first, then slowly nodded her head when Arnetta gave her a hard look.

Twenty minutes later, when my restroom group returned to the cabin, Arnetta was still talking about Troop 909. My restroom group had passed by some of the 909 girls. For the most part, they deferred to us, waving us into the restrooms, letting us go even though they'd gotten there first.

We'd seen them, but from afar, never within their orbit enough to see whether their faces were the way all white girls appeared on TV—ponytailed and full of energy, bubbling over with love and money. All I could see was that some of them rapidly fanned their faces with their hands, though the heat of the day had long passed. A few seemed to be lolling their heads in slow circles, half purposefully, as if exercising the muscles of their necks, half ecstatically, like Stevie Wonder.

"We can't let them get away with that," Arnetta said, dropping her voice to a laryngitic whisper. "We can't let them get away with calling us niggers. I say we teach them a lesson." She sat down cross-legged on a sleeping bag, an embittered Buddha, eyes glimmering acrylic-black. "We can't go telling Mrs. Margolin, either. Mrs. Margolin'll say something about doing unto others and the path of righteousness and all. Forget that shit." She let her eyes flutter irreverently till they half closed, as though ignoring an insult not worth returning. We could all hear Mrs. Margolin outside, gathering the last of the metal campware.

Nobody said anything for a while. Usually people were quiet after Arnetta spoke. Her tone   25 had an upholstered confidence that was somehow both regal and vulgar at once. It demanded a few moments of silence in its wake, like the ringing of a church bell or the playing of taps. Sometimes Octavia would ditto or dissent to whatever Arnetta had said, and this was the signal that others could speak. But this time Octavia just swirled a long cord of hair into pretzel shapes.

"Well?" Arnetta said. She looked as if she had discerned the hidden severity of the situation and was waiting for the rest of us to catch up. Everyone looked from Arnetta to Daphne. It was, after all, Daphne who had supposedly been called the name, but Daphne sat on the bare cabin floor, flipping through the pages of the Girl Scout handbook, eyebrows arched in mock wonder, as if the handbook were a catalogue full of bright and startling foreign costumes. Janice broke the silence. She clapped her hands to broach her idea of a plan.

"They gone be sleeping," she whispered conspiratorially, "then we gone sneak into they cabin, then we'll put daddy longlegs in they sleeping bags. Then they'll wake up. Then we gone beat 'em up till they're as flat as frying pans!" She jammed her fist into the palm of her hand, then made a sizzling sound.

Janice's country accent was laughable, her looks homely, her jumpy acrobatics embarrassing to behold. Arnetta and Octavia volleyed amused, arrogant smiles whenever Janice opened her mouth, but Janice never caught the hint, spoke whenever she wanted, fluttered around Arnetta and Octavia futilely offering her opinions to their departing backs. Whenever Arnetta and Octavia shooed her away, Janice loitered until the two would finally sigh and ask, "What *is* it, Miss Caucausoid? What do you *want?*"

"Shut up, Janice," Octavia said, letting a fingered loop of hair fall to her waist as though just the sound of Janice's voice had ruined the fun of her hair twisting.

30   Janice obeyed, her mouth hung open in a loose grin, unflappable, unhurt.

"All right," Arnetta said, standing up. "We're going to have a secret meeting and talk about what we're going to do."

Everyone gravely nodded her head. The word "secret" had a built-in importance, the modifier form of the word carried more clout than the noun. A secret meant nothing; it was like gossip: just a bit of unpleasant knowledge about someone who happened to be someone other than yourself. A secret *meeting,* or a secret *club* was entirely different.

That was when Arnetta turned to me as though she knew that doing so was both a compliment and a charity.

"Snot, you're not going to be a bitch and tell Mrs. Margolin, are you?"

35   I had been called "Snot" ever since first grade, when I'd sneezed in class and two long ropes of mucus had splattered a nearby girl.

"Hey," I said. "Maybe you didn't hear them right—I mean—"

"Are you gonna tell on us or not?" was all Arnetta wanted to know, and by the time the question was asked, the rest of our Brownie troop looked at me as though they'd already decided their course of action, me being the only impediment.

Camp Crescendo used to double as a high-school-band and field-hockey camp until an arcing field hockey ball landed on the clasp of a girl's metal barrette, knifing a skull nerve and paralyzing the right side of her body. The camp closed down for a few years and the girl's teammates built a memorial, filling the spot on which the girl fell with hockey balls, on which they had painted—all in nail polish—get-well tidings, flowers, and hearts. The balls were still stacked there, like a shrine of ostrich eggs embedded in the ground.

On the second day of camp, Troop 909 was dancing around the mound of hockey balls, their limbs jangling awkwardly, their cries like the constant summer squeal of an amusement park. There was a stream that bordered the field hockey lawn, and the girls from my troop settled next to it, scarfing down the last of lunch: sandwiches made from salami and slices of tomato that had gotten waterlogged from the melting ice in the cooler. From the stream bank, Arnetta eyed the Troop 909 girls, scrutinizing their movements to glean inspiration for battle.

40   "Man," Arnetta said, "we could bumrush them right now if that damn lady would *leave.*"

The 909 troop leader was a white woman with the severe pageboy hairdo of an ancient Egyptian. She lay on a picnic blanket, sphinx-like, eating a banana, sometimes holding it out in front of her like a microphone. Beside her sat a girl slowly flapping one hand like a bird with a broken wing. Occasionally, the leader would call out the names of girls who'd attempted leapfrogs and flips, or of girls who yelled too loudly or strayed far from the circle.

"I'm just glad Big Fat Mama's not following us here," Octavia said. "At least we don't have to worry about her." Mrs. Margolin, Octavia assured us, was having her Afternoon Devotional, shrouded in mosquito netting, in a clearing she'd found. Mrs. Hedy was cleaning mud from her espadrilles in the cabin.

"I handled them." Arnetta sucked on her teeth and proudly grinned. "I told her we was going to gather leaves."

"Gather leaves," Octavia said, nodding respectfully. "That's a good one. Especially since they're so mad-crazy about this camping thing." She looked from ground to sky, sky to ground. Her hair hung down her back in two braids like a squaw's. "I mean, I really don't know why it's even called *camping*—all we ever do with Nature is find some twigs and say something like, 'Wow, this fell from a tree.'" She then studied her sandwich. With two disdainful fingers, she picked out a slice of dripping tomato, the sections congealed with red slime. She pitched it into the stream embrowned with dead leaves and the murky effigies of other dead things, but in the opaque water, a group of small silver-brown fish appeared. They surrounded the tomato and nibbled.

"Look!" Janice cried. "Fishes! Fishes!" As she scrambled to the edge of the stream to watch, a covey of insects threw up tantrums from the wheatgrass and nettle, a throng of tiny electric machines, all going at once. Octavia sneaked up behind Janice as if to push her in. Daphne and I exchanged terrified looks. It seemed as though only we knew that Octavia was close enough—and bold enough—to actually push Janice into the stream. Janice turned around quickly, but Octavia was already staring serenely into the still water as though she was gathering some sort of courage from it. "What's so funny?" Janice said, eyeing them all suspiciously. 45

Elise began humming the tune to "Karma Chameleon,"° all the girls joining in, their hums light and facile. Janice also began to hum, against everyone else, the high-octane opening chords of "Beat It."°

"I love me some Michael Jackson," Janice said when she'd finished humming, smacking her lips as though Michael Jackson were a favorite meal. "I *will* marry Michael Jackson."

Before anyone had a chance to impress upon Janice the impossibility of this, Arnetta suddenly rose, made a sun visor of her hand, and watched Troop 909 leave the field hockey lawn.

"Dammit!" she said. "We've got to get them *alone.*"

"They won't ever be alone," I said. All the rest of the girls looked at me, for I usually kept quiet. If I spoke even a word, I could count on someone calling me Snot. Everyone seemed to think that we could beat up these girls; no one entertained the thought that they might fight *back*. "The only time they'll be unsupervised is in the bathroom." 50

"Oh shut up, Snot," Octavia said.

But Arnetta slowly nodded her head. "The bathroom," she said. "The bathroom," she said, again and again. "The bathroom! The bathroom!"

According to Octavia's watch, it took us five minutes to hike to the restrooms, which were midway between our cabin and Troop 909's. Inside, the mirrors above the sinks returned only the vaguest of reflections, as though someone had taken a scouring pad to their surfaces to obscure the shine. Pine needles, leaves, and dirty, flattened wads of chewing gum covered the floor like a mosaic. Webs of hair matted the drain in the middle of the floor. Above the sinks and below the mirrors, stacks of folded white paper towels lay on a long metal counter. Shaggy white balls of paper towels sat on the sinktops in a line like corsages on display. A thread of floss snaked from a wad of tissues dotted with the faint red-pink of blood. One of those white girls, I thought, had just lost a tooth.

Karma Chameleon: song by the British group Culture Club (1983).
Beat It: song by Michael Jackson (1982).

Though the restroom looked almost the same as it had the night before, it somehow seemed stranger now. We hadn't noticed the wooden rafters coming together in great V's. We were, it seemed, inside a whale, viewing the ribs of the roof of its mouth.

55   "Wow. It's a mess," Elise said.

"You can say that again."

Arnetta leaned against the doorjamb of a restroom stall. "This is where they'll be again," she said. Just seeing the place, just having a plan seemed to satisfy her. "We'll go in and talk to them. You know, 'How you doing? How long'll you be here?' That sort of thing. Then Octavia and I are gonna tell them what happens when they call anyone of us a nigger."

"I'm going to say something, too," Janice said.

Arnetta considered this. "Sure," she said. "Of course. Whatever you want."

60   Janice pointed her finger like a gun at Octavia and rehearsed the line she'd thought up, "'We're gonna teach you a *lesson!*' That's what I'm going to say." She narrowed her eyes like a TV mobster. "'We're gonna teach you little girls a lesson!'"

With the back of her hand, Octavia brushed Janice's finger away. "You couldn't teach me to shit in a toilet."

"But," I said, "what if they say, 'We didn't say that? We didn't call anyone an N-I-G-G-E-R.'"

"Snot," Arnetta said, and then sighed. "Don't think. Just fight. If you even know how."

Everyone laughed except Daphne. Arnetta gently laid her hand on Daphne's shoulder. "Daphne. You don't have to fight. We're doing this for you."

65   Daphne walked to the counter, took a clean paper towel, and carefully unfolded it like a map. With it, she began to pick up the trash all around. Everyone watched.

"C'mon," Arnetta said to everyone. "Let's beat it." We all ambled toward the doorway, where the sunshine made one large white rectangle of light. We were immediately blinded, and we shielded our eyes with our hands and our forearms.

"Daphne?" Arnetta asked. "Are you coming?"

We all looked back at the bending girl, the thin of her back hunched like the back of a custodian sweeping a stage, caught in limelight. Stray strands of her hair were lit near—transparent, thin fiber-optic threads. She did not nod yes to the question, nor did she shake her head no. She abided, bent. Then she began again, picking up leaves, wads of paper, the cotton fluff innards from a torn stuffed toy. She did it so methodically, so exquisitely, so humbly, she must have been trained. I thought of those dresses she wore, faded and old, yet so pressed and clean. I then saw the poverty in them; I then could imagine her mother, cleaning the houses of others, returning home, weary.

"I guess she's not coming."

70   We left her and headed back to our cabin, over pine needles and leaves, taking the path full of shade.

"What about our secret meeting?" Elise asked.

Arnetta enunciated her words in a way that defied contradiction: "We just had it."

It was nearing our bedtime, but the sun had not yet set.

"Hey, your mama's coming," Arnetta said to Octavia when she saw Mrs. Hedy walk toward the cabin, sniffling. When Octavia's mother wasn't giving bored, parochial orders, she sniffled continuously, mourning an imminent divorce from her husband. She might begin a sentence, "I don't know what Robert will do when Octavia and I are gone. Who'll buy him cigarettes?" and Octavia would hotly whisper, *"Mama,"* in a way that meant: Please don't talk about our problems in front of everyone. Please shut up.

75   But when Mrs. Hedy began talking about her husband, thinking about her husband, seeing clouds shaped like the head of her husband, she couldn't be quiet, and no one could dislodge her from the comfort of her own woe. Only one thing could perk her up—Brownie songs. If the girls were quiet, and Mrs. Hedy was in her dopey, sorrowful

mood, she would say, "Y'all know I like those songs, girls. Why don't you sing one?" Everyone would groan, except me and Daphne. I, for one, liked some of the songs.

"C'mon, everybody," Octavia said drearily. "She likes the Brownie song best."

We sang, loud enough to reach Mrs. Hedy:

> "I've got something in my pocket;
> It belongs across my face.
> And I keep it very close at hand
>   in a most convenient place.
> I'm sure you couldn't guess it
> If you guessed a long, long while.
> So I'll take it out and put it on—
> It's a great big Brownie smile!"

The Brownie song was supposed to be sung cheerfully, as though we were elves in a workshop, singing as we merrily cobbled shoes, but everyone except me hated the song so much that they sang it like a maudlin record, played on the most sluggish of rpms.

"That was good," Mrs. Hedy said, closing the cabin door behind her. "Wasn't that nice, Linda?"

"Praise God," Mrs. Margolin answered without raising her head from the chore of   80 counting out Popsicle sticks for the next day's craft session.

"Sing another one," Mrs. Hedy said. She said it with a sort of joyful aggression, like a drunk I'd once seen who'd refused to leave a Korean grocery.

"God, Mama, get over it," Octavia whispered in a voice meant only for Arnetta, but Mrs. Hedy heard it and started to leave the cabin.

"Don't go," Arnetta said. She ran after Mrs. Hedy and held her by the arm. "We haven't fin-ished singing." She nudged us with a single look. "Let's sing the 'Friends Song.' For Mrs. Hedy."

Although I liked some of the songs, I hated this one:

> Make new friends
> But keep the o-old,
> One is silver
> And the other gold.

If most of the girls in the troop could be any type of metal, they'd be bunched-up wads   85 of tinfoil, maybe, or rusty iron nails you had to get tetanus shots for.

"No, no, no," Mrs. Margolin said before anyone could start in on the "Friends Song."

"An uplifting song. Something to lift her up and take her mind off all these earthly burdens."

Arnetta and Octavia rolled their eyes. Everyone knew what song Mrs. Margolin was talking about, and no one, no one, wanted to sing it.

"Please, no," a voice called out. "Not 'The Doughnut Song,'" "Please not 'The Doughnut Song,'" Octavia pleaded.

"I'll brush my teeth two times if I don't have to sing 'The Doughnut—'"   90

"Sing!" Mrs. Margolin demanded.

We sang:

> Life without Jesus is like a do-ough-nut!
> Like a do-ooough-nut!
> Like a do-ooough-nut!
> Life without Jesus is like a do-ough-nut!
> There's a hole in the middle of my soul!"

There were other verses, involving other pastries, but we stopped after the first one and cast glances toward Mrs. Margolin to see if we could gain a reprieve. Mrs. Margolin's eyes fluttered blissfully. She was half asleep.

"Awww," Mrs. Hedy said, as though giant Mrs. Margolin were a cute baby. "Mrs. Margolin's had a long day."

"Yes indeed," Mrs. Margolin answered. "If you don't mind, I might just go to the lodge where the beds are. I haven't been the same since the operation."

95   I had not heard of this operation, or when it had occurred, since Mrs. Margolin had never missed the once-a-week Brownie meetings, but I could see from Daphne's face that she was concerned, and I could see that the other girls had decided that Mrs. Margolin's operation must have happened long ago in some remote time unconnected to our own. Nevertheless, they put on sad faces. We had all been taught that adulthood was full of sorrow and pain, taxes and bills, dreaded work and dealings with whites, sickness and death. I tried to do what the others did. I tried to look silent.

"Go right ahead, Linda," Mrs. Hedy said. "I'll watch the girls." Mrs. Hedy seemed to forget about divorce for a moment; she looked at us with dewy eyes, as if we were mysterious, furry creatures. Meanwhile, Mrs. Margolin walked through the maze of sleeping bags until she found her own. She gathered a neat stack of clothes and pajamas slowly, as though doing so was almost painful. She took her toothbrush, her toothpaste, her pillow. "All right!" Mrs. Margolin said, addressing us all from the threshold of the cabin. "Be in bed by nine." She said it with a twinkle in her voice, letting us know she was allowing us to be naughty and stay up till nine-fifteen.

"C'mon everybody," Arnetta said after Mrs. Margolin left. "Time for us to wash up."

Everyone watched Mrs. Hedy closely, wondering whether she would insist on coming with us since it was night, making a fight with Troop 909 nearly impossible. Troop 909 would soon be in the bathroom, washing their faces, brushing their teeth—completely unsuspecting of our ambush.

"We won't be long," Arnetta said. "We're old enough to go to the restrooms by ourselves."

100   Mrs. Hedy pursed her lips at this dilemma. "Well, I guess you Brownies are almost Girl Scouts, right?"

"Right!"

"Just one more badge," Drema said.

"And about," Octavia droned, "a million more cookies to sell." Octavia looked at all of us, *Now's our chance,* her face seemed to say, but our chance to do *what,* I didn't exactly know.

Finally, Mrs. Hedy walked to the doorway where Octavia stood dutifully waiting to say goodbye but looking bored doing it. Mrs. Hedy held Octavia's chin. "You'll be good?"

105   "Yes, Mama."

"And remember to pray for me and your father? If I'm asleep when you get back?"

"Yes, Mama."

When the other girls had finished getting their toothbrushes and washcloths and flashlights for the group restroom trip, I was drawing pictures of tiny birds with too many feathers. Daphne was sitting on her sleeping bag, reading.

"You're not going to come?" Octavia asked.

110   Daphne shook her head.

"I'm gonna stay, too," I said. "I'll go to the restroom when Daphne and Mrs. Hedy go."

Arnetta leaned down toward me and whispered so that Mrs. Hedy, who'd taken over Mrs. Margolin's task of counting Popsicle sticks, couldn't hear. "No, Snot. If we get in trouble, you're going to get in trouble with the rest of us."

We made our way through the darkness by flashlight. The tree branches that had shaded us just hours earlier, along the same path, now looked like arms sprouting menacing hands. The stars sprinkled the sky like spilled salt. They seemed fastened to the darkness, high up and holy, their places fixed and definite as we stirred beneath them.

Some, like me, were quiet because we were afraid of the dark; others were talking like crazy for the same reason.

115   "Wow!" Drema said, looking up. "Why are all the stars out here? I never see stars back on Oneida Street."

"It's a camping trip, that's why," Octavia said. "You're supposed to see stars on camping trips.

Janice said, "This place smells like my mother's air freshener."

"These woods are *pine*," Elise said. "Your mother probably uses *pine* air freshener."

Janice mouthed an exaggerated "Oh," nodding her head as though she just then understood one of the world's great secrets.

No one talked about fighting. Everyone was afraid enough just walking through the   120
infinite deep of the woods. Even though I didn't fight to fight, was afraid of fighting, I felt
I was part of the rest of the troop; like I was defending something. We trudged against the
slight incline of the path, Arnetta leading the way.

"You know," I said, "their leader will be there. Or they won't even be there. It's dark already. Last night the sun was still in the sky. I'm sure they're already finished."

Arnetta acted as if she hadn't heard me. I followed her gaze with my flashlight, and that's when I saw the squares of light in the darkness. The bathroom was just ahead.

But the girls were there. We could hear them before we could see them.

"Octavia and I will go in first so they'll think there's just two of us, then wait till I say, 'We're gonna teach you a lesson,'" Arnetta said. "Then, bust in. That'll surprise them."

"That's what I was supposed to say," Janice said.   125

Arnetta went inside, Octavia next to her. Janice followed, and the rest of us waited outside.

They were in there for what seemed like whole minutes, but something was wrong. Arnetta hadn't given the signal yet. I was with the girls outside when I heard one of the Troop 909 girls say, "NO. That did NOT happen!"

That was to be expected, that they'd deny the whole thing. What I hadn't expected was *the voice* in which the denial was said. The girl sounded as though her tongue were caught in her mouth. "That's a BAD word!" the girl continued. "We don't say BAD words!"

"Let's go in," Elise said.

"No," Drema said, "I don't want to. What if we get beat up?"   130

"Snot?" Elise turned to me, her flashlight blinding. It was the first time anyone had asked my opinion, though I knew they were just asking because they were afraid.

"I say we go inside, just to see what's going on."

"But Arnetta didn't give us the signal," Drema said. "She's supposed to say, 'We're gonna teach you a lesson,' and I didn't hear her say it."

"C'mon," I said. "Let's just go in."

We went inside. There we found the white girls—about five girls huddled up next to one   135
big girl. I instantly knew she was the owner of the voice we'd heard. Arnetta and Octavia
inched toward us as soon as we entered.

"Where's Janice?" Elise asked, then we heard a flush. "Oh."

"I think," Octavia said, whispering to Elise, "they're retarded."

"We ARE NOT retarded!" the big girl said, though it was obvious that she was. That they all were. The girls around her began to whimper.

"They're just pretending," Arnetta said, trying to convince herself. "I know they are."

Octavia turned to Arnetta. "Arnetta. Let's just leave."   140

Janice came out of a stall, happy and relieved, then she suddenly remembered her line,
pointed to the big girl, and said, "We're gonna teach you a lesson."

"Shut up, Janice," Octavia said, but her heart was not in it. Arnetta's face was set in a lost, deep
scowl. Octavia turned to the big girl and said loudly, slowly, as if they were all deaf, "We're going
to leave. It was nice meeting you, O.K.? You don't have to tell anyone that we were here. O.K.?"

"Why not?" said the big girl, like a taunt. When she spoke, her lips did not meet, her
mouth did not close. Her tongue grazed the roof of her mouth, like a little pink fish. "You'll
get in trouble. I know. *I know.*"

Arnetta got back her old cunning. "If you said anything, then you'd be a tattletale."

145   The girl looked sad for a moment, then perked up quickly. A flash of genius crossed her face. "I *like* tattletale."

"It's all right, girls. It's gonna be all right!" the 909 troop leader said. All of Troop 909 burst into tears. It was as though someone had instructed them all to cry at once. The troop leader had girls under her arm, and all the rest of the girls crowded about her. It reminded me of a hog I'd seen on a field trip, where all the little hogs gathered about the mother at feeding time, latching onto her teats. The 909 troop leader had come into the bathroom, shortly after the big girl had threatened to tell. Then the ranger came, then, once the ranger had radioed the station, Mrs. Margolin arrived with Daphne in tow.

The ranger had left the restroom area, but everyone else was huddled just outside, swatting mosquitoes.

"Oh. They *will* apologize," Mrs. Margolin said to the 909 troop leader, but she said this so angrily, I knew she was speaking more to us than to the other troop leader. "When their parents find out, every one a them will be on punishment."

"It's all right, it's all right," the 909 troop leader reassured Mrs. Margolin. Her voice lilted in the same way it had when addressing the girls. She smiled the whole time she talked. She was like one of those TV-cooking-show women who talk and dice onions and smile all at the same time.

150   "See. It could have happened. I'm not calling your girls fibbers or anything." She shook her head ferociously from side to side, her Egyptian-style pageboy flapping against her cheeks like heavy drapes. "It *could* have happened. See. Our girls are *not* retarded. They are *delayed* learners." She said this in a syrupy instructional voice, as though our troop might be delayed learners as well. "We're from the Decatur Children's Academy. Many of them just have special needs."

"Now we won't be able to walk to the bathroom by ourselves!" the big girl said.

"Yes you will," the troop leader said, "but maybe we'll wait till we get back to Decatur—"

"I don't want to wait!" the girl said. "I want my Independence badge!"

The girls in my troop were entirely speechless. Arnetta looked stoic, as though she were soon to be tortured but was determined not to appear weak. Mrs. Margolin pursed her lips solemnly and said, "Bless them, Lord. Bless them."

155   In contrast, the Troop 909 leader was full of words and energy. "Some of our girls are echolalic—" She smiled and happily presented one of the girls hanging onto her, but the girl widened her eyes in horror, and violently withdrew herself from the center of attention, sensing she was being sacrificed for the village sins. "Echolalic," the troop leader continued. "That means they will say whatever they hear, like an echo—that's where the word comes from. It comes from 'echo.'" She ducked her head apologetically, "I mean, not all of them have the most *progressive* of parents, so if they heard a bad word, they might have repeated it. But I guarantee it would not have been *intentional*."

Arnetta spoke. "I saw her say the word. I heard her." She pointed to a small girl, smaller than any of us, wearing an oversized T-shirt that read: "Eat Bertha's Mussels."

The troop leader shook her head and smiled, "That's impossible. She doesn't speak. She can, but she doesn't."

Arnetta furrowed her brow. "No. It wasn't her. That's right. It was *her*."

The girl Arnetta pointed to grinned as though she'd been paid a compliment. She was the only one from either troop actually wearing a full uniform: the mocha-colored A-line shift, the orange ascot, the sash covered with badges, though all the same one—the Try-It patch. She took a few steps toward Arnetta and made a grand sweeping gesture toward the sash. "See," she said, full of self-importance, "I'm a Brownie." I had a hard time imagining this girl calling anyone a "nigger"; the girl looked perpetually delighted, as though she would have cuddled up with a grizzly if someone had let her.

160   On the fourth morning, we boarded the bus to go home.

The previous day had been spent building miniature churches from Popsicle sticks. We hardly left the cabin. Mrs. Margolin and Mrs. Hedy guarded us so closely, almost no one talked for the entire day.

Even on the day of departure from Camp Crescendo, all was serious and silent. The bus ride began quietly enough. Arnetta had to sit beside Mrs. Margolin; Octavia had to sit beside her mother. I sat beside Daphne, who gave me her prize journal without a word of explanation.

"You don't want it?"

She shook her head no. It was empty.

Then Mrs. Hedy began to weep. "Octavia," Mrs. Hedy said to her daughter without looking at her, "I'm going to sit with Mrs. Margolin. All right?"

Arnetta exchanged seats with Mrs. Hedy. With the two women up front, Elise felt it safe to speak. "Hey," she said, then she set her face into a placid, vacant stare, trying to imitate that of a Troop 909 girl. Emboldened, Arnetta made a gesture of mock pride toward an imaginary sash, the way the girl in full uniform had done. Then they all made a game of it, trying to do the most exaggerated imitations of the Troop 909 girls, all without speaking, all without laughing loud enough to catch the women's attention.

Daphne looked down at her shoes, white with sneaker polish. I opened the journal she'd given me. I looked out the window, trying to decide what to write, searching for lines, but nothing could compare with what Daphne had written, *"My father, the veteran,"* my favorite line of all time. It replayed itself in my head, and I gave up trying to write.

By then, it seemed that the rest of the troop had given up making fun of the girls in Troop 909. They were now quietly gossiping about who had passed notes to whom in school. For a moment the gossiping fell off, and all I heard was the hum of the bus as we sped down the road and the muffled sounds of Mrs. Hedy and Mrs. Margolin talking about serious things.

"You know," Octavia whispered, "why did *we* have to be stuck at a camp with retarded girls? You know?"

"You know why," Arnetta answered. She narrowed her eyes like a cat. "My mama and I were in the mall in Buckhead, and this white lady just kept looking at us. I mean, like we were foreign or something. Like we were from China."

"What did the woman say?" Elise asked.

"Nothing," Arnetta said. "She didn't say nothing."

A few girls quietly nodded their heads.

"There was this time," I said, "when my father and I were in the mall and—"

"Oh shut up, Snot," Octavia said.

I stared at Octavia, then rolled my eyes from her to the window. As I watched the trees blur, I wanted nothing more than to be through with it all: the bus ride, the troop, school— all of it. But we were going home. I'd see the same girls in school the next day. We were on a bus, and there was nowhere else to go.

"Go on, Laurel," Daphne said to me. It seemed like the first time she'd spoken the whole trip, and she'd said my name. I turned to her and smiled weakly so as not to cry, hoping she'd remember when I'd tried to be her friend, thinking maybe that her gift of the journal was an invitation of friendship. But she didn't smile back. All she said was, "What happened?"

I studied the girls, waiting for Octavia to tell me to shut up again before I even had a chance to utter another word, but everyone was amazed that Daphne had spoken. The bus was silent. I gathered my voice. "Well," I said. "My father and I were in this mall, but I was the one doing the staring." I stopped and glanced from face to face. I continued. "There were these white people dressed like Puritans or something, but they weren't Puritans. They were Mennonites.° They're these people who, if you ask them to do a favor, like paint your porch or something, they have to do it. It's in their rules."

Mennonites: members of the Mennonite Church, USA, which has a number of related groups such as the Amish. Mennonite members are devoted to church, a simple lifestyle, an avoidance of modern conveniences, and service to others.

"That sucks," someone said.

180   "C'mon," Arnetta said. "You're lying."

"I am not."

"How do you know that's not just some story someone made up?" Elise asked, her head cocked full of daring. "I mean, who's gonna do whatever you ask?"

"It's not made up. I know because when I was looking at them, my father said, 'See those people? If you ask them to do something, they'll do it. Anything you want.'"

No one would call anyone's father a liar—then they'd have to fight the person. But Drema parsed her words carefully. "How does your *father* know that's not just some story? Huh?"

185   "Because," I said, "he went up to the man and asked him would he paint our porch, and the man said yes. It's their religion."

"Man, I'm glad I'm a Baptist," Elise said, shaking her head in sympathy for the Mennonites.

"So did the guy do it?" Drema asked, scooting closer to hear if the story got juicy.

"Yeah," I said. "His whole family was with him. My dad drove them to our house. They all painted our porch. The woman and girl were in bonnets and long, long skirts with buttons up to their necks. The guy wore this weird hat and these huge suspenders."

"Why," Arnetta asked archly, as though she didn't believe a word, "would someone pick a *porch*? If they'll do anything, why not make them paint the whole *house*? Why not ask for a hundred bucks?"

190   I thought about it, and then remembered the words my father had said about them painting our porch, though I had never seemed to think about his words after he'd said them.

"He said," I began, only then understanding the words as they uncoiled from my mouth, "it was the only time he'd have a white man on his knees doing something for a black man for free."

I now understood what he meant, and why he did it, though I didn't like it. When you've been made to feel bad for so long, you jump at the chance to do it to others. I remembered the Mennonites bending the way Daphne had bent when she was cleaning the restroom. I remembered the dark blue of their bonnets, the black of their shoes. They painted the porch as though scrubbing a floor. I was already trembling before Daphne asked quietly, "Did he thank them?"

I looked out the window. I could not tell which were the thoughts and which were the trees. "No," I said, and suddenly knew there was something mean in the world that I could not stop.

Arnetta laughed. "If I asked them to take off their long skirts and bonnets and put on some jeans, would they do it?"

195   And Daphne's voice, quiet, steady: "Maybe they would. Just to be nice."

QUESTIONS

1. Why is this story titled "Brownies"? Brownie/Girl Scouts, between the ages of 7 to 9, also sometimes called Girl Guides, are dedicated to taking care of the world around them. To what degree does this principle apply to the girls of Laurel's group, and to the girls of Troop 909? What might the situation of this story be like if the girls were considerably older than the girls in the Brownie troops?

2. How many major characters does the story have? Why is the narrator called "Snot" by the other girls? What is Snot's real name? When do we learn this? In the discussions about how to deal with the girls of Troop 909, what ideas does she present? Why does she not want to accompany the other girls as they go to meet Troop 909?

3. How does the story deal with problems in racism? What is the principal racist incident in the story? How is the incident resolved in the story?

4. What is the relationship between racism and Laurel's father's experience with the Mennonites? Analyze this section of the story in paragraphs 177–192. What is meant by Laurel's comment that "there was something mean in the world that I could not stop"?

5. In paragraph 193, Laurel, the narrator, says "I could not tell which were the thoughts and which were the trees." What does she mean by this observation? How might her comment be applicable to the thoughts of an older person? How might it indicate that racism is not easily erased from the consciousness of human beings?

WRITING ABOUT POINT OF VIEW

In an essay about point of view, you should explain how point of view contributes to making the work exactly as it is. As you prepare to write, therefore, consider language, authority and opportunity for observation, the involvement or detachment of the speaker, the selection of detail, interpretive commentaries, and narrative development. The following questions will help you get started.

Questions for Discovering Ideas

- How is the narration made to seem real or probable? Are the actions and speeches reported authentically, as they might be seen and reported in life?
- Is the narrator/speaker identifiable? What are the narrator's qualifications as an observer? How much of the story seems to result from the imaginative or creative powers of the narrator?
- How does the narrator/speaker perceive the time of the actions? If the predominant tense is the past, what relationship, if any, does the narrator establish between the past and the present (e.g., providing explanations, making conclusions)? If the tense is present, what effect does this tense have on your understanding of the story?
- To what extent does the point of view make the work interesting and effective?

First-Person Point of View

- What situation prompts the speaker to tell the story or explain the situation? What does the story tell us about the experience and interests of the narrator/speaker?
- Is the speaker talking to the reader, a listener, or herself? How does her audience affect what she is saying? Is the level of language appropriate to her and the situation? How much does she tell about herself?
- To what degree is the narrator involved in the action (i.e., as a major participant or major mover, minor participant, or nonparticipating observer)? Does he make himself the center of humor or admiration? How? Does he seem aware of changes he undergoes?

- Does the speaker criticize other characters? Why? Does she seem to report fairly and accurately what others have told her?
- How reliable is the speaker? Does the speaker seem to have anything to hide? Does it seem that he may be using the story for self-justification or exoneration? What effect does this complexity have on the story?

Second-Person Point of View

- What situation prompts the use of the second person? How does the speaker acquire the authority to explain things to the listener? How directly involved is the listener? What is the relationship between the speaker and listener? If the listener is indefinite, why does the speaker choose to use "you" as the basis of the narration?

Third-Person Point of View

- Does the author speak in an authorial voice, or does it seem that the author has adopted a special but unnamed voice for the work?
- What is the speaker's level of language (e.g., formal and grammatical, informal or intimate and ungrammatical)? Are actions, speeches, and explanations made fully or sparsely?
- From what apparent vantage point does the speaker report action and speeches? Does this vantage point make the characters seem distant or close? How much sympathy does the speaker express for the characters?
- To what degree is your interest centered on a particular character? Does the speaker give you thoughts and responses of this character (limited third person)?
- If the work is third-person omniscient, how extensive is this omniscience (e.g., all the characters or just a few)? Generally, what limitations or freedoms can be attributed to this point of view?
- What special kinds of knowledge does the narrator assume that the listeners or readers possess (e.g., familiarity with art, religion, politics, history, navigation, music, current or past social conditions)?
- How much dialogue is used in the story? Is the dialogue presented directly, as dramatic speech, or indirectly, as past-tense reports of speeches? What is your perception of the story's events as a result of the use of dialogue?

Tense

- What tense is mainly used throughout the story? If a single tense is used throughout (e.g., present, past), what is the effect of this constant use of tense?
- Does the story demonstrate a mixture of tenses? Why are the tenses mixed? What purpose is served by these variations? What is the effect of this mixture?
- Is any special use made of the future tense? What is the effect of this use on the present and past circumstances of the characters?

Organizing Your Essay About Point of View

Throughout your essay, you should develop your analysis of how the point of view determines such aspects as situation, form, general content, and language. The questions in the preceding section should help you decide how the point of view interacts with these other elements.

Begin by briefly stating the major influence of the point of view on the work. (*Examples:* "The omniscient point of view permits many insights into the major character," or "The first-person point of view makes the work seem like an exposé of backroom political deals.") How does the point of view make the work interesting and effective? How will your analysis support your central idea?

A fruitful and imaginative way to build your analysis and argument is to explore how changing the point of view might affect the presentation of the story. Let us consider Welty's "A Worn Path" (Chapter 5), which limits its third-person point of view to the circumstances of Phoenix Jackson, whose walk to Natchez is a mission of mercy for her invalid grandson. With the third-person limited focus as we have it, we derive just enough information about Phoenix to understand and sympathize deeply with her plight. If she herself were the narrator, however, we would get not an objective but rather a personalized view of her circumstances—and also perhaps a scattered and unfocused one—and the story would not be as powerful as it is. (Or it might become powerful through different means.) Two stories that would be vastly different if told from alternative perspectives are Oates's "Where Are You Going, Where Have you Been" and Tan's "Two Kinds" (Chapter 3). Just suppose—for a moment—that "Where Are You Going, Where Have You Been" were to have been written in the first person, not the third person, as though Connie or Arnold were telling the story. Either speaker would likely slant the narration and focus more on their individual feelings than on the action of the story and its outcome. Or, suppose that "Two Kinds" (Chapter 3), which is the first-person narration of Jing-Mei, were rather to be told in the first person by Jing-Mei's mother. Certainly the mother would explain her ambitions for her daughter fully and reasonably, and Jing-Mei herself would not be as comprehensible to readers as she is in the story as we have it.

You can see that this alternative approach to point of view requires creative imagination, for to carry it out you must, as it were, invade the author's space and speculate about the results of a point of view that the author did not choose. Considering such hypothetical alternative points of view deeply, however, will greatly enhance your analytical and critical abilities.

In your conclusion, evaluate the success of the point of view. Is it consistent, effective, truthful? What does it contribute to the nature and quality of the story? What particular benefits does the writer gain or lose (if anything) as a result of the point of view?

Illustrative Student Essay

Although underlined sentences are not recommended by MLA style, they are used in this illustrative essay as teaching tools to emphasize the central idea, thesis sentence, and topic sentences.

Garcia 1

Ashley Garcia

Professor Sutton

English 243

10 October 2014

Shirley Jackson's Dramatic Point of View in "The Lottery"°

[1]   The dramatic point of view in Shirley Jackson's "The Lottery" is essential to her success in rendering horror in the midst of the ordinary.* The story, however, is not only about horror: It may also be called a surprise story, an allegory, or a portrayal of human insensitivity and cruelty. But the validity of all other claims for "The Lottery" hinges on the author's control over point of view to make the events develop out of a seemingly everyday, matter-of-fact situation—a control that could not be easily maintained with another point of view. The success of Jackson's point of view is achieved through her characterization, selection of details, and diction.†

[2]   Because of the dramatic point of view, Jackson succeeds in presenting the villagers as ordinary folks attending a normal, festive event—in contrast to the horror of their real purpose. The contrast depends on Jackson's speaker, who is emotionally uninvolved and who tells only enough about the three hundred townsfolk and their customs to permit the conclusion that they are normal, common people. The principal character is a local housewife, Tessie Hutchinson, but the speaker presents little about her except that she is just like everyone else—an important characteristic when she, like any other person being singled out for punishment, objects not to the lottery itself but to the "unfairness" of the drawing. The same commonness applies also to the other characters, whose brief conversations are recorded but not analyzed. This

°This story appears on pages 130–39.
*Central idea.
†Thesis sentence.

Garcia 2

detached, reportorial method of making the villagers seem common and one-dimensional is fundamental to Jackson's dramatic point of view, and the cruel twist of the ending depends on the method.

<u>While there could be much description, Jackson's speaker omits some of the important details to conceal the lottery's horrifying purpose.</u> For example, the speaker presents enough information about the lottery to permit readers to understand its rules but does not disclose the grim prize for the "winner." The short saying "Lottery in June, corn be heavy soon" is mentioned as a remnant of a long-forgotten ritual, but the speaker does not explain anything more about this connection with scapegoatism and human sacrifice (142). None of these references seems unusual as the narrator first presents them, and it is only the conclusion that reveals, in reconsideration, their shocking ghastliness.

[3]

<u>Without doubt, a point of view other than the dramatic would spoil Jackson's concluding horror because it would require more explanatory detail.</u> A first-person speaker, for example, would not be credible without explaining the situation and revealing feelings that would give away the ending. Such an "I" speaker would need to say something like "The little boys gathered rocks but seemed not to be thinking about their forthcoming use in the stoning." But how would such detail affect the reader's response to the terrifying conclusion? Similarly, an omniscient narrator would need to include details about people's reactions (how could he or she be omniscient otherwise?). A more suitable alternative might be a limited omniscient point of view confined to, say, a stranger in town or one of the local children. But any intelligent stranger would be asking "giveaway" questions, and any child but a tiny tot would know about the lottery's sinister outcome. Either hypothetical point-of-view character would therefore require revealing the information too soon. The only conclusion is that Jackson's point of view—the dramatic—is best for this story. Because it permits her naturally to hold back crucial details, it is essential for the suspenseful delay of horror.

[4]

Garcia 3

[5]   Appropriate both to the suspenseful ending and also to the simple
character of the villagers is the speaker's language. The words are accurate
and descriptive but not elaborate. When Tessie Hutchinson appears, for
example, she dries "her hands on her apron" (141)—words that define
her role as a housewife. Most of these simple, bare words may be seen
as part of Jackson's technique of withholding detail to delay the reader's
understanding. A prime example is the pile of stones, which is in truth
a thoughtless and cruel preparation for the stoning, yet this conclusion
cannot be drawn from the easy words describing it:

> Bobby Martin had already stuffed his pockets full of stones, and the
> other boys soon followed his example, selecting the smoothest and
> roundest stones; Bobby and Harry Jones and Dickie Delacroix—the
> villagers pronounced this name "Dellacroy"—eventually made a great
> pile of stones in one corner of the square and guarded it against the
> raids of the other boys. (139)

[6]   Both the nicknames and the connotation of boyhood games divert
attention and obscure the horrible purpose of the stones. Even at the
end, the speaker uses the word "pebbles" to describe the stones given
to Tessie's son Davy (144). The implication is that Davy is playing a
game, not participating in the ritual stoning of his own mother!

[7]   Such masterly control over point of view is a major cause of
Jackson's success in "The Lottery." Her narrative method is to
establish the appearance of everyday, uneventful reality, which she
maintains up to the beginning of the last scene. She is so successful
that a reader's first response to the stoning is "Such an event could
not take place among such common, earthy folks." Yet it is this reality
that validates Jackson's vision. Horror is not to be found on moors
and in haunted castles but among everyday people like Jackson's three
hundred villagers. Without her control of the dramatic point of view,
there could be little of this power of suggestion, and it would not be
possible to claim such success for the story.

Garcia 4

Work Cited

Jackson, Shirley. "The Lottery." *Literature: An Introduction to Reading and Writing, Compact Edition*. Ed. Edgar V. Roberts and Robert Zweig. 6th ed. New York: Pearson, 2015. 130–39. Print.

Commentary on the Essay

The strategy of this essay is to argue for the importance of Jackson's dramatic point of view in building toward the shocking ending. Words of tribute throughout the essay are "success," "control," "essential," "appropriate," and "masterly." The introductory paragraph sets out three areas for exploration in the body: character, detail, and diction.

The body begins with paragraph 2, in which the aim is not to present a full character study (since the essay is not about character but point of view), but rather to discuss the ways in which the dramatic point of view enables the characters to be rendered. The argument of the paragraph is that the villagers are to be judged not as complete human beings but as "ordinary folks."

The second part of the body (paragraphs 3 and 4) emphasizes that the sparseness of detail permitted by the dramatic point of view aids Jackson in deferring conclusions about the horror of the drawing. Paragraph 4, which continues the topic of paragraph 3, shows how talking about alternative points of view may aid understanding of the story's actual point of view (see paragraph 4). The material for the paragraph is derived from notes speculating about whether Jackson's technique of withholding detail to build toward the concluding horror (the topic of paragraph 3) could be maintained with differing points of view. A combination of analysis and imagination is therefore at work in the paragraph.

The third section of the body (paragraph 5) emphasizes the idea that the flat, colorless diction defers awareness of what is happening; therefore the point of view is vital in the story's surprise and horror. The concluding paragraph (6) emphasizes the way in which general response to the story, and also its success, are conditioned by the detached, dramatic point of view.

USING SOURCES EFFECTIVELY

SUMMARY

Summary is a skill you will employ often in academic writing as you incorporate sources into your work. Sometimes, especially when discussing a secondary source your audience may not have read, summary provides the reader with an efficient general understanding of a work's elements and traits that is crucial in order for them to understand the point you are trying to make. When writing about a work of literature—a source your audience is likely very familiar with—your purpose is to provide a context for *your* reading of that work.

In writing about point of view in "The Lottery," Ashley Garcia chooses to summarize how an important general characteristic she observes permeates the story. In paragraph 3, she presents a broad picture of how Shirley Jackson uses spare, unemotional, everyday language to heighten the tension between the mundane surface facts of the plot and the terrible reality of what happens.

While there could be much description, Jackson's speaker omits some of the important details to conceal the lottery's horrifying purpose.

Garcia summarizes how the information is presented, basically highlighting what the author does *not* say, what she chooses to leave out.

For example, the speaker presents enough information about the lottery to permit readers to understand its rules but does not disclose the grim prize for the "winner." The short saying, "Lottery in June, corn be heavy soon" is mentioned as a remnant of a long-forgotten ritual, but the speaker does not explain anything more about this connection with scapegoatism and human sacrifice (142). None of these references seems unusual as the narrator first presents them, and it is only the conclusion that reveals, in reconsideration, their shocking ghastliness.

This brief quote is completely innocuous—reinforcing the point made by the summary.

The second and third sentences in Garcia's essay simply catalogue the plain facts of the story—not her opinions—presented to give readers a brief synopsis of the story in light of the author's technique. In the final sentence, she offers her analysis of how this becomes "shocking" at the story's conclusion. Writers must be sure that summaries are in their own words and do not stick too closely to the language of the work itself. Also, although summaries may provide context, they should not include opinions or interpretations. After providing a broader overview of the action or the characters, as depicted in the story, the writer may offer some informed analysis on what the work has attempted or achieved. (For more information on using summary when writing about fiction, see page 509.)

Writing Topics About Point of View

Writing Paragraphs

1. Write a narrative paragraph from the first-person point of view of one of these characters:

    a. Old Man Warner in "The Lottery": People ain't the way they used to be.

    b. Faith in "Young Goodman Brown" (Chapter 7): I don't understand why my husband is so sour and sullen all the time.

    c. Robert, the blind man, in "Cathedral": I met an interesting man tonight, but I don't know how he feels about me.

2. Consider the narrator of "Where Are You Going, Where Have You Been?" How does this person know about what Connie really thinks, regardless of what she says? Write a paragraph that sums up what the narrator seems to know about Connie's thoughts, fears, and desires.

Writing Essays

1. Write an essay about the proposition that people often have something to gain when they speak, and that therefore we need to be critical about what others tell us. Are they trying to change our judgments and opinions? Are they telling the truth? Are they leaving out any important details? Are they trying to sell us something? In your discussion, you may strengthen your ideas by referring to stories that you have been reading.

2. Write an essay about how Hawthorne's story "Young Goodman Brown" (Chapter 7) would be affected if told by a narrator with different knowledge, different interests, and different purposes for telling the story, such as the narrators of "A Worn Path" (Chapter 5) or Bierce's "An Occurrence at Owl Creek Bridge" (Chapter 1).

Creative Writing Assignment

1. Recall a childhood occasion on which you were punished. Write an explanation of the punishment as though you were the adult who was in the position of punishing you. Be sure to consider your childhood self objectively, in the third person. Present things from the viewpoint of the adult, and try to determine how the adult would have learned about your action, judged it, and decided on your punishment.

Library Assignment

1. In the reference section of your library, find two books on literary terms and concepts. How completely and clearly do these works explain the concept of point of view? With the aid of these books, together with the materials in this chapter, describe the interests and views of the narrators in Updike's "A & P" (Chapter 6), Bierce's "An Occurrence at Owl Creek Bridge," or another story of your choice. You should also consult Google, under "Glossary of Literary Terms," to see some of the many online resources available to you.

Chapter 3
Characters: The People in Fiction

AFTER STUDYING THIS MATERIAL, YOU SHOULD BE ABLE TO DO THE FOLLOWING:

- Understand the term *character* and the idea of character traits
- Describe how speeches illustrate character
- Illustrate how action reveals character traits
- Analyze how authors represent major and minor characters

Writers of fiction create narratives that enhance and deepen our understanding of human character and human life. In our own day, under the influences of such pioneers as Freud (1856–1939), Jung (1875–1961), and Skinner (1904–1990), the science of psychology has influenced both the creation and the study of literature. It is well known that Freud reinforced some of his psychological conclusions by referring to literary works, especially plays by Shakespeare. Widely known films such as *The Silence of the Lambs* (1991) and *American Psycho* (2000), together with the *Dexter* series on Showtime, have popularized the relationships between literary character and psychology. Without doubt, the presentation and understanding of character are two of the major aims of fiction, and literature generally.

In literature, a **character** is a verbal representation of a human being. Through action, speech, description, and commentary, authors portray characters who are worth caring about, cheering for, and even loving, although there are also characters you may laugh at, dislike, or even hate.

In a story or play emphasizing a major character, you may expect that each action or speech, no matter how small, is part of a total presentation of the complex combination of both the inner and the outer self that constitutes a human being. Whereas in life things may "just happen," in literature all actions, interactions, speeches, and observations are deliberate. Thus, you read about important actions like a long period of work and sacrifice (Maupassant's "The Necklace" in Part I), the uncertain relationship between a husband and wife (Carver's "Cathedral" in Chapter 2), acts of defiance and retribution (Poe's "The Masque of the Red Death" in Chapter 9). or a young man's poignant dream of freedom (Bierce's "An Occurrence at Owl Creek Bridge" in Chapter 1). By making such actions interesting, authors help you understand and appreciate not only their major characters but also life itself.

Character Traits

In studying a literary character, try to determine the character's outstanding *traits*. A **trait** is a quality of mind or habitual mode of behavior that is evident in both positive and negative ways, such as supplying moral support to friends and loved ones, being a person on whom people always rely, always wearing a sunny smile, listening to the thoughts and problems of others, avoiding eye contact, never repaying borrowed money, taking the biggest portions, or always thinking oneself the center of attention. Similarly, artists utilize elements such as facial characteristics and expressions to convey their judgments about the characteristics of their human subjects. If we study the facial expression of the bust of Lorenzo de Medici by Andrea del Verrocchio (c. 1435–1488), for example, we can see that Verrocchio is presenting a negative view of his subject. Lorenzo's firm mouth, his fixed stare, and his closely knit eyebrows suggest a high degree of pride and ruthlessness.

Sometimes, of course, the traits we encounter are minor and insignificant, but often a trait may be a person's *primary* characteristic (not only in fiction but also in life). Thus, characters may be ambitious or lazy, calm or anxious, aggressive or fearful, thoughtful or inconsiderate, open or secretive, confident or self-doubting, kind or cruel, quiet or noisy, idealistic or practical, careful or careless, impartial or biased, straightforward or underhanded, "winners" or "losers," and so on.

"Bust of Lorenzo de Medici," Florentine, fifteenth or sixteenth century, probably after a model by Andrea del Verrocchio and Orsino Benintendi. (*Photograph © Board of Trustees, National Gallery of Art, Washington, D.C. Samuel H. Kress Collection.*)

With this sort of list, to which you may add at will, you can analyze and develop conclusions about character. For example, Mathilde in Maupassant's "The Necklace" (Part I) indulges in thoughts of unattainable wealth and comfort, and is so swept up in her dreams that she scorns the comparatively good life she has with her reliable but dull husband. It is fair to say that this denial of reality is her major trait. It is also a major weakness, because Maupassant shows that her dream life harms her real life. Comparably, the character Miss Brill in Mansfield's "Miss Brill" (this chapter) is totally taken up by her unrealistically imaginary perceptions of her surroundings. All the actions she witnesses are filtered through these perceptions, and hence she is disconnected from her true circumstances. A contrast between a mother's dreams and a daughter's realism is brought out by Amy Tan in "Two Kinds" (this chapter). By similarly analyzing the thoughts, actions, and speeches of the literary characters you encounter, you can also draw conclusions about their nature and their qualities.

Distinguishing Between Circumstances and Character Traits

When you study a fictional person, distinguish between circumstances and character, for circumstances have value *only if you show that they demonstrate important traits*. Thus, if our good friend Sam wins a lottery, let us congratulate him on his luck; but the win does not say much about his *character*—not much, that is, unless you also point out that for years he has been regularly spending hundreds of dollars each week for lottery tickets. In other words, making the effort to win a lottery *is* a character trait but winning (or losing) *is not*.

Or, let us suppose that an author stresses the neatness of one character and the sloppiness of another. If you accept the premise that people care for their appearance according to choice—and that choices develop from character—you can use these details to make conclusions about a person's self-esteem or the lack of it. In short, when reading about characters in literature, look beyond circumstances, actions, and appearances, and try to determine what these things show about character. Always try to get from the outside to the inside, for it is the internal qualities of character that determine external behavior.

How Authors Disclose Character in Literature

Basically, authors rely on five ways of bringing characters to life. Remember that you can draw on your own knowledge and experience to make judgments about the qualities of the characters.

The Actions of Characters Reveal Their Qualities

What characters *do* is our best clue to understanding what they *are*. For example, inviting a wife's former boss to dinner may seem like an ordinary social event and most people will act courteously in such a situation. However, the husband in Carver's "Cathedral" shows the former boss both rudeness and kindness, revealing himself to be a far more interesting and complicated personality.

At the end, he struggles to make sense of the experience and is not sure how he feels about it. By contrast, in Tan's "Two Kinds," the narrator Jing-Mei, after her difficult childhood opposition to her mother's influences, reaches an emotional reconciliation when playing the piano her mother had bought for her and given to her.

Like most of us, fictional characters do not always understand why they do what they do, or why they think what they think. Nevertheless, their actions and thoughts provide insights into their characters. Miss Brill, of Mansfield's "Miss Brill" (this chapter), is alone on a Sunday afternoon—always alone—and she goes to a nearby public park to enjoy the passing crowds—her only weekly excitement. She eavesdrops on people sitting nearby, and draws silent conclusions about others, and in this way she imagines that she is a part of their lives. She even supposes that all those in the park are actors, along with herself, performing in a massive drama of life. Her unrealistic daydreams reveal her habitual solitude and pathetic vulnerability.

Actions may also signal qualities such as naiveté, weakness, deceit, a scheming personality, strong inner conflicts, sudden comprehension, or other growth or change. In Luke's "Parable of the Prodigal Son" (Chapter 7), the father's demonstrations of love toward his returning son illustrate his capacity for forgiveness. The intellectual boy in the dentist's office in Gaines's "The Sky is Gray" (this chapter) demonstrates an earnest commitment to ideas in which he believes. As he turns his cheek to permit the angry preacher to strike him a second time, he frustrates the preacher and emphatically asserts the value of his own intellect.

The Author's Descriptions Tell Us About Characters

Appearance and environment reveal much about a character's social and economic status, and they also tell us about character traits. Although Mathilde's dreams in Maupassant's "The Necklace" (Part I) are unrealizable and destructive, they also bring about her character strength that emerges in the story. Similarly, in Oates's "Where Are You Going, Where Have You Been" (Chapter 2) Connie's descriptions of her interactions with her mother and sister suggest her feelings about her place in the family, just as Arthur's clothes, car, and attitude indicate that he may be quirky, untrustworthy, or even dangerous.

What Characters Say Reveals What They Are Like

Although the speeches of most characters are functional—essential to keeping the action moving along—they provide material from which you may draw conclusions. When the second traveler of Hawthorne's "Young Goodman Brown" (Chapter 7) speaks, for example, he reveals his devious and deceptive nature even though outwardly he appears friendly. Jackie's parents and sister in O'Connor's "First Confession" (Chapter 6) speak angrily to Jackie, the stubborn child who, as an older person, is the story's narrator. Their anger suggests that they have little interest in Jackie's thoughts or concerns, but view their world through nothing more than ordinary and limited eyes. It is because of the unsympathetic nature of his family that Jackie is so delighted by the priest, who shows enough interest in Jackie to listen to him.

Often, characters use speech to hide their motives from others. The traveling pot mender in Steinbeck's "The Chrysanthemums" (Chapter 7) is deceptive and guileful. His sole aim is to have Elisa give him some work to do, and we may consequently believe nothing of what he says. The Federal scout in Bierce's "An Occurrence at Owl Creek Bridge" (Chapter 1) is pretending to be a Confederate soldier, and in speaking with the major character Farquhar, who is a landowner and a Confederate loyalist, he speaks confidentially but deceivingly. The result of the scout's lies is that Farquhar is fooled into believing that he will be safe if he sabotages the bridge at Owl Creek.

What Others Say Tells Us About a Character

By studying what characters say about each other, you can enhance your understanding not only of the character being discussed but also about the characters doing the talking.

Ironically, speeches often indicate something other than what the speakers intend, perhaps because of prejudice, stupidity, or foolishness. Nora, in O'Connor's "First Confession" (Chapter 6), tells about Jackie's lashing out at her with a butter knife, but in effect she describes the boy's individuality just as she also discloses her own spitefulness.

The Author, Speaking as a Storyteller or an Observer, May Present Judgments About Characters

What the author, speaking as a work's authorial voice, says about a character is usually accurate, and the authorial voice can be accepted factually. However, when the authorial voice interprets actions and characteristics, as in Hawthorne's "Young Goodman Brown" (Chapter 7), the author himself or herself assumes the role of a reader or critic, whose opinions are therefore open to question. For this reason, authors frequently avoid interpretations and devote their skill to arranging events and speeches so that readers can draw their own conclusions.

Types of Characters: Round and Flat

No writer can present an entire life history of a protagonist, nor can each character in a story get "equal time" for development. Accordingly, some characters grow to be full and alive, while others remain shadowy. The British novelist and critic E. M. Forster, in *Aspects of the Novel* (1927), calls the two major types "round" and "flat."

Round Characters Are Three-Dimensional and Lifelike

The basic trait of **round characters** is that we are told enough about them to permit the conclusion that they are three-dimensional, rounded, authentic, memorable, original, and true to life. They are the centers of our attention in most works of fiction. Their roundness and fullness are characterized by both individuality and unpredictability. It is true that, like all human beings, round characters have inner and sometimes hidden qualities that the circumstances of a story bring out, and therefore their full realization as characters is directly connected to the stories in which they live their lives. Mabel, of Lawrence's "The Horse Dealer's Daughter" (Chapter 8), is a round character. She has spent her life taking care of her father and his affairs, but following her father's death she sees no value in continuing to live. It is when she discovers a favorable change in her life that she becomes restored. Along with her new direction, however, she also anticipates new complications, and it is this complexity of response that especially marks the roundness and fullness of her character.

A complementary quality about round characters is that they are dynamic. **Dynamic characters** *recognize, change with*, or *adjust to* circumstances. Such changes may be shown in (1) an action or actions, (2) the realization of new strength and therefore the affirmation of previous decisions, (3) the acceptance of new conditions and the need for making changes, (4) the discovery of unrecognized truths, or (5) the reconciliation of the character to adverse conditions. A case in point is Farquhar in Bierce's "An Occurrence at Owl Creek Bridge" (Chapter 1). Although he is a "well-to-do" southern planter during the Civil War, for a number of reasons he has not been called to service in the Confederate Army. His life as a planter and slaveholder is stable, and would continue so; but when he learns about the possibility of dynamiting the bridge, he goes ahead and does it. By this action he undergoes change and growth; he is dynamic. Usually, dynamic character growth like this is good, but such growth, under some conditions, may bring a dynamic character to ruin, such as that experienced by Farquhar.

This is not to say that only round characters are dynamic, for less significant characters in a story may also undergo alteration as their circumstances change, as with Uncle Apolonio in Arredondo's "The Shunammite (Chapter 1) who develops from the loving, generous figure that raised Luisa into a more selfish, exploitative person who cares more about his own desires and comfort than about his niece. Often, dynamic character growth can be good, but such growth, under some conditions, may bring a dynamic character to ruin—a situation, as we have just seen, experienced by Farquhar of "An Occurrence at Owl Creek Bridge."

Because a round character plays a major role in a story, he or she is often called the **hero** or **heroine.** Some round characters are not particularly heroic, however, so it is preferable to use the more neutral word **protagonist** (the "first actor"). The protagonist is central to the action, moves against an **antagonist** (the "opposing actor"), and exhibits the ability to adapt to new situations.

Flat Characters Are Simple and One-Dimensional

Unlike round characters, **flat characters** are not complex, but are simple and one-dimensional. They may have no more than a single role to perform in a story, or they may be associated with no more than a single dominating idea. Most flat characters end pretty much where they begin, and for this reason we may think of them as **static,** not dynamic. Often their absence of growth or development results from lack of knowledge or understanding, or even from stupidity or insensitivity. Flat characters are not worthless in fiction, however, for they high-light the development of the round characters. In Joyce's "Araby" (Chapter 4), there is no character growth in Mangan's sister, and yet her presence is the major reason for the narrator's attitudes, and he travels to the Saturday night bazaar in order to please her.

Usually, flat characters are minor (e.g., relatives, acquaintances, functionar-ies), but not all minor characters are necessarily flat. Sometimes flat characters are prominent in certain types of literature, such as cowboy, police, and detective stories, where the focus is less on character than on performance. Such charac-ters might be lively and engaging, even though they do not undergo significant change and development. They must be strong, tough, and clever enough to per-form recurring tasks such as solving a crime, boxing with the major character, overcoming a villain, or finding a treasure. The term **stock character** is often used to describe characters in these repeating situations. To the degree that stock char-acters have many common traits, they are **representative** of their class or group. Such characters, with variations in names, ages, and sexes, have been constant in literature since the ancient Greeks. Some regular stock or representative char-acters are the insensitive father, the interfering mother, the sassy younger sister or brother, the greedy politician, the harassed boss, the resourceful cowboy or detective, the overbearing or henpecked husband, the submissive or nagging wife, the absent-minded professor, the angry police captain, the lovable drunk, and the town do-gooder.

Stock characters are usually also flat as long as they do no more than per-form their roles and exhibit conventional and nonindividual traits. Because they possess no attitudes except those of their class, they are often called **ste-reotype characters,** or characters who all seem to have been cast in the same mold.

When authors bring characters into strong focus, however, no matter what roles they perform, the characters emerge from flatness and move into roundness. For example, Maggie, in Alice Walker's "Everyday Use" (Chapter 10) initially appears to be a nondescript, unintelligent person of little interest, but as the story proceeds, we come to appreciate her depth of feeling and practical intelligence much more than we first did. At the same time, her sister, Dee (now Wangero), seems to be more successful and colorful than her family members but she even-tually shows herself to be selfish and inauthentic as she dismisses her family's importance as people in her quest to find a new, persona for herself. The evolution of these traits as the story progresses demonstrates the how writers can make flat characters develop into round characters.

Reality and Probability: Verisimilitude

Characters in fiction should be true to life. Therefore their actions, statements, and thoughts must all be what human beings are *likely* to do, say, and think under the conditions presented in the literary work. This is the standard of **verisimilitude, probability,** or **plausibility.** One may readily admit that there are people *in life* who perform tasks or exhibit characteristics that are difficult or seemingly impos-sible (such as always leading the team to victory, always getting A+'s on every

test, always being cheerful and helpful, or always understa
ers). However, such characters in fiction would not be true to
not fit within normal or usual behavior.

You should therefore distinguish between what characters ma
and what they *most frequently* or *most usually* do. Thus, in Maupassa
Necklace" (Part I), it is possible that Mathilde could be truthful and tell he
Jeanne Forrestier about the lost necklace. In light of Mathilde's pride and con
of self-respect, however, it is more in character for her and her husband to hide
the loss and borrow money for a replacement, even though they endure disastrous
financial hardship for ten years. Granted the possibilities of the story (either self-
sacrifice or the admission of fault or of a possible crime), the decision she makes
with her husband is the more *probable* one.

Nevertheless, probability does not rule out surprise or even exaggeration.
In Katherine Anne Porter's "The Jilting of Granny Weatherall" (Chapter 7), the
accomplishments of Granny—such as fencing a hundred acres of farmland all
by herself—do not seem impossible even if they do seem unlikely. But we learn
that when she was young she became compulsively determined to overcome the
shame of having been betrayed and left at the altar by her fiancé. It is therefore
probable, or at least not improbable, that she would be capable of the heavy labor
of building the fence.

Writers render probability of character in many ways. Works that attempt
to mirror life—realistic, naturalistic, or "slice of life" stories like Joyce's "Araby"
(Chapter 4)—set up a pattern of ordinary, everyday probability. Less realistic
conditions establish different frameworks of probability, in which characters are
expected to be unusual, as in Hawthorne's "Young Goodman Brown" (Chapter 7).
Because a major way of explaining this story is that Brown is having a nightmarish
psychotic trance, his bizarre and unnatural responses are probable.

You might also encounter works containing *supernatural* figures, such as the
second traveler in "Young Goodman Brown" (Chapter 7) and the unannounced
guest in Poe's "The Masque of the Red Death" (Chapter 9). You may wonder
whether such characters are probable or improbable. Usually, gods and goddesses
embody qualities of the best and most moral human beings, and devils like Hawthorne's guide take on attributes of the worst. However, you might remember that
the devil is often given dashing and engaging qualities so that he can deceive gull-
ible sinners and then drag them screaming into the fiery pits of hell. The friendliness of Brown's guide is therefore not an improbable trait. In judging characters
of this or any other type, your best standards are probability, consistency, and
believability.

Stories for Study

Ernest J. Gaines . . . . The Sky Is Gray, 184
Susan Glaspell . . . . A Jury of Her Peers, 202
Zora Neale Hurston. . . . . Spunk, 214
Katherine Mansfield . . . . Miss Brill, 218
Amy Tan. . . . . Two Kinds, 222

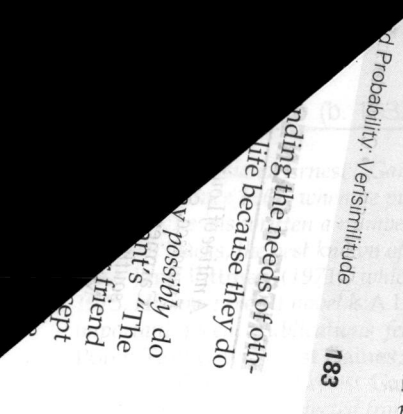

... has spent much of his life in San ... ished his first novel, Catherine ... f novels chronicling the lives of ... which is The Autobiography of ... was translated into German in ... sson Before Dying (1993). Two ... turing interviews with him are ... edited by Marcia Gau (1990), and ... ines, edited by John Lowe (1995). ... n his 1968 collection of stories, Bloodlines.

The Sky Is Gray (1968)

1

Go'n be coming in a few minutes. Coming round that bend down there full speed. And I'm go'n get out my handkerchief and wave it down, and we go'n get on it and go.

I keep on looking for it, but Mama don't look that way no more. She's looking down the road where we just come from. It's a long old road, and far 's you can see you don't see nothing but gravel. You got dry weeds on both sides, and you got trees on both sides, and fences on both sides, too. And you got cows in the pastures and they standing close together. And when we was coming out here to catch the bus I seen the smoke coming out of the cows's noses.

I look at my mama and I know what she's thinking. I been with Mama so much, just me and her, I know what she's thinking all the time. Right now it's home—Auntie and them. She's thinking if they got enough wood—if she left enough there to keep them warm till we get back. She's thinking if it go'n rain and if any of them go'n have to go out in the rain. She's thinking 'bout the hog—if he go'n get out, and if Ty and Val be able to get him back in. She always worry like that when she leaves the house. She don't worry too much if she leave me there with the smaller ones, 'cause she know I'm go'n look after them and look after Auntie and everything else. I'm the oldest and she say I'm the man.

I look at my mama and I love my mama. She's wearing that black coat and that black hat and she's looking sad. I love my mama and I want put my arm round her and tell her. But I'm not supposed to do that. She say that's weakness and that's crybaby stuff, and she don't want no crybaby round her. She don't want you to be scared, either. 'Cause Ty's scared of ghosts and she's always whipping him. I'm scared of the dark, too, but I make 'tend I ain't. I make 'tend I ain't 'cause I'm the oldest, and I got to set a good sample for the rest. I can't ever be scared and I can't ever cry. And that's why I never said nothing 'bout my teeth. It's been hurting me and hurting me close to a month now, but I never said it. I didn't say it 'cause I didn't want act like a crybaby, and 'cause I know we didn't have enough money to go have it pulled. But, Lord, it been hurting me. And look like it wouldn't start till at night when you was trying to get yourself little sleep. Then soon 's you shut your eyes—ummm-ummm, Lord, look like it go right down to your heartstring.

5   "Hurting, hanh?" Ty'd say.

I'd shake my head, but I wouldn't open my mouth for nothing. You open your mouth and let that wind in, and it almost kill you.

I'd just lay there and listen to them snore. Ty there, right 'side me, and Auntie and Val over by the fireplace. Val younger than me and Ty, and he sleeps with Auntie. Mama sleeps round the other side with Louis and Walker.

I'd just lay there and listen to them, and listen to that wind out there, and listen to that fire in the fireplace. Sometimes it'd stop long enough to let me get little rest. Sometimes it just hurt, hurt, hurt. Lord, have mercy.

2

Auntie knowed it was hurting me. I didn't tell nobody but Ty, 'cause we buddies and he ain't go'n tell nobody. But some kind of way Auntie found out. When she asked me, I told her no, nothing was wrong. But she knowed it all the time. She told me to mash up a piece of aspirin and wrap it in some cotton and jugg it down in that hole. I did it, but it didn't do no good. It stopped for a little while, and started right back again. Auntie wanted to tell Mama, but I told her, "Uh-uh." 'Cause I knowed we didn't have any money, and it just was go'n make her mad again. So Auntie told Monsieur Bayonne, and Monsieur Bayonne came over to the house and told me to kneel down 'side him on the fireplace. He put his finger in his mouth and made the Sign of the Cross on my jaw. The tip of Monsieur Bayonne's finger is some hard, 'cause he's always playing on that guitar. If we sit outside at night we can always hear Monsieur Bayonne playing on his guitar. Sometimes we leave him out there playing on the guitar.

Monsieur Bayonne made the Sign of the Cross over and over on my jaw, but that didn't do no good. Even when he prayed and told me to pray some, too, that tooth still hurt me. 10

"How you feeling?" he say.

"Same," I say.

He kept on praying and making the Sign of the Cross and I kept on praying, too.

"Still hurting?" he say.

"Yes, sir." 15

Monsieur Bayonne mashed harder and harder on my jaw. He mashed so hard he almost pushed me over on Ty. But then he stopped.

"What kind of prayers you praying, boy?" he say.

"Baptist," I say.

"Well, I'll be—no wonder that tooth still killing him. I'm going one way and he pulling the other. Boy, don't you know any <u>Catholic prayers</u>?"

"I know '<u>Hail Mary</u>,'" I say. 20

"Then you better start saying it."

"Yes, sir."

He started mashing on my jaw again, and I could hear him praying at the same time. And, sure enough, <del>after while it stopped hurting me.</del>

Me and Ty went outside where Monsieur Bayonne's two hounds was and we started playing with them. "Let's go hunting," Ty say. "All right," I say; and we went on back in the pasture. Soon the hounds got on a trail, and me and Ty followed them all 'cross the pasture and then back in the woods, too. And then they cornered this little old rabbit and killed him, and me and Ty made them get back, and we picked up the rabbit and started on back home. But my tooth had started hurting me again. It was hurting me plenty now, but I wouldn't tell Monsieur Bayonne. That night I didn't sleep a bit, and first thing in the morning Auntie told me to go back and let Monsieur Bayonne pray over me some more. Monsieur Bayonne was in his kitchen making coffee when I got there. Soon 's he seen me he knowed what was wrong.

"All right, kneel down there 'side that stove," he say. "And this time make sure you pray 25 Catholic. I don't know nothing 'bout that Baptist, and I don't want know nothing 'bout him."

3

Last night Mama say, "Tomorrow we going to town."

"It ain't hurting me no more," I say. "I can eat anything on it."

"<u>Tomorrow we going to town</u>," she say.

And after she finished eating, she got up and went to bed. She always go to bed early now. 'Fore Daddy went in the Army,° she used to stay up late. All of us sitting out on the gallery or round the fire. But now, look like soon 's she finish eating she go to bed.

30   This morning when I woke up, her and Auntie was standing 'fore the fireplace. She say: "Enough to get there and back. Dollar and a half to have it pulled. Twenty-five for me to go, twenty-five for him. Twenty-five for me to come back, twenty-five for him. Fifty cents left. Guess I get little piece of salt meat with that."

"Sure can use it," Auntie say. "White beans and no salt meat ain't white beans."

"I do the best I can," Mama say.

They was quiet after that, and I made 'tend I was still asleep.

"James, hit the floor," Auntie say.

35   I still made 'tend I was asleep. I didn't want them to know I was listening.

"All right," Auntie say, shaking me by the shoulder. "Come on. Today's the day."

I pushed the cover down to get out, and Ty grabbed it and pulled it back.

"You, too, Ty," Auntie say.

"I ain't getting no teef pulled," Ty say.

40   "Don't mean it ain't time to get up," Auntie say. "Hit it, Ty."

Ty got up grumbling.

"James, you hurry up and get in your clothes and eat your food," Auntie say. "What time y'all coming back?" she say to Mama.

"That 'leven o'clock bus," Mama say. "Got to get back in that field this evening."

"Get a move on you, James," Auntie say.

45   I went in the kitchen and washed my face, then I ate my breakfast. I was having bread and syrup. The bread was warm and hard and tasted good. And I tried to make it last a long time.

Ty came back there grumbling and mad at me.

"Got to get up," he say. "I ain't having no teefes pulled. What I got to be getting up for?"

Ty poured some syrup in his pan and got a piece of bread. He didn't wash his hands, neither his face, and I could see that white stuff in his eyes.

"You the one getting your teef pulled," he say. "What I got to get up for. I bet if I was getting a teef pulled, you wouldn't be getting up. Shucks; syrup again. I'm getting tired of this old syrup. Syrup, syrup, syrup. I'm go'n take with the sugar diabetes. I want me some bacon sometime."

50   "Go out in the field and work and you can have your bacon," Auntie say. She stood in the middle door looking at Ty. "You better be glad you got syrup. Some people ain't got that—hard's time is."

"Shucks," Ty say. "How can I be strong."

"I don't know too much 'bout your strength," Auntie say; "but I know where you go'n be hot at, you keep that grumbling up. James, get a move on you; your mama waiting."

I ate my last piece of bread and went in the front room. Mama was standing 'fore the fireplace warming her hands. I put on my coat and my cap, and we left the house.

4

I look down there again, but it still ain't coming. I almost say, "It ain't coming yet," but I keep my mouth shut. 'Cause that's something else she don't like. She don't like for you to say something just for nothing. She can see it ain't coming. I can see it ain't coming, so why

---

°*Daddy went in the Army*: The time of the story is about 1942, early in World War II, when millions of men were being drafted into the armed services.

say it ain't coming. I don't say it, I turn and look at the river that's back of us. It's so cold the smoke's just raising up from the water. I see a bunch of pool-doos° not too far out—just on the other side of the lilies. I'm wondering if you can eat pool-doos. I ain't too sure, 'cause I ain't never ate none. But I done ate owls and blackbirds, and I done ate redbirds,° too. I didn't want kill the redbirds, but she made me kill them. They had two of them back there. One in my trap, one in Ty's trap. Me and Ty was go'n play with them and let them go, but she made me kill them 'cause we needed the food.

"I can't," I say. "I can't."   55

"Here," she say. "Take it."

"I can't," I say. "I can't. I can't kill him, Mama, please."

"Here," she say. "Take this fork, James."

"Please, Mama, I can't kill him," I say.

I could tell she was go'n hit me. I jerked back, but I didn't jerk back soon enough.   60

"Take it," she say.

I took it and reached in for him, but he kept on hopping to the back.

"I can't, Mama," I say. The water just kept on running down my face. "I can't," I say.

"Get him out of there," she say.

I reached in for him and he kept on hopping to the back. Then I reached in farther, and   65
he pecked me on the hand.

"I can't, Mama," I say.

She slapped me again.

I reached in again, but he kept on hopping out my way. Then he hopped to one side and I reached there. The fork got him on the leg and I heard his leg pop. I pulled my hand out 'cause I had hurt him.

"Give it here," she say, and jerked the fork out my hand.

She reached in and got the little bird right in the neck. I heard the fork go in his neck, and   70
I heard it go in the ground. She brought him out and helt him right in front of me.

"That's one," she say. She shook him off and gived me the fork. "Get the other one."

"I can't, Mama," I say, "I'll do anything, but don't make me do that."

She went to the corner of the fence and broke the biggest switch over there she could find. I knelt 'side the trap, crying.

"Get him out of there," she say.

"I can't, Mama."   75

She started hitting me 'cross the back. I went down on the ground, crying.

"Get him," she say.

"Octavia?" Auntie say.

'Cause she had come out of the house and she was standing by the tree looking at us.

"Get him out of there," Mama say.   80

"Octavia," Auntie say, "explain to him. Explain to him. Just don't beat him. Explain to him."

But she hit me and hit me and hit me.

I'm still young—I ain't no more than eight; but I know now; I know why I had to do it. (They was so little, though. They was so little. I 'member how I picked the feathers off them and cleaned them and helt them over the fire. Then we all ate them. Ain't had but a little bitty piece each, but we all had a little bitty piece, and everybody just looked at me 'cause they was so proud.) Suppose she had to go away? That's why I had to do it. Suppose she

---

°*pool-doos: Pool-doo* is a local Louisiana pronunciation of French *poule d'eau*, or "bird of water." It refers to a marsh hen, or bird of the rail family—most likely the American coot.
°*redbirds:* cardinals.

had to go away like Daddy went away? Then who was go'n look after us? They had to be somebody left to carry on. I didn't know it then, but I know it now. Auntie and Monsieur Bayonne talked to me and made me see.

5

Time I see it I get out my handkerchief and start waving. It's still 'way down there, but I keep waving anyhow. Then it come up and stop and me and Mama get on. Mama tell me go sit in the back while she pay. I do like she say, and the people look at me. When I pass the little sign that say "White" and "Colored," I start looking for a seat. I just see one of them back there, but I don't take it, 'cause I want my mama to sit down herself. She comes in the back and sit down, and I lean on the seat. They got seats in the front, but I know I can't sit there, 'cause I have to sit back of the sign. Anyhow, I don't want sit there if my mama go'n sit back here.

85   They got a lady sitting 'side my mama and she looks at me and smiles little bit. I smile back, but I don't open my mouth, 'cause the wind'll get in and make that tooth ache. The lady take out a pack of gum and reach me a slice, but I shake my head. The lady just can't understand why a little boy'll turn down gum, and she reach me a slice again. This time I point to my jaw. The lady understands and smiles little bit, and I smile little bit, but I don't open my mouth, though.

They got a girl sitting 'cross from me. She got on a red overcoat and her hair's plaited in one big plait. First, I make 'tend I don't see her over there, but then I start looking at her little bit. She make 'tend she don't see me, either, but I catch her looking that way. She got a cold, and every now and then she h'ist that little handkerchief to her nose. She ought to blow it, but she don't. Must think she's too much a lady or something.

Every time she h'ist that little handkerchief, the lady 'side her say something in her ear. She shakes her head and lays her hands in her lap again. Then I catch her kind of looking where I'm at. I smile at her little bit. But think she'll smile back? Uh-uh. She just turn up her little old nose and turn her head. Well, I show her both of us can turn us head. I turn mine too and look out at the river.

The river is gray. The sky is gray. They have pool-doos on the water. The water is wavy, and the pool-doos go up and down. The bus go round a turn, and you got plenty trees hiding the river. Then the bus go round another turn, and I can see the river again.

I look toward the front where all the white people sitting. Then I look at that little old gal again. I don't look right at her, 'cause I don't want all them people to know I love her. I just look at her little bit, like I'm looking out that window over there. But she knows I'm looking that way, and she kind of look at me, too. The lady sitting 'side her catch her this time, and she leans over and says something in her ear.

90   "I don't love him nothing," that little old gal says out loud.

Everybody back there hear her mouth, and all of them look at us and laugh.

"I don't love you, either," I say. "So you don't have to turn up your nose, Miss."

"You the one looking," she say.

"I wasn't looking at you," I say. "I was looking out that window, there."

95   "Out that window, my foot," she say. "I seen you. Everytime I turned round you was looking at me."

"You must of been looking yourself if you seen me all them times," I say.

"Shucks," she say, "I got me all kind of boyfriends."

"I got girlfriends, too," I say.

"Well, I just don't want you getting your hopes up," she say.

100   I don't say no more to that little old gal 'cause I don't want have to bust her in the mouth. I lean on the seat where Mama sitting, and I don't even look that way no more. When we get to Bayonne, she jugg her little old tongue out at me. I make 'tend I'm go'n hit her, and she duck down 'side her mama. And all the people laugh at us again.

6

Me and Mama get off and start walking in town. Bayonne is a little bitty town. Baton Rouge is a hundred times bigger than Bayonne. I went to Baton Rouge once—me, Ty, Mama, and Daddy. But that was 'way back yonder, 'fore Daddy went in the Army. I wonder when we go'n see him again. I wonder when. Look like he ain't ever coming back home. . . . Even the pavement all cracked in Bayonne. Got grass shooting right out the sidewalk. Got weeds in the ditch, too; just like they got at home.

It's some cold in Bayonne. Look like it's colder than it is home. The wind blows in my face, and I feel that stuff running down my nose. I sniff. Mama says use that handkerchief. I blow my nose and put it back.

We pass a school and I see them white children playing in the yard. Big old red school, and them children just running and playing. Then we pass a café, and I see a bunch of people in there eating. I wish I was in there 'cause I'm cold. Mama tells me keep my eyes in front where they belong.

We pass stores that's got dummies, and we pass another café, and then we pass a shoe shop, and that bald-head man in there fixing on a shoe. I look at him and I butt into that white lady, and Mama jerks me in front and tells me stay there.

We come up to the courthouse, and I see the flag waving there. This flag ain't like the   105
one we got at school. This one here ain't got but a handful of stars.° One at school got a big pile of stars—one for every state. We pass it and we turn and there it is—the dentist office. Me and Mama go in, and they got people sitting everywhere you look. They even got a little boy in there younger than me.

Me and Mama sit on that bench, and a white lady come in there and ask me what my name is. Mama tells her and the white lady goes on back. Then I hear somebody hollering in there. Soon 's that little boy hear him hollering, he starts hollering, too. His mama pats him and pats him, trying to make him hush up, but he ain't thinking 'bout his mama.

The man that was hollering in there comes out holding his jaw. He is a big old man and he's wearing overalls and a jumper.

"Got it, hanh?" another man asks him.

The man shakes his head—don't want open his mouth.

"Man, I thought they was killing you in there," the other man says. "Hollering like a pig   110
under a gate."

The man don't say nothing. He just heads for the door, and the other man follows him.

"John Lee," the white lady says. "John Lee Williams."

The little boy juggs his head down in his mama's lap and holler more now. His mama tells him go with the nurse, but he ain't thinking 'bout his mama. His mama tells him again, but he don't even hear her. His mama picks him up and takes him in there, and even when the white lady shuts the door I can still hear little old John Lee.

"I often wonder why the Lord let a child like that suffer," a lady says to my mama. The lady's sitting right in front of us on another bench. She's got on a white dress and a black sweater. She must be a nurse or something herself, I reckon.

"Not us to question," a man says.   115

"Sometimes I don't know if we shouldn't," the lady says.

"I know definitely we shouldn't," the man says. The man looks like a preacher. He's big and fat and he's got on a black suit. He's got a gold chain, too.

"Why?" the lady says.

"Why anything?" the preacher says.

°*handful of stars:* The Confederate flag contains thirteen stars. At the time of the story, the American flag had forty-eight.

120   "Yes," the lady says. "Why anything?"

"Not us to question," the preacher says.

The lady looks at the preacher a little while and looks at Mama again.

"And look like it's the poor who suffers the most," she says. "I don't understand it."

"Best not to even try," the preacher says. "He works in mysterious ways—wonders to perform."°

125   Right then little John Lee bust out hollering, and everybody turn they head to listen.

"He's not a good dentist," the lady says. "Dr. Robillard is much better. But more expensive. That's why most of the colored people come here. The white people go to Dr. Robillard. Y'all from Bayonne?"

"Down the river," my mama says. And that's all she go'n say, 'cause she don't talk much. But the lady keeps on looking at her, and so she says, "Near Morgan."

"I see," the lady says.

7

"That's the trouble with the black people in this country today," somebody else says. This one here's sitting on the same side me and Mama's sitting, and he is kind of sitting in front of that preacher. He looks like a teacher or somebody that goes to college. He's got on a suit, and he's got a book that he's been reading. "We don't question is exactly our problem," he says. "We should question and question and question—question everything."

130   The preacher just looks at him a long time. He done put a toothpick or something in his mouth, and he just keeps on turning it and turning it. You can see he don't like that boy with that book.

"Maybe you can explain what you mean," he says.

"I said what I meant," the boy says. "Question everything. Every stripe, every star, every word spoken. Everything."

"It 'pears to me that this young lady and I was talking 'bout God, young man," the preacher says.

"Question Him, too," the boys says.

135   "Wait," the preacher says. "Wait now."

"You heard me right," the boy says. "His existence as well as everything else. Everything."

The preacher just looks across the room at the boy. You can see he's getting madder and madder. But mad or no mad, the boy ain't thinking 'bout him. He looks at that preacher just 's hard 's the preacher looks at him.

"Is this what they coming to?" the preacher says. "Is this what we educating them for?"

"You're not educating me," the boy says. "I wash dishes at night so that I can go to school in the day. So even the words you spoke need questioning."

140   The preacher just looks at him and shakes his head.

"When I come in this room and seen you there with your book, I said to myself, 'There's an intelligent man.' How wrong a person can be."

"Show me one reason to believe in the existence of a God," the boy says.

"My heart tells me," the preacher says.

"'My heart tells me,'" the boys says. "'My heart tells me.' Sure, 'My heart tells me.' And as long as you listen to what your heart tells you, you will have only what the white man gives you and nothing more. Me, I don't listen to my heart. The purpose of the heart is to pump blood throughout the body, and nothing else."

°*He works . . . perform*: an allusion to the well-known hymn "God moves in a mysterious way / His wonders to perform," by William Cowper (1731–1800).

"Who's your paw, boy?" the preacher says.   145

"Why?"

"Who is he?"

"He's dead."

"And you mom?"

"She's in Charity Hospital with pneumonia. Half killed herself, working for nothing."   150

"And 'cause he's dead and she's sick, you mad at the world?"

"I'm not mad at the world. I'm questioning the world. I'm questioning it with cold logic, sir. What do words like Freedom, Liberty, God, White, Colored mean? I want to know. That's why you are sending us to school, to read and to ask questions. And because we ask these questions, you call us mad. No sir, it is not us who are mad."

"You keep saying 'us'?"

"'Us.' Yes—us. I'm not alone."

The preacher just shakes his head. Then he looks at everybody in the room—everybody.   155
Some of the people look down at the floor, keep from looking at him. I kind of look 'way myself, but soon 's I know he done turn his head, I look that way again.

"I'm sorry for you," he says to the boy.

"Why?" the boy says. "Why not be sorry for yourself? Why are you so much better off than I am? Why aren't you sorry for these other people in here? Why not be sorry for the lady who had to drag her child into the dentist office? Why not be sorry for the lady sitting on that bench over there? Be sorry for them. Not for me. Some way or the other I'm going to make it."

"No, I'm sorry for you," the preacher says.

"Of course, of course," the boy says, nodding his head. "You're sorry for me because I rock that pillar you're leaning on."

"You can't ever rock the pillar I'm leaning on, young man. It's stronger than anything   160
man can ever do."

"You believe in God because a man told you to believe in God," the boy says. "A white man told you to believe in God. And why? To keep you ignorant so he can keep his feet on your neck."

"So now we the ignorant?" the preacher says.

"Yes," the boy says. "Yes." And he opens his book again.

The preacher just looks at him sitting there. The boy done forgot all about him. Everybody else make 'tend they done forgot the squabble, too.

Then I see that preacher getting up real slow. Preacher's a great big old man and he got   165
to brace himself to get up. He comes over where the boy is sitting.

He just stands there a little while looking down at him, but the boy don't raise his head.

"Get up, boy," preacher says.

The boy looks up at him, then he shuts his book real slow and stands up. Preacher just hauls back and hit him in the face. The boy falls back 'gainst the wall, but he straightens himself up and looks right back at that preacher.

"You forgot the other cheek°," he says.

The preacher hauls back and hit him again on the other side. But this time the boy braces   170
himself and don't fall.

"That hasn't changed a thing," he says.

The preacher just looks at the boy. The preacher's breathing real hard like he just run up a big hill. The boy sits down and opens his book again.

°*other cheek:* Matthew 5:39.

"I feel sorry for you," the preacher says. "I never felt so sorry for a man before."

The boy makes 'tend he don't even hear that preacher. He keeps on reading his book. The preacher goes back and gets his hat off the chair.

175 "Excuse me," he says to us. "I'll come back some other time. Y'all, please excuse me."

And he looks at the boy and goes out the room. The boy h'ist his hand up to his mouth one time to wipe 'way some blood. All the rest of the time he keeps on reading. And nobody else in there say a word.

8

Little John Lee and his mama come out the dentist office, and the nurse calls somebody else in. Then little bit later they come out, and the nurse calls another name. But fast 's she calls somebody in there, somebody else comes in the place where we sitting, and the room stays full.

The people coming in now, all of them wearing big coats. One of them says something 'bout sleeting, another one says he hope not. Another one says he think it ain't nothing but rain. 'Cause, he says, rain can get awful cold this time of year.

All round the room they talking. Some of them talking to people right by them, some of them talking to people clear 'cross the room, some of them talking to anybody'll listen. It's a little bitty room, no bigger than us kitchen, and I can see everybody in there. The little old room's full of smoke, 'cause you got two old men smoking pipes over by that side door. I think I feel my tooth thumping me some, and I hold my breath and wait. I wait and wait, but it don't thump me no more. Thank God for that.

180 I feel like going to sleep, and I lean back 'gainst the wall. But I'm scared to go to sleep. Scared 'cause the nurse might call my name and I won't hear her. And Mama might go to sleep, too, and she'll be mad if neither one of us heard the nurse.

I look up at Mama. I love my mama. I love my mama. And when cotton come I'm go'n get her a new coat. And I ain't go'n get a black one, either. I think I'm go'n get her a red one.

"They got some books over there," I say. "Want read one of them?"

Mama looks at the books, but she don't answer me.

"You got yourself a little man there," the lady says.

185 Mama don't say nothing to the lady, but she must've smiled, 'cause I seen the lady smiling back. The lady looks at me a little while, like she's feeling sorry for me.

"You sure got that preacher out here in a hurry," she says to that boy.

The boy looks up at her and looks in his book again. When I grow up I want be just like him. I want clothes like that and I want keep a book with me, too.

"You really don't believe in God?" the lady says.

"No," he says.

190 "But why?" the lady says.

"Because the wind is pink," he says.

"What?" the lady says.

The boy don't answer her no more. He just reads in his book.

"Talking 'bout the wind is pink," that old lady says. She's sitting on the same bench with the boy and she's trying to look in his face. The boy makes 'tend the old lady ain't even there. He just keeps on reading. "Wind is pink," she says again. "Eh, Lord, what children go'n be saying next?"

195 The lady 'cross from us bust out laughing.

"That's a good one," she says. "The wind is pink. Yes sir, that's a good one."

"Don't you believe the wind is pink?" the boy says. He keeps his head down in the book.

"Course I believe it, honey," the lady says. "Course I do." She looks at us and winks her eye. "And what color is grass, honey?"

"Grass? Grass is black."

She bust out laughing again. The boy looks at her.

"Don't you believe grass is black?" he says.

The lady quits her laughing and looks at him. Everybody else looking at him, too. The place quiet, quiet.

"Grass is green, honey," the lady says. "It was green yesterday, it's green today, and it's go'n be green tomorrow."

"How do you know it's green?"

"I know because I know."

"You don't know it's green," the boy says. "You believe it's green because someone told you it was green. If someone had told you it was black you'd believe it was black."

"It's green," the lady says. "I know green when I see green."

"Prove it's green," the boy says.

"Sure, now," the lady says. "Don't tell me it's coming to that."

"It's coming to just that," the boy says. "Words mean nothing. One means no more than the other."

"That's what it all coming to?" that old lady says. That old lady got on a turban and she got on two sweaters. She got a green sweater under a black sweater. I can see the green sweater 'cause some of the buttons on the other sweater's missing.

"Yes, ma'am," the boy says. "Words mean nothing. Action is the only thing. Doing. That's the only thing."

"Other words, you want the Lord to come down here and show Hisself to you?" she says.

"Exactly, ma'am," he says.

"You don't mean that, I'm sure?" she says.

"I do, ma'am," he says.

"Done, Jesus," the old lady says, shaking her head.

"I didn't go 'long with that preacher at first," the other lady says; "but now—I don't know. When a person say the grass is black, he's either a lunatic or something's wrong."

"Prove to me that it's green," the boy says.

"It's green because the people say it's green."

"Those same people say we're citizens of these United States," the boy says.

"I think I'm a citizen," the lady says.

"Citizens have certain rights," the boy says. "Name me one right that you have. One right, granted by the Constitution, that you can exercise in Bayonne."

The lady don't answer him. She just looks at him like she don't know what he's talking 'bout. I know I don't.

"Things changing," she says.

"Things are changing because some black men have begun to think with their brains and not their hearts," the boy says.

"You trying to say these people don't believe in God?"

"I'm sure some of them do. Maybe most of them do. But they don't believe that God is going to touch these white people's hearts and change things tomorrow. Things change through action. By no other way."

Everybody sit quiet and look at the boy. Nobody says a thing. Then the lady 'cross the room from me and Mama just shakes her head.

"Let's hope that not all your generation feel the same way you do," she says.

"Think what you please, it doesn't matter," the boy says. "But it will be men who listen to their heads and not their hearts who will see that your children have a better chance than you had."

"Let's hope they ain't all like you, though," the old lady says. "Done forgot the heart absolutely."

"Yes ma'am, I hope they aren't all like me," the boy says. "Unfortunately, I was born too late to believe in your God. Let's hope that the ones who come after will have your faith—if not in your God, then in something else, something definitely that they can lean on. I haven't anything. For me, the wind is pink, the grass is black."

9

235   The nurse comes in the room where we all sitting and waiting and says the doctor won't take no more patients till one o'clock this evening.° My mama jumps up off the bench and goes up to the white lady.

"Nurse, I have to go back in the field this evening," she says.

"The doctor is treating his last patient now," the nurse says. "One o'clock this evening."

"Can I at least speak to the doctor?" my mama asks.

"I'm his nurse," the lady says.

240   "My little boy's sick," my mama says. "Right now his tooth almost killing him."

The nurse looks at me. She's trying to make up her mind if to let me come in. I look at her real pitiful. The tooth ain't hurting me at all, but Mama say it is, so I make 'tend for her sake.

"This evening," the nurse says, and goes on back in the office.

"Don't feel 'jected, honey," the lady says to Mama. "I been round them a long time—they take you when they want to. If you was white, that's something else; but we the wrong color."

Mama don't say nothing to the lady, and me and her go outside and stand 'gainst the wall. It's cold out there. I can feel that wind going through my coat. Some of the other people come out of the room and go up the street. Me and Mama stand there a little while and we start walking. I don't know where we going. When we come to the other street we just stand there.

245   "You don't have to make water, do you?" Mama says.

"No, ma'am," I say.

We go on up the street. Walking real slow. I can tell Mama don't know where she's going. When we come to a store we stand there and look at the dummies. I look at a little boy wearing a brown overcoat. He's got on brown shoes, too. I look at my old shoes and look at his'n again. You wait till summer, I say.

Me and Mama walk away. We come up to another store and we stop and look at them dummies, too. Then we go on again. We pass a café where the white people in there eating. Mama tells me keep my eyes in front where they belong, but I can't help from seeing them people eat. My stomach starts to growling 'cause I'm hungry. When I see people eating, I get hungry; when I see a coat, I get cold.

A man whistles at my mama when we go by a filling station. She makes 'tend she don't even see him. I look back and I feel like hitting him in the mouth. If I was bigger, I say; if I was bigger, you'd see.

250   We keep on going. I'm getting colder and colder, but I don't say nothing. I feel that stuff running down my nose and I sniff.

"That rag," Mama says.

I get it out and wipe my nose. I'm getting cold all over now—my face, my hands, my feet, everything. We pass another little café, but this'n for white people, too, and we can't go in there, either. So we just walk. I'm so cold now I'm 'bout ready to say it. If I knowed where we was going I wouldn't be so cold, but I don't know where we going. We go, we go, we go. We walk clean out of Bayonne. Then we cross the street and we come back. Same thing

---

°evening: local dialect for *afternoon*.

I seen when I got off the bus this morning. Same old trees, same old walk, same old weeds, same old cracked pave—same old everything.

I sniff again.

"That rag," Mama says.

I wipe my nose real fast and jugg that handkerchief back in my pocket 'fore my hand 255
gets too cold. I raise my head and I can see David's hardware store. When we come up to it, we go in. I don't know why, but I'm glad.

It's warm in there. It's so warm in there you don't ever want to leave. I look for the heater, and I see it over by them barrels. Three white men standing round the heater talking in Creole.° One of them comes over to see what my mama want.

"Got any axe handles?" she says.

Me, Mama and the white man start to the back, but Mama stops me when we come up to the heater. She and the white man go on. I hold my hands over the heater and look at them. They go all the way to the back, and I see the white man pointing to the axe handles 'gainst the wall. Mama takes one of them and shakes it like she's trying to figure how much it weighs. Then she rubs her hand over it from one end to the other end. She turns it over and looks at the other side, then she shakes it again, and shakes her head and puts it back. She gets another one and she does it just like she did the first one, then she shakes her head. Then she gets a brown one and do it that, too. But she don't like this one, either. Then she gets another one, but 'fore she shakes it or anything, she looks at me. Look like she's trying to say something to me, but I don't know what it is. All I know is I done got warm now and I'm feeling right smart better. Mama shakes this axe handle just like she did the others, and shakes her head and says something to the white man. The white man just looks at his pile of axe handles, and when Mama pass him to come to the front, the white man just scratch his head and follows her. She tells me come on and we go on out and start walking again.

We walk and walk, and no time at all I'm cold again. Look like I'm colder now 'cause I can still remember how good it was back there. My stomach growls and I suck it in to keep Mama from hearing it. She's walking right 'side me, and it growls so loud you can hear it a mile. But Mama don't say a word.

10

When we come up to the courthouse, I look at the clock. It's got quarter to twelve. Mean we 260
got another hour and a quarter to be out here in the cold. We go and stand 'side a building. Something hits my cap and I look up at the sky. Sleet's falling.

I look at Mama standing there. I want stand close 'side her, but she don't like that. She say that's crybaby stuff. She say you got to stand for yourself, by yourself.

"Let's go back to that office," she says.

We cross the street. When we get to the dentist office I try to open the door, but I can't. I twist and twist, but I can't. Mama pushes me to the side and she twist the knob, but she can't open the door, either. She turns 'way from the door. I look at her, but I don't move and I don't say nothing. I done seen her like this before and I'm scared of her.

"You hungry?" she says. She says it like she's mad at me, like I'm the cause of everything.

"No, ma'am," I say. 265

"You want eat and walk back, or you rather don't eat and ride?"

"I ain't hungry," I say.

I ain't just hungry, but I'm cold, too. I'm so hungry and cold I want to cry. And look like I'm getting colder and colder. My feet done got numb. I try to work my toes, but I don't

---

°*Creole:* the French Cajun dialect in Louisiana.

even feel them. Look like I'm go'n die. Look like I'm go'n stand right here and freeze to death. I think 'bout home. I think 'bout Val and Auntie and Ty and Louis and Walker. It's 'bout twelve o'clock and I know they eating dinner now. I can hear Ty making jokes. He done forgot 'bout getting up early this morning and right now he's probably making jokes. Always trying to make somebody laugh. I wish I was right there listening to him. Give anything in the world if I was home round the fire.

"Come on," Mama says.

270   We start walking again. My feet so numb I can't hardly feel them. We turn the corner and go on back up the street. The clock on the courthouse starts hitting for twelve.

The sleet's coming down plenty now. They hit the pave and bounce like rice. Oh, Lord; oh, Lord, I pray. Don't let me die, don't let me die, don't let me die, Lord.

11

Now I know where we going. We going back of town where the colored people eat. I don't care if I don't eat. I been hungry before. I can stand it. But I can't stand the cold.

I can see we go'n have a long walk. It's 'bout a mile down there. But I don't mind. I know when I get there I'm go'n warm myself. I think I can hold out. My hands numb in my pockets and my feet numb, too, but if I keep moving I can hold out. Just don't stop no more, that's all.

The sky's gray. The sleet keeps on falling. Falling like rain now—plenty, plenty. You can hear it hitting the pave. You can see it bouncing. Sometimes it bounces two times 'fore it settles.

275   We keep on going. We don't say nothing. We just keep on going, keep on going.

I wonder what Mama's thinking. I hope she ain't mad at me. When summer come I'm go'n pick plenty cotton and get her a coat. I'm go'n get her a red one.

I hope they'd make it summer all the time. I'd be glad if it was summer all the time—but it ain't. We got to have winter, too. Lord, I hate the winter. I guess everybody hate the winter.

I don't sniff this time. I get out my handkerchief and wipe my nose. My hand's so cold I can hardly hold the handkerchief.

I think we getting close, but we ain't there yet. I wonder where everybody is. Can't see a soul but us. Look like we the only two people moving round today. Must be too cold for the rest of the people to move round in.

280   I can hear my teeth. I hope they don't knock together too hard and make that bad one hurt. Lord, that's all I need, for that bad one to start off.

I hear a church bell somewhere. But today ain't Sunday. They must be ringing for a funeral or something.

I wonder what they doing at home. They must be eating. Monsieur Bayonne might be there with his guitar. One day Ty played with Monsieur Bayonne's guitar and broke one of the strings. Monsieur Bayonne was some mad with Ty. He say Ty wasn't go'n ever 'mount to nothing. Ty can go just like Monsieur Bayonne when he ain't there. Ty can make everybody laugh when he starts to mocking Monsieur Bayonne.

I used to like to be with Mama and Daddy. We used to be happy. But they took him in the Army. Now, nobody happy no more . . . I be glad when Daddy comes home.

Monsieur Bayonne say it wasn't fair for them to take Daddy and give Mama nothing and give us nothing. Auntie say, "Shhh, Etienne. Don't let them hear you talk like that." Monsieur Bayonne say, "It's God truth. What they giving his children? They have to walk three and a half miles to school hot or cold. That's anything to give for a paw? She's got to work in the field rain or shine just to make ends meet. That's anything to give for a husband?" Auntie say, "Shhh, Etienne, shhh." "Yes, you right," Monsieur Bayonne say.

"Best don't say it in front of them now. But one day they go'n find out. One day." "Yes, I suppose so," Auntie say. "Then what, Rose Mary?" Monsieur Bayonne say. "I don't know, Etienne," Auntie say. "All we can do is us job, and leave everything else in His hand . . ."

We getting closer, now. We getting closer. I can even see the railroad tracks.   285

We cross the tracks, and now I see the café. Just to get in there, I say. Just to get in there. Already I'm starting to feel little better.

12

We go in. Ahh, it's good. I look for the heater; there 'gainst the wall. One of them little brown ones. I just stand there and hold my hands over it. I can't open my hands too wide 'cause they almost froze.

Mama's standing right 'side me. She done unbuttoned her coat. Smoke rises out of the coat, and the coat smells like a wet dog.

I move to the side so Mama can have more room. She opens out her hands and rubs them together. I rub mine together, too, 'cause this keeps them from hurting. If you let them warm too fast, they hurt you sure. But if you let them warm just little bit at a time, and you keep rubbing them, they be all right every time.

They got just two more people in the café. A lady back of the counter, and a man on this   290
side the counter. They been watching us even since we come in.

Mama gets out the handkerchief and count up the money. Both of us know how much money she's got there. Three dollars. No, she ain't got three dollars, 'cause she had to pay us way up here. She ain't got but two dollars and a half left. Dollar and a half to get my tooth pulled, and fifty cents for us to go back on, and fifty cents worth of salt meat.

She stirs the money round with her finger. Most of the money is change 'cause I can hear it rubbing together. She stirs it and stirs it. Then she looks at the door. It's still sleeting. I can hear it hitting 'gainst the wall like rice.

"I ain't hungry, Mama," I say.

"Got to pay them something for they heat," she says.

She takes a quarter out the handkerchief and ties the handkerchief up again. She looks   295
over her shoulder at the people, but she still don't move. I hope she don't spend the money. I don't want her spending it on me. I'm hungry, I'm almost starving I'm so hungry, but I don't want her spending the money on me.

She flips the quarter over like she's thinking. She's must be thinking 'bout us walking back home. Lord, I sure don't want walk home. If I thought it'd do any good to say something, I'd say it. But Mama makes up her own mind 'bout things.

She turns 'way from the heater right fast, like she better hurry up and spend the quarter 'fore she change her mind. I watch her go toward the counter. The man and the lady look at her, too. She tells the lady something and the lady walks away. The man keeps on looking at her. Her back's turned to the man, and she don't even know he's standing there.

The lady puts some cakes and a glass of milk on the counter. Then she pours a cup of coffee and sets it 'side the other stuff. Mama pays her for the things and comes on back where I'm standing. She tells me sit down at the table 'gainst the wall.

The milk and the cake's for me; the coffee's for Mama. I eat slow and I look at her. She's looking outside at the sleet. She's looking real sad. I say to myself, I'm go'n make all this up one day. You see, one day, I'm go'n make all this up. I want say it now; I want tell her how I feel right now; but Mama don't like for us to talk like that.

"I can't eat all this," I say.
    300
They ain't got but just three little old cakes there. I'm so hungry right now, the Lord knows I can eat a hundred times three, but I want my mama to have one.

Mama don't even look my way. She knows I'm hungry, she knows I want it. I let it stay there a little while, then I get it and eat it. I eat just on my front teeth, though, 'cause if cake touch that back tooth I know what'll happen. Thank God it ain't hurt me at all today.

After I finish eating I see the man go to the juke box. He drops a nickel in it, then he just stand there a little while looking at the record. Mama tells me keep my eyes in front where they belong. I turn my head like she say, but then I hear the man coming toward us.

"Dance, pretty?" he says.

305 Mama gets up to dance with him. But 'fore you know it, she done grabbed the little man in the collar and done heaved him 'side the wall. He hit the wall so hard he stop the juke box from playing.

"Some pimp," the lady back of the counter says. "Some pimp."

The little man jumps up off the floor and starts toward my mama. 'Fore you know it, Mama done sprung open her knife and she's waiting for him.

"Come on," she says. "Come on. I'll gut you from your neighbo° to your throat. Come on."

I go up to the little man to hit him, but Mama makes me come and stand 'side her. The little man looks at me and Mama and goes on back to the counter.

310 "Some pimp," the lady back of the counter says. "Some pimp." She starts laughing and pointing at the little man. "Yes sir, you a pimp, all right. Yes sirree."

13

"Fasten that coat, let's go," Mama says.

"You don't have to leave," the lady says.

Mama don't answer the lady, and we right out in the cold again. I'm warm right now—my hands, my ears, my feet—but I know this ain't go'n last too long. It done sleet so much now you got ice everywhere you look.

We cross the railroad tracks, and soon's we do, I get cold. That wind goes through this little old coat like it ain't even there. I got on a shirt and a sweater under the coat, but that wind don't pay them no mind. I look up and I can see we got a long way to go. I wonder if we go'n make it 'fore I get too cold.

315 We cross over to walk on the sidewalk. They got just one sidewalk back here, and it's over there.

After we go just a little piece, I smell bread cooking. I look, then I see a baker shop. When we get closer, I can smell it more better. I shut my eyes and make 'tend I'm eating. But I keep them shut too long and I butt up 'gainst a telephone post. Mama grabs me and see if I'm hurt. I ain't bleeding or nothing and she turns me loose.

I can feel I'm getting colder and colder, and I look up to see how far we still got to go. Uptown is 'way up yonder. A half mile more, I reckon. I try to think of something. They say think and you won't get cold. I think of that poem, "Annabel Lee."° I ain't been to school in so long—this bad weather—I reckon they done passed "Annabel Lee" by now. But passed it or not, I'm sure Miss Walker go'n make me recite it when I get there. That woman don't never forget nothing. I ain't never seen nobody like that in my life.

I'm still getting cold. "Annabel Lee" or no "Annabel Lee," I'm still getting cold. But I can see we getting closer. We getting there gradually.

Soon 's we turn the corner, I see a little old white lady up in front of us. She's the only lady on the street. She's all in black and she's got a long black rag over her head.

°*neighbo*: navel.
°*"Annabel Lee"*: poem (1849) by Edgar Allan Poe (1809–1849) (see pp. 930–31).

"Stop," she says.   320

Me and Mama stop and look at her. She must be crazy to be out in all this bad weather. Ain't got but a few other people out there, and all of them's men.

"Y'all done ate?" she says.

"Just finish," Mama says.

"Y'all must be cold then?" she says.

"We headed for the dentist," Mama says. "We'll warm up when we get there."   325

"What dentist?" the old lady says. "Mr. Bassett?"

"Yes, ma'am," Mama says.

"Come on in," the old lady says. "I'll telephone him and tell him y'all coming."

Me and Mama follow the old lady in the store. It's a little bitty store, and it don't have much in there. The old lady takes off her head rag and folds it up.

"Helena?" somebody calls from the back.   330

"Yes, Alnest?" the old lady says.

"Did you see them?"

"They're here. Standing beside me."

"Good. Now you can stay inside."

The old lady looks at Mama. Mama's waiting to hear what she brought us in here for. 335
I'm waiting for that, too.

"I saw y'all each time you went by," she says. "I came out to catch you, but you were gone."

"We went back of town," Mama says.

"Did you eat?"

"Yes, ma'am."

The old lady looks at Mama a long time, like she's thinking Mama might be just saying 340
that. Mama looks right back at her. The old lady looks at me to see what I have to say. I don't say nothing. I sure ain't going 'gainst my mama.

"There's food in the kitchen," she says to Mama. "I've been keeping it warm."

Mama turns right around and starts for the door.

"Just a minute," the old lady says. Mama stops. "The boy'll have to work for it. It isn't free."

"We don't take no handout," Mama says.

"I'm not handing out anything," the old lady says. "I need my garbage moved to the   345
front. Ernest has a bad cold and can't go out there."

"James'll move it for you," Mama says.

"Not unless you eat," the old lady says. "I'm old, but I have my pride, too, you know."

Mama can see that she ain't go'n beat this old lady down, so she just shakes her head.

"All right," the old lady says. "Come into the kitchen."

She leads the way with that rag in her hand. The kitchen is a little bitty little old thing, 350
too. The table and the stove just 'bout fill it up. They got a little room to the side. Somebody in there laying 'cross the bed—'cause I can see one of his feet. Must be the person she was talking to: Ernest or Alnest—something like that.

"Sit down," the old lady says to Mama. "Not you," she says to me. "You have to move the cans."

"Helena?" the man says in the other room.

"Yes, Alnest?" the old lady says.

"Are you going out there again?"

"I must show the boy where the garbage is, Alnest," the old lady says.   355

"Keep that shawl over your head," the old man says.

"You don't have to remind me, Alnest. Come, boy," the old lady says.

We go out in the yard. Little old back yard ain't no bigger than the store or the kitchen. But it can sleet here just like it can sleet in any big back yard. And 'fore you know it, I'm trembling.

"There," the old lady says, pointing to the cans. I pick up one of the cans and set it right back down. The can's so light, I'm go'n see what's inside of it.

360   "Here," the old lady says. "Leave that can alone."

I look back at her standing there in the door. She's got that black rag wrapped round her shoulders, and she's pointing one of her little old fingers at me.

"Pick it up and carry it to the front," she says. I go by her with the can, and she's looking at me all the time. I'm sure the can's empty. I'm sure she could've carried it herself—maybe both of them at the same time. "Set it on the sidewalk by the door and come back for the other one," she says.

I go and come back, and Mama looks at me when I pass her. I get the other can and take it to the front. It don't feel a bit heavier than that first one. I tell myself I ain't go'n be nobody's fool, and I'm go'n look inside this can to see just what I been hauling. First, I look up the street, then down the street. Nobody coming. Then I look over my shoulder toward the door. That little old lady done slipped up there quiet 's mouse, watching me again. Look like she knowed what I was go'n do.

"Ehh, Lord," she says. "Children, children. Come in here, boy, and go wash your hands."

365   I follow her in the kitchen. She points toward the bathroom, and I go in there and wash up. Little bitty old bathroom, but it's clean, clean. I don't use any of her towels; I wipe my hands on my pants legs.

When I come back in the kitchen, the old lady done dished up the food. Rice, gravy, meat—and she even got some lettuce and tomato in a saucer. She even got a glass of milk and a piece of cake there, too. It looks so good, I almost start eating 'fore I say my blessing.

"Helena?" the old man says.

"Yes, Alnest?"

"Are they eating?"

370   "Yes," she says.

"Good," he says. "Now you'll stay inside."

The old lady goes in there where he is and I can hear them talking. I look at Mama. She's eating slow like she's thinking. I wonder what's the matter now. I reckon she's thinking 'bout home.

The old lady comes back in the kitchen.

"I talked to Dr. Bassett's nurse," she says. "Dr. Bassett will take you as soon as you get there."

375   "Thank you, ma'am," Mama says.

"Perfectly all right," the old lady says. "Which one is it?"

Mama nods toward me. The old lady looks at me real sad. I look sad, too.

"You're not afraid, are you?" she says.

"No, ma'am," I say.

380   "That's a good boy," the old lady says. "Nothing to be afraid of. Dr. Bassett will not hurt you."

When me and Mama get through eating, we thank the old lady again.

"Helena, are they leaving?" the old man says.

"Yes, Alnest."

"Tell them I say good-bye."

385   "They can hear you, Alnest."

"Good-bye both mother and son," the old man says. "And may God be with you."

Me and Mama tell the old man good-bye, and we follow the old lady in the front room. Mama opens the door to go out, but she stops and comes back in the store.

"You sell salt meat?" she says.

"Yes."

"Give me two bits worth."   390

"That isn't very much salt meat," the old lady says.

"That's all I have," Mama says.

The old lady goes back of the counter and cuts a big piece off the chunk. Then she wraps it up and puts it in a paper bag.

"Two bits," she says.

"That looks like awful lot of meat for a quarter," Mama says.   395

"Two bits," the old lady says. "I've been selling salt meat behind this counter twenty-five years. I think I know what I'm doing."

"You got a scale there," Mama says.

"What?" the old lady says.

"Weigh it," Mama says.

"What?" the old lady says. "Are you telling me how to run my business?"   400

"Thanks very much for the food," Mama says.

"Just a minute," the old lady says.

"James," Mama says to me. I move toward the door.

"Just one minute, I said," the old lady says.

Me and Mama stop again and look at her. The old lady takes the meat out of the bag and   405
unwraps it and cuts 'bout half of it off. Then she wraps it up again and juggs it back in the
bag and gives the bag to Mama. Mama lays the quarter on the counter.

"Your kindness will never be forgotten," she says. "James," she says to me.

We go out, and the old lady comes to the door to look at us. After we go a little piece I look back, and she's still there watching us.

The sleet's coming down heavy, heavy now, and I turn up my coat collar to keep my neck warm. My mama tells me turn it right back down.

"You not a bum," she says. "You a man."

QUESTIONS

1. What does Gaines establish by using the eight-year-old boy, James, as the narrator who tells the story in the present tense and in his own dialect?

2. Why does James describe the family's need to kill and eat the small birds?

3. What is the major action in the story? What is the result of James and his mother Octavia taking the trip to the dentist? What is gained by the delays, which require the boy and his mother to wait in the office and then to walk out into the cold and sleet?

4. What is the significance of the discussions of suffering occasioned by the protesting child in the dentist's office? What ideas does the young man present (section 7)? When the minister hits him and reproaches him, what is demonstrated about the old and new ideas professed by African-Americans?

5. What values are represented by the elderly couple in the store? Why doesn't the woman phone Dr. Robillard, the "better" but "more expensive" dentist? Why doesn't Octavia accept the portion of salt meat the woman first offers her? What causes the woman to cut the salt meat in half?

SUSAN GLASPELL (1882–1948)

For a brief biography and photo, see Chapter 20, page 982.

A Jury of Her Peers° (1917)

When Martha Hale opened the storm-door and got a cut of the north wind, she ran back for her big woolen scarf. As she hurriedly wound that round her head her eye made a scandalized sweep of her kitchen. It was no ordinary thing that called her away—it was probably further from ordinary than anything that had ever happened in Dickson County. But what her eye took in was that her kitchen was in no shape for leaving: her bread all ready for mixing, half the flour sifted and half unsifted.

She hated to see things half done; but she had been at that when the team from town stopped to get Mr. Hale, and then the sheriff came running in to say his wife wished Mrs. Hale would come too—adding, with a grin, that he guessed she was getting scary and wanted another woman along. So she had dropped everything right where it was.

"Martha!" now came her husband's impatient voice. "Don't keep folks waiting out here in the cold."

She again opened the storm-door, and this time joined the three men and the one woman waiting for her in the big two-seated buggy.

5   After she had the robes tucked around her she took another look at the woman who sat beside her on the back seat. She had met Mrs. Peters the year before at the county fair, and the thing she remembered about her was that she didn't seem like a sheriff's wife. She was small and thin and didn't have a strong voice. Mrs. Gorman, sheriff's wife before Gorman went out and Peters came in, had a voice that somehow seemed to be backing up the law with every word. But if Mrs. Peters didn't look like a sheriff's wife, Peters made it up in looking like a sheriff. He was to a dot the kind of man who could get himself elected sheriff—a heavy man with a big voice, who was particularly genial with the law-abiding, as if to make it plain that he knew the difference between criminals and non-criminals. And right there it came into Mrs. Hale's mind, with a stab, that this man who was so pleasant and lively with all of them was going to the Wrights' now as a sheriff.

"The country's not very pleasant this time of year," Mrs. Peters at last ventured, as if she felt they ought to be talking as well as the men.

Mrs. Hale scarcely finished her reply, for they had gone up a little hill and could see the Wright place now, and seeing it did not make her feel like talking. It looked very lonesome this cold March morning. It had always been a lonesome-looking place. It was down in a hollow, and the poplar trees around it were lonesome-looking trees. The men were looking at it and talking about what had happened. The county attorney was bending to one side of the buggy, and kept looking steadily at the place as they drew up to it.

"I'm glad you came with me," Mrs. Peters said nervously, as the two women were about to follow the men in through the kitchen door.

Even after she had her foot on the door-step, her hand on the knob, Martha Hale had a moment of feeling she could not cross that threshold. And the reason it seemed she couldn't cross it now was simply because she hadn't crossed it before. Time and time again it had been in her mind, "I ought to go over and see Minnie Foster"—she still thought of her as Minnie Foster, though for twenty years she had been Mrs. Wright. And then there was always something to do and Minnie Foster would go from her mind. But *now* she could come.

°Glaspell's play *Trifles*, with which this story may be compared, appears in Chapter 20.

The men went over to the stove. The women stood close together by the door. Young
Henderson, the county attorney, turned around and said, "Come up to the fire, ladies."

Mrs. Peters took a step forward, then stopped. "I'm not—cold," she said.

And so the two women stood by the door, at first not even so much as looking around
the kitchen.

The men talked for a minute about what a good thing it was the sheriff had sent his
deputy out that morning to make a fire for them, and then Sheriff Peters stepped back from
the stove, unbuttoned his outer coat, and leaned his hands on the kitchen table in a way
that seemed to mark the beginning of official business. "Now, Mr. Hale," he said in a sort of
semi-official voice, "before we move things about, you tell Mr. Henderson just what it was
you saw when you came here yesterday morning."

The county attorney was looking around the kitchen.

"By the way," he said, "has anything been moved?" He turned to the sheriff. "Are things   15
just as you left them yesterday?"

Peters looked from cupboard to sink; from that to a small worn rocker a little to one side
of the kitchen table.

"It's just the same."

"Somebody should have been left here yesterday," said the county attorney.

"Oh—yesterday," returned the sheriff, with a little gesture as of yesterday having been
more than he could bear to think of. "When I had to send Frank to Morris Center for that
man who went crazy—let me tell you. I had my hands full *yesterday*. I knew you could get
back from Omaha by today, George, and as long as I went over everything here myself—"

"Well, Mr. Hale," said the county attorney, in a way of letting what was past and gone   20
go, "tell just what happened when you came here yesterday morning."

Mrs. Hale, still leaning against the door, had that sinking feeling of the mother whose
child is about to speak a piece. Lewis often wandered along and got things mixed up in a
story. She hoped he would tell this straight and plain, and not say unnecessary things that
would just make things harder for Minnie Foster. He didn't begin at once, and she noticed
that he looked queer—as if standing in that kitchen and having to tell what he had seen
there yesterday morning made him almost sick.

"Yes, Mr. Hale?" the county attorney reminded.

"Harry and I had started to town with a load of potatoes," Mrs. Hale's husband began.

Harry was Mrs. Hale's oldest boy. He wasn't with them now, for the very good reason
that those potatoes never got to town yesterday and he was taking them this morning, so
he hadn't been home when the sheriff stopped to say he wanted Mr. Hale to come over to
the Wright place and tell the county attorney his story there, where he could point it all out.
With all Mrs. Hale's other emotions came the fear now that maybe Harry wasn't dressed
warm enough—they hadn't any of them realized how that north wind did bite.

"We come along this road," Hale was going on, with a motion of his hand to the road   25
over which they had just come, "and as we got in sight of the house I says to Harry, 'I'm
goin' to see if I can't get John Wright to take a telephone.' You see," he explained to Henderson, "unless I can get somebody to go in with me they won't come out this branch road
except for a price I can't pay. I'd spoke to Wright about it once before; but he put me off,
saying folks talked too much anyway, and all he asked was peace and quiet—guess you
know about how much he talked himself. But I thought maybe if I went to the house and
talked about it before his wife, and said all the women-folks liked the telephones, and that
in this lonesome stretch of road it would be a good thing—well, I said to Harry that that was
what I was going to say—though I said at the same time that I didn't know as what his wife
wanted made much difference to John—"

Now there he was!—saying things he didn't need to say. Mrs. Hale tried to catch her
husband's eye, but fortunately the county attorney interrupted with:

"Let's talk about that a little later, Mr. Hale. I do want to talk about that, but I'm anxious now to get along to just what happened when you got here."

When he began this time, it was very deliberately and carefully:

"I didn't see or hear anything. I knocked at the door. And still it was all quiet inside. I knew they must be up—it was past eight o'clock. So I knocked again, louder, and I thought I heard somebody say, 'Come in.' I wasn't sure—I'm not sure yet. But I opened the door—this door," jerking a hand toward the door by which the two women stood, "and there, in that rocker"—pointing to it—"sat Mrs. Wright."

30 Everyone in the kitchen looked at the rocker. It came into Mrs. Hale's mind that that rocker didn't look in the least like Minnie Foster—the Minnie Foster of twenty years before. It was a dingy red, with wooden rungs up the back, and the middle rung was gone, and the chair sagged to one side.

"How did she—look?" the county attorney was inquiring.

"Well," said Hale, "she looked—queer."

"How do you mean—queer?"

As he asked it he took out a note-book and pencil. Mrs. Hale did not like the sight of that pencil. She kept her eye fixed on her husband, as if to keep him from saying unnecessary things that would go into that note-book and make trouble.

35 Hale did speak guardedly, as if the pencil had affected him too.

"Well, as if she didn't know what she was going to do next. And kind of—done up."

"How did she seem to feel about your coming?"

"Why, I don't think she minded—one way or other. She didn't pay much attention. I said, 'Ho' do, Mrs. Wright? It's cold, ain't it?' And she said. 'Is it?'—and went on pleatin' at her apron.

"Well, I was surprised. She didn't ask me to come up to the stove, or to sit down, but just set there, not even lookin' at me. And so I said: 'I want to see John.'

40 "And then she—laughed. I guess you would call it a laugh.

"I thought of Harry and the team outside, so I said, a little sharp, 'Can I see John?' 'No,' says she—kind of dull like. 'Ain't he home?' says I. Then she looked at me. 'Yes,' says she, 'he's home.' 'Then why can't I see him?' I asked her, out of patience with her now. ''Cause he's dead' says she, just as quiet and dull—and fell to pleatin' her apron. 'Dead?' says I, like you do when you can't take in what you've heard.

"She just nodded her head, not getting a bit excited, but rockin' back and forth.

"'Why—where is he?' says I, not knowing *what* to say.

"She just pointed upstairs—like this"—pointing to the room above.

45 "I got up, with the idea of going up there myself. By this time I—didn't know what to do. I walked from there to here; then I says: 'Why, what did he die of?'

"'He died of a rope around his neck,' says she; and just went on pleatin' at her apron."

Hale stopped speaking, and stood staring at the rocker, as if he were still seeing the woman who had sat there the morning before. Nobody spoke; it was as if every one were seeing the woman who had sat there the morning before.

"And what did you do then?" the county attorney at last broke the silence.

"I went out and called Harry. I thought I might—need help. I got Harry in, and we went upstairs." His voice fell almost to a whisper. "There he was—lying over the—"

50 "I think I'd rather have you go into that upstairs," the county attorney interrupted, "where you can point it all out. Just go on now with the rest of the story."

"Well, my first thought was to get that rope off. It looked—"

He stopped, his face twitching.

"But Harry, he went up to him, and he said. 'No, he's dead all right, and we'd better not touch anything.' So we went downstairs.

"She was still sitting that same way. 'Has anybody been notified?' I asked. 'No,' says she, unconcerned.

"'Who did this, Mrs. Wright?' said Harry. He said it businesslike, and she stopped   55
pleatin' at her apron. 'I don't know,' she says. 'You don't *know*?' says Harry. 'Weren't you
sleepin' in the bed with him?' 'Yes,' says she, 'but I was on the inside.' 'Somebody slipped
a rope round his neck and strangled him, and you didn't wake up?' says Harry. 'I didn't
wake up,' she said after him.

"We may have looked as if we didn't see how that could be, for after a minute she said,
'I sleep sound.'

"Harry was going to ask her more questions, but I said maybe that weren't our business;
maybe we ought to let her tell her story first to the coroner or the sheriff. So Harry went fast
as he could over to High Road—the Rivers' place, where there's a telephone."

"And what did she do when she knew you had gone for the coroner?" The attorney got
his pencil in his hand all ready for writing.

"She moved from that chair to this one over here"—Hale pointed to a small chair in the
corner—"and just sat there with her hands held together and looking down. I got a feeling that I ought to make some conversation, so I said I had come in to see if John wanted
to put in a telephone; and at that she started to laugh, and then she stopped and looked at
me—scared."

At the sound of a moving pencil the man who was telling the story looked up.   60

"I dunno—maybe it wasn't scared," he hastened: "I wouldn't like to say it was. Soon
Harry got back, and then Dr. Lloyd came, and you, Mr. Peters, and so I guess that's all I
know that you don't."

He said that last with relief, and moved a little, as if relaxing. Everyone moved a little.
The county attorney walked toward the stair door.

"I guess we'll go upstairs first—then out to the barn and around there."

He paused and looked around the kitchen.

"You're convinced there was nothing important here?" he asked the sheriff. "Nothing   65
that would—point to any motive?"

The sheriff too looked all around, as if to re-convince himself.

"Nothing here but kitchen things," he said, with a little laugh for the insignificance of
kitchen things.

The county attorney was looking at the cupboard—a peculiar, ungainly structure,
half closet and half cupboard, the upper part of it being built in the wall, and the lower
part just the old-fashioned kitchen cupboard. As if its queerness attracted him, he got a
chair and opened the upper part and looked in. After a moment he drew his hand away
sticky.

"Here's a nice mess," he said resentfully.

The two women had drawn nearer, and now the sheriff's wife spoke.   70

"Oh—her fruit," she said, looking to Mrs. Hale for sympathetic understanding. She
turned back to the county attorney and explained: "She worried about that when it turned
so cold last night. She said the fire would go out and her jars might burst."

Mrs. Peters' husband broke into a laugh.

"Well, can you beat the woman! Held for murder, and worrying about her preserves!"

The young attorney set his lips.

"I guess before we're through with her she may have something more serious than   75
preserves to worry about."

"Oh, well," said Mrs. Hale's husband, with good-natured superiority, "women are used
to worrying over trifles."

The two women moved a little closer together. Neither of them spoke. The county
attorney seemed suddenly to remember his manners—and think of his future.

"And yet," said he, with the gallantry of a young politician, "for all their worries, what
would we do without the ladies?"

The women did not speak, did not unbend. He went to the sink and began washing his hands. He turned to wipe them on the roller towel—whirled it for a cleaner place.

80   "Dirty towels! Not much of a housekeeper, would you say, ladies?"

He kicked his foot against some dirty pans under the sink.

"There's a great deal of work to be done on a farm," said Mrs. Hale stiffly.

"To be sure. And yet"—with a little bow to her—"I know there are some Dickson County farm-houses that do not have such roller towels." He gave it a pull to expose its full length again.

"Those towels get dirty awful quick. Men's hands aren't always as clean as they might be."

85   "Ah, loyal to your sex, I see," he laughed. He stopped and gave her a keen look. "But you and Mrs. Wright were neighbors. I suppose you were friends, too."

Martha Hale shook her head.

"I've seen little enough of her of late years. I've not been in this house—it's more than a year."

"And why was that? You didn't like her?"

"I liked her well enough," she replied with spirit. "Farmers' wives have their hands full, Mr. Henderson. And then—" She looked around the kitchen.

90   "Yes?" he encouraged.

"It never seemed a very cheerful place," said she, more to herself than to him.

"No," he agreed; "I don't think anyone would call it cheerful. I shouldn't say she had the home-making instinct."

"Well, I don't know as Wright had, either," she muttered.

"You mean they didn't get on very well?" he was quick to ask.

95   "No; I don't mean anything," she answered, with decision. As she turned a little away from him, she added: "But I don't think a place would be any the cheerfuller for John Wright's bein' in it."

"I'd like to talk to you about that a little later, Mrs. Hale," he said. "I'm anxious to get the lay of things upstairs now."

He moved toward the stair door, followed by the two men.

"I suppose anything Mrs. Peters does'll be all right?" the sheriff inquired. "She was to take in some clothes for her, you know—and a few little things. We left in such a hurry yesterday."

The county attorney looked at the two women whom they were leaving alone there among the kitchen things.

100   "Yes—Mrs. Peters," he said, his glance resting on the woman who was not Mrs. Peters, the big farmer woman who stood behind the sheriff's wife. "Of course Mrs. Peters is one of us," he said, in a manner of entrusting responsibility. "And keep your eye out, Mrs. Peters, for anything that might be of use. No telling; you women might come upon a clue to the motive—and that's the thing we need."

Mr. Hale rubbed his face after the fashion of a showman getting ready for a pleasantry.

"But would the women know a clue if they did come upon it?" he said; and, having delivered himself of this, he followed the others through the stair door.

The women stood motionless and silent, listening to the footsteps, first upon the stairs, then in the room above them.

Then, as if releasing herself from something strange, Mrs. Hale began to arrange the dirty pans under the sink, which the county attorney's disdainful push of the foot had deranged.

105   "I'd hate to have men comin' into my kitchen," she said testily—"snoopin' round and criticizin'."

"Of course it's no more than their duty," said the sheriff's wife, in her manner of timid acquiescence.

"Duty's all right," replied Mrs. Hale bluffly; "but I guess that deputy sheriff that come out to make the fire might have got a little of this on." She gave the roller towel a pull. "Wish I'd thought of that sooner! Seems mean to talk about her for not having things slicked up, when she had to come away in such a hurry."

She looked around the kitchen. Certainly it was not "slicked up." Her eye was held by a bucket of sugar on a low shelf. The cover was off the wooden bucket, and beside it was a paper bag—half full.

Mrs. Hale moved toward it.

"She was putting this in there," she said to herself—slowly. 110

She thought of the flour in her kitchen at home—half sifted, half not sifted. She had been interrupted, and had left things half done. What had interrupted Minnie Foster? Why had that work been left half done? She made a move as if to finish it,—unfinished things always bothered her,—and then she glanced around and saw that Mrs. Peters was watching her—and she didn't want Mrs. Peters to get that feeling she had got of work begun and then—for some reason—not finished.

"It's a shame about her fruit," she said, and walked toward the cupboard that the county attorney had opened, and got on the chair, murmuring: "I wonder if it's all gone."

It was a sorry enough looking sight, but "Here's one that's all right," she said at last. She held it toward the light. "This is cherries, too." She looked again. "I declare I believe that's the only one."

With a sigh, she got down from the chair, went to the sink, and wiped off the bottle.

"She'll feel awful bad, after all her hard work in the hot weather. I remember the after- 115
noon I put up my cherries last summer."

She set the bottle on the table, and, with another sigh, started to sit down in the rocker. But she did not sit down. Something kept her from sitting down in that chair. She straightened—stepped back, and, half turned away, stood looking at it, seeing the woman who had sat there "pleatin' at her apron."

The thin voice of the sheriff's wife broke in upon her: "I must be getting those things from the front-room closet." She opened the door into the other room, started in, stepped back. "You coming with me, Mrs. Hale?" she asked nervously. "You—you could help me get them."

They were soon back—the stark coldness of that shut-up room was not a thing to linger in.

"My!" said Mrs. Peters, dropping the things on the table and hurrying to the stove.

Mrs. Hale stood examining the clothes the woman who was being detained in town had 120
said she wanted.

"Wright was close!"° she exclaimed, holding up a shabby black skirt that bore the marks of much making over. "I think maybe that's why she kept so much to herself. I s'pose she felt she couldn't do her part; and then, you don't enjoy things when you feel shabby. She used to wear pretty clothes and be lively—when she was Minnie Foster, one of the town girls, singing in the choir. But that—oh, that was twenty years ago."

With a carefulness in which there was something tender, she folded the shabby clothes and piled them at one corner of the table. She looked up at Mrs. Peters, and there was something in the other woman's look that irritated her.

"She don't care," she said to herself. "Much difference it makes to her whether Minnie Foster had pretty clothes when she was a girl."

Then she looked again, and she wasn't so sure; in fact, she hadn't at any time been perfectly sure about Mrs. Peters. She had that shrinking manner, and yet her eyes looked as if they could see a long way into things.

°*close:* that is, frugal, tightfisted.

125   "This all you was to take in?" asked Mrs. Hale.

"No," said the sheriff's wife; "she said she wanted an apron. Funny thing to want," she ventured in her nervous little way, "for there's not much to get you dirty in jail, goodness knows. But I suppose just to make her feel more natural. If you're used to wearing an apron—. She said they were in the bottom drawer of this cupboard. Yes—here they are. And then her little shawl that always hung on the stair door."

She took the small gray shawl from behind the door leading upstairs, and stood a minute looking at it.

Suddenly Mrs. Hale took a quick step toward the other woman.

"Mrs. Peters!"

130   "Yes, Mrs. Hale?"

"Do you think she—did it?"

A frightened look blurred the other thing in Mrs. Peters' eyes.

"Oh, I don't know," she said, in a voice that seemed to shrink away from the subject.

"Well, I don't think she did," affirmed Mrs. Hale stoutly.

135   "Asking for an apron, and her little shawl. Worryin' about her fruit."

"Mr. Peters says—." Footsteps were heard in the room above; she stopped, looked up, then went on in a lowered voice: "Mr. Peters says—it looks bad for her. Mr. Henderson is awful sarcastic in a speech, and he's going to make fun of her saying she didn't—wake up."

For a moment Mrs. Hale had no answer. Then, "Well, I guess John Wright didn't wake up—when they was slippin' that rope under his neck," she muttered.

"No, it's *strange*," breathed Mrs. Peters. "They think it was such a—funny way to kill a man."

She began to laugh; at sound of the laugh, abruptly stopped.

140   "That's just what Mr. Hale said," said Mrs. Hale, in a resolutely natural voice. "There was a gun in the house. He says that's what he can't understand."

"Mr. Henderson said, coming out, that what was needed for the case was a motive. Something to show anger—or sudden feeling."

"Well, I don't see any signs of anger around here," said Mrs. Hale, "I don't—" She stopped. It was as if her mind tripped on something. Her eye was caught by a dish-towel in the middle of the kitchen table. Slowly she moved toward the table. One half of it was wiped clean, the other half messy. Her eyes made a slow, almost unwilling turn to the bucket of sugar and the half empty bag beside it. Things begun—and not finished.

After a moment she stepped back, and said, in that manner of releasing herself:

"Wonder how they're finding things upstairs? I hope she had it a little more redd up° up there. You know,"—she paused, and feeling gathered,—"it seems kind of *sneaking*: locking her up in town and coming out here to get her own house to turn against her!"

145   "But, Mrs. Hale," said the sheriff's wife, "the law is the law."

"I s'pose 'tis," answered Mrs. Hale shortly.

She turned to the stove, saying something about that fire not being much to brag of. She worked with it a minute, and when she straightened up she said aggressively:

"The law is the law—and a bad stove is a bad stove. How'd you like to cook on this?"—pointing with the poker to the broken lining. She opened the oven door and started to express her opinion of the oven; but she was swept into her own thoughts, thinking of what it would mean, year after year, to have that stove to wrestle with. The thought of Minnie Foster trying to bake in that oven—and the thought of her never going over to see Minnie Foster—.

She was startled by hearing Mrs. Peters say: "A person gets discouraged—and loses heart."

°*redd up*: neat.

The sheriff's wife had looked from the stove to the sink—to the pail of water which   150
had been carried in from outside. The two women stood there silent, above them the
footsteps of the men who were looking for evidence against the woman who had worked
in that kitchen. That look of seeing into things, of seeing through a thing to something
else, was in the eyes of the sheriff's wife now. When Mrs. Hale next spoke to her, it was
gently:

"Better loosen up your things, Mrs. Peters. We'll not feel them when we go out."

Mrs. Peters went to the back of the room to hang up the fur tippet she was wearing. A
moment later she exclaimed, "Why, she was piecing a quilt," and held up a large sewing
basket piled high with quilt pieces.

Mrs. Hale spread some of the blocks on the table.

"It's a log-cabin pattern," she said, putting several of them together, "Pretty, isn't it?"

They were so engaged with the quilt that they did not hear the footsteps on the stairs.   155
Just as the stair door opened Mrs. Hale was saying:

"Do you suppose she was going to quilt it or just knot it?"

The sheriff threw up his hands.

"They wonder whether she was going to quilt it or just knot it!"

There was a laugh for the ways of women, a warming of hands over the stove, and then
the county attorney said briskly:

"Well, let's go right out to the barn and get that cleared up."   160

"I don't see as there's anything so strange," Mrs. Hale said resentfully, after the outside
door had closed on the three men—"our taking up our time with little things while we're
waiting for them to get the evidence. I don't see as it's anything to laugh about."

"Of course they've got awful important things on their minds," said the sheriff's wife
apologetically.

They returned to an inspection of the block for the quilt. Mrs. Hale was looking at the
fine, even sewing, and preoccupied with thoughts of the woman who had done that sewing,
when she heard the sheriff's wife say, in a queer tone:

"Why, look at this one."

She turned to take the block held out to her.   165

"The sewing," said Mrs. Peters, in a troubled way, "All the rest of them have been so nice
and even—but—this one. Why, it looks as if she didn't know what she was about!"

Their eyes met—something flashed to life, passed between them; then, as if with an
effort, they seemed to pull away from each other. A moment Mrs. Hale sat there, her hands
folded over that sewing which was so unlike all the rest of the sewing. Then she had pulled
a knot and drawn the threads.

"Oh, what are you doing, Mrs. Hale?" asked the sheriff's wife, startled.

"Just pulling out a stitch or two that's not sewed very good," said Mrs. Hale mildly.

"I don't think we ought to touch things," Mrs. Peters said, a little helplessly.   170

"I'll just finish up this end," answered Mrs. Hale, still in that mild, matter-of-fact fashion.

She threaded a needle and started to replace bad sewing with good. For a little while she
sewed in silence. Then, in that thin, timid voice, she heard:

"Mrs. Hale!"

"Yes, Mrs. Peters?"

"What do you suppose she was so—nervous about?"   175

"Oh, I don't know," said Mrs. Hale, as if dismissing a thing not important enough to
spend much time on. "I don't know as she was—nervous. I sew awful queer sometimes
when I'm just tired."

She cut a thread, and out of the corner of her eye looked up at Mrs. Peters. The small, lean
face of the sheriff's wife seemed to have tightened up. Her eyes had that look of peering into
something. But next moment she moved, and said in her thin, indecisive way:

"Well, I must get those clothes wrapped. They may be through sooner than we think. I wonder where I could find a piece of paper—and string."

"In that cupboard, maybe," suggested to Mrs. Hale, after a glance around.

180 One piece of the crazy sewing remained unripped. Mrs. Peter's back turned, Martha Hale now scrutinized that piece, compared it with the dainty, accurate sewing of the other blocks. The difference was startling. Holding this block made her feel queer, as if the distracted thoughts of the woman who had perhaps turned to it to try and quiet herself were communicating themselves to her.

Mrs. Peters' voice roused her.

"Here's a bird-cage," she said. "Did she have a bird, Mrs. Hale?"

"Why, I don't know whether she did or not." She turned to look at the cage Mrs. Peters was holding up. "I've not been here in so long." She sighed. "There was a man round last year selling canaries cheap—but I don't know as she took one. Maybe she did. She used to sing real pretty herself."

Mrs. Peters looked around the kitchen.

185 "Seems kind of funny to think of a bird here." She half laughed—an attempt to put up a barrier. "But she must have had one—or why would she have a cage? I wonder what happened to it."

"I suppose maybe the cat got it," suggested Mrs. Hale, resuming her sewing.

"No; she didn't have a cat. She's got that feeling some people have about cats—being afraid of them. When they brought her to our house yesterday, my cat got in the room, and she was real upset and asked me to take it out."

"My sister Bessie was like that," laughed Mrs. Hale.

The sheriff's wife did not reply. The silence made Mrs. Hale turn round. Mrs. Peters was examining the bird-cage.

190 "Look at this door," she said slowly. "It's broke. One hinge has been pulled apart."

Mrs. Hale came nearer.

"Looks as if someone must have been—rough with it."

Again their eyes met—startled, questioning, apprehensive. For a moment neither spoke nor stirred. Then Mrs. Hale, turning away, said brusquely:

"If they're going to find any evidence, I wish they'd be about it. I don't like this place."

195 "But I'm awful glad you came with me, Mrs. Hale." Mrs. Peters put the bird-cage on the table and sat down. "It would be lonesome for me—sitting here alone."

"Yes, it would, wouldn't it?" agreed Mrs. Hale, a certain determined naturalness in her voice. She had picked up the sewing, but now it dropped in her lap, and she murmured in a different voice: "But I tell you what I *do* wish, Mrs Peters. I wish I had come over sometimes when she was here. I wish—I had."

"But of course you were awful busy, Mrs. Hale. Your house—and your children."

"I could've come," retorted Mrs. Hale shortly. "I stayed away because it weren't cheerful—and that's why I ought to have come. I"—she looked around—"I've never liked this place. Maybe because it's down in a hollow and you don't see the road. I don't know what it is, but it's a lonesome place, and always was. I wish I had come over to see Minnie Foster sometimes. I can see now—" She did not put it into words.

"Well, you mustn't reproach yourself," counseled Mrs. Peters. "Somehow, we just don't see how it is with other folks till—something comes up."

200 "Not having children makes less work," mused Mrs. Hale, after a silence, "but it makes a quiet house—and Wright out to work all day—and no company when he did come in. Did you know John Wright, Mrs. Peters?"

"Not to know him. I've seen him in town. They say he was a good man."

"Yes—good," conceded John Wright's neighbor grimly. "He didn't drink, and kept his word as well as most, I guess, and paid his debts. But he was a hard man, Mrs. Peters. Just to pass the time of day with him—." She stopped, shivered a little. "Like a raw wind that gets to the bone." Her eye fell upon the cage on the table before her, and she added, almost bitterly: "I should think she would've wanted a bird!"

Suddenly she leaned forward, looking intently at the cage. "But what do you s'pose went wrong with it?"

"I don't know," returned Mrs. Peters; "unless it got sick and died."

But after she said it she reached over and swung the broken door. Both women watched it as if somehow held by it.   205

"You didn't know—her?" Mrs. Hale asked, a gentler note in her voice.

"Not till they brought her yesterday," said the sheriff's wife.

"She—come to think of it, she was kind of like a bird herself. Real sweet and pretty, but kind of timid and—fluttery. How—she—did—change."

That held her for a long time. Finally, as if struck with a happy thought and relieved to get back to everyday things, she exclaimed:

"Tell you what, Mrs. Peters, why don't you take the quilt in with you? It might take up   210
her mind."

"Why, I think that's a real nice idea, Mrs. Hale," agreed the sheriff's wife, as if she too were glad to come into the atmosphere of a simple kindness. "There couldn't possibly be any objection to that, could there? Now, just what will I take? I wonder if her patches are in here—and her things?"

They turned to the sewing basket.

"Here's some red," said Mrs. Hale, bringing out a roll of cloth. Underneath that was a box. "Here, maybe her scissors are in here—and her things." She held it up. "What a pretty box! I'll warrant that was something she had a long time ago—when she was a girl."

She held it in her hand a moment; then, with a little sigh, opened it.

Instantly her hand went to her nose.   215

"Why—!"

Mrs. Peters drew nearer—then turned away.

"There's something wrapped up in this piece of silk," faltered Mrs. Hale.

"This isn't her scissors," said Mrs. Peters, in a shrinking voice.

Her hand not steady, Mrs. Hale raised the piece of silk. "Oh, Mrs. Peters!" she cried.   220
"It's—"

Mrs. Peters bent closer.

"It's the bird," she whispered.

"But, Mrs. Peters!" cried Mrs. Hale. "*Look* at it! Its *neck*—look at its neck! It's all—other side *to*."

She held the box away from her.

The sheriff's wife again bent closer.   225

"Somebody wrung its neck," said she, in a voice that was slow and deep.

And then again the eyes of the two women met—this time clung together in a look of dawning comprehension, of growing horror. Mrs. Peters looked from the dead bird to the broken door of the cage. Again their eyes met. And just then there was a sound at the outside door.

Mrs. Hale slipped the box under the quilt pieces in the basket, and sank into the chair before it. Mrs. Peters stood holding to the table. The county attorney and the sheriff came in from outside.

"Well, ladies," said the county attorney, as one turning from serious things to little pleasantries, "have you decided whether she was going to quilt it or knot it?"

"We think," began the sheriff's wife in a flurried voice, "that she was going to—knot it."   230

He was too preoccupied to notice the change that came in her voice on that last.

"Well, that's very interesting, I'm sure," he said tolerantly. He caught sight of the birdcage. "Has the bird flown?"

"We think the cat got it," said Mrs. Hale in a voice curiously even.

He was walking up and down, as if thinking something out.

235   "Is there a cat?" he asked absently.

Mrs. Hale shot a look up at the sheriff's wife.

"Well, not *now*," said Mrs. Peters. "They're superstitious, you know; they leave."

She sank into her chair.

The county attorney did not heed her. "No sign at all of anyone having come in from the outside," he said to Peters, in the manner of continuing an interrupted conversation. "Their own rope. Now let's go upstairs again and go over it, piece by piece. It would have to have been someone who knew just the—"

240   The stair door closed behind them and their voices were lost.

The two women sat motionless, not looking at each other, but as if peering into something and at the same time holding back. When they spoke now it was as if they were afraid of what they were saying, but as if they could not help saying it.

"She liked the bird," said Martha Hale, low and slowly. "She was going to bury it in that pretty box."

"When I was a girl," said Mrs. Peters, under her breath, "my kitten—there was a boy took a hatchet, and before my eyes—before I could get there—" She covered her face an instant. "If they hadn't held me back I would have"—she caught herself, looked upstairs where footsteps were heard, and finished weakly—"hurt him."

Then they sat without speaking or moving.

245   "I wonder how it would seem," Mrs. Hale at last began, as if feeling her way over strange ground—"never to have had any children around?" Her eyes made a slow sweep of the kitchen, as if seeing what that kitchen had meant through all the years. "No, Wright wouldn't like the bird," she said after that—"a thing that sang. She used to sing. He killed that too." Her voice tightened.

Mrs. Peters moved uneasily.

"Of course we don't know who killed the bird."

"I knew John Wright," was Mrs. Hale's answer.

"It was an awful thing was done in this house that night, Mrs. Hale," said the sheriff's wife. "Killing a man while he slept—slipping a thing round his neck that choked the life out of him."

250   Mrs. Hale's hand went out to the bird cage.

"His neck. Choked the life out of him."

"We don't *know* who killed him," whispered Mrs. Peters wildly. "We don't *know*."

Mrs. Hale had not moved. "If there had been years and years of—nothing, then a bird to sing to you, it would be awful—still—after the bird was still."

It was as if something within her not herself had spoken, and it found in Mrs. Peters something she did not know as herself.

255   "I know what stillness is," she said, in a queer, monotonous voice. "When we homesteaded in Dakota, and my first baby died—after he was two years old—and me with no other then—"

Mrs. Hale stirred.

"How soon do you suppose they'll be through looking for the evidence?"

"I know what stillness is," repeated Mrs. Peters, in just that same way. Then she too pulled back. "The law has got to punish crime, Mrs. Hale," she said in her tight little way.

"I wish you'd seen Minnie Foster," was the answer, "when she wore a white dress with blue ribbons, and stood up there in the choir and sang."

The picture of that girl, the fact that she had lived neighbor to that girl for twenty years,   260
and had let her die for lack of life, was suddenly more than she could bear.

"Oh, I *wish* I'd come over here once in a while!" she cried. "That was a crime! Who's
going to punish that?"

"We mustn't take on," said Mrs. Peters, with a frightened look toward the stairs.

"I might 'a' *known* she needed help! I tell you, it's *queer*, Mrs. Peters. We live close
together, and we live far apart. We all go through the same things—it's all just a different
kind of the same thing! If it weren't—why do you and I *understand?* Why do we *know*—
what we know this minute?"

She dashed her hand across her eyes. Then, seeing the jar of fruit on the table, she reached
for it and choked out:

"If I was you I wouldn't *tell* her her fruit was gone! Tell her it *ain't*. Tell her it's all right—   265
all of it. Here—take this in to prove it to her! She—she may never know whether it was
broke or not."

She turned away.

Mrs. Peters reached out for the bottle of fruit as if she were glad to take it—as if touching a familiar thing, having something to do, could keep her from something else. She got
up, looked about for something to wrap the fruit in, took a petticoat from the pile of clothes
she had brought from the front room, and nervously started winding that round the bottle.

"My!" she began, in a high, false voice, "it's a good thing the men couldn't hear us! Getting all stirred up over a little thing like a—dead canary." She hurried over that. "As if that
could have anything to do with—with—My, wouldn't they *laugh?*"

Footsteps were heard on the stairs.

"Maybe they would," muttered Mrs. Hale—"maybe they wouldn't."   270

"No, Peters," said the county attorney incisively; "it's all perfectly clear, except the reason for doing it. But you know juries when it comes to women. If there was some definite
thing—something to show. Something to make a story about. A thing that would connect
up with this clumsy way of doing it."

In a covert way Mrs. Hale looked at Mrs. Peters. Mrs. Peters was looking at her. Quickly
they looked away from each other. The outer door opened and Mr. Hale came in.

"I've got the team° round now," he said. "Pretty cold out there."

"I'm going to stay here awhile by myself," the county attorney suddenly announced.
"You can send Frank out for me, can't you?" he asked the sheriff. "I want to go over everything. I'm not satisfied we can't do better."

Again, for one brief moment, the two women's eyes found one another.   275

The sheriff came up to the table.

"Did you want to see what Mrs. Peters was going to take in?"

The county attorney picked up the apron. He laughed.

"Oh, I guess they're not very dangerous things the ladies have picked out."

Mrs. Hale's hand was on the sewing basket in which the box was concealed. She felt that   280
she ought to take her hand off the basket. She did not seem able to. He picked up one of the
quilt blocks which she had piled on to cover the box. Her eyes felt like fire. She had a feeling
that if he took up the basket she would snatch it from him.

But he did not take it up. With another little laugh, he turned away, saying:

"No; Mrs. Peters doesn't need supervising. For that matter, a sheriff's wife is married to
the law. Ever think of it that way, Mrs. Peters?"

Mrs. Peters was standing beside the table. Mrs. Hale shot a look up at her; but she could
not see her face. Mrs. Peters had turned away. When she spoke, her voice was muffled.

°*team:* team of horses pulling the buggy or sleigh in which the group had come.

"Not—just that way," she said.

285 "Married to the law!" chuckled Mrs. Peters' husband. He moved toward the door into the front room, and said to the county attorney:

"I just want you to come in here a minute, George. We ought to take a look at these windows."

"Oh—windows," said the county attorney scoffingly.

"We'll be right out, Mr. Hale," said the sheriff to the farmer, who was still waiting by the door.

Hale went to look after the horses. The sheriff followed the county attorney into the other room. Again—for one final moment—the two women were alone in that kitchen.

290 Martha Hale sprang up, her hands tight together, looking at that other woman, with whom it rested. At first she could not see her eyes, for the sheriff's wife had not turned back since she turned away at that suggestion of being married to the law. But now Mrs. Hale made her turn back. Her eyes made her turn back. Slowly, unwillingly, Mrs. Peters turned her head until her eyes met the eyes of the other woman. There was a moment when they held each other in a steady, burning look in which there was no evasion nor flinching. Then Martha Hale's eyes pointed the way to the basket in which was hidden the thing that would make certain the conviction of the other woman—that woman who was not there and yet who had been there with them all through that hour.

For a moment Mrs. Peters did not move. And then she did it. With a rush forward, she threw back the quilt pieces, got the box, tried to put it in her handbag. It was too big. Desperately she opened it, started to take the bird out. But there she broke—she could not touch the bird. She stood there helpless, foolish.

There was the sound of a knob turning in the inner door. Martha Hale snatched the box from the sheriff's wife, and got it in the pocket of her big coat just as the sheriff and the county attorney came back into the kitchen.

"Well, Henry," said the county attorney facetiously, "at least we found out that she was not going to quilt it. She was going to—what is it you call it, ladies?"

Mrs. Hale's hand was against the pocket of her coat.

295 "We call it—knot it, Mr. Henderson."

QUESTIONS

1. Who is the central character? That is, on whom does the story focus? What do you learn about her? What are her circumstances of life? Why does she explain her actions as she does?

2. Describe the differences between Mrs. Hale and Mrs. Peters, in terms of their status, backgrounds, and comparative qualities and strengths of character.

3. Why do the two women not voice their conclusions about the murderer? How does Glaspell show that they both know the murderer's identity, the reasons, and the method? At the story's conclusion, why do they silently "cover up" the clues they have discovered?

ZORA NEALE HURSTON (1891–1960)

Zora Neale Hurston grew up in Eatonville, Florida, the first incorporated all-black community in America. Her father, a Baptist preacher, was the mayor, but the family was poor. "Mama," she said, "exhorted her children at every opportunity to 'jump at de sun.' We might not land on the sun, but at least we would get off the ground." She won a scholarship to Barnard College, studied anthropology, and

became a prominent member of the black cultural revival known as the Harlem Renaissance. Although a noted author and folklorist, she alienated so many people by her opposition to the civil rights movement that she died in 1960 in poverty and obscurity.

Spunk (1925)

1

A giant of a brown-skinned man sauntered up the one street of the village and out into the palmetto thickets with a small pretty woman clinging lovingly to his arm.

"Looka theah, folkses!" cried Elijah Mosley, slapping his leg gleefully. "Theah they go, big as life an' brassy as tacks."

All the loungers in the store tried to walk to the door with an air of nonchalance but with small success.

"Now pee-eople!" Walter Thomas gasped. "Will you look at 'em!"

"But that's one thing Ah likes about Spunk Banks—he ain't skeered of nothin' on God's   5
green footstool— *nothin*'! He rides that log down at saw-mill jus' like he struts 'round wid another man's wife—jus' don't give a kitty. When Tes' Miller got cut to giblets on that circle-saw, Spunk steps right up and starts ridin'. The rest of us was skeered to go near it."

A round-shouldered figure in overalls much too large came nervously in the door and the talking ceased. The men looked at each other and winked.

"Gimme some soda-water. Sass'prilla. Ah reckon," the newcomer ordered, and stood far down the counter near the open pickled pig-feet tub to drink it.

Elijah nudged Walter and turned with mock gravity to the newcomer.

"Say, Joe, how's everything up yo' way? How's yo' wife?"

Joe started and all but dropped the bottle he was holding. He swallowed several times   10
painfully and his lips trembled.

"Aw 'Lige, you oughtn't to do nothin' like that," Walter grumbled. Elijah ignored him.

"She jus' passed heah a few minutes ago goin' thata way," with a wave of his hand in the direction of the woods.

Now Joe knew his wife had passed that way. He knew that the men lounging in the general store had seen her; moreover, he knew that the men knew *he* knew. He stood there silent for a long moment staring blankly, with his Adam's apple twitching nervously up and down his throat. One could actually *see* the pain he was suffering, his eyes, his face, his hands, and even the dejected slump of his shoulders. He set the bottle down upon the counter. He didn't bang it, just eased it out of his hand silently and fiddled with his suspender buckle.

"Well, Ah'm goin' after her to-day. Ah'm goin' an' fetch her back, Spunk's done gone too fur."

He reached deep down into his trouser pocket and drew out a hollow ground razor,   15
large and shiny, and passed his moistened thumb back and forth over the edge.

"Talkin' like a man, Joe. 'Course that's yo' fambly affairs, but Ah like to see grit in anybody."

Joe Kanty laid down a nickel and stumbled out into the street.

Dusk crept in from the woods. Ike Clarke lit the swinging oil lamp that was almost immediately surrounded by candle-flies. The men laughed boisterously behind Joe's back as they watched him shamble woodward.

"You oughtn't to said whut you said to him, 'Lige—look how it worked him up," Walter chided.

"And Ah hope it did work him up. Tain't even decent for a man to take and take like he   20
do."

"Spunk will sho' kill him."

"Aw, Ah doan know. You never kin tell. He might turn him up an' spank him fur gettin' in the way, but Spunk wouldn't shoot no unarmed man. Dat razor he carried outa heah ain't gonna run Spunk down an' cut him, an' Joe ain't got the nerve to go to Spunk with it knowin' he totes that Army .45. He makes that break outa heah to bluff us. He's gonna hide that razor behind the first palmetto root and sneak back home to bed. Don't tell me nothin' 'bout that rabbit-foot colored man. Didn't he meet Spunk an' Lena face to face one day las' week an' mumble sumthin' to Spunk 'bout lettin' his wife alone?"

"What did Spunk say?" Walter broke in. "Ah like him fine but tain't right the way he carries on wid Lena Kanty, jus' 'cause Joe's timid 'bout fightin'."

"You wrong theah, Walter. Tain't 'cause Joe's timid at all, it's 'cause Spunk wants Lena. If Joe was a passle of wile cats Spunk would tackle the job just the same. He'd go after *any-thing* he wanted the same way. As Ah wuz sayin' a minute ago, he tole Joe right to his face that Lena was his. 'Call her and see if she'll come. A woman knows her boss an' she answers when he calls.' 'Lena, ain't I yo' husband?' Joe sorter whines out. Lena looked at him real disgusted but she don't answer and she don't move outa her tracks. Then Spunk reaches out an' takes hold of her arm an' says: 'Lena, youse mine. From now on Ah works for you an' fights for you an' Ah never wants you to look to nobody for a crumb of bread, a stitch of close or a shingle to go over yo' head, but me long as Ah live. Ah'll git the lumber foh owah house to-morrow. Go home an' git yo' things together!'

25   "'Thass mah house,' Lena speaks up. 'Papa gimme that.'

"'Well,' says Spunk, 'doan give up whut's yours, but when youse inside doan forgit youse mine, an' let no other man git outa his place wid you!'

"Lena looked up at him with her eyes so full of love that they wuz runnin' over, an' Spunk seen it an' Joe seen it too, and his lip started to tremblin' and his Adam's apple was galloping up and down his neck like a race horse. Ah bet he's wore out half a dozen Adam's apples since Spunk's been on the job with Lena. That's all he'll do. He'll be back heah after while swallowin' an' workin' his lips like he wants to say somethin' an' can't."

"But didn't he do nothin' to stop 'em?"

"Nope, not a frazzlin' thing—jus' stood there. Spunk took Lena's arm and walked off jus' like nothin' ain't happened and he stood there gazin' after them till they was outa sight. Now you know a woman don't want no man like that. I'm jus' waitin' to see whut he's goin' to say when he gits back."

2

30   But Joe Kanty never came back, never. The men in the store heard the sharp report of a pistol somewhere distant in the palmetto thicket and soon Spunk came walking leisurely, with his big black Stetson set at the same rakish angle and Lena clinging to his arm, came walking right into the general store. Lena wept in a frightened manner.

"Well," Spunk announced calmly, "Joe came out there wid a meat axe an' made me kill him."

He sent Lena home and led the men back to Joe—crumpled and limp with his right hand still clutching his razor.

"See mah back? Mah close cut clear through. He sneaked up an' tried to kill me from the back, but Ah got him, an' got him good, first shot," Spunk said.

The men glared at Elijah, accusingly.

35   "Take him up an' plant him in Stony Lonesome," Spunk said in a careless voice. "Ah didn't wanna shoot him but he made me do it. He's a dirty coward, jumpin' on a man from behind."

Spunk turned on his heel and sauntered away to where he knew his love wept in fear for him and no man stopped him. At the general store later on, they all talked of locking him up until the sheriff should come from Orlando, but no one did anything but talk.

A clear case of self-defense, the trial was a short one, and Spunk walked out of the court house to freedom again. He could work again, ride the dangerous log-carriage that fed the singing, snarling, biting circle-saw; he could stroll the soft dark lanes with his guitar. He was free to roam the woods again; he was free to return to Lena. He did all these things.

3

"Whut you reckon, Walt?" Elijah asked one night later, "Spunk's gittin' ready to marry Lena!"

"Naw! Why, Joe ain't had time to git cold yit. Nohow Ah didn't figger Spunk was the marryin' kind."

"Well, he is," rejoined Elijah. "He done moved most of Lena's things—and her along wid 'em—over to the Bradley house. He's buying it. Jus' like Ah told yo' all right in heah the night Joe was kilt. Spunk's crazy 'bout Lena. He don't want folks to keep on talkin' 'bout her—thass reason he's rushin' so. Funny thing 'bout that bob-cat, wan't it?"

"What bob-cat, 'Lige? Ah ain't heered 'bout none."

"Ain't cher? Well, night befo' las' as they was goin' to bed, a big black bob-cat, black all over, you hear me, *black*, walked round and round that house and howled like forty, an' when Spunk got his gun an' went to the winder to shoot it, he says it stood right still an' looked him in the eye, an' howled right at him. The thing got Spunk so nervoused up he couldn't shoot. But Spunk says twan't no bob-cat nohow. He says it was Joe done sneaked back from Hell!"

"Humph!" sniffed Walter, "he oughter be nervous after what he done: Ah reckon Joe come back to dare him to marry Lena, or to come out an' fight. Ah bet he'll be back time and again, too. Known what Ah think? Joe wuz a braver man than Spunk."

There was a general shout of derision from the group.

"Thass a fact," went on Walter. "Lookit whut he done; took a razor an' went out to fight a man he knowed toted a gun an' wuz a crack shot, too; 'nother thing he wuz skeered of Spunk, skeered plumb stiff! But he went jes' the same. It took him a long time to get his nerve up. Tain't nothin' for Spunk to fight when he ain't skeered of nothin'. Now, Joe's done come back to have it out wid the man that's got all he ever had. Y'all know Joe ain't never had nothin' nor wanted nothin' besides Lena. It musta been a h'ant 'cause ain't nobody never seen no black bob-cat."

" 'Nother thing," cut in one of the men, "Spunk was cussin' a blue streak to-day 'cause he 'lowed dat saw wuz wobblin'—almos' got 'im once. The machinist come, looked it over an' said it wuz alright. Spunk musta been leanin' t'wards it some. Den he claimed somebody pushed 'im but twan't nobody close to 'im. Ah wuz glad when knockin' off time came. I'm skeered of dat man when he gits hot. He'd beat you full of button holes as quick as he'd look atcher."

4

The men gathered the next evening in a different mood, no laughter. No badinage this time.

"Look, 'Lige, you goin' to set up wid Spunk?"

"Naw, Ah reckon not, Walter. Tell yuh the truth, Ah'm a li'l bit skittish. Spunk died too wicket—died cussin' he did. You know he thought he was done outa life."

"Good Lawd, who'd he think done it?"

"Joe."

"Joe Kanty? How come?"

"Walter, Ah b'leeve Ah will walk up thata way an' set. Lena would like it Ah reckon."

"But whut did he say, 'Lige?"

Elijah did not answer until they had left the lighted store and were strolling down the dark street.

"Ah wuz loadin' a wagon wid scantlin' right near the saw when Spunk fell on the carriage but 'fore Ah could git to him the saw got him in the body—awful sight. Me an' Skint Miller got him off but it was too late. Anybody could see that. The fust thing he said wuz: 'He pushed me, 'Lige—the dirty hound pushed me in the back!'—he was spittin' blood at ev'ry breath. We laid him on the sawdust pile with his face to the East so's he could die easy. He helt mah han' till the last, Walter, and said: 'It was Joe, 'Lige . . . the dirty sneak shoved me . . . he didn't dare come to mah face . . . but Ah'll git the son-of-a-wood louse soon's Ah get there an' make hell too hot for him . . . Ah felt him shove me . . . !' Thass how he died."

"If spirits kin fight, there's a powerful tussle goin' on somewhere ovah Jordan,° cause Ah b'leeve Joe's ready for Spunk an' ain't skeered any more—yas, Ah b'leeve Joe pushed 'im mahself."

They had arrived at the house. Lena's lamentations were deep and loud. She had filled the room with magnolia blossoms that gave off a heavy sweet odor. The keepers of the wake tipped about whispering in frightened tones. Everyone in the village was there, even old Jeff Kanty, Joe's father, who a few hours before would have been afraid to come within ten feet of him, stood leering triumphantly down upon the fallen giant as if his fingers had been the teeth of steel that laid him low.

The cooling board consisted of three sixteen-inch boards on saw horses, a dingy sheet was his shroud.

60   The women ate heartily of the funeral baked meats and wondered who would be Lena's next. The men whispered coarse conjectures between guzzles of whiskey.

QUESTIONS

1. How is revenge different from justice? Can you think of any actions you have taken out of revenge? How did you feel about what you did afterward?

2. What function do the characters other than Joe and Spunk play in the story? Do they interpret the events in the story properly?

3. Spunk is let off at his trial because of a "clear case of self-defense, . . . " Were you convinced that this was the correct verdict? Is there any evidence that he may have not acted in self-defense?

4. Why do you think the story was divided in four distinct and numbered sections? How would you summarize what happens in each one? How does each section relate to the other sections?

5. Is it possible that the events following the death of Joe are due to Spunk's feeling of guilt? Explain.

KATHERINE MANSFIELD (1888–1923)

"Katherine Mansfield" was the pen name of Kathleen Mansfield Beauchamp Murry. She was brought up in a prosperous household in New Zealand, and in the early years of the twentieth century she went to England to study at Queen's College. An accomplished cellist, she had been a serious student of music, but she was discouraged from that profession by her father. She then turned to writing. Before she was thirty she realized that she was afflicted with tuberculosis,

---

°*Jordan:* Crossing the River Jordan means passing into the Promised Land, here seen as the hereafter.

and spent many of her remaining years desperately seeking a cure. Without the benefit of modern antibiotics, however, her doom was sealed, and she succumbed to the disease in her thirty-fifth year. During her lifetime her collections were In a German Pension *(1911),* Bliss and Other Stories *(1920), and* The Garden Party and Other Stories *(1922), which included "Miss Brill." Her posthumous collections were* The Dove's Nest *(1923) and* Something Childish *(1924). Her husband and literary executor, the critic John Middleton Murry, arranged for a number of other publications after her death, including her letters and selections from her journals.*

Miss Brill (1920)

Although it was so brilliantly fine—the blue sky powdered with gold and great spots of light like white wine splashed over the Jardins Publiques° —Miss Brill° was glad that she had decided on her fur. The air was motionless, but when you opened your mouth there was just a faint chill, like a chill from a glass of iced water before you sip, and now and again a leaf came drifting—from nowhere, from the sky. Miss Brill put up her hand and touched her fur. Dear little thing! It was nice to feel it again. She had taken it out of its box that afternoon, shaken out the moth-powder, given it a good brush, and rubbed the life back into the dim little eyes. "What has been happening to me?" said the sad little eyes. Oh, how sweet it was to see them snap at her again from the red eiderdown! . . . But the nose, which was of some black composition, wasn't at all firm. It must have had a knock, somehow. Never mind—a little dab of black sealing-wax when the time came—when it was absolutely necessary. . . . Little rogue! Yes, she really felt like that about it. Little rogue biting its tail just by her left ear. She could have taken it off and laid it on her lap and stroked it. She felt a tingling in her hands and arms, but that came from walking, she supposed. And when she breathed, something light and sad—no, not sad, exactly—something gentle seemed to move in her bosom.

There were a number of people out this afternoon, far more than last Sunday. And the band sounded louder and gayer. That was because the Season had begun. For although the band played all the year round on Sundays, out of season it was never the same. It was like someone playing with only the family to listen; it didn't care how it played if there weren't any strangers present. Wasn't the conductor wearing a new coat, too? She was sure it was new. He scraped with his foot and flapped his arms like a rooster about to crow, and bandsmen sitting in the green rotunda blew out their cheeks and glared at the music. Now there came a little "flutey" bit—very pretty!—a little chain of bright drops. She was sure it would be repeated. It was; she lifted her head and smiled.

Only two people shared her "special" seat: a fine old man in a velvet coat, his hands clasped over a huge carved walking-stick, and a big old woman, sitting upright, with a roll of knitting on her embroidered apron. They did not speak. This was disappointing, for Miss Brill always looked forward to the conversation. She had become really quite expert, she thought, at listening as though she didn't listen, at sitting in other people's lives just for a minute while they talked round her.

She glanced, sideways, at the old couple. Perhaps they would go soon. Last Sunday, too, hadn't been as interesting as usual. An Englishman and his wife, he wearing a dreadful Panama hat and she button boots. And she'd gone on the whole time about how she ought to wear spectacles; she knew she needed them; but that it was no good getting any; they'd be sure to break and they'd never keep on. And he'd been so patient. He'd suggested everything—gold rims, the kind that curved round your ears, little pads inside the bridge.

°*Jardins Publiques:* public gardens or park. The setting of the story is apparently a French seaside town.
°*Miss Brill:* Brill is the name of a common deep-sea flatfish.

No, nothing would please her. "They'll always be sliding down my nose!" Miss Brill had wanted to shake her.

5   The old people sat on the bench, still as statues. Never mind, there was always the crowd to watch. To and fro, in front of the flower-beds and the band rotunda, the couples and groups paraded, stopped to talk, to greet, to buy a handful of flowers from the old beggar who had his tray fixed to the railings. Little children ran among them, swooping and laughing; little boys with big white silk bows under their chins, little girls, little French dolls, dressed up in velvet and lace. And sometimes a tiny staggerer came suddenly rocking into the open from under the trees, stopped, stared, as suddenly sat down "flop," until its small high-stepping mother, like a young hen, rushed scolding to its rescue. Other people sat on the benches and green chairs, but they were nearly always the same, Sunday after Sunday, and—Miss Brill had often noticed—there was something funny about nearly all of them. They were odd, silent, nearly all old, and from the way they stared they looked as though they'd just come from dark little rooms or even—even cupboards!

Behind the rotunda the slender trees with yellow leaves down drooping and through them just a line of sea, and beyond the blue sky with gold-veined clouds.

Tum-tum-tum tiddle-um! tiddle-um! tum tiddle-um tum ta! blew the band.

Two young girls in red came by and two young soldiers in blue met them, and they laughed and paired and went off arm-in-arm. Two peasant women with funny straw hats passed, gravely, leading beautiful smoke-coloured donkeys. A cold, pale nun hurried by. A beautiful woman came along and dropped her bunch of violets, and a little boy ran after to hand them to her, and she took them and threw them away as if they'd been poisoned. Dear me! Miss Brill didn't know whether to admire that or not! And now an ermine toque° and a gentleman in grey met just in front of her. He was tall, stiff, dignified and she was wearing the ermine toque she'd bought when her hair was yellow. Now everything, her hair, her face, even her eyes, was the same colour as the shabby ermine, and her hand, in its cleaned glove, lifted to dab her lips, was a tiny yellowish paw. Oh, she was so pleased to see him— delighted! She rather thought they were going to meet that afternoon. She described where she'd been—everywhere, here, there, along by the sea. The day was so charming—didn't he agree? And wouldn't he, perhaps? . . . But he shook his head, lighted a cigarette, slowly breathed a great deep puff into her face, and, even while she was still talking and laughing, flicked the match away and walked on. The ermine toque was alone; she smiled more brightly than ever. But even the band seemed to know what she was feeling and played more softly, played tenderly, and the drum beat, "The Brute! The Brute!" over and over. What would she do? What was going to happen now? But as Miss Brill wondered, the ermine toque turned, raised her hand as though she'd seen some one else, much nicer, just over there, and pattered away. And the band changed again and played more quickly, more gaily than ever, and the old couple on Miss Brill's seat got up and marched away, and such a funny old man with long whiskers hobbled along in time to the music and was nearly knocked over by four girls walking abreast.

Oh, how fascinating it was! How she enjoyed it! How she loved sitting here, watching it all! It was like a play. It was exactly like a play. Who could believe the sky at the back wasn't painted? But it wasn't till a little brown dog trotted on solemn and then slowly trotted off, like a little "theatre" dog, a little dog that had been drugged, that Miss Brill discovered what it was that made it so exciting. They were all on the stage. They weren't only the audience, not only looking on; they were acting. Even she had a part and came every Sunday. No doubt somebody would have noticed if she hadn't been there; she was part of the performance

---

°*ermine toque:* close-fitting hat made of the white fur of an ermine; here the phrase stands for the woman wearing the hat.

after all. How strange she'd never thought of it like that before! And yet it explained why she made such a point of starting from home at just the same time each week—so as not to be late for the performance—and it also explained why she had quite a queer, shy feeling at telling her English pupils how she spent her Sunday afternoons. No wonder! Miss Brill nearly laughed out loud. She was on the stage. She thought of the old invalid gentleman to whom she read the newspaper four afternoons a week while he slept in the garden. She had got quite used to the frail head on the cotton pillow, the hollowed eyes, the open mouth and the high pinched nose. If he'd been dead she mightn't have noticed for weeks; she wouldn't have minded. But suddenly he knew he was having the paper read to him by an actress! "An actress!" The old head lifted; two points of light quivered in the old eyes. "An actress—are ye?" And Miss Brill smoothed the newspaper as though it were the manuscript of her part and said gently: "Yes, I have been an actress for a long time."

The band had been having a rest. Now they started again. And what they played was warm, sunny, yet there was just a faint chill—a something, what was it?—not sadness—no, not sadness—a something that made you want to sing. The tune lifted, lifted, the light shone; and it seemed to Miss Brill that in another moment all of them, all the whole company, would begin singing. The young ones, the laughing ones who were moving together, they would begin, and the men's voices, very resolute and brave, would join them. And then she too, she too, and the others on the benches—they would come in with a kind of accompaniment— something low, that scarcely rose or fell, something so beautiful—moving. . . . And Miss Brill's eyes filled with tears and she looked smiling at all the other members of the company. Yes, we understand, we understand, she thought—though what they understood she didn't know. [10]

Just at the moment a boy and girl came and sat down where the old couple had been. They were beautifully dressed; they were in love. The hero and heroine, of course, just arrived from his father's yacht. And still soundlessly singing, still with that trembling smile, Miss Brill prepared to listen.

"No, not now," said the girl, "Not here, I can't."

"But why? Because of that stupid old thing at the end there?" asked the boy. "Why does she come here at all—who wants her? Why doesn't she keep her silly old mug at home?"

"It's her fu-fur which is so funny," giggled the girl. "It's exactly like a fried whiting."

"Ah, be off with you!" said the boy in an angry whisper. Then: "Tell me, ma petite chérie—" [15]

"No, not here," said the girl, "Not *yet*."

On her way home she usually bought a slice of honeycake at the baker's. It was her Sunday treat. Sometimes there was an almond in her slice, sometimes not. It made a great difference. If there was an almond it was like carrying home a tiny present—a surprise— something that might very well not have been there. She hurried on the almond Sundays and struck the match for the kettle in quite a dashing way.

But to-day she passed the baker's by, climbed the stairs, went into the little dark room— her room like a cupboard—and sat down on the red eiderdown. She sat there for a long time. The box that the fur came out of was on the bed. She unclasped the necklet quickly; quickly, without looking, laid it inside. But when she put the lid on she thought she heard something crying.

QUESTIONS

1. Describe the scene in which the action of this story occurs.

2. What details about the life of Miss Brill do we learn from the story? What sort of life does she live? How often does she come to the park? How is her life comparable to the lives of the old people sitting on the benches as described in paragraph 5?

3. Miss Brill observes a number of people who are walking in the park, and she overhears some of their conversations. Why does Mansfield described these scenes, or vignettes, in so detailed a way?

4. What is the significance of the young couple near the story's end? What is Miss Brill's response to them? What is happening to Miss Brill as the story ends?

AMY TAN (b. 1952)

Amy Tan was born in Oakland, California, several years after her parents had left their native China to settle in the San Francisco Bay Area. Early in her life she exhibited talent as a writer, winning a first prize for essay writing at the age of eight. Her family endured the untimely deaths of her father and brother in 1967 and 1968, and the remaining family spent time afterward in Switzerland. She attended a number of U.S. colleges, including San Jose State University, where she graduated with honors in 1972 and received an MA in 1973. After graduating she did freelance business writ-
ing for companies such as IBM and Pacific Bell. By 1985 she had decided to devote herself to the writing of fiction, and she launched her career in 1986 with the publication of her first short story, "End Game." In 1989 her The Joy Luck Club, *an interlinked collection of stories, was published and enjoyed forty weeks on the* New York Times *best-sellers list. Her other major books are* The Kitchen God's Wife *(1991),* The Hundred Secret Senses *(1995),* The Bonesetter's Daughter *(2001), which had been earlier excerpted for publication in* The New Yorker, Saving Fish from Drowning *(2005), and* The Valley of Amazement *(2013). Tan has also written two children's books,* The Moon Lady *(1992) and* SAGWA The Chinese Siamese Cat *(1994). She collaborates with novelist Stephen King, cartoonist Matt Groening, novelist Barbara Kingsolver, and humorist Dave Barry in a "literary garage band, the Rock Bottom Remainders," which raises money for literacy causes and also for groups devoted to First Amendment rights. "Two Kinds" is taken from* The Joy Luck Club.

Two Kinds (1989)

My mother believed you could be anything you wanted to be in America. You could open a restaurant. You could work for the government and get good retirement. You could buy a house with almost no money down. You could become rich. You could become instantly famous.

"Of course you can be prodigy, too," my mother told me when I was nine. "You can be best anything. What does Auntie Lindo know? Her daughter, she is only best tricky."

America was where all my mother's hopes lay. She had come here in 1949 after losing everything in China: her mother and father, her family home, her first husband, and two daughters, twin baby girls. But she never looked back with regret. There were so many ways for things to get better.

We didn't immediately pick the right kind of prodigy. At first my mother thought I could be a Chinese Shirley Temple. We'd watch Shirley's old movies on TV as though they were training films. My mother would poke my arm and say, "Ni kan"—You watch. And I would see Shirley tapping her feet, or singing a sailor song, or pursing her lips into a very round O while saying, "Oh my goodness."

5   "Ni kan," said my mother as Shirley's eyes flooded with tears. "You already know how. Don't need talent for crying!"

Soon after my mother got this idea about Shirley Temple, she took me to a beauty training school in the Mission district and put me in the hands of a student who could barely hold the scissors without shaking. Instead of getting big fat curls, I emerged with an uneven mass of crinkly black fuzz. My mother dragged me off to the bathroom and tried to wet down my hair.

"You look like Negro Chinese," she lamented, as if I had done this on purpose.

The instructor of the beauty training school had to lop off these soggy clumps to make my hair even again. "Peter Pan is very popular these days," the instructor assured my mother. I now had hair the length of a boy's, with straight-across bangs that hung at a slant two inches above my eyebrows. I liked the haircut and it made me actually look forward to my future fame.

In fact, in the beginning, I was just as excited as my mother, maybe even more so. I pictured this prodigy part of me as many different images, trying each one on for size. I was a dainty ballerina girl standing by the curtains, waiting to hear the right music that would send me floating on my tiptoes. I was like the Christ child lifted out of the straw manger, crying with holy indignity. I was Cinderella stepping from her pumpkin carriage with sparkly cartoon music filling the air.

In all of my imaginings, I was filled with a sense that I would soon become *perfect*. My 10 mother and father would adore me. I would be beyond reproach. I would never feel the need to sulk for anything.

But sometimes the prodigy in me became impatient. "If you don't hurry up and get me out of here, I'm disappearing for good," it warned. "And then you'll always be nothing."

• • •

Every night after dinner, my mother and I would sit at the Formica kitchen table. She would present new tests, taking her examples from stories of amazing children she had read in *Ripley's Believe It or Not*, or *Good Housekeeping, Reader's Digest*, and a dozen other magazines she kept in a pile in our bathroom. My mother got these magazines from people whose houses she cleaned. And since she cleaned many houses each week, we had a great assortment. She would look through them all, searching for stories about remarkable children.

The first night she brought out a story about a three-year-old boy who knew the capitals of all the states and even most of the European countries. A teacher was quoted as saying the little boy could also pronounce the names of the foreign cities correctly.

"What's the capital of Finland?" my mother asked me, looking at the magazine story.

All I knew was the capital of California, because Sacramento was the name of the street 15 we lived on in Chinatown. "Nairobi!" I guessed, saying the most foreign word I could think of. She checked to see if that was possibly one way to pronounce "Helsinki" before showing me the answer.

The tests got harder—multiplying numbers in my head, finding the queen of hearts in a deck of cards, trying to stand on my head without using my hands, predicting the daily temperatures in Los Angeles, New York, and London.

One night I had to look at a page from the Bible for three minutes and then report everything I could remember. "Now Jehoshaphat had riches° and honor in abundance and . . . that's all I remember, Ma," I said.

And after seeing my mother's disappointed face once again, something inside of me began to die. I hated the tests, the raised hopes and failed expectations. Before going to bed

---

°*Now Jehoshaphat had riches*: Jing-Mei had been told to report on the Hebrew monarch Jehoshaphat as narrated in the eighteenth chapter of II Chronicles.

that night, I looked in the mirror above the bathroom sink and when I saw only my face staring back—and that it would always be this ordinary face—I began to cry. Such a sad, ugly girl! I made high-pitched noises like a crazed animal, trying to scratch out the face in the mirror.

And then I saw what seemed to be the prodigy side of me—because I had never seen that face before. I looked at my reflection, blinking so I could see more clearly. The girl staring back at me was angry, powerful. This girl and I were the same. I had new thoughts, willful thoughts, or rather thoughts filled with lots of won'ts. I won't let her change me, I promised myself. I won't be what I'm not.

20   So now on nights when my mother presented her tests, I performed listlessly, my head propped on one arm. I pretended to be bored. And I was. I got so bored I started counting the bellows of the foghorns out on the bay while my mother drilled me in other areas. The sound was comforting and reminded me of the cow jumping over the moon. And the next day, I played a game with myself, seeing if my mother would give up on me before eight bellows. After a while I usually counted only one, maybe two bellows at most. At last she was beginning to give up hope.

Two or three months had gone by without any mention of my being a prodigy again. And then one day my mother was watching *The Ed Sullivan Show*° on TV. The TV was old and the sound kept shorting out. Every time my mother got halfway up from the sofa to adjust the set, the sound would go back on and Ed would be talking. As soon as she sat down, Ed would go silent again. She got up, the TV broke into loud piano music. She sat down. Silence. Up and down, back and forth, quiet and loud. It was like a stiff embraceless dance between her and the TV set. Finally she stood by the set with her hand on the sound dial.

She seemed entranced by the music, a little frenzied piano piece with this mesmerizing quality, sort of quick passages and then teasing lilting ones before it returned to the quick playful parts.

"*Ni kan*," my mother said, calling me over with hurried hand gestures, "Look here."

I could see why my mother was fascinated by the music. It was being pounded out by a little Chinese girl, about nine years old, with a Peter Pan haircut. The girl had the sauciness of a Shirley Temple. She was proudly modest like a proper Chinese child. And she also did this fancy sweep of a curtsy, so that the fluffy skirt of her white dress cascaded slowly to the floor like the petals of a large carnation.

25   In spite of these warning signs, I wasn't worried. Our family had no piano and we couldn't afford to buy one, let alone reams of sheet music and piano lessons. So I could be generous in my comments when my mother bad-mouthed the little girl on TV.

"Play note right, but doesn't sound good! No singing sound," complained my mother.

"What are you picking on her for?" I said carelessly. "She's pretty good. Maybe she's not the best, but she's trying hard." I knew almost immediately I would be sorry I said that.

"Just like you," she said. "Not the best. Because you not trying." She gave a little huff as she let go of the sound dial and sat down on the sofa.

The little Chinese girl sat down also to play an encore of "Anitra's Dance" by Grieg.° I remember the song, because later on I had to learn how to play it.

30   Three days after watching *The Ed Sullivan Show*, my mother told me what my schedule would be for piano lessons and piano practice. She had talked to Mr. Chong, who lived on

---

°*The Ed Sullivan Show:* Ed Sullivan (1902–1974), originally a newspaper columnist, hosted this popular variety television show from 1948 to 1971.
°*"Anitra's Dance" by Grieg:* a portion of the suite composed for Ibsen's *Peer Gynt* by Norwegian composer Edvard Grieg (1843–1907).

the first floor of our apartment building. Mr. Chong was a retired piano teacher and my mother had traded housecleaning services for weekly lessons and a piano for me to practice on every day, two hours a day, from four until six.

When my mother told me this, I felt as though I had been sent to hell. I whined and then kicked my foot a little when I couldn't stand it anymore.

"Why don't you like me the way I am? I'm *not* a genius! I can't play the piano. And even if I could, I wouldn't go on TV if you paid me a million dollars!" I cried.

My mother slapped me. "Who ask you be genius?" she shouted. "Only ask you be you best. For you sake. You think I want you be genius? Hnnh! What for! Who ask you!"

"So ungrateful," I heard her mutter in Chinese. "If she had as much talent as she has temper, she would be famous now."

Mr. Chong, whom I secretly nicknamed Old Chong, was very strange, always tapping   35 his fingers to the silent music of an invisible orchestra. He looked ancient in my eyes. He had lost most of the hair on top of his head and he wore thick glasses and had eyes that always looked tired and sleepy. But he must have been younger than I thought, since he lived with his mother and was not yet married.

I met Old Lady Chong once and that was enough. She had this peculiar smell like a baby that had done something in its pants. And her fingers felt like a dead person's, like an old peach I once found in the back of the refrigerator; the skin just slid off the meat when I picked it up.

I soon found out why Old Chong had retired from teaching piano. He was deaf. "Like Beethoven!" he shouted to me. "We're both listening only in our head!" And he would start to conduct his frantic silent sonatas.

Our lessons went like this. He would open the book and point to different things, explaining their purpose: "Key! Treble! Bass! No sharps or flats! So this is C major! Listen now and play after me!"

And then he would play the C scale a few times, a simple chord, and then, as if inspired by an old, unreachable itch, he gradually added more notes and running trills and a pounding bass until the music was really something quite grand.

I would play after him, the simple scale, the simple chord, and then I just played   40 some nonsense that sounded like a cat running up and down on top of garbage cans. Old Chong smiled and applauded and then said, "Very good! But now you must learn to keep time!"

So that's how I discovered that Old Chong's eyes were too slow to keep up with the wrong notes I was playing. He went through the motions in half-time. To help me keep rhythm, he stood behind me, pushing down on my right shoulder for every beat. He balanced pennies on top of my wrists so I would keep them still as I slowly played scales and arpeggios. He had me curve my hand around an apple and keep that shape when playing chords. He marched stiffly to show me how to make each finger dance up and down, staccato like an obedient little soldier.

He taught me all these things, and that was how I also learned I could be lazy and get away with mistakes, lots of mistakes. If I hit the wrong notes because I hadn't practiced enough, I never corrected myself. I just kept playing in rhythm. And Old Chong kept conducting his own private reverie.

So maybe I never really gave myself a fair chance. I did pick up the basics pretty quickly, and I might have become a good pianist at that young age. But I was so determined not to try, not to be anybody different that I learned to play only the most earsplitting preludes, the most discordant hymns.

Over the next year, I practiced like this, dutifully in my own way. And then one day I heard my mother and her friend Lindo Jong both talking in a loud bragging tone of voice so others could hear. It was after church, and I was leaning against the brick wall wearing a dress with stiff white petticoats. Auntie Lindo's daughter, Waverly, who was about my age, was standing farther down the wall about five feet away. We had grown up together and shared all the closeness of two sisters squabbling over crayons and dolls. In other words, for the most part, we hated each other. I thought she was snotty. Waverly Jong had gained a certain amount of fame as "Chinatown's Littlest Chinese Chess Champion."

45 "She bring home too many trophy," lamented Auntie Lindo that Sunday. "All day she play chess. All day I have no time do nothing but dust off her winnings." She threw a scolding look at Waverly, who pretended not to see her.

"You lucky you don't have this problem," said Auntie Lindo with a sigh to my mother.

And my mother squared her shoulders and bragged: "Our problem worser than yours. If we ask Jing-Mei wash dish, she hear nothing but music. It's like you can't stop this natural talent."

And right then, I was determined to put a stop to her foolish pride.

A few weeks later, Old Chong and my mother conspired to have me play in a talent show which would be held in the church hall. By then, my parents had saved up enough to buy me a secondhand piano, a black Wurlitzer spinet with a scarred bench. It was the showpiece of our living room.

50 For the talent show, I was to play a piece called "Pleading Child" from Schumann's *Scenes from Childhood*.° It was a simple, moody piece that sounded more difficult than it was. I was supposed to memorize the whole thing, playing the repeat parts twice to make the piece sound longer. But I dawdled over it, playing a few bars and then cheating, looking up to see what notes followed. I never really listened to what I was playing. I daydreamed about being somewhere else, about being someone else.

The part I liked to practice best was the fancy curtsy: right foot out, touch the rose on the carpet with a pointed foot, sweep to the side, left leg bends, look up and smile.

My parents invited all the couples from the Joy Luck Club to witness my debut. Auntie Lindo and Uncle Tin were there. Waverly and her two older brothers had also come. The first two rows were filled with children both younger and older than I was. The littlest ones got to go first. They recited simple nursery rhymes, squawked out tunes on miniature violins, twirled Hula Hoops, pranced in pink ballet tutus, and when they bowed or curtsied, the audience would sigh in unison, "Awww," and then clap enthusiastically.

When my turn came, I was very confident. I remember my childish excitement. It was as if I knew, without a doubt, that the prodigy side of me really did exist. I had no fear whatsoever, no nervousness. I remember thinking to myself, This is it! This is it! I looked out over the audience, at my mother's blank face, my father's yawn. Auntie Lindo's stiff-lipped smile, Waverly's sulky expression. I had on a white dress layered with sheets of lace, and a pink bow in my Peter Pan haircut. As I sat down I envisioned people jumping to their feet and Ed Sullivan rushing up to introduce me to everyone on TV.

And I started to play. It was so beautiful. I was so caught up in how lovely I looked that at first I didn't worry how I would sound. So it was a surprise to me when I hit the first wrong note and I realized something didn't sound quite right. And then I hit another and another followed that. A chill started at the top of my head and began to trickle down. Yet I couldn't stop playing, as though my hands were bewitched. I kept thinking my fingers would adjust themselves back, like a train switching to the right track. I played this strange jumble through two repeats, the sour notes staying with me all the way to the end.

55 When I stood up, I discovered my legs were shaking. Maybe I had just been nervous and the audience, like Old Chong, had seen me go through the right motions and had not

---

°*Scenes from Childhood: Scenes from Childhood*, or *Kinderszenen* (1836), is one of the best-known works for piano by Robert Schumann (1810–1856).

heard anything wrong at all. I swept my right foot out, went down on my knee, looked up and smiled. The room was quiet, except for Old Chong, who was beaming and shouting, "Bravo! Bravo! Well done!" But then I saw my mother's face, her stricken face. The audience clapped weakly, and as I walked back to my chair, with my whole face quivering as I tried not to cry, I heard a little boy whisper loudly to his mother, "That was awful," and the mother whispered back, "Well, she certainly tried."

And now I realized how many people were in the audience, the whole world it seemed. I was aware of eyes burning into my back. I felt the shame of my mother and father as they sat stiffly throughout the rest of the show.

We could have escaped during intermission. Pride and some strange sense of honor must have anchored my parents to their chairs. And so we watched it all: the eighteen-year-old boy with a fake mustache who did a magic show and juggled flaming hoops while riding a unicycle. The breasted girl with white makeup who sang from *Madama Butterfly*° and got honorable mention. And the eleven-year-old boy who won first prize playing a tricky violin song that sounded like a busy bee.°

After the show, the Hsus, the Jongs, and the St. Clairs from the Joy Luck Club came up to my mother and father.

"Lots of talented kids," Auntie Lindo said vaguely, smiling broadly.

"That was somethin' else," said my father, and I wondered if he was referring to me in a   60
humorous way, or whether he even remembered what I had done.

Waverly looked at me and shrugged her shoulders. "You aren't a genius like me," she said matter-of-factly. And if I hadn't felt so bad, I would have pulled her braids and punched her stomach.

But my mother's expression was what devastated me: a quiet, blank look that said she had lost everything. I felt the same way, and it seemed as if everybody were now coming up, like gawkers at the scene of an accident, to see what parts were actually missing. When we got on the bus to go home, my father was humming the busy-bee tune and my mother was silent. I kept thinking she wanted to wait until we got home before shouting at me. But when my father unlocked the door to our apartment, my mother walked in and then went to the back, into the bedroom. No accusations. No blame. And in a way, I felt disappointed. I had been waiting for her to start shouting, so I could shout back and cry and blame her for all my misery.

I assumed my talent-show fiasco meant I never had to play the piano again. But two days later, after school, my mother came out of the kitchen and saw me watching TV.

"Four clock," she reminded me as if it were any other day. I was stunned, as though she were asking me to go through the talent-show torture again. I wedged myself more tightly in front of the TV.

"Turn off TV," she called from the kitchen five minutes later.   65

I didn't budge. And then I decided. I didn't have to do what my mother said anymore. I wasn't her slave. This wasn't China. I had listened to her before and look what happened. She was the stupid one.

She came out from the kitchen and stood in the arched entryway of the living room. "Four clock," she said once again, louder.

"I'm not going to play anymore," I said nonchalantly. "Why should I? I'm not a genius."

She walked over and stood in front of the TV. I saw her chest was heaving up and down in an angry way.

°*Madama Butterfly:* The girl probably sang "Un Bel Di," the signature soprano aria from the opera *Madama Butterfly* by Giacomo Puccini (1858–1924).
°*busy bee:* probably the well-known "Flight of the Bumblebee" by Nikolay Rimsky-Korsakov (1844–1908) from the opera *Tale of Tsar Saltan* (1900).

70   "No!" I said, and I now felt stronger, as if my true self had finally emerged. So this was what had been inside me all along.

"No! I won't!" I screamed.

She yanked me by the arm, pulled me off the floor, snapped off the TV. She was frighteningly strong, half pulling, half carrying me toward the piano as I kicked the throw rugs under my feet. She lifted me up and onto the hard bench. I was sobbing by now, looking at her bitterly. Her chest was heaving even more and her mouth was open, smiling crazily as if she were pleased I was crying.

"You want me to be someone that I'm not!" I sobbed. "I'll never be the kind of daughter you want me to be!"

"Only two kinds of daughters," she shouted in Chinese. "Those who are obedient and those who follow their own mind! Only one kind of daughter can live in this house. Obedient daughter!"

75   "Then I wish I wasn't your daughter. I wish you weren't my mother," I shouted. As I said these things I got scared. It felt like worms and toads and slimy things crawling out of my chest, but it also felt good, as if this awful side of me had surfaced, at last.

"Too late change this," said my mother shrilly.

And I could sense her anger rising to its breaking point. I wanted to see it spill over. And that's when I remembered the babies she had lost in China, the ones we never talked about. "Then I wish I'd never been born!" I shouted. "I wish I were dead! Like them."

It was as if I had said the magic words. Alakazam!—and her face went blank, her mouth closed, her arms went slack, and she backed out of the room, stunned, as if she were blowing away like a small brown leaf, thin, brittle, lifeless.

It was not the only disappointment my mother felt in me. In the years that followed, I failed her so many times, each time asserting my own will, my right to fall short of expectations. I didn't get straight As. I didn't become class president. I didn't get into Stanford. I dropped out of college.

80   For unlike my mother, I did not believe I could be anything I wanted to be. I could only be me.

And for all those years, we never talked about the disaster at the recital or my terrible accusations afterward at the piano bench. All that remained unchecked, like a betrayal that was now unspeakable. So I never found a way to ask her why she had hoped for something so large that failure was inevitable.

And even worse, I never asked her what frightened me the most: Why had she given up hope?

For after our struggle at the piano, she never mentioned my playing again. The lessons stopped. The lid to the piano was closed, shutting out the dust, my misery, and her dreams.

So she surprised me. A few years ago, she offered to give me the piano, for my thirtieth birthday. I had not played in all those years. I saw the offer as a sign of forgiveness, a tremendous burden removed.

85   "Are you sure?" I asked shyly. "I mean, won't you and Dad miss it?"

"No, this your piano," she said firmly. "Always your piano. You only one can play."

"Well, I probably can't play anymore," I said. "It's been years."

"You pick up fast," said my mother, as if she knew this was certain. "You have natural talent. You could been genius if you want to."

"No I couldn't."

90   "You just not trying," said my mother. And she was neither angry nor sad. She said it as if to announce a fact that could never be disproved. "Take it," she said.

But I didn't at first. It was enough that she had offered it to me. And after that, every time I saw it in my parents' living room, standing in front of the bay windows, it made me feel proud, as if it were a shiny trophy I had won back.

Last week I sent a tuner over to my parents' apartment and had the piano recondi-
tioned, for purely sentimental reasons. My mother had died a few months before and I had
been getting things in order for my father, a little bit at a time. I put the jewelry in special
silk pouches. The sweaters she had knitted in yellow, pink, bright orange—all the colors I
hated—I put those in moth-proof boxes. I found some old Chinese silk dresses, the kind
with little slits up the sides. I rubbed the old silk against my skin, then wrapped them in
tissue and decided to take them home with me.

After I had the piano tuned, I opened the lid and touched the keys. It sounded even
richer than I remembered. Really, it was a very good piano. Inside the bench were the same
exercise notes with handwritten scales, the same secondhand music books with their covers
held together with yellow tape.

I opened up the Schumann book to the dark little piece I had played at the recital. It was
on the left-hand side of the page, "Pleading Child." It looked more difficult than I remembered. I played a few bars, surprised at how easily the notes came back to me.

And for the first time, or so it seemed, I noticed the piece on the right-hand side. It was   95
called "Perfectly Contented." I tried to play this one as well. It had a lighter melody but the
same flowing rhythm and turned out to be quite easy. "Pleading Child" was shorter but
slower; "Perfectly Contented" was longer, but faster. And after I played them both a few
times, I realized they were two halves of the same song.

QUESTIONS

1. What major characteristics about the narrator, Jing-Mei, are brought out in the story?
2. Describe the relationship between Jing-Mei and her mother. Why does Jing-Mei resist
   all efforts to develop her talents?
3. Characterize the mother. To what degree is she sympathetic? Unsympathetic? At the
   story's end, how does Jing-Mei feel about her mother?
4. What general details about the nature of first- and second-generation immigrants are
   presented in the story?

WRITING ABOUT CHARACTER

Usually your topic will be a major character in a story or drama, although you
might also study one or more minor characters. After your customary overview, begin taking notes. List as many traits as you can, and also determine
how the author presents details about the character through actions, appearances, speeches, comments by others, or authorial explanations. If you discover unusual traits, determine what they show. The following suggestions
and questions will help you get started.

Questions for Discovering Ideas

- Who is the major character? What do you learn about this character from
  his or her actions and speeches? From the speeches and actions of other
  characters? How else do you learn about the character?
- How important is the character to the work's principal action? Which
  characters oppose the major character? How do the major character and

the opposing antagonist(s) interact? What effects do these interactions create?

- What actions bring out important traits of the main character? To what degree does the character simply respond to events? To what degree does he or she create and influence events?
- Describe the main character's actions: Are they good or bad, intelligent or stupid, deliberate or spontaneous? How do they help you understand her or him? What do they show about the character as a person?
- Describe and explain the traits, both major and minor, of the character you plan to discuss. To what extent do the traits permit you to judge the character? What is your judgment?
- What descriptions (if any) of how the character looks do you discover in the story? What does this appearance demonstrate about him or her?
- In what ways is the character's major trait a strength—or a weakness? As the story progresses, to what degree does the trait become more (or less) prominent?
- How does the character recognize, change with, or adjust to circumstances? Is the character round and dynamic, or flat and passive?
- If the character you are analyzing is flat or passive, and minor, what function does he or she perform in the story (for example, by doing a task or by bringing out qualities of the major character)?
- If the character is a stereotype, to what type does he or she belong? To what degree does the character stay in the stereotypical role or rise above it? How?
- What do any of the other characters do, say, or think to give you understanding of the character you are analyzing? What does the character say or think about himself or herself? What does the storyteller or narrator say? How valid are these comments and insights? How helpful are they in providing insights into the character?
- Is the character lifelike or unreal? Consistent or inconsistent? Believable or not believable?

Strategies for Organizing Ideas

Sometimes when you have begun discussing a character you may find it easy to lapse into doing no more than presenting details of action without tying the actions to the character's traits and qualities. This is a trap to be avoided. Remember always to connect the actions and circumstances directly to characteristics—in other words to the *character* of the character. Do not be satisfied just to say what the character is doing, but tell your reader what the actions show about the character *as a person*—as a living, breathing individual with particular distinctness and unique identity. Always keep these thoughts in your mind when you discuss a literary character.

In your developing essay, identify the character you are studying, and refer to noteworthy problems in determining this character's qualities. Use your central idea and thesis statement to form the body of your essay. Consider one of the following approaches to organize your ideas.

1. *Develop a central trait or major characteristic,* such as "a determination to preserve her children despite the constant threats around her" (Rosa of Ozick's "The Shawl" in Chapter 4) or "the habit of remaking the world through one's own eyes alone" (Miss Brill in Mansfield's "Miss Brill" in this chapter). This kind of structure should be organized to show how the work brings out the trait. For example, one story might use selected speeches and actions to bring the character to life (the mother in Tan's "Two Kinds" in this chapter). Another story might employ the character's speeches and actions alone (Tessie Hutchinson of Jackson's "The Lottery" in Chapter 2). Studying the trait thus enables you to focus on the ways in which the author presents the character, and it also enables you to focus on separate parts of the work.

2. *Explain a character's growth or change.* This type of essay describes a character's traits at the work's beginning and then analyzes changes or developments. It is important to stress the actual alterations as they emerge, but at the same time to avoid retelling the story. Additionally, you should not only describe the changing traits but also analyze how they are brought out within the work (such as the unnamed narrator's drawing of a cathedral in Carver's "Cathedral" in Chapter 2 the dream of Goodman Brown in Hawthorne's "Young Goodman Brown" in Chapter 7, or Mathilde Loisel's ten-year economic ordeal in "The Necklace" in Part I).

3. *Organize your essay around a number of important but separate events, objects, or characteristics.* Most major characters exhibit not just one but many separate traits and qualities. Thus, for example, Updike's Sammy of "A & P" (Chapter 6), appears at first to be just an ordinary young man. He seems lively but does not show any more than ordinary postadolescent interests and ordinary views on life. When a key incident occurs in the grocery store, however, he suddenly illustrates his capacity to make a significant moral gesture. His character might be studied on the basis of the separate characteristics he shows—provided, of course, that they are connected within the essay. (See the illustrative essay that follows here for this type of development.)

4. *Organize your essay around central actions, objects, or quotations that reveal primary characteristics.* Key incidents may stand out (such as falling inadvertently into a ditch), along with objects closely associated with the character being analyzed (such as a falling hair ribbon). There may be important quotations spoken by the character or by someone else in the work. Show how such elements serve as signposts or guides to understanding the character.

5. *Develop qualities of a flat character or characters.* If the character is flat (such as Homer Barron in Faulkner's "A Rose for Emily" (Chapter 1), or Jackie's sister in Frank O'Connor's "First Confession" in Chapter 6, or the nurses

in the medical station in Welty's "A Worn Path" in Chapter 5), you might develop topics such as the function and relative significance of the character, the group the character represents, the relationship of the flat character to the round ones, the importance of this relationship, and any additional qualities or traits. For a flat character, you should explain the circumstances or characteristics that keep the character from seeming round and full, as well as the importance of these shortcomings in the author's presentation of character.

In your conclusion, show how the character's traits are related to the work as a whole. If the person was good but came to a bad end, does this misfortune make him or her seem especially worthy? If the person suffers, does the suffering suggest any attitudes about the class or type of which he or she is a part? Or does it illustrate the author's general view of human life? Or both? Do the characteristics explain why the person helps or hinders other characters? How does your essay help to clear up things that you did not understand on your first reading?

Illustrative Student Essay

Although underlined sentences are not recommended by MLA style, they are used in this illustrative essay as teaching tools to emphasize the central idea, thesis sentence, and topic sentences.

Hernandez 1

Ali Hernandez

Professor Lee

English 201

17 October 2014

The Character of Minnie Wright in Glaspell's "A Jury of Her Peers"°

[1]   Minnie Wright is Susan Glaspell's major character in "A Jury of Her Peers." She is the center, the focus, of the story. We do not learn about her first-hand, however, because she is not an actual speaking and acting character. Rather, we get all our information from the speeches of the actual characters in the story, who talk about her constantly. Lewis Hale, a neighboring farmer, tells about Minnie's behavior after the body of her

°This story appears on pages 202–214.

Hernandez 2

husband, John, was found strangled, in bed. Mrs. Martha Hale, Hale's wife,
tells about Minnie's young womanhood and about how she became alienated
from her nearest neighbors because of John's stingy and unfriendly ways.
Both Mrs. Hale and Mrs. Peters, the sheriff's wife, make observations about
Minnie based on the condition of her kitchen. <u>From this information we
get a full portrait of Minnie, who has changed from passivity to destructive
assertiveness.</u>* Her change in character is indicated by her clothing, her dead
canary, and her unfinished patchwork quilt.†

　　<u>The clothes that Minnie wore in the past and has worn in the present</u>   [2]
<u>indicate her character as a person of charm who has withered under neglect
and contempt.</u> Martha Hale mentions Minnie's attractive and colorful dresses
as a young woman, even recalling a "white dress with blue ribbons" (212).
Martha also recalls that Minnie, when young, was "sweet and pretty, but
kind of timid and—fluttery" (211). In the light of these recollections, Martha
observes that Minnie had changed, and changed for the worse, during her
dreary years of marriage with John Wright, who is characterized as a "raw
wind that gets to the bone" (211). As more evidence for Minnie's acceptance
of her drab life, Mrs. Peters says that Minnie asks for no more than an apron
and shawl when under arrest in the sheriff's home. This modest and shabby
clothing, as contrasted with the colorful dresses of her youth, suggests her
suppression of spirit.

　　<u>It is the discovery of her dead canary that clearly marks the emergence</u>   [3]
<u>of Minnie's rage to the point of actually killing her miserable husband.</u> We
learn that she, who when young had been in love with music, had endured her
cheerless farm home for thirty years. During this time her husband's contempt
made her life solitary, cheerless, unmusical, and depressingly impoverished.
But her buying the canary (211) suggests the reemergence of her love of song,
just as it also suggests her growth toward self-assertion. That her husband
(obviously her husband) had wrung the bird's neck may thus be seen as the
cause not only of her immediate sorrow (shown by the dead bird in a "pretty

*Central idea.
†Thesis sentence.

box" (212) but also of the anger that marks her change from a stock, obedient wife to a person angry enough to commit murder.

[4]   Like her love of song, her unfinished quilt indicates her creativity. In thirty years on the farm, never having had children, she has had nothing creative to do except for needlework like the quilt. Martha Hale comments on the beauty of Minnie's log-cabin design, and Mrs. Peters draws attention to the pieces in the sewing basket (209). The inference is that even though Minnie's life has been bleak, she has been able to indulge her characteristic love of color and form—and also of warmth, granted the purpose of a quilt.

[5]   Ironically, the quilt also shows Minnie's creativity in committing her act of murder. Both Mrs. Hale and Mrs. Peters interpret the breakdown of her stitching on the quilt as signs of distress about the dead canary and also of her nervousness in planning revenge. Further, even though nowhere in the story is it said that John is strangled with a quilting knot, this conclusion is inescapable. Both Mrs. Hale and Mrs. Peters agree that Minnie probably intended to knot the quilt rather than sew it in a quilt stitch, and Glaspell pointedly causes the men to learn this detail also, even though they scoff at it and ignore it, thus showing their incompetence at recognizing evidence (209). In other words, we learn that Minnie's only outlet for creativity— needlework—had enabled her to perform the murder in the only way she could, by strangling John with a slipproof quilting knot. Even though her plan for the murder is deliberate—Mrs. Peters observes that the arrangement of the rope was "strange" and a "funny way to kill" (208)—Minnie is not cold or remorseless. Her passivity after the crime demonstrates that planning to evade guilt, beyond simple denial, is not in her character. She is not so diabolically creative that she plans or even understands the irony of her having used a quilting knot to kill her husband (remember that he killed the bird by wringing its neck). Glaspell, however, makes the irony plain.

[6]   It is important to stress once more that we learn about Minnie from others. Nevertheless, Minnie is fully realized, round, and poignant. For the greater part of her adult life, she patiently endured her drab and

Hernandez 4

colorless marriage even though it was so cruelly different from her youthful
expectations. In the dreary surroundings of the Wright farm, she suppressed
her grudges, just as she suppressed her prettiness, creativity, and love of
color and beauty. In short, she had been nothing more than a flat character.
The killing of the canary, however, causes her to change and to destroy her
husband in an assertive rejection of her stock role as the suffering wife. She is a
patient woman whose patience finally reaches the breaking point.

Hernandez 5

Work Cited

Glaspell, Susan. "A Jury of Her Peers." *Literature: An Introduction to
Reading and Writing, Compact Edition.* Ed. Edgar V. Roberts and
Robert Zweig. 6th ed. New York: Pearson, 2015. 202–14. Print.

Commentary on the Essay

The strategy of this essay is to support the central idea that Minnie Wright is a
round, developing character. Hence the essay illustrates one of the types described
in strategy 3 on page 231. Other plans of organization could also have been chosen,
such as the qualities of acquiescence, fortitude, and potential for anger (strategy 1);
the change in Minnie from submission to vengefulness (strategy 2); or the reported
actions of Minnie's singing, knotting quilts, and sitting in the kitchen on the morning after the murder (another way to use strategy 3).

Because Minnie does not appear in the story but is described only in the words
of the major characters, the introductory paragraph of the illustrative essay deals
with the way readers learn about her. The essay thus highlights how Glaspell uses
strategies 2 and 4 in the introductory section of this chapter (see page 231) as the
ways of rendering the story's main character, while omitting strategies 1, 3, and 5.

The essay's argument is developed through inferences made from details in
the story—namely, Minnie's clothing (paragraph 2), her canary (paragraph 3), and
her quilt (paragraphs 4 and 5). The concluding paragraph summarizes a number of
these details, and it also considers how Minnie transcends the stock qualities of her
role as a farm wife and gains roundness of character as a result of this emergence.

As a study in composition, paragraph 3 demonstrates how discussion of a specific character trait, together with related details, can contribute to the essay's main argument. The trait is Minnie's love of music (shown by her canary). The connecting details, selected from study notes, are her isolation as a farm wife, her lack of pretty clothing, the contemptibility of her husband, her grief when putting the dead bird into the box, and the loss of music in her life. In short, the paragraph weaves together enough material to show the relationship between Minnie's trait of loving music and the crisis of her developing anger—a change that marks her as a round character.

Writing Topics About Character

Writing Paragraphs

1. Write a paragraph in which you compare the ways in which actions (or speeches, or the comments of others) are used to bring out the character traits in one of the following characters: Jing-Mei in "Two Kinds" (this chapter); Jackie in "First Confession" (Chapter 6); Miss Brill in "Miss Brill" (this chapter).

2. Write a paragraph in which you compare the parent-child relationships in "Two Kinds," and "The Parable of the Prodigal Son" (Chapter 7), or between "The Sky is Gray" and "First Confession" (Chapter 6).

3. Write a paragraph on one of the following:

   a. It often seems that fictional characters are under stress and also that they lead lives of great difficulty. How true is this claim? To what degree do the difficulties that characters experience bring out either good or bad qualities, or both?

   b. Discuss this point: To our friends and close relatives, we are round, but to ourselves and most other people, we are flat.

Writing Essays

1. Write a brief essay comparing the changes or developments of two major or *round* characters in stories included in this chapter or elsewhere in the book. You might deal with issues such as what the characters are like at the beginning; what conflicts they confront, deal with, or avoid; what qualities are brought out that signal the characters' changes or developments; and so on.

2. Write an essay in which you compare the qualities and functions of two or more flat characters (e.g., Mangan's sister in Joyce's "Araby" in Chapter 4, the father and Old Chong in Tan's "Two Kinds," in this chapter, the hunter in "A Worn Path" in Chapter 5). How do the flat characters bring out qualities of the major characters? What do you discover about their own character traits?

3. Using the narrator of "Battle Royal" (Chapter 5), and Jing-Mei (in Tan's "Two Kinds" in this chapter) as examples, write an essay in which you describe the effects of circumstance on character. Under the rubric "circumstance" you may consider elements such as education, family, economic and social status, cultural background, and geographic isolation.

Creative Writing Assignment

1. Write a brief story about an important decision you have made (e.g., choosing a school, beginning or leaving a job, declaring a major, starting or ending a friendship). Show how your qualities of character (to the extent that you understand yourself), together with your experiences, have gone into the decision. You may write more comfortably if you give yourself another name and describe your actions in the third person. Try that.

Library Assignment

1. Google "Topic of Characters in Literature" (there are more than 45,000,000 entries in Google). Make a selection of topics: What information can you gather from "flat and round," "favorite classic characters," "the image of women in early British literature," and so on? How thoroughly do the entries explore the topics? Make a report on your discoveries.

Chapter 4
Setting: The Background of Place, Objects, and Culture in Stories

AFTER STUDYING THIS MATERIAL, YOU SHOULD BE ABLE TO DO THE FOLLOWING:

- Understand the three basic types of setting used in literary works
- Define the nature and importance of setting in fiction
- Describe the relationship of literary settings to character development
- Analyze the importance of setting to the development of a story's ideas

Like all human beings, literary characters do not exist in isolation. Just as they become human by interacting with other characters, they gain identity because of their cultural and political allegiances, their possessions, their jobs, and where they live and move and undergo experiences. They are usually involved deeply with their environments, and their surroundings are causes of much of their motivation and many of their possible conflicts. Plays, stories, and narrative poems must therefore necessarily include descriptions of places, objects, and backgrounds—the setting.

What Is Setting?

Setting is the natural, manufactured, political, cultural, and temporal environment, including everything that characters know, own, and otherwise experience. Characters may be either helped or hurt by their surroundings, and they may oppose each other and even fight about possessions and goals. Further, as characters speak with each other, they reveal the degree to which they share the customs and ideas of their times.

Three Basic Types of Settings

Settings may be indoor places that are either private or public, together with all outdoor places. In addition, we may also consider historical and cultural circumstances as a vital aspect of setting.

PUBLIC AND PRIVATE PLACES, TOGETHER WITH VARIOUS POSSESSIONS, ARE IMPORTANT IN FICTION, AS IN LIFE. To reveal or highlight qualities of character, and also to make literature lifelike, authors include many details about objects and places of human manufacture, construction, and maintenance. Houses, both interiors and exteriors, are common, as are streets, alleys, public parks, park benches, garden paths, fences, confessionals, offices, hallways, steamships, sailboats, terraces, cemeteries, railway cars, trolley cars, historical landmarks, grocery stores, recital rooms, bridges, and the like. In addition, writers include references to objects such as walking sticks, baseballs, books, phonograph records, necklaces, money, guns, shawls, clocks, wallpaper, or hair ribbons. In Maupassant's "The Necklace" (Part I), the loss of a comfortable home brings out the best in the major character by causing her to adjust to her economic reversal, whereas in Lawrence's "The Horse Dealer's Daughter" (Chapter 8), such a loss leads a major character to depression and attempted suicide.

Objects also enter directly into fictional action and character. The lives of the men in O'Brien's "The Things They Carried" (Chapter 1) depend on the countless objects they must carry on their military missions. A seemingly random strand of hair upon a pillow indicates extremely dark behavior in Faulkner's "A Rose for Emily" (Chapter 1). A falling hair ribbon reveals the inadequate relationship between Brown and Faith in Hawthorne's "Young Goodman Brown" (Chapter 7).

OUTDOOR PLACES ARE SCENES OF MANY FICTIONAL ACTIONS.   The natural world is an obvious location for the action of many narratives and plays. It is therefore important to note natural surroundings (hills, shorelines, valleys, mountains, meadows, fields, trees, lakes, streams), living creatures (birds, dogs, horses, sharks, snakes), and also the times, seasons, and conditions in which things happen (morning or night, summer or winter, sunlight or cloudiness, wind or calmness, rain or shine, sunlight or darkness, summer or winter, snowfall or blizzard, heat or cold)—any or all of which may influence and interact with character, motivation, and conduct. Without the forest in Hawthorne's "Young Goodman Brown," there could be no story, for the events in the story could not have taken place anywhere else just as Hawthorne presents them.

CULTURAL AND HISTORICAL CIRCUMSTANCES ARE OFTEN IMPORTANT IN LITERATURE. Just as physical setting influences characters, so do historical and cultural conditions and assumptions. The broad cultural setting of Jackson's "The Lottery" (Chapter 2) is built on the persistence of a primitive belief despite the sophistication of our own modern and scientific age. The brutal concentration-camp conditions in Ozick's "The Shawl" (this chapter) cause the major character to conceal a small child as the only way to keep that child alive. In Mansfield's "Miss Brill" (Chapter 3), we see that the shabbiness of a favorite article of clothing suggests the isolation of the principal character. Bear in mind that settings are frequently important in poetry and also (especially) in drama.

The Literary Uses of Setting

Writers manipulate literary locations in a comparable way. For example, in Hawthorne's "Young Goodman Brown" (Chapter 7), a woodland path that is difficult to follow and filled with obstacles is a major geographical feature. The path is of course no more than ordinary, granted the time and circumstances of the story, but it also conveys the idea that life is difficult, unpredictable, risky, deceiving, and mysterious. Similarly, in O'Brien's "The Things They Carried" (Chapter 1), the constant attention to details indicates the exceedingly difficult and dangerous lives that were led by American soldiers during the Vietnam War.

The Setting Is Usually Essential and Vital in a Story

To study the setting in a narrative (or play), discover the important details and then try to explain their function. Depending on the author's purpose, the amount of detail may vary. Poe provides many graphic and also impressionistic details in "The Masque of the Red Death" (Chapter 9) so that we can follow, almost visually, the bizarre action at the story's end. In some works the setting is so intensely present, like the various Dublin scenes in Joyce's "Araby" (this chapter), that it is almost literally an additional participant in the action.

Setting Enhances a Work's Realism and Credibility

One of the major purposes of literary setting is to establish **realism,** or **verisimilitude.** As the description of location and objects becomes particular and detailed, the events of the work become more believable. Maupassant places "The Necklace" (Part I) in real locations in late-nineteenth-century France, and for this reason the story has all the appearance of having actually happened, in reality. Even futuristic, symbolic, and fantastic stories, as well as ghost stories, seem more believable if they include places and objects from everyday experience. Hawthorne's "Young Goodman Brown" (Chapter 7) is such a story, as is Poe's "The Masque of the Red Death" (Chapter 9). Although these stories are by no means realistic, their credibility is enhanced because they take place in settings that have a basis in the world of reality.

Setting May Accentuate Qualities of Character

Setting may intersect with character as a means by which authors underscore the influence of place, circumstance, and time on human growth and change. The dry Southwestern desert setting in Silko's "The Man to Send Rain Clouds" (this chapter) provides a necessary context for the characters' conflicting values, as exemplified by the holy water used for burial and the impending rainstorm, needed to sustain life in this harsh land.

The ways that characters respond and adjust to the world around them can reveal their qualities. Peyton Farquhar's scheme to escape from his fate, even when it is literally dangling in front of him, suggests that he is a character of great strength but also of powerful imagination (Bierce's "An Occurrence at Owl Creek Bridge" in Chapter 1). In contrast, Goodman Brown's Calvinistic religious conviction that human beings are evil at the time of their birth, and are evil throughout their lives, which is confirmed to him by his nightmarish encounter, indicates the weakness and gullibility of his character (Hawthorne's "Young Goodman Brown" in Chapter 7).

Setting Is a Means by Which Authors Structure and Shape Their Works

Authors often use setting as one of the means of organizing their stories, as in Maupassant's "The Necklace" (Part I). The story's final scene is believable because Mathilde leaves her impoverished home to take a nostalgic stroll on the Champs-Elysées, the most fashionable street in Paris. Without this change of setting, she could not have encountered Jeanne Forrestier again, for their usual ways of life would have in fact separated them. In short, the structure of the story depends on a normal and natural change of scene.

Another organizational application of place, time, and object is a **framing** or **enclosing setting,** when an author opens with a particular description and then returns to the same setting at the end. An example is Steinbeck's "The Chrysan-themums" (Chapter 7), which begins with the major character tending her flowers and ends with her seeing the destruction of some of these same flowers that she had given away. A comparable use of framing occurs in Welty's "A Worn Path" (Chapter 5), in which the walking trips taken by the main character open and close the story—to the town and then away from the town. By such means, framing creates a formal completeness, just as it may underscore the author's depiction of the human condition.

Various Settings May Be Symbolic

If the scenes and materials of setting are highlighted or emphasized, they also may be taken as symbols through which the author expresses ideas. Such an emphasis is made in Ozick's "The Shawl," in which the shawl has the ordinary function of providing cover and warmth for a baby. Because it is so prominent, however, the shawl also may be taken as a symbol of the attempt to preserve future generations; and because its loss also produces a human loss, it symbolizes the helplessness of the victims in Nazi extermination camps during World War II. In O'Brien's "The Things They Carried" (Chapter 1), the constant references to the weights of the objects symbolize how the men's lives depend on their own resources—their carried burdens.

Setting Is Used in the Creation of Atmosphere and Mood

Most actions *require* no more than a functional description of setting. Thus, taking a walk in a forest needs just the statement that there are many, or few, trees. However, if you find descriptions of shapes, light and shadows, animals, wind, and sounds, you may be sure that the author is creating an **atmosphere** or **mood** for the action (as in Gilman's "The Yellow Wallpaper" in Chapter 10 and Joyce's "Araby" in this chapter). There are many ways to develop moods. Descriptions of bright colors (red, orange, yellow) may contribute to a mood of happiness. The same colors in dim or eerie light, like the rooms in Poe's "The Masque of the Red Death" (Chapter 9), invoke gloom or intensify hysteria. References to smells and sounds bring the setting to life further by asking additional sensory responses from the reader. The setting of a story in a small town or large city, in green or snow-covered fields, or in middle-class or lower-class residences may evoke responses to these places that contribute to the work's atmosphere.

Setting May Underscore a Work's Irony

Just as setting may reinforce character and theme, so it may establish expectations that are the opposite of what occurs. At the beginning of "The Lottery" (Chapter 2), for example, Jackson describes the plainness and folksiness of the assembling townspeople—details that make the conclusion ironic, for it is these same everyday folks who bring about the final horror. Irony is also a motif in Chopin's "The Story of an Hour" (Chapter 6) inasmuch as the major characters in the story are unable to prevent the final outcome, even though their intentions aim toward the opposite result. The ironic use of setting is by no means limited only to fiction, because it may also be significantly important in plays and poems. The case of dueling pistols in Chekhov's *The Bear* (Chapter 23) brings out the developing love between Smirnov and Mrs. Popov, for instead of separating these characters through death, the pistols bring them into passionate direct contact. Thomas Hardy creates a heavily ironic situation in the poem "Channel Firing"(Chapter 13) when the noise of large guns at sea "wakens" the skeletons buried in an English churchyard. The irony is that those engaged in the gunnery practice, if "red war" gets "yet redder," will soon be numbered among the skeletons in the graveyard.

Stories for Study

James Joyce . . . . Araby, 242
Cynthia Ozick . . . . The Shawl, 246
Edgar Allan Poe. . . . . The Cask of Amontillado, 249
Leslie Marmon Silko . . . . The Man to Send Rain Clouds, 254

JAMES JOYCE (1882–1940)

James Joyce, one of the great twentieth-century writers, was born in Ireland and received a vigorous and thorough education there. He left Ireland in 1902 and spent most of the rest of his life in Switzerland and France. His best-known works are Dubliners *(1914),* A Portrait of the Artist as a Young Man *(1914–1915),* Ulysses *(1922), and* Finnegans Wake *(1939). Much of his work has been called "fictionalized autobiography," a quality shown in "Araby," which is selected from* Dubliners*. As a young child, Joyce had lived on North Richmond Street, just like the narrator of the story. The bazaar that the narrator visits actually did take place in Dublin, from May 14 to 19, 1894, when Joyce was the same age as the narrator. It was called "Araby in Dublin" and was advertised as a "Grand Oriental Fete."*

Araby (1914)

North Richmond Street,° being blind,° was a quiet street except at the hour when the Christian Brothers' School set the boys free. An uninhabited house of two storeys stood at the blind end, detached from its neighbours in a square ground. The other houses of the street, conscious of decent lives within them, gazed at one another with brown imperturbable faces.

The former tenant of our house, a priest, had died in the back drawing room. Air, musty from having long been enclosed, hung in all the rooms, and the waste room behind the

---

°*North Richmond Street:* name of a real street in Dublin on which Joyce lived as a boy.
°*blind:* dead-end street.

kitchen was littered with old useless papers. Among these I found a few paper-covered books, the pages of which were curled and damp: *The Abbott*, by Walter Scott, *The Devout Communicant*° and *The Memoirs of Vidocq*.° I liked the last best because its leaves were yellow. The wild garden behind the house contained a central apple-tree and a few straggling bushes under one of which I found the late tenant's rusty bicycle-pump. He had been a very charitable priest; in his will he had left all his money to institutions and the furniture of his house to his sister.

When the short days of winter came dusk fell before we had well eaten our dinners. When we met in the street the houses had grown sombre. The space of sky above us was the colour of ever-changing violet and towards it the lamps of the street lifted their feeble lanterns. The cold air stung us and we played till our bodies glowed. Our shouts echoed in the silent street. The career of our play brought us through the dark muddy lanes behind the houses where we ran the gauntlet of the rough tribes from the cottages, to the back doors of the dark dripping gardens where odors arose from the ashpits, to the dark odorous stables where a coachman smoothed and combed the horse or shook music from the buckled harness. When we returned to the street light from the kitchen windows had filled the areas. If my uncle was seen turning the corner we hid in the shadow until we had seen him safely housed. Or if Mangan's sister came out on the doorstep to call her brother in to his tea we watched her from our shadow peer up and down the street. We waited to see whether she would remain or go in and, if she remained, we left our shadow and walked up to Mangan's steps resignedly. She was waiting for us, her figure defined by the light from the half-opened door. Her brother always teased her before he obeyed and I stood by the railings looking at her. Her dress swung as she moved her body and the soft rope of her hair tossed from side to side.

Every morning I lay on the floor in the front parlor watching her door. The blind was pulled down within an inch of the sash so that I could not be seen. When she came out on the doorstep my heart leaped. I ran to the hall, seized my books and followed her. I kept her brown figure always in my eye and, when we came near the point at which our ways diverged, I quickened my pace and passed her. This happened morning after morning. I had never spoken to her, except for a few casual words, and yet her name was like a summons to all my foolish blood.

Her image accompanied me even in places the most hostile to romance. On Saturday evenings when my aunt went marketing I had to go to carry some of the parcels. We walked through the flaring street, jostled by drunken men and bargaining women, amid the curses of laborers, the shrill litanies of shop-boys who stood on guard by the barrels of pigs' cheeks, the nasal chanting of street singers, who sang a *come-all-you* about O'Donovan Rossa,° or a ballad about the troubles in our native land. These noises converged in a single sensation of life for me: I imagined that I bore my chalice safely through the throng of foes. Her name sprang to my lips at moments in strange prayers and praises which I myself did not understand. My eyes were often full of tears (I could not tell why) and at times a flood from my heart seemed to pour itself out into my bosom. I thought little of the future. I did not know whether I would ever speak to her or not or, if I spoke to her, how I could tell her of my confused adoration. But my body was like a harp and her words and gestures were like fingers running upon the wires.

5

°*The Devout Communicant:* a book of meditations by Pacificus Baker, published 1873.
°*The Memoirs of Vidocq:* published 1829, the story of François Vidocq, a Parisian chief of detectives.
°*O'Donovan Rossa:* popular ballad about Jeremiah O'Donovan (1831–1915), a leader in the movement to free Ireland from English control. He was called "Dynamite Rossa."

One evening I went into the back drawing-room in which the priest had died. It was a dark rainy evening and there was no sound in the house. Through one of the broken panes I heard the rain impinge upon the earth, the fine incessant needles of water playing in the sodden beds. Some distant lamp or lighted window gleamed below me. I was thankful that I could see so little. All my senses seemed to desire to veil themselves and, feeling that I was about to slip from them, I pressed the palms of my hands together until they trembled, murmuring: *O love! O love!* many times.

At last she spoke to me. When she addressed the first words to me I was so confused that I did not know what to answer. She asked me was I going to *Araby.*° I forget whether I answered yes or no. It would be a splendid bazaar, she said; she would love to go.

—And why can't you? I asked.

While she spoke she turned a silver bracelet round and round her wrist. She could not go, she said, because there would be a retreat° that week in her convent. Her brother and two other boys were fighting for their caps and I was alone at the railings. She held one of the spikes, bowing her head towards me. The light from the lamp opposite our door caught the white curve of her neck, lit up her hair that rested there and, falling, lit up the hand upon the railing. It fell over one side of her dress and caught the white border of a petticoat, just visible as she stood at ease.

10   —It's well for you, she said.

—If I go, I said, I will bring you something.

What innumerable follies laid waste my waking and sleeping thoughts after that evening! I wished to annihilate the tedious intervening days. I chafed against the work of school. At night in my bedroom and by day in the classroom her image came between me and the page I strove to read. The syllables of the word *Araby* were called to me through the silence in which my soul luxuriated and cast an Eastern enchantment over me. I asked for leave to go to the bazaar on Saturday night. My aunt was surprised and hoped it was not some Freemason° affair. I answered few questions in class. I watched my master's face pass from amiability to sternness; he hoped I was not beginning to idle. I could not call my wandering thoughts together. I had hardly any patience with the serious work of life which, now that it stood between me and my desire, seemed to me child's play, ugly monotonous child's play.

On Saturday morning I reminded my uncle that I wished to go to the bazaar in the evening. He was fussing at the hall-stand, looking for the hatbrush, and answered me curtly:

—Yes, boy, I know.

15   As he was in the hall I could not go into the front parlour and lie at the window. I left the house in bad humour and walked slowly towards the school. The air was pitilessly raw and already my heart misgave me.

When I came home to dinner my uncle had not yet been home. Still, it was early. I sat staring at the clock for some time and, when its ticking began to irritate me, I left the room. I mounted the staircase and gained the upper part of the house. The high cold empty gloomy rooms liberated me and I went from room to room singing. From the front window I saw my companions playing below in the street. Their cries reached me weakened and indistinct and, leaning my forehead against the cool glass, I looked over at the dark house where she lived. I may have stood there for an hour, seeing nothing but the brown-clad figure cast by my imagination, touched discreetly by the lamplight at the curved neck, at the hand upon the railing and at the border below the dress.

°*Araby:* the bazaar held in Dublin from May 14 to 19, 1894.
°*retreat:* a special time set aside for concentrated religious instruction, discussion, and prayer.
°*Freemason:* and therefore Protestant.

When I came downstairs again I found Mrs. Mercer sitting at the fire. She was an old garrulous woman, a pawnbroker's widow, who collected used stamps for some pious purpose. I had to endure the gossip of the tea-table. The meal was prolonged beyond an hour and still my uncle did not come. Mrs. Mercer stood up to go: she was sorry she couldn't wait any longer, but it was after eight o'clock and she did not like to be out late, as the night air was bad for her. When she had gone I began to walk up and down the room, clenching my fists. My aunt said:

—I'm afraid you may put off your bazaar for this night of Our Lord.

At nine o'clock I heard my uncle's latchkey in the halldoor. I heard him talking to himself and heard the hall-stand rocking when it had received the weight of his overcoat. I could interpret these signs. When he was midway through his dinner I asked him to give me the money to go to the bazaar. He had forgotten.

—The people are in bed and after their first sleep now, he said.   20

I did not smile. My aunt said to him energetically:

—Can't you give him the money and let him go? You've kept him late enough as it is.

My uncle said he was very sorry he had forgotten. He said he believed in the old saying: *All work and no play makes Jack a dull boy*. He asked me where I was going and, when I had told him a second time he asked me did I know *The Arab's Farewell to his Steed*.° When I left the kitchen he was about to recite the opening lines of the piece to my aunt.

I held a florin° tightly in my hand as I strode down Buckingham Street towards the station. The sight of the streets thronged with buyers and glaring with gas recalled to me the purpose of my journey. I took my seat in a third-class carriage of a deserted train. After an intolerable delay the train moved out of the station slowly. It crept onward among ruinous houses and over the twinkling river. At Westland Row Station a crowd of people pressed to the carriage doors; but the porters moved them back, saying that it was a special train for the bazaar. I remained alone in the bare carriage. In a few minutes the train drew up beside an improvised wooden platform. I passed out on to the road and saw by the lighted dial of a clock that it was ten minutes to ten. In front of me was a large building which displayed the magical name.

I could not find any sixpenny entrance and, fearing that the bazaar would be closed, I   25
passed in quickly through a turnstile, handing a shilling to a weary-looking man. I found myself in a big hall girdled at half its height by a gallery. Nearly all the stalls were closed and the greater part of the hall was in darkness. I recognized a silence like that which pervades a church after a service. I walked into the centre of the bazaar timidly. A few people were gathered about the stalls which were still open. Before a curtain, over which the words *Café Chantant* were written in coloured lamps, two men were counting money on a salver. I listened to the fall of the coins.

Remembering with difficulty why I had come I went over to one of the stalls and examined porcelain vases and flowered tea-sets. At the door of the stall a young lady was talking and laughing with two young gentlemen. I remarked their English accents and listened vaguely to their conversation.

—O, I never said such a thing!

—O, but you did!

—O, but I didn't!

—Didn't she say that?   30

—Yes I heard her.

—O, there's a . . . fib!

°*The Arab's Farewell to his Steed*: poem by Caroline Norton (1808–1877).
°*florin*: a two-shilling coin in the 1890s (when the story takes place), worth perhaps twenty dollars in today' money.

Observing me the young lady came over and asked me did I wish to buy anything. The tone in her voice was not encouraging; she seemed to have spoken to me out of a sense of duty. I looked humbly at the great jars that stood like eastern guards at either side of the dark entrance to the stall and murmured:

—No, thank you.

35 The young lady changed the position of one of the vases and went back to the two young men. They began to talk of the same subject. Once or twice the young lady glanced at me over her shoulder.

I lingered before her stall, though I knew my stay was useless, to make my interest in her wares seem the more real. Then I turned away slowly and walked down the middle of the bazaar. I allowed the two pennies to fall against the sixpence in my pocket. I heard a voice call from one end of the gallery that the light was out. The upper part of the hall was now completely dark.

Gazing up into the darkness I saw myself as a creature driven and derided by vanity; and my eyes burned with anguish and anger.

QUESTIONS

1. Describe what you consider to be the story's major idea.
2. How might the bazaar, "Araby," be considered symbolically in the story? To what extent does this symbol embody the story's central idea?
3. Consider the attitude of the speaker toward his home as indicated in the first paragraph. Why do you think the speaker uses the word *blind* to describe the dead-end street? What relationship exists between the speaker's pain at the end of the story to the ideas in the first paragraph?
4. Who is the narrator? About how old is he at the time of the story? About how old when he tells the story? What effect is produced by this difference in age between narrator-as-character and narrator-as-storyteller?

CYNTHIA OZICK (b. 1928)

Cynthia Ozick has published three novels, Trust *(1966),* The Cannibal Galaxy *(1983), and* The Messiah of Stockholm *(1987); four short-story collections,* The Pagan Rabbi *(1971),* Bloodshed *(1976),* Levitation *(1982), and* Collected Stories *(2006); and frequent essays and reviews, among which is the collection* Fame and Folly *(1996). Among her many recognitions and awards, she serves on the Board of Advisers of the* American Poetry Review. *Her 1990 novella "Puttermesser Paired" was the first story featured in* Prize Stories 1992: The O. Henry Awards, *edited by William Abrahams. "The Shawl," first published in* The New Yorker *in 1980, was republished in* The Shawl *in 1989, with a companion story describing the heroine's experiences in the United States after surviving the death camp. "The Shawl" was also adapted as a play in 1996.*

🍃 The Shawl (1980)

Stella, cold, cold the coldness of hell. How they walked on the roads together, Rosa with Magda curled up between sore breasts, Magda wound up in the shawl. Sometimes Stella carried Magda. But she was jealous of Magda. A thin girl of fourteen, too small, with thin breasts of her own, Stella wanted to be wrapped in a shawl, hidden away, asleep, rocked by the march, a baby, a round infant in arms. Magda took Rosa's nipple, and Rosa never stopped walking, a walking cradle. There was not enough milk; sometimes Magda sucked air; then she screamed. Stella was ravenous. Her knees were tumors on sticks, her elbows chicken bones.

Rosa did not feel hunger; she felt light, not like someone walking but like someone in a faint, in trance, arrested in a fit, someone who is already a floating angel, alert and seeing everything, but in the air, not there, not touching the road. As if teetering on the tips of her fingernails. She looked into Magda's face through a gap in the shawl: a squirrel in a nest, safe, no one could reach her inside the little house of the shawl's windings. The face, very round, a pocket mirror of a face: but it was not Rosa's bleak complexion, dark like cholera, it was another kind of face altogether, eyes blue as air, smooth feathers of hair nearly as yellow as the Star sewn into Rosa's coat. You could think she was one of *their* babies.

Rosa, floating, dreamed of giving Magda away in one of the villages. She could leave the line for a minute and push Magda into the hands of any woman on the side of the road. But if she moved out of line they might shoot. And even if she fled the line for half a second and pushed the shawl-bundle at a stranger, would the woman take it? She might be surprised, or afraid; she might drop the shawl, and Magda would fall out and strike her head and die. The little round head. Such a good child, she gave up screaming, and sucked now only for the taste of the drying nipple itself. The neat grip of the tiny gums. One mite of a tooth tip sticking up in the bottom gum, how shining, an elfin tombstone of white marble gleaming there. Without complaining, Magda relinquished Rosa's teats, first the left, then the right; both were cracked, not a sniff of milk. The duct crevice extinct, a dead volcano, blind eye, chill hole, so Magda took the corner of the shawl and milked it instead. She sucked and sucked, flooding the threads with wetness. The shawl's good flavor, milk of linen.

It was a magic shawl, it could nourish an infant for three days and three nights. Magda did not die, she stayed alive, although very quiet. A peculiar smell, of cinnamon and almonds, lifted out of her mouth. She held her eyes open every moment, forgetting how to blink or nap, and Rosa and sometimes Stella studied their blueness. On the road they raised one burden of a leg after another and studied Magda's face. "Aryan," Stella said, in a voice grown as thin as a string; and Rosa thought how Stella gazed at Magda like a young cannibal. And the time that Stella said "Aryan," it sounded to Rosa as if Stella had really said "Let us devour her."

But Magda lived to walk. She lived that long, but she did not walk very well, partly   5
because she was only fifteen months old, and partly because the spindles of her legs could not hold up her fat belly. It was fat with air, full and round. Rosa gave almost all her food to Magda, Stella gave nothing; Stella was ravenous, a growing child herself, but not growing much. Stella did not menstruate. Rosa did not menstruate. Rosa was ravenous, but also not; she learned from Magda how to drink the taste of a finger in one's mouth. They were in a place without pity, all pity was annihilated in Rosa, she looked at Stella's bones without pity. She was sure that Stella was waiting for Magda to die so she could put her teeth into the little thighs.

Rosa knew Magda was going to die very soon; she should have been dead already, but she had been buried away deep inside the magic shawl, mistaken there for the shivering mound of Rosa's breasts; Rosa clung to the shawl as if it covered only herself. No one took it away from her. Magda was mute. She never cried. Rosa hid her in the barracks, under the shawl, but she knew that one day someone would inform; or one day someone, not even Stella, would steal Magda to eat her. When Magda began to walk Rosa knew that Magda was going to die very soon, something would happen. She was afraid to fall asleep; she slept with the weight of her thigh on Magda's body; she was afraid she would smother Magda under her thigh. The weight of Rosa was becoming less and less; Rosa and Stella were slowly turning into air.

Magda was quiet, but her eyes were horribly alive, like blue tigers. She watched. Sometimes she laughed—it seemed a laugh, but how could it be? Magda had never seen anyone laugh. Still, Magda laughed at her shawl when the wind blew its corners, the bad wind with pieces of black in it, that made Stella's and Rosa's eyes tear. Magda's eyes were always clear and tearless. She watched like a tiger. She guarded her shawl. No one could touch it; only Rosa could touch it. Stella was not allowed. The shawl was Magda's own baby, her pet, her little sister. She tangled herself up in it and sucked on one of the corners when she wanted to be very still.

Then Stella took the shawl away and made Magda die.

Afterward Stella said: "I was cold."

10   And afterward she was always cold, always. The cold went into her heart: Rosa saw that Stella's heart was cold. Magda flopped onward with her little pencil legs scribbling this way and that, in search of the shawl; the pencils faltered at the barracks opening, where the light began. Rosa saw and pursued. But already Magda was in the square outside the barracks, in the jolly light. It was the roll-call arena. Every morning Rosa had to conceal Magda under the shawl against a wall of the barracks and go out and stand in the arena with Stella and hundreds of others, sometimes for hours, and Magda, deserted, was quiet under the shawl, sucking on her corner. Every day Magda was silent, and so she did not die. Rosa saw that today Magda was going to die, and at the same time a fearful joy ran into Rosa's two palms, her fingers were on fire, she was astonished, febrile: Magda, in the sunlight, swaying on her pencil legs, was howling. Ever since the drying up of Rosa's nipples, ever since Magda's last scream on the road, Magda had been devoid of any syllable; Magda was a mute. Rosa believed that something had gone wrong with her vocal cords, with her windpipe, with the cave of her larynx; Magda was defective, without a voice; perhaps she was deaf; there might be something amiss with her intelligence; Magda was dumb. Even the laugh that came when the ash-stippled wind made a clown out of Magda's shawl was only the air-blown showing of her teeth. Even when the lice, head lice and body lice, crazed her so that she became as wild as one of the big rats that plundered the barracks at daybreak looking for carrion, she rubbed and scratched and kicked and bit and rolled without a whimper. But now Magda's mouth was spilling a long viscous rope of clamor.

"Maaaa—"

It was the first noise Magda had ever sent out from her throat since the drying up of Rosa's nipples.

"Maaaa . . . aaa!"

Again! Magda was wavering in the perilous sunlight of the arena, scrabbling on such pitiful little bent shins. Rosa saw. She saw that Magda was grieving for the loss of her shawl, she saw that Magda was going to die. A tide of commands hammered in Rosa's nipples: Fetch, get, bring! But she did not know which to go after first, Magda or the shawl. If she jumped out into the arena to snatch Magda up, the howling would not stop, because Magda would still not have the shawl; but if she ran back into the barracks to find the shawl, and if she found it, and if she came after Magda holding it and shaking it, then she would get Magda back, Magda would put the shawl in her mouth and turn dumb again.

15   Rosa entered the dark. It was easy to discover the shawl. Stella was heaped under it, asleep in her thin bones. Rosa tore the shawl free and flew—she could fly, she was only air—into the arena. The sunheat murmured of another life, of butterflies in summer. The light was placid, mellow. On the other side of the steel fence, far away, there were green meadows speckled with dandelions and deep-colored violets; beyond them, even farther, innocent tiger lilies, tall, lifting their orange bonnets. In the barracks they spoke of "flowers," of "rain": excrement, thick turd-braids, and the slow stinking maroon waterfall that slunk down from the upper bunks, the stink mixed with a bitter fatty floating smoke that greased Rosa's skin. She stood for an instant at the margin of the arena. Sometimes the electricity inside the fence would seem to hum; even Stella said it was only an imagining, but Rosa heard real sounds

in the wire: grainy sad voices. The farther she was from the fence, the more clearly the voices crowded at her. The lamenting voices strummed so convincingly, so passionately, it was impossible to suspect them of being phantoms. The voices told her to hold up the shawl, high; the voices told her to shake it, to whip with it, to unfurl it like a flag. Rosa lifted, shook, whipped, unfurled. Far off, very far, Magda leaned across her air-fed belly, reaching out with the rods of her arms. She was high up, elevated, riding someone's shoulder. But the shoulder that carried Magda was not coming toward Rosa and the shawl, it was drifting away, the speck of Magda was moving more and more into the smoky distance. Above the shoulder a helmet glinted. The light tapped the helmet and sparkled it into a goblet. Below the helmet a black body like a domino and a pair of black boots hurled themselves in the direction of the electrified fence. The electric voices began to chatter wildly. "Maa-maa, maaa-maaa," they all hummed together. How far Magda was from Rosa now, across the whole square, past a dozen barracks, all the way on the other side! She was no bigger than a moth.

All at once Magda was swimming through the air. The whole of Magda traveled through loftiness. She looked like a butterfly touching a silver vine. And the moment Magda's feathered round head and her pencil legs and balloonish belly and zigzag arms splashed against the fence, the steel voices went mad in their growling, urging Rosa to run and run to the spot where Magda had fallen from her flight against the electrified fence; but of course Rosa did not obey them. She only stood, because if she ran they would shoot, and if she tried to pick up the sticks of Magda's body they would shoot, and if she let the wolf's screech ascending now through the ladder of her skeleton break out, they would shoot; so she took Magda's shawl and filled her own mouth with it, stuffed it in and stuffed it in, until she was swallowing up the wolf's screech and tasting the cinnamon and almond depth of Magda's saliva; and Rosa drank Magda's shawl until it dried.

QUESTIONS

1. Describe how Ozick presents the setting. Why do you not receive a clear picture of how things look? Why does Ozick present the details as she does?

2. In paragraph 15, what is on the other side of the fence? Explain Ozick's description here. Why does Ozick include these details so close to the story's end?

3. What character is the center of interest in "The Shawl"? Why is she being treated as she is? What are her impressions of the conditions and circumstances around her? What are her responses to her hunger and deprivation?

4. Explain the function of the more unpleasant and brutal details. What do you need to know about the circumstances of the story to respond to these details?

EDGAR ALLAN POE (1809–1849)

Edgar Allan Poe was born in Boston in January 1809 to parents who separated before he was a year old. In 1826, at the age of 17, he enrolled at the University of Virginia.

Although Poe was a natural student, personal problems upset his studies. Within a year he left college and went to Boston, where he published his first volume of poetry in 1827 (Tamerlane and Other Poems). In the same year he joined the army and quickly gained the highest rank of noncommissioned officers, although he left the service in 1829. Poe then secured an appointment to West Point but, lacking the financial help that he needed to maintain his life as a cadet, he got himself expelled in 1931. Now totally dependent on his own resources, he embarked on a career as a writer.

In the following years he struggled constantly against poverty. He also struggled against alcohol, and excessive drinking caused him to lose some of his positions. Though the loss of his wife, Virginia "Sissy" Clemm, in 1847 marked a low point in his life, he continued writing, reviewing, and lecturing. Though in September 1849, he proposed to Sarah Elmira Royster Shelton, a wealthy widow and the sweetheart of his youth. She accepted and the couple set a date in mid-October 1849 for the wedding. Though at this time his lectures were increasingly popular and he was offered an editing job in Philadelphia. Poe was found on October 3, 1849, a few days after leaving for Philadelphia, in Baltimore. He was drunken, incoherent, robbed, and possibly beaten. He was taken to a local hospital where his condition worsened and on October 7 he died.

The Cask of Amontillado (1846)

The thousand injuries of Fortunato I had borne as I best could; but when he ventured upon insult, I vowed revenge. You, who so well know the nature of my soul, will not suppose, however, that I gave utterance to a threat. *At length* I would be avenged; this was a point definitively settled—but the very definitiveness with which it was resolved, precluded the idea of risk. I must not only punish, but punish with impunity. A wrong is unredressed when retribution overtakes its redresser. It is equally unredressed when the avenger fails to make himself felt as such to him who has done the wrong.

It must be understood, that neither by word nor deed had I given Fortunato cause to doubt my good will. I continued, as was my wont, to smile in his face, and he did not perceive that my smile *now* was at the thought of his immolation.

He had a weak point—this Fortunato—although in other regards he was a man to be respected and even feared. He prided himself on his connoisseurship in wine. Few Italians have the true virtuoso spirit. For the most part their enthusiasm is adopted to suit the time and opportunity—to practice imposture upon the British and Austrian *millionaires.* In painting and gemmary, Fortunato, like his countrymen, was a quack—but in the matter of old wines he was sincere. In this respect I did not differ from him materially: I was skilful in the Italian vintages myself, and bought largely whenever I could.

It was about dusk, one evening during the supreme madness of the carnival season, that I encountered my friend. He accosted me with excessive warmth, for he had been drinking much. The man wore motley. He had on a tight-fitting parti-striped dress, and his head was surmounted by the conical cap and bells. I was so pleased to see him, that I thought I should never have done wringing his hand.

5   I said to him—"My dear Fortunato, you are luckily met. How remarkably well you are looking to-day! But I have received a pipe of what passes for Amontillado, and I have my doubts."

"How?" said he. "Amontillado? A pipe? Impossible! And in the middle of the carnival!"

"I have my doubts," I replied; "and I was silly enough to pay the full Amontillado price without consulting you in the matter. You were not to be found, and I was fearful of losing a bargain."

"Amontillado!"

"I have my doubts."

10   "Amontillado!"

"And I must satisfy them."

"Amontillado!"

"As you are engaged, I am on my way to Luchesi. If any one has a critical turn, it is he. He will tell me—"

"Luchesi cannot tell Amontillado from Sherry."

15   "And yet some fools will have it that his taste is a match for your own."

"Come, let us go."

"Whither?"

"To your vaults."

"My friend, no; I will not impose upon your good nature. I perceive you have an engagement. Luchesi—"

"I have no engagement;—come."

"My friend, no. It is not the engagement, but the severe cold with which I perceive you are afflicted. The vaults are insufferably damp. They are encrusted with nitre."

"Let us go, nevertheless. The cold is merely nothing. Amontillado! You have been imposed upon. And as for Luchesi, he cannot distinguish Sherry from Amontillado."

Thus speaking, Fortunato possessed himself of my arm. Putting on a mask of black silk, and drawing a *roquelaire*° closely about my person, I suffered him to hurry me to my palazzo.

There were no attendants at home; they had absconded to make merry in honor of the time. I had told them that I should not return until the morning, and had given them explicit orders not to stir from the house. These orders were sufficient, I well knew, to insure their immediate disappearance, one and all, as soon as my back was turned.

I took from their sconces two flambeaux, and giving one to Fortunato, bowed him through several suites of rooms to the archway that led into the vaults. I passed down a long and winding staircase, requesting him to be cautious as he followed. We came at length to the foot of the descent, and stood together on the damp ground of the catacombs of the Montresors.

The gait of my friend was unsteady, and the bells upon his cap jingled as he strode.

"The pipe," said he.

"It is farther on," said I; "but observe the white web-work which gleams from these cavern walls."

He turned towards me, and looked into my eyes with two filmy orbs that distilled the rheum of intoxication.

"Nitre?" he asked, at length.

"Nitre," I replied. "How long have you had that cough?"

"Ugh! ugh! ugh!—ugh! ugh! ugh!—ugh! ugh! ugh!—ugh! ugh! ugh!—ugh! ugh! ugh!"

My poor friend found it impossible to reply for many minutes.

"It is nothing," he said, at last.

"Come," I said, with decision, "we will go back; your health is precious. You are rich, respected, admired, beloved; you are happy, as once I was. You are a man to be missed. For me it is no matter. We will go back; you will be ill, and I cannot be responsible. Besides, there is Luchesi—"

"Enough," he said; "the cough is a mere nothing; it will not kill me. I shall not die of a cough."

"True—true," I replied; "and, indeed, I had no intention of alarming you unnecessarily— but you should use all proper caution. A draught of this Medoc will defend us from the damps."

Here I knocked off the neck of a bottle which I drew from a long row of its fellows that lay upon the mould.

"Drink," I said, presenting him the wine.

He raised it to his lips with a leer. He paused and nodded to me familiarly, while his bells jingled.

"I drink," he said, "to the buried that repose around us."

"And I to your long life."

He again took my arm, and we proceeded.

"These vaults," he said, "are extensive."

"The Montresors," I replied, "were a great and numerous family."

"I forget your arms."

°*roquelaire*: a type of cloak.

"A huge human foot d'or, in a field azure; the foot crushes a serpent rampant whose fangs are imbedded in the heel."

"And the motto?"

"*Nemo me impune lacessit.*"°

50   "Good!" he said.

The wine sparkled in his eyes and the bells jingled. My own fancy grew warm with the Medoc. We had passed through walls of piled bones, with casks and puncheons intermingling, into the inmost recesses of the catacombs. I paused again, and this time I made bold to seize Fortunato by an arm above the elbow.

"The nitre!" I said: "see, it increases. It hangs like moss upon the vaults. We are below the river's bed. The drops of moisture trickle among the bones. Come, we will go back ere it is too late. Your cough—"

"It is nothing," he said; "let us go on. But first, another draught of the Medoc."

I broke and reached him a flagon of De Grave. He emptied it at a breath. His eyes flashed with a fierce light. He laughed and threw the bottle upwards with a gesticulation I did not understand.

55   I looked at him in surprise. He repeated the movement—a grotesque one.

"You do not comprehend?" he said.

"Not I," I replied.

"Then you are not of the brotherhood."

"How?"

60   "You are not of the masons."

"Yes, yes," I said, "yes, yes."

"You? Impossible! A mason?"

"A mason," I replied.

"A sign," he said.

65   "It is this," I answered, producing a trowel from beneath the folds of my *roquelaire.*

"You jest," he exclaimed, recoiling a few paces. "But let us proceed to the Amontillado."

"Be it so," I said, replacing the tool beneath the cloak, and again offering him my arm. He leaned upon it heavily. We continued our route in search of the Amontillado. We passed through a range of low arches, descended, passed on, and descending again, arrived at a deep crypt, in which the foulness of the air caused our flambeaux rather to glow than flame.

At the most remote end of the crypt there appeared another less spacious. Its walls had been lined with human remains, piled to the vault overhead, in the fashion of the great catacombs of Paris. Three sides of this interior crypt were still ornamented in this manner. From the fourth the bones had been thrown down, and lay promiscuously upon the earth, forming at one point a mound of some size. Within the wall thus exposed by the displacing of the bones, we perceived a still interior recess, in depth about four feet, in width three, in height six or seven. It seemed to have been constructed for no especial use in itself, but formed merely the interval between two of the colossal supports of the roof of the catacombs, and was backed by one of their circumscribing walls of solid granite.

It was in vain that Fortunato, uplifting his dull torch, endeavored to pry into the depths of the recess. Its termination the feeble light did not enable us to see.

70   "Proceed," I said; "herein is the Amontillado. As for Luchesi—"

"He is an ignoramus," interrupted my friend, as he stepped unsteadily forward, while I followed immediately at his heels. In an instant he had reached the extremity of the niche, and finding his progress arrested by the rock, stood stupidly bewildered. A moment more and I had fettered him to the granite. In its surface were two iron staples, distant from each other about two feet, horizontally. From one of these depended a short chain, from the other

---

°*Nemo me impune lacessit:* No one attacks me with impunity.

a padlock. Throwing the links about his waist, it was but the work of a few seconds to secure it. He was too much astounded to resist. Withdrawing the key I stepped back from the recess.

"Pass your hand," I said, "over the wall; you cannot help feeling the nitre. Indeed it is *very* damp. Once more let me *implore* you to return. No? Then I must positively leave you. But I must first render you all the little attentions in my power."

"The Amontillado!" ejaculated my friend, not yet recovered from his astonishment.

"True," I replied; "the Amontillado."

As I said these words I busied myself among the pile of bones of which I have before spoken. 75
Throwing them aside, I soon uncovered a quantity of building stone and mortar. With these materials and with the aid of my trowel, I began vigorously to wall up the entrance of the niche.

I had scarcely laid the first tier of my masonry when I discovered that the intoxication of Fortunato had in a great measure worn off. The earliest indication I had of this was a low moaning cry from the depth of the recess. It was *not* the cry of a drunken man. There was then a long and obstinate silence. I laid the second tier, and the third, and the fourth; and then I heard the furious vibrations of the chain. The noise lasted for several minutes, during which, that I might hearken to it with the more satisfaction, I ceased my labors and sat down upon the bones. When at last the clanking subsided, I resumed the trowel, and finished without interruption the fifth, the sixth, and the seventh tier. The wall was now nearly upon a level with my breast. I again paused, and holding the flambeaux over the mason-work, threw a few feeble rays upon the figure within.

A succession of loud and shrill screams, bursting suddenly from the throat of the chained form, seemed to thrust me violently back. For a brief moment I hesitated—I trembled. Unsheathing my rapier, I began to grope with it about the recess: but the thought of an instant reassured me. I placed my hand upon the solid fabric of the catacombs, and felt satisfied. I reapproached the wall. I replied to the yells of him who clamored. I re-echoed—I aided—I surpassed them in volume and in strength. I did this, and the clamorer grew still.

It was now midnight, and my task was drawing to a close. I had completed the eighth, the ninth, and the tenth tier. I had finished a portion of the last and the eleventh; there remained but a single stone to be fitted and plastered in. I struggled with its weight; I placed it partially in its destined position. But now there came from out the niche a low laugh that erected the hairs upon my head. It was succeeded by a sad voice, which I had difficulty in recognizing as that of the noble Fortunato. The voice said—

"Ha! ha! ha!—he! he!—a very good joke indeed—an excellent jest. We will have many a rich laugh about it at the palazzo—he! he! he!—over our wine—he! he! he!"

"The Amontillado!" I said.
80
"He! he! he!—he! he! he!—yes, the Amontillado. But is it not getting late? Will not they be awaiting us at the palazzo, the Lady Fortunato and the rest? Let us be gone."

"Yes," I said, "let us be gone."

"For the love of God, Montresor!"

"Yes," I said, "for the love of God!"

But to these words I hearkened in vain for a reply. I grew impatient. I called aloud—
85
"Fortunato!"

No answer. I called again—

"Fortunato!"

No answer still. I thrust a torch through the remaining aperture and let it fall within. There came forth in return only a jingling of the bells. My heart grew sick—on account of the dampness of the catacombs. I hastened to make an end of my labor. I forced the last stone into its position; I plastered it up. Against the new masonry I re-erected the old rampart of bones. For the half of a century no mortal has disturbed them. *In pace requiescat!*°

°*In pace requiescat:* May he rest in peace.

QUESTIONS

1. In what ways is this story typical of Poe's theory of the brief prose tale? How would you describe the effect or effects of the story?

2. Describe Poe's use of setting in "The Cask of Amontillado" (the cap and bells, Fortunato's motley clothing, the interior recess in which Fortunato is pinioned, etc.).

3. To whom is Montresor, the narrator, speaking? What is the purpose of his saying "May he rest in peace" at the story's end? Why is the nature of Fortunato's insult against Montresor not explained in detail?

4. What do you learn about Montresor from his description of revenge and from his family's coat of arms?

5. How does Montresor manipulate Fortunato so that Fortunato seems to be the originator of the trip to examine the Amontillado? Who is Luchesi? What does Fortunato think of him?

LESLIE MARMON SILKO (b. 1948)

Leslie Marmon Silko is a writer of the American Southwest, having been brought up on the Laguna Pueblo Reservation in New Mexico, followed by attendance at the University of New Mexico. With an obvious sense of mission about telling her Laguna Pueblo heritage, she began writing and publishing poetry and short stories when she was in her early twenties. She has gained continued recognition, not only because of her works in English but also because of the translations of a number of works in Italian, German, and Korean. Published early in her career, "The Man to Send Rain Clouds" gained early acclaim for Silko and has continued to achieve wide praise up to the present time.

The Man to Send Rain Clouds (1969/1981)

They found him under a big cottonwood tree. His Levi jacket and pants were faded light blue so that he had been easy to find. The big cottonwood tree stood apart from a small grove of winterbare cottonwoods which grew in the wide, sandy arroyo. He had been dead for a day or more, and the sheep had wandered and scattered up and down the arroyo. Leon and his brother-in-law, Ken, gathered the sheep and left them in the pen at the sheep camp before they returned to the cottonwood tree. Leon waited under the tree while Ken drove the truck through the deep sand to the edge of the arroyo. He squinted up at the sun and unzipped his jacket—it sure was hot for this time of year. But high and northwest the blue mountains were still in snow. Ken came sliding down the low, crumbling bank about fifty yards down, and he was bringing the red blanket.

Before they wrapped the old man, Leon took a piece of string out of his pocket and tied a small gray feather in the old man's long white hair. Ken gave him the paint. Across the brown wrinkled forehead he drew a streak of white and along the high cheekbones he drew a strip of blue paint. He paused and watched Ken throw pinches of corn meal and pollen into the wind that fluttered the small gray feather. Then Leon painted with yellow under the old man's broad nose, and finally, when he had painted green across the chin, he smiled.

"Send us rain clouds, Grandfather." They laid the bundle in the back of the pickup and covered it with a heavy tarp before they started back to the pueblo.

They turned off the highway onto the sandy pueblo road. Not long after they passed the store and post office they saw Father Paul's car coming toward them. When he recognized their faces he slowed his car and waved for them to stop. The young priest rolled down the car window.

"Did you find old Teofilo?" he asked loudly.   5

Leon stopped the truck. "Good morning, Father. We were just out to the sheep camp. Everything is O.K. now."

"Thank God for that. Teofilo is a very old man. You really shouldn't allow him to stay at the sheep camp alone."

"No, he won't do that any more now."

"Well, I'm glad you understand. I hope I'll be seeing you at Mass this week—we missed you last Sunday. See if you can get old Teofilo to come with you." The priest smiled and waved at them as they drove away.

Louise and Teresa were waiting. The table was set for lunch, and the coffee was boiling   10
on the black iron stove. Leon looked at Louise and then at Teresa.

"We found him under a cottonwood tree in the big arroyo near sheep camp. I guess he sat down to rest in the shade and never got up again." Leon walked toward the old man's bed. The red plaid shawl had been shaken and spread carefully over the bed, and a new brown flannel shirt and pair of stiff new Levi's were arranged neatly beside the pillow. Louise held the screen door open while Leon and Ken carried in the red blanket. He looked small and shriveled, and after they dressed him in the new shirt and pants he seemed more shrunken.

It was noontime now because the church bells rang the Angelus. They ate the beans with hot bread, and nobody said anything until after Teresa poured the coffee.

Ken stood up and put on his jacket. "I'll see about the gravediggers. Only the top layer of soil is frozen. I think it can be ready before dark."

Leon nodded his head and finished his coffee. After Ken had been gone for a while, the neighbors and clanspeople came quietly to embrace Teofilo's family and to leave food on the table because the gravediggers would come to eat when they were finished.

The sky in the west was full of pale yellow light. Louise stood outside with her hands   15
in the pockets of Leon's green army jacket that was too big for her. The funeral was over, and the old men had taken their candles and medicine bags and were gone.

She waited until the body was laid into the pickup before she said anything to Leon. She touched his arm, and he noticed that her hands were still dusty from the corn meal that she had sprinkled around the old man. When she spoke, Leon could not hear her.

"What did you say? I didn't hear you."

"I said that I had been thinking about something."

"About what?"

"About the priest sprinkling holy water for Grandpa. So he won't be thirsty."   20

Leon stared at the new moccasins that Teofilo had made for the ceremonial dances in the summer. They were nearly hidden by the red blanket. It was getting colder, and the wind pushed gray dust down the narrow pueblo road. The sun was approaching the long mesa where it disappeared during the winter. Louise stood there shivering and watching his face. Then he zipped up his jacket and opened the truck door. "I'll see if he's there."

Ken stopped the pickup at the church, and Leon got out; and then Ken drove down the hill to the graveyard where people were waiting. Leon knocked at the old carved door with its symbols of the Lamb. While he waited he looked up at the twin bells from the king of Spain with the last sunlight pouring around them in their tower.

The priest opened the door and smiled when he saw who it was. "Come in! What brings you here this evening?"

The priest walked toward the kitchen, and Leon stood with his cap in his hand, playing with the earflaps and examining the living room—the brown sofa, the green armchair, and the brass lamp that hung down from the ceiling by links of chain. The priest dragged a chair out of the kitchen and offered it to Leon.

25   "No thank you, Father. I only came to ask you if you would bring your holy water to the graveyard."

The priest turned away from Leon and looked out the window at the patio full of shadows and the dining-room windows of the nuns' cloister across the patio. The curtains were heavy, and the light from within faintly penetrated; it was impossible to see the nuns inside eating supper. "Why didn't you tell me he was dead? I could have brought the Last Rites anyway."

Leon smiled. "It wasn't necessary, Father."

The priest stared down at his scuffed brown loafers and the worn hem of his cassock. "For a Christian burial it was necessary."

His voice was distant, and Leon thought that his blue eyes looked tired.

30   "It's O.K., Father, we just want him to have plenty of water."

The priest sank down into the green chair and picked up a glossy missionary magazine. He turned the colored pages full of lepers and pagans without looking at them.

"You know I can't do that, Leon. There should have been the Last Rites and a funeral Mass at the very least."

Leon put on his green cap and pulled the flaps down over his ears. "It's getting late, Father. I've got to go."

When Leon opened the door Father Paul stood up and said, "Wait." He left the room and came back wearing a long brown overcoat. He followed Leon out the door and across the dim churchyard to the adobe steps in front of the church. They both stooped to fit through the low adobe entrance. And when they started down the hill to the graveyard only half of the sun was visible above the mesa.

35   The priest approached the grave slowly, wondering how they had managed to dig into the frozen ground; and then he remembered that this was New Mexico, and saw the pile of cold loose sand beside the hole. The people stood close to each other with little clouds of steam puffing from their faces. The priest looked at them and saw a pile of jackets, gloves, and scarves in the yellow, dry tumbleweeds that grew in the graveyard. He looked at the red blanket, not sure that Teofilo was so small, wondering if it wasn't some perverse Indian trick—something they did in March to ensure a good harvest—wondering if maybe old Teofilo was actually at sheep camp corralling the sheep for the night. But there he was, facing into a cold dry wind and squinting at the last sunlight, ready to bury a red wool blanket while the faces of his parishioners were in shadow with the last warmth of the sun on their backs.

His fingers were stiff, and it took him a long time to twist the lid off the holy water. Drops of water fell on the red blanket and soaked into dark icy spots. He sprinkled the grave and the water disappeared almost before it touched the dim, cold sand; it reminded him of something—he tried to remember what it was, because he thought if he could remember he might understand this. He sprinkled more water; he shook the container until it was empty, and the water fell through the light from sundown like August rain that fell while the sun was still shining, almost evaporating before it touched the wilted squash flowers.

The wind pulled at the priest's brown Franciscan robe and swirled away the corn meal and pollen that had been sprinkled on the blanket. They lowered the bundle into the ground, and they didn't bother to untie the stiff pieces of new rope that were tied around the ends of the blanket. The sun was gone, and over on the highway the east-bound lane was full of headlights. The priest walked away slowly. Leon watched him climb the hill, and when he had disappeared within the tall, thick walls, Leon turned to look up at the high blue mountains in the deep snow that reflected a faint red light from the west. He felt good because it was finished, and he was happy about the sprinkling of the holy water; now the old man could send them big thunderclouds for sure.

QUESTIONS

1. What did Ken and Leon do when they found the dead man's body? What was your reaction to their actions?
2. How does this story illustrate a conflict between two cultures? What specific instances can you point to that show the conflict?
3. Why does Father Paul hesitate to sprinkle the holy water over the dead body? What rituals reflect Indian culture?
4. What is the tone of the story? Is there a conflict between the tone of the story and the plot?

WRITING ABOUT SETTING

In preparing to write about setting, determine the number and importance of locations, artifacts, and customs. Ask questions such as the following:

- How extensive are the visual descriptions? Does the author provide such vivid and carefully arranged detail about surroundings that you could draw a map or plan? Or is the scenery vague and difficult for you to reconstruct imaginatively? In either case, why?
- What connections, if any, are apparent between locations and characters? Do the locations bring characters together, separate them, facilitate their privacy, make intimacy and conversation difficult?
- How fully are objects described? How vital are they to the action? How important are they in the development of the plot or idea? How are they connected to the mental states of the characters?
- How important to plot and character are shapes, colors, times of day, clouds, storms, light and sun, seasons of the year, and conditions of vegetation?
- Are the characters poor, moderately well off, or rich? How does their economic condition affect what happens to them, and how does it affect their actions and attitudes?
- What cultural, religious, and political conditions are brought out in the story? How do the characters accept and adjust to these conditions? How do the conditions affect the characters' judgments and actions?
- What is the state of houses, furniture, and objects (e.g., polished and new, old and worn, ragged and torn)? What connections can you find between these conditions and the outlook and behavior of the characters?
- How important are sounds or silences? To what degree is music or other sound important in the development of character and action?
- Do characters respect or mistreat the environment? If there is an environmental connection, how central is it to the story?
- What conclusions do you think the author expects you to draw as a result of the neighborhood, culture, and larger world of the story?

Strategies for Organizing Ideas

Begin by making a brief description of the setting or scenes of the work, specifying the amount and importance of detail. Choosing one of the approaches in the following list, describe the approach you plan to develop. As you gather material for your essay, however, you may need to combine your major approach with one or more of the others. Whatever approach for development you choose, be sure to consider setting not as an end in itself but rather as illustration and evidence for claims you are making about the particular story.

1. *Setting and action.* Explore the importance of setting in the work. How extensively is the setting described? Are locations essential or incidental to the actions? Does the setting serve as part of the action (e.g., places of flight or concealment; public places where people meet openly, or hidden places where they meet privately; natural or environmental conditions; seasonal conditions such as searing heat or numbing cold; customs and conventions)? Do any objects cause inspiration, difficulty, or conflict (such as a bridge, a farm, a walking stick, a necklace, a fence, a hair ribbon, a frozen lake, a bizarre party, a hat floating in water)? How directly do these objects influence the action?

2. *Setting and organization.* How is the setting connected to the various parts of the work? Does it undergo any changes as the action develops? Why are some parts of the setting more important than others? Is the setting used as a structural frame or enclosure for the story? Describe the effect and purpose of such a structural use of setting. How do objects such as money, appliances, property, or physical location (e.g., a subway platform, a prison camp, a winter scene on a lake) influence the characters? How do descriptions made at the start become important in the action later on?

3. *Setting and character.* (For examples of this approach, see the two drafts of the illustrative essay in Part I.) Analyze the degree to which setting influences and interacts with character. Are the characters happy or unhappy where they live? Do they get into discussions or arguments about their home environments? Do they want to stay or leave? Do the economic, philosophical, religious, or ethnic aspects of the setting make the characters undergo changes? What jobs do the characters perform because of their ways of life? What freedoms or restraints do these jobs cause? How does the setting influence their decisions, transportation, speech habits, eating habits, attitudes about love and honor, and general behavior?

4. *Setting and atmosphere.* To what extent does setting contribute to mood? Does the setting go beyond the minimum needed for action or character? How do descriptive words paint verbal pictures and evoke moods through references to colors, shapes, sounds, smells, or tastes? Does the setting establish a mood, say, of joy or hopelessness, plenty or scarcity? What is the effect of daylight or nighttime upon events in the story? Do

the locations and activities of the characters suggest permanence or im-permanence (like returning home, creating figures out of mud, repairing a battered boat, perceiving ocean currents, being confined within a room)? Are things warm and pleasant, or cold and harsh? What connection do you find between the atmosphere and the author's expressed or apparent thoughts about existence?

5. *Setting and other aspects of the story.* Does the setting reinforce the story's meaning? Does it establish irony about the circumstances and ideas in the story? If you choose this approach, consult the introductory paragraph in "The Literary Uses of Setting" earlier in this chapter. If you are interested in writing about the symbolic implications of a setting, consult Chapter 7.

To conclude, summarize your major points or write about related aspects of setting that you have not considered. Thus, if your essay treats the relationship of setting and action, your conclusion might mention connections of the setting with character or atmosphere. You might also point out whether your central idea about setting also applies to other major aspects of the story.

Illustrative Student Essay

Although underlined sentences are not recommended by MLA style, they are used in this illustrative essay as teaching tools to emphasize the central idea, thesis sentence, and topic sentences.

Jani 1

Sonal Jani

Professor Addas

English 200

1 March 2014

The Interaction of Story and Setting in James Joyce's "Araby"°

The narrator of Joyce's "Araby" is a young man telling a story [1] about himself as an early adolescent first experiencing the overwhelming emotions that accompany sexual development. This intensely imaginative boy attaches his powerful feelings to the unnamed sister of Mangan, one of his playmates. Although he mainly worships her from afar, the two finally

°**This story appears on pages 242–246.**

do speak, and he promises her that he will go to a Dublin bazaar called "Araby" and buy something for her. To him, the gift will be virtually a holy gift. In telling this boy's story Joyce closely integrates the events themselves with the places in which they occur. The setting not only serves as the place of the actions, but it is also suggestive of the narrator's intense but confused emotions.* The aspects of setting are the outside scenes and the interior of his home, and also the negative views of the environment near his home and at the bazaar.†

[2]   Even before the narrator tells about going to the bazaar, a number of elements of setting establish his ardent but silent affection for Mangan's sister. When she is first introduced, the narrator and his friend Mangan are standing in "shadow," while she is described as standing in the light—"her figure defined by the light from the half-opened door" of her house—as though she is surrounded by a halo (243). When she and the narrator first speak together about the Araby bazaar, the narrator says, "The light from the lamp opposite our door caught the white curve of her neck, lit up her hair that rested there and falling, lit up the hand upon the railing" (244). These words of love and worship blend setting and subject matter, for the narrator's feelings stem out of his vision of Mangan's sister at the entrance of the house. The interior light and the lamplight, which illuminate her in these two scenes, provide for him the hopeful vision that he might move permanently out of the shadow to be with her. Place, object, illumination, and imagination all blend in these early scenes and seem, as setting, to offer him the opportunities which he dreams that he might realize.

[3]   Additional aspects of setting also point to the narrator's idealized feelings for the girl. The first of these is the local marketplace, where he accompanies his aunt to help carry parcels (his aunt and uncle are apparently his guardians). The circumstances here are "hostile to romance" (243), for the streets are swarming with "drunken men and

*Central idea.
†Thesis sentence.

Jani 3

bargaining women, amid the curses of laborers [. . . and] the shrill litanies
of shop-boys" (243). Despite this loud and boisterous environment, the
narrator confesses that he indulges himself in the daydream of acting out
his great love and devotion to Mangan's sister. "I imagined," he says,
"that I bore my chalice safely through the throng of foes" (243). In these
passages the word *chalice*, and also the word *litanies*, reveals the religious
overtones about the intensity of the narrator's boyhood love. Another
significant location of setting is the back drawing room of his home, where
a priest who once owned the house had died. In the total privacy of this
room, listening to the sound of the rain hit the earth outside, the narrator
as a boy experiences great depths of emotion that are mixed with religious
fervor and prayer: "All my senses seemed to desire to veil themselves and,
feeling that I was about to slip from them, I pressed the palms of my hands
together until they trembled, murmuring: *O love! O love!* many times" (244).

An alternative pattern of settings in the story, however, complements   **[4]**
the narrator's misgivings and disillusionment about his feelings. The
very first sentence explains that the street on which he lived as a boy was
"blind," a term meaning "dead-end" (242). Even here at the beginning,
then, the setting casts a pall over the narrator's idealized love, the
implication of the setting being that the narrator's youthful imaginative
power could have no outlet. In addition, the streets and alleys around
his house are described as "dark," a word that Joyce uses three times to
describe the scenes of early winter nights when the narrator and his friends
play their childhood games of chase (243). Darkness also pervades both
the "gloomy rooms" of the narrator's house and the home of Mangan's
sister (244). The darkness constantly surrounding the narrator suggests the
uncertainty and lack of direction of his feelings, and he explains that his
attitudes were those of "confused adoration" (243). This lack of knowledge
and experience is reinforced by the "uninhabited house" at the end of his
street, which is "detached from its neighbours" (242), and by the "deserted"
and "bare" third-class train car that carries him to the Araby bazaar (245).

Jani 4

[5]   The setting within the bazaar is strongly influential in the narrator's disillusionment. His aim has been to purchase "something" for Mangan's sister, a gesture that he believes is on the level of a holy obligation. But when he enters the building with the "magical name" (245), he is struck not by the romance of the setting and the possibility of realizing his dreams, but rather by the closed stalls and the pervading darkness (245). In addition, he finds that the place is bathed in "a silence like that which pervades a church after a service" (245). Here the setting illustrates the narrator's memory of growing frustration and anger. When he goes to one of the few open stalls to shop for a gift, he notices "the great jars that stood like eastern guards at either side of the dark entrance to the stall" (246). The young saleswoman there, who is rather unintelligent, is flirting with two men, but she leaves her flirtation to ask if she can help him. Interestingly, as she leaves him she changes "the position of one of the vases" (246). This alteration of setting suggests a similar alteration in the boy's romantic ideals, for he concludes that his trip has been "useless" (246). The darkness that immediately comes over the upper part of the hall is suggestive of his "vanity" (246) and it also suggests that his idealized love has fled to an emotional equivalent of the shadow where, earlier, he and Mangan waited for Mangan's sister to appear.

[6]   Without question the narrator as a boy is capable of intense imagination and the most deeply felt romantic enthusiasm, as is shown by the setting of doorlight and lamplight which forms a halo around Mangan's sister. But the negative objects and locations of setting, together with the narrator's youth, suggest the impossibility of his ever realizing his dreams. Ultimately, he concludes that he is a "creature driven and derided by vanity," a realization that overwhelms him with "anguish and anger" (246). The story ends on this note, and Joyce's use of setting throughout the story points toward the same conclusion.

Jani 5

Work Cited

Joyce, James. "Araby." *Literature: An Introduction to Reading and Writing*,

   Compact Edition. Ed. Edgar V. Roberts and Robert Zweig. 6th ed.

   New York: Pearson, 2015. 242–46. Print.

Commentary on the Essay

Because the topic of this essay is the setting of Joyce's "Araby," it is most important to note that, after a few sentences briefly describing the narrative, the essay focuses not on character, or point of view, but on setting. Setting is foremost. Whenever other aspects of the story become significant, the point of the essay is to emphasize these additional aspects to the story's setting.

The central idea of the essay is that the locations and some of the objects described in the story are linked with the major character's developing emotions. In its consideration of action and setting, the essay illustrates some aspects of strategy 1 described on page 258. In showing the connection between setting, character, and ideas, it illustrates strategies 3 and 5.

The introductory paragraph indicates the closeness of setting and story and lays out the areas to be developed. Paragraph 2 contains details showing the ways in which place and conditions of light establish the narrator's affections when he was a boy. Paragraph 3 brings out two major additional details of setting that illustrate the force of the narrator's boyhood emotions: in public, where he indulges his daydreams, and in private, where his desires take on an almost religious fervor. Paragraph 4 introduces a contrary patterning of setting in and around the boy's home that reinforces the negative aspects of the narrator's childhood love. Paragraph 5 does the same for the setting of the Araby bazaar itself. The concluding paragraph encapsulates both the positive and negative aspects of setting, and focuses on the story's conclusion as the climax of the narrator's boyhood disillusionment.

Writing Topics About Setting

Writing Paragraphs

1. Write a paragraph in which you compare and contrast how details of setting establish qualities and traits of one of the following female characters: Stella of "The Shawl" (this chapter) or Miss Brill of "Miss Brill" (Chapter 3).

2. Write a paragraph in which you consider the significance of place to character in "The Man to Send Rain Clouds" or "Araby" (both in this chapter).

Writing Essays

1. In what ways might we say that both "The Masque of the Red Death" (Chapter 9) and "The Shawl" (this chapter) are inseparable from their settings? Write an essay in which you consider the relationship of character to place and circumstance in order to answer this question. How could the actions of the stories happen without the locations in which they occur?

Creative Writing Assignment

1. Write a short narrative as though it is part of a story (which you may also wish to write for the assignment), using option (a) and/or (b).

   a. Relate a natural setting or type of day to a mood—for example, a nice day to happiness and satisfaction, or a cold, cloudy, rainy day to sadness. Or create irony by relating the nice day to sadness or the rainy day to happiness.

   b. Indicate how an object or circumstance becomes the cause of conflict or reconciliation (such as the shawl in "The Shawl" in this chapter or the newly tuned piano in "Two Kinds" in Chapter 3).

2. Choose one story included in this chapter and rewrite a page or two, taking the characters out of their setting and placing them in an entirely new setting or in the setting of another story (you choose). Then write a brief analysis dealing with questions like these: How do you think your characters would be affected by their new settings? Do you make them change slowly or rapidly? Why? As a result of your rewriting, what can you conclude about the uses of setting in fiction?

Library Assignment

1. Locate two books or Internet sources on the career of James Joyce. On the basis of information you find in these sources, write a brief account of Joyce's use of setting and place to evoke atmosphere and to bring out qualities of human character.

Chapter 5
Structure: The Organization of Stories

AFTER STUDYING THIS MATERIAL, YOU SHOULD BE ABLE TO DO THE FOLLOWING:

- Understand the general methods of organization in stories
- Recognize the concepts of exposition, complication, crisis, and resolution
- Compare and contrast the structural methods of various stories
- Evaluate how a story's structure affects its meaning and impact on readers

S**tructure** refers to the ways in which writers arrange materials in accord with the general ideas and purposes of their works. Unlike plot, which is focused on conflict or conflicts (see Chapter 1), structure defines the layouts of works—the ways the story, play, or poem is shaped. Structure is about matters such as placement, balance, recurring themes, true and misleading conclusions, suspense, and the imitation of models or forms such as reports, letters, conversations, or confessions. A work might be divided into numbered sections or parts, or it might begin in a countryside (or one state) and conclude in a city (or another state), or it might develop a relationship between two people from their first introduction to their falling in love.

Formal Categories of Structure

Many aspects of structure are common to all genres of literature. Particularly for stories and plays, however, the following aspects form a skeleton, a pattern of development.

The Exposition Provides the Materials Necessary to Put the Plot into Operation

Exposition is the laying out, the putting forth, of the materials in the story—the main characters, their backgrounds, their characteristics, interests, goals, limitations, potentials, and basic assumptions. Exposition may not be limited to the beginning of the work, where it is most expected, but may be found anywhere. Thus, intricacies, twists, turns, false leads, blind alleys, surprises, and other quirks may be introduced to interest, intrigue, perplex, mystify, and please readers. Whenever something new arises, to the degree that it is new it is a part of exposition.

The Complication Marks the Beginning and the Growth of the Conflict

The **complication** is the onset and development of the major conflict—the plot. The major participants are the protagonist and antagonist, together with whatever ideas and values they represent, such as good or evil, freedom or oppression, independence or dependence, love or hate, intelligence or stupidity, and knowledge or ignorance.

The Crisis Marks the Decisions Made to End the Conflict

The **crisis** (the Greek word for *judgment* or *separation*—a separating, distinguishing, or turning point) marks that part of the action where the conflict reaches its greatest tension. During the crisis, a decision or an action is undertaken to resolve the complication or complications, and therefore the crisis is that point at which uncertainty and anxiety are greatest. Usually the crisis is followed closely by the next stage, the *climax*. In fact, the two often occur so near each other that they are considered the same.

The Climax Is the Conclusion of the Conflict

Because the **climax** (the Greek word for *ladder*) is a consequence of the crisis, it is the story's *high point* (from the idea of a ladder) and may take the shape of an action, a decision, an affirmation or denial, or an illumination or realization. It is the logical conclusion of the preceding actions; no new major developments follow it. In most stories, the climax occurs at the end or close to it. For example, in Edgar Allan Poe's "The Cask of Amontillado" (Chapter 4), the narrator, Montresor, begins the story by describing briskly how he had come to hate Fortunato and resolved to seek his revenge. The rest of the story is a fairly straightforward narrative of their journey across Paris and into the deeps of the old family wine cellar where Fortunato is to taste the much-prized wine. It is only at the very end of the story, when we realize, at the climax, how Montresor has calmly and methodically exacted his revenge.

The Resolution or Dénouement Finishes the Work and Releases the Tension

The **resolution** (the Latin word for *untying* or *releasing*) or **dénouement** (the French word for *untying* or *undoing*) is the completing of the story or play after the climax; for once the climax has occurred, the work's tension and uncertainty are finished, and most authors conclude quickly to avoid losing their readers' interest. For instance, Poe ends "The Masque of the Red Death" (Chapter 9) by asserting that the "illimitable" power of the Red Death has overcome the earth and all its occupants. In other words, after the story's major conflicts are finished, the dénouement brings the work to a satisfying and rapid ending.

Formal and Actual Structure

The structure just described is a *formal* one, an ideal pattern that moves directly from beginning to end. Few narratives and dramas follow this pattern exactly, however. A mystery story might hold back crucial details of exposition (because the goal is to mystify); a suspense story might keep the protagonist ignorant but provide readers with abundant details in order to maximize concern and tension about the outcome.

More realistic, less "artificial" stories might also contain structural variations. For example, Welty's "A Worn Path" (this chapter) produces a *double take* because of unique structuring. During most of the story the major character, Phoenix, seems to be in conflict with age, poverty, and environment. At the end, however, the story brings out an additional difficulty—a new conflict that enlarges our responses to include not just concern but also heartfelt anguish. "A Worn Path" is just one example of how a structural variation maximizes the impact of a work.

There are many other possible variants in structure. One of these is called **flashback,** or **selective recollection,** in which present circumstances are explained by the selective introduction of past events. The moment at which the flashback is introduced may be a part of the resolution of the plot, and the flashback might lead you into a moment of climax but then go from there to develop the details that are more properly part of the exposition. In this structure the action begins and remains in the present. Important parts of the past flood the protagonist's memory in flashback, though perhaps not in the order in which they happened. Memory might be used structurally in other ways. An example is Katherine Anne Porter's "The Jilting of Granny Weatherall" (Chapter 7), an intense story that is developed within the dying imaginings of an aged woman, Granny Weatherall. As she passes in and out of consciousness on her deathbed, we follow her recollection of major events in her life, such as being deserted on her wedding day, remarrying and bringing up her children, enduring her long widowhood, losing a favorite daughter, and retaining her lifelong obligation to her church. In short, this story builds its chronology through a series of apparently disconnected but closely unified flashbacks.

Each narrative or drama has its own unique structure. Some stories may be organized according to simple geography, as in Joyce's "Araby" (Chapter 4), which follows a young man on a trip from the neighborhood to the town bazaar, or Hawthorne's "Young Goodman Brown" (Chapter 7), where the main character travels from his safe home to the haunted forest. Parts or scenes might be carried on through conversations, as in Carver's "Cathedral" (Chapter 2), or through a period of dying fantasy, as in Ambrose Bierce's "An Occurrence at Owl Creek Bridge" (Chapter 1). Additionally, parts of a work may be set out as fragments of conversation, as in Luke's "The Parable of the Prodigal Son" (Chapter 7), or as a ceremony, as in Hawthorne's "Young Goodman Brown" (Chapter 7), or as an announcement of a party, as in "The Necklace" (Part I). The possible variations in literary structures are infinite.

Stories for Study

Ralph Ellison . . . . Battle Royal, 268
Geri Lipschultz. . . . . Slow Dance of the Heart, 277
Daniel Orozco . . . . Orientation, 284
Eudora Welty. . . . . A Worn Path, 288

RALPH ELLISON (1914–1994)

Ralph Ellison was born in Oklahoma seven years after it became a state. As a youth he was attracted to music, particularly jazz; and at one point he planned on becoming a classical music compos-er, his ideal being Richard Wagner, the giant among nineteenth-century German operatic composers. In 1933 Ellison went to Alabama's Tuskegee Institute, but after three years he left for New York with a plan to become a sculptor. Once in New York, he met Richard Wright (1908–1960), and with Wright's encouragement and influence he began writing essays and stories for magazines such as New Challenge *and* New Masses. *Before he published* Invisible Man *in 1952, his best known works were the stories "King of the Bingo Game" and "Flying Home." With* Invisible Man, *which won a National Book Award in 1953, his work became widely read and taught. In 1964 he published* Shadow and Act, *a collection of essays, and in 1985 he published* Going to the Territory, *a book of essays and interviews. In later years he held a chair in humanities at New York University. His works published posthumously are* The Collected Essays of Ralph Ellison *(1995),* Flying Home and Other Stories *(1996), and the novel* Juneteenth *(1999).*

Battle Royal (1952)

It goes a long way back, some twenty years. All my life I had been looking for something, and everywhere I turned someone tried to tell me what it was. I accepted their answers too, though they were often in contradiction and even self-contradictory. I was naïve. I was looking for myself and asking everyone except myself questions which I, and only I, could answer. It took me a long time and much painful boomeranging of my expectations to achieve a realization everyone else appears to have been born with: That I am nobody but myself. But first I had to discover that I am an invisible man!

And yet I am no freak of nature, nor of history. I was in the cards, other things having been equal (or unequal) eighty-five years ago. I am not ashamed of my grandparents for having been slaves. I am only ashamed of myself for having at one time been ashamed. About eighty-five years ago they were told that they were free, united with others of our country in everything pertaining to the common good, and, in everything social, separate like the fingers of the hand.

And they believed it. They exulted in it. They stayed in their place, worked hard, and brought up my father to do the same. But my grandfather is the one. He was an odd old guy, my grandfather, and I am told I take after him. It was he who caused the trouble. On his deathbed he called my father to him and said, "Son, after I'm gone I want you to keep up the good fight. I never told you, but our life is a war and I have been a traitor all my born days, a spy in the enemy's country ever since I gave up my gun back in the Reconstruction. Live with your head in the lion's mouth. I want you to overcome 'em with yeses, undermine 'em with grins, agree 'em to death and destruction, let 'em swallow you till they vomit or bust wide open." They thought the old man had gone out of his mind. He had been the meekest of men. The younger children were rushed from the room, the shades drawn and the flame of the lamp turned so low that it sputtered on the wick like the old man's breath-ing. "Learn it to the younguns," he whispered fiercely; then he died.

But my folks were more alarmed over his last words than over his dying. It was as though he had not died at all, his words caused so much anxiety. I was warned emphati-cally to forget what he had said and, indeed, this is the first time it has been mentioned out-side the family circle. It had a tremendous effect upon me, however. I could never be sure of what he meant. Grandfather had been a quiet old man who never made any trouble, yet on his deathbed he had called himself a traitor and a spy, and he had spoken of his meekness as a dangerous activity. It became a constant puzzle which lay unanswered in the back of my mind. And whenever things went well for me I remembered my grandfather and felt guilty and uncomfortable. It was as though I was carrying out his advice in spite of myself. And to make it worse, everyone loved me for it. I was praised by the most lily-white men of the town. I was considered an example of desirable conduct—just as my grandfather had been. And what puzzled me was that the old man had defined it as *treachery*. When I was praised for my conduct I felt a guilt that in some way I was doing something that was really against the wishes of the white folks, that if they had understood they would have desired me to act just the opposite, that I should have been sulky and mean, and that that really would have been what they wanted, even though they were fooled and thought they wanted me to act as I did. It made me afraid that some day they would look upon me as a traitor and I would be lost. Still I was more afraid to act any other way because they didn't like that at all. The old man's words were like a curse. On my graduation day I delivered an oration in which I showed that humility was the secret, indeed, the very essence of progress. (Not that I believed this—how could I, remembering my grandfather?—I only believed that it worked.) It was a great success. Everyone praised me and I was invited to give the speech at a gathering of the town's leading white citizens. It was a triumph for our whole community.

It was in the main ballroom of the leading hotel. When I got there I discovered that it was on the occasion of a smoker, and I was told that since I was to be there anyway I might as well take part in the battle royal to be fought by some of my schoolmates as part of the entertainment. The battle royal came first.

All of the town's big shots were there in their tuxedoes, wolfing down the buffet foods, drinking beer and whiskey and smoking black cigars. It was a large room with a high ceiling. Chairs were arranged in neat rows around three sides of a portable boxing ring. The fourth side was clear, revealing a gleaming space of polished floor. I had some misgivings over the battle royal, by the way. Not from a distaste for fighting, but because I didn't care too much for the other fellows who were to take part. They were tough guys who seemed to have no grandfather's curse worrying their minds. No one could mistake their toughness. And besides, I suspected that fighting a battle royal might detract from the dignity of my speech. In those pre-invisible days I visualized myself as a potential Booker T. Washington.° But the other fellows didn't care too much for me either, and there were nine of them. I felt superior to them in my way, and I didn't like the manner in which we were all crowded together into the servants' elevator. Nor did they like my being there. In fact, as the warmly lighted floors flashed past the elevator we had words over the fact that I, by taking part in the fight, had knocked one of their friends out of a night's work.

We were led out of the elevator through a rococo hall into an anteroom and told to get into our fighting togs. Each of us was issued a pair of boxing gloves and ushered out into the big mirrored hall, which we entered looking cautiously about us and whispering, lest we might accidentally be heard above the noise of the room. It was foggy with cigar smoke. And already the whiskey was taking effect. I was shocked to see some of the most important men of the town quite tipsy. They were all there—bankers, lawyers, judges, doctors, fire chiefs, teachers, merchants. Even one of the more fashionable pastors. Something we could not see was going on up front. A clarinet was vibrating sensuously and the men were standing up and moving eagerly forward. We were a small tight group, clustered together, our bare upper bodies touching and shining with anticipatory sweat; while up front the big shots were becoming increasingly excited over something we still could not see. Suddenly

°*Booker T. Washington:* Booker T. Washington (1856–1915) was born a slave, but ultimately he became widely recognized as an educator, and served as president of the Tuskeegee Institute.

I heard the school superintendent, who had told me to come, yell, "Bring up the shines gentlemen! Bring up the little shines!"

We were rushed up to the front of the ballroom, where it smelled even more strongly of tobacco and whiskey. Then we were pushed into place. I almost wet my pants. A sea of faces, some hostile, some amused, ringed around us, and in the center, facing us, stood a magnificent blonde—stark naked. There was dead silence. I felt a blast of cold air chill me. I tried to back away, but they were behind me and around me. Some of the boys stood with lowered heads, trembling. I felt a wave of irrational guilt and fear. My teeth chattered, my skin turned to goose flesh, my knees knocked. Yet I was strongly attracted and looked in spite of myself. Had the price of looking been blindness, I would have looked. The hair was yellow like that of a circus kewpie doll, the face heavily powdered and rouged, as though to form an abstract mask, the eyes hollow and smeared a cool blue, the color of a baboon's butt. I felt a desire to spit upon her as my eyes brushed slowly over her body. Her breasts were firm and round as the domes of East Indian temples, and I stood so close as to see the fine skin texture and beads of pearly perspiration glistening like dew around the pink and erected buds of her nipples. I wanted at one and the same time to run from the room, to sink through the floor, or go to her and cover her from my eyes and the eyes of the others with my body; to feel the soft thighs, to caress her and destroy her, to love her and murder her, to hide from her, and yet to stroke where below the small American flag tattooed upon her belly her thighs formed a capital V. I had a notion that of all in the room she saw only me with her impersonal eyes.

And then she began to dance, a slow sensuous movement; the smoke of a hundred cigars clinging to her like the thinnest of veils. She seemed like a fair bird-girl girdled in veils calling to me from the angry surface of some gray and threatening sea. I was transported. Then I became aware of the clarinet playing and the big shots yelling at us. Some threatened us if we looked and others if we did not. On my right I saw one boy faint. And now a man grabbed a silver pitcher from a table and stepped close as he dashed ice water upon him and stood him up and forced two of us to support him as his head hung and moans issued from his thick bluish lips. Another boy began to plead to go home. He was the largest of the group, wearing dark red fighting trunks much too small to conceal the erection which projected from him as though in answer to the insinuating low-registered moaning of the clarinet. He tried to hide himself with his boxing gloves.

10   And all the while the blonde continued dancing, smiling faintly at the big shots who watched her with fascination, and faintly smiling at our fear. I noticed a certain merchant who followed her hungrily, his lips loose and drooling. He was a large man who wore diamond studs in a shirtfront which swelled with the ample paunch underneath, and each time the blonde swayed her undulating hips he ran his hand through the thin hair of his bald head and, with his arms upheld, his posture clumsy like that of an intoxicated panda, wound his belly in a slow and obscene grind. This creature was completely hypnotized. The music had quickened. As the dancer flung herself about with a detached expression on her face, the men began reaching out to touch her. I could see their beefy fingers sink into her soft flesh. Some of the others tried to stop them and she began to move around the floor in graceful circles, as they gave chase, slipping and sliding over the polished floor. It was mad. Chairs went crashing, drinks were spilt, as they ran laughing and howling after her. They caught her just as she reached a door, raised her from the floor, and tossed her as college boys are tossed at a hazing, and above her red, fixedsmiling lips I saw the terror and disgust in her eyes, almost like my own terror and that which I saw in some of the other boys. As I watched, they tossed her twice and her soft breasts seemed to flatten against the air and her legs flung widely as she spun. Some of the more sober ones helped her to escape. And I started off the floor, heading for the anteroom with the rest of the boys.

Some were still crying and in hysteria. But as we tried to leave we were stopped and ordered to get into the ring. There was nothing to do but what we were told. All ten of us climbed under the ropes and allowed ourselves to be blindfolded with broad bands of white cloth. One of the men seemed to feel a bit sympathetic and tried to cheer us up as we stood with our backs against the ropes. Some of us tried to grin. "See that boy over there?" one of the men said. "I want you to run across at the bell and give it to him right in the belly. If you don't get him, I'm going to get you. I don't like his looks." Each of us was told the same. The blindfolds were put on. Yet even then I had been going over my speech. In my mind each word was as bright as flame. I felt the cloth pressed into place, and frowned so that it would be loosened when I relaxed.

But now I felt a sudden fit of blind terror. I was unused to darkness. It was as though I had suddenly found myself in a dark room filled with poisonous cottonmouths. I could hear the bleary voices yelling insistently for the battle royal to begin.

"Get going in there!"

"Let me at that big nigger!"

I strained to pick up the school superintendent's voice, as though to squeeze some security out of that slightly more familiar sound.   15

"Let me at those black sonsabitches!" someone yelled.

"No, Jackson, no!" another voice yelled. "Here, somebody, help me hold Jack."

"I want to get at that ginger-colored nigger. Tear him limb from limb," the first voice yelled.

I stood against the ropes trembling. For in those days I was what they called ginger-colored, and he sounded as though he might crunch me between his teeth like a crisp ginger cookie.

Quite a struggle was going on. Chairs were being kicked about and I could hear voices   20 grunting as with a terrific effort. I wanted to see, to see more desperately than ever before. But the blindfold was as tight as a thick skinpuckering scab and when I raised my gloved hands to push the layers of white aside a voice yelled, "Oh, no you don't, black bastard! Leave that alone!"

"Ring the bell before Jackson kills him a coon!" someone boomed in the sudden silence. And I heard the bell clang and the sound of the feet scuffling forward.

A glove smacked against my head. I pivoted, striking out stiffly as someone went past, and felt the jar ripple along the length of my arm to my shoulder. Then it seemed as though all nine of the boys had turned upon me at once. Blows pounded me from all sides while I struck out as best I could. So many blows landed upon me that I wondered if I were not the only blindfolded fighter in the ring, or if the man called Jackson hadn't succeeded in getting me after all.

Blindfolded, I could no longer control my motions. I had no dignity. I stumbled about like a baby or a drunken man. The smoke had become thicker and with each new blow it seemed to sear and further restrict my lungs. My saliva became like hot bitter glue. A glove connected with my head, filling my mouth with warm blood. It was everywhere. I could not tell if the moisture I felt upon my body was sweat or blood. A blow landed hard against the nape of my neck. I felt myself going over, my head hitting the floor. Streaks of blue light filled the black world behind the blindfold. I lay prone, pretending that I was knocked out, but felt myself seized by hands and yanked to my feet. "Get going, black boy! Mix it up!" My arms were like lead, my head smarting from blows. I managed to feel my way to the ropes and held on, trying to catch my breath. A glove landed in my midsection and I went over again, feeling as though the smoke had become a knife jabbed into my guts. Pushed this way and that by the legs milling around me, I finally pulled erect and discovered that I could see the black, sweat-washed forms weaving in the smoky-blue atmosphere like drunken dancers weaving to the rapid drum-like thuds of blows.

Everyone fought hysterically. It was complete anarchy. Everybody fought everybody else. No group fought together for long. Two, three, four, fought one, then turned to fight each other, were themselves attacked. Blows landed below the belt and in the kidney, with the gloves open as well as closed, and with my eye partly opened now there was not so much terror. I moved carefully, avoiding blows, although not too many to attract attention, fighting from group to group. The boys groped about like blind, cautious crabs crouching to protect their midsections, their heads pulled in short against their shoulders, their arms stretched nervously before them, with their fists testing the smoke-filled air like the knobbed feelers of hypersensitive snails. In one corner I glimpsed a boy violently punching the air and heard him scream in pain as he smashed his hand against a ring post.

25   For a second I saw him bent over holding his hand, then going down as a blow caught his unprotected head. I played one group against the other, slipping in and throwing a punch then stepping out of range while pushing the others into the melee to take the blows blindly aimed at me. The smoke was agonizing and there were no rounds, no bells at three minute intervals to relieve our exhaustion. The room spun round me, a swirl of lights, smoke, seating bodies surrounded by tense white faces. I bled from both nose and mouth, the blood spattering upon my chest.

The men kept yelling, "Slug him, black boy! Knock his guts out!"

"Uppercut him! Kill him! Kill that big boy!"

Taking a fake fall, I saw a boy going down heavily beside me as though we were felled by a single blow, saw a sneaker-clad foot shoot into his groin as the two who had knocked him down stumbled upon him. I rolled out of range, feeling a twinge of nausea.

The harder we fought the more threatening the men became. And yet, I had begun to worry about my speech again. How would it go? Would they recognize my ability? What would they give me?

30   I was fighting automatically and suddenly I noticed that one after another of the boys was leaving the ring. I was surprised, filled with panic, as though I had been left alone with an unknown danger. Then I understood. The boys had arranged it among themselves. It was the custom for the two men left in the ring to slug it out for the winner's prize. I discovered this too late. When the bell sounded two men in tuxedoes leaped into the ring and removed the blindfold. I found myself facing Tatlock, the biggest of the gang. I felt sick at my stomach. Hardly had the bell stopped ringing in my ears than it clanged again and I saw him moving swiftly toward me. Thinking of nothing else to do I hit him smash on the nose. He kept coming, bringing the rank sharp violence of stale sweat. His face was a black blank of a face, only his eyes alive—with hate of me and aglow with a feverish terror from what had happened to us all. I became anxious. I wanted to deliver my speech and he came at me as though he meant to beat it out of me. I smashed him again and again, taking his blows as they came. Then on a sudden impulse I struck him lightly and as we clinched, I whispered, "Fake like I knocked you out, you can have the prize."

"I'll break your behind," he whispered hoarsely.

"For *them?*"

"For *me*, sonofabitch!"

They were yelling for us to break it up and Tatlock spun me half around with a blow, and as a joggled camera sweeps in a reeling scene, I saw the howling red faces crouching tense beneath the cloud of blue-gray smoke. For a moment the world wavered, unraveled, flowed, then my head cleared and Tatlock bounced before me. That fluttering shadow before my eyes was his jabbing left hand. Then falling forward, my head against his damp shoulder, I whispered,

35   "I'll make it five dollars more."

"Go to hell!"

But his muscles relaxed a trifle beneath my pressure and I breathed, "Seven!"

"Give it to your ma," he said, ripping me beneath the heart.

And while I still held him I butted him and moved away. I felt myself bombarded with punches. I fought back with hopeless desperation. I wanted to deliver my speech more than anything else in the world, because I felt that only these men could judge truly my ability, and now this stupid clown was ruining my chances. I began fighting carefully now, moving in to punch him and out again with my greater speed. A lucky blow to his chin and I had him going too—until I heard a loud voice yell, "I got my money on the big boy."

Hearing this, I almost dropped my guard. I was confused: Should I try to win against the voice out there? Would not this go against my speech, and was not this a moment for humility, for nonresistance? A blow to my head as I danced about sent my right eye popping like a jack-in-the-box and settled my dilemma. The room went red as I fell. It was a dream fall, my body languid and fastidious as to where to land, until the floor became impatient and smashed up to meet me. A moment later I came to. An hypnotic voice said FIVE emphatically. And I lay there, hazily watching a dark red spot of my own blood shaping itself into a butterfly, glistening and soaking into the soiled gray world of the canvas.

When the voice drawled TEN I was lifted up and dragged to a chair. I sat dazed. My eye pained and swelled with each throb of my pounding heart and I wondered if now I would be allowed to speak. I was wringing wet, my mouth still bleeding. We were grouped along the wall now. The other boys ignored me as they congratulated Tatlock and speculated as to how much they would be paid. One boy whimpered over his smashed hand. Looking up front, I saw attendants in white jackets rolling the portable ring away and placing a small square rug in the vacant space surrounded by chairs. Perhaps, I thought, I will stand on the rug to deliver my speech.

Then the M.C. called to us, "Come on up here boys and get your money."

We ran forward to where the men laughed and talked in their chairs, waiting. Everyone seemed friendly now.

"There it is on the rug," the man said. I saw the rug covered with coins of all dimensions and a few crumpled bills. But what excited me, scattered here and there, were the gold pieces.

"Boys, it's all yours," the man said. "You get all you grab."

"That's right, Sambo," a blond man said, winking at me confidentially.

I trembled with excitement, forgetting my pain. I would get the gold and the bills, I thought. I would use both hands. I would throw my body against the boys nearest me to block them from the gold.

"Get down around the rug now," the man commanded, "and don't anyone touch it until I give the signal."

"This ought to be good," I heard.

As told, we got around the square rug on our knees. Slowly the man raised his freckled hand as we followed it upward with our eyes.

I heard, "These niggers look like they're about to pray!"

Then, "Ready," the man said. "Go!"

I lunged for a yellow coin lying on the blue design of the carpet, touching it and sending a surprised shriek to join those rising around me. I tried frantically to remove my hand but could not let go. A hot, violent force tore through my body, shaking me like a wet rat. The rug was electrified. The hair bristled up on my head as I shook myself free. My muscles jumped, my nerves jangled, writhed. But I saw that this was not stopping the other boys. Laughing in fear and embarrassment, some were holding back and scooping up the coins knocked off by the painful contortions of the others. The men roared above us as we struggled.

"Pick it up, goddamnit, pick it up!" someone called like a bass-voiced parrot. "Go on, get it!"

55   I crawled rapidly around the floor, picking up the coins, trying to avoid the coppers and to get greenbacks and the gold. Ignoring the shock by laughing, as I brushed the coins off quickly, I discovered that I could contain the electricity—a contradiction, but it works. Then the men began to push us onto the rug. Laughing embarrassedly, we struggled out of their hands and kept after the coins. We were all wet and slippery and hard to hold. Suddenly I saw a boy lifted into the air, glistening with sweat like a circus seal, and dropped, his wet back landing flush upon the charged rug, heard him yell and saw him literally dance upon his back, his elbows beating a frenzied tattoo upon the floor, his muscles twitching like the flesh of a horse stung by many flies. When he finally rolled off, his face was gray and no one stopped him when he ran from the floor amid booming laughter.

"Get the money," the M.C. called. "That's good hard American cash!"

And we snatched and grabbed, snatched and grabbed. I was careful not to come too close to the rug now, and when I felt the hot whiskey breath descend upon me like a cloud of foul air I reached out and grabbed the leg of a chair. It was occupied and I held on desperately.

"Leggo, nigger! Leggo!"

The huge face wavered down to mine as he tried to push me free. But my body was slippery and he was too drunk. It was Mr. Colcord, who owned a chain of movie houses and "entertainment palaces." Each time he grabbed me I slipped out of his hands. It became a real struggle. I feared the rug more than I did the drunk, so I held on, surprising myself for a moment by trying to topple him upon the rug. It was such an enormous idea that I found myself actually carrying it out. I tried not to be obvious, yet when I grabbed his leg, trying to tumble him out of the chair, he raised up roaring with laughter, and, looking at me with soberness dead in the eye, kicked me viciously in the chest. The chair leg flew out of my hand. I felt myself going and rolled. It was as though I had rolled through a bed of hot coals. It seemed a whole century would pass before I would roll free, a century in which I was scared through the deepest levels of my body to the fearful breath within me and the breath seared and heated to the point of explosion. It'll all be over in a flash, I thought as I rolled clear. It'll all be over in a flash.

60   But not yet, the men on the other side were waiting, red faces swollen as though from apoplexy as they bent forward in their chairs. Seeing their fingers coming toward me I rolled away as a fumbled football rolls off the receiver's fingertips, back into the coals. That time I luckily sent the rug sliding out of place and heard the coins ringing against the floor and the boys scuffling to pick them up and the M.C. calling, "All right, boys, that's all. Go get dressed and get your money."

I was limp as a dish rag. My back felt as though it had been beaten with wires.

When we had dressed the M.C. came in and gave us each five dollars, except Tatlock, who got ten for being last in the ring. Then he told us to leave. I was not to get a chance to deliver my speech, I thought. I was going out into the dim alley in despair when I was stopped and told to go back. I returned to the ballroom, where the men were pushing back their chairs and gathering in groups to talk.

The M.C. knocked on a table for quiet. "Gentlemen," he said, "we almost forgot an important part of the program. A most serious part, gentlemen. This boy was brought here to deliver a speech which he made at his graduation yesterday. . . ."

"Bravo!"

65   "I'm told that he is the smartest boy we've got out there in Greenwood. I'm told that he knows more big words than a pocket-sized dictionary."

Much applause and laughter.

"So now, gentlemen, I want you to give him your attention."

There was still laughter as I faced them, my mouth dry, my eye throbbing. I began slowly, but evidently my throat was tense, because they began shouting, "Louder! Louder!"

"We of the younger generation extol the wisdom of that great leader and educator," I shouted, "who first spoke these flaming words of wisdom: 'A ship lost at sea for many days suddenly sighted a friendly vessel. From the mast of the unfortunate vessel was seen a signal: "Water, water; we die of thirst!" The answer from the friendly vessel came back: "Cast down your bucket where you are." The captain of the distressed vessel, at last heeding the injunction, cast down his bucket, and it came up full of fresh sparkling water from the mouth of the Amazon River.' And like him I say, and in his words, 'To those of my race who depend upon bettering their condition in a foreign land, or who underestimate the importance of cultivating friendly relations with the Southern white man, who is his next-door neighbor, I would say: "Cast down your bucket where you are"—cast it down in making friends in every manly way of the people of all races by whom we are surrounded. . . .'"

I spoke automatically and with such fervor that I did not realize that the men were   70
still talking and laughing until my dry mouth, filling up with blood from the cut, almost strangled me. I coughed, wanting to stop and go to one of the tall brass, sand-filled spittoons to relieve myself, but a few of the men, especially the superintendent, were listening and I was afraid. So I gulped it down, blood, saliva and all, and continued. (What powers of endurance I had during those days! What enthusiasm! What a belief in the rightness of things!) I spoke even louder in spite of the pain. But still they talked and still they laughed, as though deaf with cotton in dirty ears. So I spoke with greater emotional emphasis. I closed my ears and swallowed blood until I was nauseated. The speech seemed a hundred times as long as before, but I could not leave out a single word. All had to be said, each memorized nuance considered, rendered. Nor was that all. Whenever I uttered a word of three or more syllables a group of voices would yell for me to repeat it. I used the phrase "social responsibility" and they yelled:

"What's the word you say, boy?"

"Social responsibility," I said.

"What?"

"Social . . ."

"Louder."   75

". . . responsibility."

"More!"

"Respon—"

"Repeat!"

"—sibility."   80

The room filled with the uproar of laughter until, no doubt, distracted by having to gulp down my blood, I made a mistake and yelled a phrase I had often seen denounced in newspaper editorials, heard debated in private.

"Social . . ."

"What?" they yelled.

". . . equality—"

The laughter hung smokelike in the sudden stillness. I opened my eyes, puzzled. Sounds   85
of displeasure filled the room. The M.C. rushed forward. They shouted hostile phrases at me. But I did not understand.

A small dry mustached man in the front row blared out, "Say that slowly, son!"

"What sir?"

"What you just said!"

"Social responsibility, sir," I said.

"You weren't being smart, were you, boy?" he said, not unkindly.   90

"No, sir!"

"You sure that about 'equality' was a mistake?"

"Oh, yes, sir," I said. "I was swallowing blood."

"Well, you had better speak more slowly so we can understand. We mean to do right by you, but you've got to know your place at all times. All right, now, go on with your speech."

95   I was afraid. I wanted to leave but I wanted also to speak and I was afraid they'd snatch me down.

"Thank you, sir," I said, beginning where I had left off, and having them ignore me as before.

Yet when I finished there was a thunderous applause. I was surprised to see the superintendent come forth with a package wrapped in white tissue paper, and, gesturing for quiet, address the men.

"Gentlemen, you see that I did not overpraise this boy. He makes a good speech and some day he'll lead his people in the proper paths. And I don't have to tell you that that is important in these days and times. This is a good, smart boy, and so to encourage him in the right direction, in the name of the Board of Education I wish to present him a prize in the form of this . . ."

He paused, removing the tissue paper and revealing a gleaming calfskin brief case.

100   ". . . in the form of this first-class article from Shad Whitmore's shop."

"Boy," he said, addressing me, "take this prize and keep it well. Consider it a badge of office. Prize it. Keep developing as you are and some day it will be filled with important papers that will help shape the destiny of your people."

I was so moved that I could hardly express my thanks. A rope of bloody saliva forming a shape like an undiscovered continent drooled upon the leather and I wiped it quickly away. I felt an importance that I had never dreamed.

"Open it and see what's inside," I was told.

My fingers a-tremble, I complied, smelling the fresh leather and finding an official-looking document inside. It was a scholarship to the state college for Negroes. My eyes filled with tears and I ran awkwardly off the floor.

105   I was overjoyed; I did not even mind when I discovered that the gold pieces I had scrambled for were brass pocket tokens advertising a certain make of automobile.

When I reached home everyone was excited. Next day the neighbors came to congratulate me. I even felt safe from grandfather, whose deathbed curse usually spoiled my triumphs. I stood beneath his photograph with my brief case in hand and smiled triumphantly into his stolid black peasant's face. It was a face that fascinated me. The eyes seemed to follow everywhere I went.

That night I dreamed I was at a circus with him and that he refused to laugh at the clowns no matter what they did. Then later he told me to open my brief case and read what was inside and I did, finding an official envelope stamped with the state seal; and inside the envelope I found another and another, endlessly, and I thought I would fall of weariness. "Them's years," he said. "Now open that one." And I did and in it I found an engraved document containing a short message in letters of gold. "Read it," my grandfather said. "Out loud."

"To Whom It May Concern," I intoned. "Keep This Nigger-Boy Running."

I awoke with the old man's laughter ringing in my ears.

110   (It was a dream I was to remember and dream again for many years after. But at the time I had no insight into its meaning. First I had to attend college.)

QUESTIONS

1. Describe the narrator. How old is he? What are the circumstances that lead him to the "gathering of the town's leading white citizens"? What conclusions do you draw about the mental and moral qualities of these citizens?
2. What is the significance of the advice given by the narrator's grandfather? What is the connection between the narrator's dream and the grandfather's advice?

3. What is a battle royal? What is the narrator's attitude toward the battle in which he is to participate? Why does he have this attitude? To what indignities are the boys subjected as a result of their appearance before the assembled townsmen? In what way is the female dancer's plight like that of the boys?

4. Describe how the story's structure underlies the story's attack on racism.

5. What special indignities are imposed on the narrator? Why does he have difficulty in delivering his speech? Why is he reminded that "you've got to know your place at all times" (paragraph 93)?

GERI LIPSCHULTZ (b. 1951)

Geri Lipschultz was born in Newark and raised in Park Ridge, New Jersey. She has a BA from University of Massachusetts-Amherst, an MFA in fiction from the Iowa Writers' Workshop, and a PhD in English and creative writing from Ohio University/Athens. She has lived most of her life in metropolitan New York, teaching literature and writing in a number of schools, including Hunter College, Baruch College, Suffolk Community College, C. W. Post, and Borough of Manhattan Community College. She performed in her one-woman show, "Once Upon the Present Time," produced by Woodie King Jr. at the New Federal Theatre in New York City. She was awarded a Creative Artists in Public Service (CAPS) grant from New York State for her fiction, and she has published stories in the New York Times, College English, Kalliope, Black Warrior Review, *and other publications. "Slow Dance of the Heart" was first published in* So to Speak: A Feminist Journal of Language and Art, *where it won the fiction 2012 award.*

Slow Dance of the Heart (2012)

"Guess who?" I hear it.

"Guess who is here?"

"You," I say. My eldest, Stuart, standing there, putting on his best doctor's face, his eyes pinched. Winston, next in line—not so serious, a little grin there, as he glances at his wife, Marie. Marie looks at me and smiles as if I'm already a corpse. And then in the back there, I see you, Rachel. She catches my eye when she sees me spying on her. Lucky, my youngest and biggest, stands beside Stuart's son, William. "A lot of people for one room," I say.

"Yes."

"You hungry? We can get some take-out down the street. Nothing fancy." Nobody   5
moves. They nod, smile. On either side of me, a granddaughter, each holding one of my hands. I look at my oldest granddaughter, Cassandra, tall, slender, and elegant enough to be in the movies. And then Aurora, the little one who is now not so little. Where did those braids go? Eyebrows arched high just like mine. Watch out what they will do to you.

"What did you say?"

"Watch out," I say.

"Watch out for what, Grandma?" Aurora says.

"Watch out for the boys."

"How are you, Mom?"   10

"I am hiding somewhere," I say.

Suddenly, it's Lucky pretending my back is like clay.

I groan, a good groan.

"This feel good, Mom?"

15   "I'm in a million pieces," I say. "Give me a dollar for each piece, I'll be a millionaire."

They laugh, tell me I'm funny. I am grateful for that, burst out laughing, and soon I am crying. Aurora puts her arms around me. Cassandra softly whispers words in my ear. "It's okay, Grandma. It's okay."

"Please take me home, now." Nobody says anything. I watch them looking away. All except Rachel. Rachel comes up to me. Starts talking softly. I am not listening to a single word she says. Finally, she steps back. "Tired," I say.

"You want us to leave?" Stuart asks.

They kiss me.

20   I just smile. Wheeling me around, now. Who is it? Did they leave so soon?

"Where are my children?" I ask the nurse.

"Gone now," she says. She is ready to take care of me. She picks me up, puts my arms and legs in their place.

I groan. Oh, it's this one. She is nice, but she is not gentle.

"Sorry, Mrs. Teng," the nurse says.

25   "My son gave me a backrub," I say.

"How many sons do you have? I thought I saw four big guys there."

"I have five sons. I have seven grandchildren and one great grandchild."

"You have a great grandchild?"

"Yes."

30   "Is that so, Mrs. Teng? Tell me more. You're so quiet, Mrs. Teng."

I warm up to her. I say, "I don't mind if you call me Dottie."

"You have lived a long time, Dottie," she says. "You must have seen a lot of changes in this world."

"Yes."

"You told me about your house in Hong Kong."

35   "Yes."

"You must have been rich."

"We had servants helping us. I never had to wash a dish."

"It must have been wonderful."

"We own buildings there."

40   "Yes, you told me. You told me you owned three buildings."

"My grandfather. He bought the buildings."

"Must have been beautiful."

"Yes."

"And then you have a house in Queens."

45   "Yes."

"I've never been to the Orient."

"You should go sometime."

"Where should I go?"

"Wherever you like."

50   "Did you go back to visit?"

"No. My home is here."

"Do you miss it?"

"Too many questions," I say.

"I'm so sorry. I don't mean to make you uncomfortable. I thought maybe you wanted to talk some more. Shall I wheel you into the television room? It's almost dinner time."

55   "Sure," I say. Nobody's business what I am thinking.

The smell of porkchops hangs in the air. They wheel me right along, a little locomotive. I am passing a sea of sad faces. That one there holding a stuffed goat, the one with no teeth, she's always talking. She smells like liver. She cries, too. Gives the nurses a hard time. Nobody comes to see her. The other one stretched out there, her white hair flying like an avalanche, she's hollering for her mother. The man, there, he's Chinese also, like me. Except, he speaks no English. They give him and me some version of Chinese food. I don't touch it. He eats away, food dripping from his mouth. Food drips from my mouth, too, sometimes. Probably a hundred times a day, I think this: how do I kill myself.

They wheel me back to my room. Sit there. "I'm fine," I say. "Now hungry." I see him there. Daddy. He sits there in the cushioned chair. Not looking at me. A cigarette.

"They let you smoke in here?"

"Can't stop me," King says. The edge of sarcasm in his voice. He laughs, starts choking.

"Hush," I say. I am giggling. "What if someone comes?"   60

"Let them come," he says, in between the coughs. He looks away. He's wearing the hat Stuart bought him for Christmas.

Daddy and I, we wanted to tell the kids all our stories, but we forgot. Up there on the roof of my building, we told story after story.

"We didn't tell the story," I say. "I didn't have time today."

"Go ahead."

"I should jump off right now," I say.   65

"You say that," he says. "You didn't do it."

"I wish I did," I say.

"No."

"No, I didn't do it then. And I can't do it now."

King starts laughing. "Life is cruel, isn't it," he says.   70

"Daddy," I tell my husband. "You were never one for small talk."

"I could jump off right now," I told him. "I could jump off right now, and it would be better than my story."

"Oh, it cannot be that bad."

"As bad as your story is, mine is much worse."

"Cannot be."   75

"Once I tell you my story, you will tell me to jump. You will push me off."

"Never."

"You were a kind man, Daddy."

"Not anymore."

"I'm not who I am anymore either."   80

"Welcome," he says. "Welcome."

"We met in secret," I say.

He laughs, that cigarette laugh, "We are still meeting in secret." He coughs, takes the romance right out of it.

"We stood there. Midnight or later it was. My hands on the railing. Your arm around my shoulder. I see it now, a hundred million stars. Like fireworks that got caught in the branches. Blinking like shy eyes. Peaceful, even though everywhere else below city noise. People killing, stealing, shouting—from one end of the city to the other. I didn't hear any of it. I was so happy. I could block out the world."

And now, he's gone. "Where did you go, Daddy?"   85

A nurse comes in here. "Time to take me home?" I say.

"Not today," she says.

"You are very strong," I say. "It's a good thing you are gentle."

"Mrs. Teng," she says. "You are very light."

90   "But I break easy," I say.

"I know," she says. This nurse doesn't feel the need to make small talk, and neither do I.

I am lying down now. You would think I could go to sleep. They brought old photographs, my sons. They are going through my house, it means. They held the photograph in front of me, the shiny black and white. They were afraid to leave it here. I was holding hands with my brother. I was not even five years old. His chubby little fist in mine. My brother. If he weren't dead already, I could kill him. Sometimes I wonder why I am not yet dead. Must be all that ginseng. Makes Grandma a high-powered battery. What keeps me going? Then I think, it's this. I have to tell them my story, but each time I try, I get too choked up. Maybe I should let my story die with me, take it into the ground with me. That is what stops me. And what will they think of their mother.

"Okay, Mrs. Teng," she says. "I will turn out the lights now. Okay?"

"Yes," I say.

95   Lights out, the window shows a sky out there. It's a rectangle of gray. New York sky, the Hong Kong sky. My story comes back, as if it ever left. Looking out into the night. I am remembering how King held me. That cigarette in his hands. I was telling my story to the stars. The stars knew my story. I did not look at him.

"You know the history of this city," I said. "It wasn't always like this, noisy but still safe."

"I know," he said. "I know about the Japanese. I know my history."

Unlike me, he was a country boy. Except that he had gone to America—he lived there, now. Was just visiting. He was going back. Maybe I wanted to go back with him?

He asked me this. He told me that America wanted to make him a soldier, how he managed to stay in the States by making himself sick with cigarettes, chain-smoking. Instead of killing people in Japan or Germany, he is sitting in an office in Tennessee. That is how he started with cigarettes. The cigarettes kept him alive, he said. Alive so he could be here with me. So he could listen to my story. I told him that my story started when the soldiers came to our door. We knew they were all the time on horseback in the streets. We could hear the galloping, and we would hold our breath, listening, and pray they keep going. It was just women in our house. A big building. All ours. We had tenants, in this one and in the others. They paid us rent. But not when the Japanese came. When the Japanese came, they fought and they won. In our house was only my grandmother, my mother, and me. And my brother, too. But my brother was worthless. Spoiled. Selfish. What I wonder about is what would have happened if my father were there. My father was in America, in Boston. He owned restaurants there. He worked hard, saved up. Started as a waiter. If my father were there something else would have happened. But not this. No, never. Maybe we'd all be dead. Dismembered. Tied up. Tortured, one by one. That's what they did. Always how it was. We all knew the Japanese were brutal, but we didn't think it would happen to us.

100   "What happened, what happened, what happened?" It must have been twenty times he asked me this question.

I stopped telling the story for a little while. We kissed. I wondered if he could see that I knew very well how to kiss a man.

Then big hard knocks on the door. Lots of loud voices in Japanese. "Open up. Open up." First we don't open, but then my grandmother says to my mother, open up, or else they will break it down. I run, run, run behind a door. Two men screaming at my mother and my grandmother. My brother there, too. My brother was six when my father left. I was eight. We never saw him after that. Just letters. Letters back and forth. Photographs. My father was tall. That is why my sons are tall and my grandsons are tall. My brother was tall, but not then. Then, he was maybe twelve years old. I was fourteen. He sits there, until the man waves him off. "Get him out of here," he says, and my brother runs out of the room. Both of us now behind the door. They talk. I know what it's about because my friends at school talk. Everybody knows the Japanese are controlling Hong Kong now. People are leaving. The Japanese are taking away people's houses. That is what they say. My friends at school are disappearing. Who knows where they are going. Some to America, some to China, some to South America. That's what people say. The Japanese soldiers, they make us use the yen, Japanese money. You see soldiers everywhere. You hear the Japanese language. Before long, you understand the words. You figure out what they are going to take from you. "They came here before," my brother says, "when you were at school."

I get a bad feeling in my stomach, worse than the feeling I get before my mother beats me, worse than when she ties me up. It's so bad, I go into the bathroom. I throw up.

"You want to hear this?" I say to the man who will be with me for the rest of his life, but neither of us knows that then. Neither of us knows we are going to have five boys. Neither of us knows we are going to have three handfuls of grandchildren, have doctors and lawyers and artists for sons. All we know is that we are in love, and we have suffered. "I'm not a virgin," I say to this man. "I'll tell you that for starters. Now are you sure you want to hear more?"

"I'll kill them," he says.   105

"You can't, I say.

"I'll find them. You remember their names?"

"Too many of them. I can't count."

"How can that be?"

"You sure you want to hear this story?"   110

"I must hear the story," he says. "I must hear every word of it. Don't spare me one detail." That's the kind of man Daddy is. He listens, and then he cries. He hears the words and he feels the feelings, and he smokes and smokes.

"Okay," I say. "You are in for it."

This is a story that always comes to haunt me. I tell this story to myself many times, but aloud, only once. I will tell it to him, only after I tell him the other one, the one where I have run, run, run away from the man my mother married me to. An old, stinky man. A man who got his money back. How many times can you sell the same girl?

"She sold you? Your mother sold you?"

"Yes," I say. "You'll see why. You'll see if she had a choice. Did she have a choice?" I   115
always wonder something. I wonder it now. I did not wonder it then. Did something happen to her, too? Did something happen to my grandmother? Did something happen to my brother? I never ask these things. She never asked me, either. My brother never asked me, either. They didn't want to hear the answer, but this man who will become my husband, he wants to know every single detail.

I ask him why he wants to know all this.

"I think maybe you will feel better when you tell me," he says. "I don't care for myself. I don't care what happened to you, but I want to know how to take care of you."

So I go on. I give him the details, I tell him what I've been telling myself for three years. I go over and over it again, where it starts. And I tell him about the sounds because sounds tell you everything. Sounds are the first thing that gives you a hint of what's coming. I tell him that I hear my grandmother. She's sobbing. Big, loud, ugly sobs. Not my mother. Her voice rings out like a gong. "Bring me Mei Lin. Now." I am hiding. Like a child. I am in the bathroom. The door is locked. I hear her call out my brother's name. They told my brother to tell me to pack my clothes and bring me to these men.

My brother finds me. He's standing there. I look at him straight in the eye. He looks away. He says, "You'd better go pack your bags."

120   I say, "You'd better get a good look at me. If I go with them, you'll never see me again."

My brother says, "Whatever you do, don't cause trouble. If you cause trouble, they'll kill you. If you listen to them, you'll come back alive."

We are whispering. I am hissing at him. "You are a simpleton. You are a fool. You know nothing but what's good for you. You've sold me out before, and you'll sell me out again." I walk past him. I go get my bags.

"Up till this moment in my life," I tell the man who is going to be my husband. "Up till this very moment, I always looked back and wished I had jumped then. I wished I'd gone up to the roof and jumped."

If I'd jumped then, no brothel. No disgusting Japanese men. But also, no children, no husband, no grandchildren, no life, no this. See, life is not simple. Now I come to another part of my life, I would jump out here. One jump, and that's it. It's all over. Here it's high up, too. You look out, you see the water. Sometimes you see the Statue of Liberty. Here, it's different. Here, if I could walk, if I could move my legs, I would jump. Good thing I can't move.

125   At night they come for me. I can't scream. My voice so weak. They touch me and poke me. One after the other. They crush me. I close my eyes. Where are the other girls? Next to me, another girl. She's also Chinese. Sometimes we speak. Only a little. Mandarin. Whisper. They come for her, too. They pull the curtain around us. I hear her cry. I hear her scream. I know those sounds. My children, they've put me in a whorehouse.

I feel someone's arms around me. I am struggling, struggling.

"Please, Mrs. Teng," she says. The night nurse is giving me a hug. "It's okay. You know that no one wants to hurt/hunt you."

"I don't know that," I tell her.

"I am telling you that," she says.

130   "You promise?"

"I promise," she says. "Would you like to tell me what's bothering you?"

"No, thank you," I say.

After a while, she collects herself, straightens up the bed, snaps me in, lifts up the railings. Grandma is like a little baby.

"Are you sure? If you want to talk, I am here all night, now Mrs. Teng. You know how to call me."

135   "Yes," I say. "I know."

Nobody's business. They will have to take a hammer to my brain and bang bang bang. See what they get. Now I'm lying down in the bed. I am alone. I hear the woman next to me. She snores. She is alone, too. This whole place is humming in the dark. Outside it's nighttime. Inside here, we are trying to sleep. Lights still, not dimmed enough. I can't fall asleep. Most of the time when they have me in the chair, I'm drooping, all curled up. My head falling on my belly like a rag doll. Here I am flat. They tie me in now. Don't want me to escape. Don't want me to jump. Don't want me to fall. I don't know what they want from me. All I know is what they don't want.

The rooftop on my building in Hong Kong was like the top of the world.

"A whole world out there." That's what Daddy said to me. "You don't want to jump."

This is a man I lived with for my life, and when he gets sick, I nurse him until he's dead

on the floor. It just happens that after that, my body starts falling apart, and my mind—I
start seeing them, the villains. Oh, I miss him. I cry for him. I cry for myself.

"Stop crying," someone says. I think I know.   140

"Who are you?" I say this, but I smell the cigarette.

"Are you here?" I say. My words hang there. So quiet it begins to sound suspicious.

"Where else should I be," he says. A familiar laugh, a cough, the tobacco burning. "You
come dance with me now?"

That sounds like King.

"Daddy?"   145

"What do you think?"

Seems everybody wants to know that.

"Why are you standing above me like that?"

"I am asking you to dance."

"I don't like to dance."   150

"Dance with me, Mei Lin."

"Daddy, you are going to make me cry, again."

"Why you won't dance with me?"

"I . . . can't. I . . . can't."

"Real slow," he says. He's lying down here with me. "See," he says. "You can dance. You   155
can dance. You can dance."

"Mom? Mom? You know who I am?"

I hear that voice. Other voices, too. A thousand other voices. Faces around my bed. Has it
happened. No, too painful. Can't be heaven. Can't be hell. It's not my fault. I had no choice. Oh,
my voice. I'm waking up. I'm asleep and awake at the same time. These are my kids. Big guys.

"Oh, it's you." They go through their game of Guess Who Is Here.

"Guess who," I say. "Guess who."

They laugh. My boys are here. Ah, I think life is good. I'm glad to be here this minute.   160
Don't talk to me about the next one.

QUESTIONS

1. What kinds of stories do you tell yourself? What is the purpose of telling stories to
   yourself? Dottie is haunted by her stories, yet she keeps telling them to herself. What
   are the stories she tells herself? What function do they serve for her at this moment in
   her life?

2. This story has been given the title "Slow Dance of the Heart," which may be looked at
   as holding a symbol, as there is really little opportunity for dancing in this story of a
   woman whose life has been reduced to a wheelchair in a nursing home, or home for
   the aged. How do you read a title such as this? How does the title serve to illuminate
   or introduce the story?

3. The structure of this story is one that makes it possible to move forward from several
   points in time. How would you describe the structure, and what do you think a story
   like this is saying about time? How does the structure of this story help us to understand and to mirror what is happening in the mind of Dottie Teng?

4. In a sense this is a story that holds much of the entire life story of Dottie Teng. The stories she entertains herself with offer clues to her character. Several times, she mentions
   a desire to kill herself, but indeed she does not. Why not? Is this a sign of strength or
   weakness? What is it about her that has kept her from committing suicide, and what
   does this say about her character?

DANIEL OROZCO (b. c. 1957)

A native of San Francisco, Daniel Orozco studied at the University of Washington, where he earned a master's degree in fine arts. He also studied at Stanford University, where he was a Scowcroft and L'Heureux Fiction Fellow, and also a Jones Lecturer in Fiction in the Creative Writing Program. In 2005 he was a MacDowell Colony Fellow. He has become a prolific writer of stories, having published in collections such as The Best American Short Stories, The Best American Mystery Stories, *the* Pushcart Prize Anthology *of 2005,* Harper's Magazine, Zoetrope: All Story, Story Quarterly, *and* McSweeney's. *His story "Samoza's Dream" was one of the finalists in the competition for a 2006 National Magazine Award in fiction. He currently teaches creative writing at the University of Idaho. "Orientation," one of his best-known stories, first appeared in* The Seattle Review. *It was chosen by Jane Smiley for* The Best American Short Stories, *1995.*

Orientation (1994)

Those are the offices and these are the cubicles. That's my cubicle there, and this is your cubicle. This is your phone. Never answer your phone. Let the Voicemail System answer it. This is your Voicemail System Manual. There are no personal phone calls allowed. We do, however, allow for emergencies. If you must make an emergency phone call, ask your supervisor first. If you can't find your supervisor, ask Phillip Spiers, who sits over there. He'll check with Clarissa Nicks, who sits over there. If you make an emergency phone call without asking, you may be let go.

These are your IN and OUT boxes. All the forms in your IN box must be logged in by the date shown in the upper left-hand corner, initialed by you in the upper right-hand corner, and distributed to the Processing Analyst whose name is numerically coded in the lower left-hand corner. The lower right-hand corner is left blank. Here's your Processing Analyst Numerical Code Index. And here's your Forms Processing Procedures Manual.

You must pace your work. What do I mean? I'm glad you asked that. We pace our work according to the eight-hour workday. If you have twelve hours of work in your IN box, for example, you must compress that work into the eight-hour day. If you have one hour of work in your IN box, you must expand that work to fill the eight hour day. That was a good question. Feel free to ask questions. Ask too many questions, however, and you may be let go.

That is our receptionist. She is a temp. We go through receptionists here. They quit with alarming frequency. Be polite and civil to the temps. Learn their names, and invite them to lunch occasionally. But don't get close to them, as it only makes it more difficult when they leave. And they always leave. You can be sure of that.

5   The men's room is over there. The women's room is over there. John LaFountaine, who sits over there, uses the women's room occasionally. He says it is accidental. We know better, but we let it pass. John LaFountaine is harmless, his forays into the forbidden territory of the women's room simply a benign thrill, a faint blip on the dull flat line of his life.

Russell Nash, who sits in the cubicle to your left, is in love with Amanda Pierce, who sits in the cubicle to your right. They ride the same bus together after work. For Amanda Pierce, it is just a tedious bus ride made less tedious by the idle nattering of Russell Nash. But for Russell Nash, it is the highlight of his day. It is the highlight of his life. Russell Nash has put on forty pounds, and grows fatter with each passing month, nibbling on chips and cookies while peeking glumly over the partitions at Amanda

Pierce, and gorging himself at home on cold pizza and ice cream while watching adult videos on TV.

Amanda Pierce, in the cubicle to your right, has a six-year-old son named Jamie, who is autistic. Her cubicle is plastered from top to bottom with the boy's crayon artwork—sheet after sheet of precisely drawn concentric circles and ellipses, in black and yellow. She rotates them every other Friday. Be sure to comment on them. Amanda Pierce also has a husband, who is a lawyer. He subjects her to an escalating array of painful and humiliating sex games, to which Amanda Pierce reluctantly submits. She comes to work exhausted and freshly wounded each morning, wincing from the abrasions on her breasts, or the bruises on her abdomen, or the second-degree burns on the backs of her thighs.

But we're not supposed to know any of this. Do not let on. If you let on, you may be let go.

Amanda Pierce, who tolerates Russell Nash, is in love with Albert Bosch, whose office is over there. Albert Bosch, who only dimly registers Amanda Pierce's existence, has eyes only for Ellie Tapper, who sits over there. Ellie Tapper, who hates Albert Bosch, would walk through fire for Curtis Lance. But Curtis Lance hates Ellie Tapper. Isn't the world a funny place? Not in the ha-ha sense, of course.

Anika Bloom sits in that cubicle. Last year, while reviewing quarterly reports in a meeting with Barry Hacker, Anika Bloom's left palm began to bleed. She fell into a trance, stared into her hand, and told Barry Hacker when and how his wife would die. We laughed it off. She was, after all, a new employee. But Barry Hacker's wife is dead. So unless you want to know exactly when and how you'll die, never talk to Anika Bloom. 10

Cohn Heavey sits in that cubicle over there. He was new once, just like you. We warned him about Anika Bloom. But at last year's Christmas Potluck, he felt sorry for her when he saw that no one was talking to her. Cohn Heavey brought her a drink. He hasn't been himself since. Cohn Heavey is doomed. There's nothing he can do about it, and we are powerless to help him. Stay away from Cohn Heavey. Never give any of your work to him. If he asks to do something, tell him you have to check with me. If he asks again, tell him I haven't gotten back to you.

This is the Fire Exit. There are several on this floor, and they are marked accordingly. We have a Floor Evacuation Review every three months, and an Escape Route Quiz once a month. We have our Biannual Fire Drill twice a year, and our Annual Earthquake Drill once a year. These are precautions only. These things never happen.

For your information, we have a comprehensive health plan. Any catastrophic illness, any unforeseen tragedy is completely covered. All dependents are completely covered. Larry Bagdikian, who sits over there, has six daughters. If anything were to happen to any of his girls, or to all of them, if all six were to simultaneously fall victim to illness or injury—stricken with a hideous degenerative muscle disease or some rare toxic blood disorder, sprayed with semiautomatic gunfire while on a class field trip, or attacked in their bunk beds by some prowling nocturnal lunatic—if any of this were to pass, Larry's girls would all be taken care of. Larry Bagdikian would not have to pay one dime. He would have nothing to worry about.

We also have a generous vacation and sick leave policy. We have an excellent disability insurance plan. We have a stable and profitable pension fund. We get group discounts for the symphony, and block seating at the ballpark. We get commuter ticket books for the bridge. We have Direct Deposit. We are all members of Costco.

This is our kitchenette. And this, this is our Mr. Coffee. We have a coffee pool, into which 15 we each pay two dollars a week for coffee, filters, sugar, and CoffeeMate. If you prefer Cremora or half-and-half to CoffeeMate, there is a special pool for three dollars a week. If you prefer Sweet'n Low to sugar, there is a special pool for two-fifty a week. We do not do decaf. You are allowed to join the coffee pool of your choice, but you are not allowed to touch the Mr. Coffee.

This is the microwave oven. You are allowed to heat food in the microwave oven. You are not, however, allowed to cook food in the microwave oven.

We get one hour for lunch. We also get one fifteen-minute break in the morning, and one fifteen-minute break in the afternoon. Always take your breaks, if you skip a break, it is gone forever. For your information, your break is a privilege, not a right. If you abuse the break policy, we are authorized to rescind your breaks. Lunch, however, is a right, not a privilege. If you abuse the lunch policy, our hands will be tied, and we will be forced to look the other way. We will not enjoy that.

This is the refrigerator. You may put your lunch in it. Barry Hacker, who sits over there, steals food from this refrigerator. His petty theft is an outlet for his grief. Last New Year's Eve, while kissing his wife, a blood vessel burst in her brain. Barry Hacker's wife was two months pregnant at the time, and lingered in a coma for half a year before dying. It was a tragic loss for Barry Hacker. He hasn't been himself since. Barry Hacker's wife was a beautiful woman. She was also completely covered. Barry Hacker did not have to pay one dime. But his dead wife haunts him. She haunts all of us. We have seen her, reflected in the monitors of our computers, moving past our cubicles. We have seen the dim shadow of her face in our photocopies. She pencils herself in the receptionist's appointment book, with the notation: To see Barry Hacker. She has left messages in the receptionist's Voicemail box, messages garbled by the electronic chirrups and buzzes in the phone line, her voice echoing from an immense distance within the ambient hum. But the voice is hers. And beneath her voice, beneath the tidal whoosh of static and hiss, the gurgling and crying of a baby can be heard.

In any case, if you bring a lunch, put a little something extra in the bag for Barry Hacker. We have four Barrys in this office. Isn't that a coincidence?

20   This is Matthew Payne's office. He is our Unit Manager, and his door is always closed. We have never seen him, and you will never see him. But he is here. You can be sure of that. He is all around us.

This is the Custodian's Closet. You have no business in the Custodian's Closet.

And this, this is our Supplies Cabinet. If you need supplies, see Curtis Lance. He will log you in on the Supplies Cabinet Authorization Log, then give you a Supplies Authorization Slip. Present your pink copy of the Supplies Authorization Slip to Ellie Tapper. She will log you in on the Supplies Cabinet Key Log, then give you the key. Because the Supplies Cabinet is located outside the Unit Manager's office, you must be very quiet. Gather your supplies quietly. The Supplies Cabinet is divided into four sections. Section One contains letterhead stationery, blank paper and envelopes, memo and note pads, and so on. Section Two contains pens and pencils and typewriter and printer ribbons, and the like. In Section Three we have erasers, correction fluids, transparent tapes, glue sticks, et cetera. And in Section Four we have paper clips and push pins and scissors and razor blades. And here are the spare blades for the shredder. Do not touch the shredder, which is located over there. The shredder is of no concern to you.

Gwendolyn Stich sits in that office there. She is crazy about penguins, and collects penguin knickknacks: penguin posters and coffee mugs and stationery, penguin stuffed animals, penguin jewelry, penguin sweaters and T-shirts and socks. She has a pair of penguin fuzzy slippers she wears when working late at the office. She has a tape cassette of penguin sounds which she listens to for relaxation. Her favorite colors are black and white. She has personalized license plates that read PEN GWEN. Every morning, she passes through all the cubicles to wish each of us a good morning. She brings Danish on Wednesdays for Hump Day morning break, and doughnuts on Fridays for TGIF afternoon break. She organizes the Annual Christmas Potluck, and is in charge of the Birthday List. Gwendolyn

Stich's door is always open to all of us. She will always lend an ear, and put in a good word for you; she will always give you a hand, or the shirt off her back, or a shoulder to cry on. Because her door is always open, she hides and cries in a stall in the women's room. And John LaFountaine—who, enthralled when a woman enters, sits quietly in his stall with his knees to his chest—John LaFountaine has heard her vomiting in there. We have come upon Gwendolyn Stich huddled in the stairwell, shivering in the updraft, sipping a Diet Mr. Pibb and hugging her knees. She does not let any of this interfere with her work. If it interfered with her work, she might have to be let go.

Kevin Howard sits in that cubicle over there. He is a serial killer, the one they call the Carpet Cutter, responsible for the mutilations across town. We're not supposed to know that, so do not let on. Don't worry. His compulsion inflicts itself on strangers only, and the routine established is elaborate and unwavering. The victim must be a white male, a young adult no older than thirty, heavyset, with dark hair and eyes, and the like. The victim must be chosen at random, before sunset, from a public place; the victim is followed home, and must put up a struggle; et cetera. The carnage inflicted is precise: the angle and direction of the incisions; the layering of skin and muscle tissue; the rearrangement of the visceral organs; and so on. Kevin Howard does not let any of this interfere with his work. He is, in fact, our fastest typist. He types as if he were on fire. He has a secret crush on Gwendolyn Stich, and leaves a red-foil-wrapped Hershey's Kiss on her desk every afternoon. But he hates Anika Bloom, and keeps well away from her. In his presence, she has uncontrollable fits of shaking and trembling. Her left palm does not stop bleeding.

In any case, when Kevin Howard gets caught, act surprised. Say that he seemed like a   25 nice person, a bit of a loner, perhaps, but always quiet and polite.

This is the photocopier room. And this, this is our view. It faces southwest. West is down there, toward the water. North is back there. Because we are on the seventeenth floor, we are afforded a magnificent view. Isn't it beautiful? It overlooks the park, where the tops of those trees are. You can see a segment of the bay between those two buildings there. You can see the sun set in the gap between those two buildings over there. You can see this building reflected in the glass panels of that building across the way. There. See? That's you, waving. And look there. There's Anika Bloom in the kitchenette, waving back.

Enjoy this view while photocopying. If you have problems with the photocopier, see Russell Nash. If you have any questions, ask your supervisor. If you can't find your supervisor, ask Phillip Spiers. He sits over there. He'll check with Clarissa Nicks. She sits over there. If you can't find them, feel free to ask me. That's my cubicle. I sit in there.

QUESTIONS

1. What is the situation throughout this story? Who is talking? To whom is he talking? Does the listener have any chance to comment on the speaker's discourse?

2. In the first four paragraphs, is there anything unusual about the speaker's language? What does Orozco have the speaker say in paragraph 5 that alerts you to the unusual nature of the persons in the office?

3. Is there anything funny about the situations of fellow employees in the office? If not, how does one account for the fact that the story is comic? How do the speaker's controlled descriptions of the plights of the various office workers contribute to the story's comic tone?

4. Why is Kevin Howard the last one to be described by the speaker? Of what is Kevin guilty? What might the story be like if Kevin Howard had been mentioned first? Describe the comic technique of paragraph 25.

EUDORA WELTY (1909–2001)

One of the major southern writers, Welty was born in Jackson, Mississippi. She attended the Mississippi State College for Women and the University of Wisconsin, and she began her writing career during the Great Depression. By 1943 she had published two major story collections, Curtain of Green *(1941, including "A Worn Path") and* The Wide Net *(1943). She was the author of many stories and was awarded the Pulitzer Prize in 1973 for her short novel* The Optimist's Daughter *(1972). "A Worn Path" received an O. Henry Award in 1941.*

A Worn Path°(1941)

It was December—a bright frozen day in the early morning. Far out in the country there was an old Negro woman with her head tied in a red rag, coming along a path through the pinewoods. Her name was Phoenix Jackson. She was very old and small and she walked slowly in the dark pine shadows, moving a little from side to side in her steps, with the balanced heaviness and lightness of a pendulum in a grandfather clock. She carried a thin, small cane made from an umbrella, and with this she kept tapping the frozen earth in front of her. This made a grave and persistent noise in the still air, that seemed meditative like the chirping of a solitary little bird.

She wore a dark striped dress reaching down to her shoe tops, and an equally long apron of bleached sugar sacks, with a full pocket: all neat and tidy, but every time she took a step she might have fallen over her shoelaces, which dragged from her unlaced shoes. She looked straight ahead. Her eyes were blue with age. Her skin had a pattern all its own of numberless branching wrinkles and as though a whole little tree stood in the middle of her forehead, but a golden color ran underneath, and the two knobs of her cheeks were illuminated by a yellow burning under the dark. Under the rag her hair came down on her neck in the frailest of ringlets, still black, and with an odor like copper.

Now and then there was a quivering in the thicket. Old Phoenix said, "Out of my way, all you foxes, owls, beetles, jack rabbits, coons and wild animals! . . . Keep out from under these feet, little bob-whites. . . . Keep the big wild hogs out of my path. Don't let none of those come running my direction. I got a long way." Under her small black-freckled hand her cane, limber as a buggy whip, would switch at the brush as if to rouse up any hiding things.

On she went. The woods were deep and still. The sun made the pine needles almost too bright to look at, up where the wind rocked. The cones dropped as light as feathers. Down in the hollow was the mourning dove—it was not too late for him.

5   The path ran up a hill. "Seem like there is chains about my feet, time I get this far," she said, in the voice of argument old people keep to use with themselves. "Something always take a hold of me on this hill—pleads I should stay."

After she got to the top she turned and gave a full, severe look behind her where she had come. "Up through pines," she said at length. "Now down through oaks."

Her eyes opened their widest, and she started down gently. But before she got to the bottom of the hill a bush caught her dress.

Her fingers were busy and intent, but her skirts were full and long, so that before she could pull them free in one place they were caught in another. It was not possible to allow

---

°"A Worn Path," from *A Curtain of Green and Other Stories*. Copyright 1941 and renewed 1969 by Eudora Welty, reprinted by permission of Harcourt, Inc.

the dress to tear. "I in the thorny bush," she said. "Thorns, you doing your appointed work. Never want to let folks pass, no sir. Old eyes thought you was a pretty little *green* bush."

Finally, trembling all over, she stood free, and after a moment dared to stoop for her cane.

"Sun so high!" she cried, leaning back and looking, while the thick tears went over her eyes. "The time getting all gone here."

At the foot of this hill was a place where a log was laid across the creek.

"Now comes the trial," said Phoenix.

Putting her right foot out, she mounted the log and shut her eyes. Lifting her skirt, leveling her cane fiercely before her, like a festival figure in some parade, she began to march across. Then she opened her eyes and she was safe on the other side.

"I wasn't as old as I thought," she said.

But she sat down to rest. She spread her skirts on the bank around her and folded her hands over her knees. Up above her was a tree in a pearly cloud of mistletoe. She did not dare to close her eyes, and when a little boy brought her a plate with a slice of marble-cake on it she spoke to him. "That would be acceptable," she said. But when she went to take it there was just her own hand in the air.

So she left that tree, and had to go through a barbed-wire fence. There she had to creep and crawl, spreading her knees and stretching her fingers like a baby trying to climb the steps. But she talked loudly to herself: she could not let her dress be torn now, so late in the day, and she could not pay for having her arm or leg sawed off if she got caught fast where she was.

At last she was safe through the fence and risen up out in the clearing. Big dead trees, like black men with one arm, were standing in the purple stalks of the withered cotton field. There sat a buzzard.

"Who you watching?"

In the furrow she made her way along.

"Glad this is not the season for bulls," she said, looking sideways, "and the good Lord made his snakes to curl up and sleep in the winter. A pleasure I don't see no two-headed snake coming around that tree, where it come once. It took a while to get by him, back in the summer."

She passed through the old cotton and went into a field of dead corn. It whispered and shook and was taller than her head. "Through the maze now," she said, for there was no path.

Then there was something tall, black, and skinny there, moving before her.

At first she took it for a man. It could have been a man dancing in the field. But she stood still and listened, and it did not make a sound. It was as silent as a ghost.

"Ghost," she said sharply, "who be you the ghost of? For I have heard of nary death close by."

But there was no answer—only the ragged dancing in the wind.

She shut her eyes, reached out her hand, and touched a sleeve. She found a coat and inside that an emptiness, cold as ice.

"You scarecrow," she said. Her face lighted. "I ought to be shut up for good," she said with laughter. "My senses is gone. I too old, I the oldest people I ever know. Dance, old scarecrow," she said, "while I dancing with you."

She kicked her foot over the furrow, and with mouth drawn down, shook her head once or twice in a little strutting way. Some husks blew down and whirled in steamers about her skirts.

Then she went on, parting her way from side to side with the cane, through the whispering field. At last she came to the end, to a wagon track where the silver grass blew between the red ruts. The quail were walking around like pullets, seeming all dainty and unseen.

"Walk pretty," she said. "This is the easy place. This the easy going."

She followed the track, swaying through the quiet bare fields, through the little strings of trees silver in their dead leaves, past cabins silver from weather, with the doors and windows boarded shut, all like old women under a spell sitting there. "I walking in their sleep," she said, nodding her head vigorously.

In a ravine she went where a spring was silently flowing through a hollow log. Old Phoenix bent and drank. "Sweet-gum makes the water sweet," she said, and drank more. "Nobody know who made this well, for it was here when I was born."

The track crossed a swampy part where the moss hung as white as lace from every limb. "Sleep on, alligators, and blow your bubbles." Then the track went into the road.

Deep, deep the road went down between the high green-colored banks. Overhead the live-oaks met, and it was as dark as a cave.

35   A black dog with a lolling tongue came up out of the weeds by the ditch. She was meditating, and not ready, and when he came at her she only hit him a little with her cane. Over she went in the ditch, like a little puff of milkweed.

Down there, her sense drifted away. A dream visited her, and she reached her hand up, but nothing reached down and gave her a pull. So she lay there and presently went to talking. "Old woman," she said to herself, "that black dog come up out of the weeds to stall you off, and now there he sitting on his fine tail smiling at you."

A white man finally came along and found her—a hunter, a young man, with his dog on a chain.

"Well, Granny!" he laughed. "What are you doing there?"

"Lying on my back like a June-bug waiting to be turned over, mister," she said, reaching up her hand.

40   He lifted her up, gave her a swing in the air, and set her down. "Anything broken, Granny?"

"No sir, them old dead weeds is springy enough," said Phoenix, when she had got her breath. "I thank you for your trouble."

"Where do you live, Granny?" he asked, while the two dogs were growling at each other.

"Away back yonder, sir, behind the ridge. You can't even see it from here."

"On your way home?"

45   "No sir, I goin to town."

"Why, that's too far! That's as far as I walk when I come out myself, and I get something for my trouble." He patted the stuffed bag he carried, and there hung down a little closed claw. It was one of the bob-whites, with its beak hooked bitterly to show it was dead. "Now you go on home, Granny!"

"I bound to go to town, mister," said Phoenix. "The time come around."

He gave another laugh, filling the whole landscape. "I know you old colored people! Wouldn't miss going to town to see Santa Claus!"

But something held old Phoenix very still. The deep lines in her face went into a fierce and different radiation. Without warning, she had seen with her own eyes a flashing nickel fall out of the man's pocket onto the ground.

"How old are you, Granny?" he was saying.

50   "There is no telling, mister," she said, "no telling."

Then she gave a little cry and clapped her hands and said, "Git on away from here, dog! Look! Look at that dog!" She laughed as if in admiration. "He ain't scared of nobody. He a big black dog." She whispered, "Sic him!"

"Watch me get rid of that cur," said the man. "Sic him, Pete! Sic him!"

Phoenix heard the dogs fighting, and heard the man running and throwing sticks. She even heard a gunshot. But she was slowly bending forward by that time, further and further forward, the lids stretched down over her eyes, as if she were doing this in her sleep. Her chin was lowered almost to her knees. The yellow palm of her hand came out from the fold of her apron. Her fingers slid down and along the ground under the piece of money with the grace and care they would have in lifting an egg from under a setting hen. Then she slowly straightened up, she stood erect, and the nickel was in her apron pocket. A bird flew by. Her lips moved. "God watching me the whole time. I come to stealing."

The man came back, and his own dog panted about them. "Well, I scared him off that time," he said, and then he laughed and lifted his gun and pointed it at Phoenix.

She stood straight and faced him.

"Doesn't the gun scare you?" he said, still pointing it.

"No sir. I seen plenty go off closer by, in my day, and for less than what I done," she said, holding utterly still.

He smiled, and shouldered the gun. "Well, Granny," he said, "you must be a hundred years old, and scared of nothing. I'd give you a dime if I had any money with me. But you take my advice and stay home, and nothing will happen to you."

"I bound to go on my way, mister," said Phoenix. She inclined her head in the red rag. Then they went in different directions, but she could hear the gun shooting again and again over the hill.

She walked on. The shadows hung from the oak trees to the road like curtains. Then she smelled wood-smoke, and smelled the river, and she saw a steeple and the cabins on their steep steps. Dozens of little black children whirled around her. There ahead was Natchez shining. Bells were ringing. She walked on.

In the paved city it was Christmas time. There were red and green electric lights strung and crisscrossed everywhere, and all turned on in the daytime. Old Phoenix would have been lost if she had not distrusted her eyesight and depended on her feet to know where to take her.

She paused quietly on the sidewalk where people were passing by. A lady came along in the crowd, carrying an armful of red-, green-, and silver-wrapped presents; she gave off perfume like the red roses in hot summer, and Phoenix stopped her.

"Please, missy, will you lace up my shoe?" She held up her foot.

"What do you want, Grandma?"

"See my shoe," said Phoenix. "Do all right for out in the country, but wouldn't look right to go in a big building."

"Stand still then, Grandma," said the lady. She put her packages down on the sidewalk beside her and laced and tied both shoes tightly.

"Can't lace 'em with a cane," said Phoenix. "Thank you, missy. I doesn't mind asking a nice lady to tie up my shoe, when I gets out on the street."

Moving slowly and from side to side, she went into the big building, and into a tower of steps, where she walked up and around and around until her feet knew to stop.

She entered a door, and there she saw nailed up on the wall the document that had been stamped with the gold seal and framed in the gold frame, which matched the dream that was hung up in her head.

"Here I be," she said. There was a fixed and ceremonial stiffness over her body.

"A charity case, I suppose," said an attendant who sat at the desk before her.

But Phoenix only looked above her head. There was sweat on her face, the wrinkles in her skin shone like a bright net.

"Speak up, Grandma," the woman said, "What's your name? We must have your history, you know. Have you been here before? What seems to be the trouble with you?"

Old Phoenix only gave a twitch to her face as if a fly were bothering her.

"Are you deaf?" cried the attendant.

But then the nurse came in.

"Oh, that's just old Aunt Phoenix," she said. "She doesn't come for herself—she has a little grandson. She makes these trips just as regular as clockwork. She lives away back off the Old Natchez Trace." She bent down. "Well, Aunt Phoenix, why don't you just take a seat? We won't keep you standing after your long trip." She pointed.

The old woman sat down, bolt upright in the chair.

"Now, how is the boy?" asked the nurse.

80 Old Phoenix did not speak.

"I said, how is the boy?"

But Phoenix only waited and stared straight ahead, her face very solemn and withdrawn into rigidity.

"Is his throat any better?" asked the nurse. "Aunt Phoenix, don't you hear me? Is your grandson's throat any better since the last time you came for the medicine?"

With her hands on her knees, the old woman waited, silent, erect, and motionless, just as if she were in armor.

85 "You mustn't take up our time this way, Aunt Phoenix," the nurse said. "Tell us quickly about your grandson, and get it over. He isn't dead, is he?"

At last there came a flicker and then a flame of comprehension across her face, and she spoke.

"My grandson. It was my memory had left me. There I sat and forgot why I made my long trip."

"Forgot?" the nurse frowned. "After you came so far?"

Then Phoenix was like an old woman begging a dignified forgiveness for waking up frightened in the night. "I never did go to school, I was too old at the Surrender," she said in a soft voice. "I'm an old woman without an education. It was my memory fail me. My little grandson, he is just the same, and I forgot it in the coming."

90 "Throat never heals, does it?" said the nurse, speaking in a loud, sure voice to old Phoenix. By now she had a card with something written on it, a little list. "Yes. Swallowed lye. When was it—January—two, three years ago—"

Phoenix spoke unasked now. "No missy, he not dead, he just the same. Every little while his throat begin to close up again, and he not able to swallow. He not get his breath. He not able to help himself. So the time come around, and I go on another trip for the soothing medicine."

"All right. The doctor said as long as you came to get it, you could have it," said the nurse. "But it's an obstinate case."

"My little grandson, he sit up there in the house all wrapped up, waiting by himself," Phoenix went on. "We is the only two left in the world. He suffer and it don't seem to put him back at all. He got a sweet look. He going to last. He wear a little patch quilt and peep out holding his mouth open like a little bird. I remembers so plain now. I not going to forget him again, no, the whole enduring time. I could tell him from all the others in creation."

"All right." The nurse was trying to hush her now. She brought her a bottle of medicine. "Charity," she said, making a check mark in a book.

Old Phoenix held the bottle close to her eyes, and then carefully put it into her pocket.

"I thank you," she said.

95 "It's Christmas time, Grandma," said the attendant. "Could I give you a few pennies out of my purse?"

"Five pennies is a nickel," said Phoenix stiffly.

"Here's a nickel," said the attendant.

Phoenix rose carefully and held out her hand. She received the nickel and then fished the other nickel out of her pocket and laid it beside the new one. She stared at her palm closely, with her head on one side.

100 Then she gave a tap with her cane on the floor.

"This is what come to me to do," she said, "I going to the store and buy my child a little windmill they sells, made out of paper. He going to find it hard to believe there such a thing in the world. I'll march myself back where he waiting, holding it straight up in this hand."

She lifted her free hand, gave a little nod, turned around, and walked out of the doctor's office. Then her slow step began on the stairs, going down.

QUESTIONS

1. From the description of Phoenix, what do you conclude about her economic condition? How do you know that she has taken the path through the woods before? Is she accustomed to being alone? What do you make of her speaking to animals, and of her imagining a boy offering her a piece of cake? What does her speech show about her education and background?

2. Describe the form of the story. With Phoenix as the protagonist, what are the obstacles ranged against her? How might the story be considered as a succession of obstacles that Phoenix encounters on the "worn path"? How might Phoenix be considered to be in the grip of large and indifferent social and political forces?

3. Why is the existence and condition of Phoenix's grandson not introduced until the very end? How does this knowledge shed light on Phoenix's walk to town?

4. Comment on the meaning of this dialogue between Phoenix and the hunter:

   "Doesn't the gun scare you?" he said, still pointing it.

   "No, sir. I seen plenty go off closer by, in my day, and for less than what I done," she said, holding utterly still.

5. A number of responses might be made to this story, among them admiration for Phoenix, pity for her and her grandson and for the downtrodden generally, anger at her impoverished condition, and apprehension about her approaching senility. Do you share in any of these responses? Do you have any others?

WRITING ABOUT STRUCTURE IN A STORY

Your essay should concern arrangement and shape. In form, the essay should not restate or summarize the part-by-part unfolding of the narrative or argument. Rather, it should explain why things are where they are: "Why is this here and not there?" is the fundamental question you need to answer. Thus it is possible to begin with a consideration of a work's crisis, and then to consider how the exposition and complication have built up to it. A vital piece of information, for example, might have been withheld in the story's earlier exposition (as in Bierce's "An Occurrence at Owl Creek Bridge" in Chapter 1 and Faulkner's "A Rose for Emily" in Chapter 1) and introduced only at or near the conclusion. Therefore the crisis might be heightened because there would have been less suspense if the detail had been introduced earlier. Consider the following questions in planning to write about the story's structure.

Questions for Discovering Ideas

* If spaces or numbers divide the story into sections or parts, what structural importance do these parts have?
* If there are no marked divisions, what major sections can you find? (You might make divisions according to places where actions occur, various times of day, changing weather, or increasingly important events.)
* If the story departs in major ways from the formal structure of exposition, complication, crisis, climax, and resolution, what purpose do these departures serve?
* What variations in chronological order, if any, appear in the story (for example, gaps in the time sequence; flashbacks or selective recollection)? What effects are achieved by these variations?
* Does the story delay any crucial details of exposition? Why? What effect is achieved by the delay?
* Where does an important action or a major section (such as the climax) begin? End? How is it related to the other formal structural elements, such as the crisis? Is the climax an action, a realization, or a decision? To what degree does it relieve the work's tension? What is the effect of the climax on your understanding of the characters involved in it? How is this effect related to the arrangement of the climax?

Strategies for Organizing Ideas

Your essay should show why an entire story is arranged the way it is—to reveal the nature of a character's situation, to create surprise, or to evoke sympathy, reveal nobility (or depravity) of character, unravel apparently insoluble puzzles, express philosophical or political values, or bring out maximum humor. You might also, however, explain the structure of no more than a part of the story, such as the climax or the complication.

The essay is best developed in concert or agreement with what the work contains. The location of scenes is an obvious organizing element. Thus, essays on the structure of Hawthorne's "Young Goodman Brown" (Chapter 7) and Silko's "The Man to Send Rain Clouds" (Chapter 4) might be based on the fact that both take place outdoors (a dark forest for one and a rural desert location in the American Southwest in the other). Similarly, an essay might explore the structure of Maupassant's "The Necklace" (Part I) by contrasting the story's indoor and outdoor locations. Other ways to consider structure may be derived from a work's notable aspects, such as the growing suspense of Jackson's "The Lottery" (Chapter 2) or the revelations about the "sinfulness" of Goodman Brown's father and neighbors in Hawthorne's "Young Goodman Brown" (Chapter 7).

The conclusion should highlight the main parts of your essay. You may also deal briefly with the relationship of structure to the plot. If the work you have analyzed departs from chronological order, you might explain the causes and effects of this departure. Your aim should be to focus on the success of the work as it has been brought about by the author's choices in development.

Illustrative Student Essay

Although underlined sentences are not recommended by MLA style, they are used in this illustrative essay as teaching tools to emphasize the central idea, thesis sentence, and topic sentences.

Flores 1

Jeannette Flores

Professor Iacovelli

English 120

29 January 2014

The Structure of Eudora Welty's "A Worn Path"°

The narrative of Welty's "A Worn Path" is not difficult to follow.   [1]
Events occur in sequence. The main character is Phoenix Jackson, an old
and poor woman. She walks from her rural home in Mississippi through
the woods to Natchez to get a free bottle of medicine for her grandson,

°This story appears on pages 288–92.

Flores 2

who is a hopeless invalid. Everything takes place in just a few hours. <u>This
action is only the frame, however, for a skillfully structured plot.</u>* The
<u>masterly control of structure is shown in the story's locations, and in the way
in which the delayed revelation produces both mystery and complexity.</u>†

[2]   <u>The locations in the story coincide with the increasing difficulties that
Phoenix encounters.</u> The first and most obvious worn path is the rural woods with
all its natural difficulties. For most people the obstacles would not be challenging,
but for an old woman they are formidable. In Natchez, the location of the next
part of the story, Phoenix's inability to bend over to tie her shoe demonstrates
the lack of flexibility of old age. In the medical office, where the final scene
takes place, two major difficulties of the plot are brought out. One is Phoenix's
increasing senility, and the other is the disclosure that her grandson is an incurable
invalid. This set of oppositions, the major conflicts in the plot, thus coincides with
locations or scenes and show the powerful forces opposing Phoenix.

       <u>The strongest of these conditions, the revelation about the grandson,</u>

[3]   <u>makes the story something like a mystery.</u> Because detail about the boy is
delayed until the end, the reader wonders for most of the story what bad
thing might happen next. In fact, some parts of the story are false leads.
For example, the episode with the hunter's dog is threatening, but it leads
nowhere: Phoenix, with the aid of the hunter, is unharmed. That she picks up
and keeps the nickel dropped by the hunter might seem at first to be cause for
punishment. In fact, she thinks it does, as this scene with the hunter shows:

> [H]e laughed and lifted his gun and pointed it at Phoenix.
> She stood straight and faced him.
> "Doesn't the gun scare you?" he said, still pointing it.
> "No, sir, I seen plenty go off closer by, in my day, and for less than what I
> done," she said, holding utterly still. (291)

But the young hunter does not notice that the coin is missing, and he does not
accuse her. Right up to the moment of her entering the medical building, in
fact, the reader is still wondering what might happen.

---

*Central idea.
†Thesis sentence.

Flores 3

Therefore the details about the grandson, carefully concealed until the end,   **[4]**
make the story more complex than it at first seems. Because of this concluding
revelation, the reader must do a double take and reconsider what has gone
on before. Phoenix's difficult walk into town must be seen not as an ordinary
errand but as a hopeless mission of mercy. Her character also bears reevaluation:
She is not just a funny old woman who speaks to the woods and the animals
in it, but she is also a brave woman carrying on against crushing odds. These
conclusions are not apparent for most of the story, and the late emergence of the
carefully concealed details makes "A Worn Path" both forceful and powerful.

    Thus the parts of "A Worn Path," while simple at first, are skillfully   **[5]**
arranged. The key to the double take and reevaluation is Welty's withholding
of the crucial detail of exposition until the very end. The result is that parts of
the exposition and complication, through the speeches of the attendant and the
nurse, merge with the climax near the story's end. In some respects, the detail
makes it seem as though Phoenix's entire existence is a crisis, although she is
not aware of this condition as she leaves the office to buy the paper windmill.
It is this complex buildup and emotional peak that make the structure of "A
Worn Path" the creation of a master writer.

Flores 4

Work Cited

Welty, Eudora. "A Worn Path." *Literature: An Introduction to Reading and
    Writing, Compact Edition.* Ed. Edgar V. Roberts and Robert Zweig.
    6th ed. New York: Pearson, 2015. 288–92. Print.

Commentary on the Essay

Essays about either plot (Chapter 2) or structure are concerned with the conflicts of
the story, but the essay on plot concentrates on the opposing forces whereas the essay on structure focuses on the placement and arrangement of the story's details.

Notice here that an essay on structure, like an essay on plot, does not simply retell the story event by event. That is not the concern of analytical writing. Instead, essays on both plot and structure explain the *conflict* (for plot) and the *arrangement and layout* (for structure). In both essays, the writer's assumption is that the reader has read the story, and therefore there is no need to include a retelling of the story in an essay.

The introductory paragraph of this essay on the structure of "A Worn Path" points out that the masterly structure accounts for the story's power. Paragraph 2 develops the topic that the geographical locations are arranged climactically to demonstrate the forces against the major character. Paragraph 3 considers how the early exposition about the grandson creates uncertainty about the issues and direction of the story. As supporting evidence, the paragraph cites two important details—the danger from the hunter's dog and the theft of his nickel—as structural false leads about Phoenix's troubles. Paragraph 4 deals with the complexity brought about by the delayed information: the necessary reevaluation of Phoenix's character and her mission to town. The concluding paragraph also considers this complexity, accounting for the story's power by pointing out how a number of plot elements merge near the end to bring things out swiftly and powerfully.

Writing Topics About Structure

Writing Paragraphs

1. Consider the surprises in Oates's "Where Are You Going, Where Have You Been?" (Chapter 2), Maupassant's "The Necklace" (Part I), Faulkner's "A Rose for Emily" (Chapter 1), Bierce's "An Occurrence at Owl Creek Bridge" (Chapter 1), and Chopin's "The Story of an Hour" (Chapter 6). Write a paragraph about one of these stories. How much preparation is made, structurally, for the surprise in this story? In retrospect, to what degree is the surprise not a surprise at all but rather necessary outcomes of the preceding parts of the work?

2. Write a paragraph about what kind of story "A Worn Path" might be, structurally, if the detail about the invalid grandson were introduced at the start, before Phoenix begins her walk to town.

Writing Essays

1. Write an essay in which you compare the structuring of the interior scenes in Geri Lipschultz's "Slow Dance of the Heart" and Oates's "Where Are You Going, Where Have You Been?" How do these scenes bring out the various conflicts of the stories? How does the presence of characters in the individual rooms contribute to the organization of the stories? What is the relationship of these characters to the major actions of the stories?

2. Write an essay in which you compare Tan's "Two Kinds" (Chapter 3) and Silko's "The Man to Send Rain Clouds" (Chapter 4) as stories about clashing racial and social values. What are the comparative values? How do the stories develop, structurally, as a result of these clashes?

Creative Writing Assignment

1. Select a circumstance in your life that caused you doubt, difficulty, and conflict. Making yourself anonymous (give yourself a fictitious name and put yourself in a fictitious location if you wish), write a brief story about the occasion, stressing how your conflict began, how it affected you, and how you resolved it. You might choose to begin your story in the present tense and introduce details in flashback.

Library Assignment

1. Go online to investigate two of the following structural terms:

> adventure novel
> chiastic structure
> detective fiction
> dramatic structure: tragedy and comedy
> epistolary structure
> narrative structure
> stream of consciousness

Write a short report on your discoveries. Be sure to include definitions of the terms and descriptions of how the structures are important in various fictional works.

Chapter 6
Tone and Style: The Words That Convey Attitudes in Fiction

AFTER STUDYING THIS MATERIAL, YOU SHOULD BE ABLE TO DO THE FOLLOWING:

- Understand the components of literary tone
- Explain the concepts of formal and informal language
- Recognize specific-general and concrete-abstract language
- Define and illustrate denotative and connotative words
- Recognize the uses of irony and humor
- Describe how a work's tone and style affect its meaning and impact on readers

Tone refers to the methods by which writers and speakers reveal attitudes or feelings—toward the material, toward their readers, and toward the general situation they are describing or analyzing. It is an aspect of all spoken and written statements, whether serious analyses of political campaigns, earnest declarations of love, requests to pass a dinner dish, descriptions of social or athletic events, letters from students asking parents for money, or official government notices threatening penalties if fines and taxes are not paid. The attitudes expressed in each of these situations are usually readily apparent. When we speak about tone here, we refer to a variety of similar and dissimilar attitudes, but, in addition, and more importantly, we stress those modes of expression that create and shape those attitudes.

Although tone is a vast subject that can involve large matters of action and situation, in this chapter we will treat the interconnectedness of tone and style. **Style** refers to the ways in which writers assemble words to tell the story, to develop the argument, to dramatize the play, or to compose the poem. Sometimes style is distinguished from content, but actually style is best considered as the choice of words in the *service* of content. The written expression of an action or scene, in other words, cannot be separated from the action or scene itself, nor can it be separated from the impressions and attitudes it creates.

By reading a story carefully, we may deduce the author's attitude or attitudes toward the subject matter and toward readers. In "The Story of an Hour," for example (this chapter), Kate Chopin sympathetically portrays a young wife's secret wishes for freedom, just as Chopin also satirically reveals the unwitting smugness that often pervades men's relationships with women.

Words and subject matter may also indicate the writer's assessment of readers. When Hawthorne's woodland guide in "Young Goodman Brown" (Chapter 7) refers to "King Philip's War," for example, Hawthorne clearly assumes that his readers know that this war in seventeenth-century New England was notoriously cruel and inhumane. In this way he indicates respect for the knowledge of his readers, and he also assumes that they will assent to his interpretation. Authors always make such considerations about readers by implicitly complimenting them on their capacity to recognize and understand the ways in which materials are presented.

Diction: The Writer's Choice and Control of Words

Control over style and tone is highly individual, because all authors put words together uniquely to fit the specific circumstances of specific works. We may therefore speak of the *style* of Ernest Hemingway and the *style* of Alice Walker, even though both writers adapt words to situations. An author may have a distinct style for narrative and descriptive passages, but a very different style for dialogue.

The essential aspect of style is **diction,** the writer's selection of words. First, words must be accurate and comprehensive, so that all actions, scenes, and ideas are perfectly understandable to readers. If a writer's work is effective—if it portrays an action graphically and clearly, explains ideas accurately, and indicates the conditions of human relationships among the major characters—we may confidently say that the words are right. Additionally, right words bear the burden of controlling the ways in which readers respond to the material. Thus, a passage of action should verbally create the action and the place or places in which things happen, and it should also cause readers to be interested and involved. Similarly, explanatory or reflective passages should be clear but should also spark the curiosity and satisfy the understanding of readers. In short, the writer should make all efforts to control the work's tone.

Formal, Neutral, and Informal Diction Create Unique Effects

As a guide to the types of words authors use to control tone, a major classification of diction can be made according to three degrees of formality or informality: **formal** or *high*, **neutral** or *middle*, and **informal** or *low*.

Formal or *high* diction bestows major importance to the characters and actions being described. It consists of standard and also "elegant" words (frequently polysyllabic), correct word order, and the absence of contractions. The sentence "It is I," for example, is formal, for this expression is more "elegant" and grammatically correct than most American speakers normally now prefer. An example of formal diction may be seen in the narrative sections of Hawthorne's "Young Goodman Brown."

Neutral or *middle* diction is ordinary, everyday standard vocabulary, shunning longer words and using contractions when necessary. The sentence "It's me" is an example of what many American speakers naturally say in preference to the formal "It is I." Neutral words may be thought of as clear window glass, while words in the formal or high style are more decorative, like stained glass. Neutral diction is appropriate for stories about everyday, ordinary people going through situations they encounter or can imagine encountering in their lives. Generally, today's writers favor neutral diction as a means of putting their characters in a light that is normal and appropriate but also respectful.

Informal or *low* diction may range from *colloquial*—the language of relaxed, common activities—to the level of *substandard* or *slang* expressions. A person speaking to a close friend uses diction that would not be appropriate in public and formal situations and even in some social situations. Informal or low diction is thus appropriate for some narrative dialogue, depending, of course, on individual speakers. It is also a natural choice for stories told in the first-person point of view as though the speaker is talking directly to sympathetic and relaxed close friends—"pals." The following sentence from Bambara's "The Lesson" (Chapter 8) illustrates informal, low diction:

> And school suppose to let up in summer I heard, but she don't never let up.

Note the ungrammatical "don't never," a double negative often used in informal or low speech but frowned upon in writing. Note also that the *d* has been dropped in the participle "suppose," that the word "is" before "suppose" is omitted, and that "I heard" follows and does not precede the clause "And school suppose to let up in summer." The purpose of these substandard usages is clearly to establish the voice of the speaker, Sylvia, and to encourage us to listen attentively to her story.

Authors Use Specific-General and Concrete-Abstract Language to Guide Readers to Perceptions of Numbers and Qualities

Another aspect of language is its degree of exactness. **Specific language** refers to words that bring to mind images from the real world. "My dog Teddie is barking" is specific. **General language** refers to broad classes, such as "All people like pets" and "Dogs make good pets." There is an ascending order of generality from (1) very specific, to (2) less specific, to (3) general, as though the words themselves are climbing a ladder. Thus *peach* is a specific fruit. *Fruit* is specific but more general because it may also include apples, oranges, and all other fruits. *Dessert* is a still more general word, which can include all sweets, including fruits and peaches, and also other confections, such as ice cream. *Food* is more general yet, for it is a comprehensive word that describes everything we eat.

While *specific–general* refers to categories, *concrete–abstract* refers to qualities or conditions. **Concrete diction** describes qualities of immediate perception. If you say, "Ice cream is cold," the word *cold* is concrete because it describes a condition that you can feel, just as you can taste ice cream's *sweetness* and feel its *creamy* texture in your mouth. **Abstract diction** refers to broader and less concrete qualities; the words may therefore apply to many separate things. If we describe ice cream as *good*, our word is abstract because *good* is far removed from ice cream itself and conveys no descriptive information about it. A vast number of things may be *good*, just as they may be *bad, fine*, "cool," *excellent*, and so on.

Usually, narrative and descriptive writing features specific and concrete words that are intended to help us visualize actions, scenes, and objects, for with more specificity and concreteness there is less ambiguity. Because exactness and vividness are goals of most fiction, specific and concrete words are the fiction writer's basic tools, with general and abstract words being used sparingly.

The point, however, is not that abstract and general words have no place at all, but rather that *words should be appropriate in the context*. Good writers control style in the interests of tone as well as description. Observe, for example, Hemingway's diction in "Hills Like White Elephants" (this chapter). This brief story takes place at a railway station in Spain, and it consists largely of conversation between the "American and the girl with him" as they are waiting for a train. The two speak idly about details of the day, the appearance of the nearby hills, and the drinks they are having as they wait. The language here is all quite specific, but at a certain point the specifics bring out an obvious issue of contention the two had been discussing before the story opens. About a third of the way through the story, the man speaks about an operation that is "not really an operation at all." It is clear that the operation he wants "Jig" (the woman's nickname) to have is an abortion. In the rest of the story, the dialogue takes a more negative turn. Even when he says that he doesn't want her to go through with it unless she wants it, she understands his words as an expression of the anger her refusal would cause. Her many questions about their relationship after such an operation indicate her worries not only about the procedure but also her increasing disappointment in the American. The height of the American's generalized view of abortion is his claim to have known "lots of people that have done it." Her response, at the same level of generalization, but with cutting irony, marks the height of their dispute: "So have I," said the girl. "And afterward they were all so happy." Through such passages, mixing appropriate specific details with general observations, Hemingway skillfully points readers toward great understanding of the life these two characters have shared together.

Authors Use Denotation and Connotation to Control Meaning and Suggestion

Another way to understand the connection of style and tone is to study the author's management of *denotation* and *connotation*. **Denotation** is a limiting term, referring to what a word means, and **connotation** is a broader word, referring to what the word suggests. For example, if a person in a social situation behaves in ways that are *friendly, warm, polite,* or *cordial,* these words are different in tone because they have different connotations. Similarly, both *cat* and *kitten* are close to each other denotatively, but *kitten* connotes more playfulness and cuteness than *cat.* Consider the connotations of words describing physical appearance. It is one thing to call a person *thin,* for example, but another to use such words as *skinny, gaunt, scrawny,* and *skeletal,* and still something else to say *fit, trim, svelte, slim,* and *slender.*

Through the careful choice of words, not only for denotation but also for connotation, writers control tone even though they might be describing similar or even identical situations. Let us look briefly at Cynthia Ozick's opening paragraph of "The Shawl" (Chapter 4).

Stella, cold, cold the coldness of hell. How they walked on the roads together, Rosa with Magda curled up between sore breasts, Magda wound up in the shawl. Sometimes Stella carried Magda. But she was jealous of Magda. A thin girl of fourteen, too small, with thin breasts of her own, Stella wanted to be wrapped in a shawl, hidden away, asleep, rocked by the march, a baby, a round infant in arms. Magda took Rosa's nipple, and Rosa never stopped walking, a walking cradle. There was not enough milk; sometimes Magda sucked air; then she screamed. Stella was ravenous. Her knees were tumors on sticks, her elbows chicken bones. (246, paragraph 1)

This short but complex paragraph conveys a grisly close-up experience of horror during the enforced death marches of Nazi prisoners during the closing months of World War II. Many of the words here would be totally appropriate to the peaceful mothering and nurturing of an infant, but in the context of the paragraph these words dissolve into the bleakness and despair described in the passage. Stella, the thin fourteen-year-old girl who is forced to walk while carrying her infant sister, is "ravenous," a word suggesting her desperation for food, rather than "hungry," a word that connotes normal life in which meals are taken for granted. In addition, because of the march and her starved condition her knees have come to resemble "tumors on sticks" and her elbows are "chicken bones." Babies cry all the time, and the word *cry* would describe a baby under normal circumstances, but this paragraph conveys the unspeakably cruel treatment of innocent prisoners, and therefore Magda, Rosa's baby, "screamed." The brief discussion of these words shows how an author's skillful use of connotation shapes the tone of individual passages and, beyond that, of entire works.

Tone, Irony, and Style

The capacity to have more than one attitude toward someone or something is a uniquely human trait. We know that people are not perfect, but we love a number of them anyway. Therefore, we speak to them not only with love and praise but also with banter and criticism. On occasion, you may have given mildly insulting greeting cards to your loved ones, not to offend them but to amuse them. You share smiles and laughs at these negative words on your cards, but at the same time you remind your loved ones of your affection.

The word **irony,** specifically **verbal irony,** describes such contradictory statements, in which one thing is said and the opposite is meant. There are important types of verbal irony. In **understatement** the expression does not fully describe the importance of a situation, and therefore makes its point by implication. For example, in Bierce's "An Occurrence at Owl Creek Bridge" (Chapter 1) the condemned man, Farquhar, contemplates the device designed by the soldiers to hang him. After considering the method, Farquhar's response is described by the narrator: "The arrangement commended itself to his judgment as simple and effective" (88, paragraph 4). These words would be appropriate for ordinary machinery, perhaps, but because the apparatus is soon to cause Farquhar's death, the understated observation is ironic.

By contrast, in **hyperbole** or **overstatement**, the words are far in excess of the situation, and readers or listeners therefore understand that the true meaning is considerably less than what is said. An example is the priest's exaggerated dialogue with Jackie in "First Confession" (this chapter). Though the priest makes exaggerated comments on Jackie's plans for slaughtering his grandmother, readers automatically know he means no such thing. The gulf between what is said and what is meant creates smiles and chuckles.

Often verbal irony is ambiguous, having double meaning or **double entendre.** Midway through "Young Goodman Brown" (Chapter 7), for example, the woodland guide leaves Brown alone while stating, "[W]hen you feel like moving again, there is my staff to help you along" (345, paragraph 40). The word "staff" is ambiguous, for it refers to the staff that resembles a serpent (343, paragraph 13). The word therefore suggests that the devilish guide is leaving Brown not only with a real staff but also with the spirit of evil (unlike the divine "staff" of Psalm 23:4 that gives comfort). Ambiguity of course may be used in relation to any topic. Quite often double entendre is used in statements about sexuality, and on such occasions it is intended for the amusement of listeners or readers.

Tone, Humor, and Style

A major aspect of tone is humor and laughter. Everyone likes to laugh, and shared laughter is part of good human relationships. As common and enjoyable as laughter is, however, not many people can adequately explain why some things are funny. Even when reasons for laughter are analyzed and explained, it always seems that they do not answer all our questions. Explanation, however, is a goal worthy of pursuit. It seems that a common element in laughter is that it depends on our seeing something familiar in a new light, or in encountering something surprisingly new or unique. It also seems that whenever we laugh—perhaps in the company of our friends or as a result of our reading or looking at films and television shows—we likely find that laughter is most often unplanned, personal, unique, and unpredictable.

A primary ingredient in humor is something to laugh at—a person, thing, situation, custom, habit of speech or dialect, or arrangement of words. But once we have this ingredient we must also have *disproportion* or *incongruity*; that is, something happens or is said that violates what we might normally expect. It is such jarring juxtapositions that provide the comic newness prompting the occasion of laughter. In O'Connor's "First Confession" (this chapter) we might expect that Mrs. Ryan's discourse about enduring the agonizing pain of hellfire for all eternity might have made Jackie, the narrator, fearful. But is this what happens? Let us look:

> She lit a candle, took out a new half-crown [a valuable coin], and offered it to the first boy who would hold one finger—only one finger!—in the flame for five minutes by the school clock. Being always very ambitious I was tempted to volunteer, but I thought it might look greedy. Then she asked were we afraid of holding one finger—only one finger!—in a little candle flame for five minutes and not afraid of burning all over in roasting hot furnaces for all eternity. "All eternity! Just think of that! A whole lifetime goes by and it's nothing, not even a drop in the ocean of your sufferings." The woman was really interesting about hell, but my attention was all fixed on the half-crown. . . . (315, paragraph 5)

Jackie's response shows that Mrs. Ryan's challenge has not even dented his boyhood problems, which have nothing to do with eternal punishment. For him, punishment is a matter of things happening day by day: the "flaking" administered by his father and also the family disruptions caused by his grandmother. Eternity, for him as a little boy, is not even a remote concern. It is comparable incongruities in Jackie's responses that characterize the comic method in O'Connor's story. Situations producing laughter in most other works are not dissimilar to the situation of "First Confession."

In addition, the language itself may be used for incongruity. A well-known example is the traditional stand-up comedian's statement, "One day I was walking in the local shopping mall, and I turned into a drugstore." Here the comedian causes laughter through the ambiguous meaning of "turned into," thus verbally changing an ordinary walk into a miraculously comic event. Another verbal incongruity is this one: "Barking loudly, I was awakened by my dog." Here the humor depends on the juggling of grammar: the modifier "barking loudly" is misplaced, and the resulting sentence seems to say incongruously that the speaker, and not the dog, is barking. A real-life speaker, who will be nameless here, once stated that he had trouble understanding the "*congregation* of verbs," not quite catching up to the word *conjugation*. Here the inadvertent pun creates the humor of the sentence. We laugh *at* the pun, and we also laugh *at* the speaker whose verbal mistake has produced the pun. The same speaker also described the grammatical parts of speech as "nouns, verbs, and *proverbs*." We conclude that he intended to say (maybe) either *pronouns* or *adverbs*, but somehow his understanding slipped and he created a comic incongruity. If we discover such verbal errors in a story, the author is controlling tone by directing humor against the speaker and his or her language, for the amusement of both readers and author alike.

It is such flashes of insight, or sudden revelations like these, that create the newness and spontaneity underlying humor. Indeed, the task of the writer is to develop ordinary materials to that point when spontaneity brings us to the explosiveness of laughter. This is not to say that works that you already know are not spontaneous or new. You can read O'Connor's "First Confession" and laugh, and read it again and laugh again, because even though you know what happens, the story shapes your acceptance of how Jackie maintains his natural innocence despite the fact that the older people around him, except for the priest, are pushing him to accept their own fears and anxieties. Jackie's experience is and always will be comic—and new—because it is so incongruous and so spontaneous.

Stories for Study

Kate Chopin. . . . . The Story of an Hour, 306
Dagoberto Gilb . . . . Love in L.A., 309
Ernest Hemingway . . . . Hills Like White Elephants, 311
Frank O'Connor. . . . . First Confession, 315
John Updike . . . . A & P, 320

KATE CHOPIN (1851–1904)

Born in St. Louis, Missouri, Kate Chopin lived in Louisiana from the time of her marriage until 1882. After her husband's death she returned to St. Louis and began to write. She published two collections of stories based on the life she had known back in Louisiana: Bayou Folk (1894) *and* A Night in Acadie (1897). *However, she became best known for her major novel,* The Awakening (1899), *which aroused negative reactions because it mentioned taboo subjects like adultery and miscegenation. Indeed, the critical disapproval was so intense that Chopin published no further works, even though she was at the height of her literary power and lived five years after the controversy.*

The Story of an Hour (1894)

Knowing that Mrs. Mallard was afflicted with a heart trouble, great care was taken to break to her as gently as possible the news of her husband's death.

It was her sister Josephine who told her, in broken sentences: veiled hints that revealed in half concealing. Her husband's friend Richards was there, too, near her. It was he who had been in the newspaper office when intelligence of the railroad disaster was received, with Brently Mallard's name leading the list of "killed." He had only taken the time to assure himself of its truth by a second telegram, and had hastened to forestall any less careful, less tender friend in bearing the sad message.

She did not hear the story as many women have heard the same, with a paralyzed inability to accept its significance. She wept at once, with sudden, wild abandonment, in her sister's arms. When the storm of grief had spent itself she went away to her room alone. She would have no one follow her.

There stood, facing the open window, a comfortable, roomy armchair. Into this she sank, pressed down by a physical exhaustion that haunted her body and seemed to reach into her soul.

She could see in the open square before her house the tops of trees that were all aquiver   5
with the new spring life. The delicious breath of rain was in the air. In the street below a peddler was crying his wares. The notes of a distant song which some one was singing reached her faintly, and countless sparrows were twittering in the eaves.

There were patches of blue sky showing here and there through the clouds that had met and piled one above the other in the west facing her window.

She sat with her head thrown back upon the cushion of the chair, quite motionless, except when a sob came up into her throat and shook her, as a child who has cried itself to sleep continues to sob in its dreams.

She was young, with a fair, calm face, whose lines bespoke repression and even a certain strength. But now there was a dull stare in her eyes, whose gaze was fixed away off yonder on one of those patches of blue sky. It was not a glance of reflection, but rather indicated a suspension of intelligent thought.

There was something coming to her and she was waiting for it, fearfully. What was it? She did not know; it was too subtle and elusive to name. But she felt it, creeping out of the sky, reaching toward her through the sounds, the scents, the color that filled the air.

Now her bosom rose and fell tumultuously. She was beginning to recognize this thing   10
that was approaching to possess her, and she was striving to beat it back with her will—as powerless as her two white slender hands would have been.

When she abandoned herself a little whispered word escaped her slightly parted lips. She said it over and over under her breath: "free, free, free!" The vacant stare and the look of terror that had followed it went from her eyes. They stayed keen and bright. Her pulses beat fast, and the coursing blood warmed and relaxed every inch of her body.

She did not stop to ask if it were or were not a monstrous joy that held her. A clear and exalted perception enabled her to dismiss the suggestion as trivial.

She knew that she would weep again when she saw the kind, tender hands folded in death; the face that had never looked save with love upon her, fixed and gray and dead. But she saw beyond that bitter moment a long procession of years to come that would belong to her absolutely. And she opened and spread her arms out to them in welcome.

There would be no one to live for during those coming years; she would live for herself. There would be no powerful will bending hers in that blind persistence with which men and women believe they have a right to impose a private will upon a fellow-creature. A kind intention or a cruel intention made the act seem no less a crime as she looked upon it in that brief moment of illumination.

15 And yet she had loved him—sometimes. Often she had not. What did it matter! What could love, the unsolved mystery, count for in face of this possession of self-assertion which she suddenly recognized as the strongest impulse of her being!

"Free! Body and soul free!" she kept whispering.

Josephine was kneeling before the closed door with her lips to the keyhole, imploring for admission. "Louise, open the door! I beg; open the door—you will make yourself ill. What are you doing, Louise? For heaven's sake open the door."

"Go away. I am not making myself ill." No; she was drinking in a very elixir of life through that open window.

Her fancy was running riot along those days ahead of her. Spring days, and summer days, and all sorts of days that would be her own. She breathed a quick prayer that life might be long. It was only yesterday she had thought with a shudder that life might be long.

20 She arose at length and opened the door to her sister's importunities. There was a feverish triumph in her eyes, and she carried herself unwittingly like a goddess of Victory. She clasped her sister's waist, and together they descended the stairs. Richards stood waiting for them at the bottom.

Someone was opening the front door with a latchkey. It was Brently Mallard who entered, a little travel-stained, composedly carrying his grip-sack and umbrella. He had been far from the scene of the accident, and did not even know there had been one. He stood amazed at Josephine's piercing cry: at Richards' quick motion to screen him from the view of his wife.

But Richards was too late.

When the doctors came they said she had died of heart disease—of joy that kills.

QUESTIONS

1. What do we learn about Louise's husband? How has he justified her responses? How are your judgments about him controlled by the context of the story?

2. Analyze the tone of paragraph 5. How is the imagery here (and in the following paragraphs) appropriate for her developing mood?

3. What is the apparent attitude of the narrator toward the institution of marriage, and what elements of tone make this apparent?

4. What do Louise's sister and Richards have in common? How do their attitudes contribute to the irony of the story?

5. Consider the tone of the last paragraph. What judgment is being made about how men view their importance to women?

DAGOBERTO GILB (b. 1950)

Born in Los Angeles, Dagoberto Gilb was educated in that city's public school system, and he received degrees from the University of California at Santa Barbara. After graduating he began writing, sending manuscripts "into the wind" and meeting with little financial success. He found that he needed to support himself in a more reliable way and went to work for more than a dozen years in the building trades as a carpenter, laborer, and occasional stonemason. He did not start receiving acclaim as a writer until he was
in his mid-thirties, but since then he has received much recognition, including a Guggenheim Fellowship, the PEN/Hemingway Award, and an NEA fellowship. On his way to establishing

himself as a writer, he taught at a number of schools in the West, including Texas State University at San Marcos, and more recently at the University of Houston. His most notable books are Winners on the Pass Line and Other Stories *(1985),* The Magic of Blood *(1993),* The Last Known Residence of Mickey Acuna *(1994),* Woodcuts of Women *(2001), and* The Flowers *(2008). "Love in L.A." first appeared in* Winners on the Pass Line *in 1985; its first title was "The Short Life and Quick Death of Love in L.A."*

Love in L.A. (1985)

Jake slouched in a clot of near motionless traffic, in the peculiar gray of concrete, smog, and early morning beneath the overpass of the Hollywood Freeway on Alvarado Street. He didn't really mind because he knew how much worse it could be trying to make a left onto the onramp. He certainly didn't do that every day of his life, and he'd assure anyone who'd ask that he never would either. A steady occupation had its advantages and he couldn't deny thinking about that too. He needed an FM radio in something better than this '58 Buick he drove. It would have crushed velvet interior with electric controls for the L.A. summer, a nice warm heater and defroster for the winter drives at the beach, a cruise control for those longer trips, mellow speakers front and rear of course, windows that hum closed, snuffing out that nasty exterior noise of freeways. The fact was that he'd probably have to change his whole style. Exotic colognes, plush, dark night-clubs, mai-tais and daiquiris, necklaced ladies in satin gowns, misty and sexy like in a tequila ad. Jake could imagine lots of possibilities when he let himself, but none that ended up with him pressed onto a stalled freeway.

Jake was thinking about this freedom of his so much that when he glimpsed its green light he just went ahead and stared bye-bye to the steadily employed. When he turned his head the same direction his windshield faced, it was maybe one second too late. He pounced the brake pedal and steered the front wheels away from the tiny brake lights but the smack was unavoidable. Just one second sooner and it would only have been close. One second more and he'd be crawling up the Toyota's trunk. As it was, it seemed like only a harmless smack, much less solid than the one against his back bumper.

Jake considered driving past the Toyota but was afraid the traffic ahead would make it too difficult. As he pulled up against the curb a few car lengths ahead, it occurred to him that the traffic might have helped him get away too. He slammed the car door twice to make sure it was closed fully and to give himself another second more, then toured front and rear of his Buick for damage on or near the bumpers. Not an impressionable scratch even in the chrome. He perked up. Though the car's beauty was secondary to its ability to start and move, the body and paint were clean except for a few minor dings. This stood out as one of his few clearcut accomplishments over the years.

Before he spoke to the driver of the Toyota, whose looks he could see might present him with an added complication, he signaled to the driver of the car that hit him, still in his car and stopped behind the Toyota, and waved his hands and shook his head to let the man know there was no problem as far as he was concerned. The driver waved back and started his engine.

"It didn't even scratch my paint," Jake told her in that way of his. "So how you doin'? Any damage to the car? I'm kinda hoping so, just so it takes a little more time and we can talk some. Or else you can give me your phone number now and I won't have to lay my regular b.s. on you to get it later."

He took her smile as a good sign and relaxed. He inhaled her scent like it was clean air and straightened out his less than new but not unhip clothes.

"You've got Florida plates. You look like you must be Cuban."

"My parents are from Venezuela."

"My name's Jake." He held out his hand.

10   "Mariana." They shook hands like she'd never done it before in her life.

"I really am sorry about hitting you like that." He sounded genuine. He fondled the wide dimple near the cracked taillight. "It's amazing how easy it is to put a dent in these new cars. They're so soft they might replace waterbeds soon." Jake was confused about how to proceed with this. So much seemed so unlikely, but there was always possibility. "So maybe we should go out to breakfast somewhere and talk it over."

"I don't eat breakfast."

"Some coffee then."

"Thanks, but I really can't."

15   "You're not married, are you? Not that that would matter that much to me. I'm an open-minded kinda guy."

She was smiling. "I have to get to work."

"That sounds boring."

"I better get your driver's license," she said.

20   Jake nodded, disappointed.

"One little problem," he said. "I didn't bring it. I just forgot it this morning. I'm a musician," he exaggerated greatly, "and, well, I dunno, I left my wallet in the pants I was wearing last night. If you have some paper and a pen I'll give you my address and all that."

He followed her to the glove compartment side of her car.

"What if we don't report it to the insurance companies? I'll just get it fixed for you."

"I don't think my dad would let me do that."

25   "Your dad? It's not your car?"

"He bought it for me. And I live at home."

"Right." She was slipping away from him. He went back around to the back of her new Toyota and looked over the damage again. There was the trunk lid, the bumper, a rear panel, a taillight.

"You do have insurance?" she asked, suspicious, as she came around the back of the car.

"Oh yeah," he lied.

30   "I guess you better write the name of that down too."

He made up a last name and address and wrote down the name of an insurance company an old girlfriend once belonged to. He considered giving a real phone number but went against that idea and made one up.

"I act too," he lied to enhance the effect more. "Been in a couple of movies." She smiled like a fan.

"So how about your phone number?" He was rebounding maturely. She gave it to him.

"Mariana, you are beautiful," he said in his most sincere voice.

35   "Call me," she said timidly.

Jake beamed. "We'll see you, Mariana," he said holding out his hand. Her hand felt so warm and soft he felt like he'd been kissed.

Back in his car he took a moment or two to feel both proud and sad about his performance. Then he watched the rear view mirror as Mariana pulled up behind him. She was writing down the license plate numbers on his Buick, ones that he'd taken off a junk because the ones that belonged to his had expired so long ago. He turned the ignition key and revved the big engine and clicked into drive. His sense of freedom swelled as he drove into the now moving street traffic, though he couldn't stop the thought about that FM stereo radio and crushed velvet interior and the new car smell that would even make it better.

QUESTIONS

1. Describe the point of view of this story. Who is the central character? What is he like? What sorts of things seem to occupy his waking thoughts? Is he a comic or serious character? What do his thoughts at the end of the story reveal about him?

2. Who is Mariana? How do she and Jake meet? What seems to be Jake's interest in Mariana? Does she seem accustomed to characters like Jake? Why does she write down his plate number after the accident? Why does Jake not seem worried about her taking the number?

3. How might the acquaintanceship of Jake and Mariana be considered sufficiently important to justify the word "Love" in the title? If you do not think that love is that important, explain why it is possible to consider that the word "Love" in the title is being used ironically?

4. The original title of this story was "The Short Life and Quick Death of Love in L.A." In your judgment, which title is more appropriate? Which title do you prefer? Why?

ERNEST HEMINGWAY (1899–1961)

Ernest Hemingway was born in Illinois. During World War I he served in the Ambulance Corps in France, where he was wounded. In the 1920s he published The Sun Also Rises *(1926) and* A Farewell to Arms *(1929), and the resulting critical fame made him a major literary celebrity. He developed a sparse style, in keeping with the elemental, stark lives of the characters he depicted. "Hills Like White Elephants," from the collection* Men Without Women *(1927), typifies that pared, annealed style. Of particular note in this story is the way in which Hemingway, by carefully controlling the various speeches of his two characters without providing any extra prose guidance, enables readers clearly to identify the speakers and to follow their interests about the topics of concern.*

⬩ Hills Like White Elephants° (1927)

The hills across the valley of the Ebro° were long and white. On this side there was no shade and no trees and the station was between two lines of rails in the sun. Close against the side of the station there was the warm shadow of the building and a curtain, made of strings of bamboo beads, hung across the open door into the bar, to keep out flies. The American and the girl with him sat at a table in the shade, outside the building. It was very hot and the express from Barcelona would come in forty minutes. It stopped at this junction for two minutes and went on to Madrid.

"What should we drink?" the girl asked. She had taken off her hat and put it on the table.

"It's pretty hot," the man said.

"Let's drink beer."

"Dos cervezas," the man said into the curtain.

5

°*Ebro*: a river in Spain.

"Big ones?" a woman asked° from the doorway.

"Yes. Two big ones."

The woman brought two glasses of beer and two felt pads. She put the felt pads and the beer glasses on the table and looked at the man and the girl. The girl was looking off at the line of hills. They were white in the sun and the country was brown and dry.

"They look like white elephants," she said.

10   "I've never seen one," the man drank his beer.

"No, you wouldn't have."

"I might have," the man said. "Just because you say I wouldn't have doesn't prove anything."

The girl looked at the bead curtain. "They've painted something on it," she said. "What does it say?"

"Anis del Toro. It's a drink."

15   "Could we try it?"

The man called "Listen" through the curtain. The woman came out from the bar.

"Four reales."°

"We want two Anis del Toro."

"With water?"

20   "Do you want it with water?"

"I don't know," the girl said. "Is it good with water?"

"It's all right."

"You want them with water?" asked the woman.

"Yes, with water."

25   "It tastes like licorice," the girl said and put the glass down.

"That's the way with everything."

"Yes," said the girl. "Everything tastes of licorice. Especially all the things you've waited so long for, like absinthe."

"Oh, cut it out."

"You started it," the girl said. "I was being amused. I was having a fine time."

30   "Well, let's try and have a fine time."

"All right. I was trying. I said the mountains looked like white elephants. Wasn't that bright?"

"That was bright."

"I wanted to try this new drink. That's all we do, isn't it—look at things and try new drinks?"

"I guess so."

35   The girl looked across at the hills.

"They're lovely hills," she said. "They don't really look like white elephants. I just meant the coloring of their skin through the trees."

"Should we have another drink?"

"All right."

The warm wind blew the bead curtain against the table.

40   "The beer's nice and cool," the man said.

"It's lovely," the girl said.

"It's really an awfully simple operation, Jig," the man said. "It's not really an operation at all."

The girl looked at the ground the table legs rested on.

"I know you wouldn't mind it, Jig. It's really not anything. It's just to let the air in."

45   The girl did not say anything.

°*a woman asked*: The waitress speaks in Spanish. The American man understands Spanish, but the girl does not. The man therefore translates for her throughout the story, when necessary.

°*reales*: a *real* was a silver Spanish coin.

"I'll go with you and I'll stay with you all the time. They just let the air in and then it's all perfectly natural."

"Then what will we do afterward?"

"We'll be fine afterward. Just like we were before."

"What makes you think so?"

"That's the only thing that bothers us. It's the only thing that's made us unhappy."   50

The girl looked at the bead curtain, put her hand out and took hold of two of the strings of beads.

"And you think then we'll be all right and be happy."

"I know we will. You don't have to be afraid. I've known lots of people that have done it."

"So have I," said the girl. "And afterward they were all so happy."

"Well," the man said, "if you don't want to you don't have to. I wouldn't have you do it   55
if you didn't want to. But I know it's perfectly simple."

"And you really want to?"

"I think it's the best thing to do. But I don't want you to do it if you don't really want to."

"And if I do it you'll be happy and things will be like they were and you'll love me?"

"I love you now. You know I love you."

"I know. But if I do it, then it will be nice again if I say things are like white elephants,   60
and you'll like it?"

"I'll love it. I love it now but I just can't think about it. You know how I get when I worry."

"If I do it you won't ever worry?"

"I won't worry about that because it's perfectly simple."

"Then I'll do it. Because I don't care about me."

"What do you mean?"   65

"I don't care about me."

"Well, I care about you."

"Oh, yes. But I don't care about me. And I'll do it and then everything will be fine."

"I don't want you to do it if you feel that way."

The girl stood up and walked to the end of the station. Across, on the other side, were   70
fields of grain and trees along the banks of the Ebro. Far away, beyond the river, were mountains. The shadow of a cloud moved across the field of grain and she saw the river through the trees.

"And we could have all this," she said. "And we could have everything and every day we make it more impossible."

"What did you say?"

"I said we could have everything."

"We can have everything."

"No, we can't."

"We can have the whole world."   75

"No, we can't."

"We can go everywhere."

"No, we can't. It isn't ours any more."

"It's ours."

"No, it isn't. And once they take it away, you never get it back."   80

"But they haven't taken it away."

"We'll wait and see."

"Come on back in the shade," he said. "You mustn't feel that way."

"I don't feel any way," the girl said. "I just know things."

"I don't want you to do anything that you don't want to do—"   85

"Nor that isn't good for me," she said. "I know. Could we have another beer?"

"All right. But you've got to realize—"

"I realize," the girl said. "Can't we maybe stop talking?"

90   They sat down at the table and the girl looked across at the hills on the dry side of the valley and the man looked at her and at the table.

"You've got to realize," he said, "that I don't want you to do it if you don't want to. I'm perfectly willing to go through with it if it means anything to you."

"Doesn't it mean anything to you? We could get along."

"Of course it does. But I don't want anybody but you. I don't want any one else. And I know it's perfectly simple."

"Yes, you know it's perfectly simple."

95   "It's all right for you to say that, but I do know it."

"Would you do something for me now?"

"I'd do anything for you."

"Would you please please please please please please please stop talking?"

He did not say anything but looked at the bags against the wall of the station. There were labels on them from all the hotels where they had spent nights.

100   "But I don't want you to," he said, "I don't care anything about it."

"I'll scream," the girl said.

The woman came out through the curtains with two glasses of beer and put them down on the damp felt pads. "The train comes in five minutes," she said.

"What did she say?" asked the girl.

"That the train is coming in five minutes."

105   The girl smiled brightly at the woman, to thank her.

"I'd better take the bags over to the other side of the station," the man said. She smiled at him.

"All right. Then come back and we'll finish the beer."

He picked up the two heavy bags and carried them around the station to the other tracks. He looked up the tracks but could not see the train. Coming back, he walked through the barroom, where people waiting for the train were drinking. He drank an Anis at the bar and looked at the people. They were all waiting reasonably for the train. He went out through the bead curtain. She was sitting at the table and smiled at him.

"Do you feel better?" he asked.

110   "I feel fine," she said. "There's nothing wrong with me. I feel fine."

QUESTIONS

1. Who are the major characters in this story? What is the principal problem that they are facing? What does "Jig" want to do? What does "the American" want her to do?

2. What are her responses to his wishes? In what ways can you determine what her wishes are? What is happening to her judgment about the American?

3. Describe Hemingway's handling of the dialogue. Stylistically, how does Hemingway make it plain who is speaking, without the many "he said" and "she said" statements that you might find in other stories?

4. Why does the American stop in the station barroom to have another Anis, to which "Jig" has voiced what seems to be an objection?

5. What evidence do you find in the dialogue about the relationship between the American and "Jig" before the story has opened? Explain Hemingway's use of irony in Jig's speeches after paragraph 53. How do the speeches of Jig and the American let you know about their attitudes toward the future of their relationship? How does Jig seem to be growing psychologically as the story unfolds? How believable is her final statement, that she "feels fine"?

FRANK O'CONNOR (1903–1966)

Frank O'Connor, the nom de plume of Michael O'Donovan, was an only child of poor parents in County Cork, Ireland. He began writing when young, and for a time he was a director of Ireland's national theater. His output as a writer was considerable, with sixty-seven stories appearing in the posthumous Collected Stories *of 1981. A meticulous writer, he was constantly revising his work. "First Confession," for example, went through a number of stages before the final version included here.*

First Confession (1951)

All the trouble began when my grandfather died and my grandmother—my father's mother—came to live with us. Relations in the one house are a strain at the best of times, but, to make matters worse, my grandmother was a real old countrywoman and quite unsuited to the life in town. She had a fat, wrinkled old face, and, to Mother's great indignation, went round the house in bare feet—the boots had her crippled, she said. For dinner she had a jug of porter° and a pot of potatoes with—sometimes—a bit of salt fish, and she poured out the potatoes on the table and ate them slowly, with great relish, using her fingers by way of a fork.

Now, girls are supposed to be fastidious, but I was the one who suffered most from this. Nora, my sister, just sucked up to the old woman for the penny she got every Friday out of the old-age pension, a thing I could not do. I was too honest, that was my trouble; and when I was playing with Bill Connell, the sergeant-major's son, and saw my grandmother steering up the path with the jug of porter sticking out from beneath her shawl I was mortified. I made excuses not to let him come into the house, because I could never be sure what she would be up to when we went in.

When Mother was at work and my grandmother made the dinner I wouldn't touch it. Nora once tried to make me, but I hid under the table from her and took the bread-knife with me for protection. Nora let on to be very indignant (she wasn't, of course, but she knew Mother saw through her, so she sided with Gran) and came after me. I lashed out at her with the bread-knife, and after that she left me alone. I stayed there till Mother came in from work and made my dinner, but when Father came in later Nora said in a shocked voice: "Oh, Dadda, do you know what Jackie did at dinner-time?" Then, of course, it all came out; Father gave me a flaking; Mother interfered, and for days after that he didn't speak to me and Mother barely spoke to Nora. And all because of that old woman! God knows, I was heart-scalded.

Then, to crown my misfortune, I had to make my first confession and communion. It was an old woman called Ryan who prepared us for these. She was about the one age with Gran; she was well-to-do, lived in a big house on Montenotte, wore a black cloak and bonnet, and came every day to school at three o'clock when we should have been going home, and talked to us of hell. She may have mentioned the other place as well, but that could only have been by accident, for hell had the first place in her heart.

She lit a candle, took out a new half-crown, and offered it to the first boy who would   5
hold one finger—only one finger!—in the flame for five minutes by the school clock. Being always very ambitious I was tempted to volunteer, but I thought it might look greedy. Then she asked were we afraid of holding one finger—only one finger!—in a little candle flame for five minutes and not afraid of burning all over in roasting hot furnaces for all eternity.

°*porter:* a dark-brown beer.

"All eternity! Just think of that! A whole lifetime goes by and it's nothing, not even a drop in the ocean of your sufferings." The woman was really interesting about hell, but my attention was all fixed on the half-crown. At the end of the lesson she put it back in her purse. It was a great disappointment; a religious woman like that, you wouldn't think she'd bother about a thing like a half-crown.

Another day she said she knew a priest who woke one night to find a fellow he didn't recognize leaning over the end of his bed. The priest was a bit frightened—naturally enough—but he asked the fellow what he wanted, and the fellow said in a deep, husky voice that he wanted to go to confession. The priest said it was an awkward time and wouldn't it do in the morning, but the fellow said that last time he went to confession, there was one sin he kept back, being ashamed to mention it, and now it was always on his mind. Then the priest knew it was a bad case, because the fellow was after making a bad confession and committing a mortal sin. He got up to dress, and just then the cock crew in the yard outside, and—lo and behold!—when the priest looked round there was no sign of the fellow, only a smell of burning timber, and when the priest looked at his bed didn't he see the print of two hands burned in it? That was because the fellow had made a bad confession. This story made a shocking impression on me.

But the worst of all was when she showed us how to examine our conscience. Did we take the name of the Lord, our God, in vain? Did we honour our father and our mother? (I asked her did this include grandmothers and she said it did.) Did we love our neighbours as ourselves? Did we covet our neighbour's goods? (I thought of the way I felt about the penny that Nora got every Friday.) I decided that, between one thing and another, I must have broken the whole ten commandments, all on account of that old woman, and so far as I could see, so long as she remained in the house I had no hope of ever doing anything else.

I was scared to death of confession. The day the whole class went I let on to have a toothache, hoping my absence wouldn't be noticed; but at three o'clock, just as I was feeling safe, along comes a chap with a message from Mrs. Ryan that I was to go to confession myself on Saturday and be at the chapel for communion with the rest. To make it worse, Mother couldn't come with me and sent Nora instead.

Now, that girl had ways of tormenting me that Mother never knew of. She held my hand as we went down the hill, smiling sadly and saying how sorry she was for me, as if she were bringing me to the hospital for an operation.

10   "Oh, God help us!" she moaned. "Isn't it a terrible pity you weren't a good boy? Oh, Jackie, my heart bleeds for you! How will you ever think of all your sins? Don't forget you have to tell him about the time you kicked Gran on the shin."

"Lemme go!" I said, trying to drag myself free of her. "I don't want to go to confession at all."

"But sure, you'll have to go to confession, Jackie," she replied in the same regretful tone. "Sure, if you didn't the parish priest would be up to the house, looking for you. 'Tisn't, God knows, that I'm not sorry for you. Do you remember the time you tried to kill me with the bread-knife under the table? And the language you used to me? I don't know what he'll do with you at all, Jackie. He might have to send you up to the bishop."

I remember thinking bitterly that she didn't know the half of what I had to tell—if I told it. I knew I couldn't tell it, and understood perfectly why the fellow in Mrs. Ryan's story made a bad confession; it seemed to me a great shame that people wouldn't stop criticizing him. I remember that steep hill down to the church, and the sunlit hillsides beyond the valley of the river, which I saw in the gaps between the houses like Adam's last glimpse of Paradise.°

Then, when she had maneuvered me down the long flight of steps to the chapel yard, Nora suddenly changed her tone. She became the raging malicious devil she really was.

°*Adam's last glimpse of Paradise:* Genesis 3:23–24.

"There you are!" she said with a yelp of triumph, hurling me through the church door.   15
"And I hope he'll give you the penitential psalms, you dirty little caffler."

I knew then I was lost, given up to eternal justice. The door with the coloured-glass panels swung shut behind me, the sunlight went out and gave place to deep shadow, and the wind whistled outside so that the silence within seemed to crackle like ice under my feet. Nora sat in front of me by the confession box. There were a couple of old women ahead of her, and then a miserable-looking poor devil came and wedged me in at the other side, so that I couldn't escape even if I had the courage. He joined his hands and rolled his eyes in the direction of the roof, muttering aspirations in an anguished tone, and I wondered had he a grandmother too. Only a grandmother could account for a fellow behaving in that heartbroken way, but he was better off than I, for he at least could go and confess his sins; while I would make a bad confession and then die in the night and be continually coming back and burning people's furniture.

Nora's turn came, and I heard the sound of something slamming, and then her voice as if butter wouldn't melt in her mouth, and then another slam, and out she came. God, the hypocrisy of women! Her eyes were lowered, her head was bowed, and her hands were joined very low down on her stomach, and she walked up the aisle to the side altar looking like a saint. You never saw such an exhibition of devotion, and I remembered the devilish malice with which she had tormented me all the way from our door, and wondered were all religious people like that, really. It was my turn now. With the fear of damnation in my soul I went in, and the confessional door closed of itself behind me.

It was pitch-dark and I couldn't see the priest or anything else. Then I really began to be frightened. In the darkness it was a matter between God and me, and He had all the odds. He knew what my intentions were before I even started; I had no chance. All I had ever been told about confession got mixed up in my mind, and I knelt to one wall and said: "Bless me, father, for I have sinned; this is my first confession." I waited for a few minutes, but nothing happened, so I tried it on the other wall. Nothing happened there either. He had me spotted all right.

It must have been then that I noticed the shelf at about one height with my head. It was really a place for grown-up people to rest their elbows, but in my distracted state I thought it was probably the place you were supposed to kneel. Of course, it was on the high side and not very deep, but I was always good at climbing and managed to get up all right. Staying up was the trouble. There was room only for my knees, and nothing you could get a grip on but a sort of wooden moulding a bit above it. I held on to the moulding and repeated the words a little louder, and this time something happened all right. A slide was slammed back; a little light entered the box, and a man's voice said: "Who's there?"

"'Tis me, father," I said for fear he mightn't see me and go away again. I couldn't see him   20
at all. The place the voice came from was under the moulding, about level with my knees, so I took a good grip of the moulding and swung myself down till I saw the astonished face of a young priest looking up at me. He had to put his head on one side to see me, and I had to put mine on one side to see him, so we were more or less talking to one another upside-down. It struck me as a queer way of hearing confessions, but I didn't feel it my place to criticize.

"Bless me, father, for I have sinned; this is my first confession," I rattled off all in one breath, and swung myself down the least shade more to make it easier for him.

"What are you doing up there?" he shouted in an angry voice, and the strain the politeness was putting on my hold of the moulding, and the shock of being addressed in such an uncivil tone, were too much for me. I lost my grip, tumbled, and hit the door an unmerciful wallop before I found myself flat on my back in the middle of the aisle. The people who had been waiting stood up with their mouths open. The priest opened the door of the middle box and came out, pushing his biretta back from his forehead; he looked something terrible. Then Nora came scampering down the aisle.

"Oh, you dirty little caffler!" she said. "I might have known you'd do it. I might have known you'd disgrace me. I can't leave you out of my sight for one minute."

Before I could even get to my feet to defend myself she bent down and gave me a clip across the ear. This reminded me that I was so stunned I had even forgotten to cry, so that people might think I wasn't hurt at all, when in fact I was probably maimed for life. I gave a roar out of me.

25   "What's all this about?" the priest hissed, getting angrier than ever and pushing Nora off me. "How dare you hit the child like that, you little vixen?"

"But I can't do my penance with him, father," Nora cried, cocking an outraged eye up to him.

"Well, go and do it, or I'll give you some more to do," he said, giving me a hand up. "Was it coming to confession you were, my poor man?" he asked me.

"'Twas, father," said I with a sob.

"Oh," he said respectfully, "a big hefty fellow like you must have terrible sins. Is this your first?"

30   "'Tis, father," said I.

"Worse and worse," he said gloomily. "The crimes of a lifetime. I don't know will I get rid of you at all today. You'd better wait now till I'm finished with these old ones. You can see by the looks of them they haven't much to tell."

"I will, father," I said with something approaching joy.

The relief of it was really enormous. Nora stuck out her tongue at me from behind his back, but I couldn't even be bothered retorting. I knew from the very moment that man opened his mouth that he was intelligent above the ordinary. When I had time to think, I saw how right I was. It only stood to reason that a fellow confessing after seven years would have more to tell than people that went every week. The crimes of a lifetime, exactly as he said. It was only what he expected, and the rest was the cackle of old women and girls with their talk of hell, the bishop, and the penitential psalms. That was all they knew. I started to make my examination of conscience, and barring the one bad business of my grandmother it didn't seem so bad.

The next time, the priest steered me into the confession box himself and left the shutter back the way I could see him get in and sit down at the further side of the grille from me.

35   "Well, now," he said, "what do they call you?"

"Jackie, father," said I.

"And what's a-trouble to you, Jackie?"

"Father," I said, feeling I might as well get it over while I had him in good humour, "I had it all arranged to kill my grandmother."

He seemed a bit shaken by that, all right, because he said nothing for quite a while.

40   "My goodness," he said at last, "that'd be a shocking thing to do. What put that into your head?"

"Father," I said, feeling very sorry for myself, "she's an awful woman."

"Is she?" he asked. "What way is she awful?"

"She takes porter, father," I said, knowing well from the way Mother talked of it that this was a mortal sin, and hoping it would make the priest take a more favourable view of my case.

"Oh, my!" he said, and I could see he was impressed.

45   "And snuff, father," said I.

"That's a bad case, sure enough, Jackie," he said.

"And she goes round in her bare feet, father," I went on in a rush of self-pity, "and she knows I don't like her, and she gives pennies to Nora and none to me, and my da sides with her and flakes me, and one night I was so heart-scalded I made up my mind I'd have to kill her."

"And what would you do with the body?" he asked with great interest.

"I was thinking I could chop that up and carry it away in a barrow I have," I said.

50   "Begor, Jackie," he said, "do you know you're a terrible child?"

"I know, father," I said, for I was just thinking the same thing myself. "I tried to kill Nora too with a bread-knife under the table, only I missed her."

"Is that the little girl that was beating you just now?" he asked.

"'Tis, father."

"Someone will go for her with a bread-knife one day, and he won't miss her," he said rather cryptically. "You must have great courage. Between ourselves, there's a lot of people I'd like to do the same to but I'd never have the nerve. Hanging is an awful death."

"Is it, father?" I asked with the deepest interest—I was always very keen on hanging. "Did you ever see a fellow hanged?"

"Dozens of them," he said solemnly. "And they all died roaring."

"Jay!" I said.

"Oh, a horrible death!" he said with great satisfaction. "Lots of fellows I saw killed their grandmothers too, but they all said 'twas never worth it."

He had me there for a full ten minutes talking, and then walked out the chapel yard with me. I was genuinely sorry to part with him, because he was the most entertaining character I'd ever met in the religious line. Outside, after the shadow of the church, the sunlight was like the roaring of waves on a beach; it dazzled me; and when the frozen silence melted and I heard the screech of trams on the road my heart soared. I knew now I wouldn't die in the night and come back, leaving marks on my mother's furniture. It would be a great worry to her, and the poor soul had enough.

Nora was sitting on the railing, waiting for me, and she put on a very sour puss when she saw the priest with me. She was made jealous because a priest had never come out of the church with her.

"Well," she asked coldly, after he left me, "what did he give you?"

"Three Hail Marys," I said.

"Three Hail Marys," she repeated incredulously. "You mustn't have told him anything."

"I told him everything," I said confidently.

"About Gran and all?"

"About Gran and all."

(All she wanted was to be able to go home and say I'd made a bad confession.)

"Did you tell him you went for me with the bread-knife?" she asked with a frown.

"I did to be sure."

"And he only gave you three Hail Marys?"

"That's all."

She slowly got down from the railing with a baffled air. Clearly, this was beyond her. As we mounted the steps back to the main road she looked at me suspiciously.

"What are you sucking?" she asked.

"Bullseyes."

"Was it the priest gave them to you?"

"'Twas."

"Lord God," she wailed bitterly, "some people have all the luck! 'Tis no advantage to anybody trying to be good. I might just as well be a sinner like you."

QUESTIONS

1. Describe Jackie as a narrator. What is the level of his language? To whom does he seem to be speaking or writing? What elements of language do you find in the story that seem characteristically Irish?

2. Describe Jackie's character. How old do you think he is at the time of the narration? Is there evidence that he has grown as a person since the time of the story's events? Do you think his attitudes have changed about his grandmother? His parents? His sister? Mrs. Ryan? The priest?

3. Is Jackie's confession a "good" one? Whose religion seems more appealing, Mrs. Ryan's or the priest's?

4. To what degree do the relationships within Jackie's family seem either ordinary or unusual?

5. "First Confession" is a funny story. What contributions are made to the humor by the situations? The language?

JOHN UPDIKE (1932–2009)

John Updike was born and reared in Pennsylvania during the Great Depression. His parents were diligent about his education, and in 1950 he received a scholarship for study at Harvard, graduating in 1954. He worked for The New Yorker *for two years before deciding to devote himself exclusively to his own writing, but since then he has remained a frequent contributor of stories and poems to that magazine. In 1959, he published his first story collection,* The Same Door, *and his first novel,* The Poorhouse Fair. *In 1960, with* Rabbit, Run, *he began his extensive Rabbit chronicles. In 1981 he received the Pulitzer Prize for* Rabbit Is Rich. *His collected poems were published in 1993, and he was continually productive in writing new stories and poems. He is considered one of the best of America's major writers of fiction and poetry.*

A & P° (1961)

In walks these three girls in nothing but bathing suits. I'm in the third checkout slot, with my back to the door, so I don't see them until they're over by the bread. The one that caught my eye first was the one in the plaid green two-piece. She was a chunky kid, with a good tan and a sweet broad soft-looking can with those two crescents of white just under it, where the sun never seems to hit, at the top of the backs of her legs. I stood there with my hand on a box of HiHo crackers trying to remember if I rang it up or not. I ring it up again and the customer starts giving me hell. She's one of these cash-register-watchers, a witch about fifty with rouge on her cheekbones and no eyebrows, and I know it made her day to trip me up. She'd been watching cash registers for fifty years and probably never seen a mistake before.

By the time I got her feathers smoothed and her goodies into a bag—she gives me a little snort in passing, if she'd been born at the right time they would have burned her over in Salem—by the time I get her on her way the girls had circled around the bread and were coming back, without a pushcart, back my way along the counters, in the aisle between the checkouts and the Special bins. They didn't even have shoes on. There was this chunky one, with the two-piece—it was bright green and the seams on the bra were still sharp and her belly was still pretty pale so I guessed she just got it (the suit)—there was this one, with one of those chubby berry-faces, the lips all bunched together under her nose, this one, and a tall one, with black hair that hadn't quite frizzed right, and one of these sunburns right across under the eyes, and a chin that was too long—you know, the kind of girl other girls think is very "striking" and "attractive" but never quite makes it, as they very well know, which is why they like her so much—and then the third one, that wasn't quite so tall. She was the queen. She kind of led them, the other two peeking around and making their shoulders round. She didn't look around, not this queen, she just walked straight on slowly, on these long white prima-donna legs. She came down a little hard on her heels, as if she didn't walk in her bare feet that much, putting down her heels and then letting the weight move along

---

°A & P: the Great Atlantic and Pacific Tea Company, a large grocery chain established in 1859 and still flourishing in 18 states, with more than 800 A & P stores in the United States and 200 in Canada.

to her toes as if she was testing the floor with every step, putting a little deliberate extra action into it. You never know for sure how girls' minds work (do you really think it's a mind in there or just a little buzz like a bee in a glass jar?) but you got the idea she had talked the other two into coming in here with her, and now she was showing them how to do it, walk slow and hold yourself straight.

She had on a kind of dirty-pink—beige, maybe, I don't know—bathing suit with a little nubble all over it and, what got me, the straps were down. They were off her shoulders looped loose around the cool tops of her arms, and I guess as a result the suit had slipped a little on her, so all around the top of the cloth there was this shining rim. If it hadn't been there you wouldn't have known there could have been anything whiter than those shoulders. With the straps pushed off, there was nothing between the top of the suit and the top of her head except just *her*, this clean bare plane of the top of her chest down from the shoulder bones like a dented sheet of metal tilted in the light. I mean, it was more than pretty.

She had sort of okay hair that the sun and salt had bleached, done up in a bun that was unraveling, and a kind of prim face. Walking into the A & P with your straps down, I suppose it's the only kind of face you *can* have. She held her head so high her neck, coming up out of those white shoulders, looked kind of stretched, but I didn't mind. The longer her neck was, the more of her there was.

She must have felt in the corner of her eye me and over my shoulder Stokesie in the second slot watching, but she didn't tip. Not this queen. She kept her eyes moving across the racks, and stopped, and turned so slow it made my stomach rub the inside of my apron, and buzzed to the other two, who kind of huddled against her for relief, and then they all three of them went up the cat-and-dog-food-breakfast-cereal-macaroni-rice-raisins-seasonings-spreads-spaghetti-soft-drinks-crackers-and-cookies aisle. From the third slot I look straight up this aisle to the meat counter, and I watched them all the way. The fat one with the tan sort of fumbled with the cookies, but on second thought she put the package back. The sheep pushing their carts down the aisle—the girls were walking against the usual traffic (not that we have one-way signs or anything)—were pretty hilarious. You could see them, when Queenie's white shoulders dawned on them, kind of jerk, or hop, or hiccup, but their eyes snapped back to their own baskets and on they pushed. I bet you could set off dynamite in an A & P and the people would by and large keep reaching and checking oatmeal off their lists and muttering "Let me see, there was a third thing, began with A, asparagus, no ah, yes, applesauce!" or whatever it is they do mutter. But there was no doubt, this jiggled them. A few houseslaves in pin curlers even looked around after pushing their carts past to make sure what they had seen was correct.

You know, it's one thing to have a girl in a bathing suit down on the beach, where what with the glare nobody can look at each other much anyway, and another thing in the cool of the A & P, under the fluorescent lights, against all those stacked packages, with her feet paddling along naked over our checkerboard green-and-cream rubber-tile floor.

"Oh Daddy," Stokesie said beside me. "I feel so faint."

"Darling," I said. "Hold me tight." Stokesie's married, with two babies chalked up on his fuselage already, but as far as I can tell that's the only difference. He's twenty-two, and I was nineteen this April.

"Is it done?" he asks, the responsible married man finding his voice. I forgot to say he thinks he's going to be manager some sunny day, maybe in 1990 when it's called the Great Alexandrov and Petrooshki° Tea Company or something.

°*Great Alexandrov and Petrooshki:* apparently a reference to the possibility that some day Russia might rule the United States.

10   What he meant was, our town is five miles from the beach, with a big summer colony out on the Point, but we're right in the middle of town, and the women generally put on a shirt or shorts or something before they get out of the car into the street. And anyway these are usually women with six children and varicose veins mapping their legs and nobody, including them, could care less. As I say, we're right in the middle of town, and if you stand at our front doors you can see two banks and the Congregational church and the newspaper store and three real-estate offices and about twenty-seven old freeloaders tearing up Central Street because the sewer broke again. It's not as if we're on the Cape,° we're north of Boston and there's people in this town haven't seen the ocean for twenty years.

The girls had reached the meat counter and were asking McMahon something. He pointed, they pointed, and they shuffled out of sight behind a pyramid of Diet Delight peaches. All that was left for us to see was old McMahon patting his mouth and looking after them sizing up their joints. Poor kids, I began to feel sorry for them, they couldn't help it.

Now here comes the sad part of the story, at least my family says it's sad, but I don't think it's so sad myself. The store's pretty empty, it being Thursday afternoon, so there was nothing much to do except lean on the register and wait for the girls to show up again. The whole store was like a pinball machine and I didn't know which tunnel they'd come out of. After a while they come around out of the far aisle, around the light bulbs, records at discount of the Caribbean Six or Tony Martin Sings or some such gunk you wonder they waste the wax on, sixpacks of candy bars, and plastic toys done up in cellophane that fall apart when a kid looks at them anyway. Around they come, Queenie still leading the way, and holding a little gray jar in her hand. Slots Three through Seven are unmanned and I could see her wondering between Stokes and me, but Stokesie with his usual luck draws an old party in baggy gray pants who stumbles up with four giant cans of pineapple juice (what do these bums *do* with all that pineapple juice? I've often asked myself) so the girls come to me. Queenie puts down the jar and I take it into my fingers icy cold. Kingfish Fancy Herring Snacks in Pure Sour Cream: 49¢. Now her hands are empty, not a ring or a bracelet, bare as God made them, and I wonder where the money's coming from. Still with that prim look she lifts a folded dollar bill out of the hollow at the center of her nubbed pink top. The jar went heavy in my hand. Really, I thought that was so cute.

Then everybody's luck begins to run out. Lengel comes in from haggling with a truck full of cabbages on the lot and is about to scuttle into that door marked MANAGER behind which he hides all day when the girls touch his eye. Lengel's pretty dreary, teaches Sunday school and the rest, but he doesn't miss that much. He comes over and says, "Girls, this isn't the beach."

Queenie blushes, though maybe it's just a brush of sunburn I was noticing for the first time, now that she was so close. "My mother asked me to pick up a jar of herring snacks." Her voice kind of startled me, the way voices do when you see the people first, coming out so flat and dumb yet kind of tony, too, the way it ticked over "pick up" and "snacks." All of a sudden I slid right down her voice into her living room. Her father and the other men were standing around in ice-cream coats and bow ties and the women were in sandals picking up herring snacks on toothpicks off a big glass plate and they were all holding drinks the color of water with olives and sprigs of mint in them. When my parents have somebody over they get lemonade and if it's a real racy affair Schlitz in tall glasses with "They'll Do It Every Time"° cartoons stenciled on.

15   "That's all right," Lengel said. "But this isn't the beach." His repeating this struck me as funny, as if it had just occurred to him, and he had been thinking all these years the A & P was a great big dune and he was the head lifeguard. He didn't like my smiling—as I say he doesn't miss much—but he concentrates on giving the girls that sad Sunday-school-superintendent stare.

°*the Cape*: Cape Cod, the southeastern area of Massachusetts, a place of many resorts and beaches.
° *"They'll Do It Every Time"*: syndicated daily and Sunday cartoon created by Jimmy Hatlo.

Queenie's blush is no sunburn now, and the plump one in plaid, that I liked better from the back—a really sweet can—pipes up, "We weren't doing any shopping. We just came in for the one thing."

"That makes no difference," Lengel tells her, and I could see from the way his eyes went that he hadn't noticed she was wearing a two-piece before. "We want you decently dressed when you come in here."

"We *are* decent," Queenie says suddenly, her lower lip pushing, getting sore now that she remembers her place, a place from which the crowd that runs the A & P must look pretty crummy. Fancy Herring Snacks flashed in her very blue eyes.

"Girls, I don't want to argue with you. After this come in here with your shoulders covered. It's our policy." He turns his back. That's policy for you. Policy is what the kingpins want. What the others want is juvenile delinquency.

All this while, the customers had been showing up with their carts but, you know, sheep, seeing a scene, they had all bunched up on Stokesie, who shook open a paper bag as gently as peeling a peach, not wanting to miss a word. I could feel in the silence everybody getting nervous, most of all Lengel, who asks me, "Sammy, have you rung up their purchase?"   20

I thought and said "No" but it wasn't about that I was thinking. I go through the punches, 4, 9, GROC, TOT—it's more complicated than you think, and after you do it often enough, it begins to make a little song, that you hear words to, in my case "Hello (*bing*) there, you (*gung*) hap-py *pee*-pul (*splat*)!"—the *splat* being the drawer flying out. I uncrease the bill, tenderly as you may imagine, it just having come from between the two smoothest scoops of vanilla I had ever known were there, and pass a half and a penny into her narrow pink palm, and nestle the herrings in a bag and twist its neck and hand it over, all the time thinking.

The girls, and who'd blame them, are in a hurry to get out, so I say "I quit" to Lengel quick enough for them to hear, hoping they'll stop and watch me, their unsuspected hero. They keep right on going, into the electric eye; the door flies open and they flicker across the lot to their car, Queenie and Plaid and Big Tall Goony-Goony (not that as raw material she was so bad), leaving me with Lengel and a kink in his eyebrow.

"Did you say something, Sammy?"

"I said I quit."

"I thought you did."

"You didn't have to embarrass them."   25

"It was they who were embarrassing us."

I started to say something that came out "Fiddle-de-doo." It's a saying of my grandmother's, and I know she would have been pleased.

"I don't think you know what you're saying," Lengel said.

"I know you don't," I said. "But I do." I pull the bow at the back of my apron and start shrugging it off my shoulders. A couple customers that had been heading for my slot begin to knock against each other, like scared pigs in a chute.   30

Lengel sighs and begins to look very patient and old and gray. He's been a friend of my parents for years. "Sammy, you don't want to do this to your Mom and Dad," he tells me. It's true, I don't. But it seems to me that once you begin a gesture it's fatal not to go through with it. I fold the apron, "Sammy" stitched in red on the pocket, and put it on the counter, and drop the bow tie on top of it. The bow tie is theirs, if you've ever wondered. "You'll feel this for the rest of your life," Lengel says, and I know that's true, too, but remembering how he made that pretty girl blush makes me so scrunchy inside I punch the No Sale tab and the machine whirs "pee-pul" and the drawer splats out. One advantage to this scene taking place in summer, I can follow this up with a clean exit, there's no fumbling around getting your coat and galoshes, I just saunter into the electric eye in my white shirt that my mother ironed the night before, and the door heaves itself open, and outside the sunshine is skating around on the asphalt.

I look around for my girls, but they're gone, of course. There wasn't anybody but some young married screaming with her children about some candy they didn't get by the door of a powder-blue Falcon° station wagon. Looking back in the big windows, over the bags of peat moss and aluminum lawn furniture stacked on the pavement, I could see Lengel in my place in the slot, checking the sheep through. His face was dark gray and his back stiff, as if he'd just had an injection of iron, and my stomach kind of fell as I felt how hard the world was going to be to me hereafter.

QUESTIONS

1. From Sammy's language, what do you learn about his view of himself? About his educational and class level? The first sentence, for example, is grammatically incorrect in standard English but not uncommon in colloquial English. Point out and explain similar passages.

2. Consider the first eleven paragraphs as exposition, in which you learn about the location, the issues, and the participants in the story's conflict. Is there anything inessential in this section? Do you learn enough to understand the story? How might someone other than Sammy present the material?

3. How do you learn that Sammy is an experienced "girl watcher"? What does *he think* he thinks about most girls? To what degree is this estimate inconsistent with what he finally does after the girls leave?

4. Why does Sammy say "I quit" so abruptly? What does he mean when he says that the world is going to be hard to him after his experience at the A & P?

WRITING ABOUT TONE AND STYLE

The task of writing about tone and style is to identify attitudes that you find in the work and then to explain how attitudes are made obvious by the author's style. How do words describing characters, scenes, thoughts, and actions indicate attitude? In Poe's "The Masque of the Red Death" (Chapter 9), for example, do the descriptions of the dimly lit rooms evoke fear or tension, or do they seem exaggerated? Depending on the story, your devising and answering such questions will help you understand an author's control over tone.

Questions for Discovering Ideas

- Use a dictionary to discover the meaning of any words you do not immediately know. Are there any unusual words? Any especially difficult or uncommon ones? Do any of the words distract you as you read?
- How strongly do you respond to the story? What words bring out your interest, concern, indignation, fearfulness, anguish, amusement, or sense of affirmation?
- Does the diction seem unusual or noteworthy, such as words in dialect, polysyllabic words, or foreign words or phrases that the author assumes you know? Are there any especially connotative or emotive words? What do these words suggest concerning the author's apparent assumptions about readers?

°*Falcon*: small car that had recently been introduced by the Ford Motor Company.

- Can you easily visualize and imagine the situations described by the words? If you find it easy, or hard, to what degree does your success or difficulty stem from the level of diction?
- For passages describing action, how vivid are the words? How do they help you picture the action? How do they hold your attention?
- For passages describing exterior or interior scenes, how specific are the words? How much detail does the writer provide? Should there be more or fewer words? How vivid are the descriptions? How successfully does the author locate scenes spatially? How many words are devoted to colors, shapes, sizes, and so on? What is the effect of such passages?
- For passages of dialogue, what does the level of speech indicate about the characters? How do a person's speeches help to establish her or his character? For what purposes does the author use formal or informal diction? How much slang (low or informal language) do you find? Why is it there? How does dialogue shape your responses to the characters and to the actions?
- What role does the narrator/speaker play in your attitudes toward the story material? Does the speaker seem intelligent/stupid, friendly/unfriendly, sane/insane, or idealistic/pragmatic?
- What verbal irony do you find in the story? How is the irony connected to philosophies of marriage, family, society, politics, religion, or morality? How do you think you are expected to respond to the irony?
- Did anything in the story make you laugh? What placement of words brought out the humor? Explain how the word arrangement caused your laughter.

Strategies for Organizing Ideas

Begin with a careful reading, noting particularly those elements of language that convey attitudes. How does the author establish the dominant moods of the story (e.g., the humor of "First Confession," the tension in "Hills Like White Elephants")? Some possibilities are the use or misuse of language, the exposé of a pretentious speaker, the use of exact and specific descriptions, the isolation of a major character, the failure of plans, and the continuance of na-iveté in a disillusioned world.

Here are some of the things to discuss.

1. *How is the work's tone affected by situation, characters, action, and audience?* Does the speaker directly address any person or group? What attitude is expressed (love, respect, condescension, confidentiality, confidence, etc.)? What is the basic situation in the story? Do you find instances of verbal irony? What do these show (optimism or pessimism, for example)? How is the situation of the story controlled to shape your responses? That is, can actions, situations, or characters be seen as expressions of attitude, or as embodiments of certain favorable or unfavorable ideas or positions? What sort of person is the narrator or persona? Why does the narrator speak exactly as he or she does? How is the narrator's character manipulated to show apparent authorial attitude and to elicit reader response? Does the story promote respect, admiration, dislike, or other feelings about character or situation? How?

2. *What do diction and descriptions contribute to the tone?* Your concern here is not to analyze descriptions or diction for themselves alone, but to relate these matters to attitude. *For descriptions*: Do descriptions of natural scenery and conditions (snowstorms, cold, rain, ice, intense sunlight) complement or oppose the circumstances of the characters? Are there any systematic references to colors, sounds, or noises that collectively reflect an attitude? *For diction*: Do connotative meanings of words control response in any way? Does the diction require readers to have a large or technical vocabulary? Do speech patterns or the use of dialect evoke attitudes about speakers or their condition of life? Is the level of diction formal, middle, or informal? Do you find any substandard or slang expressions? What effect do these create? Are there unusual or particularly noteworthy expressions? If so, what attitudes do these show?

3. *To what degree does the story contain humor?* Is the story funny? How funny, how intense? How is the humor achieved? How does the language bring out the incongruity of funny situations? Are the objects of laughter still respected or even loved even though the story's treatment of them causes amusement?

4. *How does the expression of ideas shape the work's tone?* Are any ideas advocated, defended mildly, or attacked? How does the author clarify his or her attitude toward these ideas—directly, by statement, or indirectly, through understatement, overstatement, or a character's speeches? In what ways does the story assume agreement between author and readers? What common religious views can you find? What political views, moral and behavioral standards, and so on?

In concluding, first summarize your main points and then go on to definitions, explanations, or afterthoughts, together with ideas reinforcing earlier points. To what extent has your analysis increased or reinforced your appreciation of the author's technique? Does the passage take on added importance as a result of your study? Is there anything else in the work comparable to the content, words, or ideas you have discussed in the passage?

Numbering Your Passage for Easy Reference

To focus on specifics of style and tone, the assignment visualized here is to analyze a passage—either short or long—from a story. After you have selected a passage, include a copy at the beginning of your essay, as in the example. For your reader's convenience, number the sentences in the passage, and use these numbers when you refer to them. To focus your essay, either single out one aspect of style and tone, or discuss everything, depending on the length of the assignment. Be sure to consider relationships that you can discover between tone and *levels of diction, specific and general words, concrete and abstract words, denotation and connotation, irony, and humor*.

Illustrative Student Essay

Although underlined sentences are not recommended by MLA style, they are used in this illustrative essay as teaching tools to emphasize the central idea, thesis sentence, and topic sentences.

Elizabeth Torres

Professor Moorhouse

English 24

15 December 2014

Frank O'Connor's Control of Tone and Style in "First Confession"°

> [1] Nora's turn came, and I heard the sound of something slamming, and then her voice as if butter wouldn't melt in her mouth, and then another slam, and out she came. [2] God, the hypocrisy of women! [3] Her eyes were lowered, her head was bowed, and her hands were joined very low down on her stomach, and she walked up the aisle to the side altar looking like a saint. [4] You never saw such an exhibition of devotion, and I remembered the devilish malice with which she had tormented me all the way from our door, and wondered were all religious people like that, really. [5] It was my turn now. [6] With the fear of damnation in my soul I went in, and the confessional door closed of itself behind me (317).

This paragraph from O'Connor's "First Confession" appears midway in   [1]
the story. It is transitional, coming between Jackie's "heartscalded" memories
of family troubles and his happier memory of the confession itself. Though
mainly narrative, the passage is punctuated by Jackie's recollections of disgust
with his sister and fear of eternal punishment for his childhood "sins." It is the
controlled contrast of these attitudes that creates the humor of the passage.* In
all respects—brevity, word level, concreteness, and grammatical control—the
passage is typical of the story's humor.†

°**This story appears on pages 315–319.**
***Central idea.**
†**Thesis sentence.**

Torres 2

[2]   The actions and responses of the paragraph are described briefly and accurately. The first four sentences convey Jackie's exaggerated reactions to Nora's confession. Sentence 1 describes his recollections of her voice in the confessional, and the tone of sentence 3 makes his judgment clear about the hypocrisy of her pious appearance when she leaves for the altar. Each of these descriptive sentences is followed by Jackie's angry reactions, at which readers smile, at least, if they do not laugh. This depth of feeling is transformed to "fear of damnation" at the beginning of sentence 6, which describes Jackie's own entry into the confessional, with the closing door suggesting that he is being shut off from the world and thrown into hell. In other words, the paragraph succinctly presents the sounds, reactions, sights, and confusion of the scene itself, all of which furnish readers with a brief and comic drama.

[3]   The humorous action of the passage is augmented by O'Connor's neutral level of diction, which enables readers to concentrate fully on Jackie's responses. Jackie is recalling an unpleasant childhood memory, and the neutral, middle diction enables readers both to sympathize with him and to be amused by him. His words are neither unusual nor difficult. What could be more ordinary, for example, than "butter," "slam," "out," "hands," "joined," "low," "people," and "closed"? Even Jackie's moral and religious words fall within the vocabulary of ordinary discussions about sin and punishment: "hypocrisy," "exhibition," "devilish," "malice," "tormented," and "damnation." In the passage, therefore, the diction accurately conveys Jackie's vision of the oppressive religious forces which he dislikes, and which he also exaggerates. Readers follow these words easily and with amusement.

[4]   Additionally, the words of the paragraph are appropriate to Jackie's boyhood anger because they are specific and concrete. When he tells about Nora going into the confessional, he says specifically that he "heard the sound of something slamming," followed by the sound of Nora's "voice," "another slam," and then her appearance as "she came" out of the confessional. Equally specific, and equally comic, is his description of Nora's appearance as she leaves. Readers can easily visualize her "bowed" head, her "lowered" eyes, and her prayerful hands, and are amused by the scene just as Jackie, as a child, was annoyed by it. In addition to these specific descriptions, sentences 2 and 4

contain Jackie's angry responses, which also provoke amusement. Sentence 4
presents the greater number of connotative abstractions—first the "exhibition
of devotion," and second the "devilish malice with which she had tormented
me." But these define Jackie's childhood conclusions about his sister, not his
adult ones, and their incongruity furnishes readers with a realistic basis for
laughter.

    A major element contributing to Jackie's remembrance of his boyhood   [5]
attitudes is the control over grammar that O'Connor gives to him. At the time
of the narrative Jackie is presumably no longer angry, even though as a child
he felt misunderstood and unfairly treated. He therefore does not need to recall
his story in angry outbursts, despite his exclamation about the "hypocrisy of
women," but rather he presents details with grammatical correctness. The very
first sentence, for example, contains three parallel grammatical direct objects
("sound," "voice," "slam"), thereby using a minimal number of words while
still detailing the major sounds of Nora's confession. The grammar of the third
sentence illustrates the swiftness and sparseness of O'Connor's (and Jackie's)
narrative style. The first three parallel clauses are each made up of four words
("her eyes were lowered," "her head was bowed," and "her hands were joined").
These clauses give Jackie the opportunity to introduce his sarcastic and amusing
phrase "looking like a saint" at the end to express his disgust over his sister's
"hypocrisy." This control shapes the developing comedy of the paragraph.

    In all respects, the passage shows the right use of words and exactly   [6]
the right tone. Jackie's accurate descriptions are mixed with his expressions
of childhood emotions—all important aspects of O'Connor's good humor.
In retrospect, Jackie's anger and disgust were unnecessary, but they were
important to him as a child—so much so that his exaggerations make him
the center of the story's comedy. The words that O'Connor skillfully puts
in Jackie's mouth (or on his page) enable readers to share this particular
experience of a first confession but to do so while smiling. Jackie's bittersweet
memories are successfully rendered and made comic through O'Connor's
control over style and tone.

Torres 4

Work Cited

O'Connor, Frank. "First Confession." *Literature: An Introduction to Reading and Writing, Compact.* Ed. Edgar V. Roberts and Robert Zweig. 6th ed. New York: Pearson, 2015. 315–19. Print.

Commentary on the Essay

Paragraph 1 demonstrates how a passage being studied may be related to the entire work of which it is a part. The central idea connects the story's comic tone to O'Connor's control over situation and diction. Throughout the essay, the connection of style and humor are emphasized. The thesis sentence presents four topics that the essay will develop. Any one of these topics, if necessary, could also be treated separately.

In the body of the essay, the writer stresses the way O'Connor creates the story's tone by the careful manipulation of words and expressions. Paragraph 2 indicates O'Connor's verbal economy in describing the actions and reactions of the passage. Paragraph 3 deals with the level of diction, noting that the words are appropriate both to the action and to Jackie's anger when recollecting it. In paragraph 4 the topic is O'Connor's use of specific and concrete diction, a quality that makes for easy visualization of the details. This paragraph also considers the small number of abstract and general words that appear in O'Connor's sentences 2 and 4.

Paragraph 5 connects O'Connor's grammatical control with the speaker's recollected boyhood anger. Examples of parallelism are three direct objects in sentence 1 and the first three clauses in sentence 3. Paragraph 6, the conclusion of the essay, summarizes the means by which O'Connor uses style to create the comedy of Jackie and his recollected feelings.

Writing Topics About Tone and Style

Writing Paragraphs

1. In "First Confession" the adult narrator is describing events that happened to him as a child. Write a paragraph in which you consider the following questions. To what degree has this narrator, Jackie, separated himself from his childish emotions? What does he say that might be considered residual childhood responses? What effect, if any, do such comments create? For an additional dimension to this topic you might compare Jackie as a narrator with the unnamed narrator of Joyce's "Araby" (Chapter 4).

2. In "Hills Like White Elephants" (this chapter) how does Hemingway's style shape your responses to the two main characters? How much description do you find in the story? How much dialogue? Write a paragraph in which you consider these questions.

3. Write a paragraph in which you show how Chopin conveys attitudes toward the marital role of women and men in "The Story of an Hour" (this chapter). Consider Louise's reactions to the news that her husband has been killed, and also consider Josephine's responses.

Writing Essays

1. Gilman's "The Yellow Wallpaper" (Chapter 10) probes the psychological makeup of the major characters. Write an essay about the nature and effect of the language of character depiction in these stories.

2. Consider a short story in which the narrator is the central character, for example, "The Lesson" (Chapter 8), "First Confession" (this chapter), and "A & P" (this chapter). Write an essay showing how the language of the narrator affects your attitudes toward him or her (that is, your sympathy for the narrator, your interest in the narrative, your feelings toward the other characters and what they do). Be sure to emphasize the relationship between the language of the narrators and the attitudes they demonstrate and elicit.

3. In "Barn Burning" (Chapter 10), how does Faulkner make it plain that Sarty's father and brother do not trust Sarty? Why do they have this attitude? On what evidence is their distrust confirmed? Write an essay in which you argue that their attitudes make Sarty a likeable (or not likeable) character.

Creative Writing Assignment

1. Write two brief character sketches, or a description of an action, to be included in a longer story. Make the first favorable, and the second negative. Analyze your word choices in the contrasting accounts: What kinds of words do you select, and on what principles do you select them? What kinds of words might you select if you wanted to create a neutral account? On the basis of your answers, what can you conclude about the development of a fiction writer's style?

Library Assignment

1. In your school library, or online, consult the most recent copy of the *MLA International Bibliography of Books and Articles on the Modern Languages and Literatures*, and make a short list of books and articles on Kate Chopin, Ernest Hemingway, John Updike, Frank O'Connor, or Dagoberto Gilb (just one, not all). Consult at least two of the works, and with these, together with your own insights, write a short description of the writer's irony (comic or serious) and social criticism.

Chapter 7
Symbolism and Allegory: Keys to Extended Meaning

AFTER STUDYING THIS MATERIAL, YOU SHOULD BE ABLE TO DO THE FOLLOWING:

- Recognize and explain cultural and contextual symbolism
- Explore the nature and function of literary symbolism
- Explain the meanings of fables, parables, and myths
- Identify and interpret literary allusions
- Analyze how symbolism and allegory affect a work's meaning and impact on readers

Symbolism and **allegory,** like metaphors and similes (see Chapter 14) are modes that expand meaning. They are literary devices developed from the connections that real-life people make between their own existence and particular objects, places, or occurrences, through either experience or reading: A young woman might recall a number of childhood difficulties with her mother, but realize that her mother acted out of love. A college student might remember the quiet satisfaction of returning home after a turbulent time spent away at a distant university. A war veteran might recall the crushing burdens that he and his fellow soldiers carried in combat. An elderly woman on her deathbed might consider the value of her life even though she sustained a crushing disappointment when she was young. The significance of details like these can be meaningful not just at a single moment but also throughout an entire lifetime. Merely bringing them to mind or speaking about them unlocks their meanings, implications, and consequences. It is as though the reference alone can be the equivalent of pages of explanation and analysis.

From this principle, both symbolism and allegory are derived. By highlighting details as *symbols*, and stories or parts of stories as *allegories*, writers expand their meaning while keeping their works within reasonable lengths.

Symbolism

The words **symbol** and **symbolism** are derived from the Greek word meaning "to throw together" (*syn*, "together," and *ballein*, "to throw"). A symbol creates a direct meaningful equation between (1) a specific object, scene, character, or action and (2) ideas, values, persons, or ways of life. In effect, a symbol is a *substitute* for the elements being signified, much as the flag stands for the ideals of the nation.

When we first encounter a symbol in a story (also in poems and plays), it may seem to carry no more weight than its surface or obvious meaning. It can be a description of a character, an object, a place, an action, or a situation, and it may function normally and usefully in this capacity. What makes a symbol symbolic, however, is its capacity to signify additional levels of meaning—major ideas, simple or complex emotions, or philosophical or religious qualities or values. There are two types of symbols—*cultural* and *contextual*.

Cultural Symbols Are Derived from Our Cultural and Historical Heritage

Many symbols are *generally or universally* recognized and are therefore **cultural** (also called **universal**). They embody ideas and emotions that writers and readers share as heirs of the same historical and cultural tradition. When using cultural symbols, a writer assumes that readers already know what the symbols represent. An example is the character Sisyphus of ancient Greek myth. As a punishment for trying to overcome death not just once but twice, Sisyphus is doomed by the underworld gods to roll a large boulder up a high hill forever. Just as he gets the boulder to the top, it rolls down, and then he is fated to roll it up again—and again—and again—because the boulder always rolls back. The plight of Sisyphus has been interpreted as a symbol of the human condition: In spite of constant struggle, a person rarely if ever completes anything. Work must always be done over and over from day to day and from generation to generation, and the same problems confront humanity throughout all time. Because of such fruitless effort, life seems to have little or no meaning. Nevertheless, there is hope: People who confront their tasks, as Sisyphus does, stay involved and active, and their tasks make their lives meaningful. A writer referring to Sisyphus would expect us to understand that this ancient mythological figure symbolizes these conditions.

Similarly, ordinary water, because living creatures cannot live without it, is recognized as a symbol of life. It has this meaning in the ceremony of baptism, and it conveys this meaning and dimension in a variety of literary contexts. Thus, a spouting fountain might symbolize optimism (as upwelling, bubbling life), and a stagnant pool might symbolize the pollution and decline of life. Water is also a universal symbol of sexuality, and its condition or state can symbolize various romantic relationships. For instance, stories in which lovers meet near a turbulent stream, a roaring waterfall, a mud puddle, a beach with high breakers, a stormy sea, a calm lake, or a wide and gently flowing river symbolically represent love relationships that range from uncertainty to serenity.

Contextual Symbols Are Symbolic Only in Individual Works

Objects and descriptions that are not universal symbols can be symbols *only if they are made so within individual works.* These are **contextual, private,** or **authorial symbols.** Unlike cultural symbols, contextual symbols derive their meanings from the context and circumstances of individual works. For example, the standing clock in Poe's "The Masque of the Red Death" (Chapter 9) is a large timepiece that in the story symbolizes not only the passage of time but also the dark forces of death. Similarly, Elisa's chrysanthemums in Steinbeck's "The Chrysanthemums" (this chapter) seem at first nothing more than prized flowers. As the story progresses, however, they gain symbolic significance. The traveling tinsmith's apparent interest in them is the wedge he uses to coax a small mending job from Elisa. Her description of the care needed in planting and tending them suggests that they symbolize her kindness, love, orderliness, femininity, and motherliness.

Like Poe's clock, Steinbeck's chrysanthemums are a major contextual symbol. But there is not necessarily any carryover of symbolic meaning. In other stories, clocks and flowers are not symbolic unless the authors of these stories deliberately give them a symbolic charge. Further, if they are symbolic, they can be given different meanings than in the Poe and Steinbeck stories.

Determine What Is Symbolic (and Not Symbolic)

In determining whether a particular object, action, or character is a symbol, you need to judge the importance that the author gives to it. If the element is prominent and also maintains a constancy of meaning, you can justify interpreting it as a symbol. In Coleman's "Unfinished Masterpieces" (this chapter), we are told about how as a child, Dora Johns made things "out of mud." These little figures—"dolls and toys, flying birds and trotting horses, frisking dogs and playing kittens"—are remembered by the narrator as "drying in the sun," but they are intensely fragile. When wet, their shapes can be destroyed by a touch, and when dry they can fall and break. Although these figures are made of ordinary mud, they symbolize the suppressing of talent among minorities. It is the importance that Coleman gives to Dora's shaped figures that invests them with symbolic meaning. Importance is therefore a key to the determination of symbolism, as at the end of Welty's "A Worn Path" (Chapter 5). Phoenix, Welty's major character, plans to spend all her money—ten cents—for a toy windmill for her sick grandson. Readers will note that the windmill is small and fragile, like Phoenix's life and that of her grandson, but that she wants to give the boy a little happiness despite their poor and hopeless circumstances. For these reasons the windmill is a contextual or authorial symbol of Phoenix's loving character, bravery, generous nature, and touching existence.

Allegory

An **allegory** is like a symbol because it transfers and broadens meaning. The term is derived from the Greek word *allegorein* (from *allos*, "other," and *agoreuein*, "to speak in public"), which means "to say something beyond what is commonly understood." Allegory, however, is more sustained than symbolism. An allegory is to a symbol as a motion picture is to a still picture. In form, an allegory is a complete and self-sufficient narrative, but it also signifies another series of conditions or events. Although some stories are allegories from beginning to end, many stories that are not allegories nevertheless may contain brief sections or episodes that are *allegorical*. Allegories are often concerned with morality and especially with religion, but we may also find political and social allegories. To the degree that literary works are true not only because of the lives of their main characters but also because of life generally, we might maintain that much literature may be considered allegorical even though the authors did not plan their works as allegories.

Understand the Applications and Meaning of Allegory

Allegories and the allegorical method are more than literary exercises. Without question, readers and listeners learn and memorize stories and tales more easily than moral lessons, and therefore allegory is a favorite method of teaching morality. In addition, thought and expression have not always been free and safe, as we hope they are today in the United States. At times in other nations, under sometimes repressive political systems, the threat of censorship and the danger of political or economic reprisal have prompted authors to express their views indirectly in the form of allegory rather than to name names and write openly, thereby risking political persecution, accusations of libel, or even bodily harm. Hence, the double meanings of many allegories are based not just in the literary form but also in the reality of circumstances in our difficult world.

In studying allegory, determine whether all or part of a work can have an extended, allegorical meaning. The popularity of George Lucas's film *Star Wars* and its sequels and also its "prequels," for example, is attributable at least partly to its being an allegory about the conflict between good and evil. Obi Wan Kenobi (intelligence) assists Luke Skywalker (heroism, boldness) and instructs him in "the Force" (moral or religious faith). Thus armed and guided, Skywalker opposes the powers of Darth Vader (evil) to rescue Princess Leia (purity and goodness) with the aid of the latest spaceships and weaponry (technology). The story has produced a set of popular adventure films, accompanied by dramatic music and ingenious visual and sound effects. With the obvious allegorical overtones, however, it stands for any person's quest for self-fulfillment.

To apply a part of the allegory more specifically, consider that for a time the evil Vader imprisons Skywalker and that Skywalker must exert all his skill and strength to get free and overcome Vader. In the allegorical application of the episode, this imprisonment may be taken to signify those moments of doubt, discouragement, and depression that people experience while trying to better themselves through education, work, self-improvement, friendship, marriage, and so on.

Almost from the beginning of recorded literature, similar heroic deeds have been represented in allegorical forms. From ancient Greece, the allegorical hero Jason sails the *Argo* to distant lands to gain the Golden Fleece (those who take risks are rewarded). From Anglo-Saxon England, the hero Beowulf saves King Hrothgar's throne by killing the monster Grendel and his even more monstrous mother (victory comes to those who rely on the forces of good). From seventeenth-century England, Bunyan's *The Pilgrim's Progress* tells how the hero Christian overcomes difficulties and temptations while traveling from this world to the next (belief, perseverance, and resistance to temptation save the faithful). As long as the parallel connections are close and consistent, such as those mentioned here, an allegorical interpretation is valid.

Fable, Parable, and Myth

Closely related to symbolism and allegory in the ability to extend and expand meaning are three additional forms—*fable, parable,* and *myth*.

A Fable Is a Short Tale with a Pointed Moral

The **fable** (from the Latin word *fabula*, a story or narration) is an old, brief, and popular form. Often but not always, fables are about animals that possess human traits (such fables are called **beast fables**). Past collectors and editors of fables have attached "morals" or explanations to the brief stories, as is the case with Aesop, the most enduringly popular of fable writers. Tradition has it that Aesop was a slave who composed fables in ancient Greece. His fable "The Fox and the Grapes" (this chapter) signifies the trait of belittling things we cannot have. Other popular contributions to the fable tradition include Walt Disney's Mickey Mouse, and Wile E. Coyote, Road Runner, and Bugs Bunny of Warner Brothers. The adjective *fabulous* refers to the collective body of fables of all sorts, even though the word is often overused as little more than a routine term of approval.

A Parable Is a Short Narrative Illustrating a Religious Concept

A **parable** (from the Greek word *parabolé*, a "setting beside" or comparison) is a short, simple story with a moral or religious thrust. Parables are most often associated with Jesus, who used them to embody unique religious insights and truths. For example, his parables "The Prodigal Son" (this chapter) and "The Good Samaritan," as recorded by Luke, are interpreted to show God's understanding, forgiveness, concern, and love.

A Myth Is a Tale with Social, Political, Religious, or Philosophical Meanings

A **myth** (from the Greek word *muthos*, a "story" or "plot") is a traditional story that reflects and embodies the religious, philosophical, and cultural values of the civilization in which it is composed. Usually the central figures of mythical stories are heroes, gods, and demigods, such as the ancient figures Aeneas, Zeus, Hera, Prometheus, Athena, Dionysus, Sisyphus, Oedipus, Atalanta, Hercules, and Venus. Most myths are of course fictional, but some are based in historical truth. They are by no means confined to the past, for the word *myth* can also refer to beliefs and ideas that people today hold collectively, such as the concept of never-ending economic growth or the idea that the earth can endlessly sustain all human exploitation and activities with no adverse effects. Sometimes the words *myth* and *mythical* are used with the meaning "fanciful" or "untrue." Such detraction is misleading because the truths of mythology are not to be found literally in the myths themselves but rather in their symbolic and allegorical interpretations.

Allusion in Symbolism and Allegory

Cultural or universal symbols and allegories often involve **allusions** to other works from our cultural heritage, such as the Bible, ancient history and literature, and works of the British and American traditions. Sometimes understanding a story may require knowledge of history and current politics.

If the meaning of a symbol is not immediately clear to you, you will need a dictionary or other reference work. The scope of your college dictionary will surprise you. If you cannot find an entry there, however, try one of the major print or online encyclopedias, or ask your reference librarian, who can direct you to helpful books or online references. A few excellent guides, which are frequently reprinted, are *The Oxford Companion to Classical Literature* (ed. M. C. Howatson and Ian Chilvers); *The Oxford Companion to English Literature* (ed. Margaret Drabble); *Benét's Reader's Encyclopedia*, 5th edition; Timothy Gantz's *Early Greek Myth: A Guide to Literary and Artistic Sources*; Barry B. Powell's *Classical Myth* (with translations by Herbert M. Howe); and Richmond Y. Hathorn's *Greek Mythology*.

Useful aids in finding biblical references are *Cruden's Complete Concordance*, which in various editions has been a reliable guide since 1737 (yes, 1737), and *Strong's Exhaustive Concordance of the Bible*, which has been revised and expanded regularly—and renamed (as *The Strongest Strong's Exhaustive Concordance of the Bible*)—since it was first published in 1890. These concordances list all the major words used in the Bible (usually the King James Version), so you can easily locate the chapter and verse of any and all biblical passages. If you still have trouble after using sources like these, be sure to see your instructor.

Stories for Study

Aesop . . . . The Fox and the Grapes, 337
Anonymous . . . . The Myth of Atalanta, 338
Anita Scott Coleman . . . . Unfinished Masterpieces, 339
Nathaniel Hawthorne . . . . Young Goodman Brown, 342
Luke . . . . The Parable of the Prodigal Son, 350
Katherine Anne Porter . . . . The Jilting of Granny Weatherall, 352
John Steinbeck . . . . The Chrysanthemums, 358

AESOP (c. 620–560 BCE)

Not much is known about the ancient fabulist Aesop. According to tradition, he was a freed slave who lived from about 620 to 560 BCE. Aristotle claimed that he had been a public defender, but there is no other evidence that he existed at all. In fact, versions of some of the fables were known a millennium before his time. Aesop might therefore be considered as much a collector as a creator of fables.

 ### The Fox and the Grapes (c. 6th century BCE)

From a painting by Diego Velasquez (1599–1660)

A hungry Fox came into a vineyard where there hung delicious clusters of ripe Grapes; his mouth watered to be at them; but they were nailed up to a trellis so high, that with all his springing and leaping he could not reach a single bunch. At last, growing tired and disappointed, "Let who will take them!" says he, "they are but green and sour; so I'll e'en let them alone."

QUESTIONS

1. How much do you learn about the character of the fox? How are his characteristics related to the moral or message of the fable?
2. What is the conflict in the fable? What is the resolution?
3. In your own words, explain the meaning of the fable. Is the "sour grapes" explanation a satisfactory excuse, or is it a rationalization for failure?
4. From your reading of "The Fox and the Grapes," explain the characteristics of the fable as a type of literature.

ANONYMOUS (ANCIENT WRITER)

The story of Atalanta is an anonymous myth that was known throughout both the ancient Greek and Roman worlds. Because communication in ancient times was uncertain, there were variations in some of the details of the story, such as the names of Atalanta's father and her suitors. However, there was general agreement about the details of her story, which was told by many different writers, such as Apollodorus, Aelian, and Pacuvius. The best-known ancient text of the story appears in Ovid's Metamorphoses. *The story included here is slightly adapted from the brief but comprehensive version by Richmond Y. Hathorn (Greek Mythology, 1977).*

The Myth of Atalanta (5th–1st century BCE)

There was once a man from Arcadia, in southern Greece, who hoped very much for a son, and when his wife gave birth to a daughter, he abandoned the child in the woods. A she-bear that lived there suckled the baby, until some hunters chanced on the child and reared it, calling it Atalanta [i.e., "the invincible one"]. Atalanta grew up to be a true daughter of the wilderness, an incomparable hunter, being instructed by the Goddess of the Hunt, Artemis, herself. Atalanta was a runner who could outrace any man, and a skillful wrestler, on one occasion defeating the hero Peleus at Pelias' funeral games. She tried also to go on the expedition with the Argonauts to recover the Golden Fleece, but she was turned away by Jason, who was afraid of the trouble a beautiful young woman might cause in a crew of young men.

Then Atalanta took part in the hunting of the Calydonian Boar, falling in love with the Calydonian Prince Meleager and being loved in return. But as this love brought about Meleager's death and as Atalanta was already inclined toward celibacy because of her allegiance to Artemis, she resolved on leading a solitary manless life henceforth, especially because the oracle at Delphi warned her that marriage would cause her whole nature to be changed. So when she gave birth to Meleager's child on her way back from Calydon to Arcadia, she kept it a secret and exposed the baby boy on Mount Parthenion. This child, called Parthenopaeous, was found by the same shepherds who had found and reared Telephus (the son of Hercules and the Princess Auge), and he grew up to be Telephus' companion in early adventures. Eventually Parthenopaeous met his death in the war of the Seven against Thebes.

Meanwhile Atalanta had returned to her old hunting haunts, fighting off attacks of satyrs and discouraging the proposals of mortal men by stipulating that each suitor should compete with her in a race, in which she would be armed with a spear. The condition was that if she overtook her opponent she might stab him to death. And in this way she had disposed of three suitors, cutting off their heads and displaying them beside the racecourse.

There was a young Arcadian named Milanion, who hated women as much as Atalanta hated men, and who was as fond of the chase as she was. He encountered Atalanta frequently during his hunts, and imperceptibly he fell in love with her. More and more he put himself in her way, until he was faithfully following her around, carrying her hunting-nets and enduring her endless disdain. Once when a centaur, Hylaeus, whom Atalanta had rejected, attacked her in anger, Milanion intervened, receiving the blows of the centaur's club and even being wounded by one of the centaur's arrows while protecting Atalanta with his body. Atalanta killed the man-beast, and then nursed the injured Milanion back to health, her feeling for him growing warmer all the while.

Still there was no way of winning Atalanta short of defeating her in the footrace; so in spite of all her discouragements Milanion challenged her. But before the day of the race he prayed to Aphrodite, the Goddess of Love, for aid, and the Goddess plucked three golden apples from the Garden of the Hesperides and instructed him in their use. When the race had begun and Atalanta was drawing near, Milanion dropped one golden apple and the young woman stopped to pick it up. Again she drew near, and again he dropped an apple, the Goddess causing them to weigh heavily in Atalanta's bosom. So when the third apple was dropped and picked up, Milanion was able to reach the goal unscathed and to claim Atalanta as his bride.

But in the flush of his victory and her willing defeat they both forgot to give thanks to Aphrodite. The Goddess punished them by inflicting a rage of lust on both of them, so that they lost all control of themselves. Passing by a sanctuary of Cybele, the Great Mother of Gods, they fell immediately to lovemaking in the holy grotto near the holy temple. They behaved with such abandon that the very statues averted their eyes. The Great Mother was incensed and thought of killing them at once, but instead she changed Milanion into a Lion and Atalanta into a lioness and made them the team that draws her chariot.

QUESTIONS

1. What abilities does Atalanta have? How does she try to preserve her independence?
2. Why does Atalanta vow to shun men? What causes her to change her mind? What finally happens to her?
3. Consider the symbolic significance of Atalanta's name, the golden apples, the chopping off of the heads of slow running suitors, the father's abandonment of Atalanta, the exposure of the infant Parthenopaeus, the battle with the centaur, the way in which Atalanta loses the race, and the lovemaking in the holy grotto of the Great Mother of Gods.

ANITA SCOTT COLEMAN (1890–1960)

Anita Scott Coleman, a writer of stories, poems, and essays, was born in Mexico and educated in New Mexico. Her mother had been a slave who had been bought out of slavery by her father. She published mainly in magazines. "Unfinished Masterpieces," for example, was published in Crisis: A Record of the Darker Races, *the magazine begun in 1910 that heralded the development of the Harlem Renaissance.*

Unfinished Masterpieces (1927)

There are days which stand out clearly like limpid pools beside the dusty road; when your thoughts, crystal clear as water, are pinioned in loveliness like star-points. Solitary days, which come often, if you are given to browsing in fields of past adventure; or rarely, if you are seldom retrospective; and not at all, if you are too greatly concerned with rushing onward to a nebulous future. Days whereupon your experiences glimmer before you waveringly like motion pictures and the people you have known stroll through the lanes of memory, arrayed in varicolored splendor or in amusing disarray. Days like these are to be revered, for they have their humors and their whimsicalities. Hurry your thoughts and the gathering imageries take flight. Perplexity but makes the lens of introspection blur. And of annoyance beware, for it is an evil vapor that disseminates and drowns the visions in the sea of grim realities. Such days must be cultivated. Scenes for their reception must be set. Cushions perhaps, and warmth of fire. Above all, the warmth of sweet content. Ease and comfort, comfort and ease and moods of receptivity. Then hither, come hither the places and the people we have known, the associations that withstand time's effacements. Backward ho, through the mazes of the past.

stop! "Why howdy, Dora Johns." Darling playmate of my child-years. With wooly hair a length too short for even pigtails. Mud-spatters upon your funny black face. Mud-spatters all over your dress and your little black hands mud-spattered too.

Why? What? Come on and see. And lo! I am a child again.

Hand in hand, unmindful of her muddy ones, we skip around the old ramshackle house, back to the furthest corner of an unkempt yard, impervious to the tin cans, the ash-heap, the litter, the clutter that impedes our way, our eyes upon, our thoughts bent upon one small clean-swept corner, where there is mud. More mud and water in a battered tin can. And row after row of mud. No, not mud—not merely mud, but things made out of mud. Row on row, drying in the sun.

5   Carefully, I sit down, doubling up, to be as small as possible, for only this corner where mud things are drying is clean and corners are seldom, if ever, quite large enough. Besides, I must not touch the things made out of mud. If the dried ones fall, they break. If the moist ones are molested, be it with ever so gentle a finger, they lose their shape. Moreover I must not disturb Dora.

Her little hands are busied with the mud. Little moulder's fingers are deftly playing their skill. Her child's face is alight. What has splashed her grave child's face with such a light? I wondered. I wonder now. The glitter of brittle talent, a gleam of sterling genius or the glow from artistic fires burning within the soul of a little black child?

Little Dora shaping figures out of mud. Vases and urns, dolls and toys, flying birds and trotting horses, frisking dogs and playing kittens, marvelous things out of mud. Crying aloud as though dealt a blow if one of the dried mud-figures is broken. Working in mud for endless hours, while the neighbor children play. Their hilarious merriment dropping like bombs into the quiet of our clean-swept corner. Deadly missiles seeking to find a mark. The insistent halloes of futile mirth forever bubbling on the other side of a high-board fence. The dividing fence and upon one side the clean-swept corner and the row on row of mud things drying in the sun. And Dora seeming not to heed the seething bubbles upon the other side, shaping, shaping marvelous things out of mud.

Yet, Oh Dora, now that the day is ours, will you not say, "When did the bombs of futile mirth strike their target? When did the tin cans and the rags and the old ash-heap crowd you out from your clean-swept corner? What rude hand caused the dried mud shapes to fall and break? Who set a ruthless foot in the midst of your damp mud things?" Or were you too plastic, as plastic as your mud? You dare not tell. Only this you can whisper into the mists of our today. You are one of the Master's unfinished shapes which He will some day gather to mould anew into the finished masterpiece.

A lump of mud. Now, there is a sobriquet for you—you funny, funny man. Mr. William Williams. I saw you but once. We chanced to meet in the home of a mutual friend. I thought you so very funny then. Uncouth and very boorish, but ever, when these pageants of the past, these dumb shows of inarticulate folks arise before me upon retrospective days, you appear garbed in the tatters of pathos.

"I am fifty-one years old," you kept repeating. How pitiful those fifty-one years are. You wear a child's simplicity, the sort that is so sad to see upon a man. Fifty-one and penniless. Fifty-one and possessed of naught else but the clothing you wore. Fifty-one and no place on earth you might call home. You confessed to being a vagabond though "bum" was the term you used and you were very proud of your one accomplishment, an ability to avoid all labour.

"I've given no man a full day's honest work in all my fifty-one years," you boasted. "I gambles. I ain't no cotton-pickin' nigger." Your one and only boast after holding life, the fathomless fountain of eternal possibilities, in your possession for fifty-one priceless years.

Nevertheless you have lived and so intensely. You held us against our will. Clustered around you, listening to you talk. Relating clippings as it were from the scrapbook of your life.

Tales of the road, of the only places you knew. Roads leading away from plantations where the cotton waited to be picked by numberless "cotton-pickin' niggers." Roads leading to pool halls and gambling dens. Roads beginning and roads ending in "riding the roads," carrying backward and forward, here and yon through the weird goblin land of the South's black belt.

With a hardened casualness you told stories that revolted and at the same time cheered us with an all sufficing glow of thankfulness that life had spared us the sordidness of yours. Offhandedly, you gave us humorous skits that tempered our laughter with wishes that we might know at least a bit of such a droll existence as had been yours. With magical words you painted pictures so sharply they cut scars upon our hearts. You drew others so filled with rollicking delight their gladsomeness was contagious. With the nonchalance of a player shuffling cards you flipped your characters before us, drawn directly from the cesspool of your contacts and spellbound we listened.

Someone remarked how wonderful you talked and you replied, "Once, I sorter wanted to write books. Once, I uster read a heaps. See times when I was broke and nobody would stake me for a game. I'd lay around and read. I've read the Bible through and through and every Police Gazette I could lay my hands on. Yes, suh, I've read a heap. And I've wished a lot'er times I'd sense enough to write a book."

Lump of mud. Containing the you, the splendid artist in you, the soul of you, the unfinished you in the ungainly lump of you, awaiting the gathering-up to be molded anew into the finished masterpiece.

What a day! Here is my friend at whose fire-side I have lingered beholding Mr. William Williams, great lump of mud. To be sure, she also is an unfinished production. Though it is apparent that the Master had all but done when she slipped from his hands and dropped to earth to lie groping like the rest of us thereon.

Let us sit here together, friend, and enjoy this day.

I shall try to discover what recent gift you have given to the poor the while you are quietly stitching upon the garments, linens and scarlet, with which to clothe your household. Sit here and smile with the welcoming light in your eyes, knowing that your door is open to such as William Williams and Dora Johns, the Dora who is become as the mud beneath one's feet. Kind mistress of the widely opened door where white and black, rich and poor, of whatever caste or creed may enter and find comfort and ease and food and drink.

QUESTIONS

1. What talents do Dora and William possess? Why have they not lived up to their talents? What has kept them down? Why are they "unfinished masterpieces"?

2. How may Dora and William be seen as symbols? What do they symbolize?

3. Characterize the narrator. What attitude does she exhibit toward the lack of fulfillment of the major characters (see particularly paragraph 19)? How might the story have been different if the narrator had shown hostility, for example, or extreme bitterness?

NATHANIEL HAWTHORNE (1804–1864)

Nathaniel Hawthorne, a friend and associate of the fourteenth president of the United States, Franklin Pierce, is one of the great American writers of the nineteenth century. His most famous work is The Scarlet Letter *(1850), the sale of which gave him a degree of independence. During the administration of President Pierce (1853–1857), Hawthorne served as American consul in Liverpool, England, and this opportunity enabled him to travel extensively in Europe. Throughout his writing there runs a conflict between freedom and conventionality, with those choosing freedom sometimes suffering from the guilt that their choice brings. "Young Goodman Brown," which is one of the early stories that he included in* Twice-Told Tales *(1837, 1842), embodies this conflict.*

Young Goodman Brown (1835)

Young Goodman Brown came forth at sunset, into the street of Salem village,° but put his head back, after crossing the threshold, to exchange a parting kiss with his young wife. And Faith, as the wife was aptly named, thrust her own pretty head into the street, letting the wind play with the pink ribbons of her cap, while she called to Goodman Brown.

"Dearest heart," whispered she, softly and rather sadly, when her lips were close to his ear, "prithee, put off your journey until sunrise, and sleep in your own bed tonight. A lone woman is troubled with such dreams and such thoughts, that she's afeared of herself, sometimes. Pray, tarry with me this night, dear husband, of all nights in the year!"

"My love and my Faith," replied young Goodman Brown, "of all nights in the year, this one night must I tarry away from thee. My journey, as thou callest it, forth and back again, must needs be done 'twixt now and sunrise. What, my sweet, pretty wife, dost thou doubt me already, and we but three months married!"

"Then God bless you!" said Faith with the pink ribbons, "and may you find all well, when you come back."

5   "Amen!" cried Goodman Brown. "Say thy prayers, dear Faith, and go to bed at dusk, and no harm will come to thee."

So they parted; and the young man pursued his way, until, being about to turn the corner by the meeting-house, he looked back and saw the head of Faith still peeping after him, with a melancholy air, in spite of her pink ribbons.

"Poor little Faith!" thought he, for his heart smote him. "What a wretch am I, to leave her on such an errand! She talks of dreams, too. Methought, as she spoke, there was trouble in her face, as if a dream had warned her what work is to be done tonight. But no, no! 't would kill her to think it. Well; she's a blessed angel on earth; and after this one night, I'll cling to her skirts and follow her to Heaven."

°*Salem village:* in Massachusetts, about 15 miles north of Boston. The time of the story is the late seventeenth or early eighteenth century.

With this excellent resolve for the future, Goodman Brown felt himself justified in making more haste on his present evil purpose. He had taken a dreary road, darkened by all the gloomiest trees of the forest, which barely stood aside to let the narrow path creep through, and closed immediately behind. It was all as lonely as could be; and there is this peculiarity in such a solitude, that the traveller knows not who may be concealed by the innumerable trunks and the thick boughs overhead; so that, with lonely footsteps, he may yet be passing through an unseen multitude.

"There may be a devilish Indian behind every tree," said Goodman Brown to himself; and he glanced fearfully behind him, as he added, "What if the devil himself should be at my very elbow!"

His head being turned back, he passed a crook of the road, and looking forward again, 10 beheld the figure of a man, in grave and decent attire, seated at the foot of an old tree. He arose at Goodman Brown's approach, and walked onward, side by side with him.

"You are late, Goodman Brown," said he. "The clock of the Old South° was striking, as I came through Boston; and that is full fifteen minutes agone."

"Faith kept me back awhile," replied the young man, with a tremor in his voice, caused by the sudden appearance of his companion, though not wholly unexpected.

It was now deep dusk in the forest, and deepest in that part of it where these two were journeying. As nearly as could be discerned, the second traveller was about fifty years old, apparently in the same rank of life as Goodman Brown, and bearing a considerable resemblance to him, though perhaps more in expression than features. Still, they might have been taken for father and son. And yet, though the elder person was as simply clad as the younger, and as simple in manner too, he had an indescribable air of one who knew the world, and would not have felt abashed at the governor's dinner-table, or in King William's° court, were it possible that his affairs should call him thither. But the only thing about him that could be fixed upon as remarkable, was his staff, which bore the likeness of a great black snake, so curiously wrought, that it might almost be seen to twist and wriggle itself like a living serpent. This, of course, must have been an ocular deception, assisted by the uncertain light.

"Come, Goodman Brown!" cried his fellow-traveller, "this is a dull pace for the beginning of a journey. Take my staff, if you are so soon weary."

"Friend," said the other, exchanging his slow pace for a full stop, "having kept covenant 15 by meeting thee here, it is my purpose now to return whence I came. I have scruples, touching the matter thou wot'st of.°"

"Sayest thou so?" replied he of the serpent, smiling apart. "Let us walk on, nevertheless, reasoning as we go, and if I convince thee not, thou shalt turn back. We are but a little way in the forest, yet."

"Too far, too far!" exclaimed the goodman, unconsciously resuming his walk. "My father never went into the woods on such an errand, nor his father before him. We have been a race of honest men and good Christians, since the days of the martyrs.° And shall I be the first of the name of Brown that ever took this path and kept—"

"Such company, thou wouldst say," observed the elder person, interrupting his pause. "Well said, Goodman Brown! I have been as well acquainted with your family as ever a one among the Puritans; and that's no trifle to say. I helped your grandfather, the constable,

---

°*Old South:* The Old South Church, in Boston, is still there.
°*King William:* William III was king of England from 1688 to 1701 (the time of the story). William IV was king from 1830 to 1837 (the period when Hawthorne wrote the story).
°*thou wot'st:* you know (thou knowest).
°*days of the martyrs:* the martyrdoms of Protestants in England during the reign of Queen Mary (1553–1558).

when he lashed the Quaker woman so smartly through the streets of Salem. And it was I that brought your father a pitch-pine knot, kindled at my own hearth, to set fire to an Indian village, in King Philip's war.° They were my good friends, both; and many a pleasant walk have we had along this path, and returned merrily after midnight. I would fain be friends with you, for their sake."

"If it be as thou sayest," replied Goodman Brown, "I marvel they never spoke of these matters. Or, verily, I marvel not, seeing that the least rumor of the sort would have driven them from New England. We are a people of prayer, and good works to boot, and abide no such wickedness."

20   "Wickedness or not," said the traveller with twisted staff, "I have a very general acquaintance here in New England. The deacons of many a church have drunk the communion wine with me; the selectmen, of divers towns, make me their chairman; and a majority of the Great and General Court are firm supporters of my interest. The governor and I, too—but these are state secrets."

"Can this be so!" cried Goodman Brown, with a stare of amazement at his undisturbed companion. "Howbeit, I have nothing to do with the governor and council; they have their own ways, and are no rule for a simple husbandman like me. But, were I to go on with thee, how should I meet the eye of that good old man, our minister, at Salem village? Oh, his voice would make me tremble, both Sabbath-day and lecture-day!"°

Thus far, the elder traveller had listened with due gravity, but now burst into a fit of irrepressible mirth, shaking himself so violently, that his snakelike staff actually seemed to wriggle in sympathy.

"Ha! ha! ha!" shouted he, again and again; then composing himself, "Well, go on, Goodman Brown, go on; but, prithee, don't kill me with laughing!"

"Well, then, to end the matter at once," said Goodman Brown, considerably nettled, "there is my wife, Faith. It would break her dear little heart; and I'd rather break my own!"

25   "Nay, if that be the case," answered the other, "e'en go thy ways, Goodman Brown. I would not, for twenty old women like the one hobbling before us, that Faith should come to any harm."

As he spoke, he pointed his staff at a female figure on the path, in whom Goodman Brown recognized a very pious and exemplary dame, who had taught him his catechism in youth, and was still his moral and spiritual adviser, jointly with the minister and Deacon Gookin.

"A marvel, truly, that Goody° Cloyse should be so far in the wilderness, at nightfall!" said he. "But, with your leave, friend, I shall take a cut through the woods, until we have left this Christian woman behind. Being a stranger to you, she might ask whom I was consorting with, and whither I was going."

"Be it so," said his fellow-traveller. "Betake you to the woods, and let me keep the path."

Accordingly, the young man turned aside, but took care to watch his companion, who advanced softly along the road, until he had come within a staff's length of the old dame. She, meanwhile, was making the best of her way, with singular speed for so aged a woman, and mumbling some indistinct words, a prayer, doubtless, as she went. The traveller put forth his staff, and touched her withered neck with what seemed the serpent's tail.

°*King Philip's war:* This war (1675–1676), infamous for the atrocities committed by the New England settlers, resulted in the suppression of Indian tribal life and prepared the way for unlimited settlement of New England by European immigrants. "Philip" was the English name of Chief Metacomet of the Wampanoag tribe.
°*Sabbath-day and lecture-day:* "Sabbath-day" is Sunday. "Lecture-day" refers to Thursday lectures on biblical and moral topics.
°*Goody:* shortened form of "goodwife," a respectful name for a married woman of low rank. A "Goody Cloyse" was one of the women sentenced to execution by Hawthorne's great-grandfather, Judge John Hathorne.

"The devil!" screamed the pious old lady.   30

"Then Goody Cloyse knows her old friend?" observed the traveller, confronting her, and leaning on his writhing stick.

"Ah, forsooth, and is it your worship, indeed?" cried the good dame. "Yea, truly is it, and in the very image of my old gossip,° Goodman Brown, the grandfather of the silly fellow that now is. But, would your worship believe it? My broomstick hath strangely disappeared, stolen, as I suspect, by that unhanged witch, Goody Cory,° and that, too, when I was all anointed with the juice of smallage and cinquefoil and wolf's-bane—"°

"Mingled with fine wheat and the fat of a new-born babe," said the shape of old Goodman Brown.

"Ah, your worship knows the recipe," cried the old lady, cackling aloud. "So, as I was saying, being all ready for the meeting, and no horse to ride on, I made up my mind to foot it; for they tell me there is a nice young man to be taken into communion tonight. But now your good worship will lend me your arm, and we shall be there in a twinkling."

"That can hardly be," answered her friend. "I will not spare you my arm, Goody Cloyse,   35 but here is my staff, if you will."

So saying, he threw it down at her feet, where, perhaps, it assumed life, being one of the rods which its owner had formerly lent to the Egyptian Magi.° Of this fact, however, Goodman Brown could not take cognizance. He had cast up his eyes in astonishment, and looking down again, beheld neither Goody Cloyse nor the serpentine staff, but his fellow-traveller alone, who waited for him as calmly as if nothing had happened.

"That old woman taught me my catechism!" said the young man; and there was a world of meaning in this simple comment.

They continued to walk onward, while the elder traveller exhorted his companion to make good speed and persevere in the path, discoursing so aptly, that his arguments seemed rather to spring up in the bosom of his auditor, than to be suggested by himself. As they went he plucked a branch of maple, to serve for a walking-stick, and began to strip it of the twigs and little boughs, which were wet with evening dew. The moment his fingers touched them, they became strangely withered and dried up, as with a week's sunshine. Thus the pair proceeded, at a good free pace, until suddenly, in a gloomy hollow of the road, Goodman Brown sat himself down on the stump of a tree, and refused to go any farther.

"Friend," said he, stubbornly, "my mind is made up. Not another step will I budge on this errand. What if a wretched old woman do choose to go to the devil, when I thought she was going to Heaven! Is that any reason why I should quit my dear Faith, and go after her?"

"You will think better of this by and by," said his acquaintance, composedly. "Sit here   40 and rest yourself a while; and when you feel like moving again, there is my staff to help you along."

Without more words, he threw his companion the maple stick, and was as speedily out of sight as if he had vanished into the deepening gloom. The young man sat a few moments by the roadside, applauding himself greatly, and thinking with how clear a conscience he should meet the minister, in his morning walk, nor shrink from the eye of good old Deacon Gookin. And what calm sleep would be his, that very night, which was to have been spent so wickedly, but purely and sweetly now, in the arms of Faith! Amidst these pleasant and praiseworthy meditations, Goodman Brown heard the tramp of horses along the road, and

---

°*gossip:* from "good sib" or "good relative."
°*Goody Cory:* name of a woman who was also sent to execution by Judge Hathorne.
°*smallage and cinquefoil and wolf's-bane:* plants commonly used by witches in making ointments.
°*lent to the Egyptian Magi:* See Exodus 7:10–12.

deemed it advisable to conceal himself within the verge of the forest, conscious of the guilty purpose that had brought him thither, though now so happily turned from it.

On came the hoof-tramps and the voices of the riders, two grave old voices, conversing soberly as they drew near. These mingled sounds appeared to pass along the road, within a few yards of the young man's hiding-place; but owing, doubtless, to the depth of the gloom, at that particular spot, neither the travellers nor their steeds were visible. Though their figures brushed the small boughs by the wayside, it could not be seen that they intercepted, even for a moment, the faint gleam from the strip of bright sky, athwart which they must have passed. Goodman Brown alternately crouched and stood on tiptoe, pulling aside the branches, and thrusting forth his head as far as he durst, without discerning so much as a shadow. It vexed him the more, because he could have sworn, were such a thing possible, that he recognized the voices of the minister and Deacon Gookin, jogging° along quietly, as they were wont to do, when bound to some ordination or ecclesiastical council. While yet within hearing, one of the riders stopped to pluck a switch.

"Of the two, reverend Sir," said the voice like the deacon's, "I had rather miss an ordination dinner than to-night's meeting. They tell me that some of our community are to be here from Falmouth and beyond, and others from Connecticut and Rhode Island; besides several of the Indian powwows,° who, after their fashion, know almost as much deviltry as the best of us. Moreover, there is a goodly young woman to be taken into communion."

"Mighty well, Deacon Gookin!" replied the solemn old tones of the minister. "Spur up, or we shall be late. Nothing can be done, you know, until I get on the ground."

45   The hoofs clattered again, and the voices, talking so strangely in the empty air, passed on through the forest, where no church had ever been gathered, nor solitary Christian prayed. Whither, then, could these holy men be journeying, so deep into the heathen wilderness? Young Goodman Brown caught hold of a tree, for support, being ready to sink down on the ground, faint and over-burthened with the heavy sickness of his heart. He looked up to the sky, doubting whether there really was a Heaven above him. Yet, there was the blue arch, and the stars brightening in it.

"With Heaven above, and Faith below, I will yet stand firm against the devil!" cried Goodman Brown.

While he still gazed upward, into the deep arch of the firmament, and had lifted his hands to pray, a cloud, though no wind was stirring, hurried across the zenith, and hid the brightening stars. The blue sky was still visible, except directly overhead, where this black mass of cloud was sweeping swiftly northward. Aloft in the air, as if from the depths of the cloud, came a confused and doubtful sound of voices. Once, the listener fancied that he could distinguish the accents of town's people of his own, men and women, both pious and ungodly, many of whom he had met at the communion-table, and had seen others rioting at the tavern. The next moment, so indistinct were the sounds, he doubted whether he had heard aught but the murmur of the old forest, whispering without a wind. Then came a stronger swell of those familiar tones, heard daily in the sunshine, at Salem village, but never, until now, from a cloud at night. There was one voice, of a young woman, uttering lamentations, yet with an uncertain sorrow, and entreating for some favor, which, perhaps, it would grieve her to obtain. And all the unseen multitude, both saints and sinners, seemed to encourage her onward.

"Faith!" shouted Goodman Brown, in a voice of agony and desperation; and the echoes of the forest mocked him, crying—"Faith! Faith!" as if bewildered wretches were seeking her, all through the wilderness.

°*jogging*: riding a horse at a slow trot, not to be confused with today's meaning of "jogging."
°*powwow*: a Narragansett Indian word describing a priest or cult leader who led ritual ceremonies of dance, incantation, and magic.

The cry of grief, rage, and terror was yet piercing the night, when the unhappy husband held his breath for a response. There was a scream, drowned immediately in a louder murmur of voices fading into far-off laughter, as the dark cloud swept away, leaving the clear and silent sky above Goodman Brown. But something fluttered lightly down through the air, and caught on the branch of a tree. The young man seized it and beheld a pink ribbon.

"My Faith is gone!" cried he, after one stupefied moment. "There is no good on earth,   50
and sin is but a name. Come, devil! for to thee is this world given."

And maddened with despair, so that he laughed loud and long, did Goodman Brown grasp his staff and set forth again, at such a rate, that he seemed to fly along the forest path, rather than to walk or run. The road grew wilder and drearier, and more faintly traced, and vanished at length, leaving him in the heart of the dark wilderness, still rushing onward, with the instinct that guides mortal man to evil. The whole forest was peopled with frightful sounds; the creaking of the trees, the howling of wild beasts, and the yell of Indians; while, sometimes, the wind tolled like a distant church bell, and sometimes gave a broad roar around the traveller, as if all Nature were laughing him to scorn. But he was himself the chief horror of the scene, and shrank not from its other horrors.

"Ha! ha! ha!" roared Goodman Brown, when the wind laughed at him. "Let us hear which will laugh loudest! Think not to frighten me with your deviltry! Come witch, come wizard, come Indian powwow, come devil himself! and here comes Goodman Brown. You may as well fear him as he fear you!"

In truth, all through the haunted forest, there could be nothing more frightful than the figure of Goodman Brown. On he flew, among the black pines, brandishing his staff with frenzied gestures, now giving vent to an inspiration of horrid blasphemy, and now shouting forth such laughter, as set all the echoes of the forest laughing like demons around him. The fiend in his own shape is less hideous than when he rages in the breast of man. Thus sped the demoniac on his course, until, quivering among the trees, he saw a red light before him, as when the felled trunks and branches of a clearing have been set on fire, and throw up their lurid blaze against the sky, at the hour of midnight. He paused, in a lull of the tempest that had driven him onward, and heard the swell of what seemed a hymn, rolling solemnly from a distance, with the weight of many voices. He knew the tune. It was a familiar one in the choir of the village meeting-house. The verse died heavily away, and was lengthened by a chorus, not of human voices, but of all the sounds of the benighted wilderness, pealing in awful harmony together. Goodman Brown cried out; and his cry was lost to his own ear, by its unison with the cry of the desert.

In the interval of silence, he stole forward, until the light glared full upon his eyes. At one extremity of an open space, hemmed in by the dark wall of the forest, arose a rock, bearing some rude, natural resemblance either to an altar or a pulpit, and surrounded by four blazing pines, their tops aflame, their stems untouched, like candles at an evening meeting. The mass of foliage, that had overgrown the summit of the rock, was all on fire, blazing high into the night, and fitfully illuminating the whole field. Each pendent twig and leafy festoon was in a blaze. As the red light arose and fell, a numerous congregation alternately shone forth, then disappeared in shadow, and again grew, as it were, out of the darkness, peopling the heart of the solitary woods at once.

"A grave and dark-clad company!" quoth Goodman Brown.   55

In truth, they were such. Among them, quivering to-and-fro, between gloom and splendor, appeared faces that would be seen, next day, at the council-board of the province, and others which, Sabbath after Sabbath, looked devoutly heavenward, and benignantly over the crowded pews, from the holiest pulpits in the land. Some affirm that the lady of the governor was there. At least, there were high dames well known to her, and wives of honored husbands, and widows a great multitude, and ancient maidens, all of excellent repute, and fair young girls, who trembled lest their mothers should espy them. Either the sudden gleams of light, flashing over the obscure field, bedazzled Goodman Brown, or he recognized a score of the church members of Salem village, famous for their especial sanctity. Good old Deacon Gookin had arrived, and waited at the skirts of that venerable saint, his reverend pastor. But, irreverently consorting with these grave, reputable, and pious people, these elders of the church, these chaste dames and dewy virgins, there were men of dissolute lives and women of spotted fame, wretches given over to all mean and filthy vice, and suspected even of horrid crimes. It was strange to see, that the good shrank not from the wicked, nor were the sinners abashed by the saints. Scattered, also, among their pale-faced enemies, were the Indian priests, or powwows, who had often scared their native forest with more hideous incantations than any known to English witchcraft.

"But, where is Faith?" thought Goodman Brown; and, as hope came into his heart, he trembled.

Another verse of the hymn arose, a slow and mournful strain, such as the pious love, but joined to words which expressed all that our nature can conceive of sin, and darkly hinted at far more. Unfathomable to mere mortals is the lore of fiends. Verse after verse was sung, and still the chorus of the desert swelled between, like the deepest tone of a mighty organ. And, with the final peal of that dreadful anthem, there came a sound, as if the roaring wind, the rushing streams, the howling beasts, and every other voice of the unconverted wilderness were mingling and according with the voice of guilty man, in homage to the prince of all. The four blazing pines threw up a loftier flame, and obscurely discovered shapes and visages of horror on the smoke-wreaths, above the impious assembly. At the same moment, the fire on the rock shot redly forth, and formed a glowing arch above its base, where now appeared a figure. With reverence be it spoken, the apparition bore no slight similitude, both in garb and manner, to some grave divine of the New England churches.

"Bring forth the converts!" cried a voice, that echoed through the field and rolled into the forest.

60 At the word, Goodman Brown stepped forth from the shadow of the trees, and approached the congregation, with whom he felt a loathful brotherhood, by the sympathy of all that was wicked in his heart. He could have well-nigh sworn, that the shape of his own dead father beckoned him to advance, looking downward from a smoke-wreath, while a woman, with dim features of despair, threw out her hand to warn him back. Was it his mother? But he had no power to retreat one step, nor to resist, even in thought, when the minister and good old Deacon Gookin seized his arms, and led him to the blazing rock. Thither came also the slender form of a veiled female, led between Goody Cloyse, that pious teacher of the catechism, and Martha Carrier, who had received the devil's promise to be queen of hell. A rampant hag was she! And there stood the proselytes, beneath the canopy of fire.

"Welcome, my children," said the dark figure, "to the communion of your race! Ye have found, thus young, your nature and your destiny. My children, look behind you!"

They turned; and flashing forth, as it were, in a sheet of flame, the fiend-worshippers were seen; the smile of welcome gleamed darkly on every visage.

"There," resumed the sable form, "are all whom ye have reverenced from youth. Ye deemed them holier than yourselves, and shrank from your own sin, contrasting it with their lives of righteousness and prayerful aspirations heavenward. Yet, here are they all, in my worshipping assembly! This night it shall be granted you to know their secret deeds; how hoary-bearded elders of the church have whispered wanton words to the young maids of their households; how many a woman, eager for widow's weeds, has given her husband a drink at bedtime, and let him sleep his last sleep in her bosom; how beardless youths have made haste to inherit their father's wealth; and how fair damsels—blush not, sweet ones!— have dug little graves in the garden, and bidden me, the sole guest, to an infant's funeral. By the sympathy of your human hearts for sin, ye shall scent out all the places—whether in church, bed-chamber, street, field, or forest—where crime has been committed, and shall exult to behold the whole earth one stain of guilt, one mighty blood-spot. Far more than this! It shall be yours to penetrate, in every bosom, the deep mystery of sin, the fountain of all wicked arts, and which inexhaustibly supplies more evil impulses than human power—than my power, at its utmost!—can make manifest in deeds. And now, my children, look upon each other."

They did so; and, by the blaze of the hell-kindled torches, the wretched man beheld his Faith, and the wife her husband, trembling before that unhallowed altar.

"Lo! there ye stand, my children," said the figure, in a deep and solemn tone, almost sad, with its despairing awfulness, as if his once angelic nature° could yet mourn for our miserable race. "Depending upon one another's hearts, ye had still hoped that virtue were not all a dream! Now are ye undeceived!—Evil is the nature of mankind. Evil must be your only happiness. Welcome, again, my children, to the communion of your race!"

"Welcome!" repeated the fiend-worshippers, in one cry of despair and triumph.

And there they stood, the only pair, as it seemed, who were yet hesitating on the verge of wickedness, in this dark world. A basin was hollowed, naturally, in the rock. Did it contain water, reddened by the lurid light? or was it blood? or, perchance, a liquid flame? Herein did the Shape of Evil dip his hand, and prepare to lay the mark of baptism upon their foreheads, that they might be partakers of the mystery of sin, more conscious of the secret guilt of others, both in deed and thought, than they could now be of their own. The husband cast one look at his pale wife, and Faith at him. What polluted wretches would the next glance show them to each other, shuddering alike at what they disclosed and what they saw!

"Faith! Faith!" cried the husband. "Look up to Heaven, and resist the Wicked One!"

Whether Faith obeyed, he knew not. Hardly had he spoken, when he found himself amid calm night and solitude, listening to a roar of the wind, which died heavily away through the forest. He staggered against the rock, and felt it chill and damp, while a hanging twig, that had been all on fire, besprinkled his cheek with the coldest dew.

The next morning, young Goodman Brown came slowly into the street of Salem village staring around him like a bewildered man. The good old minister was taking a walk along the grave yard, to get an appetite for breakfast and meditate his sermon, and bestowed a blessing, as he passed, on Goodman Brown. He shrank from the venerable saint, as if to avoid an anathema. Old Deacon Gookin was at domestic worship, and the holy words of his prayer were heard through the open window. "What God doth the wizard pray to?" quoth Goodman Brown. Goody Cloyse, that excellent old Christian, stood in the early sunshine, at her own lattice, catechising a little girl, who had brought her a pint of morning's milk. Goodman Brown snatched away the child, as from the grasp of the fiend himself. Turning the corner by the meetinghouse, he spied the head of Faith, with the pink ribbons, gazing anxiously forth, and bursting into such joy at the sight of him that she skipt along the street, and almost kissed her husband before the whole village. But Goodman Brown looked sternly and sadly into her face, and passed on without a greeting.

Had Goodman Brown fallen asleep in the forest, and only dreamed a wild dream of a witch-meeting?

Be it so, if you will. But, alas! it was a dream of evil omen for young Goodman Brown. A stern, a sad, a darkly meditative, a distrustful, if not a desperate man did he become, from the night of that fearful dream. On the Sabbath day, when the congregation were singing a holy psalm, he could not listen, because an anthem of sin rushed loudly upon his ear, and drowned all the blessed strain. When the minister spoke from the pulpit, with power and fervid eloquence, and with his hand on the open Bible, of the sacred truths of our religion, and of saint-like lives and triumphant deaths, and of future bliss or misery unutterable,

---

°*once angelic nature:* Lucifer ("light bearer"), another name for the Devil, led the traditional revolt of the angels and was thrown into hell as his punishment. See Isaiah 14:12–15.

then did Goodman Brown turn pale, dreading lest the roof should thunder down upon the gray blasphemer and his hearers. Often, awaking suddenly at midnight, he shrank from the bosom of Faith, and at morning or eventide, when the family knelt down in prayer, he scowled, and muttered to himself, and gazed sternly at his wife, and turned away. And when he had lived long, and was borne to his grave, a hoary corpse, followed by Faith, an aged woman, and children and grandchildren, a goodly procession, besides neighbors not a few, they carved no hopeful verse upon his tombstone; for his dying hour was gloom.

QUESTIONS

1. Near the end of the story the narrator asks the following: "Had Goodman Brown fallen asleep in the forest, and only dreamed a wild dream of a witch-meeting?" What is the answer? If Goodman Brown's visions come out of his own dreams (mind, subconscious), what do they tell us about him?

2. Is Goodman Brown round or flat? To what extent is he a symbolic "everyman" or representative of humankind?

3. Consider Hawthorne's use of symbolism, such as sunset and night, the walking sticks, the witches' sabbath, the marriage to Faith, and the vague shadows amid darkness, together with other symbols that you may find.

4. What details establish the two settings? What characterizes Salem? The woods? Why might we be justified in seeing the forest as a symbolic setting?

5. To what extent are the people, objects, and events in Goodman Brown's adventure invested with enough *consistent* symbolic resonance to justify calling his episode in the woods an allegory? Consider Brown's wife, Faith, as an allegorical figure. What do you make of Brown's statements "I'll cling to her skirts and follow her to Heaven" (paragraph 7) and "Faith kept me back awhile" (paragraph 12)? In this same light, consider the other characters Brown meets in the forest, the sunset, the walk into the forest, and the staff "which bore the likeness of a great black snake" (paragraph 13).

LUKE (1st century CE)

Although little is known about Luke, evidence in Colossians, Philemon, and 2 Timothy indicates that a man named Luke was the "beloved physician" and traveling companion of the apostle Paul, who journeyed in the Mediterranean area during the middle of the first century CE. Scholars indicate that Luke built his gospel from the Gospel of St. Mark and also from written sources known as "Q," some of which were also used by St. Matthew. Luke also relied on other sources that were available only to him. In addition to his gospel, Luke is also accepted as the author of the Acts of the Apostles.

The Parable of the Prodigal Son° (c. 90 CE)

¹¹ And he [Jesus] said, A certain man had two sons:

¹² And the younger of them said to *his* father, Father, give me the portion of goods that falleth to me. And he divided unto them *his* living.°

°Luke 15:11–32
°*divided . . . his living:* one-third of the father's estate; the son had to renounce all further claim.

¹³ And not many days after the younger son gathered all together, and took his journey into a far country,° and there wasted his substance with riotous living.

¹⁴ And when he had spent all, there arose a mighty famine in that land; and he began to be in want.

¹⁵ And he went and joined himself to a citizen of that country; and he sent him into his fields to feed swine.°

¹⁶ And he would fain have filled his belly with the husks° that the swine did eat: and no man gave unto him.

¹⁷ And when he came to himself, he said, How many hired servants of my father's have bread enough and to spare, and I perish with hunger!

¹⁸ I will arise and go to my father, and will say unto him, Father, I have sinned against heaven, and before thee.

¹⁹ And am no more worthy to be called thy son: make me as one of thy hired servants.

²⁰ And he arose, and came to his father. But when he was yet a great way off, his father saw him, and had compassion, and ran, and fell on his neck, and kissed him.

²¹ And the son said unto him, Father, I have sinned against heaven, and in thy sight, and am no more worthy to be called thy son.

²² But the father said to his servants, Bring forth the best robe, and put *it* on him; and put a ring on his hand, and shoes on *his* feet:

²³ And bring hither the fatted calf,° and kill *it;* and let us eat, and be merry:

²⁴ For this my son was dead, and is alive again; he was lost, and is found. And they began to be merry.

²⁵ Now his elder son was in the field: and as he came and drew nigh to the house, he heard music and dancing.

²⁶ And he called one of the servants, and asked what these things meant.

²⁷ And he said unto him, Thy brother is come; and thy father hath killed the fatted calf, because he hath received him safe and sound.

²⁸ And he was angry, and would not go in: therefore came his father out, and intreated him.

²⁹ And he answering said to *his* father, Lo, these many years do I serve thee, neither transgressed I at any time thy commandment: and yet thou never gavest me a kid, that I might make merry with my friends:

³⁰ But as soon as this thy son was come, which hath devoured thy living with harlots, thou hast killed for him the fatted calf.

³¹ And he said unto him, Son, thou art ever with me, and all that I have is thine.

³² It was meet° that we should make merry, and be glad: for this thy brother was dead, and is alive again: and was lost, and is found.

QUESTIONS

1. Describe the character of the Prodigal Son. Is he flat or round, representative or individual? Why is it necessary that the character be considered representatively, even though he has individual characteristics? Who or what does the Prodigal Son symbolize?

°*far country:* countries of the Jewish dispersal, or diaspora, in the areas bordering the Mediterranean Sea.
°*feed swine:* in Jewish custom, pigs were unclean.
°*husks:* pods of the carob tree, the eating of which was thought to be penitential.
°*fatted calf:* grain-fed calf.
°*meet:* appropriate.

2. What is the plot? What is the antagonism against which the Prodigal Son contends? Why is it necessary that the brother resent the brother's return?

3. What is the resolution of the parable? Why is there no "they lived happily ever after" ending?

4. Using verse numbers, analyze the structure of the parable. What determines your division of the parts? Do these parts coincide with the development of the plot? Describe the relationship of plot to structure in the parable.

5. What is the point of view here? How does the emphasis shift with verse 22?

6. On the basis of the fact that there are many characteristics here of many stories you have read, write a description of the parable as a type of literature.

KATHERINE ANNE PORTER (1890–1980)

Katherine Anne Porter was a native of Texas but made her home in many places during her life, spending considerable time in Mexico and Germany. She established her reputation with her early collections Flowering Judas *(1930) and* Pale Horse, Pale Rider *(1939), which gained praise for her analyses and insights into human character. A later collection of stories was* The Leaning Tower *(1944). Her major novel,* Ship of Fools, *appeared in 1962 and was made into a motion picture. She was awarded the Pulitzer Prize for Fiction and also the National Book Award in 1966 for her* The Collected Stories. *"The Jilting of Granny Weatherall" first appeared in* Flowering Judas.

The Jilting of Granny Weatherall (1930)

She flicked her wrist neatly out of Doctor Harry's pudgy careful fingers and pulled the sheet up to her chin. The brat ought to be in knee breeches. Doctoring around the country with spectacles on his nose! "Get along now, take your schoolbooks and go. There's nothing wrong with me."

Doctor Harry spread a warm paw like a cushion on her forehead where the forked green vein danced and made her eyelids twitch. "Now, now, be a good girl, and we'll have you up in no time."

"That's no way to speak to a woman nearly eighty years old just because she's down. I'd have you respect your elders, young man."

"Well, Missy, excuse me." Doctor Harry patted her cheek. "But I've got to warn you, haven't I? You're a marvel, but you must be careful or you're going to be good and sorry."

5   "Don't tell me what I'm going to be. I'm on my feet now, morally speaking. It's Cornelia. I had to go to bed to get rid of her."

Her bones felt loose, and floated around in her skin, and Doctor Harry floated like a balloon around the foot of the bed. He floated and pulled down his waistcoat and swung his glasses on a cord. "Well, stay where you are, it certainly can't hurt you."

"Get along and doctor your sick," said Granny Weatherall. "Leave a well woman alone. I'll call for you when I want you. . . . Where were you forty years ago when I pulled through milk-leg and double pneumonia? You weren't even born. Don't let Cornelia lead you on," she shouted, because Doctor Harry appeared to float up to the ceiling and out. "I pay my own bills, and I don't throw my money away on nonsense!"

She meant to wave good-by, but it was too much trouble. Her eyes closed of themselves, it was like a dark curtain drawn around the bed. The pillow rose and floated under her, pleasant as a hammock in a light wind. She listened to the leaves rustling outside the window. No, somebody was swishing newspapers: no, Cornelia and Doctor Harry were whispering together. She leaped broad awake, thinking they whispered in her ear.

"She was never like this, *never* like this!" "Well, what can we expect?" "Yes, eighty years old. . . ."

Well, and what if she was? She still had ears. It was like Cornelia to whisper around   10
doors. She always kept things secret in such a public way. She was always being tactful and kind. Cornelia was dutiful; that was the trouble with her. Dutiful and good: "So good and dutiful," said Granny, "that I'd like to spank her." She saw herself spanking Cornelia and making a fine job of it.

"What'd you say, Mother?"

Granny felt her face tying up in hard knots.

"Can't a body think, I'd like to know?"

"I thought you might want something."

"I do. I want a lot of things. First off, go away and don't whisper."   15

She lay and drowsed, hoping in her sleep that the children would keep out and let her rest a minute. It had been a long day. Not that she was tired. It was always pleasant to snatch a minute now and then. There was always so much to be done, let me see: tomorrow.

Tomorrow was far away and there was nothing to trouble about. Things were finished somehow when the time came; thank God there was always a little margin over for peace: then a person could spread out the plan of life and tuck in the edges orderly. It was good to have everything clean and folded away, with the hair brushes and tonic bottles sitting straight on the white embroidered linen: the day started without fuss and the pantry shelves laid out with rows of jelly glasses and brown jugs and white stone-china jars with blue whirligigs and words painted on them: coffee, tea, sugar, ginger, cinnamon, allspice: and the bronze clock with the lion on top nicely dusted off. The dust that lion could collect in twenty-four hours! The box in the attic with all those letters tied up, well she'd have to go through that tomorrow. All those letters—George's letters and John's letters and her letters to them both—lying around for the children to find afterwards made her uneasy. Yes, that would be tomorrow's business. No use to let them know how silly she had been once.

While she was rummaging around she found death in her mind and it felt clammy and unfamiliar. She had spent so much time preparing for death there was no need for bringing it up again. Let it take care of itself now. When she was sixty she had felt very old, finished, and went around making farewell trips to see her children and grandchildren, with a secret in her mind: This is the very last of your mother, children! Then she made her will and came down with a long fever. That was all just a notion like a lot of other things, but it was lucky too, for she had once for all got over the idea of dying for a long time. Now she couldn't be worried. She hoped she had better sense now. Her father had lived to be one hundred and two years old and had drunk a noggin of strong hot toddy on his last birthday. He told the reporters it was his daily habit, and he owed his long life to that. He had made quite a scandal and was very pleased about it. She believed she'd just plague Cornelia a little.

"Cornelia! Cornelia!" No footsteps, but a sudden hand on her cheek. "Bless you, where have you been?"

"Here, mother."   20

"Well, Cornelia, I want a noggin of hot toddy."

"Are you cold, darling?"

"I'm chilly, Cornelia. Lying in bed stops the circulation. I must have told you that a thousand times."

Well, she could just hear Cornelia telling her husband that Mother was getting childish and they'd have to humor her. The thing that most annoyed her was that Cornelia thought she was deaf, dumb, and blind. Little hasty glances and tiny gestures tossed around her and over her head saying, "Don't cross her, let her have her way, she's eighty years old," and she sitting there as if she lived in a thin glass cage. Sometimes Granny almost made up her mind to pack up and move back to her own house where nobody could remind her every minute that she was old. Wait, wait, Cornelia, till your own children whisper behind your back!

25   In her day she had kept a better house and had got more work done. She wasn't too old yet for Lydia to be driving eighty miles for advice when one of the children jumped the track, and Jimmy still dropped in and talked things over: "Now, Mammy, you've a good business head, I want to know what you think of this? . . ." Old Cornelia couldn't change the furniture around without asking. Little things, little things! They had been so sweet when they were little. Granny wished the old days were back again with the children young and everything to be done over. It had been a hard pull, but not too much for her. When she thought of all the food she had cooked, and all the clothes she had cut and sewed, and all the gardens she had made—well, the children showed it. There they were, made out of her, and they couldn't get away from that. Sometimes she wanted to see John again and point to them and say, Well, I didn't do so badly, did I? But that would have to wait. That was for tomorrow. She used to think of him as a man, but now all the children were older than their father, and he would be a child beside her if she saw him now. It seemed strange and there was something wrong in the idea. Why, he couldn't possibly recognize her. She had fenced in a hundred acres once, digging the post holes herself and clamping the wires with just a negro boy to help. That changed a woman. John would be looking for a young woman with the peaked Spanish comb in her hair and the painted fan. Digging post holes changed a woman. Riding country roads in the winter when women had their babies was another thing: sitting up nights with sick horses and sick negroes and sick children and hardly ever losing one. John, I hardly ever lost one of them! John would see that in a minute, that would be something he could understand, she wouldn't have to explain anything!

It made her feel like rolling up her sleeves and putting the whole place to rights again. No matter if Cornelia was determined to be everywhere at once, there were a great many things left undone on this place. She would start tomorrow and do them. It was good to be strong enough for everything, even if all you made melted and changed and slipped under your hands, so that by the time you finished you almost forgot what you were working for. What was it I set out to do? she asked herself intently, but she could not remember. A fog rose over the valley, she saw it marching across the creek swallowing the trees and moving up the hill like an army of ghosts. Soon it would be at the near edge of the orchard, and then it was time to go in and light the lamps. Come in children, don't stay out in the night air.

Lighting the lamps had been beautiful. The children huddled up to her and breathed like little calves waiting at the bars in the twilight. Their eyes followed the match and watched the flame rise and settle in a blue curve, then they moved away from her. The lamp was lit, they didn't have to be scared and hang on to mother any more. Never, never, never more. God, for all my life I thank Thee. Without Thee, my God, I could never have done it. Hail, Mary, full of grace.

I want you to pick all the fruit this year and see that nothing is wasted. There's always someone who can use it. Don't let good things rot for want of using. You waste life when you waste good food. Don't let things get lost. It's bitter to lose things. Now, don't let me get to thinking, not when I am tired and taking a little nap before supper. . . .

The pillow rose about her shoulders and pressed against her heart and the memory was being squeezed out of it: oh, push down the pillow, somebody: it would smother her if she tried to hold it. Such a fresh breeze blowing and such a green day with no threats in it. But he had not come, just the same. What does a woman do when she has put on the white veil and set out the white cake for a man and he doesn't come? She tried to remember. No, I swear he never harmed me but in that. He never harmed me but in that . . . and what if he did? There was the day, the day, but a whirl of dark smoke rose and covered it, crept up and over into the bright field where everything was planted so carefully in orderly rows. That was hell, she knew hell when she saw it. For sixty years she had prayed against remembering him and against losing her soul in the deep pit of hell, and now the two things were mingled in one and the thought of him was a smoky cloud from hell that moved and crept in her head when she had just got rid of Doctor Harry and was trying to rest a minute. Wounded vanity, Ellen, said a sharp voice in the top of her mind. Don't let your wounded vanity get the upper hand of you. Plenty of girls get jilted. You were jilted, weren't you. Then stand up to it. Her eyelids wavered and let in streamers of blue-gray light like tissue paper over her eyes. She must get up and pull the shades down or she'd never sleep. She was in bed again and the shades were not down. How could that happen? Better turn over, hide from the light, sleeping in the light gave you nightmares. "Mother, how do you feel now?" and a stinging wetness on her forehead. But I don't like having my face washed in cold water!

Hapsy? George? Lydia? Jimmy? No, Cornelia, and her features were swollen and full of little puddles. "They're coming, darling, they'll all be here soon." Go wash your face, child, you look funny.   30

Instead of obeying, Cornelia knelt down and put her head on the pillow. She seemed to be talking but there was no sound. "Well, are you tongue-tied? Whose birthday is it? Are you going to give a party?"

Cornelia's mouth moved urgently in strange shapes. "Don't do that, you bother me, daughter."

"Oh, no, Mother, Oh, no . . ."

Nonsense. It was strange about children. They disputed your every word. "No what, Cornelia?"

"Here's Doctor Harry."   35

"I won't see that boy again. He just left five minutes ago."

"That was this morning, Mother. It's night now. Here's the nurse."

"This is Doctor Harry, Mrs. Weatherall. I never saw you look so young and happy!"

"Ah, I'll never be young again—but I'd be happy if they'd let me lie in peace and get rested."

She thought she spoke up loudly, but no one answered. A warm weight on her forehead, a warm bracelet on her wrist, and a breeze went on whispering, trying to tell her something.   40 A shuffle of leaves in the everlasting hand of God. He blew on them and they danced and rattled. "Mother, don't mind, we're going to give you a little hypodermic." "Look here, daughter, how do ants get in this bed? I saw sugar ants yesterday." Did you send for Hapsy too?

It was Hapsy she really wanted. She had to go a long way back through a great many rooms to find Hapsy standing with a baby on her arm. She seemed to herself to be Hapsy also, and the baby on Hapsy's arm was Hapsy and himself and herself, all at once, and there was no surprise in the meeting. Then Hapsy melted from within and turned flimsy as gray gauze and the baby was a gauzy shadow, and Hapsy came up close and said, "I thought you'd never come," and looked at her very searchingly and said, "You haven't changed a bit!" They leaned forward to kiss, when Cornelia began whispering from a long way off, "Oh, is there anything you want to tell me? Is there anything I can do for you?"

Yes, she had changed her mind after sixty years and she would like to see George. I want you to find George. Find him and be sure to tell him I forgot him. I want him to know I had my husband just the same and my children and my house like any other woman. A good house too and a good husband that I loved and fine children out of him. Better than I hoped for even. Tell him I was given back everything he took away and more. Oh, no, oh, God, no, there was something else besides the house and the man and the children. Oh, surely they were not all? What was it? Something not given back. . . . Her breath crowded down under her ribs and grew into a monstrous frightening shape with cutting edges; it bored up into her head, and the agony was unbelievable: Yes, John, get the doctor now, no more talk, my time has come.

When this one was born it should be the last. The last. It should have been born first, for it was the one she had truly wanted. Everything came in good time. Nothing left out, left over. She was strong, in three days she would be as well as ever. Better. A woman needed milk in her to have her full health.

"Mother, do you hear me?"

45   "I've been telling you—"

"Mother, Father Connolly's here."

"I went to Holy Communion only last week. Tell him I'm not so sinful as all that."

"Father just wants to speak to you."

He could speak as much as he pleased. It was like him to drop in and inquire about her soul as if it were a teething baby, and then stay on for a cup of tea and a round of cards and gossip. He always had a funny story of some sort, usually about an Irishman who made his little mistakes and confessed them, and the point lay in some absurd thing he would blurt out in the confessional showing his struggles between native piety and original sin. Granny felt easy about her soul. Cornelia, where are your manners? Give Father Connolly a chair. She had her secret comfortable understanding with a few favorite saints who cleared a straight road to God for her. All as surely signed and sealed as the papers for the new Forty Acres. Forever . . . heirs and assigns forever. Since the day the wedding cake was not cut, but thrown out and wasted. The whole bottom dropped out of the world, and there she was blind and sweating with nothing under her feet and the walls falling away. His hand had caught her under the breast, she had not fallen, there was the freshly polished floor with the green rug on it, just as before. He had cursed like a sailor's parrot and said, "I'll kill him for you." Don't lay a hand on him, for my sake leave something to God. "Now, Ellen, you must believe what I tell you . . ."

50   So there was nothing, nothing to worry about any more, except sometimes in the night one of the children screamed in a nightmare, and they both hustled out shaking and hunting for the matches and calling, "There, wait a minute, here we are!" John, get the doctor now. Hapsy's time has come. But there was Hapsy standing by the bed in a white cap. "Cornelia, tell Hapsy to take off her cap. I can't see her plain."

Her eyes opened very wide and the room stood out like a picture she had seen somewhere. Dark colors with the shadow rising towards the ceiling in long angles. The tall black dresser gleamed with nothing on it but John's picture, enlarged from a little one, with John's eyes very black when they should have been blue. You never saw him, so how do you know how he looked? But the man insisted the copy was perfect, it was very rich and handsome. For a picture, yes, but it's not my husband. The table by the bed had a linen cover and a candle and a crucifix. The light was blue from Cornelia's silk lampshades. No sort of light at all, just frippery. You had to live forty years with kerosene lamps to appreciate honest electricity. She felt very strong and she saw Doctor Harry with a rosy nimbus around him.

"You look like a saint, Doctor Harry, and I vow that's as near as you'll ever come to it."

"She's saying something."

"I heard you, Cornelia. What's all this carrying-on?"

55   "Father Connolly's saying—"

Cornelia's voice staggered and bumped like a cart in a bad road. It rounded corners and turned back again and arrived nowhere. Granny stepped up in the cart very lightly and reached for the reins, but a man sat beside her and she knew him by his hands, driving the cart. She did not look in his face, for she knew without seeing, but looked instead down the road where the trees leaned over and bowed to each other and a thousand birds were singing a Mass. She felt like singing too, but she put her hand in the bosom of her dress and pulled out a rosary, and Father Connolly murmured Latin in a very solemn voice and tickled her feet. My God, will you stop that nonsense? I'm a married woman. What if he did run away and leave me to face the priest by myself? I found another a whole world better. I wouldn't have exchanged my husband for anybody except St. Michael himself, and you may tell him that for me with a thank you in the bargain.

Light flashed on her closed eyelids, and a deep roaring shook her. Cornelia, is that lightning? I hear thunder. There's going to be a storm. Close all the windows. Call the children in . . . "Mother, here we are, all of us." "Is that you, Hapsy?" "Oh, no, I'm Lydia. We drove as fast as we could." Their faces drifted above her, drifted away. The rosary fell out of her hands and Lydia put it back. Jimmy tried to help, their hands fumbled together, and Granny closed two fingers around Jimmy's thumb. Beads wouldn't do, it must be something alive. She was so amazed her thoughts ran round and round. So, my dear Lord, this is my death and I wasn't even thinking about it. My children have come to see me die. But I can't, it's not time. Oh, I always hated surprises. I wanted to give Cornelia the amethyst set—Cornelia, you're to have the amethyst set, but Hapsy's to wear it when she wants, and, Doctor Harry, do shut up. Nobody sent for you. Oh, my dear Lord, do wait a minute. I meant to do something about the Forty Acres, Jimmy doesn't need it and Lydia will later on with that worthless husband of hers. I meant to finish the altar cloth and send six bottles of wine to Sister Borgia for her dyspepsia. I want to send six bottles of wine to Sister Borgia, Father Connolly, now don't let me forget.

Cornelia's voice made short turns and tilted over and crashed. "Oh, Mother, oh, Mother, oh, Mother. . . ."

"I'm not going, Cornelia. I'm taken by surprise. I can't go."

You'll see Hapsy again. What about her? "I thought you'd never come." Granny made   60
a long journey outward, looking for Hapsy. What if I don't find her? What then? Her heart sank down and down, there was no bottom to death, she couldn't come to the end of it. The blue light from Cornelia's lampshade drew into a tiny point in the center of her brain, it flickered and winked like an eye, quietly it fluttered and dwindled. Granny lay curled down within herself, amazed and watchful, staring at the point of light that was herself; her body was now only a deeper mass of shadow in an endless darkness and this darkness would curl around the light and swallow it up. God, give a sign!

For the second time there was no sign. Again no bridegroom and the priest in the house. She could not remember any other sorrow because this grief wiped them all away. Oh, no, there's nothing more cruel than this—I'll never forgive it. She stretched herself with a deep breath and blew out the light.

QUESTIONS

1. What are Granny's circumstances in the story? What is happening to her? How do we learn about her and her past life? What evidence do you see in the story that Granny is hallucinating and becoming delirious?

2. What sort of person is Granny? Would you call her admirable? Why or why not? In what way is light symbolic in the story? In what ways is Granny associated with light? Would it be fair to claim that Granny has been a giver of light during her life?

3. What is the meaning of "jilting" as it applies to Granny? To what degree does Granny feel "jilted" at the end of her life? How has jilting colored and symbolized her life? How has she lived to overcome it?

4. Explain the story's point of view. (See also Chapter 2.) To what degree does the narrator enter Granny's mind to explain what is happening to her?

5. Who is Hapsy? What is the significance of Hapsy to Granny? What has apparently happened to Hapsy?

JOHN STEINBECK (1902–1968)

John Steinbeck was born in Salinas, California, and for a time attended Stanford University. In the 1920s, while working at jobs such as surveying, picking fruit, and hatching trout, he began his writing career. A number of stories and novels preceded his best-known novel, The Grapes of Wrath *(1939), for which he was awarded the Pulitzer Prize in 1940. He received the Nobel Prize in Literature in 1962. His fiction, often set in rural areas, features a realistic and pessimistic view of life. A number of his novels have been made into films, the best known of which is* The Grapes of Wrath *(1940, directed by John Ford). His home in Salinas is open to the visiting public.*

The Chrysanthemums (1937)

The high grey-flannel fog of winter closed off the Salinas Valley° from the sky and from all the rest of the world. On every side it sat like a lid on the mountains and made of the great valley a closed pot. On the broad, level land floor the gang plows bit deep and left the black earth shining like metal where the shares had cut. On the foothill ranches across the Salinas River, the yellow stubble fields seemed to be bathed in pale cold sunshine, but there was no sunshine in the valley now in December. The thick willow scrub along the river flamed with sharp and positive yellow leaves.

It was a time of quiet and of waiting. The air was cold and tender. A light wind blew up from the southwest so that the farmers were mildly hopeful of a good rain before long; but fog and rain do not go together.

Across the river, on Henry Allen's foothill ranch there was little work to be done, for the hay was cut and stored and the orchards were plowed up to receive the rain deeply when it should come. The cattle on the higher slopes were becoming shaggy and rough-coated.

Elisa Allen, working in her flower garden, looked down across the yard and saw Henry, her husband, talking to two men in business suits. The three of them stood by the tractor shed, each man with one foot on the side of the little Fordson.° They smoked cigarettes and studied the machines as they talked.

5   Elisa watched them for a moment and then went back to her work. She was thirty-five. Her face was lean and strong and her eyes were as clear as water. Her figure looked blocked and heavy in her gardening costume, a man's black hat pulled low down over her eyes, clodhopper shoes, a figured print dress almost completely covered by a big corduroy apron with four big pockets to hold the snips, the trowel and scratcher, the seeds and the knife she worked with. She wore heavy leather gloves to protect her hands while she worked.

She was cutting down the old year's chrysanthemum stalks with a pair of short and powerful scissors. She looked down toward the men by the tractor shed now and then. Her face was eager and mature and handsome; even her work with the scissors was over-eager, over-powerful. The chrysanthemum stems seemed too small and easy for her energy.

She brushed a cloud of hair out of her eyes with the back of her glove, and left a smudge of earth on the cheek in doing it. Behind her stood the neat white farm house with red geraniums close-banked around it as high as the windows. It was a hard-swept looking little house, with hard-polished windows, and a clean mud-mat on the front steps.

°*Salinas Valley:* in Monterey County, California, about 50 miles south of San Jose.
°*Fordson:* a relatively small tractor manufactured in the days before World War II by the Ford Motor Company, with large steel-lugged rear wheels.

Elisa cast another glance toward the tractor shed. The strangers were getting into their Ford coupe. She took off a glove and put her strong fingers down into the forest of new green chrysanthemum sprouts that were growing around the old roots. She spread the leaves and looked down among the close-growing stems. No aphids were there, no sowbugs or snails or cutworms. Her terrier fingers destroyed such pests before they could get started.

Elisa started at the sound of her husband's voice. He had come near quietly, and he leaned over the wire fence that protected her flower garden from cattle and dogs and chickens.

"At it again," he said. "You've got a strong new crop coming."   10

Elisa straightened her back and pulled on the gardening glove again. "Yes. They'll be strong this coming year." In her tone and on her face there was a little smugness.

"You've got a gift with things," Henry observed. "Some of those yellow chrysanthemums you had this year were ten inches across. I wish you'd work out in the orchard and raise some apples that big."

Her eyes sharpened. "Maybe I could do it, too. I've a gift with things, all right. My mother had it. She could stick anything in the ground and make it grow. She said it was having planters' hands that knew how to do it."

"Well, it sure works with flowers," he said.

"Henry, who were those men you were talking to?"   15

"Why, sure, that's what I came to tell you. They were from the Western Meat Company. I sold those thirty head of three-year-old steers. Got nearly my own price, too."

"Good," she said. "Good for you."

"And I thought," he continued, "I thought how it's Saturday afternoon, and we might go to Salinas for dinner at a restaurant, and then to a picture show—to celebrate, you see."

"Good," she repeated. "Oh, yes. That will be good."

Henry put on his joking tone. "There's fights tonight. How'd you like to go to the fights?"   20

"Oh, no," she said breathlessly. "No, I wouldn't like fights."

"Just fooling, Elisa. We'll go to a movie. Let's see. It's two now. I'm going to take Scotty and bring down those steers from the hill. It'll take us maybe two hours. We'll go in town about five and have dinner at the Cominos Hotel. Like that?"

"Of course I'll like it. It's good to eat away from home."

"All right, then. I'll go get up a couple of horses."

She said, "I'll have plenty of time to transplant some of these sets, I guess."   25

She heard her husband calling Scotty down by the barn. And a little later she saw the two men ride up the pale yellow hillside in search of the steers.

There was a little square sandy bed kept for rooting the chrysanthemums. With her trowel she turned the soil over and over, and smoothed it and patted it firm. Then she dug ten parallel trenches to receive the sets. Back at the chrysanthemum bed she pulled out the little crisp shoots, trimmed off the leaves of each one with her scissors and laid it on a small orderly pile.

A squeak of wheels and plod of hoofs came from the road. Elisa looked up. The country road ran along the dense bank of willows and cottonwoods that bordered the river, and up this road came a curious vehicle, curiously drawn. It was an old springwagon, with a round canvas top on it like the cover of a prairie schooner. It was drawn by an old bay horse and a little grey-and-white burro. A big stubble-bearded man sat between the cover flaps and drove the crawling team. Underneath the wagon, between the hind wheels, a lean and rangy mongrel dog walked sedately. Words were painted on the canvas in clumsy, crooked letters. "Pots, pans, knives, sisors, lawn mores. Fixed." Two rows of articles and the triumphantly definitive "Fixed" below. The black paint had run down in little sharp points beneath each letter.

Elisa, squatting on the ground, watched to see the crazy, loose-jointed wagon pass by. But it didn't pass. It turned into the farm road in front of her house, crooked old wheels skirling and squeaking. The rangy dog darted from between the wheels and ran ahead. Instantly the two ranch shepherds flew out at him. Then all three stopped, and with stiff and quivering tails, with taut straight legs, with ambassadorial dignity, they slowly circled, sniffing daintily. The caravan pulled up to Elisa's wire fence and stopped. Now the new-comer dog, feeling outnumbered, lowered his tail and retired under the wagon with raised hackles and bared teeth.

30   The man on the wagon seat called out. "That's a bad dog in a fight when he gets started."

Elisa laughed. "I see he is. How soon does he generally get started?"

The man caught up her laughter and echoed it heartily. "Sometimes not for weeks and weeks," he said. He climbed stiffly down, over the wheel. The horse and the donkey dropped like unwatered flowers.

Elisa saw that he was a very big man. Although his hair and beard were greying, he did not look old. His worn black suit was wrinkled and spotted with grease. The laughter had disappeared from his face and eyes the moment his laughing voice ceased. His eyes were dark and they were full of the brooding that gets in the eyes of teamsters and of sailors. The calloused hands he rested on the wire fence were cracked, and every crack was a black line. He took off his battered hat.

"I'm off my general road, ma'am," he said. "Does this dirt road cut over across the river to the Los Angeles highway?"

35   Elisa stood up and shoved the thick scissors in her apron pocket. "Well, yes, it does, but it winds around and then fords the river. I don't think your team could pull through the sand."

He replied with some asperity, "It might surprise you what them beasts can pull through."

"When they get started?" she asked.

He smiled for a second. "Yes. When they get started."

"Well," said Elisa, "I think you'll save time if you go back to the Salinas road and pick up the highway there."

40   He drew a big finger down the chicken wire and made it sing. "I ain't in any hurry, ma'am. I go from Seattle to San Diego and back every year. Takes all my time. About six months each way. I aim to follow nice weather."

Elisa took off her gloves and stuffed them in the apron pocket with the scissors. She touched the under edge of her man's hat, searching for fugitive hairs. "That sounds like a nice kind of a way to live," she said.

He leaned confidentially over the fence. "Maybe you noticed the writing on my wagon. I mend pots and sharpen knives and scissors. You got any of them things to do?"

"Oh, no," she said quickly. "Nothing like that." Her eyes hardened with resistance.

"Scissors is the worst thing," he explained. "Most people just ruin scissors trying to sharpen 'em, but I know how. I got a special tool. It's a little bobbit kind of thing, and pat-ented. But it sure does the trick."

45   "No. My scissors are all sharp."

"All right, then. Take a pot," he continued earnestly, "a bent pot, or a pot with a hole. I can make it like new so you don't have to buy no new ones. That's saving for you."

"No," she said shortly. "I tell you I have nothing like that for you to do."

His face fell to an exaggerated sadness. His voice took on a whining undertone. "I ain't had a thing to do today. Maybe I won't have no supper tonight. You see I'm off my regular road. I know folks on the highway clear from Seattle to San Diego. They save their things for me to sharpen up because they know I do it so good and save them money."

"I'm sorry," Elisa said irritably. "I haven't anything for you to do."

His eyes left her face and fell to searching the ground. They roamed about until they came to the chrysanthemum bed where she had been working. "What's them plants, ma'am?" 50

The irritation and resistance melted from Elisa's face. "Oh, those are chrysanthemums, giant whites and yellows. I raise them every year, bigger than anybody around here."

"Kind of a long-stemmed flower? Looks like a quick puff of colored smoke?" he asked.

"That's it. What a nice way to describe them."

"They smell kind of nasty till you get used to them," he said.

"It's a good bitter smell," she retorted, "not nasty at all." 55

He changed his tone quickly. "I like the smell myself."

"I had ten-inch blooms this year," she said.

The man leaned farther over the fence. "Look. I know a lady down the road a piece, has got the nicest garden you ever seen. Got nearly every kind of flower but no chrysanthemums. Last time I was mending a copper-bottom washtub for her (that's hard job but I do it good), she said to me, 'If you ever run across some nice chrysantheums I wish you'd try to get me a few seeds.' That's what she told me."

Elisa's eyes grew alert and eager. "She couldn't have known much about chrysanthemums. You can raise them from seed, but it's much easier to root the little sprouts you see there."

"Oh," he said. "I s'pose I can't take none to her, then?" 60

"Why yes you can," Elisa cried. "I can put some in damp sand, and you can carry them right along with you. They'll take root in the pot if you keep them damp. And then she can transplant them."

"She'd sure like to have some, ma'am. You say they're nice ones?"

"Beautiful," she said. "Oh, beautiful." Her eyes shone. She tore off the battered hat and shook out her dark pretty hair. "I'll put them in a flower pot, and you can take them right with you. Come into the yard."

While the man came through the picket gate Elisa ran excitedly along the geranium-bordered path to the back of the house. And she returned carrying a big red flower pot. The gloves were forgotten now. She kneeled on the ground by the starting bed and dug up the sandy soil with her fingers and scooped it into the bright new flower pot. Then she picked up the little pile of shoots she had prepared. With her strong fingers she pressed them into the sand and tamped around them with her knuckles. The man stood over her. "I'll tell you what to do," she said. "You remember so you can tell the lady."

"Yes, I'll try to remember." 65

"Well, look. These will take root in about a month. Then she must set them out, about a foot apart in good rich earth like this, see?" She lifted a handful of dark soil for him to look at. "They'll grow fast and tall. Now remember this. In July tell her to cut them down, about eight inches from the ground."

"Before they bloom?" he asked.

"Yes, before they bloom." Her face was tight with eagerness. "They'll grow right up again. About the last of September the buds will start."

She stopped and seemed perplexed. "It's the budding that takes the most care," she said hesitantly. "I don't know how to tell you." She looked deep into his eyes, searchingly. Her mouth opened a little, and she seemed to be listening. "I'll try to tell you," she said. "Did you ever hear of planting hands?"

"Can't say I have, ma'am." 70

"Well, I can only tell you what it feels like. It's when you're picking off the buds you don't want. Everything goes right down into your fingertips. You watch your fingers work. They do it themselves. You can feel how it is. They pick and pick the buds. They never make a mistake. They're with the plant. Do you see? Your fingers and the plant. You can feel that, right up your arm. They know. They never make a mistake. You can feel it. When you're like that you can't do anything wrong. Do you see that? Can you understand that?"

She was kneeling on the ground looking up at him. Her breast swelled passionately.

The man's eyes narrowed. He looked away self-consciously. "Maybe I know," he said. "Sometimes in the night in the wagon there—"

Elisa's voice grew husky. She broke in on him. "I've never lived as you do, but I know what you mean. When the night is dark—why, the stars are sharp-pointed, and there's quiet. Why, you rise up and up! Every pointed star gets driven into your body. It's like that. Hot and sharp and—lovely."

75 Kneeling there, her hand went out toward his legs in the greasy black trousers. Her hesitant fingers almost touched the cloth. Then her hand dropped to the ground. She crouched low like a fawning dog.

He said, "It's nice, just like you say. Only when you don't have no dinner, it ain't."

She stood up then, very straight, and her face was ashamed. She held the flower pot out to him and placed it gently in his arms. "Here. Put it in your wagon, on the seat, where you can watch it. Maybe I can find something for you to do."

At the back of the house she dug in the can pile and found two old and battered aluminum saucepans. She carried them back and gave them to him. "Here, maybe you can fix these."

His manner changed. He became professional. "Good as new I can fix them." At the back of his wagon he set a little anvil, and out of an oily tool box dug a small machine hammer. Elisa came through the gate to watch him while he pounded out the dents in the kettles. His mouth grew sure and knowing. At a difficult part of the work he sucked his under-lip.

80 "You sleep right in the wagon?" Elisa asked.

"Right in the wagon, ma'am. Rain or shine. I'm dry as a cow in there."

"It must be nice," she said. "It must be very nice. I wish women could do such things."

"It ain't the right kind of a life for a woman."

Her upper lip raised a little, showing her teeth. "How do you know? How can you tell?" she said.

85 "I don't know ma'am," he protested. "Of course I don't know. Now here's your kettles, done. You don't have to buy no new ones."

"How much?"

"Oh, fifty cents'll do. I keep my prices down and my work good. That's why I have all them satisfied customers up and down the highway."

Elisa brought him a fifty-cent piece from the house and dropped it in his hand. "You might be surprised to have a rival some time. I can sharpen scissors, too. And I can beat the dents out of little pots. I could show you what a woman might do."

He put his hammer back in the oily box and shoved the little anvil out of sight. "It would be a lonely life for a woman, ma'am, and a scarey life, too, with animals creeping under the wagon all night." He climbed over the single-tree, steadying himself with a hand on the burro's white rump. He settled himself in the seat, picked up the lines. "Thank you kindly, ma'am," he said. "I'll do like you told me; I'll go back and catch the Salinas road."

90 "Mind," she called, "if you're long in getting there, keep the sand damp."

"Sand, ma'am? . . . Sand? Oh, sure. You mean round the chrysanthemums. Sure I will." He clucked his tongue. The beasts leaned luxuriously into their collars. The mongrel dog took his place between the back wheels. The wagon turned and crawled out the entrance road and back the way it had come, along the river.

Elisa stood in front of her wire fence watching the slow progress of the caravan. Her shoulders were straight, her head thrown back, her eyes half-closed, so that the scene came vaguely into them. Her lips moved silently, forming the words "Good-bye—good-bye." Then she whispered, "That's a bright direction. There's a glowing there." The sound of her whisper startled her. She shook herself free and looked about to see whether anyone had been listening. Only the dogs had heard. They lifted their heads toward her from their sleeping in the dust, and then stretched out their chins and settled asleep again. Elisa turned and ran hurriedly into the house.

In the kitchen she reached behind the stove and felt the water tank. It was full of hot water from the noonday cooking. In the bathroom she tore off her soiled clothes and flung them into the corner. And then she scrubbed herself with a little block of pumice, legs and thighs, loins and chest and arms, until her skin was scratched and red. When she had dried herself she stood in front of a mirror in her bedroom and looked at her body. She tightened her stomach and threw out her chest. She turned and looked over her shoulder at her back.

After a while she began to dress, slowly. She put on her newest under-clothing and her nicest stockings and the dress which was the symbol of her prettiness. She worked carefully on her hair, pencilled her eyebrows and rouged her lips.

Before she was finished she heard the little thunder of hoofs and the shouts of Henry and his helper as they drove the red steers into the corral. She heard the gate bang shut and set herself for Henry's arrival.

His step sounded on the porch. He entered the house calling "Elisa, where are you?"

"In my room, dressing. I'm not ready. There's hot water for your bath. Hurry up. It's getting late."

When she heard him splashing in the tub, Elisa laid his dark suit on the bed, and shirt and socks and tie beside it. She stood his polished shoes on the floor beside the bed. Then she went to the porch and sat primly and stiffly down. She looked toward the river road where the willow-line was still yellow with frosted leaves so that under the high grey fog they seemed a thin band of sunshine. This was the only color in the grey afternoon. She sat unmoving for a long time. Her eyes blinked rarely.

Henry came banging out of the door, shoving his tie inside his vest as he came. Elisa stiffened and her face grew tight. Henry stopped short and looked at her. "Why—why, Elisa. You look so nice!"

"Nice? You think I look nice? What do you mean by 'nice'?"

Henry blundered on. "I don't know. I mean you look different, strong and happy."

"I am strong? Yes, strong. What do you mean 'strong'?"

He looked bewildered. "You're playing some kind of a game," he said helplessly. "It's a kind of a play. You look strong enough to break a calf over your knee, happy enough to eat it like watermelon."

For a second she lost her rigidity. "Henry! Don't talk like that. You didn't know what you said." She grew complete again. "I'm strong," she boasted. "I never knew before how strong."

Henry looked down toward the tractor shed, and when he brought his eyes back to her, they were his own again. "I'll get out the car. You can put on your coat while I'm starting."

Elisa went into the house. She heard him drive to the gate and idle down his motor, and then she took a long time to put on her hat. She pulled it here and pressed it there. When Henry turned the motor off she slipped into her coat and went out.

The little roadster bounced along on the dirt road by the river, raising the birds and driving the rabbits into the brush. Two cranes flapped heavily over the willow-line and dropped into the river-bed.

Far ahead on the road Elisa saw a dark speck. She knew.

She tried not to look as they passed it, but her eyes would not obey. She whispered to herself sadly. "He might have thrown them off the road. That wouldn't have been much trouble, not very much. But he kept the pot," she explained. "He had to keep the pot. That's why he couldn't get them off the road."

The roadster turned a bend and she saw the caravan ahead. She swung full around toward her husband so she could not see the little covered wagon and the mismatched team as the car passed them.

In a moment it was over. The thing was done. She did not look back. She said loudly, to be heard above the motor, "It will be good, tonight, a good dinner."

"Now you're changed again," Henry complained. He took one hand from the wheel and patted her knee. "I ought to take you in to dinner oftener. It would be good for both of us. We get so heavy out on the ranch."

"Henry," she asked, "could we have wine at dinner?"

"Sure we could. Say! That will be fine."

115   She was silent for a little while; then she said, "Henry, at those prize fights, do the men hurt each other very much?"

"Sometimes a little, not often. Why?"

"Well, I've read how they break noses, and blood runs down their chests. I've read how the fighting gloves get heavy and soggy with blood."

He looked around at her. "What's the matter, Elisa? I didn't know you read things like that." He brought the car to a stop, then turned to the right over the Salinas River bridge.

"Do any women ever go to the fights?" she asked.

120   "Oh, sure, some. What's the matter, Elisa? Do you want to go? I don't think you'd like it, but I'll take you if you really want to go."

She relaxed limply in the seat. "Oh, no. No. I don't want to go. I'm sure I don't." Her face was turned away from him. "It will be enough if we can have wine. It will be plenty." She turned up her coat collar so he could not see that she was crying weakly—like an old woman.

QUESTIONS

1. What point of view is used in the story? What are the advantages of this point of view?

2. Consider the symbolism of the setting in this story with respect to the Salinas Valley, the time of year, and the description of the Allen house. What do these things tell us about Elisa Allen and her world?

3. To what extent is Steinbeck's description of Elisa in paragraphs 5 and 6 symbolic? What is she wearing? What do her clothes hide or suppress?

4. What do the chrysanthemums symbolize for Elisa? What do they symbolize *about* her? What role do these flowers play in her life?

5. How does Elisa's character or sense of self change during the episode in which she washes and dresses for dinner? To what extent is this washing-dressing episode symbolic? How would you explain the symbolism?

6. Consider the symbolic impact of Elisa's seeing the chrysanthemum sprouts at the roadside. What does her reaction tell us about her values?

WRITING ABOUT SYMBOLISM AND ALLEGORY

To discover possible parallels that determine the presence of symbolism or allegory, consider the following questions.

Questions for Discovering Ideas

SYMBOLISM

- What cultural or universal symbols can you discover in names, objects, places, situations, or actions in a work (e.g., the character Faith, the woods, and the walking stick in "Young Goodman Brown"; the bleakness of the weather in "The Chrysanthemums"; or the straying son in "The Parable of the Prodigal Son")?

- What contextual symbolism can be found in a work? What leads you to conclude that it is symbolic? What is being symbolized? How definite or direct is the symbolism? How systematically is it used? How necessary to the work is it? To what degree does it strengthen the work? How strongly does the work stand on its own without the reading for symbolism?
- Is it possible to make parallel lists to show how qualities of a particular symbol match the qualities of a character or action? Here is such a list for the toy windmill in Welty's "A Worn Path"(Chapter 5):

Qualities of the Windmill	Comparable Qualities in Phoenix and Her Life
1. Cheap	1. Poor, but she gives all her money for the windmill
2. Breakable	2. Old, and not far from death
3. A gift	3. Generous
4. Not practical	4. Needs relief from reality and practicality
5. Colorful	5. Needs something new and cheerful

ALLEGORY

- How clearly does the author point you toward an allegorical reading (i.e., through names and allusions, consistency of narrative, literary context)?
- How consistent is the allegorical application? Does the entire work, or only a part, embody the allegory? On what basis do you draw these conclusions?
- How complete is the allegorical reading? How might the allegory yield to a diagram such as the one shown below on Hawthorne's "Young Goodman Brown," which shows how characters, actions, objects, and ideas correspond allegorically?

Young Goodman Brown	Brown Himself	Citizens of the Village	The Forest Figure (Father), the Devil	Faith	The Forest Meeting	Retreat into Suspicion and Distrust
Allegorical application to morality and faith	Potential for good	Culture and religious reinforcement	Forces of evil and deceit	Salvation and love; ideals to be rescued and preserved	Attack on ideals; incentive to disillusionment	Destruction of faith; doubt, spiritual negligence, loss of certainty, increase of gloom and suspicion
Allegorical application to personal and general concerns	Individual in pursuit of goals	External support for personal strength and growth	Obstacles to overcome, or by which to be overcome	Personal involvement, steadiness, happiness, religious conviction	Susceptibility to deceit, lack of conviction, misunderstanding, misinterpretation of others	Failure, depression, discouragement, disappointment, bitterness

OTHER FORMS

• What enables you to identify the story as a parable or fable? What lesson or moral is either clearly stated or implicit?

• What mythological identification is established in the work? What do you find in the story (names, situations, etc.) that enables you to determine its mythological significance? How is the myth to be understood? What symbolic value does the myth have? What current and timeless application does it have?

Strategies for Organizing Ideas

Relate the central idea of your essay to the meaning of the major symbols or allegorical thrust of the story. An idea about Goodman Brown, for example, is that fanaticism darkens and limits the human soul. An early incident in the story provides symbolic support for this idea. Specifically, when Goodman Brown enters the woods, he resolves "to stand firm against the devil," and he then looks up toward "Heaven above him." As he looks, a "black mass of cloud" appears to hide the "brightening stars" (page 346, paragraph 47). Within the limits of our central idea, the cloud can be seen as a symbol, just like the widening path or the night walk itself. Look for ways to make solid connections like this when you designate something as a symbol or allegory.

Also, your essay will need to include justifications for your symbols or allegorical parallels. In Poe's "The Masque of the Red Death" (Chapter 9), for example, Prince Prospero's seemingly impregnable "castellated abbey" is a line of defense against the plague. But the Red Death in a human shape easily invades the castle and conquers Prospero and his ill-fated guests. If you treat the abbey as a symbol, it is important to apply it to measures that people take (medicine, escapist activity, etc.) to keep death distant and remote. In the same way, in describing the allegorical elements in "Young Goodman Brown," you need to establish a comprehensive statement such as the following: People lose ideals and forsake principles not because they are evil but because they misunderstand the people around them (see the second illustrative essay that follows).

For the body of your essay there are a number of strategies for discussing symbolism and allegory. You might use one exclusively or a combination.

SYMBOLISM If you want to write about symbolism, you might consider the following points:

1. *The meaning of a major symbol.* Identify the symbol and what it stands for. Then answer questions such as these: Is the symbol cultural or contextual? How do you decide? How do you derive your interpretation of the symbolic meaning? What is the extent of the meaning? Does the symbol undergo modification or new applications if it reappears in the work? How does the symbol affect your understanding of the work? Does the symbol bring out any ironies? How does the symbol add strength and depth to the work?

2. *The development and relationship of symbols.* For two or more symbols, consider issues such as these: How do the symbols connect with each other (like night and the cloud in "Young Goodman Brown" as symbols of a darkening mind)? What additional meanings do the symbols provide? (The windmill and the medicine in "A Worn Path," for example, are ironic because the windmill suggests cheer while the medicine suggests hopelessness.) Do the symbols control the form of the work? How? (For example, at the beginning of Steinbeck's "The Chrysanthemums" the barren wintry countryside is compared to a "closed pot," and at the ending Elisa learns that the tinsmith has dumped the earth out of the flower pot that she had given to him as a gift. In a similar vein, Joyce's "Araby" in Chapter 4 begins with the "blind" or dead-end street and ends with the darkness of the closed bazaar.) Can these comparable objects and conditions be viewed symbolically in relationship to the development of the two stories? Other issues are whether the symbols fit naturally or artificially into the context of the story or whether and how the writer's symbols create a unique quality or excellence.

ALLEGORY When writing about allegory, you might use one of the following approaches.

1. *The application and meaning of the allegory.* What is the subject of the story (allegory, fable, parable, myth)? How can it be more generally applied to ideas or to qualities of human character, not only of its own time but also of our own? What other versions of the story do you know, if any? Does it illustrate, either closely or loosely, particular philosophies or religious views? If so, what are these? How do you know?

2. *The consistency of the allegory.* Is the allegory used consistently throughout the story, or is it used intermittently? Explain and illustrate this use. Would it be correct to call your story allegorical rather than an allegory? Can you determine how parts of the story are introduced for their allegorical importance? Examples are the increasingly dark pathway leading to home in Bierce's "An Occurrence at Owl Creek Bridge" (Chapter 1), which indicates the weakening hold that Farquhar has on life, the shabby fur muff in Mansfield's "Miss Brill" (Chapter 3), which suggest the comparably dismal circumstances of Miss Brill herself, and the Champs Elysées, the fashionable Parisian street in Maupassant's "The Necklace" (Part I), which corresponds to Mathilde's constant temptation to live beyond her means.

In concluding, you might summarize main points, describe general impressions, explain the impact of the symbolic or allegorical methods, indicate personal responses, or suggest further lines of thought and application. You might also assess the quality and appropriateness of the symbolism or allegory (such as Hawthorne's "Young Goodman Brown" opening at sunset and closing in gloom).

Illustrative Student Essay (Symbolism)

Although underlined sentences are not recommended by MLA style, they are used in this illustrative essay as teaching tools to emphasize the central idea, thesis sentence, and topic sentences.

Raj 1

Michael Raj

Professor Thomas

English 320

27 January, 2014

Symbols of Light and Darkness in Porter's "The Jilting of Granny Weatherall"°

[1]   In Katherine Anne Porter's "The Jilting of Granny Weatherall," Ellen Weatherall—Granny Weatherall—is lying on her deathbed, and things in the story are described as they are being filtered through her conscious and unconscious mind. For sixty of her eighty years Granny has been a tower of strength to those around her, but now she is succumbing to a series of powerful strokes, climaxed by the "deep roaring" of the terminal, killing stroke (357). As she gets closer and closer to her last moments she fades in and out of awareness, and she finally loses direct awareness of her adult children who are keeping vigil around her. Near the end, as she receives last rites from her priest, she does not understand what is happening to her (357). While she sometimes makes at least some contact with those around her, her mind wanders and touches base with her lifelong beliefs, hopes, plans, fears, embarrassments, sorrows, intentions, and convictions. Her mental associations reveal her personality as a valiant and triumphant woman who has met and overcome the major obstacles and challenges of her life.

[2]   She has been constant in her religious duties, and religious concerns are never far from her mind. For example, one of her last thoughts is that she wants to send six bottles of wine to a Sister Borgia (357). In her delirium her thoughts touch on her gratefulness for her life of hard work and service, and also on her love for her children, even including a child,

°**This story appears on pages 352–357.**

Raj 2

Hapsy, whom she apparently lost in childbirth but whom she imagines as having lived to adulthood (Hapsy seems to be the "something not given back" that she tries to remember [355]). Significantly, as Granny's thoughts "spread the plan of life and tuck in the edges orderly" (353), her memories are dominated by biblical symbols of light and darkness.* The symbols of light crystallize her convictions and ideals, while the symbols of darkness express her lifelong fears and anxieties.†

Light, whiteness, and brightness symbolize the security and inner peace   [3]
that Granny has sought but not always found. Several times she recalls that during her lifetime she made a ceremony out of lighting the household lamps to dispel the darkness, thus acting out many actions reminiscent of the Bible, such as the books of Genesis and Exodus. She remembers that when fog began to move toward her house, "marching across the creek swallowing the trees and moving up the hill like an army of ghosts," her regular reaction was "to go in and light the lamps" (354). She also remembers that "lighting the lamps had been beautiful" when her children were small (354). After the rooms had been illuminated, the children would no longer be frightened: "they didn't have to be scared and hang on to mother any more. Never, never, never more" (354). Furthermore, when Granny contemplates having chased the darkness of their fears away with light, she associates the light with divine protection and guidance. She likes strong, bright light, not the blue light shining from her daughter Cornelia's silk lampshades, which she believes are "[no] sort of light at all, just frippery" (356). Although darkness has always loomed near her, Granny constantly found comfort in light and brightness symbols that reflect her need for order and peace of mind.

In contrast, images of darkness, smoke, and fog suggest the fear, doubt,   [4]
and instability that Granny associates with uncertainty and abandonment. We learn that at the age of twenty she experienced the most crushing event of her life. On the day of her intended marriage, her fiancé, George, jilted her at the altar. She was inconsolable, and "The whole bottom dropped out of the world,

---

*Central idea.
†Thesis sentence.

Raj 3

and there she was blind and sweating and nothing under her feet and the walls falling away" (356). When she recalls this betrayal, dark images flow into her mind—disturbing symbols of horror and rejection: "There was the day, the day, but a whirl of dark smoke rose and covered it, crept up and over into the bright field. [. . .] That was hell, she knew hell when she saw it" (355). Even her marriage with John, who died young and left her as a widow to rear their children, has not lessened her pain and regret. On her deathbed, after sixty years of "pray[ing] against remembering him [George] and against losing her soul in the deep pit of hell" (355), another symbol of darkness indicates that she has never truly recovered from being rejected: "the thought of him was a smoky cloud from hell that moved and crept in her head" (355). These symbols of darkness bring out the shattering anguish of Granny's memory.

[5]   At the end of the story, the combination of references to light and dark symbolizes the second "jilting" that Granny has experienced in her life. After Porter establishes that darkness symbolizes doubt and despair and that light symbolizes safety and security, she uses both symbols to show Granny's state of mind during her final moments. Granny visualizes a "point of light that was herself" which is being consumed by darkness (357). Through repetition, Porter stresses the negative symbolism of darkness, for Granny's "body was now only a deeper mass of shadow in an endless darkness and this darkness would curl around the light and swallow it up" (357). As the darkness overwhelms her, she cries out to God to give her a saving and healing sign of divine presence. But "[f]or the second time there was no sign" (357)—a direct echo of Matthew 12:39 ("there shall no sign be given"). It is safe to assume that Granny feels the despair of darkness as she dies, for her thoughts of George as bridegroom merge with her thoughts of God as bridegroom, and she feels jilted by the second just as by the first. Despite her despair, however, the true status of her soul is demonstrated by what we have learned throughout the story about the energy and devotion of her life. Her achievement as the center of her family is summed up by her brief prayer

Raj 4

as she remembers lighting the lamps, which is to her the symbol of divine love:

"God, for all my life I thank thee. Without Thee, my God, I could never have
done it" (354).

    The symbols are of course not only symbols, but they also have a basis   [6]
in the actual reality of light and darkness. Thus at one point Granny remarks
that she should "hide from the light" and that "sleeping in the light gave you
nightmares". It appears that here, at least, reality is more significant than
symbolism. When Granny approaches the very end of the "hard pull" of her life,
she despairs because of the "cruel" realization that she has received no divine
sign. The last words of the story describe her last moment: "She stretched herself
with a deep breath and blew out the light." This ending is final, and at first we
might think that Granny's light is gone and that the darkness she feared has
overcome her. Another biblical quotation, however, may put the two symbols
into additional perspective, for we learn in Isaiah that in the long run both light
and darkness are divine, for God says, "I form the light, and create darkness"
(Isaiah 45:7). This is a dimension of Granny's life that goes beyond symbolism.

Raj 5

Work Cited

Porter, Katherine Anne. "The Jilting of Granny Weatherall." *Literature:*
    An Introduction to Reading and Writing, Compact Edition. Ed. Edgar
    V. Roberts and Robert Zweig. 6th ed. New York: Pearson, 2015.
    352–57. Print.

Commentary on the Essay About Symbolism

This essay illustrates the principles of analysis described in the second part of the
guide for considering symbolism. Connection within the essay may be seen in the
continuity of topic from paragraph 1 to paragraph 2, and also from paragraph 4 to
paragraph 5. Additionally, some of the individual words and phrases providing continuity are "in contrast," "another," "despite," "however," and "not only . . . but also."

Paragraph 1 establishes the nature of the story and also the qualities of the major character, Granny Weatherall. Paragraph 2 introduces her religious outlook, and it also contains the central idea, about the significance of symbolic light and darkness in the story. The concluding thesis sentence indicates that the body of the essay will treat the meanings of both symbols.

In the body, paragraph 3 introduces the idea that both symbols are common in the Bible, and that therefore they are a natural function of Granny's religiosity. Paragraph 4 is in contrast to paragraph 3 because it explains that Granny was jilted at age twenty and that she has always associated this horrible memory with darkness. Paragraph 5 emphasizes that to Granny, the darkness seems to be victorious as she assumes that God has deserted her just as she had been jilted when she was young. Paragraph 6 concludes the essay by (1) treating the reality of light and dark in the story, thereby pointing out that the symbols are not consistently used symbolically, and (2) introducing the biblical idea that Granny is in divine hands, whether in lightness or darkness.

Second Illustrative Student Essay (Allegory)

Although underlined sentences are not recommended by MLA style, they are used in this illustrative essay as teaching tools to emphasize the central idea, thesis sentence, and topic sentences.

Murphy 1

Heather Murphy

Professor Thomas

English 2B

10 December 2014

The Allegory of Hawthorne's "Young Goodman Brown"°

[1]   Nathaniel Hawthorne's "Young Goodman Brown" is a nightmarish narrative. It allegorizes the process by which something good—religion— becomes a justification for intolerance and prejudice. The major character, Young Goodman Brown of colonial Salem, begins as a pious and holy person, but he takes a walk into a nearby darkening forest of suspicion. The process is portrayed by Hawthorne as something created by the devil himself, who leads Goodman Brown into the increasingly evil and sinful

°**This story appears on pages 342–350.**

Murphy 2

night. By the end of the allegory, Brown is transformed into an unforgiving, antisocial, dour, and dreary misanthrope.

Hawthorne's choice of the story's location reminds us that it was in [2] Salem, in the late seventeenth century, that religious zealousness became so extreme that a number of witch trials and public hangings took place solely on the basis of suspicion and false accusation. This setting indicates that Hawthorne's immediate allegorical target is the overzealous pursuit of religious principles. And so Goodman Brown's trip not only takes him into the gloom of night, but also marks a descent into the darkest dungeons of his soul.*

While the story presents Brown's embarkation into religious zealotry, [3] Hawthorne's allegory may also be applied generally to the ways in which people uncritically follow *any* ideal which leads them to distrust and suspect others. The allegory thus applies to those who swallow political slogans, who believe in their own racial or ethnic superiority, or who justify super-patriotism and super-nationalism. Thus convinced of their own supremacy, people ignore the greater need for love, understanding, toleration, cooperation, and forgiveness. Hawthorne's allegory is a realistic portrait of how people get into such a mental state, with Goodman Brown as the major example. Such people push ahead even against their own good nature and background, and they become prejudiced through delusion and suspicion.†

Young Goodman Brown's pathway into the night is not a direct plunge, [4] but first Hawthorne shows that Brown does not begin without good nature. Many times early in the story we learn that Brown has doubts about the "evil purpose" of his allegorical walk. At the very beginning, Faith calls him back and pleads with him to stay with her, but even so, he leaves her. As he walks away he thinks of himself as "a wretch" for doing so (342). He excuses himself with a promise that once the evening is over he will stick with Faith forever after—an "excellent resolve for the future," as the narrator ironically states (343). When Goodman Brown is reproached by the devil for being late, he

*Central idea.
†Thesis sentence.

Murphy 3

gives the excuse "Faith kept me back a while" (343), a sentence of ironic double meaning. Once he has kept his appointment with the devil, he states his intention to go no farther because he has "scruples" which remind him that "it is my purpose now to return whence I came" (343). When he refers to his family's proud and virtuous heritage, the devil is amused by his naivety. Even when Brown is standing before the altar of profanation deep within the forest, he appeals to Faith, "Look up to Heaven, and resist the Wicked One!" (349). All this hesitation represents a true conscience in Goodman Brown even though he ignores it as he progresses deeper into the forest of sin. His failure— and failure it is—is his inability or unwillingness to persist in making his own insight and conscience his guides of conduct.

[5]   It is important to remember that Goodman Brown is favored by his background, which should have kept him on a true path of goodness. Almost as a claim of entitlement he cries out, "With Heaven above, and Faith below, I will yet stand firm against the devil" (346). He also cries out for Faith even when he hears a voice resembling hers that is "uttering lamentations" within the darkening woods (346). When he sees Faith's pink ribbon fluttering down, he exclaims, "My Faith is gone!" (347). These instances show allegorically that Goodman Brown's previous way of life has given him proper spiritual guidance. Even as he is tempted before the "unhallowed altar" (349), he asks the question "But, where is Faith?" as though he could reclaim his previous innocence (349). Just as he ignores his conscience, he also ignores the power of his background, and it is this neglect that fuels his change into the "demoniac" who abandons himself to "the instinct that guides mortal man to evil" (347).

[6]   Another major element in Goodman Brown's allegorical path to darkness is that he persuades himself that virtually all the people he knows have yielded their lives to sin. In the grips of this distorted view of others, he believes not what he sees but what he thinks he is seeing. Thus he witnesses the encounter between the devil and Goody Cloyse shortly after he enters the forest, but what he sees is not the good woman who taught him his catechism but rather

Murphy 4

a witch who is bent on evil and who is friendly with the devil. He ignores the fact that he too is friendly with the devil (the image of his own father) and therefore, while ignoring the log in his own eye, he condemns Goody Cloyse for the speck in hers. After his transformation, when he walks back into his village from his allegorical walk into evil, he "snatche[s] away" a child from Goody as though she were preaching the words of the devil (349). He cannot believe that others possess goodness as long as he is convinced by the devil's words that "the whole earth [is] one stain of guilt, one mighty blood-spot" (349). For this reason he condemns both his minister and Deacon Gookin, whose conspiratorial voices he imagines that he overhears on the pathway through the forest. In short, the process of Hawthorne's allegory about the growth of harmful pietism demonstrates that travelers on the pathway to prejudice accept suspicion and mistrust without trying to get at the whole truth and without recognizing that judgment is not in human but rather is in divine hands.

As Hawthorne allegorizes the development of religious discrimination he [7] makes clear that mistrust and suspicion form its basis. Certainly, as the devil claims, human beings commit many criminal and depraved sins (348), but this does not mean that all human beings are equally at fault, and that they are beyond love and redemption. The key for Goodman Brown is that he exceeds his judgmental role and condemns others solely on his own hasty conclusions. As long as he has faith he will not falter, but when he leaves his faith, or believes that he has lost his faith, he is adrift and will see only evil wherever he looks. For this reason he permits suspicion and loathing to distort his previous love for his wife and neighbors, and he becomes harsh and desperate. Hawthorne devotes the concluding paragraph of the story to a brief summary of Brown's life after the fateful night. This conclusion completes the allegorical cycle beginning with Brown's initiation into evil and extending to his "dying hour" of "gloom" and his unhopeful tombstone (349).

Hawthorne's "Young Goodman Brown" allegorizes the paradox of how [8] noble beliefs become ignoble. Goodman Brown dies in gloom because he believes that his wrong vision is true. His form of evil is the hardest to stop because wrongdoers who are convinced of their own goodness are beyond reach. In view of such self-righteous evil, whether cloaked in the apparent virtues of Puritanism or of some other blindly rigorous doctrine, Hawthorne writes, "the fiend in his own shape is less hideous than when he rages in the breast of man". Young Goodman Brown is one of the many who create darkness but are convinced that they alone walk in light.

Work Cited

Hawthorne, Nathaniel. "Young Goodman Brown." *Literature: An Introduction to Reading and Writing, Compact Edition.* Ed. Edgar V. Roberts and Robert Zweig. 6th ed. New York: Pearson, 2015. 342–50. Print.

Commentary on the Essay About Allegory

This essay deals with a major idea in "Young Goodman Brown," and it therefore illustrates the first approach described earlier (p. 365). Unity in the essay is achieved by a number of means. For example, paragraph 2 extends a topic in paragraph 1. Also, a phrase in sentence 2 of paragraph 1 is echoed in sentence 1 of paragraph 8. Making additional connections within the essay are individual words such as "another," "while," "therefore," and the repetition of words throughout the essay that are contained in the thesis sentence.

The first three paragraphs of the essay constitute an extended introduction to the topics of paragraphs 4 through 8, for they establish "Young Goodman Brown" as an allegory. Paragraph 1 briefly treats the allegorical nature of the narrative. Paragraph 2 relates the historical basis of the topic to Hawthorne's purpose in writing the story, and it concludes with the essay's central idea. Paragraph 3 broadens the scope of Hawthorne's allegory by showing that it includes zealousness wherever it might appear. Paragraph 3 also concludes with the essay's thesis sentence.

Paragraph 4, the first in the body, deals with an important aspect of the allegory, and one that makes it particularly relevant and timely even today—namely, that people of goodwill may become evil under the pretense of goodness.

Similarly, paragraph 5 points out that such people usually come from good backgrounds and have benefited from good influences during their lives.

Paragraphs 6 and 7 locate the origins of evil in two major human qualities—first, the belief in one's own delusions; and second, the mental confusion that results from the conviction that appearance is more real and believable than reality itself. Paragraph 8 concludes the essay on the note that the finished "product"—a person who has become suspicious and misguided—demonstrates how good ideas, when pushed to the extreme by false imagination, can backfire.

Writing Topics About Symbolism and Allegory

Writing Paragraphs

1. Why do writers who advocate moral, philosophical, or religious issues frequently use symbolism or allegory? Write a paragraph in which you answer this question. In treating this question, you might introduce references from "The Parable of the Prodigal Son" and Hawthorne's "Young Goodman Brown."

Writing Essays

1. Write an essay in which you compare and contrast the symbolism in Porter's "The Jilting of Granny Weatherall" (this chapter), Faulkner's "A Rose for Emily" (Chapter 1), and Steinbeck's "The Chrysanthemums" (this chapter). To what degree do the stories rely on contextual symbols? On universal symbols? On the basis of your comparison, what is the case for asserting that realism and fantasy are directly related to the nature of the symbolism employed by the writer?

2. Write an essay on the allegorical method of one or more of the parables included in the Gospel of St. Luke, such as "The Bridegroom" (5:34–35), "The Garments and the Wineskins" (5:36–39), "The Sower" (8:4–15), "The Good Samaritan" (10:25–37), "The Prodigal Son" (15:11–32), "The Ox in the Well" (14:5–6), "The Watering of Animals on the Sabbath" (13:15–17), "The Rich Fool" (12:16–21), "Lazarus" (16:19–31), "The Widow and the Judge" (18:1–8), and "The Pharisee and the Publican" (18:9–14).

Creative Writing Assignment

1. Write your own brief story using a widely recognized cultural symbol such as the flag (patriotism, love of country, a certain type of politics), water (life, sexuality, regeneration), or the population explosion (the end of life on earth). By arranging actions and dialogue, make clear the issues conveyed by your symbol, and also try to resolve conflicts the symbol might raise among your characters.

2. Write a brief story in which you develop your own contextual symbol. You might, for example, demonstrate how holding a job brings out character strengths that are not at first apparent or how neglecting to care for the inside

or outside of a house indicates a character's decline. The principle is to take something that can at first seem normal and ordinary and then to make that thing symbolic as you develop your story.

Library Assignment

1. Using the catalog system of your library, discover a recent critical-biographical book or books about Hawthorne. Explain what the book says about Hawthorne's uses of symbolism. To what extent does the book relate Hawthorne's symbolism to his religious and family heritage?

Chapter 8
Idea or Theme: The Meaning and the Message in Fiction

380

AFTER READING THIS MATERIAL, YOU SHOULD BE ABLE TO DO THE FOLLOWING:

- Explain the concept and importance of a work's idea or theme
- Illustrate the formulation of ideas as assertions
- Distinguish between issues and values as they relate to literary ideas
- Discuss how effectively ideas are expressed in literary works

The word **idea** refers to the result or results of general and abstract thinking. Synonymous words are *concept, thought, opinion,* and *principle*. In literary study the consideration of ideas relates to *meaning, interpretation, explanation,* and *significance*. Although ideas are usually extensive and complex, separate ideas can be described by individual words such as *right, good, love, piety, liberty, causation, wilderness,* and, not surprisingly, *idea* itself.

Ideas and Assertions

Although single words alone can name ideas, we must put these words into operation in *sentences* or *assertions* before they can advance our understanding. Good operational sentences about ideas are not the same as ordinary conversational statements such as "It's a nice day." An observation of this sort may be true (depending on the weather), but it gives us no ideas and does not stimulate our minds. Rather, a sentence asserting an idea about a nice day should initiate a thought or argument about the day's quality, such as "A nice day requires light breezes, blue sky, a warm sun, and relaxation." Because this sentence makes an assertion about the word *nice*, it allows us to consider and develop the idea of a nice day.

In studying literature, always express ideas as assertions. For example, you might state that an idea in Lawrence's "The Horse Dealer's Daughter" (this chapter) is "love," but it would be difficult to discuss anything more unless you make an assertion that promises an argument, such as "This story demonstrates the idea that love is irresistible and irrational." This assertion would lead you to explain the unlikely love that bursts out in the story. Similarly, for Welty's "A Worn Path" (Chapter 5) an assertion like the following would advance further argument: "Phoenix embodies the idea that caring for others gives no reward but the continuation of the duty itself."

Although we have noted only one idea in these two works, most stories contain many ideas. When one of the ideas seems to be the major one, which recurs throughout the work, it is called the **theme.** In practice, the words *theme* and *major idea* are the same.

Ideas and Issues

A word that is often used as an equivalent to idea is **issue,** which may be defined as an open and unsettled point or concern about which there may be argument or contention. On political matters, issues are usually about what courses of action to take, such as whether a new bridge should be built, or whether more money should be spent on schools. Often, however, the issues revolve about the theoretical basis on which to proceed. To this extent, issues are very close in meaning to ideas, but also to problems and to difficulties that require some sort of solution. The nature of issue as a concept—because issues develop out of situations—is particularly helpful in the study of literature. Sometimes issues are not stated and we as readers draw conclusions from the work or works we are discussing. What do we find there? What do we take away from that work? Have we understood the issue properly? How do we define the issue as an idea? The answers to such questions frequently lead us directly into discussions of ideas. Chopin's "The Story of an Hour" (Chapter 6) deals with a woman's unexpected thoughts when she is (mistakenly) told that her husband has died, and through her thoughts the story raises the issue of what a woman's role should be in marriage. In Bambara's "The Lesson" (this chapter) we find the issue of economic inequality and political injustice. Here the idea is that economic inequality results in an unacceptably high human cost.

Ideas and Values

Literature embodies **values** along with ideas. *Value*, of course, commonly refers to the price of something, but in the realm of ideas and principles, it is a standard of what is desired, sought, esteemed, and treasured. For example, *democracy* refers to our political system, but it is also a complex idea of representative government that we prize most highly, and so also do we esteem concepts such as *honor, cooperation, generosity,* and *love.* A vital idea/value is *justice*, which, put most simply, involves equality before the law and also the fair evaluation of conduct that is deemed unacceptable or illegal. Literature embodies values along with ideas. This means that ideas imply that certain conditions and standards should be—or should not be—highly esteemed. For example, the idea of *justice* may be considered abstractly and broadly, as Plato does in his *Republic* when developing his concept of a just government. In comparison, justice is also a subject of Susan Glaspell's story "A Jury of Her Peers" (Chapter 3; see also the story's companion piece, the play *Trifles* in Chapter 20). Glaspell treats the value of justice very practically, as a problem that arises when two women, wives of men investigating a murder, discover circumstantial evidence in a dreary farm kitchen that a housewife has strangled her husband in his sleep. One of the women is familiar with the woman and the situation of her miserable marriage, and as a result both women together hide the incriminating evidence. With the freedom of their opportunity, in other words, the women choose to excuse the farm wife, while denying the validity of the strictly legal case against her. By their action they have engaged in their own "jury nullification," by which they find the farm wife not guilty. In their judgment, which they act on but do not discuss, justice is better served by suppressing the evidence they have found in preference to bringing it forward. The idea of justice underlying Glaspell's "A Jury of Her Peers," in short, also involves a deeply held value.

The Place of Ideas in Literature

Because writers of poems, plays, and stories are usually not systematic philosophers, it is not appropriate to go "message hunting" as though their works contained nothing but ideas. Indeed, there is great benefit and pleasure to be derived from just savoring a work—getting engrossed in the story, following the patterns of narrative and conflict, getting to like the characters, understanding the work's implications and suggestions, and listening to the sounds of the author's words—to name only a few of the reasons for which literature is treasured.

Nevertheless, ideas are vital to understanding and appreciating not just fiction but all literature. Writers have ideas and want to communicate them to you. For example, in "The Horse Dealer's Daughter" (this chapter) Lawrence tells the story of a man and a woman who fall unpredictably but passionately in love. This love is unlikely but real, and the story is therefore effective, but the story is also provocative because it develops the idea that love has the power to override all other personal emotions and decisions. Paredes's narrator in "The Hammon and the Beans" (this chapter) tells the story of a little Mexican girl, with great potential but no opportunities at all, who dies from an undisclosed illness produced by her family's impoverishment and medical neglect. Through this event the story conveys the idea that massive humanitarian damage is a major result of economic hardship. In these works, the ideas of the authors both underlie and connect the various narrative details.

Distinguish Between Ideas and Actions

As you analyze works for ideas, it is important to avoid the trap of confusing ideas and actions. Such a trap is contained in the following sentence about O'Connor's "First Confession" (Chapter 6): "The major character, Jackie, misbehaves at home and tries to stab his sister with a bread knife." This sentence successfully describes a major action in the story, but it does not express an *idea* that connects characters and events, and for this reason it obstructs understanding. Some possible connections might be achieved with sentences like these: "'First Confession' illustrates the idea that family life may produce anger and potential violence" or "'First Confession' shows that compelling children to accept authority may produce effects that are the opposite of adult intentions." A study based on these connecting formulations could be focused on ideas and would not be sidetracked into doing no more than retelling O'Connor's story.

Distinguish Between Ideas and Situations

You should also distinguish between ideas and situations. For example, in Joyce's "Araby" (Chapter 4) the narrator describes his frustration and embarrassment when he arrives late at the Araby bazaar in Dublin. This is a *situation*, but it is not the *idea* brought out by the situation. Joyce's idea here is rather that immature love causes unreal dreams and hopes that result in disappointment and self-criticism. If you are able to distinguish a story's various situations from the writer's major idea or ideas, you will be able to focus on ideas and therefore sharpen your own thinking.

How to Find Ideas

Ideas are not as obvious as characters or setting. To determine an idea, you need to consider the meaning of what you read and then to develop explanatory and comprehensive assertions. Your assertions need not be the same as those that others might make. People notice different things, and individual formulations vary. In Chopin's "The Story of an Hour" (Chapter 6), for example, an initial expression of some of the story's ideas might take any of the following forms: (1) Partners in even a good marriage can have ambivalent feelings about their lives together. (2) An unforeseen event can lead a wife to develop negative but previously unrecognized thoughts. (3) Even those closest to a person may never realize this person's innermost feelings. Although any one of these choices could be a basic idea in the study of "The Story of an Hour," they have in common the main character's surprising feelings of release when she is told that her husband has been killed in an accident. In discovering ideas, you should follow a similar process—making a number of formulations for an idea and then selecting one for further development.

As you read, be alert to the different ways in which authors convey ideas. One author might prefer an indirect way through a character's speeches, whereas another may prefer direct statements. In practice, authors can employ any or all of the following methods.

1. *Study the authorial voice.* Although authors mainly render action, dialogue, and situation, they sometimes state ideas to guide us and deepen our understanding. In the second paragraph of Maupassant's "The Necklace" (Part I), for example, the authorial voice presents the idea that women have only charm and beauty to get on in the world. Ironically, Maupassant uses the story to show that for the major character, Mathilde, nothing is effective, for her charm cannot prevent disaster. Hawthorne, in "Young Goodman Brown" (Chapter 7), expresses this powerful idea: "The fiend in his own shape is less hideous than when he rages in the breast of man" (p. 347, paragraph 53). The narrator makes this statement just when the major character, Goodman Brown, is speeding through "the benighted wilderness" on his way to the satanic ritual. Although the idea is complex and will sustain extensive discussion, its essential aspect is that the causes of evil originate within human beings themselves, and the implication is that we alone are responsible for all our actions, whether good or evil.

2. *Study the first-person speaker.* First-person narrators or speakers frequently express ideas along with their depiction of actions and situations, and they also make statements from which you can make inferences about ideas. (See

also Chapter 2, on point of view.) Because what they say is part of a dramatic presentation, they can be right or wrong, well-considered or thoughtless, good or bad, or brilliant or half-baked, depending on the speaker. A somewhat half-baked speaker, yet an interesting one, is Sammy, the narrator of Updike's "A & P" (Chapter 6), who seems to have accepted many intellectual commonplaces, particularly his attitude about the intelligence of women. In his defense, however, Sammy *acts* on the worthy idea that people have private rights. If the speaker seems to possess limited understanding or inadequate consideration of what he or she is saying, like Jackie, sometimes, in Frank O'Connor's "First Confession" (Chapter 6), you may nevertheless still study and evaluate such a speaker's ideas. Jackie, for example, maintains some of his childhood attitudes even though at the time of the narration he is an older and presumably mature narrator. Mrs. Johnson, the simple but mature narrator of Walker's "Everyday Use" describes her reunion with her daughter matter-of-factly, but her narrative voice provides subtle hints that she wisely sees through Dee's pretentious posturing. The first-person narrator of Gilman's "The Yellow Wallpaper" (Chapter 10) is increasingly delusional, yet an idea we can derive from her speech and circumstances is that people with her illness need less harsh and more humane treatment. In Tan's "Two Kinds" (Chapter 3) the narrator describes the negative behavior that stemmed from her childhood conflicts with her mother. An idea that may be taken from this narration is that adult composure is reached only through tortuous childhood paths. If the speaker seems to possess incomplete or limited understanding of what he or she is saying, you may nevertheless still study and evaluate this speaker's ideas. In Bambara's "The Lesson" (this chapter), for example, the narrator, Sylvia, is a child who speaks the language of the streets but who nevertheless exhibits natural analytical skills befitting an astute political scientist.

3. *Study the statements made by characters.* In many stories, characters express their own views, which can be right or wrong, admirable or contemptible. When you consider such dramatic speeches, you must do considerable interpreting and evaluating yourself. Old Man Warner in Jackson's "The Lottery" (Chapter 2) states that the lottery is valuable even though we learn from the narrator that the beliefs underlying it have long been forgotten. Because Warner is an uninformed but insistent person, however, his words show that outdated ideas continue to do harm even when there is strong reason to reevaluate and abandon them.

4. *Study the work's figurative language.* Figurative language is one of the major components of poetry, but it also abounds in prose fiction (see also Chapter 14). In Joyce's "Araby," for example (Chapter 4), the narrator uses a beautiful comparison to describe his youthful admiration for his friend Mangan's sister. He says that his body "was like a harp and her words and gestures were like fingers running upon the wires" (paragraph 5). A less complimentary figure is seen in D. H. Lawrence's "The Horse Dealer's Daughter." Lawrence develops the comparison through the Pervin family. Joe Pervin, one of Mabel's brothers, is demeaning himself by accepting his future role as no more than a subordinate worker for his future father-in-law. Lawrence's idea is that financial security alone involves the sacrifice of personal freedom, and so the

comparison shows that Joe is no different from the great draft horses on the Pervin estate: "He [Joe] would marry and go into harness. His life was over, he would be a subject animal now" (393, paragraph 7).

5. *Study how characters stand for ideas.* Characters and their actions can often be equated with certain ideas and values. The power of Mathilde's story in Maupassant's "The Necklace" (Part I) emphasizes the idea that unrealizable dreams can invade and damage the real world. Two diverse or opposed characters can embody contrasting ideas, as with Louise and Josephine of Chopin's "The Story of an Hour" (Chapter 6). Each woman can be taken to represent differing views about the role of women in marriage. In effect, characters who stand for ideas can assume symbolic status, as in Hawthorne's "Young Goodman Brown" (Chapter 7) where the protagonist symbolizes the alienation accompanying zealousness, or in Ozick's "The Shawl" (Chapter 4) where the small child Magda embodies the vulnerability and helplessness of human beings in the face of dehumanizing state brutality. Such characters can be equated directly with particular ideas, and to talk about them is a shorthand way of talking about the ideas.

6. *Study the work itself as an embodiment of ideas.* One of the most important ways in which authors express ideas is to interlock them within all parts and aspects of the work. When a work is considered in its totality, the various parts collectively can embody major ideas, as in Bierce's "An Occurrence at Owl Creek Bridge" (Chapter 1), where Bierce dramatizes the idea that under great stress the human mind operates with lightning speed. Most works represent ideas in a similar way. Even "escape literature," which at first glance enables readers to forget immediate problems, contains conflicts between good and evil, love and hate, good spies and bad, earthlings and aliens, and so on. Such works *do* thereby embody ideas, even though their avowed intention is not to make readers think but rather to help them forget.

Stories for Study

Margaret Atwood . . . . Happy Endings, 384
Toni Cade Bambara . . . . The Lesson, 387
D. H. Lawrence . . . . The Horse Dealer's Daughter, 392
Américo Paredes . . . . The Hammon and the Beans, 402

MARGARET ATWOOD (b. 1939)

Margaret Atwood is one of Canada's premier writers, having published many books of poetry, novels, and short stories, and a number of critical works. In addition, she is editor of The New Oxford Book of Canadian Verse in English (1982). One of her most recognized works is the anti-Utopian novel, The Handmaid's Tale (1986), which describes a futuristic nightmare society of fear and repression for women and which was adapted as a movie in 1990. The stories in the collection Wilderness Tips (1992) reflect regret and diminished hopes, unlike the more comic topics of her story "Rape Fantasies"

and her poem "Siren Song." The scope of her work may be inferred from just a few of her many other publications, such as The Robber Bride *(1993),* Good Bones and Simple Murders *(1994),* Poems *(1994),* Princess Prunella and the Purple Peanut *(1994), and* Morning in the Burned House *(1995).*

Happy Endings (1983)

John and Mary meet.
What happens next?
If you want a happy ending, try A.

A

John and Mary fall in love and get married. They both have worthwhile and remunerative jobs which they find stimulating and challenging. They buy a charming house. Real estate values go up. Eventually, when they can afford live-in help, they have two children, to whom they are devoted. The children turn out well. John and Mary have a stimulating and challenging sex life and worthwhile friends. They go on fun vacations together. They retire. They both have hobbies which they find stimulating and challenging. Eventually they die. This is the end of the story.

B

Mary falls in love with John but John doesn't fall in love with Mary. He merely uses her body for selfish pleasure and ego gratification of a tepid kind. He comes to her apartment twice a week and she cooks him dinner, you'll notice that he doesn't even consider her worth the price of a dinner out, and after he's eaten the dinner he fucks her and after that he falls asleep, while she does the dishes so he won't think she's untidy, having all those dirty dishes lying around, and puts on fresh lipstick so she'll look good when he wakes up, but when he wakes up he doesn't even notice, he puts on his socks and his shorts and his pants and his shirt and his tie and his shoes, the reverse order from the one in which he took them off. He doesn't take off Mary's clothes, she takes them off herself, she acts as if she's dying for it every time, not because she likes sex exactly, she doesn't, but she wants John to think she does because if they do it often enough surely he'll get used to her, he'll come to depend on her and they will get married, but John goes out the door with hardly so much as a goodnight and three days later he turns up at six o'clock and they do the whole thing over again.

Mary gets rundown. Crying is bad for your face, everyone knows that and so does Mary but she can't stop. People at work notice. Her friends tell her John is a rat, a pig, a dog, he isn't good enough for her, but she can't believe it. Inside John, she thinks, is another John, who is much nicer. This other John will emerge like a butterfly from a cocoon, a Jack from a box, a pit from a prune, if the first John is only squeezed enough.

One evening John complains about the food. He has never complained about the food before. Mary is hurt.

Her friends tell her they've seen him in a restaurant with another woman, whose name is Madge. It's not even Madge that finally gets to Mary; it's the restaurant. John has never taken Mary to a restaurant. Mary collects all the sleeping pills and aspirins she can find, and takes them and a half a bottle of sherry. You can see what kind of a woman she is by the fact that it's not even whiskey. She leaves a note for John. She hopes he'll discover her and get her to the hospital in time and repent and then they can get married, but this fails to happen and she dies.

John marries Madge and everything continues as in A.

C

10   John, who is an older man, falls in love with Mary, and Mary, who is only twenty-two, feels sorry for him because he's worried about his hair falling out. She sleeps with him even though she's not in love with him. She met him at work. She's in love with someone called James, who is twenty-two also and not yet ready to settle down.

John on the contrary settled down long ago: this is what is bothering him. John has a steady, respectable job and is getting ahead in his field, but Mary isn't impressed by him, she's impressed by James, who has a motorcycle and a fabulous record collection. But James is often away on his motorcycle, being free. Freedom isn't the same for girls, so in the meantime Mary spends Thursday evenings with John. Thursdays are the only days John can get away.

John is married to a woman called Madge and they have two children, a charming house which they bought just before the real estate values went up, and hobbies which they find stimulating and challenging, when they have the time. John tells Mary how important she is to him, but of course, he can't leave his wife because a commitment is a commitment. He goes on about this more than is necessary and Mary finds it boring, but older men can keep it up longer so on the whole she has a fairly good time.

One day James breezes in on his motorcycle with some top-grade California hybrid and James and Mary get higher than you'd believe possible and they climb into bed. Everything becomes very underwater, but along comes John, who has a key to Mary's apartment. He finds them stoned and entwined. He's hardly in any position to be jealous, considering Madge, but nevertheless he's overcome with despair. Finally he's middle-aged, in two years he'll be bald as an egg and he can't stand it. He purchases a handgun, saying he needs it for target practice—this is the thin part of the plot, but it can be dealt with later—and shoots the two of them and himself.

Madge, after a suitable period of mourning, marries an understanding man called Fred and everything continues as in A, but under different names.

D

15   Fred and Madge have no problems. They get along exceptionally well and are good at working out any little difficulties that may arise. But their charming house is by the sea-shore and one day a giant tidal wave approaches. Real estate values go down. The rest of the story is about what caused the tidal wave and how they escape from it. They do, though thousands drown, but Fred and Madge are virtuous and lucky. Finally on high ground they clasp each other, wet and dripping and grateful, and continue as in A.

E

Yes, but Fred has a bad heart. The rest of the story is about how kind and understanding they both are until Fred dies. Then Madge devotes herself to charity work until the end of A. If you like, it can be "Madge," "cancer," "guilty and confused," and "bird watching."

F

If you think this is all too bourgeois, make John a revolutionary and Mary a counterespionage agent and see how far that gets you. Remember, this is Canada. You'll still end up with A, though in between you may get a lustful brawling saga of passionate involvement, a chronicle of our times, sort of.

You'll have to face it, the endings are the same however you slice it. Don't be deluded by any other endings, they're all fake, either deliberately fake, with malicious intent to deceive, or just motivated by excessive optimism if not by downright sentimentality.

The only authentic ending is the one provided here:

John and Mary die. John and Mary die. John and Mary die.

So much for endings. Beginnings are always more fun. True connoisseurs, however, are known to favor the stretch in between, since it's the hardest to do anything with.

That's about all that can be said for plots, which anyway are just one thing after another, a what and a what and a what.

Now try How and Why.

QUESTIONS

1. All the stories Atwood relates about marriage end with a happy ending. Which of the stories is the most realistic? Which is the least? What is your definition of a happy marriage with a happy ending?

2. What is the relationship between the theme of "Happy Endings" and the way it is divided in sections?

3. What do you think Atwood means by "That's about all that can be said for plots"? What does she mean by the last sentence, "Now try How and Why."

4. What do you think Atwood means by "So much for endings. Beginnings are always more fun." Do you agree?

TONI CADE BAMBARA (1939–1995)

Bambara (an African tribal name that Toni Cade appropriated from an old manuscript) was brought up in Harlem and Bedford Stuyvesant in New York. She received a BA from Queens College and an MA in American Studies from the City College of New York. For a time she was a social worker, and later she taught at many schools, including Rutgers, Duke, and the Scribe Video Center in Philadelphia. She also collaborated in the writing of television documentaries, including a life of W. E. B. Du Bois. In her fiction she treats the subjects of the black and also the female experience. She avoids using this material for political purposes, however, even though the subjects could easily fall within the political realm. Instead, she deals with her characters on the human level, trying to offer her readers "nourishment." Story collections are Gorilla, My Love *(1972), from which "The Lesson" is taken, and* The Sea Birds Are Still Alive *(1977). Her novels are* The Salt Eaters *(1980) and* If Blessing Comes *(1987).*

The Lesson (1972)

Back in the days when everyone was old and stupid or young and foolish and me and Sugar were the only ones just right, this lady moved on our block with nappy hair and proper speech and no makeup. And quite naturally we laughed at her, the way we did at the junk man who went about his business like he was some big-time president and his sorry-ass horse his secretary. And we kinda hated her too, hated the way we did the winos who cluttered up our parks and pissed on our handball walls and stank up our hallways and stairs so you couldn't halfway play hide-and-seek without a goddamn gas mask. Miss Moore was her name. The only woman on the block with no first name. And she was black as hell, cept for her feet, which were fish-white and spooky. And she was always planning these boring-ass things for us to do, us being my cousin, mostly, who lived on the block cause we all moved North the same time and to the same apartment then spread out gradual to breathe. And our parents would yank our heads into some kinda shape and crisp up our clothes so we'd be presentable for travel with Miss Moore, who always looked like she was going to church, though she never did. Which is just one of the things the grown-ups talked about when they talked behind her back like a dog. But when she came calling with some sachet she'd sewed up or some gingerbread she'd made or some book, why then they'd all be too embarrassed to turn her down and we'd get handed over all spruced up. She'd been to college and said it was only right that she should take responsibility for the young ones education, and she not even related by marriage or blood. So they'd go for it. Specially Aunt Gretchen. She was the main gofer in the family. You got some ole dumb shit foolishness you want somebody to go for, you send for Aunt Gretchen. She been screwed into the go-along for so long, it's a blood-deep natural thing with her. Which is how she got saddled with me and Sugar and Junior in the first place while our mothers were in a la-de-da apartment up the block having a good ole time.

So this one day Miss Moore rounds us all up at the mailbox and it's purdee° hot and she's knockin herself out about arithmetic. And school suppose to let up in summer I heard, but she don't never let up. And the starch in my pinafore scratching the shit outta me and I'm really hating this nappy-head bitch and her goddamn college degree. I'd much rather go to the pool or to the show where it's cool. So me and Sugar leaning on the mailbox being surly, which is a Miss Moore word. And Flyboy checking out what everybody brought for lunch. And Fat Butt already wasting his peanut-butter-and-jelly sandwich like the pig he is. And Junebug punchin on Q.T.'s arm for potato chips. And Rosie Giraffe shifting from one hip to the other waiting for somebody to step on her foot or ask her if she from Georgia so she can kick ass, preferably Mercedes'. And Miss Moore asking us do we know what money is, like we a bunch of retards. I mean real money, she say, like it's only poker chips or Monopoly papers we lay on the grocer. So right away I'm tired of this and say so. And would much rather snatch Sugar and go to the Sunset and terrorize the West Indian kids and take their hair ribbons and their money too. And Miss Moore files that remark away for next week's lesson on brotherhood, I can tell. And finally I say we oughta get to the subway cause it's cooler and besides we might meet some cute boys. Sugar done swiped her mama's lipstick, so we ready.

So we heading down the street and she's boring us silly about what things cost and what our parents make and how much goes for rent and how money ain't divided up right in this country. And then she gets to the part about we all poor and live in the slums, which I don't feature. And I'm ready to speak on that, but she steps out in the street and hails two cabs just like that. Then she hustles half the crew in with her and hands me a five-dollar bill and tells me to calculate 10 percent tip for the driver. And we're off. Me and Sugar and Junebug and Flyboy hangin out the window and hollering to everybody, putting lipstick on each other cause Flyboy a faggot anyway, and making farts with our sweaty armpits. But I'm mostly trying to figure how to spend this money. But they all fascinated with the meter ticking and Junebug starts laying bets as to how much it'll read when Flyboy can't hold his breath no more. Then Sugar lays bets as to how much it'll be when we get there. So I'm stuck. Don't nobody want to go for my plan, which is to jump out at the next light and run off to the first bar-b-que we can find. Then the driver tells us to get the hell out cause we there already. And the meter reads eighty-five cents. And I'm stalling to figure out the tip and Sugar say give him a dime. And I decide he don't need it bad as I do, so later for him. But then he tries to take off with Junebug foot still in the door so we talk about his mama something ferocious. Then we check out that we on Fifth Avenue and everybody dressed up in stockings. One lady in a fur coat, hot as it is. White folks crazy.

"This is the place," Miss Moore say, presenting it to us in the voice she uses at the museum. "Let's look in the windows before we go in."

°*purdee:* pretty.

"Can we steal?" Sugar asks very serious like she's getting the ground rules squared away before she plays. "I beg your pardon," say Miss Moore, and we fall out. So she leads us around the windows of the toy store and me and Sugar screamin, "This is mine, that's mine, I gotta have that, that was made for me, I was born for that," till Big Butt drowns us out.

"Hey, I'm going to buy that there."

"That there? You don't even know what it is, stupid."

"I do so," he say punchin on Rosie Giraffe. "It's a microscope."

"Whatcha gonna do with a microscope, fool?"

"Look at things."

"Like what, Ronald?" ask Miss Moore. And Big Butt ain't got the first notion. So here go Miss Moore gabbing about the thousands of bacteria in a drop of water and the somethin-or other in a speck of blood and the million and one living things in the air around us is invisible to the naked eye. And what she say that for? Junebug go to town on that "naked" and we rolling. Then Miss Moore ask what it cost. So we all jam into the window smudgin it up and the price tag say $300. So then she ask how long'd take for Big Butt and Junebug to save up their allowances. "Too long," I say. "Yeh," adds Sugar, "outgrown it by that time." And Miss Moore say no, you never outgrow learning instruments. "Why, even medical students and interns and," blah, blah, blah. And we ready to choke Big Butt for bringing it up in the first damn place.

"This here costs four hundred eighty dollars," say Rosie Giraffe. So we pile up all over her to see what she pointin out. My eyes tell me it's a chunk of glass cracked with something heavy, and different-color inks dripped into the splits, then the whole thing put into a oven or something. But for $480 it don't make sense.

"That's a paperweight made of semi-precious stones fused together under tremendous pressure," she explains slowly, with her hands doing the mining and all the factory work.

"So what's a paperweight?" asks Rosie Giraffe.

"To weigh paper with, dumbbell," say Flyboy, the wise man from the East.

"Not exactly," say Miss Moore, which is what she say when you warm or way off too. "It's to weigh paper down so it won't scatter and make your desk untidy." So right away me and Sugar curtsy to each other and then to Mercedes who is more the tidy type.

"We don't keep paper on top of the desk in my class," say Junebug, figuring Miss Moore crazy or lyin one.

"At home, then," she say. "Don't you have a calendar and a pencil case and a blotter and a letter-opener on your desk at home where you do your homework?" And she know damn well what our homes look like cause she nosys around in them every chance she gets.

"I don't even have a desk," say Junebug. "Do we?"

"No. And I don't get no homework neither," says Big Butt.

"And I don't even have a home," say Flyboy like he do at school to keep the white folks off his back and sorry for him. Send this poor kid to camp posters, is his specialty.

"I do," says Mercedes. "I have a box of stationery on my desk and a picture of my cat. My godmother bought the stationery and the desk. There's a big rose on each sheet and the envelopes smell like roses."

"Who wants to know about your smelly-ass stationery," say Rosie Giraffe fore I can get my two cents in.

"It's important to have a work area all your own so that. . . ."

"Will you look at this sailboat, please," say Flyboy, cuttin her off and pointin to the thing like it was his. So once again we tumble all over each other to gaze at this magnificent thing in the toy store which is just big enough to maybe sail two kittens across the pond if you strap them to the posts tight. We all start reciting the price tag like we in assembly. "Hand-crafted sailboat of fiberglass at one thousand one hundred ninety-five dollars."

"Unbelievable," I hear myself say and am really stunned. I read it again for myself just in case the group recitation put me in a trance. Same thing. For some reason this pisses me off. We look at Miss Moore and she lookin at us, waiting for I dunno what.

"Who'd pay all that when you can buy a sailboat set for a quarter at Pop's, a tube of glue for a dime, and a ball of string for eight cents? It must have a motor and a whole lot else besides," I say. "My sailboat cost me about fifty cents."

"But will it take water?" say Mercedes with her smart ass.

"Took mine to Alley Pond Park once," say Flyboy. "String broke. Lost it. Pity."

30   "Sailed mine in Central Park and it keeled over and sank. Had to ask my father for another dollar."

"And you got the strap," laughed Big Butt. "The jerk didn't even have a string on it. My old man wailed on his behind."

Little Q.T. was staring hard at the sailboat and you could see he wanted it bad. But he too little and somebody'd just take it from him. So what the hell. "This boat for kids, Miss Moore?"

"Parents silly to buy something like that just to get all broke up," say Rosie Giraffe.

"That much money it should last forever," I figure.

35   "My father'd buy it for me if I wanted it."

"Your father, my ass," say Rosie Giraffe getting a chance to finally push Mercedes.

"Must be rich people shop here," say Q.T.

"You are a very bright boy," say Flyboy. "What was your first clue?" And he rap him on the head with the back of his knuckles, since Q.T. the only one he could get away with. Though Q.T. liable to come up behind you years later and get his licks in when you half expect it.

"What I want to know is," I says to Miss Moore though I never talk to her, I wouldn't give the bitch that satisfaction, "is how much a real boat costs? I figure a thousand'd get you a yacht any day."

40   "Why don't you check that out," she says, "and report back to the group?" Which really pains my ass. If you gonna mess up a perfectly good swim day least you could do is have some answers. "Let's go in," she say like she got something up her sleeve. Only she don't lead the way. So me and Sugar turn the corner to where the entrance is, but when we get there I kinda hang back. Not that I'm scared, what's there to be afraid of, just a toy store. But I feel funny, shame. But what I got to be shamed about? Got as much right to go in as anybody. But somehow I can't seem to get hold of the door, so I step away from Sugar to lead. But she hangs back too. And I look at her and she looks at me and this is ridiculous. I mean, damn, I have never ever been shy about doing nothing or going nowhere. But then Mercedes steps up and then Rosie Giraffe and Big Butt crowd in behind and shove, and next thing we all stuffed into the doorway with only Mercedes squeezing past us, smoothing out her jumper and walking right down the aisle. Then the rest of us tumble in like a glued-together jigsaw done all wrong. And people lookin at us. And it's like the time me and Sugar crashed into the Catholic church on a dare. But once we got in there and everything so hushed and holy and the candles and the bowin and the handkerchiefs on all the drooping heads, I just couldn't go through with the plan. Which was for me to run up to the altar and do a tap dance while Sugar played the nose flute and messed around in the holy water. And Sugar kept givin me the elbow. Then later teased me so bad I tied her up in the shower and turned it on and locked her in. And she'd be there till this day if Aunt Gretchen hadn't finally figured I was lyin about the boarder takin a shower.

Same thing in the store. We all walkin on tiptoe and hardly touchin the games and puzzles and things. And I watched Miss Moore who is steady watchin us like she waitin for a sign. Like Mama Drewery watches the sky and sniffs the air and takes note of just how much slant is in the bird formation. Then me and Sugar bump smack into each other, so busy gazing at the toys, 'specially the sailboat. But we don't laugh and go into our fat-lady bump-stomach routine. We just stare at that price tag. Then Sugar run a finger over the whole boat. And I'm jealous and want to hit her. Maybe not her, but I sure want to punch somebody in the mouth.

"Whatcha bring us here for, Miss Moore?"

"You sound angry, Sylvia. Are you mad about something?" Givin me one of them grins like she tellin a grown-up joke that never turns out to be funny. And she's lookin very closely at me like maybe she plannin to do my portrait from memory. I'm mad, but I won't give her that satisfaction. So I slouch around the store bein very bored and say, "Let's go."

Me and Sugar at the back of the train watchin the tracks whizzin by large then small then gettin gobbled up in the dark. I'm thinking about this tricky toy I saw in the store. A clown that somersaults on a bar then does chin-ups just cause you yank lightly at his leg. Cost $35. I could see me askin my mother for a $35 birthday clown. "You wanna who that costs what?" she'd say, cocking her head to the side to get a better view of the hole in my head. Thirty-five dollars could buy new bunk beds for Junior and Gretchen's boy. Thirty-five dollars and the whole household could go visit Granddaddy Nelson in the country. Thirty-five dollars would pay for the rent and the piano bill too. Who are these people that spend that much for performing clowns and $1000 for toy sailboats? What kinda work they do and how they live and how come we ain't in on it? Where we are is who we are. Miss Moore always pointin out. But it don't necessarily have to be that way, she always adds then waits for somebody to say that poor people have to wake up and demand their share of the pie and don't none of us know what kind of pie she talking about in the first damn place. But she ain't so smart cause I still got her four dollars from the taxi and she sure ain't gettin it. Messin up my day with this shit. Sugar nudges me in my pocket and winks.

Miss Moore lines us up in front of the mailbox where we started from, seem like years ago, and I got a headache for thinkin so hard. And we lean all over each other so we can hold up under the draggy-ass lecture she always finishes us off with at the end before we thank her for borin us to tears. But she just looks at us like she readin tea leaves. Finally she say, "Well, what did you think of F.A.O. Schwarz?"

Rosie Giraffe mumbles, "White folks crazy."

"I'd like to go there again when I get my birthday money," says Mercedes, and we shove her out the pack so she has to lean on the mailbox by herself.

"I'd like a shower. Tiring day," say Flyboy.

Then Sugar surprises me by sayin, "You know, Miss Moore, I don't think all of us here put together eat in a year what that sailboat costs." And Miss Moore lights up like some-body goosed her. "And?" she say, urging Sugar on. Only I'm standin on her foot so she don't continue.

"Imagine for a minute what kind of society it is in which some people can spend on a toy what it would cost to feed a family of six or seven. What do you think?"

"I think," say Sugar pushing me off her feet like she never done before, cause I whip her ass in a minute, "that this is not much of a democracy if you ask me. Equal chance to pursue happiness means an equal crack at the dough, don't it?" Miss Moore is besides herself and I am disgusted with Sugar's treachery. So I stand on her foot one more time to see if she'll shove me. She shuts up, and Miss Moore looks at me, sorrowfully I'm thinkin. And some-thin weird is goin on, I can feel it in my chest.

"Anybody else learn anything today?" lookin dead at me. I walk away and Sugar has to run to catch up and don't even seem to notice when I shrug her arm off my shoulder.

"Well, we got four dollars anyway," she says.

"Uh hunh."

"We could go to Hascombs and get half a chocolate layer and then go to the Sunset and still have plenty money for potato chips and ice cream sodas."

"Uh hunh."

"Race you to Hascombs," she say.

We start down the block and she gets ahead which is O.K. by me cause I'm going to the West End and then over to the Drive to think this day through. She can run if she want to and even run faster. But ain't nobody gonna beat me at nuthin.

QUESTIONS

1. Who is Miss Moore? Why does she take an interest in the neighborhood children? Where does she take them? How does she attempt to teach them?

2. Describe Sylvia, the narrator, as a character. Why does she keep $4 of the five-dollar bill given her by Miss Moore? What does she mean by saying "ain't nobody gonna beat me at nuthin" in the story's final paragraph?

3. Describe the level of language of the narrator. Is she writing the story or speaking it? How do you know?

4. Consider paragraphs 44–50. What ideas about equality and inequality are brought out in the story? Do you think the children will remember the "lesson" or that they will forget it? Why?

D. H. LAWRENCE (1885–1930)

Lawrence was born in an English mining community, but he received a sufficient education to enable him to become a teacher and writer. He fictionalized the early years of his life in the novel Sons and Lovers *(1913). His most controversial work,* Lady Chatterley's Lover, *was printed privately in Italy in 1928 but was not published in an uncut version in the United States until the 1960s. He shocked his contemporaries with his emphasis on the importance of sexuality, an idea that is central to "The Horse Dealer's Daughter." He was afflicted with tuberculosis and lived in a number of warm, sunny places, including Italy, New Zealand, and New Mexico, in an attempt to restore his health. Nevertheless, his illness claimed him in 1930, when he was only forty-five years old.*

The Horse Dealer's Daughter (1922)

"Well, Mabel, and what are you going to do with yourself?" asked Joe, with foolish flippancy. He felt quite safe himself. Without listening for an answer, he turned aside, worked a grain of tobacco to the tip of his tongue, and spat it out. He did not care about anything, since he felt safe himself.

The three brothers and the sister sat round the desolate breakfast table, attempting some sort of desultory consultation. The morning's post had given the final tap to the family fortunes, and all was over. The dreary dining-room itself, with its heavy mahogany furniture, looked as if it were waiting to be done away with.

But the consultation amounted to nothing. There was a strange air of ineffectuality about the three men, as they sprawled at table, smoking and reflecting vaguely on their own condition. The girl was alone, a rather short, sullen-looking young woman of twenty-seven. She did not share the same life as her brothers. She would have been good-looking, save for the impassive fixity of her face, "bulldog," as her brothers called it.

There was a confused tramping of horses' feet outside. The three men all sprawled round in their chairs to watch. Beyond the dark holly-bushes that separated the strip of lawn from the high-road, they could see a cavalcade of shire horses swinging out of their own yard, being taken for exercise. This was the last time. These were the last horses that would go through their hands. The young men watched with critical, callous look. They were all frightened at the collapse of their lives, and the sense of disaster in which they were involved left them no inner freedom.

Yet they were three fine, well-set fellows enough. Joe, the eldest, was a man of thirty-three, broad and handsome in a hot, flushed way. His face was red, he twisted his black moustache over a thick finger, his eyes were shallow and restless. He had a sensual way of uncovering his teeth when he laughed, and his bearing was stupid. Now he watched the horses with a glazed look of helplessness in his eyes, a certain stupor of downfall.

The great draught-horses swung past. They were tied head to tail, four of them, and they heaved along to where a lane branched off from the highroad, planting their great hoofs floutingly in the fine black mud, swinging their great rounded haunches sumptuously, and trotting a few sudden steps as they were led into the lane, round the corner. Every movement showed a massive, slumbrous strength, and a stupidity which held them in subjection. The groom at the head looked back, jerking the leading rope. And the cavalcade moved out of sight up the lane, the tail of the last horse, bobbed up tight and stiff, held out taut from the swinging great haunches as they rocked behind the hedges in a motionlike sleep.

Joe watched with glazed hopeless eyes. The horses were almost like his own body to him. He felt he was done for now. Luckily, he was engaged to a woman as old as himself, and therefore her father, who was steward of a neighbouring estate, would provide him with a job. He would marry and go into harness. His life was over, he would be a subject animal now.

He turned uneasily aside, the retreating steps of the horses echoing in his ears. Then, with foolish restlessness, he reached for the scraps of bacon-rind from the plates, and making a faint whistling sound, flung them to the terrier that lay against the fender. He watched the dog swallow them, and waited till the creature looked into his eyes. Then a faint grin came on his face, and in a high, foolish voice he said:

"You won't get much more bacon, shall you, you little b—?"

The dog faintly and dismally wagged its tail, then lowered its haunches, circled round, and lay down again.

There was another helpless silence at the table. Joe sprawled uneasily in his seat, not willing to go till the family conclave was dissolved. Fred Henry, the second brother, was erect, clean-limbed, alert. He had watched the passing of the horses with more *sang-froid*.° If he was an animal, like Joe, he was an animal which controls, not one which is controlled. He was master of any horse, and he carried himself with a well-tempered air of mastery. But he was not master of the situations of life. He pushed his coarse brown moustache upwards, off his lip, and glanced irritably at his sister, who sat impassive and inscrutable.

"You'll go and stop with Lucy for a bit, shan't you?" he asked. The girl did not answer.

"I don't see what else you can do," persisted Fred Henry.

"Go as a skivvy,"° Joe interpolated laconically.

The girl did not move a muscle.

"If I was her, I should go in for training for a nurse," said Malcolm, the youngest of them all. He was the baby of the family, a young man of twenty-two, with a fresh, jaunty *museau*.°

But Mabel did not take any notice of him. They had talked at her and round her for so many years, that she hardly heard them at all.

The marble clock on the mantel-piece softly chimed the half-hour, the dog rose uneasily from the hearthrug and looked at the party at the breakfast table. But still they sat on in ineffectual conclave.

"Oh, all right," said Joe suddenly, *à propos* of nothing. "I'll get a move on."

°*sang-froid*: unconcern (literally, cold blood).
°*skivvy*: British slang for housemaid.
°*museau*: French for nose, snout (muzzle).

20   He pushed back his chair, straddled his knees with a downward jerk, to get them free, in horsey fashion, and went to the fire. Still he did not go out of the room; he was curious to know what the others would do or say. He began to charge his pipe, looking down at the dog and saying, in a high, affected voice:

"Going wi' me? Going wi' me are ter? Tha'rt goin' further than tha counts on just now, dost hear?"

The dog faintly wagged its tail, the man stuck out his jaw and covered his pipe with his hands, and puffed intently, losing himself in the tobacco, looking down all the while at the dog, with an absent brown eye. The dog looked up at him in mournful distrust. Joe stood with his knees stuck out, in real horsey fashion.

"Have you had a letter from Lucy?" Fred Henry asked of his sister.

"Last week," came the neutral reply.

25   "And what does she say?"

There was no answer.

"Does she *ask* you to go and stop there?" persisted Fred Henry.

"She says I can if I like."

"Well, then, you'd better. Tell her you'll come on Monday."

30   This was received in silence.

"That's what you'll do then, is it?" said Fred Henry, in some exasperation.

But she made no answer. There was a silence of futility and irritation in the room. Malcolm grinned fatuously.

"You'll have to make up your mind between now and next Wednesday," said Joe loudly, "or else find yourself lodgings on the kerbstone."

The face of the young woman darkened, but she sat on immutable.

35   "Here's Jack Fergusson!" exclaimed Malcolm, who was looking aimlessly out of the window.

"Where?" exclaimed Joe, loudly.

"Just gone past."

"Coming in?"

Malcolm craned his neck to see the gate.

40   "Yes," he said.

There was a silence. Mabel sat on like one condemned, at the head of the table. Then a whistle was heard from the kitchen. The dog got up and barked sharply. Joe opened the door and shouted:

"Come on."

After a moment, a young man entered. He was muffled up in overcoat and a purple woolen scarf, and his tweed cap, which he did not remove, was pulled down on his head. He was of medium height, his face was rather long and pale, his eyes looked tired.

"Hello, Jack! Well, Jack!" exclaimed Malcolm and Joe. Fred Henry merely said "Jack!"

45   "What's doing?" asked the newcomer, evidently addressing Fred Henry.

"Same. We've got to be out by Wednesday—Got a cold?"

"I have—got it bad, too."

"Why don't you stop in?"

"*Me* stop in? When I can't stand on my legs, perhaps I shall have a chance." The young man spoke huskily. He had a slight Scotch accent.

50   "It's a knock-out, isn't it," said Joe boisterously, "if a doctor goes round croaking with a cold. Looks bad for the patients, doesn't it?"

The young doctor looked at him slowly.

"Anything the matter with *you*, then?" he asked, sarcastically.

"Not as I know of. Damn your eyes, I hope not. Why?"

"I thought you were very concerned about the patients, wondered if you might be one yourself."

"Damn it, no, I've never been patient to no flaming doctor, and hope I never shall be," returned Joe. 55

At this point Mabel rose from the table, and they all seemed to become aware of her existence. She began putting the dishes together. The young doctor looked at her, but did not address her. He had not greeted her. She went out of the room with the tray, her face impassive and unchanged.

"When are you off then, all of you?" asked the doctor.

"I'm catching the eleven-forty," replied Malcolm. "Are you goin' down wi' th' trap,° Joe?"

"Yes, I've told you I'm going down wi' th' trap, haven't I?"

"We'd better be getting her in then.—So long, Jack, if I don't see you before I go," said 60 Malcolm, shaking hands.

He went out, followed by Joe, who seemed to have his tail between his legs.

"Well, this is the devil's own," exclaimed the doctor, when he was left alone with Fred Henry. "Going before Wednesday, are you?"

"That's the orders," replied the other.

"Where, to Northampton?" 65

"That's it."

"The devil!" exclaimed Fergusson, with quiet chagrin.

And there was silence between the two.

"All settled up, are you?" asked Fergusson.

"About."

There was another pause.

"Well, I shall miss yer, Freddy boy," said the young doctor. 70

"And I shall miss thee, Jack," returned the other.

"Miss you like hell," mused the doctor.

Fred Henry turned aside. There was nothing to say. Mabel came in again, to finish clearing the table.

"What are *you* going to do then, Miss Pervin?" asked Fergusson. "Going to your sister's, 75 are you?"

Mabel looked at him with her steady, dangerous eyes, that always made him uncomfortable, unsettling his superficial ease.

"No," she said.

"Well, what in the name of fortune *are* you going to do? Say what you *mean* to do," cried Fred Henry, with futile intensity.

But she only averted her head, and continued her work. She folded the white table-cloth, and put on the chenille cloth.

"The sulkiest bitch that ever trod!" muttered her brother. 80

But she finished her task with perfectly impassive face, the young doctor watching her interestedly all the while. Then she went out.

Fred Henry stared after her, clenching his lips, his blue eyes fixing in sharp antagonism, as he made a grimace of sour exasperation.

"You could bray her into bits, and that's all you'd get out of her," he said, in a small, narrowed tone.

The doctor smiled faintly.

"What's she *going* to do then?" he asked.

"Strike me if *I* know!" returned the other. 85

°*trap*: small wagon.

There was a pause. Then the doctor stirred.

"I'll be seeing you to-night, shall I?" he said to his friend.

"Ay—where's it to be? Are we going over to Jessdale?"

90 "I don't know. I've got such a cold on me. I'll come round to the Moon and Stars, anyway."

"Let Lizzie and May miss their night for once, eh?"

"That's it—if I feel as I do now."

"All's one—"

The two young men went through the passage and down to the back door together. The house was large, but it was servantless now, and desolate. At the back was a small bricked house-yard, and beyond that a big square, gravelled fine and red, and having stables on two sides. Sloping, dank, winter-dark fields stretched away on the open sides.

95 But the stables were empty. Joseph Pervin, the father of the family, had been a man of no education, who had become a fairly large horse dealer. The stables had been full of horses, there was a great turmoil and come-and-go of horses and of dealers and grooms. Then the kitchen was full of servants. But of late things had declined. The old man had married a second time, to retrieve his fortunes. Now he was dead and everything was gone to the dogs, there was nothing but debt and threatening.

For months, Mabel had been servantless in the big house, keeping the home together in penury for her ineffectual brothers. She had kept house for ten years. But previously, it was with unstinted means. Then, however brutal and coarse everything was, the sense of money had kept her proud, confident. The men might be foul-mouthed, the women in the kitchen might have bad reputations, her brothers might have illegitimate children. But so long as there was money, the girl felt herself established, and brutally proud, reserved.

No company came to the house, save dealers and coarse men. Mabel had no associates of her own sex, after her sister went away. But she did not mind. She went regularly to church, she attended to her father. And she lived in the memory of her mother, who had died when she was fourteen, and whom she had loved. She had loved her father, too, in a different way, depending upon him, and feeling secure in him, until at the age of fifty-four he married again. And then she had set hard against him. Now he had died and left them all hopelessly in debt.

She had suffered badly during the period of poverty. Nothing, however, could shake the curious sullen, animal pride that dominated each member of the family. Now, for Mabel, the end had come. Still she would not cast about her. She would follow her own way just the same. She would always hold the keys of her own situation. Mindless and persistent, she endured from day to day. Why should she think? Why should she answer anybody? It was enough that this was the end, and there was no way out. She need not pass any more darkly along the main street of the small town, avoiding every eye. She need not demean herself any more, going into the shops and buying the cheapest food. This was at an end. She thought of nobody, not even of herself. Mindless and persistent, she seemed in a sort of ecstasy to be coming nearer to her fulfilment, her own glorification, approaching her dead mother, who was glorified.°

In the afternoon she took a little bag, with shears and sponge and a small scrubbing brush, and went out. It was a grey, wintry day, with saddened, dark-green fields and an atmosphere blackened by the smoke of foundries not far off. She went quickly, darkly along the causeway, heeding nobody, through the town to the churchyard.

100 There she always felt secure, as if no one could see her, although as a matter of fact she was exposed to the stare of everyone who passed along under the churchyard wall. Nevertheless, once under the shadow of the great looming church, among the graves, she felt immune from the world, reserved within the thick churchyard wall as in another country.

°*who was glorified:* See Romans 8:17, 30.

Carefully she clipped the grass from the grave, and arranged the pinky-white, small chrysanthemums in the tin cross. When this was done, she took an empty jar from a neighbouring grave, brought water, and carefully, most scrupulously sponged the marble headstone and the coping-stone.

It gave her sincere satisfaction to do this. She felt in immediate contact with the world of her mother. She took minute pains, went through the park in a state bordering on pure happiness, as if in performing this task she came into a subtle, intimate connection with her mother. For the life she followed here in the world was far less real than the world of death she inherited from her mother.

The doctor's house was just by the church. Fergusson, being a mere hired assistant, was slave to the countryside. As he hurried now to attend to the outpatients in the surgery, glancing across the graveyard with his quick eye, he saw the girl at her task at the grave. She seemed so intent and remote, it was like looking into another world. Some mystical element was touched in him. He slowed down as he walked, watching her as if spell-bound.

She lifted her eyes, feeling him looking. Their eyes met. And each looked again at once, each feeling, in some way, found out by the other. He lifted his cap and passed on down the road. There remained distinct in his consciousness, like a vision, the memory of her face, lifted from the tombstone in the churchyard, and looking at him with slow, large, portentous eyes. It *was* portentous, her face. It seemed to mesmerise him. There was a heavy power in her eyes which laid hold of his whole being, as if he had drunk some powerful drug. He had been feeling weak and done before. Now the life came back into him, he felt delivered from his own fretted, daily self.

He finished his duties at the surgery as quickly as might be, hastily filling up the bottles of the waiting people with cheap drugs. Then, in perpetual haste, he set off again to visit several cases in another part of his round, before teatime. At all times he preferred to walk, if he could, but particularly when he was not well. He fancied the motion restored him.

The afternoon was falling. It was grey, deadened, and wintry, with a slow, moist, heavy coldness sinking in and deadening all the faculties. But why should he think or notice? He hastily climbed the hill and turned across the dark-green fields, following the black cinder-track. In the distance, across a shallow dip in the country, the small town was clustered like smouldering ash, a tower, a spire, a heap of low, raw, extinct houses. And on the nearest fringe of the town, sloping into the dip, was Oldmeadow, the Pervins' house. He could see the stables and the outbuildings distinctly, as they lay towards him on the slope. Well, he would not go there many more times! Another resource would be lost to him, another place gone: the only company he cared for in the alien, ugly little town he was losing. Nothing but work, drudgery, constant hastening from dwelling to dwelling among the colliers and the iron-workers. It wore him out, but at the same time he had a craving for it. It was a stimulant to him to be in the homes of the working people, moving as it were through the innermost body of their life. His nerves were excited and gratified. He could come so near, into the very lives of the rough, inarticulate, powerfully emotional men and women. He grumbled, he said he hated the hellish hole. But as a matter of fact it excited him, the contact with the rough, strongly-feeling people was a stimulant applied direct to his nerves.

Below Oldmeadow, in the green, shallow, soddened hollow of fields, lay a square, deep pond. Roving across the landscape, the doctor's quick eye detected a figure in black passing through the gate of the field, down towards the pond. He looked again. It would be Mabel Pervin. His mind suddenly became alive and attentive.

Why was she going down there? He pulled up on the path on the slope above, and stood staring. He could just make sure of the small black figure moving in the hollow of the failing day. He seemed to see her in the midst of such obscurity, that he was like a clairvoyant, seeing rather with the mind's eye than with ordinary sight. Yet he could see her positively enough, whilst he kept his eye attentive. He felt, if he looked away from her, in the thick, ugly falling dusk, he would lose her altogether.

105

He followed her minutely as she moved, direct and intent, like something transmitted rather than stirring in voluntary activity, straight down the field towards the pond. There she stood on the bank for a moment. She never raised her head. Then she waded slowly into the water.

110 He stood motionless as the small black figure walked slowly and deliberately towards the centre of the pond, very slowly, gradually moving deeper into the motionless water, and still moving forward as the water got up to her breast. Then he could see her no more in the dusk of the dead afternoon.

"There!" he exclaimed. "Would you believe it?"

And he hastened straight down, running over the wet, soddened fields, pushing through the hedges, down into the depression of callous wintry obscurity. It took him several minutes to come to the pond. He stood on the bank, breathing heavily. He could see nothing. His eyes seemed to penetrate the dead water. Yes, perhaps that was the dark shadow of her black clothing beneath the surface of the water.

He slowly ventured into the pond. The bottom was deep, soft clay, he sank in, and the water clasped dead cold round his legs. As he stirred he could smell the cold, rotten clay that fouled up into the water. It was objectionable in his lungs. Still, repelled and yet not heeding, he moved deeper into the pond. The cold water rose over his thighs, over his loins, upon his abdomen. The lower part of his body was all sunk in the hideous cold element. And the bottom was so deeply soft and uncertain, he was afraid of pitching with his mouth underneath. He could not swim, and was afraid.

He crouched a little, spreading his hands under the water and moving them round, trying to feel for her. The dead cold pond swayed upon his chest. He moved again, a little deeper, and again, with his hands underneath, he felt all around under the water. And he touched her clothing. But it evaded his fingers. He made a desperate effort to grasp it.

115 And so doing he lost his balance and went under, horribly, suffocating in the foul earthy water, struggling madly for a few moments. At last, after what seemed an eternity, he got his footing, rose again into the air and looked around. He gasped, and knew he was in the world. Then he looked at the water. She had risen near him. He grasped her clothing, and drawing her nearer, turned to take his way to land again.

He went very slowly, carefully, absorbed in the slow progress. He rose higher, climbing out of the pond. The water was now only about his legs; he was thankful, full of relief to be out of the clutches of the pond. He lifted her and staggered on to the bank, out of the horror of wet, grey clay.

He laid her down on the bank. She was quite unconscious and running with water. He made the water come from her mouth, he worked to restore her. He did not have to work very long before he could feel the breathing begin again in her; she was breathing naturally. He worked a little longer. He could feel her live beneath his hands; she was coming back. He wiped her face, wrapped her in his overcoat, looked round into the dim, dark-grey world, then lifted her and staggered down the bank and across the fields.

It seemed an unthinkably long way, and his burden so heavy he felt he would never get to the house. But at last he was in the stable-yard, and then in the house-yard. He opened the door and went into the house. In the kitchen he laid her down on the hearthrug, and called. The house was empty. But the fire was burning in the grate.

Then again he kneeled to attend to her. She was breathing regularly, her eyes were wide open as if conscious, but there seemed something missing in her look. She was conscious in herself, but unconscious of her surroundings.

120 He ran upstairs, took blankets from a bed, and put them before the fire to warm. Then he removed her saturated, earthy-smelling clothing, rubbed her dry with a towel, and wrapped her naked in the blankets. Then he went into the dining-room, to look for spirits. There was a little whiskey. He drank a gulp himself, and put some into her mouth.

The effect was instantaneous. She looked full into his face, as if she had been seeing him for some time, and yet had only just become conscious of him.

"Dr. Fergusson?" she said.

"What?" he answered.

He was divesting himself of his coat, intending to find some dry clothing upstairs. He could not bear the smell of the dead, clayey water, and he was mortally afraid for his own health.

"What did I do?" she asked. 125

"Walked into the pond," he replied. He had begun to shudder like one sick, and could hardly attend to her. Her eyes remained full on him, he seemed to be going dark in his mind, looking back at her helplessly. The shuddering became quieter in him, his life came back in him, dark and unknowing, but strong again.

"Was I out of my mind?" she asked, while her eyes were fixed on him all the time.

"Maybe, for the moment," he replied. He felt quiet, because his strength had come back. The strange fretful strain had left him.

"Am I out of my mind now?" she asked.

"Are you?" he reflected a moment. "No," he answered truthfully, "I don't see that you 130 are." He turned his face aside. He was afraid, now, because he felt dazed, and felt dimly that her power was stronger than his, in this issue. And she continued to look at him fixedly all the time. "Can you tell me where I shall find some dry things to put on?" he asked.

"Did you dive into the pond for me?" she asked.

"No," he answered. "I walked in. But I went in overhead as well."

There was silence for a moment. He hesitated. He very much wanted to go upstairs to get into dry clothing. But there was another desire in him. And she seemed to hold him. His will seemed to have gone to sleep, and left him, standing there slack before her. But he felt warm inside himself. He did not shudder at all, though his clothes were sodden on him.

"Why did you?" she asked.

"Because I didn't want you to do such a foolish thing," he said. 135

"It wasn't foolish," she said, still gazing at him as she lay on the floor, with a sofa cushion under her head. "It was the right thing to do. I knew best, then."

"I'll go and shift these wet things," he said. But still he had not the power to move out of her presence, until she sent him. It was as if she had the life of his body in her hands, and he could not extricate himself. Or perhaps he did not want to.

Suddenly she sat up. Then she became aware of her own immediate condition. She felt the blankets about her, she knew her own limbs. For a moment it seemed as if her reason were going. She looked round, with wild eye, as if seeking something. He stood still with fear. She saw her clothing lying scattered.

"Who undressed me?" she asked, her eyes resting full and inevitable on his face.

"I did," he replied, "to bring you round." 140

For some moments she sat and gazed at him awfully, her lips parted.

"Do you love me then?" she asked.

He only stood and stared at her, fascinated. His soul seemed to melt.

She shuffled forward on her knees, and put her arms round him, round his legs, as he stood there, pressing her breasts against his knees and thighs, clutching him with strange, convulsive certainty, pressing his thighs against her, drawing him to her face, her throat, as she looked up at him with flaring, humble eyes of transfiguration, triumphant in first possession.

"You love me," she murmured, in strange transport, yearning and triumphant and con- 145 fident. "You love me. I know you love me, I know."

And she was passionately kissing his knees, through the wet clothing, passionately and indiscriminately kissing his knees, his legs, as if unaware of everything.

He looked down at the tangled wet hair, the wild, bare, animal shoulders. He was amazed, bewildered, and afraid. He had never thought of loving her. He had never wanted to love her. When he rescued her and restored her, he was a doctor, and she was a patient. He had had no single personal thought of her. Nay, this introduction of the personal element was very distasteful to him, a violation of his professional honour. It was horrible to have her there embracing his knees. It was horrible. He revolted from it, violently. And yet—and yet—he had not the power to break away.

She looked at him again, with the same supplication of powerful love, and that same transcendent, frightening light of triumph. In view of the delicate flame which seemed to come from her face like a light, he was powerless. And yet he had never intended to love her. He had never intended. And something stubborn in him could not give way.

"You love me," she repeated, in a murmur of deep, rhapsodic assurance. "You love me."

150   Her hands were drawing him, drawing him down to her. He was afraid, even a little horrified. For he had, really, no intention of loving her. Yet her hands were drawing him towards her. He put out his hand quickly to steady himself, and grasped her bare shoulder. A flame seemed to burn the hand that grasped her soft shoulder. He had no intention of loving her: his whole will was against his yielding. It was horrible—And yet wonderful was the touch of her shoulder, beautiful the shining of her face. Was she perhaps mad? He had a horror of yielding to her. Yet something in him ached also.

He had been staring away at the door, away from her. But his hand remained on her shoulder. She had gone suddenly very still. He looked down at her. Her eyes were now wide with fear, with doubt, the light was dying from her face, a shadow of terrible greyness was returning. He could not bear the touch of her eyes' question upon him, and the look of death behind the question.

With an inward groan he gave way, and let his heart yield towards her. A sudden gentle smile came on his face. And her eyes, which never left his face, slowly, slowly filled with tears. He watched the strange water rise in her eyes, like some slow fountain coming up. And his heart seemed to burn and melt away in his breast.

He could not bear to look at her any more. He dropped on his knees and caught her head with his arms and pressed her face against his throat. She was very still. His heart, which seemed to have broken, was burning with a kind of agony in his breast. And he felt her slow, hot tears wetting his throat. But he could not move.

He felt the hot tears wet his neck and the hollows of his neck, and he remained motionless, suspended through one of man's eternities. Only now it had become indispensable to him to have her face pressed close to him; he could never let her go again. He could never let her head go away from the close clutch of his arm. He wanted to remain like that for ever, with his heart hurting him in a pain that was also life to him. Without knowing, he was looking down on her damp, soft brown hair.

155   Then, as it were suddenly, he smelt the horrid stagnant smell of the water. And at the same moment she drew away from him and looked at him. Her eyes were wistful and unfathomable. He was afraid of them, and he fell to kissing her, not knowing what he was doing. He wanted her eyes not to have that terrible, wistful, unfathomable look.

When she turned her face to him again, a faint delicate flush was glowing, and there was again dawning that terrible shining of joy in her eyes, which really terrified him, and yet which he now wanted to see, because he feared the look of doubt still more.

"You love me?" she said, rather faltering.

"Yes." The word cost him a painful effort. Not because it wasn't true. But because it was too newly true, the *saying* seemed to tear open again his newly-torn heart. And he hardly wanted it to be true, even now.

She lifted her face to him, and he bent forward and kissed her on the mouth gently, with the one kiss that is an eternal pledge. And as he kissed her his heart strained again in his breast. He never intended to love her. But now it was over. He had crossed over the gulf to her, and all that he had left behind had shrivelled and become void.

After the kiss, her eyes again slowly filled with tears. She sat still, away from him, with her face drooped aside, and her hands folded in her lap. The tears fell very slowly. There was complete silence. He too sat there motionless and silent on the hearthrug. The strange pain of his heart that was broken seemed to consume him. That he should love her? That this was love! That he should be ripped open in this way!—Him, a doctor!—How they would all jeer if they knew!—It was agony to him to think they might know.

In the curious naked pain of the thought he looked again to her. She was sitting there drooped into a muse. He saw a tear fall, and his heart flared hot. He saw for the first time that one of her shoulders was quite uncovered, one arm bare, he could see one of her small breasts; dimly, because it had become almost dark in the room.

"Why are you crying?" he asked, in an altered voice.

She looked up at him, and behind her tears the consciousness of her situation for the first time brought a dark look of shame to her eyes.

"I'm not crying, really," she said, watching him half frightened.

He reached his hand, and softly closed it on her bare arm.

"I love you! I love you!" he said in a soft, low vibrating voice, unlike himself.

She shrank, and dropped her head. The soft, penetrating grip of his hand on her arm distressed her. She looked up at him.

"I want to go," she said. "I want to go and get you some dry things."

"Why?" he said. "I'm all right."

"But I want to go," she said. "And I want you to change your things."

He released her arm, and she wrapped herself in the blanket, looking at him rather frightened. And still she did not rise.

"Kiss me," she said wistfully.

He kissed her, but briefly, half in anger.

Then, after a second, she rose nervously, all mixed up in the blanket. He watched her in her confusion, as she tried to extricate herself and wrap herself up so that she could walk. He watched her relentlessly, as she knew.

And as she went, the blanket trailing, and as he saw a glimpse of her feet and her white leg, he tried to remember her as she was when he had wrapped her in the blanket. But then he didn't want to remember, because she had been nothing to him then, and his nature revolted from remembering her as she was when she was nothing to him.

A tumbling muffled noise from within the dark house startled him. Then he heard her voice:—"There are clothes." He rose and went to the foot of the stairs, and gathered up the garments she had thrown down. Then he came back to the fire, to rub himself down and dress. He grinned at his own appearance, when he had finished.

The fire was sinking, so he put on coal. The house was now quite dark, save for the light of a street-lamp that shone in faintly from beyond the holly trees. He lit the gas with matches he found on the mantel-piece. Then he emptied the pockets of his own clothes, and threw all his wet things in a heap into the scullery. After which he gathered up her sodden clothes, gently, and put them in a separate heap on the copper-top in the scullery.

It was six o'clock on the clock. His own watch had stopped. He ought to be back to the surgery. He waited, and still she did not come down. So he went to the foot of the stairs and called:

"I shall have to go."

Almost immediately he heard her coming down. She had on her best dress of black voile, and her hair was tidy, but still damp. She looked at him—and in spite of herself, smiled.

"I don't like you in those clothes," she said.

"Do I look a sight?" he answered.

They were shy of one another.

"I'll make you some tea," she said.

185   "No, I must go."

"Must you?" And she looked at him again with the wide, strained, doubtful eyes. And again, from the pain of his breast, he knew how he loved her. He went and bent to kiss her, gently, passionately, with his heart's painful kiss.

"And my hair smells so horrible," she murmured in distraction. "And I'm so awful, I'm so awful! Oh, no, I'm too awful." And she broke into bitter, heartbroken sobbing. "You can't want to love me, I'm horrible."

"Don't be silly, don't be silly," he said, trying to comfort her, kissing her, holding her in his arms. "I want you, I want to marry you, we're going to be married, quickly, quickly— tomorrow if I can."

But she only sobbed terribly, and cried.

190   "I feel awful. I feel awful. I feel I'm horrible to you."

"No, I want you, I want you," was all he answered blindly, with that terrible intonation which frightened her almost more than her horror lest he should *not* want her.

QUESTIONS

1. What idea does Lawrence seem to be illustrating by the breakup of the Pervin household?

2. What does the comparison of Joe Pervin and the draft horses (paragraphs 6, 7) mean with regard specifically to Joe, and generally to people without love?

3. What kind of person is Mabel? How do her brothers treat her? How does she feel about her brothers? What dilemma does she face as the story begins?

4. What effect does Mabel have on Fergusson as he watches her in her home, in the church-yard, and at the pond? What does this effect contribute to Lawrence's ideas about love?

5. What do Mabel and Fergusson realize as he revives and warms her (paragraphs 113–142)? How do their responses signify their growth as characters?

6. In this story, there is an extensive exploration of the ambiguous feelings of both Fergusson and Mabel after they realize their love. Why does Lawrence explore these feelings so extensively? For example, why does the narrator tell us that Fergusson does not want to remember Mabel as she was when "she had been nothing" to him (para-graph 175)? And why does Mable hear, in Fergusson's concluding speech, a "terrible intonation which frightened her almost more than her horror lest he should *not* want her "(paragraph 191)?

AMÉRICO PAREDES (1915–1999)

Américo Paredes was a Mexican American storyteller, folklorist, es-sayist, and poet, closely identified with Mexican Americans living in Texas, his native state. He received his PhD at the University of Texas in 1956 and also taught there for many years. His dissertation was published in 1958 as With His Pistol in His Hand, *a study of an early-twentieth-century popular ballad about a fugitive, Gregorio Cortés. Deeply interested in the culture of the "lower border," he was one of the leaders of the Chicano movement in cultural-literary studies. He edited the* Journal of American Folklore *and also edited* Folklore and Culture on the Texas-Mexican Border *(1993). Among his honors was a Guggenheim Fel-lowship in 1962 and the Aztec Eagle medal from the Mexican government in 1991. "The Hammon and the Beans" was first published in the* Texas Observer *in 1963 and was republished in* The Hammon and the Beans and Other Stories *in 1994.*

The Hammon and the Beans (1963)

Once we lived in one of my grandfather's houses near Fort Jones.° It was just a block from the parade grounds, a big frame house painted a dirty yellow. My mother hated it, especially because of the pigeons that cooed all day about the eaves. They had fleas, she said. But it was a quiet neighborhood at least, too far from the center of town for automobiles and too near for musical, night-roaming drunks.

At this time Jonesville-on-the-Grande was not the thriving little city that it is today. We told off our days by the routine on the post. At six sharp the flag was raised on the parade grounds to the cackling of the bugles, and a field piece thundered out a salute. The sound of the shot bounced away through the morning mist until its echoes worked their way into every corner of town. Jonesville-on-the-Grande woke to the cannon's roar, as if to battle, and the day began.

At eight the whistle from the post laundry sent us children off to school. The whole town stopped for lunch with the noon whistle, and after lunch everybody went back to work when the post laundry said that it was one o'clock, except for those who could afford to be old-fashioned and took the siesta. The post was the town's clock, you might have said, or like some insistent elder person who was always there to tell you it was time.

At six the flag came down, and we went to watch through the high wire fence that divided the post from the town. Sometimes we joined in the ceremony, standing at salute until the sound of the cannon made us jump. That must have been when we had just studied about George Washington in school, or recited "The Song of Marion's Men"° about Marion the Fox and the British cavalry that chased him up and down the broad Santee. But at other times we stuck out our tongues and jeered at the soldiers. Perhaps the night before we had hung at the edges of a group of old men and listened to tales about Aniceto Pizaña and the "border troubles,"° as the local paper still called them when it referred to them gingerly in passing.

It was because of the border troubles, ten years or so before, that the soldiers had come ⁵ back to old Fort Jones. But we did not hate them for that; we admired them even, at least sometimes. But when we were thinking about the border troubles instead of Marion the Fox we hooted them and the flag they were lowering, which for the moment was theirs alone, just as we would have jeered an opposing ball team, in a friendly sort of way. On these occasions even Chonita would join in the mockery, though she usually ran home at the stroke of six. But whether we taunted or saluted, the distant men in khaki uniforms went about their motions without noticing us at all.

The last word from the post came in the night when a distant bugle blew. At nine it was all right because all the lights were on. But sometimes I heard it at eleven when everything was dark and still, and it made me feel that I was all alone in the world. I would even doubt that I was me, and that put me in such a fright that I felt like yelling out just to make sure I was really there. But next morning the sun shone and life began all over again. With its whistles and cannon shots and bugles blowing. And so we lived, we and the post, side by side with the wire fence in between.

°*Fort Jones:* The setting of Fort Jones and Jonesville-on-the-Grande in Texas is fictional. The story takes place in the mid-1920s, one of the most turbulent periods of Mexican history and only a few years after the deaths of two of the greatest heroes of the Mexican revolution—Pancho Villa (1877–1923) and Emiliano Zapata (c. 1879–1919).
°*"Song of Marion's Men":* a poem by William Cullen Bryant (1794–1878) about Colonel Francis Marion (c. 1732–1795), who was a leader of irregular guerrilla forces in South Carolina during the Revolutionary War. Because of his hit-and-run tactics, involving his hiding in the swamps near the "broad Santee" river in South Carolina, Marion was nicknamed the "Swamp Fox."
°*border troubles:* The most serious border incidents occurred in 1916, when Pancho Villa was responsible for deaths of Americans on both sides of the border. He made repeated raids into New Mexico and Texas.

The wandering soldiers whom the bugle called home at night did not wander in our neighborhood, and none of us ever went into Fort Jones. None except Chonita. Every evening when the flag came down she would leave off playing and go down towards what was known as the "lower" gate of the post, the one that opened not on Main Street but against the poorest part of town. She went into the grounds and to the mess halls and pressed her nose against the screens and watched the soldiers eat. They sat at long tables calling to each other through food-stuffed mouths.

"Hey bud, pass the coffee!"

"Give me the ham!"

10 "Yeah, give me the beans!"

After the soldiers were through the cooks came out and scolded Chonita, and then they gave her packages with things to eat.

Chonita's mother did our washing, in gratefulness—as my mother put it—for the use of a vacant lot of my grandfather's which was a couple of blocks down the street. On the lot was an old one-room shack which had been a shed long ago, and this Chonita's father had patched up with flattened-out pieces of tin. He was a laborer. Ever since the end of the border troubles there had been a development boom in the Valley, and Chonita's father was getting his share of the good times. Clearing brush and building irrigation ditches he sometimes pulled down as much as six dollars a week. He drank a good deal of it up, it was true. But corn was just a few cents a bushel in those days. He was the breadwinner, you might say, while Chonita furnished the luxuries.

Chonita was a poet too. I had just moved into the neighborhood when a boy came up to me and said, "Come on! Let's go hear Chonita make a speech."

She was already on top of the alley fence when we got there, a scrawny little girl of about nine, her bare dirty feet clinging to the fence almost like hands. A dozen other kids were there below her, waiting. Some were boys I knew at school; five or six were her younger brothers and sisters.

15 "Speech! Speech!" they all cried. "Let Chonita make a speech! Talk in English, Chonita!"

They were grinning and nudging each other except for her brothers and sisters, who looked up at her with proud serious faces. She gazed out beyond us all with a grand, distant air and then she spoke.

"Give me the hammon and the beans!" she yelled. "Give me the hammon and the beans!"

She leaped off the fence and everybody cheered and told her how good it was and how she could talk English better than the teachers at the grammar school.

I thought it was a pretty poor joke. Every evening almost, they would make her get up on the fence and yell, "Give me the hammon and the beans!" And everybody would cheer and make her think she was talking English. As for me, I would wait there until she got it over with so we could play at something else. I wondered how long it would be before they got tired of it all. I never did find out because just about that time I got the chills and fever, and when I got up and around Chonita wasn't there anymore.

20 In later years I thought of her a lot, especially during the thirties when I was growing up. Those years would have been just made for her. Many's the time I have seen her in my mind's eyes, in the picket lines demanding not bread, not cake, but the hammon and the beans. But it didn't work out that way.

One night Doctor Zapata came into our kitchen through the back door. He set his bag on the table and said to my father, who had opened the door for him, "Well, she is dead."

My father flinched. "What was it?" he asked.

The doctor had gone to the window and he stood with his back to us, looking out toward the light of Fort Jones. "Pneumonia, flu, malnutrition, worms, the evil eye," he said without turning around. "What the hell difference does it make?"

"I wish I had known how sick she was," my father said in a very mild tone. "Not that it's really my affair, but I wish I had."

The doctor snorted and shook his head.

My mother came in and I asked her who was dead. She told me. It made me feel strange but I did not cry. My mother put her arm around my shoulders. "She is in Heaven now," she said. "She is happy."

I shrugged her arm away and sat down in one of the kitchen chairs.

"They're like animals," the doctor was saying. He turned round suddenly and his eyes glistened in the light. "Do you know what that brute of a father was doing when I left? He was laughing! Drinking and laughing with his friends."

"There's no telling what the poor man feels," my mother said.

My father made a deprecatory gesture. "It wasn't his daughter anyway."

"No?" the doctor said. He sounded interested.

"This is the woman's second husband," my father explained. "First one died before the girl was born, shot and hanged from a mesquite limb. He was working too close to the tracks the day the Olmito train was derailed."

"You know what?" the doctor said. "In classical times they did things better. Take Troy, for instance. After they stormed the city they grabbed the babies by the heels and dashed them against the wall. That was more humane."

My father smiled. "You sound very radical. You sound just like your relative down there in Morelos."°

"No relative of mine," the doctor said. "I'm a conservative, the son of a conservative, and you know that I wouldn't be here except for that little detail."

"Habit," my father said. "Pure habit, pure tradition. You're a radical at heart."

"It depends on how you define radicalism," the doctor answered. "People tend to use words too loosely. A dentist could be called a radical, I suppose. He pulls up things by the roots."

My father chuckled.

"Any bandit in Mexico nowadays can give himself a political label," the doctor went on, "and that makes him respectable. He's a leader of the people."

"Take Villa, now—" my father began.

"Villa was a different type of man," the doctor broke in.

"I don't see any difference."

The doctor came over to the table and sat down. "Now look at it this way," he began, his finger in front of my father's face. My father threw back his head and laughed.

"You'd better go to bed and rest," my mother told me. "You're not completely well, you know."

So I went to bed, but I didn't go to sleep, not right away. I lay there for a long time while behind my darkened eyelids Emiliano Zapata's cavalry charged down to the broad Santee, where there were grave men with hoary hairs.° I was still awake at eleven when the cold voice of the bugle went gliding in and out of the dark like something that couldn't find its way back to wherever it had been. I thought of Chonita in Heaven, and I saw her in her torn and dirty dress, with a pair of bright wings attached, flying round and round like a butterfly shouting, "Give me the hammon and the beans!"

Then I cried. And whether it was the bugle, or whether it was Chonita or what, to this day I do not know. But cry I did, and I felt much better after that.

°*Morelos:* the home state of Zapata.
°*grave men with hoary hairs:* cf. lines 49–52 of Bryant's "Song of Marion's Men":
    Grave men there are by broad Santee,
      Grave men with hoary hairs;
    Their hearts are all with Marion,
      For Marion are their prayers.

QUESTIONS

1. How does the tale of Chonita's brief life and her death fit into the political, social, and broadly human framework of the story? What particular idea or ideas does Paredes illustrate by the brief life of Chonita?
2. How does Paredes establish the setting of the story? What is the significance of the fort? Of the "dirty yellow" paint? Of the vacant lot and the shack?
3. Is Chonita a round or flat character? To what extent does the author make her symbolic and representative? Why?
4. What is the tone of the story (some possibilities: ironic, cynical, resigned, bitter, resentful)? What techniques does Paredes use to control the tone?
5. How does Doctor Zapata's attitude toward Chonita's death, along with the words he uses to announce it, contribute to the major ideas of the story?
6. Near the end of William Cullen Bryant's "Song of Marion's Men" (lines 53–56) the following four lines appear:

> And lovely ladies greet our band [i.e., of soldiers]
> With kindliest welcoming,
> And smiles like those of summer,
> And tears like those of spring.

Contrast these lines with the narrator's vision of Chonita in heaven.

WRITING ABOUT A MAJOR IDEA IN FICTION

Most likely you will write about a major idea or theme, but you may also get interested in one of your story's other ideas. As you begin brainstorming and developing your first drafts, consider questions such as the following.

Questions for Discovering Ideas

GENERAL IDEAS

- What ideas do you discover in the work? How do you discover them (through action, character description, scenes, figurative language)?
- To what do the ideas pertain? To individuals themselves? To individuals and society? To religion? To social, political, or economic circumstances? To fairness? To inequality? To justice?
- How balanced are the ideas? If a particular idea is strongly presented, what conditions and qualifications are also presented (if any)? What contradictory ideas are presented?
- Are the ideas limited to members of any groups represented by the characters (age, race, nationality, personal status)? Or are the ideas applicable to general conditions of life? Explain.
- Which characters in their own right represent or embody ideas? How do their actions and speeches bring out these ideas?
- If characters state ideas directly, how persuasive is their expression, how intelligent and well considered? How germane are the ideas to the work? How germane to more general conditions?

- With children, young adults, or the old, how do the circumstances express or embody an idea?

A SPECIFIC IDEA

- What idea seems particularly important in the work? Why? How is it presented? Is it asserted directly, indirectly, dramatically, ironically? Does any one method predominate? Why?
- How pervasive in the work is the idea (throughout or intermittent)? To what degree is it associated with a major character or action? How does the structure of the work affect or shape your understanding of the idea?
- What value or values are embodied in the idea? Of what importance are the values to the work's meaning?
- How compelling is the idea? How could the work be appreciated without reference to any idea at all?

Strategies for Organizing Ideas

Narrative and dramatic elements have a strong bearing on ideas in well-written stories, poems, and plays. In this sense, an idea is like a key in music or like a continuous thread tying together actions, characters, statements, symbols, and dialogue. As readers, we can trace such threads throughout the entire fabric of the work.

As you write about ideas, you may find yourself relying most heavily on the direct statements of the authorial voice or on a combination of these and your interpretation of characters and action. Or you may focus exclusively on a first-person speaker and use his or her ideas to develop your analysis. Always make clear the sources of your details and distinguish the sources from your own commentary.

In your essay, your general goal is to describe an idea and show its importance in the story. Each separate work will invite its own approach, but here are a number of strategies you might use to organize your essay:

1. *Analyze the idea as it applies to character. Example:* "Chonita embodies the idea that life amid poverty leads to the loss of dignity and opportunity, and also to the loss of health and even to death itself" ("The Hammon and the Beans").

2. *Show how actions bring out the idea. Example:* "That Mabel and Dr. Fergusson fall in love rather than go their separate ways indicates Lawrence's idea that love literally rescues human lives" ("The Horse Dealer's Daughter").

3. *Show how dialogue and separate speeches bring out the idea. Example:* "The priest's responses to Jackie's confession embody the idea that kindness and understanding are the best means to encourage religious and philosophical commitment" ("First Confession" in Chapter 6).

4. *Show how the story's structure is determined by the idea. Example:* "The idea that horror can exist in ordinary things leads to a structure in which Jackson introduces seemingly commonplace people, builds suspense about an impending misfortune, and develops a conclusion of mob insensitivity and cruelty" ("The Lottery" in Chapter 2).

5. *Treat variations or differing manifestations of the idea. Example:* "The idea that zealousness leads to harm is shown in Brown's nightmarish distortion of reality, his rejection of others, and his dying gloom" ("Young Goodman Brown" in Chapter 7).

6. *Deal with a combination of these (together with any other significant aspect). Example:* "The idea in 'Araby' [Chapter 4] that devotion is complex and contradictory is shown in the narrator's romantic mission as a carrier of parcels, his outcries to love in the back room of his house, and his self-reproach and shame at the story's end." (Here the idea is traced through both speech and action.)

Your conclusion might begin with a summary, together with your evaluation of the validity or force of the idea. If you have been convinced by the author's ideas, you might say that the author has expressed the idea forcefully and convincingly, or else you might show the relevance of the idea to current conditions. If you are not persuaded by the idea, you should demonstrate its shortcomings or limitations. If you wish to mention a related idea, whether in the story you have studied or in some other story, you might introduce that here, but be sure to stress the connections.

Illustrative Student Essay

Although underlined sentences are not recommended by MLA style, they are used in this illustrative essay as teaching tools to emphasize the central idea, thesis sentence, and topic sentences.

---

de los Reyes 1

Oscar de los Reyes

Professor Garcia

English 112

8 October 2014

    D. H. Lawrence's "The Horse Dealer's Daughter" as an Expression of the

Idea That Loving Commitment Is Essential in Life.°

[1]   Lawrence's "The Horse Dealer's Daughter" is an unusual love story. We learn that the lovers—Mabel Pervin (who is "The Horse Dealer's Daughter") and Dr. Jack Fergusson—have known each other for many years but have never thought of themselves as lovers. It is not until after an almost catastrophic event that the two recognize that they love each other.

°**This story appears on pages 392–402.**

de los Reyes 2

Lawrence makes clear that this new love is about to bring new meaning and new direction to their lives. Most important about this love is that it fulfills Lawrence's idea that it is dedicated commitment that gives life meaning.* Lawrence brings out this idea first by showing characters with no sense of love or commitment and then by developing the two major characters whose lives are to be fulfilled by commitment.†

Negatively, at the story's beginning, Lawrence introduces his idea   [2] through the Pervin brothers, who have no sense of service or commitment and who therefore are leading obtuse, insensitive, somewhat cruel, and basically "ineffectual" lives (396). It is true that Joe, the oldest brother, is planning to marry, and, one might assume, is also undertaking the promises and commitments that marriage brings. But Joe is seeking marriage only to receive a job from his future father-in-law. In other words, his only duty is to himself, and even though that is a commitment of sorts, it is only a limited one.

In line with Lawrence's idea, Joe's life has little if any meaning. Lawrence's speaker dismisses Joe with the cutting words that he is not much better than the large draft horses on the Pervin farm, whose "stupidity . . . [holds] them in subjection" (393).

Lawrence's first use of his major characters, Mabel Pervin and Dr. Jack   [3] Fergusson, also embodies the negative aspect of his idea that lack of service and commitment to others leaves people aimless and unfulfilled. When Jack first enters the story his eyes look "tired" (394), and he is suffering from a severe cold. His social life seems to be confined to spending time at a nearby pub and drinking with one of the Pervin brothers, Fred Henry, and two women named "Lizzie and May" (396). These outward signs of illness and aimlessness suggest an inner lack of conviction and commitment. But nevertheless, Jack is a good doctor. He may sometimes think of himself as a "slave" to his patients (397), but he is dedicated to his work and finds excitement in it (397). Therefore he declares that he cannot take a brief rest from serving his patients even to overcome his cold (394). Clearly he

---

*Central idea.
†Thesis sentence.

de los Reyes 3

is committed to his profession, but the commitment that comes from love is lacking in his life. When he goes into the pond to rescue Mabel, it is as a professional, not as a committed lover. His action, however, will change him and point him in the path of completeness.

[4]   Mabel is in a position similar to Jack's. Lawrence introduces her as "a rather short, sullen-looking young woman" with an "impassive fixity of her face" (392). Her brothers all seem to dislike her. Like Jack, she is living only half a life, even though she has gained some little meaning through service, of a sort, to others. In the past she has been "keeping the home together" for her father and her brothers as the family fortunes declined. As long as the family had had money, her life was adequate, even if the household to which she was committed was "brutal and coarse" in many ways (396). But with the family now "hopelessly in debt," requiring the breakup of the household, her duties are vanishing, and this loss also brings the loss of the meaning that her service has brought to her (396).

[5]   In line with the idea, Lawrence makes plain that Mabel's developing despair will end her existence and that Jack's aimlessness, if unchanged, will keep him incomplete. Mabel's situation is, of course, the more critical. After completing her chores at home, thus fulfilling all her obligations there, she sets about to care for the grave of her dead mother, to whom her commitment is total (396–97). Once she finishes this loving task, she has nowhere to go, nothing more to do, and she therefore walks purposefully to the nearby pond and enters it in an attempt to drown herself (398). One can read her attempted suicide as a symbol of Lawrence's idea that once a person's commitments end, meaning is gone and life is, without dedicated love, over.

[6]   The paragraphs devoted by Lawrence to the interchanges of Mabel and Jack after he has rescued her from the pond demonstrate the connections of love and commitment. When he brings her to the shore he works "to restore her" (398). After he carries her home—an arduous and difficult task—he disrobes her and wraps her in blankets to bring back warmth and life to her. At this point his commitment to her, however, is not to a loved one but to a patient. But when Mabel recovers, her first thought is to associate her

de los Reyes 4

nakedness with a newly discovered love for her. She asks him "Do you love me then?" (399). Once she has extracted a declaration of love, her first wishes are an enactment of Lawrence's idea of the power of commitment. She wants to get him "dry things" and then to make him some tea (401). She has been awakened to a new life by a man who suddenly appears in a totally new light, and her response is immediately to begin the simple tasks that follow naturally from commitment. For his part, Jack demonstrates his newly found commitment by stating that he wants the two of them "to be married" (402). The idea is that love is for the moment, but commitment is for the long term.

    The major and most truthful aspect of Lawrence's idea is that the transformation to loving obligation is not easy but is both tentative and complex. Lawrence demonstrates this complexity by showing that both Mabel and Jack are uneasy and uncertain, for neither one can easily give up the past (even though Mabel was willing to give up everything when she tried suicide). When Jack expresses love for Mabel it is in a voice that is "unlike himself" (401), and her response is to say "I feel I'm horrible to you" (402). Difficult and fearful as the change to their new commitment is, however, it is leading them into the lives they have been designed for. Generally, people who evade such a change, like the Pervin brothers, may find life easy, but they are permanently incomplete because they lack the bravery of committed love shown by Mabel and Jack Thus, Lawrence's idea in "The Horse Dealer's Daughter" emphasizes that a full life requires love and commitment, no matter how difficult, and that without such commitment lives can be lived only in the shadows.

[7]

de los Reyes 5

Work Cited

Lawrence, D. H. "The Horse Dealer's Daughter." *Literature: An Introduction to Reading and Writing, Compact Edition*. Ed. Edgar V. Roberts
and Robert Zweig. 6th ed. New York: Pearson, 2015. 392–402. Print.

Commentary on the Essay

This essay follows strategy 6 (p. 408) by showing how separate components of the story exhibit the idea's pervasiveness. Throughout, citations of characters, actions, and speeches, together with observations about the story's organization, are used as evidence for the various conclusions. Transitions between paragraphs are effected by words and phrases like "introduces," "similar," "after he has rescued her," and "the major and most truthful aspect," all of which emphasize the continuity of the topic.

The first paragraph asserts that the story's major action—the development of love between the major characters—brings out Lawrence's idea that commitment gives meaning to life. The idea is to be developed as it applies to characters without commitment and then to those who find it.

The argument of paragraphs 2 through 4 is to show how Lawrence brings out his idea negatively by demonstrating the shortcomings of characters, including the story's two major characters, who are living without commitment. The essay thus asserts that Joe is following a path of stupidity, Jack a life of aimlessness, and Mabel an action of suicide. These details are brought out in support of the essay's central idea or argument. Paragraphs 5 and 6 treat the positive aspects of the main idea, focusing on the renewing effect of commitment for both Jack and Mabel. The last paragraph pays tribute to Lawrence's idea by demonstrating that it is realistic and true to life because both Jack and Mabel discover that their new commitments are not made easily but require profound and even disturbing changes in their lives.

Writing Topics About Ideas

Writing Paragraphs

1. Pick one of the stories from this chapter. Write a paragraph about what you think the main idea is and state it in a topic sentence. Relate that idea to specific evidence in the story to back up your claim.

Writing Essays

1. Write an essay in which you compare two stories containing similar themes. *Examples:* Faulkner's "A Rose for Emily" (Chapter 1) and Porter's "The Jilting of Granny Weatherall" (Chapter 7), Chopin's "The Story of an Hour" (Chapter 6) and Gilman's "The Yellow Wallpaper" (Chapter 10). For help in developing your essay, consult Chapter 26 on the technique of comparison-contrast.

2. Write an essay criticizing the ideas in a story in this book that you dislike or to which you are indifferent. With what statements in the story do you disagree? What actions? What characters? How do your own beliefs and values cause you to dislike the story's ideas? How might the story be changed to illustrate ideas with which you would agree?

Creative Writing Assignment

1. Select an idea that particularly interests you, and write a story showing how characters may or may not live up to the idea. If you have difficulty getting started, try one of these possible ideas:
   a. Interest and enthusiasm are hard to maintain for long.
   b. People always want more than they have or need.
   c. The concerns of adults are different from those of children.
   d. Confronting another person about a grievance is awkward.
   e. Making a romantic or career decision is hard because it requires a change in life's directions.

Library Assignment

1. Using books that you discover through the retrieval system in your college or local library, or works that you find online, search for discussions of only one of the following topics, and write a brief report on what you find.

   a. Nathaniel Hawthorne on the significance of religion, both good and bad.
   b. Ernest Hemingway on individualism and self-realization.
   c. James Joyce on the significance, good or bad, of religion.
   d. D. H. Lawrence on the power of the working classes.
   e. Cynthia Ozick on the Holocaust.
   f. The ideas underlying Poe's concept of the short story as a literary form.

Chapter 9

A Casebook of Four Stories by Edgar Allan Poe with Critical Readings for Research

AFTER STUDYING THIS MATERIAL, YOU SHOULD BE ABLE TO DO THE FOLLOWING:

- Understand Poe's life as a journalist and fiction writer
- Recognize the range of important critical works on Poe's fiction
- Synthesize major critical assessments of Poe in an essay on his work

POE'S LIFE AND CAREER (1809–1849)

Edgar Allan Poe was born in Boston in January 1809. His parents, who were actors, separated before he was a year old. Needing to make an independent living, his mother, Elizabeth Poe, went on an acting tour, taking Edgar, his infant sister, and his older brother along with her. Shortly before Poe's third birthday, Elizabeth died, and the three children were separated. Poe was rescued from a childhood of poverty when he was taken into foster care by John and Frances Allan of Richmond, Virginia, who were childless. The Allans did not make a formal adoption, but when Poe was
christened he was given Allan as his middle name. In 1815 John Allan, who was an importer, took his family to England, where they spent five years and where Poe received most of his elementary education. In 1820 the Allans returned to America and Poe resumed his studies at a private school. He was successful both as a student and as an athlete, one of his noteworthy achievements being a broad jump of 21 feet, 6 inches, a national schoolboy record at the time. In 1826, at the age of 17, he enrolled at the University of Virginia, which had recently been founded by Thomas Jefferson.

Although Poe was a natural student, personal problems—primarily an increasingly strained relationship with Allan—upset his studies. Within a year he left college and went to Boston, where he published his first volume of poetry in 1827 (Tamerlane and Other Poems). In the same year he joined the army and quickly gained the highest rank of noncommissioned officers, although he left the service in 1829. In 1830, during a truce with Allan following the death of Mrs. Allan, he was granted an appointment at the U.S. Military Academy. Unfortunately, he got into debt, and Allan refused to help him out despite having become wealthy as the result of an inheritance. In fact, Allan, who had quickly remarried and was beginning a new family, stopped supporting Poe and cut him out of his will entirely. In 1831, lacking the financial help that he needed to maintain his life as a cadet, Poe got himself expelled from West Point by deliberately refusing to follow orders. After this time he never again used Allan in his name even though he kept "A" as his middle initial. Now totally dependent on his own resources, he embarked on a career as a writer.

Despite his difficulties with Allan, Poe had been held in high esteem by his fellow West Point cadets, who took up a collection to subsidize the second edition of his poetry in 1832. In the following years, and throughout his career as a writer and editor, he struggled constantly against poverty. It was not that he did not work hard and productively. He was always writing reviews, criticism, lectures, poetry, and fiction, and he even tried his hand as a playwright. As with his college and West Point experiences, however, he was unable to stay anywhere for long. He also struggled against alcohol, and excessive drinking caused him to lose some of his positions, although at other times his jobs simply vanished through no fault of his own.

Early in his writing career he went to live in Baltimore with his aunt, Maria ("Muddy") Clemm, and her daughter Virginia ("Sissy"). In 1836, he and Sissy, who was then only 13, were married. Mrs. Clemm continued to live with the couple and also managed household affairs as Poe moved from city to city to take new editorial positions. The marriage lasted eleven years until Sissy died of tuberculosis in 1847, when the Poes were living in Fordham, New York (later incorporated into the Bronx). The house they lived in (the "Poe Cottage") still stands and is open to the public. A plan for repair and restoration of the Cottage began in 2009. It is now claimed that the Cottage "has been restored to its original appearance."

Although Sissy's death marked a low point in Poe's life, he continued his writing, reviewing, and lecturing. In September 1849, he went on an extended lecture tour, including Richmond, where he had been brought up, as one of his destinations. When there he proposed to Sarah Elmira Royster Shelton, a wealthy widow to whom he had been engaged when he was in his late teens. Elmira's father had objected to the first engagement, and now her three brothers and two children objected because they believed that Poe was an opportunistic drunkard who wanted to marry Elmira only for her money. Despite these objections, Elmira appears genuinely to have loved Poe (she wrote that he was "the dearest object on earth" to her), and she accepted his proposal. The couple set a date in mid-October 1849 for the wedding.

It seems clear that Poe was trying to build a new life. He had just taken an oath of sobriety, he was about to marry the sweetheart of his youth, his lectures were increasingly popular, and he was developing an idea for a new critical journal. He had also just received an offer of a short-term but lucrative editing job in Philadelphia. So on September 27, 1849, he left Richmond for the boat and train ride to Philadelphia, after which he was planning to go north to New York to bring Mrs. Clemm to Richmond for the wedding. However, he never reached his destination in Philadelphia, he never did the editing job, and five days after his departure from Richmond he was found in Baltimore in a drunken and incoherent state. He was no longer dressed in his traveling suit but instead was wearing cheap and worn clothing, and he no longer possessed any of the money he had been carrying (which may have been considerable). To this day, what had brought him to this condition is a mystery. Existing evidence is inconclusive and sometimes contradictory, but it seems that he may have been waylaid, robbed, beaten, and encouraged or forced to drink a huge amount of liquor. Although it does not seem that anyone made an attempt on his life, as some accounts would have it, it does appear that at some period during the unexplained lapse of time he was under the control of people who were hostile to him.

Whatever actually did happen, and for whatever reason, Poe was in grave condition on October 3, 1849, when he was found and taken to the Washington College Hospital (now Church Hospital) in Baltimore. Because he was delirious and sometimes comatose in the hospital, he was unable to tell anyone what had happened to him. He worsened, and on October 7 he died. The following day he was buried in Baltimore's Presbyterian Cemetery. The Baltimore Clipper reported that he had died of "congestion of the brain." Since then a number of possible diagnoses have been offered, including acute alcoholic poisoning, hypoglycemia, head trauma, diabetic shock, and even rabies. According to recent scholarship, however, there "simply is not enough medical evidence at hand" to determine the exact cause of death.[1] What we can safely conclude is that Poe died abruptly under mysterious, suspicious, or even sinister circumstances just when his life and career seemed to be taking a new and positive turn.

See John Evangelist Walsh, Midnight Dreary: The Mysterious Death of Edgar Allan Poe (New Brunswick: Rutgers UP, 1998), 179.

Poe's Work as a Journalist and Writer of Fiction

During his seventeen-year career as a writer, Poe did editorial work for a number of magazines in Richmond, Philadelphia, and New York, with the most important of his associations being the *Southern Literary Messenger, Burton's Magazine, Graham's Magazine,* the *Broadway Journal,* and the *New York Mirror.* He sometimes had a regular income, although the largest salary he ever received was $800 from his editorship at *Graham's Magazine* in 1841–1842. In 1845 he seemed on the way to success when he began running the *Broadway Journal,* but this publication ran out of money early in 1846 and he was once again in financial trouble.

Along with his uncertain career in journalism and editing, Poe steadily wrote fiction. As a theoretical critic, he provided a foundation for short fiction and paved the way for subsequent writers of short stories. His critical review of Hawthorne's *Twice-Told Tales* (1842) is accepted as his theory of fiction.[2] In it he tells us that the special aim of the writer of a short prose tale is to create a concentrated emotional impact. Assuming that the writing is of high quality, the impact is directly related to the brevity of the narrative, which Poe states should take the reader no more than a single sitting of an hour or perhaps two. As a practical fact of reading, he indicates, longer stories and novels diffuse the desired effect because time itself produces inevitable distractions and the need for personal business. Therefore Poe's concept of the story stresses the primacy of effect. The implication of his theory is that, to achieve maximum impact, stories should be based on swiftly moving situations and descriptions, intricate plotting, and moods of fear and horror.

As a practitioner of fiction, Poe was both original and creative. It is to him that we owe the genres of detective story, murder story, horror story, suspense story, and psychological story (sometimes overlapping in the same work). Although he apparently considered himself a poet first and a fiction writer second, his complete stories, or tales, total more than seventy. He sought to capture his readers' attention by freely including material from his wide reading and by using his vivid and often sensational and macabre imagination. Some of his better-known tales are *The Narrative of A. Gordon Pym* (one of his longest stories, sometimes called a novel, 1837), "The Fall of the House of Usher" (1839), "The Murders in the Rue Morgue" (1841), "A Descent into the Maelström" (1841), "The Pit and the Pendulum" (1842), "The Masque of the Red Death" (1842), "The Tell-Tale Heart" (1843), "The Gold Bug" (1843), "The Black Cat" (1843), "The Purloined Letter" (1844), and "The Cask of Amontillado" (1846), which is included in Chapter 4 of this book. He also assembled many of his tales into two major collections: *Tales of the Grotesque and Arabesque* (1840) and *Tales* (1845).

Because Poe as a practicing writer followed his own theory of fiction, he does not seek to create full-blown, round character development in his tales, but instead he focuses on situations, actions, and his characters' responses. His subject matter varies widely: He includes faraway, exotic, and often dismal locations such as Paris, the sea, American islands, dreary and collapsible mansions, Gothic interiors, cellars, subterranean vaults, and mythological ends of the earth. Few of his

---

See also page 3.

characters fall within the spectrum of what we think of as normal, and a number who start out as normal take a turn into the unusual or bizarre. Some characters are driven by pride and/or guilt; some commit deranged and grisly crimes; some are dead, either recently or for centuries; some of the dead are brought to life long enough to claim possession over the living. The actions in Poe's stories are uncanny and often weird, consisting of intricate punishments, self-destructiveness, live burials, mysterious substitutions of personality, journeys into unknown regions, trips to the moon, total physical and psychological collapse, and strange and sometimes comic resurrections of the dead.

Poe's Reputation

During his lifetime, Poe was not highly regarded in the United States. Perhaps his lack of recognition resulted from his own combativeness, for he regularly alienated people who might have supported him. From time to time he was involved in lawsuits, literary quarrels, and even a fistfight. He accused Henry Wadsworth Longfellow, one of the major poets of the time, of plagiarism—certainly not a way to make himself popular and respected within the nineteenth-century American literary community. He achieved success to the degree that he won a few prizes for stories, but his chief recognition was the praise heaped upon his poem "The Raven" in 1845 (for which he received little money). In 1846 he received a letter from Elizabeth Barrett Browning congratulating him on the warm reception of his works in England, and in the same year he was commended by Nathaniel Hawthorne even though he had written negative criticism of some of Hawthorne's fiction. The highest public recognition Poe received in his lifetime was his representation in *Prose Writers of America* (1847), edited by his sometime friend, Rufus Griswold, who also was his literary executor.

After Poe died, the decline of his reputation was hastened by Griswold, who published a short but poisonous biography, most of which was later included in various editions of Poe's collected works. (Griswold stated in italics that "*few will be grieved by*" Poe's death and that Poe "*had few or no friends.*") Before long the public perception of Poe was that he had been an alcoholic and brooding loner who wrote about characters beyond the fringes of sanity. Poe's works did not contradict this image, for many unsophisticated readers readily believed that some of his disturbed fictional and poetic narrators (such as those of "The Black Cat," "The Cask of Amontillado," and "The Tell-Tale Heart") were the writer himself in his own person.

His work therefore fell into relative obscurity except in France, where he was considered a brilliant and creative though eccentric visionary. In the United States his reputation as a writer was obscured by the more objectionable and unexplainable aspects of his life, principally his marriage to his 13-year-old cousin together with reports of alcoholism and drug addiction and the mysterious circumstances of his death. As his writings have become more available, and as the early opinions about him have been modified, his literary reputation has risen. He is seen today as a romantic who asserted the need for artistic individuality and integrity, and who in his works explored the exotic, the passionate, the puzzling, the intricate, the uncontrollable, the vengeful, and—in the face of human violence—the power of conscience. Because many of his works are unrealistic, grisly, and gruesome, general readers often appreciate him for the shudder of sensational horror, while critics find ample materials for readings that are symbolic, allegorical, feminist, psychological, structuralist, and formalist. Today, of all nineteenth-century American writers of fiction, Poe is the most widely published and still the most widely read. His stature as a writer was fully acknowledged in 1986 when his name was placed in the Hall of Fame of American Authors.

Bibliographic Sources

The number of books and essays about Poe is vast. The standard edition of his works is the three-volume *Collected Works of Edgar Allan Poe* (1969–1978), edited by Thomas Ollive Mabbott. The Library of America edition of Poe's *Poetry and Tales* and *Essays and Reviews* appeared in 1984 in two volumes. A convenient popular edition has been regularly available for the past seventy years in the Modern Library edition of *The Complete Tales and Poems of Edgar Allan Poe*, with an introduction by Hervey Allen (1938). This volume includes seventy-three stories and fifty-three poems. Another readily available edition is G. R. Thompson, ed., *Great Short Works of Edgar Allan Poe* (1970). A thoroughgoing edition of the stories is *The Short Fiction of Edgar Allan Poe: An Annotated Edition* (1976, rpt. 1990), edited by Stuart and Susan Levine. This volume also contains a comprehensive introduction, a useful arrangement of the stories, copious notes, and an excellent working bibliography. An interesting popular edition is *18 Best Stories by Edgar Allan Poe* (1965), edited by Vincent Price and Chandler Brossard, with an introduction by Vincent Price, a film actor who specialized in movie villains and starred in film adaptations of Poe stories. Price's introduction, though brief, is therefore of independent interest.

Biographies of Poe are Kenneth Silverman, *Edgar A. Poe: Mournful and Never-ending Remembrance* (1991); Jeffrey Meyers, *Edgar Allan Poe: His Life and Legacy* (1992); and Scott Peeples, *Edgar Allan Poe Revisited* (1998). Other excellent biographies are Arthur H. Quinn, *Edgar Allan Poe: A Critical Biography* (1941, rpt. 1998 with a new foreword by Shawn Rosenheim); and Edward Wagenknecht, *Edgar Allan Poe: The Man Behind the Legend* (1963). George E. Woodberry's biography, *Edgar Allan Poe*, originally published in 1885, was reprinted in 1980 with an introduction and evaluation by R. W. B. Lewis. To these biographies should be added Peter Ackroyd, *Poe: A Life Cut Short* (2008), and John Evangelist Walsh, *Midnight Dreary: The Mysterious Death of Edgar Allan Poe* (1998), a study of the relevant evidence concerning Poe's death.

Significant criticism and background information may be found in Kenneth Silverman, ed., *New Essays on Poe's Major Tales* (1993); William L. Howarth, ed., *Twentieth Century Interpretations of Poe's Tales* (1971); Charles E. May, *Edgar Allan Poe: A Study of the Short Fiction* (1991); Vincent Buranelli, *Edgar Allan Poe* (1961); Benjamin F. Fisher, ed., *Poe in His Own Time* (2010); A. Robert Lee, ed., *Edgar Allan Poe: The Design of Order* (1987); Kevin J. Hayes, ed., *The Cambridge Companion to Edgar Allan Poe* (2002); Eric W. Carlson, ed., *Critical*

Essays on Edgar Allan Poe (1987); Shawn Rosenheim and Stephen Rachman, eds., *The American Face of Edgar Allan* Poe (1995); J. R. Hammond, *An Edgar Allan Poe Companion* (1981); J. Gerald Kennedy, ed., *A Historical Guide to Edgar Allan Poe* (2001); Dawn B. Sova, *Edgar Allan Poe A to Z: The Essential Reference to His Life and Work* (2001); and Bonnie Szumski and Carol Prime, eds., *Readings on Edgar Allan Poe* (1998). Eric W. Carlson in *The Recognition of Edgar Allan Poe* (1966) reprints essays and portions of essays selected to show the changes and growth of Poe's reputation from the time of his death through 1965, the year of publication. Louis Broussard, *The Measure of Poe* (1969), includes a fifty-nine-page bibliography, up to date through 1969, and Charles E. May includes a ten-page bibliography, up to date through 1991. These works are complemented by the selected bibliography provided by Peeples (pp. 196–203), which reflects criticism through 1998. In 1993 a video recording was issued with the title *Homage to Edgar Allan Poe.*

Foreign interest in Poe was pioneered by the nineteenth-century French poet Charles Baudelaire, whose *Edgar Allan Poe: Sa Vie et Ses Ouvrages* of 1852 was reprinted in 1994. A relatively recent Italian work on Poe is by Giorgio Ghidetti, *Poe, L'Eresia de un Americano Maledetto* (1989).

Poe's works have been the subject of many films and musical settings. In 1960, Roger Corman produced a film adaptation of "The Fall of the House of Usher," and he also made film versions of "The Black Cat" and "The Masque of the Red Death." More than one composer has adapted "The Fall of the House of Usher" as a musical drama. Claude Debussy worked for the last twenty-eight years of his life on an opera based on "The Fall of the House of Usher," but never finished it. Another of Poe's stories, "Ligeia," has also been set to music. As one might expect, composers writing music for Poe's works have found the poetry to be of equal or greater interest than the fiction. The most significant musical version of Poe is by Sergei Rachmaninoff (1873–1943), who composed "The Bells" in 1913 for soloists, chorus, and orchestra to a Russian adaptation of the poem by Konstantin Balmont. Rachmaninoff himself considered *The Bells* as one of his very best compositions. Two additional musical versions of Poe's poems are Norman Dello Joio's chorus *The Quest* (1991) and Paul Moravec's song cycle *Evensong* (1992). Dawn B. Sova's *Edgar Allan Poe A to Z* (2001) describes many other existing film and musical versions under the titles of Poe's works.

Writing Topics About Poe

1. Poe's idea that fiction should create a single and clearly focused impression or impact on the reader.
2. Poe's explorations of the eerie and bizarre.
3. Poe's use of setting in one or more stories.
4. Poe's use of irony and humor.
5. Poe and psychology: the meaning of evil in the lives of his characters.
6. The inevitability of guilt and punishment following criminal and immoral behavior.

7. The social background of Poe's stories (the people and their ways of life, work habits, husband-wife relationships, involvement in the world at large).

8. Poe's use of symbolism and/or allegory.

9. Poe's use of dramatic dialogue and indirect discourse.

10. Poe's use of the first-person narrator.

Four Stories by Edgar Allan Poe (Chronologically Arranged)

The Fall of the House of Usher (1839) 420

The Masque of the Red Death (1842) 431

The Black Cat (1843) 435

The Tell-Tale Heart (1843/1845) 440

 ## The Fall of the House of Usher (1839)

> Son cœur est un luth suspendu;
> Sitôt qu'on le touche il résonne.°
>
> —De Béranger

During the whole of a dull, dark, and soundless day in the autumn of the year, when the clouds hung oppressively low in the heavens, I had been passing alone, on horseback, through a singularly dreary tract of country; and at length found myself, as the shades of the evening drew on, within view of the melancholy House of Usher. I know not how it was—but, with the first glimpse of the building, a sense of insufferable gloom pervaded my spirit. I say insufferable; for the feeling was unrelieved by any of that half-pleasurable, because poetic, sentiment, with which the mind usually receives even the sternest natural images of the desolate or terrible. I looked upon the scene before me—upon the mere house, and the simple landscape features of the domain—upon the bleak walls—upon the vacant eye-like windows—upon a few rank sedges—and upon a few white trunks of decayed trees—with an utter depression of soul which I can compare to no earthly sensation more properly than to the after-dream of the reveller upon opium—the bitter lapse into every-day life—the hideous dropping off of the veil. There was an iciness, a sinking, a sickening of the heart—an unredeemed dreariness of thought which no goading of the imagination could torture into aught of the sublime. What was it—I paused to think—what was it that so unnerved me in the contemplation of the House of Usher? It was a mystery all insoluble; nor could I grapple with the shadowy fancies that crowded upon me as I pondered. I was forced to fall back upon the unsatisfactory conclusion, that while, beyond doubt, there are combinations of very simple natural objects which have the power of thus affecting us, still the analysis of this power lies among considerations beyond our depth. It was possible, I reflected, that a mere different arrangement of the particulars of the scene, of the details of the picture, would be sufficient to modify, or perhaps to annihilate its capacity for sorrowful impression; and, acting upon this idea, I reined my horse to the precipitous brink of a

---

°*Son cœur . . . résonne:* a passage from the poem "Le Refus" by Pierre-Jean de Béranger (1780–1857): "His heart is a tightly strung lute; / It rings as soon as it is touched."

black and lurid tarn that lay in unruffled lustre by the dwelling, and gazed down—but with a shudder even more thrilling than before—upon the remodelled and inverted images of the grey sedge, and the ghastly tree-stems, and the vacant and eye-like windows.

Nevertheless, in this mansion of gloom I now proposed to myself a sojourn of some weeks. Its proprietor, Roderick Usher, had been one of my boon companions in boyhood; but many years had elapsed since our last meeting. A letter, however, had lately reached me in a distant part of the country—a letter from him—which, in its wildly importunate nature, had admitted of no other than a personal reply. The MS gave evidence of nervous agitation. The writer spoke of acute bodily illness—of a mental disorder which oppressed him—and of an earnest desire to see me, as his best, and indeed his only personal friend, with a view of attempting, by the cheerfulness of my society, some alleviation of his malady. It was the manner in which all this, and much more, was said—it was the apparent heart that went with his request—which allowed me no room for hesitation; and I accordingly obeyed forthwith what I still considered a very singular summons.

Although, as boys, we had been even intimate associates, yet I really knew little of my friend. His reserve had been always excessive and habitual. I was aware, however, that his very ancient family had been noted, time out of mind, for a peculiar sensibility of temperament, displaying itself, through long ages, in many works of exalted art, and manifested, of late, in repeated deeds of munificent yet unobtrusive charity, as well as in a passionate devotion to the intricacies, perhaps even more than to the orthodox and easily recognizable beauties of musical science. I had learned, too, the very remarkable fact, that the stem of the Usher race, all time-honoured as it was, had put forth, at no period, any enduring branch; in other words, that the entire family lay in the direct line of descent, and had always, with very trifling and very temporary variation, so lain. It was this deficiency, I considered, while running over in thought the perfect keeping of the character of the premises with the accredited character of the people, and while speculating upon the possible influence which the one, in the long lapse of centuries, might have exercised upon the other—it was this deficiency, perhaps, of collateral issue, and the consequent undeviating transmission, from sire to son, of the patrimony with the name, which had, at length, so identified the two as to merge the original title of the estate in the quaint and equivocal appellation of the "House of Usher"—an appellation which seemed to include, in the minds of the peasantry who used it, both the family and the family mansion.

I have said that the sole effect of my somewhat childish experiment—that of looking down within the tarn—had been to deepen the first singular impression. There can be no doubt that the consciousness of the rapid increase of my superstition—for why should I not so term it?—served mainly to accelerate the increase itself. Such, I have long known, is the paradoxical law of all sentiments having terror as a basis. And it might have been for this reason only, that, when I again uplifted my eyes to the house itself, from its image in the pool, there grew in my mind a strange fancy—a fancy so ridiculous, indeed, that I but mention it to show the vivid force of the sensations which oppressed me. I had so worked upon my imagination as really to believe that about the whole mansion and domain there hung an atmosphere peculiar to themselves and their immediate vicinity—an atmosphere which had no affinity with the air of heaven, but which had reeked up from the decayed trees, and the grey wall, and the silent tarn—a pestilent and mystic vapour, dull, sluggish, faintly discernible, and leaden-hued.

Shaking off from my spirit what must have been a dream, I scanned more narrowly the 5
real aspect of the building. Its principal feature seemed to be that of an excessive antiquity. The discoloration of ages had been great. Minute fungi overspread the whole exterior, hanging in a fine tangled web-work from the eaves. Yet all this was apart from any extraordinary dilapidation. No portion of the masonry had fallen; and there appeared to be a wild inconsistency between its still perfect adaptation of parts, and the crumbling

condition of the individual stones. In this there was much that reminded me of the specious totality of old wood-work which has rotted for long years in some neglected vault, with no disturbance from the breath of the external air. Beyond this indication of extensive decay, however, the fabric gave little token of instability. Perhaps the eye of a scrutinizing observer might have discovered a barely perceptible fissure, which, extending from the roof of the building in front, made its way down the wall in a zigzag direction, until it became lost in the sullen waters of the tarn.

Noticing these things, I rode over a short causeway to the house. A servant in waiting took my horse, and I entered the Gothic archway of the hall. A valet, of stealthy step, thence conducted me, in silence, through many dark and intricate passages in my progress to the studio of his master. Much that I encountered on the way contributed, I know not how, to heighten the vague sentiments of which I have already spoken. While the objects around me—while the carvings of the ceilings, the sombre tapestries of the walls, the ebon blackness of the floors, and the phantasmagoric armorial trophies which rattled as I strode, were but matters to which, or to such as which, I had been accustomed from my infancy—while I hesitated not to acknowledge how familiar was all this—I still wondered to find how unfamiliar were the fancies which ordinary images were stirring up. On one of the staircases, I met the physician of the family. His countenance, I thought, wore a mingled expression of low cunning and perplexity. He accosted me with trepidation and passed on. The valet now threw open a door and ushered me into the presence of his master.

The room in which I found myself was very large and lofty. The windows were long, narrow, and pointed, and at so vast a distance from the black oaken floor as to be altogether inaccessible from within. Feeble gleams of encrimsoned light made their way through the trellised panes, and served to render sufficiently distinct the more prominent objects around; the eye, however, struggled in vain to reach the remoter angles of the chamber, or the recesses of the vaulted and fretted ceiling. Dark draperies hung upon the walls. The general furniture was profuse, comfortless, antique, and tattered. Many books and musical instruments lay scattered about, but failed to give any vitality to the scene. I felt that I breathed an atmosphere of sorrow. An air of stern, deep, and irredeemable gloom hung over and pervaded all.

Upon my entrance, Usher rose from a sofa on which he had been lying at full length, and greeted me with a vivacious warmth which had much in it, I at first thought, of an overdone cordiality—of the constrained effort of the ennuye man of the world. A glance, however, at his countenance, convinced me of his perfect sincerity. We sat down; and for some moments, while he spoke not, I gazed upon him with a feeling half of pity, half of awe. Surely, man had never before so terribly altered, in so brief a period, as had Roderick Usher! It was with difficulty that I could bring myself to admit the identity of the wan being before me with the companion of my early boyhood. Yet the character of his face had been at all times remarkable. A cadaverousness of complexion; an eye large, liquid, and luminous beyond comparison; lips somewhat thin and very pallid, but of a surpassingly beautiful curve; a nose of a delicate Hebrew model, but with a breadth of nostril unusual in similar formations; a finely moulded chin, speaking, in its want of prominence, of a want of moral energy; hair of a more than web-like softness and tenuity; these features, with an inordinate expansion above the regions of the temple, made up altogether a countenance not easily to be forgotten. And now in the mere exaggeration of the prevailing character of these features, and of the expression they were wont to convey, lay so much of change that I doubted to whom I spoke. The now ghastly pallor of the skin, and the now miraculous lustre of the eye, above all things startled and even awed me. The silken hair, too, had been suffered to grow all unheeded, and as, in its wild gossamer texture, it floated rather than fell about the face, I could not, even with effort, connect its Arabesque expression with any idea of simple humanity.

In the manner of my friend I was at once struck with an incoherence—an inconsistency; and I soon found this to arise from a series of feeble and futile struggles to overcome an habitual trepidancy—an excessive nervous agitation. For something of this nature I had indeed been prepared, no less by his letter, than by reminiscences of certain boyish traits, and by conclusions deduced from his peculiar physical conformation and temperament. His action was alternately vivacious and sullen. His voice varied rapidly from a tremulous indecision (when the animal spirits seemed utterly in abeyance) to that species of energetic concision—that abrupt, weighty, unhurried, and hollow-sounding enunciation—that leaden, self-balanced and perfectly modulated guttural utterance, which may be observed in the lost drunkard, or the irreclaimable eater of opium, during the periods of his most intense excitement.

It was thus that he spoke of the object of my visit, of his earnest desire to see me, and   10
of the solace he expected me to afford him. He entered, at some length, into what he conceived to be the nature of his malady. It was, he said, a constitutional and a family evil, and one for which he despaired to find a remedy—a mere nervous affection, he immediately added, which would undoubtedly soon pass off. It displayed itself in a host of unnatural sensations. Some of these, as he detailed them, interested and bewildered me; although, perhaps, the terms, and the general manner of the narration had their weight. He suffered much from a morbid acuteness of the senses; the most insipid food was alone endurable; he could wear only garments of certain texture; the odours of all flowers were oppressive; his eyes were tortured by even a faint light; and there were but peculiar sounds, and these from stringed instruments, which did not inspire him with horror.

To an anomalous species of terror I found him a bounden slave. "I shall perish," said he, "I must perish in this deplorable folly. Thus, thus, and not otherwise, shall I be lost. I dread the events of the future, not in themselves, but in their results. I shudder at the thought of any, even the most trivial, incident, which may operate upon this intolerable agitation of soul. I have, indeed, no abhorrence of danger, except in its absolute effect—in terror. In this unnerved—in this pitiable condition—I feel that the period will sooner or later arrive when I must abandon life and reason together, in some struggle with the grim phantasm, FEAR."

I learned, moreover, at intervals, and through broken and equivocal hints, another singular feature of his mental condition. He was enchained by certain superstitious impressions in regard to the dwelling which he tenanted, and whence, for many years, he had never ventured forth—in regard to an influence whose supposititious force was conveyed in terms too shadowy here to be re-stated—an influence which some peculiarities in the mere form and substance of his family mansion, had, by dint of long sufferance, he said, obtained over his spirit—an effect which the physique of the grey walls and turrets, and of the dim tarn into which they all looked down, had, at length, brought about upon the morale of his existence.

He admitted, however, although with hesitation, that much of the peculiar gloom which thus afflicted him could be traced to a more natural and far more palpable origin—to the severe and long-continued illness—indeed to the evidently approaching dissolution—of a tenderly beloved sister—his sole companion for long years—his last and only relative on earth. "Her decease," he said, with a bitterness which I can never forget, "would leave him (him the hopeless and the frail) the last of the ancient race of the Ushers." While he spoke, the lady Madeline (for so was she called) passed slowly through a remote portion of the apartment, and, without having noticed my presence, disappeared. I regarded her with an utter astonishment not unmingled with dread—and yet I found it impossible to account for such feelings. A sensation of stupor oppressed me, as my eyes followed her retreating steps. When a door, at length, closed upon her, my glance sought instinctively and eagerly the countenance of the brother—but he had buried his face in his hands, and I could only perceive that a far more than ordinary wanness had overspread the emaciated fingers through which trickled many passionate tears.

The disease of the lady Madeline had long baffled the skill of her physicians. A settled apathy, a gradual wasting away of the person, and frequent although transient affections of a partially cataleptical character, were the unusual diagnosis. Hitherto she had steadily borne up against the pressure of her malady, and had not betaken herself finally to bed; but, on the closing in of the evening of my arrival at the house, she succumbed (as her brother told me at night with inexpressible agitation) to the prostrating power of the destroyer; and I learned that the glimpse I had obtained of her person would thus probably be the last I should obtain—that the lady, at least while living, would be seen by me no more.

15   For several days ensuing, her name was unmentioned by either Usher or myself: and during this period I was busied in earnest endeavours to alleviate the melancholy of my friend. We painted and read together; or I listened, as if in a dream, to the wild improvisations of his speaking guitar. And thus, as a closer and still closer intimacy admitted me more unreservedly into the recesses of his spirit, the more bitterly did I perceive the futility of all attempt at cheering a mind from which darkness, as if an inherent positive quality, poured forth upon all objects of the moral and physical universe, in one unceasing radiation of gloom.

I shall ever bear about me a memory of the many solemn hours I thus spent alone with the master of the House of Usher. Yet I should fail in any attempt to convey an idea of the exact character of the studies, or of the occupations, in which he involved me, or led me the way. An excited and highly distempered ideality threw a sulphurous lustre over all. His long improvised dirges will ring for ever in my ears. Among other things, I hold painfully in mind a certain singular perversion and amplification of the wild air of the last waltz of Von Weber. From the paintings over which his elaborate fancy brooded, and which grew, touch by touch, into vagueness at which I shuddered the more thrillingly, because I shuddered knowing not why;—from these paintings (vivid as their images now are before me) I would in vain endeavour to educe more than a small portion which should lie within the compass of merely written words. By the utter simplicity, by the nakedness of his designs, he arrested and overawed attention. If ever mortal painted an idea, that mortal was Roderick Usher. For me at least—in the circumstances then surrounding me—there arose out of the pure abstractions which the hypochondriac contrived to throw upon his canvas, an intensity of intolerable awe, no shadow of which felt I ever yet in the contemplation of the certainly glowing yet too concrete reveries of Fuseli.

One of the phantasmagoric conceptions of my friend, partaking not so rigidly of the spirit of abstraction, may be shadowed forth, although feebly, in words. A small picture presented the interior of an immensely long and rectangular vault or tunnel, with low walls, smooth, white, and without interruption or device. Certain accessory points of the design served well to convey the idea that this excavation lay at an exceeding depth below the surface of the earth. No outlet was observed in any portion of its vast extent, and no torch, or other artificial source of light was discernible; yet a flood of intense rays rolled throughout, and bathed the whole in a ghastly and inappropriate splendour.

I have just spoken of that morbid condition of the auditory nerve which rendered all music intolerable to the sufferer, with the exception of certain effects of stringed instruments. It was, perhaps, the narrow limits to which he thus confined himself upon the guitar, which gave birth, in great measure, to the fantastic character of the performances. But the fervid facility of his impromptus could not be so accounted for. They must have been, and were, in the notes, as well as in the words of his wild fantasias (for he not unfrequently accompanied himself with rhymed verbal improvisations), the result of that intense mental collectedness and concentration to which I have previously alluded as observable only in particular moments of the highest artificial excitement. The words of one of these rhapsodies I have easily remembered. I was, perhaps, the more forcibly impressed with it, as he gave it, because, in the under or mystic current of its meaning, I fancied that I perceived, and for the first time, a full consciousness on the part of Usher, of the tottering of his lofty reason upon her throne. The verses, which were entitled "The Haunted Palace," ran very nearly, if not accurately, thus:

I

In the greenest of our valleys,
By good angels tenanted,
Once a fair and stately palace—
Radiant palace—reared its head.
In the monarch Thought's dominion—
It stood there!
Never seraph spread a pinion
Over fabric half so fair.

II

Banners yellow, glorious, golden,
On its roof did float and flow;
(This—all this—was in the olden
Time long ago)
And every gentle air that dallied,
In that sweet day,
Along the ramparts plumed and pallid,
A winged odour went away.

III

Wanderers in that happy valley
Through two luminous windows saw
Spirits moving musically
To a lute's well tuned law,
Round about a throne, where sitting
(Porphyrogene!)
In state his glory well befitting,
The ruler of the realm was seen.

IV

And all with pearl and ruby glowing
Was the fair palace door,
Through which came flowing, flowing, flowing
And sparkling evermore,
A troop of Echoes whose sweet duty
Was but to sing,
In voices of surpassing beauty,
The wit and wisdom of their king.

V

But evil things, in robes of sorrow,
Assailed the monarch's high estate;
(Ah, let us mourn, for never morrow
Shall dawn upon him, desolate!)
And, round about his home, the glory
That blushed and bloomed
Is but a dim-remembered story,
Of the old time entombed.

VI

> And travellers now within that valley,
> Through the red-litten windows, see
> Vast forms that move fantastically
> To a discordant melody;
> While, like a rapid ghastly river,
> Through the pale door,
> A hideous throng rush out forever,
> And laugh—but smile no more.

I well remember that suggestions arising from this ballad, led us into a train of thought wherein there became manifest an opinion of Usher's which I mention not so much on account of its novelty (for other men° have thought thus,) as on account of the pertinacity with which he maintained it. This opinion, in its general form, was that of the sentience of all vegetable things. But, in his disordered fancy, the idea had assumed a more daring character, and trespassed, under certain conditions, upon the kingdom of inorganization. I lack words to express the full extent, or the earnest abandon of his persuasion. The belief, however, was connected (as I have previously hinted) with the gray stones of the home of his forefathers. The conditions of the sentience had been here, he imagined, fulfilled in the method of collocation of these stones—in the order of their arrangement, as well as in that of the many fungi which overspread them, and of the decayed trees which stood around— above all, in the long undisturbed endurance of this arrangement, and in its reduplication in the still waters of the tarn. Its evidence—the evidence of the sentience—was to be seen, he said, (and I here started as he spoke,) in the gradual yet certain condensation of an atmosphere of their own about the waters and the walls. The result was discoverable, he added, in that silent, yet importunate and terrible influence which for centuries had moulded the destinies of his family, and which made him what I now saw him—what he was. Such opinions need no comment, and I will make none.

20 Our books—the books which, for years, had formed no small portion of the mental existence of the invalid—were, as might be supposed, in strict keeping with this character of phantasm. We pored together over such works as the Ververt et Chartreuse of Gresset; the Belphegor of Machiavelli; the Heaven and Hell of Swedenborg; the Subterranean Voyage of Nicholas Klimm by Holberg; the Chiromancy of Robert Flud, of Jean D'Indagine, and of De la Chambre; the Journey into the Blue Distance of Tieck; and the City of the Sun by Campanella. One favourite volume was a small octavo edition of the Directorium Inquisitorum, by the Dominican Eymeric de Gironne; and there were passages in Pomponius Mela, about the old African Satyrs and OEgipans, over which Usher would sit dreaming for hours. His chief delight, however, was found in the perusal of an exceedingly rare and curious book in quarto Gothic—the manual of a forgotten church—the *Vigiliae Mortuorum Secundum Chorum Ecclesiae Maguntinae.*°

I could not help thinking of the wild ritual of this work, and of its probable influence upon the hypochondriac, when, one evening, having informed me abruptly that the lady Madeline was no more, he stated his intention of preserving her corpse for a fortnight, (previously to its final interment), in one of the numerous vaults within the main walls of

---

°Watson, Dr. Percival, Spallanzani, and especially the Bishop of Landaff.—See "Chemical Essays," vol. 5. [This is Poe's own note. He is citing these scientific and historical writers as support for his assertions.]
°*Our books . . . Maguntinae:* Poe's speaker characterizes the works of the writers contained in the paragraph as being "in keeping with this character of phantasm." This judgment is right; the works are about mysticism, utopias, travels to fantastic underworld countries, palmistry, and forest deities such as Pan. The concluding reference is to a 1500 publication describing ceremonies and prayers for the dead.

the building. The worldly reason, however, assigned for this singular proceeding, was one which I did not feel at liberty to dispute. The brother had been led to his resolution (so he told me) by consideration of the unusual character of the malady of the deceased, of certain obtrusive and eager inquiries on the part of her medical men, and of the remote and exposed situation of the burial-ground of the family. I will not deny that when I called to mind the sinister countenance of the person whom I met upon the staircase, on the day of my arrival at the house, I had no desire to oppose what I regarded as at best but a harmless, and by no means an unnatural, precaution.

At the request of Usher, I personally aided him in the arrangements for the temporary entombment. The body having been encoffined, we two alone bore it to its rest. The vault in which we placed it (and which had been so long unopened that our torches, half smothered in its oppressive atmosphere, gave us little opportunity for investigation) was small, damp, and entirely without means of admission for light; lying, at great depth, immediately beneath that portion of the building in which was my own sleeping apartment. It had been used, apparently, in remote feudal times, for the worst purposes of a donjon-keep, and, in later days, as a place of deposit for powder, or some other highly combustible substance, as a portion of its floor, and the whole interior of a long archway through which we reached it, were carefully sheathed with copper. The door, of massive iron, had been, also, similarly protected. Its immense weight caused an unusually sharp grating sound, as it moved upon its hinges.

Having deposited our mournful burden upon tressels within this region of horror, we partially turned aside the yet unscrewed lid of the coffin, and looked upon the face of the tenant. A striking similitude between the brother and sister now first arrested my attention; and Usher, divining, perhaps, my thoughts, murmured out some few words from which I learned that the deceased and himself had been twins, and that sympathies of a scarcely intelligible nature had always existed between them. Our glances, however, rested not long upon the dead—for we could not regard her unawed. The disease which had thus entombed the lady in the maturity of youth, had left, as usual in all maladies of a strictly cataleptical character, the mockery of a faint blush upon the bosom and the face, and that suspiciously lingering smile upon the lip which is so terrible in death. We replaced and screwed down the lid, and, having secured the door of iron, made our way, with toil, into the scarcely less gloomy apartments of the upper portion of the house.

And now, some days of bitter grief having elapsed, an observable change came over the features of the mental disorder of my friend. His ordinary manner had vanished. His ordinary occupations were neglected or forgotten. He roamed from chamber to chamber with hurried, unequal, and objectless step. The pallor of his countenance had assumed, if possible, a more ghastly hue—but the luminousness of his eye had utterly gone out. The once occasional huskiness of his tone was heard no more; and a tremulous quaver, as if of extreme terror, habitually characterized his utterance. There were times, indeed, when I thought his unceasingly agitated mind was labouring with some oppressive secret, to divulge which he struggled for the necessary courage. At times, again, I was obliged to resolve all into the mere inexplicable vagaries of madness, for I beheld him gazing upon vacancy for long hours, in an attitude of the profoundest attention, as if listening to some imaginary sound. It was no wonder that his condition terrified—that it infected me. I felt creeping upon me, by slow yet certain degrees, the wild influences of his own fantastic yet impressive superstitions.

It was, especially, upon retiring to bed late in the night of the seventh or eighth day after the placing of the lady Madeline within the donjon, that I experienced the full power of such feelings. Sleep came not near my couch—while the hours waned and waned away. I struggled to reason off the nervousness which had dominion over me. I endeavoured to believe that much, if not all of what I felt, was due to the bewildering influence of the

25

gloomy furniture of the room—of the dark and tattered draperies, which, tortured into motion by the breath of a rising tempest, swayed fitfully to and fro upon the walls, and rustled uneasily about the decorations of the bed. But my efforts were fruitless. An irrepressible tremor gradually pervaded my frame; and, at length, there sat upon my very heart an incubus of utterly causeless alarm. Shaking this off with a gasp and a struggle, I uplifted myself upon the pillows, and, peering earnestly within the intense darkness of the chamber, hearkened—I know not why, except that an instinctive spirit prompted me—to certain low and indefinite sounds which came, through the pauses of the storm, at long intervals, I knew not whence. Overpowered by an intense sentiment of horror, unaccountable yet unendurable, I threw on my clothes with haste (for I felt that I should sleep no more during the night,) and endeavoured to arouse myself from the pitiable condition into which I had fallen, by pacing rapidly to and fro through the apartment.

I had taken but few turns in this manner, when a light step on an adjoining staircase arrested my attention. I presently recognized it as that of Usher. In an instant afterwards he rapped, with a gentle touch, at my door, and entered, bearing a lamp. His countenance was, as usual, cadaverously wan—but, moreover, there was a species of mad hilarity in his eyes—an evidently restrained hysteria in his whole demeanor. His air appalled me—but anything was preferable to the solitude which I had so long endured, and I even welcomed his presence as a relief.

"And you have not seen it?" he said abruptly, after having stared about him for some moments in silence—"you have not then seen it?—but, stay! you shall." Thus speaking, and having carefully shaded his lamp, he hurried to one of the casements, and threw it freely open to the storm.

The impetuous fury of the entering gust nearly lifted us from our feet. It was, indeed, a tempestuous yet sternly beautiful night, and one wildly singular in its terror and its beauty. A whirlwind had apparently collected its force in our vicinity; for there were frequent and violent alterations in the direction of the wind; and the exceeding density of the clouds (which hung so low as to press upon the turrets of the house) did not prevent our perceiving the lifelike velocity with which they flew careering from all points against each other, without passing away into the distance. I say that even their exceeding density did not prevent our perceiving this—yet we had no glimpse of the moon or stars—nor was there any flashing forth of the lightning. But the under surfaces of the huge masses of agitated vapor, as well as all terrestrial objects immediately around us, were glowing in the unnatural light of a faintly luminous and distinctly visible gaseous exhalation which hung about and enshrouded the mansion.

"You must not—you shall not behold this!" said I, shudderingly, to Usher, as I led him, with a gentle violence, from the window to a seat. "These appearances, which bewilder you, are merely electrical phenomena not uncommon—or it may be that they have their ghastly origin in the rank miasma of the tarn. Let us close this casement;—the air is chilling and dangerous to your frame. Here is one of your favourite romances. I will read, and you shall listen;—and so we will pass away this terrible night together."

30   The antique volume which I had taken up was the "Mad Trist" of Sir Launcelot Canning;° but I had called it a favourite of Usher's more in sad jest than in earnest; for, in truth, there is little in its uncouth and unimaginative prolixity which could have had interest for the lofty and spiritual ideality of my friend. It was, however, the only book immediately at hand; and I indulged a vague hope that the excitement which now agitated the hypochondriac, might find relief (for the history of mental disorder is full of similar anomalies) even in the extremeness of the folly which I should read. Could I have judged, indeed, by the

---

°*the "Mad Trist" of Sir Launcelot Canning:* There was no Sir Launcelot Canning, unlike the authors cited in paragraph 27. The "passages" from "Canning" read by the narrator to Usher were written by Poe himself.

wild overstrained air of vivacity with which he hearkened, or apparently hearkened, to the words of the tale, I might well have congratulated myself upon the success of my design.

I had arrived at that well-known portion of the story where Ethelred, the hero of the Trist, having sought in vain for peaceable admission into the dwelling of the hermit, proceeds to make good an entrance by force. Here, it will be remembered, the words of the narrative run thus:

"And Ethelred, who was by nature of a doughty heart, and who was now mighty withal, on account of the powerfulness of the wine which he had drunken, waited no longer to hold parley with the hermit, who, in sooth, was of an obstinate and maliceful turn, but, feeling the rain upon his shoulders, and fearing the rising of the tempest, uplifted his mace outright, and, with blows, made quickly room in the plankings of the door for his gauntleted hand; and now pulling therewith sturdily, he so cracked, and ripped, and tore all asunder, that the noise of the dry and hollow-sounding wood alarmed and reverberated throughout the forest."

At the termination of this sentence I started, and for a moment, paused; for it appeared to me (although I at once concluded that my excited fancy had deceived me)—it appeared to me that, from some very remote portion of the mansion, there came, indistinctly, to my ears, what might have been, in its exact similarity of character, the echo (but a stifled and dull one certainly) of the very cracking and ripping sound which Sir Launcelot had so particularly described. It was, beyond doubt, the coincidence alone which had arrested my attention; for, amid the rattling of the sashes of the casements, and the ordinary commingled noises of the still increasing storm, the sound, in itself, had nothing, surely, which should have interested or disturbed me. I continued the story:

"But the good champion Ethelred, now entering within the door, was sore enraged and amazed to perceive no signal of the maliceful hermit; but, in the stead thereof, a dragon of a scaly and prodigious demeanour, and of a fiery tongue, which sate in guard before a palace of gold, with a floor of silver; and upon the wall there hung a shield of shining brass with this legend enwritten—

Who entereth herein, a conqueror hath bin;
Who slayeth the dragon, the shield he shall win;

And Ethelred uplifted his mace, and struck upon the head of the dragon, which fell before him, and gave up his pesty breath, with a shriek so horrid and harsh, and withal so piercing, that Ethelred had fain to close his ears with his hands against the dreadful noise of it, the like whereof was never before heard."

Here again I paused abruptly, and now with a feeling of wild amazement—for there [35] could be no doubt whatever that, in this instance, I did actually hear (although from what direction it proceeded I found it impossible to say) a low and apparently distant, but harsh, protracted, and most unusual screaming or grating sound—the exact counterpart of what my fancy had already conjured up for the dragon's unnatural shriek as described by the romancer.

Oppressed, as I certainly was, upon the occurrence of the second and most extraordinary coincidence, by a thousand conflicting sensations, in which wonder and extreme terror were predominant, I still retained sufficient presence of mind to avoid exciting, by any observation, the sensitive nervousness of my companion. I was by no means certain that he had noticed the sounds in question; although, assuredly, a strange alteration had, during the last few minutes, taken place in his demeanor. From a position fronting my own, he had gradually brought round his chair, so as to sit with his face to the door of the chamber; and thus I could but partially perceive his features, although I saw that his lips trembled as if he were murmuring inaudibly. His head had dropped upon his breast—yet I knew that he was not asleep, from the wide and rigid opening of the eye as I caught a glance of it in profile. The motion of his body, too, was at variance with this idea—for he rocked from side to side with a gentle yet constant and uniform sway. Having rapidly taken notice of all this, I resumed the narrative of Sir Launcelot, which thus proceeded:

"And now, the champion, having escaped from the terrible fury of the dragon, bethinking himself of the brazen shield, and of the breaking up of the enchantment which was upon it, removed the carcass from out of the way before him, and approached valorously over the silver pavement of the castle to where the shield was upon the wall; which in sooth tarried not for his full coming, but fell down at his feet upon the silver floor, with a mighty great and terrible ringing sound."

No sooner had these syllables passed my lips, than—as if a shield of brass had indeed, at the moment, fallen heavily upon a floor of silver—I became aware of a distinct, hollow, metallic, and clangorous, yet apparently muffled reverberation. Completely unnerved, I leaped to my feet; but the measured rocking movement of Usher was undisturbed. I rushed to the chair in which he sat. His eyes were bent fixedly before him, and throughout his whole countenance there reigned a stony rigidity. But, as I placed my hand upon his shoulder, there came a strong shudder over his whole person; a sickly smile quivered about his lips; and I saw that he spoke in a low, hurried, and gibbering murmur, as if unconscious of my presence. Bending closely over him, I at length drank in the hideous import of his words.

"Not hear it?—yes, I hear it, and have heard it. Long—long—long—many minutes, many hours, many days, have I heard it—yet I dared not—oh, pity me, miserable wretch that I am!—I dared not—I dared not speak! We have put her living in the tomb! Said I not that my senses were acute? I now tell you that I heard her first feeble movements in the hollow coffin. I heard them—many, many days ago—yet I dared not—I dared not speak! And now—to-night—Ethelred—ha! ha!—the breaking of the hermit's door, and the death-cry of the dragon, and the clangour of the shield!—say, rather, the rending of her coffin, and the grating of the iron hinges of her prison, and her struggles within the coppered archway of the vault! Oh whither shall I fly? Will she not be here anon? Is she not hurrying to upbraid me for my haste? Have I not heard her footsteps on the stair? Do I not distinguish that heavy and horrible beating of her heart? Madman!" here he sprang furiously to his feet, and shrieked out his syllables, as if in the effort he were giving up his soul—"Madman! I tell you that she now stands without the door!"

40   As if in the superhuman energy of his utterance there had been found the potency of a spell—the huge antique panels to which the speaker pointed, threw slowly back, upon the instant, their ponderous and ebony jaws. It was the work of the rushing gust—but then without those doors there DID stand the lofty and enshrouded figure of the lady Madeline of Usher. There was blood upon her white robes, and the evidence of some bitter struggle upon every portion of her emaciated frame. For a moment she remained trembling and reeling to and fro upon the threshold,—then, with a low moaning cry, fell heavily inward upon the person of her brother, and in her violent and now final death-agonies, bore him to the floor a corpse, and a victim to the terrors he had anticipated.

From that chamber, and from that mansion, I fled aghast. The storm was still abroad in all its wrath as I found myself crossing the old causeway. Suddenly there shot along the path a wild light, and I turned to see whence a gleam so unusual could have issued; for the vast house and its shadows were alone behind me. The radiance was that of the full, setting, and blood-red moon which now shone vividly through that once barely discernible fissure of which I have before spoken as extending from the roof of the building, in a zigzag direction, to the base. While I gazed, this fissure rapidly widened—there came a fierce breath of the whirlwind—the entire orb of the satellite burst at once upon my sight—my brain reeled as I saw the mighty walls rushing asunder—there was a long tumultuous shouting sound like the voice of a thousand waters—and the deep and dank tarn at my feet closed sullenly and silently over the fragments of the "House of Usher."

QUESTIONS

1. Consider Poe's use of setting in "The Fall of the House of Usher." Which details (e.g., landscape, weather, descriptive details) seem realistic? What is the condition of the house, both outside and inside? What is the relationship between the house and the Usher family?

2. Should Poe's description be taken literally or symbolically, or both? Explain.

3. What is the relationship between the narrator and Roderick Usher? Why is the narrator not named? Is he as involved in the events of the story as the unnamed narrator of "The Black Cat" or the named narrator of "The Cask of Amontillado" (Chapter 4)?

4. In what ways is Madeline a double of Usher himself? Why is Usher unwilling or unable to rescue her from the burial vault? What is the meaning of her falling on him at the end and bringing about his death?

5. Why is Usher's poem included as a part of the story? How does the poem explain the condition of the Usher household?

🖋 The Masque of the Red Death (1842)

The "Red Death" had long devastated the country. No pestilence had ever been so fatal, or so hideous. Blood was its Avatar° and its seal—the redness and the horror of blood. There were sharp pains, and sudden dizziness, and then profuse bleeding at the pores, with dissolution. The scarlet stains upon the body and especially upon the face of the victim, were the pest ban which shut him out from the aid and from the sympathy of his fellow-men. And the whole seizure, progress, and termination of the disease, were the incidents of half an hour.

But the Prince Prospero° was happy and dauntless and sagacious. When his dominions were half depopulated, he summoned to his presence a thousand hale and light-hearted friends from among the knights and dames of his court, and with these retired to the deep seclusion of one of his castellated abbeys. This was an extensive and magnificent structure, the creation of the prince's own eccentric yet august taste. A strong and lofty wall girdled it in. This wall had gates of iron. The courtiers, having entered, brought furnaces and massy hammers and welded the bolts. They resolved to leave means neither of ingress nor egress to the sudden impulses of despair or of frenzy from within. The abbey was amply provisioned. With such precautions the courtiers might bid defiance to contagion. The external world could take care of itself. In the meantime it was folly to grieve, or to think. The prince had provided all the appliances of pleasure. There were buffoons, there were improvisatori, there were ballet-dancers, there were musicians, there was Beauty, there was wine. All these and security were within. Without was the "Red Death."

It was toward the close of the fifth or sixth month of his seclusion, and while the pestilence raged most furiously abroad, that the Prince Prospero entertained his thousand friends at a masked ball of the most unusual magnificence.

It was a voluptuous scene, that masquerade. But first let me tell of the rooms in which it was held. There were seven—an imperial suite. In many palaces, however, such suites form a long and straight vista, while the folding doors slide back nearly to the walls on either hand, so that the view of the whole extent is scarcely impeded. Here the case was very different; as might have been expected from the duke's love of the *bizarre*. The apartments were so irregularly disposed that the vision embraced but little more than one at a time.

°*Avatar:* model, incarnation, manifestation.
°*Prospero:* that is, "prosperous." In Shakespeare's play *The Tempest*, the principal character is Prospero.

There was a sharp turn at every twenty or thirty yards, and at each turn a novel effect. To the right and left, in the middle of each wall, a tall and narrow Gothic window looked out upon a closed corridor which pursued the windings of the suite. These windows were of stained glass whose color varied in accordance with the prevailing hue of the decorations of the chamber into which it opened. That at the eastern extremity was hung, for example, in blue—and vividly blue were its windows. The second chamber was purple in its ornaments and tapestries, and here the panes were purple. The third was green throughout, and so were the casements. The fourth was furnished and lighted with orange—the fifth with white—the sixth with violet. The seventh apartment was closely shrouded in black velvet tapestries that hung all over the ceiling and down the walls, falling in heavy folds upon a carpet of the same material and hue. But in this chamber only, the color of the windows failed to correspond with the decorations. The panes here were scarlet—a deep blood color. Now in no one of the seven apartments was there any lamp or candelabrum, amid the profusion of golden ornaments that lay scattered to and fro or depended from the roof. There was no light of any kind emanating from lamp or candle within the suite of chambers. But in the corridors that followed the suite, there stood, opposite to each window, a heavy tripod, bearing a brazier of fire, that projected its rays through the tinted glass and so glaringly illumined the room. And thus were produced a multitude of gaudy and fantastic appearances. But in the western or black chamber the effect of the fire-light that streamed upon the dark hangings through the blood-tinted panes was ghastly in the extreme, and produced so wild a look upon the countenances of those who entered, that there were few of the company bold enough to set foot within its precincts at all.

5   It was in this apartment, also, that there stood against the western wall, a gigantic clock of ebony. Its pendulum swung to and fro with a dull, heavy, monotonous clang; and when the minute-hand made the circuit of the face, and the hour was to be stricken, there came from the brazen lungs of the clock a sound which was clear and loud and deep and exceedingly musical, but of so peculiar a note and emphasis that, at each lapse of an hour, the musicians of the orchestra were constrained to pause, momentarily, in their performance, to hearken to the sound; and thus the waltzers perforce ceased their evolutions; and there was a brief disconcert of the whole gay company; and, while the chimes of the clock yet rang, it was observed that the giddiest grew pale, and the more aged and sedate passed their hands over their brows as if in confused revery or meditation. But when the echoes had fully ceased, a light laughter at once pervaded the assembly; the musicians looked at each other and smiled as if at their own nervousness and folly, and made whispering vows, each to the other, that the next chiming of the clock should produce in them no similar emotion; and then, after the lapse of sixty minutes (which embrace three thousand and six hundred seconds of the Time that flies), there came yet another chiming of the clock, and then were the same disconcert and tremulousness and meditation as before.

But, in spite of these things, it was a gay and magnificent revel. The tastes of the duke were peculiar. He had a fine eye for colors and effects. He disregarded the *decora*° of mere fashion. His plans were bold and fiery, and his conceptions glowed with barbaric lustre. There are some who would have thought him mad. His followers felt that he was not. It was necessary to hear and see and touch him to be *sure* that he was not.

He had directed, in great part, the movable embellishments of the seven chambers, upon occasion of this great fête,° and it was his own guiding taste which had given character to the masqueraders. Be sure they were grotesque. There were much glare and glitter and piquancy and phantasm—much of what has been since seen in "Hernani."° There

---

°*decora:* schemes, patterns.
fête: party, revel.
°*Hernani:* tragedy by Victor Hugo (1802–1885), featuring elaborate scenes and costumes.

were arabesque figures with unsuited limbs and appointments. There were delirious fancies such as the madman fashions. There were much of the beautiful, much of the wanton, much of the *bizarre*, something of the terrible, and not a little of that which might have excited disgust. To and fro in the seven chambers there stalked, in fact, a multitude of dreams. And these—the dreams—writhed in and about, taking hue from the rooms, and causing the wild music of the orchestra to seem as the echo of their steps. And, anon, there strikes the ebony clock which stands in the hall of the velvet. And then, for a moment, all is still, and all is silent save the voice of the clock. The dreams are stiff-frozen as they stand. But the echoes of the chime die away—they have endured but an instant—and a light, half-subdued laughter floats after them as they depart. And now again the music swells, and the dreams live, and writhe to and fro more merrily than ever, taking hue from the many-tinted windows through which stream the rays from the tripods. But to the chamber which lies most westwardly of the seven there are now none of the maskers who venture; for the night is waning away; and there flows a ruddier light through the blood-colored panes; and the blackness of the sable drapery appalls; and to him whose foot falls upon the sable carpet, there comes from the near clock of ebony a muffled peal more solemnly emphatic than any which reaches *their* ears who indulge in the more remote gaieties of the other apartments.

But these other apartments were densely crowded, and in them beat feverishly the heart of life. And the revel went whirlingly on, until at length there commenced the sounding of midnight upon the clock. And then the music ceased, as I have told; and the evolutions of the waltzers were quieted; and there was an uneasy cessation of all things as before. But now there were twelve strokes to be sounded by the bell of the clock; and thus it happened, perhaps that more of thought crept, with more of time, into the meditations of the thoughtful among those who revelled. And thus, too, it happened, perhaps, that before the last echoes of the last chime had utterly sunk into silence, there were many individuals in the crowd who had found leisure to become aware of the presence of a masked figure which had arrested the attention of no single individual before. And the rumor of this new presence having spread itself whisperingly around, there arose at length from the whole company a buzz, or murmur, expressive of disapprobation and surprise—then, finally, of terror, of horror, and of disgust.

In an assembly of phantasms such as I have painted, it may well be supposed that no ordinary appearance could have excited such sensation. In truth the masquerade license of the night was nearly unlimited; but the figure in question had out-Heroded Herod,° and gone beyond the bounds of even the prince's indefinite decorum. There are chords in the hearts of the most reckless which cannot be touched without emotion. Even with the utterly lost, to whom life and death are equally jests, there are matters of which no jest can be made. The whole company, indeed, seemed now deeply to feel that in the costume and bearing of the stranger neither wit nor propriety existed. The figure was tall and gaunt, and shrouded from head to foot in the habiliments of the grave. The mask which concealed the visage was made so nearly to resemble the countenance of a stiffened corpse that the closest scrutiny must have had difficulty in detecting the cheat. And yet all this might have been endured, if not approved, by the mad revellers around. But the mummer had gone so far as to assume the type of the Red Death. His vesture was dabbled in *blood*—and his broad brow, with all the features of the face, was besprinkled with the scarlet horror.

When the eyes of Prince Prospero fell upon this spectral image (which, with a slow and solemn movement, as if more fully to sustain its *rôle*, stalked to and fro among the waltzers) he was seen to be convulsed, in the first moment with a strong shudder either of terror or distaste; but, in the next, his brow reddened with rage.

10

---

out-Heroded Herod: from Shakespeare's *Hamlet* (3.2.13), in reference to extreme overacting.

"Who dares"—he demanded hoarsely of the courtiers who stood near him—"who dares insult us with this blasphemous mockery? Seize him and unmask him—that we may know whom we have to hang, at sunrise, from the battlements!"

It was in the eastern or blue chamber in which stood the Prince Prospero as he uttered these words. They rang throughout the seven rooms loudly and clearly, for the prince was a bold and robust man, and the music had become hushed at the waving of his hand.

It was in the blue room where stood the prince, with a group of pale courtiers by his side. At first, as he spoke, there was a slight rushing movement of this group in the direction of the intruder, who, at the moment was also near at hand, and now, with deliberate and stately step, made closer approach to the speaker. But from a certain nameless awe with which the mad assumptions of the mummer had inspired the whole party, there were found none who put forth hand to seize him; so that, unimpeded, he passed within a yard of the prince's person; and, while the vast assembly, as if with one impulse, shrank from the centres of the rooms to the walls, he made his way uninterruptedly, but with the same solemn and measured step which had distinguished him from the first, through the blue chamber to the purple—through the purple to the green—through the green to the orange—through this again to the white—and even thence to the violet, ere a decided movement had been made to arrest him. It was then, however, that the Prince Prospero, maddening with rage and the shame of his own momentary cowardice, rushed hurriedly through the six chambers, while none followed him on account of a deadly terror that had seized upon all. He bore aloft a drawn dagger, and had approached, in rapid impetuosity, to within three or four feet of the retreating figure, when the latter, having attained the extremity of the velvet apartment, turned suddenly and confronted his pursuer. There was a sharp cry—and the dagger dropped gleaming upon the sable carpet, upon which, instantly afterward, fell prostrate in death the Prince Prospero. Then, summoning the wild courage of despair, a throng of the revellers at once threw themselves into the black apartment, and, seizing the mummer, whose tall figure stood erect and motionless within the shadow of the ebony clock, gasped in unutterable horror at finding the grave cerements and corpse-like mask, which they handled with so violent a rudeness, untenanted by any tangible form.

And now was acknowledged the presence of the Red Death. He had come like a thief in the night.° And one by one dropped the revellers in the blood-bedewed halls of their revel, and died each in the despairing posture of his fall. And the life of the ebony clock went out with that of the last of the gay. And the flames of the tripods expired. And Darkness and Decay and the Red Death held illimitable dominion over all.

QUESTIONS

1. What is happening throughout the country in this story? What does the Prince's reaction to these events tell us about him?
2. How do the details of number, color, and lighting help create the atmosphere and mood of the story?
3. Why do the color and window of the last room disturb the revellers? To what extent does this last room reflect the plot and ideas of the story?
4. What single object is located in this last room? How is this object described? What effect does its sound have on the revellers? What do you think Poe is suggesting by this object and its effects?
5. How are the nobles dressed for the masquerade? Why is the "masked figure" remarkable? How does Prospero react to him?

°*thief in the night:* 2 Peter 3:10.

The Black Cat (1843)

For the most wild, yet most homely narrative which I am about to pen, I neither expect nor solicit belief. Mad indeed would I be to expect it, in a case where my very senses reject their own evidence. Yet, mad am I not—and very surely do I not dream. But to-morrow I die, and to-day I would unburden my soul. My immediate purpose is to place before the world, plainly, succinctly, and without comment, a series of mere household events. In their consequences, these events have terrified—have tortured—have destroyed me. Yet I will not attempt to expound them. To me, they have presented little but Horror—to many they will seem less terrible than *barroques*. Hereafter, perhaps, some intellect may be found which will reduce my phantasm to the common-place—some intellect more calm, more logical, and far less excitable than my own, which will perceive, in the circumstances I detail with awe, nothing more than an ordinary succession of very natural causes and effects.

From my infancy I was noted for the docility and humanity of my disposition. My tenderness of heart was even so conspicuous as to make me the jest of my companions. I was especially fond of animals, and was indulged by my parents with a great variety of pets. With these I spent most of my time, and never was so happy as when feeding and caressing them. This peculiarity of character grew with my growth, and in my manhood, I derived from it one of my principal sources of pleasure. To those who have cherished an affection for a faithful and sagacious dog, I need hardly be at the trouble of explaining the nature or the intensity of the gratification thus derivable. There is something in the unselfish and self-sacrificing love of a brute, which goes directly to the heart of him who has had frequent occasion to test the paltry friendship and gossamer fidelity of mere *Man*.

I married early, and was happy to find in my wife a disposition not uncongenial with my own. Observing my partiality for domestic pets, she lost no opportunity of procuring those of the most agreeable kind. We had birds, gold-fish, a fine dog, rabbits, a small monkey, and *a cat*.

This latter was a remarkably large and beautiful animal, entirely black, and sagacious to an astonishing degree. In speaking of his intelligence, my wife, who at heart was not a little tinctured with superstition, made frequent allusion to the ancient popular notion, which regarded all black cats as witches in disguise. Not that she was ever *serious* upon this point—and I mention the matter at all for no better reason than that it happens, just now, to be remembered.

Pluto°—this was the cat's name—was my favorite pet and playmate. I alone fed him, and he attended me wherever I went about the house. It was even with difficulty that I could prevent him from following me through the streets.

Our friendship lasted, in this manner, for several years, during which my general temperament and character—through the instrumentality of the Fiend Intemperance—had (I blush to confess it) experienced a radical alteration for the worse. I grew, day by day, more moody, more irritable, more regardless of the feelings of others. I suffered myself to use intemperate language to my wife. At length, I even offered her personal violence. My pets, of course, were made to feel the change in my disposition. I not only neglected, but ill-used them. For Pluto, however, I still retained sufficient regard to restrain me from maltreating him, as I made no scruple of maltreating the rabbits, the monkey, or even the dog, when by accident, or through affection, they came in my way. But my disease grew upon me—for what disease is like Alcohol!—and at length even Pluto, who was now becoming old, and consequently somewhat peevish—even Pluto began to experience the effects of my ill temper.

One night, returning home, much intoxicated, from one of my haunts about town, I fancied that the cat avoided my presence. I seized him; when, in his fright at my violence, he inflicted a slight wound upon my hand with his teeth. The fury of a demon instantly

5

°*Pluto:* the Roman name of Hades, the ancient Greek God of the Underworld.

possessed me. I knew myself no longer. My original soul seemed, at once, to take its flight from my body and a more than fiendish malevolence, gin-nurtured, thrilled every fibre of my frame. I took from my waistcoat-pocket a pen-knife, opened it, grasped the poor beast by the throat, and deliberately cut one of its eyes from the socket! I blush, I burn, I shudder, while I pen the damnable atrocity.

When reason returned with the morning—when I had slept off the fumes of the night's debauch—I experienced a sentiment half of horror, half of remorse, for the crime of which I had been guilty; but it was, at best, a feeble and equivocal feeling, and the soul remained untouched. I again plunged into excess, and soon drowned in wine all memory of the deed.

In the meantime the cat slowly recovered. The socket of the lost eye presented, it is true, a frightful appearance, but he no longer appeared to suffer any pain. He went about the house as usual, but, as might be expected, fled in extreme terror at my approach. I had so much of my old heart left, as to be at first grieved by this evident dislike on the part of a creature which had once so loved me. But this feeling soon gave place to irritation. And then came, as if to my final and irrevocable overthrow, the spirit of PERVERSENESS. Of this spirit philosophy takes no account. Yet I am not more sure that my soul lives, than I am that perverseness is one of the primitive impulses of the human heart—one of the indivisible primary faculties, or sentiments, which give direction to the character of Man. Who has not, a hundred times, found himself committing a vile or a silly action, for no other reason than because he knows he should not? Have we not a perpetual inclination, in the teeth of our best judgment, to violate that which is *Law*, merely because we understand it to be such? This spirit of perverseness, I say, came to my final overthrow. It was this unfathomable longing of the soul *to vex itself*—to offer violence to its own nature—to do wrong for the wrong's sake only—that urged me to continue and finally to consummate the injury I had inflicted upon the unoffending brute. One morning, in cool blood, I slipped a noose about its neck and hung it to the limb of a tree;—hung it with the tears streaming from my eyes, and with the bitterest remorse at my heart;—hung it *because* I knew that it had loved me, and *because* I felt it had given me no reason of offence;—hung it *because* I knew that in so doing I was committing a sin—a deadly sin that would so jeopardize my immortal soul as to place it—if such a thing were possible—even beyond the reach of the infinite mercy of the Most Merciful and Most Terrible God.

10   On the night of the day on which this cruel deed was done, I was aroused from sleep by the cry of fire. The curtains of my bed were in flames. The whole house was blazing. It was with great difficulty that my wife, a servant, and myself, made our escape from the conflagration. The destruction was complete. My entire worldly wealth was swallowed up, and I resigned myself thenceforward to despair.

I am above the weakness of seeking to establish a sequence of cause and effect, between the disaster and the atrocity. But I am detailing a chain of facts—and wish not to leave even a possible link imperfect. On the day succeeding the fire, I visited the ruins. The walls, with one exception, had fallen in. This exception was found in a compartment wall, not very thick, which stood about the middle of the house, and against which had rested the head of my bed. The plastering had here, in great measure, resisted the action of the fire—a fact which I attributed to its having been recently spread. About this wall a dense crowd were collected, and many persons seemed to be examining a particular portion of it with very minute and eager attention. The words "strange!" "singular!" and other similar expressions, excited my curiosity. I approached and saw, as if graven in *bas relief* upon the white surface, the figure of a gigantic *cat*. The impression was given with an accuracy truly marvellous. There was a rope about the animal's neck.

When I first beheld this apparition—for I could scarcely regard it as less—my wonder and my terror were extreme. But at length reflection came to my aid. The cat, I remembered, had been hung in a garden adjacent to the house. Upon the alarm of fire, this garden had been immediately filled by the crowd—by some one of whom the animal must have been cut from the tree and thrown, through an open window, into my chamber. This had probably been done with the view of arousing me from sleep. The falling of other walls had compressed the victim of my cruelty into the substance of the freshly-spread plaster; the lime of which, with the flames, and the *ammonia* from the carcass, had then accomplished the portraiture as I saw it.

Although I thus readily accounted to my reason, if not altogether to my conscience, for the startling fact just detailed, it did not the less fail to make a deep impression upon my fancy. For months I could not rid myself of the phantasm of the cat; and, during this period, there came back into my spirit a half-sentiment that seemed, but was not, remorse. I went so far as to regret the loss of the animal, and to look about me, among the vile haunts which I now habitually frequented, for another pet of the same species, and of somewhat similar appearance, with which to supply its place.

One night as I sat, half stupefied, in a den of more than infamy, my attention was suddenly drawn to some black object, reposing upon the head of one of the immense hogsheads of Gin, or of Rum, which constituted the chief furniture of the apartment. I had been looking steadily at the top of this hogshead for some minutes, and what now caused me surprise was the fact that I had not sooner perceived the object thereupon. I approached it, and touched it with my hand. It was a black cat—a very large one—fully as large as Pluto, and closely resembling him in every respect but one. Pluto had not a white hair upon any portion of his body; but this cat had a large, although indefinite splotch of white, covering nearly the whole region of the breast.

Upon my touching him, he immediately arose, purred loudly, rubbed against my hand, and appeared delighted with my notice. This, then, was the very creature of which I was in search. I at once offered to purchase it of the landlord; but this person made no claim to it—knew nothing of it—had never seen it before.

I continued my caresses, and, when I prepared to go home, the animal evinced a disposition to accompany me. I permitted it to do so; occasionally stooping and patting it as I proceeded. When it reached the house it domesticated itself at once, and became immediately a great favorite with my wife.

For my own part, I soon found a dislike to it arising within me. This was just the reverse of what I had anticipated; but—I know not how or why it was—its evident fondness for myself rather disgusted and annoyed. By slow degrees, these feelings of disgust and annoyance rose into the bitterness of hatred. I avoided the creature; a certain sense of shame, and the remembrance of my former deed of cruelty, preventing me from physically abusing it. I did not, for some weeks, strike, or otherwise violently ill use it; but gradually—very gradually—I came to look upon it with unutterable loathing, and to flee silently from its odious presence, as from the breath of a pestilence.

What added, no doubt, to my hatred of the beast, was the discovery, on the morning after I brought it home, that, like Pluto, it also had been deprived of one of its eyes. This circumstance, however, only endeared it to my wife, who, as I have already said, possessed, in a high degree, that humanity of feeling which had once been my distinguishing trait, and the source of many of my simplest and purest pleasures.

With my aversion to this cat, however, its partiality for myself seemed to increase. It followed my footsteps with a pertinacity which it would be difficult to make the reader comprehend. Whenever I sat, it would crouch beneath my chair, or spring upon my knees, covering me with its loathsome caresses. If I arose to walk it would get between my feet and thus nearly throw me down, or, fastening its long and sharp claws in my dress, clamber, in this manner, to my breast. At such times, although I longed to destroy it with a blow, I was yet withheld from so doing, partly by a memory of my former crime, but chiefly—let me confess it at once—by absolute dread of the beast.

20   This dread was not exactly a dread of physical evil—and yet I should be at a loss how otherwise to define it. I am almost ashamed to own—yes, even in this felon's cell, I am almost ashamed to own—that the terror and horror with which the animal inspired me, had been heightened by one of the merest chimaeras it would be possible to conceive. My wife had called my attention, more than once, to the character of the mark of white hair, of which I have spoken, and which constituted the sole visible difference between the strange beast and the one I had destroyed. The reader will remember that this mark, although large, had been originally very indefinite; but, by slow degrees—degrees nearly imperceptible, and which for a long time my Reason struggled to reject as fanciful—it had, at length, assumed a rigorous distinctness of outline. It was now the representation of an object that I shudder to name— and for this, above all, I loathed, and dreaded, and would have rid myself of the monster *had I dared*—it was now, I say, the image of a hideous—of a ghastly thing—of the GALLOWS!—oh, mournful and terrible engine of Horror and of Crime—of Agony and of Death!

And now was I indeed wretched beyond the wretchedness of mere Humanity. And *a brute beast*—whose fellow I had contemptuously destroyed—*a brute beast* to work out for *me*—for me a man, fashioned in the image of the High God—so much of insufferable woe! Alas! neither by day nor by night knew I the blessing of Rest any more! During the former the creature left me no moment alone; and, in the latter, I started, hourly, from dreams of unutterable fear, to find the hot breath of *the thing* upon my face, and its vast weight—an incarnate Night-Mare that I had no power to shake off—incumbent eternally upon my *heart!*

Beneath the pressure of torments such as these, the feeble remnant of the good within me succumbed. Evil thoughts became my sole intimates—the darkest and most evil of thoughts. The moodiness of my usual temper increased to hatred of all things and of all mankind; while, from the sudden, frequent, and ungovernable outbursts of a fury to which I now blindly abandoned myself, my uncomplaining wife, alas! was the most usual and the most patient of sufferers.

One day she accompanied me, upon some household errand, into the cellar of the old building which our poverty compelled us to inhabit. The cat followed me down the steep stairs, and, nearly throwing me headlong, exasperated me to madness. Uplifting an axe, and forgetting, in my wrath, the childish dread which had hitherto stayed my hand, I aimed a blow at the animal which, of course, would have proved instantly fatal had it descended as I wished. But this blow was arrested by the hand of my wife. Goaded, by the interference, into a rage more than demoniacal, I withdrew my arm from her grasp and buried the axe in her brain. She fell dead upon the spot, without a groan.

This hideous murder accomplished, I set myself forthwith, and with entire deliberation, to the task of concealing the body. I knew that I could not remove it from the house, either by day or by night, without the risk of being observed by the neighbors. Many projects entered my mind. At one period I thought of cutting the corpse into minute fragments, and destroying them by fire. At another, I resolved to dig a grave for it in the floor of the cellar. Again, I deliberated about casting it in the well in the yard—about packing it in a box, as if merchandize, with the usual arrangements, and so getting a porter to take it from the house. Finally I hit upon what I considered a far better expedient than either of these. I determined to wall it up in the cellar—as the monks of the middle ages are recorded to have walled up their victims.

25   For a purpose such as this the cellar was well adapted. Its walls were loosely constructed, and had lately been plastered throughout with a rough plaster, which the dampness of the atmosphere had prevented from hardening. Moreover, in one of the walls was a projection, caused by a false chimney, or fireplace, that had been filled up, and made to resemble the red of the cellar. I made no doubt that I could readily displace the bricks at this point, insert the corpse, and wall the whole up as before, so that no eye could detect any thing suspicious. And in this calculation I was not deceived. By means of a crow-bar I easily dislodged the bricks, and, having carefully deposited the body against the inner wall, I propped it in that position, while, with little trouble, I re-laid the whole structure as it originally stood.

Having procured mortar, sand, and hair, with every possible precaution, I prepared a plaster which could not be distinguished from the old, and with this I very carefully went over the new brickwork. When I had finished, I felt satisfied that all was right. The wall did not present the slightest appearance of having been disturbed. The rubbish on the floor was picked up with the minutest care. I looked around triumphantly, and said to myself— "Here at least, then, my labor has not been in vain."

My next step was to look for the beast which had been the cause of so much wretchedness; for I had, at length, firmly resolved to put it to death. Had I been able to meet with it, at the moment, there could have been no doubt of its fate; but it appeared that the crafty animal had been alarmed at the violence of my previous anger, and forebore to present itself in my present mood. It is impossible to describe, or to imagine, the deep, the blissful sense of relief which the absence of the detested creature occasioned in my bosom. It did not make its appearance during the night—and thus for one night at least, since its introduction into the house, I soundly and tranquilly slept; aye, slept even with the burden of murder upon my soul!

The second and the third day passed, and still my tormentor came not. Once again I breathed as a freeman. The monster, in terror, had fled the premises forever! I should behold it no more! My happiness was supreme! The guilt of my dark deed disturbed me but little. Some few inquiries had been made, but these had been readily answered. Even a search had been instituted—but of course nothing was to be discovered. I looked upon my future felicity as secured.

Upon the fourth day of the assassination, a party of the police came, very unexpectedly, into the house, and proceeded again to make rigorous investigation of the premises. Secure, however, in the inscrutability of my place of concealment, I felt no embarrassment whatever. The officers bade me accompany them in their search. They left no nook or corner unexplored. At length, for the third or fourth time, they descended into the cellar. I quivered not in a muscle. My heart beat calmly as that of one who slumbers in innocence. I walked the cellar from end to end. I folded my arms upon my bosom, and roamed easily to and fro. The police were thoroughly satisfied and prepared to depart. The glee at my heart was too strong to be restrained. I burned to say if but one word, by way of triumph, and to render doubly sure their assurance of my guiltlessness.

"Gentlemen," I said at last, as the party ascended the steps, "I delight to have allayed your suspicions. I wish you all health, and a little more courtesy. By the bye, gentlemen, this—this is a very well constructed house." [In the rabid desire to say something easily, I scarcely knew what I uttered at all.]—"I may say an *excellently* well constructed house. These walls—are you going, gentlemen?—these walls are solidly put together;" and here, through the mere frenzy of bravado, I rapped heavily, with a cane which I held in my hand, upon that very portion of the brick-work behind which stood the corpse of the wife of my bosom.

But may God shield and deliver me from the fangs of the Arch-Fiend! No sooner had the reverberation of my blows sunk into silence, than I was answered by a voice from within the tomb!—by a cry, at first muffled and broken, like the sobbing of a child, and then quickly swelling into one long, loud, and continuous scream, utterly anomalous and inhuman—a howl—a wailing shriek, half of horror and half of triumph, such as might have arisen only out of hell, conjointly from the throats of the damned in their agony and of the demons that exult in the damnation.

Of my own thoughts it is folly to speak. Swooning, I staggered to the opposite wall. For one instant the party upon the stairs remained motionless, through extremity of terror and of awe. In the next, a dozen stout arms were toiling at the wall. It fell bodily. The corpse, already greatly decayed and clotted with gore, stood erect before the eyes of the spectators. Upon its head, with red extended mouth and solitary eye of fire, sat the hideous beast whose craft had seduced me into murder, and whose informing voice had consigned me to the hangman. I had walled the monster up within the tomb!

30

QUESTIONS

1. Does the first paragraph establish clarity or ambiguity about the narrator and the events he is about to describe? Explain.

2. What changes occur in the narrator's character? Is he sane? Are his explanations of the changes plausible and convincing? Why is the narrator not named?

3. What does the narrator, in considering what he does to Pluto, mean by "perverseness" (paragraph 9)? Why does Poe introduce the details about perverseness? In what ways should the house fire and the consequences be considered as punishment for the narrator's actions?

4. How does the second cat resemble the first? What does the gallows mark represent when it takes shape on the new cat (paragraph 20)?

5. When the narrator knocks on the wall (paragraph 20), should his action be considered a mark of arrogance or an admission of guilt? Explain.

The Tell-Tale Heart (1843/1845)

True!—nervous—very, very dreadfully nervous I had been and am; but why *will* you say that I am mad? The disease had sharpened my senses—not destroyed—not dulled them. Above all was the sense of hearing acute. I heard all things in the heaven and in the earth. I heard many things in hell. How, then, am I mad? Hearken! and observe how healthily— how calmly, I can tell you the whole story.

It is impossible to say how first the idea entered my brain; but once conceived, it haunted me day and night. Object there was none. Passion there was none. I loved the old man. He had never wronged me. He had never given me insult. For his gold I had no desire. I think it was his eye! yes, it was this! One of his eyes resembled that of a vulture—a pale blue eye, with a film over it. Whenever it fell upon me, my blood ran cold; and so by degrees—very gradually—I made up my mind to take the life of the old man, and thus rid myself of the eye forever.

Now this is the point. You fancy me mad. Madmen know nothing. But you should have seen *me*. You should have seen how wisely I proceeded—with what caution—with what foresight—with what dissimulation I went to work! I was never kinder to the old man than during the whole week before I killed him. And every night, about midnight, I turned the latch of his door and opened it—oh, so gently! And then, when I had made an opening sufficient for my head, I put in a dark lantern, all closed, closed, so that no light shone out, and then I thrust in my head. Oh, you would have laughed to see how cunningly I thrust it in! I moved it slowly—very, very slowly, so that I might not disturb the old man's sleep. It took me an hour to place my whole head within the opening so far that I could see him as he lay upon his bed. Ha!—would a madman have been so wise as this? And then, when my head was well in the room, I undid the lantern cautiously—oh, so cautiously—cautiously (for the hinges creaked)—I undid it just so much that a single thin ray fell upon the vulture eye. And this I did for seven long nights—every night just at midnight—but I found the eye always closed; and so it was impossible to do the work; for it was not the old man who vexed me, but his Evil Eye. And every morning, when the day broke, I went boldly into the chamber, and spoke courageously to him, calling him by name in a hearty tone, and inquiring how he had passed the night. So you see he would have been a very profound old man, indeed, to suspect that every night, just at twelve, I looked in upon him while he slept.

Upon the eighth night I was more than usually cautious in opening the door. A watch's minute hand moves more quickly than did mine. Never before that night had I *felt* the extent of my own powers—of my sagacity. I could scarcely contain my feelings of triumph. To think that there I was, opening the door, little by little, and he not even to dream of my secret deeds or thoughts. I fairly chuckled at the idea; and perhaps he heard me; for he moved on the bed suddenly, as if startled. Now you may think that I drew back—but no. His room was as black as pitch with the thick darkness (for the shutters were close fastened, through fear of robbers), and so I knew that he could not see the opening of the door, and I kept pushing it on steadily, steadily.

I had my head in, and was about to open the lantern, when my thumb slipped upon the   5
tin fastening, and the old man sprang up in the bed, crying out—"Who's there?"

I kept quite still and said nothing. For a whole hour I did not move a muscle, and in the meantime I did not hear him lie down. He was still sitting up in the bed, listening;—just as I have done, night after night, hearkening to the death watches in the wall.

Presently I heard a slight groan, and I knew it was the groan of mortal terror. It was not a groan of pain or of grief—oh, no!—it was the low stifled sound that arises from the bottom of the soul when overcharged with awe. I knew the sound very well. Many a night, just at midnight, when all the world slept, it has welled up from my own bosom, deepening, with its dreadful echo, the terrors that distracted me. I say I knew it well. I knew what the old man felt, and pitied him, although I chuckled at heart. I knew that he had been lying awake ever since the first slight noise, when he had turned in the bed. His fears had been ever since growing upon him. He had been trying to fancy them causeless, but could not. He had been saying to himself—"It is nothing but the wind in the chimney—it is only a mouse crossing the floor," or "it is merely a cricket which has made a single chirp." Yes, he had been trying to comfort himself with these suppositions; but he had found all in vain. *All in vain*; because Death, in approaching him, had stalked with his black shadow before him, and enveloped the victim. And it was the mournful influence of the unperceived shadow that caused him to feel—although he neither saw nor heard—to *feel* the presence of my head within the room.

When I had waited a long time, very patiently, without hearing him lie down, I resolved to open a little—a very, very little crevice in the lantern. So I opened it—you cannot imagine how stealthily, stealthily—until, at length, a single dim ray, like the thread of the spider, shot from out of the crevice and fell upon the vulture eye.

It was open—wide, wide open—and I grew furious as I gazed upon it. I saw it with perfect distinctness—all a dull blue, with a hideous veil over it that chilled the very marrow in my bones; but I could see nothing else of the old man's face or person: for I had directed the ray as if by instinct, precisely upon the damned spot.

And now have I not told you that what you mistake for madness is but over-acuteness   10
of the senses?—now, I say, there came to my ears a low, dull, quick sound, such as a watch makes when enveloped in cotton. I knew *that* sound well, too. It was the beating of the old man's heart. It increased my fury, as the beating of a drum stimulates the soldier into courage.

But even yet I refrained and kept still. I scarcely breathed. I held the lantern motionless. I tried how steadily I could maintain the ray upon the eye. Meantime the hellish tattoo of the heart increased. It grew quicker and quicker, and louder and louder every instant. The old man's terror *must* have been extreme! It grew louder, I say, louder every moment!—do you mark me well? I have told you that I am nervous: so I am. And now at the dead hour of the night, amid the dreadful silence of that old house, so strange a noise as this excited me to uncontrollable terror. Yet, for some minutes longer I refrained and stood still. But the beating grew louder, louder! I thought the heart must burst. And now a new anxiety seized me—the sound would be heard by a neighbor! The old man's hour had come! With a loud yell, I threw open the lantern and leaped into the room. He shrieked once—once only. In an instant I dragged him to the floor, and pulled the heavy bed over him. I then smiled gaily, to find the deed so far done. But, for many minutes, the heart beat on with a muffled sound. This, however, did not vex me; it would not be heard through the wall. At length it ceased. The old man was dead. I removed the bed and examined the corpse. Yes, he was stone, stone dead. I placed my hand upon the heart and held it there many minutes.

If still you think me mad, you will think so no longer when I describe the wise precautions I took for the concealment of the body. The night waned, and I worked hastily, but in silence. First of all I dismembered the corpse. I cut off the head and the arms and the legs.

I then took up three planks from the flooring of the chamber, and deposited all between the scantlings. I then replaced the boards so cleverly, so cunningly, that no human eye—not even *his*—could have detected anything wrong. There was nothing to wash out—no stain of any kind—no blood-spot whatever. I had been too wary for that. A tub had caught all—ha! ha!

When I had made an end of these labors, it was four o'clock—still dark as midnight. As the bell sounded the hour, there came a knocking at the street door. I went down to open it with a light heart,—for what had I *now* to fear? There entered three men, who introduced themselves, with perfect suavity, as officers of the police. A shriek had been heard by a neighbor during the night; suspicion of foul play had been aroused, information had been lodged at the police office, and they (the officers) had been deputed to search the premises.

15   I smiled,—for *what* had I to fear? I bade the gentlemen welcome. The shriek, I said, was my own in a dream. The old man, I mentioned, was absent in the country. I took my visitors all over the house. I bade them search—search *well*. I led them, at length, to *his* chamber. I showed them his treasures, secure, undisturbed. In the enthusiasm of my confidence, I brought chairs into the room, and desired them *here* to rest from their fatigues, while I myself, in the wild audacity of my perfect triumph, placed my own seat upon the very spot beneath which reposed the corpse of the victim.

The officers were satisfied. My *manner* had convinced them. I was singularly at ease. They sat, and while I answered cheerily, they chatted of familiar things. But, ere long, I felt myself getting pale and wished them gone. My head ached, and I fancied a ringing in my ears: but still they sat and still they chatted. The ringing became more distinct:—it continued and became more distinct: I talked more freely to get rid of the feeling: but it continued and gained definitiveness—until, at length, I found that the noise was *not* within my ears.

No doubt I now grew *very* pale:—but I talked more fluently, and with a heightened voice. Yet the sound increased—and what could I do? It was a *low, dull, quick sound—much such a sound as a watch makes when enveloped in cotton*. I gasped for breath—and yet the officers heard it not. I talked more quickly—more vehemently; but the noise steadily increased. I arose and argued about trifles, in a high key and with violent gesticulations; but the noise steadily increased. Why *would* they not be gone? I paced the floor to and fro with heavy strides, as if excited to fury by the observations of the men—but the noise steadily increased. Oh God! what *could* I do? I foamed—I raved—I swore! I swung the chair upon which I had been sitting, and grated it upon the boards, but the noise arose over all and continually increased. It grew louder—louder—*louder!* And still the men chatted pleasantly, and smiled. Was it possible they heard not? Almighty God!—no, no! They heard!—they suspected!—they *knew!*—they were making a mockery of my horror!—this I thought, and this I think. But anything was better than this agony! Anything was more tolerable than this derision! I could bear those hypocritical smiles no longer! I felt that I must scream or die!—and now—again!—hark! louder! louder! louder! *louder!*—

"Villains!" I shrieked, "dissemble no more! I admit the deed!—tear up the planks!—here, here!—it is the beating of his hideous heart!"

QUESTIONS

1. What is the narrator's state of mind and how might that affect his description of the story's events? How might this story be told by someone with a different perspective or feeling about the old man?

2. The narrator feels he is in the process of pulling off a perfectly planned crime? What happens? Does he make any mistakes?

3. What is the old man's crime, and what does his punishment suggest about the narrator?
4. Why do the police officers seem to the narrator to act so calmly and easy-going, especially when the sound resembling a beating heart grows so much louder? Are they trying to trick the narrator?

Edited Selections from Criticism of Poe's Stories

The following selections are intended to supply details and ideas for essays on Poe's stories. For a selective bibliography, consult the *bibliographic sources* section above (pp. 418–19), which may be augmented with your college library research facilities and the most recent volumes of the *MLA International Bibliography* available in your library's reference room. In the following selections the bracketed page numbers refer to the original pagination of the sources included here. Footnotes in the sources have been deleted.

1. Poe's Irony[3]

Poe's "serious" tales, clearly, are only apparently serious in the manner that they purport to be. The whole of Poe's Gothic fiction can be read not only as an ambivalent parody of the world of Gothic horror tales, but also as an extended grotesquerie of the human condition. Nothing quite works out for his heroes, even though they sometimes make superhuman efforts, and even though they are occasionally rescued from their predicaments. They undergo extended series of ironic reverses in fictional structures so ironically twisted that the form itself, even the very plot, approaches an absurd hoax perpetrated on the characters. The universe created in Poe's fiction is one in which the human mind tries vainly to perceive order and meaning. The universe is deceptive; its basic mode seems almost to be a constant shifting of appearances; reality is a flux variously interpreted, or even [37] created, by the individual human mind. In its deceptiveness, the universe of Poe's Gothic fiction seems not so much malevolent as mocking or "perverse." The universe is much like a gigantic hoax that God has played on man, an idea which is the major undercurrent of Poe's essay on the universe, *Eureka*. Thus, the hoaxlike irony of Poe's technique has its parallel in the dramatic world in which his characters move.

The ultimate irony of this universe, however, is the "perversity" of man's own mind. The mind, and the mind only, seems to sustain Poe's heroes in their most desperate predicaments; yet in an instant the mind is capable of slipping into confusion, hysteria, madness—even while it seems most rational. From a more "Gothicist" point of view, Edward H. Davidson, without using the term *irony*, and without reading Poe's Gothic tales ironically or satirically, comes to much the same conclusion regarding Poe's universe. "Poe's nightmare universe," Davidson writes, "is one in which . . . people . . . are condemned to live as if they are in some long aftertime of belief and morality." The evildoer is driven by "some maggot in the brain" that leaves him a kind of "moral freak" in a universe that also has some fantastic defect in it. In Poe's universe, Davidson suggests, evil and suffering are "the capacity and measure of man to feel and to know"; pain is the basis of life, and death is the only release from his "grotesque condition of 'perversity.'"

Selections 1–5 are from G. R. Thompson, ed., *Great Short Works of Edgar Allan Poe* (New York: Harper, 1970).

This view of Poe's "perverse" universe is, I think, essentially correct. Poe's fiction developed from a basically satiric mode into an ironic mode in which a tragic response to the perversities of fortune and to the treacheries of one's own mind is contrasted by a near-comic perception of the absurdity of man's condition in the universe. Such a double perception, according to the German Ironists, leads, through art, to a momentary [38] transcendence of the dark chaos of the universe. If the artist (and through him the reader) can mock man's absurd condition at the same time that he feels it deeply, he transcends earthly or finite limits in an artistic paralleling of God's infinite perception. In Poe, however, such transcendence is always at the expense of the less perceptive mind. Poe plays a constant intellectual game with his readers; he tries to draw the reader into the "Gothic" world of the mind, but he is ready at any moment to mock the simplistic Gothic vision (under the trappings of which Poe saw man's real estrangement and isolation) that contemporary readers insisted on in the popular magazines.

2. The Narrators of "The Cask of Amontillado" (Chapter 4) and "The Fall of the House of Usher"

When we come to the tales, the comic and ironic side of Poe is clearer and more emphatic. And it is here, rather than among the poems, I believe, that we find the *great* works of Poe. (All of Poe's works, except his one novel, *Arthur Gordon Pym,* are "short.") His criticism, though historically interesting in its specificity and topicality, and the best of his time (barring only Coleridge's criticism), is valuable today mainly for its precise enunciation of principles of rational control over even the wildest materials—for its enunciation of a principle, not merely of "unity," but of "totality of effect." "If [the] very first sentence," Poe wrote in his 1847 review of Hawthorne's *Twice-Told Tales,* "tend not to the outbringing of this [19] effect, then in his very first step has [the artist] committed a blunder. In the whole composition there should be no word written of which the tendency, direct *or indirect,* is not to the pre-established design" [my italics]. This principle he observed in each and every one of his tales— and not only in the well-known gothic tales and detective stories, but also in the underrated comic and satiric tales, even though in these he was "slapping" (as he said in a letter to Joseph Snodgrass in 1841) "left & right at things in general."

In Poe's characteristically intricate, even involuted patterns of dramatic irony, the apparent narrative "voice" which pervades the surface atmosphere of the work is also seen within a qualifying frame. Several of the tales (for example "The Black Cat," "The Tell-Tale Heart," "Ligeia," "The Imp of the Perverse," "The Cask of Amontillado") involve a confessional element, wherein a first-person narrator, like Montresor, seems calmly or gleefully to recount horrible deeds, but which generally implies a listener to whom the agonized soul is revealing his torment. Especially revealing of the ironic structure thus achieved is Montresor in "The Cask of Amontillado." In the surface story, Montresor seems to be chuckling over his flawlessly executed revenge upon unfortunate "Fortunato" fifty years before. But a moment's reflection suggests that the indistinct "you" whom Montresor addresses in the first paragraph is probably his death-bed confessor—for if Montresor has murdered Fortunato fifty years before, he must now be some seventy to eighty years of age. None of this is explicitly stated; it is presented dramatically, and we get the double effect of feeling the coldly calculated murder at the same time that we see the larger point that Montresor, rather than having successfully taken his revenge "with impunity," as he says, has instead suffered a fifty-year's ravage of conscience. Likewise, many of Poe's [20] gothic tales seem to involve supernatural happenings; but insinuated into them, like clues in a detective story, are details which begin to construct dramatic frames around the narrative "voice" of the work. These dramatic frames suggest the elusiveness of the experience as the first-person narrator renders it. As in Henry James and Joseph Conrad, there is often in Poe a tale within a tale within a tale; and the meaning of the whole lies in the relationship of the various implied stories and their frames rather than in the explicit meaning given to the surface story by the dramatically involved narrator.

Only within the last ten to fifteen years have critics begun to examine Poe's narrators as characters in the total design of his tales and poems, and to suspect that even his most famous Gothic works—like "Usher" and "Ligeia"—have ironic double and triple perspectives playing upon them: supernatural from one point of view, psychological from another point of view, and often burlesque from yet a third. Not only is nearly half of Poe's fiction satiric and comic in an obvious way, but the Gothic tales contain within them satiric and comic elements thematically related to the macabre elements. Poe seems very carefully to have aimed at the ironic effect of touching his readers simultaneously on an archetypal emotional level of fear and on an (almost subliminal) level of intellectual and philosophical perception of the Absurd. The result in the Gothic tales, as in many of the poems, is a kind of ambivalent mockery. We can respond to Poe's scenes of horror or despair at the same time that we are aware of their caricatural quality.

3. "The Fall of the House of Usher"

Between 1838 and 1840, the middle years of his [34] career, Poe published three of his most famous Gothic stories: "Ligeia," "The Fall of the House of Usher," and "William Wilson." Like "Ligeia," the other two tales involve "doubles" and dramatize a weird universe as perceived by a subjective mind. "Usher," despite the supernatural atmosphere, can be read as the tale of the frenzied fantasies of *both* the narrator and Usher, fantasies engendered by a vague fear that something ominous *may* happen and by the disconnected, alien environment. The overriding theme is the mechanism of fear itself, which has perversely operated on Roderick Usher before the narrator arrives, and which operates on the narrator *through* Usher afterwards. When the narrator rides his horse up to the House of Usher and gazes at its leaden-eyed aspect and at the tarn, with its sickly white stems of dead plants sticking up through the stagnant water, he is immediately seized by a vague apprehension. Later in the tale, he remarks that the "mental disorder" and "hysteria" of his friend Roderick Usher "terrified" [35] and "infected" him: "I felt creeping upon me, by slow yet certain degrees, the wild influences of his own fantastic yet impressive superstitions." The narrator's confrontation with (and submission to) a mind gone mad is imaged in the facelike appearance of the House itself, with its leaden-hued eyelike windows and its zigzag crack down the middle, and in the wild "arabesque" face of Roderick Usher. The poem "The Haunted Palace," which Usher has composed, is also a symbolic, indeed allegorical, portrait of a facelike structure. The "face" of the palace changes when the "Monarch Thought" topples from his throne within, and the palace comes to resemble the face of Usher and his House as the narrator has described them. Moreover, when the narrator first looks down into the tarn, what he should see of course is his own face since he is on its very brink, but instead he sees the inverted image of the "face" of the House of Usher. His next action is to go inside and meet Usher face to face. Immediately, his attention is arrested by certain details of Usher's face; though he does not articulate the resemblances, as such, the narrator so describes the weblike hair of Usher that we are compelled to remember the webwork of fungi about the eaves of the House.

By the time the narrator "sees" the "return" of Madeline Usher from her grave, the themes of narcissism and inversion are so clear that the relevance of the absurdist interlude, "The Mad Trist of Sir Lancelot Canning," to the story as a whole (that is, to the dramatic situation of the narrator rather than merely to Roderick's "trist" with his twin sister) is obvious. The tale is the story of the "mad trist" of the twin, hysterical personalities of the narrator and Usher. Finally, we do not know for sure *what* has happened for, as our narrator flees "aghast" from the scene, the face of the House splits apart and sinks into that tarn which first merged the images of the faces of both the House and the narrator. The tale has long been hailed as a masterpiece of [36] gothic horror; it is also a masterpiece of dramatic irony and structural symbolism.

4. "The Black Cat" and "The Tell-Tale Heart"

"The Tell-Tale Heart" (1843), a study in obsessive paranoia, is yet another story of the mind watching itself disintegrate under the stresses of delusion in an [40] alienated world. It is the perverse fortune of the narrator to become fearful of the grotesque eye of a kindly old man, whom he says he loves. With a double perversity, he gives himself away to the police at the moment of success. Yet the narrator is caught in a weird world in which [41] he loves the old man yet displays no real emotion toward him, in which he cannot let the "beloved" old man live and yet cannot kill him without remorse, in which he cannot expose his crime and yet must do so. Perhaps the final irony is that the apparent beating of his own heart which he mistakes as, first, the beating of the still-living heart of the old man, and which, second, seems to be an emblem of his own guilt (and which, finally, compels him to confess), may very well be initially the peculiar thumping sound of the wood-beetles gnawing at the walls. "The Black Cat" (1843) carries the same themes further and details more clearly the irrational desire, almost the ultimate irony, to act against oneself, with an ambiguous conclusion suggesting the agency of malevolent fortune at the same time that it suggests subconscious self-punishment. The major absurdist irony, perhaps, is that the murder which the narrator commits is the result of subconscious remorse over the *cat* he has previously mistreated.

5. "The Masque of the Red Death"

"The Masque of the Red Death" (1842), a tale of the supernatural visitation of Death himself, can [39] also be read as a tone poem about hysteria, engendered by mood and setting, with a sarcastic concluding echo from Pope's *Dunciad*. Prince Prospero's sinister stronghold, of course, contrasts directly with the enchanted island of his namesake, Prospero, the magician in Shakespeare's *The Tempest*. The ironic theme of Poe's tale focuses on the grimly perverse joke of Prospero's having walled *in* death in a frenetic attempt to wall it out.

6. Symbolism in "The Masque of the Red Death"[4]

[88] The symbolism of certain stories of Poe is rather clear, and it would be useless to insist upon it. For example, "The Masque of the Red Death" is "a parable of the inevitability and universality of death," "the human condition of man's fate, and the fate of the universe." The seven rooms are none other than the seven ages of man; the gigantic ebony clock with the "dull, heavy, monotonous clang" emphasizes the passage of time; and the spectre in the winding sheet smeared with blood is the personification of death, or "man's . . . self aroused and self-developed fear of his own mistaken concept of death."

7. "The Masque of the Red Death" as Representative of a "Diseased Age"[5]

[118] More than once, in his dialogues or critical writings, Poe describes the earth-bound, time-bound rationalism of his age as a *disease*. And that is what the Red Death signifies. Prince Prospero's flight from the Red Death is the poetic imagination's flight from temporal and worldly consciousness into dream. The thousand dancers of Prince Prospero's costume ball are just what Poe says they are—"dreams" or "phantasms," veiled and vivid creatures of Prince Prospero's rapt imagination. Whenever there is a feast, or a carnival, or costume ball in Poe, we may be sure that a dream is in progress.

But what is the gigantic ebony clock? . . . In sleep, our minds may roam beyond the temporal world, but our hearts tick on, binding us to time and mortality. Whenever the ebony clock strikes, the dancers of Prince Prospero's dream grow momentarily pale and still, in half-awareness that they and their revel must have an end; it is as if a sleeper should half-awaken, and know that he has been dreaming, and then sink back into dreams again.

The figure in blood-dabbled grave-clothes, who stalks through the terrified company and vanishes in the shadow of the clock, is waking, temporal consciousness, and his coming means the death of dreams. He breaks up Prince Prospero's ball. . . . The final confrontation between Prince Prospero and the shrouded figure is like the terrible final meeting between William Wilson and his double. Recognizing his adversary as his own worldly and mortal self, Prince Prospero gives a cry of despair which is also Poe's cry of despair: despair at the realization that only by self-destruction could the poet fully free his soul from the trammels of this world.

Poe's aesthetic, Poe's theory of the nature of art, seems to me insane. To say that art should repudiate everything [119] human and earthly, and find its subject-matter at the flickering end of dreams, is hopelessly to narrow the scope and function of art. Poe's aesthetic points toward such impoverishments as *poésie pure* and the abstract expressionist movement in painting. And yet, despite his aesthetic, Poe is a great artist, and I would rest my case for him on his prose allegories of psychic conflict. In them, Poe broke wholly new ground, and they remain the best things of their kind in our literature. Poe's mind may have been a strange one; yet all minds are alike in their general structure; therefore we can understand him, and I think that he will have something to say to us as long as there is civil war in the palaces of men's minds.

From Georges Zayed, "Symbolism in Poe's Tales." *Readings on Edgar Allan Poe,* ed. Bonnie Szumski and Carol Prime (San Diego: Greenhaven Press, 1998) 82–91.

From Richard Wilbur, "Poe's Use of Allegory." *Readings on Edgar Allan Poe,* ed. Bonnie Szumski and Carol Prime (San Diego: Greenhaven Press, 1998) 110–119.

8. Sources and Analogues of "The Cask of Amontillado"[6]

"[93] The Cask of Amontillado" (Chapter 4) is a prime example of Poe's ability to sculpt materials from popular literature and culture into a masterwork of terror. At once derivative and freshly individualistic, the tale enacts Poe's belief that "the truest and surest test of *originality* is the manner of handling a hackneyed subject."

It has long been surmised that this story of murderous revenge reflects Poe's vindictive hatred of two prominent New York literary figures, the author Thomas Dunn English and the newspaper editor Hiram Fuller. If "The Cask" is on some level, a retaliatory document, surely Poe could not have envisioned a more ghoulish type of retaliation. Seen against the background of the war of the literati, the narrator Montresor (Poe) gets back at his enemy Fortunato (English) for a recent insult, using their mutual friend Luchesi (Fuller) as a foil in his scheme. Although we know from the start that Montresor is bent on revenge, and we have ominous feelings as he takes his foe into the depths of his skeleton-filled wine vaults, the tale's atmosphere is deceptively convivial; the two connoisseurs banter and drink as they go in search of the cask of Amontillado (a fine Spanish sherry) Montresor says he has received. Only when Montresor lures Fortunato into a small niche, quickly chains up his stupefied victim, and proceeds to wall up the niche with bricks and mortar are we overwhelmed by the horrifying fact of live burial.

Poe's animus against the literati may have motivated the revenge theme, but it fails to account for specific details of plot, character, and imagery. For those we must look to the tale's popular cultural context. Poe was a great borrower, and he had an eye on the [94] popular market. On one level, his terror tales were clearly designed to cater to a public increasingly enamored of horror and sensationalism. Writing in the era of the crime-filled penny papers and mass-produced pamphlet novels, he was well aware of the demands of the sensation-loving public. His letters are peppered with excited boasts about some work of his that has made a "sensation" or a "hit." In his tale "The Psyche Zenobia," he had the editor of a popular magazine declare: "Sensations are the great thing after all. Should you ever be drowned or hung, be sure and make a note of your sensations—they will be worth to you ten guineas a sheet." Following the lead of the sensation mongers, Poe made use of some of the wildest situations imaginable.

One such situation was live burial. In "The Premature Burial" Poe wrote that "*no* event is so terribly well adapted to inspire the supremeness of bodily and of mental distress, as is burial before death," a topic that creates "a degree of appalling and intolerable horror from which the most daring imagination must recoil." The specific work which established the premise of "The Cask of Amontillado" was Joel Tyler Headley's "A Man Built in a Wall," first published in the *Columbian Magazine* in 1844 and collected in Headley's *Letters from Italy* (1845). Headley reports having visited an Italian church containing a niche in which was discovered the skeleton of a man who had been buried alive by a workman under the direction of the man's smirking archenemy. After a detailed description of the grotesque posture of the skeleton, suggesting an excruciatingly painful death, Headley recreates the murder:

From David S. Reynolds, "Poe's Art of Transformation: 'The Cask of Amontillado' in Its Cultural Context," *New Essays on Poe's Major Tales*, ed. Kenneth Silverman, (New York: Cambridge, 1993) 93–112.

The workman began at the feet, and with his mortar and trowel built up with the same carelessness he would exhibit in filling any broken wall. The successful enemy stood leaning on his sword—a smile of scorn and revenge on his features—and watched the face of the man he hated, but no longer feared. . . . It was slow work fitting the pieces nicely, so as to close up the aperture with precision. . . . With care and precision the last stone was fitted in the narrow space—the trowel passed smoothly over it—a stifled groan as if from the centre of a rock, broke the stillness—one strong shiver and all was over. The agony had passed—revenge was satisfied, and a secret locked up for the great revelation day.

Several details in Headley's piece—the premise of live burial in a hidden niche, the careful placement of the bricks, the revenge motive, the victim's [95] agonized groaning and numbed stillness—anticipate "The Cask of Amontillado."

Also analogous to Poe's story is Honoré de Balzac's "La Grande Bretêche," an adaptation of which appeared in the *Democratic Review* in November 1843. Balzac describes a jealous husband who, on discovering that his wife's lover is hiding in her closet, has the closet walled up as the lady watches. Poe most likely also knew the story "Apropos of Bores" (*New York Mirror*, December 2, 1837), in which a man at a party tells of going with a porter into the vast wine vaults of Lincoln's Inn to view several pipes of Madeira that were stored there. They found the pipes in good condition but had a terrifying accident: When their candle was extinguished, they groped to the cellar door only to have the key break off in the lock. They impulsively decided to forget their sorrows by staving in a wine pipe and getting drunk in order to forget "the horrible death that awaits us." Giving up this impulse, they soberly faced the fact that their remains would not be discovered until all traces of identity were destroyed. We never learn the outcome of the tale, for the narrator and his listeners are called to tea before he is finished.

Another predecessor of Poe's tale, hitherto unacknowledged, was the sensational best-seller *The Quaker City; or The Monks of Monk Hall* (1845) by George Lippard, Poe's friend from his Philadelphia days. Monk Hall, a huge mansion where Philadelphia's prominent citizens gather in secret revels and debauchery, has below it a so-called "deadvault," a vast cellar with labyrinthine passages and hidden recesses. The cellar is anticipatory of the vast vault beneath Montresor's mansion in several ways: It is lined with countless skeletons, its walls are clammy with moisture, and it is the scene of live burial. One critic has called "absurd" Poe's notion in "Cask" of "an ossuary . . . gruesomely combined with the appurtenances of a wine cellar," but many of Poe's contemporary readers had been prepared for such an odd coupling by the description of Monk Hall, where not only are the wine cellar and dead-vault side-by-side but the dead-vault is littered with liquor bottles strewn amid the skeletons. In a scene that presages Montresor's long descent with his victim into the catacombs, Devil-Bug, the sadistic keeper of Monk Hall, slowly takes a victim, Luke Harvey, down an extensive staircase into the depths of the dead-vault. Hardly as subtle as Montresor, Devil-Bug mutters to his [96] victim, "I am a-goin' to bury you alive! D'ye hear that? I'm a-goin' to bury you alive! "Just as Montresor howls and laughs at the enchained Fortunato, so Devil-Bug takes noisy pleasure in the sufferings of his victim. "He shrieked forth a horrible peal of laughter, more like the howl of a hyena, than the sound of a human laugh." Unlike Montresor, Devil-Bug does not succeed in his murderous scheme; his intended victim escapes. Devil-Bug, however, is haunted by the vision of a previous murder victim, just as (according to one reading) Montresor is tortured by the recollection of his crime.

A larger cultural phenomenon that influenced Poe was the temperance movement, which produced a body of literature and lectures filled with the kinds of horrifying images that fascinated him. Poe's bouts with the bottle, leading eventually to his death, are well known. Less familiar is Poe's ambiguous relationship with the American temperance movement. In the 1830s Poe had befriended the Baltimore writer John Lofland, who delivered temperance lectures even though, like several other backsliding reformers of the period, he drank and took drugs in private. Another of Poe's acquaintances, Timothy Shay Arthur, wrote some of the most popular (and darkest) temperance tales of the day, including *Six Nights with the Washingtonians* (1842) and *Ten Nights in a Barroom* (1854). In the early 1840s, the rise of the Washingtonians—reformed drunkards who told grisly tales of alcoholism in an effort to frighten listeners into signing a pledge of abstinence—brought to temperance rhetoric a new sensationalism. Walt Whitman's novel *Franklin Evans* (1842), for example, written on commission for the Washingtonians, luridly depicts the ill results of alcohol, including shattered homes, infanticide, crushing poverty that leads to crime, and delirium tremens with its nightmare visions. Poe had direct association with the Washingtonians. In 1843, after a period of heavy drinking, he promised a temperance friend from whom he hoped to gain a political appointment that he would join the Washingtonians. Whether or not he did so at that time, he did join a related group, the Sons of Temperance, in the last year of his life. When on August 31, 1849, the *Banner of Temperance* [97] announced Poe's initiation into the order, it said: "We trust his pen will sometimes be employed in its behalf. A vast amount of good might be accomplished by so pungent and forcible a writer."

What the *Banner of Temperance* neglected to say was that Poe had already written temperance fiction, or more precisely, his own version of what I would call dark temperance, a popular mode that left didacticism behind and emphasized the perverse results of alcoholism. Following the lead of many dark temperance writers who portrayed once-happy families ripped asunder by a husband's inebriety, Poe in "The Black Cat" (1843) dramatized alcohol's ravages on an initially peaceful couple. The narrator tells us that he had once been known for his docility and gentleness but that his character—"through the instrumentality of the Fiend Intemperance—had (I blush to confess it) experienced a radical alteration for the worse. I grew, day by day, more moody, more irritable, more regardless of the feelings of others." As in popular temperance literature, the first sip is followed by escalating pathological behavior. The narrator declares that "my disease grew upon me—for what disease is like Alcohol!" One night a "fiendish malevolence, gin-nurtured" impels him to cut out the eye of his cat with a penknife, a deed he tries unsuccessfully to drown in wine. Before long he has been driven by alcohol to paranoia and crime, even to the extent of murdering his wife.

"The Cask of Amontillado" also studies the diseased psyche associated with alcohol. Everything in the story revolves around alcohol obsession. The object of the descent into the vault is a pipe of wine. Both of the main characters are wine connoisseurs, as is their mentioned friend Luchesi. The narrator, Montresor, boasts, "I was skilful in the Italian vintages myself, and bought largely whenever I could." As for Fortunato, he is so vain about his knowledge of wine and so fixated on the supposed Amontillado that he goes willingly to his own destruction.

When we meet him, we learn "he had been drinking much" in the carnival revelry, and as he walks unsteadily into the vault his eyes look like "two filmy orbs that distilled the rheum of intoxication." He gets drunker after sharing the bottle of Médoc that Montresor breaks open in the cellar, and even more so when he subsequently gulps down the flacon of De Grave (one of several puns that point to his fate). [98] Fortunato's name has a double meaning: from his perspective he is "fortunate" to have an opportunity to show off his expertise in wines; from the reader's viewpoint, it is his bad "fortune" to be sucked to doom by his overriding interest in liquor. Poe's contemporary readers, accustomed to dark temperance rhetoric, would have found special significance in the interweaving of alcohol and death images in passages like this:

> The wine sparkled in his eyes and the bells jingled. My own fancy grew warm with Medoc. We had passed through walls of piled bones, with casks and puncheons intermingling, into the inmost depths of the catacombs.

The jingling of the bells reminds us of the fool Fortunato has become because of his destructive obsession. The wine-instilled agitation of Montresor's fancy reflects his role in this devilish communion, while the intermingled casks and bones, besides recalling Lippard's Monk Hall, enhance the eerie dark temperance atmosphere. After Montresor chains Fortunato to the wall, their dialogue takes on a dreary circularity that shows once again the importance of alcohol obsession to the story. "The Amontillado!" exclaims the victim; "True, the Amontillado," replies the murderer. Even after he has been walled in, the hapless Fortunato, in a desperate attempt to pass off the situation as a joke, returns to the subject of drinking:

> "We will have many a rich laugh about it at the palazzo—he! he! he!—over our wine—he! he! he!"
> "The Amontillado!" I said.
> "He! he! he!—he! he! he!—yes, the Amontillado!"

The dark temperance mode gives the tale a grim inevitability and another cultural phenomenon—anti-Masonry—contributes to its black humor and mysterious aura. At the center of the story is a dialogue that shows Poe tapping into his contemporaries' concerns about the Masons, a private all-male order widely thought to be involved in heinous crime. After drinking the bottle of De Grave, Fortunato throws it upward with a grotesque gesture Montresor does not understand. [99]

> "You do not comprehend?" he said.
> "Not I," I replied.
> "Then you are not of the brotherhood."
> "How?"
> "You are not of the masons."
> "Yes, yes," I said, "yes, yes."
> "You? Impossible! A mason?"
> "A mason," I replied.
> "A sign," he said.
> "It is this," I answered, producing a trowel from beneath the fold of my *roquelaire*.
> "You jest," he exclaimed, recoiling a few paces. "But let us proceed to the Amontillado."

This marvelous moment of black humor has a range of historical associations rooted in the anti-Masonry mania that had swept America during Poe's apprentice period. The pun on "mason" (referring both to the fraternal order and to a worker in brick and stone) seems to have a specific historical referent. At the center of the Masonry controversy was one William Morgan, a brick-and-stone mason of Batavia, New York, who in 1826, after thirty years of membership in the Masons, was determined to publish a harsh exposé of the order but was silenced before he could, most likely by vindictive members of the order. Morgan's disappearance was wreathed in mystery. One night in September 1826 he was seized, gagged, and spirited away in a carriage to the Niagara frontier, where all trace of him was lost. The story spread that a group of Masons, viewing Morgan as a traitor, had drowned him in the Niagara River. (It is perhaps meaningful, in this context, that Montresor leads his victim "below the river bed.") Anti-Masonry sentiment snowballed and became a substantial political movement, peaking in the mid-1830s and then feeding into the ascendant Whig party. The Masonic order was viewed as undemocratic and as a tangible threat to American institutions. In particular, its oath, whereby members swore to uphold rational secular values (without reference to God or Christianity), was seen as sacrilegious. When Poe has Fortunato make a "grotesque" movement signaling membership in the order, he is introducing a sign that many of his readers would have regarded as demonic. When Montresor [100] gives the sign of the trowel, he is not only foretelling the story's climax but is also summoning up the associations of brick-and-stone masonry, murderous revenge, and mysterious disappearance surrounding American Masonry.

So central is the Masonic image that the tale has been interpreted as an enactment of the historical conflict between Catholics and Masons. In this reading, Fortunato's real crime is that he is a Mason, whereas Montresor, a Roman Catholic, assumes a perverted priestly function in his ritualistic murder of his Masonic foe. It should be pointed out, however, that in the predominantly evangelical Protestant America of Poe's day *both* Masons and Catholics were held suspect. If anti-Masonic feeling feeds into the portrait of Fortunato, anti-Catholic sentiment lies behind several of the grim images in the tale. In the 1830s and 1840s, American Protestant authors, fearful of the rapid growth of the Catholic church with the sudden flood of immigrants arriving from abroad, produced a large body of lurid literature aimed at exposing alleged depravity and criminality among Catholics. In 1838 one alarmed commentator wrote of the "tales of lust, and blood, and murder . . . with which the ultra protestant is teeming." Of special interest in connection with Poe's tale is Maria Monk's best-selling *Awful Disclosures of . . . the Hotel Dieu Nunnery at Montreal* (1836), which featured a huge cellar that served as both a torture chamber and a tomb, where priests had killed some 375 people and cast their remains into a lime pit. Whether or not Poe had Maria Monk and her ilk in mind when he concocted his tale of torture behind cellar walls, it is notable that he made use of Catholic images: The story is set during the *Carnivale,* a Catholic season just before Lent; Montresor's family motto about the heel crushing the serpent refers to Genesis 3:14 (the curse upon the serpent) and historically symbolizes the Church militant triumphing over the forces of evil; the early history of the Church is recalled when the underground passages are called "catacombs"; and the final words, *"In pace requiescat!"* are the last words of a requiem mass. The Catholic connection is further strengthened if we accept the idea that Poe derived the name

Montresor from an old French Catholic family. Although not explicitly anti-Catholic, the tale combines religious [101] and criminal imagery in a way reminiscent of the anti-Catholic bestsellers of the day.

Though grounded in nineteenth-century American culture, "The Cask of Amontillado" transcends its time-specific referents because it is crafted in such a way that it remains accessible to generations of readers unfamiliar with such sources as anti-Catholicism, temperance, and live-burial literature. The special power of the tale can be understood if we take into account Poe's theories about fiction writing, developed largely in response to emerging forms of popular literature that aroused both his interest and his concern. On the one hand, as a literary professional writing for popular periodicals ("Cask" appeared in the most popular of all, *Godey's Lady's Book*) Poe had to keep in mind the demands of an American public increasingly hungry for sensation. On the other hand, as a scrupulous craftsman he was profoundly dissatisfied with the way in which other writers handled sensational topics. John Neal's volcanic, intentionally disruptive fiction seemed energetic but formless to Poe, who saw in it "no precision, no finish . . . —always an excessive force but little of refined art." Similarly, he wrote of the blackly humorous stories in Washington Irving's *Tales of a Traveller* that "the interest is subdivided and frittered away, and their conclusions are insufficiently *climacic* [sic]." George Lippard's *The Ladye Annabel*, a dizzying novel involving medieval torture and necrophilic visions, struck him as indicative of genius yet chaotic. A serial novel by Edward Bulwer-Lytton wearied him with its "continual and vexatious shifting of scene," while N. P. Willis's sensational play *Tortesa* exhibited "the great error" of "*inconsequence.* Underplot is piled on underplot," as Willis gives us "vast designs that terminate in nothing."

In his own fiction Poe tried to correct the mistakes he saw in other writers. The good plot, he argued, was that from which nothing can be taken without detriment to the whole. If, as he rightly pointed out, much sensational fiction of the day was digressive and directionless, his best tales were tightly unified. Of them all, "The Cask of Amontillado" perhaps most clearly exemplifies the unity he aimed for.

The tale's compactness becomes instantly apparent when we [102] compare it with the popular live-burial works mentioned earlier. Headley's journalistic "A Man Built in a Wall" begins with a long passage about a lonely Italian inn and ends with an account of the countryside around Florence; the interpolated story about the entombed man dwells as much on the gruesome skeleton as on the vindictive crime. Balzac's "La Grande Brêteche" is a slowly developing tale in which the narrator gets mixed accounts about an old abandoned mansion near the Loire; only in the second half of the story does he learn from his landlady that the mansion had been the scene of a live burial involving a husband's jealous revenge. The entombment in "Apropos of Bores" is purely accidental (two unlucky men find themselves trapped in a wine vault) and is reduced to frivolous chatter when the narrator breaks off at the climactic moment and his listeners crack jokes and disperse to tea. Closest in spirit to Poe, perhaps, is the "dead-vault" scene in Lippard's *The Quaker City*: There is the same ritualistic descent into an immense cellar by a sadistic murderer intent on burying his victim alive. Lippard, however, constantly interrupts the scene with extraneous descriptions (he's especially fascinated by the skeletons and caskets strewn around the cellar). In addition, this is just one of countless bloodcurdling scenes in a meandering novel light-years distant, structurally, from Poe's carefully honed tale.

• • •

So tightly woven is "The Cask" that it may be seen as an effort at literary one-upsmanship on Poe's part, designed pointedly as a contrast to other, more casually constructed live-burial pieces. In his essays on popular literature, Poe expressed particular impatience with irrelevancies of plot or character. For instance, commenting on J. H. Ingraham's perfervid best-seller *Lafitte, the Pirate of the Gulf*, he wrote: "We are surfeited with unnecessary details. . . . Of outlines there are none. Not a dog yelps, unsung."

There is absolutely no excess in "The Cask of Amontillado." Every sentence points inexorably to the horrifying climax. In the interest of achieving unity, Poe purposely leaves several questions unanswered. The tale is remarkable for what it leaves out. What are the "thousand injuries" Montresor has suffered at the hands of Fortunato? In particular, what was the "insult" that has driven Montresor to the grisly extreme of murder by live burial? What personal misfortune is he referring to when he tells his foe, "you [103] are happy, as once I was"? Like a painter who leaves a lot of suggestive white canvas, Poe sketches character and setting lightly, excluding excess material. Even so simple a detail as the location of the action is unknown. Most assume the setting is Italy, but one commentator makes a good case for France. What do we know about the main characters? As discussed, both are bibulous and proud of their connoisseurship in wines. Fortunato, besides being a Mason, is "rich, respected, admired, beloved," and there is a Lady Fortunato who will miss him. Montresor is descended from "a great and numerous family" and is wealthy enough to sustain a palazzo, servants, and extensive wine vaults.

Other than that, Poe tells very little about the two. Both exist solely to fulfill the imperatives of the plot Poe has designed. Everything Montresor does and says furthers his strategy of luring his enemy to his death. Everything Fortunato does and says reveals the fatuous extremes his vanity about wines will lead him to. Though limited, these characters are not what E. M. Forster would call flat. They swiftly come alive before our eyes because Poe describes them with acute psychological realism. Montresor is a complex Machiavellian criminal, exhibiting a full range of traits from clever ingratiation to stark sadism. Fortunato, the dupe whose pride leads to his own downfall, nevertheless exhibits enough admirable qualities that one critic has seen him as a wronged man of courtesy and good will. The drama of the story lies in the carefully orchestrated interaction between the two. Poe directs our attention away from the merely sensational and toward the psychological.

Herein lies another key difference between the tale and its precursors. In none of the popular live-burial works is the *psychology* of revenge a factor. In Headley and Lippard, the victim is unconscious and thus incognizant of the murderer's designs; similarly, in Balzac there is no communication at all between the murderer and the entombed. In Poe, the relationship between the two is, to a large degree, the story. Montresor says at the start, murder is most successful if the victim is made painfully aware of what is happening: "A wrong is unredressed . . . when the avenger fails to make himself felt as such to him who has done the wrong." By focusing on the process of vanity falling prey to sly revenge, Poe [104] shifts attention to psychological subtleties ignored by the other live-burial writers.

9. Poe's Idea of Unity and "The Fall of the House of Usher"[7]

[15] One of Poe's most characteristic ideas is unity. This is the key to the philosophy of *Eureka* and the visionary dialogues; this is the essence of his contribution to the theory and practice of the short story. In his review of Hawthorne's *Twice-Told Tales* he speaks of the need for totality, for "a certain unique single *effect* to be wrought out": every word of a piece of fiction should contribute to the realization of this aim. Many critics have noticed the intensity of the concentration on unity in "Usher"— how the opening description of the House and the narrator's reactions lead swiftly and inevitably to the final catastrophe. It is perhaps instructive to see the story's structure as three sections of about equal length: paragraphs 1 to 14 introduce the House, the circumstances of the narrator's visit, and Roderick and Madeline Usher; the movement is of entrance, of the opening of doors (there is perhaps a pun on the family name when the valet "threw open a door and ushered me into the presence of his master"). The middle section, paragraphs 15 to 29, develops the narrator's initial impressions through the analysis of Roderick's aesthetic ideas, and the application of his most abstract and intellectual madness to his relationship with his sister. The final part, paragraphs 30 to 47 logically completes these themes by building rapidly to Madeline's reappearance and the simultaneous collapse of both Ushers and their house. Here there is a final door-opening, as Madeline reels on the threshold; then the tarn finally "closes" over the fragments of the fallen house. As often in Poe's fiction, the protagonist (here the narrator and both Ushers combined) ends teetering on the verge of a supreme revelation that is also his destruction, an opening that mockingly also closes everything.

Poe attains an effect of structural symmetry by placing certain actions and images only in [16] the first and third parts: the sullen tarn; the appearances of Madeline in the apartment; and the speeches of Roderick (there is little dialogue; Roderick speaks only twice at length, once early in the story to confirm his "intolerable agitation of soul," and then at the end to announce, *"We have put her living in the tomb!"*).

This unity of structure is reinforced by the style. From the magnificent opening sentences to the end, Poe's language is highly charged with emotion, but at the same time, quite abstract: for instance, the narrator remarks at the beginning, "a sense of insufferable gloom pervaded my spirit." Instead of simple, direct description, we experience the narrator's *sense* of things. *Pervaded* is also a key word, evoking the notorious "atmosphere" of the House, the "condensation" of "vapours" from the tarn. As Poe's note about "sentience" suggests, he seeks credibility for his psychological claims by using the vocabulary of nineteenth-century chemistry. *Pervaded* is also important in introducing the theme of *oppression*, which recurs throughout: something sinister presses down on the mind, anticipating the collapse of the House. Later the narrator says: "An irrepressible terror pervaded my frame; and, at length, there sat upon my very heart an incubus of utterly causeless alarm." *Frame* hints at the identity of the human body with the building, as does the similarity of appearance between Roderick's head and the House, and the imagery of

From Thomas Woodson, ed., *Twentieth-Century Interpretations of "The Fall of the House of Usher"* (Englewood Cliffs, NJ: Prentice Hall, 1969) 15–17.

his poem, "The Haunted Palace." In fact, a close study of the story's style reveals a very high degree of recurrence of a rather small and special vocabulary. The effect of this stylistic narrowness is to bring together, almost to the verge of solipsism, the sensations of both Roderick and the narrator, and the "sentience" of Madeline and the House, Madeline being less a character than an object to be perceived.

Another peculiarity of Poe's diction is his emphasis on the negative. In the first paragraph alone we find, in addition to *insufferable,* these adjectives and verbs: *unrelieved, unredeemed, unnerved, insoluble,* and *unsatisfactory.* The story is full of words beginning with *un-* or *in* , or ending in *-less,* and expressions containing *no, not, mere,* or *scarcely.* Poe uses these words to maintain an excited, exaggerated tone, but also to evoke the results of oppression on the mind: the nightmare of a vacant, featureless world—imaged by sinking beneath the surface of the tarn—a world where meaning and value have dissolved into nothingness. [17]

Through these devices Poe has made style his weapon to redeem, as William Hedges has put it, the sensational material of popular fiction for the analysis of the soul. In the speeches of Roderick Usher this style is speeded up, intensified, almost to the point of hysterical incoherence. This style is then counterpointed to the burlesque extravagance of the "Mad Trist" of Sir Launcelot Canning, which the narrator describes as a style of "uncouth and unimaginative prolixity," portentously empty of meaning (perhaps Poe's attempt to imitate the effect of the porter's knocking on the door in *Macbeth*).

10. The Narrators of "The Cask of Amontillado" (Chapter 4) and "The Black Cat"[8]

[309] It goes without saying that Poe, like other creative men, is sometimes at the mercy of his own worst qualities. Yet the contention that he is fundamentally a bad or tawdry stylist appears to me to be rather facile and sophistical. It is based, ultimately, on the untenable and often unanalyzed assumption that Poe and his narrators are identical literary twins and that he must be held responsible for all their wild or perfervid utterances; their shrieks and groans are too often conceived as originating from Poe himself. I believe, on the contrary, that Poe's narrators possess a character and consciousness distinct from those of their creator. These protagonists, I am convinced, speak their own thoughts and are the dupes of their own passions. In short, Poe understands them far better than they can possibly understand themselves. Indeed, he often so designs his tales as to show his narrators' limited comprehension of their own problems and states of mind; the structure of many of Poe's stories clearly reveals an ironical and comprehensive intelligence critically and artistically ordering events so as to establish a vision of life and character which the narrator's very inadequacies help to "prove."

[310] The structure of Poe's stories compels realization that they are more than the effusions of their narrators' often disordered mentalities. Through the irony of his characters' self-betrayal and through the development and arrangement of his dramatic actions, Poe suggests to his readers ideas never entertained by the

---

From James W. Gargano, "The Question of Poe's Narrators," *The Recognition of Edgar Allan Poe,* ed. Eric W. Carlson (Ann Arbor: U of Michigan P, 1966) 308–16.

narrators. Poe intends his readers to keep their powers of analysis and judgment ever alert; he does not require or desire complete surrender to the experience of the sensations being felt by his characters. The point of Poe's technique, then, is not to enable us to lose ourselves in strange or outrageous emotions, but to see these emotions and those obsessed by them from a rich and thoughtful perspective. I do not mean to advocate that, while reading Poe, we should cease to feel; but feeling should be "simultaneous" with an analysis carried on with the composure and logic of Poe's great detective, Dupin. For Poe is not merely a Romanticist; he is also a chronicler of the consequences of the Romantic excesses which lead to psychic disorder, pain, and disintegration.

[313] Evidence of Poe's "seriousness" seems to me indisputable in "The Cask of Amontillado." Far from being his author's mouthpiece, the narrator, Montresor, is one of the supreme examples in fiction of a deluded rationalist who cannot glimpse the moral implications of his planned folly. Poe's fine ironic sense makes clear that Montresor, the stalker of Fortunato, is both a compulsive and pursued man; for in committing a flawless crime against another human being, he really (like Wilson and the protagonist in "The Tell-Tale Heart") commits the worst of crimes against himself. His reasoned, "cool" intelligence weaves an intricate plot which, while ostensibly satisfying his revenge, despoils him of humanity. His impeccably contrived murder, his weird mask of goodness in an enterprise of evil, and his abandonment of all his life-energies in one pet project of hate convict him of a madness which he mistakes for the inspiration of genius. The brilliant masquerade setting of Poe's tale intensifies the theme of Montresor's apparently successful duplicity; Montresor's ironic appreciation of his own deviousness seems further to justify his arrogance of intellect. But the greatest irony of all, to which Montresor is never sensitive, is that the "injuries" supposedly perpetrated by Fortunato are illusory and that the vengeance meant for the victim recoils upon Montresor himself. In immolating Fortunato, the narrator unconsciously calls him the "noble" Fortunato and confesses that his own "heart grew sick." Though Montresor attributes this sickness to "the dampness of the catacombs," it is clear that his crime has begun to "possess" him. [314] We see that, after fifty years, it remains the obsession of his life; the meaning of his existence resides in the tomb in which he has, symbolically, buried himself. In other words, Poe leaves little doubt that the narrator has violated his own mind and humanity, that the external act has had its destructive inner consequences.

The same artistic integrity and seriousness of purpose evident in "The Cask of Amontillado" can be discovered in "The Black Cat." No matter what covert meanings one may find in this much-discussed story, it can hardly be denied that the nameless narrator does not speak for Poe. Whereas the narrator, at the beginning of his "confession," admits that he cannot explain the events which overwhelmed him, Poe's organization of his episodes provides an unmistakable clue to his protagonist's psychic deterioration. The tale has two distinct, almost parallel parts: in the first, the narrator's inner moral collapse is presented in largely symbolic narrative; in the second part, the consequences of his self-violation precipitate an act of murder, punishable by society. Each section of the story deals with an ominous cat, an atrocity, and an exposé of a "crime." In the first section, the narrator's house is consumed by fire after he has mutilated and subsequently hanged Pluto, his pet cat. Blindly, he refuses to grant any connection between his violence and the fire; yet the image of a hanged cat on the one remaining wall indicates that he will be haunted and hag-ridden by his deed. The sinister figure of Pluto, seen by a crowd of neighbors, is symbolically both an accusation and a portent, an enigma to the spectators but an infallible sign to the reader.

In the second section of "The Black Cat," the reincarnated cat goads the narrator into the murder of his wife. As in "William Wilson," "The Tell-Tale Heart," and "The Cask of Amontillado," the narrator cannot understand that his assault upon another person derives from his own moral sickness and unbalance. Like his confreres, too, he seeks psychic release and freedom in a crime which completes his torture. To the end of his life he is incapable of locating the origin of his evil and damnation within himself.

The theme of "The Black Cat" is complicated for many critics by the narrator's dogged assertion that he was pushed into evil and self-betrayal by the "imp of the perverse." [315] This imp is explained, by a man who, it must be remembered, eschews explanation, as a radical, motiveless, and irresistible impulse within the human soul. Consequently, if his self-analysis is accepted, his responsibility for his evil life vanishes. Yet, it must be asked if it is necessary to give credence to the words of the narrator. William Wilson, too, regarded himself as a "victim" of a force outside himself and Montresor speaks as if he has been coerced into his crime by Fortunato. The narrator in "The Black Cat" differs from Wilson in bringing to his defense a well-reasoned theory with perhaps a strong appeal to many readers. Still, the narrator's pat explanation is contradicted by the development of the tale, for instead of being pushed into crime, he pursues a life which makes crime inevitable. He cherishes the intemperate self-indulgence which blunts his powers of self-analysis; he is guided by his delusions to the climax of damnation. Clearly, Poe does not espouse his protagonist's theory any more than he approves of the specious rationalizations of his other narrators. Just as the narrator's well constructed house has a fatal flaw, so the theory of perverseness is flawed because it really explains nothing. Moreover, even the most cursory reader must be struck by the fact that the narrator is most "possessed and maddened" when he most proudly boasts of self-control. If the narrator obviously cannot be believed at the end of the tale, what argument is there for assuming that he must be telling the truth when he earlier tries to evade responsibility for his "sin" by slippery rationalizations?

A close analysis of "The Black Cat" must certainly exonerate Poe of the charge of merely sensational writing. The final frenzy of the narrator, with its accumulation of superlatives, cannot be ridiculed as an example of Poe's style. The breakdown of the shrieking criminal does not reflect similar breakdown in the author. Poe, I maintain, is a serious artist who explores the neuroses of his characters with probing intelligence. He permits his narrator to revel and flounder in torment, but he sees beyond the torment to its causes.

In conclusion, then, the five tales I have commented on display Poe's deliberate craftsmanship and penetrating sense of irony. If my thesis is correct, Poe's narrators should not be construed as his mouthpieces; instead they should be regarded as expressing, in "charged" language indicative of their internal disturbances, [316] their own peculiarly nightmarish visions. Poe, I contend, is conscious of the abnormalities of his narrators and does not condone the intellectual ruses through which they strive, only too earnestly, to justify themselves. In short, though his narrators are often febrile or demented. Poe is conspicuously "sane." They may be "decidedly primitive" or "wildly incoherent," but Poe, in his stories at least, is mature and lucid.

11. Poe, Women, and "The Fall of the House of Usher"[9]

[340] Like the Egyptians, Poe would preserve bodies so as to prolong their historical effects. Corpses, particularly female ones, are regularly revived in Poe's tales: Ligeia, Morella, Berenice, and Eleanora all revisit the scenes of their lives. Many readers of Poe have noted the prevalence of female deaths in his work. His dictum that "the death . . . of a beautiful woman is, unquestionably, the most poetical topic in the world" has long suggested both a personal obsession with lost women—stemming from the early loss of his mother, a loss then recapitulated in the death of his young wife—and an aesthetic misogyny working to delimit and destroy women. Yet however much Poe's stories and poems seem to propel and be propelled by the deaths of women, the morbidity of his treatment of women is regularly accompanied by the imagination of their regeneration. The horror, and sometimes solace, for the husbands, brothers, and lovers of these women [341] is that they cannot be extinguished: they return as indestructible forces to haunt their partners. At the same time, these resurrected women testify to the stories their partners tell; they verify the narratives about themselves. Their regenerate corpses thus embody a principle of preservation, safeguarding the consciousnesses in which they figure as memories and thus poetic subjects.

The misogyny in Poe's representations of women consists less in his death plots than in his revivification of women in service to the history of consciousness. Poe's necrophilic interest in women quite distinctively eschews their given generative power and their role in the perpetuation of the species. He fantasizes a self that is always and only self-transmitting. . . . In the tales, he assuages the fear of termination with the notion of succession through regeneration, a regeneration of women's bodies to prolong not themselves but men's minds. The ghoulishness of Poe's portrayal of women lies in this single-minded prohibition of female generativity in order to produce evidence of a particular existence.

The anthropological and androcentric function of such figures as Ligeia, Morella, Berenice, and Eleanora is also to supply a legibility, albeit a problematic one, to death. Their returns, like Madeline's, suggest an uncertainty, both hopeful and horrific, about death. On the one hand, bodies somehow survive death, but on the other hand, bodies seem subject to many forms of death, or to conditions that seem indistinguishable from death. Madeline suffers from catalepsy. The loss of consciousness and rigidification of the muscles caused by this disease make its sufferers likely candidates for premature burial. As Poe explains in "The Premature Burial," even "the most rigorous medical tests fail to establish any material distinction between the state of the sufferer and what we conceive of absolute death."

From Gillian Brown, "The Poetics of Extinction," *The American Face of Edgar Allan Poe*, ed. Shawn Rosenheim and Stephen Rachman (Baltimore: Johns Hopkins UP, 1995.) 340–44.

Thus bodies in such states can be misread, and effectively murdered by misreading. Such fatal misreadings anticipate the eventuality of death, making it the result of human (mis)calculations. The horror of premature burial in "The Fall of the House of Usher" and other Poe tales ("Berenice," "The Cask of Amontillado," and "Loss of Breath") lies in the body's helplessness to govern interpretations of itself. Individual intention always exists [342] amidst other intentionalities, other agents. The consciousness that resurrected bodies signify is not just their own. Corpses in Poe, then, are always potential evidence of murder.

Murder narratives nicely serve Poe's anthropological purposes because they highlight the presence of some form of agency. When Madeline emerges from her premature interment, she reveals her brother's murderous mistake, literally scaring him to death. In her "now final death-agonies," she bears "him to the floor a corpse, and a victim to the terrors he had anticipated." He dies in a "struggle with the grim phantasm, FEAR," just as he had foreseen. Since Roderick's anticipation produces both deaths, the story of the extinction of his family reads as the record of his sensibility. Anticipation thus operates as an engine of transmission, disseminating the traces of human agency in death.

Not just any human agency: What survives is evidence of Roderick's consciousness, imprinted on his friend the narrator, who has shared his presentiments and aided Roderick in entombing Madeline.

12. The Deceptive Narrator of "The Black Cat"[10]

[96] Like "The Tell-Tale Heart," "The Black Cat" is not so much a confession as it is a murderer's attempt to rationalize his crime. "What disease is like Alcohol!" the narrator cries, elsewhere referring to the "Fiend Intemperance" and the "demon" that "possessed me" in order to shift responsibility from himself to his illness. Temperance crusaders sought to change public opinion on alcoholism, to treat it as a disease rather than as a moral failing or vice of the alcoholic. But . . . the story undercuts the narrator's insistence that the demon alcohol made him do it; readers see that his entire story is built on implausibilities and lame excuses, and his crime is motivated by impulses more sinister than a weakness for drink. As with "The Tell-Tale Heart," we must read against the narrator of "The Black Cat," establish which parts of his testimony should be believed and which should not, and try to discover the deeper motivations for the crime.

Once again, the concept of doubling provides a means for making sense of the narrator's strange logic. The black cat that replaces Pluto is certainly a kind of doppelgänger: uncannily, he too is missing an eye, he too is loved by the wife, and he too torments the narrator. . . . I see both cats as doubles for the wife, in the narrator's mind, at least: . . . Whenever the narrator mentions his wife, a black cat is close by. He physically abuses [97] both wife and cat, he tells us, even before hanging Pluto, and when he does hang it, its image mysteriously appears, of all places, on the wall above the unhappy couple's bed. Immediately after the second cat became "a great favorite with my wife," he explains, "For my own part, I soon found a dislike to it

From Scott Peeples, *Edgar Allan Poe Revisited*, Twayne's United States Authors Series No. 705. (New York: Twayne, 1998) 96–98.

arising within me": as soon he associates cat with wife, he begins to loathe the cat. It is his wife who calls his attention to the gallows shape of the white spot on the cat's breast—appropriately so, for the gallows not only reflects Pluto's fate but forecasts the narrator's punishment for killing his wife. Finally, he unknowingly walls up the living cat with the wife, so that the cat's crying leads the police to the wife and leads the narrator to the story's final image of the cat perched on the dead wife's head. Although the context makes clear that the narrator's literal reference is to the cat in the last sentence, one can imagine cat and wife converging in the narrator's mind when he says, "I had walled the monster up within the tomb!"

But why would the narrator want to kill his wife? For the very reason he gives for killing Pluto: "[I] hung it *because* I knew that it had loved me." He describes his wife as tender, possessing "that humanity of feeling which had once been my distinguishing trait," so it is reasonable to assume she would be affectionate and loving toward him. When the cat "spring[s] upon my knees, covering me with its loathsome caresses," or follows him closely, the narrator "long[s] to destroy it with a blow"; this exaggerated reaction to the cat's behavior leads one to suspect that the cat's expressions of love remind him of his wife's. When he does destroy his wife with a blow, his nonchalance is chilling, in contrast with his reaction to the murder of Pluto, which he calls "a deadly sin that would so jeopardize my immortal soul as to place it—if such a thing were possible—even beyond the reach of the infinite mercy of the Most Merciful and Most Terrible God." Either this guilt actually stems from his decision at that moment to kill his wife, having already killed her surrogate, or . . . he actually does kill his wife at the point when he says he killed Pluto, and in his confession fabricates the incident on the cellar stairs and the existence of a second cat. In either case, he responds to killing the cat as he ought to respond to killing his wife, a sin that is deadly and unforgivable because of his wife's innocence, because she died for loving him.

Such a paradox—death as the penalty for love—seems consistent with the contradictions that make up the narrator's initial description of his story. [98] It is "wild, yet most homely." The incidents have presented "little but Horror," yet he also refers to it as "a series of mere household events" and believes it could be perceived as "an ordinary succession of very natural causes and effects." And although he does not expect to be believed, he tries hard to explain his behavior as the result of all-too-human perverse impulses and the disease of alcoholism. One can attribute these contradictions, like the crime itself, to the narrator's madness, but again the story's network of uncanny images and plot twists warrants some consideration of how these bizarre occurrences might also be "mere household events." What the narrator does is horrible, shocking, and yet perhaps his motivations are common to marriages and other intimate relationships. . . . The narrator's hidden hatred of his wife, his unwillingness to acknowledge that hatred, his displacement of it onto the family pet, and certainly his turning to alcohol could be categorized as common "household events." His ultimate response, of course, is "wild" and "horrible"—but equally frightening is the implication that his predicament is not so uncommon, that, like the perverse impulse to do wrong for wrong's sake, the fear of intimacy is "one of the primitive impulses of the human heart—one of the indivisible primary faculties, or sentiments, which give direction to the character of Man."

Chapter 10
Collection of Stories for Additional Enjoyment and Study

William Faulkner . . . . Barn Burning, 462

Charlotte Perkins Gilman . . . . The Yellow Wallpaper, 473

Jamaica Kincaid . . . . Girl, 483

Flannery O'Connor . . . . A Good Man Is Hard to Find, 484

Alice Walker . . . . Everyday Use, 494

WILLIAM FAULKNER (1897–1962)

For a brief biographical note about Faulkner, see Chapter 1, page 95.

Barn Burning (1939)

The store in which the Justice of the Peace's court was sitting smelled of cheese. The boy, crouched on his nail keg at the back of the crowded room, knew he smelled cheese, and more; from where he sat he could see the ranked shelves close-packed with the solid, squat, dynamic shapes of tin cans whose labels his stomach read, not from the lettering which meant nothing to his mind but from the scarlet devils and the silver curve of fish—this, the cheese which he knew he smelled and the hermetic meat° which his intestines believed he smelled coming in intermittent gusts momentary and brief between the other constant one, the smell and sense just a little of fear because mostly of despair and grief, the old fierce pull of blood. He could not see the table where the Justice sat and before which his father and his father's enemy (*our enemy* he thought in that despair; *ourn! mine and his both! He's my father!*) stood, but he could hear them, the two of them that is, because his father had said no word yet:

"But what proof have you, Mr. Harris?"

"I told you. The hog got into my corn. I caught it up and sent it back to him. He had no fence that would hold it. I told him so, warned him. The next time I put the hog in my pen. When he came to get it I gave him enough wire to patch up his pen. The next time I put the hog up and kept it. I rode down to his house and saw the wire I gave him still rolled on to the spool in his yard. I told him he could have the hog when he paid me a dollar pound fee. That evening a nigger came with the dollar and got the hog. He was a strange nigger. He said, 'He say to tell you wood and hay kin burn.' I said, 'What?' 'That what he say to tell you,' the nigger said. 'Wood and hay kin burn.' That night my barn burned. I got the stock out but I lost the barn."

"Where is the nigger? Have you got him?"

"He was a strange nigger, I tell you. I don't know what became of him."

"But that's not proof. Don't you see that's not proof?"

°*hermetic meat:* canned meat.

5

"Get that boy up here. He knows." For a moment the boy thought too that the man meant his older brother until Harris said. "Not him. The little one. The boy," and, crouching, small for his age, small and wiry like his father, in patched and faded jeans even too small for him, with straight, uncombed, brown hair and eyes gray and wild as storm scud, he saw the men between himself and the table part and become a lane of grim faces, at the end of which he saw the Justice, a shabby, collarless, graying man in spectacles, beckoning him. He felt no floor under his bare feet; he seemed to walk beneath the palpable weight of the grim turning faces. His father, stiff in his black Sunday coat donned not for the trial but for the moving, did not even look at him. *He aims for me to lie,* he thought, again with that frantic grief and despair. *And I will have to do hit.*

"What's your name, boy?" the Justice said.

"Colonel Sartoris Snopes," the boy whispered.

"Hey?" the Justice said. "Talk louder. Colonel Sartoris? I reckon anybody named for Colonel Sartoris in this country can't help but tell the truth, can they?" The boy said nothing. *Enemy! Enemy!* he thought; for a moment he could not even see, could not see that the Justice's face was kindly nor discern that his voice was troubled when he spoke to the man named Harris: "Do you want me to question this boy?" But he could hear, and during those subsequent long seconds there was absolutely no sound in the crowded little room save that of quiet and intent breathing it was as if he had swung outward at the end of a grape vine, over a ravine, and at the top of the swing had been caught in a prolonged instant of mesmerized gravity, weightless in time.

"No!" Harris said violently, explosively. "Damnation! Send him out of here!" Now time, the fluid world, rushed beneath him again, the voices coming to him again through the smell of cheese and sealed meat, the fear and despair and the old grief of blood:

"This case is closed. I can't find against you, Snopes, but I can give you advice. Leave this country and don't come back to it."

His father spoke for the first time, his voice cold and harsh, level, without emphasis: "I aim to. I don't figure to stay in a country among people who . . ." he said something unprintable and vile, addressed to no one.

"That'll do," the Justice said, "Take your wagon and get out of this country before dark. Case dismissed."

His father turned, and he followed the stiff black coat, the wiry figure walking a little stiffly, from where a Confederate provost's man's musket ball had taken him in the heel on a stolen horse thirty years ago, followed the two backs now, since his older brother had appeared from somewhere in the crowd, no taller than the father but thicker, chewing tobacco steadily, between the two lines of grim-faced men and out of the store and across the worn gallery and down the sagging steps and among the dogs and half-grown boys in the mild May dust, where as he passed a voice hissed:

"Barn burner!"

Again he could not see, whirling; there was a face in a red haze, moonlike, bigger than the full moon, the owner of it half again his size, he leaping in the red haze toward the face, feeling no blow, feeling no shock when his head struck the earth, scrabbling up and leaping again, feeling no blow this time either and tasting no blood, scrabbling up to see the other boy in full flight and himself already leaping into pursuit as his father's hand jerked him back, the harsh, cold voice speaking above him: "Go get in the wagon."

It stood in a grove of locusts and mulberries across the road. His two hulking sisters in their Sunday dresses and his mother and her sister in calico and sunbonnets were already in it, sitting on and among the sorry residue of the dozen and more movings which even the boy could remember—the battered stove, the broken beds and chairs, the clock inlaid with mother-of-pearl, which would not run, stopped at some fourteen minutes past two o'clock of a dead and forgotten day and time, which had been his mother's dowry. She was crying, though when she saw him she drew her sleeve across her face and began to descend from the wagon. "Get back," the father said.

"He's hurt, I got to get some water and wash his . . ."

20   "Get back in the wagon," his father said. He got in too, over the tail-gate. His father mounted to the seat where the older brother already sat and struck the gaunt mules two savage blows with the peeled willow, but without heat. It was not even sadistic; it was exactly that same quality which in later years would cause his descendants to over-run the engine before putting a motor car into motion, striking and reining back in the same movement. The wagon went on, the store with its quiet crowd of grimly watching men dropped behind; a curve in the road hid it. *Forever* he thought. *Maybe he's done satisfied now, now that he has* . . . stopping himself, not to say it aloud even to himself. His mother's hand touched his shoulder.

"Does hit hurt?" she said.

"Naw," he said. "Hit don't hurt. Lemme be."

"Can't you wipe some of the blood off before hit dries?"

"I'll wash tonight," he said. "Lemme be, I tell you."

25   The wagon went on. He did not know where they were going. None of them ever did or ever asked, because it was always somewhere, always a house of sorts waiting for them a day or two days or even three days away. Likely his father had already arranged to make a crop on another farm before he. . . . Again he had to stop himself. He (the father) always did. There was something about his wolflike independence and even courage when the advantage was at least neutral which impressed strangers, as if they got from his latent ravening ferocity not so much a sense of dependability as a feeling that his ferocious conviction in the rightness of his own actions would be of advantage to all whose interest lay with his.

That night they camped, in a grove of oaks and beeches where a spring ran. The nights were still cool and they had a fire against it, of a rail lifted from a nearby fence and cut into lengths—a small fire, neat, niggard almost, a shrewd fire; such fires were his father's habit and custom always, even in freezing weather. Older, the boy might have remarked this and wondered why not a big one; why should not a man who had not only seen the waste and extravagance of war, but who had in his blood an inherent prodigality with material not his own, have burned everything in sight? Then he might have gone a step farther and thought that that was the reason; that niggard blaze was the living fruits of nights passed during those four years in the woods hiding from all men, blue or gray, with his strings of horses (captured horses, he called them). And older still, he might have divined the true reason: that the element of fire spoke to some deep mainspring of his father's being, as the element of steel or of powder spoke to other men, as the one weapon for the preservation of integrity, else breath were not worth the breathing, and hence to be regarded with respect and used with discretion.

But he did not think this now and he had seen those same niggard blazes all his life. He merely ate his supper beside it and was already half asleep over his iron plate when his father called him, and once more he followed the stiff back, the stiff and ruthless limp, up the slope and on to the starlit road where, turning, he could see his father against the stars but without face or depth—a shape black, flat, and bloodless as though cut from tin in the iron folds of the frockcoat which had not been made for him, the voice harsh like tin and without heat like tin:

"You were fixing to tell them. You would have told him." He didn't answer. His father struck him with the flat of his hand on the side of the head, hard but without heat, exactly as he had struck the two mules at the store, exactly as he would strike either of them with any stick in order to kill a horse fly, his voice still without heat or anger: "You're getting to be a man. You got to learn. You got to learn to stick to your own blood or you ain't going to have any blood to stick to you. Do you think either of them, any man there this morning, would? Don't you know all they wanted was a chance to get at me because they knew I had them beat? Eh?" Later, twenty years later, he was to tell himself, "If I had said they wanted only truth, justice, he would have hit me again." But now he said nothing. He was not crying. He just stood there. "Answer me," his father said.

"Yes," he whispered. His father turned.

"Get on to bed. We'll be there tomorrow."   30

Tomorrow they were there. In the early afternoon the wagon stopped before a paintless two-room house identical almost with the dozen others it had stopped before even in the boy's ten years, and again, as on the other dozen occasions, his mother and aunt got down and began to unload the wagon, although his two sisters and his father and brother had not moved.

"Likely hit ain't fitten for hawgs," one of the sisters said.

"Nevertheless, fit it will and you'll hog it and like it," his father said. "Get out of them chairs and help your Ma unload."

The two sisters got down, big, bovine, in a flutter of cheap ribbons; one of them drew from the jumbled wagon bed a battered lantern, the other a worn broom. His father handed the reins to the older son and began to climb stiffly over the wheel. "When they get unloaded, take the team to the barn and feed them." Then he said, and at first the boy thought he was still speaking to his brother: "Come with me."

"Me?" he said.   35

"Yes," his father said. "You."

"Abner," his mother said. His father paused and looked back—the harsh level stare beneath the shaggy, graying, irascible brows.

"I reckon I'll have a word with the man that aims to begin tomorrow owning me body and soul for the next eight months."

They went back up the road. A week ago—or before last night, that is—he would have asked where they were going, but not now. His father had struck him before last night but never before had he paused afterward to explain why; it was as if the blow and the following calm, outrageous voice still rang, repercussed, divulging nothing to him save the terrible handicap of being young, the light weight of his few years, just heavy enough to prevent his soaring free of the world as it seemed to be ordered but not heavy enough to keep footed solid in it, to resist it and try to change the course of its events.

Presently he could see the grove of oaks and cedars and the other flowering trees and   40 shrubs where the house would be, though not the house yet. They walked beside a fence massed with honeysuckle and Cherokee roses and came to a gate swinging open between two brick pillars, and now, beyond a sweep of drive, he saw the house for the first time and at that instant he forgot his father and the terror and despair both, and even when he remembered his father again (who had stopped) the terror and despair did not return. Because, for all the twelve movings, they had sojourned until now in a poor country, a land of small farms and fields and houses, and he had never seen a house like this before. *Hit's big as a courthouse* he thought quietly, with a surge of peace and joy whose reason he could not have thought into words, being too young for that: *They are safe from him. People whose lives are a part of this peace and dignity are beyond his touch, he no more to them than a buzzing wasp: capable of stinging for a little moment but that's all; the spell of this peace and dignity rendering even the barns and stable and cribs which belong to it impervious to the puny flames he might contrive* . . . this, the peace and joy, ebbing for an instant as he looked again at the stiff black back, the stiff and implacable limp of the figure which was not dwarfed by the house, for the reason that it had never looked big anywhere and which now, against the serene columned backdrop, had more than ever that impervious quality of something cut ruth-lessly from tin, depthless, as though, sidewise to the sun, it would cast no shadow. Watch-ing him, the boy remarked the absolutely undeviating course which his father held and saw the stiff foot come squarely down in a pile of fresh droppings where a horse had stood in the drive and which his father could have avoided by a simple change of stride. But it ebbed only for a moment, though he could not have thought this into words either, walking on in the spell of the house, which he could even want but without envy, without sorrow, certainly never with that ravening and jealous rage which unknown to him walked in the ironlike black coat before him: *Maybe he will feel it too. Maybe it will even change him now from what maybe he couldn't help but be.*

They crossed the portico. Now he could hear his father's stiff foot as it came down on the boards with clocklike finality, a sound out of all proportion to the displacement of the body it bore and which was not dwarfed either by the white door before it, as though it had attained to a sort of vicious and ravening minimum not to be dwarfed by anything—the flat, wide, black hat, the formal coat of broadcloth which had once been black but which had now that friction-glazed greenish cast of the bodies of old house flies, the lifted sleeve which was too large, the lifted hand like a curled claw. The door opened so promptly that the boy knew the Negro must have been watching them all the time, an old man with neat grizzled hair, in a linen jacket, who stood barring the door with his body, saying "Wipe yo foots, white man, fo you come in here. Major ain't home nohow."

"Get out of my way, nigger," his father said, without heat too, flinging the door back and the Negro also and entering, his hat still on his head. And now the boy saw the prints of the stiff foot on the doorsill and saw them appear on the pale rug behind the machinelike deliberation of the foot which seemed to bear (or transmit) twice the weight which the body compassed. The Negro was shouting "Miss Lula! Miss Lula!" somewhere behind them, then the boy, deluged as though by a warm wave by a suave turn of carpeted stair and a pendant glitter of chandeliers and a mute gleam of gold frames, heard the swift feet and saw her too, a lady—perhaps he had never seen her like before either—in a gray, smooth gown with lace at the throat and an apron tied at the waist and the sleeves turned back, wiping cake or biscuit dough from her hands with a towel as she came up the hall, looking not at his father at all but at the tracks on the blond rug with an expression of incredulous amazement.

"I tried," the Negro cried. "I tole him to . . . ."

"Will you please go away?" she said in a shaking voice. "Major de Spain is not at home. Will you please go away?"

His father had not spoken again. He did not speak again. He did not even look at her. He just stood stiff in the center of the rug, in his hat, the shaggy iron-gray brows twitching slightly above the pebble-colored eyes as he appeared to examine the house with brief delib-eration. Then with the same deliberation he turned; the boy watched him pivot on the good leg and saw the stiff foot drag round the arc of the turning, leaving a final long and fading smear. His father never looked at it, he never once looked down at the rug. The Negro held the door. It closed behind them, upon the hysteric and indistinguishable woman-wail. His father stopped at the top of the steps and scraped his boot clean on the edge of it. At the gate he stopped again. He stood for a moment, planted stiffly on the stiff foot, looking back at the house. "Pretty and white, ain't it?" he said. "That's sweat. Nigger sweat. Maybe it ain't white enough yet to suit him. Maybe he wants to mix some white sweat with it."

Two hours later the boy was chopping wood behind the house within which his mother and aunt and the two sisters (the mother and aunt, not the two girls, he knew that; even at this distance and muffled by walls the flat loud voices of the two girls emanated an incor-rigible idle inertia) were setting up the stove to prepare a meal, when he heard the hooves and saw the linen-clad man on a fine sorrel mare, whom he recognized even before he saw the rolled rug in front of the Negro youth following on a fat bay carriage horse—a suffused, angry face vanishing, still at full gallop, beyond the corner of the house where his father and brother were sitting in the two tilted chairs; and a moment later, almost before he could have put the axe down, he heard the hooves again and watched the sorrel mare go back out of the yard, already galloping again. Then his father began to shout one of the sisters' names, who presently emerged backward from the kitchen door dragging the rolled rug along the ground by one end while the other sister walked behind it.

"If you ain't going to tote, go on and set up the wash pot," the first said.

"You, Sarty!" the second shouted. "Set up the wash pot!" His father appeared at the door, framed against that shabbiness, as he had been against that other bland perfection, impervious to either, the mother's anxious face at his shoulder.

"Go on," the father said. "Pick it up." The two sisters stooped, broad, lethargic; stooping, they presented an incredible expanse of pale cloth and a flutter of tawdry ribbons.

"If I thought enough of a rug to have to git hit all the way from France I wouldn't keep   50
hit where folks coming in would have to tromp on hit," the first said. They raised the rug.

"Abner," the mother said. "Let me do it."

"You go back and git dinner," his father said. "I'll tend to this."

From the woodpile through the rest of the afternoon the boy watched them, the rug spread flat in the dust beside the bubbling wash pot, the two sisters stooping over it with that profound and lethargic reluctance, while the father stood over them in turn, implacable and grim, driving them though never raising his voice again. He could smell the harsh homemade lye they were using; he saw his mother come to the door once and look toward them with an expression not anxious now but very like despair; he saw his father turn, and he fell to with the axe and saw from the corner of his eye his father raise from the ground a flattish fragment of field stone and examine it and return to the pot, and this time his mother actually spoke: "Abner. Abner. Please don't. Please, Abner."

Then he was done too. It was dusk; the whippoorwills had already begun. He could smell coffee from the room where they would presently eat the cold food remaining from the mid-afternoon meal, though when he entered the house he realized they were having coffee again because there was a fire on the hearth, before which the rug now lay spread over the backs of the two chairs. The tracks of his father's foot were gone. Where they had been were now long, water-cloudy scoriations resembling the sporadic course of a Lilliputian mowing machine.

It still hung there while they ate the cold food and then went to bed, scattered without   55
order or claim up and down the two rooms, his mother in one bed, where his father would later lie, the older brother in the other, himself, the aunt, and the two sisters on pallets on the floor. But his father was not in bed yet. The last thing the boy remembered was the depthless, harsh silhouette of the hat and coat bending over the rug and it seemed to him that he had not even closed his eyes when the silhouette was standing over him, the fire almost dead behind it, the stiff foot prodding him awake. "Catch up the mule," his father said.

When he returned with the mule his father was standing in the black door, the rolled rug over his shoulder. "Ain't you going to ride?" he said.

"No. Give me your foot."

He bent his knee into his father's hand, the wiry, surprising power flowed smoothly, rising, he rising with it, on to the mule's bare back (they had owned a saddle once; the boy could remember it though not when or where) and with the same effortlessness his father swung the rug up in front of him. Now in the starlight they retraced the afternoon's path, up the dusty road rife with honeysuckle, through the gate and up the black tunnel of the drive to the lightless house, where he sat on the mule and felt the rough warp of the rug drag across his thighs and vanish.

"Don't you want me to help?" he whispered. His father did not answer and now he heard again that stiff foot striking the hollow portico with that wooden and clocklike deliberation, that outrageous overstatement of the weight it carried. The rug, hunched, not flung (the boy could tell that even in the darkness) from his father's shoulder, struck the angle of wall and floor with a sound unbelievably loud, thunderous, then the foot again, unhurried and enormous; a light came on in the house and the boy sat, tense, breathing steadily and quietly and just a little fast, though the foot itself did not increase its beat at all, descending the steps now; now the boy could see him.

60 "Don't you want to ride now?" he whispered. "We kin both ride now," the light within the house altering now, flaring up and sinking. *He's coming down the stairs now*, he thought. He had already ridden the mule up beside the horse block; presently his father was up behind him and he doubled the reins over and slashed the mule across the neck, but before the animal could begin to trot the hard, thin arm came round him, the hard, knotted hand jerking the mule back to a walk.

In the first red rays of the sun they were in the lot, putting plow gear on the mules. This time the sorrel mare was in the lot before he heard it at all, the rider collarless and even bareheaded, trembling, speaking in a shaking voice as the woman in the house had done, his father merely looking up once before stooping again to the hame he was buckling, so that the man on the mare spoke to his stooping back:

"You must realize you have ruined that rug. Wasn't there anybody here, any of your women . . ." He ceased, shaking, the boy watching him, the older brother leaning now in the stable door, chewing, blinking slowly and steadily at nothing apparently. "It cost a hundred dollars. But you never had a hundred dollars. You never will. So I'm going to charge you twenty bushels of corn against your crop. I'll add it in your contract and when you come to the commissary you can sign it. That won't keep Mrs. de Spain quiet but maybe it will teach you to wipe your feet off before you enter her house again."

Then he was gone. The boy looked at his father, who still had not spoken or even looked up again, who was now adjusting the logger-head in the hame.

"Pap," he said. His father looked at him—the inscrutable face, the shaggy brows beneath which the gray eyes glinted coldly. Suddenly the boy went toward him, fast, stopping as suddenly. "You done the best you could!" he cried. "If he wanted hit done different why didn't he wait and tell you how? He won't git no twenty bushels! He won't git none! We'll get hit and hide hit! I kin watch . . ."

65 "Did you put the cutter back in that straight stock like I told you?"

"No, sir," he said.

"Then go do it."

That was Wednesday. During the rest of that week he worked steadily, at what was within his scope and some which was beyond it, with an industry that did not need to be driven nor even commanded twice; he had this from his mother, with the difference that some at least of what he did he liked to do, such as splitting wood with the half-size axe which his mother and aunt had earned, or saved money somehow, to present him with at Christmas. In company with the two older women (and on one afternoon even one of the sisters), he built pens for the shoat and the cow which were a part of his father's contract with the landlord, and one afternoon, his father being absent, gone somewhere on one of the mules, he went to the field.

They were running a middle buster now, his brother holding the plow straight while he handled the reins, and walking beside the straining mule, the rich black soil shearing cool and damp against his bare ankles, he thought *Maybe this is the end of it. Maybe even that twenty bushels that seems hard to have to pay for just a rug will be a cheap price for him to stop forever and always from being what he used to be*; thinking, dreaming now, so that his brother had to speak sharply to him to mind the mule: *Maybe he even won't collect the twenty bushels. Maybe it will all add up and balance and vanish—corn, rug, fire; the terror and grief, the being pulled two ways like between two teams of horses—gone, done with forever and ever.*

Then it was Saturday; he looked up from beneath the mule he was harnessing and saw   70
his father in the black coat and hat. "Not that," his father said. "The wagon gear." And
then, two hours later, sitting in the wagon bed behind his father and brother on the seat, the
wagon accomplished a final curve, and he saw the weathered paintless store with its tattered
tobacco- and patent-medicine posters and the tethered wagons and saddle animals below
the gallery. He mounted the gnawed steps behind his father and brother, and there again
was the lane of quiet, watching faces for the three of them to walk through. He saw the man
in spectacles sitting at the plank table and he did not need to be told this was a Justice of the
Peace; he sent one glare of fierce, exultant, partisan defiance at the man in collar and cravat
now, whom he had seen but twice in his life, and that on a galloping horse, who now wore
on his face an expression not of rage but of amazed unbelief which the boy could not have
known was at the incredible circumstance of being sued by one of his own tenants, and came
and stood against his father and cried at the Justice: "He ain't done it! He ain't burnt . . ."

"Go back to the wagon," his father said.

"Burnt?" the Justice said. "Do I understand this rug was burned too?"

"Does anybody here claim it was?" his father said. "Go back to the wagon." But he did
not, he merely retreated to the rear of the room, crowded as that other had been, but not to
sit down this time, instead, to stand pressing among the motionless bodies, listening to the
voices:

"And you claim twenty bushels of corn is too high for the damage you did to the rug?"

"He brought the rug to me and said he wanted the tracks washed out of it. I washed the   75
tracks out and took the rug back to him."

"But you didn't carry the rug back to him in the same condition it was in before you
made the tracks on it."

His father did not answer, and now for perhaps half a minute there was no sound at all
save that of breathing, the faint, steady suspiration of complete and intent listening.

"You decline to answer that, Mr. Snopes?" Again his father did not answer. "I'm going
to find against you, Mr. Snopes. I'm going to find that you were responsible for the injury
to Major de Spain's rug and hold you liable for it. But twenty bushels of corn seems a little
high for a man in your circumstances to have to pay. Major de Spain claims it cost a hundred dollars. October corn will be worth about fifty cents. I figure that if Major de Spain can
stand a ninety-five-dollar loss on something he paid cash for, you can stand a five-dollar
loss you haven't earned yet. I hold you in damages to Major de Spain to the amount of ten
bushels of corn over and above your contract with him, to be paid to him out of your crop
at gathering time. Court adjourned."

It had taken no time hardly, the morning was but half begun. He thought they would
return home and perhaps back to the field, since they were late, far behind all other farmers. But instead his father passed on behind the wagon, merely indicating with his hand
for the older brother to follow with it, and crossed the road toward the blacksmith shop
opposite, pressing on after his father, overtaking him, speaking, whispering up at the
harsh, calm face beneath the weathered hat: "He won't git no ten bushels neither. He
won't git one. We'll . . ." until his father glanced for an instant down on him, the face
absolutely calm, the grizzled eyebrows tangled above the cold eyes, the voice almost
pleasant, almost gentle:

"You think so? Well, we'll wait till October anyway."   80

The matter of the wagon—the setting of a spoke or two and the tightening of the tires—
did not take long either, the business of the tires accomplished by driving the wagon into
the spring branch behind the shop and letting it stand there, the mules nuzzling into the
water from time to time, and the boy on the seat with the idle reins, looking up the slope
and through the sooty tunnel of the shed where the slow hammer rang and where his father
sat on an upended cypress bolt, easily, either talking or listening, still sitting there when the
boy brought the dripping wagon up out of the branch and halted it before the door.

"Take them on to the shade and hitch," his father said. He did so and returned. His father and the smith and a third man squatting on his heels inside the door were talking, about crops and animals; the boy, squatting too in the ammoniac dust and hoof-parings and scales of rust, heard his father tell a long and unhurried story out of the time before the birth of the older brother even when he had been a professional horse-trader. And then his father came up beside him where he stood before a tattered last year's circus poster on the other side of the store, gazing rapt and quiet at the scarlet horses, the incredible poisings and convolutions of tulle and tights and the painted leers of comedians, and said, "It's time to eat."

But not at home. Squatting beside his brother against the front wall, he watched his father emerge from the store and produce from a paper sack a segment of cheese and divided it carefully and deliberately into three with his pocket knife and produce crackers from the same sack. They all three squatted on the gallery and ate slowly, without talking; then in the store again, they drank from a tin dipper tepid water smelling of the cedar bucket and of living beech trees. And still they did not go home. It was a horse lot this time, a tall rail fence upon and along which men stood and sat and out of which one by one horses were led, to be walked and trotted and then cantered back and forth along the road while the slow swapping and buying went on and the sun began to slant westward, they—the three of them—watching and listening, the older brother with his muddy eyes and his steady inevitable tobacco, the father commenting now and then on certain of the animals, to no one in particular.

It was after sundown when they reached home. They ate supper by lamplight, then, sitting on the doorstep, the boy watched the night fully accomplish, listening to the whippoorwills and the frogs, when he heard his mother's voice: "Abner! No! No! Oh, God, Oh, God, Abner!" and he rose, whirled, and saw the altered light through the door where a candle stub now burned in a bottle neck on the table and his father, still in the hat and coat, at once formal and burlesque as though dressed carefully for some shabby and ceremonial violence, emptying the reservoir of the lamp back into the five-gallon kerosene can from which it had been filled, while the mother tugged at his arm until he shifted the lamp to the other hand and flung her back, not savagely or viciously, just hard, into the wall, her hands flung out against the wall for balance, her mouth open and in her face the same quality of hopeless despair as had been in her voice. Then his father saw him standing in the door.

85   "Go to the barn and get that can of oil we were oiling the wagon with," he said. The boy did not move. Then he could speak.

"What . . ." he cried. "What are you . . ."

"Go get that oil," his father said. "Go."

Then he was moving, running, outside the house, toward the stable: this the old habit, the old blood which he had not been permitted to choose for himself, which had been bequeathed him willy nilly and which had run for so long (and who knew where, battening on what of outrage and savagery and lust) before it came to him. *I could keep on,* he thought. *I could run on and on and never look back, never need to see his face again. Only I can't. I can't,* the rusted can in his hand now, the liquid sloshing in it as he ran back to the house and into it, into the sound of his mother's weeping in the next room, and handed the can to his father.

"Ain't you going to even send a nigger?" he cried. "At least you sent a nigger before!"

90   This time his father didn't strike him. The hand came even faster than the blow had, the same hand which had set the can on the table with almost excruciating care flashing from the can toward him too quick for him to follow it, gripping him by the back of his shirt and on to tiptoe before he had seen it quit the can, the face stooping at him in breathless and frozen ferocity, the cold, dead voice speaking over him to the older brother who leaned against the table, chewing with that steady, curious, sidewise motion of cows:

"Empty the can into the big one and go on. I'll catch up with you."

"Better tie him up to the bedpost," the brother said.

"Do like I told you," the father said. Then the boy was moving, his bunched shirt and the hard, bony hand between his shoulder-blades, his toes just touching the floor, across the room and into the other one, past the sisters sitting with spread heavy thighs in the two chairs over the cold hearth, and to where his mother and aunt sat side by side on the bed, the aunt's arms about the mother's shoulders.

"Hold him," the father said. The aunt made a startled movement. "Not you," the father said. "Lennie. Take hold of him. I want to see you do it." His mother took him by the wrist. "You'll hold him better than that. If he gets loose don't you know what he is going to do? He will go up yonder." He jerked his head toward the road. "Maybe I'd better tie him."

"I'll hold him," his mother whispered.   95

"See you do then." Then his father was gone, the stiff foot heavy and measured upon the boards, ceasing at last.

Then he began to struggle. His mother caught him in both arms, he jerking and wrenching at them. He would be stronger in the end, he knew that. But he had not time to wait for it. "Lemme go!" he cried. "I don't want to have to hit you!"

"Let him go!" the aunt said. "If he don't go, before God, I am going up there myself!"

"Don't you see I can't?" his mother cried. "Sarty! Sarty! No! No! Help me, Lizzie!"

Then he was free. His aunt grasped at him but it was too late. He whirled, running, his   100
mother stumbled forward on to her knees behind him, crying to the nearer sister: "Catch him, Net! Catch him!" But that was too late too, the sister (the sisters were twins, born at the same time, yet either of them now gave the impression of being, encompassing as much living meat and volume and weight as any other two of the family) not yet having begun to rise from the chair, her head, face, alone merely turned, presenting to him in the flying instant an astonishing expanse of young female features untroubled by any surprise even, wearing only an expression of bovine interest. Then he was out of the room, out of the house, in the mild dust of the starlit road and the heavy rifeness of honeysuckle, the pale ribbon unspooling with terrific slowness under his running feet, reaching the gate at last and turning in, running, his heart and lungs drumming, on up the drive toward the lighted house, the lighted door. He did not knock, he burst in, sobbing for breath, incapable for the moment of speech; he saw the astonished face of the Negro in the linen jacket without knowing when the Negro had appeared.

"De Spain!" he cried, panted. "Where's . . ." then he saw the white man too emerging from a white door down the hall. "Barn!" he cried. "Barn!"

"What?" the white man said. "Barn?"

"Yes!" the boy cried. "Barn!"

"Catch him!" the white man shouted.

But it was too late this time too. The Negro grasped his shirt, but the entire sleeve, rotten   105
with washing, carried away, and he was out that door too and in the drive again, and had actually never ceased to run even while he was screaming into the white man's face.

Behind him the white man was shouting. "My horse! Fetch my horse!" and he thought for an instant of cutting across the park and climbing the fence into the road, but he did not know the park nor how high the vine-massed fence might be and he dared not risk it. So he ran on down the drive, blood and breath roaring; presently he was in the road again though he could not see it. He could not hear either: the galloping mare was almost upon him before he heard her, and even then he held his course, as if the very urgency of his wild grief and need must in a moment more find him wings, waiting until the ultimate instant to hurl himself aside and into the weed-choked roadside ditch as the horse thundered past and on, for an instant in furious silhouette against the stars, the tranquil early summer night sky which, even before the shape of the horse and rider vanished, strained abruptly and violently upward: a long, swirling roar incredible and soundless, blotting the stars, and he springing up and into the road again, running again, knowing it was too late yet still running even after he heard the shot and, an instant later, two shots, pausing now without knowing he had ceased to run, crying "Pap! Pap!," running again before he knew he had begun to run, stumbling, tripping over something and scrabbling up again without ceasing to run, looking backward over his shoulder at the glare as he got up, running on among the invisible trees, panting, sobbing, "Father! Father!"

At midnight he was sitting on the crest of a hill. He did not know it was midnight and he did not know how far he had come. But there was no glare behind him now and he sat now, his back toward what he had called home for four days anyhow, his face toward the dark woods which he would enter when breath was strong again, small, shaking steadily in the chill darkness, hugging himself into the remainder of his thin, rotten shirt, the grief and despair now no longer terror and fear but just grief and despair. *Father. My father,* he thought. "He was brave!" he cried suddenly, aloud but not loud, no more than a whisper: "He was! He was in the war! He was in Colonel Sartoris' cav'ry!" not knowing that his father had gone to that war a private in the fine old European sense, wearing no uniform, admitting the authority of and giving fidelity to no man or army or flag, going to war as Malbrouck° himself did: for booty—it meant nothing and less than nothing to him if it were enemy booty or his own.

The slow constellations wheeled on. It would be dawn and then sun-up after a while and he would be hungry. But that would be tomorrow and now he was only cold, and walking would cure that. His breathing was easier now and he decided to get up and go on, and then he found that he had been asleep because he knew it was almost dawn, the night almost over. He could tell that from the whippoorwills. They were everywhere now among the dark trees below him, constant and inflectioned and ceaseless, so that, as the instant for giving over to the day birds drew nearer and nearer, there was no interval at all between them. He got up. He was a little stiff, but walking would cure that too as it would the cold, and soon there would be the sun. He went on down the hill, toward the dark woods within which the liquid silver voices of the birds called unceasing—the rapid and urgent beating of the urgent and quiring heart of the late spring night. He did not look back.

QUESTIONS

1. Discuss the style and tone of the final paragraph of "Barn Burning." What does it tell you about Sarty's location and the time of day? How do Faulkner's descriptions suggest that Sarty is embarking on a new phase of his life? Why does Faulkner conclude the paragraph—and the story—with the sentence "He did not look back"?

2. In the Bible (2 Samuel, Chapters 2 and 3) Abner, the cousin of King Saul, is a powerful commander, warrior, and king maker. He is loyal to the son of King Saul and fights against the supporters of King David. Abner's death makes it possible for David to become the uncontested ruler. Why do you think that Faulkner chose the name Abner for the father of the Snopes family? What actions of Abner Snopes make him seem heroic? Antiheroic? Why?

3. When and where is the story occurring? How does Faulkner convey this information to you?

4. Describe the characters of Sarty's mother and sisters. What do you learn about them? To what extent do any of them exhibit growth or development?

5. At the story's end, who is the rider of the horse? Who fires the three shots? Why does Faulkner not tell us the result of the shooting? (In Book I of *The Hamlet*, Faulkner explains that Abner and his other son, Flem, escape.)

°*Malbrouck:* hero of an old French ballad (*Malbrouck s'en va-t-en guerre*). The original Malbrouck, the English Duke of Marlborough (1650–1722), had been accused of profiteering during the War of the Spanish Succession (1702–1713).

CHARLOTTE PERKINS GILMAN (1860–1935)

*Born in 1860, Charlotte Perkins Gilman did not begin writing seri-
ously until after the birth of her daughter in the 1880s, which was
followed by her "nervous breakdown." Attempting to establish her
independence, she left her husband in 1890 and went to California,
where she launched what was to become a distinguished career as an
advocate for women's rights. For many decades she lectured and wrote
extensively, her touchstone work being* Women and Economics
*(1898), in which she championed the need for women's financial inde-
pendence. Among her many writings were* Concerning Children
(1900), Human Work *(1904), and* His Religion and Hers *(1923). In the 1930s she became
incurably ill, and with death facing her, she took her own life in 1935.*

The Yellow Wallpaper° (1892)

It is very seldom that mere ordinary people like John and myself secure ancestral halls for
the summer.

A colonial mansion, a hereditary estate, I would say a haunted house and reach the
height of romantic felicity—but that would be asking too much of fate!

Still I will proudly declare that there is something queer about it.

Else, why should it be let so cheaply? And why have stood so long untenanted?

John laughs at me, of course, but one expects that.   5

John is practical in the extreme. He has no patience with faith, an intense horror of superstition, and he scoffs openly at any talk of things not to be felt and seen and put down in
figures.

John is a physician, and *perhaps*—(I would not say it to a living soul, of course, but this
is dead paper and a great relief to my mind)—*perhaps* that is one reason I do not get well
faster.

You see, he does not believe I am sick! And what can one do?

If a physician of high standing, and one's own husband, assures friends and relatives
that there is really nothing the matter with one but temporary nervous depression—a slight
hysterical tendency—what is one to do?

My brother is also a physician, and also of high standing, and he says the same thing.   10

So I take phosphates or phosphites—whichever it is—and tonics, and air and exercise,
and journeys, and am absolutely forbidden to "work" until I am well again.

Personally, I disagree with their ideas.

Personally, I believe that congenial work, with excitement and change, would do me
good.

But what is one to do?

I did write for a while in spite of them; but it *does* exhaust me a good deal—having to be   15
so sly about it, or else meet with heavy opposition.

I sometimes fancy that in my condition, if I had less opposition and more society and
stimulus—but John says the very worst thing I can do is to think about my condition, and I
confess it always makes me feel bad.

°*The Yellow Wallpaper:* The story is based on the "rest cure" developed after the Civil War by the famous Philadelphia physician S. Weir Mitchell (1829–1914); see paragraph 83. The Mitchell treatment required confining
the patient to a hospital, hotel, or some other remote residence. Once isolated, the patient was to have complete
bed rest, increased food intake, iron supplements, exercise, and sometimes massage and electric shock therapy.
Gilman had experienced Mitchell's "cure," and sent a copy of this story to him as criticism. After receiving the
story Mitchell modified his methods.

So I will let it alone and talk about the house.

The most beautiful place! It is quite alone, standing well back from the road, quite three miles from the village. It makes me think of English places that you read about, for there are hedges and walls and gates that lock, and lots of separate little houses for the gardeners and people.

There is a *delicious* garden! I never saw such a garden—large and shady, full of box-bordered paths, and lined with long grape-covered arbors with seats under them.

20 There were greenhouses, but they are all broken now.

There was some legal trouble, I believe, something about the heirs and co-heirs; anyhow, the place has been empty for years.

That spoils my ghostliness, I am afraid, but I don't care—there is something strange about the house—I can feel it.

I even said so to John one moonlight evening, but he said what I felt was a draught, and shut the window.

I get unreasonably angry with John sometimes. I'm sure I never used to be so sensitive. I think it is due to this nervous condition.

25 But John says if I feel so I shall neglect proper self-control; so I take pains to control myself—before him, at least, and that makes me very tired.

I don't like our room a bit. I wanted one downstairs that opened onto the piazza and had roses all over the window, and such pretty old-fashioned chintz hangings! But John would not hear of it.

He said there was only one window and not room for two beds, and no near room for him if he took another.

He is very careful and loving, and hardly lets me stir without special direction.

I have a schedule prescription for each hour in the day; he takes all care from me, and so I feel basely ungrateful not to value it more.

30 He said he came here solely on my account, that I was to have perfect rest and all the air I could get. "Your exercise depends on your strength, my dear," said he, "and your food somewhat on your appetite; but air you can absorb all the time." So we took the nursery at the top of the house.

It is a big, airy room, the whole floor nearly, with windows that look all ways, and air and sunshine galore. It was nursery first, and then playroom and gymnasium, I should judge, for the windows are barred for little children, and there are rings and things in the walls.

The paint and paper look as if a boys' school had used it. It is stripped off—the paper—in great patches all around the head of my bed, about as far as I can reach, and in a great place on the other side of the room low down. I never saw a worse paper in my life. One of those sprawling, flamboyant patterns committing every artistic sin.

It is dull enough to confuse the eye in following, pronounced enough constantly to irritate and provoke study, and when you follow the lame uncertain curves for a little distance they suddenly commit suicide—plunge off at outrageous angles, destroy themselves in unheard-of contradictions.

The color is repellent, almost revolting: a smouldering unclean yellow, strangely faded by the slow-turning sunlight. It is a dull yet lurid orange in some places, a sickly sulphur tint in others.

35 No wonder the children hated it! I should hate it myself if I had to live in this room long.

There comes John, and I must put this away—he hates to have me write a word.

We have been here two weeks, and I haven't felt like writing before, since that first day.

I am sitting by the window now, up in this atrocious nursery, and there is nothing to hinder my writing as much as I please, save lack of strength.

John is away all day, and even some nights when his cases are serious.

I am glad my case is not serious!

But these nervous troubles are dreadfully depressing.

John does not know how much I really suffer. He knows there is no reason to suffer, and that satisfies him.

Of course it is only nervousness. It does weigh on me so not to do my duty in any way!

I meant to be such a help to John, such a real rest and comfort, and here I am a comparative burden already!

Nobody would believe what an effort it is to do what little I am able—to dress and entertain, and order things.

It is fortunate Mary is so good with the baby. Such a dear baby!

And yet I *cannot* be with him, it makes me so nervous.

I suppose John never was nervous in his life. He laughs at me so about this wallpaper!

At first he meant to repaper the room, but afterward he said that I was letting it get the better of me, and that nothing was worse for a nervous patient than to give way to such fancies.

He said that after the wallpaper was changed it would be the heavy bedstead, and then the barred windows, and then that gate at the head of the stairs, and so on.

"You know the place is doing you good," he said, "and really, dear, I don't care to renovate the house just for a three months' rental."

"Then do let us go downstairs," I said. "There are such pretty rooms there."

Then he took me in his arms and called me a blessed little goose, and said he would go down to the cellar, if I wished, and have it whitewashed into the bargain.

But he is right enough about the beds and windows and things.

It is as airy and comfortable a room as anyone need wish, and, of course, I would not be so silly as to make him uncomfortable just for a whim.

I'm really getting quite fond of the big room, all but that horrid paper.

Out of one window I can see the garden—those mysterious deep-shaded arbors, the riotous old-fashioned flowers, and bushes and gnarly trees.

Out of another I get a lovely view of the bay and a little private wharf belonging to the estate. There is a beautiful shaded lane that runs down there from the house. I always fancy I see people walking in these numerous paths and arbors, but John has cautioned me not to give way to fancy in the least. He says that with my imaginative power and habit of story-making, a nervous weakness like mine is sure to lead to all manner of excited fancies, and that I ought to use my will and good sense to check the tendency. So I try.

I think sometimes that if I were only well enough to write a little it would relieve the press of ideas and rest me.

But I find I get pretty tired when I try.

It is so discouraging not to have any advice and companionship about my work. When I get really well, John says we will ask Cousin Henry and Julia down for a long visit; but he says he would as soon put fireworks in my pillow-case as to let me have those stimulating people about now.

I wish I could get well faster.

But I must not think about that. This paper looks to me as if it *knew* what a vicious influence it had!

There is a recurrent spot where the pattern lolls like a broken neck and two bulbous eyes stare at you upside down.

I get positively angry with the impertinence of it and the everlastingness. Up and down and sideways they crawl, and those absurd unblinking eyes are everywhere. There is one place where two breadths didn't match, and the eyes go all up and down the line, one a little higher than the other.

I never saw so much expression in an inanimate thing before, and we all know how much expression they have! I used to lie awake as a child and get more entertainment and terror out of blank walls and plain furniture than most children could find in a toy-store.

I remember what a kindly wink the knobs of our big old bureau used to have, and there was one chair that always seemed like a strong friend.

I used to feel that if any of the other things looked too fierce I could always hop into that chair and be safe.

The furniture in this room is no worse than inharmonious, however, for we had to bring it all from downstairs. I suppose when this was used as a playroom they had to take the nursery things out, and no wonder! I never saw such ravages as the children have made here.

The wallpaper, as I said before, is torn off in spots, and it sticketh closer than a brother°— they must have had perseverance as well as hatred.

Then the floor is scratched and gouged and splintered, the plaster itself is dug out here and there, and this great heavy bed, which is all we found in the room, looks as if it had been through the wars.

But I don't mind it a bit—only the paper.

There comes John's sister. Such a dear girl as she is, and careful of me! I must not let her find me writing.

She is a perfect and enthusiastic housekeeper, and hopes for no better profession. I verily believe she thinks it is the writing which made me sick!

But I can write when she is out, and see her a long way off from these windows.

There is one that commands the road, a lovely shaded winding road, and one that just looks off over the country. A lovely country, too, full of great elms and velvet meadows.

This wallpaper has a kind of sub-pattern in a different shade, a particularly irritating one, for you can only see it in certain lights, and not clearly then.

But in the places where it isn't faded and where the sun is just so—I can see a strange, provoking, formless sort of figure that seems to skulk about behind that silly and conspicuous front design.

There's sister on the stairs!

Well, the Fourth of July is over! The people are all gone, and I am tired out. John thought it might do me good to see a little company, so we just had Mother and Nellie and the children down for a week.

Of course I didn't do a thing. Jennie sees to everything now.

But it tired me all the same.

John says if I don't pick up faster he shall send me to Weir Mitchell° in the fall.

But I don't want to go there at all. I had a friend who was in his hands once, and she says he is just like John and my brother, only more so!

Besides, it is such an undertaking to go so far.

I don't feel as if it was worthwhile to turn my hand over for anything, and I'm getting dreadfully fretful and querulous.

I cry at nothing, and cry most of the time.

Of course I don't when John is here, or anybody else, but when I am alone.

And I am alone a good deal just now. John is kept in town very often by serious cases, and Jennie is good and lets me alone when I want her to.

So I walk a little in the garden or down that lovely lane, sit on the porch under the roses, and lie down up here a good deal.

°*sticketh closer than a brother:* Proverbs 18:24.

°*Weir Mitchell:* See note on page 473.

I'm getting really fond of the room in spite of the wallpaper. Perhaps *because* of the wallpaper.

It dwells in my mind so!

I lie here on this great immovable bed—it is nailed down, I believe—and follow that pattern about by the hour. It is as good as gymnastics, I assure you. I start, we'll say, at the bottom, down in the corner over there where it has not been touched, and I determine for the thousandth time that I *will* follow that pointless pattern to some sort of a conclusion.

I know a little of the principle of design, and I know this thing was not arranged on any laws of radiation, or alternation, or repetition, or symmetry, or anything else that I ever heard of.

It is repeated, of course, by the breadths, but not otherwise.   95

Looked at in one way, each breadth stands alone; the bloated curves and flourishes—a kind of "debased Romanesque" with delirium tremens—go waddling up and down in isolated columns of fatuity.

But, on the other hand, they connect diagonally, and the sprawling outlines run off in great slanting waves of optic horror, like a lot of wallowing sea-weeds in full chase.

The whole thing goes horizontally, too, at least it seems so, and I exhaust myself trying to distinguish the order of its going in that direction.

They have used a horizontal breadth for a frieze, and that adds wonderfully to the confusion.

There is one end of the room where it is almost intact, and there, when the crosslights   100
fade and the low sun shines directly upon it, I can almost fancy radiation after all—the interminable grotesque seems to form around a common center and rush off in headlong plunges of equal distraction.

It makes me tired to follow it. I will take a nap, I guess.

I don't know why I should write this.

I don't want to.

I don't feel able.

And I know John would think it absurd. But I *must* say what I feel and think in some   105
way—it is such a relief!

But the effort is getting to be greater than the relief.

Half the time now I am awfully lazy, and lie down ever so much. John says I mustn't lose my strength, and has me take cod liver oil and lots of tonics and things, to say nothing of ale and wine and rare meat.

Dear John! He loves me very dearly, and hates to have me sick. I tried to have a real earnest reasonable talk with him the other day, and tell him how I wish he would let me go and make a visit to Cousin Henry and Julia.

But he said I wasn't able to go, nor able to stand it after I got there; and I did not make out a very good case for myself, for I was crying before I had finished.

It is getting to be a great effort for me to think straight. Just this nervous weakness, I   110
suppose.

And dear John gathered me up in his arms, and just carried me upstairs and laid me on the bed, and sat by me and read to me till it tired my head.

He said I was his darling and his comfort and all he had, and that I must take care of myself for his sake, and keep well.

He says no one but myself can help me out of it, that I must use my will and self-control and not let any silly fancies run away with me.

There's one comfort—the baby is well and happy, and does not have to occupy this nursery with the horrid wallpaper.

If we had not used it, that blessed child would have! What a fortunate escape! Why, I   115
wouldn't have a child of mine, an impressionable little thing, live in such a room for worlds.

I never thought of it before, but it is lucky that John kept me here after all; I can stand it so much easier than a baby, you see.

Of course I never mention it to them any more—I am too wise—but I keep watch for it all the same.

There are things in that wallpaper that nobody knows about but me, or ever will.

Behind that outside pattern the dim shapes get clearer every day.

120 It is always the same shape, only very numerous.

And it is like a woman stooping down and creeping about behind that pattern. I don't like it a bit. I wonder—I begin to think—I wish John would take me away from here!

It is so hard to talk with John about my case, because he is so wise, and because he loves me so.

But I tried it last night.

It was moonlight. The moon shines in all around just as the sun does.

125 I hate to see it sometimes, it creeps so slowly, and always comes in by one window or another.

John was asleep and I hated to waken him, so I kept still and watched the moonlight on that undulating wallpaper till I felt creepy.

The faint figure behind seemed to shake the pattern, just as if she wanted to get out.

I got up softly and went to feel and see if the paper *did* move, and when I came back John was awake.

"What is it, little girl?" he said. "Don't go walking about like that—you'll get cold."

130 I thought it was a good time to talk, so I told him that I really was not gaining here, and that I wished he would take me away.

"Why, darling!" said he. "Our lease will be up in three weeks, and I can't see how to leave before.

"The repairs are not done at home, and I cannot possibly leave town just now. Of course, if you were in any danger, I could and would, but you really are better, dear, whether you can see it or not. I am a doctor, dear, and I know. You are gaining flesh and color, your appetite is better, I feel really much easier about you."

"I don't weigh a bit more," said I, "nor as much; and my appetite may be better in the evening when you are here but it is worse in the morning when you are away!"

"Bless her little heart!" said he with a big hug. "She shall be as sick as she pleases! But now let's improve the shining hours by going to sleep, and talk about it in the morning!"

135 "And you won't go away?" I asked gloomily.

"Why, how can I, dear? It is only three weeks more and then we will take a nice little trip of a few days while Jennie is getting the house ready. Really, dear, you are better!"

"Better in body perhaps—" I began, and stopped short, for he sat up straight and looked at me with such a stern, reproachful look that I could not say another word.

"My darling," said he, "I beg of you, for my sake and for our child's sake, as well as for your own, that you will never for one instant let that idea enter your mind! There is nothing so dangerous, so fascinating, to a temperament like yours. It is a false and foolish fancy. Can you not trust me as a physician when I tell you so?"

So of course I said no more on that score, and we went to sleep before long. He thought I was asleep first, but I wasn't, and lay there for hours trying to decide whether that front pattern and the back pattern really did move together or separately.

140 On a pattern like this, by daylight, there is a lack of sequence, a defiance of law, that is a constant irritant to a normal mind.

The color is hideous enough, and unreliable enough, and infuriating enough, but the pattern is torturing.

You think you have mastered it, but just as you get well under way in following, it turns a back-somersault and there you are. It slaps you in the face, knocks you down, and tramples upon you. It is like a bad dream.

The outside pattern is a florid arabesque, reminding one of a fungus. If you can imagine a toadstool in joints an interminable string of toadstools, budding and sprouting in endless convolutions—why, that is something like it.

That is, sometimes!

There is one marked peculiarity about this paper, a thing nobody seems to notice but myself, and that is that it changes as the light changes.

When the sun shoots in through the east window—I always watch for that first long, straight ray—it changes so quickly than I never can quite believe it.

That is why I watch it always.

By moonlight—the moon shines in all night when there is a moon—I wouldn't know it was the same paper.

At night in any kind of light, in twilight, candlelight, lamplight, and worst of all by moonlight, it becomes bars! The outside pattern, I mean, and the woman behind it is as plain as can be.

I didn't realize for a long time what the thing was that showed behind, that dim sub-pattern, but now I am quite sure it is a woman.

By daylight she is subdued, quiet. I fancy it is the pattern that keeps her so still. It is so puzzling. It keeps me quiet by the hour.

I lie down ever so much now. John says it is good for me, and to sleep all I can.

Indeed he started the habit by making me lie down for an hour after each meal.

It is a very bad habit, I am convinced, for you see, I don't sleep.

And that cultivates deceit, for I don't tell them I'm awake—oh, no!

The fact is I am getting a little afraid of John.

He seems very queer sometimes, and even Jennie has an inexplicable look.

It strikes me occasionally, just as a scientific hypothesis, that perhaps it is the paper!

I have watched John when he did not know I was looking, and come into the room suddenly on the most innocent excuses, and I've caught him several times *looking at the paper*! And Jennie too. I caught Jennie with her hand on it once.

She didn't know I was in the room, and when I asked her in a quiet, a very quiet voice, with the most restrained manner possible, what she was doing with the paper, she turned around as if she had been caught stealing, and looked quite angry—asked me why I should frighten her so!

Then she said that the paper stained everything it touched, that she had found yellow smooches on all my clothes and John's and she wished we would be more careful!

Did not that sound innocent? But I know she was studying that pattern, and I am determined that nobody shall find it out but myself.

Life is very much more exciting now than it used to be. You see, I have something more to expect, to look forward to, to watch. I really do eat better, and am more quiet than I was.

John is so pleased to see me improve! He laughed a little the other day, and said I seemed to be flourishing in spite of my wallpaper.

I turned it off with a laugh. I had no intention of telling him it was *because* of the wallpaper—he would make fun of me. He might even want to take me away.

I don't want to leave now until I have found it out. There is a week more, and I think that will be enough.

I'm feeling so much better!

I don't sleep much at night, for it is so interesting to watch developments; but sleep a good deal during the daytime.

In the daytime it is tiresome and perplexing.

There are always new shoots on the fungus, and new shades of yellow all over it. I cannot keep count of them, though I have tried conscientiously.

It is the strangest yellow, that wallpaper! It makes me think of all the yellow things I ever saw—not beautiful ones like buttercups, but old, foul, bad yellow things.

But there is something else about that paper—the smell! I noticed it the moment we came into the room, but with so much air and sun it was not bad. Now we have had a week of fog and rain, and whether the windows are open or not, the smell is here.

It creeps all over the house.

I find it hovering in the dining-room, skulking in the parlor, hiding in the hall, lying in wait for me on the stairs.

175   It gets into my hair.

Even when I go to ride, if I turn my head suddenly and surprise it—there is that smell!

Such a peculiar odor, too! I have spent hours in trying to analyze it, to find what it smelled like.

It is not bad—at first—and very gentle, but quite the subtlest, most enduring odor I ever met.

In this damp weather it is awful. I wake up in the night and find it hanging over me.

180   It used to disturb me at first. I thought seriously of burning the house—to reach the smell.

But now I am used to it. The only thing I can think of that it is like is the *color* of the paper! A yellow smell.

There is a very funny mark on this wall, low down, near the mopboard. A streak that runs round the room. It goes behind every piece of furniture, except the bed, a long, straight, even *smooch*, as if it had been rubbed over and over.

I wonder how it was done and who did it, and what they did it for. Round and round and round—round and round and round—it makes me dizzy!

I really have discovered something at last.

185   Through watching so much at night, when it changes so, I have finally found out.

The front pattern *does* move—and no wonder! The woman behind shakes it!

Sometimes I think there are a great many women behind, and sometimes only one, and she crawls around fast, and her crawling shakes it all over.

Then in the very bright spots she keeps still, and in the very shady spots she just takes hold of the bars and shakes them hard.

And she is all the time trying to climb through. But nobody could climb through that pattern—it strangles so; I think that is why it has so many heads.

190   They get through and then the pattern strangles them off and turns them upside down, and makes their eyes white!

If those heads were covered or taken off it would not be half so bad.

I think that woman gets out in the daytime!

And I'll tell you why—privately—I've seen her!

I can see her out of every one of my windows!

195   It is the same woman, I know, for she is always creeping, and most women do not creep by daylight.

I see her in that long shaded lane, creeping up and down. I see her in those dark grape arbors, creeping all around the garden.

I see her on that long road under the trees, creeping along, and when a carriage comes she hides under the blackberry vines.

I don't blame her a bit. It must be very humiliating to be caught creeping by daylight!

I always lock the door when I creep by daylight. I can't do it at night, for I know John would suspect something at once.

200   And John is so queer now that I don't want to irritate him. I wish he would take another room! Besides, I don't want anybody to get that woman out at night but myself.

I often wonder if I could see her out of all the windows at once.

But, turn as fast as I can, I can only see out of one at a time.

And though I always see her, she *may* be able to creep faster than I can turn! I have watched her sometimes away off in the open country, creeping as fast as a cloud shadow in a wind.

If only that top pattern could be gotten off from the under one! I mean to try it, little by little.

I have found out another funny thing, but I shan't tell it this time! It does not do to trust 205 people too much.

There are only two more days to get this paper off, and I believe John is beginning to notice. I don't like the look in his eyes.

And I heard him ask Jennie a lot of professional questions about me. She had a very good report to give.

She said I slept a good deal in the daytime.

John knows I don't sleep very well at night, for all I'm so quiet!

He asked me all sorts of questions, too, and pretended to be very loving and kind. 210

As if I couldn't see through him!

Still, I don't wonder he acts so, sleeping under this paper for three months.

It only interests me, but I feel sure John and Jennie are affected by it.

• • •

Hurrah! This is the last day, but it is enough. John is to stay in town over night, and won't be out until this evening.

Jennie wanted to sleep with me—the sly thing; but I told her I should undoubtedly rest 215 better for a night all alone.

That was clever, for really I wasn't alone a bit! As soon as it was moonlight and that poor thing began to crawl and shake the pattern, I got up and ran to help her.

I pulled and she shook. I shook and she pulled, and before morning we had peeled off yards of that paper.

A strip about as high as my head and half around the room.

And then when the sun came and that awful pattern began to laugh at me, I declared I would finish it today!

We go away tomorrow, and they are moving all my furniture down again to leave things 220 as they were before.

Jennie looked at the wall in amazement, but I told her merrily that I did it out of pure spite at the vicious thing.

She laughed and said she wouldn't mind doing it herself, but I must not get tired.

How she betrayed herself that time!

But I am here, and no person touches this paper but Me—not *alive*!

She tried to get me out of the room—it was too patent! But I said it was so quiet and 225 empty and clean now that I believed I would lie down again and sleep all I could, and not to wake me even for dinner—I would call when I woke.

So now she is gone, and the servants are gone, and the things are gone, and there is nothing left but that great bedstead nailed down, with the canvas mattress we found on it.

We shall sleep downstairs tonight, and take the boat home tomorrow.

I quite enjoy the room, now it is bare again.

How those children did tear about here!

This bedstead is fairly gnawed! 230

But I must get to work.

I have locked the door and thrown the key down into the front path.

I don't want to go out, and I don't want to have anybody come in, till John comes.

I want to astonish him.

I've got a rope up here that even Jennie did not find. If that woman does get out, and 235 tries to get away, I can tie her!

But I forgot I could not reach far without anything to stand on!

This bed will *not* move!

I tried to lift and push it until I was lame, and then I got so angry I bit off a little piece at one corner—but it hurt my teeth.

Then I peeled off all the paper I could reach standing on the floor. It sticks horribly and the pattern just enjoys it! All those strangled heads and bulbous eyes and waddling fungus growths just shriek with derision!

240   I am getting angry enough to do something desperate. To jump out of the window would be admirable exercise, but the bars are too strong even to try.

Besides I wouldn't do it. Of course not. I know well enough that a step like that is improper and might be misconstrued.

I don't like to *look* out of the windows even—there are so many of those creeping women, and they creep so fast.

I wonder if they all came out of that wallpaper as I did?

But I am securely fastened now by my well-hidden rope—you don't get *me* out in the road there!

245   I suppose I shall have to get back behind the pattern when it comes night, and that is hard!

It is so pleasant to be out in this great room and creep around as I please!

I don't want to go outside. I won't, even if Jennie asks me to.

For outside you have to creep on the ground, and everything is green instead of yellow.

But here I can creep smoothly on the floor, and my shoulder just fits in that long smooch around the wall, so I cannot lose my way.

250   Why, there's John at the door!

It is no use, young man, you can't open it!

How he does call and pound!

Now he's crying to Jennie for an axe.

It would be a shame to break down that beautiful door!

255   "John, dear!" said I in the gentlest voice. "The key is down by the front steps, under a plantain leaf!"

That silenced him for a few moments.

Then he said, very quietly indeed, "Open the door, my darling!"

"I can't," said I. "The key is down by the front door under a plantain leaf!" And then I said it again, several times, very gently and slowly, and said it so often that he had to go and see, and he got it of course, and came in. He stopped short by the door.

"What is the matter?" he cried. "For God's sake, what are you doing!"

260   I kept on creeping just the same, but I looked at him over my shoulder.

"I've got out at last," said I, "in spite of you and Jane. And I've pulled off most of the paper, so you can't put me back!"

Now why should that man have fainted? But he did, and right across my path by the wall, so that I had to creep over him every time!

QUESTIONS

1. Describe the point of view of "The Yellow Wallpaper." How consistent is the point of view? How is the story told? To whom does the narrator seem to be speaking? How does the narrator change as the story progresses?

2. How much time elapses in the story? How well does this passage of time explain what is happening to the narrator?

3. What is the narrator's connection to the room's wallpaper? What has she obviously been doing in the course of the story? What does this show about her mental condition?

4. How effectively can a case be made that the "treatment" the narrator receives is actually the cause of her mental disturbance, which is so evident at the story's end?

JAMAICA KINCAID

Jamaica Kincaid was born Elaine Potter Richardson in 1949 in St. John's, capital of the West Indian island nation of Antigua and Barbuda (she adopted the name Jamaica Kincaid in 1973 because of her family's disapproval of her writing). In 1965 she was sent to Westchester County, New York, to work as an au pair (or "servant," as she prefers to describe it). She attended Franconia College in New Hampshire, but did not complete a degree. Kincaid worked as a staff writer for the New Yorker *for nearly twenty years;* Talk Stories *(2001) is a collection of seventy-seven short pieces that she wrote for the magazine. She won wide attention for* At the Bottom of the River *(1983), the volume of her stories that includes "Girl." In 1985 she published* Annie John, *an interlocking cycle of short stories about growing up in Antigua.* Lucy *(1990) was her first novel; it was followed by* The Autobiography of My Mother *(1996) and* Mr. Potter *(2002), novels inspired by the lives of her parents. Kincaid is also the author of* A Small Place *(1988), a memoir of her homeland and meditation on the destructiveness of colonialism, and* My Brother *(1997), a reminiscence of her brother Devon, who died of AIDS at thirty-three. Her most recent work is* Among Flowers: A Walk in the Himalaya *(2005), a travel book. A naturalized U.S. citizen, Kincaid has said of her adopted country: "It's given me a place to be myself—but myself as I was formed somewhere else." She currently teaches at Claremont McKenna College in Southern California.*

Girl 1983

Wash the white clothes on Monday and put them on the stone heap; wash the color clothes on Tuesday and put them on the clothesline to dry; don't walk barehead in the hot sun; cook pumpkin fritters in very hot sweet oil; soak your little cloths right after you take them off; when buying cotton to make yourself a nice blouse, be sure that it doesn't have gum on it, because that way it won't hold up well after a wash; soak salt fish overnight before you cook it; is it true that you sing benna° in Sunday school?; always eat your food in such a way that it won't turn someone else's stomach; on Sundays try to walk like a lady and not like the slut you are so bent on becoming; don't sing benna in Sunday school; you mustn't speak to wharf-rat boys, not even to give directions; don't eat fruits on the street—flies will follow you; *but I don't sing benna on Sundays at all and never in Sunday school;* this is how to sew on a button; this is how to make a buttonhole for the button you have just sewed on; this is how to hem a dress when you see the hem coming down and so to prevent yourself from looking like the slut I know you are so bent on becoming; this is how you iron your father's khaki shirt so that it doesn't have a crease; this is how you iron your father's khaki pants so that they don't have a crease; this is how you grow okra—far from the house, because okra tree harbors red ants; when you are growing dasheen, make sure it gets plenty of water or else it makes your throat itch when you are eating it; this is how you sweep a corner; this is how you sweep a whole house; this is how you sweep a yard; this is how you smile to someone you don't like too much; this is how you smile to someone you don't like at all; this is how you smile to someone you like completely; this is how you set a table for tea; this is how you set a table for dinner; this is how you set a table for dinner with an important guest; this is how you set a table for lunch; this is how you set a table for breakfast; this is how to behave in the presence of men who don't know you very well, and this way they

---

°benna: Kincaid defined this word, for two editors who inquired, as meaning "songs of the sort your parents didn't want you to sing, at first calypso and later rock and roll" (quoted by Sylvan Barnet and Marcia Stubbs, *The Little Brown Reader*, 2nd ed. [Boston: Little, Brown, 1980] 74).

won't recognize immediately the slut I have warned you against becoming; be sure to wash every day, even if it is with your own spit; don't squat down to play marbles—you are not a boy, you know; don't pick people's flowers—you might catch something; don't throw stones at blackbirds, because it might not be a blackbird at all; this is how to make a bread pudding; this is how to make doukona; this is how to make pepper pot; this is how to make a good medicine for a cold; this is how to make a good medicine to throw away a child before it even becomes a child; this is how to catch a fish; this is how to throw back a fish you don't like, and that way something bad won't fall on you; this is how to bully a man; this is how a man bullies you; this is how to love a man, and if this doesn't work there are other ways, and if they don't work don't feel too bad about giving up; this is how to spit up in the air if you feel like it, and this is how to move quick so that it doesn't fall on you; this is how to make ends meet; always squeeze bread to make sure it's fresh; *but what if the baker won't let me feel the bread?*; you mean to say that after all you are really going to be the kind of woman who the baker won't let near the bread?

QUESTIONS

1. Who is the speaker of "Girl"? Who is the listener?
2. What do we specifically know about the mother and daughter from the story? What can we infer?
3. What words of the daughter appear in the story?
4. How different do you think the story would be if the daughter were given a chance to respond?
5. Do you think the mother offers her daughter good advice?

FLANNERY O'CONNOR (1925–1964)

Mary Flannery O'Connor, a Georgia native, graduated from the Women's College of Georgia and received a master of fine arts degree from the University of Iowa in 1947. She contracted lupus, a disorder of the immune system, and was an invalid for the last ten years of her life. Despite her illness, she wrote extensively, publishing two novels and many short stories. Her first collection was A Good Man Is Hard to Find, in 1955. A posthumous collection, Everything That Rises Must Converge, was published in 1965, and Complete Stories appeared in 1971. Her works combine flat realism with grotesque situations; violence occurs without apparent reason or preparation. Many of her characters are odd, eccentric, and bizarre. Others, such as the Misfit in "A Good Man Is Hard to Find," are gratuitously cruel. Ironically, however, their cold and depraved actions highlight the need for religious awakening because they enable some of the characters, such as the grandmother in the following story, to achieve spiritual elevation.

A Good Man Is Hard to Find (1955)

The grandmother didn't want to go to Florida. She wanted to visit some of her connections in east Tennessee and she was seizing at every chance to change Bailey's mind. Bailey was the son she lived with, her only son. He was sitting on the edge of his chair at the table, bent over the orange sports section of the *Journal*. "Now look here, Bailey," she said, "see here, read this," and she stood with one hand on her thin hip and the other rattling the newspaper at his bald head. "Here this fellow that calls himself The Misfit is aloose from the Federal Pen and headed toward Florida and you read here what it says he did to these people. Just you read it I wouldn't take my children in any direction with a criminal like that aloose in it. I couldn't answer to my conscience if I did."

Bailey didn't look up from his reading so she wheeled around then and faced the children's mother, a young woman in slacks, whose face was as broad and innocent as a cabbage and was tied round with a green head-kerchief that had two points on the top like rabbit's ears. She was sitting on the sofa, feeding the baby his apricots out of a jar. "The children have been to Florida before," the old lady said. "You all ought to take them somewhere else for a change so they would see different parts of the world and be broad. They never have been to east Tennessee."

The children's mother didn't seem to hear her but the eight-year-old boy, John Wesley, a stocky child with glasses, said, "If you don't want to go to Florida, why dontcha stay at home?" He and the little girl, June Star, were reading the funny papers on the floor.

"She wouldn't stay at home to be queen for a day," June Star said without raising her yellow head.

"Yes and what would you do if this fellow, The Misfit, caught you?" the grandmother asked.   5

"I'd smack his face," John Wesley said.

"She wouldn't stay at home for a million bucks." June Star said. "Afraid she'd miss something. She has to go everywhere we go."

"All right, Miss," the grandmother said. "Just remember that the next time you want me to curl your hair."

June Star said her hair was naturally curly.

The next morning the grandmother was the first one in the car, ready to go. She had her   10 big black valise that looked like the head of a hippopotamus in one corner, and underneath it she was hiding a basket with Pitty Sing, the cat, in it. She didn't intend for the cat to be left alone in the house for three days because he would miss her too much and she was afraid he might brush against one of the gas burners and accidentally asphyxiate himself. Her son, Bailey, didn't like to arrive at a motel with a cat.

She sat in the middle of the back seat with John Wesley and June Star on either side of her. Bailey and the children's mother and the baby sat in the front and they left Atlanta at eight forty-five with the mileage on the car at 55890. The grandmother wrote this down because she thought it would be interesting to say how many miles they had been when they got back. It took them twenty minutes to reach the outskirts of the city.

The old lady settled herself comfortably, removing her white cotton gloves and putting them up with her purse on the shelf in front of the back window. The children's mother still had on slacks and still had her head tied up in a green kerchief, but the grandmother had on a navy blue straw sailor hat with a bunch of white violets on the brim and a navy blue dress with a small white dot in the print. Her collar and cuffs were white organdy trimmed with lace and at her neckline she had pinned a purple spray of cloth violets containing a sachet. In case of an accident, anyone seeing her dead on the highway would know at once that she was a lady.

She said she thought it was going to be a good day for driving, neither too hot nor too cold, and she cautioned Bailey that the speed limit was fifty-five miles an hour and that the patrolmen hid themselves behind billboards and small clumps of trees and sped out after you before you had a chance to slow down. She pointed out interesting details of the scenery: Stone Mountain; the blue granite that in some places came up to both sides of the highway; the brilliant red clay banks slightly streaked with purple; and the various crops that made rows of green lacework on the ground. The trees were full of silver-white sunlight and the meanest of them sparkled. The children were reading comic magazines and their mother had gone back to sleep.

"Let's go through Georgia fast so we won't have to look at it much," John Wesley said.

15 "If I were a little boy," said the grandmother. "I wouldn't talk about my native state that way. Tennessee has the mountains and Georgia has the hills."

"Tennessee is just a hillbilly dumping ground," John Wesley said, "and Georgia is a lousy state too."

"You said it," June Star said.

"In my time," said the grandmother, folding her thin veined fingers, "children were more respectful of their native states and their parents and everything else. People did right then. Oh look at the cute little pickaninny!" she said and pointed to a Negro child standing in the door of a shack. "Wouldn't that make a picture, now?" she asked and they all turned and looked at the little Negro out of the back window. He waved.

"He didn't have any britches on," June said.

20 "He probably didn't have any," the grandmother explained. "Little niggers in the country don't have things like we do. If I could paint, I'd paint that picture," she said.

The children exchanged comic books.

The grandmother offered to hold the baby and the children's mother passed him over the front seat to her. She set him on her knee and bounced him and told him about the things they were passing. She rolled her eyes and screwed up her mouth and stuck her leathery thin face into his smooth bland one. Occasionally he gave her a faraway smile. They passed a large cotton field with five or six graves fenced in the middle of it, like a small island. "Look at the graveyard!" the grandmother said, pointing it out. "That was the old family burying ground. That belonged to the plantation."

"Where's the plantation?" John Wesley asked.

"Gone With the Wind," said the grandmother. "Ha. Ha."

25 When the children finished all the comic books they had brought, they opened the lunch and ate it. The grandmother ate a peanut butter sandwich and an olive and would not let the children throw the box and the paper napkins out the window. When there was nothing else to do they played a game by choosing a cloud and making the other two guess what shape it suggested. John Wesley took one the shape of a cow and June Star guessed a cow and John Wesley said, no, an automobile, and June Star said he didn't play fair, and they began to slap each other over the grandmother.

The grandmother said she would tell them a story if they would keep quiet. When she told a story, she rolled her eyes and waved her head and was very dramatic. She said once when she was a maiden lady she had been courted by a Mr. Edgar Atkins Teagarden from Jasper, Georgia. She said he was a very good-looking man and a gentleman and that he brought her a watermelon every Saturday afternoon with his initials cut in it, E. A. T. Well, one Saturday, she said, Mr. Teagarden brought the watermelon and there was nobody at home and he left it on the front porch and returned in his buggy to Jasper, but she never got the watermelon, she said, because a nigger boy ate it when he saw the initials, E. A. T.! This story tickled John Wesley's funny bone and he giggled and giggled but June Star didn't think it was any good. She said she wouldn't marry a man that just brought her a watermelon on Saturday. The grandmother said she would have done well to marry Mr. Teagarden because he was a gentleman and had bought Coca-Cola stock when it first came out and that he had died only a few years ago, a very wealthy man.

They stopped at The Tower for barbecued sandwiches. The Tower was a part stucco and part wood filling station and dance hall set in a clearing outside of Timothy. A fat man named Red Sammy Butts ran it and there were signs stuck here and there on the building and for miles up and down the highway saying, TRY RED SAMMY'S FAMOUS BARBECUE. NONE LIKE FAMOUS RED SAMMY'S! RED SAM! THE FAT BOY WITH THE HAPPY LAUGH A VETERAN! SAMMY'S YOUR MAN!

Red Sammy was lying on the bare ground outside The Tower with his head under a truck while a gray monkey about a foot high, chained to a small chinaberry tree, chattered nearby. The monkey sprang back into the tree and got on the highest limb as soon as he saw the children jump out of the car and run toward him.

Inside, The Tower was a long dark room with a counter at one end and tables at the other and dancing space in the middle. They all sat down at a broad table next to the nickelodeon and Red Sam's wife, a tall burnt-brown woman with hair and eyes lighter than her skin, came and took their order. The children's mother put a dime in the machine and played "The Tennessee Waltz," and the grandmother said the tune always made her want to dance. She asked Bailey if he would like to dance but he only glared at her. He didn't have a naturally sunny disposition like she did and trips made him nervous. The grandmother's brown eyes were very bright. She swayed her head from side to side and pretended she was dancing in her chair. June Star said play something she could tap to so the children's mother put in another dime and played a fast number and June Star stepped out onto the dance floor and did her tap routine.

"Ain't she cute?" Red Sam's wife said, leaning over the counter. "Would you like to come be my little girl?"   30

"No I certainly wouldn't," June Star said. "I wouldn't live in a broken-down place like this for a million bucks!" and she ran back to the table.

"Ain't she cute?" the woman repeated, stretching her mouth politely.

"Aren't you ashamed?" hissed her grandmother.

Red Sam came in and told his wife to quit lounging on the counter and hurry with these people's order. His khaki trousers reached just to his hip bones and his stomach hung over them like a sack of meal swaying under his shirt. He came over and sat down at a table nearby and let out a combination sigh and yodel, "You can't win," he said. "You can't win," and he wiped his sweating red face with a gray handkerchief. "These days you don't know who to trust," he said. "Ain't that the truth?"

"People are certainly not nice like they used to be," said the grandmother.   35

"Two fellers come in here last week," Red Sammy said, "driving a Chrysler. It was a old beat-up car but it was a good one and these boys looked all right to me. Said they worked at the mill and you know I let them fellers charge the gas they bought? Now why did I do that?"

"Because you're a good man!" the grandmother said at once.

"Yes'm, I suppose so," Red Sam said as if he were struck with the answer.

His wife brought the orders, carrying the five plates all at once without a tray, two in each hand and one balanced on her arm. "It isn't a soul in this green world of God's that you can trust," she said. "And I don't count anybody out of that, not nobody," she repeated, looking at Red Sammy.

"Did you read about that criminal, The Misfit, that's escaped?" asked the grandmother.   40

"I wouldn't be a bit surprised if he didn't attack this place right here," said the woman. "If he hears about it being here, I wouldn't be none surprised to see him. If he hears it's two cent in the cash register, I wouldn't be a tall surprised if he . . ."

"That'll do," Red Sam said, "Go bring these people their Co'Colas," and the woman went off to get the rest of the order.

"A good man is hard to find," Red Sammy said. "Everything is getting terrible. I remember the day you could go off and leave your screen door unlatched. Not no more."

He and the grandmother discussed better times. The old lady said that in her opinion Europe was entirely to blame for the way things were now. She said the way Europe acted you would think we were made of money and Red Sam said it was no use talking about it, she was exactly right. The children ran outside into the white sunlight and looked at the monkey in the lacy chinaberry tree. He was busy catching fleas on himself and biting each one carefully between his teeth as if it were a delicacy.

45   They drove off again into the hot afternoon. The grandmother took cat naps and woke up every few minutes with her own snoring. Outside of Toombsboro she woke up and recalled an old plantation that she had visited in this neighborhood once when she was a young lady. She said the house had six white columns across the front and that there was an avenue of oaks leading up to it and two little wooden trellis arbors on either side in front where you sat down with your suitor after a stroll in the garden. She recalled exactly which road to turn off to get to it. She knew that Bailey would not be willing to lose any time looking at an old house, but the more she talked about it, the more she wanted to see it once again and find out if the little twin arbors were still standing. "There was a secret panel in this house," she said craftily, not telling the truth but wishing that she were, "and the story went that all the family silver was hidden in it when Sherman° came through but it was never found . . ."

"Hey!" John Wesley said, "Let's go see it! We'll find it! We'll poke all the woodwork and find it! Who lives there? Where do you turn off at? Hey Pop, can't we turn off there?"

"We never have seen a house with a secret panel!" June Star shrieked, "Let's go to the house with the secret panel! Hey, Pop, can't we go see the house with the secret panel!"

"It's not far from here, I know," the grandmother said. "It wouldn't take over twenty minutes."

Bailey was looking straight ahead. His jaw was as rigid as a horseshoe. "No," he said.

50   The children began to yell and scream that they wanted to see the house with the secret panel. John Wesley kicked the back of the front seat and June Star hung over her mother's shoulder and whined desperately into her ear that they never had any fun even on their vacation, and that they could never do what THEY wanted to do. The baby began to scream and John Wesley kicked the back of the seat so hard that his father could feel the blows in his kidney.

"All right!" he shouted, and drew the car to a stop at the side of the road. "Will you all shut up? Will you all just shut up for one second? If you don't shut up, we won't go anywhere."

"It would be very educational for them," the grandmother murmured.

"All right," Bailey said, "but get this: this is the only time we're going to stop for anything like this. This is the one and only time."

"The dirt road that you have to turn down is about a mile back," the grandmother directed. "I marked it when we passed."

55   "A dirt road," Bailey groaned.

After they had turned around and were headed toward the dirt road, the grandmother recalled other points about the house, the beautiful glass over the front doorway and the candle-lamp in the hall. John Wesley said that the secret panel was probably in the fireplace.

"You can't go inside this house," Bailey said. "You don't know who lives there."

"While you all talk to the people in front, I'll run around behind and get in a window," John Wesley suggested.

"We'll all stay in the car," his mother said.

60   They turned onto the dirt road and the car raced roughly along in a swirl of pink dust. The grandmother recalled the times when there were no paved roads and thirty miles was a day's journey. The dirt road was hilly and there were sudden washes in it and sharp curves on dangerous embankments. All at once they would be on a hill, looking down over the blue tops of trees for miles around, then the next minute, they would be in a red depression with the dust-coated trees looking down on them.

"This place had better turn up in a minute," Bailey said, "or I'm going to turn around."

The road looked as if no one had traveled on it in months.

°*Sherman*: William Tecumseh Sherman (1820–1892), Union general during the Civil War.

"It's not much farther," the grandmother said and just as she said it, a horrible thought came to her. The thought was so embarrassing that she turned red in the face and her eyes dilated and her feet jumped up, upsetting her valise in the corner. The instant the valise moved, the newspaper top she had over the basket under it rose with a smart and Pitty Sing, the cat, sprang onto Bailey's shoulder.

The children were thrown to the floor and their mother, clutching the baby, was thrown out the door onto the ground; the old lady was thrown into the front seat. The car turned over once and landed right-side-up in a gulch on the side of the road. Bailey remained in the driver's seat with the cat—gray-striped with a broad white face and an orange nose—clinging to his neck like a caterpillar.

As soon as the children saw they could move their arms and legs, they scrambled out   65
of the car, shouting, "We've had an ACCIDENT!" The grandmother was curled up under the dashboard, hoping she was injured so that Bailey's wrath would not come down on her all at once. The horrible thought she had had before the accident was that the house she had remembered so vividly was not in Georgia but in Tennessee.

Bailey removed the cat from his neck with both hands and flung it out the window against the side of a pine tree. Then he got out of the car and started looking for the children's mother. She was sitting against the side of the red gutted ditch, holding the screaming baby, but she only had a cut down her face and a broken shoulder. "We've had an ACCIDENT!" the children screamed in a frenzy of delight.

"But nobody's killed," June Star said with disappointment as the grandmother limped out of the car, her hat still pinned to her head but the broken front brim standing up at a jaunty angle and the violet spray hanging off the side. They all sat down in the ditch, except the children, to recover from the shock. They were all shaking.

"Maybe a car will come along," said the children's mother hoarsely.

"I believe I have injured an organ," said the grandmother, pressing her side, but no one answered her. Bailey's teeth were clattering. He had on a yellow sport shirt with bright blue parrots designed in it and his face was as yellow as the shirt. The grandmother decided that she would not mention that the house was in Tennessee.

The road was about ten feet above and they could see only the tops of the trees on the   70
other side of it. Behind the ditch they were sitting in there were more woods, tall and dark and deep. In a few minutes they saw a car some distance away on top of a hill, coming slowly as if the occupants were watching them. The grandmother stood up and waved both arms dramatically to attract their attention. The car continued to come on slowly, disappeared around a bend and appeared again, moving even slower, on top of the hill they had gone over. It was a big black battered hearse-like automobile. There were three men in it.

It came to a stop just over them and for some minutes, the driver looked down with a steady expressionless gaze to where they were sitting, and didn't speak. Then he turned his head and muttered something to the other two and they got out. One was a fat boy in black trousers and a red sweat shirt with a silver stallion embossed on the front of it. He moved around on the right side of them and stood staring, his mouth partly open in a kind of loose grin. The other had on khaki pants and a blue striped coat and a gray hat pulled down very low, hiding most of his face. He came around slowly on the left side. Neither spoke.

The driver got out of the car and stood by the side of it, looking down at them. He was an older man than the other two. His hair was just beginning to gray and he wore silver-rimmed spectacles that gave him a scholarly look. He had a long creased face and didn't have on any shirt or undershirt. He had on blue jeans that were too tight for him and was holding a black hat and a gun. The two boys also had guns.

"We've had an ACCIDENT!" the children screamed.

The grandmother had the peculiar feeling that the bespectacled man was someone she knew. His face was as familiar to her as if she had known him all her life but she could not recall who he was. He moved away from the car and began to come down the embankment, placing his feet carefully so that he wouldn't slip. He had on tan and white shoes and no socks, and his ankles were red and thin. "Good afternoon," he said. "I see you all had a little spill."

75 "We turned over twice!" said the grandmother.

"Oncet," he corrected. "We seen it happen. Try their car and see will it run, Hiram," he said quietly to the boy with the gray hat.

"What you got that gun for?" John Wesley asked. "Whatcha gonna do with that gun?"

"Lady," the man said to the children's mother, "would you mind calling them children to sit down by you? Children make me nervous. I want all you all to set down right together there where you're at."

"What are you telling us what to do for?" June Star asked.

80 Behind them the line of woods gaped like a dark, open mouth. "Come here," said their mother.

"Look here now," Bailey began suddenly, "we're in a predicament! We're in . . ."

The grandmother shrieked. She scrambled to her feet and stood staring. "You're The Misfit!" she said. "I recognized you at once."

"Yes'm," the man said, smiling slightly at if he were pleased in spite of himself to be known, "but it would have been better for all of you, lady, if you hadn't reckernized me."

Bailey turned his head sharply and said something to his mother that shocked even the children. The old lady began to cry and The Misfit reddened.

85 "Lady," he said, "don't you get upset: Sometimes a man says things he don't mean. I don't reckon he meant to talk to you thataway."

"You wouldn't shoot a lady, would you?" the grandmother said and removed a clean handkerchief from her cuff and began to slap at her eyes with it.

The Misfit pointed the toe of his shoe into the ground and made a little hole and then covered it up again. "I would hate to have to," he said.

"Listen," the grandmother almost screamed, "I know you're a good man. You don't look a bit like you have common blood. I know you must come from nice people!"

"Yes mam," he said, "finest people in the world." When he smiled he showed a row of strong white teeth. "God never made a finer woman than my mother and my daddy's heart was pure gold," he said. The boy with the red sweat shirt had come around behind them and was standing with his gun at his hip. The Misfit squatted down on the ground. "Watch them children, Bobby Lee," he said. "You know they make me nervous." He looked at the six of them huddled together in front of him and he seemed to be embarrassed as if he couldn't think of anything to say. "Ain't a cloud in the sky," he remarked, looking up at it. "Don't see no sun but don't see no cloud neither."

90 "Yes, it's a beautiful day," said the grandmother. "Listen," she said, "you shouldn't call yourself The Misfit because I know you're a good man at heart. I can just look at you and tell."

"Hush!" Bailey yelled. "Hush! Everybody shut up and let me handle this!" He was squatting in the position of a runner about to sprint forward but he didn't move.

"I pre-chate that, lady," The Misfit said and drew a little circle in the ground with the butt of his gun.

"It'll take a half a hour to fix this here car," Hiram called, looking over the raised hood of it.

"Well, first you and Bobby Lee get him and that little boy to step over yonder with you," The Misfit said, pointing to Bailey and John Wesley. "The boys want to ask you something," he said to Bailey. "Would you mind stepping back in them woods there with them?"

95 "Listen," Bailey began, "we're in a terrible predicament. Nobody realizes what this is," and his voice cracked. His eyes were as blue and intense as the parrots in his shirt and he remained perfectly still.

The grandmother reached up to adjust her hat brim as if she were going to the woods with him but it came off in her hand. She stood staring at it and after a second she let it fall to the ground. Hiram pulled Bailey up by the arm as if he were assisting an old man. John Wesley caught hold of his father's hand and Bobby Lee followed. They went off toward the woods and just as they reached the dark edge. Bailey turned and supporting himself against a gray naked pine trunk, he shouted, "I'll be back in a minute, Mamma, wait on me!"

"Come back this instant!" his mother shrilled but they all disappeared into the woods.

"Bailey Boy!" the grandmother called in a tragic voice but she found she was looking at The Misfit squatting on the ground in front of her. "I just know you're a good man," she said desperately. "You're not a bit common!"

"Nome, I ain't a good man," The Misfit said after a second as if he had considered her statement carefully, "but I ain't the worst in the world neither. My daddy said I was different breed of dog from my brothers and sisters. 'You know,' Daddy said, 'it's some that can live their whole life out without asking about it and it's others has to know why it is, and this boy is one of the latters. He's going to be into everything!'" He put on his black hat and looked up suddenly and then away deep into the woods as if he were embarrassed again. "I'm sorry I don't have on a shirt before you ladies," he said, hunching his shoulders slightly. "We buried our clothes that we had on when we escaped and we're just making do until we can get better. We borrowed these from some folks we met," he explained.

"That's perfectly all right," the grandmother said. "Maybe Bailey has an extra shirt in his suitcase." 100

"I'll look and see terrectly," the Misfit said.

"Where are they taking him?" the children's mother screamed.

"Daddy was a card himself," the Misfit said. "You couldn't put anything over on him. He never got in trouble with the Authorities though. Just had the knack of handling them."

"You could be honest too if you'd only try," said the grandmother. "Think how wonderful it would be to settle down and live a comfortable life and not have to think about somebody chasing you all the time."

The Misfit kept scratching in the ground with the butt of his gun as if he were thinking about it. "Yes'm, somebody is always after you," he murmured. 105

The grandmother noticed how thin his shoulder blades were just behind his hat because she was standing up looking down on him. "Do you ever pray?" she asked.

He shook his head. All she saw was the black hat wiggle between his shoulder blades. "Nome," he said.

There was a pistol shot from the woods, followed closely by another. Then silence. The old lady's head jerked around. She could hear the wind move through the tree tops like a long satisfied insuck of breath. "Bailey Boy!" she called.

"I was a gospel singer for a while," The Misfit said. "I been most everything. Been in the arm service, both land and sea, at home and abroad, been twicet married, been an undertaker, been with the railroads, plowed Mother Earth, been in a tornado, seen a man burnt alive oncet," and he looked up at the children's mother and the little girl who were sitting close together, their faces white and their eyes glassy; "I even seen a woman flogged," he said.

"Pray, pray," the grandmother began, "pray, pray . . . ." 110

"I never was a bad boy that I remember of," The Misfit said in an almost dreamy voice, "but somewheres along the line I done something wrong and got sent to the penitentiary. I was buried alive," and he looked up and held her attention to him by a steady stare.

"That's when you should have started to pray," she said. "What did you do to get sent to the penitentiary that first time?"

"Turn to the right, it was a wall," The Misfit said, looking up again at the cloudless sky. "Turn to the left, it was a wall. Look up it was a ceiling, look down it was a floor. I forgot what I done, lady. I set there and set there, trying to remember what it was I done and I ain't recalled it to this day. Oncet in a while, I would think it was coming to me, but it never come."

"Maybe they put you in by mistake," the old lady said vaguely.

115   "Nome," he said. "It wasn't no mistake. They had the papers on me."

"You must have stolen something," she said.

The Misfit sneered slightly. "Nobody had nothing I wanted," he said. "It was a head-doctor at the penitentiary said what I had done was kill my daddy but I know that for a lie. My daddy died in nineteen ought nineteen of the epidemic flu and I never had a thing to do with it. He was buried in the Mount Hopewell Baptist churchyard and you can go there and see for yourself."

"If you would pray," the old lady said, "Jesus would help you."

"That's right," The Misfit said.

120   "Well then, why don't you pray?" she asked trembling with delight suddenly.

"I don't want no hep," he said. "I'm doing all right by myself."

Bobby Lee and Hiram came ambling back from the woods. Bobby Lee was dragging a yellow shirt with bright blue parrots on it.

"Throw me that shirt, Bobby Lee," The Misfit said. The shirt came flying at him and landed on his shoulder and he put it on. The grandmother couldn't name what the shirt reminded her of. "No, lady," The Misfit said while he was buttoning it up. "I found out the crime don't matter. You can do one thing or you can do another, kill a man or take a tire off his car, because sooner or later you're going to forget what it was you done and just be punished for it."

The children's mother had begun to make heaving noises as if she couldn't get her breath. "Lady," he asked, "would you and that little girl like to step off yonder with Bobby Lee and Hiram and join your husband?"

125   "Yes, thank you," the mother said faintly. Her left arm dangled helplessly and she was holding the baby, who had gone to sleep, in the other. "Hep that lady up, Hiram," The Misfit said as she struggled to climb out of the ditch, "and Bobby Lee, you hold onto that little girl's hand."

"I don't want to hold hands with him," June Star said. "He reminds me of a pig."

The fat boy blushed and laughed and caught her by the arm and pulled her off into the woods after Hiram and her mother.

Alone with The Misfit, the grandmother found that she had lost her voice. There was not a cloud in the sky nor any sun. There was nothing around her but woods. She wanted to tell him that he must pray. She opened and closed her mouth several times before anything came out. Finally she found herself saying, "Jesus, Jesus," meaning Jesus will help you, but the way she was saying it, it sounded as if she might be cursing.

"Yes'm," The Misfit said as if he agreed. "Jesus thown everything off balance. It was the same case with Him as with me except He hadn't committed any crime and they could prove I had committed one because they had the papers on me. Of course," he said, "they never shown me any papers. That's why I sign myself now. I said long ago, you get you a signature and sign everything you do and keep a copy of it. Then you'll know what you done and you can hold up the crime to the punishment and see do they match and in the end you'll have something to prove you ain't been treated right. I call myself The Misfit," he said, "because I can't make what all I done wrong fit what all I gone through in punishment."

130   There was a piercing scream from the woods, followed closely by a pistol report. "Does it seem right to you, lady, that one is punished a heap and another ain't punished at all?"

"Jesus!" the old lady cried. "You've got good blood! I know you wouldn't shoot a lady! I know you come from nice people! Pray! Jesus, you ought not to shoot a lady: I'll give you all the money I've got!"

"Lady," The Misfit said, looking beyond her far into the woods, "there never was a body that give the undertaker a tip."

There were two more pistol reports and the grandmother raised her head like a parched old turkey hen crying for water and called, "Bailey Boy, Bailey Boy!" as if her heart would break.

"Jesus was the only One that ever raised the dead," The Misfit continued, "and He shouldn't have done it. He thown everything off balance. If He did what He said then it's nothing for you to do but thow away everything and follow Him, and if He didn't, then it's nothing for you to do but enjoy the few minutes you got left the best way you can—by killing somebody or burning down his house or doing some other meanness to him. No pleasure but meanness," he said and his voice had become almost a snarl.

"Maybe He didn't raise the dead," the old lady mumbled, not knowing what she   135
was saying and feeling so dizzy that she sank down in the ditch with her legs twisted under her.

"I wasn't there so I can't say He didn't." The Misfit said, "I wisht I had of been there," he said, hitting the ground with his fist. "It ain't right I wasn't there because if I had of been there I would of known. Listen lady," he said in a high voice, "if I had of been there I would of known and I wouldn't be like I am now." His voice seemed about to crack and the grandmother's head cleared for an instant. She saw the man's face twisted close to her own as if he were going to cry and she murmured, "Why you're one of my babies. You're one of my own children!" She reached out and touched him on the shoulder. The Misfit sprang back as if a snake had bitten him and shot her three times through the chest. Then he put his gun down on the ground and took off his glasses, and began to clean them.

Hiram and Bobby Lee returned from the woods and stood over the ditch, looking down at the grandmother who half sat and half lay in a puddle of blood with her legs crossed under her like a child's and her face smiling up at the cloudless sky.

Without his glasses, The Misfit's eyes were red-rimmed and pale and defenseless-looking. "Take her off and thow her where you thown the others," he said, picking up the cat that was rubbing itself against his leg.

"She was a talker, wasn't she?" Bobby Lee said, sliding down the ditch with a yodel.

"She would of been a good woman," The Misfit said, "if it had been somebody there to   140
shoot her every minute of her life."

"Some fun!" Bobby Lee said.

"Shut up, Bobby Lee," The Misfit said. "It's no real pleasure in life."

QUESTIONS

1. Describe the story's point of view. On whom is the story focused? How appealing is this character as a focal point of attention?

2. What is the function of chance in the story's development? Describe some of the chances, or unlikelihoods, in the story. Why does O'Connor develop the story through the unfolding of these unlikelihoods?

3. Who is The Misfit? Why is he given this name? To what degree is he symbolic? What might he symbolize?

4. Some have called this story a religious allegory. How might it be considered allegorical? What might the story's violence be seen to symbolize?

ALICE WALKER (b. 1944)

Walker was born in Georgia and attended Sarah Lawrence College, graduating in 1965. In addition to teaching at Yale, Wellesley, and other schools, she has edited and published fiction, poetry and biography, and she received a Guggenheim Fellowship in 1977. Her main hobby is gardening. For her collection of poems Revolutionary Petunias *(1973), she received a Wall Book Award nomination. Her best-known novel,* The Color Purple *(1982), was made into a movie that won an Academy Award in 1985. Her most recent novel is* By the Light of My Father's Smile *(1998).*

Everyday Use (1973)

I will wait for her in the yard that Maggie and I made so clean and wavy yesterday afternoon. A yard like this is more comfortable than most people know. It is not just a yard. It is like an extended living room. When the hard clay is swept clean as a floor and the fine sand around the edges lined with tiny, irregular grooves, anyone can come and sit and look up into the elm tree and wait for the breezes that never come inside the house.

Maggie will be nervous until after her sister goes; she will stand hopelessly in corners, homely and ashamed of the burn scars down her arms and legs, eyeing her sister with a mixture of envy and awe. She thinks her sister has held life always in the palm of one hand, that "no" is a word the world never learned to say to her.

You've no doubt seen those TV shows° where the child who has "made it" is confronted, as a surprise, by her own mother and father, tottering in weakly from backstage. (A pleasant surprise, of course: What would they do if parent and child came on the show only to curse out and insult each other?) On TV mother and child embrace and smile into each other's faces. Sometimes the mother and father weep, the child wraps them in her arms and leans across the table to tell how she would not have made it without their help. I have seen these programs.

Sometimes I dream a dream in which Dee and I are suddenly brought together on a TV program of this sort. Out of a dark and soft-seated limousine I am ushered into a bright room filled with many people. There I meet a smiling, gray, sporty man like Johnny Carson° who shakes my hand and tells me what a fine girl I have. Then we are on the stage and Dee is embracing me with tears in her eyes. She pins on my dress a large orchid, even though she has told me once that she thinks orchids are tacky flowers.

5   In real life I am a large, big-boned woman with rough, man-working hands. In the winter I wear flannel nightgowns to bed and overalls during the day. I can kill and clean a hog as mercilessly as a man. My fat keeps me hot in zero weather. I can work outside all day, breaking ice to get water for washing; I can eat pork liver cooked over the open fire minutes after it comes steaming from the hog. One winter I knocked a bull calf straight in the brain between the eyes with a sledge hammer and had the meat hung up to chill before nightfall. But of course all this does not show on television. I am the way my daughter would want me to be: a hundred pounds lighter, my skin like an uncooked barley pancake. My hair glistens in the hot bright lights. Johnny Carson has much to do to keep up with my quick and witty tongue.

°*TV shows:* In the early days of television (i.e., the 1950s), *This Is Your Life* was a popular show, which the narrator accurately describes here.
°Johnny Carson (1925–2005) was an amateur magician, actor, and radio announcer before he began hosting the late night television *Tonight* show, a role that he continued for thirty years. He amused and pleased huge national audiences, gained many awards, and was known as "the king of late night." He did not host *This Is Your Life.*

But that is a mistake. I know even before I wake up. Who ever knew a Johnson with a quick tongue? Who can even imagine me looking a strange white man in the eye? It seems to me I have talked to them always with one foot raised in flight, with my head turned in whichever way is farthest from them. Dee, though. She would always look anyone in the eye. Hesitation was no part of her nature.

"How do I look, Mama?" Maggie says, showing just enough of her thin body enveloped in pink skirt and red blouse for me to know she's there, hidden by the door.

"Come out into the yard," I say.

Have you ever seen a lame animal, perhaps a dog run over by some careless person rich enough to own a car, sidle up to someone who is ignorant enough to be kind to him? That is the way my Maggie walks. She has been like this, chin on chest, eyes on ground, feet in shuffle, ever since the fire that burned the other house to the ground.

Dee is lighter than Maggie, with nicer hair and a fuller figure. She's a woman now, though sometimes I forget. How long ago was it that the other house burned? Ten, twelve years? Sometimes I can still hear the flames and feel Maggie's arms sticking to me, her hair smoking and her dress falling off her in little black papery flakes. Her eyes seemed stretched open, blazed open by the flames reflected in them. And Dee, I see her standing off under the sweet gum tree she used to dig gum out of; a look of concentration on her face as she watched the last dingy gray board of the house fall in toward the red-hot brick chimney. Why don't you do a dance around the ashes? I'd wanted to ask her. She had hated the house that much.

10

I used to think she hated Maggie, too. But that was before we raised the money, the church and me, to send her to Augusta° to school. She used to read to us without pity; forcing words, lies, other folks' habits, whole lives upon us two, sitting trapped and ignorant underneath her voice. She washed us in a river of make-believe, burned us with a lot of knowledge we didn't necessarily need to know. Pressed us to her with the serious way she read, to shove us away at just the moment, like dimwits, we seemed about to understand.

Dee wanted nice things. A yellow organdy dress to wear to her graduation from high school; black pumps to match a green suit she'd made from an old suit somebody gave me. She was determined to stare down any disaster in her efforts. Her eyelids would not flicker for minutes at a time. Often I fought off the temptation to shake her. At sixteen she had a style of her own; and knew what style was.

I never had an education myself. After second grade the school was closed down. Don't ask me why: in 1927 colored asked fewer questions than they do now. Sometimes Maggie reads to me. She stumbles along good-naturedly, but can't see well. She knows she is not bright. Like good looks and money, quickness passed her by. She will marry John Thomas (who has mossy teeth in an earnest face) and then I'll be free to sit here and I guess just sing church songs to myself. Although I never was a good singer. Never could carry a tune. I was always better at a man's job. I used to love to milk till I was hooked in the side° in '49. Cows are soothing and slow and don't bother you, unless you try to milk them the wrong way.

I have deliberately turned my back on the house. It is three rooms, just like the one that burned, except the roof is tin; they don't make shingle roofs any more. There are no real windows, just some holes cut in the sides, like the portholes on a ship, but not round and not square, with rawhide holding the shutters up on the outside. This house is in a pasture, too, like the other one. No doubt when Dee sees it she will want to tear it down. She wrote me once that no matter where we "choose" to live, she will manage to come see us. But she will never bring her friends. Maggie and I thought about this and Maggie asked me, "Mama, when did Dee ever *have* any friends?"

°*Augusta:* Augusta, Georgia, the second largest city in the state, is the home of Augusta State University, and also of Paine College, traditionally a "black" school.
°*hooked in the side:* i.e., kicked by a cow.

15   She had a few. Furtive boys in pink shirts hanging about on washday after school. Nervous girls who never laughed. Impressed with her they worshiped the well-turned phrase, the cute shape, the scalding humor that erupted like bubbles in lye. She read to them.

When she was courting Jimmy T she didn't have much time to pay to us, but turned all her faultfinding power on him. He *flew* to marry a cheap city girl from a family of ignorant flashy people. She hardly had time to recompose herself.

When she comes I will meet . . . but there they are!

Maggie attempts to make a dash for the house, in her shuffling way, but I stay her with my hand. "Come back here," I say. And she stops and tries to dig a well in the sand with her toe.

It is hard to see them clearly through the strong sun. But even the first glimpse of leg out of the car tells me it is Dee. Her feet were always neat-looking, as if God himself had shaped them with a certain style. From the other side of the car comes a short, stocky man. Hair is all over his head a foot long and hanging from his chin like a kinky mule tail. I hear Maggie suck in her breath. "Uhnnnh," is what it sounds like. Like when you see the wriggling end of a snake just in front of your foot on the road. "Uhnnnh."

20   Dee next. A dress down to the ground, in this hot weather. A dress so loud it hurts my eyes. There are yellows and oranges enough to throw back the light of the sun. I feel my whole face warming from the heat waves it throws out. Earrings gold, too, and hanging down to her shoulders. Bracelets dangling and making noises when she moves her arm up to shake the folds of the dress out of her armpits. The dress is loose and flows, and as she walks closer, I like it. I hear Maggie go "Uhnnnh" again. It is her sister's hair. It stands straight up like the wool on a sheep. It is black as night and around the edges are two long pigtails that rope about like small lizards disappearing behind her ears.

"Wa-su-zo-Tean-o!"° she says, coming on in that gliding way the dress makes her move. The short stocky fellow with the hair to his navel is all grinning and he follows up with "Asalamalakim,° my mother and my sister!" He moves to hug Maggie but she falls back, tight up against the back of my chair. I feel her trembling there and when I look up I see the perspiration falling off her chin.

"Don't get up," says Dee. Since I am stout it takes something of a push. You can see me trying to move a second or two before I make it. She turns, showing white heels through her sandals, and goes back to the car. Out she peeks next with a Polaroid.° She stoops down quickly and lines up picture after picture of me sitting there in front of the house with Maggie cowering behind me. She never takes a shot without making sure the house is included. When a cow comes nibbling around the edge of the yard she snaps it and me and Maggie *and* the house. Then she puts the Polaroid in the back seat of the car, and comes up and kisses me on the forehead.

Meanwhile Asalamalakim is going through motions with Maggie's hand. Maggie's hand is as limp as a fish, and probably as cold, despite the sweat, and she keeps trying to pull it back. It looks like Asalamalakim wants to shake hands but wants to do it fancy. Or maybe he don't know how people shake hands. Anyhow, he soon gives up on Maggie.

"Well," I say, "Dee."

25   "No, Mama," she says. "Not 'Dee.' Wangero Leeewanika Kemanjo!"°

"What happened to 'Dee'?" I wanted to know.

"She's dead," Wangero said. "I couldn't bear it any longer, being named after the people who oppress me."

"You know as well as me you was named after your aunt Dicie," I said. Dicie is my sister: She named Dee. We called her "Big Dee" after Dee was born.

°*Wa-su-zo-Tean-o*: a phrase from the Lugandan dialect, meaning "Good morning," or "I hope you had a good night."
°*Asalamalakim*: Arabic phrase for "Peace be with you."
°*Polaroid*: The Polaroid Land Camera was an "instant camera" that in the 1970s and beyond provided fully developed photographs a minute after the picture was taken.
°*Wangero . . . Kemanjo*: Dee apparently mispronounces "Wanjiro" and "Kamenjo," two of her adopted African names.

"But who was *she* named after?" asked Wangero.

"I guess after Grandma Dee," I said.

"And who was she named after?" asked Wangero.

"Her mother," I said, and saw Wangero was getting tired. "That's about as far back as I can trace it," I said. Though, in fact, I probably could have carried it back beyond the Civil War through the branches.

"Well," said Asalamalakim, "there you are."

"Uhnnnh," I heard Maggie say.

"There I was not," I said, "before 'Dicie' cropped up in our family, so why should I try to trace it that far back?"

He just stood there grinning, looking down on me like somebody inspecting a Model A° car. Every once in a while he and Wangero sent eye signals over my head.

"How do you pronounce this name?" I asked.

"You don't have to call me by it if you don't want to," said Wangero.

"Why shouldn't I?" I asked. "If that's what you want us to call you, we'll call you."

"I know it might sound awkward at first," said Wangero.

"I'll get used to it," I said. "Ream it out again."

Well, soon we got the name out of the way. Asalamalakim had a name twice as long and three times as hard. After I tripped over it two or three times he told me to just call him *Hakim-a-barber.*° I wanted to ask him was he a barber, but I didn't really think he was, so I didn't ask.

"You must belong to those beef-cattle peoples down the road," I said. They said "Asalamalakim" when they met you, too, but they didn't shake hands. Always too busy: feeding the cattle, fixing the fences, putting up salt-lick shelters,° throwing down hay. When the white folks poisoned some of the herd the men stayed up all night with rifles in their hands. I walked a mile and a half just to see the sight.

Hakim-a-barber said, "I accept some of their doctrines, but farming and raising cattle is not my style." (They didn't tell me, and I didn't ask, whether Wangero (Dee) had really gone and married him.)

We sat down to eat and right away he said he didn't eat collards and pork was unclean. Wangero, though, went on through the chitlins and corn bread, the greens and everything else. She talked a blue streak over the sweet potatoes. Everything delighted her. Even the fact that we still used the benches her daddy made for the table when we couldn't afford to buy chairs.

"Oh, Mama!" she cried. Then turned to Hakim-a-barber. "I never knew how lovely these benches are. You can feel the rump prints," she said, running her hands underneath her and along the bench. Then she gave a sigh and her hand closed over Grandma Dee's butter dish. "That's it!" she said. "I knew there was something I wanted to ask you if I could have." She jumped up from the table and went over in the corner where the churn stood, the milk in it clabber° by now. She looked at the churn and looked at it.

"This churn top is what I need," she said. "Didn't Uncle Buddy whittle it out of a tree you all used to have?"

"Yes," I said.

"Uh huh," she said happily. "And I want the dasher,° too."

"Uncle Buddy whittle that, too?" asked the barber.

Dee (Wangero) looked up at me.

°*Model A:* The Ford car that replaced the Model T in the late 1920s. The Model A was proverbial for its quality and durability.
°*Hakim-a-barber:* a mistake in hearing "Hakim Akbar," meaning, in Arabic, "The wise man is great."
°*Salt-lick shelters:* Structures designed to keep rain from dissolving the large blocks of rock salt put on poles for cattle.
°*clabber:* i.e., clabbered: curdled.
°*dasher:* device used for agitating and blending together the ingredients of butter (and also ice cream).

"Aunt Dee's first husband whittled the dash," said Maggie so low you almost couldn't hear her. "His name was Henry, but they called him Stash."

"Maggie's brain is like an elephant's." Wangero said, laughing. "I can use the churn top as a centerpiece for the alcove table," she said, sliding a plate over the churn, "and I'll think of something artistic to do with the dasher."

When she finished wrapping the dasher the handle stuck out. I took it for a moment in my hands. You didn't even have to look too close to see where hands pushing the dasher up and down to make butter had left a kind of sink in the wood. In fact, there were a lot of small sinks; you could see where thumbs and fingers had sunk into the wood. It was beautiful light yellow wood, from a tree that grew in the yard where Big Dee and Stash had lived.

55   After dinner Dee (Wangero) went to the trunk at the foot of my bed and started rifling through it. Maggie hung back in the kitchen over the dishpan. Out came Wangero with two quilts. They had been pieced by Grandma Dee and then Big Dee and me had hung them on the quilt frames on the front porch and quilted them. One was in the Lone Star pattern. The other was Walk Around the Mountain. In both of them were scraps of dresses Grandma Dee had worn fifty and more years ago. Bits and pieces of Grandpa Jarrell's Paisley shirts. And one teeny faded blue piece, about the size of a penny matchbox, that was from Great Grandpa Ezra's uniform that he wore in the Civil War.

"Mama," Wangero said sweet as a bird. "Can I have these old quilts?"

I heard something fall in the kitchen, and a minute later the kitchen door slammed.

"Why don't you take one or two of the others?" I asked. "These old things was just done by me and Big Dee from some tops your grandma pieced before she died."

"No," said Wangero. "I don't want those. They are stitched around the borders by machine."

60   "That'll make them last better," I said.

"That's not the point," said Wangero. "These are all pieces of dresses Grandma used to wear. She did all this stitching by hand. Imagine!" She held the quilts securely in her arms stroking them.

"Some of the pieces, like those lavender ones, come from old clothes her mother handed down to her," I said, moving up to touch the quilts. Dee (Wangero) moved back just enough so that I couldn't reach the quilts. They already belonged to her.

"Imagine!" she breathed again, clutching them closely to her bosom.

"The truth is," I said, "I promised to give them quilts to Maggie, for when she marries John Thomas."

65   She gasped like a bee had stung her.

"Maggie can't appreciate these quilts!" she said. "She'd probably be backward enough to put them to everyday use."

"I reckon she would," I said. "God knows I been saving 'em for long enough with nobody using 'em. I hope she will!" I didn't want to bring up how I had offered Dee (Wangero) a quilt when she went away to college. Then she had told me they were old-fashioned, out of style.

"But they're *priceless*!" she was saying now, furiously, for she has a temper. "Maggie would put them on the bed and in five years they'd be in rags. Less than that!"

"She can always make some more," I said. "Maggie knows how to quilt."

70   Dee (Wangero) looked at me with hatred. "You just will not understand. The point is these quilts, *these* quilts!"

"Well," I said, stumped. "What would *you* do with them?"

"Hang them," she said. As if that was the only thing you *could* do with quilts.

Maggie by now was standing in the door. I could almost hear the sound her feet made as they scraped over each other.

"She can have them, Mama," she said, like somebody used to never winning anything, or having anything reserved for her. "I can 'member Grandma Dee without the quilts."

I looked at her hard. She had filled her bottom lip with checkerberry snuff° and it gave her face a kind of dopey, hangdog look. It was Grandma Dee and Big Dee who taught her how to quilt herself. She stood there with her scarred hands hidden in the folds of her skirt. She looked at her sister with something like fear but she wasn't mad at her. This was Maggie's portion. This was the way she knew God to work.

When I looked at her like that something hit me in the top of my head and ran down to the soles of my feet. Just like when I'm in church and the spirit of God touches me and I get happy and shout. I did something I never had done before: hugged Maggie to me, then dragged her on into the room, snatched the quilts out of Miss Wangero's hands and dumped them into Maggie's lap. Maggie just sat there on my bed with her mouth open.

"Take one or two of the others," I said to Dee.

But she turned without a word and went out to Hakim-a-barber.

"You just don't understand," she said, as Maggie and I came out to the car.

"What don't I understand?" I wanted to know.   80

"Your heritage," she said. And then she turned to Maggie, kissed her, and said, "You ought to try to make something of yourself, too, Maggie. It's really a new day for us. But from the way you and Mama still live you'd never know it."

She put on some sunglasses that hid everything above the tip of her nose and her chin.

Maggie smiled; maybe at the sunglasses. But a real smile, not scared. After we watched the car dust settle I asked Maggie to bring me a dip of snuff. And then the two of us sat there just enjoying, until it was time to go in the house and go to bed.

QUESTIONS

1. Describe the narrator, Mrs. Johnson. Who is she? What is she like? Where and how does she live? What kind of life has she had? How does the story bring out her judgments about her two daughters?

2. Describe Dee and Maggie. How are they different physically and mentally? How have their lives been different? How do they change during the story?

3. Why did Dee change her name? How is this change important, and how is it reflected in her desire for the family artifacts?

4. Describe the importance of the title "Everyday Use" in the story (paragraph 66). How does this phrase highlight the conflicting values in the story?

°*checkerberry snuff:* snuff flavored with wintergreen.

Chapter 10A
Writing a Research Essay on Fiction

AFTER STUDYING THIS MATERIAL, YOU SHOULD BE ABLE TO DO THE FOLLOWING:

- Explain the meaning of literary research
- Develop a bibliography with which to guide your own research
- Learn the more common types of bibliographies for literary research
- Take notes on published works to prepare for developing the results of your own research
- Develop your own writing ideas based on your notes
- Learn the form and use of detail from your printed sources

Broadly, **research** is systematic investigation, examination, and experimentation. It is the basic tool of intellectual inquiry for anyone working in any discipline—physics, chemistry, biology, psychology, anthropology, history, and literature, to name just a few disciplines. With research, and with the breakthroughs of knowledge that research brings, our understanding and our civilization grow; without research, they languish.

The major assumption of doing research is that the researcher is reaching out to find and master new areas of knowledge and expertise. With each assignment the researcher acquires not only the knowledge gained from the particular task but also the skills needed to undertake further research and thereby to gain further knowledge. Some research tasks are elementary, such as using a dictionary to discover the meaning of a word and thereby aiding the understanding of an important passage. Many people would not even call that research. More detailed research uses an array of resources: critical studies, biographies, introductions, bibliographies, and histories. When you begin a research task you usually have little or no knowledge of your topic, but with such resources you can acquire expert knowledge in a relatively short time.

Although research is the animating spark of all disciplines, our topic here is **literary research**—the systematic use of primary and secondary sources in studying a literary problem. In doing literary research, you consult not only individual works themselves (primary sources) but many other works that shed light on them and interpret them (secondary sources). Typical research tasks are to learn important facts about a work and about the period in which it was written; to learn about the lives, careers, and other works of authors; to discover and apply the comments and judgments of modern or earlier critics; to learn details that help explain the meaning of works; and to learn about critical and artistic taste.

Selecting a Topic

In most instances, your instructor assigns a research essay on a specific topic. Sometimes, however, the choice of a topic will be left in your hands. For such assignments, it is helpful to know the types of research essays you might find most interesting and approachable. Here are some possibilities:

1. **A particular work.** At first, this type of research essay is probably the most common one, as shown in the illustrative essay (p. 523). You might treat character (for example, "The Character of Louise in Chopin's 'The Story of an Hour'" or "The Question of Whether Young Goodman Brown Is a Hero or a Dupe in Hawthorne's 'Young Goodman Brown'") or tone and style, ideas, structure, form, and the like. A research paper on a single work is similar to an essay on the same work, except that the research paper takes into account more views and facts than those you are likely to have without the research.

2. **A particular author.** A project might focus on an idea or some facet of style, imagery, setting, or tone of the author, tracing the origins and development of the topic through a number of different stories, poems, or plays. Examples are "Joyce's Use of Local References in *Dubliners*" and "Faulkner's Use of the Yoknapatawpha Environment in His Stories." This type of essay is suitable for a number of shorter works, although it is also applicable for a single major work, such as a longer story, novel, or play.

3. **Comparison and contrast** (see Chapter 26). There are two types.
   a. *An idea or quality common to two or more authors.* Here you show points of similarity or contrast, or else you show how one author's work can be taken to criticize another's. A possible subject is "Contrasting Uses of Dialogue in Ellison's 'Battle Royal' and Tan's 'Two Kinds,'" or "The Theme of Love and Sexuality in Faulkner's 'A Rose for Emily,' Munro's 'The Found Boat,' and Joyce's 'Araby.'"
   b. *Different critical views of a particular work or body of works.* Sometimes much is to be gained from an examination of differing critical opinions on topics like "The Meaning of Poe's 'The Masque of the Red Death'" or "Various Views of Hawthorne's 'Young Goodman Brown.'" Such a study would attempt to determine the critical opinion and taste to which a work did or did not appeal, and it might also aim at conclusions about whether the work was in the advance or rear guard of its time.

4. **The influence of an idea, author, philosophy, political situation, or artistic movement on specific works of an author or authors.** An essay on influences can be specific and to the point, as in "Details of Twentieth-Century Native American Life as Reflected in Silko's 'The Man to Send Rain'" or else it can be more abstract and critical, as in "The Influence of Traditional Religion on Hawthorne's 'Young Goodman Brown.'"

5. **The origin of a particular work or type of work.** Such an essay might examine an author's biography to discover the germination and development of a work—for example, "Poe's Personal Experience with Illness and 'The Masque of the Red Death'" and "Poe's Theory of the Short Story."

If you consider these types, an idea of what to write may come to you. Perhaps you have particularly liked one author or several authors. If so, you might start to think along the lines of types 1, 2, or 3. If you are interested in influences or origins, then type 4 or 5 may suit you better.

If you still cannot decide on a topic after rereading the works you have liked, then you should carry your search for a topic into your school library. Look up your author or authors in the library's catalog. One approach is to find a relatively recent book-length critical study published by a university press. Look for a title indicating that the book is a general one dealing with the author's major works rather than just one work. Study those chapters relevant to the work or works you have chosen. Most writers of critical studies describe their purpose and plan in their introductions or first chapters, so begin with the first part of the book. If there is no separate chapter on your primary text, use the index as your guide to the relevant pages. Reading in this way will give you enough knowledge about the issues and ideas raised by the work to enable you to select a promising topic. Once you make your decision, you are ready to develop a working bibliography.

Setting Up a Working Bibliography

The first step in your research bibliography should be to create a working bibliography, a list of sources that you plan to consult during your research. A working bibliography is a tool that will evolve with you as you progress through the research process. For example, you may locate and read a source only to discover that it does not address your research topic, or you may come across a new promising source to add to your working bibliography. Many instructors may also encourage you to develop this bibliography as an annotated bibliography, a list of sources that includes your summary of the source and potentially your commentary on how this source will (or will not) be used in your essay. Either way, the goal of a working bibliography is to create a fairly comprehensive research bibliography to use as a guide when you begin to collect your sources.

Locating Sources

Through computer access, today's libraries are constantly connected to a vast array of local, national, and even international libraries, so that by using various online services, you can extend your research far beyond the capacities of your own library. Just a few years ago, the broadness of scope that electronic searches provide for most undergraduate students doing research assignments was not possible; today, it is commonplace. Even with the astounding possibilities of electronic-aided research, however, it is still necessary to read, evaluate, and take notes on your material—before you can begin and complete a research essay. This section will teach you to use today's library services to find the materials you are seeking, but these services cannot do your reading, evaluating, note taking, and writing. All that is still up to you, as it always has been for all students doing research.

Searching the Internet

Many students choose to begin their research with the Internet. While Internet research may be familiar and convenient, it is important to be aware of its limitations. Most websites lack the type of thorough review that print sources are subjected to; therefore, the content you find online may not have been held to the same quality standards as the content that you would find in traditional research sources like books or scholarly journals. In fact, with today's technology, anyone with access to the Internet and some basic software can publish a website. Therefore, it is essential that you evaluate websites carefully before trusting their content.

To search the Internet through the use of various search engines, such as Google and Bing, you simply need to enter the name of an author, a title, or a topic, upon which you will be linked to a host of resources from all over the world—home pages of specific authors, literary organizations, and works on various topics by contemporary writers. You may want to conduct your search through multiple

EVALUATING SOURCES

Evaluating sources is a two-pronged issue that involves assessing both a source's reliability and its relevance to your research topic. When evaluating sources, ask yourself the following questions:

- Who is the author of this source? Who is the publisher? Was this source created by an established author and publisher with a reputation for accuracy and reliability?
- What is the purpose of this source? To inform? To sell something? To advocate a cause? In other words, is the source biased by political or financial interests?
- Has the source been through a scholarly review process? If not, proceed with caution; ask yourself, does this source cite its own sources? Do its sources appear reliable?
- Does this source's discussion relate to your topic? How does this information address your research question?

While you must evaluate *all* sources for reliability and relevance, sources uncovered through Internet searches require extra caution on the part of the researcher. Your search-engine results will likely bring up many so-called "free essays" on literary topics that were written largely by beginners, not by scholars who have studied particular topics for many years and who have become experts in their analyses. The reason for using books and articles approved by scholarly publishers is that the works have been *refereed* by authorities in the particular field. If these authorities, or referees, have recommended a publication, you are entitled to expect that the breadth and depth of the critical analyses will be well considered and reliable. A college-level literary paper should rely on these types of refereed sources, which are found primarily through the library.

search engines, because search engines index different sites and report their results in different formats. One useful tool you may want to experiment with is a meta-search engine, such as Dogpile; metasearch engines allow you to search multiple search engines simultaneously. There are also more specialized search engines that you can utilize; for example, Google Scholar allows for broad searches of scholarly research.

The key to successful Internet searches, and really any electronic search, is utilizing appropriate search terms. A search for "Katherine Mansfield" on a general search engine may produce several thousand results, many of which may be unrelated to your topic. To avoid this type of overwhelming or disappointing result, use the advanced search options on your search engine. Most search engines will allow you to use quotation marks to indicate certain phrases, or use the search terms *AND* (searches for only sites that include both search terms), *OR* (searches for sites that include only one of the search terms), *NOT* (searches for sites that include the first term but do not include the second) to limit your results.

Using Internet research, you may quickly find a vast range of resources for your essay; however, the importance of evaluating sources found through Internet searches for reliability and relevance cannot be overstated (see the box on p. 503 on evaluating sources). Finally, an additional important caveat is that many sources remain in printed journals and magazines that may be or, more

A major university's library catalog page.

probably, may not be on the web. To make sure your searches are thorough, therefore, *you must never neglect to search for information available only through your library.*

Searching Library Resources

Libraries provide vast amounts of print and electronic resources; however, the most useful resource in your library is perhaps the reference librarian, who will be able to help you make the most of the library's resources. Be sure to consult your reference librarian for any help you may need with the research process.

Though card catalogs are still in use at some small libraries, your library's catalog is most likely electronic. Using an electronic catalog, you can search your library's holdings by author name, title, keyword, or in some catalogs, by subject.

An additional convenience is that many associated libraries have pooled their resources. Thus, if you use the services of a network of associated libraries, you can go to another library to use materials that are not accessible at your own college or branch. If distances are great, however, and your own library does not have a book that you think is important to your project, you can ask a librarian to get the book for you through the Interlibrary Loan Service. Usually, given time, the libraries will accommodate as many of your needs as they can.

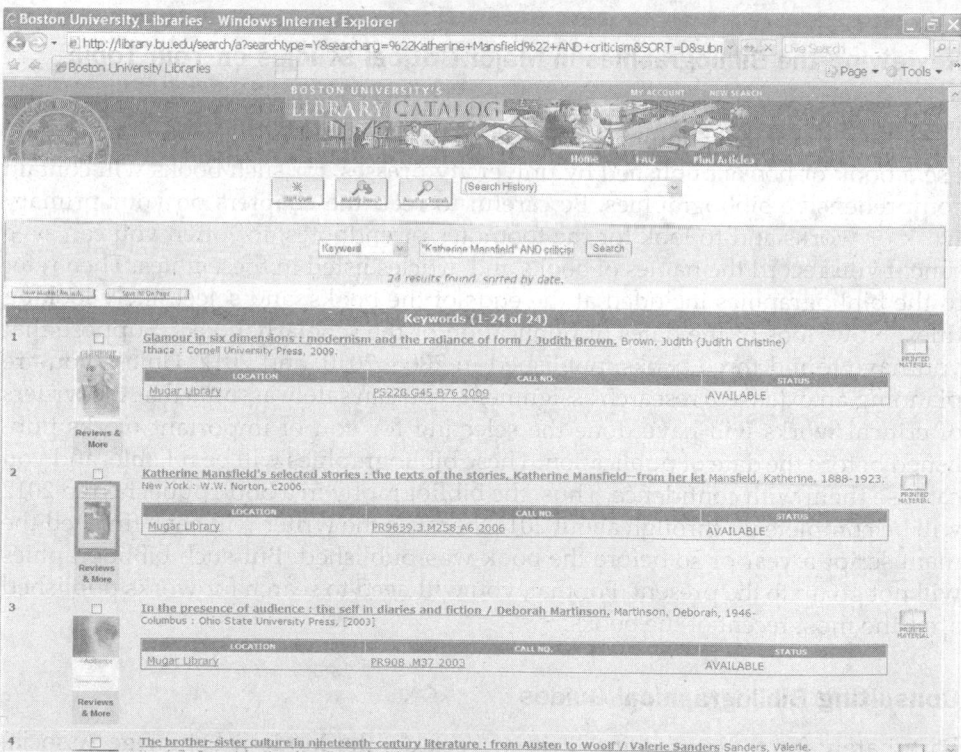

The search results for the search terms: *"Katherine Mansfield" AND criticism*. Each record lists the author, title, the type of resource, the call number (which indicates where in the library the resource can be found), and finally the availability of the resource (which indicates whether the book has been checked out or is on the shelf).

IMPORTANT CONSIDERATIONS ABOUT COMPUTER-AIDED RESEARCH

You must always remind yourself that online catalogs, such as those you might select from other colleges and universities, and from private organizations, can give you only what has been entered into them. If one university library classifies a work under "criticism and interpretation" and another classifies it under "characters," a search of "criticism and interpretation" at the first library will find the work but the same search at the second will not. Sometimes the inclusion of an author's life dates immediately following the name might throw off your search. Typographic errors in the system will cause additional search problems, although many programs try to forestall such difficulties by providing "nearby" entries to enable you to determine whether incorrectly entered topics may in fact be helpful to you.

Also, if you use online services, be careful to determine the year when the computerization began. Many libraries have a recent commencement date—1978, for example, or 1985. For completeness, therefore, you would need assistance in finding catalog entries for items published before these years.

Reviewing the Bibliographies in Major Critical Studies on Your Topic

One of the best ways to locate relevant and reliable sources for your working bibliography is to begin by finding major critical studies of the writer or writers. Again, use a book or books published by university presses, for such books will contain comprehensive bibliographies. Be careful to read the chapters on your primary work or works and to look for the footnotes or endnotes, for often you can save time if you record the names of books and articles listed in these notes. Then refer to the bibliographies included at the ends of the books, and select likely looking titles. Now, look at the dates of publication of the scholarly books. Suppose that you have found three books, published in 2006, 2010, and 2012. Unless you are planning an extensive research assignment, you can safely assume that the writers of critical works will have done the selecting for you of important works published before the date of publication. These bibliographies will be reliable, and you can use them with confidence. Thus, the bibliography in a book published in 2012 will be complete up through about 2011, because the writer will have finished the manuscript a year or so before the book was published. But such bibliographies will not go up to the present. For that, you will need to search for works published after the most recent of the books.

Consulting Bibliographical Guides

Fortunately for students doing literary research, the Modern Language Association (MLA) of America has been providing a complete bibliography of literary studies for years, not only in English and American literatures but also in the literatures of many foreign languages. This is the *MLA International Bibliography*

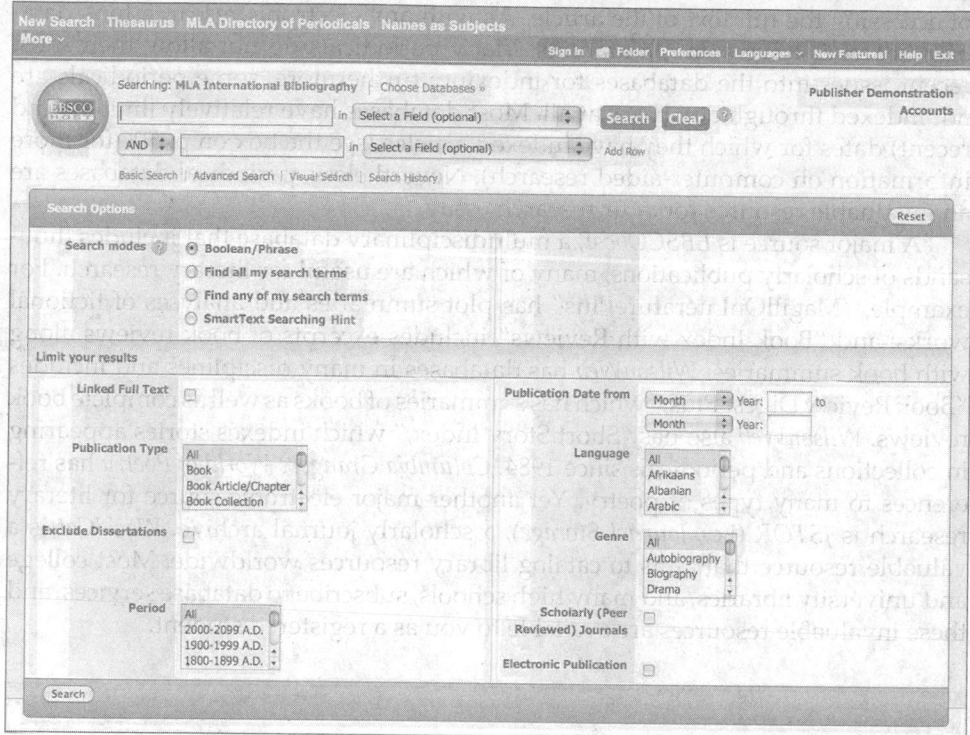

The search page for the *MLA Bibliography*. Note the many search options including the ability to limit your search by date, language, and peer-reviewed publications.

of Books and Articles on the Modern Languages and Literatures ("*MLA Bibliography*"). The *MLA Bibliography* started achieving completeness in the late 1950s. In the latest volume, dated 2008, this comprehensive bibliography lists 71,649 books and articles. The MLA discontinued production of the traditional book format of the *MLA Bibliography* in 2009. However, it may be available at university and college libraries. The most recent version of the bibliography is published electronically—accessible to you through your library services.

Using the electronic version of the *MLA Bibliography*, you can search by typing in the name of the author or subject. By whatever means you gain access to the bibliography, be sure to get the complete information—especially volume numbers and years of publication—for each article and book.

There are many other bibliographies useful for students doing literary research, such as the *Essay and General Literature Index*, the *Readers' Guide to Periodical Literature*, and various specific indexes. With over 2.1 million citations, the *MLA Bibliography* contains more than enough, however, for your present research purposes.

Gaining Access to Books and Articles Through Databases

Today's libraries subscribe to a number of academic databases that index articles from reliable scholarly journals and other periodicals. Many of these databases include abstracts (brief, nonevaluative summaries) and some even offer the option of accessing the full text of the article. As with any electronic research tool, database searches have some limitations. Many periodicals do not allow their most recent issues into the databases for indexing; furthermore, some periodicals are not indexed through databases at all. Most databases have relatively limited (and recent) dates for which they have indexed articles (see the box on p. 506 for more information on computer-aided research). Nevertheless, periodical databases are an invaluable resource for your research essay.

A major source is *EBSCOhost*, a multidisciplinary database that includes thousands of scholarly publications, many of which are useful for literary research. For example, "MagillOnLiteraturePlus" has plot summaries and analyses of fictional works; and "Book Index with Reviews" includes excerpts of book reviews along with book summaries. *WilsonWeb* has databases in many disciplines and includes "Book Review Digest Plus," which has summaries of books as well as complete book reviews. *WilsonWeb* also has "Short Story Index," which indexes stories appearing in collections and periodicals since 1984. *Columbia Grangers World of Poetry* has references to many types of poetry. Yet another major electronic source for literary research is *JSTOR* (i.e., *Journal Storage*), a scholarly journal archive. *WorldCat* is a valuable resource that aims to catalog library resources worldwide. Most college and university libraries, and many high schools, subscribe to database services, and these invaluable resources are available to you as a registered student.

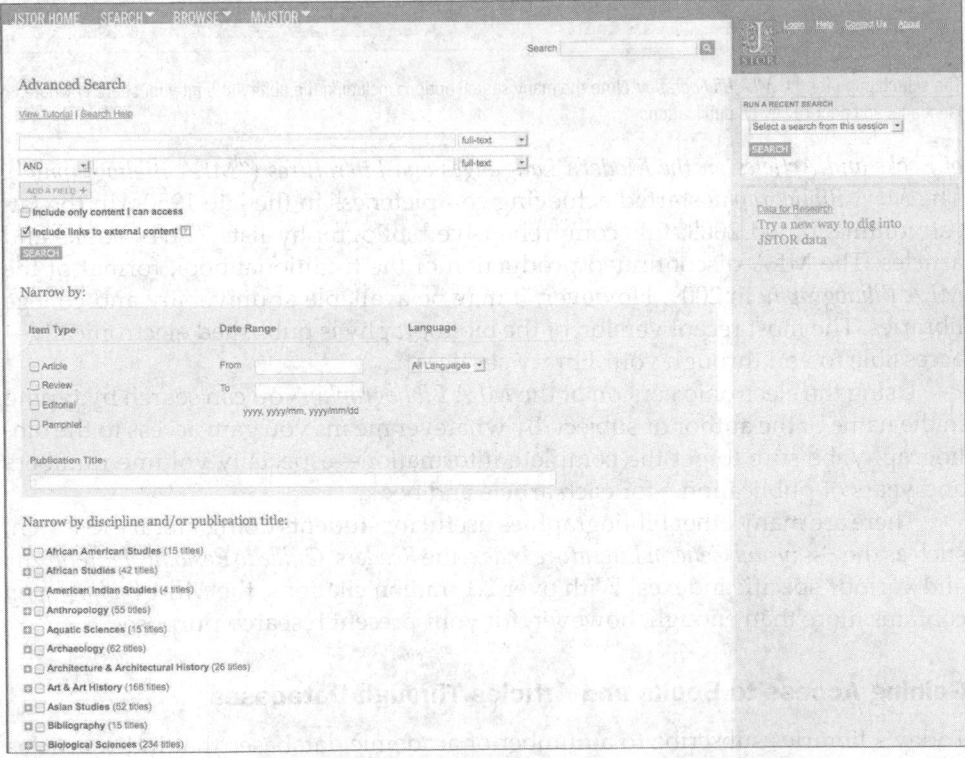

The advanced search page for *JSTOR*. While the search pages for each database differ, the skills you need to conduct a successful search are similar to those needed for other electronic searches.

Taking Notes and Paraphrasing Material

There are many ways of taking notes, but a few things are clear. Because your notes should facilitate, not hinder, your writing of the final research essay, you will need a systematic way of handling your notes. The best way is to develop a method whereby you will be able to see all your notes together, laid out in front of you. If you are taking handwritten notes, you can achieve simultaneous viewability by using note cards. If you have never used cards before, you might profit from consulting any one of a number of handbooks and special workbooks on research.[1] The principal advantage of cards is the ease with which you can see them at a glance when you lay them out on a desk or other large surface. Cards are also sturdy and will easily maintain their physical integrity as you handle them and assign them to their relevant piles. As a result, cards may be easily classified; they may be numbered and renumbered; shuffled; tried out in one place, rejected, and then used in another place (or thrown away); and arranged in order when you start to write. If you prefer taking notes on a computer, it is these same qualities—viewability and ease of finding, classifying, and reordering notes without losing information—that you should aim for in a filing system. When taking notes on the computer, you may want to consider either keeping them in one large file or organizing them in separate files by source or by topic. No matter how you decide to take notes, follow the guidelines in the next section to ease your research process and avoid plagiarism.

Taking Complete and Accurate Notes

WRITE THE SOURCE OF EACH NOTE YOU TAKE.   Be especially diligent about writing the source of your information on each card or computer note. This may seem bothersome, but it is easier than going back to the library to locate the correct source after you have begun your essay. You can save time if you take the complete data on one card or computer file—a "master card" for that source—and then create an abbreviation for the separate notes you take from the source. Here is an example, which also includes the location where the reference was originally found (library catalog, research database, Internet search, bibliography in a book, the *MLA Bibliography*, etc.). Observe that the author's last name goes first.

DONOVAN, JOSEPHINE, ED. FEMINIST	PN
Literary Criticism: Explorations	98
in Theory. 2nd ed. Lexington:	W64
UP of Kentucky. 1989	F4
DONOVAN	
CARD CATALOG, "WOMEN"	

See Muriel Harris, *Prentice Hall Reference Guide to Grammar and Usage*, 8th ed. (New York, Pearson, 2010).

If you take many notes from this book, the name "Donovan" will serve as identification. Be sure not to lose your master group of references because you will need them when you prepare your list of works cited.

RECORD THE PAGE NUMBER FOR EACH NOTE. It would be hard to guess how much exasperation has been caused by the failure to record page numbers in notes. Be sure to write the page number down first, before you begin to take your note, and, to be doubly sure, write the page number again at the end of your note. If the detail goes from one page to the next in your source, record the exact spot where the page changes, as in this example.

> HEILBRUN AND STIMSON, IN DONOVAN, PP. 63–64
>
> [63]After the raising of the feminist conscious-
> ness it is necessary to develop/ [64]"the growth
> of moral perception" through anger and the
> "amelioration of social inequities."

The reason for such care is that you may wish to use only a part of a note you have taken, and when there are two pages you will need to be accurate in locating what goes where.

RECORD ONLY ONE FACT OR OPINION ON A CARD OR COMPUTER ENTRY. Record only one major detail for each of your notes—one quotation, one paraphrase, one observation—never two or more. You might be tempted to fill up entire notes with many separate but unrelated details, but such a try at economy often gets you in trouble because you might want to use some of the details in other places. If you have only one entry per note, you will avoid such problems and also retain the freedom you need.

USE QUOTATION MARKS FOR ALL QUOTED MATERIAL. In taking notes it is extremely important—vitally important, urgently important—to distinguish copied material from your own words. Always put quotation marks around every direct quotation you copy verbatim from a source. Make the quotation marks immediately, before you forget, so that you will always know that the words of your notes within quotation marks are the words of another writer.

Often, as you write your notes, you may use some of your own words and some of the words from your source. In cases like this you should be even more cautious. *Put quotation marks around every word that you take directly from the source, even if your note looks like a picket fence.* Later, when you begin writing your essay, your memory of what is yours and not yours will be dim, and if you use another's words in your own essay without proper acknowledgment, you are risking the charge of plagiarism. Much of the time, plagiarism is caused not by deliberate deception but rather by sloppy note taking.[2]

See page 519–20 for a further discussion of plagiarism.

PLAGIARISM: AN EMBARRASSING BUT VITAL SUBJECT—AND A DANGER TO BE OVERCOME

When you are using sources as the substance of many of the details in your essay, you run the risk of *plagiarism*—using the words and ideas of other writers without their consent and without acknowledgment. Recognizing the source means being clear about the identity of other authors, together with the name or names of the works from which one gets details and ideas. When there is no recognition, readers, and the intellectual world generally, are deceived. They assume that the material they are reading is the original work and the intellectual possession of the writer. When there is no recognition, the plagiarizing author is committing intellectual theft.

This is no small matter. In the world of publications, many people who have committed plagiarism have suffered irreparable damage to their credibility and reputations as writers and authorities. Some well-known writers have found it hard if not impossible to continue their careers, and all because of the wide knowledge of their plagiarism. It does not end there. A plagiarist might be open to legal actions, and might, if the situation is grave enough, be required to supply financial restitution to the author or authors whose work has been illegally appropriated. In schools and colleges, students who plagiarize may face academic discipline. Often the discipline is a failure for the course, but it might also include suspension and expulsion.

See pages 517–22 on *how* to give recognition to your sources.

IF YOUR SOURCE IS LONG, MAKE A BRIEF AND ACCURATE PARAPHRASE. When you take notes, it is best to paraphrase the sources. A paraphrase is a restatement in your own words, and because of this it is actually a first step in the writing of your essay. A big problem in paraphrasing is to capture the idea in the source without copying the words in the source. The best way is to read and reread the passage you are noting. Turn over the book or journal—or turn away from your computer screen—and write out the idea in your own words as accurately as you can. Once you have completed this note, compare it with the original and make corrections to improve your thought and emphasis. Add a short quotation if you believe it is needed, but be sure to use quotation marks. If your paraphrase is too close to the original, throw out the note and write another one. This effort may have its own reward because often you may be able to transfer some or even all of your note, word for word, directly to the appropriate place in your research essay.

To see the problems of paraphrasing, let us look at a paragraph of criticism and then see how a student doing research might take notes on it. The paragraph is by Richard F. Peterson, from an essay entitled "The Circle of Truth: The Stories of Katherine Mansfield and Mary Lavin," published in *Modern Fiction Studies* 24 (1978): 383–94. In the passage to be quoted, Peterson is considering the structures of two Mansfield stories, "Bliss" and "Miss Brill":

> "Bliss" and "Miss Brill" are flawed stories, but not because the truth they reveal about their protagonists is too brutal or painful for the tastes of the common reader. In each story, the climax of the narrative suggests an arranged reality that leaves a lasting impression, not of life, but of the author's cleverness. This strategy of arrangement for dramatic effect or revelation, unfortunately, is common in Katherine Mansfield's fiction. Too often in her stories a dropped remark at the right or wrong moment, a chance meeting or discovery, an intrusive figure in the shape of a fat man at a ball or in the Café de Madrid, a convenient death of a hired man or a stranger dying aboard a ship, or a *deus ex machina* in the form of two doves, a dill pickle, or a fly plays too much of a role in / [386] creating a character's dilemma or deciding the outcome of the narrative. 385–386

Because taking notes forces a shortening of this or any criticism, it also requires you to discriminate, judge, interpret, and select; good note taking is not easy. The suggestions that follow will guide you, however, when you go through the many sources you uncover.

THINK ABOUT THE PURPOSE OF YOUR RESEARCH. You may not know exactly what you are "fishing for" when you start to take notes, for you cannot prejudge what your essay will contain. Research is a form of discovery. But soon you will notice subjects and issues that your sources constantly explore. If you can accept one of these as your major topic, or focus of interest, you can use that as your guide in all further note taking.

For example, suppose you start to take notes on criticism about Katherine Mansfield's "Miss Brill," and after a certain amount of reading, you decide to focus on the story's structure. This decision guides your further research and note taking. Thus, for example, Richard Peterson criticizes Mansfield's technique of arranging climaxes in her stories. With your topic being "structure," it would therefore be appropriate to write a note about Peterson's judgment. The following note is adequate as a brief reminder of the content in the passage:

> Peterson 385   structure: negative
>
> Peterson claims that Mansfield creates climaxes that are too artificial, too unlifelike, giving the impression not of reality but of Mansfield's own "cleverness." 385

Let us now suppose that you want a fuller note, in the expectation that you need not just Peterson's general idea but also some of his supporting detail. Such a note might look like this:

> Peterson 385   structure: negative
>
> Peterson thinks that "Bliss" and "Miss Brill" are "flawed" because they have contrived endings that give the impression "not of life but of" Mansfield's "cleverness." She arranges things artificially, according to Peterson, to cause the endings in many other stories. Some of these things are chance remarks, discoveries, or meetings, together with other unexpected or chance incidents and objects. These contrivances make their stories imperfect. 385

In an actual research essay, any part of this note would be useful. The words are almost all the note taker's own, and the few quotations are within quotation marks. Note that Peterson, the critic, is properly recognized as the source of the criticism, so you could adapt the note easily when you are doing your writing. The key here is that your note taking should be guided by your developing plan for your essay.

Note taking is part of your thinking and composing process. You may not always know whether you will be able to use each note that you take, and you will always exclude many notes when you write your essay. You will always find, however, that taking notes is easier once you have determined your purpose.

GIVE YOUR NOTES TITLES.   To help plan and develop the various parts of your essay, write a title for each of your notes, as in the examples in this chapter. This practice is a form of outlining. Let us continue discussing the structure of Mansfield's "Miss Brill," the actual subject of the illustrative research essay (pp. 523–29). As you do your research, you discover that there is a divergence of critical thought about how the ending of the story should be understood. Here is a note about one of the diverging interpretations:

Daly 90   Last sentence of the story

Miss Brill's "complete" "identification" with the shabby fur piece at the very end may cause readers to conclude that she is the one in tears but bravely does not recognize this fact, and also to conclude that she may never use the fur in public again because of her complete defeat. Everything may be for "perhaps the very last time." 90

Notice that the title classifies the topic of the note. If you use such classifications, a number of like-titled notes could form the basis for a section in your essay about how to understand the conclusion of "Miss Brill." Whether you use this note or not—and very often you may not, for it may not fit into your final plan for your essay—the topic itself will guide you in further study and note taking.

WRITE DOWN YOUR OWN ORIGINAL THOUGHTS, AND BE SURE TO MARK THEM AS YOUR OWN.   As you take notes, you will be acquiring your own observations and thoughts. Do not push these aside in your mind, on the chance of remembering them later, *but write them down immediately*. Often you may notice a detail that your source does not mention, or you may get a hint for an idea that the critic does not develop. Often, too, you may get thoughts that can serve as "bridges" between details in your notes or as introductions or concluding observations. Be sure to title your comments and also to mark them as your own thought. Here is such a note, which is about Katherine Mansfield's emphasis on the impoverished existence of her heroine, Miss Brill, and the many people inhabiting the park where the action of the story takes place:

My Own   About Miss Brill's "cupboard"

Mansfield's speaker avoids taking us to the homes of the other people in the park, as she does when we follow Miss Brill into her living quarters. Instead, she lets us know that the silent couple, the complaining wife and suffering husband, the unseen man rejected by the young woman dumping the flowers, the "ermine toque," and the funny gentleman, not to mention the many people resembling statues in the park, all return to loneliness and personal pain.

Observe that the substance of this note (also most of the language) is used as the basis for much of paragraph 10 in the illustrative essay (p. 527). The point here is that as you make your own observations while doing your research, you are also free to develop materials that can go directly into your final essay.

CLASSIFY YOUR NOTES, AND GROUP THEM.   If you do a careful and thorough job of taking notes, your essay will already have been forming in your mind. The titles of your notes will suggest areas to be developed as you do your planning and initial drafting. Once you have assembled a significant amount of material derived from a reasonable number of sources (your instructor may have assigned an approximate number or a minimum number), you can sort them into groups according to the topics and titles. For the illustrative research essay, after some shuffling and retitling, the notes were assembled in the following groups:

> General structure
>
> Specific structures: season, time of day, levels of cruelty, Miss Brill's own "hierarchies" of unreality
>
> The concluding paragraphs, especially the last sentence

If you look at the major sections of the illustrative essay, you will see that the topics are closely adapted from these groups of notes. In other words, the arrangement of the notes is an effective means of outlining and organizing a research essay. Be smart; do it this way.

MAKE LOGICAL ARRANGEMENTS OF THE NOTES IN EACH GROUP.   There is still much to do with each group of notes. You cannot use the details as they happen to fall randomly in your stack or file. You need to decide which notes are relevant. You might also need to retitle some notes and use them elsewhere. Those that remain will have to be arranged in a logical order for you to find use for them in your essay.

Once you have your notes in order, you can write whatever comments or transitions are needed to move from detail to detail. Write this material directly in your notes. If you are using cards, be sure to use a different color ink so that you can distinguish later between the original note and what you add. If you are using a computer, you may want to try the "Track Changes" feature to achieve a similar effect. Here is an example of such a "developed" note, with quotation and commentary distinguished by different kinds of type:

| Magalaner 39 | Structure, general |

Magalaner, using "Miss Brill" as an example, speaks of Mansfield's weaving "a myriad of threads into a rigidly patterned whole" in her stories. (39). Some of these "threads" are the fall season, the time of day, examples of unkindness, the park bench sitters from the cupboards, and Miss Brill's stages of unreality. Each of these is separate, but all work together structurally to unify the story.

By adding such commentary to your notes, you are also simplifying the writing of your first draft. In many instances, the note and whatever comments you make may be moved directly into the paper with minor adjustments (some of the content of this note appears in paragraph 6 of the illustrative essay, and almost all the topics introduced here are developed in paragraphs 9 to 14).

Being Creative and Original While Doing Research

You will not always transfer your notes directly into your essay. The major trap to avoid in a research paper is that your use of sources can become an end in itself and therefore a shortcut for your own thinking and writing. Often, students make the mistake of introducing details the way a master of ceremonies introduces performers in a variety show. This is unfortunate because it is the student whose essay will be judged, even though the sources, like the performers, do all the work. Thus, it is important to be creative and original in a research essay and to do your own thinking and writing, even though you are relying heavily on your sources. Here are five ways in which research essays may be original.

1. **Your selection of material is original with you.** In each major part of your essay you will include many details from your sources. To be creative you should select different but related details and avoid overlapping or repetition. Your completed essay will be judged on the basis of the thoroughness with which you make your points with different details (which in turn will represent the completeness of your research). Even though you are relying on published materials and cannot be original on that score, your selection can be original because you bring these materials together for the first time, and because you emphasize some details and minimize others. Inevitably, your assemblage of details from your sources will be unique and therefore original.

2. **The development of your essay is yours alone.** Your arrangement of various points is an obvious area of originality: One detail seems naturally to precede another, and certain conclusions stem from certain details. As you present the details, conclusions, and arguments from your sources, you can also add an original stamp by introducing supporting details different from those in the source material. You can also add your own emphasis to particular points—an emphasis that you do not find in your sources.

3. **The words are yours and yours alone.** Naturally, the words that you use will be original because they are yours. Your topic sentences, for example, will

all be your own. As you introduce details and conclusions, you will need to write "bridges" to get yourself from point to point. These can be introductory remarks or transitions. In other words, as you write, you are not just stringing your notes together, but rather you are actively assembling and arranging your thoughts, based on your notes, in creative and unique ways.

4. **Explaining and contrasting controversial views is an original presentation of material.** Closely related to your selection is that in your research you may have found conflicting or differing views on a topic. If you make a point to describe and distinguish these views, and explain the reasons for the differences, you are presenting material originally.

5. **Your own insights and positions are uniquely your own.** There are three possibilities here, all related to how well you have learned the primary texts on which your research in secondary sources is based.

   a. *Weave your own interpretations and ideas into your essay.* An important part of taking notes is to make your own points precisely when they occur to you. Often you can expand these as truly original parts of your essay. Your originality does not need to be extensive; it may consist of no more than a single insight. Here is such a card, which was written during research on the structure of "Miss Brill."

My Own   Miss Brill's unreality

In light of this hierarchical structure of unrealities, it is ironic that the boy and girl sit down next to her just when she is at the height of her fancy about her own importance. When she hears the girl's insults, the couple introduces objective reality to her with a vengeance, and she is plunged from rapture to pain.

   The originality here is built around the contrast between Miss Brill's exhilaration and her rapid and cruel deflation. This observation is not unusual or startling, but it nevertheless represents original thought about the story. When modified and adapted (and put into full sentences with proper punctuation), the material of the card supplies much of paragraph 13 of the illustrative essay. You can see that your development of a "My Own" note card is an important part of the prewriting stage of a research essay.

   b. *Filling gaps in the sources enables you to present original thoughts and insights.* As you read your secondary sources, you may realize that an obvious conclusion is not being made or that an important detail is not being stressed. Here is an area that you can develop on your own. Your conclusions may involve a particular interpretation or major point of comparison, or they may rest on a particularly important but understressed word or fact. For example, paragraphs 10 to 13 in the illustrative essay form an argument based on observations that critics have overlooked, or have not stressed, about the attitudes of the heroine of "Miss Brill." In your research, whenever you find such a critical "vacuum" (assuming that you cannot read all the articles about some of your topics, where your discovery may already have been made a number of times), it is right to include whatever is necessary to fill it.

c. *By disputing your sources with your own arguments, you are being original.* The originality of your disagreement is that you will be using details in a different way from that of the critic or critics whom you are disputing, and your conclusions will be your own. This area of originality is similar to the laying out of controversial critical views, except that you furnish one of the opposing views yourself. The approach is limited because it is difficult to find many substantive points of interpretation on which there are not already clearly delineated opposing views. Paragraph 13 of the illustrative research essay shows how a disagreement can lead to a different, if not original, interpretation.

Documenting Your Work

It is necessary and essential to acknowledge—to *document*—all sources from which you have quoted or paraphrased factual and interpretive information. Because of the need to avoid being challenged for plagiarism, this point cannot be overemphasized. As the means of documentation, various reference systems use parenthetical references, footnotes, or endnotes. Whatever system is used, documentation almost always includes a carefully prepared bibliography, or list of works cited.

We will first discuss the list of works cited and then review the major reference system for use in a literary research paper. Parenthetical references, preferred by the Modern Language Association (MLA) since 1984, are described in the *MLA Handbook for Writers of Research Papers*, 7th ed., 2009. We explore this style of documentation in detail below and provide an extensive list of sample works cited listings in Appendix II: MLA Recommendations for Documenting Sources. We will also discuss in brief, footnotes or endnotes, recommended by the MLA before 1984, as this system of documentation is still required by many instructors. *Always consult your instructor regarding which documentation system to use.*

Include All the Works You Have Used in a List of Works Cited (Bibliography)

The key to any reference system is a carefully prepared list of works cited that is included at the end of the essay. "Works cited" means exactly that; the list should include just those books and articles you have actually used in your essay. If, however, your instructor requires that you use footnotes or endnotes, you can extend your concluding list to be a complete bibliography both of works cited and of works consulted but not actually used. Always, always, always, follow your instructor's directions.

The list of works cited should include the following information, in each entry, in the form indicated.

FOR A BOOK

- The author's name: last name first, followed by first name and middle name or initial. Period.
- The title, italicized. Period.

- The city of publication (not state or nation), colon; publisher (easily recognized abbreviations or key words can be used unless they seem awkward or strange; see the *MLA Handbook*, pp. 233–57), comma; year of publication. Period.
- The medium of publication (Print, Web, etc.). Period.

FOR AN ARTICLE

- The author's name: last name first, followed by first name and middle name or initial. Period.
- The title of the article in quotation marks. Period.
- The title of the journal or periodical, italicized, followed by the volume and issue numbers in Arabic (not Roman) numbers with no punctuation, then the year of publication within parentheses. Colon. For a daily paper or weekly magazine, omit the parentheses and cite the date in the British style followed by a colon (day, month, year, as in 2 Feb. 2012). Inclusive page numbers (without any preceding p. or pp.). Period.
- The medium of publication (Print, Web, DVD, etc.). Period.
- If your article was obtained through a database, include the database name. If your article was obtained electronically, either through a database or on the Internet, include the date you visited the site. Period.

FOR A WEB PUBLICATION

- The author's name: last name first, followed by first name and middle name or initial. Period.
  - The title of work/site. Italicize if the document is independent or use quotation marks if it is a part of a larger work.
  - Website's name, italicized (if this is different than above).
  - Publisher. Comma. Publication Date. Use "n.d." if no publication date is available.
- The medium of publication (Print, Web, etc.). Period.
- The access date, meaning the date you viewed the site. Period.
- The URL (uniform resource locator). The MLA specifies that the URLs should no longer accompany works cited entries unless the URL is essential to locating the site. If you determine that the URL is necessary, include the full address (be absolutely accurate in reproducing the URL) and place angle brackets (< >) before and after. Period. (Note: when a URL continues from one line to the next, break it *before* punctuation.)

The works you are citing should be listed alphabetically according to the last names of authors, with unsigned articles included in the list alphabetically by titles. Bibliographical lists are begun at the left margin, with subsequent lines in a five-space hanging indentation, so that the key locating word—the author's last name or the first title word of an unsigned article—can be easily seen. Many unpredictable and complex combinations, including ways to describe works of art, musical or other performances, and films, are detailed extensively in the *MLA Handbook* (pp. 123–212). Appendix II in this book presents details on MLA recommendations for documenting sources and offers over 40 model works-cited entries.

Refer to Works Parenthetically as You Draw Details from Them

Within the text of your research essay, use parentheses in referring to works from which you are using facts and conclusions. This parenthetical citation system is recommended in the *MLA Handbook* (pp. 213–232), and its guiding principle is to provide documentation without asking readers to interrupt their reading to find footnotes or endnotes. Readers wanting to see the complete reference can easily find it in your list of works cited. With this system, you incorporate the author's last name and the relevant page number or numbers directly, whenever possible, into the body of your essay. If the author's name is mentioned in your discussion, you need to give only the page number or numbers in parentheses. Here are two examples, from a critical study of another author, the eighteenth-century poet Alexander Pope:

> Alexander Pope believed in the idea that the universe is a whole, a totally unified body, which provides a "viable benevolent system for the salvation of everyone who does good" (Kallich 24).

> Martin Kallich draws attention to Alexander Pope's belief in the idea that the universe is a whole, a totally unified body, which provides a "viable benevolent system for the salvation of everyone who does good" (24).

✒ INTEGRATING AND ATTRIBUTING YOUR SOURCES

When writing a research essay, you must be constantly aware that you need to distinguish between the sources you are using and your own work. When blending your words with the ideas from sources, **be clear about proper acknowledgments**. Most commonly, if you are simply presenting details and facts, you can write straightforwardly and let parenthetical references suffice as your authority, as in the following sentence from the illustrative research essay:

> Marvin Magalaner, using "Miss Brill" as an example, speaks of Mansfield's weaving of "a myriad of threads into a rigidly patterned whole" (39). Also noting Mansfield's control over form, Cheryl Hankin suggests that Mansfield's structuring is perhaps more "instinctive" than deliberate (474).

Here there can be no question about plagiarism, for the names of the authors of the critical sources are fully acknowledged, the page numbers are specific, and the quotation marks clearly distinguish the words of the critics from the words of the essay writer. If you grant recognition as recommended here, no confusion can result about the authority underlying your essay. The linking words obviously belong to the writer of the essay, but the parenthetical references clearly indicate that the sentence is based on two sources.

If you use an interpretation unique to a particular writer, or if you rely on a significant quotation from your source, you should make your acknowledgment an essential part of your discussion, as in this sentence.

> Saralyn Daly, referring to Miss Brill as one of Mansfield's "isolatoes"—that is, solitary persons cut off from normal human contacts—fears that the couple's callous insults have caused Miss Brill to face the outside world with her fur piece "perhaps for the very last time" (88, 90).

Here the idea of the critic is singled out for special acknowledgment. If you recognize your sources in this way, no confusion can arise about how you have used them.

Please, always keep foremost in your mind that ***the purpose of research is to acquire knowledge and details from which to advance your own thoughts and interpretations.*** You should consider your research discoveries as a kind of springboard from which you can launch yourself into your own written work. In this way, research should be creative. A test of how you use research is to determine how well you move from the details you are using to the development of your own ideas. Once you have gone forth in this way, you are using research correctly and creatively. Plagiarism will then no more be even a remote issue for you.

Use Footnotes and Endnotes—Formal and Traditional Reference Formats

As long as all you want from a reference is the page number of a quotation or paraphrase, the parenthetical system described briefly in the previous section—and detailed fully in the *MLA Handbook*—is the most suitable and convenient one you can use. However, you may wish to use footnotes (references at the bottom of each page) or endnotes (references listed numerically at the end of the essay) if you need to add more details, provide additional explanations, or refer your readers to other materials that you are not using. If your instructor wants you to use one of these formats, do the following: Make a note the first time you quote or refer to a source, with the details ordered as outlined below.

FOR A BOOK

- The author's name: first name or initials first, followed by middle name or initial, then last name. Comma.
- The title, italicized for a book, no punctuation. If you are referring to a work in a collection (article, story, poem) use quotation marks for that, but italicize the title of the book. No punctuation, but use a comma after the title if an editor, translator, or edition number follows.
- The name of the editor or translator, if relevant. Abbreviate "editor" or "edited by" as "ed.," "editors" as "eds." Use "trans." for "translator" or "translated by." No punctuation, but use a comma if an edition number follows.
- The edition (if indicated), abbreviated thus: 2nd ed., 3rd ed., and so on. No additional punctuation.
- The publication facts, within parentheses, without any preceding or following punctuation, in the following order:

City (but not the state or nation) of publication, colon.

Publisher (clear abbreviations are acceptable and desirable), comma.

Year of publication.

- The page number(s) with no "p." or "pp.," for example, 5, 6–10, 15–19, 295–307, 311–16. Period. If you are referring to longer works, such as novels or longer stories with division or chapter numbers, include these numbers for readers who may be using an edition different from yours.

FOR A JOURNAL OR MAGAZINE ARTICLE

- The author: first name or initials first, followed by middle name or initial, then last name. Comma.
- The title of the article, in quotation marks. Comma.
- The name of the journal, italicized. No punctuation.
- The volume number, in Arabic numerals. No punctuation.
- The year of publication within parentheses. Colon. For newspaper and journal articles, omit the parentheses, and include day, month, and year (in the British style: 21 May 2010). Colon.
- The page number(s) with no "p." or "pp.": 5, 6–10, 34–36, 98–102, 345–47. Period.

For later notes to the same work, use the last name of the author as the reference unless you are referring to two or more works by the same author. Footnotes are placed at the bottom of each page, and endnotes are included on separate page(s) at the end of the essay. The first lines of both footnotes and endnotes should be paragraph indented, and continuing lines should be flush with the left margin. Both endnote and footnote numbers are set in a smaller font and positioned slightly above the line (as superior numbers) like this:[12]. You can single-space footnotes and endnotes and leave a line of space between them. *Most computer programs have specially designed and consecutively numbered footnote formats. These are generally acceptable, but be sure to consult your instructor.*

Sample Footnotes

In the examples below, book titles and periodicals are italicized.

---

[3] Blanche H. Gelfant, *Women Writing in America: Voices in Collage* (Hanover: UP of New England, for Dartmouth College, 1984) 110. Print.

[1] Günter Grass, "Losses," *Granta* 42 (Winter 1992): 99. Print.

[5] John O'Meara, "Hamlet and the Fortunes of Sorrowful Imagination: A Re-examination of the Genesis and Fate of the Ghost," *Cahiers Elisabéthains* 35 (1989): 21. Print.

[8] Grass 104.

[15] Gelfant 141.

[21] O'Meara 17.

In principle, you do not need to repeat in a footnote or endnote any material you have already mentioned in your own discourse. For example, if you recognize the author and title of your source, then the footnote or endnote should give no more than the data about publication. Here is an example:

In *The Fiction of Katherine Mansfield*,[9] Marvin Magalaner points out that Mansfield was as skillful in the development of epiphanies (that is, the use of highly significant though perhaps unobtrusive actions or statements to reveal the depths of a particular character) as James Joyce himself, the "inventor" of the technique.

(Carbondale: Southern Illinois UP, 1971) 130. Print.

Follow the Requirements for Documentation Set by Other Academic Disciplines

A variety of reference systems and style manuals have been adopted by certain disciplines (e.g., mathematics, medicine, psychology) to serve their own special needs. If you receive no instructions from your instructors in other courses, you can adapt the systems described here. If you need to use the documentation methods of other fields, however, use the *MLA Handbook* (261–63) for guidance about which style manual to select.

When in Doubt, Consult Your Instructor

Whatever method you follow, you must always acknowledge sources properly. Remember that whenever you begin to write and cite references, you might forget a number of specific details about documentation, and you will certainly discover that you have many questions. Be sure, then, to ask your instructor, who is your final authority.

Strategies for Organizing Ideas in Your Research Essay

INTRODUCTION   In your research essay you may wish to expand your introduction more than usual because of the need to relate the problem of research to your topic. You may wish to bring in relevant historical or biographical information. You may also wish to summarize critical opinion or describe critical problems about your topic. The idea is to lead your reader into your topic by providing interesting and significant materials that you have found.

Because of the length of many research essays, some instructors require a topic outline, which is in effect a brief table of contents. Because the inclusion of an outline is a matter of the instructor's choice, be sure to learn whether your instructor requires it.

BODY AND CONCLUSION   As you write the body and conclusion of your research essay, its development will be governed by your choice of topic. Consult the relevant chapters in this book about what to include for whatever approach or approaches you select (setting, ideas, point of view, character, tone, etc.).

In length, the research essay can be anywhere from as few as two or three or as many as fifteen or thirty or more pages, depending on your instructor's assignment. If you narrow the scope of your topic, as suggested in the approaches described at the beginning of this chapter, you can readily keep your essay within the assigned length. The following illustrative research essay, for example, illustrates approach 1 (p. 501) by being limited to only one character in one story. Were you to write on characters in a number of other stories by Mansfield or any other writer (approach 2), you could limit your total number of pages by stressing comparative treatments and by avoiding excessive detail about problems pertaining to only one work.

Although you limit your topic yourself in consultation with your instructor, you may encounter problems because you will deal not with one source alone but with many. Naturally the sources will provide you with details and also trigger many of your ideas. The problem is to handle the many strands without piling on too many details, and also without being led into digressions. It is important therefore to keep your central idea foremost; the constant stressing of your central idea will help you both to select relevant materials and to reject irrelevant ones.

Illustrative Student Essay Using Research

Although underlined sentences are not recommended by MLA style, they are used in this illustrative essay as teaching tools to emphasize the central idea, thesis sentence, and topic sentences.

Outline

I.   Introduction. The parallel structures of "Miss Brill"

II.   Season and time as structure

III.   Insensitive or cruel actions as structure

IV.   Miss Brill's "hierarchy of unrealities" as structure

V.   The story's conclusion

VI.   Conclusion

Use 1 inch top margin, 1 inch bottom and side margin; double-space throughout.

Put identifying information in upper-left corner, double-space.

Simone Delgado

Professor Leeshock

In MLA style, the header has the student's last name and page number.

Composition 102

30 October 2014

Use 1 inch top margin, 1 inch bottom and side margin; double-space throughout.

[1]

Center title one double-space below identifying information.

The Structure of Katherine Mansfield's "Miss Brill"°

    In the story "Miss Brill," Mansfield creates an aging and emotionally vulnerable character, Miss Brill (we are given no first name), whose good feelings are dashed when she overhears some cruel and shattering personal insults. In accord with Miss Brill's emotional deflation, the story is developed through a parallel number of structures.* This parallelling demonstrates Mansfield's power generally over tight narrative control. Marvin Magalaner,

In MLA style, put only the page number in parentheses when the author is named in the text.

using "Miss Brill" as an example, speaks of Mansfield's weaving "a myriad of threads into a rigidly patterned whole" (39). Also noting Mansfield's control over form, Cheryl Hankin suggests that Mansfield's structuring is perhaps more "instinctive" than deliberate (474). Either of these observations is great praise for Mansfield. The complementary parallels, threads, stages, or "levels" of "unequal length" (Harmat uses the terms "niveaux" and "longueur inégale," 49, 51) are the fall season, the time of day, insensitive or cruel actions, Miss Brill's own unreal perceptions, and the final section or dénouement.†

[2]

    An important aspect of structure in "Miss Brill" is Mansfield's use of the season of the year. Autumn, with its propulsion toward winter, is integral to the deteriorating life of the heroine. In the first paragraph, we learn that there is a "faint chill" in the air (is the word "chill" chosen to rhyme with "Brill"?), and this phrase is repeated in paragraph 10 (217). Thus the author establishes autumn and the approaching year's end as the beginning of the downward movement toward dashed hopes. This seasonal reference is also carried out when we read that "yellow leaves" are "down drooping" in the local *Jardins Publiques* (215) and that leaves are drifting "now and again" from almost "nowhere, from the sky" (215). It is the autumn cold that has caused

°This story appears on pages 218–22.
*Central idea.
†Thesis sentence.

Delgado 2

Miss Brill to wear her shabby fur piece, which later the young girl considers
the object of contempt. The chill, together with the fur, forms a structural
setting for both the action and the mood of the story. Sewell notes that
"Miss Brill" both begins and ends with the fur, which is the direct cause of
the heroine's deep hurt at the conclusion (25).

Like the seasonal structuring, the times of day parallel Miss Brill's   [3]
darkening existence. At the beginning, the speaker points out that the day
is "brilliantly fine—the blue sky powdered with gold," and that the light
is "like white wine." This figurative language suggests the brightness and
crispness of full sunlight. In paragraph 6 (216), where we also learn of the
yellow leaves, "the blue sky with gold-veined clouds" indicates that time has
been passing as clouds accumulate during late afternoon. By the story's end,
Miss Brill has returned in sadness to her "little dark room" (217). In other
words, the time moves from day to evening, from light to darkness, as a virtual
accompaniment to Miss Brill's emotional pain.

Mansfield's most significant structural device, which is not emphasized   [4]
by critics, is the introduction of insensitive or cruel actions. It is as though the
hurt felt by Miss Brill on the bright Sunday afternoon is also being felt by many
others. Because she is the spectator who is closely related to Mansfield's narrative
voice, Miss Brill is the filter through whom these negative examples reach the
reader. Considering the patterns that emerge, one may conclude that Mansfield
intends that the beauty of the day and the joyousness of the band be taken as an
ironic contrast to the pettiness and insensitivity of the people in the park.

The first of these people are the silent couple on Miss Brill's bench and the   [5]
incompatible couple of the week before (215). Because these seem no more than
ordinary, they do not at first appear to be part of the story's pattern of cruelty
and rejection. But their incompatibility, suggested by their silence and one-way
complaining, establishes a structural parallel with the young and insensitive
couple who later insult Miss Brill. Thus the first two couples prepare the way
for the third, and all show increasing insensitivity and cruelty.

Delgado 3

[6]   Almost unnoticed as a second level of negation is the vast group of "odd, silent, nearly all old" people filling "the benches and green chairs" (216). They seem to be no more than a normal part of the Sunday afternoon landscape. But these people are significant structurally because the "dark little rooms—or even cupboards" that Miss Brill associates with them also, ironically, describe the place where she lives (216, 217). The reader may conclude from Miss Brill's quiet eavesdropping that she herself is one of these nameless and faceless ones who lead similarly dreary lives.

[7]   After Mansfield sets these levels for her heroine, she introduces characters experiencing additional rejection and cruelty. The beautiful woman who throws down the bunch of violets is the first of these (216). The story does not explain the causes of this woman's scorn, and Miss Brill does not know what to make of the incident; but the woman's actions suggest that she has been involved in a relationship that has ended in anger and bitterness.

[8]   The major figure involved in rejection, who is important enough to be considered a structural double of Miss Brill, is the woman wearing the ermine toque (216). It is clear that she, like Miss Brill, is one of "the lonely and isolated women in a hostile world" that Mansfield is so skillful in portraying (Gordon 6). This woman tries to please the "gentleman in grey," but this man insults her by blowing smoke in her face. It could be, as Peter Thorpe observes, that she is "obviously a prostitute" (661). But it is more likely that the "ermine toque" has had a broken relationship with the gentleman, or perhaps even no relationship. Being familiar with his Sunday habits, she comes to the park to meet him, as though by accident, to attempt to renew contact. After her rejection, her hurrying off to meet someone "much nicer" (there is no such person, for Mansfield uses the phrase "as though" to introduce "ermine toque's" departure) is her way of masking her hurt. Regardless of the exact situation, however, Mansfield makes it plain that the encounter demonstrates vulnerability, unkindness, and pathos, but also a certain amount of self-defense.

In MLA style, put author and page number in parentheses when the author is not named in the sentence.

[9]   Once Mansfield establishes this major incident, she introduces two additional examples of insensitivity. At the end of paragraph 8 (216), the hobbling old man "with long whiskers" is nearly knocked over by the group

Delgado 4

of four girls, who show arrogance if not contempt toward him. The final
examples involve Miss Brill herself. These are her recollections of the apparent
indifference of her students and of the old invalid "who habitually sleeps"
when she reads to him.

Although "Miss Brill" is a brief story, Mansfield creates a large number   **[10]**
of structural parallels to the sudden climax brought about by the boorishly
insensitive young couple. The boy and girl do not appear until the very end, in
other words (217), but extreme insults like theirs have been fully anticipated
in the story's earlier parts. Mansfield's speaker does not take us to the homes
of the other people in the park, as she does when we follow Miss Brill to her
wretched room. Instead, the narrative invites us to conclude that the silent
couple, the complaining wife and long-suffering husband, the unseen man
rejected by the young woman, the "ermine toque," and the funny gentleman,
not to mention the many silent and withdrawn people sitting like statues in
the park, all return to loneliness and personal pain that are comparable to the
feelings of Miss Brill.

The intricacy of the structure of "Miss Brill" does not end here. Of great   **[11]**
importance is the structural development of the protagonist herself. Peter
Thorpe notes a "hierarchy of unrealities" that govern the reader's increasing
awareness of Miss Brill's plight (661). By this measure, the story's actions
progressively bring out Miss Brill's failures of perception and understanding—
failures that in this respect make her like her namesake fish, the lowly brill
(Gargano).

These unrealities begin with Miss Brill's fanciful but harmless imaginings   **[12]**
about her shabby fur piece. This beginning sets up the pattern of her pathetic
inner life. When she imagines that the park band is a "single, responsive, and
very sensitive creature" (Thorpe 661), we realize that she is unrealistically
making too much out of a mediocre band of ordinary musicians. Although she
cannot interpret the actions of the beautiful young woman with the violets, she
does see the encounter between the "ermine toque" and the gentleman in grey
as a vision of rejection. Her response is correct, but then her belief that the
band's drumbeats are sounding out "The Brute! The Brute!" indicates

**Quotation
marks around
phrases show
that they
appeared
separately
in the source.**

Delgado 5

her vivid overdramatization of the incident. The "top of the hierarchy of unrealities" (Thorpe 661) is her fancy that Miss Brill is an actor with a vital part in a gigantic drama played by all the people in the park. The most poignant aspect of this daydream is her unreal thought that someone would miss her if she were to be absent.

[13]   In light of this hierarchical structure of unrealities, it is ironic that the boy and girl sit down next to her just when she is at the height of her fancy about her own importance. When she hears the girl's insults, the couple has introduced objective reality to her with a vengeance, and she is plunged from rapture to pain. The concluding two paragraphs of "Miss Brill" hence form a rapid dénouement to reflect her loneliness and solitude.

[14]   Of unique importance in the structure of "Miss Brill" are these final two paragraphs, in which Miss Brill, all alone, returns to her wretched little room. Saralyn Daly, referring to Miss Brill as one of Mansfield's "isolatoes"—that is, solitary persons cut off from normal human contacts—fears that the couple's callous insults have caused Miss Brill to face the outside world with her fur piece "perhaps for the very last time" (88, 90). Sydney Kaplan adds a political dimension to Miss Brill's defeat, asserting that here and in other stories Mansfield is expressing "outrage" against "a society in which privilege is . . . marked by indifference" to situations like those of Miss Brill (192).

[15]   It is clear that Mansfield is asking readers to consider not only Miss Brill alone, but also her similarity to the many park inhabitants who are like her. Miss Brill's grim existence exemplifies a common personal pattern in which the old are destroyed "by loneliness and sickness, by fear of death, by the thoughtless energy of the younger world around them" (Zinman 457). More generally, Mansfield herself considered such negative situations as "the snail under the leaf," which implies that a gnawing fate is waiting for everyone, not just those who are old (Meyers 213). With such a crushing experience for the major character, "Miss Brill" may be fitted to the structuring of Mansfield's stories described by André Maurois: "moments of beauty suddenly broken by contact with ugliness, cruelty, or death" (342–43).

Delgado 6

Works Cited

Daly, Saralyn R. *Katherine Mansfield*. New York: Twayne, 1965. Print.

Gargano, James W. "Mansfield's Miss Brill." *Explicator* 19.2 (1960): N. pag. Print.

Gordon, Ian A. "Katherine Mansfield: Overview." *Reference Guide to English Literature*. Ed. D. L. Kirkpatrick. 2nd ed. London: St. James Press, 1991. *InfoTrac*. Web. 26 March 2010.

Hankin, Cheryl. "Fantasy and the Sense of an Ending in the Work of Katherine Mansfield." *Modern Fiction Studies* 24.3 (1978): 465–74. Print.

Harmat, Andrée-Marie. "Essai D'Analyse Structurale d'une Nouvelle Lyrique Anglaise: 'Miss Brill' de Katherine Mansfield." *Les Cahiers de la Nouvelle* 1 (1983): 49–74. Print.

Kaplan, Sydney Janet. *Katherine Mansfield and the Origins of Modernist Fiction*. Ithaca: Cornell UP, 1991. *GoogleBooks*. Web. 26 March 2010.

McLaughlin, Ann L. "The Same Job: The Shared Writing Aims of Katherine Mansfield and Virginia Woolf." *Modern Fiction Studies* 24.3 (1978): 369–82. *Questia*. Web. 26 March 2010.

Magalaner, Marvin. *The Fiction of Katherine Mansfield*. Carbondale: Southern Illinois UP, 1971. Print.

—. *The Short Stories of Katherine Mansfield*. New York: Knopf, 1967. Print.

Mansfield, Katherine. "Miss Brill." *Literature: An Introduction to Reading and Writing, Compact Edition*. Ed. Edgar V. Roberts and Robert Zweig. 6th ed. New York: Pearson, 2015. 218–22. Print.

Maurois, André. *Points of View from Kipling to Graham Greene*. 1935. New York: Ungar, 1968. Print.

Meyers, Jeffrey. *Katherine Mansfield: A Darker View*. 1978. New York: Cooper Square Press, 2002. Print.

Sewell, Arthur. *Katherine Mansfield: A Critical Essay*. Auckland: Unicorn, 1936. Print.

Thorpe, Peter. "Teaching 'Miss Brill.'" *College English* 23.8 (1962): 661–63. *JSTOR*. Web. 26 March 2010.

Zinman, Toby Silverman. "The Snail Under the Leaf: Katherine Mansfield's Imagery." *Modern Fiction Studies* 24.3 (1978): 457–64. Print.

In MLA style, the list of sources, called the "Works Cited," begins a new page. Double-space throughout.

List sources in alphabetical order.

Commentary on the Essay

This essay fulfills an assignment of 1500–2000 words, with ten to fifteen sources. (There are actually fifteen.) The bibliography was developed from a college library catalog, references in books of criticism (Magalaner, Daly); the *MLA International Bibliography*; the *Essay and General Literature Index*, and the Literature Resource Center available through the Internet and a county library system (www.wls .lib.ny.us). The sources themselves were found in a college library with selective holdings, in a local public library, and in online resources. There is only one rare source, an article (Harmat) obtained in photocopy through interlibrary loan from one of only two U.S. libraries holding the journal in which it appears. The location was made through the national Online Computer Library Center (OCLC). For most semester-long or quarter-long courses, you will probably not have time to add to your sources by such a method, but the article in question refers specifically to "Miss Brill," and it was therefore desirable to examine it.

The sources consist of books, articles, and chapters or portions of books. One article (Sewell) has been published as a separate short monograph. Also, one of the sources is the story "Miss Brill" itself (with locations made by paragraph and page numbers), together with a collection of Mansfield's stories. The sources are used for facts, interpretations, reinforcement of conclusions, and general guidance and authority.

All necessary thematic devices, including overall organization and transitions, are unique to the illustrative essay. The essay also contains passages taking issue with certain conclusions in a few of the sources. Additional particulars about the handling of sources and developing a research essay are included in the discussion of note taking and related matters in this chapter.

The central idea of the essay (paragraph 1) is built out of this idea, explaining that the movement of emotions in the story is accompanied by an intricate and complementary set of structures. Paragraphs 2 through 13 examine various elements of the story for their structural relationship to Miss Brill's emotions.

Paragraphs 2 and 3 detail the structural uses of the settings of autumn and times of day, pointing out how they parallel her experiences.

The longest part, paragraphs 4 through 10, is based on an idea not found in the sources—that a number of characters are experiencing difficulties and cruelties such as those that befall Miss Brill. Paragraph 5 cites the three couples of the story, paragraph 6 the silent old people, and paragraph 7 the scornful woman with violets. Paragraph 8 is developed in disagreement with one of the sources, showing how an essay involving research may be original even though the sources form the basis of discussion. Paragraph 9 contains additional examples of insensitivity—two of them involving Miss Brill herself. Paragraph 10 summarizes the story's instances of insensitivity and cruelty, once again emphasizing parallels to Miss Brill's situation.

Paragraphs 11 through 13 of the essay are based on ideas about the story's structure found in one of the sources (Thorpe). It is hence more derivative than paragraphs 4 through 10. Paragraphs 14 and 15, the concluding paragraphs of the essay, are devoted to the story's dénouement and to the broader application of the story: Miss Brill is to be considered an example of the anonymous "isolatoes" who inhabit the park.

The list of works cited is the basis of all references in the essay, in accord with the *MLA Handbook*. By locating these references, a reader might readily examine, verify, and study any of the ideas and details drawn from the sources and developed in the essay.

USING SOURCES EFFECTIVELY

PARAPHRASING TO AVOID PLAGIARISM

Writing about literature often requires consulting secondary sources such as scholarly works of criticism, biography, and history that help make an essay more authoritative and critically balanced. However, overquoting a source or using a source's original language without proper citation make an essay less persuasive—and less "your own"—and could be regarded as plagiarism, whether intentional or unintentional. This error often occurs when a student's notes do not explicitly show what the source's exact words were. Paraphrasing is the restatement of a source's key ideas or main point in your own language, and learning how to paraphrase accurately without plagiarizing is an essential skill for any academic writing that uses sources. Your paraphrase can be slightly shorter or longer than the original, but it should always accurately convey the essence of the original using your own words. Finding your own way of expressing the ideas in the source is critical. It will not only help you to thoughtfully weigh ideas other than your own but also help you to absorb them smoothly and honestly into your larger argument.

Let's take a look at how one student used the notecard (see page 512) quoting the essay by Richard F. Peterson (with words and phrases from the original source underlined).

> In "Miss Brill" <u>the climax of the narrative suggests</u> <u>an arranged reality</u> that leaves a strong <u>impression</u> of only the author's cleverness, not of real life.

Although elements of the sentence have been rearranged, most of the language has been copied directly from the source without attribution. This is plagiarism.

Note how much of the original language is picked up from the student's note cards without any quotation marks to indicate what has been borrowed from someone else. Nor does this extract include any citation or specific reference to the critic's essay. If this passage made its way into the student's paper, she could get into serious trouble.

In a more careful paraphrase of this material, the student restated the sentence in her own words and indicated the source by using proper documentation style.

> The main plot point of "Miss Brill" indicates the author's preference for, according to critic Richard F. Peterson "an arranged reality" (385), not a realistic or believable view of the world.

This paraphrase both acknowledges the specific author of the essay and cites the page where the idea is found.

The revised version not only gives proper credit to the critic whose ideas were consulted for this essay but also grounds the essay in critical expertise and balanced academic validity. In the revision, the writer demonstrates her command of both the principles of academic inquiry and the use of paraphrase to avoid plagiarism. (For more information on avoiding plagiarism when writing research essays, see page 511.)

Writing Topics About How to Undertake a Research Essay

In beginning research on any of the following topics, follow the steps in research described in this chapter.

1. Common themes in a number of stories by Hawthorne, Poe, or Mansfield (just one, not all).
2. Various critical views of a Hemingway story.
3. Hawthorne's use of religious and moral topic material.
4. Porter's exemplification of Granny Weatherall's strength of character.
5. Views about women in Chopin, Welty, Mansfield, or Steinbeck.
6. Poe's view of the short story as represented in "The Masque of the Red Death."

PART III

Reading and Writing About Poetry

Chapter 11
Meeting Poetry:
An Overview

AFTER STUDYING THIS MATERIAL, YOU SHOULD BE ABLE TO DO THE FOLLOWING:
- Understand the general nature and shape of poetry
- Describe broadly the general history of poetry in English
- Explain the different ways to approach and study a poem
- Explicate a short English poem

Our words **poem** and **poetry** are derived from the Greek word *poiein*, "to create or make," the idea being that poetry is a created artifact, a structure that develops from the human imagination and that is expressed rhythmically in words. Although the word *poet* originally meant the writer of any kind of literature, we now use the word exclusively to mean a person who writes poems. *Poetry* and *poem* describe a wide variety of spoken and written forms, styles, and patterns, and also a wide variety of subjects. In light of this variety, we believe that the best way to understand poetry is to experience it—read it, study it, savor it, think about it, dream about it, learn it, memorize it, mull it over, talk about it with others, ask questions about it, enjoy it, love it. The more experience with poetry you have, the more you will develop your own ideas and definitions of just what poetry is, and the deeper will be your comprehension and the greater your appreciation.

The Nature of Poetry

We begin with a favorite poem based in the lives of students and teachers alike. It was written by Billy Collins, who was our American Poet Laureate from 2001 to 2003:

BILLY COLLINS (b. 1941)

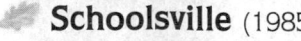 Schoolsville (1985)

Glancing over my shoulder at the past,
I realize the number of students I have taught
is enough to populate a small town.

I can see it nestled in a paper landscape,
5   chalk dust flurrying down in winter,
nights dark as a blackboard.

The population ages but never graduates.
On hot afternoons they sweat the final in the park
and when it's cold they shiver around stoves
reading disorganized essays out loud.   10
A bell rings on the hour and everybody zigzags
in the streets with their books.

I forgot all their last names first and their
first names last in alphabetical order.
But the boy who always had his hand up   15
is an alderman and owns the haberdashery.
The girl who signed her papers in lipstick
leans against the drugstore, smoking,
brushing her hair like a machine.

Their grades are sewn into their clothes   20
like references to Hawthorne.°   *i.e., The Scarlet Letter*
The A's stroll along with other A's.
The D's honk whenever they pass another D.

All the creative writing students recline
on the courthouse lawn and play the lute.   25
Wherever they go, they form a big circle.

Needless to say, I am the mayor.
I live in the white colonial at Maple and Main.
I rarely leave the house. The car deflates
in the driveway. Vines twirl around the porchswing.   30

Once in a while a student knocks on the door
with a term paper fifteen years late
or a question about Yeats or double-spacing.
And sometimes one will appear in a window pane
to watch me lecturing the wall paper,   35
quizzing the chandelier, reprimanding the air.

QUESTIONS

1. What recognizable school experiences does the poem mention? Why is "Schoolsville" the title?

2. Describe the speaker. How does he indicate affection for students?

3. What details indicate that the poem is fantasy and not reality? To what degree is the poem humorous?

4. Compare the details of this poem with those in Roethke's "Dolor" (Chapter 12). What similarities do you find in the choice and appropriateness of detail? What differences?

5. Each poem you read may help you understand, and therefore define, poetry. How might this poem help you begin making a definition?

"Schoolsville" reveals the variety and freedom of poetry. Unlike poems that are set out in strict line lengths, rhythms, and rhymes, "Schoolsville," though arranged in lines, does not follow measured rhythmical or rhyming patterns. The language is not difficult, the descriptions are straightforward, and the scenes seem both real and amusing. Many details—such as the "chalk dust flurrying down" like snow, "the girl who signed her papers in lipstick," and the students forming a circle when they meet—are genuinely funny. But the poem moves from apparent reality to something beyond reality. Unifying the poem is the fanciful idea that school life is, like life generally, at once comical, serious, memorable, and poignant.

We may contrast "Schoolsville" with the following poem, "Hope," by Lisel Mueller, which deals with a topic—hope—that is common to us all, a topic that governs both our present and future behavior. What is unique, however, is that the poet provides us with thoughts about the nature of hope that might never have occurred to us. In this sense the poem fulfills the creative goal of poetry to lead us and guide us.

LISEL MUELLER (b. 1924)

Hope (1976)

It hovers in dark corners
before the lights are turned on,
   it shakes sleep from its eyes
   and drops from mushroom gills,
5   it explodes in the starry heads
      of dandelions turned sages,
         it sticks to the wings of green angels
         that sail from the tops of maples.

It sprouts in each occluded° eye   *closed, blind*
10 of the many-eyed potato,
   it lives in each earthworm segment
   surviving cruelty,
      it is the motion that runs
      from the eyes to the tail of a dog,
15   it is the mouth that inflates the lungs
         of the child that has just been born.

It is the singular gift
we cannot destroy in ourselves,
the argument that refutes death,
20 the genius that invents the future,
all we know of God.

It is the serum which makes us swear
not to betray one another;
it is in this poem, trying to speak.

QUESTIONS

1. How does the poem illustrate the meaning of hope? How true or adequate are the specific locations where hope may be found? How do these locations provide the grounds for a broadened understanding of hope?
2. What does the poet mean by saying that hope is a "singular gift / we cannot destroy in ourselves" and that hope is a "serum" that prevents people from betraying each other?
3. According to the illustrations in the poem, how strong is the connection between hope and life? Can anything or anyone be without hope?
4. Why does the poet write "trying to speak" rather than "speaking" in the final line?

"Hope" demonstrates that poetry is inseparable from life and living. We regularly hope for fine weather, good luck, happier times, love, successful academic and athletic performance, more money, more and better friendships, successful and rewarding careers, and so on. But Mueller takes us on a new and unexpected trip. Her speaker reminds us that hope exists in common things around us where we have never even imagined it might be, such as the fluttering seeds ("angels") of maple trees, the expanding lungs of a newborn baby, and "the genius that invents the future." Hope may even be found in the blind eyes of a potato which, when planted in lowly garden dirt, possess an indomitable wish for growth. The poem makes these ordinary things extraordinary. Mueller even leaves us with a speculative and unusual conclusion, giving life to hope by stating that hope speaks simultaneously with poetry itself. All these connections, which Mueller naturally and easily creates for us, cause us to say yes, to agree that hope exists in every obscure and out-of-the-way part of existence. Like all good poetry, "Hope" leads us into thoughts that we have not only not considered, but that we have never even dreamed about.

We should always recognize that good poems, regardless of their topics, have similar power. To see this, let us look at another poem, by the seventeenth-century English poet Robert Herrick.

ROBERT HERRICK (1591–1664)

Here a Pretty Baby Lies (1648)

Here a pretty baby lies
Sung asleep with lullabies:
Pray be silent, and not stir
Th'easy earth that covers her.

QUESTIONS

1. What situation is described in this poem? To what degree is this situation either ordinary or unusual?
2. How does the final line change your perception of the first three lines? How does it change your response to the poem?
3. Consider the double meanings of the following words and phrases: "Here . . . lies"; "Sung asleep"; "lullabies"; "stir."
4. Compare this poem with Jonson's "On My First Daughter" (this chapter).

Nothing in the first three lines of this short poem seems anything other than ordinary. A scene is described that takes place over and over again everywhere in the world. A baby is sleeping quietly, and we are told to make no sounds that would awaken her. But the last line hits us with a hammer, making us realize that nothing in the poem is what we understood at first. We immediately change our initial impressions and realize that the baby is not just sleeping but dead, lying not in a cradle but in a coffin; that the lullabies are not the lullabies sung by a loving mother but the religious songs sung at a funeral ceremony; and that the stirring is not just making noise but disturbing the still-loose earth that has just been shoveled onto the baby's grave. The effect of this very simple poem has been called overwhelming; it was overwhelming when it was first written in the seventeenth century, and it is still overwhelming.

The three poems we have just seen have much in common; they are serious, engaging, original, and powerful. The first, however, is amusing and slightly perplexing; the second is serious and thought-provoking; the third is sad and deeply moving. There are no other poems like them. Once we have read them, we will never forget them. Even if we never read them again (but we should), they will echo in our minds as time passes, sometimes with great power and impact, sometimes with less. In reading them again we may rediscover our original responses, and often we may have entirely new responses to them. In short, these poems live, and as long as we too live, they will be a permanent part of our minds.

Preliminary Ideas About Poetry

As "Schoolsville," "Hope," and "Here a Pretty Baby Lies" demonstrate, all good poems are unique, and all good poems broaden our comprehension and add layers to our understandings. Like living itself, the experience of poetry is a developing process, but nevertheless, it is possible to offer a number of preliminary statements as a guide to understanding. To begin with, poems are imaginative works expressed in words that are used with the utmost compression, force, and economy. Unlike prose, which is expansive if not exhaustive, many poems are brief. But poetry is also comprehensive, offering us high points of thought, feeling, reflection, and resolution. Poems may be formed in just about any coherent and developed shape, from a line of a single word to lines of twenty, thirty, or more words; and these lines may be organized into any number of repeating or nonrepeating patterns. Some poems make us think, give us new and unexpected insights, and generally instruct us. Other poems arouse our emotions, surprise us, amuse us, and inspire us. Ideally, reading and understanding poetry should prompt us to reexamine, reinforce, and reshape our ideas, our attitudes, our feelings, and our lives. Let us hear what Robert Frost concluded about poetry: "Read it a hundred times: it will forever keep its freshness as a metal keeps its fragrance. It can never lose its sense of a meaning that once unfolded by surprise as it went."[1] Always be prepared for the surprise, and be delighted when it appears.

"The Figure a Poem Makes," in *Complete Poems of Robert Frost 1949* (New York: Holt, 1949) viii.

Poetry of the English Language

Today, most nations of the world have their own literatures, including poetry, with their own unique histories and characteristics. Name a nation, and you may be assured that it will have its own linguistic history, and its own history of literature. Let us try France, which has a history of literature and poetry that is many centuries old. Many Americans know "La Marseillaise," the French national anthem by Claude-Joseph Rouget de Lisle (1760–1836), and some may even be able to sing at least some of the lyrics. Name the Philippine Islands, the island nation on the other side of the world. The language of the Philippines is *Tagalog*, and there is a body of literature in that language. So also is it with Germany, Russia, Sweden, China, Japan, and as many nations as we might possibly name. In this anthology, however, we will be concentrating primarily on poetry in our own language by American, British, and Canadian poets. When we introduce poems from other languages, we will be relying on translations from these languages into English.

The earliest poems in English date back to the period of *Old English* (450–1100). Many of these early English poems reflect the influence of Christianity. Indeed, the most famous poem, the anonymous epic *Beowulf*, was probably interpreted as a Christian allegory even though it concerns the secular themes of adventure, courage, and war. Ever since the *Middle English* period (1100–1500), poets have written about many other subjects, although religious themes have remained important. Today, we find poetry on virtually all topics, including worship, music, love, society, sports, individuality, strong drink, sexuality, warfare, government, and politics; some poems treat special and unusual topics such as fishing, machines, buildings, computers, exotic birds, and car crashes.

In short, poetry is in a flourishing condition in all its many topics. Commonly held moral principles are instilled by the use of well-known brief poems, epigrams, rhymes, and jingles, such as "Work. / Don't shirk," "A good beginning / Is half the winning," and "A stitch in time / Saves nine." Many people, such as poets themselves and teachers, read poetry or parts of poems aloud in front of audiences of students, friends, families, and general audiences. Many others read poetry silently in private for their own benefit. Nursery rhymes are one of the important means by which children learn the vocabulary and rhythms of our language. Poems that are set to music and sung aloud are especially powerful. "The Star-Spangled Banner" by Francis Scott Key (1779–1843), who wrote the poem during the Battle of Fort McHenry in the War of 1812, is our national anthem and is sung before sports competitions and many other events. In more recent times, musical groups like the Beatles and U2, along with singer Bruce Springsteen, have given poetic expression to ideas that huge masses of people have taken to heart. Ever since the 1960s, people devoted to civil rights have been unified and strengthened by the simple lyrics of "We Shall Overcome," based on a Gospel hymn by Charles Albert Tindley (1851–1933), not only in the United States but throughout the world. During the national crisis following the attacks on the World Trade Center and the Pentagon in 2001, many people turned to "America the Beautiful" and "God Bless America" as songs that stir the heart. The strength and vitality of poetry could be similarly documented time and time again.

How to Read a Poem

With poetry, as with any other literary form, the more effort we put into under-standing, the greater will be our reward. Poems are often about subjects that we have never experienced directly. We have never met the poet, never had his or her exact experiences, and never thought about things in exactly the same way. To recapture the experience of the poem, we need to understand the language, ideas, attitudes, and frames of reference that bring the poem to life.

We must therefore read all poems carefully, thoughtfully, sympathetically. The economy and compression of poetry mean that every part of the poem must carry some of the impact and meaning, and thus every part repays careful attention. Try to interact with the poem. Do not expect the poem (or the poet) to do all the work. The poem contributes its language, imagery, rhythms, ideas, and all the other aspects that make it poetry; but you, the reader, will need to open your mind and your heart to the poem's impact. You have to use your imagination and let it happen.

There is no single technique for reading, absorbing, and appreciating poetry. In Part I we offer a number of guidelines for studying any work of literature (pp. 13–30). In addition to following the guidelines, read each poem more than once and keep in mind these objectives.

1. **Read straight through to get a general sense of the poem.** In this first reading, do not stop to puzzle out hard passages or obscure words; just read through from beginning to end. The poem is probably not as hard as you might at first think.

2. **Try to understand the poem's meaning and organization.** As you read and reread the poem, study these elements:

   • *The title.* The title is almost always informative. The title of Collins's "Schoolsville" suggests that the poem will contain a somewhat flippant treatment of school life. The title of Frost's "Stopping by Woods on a Snowy Evening" suggests that the poem will present ideas derived from a natural scene of cold and darkness.

   • *The speaker.* Poems are dramatic, having points of view just like prose fiction. First-person speakers talk from the "inside" because they are directly involved in the action (like the speaker in Collins's "Schoolsville"). Other speakers are "outside" observers demonstrating the third-person limited and omniscient points of view, as in the anonymous "Sir Patrick Spens" (see also Chapter 2 on point of view).

   • *The meanings of all words, whether familiar or unfamiliar.* The words in many poems are immediately clear, as in Herrick's "Here a Pretty Baby Lies," but other poems may contain unfamiliar words and references and you may need to consult dictionaries, encyclopedias, and other sources until you gain a grasp of the poem's content. If you have difficulty with meanings even after using your sources, ask your instructor for help.

   • *The poem's setting and situation.* Some poems establish their settings and circumstances vividly. Frost's "Stopping by Woods on a Snowy Evening" describes an evening scene in which the speaker stops his sleigh by a woods so that he can watch snow falling amid the trees. Although not all poems are so clear, you should learn as much as you can about setting and situation in every poem you read.

QUESTIONS

1. What action does the poem describe? Who are the principal individual figures? What groups of people are involved with and concerned about the action?
2. What do you learn about the principal figure, Sir Patrick Spens? Why does he follow the king's orders rather than his own judgment?
3. What conflicts do you find in the poem? Do they seem personal or political?
4. What emotions are conveyed in the last two stanzas? Since the poem does not explain why the king sends Sir Patrick and his men to sea, how might the emotions have been expressed more strongly?
5. Describe the poem's use of dialogue. How many people speak? How do the speeches assist in conveying the poem's action?

"Sir Patrick Spens" is a **narrative ballad**. A **narrative** tells a story, and the term **ballad** defines the poem's shape or form, which was originally a song for dancing (related to our word *ballet*). The first two stanzas set up the situation: The king needs a captain and crew to undertake a vital mission, and an old knight—one of the king's close advisers—suggests Sir Patrick Spens, who is obviously distinguished and reliable. The rest of the poem focuses on the feelings and eventual death of Sir Patrick and his men. The third stanza provides a transition from the king to Sir Patrick. The king orders Sir Patrick to embark on an important sea voyage, and Sir Patrick reads the order. At first he laughs—probably bitterly, because Sir Patrick's response is that an order to go to sea during an obvious time of danger is nothing more than a grim joke. But when he realizes that the order is real, he foresees disaster. Our sense of impending calamity is increased when we learn that Sir Patrick's crewmen are also frightened (lines 23–28).

The shipwreck, described in the eighth stanza, is presented with ironic understatement. There is no description of the storm or of the crew's panic, nor does the speaker describe the masts splitting or the ship sinking under the waves. Although these horrors are omitted, the floating hats are grim evidence of destruction and death. The remainder of the poem continues in this vein of understatement. In the ninth and tenth stanzas the focus shifts back to the land, and to the ladies who will wait a "long, long" time (forever) for Sir Patrick and his men to return. The poem ends with a vision of Sir Patrick and the "Scots lords" lying "fifty fathom deep."

On first reflection, "Sir Patrick Spens" tells a sad tale without complications. The subject seems to describe no more than Sir Patrick's drowning, along with his crew and the Scots noblemen. One might therefore claim that the poem does not have a clear theme. Even the irony of the floating hats and the waiting ladies is straightforward and unambiguous.

However, you might consider how the poem appeals to our imaginations through its suggestions of the contradictions and conflicts between authority and individuals. Sir Patrick knows the danger, yet he still obeys the king. In addition, in lines 5, 17–20, and 31, there is a suggestion of political infighting. The "eldern knight" is in effect responsible for dooming the ship. Moreover, the "play" being "played" suggests that a political game is happening beyond the grim game of the men caught in the deadly storm (if Sir Patrick knows the danger, would not the knight also know it, and would not this knight also know the consequences of choosing Sir Patrick?). These political motives are not spelled out, but they are implied. Thus the poem is not only a sad tale but also a poignant dramatization of how power operates, of how a loyal person responds to a tragic dilemma, and of the pitiful consequences of that response.

In reading poetry, then, let the poem be your guide. Get all the words, try to understand dramatic situations, follow the emotional cues the poet gives you, and try to explain everything that is happening. Let the poem trigger your imagination. If you find implications that you believe are important, as with the political overtones of "Sir Patrick Spens," use details from the poem to support your observations. Resist the temptation to "uncover" unusual or far-fetched elements in the poem (for example, that hope is a tiny spirit that inhabits human beings, trees, and vegetables, or that the "man he killed" was literally the speaker's brother). Draw only those conclusions that the poem itself supports.

Poems for Study

Gwendolyn Brooks . . . . The Mother, 544
Emily Dickinson . . . . Because I Could Not Stop for Death, 545
Rita Dove . . . . The House Slave, 546
Robert Francis . . . . Catch, 547
Robert Frost . . . . Stopping by Woods on a Snowy Evening, 548
Thomas Hardy . . . . The Man He Killed, 548
Joy Harjo . . . . Eagle Poem, 549
Randall Jarrell . . . . The Death of the Ball Turret Gunner, 550
Ben Jonson . . . . On My First Daughter, 550
Kenneth Koch . . . Variations on a Theme by William Carlos Williams, 551
Louis MacNeice . . . . Snow, 552
Magus Magnus . . . . An Old Soldier Cleans His Rifle for the Last Time, 552
Jim Northrup . . . . Ogichidag, 553
Naomi Shihab Nye . . . . Where Children Live, 554
Louis Simpson . . . . American Poetry, 555
William Shakespeare . . . . Sonnet 55: Not Marble, Nor the Gilded
                                                                  Monuments, 555
Elaine Terranova . . . . Rush Hour, 556
William Carlos Williams . . . . This Is Just to Say, 557
William Wordsworth . . . . Tintern Abbey, 557

GWENDOLYN BROOKS (1917–2000)

 ### The Mother (1945)

Abortions will not let you forget.
You remember the children you got that you did not get,
The damp small pulps with a little or with no hair,
The singers and workers that never handled the air.
5 You will never neglect or beat
Them, or silence or buy with a sweet.
You will never wind up the sucking-thumb

Or scuttle off ghosts that come.
You will never leave them, controlling your luscious sigh,
Return for a snack of them, with gobbling mother-eye.   10
I have heard in the voices of the wind the voices of my dim killed children.
I have contracted. I have eased
My dim dears at the breasts they could never suck.
I have said, Sweets, if I sinned, if I seized
Your luck   15
And your lives from your unfinished reach,
If I stole your births and your names,
Your straight baby tears and your games,
Your stilted or lovely loves, your tumults, your marriages, aches, and your deaths,
If I poisoned the beginnings of your breaths,   20
Believe that even in my deliberateness I was not deliberate.
Though why should I whine,
Whine that the crime was other than mine?—
Since anyhow you are dead.
Or rather, or instead,   25
You were never made.
But that too, I am afraid,
Is faulty: oh, what shall I say, how is the truth to be said?
You were born, you had body, you died.
It is just that you never giggled or planned or cried.   30

Believe me, I loved you all.
Believe me, I knew you, though faintly, and I loved, I loved you
All.

QUESTIONS

1. Describe the circumstances of the speaker. Who is she? What is the topic of her narrative? What has happened to her? What thoughts and feelings does she express about her experiences? Why does she say "how is the truth to be said" (line 28)?

2. What is the topic of this poem? What moral and political issues does the poem raise?

3. What conclusions do you think the poet wants you to draw from this poem? What "pro" and "con" positions might be derived from the poem?

4. Considering this poem, discuss what topical material might be imposed on writers of poetry? What might be considered "poetic" subject matter?

EMILY DICKINSON (1830–1886)

For a photo, see Chapter 18, page 801.

Because I Could Not Stop for Death (1890; c.1863)°

Because I could not stop for Death—
He kindly stopped for me—

°This poem was first published, 1890; written c. 1863. You will see two dates given for many poems in the book.

The Carriage held but just Ourselves—
And Immortality.

5 We slowly drove—He knew no haste
And I had put away
My labor and my leisure too,
For His Civility—

We passed the School, where Children strove
10 At Recess—in the Ring—
We passed the Fields of Gazing Grain—
We passed the Setting Sun—

Or rather—He passed Us—
The Dews drew quivering and chill—
15 For only Gossamer,° my Gown—   thin fabric
My Tippet°—only Tulle°—   cape, scarf; thin silk

We passed before a House that seemed
A Swelling of the Ground—
The Roof was scarcely visible—
20 The Cornice—in the Ground—

Since then—tis Centuries—and yet
Feels shorter than the Day
I first surmised the Horses' Heads
Were toward Eternity—

QUESTIONS

1. Who is the speaker, and what is she like? Why couldn't she stop for Death? What perspective does her present position give the poem?

2. In what unusual ways does the poem characterize death?

3. What does the carriage represent? Where is it headed? Who are the riders? What is meant by the things the carriage passes?

4. What is represented by the house in line 17? Why does the poet use the word "House" in preference to some other word?

RITA DOVE (b. 1952)

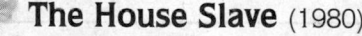 The House Slave (1980)

The first horn lifts its arm over the dew-lit grass
and in the slave quarters there is a rustling—
children are bundled into aprons, cornbread

and water gourds grabbed, a salt pork breakfast taken.
5 I watch them driven into the vague before-dawn
while their mistress sleeps like an ivory toothpick

and Massa dreams of asses, rum and slave-funk.
I cannot fall asleep again. At the second horn,
the whip curls across the backs of the laggards—

sometimes my sister's voice, unmistaken, among them.   10
"Oh! pray," she cries. "Oh! pray!" Those days
I lie on my cot, shivering in the early heat,

and as the fields unfold to whiteness,
and they spill like bees among the fat flowers,
I weep. It is not yet daylight.   15

QUESTIONS

1. Did this poem touch you on an emotional level? Why does the speaker "weep" near the end of the poem?
2. What is the relationship between the two sisters in the poem?
3. Which images stand out? How do they relate to the poem's theme?

ROBERT FRANCIS (1901–1987)

 ## Catch (1950)

Two boys uncoached are tossing a poem together,
Overhand, underhand, backhand, sleight of hand, every hand,
Teasing with attitudes, latitudes, interludes, altitudes,
High, make him fly off the ground for it, low, make him stoop,
Make him scoop it up, make him as-almost-as-possible miss it,   5
Fast, let him sting from it, now, fool him slowly,
Anything, everything tricky, risky, nonchalant,
Anything under the sun to outwit the prosy,
Over the tree and the long sweet cadence down,
Over his head, make him scramble to pick up the meaning,   10
And now, like a posy, a pretty one plump in his hands.

QUESTIONS

1. Describe the language of "Catch." How does the poet establish that there are two meanings to most of the words in the game of catch played by the "boys"?
2. How accurately does the poem describe a game of ordinary catch in which the participants are throwing a baseball? How interesting would a game of catch be if the participants stood still and merely threw the ball back and forth to each other? How interesting would poetry be if the poet did not create variety just as the catch players vary their throws?
3. How well does the analogy of the game of catch explain why poetry sometimes requires extra efforts of understanding?

ROBERT FROST (1874–1963)

For a photo, see Chapter 18, page 837.

 ## Stopping by Woods on a Snowy Evening (1923)

Whose woods these are I think I know.
His house is in the village though;
He will not see me stopping here
To watch his woods fill up with snow.

5 My little horse must think it queer
To stop without a farmhouse near
Between the woods and frozen lake
The darkest evening of the year.

He gives his harness bells a shake
10 To ask if there is some mistake.
The only other sound's the sweep
Of easy wind and downy flake.

The woods are lovely, dark and deep,
But I have promises to keep,
15 And miles to go before I sleep,
And miles to go before I sleep.

QUESTIONS

1. What do we learn about the speaker? Where is he? What is he doing?
2. What is the setting (place, weather, time) of this poem?
3. Why does the speaker want to watch the "woods fill up with snow"?
4. What evidence suggests that the speaker is embarrassed or self-conscious about stopping? Consider the words "though" in line 2 and "must" in line 5.
5. The last stanza offers two alternative attitudes and courses of action. What are they? Which does the speaker choose?

THOMAS HARDY (1840–1928)

The Man He Killed (1902)

"Had he and I but met
By some old ancient inn,
We should have sat us down to wet
Right many a nipperkin!°   *half-pint cup*

5   "But ranged as infantry,
And staring face to face,
I shot at him as he at me,
And killed him in his place.

"I shot him dead because—
    Because he was my foe.
Just so: my foe of course he was;
    That's clear enough; although   10

"He thought he'd 'list,° perhaps,   *enlist*
    Off-hand like—just as I—
Was out of work—had sold his traps°—   *possessions*   15
    No other reason why.

"Yes; quaint and curious war is!
    You shoot a fellow down
You'd treat if met where any bar is,
    Or help to half-a-crown." °   20

_____

°20 *half-a-crown*: at the time, the equivalent of $20 or $30.

QUESTIONS

1. Who and what is the speaker? What do you learn about him from his language?
2. What situation or event is the speaker recalling and relating?
3. What is the effect produced by repeating the word "because" in lines 9 and 10 and using the word "although" in line 12?
4. What is the speaker's attitude toward his "foe" and toward what he has done?
5. What point, if any, does this poem make about war? How are this poem and Jarrell's "The Death of the Ball Turret Gunner" similar and different?

JOY HARJO (b. 1951)

Eagle Poem (1990)

To pray you open your whole self
To sky, to earth, to sun, to moon
To one whole voice that is you.
And know there is more
That you can't see, can't hear,   5
Can't know except in moments
Steadily growing, and in languages
That aren't always sound but other
Circles of motion.
Like eagle that Sunday morning   10
Over Salt River. Circled in blue sky
In wind, swept our hearts clean
With sacred wings.
We see you, see ourselves and know
That we must take the utmost care   15
And kindness in all things.
Breathe in, knowing we are made of
All this, and breathe, knowing
We are truly blessed because we
Were born, and die soon within a   20

True circle of motion,
Like eagle rounding out the morning
Inside us.
We pray that it will be done
25 In beauty.
In beauty.

QUESTIONS

1. What is meant by the requirement that "to pray you open your whole self / To sky, to earth, to sun, to moon"? What is the meaning of lines 4–9?
2. Why is the eagle significant to the speaker? Of what importance is the figure that the eagle makes?
3. Why does the poet repeat the phrase "In beauty" at the poem's end?

RANDALL JARRELL (1914–1965)

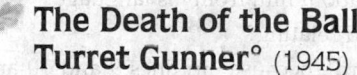 The Death of the Ball Turret Gunner° (1945)

From my mother's sleep I fell into the State
And I hunched in its belly till my wet fur froze.°
Six miles from earth, loosed from its dream of life,
I woke to black flak° and the nightmare fighters.
5 When I died they washed me out of the turret with a hose.

°*Ball Turret Gunner.* High-altitude bombers in World War II (1941–1945) contained a revolvable gun turret both at the top and at the bottom, from which a machine-gunner could shoot at attacking fighter planes. Gunners in these turrets were sometimes mutilated by the gunfire of attacking planes. °2 *froze:* The stratospheric below-zero temperatures caused the moisture in the gunner's breath to freeze as it contacted the collar of his flight jacket. °4 *flak:* the round, black explosions of antiaircraft shells fired at bombers from the ground, an acronym of the German word *Fliegerabwehrkanone.*

QUESTIONS

1. Who is the speaker? Where has he been, and what has he been doing? What has happened to him?
2. In the first line, what is the poet saying about the age of the speaker and the opportunities he had for living before he was killed? How may this line be read politically and polemically?
3. What is a turret? What is your response to the last line?

BEN JONSON (1573–1637)

On My First Daughter° (1616)

Here lies, to each her parents' ruth,°
Mary, the daughter of their youth:

°*On My First Daughter:* Jonson's infant daughter, Mary, died at the age of six months, but the year of her death is unknown. The poem was included in the 1616 edition of Jonson's *Epigrams.* °1 *ruth:* sadness, grief 3-4.

Yet all heaven's gifts, being heaven's due,
It makes the father less, to rue.°
At six month's end, she parted hence   5
With safety of her innocence;
Whose soul heaven's Queen (whose name she bears),
In comfort of her mother's tears,
Hath placed amongst her virgin-train:°
Where, while that severed° doth remain,   10
This grave partakes° the fleshly birth,
Which cover lightly, gentle earth.

°*Yet . . . rue:* i.e., because all heaven's gifts are [still] owned by heaven, the child's death takes from me, her
father, a cause of mourning.   °7–9 *Whose soul . . . virgin-train:* i.e., to comfort the tears of her mother, the Queen
of heaven, after whom [my daughter] was named, has placed her soul among her [Mary's] virgin-train.
10 *that severed:* the child's soul, which at death is separated from the body.   11 *partakes:* contains the infant's
body [until the Resurrection].

QUESTIONS

1. What is the situation of this poem? How does the speaker reconcile himself to the death of his infant daughter?

2. Compare this poem with Herrick's "Here a Pretty Baby Lies" (p. 537).

KENNETH KOCH (1925–2002)

 from **Variations on a Theme by William Carlos Williams** (1962)

1

I chopped down the house that you had been saving
to live in next summer.
I am sorry, but it was morning, and I had nothing to do
and its wooden beams were so inviting.

2

We laughed at the hollyhocks together
and then I sprayed them with lye.   5
Forgive me. I simply do not know what I am doing.

QUESTIONS

1. Why do you think Koch is imitating Williams's poem (page 557)? Do you think he is "spoofing" the poem or being serious? How do you know?

2. What do you imagine is the relationship between the speaker and the other person in each poem?

3. If Koch's poem had been written first, could Williams's poem be read as a spoof of Koch's?

LOUIS MACNEICE (1907–1963)

 **Snow** (1935)

The room was suddenly rich and the great bay-window was
Spawning snow and pink roses against it
Soundlessly collateral and incompatible:
World is suddener than we fancy it.

5   World is crazier and more of it than we think,
Incorrigibly plural. I peel and portion
A tangerine and spit the pips and feel
The drunkenness of things being various.

And the fire flames with a bubbling sound for world
10   Is more spiteful and gay than one supposes—
On the tongue on the eyes on the ears in the palms of one's hands—
There is more than glass between the snow and the huge roses.

QUESTIONS

1. Where is the speaker at the time of the poem? What is the contrast between the roses and the snow? Why is this contrast important?
2. What words describe snow in lines 1–3? What words in lines 4, 5, 6, 8, 10 describe the world generally? Why does the speaker choose these words rather than more descriptive ones?
3. What does the last line suggest?
4. What similarities and differences do you find between "Snow" and Frost's "Stopping by Woods on a Snowy Evening" (p. 000)?

MAGUS MAGNUS (1967)

An Old Soldier Cleans His Rifle for the Last Time (2011)

(holding a rifle and a rag)
   Feels right in my hands. My hands feel strong again. Like fists. Old friend, let us continue our old comradery. Rely on this shoulder to carry you. I'm old, but I've got some fight in me. Bring 'em on! With these knobby bones, can still give a good elbow into someone's ribs. Old friend, old comrade, trustiest friend: I've never let you get rusty yet. Saved my life many times. Shared with me perils of battle. Oil the rag, loving care. Smell of gunpowder. Life-giving whiff. When did I last fire you? Got that tusked boar last year. Stimulating smell of gunpowder. I've some life in me yet. Gray smudge, black grains. When I'm dust, you'll be rust; only when I'm dust. So it goes. You'll be rust, I'll be dust. Me first, though. And it won't be too long in coming. Hear that, one of my granddaughters just came in. Probably try to put me back into bed, take this out of my hands. Saying hello; pretend I don't hear. Won't turn around yet, let her wait. More of the family coming in? Keep my back to 'em, let 'em hear me.

Sons, daughters, sons-in-law, grandsons-in-law, all them, they come in here to gawk, as I lay dying. Yes, Granddad's dying; your aged, brave—disobeyed!—patriarch's on his way out. But I'm up now, I'm gonna clean my gun. Don't you dare try to drag me back to bed, like those Secesh bastards trying to take me prisoner. I don't give up so easily! Ease up, they're tender for me. They want to help me, I'll give them that. But this coddling will kill me quicker. They're too soft. You're too soft, you hear me? Take your ease, prosperity, peace, decorum! They don't think I'm talking to them. Soft in comfort and prosperity. No comprehension of what I love: the hard, my hard-earned hardness, hard warrior ways. Slogging through mud and swamps, boots falling apart. Living off groats, hardtack, spitting-bad coffee. Salted pork a treat. No one comprehends a soldier's work anymore. Outsiders—townsfolk paying their respects, church-deacons—they come over, and I overhear them amongst themselves. "A dying veteran," that's how they talk about me. They don't know a thing. Fought in the ranks with this rifle—fought well—fought for Union! Been through it. Later fought the Indians, opened up the western plains. Put an end to the massacres, abductions, slaughtering of women and children. No one comprehends a soldier's work anymore.

Take it! Take your modern soft pleasures and comforts! Your joys! I'll have the ancient ways of honor and battle-glory. This I've known and lived. Give me back my war-days! Let me see again—tough men. Also drummer boys, fighting boys in uniform, good boys all of them, all courageous men at half my sons' age, younger than my grandsons. And enemies, let me have my enemies. Proud foes, fierce, enemies I can be proud of. Return me to the sights and sounds, scenes of history and struggle. Forming the line. The smoke, the cannons, grim artillery. Scouts, reconnoitering. Galloping aides, carrying orders. Officers issuing orders. The commanding, the obeying. The trumpet!: the cavalry charges over hills, drawn sabers, horses snorting for war; the approach, the shooting, the stabbing bayonets; the smell of fresh gunpowder, the strong perfume of blood; the wounded, the fallen, somber ditch-graves; yet the deafening noise, yet the craziness, the excitement, the fear! Feeling yourself in heart and sinew ever willing and ready to answer the call to arms. Away with your peace! Your life of peace! Your concerns of peace! Again and again, give me tests, conflict, my old wild battle-life!

QUESTIONS

1. Have you ever heard someone speak about the accomplishments of his or her life? Did he or she speak of them with pride? Disappointment?

2. Could this poem be considered a short story or a play? Does it have a plot? How is it the same or different from other poems you have read?

3. In thinking back on his life, what mood does the soldier reflect?

JIM NORTHRUP (b. 1943)

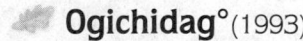
Ogichidag°(1993)

I was born in war, WW Two.
Listened as the old men told stories
of getting gassed in the trenches, WW One.
Saw my uncles come back from

°The title "Ogichidag" is the Ojibway word for "warriors."

5   Guadalcanal, North Africa,
     and the Battle of the Bulge.
     Memorized the war stories
     my cousins told of Korea.
     Felt the fear in their voices.
10   Finally it was my turn,
     my brothers too.
     Joined the marines in time
     for the Cuban Missile Crisis.
     Heard the crack of rifles
15   in the rice paddies south of Da Nang.
     Watched my friends die there
     then tasted the bitterness of
     the only war America ever lost.
     My son is now a warrior.
20   Will I listen to his war stories
     or cry into his open grave?

QUESTIONS

1. What battles are mentioned in the poem, and over what period of time do these battles extend?
2. How does the speaker state that he learned about the battles? Why is this method of gaining knowledge important? What experience has the speaker had with war?
3. Why does the speaker finish the poem by referring to his son? In relationship to the poem's structure, why is the concluding question important?

NAOMI SHIHAB NYE (b. 1952)

🖋 Where Children Live (1982)

Homes where children live exude a pleasant rumpledness,
like a bed made by a child, or a yard littered with balloons.

To be a child again one would need to shed details
till the heart found itself dressed in the coat with a hood.
5   Now the heart has taken on gloves and mufflers,
the heart never goes outside to find something to "do."
And the house takes on a new face, dignified.
No lost shoes blooming under bushes.
No chipped trucks in the drive.
10 Grown-ups like swings, leafy plants, slow-motion back and forth.
While the yard of a child is strewn with the corpses
of bottle-rockets and whistles,
anything whizzing and spectacular, brilliantly short-lived.

Trees in children's yards speak in clearer tongues.
15 Ants have more hope. Squirrels dance as well as hide.
The fence has a reason to be there, so children can go in and out.
Even when the children are at school, the yards glow

with the leftovers of their affection,
the roots of the tiniest grasses curl toward one another
like secret smiles.   20

QUESTIONS

1. How accurately does the poem present the "pleasant rumpledness" of children?
2. What is the speaker's view of the comparative dependence or independence of children? What does the speaker think of children?
3. Sometimes poems about children can be overly sentimental. How well does this poem present sentiment about children? Does it go too far, or is it about right?

LOUIS SIMPSON (1923–2012)

American Poetry (1963)

Whatever it is, it must have
A stomach that can digest
Rubber, coal, uranium, moons, poems.

Like the shark it contains a shoe.
It must swim for miles through the desert   5
Uttering cries that are almost human.

QUESTIONS

1. What do you think poems should be about? What does this poem imply about the subject matter of poetry?
2. The word "poetry" is only mentioned in the title. Why?
3. Which images stand out? What do they say about poetry?

WILLIAM SHAKESPEARE (1564–1616)

For a portrait, see Chapter 21, page 1079.

Sonnet 55: Not Marble, Nor the Gilded Monuments (1609)

Not marble, nor the gilded monuments
Of princes, shall outlive this powerful rhyme;
But you shall shine more bright in these contents
Than unswept stone, besmeared with sluttish time.
When wasteful war shall statues overturn,   5
And broils root out the work of masonry,
Nor° Mars his° sword nor war's quick fire shall burn   *Neither, Mars's*
The living record of your memory.
'Gainst death and all-oblivious enmity
Shall you pace forth; your praise shall still find room   10
Even in the eyes of all posterity

That wear this world out to the ending doom.°   *Judgment Day*
So, till the judgment that yourself arise,
You live in this, and dwell in lovers' eyes.

QUESTIONS

1. Who is the speaker of the poem, and who is being addressed?
2. What powers of destruction does the speaker mention? What, according to the speaker, will survive these powers?
3. What does "the living record of your memory" (line 8) mean?
4. What is the poem's subject? Theme?

ELAINE TERRANOVA (b. 1939)

Rush Hour (1995)

Odd, the baby's scabbed face peeking over
the woman's shoulder. The little girl
at her side with her arm in a cast,
wearing a plain taffeta party dress.
5   The woman herself who is in shorts and sunglasses
among commuters in the underground station. Her body
that sags and tenses at the same time.

The little girl has not once moved
to touch her or to be touched.
10   Even on the train, she never turns and says,
"Mommy." Sunlight bobs over her blond head
inclining toward the window. The baby
is excited now. "Loo, loo, loo, loo,"
he calls, a wet crescendo. "He's pulling
15   my hair," the little girl at last cries out.

A kind man comes up the aisle to see
the baby. He stares at those rosettes of blood
and wants to know what's wrong with him.
The woman says a dog bit him. "It must have been
20   a big dog, then." "Oh, no. A neighbor's little dog."
The man says, "I hope they put that dog to sleep."
The woman is nearly pleading. "It was an accident. He didn't
mean to do it." The conductor, taking tickets,

asks the little girl how she broke her arm.
25   But the child looks out to the big, shaded houses.
The woman says, "She doesn't like to talk
about that." No one has seen what is behind
her own dark glasses. She pulls the children to her.
Maybe she is thinking of the arm raised over them,
30   Its motion that would begin like a blessing.

QUESTIONS

1. What clues early in the poem indicate that the woman and her children are victims of domestic abuse?
2. Why does the mother not appeal for help when the two men, the "kind man" and the conductor, inquire about the injuries of the children? What is the irony of the raised arm in the last two lines? What is the pathos of the mother's situation?
3. Describe the attitude of the speaker telling the story of the poem. Why does the speaker do no more than describe details, and not actually rail against domestic abuse?

WILLIAM CARLOS WILLIAMS (1883–1963)

 ## This Is Just to Say (1934)

I have eaten
the plums
that were in
the icebox

and which   5
you were probably
saving
for breakfast

Forgive me
they were delicious   10
so sweet
and so cold

QUESTIONS

1. Do you think this poem reflects a sincere apology? Should anything else have been included in it to make it more sincere?
2. Who is the speaker addressing?
3. Why do you think Williams did not use punctuation? How would the poem be different if he had?

WILLIAM WORDSWORTH (1770–1850)

 ## Lines Composed a Few Miles Above Tintern Abbey on Revisiting the Banks of the Wye During a Tour, June 13, 1798° (1798)

Five years have past; five summers, with the length
Of five long winters! and again I hear
These waters, rolling from their mountain-springs

°Wordsworth first visited the valley of the Wye in southwest England in August 1793, at age twenty-three. On this second visit he was accompanied by his sister Dorothy (the "Friend" in line 115).

With a soft inland murmur.—Once again
5 Do I behold these steep and lofty cliffs,
That on a wild secluded scene impress
Thoughts of more deep seclusion, and connect
The landscape with the quiet of the sky.
The day is come when I again repose

10 Here, under this dark sycamore, and view
These plots of cottage-ground, these orchard-tufts,
Which at this season, with their unripe fruits,
Are clad in one green hue, and lose themselves
'Mid groves and copses. Once again I see
15 These hedge-rows, hardly hedge-rows, little lines
Of sportive wood run wild; these pastoral farms,
Green to the very door; and wreaths of smoke
Sent up, in silence, from among the trees!
With some uncertain notice, as might seem
20 Of vagrant dwellers in the houseless woods,
Or of some Hermit's cave, where by his fire
The Hermit sits alone.
                                   These beauteous forms,
Through a long absence, have not been to me
As is a landscape to a blind man's eye:
25 But oft, in lonely rooms, and 'mid the din
Of towns and cities, I have owed to them
In hours of weariness, sensations sweet,
Felt in the blood, and felt along the heart;
And passing even into my purer mind,
30 With tranquil restoration:—feelings too
Of unremembered pleasure: such, perhaps,
As have no slight or trivial influence
On that best portion of a good man's life,
His little, nameless, unremembered acts
35 Of kindness and of love. Nor less, I trust,
To them I may have owed another gift,
Of aspect more sublime; that blessed mood,
In which the burden of the mystery,
In which the heavy and the weary weight
40 Of all this unintelligible world,
Is lightened:—that serene and blessed mood,
In which the affections gently lead us on,—
Until, the breath of this corporeal frame
And even the motion of our human blood
45 Almost suspended, we are laid asleep
In body, and become a living soul:
While with an eye made quiet by the power
Of harmony, and the deep power of joy,
We see into the life of things.
                                           If this
50 Be but a vain belief, yet, oh!—how oft—
In darkness and amid the many shapes

Of joyless daylight; when the fretful stir
Unprofitable, and the fever of the world,
Have hung upon the beatings of my heart—
How oft, in spirit, have I turned to thee, 55
O sylvan Wye! thou wanderer thro' the woods,
How often has my spirit turned to thee!
And now, with gleams of half extinguished thought,
With many recognitions dim and faint,
    And somewhat of a sad perplexity, 60
The picture of the mind revives again:
While here I stand, not only with the sense
Of present pleasure, but with pleasing thoughts
That in this moment there is life and food
For future years. And so I dare to hope, 65
Though changed, no doubt, from what I was when first
I came among these hills; when like a roe
I bounded o'er the mountains, by the sides
Of the deep rivers, and the lonely streams,
Wherever nature led: more like a man 70
Flying from something that he dreads, than one
Who sought the thing he loved. For nature then
(The coarser pleasures of my boyish days,
And their glad animal movements all gone by)
To me was all in all.—I cannot paint 75
What then I was. The sounding cataract
Haunted me like a passion: the tall rock,
The mountain, and the deep and gloomy wood,
Their colours, and their forms, were then to me
An appetite; a feeling and a love, 80
That had no need of a remoter charm,
By thought supplied, nor any interest
Unborrowed from the eye.—That time is past,
And all its aching joys are now no more,
And all its dizzy raptures. Not for this 85
Faint I, nor mourn nor murmur; other gifts
Have followed; for such loss, I would believe,
Abundant recompense. For I have learned
To look on nature, not as in the hour
Of thoughtless youth; but hearing oftentimes 90
The still, sad music of humanity,
Nor harsh nor grating, though of ample power
To chasten and subdue. And I have felt
A presence that disturbs me with the joy
Of elevated thoughts; a sense sublime 95
Of something far more deeply interfused,
Whose dwelling is the light of setting suns,
And the round ocean, and the living air,
And the blue sky, and in the mind of man;
A motion and a spirit, that impels 100
All thinking things, all objects of all thought,
And rolls through all things. Therefore am I still

A lover of the meadows and the woods,
And mountains; and of all that we behold
105 From this green earth; of all the mighty world
Of eye, and ear,—both what they half create,
And what perceive; well pleased to recognize
In nature and the language of the sense,
The anchor of my purest thoughts, the nurse,
110 The guide, the guardian of my heart, and soul
Of all my moral being.
                            Nor perchance,
If I were not thus taught, should I the more
Suffer my genial spirits to decay:
For thou art with me here upon the banks
115 Of this fair river; thou my dearest Friend,
My dear, dear Friend; and in thy voice I catch
The language of my former heart, and read
My former pleasures in the shooting lights
Of thy wild eyes. Oh! yet a little while
120 May I behold in thee what I was once,
My dear, dear Sister! and this prayer I make,
Knowing that Nature never did betray
The heart that loved her; 'tis her privilege,
Through all the years of this our life, to lead
125 From joy to joy: for she can so inform
The mind that is within us, so impress
With quietness and beauty, and so feed
With lofty thoughts, that neither evil tongues,
Rash judgments, nor the sneers of selfish men,
130 Nor greetings where no kindness is, nor all
The dreary intercourse of daily life,
Shall e'er prevail against us, or disturb
Our cheerful faith that all which we behold
Is full of blessings. Therefore let the moon
135 Shine on thee in thy solitary walk;
And let the misty mountain-winds be free
To blow against thee: and, in after years,
When these wild ecstasies shall be matured
Into a sober pleasure; when thy mind
140 Shall be a mansion for all lovely forms,
Thy memory be as a dwelling-place
For all sweet sounds and harmonies; oh! then,
If solitude, or fear, or pain, or grief,
Should be thy portion, with what healing thoughts
145 Of tender joy wilt thou remember me,
And these my exhortations! Nor, perchance—
If I should be where I no more can hear
Thy voice, nor catch from thy wild eyes these gleams
Of past existence—wilt thou then forget
150 That on the banks of this delightful stream
We stood together; and that I, so long
A worshipper of Nature, hither came

Unwearied in that service: rather say
With warmer love—oh! with far deeper zeal
Of holier love. Nor wilt thou then forget,   155
That after many wanderings, many years
Of absence, these steep woods and lofty cliffs,
And this green pastoral landscape, were to me
More dear, both for themselves and for thy sake!

QUESTIONS

1. What is the opening scene, and what meaning does the poet ascribe to it?
2. To the speaker, what is the relationship of remembered scenes and the growth of moral behavior?
3. What effect does the speaker believe the present will have on his future?
4. In lines 93–111, how successfully does the speaker make concrete his ideas about moral forces?
5. What is the power that the speaker attributes to nature? What is the "cheerful faith" of lines 133–134?

WRITING A PARAPHRASE OF A POEM (PARAGRAPH LENGTH)

Paraphrasing is especially useful in the study of poetry. It fixes both the general shape and the details of a poem in your mind, and it also reveals the poetic devices at work. A comparison of the original poem with the paraphrase highlights the techniques and the language that make the poem effective.

To paraphrase a poem, rewrite it in prose, in your own words. Decide what details to include—a number that you determine partly by the length of the poem and partly by the total length of your paraphrase. When you deal with lyrics, sonnets, and other short poems, you may include all the details, and thus your paraphrase may be as long as the work, or longer. Paraphrases of long poems, however, will be shorter than the originals because some details must be summarized briefly while others may be cut entirely.

It is vital to make your paraphrase accurate and also to use *only your own words*. To make sure that your words are all your own, read through the poem several times. Then, put the poem out of sight and write your paraphrase. Once you have finished, check yourself both for accuracy and vocabulary. If you find that you have borrowed too many of the poem's words, choose other words that mean the same thing, or else use quotation marks to set off the original words (but do not overuse quotations).

Above all, remain faithful to the poem, but *avoid drawing conclusions and giving unnecessary explanations*. It would be wrong in a paraphrase of Jarrell's "The Death of the Ball Turret Gunner," for example, to state, "This poem makes a forceful argument against the brutal and wasteful deaths caused by war." This assertion states the poem's *theme*, but it *does not* describe the poem's actual content.

Organizing Your Paraphrase

The organization of your paraphrase should reflect the poem's form or development. Include material in the order in which it occurs. With short poems, organize your paraphrase to reflect the poem's development line by line or stanza by stanza. In paraphrasing Shakespeare's "Not Marble, Nor the Gilded Monuments," for example, you should deal with each four-line group in sequence and then consider the final couplet. With longer poems, look for natural divisions such as groups of related stanzas, verse paragraphs, or other possible organizational units. In every situation, the poem's shape should determine the form of your paraphrase.

Illustrative Student Paraphrase

A Paraphrase of Thomas Hardy's "The Man He Killed"°

[1]   If the man I killed had met me in a bar, we would have sat down together and had many drinks. But because we belonged to armies of warring foot soldiers lined up on a battlefield, we shot at each other, and my shot killed him.

[2]   The reason I killed him, I think, was that he and I were enemies— just that. But as I think of it, I realize that he had enlisted exactly as I did. Maybe he did it on a whim, or maybe he had lost his job and sold everything he owned. There was no other reason to enlist.

[3]   Being at war is unusual and strange. Instead of buying a man a drink, or helping him out with a little money, you have to kill him.

°This poem appears on pages 548–549.

Commentary on the Paraphrase

Because Hardy's poem is short, the paraphrase attempts to include all its details. The organization closely follows the poem's development. Paragraph 1, for example, restates the contents of the first two stanzas. Paragraph 2 restates the third and fourth stanzas. Finally, the last paragraph separately paraphrases the last stanza, which contains the reflections made by the poem's "I" speaker. This paragraph concludes the paraphrase just as the last stanza concludes the poem.

Notice that the essay does not abstract details from the poem, such as "The dead man might have become a good friend in peacetime" in paraphrasing stanza 5; nor does it extend details, such as "We would have gotten acquainted, had drinks together, told many stories, and done a lot of laughing" for stanza 1 (both stanzas, however, actually do suggest these details). Although the paraphrase reflects the poem's strong antiwar sentiments, an interpretive sentence like "By his very directness, the narrator brings out the senselessness and brutality of warfare" would be out of place. What is needed is a short restatement of the poem to demonstrate the essay writer's understanding of the poem's content, and no more.

WRITING AN EXPLICATION OF A POEM (ESSAY LENGTH)

Explication goes beyond the assimilation required for a paraphrase and thus provides you with the opportunity to show your understanding. But there is no need to explain everything in the poem. A complete, or total, explication would theoretically require you to explain the meaning and implications of each word and every line—a technique that obviously would be exhaustive (and exhausting). It would also be self-defeating, for explicating everything would prohibit you from using your judgment and deciding what is important.

A more manageable and desirable technique is therefore the *general explication*, which devotes attention to the meaning of individual parts in relationship to the entire work, as in the discussion of "Sir Patrick Spens" (p. 541–42). You might think of a general explication as your explanation or "reading" of the poem. Because it does not require you to go into exhaustive detail, you will need to be selective and to consider only those details that are significant in themselves and vital to your own thematic development.

Questions for Discovering Ideas

- What does the title contribute to the reader's understanding?
- Who is speaking? Where is the speaker when the poem is happening?
- What is the situation? What has happened in the past, or what is happening in the present, that has brought about the speech?
- What difficult, special, or unusual words does the poem contain? What references need explaining? How does an explanation assist in the understanding of the poem?
- How does the poem develop? Is it a personal statement? Is it a story?
- What is the main idea of the poem? What details make possible the formulation of the main idea?

Strategies for Organizing Ideas

Your general explication demonstrates your ability to (1) follow the essential details of the poem (the same as in a paraphrase), (2) understand the issues and the meaning the poem reveals, (3) explain some of the relationships of content to technique, and (4) note and discuss especially important or unique aspects of the poem.

In your introduction, use your central idea to express a general view of the poem, which your essay will bear out. The discussion of the anonymous "Sir Patrick Spens" (p. 543) suggests some possible central ideas—namely, that (1) the poem highlights a conflict between self-preservation and obedience to authority, and (2) innocent people may be caught in political infighting. In the following illustrative student essay explicating Hardy's "The Man He Killed," the central idea is that war is senseless.

In the body of your essay, first explain the poem's content—not with a paraphrase but with a description of the poem's major organizing elements. Hence, if the speaker of the poem is "inside" the poem as a first-person involved "I," you do not need to reproduce this voice yourself in your description. Instead, *describe* the poem in your own words, with whatever brief introductory phrases you find necessary, as in the second paragraph of the illustrative essay that follows.

Next, explicate the poem in relation to your central idea. Choose *your own* order of discussion, depending on your topics. You should, however, keep stressing your central idea with each new topic. Thus, you might wish to follow your description by discussing the poem's meaning, or even by presenting two or more possible interpretations.

You might also wish to refer to significant techniques. For example, in the anonymous "Sir Patrick Spens," a noteworthy technique is the unintroduced quotations (i.e., quotations appearing without any "he said" or "quoth he" phrases) as the ballad writer's means of dramatizing the commands and responses of Sir Patrick and his doomed crew. You might also introduce special topics, such as the crewman who explains that there will be bad luck because the new moon has "the old moon in her arm" (line 26). Such a reference to superstition might include the explanation of the crewman's assumptions, the relationship of his uneasiness to the remainder of the poem, and also how the ballad writer keeps the narrative brief. In short, discuss those aspects of meaning and technique that bear upon your central idea.

In your conclusion, you may repeat your major idea to reinforce your essay's thematic structure. Because your essay is a general explication, there will be parts of the poem that you will not have discussed. You might therefore mention what might be gained from an exhaustive discussion of various parts of the poem (do not, however, begin to exhaust any subject in the conclusion of your essay). The last stanza of Hardy's "The Man He Killed," for example, contains the words "quaint and curious" in reference to war. These words are unusual, particularly because the speaker might have chosen *hateful, senseless, destructive,* or other similarly descriptive words. Why did Hardy have his speaker make such a choice? With brief attention to such a problem, you may conclude your essay.

Illustrative Student Essay

Although underlined sentences are not recommended by MLA style, they are used in this illustrative essay as teaching tools to emphasize the central idea, thesis sentence, and topic sentences.

Steven Lagerstrom

Professor Bonner

English 110

22 September 2014

An Explication of Thomas Hardy's "The Man He Killed"°

Hardy's "The Man He Killed" deals with the senselessness of war.* It [1] does this through a silent contrast between the needs of ordinary people, as represented by a young man—the speaker—who has killed an enemy soldier in battle, and the antihuman and unnatural deaths of war. Of major note in this contrast are the speaker's circumstances, his language, his sense of identity with the dead man, and his concerns and wishes.†

The speaker begins by contrasting the circumstances of warfare with [2] those of peace. He does not identify himself, but his speech reveals that he is common and ordinary—a person who enjoys drinking in a bar and who prefers friendship and helpfulness to violence. If he and the man he killed had met in an inn, he says, they would have shared many drinks; but because they met on a battlefield they shot at each other, and he killed the other man. The speaker tries to justify the killing but can produce no stronger reason than that the dead man was his "foe." Once he states this reason, he again thinks of the similarities between himself and the dead man, and then he concludes that warfare is "quaint and curious" (line 17) because it forces a man to kill another man whom he would have befriended if they had met during peacetime.

To make the irony of warfare clear, the poem uses easy, everyday [3] language to bring out the speaker's ordinary qualities. His manner of speech is conversational, as in "We should have sat us down" (3), "'list" (for "enlist," 13),

°This poem appears on pages 548–549.
*Central idea.
†Thesis sentence.

Lagerstrom 2

and his use of "you" in the last stanza. Also, his word choices, shown in words like "nipperkin," "traps," and "fellow" (4, 15, and 18), are common and informal, at least in British usage. This language is important because it establishes that the speaker is an average man whom war has thrown into an unnatural role.

[4]   As another means of stressing the stupidity of war, the poem makes clear that the two men—the live soldier who killed and the dead soldier who was killed—were so alike that they could have been brothers or even twins. They had similar ways of life, similar economic troubles, similar wishes to help other people, and similar motives in enlisting in the army. Symbolically, the "man he killed" is the speaker himself, and hence the killing may be considered a form of suicide. The poem thus raises the question of why two people who are almost identical should be shoved into opposing battle lines in order to kill each other. This question is rhetorical, for the obvious answer is that there is no good reason.

[5]   Because the speaker (and also, very likely, the dead man) is shown as a person embodying the virtues of friendliness and helpfulness, Hardy's poem is a strong disapproval of war. Clearly, political reasons for violence as policy are irrelevant to the characters and concerns of the men who fight. They, like the speaker, would prefer to follow their own needs rather than remote and meaningless ideals. The failure of complex but irrelevant political explanations is brought out most clearly in the third stanza, in which the speaker tries to give a reason for shooting the other man. Hardy's use of punctuation—the dashes—stresses the fact that the speaker has no commitment to the cause he served when killing. Thus the speaker stops at the word "because—" and gropes for a reason (9). Not being articulate, he can say only "Because he was my foe. / Just so: my foe of course he was; / That's clear enough" (10–12). These short bursts of words indicate that he cannot explain things to himself or to anyone else except in the most obvious and trite terms, and in apparent embarrassment he inserts "of course" as a way of emphasizing hostility even though he clearly felt none toward the man he killed.

Lagerstrom 3

A reading thus shows the power of the poem's dramatic argument. Hardy   [6]
does not establish closely detailed reasons against war as a policy but rather
dramatizes the idea that all political arguments are unimportant in view of the
central and glaring brutality of war—killing. Hardy's speaker is not able to
express deep feelings; rather he is confused because he is an average sort who
wants only to live and let live and to enjoy a drink in a bar with friends. But
this very commonness stresses the point that everyone is victimized by war—
both those who die and those who kill. The poem is a powerful argument for
peace and reconciliation.

Lagerstrom 4

Work Cited

Hardy, Thomas. "The Man He Killed." *Literature: An Introduction to*
Reading and Writing, Compact Edition. Ed. Edgar V. Roberts and
Robert Zweig. 6th ed. New York: Pearson, 2015. 548–49. Print.

Commentary on the Essay

This explication begins by stating a central idea about "The Man He Killed," then
indicates the topics to follow that will develop the idea. Although nowhere does
the speaker state that war is senseless, the illustrative essay takes the position that
the poem embodies this idea. A more detailed examination of the poem's themes
might develop the idea by discussing the ways in which individuals are caught up
in social and political forces, or the contrast between individuality and the state. In
this essay, however, the simple statement of the idea is enough.

Paragraph 2 describes the major details of the poem, with guiding phrases
like "The speaker begins," "he says," and "he again thinks." Thus the paragraph
goes over the poem, like a paraphrase, but explains how things occur, as is
appropriate for an explication. Paragraph 3 is devoted to the speaker's words
and idioms, with the idea that his conversational manner is part of the poem's
contrasting method of argument. If these brief references to style were more
detailed, this topic could be more fully developed as an aspect of Hardy's implied
argument against war. (text continues on page 569)

USING SOURCES EFFECTIVELY

PARAPHRASING TO SET THE STAGE FOR ANALYSIS

Paraphrasing is an especially useful tool when writing analytically about poetry. Poems usually employ highly condensed, stylized, or metaphorical language that requires a clarifying restatement of what's happening in the work before a formal discussion of literary elements like the poet's use of language, metrics, or symbols. The box on page 561 in this chapter illustrates a "straight paraphrase" of the poem as the student writer sets down for himself the basic details of the poem's story to be sure he understands what is happening. However, in an academic essay, this straightforward restatement of the work needs to be adapted to serve the larger purpose of the essay, in this case, "An Explication of Thomas Hardy's 'The Man He Killed.'"

In the second paragraph, Steven Lagerstrom provides a smooth and accurate paraphrase of Hardy's 20-line poem. He purposely does not offer opinions of what the work "means" here, nor does he extensively reuse the language of the poem, much of which is colloquial to the English countryside, circa 1900, and somewhat obscure to contemporary readers.

> **This paraphrase does not quote words from the poem like "nipperkin." Later in the essay he does introduce Hardy's language to prove his point about the poem's characters.**
>
> The speaker begins by contrasting the circumstances of warfare with those of peace. He does not identify himself, but his speech reveals that he is common and ordinary—a person who enjoys drinking in a bar and who prefers friendship and helpfulness to violence. If he and the man he killed had met in an inn, he says, they would have shared many drinks; but because they met on a battlefield they shot
>
> **The essayist clearly details the sequence of the poem's ideas with tags like "Once he states. . . ." and "then he concludes." The paraphrase on page 562 only "translates" the poem line-by-line without making such connections.**
>
> at each other and he killed the other man. The speaker tries to justify the killing but can produce no stronger reason than that the dead man was his "foe." Once he states this reason, he again thinks of the similarities between himself and the dead man, and then he concludes that warfare is "quaint and curious" (line 17) because it forces a man to kill another man whom he would have befriended if they had met during peacetime.

Because this paraphrase clearly and simply outlines the work's complete "story," readers have a solid base from which to consider Lagerstrom's subsequent comments about why Hardy uses certain words and what the poet's actual views on warfare are. Understanding clearly who the speaker is and what the sequence of events developed in the poem is sets the stage for a more critical or analytical examination of the poet's themes and techniques in the remainder of the essay. This analysis would be less effective if Lagerstrom had not provided such a clear and concise overview of the poem before discussing the poem's diction in greater detail. (For more information on paraphrasing, see page 509.)

Paragraph 4 extends paragraph 3 inasmuch as it points out the similarities of the speaker and the man he killed. If the situation were reversed, the dead man might say exactly the same things about the present speaker. This affinity underscores the suicidal nature of war. Paragraph 5 treats the style of the poem's fourth stanza. In this context, the treatment is brief. The last paragraph reiterates the main idea and concludes with a tribute to the poem as an argument.

The entire essay therefore represents a reading and explanation of the poem's high points. It stresses a particular interpretation and briefly shows how various aspects of the poem bear it out.

Writing Topics About the Nature of Poetry

Writing Paragraphs

1. Skim the titles of poems listed in the table of contents of this book. Judging by the subjects of these poems, in a paragraph, describe and discuss the possible range of subject matter for poetry. What topics seem most suitable? Why? Do any topics seem to be ruled out? Why?

2. Besides the subject matter of the poems in this chapter, in a paragraph, describe what additional subject matter you would suggest as possible topics for poems?

3. In a paragraph, describe how accurate the proposition is that poetry is a particularly compressed form of expression. To support your position, you might refer to one of the following poems: "Because I Could Not Stop for Death," Francis's "Catch," or Frost's "Stopping by Woods on a Snowy Evening." Rita Dove's "The House Slave."

Writing Essays

1. Consider the subject of war as brought out in Jarrell's "The Death of the Ball Turret Gunner," Hardy's "The Man He Killed," and Northrop's "Ogichidag." What ideas are common to the poems? What ideas are distinct and unique? In an essay, on the basis of your comparison, argue that poetry is an excellent vehicle for the expression of moral and political ideas.

2. Consult the brief section on reader-response criticism in Chapter 26. Then write an essay about your responses to one poem, or a number of poems, in this chapter. Assume that your own experiences are valuable guides for your judgment. In the poems that you have read, what has had a bearing on your experiences? What in your own experiences has given you insights into the poems? Try to avoid being anecdotal; instead, try to find a relationship between your experiences and the poetry.

Creative Writing Assignment

1. Write two poems of your own about your future plans. In one, assume that the world is stable and will go on forever. In the other, assume that a large asteroid is out of orbit and is hurtling toward earth at great speed, and a collision six months from now will bring untold destruction and may even end life on earth. After composing your poems, write a brief explanation of how and why they differ in terms of language, references, and attitudes toward friends, family, country, religion, and so on.

Library Assignment

1. In the reference section of your library, find two books (anthologies, encyclopedias, introductions, dictionaries of literary terms) about the general subject of poetry. On the basis of how these two sources define and explain poetry, write a brief essay telling a person younger than you what to expect from the reading of poems.

Chapter 12
Words: The Building Blocks of Poetry

AFTER STUDYING THIS MATERIAL, YOU SHOULD BE ABLE TO DO THE FOLLOWING:

- Identify examples of concrete and abstract language
- Distinguish different levels of diction
- Assess the use of syntax in poetry
- Illustrate the uses of denotation and connotation
- Appraise how a poem's diction contributes to its effect

Words are the spoken and written signifiers of thoughts, objects, and actions. They are also the building blocks of both poetry and prose, but poetry is unique because by its nature it uses words with the utmost economy. The words of poetry create rhythm, rhyme, meter, and form. They define the poem's speaker, the characters, the setting, and the situation, and they also carry its ideas and emotions. For this reason, each poet searches for perfect and indispensable words, words that convey all the compressed meanings, overtones, and emotions that each poem requires, and also the words that sound right and look right.

Life—and poetry—might be simpler (but less interesting) if there were an exact one-to-one correspondence between words and the objects or ideas they signify. Such close correspondences exist in artificial language systems such as chemical equations and computer languages. This identical correlation, however, is not characteristic of English or any other natural language. Instead, words have the independent and glorious habit of attracting and expressing a vast array of different meanings.

Even if we have not thought much about language, most of us know that words are sometimes ambiguous, and that much literature is built on ambiguity. For instance, in Shakespeare's *Romeo and Juliet*, when Mercutio says, "Seek for me tomorrow and you shall find me a grave man" (3.1.97), the joke works because *grave* has two separate meanings, both of which come into play. In reading poetry, we recognize that poets rejoice in this shifting and elusive but also rich nature of language.

Choice of Diction: Specific and Concrete, General and Abstract

Because poets always try to use only the exactly right words, they constantly make conscious and subconscious decisions about diction. One of the major categories of their choice is diction that is either specific and concrete or general and abstract.

Specific language refers to objects or conditions that can be perceived or imagined; **general language** signifies broad classes of persons, objects, and phenomena. **Concrete diction** describes conditions or qualities that are exact and particular; **abstract diction** refers to qualities that are rarefied and theoretical. In practice, poems using specific and concrete words tend to be visual, familiar, and compelling. By contrast, poems that use general and abstract words tend to be detached and cerebral, and they often deal with universal questions or emotions.

Most poets employ mixtures of words in these categories because in many poems they draw general observations and abstract conclusions from specific situations and concrete responses. They therefore interweave their words to fit their situations and ideas, as in Roethke's "Dolor," which uses specific and concrete words to define a series of abstract emotional states.

Levels of Diction

Like ordinary speakers and writers of prose, poets choose words from the category of the three levels of diction: high or formal, middle or neutral, and low or informal. Often, the high and middle levels are considered standard or "right," while low language is dismissed as substandard or "wrong." In poetry, however, none of the classes is more correct than any other, for what counts is that they all function according to the poet's wishes, from broadly formal and intellectual to ordinary and popular.

High or Formal Diction Is Elevated and Elaborate

High or **formal diction** exactly follows the rules of syntax, seeking accuracy of expression even if unusually elevated or complex words are brought into play. Beyond "correctness," formal language is characterized by complex words and a lofty tone. In general, formal diction freely introduces words of French, Latin, and Greek derivation, some of which are quite long, so some people might think that formal language is "difficult." Graves uses formal diction in "The Naked and the Nude" when the speaker asserts that the terms in the title are "By lexicographers construed / As synonyms that should express / The same deficiency of dress." The Latinate words stiffen and generalize the passage: We find *lexicographers* instead of *dictionary writers*, *construed* (from Latin) instead of *thought* (native English), *express* (from Latin) instead of *say* or *show* (native English), and *deficiency* (Latin) instead of *lack* (English). It is simply a fact that our language contains thousands of words that have descended to our language from French, Latin, or Greek and that many of these are long and abstract. But not all words of this sort are necessarily long, nor are they abstract and stiff. Many of our short words, for example, are French in origin, such as *class, face, fort, paint, bat, tend, gain, cap, trace, order,* and *very*. A college-level dictionary contains brief descriptions of word origins, or etymologies; as an exercise, you might trace the origins of a number of words in a poem.

Middle or Neutral Diction Stresses Simplicity

Middle or **neutral diction** maintains the correct language and word order of formal diction but avoids elaborate words and elevated tone, just as it avoids idioms, colloquialisms, contractions, slang, jargon, and fads of speech. For example, Emily Dickinson's "Because I Could Not Stop for Death" (Chapter 11) is almost entirely in middle diction.

Low or Informal Diction Is the Language of Common, Everyday Use

Low or **informal diction** is relaxed and unselfconscious, the language of people buying groceries, gasoline, and pizza, and of people who may just be "hanging out." Poems using informal diction include common and simple words, idiomatic expressions, substandard expressions, foreign expressions, slang, "swearwords" or "cusswords," grammatical errors, and contractions. Informal diction is seen in Hardy's "The Man He Killed" (Chapter 11), in which the speaker uses words and phrases like "many a nipperkin," "He thought he'd 'list," and "off-hand like."

Special Types of Diction

Depending on their subjects and purposes, poets (and writers of prose) may wish to introduce four special types of diction into their poems: *idiom, dialect, slang,* and *jargon.*

Idiom Refers to Unique Forms of Diction and Word Order

The word *idiom,* originally meaning "making one's own," refers to words, phrases, and expressions that are common and acceptable in a particular language, even though they might, upon analysis, seem peculiar or illogical. Standard English idioms are so ingrained into our thought that we do not notice them. Poems automatically reflect these idioms. Thus, for example, a poet may "think *of*" an idea, speak of "living *in*" a house, talk of "going *out* to play," or describe a woman "lovely *as* chandeliers." Poets hardly have choices about such idioms as long as they are using standard English. Real choice occurs when poets select idioms that are unusual or even ungrammatical, as in phrases like "had he and I but met," "we was happy," and "except that You than He" (this last phrase is by Emily Dickinson). Idioms like these enable poets to achieve levels of ordinary and colloquial diction, depending on their purposes.

Dialect Refers to Regional and Group Usage and Pronunciation

Although we recognize English as a common language, in practice the language is made up of many habits of speech or **dialects** that are characteristic of many groups, regions, and nations. In addition to "general American," we can recognize many common dialects, such as Southern, Midwestern, New England, Brooklynese, American Black English, Yiddish English, and Texan, together with "upper" British, Cockney, Scottish, and Australian English. Dialect is concerned with whether we refer to a *pail* (general American) or a *bucket* (Southern); or sit down on a *sofa* (Eastern) or a *couch* (general American) or *davenport* (Midwestern); or drink *soda* (Eastern), *pop* (Midwestern), *soda pop* (a confused Midwesterner living in the East, or a confused Easterner living in the Midwest), or *tonic* (Bostonian). For example, Hardy's "The Ruined Maid" (Chapter 19) illustrates the poetic use of dialect.

Slang Refers to Informal and Substandard Vocabulary and Idiom

Much of the language that people use every day is **slang.** Usually, slang is impermanent, appearing among certain speakers and then vanishing. The use of the word *bad* to mean "good" illustrates how a new slang meaning can develop, and even stay for a time. This is not to say that slang is not persistent, for some of it is a significant part of our language. There is a continuous word stock of substandard or "impolite" words, some of which are so-called "four-letter" words, which everyone knows but speaks only privately. There are also innumerable slang expressions. For example, we have many slang phrases describing dying, such as *kick the bucket, croak, be wasted, sleep with the fishes, buy the farm, be disappeared, be whacked,* and *be offed*. A nonnative speaker of English, unfamiliar with our slang, would have difficulty understanding that a person who "kicked the bucket," "bought the farm," "croaked," or "was offed" had actually died.

Even though slang is a permanent part of our language, it is usually confined to colloquial or conversational levels. (Interestingly, people with perfect command of standard English regularly use slang in private among their friends and acquaintances.) If slang is introduced into a standard context, therefore, it mars and jars, as in Cummings's "Buffalo Bill's Defunct" (Chapter 16), where the speaker refers to Buffalo Bill as a "blueeyed boy." Because the poem deals with the universality of death, the phrase, which usually refers to a young man on the make, or moving upward in his career, ironically underscores this intention.

Jargon Is the Special Language and Terminology of Groups

Particular groups develop **jargon**—specialized words and expressions that are usually employed by members of specific professions or trades, such as astronauts, doctors, lawyers, computer experts, plumbers, and football players. Without an initiation, people ordinarily cannot understand the special meanings. Although jargon at its worst befuddles rather than informs, it is significant when it becomes part of mainstream English or is used in literature. Poets may introduce jargon for special effects. For example, Paul Zimmer, in "The Day Zimmer Lost Religion" (this chapter), wryly uses the phrase "ready for Him now," a boxing expression that describes a fighter in top condition. Linda Pastan uses "gives me an A" and "I'm dropping out," both phrases from school life, to create comic effects in "Marks" (Chapter 19). Another poem employing jargon is Hardy's "The Man He Killed" (Chapter 11), which uses commonplace terms encountered in everyday village life to establish that the dead man was just an ordinary person, reinforcing the poem's focus on the seemingly random violence of war.

Syntax

Syntax refers to word order and sentence structure. Normal English word order is fixed in a *subject-verb-object* sequence. At the simplest level, we say, "A dog (*subject*) bites (*verb*) a man (*object*)." This order is so central to our communication that any change significantly affects meaning: "A dog bites a man" is not the same as "A man bites a dog."

🌿 DECORUM: THE MATCHING OF SUBJECT AND WORD

A vital literary concept is **decorum** ("beautiful," "appropriate"); that is, words and subjects should be in perfect accord—formal words for serious subjects, and informal words for low subjects and comedy. In Shakespeare's *A Midsummer Night's Dream*, for example, the nobles usually speak poetry and the "mechanicals" speak prose (Chapter 22). When the nobility are relaxed and in the forest, however, they also speak prose. Decorum governs such choices of language.

In the eighteenth century, English writers aimed to make their language as dignified as ancient Latin, which was the international language of discourse. They therefore asserted that only formal diction was appropriate for poetry; common life and colloquial language were excluded, except in drama and popular ballads. These rules of decorum required standard and elevated language rather than common words and phrases. The development of scientific terminology during the eighteenth century also influenced language. In the scientific mode, poets of the time used descriptive phrases, like "lowing herd" for cattle (Thomas Gray) and "finny prey" for fish (Alexander Pope). In this vein, Thomas Gray observed the dependence of color on light in the line "And cheerful fields resume their green attire" from the "Sonnet on the Death of Richard West."

Pope, one of the greatest eighteenth-century poets, maintained these rules of decorum—and also made fun of them—in his mock-epic poem *The Rape of the Lock* (1714), and more fully in the mock-critical work *Peri Bathous, or The Art of Sinking in Poetry* (1715). In *The Rape of the Lock*, he refers to a scissors as a "glittering forfex" (3.147). Similarly, in an earlier couplet he elevates the simple act of pouring coffee.

> From silver spouts the grateful liquors glide,
> While China's earth receives the smoking tide. (3.109-10)

After Wordsworth transformed poetic diction early in the nineteenth century, the topics and language of people of all classes, with a special stress on common folk, have become a feature of poetry. Poets have continued to follow rules of decorum, however, inasmuch as the use of colloquial diction and even slang is a necessary consequence of popular subject matter.

Much of the time, poets follow normal word order, as in "The Lamb," where Blake creates a simple, easy order in keeping with the poem's purpose of presenting a childlike praise of God. Many modern poets, such as Mark Strand, go out of their way to create ordinary, everyday syntax, on the theory that a poem's sentence structures should not get in the way of the reader's perceptions.

Yet, just as poets always explore the limits of ideas, so also do they sometimes explore the many possibilities of syntax, as in line 7 of Donne's "Batter My Heart": "Reason, Your viceroy in me, me should defend." In prose, this sentence would read "Reason, who is Your viceroy in me, should defend me." But note that Donne drops the "who is," and that he also puts the direct object "me" before and not after the verb. The resulting emphasis on the pronoun *me* is appropriate to the personal-divine relationship that is the topic of the sonnet. The alteration also meets the demand of the poem's rhyme scheme. A set of particularly noteworthy syntactic variations occurs in Roethke's "Dolor." The poet uses an irregular and idiosyncratic combination of objects, phrases, and appositives to create ambiguity and uncertainty, underscoring the idea that school and office routines are aimless and depressing.

Some of the other means by which poets shape word order to create emphasis are an aspect of **rhetoric. Parallelism** is the most easily recognized rhetorical device. A simple form of parallelism is **repetition,** as with the question "who made thee?" in Blake's "The Lamb." Through the use of the same grammatical forms, though in different words, parallelism produces lines or portions of lines that impress our minds strongly, as in this passage from Robinson's "Richard Cory," in which there are four parallel past-tense verbs (italicized here).

> So on we *worked*, and *waited* for the light,
> And *went* without the meat, and *cursed* the bread;

The final two lines of this poem demonstrate how parallelism may embody **antithesis**—a contrasting situation or idea that brings out surprise, shock, or climax:

> And Richard Cory, one calm summer night,
> *Went* home and *put* a bullet through his head.

A major quality of parallelism is the packing of words (the *economy* and *compression* of poetry), for by using a parallel structure the poet makes a single word or phrase function a number of times, with no need for repetition. The opening verb phrase "have known" in Roethke's "Dolor," though used once, controls six parallel direct objects. At the end of Donne's "Batter My Heart," parallelism (along with antithesis) permits Donne to omit the italicized words added and bracketed in the last line here.

> for I,
> Except° You enthrall° me, never shall be free,   *unless; enslave*
> Nor [*shall I*] ever [*be*] chaste, except You ravish me.

Note also that parallelism and antithesis make possible the unique *abba* ordering of these two lines, with the pattern "enthrall" (verb), "free" (adjective), "chaste" (adjective), "ravish" (verb). This rhetorical pattern is called **antimetabole,** or **chiasmus,** and is a common pattern of creating emphasis.

Denotation and Connotation

To achieve the maximum impact, poets depend not just on the simplest, most essential meanings of words, but also on the suggestions and associations that words bring to us. For this reason, control over denotation and connotation (see also Chapter 6) is so important that it has been called the very soul of the poet's art.

Denotation Refers to Standard, Most Commonly Recognized Meanings

The ordinary dictionary meaning of a word—**denotation**—indicates conventional correspondences between words and objects or ideas. Although we might expect denotation to be straightforward, most English words have multiple denotations. The noun *house*, for example, can refer to a *building*, a *family*, a *branch of Congress*, a *theater*, a *theater audience*, a *sorority* or *fraternity*, an *astrological classification*, or a *brothel*. Although context usually makes the denotation of *house* more specific, the various meanings confer a built-in ambiguity in this simple word.

Denotation presents problems, because with the passing of time new meanings emerge and old ones are shed. In poems written in the eighteenth century and earlier, there are many words that have changed so completely that a modern dictionary is not much help. In Marvell's "To His Coy Mistress" (Chapter 17), for example, the speaker asserts that his "vegetable love should grow/ Vaster than empires, and more slow." At first reading, "vegetable" may seem to refer to something like a giant, loving turnip. When we turn to a current dictionary, we discover that *vegetable* is an adjective meaning "plantlike"; but *plantlike love* does not get us much beyond *vegetable love*. A reference to the *Oxford English Dictionary (OED)*, however, tells us that *vegetable* was used as an adjective in the seventeenth century to mean "living or growing like a plant." Thus we find out that "vegetable love" means love that grows slowly but steadily larger.

Connotation Refers to a Word's Emotional, Psychological, Social, and Historical Overtones

The life of language, and the most difficult to control, is a result of **connotation**. Almost no word is without it. For instance, according to the dictionary, the words *childish* and *childlike* denote the state of being like a child. Nevertheless, they connote or imply different sets of characteristics. *Childish* suggests a person who is bratty, stubborn, immature, silly, and petulant, whereas *childlike* suggests that a person may be innocent, charming, and unaffected. These different meanings are based entirely on connotations, for the denotations make little distinction.

Connotation affects us in almost everything we hear and read. We constantly encounter the manipulation of connotation in advertising, for example, which could not exist without the controlled management of meaning. Such manipulation may be as simple as calling a *used car* a *pre-owned car* to avoid the negative connotations of *used*. On the other hand, the manipulation may be as sophisticated as the current use of the word *lite* or *light* to describe foods and drinks. In all such products, *lite* denotes "dietetic," "low-calorie," or even "weak." The distinction—and the selling point—is found in connotation. Imagine how difficult it would be to sell a drink called "dietetic beer" or "weak beer." *Light* and *lite*, however, carry none of the negative connotations and, instead, suggest products that are pleasant, sparkling, bright, and healthy.

Poets always try to make individual words carry as many appropriate and effective denotations and connotations as possible. Put another way, poets use *packed* or *loaded* words that carry a broad range of meaning and association. With this in mind, read the following poem by Robert Graves.

ROBERT GRAVES (1895–1985)

The Naked and the Nude (1957)

For me, the naked and the nude
(By lexicographers° construed
As synonyms that should express
The same deficiency of dress
5   Or shelter) stand as wide apart
As love from lies, or truth from art.

Lovers without reproach will gaze
On bodies naked and ablaze;
The Hippocratic° eye will see
10   In nakedness, anatomy;
And naked shines the Goddess when
She mounts her lion among men.

The nude are bold, the nude are sly
To hold each treasonable eye.
15   While draping by a showman's trick
Their dishabille° in rhetoric,
They grin a mock-religious grin
Of scorn at those of naked skin.

The naked, therefore, who compete
20   Against the nude may know defeat;
Yet when they both together tread
The briary pastures of the dead,
By Gorgons° with long whips pursued,
How naked go the sometime nude!

°2 *lexicographers*: writers of dictionaries.   °9 *Hippocratic*: medical; the adjective derives from Hippocrates (c. 460–377 BCE), the ancient Greek who is considered the "father of medicine."   °16 *dishabille*: being carelessly or partly dressed.   °23 *Gorgons*: mythological female monsters with snakes for hair.

QUESTIONS

1. How does the speaker explain the denotations and connotations of "naked" and "nude" in the first stanza? What is indicated by the fact that the word *naked* is derived from Old English *nacod*, while *nude* comes from Latin *nudus*?

2. What examples of "the naked" and "the nude" do the second and third stanzas provide? What do the examples have in common?

3. How do the connotations of words like "sly," "draping," "dishabille," "rhetoric," and "grin" contribute to the poem's ideas about "the nude"?

4. What does "briary pastures of the dead" mean in line 22?

This poem explores the connotative distinctions between the title words, *naked* and *nude*, which share a common denotation. The title also suggests that the poem is about human customs; for if the speaker were considering the words alone, he would say "naked" and "nude" instead of "*the* naked and *the* nude." The speaker's use of *the* signifies a double focus on both language and human perspectives. In the first five lines, the poem establishes that the two key words should be "synonyms that should express / The same deficiency of dress" (lines 3–4). By introducing elevated and complex words such as "lexicographers" and "construed," however, Graves implies that the connection between "the naked" and "the nude" is sophisticated and artificial.

In the rest of the poem, Graves develops this distinction, linking the word *naked* to virtues of love, truth, innocence, and honesty, while connecting *nude* to artifice, hypocrisy, and deceit. At the end, he visualizes a classical underworld in which all pretentiousness will disappear, and the nude will lose their sophistication and become merged with the naked. The implication is that artifice will vanish in the face of eternal reality. A thorough study of the words in the poem bears out the consistency of Graves's idea, not only about the two words in the title, but also about the accumulated layers of history, usage, and philosophy that weigh upon human life and thought.

Poems for Study

John Ashbery . . . . The Cathedral Is, 580
Charles Baudelaire . . . . Exotic Perfume, 580
William Blake . . . . .The Lamb, 581
Lewis Carroll . . . . Jabberwocky, 581
Hayden Carruth . . . . An Apology for Using the Word "Heart" in Too Many Poems, 582
Robert Creeley . . . . I Know a Man, 583
E. E. Cummings . . . . .next to of course god america i, 584
John Donne . . . . Holy Sonnet 14: Batter My Heart, Three Personed God, 585
A. E. Housman . . . . To an Athlete Dying Young, 585
Carolyn Kizer . . . . Night Sounds, 586
Denise Levertov . . . . Of Being, 587
Geri Lipschultz . . . . In the Beginning of the End, 588
Judith Ortiz Cofe . . . . Latin Women Pray, 589
Edwin Arlington Robinson . . . . Richard Cory, 590
Theodore Roethke . . . . Dolor, 591
Kay Ryan . . . . Crib, 591
Stephen Spender . . . . I Think Continually of Those Who Were Truly Great, 592
Wallace Stevens . . . . Disillusionment of Ten O'Clock, 593
Mark Strand . . . . Eating Poetry, 593
Natasha Trethewey. . . . . White Lies, 594
William Wordsworth . . . . . Daffodils (I Wandered Lonely as a Cloud), 595
Paul Zimmer . . . . The Day Zimmer Lost Religion, 596

JOHN ASHBERY (1927)

The Cathedral Is (1979)

Slated for demolition

QUESTIONS

1. Do you think demolishing a cathedral is different from demolishing another type of building, for instance, an apartment building? Why? Does the poem imply any particular attitude toward the demolition of the cathedral?
2. Why do you think the first word of the poem is "slated?" What connotations does this word have?
3. The title and the poem make up one grammatically correct sentence. Why do you think that Ashbery did this?

CHARLES BAUDELAIRE (1821–1867)

Exotic Perfume (1857)

Translated by Jacques Leclerc

On autumn nights, eyes closed, when, sensuous,

I breathe the scent of your warm breasts, my sight
Is peopled by far shores, happy and bright,
Under a sun, warm and monotonous.
5   A lazy isle which nature, generous,
Stocks with weird trees and fruits of strange delight,
Men with lithe bodies, powerful but slight,
Women whose candid eyes flash luminous. . . .

Urged by your scent to such charmed lands at last,
10 I see a port with many a sail and mast
Still weary from the ocean's frenzied roll,
While the green tamarinds exhale their savor
To please my nostrils with a dulcet flavor,
Mingled with sailor chanteys in my soul.

QUESTIONS

1. In this poem the smell of a lover's perfume sends the speaker on an imaginative journey. Have you ever felt "transported" to another time or place by a smell or a taste?
2. What words reflect the smell of an exotic perfume?
3. Which senses are mentioned by the speaker? In which images?

Unfeasible. It is equivocal, sentimental,
　　Debatable, really a sort of lentil— 5
Neither pea nor bean. Sometimes it's a muscle,
　　Sometimes courage or at least hustle,
Sometimes a core or center, but mostly it's
　　A sound that slushily fits 10
The meters of popular songwriters without
　　Meaning anything. It is stout,
Leonine, chicken, great, hot, warm, cold,
　　Broken, whole, tender, bold,
Stony, soft, green, blue, red, white, 15
　　Faint, true, heavy, light,
Open, down, shallow, etc. No wonder
　　Our superiors thunder
Against it. And yet in spite of a million abuses
　　The word survives; its uses 20
Are such that it remains virtually indispensable
　　And, I think, defensible.
The Freudian terminology is awkward or worse,
　　And suggests so many perverse
Etiologies that it is useless; but "heart" covers 25
　　The whole business, lovers
To monks, i.e., the capacity to love in the fullest
　　Sense. Not even the dullest
Reader misapprehends it, although locating
　　It is a matter awaiting 30
Someone more ingenious than I. But given
　　This definition, driven
Though it is out of a poet's necessity, isn't
　　The word needed at present
As much as ever, if it is well written and said, 35
　　With the heart and the head?

QUESTIONS

1. How much attention is given in this poem to the meanings of the word "heart"? How accurate are the definitions? Why does the poet title the poem "An Apology . . ."?

2. Would it be fair to describe some of the definitions as "flippant"? Why? How do we know that the poet is being serious?

3. Why does Carruth say, "Not even the dullest / Reader misapprehends it" (i.e., the word "heart")? How true is this claim?

ROBERT CREELEY (1926–2005)

I Know a Man

As I sd to my
friend, because I am
always talking,—John, I

sd. which was not his
5   name, the darkness surrounds us, what

can we do against
it, or else, shall we &
why not, buy a goddamn big car,

10   drive, he sd, for
christ's sake, look
out where yr going.

QUESTIONS

1. How do people speak differently to friends, family, coworkers, fellow students? What do you think the relationship is between the two people in this poem?

2. Why are letters missing from words? How might the poem be read differently if the words were spelled out correctly?

3. What is the setting of the poem? How does the way the poem is written reflect it?

E. E. CUMMINGS (1894–1962)

next to of course god america i (1926)

"next to of course god america i
love you land of the pilgrims' and so forth oh
say can you see by the dawn's early my
country 'tis of centuries come and go
5   and are no more what of it we should worry
in every language even deafanddumb
thy sons acclaim your glorious name by gorry
by jingo by gee by gosh by gum
why talk of beauty what could be more beaut-
10   iful than these heroic happy dead
who rushed like lions to the roaring slaughter
they did not stop to think they died instead
then shall the voice of liberty be mute?"

He spoke. And drank rapidly a glass of water

QUESTIONS

1. What is the form of this poem? What is the rhyme scheme? What does Cummings achieve by not using capitalization and punctuation?

2. Who is the speaker? What characteristics and capacities does he show? How do you respond to him?

3. What ideas does the poem bring out? In what ways does the speaker parody the speakers that one is likely to hear on the Fourth of July throughout the United States? What is Cummings saying not only about the speakers but also about the crowds that listen to such speeches?

And there were the lovely times when, to the skies' cold *No*
You cried to me, *Yes!* Impaled me with affirmation.
Now when I call out in fear, not in love, there is no answer.   20
Nothing speaks in the dark but the distant voices,
A child with the moon in his face, a dog's hollow cadence.

QUESTIONS

1. To what degree may this poem be considered confessional? What is being confessed?
2. Who is the "you" of the poem? What has happened between the speaker and the "you"? With what contrasts does the speaker conclude the poem? How are these contrasts related to the relationship between the speaker and the "you"?
3. What situation and impressions are brought about by these words in the first stanza: "moonlight," "weeping," "nightmares," "tinged," "terror," "nostalgia"?
4. What is the effect of the participles in stanzas 1–4 ("living," "coaxing," "withholding," "trying," "feigning")?

DENISE LEVERTOV (1923–1997)

 Of Being (1997)

I know this happiness
Is provisional:

    the looming presences—
    great suffering, great fear—

    withdraw only   5
    into peripheral vision:

but ineluctable this shimmering
of wind in the blue leaves:

this flood of stillness
widening the lake of sky: 10

this need to dance,
this need to kneel:

    this mystery:

QUESTIONS

1. What is meant by "this happiness / Is provisional"?
2. What is it that withdraws (line 5)? How does the poet connect withdrawing with the poem's title?
3. What do the words "peripheral vision," "ineluctable," "blue leaves," "flood of stillness," and "lake of sky" contribute to your understanding of the "mystery" with which the poem closes? What is noteworthy about these words?
4. Why does the poet end the poem with a colon rather than a period?

GERI LIPSCHULTZ (1951)

For a photo, see Chapter 5, page 277.

In the Beginning of the End (1985)

<pre>
                        Freud created
      the ego and the id.
                     And the id
      was rich
5   and without form
                        and the ego worked
                                    upon the
      face
             of the darkness.
10   And Freud said,
                  "Let there be ambivalence,"
      and there was
            ambivalence.
                     And Freud saw
15   that the ambivalence
                         was good.
      And Freud said,
                  "Let there be repression and regression depression
      and suppression."
20   And there was repression and regression and depression and
      suppression.
                  And Freud heard some dreams
                     and thought them significant.
                                 And Freud divided the
25   dream from the reality.
                           And Freud called the
      unconscious a dream.
                        And the reality, Freud called
      Oedipal.
30   And Freud said, "Let there

      be a firmament
                     in the midst of the people,
                                 and let it
      divided the girlchild

35   from the boychild,

         and the son
               from his mother,

      and the daughter

            from her father,
</pre>

and the parents   40

from the grandparents,

and the children

from the grandchildren,

and the man

from the woman."   45

And that
firmament still remains.

QUESTIONS

1. How did you feel about encountering so many technical terms from psychology in this poem?
2. Even if you did not understand all the words of the poem, did you find the poem serious, funny, amusing? What do you think the speaker's attitude is toward psychology?
3. Why are the lines of the poem arranged in this way?

JUDITH ORTIZ COFER (b. 1952)

 ## Latin Women Pray (1987)

Latin women pray
In incense sweet churches
They pray in Spanish to an Anglo God
With a Jewish heritage.
And this great White Father   5
Imperturbable in his marble pedestal
Looks down upon his brown daughters
Votive candles shining like lust
In his all seeing eyes
Unmoved by their persistent prayers.   10

Yet year after year
Before his image they kneel
Margarita Josefina Maria and Isabel
All fervently hoping
That if not omnipotent   15
At least he be bilingual.

QUESTIONS

1. What is the situation described in this poem? Who are the women who pray? What do their names indicate about them? To what God do these women pray? Are they living in their native countries?

2. What words in the poem explain the contradiction implied by the speaker? What is conveyed by the term "Anglo" (line 3). What is conveyed by the terms "White Father" and "Jewish heritage" (lines 4 and 5).

3. What are votive candles? Why does the speaker state that they shine "like lust"? What does "lust" indicate in this context?

4. Describe the effect of the last line (16). In what way is the line comic? How does the line contrast with the previous part of the poem?

EDWIN ARLINGTON ROBINSON (1869–1935)

 Richard Cory (1897)

Whenever Richard Cory went down town,
We people on the pavement looked at him:
He was a gentleman from sole to crown,
Clean favored, and imperially slim.

5 And he was always quietly arrayed,
And he was always human when he talked;
But still he fluttered pulses when he said,
'Good-morning,' and he glittered when he walked.

And he was rich—yes, richer than a king—
10 And admirably schooled in every grace:
In fine, we thought that he was everything
To make us wish that we were in his place.

So on we worked, and waited for the light,
And went without the meat, and cursed the bread;
15 And Richard Cory, one calm summer night,
Went home and put a bullet through his head.

QUESTIONS

1. What is the effect of using "down town," "pavement," "meat," and "bread" in connection with the people who admire Richard Cory?

2. What are the connotations and implications of the name "Richard Cory"? Of the word "gentleman"?

3. Why does the poet use "sole to crown" instead of "head to toe" and "imperially slim" instead of "very thin" to describe Cory?

4. What effect does repetition produce in this poem? Consider especially the six lines that begin with "And."

5. What positive characteristic does Richard Cory possess (at least from the perspective of the speaker) besides wealth?

THEODORE ROETHKE (1908–1963)

 Dolor (1943)

I have known the inexorable sadness of pencils,
Neat in their boxes, dolor of pad and paper-weight,
All the misery of manila folders and mucilage,
Desolation in immaculate public places,
Lonely reception room, lavatory, switchboard,   5
The unalterable pathos of basin and pitcher,
Ritual of multigraph, paper-clip, comma,
Endless duplication of lives and objects.
And I have seen dust from the walls of institutions,
Finer than flour, alive, more dangerous than silica,   10
Sift, almost invisible, through long afternoons of tedium,
Dropping a fine film on nails and delicate eyebrows,
Glazing the pale hair, the duplicate grey standard faces.

QUESTIONS

1. What does "dolor" mean? What words objectify the concept?
2. Why does "Dolor" not contain the fourteen lines usual in a sonnet?
3. What institutions, conditions, and places does the speaker associate with "dolor"? What do these have in common?
4. Describe the relationships of sentence structures and lines in "Dolor."

KAY RYAN (b. 1945)

 Crib (1997)

From the Greek for
woven or *plaited*
which quickly translated
to *basket*. Whence the verb
crib, which meant to *filch*   5
under cover of wicker
anything—some liquor,
a cutlet.
For we want to make off
with things that are not   10
our own. There is a pleasure
theft brings, a vitality
to the home.
Cribbed objects or answers
keep their guilty shimmer   15
forever, have you noticed?
Yet religions downplay this.

Note, for instance, in our annual rehearsals of innocence,
the substitution of *manger* for *crib*—
20 as if we ever deserved that baby,
or thought we did.

QUESTIONS

1. Why do you think the poet named this poem "Crib"? In what way is the word "crib" developed in the poem?
2. Why does the speaker bring out the idea of theft in the word "crib"? What is meant by the sentence "There is a pleasure / Theft brings"? Is this true? How is the idea of theft related to the entire poem?
3. What is meant by the "annual rehearsals of innocence." What is the connection between the rehearsals of innocence and the title, "Crib," of the poem?
4. Explain the idea of the final four lines of the poem. Should we consider this poem to be about the development of words, or about the nature of religious belief, or both?

STEPHEN SPENDER (1909–1995)

I Think Continually of Those Who Were Truly Great (1934)

I think continually of those who were truly great.
Who, from the womb, remembered the soul's history
Through corridors of light where the hours are suns,
Endless and singing. Whose lovely ambition
5   Was that their lips, still touched with fire,
Should tell of the spirit clothed from head to foot in song.
And who hoarded from the spring branches
The desires falling across their bodies like blossoms.

What is precious is never to forget
10 The delight of the blood drawn from ageless springs
Breaking through rocks in worlds before our earth;
Never to deny its pleasure in the simple morning light,
Nor its grave evening demand for love;
Never to allow gradually the traffic to smother
15 With noise and fog the flowering of the spirit.

QUESTIONS

1. How does this poem cause you to reconsider what is usually understood by the word "great"? What are the principal characteristics of people "who were truly great"?
2. Why does Spender use the words "were great" rather than "are great"? What difference, if any, does this distinction make to Spender's definition of greatness?
3. What is the meaning of phrases like "delight of the blood," "in worlds before our earth," "hours are suns," "still touched with fire"? What other phrases need similar thought and explanation?
4. How practical is the advice of the poem in the light of its definitions of "great" and "precious"? Why should the practicality or impracticality of these definitions probably not be considered in your judgment of the poem?

WALLACE STEVENS (1879–1955)

 ## Disillusionment of Ten O'Clock (1923)

The houses are haunted
By white night-gowns.
None are green,
Or purple with green rings,
Or green with yellow rings,   5
Or yellow with blue rings.
None of them are strange,
With socks of lace
And beaded ceintures.°   *belts*
People are not going   10
To dream of baboons and periwinkles.
Only, here and there, an old sailor,
Drunk and asleep in his boots,
Catches tigers
In red weather.   15

QUESTIONS

1. Is the "Ten O'Clock" here morning or night? How can you tell?
2. What do "haunted" and "white night-gowns" suggest about the people who live in the houses? What do the negative images in lines 3–9 suggest?
3. To whom are these people contrasted in lines 12–15?
4. What are the connotations of "socks with lace" and "beaded ceintures"? With which character in the poem would you associate these things?
5. What is the effect of using words and images like "baboons," "periwinkles," "tigers," and "red weather" in lines 11–15? Who will dream of these things?
6. Explain the term "disillusionment" and explore its relation to the point that this poem makes about dreams, images, and imagination.

MARK STRAND (b. 1934)

 ## Eating Poetry (1968)

Ink runs from the corners of my mouth.
There is no happiness like mine.
I have been eating poetry.

The librarian does not believe what she sees.
Her eyes are sad
and she walks with her hands in her dress.   5

The poems are gone.
The light is dim.
The dogs are on the basement stairs and coming up.

10   Their eyeballs roll,
      their blond legs burn like brush.
      The poor librarian begins to stamp her feet and weep.

      She does not understand.
      When I get on my knees and lick her hand,
15   She screams.

      I am a new man.
      I snarl at her and bark.
      I romp with joy in the bookish dark.

QUESTIONS

1. In the first three lines, which words tell you the poem is not to be taken literally?
2. What is the serious topic of the poem? What words indicate its serious intent?
3. What is the comic topic? Which words tell you that the poem's action is comic?

NATASHA TRETHEWEY (1966)

🖋 White Lies (2000)

      The lies I could tell,
      when I was growing up
      light-bright, near-white,
      high-yellow, red-boned
5   in a black place,
      were just white lies.

      I could easily tell the white folks
      that we lived uptown,
      not in that pink and green
10   shanty-fied shotgun section
      along the tracks. I could act
      like my homemade dresses
      came straight out the window
      of Maison Blanche. I could even
15   keep quiet, quiet as kept,
      like the time a white girl said
      (squeezing my hand), *Now*
      we have three of us in this class.

      But I paid for it every time
20   Mama found out.
      She laid her hands on me,
      then washed out my mouth
      with Ivory soap. This
      is to purify, she said,
25   *and cleanse your lying tongue.*
      Believing her, I swallowed suds
      thinking they'd work
      from the inside out.

QUESTIONS

1. Why do people tell lies about where and how they grew up? Are these "white lies" or are they more than that?
2. What did the speaker mean when she said she believed washing her mouth out with soap would work "from the inside out"?
3. What is the significance of the word "white" in this poem?

WILLIAM WORDSWORTH (1770–1850)

For a portrait, see Chapter 11, page 557.

Daffodils (I Wandered Lonely as a Cloud)° (1807; 1804)

I wandered lonely as a cloud
That floats on high o'er vales and hills,
When all at once I saw a crowd,
A host, of golden daffodils;
Beside the lake, beneath the trees,   5
Fluttering and dancing in the breeze.

Continuous as the stars that shine
And twinkle on the milky way,
They stretched in never-ending line
Along the margin of a bay: 10
Ten thousand saw I at a glance,
Tossing their heads in sprightly dance.

The waves beside them danced; but they
Out-did the sparkling waves in glee:
A poet could not but be gay,   15
In such a jocund° company: *cheerful, merry*
I gazed—and gazed—but little thought
What wealth the show to me had brought:

For oft, when on my couch I lie
In vacant or in pensive mood,
They flash upon that inward eye   20
Which is the bliss of solitude;
And then my heart with pleasure fills,
And dances with the daffodils.

QUESTIONS

1. What is the occasion of the poem? Where was the speaker at the time he describes in the poem? What was he doing? What did he see?
2. What words does Wordsworth use to show the life and beauty of the flowers at the side of the lake? How successful are these word choices?
3. How important to the speaker is the memory of this experience?

°Wordsworth's note: "Written at Town-end, Grasmere. Daffodils grew and still grow on the margin of Ullswater, and probably may be seen to this day as beautiful in the month of March, nodding their golden heads beside the dancing and foaming waves." Wordsworth also pointed out that lines 21 and 22, the "best lines," were by his wife, Mary.

PAUL ZIMMER (b. 1934)

🔖 The Day Zimmer Lost Religion (1973)

The first Sunday I missed Mass on purpose
I waited all day for Christ to climb down
Like a wiry flyweight° from the cross and
Club me on my irreverent teeth, to wade into
5　My blasphemous gut and drop me like a
Red hot thurible,° the devil roaring in
Reserved seats until he got the hiccups.

It was a long cold way from the old days
When cassocked and surpliced° I mumbled Latin
10　At the old priest and rang his obscure bell.
A long way from the dirty wind that blew
The soot like venial sins° across the schoolyard
Where God reigned as a threatening,
One-eyed triangle high in the fleecy sky.

15　The first Sunday I missed Mass on purpose
I waited all day for Christ to climb down
Like the playground bully, the cuts and mice
Upon his face agleam, and pound me
Till my irreligious tongue hung out.
20　But of course He never came, knowing that
I was grown up and ready for Him now.

QUESTIONS

1. Why might the speaker juxtapose slang terms from boxing and playground fights with technical terms from the Catholic Mass and theology?
2. Why might the priest be described as "old" and his ringing bell "obscure"?
3. What are different ways to interpret that the speaker is "ready for him now"? Is he ready to reject, battle, or accept God? Why has missing Mass changed him?

°3 *flyweight:* a boxer weighing less than 112 pounds.　°6 *thurible:* a censer, a container in which incense is burned. °9 *cassocked and surpliced:* wearing the traditional garb of an altar boy during Mass. °12 *venial sins:* minor inadvertent sins.

WRITING ABOUT DICTION AND SYNTAX IN POETRY

Study your poem carefully, line by line, to gain a general sense of its meaning. Try to establish how diction and syntax may be connected to elements such as tone, character, and idea. As you develop your ideas, look for effective and consistent patterns of word choice, connotation, repetition, and syntactic patterns that help create and reinforce the conclusions you have drawn about the poem. Ask questions like these.

Questions for Discovering Ideas

- Who is the speaker? What is the speaker's profession or way of life? How does the speaker's background affect his or her power of observation? How does the background affect his or her level of speech?
- Who is the listener? How does the listener affect what the speaker says?
- What other characters are in the poem? How are their actions described? How accurate and fair do you think these descriptions are?
- Is the level of diction in the poem elevated, neutral, or informal; and how does this level affect your perception of the speaker, subject, and main idea or ideas?
- What patterns of diction or syntax do you discover in the poem? (*Example:* Consider words related to situation, action, setting, or particular characters.) How ordinary or unusual are these words? Which, if any, are unusual enough to warrant further examination?
- Does the poem contain many "loaded" or connotative words in connection with any single element, such as setting, speaker, or theme?
- Does the poem contain a large number of general and abstract or specific and concrete words? What is the effect of these choices?
- Does the poem contain dialect? Colloquialisms? Jargon? If so, how does this special diction shape your response to the poem?
- What is the nature of the poem's syntax? Is there any unusual word order? What seems to be the purpose or effect of syntactic variations?
- Has the poet used any striking patterns of sentence structure such as parallelism or repetition? If so, what is the effect?

Strategies for Organizing Ideas

When you narrow your examination to one or two specific areas of diction or syntax, you should list important words, phrases, and sentences. Begin grouping examples that work in similar ways or produce similar effects. Investigate the full range of meaning and effect that the examples produce. Eventually you may be able to develop the related examples as units or sections for your essay.

Your central idea should emerge from your investigation of the diction or syntax that you find most fruitful and interesting. Let the poem be your guide. Since diction and syntax contribute to the poem's impact and meaning, try to connect your thesis and examples to your other conclusions. If you are writing about Stevens's "Disillusionment of Ten O'Clock," for example, your central idea might assert that Stevens uses words describing colors (i.e., "white," "green," "purple," "yellow," "blue," "red") to contrast life's visual reality with the psychological "disillusionment" of the "houses," "People," and "old sailor." Such a formulation makes a clear connection of diction to meaning.

There are many different ways to organize your material. If you deal with only one aspect of diction, such as connotative words, you might treat these in the order in which they appear in the poem. When you deal with two or three different aspects of diction and syntax, however, you might devote a series of paragraphs to related examples of multiple denotation, then connotation, and finally jargon (assuming the presence of jargon in the poem). In such an instance, your organization would be controlled by the types of material under consideration rather than by the order in which the words occur.

Alternatively, you might deal with the impact of diction or syntax on a series of other elements, such as character, setting, or situation. Such an essay would focus on a single type of lexical or syntactic device (described earlier in this chapter) as it relates to these different elements in sequence. Thus, you might discuss the link between connotation and situation, character, and the basic situation of the poem. Whatever organization you select, keep in mind that each poem will suggest its own avenues of exploration and strategies of organization.

In your conclusion, summarize your ideas about the impact of the poem's diction or syntax. You might also consider the larger implications of your ideas in connection with the thoughts and emotions evoked by your reading.

Illustrative Student Essay

Although underlined sentences are not recommended by MLA style, they are used in this illustrative essay as teaching tools to emphasize the central idea, thesis sentence, and topic sentences.

Fitzpatrick 1

Lionel Fitzpatrick

Professor Allen

English 1B

20 October 2014

[1]   Diction and Character in Robinson's "Richard Cory"°

In "Richard Cory," Edwin Arlington Robinson dramatizes the idea that nothing can guarantee happiness. His example, and the central character in the poem, is Richard Cory, a man who apparently has everything: wealth, status, dignity, taste, and respect. Cory's suicide, however, reveals that these qualities did not make him happy. By creating a gulf between Cory and the people of the town who admire and envy him, Robinson sets us up for the surprising suicide described in the last two lines. The distinction is produced

°This poem appears on page 590.

Fitzpatrick 2

through the words that Robinson uses to demean the general populace and elevate the central character.* The speaker and his or her fellow townspeople are associated with words that indicate their ordinary existence, while Richard Cory is described in words of nobility and privilege.†

    The poem focuses on Richard Cory as perceived by the townspeople,   [2] who wish that they "were in his place" (line 12). Robinson skillfully employs words about these common folk to suggest their poverty and low status. In the first line, for example, the speaker places himself or herself and these other people "down town." The phrase refers to a central business district, but here it also carries the negative connotation of the word "down." The word implies that Cory's journey to town seems to be a descent, and that the people constantly live in this "down" condition. A similar instance of connotative diction is "pavement" (2), which can mean "sidewalk," but can also mean "street" or "roadbed." The net effect of the word "pavement" rather than "sidewalk" is to place the "people" even lower than Richard Cory—literally on the street.

    In contrast to these few words suggesting the people's lowness, the   [3] poem contains many words that glowingly describe Cory's high status. Many words and phrases suggest nobility or royalty. These implications begin with the title of the poem and the name "Richard Cory." That the word "rich" is contained within "Richard" implies Cory's wealth and privilege. It is also the name of a number of English kings, most notably Richard the Lion Hearted ("Richard Coeur de Lion"). The name "Cory" is equally connotative. It clearly suggests the "Coeur," the heart, of the famous king, and it also reminds us of "core," the central or innermost part of anything. The name thus points toward Cory's singular position and significance. Through sound, "Cory" also suggests the English word "court"—that is, a place for kings and courtiers. The name "Richard Cory" thus begins an association through sound and implication that links the central character to kingship and elegance.

---

*Central idea.
†Thesis sentence.

Fitzpatrick 3

[4]   There are other similar words in the poem's first stanza. The speaker
describes Richard Cory as "a gentleman from sole to crown" (3). "Gentleman"
refers to a civilized and well-mannered individual, but it originally also meant a
man of "high" or "noble" birth. The phrase "from sole to crown" is another way
of saying "from head to toe," but it connotes a great deal more. "Sole" means
both "the bottom of a shoe or foot" and "alone" or "singular." Thus, the word
suggests Cory's isolation and separation from the common folk. The word is also
a pun (and homophone) on "soul," implying that Cory's gentility is inward as well
as outward. The final touch is the word "crown." In context, the term denotes the
top of the head, but it also has connotations of aristocracy and royalty.

[5]   The speaker also describes Cory as "clean favored" and "imperially slim"
(4). The word "imperially," like "crown," makes an explicit connection between
Cory and emperors. "Clean favored," instead of the more common "good-
looking," connotes crisp and untouched features. More to the point, the term
"favored" also means "preferred," "elevated," "honored," and "privileged."
"Imperially slim," instead of "thin," is equally connotative of wealth and status.
While both terms denote the same physical condition, *slim* suggests elegance,
wealth, and choice, whereas "thin" suggests poverty and necessity.

[6]   Although this type of diction is mostly in the first stanza, Robinson
sustains the link between Cory and royalty by using similar terms in the rest of
the poem. In stanza 2, for example, he uses "quietly arrayed" and "glittered."
Both carry elevated and imperial connotations. "Arrayed" means "dressed,"
but it is also a word in the King James Bible that suggests elegant and heavenly
clothing (see Matthew 6:29; Acts 12:21, Revelation 7:13). "Quietly" also
suggests solitude and introversion. "Glittered" complements "quietly"; it
connotes richness of dress and manner, suggesting that the man himself is
golden. In the third stanza, the deliberate cliché "richer than a king" again
clearly links Richard Cory to royalty. The speaker also notes that Cory was
"schooled in every grace" (10). The phrase means that Cory was trained in
manners and social niceties, but "grace" connotes privilege and nobility ("Your
Grace") and also the idea of heavenly love and forgiveness ("God's Grace").

Fitzpatrick 4

It is clear, then, that Robinson uses the effects of connotation to lower the [7]

common folk and elevate the central character. The words linked to the speaker

and the other townspeople have demeaning and negative implications. At the

same time, the poet uses words and phrases about Cory that connote royalty and

privilege. This careful manipulation of diction widens the gulf between Cory and

the town. It also heightens our sense that Cory has aristocratic looks, manners,

taste, and breeding. The network of associations built through this skillful diction

makes the poem's ending powerfully shocking, and reinforces the poem's idea

that appearance, wealth, and high status do not necessarily produce happiness.

Fitzpatrick 5

Work Cited

Robinson, Edwin Arlington. "Richard Cory." *Literature: An*

Introduction to Reading and Writing, Compact Edition. Ed. Edgar V.

Roberts and Robert Zweig. 6th ed. New York: Pearson, 2015. 590. Print.

Commentary on the Essay

This essay deals with Robinson's use of connotative words to elevate the central character and demean the townspeople. The opening paragraph makes a general assertion about the poem's theme, connects character to this assertion, and argues that Robinson controls diction to make his distinctions.

The body of the essay, in five paragraphs, deals with the effects of a number of examples of word choice. The examples of connotative words are arranged to reflect partly the characters they define and partly the order in which they appear in the poem. Thus, paragraph 2 discusses the common people and the speaker in connection with two highly connotative terms: *down town* and *pavement*.

The next four paragraphs (3–6) focus on Richard Cory and words or phrases that suggest royalty and privilege. The examples of diction examined here are taken up in the order in which they appear in the poem. Thus, paragraph 3 considers Cory's name, and the fourth explores the effects of *gentleman* and *sole to crown*. Paragraphs 5 and 6 continue this process, examining instances of diction that sustain the association between Cory and nobility. Taken together, the four paragraphs devoted to this central character illustrate Robinson's consistent manipulation of diction both to ennoble and isolate Cory.

USING SOURCES EFFECTIVELY

SUMMARIZING TO PROVIDE NECESSARY BACKGROUND

Summarizing is not a substitute for true academic analysis, but it is useful in giving your reader a quick, general overview of what a literary work is about so that your academic essay can then go into further detail, using evidence from the work itself, to make your case persuasively. You should always avoid overquoting, but when you do quote, be sure it is in the service of giving a strong basis to your points. In the first draft of this student essay, the writer provided an overview of Richard Cory that included many selected phrases and words taken directly from the poem itself.

Using these quotations from the work in a summary can confuse readers who may need a clearer idea of what the work as a whole is before delving into such images.

> In "Richard Cory," Edwin Arlington Robinson dramatizes the idea that nothing can guarantee happiness. His example, and the central character in the poem, is Richard Cory, who "was a gentleman from sole to crown" and was "imperially slim." He even "glittered when he walked" and appeared to be "richer than a king." At the end of the poem, he "went home and put a bullet through his head."

Although these phrases are, to be sure, important to the poem, the first paragraph's summary should efficiently restate the major elements of the poem's story in the writer's own language. The rest of this essay will focus on the specific diction that the poet uses to create the character of Richard Cory. Using a number of examples of the poet's language in a summary does not allow for clear elaboration of the essay's points or a readily understandable translation of the basic plot of the work.

In this final version, Fitzpatrick uses clear and accessible language to give his readers a clear sense of the poem's narrative outline. The rest of the essay then delivers clear evidence from the actual work to support his thesis.

This gives a general overview of the main character qualities of Richard Cory that will be thoroughly developed and illustrated in the body of the essay.

> In "Richard Cory," Edwin Arlington Robinson dramatizes the idea that nothing can guarantee happiness. His example, and the central character in the poem, is Richard Cory, a man who apparently has everything: wealth, status, dignity, taste, and respect. Cory's suicide, however, reveals that these qualities did not make him happy.

The summary avoids using direct quotations from the poem so the reader can quickly grasp what the work is about. In the body of the essay, Fitzpatrick examines specific examples from the poem in greater depth to support his thesis that money and status cannot buy happiness. (For more information on summary, see pages 509–515.)

The conclusion reasserts that Robinson's diction not only contributes to Cory's isolation but also adds to the impact of his mysterious suicide. In this way, the words and phrases examined in the essay are linked to the poem's exploration of ideas about the human condition.

Writing Topics About the Words of Poetry

Writing Paragraphs

1. In a paragraph compare any two words describing natural scenes in Kizer's "Night Sounds" and Wordsworth's "Daffodils." Which poem seems more specific and direct in its depiction of nature?

2. In a paragraph compare and contrast John Donne "Holy Sonnet 14: Batter My Heart, Three-Personed God" and Carruth's "An Apology for Using the Word 'Heart' in Too Many Poems." What common idea about love do the poems share? What differences about love do you find?

Writing Essays

1. Write an essay considering the sound qualities of the invented words in "Jabberwocky." Some obvious choices are "brillig," "frumious," "vorpal," and "manxome," but you are free to choose any or all of them. What is the relationship between the sound and apparent meaning of these words? What effect do the surrounding normal words and normal word order have on the special words? How does Carroll succeed in creating a narrative "structure," even though the key words are, on the surface, nonsense? Argue that the poem would have had a very different meaning had Carroll not used invented words.

2. Write a brief essay discussing the use of connotation in Cummings's "next to of course god america i," Ortiz Cofer's "Latin Women Pray," Levertov's "Of Being," and "Roethke's "Dolor." What particularities of meaning do the poets introduce? How does their control of connotation contribute to the various ideas you discover in the poems?

Creative Writing Assignment

1. Write a short poem describing a violent crime and commenting on it. Then, assume that you are the "alleged perpetrator" of the crime, and write another poem on the same topic. Even though you describe the same situation, how do your words differ, and why have you made these different choices? Explain the other different word choices you have made. You might also discuss words that you considered using but rejected.

Library Assignment

1. Find a book or books in your library about the works of Blake, Roethke, Robinson, Wordsworth, or another poet represented in this chapter. How fully do these sources discuss the style of these poets? Write a brief report explaining how the writers of the book or books deal with poetic diction.

Chapter 13
Imagery: The Poem's Link to the Senses

AFTER STUDYING THIS MATERIAL, YOU SHOULD BE ABLE TO DO THE FOLLOWING:

- Understand the concept of imagery in poems
- Compare different types of imagery found in poetry
- Evaluate the use of imagery in poems

In literature, **imagery** refers to words that trigger your imagination to recall and recombine images—memories or mental pictures of sights, sounds, tastes, smells, sensations of touch, and motions. The process is active and even vigorous, for when words or descriptions produce images, you are using your personal experiences with life and language to help you understand the works you are reading. In effect, you are re-creating the work *in your own way* through the controlled stimulation produced by the writer's words. Imagery is therefore one of the strongest modes of literary expression because it provides a channel to your active imagination, and along this channel, writers bring their works directly to you and into your consciousness.

For example, reading the word *lake* may bring to your mind your literal memory of a particular lake. Your mental picture—or image—may be a distant view of calm waters reflecting blue sky, a nearby view of gentle waves rippling in the wind, a close-up view of the sandy lake bottom from a boat, or an overhead view of a sun-drenched shoreline. Similarly, the words *rose, apple, hot dog, malted milk,* and *pizza* all cause you to recollect these objects, and, in addition, may cause you to recall their smells and tastes. Active and graphic words like *row, swim,* and *dive* stimulate you to picture moving images of someone performing these actions.

Responses and the Poet's Use of Detail

In studying imagery, we try to comprehend and explain our imaginative reconstruction of the pictures and impressions evoked by the poem's images. We let the poet's words simmer and percolate in our minds. To get our imaginations stirring, we might follow a description by Samuel Taylor Coleridge in lines 37–41 of "Kubla Khan."

> A damsel with a dulcimer
> In a vision once I saw:
> It was an Abyssinian maid,
> And on her dulcimer she played
> Singing of Mount Abora.

Note that we do not read about the color of the young woman's clothing or learn anything else about her appearance except that she is playing a stringed instrument, a dulcimer, and that she is singing a song about a mountain in a foreign, remote land. But Coleridge's image is enough. From it we can visualize a vivid, exotic picture of a young woman from a distant land singing, together with impressions of the loveliness of her song (even though we never hear it or understand it). The image lives.

The Relationship of Imagery to Ideas and Attitudes

Images do more than elicit impressions. By the *authenticating* effects of the vision and perceptions underlying them, they give you new ways of seeing the world and of strengthening your old ways of seeing it. Shakespeare, in Sonnet 116: "Let Me Not to the Marriage of True Minds" (Chapter 16), develops the idea that love provides people with consistency of purpose in their lives. Rather than stating the idea directly, he uses images of a landmark or lighthouse and also of a fixed star—sights with which we as his readers are familiar.

> . . . it [love] is an ever fixèd mark
> That looks on tempests and is never shaken;
> It is the star to every wandering bark°   *boat, ship*
> Whose worth's unknown, although his° height be taken.   *its*

These images form a link with readers that is clear and also verifiable by observation. Such uses of imagery comprise one of the strongest means by which writers reinforce ideas.

In addition, as you form mental pictures and impressions from a poet's images, you respond with appropriate attitudes and feelings. Thus the phrase "Beside the lake, beneath the trees," from Wordsworth's poem "Daffodils" (Chapter 12) prompts both the visualization of a wooded lakeshore and the related pleasantness of outdoor relaxation and happiness. By using such imagery, poets create sensory vividness, and they also influence and control our attitudes as readers.

Types of Imagery

Visual Imagery Is the Language of Sight

Human beings are visual. Sight is the most significant of our senses, for it is the key to our remembrance of other sense impressions. Therefore, the most frequently occurring literary imagery is to things we can visualize either exactly or approximately—**visual imagery.** In the three-stanza poem "Cargoes," John Masefield creates mental pictures or images of ocean-going merchant vessels from three periods of human history.

JOHN MASEFIELD (1878–1967)

Cargoes (1902)

Quinquireme° of Nineveh° from distant Ophir,°
Rowing home to haven in sunny Palestine,
With a cargo of ivory,
And apes and peacocks,°
5   Sandalwood, cedarwood,° and sweet white wine.

Stately Spanish galleon coming from the Isthmus,°
Dipping through the Tropics by the palm-green shores,
With a cargo of diamonds,
Emeralds, amethysts,
10 Topazes, and cinnamon, and gold moidores.°

Dirty British coaster with a salt-caked smoke stack,
Butting through the Channel in the mad March days,
With a cargo of Tyne coal,°
Road-rails, pig-lead,
15 Firewood, iron-ware, and cheap tin trays.

°1 *quinquereme:* the largest of the ancient warships, although no wrecks are known to have survived from antiquity. Very likely a quinquereme was powered by three tiers of oars and was named "quinquereme" because five men operated each vertical oar station. The top two oars were each taken by two men, while one man alone took the bottom oar. *Nineveh:* the capital of ancient Assyria, and an "exceeding great city" (Jonah 3:3). *Ophir:* Ophir probably was in Africa and was known for its gold (1 Kings 10:22; 1 Chron. 29:4). Masefield quotes from some of the biblical verses in his first stanza. °4 *apes and peacocks:* 1 Kings 10:22; 2 Chron. 9:21. °5 *cedarwood:* 1 Kings 9:11. °6 *Isthmus:* the Isthmus of Panama. °10 *moidores:* coins used in Portugal and Brazil at the time the New World was being explored. °13 *Tyne coal:* coal from Newcastle upon Tyne, in northern England, proverbial for its coal production.

QUESTIONS

1. Consider the images of life during three periods of history: ancient Israel at the time of Solomon (c. 950 BCE), sixteenth-century Spain, and modern England. What do these images tell you about Masefield's interpretation of modern commercial life?

2. To what senses do most of the images refer (e.g., sight, taste)?

3. The poem contains no complete sentences. Why do you think Masefield included only verbals ("rowing," "dipping," "butting") to begin the second line of each stanza, rather than finite verbs?

4. In historical reality, the quinquereme was likely rowed by slaves, and the Spanish galleon likely carried riches stolen from Central American natives. How might these unpleasant details affect the impressions otherwise achieved in the first two stanzas?

Masefield's images are vivid as they stand and need no further amplification. For us to reconstruct them imaginatively, we do not need ever to have seen the ancient biblical lands or waters, or ever to have seen or handled the cheap commodities on a modern merchant ship. We have seen enough in our lives to *imagine* places and objects like these, and hence Masefield is successful in fixing his visual images in our minds.

Auditory Imagery Is the Language of Sound

Auditory images trigger our experiences with sound. For such images, let us consider Wilfred Owen's "Anthem for Doomed Youth," which is about the death of soldiers in warfare and the sorrow of their loved ones.

WILFRED OWEN (1893–1918)

Anthem for Doomed Youth (1920)

What passing-bells° for these who die as cattle?
Only the monstrous anger of the guns.
Only the stuttering rifles' rapid rattle
Can patter out their hasty orisons.°   *prayers*
No mockeries for them from prayers or bells,   5
Nor any voice of mourning save the choirs—
The shrill, demented choirs of wailing shells;
And bugles calling for them from sad shires.°

What candles may be held to speed them all?
Not in the hands of boys, but in their eyes   10
Shall shine the holy glimmers of good-byes.
The pallor of girls' brows shall be their pall;
Their flowers the tenderness of patient minds,
And each slow dusk a drawing-down of blinds.

°1 *passing-bells:* church bells tolling upon the entry of a funeral cortege into a church cemetery.   °8 *shires:* British counties.

QUESTIONS

1. What type of imagery predominates in the first eight lines? How does the imagery change in the last six lines?
2. Contrast the images of death at home and death on the battlefield. How does this contrast affect your experience and understanding of the poem?
3. Consider these images: "holy glimmers of good-byes," "pallor of girls' brows," "patient minds," "drawing-down of blinds." What relationship do the people defined by these images have to the doomed youth?

The poem begins with the question of "What passing-bells" may be tolled "for these who die as cattle." Owen's speaker is referring to the traditional tolling of a church bell to announce a burial. The images of these ceremonial sounds suggest a period of peace and order, when there is time to pay respect to the dead. But the poem points out that the only sound for those who have fallen in battle is the "rapid rattle" of "stuttering" rifles—not the solemn, dignified sounds of peace but the horrifying noises of war. Owen's auditory images evoke corresponding sounds in our imaginations, and they help us to experience the poem and to hate the uncivilized depravity of war.

Olfactory, Gustatory, and Tactile Imagery Refers to Smell, Taste, and Touch

In addition to sight and sound, you will find images from the other senses: smell, taste, and touch. Shakespeare includes an **olfactory image** of sweet perfumes in Sonnet 130: "My Mistress' Eyes Are Nothing Like the Sun," and the odor of roses is suggested in Burns's "A Red, Red Rose" (Chapter 14).

Gustatory images—taste images—are also common, though less frequent than those referring to sight and sound. Lines 5 and 10 of Masefield's "Cargoes," for example, include images of "sweet white wine" and "cinnamon." Although the poem refers to these commodities as cargoes, the words themselves also register in our minds as gustatory images because they evoke our sense of taste.

Images of touch and texture—**tactile images**—are not as common, because touch is difficult to render except in terms of effects. Tactile images are not uncommon in love poetry, where references to touch and feeling are natural.

Kinetic and Kinesthetic Imagery Refers to Motion and Activity

References to movement are also images. Images of general motion are **kinetic** (remember that *motion pictures* may be called "cinema"; note the closeness of *kine* in *kinetic* and *cine* in *cinema*), whereas the term **kinesthetic** is applied to human or animal movement. Imagery of motion is closely related to visual images, for motion is most often seen. Masefield's "British coaster" is a visual image, but when it goes "Butting through the channel," this reference to motion makes it also kinetic. When Hardy's skeletons sit upright at the beginning of "Channel Firing," the image is kinesthetic. Both types are seen at the conclusion of the following poem, Elizabeth Bishop's "The Fish."

ELIZABETH BISHOP (1911–1979)

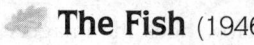 ### The Fish (1946)

I caught a tremendous fish
and held him beside the boat
half out of water, with my hook
fast in a corner of his mouth.
5   He didn't fight.
He hadn't fought at all.
He hung a grunting weight,
battered and venerable
and homely. Here and there
10   his brown skin hung in strips
like ancient wallpaper,
and its pattern of darker brown
was like wallpaper:
shapes like full-blown roses
15   stained and lost through age.
He was speckled with barnacles,
fine rosettes of lime,

and infested
with tiny white sea-lice,
and underneath two or three   20
rags of green weed hung down.
While his gills were breathing in
the terrible oxygen
—the frightening gills,
fresh and crisp with blood,   25
that can cut so badly—
I thought of the coarse white flesh
packed in like feathers,
the big bones and the little bones,
the dramatic reds and blacks   30
of his shiny entrails,
and the pink swim-bladder
like a big peony.
I looked into his eyes
which were far larger than mine   35
but shallower, and yellowed,
the irises backed and packed
with tarnished tinfoil
seen through the lenses
of old scratched isinglass.°   *a thin sheet of mica*   40
They shifted a little, but not
to return my stare.
—It was more like the tipping
of an object toward the light.
I admired his sullen face,   45
the mechanism of his jaw,
and then I saw
that from his lower lip
—if you could call it a lip—
grim, wet, and weaponlike,   50
hung five old pieces of fish-line,
or four and a wire leader
with the swivel still attached,
with all their five big hooks
grown firmly in his mouth.   55
A green line, frayed at the end
where he broke it, two heavier lines,
and a fine black thread
still crimped from the strain and snap
when it broke and he got away.   60
Like medals with their ribbons
frayed and wavering,
a five-haired beard of wisdom
trailing from his aching jaw.
I stared and stared   65
and victory filled up
the little rented boat,
from the pool of bilge
where oil had spread a rainbow

70   around the rusted engine
      to the bailer rusted orange,
      the sun-cracked thwarts,
      the oarlocks on their strings,
      the gunnels—until everything
75   was rainbow, rainbow, rainbow!
      And I let the fish go.

QUESTIONS

1. Describe the poem's images of action (kinetic, kinesthetic). What is unusual about them?
2. What impression does the fish make upon the speaker? Is the fish beautiful? Ugly? Why is the fish described in such detail?
3. What do the "five old pieces of fish-line" indicate (line 51)?
4. How is the rainbow formed around the boat's engine? Why does the speaker refer to the "pool of bilge"? What does the rainbow mean to the speaker?
5. What right does the speaker have to keep the fish? Why does she choose to relinquish this right?

The kinetic images at the end of "The Fish" are those of victory filling the boat (difficult to visualize) and the oil spreading to make a rainbow in the bilgewater (easy to visualize). The kinesthetic images are readily imagined—the speaker's staring, observing, and letting the fish go—and they are vivid and real. The final gesture is the necessary outcome of the observed contrast between the deteriorating artifacts of human beings and the natural world of the fish, and it is a vivid expression of the right of the natural world to exist without human intervention. In short, Bishop's kinetic and kinesthetic images are designed to emphasize the need for freedom not only for human beings but for all the earth and animated nature.

The areas from which kinetic and kinesthetic imagery can be derived are too varied and unpredictable to describe. Occupations, trades, professions, businesses, recreational activities—all these might furnish images. One poet introduces references from gardening, another from money and banking, another from modern real estate developments, another from the falling of leaves in autumn, another from life in the jungle, another from life in the home. The freshness, newness, and surprise of much poetry result from the many and varied areas from which writers draw their images.

Poems for Study

Elizabeth Barrett Browning. . . . . .Sonnets from the Portuguese,
                                  Number 14: If Thou Must Love Me, 611
Samuel Taylor Coleridge . . . . Kubla Khan, 612
T. S. Eliot. . . . . Preludes, 613
Louise Erdrich . . . . Indian Boarding School: The Runaways, 615
Susan Griffin. Love Should Grow Up Like a
                                        Wild Iris in the Fields, 616

Thomas Hardy. . . . . Channel Firing, 617

H. D. (Hilda Doolittle) . . . . Heat, 618

George Herbert. . . . . The Pulley, 619

Gerard Manley Hopkins. . . . . Spring, 620

Robinson Jeffers. . . . . Hurt Hawks, 620

Denise Levertov . . . . A Time Past, 621

Amy Lowell. . . . . The Taxi, 622

Thomas Lux . . . . .The Voice You Hear When
You Read Silently, 623

Marianne Moore. . . . . The Fish, 624

Pablo Neruda . . . . Every Day You Play, 625

Octavio Paz. . . . . .The Street, 626

Ezra Pound . . . . In a Station of the Metro, 627

Philip Henry Savage. . . . . Shorter Poem 13, 628

William Shakespeare . . . . Sonnet 130: My Mistress' Eyes Are
Nothing Like the Sun, 628

Charles Simic . . . . Fork, 629

James Tate . . . . Dream On, 629

David Wojahn. . . . ."It's Only Rock and Roll but I Like It":
The Fall of Saigon, 631

ELIZABETH BARRETT BROWNING (1806–1861)

Sonnets from the Portuguese, Number 14: If Thou Must Love Me (1850)

If thou must love me, let it be for nought
Except for love's sake only. Do not say
"I love her for her smile—her look—her way
Of speaking gently—for a trick of thought
That falls in well with mine, and certes° brought   *certainly*   5
A sense of pleasant ease on such a day"—
For these things in themselves, Belovèd, may
Be changed, or change for thee—and love, so wrought,°   *created*
May be unwrought so. Neither love me for
Thine own dear pity's wiping my cheeks dry—   10
A creature might forget to weep, who bore
Thy comfort long, and lose thy love thereby!
But love me for love's sake, that evermore
Thou mayst love on, through love's eternity.

QUESTIONS

1. Who is the speaker of this poem? Why might you conclude that the speaker is female?
2. What images does the speaker use to indicate possible causes for loving? What kinds of images are they? How does the speaker explain why they should be rejected?
3. How does the idea of lines 1, 13, and 14 build upon the ideas in the rest of the poem?

SAMUEL TAYLOR COLERIDGE (1772–1834)

Kubla Khan (1816)

In Xanadu did Kubla Khan
A stately pleasure dome decree:
Where Alph,° the sacred river, ran
Through caverns measureless to man
5   Down to a sunless sea.
So twice five miles of fertile ground
With walls and towers were girdled round:
And there were gardens bright with sinuous rills,
Where blossomed many an incense-bearing tree;
10 And here were forests ancient as the hills,
Enfolding sunny spots of greenery.
But oh! that deep romantic chasm which slanted
Down the green hill athwart a cedarn cover!
A savage place! as holy and enchanted
15 As e'er beneath a waning moon was haunted
By woman wailing for her demon lover!
And from this chasm, with ceaseless turmoil seething,
As if this earth in fast thick pants were breathing,
A mighty fountain momently was forced:
20 Amid whose swift half-intermitted burst
Huge fragments vaulted like rebounding hail,
Or chaffy grain beneath the thresher's flail:
And 'mid these dancing rocks at once and ever
It flung up momently the sacred river.
25 Five miles meandering with a mazy motion
Through wood and dale the sacred river ran,
Then reached the caverns measureless to man,
And sank in tumult to a lifeless ocean:
And 'mid this tumult Kubla heard from far
30 Ancestral voices prophesying war!
    The shadow of the dome of pleasure
    Floated midway on the waves;
    Where was heard the mingled measure
    From the fountain and the caves.
35 It was a miracle of rare device,
A sunny pleasure dome with caves of ice!

    A damsel with a dulcimer
    In a vision once I saw:
    It was an Abyssinian maid,
40 And on her dulcimer she played
    Singing of Mount Abora.°

°3 *Alph:* possibly a reference to the river Alpheus in Greece, as described by the ancient writers Virgil and Pausanias. °41 *Mount Abora:* a mountain of Coleridge's imagination. But see John Milton's *Paradise Lost*, IV. 268–84.

Could I revive within me
Her symphony and song,
To such a deep delight 'twould win me,
That with music loud and long,   45
I would build that dome in air,
That sunny dome! those caves of ice!
And all who heard should see them there,
And all should cry, Beware! Beware!
His flashing eyes, his floating hair!   50
Weave a circle round him thrice,
And close your eyes with holy dread,
For he on honeydew hath fed,
And drunk the milk of Paradise.

QUESTIONS

1. How many of the poem's images might be sketched or visualized? Which ones would be panoramic landscapes? Which might be close-ups?

2. What is the effect of auditory images such as "wailing," "fast thick pants," "tumult," "ancestral voices prophesying war," and "mingled measure"?

3. When Coleridge was writing this poem, he was recalling it from a dream. At line 54 he was interrupted, and when he resumed he could write no more. How might an argument be made that the poem is finished?

4. How do lines 35–36 establish the pleasure dome as a place of mysterious oddity? What is the effect of the words "miracle" and "rare"? The effect of combining the images "sunny" and "caves of ice"?

5. Why does the speaker yearn for the power of the singing Abyssinian maid? What kinesthetic images end the poem? How are these images important in the speaker's desire to reconstruct the vision of the pleasure dome?

T. S. ELIOT (1888–1965)

 ## Preludes (1910)

I

The winter evening settles down
With smell of steaks in passageways.
Six o'clock.
The burnt-out ends of smoky days.
And now a gusty shower wraps   5
The grimy scraps
Of withered leaves about your feet
And newspapers from vacant lots;
The showers beat
On broken blinds and chimney-pots,   10
And at the corner of the street

A lonely cab-horse steams and stamps.
And then the lighting of the lamps.

II

The morning comes to consciousness
15   Of faint stale smells of beer
From the sawdust-trampled street
With all its muddy feet that press
To early coffee-stands.
With the other masquerades
20   That time resumes,
One thinks of all the hands
That are raising dingy shades
In a thousand furnished rooms.

III

You tossed a blanket from the bed,
25   You lay upon your back, and waited;
You dozed, and watched the night revealing
The thousand sordid images
Of which your soul was constituted;
They flickered against the ceiling.
30   And when all the world came back
And the light crept up between the shutters
And you heard the sparrows in the gutters,
You had such a vision of the street,
As the street hardly understands;
35   Sitting along the bed's edge, where
You curled the papers from your hair,
Or clasped the yellow soles of feet
In the palms of both soiled hands.

IV

His soul stretched tight across the skies
40   That fade behind a city block,
Or trampled by insistent feet
At four and five and six o'clock;
And short square fingers stuffing pipes,
And evening newspapers, and eyes
45   Assured of certain certainties,
The conscience of a blackened street
Impatient to assume the world.

I am moved by fancies that are curled
Around these images, and cling:
50   The notion of some infinitely gentle
Infinitely suffering thing.

Wipe your hand across your mouth, and laugh;
The worlds revolve like ancient women
Gathering fuel in vacant lots.

QUESTIONS

1. From what locations are the images in the first stanza derived? How do the images shift in the second stanza? What is the connection between the images in the second and third stanzas?
2. Who is the "you" in the third stanza? What images are associated with this listener?
3. Who is the "His" of the fourth stanza? How do the images develop in this stanza? What is meant particularly in the images of lines 46–47?
4. What is the nature of the bodily imagery in the poem? The urban imagery? What impressions do these images cause?
5. In lines 48–51, what does the speaker conclude? How do the last two unnumbered stanzas constitute a contrast of attitude?

LOUISE ERDRICH (b. 1954)

🍂 Indian Boarding School: The Runaways° (1984)

Home's the place we head for in our sleep.
Boxcars stumbling north in dreams
don't wait for us. We catch them on the run.
The rails, old lacerations that we love,
shoot parallel across the face and break   5
Just under Turtle Mountains.° Riding scars
you can't get lost. Home is the place they cross.

The lame guard strikes a match and makes the dark
less tolerant. We watch through cracks in boards
as the land starts rolling, rolling till it hurts   10
to be here, cold in regulation clothes.
We know the sheriff's waiting at midrun
to take us back. His car is dumb and warm.
The highway doesn't rock, it only hums
like a wing of long insults. The worn-down welts   15
of ancient punishments lead back and forth.

All runaways wear dresses, long green ones,
the color you would think shame was. We scrub
the sidewalks down because it's shameful work.
Our brushes cut the stone in watered arcs   20
and in the soak frail outlines shiver clear
a moment, things us kids pressed on the dark
face before it hardened, pale, remembering
delicate old injuries, the spines of names and leaves.

°In the late nineteenth and early twentieth centuries, many Indian boarding schools were instituted for the education of Indian children. The principal aim of these schools was to inculcate European- and English-based knowledge and ideals, along with encouraging Indian children to forsake their own heritage. If any children left the schools without permission, as runaways, they were punished when they were captured and returned. °6 *Turtle Mountains:* the Turtle Mountain Chippewa Indian Reservation in north-central North Dakota.

QUESTIONS

1. Who is the speaker? What has she been dreaming about? For whom does she speak? For herself? For others? Why does she say that "we" head for home "in our sleep"? How have the "we" left the Indian Boarding School? In reality? In their dreams?

2. Explain the nature of the images in the first and second stanzas. Could the images in the second stanza be considered as being based in fear? How do the images in the first two stanzas differ from the imagery in the third stanza? In the light of the nature of the images, can the poem be considered as a narrative based in a sequence of dreams?

3. Compare this poem with Edward Bok Lee's play "El Santo Americano" in Chapter 23. In what ways are the main characters of these works similar? Are they all to be considered "runaways"? What does their future look like at the conclusions of the works?

SUSAN GRIFFIN (b. 1943)

Love Should Grow Up Like a Wild Iris in the Fields (1972)

Love should grow up like a wild iris in the fields,
unexpected, after a terrible storm, opening a purple
mouth to the rain, with not a thought to the future,
ignorant of the grass and the graveyard of leaves
5   around, forgetting its own beginning. Love should
grow like a wild iris
but does not.
Love more often is to be found in kitchens at the dinner hour,
tired out and hungry, lingers over tables in houses where
10   the walls record movements; while the cook is probably angry,
and the ingredients of the meal are budgeted, while
a child cries feed me now and her mother not quite
hysterical says over and over, wait just a bit, just a bit.
Love should grow up in the fields like a wild iris
15   but never does
really startle anyone, was to be expected, was to be
predicted, is almost absurd, goes on from day to day, not quite
blindly, gets taken to the cleaners every fall, sings old
songs over and over, and falls on the same piece of rug that
20   never gets tacked down, gives up, wants to hide, is not
brave, knows too much, is not like an
iris growing wild but more like
staring into space
in the street
25   not quite sure
which door it was, annoyed about the sidewalk being
slippery, trying all the doors, thinking
if love wished the world to be well, it would be well.
Love should
30   grow up like a wild iris, but doesn't, it comes from
the midst of everything else, sees like the iris
of an eye, when the light is right,

feels in blindness and when there is nothing else is
tender, blinks, and opens
face up to the skies.   35

QUESTIONS

1. Contrast the locations of the images in the first seven lines and in the next eight. How
   do the ideas of the poet depend on this contrast in locations?

2. Note the difference in the mood of the verbs, from the "should" clause in the first six
   lines to the declarative present verb in line 7. Also, note the present tense verbs from
   lines 8–13, and then the "should" again in line 14. What is the effect of this differing use
   of verbs?

3. Trace the image of the wild iris throughout the poem. Why is the iris wild, and not
   cultivated? How does the iris grow? What is the effect of the change in the image of the
   iris from the flower to the eye (line 32)?

4. How is the sentence in lines 30–31 ("it comes from / the midst of everything else")
   related to the ideas and images in the rest of the poem?

THOMAS HARDY (1840–1928)

For a photo, see Chapter 11, page 548.

 ## Channel Firing (1914)

That night your great guns, unawares,
Shook all our coffins° as we lay,
And broke the chancel window-squares,
We thought it was the Judgment Day

And sat upright. While drearisome   5
Arose the howl of wakened hounds:
The mouse let fall the altar-crumb,
The worms drew back into the mounds,

The glebe° cow drooled. Till God called, "No;
It's gunnery practice out at sea   10
Just as before you went below;
The world is as it used to be:

"All nations striving strong to make
Red war yet redder. Mad as hatters
They do no more for Christés sake   15
Than you who are helpless in such matters.

°2 *coffins:* It has been common practice in England for hundreds of years to bury certain people in the floors or
basements of churches. °9 *glebe:* a parcel of land adjoining and belonging to a church. Cows were grazed there to
keep the grass short.

"That this is not the judgment hour
For some of them's a blessed thing,
For if it were they'd have to scour
20   Hell's floor for so much threatening. . . .

"Ha, ha. It will be warmer when
I blow the trumpet (if indeed
I ever do; for you are men,
And rest eternal sorely need)."

25   So down we lay again. "I wonder,
Will the world ever saner be,"
Said one, "than when He sent us under
In our indifferent century!"

And many a skeleton shook his head.
30   "Instead of preaching forty year,"
My neighbor Parson Thirdly said,
"I wish I had stuck to pipes and beer."

Again the guns disturbed the hour,
Roaring their readiness to avenge,
35   As far inland as Stourton Tower,°
And Camelot,° and starlit Stonehenge.°

°35 *Stourton Tower*: a tower commemorating King Alfred the Great's defeat of the Danes in 879 CE. °36 *Camelot*: legendary seat of King Arthur's court. °*Stonehenge*: a group of standing stones on Salisbury Plain, probably built as a place of worship before 1000 BCE. Stonehenge is one of England's famous landmarks.

QUESTIONS

1. Who is the speaker in this poem? What is the setting? The situation?
2. To whom does the "your" in line 1 refer? The "our" in line 2?
3. What has awakened the speaker and his friends? What mistake have they made?
4. What other voices are heard in the poem? How are their traits revealed?
5. What ideas about war and the nature of humanity does this poem explore?

H. D. (HILDA DOOLITTLE) (1886–1961)

 **Heat** (1916)

O wind, rend open the heat,
cut apart the heat,
rend it to tatters.

Fruit cannot drop
5   through this thick air—
fruit cannot fall into heat
that presses up and blunts

the points of pears
and rounds the grapes.

Cut the heat—
plough through it,
turning it on either side
of your path.

10

QUESTIONS

1. What is the meaning of the images of rending and cutting in the first three lines?
2. In lines 4–9, is it literally true that fruit cannot fall? If it is not, what is the meaning of the image that heat may blunt the points of pears and make grapes round?
3. Discuss the image of a plough as a cutter and separator of heat.
4. In the light of the various images in the poem, what impression of heat does the poet succeed in expressing?

GEORGE HERBERT (1593–1633)

The Pulley (1633)

When God at first made man,
Having a glass of blessings standing by,
   "Let us," said he, "pour on him all we can.
Let the world's riches, which dispersed lie,
     Contract into a span."°

5

So strength first made a way;
Then beauty flowed, then wisdom, honor, pleasure.
   When almost all was out, God made a stay,
Perceiving that, alone of all his treasure,
     Rest° in the bottom lay.

10

   "For if I should," said he,
"Bestow this jewel also on my creature,
   He would adore my gifts instead of me.
And rest in Nature, not the God of Nature;
     So both should losers be.

15

   "Yet let him keep the rest,
But keep them with repining restlessness.
   Let him be rich and weary, that at least,
If goodness lead him not, yet weariness
     May toss him to my breast."

20

°5 *into a span:* that is, within the control of human beings. °10 *rest:* (1) repose, security; (2) all that remains.

QUESTIONS

1. Describe the dramatic scene of the poem. Who is doing what?
2. What are the particular "blessings" that God confers on humanity, according to the speaker? Why should these be considered blessings?

3. Consider the image of the pulley as the means, or device (through "repining restlessness"), by which God compels people to become worshipful.

4. Analyze and discuss the meaning of the kinetic images signified by the words "pour," "flowed," "rest," and "toss."

GERARD MANLEY HOPKINS (1844–1889)

 Spring (1877)

Nothing is so beautiful as Spring—
    When weeds, in wheels, shoot long and lovely and lush;
    Thrush's eggs look little low heavens, and thrush
Through the echoing timber does so rinse and wring
5   The ear, it strikes like lightnings to hear him sing;
    The glassy peartree leaves and blooms, they brush
    The descending blue; that blue is all in a rush
With richness; the racing lambs too have fair their fling.

What is all this juice and all this joy?
10   A strain of the earth's sweet being in the beginning
In Eden garden.— Have, get, before it cloy,
    Before it cloud, Christ, lord, and sour with sinning,
Innocent mind and Mayday in girl and boy,
    Most, O maid's child, thy choice and worthy the winning.

QUESTIONS

1. What images does the speaker mention as support for his first line, "Nothing is so beautiful as Spring"? Are these images those that you would normally expect? To what degree do they seem to be new or unusual?

2. What images of motion and activity do you find in the poem? Are these mainly static or dynamic? What do these suggest about the speaker's view of spring?

3. What is the relationship between "Eden garden" in line 11 and the scene described in lines 1–8? To what extent are spring and "Innocent mind and Mayday" a glimpse of the Garden of Eden?

4. Christ is mentioned in lines 12 and 14 (as "maid's child"). Do these references seal the poem off from readers who are not Christian? Why or why not?

ROBINSON JEFFERS (1887–1962)

 Hurt Hawks (1928)

I

The broken pillar of the wing jags from the clotted shoulder,
The wing trails like a banner in defeat,
No more to use the sky forever but live with famine
And pain a few days: cat nor coyote

Will shorten the week of waiting for death, there is game without talons.   5
He stands under the oak-bush and waits
The lame feet of salvation; at night he remembers freedom
And flies in a dream, the dawns ruin it.
He is strong and pain is worse to the strong, incapacity is worse.
The curs° of the day come and torment him   10
At distance, no one but death the redeemer will humble that head,
The intrepid readiness, the terrible eyes.
The wild God of the world is sometimes merciful to those
That ask mercy, not often to the arrogant.
You do not know him, you communal people, or you have forgotten him;   15
Intemperate and savage, the hawk remembers him;
Beautiful and wild, the hawks, and men that are dying, remember him.

II

I'd sooner, except the penalties, kill a man than a hawk; but the great redtail
Had nothing left but unable misery
From the bones too shattered for mending, the wing that trailed under his talons   20
    when he moved.
We had fed him six weeks, I gave him freedom,
He wandered over the foreland hill and returned in the evening,
    asking for death,
Not like a beggar, still eyed with the old
Implacable arrogance. I gave him the lead gift in the twilight.
    What fell was relaxed.
Owl-downy, soft feminine feathers; but what   25
Soared: the fierce rush: the night-herons by the flooded river cried
    fear at its rising
Before it was quite unsheathed from reality.

QUESTIONS

1. What are some qualities that you admire in animals? What are some qualities that humans and animals share?
2. The speaker says, "I'd sooner, except the penalties, kill a man than a hawk;" Why do you think he said that? Is the statement disturbing in any way?
3. How does the image of the "soft feminine feathers" contrast with the other images of the hawk?

DENISE LEVERTOV (1923–1997)

For a photo, see Chapter 12, page 587.

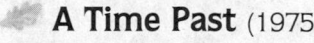 A Time Past (1975)

The old wooden steps to the front door
where I was sitting that fall morning
when you came downstairs, just awake,

and my joy at sight of you (emerging
into golden day—
5   the dew almost frost)
pulled me to my feet to tell you
how much I loved you:

those wooden steps
are gone now, decayed
10 replaced with granite,
hard, gray, and handsome.
The old steps live
only in me:
my feet and thighs
15 remember them, and my hands
still feel their splinters.
Everything else about and around that house
brings memories of others—of marriage,
of my son. And the steps do too: I recall
20 sitting there with my friend and her little son who died,
or was it the second one who lives and thrives?
And sitting there 'in my life,' often, alone or with my husband.
Yet that one instant,
your cheerful, unafraid, youthful, 'I love you too,'
25 the quiet broken by no bird, no cricket, gold leaves
spinning in silence down without
any breeze to blow them,
                      is what twines itself
in my head and body across those slabs of wood
30 that were warm, ancient, and now
wait somewhere to be burnt.

QUESTIONS

1. Describe the visual imagery of the poem. What tactile imagery is associated with the steps? What other images are part of the speaker's memory?

2. How is the image of the "old wooden steps" developed in the poem? What has happened to the wooden steps? What meaning may be derived from their having been replaced by the granite steps? How are these steps tied to the speaker's "time past"?

3. Why do you think the speaker expressly denies the recollection of any sounds of bird or cricket?

AMY LOWELL (1874–1925)

 **The Taxi** (1914)

When I go away from you
The world beats dead
Like a slackened drum.
I call out for you against the jutted stars
5 And shout into the ridges of the wind.
Streets coming fast,

One after the other,
Wedge you away from me,
And the lamps of the city prick my eyes
So that I can no longer see your face.   10
Why should I leave you,
To wound myself upon the sharp edges of the night?

QUESTIONS

1. Can you think of one image that may suggest the complexity of a relationship?
2. What do the first three lines of the poem suggest about the relationship between the speaker and "you."
3. What do you think the last lines of the poem suggest about the speaker's wishes?

THOMAS LUX (b. 1946)

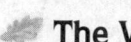 ### The Voice You Hear When You Read Silently (1997)

THE VOICE YOU HEAR WHEN YOU READ SILENTLY
is not silent, it is a speaking-
out-loud voice in your head: it is *spoken*,
a voice is *saying* it
as you read. It's the writer's words,   5
of course, in a literary sense
his or her "voice" but the sound
of that voice is the sound of *your* voice.
Not the sound your friends know
or the sound of a tape played back   10
but your voice
caught in the dark cathedral
of your skull, your voice heard
by an internal ear informed by internal abstracts
and what you know by feeling,   15
having felt. It is your voice
saying, for example, the word "barn"
that the writer wrote
but the "barn" you say
is a barn you know or knew. The voice   20
in your head, speaking as you read,
never says anything neutrally—some people
hated the barn they knew,
some people love the barn they know
so you hear the word loaded   25
and a sensory constellation
is lit: horse-gnawed stalls,
hayloft, black heat tape wrapping
a water pipe, a slippery
spilled *chirrr* of oats from a split sack,   30
the bony, filthy haunches of cows. . . .
And "barn" is only a noun—no verb

or subject has entered into the sentence yet!
The voice you hear when you read to yourself
35 is the clearest voice: you speak it
speaking to you.

QUESTIONS

1. What is meant by the "constellation" being lit when the reader reads a word, in this case "barn"? How does "constellation" explain the development of the barn image in lines 26–30?

2. Why is the "voice you hear when you read silently/ . . . not silent"?

3. Describe the meaning and associations of "the dark cathedral/of your skull" in lines 11–12. What is particularly significant about the use of "cathedral" in these lines?

MARIANNE MOORE (1887–1972)

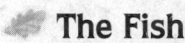 The Fish (1918)

wade
through black jade.
   Of the crow-blue mussel-shells, one keeps
   adjusting the ash-heaps;
5   opening and shutting itself like

an
injured fan.
   The barnacles which encrust the side
   of the wave, cannot hide
10   there for the submerged shafts of the

sun,
split like spun
   glass, move themselves with spotlight swiftness
   into the crevices—
15   in and out, illuminating

the
turquoise sea
   of bodies. The water drives a wedge
   of iron through the iron edge
20   of the cliff; whereupon the stars,

pink
rice-grains, ink-
   bespattered jelly fish, crabs like green
   lilies, and submarine
25   toadstools, slide each on the other.

All
external
   marks of abuse are present on this
   defiant edifice—
      all the physical features of   30

ac-
cident—lack
   of cornice, dynamite grooves, burns, and
   hatchet strokes, these things stand
      out on it; the chasm-side is   35

dead.
Repeated
   evidence has proved that it can live
   on what can not revive
      its youth. The sea grows old in it.   40

QUESTIONS

1. Why is this poem titled "The Fish"? What actual fish does the poem describe? What images of other sea creatures do you find?
2. What action is described in this poem? In what ways may this poem be contrasted with Bishop's poem "The Fish"?
3. Describe the structure of rhymes in "The Fish." What pictorial image is suggested by the shapes of the stanzas and by the fact that most of the lines ending the stanzas extend grammatically to the next stanzas?
4. What idea does the speaker seem to be developing in the last three stanzas of the poem?

PABLO NERUDA (1904–1977)

 Every Day You Play (1924)

Every day you play with the light of the universe.
Subtle visitor, you arrive in the flower and the water.
You are more than this white head that I hold tightly
as a cluster of fruit, every day, between my hands.

You are like nobody since I love you.   5
Let me spread you out among yellow garlands.
Who writes your name in letters of smoke among the stars of the south?
Oh let me remember you as you were before you existed.

Suddenly the wind howls and bangs at my shut window.
The sky is a net crammed with shadowy fish.   10
Here all the winds let go sooner or later, all of them.
The rain takes off her clothes.

The birds go by, fleeing.
The wind. The wind.

15 I can contend only against the power of men.
The storm whirls dark leaves
and turns loose all the boats that were moored last night to the sky.

You are here. Oh, you do not run away.
You will answer me to the last cry.
20 Cling to me as though you were frightened.
Even so, at one time a strange shadow ran through your eyes.

Now, now too, little one, you bring me honeysuckle,
and even your breasts smell of it.
While the sad wind goes slaughtering butterflies
25 I love you, and my happiness bites the plum of your mouth.

How you must have suffered getting accustomed to me,
my savage, solitary soul, my name that sends them all running.
So many times we have seen the morning star burn, kissing our eyes,
and over our heads the gray light unwind in turning fans.

30 My words rained over you, stroking you.
A long time I have loved the sunned mother-of-pearl of your body.
I go so far as to think that you own the universe.
I will bring you happy flowers from the mountains, bluebells,
dark hazels, and rustic baskets of kisses.

35 I want
to do with you what spring does with the cherry trees.

QUESTIONS

1. What is the situation in this poem? Who is talking to whom? What is their relationship?
2. Describe the nature of the images in this poem. What kinetic and kinesthetic images do you find? What is the effect of these images? What visual images do you find? What tactile images? Olfactory images? Gustatory images?
3. What reality is reflected in the poem's imagery? Analyze the images of lines 9–17 and their meaning.
4. What does the speaker mean by line 8, "Oh let me remember you as you were before you existed"?

EDGAR ALLAN POE (1809–1849)

For a portrait, see Chapter 4, page 249.

To Helen° (1831, 1843)

Helen, thy beauty is to me
  Like those Nicean barks° of yore,
That gently, o'er a perfumed sea,

°*Helen:* Helen of Troy, in mythology the most beautiful woman in the world, was the cause of the Trojan War.
°2 *Nicean barks:* victorious ships returning home after battle.

The weary, way-worn wanderer bore
To his own native shore.   5

On desperate seas long wont to roam,
  Thy hyacinth hair, thy classic face,
Thy Naiad° airs have brought me home
  To the glory that was Greece,
    And the grandeur that was Rome.   10

Lo! in yon brilliant window-niche
  How statue-like I see thee stand,
The agate lamp within thy hand!
  Ah, Psyche,° from the regions which
    Are Holy-Land!   15

°8 *Naiad:* in Greek mythology, beautiful river goddesses. °14 *Psyche:* a princess wed to Eros, god of love.

QUESTIONS

1. Why does the poet use a number of classical images in describing Helen's beauty? How does this comparison shape your mental image of the person Poe wrote this poem for?
2. What visual associations do you have with "the glory that was Greece,/And the grandeur that was Rome, and how might they affect your mental image of Helen?

EZRA POUND (1885–1972)

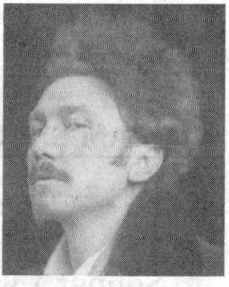

In a Station of the Metro° (1916)

The apparition of these faces in the crowd;
Petals on a wet, black bough.

°*Metro:* the Paris subway.

QUESTIONS

1. Is the image of the wet, black bough happy or sad? If the petals were on a tree in the sunlight, what would be the effect?
2. What is the meaning of the image suggested by "apparition"? Does it suggest a positive or negative view of human life?
3. This poem contains only two lines. Is it proper to consider it as a poem nevertheless? If it is not a poem, what is it?

PHILIP HENRY SAVAGE (1868-1899)

Shorter Poem 13 (1895)

The flash of sunlight from a bit of glass
Has often power to stop me as I pass;
And when I turn into the burning west
I fling me down upon the sunny grass,

Silent. I tell not all the little things
That fly to me and give my spirit wings;
The black-eyed bird, the cloud, the silver leaf,
The valley wind that passes as it sings.

And when the sun descending from the height,
Seeks in the sunken west the bath of night,
Wrapped in the darkling mantle of the sky
I wander forth and seek a new delight.

QUESTIONS

1. What does the imagery in the first stanza tell you about the speaker?
2. What is the speaker's relationship with nature? How does the imagery inform your understanding of this relationship?
3. Consider what forms of imagery (kinetic, visual, auditory…) appear in the poem. Give an example that stands out to you and explain why it is important to the poem.
4. Where do you visualize the setting of the poem? What imagery creates this setting?
5. Compare the last line of the first stanza with the last line of the last stanza. How does the imagery change during the poem?

WILLIAM SHAKESPEARE (1564–1616)

For a portrait, see Chapter 21, page 1079.

Sonnet 130: My Mistress' Eyes Are Nothing Like the Sun (1609)

My mistress' eyes are nothing like the sun;
Coral is far more red than her lips' red;
If snow be white, why then her breasts are dun;
If hairs be wires, black wires grow on her head.
5 I have seen roses damasked,° red and white,   *set in an elaborate bouquet*
But no such roses see I in her cheeks;
And in some perfumes is there more delight
Than in the breath that from my mistress reeks.
I love to hear her speak, yet well I know
10 That music hath a far more pleasing sound;

I grant I never saw a goddess go;
My mistress, when she walks, treads on the ground.
And yet, by heaven, I think my love as rare
As any she belied with false compare.

QUESTIONS

1. To what does the speaker negatively compare his mistress's eyes? Lips? Breasts? Hair? Cheeks? Breath? Voice? Walk? What kinds of images are created in these negative comparisons?

2. What conventional images does this poem ridicule? What sort of poem is Shakespeare mocking by using the negative images in lines 1–12?

3. In the light of the last two lines, do you think the speaker intends the images as insults? If not as insults, how should they be taken?

4. Are most of the images auditory, olfactory, visual, or kinesthetic? Explain.

5. What point does this poem make about love poetry? About human relationships? How does the imagery contribute to the development of both points?

CHARLES SIMIC (1938)

 Fork (1969)

This strange thing must have crept
Right out of hell.
It resembles a bird's foot
Worn around the cannibal's neck.

As you hold it in your hand,
As you stab with it into a piece of meat,   5
It is possible to imagine the rest of the bird:
Its head which like your fist
Is large, bald, beakless, and blind.

QUESTIONS

1. Have you ever thought of an unusual image to suggest a common object as Simic does?

2. What unusual images might suggest a fork?

3. Would it make any difference if the title were "The Fork" instead of "Fork"?

JAMES TATE (b. 1943)

 Dream On (1998)

Some people go their whole lives
without ever writing a single poem.

Extraordinary people who don't hesitate
to cut somebody's heart or skull open.
5   They go to baseball games with the greatest of ease
and play a few rounds of golf as if it were nothing.
These same people stroll into a church
as if that were a natural part of life.
Investing money is second nature to them.
10   They contribute to political campaigns
that have absolutely no poetry in them
and promise none for the future.
They sit around the dinner table at night
and pretend as though nothing is missing.
15   Their children get caught shoplifting at the mall
and no one admits that it is poetry they are missing.
The family dog howls all night,
lonely and starving for more poetry in his life.
Why is it so difficult for them to see
20   that, without poetry, their lives are effluvial.
Sure, they have their banquets, their celebrations,
croquet, fox hunts, their seashores and sunsets,
their cocktails on the balcony, dog races,
and all that kissing and hugging, and don't
25   forget the good deeds, the charity work,
nursing the baby squirrels all through the night,
filling the birdfeeders all winter,
helping the stranger change her tire.
Still, there's that disagreeable exhalation
30   from decaying matter, subtle but ever present.
They walk around erect like champions.
They are smooth-spoken, urbane and witty.
When alone, rare occasion, they stare
into the mirror for hours, bewildered.
35   There was something they meant to say, but didn't:
"And if we put the statue of the rhinoceros
next to the tweezers, and walk around the room three times
learn to yodel, shave our heads, call
our ancestors back from the dead—"
40   poetrywise it's still a bust, bankrupt.
You haven't scribbled a syllable of it.
You're a nowhere man misfiring
the very essence of your life, flustering
nothing from nothing and back again.
45   The hereafter may not last all that long.
Radiant childhood sweetheart,
secret code of everlasting joy and sorrow,
fanciful pen strokes beneath the eyelids:
all day, all night meditation, knot of hope,
50   kernel of desire, pure ordinariness of life,
seeking, through poetry, a benediction
or a bed to lie down on, to connect, reveal,

explore, to imbue meaning on the day's extravagant labor.
And yet it's cruel to expect too much.
It's a rare species of bird   55
That refuses to be categorized.
Its song is barely audible.
It is like a dragonfly in a dream—
Here, then there, then here again,
Low-flying amber-wing darting upward   60
and then out of sight.
And the dream has a pain in its heart
the wonders of which are manifold,
or so the story is told.

QUESTIONS

1. Characterize the images from lines 3–20. What types of images, for the most part, are these? What part do they play in the poem's argument?

2. In lines 36–42 there is a different unit of imagery. What are the characteristics and purpose of these?

3. How does the speaker use images to characterize poetry from line 54 (if we take the repetition of "it" in lines 54, 55, 57, and 58 as descriptions of poetry). How true is the idea that poetry is a dream with a pain in its heart (line 63)? What is the effect of the final line?

DAVID WOJAHN (b. 1953)

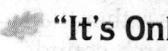 ## "It's Only Rock and Roll, but I Like It": The Fall of Saigon (1975; 1990)

The gutteral stammer of the chopper blades
Raising arabesques of dust, tearing leaves
From the orange trees lining the Embassy compound:
One chopper left, and a CBS cameraman leans
From inside its door, exploiting the artful   5
Mayhem. Somewhere a radio blares the Stones,
"I like it, like it, yes indeed. . . ." Carts full
Of files blaze in the yard. Flak-jacketed marines
Gunpoint the crowd away. The overloaded chopper strains
And blunders from the roof. An ice-cream-suited   10
Saigonese drops his briefcase; both hands
Now cling to the airborne skis. The camera gets
It all: the marine leaning out the copter bay,
His fists beating time. Then the hands giving way.

QUESTIONS

1. What actions are described in this poem? Why does the Saigonese man "cling to the airborne skis"? What happens to him?

2. Describe the poem's images of sound (auditory images). How many such images does the poem contain? What is their effect? What images of sight (visual) do you find? What other types of images?

3. Contrast the poem's title with its content.

4. Cumulatively, what is the relationship of the poem's images to the phrase "artful/ Mayhem" in lines 5–6, and also to the poem's judgment about the American presence in Vietnam?

WRITING ABOUT IMAGERY

Questions for Discovering Ideas

In preparing to write, you should develop a set of thoughtful notes dealing with issues such as the following:

- What type or types of images prevail in the work? Visual (shapes, colors)? Auditory (sounds)? Olfactory (smells)? Tactile (touch and texture)? Gustatory (taste)? Kinetic or kinesthetic (motion)? Or is the imagery a combination?

- To what degree do the images reflect either the poet's actual observation or the poet's reading and knowledge of fields such as science or history?

- How well do the images stand out? How vivid are they? How does the poet make the images vivid?

- Within a group of images—say, visual or auditory—do the images pertain to one location or area rather than another (e.g., natural scenes rather than interiors, snowy scenes rather than grassy ones, loud and harsh sounds rather than quiet and soothing ones)?

- What explanation is needed for the images? (Images might be derived from the classics or the Bible, the Vietnam War or World War II, the behaviors of four-footed creatures or birds or fish, and so on.)

- What effect do the circumstances described in the poem (e.g., conditions of brightness or darkness, warmth or cold) have on your responses to the images? What purpose do you think the poet achieves by controlling these responses?

- How well are the images integrated within the poem's argument or development?

Answering questions like these will provide you with a sizable body of material that you can organize and then discuss in your essay.

Strategies for Organizing Ideas

Connect a brief overview of the poem to your plan for the body of your essay, noting perhaps that the writer uses images to strengthen ideas about war, character, or love or that the writer relies predominantly on images of sight, sound, and action. You might deal with just one of the following aspects, or you may combine your approaches, as you wish.

1. *Images suggesting ideas and/or moods.* Such an essay should emphasize the effects of the imagery. What ideas or moods are evoked by the images? (In this chapter the auditory images beginning Owen's "Anthem for Doomed Youth," for example, all point toward a condemnation of the brutality of war. The visual images in "Spring," by Hopkins, all point toward a sense of earthly and also divine growth and lushness.) Do the images promote approval or disapproval? Cheerfulness? Melancholy? Are the images drab, exciting, vivid? How? Why? Are they conducive to humor or surprise? How does the writer achieve these effects? Are the images consistent, or are they ambiguous? (The images in Masefield's "Cargoes" indicate first approval and then disapproval, with no ambiguity. By contrast, Shakespeare's images in "My Mistress' Eyes" might be construed as insults, but in context, they are really compliments [both in this chapter].)

2. *The types of images.* Here the emphasis is on the categories of images themselves. Is there a predominance of a particular type of image (e.g., visual or auditory), or is there a blending, as in Neruda's "Every Day You Play"? Is there a bunching of types at particular points in the poem or story? If so, why? Is there any shifting as the work develops (for example, in Owen's "Anthem for Doomed Youth" [this chapter] the auditory images first suggest loudness and harshness, but later auditory images describe quietness and sorrow)? Are the images appropriate, granted the nature and apparent intent of the work? Do they assist in making the ideas seem convincing? If any images seem inappropriate, is the inappropriateness intentional or inadvertent? What is the effect of the inappropriate imagery?

3. *Systems of images.* Here the emphasis should be on the areas from which the images are drawn. This is another way of considering the appropriateness of the imagery: Is there a pattern of similar or consistent images, such as dark and dreary urban scenes (Eliot's "Preludes") or color and activity (Hopkins's "Spring")? Do all the images adhere consistently to a particular frame of reference, such as an extensive recreational forest and garden (Coleridge's "Kubla Khan"), a front stair (Levertov's "A Time Past"), or a forest at night (Blake's "The Tyger" [Chapter 14])? What is unusual or unique about the set of images? What unexpected or new responses do they produce?

Your conclusion, in addition to restating your major points, is the place for additional insights. It would not be proper to go too far in new directions here, but you might briefly take up one or more of the ideas that you have not developed in the body. In short, what have you learned from your study of imagery in the poem?

Illustrative Student Essay

Although underlined sentences are not recommended by MLA style, they are used in this illustrative essay as teaching tools to emphasize the central idea, thesis sentence, and topic sentences.

Pugh 1

Mike Pugh

Professor Skaggs

English 101

14 January 2014

The Images of Masefield's "Cargoes"°

[1] In the three-stanza poem "Cargoes," John Masefield develops contrasting imagery to create a negative impression of modern commercial life.* He does not explicitly state that modern commercialism is ugly and drab and that it affects modern human beings negatively, but he creates his word pictures to make this point for him. His first two stanzas contain idealized images of ships from ancient and Renaissance times, and his contrasting third stanza includes realistic images of a gritty and grimy modern "coaster." Masefield's images are thus both positive and lush, on the one hand, and negative and stark, on the other.†

[2] The most evocative and pleasant images in the poem are in the first stanza. The speaker asks that we imagine a "Quinquereme of Nineveh from distant Ophir" (line 1), an oceangoing, many-oared vessel loaded with treasure at the time of the biblical King Solomon. As Masefield identifies the cargo, the visual images are lush and romantic (3–5):

> With a cargo of ivory,
>
> And apes and peacocks,
>
> Sandalwood, cedarwood, and sweet white wine.

Ivory suggests richness, which is augmented by the exotic "apes and peacocks" in all their exciting strangeness. The "sandalwood, cedarwood, and sweet white

°This poem appears on page 606.
*Central idea.
†Thesis sentence.

wine" evoke pungent smells and tastes. The "sunny" light of ancient Palestine
(2) not only illuminates the imaginative scene (visual) but invites readers to
imagine the sun's warming touch (tactile). The references to animals and birds
also suggest the sounds made by these creatures (auditory). Thus, in this rich
first stanza, images derived from all the senses evoke impressions of an ideal,
romantic past.

Almost equally lush are the images of the second stanza, which completes   [3]
the poem's first part. Here the visual imagery evokes the regal splendor of a
tall-masted, full-sailed galleon (6) at the height of Spain's commercial power
in the sixteenth century. The galleon's cargo suggests wealth, with sparkling
diamonds and amethysts, and Portuguese "gold moidores" gleaming in open
chests (10). With cinnamon in the second stanza's bill of lading (10), Masefield
includes the image of an exotic, pleasant-tasting spice.

The negative images of the third stanza contrast starkly with those in   [4]
the first two stanzas. The poem asks us to imagine a modern "Dirty British
coaster" (11), which draws attention to the griminess and suffocation of
modern civilization. This spray-swept ship is loaded with materials that pollute
the earth with noise and smoke. The smoke stack of the coaster (11) and the
firewood it is carrying suggest choking smog. The Tyne coal (13) and road
rails (14) suggest the noise and smoke of puffing railroad engines. As if this
were not enough, the "pig-lead" (14) to be used in various industrial processes
indicates not just more unpleasantness but also something poisonous and
deadly. In contrast to the lush and stately imagery of the first two stanzas,
the images in the third stanza invite the conclusion that people now, when the
"Dirty British coaster" butts through the English Channel, are surrounded and
threatened by visual, olfactory, and auditory pollution.

The poem thus establishes a romantic past and ugly present through   [5]
images of sight, smell, and sound. The images of motion also emphasize this
view: In the first two stanzas the quinquereme is "rowing" and the galleon
is "dipping." These kinetic images suggest dignity and lightness. The British
coaster, however, is "butting," an image indicating bull-like hostility and stupid

Pugh 3

force. These, together with all the other images, focus the poem's negative views of modern life. The facts that existence for both ancient Palestinians and Renaissance Spaniards included slavery (of those men rowing the quinquereme) and piracy (by those Spanish "explorers" who robbed and killed the natives of the isthmus) should probably not be emphasized as a protest against Masefield's otherwise valid contrasts in images. His final commentary may hence be thought of as the banging of his "cheap tin trays" (15), which makes a percussive climax of the oppressive images filling too large a portion of modern lives.

Pugh 4

Work Cited

Masefield, John. "Cargoes." *Literature: An Introduction to Reading and Writing, Compact Edition*. Ed. Edgar V. Roberts and Robert Zweig. 6th ed. New York: Pearson, 2015. 606. Print.

Commentary on the Essay

This essay illustrates strategy 1 for writing about imagery (p. 633), using images to develop ideas and moods. All the examples—derived directly from the poem—emphasize the qualities of Masefield's images. This method permits the introduction of imagery drawn from all the senses in order to demonstrate Masefield's ideas about the past and the present. Other approaches might have concentrated exclusively on Masefield's visual images or on his images drawn from trade and commerce. Because Masefield uses auditory and gustatory images but does not develop them extensively, sound or taste might be appropriately treated in short, paragraph-length essays.

The introductory paragraph of the essay presents the central idea that Masefield uses his images contrastingly to lead to his negative view of modern commercialism. The thesis sentence indicates that the topics to be developed are those of (1) lushness and (2) starkness.

Paragraphs 2 and 3 form a unit stressing the lushness and exoticism of the first stanza and the wealth and colorfulness of the second stanza. In particular, paragraph 2 uses the words "lush," "evoke," "rich," "exotic," "pungent," "exciting," and "romantic" to characterize the pleasing mental pictures prompted by the images. Although the paragraph indicates enthusiastic responses to the images, it does not go beyond the limits of the images themselves.

Paragraph 4 stresses the contrast of Masefield's images in the third stanza with those of the first two stanzas. To this end the paragraph illustrates the imaginative reconstruction needed to develop an understanding of this contrast. The unpleasantness, annoyance, and even danger of the cargoes mentioned in the third stanza are therefore emphasized as the qualities evoked by the images.

The last paragraph demonstrates that the imagery of motion—not much stressed in the poem—is in agreement with the rest of Masefield's imagery. As a demonstration of the need for fair, impartial judgment, the conclusion introduces the possible objection that Masefield may be slanting his images by including not a full but rather a partial view of their respective historical periods. Thus the concluding paragraph adds balance to the analysis illustrated in paragraphs 2, 3, and 4.

Writing Topics About Imagery in Poetry

Writing Paragraphs

1. In a paragraph compare the images of war in Owen's "Anthem for Doomed Youth" and Hardy's "Channel Firing" (both in this chapter). Describe the differing effects of the images. How are the images used? How effectively do these images aid in the development of the attitudes toward war expressed in each poem?

2. In a paragraph write a comparison of the imagery in Elizabeth Browning's "If Thou Must Love Me" and Susan Griffin's "Love Should Grow Up Like a Wild Iris in the Fields" (pp. 611, 616). Even though the poems are on similar subjects, how does the selection of images contribute toward making each poem distinct?

Essay Writing

1. Basing your work on the poems in this chapter by Coleridge, Griffin, and Hopkins, write an essay discussing the poetic use of images drawn from the natural world. What sorts of references do the poets make? What attitudes do they express about the details they select? What is the relationship between the images and religious views? What judgments about topics such as nature, God, humanity, and friendship do the poets show by their images?

2. Considering the imagery of Tate's "Dream On" (this chapter) write an essay explaining the nature and use of imagery in poetry. As you develop your thoughts, be sure to consider the different characteristics of Tate's images and to account for the impressions and ideas that they create. You may also wish to introduce references to images from other poems that are relevant to your points.

3. Write an essay comparing and contrasting Hopkins's poem "Spring" and Pound's "In a Station of the Metro," along with other poems that you may wish to include. What similarities and differences do you find in subject matter, treatment, arrangement, and general idea?

Creative Writing Assignment

1. Write a poem describing one of these:
   a. Athletes who have just completed an exhausting run.
   b. Children getting out of school for the day.
   c. Your recollection of having been lost as a child.
   d. A cat that always sits down right on your schoolwork.
   e. A particularly good meal you had recently.
   f. The best concert you ever attended.
   g. Driving to work or school on a rainy or snowy day.

   Write an analysis of the images you selected for your poem, and explain your choices. What details stand out in your mind? What do you recall best—sight, smell, sound, action? What is the relationship between your images and the ideas you express in your poem?

Library Assignment

1. Use the retrieval system in your library or go online to research the topic of imagery in Shakespeare (see *imagery* or *style and imagery*). How many titles do you find? Over how many years have these works been published? Take out one of the books or articles, and write a brief report on your findings. What topics are discussed? What types of imagery are introduced? What relationship does the author make between imagery and content?

Chapter 14
Figures of Speech, or Metaphorical Language: A Source of Depth and Range in Poetry

AFTER STUDYING THIS MATERIAL, YOU SHOULD BE ABLE TO DO THE FOLLOWING:

- Understand the nature and function of figures of speech
- Identify similes and metaphors
- Recognize other figures of speech (such as paradox, personification, overstatement, and understatement)
- Characterize the use of figurative language in poems

Figures of speech, metaphorical language, figurative language, figurative devices, and rhetorical figures are terms describing organized patterns of comparison that deepen, broaden, extend, illuminate, and emphasize meaning. First and foremost, the use of figures of speech is a major characteristic by which great literature provides us with fresh and original ways of thinking, feeling, and understanding. Although figurative language is sometimes called "ornate," as though it were unnecessarily decorative, it is not uncommon in conversational speech, and it is essential in literary thought and expression. Unlike the writing of the social and "hard" sciences, imaginative literature is not direct and unambiguous, offering exact correspondences of words and things. Yes, literature presents specific and accurate descriptions and explanations, but it also moves in areas of implication and suggestiveness through the use of **figurative language,** which enables writers to amplify their ideas while still employing relatively small numbers of words. Such language is therefore a *sine qua non* in imaginative literature, particularly poetry, where it compresses thought, deepens understanding, and shapes response.

The two most important figures of speech, and the most easily recognized, are *metaphors* and *similes.* There are also many other metaphorical figures, some of which are *paradox, anaphora, apostrophe, personification, synecdoche* and *metonymy, pun* (or *paronomasia*), *synesthesia, overstatement,* and *understatement.* All these figures are modes of comparison, and they may be expressed in single words, phrases, clauses, or entire structures.

Metaphors and Similes: The Major Figures of Speech

A Metaphor Shows That Something Unknown Is Identical to Something Known

A **metaphor** (a "carrying out a change") equates known objects or actions with something that is unknown or to be explained (e.g., "Your words are music to my ears," "You are the sunshine of my life," "My life is a squirrel cage"). The equation of the metaphor not only explains and illuminates the thing—let us choose Judith Minty's concept of marital inseparability in "Conjoined"—but also offers distinctive and original and often startling ways of seeing it and thinking about it. Thus Minty draws her metaphor of a married couple from the joining of two onions under one onion skin. Here the metaphor is unique and surprising, and yet on examination it is right and natural, and also somewhat comic.

Metaphors are inseparable from language. In a heavy storm, for example, trees may be said to *bow* constantly as the wind blows against them. *Bow* is a metaphor because the word usually refers to performers' bending forward to acknowledge the applause of an audience and to indicate their gratitude for the audience's approval. The metaphor therefore asks us to equate our knowledge of theater life (something known) to a weather occurrence (something to be explained). A comparable reference to theater life creates one of the best-known metaphors to appear in Shakespeare's plays: "All the world's a stage, / And all the men and women merely players." Here, Shakespeare's character Jacques (JAY-queez) from Act 2, scene 7, of *As You Like It*, identifies human life exactly with stage life. In other words, the things said and done by stage actors are also said and done by living people in real life. It is important to recognize that Shakespeare's metaphor does not state that the world is *like* a stage but that it literally *is* a stage.

A Simile Shows That Something Unknown Is Similar to Something Known

A **simile** (a "showing of likeness or resemblance") illustrates the similarity or comparability of the known to something unknown or to be explained. Whereas a metaphor merges identities, a simile focuses on resemblances (e.g., "Your words are like music to me," "you are like sunshine in my life," "I feel like a squirrel in a cage"). Similes are distinguishable from metaphors because they are introduced by "like" with nouns and "as" (also "as if" and "as though") with clauses. If Minty had written that a married couple is *like* "The onion in my cupboard," her comparison would have been a simile.

Let us consider one of the best-known similes in poetry, from "A Valediction: Forbidding Mourning" by the Renaissance poet John Donne. This is a dramatic poem spoken by a lover about to go on a trip. His loved one is sorrowful, and he attempts to console her by claiming that even when he is gone, he will remain with her in spirit. The following stanza contains the famous simile embodying this idea.

> Our two souls therefore, which are one,
>   Though I must go, endure not yet
> A breach,° but an expansion   *break, separation*
>   Like gold to airy thinness beat.

The simile compares the souls of the speaker and his loved one to gold, a metal both valuable and malleable. By the simile, the speaker asserts that the impending departure will not be a separation but rather a thinning out, so that the relationship of the lovers will remain constant and fervent, even as the distance between them increases. Because the comparison is introduced by *like*, the emphasis of the figurative language is on the *similarity* of the lovers' love to gold (which is always gold, even when it is thinned out by the goldsmith's hammer), not on the *identification* of the two.

Characteristics of Metaphorical Language

In language, the words **image** and **imagery** define words that stimulate the imagination and recall memories (images) of sights, sounds, tastes, smells, sensations of touch, and motions (see Chapter 13). Metaphors and similes go beyond literal imagery to introduce perceptions and comparisons that can be unusual, unpredictable, and surprising, as in Donne's simile comparing the lovers' relationship to gold. The comparison emphasizes the bond between the two lovers; the reference to gold shows how valuable the bond is; the unusual and original comparison is one of the elements that make the poem striking and memorable.

To see metaphorical language in further operation, let us take a commonly described condition—happiness. In everyday speech, we might use the sentence "She was happy" to state that a particular character was experiencing joy and excitement. The sentence is of course accurate, but it is not interesting. A more vivid way of saying the same thing is to use an image of action, such as "She jumped for joy." But another and better way of communicating joy is the following simile: "She felt as if she had just won the lottery." Because readers easily understand the disbelief, excitement, exhilaration, and delight that such an event would bring, they also understand—and feel—the character's happiness. It is the simile that evokes this perception and enables each reader to personalize the experience, for no simple description could help a reader comprehend the same degree of emotion.

As a parallel poetic example, let us look at John Keats's sonnet "On First Looking into Chapman's Homer," which Keats wrote soon after reading the translation of Homer's great epics *The Iliad* and *The Odyssey* by the Renaissance poet George Chapman. Keats, one of the greatest of all poets himself, describes his enthusiasm about Chapman's successful and exciting work.

JOHN KEATS (1795–1821)

On First Looking into Chapman's Homer° (1816)

Much have I travell'd in the realms of gold,°   *the world of great art*
  And many goodly states and kingdoms seen:
  Round many western islands° have I been   *much ancient literature*
Which bards in fealty to Apollo° hold.
Oft of one wide expanse° had I been told   *epic poetry*   5
  That deep-brow'd Homer ruled as his demesne;°   *realm, estate*
  Yet did I never breathe its pure serene°
Till I heard Chapman speak out loud and bold:
Then felt I like some watcher of the skies
  When a new planet swims into his ken;°   *range of vision*   10

°George Chapman (c. 1560–1634) published his translations of Homer's *Iliad* in 1612 and *Odyssey* in 1614–15.
°4 *bards . . . Apollo*: writers who are sworn subjects of Apollo, the Greek god of light, music, poetry, prophecy, and the sun.   °7 *serene*: a clear expanse of air; also grandeur, clarity; rulers were also sometimes called "serene majesty."

Or like stout Cortez° when with eagle eyes
   He star'd at the Pacific—and all his men
Look'd at each other with a wild surmise°—
   Silent, upon a peak in Darien.   *conjecture, supposition*

°11 *Cortez:* Hernando Cortès (1485–1547), a Spanish general and the conqueror of Mexico. Keats confuses him with Vasco de Balboa (c. 1475–1519), the first European to see the Pacific Ocean (in 1510) from Darien, an early name for the Isthmus of Panama.

As a first step in understanding the power of metaphorical language, we can briefly paraphrase the sonnet's content.

> I have enjoyed much art and read much poetry, and I have been told that Homer is the best writer of all. However, I did not appreciate his works until I first read them in Chapman's clear and forceful translation. This discovery was exciting and awe-inspiring.

If all Keats had written had been a paragraph like this one, we would pay little attention to it, for it conveys no excitement or wonder. But the last six lines of the sonnet contain two memorable similes ("like some watcher of the skies" and "like stout Cortez") that stand out and demand a special effort of imagination. To appreciate these similes fully, we need to imagine what it would be like to be an astronomer as he or she discovers a previously unknown planet, and what it would have been like to be one of the first European explorers to see the Pacific Ocean. As we imagine ourselves in these roles, we get a sense of the amazement, excitement, exhilaration, and joy that would accompany such discoveries. With that experience comes the realization that the world is far bigger and more astonishing than we had ever dreamed. Metaphorical language, therefore, makes strong demands on our creative imaginations. It bears repeating that as we develop our own mental pictures under the stimulation of metaphors and similes, we also develop appropriately associated attitudes and feelings. Let us consider once more how Keats's metaphor "realms of gold" invites us both to imagine brilliant and shining kingdoms and also to join Keats in valuing and loving not just poetry but all literature. The metaphorical "realms of gold" act upon our minds—liberating our imaginations, directing our understanding, and evoking our feelings. In such a way, reading and responding to the works of writers like Keats produces both mental and emotional experiences that were previously hidden to us. Poets constantly give us something new, and they increase our power to think and know. They enlarge us.

🌿 VEHICLE AND TENOR

To describe the relationship between a writer's ideas and the metaphors and similes chosen to objectify them, two useful terms have been coined by I. A. Richards (in *The Philosophy of Rhetoric* [1929]). First is the **vehicle,** or the specific words of the metaphor or simile. Second is the **tenor,** which is the totality of ideas and attitudes not only of the literary speaker but also of the author. For example, the

tenor of Donne's simile in "A Valediction: Forbidding Mourning" is the inseparable love and unbreakable connection of the two lovers; the vehicle is the hammering of gold "to airy thinness." Similarly, the tenor of the similes in the sestet
of Keats's sonnet "On First Looking into Chapman's Homer" is awe and wonder;
the vehicle is the description of astronomical and geographical discovery.

Other Figures of Speech

A Paradox Uses an Apparent Error or Contradiction to Reveal Truth

A **paradox** is "a thought beyond a thought," a figurative device through which
something apparently wrong or contradictory is shown to be truthful and non-
contradictory. The phrase "I, a child, very old" in Whitman's "Facing West from
California's Shores" is a paradox. The obvious contradiction is that no one can be
old and young at the same time, but this contradiction can be reconciled if we realize that even as people get older they still retain many of the qualities of children
(such as enthusiasm and hope). Thus Whitman's contradiction is not contradictory (is this clause a paradox?) and the speaker may genuinely be "a child, very
old." The second line of Sir Thomas Wyatt's sonnet "I Find No Peace" embodies
two paradoxes. One opposes fear with hope, the other fire with ice: "I fear and
hope, I burn and freeze like ice." These paradoxes reflect the contradictory states
of people in love—wanting love ("hope," "burn"), but also being uncertain and
unsure about the relationship ("fear," "freeze"). The paradoxes thus highlight the
truth that love is a complex and often unsettling emotion.

Anaphora Provides Weight and Emphasis Through Repetition

Anaphora ("to carry again or repeat") is the repetition of the same word or phrase
throughout a work or a section of a work in order to lend weight and emphasis.
An example occurs in Blake's "The Tyger" (this chapter), when the interrogative
word *what* is used five times to emphasize the mystery of evil (italics added).

> *What* the hammer? *what* the chain?
> In *what* furnace was thy brain?
> *What* the anvil? *what* dread grasp
> Dare its deadly terrors clasp?

Anaphora is the most obvious feature of Muriel Rukeyser's "Looking at Each
Other," where the word *yes* begins each of the poem's twenty-five lines.

Apostrophe Creates the Drama of a Speaker Addressing an Audience

In an **apostrophe** (a "turning away," or redirection of attention) a speaker
addresses a real or imagined listener who is not present. It is like a public speech,
with readers as audience, and it therefore makes a poem dramatic. An apostrophe enables the speaker to develop ideas that might arise naturally on a public

occasion, as in Wordsworth's sonnet "London, 1802," which is addressed to the long dead English poet Milton. In the following sonnet by Keats, "Bright Star," the speaker addresses a distant and inanimate star, yet through apostrophe he speaks as though the star has human understanding and divine power.

JOHN KEATS (1795–1822)

Bright Star (1838; 1819)

Bright star! would I were steadfast as thou art—
   Not in lone splendor hung aloft the night,
And watching, with eternal lids apart,
   Like Nature's patient, sleepless eremite,°   *hermit, a holy presence*
The moving waters at their priestlike task
   Of pure ablution round earth's human shores,
Or gazing on the new soft-fallen mask
   Of snow upon the mountains and the moors;
No—yet still steadfast, still unchangeable,
   Pillowed upon my fair love's ripening breast,
To feel forever its soft fall and swell,
   Awake forever in a sweet unrest,
     Still, still to hear her tender-taken breath,
     And so live ever—or else swoon to death.

QUESTIONS

1. With what topic is the speaker concerned in this sonnet? How does he compare himself with the distant star?

2. What qualities does the speaker attribute specifically to the star? What role does he seem to assign to it? In light of this role, and the qualities needed to serve in it, how might the star be compared to a divine and benign presence?

3. In light of the emphasis on the words *forever* and *ever* in lines 11–14, how appropriate is the choice of the star as the subject of the apostrophe in the poem?

In this sonnet the speaker addresses the star as though it is a person or god, an object of adoration, and the poem is therefore like a petitionary prayer. The star is idealized with qualities that the speaker wishes to establish in himself—namely, steadfastness, eternal watchfulness, and fidelity. The point of the apostrophe is thus to dramatize the speaker's yearning and to stress the permanence of space and eternity as contrasted with earthly impermanence.

Personification Is the Attribution of Human Traits to Abstractions or to Nonhuman Objects

A close neighbor of apostrophe is **personification**, another dramatic figurative device through which poets explore relationships to environment, ideals, and inner lives. In "Bright Star," as we have just seen, Keats personifies the star addressed by the speaker. Donne's speaker in "Holy Sonnet 10: Death Be Not Proud" (Chapter 19) personifies death itself as he asserts the power of

Poems for Study

William Blake .... The Tyger, 647

Robert Burns .... A Red, Red Rose, 648

John Donne .... A Valediction: Forbidding Mourning, 649

Alan Dugan .... Untitled Poem, 651

Federico García Lorca .... Sonnet of the Sweet Complaint, 651

Thomas Hardy .... The Convergence of the Twain, 652

Joy Harjo.. Remember, 653

John Keats .... To Autumn, 654

Jane Kenyon .... Let Evening Come, 655

Judith Minty .... Conjoined, 656

Ogden Nash.. Exit Pursued by a Bear, 657

Pablo Neruda .... If You Forget Me, 658

Mary Oliver .... Showing the Birds, 660

Marge Piercy .... A Work of Artifice, 660

Marguerite Rivas .... Pilgrimage, 661

Muriel Rukeyser .... Looking at Each Other, 662

William Shakespeare .... Sonnet 18: Shall I Compare
Thee to a Summer's Day? 663

William Shakespeare .... Sonnet 30: When to the Sessions
of Sweet Silent Thought, 663

Alfred, Lord Tennyson .... Break, Break, Break, 664

Elizabeth Tudor, Queen Elizabeth I .... On Monsieur's Departure, 665

Mona Van Duyn .... Earth Tremors Felt in Missouri, 666

Diane Wakoski .... Inside Out, 666

Walt Whitman........................... Facing West from California's Shores, 667

William Wordsworth .... London, 1802, 668

Sir Thomas Wyatt .... I Find No Peace, 669

WILLIAM BLAKE (1757–1827)

For a portrait, see Chapter 12, page 581.

 ### The Tyger° (1794)

Tyger! Tyger! burning bright
In the forests of the night,
What immortal hand or eye
Could frame thy fearful symmetry?

In what distant deeps or skies   5
Burnt the fire of thine eyes?
On what wings dare he aspire?
What the hand, dare seize the fire?

°*"Tyger"*: refers not only to a tiger but also to any large, wild, ferocious cat.

And what shoulder, & what art,
10   Could twist the sinews of thy heart?
And when thy heart began to beat,
What dread hand? & what dread feet?

What the hammer? what the chain?
In what furnace was thy brain?
15   What the anvil? what dread grasp
Dare its deadly terrors clasp?

When the stars threw down their spears,
And water'd heaven with their tears,
Did he smile his work to see?
20   Did he who made the Lamb make thee?

Tyger! Tyger! burning bright
In the forests of the night,
What immortal hand or eye
Dare frame thy fearful symmetry?

QUESTIONS

1. What do the associations of the image of "burning" suggest? Why is the burning done at night rather than day? What does night suggest?

2. Describe the kinesthetic images of lines 5–20. What ideas is Blake's speaker representing by these images? What attributes does the speaker suggest may belong to the blacksmith-type initiator of these actions?

3. Line 20 presents the kinesthetic image of a creator. What is implied about the mixture of good and evil in the world? What answer does the poem offer? Why does Blake phrase this line as a question rather than an assertion?

4. The sixth stanza repeats the first stanza with only one change of imagery of action. Contrast these stanzas, stressing the difference between "could" (line 4) and "dare" (24).

ROBERT BURNS (1759–1796)

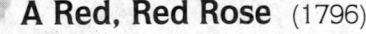 A Red, Red Rose (1796)

O my Luve's like a red, red rose,
    That's newly sprung in June:
O my Luve's like the melodie
    That's sweetly play'd in tune.

5   As fair art thou, my bonnie lass,
    So deep in luve am I;
And I will luve thee still, my Dear,
    Till a'° the seas gang° dry.   *all; go*

Till a' the seas gang dry, my Dear,
   And the rocks melt wi'° the sun: *with*   10
And I will luve thee still, my Dear,
   While the sands o'° life shall run.   *of*

And fare thee weel, my only Luve!
   And fare thee weel, awhile!
And I will come again, my Luve,   15
   Tho' it were ten thousand mile!

QUESTIONS

1. In light of the character and background of the speaker, do the two opening similes seem common or unusual? If they are just ordinary, does that fact diminish their value? How and why?

2. Describe the shift of listener envisioned after the first stanza. How are the last three stanzas related to the first?

3. Consider the metaphors concerning time and travel. How do the metaphors assist you in comprehending the speaker's character?

JOHN DONNE (1572–1631)

For a portrait, see Chapter 12, page 585.

A Valediction°: Forbidding Mourning (1633)

As virtuous men pass mildly away,
   And whisper to their souls to go,
Whilst some of their sad friends do say
   The breath goes now, and some say, No;

So let us melt, and make no noise,   5
   No tear-floods, nor sigh-tempests move,
'Twere profanation of our joys
   To tell the laity° our love.

Moving of th'earth° brings harm and fears,   *earthquakes*
   Men reckon what it did and meant: 10
But trepidation° of the spheres,
   Though greater far, is innocent.

°*Valediction:* the saying of farewell, or goodbye. °7, 8 *profanation . . . laity:* as though the lovers are priests of love, whose love is a mystery. °11 *trepidation:* Before Sir Isaac Newton explained the precession of the equinoxes, it was assumed that the positions of heavenly bodies should be constant and perfectly circular. The clearly observable irregularities (caused by the slow wobbling of the earth's axis) were explained by the concept of *trepidation,* or a trembling or oscillation that occurred in the outermost of the spheres surrounding the earth.

Dull sublunary lovers' love
 (Whose soul is sense°) cannot admit
15 Absence, because it doth remove
  Those things which elemented it.

But we by a love so much refined
 That our selves know not what it is,
Inter-assured of the mind,
20 Care less, eyes, lips, and hands to miss.

Our two souls therefore, which are one,
 Though I must go, endure not yet
A breach, but an expansion
 Like gold to airy thinness beat.°

25 If they be two, they are two so
 As stiff twin compasses° are two;
Thy soul, the fixt foot, makes no show
 To move, but doth, if th'other do.

And though it in the center sit,
30 Yet when the other far doth roam,
It leans and harkens after it,
 And grows erect, as that comes home.

Such wilt thou be to me, who must
 Like th'other foot, obliquely run;
35 Thy firmness draws my circle just,°
 And makes me end where I begun.

°14 *soul is sense:* lovers whose attraction is totally physical.　°24 gold to airy thinness beat: a reference to the malleability of gold.　°26 *compasses:* a compass used for drawing circles.　°35 *just:* perfectly round.

QUESTIONS

1. What is the situation envisioned as the occasion for the poem? Who is talking to whom? What is their relationship?
2. What is the intention of the first two stanzas? What is the effect of the phrases "tear-floods" and "sigh-tempests"?
3. Describe the effect of the opening simile about men on their deathbeds.
4. What is the metaphor of the third stanza (lines 9–12)? In what sense might the "trepidation of the spheres" be less harmful than the parting of the lovers?
5. In lines 13–20 there is a comparison making the love of the speaker and his sweetheart superior to the love of average lovers. What is the basis for the speaker's claim?
6. What is the comparison begun by the word "refined" in line 17 and continued by the simile in line 24?

ALAN DUGAN (1923–2003)

 ## Untitled Poem (1974)

Speciously individual
like a solid piece of spit
floating in a cuspidor
I dream of free bravery
but am a social being.   5
I should do something
to get out of here
but float around in the culture
wondering what it will grow.

QUESTIONS

1. Have you ever felt that you wanted to break free from some restrictions of society? If
so, which ones?

2. How is "a solid piece of spit" like someone who is "speciously individual"?

3. What does the phrase "float around" suggest about the speaker's desires?

FEDERICO GARCÍA LORCA (1898–1936)

 ## Sonnet of the Sweet Complaint (1934)

Never let me lose the marvel
of your statue eyes or the accent
that by night the solitary rose of your breath
places on my cheek.

I'm afraid to be on this shore   5
a trunk without limbs, and what I most regret
is not to have flower, pulp or clay
for the worm of my suffering.

If you are my hidden treasure,
if you are my cross and my wet sorrow,   10
if I am the dog of your dominion,

do not let me lose what I have won
and adorn the waters of your river with leaves
of my alienated autumn.

QUESTIONS

1. Do you feel that an attachment to another person may better be expressed through
metaphor or simile rather than direct speech?

2. In what ways is the speaker a "dog" and the person being addressed a "master?"

3. What does the speaker mean by being "a branchless trunk"?

THOMAS HARDY (1840–1928)

For a photo, see Chapter 11, page 548.

The Convergence of the Twain (1912)

Lines on the Loss of the "Titanic"°

I

In a solitude of the sea
Deep from human vanity,
And the Pride of Life that planned her, stilly couches she.

II

      Steel chambers, late the pyres
5   Of her salamandrine fires,°
Cold Currents thrid,° and turn to rhythmic tidal lyres.   *thread, instrumental strings*

III

Over the mirrors meant
To glass the opulent
The sea-worm crawls—grotesque, slimed, dumb, indifferent.

IV

10   Jewels in joy designed
      To ravish the sensuous mind
Lie lightless, all their sparkles bleared and black and blind.

V

Dim moon-eyed fishes near
Gaze at the gilded gear
15 And query: "What does this vaingloriousness down here?"

VI

Well: while was fashioning
This creature of cleaving wing,
The Immanent Will that stirs and urges everything

°The *Titanic*: The largest passenger ship in existence at the time, and considered unsinkable, was sunk after a collision with an iceberg on its maiden voyage in April 1912. The loss was particularly notable because some of the passengers were among the world's social elite, and 1,500 people died because there were not enough lifeboats for everyone. In 1985 the wreck of the ship was discovered on the ocean floor at a depth of 13,000 feet, and some of the ship's artifacts were recovered. The loss of the *Titanic* has become legendary. 4-5 *Steel chambers . . . salamandrine fires*: The idea here is that the "steel chambers" of the ship's furnaces were built to resist the high heat of the coal fires, much like the salamander of ancient myth, which was reputedly capable of living through fire.

VII

Prepared a sinister mate
For her—so gaily great—
A Shape of Ice, for the time far and dissociate.   20

VIII

And as the smart ship grew
In stature, grace, and hue,
In shadowy silent distance grew the Iceberg too.

IX

Alien they seemed to be: 25
No mortal eye could see
The intimate welding of their later history.

X

Or sign that they were bent
By paths coincident
On being anon twin halves of one august event.   30

XI

Till the Spinner of the Years
Said "Now!" And each one hears,
And consummation comes, and jars two hemispheres.

QUESTIONS

1. What human attributes does Hardy ascribe to the *Titanic?* What pronoun does he regularly use in reference to the ship? What is the name of this figure of speech?
2. What are the meanings of "vanity" (line 2), "Pride of Life" (line 3), and "vaingloriousness" (line 15) in relation to the speaker's judgment of the meaning of the *Titanic?*
3. Why does Hardy introduce the phrases "Spinner of the Years" (line 31) and "Immanent Will" (line 18)?
4. What is the idea of calling the iceberg the "sinister mate" of the *Titanic* (line 19)? What irony results from this phrase, and from the word "consummation" in the last line of the poem?

JOY HARJO (b. 1951)

For a photo, see Chapter 11, page 549.

Remember (1983)

Remember the sky that you were born under,
know each of the star's stories.
Remember the moon, know who she is. I met her
in a bar once in Iowa City.

5   Remember the sun's birth at dawn, that is the
strongest point of time. Remember sundown
and the giving away to night.
Remember your birth, how your mother struggled
to give you form and breath. You are evidence of
10   her life, and her mother's, and hers.
Remember your father. He is your life, also.
Remember the earth whose skin you are:
red earth, black earth, yellow earth, white earth
brown earth, we are earth.
15   Remember the plants, trees, animal life who all have their
tribes, their families, their histories, too. Talk to them,
listen to them. They are alive poems.
Remember the wind. Remember her voice. She knows the
origin of this universe. I heard her singing Kiowa war
20   dance songs at the corner of Fourth and Central once.
Remember that you are all people and that all people
are you.
Remember that you are this universe and that this
universe is you.
25   Remember that all is in motion, is growing, is you.
Remember that language comes from this.
Remember the dance that language is, that life is.
Remember.

QUESTIONS

1. How many times is the word "remember" repeated in this poem? What is the name of this figure of speech? What is the effect of the repetitions?

2. Who is the speaker, and who is the listener? What is the apparent purpose of stating all the things that the listener is being asked to remember? What is the implication of the word "remember," inasmuch as many of the things designated for remembrance happened before the listener was alive or was old enough to have a memory?

3. What is meant by "the earth whose skin you are" in line 12? Explain the paradox of "you are all people and . . . all people / are you" in lines 21–22.

JOHN KEATS (1795–1821)

For a portrait, see this chapter, page 641.

🍂 To Autumn (1820)

Season of mists and mellow fruitfulness!
   Close bosom-friend of the maturing sun;
Conspiring with him to load and bless
   With fruit the vines that round the thatch-eaves run;
5 To bend with apples the mossed cottage-trees,
   And fill all fruit with ripeness to the core;
     To swell the gourd, and plump the hazel shells

With a sweet kernel; to set budding more,
    And still more, later flowers for the bees,
      Until they think warm days will never cease,   10
        For Summer has o'erbrimmed their clammy cells.

Who hath not seen thee oft amid thy store?
    Sometimes whoever seeks abroad may find
Thee sitting careless on a granary floor,
    Thy hair soft-lifted by the winnowing wind,   15
Or on a half-reaped furrow sound asleep,
Drowsed with the fume of poppies, while thy hook
    Spares the next swath and all its twin'ed flowers;
And sometimes like a gleaner thou dost keep
    Steady thy laden head across a brook;   20
    Or by a cider-press, with patient look,
    Thou watchest the last oozings hours by hours.

Where are the songs of Spring? Ay, where are they?
    Think not of them, thou hast thy music too,—
While barr'ed clouds bloom the soft-dying day,   25
    And touch the stubble-plains with rosy hue;
Then in a wailful choir the small gnats mourn
    Among the river sallows, borne aloft
      Or sinking as the light wind lives or dies;
And full-grown lambs loud bleat from hilly bourn;   30
    Hedge-crickets sing; and now with treble soft
    The redbreast whistles from a garden-croft;
      And gathering swallows twitter in the skies.

QUESTIONS

1. How is personification used in the first stanza? How does it change in the second? What is the effect of such personification?

2. How does Keats structure the poem to accord with his apostrophe to autumn? That is, in what ways can the stanzas be distinguished by the type of discourse addressed to the season?

3. Analyze Keats's metonymy in the first stanza and synecdoche in the second. What effects does he achieve with these devices?

4. How, through the use of images, does Keats develop his idea that autumn is a season of "mellow fruitfulness"?

JANE KENYON (1947–1995)

Let Evening Come (1990)

Let the light of late afternoon
shine through chinks in the barn, moving
up the bales as the sun moves down.

Let the cricket take up chafing
5   as a woman takes up her needles
and her yarn. Let evening come.

Let dew collect on the hoe abandoned
in long grass. Let the stars appear
and the moon disclose her silver horn.

10   Let the fox go back to its sandy den.
Let the wind die down. Let the shed
go black inside. Let evening come.

To the bottle in the ditch, to the scoop
in the oats, to air in the lung
15   let evening come.

Let it come as it will, and don't
be afraid.° God does not leave us   *Matthew 28:10*
comfortless,° so let evening come.   *John 14:18*

QUESTIONS

1. This poem features the repetition of phrases beginning with the word *let*. What is this
    pattern called? How many such phrases does the poem contain? How does the pattern
    furnish strength to the poem?

2. What sorts of activities does the speaker associate with day? With night? How are these
    activities connected?

3. Describe the shift of topic in the last stanza. Does this shift occur logically or illogically
    from the earlier topic material of the poem? How does the final stanza seem to be an
    ordinary and necessary part of the activities described in the first five stanzas?

JUDITH MINTY (b. 1937)

 **Conjoined** (1981)

a marriage poem

The onion in my cupboard, a monster, actually
two joined under one transparent skin:
each half-round, then flat and deformed
where it pressed and grew against the other.

5   An accident, like the two-headed calf rooted
in one body, fighting to suck at its mother's teats;
or like those other freaks, Chang and Eng,° twins
joined at the chest by skin and muscle, doomed
to live, even make love, together for sixty years.

°7 *Chang and Eng:* born in 1811, the original and most famous Siamese twins. Although they were never separated, they nevertheless fathered twenty-two children. They died in 1874.

Do you feel the skin that binds us   10
together as we move, heavy in this house?
To sever the muscle could free one,
but might kill the other. Ah, but men
don't slice onions in the kitchen, seldom see
what is invisible. We cannot escape each other.   15

QUESTIONS

1. What are the two things—the "us" and "we" of lines 10 and 11—that are conjoined? Since this is "a marriage poem," might they be the man and the woman? Why might they also be considered as the body and soul of the speaker; or the desire to be married and subordinated, on the one hand, and to be free and in control of destiny, on the other?

2. Explore the metaphor of the onion and the similes of the two-headed calf and the Siamese twins. Why do you think the poet introduces the words "monster," "accident," and "freaks" into these figures in lines 1, 5, and 7? In what sense do you believe that these words are applicable to the nature and plight of women?

3. Is it true that *all* "men / don't slice onions in the kitchen, seldom see / what is invisible" (lines 13–15)? Explain.

4. The first stanza of this three-stanza poem contains four lines; the second contains five lines; and the third contains six. What reason, if any, can you give for why the poet added a line to each of the stanzas?

OGDEN NASH (1902–1970)

Exit, Pursued by a Bear°(1954)

Chipmunk chewing the Chippendale,°
Mice on the Meissen° shelf,
Pigeon stains on the Aubusson,°
Spider lace on the delf.°

Squirrel climbing the Sheraton,°   5
Skunk on the Duncan Phyfe,°
Silverfish in the Gobelins°
And the calfbound volumes of *Life.*

Pocks on the pink Picasso,
Dust on the four Cézannes,   10
Kit on the keys of the Steinway,
Cat on the Louis Quinze.°

°*Exit, Pursued By a Bear:* The title is a stage direction in Shakespeare's *The Winter's Tale* (act 3, scene 3, 58). The character is torn apart by the bear. When this poem was first published, the atomic bomb had existed for nine years, and the hydrogen bomb for two. In late 1953, Russia, which is sometimes symbolized by a bear, announced that it possessed the hydrogen bomb. °1 *Chippendale:* ornate furniture made by Thomas Chippendale (1718–1779). °2 *Meissen:* expensive chinaware made in Meissen, Germany. Also called "Dresden China." °3 *Aubusson:* carpet imported from France. °4 *delf:* expensive pottery made in Delft, The Netherlands. °5 *Sheraton:* furniture made by Thomas Sheraton (1751–1806). °6 *Duncan Phyfe:* furniture made by Duncan Phyfe (1768–1854), a Scotsman who came to America in 1783. °7 *Gobelins:* rare and exquisitely crafted tapestries made by Gobelin of Paris. °12 *Louis Quinze:* furniture made in France during the reign of Louis XV (1710–1774).

Rings on the Adam° mantel
From a thousand bygone thirsts,
15   Mold on the Henry Millers°
And the Ronald Firbank° firsts.

The lion and the lizard°
No heavenly harmonies hear
From the high-fidelity speaker
20   Concealed behind the Vermeer.

Jamshid° squats in a cavern
Screened by a waterfall,
Catered by Heinz and Campbell,
And awaits the fireball.

°13 *Adam*: Robert Adam (1728–1792) was one of the most famous English architects. °15 *Henry Miller*: American author (1891–1980). °16 *Ronald Firbank*: Arthur Ainsley Ronald Firbank (1886–1926), British author. °17 *The lion and the lizard*: see Edward Fitzgerald's (1809–1883) version of *The Rubaiyat of Omar Khayyam*, stanza 18, particularly in reference to Nash's last stanza. °21 *Jamshid*: a reference to the legendary Persian hero Jamshid, who lived for 700 years and found a cup containing the elixir of life. At one point in the story Jamshid remained hidden for a hundred years. Note also the reference to Fitzgerald's *Rubaiyát*, stanza 18.

QUESTIONS

1. In relationship to the serious subject matter of the poem, what is the effect of the title? What is the possible pun on the word *bear*?
2. What location is the speaker describing? How is metonymy used to suggest the wealth of the collections of household items and art? What sort of lifestyle is suggested by the metonymy?
3. What has hypothetically occurred so that the animals rather than people are living with the expensive artifacts? Judging from the evidence of line 15, how long has this situation existed?
4. How might the situation presented in the poem be considered as a paradox?
5. What fireball is expected (line 24)? In the light of this expectation, what ideas is the poet expressing about war? Compare this poem to Yeats's "The Second Coming" (p. 792) and Robinson Jeffers's "The Purse-Seine" (p. 780). What similarities and differences do you find among these works?

PABLO NERUDA (1904–1977)

For a photo, see Chapter 13, page 625.

If You Forget Me (1952; 1963)

Translated by Donald S. Walsh

I want you to know
one thing.

You know how this is:

if I look
at the crystal moon, at the red branch   5
of the slow autumn at my window,
if I touch
near the fire
the impalpable ash
or the wrinkled body of the log,   10
everything carries me to you,
as if everything that exists,
aromas, light, metals,
were little boats
that sail   15
toward those isles of yours that wait for me.

Well, now,
if little by little you stop loving me
I shall stop loving you little by little.

If suddenly   20
you forget me
do not look for me,
for I shall already have forgotten you.

If you think it long and mad,
the wind of banners   25
that passes through my life,
and you decide
to leave me at the shore
of the heart where I have roots,
remember   30
that on that day,
at that hour,
I shall lift my arms
and my roots will set off
to seek another land.   35

But
if each day,
each hour,
you feel that you are destined for me
with implacable sweetness,   40
if each day a flower
climbs up to your lips to seek me,
ah my love, ah my own,
in me all that fire is repeated,
in me nothing is extinguished or forgotten,   45
my love feeds on your love, beloved,
and as long as you live it will be in your arms
without leaving mine.

QUESTIONS

1. What similes and metaphors do you discover in this poem? Explain the paradox in the last stanza.

2. What is the nature of the love the speaker expresses? How strongly and firmly does the speaker express his love? To what degree does he state that his love must be reciprocated to continue to exist?

3. Describe the development of the speaker's thought. Why does he introduce the metaphor that he might possibly lift up his roots "to seek another land"?

MARY OLIVER (b. 1935)

 Showing the Birds° (2008)

Look, children, here is the shy,
flightless dodo; the many-colored
pigeon named the passenger, the
great auk, the Eskimo curlew, the
5   woodpecker called the Lord God Bird,
the . . .
Come children, hurry—there are so many
more wonderful things to show you in
the museum's dark drawers.

°*Birds:* Five extinct species of birds among those that were once abundant on earth are named in this poem, from the Dodo, which became extinct in the seventeenth century, to the Ivory Billed Woodpecker (the "Lord God Bird"), which has not been reliably sighted since the 1980s. Although at one time Passenger Pigeons and Eskimo Curlews numbered many millions, they were declared extinct long before the end of the twentieth century.

QUESTIONS

1. What is the dramatic situation of this poem? Who is talking to whom? Where is the action of the poem taking place?

2. Describe the effects of anaphora (repetitions) in lines 1 and 7 ("Look, children" and "Come children," and in lines 1 through 6 (the pattern beginning "the . . . ").

3. Consider the irony of the last two lines. Should "wonderful things" be found only in the "dark drawers" of the museum? What is the poem's implied idea about where wonderful things, instead, should be found?

MARGE PIERCY (b. 1936)

 A Work of Artifice (1973)

The bonsai tree
in the attractive pot
could have grown eighty feet tall
on the side of a mountain
5   till split by lightning.
But a gardener

carefully pruned it.
It is nine inches high.
Every day as he
whittles back the branches   10
the gardener croons,
It is your nature
to be small and cozy,
domestic and weak;
how lucky, little tree,   15
to have a pot to grow in.
With living creatures
one must begin very early
to dwarf their growth:
the bound feet,   20
the crippled brain,
the hair in curlers,
the hands you
love to touch.

QUESTIONS

1. What is a bonsai tree? In what ways is it an apt metaphor for women? The tree "could
   have grown eighty feet tall." What would be the comparable growth and development
   of a woman?

2. What do you make of the gardener's song (lines 12–16)? If the bonsai tree were able to
   respond, would it accept the gardener's consolation? What conclusions about women's
   lives are implied by the metaphor of the tree?

3. How does the poem shift at line 17? To what extent do the next images (lines 20–24)
   embody women's lives? How are the images metaphorical?

MARGUERITE RIVAS (1956)

 ## Pilgrimage (2012)

Our ancestors scraped the ground
and cursed the blackened potato
then ate the dirt and left the dead
by the emerald roadside
too weary for obligation   5
too starved and numb for keening.

Dragged leaden feet to the coast
and coffined their way to
a place where they deposited us—
hopeful seeds of sorrow and   10
starvation's progeny—for what?

For us to discover that
love was an empty well
where dreams lay waste

15 at the dry bottom?
No, despite the bent back,
the work-calloused hands,
and the burden of crying babies
slung on the working hip,
20 we dream of holy wells

where reflections of the past
and visions of the future
sustain us on the journey
begun beside a white thorn tree
25 and a low stone fence
over a century ago.

QUESTIONS

1. Do you think recent immigrants are more likely to look back at the country they came from or look forward to a future in their new country?
2. What phrases suggest the past and which the future?
3. Were there any unfamiliar words? If so, which ones? Why do you think they were used?

MURIEL RUKEYSER (1913–1980)

Looking at Each Other (1978)

Yes, we were looking at each other
Yes, we knew each other very well
Yes, we had made love with each other many times
Yes, we had heard music together
5 Yes, we had gone to the sea together
Yes, we had cooked and eaten together
Yes, we had laughed often day and night
Yes, we fought violence and knew violence
Yes, we hated the inner and outer oppression
10 Yes, that day we were looking at each other
Yes, we saw the sunlight pouring down
Yes, the corner of the table was between us
Yes, bread and flowers were on the table
Yes, our eyes saw each other's eyes
15 Yes, our mouths saw each other's mouth
Yes, our breasts saw each other's breasts
Yes, our bodies entire saw each other
Yes, it was beginning in each
Yes, it threw waves across our lives
20 Yes, the pulses were becoming very strong
Yes, the beating became very delicate
Yes, the calling the arousal
Yes, the arriving the coming
Yes, there it was for both entire
25 Yes, we were looking at each other

QUESTIONS

1. What is the dramatic situation of the poem? What sort of listener is the speaker addressing?
2. Describe the rhetorical device at work here. How many different words are being repeated?
3. What is the effect of the repetitions? What is their relationship to the emotions and experiences that the speaker is describing?

WILLIAM SHAKESPEARE (1564–1616)

For a portrait, see Chapter 21, page 1079. The following two sonnets are by Shakespeare.

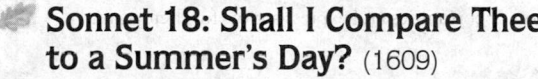 Sonnet 18: Shall I Compare Thee
to a Summer's Day? (1609)

Shall I compare thee to a summer's day?
Thou art more lovely and more temperate:
Rough winds do shake the darling° buds of May,   *dear, cherished*
And summer's lease hath all too short a date:
Sometime too hot the eye of heaven° shines   *the sun*   5
And often is his° gold complexion dimmed;   *its*
And every fair from fair sometime declines,
By chance, or nature's changing course, untrimmed;
But thy eternal summer shall not fade,
Nor lose possession of that fair thou owest;°   *owns, possess*   10
Nor shall Death brag thou wander'st in his shade,°
When in eternal lines to time thou growest:
    So long as men can breathe, or eyes can see,
    So long lives this, and this gives life to thee.

°11 *thou. . . shade:* you are wandering in Death's darkness.

QUESTIONS

1. What is the dramatic situation of the poem? Who is speaking to whom?
2. What do the metaphors in lines 1–8 assert? Why does the speaker emphasize life's brevity?
3. Describe the shift in topic beginning in line 9. How do these lines both deny and echo the subject of lines 1–8?
4. What relationship do the last two lines have to the rest of the poem? What is the meaning of "this" (line 14)? What sort of immortality does Shakespeare exalt in the sonnet?

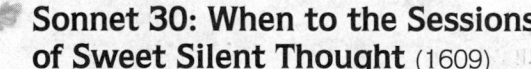 Sonnet 30: When to the Sessions
of Sweet Silent Thought (1609)

When to the sessions° of sweet silent thought   *holding of court*
I summon° up remembrance of things past,

°2 *summon:* to issue a summons to appear at a legal hearing.

I sigh the lack of many a thing I sought,
And with old woes new wail my dear time's waste:°
5   Then can I drown an eye (un-used to flow)
For precious friends hid in death's dateless° night,   *endless*
And weep afresh love's long since canceled° woe,   *paid in full*
And moan th'expense° of many a vanished sight.   *cost, loss*
Then can I grieve at grievances foregone,
10 And heavily° from woe to woe tell° o'er   *sadly; count*
The sad account of fore-bemoanèd moan,
Which I new pay, as if not paid before.
    But if the while I think on thee (dear friend)
    All losses are restored, and sorrows end.

°4 *old woes . . . waste:* revive old sorrows about lost opportunities and express sorrow for them again.

QUESTIONS

1. Explain the metaphor of "sessions" and "summon" in lines 1–2. Where are the "sessions" being held? What is a "summons" for remembrance?
2. What is the metaphor brought out by the word "canceled" in line 7? In what sense might a "woe" of love be canceled? Explain the metaphor of "expense" in line 8.
3. What type of transaction does Shakespeare refer to in the metaphor of lines 9–12? What understanding does the metaphor provide about the sadness and regret that a person feels about past mistakes and sorrows?
4. What role does the speaker assign to the "dear friend" of line 13 in relation to the metaphors of the poem?

ALFRED, LORD TENNYSON (1809–1892)

Break, Break, Break (1842)

Break, break, break,
    On thy cold gray stones, O Sea!
And I would that my tongue could utter
    The thoughts that arise in me.

5   O, well for the fisherman's boy,
    That he shouts with his sister at play!
O, well for the sailor lad,
    That he sings in his boat on the bay!

And the stately ships go on
10   To their haven under the hill;
But O for the touch of a vanish'd hand,
    And the sound of a voice that is still!

Break, break, break,
    At the foot of thy crags, O Sea!
15 But the tender grace of a day that is dead
    Will never come back to me.

QUESTIONS

1. Why does Tennyson begin and end the poem with an apostrophe to the Sea? How may this apostrophe be related to the structure of the poem?
2. What is the meaning and effect of the use of synecdoche in lines 5-10? How do these examples contrast with the synecdoche intended by *hand* (line 11), *voice* (line 12), and *day* (line 15)? What effect is achieved by this contrast?
3. What symbolic relationship is there between the breaking of the waves and the feelings of the poet? What human organ is thought to break, and how does this organ apply metonymically to human emotions?
4. Rhetorical considerations aside, why is "Break, Break, Break" a beautiful poem?

ELIZABETH TUDOR, QUEEN ELIZABETH I (1533–1603)

On Monsieur's Departure (c. 1560; 1964)

I grieve° and dare not show my discontent,   *I am unhappy*
I love and yet am forced to seem to hate,
I do, yet dare not say I ever meant,
I seem stark mute but inwardly do prate.°   *chatter endlessly*
   I am and not, I freeze and yet am burned,   5
   Since from myself another self I turned.

My care° is like my shadow in the sun,   *loved one*
Follows me flying, flies when I pursue it,
Stands and lies by me, doth what I have done.
His too familiar care° doth make me rue it.   *alternativeness, love*   10
   No means I find to rid him from my breast,
   Till by the end of things it be supprest.

Some gentler passion slide into my mind,
For I am soft and made of melting snow;
Or be more cruel, love, and so be kind.   15
Let me or float or sink, be high or low.
   Or let me live with some more sweet content.
   Or die and so forget what love ere meant.

QUESTIONS

1. What is the significance of "Monsieur's Departure"? How does this detail prompt the patterns of thought in the poem?
2. Explain the speaker's use of antithesis in the poem to explain her ambivalent situation. How seriously should we take the ideas in lines 12 and 18? Assuming that this is a deeply personal and private lyric, why, granted the speaker's royal status, does she express such contradictory feelings?
3. What is the meaning of the shadow simile in lines 7–10? How well does this comparison reveal her situation?
4. What is explained by the paradoxes in lines 5 and 15?

MONA VAN DUYN (1921–2004)

Earth Tremors Felt in Missouri (1964)

The quake last night was nothing personal,
you told me this morning. I think one always wonders,
unless, of course, something is visible: tremors
that take us, private and willy-nilly, are usual.
5   But the earth said last night that what I feel,
you feel; what secretly moves you, moves me.
One small, sensuous catastrophe
makes inklings letters, spelled in a worldly tremble.

The earth, with others on it, turns in its course
10   as we turn toward each other, less than ourselves, gross,
mindless, more than we were. Pebbles, we swell
to planets, nearing the universal roll,
in our conceit even comprehending the sun,
whose bright ordeal leaves cool men woebegone.

QUESTIONS

1. In what ways is this poem intensely personal, a "confessional" poem? How does the poem develop materials that might be considered less personal and more public?

2. Why does the speaker equate herself and her listener with the earth? Granted that this metaphor is apt, what is then meant by "earth tremors," "quake last night," "Pebbles, we swell/to planets," and "comprehending the sun"?

3. What feelings are brought out in the last line through the words "ordeal" and "woebegone"?

DIANE WAKOSKI (b. 1937)

Inside Out (1969)

I walk the purple carpet into your eye,
carrying the silver butter server,
but a truck rumbles by,
            leaving its black tire prints on my foot,
5   and old images–
            the sound of banging screen doors on hot afternoons
            and a fly buzzing over Kool-Aid spilled on the sink–
flicker, as reflections on the metal surface.

Come in, you said,
10   inside your paintings, inside the blood factory, inside the
old songs that line your hands, inside
eyes that change like a snowflake every second,

inside spinach leaves holding that one piece of gravel,

inside the whiskers of a cat,

inside your old hat, and most of all inside your mouth where you   15
grind the pigments with your teeth, painting
with a broken bottle on the floor, and painting
with an ostrich feather on the moon that rolls out of my mouth.

You cannot let me walk inside you too long
inside the veins where my small feet touch   20
bottom.
You must reach inside and pull me
like a silver bullet°
from your arm.

°23 *silver bullet:* According to legend, silver bullets were used to kill vampires. The Lone Ranger, of the radio and television series popular in the 1940s and 1950s, always used silver bullets as a trademark of his pursuit of justice.

QUESTIONS

1. Who is the speaker? Who is the person being addressed? From what the speaker says in lines 15–19, what is the profession of the addressee? What sort of relationship does the speaker have with him? How close, how intimate, are they? What knowledge of domestic details do they have in common? How may this knowledge be used in the drawing of conclusions about their relationship?

2. What "inside out" details of the listener's anatomy does the speaker mention? What do you think is meant by the poem's title?

3. Consider details of the eye and the veins as synecdoche, and the paintings and the old hat as metonymy. In the determination of the poem's characterization of the "you" inside the poem, what do these details stand for?

4. Consider the truck's black tire prints on the speaker's foot (lines 3–4) as an instance of synesthesia, that is, the application of one set of sensuous references to another sense. What might this figure mean? Do the same for the mouth with the ground pigments (lines 15–16), the ostrich feather and the rolling moon (line 18), and the walk inside the veins (lines 19–20).

5. What is meant by lines 19–24? Why, after the establishment of so personal and intimate a relationship, might the speaker express the reservations that are contained here? How might these lines be interpreted as a reflection upon the paradoxical nature of the love relationship generally?

6. Describe the paradox implicit in the speaker's mentioning the red carpet in line 1 and the silver butter sever in line 2.

WALT WHITMAN (1819–1892)

Facing West from California's Shores (1860)

Facing west from California's shores,
Inquiring, tireless, seeking what is yet unfound,
I, a child, very old, over waves, towards the house of maternity,°
    the land of migrations, look afar,

°3 *house of maternity:* Asia, then considered the cradle of human civilization.

Look off the shores of my Western sea, the circle almost circled;
5 For starting westward from Hindustan,° from the vales of Kashmir,
From Asia, from the north, from the God, the sage, and the hero,
From the south, from the flowery peninsulas° and the spice islands,°
Long having wandered since, round the earth having wandered
Now I face home again, very pleased and joyous.
10 (But where is what I started for so long ago?
And why is it yet unfound?)

°5 *Hindustan:* India. °7 *flowery peninsulas:* south India, south Burma, and the Maylay peninsula. °7 *spice islands:* the Molucca Islands of Indonesia.

QUESTIONS

1. What major paradox, or apparently contradictory situation, is described in this poem? How does the poet bring out this paradox? What has the speaker been seeking? Where has he looked for it?

2. Describe the meaning of the phrases "a child, very old"; "where is what I started for"; "the circle almost circled." In what ways are these phrases paradoxical?

3. Why does the speaker twice use the word "unfound" (lines 2, 11)? How might the word be considered a theme of the poem?

WILLIAM WORDSWORTH (1770–1850)

For a portrait, see Chapter 11, page 557.

 ## London, 1802 (1802; 1807)

Milton! thou should'st be living at this hour:
England hath need of thee: she is a fen°   bog, marsh
Of stagnant waters: altar, sword, and pen,
Fireside, the heroic wealth of hall and bower,
5 Have forfeited their ancient English dower°   widow's inheritance
Of inward happiness. We are selfish men;
Oh! raise us up, return to us again;
And give us manners,° virtue, freedom, power.
Thy soul was like a star, and dwelt apart:
10 Thou hadst a voice whose sound was like the sea:
Pure as the naked heavens, majestic, free,
So didst thou travel on life's common way,
In cheerful godliness; and yet thy heart
The lowliest duties on herself did lay.

°8 *manners:* customs, moral codes of social and political conduct.

QUESTIONS

1. What is the effect of Wordsworth's apostrophe to Milton? What elements of Milton's career as a writer does Wordsworth emphasize?

2. In lines 3 and 4, the device of metonymy is used. How does Wordsworth judge the respective institutions represented by the details?

3. Consider the use of overstatement, or hyperbole, from lines 2–6. What effect does Wordsworth achieve by using the device as extensively as he does here?

4. What effect does Wordsworth make through his use of overstatement in his praise of Milton in lines 9–14? What does he mean by the metonymic references to "soul" (line 9) and "heart" (line 13)?

SIR THOMAS WYATT (1503–1542)

I Find No Peace (1557)

<pre>
I find no peace, and all my war is done,
    I fear and hope, I burn and freeze like ice;
    I fly above the wind yet can I not arise;
    And naught I have and all the world I season.
That looseth nor locketh holdeth me in prison,°   5
    And holdeth me not, yet I can scape° nowise;   escape
    Nor letteth me live nor die at my devise,°   choice
    And yet of death it giveth none occasion.
Without eyen° I see, and without tongue I plain;°   eyes
    I desire to perish, and yet I ask health;   10
    I love another, and thus I hate myself;
I feed me in sorrow, and laugh in all my pain.
    Likewise displeaseth me both death and life°
    And my delight is causer of this strife.
</pre>

°5 *that . . . prison:* that is, "that which neither lets me go nor contains me holds me in prison." At the time of Wyatt, *-eth* was used for the third person singular present tense.   °9 *plain:* express desires about love.   °13 *Likewise . . . life:* literally, "it is displeasing to me, in the same way, both death and life." That is, "both death and life are equally distasteful to me."

QUESTIONS

1. What situation is the speaker reflecting upon? What metaphors and similes express his feelings? How successful are these figures?

2. How many paradoxes are in the poem? What is their cumulative effect? What is the topic of the paradoxes in lines 1–4? In lines 5–8? Why does the speaker declare that hating himself is a consequence of loving another? Why is it ironic that his "delight" is the "causer of this strife"?

3. To what extent do you think the paradoxes express the feelings of a person in love, particularly because in the sixteenth century free and unchaperoned meetings of lovers were not easily arranged?

WRITING TOPICS ABOUT FIGURES OF SPEECH

Begin by determining the use, line by line, of metaphors, similes, or other rhetorical figures. Obviously, similes are the easiest figures to recognize because they introduce comparisons with the words *like* or *as*. Metaphors can be recognized because the topics are discussed not as themselves but as other topics. If the poems speak of falling leaves or law courts but the subjects involve memory or increasing age, you are looking at metaphors. Similarly, if the poet is addressing an absent person or a natural object, or if you find clear double meanings in words, you may have apostrophe, personification, or puns.

Questions for Discovering Ideas

- What figures of speech does the work contain? Where do they occur? Under what circumstances? How extensive are they?
- How do you recognize them? Are they signaled by a single word or phrase, such as "desert places" in Frost's "Desert Places" (Chapter 16); or are they more extensively detailed, as in Shakespeare's Sonnet 30, "When to the Sessions of Sweet Silent Thought"?
- How vivid are the figures? How obvious? How unusual? What kind of effort is needed to understand them in context?
- Structurally, how are the figures developed? How do they rise out of the situation envisioned in the poem? To what degree are the figures integrated into the poem's development of ideas? How do they relate to other aspects of the poem?
- Is one type of figure used in a particular section while another type predominates in another section? Why?
- If you have discovered a number of figures, what relationships can you find among them (such as the judicial and financial connections in Shakespeare's "When to the Sessions of Sweet Silent Thought")?
- How do the figures of speech broaden, deepen, or otherwise assist in making the ideas in the poem forceful?
- In general, how appropriate and meaningful are the figures of speech in the poem? What effect do the figures have on the poem's tone, and on your understanding and appreciation of the poem?

Strategies for Organizing Ideas

For this essay, you might choose one of two types of compositions. One is a full-length essay. The other, because some rhetorical figures may occupy only a small part of the poem, is a single paragraph. Let us consider the single paragraph first.

1. *A paragraph.* For a single paragraph you need only one topic, such as the hyperbole used in the opening of Wordsworth's sonnet "London, 1802." The goal is to deal with the single figure and its relationship to the poem's main idea. Thus the essay should describe the figure and discuss

its meaning and implications. It is important to begin with a comprehensive topic sentence, such as one that explains the cleverness of the puns in Gay's "Let Us Take the Road," or the use of paradox in Wyatt's "I Find No Peace."

2. *A full-length essay.* One type of essay might examine just one figure, if the figure is pervasive enough in the poem to justify a full treatment. Most often, the poet's use of metaphors and similes is suitable for extensive discussion. A second type of essay might explore the meaning and effect of two or more figures, with the various parts of the body of the essay being taken up with each figure. The unity of this second kind of essay is achieved by linking a series of two or three different rhetorical devices to a single idea or emotion.

In the introduction, relate the quality of the figures to the general nature of the work. Thus, metaphors and similes of suffering might be appropriate to a religious, redemptive work, while those of sunshine, cheer, and flowers might be right for a romantic one. If there is any discrepancy between the metaphorical language and the topic, you could consider that contrast as a possible central idea, for it would clearly indicate the writer's ironic perspective. Suppose that the topic of the poem is love, but the figures put you in mind of darkness and cold: What might the poet be saying about the quality of love? You should also try to justify any claims that you make about the figures. For example, one of the similes in Coleridge's "Kubla Khan" (Chapter 13) compares the sounds of a "mighty fountain" to the breathing of the earth in "fast thick pants." How is this simile to be taken? As a reference to the animality of the earth? As a suggestion that the fountain, and the earth, are dangerous? Or simply as a comparison suggesting immense, forceful noise? How do you explain your answer or answers? Your introduction is the place to establish ideas and justifications of this sort.

The following approaches for discussing rhetorical figures are not mutually exclusive, and you may combine them as you wish. Most likely, your essay will bring in most of the following classifications.

1. *Interpret the meaning and effect of the figures.* Here you explain how the figures enable you to make an interpretation. In the second stanza of "A Valediction: Forbidding Mourning," for example, the following metaphor introduces church hierarchy and religious mystery to explain lovers and their love.

'Twere profanation of our joys
To tell the laity our love.

Here Donne emphasizes the mystical relationship of two lovers, drawing the metaphor from the religious tradition whereby any popular explanation of religious mysteries is considered a desecration. A directly explanatory approach such as this requires that metaphors, similes, or other figures be expanded and interpreted, including the explanation of necessary references and allusions.

2. *Analyze the frames of reference and their appropriateness to the subject matter.* Here you classify and locate the sources and types of the references and determine the appropriateness of these to the poem's subject matter. Ask questions similar to those you might ask in a study of imagery: Does the writer refer extensively to nature, science, warfare, politics, business, reading (e.g., Shakespeare's metaphor equating personal reverie with courtroom proceedings)? Does the metaphor seem appropriate? How? Why?

3. *Focus on the interests and sensibilities of the poet.* In a way this approach is like strategy 2, but the emphasis here is on what the selectivity of the writer might show about his or her vision and interests. You might begin by listing the figures in the poem and then determining the sources, just as you would do in discussing the sources of images generally. But then you should raise questions like the following: Does the writer use figures derived from one sense rather than another (i.e., sight, hearing, taste, smell, touch)? Does he or she record color, brightness, shadow, shape, depth, height, number, size, slowness, speed, emptiness, fullness, richness, drabness? Has the writer relied on the associations of figures of sense? Do metaphors and similes referring to green plants and trees, to red roses, or to rich fabrics, for example, suggest that life is full and beautiful, or do references to touch suggest amorous warmth? This approach is designed to help you draw conclusions about the author's taste or sensibility.

4. *Examine the effect of one figure on the other figures and ideas of the poem.* The assumption of this approach is that each literary work is unified and organically whole, so that each part is closely related and inseparable from everything else. Usually it is best to pick a figure that occurs at the beginning of the poem and then determine how this figure influences your perception of the rest of the poem. Your aim is to consider the relationship of part to parts and part to whole. The beginning of Donne's "A Valediction: Forbidding Mourning," for example, contains a simile comparing the parting of the speaker and his listener to the quiet dying of "virtuous men." What is the effect of this comparison upon the poem? To help you with questions like this, you might substitute a totally different detail, such as, here, the violent death of a condemned criminal, or the slaughter of a domestic animal, rather than the deaths of "virtuous men." Such suppositions, which would clearly be out of place, may help you understand and then explain the poet's figures of speech.

In your conclusion, summarize your main points, describe your general impressions, try to describe the impact of the figures, indicate your personal responses, or show what might further be done along the lines you have been developing. If you know other works by the same writer, or other works by other writers who use comparable or contrasting figures, you might explain the relationship of the other work or works to your present analysis.

Illustrative Student Paragraph

Wordsworth's Use of Overstatement in "London, 1802"°

Through overstatement in "London, 1802," Wordsworth emphasizes his tribute to Milton as a master of idealistic thought.* The speaker's claim that England is "a fen/Of stagnant waters" (lines 2–3) is overstated, as is the implication that people ("We") in England have no "manners, virtue, freedom, power" (6, 8). With the overstatements, however, Wordsworth implies that the nation's well-being depends on the constant flow of creative thoughts by persons of great ideas. Because Milton was clearly the greatest of these, in the view of Wordsworth's speaker, the overstatements stress the need for leadership. Milton is the model, and the overstated criticism lays the foundation in the real political and moral world for the rebirth of another Milton. Thus, through overstatement, Wordsworth emphasizes Milton's importance and in this way pays tribute to him.

°This poem appears on page 667.
*Central idea.

Commentary on the Paragraph

This paragraph deals with a single rhetorical figure, in this case Wordsworth's overstatements in "London, 1802." Although most often the figure of speech will be fairly obvious, as this one in "London, 1802" is, prominence is not a requirement. In addition, there is no need to write an excessively long paragraph. The goal here is not to describe all the details of Wordsworth's overstatement but to show how the figure affects his tribute to Milton. For this reason the paragraph illustrates clear and direct support of the major point.

Illustrative Student Essay

Although underlined sentences are not recommended by MLA style, they are used in this illustrative essay as teaching tools to emphasize the central idea, thesis sentence, and topic sentences.

Carter 1

David Carter

Professor Hernandez

English 123

17 December 2014

A Study of Shakespeare's Metaphors in Sonnet 30:

"When to the Sessions of Sweet Silent Thought"°

[1]   In this sonnet Shakespeare's speaker stresses the sadness and regret of remembered experience, but he states that a person with these feelings may be cheered by the thought of a friend. His metaphors, cleverly used, create new and fresh ways of seeing personal life in this perspective.* He presents metaphors drawn from the public and business world of law courts, money, and banking or money-handling.†

[2]   The courtroom metaphor of the first four lines shows that memories of past experience are constantly present and influential. Like a judge commanding defendants to appear in court, the speaker "summon[s]" his memory of "things past" to appear on trial before him. This metaphor suggests that people are their own judges and that their ideals and morals are like laws by which they measure themselves. The speaker finds himself guilty of wasting his time in the past. Removing himself, however, from the strict punishment that a real judge might require, he does not condemn himself for his "dear time's waste," but instead laments it (4). The metaphor is thus used to indicate that a person's consciousness is made up just as much of self-doubt and reproach as by more positive qualities.

[3]   With the closely related reference of money in the next group of four lines, Shakespeare shows that living is a lifelong investment and is greatly valuable for this reason. According to the money metaphor, living requires the spending of emotions

°This poem appears on page 663.
*Central idea.
†Thesis sentence.

Carter 2

and commitment to others. When friends move away and loved ones die, it is as though a fortune has been lost. Thus, the speaker's dead friends are "precious" because he invested time and love in them, and the "sights" that have "vanished" from his eyes make him "moan" because he went to great "expense" for them (8).

Like the money metaphor, the metaphor of banking or money-handling in the next four lines emphasizes that memory is a bank in which life's experiences are deposited. The full emotions surrounding experience are recorded there, and may be withdrawn in moments of "sweet silent thought" just as a depositor may withdraw money. Thus the speaker states that he counts out the sad parts of his experience—his woe—just as a merchant or banker counts money: "And heavily from woe to woe tell o'er" (10). Because strong emotions still accompany his memories of past mistakes, the metaphor extends to borrowing and the payment of interest. The speaker thus says that he pays again with "new" woe the accounts that he had already paid with old woe. The metaphor suggests that the past is so much a part of the present that a person never stops feeling pain and regret.

[4]

The legal, financial, and money-handling metaphors combine in the last two lines to show how a healthy present life may overcome past regrets. The "dear friend" being addressed in these lines has the resources (financial) to settle all the emotional judgments that the speaker as a self-judge has made against himself (legal). It is as though the friend is a rich patron who rescues him from emotional bankruptcy (legal and financial) and the possible doom resulting from the potential sentence of emotional misery and depression (legal).

[5]

In these metaphors, therefore, Shakespeare's references are drawn from everyday public and business actions, but his use of them is creative and brilliant. In particular, the idea of line 8 ("And moan th'expense of many a vanished sight") stresses that people spend much emotional energy in preserving their friendships. Without such personal commitment, one cannot have precious friends and loved ones. In keeping with this metaphor of money and investment, one could measure life not in months or years, but in the spending of emotion and involvement in personal relationships. Shakespeare, by inviting readers to explore the values brought out by his metaphors, gives new insights into the nature and value of life.

[6]

Carter 3

Work Cited

Shakespeare, William. "Sonnet 30: When to the Sessions of Sweet Silent
Thought." *Literature: An Introduction to Reading and Writing, Compact
Edition.* Ed. Edgar V. Roberts and Robert Zweig. 6th ed. New York:
Pearson, 2015. 663. Print.

Commentary on the Essay

This essay treats the three classes of metaphors that Shakespeare introduces in
Sonnet 30. It thus illustrates the second strategy described on page 671. But the aim
of the discussion is not to explore the extent and nature of the comparison between
the metaphors and the personal situations described in the sonnet. Instead, the
object is to explain how the metaphors develop Shakespeare's meaning. This essay
therefore also illustrates the first strategy described on page 672.

In addition to providing a brief description of the sonnet, the introduction brings out the central idea and the thesis sentence. Paragraph 2 deals with
the meaning of Shakespeare's courtroom metaphor. His money metaphor is
explained in paragraph 3. Paragraph 4 considers the banking or money-handling
figure. Paragraph 5 shows how Shakespeare's last two lines bring together the
three strands of metaphor. The conclusion comments generally on the creativity
of Shakespeare's metaphors, and it also amplifies the way in which the money
metaphor leads toward an increased understanding of life.

Throughout the essay, transitions are brought about by the linking words in
the topic sentences. In paragraph 3, for example, the words "closely related" and
"next group" move the reader from paragraph 2 to the new content. In paragraph 4,
the words effecting the transition are "like the money metaphor" and "the next
four lines." The opening sentence of paragraph 5 refers collectively to the subjects
of paragraphs 2, 3, and 4, thereby focusing them on the new topic of paragraph 5.

Writing Topics About Figures of Speech in Poetry

Writing Paragraphs

1. Consider one metaphor or simile from a poem in this chapter. Write a paragraph
   in which you answer the following questions. How effective is this metaphor or
   simile? How does the metaphor or simile help you to better understand the poem?

Writing Essays

1. Study the simile of the "stiff twin compasses" in Donne's "A Valediction:
   Forbidding Mourning." Using such a compass or a drawing of one, write an

essay that demonstrates the accuracy, or lack of it, of Donne's descriptions. What light does the simile shed on the relationship of two lovers? How does it emphasize any or all of these aspects of love: closeness, immediacy, extent, importance, duration, intensity?

2. Consider some of the metaphors and similes in various poems in which you are interested. Write an essay that answers the following questions. How effective are the figures you select? (Examples: a rose [Burns], the sunken *Titanic* [Hardy], the summer's day [Shakespeare].) What insights do the figures provide within the contexts of their respective poems? How appropriate are they? Might they be expanded more fully, and if they were, what would be the effect?

3. Consider some of the other rhetorical figures in the poems of this chapter. Write an essay describing the importance of figures of speech in creating emphasis and in extending and deepening the ideas of poetry. Here are some possible topics, all on poems in this chapter.

   a. Paradox in Wyatt's "I Find No Peace" or Whitman's "Facing West from California's Shores."

   b. Metaphor in Minty's "Conjoined" or Piercy's "A Work of Artifice."

   c. Metaphor and simile in Hardy's "The Convergence of the Twain."

   d. Anaphora in Rukeyser's "Looking at Each Other," Harjo's "Remember," Kenyon's "Let Evening Come," or Oliver's "Showing the Birds."

   e. A comparison of contrasts and paradoxes in Queen Elizabeth's "On Monsieur's Departure" and Wyatt's "I Find No Peace."

   f. Similes in Donne's "A Valediction: Forbidding Mourning," personification in the poems by Wordsworth or Keats; metonymy in Keats's "To Autumn."

Creative Writing Assignment

1. Write a poem in which you create a governing metaphor or simile. Examples: "My girlfriend/boyfriend is like (a) an opening flower, (b) a difficult book, (c) an insoluble mathematical problem, (d) a bill that cannot be paid, (e) a slow-moving chess game." "Teaching a person how to do a particular job is like (a) shoveling heavy snow, (b) climbing a mountain during a landslide, (c) having someone force you underwater when you're gasping for breath." When you finish, describe the relationship between your comparison and the development and structure of your poem.

Library Assignment

1. In your library's reference section, find the third edition of J. A. Cuddon's *A Dictionary of Literary Terms and Literary Theory* (1991) or some other dictionary of literary terms that you find under "list of literary terms" on Google. Study the entries for *metaphysical* and *conceit*, and write a brief report on these sections. You might attempt to answer questions like these: What is meant by the word *conceit*? What are some of the kinds of conceit the reference work discusses? What is a metaphysical conceit? Who are some of the writers considered metaphysical? In the "metaphysical" entry, of what importance is John Donne?

Chapter 15
Tone: The Creation of Attitude in Poetry

AFTER STUDYING THIS MATERIAL, YOU SHOULD BE ABLE TO DO THE FOLLOWING:

- Understand the concept of tone and its use in poems
- Recognize different types of irony in poetry
- Assess the impact of tone on poems

Tone, a concept derived from the phrase *tone of voice,* describes the shaping of attitudes in poetry (see also Chapter 6, on tone and style in fiction). Each poet's choice of words governs the reader's responses, as do the participants and situations in the poem. In addition, the poet shapes responses through denotation and connotation, seriousness or humor, irony, metaphors, similes, understatement, overstatement, and other figures of speech (see Chapter 14). Of major importance is the poem's speaker. How much self-awareness does the speaker show? What is his or her background? What relationship does the speaker establish with listeners and readers? What does the speaker assume about the readers and about their knowledge? How do these assumptions affect the ideas and the diction?

Sentences must be just long enough to achieve the poet's intended effect—no shorter and no longer. In a conversational style there should be few if any formal words, just as in a formal style there should be no slang, no rollicking rhythms, and no frivolous rhymes—that is, unless the poet deliberately wants readers to be startled or shocked. In all the features that contribute to a poem's tone, the poet's consistency of intention is primary. Any unintentional deviations will cause the poem to sink and the poet to fail.

Tone, Choice, and Response

Remember that a major objective of poets is to stimulate, enrich, and inspire readers. Poets may begin their poems with a brief idea, a vague feeling, or a fleeting impression. Then, in the light of their developing design, they *choose* what to say—the form of their material and the words and phrases to express their ideas. The poem "Theme for English B" by Langston Hughes illustrates this process in almost outline form (see Chapter 18, p. 861). Hughes's speaker lays out many interests that he shares with his intended reader, his English teacher, for the poem is imagined to be a response to a classroom assignment. In this way Hughes encourages all readers to accept his ideas of human equality.

In the long run, readers might not accept all the ideas in any poem, but the successful poem gains agreement—at least for a time—because the poet's control over tone is right. Each poem attempts to evoke total responses, which might be destroyed by any lapses in tone. Let us look at a poem in which the tone misses, and misses badly.

CORNELIUS WHUR (1782–1853)

The First-Rate Wife (1837)

This brief effusion I indite,
   And my vast wishes send,
That thou mayst be directed right,
And have ere long within thy sight
   A most *enchanting* friend!   5

The *maiden* should have *lovely face*,
   And be of *genteel mien*;
If not, within thy dwelling place,
There may be vestige of disgrace,
   Not much admired—when seen.   10

Nor will thy dearest be complete
   Without *domestic* care;
If otherwise, howe'er discreet,
Thine eyes will very often meet
   What none desire to share!   15

And further still—thy future *dear*,
   Should have some *mental* ray;
If not, thou mayest drop a tear,
Because no *real sense* is there
   To charm life's dreary day!   20

QUESTIONS

1. What kind of person is the poem's speaker? What is the situation? What requirements does the speaker create for the "first-rate wife"?
2. Describe the poem's tone. How does the speaker's character influence the tone? In light of the tone, to what degree can the poem be considered insulting?
3. How might lines 14 and 15 be interpreted as a possible threat if the woman as a wife does not keep the house clean and straight?

In this poem the speaker is talking to a friend or associate and is explaining his requirements for a "first-rate wife." From his tone, he clearly regards getting married as little more than hiring a pretty housekeeper. In the phrase "some *mental* ray," for example, the word *some* does not mean "a great deal" but is more like "*at least* some," as though nothing more could be expected of a woman. Even allowing for the fact that the poem was written early in the nineteenth century and represents a benighted view of women and marriage, "The First-Rate Wife" offends most readers. Do you wonder why you've never heard of Cornelius Whur before?

Tone and the Need for Control

"The First-Rate Wife" demonstrates the need for the poet to be in control over all facets of the poem. The speaker must be aware of his or her situation and should not, like Whur's speaker, demonstrate any smugness or insensitivity, unless the poet is deliberately revealing the shortcomings of the speaker by dramatizing them for the reader's amusement, as E. E. Cummings does in the poem "next to of course god america i" (Chapter 12). In a poem with well-controlled tone, details and situations should be factually correct; observations should be logical and fair, and also comprehensive and generally applicable. The following poem, based on battlefield conditions in World War I, illustrates a masterly control over tone.

WILFRED OWEN (1893–1918)

Dulce et Decorum Est° (1920)

Bent double, like old beggars under sacks,
Knock-kneed, coughing like hags, we cursed through sludge,
Till on the haunting flares we turned our backs
And towards our distant rest began to trudge.
5 Men marched asleep. Many had lost their boots
But limped on, blood-shod. All went lame; all blind;
Drunk with fatigue; deaf even to the hoots
Of tired, outstripped Five-Nines° that dropped behind.

Gas!° GAS! Quick, boys!—An ecstasy of fumbling,
10 Fitting the clumsy helmets° just in time;
But someone still was yelling out and stumbling
And flound'ring like a man in fire or lime . . .
Dim, through the misty panes and thick green° light,
As under a green sea, I saw him drowning.

15 In all my dreams, before my helpless sight,
He plunges at me, guttering, choking, drowning.
If in some smothering dreams you too could pace
Behind the wagon that we flung him in,
And watch the white eyes writhing in his face,
20 His hanging face, like a devil's sick of sin;

°The Latin title is taken from Horace's *Odes*, Book 3, line 13: *Dulce et decorum est pro patria mori* ("It is sweet and honorable to die for the fatherland"). °8 *Five-Nines:* A "five-nine" was a 5.9-inch German high-explosive artillery shell that made a hooting sound before landing. °9 *Gas:* Chlorine gas was used as an antipersonnel weapon in 1915 by the Germans at Ypres, in Belgium. °10 *helmets:* Soldiers of World War I carried gas masks as normal battle equipment. °13 *thick green:* The deadly chlorine gas used in gas attacks has a greenish-yellow color.

If you could hear, at every jolt, the blood
Come gargling from the froth-corrupted lungs,
Obscene as cancer, bitter as the cud
Of vile, incurable sores on innocent tongues.—
My friend, you would not tell with such high zest   25
To children ardent for some desperate glory,
The old Lie: *Dulce et decorum est*
Pro patria mori.

QUESTIONS

1. What is the scene described in lines 1–8? What expressions does the speaker use to indicate his attitude toward the conditions?
2. What does the title of the poem mean? What attitude or conviction does it embody?
3. Does the speaker really mean "my friend" in line 25? In what tone of voice might this phrase be spoken?
4. What is the tonal relationship between the patriotic fervor of the Latin phrase and the images of the poem? How does the tonal contrast create the dominant tone of the poem?

The tone of "Dulce et Decorum Est" never lapses. The poet intends the description to evoke a response of horror and shock, for he contrasts the strategic goals of warfare with the speaker's personal experience of terror in battle. The speaker's language skillfully emphasizes first the dreariness and fatigue of warfare (with words like "sludge," "trudge," "lame," and "blind") and second the agony of violent death from chlorine gas (embodied in the participles "guttering," "choking," "drowning," "smothering," and "writhing"). With these details established, the concluding attack against the "glory" of war is difficult to refute, even if warfare is undertaken to defend or preserve one's country. Although the details about the agonized death may distress or discomfort a sensitive reader, they are not designed to do that alone but instead are integral to the poem's argument. Ultimately, it is the contrast between the high ideals of the Latin phrase and the ugliness of battlefield death that creates the dominant tone of the poem. The Latin phrase treats war and death in the abstract; the poem makes images of battle and death vividly real. The resultant tone is that of controlled bitterness and irony.

Tone and Common Grounds of Assent

Not all those reading Owen's poem will deny that war is sometimes necessary; the issues of politics and warfare are far too complex for that. But the poem does show another important aspect of tone—namely, the degree to which the poet judges and tries to control responses through the establishment of a *common ground of assent*. An appeal to a bond of commonly held interests, concerns, and assumptions is essential if a poet is to maintain an effective tone. Owen, for example, does not create arguments against the necessity of a just war. Instead, he bases the poem on realistic details about the choking, writhing, spastic death suffered by the speaker's comrade; he also appeals to emotions that everyone, pacifist and militarist alike, would feel—horror at the contemplation of violent death. Even assuming a widely divergent audience, in other words, the *tone* of the poem is successful because it is based on commonly acknowledged facts and commonly felt emotions. Knowing a poem like this one, even advocates of a strong military would need to defend their ideas on the grounds of *preventing* just such needless, ugly deaths. Owen carefully considers the responses of his readers, and he regulates speaker, situation, detail, and argument in order to make the poem acceptable for the broadest possible spectrum of opinion.

TONE IN CONVERSATION AND POETRY

Many readers think that tone is a subtle and difficult subject, but it is nevertheless true that in ordinary situations we master tone easily and expertly (see Chapter 6). We constantly use standard questions and statements that deal with tone, such as "What do you mean by that?" "What I'm saying is this . . . ," and "Did I hear you correctly?" together with other comments that extend to humor and, sometimes, to hostility. In poetry we do not have everyday speech situations; we have only the poems themselves and are guided by the materials they provide us. Some poems are straightforward and unambiguous, but in other poems feeling and mood are essential to our understanding. In Hardy's "The Workbox" (this chapter), for example, the husband's hand-made gift to his wife indicates not love but suspicion. Also, the husband's relentless linking of the dead man's coffin to the gift reveals both doubt and anger. In Komunyakaa's "Facing It" (this chapter), the speaker assumes a tone that suggests his struggle to exhibit mental toughness and emotional control, which he finds difficult to maintain as he confronts the great human tragedy symbolized by the Vietnam Veterans Memorial Wall:

> I said I wouldn't,
> dammit: No tears.
> I'm stone. I'm flesh.

Of course, poems may also reveal respect and wonder, as shown in the last six lines of Keats's "On First Looking into Chapman's Homer" (Chapter 14). By attending carefully to the details of such poems, you can draw conclusions about poetic tone that are as accurate as those you draw in normal speech situations.

Tone and Irony

Irony is a mode of indirection, a means of making a point by emphasizing a discrepancy or opposite (see also Chapter 6). Thus Owen uses the title "Dulce et Decorum Est" to emphasize that death in warfare is not sweet and honorable but rather demeaning and horrible. The title ironically reminds us of eloquent holiday speeches at the tombs of unknown soldiers, but as we have seen, it also reminds us of the reality of the agonized death of Owen's soldier. As an aspect of tone, therefore, irony is a powerful way of conveying attitudes, for it draws your attention to at least two ways of seeing a situation, enabling you not only to *understand* but also to *experience*. Poetry shares with fiction the three primary kinds of ironies that afflict human beings: *verbal irony*, *situational irony*, and *dramatic irony*.

Verbal Irony, Through Word Selection, Emphasizes Ambiguities and Discrepancies

At almost any point in a poem, a poet may introduce the ironic effects of language itself—**verbal irony.** Cummings's poem "she being Brand/-new" is built on the double meanings derived from the procedures of breaking in a new car. Indeed, the entire poem is a virtuoso piece of double entendre. Another example of verbal irony occurs in Theodore Roethke's "My Papa's Waltz," in which the speaker uses the name of this graceful and stately dance to describe his childhood memories of his father's whirling him around the kitchen in wild, boisterous drunkenness.

Life's Anomalies and Uncertainties Underlie Situational Irony

Situational irony is derived from the discrepancies between the ideal and the actual. People would like to live their lives in terms of a standard of love, friendship, honor, success, and general excellence, but the irony is that the reality of their lives often falls far short of such standards. Whereas in fiction ironic situations emerge from extended narrative, in poetry such situations are usually at a high point or climax, and we must infer the narrative circumstances that have gone on before. Thomas Hardy, in "The Workbox," skillfully exploits an ironic situation between a husband and a wife.

THOMAS HARDY (1840–1928)

For a photo, see Chapter 11, page 548.

 The Workbox (1914)

"See, here's the workbox, little wife,
    That I made of polished oak."
He was a joiner,° of village° life;   cabinetmaker
    She came of borough° folk.

He holds the present up to her   5
    As with a smile she nears
And answers to the profferer,
    " 'Twill last all my sewing years!"

"I warrant it will. And longer too.
    'Tis a scantling° that I got   10
Off poor John Wayward's coffin, who
    Died of they knew not what.

°3, 4 *village, borough:* An English village was small and rustic; a borough was larger and more sophisticated.
°10 *scantling:* a small leftover piece of wood.

"The shingled pattern that seems to cease
    Against your box's rim
15 Continues right on in the piece
    That's underground with him.

"And while I worked it made me think
    Of timber's varied doom:
One inch where people eat and drink,
20   The next inch in a tomb.

"But why do you look so white, my dear,
    And turn aside your face?
You knew not that good lad, I fear,
    Though he came from your native place?"

25 "How could I know that good young man,
    Though he came from my native town,
When he must have left far earlier than
    I was a woman grown?"

"Ah, no. I should have understood!
30   It shocked you that I gave
To you one end of a piece of wood
    Whose other is in a grave?"

"Don't, dear, despise my intellect.
    Mere accidental things
35 Of that sort never have effect
    On my imaginings."

Yet still her lips were limp and wan,
    Her face still held aside,
As if she had known not only John,
40   But known of what he died.

QUESTIONS

1. Who does most of the speaking? What does the speaker's tone show about the characters of the husband and the wife? What does the tone indicate about the poet's attitude toward them?

2. What do lines 21–40 indicate about the wife's knowledge of John and about her earlier relationship with him? Why does she deny such knowledge? What does the last stanza show about her? Why is John's death kept a mystery?

3. In lines 17–20, what irony is suggested by the fact that the wood was used both for John Wayward's coffin and the workbox?

4. Why is the husband's irony more complex than he realizes? What do his words and actions show about his character?

5. The narrator, or poet, speaks only in lines 3–7 and 37–40. How much of his explanation is essential? How much shows his attitude? How might the poem have been more effectively concluded?

"The Workbox" is a domestic drama of deception, cruelty, and sadness. The complex details are evidence of situational irony, that is, an awareness that human beings do not control their lives but are rather controlled by powerful forces—in this case by both death and earlier feelings and commitments. Beyond this domestic irony, Hardy also emphasizes symbolically the direct connection that death has with the living. As a result of the husband's gift made of the wood with which he has also made a coffin for the dead man, the wife will never escape being reminded of this man. Within the existence imagined in the poem, she will have to live with regret and the constant need to deny her true emotions, and her situation is therefore endlessly ironic.

Dramatic Irony Is Built on the Ignorance of Characters and the Greater Knowledge of Readers

In addition to the situational irony of "The Workbox," the wife's deception reveals that the husband is in a situation of **dramatic irony.** He does not know the circumstances of his wife's past, and he does not actually *know*—though he suspects—that his wife is not being truthful about her earlier relationship with the dead man; but the poem is sufficient to enable readers to draw the right conclusions. By emphasizing the wood, the husband is apparently trying to make his wife uncomfortable, even to the point of extracting a confession from her; but he has only his suspicions, and he therefore remains unsure of the truth and also of his wife's feelings. Because of these uncertainties, Hardy has deftly used dramatic irony to create a poem of great complexity and pathos.

Tone and Satire

Satire, a vital genre in the study of tone, is designed to expose human follies and vices. In method, a satiric poem may be bitter and vituperative, but often it employs humor and irony, on the grounds that anger turns readers away while a comic tone more easily wins interest and agreement. The speaker of a satiric poem may either attack folly and vice directly, or may dramatically embody the folly or vice himself or herself and thus serve as an illustration of the satiric subject. An example of the first type is the following short poem by Alexander Pope, in which the speaker directly attacks a listener who has claimed to be a poet but whom the speaker considers both a bad poet and a fool. The speaker cleverly uses insult as the method of attack.

ALEXANDER POPE (1688–1744)

The following two poems are by Alexander Pope.

 ### Epigram from the French (1732)

Sir, I admit your general rule
That every poet is a fool:
But you yourself may serve to show it,
That every fool is not a poet.

QUESTIONS

1. What has the listener said before the poem begins? How does the speaker build on the listener's previous comment?
2. Considering this poem as a brief satire, describe the nature of satiric attack and the corresponding tone of attack.
3. Look at the pattern "poet," "fool," "fool," "poet." This is a rhetorical pattern (*a, b, b, a*) called *chiasmus* or *antimetabole*. What does the pattern contribute to the poem's effectiveness?

An example of the second type of satiric poem is another of Pope's epigrams, in which the speaker is an actual embodiment of the subject being attacked.

Epigram, Engraved on the Collar of a Dog Which I Gave to His Royal Highness (1738)

I am his Highness' dog at Kew:°   *the royal palace near London*
Pray tell me sir, whose dog are you?

QUESTIONS

1. Who or what is the subject of the satiric attack?
2. What attitude is expressed toward social pretentiousness?

Here the speaker is, comically, the king's dog, and the listener is an unknown dog. Pope's satire is directed not against canines, however, but against human beings who overemphasize the significance of social class. The first line ridicules those who claim social status that is derived, not earned. The second implies an unwillingness to recognize the listener until the question of rank is resolved. Pope, by using the dog as a speaker, reduces such snobbishness to an absurdity. A similar satiric poem attacking pretentiousness is "next to of course god america i" by Cummings (Chapter 12). In this poem the speaker voices a set of patriotic platitudes, and in doing so illustrates Cummings's satiric point that most speeches of this sort are empty-headed. Satiric tone may thus range widely, being sometimes objective, comic, and distant; sometimes deeply concerned and scornful; and sometimes dramatic, ingenuous, and revelatory. Always, however, the satiric mode aims toward confrontation and exposé.

Poems for Study

W. H. Auden . . . . The Unknown Citizen, 687

William Blake . . . . On Another's Sorrow, 688

Jimmy Carter . . . . I Wanted to Share My Father's World, 689

Lucille Clifton . . . . homage to my hips, 690

Billy Collins . . . . The Names, 691

Countee Cullen . . . . Yet Do I Marvel, 692

E. E. Cummings . . . . she being Brand / -new, 693

Martín Espada . . . . Bully, 694

Mari Evans . . . . I Am a Black Woman, 695

Seamus Heaney . . . . Mid-Term Break, 697

William Ernest Henley . . . . When You Are Old, 697

David Ignatow . . . . The Bagel, 698

Yusef Komunyakaa . . . . Facing It, 699

Abraham Lincoln . . . . My Childhood's Home, 700

Christopher Okigbo . . . . Bright, 701

Sharon Olds . . . . The Planned Child, 702

Arthur O'Shaughnessy . . . . A Love Symphony, 702

Robert Pinsky . . . . Dying, 703

Salvatore Quasímodo . . . . Auschwitz, 704

Theodore Roethke . . . . My Papa's Waltz, 706

William Shakespeare . . . . Fear No More the Heat o' th' Sun, 707

Cathy Song . . . . Lost Sister, 708

C. K. Williams . . . . Dimensions, 709

William Wordsworth . . . . The Solitary Reaper, 710

James Wright . . . . Autumn Begins at Martin's Ferry, Ohio, 711

James Wright . . . . Two Hangovers, 712

William Butler Yeats . . . . When You Are Old, 713

W. H. AUDEN (1907–1973)

For a photo, see Chapter 19, page 888.

 ## The Unknown Citizen (1940)

(To JS/07/M/378
This Marble Monument Is Erected by the State)

He was found by the Bureau of Statistics to be
One against whom there was no official complaint,
And all the reports on his conduct agree
That, in the modern sense of an old-fashioned word, he was a saint,
For in everything he did he served the Greater Community.   5

Except for the War till the day he retired
He worked in a factory and never got fired,
But satisfied his employers, Fudge Motors Inc.
Yet he wasn't a scab° or odd in his views.   *strikebreaker*
For his Union reports that he paid his dues,   10
(Our report on his Union shows it was sound)
And our Social Psychology workers found
That he was popular with his mates° and liked a drink.   *co-workers*
The Press are convinced that he bought a paper every day
And that his reactions to advertisements were normal in every way.   15
Policies taken out in his name prove that he was fully insured,
And his Health-card shows he was once in hospital but left it cured.

Both Producers Research and High-Grade Living declare
He was fully sensible to the advantages of the Installment Plan
20   And had everything necessary to the Modern Man,
A phonograph, a radio, a car and a frigidaire.
Our researchers into Public Opinion are content
That he held the proper opinions for the time of year;
When there was peace, he was for peace; when there was war, he went.
25   He was married and added five children to the population,
Which our Eugenist says was the right number for a parent of his generation,
And our teachers report that he never interfered with their education.
Was he free? Was he happy? The question is absurd:
Had anything been wrong, we should certainly have heard.

QUESTIONS

1. Can you judge a person's happiness or sense of freedom by how he or she appears to others? What do you need to know to decide if a person is happy or feels free?

2. Do you think that Auden agrees with the speaker's conclusions?

3. Are there any statistics cited that might lead you to believe that the "unknown citizen" was happy?

WILLIAM BLAKE (1757–1827)

For a portrait, see Chapter 12, page 581.

On Another's Sorrow (1789)

Can I see another's woe,
And not be in sorrow too.
Can I see another's grief,
And not seek for kind relief.

5   Can I see a falling tear,
And not feel my sorrows share,
Can a father see his child
Weep, nor be with sorrow filled.

Can a mother sit and hear,
10 An infant groan an infant fear—
No never can it be.
Never never can it be.

And can he who smiles on all
Hear the wren with sorrows small,
15 Hear the small birds grief & care
Hear the woes that infants bear—

And not sit beside the nest
Pouring pity in their breast,
And not sit the cradle near
20 Weeping tear on infants tear.

And not sit both night & day,
Wiping all our tears away.
O! no never can it be.
Never never can it be.

He doth give his joy to all.   25
He becomes an infant small.
He becomes a man of woe
He doth feel the sorrow too.

Think not, thou canst sigh a sigh,
And thy maker is not by.   30
Think not, thou canst weep a tear,
And thy maker is not near.

O! he gives to us his joy,
That our grief he may destroy
Till our grief is fled & gone   35
He doth sit by us and moan.

QUESTIONS

1. Describe the character of this poem's speaker. What is he like? What are the circumstances of the persons in need of sympathy?

2. Describe the tone of the poem. What connection with human suffering does the speaker establish with human sympathy and with the divine "maker"?

3. Why do you think Blake uses the word "maker" (line 32) rather than God? According to the poem, what are the continuing roles of the maker among human beings? What assurances do people in sorrow have from their belief in divinity?

JIMMY CARTER (b. 1924)

 I Wanted to Share My Father's World (1995)

This is a pain I mostly hide,
but ties of blood, or seed, endure,
and even now I feel inside
the hunger for his outstretched hand,
a man's embrace to take me in,   5
the need for just a word of praise.

I despised the discipline
he used to shape what I should be,
not owning up that he might feel
his own pain when he punished me.   10

I didn't show my need to him,
since his response to an appeal
would not have meant as much to me,
or been as real.

15   From those rare times when we did cross
     the bridge between us, the pure joy
     survives.
           I never put aside
     the past resentments of the boy
20   until, with my own sons, I shared
     his final hours, and came to see
     what he'd become, or always was—
     the father who will never cease to be
     alive in me.

QUESTIONS

1. This poem is about the remembered attitudes of President Carter's speaker toward his father. What is the nature of these attitudes? To what degree are these attitudes of sons to fathers either usual or unusual? Why does the speaker state in line 1, "This is a pain I mostly hide"?

2. Why does the speaker use the words "despised" (line 7) and "resentments" (line 18)? Why does he mention "those rare times" in line 15?

3. What is the tone of the last stanza? Why does the speaker refer to going with his own sons to share the "final hours" of his father? What is the tone of the final two lines?

LUCILLE CLIFTON (1936–2010)

🖋 homage to my hips (1987)

these hips are big hips
they need space to
move around in.
they don't fit into little
5 petty places, these hips
are free hips.
they don't like to be held back.
these hips have never been enslaved.
they go where they want to go.
10 they do what they want to do.
these hips are mighty hips.
these hips are magic hips.
i have known them
to put a spell on a man and
15 spin him like a top!

QUESTIONS

1. What is unusual about the subject matter? Considering that some people are embarrassed to mention their hips, what attitudes does the speaker express here?

2. How do the words "enslaved," "want to go," "want to do," "mighty," and "spell" define the poem's ideas about the relationship between mentality and physicality?

3. To what degree is this a comic poem? What about the subject and the diction makes the poem funny?

BILLY COLLINS (b. 1941)

For a photo, see Chapter 11, page 534.

The Names° (2002)

Yesterday, I lay awake in the palm of the night.
A fine rain stole in, unhelped by any breeze,
And when I saw the silver glaze on the windows,
I started with A, with Ackerman, as it happened,
Then Baxter and Calabro,   5
Davis and Eberling, names falling into place
As droplets fell through the dark.

Names printed on the ceiling of the night.
Names slipping around a watery bend.
Twenty-six willows on the banks of a stream.   10

In the morning, I walked out barefoot
Among thousands of flowers
Heavy with dew like the eyes of tears,
And each had a name—
Fiori inscribed on a yellow petal   15
Then Gonzalez and Han, Ishikawa and Jenkins.

Names written in the air
And stitched into the cloth of the day.
A name under a photograph taped to a mailbox.
Monogram on a torn shirt,   20
I see you spelled out on storefront windows
And on the bright unfurled awnings of this city.
I say the syllables as I turn a corner—
Kelly and Lee,
Medina, Nardella, and O'Connor.   25
When I peer into the woods,
I see a thick tangle where letters are hidden
As in a puzzle concocted for children.
Parker and Quigley in the twigs of an ash,
Rizzo, Schubert, Torres, and Upton,   30
Secrets in the boughs of an ancient maple.

Names written in the pale sky.
Names rising in the updraft amid buildings.

Names silent in stone
Or cried out behind a door.   35
Names blown over the earth and out to sea.
In the evening—weakening light, the last swallows.

°*The Names:* This poem was read by Professor Collins before a joint session of the U.S. Congress held in New York City on September 6, 2002. It was first published earlier that day in the *New York Times.*

A boy on a lake lifts his oars.
A woman by a window puts a match to a candle,
40   And the names are outlined on the rose clouds—
Vanacore and Wallace,
(let X stand, if it can, for the ones unfound)
Then Young and Ziminsky, the final jolt of Z.

Names etched on the head of a pin.
45   One name spanning a bridge, another undergoing a tunnel.
A blue name needled into the skin.
Names of citizens, workers, mothers and fathers,
The bright-eyed daughter, the quick son.
Alphabet of names in green rows in a field.
50   Names in the small tracks of birds.
Names lifted from a hat
Or balanced on the tip of the tongue.
Names wheeled into the dim warehouse of memory.
So many names, there is barely room on the walls of the heart.

N.B. In light of the topic of this poem, questions seem superfluous.

COUNTEE CULLEN (1903–1946)

Yet Do I Marvel (1925)

I doubt not God is good, well-meaning, kind,
And did He stoop to quibble could tell why
The little buried mole continues blind,
Why flesh that mirrors Him must some day die,
5   Make plain the reason tortured Tantalus°
Is baited by the fickle fruit, declare
If merely brute caprice dooms Sisyphus°
To struggle up a never-ending stair.
Inscrutable His ways are, and immune
10   To catechism by a mind too strewn
With petty cares to slightly understand
What awful brain compels His awful hand.
Yet do I marvel at this curious thing:
To make a poet black, and bid him sing!

°5 *Tantalus*: a figure in Greek mythology condemned to eternal hunger and thirst. He stood in Hades chin deep in water with a fruit-laden branch just above his head, but could never eat or drink. °7 *Sisyphus*: a figure in Greek mythology condemned to eternally useless labor. He was fated to roll a huge boulder up a hill in Hades, but each time he neared the top, the stone slipped and he had to begin anew.

QUESTIONS

1. What poetic form does Cullen use for "Yet Do I Marvel"? What rhyme scheme does he use in the poem? How does he vary the rhyming lines in accord with the poem's ideas?

2. Why does Cullen begin the poem with the idea that God is "good, well-meaning, kind." Show how Cullen develops the thought of the poem from the idea that God is too busy to "stoop to quibble" (i.e., "if He could take the time to explain things."

What very great puzzles, or mysteries, are brought out in lines 3 through 9? Personally, have you yourself ever considered circumstances as complex and difficult as these? Does this poem shed any light for you in these lines? If so, how so?

3. What might be considered comically ironic about the idea that God is too busy (taking care of the Universe?) to explain the imponderable questions that beset (some) human beings?

4. What is the "curious thing" that causes the speaker to "marvel" at the close of the poem? How might one say that the poem ends on a positive note, even though it may also be considered a questioning as well as a "curious" one?

E. E. CUMMINGS (1894–1962)

For a photo, see Chapter 12, page 584.

she being Brand / -new (1926)

she being Brand

-new;and you
know consequently a
little stiff i was
careful of her and (having   5

thoroughly oiled the universal
joint tested my gas felt of
her radiator made sure her springs were O.

K.)i went right to it flooded-the-carburetor cranked her

up, slipped the   10
clutch (and then somehow got into reverse she
kicked what
the hell) next
minute i was back in neutral tried and

again slo-wly;bare, ly nudg. ing (my   15

lev-er Right-
oh and her gears being in
A 1 shape passed
from low through
second-in-to-high like
greasedlightning) just as we turned the corner of Divinity   20

avenue i touched the accelerator and give

her the juice, good

        (it

was the first ride and believe i we was   25
happy to see how nice she acted right up to
the last minute coming back down by the Public
Gardens i slammed on

the
30   internalexpanding
&
externalcontracting

brakes Bothatonce and
brought allofher tremB
35   -ling
to a:dead.

stand-
;Still)

QUESTIONS

1. How extensive is the verbal irony, the double entendre, in this poem? This poem is considered comic. Do you agree? Why or why not? This poem might also be considered
   sexist. Do you agree? Why or why not?

2. How do the spacing and alignment affect your reading of the poem? How does the
   unexpected and sometimes absent punctuation—such as in line 15, "again slo-wly;bare,
   ly nudg. ing (my"—contribute to the humor?

3. Can this poem in any respect be called off-color or bawdy? How might you refute such
   charges in light of the tone the speaker uses to equate a first sexual experience with the
   breaking in of a new car?

MARTÍN ESPADA (b. 1957)

 **Bully°** (1990)

Boston, Massachusetts, 1987

In the school auditorium
the Theodore Roosevelt statue
is nostalgic
for the Spanish-American War,
5   each fist lonely for a saber
or the reins of anguish-eyed horses,
or a podium to clatter with speeches
glorying in the malaria of conquest.

But now the Roosevelt school
10   is pronounced *Hernández.*
Puerto Rico has invaded Roosevelt
with its army of Spanish-singing children
in the hallways,

°Theodore Roosevelt led his victorious troop of "Rough Riders" against Spanish opponents at the Battle of San
Juan Hill, in southeast Cuba, in 1898. He later claimed that this was a "bully" fight.

brown children devouring
the stockpiles of the cafeteria,   15
children painting *Taíno°* ancestors
that leap naked across murals.

Roosevelt is surrounded
by all the faces
he ever shoved in eugenic spite   20
and cursed as mongrels, skin of one race,
hair and cheekbones of another.

Once Marines tramped
from the newsreel of his imagination;
now children plot to spray graffiti   25
in parrot-brilliant colors
across the Victorian mustache
and monocle.

°16 *Taíno:* The Pre-Columbian people of the Caribbean islands. When European explorers first came to the Caribbean area, they reported that the Taíno natives wore no clothes.

QUESTIONS

1. What summary can you make of Espada's argument in this poem? Is his argument that the ideals of Theodore Roosevelt were wrong? That Roosevelt's sense of American supremacy over Spanish subjects during the Spanish American War was racist and imperialistic? That time has passed by the period of American supremacy represented by the American defeat of Spain in the war? That modern Spanish residents in the United States have made the views of Roosevelt and others like him obsolete? Write an essay arguing for one of these views, or for another view that you wish to uphold.

2. Considering the details of the poem, describe the speaker's tone. What do you think is his attitude toward Roosevelt personally, as supported by the details of the poem? What attitude is expressed by the phrase "glorying in the malaria of conquest"?

3. Consider the tone of the final stanza (lines 23–28). What might the speaker be suggesting by the phrase "parrot-brilliant colors"?

4. How can the poem's title, "Bully," be considered ambiguously? What are the political implications of this ambiguity?

MARI EVANS (b. 1923)

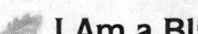 I Am a Black Woman (1970)

I am a black woman
the music of my song
some sweet arpeggio of tears
is written in a minor key

5 and I
can be heard humming in the night
Can be heard
    humming
in the night

10 I saw my mate leap screaming to the sea
and I / with these hands / cupped the lifebreath
from my issue in the canebreak
I lost Nat's swinging body° in a rain of tears

and heard my son scream all the way from Anzio°
15 for Peace he never knew . . . I

learned Da Nang° and Pork Chop Hill°
in anguish
Now my nostrils know the gas
and these trigger tire / d fingers
20 seek the softness in my warrior's beard
I
am a black woman
tall as a cypress
strong
25 beyond all definition still
defying place
and time
and circumstance
    assailed
30   impervious
          indestructible

Look
    on me and be
renewed

°13 *Nat's swinging body*: Nat Turner was hanged in 1831 for leading a slave revolt in Southampton, Virginia.
°14 *Anzio*: seacoast town in Italy, the scene of fierce fighting between the Allies and the Germans in 1943 during
World War II. °16 *Da Nang*: major American military base in South Vietnam, frequently attacked during the
Vietnam War. °*Pork Chop Hill*: site of a bloody battle between UN and Communist forces during the Korean
War (1950–1953).

QUESTIONS

1. What attitude is indicated by the phrase "sweet arpeggio of tears"? How does "in a minor key" complete both the idea and the comparison?

2. What phrases and descriptions does the speaker use to indicate her attitudes of anguish, despair, pain, and indignation?

3. In the last fourteen lines, what contrasting attitude is expressed? How does the speaker make this attitude clear? On balance, is the poem optimistic or pessimistic? Why?

SEAMUS HEANEY (b. 1939)

Mid-Term Break (1966)

I sat all morning in the college sick bay
Counting bells knelling classes to a close.
At two o'clock our neighbors drove me home.

In the porch I met my father crying—
He had always taken funerals in his stride—   5
And Big Jim Evans saying it was a hard blow.

The baby cooed and laughed and rocked the pram
When I came in, and I was embarrassed
By old men standing up to shake my hand

And tell me they were "sorry for my trouble,"   10
Whispers informed strangers I was the eldest,
Away at school, as my mother held my hand

In hers and coughed out angry tearless sighs.
At ten o'clock the ambulance arrived
With the corpse, stanched and bandaged by the nurses.   15

Next morning I went up into the room. Snowdrops
And candles soothed the bedside; I saw him
For the first time in six weeks. Paler now,

Wearing a poppy bruise on his left temple,
He lay in the four foot box as in his cot.   20
No gaudy scars, the bumper knocked him clear.

A four foot box, a foot for every year.

QUESTIONS

1. What is the situation of the poem? Who is the speaker? Why has he been called to come home? What are his responses to the circumstances at home?

2. How old was the speaker's brother at the time of the accident? How do you know? When you read line 19, what do you at first make of the "poppy bruise"?

3. Describe your responses to the last four lines of the poem the first time you read them. What clues in the earlier part of the poem prepare you for these final three lines? Do they sufficiently prepare you, or does the final line come as a surprise? Why is the poem unrhymed until the final two lines?

WILLIAM ERNEST HENLEY (1849–1903)

When You Are Old (1888)

When you are old, and I am passed away—
Passed, and your face, your golden face, is gray—

I think whate'er the end, this dream of mine,
Comforting you, a friendly star will shine
5   Down the dim slope where still you stumble and stray.
So may it be: that so dead Yesterday,
No sad-eyed ghost but generous and gay,
May serve you memories like almighty wine,
        When you are old!
10 Dear Heart, it shall be so. Under the sway
Of death the past's enormous disarray
Lies hushed and dark. Yet though there come no sign,
Live on well pleased; immortal and divine
Love shall still tend you, as God's angels may,
15   When you are old.

QUESTIONS

1. Describe the organization of thought as it is affected by time. How much attention is given to a visualization of the old age of the listener? What does the speaker imagine will have happened to him? What consolation does the speaker believe the listener will have in this future period?

2. What comfort does the speaker say will justify the listener's living on "well pleased" (line 13)? What "shall still tend" the listener? Why does the speaker say "God's angels may" rather than "God's angels will"?

DAVID IGNATOW (1914–1997)

The Bagel (1993)

I stopped to pick up the bagel
rolling away in the wind,
annoyed with myself
for having dropped it
5   as if it were a portent.
Faster and faster it rolled,
with me running after it
bent low, gritting my teeth,
and I found myself doubled over
10 and rolling down the street
head over heels, one complete somersault
after another like a bagel
and strangely happy with myself.

QUESTIONS

1. What situation does the speaker describe in this poem? Does it make sense? If it doesn't, what is the real situation that the speaker describes?

2. Considering the tone of the poem, how reasonable is it to conclude that some poems, like some activities, exist solely so that readers—and writer—might simply be made happy and be amused.

YUSEF KOMUNYAKAA (b. 1947)

Facing It (1988)

My black face fades,
hiding inside the black granite.°
I said I wouldn't,
dammit: No tears.
I'm stone. I'm flesh.   5
My clouded reflection eyes me
like a bird of prey, the profile of night
slanted against morning. I turn
this way—the stone lets me go.
I turn that way—I'm inside   10
the Vietnam Veterans Memorial
again, depending on the light
to make a difference.
I go down the 58,022° names,
half-expecting to find   15
my own in letters like smoke.
I touch the name Andrew Johnson;
I see the booby trap's white flash.
Names shimmer on a woman's blouse
but when she walks away   20
the names stay on the wall.
Brushstrokes flash, a red bird's
wings cutting across my stare.
The sky. A plane in the sky.
A white vet's image floats   25
closer to me, then his pale eyes
look through mine. I'm a window.
He's lost his right arm
inside the stone. In the black mirror
a woman's trying to erase names: 30
No, she's brushing a boy's hair.

°2 *black granite:* The Vietnam Veterans Memorial Wall in Washington, D.C., designed by the sculptor Maya Lin (b. 1959), and dedicated in 1982, is composed of polished black granite. Carved into the panels are lists of the names of all the military personnel who died during the Vietnamese War. °14 *58, 002:* In 2007, the list had grown to 58,256 names.

QUESTIONS

1. What sights and actions does the speaker describe in the poem? What does he see? Why does he state that his "black face" fades and is hiding inside the black granite? What is meant by the vet's having "lost his right arm / inside the stone" (lines 28–29)?
2. What other people are at the memorial? What is the significance of what they are doing?
3. Considering the actions of the speaker and the other visitors, how would you characterize the tone of the poem?
4. Compare this poem with "The Vietnam Wall" by Alberto Ríos in Chapter 19.

ABRAHAM LINCOLN (1809–1865)

My Childhood's Home° (1844)

My childhood's home I see again,
    And sadden with the view;
And still, as memory crowds my brain,
    There's pleasure in it too.

5   O Memory! thou midway world
       'Twixt earth and paradise,
Where things decayed and loved ones lost
       In dreamy shadows rise,

And, freed from all that's earthly vile,
10   Seem hallowed, pure, and bright,
Like scenes in some enchanted isle
       All bathed in liquid light.

As dusky mountains please the eye
       When twilight chases day;
15   As bugle-notes that, passing by,
       In distance die away.

As leaving some grand waterfall,
       We, lingering, list its roar—
So memory will hallow all
20   We've known, but know no more.

Near twenty years have passed away
       Since here I bid farewell
To woods and fields, and scenes of play,
       And playmates loved so well.

25   Where many were, but few remain
       Of old familiar things;
But seeing them, to mind again
       The lost and absent brings.

The friends I left the parting day,
30   How changed, as time has sped!
Young childhood grown, strong manhood gray,
       And half of all are dead.

I hear the loved survivors tell
       How nought from death could save
35   Till every sound appears a knell,
       And every spot a grave.

°In 1844, while on a political campaign in Indiana, Lincoln visited the home where he had been raised and where his mother and sister were buried. The occasion prompted him to write this poem.

I range the fields with pensive tread
   And pace the hollow rooms,
And feel (companion of the dead)
   I'm living in the tombs.   40

QUESTIONS

1. How does Lincoln's speaker explain the importance of memory? How is the sentence "So memory will hallow all / We've known, but know no more" (lines 19–20) related to the descriptions and ideas that follow?
2. Do stanzas 6 and 7 seem exaggerated, self-indulgent, or sentimental? What seems to forestall this criticism of the ideas here?
3. What leads the speaker to the conclusion he makes in the last two lines?

CHRISTOPHER OKIGBO (1930–1967)

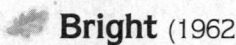 **Bright** (1962)

Bright
with the armpit-dazzle of a lioness,
she answers,

wearing white light about her;

and the waves escort her,   5
my lioness,
crowned with moonlight.

So brief her presence—
match-flare in wind's breath—
so brief with mirrors around me.   10

Downward . .
The waves distil her;
gold crop
sinking ungathered.

Watermaid of the salt-emptiness,   15
grown are the ears of the secret.

QUESTIONS

1. Have you ever seen the image of a human form in nature? What effect did this have on you?
2. What is the speaker's attitude toward the images he sees?
3. What is the "secret" mentioned at the end of the poem?

SHARON OLDS (b. 1942)

🍂 The Planned Child (1996)

I hated the fact that they had planned me, she had taken
a cardboard out of his shirt from the laundry
as if sliding the backbone up out of his body,
and made a chart of the month and put
5   her temperature on it, rising and falling
to know the day to make me—I would have
liked to have been conceived in heat,
in haste, by mistake, in love, in sex,
not on cardboard, the little x on the
10 rising line that did not fall again.

But when a friend was pouring wine
and said that I seem to have been a child who had been wanted,
I took the wine against my lips
as if my mouth were moving along
15 that valved wall in my mother's body, she was
bearing down, and then breathing from the mask, and then
bearing down, pressing me out into
the world that was not enough for her without me in it,
not the moon, the sun, Orion
20 cartwheeling across the dark, not
the earth, the sea—none of it
was enough, for her, without me.

QUESTIONS

1. Who is the speaker? What is she like? What is she talking about? Why does she begin the poem talking about something she hated?

2. What change of attitudes is described by the poem? Why does the poem seem to require such a change?

3. What attitude is expressed in the concluding global, planetary, solar, and stellar references? Why does the speaker state that, to her mother, she has more value than this image?

4. What unique qualities of perception and expression does the speaker exhibit? Have you ever read a poem before in which details about conception and childbirth have been so prominent? Why are these details included in this poem?

ARTHUR O'SHAUGHNESSY (1844–1881)

🍂 A Love Symphony (1881)

Along the garden° ways just now   *a green area*
    I heard the flowers speak;
The white rose told me of your brow,
    The red rose of your cheek;

The lily of your bended head,
 The bindweed of your hair;
Each looked its loveliest and said
 You were more fair.   5

I went into the wood anon,°   *later, soon after*
 And heard the wild birds sing   10
How sweet you were; they warbled on,
 Piped, trilled the self-same thing,
Thrush, blackbird, linnet, without pause
 The burden did repeat,
And still began again because   15
 You were more sweet.

And then I went down to the sea,
 And heard it murmuring too,
Part of an ancient mystery,
 All made of me and you.   20
How many a thousand years ago
 I loved, and you were sweet—
Longer I could not stay, and so
 I fled back to your feet.

QUESTIONS

1. What is the "symphony" of love? What is the tone of the speaker's descriptions of the symphony as coming from flowers, birds, and the sea?

2. What is the tone of the phrase "ancient mystery / All made of me and you" (lines 19–20)? Compare this use of the idea of religious mysteriousness and love with the use in John Donne's "The Canonization" (p, 877). What common attitudes about love do these poems contain? What differences?

3. What tone is expressed about the loved one in lines 23–24? In the light of his tone in describing her qualities, what sort of relationship is he celebrating?

ROBERT PINSKY (b. 1940)

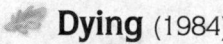 **Dying** (1984)

Nothing to be said about it, and everything—
The change of changes, closer or further away:
The Golden Retriever next door, Gussie, is dead,

Like Sandy, the Cocker Spaniel from three doors down
Who died when I was small; and every day   5
Things that were in my memory fade and die.

Phrases die out: first, everyone forgets
What doornails are; then after certain decades
As a dead metaphor, *"dead as a doornail"* flickers

10   And fades away. But someone I know is dying—
      And though one might say glibly, "everyone is,"
      The different pace makes the difference absolute.

      The tiny invisible spores in the air we breathe,
      That settle harmlessly on our drinking water
15   And on our skin, happen to come together,

      With certain conditions on the forest floor,
      Or even a shady corner of the lawn—
      And overnight the fleshy, pale stalks gather,

      The colorless growth without a leaf or flower;
20   And around the stalks, the summer grass keeps growing
      With steady pressure, like the insistent whiskers

      That grow between shaves on a face, the nails
      Growing and dying from the toes and fingers
      At their own humble pace, oblivious

25   As the nerveless moths, that live their night or two—
      Though like a moth a bright soul keeps on beating,
      Bored and impatient in the monster's mouth.

QUESTIONS

1. What details about death does the poem introduce? How are they connected in the poem's development? What is the effect of these details on the tone of the poem?

2. What is meant by line 12, "The different pace makes the difference absolute"? How strongly does this statement counter the phrase "everyone is" in line 11?

3. Up until line 25 this poem can be considered negative or even despairing. What is the effect of lines 26 and 27 on this negative tone? What is the meaning of the phrase "monster's mouth" in these last two lines?

SALVATORE QUASÍMODO (1901–1968)

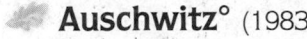 ### Auschwitz° (1983)

Translated by Jack Bevan

Far from the Vistula,° along the northern plain,
love, in a death-camp there at Auschwitz:
on the pole's rust and tangled fencing, rain
funeral cold.
5   No tree, no birds in the grey air

°*Auschwitz:* the German name for the town of Oswiecim in southern Poland, site of the most notorious of the German concentration-extermination camps in World War II. There were two major camps—Auschwitz itself, a former Polish army garrison, and nearby Birkenau, which contained many temporary barracks for worker-prisoners, together with gas chambers and crematoria for the extermination of hundreds of thousands of victims. See pages 69–76. °1 *Vistula:* The Vistula River rises in the northern Carpathian Mountains, south of Auschwitz.

or above our thought, but limp
pain that memory leaves
to its silence without irony or anger.
You ask no elegies or idylls: only
the meaning of our destiny, you, here,   10
hurt by the mind's war,
uncertain at the clear
presence of life. For life is here
in every No that seems a certainty:
here we shall hear the angel weep, the monster, hear   15
our future time
beating the hereafter that is here, forever
in motion, not an image
of dreams, of possible pity.
Here are the myths, the metamorphoses.   20
Lacking the name of symbols or a god,
they are history, earth places,
they are Auschwitz, love. How suddenly
the dear forms of Alpheus and Arethusa°
changed into shadow-smoke!   25

Out of that hell hung with a white
inscription "work will make you free"°
there came the endless smoke
of many thousand women thrust at dawn
out of the kennels up to the firing-wall,   30
or, screaming for mercy to water, choked,
their skeleton mouths under the jets of gas.

You, soldier, will find them in your annals
taking the forms of animals and rivers,
or are you too, now, ash of Auschwitz,   35
medal of silence?
Long tresses in glass urns can still be seen
bound up with charms, and an infinity
of ghostly little shoes and shawls of Jews:°
relics of a time of wisdom,   40
of man whose knowledge takes the shape of arms,
they are the myths, our metamorphoses.
Over the plains where love and sorrow
and pity rotted, there in the rain
a No inside us beat;   45
a No to death that died at Auschwitz
never from the pit of ashes
to show itself again.

°24 *Alpheus and Arethusa:* a river and fountain in Greece. In ancient mythology, Alpheus, who loved Arethusa, was transformed into the river (bearing his name) to be united with Arethusa, who was transformed into the fountain (bearing her name). °27 *work will make you free:* a translation of the large metal sign *Arbeit macht frei,* which crested the main gate of Auschwitz and is still on display there. A copy of the sign is displayed in the Holocaust Museum in Washington, D.C. °37–39 *Long tresses . . . shawls of Jews:* Today the barracks at Auschwitz house permanent displays that include the hair, shoes, eyeglasses, luggage, and clothing of thousands of the victims.

QUESTIONS

1. Compare the tone of the first ten lines with that of the last six. What differences do you notice? How does the idea of the last three lines answer the question posed in lines 9 and 10?

2. Even though the speaker is referring to the deadliest of all the camps, what does he mean by "For life is here / in every No that seems a certainty" (lines 13–14)?

3. In line 20 the speaker mentions ancient myths about metamorphoses or transformations. What type of metamorphosis is linked to the death camps in lines 26–42? What attitudes are brought out by this linkage?

THEODORE ROETHKE (1907–1963)

For a photo, see Chapter 12, page 591.

 ## My Papa's Waltz (1942)

The whiskey on your breath
Could make a small boy dizzy;
But I hung on like death:
Such waltzing was not easy.

5 We romped until the pans
Slid from the kitchen shelf;
My mother's countenance
Could not unfrown itself.

The hand that held my wrist
10 Was battered on one knuckle;
At every step you missed
My right ear scraped a buckle.

You beat time on my head
With a palm caked hard by dirt,
15 Then waltzed me off to bed
Still clinging to your shirt.

QUESTIONS

1. What is the tone of the speaker's opening description of his father? What is the tone of the phrases "like death" and "such waltzing"?

2. What is the "waltz" the speaker describes? What is the tone of his words describing it in lines 5–15?

3. What does the reference to his "mother's countenance" contribute to the tone? What situation is suggested by the selection of the word "unfrown"?

4. What does the tone of the physical descriptions of the father contribute to your understanding of the speaker's attitude toward his childhood experiences as his father's dance partner?

WILLIAM SHAKESPEARE (1564–1616)

For a portrait, see Chapter 21, page 1079.

Fear No More the Heat o' th' Sun°—1623 (c. 1610–11)

Fear no more the heat o' th' sun;
Nor the furious winter's rages.
Thou thy worldly task hast done,
Home art gone, and ta'en° thy wages;   *taken*
Golden lads and girls all must,   5
As° chimney sweepers come to dust.   *like*

Fear no more the frown o' th' great,
Thou art past the tyrant's stroke:
Care no more to clothe and eat;
To thee the reed is as the oak: 10
The sceptre, learning, physic, must
All follow this, and come to dust.

Fear no more the lightning flash,
Nor th' all-dread thunder-stone;°
Fear not slander, censure rash;   15
Thou hast finished joy and moan;°   *sadness*
All lovers young, all lovers must
Consign to thee and come to dust.

No exorcisor harm thee.
Nor no witchcraft charm thee.   20
Ghost unlaid forbear thee.
Nothing ill come near thee.
Quiet consummation have,
And renownéd be thy grave.

°*Fear No More:* This poem is a dirge or lament spoken (but not sung) over the supposedly dead body of Innogen in Act IV of Shakespeare's *Cymbeline* (she has taken a potion which makes her appear to be dead). The speakers/ singers are Guiderius and Arviragus, who are the actual brothers of Innogen, although at this time neither the brothers nor the sister know of their relationship. °14 *thunder-stone:* The sound of thunder was believed in Elizabethan times to be caused by stones falling from the sky.

QUESTIONS

1. Describe the attitude of the speakers toward death. How do they try to soften the bitterness of death?

2. In what ways is the fourth stanza a climax to the poem? How does it differ from the first three stanzas?

3. In the play Guiderius and Arviragus, though princes, have been deprived of their status and rights, and have been brought up simply. How does the language of the song reflect their rustic nature?

CATHY SONG (b. 1955)

Lost Sister (1983)

1

In China,
even the peasants
named their first daughters
Jade°—
5   the stone that in the far fields
could moisten the dry season,
could make men move mountains
for the healing green of the inner hills
glistening like slices of winter melon.
10   And the daughters were grateful:
they never left home.
To move freely was a luxury
stolen from them at birth.
Instead, they gathered patience,
15   learning to walk in shoes
the size of teacups,°
without breaking—
the arc of their movements
as dormant as the rooted willow,
20   as redundant as the farmyard hens.
But they traveled far
in surviving,
learning to stretch the family rice,
to quiet the demons,
25   the noisy stomachs.

2

There is a sister
across the ocean,
who relinquished her name,
diluting jade green
30   with the blue of the Pacific.
Rising with a tide of locusts,
she swarmed with others
to inundate another shore.
In America,
35   there are many roads
and women can stride along with men.

But in another wilderness,
the possibilities,

°4 *Jade:* In China, both the mineral and the name are considered signs of health and good fortune. °16 *teacups:* Traditionally in China, girls' feet were bound at the age of seven because minuscule feet were considered beautiful and aristocratic. The binding inhibited the natural growth of the feet and made it painful to walk.

the loneliness,
can strangulate like jungle vines.
The meager provisions and sentiments   40
of once belonging—
fermented roots, Mah-Jongg° tiles and firecrackers—
set but a flimsy household
in a forest of nightless cities.   45
A giant snake rattles above,
spewing black clouds into your kitchen.
Dough-faced landlords
slip in and out of your keyholes,
making claims you don't understand   50
tapping into your communication systems
of laundry lines and restaurant chains.

You find you need China:
your one fragile identification,
a jade link
handcuffed to your wrist.   55
You remember your mother
who walked for centuries,
footless—
and like her,
you have left no footprints,   60
but only because
there is an ocean in between,
the unremitting space of your rebellion.

°43 *Mah-Jongg*: a Chinese game played with 144 domino-like tiles marked in suits, counters, and dice.

QUESTIONS

1. Why is the poem titled "Lost Sister"? Why is it not titled something like "Lucky Sister"?

2. In light of the poem's title, what is the speaker's evaluation of the circumstances of women's life in historical China, and her attitude toward the life of a physically freer woman who has emigrated to the United States?

3. What is meant by the speaker's assertion that both mother and daughter (the "lost sister") have "left no footprints" (line 61). What does the speaker find to praise both the women who stayed in China, and the woman who came to America?

C. K. WILLIAMS (b. 1936)

Dimensions (1969)

There is a world somewhere else that is unendurable.
Those who live in it are helpless in the hands of the elements,
they are like branches in the deep woods in wind

that whip their leaves off and slice the heart of the night
5 and sob. They are like boats bleating wearily in fog.

But here, no matter what, we know where we stand.
We know more or less what comes next. We hold out.
Sometimes a dream will shake us like little dogs, a fever
hang on so we're not ourselves or love wring us out,
10 but we prevail, we certify and make sure, we go on.

There is a world that uses its soldiers and widows
for flour, its orphans for building stone, its legs for pens.
In that place, eyes are softened and harmless like God's
and all blend in the traffic of their tragedy and pass by
15 like people. And sometimes one of us, losing the way,
will drift over the border and see them there, dying,
laughing, being revived. When we come home, we are half way.
Our screams heal the torn silence. We are like scars.

QUESTIONS

1. Why should this poem be called ironic? Should the irony be called situational? Cosmic? Why?
2. What is intended by the poem's title? What is the implication of the first line? What irony does the line bring out? Describe the irony of the second stanza (lines 6–10).
3. What is meant by "losing the way" and drifting "over the border" (lines 15–16)? What is the meaning and irony of the last three lines? What does it mean to be "like scars" (line 18)?

WILLIAM WORDSWORTH (1770–1850)

For a portrait, see Chapter 11, page 557.

The Solitary Reaper (1807)

Behold her, single in the field,
Yon solitary Highland Lass!
Reaping and singing by herself;
Stop here, or gently pass!

5 Alone she cuts and binds the grain,
And sings a melancholy strain;
O listen! for the Vale profound
Is overflowing with the sound.

No Nightingale did ever chaunt
10 More welcome notes to weary bands
Of travelers in some shady haunt,
Among Arabian sands;
A voice so thrilling ne'er was heard
In springtime from the Cuckoo bird,
15 Breaking the silence of the seas
Among the farthest Hebrides.°

Will no one tell me what she sings?°
Perhaps the plaintive numbers flow
For old, unhappy, far-off things,
And battles long ago;   20
Or is it some more humble lay,
Familiar matter of today?
Some natural sorrow, loss, or pain,
That has been, and may be again?

Whate'er the theme, the Maiden sang
As if her song could have no ending;   25
I saw her singing at her work,
And o'er the sickle bending—

I listened, motionless and still;
And, as I mounted up the hill,   30
The music in my heart I bore,
Long after it was heard no more.

°16 *Hebrides:* a group of islands off the west coast of Scotland. °17 *Will . . . sings:* The speaker does not understand Scots Gaelic, the language in which the woman sings.

QUESTIONS

1. What is the scene described in the poem? Where is the speaker? What actions does he describe?
2. Why does the poet shift from present tense to the past tense at line 25? What is gained by this shift?
3. What speculations does the speaker make about the meaning of the woman's song? What conclusions does he make? What do you conclude from his observations?

JAMES WRIGHT (1927-1980)

 ### Autumn Begins in Martins Ferry, Ohio (1963)

In the Shreve High football stadium,
I think of Polacks nursing long beers in Tiltonsville,
And gray faces of Negroes in the blast furnace at Benwood,
And the ruptured night watchman of Wheeling Steel,
Dreaming of heroes.   5

All the proud fathers are ashamed to go home.
Their women cluck like starved pullets,
Dying for love.

Therefore,
Their sons grow suicidally beautiful   10
At the beginning of October,
And gallop terribly against each other's bodies.

QUESTIONS

1. Have you ever imagined what private lives people lead when you simply see them? Do your thoughts about them have to do with how they look, where they live, how they dress, how they speak? Any other factors?
2. What is the speaker's attitude about the town he is describing?
3. What do the details of the first stanza tell you about the town being described?

Two Hangovers (1963)

NUMBER ONE
I slouch in bed.
Beyond the streaked trees of my window,
All groves are bare.
5   Locusts and poplars change to unmarried women
Sorting slate from anthracite
Between railroad ties:
The yellow-bearded winter of the depression
Is still alive somewhere, an old man
10   Counting his collection of bottle caps
In a tarpaper shack under the cold trees
Of my grave.

I still feel half drunk,
And all those old women beyond my window
15   Are hunching toward the graveyard.

Drunk, mumbling Hungarian,
The sun staggers in,
And his big stupid face pitches
Into the stove.
20   For two hours I have been dreaming
Of green butterflies searching for diamonds
In coal seams;
And children chasing each other for a game
Through the hills of fresh graves.
25   But the sun has come home drunk from the sea,
And a sparrow outside
Sings of the Hanna Coal Co. and the dead moon.
The filaments of cold light bulbs tremble
In music like delicate birds.
30   Ah, turn it off.

NUMBER TWO: I TRY TO WAKEN AND GREET THE WORLD ONCE AGAIN
In a pine tree,
A few yards away from my window sill,
A brilliant blue jay is springing up and down, up and down,

On a branch.   35
I laugh, as I see him abandon himself
To entire delight, for he knows as well as I do
That the branch will not break.

QUESTIONS

1. What do we learn about the speaker in hangover "Number One"? What is his physical condition? Where is he? What is he trying to do?

2. How does the speaker's condition affect the way he views the trees outside his window? The world? His own life?

3. Who or what is drunk and "mumbling Hungarian" in line 16?

4. Do you think the sun really "staggers in" and falls "into the stove"? What does the sun stand for in "Number One"?

5. Find all the images of death and desolation that you can in "Number One." Why do you suppose these images are so dominant?

6. Why is hangover "Number Two" so much shorter than "Number One"?

7. How does the speaker's mood, attitude, perspective, or tone of voice change from hangover "Number One" to hangover "Number Two"? How do you account for this shift?

WILLIAM BUTLER YEATS (1865–1939)

 ## When You Are Old (1893)

When you are old and grey and full of sleep,
And nodding by the fire, take down this book,
And slowly read, and dream of the soft look
Your eyes had once, and of their shadows deep;

How many loved your moments of glad grace,   5
And loved your beauty with love false or true,
But one man loved the pilgrim soul in you,
And loved the sorrows of your changing face;

And bending down beside the glowing bars,
Murmur, a little sadly, how Love fled   10
And paced upon the mountains overhead
And hid his face amid a crowd of stars.

QUESTIONS

1. What is the speaker of this poem like? How does the speaker describe himself?

2. To whom is the speaker speaking? What are you asked to conclude about the past relationship between the speaker and the listener?

3. Describe the dominant attitudes expressed by the speaker. What words might describe the poem's tone?

4. Compare the tone of this poem with that of Henley's "When You Are Old" (p. 557).

WRITING ABOUT TONE IN POETRY

Be careful to note those elements of the work that touch particularly on attitudes or authorial consideration. For example, you may be studying Hughes's "Theme for English B," where it is necessary to consider the force of the poet's claim for equality (see Chapter 18). How serious is the claim? Does the speaker's apparent matter-of-factness make him seem less than enthusiastic? Or does this tone indicate that equality is so fundamental a right that its realization should be an everyday part of life? Devising and answering such questions can help you understand the degree to which authors show control of tone. Similar questions apply when you study internal qualities such as style and characterization.

Questions for Discovering Ideas

- What is the speaker like? Is he or she intelligent, observant, friendly, idealistic, realistic, trustworthy? How do you think you should respond to the speaker's characteristics?
- Do all the speeches seem right for the speaker and situation? Are all descriptions appropriate, all actions believable?
- If the work is comic, at what is the comedy directed? At situations? At characters? At the speaker himself or herself? What is the poet's apparent attitude toward the comic objects?
- Does the writer ask you to (1) sympathize with those in misfortune, (2) rejoice with those who have found happiness, (3) lament the human condition, (4) become angry against unfairness and inequality, (5) admire examples of noble human behavior, or (6) have another appropriate emotional response?
- Do any words seem unusual or especially noteworthy, such as dialect, polysyllabic words, foreign words or phrases that the author assumes you know, or especially connotative words? What is the effect of such words on the poem's tone?

Strategies for Organizing Ideas

The goal of your essay is to examine all aspects bearing on the tone. Consider the following topics.

1. *The audience, situation, and characters.* Is any person or group directly addressed by the speaker? What attitude is expressed (love, respect, condescension, confidentiality, confidence, etc.)? What is the basic situation in the work? What is the nature of the speaker or persona? What is the relationship of the speaker to the material? What is the basis of the speaker's authority? Does the speaker give you the whole truth? Is he or she trying to withhold anything? Why? How is the speaker's character manipulated to show apparent authorial attitude and to stimulate responses? Do you find any of the various sorts of irony? If so, what does the irony show (optimism or pessimism, for example)? How is the situation controlled to shape your responses? That is, can actions, situations, or characters be seen as expressions of attitude or as embodiments of certain favorable

or unfavorable ideas or positions? How does the work promote respect, admiration, dislike, or other feelings about character or situation?

2. *Descriptions and diction.* Your concern here is to relate attitudes to the poet's use of language and description. Are there any systematic references, such as to colors, sounds, noises, natural scenes, and so on, that collectively reflect an attitude? Do connotative meanings of words control response in any way? Is any special knowledge of references or unusual words expected of readers? What is the extent of this knowledge? Do speech or dialect patterns indicate attitudes about speakers or their condition of life? Are speech patterns normal and standard or slang and substandard? What is the effect of these patterns? Are there unusual or particularly noteworthy expressions? If so, what attitudes do these show? Does the author use verbal irony? To what effect?

3. *Humor.* Is the work funny? How funny, how intense? How is the humor achieved? Does the humor develop out of incongruous situations or language, or both? Is there an underlying basis of attack in the humor, or are the objects of laughter still respected or even loved despite having humor directed against them?

4. *Ideas.* Ideas may be advocated, defended mildly, attacked, or ridiculed. Which attitude is present in the work you have been studying? How does the poet make his or her attitude clear—directly, by statement, or indirectly, through understatement, overstatement, or the language of a character? In what ways does the work assume a common ground of assent between author and reader? That is, are there apparently common assumptions about religious views, political ideas, moral and behavioral standards, and so on? Are these common ideas readily acceptable, or is any concession needed by the reader to approach the work? For example, a major subject of Arnold's "Dover Beach" (Chapter 19) is that absolute belief in the truth of organized religion has been lost. This subject may not be important to everyone, but even an irreligious reader or a follower of another faith may find common ground in the poem's psychological situation or in the desire to learn as much as possible about so important an institution as religion.

5. *Unique characteristics.* Each work has unique properties that contribute to the tone. For example, Roethke's "My Papa's Waltz" is a brief narrative in which the speaker's recollected feelings about his father's boisterously drunken behavior must be inferred from understatement. Hardy's "Channel Firing" (Chapter 13) develops from the comic and absurd joke that the sounds of cannons being fired from ships at sea are so loud they could waken the dead. Be alert for such special circumstances in the poem you are considering, and as you plan and develop your essay, take them into account.

Your conclusion may summarize your main points and from there go on to any needed definitions, explanations, or afterthoughts, together with ideas reinforcing earlier points. If you have changed your mind or have made new realizations, briefly explain these. Finally, you might mention some other major aspect of the work's tone that you did not develop in the body.

Illustrative Student Essay

Although underlined sentences are not recommended by MLA style, they are used in this illustrative essay as teaching tools to emphasize the central idea, thesis sentence, and topic sentences.

Regal 1

Willa Regal

Professor Tyler

English 102

18 May 2014

The Speaker's Attitudes in Sharon Olds's "The Planned Child"°

[1]   "The Planned Child" is unusual and striking because in it Sharon Olds deals so frankly with her speaker's concern about the circumstances of her conception and birth. Few people ever learn about how they were conceived, and even fewer ever think about it enough to criticize it, and yet the poem's details concern this topic. As unusual as such details are, however, the poem's power results from the way the speaker traces the development of her attitudes towards her origins—from hate, to uncertainty, to acceptance.* These attitudes may be traced in the poem's two stanzas, its ordinary diction, and the way its use of the first-person pronoun indicates the speaker's importance.†

[2]   Olds's first stanza contrasts the speaker's hatred for planning and organization and her preference for disorganization. The stanza is arresting, if not shocking, because in it the speaker goes into the past to describe her feelings about how her mother calculated ovulation times to insure conception. Rather than finding it comical that she owes her existence to the chart her mother made on a laundry cardboard, the speaker says she hated this planned record keeping. She explains this attitude because the planning, to her way of thinking, reduced her to little more than an X on a rising graph line and by implication, therefore, it seemed cold and impersonal. From the description the speaker makes of conception in lines 7 and 8, it seems that spontaneous and

°This poem appears on page 702.
*Central idea.
†Thesis sentence.

Regal 2

disorganized love by her parents would have created a warmer, more welcoming reason for her existence.

The second stanza is continuous with the first because it stems out of feelings occasioned by an unplanned but significant moment. A friend serves wine to the speaker and tells her that she seems to have been "a child who had been *wanted*" (line 12, italics added). This casual social event is symbolic (is it similar to an experience of communion?) because it gives the speaker a lifegiving insight into her existence. The conclusion of the poem is then devoted to the speaker's newly created feelings of involvement with her mother. She finds affection for her mother in the details of childbirth—bearing down, breathing, pressing, and the emergence into life of the speaker herself. The poem's climax is the speaker's apparently amazed realization that she herself was actually *wanted*. The *X* on the graph therefore was a means of achieving a far greater goal, for her mother valued her more than the world or the galaxy. As the speaker imagines her mother's lifegiving act, she imagines how loving it was, and therefore she senses her own importance.   [3]

With such an unusual topic, one might expect a fair amount of abstract and medical diction, but such is not the case. Most of the words are flat and ordinary (e.g., "a friend was pouring wine"). Despite their simplicity, however, the diction confronts readers with direct physical details of planned conception and the labor of childbirth. The speaker refers matter-of-factly to a temperature chart, the birth canal, and breathing into a mask and bearing down during labor. Of major note is the intensity that Olds achieves through the selection of simple but strong verbs and verbals ("hated," "planned," "had taken," "sliding," "made," "pouring," "were moving," "bearing down," "breathing," "pressing," and "cartwheeling"). All these words fit the poet's aim to connect with one of life's first facts—being conceived and then delivered.   [4]

As this basic detail indicates, the central figure of the poem is the speaker and her attitudes. This centrality is emphasized by the frequent use of the first person pronoun throughout the poem. A form of the pronoun appears twelve times, and the poem begins with "I" and concludes with "me." This number may not seem high in a personal poem of twenty-two lines, but it is   [5]

Regal 3

high enough to support the idea that the poem is about attitudes toward self-realization. The poem explores some vital personal questions: Could the speaker love herself knowing that she was planned and not spontaneous? Not when these calculations seemed to result from nothing more than cold science. But could she love herself after learning that the calculations were preceded by love for her? Yes, and as a result the speaker makes inferences from this new information. She imagines that nothing in the world was more important to her mother than she. She therefore has more value than the earth and stars themselves, and this vision closes the poem on a strongly positive and affirmative note:

> not the moon, the sun, Orion
>
> cartwheeling across the dark, not
>
> the earth, the sea—none of it
>
> was enough, for her, without me. (20–22)

[6] Thus, an examination of "The Planned Child" reveals both the need and difficulty of self-understanding. The poem is a confession of changing attitudes in the light of a growing sense of personal origin. Olds makes this point through the commonness and universality of details about birth. Yet the poem is not personal or egocentric because it is about the need of discovering who one is. Without this knowledge the poem's speaker is uncertain and hostile. But once she can see that she is part of a pattern of love and creativity, she becomes positive and assertive. The tone of "The Planned Child" reflects the speaker's growing confidence that results from her increased knowledge and awareness.

Regal 4

Work Cited

Olds, Sharon. "The Planned Child." *Literature: An Introduction to Reading and Writing, Compact Edition.* Ed. Edgar V. Roberts and Robert Zweig. 6th ed. New York: Pearson, 2015. 702. Print.

Commentary on the Essay

Because this essay embodies a number of approaches by which tone may be studied in any work (situation, diction, special characteristics), it is typical of many essays that use a combined approach. The central idea, expressed in the first paragraph, is that the dominant attitudes in "The Planned Child" are the speaker's change from hostility to certainty.

Paragraph 2 considers the poem's first section, in which the speaker explains why a preference for spontaneity caused her initial hatred of how she came into being (strategy 4, p. 715). Paragraph 3 shows how the explanation of a unique situation can be seen as a feature of tone (strategy 5, p. 715). The paragraph pursues the speaker's thoughts that develop from an unexpected comment from a friend. In this sense, a casual moment explains how the speaker's relative confusion shifts to the greater self-confidence and acceptance of her mother's labors to bring her into the world.

Paragraph 4 concerns the poem's treatment of the unusual subject matter through comparatively simple diction (strategy 1, p. 714). Words in the paragraph that indicate attitudes are "confronts," "matter-of-factly," "intensity," and "desire." Paragraph 5 considers how Olds's use of the first-person pronoun fits into the poem's recognition of the speaker's importance (strategy 2, p 715). The paragraph asserts that the poem's positive conclusion is augmented by images on a planetary, solar, galactic, geographic, and marine scale (strategy 5).

The concluding paragraph points out that the speaker's concern with her origins is not simply a matter of egocentrism but rather results from her need to connect with an attitude that is more human and loving than the act of planning at first seems to convey.

Writing Topics About Tone in Poetry

Writing Paragraphs

1. Consider the tone of Roethke's "My Papa's Waltz." Some readers have concluded that the speaker is expressing fond memories of his childhood experiences with his father. Others believe that the speaker is ambiguous about the father and that he suppresses childhood pain as he describes the father's boisterousness in the kitchen. Basing your conclusion on the tone of the poem alone, write a paragraph about how you believe the poem should be interpreted.

Writing Essays

1. Consider Clifton's "homage to my hips," Cummings's "she being Brand / -new," Hardy's "The Workbox," Whur's "The First-Rate Wife," and Henley's "When You Are Old" as poems about love. Write an essay that answers the following questions. What similarities do you find? That is, do the poets state that love creates joy, satisfaction, distress, embarrassment, trouble? How does the tone of each of the poems enable you to draw your conclusions? What differences do you find in the ways the poets either control or do not control tone?

2. Consider these same poems (from question 1) from a feminist viewpoint (see Chapter 24). What importance and value do the poems give to women? How do they view women's actions? Write an essay arguing that any of these poems deserves praise or blame because of their treatment of women.

3. Quasímodo's "Auschwitz" (p. 704) concerns one of the twentieth century's central evils, the most abhorrent of the Nazi death camps, about which people have expressed anger, horror, indignation, outrage, disgust, hatred, and vengefulness. Write an essay in which you discuss to what degree you find these attitudes in Quasímodo's poem. How do such attitudes, or others, govern the poem's tone?

Creative Writing Assignment

1. Write a poem about a person or occasion that has made you either glad or angry. Try to create the same feelings in your reader, but create these feelings through your rendering of situation and your choices of the right words. (*Possible topics:* a social injustice; an unfair grade; a compliment you have received on a task well done; the landing of a good job; the winning of a game; a rise in the price of gasoline; a good book or movie.)

Library Assignment

1. From resources in your library or online, find two critical biographies about Theodore Roethke published by university presses. What do these works disclose about Roethke's childhood and his family, particularly his father? On the basis of what you learn, should your interpretation of the tone of "My Papa's Waltz" be changed or unchanged? Why?

Chapter 16
Form: The Shape of Poems

AFTER STUDYING THIS MATERIAL, YOU SHOULD BE ABLE TO DO THE FOLLOWING:

- Define various types of closed-form poetry
- Identify various types of open-form poetry
- Demonstrate how a poem's form relates to its sense

Because poetry is compressed and highly rhythmical, it always exists under self-imposed restrictions, or conventions. Traditionally, many poets have chosen a variety of clearly recognizable shapes or forms—*closed-form poetry*. Since the middle of the nineteenth century, however, many poets have rejected regular patterns in favor of poems that appear more free and spontaneous—*open-form poetry*. Both terms refer to the structure and technique of the poems, not to the content or ideas.

Closed-Form Poetry

Closed-form poetry is written in specific and traditional patterns of lines produced through *line length, meter, rhyme,* and *line groupings.* In the closed form (and also in the open form), the **line** is, loosely, the poetic equivalent of the prose sentence. A prime characteristic of the closed-form line, as opposed to a sentence, is that its length is usually measured or restricted. Various numbers of lines may be grouped together through rhyme and other means to form a **stanza,** which is the poetic equivalent of a paragraph in prose. Individual lines may coincide exactly with sentences, although quite often sentences stretch out over two or more lines. Stanzas consist of groups of lines that are both connected and also separated by developments of subject, idea, or expression of feeling.

Over the centuries English and American poets have appropriated and evolved many closed forms. Among the most important of these are *blank verse,* the *couplet,* the *tercet* or *triplet, terza rima,* the *villanelle,* the *quatrain,* the *sonnet,* the *song* or *lyric,* the *ode,* the *ballad,* the *elegy,* and *common measure* or the *hymnal stanza,* together with forms like the *haiku,* the *epigram,* the *epitaph,* the *limerick,* the *clerihew,* and the *double dactyl.*

Blank Verse Consists of Five Unrhymed Iambic Lines

One of the most common closed forms in English is **blank verse,** or unrhymed iambic pentameter, which represents the adaptation and fusion of sentences to poetic form. The great advantage of blank verse is that it resembles normal speech but at the same time it maintains poetic identity. It is suitable for relatively short poems, but it may also extend for hundreds or even thousands of lines. It is the most adaptable line of English poetry. The master of blank verse is Shakespeare, who used it extensively in his plays. Since Shakespeare, poets of English have used blank verse again and again. Milton used it in his masterly long epic *Paradise Lost*. Wordsworth was fond of blank verse and used it in some of his best-known poems. Let us look at a passage from his autobiographical poem *The Prelude* (1850) to see his blank verse—which has been praised as "conversational," "flexible," and "majestic"—in action (for another example, see his "Tintern Abbey," Chapter 11, pp. 557–561).

> Wisdom and Spirit of the universe!
> Thou Soul that art the eternity of thought,
> That givest to forms and images a breath
> And everlasting motion, not in vain
> By day or star-light thus from my first dawn
> Of childhood didst thou intertwine for me
> The passions that build up our human soul;
> Not with the mean and vulgar works of man,
> But with high objects, with enduring things—
> With life and nature, purifying thus
> The elements of feeling and of thought,
> And sanctifying, by such discipline,
> Both pain and fear, until we recognize
> A grandeur in the beatings of the heart. (Book I, lines 401–14)

The development of these lines takes place through a simultaneous blending of line lengths and grammatical coherence. Wordsworth expresses his ideas enthusiastically within his chosen iambic rhythm, which is both restricting and liberating, and by this means he brings about the "majestic" elevation that is characteristic of his poetry.

The Couplet Consists of Two Lines Connected by Thought and Rhyme

The **couplet** contains two rhyming lines and is the shortest distinct closed form. The two lines are usually identical in length and meter. Some couplets are short. Even lines in monometer (one major stress), like "I sing / Each spring," can make up a couplet. However, most English couplets are in iambic tetrameter (four stresses) or iambic pentameter (five stresses), and they have been a regular feature of English poetry ever since Chaucer used them in the fourteenth century. In the seventeenth and eighteenth centuries, the iambic-pentameter couplet was considered appropriate for epic, or heroic, poetry. For this reason it is often called the **heroic couplet.** Because these centuries are considered the "neoclassic" age of literature, the form is also called the **neoclassic couplet.** It was used with consummate skill by John Dryden (1631–1700) and Alexander Pope (1688–1744).

Usually, the heroic couplet expresses a complete idea and is grammatically self-sufficient. It thrives on the rhetorical strategies of **parallelism** and **antithesis.** Look, for example, at these two couplets from "The Rape of the Lock," Pope's well-known mock-epic poem (1711):

> Here Britain's statesmen oft the fall foredoom
> Of foreign tyrants, and of nymphs at home;
> Here thou, great Anna! whom three realms obey,
> Dost sometimes counsel take—and sometimes tea.

These lines describe activities at Hampton Court, the royal palace and residence of Queen Anne (reigned 1701–1714). Notice that the first couplet allows Pope to link "Britain's statesmen" with two parallel but also antithetical events: the fall of nations and the "fall" of young women. Similarly, the second heroic couplet allows for the parallel and comic linking of royal meetings of state ("counsel") and teatime (in the early eighteenth century, *tea* was pronounced "tay"). The example thus demonstrates how the heroic couplet may contrast amusing and ironic actions and situations.

The Tercet or Triplet Consists of Three Lines

A three-line stanza is called a **tercet** or **triplet.** Tercets may be written in any uniform line length or meter and most commonly contain three rhymes (*aaa, bbb,* and so on), which are, in effect, short stanzas. The following poem by Tennyson is in iambic tetrameter triplets.

ALFRED, LORD TENNYSON (1809–1892)

For a photo, see Chapter 14, page 664.

 The Eagle (1851)

He clasps the crag with crooked hands;
Close to the sun in lonely lands,
Ring'd with the azure world, he stands.

The wrinkled sea beneath him crawls;
He watches from his mountain walls,
And like a thunderbolt he falls.

5

In the first tercet, we view the eagle as though at a distance. In the second, the perspective shifts, and we see through the eagle's eyes and follow his actions. In this tercet the verbs are active: the sea "crawls" and the eagle "falls." While the two tercets and the shift in perspective divide the poem, alliteration pulls things back together. This is especially true of the *k* sound in "clasps," "crag," "crooked," "close," and "crawls" and the *w* sound in "with," "world," "watches," and "walls."

TERZA RIMA.   There are two important variations on the tercet pattern, each requiring a high degree of ingenuity and control. The first tercet variation is **terza rima,** in which stanzas are interlocked through a pattern that requires the center termination in one tercet to be rhymed twice in the next: *aba bcb cdc ded*, and so on.

THE VILLANELLE.   The most complex variation of the tercet pattern is the **villanelle,** a nineteen-line form containing five tercets, rhymed *aba*, and concluded by four lines. The first and third lines of the first tercet are repeated alternately in subsequent tercets as a refrain, and they are also used in the concluding four lines. For examples in this chapter, see Elizabeth Bishop's "One Art," Theodore Roethke's "The Waking," and Dylan Thomas's "Do Not Go Gentle into That Good Night."

The Quatrain Is a Unit of Four Lines

The most common and adaptable stanzaic building block is the four-line **quatrain.** This stanza has been popular for hundreds of years and has lent itself to many variations. Like couplets and tercets, quatrains may be written in any line length and meter; even the line lengths within a quatrain may vary. The determining factor is the rhyme scheme, and even that is variable, depending on the form and the poet's aims. Quatrains may be rhymed *aaaa*, but they can also be rhymed *abab, abba, aaba,* or even *abcb*. Quatrains are basic components of many traditional closed forms, most notably ballads and sonnets, and they are significant in many religious hymns.

The Sonnet Is a Versatile Poem of Fourteen Lines

The **sonnet,** consisting of fourteen lines, is one of the most popular and durable closed poetic forms. Initially it was an Italian form (*sonnetto* means "little song") created by the medieval Italian poet Petrarch (1304–1374), who wrote collections or *cycles* of sonnets. The sonnet form as made famous by Petrarch is called the **Italian sonnet** or **Petrarchan sonnet** in Petrarch's honor. The form and style of Petrarchan sonnets were adapted to English poetry in the early sixteenth century, and with variations they have been used ever since. As a form, the Petrarchan sonnet is in iambic pentameter, and it contains two quatrains (the **octave**) and two tercets (the **sestet**). In structure and meaning, the octave presents a problem or situation that is resolved in the sestet, as in Milton's "On His Blindness." The rhyme scheme of the Petrarchan octave is fixed in an *abba, abba* pattern. The sestet offers a number of different rhyming possibilities, including *cdc cdc* and *cde cde*.

THE SHAKESPEAREAN SONNET OR ENGLISH SONNET.   Shakespeare was the most original adapter of the sonnet tradition. Recognizing that there are fewer rhyming words in English than in Italian, he developed the **Shakespearean sonnet** or **English sonnet,** based on seven rhymes (in the pattern *abab cdcd efef gg*) rather than the usual five rhymes of the Italian sonnet. As indicated by the rhyme scheme, the Shakespearean sonnet contains three quatrains and a concluding couplet. The pattern of thought therefore shifts from the octave-sestet organization of the Italian sonnet to a four-part argument on a single thought or emotion. Each Shakespearean quatrain contains a separate development of the sonnet's central idea or problem, and the couplet provides a climax and resolution.

The Song or Lyric Is a Stanzaic Poem of Variable Measure and Length

The **song** or **lyric** is a stanzaic form that was originally designed to be sung to a repeating melody, although few lyrics today are written specifically for music. Even so, the line lengths and rhyme schemes of the first stanza are duplicated in subsequent stanzas, as though for repeated singing to the same tune. The stanzas of a lyric may be built from any combination of single lines, couplets, triplets, and quatrains. The line lengths may shift, and a great deal of metrical variation is common.

The lyric is one of the most adaptable and variable of all verse forms at the present time. In fact, the lyric is one of the forms most commonly used by contemporary poets. The form may be personal, public, philosophical, religious, or political, in addition to its use as a vehicle to express love and other emotions. There is theoretically no limit to the number of stanzas in a lyric, although these poems are typically briefer. A. E. Housman's "To An Athlete Dying Young" (Chapter 12), for example, is a lyric made up of seven quatrains containing two couplets each. It is in iambic tetrameter and it rhymes *aabb*. Lyrics often feature quite complex and ingenious stanzaic structures. Donne's "The Canonization" (Chapter 17), for instance, contains five stanzas, each of which follows the iambic pattern *5a4b5b5a4c4c4c4a3a*. This nine-line stanza contains three different rhymes and three different line lengths. Nevertheless, the same intricate pattern is repeated in each of the five stanzas.

The Ode Is a Complex and Extensive Stanzaic Poem

The **ode** is a more variable stanzaic form than the lyric, with varying line lengths and intricate rhyme schemes. Usually the topics of odes are meditative and philosophical, but there is no set topic material, just as there is no set form. Some odes have repeating patterns, while others offer no duplication and introduce a new structure in each stanza. Poets have developed their own structures according to their needs. Keats's great odes were particularly congenial to his ideas, as in "Ode to a Nightingale," which consists of eight stanzas in iambic pentameter with the repeating form *ababcde3cde*. Although many odes have been set to music, most do not fit repeating melodies.

The Elegy Is a Poem About Death and Its Meaning for the Living

The **elegy** ("lament," or "mournful song") has had a long and rich history in other languages extending back to ancient times, and it has defined a number of topics, but for our purposes it is a poem of lamentation. Usually the topic is the death of a specific person, but it is also generally concerned with mortality and the negative and tragic aspects of life. In English the most notable elegy is Milton's "Lycidas" (1638), which he wrote in observance of the death by drowning of a "learned friend" with whom he had gone to school. Milton also composed this poem as a

pastoral, that is, a poem describing rural lives and concerns, with direct allegorical implications for the lives of city-dwellers. So that you may get a sense of this poem, here are the opening twenty-four lines.

Yet once more, O ye laurels, and once more
Ye myrtles brown, with ivy never sere,°   *dry, withered*
I come to pluck your berries° harsh and crude,   *to write this poem*
And with forced fingers rude,
5   Shatter your leaves before the mellowing year.
Bitter constraint, and sad occasion dear,
Compels me to disturb your season due;
For Lycidas is dead, dead ere his prime,
Young Lycidas, and hath° not left his peer: *who hath*
10 Who would not sing for Lycidas? he knew
Himself to sing, and build the lofty rhyme.
He must not float upon his watery bier
Unwept, and welter to the parching wind,
Without the meed° of some melodious tear.   *gift, honor*
15   Begin then, sisters° of the sacred well,   *the muses*
That from beneath the seat of Jove° doth spring,   *God (Jupiter)*
Begin, and somewhat loudly sweep the string.
Hence with denial vain, and coy excuse,
So may some gentle muse
20 With lucky° words favor my destined urn,   *providential, inspired*
And as he passes turn,
And bid fair peace be to my sable shroud.
For we were nursed upon the self-same hill,
Fed the same flock; by fountain, shade, and rill.°   *i.e., we went to the same school*

Today few people think of the traditional formalities of elegiac writing, and prefer to understand poems as elegies if they concern death, mortality, and grief. Thus, Collins's "The Names" (Chapter 15), Dryden's "To the Memory of Mr. Oldham" (this chapter), Pinsky's "Dying" (Chapter 15), Cummings's "Buffalo Bill's Defunct" (this chapter), and Dickinson's "The Bustle in a House" (Chapter 18), to name just a few poems in this book, might, broadly, all be considered elegies.

A Ballad Consists of Many Narrative Quatrains

The **ballad,** which fuses narrative description with dramatic dialogue, originated in folk literature and is one of the oldest closed forms in English poetry. Ballads consist of many quatrains in which lines of iambic tetrameter alternate with iambic trimeter. Normally, only the second and fourth lines of each stanza rhyme, in the pattern *xaxa xbxb xcxc* and so on. The ballad was designed for singing, like the anonymous "Sir Patrick Spens" (Chapter 11). Popular ballad tunes were used over and over again by later balladeers, often as many as forty and fifty times, or more, and many of the tunes have survived to the present day and are still well known. The music to folk ballads like "Greensleeves" and "Waly Waly" (not in this collection) has been known now for the past 400 years in both England and America, and many balladeers have written words to be sung to this music.

Common Measure, or the Hymnal Stanza, Is a Poem Consisting of a Number of Quatrains

Common measure, a quatrain form, is similar to the ballad stanza. It shares with the ballad the alternation of four-beat and three-beat iambic lines but adds a second rhyme to the first and third lines of each quatrain: *abab cdcd* and so on. Because the measure is often used in hymns, it is sometimes called the **hymnal stanza.** Many of Emily Dickinson's poems, including "Because I Could Not Stop for Death" (Chapter 11), are in common measure.

The Haiku Is a Complete Poem of Seventeen Syllables

The **haiku** originated in Japan, where it has been a favorite genre for hundreds of years. It traditionally imposes strict rules on the writer: (1) There should be three lines (a tercet) of five, seven, and five syllables per line, for a total of seventeen syllables. (2) The topic should be derived from nature. (3) The poem should embody a unique observation or insight. Today, English-language poets have adapted the haiku but have taken liberties with the subject matter and have often reduced the syllable count. Whether the traditional pattern is varied or not, however, the haiku must be short, simple, objective, clear, and (often) symbolic. The following anonymous haiku illustrates some of these qualities.

 ## Spun in High, Dark Clouds

Spun in high, dark clouds,
Snow forms vast webs of white flakes
And drifts lightly down.

In the tradition of haiku, the subject is derived from nature, and the syllable pattern is 5–7–5. The central metaphor equates gathering snow with the webs of silkworms or spiders. To supply tension, the lines contrast "high" with "down" and "dark" with "white." Because of the enforced brevity, the diction is simple and, except for the word "forms," of English derivation (our word *form* is of Latin origin). In addition, most of the words are monosyllabic, and through this means the poem fills the seventeen-syllable form with sixteen words.

There Are Additional but Less Significant Closed-Form Types

Many other closed forms have enjoyed long popularity. One of these, the **epigram,** is a short and witty poem that usually makes a humorous or satiric point. Epigrams are two to four lines long and are often written in couplets. The form was developed by the Roman poet Martial (Marcus Valerius Martialis, c. 40–103 CE) and has always been popular. Humorous and sometimes irreverent **epitaphs,** brief poems composed to mark the death of someone, can also be epigrams.

Another popular type is the **limerick,** a five-line form popularized by the English artist and humorist Edward Lear (1812–1888). Like the epigram, limericks are comic, their humor being reinforced by falling rhymes. Usually, they are bawdy.

Comic closed forms continue to be devised by enterprising writers. The **clerihew,** a two-couplet form invented in the late nineteenth century by Edmund Clerihew Bentley (1875–1956), is related to the epigram. A final illustration of closed-form humor is the **double dactyl,** devised in the 1960s by Anthony Hecht and Paul Pascal. The form is related to the epigram, limerick, and clerihew, and it has rules that govern the meter, line length, and specific topic material.

Poets Use the Closed Form to Shape and Polish Meaning

Although many contemporary poets consider closed forms restrictive and even stultifying, the closed form has always provided both a framework and a challenge for poets to express new and fresh ideas, attitudes, and feelings. Let us look at the way Shakespeare uses the sonnet form to shape thoughts and emotions:

WILLIAM SHAKESPEARE (1564–1616)

For a portrait, see Chapter 21, page 1079.

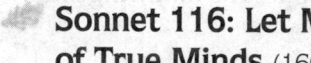 Sonnet 116: Let Me Not to the Marriage of True Minds (1609)

Let me not to the marriage of true minds
Admit impediments.° Love is not love
Which alters when it alteration finds,
Or bends with the remover to remove:
5 Oh, no! it is an ever-fixèd mark,
That looks on tempests and is never shaken;
It is the star to every wandering bark,
Whose worth's unknown, although his height° be taken.   *its altitude*
Love's not Time's fool,° though rosy lips and cheeks   *slave*
10 Within his° bending sickle's compass come;   *Time's*
Love alters not with his brief hours and weeks,
But bears it out even to the edge of doom.°   *the Last Judgment*
If this be error and upon me proved,
I never writ, nor no man ever loved.

°2 *impediments:* a reference to "The Order of Solemnization of Matrimony" in the Anglican Church's *Book of Common Prayer:* "I require that if either of you know of any impediment why ye may not be lawfully joined together in Matrimony, ye do now confess it."

QUESTIONS

1. Describe the restrictions of this closed form. How is the poem's argument structured by the form?
2. What is the poem's meter? Rhyme scheme? Structure?
3. Describe the varying ideas about love explored in the three quatrains.
4. What does the concluding couplet contribute to the poem's argument about love?

Even if we did not know that the poem is Shakespeare's, we would recognize it as a Shakespearean sonnet. It is in iambic pentameter and contains three quatrains and a concluding couplet, rhyming *abab cdcd efef gg*. The sonnet form provides the organization for the poem's argument—that real love is a "marriage of true minds" existing independent of earthly time and change. Each quatrain advances a new perspective on this idea.

This is not to say that Shakespeare exhausts the subject or that he wants to. The ideas in the third quatrain, for example, about how love transcends time, could be greatly expanded. A philosophical analysis of the topic might deal extensively with Platonic ideas about reality—whether it exists in *particulars* or *universals*. Similarly, the poem's very last line, if it were to become the topic of a prose discourse, might include the introduction of evidence about the poet's own writing, and also about many examples of human love. But the two lines are enough, granted the restrictions of the form, and more would be superfluous. One might add that most readers find Shakespeare's poem interesting and vital, while extensive philosophical discourses often drop into laps as readers fall asleep.

The closed poetic form therefore may be viewed as a complex consequence of poetic compression. No matter what form a poet chooses—couplet, sonnet, song, ballad, ode—that form imposes restrictions, and it therefore challenges and shapes the poet's thought. The poet of the closed form shares with all writers the need to make ideas seem logical and well supported, but the challenge of the form is to make all this happen *within the form itself*. The thought must be developed clearly and also fully, and there should be no lingering doubts once the poem is completed. The words must be the most fitting and exact ones that could be selected. When we look at good poems in the closed form, in short, we may be sure that they represent the ultimate degree of poetic thought, discipline, and skill.

Open-Form Poetry

Among the closed forms, as we have seen, the ode is the form that gives poets great opportunity for variability and expansion. The ode is thus the closed form that is most nearly related, in spirit, to **open-form poetry,** but the open form eliminates the restrictions of the closed form. Each open-form poem is unique and unpredictable. Poetry of this type was once termed **free verse** (from the French *vers libre*) to signify its liberation from regular metrics and its embrace of spoken rhythms. But open-form poetry is not therefore disorganized or chaotic. Open-form poets have instead created new and original ways to arrange words and lines—new ways to express thoughts and feelings, and new ways to order poetic experience.

Poets writing in the open form attempt to fuse form and content by stressing speechlike rhythms, creating a natural and easy-flowing word order, altering and varying line lengths according to the importance of ideas, and creating emphasis through the control of shorter and longer pauses. They often isolate individual words, phrases, and clauses as single lines, freely emphasize their ideas through the manipulation of spaces separating words and sentences, and sometimes even break up individual words in separate lines to highlight their importance.

Sometimes they create poems that look exactly like prose and that are printed in blocks and paragraphs instead of stanzas or lines. Such **prose poems** rely on a progression of images and the cadences of language.

Open-Form Poetry Is Free in Form and Variable in Content

An early example of open-form poetry is Walt Whitman's "When I Heard the Learned Astronomer." This poem was included in *Drum Taps,* a collection of poems about the poet's experiences during the Civil War and his reactions "to the Time and Land we swim in."

WALT WHITMAN (1819–1892)

For a photograph, see Chapter 14, page 667.

When I Heard the Learn'd Astronomer (1865)

When I heard the Learn'd astronomer,
When the proofs, the figures, were ranged in columns before me,
When I was shown the charts and diagrams, to add, divide, and measure them,
When I sitting heard the astronomer where he lectured with much applause in
     the lecture-room,
5   How soon unaccountable I became tired and sick,
Till rising and gliding out I wander'd off by myself,
In the mystical moist night-air, and from time to time,
Look'd up in perfect silence at the stars.

QUESTIONS

1. Explain why you consider the form of this poem closed or open.
2. How does Whitman use line lengths, cadences, and punctuation to create rhythm?
3. What are the effects produced by lists, repetition, and alliteration here?
4. What two worlds and ways of thinking are contrasted in this poem? Try to list the qualities of each world that are mentioned in the poem.

VISUALIZING POETRY

Poetry and Artistic Expression: Visual Poetry, Concrete Poetry, and Prose Poems

Along with the fact that many poets have rejected traditional closed-form patterns, they have moved in new directions with the open form. The idea has been to allow poetry to follow a wide range of poetic shapes, including avenues of experimentation. Poets have continued to express ideas about the topics we usually associate with poetry—which really means just about everything— but in addition, they have imaginatively invented new looks for their poems on the actual page. Some poets may indulge in creative playfulness by fashion-ing visual surprises, thus focusing on the medium itself, in which each poem starts its life, waiting patiently for readers. In fact, some poets give almost as much attention to their visual arrangement of letters, words, lines, and white space as they do to the content of their poems. To draw attention to particular thoughts, many poets deliberately alter the spellings of certain words; or they may run a number of words together, without spaces between them, to set them apart; or they may abandon the traditional capitalization of each new line; or, for that matter, they may simply reject some or all capitalization. We may see some of these characteristics in E. E. Cummings's poem "Buffalo Bill's Defunct," in which Cummings uses stretched-out lines in contrast with shorter lines, runs successive words together, and varies the placement of line beginnings, all as the means of guiding readers to see, hear, and comprehend the poem in accordance with his wishes.

E. E. CUMMINGS (1894–1962)

For a photo, see Chapter 12, page 584.

Buffalo Bill's Defunct° (1923)

Buffalo Bill's
defunct
    who used to
        ride a watersmooth-silver
                    stallion   5
and break onetwothreefourfive pigeonsjustlikethat
                              Jesus
he was a handsome man
              and what i want to know is
how do you like your blueeyed boy   10
Mister Death

°The poem has no title; it is usually referred to as "Portrait" or by its first two lines. Buffalo Bill (William F. Cody, 1846–1917) was an American plainsman, hunter, army scout, sharpshooter, and showman whose Wild West show began touring the world in 1883; he became a symbol of the Wild West.

QUESTIONS

1. What is the effect of devoting a whole line to "Buffalo Bill's" (line 1), "defunct" (line 2), "stallion" (line 5), "Jesus" (line 7), and "Mister Death" (line 11)? How does this tech-nique reflect and emphasize the content of the poem?

2. How does the typographical arrangement of line 6 contribute to the fusion of sound and sense? What other examples of this technique do you find?

3. Explain the denotations and connotations of *defunct*. What would be lost (or gained) by using the term *dead* or *deceased* instead?

4. To what extent is this poem a "portrait" of Buffalo Bill? What do we learn about him? Is the portrait respectful, mocking, or something in between?

Visual poetry, also called **shaped verse** and sometimes **picture poetry,** is alive and well today. Within this form, poets not only emphasize the idea and emotion of their subjects but also fashion their poems into a generalized or pictorial shape on the page, using words, lines, and spaces. In writing about visual and concrete poems, you should seek correspondences between images and poetic ideas. Describe the shape of the poem and the figures it resembles. Determine how varying line lengths, the placement of individual words and phrases, and the use of space all contribute to the visual effect.

Many patterns of visual form may be variable and, sometimes, surprising. William Heyen creates a unique form in his poem "Mantle," which presents his reflections about the brilliant professional career of Mickey Mantle, who is fondly remembered by sports fans as one of the superior home-run sluggers in baseball history. Many students experience a great joy of discovery when they recognize the shape that Heyen is simulating here with his poetic stanzas.

WILLIAM HEYEN (b. 1940)

 **Mantle°** (1980)

> Mantle ran so hard, they said,
> he tore his legs to pieces,
> What is this but spirit?
>
> 52 homers in '56, the triple crown.
> 5   I was a high school junior, batting
> fourth behind him in a dream.
>
> I prayed for him to quit, before
> his lifetime dropped below .300.
> But he didn't, and it did.
>
> 10   He makes Brylcreem commercials now,
> models with open mouths draped around him
> as they never were in Commerce, Oklahoma,
>
> where the sandy-haired, wide-shouldered boy
> stood up against his barn,
> 15   lefty for an hour (Ruth, Gehrig),
>
> then righty (DiMaggio),
> as his father winged them in,
> and the future blew toward him,
>
> now a fastball, now a slow
> 20   curve hanging
> like a model's smile.

°Mickey Mantle (1931–1995), a Yankee outfielder from 1951–1968. A switch hitter, he hit eighteen World Series home runs (a record) and 536 career home runs. He was the American League's most valuable player in 1956, the year he won the triple crown (line 4).

QUESTIONS

1. Describe the shape of the poem, being careful to study the last stanza. Why is this shape appropriate for a famous baseball player?
2. How does the poet use Mantle as a symbol in this poem?
3. Who are Ruth, Gehrig, and DiMaggio? In what ways are they like Mantle?

Just as some visual art is abstract and suggestive, rather than pictorial, so also may be the forms created by writers of visual poems. Such a poem is May Swenson's "Women," which is suggestive of feminine rhythm and movement. It is almost as though the poem itself is a dancing and gently swaying figure.

MAY SWENSON (1919–1989)

Women (1968)

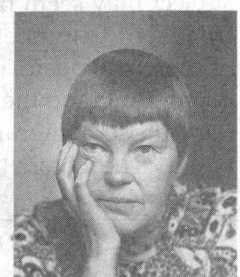

Women	Or they	
should be	should be	
pedestals	little horses	
moving	those wooden	
pedestals	sweet	5
moving	oldfashioned	
to the	painted	
motions	rocking	
of men	horses	
the gladdest things in the toyroom		10
The	feelingly	
pegs	and then	
of their	unfeelingly	
ears	To be	
so familiar	joyfully	15
and dear	ridden	
to the trusting	rockingly	
fists	ridden until	
To be chafed	the restored	
egos dismount and the legs stride away		20
Immobile	willing	
sweetlipped	to be set	
sturdy	into motion	
and smiling	Women	
women	should be	25
should always	pedestals	
be waiting	to men	

QUESTIONS

1. Is this poem an instance of closed-form, open-form, or visual poetry? In what different ways or sequences can it be read? How do the different sequences change the meaning?
2. How well does the image of the poem reinforce its meaning? Would the effect be different if the columns of words were straight instead of undulating?

3. To what extent do repetition and alliteration help to organize the poem and underscore its sense? Note especially *w*, *m*, *f*, *r*, and *s* sounds.

4. What does this poem *say* that women should be? Does it mean what it says? How are men characterized? In what way is this poem ironic?

Another and somewhat less graphic type of free verse is called the "prose poem." This phrase may seem like a contradiction in terms, but the idea that poets can write poems in the shape of prose is not surprising, granted that many modern poets are committed to principles of poetic freedom.[1] Some topics might possibly be more suitable to a prose form because they may seem less connected to poetry than to local or international news events, or they may involve the poet in reflections about politics, or about moral or religious matters. Sometimes the subject may seem problematic, and therefore more appropriate for a less formal treatment than poetry might offer. Above all, however, the major characteristic of the prose poem is that it should have the compactness and intensity of poetry, even though on the page, from a distance, it may at first seem just like any ordinary prose paragraph. Carolyn Forché creates such poetic intensity in her prose poem "The Colonel."

See David Lehman, ed., *Great American Prose Poems: From Poe to the Present* (New York: Scribner, 2003).

CAROLYN FORCHÉ (b. 1950)

The Colonel (1978)

What you have heard is true. I was in his house. His wife carried a tray of coffee and sugar. His daughter filed her nails, his son went out for the night. There were daily papers, pet dogs, a pistol on the cushion beside him. The moon swung bare on its black cord over the house. On the television was a cop show. It was in English. Broken
5 bottles were embedded in the walls around the house to scoop the kneecaps from a man's legs or cut his hands to lace. On the windows there were gratings like those in liquor stores. We had dinner, rack of lamb, good wine, a gold bell was on the table for calling the maid. The maid brought green mangoes, salt, a type of bread. I was asked how I enjoyed the country. There was a brief commercial in Spanish. His wife took
10 everything away. There was some talk then of how difficult it had become to govern. The parrot said hello on the terrace. The colonel told it to shut up, and pushed himself from the table. My friend said to me with eyes: say nothing. The colonel returned with a sack used to bring groceries home. He spilled many human ears on the table. They were like dried peach halves. There is no other way to say this. He took one of them
15 in his hands, shook it in our faces, dropped it into a water glass. It came alive there. I am tired of fooling around he said. As for the rights of anyone, tell your people they can go fuck themselves. He swept the ears to the floor with his arm and held the last of his wine in the air. Something for your poetry, no? he said. Some of the ears on the floor caught this scrap of his voice. Some of the ears on the floor were pressed to the
20 ground.

QUESTIONS

1. Why does the poet use the prose poem form for this poem?
2. What is the character of the colonel? How can he be gracious, and then abusive, at the same time? What atrocities has he committed or ordered committed?
3. Why does the speaker include details about the walls about the house? What do the walls show about the mentality of those within the walls? Explain the meaning of the last sentence.

As you explore modern poems, you will regularly encounter many different forms. Most poems will appear to be no more than slight variations of traditional poetic lines, but many will stretch and alter normal and expected linear patterns. And some will aim at fusing words and pictures, such as those we have examined briefly here. Modern writers seek to explore ideas and to blend their own new thoughts and insights with the poetic medium of new and original patterns of development. In addition to the poets mentioned here, many other modern poets have worked similarly with free forms. Some of these poets, included elsewhere in this volume, are Robinson Jeffers, Marge Piercy, Alberto Ríos, Sonia Sanchez, and C. K. Williams.

Poems for Study

John Berryman . . . . Dream Song 14, 736
Elizabeth Bishop . . . . One Art, 736
Elizabeth Bishop . . . . Sestina, 737
Billy Collins . . . . Sonnet, 738
John Dryden . . . . To the Memory of Mr. Oldham, 739
Lawrence Ferlinghetti . . . . Constantly Risking Absurdity, 740
Robert Frost . . . . Desert Places, 741
Allen Ginsberg . . . . A Supermarket In California, 742
George Herbert . . . . Virtue, 743
Ben Jonson . . . . To Celia, 744
John Keats . . . . Ode to a Nightingale, 745
Yusef Komunyakaa . . . . Grenade, 747
Claude McKay . . . . In Bondage, 748
John Milton . . . . On His Blindness (When I Consider
                                           How My Light Is Spent), 749
Dudley Randall . . . . Ballad of Birmingham, 749
Theodore Roethke . . . . The Waking, 751
Percy Bysshe Shelley . . . . Ozymandias, 751
Dylan Thomas . . . . Do Not Go Gentle into That Good Night, 752
Jean Toomer . . . . Reapers, 753
Phyllis Webb . . . . Poetics Against the Angel of Death, 753
Walt Whitman . . . . Reconciliation, 754
William Carlos Williams . . . . The Dance, 754

JOHN BERRYMAN (1914–1972)

Dream Song 14 (1964)

Life, friends, is boring. We must not say so.
After all, the sky flashes, the great sea yearns,
we ourselves flash and yearn,
and moreover my mother told me as a boy
5   (repeatedly) "Ever to confess you're bored
means you have no

Inner Resources." I conclude now I have no
inner resources, because I am heavy bored.
Peoples bore me,
10   literature bores me, especially great literature,
Henry bores me, with his plight & gripes
as bad as achilles,

who loves people and valiant art, which bores me.
And the tranquil hills, & gin, look like a drag
15   and somehow a dog
has taken itself & its tail considerably away
into mountains or sea or sky, leaving
behind: me, wag.

QUESTIONS

1. Why do you think people get bored? What advice might you give someone who says he or she is bored?
2. Who or what does the speaker blame for his boredom?
3. Why do you think the speaker does not always speak in "proper" English? How appropriate is this improper speech in relation to the theme of the poem?

ELIZABETH BISHOP (1911–1979)

One Art (1976)

The art of losing isn't hard to master;
so many things seem filled with the intent
to be lost that their loss is no disaster.

Lose something every day. Accept the fluster
5   of lost door keys, the hour badly spent.
The art of losing isn't hard to master.

Then practice losing farther, losing faster;
places, and names, and where it was you meant
to travel. None of these will bring disaster.

I lost my mother's watch. And look! my last, or   10
next-to-last, of three loved houses went.
The art of losing isn't hard to master.

I lost two cities, lovely ones. And, vaster,
some realms I owned, two rivers, a continent.
I miss them, but it wasn't a disaster.   15

—Even losing you (the joking voice, a gesture
I love) I shan't have lied. It's evident
the art of losing's not too hard to master
though it may look like (*Write* it!) like disaster.

QUESTIONS

1. This poem is written in a traditional closed form called the *villanelle* (originally an Italian peasant song), which was developed in France during the Middle Ages. A villanelle is nineteen lines long. Fairly strict rules govern the length and structure of stanzas, the rhyme scheme, and the repetition of complete lines. Try to formulate these rules. For comparison, see Roethke's "The Waking" and Thomas's "Do Not Go Gentle into That Good Night."

2. On what idea is the poem based? What evidence does the speaker produce about losing? What feelings does she express about her losses?

3. How could the speaker have lost "two cities"? What other things has she lost that justify her claim that "the art of losing isn't hard to master"? What might she mean by having lost the "you" to whom the poem is addressed?

ELIZABETH BISHOP (1911–1979)

 ## Sestina (1965)

September rain falls on the house.
In the failing light, the old grandmother
sits in the kitchen with the child
beside the Little Marvel Stove,
reading the jokes from the almanac,   5
laughing and talking to hide her tears.

She thinks that her equinoctial tears
and the rain that beats on the roof of the house
were both foretold by the almanac,
but only known to a grandmother.   10
The iron kettle sings on the stove.
She cuts some bread and says to the child,

It's time for tea now; but the child
is watching the teakettle's small hard tears
dance like mad on the hot black stove,   15
the way the rain must dance on the house.

Tidying up, the old grandmother
hangs up the clever almanac

on its string. Birdlike, the almanac
20   hovers half open above the child,
hovers above the old grandmother
and her teacup full of dark brown tears.
She shivers and says she thinks the house
feels chilly, and puts more wood in the stove.

25   *It was to be,* says the Marvel Stove.
I know what I know, says the almanac.
With crayons the child draws a rigid house
and a winding pathway. Then the child
puts in a man with buttons like tears
30   and shows it proudly to the grandmother.

But secretly, while the grandmother
busies herself about the stove,
the little moons fall down like tears
from between the pages of the almanac
35   into the flower bed the child
has carefully placed in the front of the house.

Time to plant tears, says the almanac.
The grandmother sings to the marvellous stove
and the child draws another inscrutable house.

Sᴇsᴛɪɴᴀ. As its title indicates, this poem is written in the trickiest of medieval fixed forms, that of the **sestina** (or "song of sixes"), said to have been invented in Provence in the thirteenth century by the troubadour poet Arnaut Daniel. In six six-line stanzas, the poet repeats six end-words (in a prescribed order), then reintroduces the six repeated words (in any order) in a closing **envoy** of three lines. Elizabeth Bishop strictly follows the troubadour rules for the order in which the end-words recur. (If you care, you can figure out the formula: in the first stanza, the six words are arranged A B C D E F; in the second, F A E B D C; and so on.)

QUESTIONS

1. Have you ever made up a make-believe friend or situation as a child? Why do you think children make such things up?
2. Which words are repeated throughout the poem? What is the effect of this repetition?
3. What is the relationship between the grandmother and the child?

BILLY COLLINS (b. 1941)

For a photo, see Chapter 11, page 534.

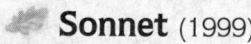 ## Sonnet (1999)

All we need is fourteen lines, well, thirteen now,
and after this next one just a dozen

to launch a little ship on love's storm-tossed seas,
then only ten more left like rows of beans.
How easily it goes unless you get Elizabethan   5
and insist the iambic bongos must be played
and rhymes positioned at the ends of lines,
one for every station of the cross.
But hang on here while we make the turn
into the final six where all will be resolved,   10
where longing and heartache will find an end,
where Laura will tell Petrarch to put down his pen,
take off those crazy medieval tights,
blow out the lights, and come at last to bed.

QUESTIONS

1. Why is this poem amusing? What makes it amusing?
2. What is the effect of lines 6 and 7? Why does the speaker refer to "every station of the cross" in line 8?
3. What is the "little ship" that is to be launched on "love's storm-tossed seas"? To what tradition of the sonnet form is this a reference?
4. Why does the poet conclude the poem with a description of a scene between Petrarch and Laura?

JOHN DRYDEN (1631–1700)

To the Memory of Mr. Oldham° (1684)

Farewell, too little and too lately known,
Whom I began to think and call my own:
For sure our souls were near allied, and thine
Cast in the same poetic mold with mine.
One common note on either lyre did strike,   5
And knaves and fools we both abhorred alike.
To the same goal did both our studies drive;
The last set out the soonest did arrive.
Thus Nisus° fell upon the slipp'ry place,
While his young friend performed and won the race.   10
O early ripe! to thy abundant store
What could advancing age have added more?
It might (what nature never gives the young)
Have taught the numbers of thy native tongue.
But satire needs not those, and wit will shine   15
Through the harsh cadence of a rugged line;
A noble error, and but seldom made,

°John Oldham (1653–1683) was a young poet whom Dryden admired. °9 *Nisus*: a character in Virgil's *Aeneid* who slipped in a pool of blood while running a race, thus allowing his best friend to win.

When poets are by too much force betrayed.
Thy gen'rous fruits, though gathered ere their prime,
20   Still showed a quickness; and maturing time
But mellows what we write to the dull sweets of rhyme.
Once more, hail and farewell;° farewell, thou young.
But ah too short, Marcellus° of our tongue;
Thy brows with ivy and with laurels° bound;
25   But fate and gloomy night encompass thee around.

°22 *hail and farewell*: an echo of the Latin phrase "*ave atque vale*"; see Catullus, *Poem* 101.10 ("and for eternity, brother, hail and farewell"). °23 *Marcellus*: a Roman general who was adopted by the Emperor Augustus as his successor but died at the age of twenty. °24 *laurels*: a plant sacred to Apollo, the Greek god of poetry; the traditional prize given to poets is a wreath of laurel.

QUESTIONS

1. What is the meter of this poem? Rhyme scheme? Closed form? How does the form control the tempo? Why is this tempo appropriate?

2. What does the speaker reveal about himself in lines 1–10? About Oldham? About his relationship with Oldham? What did the two have in common?

3. What is the effect of Dryden's frequent classical allusions? What pairs of rhyming words most effectively clinch ideas?

LAWRENCE FERLINGHETTI (b. 1919)

Constantly Risking Absurdity (1958)

Constantly risking absurdity
                    and death
         whenever he performs
                    above the heads
5   of his audience
      the poet like an acrobat
                    climbs on rime
                    to a high wire of his own making
      and balancing on eyebeams
10   above a sea of faces
         paces his way
                    to the other side of the day
      performing entrechats
                    and sleight-of-foot tricks
15   and other high theatrics
                    and all without mistaking
         any thing
                    for what it may not be
         For he's the super realist
20   who must perforce perceive

> taut truth
>> before the taking of each stance or step
> in his supposed advance
>>> toward that still higher perch
> where Beauty stands and waits   25
>> with gravity
>>> to start her death-defying leap
> And he
>> a little charleychaplin man
>>> who may or may not catch
> her fair eternal form   30
>> spreadeagled in the empty air
> of existence

QUESTIONS

1. Why do you think people enjoy watching and participating in risky behavior.
2. How is walking a tightrope like writing poetry?
3. Ferlinghetti establishes rhythm in the poem by having a constant number of stresses in each line. In what way does this pattern reflect writing poetry?

ROBERT FROST (1874–1963)

For a photo, see Chapter 18, page 837.

Desert Places (1936)

Snow falling and night falling fast, oh, fast
In a field I looked into going past,
And the ground almost covered smooth in snow,
But a few weeds and stubble showing last.

The woods around it have it—it is theirs.   5
All animals are smothered in their lairs.
I am too absent-spirited to count;
The loneliness includes me unawares.

And lonely as it is that loneliness
Will be more lonely ere it will be less—   10
A blanker whiteness of benighted snow
With no expression, nothing to express.

They cannot scare me with their empty spaces
Between stars—on stars where no human race is.
I have it in me so much nearer home   15
To scare myself with my own desert places.

QUESTIONS

1. What is the meter? The rhyme scheme? The form?

2. What setting and situation are established in lines 1–4? What does the snow affect here? What does it affect in lines 5–8? In lines 9–12?

3. What different kinds of "desert places" is this poem about? Which kind is the most important? Most frightening?

4. How does the type of rhyme (rising or falling) change in the last stanza? How does this change affect the tone and impact of the poem?

5. How does the stanzaic pattern of this poem organize the progression of the speaker's thoughts, feelings, and conclusions?

ALLEN GINSBERG (1926–1997)

A Supermarket in California (1955)

What thoughts I have of you tonight, Walt Whitman,° for
I walked down the sidestreets under the trees with a headache
self-conscious looking at the full moon.
   In my hungry fatigue, and shopping for images, I went
5 into the neon fruit supermarket, dreaming of your
   enumerations!°
What peaches and what penumbras! Whole families
shopping at night! Aisles full of husbands! Wives in the
avocados, babies in the tomatoes!—and you, Garcia Lorca,° what
10 were you doing down by the watermelons?
   I saw you, Walt Whitman, childless, lonely old grubber,
poking among the meats in the refrigerator and eyeing the grocery boys.
   I heard you asking questions of each: Who killed the pork
chops? What price bananas? Are you my Angel?
15   I wandered in and out of the brilliant stacks of cans
following you, and followed in my imagination by the store detective.
   We strode down the open corridors together in our solitary
fancy tasting artichokes, possessing every frozen delicacy, and
never passing the cashier.

20   Where are we going, Walt Whitman? The doors close in
an hour. Which way does your beard point tonight?
   (I touch your book and dream of our odyssey in the supermarket
and feel absurd.)
   Will we walk all night through solitary streets? The trees
25 add shade to shade, lights out in the houses, we'll both be lonely.

°1 *Walt Whitman*: American poet (1819–1892) who experimented with open forms and significantly influenced the development of twentieth-century poetry.   °6 *enumerations*: Many of Whitman's poems contain long lists.
°9 *Garcia Lorca*: Spanish surrealist poet and playwright (1896–1936) whose later poetry became progressively more like prose.

Will we stroll dreaming of the lost America of love past blue
automobiles in driveways, home to our silent cottage?
   Ah, dear father, graybeard, lonely old courage-teacher,
what America did you have when Charon° quit poling his ferry
and you got out on a smoking bank and stood watching the   30
boat disappear on the black waters of Lethe?°

°29 *Charon:* boatman in Greek mythology who ferried the souls of the dead across the river Styx into Hades, the underworld. °31 *Lethe:* the river of forgetfulness in Hades. The dead drank from this river and forgot their former lives.

QUESTIONS

1. Where is the speaker? What is he doing? What is his condition?
2. What effect is produced by placing Whitman and Lorca in the market?
3. To what extent do we find Whitman-like enumerations in this work? What is the effect of such enumerations?
4. Why is this a poem? What poetic devices are employed here? To what extent might it make more sense to consider this prose rather than poetry?

GEORGE HERBERT (1593–1633)

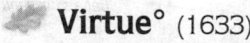 Virtue° (1633)

Sweet day, so cool, so calm, so bright,
The bridal of the earth and sky:
The dew shall weep thy fall tonight;
   For thou must die.

Sweet rose, whose hue, angry° and brave,°   *red; splendid* 5
Bids the rash° gazer wipe his eye:
Thy root is ever in its grave,
   And thou must die.

Sweet spring, full of sweet days and roses,
A box where sweets° compacted lie: *perfumes* 10
My music shows ye have your closes,°
   And all must die.

Only a sweet and virtuous soul,
Like seasoned timber, never gives;°
But though the whole world turn to coal,°   15
   Then chiefly lives.

°The title can allude to (a) divine Power operating both outside and inside an individual; (b) a characteristic quality or property; (c) conformity to divine and moral laws. °6 *rash:* eager or sympathetic. °11 *closes:* A close is the conclusion of a musical composition. °14 *never gives:* i.e., never gives in, never deteriorates and collapses (like rotted timber). °15 *turn to coal:* the burned-out residue of the earth after the universal fire on Judgment Day.

QUESTIONS

1. What is the rhyme scheme of this poem? The meter? The form?

2. What points does the speaker make about the day, the rose, spring, and the "sweet and virtuous soul"?

BEN JONSON (1572–1632)

For a portrait, see Chapter 11, page 551.

 ## To Celia° (1606)

Come my Celia, let us prove,°   *try*
While we may, the sports of love;
Time will not be ours forever;
He at length our good will sever.
5   Spend not then his gifts in vain.
Suns that set may rise again;
But if once we lose this light.
'Tis with us perpetual night.
Why should we defer our joys?
10 Fame° and rumor are but toys.   *reputation*
Cannot we delude the eyes
Of a few poor household spies,
Or his° easier ears beguile,   *Celia's husband*
So removed by our wile?
15 'Tis no sin love's fruit to steal;
But the sweet theft to reveal,
To be taken, to be seen,
These have crimes accounted been.

_____

°The poem is from Jonson's play *Volpone*; it is spoken by Volpone (the name means "the fox") to Celia, a married woman whom he is trying to seduce.

QUESTIONS

1. What is the speaker like? What is his attitude toward time? Love? Celia?

2. What is personified in lines 3–5? What power does this force have?

3. This type of poem (and the specific argument in lines 1–8) is called *carpe diem* (Latin for "seize the day"). How is the idea of "seizing the day" relevant to the first eight lines of this poem?

4. How does the speaker's argument change in the last ten lines (9–18)? What does he claim that he and Celia can do? What assertions does he (and the poem) make about time, love, reputation, and crime?

5. How consistent is the speaker's argument? How convincing? How moral?

6. What is the tone of the poem? How is it created? How does it affect the total meaning of the poem?

JOHN KEATS (1795–1821)

For a portrait, see Chapter 14, page 641.

🍂 Ode to a Nightingale (1819)

1

My heart aches, and a drowsy numbness pains
  My sense, as though of hemlock° I had drunk,   *a poisonous herb*
Or emptied some dull opiate to the drains
  One minute past, and Lethe-wards° had sunk:
'Tis not through envy of thy happy lot,   5
  But being too happy in thine happiness,—
      That thou, light-winged Dryad° of the trees,
        In some melodious plot
      Of beechen green, and shadows numberless,
  Singest of summer in full-throated ease.   10

2

O, for a draught of vintage! that hath been
  Cool'd a long age in the deep-delved earth,
Tasting of Flora° and the country green,
  Dance, and Provençal song, and sunburnt mirth!
O for a beaker full of the warm South,   15
  Full of the true, the blushful Hippocrene,°
      With beaded bubbles winking at the brim,
        And purple-stainèd mouth;
      That I might drink, and leave the world unseen,
  And with thee fade away into the forest dim: 20

3

Fade far away, dissolve, and quite forget
  What thou among the leaves hast never known,
The weariness, the fever, and the fret
  Here, where men sit and hear each other groan;
Where palsy shakes a few, sad, last gray hairs,   25
  Where youth grows pale, and spectre-thin, and dies;
      Where but to think is to be full of sorrow
        And leaden-eyed despairs,
      Where Beauty cannot keep her lustrous eyes,
  Or new Love pine at them beyond to-morrow.   30

°4 *Lethe-wards:* toward the river of forgetfulness in Hades, the underworld of Greek mythology. °7 *Dryad:* in Greek mythology, a semidivine tree spirit. °13 *Flora:* the Roman goddess of flowers. °16 *Hippocrene:* the fountain of the Muses on Mt. Helicon in Greek mythology; the phrase thus refers to both the waters of poetic inspiration and a cup of wine.

4

Away! away! for I will fly to thee,
   Not charioted by Bacchus° and his pards,°   *leopards*
But on the viewless wings of Poesy,°   *poetry*
   Though the dull brain perplexes and retards:
35 Already with thee! tender is the night,
   And haply the Queen-Moon is on her throne,
      Cluster'd around by all her starry Fays;°   *fairies*
      But here there is no light,
   Save what from heaven is with the breezes blown
40   Through verdurous glooms and winding mossy ways.

5

I cannot see what flowers are at my feet,
   Nor what soft incense hangs upon the boughs,
But, in embalmed° darkness, guess each sweet   *fragrant*
   Wherewith the seasonable month endows
45 The grass, the thicket, and the fruit-tree wild;
   White hawthorn, and the pastoral eglantine;°   *honeysuckle*
      Fast fading violets cover'd up in leaves;
        And mid-May's eldest child,
      The coming musk-rose, full of dewy wine,
50   The murmurous haunt of flies on summer eves.

6

Darkling° I listen; and, for many a time   *in the dark*
   I have been half in love with easeful Death,
Call'd him soft names in many a musèd rhyme,
   To take into the air my quiet breath;
55 Now more than ever seems it rich to die,
   To cease upon the midnight with no pain,
      While thou art pouring forth thy soul abroad
        In such an ecstasy!
   Still wouldst thou sing, and I have ears in vain—
60   To thy high requiem become a sod.

7

Thou wast not born for death, immortal Bird!
   No hungry generations tread thee down;
The voice I hear this passing night was heard
   In ancient days by emperor and clown:
65 Perhaps the self-same song that found a path
Through the sad heart of Ruth,° when, sick for home,
      She stood in tears amid the alien corn;°   *wheat, grain*
        The same that oft-times hath
Charm'd magic casements, opening on the foam
70   Of perilous seas, in faery lands forlorn.

°32 *Bacchus:* Dionysus, the Greek god of fertility and power, and, as Bacchus, the god of Wine; see Chapter 21.
66 *Ruth:* the widow of Boaz in the biblical Book of Ruth.

8

Forlorn! the very word is like a bell
　　To toll me back from thee to my sole self!
Adieu! the fancy° cannot cheat so well   *imagination*
　　As she is fam'd to do, deceiving elf.
Adieu! adieu! thy plaintive anthem fades   75
　　Past the near meadows, over the still stream,
　　　　Up the hill-side; and now 'tis buried deep
　　　　　　In the next valley-glades:
Was it a vision, or a waking dream?
　　Fled is that music:—Do I wake or sleep?   80

QUESTIONS

1. Formulate the structure (meter of each line and rhyme scheme) of the stanzas. What traditional form is employed here?

2. What is the speaker's mental and emotional state in stanza 1? What similes are employed to describe this condition?

3. What does the speaker want in stanza 2? Whom does he want to join? Why? From what aspects of the world (stanza 3) does he want to escape?

4. How do the speaker's mood and perspective change in stanza 4? How does he achieve this transition? What characterizes the world that the speaker enters in stanza 5? What senses are employed to describe this world?

5. What does the speaker establish about the nightingale's song in stanza 7? What does the song come to symbolize?

YUSEF KOMUNYAKAA (b. 1947)

Grenade (2008)

There's no rehearsal to turn flesh into dust so quickly. A hair trigger, a cocked hammer in the brain, a split second between a man & infamy. It lands on the ground—a few soldiers duck & the others are caught in a half-run—& one throws himself down on the grenade. All the watches stop. A flash. Smoke. Silence. The sound fills the whole day. Flesh & earth fall into the eyes & mouths of the men. A dream trapped in midair. They   5
touch their legs & arms, their groins, ears, & noses, saying, What happened? Some are crying. Others are laughing. Some are almost dancing. Someone tries to put the dead man back together. "He just dove on the damn thing, sir!" A flash. Smoke. Silence. The day blown apart. For those who can walk away, what is their burden? Shreds of flesh & bloody rags gathered up & stuffed into a bag. Each breath belongs to him. Each   10
song. Each curse. Every prayer is his. Your body doesn't belong to your mind & soul. Who are you? Do you remember the man left in the jungle? The others who owe their lives to this phantom, do they feel like you? Would his loved ones remember him if that little park or statue erected in his name didn't exist, & does it enlarge their lives?

15 You wish he'd lie down in that closed coffin, & not wander the streets or enter your bedroom at midnight. The woman you love, she'll never understand. Who would? You remember what he used to say: "If you give a kite too much string, it'll break free." That unselfish certainty. But you can't remember when you began to live his unspoken dreams.

QUESTIONS

1. What has happened? What do we learn that the dead man has done? Where did this event most likely occur?

2. Who does the speaker seem to be? How did he learn of the event? Is the poem less about the dead man than about him, the speaker? Why?

3. What are the first reactions of those who were near the dead man? Are these reactions to be expected? What does one of the men try to do?

4. What does the speaker say about the dead man, the one who made the sacrifice? Why does he say that he wishes the dead man would "not wander the streets or enter your bedroom at midnight"? What is meant by this language? What might be symbolized by what the dead man used to say: "If you give a kite too much string, it'll break free"?

5. Why do you think that Komunyakaa wrote this poem as a prose poem rather than as a more traditional poem?

CLAUDE McKAY (1890–1948)

 In Bondage (1922)

I would be wandering in distant fields
Where man, and bird, and beast, live leisurely,
And the old earth is kind, and ever yields
Her goodly gifts to all her children free;
5 Where life is fairer, lighter, less demanding,
And boys and girls have time and space for play
Before they come to years of understanding—
Somewhere I would be singing, far away.
For life is greater than the thousand wars
10 Men wage for it in their insatiate lust,
And will remain like the eternal stars,
When all that shines to-day is drift and dust.

But I am bound with you in your mean graves,
O black men, simple slaves of ruthless slaves.

QUESTIONS

1. What is the meter of this poem? The rhyme scheme? The form? To what extent does the form organize the speaker's thoughts?

2. Lines 1–8 present a conditional (rather than actual) situation that the speaker desires. What word signals this nature? What is the speaker's wish?

3. What point does the speaker make about life in lines 9–12?

4. How does the couplet undermine the rest of the poem? What single word conveys this reversal? How effectively do the rhymes clinch the poem's meaning? What is the speaker telling us about the lives of African Americans?

JOHN MILTON (1608–1674)

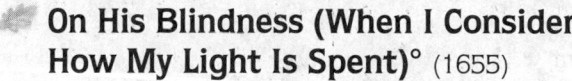 **On His Blindness (When I Consider How My Light Is Spent)°** (1655)

When I consider how my light is spent
   Ere half my days, in this dark world and wide,
   And that one talent° which is death to hide,
   Lodged with me useless, though my soul more bent
To serve therewith my Maker, and present   5
   My true account, lest he returning chide;
   "Doth God exact day-labor, light denied?"
   I fondly° ask; but Patience to prevent°   *foolishly; forestall*
That murmur, soon replies, "God doth not need
   Either man's work or his own gifts; who best   10
   Bear his mild yoke, they serve him best. His state
Is kingly. Thousands at his bidding speed
   And post o'er land and ocean without rest;
   They also serve who only stand and wait."

°Milton began to go blind in the late 1640s and was completely blind by 1651. °3 *talent:* both a skill and a reference to the talents discussed in the parable in Matthew 25:14–30.

QUESTIONS

1. What is the meter of this poem? The rhyme scheme? The closed form?

2. To what extent do the two major divisions of this form organize the poem's ideas?

3. What problem is raised in the octave? What are the speaker's complaints? Who is the speaker in the sestet? How are the earlier conflicts resolved?

4. Explore the word *talent* and relate its various meanings to the poem as a whole.

DUDLEY RANDALL (1914–2000)

 **Ballad of Birmingham°** (1966)

(On the bombing of a church in Birmingham, Alabama, 1963)

"Mother dear, may I go downtown
Instead of out to play,

°Four black children were killed when the 16th Street Baptist Church in Birmingham, Alabama, was bombed in 1963. A man was finally indicted for the murders in 1977 and convicted in 1982. There was an additional conviction in 2002.

And march the streets of Birmingham
In a Freedom March today?"

5   "No, baby, no, you may not go,
For the dogs are fierce and wild,
And clubs and hoses, guns and jails
Aren't good for a little child."

"But, mother, I won't be alone.
10 Other children will go with me,
And march the streets of Birmingham
To make our country free."

"No, baby, no, you may not go,
For I fear those guns will fire.
15 But you may go to church instead
And sing in the children's choir."

She has combed and brushed her night-dark hair,
And bathed rose petal sweet,
And drawn white gloves on her small brown hands,
20 And white shoes on her feet.

The mother smiled to know her child
Was in the sacred place,
But that smile was the last smile
To come upon her face.

25 For when she heard the explosion,
Her eyes grew wet and wild.
She raced through the streets of Birmingham
Calling for her child.

She clawed through bits of glass and brick,
30 Then lifted out a shoe
"Oh, here's the shoe my baby wore,
But, baby, where are you?"

QUESTIONS

1. Formulate the structure (meter, rhyme scheme, stanza form) of this poem. What traditional closed form is employed here?
2. Who is the speaker in stanzas 1 and 3? In stanzas 2 and 4? How are quotation and
   repetition employed to create tension?
3. What ironies do you find in the mother's assumptions? In the poem as a whole? In the
   society pictured in the poem?
4. Compare the poem to "Sir Patrick Spens" (p. 541). How are the structures of all three
   alike? To what extent do all three deal with the same type of subject matter?

THEODORE ROETHKE (1908–1963)

For a photo, see Chapter 12, page 591.

 ## The Waking (1953)

I wake to sleep, and take my waking slow.
I feel my fate in what I cannot fear.
I learn by going where I have to go.

We think by feeling. What is there to know?
I hear my being dance from ear to ear.   5
I wake to sleep, and take my waking slow.

Of those so close beside me, which are you?
God bless the Ground! I shall walk softly there,
And learn by going where I have to go.

Light takes the Tree; but who can tell us how?   10
The lowly worm climbs up a winding stair;
I wake to sleep, and take my waking slow.

Great Nature has another thing to do
To you and me; so take the lively air,
And, lovely, learn by going where to go.   15

This shaking keeps me steady. I should know.
What falls away is always. And is near.
I wake to sleep, and take my waking slow.
I learn by going where I have to go.

QUESTIONS

1. Compare the form of this poem with the poems by Bishop and Thomas in this chapter.
2. In what way or ways does the speaker "wake to sleep"? What other apparent contradictions does the speaker develop in this poem? Why might a reader conclude that the poem is positive rather than negative?
3. What does the speaker mean by saying that he learns "by going where I have to go"? In what way does "always" fall away (line 17)?

PERCY BYSSHE SHELLEY (1792–1822)

 ## Ozymandias (1818)

I met a traveller from an antique land,
Who said—"Two vast and trunkless legs of stone
Stand in the desert. . . . Near them, on the sand,
Half sunk, a shattered visage lies, whose frown,
And wrinkled lip, and sneer of cold command,   5

Tell that its sculptor well those passions read
Which yet survive, stamped on these lifeless things,
The hand that mocked them, and the heart that fed;
And on the pedestal, these words appear;
10   'My name is Ozymandias, King of Kings,
Look on my Works, ye Mighty, and despair!'
Nothing beside remains. Round the decay
Of that colossal Wreck, boundless and bare
The lone and level sands stretch far away."

QUESTIONS

1. What is the meter of this poem? The rhyme scheme? What traditional closed form is modified here? How do the modifications affect the poem?

2. To what extent are content and meaning shaped by the closed form? What is described in the octave? In the sestet?

3. Characterize Ozymandias (thought to be Ramses II, pharaoh of Egypt, who died in 1225 BCE) from the way he is portrayed in this poem.

DYLAN THOMAS (1914–1953)

Do Not Go Gentle into That Good Night (1951)

Do not go gentle into that good night,
Old age should burn and rave at close of day;
Rage, rage against the dying of the light.

Though wise men at their end know dark is right,
5   Because their words had forked no lightning they
Do not go gentle into that good night.

Good men, the last wave by, crying how bright
Their frail deeds might have danced in a green bay,
Rage, rage against the dying of the light.

10   Wild men who caught and sang the sun in flight,
And learn, too late, they grieved it on its way,
Do not go gentle into that good night.

Grave men, near death, who see with blinding sight
Blind eyes could blaze like meteors and be gay,
15   Rage, rage against the dying of the light.

And you, my father, there on the sad height,
Curse, bless, me now with your fierce tears, I pray.
Do not go gentle into that good night.
Rage, rage against the dying of the light.

QUESTIONS

1. What conclusions do you make about the poem's speaker, listener, and situation?
2. What connotative words do you find here? Consider "dying," the "good" of "good night," "gentle," "Curse, bless, me now with your fierce tears, I pray," and "grave."
3. What five different kinds of men does the speaker discuss in stanzas 2–5? What do they have in common? Of what value are they to the speaker's father (line 16)?
4. Compare the form of this poem with the poems by Bishop and Roethke in this chapter.

JEAN TOOMER (1894–1967)

Reapers (1923)

Black reapers with the sound of steel on stones
Are sharpening scythes. I see them place the hones
In their hip-pockets as a thing that's done,
And start their silent swinging, one by one.
Black horses drive a mower through the weeds,   5
And there, a field rat, startled, squealing bleeds,
His belly close to ground. I see the blade,
Blood-stained, continue cutting weeds and shade.

QUESTIONS

1. What is the poem's meter? The rhyme scheme? What is the difference between Toomer's use of the rhyming pattern and Dryden's?
2. How do the images of this poem relate to each other? How does the image of the bleeding field rat and the "blood-stained" blade heighten the impact?
3. How does alliteration unify this poem and make sound echo sense? Note especially the *s* and *b* sounds and the phrase "silent swinging."

PHYLLIS WEBB (b. 1927)

Poetics Against the Angel of Death° (1962)

I am sorry to speak of death again
(some say I'll have a long life)
but last night Wordsworth's 'Prelude'°
suddenly made sense—I mean the measure,
the elevated tone, the attitude   5
of private Man speaking to public men.
Last night I thought I would not wake again
but now with this June morning I run ragged to elude
the Great Iambic Pentameter
who is the Hound of Heaven° in our stress   10
because I want to die

°3 *Wordsworth's 'Prelude'*: See this chapter, page 722. °10 *Hound of Heaven* (*The*): a long poem (1893) by Francis Thompson (1859–1907) about attempting to evade God's love.

QUESTIONS

1. In the poem itself, what is meant by the "Angel of Death"?
2. What attitude does the speaker express about iambic pentameter? How does the speaker explain this attitude? How defensible is the attitude?
3. For what poetic forms does the speaker express a preference? Why? How does the form of this poem bear out the preference?

WALT WHITMAN (1819–1892)

For a photograph, see Chapter 14, page 667.

 Reconciliation (1865, 1881)

Word over all, beautiful as the sky,
Beautiful that war and all its deeds of carnage must in time be utterly lost,
That the hands of the sisters Death and Night incessantly softly wash again, and
   ever again, this soil'd world;
For my enemy is dead, a man divine as myself is dead,
5 I look where he lies white-faced and still in the coffin—I draw near,
Bend down and touch lightly with my lips the while face in the coffin.

QUESTIONS

1. How do individual lines, varying line lengths, punctuation, pauses, and cadences create rhythm and organize the images and ideas in this poem?
2. To what extent do alliteration, assonance, and the repetition of words unify the poem and reinforce its content?
3. What is the "word" referred to in line 1? What does the speaker find "beautiful" about this "word" and the passage of time?
4. What instances of personification can you find? What do these personified figures do? What does the speaker do in lines 5–6? Why does he do this?

WILLIAM CARLOS WILLIAMS (1883–1963)

 The Dance (1944)

In Brueghel's° great picture, The Kermess,°
the dancers go round, they go round and
around, the squeal and the blare and the
tweedle of bagpipes, a bugle and fiddles
5 tipping their bellies (round as the thick-sided
glasses whose wash they impound)
their hips and their bellies off balance
to turn them. Kicking and rolling about

°1 *Brueghel's:* Pieter Brueghel (c. 1525–1569), a Flemish painter. °The Kermess: *Peasants' Dance (The Kermess)* shows peasants dancing in celebration of the anniversary of the founding of a church (*church mass*).

the Fair Grounds, swinging their butts, those
shanks must be sound to bear up under such
rollicking measures, prance as the dance
in Brueghel's great picture, The Kermess.

10

QUESTIONS

1. What effect is produced by repeating the first line as the last line?
2. How do repetition, alliteration, assonance, onomatopoeia, and internal rhyme affect the tempo, feeling, and meaning of the poem? How do the numerous participles (like "tipping," "kicking," "rolling") make sound echo sense?
3. What words are capitalized? What effect is produced by omitting the capital letters at the beginning of each line? How does this typographical choice reinforce the sound and the sense of the poem?
4. Most of the lines of this poem are run-on rather than end-stopped, and many of them end with fairly weak words such as *and, the, about,* and *such.* What effect is produced through these techniques?
5. How successful is Williams in making the words and sentence rhythms echo the visual rhythms in Brueghel's painting? Why is this open form more appropriate to the images of the poem than any closed form could be?

WRITING ABOUT FORM IN POETRY

An essay about form in poetry should demonstrate a relationship between a poem's sense and its form. Do not discuss form or shape in isolation, for such an essay would be no more than a detailed description. The first thing to do as you go about determining what you want to say is to examine the poem's main ideas. Consider the various elements that contribute to the poem's impact and effectiveness: the speaker, listener, setting, situation, diction, imagery, and rhetorical devices. Once you understand these, it will be easier to establish a connection between form and content.

You will find it helpful to prepare a work sheet that highlights the elements you are deciding that you wish to discuss. For closed forms, these elements will be rhyme scheme, meter, line lengths, and stanzaic patterns. They may also include significant words and phrases that connect stanzas. The work sheet for an open-form poem should indicate variables such as rhythm and phrases; the use of pauses; significant words that are isolated or emphasized through typography; patterns of repeated sounds, words, phrases, and images; and, if relevant, the relationship of the poem's content and any special visual effects.

Questions for Discovering Ideas

CLOSED FORM

*   What is the principal meter? Line length? Rhyme scheme? To what extent do these establish and/or reinforce the form?

- What is the form of each stanza or unit? How many stanzas or divisions does the poem contain? How does the poem establish a pattern? How does the pattern control the poem's developing content?
- What is the form of the poem (e.g., couplet, tercet, ballad, villanelle, sonnet)? In what ways is the poem traditional, and what variations does it introduce? What is the effect of the variations?
- How effectively does the structure create or reinforce the poem's internal logic? What topical, logical, or thematic progressions unite the various parts of the poem?
- To what extent does the form organize the images of the poem? How does the poet develop images within single units or stanzas? Do images recur in more than one section? What is the purpose and effect of this recurrence?
- To what extent does the form organize and bring out the poem's ideas or emotions?

OPEN FORM

- What does the poem look like on the page? What is the relationship of its shape to its meaning?
- How does the poet use variable line lengths, spaces, punctuation, capitalization, and the like to shape the poem? How do these variables contribute to the poem's sense and impact?
- What rhythms are built into the poem through language or typography? How are these relevant to the poem's content?
- What is the poem's progression of ideas, images, and/or emotions? How is the logic created, and what does it contribute?
- How does form or typography isolate or unite, and thus emphasize, various words and phrases? What is the effect of such emphasis?
- What patterns do you discover of words and sounds? To what degree do the patterns create order and structure? How are they related to the sense of the poem?

Strategies for Organizing Ideas

In developing your central idea, you should illustrate the connections between form and meaning. For example, in planning an essay on Randall's "Ballad of Birmingham" you might develop your ideas according to the speeches that are a normal feature of the ballad form. The poem's first part is a dialogue between mother and child about the hazard of the local streets and the safety of the local church. In the second part, after the explosion, the mother runs toward the church and calls for her child, who, ironically, will never again engage with her in further dialogue. Another plan would be needed for a discussion of Heyen's "Mantle," the form of which requires enough stanzas of approximately equal length to make up the pattern of a pitched ball. (What is this pattern?)

Your introduction should contain general remarks about the poem, but it should, above that, focus on the connection between form and substance.

Describe the ways in which structure and content interact together, with a brief listing of your specific topics.

Early in the body, describe the formal characteristics of your poem, using schemes and numbers (as in paragraph 2 of the illustrative student essay). With closed forms, your description should detail such standard features as the traditional form, meter, rhyme scheme, stanzaic structure, and number of stanzas. With open-form poetry, you should focus on the most striking and significant features of the verse).

Be sure to integrate your discussion of both form and content. It may be that you have uncovered a good deal of information about technical features such as alliteration or rhyme, or you may wish to stress that words, phrases, and clauses develop a pattern of ideas. Remember that you are not making a paraphrase or a general explication, but instead are showing how the poet uses form—either an open or a closed one—in the service of meaning. The order in which you deal with your topics is entirely up to you.

The conclusion of your essay might contain additional relevant observations about shape or structure. It might also summarize your argument. Here, as in all essays about literature, make sure to reach an actual conclusion rather than simply a stopping point.

Illustrative Student Essay

Although underlined sentences are not recommended by MLA style, they are used in this illustrative essay as teaching tools to emphasize the central idea, thesis sentence, and topic sentences.

Adams 1

Kimberly Adams

Professor Patter

English 102

20 February 2014

Form and Meaning in George Herbert's "Virtue"°

Herbert's devotional four-stanza poem "Virtue" (1633) contrasts the [1]

mortality of worldly things with the immortality of the "virtuous soul." This is not

an uncommon topic in religious poetry and hymns, and there is nothing unusual

about this contrast. What is unusual, however, is the simplicity and directness

of Herbert's expressions and the way in which he integrates his ideas

°This poem appears on page 743.

within his stanzaic song pattern. Each part of the poem organizes the images logically and underscores the supremacy of life over death.* Through control over line and stanza groupings, rhyme scheme, and repeated sounds and words, Herbert's stanzas create a structural and visual distinction between the"sweet" soul and the rest of creation.†

[2]   Herbert's control over lines within the stanzas is particularly strong. Each stanza follows the same *abab* rhyme scheme. Because some rhyme sounds and words are repeated throughout the first three stanzas, however, the structure of the poem can be formulated as *4a4b4a2b 4c4b4c2b 4d4b4d2b 4e4f4e2f*. Each stanza thus contains three lines of iambic tetrameter with a final line of iambic dimeter—an unusual pattern that creates a unique emphasis. In the first three stanzas, the dimeter lines repeat the phrase "must die," while in the last stanza the contrast is made on the words "Then chiefly lives." These rhythms require a sensitive reading, and they powerfully underscore Herbert's idea that death is conquered by eternal life.

[3]   Like individual lines, Herbert's stanzaic structure provides the poem's pattern of organization and logic. The first stanza focuses on the image of the "Sweet day," comparing the day to "The bridal of the earth and sky" (line 2) and asserting that the day inevitably "must die." Similarly, the second stanza focuses on the image of a "Sweet rose" and asserts that it too "must die." The third stanza shifts to the image of "Sweet spring." Here the poet blends the images of the first two stanzas into the third by noting that the "Sweet spring" is "full of sweet days and roses" (9). The stanza concludes with the summarizing claim that "all must die." In this way, the third stanza is the climax of Herbert's imagery of beauty and mortality. The last stanza introduces a new image—"a sweet and virtuous soul"—and an assertion that is contrasted with the ideas expressed in the previous three stanzas. Although the day, the rose, and the spring "must die," the soul "never" deteriorates, but "chiefly lives" even "though the whole world turn to coal" (15). With its key image of the "virtuous soul," this last stanza marks the logical conclusion of Herbert's argument. His pattern of organization allows this key

---

*Central idea.
†Thesis sentence.

Adams 3

image of permanence to be separated structurally from the images of
impermanence.

This structural organization of images and ideas is repeated and   [4]
reinforced by other techniques. Herbert's rhyme scheme, for example, links the
first three stanzas while isolating the fourth. That the *b* rhyme is repeated at
the ends of the second and fourth lines of each of the first three stanzas makes
these stanzas into a complete unit. The fourth stanza, however, is different in
both content and rhyme. The stanza introduces the concept of immortality,
and it also introduces entirely new rhymes, replacing the *b* rhyme with an *f*
rhyme. Thus the rhyme scheme, by sound alone, parallels the poem's imagery
and logic.

As a complement to the rhyming sounds, the poem also demonstrates   [5]
organizing patterns of assonance. Most notable is the *oo* sound, which is
repeated throughout the first three stanzas in the words "cool," "dew,"
"whose," "hue," "root," and "music." The *oo* sound might also have still been
prominent in the word "thou," so that in the first three stanzas the *oo*, which
is suggestive of a moan (certainly appropriate to things that die), is repeated
eight times. In the last stanza there is a stress on the *o* sound, in "only," "soul,"
"though," "whole," and "coal." While *oh* may also be a moan, in this context
it is more like an exclamation, in keeping with the triumph contained in the
final line.

Herbert's repetition of key words and phrases also distinguishes the   [6]
first three stanzas from the last stanza. Each of the first three stanzas begins
with "sweet" and ends with "must die." These repetitions stress both the
beauty and the mortality of worldly things. In the last stanza, however, this
repetition is abandoned, just as the stress on immortality transcends mortality.
The "Sweet" that begins each of the first three stanzas is replaced by "Only"
(13). Similarly, "must die" is replaced with "chiefly lives." Both substitutions
separate this final stanza from the three previous stanzas. More importantly,
the shift in the verbal pattern emphasizes the transition from death to the
virtuous soul's immortality.

Adams 4

[7]   The lyric form of Herbert's "Virtue" provides an organizational pattern for the poem's images and ideas. At the same time, the stanzaic pattern and the rhyme scheme allow the poet to draw a strong distinction between the corruptible world and the immortal soul. The closed form of this poem is not arbitrary or incidental; it is an integral way of asserting the importance of the key image—the "sweet and virtuous soul."

Adams 5

Work Cited

Herbert, George. "Virtue." *Literature: An Introduction to Reading and Writing, Compact Edition.* Ed. Edgar V. Roberts and Robert Zweig. 6th ed. New York: Pearson, 2015. 743. Print.

Commentary on the Essay

The introductory paragraph establishes the groundwork of the essay—the treatment of form in relationship to content. The main idea is that each part of the poem represents a complete blending of image, logic, and meaning.

Paragraph 2, the first in the body, demonstrates how the poem's schematic formulation is integrated into Herbert's contrast of death and life. In this respect the paragraph demonstrates how a formal enumeration can be integrated within an essay's thematic development.

The focus of paragraph 3 is the organization of both images and ideas from stanza to stanza. Paragraph 4 begins with a transitional sentence that repeats part of the essay's central idea and, at the same time, connects it to paragraph 3. In the same way, paragraph 4 is closely tied to both paragraphs 1 and 3. The main topic here, the rhyme scheme of "Virtue," is introduced in the second sentence. This paragraph asserts that rhythm also reinforces the division between mortality and immortality. On much the same topic, paragraph 5 introduces Herbert's use of assonance, which can be seen as integral in the poem's blending of form and content.

Paragraph 6 takes up the last structural element described in the introduction—repeated key words and phrases. The idea is that these repetitions emphasize the distinction in the poem between mortality and immortality.

Paragraph 7, the conclusion, provides a brief overview and summation of the essay's argument. In addition, it concludes that form in "Virtue" is neither arbitrary nor incidental but rather an integral part of the poem's meaning.

Writing Topics About Poetic Form

Writing Paragraphs

1. Consider any closed-form poem in this chapter. In a paragraph discuss the appropriateness of this form in relation to the poem's meaning.

2. Consider any open-form poem in this chapter. In a paragraph discuss why you believe open form to be appropriate—or not appropriate—for this poem.

Writing Essays

1. In an essay describe the use of the ode form as exemplified by Keats's "Ode on a Grecian Urn" (Chapter 19) and his "Ode to a Nightingale" (this chapter). What similarities of pattern do you find? What differences do you find in the form and content of the poems? Are their noticeably different moods expressed in each poem?

2. In an essay discuss how Cummings, Dryden, Randall, and Thomas use different forms to consider the subject of death (in "Buffalo Bill's Defunct," "To the Memory of Mr. Oldham," "Ballad of Birmingham," and "Do Not Go Gentle into That Good Night")? What differences in form and treatment do you find? What similarities do you find, despite these differences?

3. In an essay compare and contrast the use of the villanelle by Bishop ("One Art"), Roethke ("The Waking"), and Thomas ("Do Not Go Gentle into That Good Night"). What topics do the poets develop? Why do the poets choose the villanelle as their poetic form? What lines do they repeat? What is the effect of this repetition?

4. In an essay compare the sonnets in this chapter by McKay, Shelley, Milton, and Collins. In what ways are the poetic forms of these poets similar? Different? How may Collins's poem be read as a commentary on the sonnet forms of the other poets?

Creative Writing Assignment

1. Write a visual poem, and explain the principles on which you develop your lines. Here are some possible topics (just to get you started): a telephone, a cat, a dog, a car, a football, a snow shovel, a giraffe. After finishing your poem, write a short essay that considers the following and other questions: What are the strengths and limitations of the visual form, according to your experience? How does the form help make your poem serious or comic? How does it encourage creative language and original development of ideas?

2. Write a haiku. Be sure to fit your poem to the 5–7–5 pattern of syllables. What challenges and problems do you encounter in this form? Once you have completed your haiku (which, to be traditional, should be on a topic concerned with nature), try to cut the number of syllables to 4–5–4. Explain how you establish the first haiku pattern, and also explain how you go about cutting the total number of syllables. Be sure to explain what kinds of words you use (length, choice of diction, etc.).

Library Assignment

1. Using an online reference system or the regular card catalog, depending on availability in your college library, look up one of the following topics: "ballads, England," "concrete poetry," or "blank verse." How many references are included under these listings? What sorts of topics are included under the basic topic?

Chapter 17
Symbolism and Allusion: Windows to Wide Expanses of Meaning

AFTER STUDYING THIS MATERIAL, YOU SHOULD BE ABLE TO DO THE FOLLOWING:

- Define symbolism and allusion and their place in poetic expression
- Identify connections between symbols and allusions and meaning
- Evaluate a poem's use of symbolism and allusion

Symbolism refers to the use of symbols in works of art and in all other forms of expression. As we note in Chapter 7, a **symbol** has meaning in and of itself, but it is also understood to represent something else, like the flag for the country or the school song for the school. Symbols occur in stories as well as in poems, but poetry relies more heavily on symbols because it is more concise and because it comprises more forms than fiction, which is restricted to narratives.

Most of the words we use every day are symbols, for they stand for various objects without actually being those objects. When we say *horse*, for example, or *tree*, or *run*, these words are symbols of horses (perhaps munching hay), and trees (in a woods, perhaps, or on a lawn), and people (or animals) running. They direct our minds to real horses, real trees, and real actions in the real world that we have seen and can therefore easily imagine. In literature, however, symbolism implies a special relationship that expands our ordinary understanding of words, descriptions, and arguments.

Symbolism and Meanings

Symbolism goes beyond the close referral of word to thing; it is more like a window through which one can glimpse the extensive world outside. Because poetry is compact, its descriptions and portrayals of experience are brief. Symbolism is therefore one of the primary characteristics of poetry. It is a shorthand way of referring to extensive ideas or attitudes that otherwise would be inappropriate to include in the brief format of a poem.

Symbolism Extends Meaning Beyond Normal Connotation

The use of symbols is a way of moving outward, a means of extending and crystallizing information and ideas. For example, at the time of William Blake (1757–1827), the word *tiger* meant both a large, wild cat and also the specific animal we know today as a tiger. The word's connotation therefore links it with wildness and predation. As a symbol in "The Tyger" (Chapter 14), however, Blake uses the animal as a stand-in for what he considers cosmic negativism—the savage, wild forces that undermine the progress of civilization. Thus the tiger as a symbol is more meaningful than either the denotation or the connotation of the word would indicate.

Cultural or Universal Symbols Are Widely Recognized

Many symbols, wherever they are used, possess a ready-made, clearly agreed upon meaning. These are **cultural** or **universal symbols** (also discussed in Chapter 7). Many such symbols, like the tiger, are taken directly from nature. Other natural universal symbols are springtime and morning, which signify beginnings, growth, hope, optimism, and love. If such symbols were to be introduced into a poem about the suddenness and irrevocability of death, however, they would be ironic, for their presence would emphasize the contrast between death and life.

Cultural symbols are drawn from history and custom, such as the many Judeo-Christian religious symbols that appear in poetry. References to the lamb, Eden, Egyptian bondage, shepherds, exile, the Temple, blood, water, bread, the cross, and wine—all Jewish and/or Christian symbols—occur over and over again. Sometimes these symbols are prominent in a purely devotional context. In other contexts, however, they may be contrasted with symbols of warfare and corruption to show how extensively people neglect their moral and religious obligations.

Contextual, Private, or Authorial Symbols Are Operative as Symbols Only Within Individual Works

Symbols that are not widely or universally recognized are termed **contextual, private**, or **authorial symbols** (also discussed in Chapter 7). Some of these have a natural relationship with the objects and ideas being symbolized. Let us consider snow, which is cold and white and covers everything when it falls. A poet can exploit this quality and make snow a symbol. At the beginning of the long poem "The Waste Land," T. S. Eliot does exactly that; he refers to snow as a symbol of retreat from life, a withdrawal into an intellectual and moral hibernation. Another poem symbolizing snow is the following one. Here the poet refers to snow as both a literal and figurative link between the living and the dead.

VIRGINIA SCOTT (b. 1938)

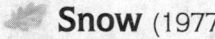 **Snow** (1977)

A doe stands at the roadside,
spirit of those who have lived here
and passed known through our memory.
The doe stands at the edge of the icy road,
5   then darts back into the woods.

Snow falling,
mother-spirit hovering,
white on the drops in the road and fields,
light from the windows
of the old house   10
brightening the snow.

Presences: mother,
grandmother,
here in their place
at the foot of *ben lomond,*°   *A Canadian mountain*   15
green trees black in the hemlock night.

The doe stands at the edge of the icy road,
then darts back into the woods.

Golden Grove, New Brunswick, Canada
January 5, 1977

QUESTIONS

1. How is snow described in the poem? How and where is it seen? As a symbol, what does it signify in relationship to the doe, the memory of other people, the mother-spirit, the old house, the light, the presences, the mountains, and the trees?

2. Explain the structural purpose for which the doe is mentioned three times in the poem, with lines 17 and 18 repeating 4 and 5. As a symbol, what do you think the doe signifies?

3. What are the relationships described in the poem between memory of the past and existence in the present? What does the symbolism contribute to your understanding of these relationships?

This poem describes a real circumstance at a real place at a real time; the poet has even provided an actual location and date, just as we do when writing a letter. We can therefore presume that the snow is real snow, falling in the evening just as lights go on in the nearby houses. This detail by itself would be sufficient as a realistic image, but as Scott develops the poem, the snow symbolizes the link between the speaker's memory of the past and perception of the present. The reality of the moment is suffused with the memory of the people—"mother, / grandmother"—who "lived here." The poet is meditating on the idea that individuals, though they may often be by themselves, like the speaker, are never alone as long as they have a vivid memory of the past. Symbolically, the past and present are always connected, just as the snow covers the scene.

At the poem's conclusion, the doe darting into the woods suggests a linking of present and future (i.e., as long as there are woods, does will dart into them). Both the snow and the deer are private and contextual symbols, for they are established and developed within the poem, and they do not necessarily have the same symbolic value elsewhere. Through the symbolism, therefore, the poet has converted a private moment into an idea of general significance.

Similarly, references to other ordinary materials may be symbolic if the poet emphasizes them sufficiently, as in Keats's "La Belle Dame Sans Merci," which opens and closes with the image of withered sedge, or grass (p. 781). What might seem like nothing more than a natural detail becomes additionally important because it can be understood to symbolize the loss and bewilderment felt by people when loved ones seem to be faithless and destructive rather than loyal and supportive.

The meanings of symbols may be placed on a continuum of qualities from good to bad, high to low, favorable to unfavorable. For example, the bird in Frost's "Oven Bird" (Chapter 18) is a positive symbol for the ability to accept and endure life's travails. In contrast, outright horror is suggested by the symbol of the rough beast slouching toward Bethlehem in Yeats's "The Second Coming" (p. 792). Although this mythical beast shares the same traditional birthplace with Jesus, the commonality is ironic because the beast represents the extremes of anger, hatred, and brutality that in Yeats's judgment have been dominant in modern national politics, regardless of country.

The Function of Symbolism in Poetry

Poets do not simply jam symbols into a poem artificially and arbitrarily. Rather, symbols are structurally important and meaningful first, and are then, simultaneously, symbolic. We therefore find symbols in single words, and also in actions, scenes and settings, characters and characterizations, and various situations.

Many Words Are Automatically Symbolic

With general and universal symbols, a single word is often sufficient, as with references to the lamb, shepherd, cross, blood, bread, and wine; or to summer and winter; or to drought and flood, morning and night, heat and shade, storm and calm, or feast and famine. One of the most famous of all birds, the nightingale, is an example of a single word being instantly symbolic. Because of this bird's beautiful song, it symbolizes natural, unspoiled beauty as contrasted with the contrived attempts by human beings to create beauty. Keats refers to the bird in this way in his "Ode to a Nightingale" (Chapter 16), and his speaker compares human mortality with the virtually eternal beauty of this singer.

Another symbolic bird is the goose. Because migratory Canada geese fly south in the fall, they symbolize the loss of summer abundance, seasonal change, alteration, and loss, with accompanying feelings of regret and sorrow. Because they return north in the spring, however, they also symbolize regeneration, newness, anticipation, and hope. These contrasting symbolic values are important in Mary Oliver's "Wild Geese." Oliver emphasizes geese as symbols of renewal, for the geese returning in spring suggest that "the world offers itself to your imagination" (p. 786).

Symbolism Is to Be Seen in Actions

Not only words but also actions may be presented as symbols. In Scott's "Snow," as we have just observed, the doe darting into the darkening woods symbolizes renewal and the mystery of life. In Hardy's "In Time of 'The Breaking of Nations,'" the action of the man plowing a field symbolizes the continued life and vitality of the folk, the people, despite the political wrangling and endless brutality that are constantly occurring in the world (p. 778).

Symbolism Is to Be Seen in Settings and Scenes

While settings and scenes may be no more than just that—settings and scenes—the poet may develop them as symbols. We may note a symbolic setting in Wilbur's "Year's End" (this chapter). Wilbur draws our attention to a little dog, curled up as if sleeping, and its (presumable) owners, all of whom were killed by falling lava when the eruption of Mount Vesuvius destroyed Pompeii, the ancient Roman town in southern Italy, in 79 CE. In the poem's context, this scene symbolizes the incompleteness of human achievements, a condition not only of present life but also of ancient life. Keats, in "La Belle Dame Sans Merci," introduces the "elfin grot" (grotto) of the "lady in the meads." This grotto is an unreal, magical, womblike location symbolizing both the allure and the disappointment that on occasion characterize sexual attraction.

Symbolism Is to Be Seen in Characters

Poets also devise characters or people as symbols of ideas or values, like the speaker in Herbert's "The Collar" (this chapter). This speaker describes his fierce reluctance against committing himself to God's service, but his anger vanishes when he thinks he hears a soothingly divine voice calling "Child." In this way he himself becomes a symbol of devoted obedience. In Keats's "La Belle Dame Sans Merci" (this chapter), the "fairy's child" is a symbol of the mystery of love. The figures in Hardy's "In Time of 'The Breaking of Nations'" (this chapter) symbolize the power of average, ordinary people to endure even "Though Dynasties pass."

Symbolism Is to Be Seen in Situations

A poem's situations, circumstances, and conditions may also be symbolic. The position of the young gunner in the World War II bomber, six miles above the earth in Jarrell's "The Death of the Ball Turret Gunner" (Chapter 11), makes him vulnerable and helpless, and his death symbolizes the condition of humankind in the modern age of fear and anxiety, when life is threatened by global war and technologically (and also diabolically) expert destructiveness. In "she being Brand / -new" (Chapter 15), Cummings cleverly uses the situation of the speaker's breaking in a new automobile as the symbol of another kind of encounter involving the speaker.

Allusions and Meaning

Just as symbolism enriches meaning, so too does **allusion** (see also Chapter 7) that takes the form of (1) unacknowledged brief quotations from other works and (2) references to historical events and any aspect of human culture—art, music, literature, and so on. The use of allusions is a means of connecting new literary works with the broader cultural tradition of which the works are a part. In addition, allusions presuppose a common bond of knowledge between the poet and the reader. On the one hand, poets making allusions compliment the past, and on the other, they salute readers able to discover how the meanings of the allusions are transformed in the new context.

Allusions Add Dimension to Poetry

An allusion carries with it the entire context of the work from which it is drawn. Perhaps the richest sources of references and stories are the King James Bible and the plays of Shakespeare. Keats introduces a biblical allusion in "Ode to a Nightingale" (Chapter 16), where he refers to the story of Ruth, who was "sick for home" while standing "in tears amid the alien corn." This allusion is particularly rich, because Ruth became the mother of Jesse. According to the Gospel of Matthew, it was from the line of Jesse that King David was born, and it was from the house of David that Jesus was born. Thus Keats's nightingale is not only a symbol of natural beauty, but through the biblical allusion it symbolizes regeneration and redemption, much in keeping with Keats's assertion that the bird is "not born for death." A reader might pursue this symbolism further, perhaps in another context. In Yeats's "The Second Coming," we encounter an allusion to Shakespeare's *Macbeth*. Yeats uses the phrase "blood-dimmed tide," which refers to Macbeth's soliloquy in the second act of *Macbeth*. In the play, after murdering Duncan, Macbeth asks if there is enough water in Neptune's ocean to wash the blood from his hands. His immediate, guilt-ridden response is that Duncan's blood will instead turn the green water to red (*Macbeth:* 2.2.63–66). This image of crime being bloody enough to stain the ocean's water is thus the allusive context of Yeats's "blood-dimmed tide."

Once works become well known, as with the Bible and the plays of Shakespeare, they may in turn become a source of allusions for subsequent writers. Such a well-known work is Frost's "Stopping by Woods on a Snowy Evening" (Chapter 11), which contains an oft-quoted last line: "And miles to go before I sleep." This line is so universally recognized that it is now considered as a symbol of the need to complete tasks and fulfill obligations.

Allusions may be discovered in no more than a single word or phrase in a poem, provided that the expression is unusual enough or associative enough to bear the weight of the reference. Scott's "Snow," for example, speaks of "green trees black in the hemlock night." Of course, the word *hemlock* refers to a common evergreen tree observed by the speaker, but a distillation of hemlock was also the poison drunk by Socrates when the ancient Athenians executed him, as described in Plato's *Phaedo*. Because of this association, any use of the word *hemlock* can be construed as an allusion to the death of Socrates and the abuse of legal authority, depending, of course, on context. Another allusion to hemlock occurs in the beginning lines of "Ode to a Nightingale" (Chapter 16), in which Keats refers to hemlock. His speaker declares that a "drowsy numbness" has overtaken him "as though of hemlock . . . [he] had drunk." As the poem continues, we realize that Keats's allusion refers to the way in which death might open a new plane of existence for the speaker—a life of immortal beauty. Thus Keats builds the single-word allusion into new speculation about the possible connection of life and death.

Allusions are therefore an important means by which poets broaden context and deepen meaning. The issues a poet raises in a new poem, in other words, are important not only there but are linked through allusion to issues raised earlier by other thinkers or brought out by previous events, places, or persons. With connections made through allusions, poets clarify their own ideas. Allusion is hence not literary "theft" but is rather a means of enrichment.

Studying for Symbols and Allusions

As you study poetry, remember that symbols and allusions do not come marked with special notice and fanfare. You can expect no brass band to let you know. Your decision to call something symbolic must be based on the circumstances of the poem. Let us say that the poet introduces a major item of importance at a climactic part of the poem, or that the poet introduces a description that is unusual or noteworthy, such as the connection between "stony sleep" and the "rough beast" in Yeats's "The Second Coming." When such a connection occurs, the element may no longer be taken literally but should be read as a symbol.

Even after you have found a connection such as this, however, you will need to discover and understand symbolic meaning. For instance, in the context of Yeats's "The Second Coming," the phrase "rough beast" might refer to the person or persons hinted at in traditional interpretations of the New Testament as the "Antichrist." In a secular frame of reference, the associations of blankness and pitilessness suggest brutality and suppression. Still further, however, if the last hundred years had not been a period in which millions of people were persecuted and exterminated in military and secret police operations, even these associations might make the "rough beast" quizzical but not necessarily symbolic. But because of the rightness of the application, together with the traditional biblical associations, the figure clearly should be construed as a symbol of heartless persecution and brutality.

As you can see, the interpretation of a symbol requires that you consider, in some depth, the person, object, situation, or action being considered as symbolic. If the element can be seen as general and representative—characteristic of the condition of a large number of human beings—it assumes symbolic significance. As a rule, the more ideas that you can associate with the element, the more likely it is to be a symbol.

As for allusions, the identification of an allusion is usually simple. A word, situation, or phrase either is an allusion or it is not, and hence the matter is easily settled once a source is located. The problem comes in determining how the allusion affects the context of the poem you are reading. Thus we understand that in the poem "Snow," Scott alludes to Frost's "Desert Places" (Chapter 16) by borrowing Frost's phrase "Snow falling." Once this allusion is established, its purpose must still be learned. Thus, on the one hand, the allusion might mean that the situation in "Snow" is the same as in Frost's poem—namely, that the speaker is making observations about interior blankness—the "desert places" of the mind, or soul. On the other hand, the poet may be using the allusion in a new sense, and such is indeed the case. Whereas Frost uses the falling snow to suggest coldness of spirit, Scott uses it, more warmly, to connect the natural scene to the memory of family. In other words, once the presence of an allusion is established, the challenge of reading and understanding goes on.

Poems for Study

Amiri Baraka . . . . Legacy, 770
Emily Brontë . . . . No Coward Soul Is Mine, 771
Marilyn Chin . . . . Autumn Leaves, 772
Lucille Clifton . . . . cutting greens, 772
Arthur Hugh Clough . . . . Say Not the Struggle Nought Availeth, 773
John Donne . . . . The Canonization, 774
Stephen Dunn . . . . Hawk, 776
Isabella Gardner . . . . Collage of Echoes, 777
Dan Georgakas . . . . Hiroshima Crewman, 777
Thomas Hardy . . . . In Time of "The Breaking of Nations," 778
George Herbert . . . . The Collar, 778
Robinson Jeffers . . . . The Purse-Seine, 780
John Keats . . . . La Belle Dame Sans Merci: A Ballad, 781
X. J. Kennedy . . . . Old Men Pitching Horseshoes, 783
Andrew Marvell . . . . To His Coy Mistress, 784
Carol Muske-Dukes . . . . Real Estate, 785
Mary Oliver . . . . Wild Geese, 786
Kay Ryan . . . . We're Building the Ship as We Sail It, 787
Gary Snyder . . . . Milton by Firelight, 788
Judith Viorst . . . . A Wedding Sonnet for the Next Generation, 789
Walt Whitman . . . . A Noiseless Patient Spider, 790
Richard Wilbur . . . . Year's End, 790
William Butler Yeats . . . . The Second Coming, 792

AMIRI BARAKA (1934)

 Legacy (1969)

(For Blues People)

In the south, sleeping against
the drugstore, growling under
the trucks and stoves, stumbling
through and over the cluttered eyes
5   of early mysterious night. Frowning
drunk waving moving a hand or lash.
Dancing kneeling reaching out, letting
a hand rest in shadows. Squatting
to drink or pee. Stretching to climb
10 pulling themselves onto horses near
where there was sea (the old songs
lead you to believe). Riding out
from this town, to another, where
it is also black. Down a road
15 where people are asleep. Towards
the moon or the shadows of houses.
Towards the songs' pretended sea.

QUESTIONS

1. Did you ever imagine escaping to an imaginary place? What did you imagine it was like?
2. What do you think the road and the "pretended sea" symbolize?
3. What is the poem's setting? Why is this important to know?

EMILY BRONTË (1818–1848)

 ## No Coward Soul Is Mine (1850; 1846)

No coward soul is mine,
No trembler in the world's storm-troubled sphere:
   I see Heaven's glories shine,
And faith shines equal, arming me from fear.

   O God within my breast,   5
Almighty, ever-present Deity
   Life—that in me has rest,
As I—undying Life—have power in Thee!

   Vain are the thousand creeds
That move men's hearts, unutterably vain,   10
   Worthless as withered weeds,
Or idle froth amid the boundless main,°   *i.e., oceans throughout the world*

   To waken doubt in one
Holding so fast by Thine infinity;
   So surely anchored on   15
The steadfast rock of immortality.

   With wide-embracing love
Thy spirit animates eternal years,
   Pervades and broods above,
Changes, sustains, dissolves, creates, and rears.   20

   Though earth and man were gone,
And suns and universes ceased to be,
   And Thou wert left alone,°   *if Thou were to be left (totally) alone*
Every existence would exist in Thee.

   There is not room for Death,   25
Nor atom that his might could render void:
   Thou—THOU art Being and Breath,
And what THOU art may never be destroyed.

QUESTIONS

1. Why does the speaker assert in the first stanza that "No coward soul is mine"? Why does she raise this issue? Why might someone consider a soul like hers cowardly? Does the speaker make a convincing argument for the poem's first line?

2. Who is "God within my breast" of the poem? What connection or lack of connection does this "Thee/THOU/THY" have with the "thousand creeds / That move men's hearts" of lines 9 and 10?

3. In general, what are the breadth and scope of the symbolic references in this poem? Compare the symbolism of the "storm-troubled sphere" in stanza 1, and of the vanished world, suns, universes, and even humanity in stanza 6.

4. What is the meaning and connection of the symbols "withered weeds" (line 11) and "idle froth" (line 12)? To what extent does the speaker, in lines 9–12, seem to be denigrating conventional religious faiths? How does the grammatical connection between stanzas 3 and 4 help in the understanding of these stanzas?

5. What does the speaker apparently mean, in lines 23–24, by the statement "And Thou wert left alone, / Every existence would exist in Thee"?

6. Describe the symbolism implied in the word "arming" in the first stanza. Against what does the speaker need arming? Who or what is arming her soul? What do "infinity" (line 14) and "immortality" (line 16) contribute to her expressed sense of her own personal strength?

MARILYN CHIN (1955)

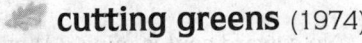 Autumn Leaves (1994)

The dead piled up, thick, fragrant, on the fire escape.
My mother ordered me again, and again, to sweep it clean.
All that blooms must fall. I learned this not from the Tao,
    but from high school biology.

Oh, the contradictions of having a broom and not a dustpan
5 I swept the leaves down, down through the iron grille
and let the dead rain over the Wong family's patio.

And it was Achilles Wong who completed the task.
    We called her:
The-one-who-cleared-away-another-family's-autumn.
She blossomed, tall, benevolent, notwithstanding.

QUESTIONS

1. What simple tasks were assigned to you as a child? Why do you think you were chosen for those tasks?

2. Why is the name "Achilles Wong" assigned to the person who sweeps the leaves?

3. Why does the poem end with the word *notwithstanding*?

LUCILLE CLIFTON (1936–2010)

For a photo, see Chapter 15, page 690.

cutting greens (1974)

curling them around
i hold their bodies in obscene embrace
thinking of everything but kinship.

collards and kale
strain against each strange other   5
away from my kissmaking hand and
the iron bedpot.
the pot is black,
the cutting board is black,
my hand,   10
and just for a minute
the greens roll black under the knife,
and the kitchen twists dark on its spine
and i taste in my natural appetite
the bond of live things everywhere.   15

QUESTIONS

1. Have you ever been involved in a simple activity as in the poem "cutting greens" and thought about how your activity revealed something important about your life?
2. What is symbolic to Clifton about cutting the greens? What do you think Clifton means by "the bond of living things everywhere"?
3. Why do you think no capitalization is used either in the title or in the poem?

ARTHUR HUGH CLOUGH (1819–1861)

 ## Say Not the Struggle Nought Availeth (1849)

Say not the struggle nought availeth,
   The labour and the wounds are vain,
The enemy faints not, nor faileth,°   See Isaiah 40:28–31
   And as things have been they remain.°

If hopes were dupes, fears may be liars;°   5
   It may be, in yon smoke concealed,
Your comrades chase e'en now the fliers,°   *soldiers in retreat*
   And, but for you, possess the field.°   *have control over the battlefield*

For while the tired waves, vainly breaking,
   Seem here no painful inch to gain,   10
Far back, through creeks and inlets making,
   Comes silent, flooding in, the main.°   *i.e., the ocean*

And not by eastern windows only,
   When daylight comes, comes in the light,
In front, the sun climbs slow, how slowly,   15
   But westward, look, the land is bright.

°1–4 *Say . . . remain:* In more direct syntax, the title sentence may be construed as "Do not say that the struggle [of life] is of no value." Lines 2, 3, and 4 are each direct objects of the opening verb "Say not." °5 *If hopes . . . liars:* i.e., if one grants that hope is unreal and therefore deceptive, one may also grant that fear is unreal and therefore equally deceptive.

QUESTIONS

1. How many separate symbols are there in this poem? From what topics are they drawn? Why does Clough allude to some of the words in Isaiah?

2. Consider this poem as a persuasive argument against feelings of personal depression and desolation. How does Clough use symbols as the basis of his argument that the listener should overcome his or her despair?

3. Why does Clough end the poem, in line 16, with the observation that the sun shining in the East illuminates the West? Why does Clough draw attention to the slowness of the ascendant sun? Additionally, to what degree might "westward" be considered as a symbol of immortality because it is the location of the setting sun?

JOHN DONNE (1572–1631)

For a portrait, see Chapter 12, page 585.

The Canonization° (1633)

For Godsake hold your tongue, and let me love,
    Or chide my palsy, or my gout,
My five gray hairs, or ruin'd fortune flout,
    With wealth your state, your mind with Arts improve,°
5   Take you a course,° get you a place,°
        Observe His Honor,° or his grace,°
Or the King's real, or his stampèd face
    Contemplate,° what you will, approve,°
    So you will let me love.

10   Alas, alas, who's injured by my love?
    What merchant's ships have my sighs drown'd?
Who says my tears have overflow'd his ground?
    When did my colds a forward spring° remove?
        When did the heats which my veins fill°
15   Add one more to the plaguy Bill?°
Soldiers find wars, and Lawyers find out still
    Litigious men, which quarrels move,
    Though she and I do love.

Call us what you will, we are made such by love;
20   Call her one, me another fly,°
We're Tapers° too, and at our own cost die,°   *candles*

°*Canonization* is the making of saints. °4 *With wealth . . . improve:* i.e., Improve your state with wealth and your mind with arts. °5 *Take you a course:* take up a career. *place:* a political appointment. °6 *His Honor:* any important courtier. *his grace:* a person of greatest eminence, such as a bishop or the king. °7, 8 *Or . . . contemplate:* i.e., Or contemplate either the king's real face (at court) or stamped face (on coins). °8 *What . . . approve:* Try anything you like (i.e., "Mind your own business"). °13 *a forward spring:* an early spring (season). °14 *the heats . . . fill:* i.e., "the heats (fevers) that fill my veins." Donne apparently wrote this line before the discovery of blood circulation was announced by William Harvey in 1616. °15 *plaguy Bill:* a regularly published list of deaths caused by the plague. °20 *fly:* a butterfly or moth (and apparently superficial and light-headed). °21 *at . . . die:* It was supposed that sexual climax shortened life.

And we in us find the Eagle and the Dove.°
   The Phoenix riddle° hath more wit
   By us, we two, being one, are it.
So, to one neutral thing both sexes fit,   25
   We die and rise the same, and prove
   Mysterious° by this love.

We can die by it, if not live by love,
   And if unfit for tombs and hearse
Our legend be, it will be fit for verse;   30
   And if no piece of Chronicle we prove,
     We'll build in sonnets pretty rooms;
     As well a well wrought run becomes
The greatest ashes, as half-acre tombs,
   And by these hymns, all shall approve   35
   Us *Canoniz'd* for love:°

And thus invoke° us; "You whom reverend love   *pray to saints*
   Made one another's hermitage;°
You, to whom love was peace, that now is rage;
   Who did the whole world's soul extract, and drove   40
     Into the glasses of your eyes
     So made such mirrors, and such spies,
That they did all to you epitomize,°
   Countries, towns, courts: Beg from above
   A pattern of your love!"   45

°22 *the Eagle and the Dove*: masculine and feminine symbols. °23 *Phoenix riddle*: In ancient times the phoenix, a mythical bird that lived for a thousand years, was supposed to die and rise five hundred years later from its own ashes; hence the phoenix symbolized immortality and the renewal of life and desire. °27 *Mysterious*: unknowable to anyone but God, and therefore quintessentially holy. °35, 36 *by these hymns . . . Canoniz'd for love*: The idea is that later generations will remember the lovers and elevate them to the sainthood of a religion of love. Because the lovers' love is recorded so powerfully in the speaker's poems ("sonnets" in line 33), these later generations will use the poems as hymns in their worship of love. °38 *Made . . . hermitage*: made a religious retreat for each other. °40–43 *Who did . . . epitomize*: An allusion to reputed alchemical processes, and therefore to be understood approximately like this: "Who extracted the whole world's soul and, through your eyes, assimilated this soul into yours, so that you, whose eyes saw and reflected each other, embodied the love and desire felt by all human beings."

QUESTIONS

1. What is the situation of the poem? Whom is the speaker addressing? Why does he begin as he does? How does he defend his love? Why does each stanza begin and end with the word "love"?

2. What symbols do you find in the poem? What are the symbols? What is being symbolized?

3. What mythic and religious mysteries are linked with sexual love in the third stanza? What does "canonization" mean? What canonizes and immortalizes the lovers? How does the "canonization" symbolize the poem's idea about the nature of love?

4. What will future lovers ask of these saints of love? Of what use will the speaker's poem be at that time? What do you think of the speaker's claim about love?

STEPHEN DUNN (b. 1939)

Hawk (1989)

What a needy, desperate thing
to claim what's wild for oneself,
yet the hawk circling above the pines
looks like the same one I thought

5   might become mine after it crashed
into the large window and lay
one wing spread, the other loosely
tucked, then no, not dead, got up

dazed, and in minutes was gone.
10 Now once again
this is its sky, this its woods.
The tasty small birds it loves

have seen their God and know
the suddenness of such love
15 as we know lightning or flash flood.
If hawks can learn, this hawk learned

what's clear can be hard
down where the humans live,
and that the hunting isn't good
20 where the air is such a lie.

It glides above the pines and I
turn back into the room, the hawk book
open on the cluttered table
to Cooper's Hawk

25 and the unwritten caption
that to be wild
means nothing you do or have done
needs to be explained.

QUESTIONS

1. Why does the speaker consider the issue of owning or not owning the hawk that crashed into his window?

2. In what way is the hawk significant? How can a reader justify considering it as a symbol? What does the bird symbolize?

3. What is the meaning of the final four lines? How true are the lines? If "to be wild" needs no explanation, what does it mean, in contrast, to be civilized?

ISABELLA GARDNER (1915–1981)

 ### Collage of Echoes (1979)

I have no promises to keep
Nor miles to go before I sleep,°
For miles of years I have made promises
and (mostly) kept them.
    It's time I slept.   5
Now I lay me down to sleep°
With no promises to keep.
    My sleaves are ravelled°
    I have travelled.°

°2 *miles to go before I sleep:* See Robert Frost, "Stopping by Woods on a Snowy Evening" (p. 548), lines 13–16.
°6 *Now I lay me down to sleep:* from the child's prayer: Now I lay me down to sleep; / I pray the Lord my soul to keep. / If I should die before I wake, / I pray the Lord my soul to take.   °8 *My sleaves are ravelled:* See *Macbeth*, 11.2.37: "Sleep that knits up the ravelled sleave of care."   °9 *I have travelled:* See Keats, "On First Looking into Chapman's Homer" (p. 641).

QUESTIONS

1. Given the allusions in the poem, what do you conclude about the speaker's judgment of the reader's knowledge of literature?

2. How reliant is "Collage of Echoes" upon the contexts being echoed? How do the echoes assist in enabling enjoyment and appreciation of the poem?

3. In relation to the speaker's character as demonstrated in the poem, consider the phrases "(mostly) kept them," "With no promises to keep," and "My sleaves are ravelled." What do they show about the speaker's self-assessment? In what way might these phrases be considered comic?

DAN GEORGAKAS (b. 1938)

Hiroshima Crewman (1969)

Somewhere in California
his body humbled by a hair shirt,
a vow of silence on his lips,
a Hiroshima crewman tries to find a life.
If he should ever choose to break his peace,   5
he might speak of death by fire
no Nazi ordered; he might tell how
war produces many brands of Auschwitz soap and Dachau lampshade.

QUESTIONS

1. Explain the meaning and purpose of the poem's title. In what way is a "hair shirt" symbolic? What does it symbolize?

2. Why is the principal figure called a "Hiroshima Crewman"? What has happened to him since August 6, 1945, the date of the atomic bombing of Hiroshima? What is the Crewman now doing, according to the poem?

3. Describe the symbolism of "death by fire" and "Auschwitz soap and Dachau lampshade." What are the human and political implications of this symbolism?

THOMAS HARDY (1840–1928)

For a photo, see Chapter 11, page 548.

 ## In Time of "The Breaking of Nations"° (1916; 1915)

Only a man harrowing clods
   In a slow silent walk,
With an old horse that stumbles and nods
   Half asleep as they stalk.

5 Only thin smoke without flame
   From the heaps of couch grass:°   *quack grass*
Yet this will go onward the same
   Though Dynasties pass.

Yonder a maid and her wight°   *fellow*
10   Come whispering by;
War's annals will fade into night
   Ere their story die.

_____

°See Jeremiah 51:20, "with you I break nations in pieces."

QUESTIONS

1. What does Hardy symbolize by the man, horse, smoke, and couple? How realistic and vivid are these symbols? Are they universal or contextual?

2. How does Hardy show that the phrase "breaking of nations" is to be taken symbolically? What meaning is gained by the biblical allusion of this phrase?

3. Contrast the structure of stanza 1 with that of stanzas 2 and 3. How does the form of stanzas 2 and 3 enable Hardy to emphasize the main idea?

4. How does the speaker show his evaluation of the life of the common people? You might consider that at the time (1915) World War I was raging in Europe.

GEORGE HERBERT (1593–1633)

The Collar° (1633)

I struck the board, and cry'd "No more;
   I will abroad!

_____

°*collar:* (a) the collar worn by a member of the clergy; (b) the collar of the harness of a draft animal such as a horse; (c) a restraint placed on prisoners; (d) a pun on *choler* (yellow bile), a bodily substance that was thought to cause quick rages.

What? shall I ever sigh and pine?
My lines and life are free; free as the road,
   Loose as the wind, as large as store,   5
     Shall I be still in suit?°
Have I no harvest but a thorn°
To let me blood, and not restore
What I have lost with cordial fruit?
     Sure there was wine   10
   Before my sighs did dry it: there was corn
     Before my tears did drown it.
Is the year only lost to me?
     Have I no bays° to crown it?
No flowers, no garlands gay? all blasted?   15
      All wasted?
Not so, my heart: but there is fruit,
     And thou hast hands.
   Recover all thy sight-blown age   20
On double pleasures: leave thy cold dispute
Of what is fit, and not; forsake thy cage;
     Thy rope of sands,
Which petty thoughts have made, and made to thee
   Good cable, to enforce and draw,
     And be thy law,   25
   While thou didst wink and wouldst not see.
     Away; take heed:
     I will abroad.
Call in thy death's head there: tie up thy fears.
     He that forbears   30
  To suit° and serve his need,   *follow*
     Deserves his load."
But as I rav'd and grew more fierce and wild
     At every word,
  Me thought I heard one calling, "Child:"   35
     And I replied, *My Lord.*

°6 *in suit:* waiting upon a person of power to gain favor or position. °7 *thorn:* See Mark 15:17. °14 *bays:* laurel
crowns to signify victory and honor.

QUESTIONS

1. What is the opening situation? Why is the speaker angry? Against what role in life is he
   complaining?
2. In light of the many possible meanings of *collar* (see note), explain the title as a symbol
   in the poem.
3. Explain the symbolism of the thorn (line 7), blood (line 8), wine (line 10), bays (line 14),
   flowers and garlands (line 15), cage (line 27), rope of sands (line 22), death's head (line 29),
   and the dialogue in lines 35 and 36.

ROBINSON JEFFERS (1887–1962)

The Purse-Seine (1937)

1

Our sardine fishermen work at night in the dark of the moon;
        daylight or moonlight
They could not tell where to spread the net, unable to see the
        phosphorescence of the shoals of fish.
They work northward from Monterey, coasting Santa Cruz;
        off New Year's Point or off Pigeon Point
The look-out man will see some lakes of milk-color light on the seas's
        night-purple; he points, and the helmsman
5 Turns the dark prow, the motorboat circles the gleaming shoal and drifts out
        her seine-net. They close the circle
And purse the bottom of the net, then with great labor haul it in.

2

                                                        I cannot tell you
How beautiful the scene is, and a little terrible, then, when the crowded fish
Know they are caught, and wildly beat from one wall to the other of their closing destiny
        the phosphorescent
Water to a pool of flame, each beautiful slender body sheeted with flame, like a
10   live rocket
A comet's tail wake of clear yellow flame; while outside the narrowing
Floats and cordage of the net great sea-lions come up to watch, sighing in the dark; the
        vast walls of night
Stand erect to the stars.

3

                                        Lately I was looking from a night mountain-top
15 On a wide city, the colored splendor, galaxies of light; how could I help but recall the
        seine-net
Gathering the luminous fish? I cannot tell you how beautiful the city appeared, and a
        little terrible.
I thought, We have geared the machines and locked all together into interdependence;
        we have built the great cities; now
There is no escape. We have gathered vast populations incapable of free survival,
        insulated
From the strong earth, each person in himself helpless, on all dependent. The circle is
        closed, and the net
Is being hauled in. They hardly feel the cords drawing, yet they shine already. The
20   inevitable mass-disasters
Will not come in our time nor in our children's, but we and our children
Must watch the net draw narrower, government take all powers—or revolution, and
        the new government
Take more than all, add to kept bodies kept souls—or anarchy, the mass-disasters.

4

These things are Progress;
Do you marvel our verse is troubled or frowning, while it keeps its reason? Or it lets go,
    lets the mood flow 25
In the manner of the recent young men into mere hysteria, splintered gleams, crackled
    laughter. But they are quite wrong.
There is no reason for amazement; surely one always knew that cultures decay, and life's
    end is death.

QUESTIONS

1. Describe how the purse-seine is used to haul in the sardines. What is the speaker's reaction to the scene as described in stanza 2?

2. How does the speaker explain that the purse-seine is a symbol? What does it symbolize? What do the sardines symbolize?

3. Compare the ideas of Jeffers with those of Yeats in "The Second Coming" (p. 792). Are the ideas of Jeffers more or less methodical?

4. Is the statement at the end to be taken as a fact or as a resigned acceptance of that fact? Does the poem offer any solution to the problem?

5. How can the sea-lions of line 12, and their sighs, be construed as a symbol?

JOHN KEATS (1795–1821)

For a portrait, see Chapter 14, page 641.

 La Belle Dame Sans Merci: A Ballad° (1820; 1819)

1

O what can ail thee, knight at arms,
    Alone and palely loitering?
The sedge has wither'd from the lake,
    And no birds sing.

2

O what can ail thee, knight at arms, 5
    So haggard and so woe-begone?
The squirrel's granary is full,
    And the harvest's done.

3

I see a lily on thy brow
    With anguish moist and fever dew, 10
And on dry cheeks a fading rose
    Fast withereth too.

°"La Belle Dame Sans Merci" is French for "The beautiful lady without pity" (that is, "The heartless woman"). This is also the title of a medieval poem by Alain Chartier; Keats's poem bears no other relationship to the medieval poem, which was thought at the time to have been by Chaucer.

4

I met a lady in the meads,°   *meadows*
    Full beautiful, a fairy's child;
15 Her hair was long, her foot was light,
    And her eyes were wild.

5

I made a garland for her head,
    And bracelets too, and fragrant zone;°   *belt*
She look'd at me as she did love,
20   And made sweet moan.

6

I set her on my pacing steed,
    And nothing else saw all day long,
For sidelong would she bend, and sing
    A fairy's song.

7

25 She found me roots of relish° sweet,   *magical potion*
    And honey wild, and manna° dew,   *See Exodus 16:14–36*
And sure in language strange she said—
    I love thee true.

8

She took me to her elfin grot,°   *grotto*
30   And there she wept, and sigh'd full sore,
And there I shut her wild wild eyes
    With kisses four.

9

And there she lullèd me asleep,
    And there I dream'd—Ah! woe betide!
35 The latest° dream I ever dream'd   *last*
    On the cold hill's side.

10

I saw pale kings, and princes too,
    Pale warriors, death pale were they all;
They cried—"La belle dame sans merci
40   Hath thee in thrall!"°   *slavery*

11

I saw their starv'd lips in the gloom
    With horrid warning gapèd wide,
And I awoke and found me here
    On the cold hill's side.

12

And this is why I sojourn here,   45
    Alone and palely loitering,
Though the sedge is wither'd from the lake,
    And no birds sing.

QUESTIONS

1. Who is the speaker of stanzas 1–3? Who speaks after that?
2. In light of the dreamlike content of the poem, how can the knight's experience be viewed as symbolic? What is being symbolized?
3. Consider "relish" (line 25), "honey" (line 26), and "manna" (line 26) as symbols. Are they realistic or mythical? What does the allusion to manna signify? What is symbolized by the "pale kings, and princes too" and "Pale warriors" (lines 37–38)?
4. Consider the poem's setting as symbols of the knight's state of mind.

X. J. KENNEDY (b. 1929)

 ## Old Men Pitching Horseshoes (1985)

Back in a yard where ringers groove a ditch,
These four in shirtsleeves congregate to pitch
Dirt-burnished iron. With appraising eye,
One sizes up a peg, hoists and lets fly—
A clang resounds as though a smith had struck   5
Fire from a forge. His first blow, out of luck,
Rattles in circles. Hitching up his face,
He swings, and weight once more inhabits space,
Tumbles as gently as a new-laid egg.
Extended iron arms surround their peg   10
Like one come home to greet a long-lost brother.
Shouts from one outpost. Mutters from the other.
Now changing sides, each withered pitcher moves
As his considered dignity behooves
Down the worn path of earth where August flies   15
And sheaves of air in warm distortions rise.
To stand ground, fling, kick dust with all the force
Of shoes still hammered to a living horse.

QUESTIONS

1. How does the poet indicate that the pitching of horseshoes is symbolic? As symbols, why are old men chosen rather than young men?
2. Discuss the effects of the words "congregate," "outpost," "withered," "sheaves," "kick dust," and "force." What do these words contribute to the poem's symbolism?

ANDREW MARVELL (1621–1678)

To His Coy Mistress (1681)

Had we but world enough, and time,
This coyness, lady, were no crime.
We would sit down, and think which way
To walk, and pass our long love's day.

5 Thou by the Indian Ganges° side
Shouldst rubies find; I by the tide
Of Humber° would complain. I would
Love you ten years before the flood,°   *Noah's flood*
And you should, if you please, refuse
10 Till the conversion of the Jews.°
My vegetable love should grow
Vaster than empires and more slow;
An hundred years should go to praise
Thine eyes, and on thy forehead gaze;
15 Two hundred to adore each breast,
But thirty thousand to the rest;
An age at least to every part,
And the last age should show your heart.
For, lady, you deserve this state,
20 Nor would I love at lower rate.
    But at my back I always hear
Time's wingèd chariot hurrying near;
And yonder all before us lie
Deserts of vast eternity.
25 Thy beauty shall no more be found,
Nor, in thy marble vault, shall sound
My echoing song, then worms shall try
That long-preserved virginity,
And your quaint honor turn to dust,
30 And into ashes all my lust;
The grave's a fine and private place,
But none, I think, do there embrace.
    Now therefore, while the youthful hue
Sits on thy skin like morning dew,
35 And while thy willing soul transpires
At every pore with instant fires,
Now let us sport us while we may,
And now, like amorous birds of prey,
Rather at once our time devour
40 Than languish in his slow-chapped° power.   *slow-jawed*
Let us roll all our strength and all
Our sweetness up into one ball,

°5 *Ganges:* a large river than runs across most of India. °7 *Humber:* a small river that runs through northern England to the North Sea. °10 *Jews:* Traditionally, this conversion is supposed to occur just before the Last Judgment.

And tear our pleasures with rough strife
Thorough° the iron gates of life: *through*
Thus, though we cannot make our sun   45
Stand still, yet we will make him run.

QUESTIONS

1. In lines 1–20 the speaker sets up a hypothetical situation and the first part of a pseu-
dological proof: If *A* then *B*. What specific words indicate the logic of this section? What
hypothetical situation is established?
2. How do geographic and biblical allusions affect our sense of time and place?
3. In lines 21–32 the speaker refutes the hypothetical condition set up in the first twenty
lines. What word indicates that this is a refutation? How do symbols of death create
and reinforce meaning here?
4. The last part of the poem (lines 33–46) presents the speaker's "logical" conclusion.
What words indicate that this is a conclusion? What is the conclusion?

CAROL MUSKE-DUKES (b. 1945)

Real Estate (1981)

You think you earned this space on earth,
but look at the gold face of the teen-age
pharaoh,° smug as a Shriner, in his box

with no diploma, a plot flashy enough
for Manhattan.° Early death, then what.   5
a task dragging a sofa into the grave,
a couple of floor lamps, the alarm set

for another century. Someday we'll heed
the testament of that paid escort watching
himself in all the ballroom mirrors: slide   10

with each slide of the old trombone,
be good to the bald, press up against
the ugly duck-like.° Time is never old,

never lies. What a past you'd have
if you'd only admit to it: the real estate   15
your family dabbled in for generations,
the vacant lots° developed like the clan

°3 *pharaoh*: Tutankhamen, the "boy king" of the fourteenth century BCE of ancient Egypt. The discovery of his
tomb in 1922, when hundreds of precious household objects were found with the sarcophagus, showed the lav-
ishness of Egyptian royal burials. The mummy of King Tut was covered with a mask of gold and colored metals.
°5. *Manhattan*: In 1981 a large number of treasures from Tutankhamen's tomb were being displayed at the Metropolitan Museum of Art in Manhattan.   °13 *ugly duck-like*: The Ugly Duckling is a children's story by Hans
Christian Andersen.   °17 *vacant lots*: see T. S. Eliot, "Preludes" concluding (p. 614).

overbite—through years of sudden
foreclosure. Who knows what it costs?
20 First you stand for the national anthem,

then you start waltzing around without
strings, reminding yourself of yourself,
expecting to live in that big city
against daddy's admonition: buy land

25 get some roots down under those spike
heels, let the river bow and scrape as
it enters the big front door of your property.

QUESTIONS

1. Who is speaking? Who is being addressed? What sort of person is the speaker? What
    does she think of old age? Of sex? What advice does she offer as a security against ad-
    vancing age?
2. What does "the teen-age pharaoh" symbolize? Why does the poet mention a modern
    set of objects that might be found in a comparable tomb of a person of the twentieth
    century? What might these things symbolize? How do the things contrast?
3. What does the "paid escort" (line 9) symbolize? What does the "old trombone" sym-
    bolize? What does the choice of these symbolize about the traditional role of women
    with regard to men? What attitude is conveyed by this choice?
4. Consider the ambiguity of lines 25–27. What might "roots" and "property" mean as
    the means of causing the "river" to "bow and scrape"? Why is it difficult to understand
    these lines without resorting to symbolic explanations?

MARY OLIVER (b. 1935)

Wild Geese (1986)

You do not have to be good.
You do not have to walk on your knees
for a hundred miles through the desert, repenting
You only have to let the soft animal of your body
5   love what it loves.
Tell me about despair, yours, and I will tell you mine.
Meanwhile the world goes on.
Meanwhile the sun and the clear pebbles of the rain
are moving across the landscapes,
10   over the prairies and the deep trees,
the mountains and the rivers.
Meanwhile the wild geese, high in the clean blue air,
are heading home again.
Whoever you are, no matter how lonely,
15   the world offers itself to your imagination,

calls to you like the wild geese, harsh and exciting—
over and over announcing your place
in the family of things.

QUESTIONS

1. What idea is contained in the first five lines? What ideas are expressed in lines 6–12? In what ways are lines 13–17 a climax of the poem? How does this last section build on the poem's earlier parts?
2. What is symbolized by the references to "the sun and the clear pebbles of the rain," and so on, in lines 7–10? Do these symbols suggest futility or hope?
3. What do the wild geese symbolize (lines 11–12, 15)? How is the symbol of the geese a response to the poem's first six lines? How well would the words *acceptance, self-knowledge,* or *adjustment* describe the poem's ideas? What other words would be better or more suitable? Why?

KAY RYAN (b. 1945)

For a photo, see Chapter 12, page 591.

We're Building the Ship as We Sail It (2010)

The first fear
being drowning, the
ship's first shape
was a raft, which
was hard to unflatten   5
after that didn't
happen. It's awkward
to have to do one's
planning *in extremis*°   under the threat of death
in the early years—   10
so hard to hide later:
sleekening the hull,
making things
more gracious.

QUESTIONS

1. In the poem's title, what does the ship symbolize? What does making a raft symbolize? What is symbolized by planning and "making things / more gracious"?
2. What does the poet mean here by the phrase "sleekening the hull" (line 12)? How is this word related to the central symbol of "the Ship"?
3. Compare this poem with Theodore Roethke's "The Waking" in Chapter 16 (p. 751). What similar ideas do the two poems have? What are the differences?

GARY SNYDER (b. 1930)

Milton by Firelight (1955)

Piute Creek, August 1955°

"O Hell, what doe mine eyes with grief behold?"°
Working with an old
Singlejack° miner, who can sense
The vein and cleavage
5   In the very guts of rock, can
Blast granite, build
Switchbacks° that last for years   *trails, or roads*
Under the beat of snow, thaw, mule-hooves.
What use, Milton, a silly story
10   Of our lost general parents,
eaters of fruit?°   *See 4.331–35 of Paradise Lost*

The Indian, the chainsaw boy,
And a string of six mules
Came riding down to camp
15   Hungry for tomatoes and green apples.
Sleeping in saddle-blankets
Under a bright night-sky
Han River slantwise° by morning.
Jays squall
20   Coffee boils

In ten thousand years the Sierras
Will be dry and dead, home of the scorpion.
Ice-scratched slabs and bent trees.
No paradise, no fall,
25   Only the weathering land
The wheeling sky,
Man, with his Satan
Scouring the chaos of the mind.
Oh Hell!

30   Fire down
Too dark to read, miles from a road
The bell-mare° clangs in the meadow

°*Piute Creek:* a creek and spring in the Sierra Nevada Mountains in Yosemite Park in California. During the summer of 1955, Snyder was working with a Yosemite trail crew, and became familiar with the tasks and tools of making hiking trails. °1 *O Hell! . . . behold:* from Milton's *Paradise Lost* (1667), Book 4, line 358. The line begins Satan's speech about his own fallen condition, which he contrasts with the prelapsarian state of paradise which Adam and Eve at that time enjoyed. It is in this speech that Satan plans to avenge his own fall by bringing both death and the loss of innocence to Adam and Eve, and, of course, to all of humanity. Snyder's speaker describes the biblical story made epic by Milton—which he calls "a silly story"—in lines 11–13 of this poem. °3 *Singlejack:* a wooden wedge that, when soaked with water, swells in size to split large rocks. °18 *Han River slantwise:* perhaps the meaning is that the men slept so soundly that when they woke, their eyes seemed to appear Asiatic, as though they were from the Han River area in Korea. °32 *bell-mare:* pack trains in the West were led by a mare with a bell around her neck. The mules and horses of the train would obediently line up behind the bell and follow its sound wherever the bell-mare went. One of the many paintings of the West by Frederic Remington (1861–1909) is *The Bell Mare* (1904).

That packed dirt for a fill-in
Scrambling through loose rocks
On an old trail
All of a summer's day.°   35

°36 *summer's day:* See Shakespeare's "Sonnet 18" (p. 663).

QUESTIONS

1. Why does the speaker contrast the future of the Sierra Nevada Mountains with human concerns about Satan? What is the purpose of the oath in line 28?

2. In Book 4 of *Paradise Lost*, Milton states that the home of Adam and Eve is totally clean and devoid of "Beast, Bird, Insect, or Worm." Why does Snyder draw attention to the future when the Sierras will be "home of the scorpion" (line 22)? What does the scorpion symbolize? In what other ways does Snyder criticize realistic and idealistic conceptions of human and earthly perfection?

3. In what way is the final line, "All of a summer's day," symbolic?

JUDITH VIORST (b. 1931)

A Wedding Sonnet for the Next Generation (2000)

He might compare you to a summer's day,°
Declaring you're far fairer in his eyes.
She might, with depth and breadth and many sighs,
Count all the ways she loves you, way by way.°

He might say when you're old and full of sleep,   5
He'll cherish still the Pilgrim soul in you.°
She might— oh, there are poems so fine, so true,
To help you speak of love and vows to keep.

Words help. And you are writing your own poem.
It doesn't always scan or always rhyme.   10
It mingles images of the sublime
With plainer words: Respect. Trust. Comfort. Home.
How very rich is love's vocabulary
When friends, dear friends, best friends decide to marry.

°1 *summer's day:* See Shakespeare's "Sonnet 18" p. 663. °3, 4 *She might . . . way by way:* See Elizabeth Barrett Browning, "How Do I Love Thee" (Chapter 19). °5, 6 *He might say . . . Pilgrim soul in you:* See Yeats, "When You Are Old" (Chapter 15).

QUESTIONS

1. Why does the poem speak of "the Next Generation" in the title? What is the form of the poem? Why do the first lines alternate between "he" and "she"?

2. What is the meaning and effect of the allusions in lines 1–6? Why does Viorst introduce these allusions? What assumptions does she make about her audience for this poem?

3. How does the poem change in the last six lines? How does the language shift in these lines?
4. What does it mean to say "you are writing your own poem"? How are the final two lines related to the previous parts of the poem?

WALT WHITMAN (1819–1892)

For a photo, see Chapter 14, page 667.

 ### A Noiseless Patient Spider (1868)

A noiseless patient spider,
I marked where on a little promontory it stood isolated,
Marked how to explore the vacant vast surrounding,
It launched forth filament, filament, filament out of itself,
5   Ever unreeling them, ever tirelessly speeding them.

And you O my soul where you stand,
Surrounded, detached, in measureless oceans of space,
Ceaselessly musing, venturing, throwing, seeking the spheres
      to connect them,
Till the bridge you will need be formed, till the ductile anchor hold,
10 Till the gossamer thread you fling catch somewhere, O my soul.

QUESTIONS

1. The subject of the second stanza is seemingly unrelated to the subject of the first. How are these stanzas related?
2. In what way does the spider's web symbolize the soul and the poet's view of the isolation of human beings? How does the web symbolize the soul's ceaseless "musing . . . seeking" and the attempt "to connect"?
3. Explain why the second stanza is not a complete sentence. How might this grammatical feature be related to the spider's web? To the poet's idea that life requires striving but does not offer completeness?

RICHARD WILBUR (b. 1921)

 ### Year's End (1950)

Now winter downs the dying of the year,
And Night is all a settlement of snow;
From the soft street the rooms of houses show
A gathered light, a shapen atmosphere,
5   Like frozen-over lakes whose ice is thin
And still allows some stirring down within.

I've known the wind by water banks to shake
The late leaves down, which frozen where they fell
And held in ice as dancers in a spell
Fluttered all winter long into a lake; 10
Graved on the dark in gestures of descent,
They seemed their own most perfect monument.

There was perfection in the death of ferns
Which laid their fragile cheeks against the stone
A million years. Great mammoths overthrown 15
Composedly have made their long sojourns,
Like palaces of patience, in the gray
And changeless lands of ice. And at Pompeii°

The little dog lay curled and did not rise
But slept the deeper as the ashes rose 20
And found the people incomplete, and froze
The random hands, the loose unready eyes
Of men expecting yet another sun
To do the shapely thing they had not done.

These sudden ends of time must give us pause. 25
We fray into the future, rarely wrought
Save in the tapestries of afterthought.
More time, more time. Barrages of applause
Come muffled from a buried radio.
The New-year bells are wrangling with the snow. 30

°18 *Pompeii:* the southern Italian Roman city buried by lava during the eruption of Mount Vesuvius in 79 CE. Many people and animals died trying to escape the lava flow and were covered over where they fell. Modern excavators created statues of these fallen figures by using plaster to fill in cavities left by their bodies. One of these was the "little dog" mentioned in line 19.

QUESTIONS

1. What natural and historical symbols does Wilbur introduce in the poem? What ideas do the symbols present about time and the use people make of time?

2. Describe Wilbur's use of two-word groups united by assonance and consonance in the poem (e.g., "People incomplete," downs the dying," "still . . . stirring"). How effective are these groups in drawing your attention to Wilbur's meaning?

3. Describe the symbols in the final stanza ("fray into the future," "tapestries of afterthought," "muffled from a buried radio"). Why does the poem conclude with the symbols of "New-year bells" and "snow"?

4. Consider the meaning of line 25. How can this line be interpreted so that the poem may have either positive or negative views of human activity?

WILLIAM BUTLER YEATS (1865–1939)

For a photo, see Chapter 15, page 713.

The Second Coming° (1920; 1919)

Turning and turning in the widening gyre°
The falcon cannot hear the falconer;
Things fall apart; the center cannot hold;
Mere anarchy is loosed upon the world,
5 The blood-dimmed tide° is loosed, and everywhere
The ceremony of innocence is drowned;
The best lack all conviction, while the worst
Are full of passionate intensity.
Surely some revelation is at hand;
10 Surely the Second Coming is at hand.
The Second Coming! Hardly are those words out
When a vast image out of *Spiritus Mundi*°
Troubles my sight; somewhere in sands of the desert
A shape with lion body and the head of a man,°
15 A gaze blank and pitiless as the sun,
Is moving its slow thighs, while all about it
Reel shadows of the indignant desert birds.
The darkness drops again; but now I know
That twenty centuries of stony sleep
20 Were vexed to nightmare by a rocking cradle,
And what rough beast, its hour come round at last,
Slouches towards Bethlehem to be born?

°The phrase "second coming" has been used traditionally to refer to expectations of the return of Jesus for the salvation of believers, as described in the New Testament. The prophecies foretold that Christ's return would be preceded by famine, epidemics, wars between nations, and general civil disturbance. Yeats believed that human history could be measured in cycles of approximately 2,000 years (see line 19, "twenty centuries"). According to this system, the birth of Jesus ended the Greco-Roman cycle and in 1919, when Yeats wrote "The Second Coming," it appeared to him that the Christian period was ending and a new era was about to take its place. The New Testament expectation was that Jesus would reappear. Yeats, by contrast, holds that the disruptions of the twentieth century were preceding a takeover by the forces of evil. °1 *gyre:* a radiating spiral, cone, or vortex. Yeats used the intersecting of two of these shapes as a visual symbol of his cyclic theory. As one gyre spiraled and widened out, to become dissipated, one period of history would end; at the same time a new gyre, closer to the center, would begin and spiral in a reverse direction to the starting point of the old gyre. A drawing of this plan looks like this:

°The falcon of line 2 is at the broadest, centrifugal point of one gyre, symbolically illustrating the end of a cycle. The "indignant desert birds" of line 17 "reel" in a tighter circle, symbolizing the beginning of the new age in the new gyre.
°5 *blood-dimmed tide:* quotation from Shakespeare's *Macbeth*, 2.2.60–63. °12 *Spiritus Mundi:* literally, the spirit of the world, a collective human consciousness that furnished writers and thinkers with a common fund of images and symbols. Yeats referred to this collective repository as "a great memory passing on from generation to generation." °14 *lion body and the head of a man:* that is, the Sphinx, which in ancient Egypt symbolized the pharaoh as a spirit of the sun. Because of this pre-Christian origin, the reincarnation of a sphinx could therefore represent qualities associated in New Testament books like Revelation (11, 13, 17), Mark (13:14–20), and 2 Thessalonians (2:1–12) with a monstrous, superhuman, satanic figure.

QUESTIONS

1. Consider the following as symbols: the "gyre," the "falcon," the "blood-dimmed tide," the "ceremony of innocence," the "worst" who are "full of passionate intensity." What ideas and values do these symbolize in the poem?

2. Why does Yeats capitalize the phrase "Second Coming"? To what does this phrase refer? Explain the irony of Yeats's use of the phrase in this poem.

3. Contrast the symbols of the falcon of line 2 and the desert birds of line 17. Considering that these are realistically presented, how does the realism contribute to their identity as symbols?

4. What is symbolized by the sphinx being revealed as a "rough beast"? What is the significance of the beast's going "towards Bethlehem to be born"?

WRITING ABOUT SYMBOLISM AND ALLUSION IN POETRY

As you read the assigned poem, take careful and accurate notes, and make observations about the presence of symbols or allusions or both. Explanatory notes will help you establish basic information, but you also need to explain meanings and create interpretations in your own words. Use a dictionary for understanding words or phrases that require further study. For allusions, you might check out original sources to determine original contexts. Use the explanations supplied in your text, and ask your instructor when you need more information. Try to determine the ways in which your poem is similar to, or different from, the original work or source, and then determine the purpose served by the allusion.

Questions for Discovering Ideas

CULTURAL OR UNIVERSAL SYMBOLS

- What symbols that you can characterize as cultural or universal can you discover in names, objects, places, situations, or actions in the poem (e.g., nightingales, hemlock, a thorn, two lovers, Bethlehem)?
- How are these symbols used? What do they mean, both specifically, in the poem, and universally, in a broader context? What would the poem be like without the symbolic meaning?

CONTEXTUAL SYMBOLS

- What contextual symbols can you locate in the poem (e.g., withered sedge, a flock of birds, a doe running into a woods)? How are these symbols used specifically in the poem? What would the poem be like if the contextual symbol were not taken to be symbolic?
- What causes you to conclude that the symbols are truly symbolic? What is being symbolized? What do the symbols mean? How definite or direct is the symbolism?
- Is the symbolism used systematically throughout the poem, or is it used only once? How does the symbolism affect the poem's ideas or emotions?

ALLUSIONS

- Granted your knowledge of literature, science, geography, television, the Bible, film, popular culture, and other fields of knowledge, what allusions do you recognize?
- Do you find other references in these or other categories? What do the allusions mean in their original context? What do they mean within the poem?
- Do you see any possible allusions that you are not sure about? What help do you find in the explanatory notes in the text you are using? Consult a dictionary, such as *The Oxford Dictionary of Allusions*, or another reference work to discover the nature of these allusions. Refer also to Chapter 7. If you have questions, be sure to ask your reference librarian for assistance.

Strategies for Organizing Ideas

Begin with a brief description of the poem and of the symbolism or allusions in it. A symbol might be central to the poem, or an allusion might be introduced at a particularly important point. Your central idea might take you in a number of directions: You might conclude that the symbolism is based on objects like flowers and natural scenes, or that it stems out of an action or set of actions, or that it is developed from an initial situation such as a time of the day or year. The symbols may be universal or contextual; they may be applicable particularly to personal life or to political or social life. Allusions may emphasize the differences between your poem and the work or event to which the allusion refers, or they may highlight the circumstances of your poem. In addition, you might make a point that the symbols and/or allusions make the poem seem optimistic, or pessimistic, and so on.

Here are some possible approaches for your essay, which may be combined as need arises.

1. *The meaning of symbols or allusions.* This approach is the most natural one to take for an essay on symbolism or allusion. If you have discovered a symbol or symbols, or allusions, explain the meaning as best you can. What is the poem's major idea? How do you know that your interpretation is valid? How do the poem's symbols and allusions contribute to your interpretation? How pervasive, how applicable, are these devices? If you have discovered many symbols and allusions, which ones predominate? What do they mean? Why are some more important than others? What connects them with each other and with the poem's main ideas? How are you able to make conclusions about all this?

2. *The effect of symbols or allusions on the poem's form.* Here the goal is to determine how symbolism or allusion is related to the poetic structure. Where does the symbol occur? If it is early in the poem, how do the subsequent parts relate to the ideas borne by the symbol? What logical

or chronological function does the symbol serve in the poem's development? Is the symbol repeated, and if so, to what effect? If the symbol is introduced later, has it been anticipated earlier? How do you know? Can the symbol be considered climactic? What might the structure of the poem have been like if the symbolism had not been used? (Answering this question can help you judge how the symbol influences the poem's structure.) Many of these same questions might also be applied to an allusion or allusions. In addition, for an allusion, it is important to compare the contexts of the work you are studying and the original to determine how the poet uses the allusion as a part of the poem's form or structure.

3. *The relationship between the literal and the symbolic.* The object here is to describe the literal nature of the symbols, and then to determine their appropriateness to the poem's context. If the symbol is part of a narrative, what is its literal function? If the symbol is a person, object, or setting, what physical aspects are described? Are colors included? Shapes? Sizes? Sounds? In light of this description, how applicable is the symbol to the ideas it embodies? How appropriate is the literal condition to the symbolic condition? The answers to questions like these should lead not so much to a detailed account of the meaning of the symbols but rather to an account of their appropriateness to the topics and ideas of the poem.

4. *The implications and resonances of symbols and allusions.* This type of essay is more personal than the others, for it is devoted to the suggestions and associations—the "implications and resonances"—that the poem's symbols and allusions bring out. The object of the essay is to describe your own responses or chain of thinking that the poem sets in motion. You are therefore free to move in your own direction as long as you base your discussion on the symbols and allusions in the poem. If the poet is speaking in general terms about the end of an era, for example, as with the symbol of the "rough beast" in Yeats's "The Second Coming" and the giant fishnets in Jeffers's "The Purse-Seine," then you could apply these symbols to your own thinking.

Your conclusion might contain a summary of your main points. If your poem is rich in symbols or allusions, you might also consider some of the elements that you have not discussed in the body and try to tie these together with those you have already discussed. It would also be appropriate to introduce any new ideas you developed as a result of your study.

Illustrative Student Essay

Although underlined sentences are not recommended by MLA style, they are used in this illustrative essay as teaching tools to emphasize the central idea, thesis sentence, and topic sentences.

Jani 1

Sonal Jani

Professor Barack

English 212

20 March 2014

Symbolism in Oliver's "Wild Geese"°

[1]   Mary Oliver's "Wild Geese" can be understood as an extended answer to the issue raised in its first line. This idea, to be refuted, is unusual—one might almost say startling—because it is stated so baldly: "You do not have to be good." It does not seem that many poems begin with a line like that. The rest of the poem is developed through a series of symbols asserting the idea that there is a more significant kind of goodness.* Oliver's argument is to shun traditional habits of contrition and repentance, and instead to emphasize that goodness exists in the animal and human spirit within oneself, and also everywhere in Nature. She asserts this idea first through a traditional but negative symbol, and second through a series of positive symbols of the natural world.†

[2]   The first symbol in the poem negatively symbolizes traditional but ineffective approaches to creating goodness within oneself. The picture is that of a hermit-like person actively suffering for contrition's sake:

> You do not have to walk on your knees
>
> for a hundred miles through the desert, repenting. (lines 2–3)

The notion of "repenting" symbolizes the tradition that human beings must endure punishment to atone for guilt and sins. The vision of knees in the desert

---

°**This poem appears on page 786.**
*Central idea.
†**Thesis sentence.**

Jani 2

thus symbolizes the deeply ingrained idea that self-denial and suffering are needed to achieve goodness and inner peace.

Before going on with the more detailed symbolism of the poem, Oliver introduces another element of the presumed discussion the speaker is having with a listener who has spoken before the poem begins, but who now just listens. The idea is that goodness can be found within "the soft animal of your body":   [3]

> You only have to let the soft animal of your body
>
> love what it loves. (4–5)

It is not clear just what sort of animal is described, but the word "animal" is based on the action of breathing, the essential characteristic of living beings. The essence of life is therefore the "soft animal" (not a vicious animal) of the self, which here symbolizes the ethics that are a consequence of love.

A second part of the poem begins with the seventh line, "Meanwhile the world goes on." The idea here is that there is a larger existence than the one that is defined by human concepts of goodness or repentance, guilt or despair. The speaker's argument is carried out with a cumulative set of symbols derived from the natural world. These are "the sun and the clear pebbles of the rain" which are visualized as "moving across" the world—over "prairies," "deep trees," "mountains," and "rivers" (8–11), all of which describe vast expanses of land and wilderness. Because of their virtual infiniteness, these natural objects make human concerns seem small and insignificant. Thus, as symbols, they signify the need for a larger perspective and a more broad dedication than human beings usually make.   [4]

In this context the poet introduces the symbol of "the wild geese, high in the clean blue air" (12). The geese, part of the general symbol of the world going on, are migrating homeward. The idea seems mystical, but nevertheless the symbolism provides a clear analogy for human beings living in our modern troubled and troubling civilization. We are part of the universe, the world. We live here and belong here, just as the wild geese do. We tend to forget our place here, however, as we lose perspective and become enmeshed in cultural concerns   [5]

Jani 3

which lead us only to guilt and loneliness (14). The need is to listen to the inner animal, the outer world, which has a strong pull on our imaginations, just as the wild geese symbolize a natural power that restores the world's creatures to home and to a sense of belonging.

[6]   The "world," in the symbolic fabric of Oliver's poem, is an active participant in the process. It "offers itself to your imagination, / calls to you like the wild geese, harsh and exciting—" (15, 16). The idea of the symbol is that we, like the wild geese, should let our imaginations follow the call. While people are traditionally preoccupied with despair, the sentient and nonsentient elements of nature are simply *being*. We could be like that if only we could perceive the symbolic meaning of the world around us. If we follow the morality of the trees and the sun and the rain, we too will experience the strength of being a part of nature. Our morality will then flow to us as a matter of course because we will have acknowledged our place "in the family of things" (18) just as the geese return home to lead their lives in the landscapes of the world.

Jani 4

Work Cited

Oliver, Mary. "Wild Geese." *Literature: An Introduction to Reading and Writing, Compact Edition*. Ed. Edgar V. Roberts and Robert Zweig. 6th ed. New York: Pearson, 2015. 786. Print

Commentary on the Essay

This essay conforms to the first strategy for writing about symbolism (p. 793) inasmuch as it involves a concentrated explanation of the symbolism in Oliver's "Wild Geese"—symbolism that is mainly drawn from the world of Nature.

The introduction briefly characterizes Oliver's confrontational opening line and goes on to assert that the rest of the poem is developed through a succession of symbols. The central idea is responsive to the opening line—namely, that the poem is to introduce symbols of "a more significant kind of goodness"—and the thesis sentence states that in the body there will be a discussion of a negative symbol and a set of more positive symbols.

Paragraphs 3 through 5 consider the meanings of the poem's three major symbols—the "soft animal" (3), rain, land, and wilderness (4), and the "wild geese" (5). The final paragraph deals with the issue of goodness and the different kind of "good" brought out in the poem's symbolism (that is, being part of the "family of things").

Writing Topics About Symbolism and Allusion in Poetry

Writing Paragraphs

1. In a paragraph describe the nature of the symbols in Hardy's "In Time of 'The Breaking of Nations'" or in Whitman's "A Noiseless Patient Spider." How appropriate are the symbols in bringing forth the major theme of the poem?

2. In a paragraph compare one symbol in Hardy's "In Time of 'The Breaking of Nations'" with one symbol in Whitman's "A Noiseless Patient Spider." What parallels in general topic matter do you discover? How do the poets make the poems diverge, despite the common qualities of the symbols?

3. In a paragraph compare the use of religious symbols in Donne's "The Canonization" and Herbert's "The Collar." What are the locations from which the poets draw their symbols? How do the symbols figure into the major ideas and arguments of the poems?

Writing Essays

1. In an essay analyze the ways in which Keats, Herbert, and Jeffers use symbols to convey the fact and idea of capture and thralldom in "La Belle Dame Sans Merci," "The Collar," and "The Purse-Seine." What major symbols do the three poets use? How appropriate is each symbol in its respective poem? How do the poets use the symbols to focus on the problems they present in their poems?

2. Describe the differences in the ways in which Viorst and Yeats use allusions in "A Wedding Sonnet for the Next Generation," and "The Second Coming." How completely can we understand these poems without an explanation of the allusions? How extensive should explanations be? In an essay argue that the allusiveness of the poem makes the poem enriching and interesting.

3. Write an essay describing the use of animals and birds as symbols in this chapter's poems by Jeffers, Oliver, and Whitman. How do the poets show the symbolic connection of the animals to human affairs? How faithfully do they consider the animals as animals?

Creative Writing Assignment

1. Write a poem in which you develop a major symbol, as Jeffers does in "The Purse-Seine" and Herbert does in "The Pulley" (Chapter 13). To get yourself started, you might consider symbols like these:

- A littered street or sidewalk
- A new SUV, or an all-terrain vehicle, or a hybrid
- Coffee-hour after religious services
- An athletic competition
- A computer
- The checkout counter at the neighborhood supermarket
- The family dog looking out a front window as the children leave for school
- A handgun

Write an essay describing the process of your creation. How do you begin? How much detail is necessary? How many conclusions do you need to bring out about your symbol? When do you think you have said enough? Too much? How do you decide?

2. Write a poem in which you make your own allusions to your own experiences, such as attending school, participating in an activity, joining a team, reading a book, identifying with a fictional or a movie character, recalling a passage from a popular song or a poem or story you have read, or going to a recent artistic or political event. What assumptions do you make about your reader when you bring out your allusions? How do you make the allusion (i.e., by a quotation, a name, a title, an indirect reference)? How does your allusion deepen your meaning? How does your allusion increase your own power of expression?

Library Assignment

1. From your library, take out a university press study of Yeats or Jeffers. How much detail is devoted in the study to either poet's use of symbols? How pervasively is symbolism employed by the poet? How does the poet use symbolism to express ideas about science or nationalism? What other use or uses does the poet make of symbolism?

Chapter 18
Four Major American Poets: Emily Dickinson, Robert Frost, Langston Hughes, and Sylvia Plath

AFTER STUDYING THIS MATERIAL, YOU SHOULD BE ABLE TO DO THE FOLLOWING:

- Identify similarities, differences, and other notable relationships across a number of works by a single poet
- Synthesize a number of critical approaches to a single poet's work
- Assess the influence of an author's life upon his or her work

In Chapters 11 through 17 we have considered poetry in terms of its elements and effects. In this chapter we present collections of poems by four major American poets: Emily Dickinson (1830–1886), Robert Frost (1874–1963), Langston Hughes (1902–1967), and Sylvia Plath (1932–1963). As both history and chance would have it, Dickinson, Frost, and Plath were New Englanders, although Plath spent four of her last six years living in England. Hughes was born and raised in the Midwest, but came to New York as an adult, and stayed. Dickinson is one of the most prominent poetic voices of the nineteenth century. Both Frost and Hughes are recognized as poetic giants of the twentieth century. Plath's poetic career was unfortunately cut short, but the posthumous edition of her poems received the honor of a Pulitzer Prize when it was published in 1982, almost twenty years after her death.

Although the poems included here comprise only a small part of the work of these poets, our hope is that there are enough poems to illustrate the typical concerns and major characteristics that are to be found in the study of their poetic careers.

EMILY DICKINSON'S LIFE AND WORK
(1830–1886)

Emily Elizabeth Dickinson, who is acknowledged today as one of America's greatest poets, was born on December 10, 1830. She was raised in Amherst, Massachusetts, which in the nineteenth century was a small and tradition-bound town. Dominating the Dickinson family was Emily's father, Edward, a lawyer, a legislator, and a rigorous Calvinist, whose concept of life was stern religious observance and obedience to God's laws as derived from the Bible. Emily was taken to Sunday School, but late in her teens she declined to pronounce herself a believing Christian. She spent a number of years at primary school and eventually studied

Emily Dickinson's room at the family homestead in Amherst, Massachusetts, where she wrote much of her poetry.

classics at Amherst Academy. She also enrolled at the South Hadley Seminary for Women (now Mount Holyoke College), but her parents withdrew her after a year because of ill health.[1]

During these years of childhood and youth, she led a normally active life. She saw many people, liked school and her teachers, wrote essays, acquired a number of good friends, gossiped, sang at the piano to her own accompaniment, treasured spring flowers, amused her friends with impromptu stories, studied theology, read Pope's *An Essay on Man*, did a good deal more reading, and planned to become the "Belle of Amherst" at the age of seventeen. She also began writing poetry, which consisted mainly of occasional verses and Valentines.

After leaving school she returned home. She was to spend the rest of her life there, sharing in family and household duties. In 1856 she won a second prize at the local fair for her recipe for Rye and Indian Bread. She took occasional trips, including long stays in Boston in 1864 and 1865 to be treated for an undisclosed eye ailment. Eventually, however, she stopped traveling altogether.

---

[1] It would appear that there are four reliable likenesses of Emily Dickinson. The first is a painting of her and her brother and sister, done by Otis A. Bullard in about 1840, showing Emily at the age of about nine. There is a silhouette of her at the age of about fourteen. The first and most reliable photo is a daguerreotype taken of her at about the age of sixteen. This is the photo that is always duplicated. Still another photograph has come to light that may show Dickinson at the age of about thirty to thirty-five. As yet the photo, an albumen print with Dickinson's name on the back, has not been authenticated, but it is fair to say that its resemblance to the authentic photo is uncanny. (See *The New Yorker*, May 22, 2000, pp. 30–31.) This photo is included in Alfred Habegger, *My Wars Are Laid Away in Books* (2001), where all the likenesses are included. Habegger believes that the photo is authentic. Richard B. Sewall includes a photograph of a young woman as the frontispiece to the second volume of his *The Life of Emily Dickinson* (1974), and he duplicates this same photo on page 752 of the one-volume *Life* of 1980. On the back of the original is written "Emily Dickenson [sic] 1860" in an unknown hand, and the features of the portrayed woman are consistent with those in the daguerreotype of Dickinson at sixteen. Although it is tempting to consider this photograph genuine, the attribution has not been validated.

Although Dickinson had written poems since her school days, she did not devote herself to poetry until her late twenties—beginning in about 1858. After this time her poetic output expanded, almost miraculously. Many of her poems are quite short, consisting of no more than a single stanza, but some are much longer. No more than ten of them were published during her lifetime, mostly against her wishes. Instead, her "publication" consisted of making fair copies of the poems in handwriting that is difficult to read. In the privacy of her own room she put numbers of poems together in "fascicles," which consist of folded sheets of stationery bound with thread. These handwritten copies were for her eyes only, although she frequently sent copies in letters and also sent batches of poems to friends. The poems she didn't prepare carefully for her fascicles were kept in little packets. She locked away all these private literary treasures, which were discovered only after her death.

In total, 1,775 to 1,789 of her poems have been recovered. The figure 1,775 is the number of poems included by Thomas H. Johnson in *The Complete Poems of Emily Dickinson* (1955), the first major complete edition of Dickinson's poetry. The figure 1,789 is the number included by Ralph W. Franklin in *The Poems of Emily Dickinson: Variorum Edition* (1998). Both editions are based on exhaustive studies of all the documentary evidence available at the times when the editors were doing their research. Beyond these major scholarly editions, a number of brief poems have been mined from Dickinson's letters, and these were published, in 1993, as 498 new poems, on the theory that parts of the letters reach a succinctness and rhythm more characteristic of poetry than prose. These poems are short, some being no more than two lines long. If one accepts them as additional Dickinson poems, they bring the total count above 2,280.

Although a surprising amount of biographical information is available about Dickinson, the connections between events in her life and her poems are missing. For example, it seems obvious that a real and powerful sadness underlies the poignant conclusion of "I Cannot Live with You," just as a sense of personal inadequacy or reproach may have caused her to write "I Felt a Funeral in My Brain." We can only guess, however, about the specific situations, if any, that led her to write such a poem.

Nevertheless, the general occasions inspiring some of her poems are clear. The world she lived in was small, and she found subjects in her surroundings: house, garden, yard, and village. A lowly snake is the topic of one of her poems—one of the few published when she was alive—as are butterflies, and a vibrating hummingbird. She even wrote a poem about the railroad locomotives servicing her home town of Amherst. Sometimes no more than a recollection, a single word, a concept, or a paradox that arose from her own interior monologue enabled her to originate poems. Such inspirations account for topics such as a haunted mind, a memory, a state of solitude, the nature of truth and beauty, the condition of self-reliance, the angle of winter light.

Dickinson's poems on death and dying probably had occasional sources also, even though these sources may be far removed from the time and circumstance of the poems. One of Dickinson's dearest childhood friends was Sophia Holland, who died in 1844. Perhaps the loss of Sophia was one of her memories when she wrote "I Never Lost as Much But Twice," and "The Bustle in a House," together with her other poems on death.

Much of her other poetry may have a similar occasional origin. She wrote poems about love and the psychology of personal relationships, even though she never married or had a love affair that we know about. We may therefore wonder about the internal necessity that caused her to write poems like "Wild Nights–Wild Nights!" and "I Cannot Live with You," which portray states of sexual ecstasy and final renunciation. And what sorts of personal experience and introspection underlay such poems as "After Great Pain, a Formal Feeling Comes," "The Soul Selects Her Own Society," and "I Dwell in Possibility"?

In the absence of specific details linking her life to her poetry, therefore, the occasions of her poems must remain no more than peripherally relevant—themselves unseen, though in the effects they remain. We are left to conclude that her inspiration rose from within herself. She is a contemplative and personal poet, whether she herself is the omnipresent "I" of her poems or whether the "I" is an objective speaker to whom she assigns all the strength of her imagination and her dreams. This speaker possesses bright wit, clever and engaging playfulness, acute powers of observation, deep sensitivity, intense introspection, and tender responsiveness. She is alive, quick, and inventive. She enjoys riddles. She leads readers into new and unexplored regions of thought and feeling.

All these characteristics are to be discovered everywhere in her poetry. Her speaker expresses a vital joy and delirious energy in the quizzical poem "I Taste a Liquor Never Brewed," an insouciant bluffness in "Some Keep the Sabbath Going to Church," and overwhelming tenderness and regret at the end of "The Bustle in a House." In the last stanza of "I Cannot Live with You" she captures the deep anguish of a relationship that is ending:

> So We must meet apart –
> You there – I – here –
> With just the Door ajar
> That Oceans are – and Prayer –
> And that White Sustenance –
> Despair –

She is also reverent, and a number of poems introduce the topics of God, immortality, scripture, and the final judgment. But she is sometimes saucy and flippant about religion. Going to church on Sunday, for example, was expected of the dutiful Christian, but she explains why she prefers staying home with "a Bobolink for a Chorister."

> So instead of getting to Heaven, at last –
> I'm going, all along.

Undeniably, Dickinson's external daily life was uneventful. Her inner life was anything but uneventful, however, for she was always reflecting and thinking. What we know about her is that her inquiring and restless mind was the source of her compulsive poetic strength, and that her poetry expresses the vital personal feelings and psychological insights that emerged from her thoughts about life, love, death, Nature, and God. It is not possible to read her poems without revering her as a person and as a poet.

After Emily Dickinson died, in 1886, her sister, Lavinia, was astonished to find the many fascicles and packets of poems that she had left. Lavinia recognized the significance of this work and eventually turned much of it over to Thomas Higginson and Mabel L. Todd for editing and publication. They published three separate volumes of Dickinson's verse (in 1890, 1891, and 1896), each containing about a hundred poems. In these volumes, the editors eliminated slant rhymes, smoothed out the meter, revised those metaphors that struck them as outrageous, and regularized the punctuation.

These well-intentioned editorial "adjustments" remained intact until 1955, when the Harvard University Press published Thomas H. Johnson's three-volume complete edition. Johnson also published a single-volume edition of the poems in 1961 and, in addition, a paperback selection titled *Final Harvest: Emily Dickinson's Poems* (1961). Johnson's pioneering edition has been followed by the ambitious and comprehensive *The Poems of Emily Dickinson: Variorum Edition* in three volumes (Cambridge: Harvard UP, 1998), edited by Ralph W. Franklin, who also edited the facsimile edition of the handwritten poems, *The Manuscript Books of Emily Dickinson* (Cambridge: Harvard UP, 1981). Franklin's edition has also been published in one volume as *The Poems of Emily Dickinson: Reading Edition* (Cambridge: Harvard UP, 1999). The poems that have been extracted from Dickinson's letters were edited by William H. Shurr, with Anna Dunlap and Emily Grey Shurr, as *New Poems of Emily Dickinson* (Chapel Hill: U of North Carolina P, 1993).

Definitive biographies of Dickinson are Richard B. Sewall, *The Life of Emily Dickinson* (New York: Farrar, 1974; rpt. [Harvard UP] 1980; rpt. 1994); Alfred Habegger, *My Wars Are Laid Away in Books: The Life of Emily Dickinson* (New York: Random House, 2001); and Cynthia Griffin Wolff, *Emily Dickinson* (New York: Knopf, 1986). Interesting details are contained in Brenda Wineapple, *White Heat: The Friendship of Emily Dickinson and Thomas Wentworth Higginson* (New York: Knopf, 2008) and Lyndall Gordon, *Lives Like Loaded Guns: Emily Dickinson and Her Family's Feuds* (New York: Viking, 2010). A useful book containing biographical, critical, and many other details is Jane Donahue Eberwein, ed., *An Emily Dickinson Encyclopedia* (Westport: Greenwood, 1998). The numbers of important critical studies are legion. Some of these are Albert J. Gelpi, *Emily Dickinson: The Mind of the Poet* (Cambridge: Harvard UP, 1966); Joanne F. Diehl, *Dickinson and the Romantic Imagination* (Princeton: Princeton UP, 1981); David Porter, *Dickinson, the Modern Idiom* (Cambridge: Harvard UP, 1981); Susan Juhasz, *The Undiscovered Continent: Emily Dickinson and the Space of the Mind* (Bloomington: U of Indiana P, 1983); Donna Dickenson, *Emily Dickinson* (Leamington Spa: Berg, 1985); Sharon Leder and Andrea Abbott, *The Language of Exclusion: The Poetry of Emily Dickinson and Christina Rossetti* (New York: Greenwood, 1987); Cristanne Miller, *Emily Dickinson: A Poet's Grammar* (Cambridge: Harvard UP, 1987); Joanne Dobson, *Dickinson and the Strategies of Reticence* (Bloomington: U of Indiana P, 1989); Paula Bennett, *Emily Dickinson: Woman Poet* (Iowa City: U of Iowa P, 1990); Gary Lee Stonum, *The Dickinson Sublime* (Madison: U of Wisconsin P, 1990); Joan Kirkby, *Emily Dickinson* (New York: St. Martin's, 1991); Judith Farr, *The Passion of Emily Dickinson* (Cambridge: Harvard UP, 1992); Claudia Ottlinger, *The Death-Motif in the*

Poetry of Emily Dickinson and Christina Rossetti (Frankfurt: Lang, 1996); and Paul Crumbley, *Inflections of the Pen: Dash and Voice in Emily Dickinson* (Lexington: U of Kentucky P, 1996).

Collections of essays on Dickinson are Paul J. Ferlazzo, ed., *Critical Essays on Emily Dickinson* (Boston: Hall, 1958, a historical collection); Richard B. Sewall, ed., *Emily Dickinson: A Collection of Critical Essays* (Englewood Cliffs: Prentice Hall, 1963); Judith Farr, ed., *Emily Dickinson: A Collection of Critical Essays* (Upper Saddle River: Prentice Hall, 1996); and Gudrun Grabher et al., eds. *The Emily Dickinson Handbook* (Amherst: U of Massachusetts P, 1998). One of the hour-long programs in the PBS *Voices and Visions* series (1987) features Dickinson's work.

Topics for Writing About the Poetry of Emily Dickinson

1. Dickinson's characteristic brevity in the explanation of situations and the expression of ideas.
2. Dickinson's use of personal but not totally disclosed subject matter.
3. Dickinson's use of imagery and symbolism: sources, types, meanings.
4. Dickinson's humor and irony.
5. Dickinson's ideas about love, separation, personal pain, war, death, faith, religion, science, the soul.
6. Dickinson's power as a poet.
7. Dickinson's poems as they appear on the page: the relationship of meaning to lines, stanzas, capitalization, punctuation, the use of the dash.
8. The structuring of a number of Dickinson's poems: subject, development, conclusions.
9. The character of the speaker in a number of Dickinson's poems: personality, things noticed, accuracy of conclusions. If there appears to be a listener in the poems, what effect does this listener have on the speaker?
10. Dickinson's verse forms and use of rhymes.
11. Themes of exhilaration, sorrow, pity, triumph, and regret in Dickinson.

Poems by Emily Dickinson (Alphabetically Arranged)

For ease in locating the selections included here, the poems are arranged alphabetically by the first significant word in the first line. There are two numbers following the title of each poem. The first number (e.g., J501) refers to the poem numbers in Thomas H. Johnson's *The Complete Poems of Emily Dickinson*. Critics since Johnson's edition have unanimously employed these numbers. The second number (e.g., F373) refers to the new numbering in Ralph W. Franklin's *The Poems of Emily Dickinson: Variorum Edition*. It would appear that future Dickinson criticism will need to include both numbers if the poem under discussion is to be properly identified, as with the following title: *After Great Pain, a Formal Feeling Comes (J341, F372).*

A single mark resembling a hyphen or short dash, following a brief space, was Dickinson's most-used punctuation. For Dickinson's poems appearing in this book, the mark is represented by an en dash (–).

A Narrow Fellow in the Grass (J986, F1096) 807
After Great Pain, a Formal Feeling Comes (J341, F372) 808
Because I Could Not Stop for Death (J712, F479)
   (See Chapter 11, p. 545)
The Bustle in a House (J1078, F1108) 808
"Faith" Is a Fine Invention (J185, F202) 809
I Cannot Live with You (J640, F706) 809
I Died for Beauty – But Was Scarce (J449, F448) 810
I Dwell in Possibility (F466, J657) 810
I Felt a Funeral, in My Brain (J280, F340) 811
I Heard a Fly Buzz – When I Died (J465, F591) 811
I Like to See It Lap the Miles (J585, F383) 812
I'm Nobody! Who Are You? (J288, F260) 812
I Never Lost as Much but Twice (J49, F39) 812
I Taste a Liquor Never Brewed (J214, F207) 813
Much Madness Is Divinest Sense (J435, F620) 813
My Life Closed Twice Before Its Close (J1732, F1773) 813
One Need Not Be a Chamber – To Be Haunted (J670, F407) 814
Safe in Their Alabaster Chambers (J216, F124) 814
Some Keep the Sabbath Going to Church (J324, F236) 814
The Soul Selects Her Own Society (J303, F409) 815
Success Is Counted Sweetest (J67, F112) 815
Tell All the Truth but Tell It Slant (J1129, F1263) 816
There Is No Frigate Like a Book (J1263, F1286) 816
There's a Certain Slant of Light (J258, F320) 816
Triumph May Be of Several Kinds (J455, F680), ... 817
Wild Nights – Wild Nights! (J249, F269) 817

A Narrow Fellow in the Grass (J986, F1096) (1891, c.1865)

A narrow Fellow In the Grass
Occasionally rides –
You may have met Him – did you not
His notice sudden is –

The Grass divides as with a Comb –   5
A spotted shaft is seen –
And then it closes at your feet
And opens further on –

He likes a Boggy Acre
A Floor too cool for Corn –   10
Yet when a Boy, and barefoot –

I more than once at Noon
Have passed, I thought, a Whip lash
Unbraiding in the Sun
15 When stooping to secure it
It wrinkled, and was gone –

Several of Nature's People
I know, and they know me –
I feel for them a transport
20 Of cordiality –

But never met this Fellow
Attended, or alone
Without a tighter breathing
And Zero at the Bone –

After Great Pain, a Formal Feeling Comes (J341, F372) (1929, c.1862)

After great pain, a formal feeling comes –
The Nerves sit ceremonious, like Tombs –
The Stiff Heart questions 'was it He, that bore,'
And 'Yesterday, or Centuries before'?

5 The Feet, mechanical, go round –
A Wooden way
Of Ground, or Air, or Ought° –   *anything, nothing*
Regardless grown,
A Quartz contentment, like a stone –

10 This is the Hour of Lead –
Remembered, if outlived,
As Freezing persons, recollect the Snow –
First – Chill – then Stupor – then the letting go –

Because I Could Not Stop for Death (J712, F479)

(See Chapter 11, p. 545)

The Bustle in a House (J1078, F1108) (1890, c.1865)

The Bustle in a House
The Morning after Death
Is solemnest of industries
Enacted upon Earth –

5 The Sweeping up the Heart
And putting Love away
We shall not want to use again
Until Eternity –

"Faith" Is a Fine Invention (J185, F202) (1891, c.1860)

"Faith" is a fine invention
When Gentlemen can *see* –
But Microscopes are prudent
In an Emergency.

 ## I Cannot Live with You (J640, F706) (1890, c.1863)

I cannot live with You –
It would be Life –
And Life is over there –
Behind the Shelf

The Sexton keeps the Key to –   5
Putting up
Our Life – His Porcelain –
Like a Cup –

Discarded of the Housewife –
Quaint – or Broke –   10
A newer Sevres° pleases –   *a fine French porcelain*
Old Ones crack –

I could not die – with You –
For One must wait
To shut the Other's Gaze down –   15
You – could not –

And I – Could I stand by
And see You – freeze –
Without my Right of Frost –
Death's privilege?   20

Nor could I rise – with You –
Because Your Face
Would put out Jesus' –
That New Grace

Glow plain – and foreign   25
On my homesick eye –
Except that You than He
Shone closer by –

They'd judge Us – How –
For You – served Heaven – You know,   30
Or sought to –
I could not –

Because You saturated sight –
And I had no more eyes
For sordid excellence   35
As Paradise

And were You lost, I would be –
Though my name
Rang loudest
40   On the Heavenly fame –

And were You – saved –
And I – condemned to be
Where You were not
That self – were Hell to Me –

45   So We must meet apart –
You there – I – here –
With just the Door ajar
That Oceans are – and Prayer –
And that White Sustenance –
50   Despair –

I Died for Beauty – but Was Scarce (J449, F448) (1890, c.1862)

I died for Beauty – but was scarce
Adjusted in the Tomb
When One who died for Truth, was lain
In an adjoining Room –

5   He questioned softly "Why I failed"?
"For Beauty," I replied –
"And I – for Truth – Themselves are One –
We Brethren, are," He said –

And so, as Kinsmen, met a Night –
10   We talked between the Rooms –
Until the Moss had reached our lips –
And covered up – Our names –

I Dwell in Possibility (F466, J657) (1929, c.1862)

I dwell in Possibility –
A fairer House than Prose –
More numerous of Windows –
Superior – for Doors –

5   Of Chambers as the Cedars –
Impregnable of eye –
And for an everlasting Roof
The Gambrels of the Sky –

Of Visitors – the fairest –
10   For Occupation – This –
The spreading wide my narrow Hands
To gather Paradise –

🌿 I Felt a Funeral in My Brain (J280, F340) (1896, c.1862)

I felt a Funeral, in my Brain,
And Mourners to and fro
Kept treading – treading – till it seemed
That Sense was breaking through –

And when they all were seated,   5
A Service, like a Drum –
Kept beating – beating – till I thought
My mind was going numb –

And then I heard them lift a Box
And creak across my Soul   10
With those same Boots of Lead, again,
Then Space – began to toll,

As all the Heavens were a Bell,
And Being, but an Ear,
And I, and Silence, some strange Race   15
Wrecked, solitary, here –

And then a Plank in Reason, broke,
And I dropped down, and down –
And hit a World, at every plunge,
And Finished knowing – then –   20

🌿 I Heard a Fly Buzz – When I Died (J465, F591) (1896, c.1863)

I heard a Fly buzz – when I died –
The Stillness in the Room
Was like the Stillness in the Air –
Between the Heaves of Storm –

The Eyes around – had wrung them dry –   5
And Breaths were gathering firm
For that last Onset – when the King
Be witnessed – in the Room –

I willed my Keepsakes – Signed away
What portion of me be   10
Assignable – and then it was
There interposed a Fly –

With Blue – uncertain – stumbling Buzz –
Between the light – and me –
And then the Windows failed – and then   15
I could not see to see –

✏ I Like to See It Lap the Miles (J585, F383) (1891, c.1862)

I like to see it lap the Miles –
And lick the Valleys up –
And stop to feed itself at Tanks –
And then – prodigious step

5 Around a Pile of Mountains –
And supercilious peer
In Shanties – by the sides of Roads –
And then a Quarry pare

To fit its sides
10 And crawl between
Complaining all the while
In horrid – hooting stanza –
Then chase itself down Hill –

And neigh like Boanerges° –
15 Then – prompter than a Star
Stop – docile and omnipotent
At its own stable door –

————————————————

°14 *Boanerges*: a surname meaning "the sons of thunder" that appears in Mark 3:17.

✏ I'm Nobody! Who Are You? (J288, F260) (1891, c.1861)

I'm Nobody! Who are you?
Are you – Nobody – too?
Then there's a pair of us!
Don't tell! they'd banish us – you know!

5 How dreary – to be – Somebody!
How public – like a Frog –
To tell your name – the livelong June –
To an admiring Bog!

✏ I Never Lost as Much but Twice (J49, F39) (1890; c.1858)

I never lost as much but twice –
And that was in the sod.
Twice have I stood a beggar
Before the door of God!

5 Angels – twice descending
Reimbursed my store –
Burglar! Banker – Father!
I am poor once more!

I Taste a Liquor Never Brewed (J214, F207)
(1861; c.1860)

I taste a liquor never brewed –
From Tankards scooped in Pearl –
Not all the Frankfort Berries°   *grapes*
Yield such an Alcohol!

Inebriate of Air – am I –   5
And Debauchee of Dew –
Reeling – thro endless summer days –
From inns of Molten Blue –

When "Landlords" turn the drunken Bee
Out of the Foxglove's door –   10
When Butterflies – renounce their "drams" –
I shall but drink the more!

Till Seraphs swing their Snowy Hats –
And Saints – to windows run –
To see the little Tippler   15
From Manzanilla° come

---

16 *Manzanilla*: a pale sherry from Spain. Dickinson may also have been thinking of Manzanillo, a Cuban city known for rum.

 ## Much Madness Is Divinest Sense (J435, F620) (1890; c.1863)

Much Madness is divinest Sense –
To a discerning Eye –
Much Sense – the starkest Madness –
'Tis the Majority

In this, as all, prevail –   5
Assent – and you are sane –
Demur – you're straightway dangerous –
And handled with a Chain –

 ## My Life Closed Twice Before Its Close
(J1732, F1773) (1896)

My life closed twice before its close;
It yet remains to see
If Immortality unveil
A third event to me,

So huge, so hopeless to conceive   5
As these that twice befell.
Parting is all we know of heaven,
And all we need of hell.

One Need Not Be a Chamber – To Be Haunted (J670, F407) (1891; c.1862)

One need not be a chamber – to be Haunted –
One need not be a House –
The Brain has Corridors – surpassing
Material Place –

5 Far safer, of a midnight meeting
External Ghost
Than it's interior confronting –
That cooler Host –

Far safer, through an Abbey gallop,
10 The Stones a'chase –
Than unarmed, one's a'self encounter –
In lonesome Place –

Ourself behind ourself, concealed –
Should startle most –
15 Assassin hid in our Apartment
Be Horror's least –

The Body – borrows a Revolver –
He bolts the Door –
O'erlooking a superior spectre –
20 Or More –

Safe in Their Alabaster Chambers (J216, F124) (1862; c.1859)

Safe in their Alabaster Chambers –
Untouched by Morning –
And untouched by Noon –
Lie the meek members of the Resurrection –
5 Rafter of Satin – and Roof of Stone!

Grand go the Years – in the Crescent – above them –
Worlds scoop their Arcs –
And Firmaments – row –
Diadems – drop – and Doges° – surrender –
10 Soundless as dots – on a Disc of snow –

---

9 *Doges:* Rulers of Venice and Genoa, Italian city-states during the Renaissance.

Some Keep the Sabbath Going to Church (J324, F236) (1864; c.1861)

Some keep the Sabbath going to Church –
I keep it, staying at Home –

With a Bobolink for a Chorister –
And an Orchard, for a Dome –

Some keep the Sabbath in Surplice –   5
I, just wear my Wings –
And instead of tolling the Bell, for Church,
Our little Sexton – sings.

God preaches, a noted Clergyman –
And the sermon is never long.   10
So instead of getting to Heaven, at last –
I'm going, all along.

The Soul Selects Her Own Society
(J303, F409) (1890; c.1862)

The Soul selects her own Society –
Then – shuts the Door –
To her divine Majority –
Present no more –

Unmoved – she notes the Chariots – pausing –   5
At her low Gate –
Unmoved – an Emperor be kneeling
Opon° her Mat –   *upon*

I've known her – from an ample nation –
Choose One –   10
Then – close the Valves of her attention –
Like Stone –

Success Is Counted Sweetest (J67, F112) (1864; c.1859)

Success is counted sweetest
By those who ne'er succeed.
To comprehend a nectar
Requires sorest need.

Not one of all the purple Host   5
Who took the Flag today
Can tell the definition
So clear of Victory

As he defeated – dying –
On whose forbidden ear   10
The distant strains of triumph
Burst agonized and clear!

Tell All the Truth but Tell It Slant
(J1129, F1263) (1945; c.1872)

Tell all the truth but tell it slant –
Success in Circuit lies
Too bright for our infirm Delight
The Truth's superb surprise
5   As Lightning to the Children eased
With explanation kind
The Truth must dazzle gradually
Or every man be blind –

There Is No Frigate Like a Book
(J1263, F1286) (1891, c.1873)

There is no Frigate like a Book
To take us Lands away
Nor any Coursers like a Page
Of prancing Poetry –
5   This Traverse may the poorest take
Without oppress of Toll –
How frugal is the Chariot
That bears the Human soul.

There's a Certain Slant of Light (J258, F320) (1890; c.1862)

There's a certain Slant of light,
Winter Afternoons –
That oppresses, like the Heft
Of Cathedral Tunes –

5   Heavenly Hurt, it gives us –
We can find no scar,
But internal difference –
Where the Meanings, are –

None may teach it – Any –
10   'Tis the Seal Despair –
An imperial affliction
Sent us of the Air –

When it comes, the Landscape listens –
Shadows – hold their breath –
15   When it goes, 'tis like the Distance
On the look of Death –

Triumph May Be of Several Kinds (J455, F680) (c. 1863)

Triumph – may be of several kinds –
There's Triumph in the Room
When that Old Imperator – Death –
By Faith – be overcome –

There's Triumph of the finer mind   5
When Truth – affronted long –
Advance unmoved – to her Supreme –
Her God – Her only Throng –

A Triumph – when Temptation's Bribe
Be slowly handed back –   10
One eye opon° the Heaven renounced –
And One – opon the Rack –

Severer Triumph – by Himself
Experienced – who pass
Acquitted – from that Naked Bar –   15
Jehovah's Countenance –

°11 *opon:* sic.

Wild Nights – Wild Nights! (J249, F269) (1891; c.1861)

Wild Nights – Wild Nights!
Were I with thee
Wild Nights should be
Our luxury!

Futile – the winds –   5
To a Heart in port –
Done with the Compass –
Done with the Chart!

Rowing in Eden –
Ah – the Sea!   10
Might I but moor – tonight –
In thee!

Edited Selections from Criticism of Dickinson's Poems

The following selections are intended to supply details and ideas for essays on Dickinson's poems. For a selective bibliography, consult the bibliography in this chapter section (p. 805), which may be augmented with your college library catalogue and the most recent editions of the *MLA International Bibliography*. Footnotes in the sources have been omitted.

1. From "Orthodox Modernisms"[2]

Dickinson's power derives partly from a cluster of techniques, from certain themes, and from tonal qualities that we consider modern and admire for their apparent newness. Her work is a catalogue of these modernisms, conventional to us now in their familiarity and so commonly known in her repertoire that a summary here will suffice. She possessed an intuitive knack for exploiting the capacity of language under certain distortions or tensions to arrest, illuminate, pierce, astonish. Her wonderfully engaging first lines range from the controlled audacity of flatness and understatement ("Before I got my eye put out") to marvelous lines of great syntactic pressure involving mystery, lure, expectation, and which play sophisticatedly with line-end novelty and grammatical deception.

The animated lexical selection that is the heart of her craft comprises violations sometimes of great daring. She surprised with her language and, when it was not so deliberately concocted as to be coy or patent, it brings off its risks and shocks in a modern way. A corpse in poem 287 [J287, F259] is "This Pendulum of snow" and death's finality is in "Decades of Arrogance." Elsewhere her lexical surprises manage a careful deflation and austerity that dehumanize, objectify, as in these sciential lines about a corpse:

> The busy eyes – congealed –
> It straightened – that was all . . .
> It multiplied indifference

Dry and hard, spare in a Poundian sense, this cold language forms into an analytical instrument of great accuracy. There is also word parading of the sort we now admire as well in Marianne Moore. In Dickinson's little known poem about a June bug, the polysyllables thump against the single-syllable vernacular:

> From Eminence remote
> Drives ponderous perpendicular
>
> . . . . .
> Depositing his Thunder
> He hoists abroad again –
> A Bomb upon the Ceiling
> Is an improving thing
> It keeps conjecture flourishing –   [J1128, F1150]

Dickinson interrupted nineteenth-century poetic discourse with a vernacular so direct it seemed crude to her first public. She disarmingly called it in poem 373 [J373, F575] "my simple speech" and "plain word." It was in fact flattened speech, a *talking* that was depoetizing; and an escape from pomposity. Into her poems and particularly into those outrageous first lines came a natural breath and diction that created the illusion and the impact of real speech acts. . . .

From David Porter, *Dickinson: The Modern Idiom* (Cambridge: Harvard University Press, 1981), from the section entitled "Orthodox Modernisms."

Most modern, perhaps, among Dickinson's techniques is her use of language realms as constitutive elements in analytical structure. She makes the language medium itself objective and able to cut like a tool, managing this in at least three ways: vernacular diction inserted in formal language for its cross-cut effect; deploying Anglo-Saxon abruptness against the formalities of Latinate diction (this has been much noticed); and cleverly treating a subject with an alien lexical set. An instance of this last, as I have noted elsewhere, is characterizing God in the language of law or commerce. Dickinson, intuitively audacious in this, makes one language subset cut against and criticize another level of lexical selection, making a drama of language itself as if lexicons were themselves characters. Here is God silently measured by cold legalisms.

> I read my sentence – steadily –
> Reviewed it with my eyes,
> To see that I made no mistake
> In its extremest clause –
> The Date, and manner, of the shame –
> And then the Pious Form
> That "God have mercy" on the Soul
> The Jury voted Him –   [J412, F432]

Besides such strategies of diction choice at which she was so adept, Dickinson employed other techniques that we call modern. As noted, she elided syntax (for various reasons), omitted transitions, and dropped structural and even syntactical copulas. This habit of withholding connective material produces curiously vexatious ways we now choose to see as modern: discontinuity of structure and story, and remystification of phenomena that seem simple and clear, and those extinguishings of meaning by which we experience complexity and feel the intractable quality of existence again. Beyond this, Dickinson's habitual brevity seems modern in its glimpses and incompleteness. These are notes raised to literature, notation as authentic response. Wayward in punctuation, the poems disregard nicety and neglect finish. They have an aura of spontaneity and the status of randomness, which, as when we look at impressionist or action painting, we find congenial and not a counterfeiting of sensation and reality. Like Hardy, but apparently less knowingly, her poetry was revolutionary because it avoided the jeweled line. It was more a making of the irregular line through a rough simplicity and by drastic reduction. Indeed, sometimes the print version of her manuscripts unavoidably makes a modern line disposition.

> And Life was not so
> Ample I
> Could finish – Enmity –   [J478, F763]

Her partial rhymes and the structural instability and shifts in poems contribute to this impatient art.

Dickinson's rift vision, the ability to make language cut into the disparities between concept and reality, between the expectation and the actuality—this creation in language of cruel parallax—effects a disruption and penetration that we also call modern. It appeals to our suspicion of wholeness and seamless compatible meaning. This effect is behind Harold Bloom's accurate observation that Dickinson, as much as any modern, made the visible world a little hard to see.

The several techniques emphasized here as modern are well known and often displayed as the true source of Dickinson's modernity. Yet we shall see that her modernity operated at a more fundamental level than this. For now it is clear that these several conventional modernisms, what have now become part of the technical orthodoxy of modernist verse in English, contribute to the powerful effect that is indubitably of our time: the estrangement from outer reality and the resistance of common words to definitive meaning. The estrangement is accomplished by the compact, unsustained, raw power of language at the surface of her clipped-off poems.

In her themes, as well, Dickinson is with the moderns. Her language, animated by her selective cleverness, together with the snapshot brevity of her hymn form, courted instability and change and spotted the vulnerability of settled states. This is why sunsets evoked some of her best imagistic effort. The spectacle of day's end was intensely, exaggeratedly visual, it was naturally associated with death, and it was recurrent novelty, change taking place before the eyes. The sunset was thus a visual allegory for what most centrally engaged this poet.

Her preoccupation with change led to more desperate visions of mutability where the price of each moment of transport qualified every ecstasy, showing by her allegorical terms the furrow that threatens every glow. Unlike Emerson and Whitman, Dickinson brought into view with her strange and critical metaphors the opaque being of man, the "mysterious peninsula" as she called it, the unmanageable, excruciatingly sensitive, and needful portion that was her preoccupation.

She possessed a modernist knowledge of the mind's hidden places, what she called "That awful stranger Consciousness," terrifying to face. Equipped with her estranging language, she raised to the reader's awareness the intricate workings out of sight, careful not to "Mistake the Outside for the in" as she said. It is this interior life, in (for this recluse) the inevitable metaphor of the house, that is "haunted" and is the crucial spot where we enact our ignorance of ourselves and the world. Here is the "interior Confronting," where "Unarmed, one's a'self encounter." Now become an orthodox element of modern themes—what Irving Howe has called a modern fondness for the signs of psychic division—the interior life and the language to see it were the particular loci of Dickinson's attention. Encountering the self both dictated the strategies of her language and was the act in which her language had its circumstantial reflection.

"I felt a Funeral, in my Brain" [J280, F340] is the first coolly targeted modern interior in American poetry, and it is handled adroitly with modernist attention not to moral judgment but to judgment-free description. There is no emotional slither, to use Pound's term, or didactic assertion as in other poems such as "Bound – a trouble / And lives can bear it!" or "A Weight with Needles on the pounds," but rather psychological interiority seen minutely. The funeral-in-the-brain poem, representative of a substantial cluster of Dickinson's works on psychic distress, manifested two generations in advance the doctrine of imagism that Pound defined as the transfer of a complex of emotions in an instant of time.

It was Dickinson diving into the wreck and her devastated speaker indeed "wrecked" in the poem. Assurance of diction and line is firm. The poem has structure and lexical cohesion of a high order for Dickinson, and it is this firmness that operates so effectively against the subject matter of instability and disintegration. It is a superb performance, thoroughly modernist in its dark vision clinically portrayed.

Such language . . . made visible a new category of psychic suffering. Minutely observant, its figure of the interior funeral sustained, the poem moves with impressive directness into its surrealist transformation at the line "Then Space – began to toll." The familiar terms make new equations: Heaven is a Bell, Being an ear, and Silence a strange Race, and the wreck itself an annihilating silence. The surreal landscape, haunted with Dickinson's sense of exclusion and ignorance, unfolds, at least to the somewhat redundant last stanza, with a sure finality of language and wholeness of vision. In its cold-blooded, unflinching way as well as in the interior location of its action, the poem is supremely modernist. From the broader view of the Dickinson canon, we see how her concern with the interior reflects an equally modern concern with intense self-consciousness extending even to self-torture and the poetry of breakdown. . . .

The protomodernist image of the durable face of technological violence, of assault masked by dehumanized visages, is related in terror to another theme of Dickinson's that is hardly depictable by such momentary frissons. That is her vision of the *absence of an end*. I find this the most frightful of all Dickinson's modernist themes because it involves the pathological extremity of her familiar images such as this, of death in life, that ends an eight-line poem of utter inertness.

> Henceforth I take my living place
> As one commuted led –
> A Candidate for Morning Chance
> But dated with the Dead.   [J1194, F1209]

The smell of nihilism rises from more than a few poems, sometimes in a complete flatness of tune where her theme is the loss that drains every gain: note the eight lines that tick off loss beginning "Finding is the first Act / The second, loss" [J870, F910]. Associated with this theme of lost purpose and the absence of an end is a fearful corollary: the prevention of ripeness, of completion and thereby of knowledge and identity. It is the vision we saw in "What ripeness after that": that is, a life of incompletion, of ignorance, of need without assuaging. It can stand for the quintessential modernist condition—until with Dickinson we find ourselves going deeper. . . .

Particular tones in Dickinson's poetry are also part of her commonly recognized modernism. Currents of doubt and the snowman moments give certain poems a psychological desperation that was unfamiliar to much nineteenth-century poetry. The sharply discrepant tone in the poems, their directness of statement, and the audacity of their attack on conventional belief and easy-going piety are elements that would have given offense in her own time and so did not appear in the first editions of her poetry in the 1890s. Her colloquial and irreverently casual heresy at times ("It's easy to invent a Life"), her deliberate inelegance in a primitive offbeat diction ("It is simple to ache in the Bone or the Rind"), and the seemingly sophisticated skepticism in offhand phrases ("Our Savior, by a Hair") combine to give a considerable portion of the poetry a discordant tone that undercuts the poetry of unquestioned assent with which her contemporaries filled the verse books of the day.

Satire and irreverence along a gamut from mild asides to bitter attack are also modernist elements that form part of our critical orthodoxy and the surfaces by which Dickinson can be labeled a modern. In the poem beginning "There's been a Death, in the opposite house" [J389, F547] she creates a gentle satire on the impersonal organization that swings into action at a death, with its ritual movements and the professional mourners who take charge. In such verse of casual irreverence, the understatement and vernacular ease effectively counterpoint the regular common meter that arranges them. Deft lexical selection provides the edge that cuts in in the modern way. Her lines on the aurora borealis, where the common expectation would be for "paint" and "tint," Dickinson slips all askew by substituting "infection" and "taint":

> The North – Tonight . . .
> Infects my simple spirit
> With Taints of Majesty   [J290, F319]

She deflated a generically solemn occasion by unobtrusive negation and the one unexpected word "soldered":

> I've seen a Dying Eye
> Run round and round a Room . . .
> And then – be soldered down
> Without disclosing what it be
> 'Twere blessed to have seen   [J547, F648]

Her language pierced theological pomposities with strokes of marvelous wit, as here with out-of-place words from the public hall set off against Resurrection:

> No crowd that has occurred
> Exhibit – I suppose
> That General Attendance
> That Resurrection – does   [J515, F653]

Dickinson's modernist tones include the confessional one. She excelled in creating a sense of private immediacy because, by the strategy of seemingly autobiographical speech acts, she reproduced in writing the speaking voice. Archibald MacLeish has written most knowingly on the unique voice by which we identify her. It is language signifying emotional experience close at hand that impresses us. The voice, quotation marks invisible, contradicts a reader's conscious awareness of the deliberately written text. This way in which Dickinson *did* speak out to strangers produces what we take to be an immediate proximity to the mind. The flattened conversational tone depoetizes experience and gives it a confessional authenticity of the sort we are familiar with in our own time.

> To Ache is human – not polite –
> The Film upon the eye
> Mortality's Old Custom –
> Just locking up – to Die   [J479, F458]

Toughness of attitude and candor couched in unstudied inelegance are further tonal qualities by which twentieth-century readers have assigned Dickinson to the origins of modernism along with Whitman. The blunt tones sound frequently along her lines, as here in this bald assertion that seems to have no poetic pretensions: "Men die – externally – / It is a truth – of Blood" [J531, F584].

Boldly secular content and skeptical tone quite disjunct from the orderly arrangement of the hymn form make an ironic combination. The poems produce that most modern of all attitudes, the ironicalization of experience. Beyond that, the disjunction and tonal qualities together effect a modernist estrangement, dissonance, and thus a critical perspective. Her bruskness deromanticizes, as in the moon poem that begins "I watched the Moon around the House." Dickinson's daring comes out most clearly if her moon is put alongside the famous protoimagist poem on the moon by T. E. Hulme. Dickinson's lines have in their more compact shape a greater bravado. It is part of what she shares with poets who followed her.

> like a Head – a Guillotine
> Slide carelessly away –
> like a Stemless Flower –
> Upheld in rolling Air –   [J629, F593]

The best summing up of these tonal qualities we now see as a modern set is in that phrase *the ironicalization of experience*. The tonal undercutting, the evasion of stock sincerity, the protective irreverence and throwaway understatement, thus making the hymn form play a different tune: all these effects, even if there were behind them no perspective of mind much more fundamental, would withal make Dickinson a modern. Neither sophisticated nor sustained, hers was a poetic cunning working by stealth of language and subversion of form to create surprise by strangeness. Out of these strategies came a disordering of experience, a new confession of our precarious status.

2. From "The Landscape of the Spirit"[3]

Dickinson's poems frequently assert her sense of the mind's actuality with images of caverns and corridors [J777, F877; J670, F407], windows and doors [J303, F409; J657, F466], even cellars [J1182, F1234]. Because she took the mind to be her dwelling place, it is appropriate that she use these domestic figurative correspondences to describe it. Yet her poems using such architectural analogues go beyond pointing out how a mind might be like a house. They set out to show, as well, what happens in a mind that is as a house, so that the solidity that door and window frame provide grants substance both to the setting and to the events occurring within. The architectural vocabulary usually portrays

---

From Suzanne Juhasz, *"The Undiscovered Continent": Emily Dickinson and the Space of the Mind* (Bloomington: Indiana University Press, 1983), from the chapter entitled "The Landscape of the Spirit."

the mind as an enclosed space, its confinement responsible for power, safety, yet fearful confrontation.

Poem 303 [J303, F409] is a strong statement about the power of the self alone. The soul is shown living within a space defined by door, gate, and mat. The external world, with its nations and their rulers, is kept outside.

> The soul selects her own Society –
> Then – shuts the Door –
> To her divine Majority –
> Present no more –
>
> Unmoved – she notes the Chariots – pausing –
> At her low Gate –
> Unmoved – an Emperor be kneeling
> Upon her Mat –
>
> I've known her – from an ample nation –
> Choose One –
> Then – close the Valves of her attention –
> Like Stone –

Traditional ideas about power are reversed here. Not control over vast populations but the ability to construct a world for oneself comprises the greatest power, a god-like achievement, announces the opening stanza. Not only is the soul alone "divine," but it is also identified as "Society" and "Majority": the poem also challenges our ideas about what constitutes a social group. Consequently, the enclosed space of the soul's house is more than adequate for a queenly life, and ambassadors of the external world's glories, even emperors, can easily be scorned. Yet while the speaker claims her equality with those most powerful in the outer world—they may be emperors, but she is "divine Majority," at the same time she asserts her difference from them; for her domestic vocabulary of door, low gate and mat establishes her dwelling as not a grand palace but rather a simple house.

While associating power with the enclosed space of the mind, the poem also implies how isolation is confinement, too. When the soul turns in upon her own concerns, she closes "the Valves of her attention – / Like Stone –."

Valves permit the flow of whatever they regulate in one direction only: here from outside to inside. Either of the halves of a double door or any of the leaves of a folding door are valves. Valves seen as doors reinforce the poem's house imagery, while their association with stone makes the walls separating soul from world so solid as to be, perhaps, prison-like.

Prison-like because they allow no escape from the kinds of conflict, the kinds of terror, even, that must occur within. Poem 670 [J670, F407] exaggerating the architectural vocabulary, compares the chambers of the mind to the haunted castle of gothic fiction, a stereotypical setting for horror.

> One need not be a Chamber – to be Haunted –
> One need not be a House –
> The Brain has Corridors – surpassing
> Material Place –

Far safer, of a Midnight Meeting
External Ghost
Than its interior Confronting –
That Cooler Host.

Far safer, through an Abbey gallop,
The stones a'chase –
Than Unarmed, one's a'self encounter –
In lonesome Place –

Ourself behind ourself, concealed –
Should startle most –
Assassin hid in our Apartment
Be Horror's least.

The Body – borrows a Revolver –
He bolts the Door –
O'erlooking a superior spectre –
Or More –

The poem assumes that the mind is substantial, possessing corridors and chambers, because it is the dwelling place of "oneself." The extended comparison that is developed, between two kinds of dwellings, two binds of hauntings, is for the purpose of dramatizing how there can be something more frightening than the most frightening situation usually imaginable.

Both the second and third stanzas begin with the same phrase: "Far safer." Safer are the supernatural events of gothic castles, meeting ghosts at midnight; we are warned about "interior confronting," the everyday moments of the mind, another lonesome place, when "one's a'self encounter." One clue to the degree of difference in horror is the word, "Unarmed." We come prepared to find ghosts in spooky old castles, but not in what Dickinson calls in another poem "That polar privacy / A soul admitted to itself" [J1695, F1696].

There is, in fact, no way one can be armed against this particular kind of ghost. The murderer seeking to kill the body can be vanquished—one can borrow a revolver, bolt the door. But this assassin is hidden within oneself—is oneself. There is no escape. As Dickinson comments in poem 894 [J894, F1076], "Of Consciousness, her awful Mate / The Soul cannot be rid."

In the final stanza [of poem J670, F407] the quintessence of this horror is revealed. The rhetoric of the poem has been dramatic as well as concrete. Two dramas, in fact, have been enacted and contrasted. The external self has been venturing into lonesome abbeys, discovering hidden assassins in her chamber, even as the internal self has become aware of the existence of the "Cooler Host." Now the two plots turn into one. The self, who is, after all, body and mind at once, bolts the door, only to discover that she has locked herself in with herself. Adventuring in the external world, one need not confront one's own consciousness. But when one turns from "Horror's least" to live in the mind, that "superior spectre" can never be avoided again.

Because consciousness is self-confrontation, it establishes a "society" within, of "ourself" with "ourself." To represent the conflict and struggle engendered here, poem 642 uses an architectural vocabulary that provides a setting, fortress, for a drama of siege and defense. Yet even as "One need not be a Chamber – to be Haunted –" constructs a comparison between external and internal ghost stories only to conflate them, so the following poem's distinctions between inner and outer, protagonist and antagonist, turn out to be fictions.

> Me from Myself – to banish –
> Had I Art –
> Impregnable my Fortress
> Unto All Heart –
>
> But since Myself – assault Me –
> How have I peace
> Except by subjugating
> Consciousness?
>
> And since We're mutual Monarch
> How this be
> Except by Abdication –
> Me – of Me – ?   [J642, F709]

The speaker of the poem "Myself" wishes for the ability to banish from her castle an enemy, called "Me." In the second stanza she admits to the complexity of the problem; more than skill is required to maintain the defense, because there is a profound connection between the combatants. Reversing their titles—"Me" is now the speaker, "Myself" the opponent—the poem acknowledges their interchangeability while at the same time continuing to deal with them as separate entities. The enemy is also identified as "Heart" in the first stanza, "Consciousness" in the second. That these are as much aspects of "Me" as they are of "Myself" the poem will not yet admit.

Although we know that the poem is discussing one person and not two, its dramatic fiction of attacker and attacked creates a situation that is surely war, albeit civil. When the dichotomy itself is collapsed in the final stanza, the effect is to intensify the situation, the pain, the impossibility of victory. "Mutual Monarch," the antagonists are revealed to be in actuality both within. There is nobody without. Without doesn't matter. Victory is impossible, is not a mere matter of "art," because enemy and friend are one. "Consciousness" is the self's awareness of itself and could be vanquished only through the annihilation of self, which would leave no victor, since no self is left. The very naming of the characters in this drama articulates and also anticipates this conclusion. If in stanza one the defender was Myself, the attacker, Me; and in stanza two the attacker was Myself, the defender, Me; in the final stanza they, as mutual Monarch, are "Me" and "Me."

The poem's structure dramatizes an experienced conflict. If the fictional dichotomy of within and without is necessary so that we might understand the problem, so is the final denial of the fiction, that we might better understand the conclusion: that self-consciousness means precisely the encounter of the self with itself, and that this is a perpetual struggle.

3. From "The American Plain Style"[4]

In a still broader sense of influence, the American idiom itself, in both its literary and daily forms, may have contributed to Dickinson's use of a style that is biblical in origin. By the mid-nineteenth century Puritan "plain style" had become the language of self-expression, the trusted idiom in America, although—or perhaps because—it had lost its bolstering doctrinal and political contexts. According to Perry Miller's "An American Language" [In *Nature's Nation* (Cambridge: Harvard UP, 1967, 208–40)], the plain style's demand that one speak from personal knowledge and as comprehensibly as possible made it the natural mode of discourse for a people living "in the wilderness:" and, by the late eighteenth century, attempting to form a democracy. All American writers, he claims, have had to deal with the consequences of this wholesale adoption of the principles and techniques of plain style. Because of its pervasiveness, Dickinson would inevitably have used language to some extent within its dictates. For epistemological reasons also, Dickinson may have felt some affinity for this style. Miller describes the plain style as inherently "defiant"—a style that both proclaims authority for the word and places the word's authority in individuals' articulate examinations of the truth; the style encourages practical discourse on theoretical or spiritual truths. Hence, it can as easily be turned against the idea of an authoritative God as it can be used to support that idea. Authority of language lies with the "plainest" (that is, apparently most artless yet still most commanding) speaker. The Puritans kept the style's implicit defiance in check by subordinating their word to God's Word; the latter was the law that theirs attempted to interpret and reflect. Emerson, Miller claims, partially maintained this check on defiance through his romantic belief in Nature as the origin of language, while Thoreau released the defiance of this style in his prose, "glory[ing] in his participation in the community of sin."

More covertly than Thoreau, Dickinson does the same. Her very disguise of defiance, however, may also stem in part from inherent characteristics of the plain style, which demands the simplicity reflected in its name but paradoxically also a kind of reticence that may prevent its complete message from being articulated. Ideally, the plain speaker "convey[s] the emphasis, the hesitancies, the searchings of language as it is spoken"; plainness lies in the apparent artlessness of the speaker's or writer's use of the word. Partly as a consequence, writers in the plain style leave much unsaid, and they claim that their discourse says even less than it does. Using words sparingly leaves much to implication, and making modest claims for a text may disguise the authority its author in fact feels. Thus the plain style frequently underplays its own importance and seriousness; even when it most anarchically expresses the perception of the individual, it maintains the guise of saying little, and that only matter-of-factly. Hence, while speaking "plain" truth, an individual may confound every doctrine that the Puritans held true and believed the plain style must express. As Miller puts it: "The forthright method [plain style] proved to be . . . the most subversive power that the wicked

From Cristanne Miller, *Emily Dickinson: A Poet's Grammar* (Cambridge: Harvard University Press, 1987), from the section entitled "The American Plain Style."

could invoke against those generalities it had, long ago, been designed to protect." Through reticence, indirection, and disguised claims for the authority of her word, Dickinson manipulates characteristics of the plain use of language in poetry that contradict Puritan convictions about the individual's relation to God and His Word. The style that affirms God's truth for the Puritans, and denies that God's power is the only good (while still celebrating it) for Thoreau, becomes ironic with Dickinson: while appearing to affirm or naively question, she denies the trustworthiness of any superhuman power. . . .

It is in her attitude toward language and toward communication itself as much as in her characteristic manipulations of the word that Dickinson differs from her contemporaries and predecessors who wrote in plain style. Like them, she emphasizes the bare force of the word, eschewing elaborate syntax, modifiers, and extended conceits. Like them, she tends to stress the word's direct mediation between the individual and the world (for them, God). Like them, but to an unusual extreme, she makes small claims for her writing: her poems are "a letter to the World"; she is often a girl, or (like) a daisy, bird, spider, or gnat. Even when she has volcanic power, she generally appears harmless and unimportant: "A meditative spot – / An acre for a Bird to choose / Would be the General thought –" [J1677, F1743]. Dickinson, however, senses a different need for both plainness and reticence from those who believe in a natural or divine law of language. The word has two faces for her. Its effect may be epiphanic and it may come to her as a "gift," revealing "That portion of the Vision" she could not find without the help of "Cherubim" [J1126, F1243]. This is the language of poetry, of pure communication, "Like signal esoteric sips / Of the communion Wine" [J1452, F1476], or a "word of Gold" [J430, F388]. At other times the word is all but meaningless—an "Opinion" [J797, F849], an empty term. In a letter to Bowles she writes: "The old words are *numb* – and there *a'nt* any *new* ones – Brooks – are useless – in *Freshettime* –" (L 252). Her trick as poet is to make the old words new. To do this, she trusts "Philology," not God or Nature, and when she succeeds in doing this she feels that she has been lucky.

To Dickinson's mind, success in speaking plainly, in creating a word "that breathes" [J1651, F1715] does not prove spiritual salvation or make her a candidate for fame, partly because her sense of moral superiority depends on overthrowing the notion that God or the world can save her. The economical use of the words of ordinary life gives language its power. Speaking indirectly or subversively disguises the poet's usurpation of moral judgment from divine or human law, and thus saves her to speak again. As Perry Miller suggests, in Dickinson's poetry the pull between plainness and reticence subverts the whole idea of plainness. Because her meanings are not plain, they cannot be expressed plainly despite her use of simple words; her plainest speech *is* that of indirection.

As this conception of language implies, for Dickinson there is no stable relation between spiritual truth, the facts of existence, and the terms of language. Names are not adequate to things, and the function of language is not primarily to name. Things are perceived and understood through their relations to the rest of the world and by the process of cumulative, even contradictory, definition rather than by categorization or labeling. Dickinson has greater affinity with the lexicographer, the scientist of language seeking to clarify each word's various meanings, than she does with the Romantic *Ur*-poet Adam. Her language stresses the relation between object and its effects or relations in an active world; meaning, for her, is not fixed by rules or even by her own previous perception of the world. The principles of Dickinson's world do not have to do with immutable properties and distinctions.

Dickinson manifests her belief in the flux or instability of relationship in the narratives of her poems more obviously than in her use of language. For example, the figures of her poems often change positions relative to each other, or prove to be undifferentiable rather than separate identities. In "The Moon is distant from the Sea," first "She" is the moon and "He" the water, then she becomes "the distant Sea –" and his are the ordering "Amber Hands –" of light [J429, F387]; the "single Hound" attending the Soul proves to be "It's own identity." [J822, F817]; in an early poem, she and her playmate Tim turn out to be "I – 'Tim'– and – Me!" [J196, F231]. In a late poem, desired object, self, and "Messenger" are indistinguishable in both their presence and their absence; in a mockery of simplicity, all have the same name:

> We send the Wave to find the Wave –
> An Errand so divine,
> The Messenger enamored too,
> Forgetting to return,
> We make the wise distinction still,
> Soever made in vain,
> The sagest time to dam the sea is when the sea is gone –   [J1604, F1643]

Although this poem may be read as an elaboration of a truism—that one must give to receive, or that some losses cannot be prevented—it also ironically suggests that distinguishing present and absent sea (loved "Wave" from our own) is "vain." The "wise distinction" persists in failing to recognize the absurdity of damming what is not there and cannot be kept anyway. We attempt to conserve only what we have already lost.

Similarly, in "The Sea said 'Come' to the Brook" [J1210, F1275], the grown Brook takes the same form and title as the Sea that wanted to keep it small, as if to prove that the existence of one sea does not prevent the growth of innumerable physically indistinguishable others. In the last stanza it is not immediately clear which "Sea" is which:

> The Sea said "Go" to the Sea –
> The Sea said "I am he
> You cherished"– "Learned Waters –
> Wisdom is stale – to Me"

In countless other poems, unspecified and multiply referential "it" or "this" is as meaningful a subject for speculation as any clearly delineated event or object. Metaphor serves as the primary tool of definition and explanation because it allows for the greatest flexibility in its reference to fact.

4. From "The Histrionic Imagination"[5]

Dickinson recognized, early in her career, the value of the dramatic monologue and learned to use it with skill. A well-known poem, dated about 1858 or 1859 when the apprenticeship was nearing its end, serves both as an example in which she has not quite mastered the form but is alert to its efficacy and as a work in which she draws on her own experience but changes it in the act of speaking about it.

> I never lost as much but twice,
> And that was in the sod.
> Twice have I stood a beggar
> Before the door of God!
>
> Angels – twice descending
> Reimbursed my store –
> Burglar! Banker – Father!
> I am poor once more!   [J49, F39]

The story line of the verse is addressed to an imagined interlocutor on the subject of the power of God; when the poet allows the speaker to address God directly, however, the break in point of view discloses that Dickinson has not yet learned to integrate narration and drama. The austerely restricted language of the narrative is right for the recollection of painful loss in contrast to the defiant and improvident moment when the persona forgets the unidentified listener and turns in line seven to revile God directly, but an experienced poet does not lose awareness of the audience assumed in a monologue even when the character being depicted rages on.

Despite the violation of point of view, or perhaps because of it, the supplicant's outburst continues to reverberate in our ears as we listen to the falling strain of a voice quickly regaining control and we believe we have overheard Emily Dickinson herself quarreling with God. When we find in a second poem, "Going to Heaven!" (#79, [J79, F128] c. 1859), that the persona, a young girl who both hopes to go and is glad she isn't going to heaven, says, "If you sh'd get there first / Save just a little place for me / Close to the two I lost –," we look elsewhere for the experiences about which *she* is talking in the angry indictment of God. Who, among the people she loved, we ask, died during Dickinson's childhood and youth? And what other personal loss is of the enormity of death? Because neither poem gives any clues, we search the biography for them.

There was more anguish in the life of young Emily Dickinson than "I never lost as much but twice" enumerates. She recalled, in a letter of March 28, 1846, to Abiah Root, whose schoolmate had just died, an experience of early sorrow. The opening words of the recollection prefigure the idiomatic cadence in which the poem begins. She wrote: "I have never lost but one friend near my age & with whom my thoughts & her own were the same. It was before you came to Amherst. My friend was Sophia Holland. She was too lovely for earth & she was transplanted

---

From Elizabeth Phillips, *Emily Dickinson: Personae and Performance* (University Park: Pennsylvania State University Press, 1988), from the chapter entitled "The Histrionic Imagination."

from earth to heaven. . . . Then it seemed to me I should die too." Emily, who was fourteen at the time of the death of her friend in the spring of 1844, gave way to "a fixed melancholy," told no one the cause of her grief, and was not well. Her parents sent her to Boston, where she stayed with relatives for a month and her health improved so that her "spirits were better." In May 1846, her maternal grandfather, Joel Norcross, died; there is no record of how she felt about him, but she went again in August to Boston for her health. In May 1848, during her seventeenth year, Jacob Holt, a friend about whom she anxiously asked more than once in letters from Holyoke, died at the age of twenty-six; he wrote some rather commonplace poems, one of which she copied in her Bible. There were, also, other persons who are usually suggested as "the two" she lost in death. Since the emotions of loss became more complex as she matured, they well may be fused beyond one's ability to extricate them in the poem.

Leonard Humphrey, who was principal of the Amherst Academy in 1846–1847, Emily's last year there, died at the age of twenty-six in November 1850; reporting the death of her "master" to Abiah, Emily mourned but did not give way to melancholy: "my rebellious thoughts," she asserted, "are many." Thereafter, Ben Newton, who introduced her to Emerson's poetry in 1850, left Amherst for Worcester, married in 1851, and died at the age of thirty-two on March 24, 1853. He taught her to read, she said, and was, "the first of my own friends." Had she forgotten Sophia Holland, who has not counted in explanations of the poet's loss?

Additional comments in the letters seem to lend support to readers who identify "the two she lost as Humphrey and Newton (Or are they "three": Holt, Humphrey, and Newton?) Writing on April 25, 1862, to Higginson, the poet said: "When a little Girl, I had a friend who taught me Immortality – but venturing too near, himself – he never returned – Soon after, my Tutor, died – and for several years, my Lexicon was my only companion." As if she were explaining "I never lost as much but twice," which Higginson had not seen, she added: "Then I found one more – but he was not contented I be his scholar – so he left the Land." This remark causes further speculation about whether the final loss in the poem is a kind different from that "in the sod." Casual readers then want to hear a name such as Charles Wadsworth or Samuel Bowles, neither of whom had "left the land" before or during the year in which Dickinson made a final copy of the verse ending with the dramatic cry: "Burglar! Banker – Father! / I am poor once more!"

There is not only too much evidence but too much uncertainty about what to choose from it for ascertaining the specific provocations of the poem's dramatic script. Nevertheless, if the letters to Abiah Root began the account of the incremental sorrow that is Dickinson's subject, one can say the soliloquy depends on events that are autobiographical but is not a literal recording of any one among them. The poet was rather finding words to make emotions *sound* true.

The recurrent experience of separations and loss may well be the source of another poem, which is more lyrical than dramatic. The emphasis is again on emotions related to a life "closed twice," but beyond the term "parting" there is no evidence that permits one to identity the events to which the persona refers. If the experiences are personal, they have been transmuted into flawless lines:

My life closed twice before its close –
It yet remains to see
If Immortality unveil
A third event to me

So huge, so hopeless to conceive
As these that twice befell.
Parting is all we know of heaven,
And all we need of hell.   [J1732, F1773, n.d.]

Although there is no autograph copy or date of composition for this justly famous poem, it points up Dickinson's practice of trying out different aspects of a theme in order to realize the perfection of form inherent in it. The poet ceased, moreover, to be an amateur in exploiting the possibilities of the dramatic monologue, which became the genre for a number of equally memorable Dickinson texts.

5. From "The Gothic Mode: 'Tis so appalling – it exhilarates –'"[6]

Emily Dickinson's gothic poems are perhaps her most startling challenge to the symbolic order. They are transgressive poems of great energy that explore taboo states usually excluded from consideration. In these poems the speakers spare the reader no excess in their relish of the macabre, as a selection of first lines suggests: "As by the dead we love to sit" [J88, F78]; "Do People moulder equally, / They bury, in the Grave?" [J432, F390] or "If I may have it, when it's dead," [J577, F431]. In many poems, the dead simply refuse to Lie down; witty, garrulous corpses relentlessly address the reader from deathbed or grave: "Twas just this time, last year, I died" [J445, F344]; "I heard a Fly buzz – when I died –" [J465, F591]; "I died for Beauty –" [J449, F448]. In others the speaker confronts an unknown self and experiences "A doubt if it be Us" [J859, F903].

The Gothic poems fall into three main categories: those in which the speaker encounters unknown forces within the self; those in which the walking dead are women and continue Dickinson's explorations of gender; and those in which death is welcomed as a liberation from the confinements of the symbolic order. These poems challenge the ideals and propriety of the social order; they are disturbing because they question the certainty and rightness of its interpretations of the world. Madness suggests that there are forces within that are beyond its jurisdiction; human identity is not ultimately fixed, coherent, controlled, knowable. The dissolution of death is a permanent reminder of the fragility and artificiality of the social order and its rigid conventions.

The nineteenth century saw the articulation of the idea of the unconscious and Dickinson's poems participate in that impulse. Dickinson was acutely aware of what Edward Young had referred to as "the stranger within thee." In his book *Night Thoughts* (1742–1745), which was used as one of the textbooks at Amherst Academy, Young writes that reason is but "a baffled counsellor": man looks within and finds "an awful stranger." Dickinson was similarly aware of an

---

From Joan Kirkby, *Emily Dickinson* (New York: St. Martin's Press, 1991), from the chapter entitled "The Gothic Mode: 'Tis so appalling – it exhilarates.'"

alien aspect to consciousness, writing in Poem 894: "Of Consciousness, her awful Mate / The Soul cannot be rid –" [J894, F1076]. Sometimes consciousness was an oppressive companion:

> I do not know the man so bold
> He dare in lonely Place
> That awful stranger Consciousness
> Deliberately face –   [J1323, F1325]

Several poems explore the encounter of the self with a stranger within. In Poem 670 [J670, F407], the internal ghost is an awesome force to be reckoned with:

> One need not be a Chamber – to be Haunted –
> One need not be a House –
> The Brain has Corridors – surpassing
> Material Place –
> Far safer, of a Midnight Meeting
> External Ghost
> Than its interior Confronting –
> That Cooler Host.
>
> Far safer, through an Abbey gallop,
> The Stones a'chase –
> Than Unarmed, one's a'self encounter –
> In lonesome Place –
>
> Ourself behind ourself, concealed –
> Should startle most –
> Assassin hid in our Apartment
> Be Horror's least.
>
> The Body – borrows a Revolver –
> He bolts the Door–
> O'erlooking a superior spectre –
> Or More –

In this poem the mind itself is seen as more terrifying and dangerous than a haunted house; it has dark, unknown corridors surpassing "Material place." The encounter with one's concealed self is more dangerous than ghost, or graveyard, or assassin; they are "Horror's least." These could be fled on horseback, locked out or vanquished with revolver, but there is no escape from the self. Indeed the self hidden within the self is "a superior spectre –/Or More –," suggesting some terror greater than any hitherto conceived. The mind has within itself the potential for insurrection and dissolution....

Dickinson's most famous Poem 712 [J712, F479] "Because I could not stop for Death –" deals with a similar moment in which a woman is severed from her chosen tasks and carried off by an anonymous gentleman called "Death." Once again the fair theme of love is associated with "a thought so mean." However, this poem makes explicit the fact that the advent of the gentleman caller is nothing short of death for the woman. While this poem is usually read as a poem about death, revealing Dickinson's playfully macabre vision of death as a gentleman caller, it is a poem that identifies the gentleman caller as death; for him woman is expected to put away both her labour and her leisure. Like the woman in Poem 732 [J732, F857] she is expected to rise "to His Requirement" and drop "The Playthings of Her Life / To take the honorable Work / Of Woman, and of Wife –."

> Because I could not stop for Death –
> He kindly stopped for me
> The Carriage held but just Ourselves –
> And Immortality.
>
> We slowly drove – He knew no haste
> And I had put away
> My labor and my leisure too,
> For His Civility –
>
> We passed the School, where Children strove
> At Recess – in the Ring –
> We passed the Fields of Gazing Grain –
> We passed the Setting Sun –
>
> Or rather – He passed Us –
> The Dews drew quivering and chill –
> For only Gossamer, my Gown –
> My Tippet – only Tulle –
>
> We paused before a House that seemed
> A Swelling of the Ground –
> The Roof was scarcely visible –
> The Cornice – in the Ground –
>
> Since then – 'tis Centuries – and yet
> Feels shorter than the Day
> I first surmised the Horses' Heads
> Were toward Eternity –

The first stanza suggests that the female speaker is so deeply engaged in her own life that she does not wish to stop, but it also suggests the passivity of female desire. Courting is a male prerogative; she must wait to be called upon, but once chosen a surrender that is both quick and total is expected. She must give up her work and her leisure "For His Civility." He has all the privileges of authority; he nominates the time of execution but is regarded as "kindly" and civil. That the death coach contains the new couple— "And Immortality"—suggests something of the enormous duration of the marriage journey. However, it also suggests that male authority extends into eternity; both earthly life and after life are in his hands; indeed that hypothesis underpins his authority here.

The second stanza highlights the slowness and solemnity of this journey to a bridal house that strongly resembles a grave. Like the anonymous "He" in Poem 315 [J315, F477] "He fumbles at your Soul," "He knew no haste." She is assumed to have no interest or activity separate from his. Rather like the woman in Poem

273 [J273, F330] "He put the Belt around my life –," she begins to sense her "Life-time folding up –." As the journey progresses the speaker becomes increasingly aware that she has lost all agency and volition. Like the woman in Poem 443 [J443, F522] her "ticking" has stopped. The fields of grain are "gazing" at her; the setting sun "passed Us." In her bridal finery she experiences a mortal chill: "For only Gossamer, my Gown – / My Tippet – only Tulle –." Indeed the fine silk veil around her neck is a kind of noose; like the bride in Poem 1072 [J1072, F194] she is "Born – Bridalled – Shrouded – / In a day –." The wedding house turns out to be her grave; it is lowly and scarcely undifferentiated from the ground. Since this deathly bridal day, it seems like an "Eternity." Dickinson's poem suggests the eternity of death-in-life endured after marriage, what the woman in Poem 443 [J443, F522] refers to as "Miles on Miles of Nought –."

In this poem woman is interrupted from her independent activities and brought to a house that seems "A Swelling of the Ground," inevitably suggesting the house of biological destiny, the womb as tomb. There is the suggestion in the poem that female autonomy would threaten the existing order; a woman with her own work and her own leisure may be too busy "to stop" for connubial death. In Poem 1445 [J1445, F1470] "Death is the supple Suitor," images of death and court-ship are intertwined in similar fashion; it is "a stealthy Wooing"; a coach carries the woman away to "Troth unknown" and "Kindred as responsive / As Porcelain."

Dickinson's most striking gothic poems are those in which the dead address the speaker from deathbed or grave. These poems bear out Gillian Beer's view that "Ghost stories are to do with the insurrection, not the resurrection of the dead." It is the element of "the insurrectionary" and "the uncontrollable" that confounds. It goes without saying that these poems are disconcerting. Death is the ultimate taboo and the corpse "the ultimate impurity," "the most sickening waste." Yet Dickinson's speakers provocatively play on graves, sit by the dead, wonder if corpses moulder equally. In drawing near the corpse, the object that marks the limit between life and death, Dickinson invokes a place that is outside the rule of the symbolic order. In these poems, death marks the dissolution of the social order and becomes an emblem of liberation from its oppressive and artificial conventions. The corpse highlights the frailty of the symbolic order. As Julia Kristeva writes, a "decaying body, lifeless, completely turned into dejection, blurred between the inanimate and the inorganic . . . the corpse represents fundamental pollution." It is "above all the opposite of the spiritual, of the symbolic, and of divine law."

In Poem 465 [J465, F591] Dickinson presents a speaker beyond the limit of the symbolic order; she has "Signed away / What portion of me be / Assignable –" and is henceforth to nature, a decomposing body subject only to the fly. The poem highlights the radical distance between the dying, who awaits the dissolution of the human into the undifferentiated matter of the corpse, and the living, who remain entirely bound up in the trappings of the social order, property, keepsakes, and the law of the father—"the King" who is to be "witnessed – in the Room –."

> I heard a Fly buzz – when I died –
> The Stillness in the Room
> Was like the Stillness in the Air –
> Between the Heaves of Storm –

> The Eyes around – had wrung them dry –
> And Breaths were gathering firm
> For that last Onset – when the King
> Be witnessed – in the Room –
>
> I willed my Keepsakes – Signed away
> What portion of me be
> Assignable – and then it was
> There interposed a Fly –
>
> With Blue – uncertain stumbling Buzz –
> Between the light – and me –
> And then the Windows failed – and then
> I could not see to see –   [J465, F591]

At the moment of death, the speaker's attention is deflected by the buzz of a fly, lowly earthly representative of physical decay. For the dying person that simple presence erases all other concerns, social and religious alike. However, the living reaffirm their allegiance to the symbolic order. They turn their attention away from the dying person and what is represented by death to an affirmation of their faith; they prepare themselves to witness God's presence in the room, his taking of the dying person.

While the living await the "King" and the re-inscription of the social order, the dying person awaits the fly and a decomposition of the self into corporeal waste. She has willed her keepsakes and signed away the portion of her with meaning in the social order, that is property, gender, social identity. The use of sign and assignable is significant in this context. In death the subject relinquishes the power to sign, to signify, to mark with characters, and to assign, to transfer or designate by writing. The corpse is outside the sign, outside the system of differences inscribed by the social order. The dead body is disconcertingly free of its rules, systems, distinctions and limits. In death there is also a dissolution of the gender-marked body. The corpse is an "it," as the speaker notes in Poem 389 [J389, F547] "There's been a Death, in the Opposite House":

> Somebody flings a Mattress out –
> The Children hurry by –
> They wonder if *it* died – on that
> I used to – when a Boy –

The buzzing fly blocks out the light of distinction and differentiation. The buzz of the fly is the antithesis of human language with its discrete units of modulated sounds. That the blue of the sky is transposed to the buzz of the fly suggests a further scrambling of the senses. Indeed the windows fail, which suggests a total breakdown of the social framing of experience. Windows are artificial barriers between inside and outside, nature and culture; windows frame and limit vision. However, in death the social framing of experience ends. There is darkness and a dissolution of all the restricting categories and hierarchies on which the social order is based.

A similar dynamics informs Poem 449 [J449, F448], which is Dickinson's witty retort to the closing lines of Keats' "Ode on a Grecian Urn": "Beauty is Truth, Truth Beauty, – that is all / Ye know on earth and all ye need to know." In Dickinson's poem death deposes pomp.

> I died for Beauty – but was scarce
> Adjusted in the Tomb
> When One who died for Truth, was lain
> In an adjoining Room –
>
> He questioned softly "Why I failed"?
> "For Beauty," I replied –
> "And I – for Truth – Themself are One –
> We Brethren, are," He said –
>
> And so, as Kinsmen, met a Night –
> We talked between the Rooms –
> Until the Moss had reached our lips –
> And covered up – our names –

The concepts and abstractions of the symbolic order avail for little here. The fact of physical decomposition overtakes the speaker practically in mid sentence. The moss covers up the speakers' names and makes the differences for which they died irrelevant. Each corpse has died as she thought in significance, for a large life ordering abstraction whose significance would continue after death. However, death marks the dissolution of the whole system of differences on which the social order is based. The moss like the fly signals the dissolution of the symbolic order as well as the decay of the body; the moss seals the lips, the locus of speech, and covers up "our names –."

ROBERT FROST'S LIFE AND WORK (1874–1963)

Robert Lee Frost published his first book of poems, *A Boy's Will*, when he was living in England in 1913. At this time he was unrecognized and unknown in the United States. Ezra Pound wrote that "it is a sinister thing that so American . . . a talent . . . should have to be exported before it can find due encouragement and recognition." Time, of course, made Frost the most visible and admired American poet of his day. He eventually received twenty-five honorary degrees  and four Pulitzer Prizes. Although there was no officially recognized national poet until the 1980s, when the poet laureateships were established through the Library of Congress, he came as close as possible to being America's official poet when he read "The Gift Outright" at the inauguration of President John F. Kennedy in January 1961. Writing in 1999, Joyce Carol Oates stated, "Frost's influence is so pervasive in American poetry, like Whitman's, as to be beyond assessment."[7] His collected poetic works continue to earn him this recognition.

American Poetry Review 28.6 (1999): 9.

Although in his person, and in his poetry, Frost presented himself as the quintessential New Englander, he was born on March 26, 1874, in California, where he spent his first ten years of life. His father, William Frost, had gone to San Francisco to take a job with the *San Francisco Bulletin*, and he and his wife, Belle, had their two children there. When William died in 1885, Frost's mother returned east to Lawrence, Massachusetts, where Frost attended high school, studied classics, and began writing poetry. He graduated in 1892 as co-valedictorian with Elinor White, whom he married in 1895. After high school he attended Dartmouth College for seven weeks and then turned to newspaper work and teaching school. Two years after his marriage, he enrolled at Harvard (1897–1899), aiming at a specialty in classical literature. He had hoped to take courses with William James, but he was disappointed because James was on leave during the years of Frost's attendance. However, Frost was able to take a class taught by the famous philosopher George Santayana. Personal reasons, including an unwillingness to submit to rigorous academic discipline, led him to end his student days at Harvard without a degree.

The image that one gains of Frost at this time is that he had enormous capability, powerful energy, much anxiety and self-doubt, and uncertain focus. In later years he stated that his early interests inclined him toward a number of separate careers: archaeology, astronomy, farming, or teaching Latin. It does not seem that he had any vision of himself as the poet and man of letters he was to become. Even at the height of his fame he minimized his poetic achievement by telling an audience at Amherst College that all he ever wanted from his poetic career was to be successful in writing "a few little poems it'd be hard to get rid of. That's all I ask."[8]

Much of Frost's early uncertainty resulted from his need to support his growing family. He gravitated toward farming as a way of life that would take up his physical energies and also give him the chance to think and to write. Fortunately, he had a supportive grandfather, William Frost Sr., who backed up his grandfatherly affection with financial support. In 1900 William Senior gave Robert a farm in Derry, New Hampshire, and for the next twelve years the poet lived in Derry, raised chickens and apples, wrote poetry, and taught English, from 1906 to 1911, at Pinkerton Academy in Derry. His life was hard but satisfying, but, as he later said, he was "not much of a farmer." He preferred to sit up late at night reading and studying, and then sleeping until noon. He did not see it as his obligation to get up with the sun and then go about the endless tasks and chores needed for successful farming. He was also an unusual farmer because he had been acquiring an immense amount of erudition, including the study of Latin and Greek poets and large numbers of Shakespeare's sonnets. It was during this time in Derry, in the first decade of the twentieth century, that he wrote many of his most famous poems, either in completed form or in draft. He sent many of these poems to magazines, but he got no publications and many rejection slips.

By 1912 he was aching to devote himself to writing but was extremely discouraged about the way things were going. According to the terms of Grandfather Frost's gift, however, he was permitted to sell the farm and use the money for his own purposes. Because he believed that he might make a better start abroad, he decided to move to England, one of the many moves he was to make during his lifetime.

Amherst Alumni News (April 1954), quoted in Jay Parini, *Robert Frost: A Life* (New York: Holt, 1999), 391.

He joked that he might live in poverty abroad without embarrassing his relatives and friends in the United States. Once he landed in England, his poetic career was energized. He found a publisher who liked his poems and put him under contract. Almost overnight he emerged from obscurity through the publication of his first two poetic volumes, *A Boy's Will* (1913) and *North of Boston* (1914), which were favorably reviewed and which started to earn him acclaim in the United States. He also met a number of emerging and established poets, including Pound, Eliot, and Yeats.

Just as in 1913 he had been anxious to move abroad, however, early in 1915 he was anxious to return home. In 1914, World War I had been declared, and he believed life would be better and safer in the United States. Once he got back he took up residence on a farm near Franconia, New Hampshire. His life after this time was one of increasing professional success together with a heavy burden of personal anxiety and grief. He and his wife lost two of their children in infancy. In addition, in later years their daughter Marjorie died (in 1934), and their son Carol, who suffered severe bouts of depression, committed suicide (in 1940). Elinor herself died in 1938, and daughter Irma was institutionalized in 1949. In addition, Frost was constantly stretching his finances to help his remaining adult children as they attempted to create their own lives. There is no question that Frost, who was becoming the most celebrated poet of his generation, suffered intensely in private.

But it must be emphasized that his career as a poet flourished beyond his early hopes. In 1916 he published *Mountain Interval,* a book containing "The Road Not Taken," "Birches," and "Out, Out—." He soon was in constant demand as a teacher and speaker. Amherst College created the position of poet-in-residence for him, an honor that would continue for much of his life. He also regularly lectured at Michigan, Harvard, Yale, and Dartmouth. Stories abound about his brilliance in front of audiences, both large and small. Seminars that he began teaching in the afternoon would stretch late into the evening as he captivated his students with his insights and his immense knowledge. Moreover, when television blossomed as a medium after 1950, he enthusiastically widened his national audience. With his memorably rumpled appearance, white hair, and cultivated New England voice, he was interviewed on many early television shows, and as a result he became perhaps the most widely recognizable poet in the history of literature.

As he gained all these successes as a teacher and lecturer, his poetic output remained constant and regular. In 1923 he published *Selected Poems* and *New Hampshire. New Hampshire,* for which he won a Pulitzer Prize, contains some of his best-known work: "Stopping by Woods on a Snowy Evening," "Fire and Ice," and "Nothing Gold Can Stay." Throughout his career there were many additional collections. *West Running Brook* appeared in 1928, *Collected Poems* in 1930. Additional collections were *A Further Range* (1936), *A Witness Tree* (1942), *Steeple Bush* (1947), *Complete Poems* (1949), *Aforesaid* (1954), and *In the Clearing* (1962).

Early in his career and throughout his long public experience as a speaker and lecturer, Frost cultivated his persona as a philosophical, wry, and wise country poet. This is the friendly, avuncular voice we most regularly hear, the one that expresses knowledge and concern for the land, history, and human nature. Even with this genial persona, however, there are complicated undertones of wit and irony. There is also what Randall Jarrell called "The Other Frost," the often agonized and troubled spirit whose voice is heard in poems such as "Acquainted with the Night," "Desert Places," and "Fire and Ice."

Regardless of the voice we hear, Frost preferred traditional poetic forms and rhythms, and he disapproved of free verse so strongly that he once asserted that writing it was like playing tennis without a net. He possessed complete knowledge of traditional forms (he knew much Latin poetry by heart). We therefore find, in much of his poetry, that he uses conventional rhyme schemes and clear meters with traditional metrical substitutions, together with closed forms such as couplets, sonnets (with interesting varying rhyme patterns), terza rima, quatrains, stanzas, and blank verse (see Chapter 16). Tension in the poems is created through the contrast of traditional form and Frost's characteristic conversational style. His diction is informal, plain, and colloquial, and his phrases are simple and direct. He uses and refines the natural speech patterns and rhythms of New England, polishing the language of everyday life and blending speech and formal patterns into a compact and unique poetic texture.

Structurally, Frost's poems typically move in a smooth, uninterrupted flow from an event or an object, through a metaphor, to an idea. Within this pattern, he usually describes a complete event rather than a single vision. The heart of the process is image or metaphor. Frost's metaphors are sparse and careful; they are brought sharply into focus and skillfully interwoven within each poem. Frost himself saw metaphors as the beginning of the process. In *Education by Poetry* (1931) he states, "poetry begins in trivial metaphors, pretty metaphors, 'grace' metaphors, and goes on to the profoundest thinking that we have. Poetry provides the one permissible way of saying one thing and meaning another." In "The Figure a Poem Makes," a brief essay that he wrote as the Preface to *The Complete Poems of Robert Frost* of 1949, he goes on further to describe what to him was the poetic process: "The figure a poem makes. It begins in delight and ends in wisdom. The figure is the same as for love. No one can really hold that the ecstasy should be static and stand still in one place. It begins in delight, it inclines to the impulse, it assumes direction with the first line laid down, it runs a course of lucky events, and ends in a clarification of life—not necessarily a great clarification, such as sects and cults are founded on, but in a momentary stay against confusion."

Frost's poems are usually based in everyday life and rural settings. Poems are occasioned by flowers, stone fences, rain, snow, birch trees, falling leaves, a spider, a tree branch, birds, a hired man, a garden, children, wood chopping, apple picking, piano playing, sleigh riding, and hay cutting, to name just a few of Frost's topics. However, the Frostian poetic structure always moves from such subjects toward philosophical implications about life and death, survival and responsibility, and nature and humanity. As he said in "The Figure a Poem Makes," the "delight" of poetry "is in the surprise of remembering something I didn't know I knew."

One of Frost's major appeals is that his poems are easily accessible. They are by no means simplistic, however, but run deep, as may be seen in such poems as "The Road Not Taken" and "Misgiving." They are often complex and ambiguous, as in "Mending Wall," in which the philosophies of the speaker and his fence-repairing neighbor are memorably presented and contrasted. Readers often conclude that the speaker's wish to remove barriers is this poem's major idea, but the neighbor's argument for maintaining them is equally strong. Further, in "Desert Places" (Chapter 16) we are presented with a chilling view of the infinite desert within the human spirit. In "Acquainted with the Night," Frost's sophisticated urban speaker tells us of the night of the city and also presents hints about the dark night of the soul.

Frost's complete works are in Richard Poirier and Mark Richardson, eds., *Robert Frost: Collected Poems, Prose, and Plays* (1995), and in Edward Connery Lathem, ed., *The Poetry of Robert Frost: The Collected Poems* (1969, frequently reprinted), which is also available in a paperback edition (2002). Of great use is Edward Connery Lathem's *A Concordance to the Poetry of Robert Frost* (rpt. 1994). Twelve of Frost's lectures have been preserved in Reginald Cook, *Robert Frost, A Living Voice* (Amherst: U of Massachusetts P, 1974). The standard biography, although often hostile, is by Lawrance Thompson, in three volumes: *Robert Frost: The Early Years*; *The Years of Triumph*; and *The Later Years* (New York: Holt Rinehart, 1966–1977). The last volume was completed after Thompson's death by Roy H. Winnick. An excellent biography is Jay Parini, *Robert Frost: A Life* (New York: Holt, 1999).

Useful criticism includes George Nitchie, *Human Values in the Poetry of Robert Frost* (Durham: Duke UP, 1960); Reuben Brower, *The Poetry of Robert Frost: Constellations of Intention* (New York: Oxford UP, 1963); Philip L. Gerber, *Robert Frost* (Boston: Twayne, 1966, rpt. 1982); Richard Poirier, *Robert Frost: The Work of Knowing* (Palo Alto: Stanford UP, 1990); John Kemp, *Robert Frost and New England: The Poet as Regionalist* (Princeton: Princeton UP, 1979); Richard Wakefield, *Robert Frost and the Opposing Lights of the Hour* (New York: Lang, 1985); James Potter, *A Robert Frost Handbook* (University Park: Pennsylvania State UP, 1980); Harold Bloom, ed., *Robert Frost*, Bloom's Modern Critical Views (New York: Chelsea House, 2003; a collection of critical essays); George Monteiro, *Robert Frost and the New England Renaissance* (Lexington: UP of Kentucky, 1988); Judith Oster, *Toward Robert Frost: The Reader and the Poet* (Athens: U of Georgia P, 1991); George F. Bagby, *Frost and the Book of Nature* (Knoxville: U of Tennessee P, 1993); and Katherine Kearns, *Robert Frost and a Poetics of Appetite* (New York: Cambridge UP, 1994). One of the programs in the PBS *Voices and Visions* series (1987) features his work.

Writing Topics About the Poetry of Robert Frost

1. Encounters with the natural world (situations, scenes, actions) and Frost's use of them for observation, narration, and metaphor.

2. Frost's assessment of the human situation: work, love, death, choices, diminution of life, stoicism, keeping or not keeping boundaries.

3. Frost's speaker: character, experiences, recollections, and reflections. In developing his subjects, to what degree does the speaker take a possible listener into account?

4. Frost as a poet of ideas. His vision of the way things are or should be.

5. Frost as a "confessional" poet: misgivings, the admission of personal error and personal fears.

6. Frost's use of narration and description in his poetry.

7. The structuring of Frost's poems: situation, observation, and generalization.

8. Frost's poetic diction: level and relationship to topic; conversational style.

9. Poetic forms in Frost: rhythm, meter, rhyme, and line and stanza patterns.

10. Frost's wry humor.

Poems by Robert Frost (Chronologically Arranged)

In White (An Early Version of "Design," p. 848) (1912) 842
Mending Wall (1914) 842
After Apple-Picking (1915) 843
Birches (1915) 844
The Road Not Taken (1915) 845
"Out, Out—" (1916) 846
The Oven Bird (1916) 847
Fire and Ice (1920) 847
Stopping by Woods on a Snowy Evening (1923)
    (See Chapter 11, p.548)
Nothing Gold Can Stay (1923) 847
Acquainted with the Night (1928) 848
Desert Places (1936)
    (See Chapter 16 p. 741)
Design (1936) 848
The Silken Tent (1936) 848
The Gift Outright (1941) 849

In White (An Early Version of "Design," p. 848) (1912)

A dented spider like a snow drop white
On a white Heal-all, holding up a moth
Like a white piece of lifeless satin cloth—
Saw ever curious eye so strange a sight?
5 Portent in little, assorted death and blight
Like the ingredients of a witches' broth?
The beady spider, the flower like a froth,

And the moth carried like a paper kite.
What had that flower to do with being white,
10 The blue Brunella every child's delight.
What brought the kindred spider to that height?
(Make we no thesis of the miller's plight.)
What but design of darkness and of night?
Design, design! Do I use the word aright?

Mending Wall (1914)

Something there is that doesn't love a wall,
That sends the frozen-ground-swell under it,
And spills the upper boulders in the sun;
And makes gaps even two can pass abreast.
5 The work of hunters is another thing:
I have come after them and made repair
Where they have left not one stone on a stone,
But they would have the rabbit out of hiding,
To please the yelping dogs. The gaps I mean,

No one has seen them made or heard them made,   10
But at spring mending-time we find them there.
I let my neighbor know beyond the hill;
And on a day we meet to walk the line
And set the wall between us once again.
We keep the wall between us as we go.   15
To each the boulders that have fallen to each.
And some are loaves and some so nearly balls
We have to use a spell to make them balance:
'Stay where you are until our backs are turned!'
We wear our fingers rough with handling them.   20
Oh, just another kind of outdoor game,
One on a side. It comes to little more:
There where it is we do not need the wall:
He is all pine and I am apple orchard.
My apple trees will never get across   25
And eat the cones under his pines, I tell him.
He only says, "Good fences make good neighbors."
Spring is the mischief in me, and I wonder
If I could put a notion in his head:
"*Why* do they make good neighbors? Isn't it   30
Where there are cows? But here there are no cows."
Before I built a wall I'd ask to know
What I was walling in or walling out,
And to whom I was like to give offense.
Something there is that doesn't love a wall,   35
That wants it down. I could say "Elves" to him,
But it's not elves exactly, and I'd rather
He said it for himself. I see him there
Bringing a stone grasped firmly by the top
In each hand, like an old-stone savage armed.   40
He moves in darkness as it seems to me,
Not of woods only and the shade of trees.
He will not go behind his father's saying,
And he likes having thought of it so well
He says again, "Good fences make good neighbors."   45

🍎 After Apple-Picking (1915)

My long two-pointed ladder's sticking through a tree
Toward heaven still,
And there's a barrel that I didn't fill
Beside it, and there may be two or three
Apples I didn't pick upon some bough.   5
But I am done with apple-picking now.
Essence of winter sleep is on the night,
The scent of apples: I am drowsing off.
I cannot rub the strangeness from my sight
I got from looking through a pane of glass   10
I skimmed this morning from the drinking trough
And held against the world of hoary grass.

It melted, and I let it fall and break.
But I was well
15   Upon my way to sleep before it fell,
And I could tell
What form my dreaming was about to take.
Magnified apples appear and disappear,
Stem end and blossom end.
20   And every fleck of russet showing clear.
My instep arch not only keeps the ache,
It keeps the pressure of a ladder-round.
I feel the ladder sway as the boughs bend.
And I keep hearing from the cellar bin
25   The rumbling sound
Of load on load of apples coming in.
For I have had too much
Of apple-picking: I am overtired
Of the great harvest I myself desired.
30   There were ten thousand thousand fruit to touch,
Cherish in hand, lift down, and not let fall.
For all
That struck the earth,
No matter if not bruised or spiked with stubble,
35   Went surely to the cider-apple heap
As of no worth.
One can see what will trouble
This sleep of mine, whatever sleep it is.
Were he not gone,
40   The woodchuck could say whether it's like his
Long sleep, as I describe its coming on,
Or just some human sleep.

Birches (1915)

When I see birches bend to left and right
Across the lines of straighter darker trees,
I like to think some boy's been swinging them.
But swinging doesn't bend them down to stay
5   As ice-storms do. Often you must have seen them
Loaded with ice a sunny winter morning
After a rain. They click upon themselves
As the breeze rises, and turn many-colored
As the stir cracks and crazes their enamel.
10   Soon the sun's warmth makes them shed crystal shells
Shattering and avalanching on the snow-crust—
Such heaps of broken glass to sweep away
You'd think the inner dome of heaven had fallen.
They are dragged to the withered bracken by the load,
15   And they seem not to break; though once they are bowed
So low for long, they never right themselves:
You may see their trunks arching in the woods

Years afterwards, trailing their leaves on the ground
Like girls on hands and knees that throw their hair
Before them over their heads to dry in the sun.   20
But I was going to say when Truth broke in
With all her matter-of-fact about the ice-storm
I should prefer to have some boy bend them
As he went out and in to fetch the cows—
Some boy too far from town to learn baseball,   25
Whose only play was what he found himself,
Summer or winter, and could play alone.
One by one he subdued his father's trees
By riding them down over and over again
Until he took the stiffness out of them,   30
And not one but hung limp, not one was left
For him to conquer. He learned all there was
To learn about not launching out too soon
And so not carrying the tree away
Clear to the ground. He always kept his poise   35
To the top branches, climbing carefully
With the same pains you use to fill a cup
Up to the brim, and even above the brim.
Then he flung outward, feet first, with a swish,
Kicking his way down through the air to the ground.   40
So was I once myself a swinger of birches.
And so I dream of going back to be.
It's when I'm weary of considerations,
And life is too much like a pathless wood
Where your face burns and tickles with the cobwebs   45
Broken across it, and one eye is weeping
From a twig's having lashed across it open.
I'd like to get away from earth awhile
And then come back to it and begin over.
May no fate willfully misunderstand me   50
And half grant what I wish and snatch me away
Not to return. Earth's the right place for love:
I don't know where it's likely to go better.
I'd like to go by climbing a birch tree,
And climb black branches up a snow-white trunk   55
Toward Heaven, till the tree could bear no more,
But dipped its top and set me down again.
That would be good both going and coming back.
One could do worse than be a swinger of birches.

The Road Not Taken (1915)

Two roads diverged in a yellow wood,
And sorry I could not travel both
And be one traveler, long I stood
And looked down one as far as I could
To where it bent in the undergrowth;   5

Then took the other, as just as fair,
And having perhaps the better claim,
Because it was grassy and wanted wear;
Though as for that the passing there
10 Had worn them really about the same,

And both that morning equally lay
In leaves no step had trodden black.
Oh, I kept the first for another day!
Yet knowing how way leads on to way,
15 I doubted if I should ever come back.

I shall be telling this with a sigh
Somewhere ages and ages hence:
Two roads diverged in a wood, and I —
I took the one less traveled by,
20 And that has made all the difference.

"Out, Out—" (1916)

The buzz saw snarled and rattled in the yard
And made dust and dropped stove-length sticks of wood,
Sweet-scented stuff when the breeze drew across it.
And from there those that lifted eyes could count
5 Five mountain ranges one behind the other
Under the sunset far into Vermont.
And the saw snarled and rattled, snarled and rattled,
As it ran light, or had to bear a load.
And nothing happened: day was all but done.
10 Call it a day, I wish they might have said
To please the boy by giving him the half hour
That a boy counts so much when saved from work.
His sister stood beside them in her apron
To tell them "Supper." At the word, the saw,
15 As if to prove saws knew what supper meant,
Leaped out at the boy's hand, or seemed to leap—
He must have given the hand. However it was,
Neither refused the meeting. But the hand!
The boy's first outcry was rueful laugh,
20 As he swung toward them holding up the hand
Half in appeal, but half as if to keep
The life from spilling. Then the boy saw all—
Since he was old enough to know, big boy
Doing a man's work, though a child at heart—
25 He saw all spoiled. "Don't let him cut my hand off—
The doctor, when he comes. Don't let him, sister!"
So. But the hand was gone already.
The doctor put him in the dark of ether.
He lay and puffed his lips out with his breath.
30 And then—the watcher at his pulse took fright.

No one believed. They listened at his heart.
Little—less—nothing!—and that ended it.
No more to build on there. And they, since they
Were not the one dead, turned to their affairs.

 ## The Oven Bird (1916)

There is a singer everyone has heard,
Loud, a mid-summer and a mid-wood bird,
Who makes the solid tree trunks sound again.
He says that leaves are old and that for flowers
Mid-summer is to spring as one to ten.   5
He says the early petal-fall is past
When pear and cherry bloom went down in showers
On sunny days a moment overcast;
And comes that other fall we name the fall.
He says the highway dust is over all.   10
The bird would cease and be as other birds
But that he knows in singing not to sing.
The question that he frames in all but words
Is what to make of a diminished thing.

 ## Fire and Ice (1920)

Some say the world will end in fire,
Some say in ice.
From what I've tasted of desire
I hold with those who favor fire.
But if it had to perish twice,   5
I think I know enough of hate
To say that for destruction ice
Is also great
And would suffice.

 ## Stopping by Woods on a Snowy Evening (1923)

(See Chapter 11, p. 548)

Nothing Gold Can Stay (1923)

Nature's first green is gold,
Her hardest hue to hold.
Her early leaf's a flower;
But only so an hour.
Then leaf subsides to leaf.   5
So Eden sank to grief,
So dawn goes down to day.
Nothing gold can stay.

 Acquainted with the Night (1928)

I have been one acquainted with the night.
I have walked out in rain—and back in rain.
I have outwalked the furthest city light.
I have looked down the saddest city lane.
5   I have passed by the watchman on his beat
And dropped my eyes, unwilling to explain.

I have stood still and stopped the sound of feet
When far away an interrupted cry
Came over houses from another street,
10 But not to call me back or say good-by,
And further still at an unearthly height,
One luminary clock against the sky

Proclaimed the time was neither wrong nor right.
I have been one acquainted with the night.

Desert Places (1936)

(See Chapter 16, p. 741)

Design (1936)

I found a dimpled spider, fat and white,
On a white heal-all,° holding up a moth
Like a white piece of rigid satin cloth—
Assorted characters of death and blight
5   Mixed ready to begin the morning right,
Like the ingredients of a witches' broth—
A snow-drop spider, a flower like a froth,
And dead wings carried like a paper kite.

What had that flower to do with being white,
10 The wayside blue and innocent heal-all?
What brought the kindred spider to that height,
Then steered the white moth thither in the night?
What but design of darkness to appall?—
If design govern in a thing so small.

°2 *heal-all:* a flower, usually blue, thought to have healing powers.

The Silken Tent (1936)

She is as in a field a silken tent
At midday when a sunny summer breeze
Has dried the dew and all its ropes relent,
So that in guys it gently sways at ease,
5   And its supporting central cedar pole,

That is its pinnacle to heavenward
And signifies the sureness of the soul,
Seems to owe naught to any single cord,
But strictly held by none, is loosely bound
By countless silken ties of love and thought   10
To everything on earth the compass round,
And only by one's going slightly taut
In the capriciousness of summer air
Is of the slightest bondage made aware.

The Gift Outright (1941)

The land was ours before we were the land's.
She was our land more than a hundred years
Before we were her people. She was ours
In Massachusetts, in Virginia,
But we were England's, still colonials,   5
Possessing what we still were unpossessed by,
Possessed by what we now no more possessed.
Something we were withholding made us weak
Until we found out that it was ourselves
We were withholding from our land of living,   10
And forthwith found salvation in surrender.
Such as we were we gave ourselves outright
(The deed of gift was many deeds of war)
To the land vaguely realizing westward,
But still unstoried, artless, unenhanced,   15
Such as she was, such as she would become.

LANGSTON HUGHES'S LIFE AND WORK
(1902–1967)

> For a discussion of Hughes and his work in drama, see Chapter 23,
> pages 1349–51.

James Mercer Langston Hughes was born in Missouri in 1902.
His childhood was characterized by uncertainty and instability. When his parents became estranged, he was cared for by
his maternal grandmother, but he also lived with friends of his
parents and was moved, among other places to, Kansas, Illinois, and Ohio, where he
received his primary and secondary schooling. He began writing early, and while in
grade school in Lincoln, Illinois, he was declared class poet. Upon graduation from
high school in Ohio, he lived for a year in Mexico. His father supported him when
he promised to study engineering at Columbia, but he left after a year because he
objected to the racism he perceived there. For a time after that he went from job to job
without much purpose. At one point he was a seaman, then a cook in a nightclub in
Paris, then a bouncer, and then a busboy in a hotel in Washington, D.C. During those
Washington years, Hughes worked for a brief time as an assistant to Dr. Carter G.

Woodson, known today as the "father" of Black History, and the founder, in 1926, of what has become Black History Week, celebrated each year. It was in Washington that he submitted his earliest poems to the poet Vachel Lindsay (1879–1931), who was a resident of the hotel. Lindsay quickly became a champion of the increasing body of Hughes's poetry, and introduced the young man to various publishers. One of the earliest major results of this association was the publication of Hughes's first collection of poetry, *The Weary Blues*, in 1926, which included "The Negro Speaks of Rivers."

With such encouragement Hughes went back to school in earnest, graduating in 1929 from Lincoln University in Pennsylvania, from which he later received an honorary doctorate. In the wake of the stock market crash in 1929 and the Great Depression that followed, Hughes was hard put to make his living as a thinker and writer. It was also during this time that he became radicalized. He visited Haiti and Cuba, and as a result of his experiences there he attacked what he considered to be American imperialist foreign policy in the Caribbean area. He also translated the poetry of a number of Cuban and Haitian writers. He was able to spend a year in Soviet Russia, assisting in the preparation of a film exposing racial prejudice in the United States. He continued to write and publish, and soon he became recognized as one of the leading figures of the Harlem Renaissance—an energetic burst of African American literary creativity that also included Claude McKay and Jean Toomer. It has been observed that Hughes was the first African American to make his living as a writer. Make his living he did, but he was not a recipient of the public acclaim that created opulence for many subsequent writers.

During the following forty years of his writing career, Hughes was to write in every major literary genre, including translations, regular newspaper columns, and, in the late thirties, reports on the Spanish Civil War. He published a total of thirty-five books. Along with other early works were poems that he published in *Crisis*, the official journal of the National Association for the Advancement of Colored People. In his first collection of short stories, *The Ways of White Folks* (1934), he fictionalized his disaffection with the condition of both southern and northern African Americans. One of the stories in this collection was "Father and Son," a version of the material that he turned into the two-act play *Mulatto*, which was produced at the Vanderbilt Theater in New York in October 1935. The play had a run of 373 performances, the record at that time for a Broadway play by an African American dramatist (see also Chapter 24, where *Mulatto* is included).

Hughes's own description of his calling as an author was to write about "Negro life in America." In addition to three short-story collections, he eventually published sixteen books of poems and two novels, together with twenty plays and texts for musical plays. He also edited a number of anthologies of the works of other African American writers, in addition to his constant production of articles and reviews. His total output was indeed voluminous. A few of his poetry collections, after *The Weary Blues* in 1926, were *The Dream Keeper* (1932), *Montage of a Dream Deferred* (1951), *The First Book of Jazz* (1955), and *Selected Poems* (1959). He published more than 860 poems during his lifetime.

His poetry develops from the idea of observing and celebrating Negro life in America. To achieve this goal, Hughes adopts a number of voices—not one voice, as in most of the poems of Dickinson and Frost, but a number of voices. His diction therefore is characterized by variety. Sometimes the words are straightforward and eloquent, as in "Let America Be America Again." We also encounter varieties of speech, from that of Hughes's beloved Harlem to the words to be found in the blues that Hughes also loved so dearly. In the poem "125th Street," he deals with the potentiality of blacks, who are both beautiful and capable. The underlying idea is that the American Dream has not been fulfilled for blacks, and that America, as a nation dedicated to equality, therefore remains unfulfilled and incomplete.

It is from such thinking that Hughes employs poetry, and literature generally, as a medium for political criticism. In "Negro" (1958), for example, Hughes asserts that Negroes, from the very beginnings of human history, have been enslaved and economically handicapped, and have suffered from all the cruelty that slavery and inequality have entailed. Thus, in the days of ancient Egypt, and Rome, the speaker's forebears were enslaved. In America, George Washington, the father of the country, kept slaves at Mount Vernon, just as Caesar had kept slaves on his estate in the first century BCE, and just as blacks, in inferior positions of heavy labor, made mortar so that the men who constructed the Woolworth Building in New York might practice their skills of craftsmanship, which they gained because of their racial privilege. Going on with the poem, in the nineteenth century, the age of colonialism, the men who exploited the Belgian Congo for profit also cruelly subjugated and exploited their slaves, just as in the twentieth-century agrarian South there was violent and cruel racial suppression—a topic Hughes more fully considers in the play *Mulatto* (see p. 1349). Hughes fills his poetry with the voices of modern African Americans who are the living heirs of this age-old inequality and prejudice. Thus the speaker of "The Weary Blues" is tired of life, and the speaker of "Po' Boy Blues" claims that "I's so weary / I wish I'd never been born." A more violent avenue of response is seen in the legendary poem "Harlem," in which the speaker considers the possibility that a "raisin in the sun" might "explode" (in violence against the cumulative suppression of centuries). A more subdued but ultimately more powerful response is that of education, which Hughes considers in "Theme for English B." Here, the speaker is a black who is obviously successful in the sphere of education. Even though this speaker recognizes his lack of equality, he is prepared to compete equally in the society that is producing resignation and possible violence among others of his race.

In looking at Hughes's poetry, then, we may discover the many aspects that typified the experiences of being black in America. There are expressions of religious renunciation, feelings of personal unease, rationalizations for personal cruelty, observations about funerals (i.e., the death of a "cool bop daddy" [or "re-bop daddy"]), descriptions of the depraved horror of lynchings, anticipation of a future of equality, uneasiness about being castigated by angry parents, the irony of naming a movie theater after Lincoln but not after John Brown, the irony of uncontrolled population growth, a sense of personal loneliness, the excitement of Harlem night life, the beauties of jukebox love songs, and the difficulty of being both loving and nurturing. In short, we may find in the poetry of Hughes the reflections about life that he believed represented not only the voice but also the soul of his people.

The complete poems of Langston Hughes are contained in Arnold Rampersad, ed., *The Collected Poems of Langston Hughes* (New York: Knopf, 1994). Rampersad is the general editor of *The Collected Works of Langston Hughes* (Columbia: Missouri UP, 2001). Hughes himself was involved in selecting the works for inclusion in *The Langston Hughes Reader: The Selected Writings of Langston Hughes* (New York: Braziller, 1958). This book is unique because it contains much introductory and explanatory commentary by Hughes. Biographies of Hughes include Milton Meltzer, *Langston Hughes* (New York: Crowell, 1968), and Arnold Rampersad, *The Life of Langston Hughes,* 2 vols. (Oxford: Oxford UP, 2002). Works of poetry criticism include Onwuchekwa Jemie, *Langston Hughes: An Introduction to the Poetry* (New York: Columbia, 1976); Steven C. Tracy, *Langston Hughes and the Blues* (Urbana: U of Illinois P, 1988, rpt 2001); and Harold Bloom, *Langston Hughes* (New York: Chelsea House, 2002). More general books of criticism of Hughes are Henry L. Gates, *Langston Hughes: Critical Perspectives Past and Present* (New York: Amistad, 1993); Harold Bloom, *Langston Hughes: Comprehensive Research and Study Guide* (New York: Chelsea House, 1999); Harold Bloom, *Langston Hughes* (New York: Chelsea House, 2007); and Steven C. Tracy, ed., *A Historical Guide to Langston Hughes* (Oxford: Oxford UP, 2004). This last volume contains a short biography of Hughes by R. Baxter Miller.

Writing Topics About the Poetry of Langston Hughes

1. Direct and indirect political implications in Hughes's poetry: social and political protest. Many of Hughes's poems reflect his concern with injustice in America and make reference to historical events. For instance, *The Negro Speaks of Rivers* makes reference to Abraham Lincoln's visit to New Orleans that influenced his decision to end slavery. Do you think that reading one of Hughes's poems may have an effect on how people think about this issue? Is there anything about America at the time Hughes was writing that you didn't know?

2. The dramatic use of speakers in the poems: different individuals, different concerns, different voices, one poet.

3. Hughes's use of geographical place and regionalism in the poetry.

4. Hughes's diction in the poems: levels of diction, standard and substandard speech. Hughes often uses everyday speech, common words, and slang. In which poems do you find this characteristic most predominant? How might the poems be different if they were written in standard English?

5. The treatment of racial cruelty in the poems: For a comparison on this topic, you might also want to consider Hughes's *Mulatto*, on page 1351.

6. The connection of the blues to the content and to the points of view in the poems: Following the pattern of songs, such as blues patterns in "Po' Boy Blues," many of the poems repeat lines, sometimes with slight variation. What is the effect of these repetitions? How are the lyrics of songs and poems different or the same?

7. "Weariness" and resignation as a recurring topic in the poems.

8. Hughes's ideas about what should be and what really exists: the ideal versus the actual in the poems.

9. The sense of humor in the poems: laughing to keep from crying (which is the title of a collection of short stories published by Hughes in 1952).

Poems by Langston Hughes
(Alphabetically Arranged)

Bad Man 853
Ballad of the Landlord 853
Dead in There 854
Dream Boogie 855
Dream Variations 855
Harlem 856
I, Too 856
Let America Be America Again 857
Negro 859
The Negro Speaks of Rivers 859
125th Street 860
Po' Boy Blues 860
Subway Rush Hour 860
Theme for English B 861
The Weary Blues 862

 ## Bad Man (1927)

I'm a bad, bad man
Cause everybody tells me so.
I'm a bad, bad man.
Everybody tells me so.
I takes my meanness and ma licker   5
Everywhere I go.

I beats my wife an'
I beats ma side fall too.
Beats my wife an'
Beats my side gall too.   10
Don't know why I do it but
It keeps me from feelin' blue.

I'm so bad I
Don't even want to be good.
So bad, bad, bad I   15
Don't even want to be good.
I'm goin' to da devil an'
I wouldn't go to heaven if I could.

 ## Ballad of the Landlord (1940, 1943)

Landlord, landlord,
My roof has sprung a leak.
Don't you 'member I told you about it
Way last week?

5   Landlord, landlord,
These steps is broken down.
When you come up yourself
It's a wonder you don't fall down.

10   Ten Bucks you say I owe you?
Ten Bucks you say is due?
Well, that's Ten Bucks more' n I'll pay you
Till you fix this house up new.

What? You gonna get eviction orders?
You gonna cut off my heat?
15   You gonna take my furniture and
Throw it in the street?

Um-huh! You talking high and mighty.
Talk on—till you get through.
You ain' t gonna be able to say a word
20   If I land my fist on you.

Police! Police!
Come and get this man!
He's trying to ruin the government
And overturn the land!

25   Copper's Whistle!
Patrol bell!
Arrest.

Precinct Station.
Iron cell.
Headlines in press:

MAN THREATENS LANDLORD

.
. .

TENANT HELD NO BAIL

.
. .

JUDGE GIVES NEGRO 90 DAYS IN COUNTY JAIL

Dead in There (1951)

Sometimes
A night funeral
Going by
Carries home
5   A cool bop daddy.

Hearse and flowers
Guarantee
He'll never hype
Another paddy.

It's hard to believe,
But dead in there,
He'll never lay a
Hype nowhere!   10

He's my ace-boy,
Gone away.   15
Wake up and live!
He used to say.

Squares
Who couldn't dig him,
Plant him now—
Out where it makes   20
No diff' no how.

🍂 Dream Boogie (1951)

Good morning, daddy!
Ain't you heard
The boogie-woogie rumble
Of a dream deferred?

Listen closely:
You'll hear their feet
Beating out and beating out a—   5

    You think
    It's a happy beat?

Listen to it closely:
Ain't you heard   10
something underneath
like a—

    What did I say?

Sure,   15
I'm happy!
Take it away!

    Hey, pop!
    Re-bop!
    Mop!   20

    Y-e-a-h!

🍂 Dream Variations (1924, 1926)

To fling my arms wide
In some place of the sun,
To whirl and to dance
Till the white day is done.

5 Then rest at cool evening
Beneath a tall tree
While night comes on gently,
    Dark like me—
This is my dream!
10 To fling my arms wide
In the face of the sun,
Dance! Whirl! Whirl!
Till the quick day is done.
Rest at pale evening . . .
15 A tall, slim tree . . .
Night coming tenderly
    Black like me.

Harlem (1951)

What happens to a dream deferred?
Does it dry up
like a raisin in the sun?
Or fester like a sore—
5 And then run?
Does it stink like rotten meat?
Or crust and sugar over—
like a syrupy sweet?

Maybe it just sags
10 like a heavy load.

Or does it explode?

I, Too (1926)

I, too, sing America.

I am the darker brother.
They send me to eat in the kitchen
When company comes,
5 But I laugh,
And eat well,
And grow strong.

Tomorrow,
I'll be at the table
10 When company comes.
Nobody'll dare
Say to me,
"Eat in the kitchen,"
Then.

Besides,
They'll see how beautiful I am
And be ashamed—

I, too, am America.

Let America Be America Again (1936)

Let America be America again.
Let it be the dream it used to be.
Let it be the pioneer on the plain
Seeking a home where he himself is free.

(America never was America to me.)

Let America be the dream the dreamers dreamed—
Let it be that great strong land of love
Where never kings connive nor tyrants scheme
That any man be crushed by one above.

(It never was America to me.)

O, let my land be a land where Liberty
Is crowned with no false patriotic wreath,
But opportunity is real, and life is free,
Equality is in the air we breathe.

(There's never been equality for me,
Nor freedom in this "homeland of the free.")

Say who are you that mumbles in the dark?
And who are you that draws your veil across the stars?
I am the poor white, fooled and pushed apart,
I am the Negro bearing slavery's scars.
I am the red man driven from the land,
I am the immigrant clutching the hope I seek—
And finding only the same old stupid plan
Of dog eat dog, of mighty crush the weak.
I am the young man, full of strength and hope,
Tangled in that ancient endless chain
Of profit, power, gain, of grab the land!
Of grab the gold! Of grab the ways of satisfying need!
Of work the men! Of take the pay!
Of owning everything for one's own greed!

I am the farmer, bondsman to the soil.
I am the worker sold to the machine.
I am the Negro, servant to you all.
I am the people, worried, hungry, mean—
Hungry yet today despite the dream.

15

5

10

15

20

25

30

35

Beaten yet today—O, Pioneers!
I am the man who never got ahead,
The poorest worker bartered through the years.

Yet I'm the one who dreamt our basic dream
40 In the Old World while still a serf of kings,
Who dreamt a dream so strong, so brave, so true,
That even yet its mighty daring sings
In every brick and stone, in every furrow turned
That's made America the land it has become.
45 O, I'm the man who sailed those early seas
In search of what I meant to be my home—
For I'm the one who left dark Ireland's shore,
And Poland's plain, and England's grassy lea,
And torn from Black Africa's strand I came
50 To build a "homeland of the free."
The free?

A dream—
Still beckoning to me!

O, let America be America again—
55 The land that never has been yet—
And yet must be—
The land where every man is free.
The land that's mine—
The poor man's, Indian's, Negro's, ME—
60 Who made America,
Whose sweat and blood, whose faith and pain,
Whose hand at the foundry, whose plow in the rain,
Must bring back our mighty dream again.
Sure, call me any ugly name you choose—
65 The steel of freedom does not stain.
From those who live like leeches on the people's lives,
We must take back our land again,
America!

O, yes;
70 I say it plain,
America never was America to me,
And yet I swear this oath—
America will be!
An ever-living seed,
75 Its dream
Lies deep in the heart of me.

We, the people, must redeem
Our land, the mines, the plants, the rivers,
The mountains and the endless plain—
80 All, all the stretch of these great green states—
And make America again!

Negro (1958)

I am a Negro:
    Black as the night is black,
    Black like the depths of my Africa.

I've been a slave:
    Caesar told me to keep his door-steps clean.   5
    I brushed the boots of Washington.

I've been a worker:
    Under my hand the pyramids arose.
    I made mortar for the Woolworth Building.

I've been a singer: 10
    All the way from Africa to Georgia
    I carried my sorrow songs.
    I made ragtime.

I've been a victim:
    The Belgians cut off my hands in the Congo.   15
    They lynch me still in Mississippi.

I am a Negro:
    Black as the night is black,
    Black like the depths of my Africa.

The Negro Speaks of Rivers (1926)

I've known rivers:
I've known rivers ancient as the world and older than the flow of human blood in human
    veins.

My soul has grown deep like the rivers.

I bathed in the Euphrates when dawns were young.
I built my hut near the Congo and it lulled me to sleep.   5

I looked upon the Nile and raised the pyramids above it.
I heard the singing of the Mississippi when Abe Lincoln went down to New Orleans, and
    I've seen its muddy bosom turn all golden in the sunset.

I've known rivers:
Ancient, dusky rivers.

My soul has grown deep like the rivers.   10

125th Street (1951)

Face like a chocolate bar
Full of nuts and sweet.

Face like a jack-o'-lantern,
Candle inside.

5   Face like slice of melon
Grin that wide.

Po' Boy Blues (1926, 1927)

When I was home de
Sunshine seemed like gold.
When I was home de
Sunshine seemed like gold.
5   Since I come up North de
Whole damn world's turned cold.

I was a good boy,
Never done no wrong.
Yes, I was a good boy,
10   Never done no wrong,
But this world is weary
An' de road is hard an' long.

I fell in love with
A gal I thought was kind.
15   Fell in love with
A gal I thought was kind.
She made me lose ma money
An' almost lose ma mind.

Weary, weary,
20   Weary early in de morn.
Weary, weary,
Early, early in de morn.
I's so weary
I wish I'd never been born.

Subway Rush Hour (1951)

Mingled
breath and smell
so close
mingled
5   black and white
so near
no room for fear.

Theme for English B (1959)

The instructor said,

> Go home and write
> a page tonight.
> And let that page come out of you—
> Then, it will be true.   5

I wonder if it's that simple?

I am twenty-two, colored, born in Winston-Salem.
I went to school there, then Durham, then here
to this college on the hill above Harlem.°
I am the only colored student in my class.   10
The steps from the hill lead down to Harlem,
through a park, then I cross St. Nicholas,
Eighth Avenue, Seventh, and I come to the Y,
the Harlem Branch Y, where I take the elevator
up to my room, sit down, and write this page: 15

It's not easy to know what is true for you or me
at twenty-two, my age. But I guess I'm what
I feel and see and hear. Harlem, I hear you:
hear you, hear me—we two—you, me talk on this page.
(I hear New York, too.) Me—who?   20

Well, I like to eat, sleep, drink, and be in love.
I like to work, read, learn, and understand life.
I like a pipe for a Christmas present,
or records—Bessie,° bop,° or Bach.°

I guess being colored doesn't make me not like   25
the same things other folks like who are other races.
So will my page be colored that I write?
Being me, it will not be white.
But it will be
a part of you, instructor.   30
You are white—
yet a part of me, as I am a part of you.
That's American.

Sometimes perhaps you don't want to be a part of me.
Nor do I often want to be a part of you.   35
But we are, that's true!

---

9 *college . . . Harlem:* a reference to Columbia University in the Columbia Heights section of New York City. The other streets and buildings mentioned in lines 11–14 refer to specific places in the same vicinity. 24 *Bessie:* Bessie Smith (c. 1898–1937), American jazz singer, famed as the "Empress of the Blues." *bop:* a type of popular music that was in vogue in the 1940s through the 1960s. *Bach:* Johann Sebastian Bach (1685–1750), German composer, considered the master of the baroque style of music.

As I learn from you,
I guess you learn from me—
although you're older—and white—
40   and somewhat more free.

This is my page for English B.

The Weary Blues (1923, 1926)

Droning a drowsy syncopated tune,
Rocking back and forth to a mellow croon,
    I heard a Negro play.
Down on Lenox Avenue the other night
5   By the pale dull pallor of an old gas light
        He did a lazy sway . . .
        He did a lazy sway . . .
To the tune o' those Weary Blues.
With his ebony hands on each ivory key
10 He made that poor piano moan with melody.
        O Blues!
Swaying to and fro on his rickety stool
He played that sad raggy tune like a musical fool.
        Sweet Blues!
15 Coming from a black man's soul.
        O Blues!
In a deep song voice with a melancholy tone
I heard that Negro sing, that old piano moan—
        "Ain't got nobody in all this world,
20   Ain't got nobody but ma self.
        I's gwine to quit ma frownin'
        And put ma troubles on the shelf."
Thump, thump, thump, went his foot on the floor.
He played a few chords then he sang some more—
25   "I got the Weary Blues
        And I can't be satisfied.
        Got the Weary Blues
        And can't be satisfied—
        I ain't happy no mo'
30   And I wish that I had died."
And far into the night he crooned that tune.
The stars went out and so did the moon.
The singer stopped playing and went to bed
While the Weary Blues echoed through his head.
35 He slept like a rock or a man that's dead.

SYLVIA PLATH'S LIFE AND WORK (1932–1963)

Sylvia Plath is one of those poets about whom the life facts are integrally connected to her works. She is considered a "confessional" poet, the basis of whose work lies in her own personal experiences, with all their difficulties, uncertainties, and personal pain. Her confessions, however, are not intended as expressions of complaint or as descriptions of intimate details. Instead, she is confessional in that she attempts to demonstrate her relationship to the many unique and often adverse situations she encountered in life. In historical comparison, the *Confessions* of St. Augustine (354–430) were composed to reveal the power and beneficence of God. John Bunyan (1628–1688) wrote his *Grace Abounding to the Chief of Sinners* as testimony of the bountiful forgiveness of God. Jean-Jacques Rousseau (1712–1778) wrote his autobiographical *Confessions*, perhaps partially to shock readers, but also to show the particular links that together make up the whole person.

In all these instances of confessional literature, confession itself is based in the admission of some sorts of transgression—usually in the form of self-indulgence—but the confession is also put in a wider context. As a twentieth-century confessional poet, Plath is ranked with fellow American poets Robert Lowell (one of Plath's teachers), Anne Sexton (a friend and confidante of Plath, and a fellow student in Lowell's class), D. W. Snodgrass, and John Berryman. Plath was a tormented soul, tortured at times, but she was a poet of great ability and brilliance, of extremes of happiness and depression—alternatively charming and blunt, but never dull. That her poems were not unrelievedly concerned with the negative aspects of confession may be seen in her "Song for a Summer's Day" and "Metaphors"—poems that would not seem unusual or special in the work of any other lyric poet. But in the poems Plath wrote during the final years of her life, we can see evidence of deeper discontent and anger. At times she refers to direct autobiographical details, or else she presents inferences based on such details. As a result, events of her brief life and lamentable death are definitely relevant to her poetry.

Sylvia Plath was born in 1932. Her father, Otto Plath, was a naturalized citizen whose native country was Germany. He was a professor at Boston University, an entomologist, and an authority on bees. Her mother, Aurelia Schober, was much younger than Otto and was from Austria. She also eventually taught at Boston University. Plath's father was diabetic, but was in denial about his affliction. In 1940 he was hospitalized for a foot infection. The foot was amputated, but the infection was rampant. It metastasized and caused his death when Sylvia was just eight years old. It then fell to her mother, Aurelia, to take over the management of her household and children—Sylvia and her brother, Warren.

Sylvia was deeply grieved by her father's death, and upon being told of it, swore that she could no longer believe in God. One of her first responses was an unsuccessful and perhaps accidental suicide attempt when she was ten, using a razor blade to gash her throat. Her adolescent responses were less destructive, but there can be no doubt that the loss of her father afflicted her deeply for the rest of her brief life. Her later experiences with insomnia, her frequent respiratory infections, and her depression perhaps had their own etiology, but the loss of her father was always there, undermining her struggle for normality. She compensated for her loss by becoming an exceedingly fine student, regularly receiving A's in her courses. As she achieved academic excellence and advancement, she also, at an early age, began sending her writings, primarily poems, to various publications, hoping for the national acceptance that would demonstrate that others recognized her precociousness. Throughout her school years she continued the arduous process of submission and publication, and by the time she matriculated at Smith College in 1952, she had developed an impressive list of academic prizes and local publications. She was tops in her high school graduating class, and she published essays, stories, and poems in publications like *Mademoiselle* and the *Christian Science Monitor*. Eventually she signed a contract with *The New Yorker* agreeing that she would give that magazine the right of first submission for any and all of her new poems.

Despite such successes, however, she regularly received rejection slips—not at all uncommon for beginning writers—and these weighed heavily upon her self-image. She became so despondent that she once again attempted suicide. In 1953, she hid herself in the crawl space under her mother's house, and swallowed almost the entire contents of a bottle of sleeping pills, many of which she fortunately regurgitated. She was, however, rendered unconscious. Everyone thought she had been abducted, and her disappearance made headlines in the Boston area. After a few days her brother heard her groaning under the house, and she was taken to the hospital for treatment and recovery. After that she underwent electric shock therapy, which in the 1950s was a standard medical treatment for depression and attempted suicide. She describes this experience in her well-received *roman à clef*, *The Bell Jar*, early in 1963, and she also alludes to it in her poem "Lady Lazarus," which she wrote just four months before her actual suicide in February 1963:

> Dying
> Is an art, like everything else,
> I do it exceptionally well.

She recovered, took heart, and went on to graduate from Smith *summa cum laude*. In 1955, as a new graduate, she applied for a Fulbright Scholarship for study in England. She won the award, and matriculated at Newnham College, Cambridge, for the year 1955–1956, which was extended to 1956–1957. The winning of a Fulbright was an inestimable honor for those who received it, but the allowances were quite low—just about $1,450 for all the living expenses of an entire year. Needless to say, Sylvia was regularly hurting for money.

During her days at Cambridge, Plath met Ted Hughes, then a striving poet, who later became English Poet Laureate (1984–1998). It was at this point that she decided to try achieving excellence through marriage and children. The two married in 1956, and their marriage continued for six years, two of which they spent in the United States after Sylvia had finished the period of her Fulbright Scholarship. When she became pregnant, the couple returned to England, where childbirth was paid for by the English National Health Service. Although the Hugheses had two children, born in 1960 and 1962, and although there were long periods of peace, tenderness, and constructive and peaceful cooperation between the two, their relationship also generated conflict and bitterness. Indeed, they once came to blows and scratches against each other. They separated in 1962. Sylvia became guardian of the children, and took up residence in rooms in a London house where William Butler Yeats had one time lived. Although she was encouraged by the connection with Yeats, she became unconquerably depressed during the bitterly cold winter of 1962–1963. Early in the morning of February 11, 1963, in the throes of deep and final anguish, she sealed the cracks in the doors of the bedroom of her sleeping children, to protect them, and left milk and cookies for them. She went to her kitchen, and turned on the gas. Despite her intellectual power and desire to excel, she had never been able to escape the demon of depression. She died at the age of thirty—her life cut regrettably short, her full potential never to be realized or recognized.

When she died, Sylvia Plath had not yet gained a major reputation. Just a few weeks before her death, her novel *The Bell Jar* appeared. Although the work was well received, she had written it under a *nom de plume* ("Victoria Lucas") and she had not yet received the public recognition that was to follow. Ever since the 1960s, however, her reputation has been elevated posthumously to the point where some critics have called her one of the greatest poets of the twentieth century. The story of her life has also made her rather much of a *cause célèbre* of the feminist movement. The idea is that during her last years her star was falling just as the star of her husband was rising. And as she necessarily became enmeshed in the endless tasks of caring for her baby and her toddler, he looked elsewhere for companionship. After Plath's suicide, there were people who accused him of having brought about her death. On her gravestone, her married name, "Hughes," was chiseled out, and then was chiseled out again when a new stone was reinstalled over the grave. When Hughes, even as Poet Laureate, would have a speaking engagement in the thirty-five years after her death, hecklers would sometimes try to drown him out. He was never able to live down the circumstances of Plath's suicide.

Plath's poems, grounded as they are in her own experiences, do not necessarily make for easy reading, because they frequently describe reactions to specific details known by the speaker, but unknown by the reader. The result is that some of the poems seem obscure. Let us take the opening three lines from "Ariel," the poem that Plath wrote on her birthday, October 27, 1962: "Stasis in darkness. / Then the substanceless blue / Pour of tor and distances." As readers we accept these details as meaningful, even though the process of mind that produced the lines is not known. "Tor" is a venerable English word for a high hill, probably borrowed from the Celts, who lived in the land before the Angles and the Saxons took the country over militarily in the fifth century. "Pour" suggests figuratively how the hill emerges in the landscape of early morning as though it is being poured out to the viewer's eye. A further probe seems in order. A biographical detail is that "Ariel," the poem's title, was the name of a horse that Plath had ridden frequently in 1957, during the earlier and happier years of her marriage. It would appear that riding had given her a sense of freedom and fulfillment. In addition, Ariel is also a spirit/fairy that serves Prospero in Shakespeare's *The Tempest* (1611). At the play's end, when Prospero is bidding farewell to his magical powers, he gives Ariel his freedom. We may therefore conclude that the reference to Ariel is Plath's dominating image of a desire for release from restrictions and a wish for the freedom of rolling hills, far distances, and the endless blue of the air. Somewhere, one can find a better existence than the one we know here on earth, although, from the poem's last line, it could also be a "cauldron" that creates difficulty and causes other problems. And so "Ariel" the poem may be taken as an expression of yearning and not unmixed hope.

Comparably, one of Plath's best known confessional poems is "Daddy." It was only natural that she could not ever have totally overcome her grief at losing her father, despite all her compensating excellences during her adolescence and college years. When she and Ted Hughes became parents themselves, she became "Mommy" and he "Daddy." Most young parents, in delight at having their own children, rejoice in using these pet names for each other. It would therefore appear that when Plath wrote "Daddy," she was thinking of both Daddies together. She never was given the time to know her own father well, and may even have subconsciously condemned him for the neglect of his own illness and his consequent culpability for deserting the Plath family. Such a response is not unusual among survivors of a family loss. In addition to this grievance, she had profoundly loved and admired her children's Daddy, but he had caused her extreme anger, grief, and bitterness. She wrote the poem "Daddy" on October 12, 1962, just at the time when she and Hughes were undergoing what was appearing to be their final separation. In the poem, Plath's speaker castigates the Daddy virtually as a persecuting Nazi. Nothing even remotely like this was true, of course, but nevertheless the speaker talks of her anguish as though the details about Nazism were factual. Thus this major detail of the poem is imaginary, but Plath's mental anguish was real, and her anger was real. It is for the power and the expression of such personal insights that Plath is today valued so highly as a lyric and confessional poet.

The most comprehensive edition of Plath's poems is Ted Hughes, ed., *The Collected Poems: Sylvia Plath*. (Cambridge: HarperCollins, 1981). The appearance of this volume in 1981 posthumously earned Plath the Pulitzer Prize for Poetry in 1982. Before she died, Plath planned a volume of "Ariel" poems. Her intended collection is included in *Ariel: The Restored Edition. A Facsimile of Plath's Manuscript, Reinstating Her Original Selection and Arrangements* (New York: Harper, 2005). Susan R. Van Dine's *Revising Life: Sylvia Plath's Ariel Poems* (Chapel Hill: U of North Carolina P, 1994) considers these poems. Plath's journals are published in *The Unabridged Journals of Sylvia Plath*, Karen V. Kukil, ed. (New York: Anchor Books, 2000), a very lengthy volume. Well-detailed biographies of Plath are Linda Wagner-Martin, *Sylvia Plath: A Biography* (New York: St. Martin's, 1988), and Anne Stevenson, *Bitter Fame: A Life of Sylvia Plath* (Boston: Houghton Mifflin, 1990). A blending of biography and criticism is Wagner-Martin's *Sylvia Plath: A Literary Life* (New York: Palgrave Macmillan, 2003). Critical works are Tim Kendall, *Sylvia Plath: A Critical Study* (London: Faber, 2001), and Lynda K. Bundtzen, *The Other Ariel* (Amherst: U of Massachusetts P, 2001). A significant number of critical essays are included in Jo Gill, ed., *The Cambridge Companion to Sylvia Plath* (Cambridge: Cambridge UP, 2006). A detailed review of criticism on Plath is Claire Brennan, ed., *The Poetry of Sylvia Plath* (New York: Columbia UP, 2001).

Writing Topics About the Poetry of Sylvia Plath

1. Plath as a "confessional" poet: What is she confessing? How much is personal? How much seems objective description and discussion? What problems and concerns does she confess?

2. Plath's references to death in her poems: What is her attitude toward her own suicide attempts? What is the relationship of "Cut" to "Last Words" and to "Lady Lazarus"?

3. The problems of "Daddy": Who is the Daddy whom she addresses? What objective criticism does she make of Daddy? What do you make of the concluding lines? Why does Plath introduce references to Nazi cruelties, here and in "Lady Lazarus"?

4. Plath's use of comparisons: How expected are her comparisons? What causes the uniqueness and surprise of her best comparisons?

5. Plath's poetic rhythms: What use does she make of adjoining heavy accents (spondees)? What is the relationship of her rhythms to her ideas?

6. Plath's use of rhymes, assonance, and alliteration: How do these rhythms and sounds undergird her ideas?

7. Write an explication of any one of Plath's poems.

8. The meaning of "Mirror": Explain the concluding image.

9. Plath's more cheerful poems: What do poems such as "Metaphors" and "Song for a Summer's Day" suggest about her ideas of what most people probably think of about happiness?

Poems by Sylvia Plath (Alphabetically Arranged)

Ariel 867
The Colossus 868
Cut 869
Daddy 870
Edge 872
The Hanging Man 873
Lady Lazarus 873
Last Words 876
Metaphors 876
Mirror 877
The Rival 877
Song for a Summer's Day 878
Tulips 878

Note: The numbers preceding each of the poems that follow refer to the numerical system used by Ted Hughes in *The Collected Poems: Sylvia Plath* (New York: HarperCollins, 1981). The dates following some of the poems indicate the dates on which Plath either wrote the poems, or completed them.

 Ariel (1962)

194

Stasis in darkness.
Then the substanceless blue
Pour of tor and distances.

God's lioness,
5   How one we grow,
Pivot of heels and knees!—The furrow

Splits and passes, sister to
The brown arc
Of the neck I cannot catch,

10 Nigger-eye
Berries cast dark
Hooks—

Black sweet blood mouthfuls,
Shadows.
15 Something else

Hauls me through air—
Thighs, hair;
Flakes from my heels.

White
20 Godiva, I unpeel—
Dead hands, dead stringencies.

And now I
Foam to wheat, a glitter of seas.
The child's cry

25 Melts in the wall.
And I
Am the arrow,

The dew that flies
Suicidal, at one with the drive
30 Into the red

Eye, the cauldron of morning.
                27 October 1962

The Colossus° (1959)

117

I shall never get you put together entirely,
Pieced, glued, and properly jointed.
Mule-bray, pig-grunt and bawdy cackles
Proceed from your great lips.
5 It's worse than a barnyard.

Perhaps you consider yourself an oracle,
Mouthpiece of the dead, or of some god or other.
Thirty years now I have labored

To dredge the silt from your throat.
I am none the wiser.   10

Scaling little ladders with gluepots and pails of lysol
I crawl like an ant in mourning
Over the weedy acres of your brow
To mend the immense skull-plates and clear
The bald, white tumuli° of your eyes.   *grave mounds*   15

A blue sky out of the Oresteia
Arches above us. O father, all by yourself
You are pithy and historical as the Roman Forum
I open my lunch on a hill of black cypress.
Your fluted bones and acanthine hair° are littered   20

In their old anarchy to the horizon-line.
It would take more than a lightning-stroke
To create such a ruin.
Nights, I squat in the cornucopia
Of your left ear, out of the wind.   25

Counting the red stars and those of plum-color.
The sun rises under the pillar of your tongue.
My hours are married to shadow.
No longer do I listen for the scrape of a keel
On the blank stones of the landing.   30

At the harbor of the Aegean island of Rhodes, the ancient Rhodians erected a gigantic statue of Apollo, the "Colossus," which was considered one of the seven wonders of the ancient world. When earthquakes later hit the city, the Colossus was destroyed. Modern marine archaeologists have discovered fragments of the statue in the harbor waters. 20 *fluted bones and acanthine hair:* The design of ancient temple columns was not smooth, but rather fluted. In the Corinthian style, the most elaborate columnar design, capitals atop the fluted columns were modeled on the acanthus plant.

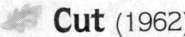 **Cut** (1962)

For Susan O'Neill Roe°

191

What a thrill –
My thumb instead of an onion.
The top quite gone
Except for a sort of a hinge

Of skin,   5
A flap like a hat,
Dead white.
Then that red plush.

Susan O'Neill Roe was Plath's nanny and babysitter.

Little pilgrim,
10   The Indian's axed your scalp.
Your turkey wattle
Carpet rolls

Straight from the heart.
I step on it,
15   Clutching my bottle
Of pink fizz.

A celebration, this is.
Out of a gap
A million soldiers run,
20   Redcoats, every one.

Whose side are they on?
O my
Homunculus,° I am ill.   *a tiny human being*
I have taken a pill to kill

25   The thin
Papery feeling.
Saboteur,
Kamikaze man—

The stain on your
30   Gauze Ku Klux Klan
Babushka
Darkens and tarnishes and when

The balled
Pulp of your heart
35   Confronts its small
Mill of silence

How you jump—
Trepanned° veteran,   *i.e., trephined, usually the result of an operation opening skull bone*
Dirty girl,
40   Thumb stump.
        24 October 1962

Daddy (1962)

183

You do not do, you do not do
Any more, black shoe
In which I have lived like a foot
For thirty years, poor and white
5   Barely daring to breathe or Achoo.

Daddy, I have had to kill you.
You died before I had time—
Marble-heavy, a bag full of God,
Ghastly statue with one gray toe
Big as a Frisco seal   10

And a head in the freakish Atlantic
Where it pours bean green over blue
In the waters off beautiful Nauset.
I used to pray to recover you.
Ach, du.   15

In the German tongue, in the Polish town
Scraped flat by the roller
Of wars, wars, wars.
But the name of the town is common.
My Polack friend   20

Says there are a dozen or two.
So I never could tell where you
Put your foot, your root,
I never could talk to you.
The tongue stuck in my jaw.   25

It stuck in a barb wire snare.
Ich, ich, ich, ich,
I could hardly speak.
I thought every German was you.
And the language obscene   30

An engine, an engine
Chuffing me off like a Jew.
A Jew to Dachau, Auschwitz, Belsen.
I began to talk like a Jew.
I think I may well be a Jew.   35

The snows of the Tyrol, the clear beer of Vienna
Are not very pure or true.
With my gipsy ancestress and my weird luck
And my Taroc pack and my Taroc pack
I may be a bit of a Jew.   40

I have always been scared of *you*,
With your Luftwaffe, your gobbledygoo.
And your neat mustache
And your Aryan eye, bright blue.
Panzer-man, panzer-man, O You—   45

Not God but a swastika
So black no sky could squeak through.

Every woman adores a Fascist,
The boot in the face, the brute
50   Brute heart of a brute like you.

You stand at the blackboard, daddy,
In the picture I have of you,
A cleft in your chin instead of your foot
But no less a devil for that, no not
55   Any less the black man who

Bit my pretty red heart in two.
I was ten when they buried you.
At twenty I tried to die
And get back, back, back to you.
60   I thought even the bones would do.

But they pulled me out of the sack,
And they stuck me together with glue.
And then I knew what to do.
I made a model of you,
65   A man in black with a Meinkampf look

And a love of the rack and the screw.
And I said I do, I do.
So daddy, I'm finally through.
The black telephone's off at the root,
70   The voices just can't worm through.

If I've killed one man, I've killed two—
The vampire who said he was you
And drank my blood for a year,
Seven years, if you want to know.
75   Daddy, you can lie back now.

There's a stake in your fat black heart
And the villagers never liked you.
They are dancing and stamping on you.
They always *knew* it was you.
80   Daddy, daddy, you bastard, I'm through.

12 October 1962

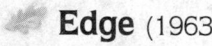 Edge (1963)

224

The woman is perfected.
Her dead

Body wears the smile of accomplishment,
The illusion of a Greek necessity

5   Flows in the scrolls of her toga,
Her bare

Feet seem to be saying:
We have come so far, it is over.

Each dead child coiled, a white serpent, 10
One at each little

Pitcher of milk, now empty.
She has folded

Them back into her body as petals
Of a rose close when the garden

Stiffens and odors bleed 15
From the sweet, deep throats of the night flower.

The moon has nothing to be sad about,
Staring from her hood of bone.

She is used to this sort of thing.
Her blacks crackle and drag. 20
                    5 February 1963

 ## The Hanging Man (1960)

123

By the roots of my hair some god got hold of me.
I sizzled in his blue volts like a desert prophet.

The nights snapped out of sight like a lizard's eyelid:
A world of bald white days in a shadeless socket.

A vulturous boredom pinned me in this tree. 5
If he were I, he would do what I did.
                    27 June 1960

 ## Lady Lazarus (1962)

198

I have done it again.
One year in every ten
I manage it—

A sort of walking miracle, my skin
Bright as a Nazi lampshade, 5
My right foot

A paperweight,
My face a featureless, fine
Jew linen.

10   Peel off the napkin
    O my enemy.
    Do I terrify?—

    The nose, the eye pits, the full set of teeth?
    The sour breath
15   Will vanish in a day.

    Soon, soon the flesh
    The grave cave ate will be
    At home on me

    And I a smiling woman.
20   I am only thirty.
    And like the cat I have nine times to die.

    This is Number Three.
    What a trash
    To annihilate each decade.

25   What a million filaments.
    The peanut-crunching crowd
    Shoves in to see

    Them unwrap me hand and foot
    The big strip tease.
30   Gentlemen, ladies

    These are my hands
    My knees.
    I may be skin and bone,

    Nevertheless, I am the same, identical woman.
35   The first time it happened I was ten.
    It was an accident.

    The second time I meant
    To last it out and not come back at all.
    I rocked shut

40   As a seashell.
    They had to call and call
    And pick the worms off me like sticky pearls.

    Dying
    Is an art, like everything else,
    I do it exceptionally well.

    I do it so it feels like hell.
    I do it so it feels real.
    I guess you could say I've a call.

It's easy enough to do it in a cell.
It's easy enough to do it and stay put.
It's the theatrical   50

Comeback in broad day
To the same place, the same face, the same brute
Amused shout:

"A miracle!"   55
That knocks me out.
There is a charge

For the eyeing of my scars, there is a charge
For the hearing of my heart—
It really goes.   60

And there is a charge, a very large charge
For a word or a touch
Or a bit of blood

Or a piece of my hair or my clothes.
So, so, Herr Doktor.   65
So, Herr Enemy.

I am your opus,
I am your valuable,
The pure gold baby

That melts to a shriek.   70
I turn and burn.
Do not think I underestimate your great concern.

Ash, ash—
You poke and stir.
Flesh, bone, there is nothing there—   75

A cake of soap,
A wedding ring,
A gold filling.

Herr God, Herr Lucifer
Beware   80
Beware.

Out of the ash
I rise with my red hair
And I eat men like air.

                    23–29 October 1962

Last Words (1961)

152

I do not want a plain box, I want a sarcophagus
With tigery stripes, and a face on it
Round as the moon, to stare up.
I want to be looking at them when they come
5   Picking among the dumb minerals, the roots
I see them already—the pale, star-distance faces.
Now they are nothing, they are not even babies.
Imagine them without fathers or mothers, like the first gods.
They will wonder if I was important.
10   I should sugar and preserve my days like fruit!
My mirror is clouding over—
A few more breaths, and it will reflect nothing at all.
The flowers and the faces whiten to a sheet.

I do not trust the spirit. It escapes like steam
15   In dreams, through mouth-hole or eye-hole. I can't stop it.
One day it won't come back. Things aren't like that.
They stay, their little particular lusters
Warmed by much handling. They almost purr.
When the soles of my feet grow cold,
20   The blue eye of my turquoise will comfort me.
Let me have my copper cooking pots, let my rouge pots
Bloom about me like night flowers, with a good smell.
They will roll me up in bandages, they will store my heart
Under my feet in a neat parcel.
25   I shall hardly know myself. It will be dark,
And the shine of these small things sweeter than the face of Ishtar.°

21 October 1961

_____

26 *Ishtar*. In ancient Babylonian and Assyrian mythology, the principal goddess of fertility, love, and war.

Metaphors (1959)

102

I'm a riddle in nine syllables,
An elephant, a ponderous house,
A melon strolling on two tendrils.
O red fruit, ivory, fine timbers!
5   This loaf's big with its yeasty rising.
Money's new-minted in this fat purse.
I'm a means, a stage, a cow in calf.
I've eaten a bag of green apples,
Boarded the train there's no getting off.

20 March 1959

Mirror (1961)

154

I am silver and exact. I have no preconceptions.
Whatever I see, I swallow immediately.
Just as it is, unmisted by love or dislike
I am not cruel, only truthful—
The eye of a little god, four-cornered.   5
Most of the time I meditate on the opposite wall.
It is pink, with speckles. I have looked at it so long
I think it is a part of my heart. But it flickers.
Faces and darkness separate us over and over.
Now I am a lake. A woman bends over me.   10
Searching my reaches for what she really is.
Then she turns to those liars, the candles or the moon.
I see her back, and reflect it faithfully
She rewards me with tears and an agitation of hands.
I am important to her. She comes and goes.   15
Each morning it is her face that replaces the darkness.
In me she has drowned a young girl, and in me an old woman
Rises toward her day after day, like a terrible fish.

23 October 1961

The Rival (1961)

147

If the moon smiled, she would resemble you.
You leave the same impression
Of something beautiful, but annihilating.
Both of you are great light borrowers.
Her O-mouth grieves at the world; yours is unaffected,   5
And your first gift is making stone out of everything.
I wake to a mausoleum; you are here,
Ticking your fingers on the marble table, looking for cigarettes,
Spiteful as a woman, but not so nervous,
And dying to say something unanswerable.   10

The moon, too, abases her subjects,
But in the daytime she is ridiculous.
Your dissatisfactions, on the other hand,
Arrive through the mailslot with loving regularity,
White and blank, expansive as carbon monoxide.   15

No day is safe from news of you,
Walking about in Africa maybe, but thinking of me.

July 1961

Song for a Summer's Day (1956)

12

Through fen and farmland walking
With my own country love
I saw slow flocked cows move
White hulks on their day's cruising;
5   Sweet grass sprang for their grazing.

The air was bright for looking:
Most far in blue, aloft,
Clouds steered a burnished drift;
Larks' nip and tuck arising
10   Came in for my love's praising.

Sheen of the noon sun striking
Took my heart as if
It were a green-tipped leaf
Kindled by my love's pleasing
15   Into an ardent blazing.

And so, together, talking,
Through Sunday's honey-air
We walked (and still walk there—
Out of the sun's bruising)
20   Till the night mists came rising.

Tulips (1961)

142

The tulips are too excitable, it is winter here.
Look how white everything is, how quiet, how snowed-in.
I am learning peacefulness, lying by myself quietly
As the light lies on these white walls, this bed, these hands.
5   I am nobody; I have nothing to do with explosions.
I have given my name and my day-clothes up to the nurses
And my history to the anesthetist and my body to surgeons.

They have propped my head between the pillow and the sheet-cuff
Like an eye between two white lids that will not shut.
10   Stupid pupil, it has to take everything in.
The nurses pass and pass, they are no trouble,
They pass the way gulls pass inland in their white caps,
Doing things with their hands, one just the same as another,
So it is impossible to tell how many there are.

15   My body is a pebble to them, they tend it as water
Tends to the pebbles it must run over, smoothing them gently.
They bring me numbness in their bright needles, they bring me sleep.

Now I have lost myself I am sick of baggage—
My patent leather overnight case like a black pillbox,
My husband and child smiling out of the family photo;   20
Their smiles catch onto my skin, little smiling hooks.

I have let things slip, a thirty-year-old cargo boat
Stubbornly hanging on to my name and address.
They have swabbed me clear of my loving associations.
Scared and bare on the green plastic-pillowed trolley   25
I watched my tea set, my bureaus of linen, my books
Sink out of sight, and the water went over my head.
I am a nun now, I have never been so pure.

I didn't want any flowers, I only wanted
To lie with my hands turned up and be utterly empty.   30
How free it is, you have no idea how free—
The peacefulness is so big it dazes you,
And it asks nothing, a name tag, a few trinkets.
It is what the dead close on, finally; I imagine them
Shutting their mouths on it, like a Communion tablet.   35

The tulips are too red in the first place, they hurt me.
Even through the gift paper I could hear them breathe
Lightly, through their white swaddlings, like an awful baby.
Their redness talks to my wound, it corresponds.
They are subtle: they seem to float, though they weigh me down,   40
Upsetting me with their sudden tongues and their color,
A dozen red lead sinkers round my neck.

Nobody watched me before, now I am watched.
The tulips turn to me, and the window behind me
Where once a day the light slowly widens and slowly thins,   45
And I see myself, flat, ridiculous, a cut-paper shadow
Between the eye of the sun and the eyes of the tulips,
And I have no face, I have wanted to efface myself.
The vivid tulips eat my oxygen.

Before they came the air was calm enough,   50
Coming and going, breath by breath, without any fuss.
Then the tulips filled it up like a loud noise.
Now the air snags and eddies round them the way a river
Snags and eddies round a sunken rust-red engine.
They concentrate my attention, that was happy   55
Playing and resting without committing itself.

The walls, also, seem to be warming themselves.
The tulips should be behind bars like dangerous animals;
They are opening like the mouth of some great African cat,
And I am aware of my heart: it opens and closes   60
Its bowl of red blooms out of sheer love of me.
The water I taste is warm and salt, like the sea,
And comes from a country far away as health.
                                      18 March 1961

Chapter 19
Collection of Poems for Additional Enjoyment and Study

Ai (Florence Anthony) . . . . Conversation, 882

Anna Akhmatova . . . . Willow, 883

Sherman Alexie . . . . . On the Amtrak from Boston to New York City, 883

Agha Shahid Ali . . . . Postcard from Kashmir, 883

Julia Alvarez . . . . Woman's Work, 884

Maya Angelou . . . . Still I Rise, 885

Anonymous (Navajo) . . . . . . Healing Prayer from the Beautyway Chant, 886

Matthew Arnold . . . . Dover Beach, 887

Margaret Atwood . . . . You fit into me, 888

W. H. Auden . . . . Musée des Beaux Arts, 888

Louise Bogan . . . . Women, 888

Jorge Luis Borges . . . . The Art of Poetry, 889

Anne Bradstreet . . . . The Author to Her Book, 890

Anne Bradstreet . . . . To My Dear and Loving Husband, 890

Emily Brontë . . . . Love and Friendship, 891

Gwendolyn Brooks . . . . We Real Cool, 891

Elizabeth Barrett Browning . . . . Sonnets from the Portuguese:
Number 43, How Do I Love Thee? 892

Robert Browning . . . . My Last Duchess, 892

George Gordon, Lord Byron . . . . She Walks in Beauty, 893

Billy Collins . . . . Days, 894

Stephen Crane . . . . Do Not Weep, Maiden, for War Is Kind, 895

E. E. Cummings . . . . anyone lived in a pretty how town, 895

E. E. Cummings . . . . if there are any heavens, 896

John Donne . . . . Holy Sonnet 10: Death Be Not Proud, 897

Rita Dove . . . . Daystar, 897

Sir Edward Dyer . . . . My Mind to Me a Kingdom Is, 898

Bob Dylan . . . . The Times They Are a-Changin', 899

T. S. Eliot . . . . The Love Song of J. Alfred Prufrock, 900

Martín Espada . . . . Latin Night at the Pawnshop, 904

Rhina Espaillat . . . . Bilingual/Bilingue, 904

Chief Dan George . . . . The Beauty of the Trees, 905

Nikki Giovanni . . . . Poetry, 905

Daniel Halpern . . . . Snapshot of Hué, 906

Thomas Hardy . . . . The Ruined Maid, 907

Frances E. W. Harper . . . . She's Free! 907

Robert Hass . . . . Spring Rain, 908

Robert Hayden . . . . Those Winter Sundays, 909

Robert Herrick . . . . Corinna's Going A-Maying, 909

Janet Holmes. . . . . Cinquains for Rocky, 910

A. D. Hope. . . . . Advice to Young Ladies, 911

Gerard Manley Hopkins . . . . Pied Beauty, 912

A. E. Housman. . . . . When I was one-and-twenty, 913

Robinson Jeffers . . . . The Answer, 913

Donald Justice . . . . On the Death of Friends in Childhood, 914

Donald Justice. . . . . Order in the Streets, 914

John Keats. . . . . .Ode on a Grecian Urn, 914

Galway Kinnell . . . . After Making Love We Hear Footsteps, 917

Yahia Lababidi . . . . What Do Animals Dream? 917

Philip Larkin. . . . . Talking in Bed, 918

Li-Young Lee . . . . .A Final Thing, 919

Audre Lorde . . . . Now that I Am Forever with Child, 920

Amy Lowell . . . . Patterns, 921

Magus Magnus . . . . Antaeus/Anchises, 923

Edna St. Vincent Millay. . . . . Travel, 924

Edna St. Vincent Millay. . . . . What Lips My Lips Have Kissed,
and Where, and Why, 924

N. Scott Momaday. . . . . .The Bear, 924

Howard Nemerov . . . . Life Cycle of Common Man, 925

Jim Northrup. . . . . wahbegan, 926

Sharon Olds . . . . The Moment the Two Worlds Meet, 927

Simon Ortiz . . . . A Story of How a Wall Stands, 927

Dorothy Parker . . . . Afternoon, 928

Dorothy Parker . . . . Résumé, 929

Linda Pastan . . . . Marks, 929

Marge Piercy . . . . The Secretary Chant, 929

Edgar Allan Poe . . . . Annabel Lee, 930

Edgar Allan Poe . . . . The Raven, 931

Ezra Pound . . . . A Girl, 933

Adrienne Rich . . . . Aunt Jennifer's Tigers, 934

Adrienne Rich . . . . Living in Sin, 934

Alberto Ríos . . . . The Vietnam Wall, 935

Luis Omar Salinas . . . . In a Farmhouse, 936

Carl Sandburg . . . . Chicago, 936

Siegfried Sassoon . . . . Dreamers, 937

Brenda Serotte . . . . My Mother's Face, 938

Anne Sexton . . . . Cinderella, 938

William Shakespeare . . . . .Sonnet 29: When in Disgrace
with Fortune and Men's Eyes, 941

Karl Shapiro . . . . Auto Wreck, 941

Stevie Smith . . . . Not Waving but Drowning, 942

Gary Soto . . . . Mexicans Begin Jogging, 942

Gary Soto. . . . . .Oranges, 943

William Stafford . . . . .Traveling Through the Dark, 944

Wallace Stevens . . . . The Emperor of Ice-Cream, 945
May Swenson . . . . Question, 945
Dylan Thomas . . . . A Refusal to Mourn the Death,
                                           by Fire, of a Child in London, 946
John Updike . . . . Perfection Wasted, 947
Alice Walker . . . . Revolutionary Petunias, 947
Phillis Wheatley . . . . On Being Brought from Africa to America, 948
Walt Whitman . . . . Beat! Beat! Drums! 948
Walt Whitman . . . . Full of Life Now, 949
Walt Whitman . . . . I Hear America Singing, 949
Richard Wilbur . . . . Love Calls Us to the Things of This World, 949
William Carlos Williams . . . . The Red Wheelbarrow, 950

Ai (FLORENCE ANTHONY) (1947–2010)

Conversation (1986)

We smile at each other
and I lean back against the wicker couch.
How does it feel to be dead? I say.
You touch my knees with your blue fingers.
5 And when you open your mouth,
a ball of yellow light falls to the floor
and burns a hole through it.
Don't tell me, I say. I don't want to hear.
Did you ever, you start,
10 wear a certain kind of dress
and just by accident,

so inconsequential you barely notice it,
your fingers graze that dress
and you hear the sound of a knife cutting paper,
15 you see it too
and you realize how that image
is simply the extension of another image,
that your own life
is a chain of words
20 that one day will snap.
Words, you say, young girls in a circle, holding hands,
and beginning to rise heavenward
in their confirmation dresses,
like white helium balloons,
25 the wreaths of flowers on their heads spinning,
and above all that,
that's where I'm floating,
and that's what it's like
only ten times clearer,
30 ten times more horrible.
Could anyone alive survive it?

ANNA AKHMATOVA (1889–1966)

 ## Willow (1940)

Translated by Judith Hemschemeyer

And I grew up in patterned tranquility,
In the cool nursery of the young century.
And the voice of man was not dear to me,
But the voice of the wind I could understand.
But best of all the silver willow.   5
And obligingly, it lived
With me all my life; its weeping branches
Fanned my insomnia with dreams.
And strange!—I outlived it.
There the stump stands; with strange voices   10
Other willows are conversing
Under our, under those skies.
And I am silent. . . . As if a brother had died.

SHERMAN ALEXIE (b. 1966)

 ## On the Amtrak from Boston
to New York City

The white woman across the aisle from me says "Look,
look at all the history, that house
on the hill there is over two hundred years old,"
as she points out the window past me

into what she has been taught. I have learned   5
little more about American history during my few days
back East than what I expected and far less
of what we should all know of the tribal stories

whose architecture is 15,000 years older
than the corners of the house that sits   10
museumed on the hill. "Walden Pond,"
the woman on the train asks, "Did you see Walden Pond?"

and I don't have a cruel enough heart to break
her own by telling her there are five Walden Ponds
on my little reservation out West   15
and at least a hundred more surrounding Spokane,

the city I pretended to call my home. "Listen,"
I could have told her. "I don't give a shit
about Walden. I know the Indians were living stories
around that pond before Walden's grandparents were born   20

and before his grandparents' grandparents were born.
I'm tired of hearing about Don-fucking-Henley saving it, too,
because that's redundant. If Don Henley's brothers and sisters
and mothers and father hadn't come here in the first place

25 then nothing would need to be saved."
But I didn't say a word to the woman about Walden
Pond because she smiled so much and seemed delighted
that I thought to bring her an orange juice

back from the food car. I respect elders
30 of every color. All I really did was eat
my tasteless sandwich, drink my Diet Pepsi
and nod my head whenever the woman pointed out

another little piece of her country's history
while I, as all Indians have done
35 since this war began, made plans
for what I would do and say the next time

somebody from the enemy thought I was one of their own.

AGHA SHAHID ALI (1949–2001)

Postcard from Kashmir (1987)

Kashmir shrinks into my mailbox,
my home a neat four by six inches.
I always loved neatness. Now I hold
the half-inch Himalayas in my hand.

5 This is home. And this the closest
I'll ever be to home. When I return,
the colors won't be so brilliant,
the Jhelum's waters so clean,
so ultramarine. My love
10 so overexposed.

And my memory will be a little
out of focus, in it
a giant negative, black
and white, still undeveloped.
15 and white, still undeveloped.

JULIA ALVAREZ (b. 1950)

Woman's Work (1996)

Who says a woman's work isn't high art?
She'd challenge as she scrubbed the bathroom tiles.
Keep house as if the address were your heart.

We'd clean the whole upstairs before we'd start
downstairs. I'd sigh, hearing my friends outside.   5
Doing her woman's work was a hard art

to practice when the summer sun would bar
the floor I swept till she was satisfied.
She kept me prisoner in her housebound heart.

She'd shine the tines of forks, the wheels of carts,   10
cut lacy lattices for all her pies.
Her woman's work was nothing less than art.

And, I, her masterpiece since I was smart,
was primed, praised, polished, scolded and advised
to keep a house much better than my heart.   15

I did not want to be her counterpart!
I struck out . . . but became my mother's child:
a woman working at home on her art,
housekeeping paper as if it were her heart.

MAYA ANGELOU (b. 1928)

 ## Still I Rise (1987)

You may write me down in history
With your bitter, twisted lies,
You may trod me in the very dirt
But still, like dust, I'll rise.

Does my sassiness upset you?   5
Why are you beset with gloom?
'Cause I walk like I've got oil wells
Pumping in my living room.

Just like moons and like suns,
With the certainty of tides,   10
Just like hopes springing high,
Still I'll rise.

Did you want to see me broken?
Bowed head and lowered eyes?
Shoulders falling down like teardrops.   15
Weakened by my soulful cries.

Does my haughtiness offend you?
Don't you take it awful hard
'Cause I laugh like I've got gold mines
Diggin' in my own back yard.   20

You may shoot me with your words,
You may cut me with your eyes,
You may kill me with your hatefulness,
But still, like air, I'll rise.

25 Does my sexiness upset you?
Does it come as a surprise
That I dance like I've got diamonds
At the meeting of my thighs?

Out of the huts of history's shame
30 I rise
Up from a past that's rooted in pain
I rise
I'm a black ocean, leaping and wide,
Welling and swelling I bear in the tide.
35 Leaving behind nights of terror and fear
I rise
Into a daybreak that's wondrously clear
I rise
Bringing the gifts that my ancestors gave,
40 I am the dream and the hope of the slave.
I rise
I rise
I rise.

ANONYMOUS (NAVAJO)

Healing Prayer from the Beautyway Chant
(traditional nineteenth century)

Out of the East, Beauty has come home,
Out of the South, Beauty has come home,
Out of the West, Beauty has come home,
Out of the North, Beauty has come home,
5 Out of the highest heavens and the lowest lands,
     Beauty has come home.
     Everywhere around us, Beauty has come home.
As we live each day, everything evil will leave us.
     We will be entirely healed,
10   Our bodies will exult in the fresh winds,
     Our steps will be firm.
As we live each day,
     Everything before us will be Beautiful;
     Everything behind us will be Beautiful;
15   Everything above us will be Beautiful;
     Everything below us will be Beautiful;
     Everything around us will be Beautiful;
     All our thoughts will be Beautiful;

All our words will be Beautiful;
   All our dreams will be Beautiful.   20
We will be forever restored, forever whole.
All things will be Beautiful forever.

MATTHEW ARNOLD (1822–1888)

Dover Beach (1867; 1849)

The sea is calm tonight.
The tide is full, the moon lies fair
Upon the straits—on the French coast the light
Gleams and is gone; the cliffs of England stand,
Glimmering and vast, out in the tranquil bay.   5
Come to the window, sweet is the night air!
Only, from the long line of spray
Where the sea meets the moon-blanched land,
Listen! you hear the grating roar
Of pebbles which the waves draw back, and fling,   10
At their return, up the high strand,
Begin, and cease, and then again begin,
With tremulous cadence slow, and bring
The eternal note of sadness in.

Sophocles long ago   15
Heard it on the Aegean, and it brought
Into his mind the turbid ebb and flow
Of human misery; we
Find also in the sound a thought,
Hearing it by this distant northern sea.   20

The Sea of Faith
Was once, too, at the full, and round earth's shore
Lay like the folds of a bright girdle furled.
But now I only hear
Its melancholy, long, withdrawing roar,   25
Retreating, to the breath
Of the night wind, down the vast edges drear
And naked shingles° of the world.   *beaches*

Ah, love, let us be true
To one another! for the world, which seems   30
To lie before us like a land of dreams,
So various, so beautiful, so new,
Hath really neither joy, nor love, nor light,
Nor certitude, nor peace, nor help for pain;
And we are here as on a darkling plain   35
Swept with confused alarms of struggle and flight,
Where ignorant armies clash by night.

MARGARET ATWOOD (b. 1939)

For a photo, see Chapter 8, page 384.

 ### You fit into me (1971)

you fit into me
like a hook into an eye

a fish hook
an open eye

W. H. AUDEN (1907–1973)

 ### Musée des Beaux Arts° (1940)

About suffering they were never wrong,
The Old Masters: how well they understood
Its human position; how it takes place
While someone else is eating or opening a window or just
    walking dully along;
5 How, when the aged are reverently, passionately waiting
For the miraculous birth, there always must be
Children who did not specially want it to happen, skating
On a pond at the edge of the wood:
They never forgot
10 That even the dreadful martyrdom must run its course
Anyhow in a corner, some untidy spot
Where the dogs go on with their doggy life and the torturer's horse
Scratches its innocent behind on a tree.

In Brueghel's *Icarus,* for instance: how everything turns away
15 Quite leisurely from the disaster; the ploughman may
Have heard the splash, the forsaken cry,
But for him it was not an important failure; the sun shone
As it had to on the white legs disappearing into the green
Water; and the expensive delicate ship that must have seen
20 Something amazing, a boy falling out of the sky,
Had somewhere to get to and sailed calmly on.

°Museum of Fine Arts (French).

LOUISE BOGAN (1897–1970)

 ### Women (1923)

Women have no wilderness in them,
They are provident instead,
Content in the tight hot cell of their hearts
To eat dusty bread.

They do not see cattle cropping red winter grass,   5
They do not hear
Snow water going down under culverts
Shallow and clear.

They wait, when they should turn to journeys,
They stiffen, when they should bend.   10
They use against themselves that benevolence
To which no man is friend.

They cannot think of so many crops to a field
Or of clean wood cleft by an axe.
Their love is an eager meaninglessness   15
Too tense, or too lax.

They hear in every whisper that speaks to them
A shout and a cry.
As like as not, when they take life over their door-sills
They should let it go by.   20

JORGE LUIS BORGES (1899–1986)

 ## The Art of Poetry (1964)

Translated by Anthony Kerrigan

To gaze at a river made of time and water
And remember Time is another river.
To know we stray like a river
and our faces vanish like water.

To feel that waking is another dream   5
that dreams of not dreaming and that the death
we fear in our bones is the death
that every night we call a dream.

To see in every day and year a symbol
of all the days of man and his years,   10
and convert the outrage of the years
into a music, a sound, and a symbol.

To see in death a dream, in the sunset
a golden sadness—such is poetry,
humble and immortal, poetry,   15
returning, like dawn and the sunset.

Sometimes at evening there's a face
that sees us from the deeps of a mirror.
Art must be that sort of mirror,
disclosing to each of us his face.   20

They say Ulysses, wearied of wonders,
wept with love on seeing Ithaca,
humble and green. Art is that Ithaca,
a green eternity, not wonders.

25   Art is endless like a river flowing,
passing, yet remaining, a mirror to the same
inconstant Heraclitus,° who is the same
and yet another, like the river flowing.

°27 *Heraclitus:* Heracleitus of Ephesus (c. 540–480 BCE), who maintained that the world was in a state of tension and balance between opposing forces.

ANNE BRADSTREET (1612–1672)

The following two poems are by Anne Bradstreet.

🍃 The Author to Her Book (1678)

Thou ill-formed offspring of my feeble brain,
Who after birth did'st by my side remain,
Till snatched from thence by friends, less wise than true,
Who thee abroad exposed to public view;
5   Made thee in rags, halting, to the press to trudge,
Where errors were not lessened, all may judge.
At thy return my blushing was not small,
My rambling brat (in print) should mother call;
I cast thee by as one unfit for light,
10   Thy visage was so irksome in my sight;
Yet being mine own, at length affection would
Thy blemishes amend, if so I could:
I washed thy face, but more defects I saw,
And rubbing off a spot, still made a flaw.
15   I stretched thy joints to make thee even feet,
Yet still thou run'st more hobbling than is meet;
In better dress to trim thee was my mind,
But nought save homespun cloth in the house I find.
In this array, 'mongst vulgars may'st thou roam;
20   In critics' hands beware thou dost not come;
And take thy way where yet thou are not known.
If for thy Father asked, say thou had'st none;
And for thy Mother, she alas is poor,
Which caused her thus to send thee out of door.

🍃 To My Dear and Loving Husband (1678)

If ever two were one, then surely we.
If ever man were loved by wife, then thee;
If ever wife was happy in a man,
Compare with me ye women if you can.

I prize thy love more than whole mines of gold,   5
Or all the riches that the East doth hold.
My love is such that rivers cannot quench,
Nor ought but love from thee give recompense.
Thy love is such I can no way repay;
The heavens reward thee manifold, I pray.   10
Then while we live, in love let's so persever,
That when we live no more we may live ever.

EMILY BRONTË (1818–1848)

Love and Friendship (1846)

Love is like the wild rose-briar,
Friendship like the holly-tree
The holly is dark when the rose-briar blooms
But which will bloom most constantly?

The wild-rose briar is sweet in the spring,   5
Its summer blossoms scent the air;
Yet wait till winter comes again
And who will call the wild-briar fair?

Then scorn the silly rose-wreath now
And deck thee with the holly's sheen,   10
That when December blights thy brow
He may still leave thy garland green.

GWENDOLYN BROOKS (1917–2000)

For a photo, see Chapter 11, page 544.

We Real Cool (1959)

The Pool Players.
Seven at the Golden Shovel.

We real cool. We
Left school. We

Lurk late. We
Strike straight. We

Sing sin. We   5
Thin gin. We

Jazz June. We
Die soon.

ELIZABETH BARRETT BROWNING (1806–1861)

Sonnets from the Portuguese: Number 43, How Do I Love Thee? (1850)

How do I love thee? Let me count the ways.
I love thee to the depth and breadth and height
My soul can reach, when feeling out of sight
For the ends of Being and ideal Grace.
5   I love thee to the level of every day's
Most quiet need, by sun and candlelight.
I love thee freely, as men strive for Right;
I love thee purely, as they turn from Praise.
I love thee with the passion put to use
10 In my old griefs, and with my childhood's faith.
I love thee with a love I seemed to lose
With my lost saints,—I love thee with the breath,
Smiles, tears, of all my life!—and, if God choose,
I shall but love thee better after death.

ROBERT BROWNING (1812–1889)

My Last Duchess° (1842)

Ferrara

That's my last Duchess painted on the wall,
Looking as if she were alive. I call
That piece a wonder, now: Frà Pandolf's° hands
Worked busily a day, and there she stands.
5   Will't please you sit and look at her? I said
"Frà Pandolf" by design, for never read
Strangers like you that pictured countenance,
The depth and passion of its earnest glance,
But to myself they turned (since none puts by
10 The curtain I have drawn for you, but I)
And seemed as they would ask me, if they durst,°   *dared*
How such a glance came there; so, not the first
Are you to turn and ask thus. Sir, 'twas not
Her husband's presence only, called that spot
15 Of joy into the Duchess' cheek: perhaps
Frà Pandolf chanced to say "Her mantle laps
Over my lady's wrist too much," or "Paint
Must never hope to reproduce the faint
Half-flush that dies along her throat": such stuff
20 Was courtesy, she thought, and cause enough

°The poem "My Last Duchess" is based on incidents in the life of Alfonso II, Duke of Ferrara, whose first wife died in 1561. Some claimed she was poisoned. The duke negotiated his second marriage to the daughter of the Count of Tyrol through an agent. °3 *Frà Pandolf:* an imaginary painter who is also a monk.

For calling up that spot of joy. She had
A heart—how shall I say?—too soon made glad,
Too easily impressed; she liked whate'er
She looked on, and her looks went everywhere.
Sir, 'twas all one! My favor at her breast,   25
The dropping of the daylight in the West,
The bough of cherries some officious fool
Broke in the orchard for her, the white mule
She rode with round the terrace—all and each
Would draw from her alike the approving speech,   30
Or blush, at least. She thanked men—good! but thanked
Somehow—I know not how—as if she ranked
My gift of a nine-hundred-years-old name
With anybody's gift. Who'd stoop to blame
This sort of trifling? Even had you skill   35
In speech—(which I have not)—to make your will
Quite clear to such a one, and say, "Just this
Or that in you disgusts me; here you miss,
Or there exceed the mark"—and if she let
Herself be lessoned so, nor plainly set   40
Her wits to yours, forsooth, and made excuse
—E'en then would be some stooping; and I choose
Never to stoop. Oh sir, she smiled, no doubt,
Whene'er I passed her; but who passed without
Much the same smile? This grew; I gave commands;   45
Then all smiles stopped together. There she stands
As if alive. Will't please you rise? We'll meet
The company below, then. I repeat,
The Count your master's known munificence
Is ample warrant that no just pretense   50
Of mine for dowry will be disallowed;
Though his fair daughter's self, as I avowed
At starting, is my object. Nay, we'll go
Together down, sir. Notice Neptune,° though,
Taming a sea horse, thought a rarity,   55
Which Claus of Innsbruck° cast in bronze for me!

°54 *Neptune*: Roman god of the sea. °56 *Claus of Innsbruck*: an imaginary sculptor.

GEORGE GORDON, LORD BYRON (1788–1824)

🌿 She Walks in Beauty (1815)

She walks in beauty, like the night
   Of cloudless climes and starry skies;
And all that's best of dark and bright
   Meet in her aspect and her eyes:
Thus mellow'd to that tender light   5
   Which heaven to gaudy day denies.

One shade the more, one ray the less,
    Had half impair'd the nameless grace
Which waves in every raven tress,
10   Or softly lightens o'er her face;
Where thoughts serenely sweet express
    How pure, how dear their dwelling-place.

And on that cheek, and o'er that brow,
    So soft, so calm, yet eloquent,
15 The smiles that win, the tints that glow,
    But tell of days in goodness spent,
A mind at peace with all below,
    A heart whose love is innocent!

BILLY COLLINS (b. 1941)

For a photo, see Chapter 11, page 534.

Days (1995)

Each one *is* a gift, no doubt.
mysteriously placed in your waking hand
or set upon your forehead
moments before you open your eyes.

5 Today begins cold and bright,
the ground heavy with snow
and the thick masonry of ice,
the sun glinting off the turrets of clouds.

Through the calm eye of the window
10 everything is in its place
but so precariously
this day might be resting somehow

on the one before it,
all the days of the past stacked high
15 like the impossible tower of dishes
entertainers used to build on stage.

No wonder you find yourself
perched on the top of a tall ladder
hoping to add one more.
20 Just another Wednesday

you whisper,
then holding your breath,
place this cup on yesterday's saucer
without the slightest clink.

STEPHEN CRANE (1871–1900)

Do Not Weep, Maiden, for War Is Kind (1896; 1895)

Do not weep, maiden, for war is kind.
Because your lover threw wild hands toward the sky
And the affrighted steed ran on alone,
Do not weep.
War is kind.   5

    Hoarse, booming drums of the regiment
    Little souls who thirst for fight,
    These men were born to drill and die
    The unexplained glory flies above them
    Great is the battle-god, great, and his kingdom—   10
    A field where a thousand corpses lie.

Do not weep, babe, for war is kind.
Because your father tumbled in the yellow trenches,
Raged at his breast, gulped and died,
Do not weep.   15
War is kind.

    Swift, blazing flag of the regiment
    Eagle with crest of red and gold,
    These men were born to drill and die
    Point for them the virtue of slaughter   20
    Make plain to them the excellence of killing
    And a field where a thousand corpses lie.

Mother whose head hung humble as a button
On the bright splendid shroud of your son,
Do not weep.   25
War is kind.

E. E. CUMMINGS (1894–1962)

The following two poems are by E. E. Cummings. For a photo, see Chapter 12, page 584.

anyone lived in a pretty how town (1940)

anyone lived in a pretty how town
(with up so floating many bells down)
spring summer autumn winter
he sang his didn't he danced his did.

Women and men(both little and small)   5
cared for anyone not at all
they sowed their isn't they reaped their same
sun moon stars rain

10 children guessed(but only a few
and down they forgot as up they grew
autumn winter spring summer)
that noone loved him more by more

when by now and tree by leaf
she laughed his joy she cried his grief
15 bird by snow and stir by still
anyone's any was all to her

someones married their everyones
laughed their cryings and did their dance
(sleep wake hope and then)they
20 said their nevers they slept their dream

stars rain sun moon
(and only the snow can begin to explain
how children are apt to forget to remember
with up so floating many bells down)

25 one day anyone died i guess
(and noone stooped to kiss his face)
busy folk buried them side by side
little by little and was by was

all by all and deep by deep
30 and more by more they dream their sleep
noone and anyone earth by april
wish by spirit and if by yes.

Women and men(both dong and ding)
summer autumn winter spring
35 reaped their sowing and went their came
sun moon stars rain

if there are any heavens (1931)

if there are any heavens my mother will(all by herself)have
one. It will not be a pansy heaven nor
a fragile heaven of lilies-of-the-valley but
it will be a heaven of blackred roses

5 my father will be (deep like a rose
tall like a rose)
standing near my

swaying over her
(silent)
10 with eyes which are really petals and see

nothing with the face of a poet really which
is a flower and not a face with

hands
which whisper
This is my beloved my   15

        (suddenly in sunlight

he will bow,

& the whole garden will bow)

JOHN DONNE (1572–1631)

For a portrait, see Chapter 12, page 585.

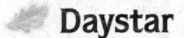 Holy Sonnet 10: Death Be Not Proud (1633)

Death, be not proud, though some have callèd thee
Mighty and dreadful, for thou art not so;
For those whom thou think'st thou dost overthrow
Die not, poor Death, nor yet canst thou kill me.
From rest and sleep, which but thy pictures° be,   *imitations*   5
Much pleasure; then from thee much more must flow,
And soonest our best men with thee do go,
Rest of their bones, and soul's delivery.
Thou art slave to fate, chance, kings, and desperate men,
And dost with poison, war, and sickness dwell,   10
And poppy° or charms can make us sleep as well   *opium*
And better than thy stroke; why swell'st° thou then?   *puff up with pride*
One short sleep past, we wake eternally°   *i.e., we will live eternally*
And death shall be no more; Death, thou shalt die.

RITA DOVE (b. 1952)

For a photo, see Chapter 11, page 546.

Daystar (1986)

She wanted a little room for thinking:
but she saw diapers steaming on the line,
a doll slumped behind the door.

So she lugged a chair behind the garage
to sit out the children's naps.   5

Sometimes there were things to watch—
the pinched armor of a vanished cricket,
a floating maple leaf. Other days
she stared until she was assured
when she closed her eyes   10
she'd see only her own vivid blood.

She had an hour, at best, before Liza appeared
pouting from the top of the stairs.
15 And just *what* was mother doing
out back with the field mice? Why,

building a palace. Later
that night when Thomas rolled over and
lurched into her, she would open her eyes
20 and think of the place that was hers
for an hour—where
she was nothing,
pure nothing, in the middle of the day.

SIR EDWARD DYER (1540–1607)

🖊 My Mind to Me a Kingdom Is (1588)

My mind to me a kingdom is;
    Such present joys therein I find
That it excells all other bliss
    That earth affords° or grows by kind.   *offers*
5   Though much I want which most would have,
Yet still my mind forbids to crave.

No princely pomp, no wealthy store,
    No force to win the victory,
No wily wit to salve a sore,
10   No shape to feed a loving eye;
To none of these I yield as thrall.°   *captive*
For why° my mind doth serve for all.   *because*

I see how plenty suffers oft,
    And hasty climbers soon do fall;
15 I see that those which are aloft
    Mishap doth threaten most of all;
They get with toil, they keep with fear.
Such cares my mind could never bear.

Content I live, this is my stay;
20   I seek no more than may suffice;
I press to bear no haughty sway;°   *influence*
    Look, what I lack my mind supplies;
Lo, thus I triumph like a king,
Content with that my mind doth bring.

25 Some have too much, yet still do crave;
    I little have, and seek no more.
They are but poor, though much they have,
    And I am rich with little store.
They poor, I rich; they beg, I give;
30 They lack, I leave; they pine, I live.

I laugh not at another's loss;
   I grudge not at another's gain;
No worldly waves my mind can toss;
   My state at one doth still remain.
I fear no foe, I fawn° no friend;   *flatter*   35
I loathe not life, nor dread my end.

Some weight their pleasures by their lust,
   Their wisdom by their rage of will;
Their treasure is their only trust;
   A cloaked craft their store of skill.   40
But all the pleasures that I find
Is to maintain a quiet mind.

My wealth is health and perfect ease;
   My conscience clear my choice° defense;   *best*
I neither seek by bribes to please,   45
   Nor by deceit to breed offense.
Thus do I live; thus will I die.
Would all did so as well as I.

BOB DYLAN (b. 1941)

🍃 The Times They Are a-Changin' (1963)

Come gather 'round people
Wherever you roam
And admit that the waters
Around you have grown
And accept it that soon   5
You'll be drenched to the bone.
If your time to you
Is worth savin'
Then you better start swimmin'
Or you'll sink like a stone   10
For the times they are a-changin'.

Come writers and critics
Who prophesize with your pen
And keep your eyes wide
The chance won't come again   15
And don't speak too soon
For the wheel's still in spin
And there's no tellin' who
That it's namin'.
For the loser now   20
Will be later to win
For the times they are a-changin'.

Come senators, congressmen
Please heed the call
Don't stand in the doorway   25

    Don't block up the hall
    For he that gets hurt
    Will be he who has stalled
    There's a battle outside
30   And it is ragin'.
    It'll soon shake your windows
    And rattle your walls
    For the times they are a-changin'.

    Come mothers and fathers
35   Throughout the land
    And don't criticize
    What you can't understand
    Your sons and your daughters
    Are beyond your command
40   Your old road is
    Rapidly agin'
    Please get out of the new one
    If you can't lend your hand
    For the times they are a-changin'.

45   The line it is drawn
    The curse it is cast
    The slow one now
    Will later be fast
    As the present now
50   Will later be past
    The order is
    Rapidly fadin'.
    And the first one now
    Will later be last
55   For the times they are a-changin'.

T. S. ELIOT (1888–1965)

For a photo, see Chapter 13, page 613.

The Love Song of J. Alfred Prufrock° (1915; 1911)

S'io credesse che mia risposta fosse
A persona che mai tornasse al mondo,
Questa fiamma staria senza piu scosse.
Ma per ciò che giammai di questo fondo
Non tornò vivo alcun, s'i'odo il vero,
Senza tema d'infamia ti rispondo.

°The poem is a monologue spoken by Prufrock; the name is invented but suggests a businessman. The Italian epigraph is quoted from Dante's *Inferno* (Canto 27, lines 61–66) and is spoken by a man who relates his evil deeds to Dante because he assumes that Dante will never return to the world: "If I believed that my response were made to a person who would ever revisit the world, this flame would stand motionless. But since none has ever returned from this depth alive, if I hear the truth, I answer you without fear of exposure."

Let us go then, you and I
When the evening is spread out against the sky
Like a patient etherized upon a table;
Let us go, through certain half-deserted streets,
The muttering retreats   5
Of restless nights in one-night cheap hotels
And sawdust restaurants with oyster shells;
Streets that follow like a tedious argument
Of insidious intent
To lead you to an overwhelming question . . .   10
Oh, do not ask, "What is it?"
Let us go and make our visit.

In the room the women come and go
Talking of Michelangelo.°
The yellow fog that rubs its back upon the windowpanes,   15
The yellow smoke that rubs its muzzle on the windowpanes
Licked its tongue into the corners of the evening,
Lingered upon the pools that stand in drains,
Let fall upon its back the soot that falls from chimneys,
Slipped by the terrace, made a sudden leap,   20
And seeing that it was a soft October night,
Curled once about the house, and fell asleep.

And indeed there will be time
For the yellow smoke that slides along the street,
Rubbing its back upon the windowpanes;   25
There will be time, there will be time°
To prepare a face to meet the faces that you meet;
There will be time to murder and create,
And time for all the works and days° of hands
That lift and drop a question on your plate;   30
Time for you and time for me,
And time yet for a hundred indecisions,
And for a hundred visions and revisions,
Before the taking of a toast and tea.

In the room the women come and go   35
Talking of Michelangelo.

And indeed there will be time
To wonder, "Do I dare?" and, "Do I dare?"

°14 *Michelangelo:* one of the greatest Italian Renaissance painters and sculptors (1475–1564). The name suggests that the women are cultured, or at least pretending to be so. °26 *time:* an allusion to Andrew Marvell's "To His Coy Mistress" (p. 784). °29 *works and days:* an allusion to a long poem, *Works and Days,* by the Greek poet Hesiod in the eighth century BCE. It is the primary source of the myth of Pandora (i.e., one who receives "all gifts"), who was considered to be "the first mortal female that ever lived" (Lemprière). Hesiod claims that Zeus, who was enraged by the theft of fire by Prometheus, created womankind, symbolized by Pandora, as his revenge on mankind, and to this end he directed Hermes to give her "a shameless mind and a deceitful nature" (tr. Hugh G. Evelyn-White, *Works and Days* 57–59, 68). We thank Professor Donald Tuthill for his work and helpfulness in the writing of this note.

Time to turn back and descend the stair,
40 With a bald spot in the middle of my hair—
    (They will say: "How his hair is growing thin!")
    My morning coat, my collar mounting firmly to the chin,
    My necktie rich and modest, but asserted by a simple pin—
    (They will say: "But how his arms and legs are thin!")
45 Do I dare
    Disturb the universe?
    In a minute there is time
    For decisions and revisions which a minute will reverse.

    For I have known them all already, known them all—
50 Have known the evenings, mornings, afternoons,
    I have measured out my life with coffee spoons;
    I know the voices dying with a dying fall°
    Beneath the music from a farther room.
        So how should I presume?

55 And I have known the eyes already, known them all—
    The eyes that fix you in a formulated phrase,
    And when I am formulated, sprawling on a pin,
    When I am pinned and wriggling on the wall,
    Then how should I begin
60 To spit out all the butt-ends of my days and ways?
    And how should I presume?

    And I have known the arms already, known them all—
    Arms that are braceleted and white and bare
    (But in the lamplight, downed with light brown hair!)
65 Is it perfume from a dress
    That makes me so digress?
    Arms that lie along a table, or wrap about a shawl.
        And should I then presume?
        And how should I begin?

* * * * *

    Shall I say, I have gone at dusk through narrow streets
70 And watched the smoke that rises from the pipes
    Of lonely men in shirt-sleeves, leaning out of windows? . . .
    I should have been a pair of ragged claws
    Scuttling across the floors of silent seas.

* * * * *

75 And the afternoon, the evening, sleeps so peacefully!
    Smoothed by long fingers,
    Asleep . . . tired . . . or it malingers,°
    Stretched on the floor, here beside you and me.

°52 *dying fall:* an allusion to a speech by Orsino in Shakespeare's *Twelfth Night* (1.1.4). °77 *malingers:* pretends
to be ill.

Should I, after tea and cakes and ices,
Have the strength to force the moment to its crisis?
But though I have wept and fasted, wept and prayed,
Though I have seen my head (grown slightly bald) brought in upon a platter,°
I am no prophet—and here's no great matter;
I have seen the moment of my greatness flicker,
And I have seen the eternal Footman hold my coat, and snicker,
And in short, I was afraid.

And would it have been worth it, after all,
After the cups, the marmalade, the tea,
Among the porcelain, among some talk of you and me,
Would it have been worth while,
To have bitten off the matter with a smile,
To have squeezed the universe into a ball°
To roll it toward some overwhelming question,
To say: "I am Lazarus,° come from the dead,
Come back to tell you all, I shall tell you all"—
If one, setling a pillow by her head,
    Should say: "That is not what I meant at all.
    That is not it, at all."

And would it have been worth it, after all,
Would it have been worth while,
After the sunsets and the dooryards and the sprinkled streets,
After the novels, after the teacups, after the skirts that trail along the floor—
And this, and so much more?—
It is impossible to say just what I mean!
But as if a magic lantern threw the nerves in patterns on a screen:
Would it have been worth while
If one, setling a pillow or throwing off a shawl,
And turning toward the window, should say:
    "That is not it at all,
    That is not what I meant, at all."

* * * * *

No! I am not Prince Hamlet,° nor was meant to be;
Am an attendant lord, one that will do
To swell a progress,° start a scene or two,
Advise the prince; no doubt, an easy tool,
Deferential, glad to be of use,
Politic, cautious, and meticulous;
Full of high sentence,° but a bit obtuse;
At times, indeed, almost ridiculous—
Almost, at times, the Fool.

I grow old . . . I grow old . . .

80

85

90

95

100

105

110

115

120

°82 *platter:* as was the head of John the Baptist; see Mark 6:17–28 and Matthew 14:3–11. °92 *ball:* another allusion to Marvell's "Coy Mistress." °94 *Lazarus:* See John 11:1–44. °111 *Prince Hamlet:* the hero of Shakespeare's play *Hamlet.* °113 *swell a progress:* enlarge a royal procession. °117 *sentence:* ideals, opinions, sentiment.

I shall wear the bottoms of my trousers rolled.°

Shall I part my hair behind? Do I dare to eat a peach?
I shall wear white flannel trousers, and walk upon the beach.
I have heard the mermaids singing, each to each.

125   I do not think that they will sing to me.

I have seen them riding seaward on the waves
Combing the white hair of the waves blown back
When the wind blows the water white and black.
We have lingered in the chambers of the sea
130   By sea-girls wreathed with seaweed red and brown
Till human voices wake us, and we drown.

°121 *rolled:* a possible reference to pants cuffs, which were becoming fashionable in 1910.

MARTÍIN ESPADA (b. 1957)

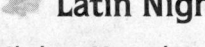 Latin Night at the Pawnshop (1990)

Chelsea, Massachusetts
Christmas, 1987

The apparition of a salsa band
gleaming in the Liberty Loan
pawnshop window:

golden trumpet,
5   silver trombone,
congas, maracas, tambourine,
all with price tags dangling
like the city morgue ticket
on a dead man's toe.

RHINA ESPAILLAT (b. 1932)

Bilingual/Bilingüe (1998)

My father liked them separate, one there,
one here (*allá y aquí*), as if aware

that words might cut in two his daughter's heart
(*el corazón*) and lock the alien part

5   to what he was—his memory, his name
(*su nombre*)—with a key he could not claim.

"English outside this door, Spanish inside,"
he said, "*y basta.*" But who can divide

the world, the word (*mundo y palabra*) from
any child? I knew how to be dumb   10

and stubborn (*testaruda*); late, in bed,
I hoarded secret syllables I read

until my tongue (*mi lengua*) learned to run
where his stumbled. And still the heart was one.

I like to think he knew that, even when,   15
proud (*orgulloso*) of his daughter's pen,

he stood outside *mis versos*, half in fear
of words he loved but wanted not to hear.

CHIEF DAN GEORGE (1899–1981)

 ### The Beauty of the Trees (1974)

The beauty of the trees,
the softness of the air,
the fragrance of the grass,
    speaks to me.

The summit of the mountain,   5
the thunder of the sky,
the rhythm of the sea,
    speaks to me.

The faintness of the stars,
the freshness of the morning,   10
the dewdrop on the flower,
    speaks to me.

The strength of fire,
the taste of salmon,
the trail of the sun,   15
and the life that never goes away,
    they speak to me.

And my heart soars.

NIKKI GIOVANNI (b. 1943)

Poetry (1996)

poetry is motion graceful
as a fawn
gentle as a teardrop
strong like the eye
finding peace in a crowded room   5

we poets tend to think
our words are golden
though emotion speaks too
loudly to be defined
10   by silence
sometimes after midnight or just before
the dawn
we sit typewriter in hand
pulling loneliness around us
15   forgetting our lovers or children
who are sleeping
ignoring the weary wariness
of our own logic
to compare a poem
20   no one understands it
it never says "love me" for poets are
beyond love
it never says "accept me" for poems seek not
acceptance but controversy
25   it only says "I am" and therefore
i concede that you are too

a poem is pure energy
horizontally contained
between the mind
30   of the poet and the ear of the reader
if it does not sing discard the ear
for poetry is song
if it does not delight discard
the heart for poetry is joy
35   if it does not inform then close
off the brain for it is dead
if it cannot heed the insistent message
that life is precious

which is all we poets
40   wrapped in our loneliness
are trying to say

DANIEL HALPERN (b. 1945)

Snapshot of Hué (1982)

For Robert Stone

They are riding bicycles on the other side
of the Perfume River.

A few months ago the bridges were down
and there was no one on the streets.

5   There were the telling piles on corners,
debris that contained a little of everything.

There was nothing not under cover—
even the sky remained impenetrable

day after day. And if you were seen
on the riverbank you were knocked down.   10

It is clear today. The litter in the streets
has been swept away. It couldn't have been

that bad, one of us said, the river barely moving,
the bicycles barely moving, the sun posted above.

THOMAS HARDY (1840–1928)

For a photo, see Chapter 11, page 548.

The Ruined Maid (1866)

"O 'melia,° my dear, this does everything crown!;°   *i.e., Amelia*
Who could have supposed I should meet you in Town?
And whence such fair garments, such prosperi-ty"—
"O didn't you know I'd been ruined," said she.

—"You left us in tatters, without shoes or socks,   5
Tired of digging potatoes, and spudding up docks;°   *digging up weeds*
And now you've gay bracelets and bright feathers three!"
"Yes: that's how we dress when we're ruined," said she.

—"At home in the barton° you said 'thee' and 'thou,'
And 'thik oon,' and 'theäs oon,' and 't'other';° but now   10
Your talking quite fits 'ee° for high compa-ny!"—   *thee*
"Some polish is gained with one's ruin," said she.

—"Your hands were like paws then, your face blue and bleak
But now I'm bewitched by your delicate cheek,
And your little gloves fit as on any la-dy!"—   15
"We never do work when we're ruined," said she.

—"You used to call home-life a hag-ridden dream,
And you'd sigh, and you'd sock;° but at present you seem   *moan, groan*
To know not of megrims° or melancho-ly!"—   *migraine headaches*
"True. One's pretty lively when ruined," said she.   20

—"I wish I had feathers, a fine sweeping gown,
And a delicate face, and could strut about Town!"—
"My dear—a raw country girl, such as you be,
Cannot quite expect that. You ain't ruined," said she.

°1 *does everything crown:* crowns everything; is a great surprise. °9 *At home in the barton:* when you lived at home on the farm. °9–10 *'thee'* . . . *'t'other':* i.e., you spoke familiarly in the country dialect (using the second-person pronoun), saying "thik oon" for "that one" and "theäs oon" for "this one."

FRANCES E. W. HARPER (1825–1911)

She's Free! (1854)

How say that by law we may torture and chase
A woman whose crime is the hue of her face?—
With her step on the ice, and her arm on her child,
The danger was fearful, the pathway was wild. . . .
5 But she's free! yes, free from the land where the slave,
From the hand of oppression, must rest in the grave;
Where bondage and blood, where scourges and chains,
Have placed on our banner indelible stains. . . .
The bloodhounds have miss'd the scent of her way,
10 The hunter is rifled and foiled of his prey,
The cursing of men and clanking of chains
Make sounds of strange discord on Liberty's plains. . . .
Oh! poverty, danger and death she can brave,
For the child of her love is no longer a slave.

ROBERT HASS (b. 1941)

Spring Rain (1989)

Now the rain is falling, freshly, in the intervals between sunlight,

a Pacific squall started no one knows where, drawn east as the drifts of
warm air make a channel;

it moves its own way, like water or the mind,
5 and spills this rain passing over. The Sierras will catch it as last snow
flurries before summer, observed only by the wakened marmots at ten
thousand feet,

and we will come across it again as larkspur and penstemon sprouting
along a creek above Sonora Pass next August,

10 where the snowmelt will have trickled into Dead Man's Creek and the
creek spilled into the Stanislaus and the Stanislaus into the San Joaquin
and the San Joaquin into the slow salt marshes of the bay.

That's not the end of it: the gray jays of the mountains eat larkspur seeds,
which cannot propagate otherwise.

15 To simulate the process, you have to soak gathered seeds all night in the
acids of coffee

and then score them gently with a very sharp knife before you plant them
in the garden.

ROBERT HAYDEN (1913–1980)

Those Winter Sundays (1962)

Sundays too my father got up early
and put his clothes on in the blueblack cold,
then with cracked hands that ached
from labor in the weekday weather made
banked fires blaze. No one ever thanked him.   5
I'd wake and hear the cold splintering, breaking,
When the rooms were warm, he'd call,
and slowly I would rise and dress,
fearing the chronic angers of that house,
Speaking indifferently to him,   10
who had driven out the cold
and polished my good shoes as well.
What did I know, what did I know
of love's austere and lonely offices?

ROBERT HERRICK (1591–1674)

Corinna's Going A-Maying (1648)

Get up! get up for shame! the blooming morn
Upon her wings presents the god unshorn°   *Apollo, god of the sun*
  See how Aurora° throws her fair   *Roman goddess of dawn*
  Fresh-quilted colors through the air:
  Get up, sweet slug-a-bed, and see   5
  The dew bespangling herb and tree.
Each flower has wept and bowed toward the east
Above an hour since, yet you not dressed;
  Nay, not so much as out of bed?
  When all the birds have matins° said,   *morning prayers*   10
  And sung their thankful hymns, 'tis sin,
  Nay, profanation to keep in,
Whenas a thousand virgins on this day
Spring, sooner than the lark, to fetch in May.°   *May Day*

Rise, and put on your foliage, and be seen   15
To tome forth, like the springtime, fresh and green,
  And sweet as Flora.° Take no care   *Roman goddess of flowers*
  For jewels for your gown or hair;
  Fear not; the leaves will strew
  Gems in abundance upon you;   20
Besides, the childhood of the days has kept,
Against you come, some orient° pearls unwept;   *eastern*
  Come and receive them while the light
  Hangs on the dew-locks of the night,
  And Titan° on the eastern hill   *the sun*   25
  Retires himself, or else stands still
Till you come forth. Wash, dress, be brief in praying:
Few beads° are best when once we go a-Maying.   *prayers, rosaries*

Come, my Corinna, come; and, coming, mark°   *note*
30 How each field turns° a street, each street a park   *turns into*
    Made green and trimmed with trees: see how
    Devotion gives each house a bough
    Or branch: each porch, each door ere this,
    An ark, a tabernacle is,
35 Made up of whitethorn neatly interwove,
    As if here were those cooler shades of love.
    Can such delights be in the street
    And open fields, and we not see 't?
    Come, we'll abroad; and let's obey
40   The proclamation made for May,
    And sin no more, as we have done, by staying;
    But, my Corinna, come, let's go a-Maying.

    There's not a budding boy or girl this day
    But is got up and gone to bring in May;
45 A deal° of youth, ere this, is come   *great many*
    Back, and with whitethorn laden home.
    Some have dispatched their cakes and cream
    Before that we have left to dream;
    And some have wept, and wooed, and plighted troth.
50 And chose their priest, ere we can cast off sloth.
    Many a green-gown° has been given,   *green with grass stains*
    Many a kiss, both odd and even;
    Many a glance, too, has been sent
    From out the eye, love's firmament;
55 Many a jest told of the keys betraying
    This night, and locks picked; yet we're not a-Maying.

    Come, let us go while we are in our prime,
    And take the harmless folly of the time.
    We shall grow old apace, and die
60   Before we know our liberty.
    Our life is short, and our days run
    As fast away as does the sun;
    And, as a vapor or a drop of rain
    Once lost, can ne'er be found again;
65   So when or you or I are made
    A fable, song, or fleeting shade,
    All love, all liking, all delight
    Lies drowned with us in endless night.
    Then while time serves, and we are but decaying,
70 Come, my Corinna, come, let's go a-Maying.

JANET HOLMES (b. 1956)

Cinquains for Rocky (1994)

You want
a word that means

separating two things
by bringing them closer. "What for?"
she asks.   5

"Doesn't
make sense." It does,
you tell her, when one speaks
about relationships—about
you two.   10

A. D. HOPE (1907–2000)

 ### Advice to Young Ladies (1970)

A.U.C.° 334: about this date
For a sexual misdemeanor, which she denied,
The vestal virgin Postumia was tried.
Livy records it among affairs of state.°

They let her off: it seems she was perfectly pure;   5
The charge arose because some thought her talk
Too witty for a young girl, her ways, her walk
Too lively, her clothes too smart to be demure.

The Pontifex Maximus, summing up the case,
Warned her in future to abstain from jokes,   10
To wear less modish and more pious frocks.
She left the court reprieved, but in disgrace.

What then? With her the annalist is less
Concerned than what the men achieved that year;
Plots, quarrels, crimes, with oratory to spare!   15
I see Postumia with her dowdy dress,

Stiff mouth and listless step; I see her strive
To give dull answers. She had to knuckle down.
A vestal virgin who scandalized that town
Had fair trial, then they buried her alive.   20

Alive, bricked up in suffocating dark,
A ration of bread, a pitcher if she was dry,
Preserved the body they did not wish to die
Until her mind was quenched to the last spark.

How many the black maw has swallowed in its time!   25
Spirited girls who would not know their place.
Talented girls who found that the disgrace
Of being a woman made genius a crime;

°1 A.U.C.: *ab urbe condita*, "from the founding of the city" (Latin); 334 years after the founding of ancient Rome.
°4 *Titus Livius: The History of Rome*, Vol. I. Electronic Text Center, U of Virginia Library. 4.44.

      How many others, who would not kiss the rod
30   Domestic bullying broke, or public shame?
      Pagan or Christian, it was much the same:
      Husbands, Saint Paul declared, rank next to God.

      Livy and Paul, it may be, never knew
      That Rome was doomed; each spoke of her with pride.
35   Tacitus, writing after both had died,
      Showed that whole fabric rotten through and through.

      Historians spend their lives and lavish ink
      Explaining how great commonwealths collapse
      From great defects of policy—perhaps
40   The cause is sometimes simpler than they think.

      It may not seem so grave an act to break
      Postumia's spirit as Galileo's, to gag
      Hypatia° as crush Socrates, or drag
      Joan as Giordano Bruno to the stake.

45   Can we be sure: Have more states perished, then,
      For having shackled the enquiring mind,
      Than those who, in their folly not less blind,
      Trusted the servile womb to breed free men?

---

43 *Hypatia:* Hypatia of Alexandria (c. 370–415 CE). She was a scholar and teacher who was brutally murdered by a mob of religious fanatics.

GERARD MANLEY HOPKINS (1844–1889)

For a photo, see Chapter 13, page 620.

Pied Beauty (1918, 1877)

Glory be to God for dappled things—
    For skies of couple-colour as a brinded° cow;
      For rose-moles all in stipple upon trout that swim;
Fresh-firecoal chestnut-falls;° finches' wings;
5   Landscape plotted and pieced°—fold,° fallow,° and plough;
      And áll trádes, their gear and tackle and trim.

All things counter,° original, spare,° strange;
    Whatever is fickle, freckled (who knows how?)
      With swift, slow; sweet, sour; adazzle, dim;
10 He fathers-forth whose beauty is past change:
    Praise him.

°2 *brinded:* brindled, that is, gray with dark spots. °4 *chestnut-falls:* the meat of a roasted chestnut. °5 *pieced:* divided into fields of different colors, depending on the crops or use. fold: an enclosed field for animals. fallow: a plowed but unplanted field. °7 *counter:* opposed, as in contrasting patterns. *spare:* rare.

A. E. HOUSMAN (1859–1936)

 When I was one-and-twenty (1896)

When I was one-and-twenty
   I heard a wise man say,
"Give crowns and pounds and guineas
   But not your heart away;
Give pearls away and rubies   5
   But keep your fancy free."
But I was one-and-twenty,
   No use to talk to me.

When I was one-and-twenty
   I heard him say again,   10
"The heart out of the bosom
   Was never given in vain;
'Tis paid with sighs a plenty
   And sold for endless rue."
And I am two-and-twenty,   15
   And oh, 'tis true, 'tis true.

ROBINSON JEFFERS (1887–1962)

For a photo, see Chapter 17, page 780.

 The Answer (1937)

Then what is the answer?—Not to be deluded by dreams.
To know that great civilizations have broken down into violence, and their tyrants come,
   many times before.
When open violence appears, to avoid it with honor or choose the least ugly faction; these
   evils are essential.
To keep one's own integrity, be merciful and uncorrupted and not wish for evil; and not be
   duped
By dreams of universal justice or happiness. These dreams will not be fulfilled.   5
To know this, and know that however ugly the parts appear the whole remains beautiful. A
   severed hand
Is an ugly thing, and man dissevered from the earth and stars and his history . . . for con-
   templation or in fact . . .

Often appears atrociously ugly. Integrity is wholeness, the greatest beauty is
Organic wholeness, the wholeness of life and things, the divine beauty of the universe. Love
   that, not man
Apart from that, or else you will share man's pitiful confusions, or drown in despair when   10
   his days darken.

DONALD JUSTICE (1925–2004)

The following two poems are by Donald Justice.

 On the Death of Friends in Childhood (1960)

We shall not ever meet them bearded in heaven,
Nor sunning themselves among the bald of hell;
If anywhere, in the deserted schoolyard at twilight,
Forming a ring, perhaps, or joining hands
5 In games whose very names we have forgotten,
Come, memory, let us seek them there in the shadows.

Order in the Streets (1969)

*(From instructions printed on a child's toy, Christmas 1968,
as reported in the* New York Times)

1. 2. 3.
Switch on.

Jeep rushes
to the scene
5 of riot

Jeep goes
in all directions
by mystery action.

Jeep stops periodically
10 to turn hood over

machine gun appears
with realistic
shooting noise.

After putting down riot,
15 jeep goes
back to the headquarters.

JOHN KEATS (1795–1821)

For a portrait, see Chapter 14, page 641.

Ode on a Grecian Urn° (1820; 1819)

1

Thou still unravish'd bride of quietness,
    Thou foster-child of silence and slow time,
Sylvan historian, who canst thus express

A flowery tale more sweetly than our rhyme:
What leaf-fring'd legend° haunts about thy shape   *border and tale*   5
    Of deities or mortals, or of both,
      In Tempe° or the dales of Arcady?°
    What men or gods are these? What maidens loth?
What mad pursuit? What struggle to escape?
    What pipes and timbrels? What wild ecstasy?   10

2

Heard melodies are sweet, but those unheard
    Are sweeter; therefore, ye soft pipes, play on;
Not to the sensual ear, but, more endear'd,
    Pipe to the spirit ditties of no tone:
Fair youth, beneath the trees, thou canst not leave   15
    Thy song, nor ever can those trees be bare;
      Bold lover, never, never canst thou kiss,
Though winning near the goal—yet, do not grieve;
      She cannot fade, though thou hast not thy bliss,
For ever wilt thou love, and she be fair!   20

3

Ah, happy, happy boughs! that cannot shed
    Your leaves, nor ever bid the spring adieu;
And, happy melodist, unwearied,
    For ever piping songs for ever new;
More happy love! more happy, happy love!   25
    For ever warm and still to be enjoy'd,
      For ever panting, and for ever young;
All breathing human passion far above,
    That leaves a heart high-sorrowful and cloy'd,
A burning forehead, and a parching tongue.   30

4

Who are these coming to the sacrifice?
    To what green altar, O mysterious priest,
Lead'st thou that heifer lowing at the skies,
    And all her silken flanks with garlands drest?
What little town by river or sea shore,   35
    Or mountain-built° with peaceful citadel,   *built on a mountain*
      Is emptied of this folk, this pious morn?
And, little town, thy streets for evermore
    Will silent be; and not a soul to tell
      Why thou art desolate, can e'er return.   40

°The imaginary Grecian urn to which the poem is addressed combines design motifs from many different existing
urns. This imaginary one is decorated with a border of leaves and trees, men (or gods) chasing women, a young musician sitting under a tree, lovers, and a priest and congregation leading a heifer to sacrifice. °7 *Tempe:* a beautiful
rustic valley in Greece. *Arcady:* refers to the valleys of Arcadia, a state in ancient Greece known for its beauty
and peacefulness.

"The Krater of Tanagra," fourth century , showing a wedding procession and musicians. National Archaeological Museum, Athens, Greece. Alinari/Art Resource, NY.

5

O Attic shape! Fair attitude! with brede°   *braid, pattern*
   Of marble men and maidens overwrought,°   *ornamented*
With forest branches and the trodden weed;
   Thou, silent form, dost tease us out of thought
45 As doth eternity: Cold Pastoral!
   When old age shall this generation waste,
Thou shalt remain, in midst of other woe
Than ours, a friend to man, to whom thou say'st,
"Beauty is truth, truth beauty,"—that is all
50 Ye know on earth, and all ye need to know.

GALWAY KINNELL (b. 1927)

After Making Love We Hear Footsteps (1980)

For I can snore like a bullhorn
or play loud music
or sit up talking with any reasonably sober Irishman
and Fergus will only sink deeper
into his dreamless sleep, which goes by all in one flash,   5
but let there be that heavy breathing
or a stifled come-cry anywhere in the house
and he will wrench himself awake
and make for it on the run—as now, we lie together,
after making love, quiet, touching along the length of our bodies,   10
familiar touch of the long-married,
and he appears—in his baseball pajamas, it happens,
the neck opening so small
he has to screw them on, which one day may make him wonder
about the mental capacity of baseball players—   15
and flops down between us and hugs us and snuggles himself to sleep,
his face gleaming with satisfaction at being this very child.

In the half darkness we look at each other
and smile
and touch arms across his little, startlingly muscled body—   20
this one whom habit of memory propels to the ground of his making,
sleeper only the mortal sounds can sing awake,
this blessing love gives again into our arms.

YAHIA LABABIDI (b. 1973)

What Do Animals Dream? (2006)

Do they dream of past lives and unlived dreams
unspeakably human or unimaginably bestial?

Do they struggle to catch in their slumber
what is too slippery for the fingers of day?

Are there subtle nocturnal intimations   5
to illuminate their undreaming hours?

Are they haunted by specters of regret
do they visit their dead in drowsy gratitude?

Or are they revisited by their crimes
transcribed in tantalizing hieroglyphs?   10

Do they retrace the outline of their wounds
or dream of transformation, instead?

Do they tug at obstinate knots
inassimilable longings and thwarted strivings?

15   Are there agitations, upheavals or mutinies
against their perceived selves or fate?

Are they free of strengths and weaknesses peculiar
to horse, deer, bird, goat, snake, lamb or lion?

Are they ever neither animal nor human
20   but creature and Being?

Do they have holy moments of understanding
deep in the seat of their entity?

Do they experience their existence more fully
relieved of the burden of wakefulness?

25   Do they suspect, with poets, that all we see or seem
is but a dream within a dream?

Or is it merely a small dying
a little taste of nothingness that gathers in their mouths?

PHILIP LARKIN (1922–1985)

Talking in Bed (1964)

Talking in bed ought to be easiest,
Lying together there goes back so far,
An emblem of two people being honest.

Yet more and more time passes silently,
5   Outside, the wind's incomplete unrest
Builds and disperses clouds about the sky,

And dark towns heap up on the horizon,
None of this cares for us. Nothing shows why
At this unique distance from isolation

10   It becomes still more difficult to find
Words at once true and kind,
Or not untrue and not unkind.

LI-YOUNG LEE (b. 1957)

A Final Thing (1990)

I am that last, that
final thing, the body
in a white sheet listening,

the whole of me trained,
curled like one great ear on   5
a sound, a noise I know, a

woman talking
in another room,
the woman I love; and

though I can't hear   10
her words, by their voicing
I can guess

she is telling a story,

using a voice which speaks to another,
weighted with that other's attention,   15
and avowing it
by deepening in intention.

Rich with the fullness of what's declared,
this voice points
away from itself   20
to some place

in the hearer,
sends the hearer back
to himself
to find what he knows.   25

A saying full of hearing,
a murmuring full of telling
and compassion for the listener
and for what's told,

now interrupted by a second voice,   30

thinner, higher, uncertain,
Querying, it seems
an invitation to be met,
stirring anticipation, embodying
incompletion of time and the day.   35

My son, my first-born, and his mother
are involved in a story no longer only theirs,

for I am implicated,
all three of us now
40   clinging to expectancy, riding sound and air.

Will my first morning of heaven be this?
No. And this is not
my last morning on earth.
I am simply last
45   in my house

to waken, and the first
sound I hear
is the voice of one I love
speaking to one we love.
50   I hear it through the bedroom wall;

something, someday, I'll close my eyes to recall.

AUDRE LORDE (1934–1992)

Now that I Am Forever with Child (1976)

How the days went
While you were blooming within me
I remember each upon each—
The swelling changed planes of my body—
5   And how you first fluttered, then jumped
And I thought it was my heart.

How the days wound down
And the turning of winter
I recall, with you growing heavy
10   Against the wind. I thought
Now her hands
Are formed, and her hair
Has started to curl
Now her teeth are done
15   Now she sneezes.
Then the seed opened.
I bore you one morning just before spring—
My head rang like a firey piston
My legs were towers between which
20   A new world was passing.

From then
I can only distinguish
One thread within running hours
You . . . flowing through selves
25   Towards you.

AMY LOWELL (1874–1925)

Patterns (1916)

I walk down the garden paths,
And all the daffodils
Are blowing, and the bright blue squills.
I walk down the patterned garden-paths
In my stiff, brocaded gown.   5
With my powdered hair and jewelled fan,
I too am a rare
Pattern. As I wander down
The garden paths.
My dress is richly figured,   10
And the train
Makes a pink and silver stain
On the gravel, and the thrift
Of the borders.
Just a plate of current fashion   15
Tripping by in high-heeled, ribboned shoes.
Not a softness anywhere about me,
Only whalebone° and brocade.
And I sink on a seat in the shade
Of a lime tree. For my passion   20
Wars against the stiff brocade.
The daffodils and squills
Flutter in the breeze
As they please.
And I weep;   25
For the lime-tree is in blossom
And one small flower has dropped upon my bosom.

And the plashing of waterdrops
In the marble fountain
Comes down the garden-paths.   30
The dripping never stops.
Underneath my stiffened gown
Is the softness of a woman bathing in a marble basin,
A basin in the midst of hedges grown
So thick, she cannot see her lover hiding,   35
But she guesses he is near,
And the sliding of the water
Seems the stroking of a dear
Hand upon her.
What is Summer in a fine brocaded gown!   40
I should like to see it lying in a heap upon the ground.
All the pink and silver crumpled up on the ground.

°18 *whalebone:* Baleen from whales was used to make corsets for women because it was strong and flexible, like
an early plastic.

I would be the pink and silver as I ran along the paths,
And he would stumble after,
45   Bewildered by my laughter.
I should see the sun flashing from his sword-hilt and buckles on his shoes.
I would choose
To lead him in a maze along the patterned paths,
A bright and laughing maze for my heavy-booted lover.
50   Till he caught me in the shade,
And the buttons of his waistcoat bruised my body as he clasped me,
Aching, melting, unafraid.
With the shadows of the leaves and the sundrops,
And the plopping of the waterdrops,
55   All about us in the open afternoon—
I am very like to swoon
With the weight of this brocade,
For the sun sifts through the shade.

Underneath the fallen blossom
60   In my bosom,
Is a letter I have hid.
It was brought to me this morning by a rider from the Duke.
Madam, we regret to inform you that Lord Hartwell
Died in action Thursday se'nnight.°
65   As I read it in the white, morning sunlight,
The letters squirmed like snakes.
"Any answer, Madam," said my footman.
"No," I told him.
"See that the messenger takes some refreshment.

70   No, no answer."
And I walked into the garden,
Up and down the patterned paths,
In my stiff, correct brocade.
The blue and yellow flowers stood up proudly in the sun,
75   Each one.
I stood upright too,
Held rigid to the pattern
By the stiffness of my gown.
Up and down I walked.
80   Up and down.

In a month he would have been my husband.
In a month, here, underneath this lime,
We would have broken the pattern;
He for me, and I for him,
85   He as Colonel, I as Lady,
On this shady seat.
He had a whim
That sunlight carried blessing.

°64 *se'nnight:* seven nights, hence a week ago.

And I answered, "It shall be as you have said."
Now he is dead.   90

In Summer and in Winter I shall walk
Up and down
The patterned garden-paths
In my stiff, brocaded gown.
The squills and daffodils   95
Will give place to pillared roses, and to asters, and to snow.
I shall go
Up and down,
In my gown.
Gorgeously arrayed,   100
Boned and stayed.
And the softness of my body will be guarded from embrace
By each button, hook, and lace.
For the man who should loose me is dead,
Fighting with the Duke in Flanders,°   105
In a pattern called a war.
Christ! What are patterns for?

°105 *Flanders:* A place of frequent warfare in Belgium. The speaker's clothing (lines 5, 6) suggests the time of the Duke of Marlborough's Flanders campaigns of 1702–1710. The Battle of Waterloo (1815) was also fought nearby under the Duke of Wellington. During World War I, fierce fighting against the Germans occurred in Flanders in 1914 and 1915, with great loss of life.

MAGUS MAGNUS (b. 1967)

For a photo, see Chapter 11, page 552.

Antaeus / Anchises (2008)

The Giant of Greek myth was an invincible wrestler because when he touched the Earth, his mother, his strength was renewed. Hercules killed him by holding him aloft and throttling him.

At the fall of Troy, in an act millennially-famous for its filial piety, Aeneas carried his father to safety on his shoulders. It is said the fires gave way to make a path for them.

The Giant's father was the sea, Poseidon, and his mother the Earth, Gaea. The old man was beloved of Aphrodite as a youth, and they gave birth to the destined Father of Rome, a fled son of destroyed Troy.

At the birth of my son I am long estranged from my father, and I hear he's seriously ailing. I hate him for this, and for more than this.

EDNA ST. VINCENT MILLAY (1892–1950)

The following two poems are by Edna St. Vincent Millay.

Travel (1921)

The railroad track is miles away,
   And the day is loud with voices speaking,
Yet there isn't a train goes by all day
   But I hear its whistle shrieking.

5   All night there isn't a train goes by,
   Though the night is still for sleep and dreaming,
But I see its cinders red on the sky,
   And hear its engine steaming.

My heart is warm with the friends I make,
10   And better friend I'll not be knowing;
Yet there isn't a train I wouldn't take,
   No matter where it's going.

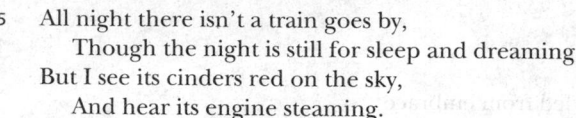 What Lips My Lips Have Kissed, and Where, and Why (1923)

What lips my lips have kissed, and where, and why,
I have forgotten, and what arms have lain
Under my head till morning; but the rain
Is full of ghosts tonight, that tap and sigh
5 Upon the glass and listen for reply,
And in my heart there stirs a quiet pain
For unremembered lads that not again
Will turn to me at midnight with a cry.
Thus in the winter stands the lonely tree,
10 Nor knows what birds have vanished one by one,
Yet knows its boughs more silent than before:
I cannot say what loves have come and gone,
I only know that summer sang in me
A little while, that in me sings no more.

N. SCOTT MOMADAY (b. 1934)

The Bear (1992)

   What ruse of vision,
escarping the wall of leaves,
   rending incision
into countless surfaces,

5   would cull and color
his somnolence, whose old age

has outworn valor,
all but the fact of courage?

    Seen, he does not come,
move, but seems forever there,   10
    dimensionless, dumb
in the windless noon's hot glare.

    More scarred than others
these years since the trap maimed him,
    pain slants his withers,   15
drawing up the crooked limb.

    Then he is gone, whole,
without urgency, from sight,
    as buzzards control,
imperceptibly, their flight.   20

HOWARD NEMEROV (1920–1991)

Life Cycle of Common Man (1960)

Roughly figured, this man of moderate habits,
This average consumer of the middle class,
Consumed in the course of his average life span
Just under half a million cigarettes,
Four thousand fifths of gin and about   5
A quarter as much vermouth; he drank
Maybe a hundred thousand cups of coffee,
And counting his parents' share it cost
Something like half a million dollars
To put him through life. How many beasts   10
Died to provide him with meat, belt and shoes
Cannot be certainly said.

                    But anyhow,
It is in this way that a man travels through time,
Leaving behind him a lengthening trail   15
Of empty bottles and bones, of broken shoes,
Frayed collars and worn out or outgrown
Diapers and dinnerjackets, silk ties and slickers.

Given the energy and security thus achieved,
He did . . . ? What? The usual things, of course,   20
The eating, dreaming, drinking and begetting,
And he worked for the money which was to pay
For the eating, et cetera, which were necessary
If he were to go on working for the money, et cetera,
But chiefly he talked. As the bottles and bones   25
Accumulated behind him, the words proceeded
Steadily from the front of his face as he

Advanced into the silence and made it verbal.
Who can tally the tale of his words? A lifetime
30 Would barely suffice for their repetition;
If you merely printed all his commas the result
Would be a very large volume, and the number of times
He said "thank you" or "very little sugar, please,"
Would stagger the imagination. There were also
35 Witticisms, platitudes, and statements beginning
"It seems to me" or "As I always say."
Consider the courage in all that, and behold the man
Walking into deep silence, with the ectoplastic
Cartoon's balloon of speech proceeding
40 Steadily out of the front of his face, the words
Borne along on the breath which is his spirit
Telling the numberless tale of his untold Word
Which makes the world his apple, and forces him to eat.

JIM NORTHRUP (b. 1943)

🍂 wahbegan° (1993)

Didja ever hear a sound
smell something
taste something
that brought you back
5 to Vietnam, instantly?
Didja ever wonder
when it would end?
It ended for my brother.
He died in the war
10 but didn't fall down
for fifteen tortured years.
His flashbacks are over,
another casualty whose name
will never be on the Wall.
15 Some can find peace
only in death.
The sound of his
family crying hurt.
The smell of the flowers
20 didn't comfort us.
The bitter taste
in my mouth
still sours me.
How about a memorial
25 for those who made it
through the war
but still died
before their time?

°The title "wahbegan" is an Ojibway name.

SHARON OLDS (b. 1942)

For a photo, see Chapter 15, page 702.

 ### The Moment the Two Worlds Meet (1987)

That's the moment I always think of—when the
slick, whole body comes out of me,
when they pull it out, not pull it but steady it
as it pushes forth, not catch it but keep their
hands under it as it pulses out,   5
they are the first to touch it,
and it shines, it glistens with the thick liquid on it.
That's the moment, while it's sliding, the limbs
compressed close to the body, the arms
bent like a crab's rosy legs, the   10
thighs closely packed plums in heavy syrup, the
legs folded like the white wings of a chicken—
that is the center of life, that moment when the
juiced bluish sphere of the baby is
sliding between the two worlds,   15
wet, like sex, it *is* sex,
it is my life opening back and back
as you'd strip the reed from the bud, not strip it but
watch it thrust so it peels itself and the
flower is there, severely folded, and   20
then it begin to open and dry
but by then the moment is over,
they wipe off the grease and wrap the child in a blanket and
hand it to you entirely in this world.

SIMON ORTIZ (b. 1941)

A Story of How a Wall Stands (1976)

> *At Aacqu there is a wall almost 400 years old which
> supports hundreds of tons of dirt and bones—it's a
> graveyard built on a steep incline—and it looks like
> it's about to fall down the incline but will not for a long time.*

My father, who works with stone,
says, "That's just the part you see,
the stones which seem to be
just packed in on the outside,"
and with his hands put the stone and mud   5
in place. "Underneath
what looks like loose stone,
there is stone woven together."

He ties one hand over the other,
10 fitting like the bones of his hands
    and fingers. "That's what is
    holding it together."

    "It is built that carefully,"
    he says, "the mud mixed
15 to a certain texture," patiently
    "with the fingers," worked
    in the palm of his hand. "So that
    placed between the stones, they hold
    together for a long, long time."

20 He tells me those things,
    the story of them worked
    with his fingers, in the palm
    of his hands, working the stone
    and the mud until they become
    the wall that stands a long, long time.

DOROTHY PARKER (1893–1967)

The following two poems are by Dorothy Parker.

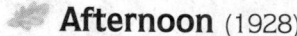 Afternoon (1928)

When I am old, and comforted,
    And done with this desire,
With Memory to share my bed
    And Peace to share my fire,

5   I'll comb my hair in scalloped bands
        Beneath my laundered cap,
    And watch my cool and fragile hands
        Lie light upon my lap.

    And I will have a sprigged gown
10   With lace to kiss my throat;
    I'll draw my curtain to the town,
        And hum a purring note.

    And I'll forget the way of tears,
        And rock, and stir my tea.
15 But oh, I wish those blessed years
        Were further than they be!

Résumé (1936)

Razors pain you;
Rivers are damp;
Acids stain you;
And drugs cause cramp.
Guns aren't lawful;   5
Nooses give;
Gas smells awful;
You might as well live.

LINDA PASTAN (b. 1932)

 ## Marks (1978)

My husband gives me an A
for last night's supper,
an incomplete for my ironing,
a B plus in bed.
My son says I am average,   5
an average mother, but if
I put my mind to it
I could improve.
My daughter believes
in Pass/Fail and tells me   10
I pass. Wait 'til they learn
I'm dropping out.

MARGE PIERCY (b. 1936)

For a photo, see Chapter 14, page 660.

The Secretary Chant (1973)

My hips are a desk.
From my ears hang
chains of paper clips.
Rubber bands form my hair.
My breasts are wells of mimeograph ink.   5
My feet bear casters.
Buzz. Click.
My head is a badly organized file.
My head is a switchboard
where crossed lines crackle.   10
Press my fingers
and in my eyes appear
credit and debit.

Zing. Tinkle.
15 My navel is a reject button.
From my mouth issue canceled reams.
Swollen, heavy, rectangular
I am about to be delivered
of a baby
20 Xerox machine.
File me under W
because I wonce
was
a woman.

EDGAR ALLAN POE (1809–1849)

For a portrait, see Chapter 4, page 249. The following two poems are by Edgar Allan Poe.

Annabel Lee (1849)

It was many and many a year ago,
  In a kingdom by the sea,
That a maiden there lived whom you may know
  By the name of Annabel Lee;
5 And this maiden she lived with no other thought
  Than to love and be loved by me.

I was a child and *She* was a child,
  In this kingdom by the sea,
But we loved with a love that was more than love—
10 I and my Annabel Lee—
With a love that the wingéd seraphs of Heaven
  Coveted her and me.

And this was the reason that, long ago,
  In this kingdom by the sea,
15 A wind blew out of a cloud by night
  Chilling my Annabel Lee;
So that her high-born kinsmen came
  And bore her away from me,
To shut her up in a sepulchre
20 In this kingdom by the sea.

The angels, not half so happy in Heaven,
  Went envying her and me:—
Yes! that was the reason (as all men know,
  In this kingdom by the sea)
25 That the wind came out of the cloud chilling
  And killing my Annabel Lee.

But our love it was stronger by far than the love
  Of those who were older than we—
  Of many far wiser than we—

And neither the angels in Heaven above   30
   Nor the demons down under the sea
   Can ever dissever my soul from the soul
   Of the beautiful Annabel Lee:—
For the moon never beams without bringing me dreams
   Of the beautiful Annabel Lee;   35
And the stars never rise but I feel the bright eyes
   Of the beautiful Annabel Lee:
And so all the night-tide, I lie down by the side
Of my darling, my darling, my life and my bride
   In her sepulchre there by the sea—   40
   In her tomb by the side of the sea.

The Raven (1845)

Once upon a midnight dreary, while I pondered, weak and weary,
Over many a quaint and curious volume of forgotten lore—
While I nodded, nearly napping, suddenly there came a tapping,
As of some one gently rapping, rapping at my chamber door.
"'Tis some visitor," I muttered, "tapping at my chamber door—   5
   Only this and nothing more."

Ah, distinctly I remember it was in the bleak December;
And each separate dying ember wrought its ghost upon the floor.
Eagerly I wished the morrow;—vainly I had sought to borrow
From my books surcease of sorrow—sorrow for the lost Lenore—   10
For the rare and radiant maiden whom the angels name Lenore—
   Nameless *here* for evermore.

And the silken, sad, uncertain rustling of each purple curtain
Thrilled me—filled me with fantastic terrors never felt before;
So that now, to still the beating of my heart, I stood repeating   15
"'Tis some visitor entreating entrance at my chamber door—
Some late visitor entreating entrance at my chamber door;—
   This it is and nothing more."

Presently my soul grew stronger; hesitating then no longer,
"Sir," said I, "or Madam, truly your forgiveness I implore;   20
But the fact is I was napping, and so gently you came rapping,
And so faintly you came tapping, tapping at my chamber door,
That I scarce was sure I heard you"—here I opened wide the door;
   Darkness there and nothing more.

Deep into that darkness peering, long I stood there wondering, fearing,   25
Doubting, dreaming dreams no mortal ever dared to dream before;
But the silence was unbroken, and the stillness gave no token,
And the only word there spoken was the whispered word, "Lenore!"
This I whispered, and an echo murmured back the word "Lenore!"
   Merely this and nothing more.   30

Back into the chamber turning, all my soul within me burning,
Soon again I heard a tapping somewhat louder than before.
"Surely," said I, "surely that is something at my window lattice;
Let me see, then, what thereat is, and this mystery explore—
35 Let my heart be still a moment and this mystery explore;—
    'Tis the wind and nothing more!"

Open here I flung the shutter, when, with many a flirt and flutter,
In there stepped a stately Raven of the saintly days of yore.
Not the least obeisance made he; not a minute stopped or stayed he;
40 But, with mien of lord or lady, perched above my chamber door—
Perched upon a bust of Pallas just above my chamber door—
    Perched, and sat, and nothing more.

Then this ebony bird beguiling my sad fancy into smiling,
By the grave and stern decorum of the countenance it wore,
45 "Though thy crest be shorn and shaven, thou," I said, "art sure no craven,
Ghastly grim and ancient Raven wandering from the Nightly shore—
Tell me what thy lordly name is on the Night's Plutonian shore!"
    Quoth the Raven "Nevermore."

Much I marvelled this ungainly fowl to hear discourse so plainly,
50 Though its answer little meaning—little relevancy bore;
For we cannot help agreeing that no living human being
Ever yet was blessed with seeing bird above his chamber door—
Bird or beast upon the sculptured bust above his chamber door,
    With such name as "Nevermore."

55 But the Raven, sitting lonely on the placid bust, spoke only
That one word, as if his soul in that one word he did outpour.
Nothing farther then he uttered—not a feather then he fluttered—
Till I scarcely more than muttered "Other friends have flown before—
On the morrow he will leave me, as my hopes have flown before."
60   Then the bird said "Nevermore."

Startled at the stillness broken by reply so aptly spoken,
"Doubtless," said I, "what it utters is its only stock and store
Caught from some unhappy master whom unmerciful Disaster
Followed fast and followed faster till his songs one burden bore—
65 Till the dirges of his Hope that melancholy burden bore
    Of "Never—nevermore."

But the Raven still beguiling all my fancy into smiling,
Straight I wheeled a cushioned seat in front of bird and bust and door;
Then upon the velvet sinking, I betook myself to linking
70 Fancy unto fancy, thinking what this ominous bird of yore—
What this grim, ungainly, ghastly, gaunt, and ominous bird of yore
    Meant in croaking "Nevermore."

This I sat engaged in guessing, but no syllable expressing
To the fowl whose fiery eyes now burned into my bosom's core;
75 This and more I sat divining, with my head at ease reclining
On the cushion's velvet lining that the lamp-light gloated o'er,

But whose velvet violet lining with the lamp-light gloating o'er,
    She shall press, ah, nevermore!

Then, methought, the air grew denser, perfumed from an unseen censer
Swung by Seraphim whose foot-falls tinkled on the tufted floor.   80
"Wretch," I cried, "thy God hath lent thee—by these angels he hath sent thee
Respite—respite and nepenthe° from thy memories of Lenore;
Quaff, oh quaff this kind nepenthe and forget this lost Lenore!"
    Quoth the Raven "Nevermore."

"Prophet!" said I, "thing of evil! prophet still, if bird or devil!—   85
Whether Tempter sent, or whether tempest tossed thee here ashore,
Desolate yet all undaunted, on this desert land enchanted—
On this home by Horror haunted—tell me truly, I implore—
Is there—*is* there balm in Gilead?°—tell me—tell me, I implore!"
    Quoth the Raven "Nevermore."   90

"Prophet!" said I, "thing of evil!—prophet still, if bird or devil!
By that Heaven that bends above us—by that God we both adore
Tell this soul with sorrow laden if, within the distant Aidenn,°
It shall clasp a sainted maiden whom the angels name Lenore—
Clasp a rare and radiant maiden whom the angels name Lenore."   95
    Quoth the Raven "Nevermore."

"Be that word our sign of parting, bird or fiend!" I shrieked, upstarting—
"Get thee back into the tempest and the Night's Plutonian shore!
Leave no black plume as a token of that lie thy soul hath spoken!
Leave my loneliness unbroken!—quit the bust above my door!   100
Take thy beak from out my heart, and take thy form from off my door!"
    Quoth the Raven "Nevermore."

And the Raven, never flitting, still is sitting, *still* is sitting
On the pallid bust of Pallas just above my chamber door;
And his eyes have all the seeming of a demon's that is dreaming,   105
And the lamp-light o'er him streaming throws his shadow on the floor;
And my soul from out that shadow that lies floating on the floor
    Shall be lifted—nevermore!

°82 *nepenthe:* an ancient drug said to cure a person of grief. °89 *balm in Gilead:* Gilead was an ancient biblical region known for its physicians and healing balms; see Jeremiah 8:22. °93 *Aidenn:* Eden, the Garden of Eden. Poe apparently took the form from his reading in Arabic literature.

EZRA POUND (1885–1972)

For a photo, see Chapter 13, page 627.

 A Girl (1987)

The tree has entered my hands,
The sap has ascended my arms,

The tree has grown in my breast—
Downward,
5 The branches grow out of me, like arms.

Tree you are,
Moss you are,
You are violets with wind above them.
A child—*so* high—you arc,
10 And all this is folly to the world.

ADRIENNE RICH (b. 1929)

The following two poems are by Adrienne Rich.

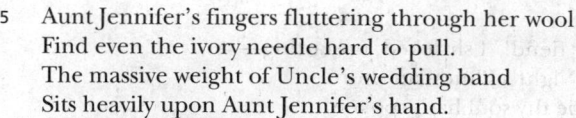

Aunt Jennifer's Tigers (1951)

Aunt Jennifer's tigers prance across a screen,
Bright topaz denizens of a world of green.
They do not fear the men beneath the tree;
They pace in sleek chivalric certainty.

5 Aunt Jennifer's fingers fluttering through her wool
Find even the ivory needle hard to pull.
The massive weight of Uncle's wedding band
Sits heavily upon Aunt Jennifer's hand.

When Aunt is dead, her terrified hands will lie
10 Still ringed with ordeals she was mastered by.
The tigers in the panel that she made
Will go on prancing, proud and unafraid.

 ## Living in Sin (1955)

She had thought the studio would keep itself;
no dust upon the furniture of love.
Half heresy, to wish the taps less vocal,
the panes relieved of grime. A plate of pears
5 a piano with a Persian shawl, a cat
stalking the picturesque amusing mouse
had risen at his urging.
Not that at five each separate stair would writhe
under the milkman's tramp; that morning light
10 so coldly would delineate the scraps
of last night's cheese and three sepulchral bottles;
that on the kitchen shelf among the saucers
a pair of beetle-eyes would fix her own—
envoy from some village in the moldings . . .
15 Meanwhile, he, with a yawn,

sounded a dozen notes upon the keyboard,
declared it out of tune, shrugged at the mirror,
rubbed at his beard, went out for cigarettes;
while she, jeered by the minor demons,
pulled back the sheets and made the bed and found   20
a towel to dust the table-top,
and let the coffee-pot boil over on the stove.
By evening she was back in love again,
though not so wholly but throughout the night
she woke sometimes to feel the daylight coming   25
like a relentless milkman up the stairs.

ALBERTO RÍOS (b. 1952)

The Vietnam Wall (1988)

I
Have seen it
And I like it. The magic,
The way like cutting onions
It brings water out of nowhere.   5
Invisible from one side, a scar
Into the skin of the ground
From the other, a black winding
Appendix line.
      A dig.   10
      An archaeologist can explain.
The walk is slow at first,
Easy, a little black marble wall
Of a dollhouse,
A smoothness, a shine   15
The boys in the street want to give.
One name. And then more
Names, long lines, lines of names until
They are the shape of the U.N. Building
Taller than I am: I have walked   20
Into a grace.
And everything I expect has been taken away, like that, quick:
      The names are not alphabetized.
      They are in the order of dying,
      An alphabet of—somewhere—screaming.   25
I start to walk out. I almost leave
But stop to look up names of friends,
My own name. There is somebody
Severiano Ríos.
Little kids do not make the same noise   30
Here, junior high school boys don't run
Or hold each other in headlocks.
No rules, something just persists
Like pinching on St. Patrick's Day

35 Every year for no green.
　　　　No one knows why.
Flowers are forced
Into the cracks
Between sections
40 Men have cried
At this wall.
I have
Seen them.

LUIS OMAR SALINAS (b. 1937)

 ### In a Farmhouse (1973)

Fifteen miles
out of Robstown
with the Texas sun
fading in the distance
5 I sit in the bedroom
profoundly,
animated by the day's work
in the cottonfields.

I made two dollars and
10 thirty cents today
I am eight years old
and I wonder
how the rest of the Mestizos°
do not go hungry
15 and if one were to die
of hunger
what an odd way
to leave for heaven.

°13 *Mestizos*: persons of mixed Spanish and Amerindian ancestry.

CARL SANDBURG (1878–1967)

Chicago (1916)

Hog Butcher for the World,
Tool Maker, Stacker of Wheat,
Player with Railroads and the Nation's Freight Handler;
Stormy, husky, brawling,
5 City of the Big Shoulders:

They tell me you are wicked and I believe them, for I have
　　seen your painted women under the gas lamps luring
　　the farm boys.

And they tell me you are crooked and I answer: Yes, it is true I have seen the gunman kill and go free to kill again.

And they tell me you are brutal and my reply is: On the faces of women and children I have seen the marks of wanton hunger.

And having answered so I turn once more to those who sneer at this my city, and I give them back the sneer and say to them:

Come and show me another city with lifted head singing so proud to be alive and coarse and strong and cunning.   10

Flinging magnetic curses amid the toil of piling job on job, here is a tall bold slugger set vivid against the little soft cities;

Fierce as a dog with tongue lapping for action, cunning as a savage pitted against the wilderness,

    Bareheaded,

    Shoveling,

    Wrecking,   15

    Planning,

    Building, breaking, rebuilding,

Under the smoke, dust all over his mouth, laughing with white teeth,

Under the terrible burden of destiny laughing as a young man laughs,

Laughing even as an ignorant fighter laughs who has never lost a battle,   20

Bragging and laughing that under his wrist is the pulse, and under his ribs the heart of the people,

      Laughing!

Laughing the stormy, husky, brawling laughter of Youth, half-naked, sweating, proud to be Hog Butcher, Tool Maker, Stacker of Wheat, Player with Railroads and Freight Handler to the Nation.

SIEGFRIED SASSOON (1886–1967)

🪶 Dreamers (1918)

Soldiers are citizens of death's grey land,
   Drawing no dividend from time's to-morrows.
In the great hour of destiny they stand,
   Each with his feuds, and jealousies, and sorrows.

Soldiers are sworn to action; they must win   5
   Some flaming, fatal climax with their lives.
Soldiers are dreamers; when the guns begin
   They think of firelit homes, clean beds, and wives.

I see them in foul dug-outs, gnawed by rats,
   And in the ruined trenches, lashed with rain,   10
Dreaming of things they did with balls and bats,
   And mocked by hopeless longing to regain
Bank-holidays,° and picture shows, and spats,
   And going to the office in the train.

°13 *Bank-holidays*: legal holidays in Great Britain.

BRENDA SEROTTE (b. 1946)

My Mother's Face (1991)

Dressing for work
I glanced in the mirror
startled to see my mother's face
white, with the mouth turned down
5   her red frizzled hair
wild in all directions.
She turned sideways
to study my dress
standing tiptoe like I do
10   craning her long neck
in a futile attempt to see my feet.
Then without warning, the tears
rolling from the outer corners down
past slightly pitted cheeks
15   past that inverted smile
into the cave of her bosom
which heaved a sigh so forlorn
so weighted with loss
that had I not been standing silent
20   I would have surely thought it was me.

ANNE SEXTON (1928–1974)

Cinderella (1971)

You always read about it:
the plumber with twelve children
who wins the Irish Sweepstakes.
From toilets to riches.
5   That story.

Or the nursemaid,
some luscious sweet from Denmark
who captures the oldest son's heart.
From diapers to Dior.
10   That story.

Or a milkman who serves the wealthy,
eggs, cream, butter, yogurt, milk,
the white truck like an ambulance
who goes into real estate
15   and makes a pile.
From homogenized to martinis at lunch.

Or the charwoman
who is on the bus when it cracks up

and collects enough from the insurance.
From mops to Bonwit Teller.   20
That story.

Once
the wife of a rich man was on her deathbed
and she said to her daughter Cinderella:
Be devout. Be good. Then I will smile   25
down from heaven in the seam of a cloud.
The man took another wife who had
two daughters, pretty enough
but with hearts like blackjacks.
Cinderella was their maid.   30
She slept on the sooty hearth each night
and walked around looking like Al Jolson.
Her father brought presents home from town,
jewels and gowns for the other women
but the twig of a tree for Cinderella.   35
She planted that twig on her mother's grave
and it grew to a tree where a white dove sat.
Whenever she wished for anything the dove
would drop it like an egg upon the ground.
The bird is important, my dears, so heed him.   40

Next came the ball, as you all know.
It was a marriage market.
The prince was looking for a wife.
All but Cinderella were preparing
and gussying up for the big event.   45
Cinderella begged to go too.
Her stepmother threw a dish of lentils
into the cinders and said: Pick them
up in an hour and you shall go.
The white dove brought all his friends;   50
all the warm wings of the fatherland came,
and picked up the lentils in a jiffy.
No, Cinderella, said the stepmother,
you have no clothes and cannot dance.
That's the way with stepmothers.   55

Cinderella went to the tree at the grave
and cried forth like a gospel singer:
Mama! Mama! My turtledove,
send me to the prince's ball!
The bird dropped down a golden dress   60
and delicate little gold slippers.
Rather a large package for a simple bird.
So she went. Which is no surprise.
Her stepmother and sisters didn't
recognize her without her cinder face   65
and the prince took her hand on the spot

and danced with no other the whole day.
As nightfall came she thought she'd better
get home. The prince walked her home
70 and she disappeared into the pigeon house
and although the prince took an axe and broke
it open she was gone. Back to her cinders.

These events repeated themselves for three days.
However on the third day the prince
75 covered the palace steps with cobbler's wax
and Cinderella's gold shoe stuck upon it.
Now he would find whom the shoe fit
and find his strange dancing girl for keeps.
He went to their house and the two sisters
80 were delighted because they had lovely feet.
The eldest went into a room to try the slipper on
but her big toe got in the way so she simply
sliced it off and put on the slipper.
The prince rode away with her until the white dove
85 told him to look at the blood pouring forth.
That is the way with amputations.
They don't just heal up like a wish.
The other sister cut off her heel
but the blood told as blood will.
90 The prince was getting tired.
He began to feel like a shoe salesman.
But he gave it one last try.
This time Cinderella fit into the shoe
like a love letter into its envelope.

95 At the wedding ceremony
the two sisters came to curry favor
and the white dove pecked their eyes out.
Two hollow spots were left
like soup spoons.

100 Cinderella and the prince
lived, they say, happily ever after,
like two dolls in a museum case
never bothered by diapers or dust,
never arguing over the timing of an egg,
105 never telling the same story twice,
never getting a middle-aged spread,
their darling smiles pasted on for eternity.
Regular Bobbsey Twins.
That story.

WILLIAM SHAKESPEARE (1564–1616)

For a portrait, see Chapter 21, page 1079.

 Sonnet 29: When in Disgrace with Fortune and Men's Eyes (1609)

When, in disgrace with Fortune and men's eyes,
I all alone beweep my outcast state,
And trouble deaf heaven with my bootless° cries,   *futile, useless*
And look upon myself and curse my fate,
Wishing me like to one more rich in hope,   5
Featured like him, like him with friends possessed,
Desiring this man's art and that man's scope,
With what I most enjoy contented least;
Yet in these thoughts myself almost despising,
Haply I think on thee, and then my state,   10
Like to the lark at break of day arising
From sullen earth, sings hymns at heaven's gate;
For thy sweet love remembered such wealth brings
That then I scorn to change my state with kings.

KARL SHAPIRO (1913–2000)

 Auto Wreck (1941)

Its quick soft silver bell beating, beating,
And down the dark one ruby flare
Pulsing out red light like an artery,
The ambulance at top speed floating down
Past beacons and illuminated clocks   5
Wings in a heavy curve, dips down,
And brakes speed, entering the crowd.
The doors leap open, emptying light;
Stretchers are laid out, the mangled lifted
And stowed into the little hospital.   10
Then the bell, breaking the hush, tolls once,
And the ambulance with its terrible cargo
Rocking, slightly rocking, moves away,
As the doors, an afterthought, are closed.
We are deranged, walking among the cops   15
Who sweep glass and are large and composed.
One is still making notes under the light.
One with a bucket douches ponds of blood
Into the street and gutter.
One hangs lanterns on the wrecks that cling,   20
Empty husks of locusts, to iron poles.
Our throats were tight as tourniquets,
Our feet were bound with splints, but now,

Like convalescents intimate and gauche,
25 We speak through sickly smiles and warn
With the stubborn saw of common sense,
The grim joke and the banal resolution.
The traffic moves around with care,
But we remain, touching a wound
30 That opens to our richest horror.
Already old, the question Who shall die?
Becomes unspoken Who is innocent?
For death in war is done by hands;
Suicide has cause and stillbirth, logic;
35 And cancer, simple as a flower, blooms.
But this invites the occult mind,
Cancels our physics with a sneer,
And spatters all we knew of dénouement
Across the expedient and wicked stones.

STEVIE SMITH (1902–1971)

🌿 Not Waving but Drowning (1957)

Nobody heard him, the dead man,
But still he lay moaning:
I was much further out than you thought
And not waving but drowning.

5 Poor chap, he always loved larking
And now he's dead
It must have been too cold for him his heart gave way,
They said.

Oh, no no no, it was too cold always
10 (Still the dead one lay moaning)
I was much too far out all my life
And not waving but drowning.

GARY SOTO (b. 1952)

The following two poems are by Gary Soto.

🌿 Mexicans Begin Jogging (1981)

At the factory I worked
In the fleck of rubber, under the press
Of an oven yellow with flame,
Until the border patrol opened
5 Their vans and my boss waved for us to run.

"Over the fence, Soto," he shouted,
And I shouted that I was American.
"No time for lies," he said, and pressed
A dollar in my palm, hurrying me
Through the back door.   10
Since I was on his time, I ran
And became the wag to a short tail of Mexicans—
Ran past the amazed crowds that lined
The streets and blurred like photographs, in rain.
I ran from that industrial road to the soft   15
Houses where people paled at the turn of an autumn sky.
What could I do but yell *vivas*
To baseball, milkshakes, and those sociologists
Who would clock me
As I jog into the next century   20
On the power of a great, silly grin.

🍃 Oranges (1984)

The first time I walked
With a girl, I was twelve,
Cold, and weighted down
With two oranges in my jacket.
December. Frost cracking   5
Beneath my steps, my breath
Before me, then gone,
As I walked toward
Her house, the one whose
Porch light burned yellow   10
Night and day, in any weather.
A dog barked at me, until
She came out pulling
At her gloves, face bright
With rouge. I smiled,   15
Touched her shoulder, and led
Her down the street, across
A used car lot and a line
Of newly planted trees,
Until we were breathing   20
Before a drugstore. We
Entered, the tiny bell
Bringing a saleslady
Down a narrow aisle of goods.
I turned to the candies   25
Tiered like bleachers,
And asked what she wanted—
Light in her eyes, a smile
Starting at the corners
Of her mouth. I fingered   30
A nickel in my pocket,
And when she lifted a chocolate

That cost a dime,
I didn't say anything.
35 I took the nickel from
My pocket, then an orange,
And set them quietly on
The counter. When I looked up,
The lady's eyes met mine,
40 And held them, knowing
Very well what it was all
About.
        Outside,
A few cars hissing past,
45 Fog hanging like old
Coats between the trees.
I took my girl's hand
In mine for two blocks,
Then released it to let
50 Her unwrap the chocolate.
I peeled my orange
That was so bright against
The gray of December
That, from some distance,
55 Someone might have thought
I was making a fire in my hands.

WILLIAM STAFFORD (1914–1993)

Traveling Through the Dark (1960)

Traveling through the dark I found a deer
dead on the edge of the Wilson River road.
It is usually best to roll them into the canyon:
that road is narrow; to swerve might make more dead.

5   By glow of the tail-light I stumbled back of the car
and stood by the heap, a doe, a recent killing;
she had stiffened already, almost cold.
I dragged her off; she was large in the belly.

My fingers touching her side brought me the reason—
10 her side was warm; her fawn lay there waiting,
alive, still, never to be born.
Beside that mountain road I hesitated.

The car aimed ahead its lowered parking lights;
under the hood purred the steady engine.
15 I stood in the glare of the warm exhaust turning red;
around our group I could hear the wilderness listen.
I thought hard for us all—my only swerving—,
then pushed her over the edge into the river.

WALLACE STEVENS (1879–1955)

For a photo, see Chapter 12, page 593.

The Emperor of Ice-Cream (1923)

Call the roller of big cigars,
The muscular one, and bid him whip
In kitchen cups concupiscent curds.
Let the wenches dawdle in such dress
As they are used to wear, and let the boys   5
Bring flowers in last month's newspapers.
Let be be finale° of seem.
The only emperor is the emperor of ice-cream.
Take from the dresser of deal,°
Lacking the three glass knobs, that sheet   10
On which she embroidered fantails° once

And spread it so as to cover her face.
If her horny feet protrude, they come
To show how cold she is, and dumb.
Let the lamp affix its beam.   15
The only emperor is the emperor of ice-cream.

°7 *finale:* the grand conclusion. °9 *deal:* unfinished pine or fir used to make cheap furniture. °11 *fantails:* fantail pigeons.

MAY SWENSON (1919–1989)

For a photo, see Chapter 16, page 733.

Question (1978)

Body my house
my horse my hound
what will I do
when you are fallen

Where will I sleep   5
How will I ride
What will I hunt

Where can I go
without my mount
all eager and quick   10

How will I know
in thicket ahead

is danger or treasure
when Body my good
15 bright dog is dead

How will it be
to lie in the sky
without roof or door
and wind for an eye

20 With cloud for shift
how will I hide?

DYLAN THOMAS (1914–1953)

For a photo, see Chapter 16, page 752.

A Refusal to Mourn the Death, by Fire, of a Child in London (1946)

Never until the mankind making
Bird beast and flower
Fathering and all humbling darkness
Tells with silence the last light breaking
5 And the still hour
Is come of the sea tumbling in harness

And I must enter again the round
Zion of the water bead
And the synagogue of the ear of corn
10 Shall I let pray the shadow of a sound
Or sow my salt seed
In the least valley of sackcloth to mourn

The majesty and burning of the child's death.
I shall not murder
15 The mankind of her going with a grave truth
Nor blaspheme down the stations of the breath
With any further
Elegy of innocence and youth.

Deep with the first dead lies London's daughter,
20 Robed in the long friends,
The grains beyond age, the dark veins of her mother,
Secret by the unmourning water
Of the riding Thames.°
After the first death, there is no other.

°23 *Thames:* the river Thames, which flows through London.

JOHN UPDIKE (1932–2009)

For a photo, see Chapter 6, page 320.

Perfection Wasted (1990)

And another regrettable thing about death
is the ceasing of your own brand of magic,
which took a whole life to develop and market—
the quips, the witticisms, the slant
adjusted to a few, those loved ones nearest   5
the lip of the stage, their soft faces blanched
in the footlight glow, their laughter close to tears,
their tears confused with their diamond earrings,
their warm pooled breath in and out with your heartbeat,
their response and your performance twinned.   10
The jokes over the phone. The memories packed
in the rapid-access file. The whole act.
Who will do it again? That's it: no one;
imitators and descendants aren't the same.

ALICE WALKER (b. 1944)

For a photo see Chapter 10, page 494.

Revolutionary Petunias (1972)

Sammy Lou of Rue
sent to his reward
the exact creature who
murdered her husband,
using a cultivator's hoe   5
with verve and skill;
and laughed fit to kill
in disbelief
at the angry, militant
pictures of herself   10
the Sonneteers quickly drew:
not any of them people that
she knew.
A backwoods woman
her house was papered with   15
funeral home calendars and
faces appropriate for a Mississippi
Sunday School. She raised a George,
a Martha, a Jackie and a Kennedy. Also
a John Wesley Junior.°   20

°18–20 *George . . . Junior:* The children are named after George and Martha Washington, Jackie and John Fitzgerald Kennedy (1917–1963, thirty-fifth U.S. president), and John Wesley (1703–1791), English evangelical preacher who founded Methodism.

"Always respect the word of God,"
she said on her way to she didn't
know where, except it would be by
electric chair, and she continued
25   "Don't yall forgit to *water*
my purple petunias."

PHILLIS WHEATLEY (1754–1784)

On Being Brought from Africa to America (1773)

'Twas mercy brought me from my *Pagan* land,
Taught my benighted soul to understand
That there's a God, that there's a *Saviour* too:
Once I redemption neither sought nor knew.
Some view our sable race with scornful eye,
5   "Their colour is a diabolic die."
Remember, *Christians*, *Negroes*, black as *Cain*,
May be refin'd, and join th' angelic train.

WALT WHITMAN (1819–1892)

For a photo, see Chapter 14, page 667. The following three poems are by Walt Whitman.

Beat! Beat! Drums! (1861)

Beat! beat! drums!—blow! bugles! blow!
Through the windows—through doors—burst like a ruthless force,
Into the solemn church, and scatter the congregation,
Into the school where the scholar is studying;
5   Leave not the bridegroom quiet—no happiness must he have now with his bride,
Nor the peaceful farmer any peace, plowing his field or gathering his grain,
So fierce you whir and pound you drums—so shrill you bugles blow.

Beat! beat! drums!—blow! bugles! blow!
Over the traffic of cities—over the rumble of wheels in the streets;
Are beds prepared for sleepers at night in the houses? no sleepers must sleep in
10   those beds,
No bargainers' bargains by day—no brokers or speculators—would they continue?
Would the talkers be talking? would the singer attempt to sing?
Would the lawyer rise in the court to state his case before the judge?
Beat! beat! drums—blow! bugles! blow!

15   Then rattle quicker, heavier drums—you bugles wilder blow.
Make no parley—stop for no expostulation,
Mind not the timid—mind not the weeper or prayer,
Mind not the old man beseeching the young man,
Let not the child's voice be heard, nor the mother's entreaties,
20   Make even the trestles to shake the dead where they lie awaiting the hearses,
So strong you thump O terrible drums—so loud you bugles blow.

Full of Life Now (1857)

Full of life now, compact, visible,
I, forty years old the eighty-third year of the States,
To one a century hence or any number of centuries hence,
To you yet unborn these, seeking you.

When you read these I that was visible am become invisible,   5
Now it is you, compact, visible, realizing my poems, seeking me,
Fancying how happy you were if I could be with you and become your comrade;
Be it as if I were with you. (Be not too certain but I am now with you.)

I Hear America Singing (1867)

I hear America singing, the varied carols I hear:
Those of mechanics—each one singing his, as it should be, blithe and strong;
The carpenter singing his, as he measures his plank or beam,
The mason singing his, as he makes ready for work, or leaves off work;
The boatman singing what belongs to him in his boat—the deckhand singing on the
        steamboat deck;   5
The shoemaker singing as he sits on his bench—the hatter singing as he stands;
The wood cutter's song—the ploughboy's on his way in the morning, or at noon
        intermissions, or at sundown;
The delicious singing of the mother—or of the young wife at work—or of the girl sewing or
        washing—
Each singing what belongs to him or her and to none else;
The day what belongs to the day—at night, the part of young fellows, robust, friendly,   10
Singing, with open mouths, their strong melodious songs.

RICHARD WILBUR (b. 1921)

For a photo, see Chapter 17, page 790.

Love Calls Us to the Things of This World (1956)

The eyes open to a cry of pulleys,
And spirited from sleep, the astounded soul
Hangs for a moment bodiless and simple
As false dawn.
Outside the open window   5
The morning air is all awash with angels.

Some are in bed-sheets, some are in blouses,
Some are in smocks: but truly there they are.
Now they are rising together in calm swells
Of halcyon feeling, filling whatever they wear   10
With the deep joy of their impersonal breathing;

Now they are flying in place, conveying
The terrible speed of their omnipresence, moving
And staying like white water; and now of a sudden
15 They swoop down into so rapt a quiet
That nobody seems to be there.
The soul shrinks

From all that is about to remember,
From the punctual rape of every blessed day,
   And cries
"Oh, let there be nothing on earth but laundry,
Nothing but rosy hands in the rising steam
And clear dances done in the sight of heaven."

   Yet, as the sun acknowledges
   With a warm look the world's hunks and colors,
The soul descends once more in bitter love
To accept the waking body, saying now
In a changed voice as the man yawns and rises,

"Bring them down from their ruddy gallows;
30 Let there be clean linen for the backs of thieves;
Let lovers go fresh and sweet to be undone,
And the heaviest nuns walk in a pure floating
Of dark habits,
   keeping their difficult balance."

WILLIAM CARLOS WILLIAMS (1883–1963)

For a photo, see Chapter 16, page 754

The Red Wheelbarrow (1923)

so much depends
upon

a red wheel
barrow

glazed with rain
water

beside the white
chickens.

Chapter 19A
Writing a Research Essay on Poetry

The end of the fiction section of this book, Chapter 10A (p. 500) contains a chapter on the use of research as the basis of an essay of term-paper length on fiction. Because the objects and goals of research are general, most of the materials in Chapter 10 are also essential for research projects in all the genres. It is therefore necessary to consult Chapter 10 for many relevant ways to engage in detailed research, which you can apply not only to writing about fiction but also to writing about both poetry and drama.

Here, however, our concern is to suggest a more limited use of research for the development of essays on the topic of poetry. Any of the essay assignments on poetry described in Chapters 11 to 18 can serve as the basic topic for the introduction of helpful research materials. Because of the general nature of research, the use of research for writing about poetry is not essentially different from research used in writing about fiction and drama.

Topics to Discover in Research

There are some general objectives in the use of research, but your goal should always be to discover materials that have a meaningful bearing on the poem or poems about which you are writing. Here are some things to look for:

- *The period of time when a poem was written, together with significant events*. In this chapter, the illustrative essay about Whitman cites the American Civil War (1861–1865) as the dominating national event occurring at the time of the poems (pp. 952 and 956). Comparably, Hardy's "The Convergence of the Twain" in Chapter 14 (p. 652) was written as a commentary on the sinking of the British liner *Titanic* in 1912. Komunyakaa's "Facing It" in Chapter 15 (p. 699) uses the Vietnam Veterans Memorial Wall to reflect upon the violence of that war and its bitter legacy.
- *Social, natural, and/or political circumstances at the time of the poem*. What was the dominant political situation at the time? Who were the sorts of persons in political power? What attitudes were prevalent at the time with regard to the circumstances of nature? Wordsworth, for example, often creates an implicit comparison between the natural world at peace and negative human activities that are at odds with it.
- *Biographical details about a poet*. At what time in his or her life did the poet write a particular poem? What kind of work was he or she doing at the time, and which of the poet's particular concerns might be relevant to our understanding of the poem? Did the poet write anything about the poem in his or her

951

personal correspondence? What was this? Are there any results of interviews with the poet that might be introduced to explain the poem? What were the poet's aims in creating a particular poem?

• *Specific or general thoughts by the poet that are relevant to the poem.* Sometimes there might be details about a poet's thoughts on the thinking and reading he or she was doing, or on works of art, or on religious or philosophical musings. Langston Hughes was deeply concerned about the circumstances of African Americans in the United States and wrote many poems on this topic. Elaine Terranova was equally concerned with the condition of women and families, and her "Rush Hour" is an expression of this deep concern (Chapter 11, p. 556).

In planning your approach, you should aim at an essay that is relevant to the poem or poems you have chosen. Thus, your topic may be the nature of the poem's speaker, such as "The Character of Mueller's Speaker in 'Alive Together,'" or "Cummings's Use of the Speaker to Control Tone in 'if there are any heavens.'" Or it may be the poet's use of images, or metaphors, or symbols, such as "Shakespeare's Widely Varied Imagery in His Sonnets." Or you may want to write about a poet's use of allusions or the use of mythical materials. A rich field for discussion might be the comparison of poems or poets, such as "The Topic of Death in Frost's 'Out, Out—' and Sassoon's 'Dreamers,'" or "The Treatment of Love and Sexuality by Peacock in 'Desire' and Donne in 'The Sun Rising.'" The possibilities are endless. Of even greater significance than your choice of topic—which should be basically the same whether you are using or not using research—is your integration of research discoveries into the development of your essay.

Illustrative Student Essay Written with the Aid of Research

Although underlined sentences are not recommended by MLA style, they are used in this illustrative essay as teaching tools to emphasize the central idea, thesis sentence, and topic sentences.

Zweig 1

Micol Zweig

Put identifying information in upper left corner, double space.

Professor Melvin

English 112 25

25 April 2014

"Beat! Beat! Drums!" and "I Hear America Singing":

Two Whitman Poems Spanning the Civil War°

[1]   Comparing two of Walt Whitman's poems, "Beat! Beat! Drums!" and

"I Hear America Singing," alongside the historical background informing his

°These poems appear on pages 948 and 949.

Zweig 2

writing, helps in the understanding of both poems.* Walt Whitman was born in 1819, when American democracy was in its infancy. He held many jobs as a young man; at various times he worked as a printer, editor, and teacher, and in 1840 he even campaigned for future President Martin Van Buren (Callow 365).

As a keen observer, Whitman took many notes about what he saw. He started to write in celebration of America's potential. He wrote many poems about the people and places of his immediate environment, and these poems gave birth to his famous collection, *Leaves of Grass* (1855). Many critics have pointed out that Whitman was uncertain about his poetic skills before he began this collection. One critic remarks that "Whitman was not really a poet at all, but a man of the people with his eyes open and his senses hungry for experience" (Zweig 113). By the time of the Civil War in 1861, he had written many of his best known poems, but the experience of war was to transform him.

His "Beat! Beat! Drums!" was written in 1861 at the beginning of the Civil War. In this poem, Whitman expresses his disfavor of the war, claiming that the pounding of the drums, which represents the fierceness of war itself, is an egregious disruption of ordinary American life. His 1860 poem, "I Hear America Singing"—also published again in *Leaves of Grass* after the war had ended—serves as a sharp contrast to "Beat! Beat! Drums!" In this more tranquil poem, music is transformed to symbolize peace. Both poems serve as examples of how similar motifs may be used to exemplify very different moods and tones. Whitman's tone and his use of musical imagery demonstrate the difference between America at peace and America at war.†

Whitman's attitude towards the war was complex. As the war developed, he saw it as an opportunity for America to develop its own identity, but he also feared impending horrors of combat. "Beat! Beat! Drums!" reflects both the ominous nature of war and also the "patriotic fervor which swept the North" (Allen 75). In contrast, "I Hear America Singing" reflects the optimism in Whitman's poetry both before and after his many disturbing experiences during the war. "From the time Whitman visited his wounded

[2]

In MLA style, put author and page number in parentheses when author is not named in the sentence.

[3]

In MLA style, the header has the student's last name and page number.

[4]

*Central idea.
†Thesis sentence.

Zweig 3

brother George in Virginia in the spring of 1862 until the end of the war . . .

he visited thousands of soldiers in army hospitals" (Allen 84). On these visits

he sometimes saw people dying right in front of him, and he also saw piles of

amputated limbs that were decaying in the sun. "Beat! Beat! Drums!" describes

the high-pitched "ruthless force" (line 2) that he had perceived. "I Hear

America Singing," although first written before the war, was republished at a

time when Whitman's best work was behind him, when "there was not silence

but sporadic effort, sparse and diminished" (Zweig 345). Seen in this light, "I

Hear America Singing" can be seen as a looking back to earlier times in its

vision of a whole nation singing as individuals—yet as one—and a looking

forward to a hopeful future.

[5]   Though references to music form recurring images of sound in both

poems, they are used in each to symbolize different states. In "Beat! Beat!

Drums!" the blowing of the bugles and the beating of the drums are a warning

of the terrible and all-encompassing aspects of war. In this poem, the speaker

commands the fierce and pounding noises invoking the startling sound of

drums and bugles to serve as a warning of impending war. "Beat! beat!

drums!—blow! bugles! blow!" (1, 8, 14) is repeated every six to seven lines,

punctuating the flow of disturbing imagery in the lines surrounding them.

These repeated lines, with the exception of one word ("bugles") all have one

syllable, making the lines themselves sound like the military rhythm of a snare

drum which is a sharp contrast to the "varied carols" that each American

possesses in "I Hear America Singing." While the sounds of "Beat! Beat!

Drums!" attempt to unite and alert different people to the oncoming conflict,

the music in "I Hear America Singing" focuses on the idea that differences

are both the strength and hallmark of America. The speaker's admonition in

"Beat! Beat! Drums!" to increase the intensity of sound—"Then rattle quicker,

heavier drums—you bugles wilder blow" (15)—may be contrasted with the

varied rhythms of "I Hear America Singing," which come together as "strong

melodious songs" (11). This harmonious resolution of diverse songs sets a

When citing poetry in MLA style, cite the line number for the poem.

Zweig 4

very different tone from the one at the end of "Beat! Beat! Drums!," when the speaker's command has been realized: "So strong you thump O terrible drums—so loud you bugles blow" (21). The symbolic sounds of both poems convey contrasting states of mind.

In each of the Whitman poems, images of sound emphasize tone and   [6]
mood. "Beat! Beat! Drums!" conveys a tone of serious urgency. Where life had been going on peacefully before the outbreak of war, the drums and bugles "burst like a ruthless force" (2) through doors and windows, now rendering a peaceful existence impossible. These jarring sounds disrupt the studying scholar and "scatter the congregation" of "the solemn church" (3). The mood of the poem conveys hopelessness as the speaker wonders if life will be able to continue amidst the din. He asks, "Would the talkers be talking? would the singer attempt to sing?" (12). "I Hear America Singing" conveys the opposite tone, one of peaceful contentment and proud patriotism as the poet becomes an approving listener of the harmonies around him. There is a predominant feeling of optimism in this poem as the mechanics, carpenters, masons, and all others sing their respective songs. The reader gets a sense of America's strength and hope, unlike the lives of Americans during the disruption and strife of war, as all different types of people cheerfully sing "what belongs to him or her and none else" (9), and then at night these same people gather to sing melodiously together. "I Hear America Singing" stresses the individualism and optimism of a country emerging from the all-encompassing strife indicated by the incessant beating drums and blaring bugles of "Beat! Beat! Drums!"

As the poet of American democracy Whitman wrote about the great   [7]
events of his time. "Beat! Beat! Drums!" paints a disturbing picture for the reader, the image of an unstoppable army playing the shrieking music of destruction that affects everything in its path, leaving the bridegroom unhappy and the "peaceful farmer" without "any peace" (6). "I Hear America Singing" announces the significance of the individual—the "I" that is part of the melody of a large and prosperous nation at peace. In Walt Whitman's most famous and ambitious poem, "Song of Myself," the symbolic singing

Zweig 5

of "myself" announces the pride and exuberant presence of the speaker's ego amidst the diversity of a democratic nation. In "Beat! Beat! Drums!" and "I Hear America Singing" the images of sound are used to convey very different aspects of American life. While to some critics "Whitman's art as a poet" may be a matter of mystery (Van Doren xxiii) there is little doubt of his intense feelings about the Civil War and what he wrote about it. Reading the poems together, along with knowing about Whitman's life, brings greater meaning to each poem.

Zweig 6

Works Cited

In MLA style, the list of sources, called the works cited, begins a new page. Double space throughout.

Allen, Gay Wilson. *A Reader's Guide to Walt Whitman*. New York: Farrar, Straus and Giroux, 1970. Print.

Callow, Philip. *From Noon to Starry Night; A Life of Walt Whitman*. Chicago: Ivan R. Dee, 1992. Print.

Doren, Mark Van, ed. *The Portable Walt Whitman*. New York: Viking, 1973. Print.

Whitman, Walt. "Beat! Beat! Drums!" and "I Hear America Singing." *Literature: An Introduction to Reading and Writing, Compact Edition*.

List sources in alphabetical order.

Ed. Edgar V. Roberts and Robert Zweig. 6th ed. New York: Pearson, 2015. 948, 949. Print.

Zweig, Paul. *Walt Whitman: The Making of the Poet*. New York: Basic, 1984. Print.

Commentary on the Essay

The research objective of this essay is the introduction of biographical details as informational support for the topic of comparison and contrast. The opening paragraph, citing one research reference, places the two poems in the context of Whitman's life. In paragraph 2, the writer connects the poems to Whitman's unique qualities as an observer, citing a research reference in support of this capacity. In paragraph 3, the writer locates the poems in the time of the Civil War, pointing out how the poems deal with opposites of American life. Paragraph 4 introduces three research references that support the details of Whitman's actual Civil War experiences. Paragraphs 5 and 6, based on the texts of the two poems themselves, grow out of paragraph 4, for they deal with the opposing music of harshness, on the one hand, and "peaceful contentment and proud patriotism," on the other. In the final paragraph, 7, the writer introduces two additional research references, while stressing Whitman's intense feelings about the subject matter of the two poems.

USING SOURCES EFFECTIVELY

QUOTING TEXTS TO ILLUSTRATE YOUR POINT

Writing effectively about a literary work requires specific reference to the work itself—precise and carefully chosen quotations that help you make your case clearly and powerfully. This is especially true when writing about poems, where the specific words and how they are arranged are so important to a work's meaning and effect. At the same time, an accomplished writer will not overquote and expect the work to "explain itself" or to convey the essay's point or primary interpretation. Think of the writer's task as being a "curator" of an archive of valuable works of art who must display these works in a sequence and in a setting that allow them to shine.

For example, in paragraph 6, Micol Zweig's first draft quote from Whitman's poem reproduces the language but provides little context.

In each of the Whitman poems, images of sound emphasize tone and mood. For example, "Beat! Beat! Drums!" sets the scene:

Through the windows—through the doors—
burst like a restless force,
Into the solemn church, and scatter the
congregation,
Into the school where the scholar is studying:
Leave not the bridegroom quiet—no happiness
must he have now with his bride, ... (2–5)

This summation follows a quote that lacks focus and doesn't allow the writer to "own" his main idea. → Whitman here describes how many things have been disturbed by the war, and how no one is immune.

In revising this paragraph, Zweig realizes that simply reproducing a long passage from the poem here did not convey his interpretation very persuasively. Instead, he judiciously chooses a handful of key phrases that he relates directly to the tone and mood Whitman wants to capture, documents them correctly with quotation marks and the line numbers from the work, and uses them in the service of his primary argument. He embeds the quotations smoothly into his critical of the work, and they provide authentic evidence of what Zweig finds in the poem, allowing him to comment effectively on what Whitman is trying to achieve.

By carefully selecting key words and phrases from the poem, the writer provides real evidence supporting his thesis.

> In each of the Whitman poems, images of sound emphasize tone and mood. "Beat! Beat! Drums!" conveys a tone of serious urgency. Where life had been going on peacefully before the outbreak of war, the drums and bugles "burst like a ruthless force" (2) through doors and windows, now rendering a peaceful existence impossible. These jarring sounds disrupt the studying scholar and "scatter the congregation" of "the solemn church" (3). The mood of the poem conveys hopelessness as the speaker wonders if life will be able to continue amidst the din. He asks, "Would the talkers be talking? would the singer attempt to sing?" (12).

By using quotations selectively and strategically, Zweig not only gains authority for his argument from the work itself but also imbues his essay with greater rhetorical power by employing Whitman's exquisite phrases to illustrate his thesis. (For more information on quotations, see pages 54–56.)

PART IV
Reading and Writing About Drama

Chapter 20
The Dramatic Vision:
An Overview

AFTER STUDYING THIS MATERIAL, YOU SHOULD BE ABLE TO DO THE FOLLOWING:

- Distinguish between written drama (drama as text) and drama that is performed on stage
- Explain the development of dramatic character types
- Describe dramatic action, conflict, and plot
- Understand the general history of tragedy and comedy in performance
- Evaluate theatrical and literary elements of plays

Drama has much in common with the other genres of literature. Like fiction, drama focuses on one or a few major characters who enjoy success or endure failure as they face challenges and deal with other characters. Many plays are written in prose, as is fiction, on the principle that the language of drama should resemble the language of life as much as possible. Drama is also like poetry because both genres develop situations through speech and action. Indeed, a great number of plays, particularly those of past ages, exist as poetry. The dramatists of ancient Athens employed intricate poetic forms in their plays. Many European plays from the Renaissance through the nineteenth century were written in blank verse or rhymed couplets, a tradition of poetic drama preserved by contemporary dramatists such as Christopher Fry and T. S. Eliot.

As separate genres, however, drama, fiction, and poetry have major differences. Fiction is distinguished from drama because the essence of fiction is narration: the making known or relating or recounting of a sequence of events or actions—the actual telling of a story. Poetry is unlike both drama and fiction because it exists in many formal and informal shapes, and it is the shortest of the genres. Although we usually read poetry silently and alone, it is also frequently read aloud before groups. Unlike both fiction and poetry, drama is literature designed for impersonation by people—actors—for the benefit and delight of other people—an audience.

Drama as Literature

Drama is a unique genre because it can be presented and discussed both as literature—drama itself—and as performance—the production of plays in the theater. The major literary aspects of drama are the *text, language, characters, plot, structure, point of view, tone, symbolism,* and *theme* or *meaning.* All these elements have remained constant throughout the history of drama. In addition, drama written in poetic forms, such as Shakespeare's *Hamlet* (Chapter 21) and *A Midsummer Night's Dream* (Chapter 22), includes elements such as meter and rhyme.

The Text Is the Printed (or Handwritten) Play

The text of a play is a plan for bringing the play into action on the stage. The most notable features of the text are *dialogue, monologue,* and *stage directions.* **Dialogue** is the conversation of two or more characters. A **monologue** is spoken by a single character who is usually alone onstage. **Stage directions** are the playwright's instructions about facial and vocal expression, movement and action, gesture and "body language," stage appearance, lighting, and similar matters. In addition, some dramatists, such as George Bernard Shaw and Tennessee Williams, provide introductions and explanations for their plays. Such material may be considered additional directions for interpretation and staging.

Language, Imagery, and Style Bring the Play to Life

What we learn about characters, relationships, and conflicts is conveyed in dramatic language. Through dialogue, and sometimes through soliloquy and aside, characters use language to reveal intimate details about their lives and their deepest thoughts—their loves, hatreds, hopes, and plans.

To bring such revelations before the audience, dramatists employ words that have wide-ranging connotations and that acquire many layers of meaning. Such is the case with the words "beautiful" and "pretty" in Jane Martin's *Beauty* (this chapter). Similarly, playwrights can introduce metaphors and symbols that contribute significantly to a play's meaning and impact, as with the broken birdcage in Glaspell's *Trifles* (this chapter), and the curtain pulled back to reveal the empty tomb in *The Visit to the Sepulcher* (this chapter).

Dramatists also make sure that the words of their characters fit the circumstances, the time, and the place of the play. O'Neill's Mrs. Rowland illustrates the language of early twentieth-century America, and Shakespeare's Hamlet speaks Elizabethan blank verse, almost academic prose, and "one-liner" remarks. Benjamin and Ronnie in Hwang's *Trying to Find Chinatown* (this chapter) speak with the diction used by many people of their age and of their time. In addition, dramatists employ accents, dialects, idiom, jargon, and clichés to indicate character traits. The gravediggers in *Hamlet* speak in a Renaissance English lower-class dialect that distinguishes them from the aristocratic characters in the play.

Characters Talk Themselves Alive Through Speech and Action

Drama necessarily focuses on its **characters,** who are persons the playwright creates to embody the play's actions, ideas, and attitudes. Of course, characters are characters, no matter where we find them, and many of the character types that populate drama are also inhabitants of fiction. The major quality of characters in drama, however, is that they come alive through their speeches and actions. To understand them, we must listen to their words and watch and interpret how they react both to their circumstances and to the characters around them. They are also sometimes described and discussed by other characters, but primarily they are rendered dramatically.

Drama is not designed to present the full life stories of its characters. Rather, the plots of drama bring out intense and highly focused oppositions or conflicts in which the characters are engaged. In accord with such conflicts, most major dramatic characters are considered as *protagonists* and *antagonists*. The **protagonist** (the first or leading struggler or actor), usually the central character, is opposed by the **antagonist** (the one who struggles against). A classic conflict is seen in Shakespeare's *Hamlet,* in which Prince Hamlet, the protagonist, tries first to confirm and then to punish the crime committed by King Claudius, his uncle and the play's antagonist.

Just as in fiction, drama presents us with both *round* and *flat* characters. A **round, dynamic, developing,** and **growing character,** like Shakespeare's Hamlet and Ibsen's Nora, possesses great **motivation.** The round character profits from experience and undergoes a development in awareness, insight, understanding, moral capacity, and the ability to make decisions. A **flat, static, fixed,** and **unchanging character** does not undergo any change or growth. There is no rule, however, that flat characters must be dull. They can be charming, vibrant, entertaining, and funny, but even if they are memorable in these ways, they remain fixed and static.

Dramatic characters can also be considered as *realistic, nonrealistic, stereotyped* (or *stock*), *ancillary,* and *symbolic.* **Realistic characters** are designed to seem like individualized women and men; the dramatist gives them thoughts, desires, motives, personalities, and lives of their own. **Nonrealistic characters** are often undeveloped and symbolic. An interesting example is Torvald Helmer of Ibsen's *A Dollhouse* (Chapter 24). In terms of his assumptions and expectations, he is nonrealistic for most of the play, but he becomes sadly realistic when he recognizes the disastrous effects of his previous outlook on life and marriage. He is unique because he does not so much grow as undergo an almost instant change.

Throughout the ages, drama and other types of literature have relied on **stereotype** or **stock characters**—that is, unindividualized characters whose actions and speeches make them seem to have been taken from a mold. The general types developed in the comedy of ancient Athens and Rome, and in the drama of the Renaissance, are the *stubborn father,* the *romantic hero* and *heroine,* the *clever male servant,* the *saucy maidservant,* the *braggart soldier,* the *bumpkin,* the *trickster,* the *victim,* the *insensitive husband,* the *shrewish wife,* and the *lusty youth.* Modern drama continues these stereotypes, and it has also invented many of its own, such as the *private eye,* the *stupid bureaucrat,* the *corrupt politician,* the *independent pioneer,* the *kindly prostitute,* the *loner cowboy,* and the *town sheriff who never loses the draw in a showdown.*

There are also **ancillary characters** who set off or highlight the protagonist and who provide insight into the action. The first type, the **foil,** has been a feature of drama since its beginnings in ancient Athens. The foil is a character who is to be compared and contrasted with the protagonist. Laertes and Fortinbras are foils in *Hamlet.* Because of the play's circumstances, Laertes is swept into destruction along with Hamlet, whereas Fortinbras picks up the pieces and gets life moving again after the final death scene. The second type is the **choric figure,** who is loosely connected to the choruses of ancient drama. Usually the choric figure is a single character, often a confidant of the protagonist, such as Hamlet's friend

Horatio. When the choric figure expresses ideas about the play's major issues and actions, he or she is called a **raisonneur** (the French word meaning "reasoner" [but also "quibbler"]) or **commentator.**

Any of the foregoing types of characters can also be **symbolic** in the context of individual plays. They can symbolize ideas, moral values, religious concepts, ways of life, or some other abstraction. For instance, Fred Higgins in *Mulatto* (Chapter 23), by Langston Hughes, symbolizes the cynicism, indifference, cruelty, and misuse of responsibility that accompany the concept of racial supremacy. Ronnie from Hwang's *Trying to Find Chinatown* elucidates many prejudices about how people feel about Asian Americans.

Action, Conflict, and Plot Make Up a Play's Development

Plays are made up of a series of sequential and related **actions** or **incidents.** The actions are connected by **chronology**—the logic of time—and the term given to the principles underlying this ordered chain of actions and reactions is **plot,** which is a connected plan or pattern of causation. The impulse controlling the connections is **conflict,** which refers to people or circumstances—the antagonist—that the pro-tagonist tries to overcome. Most dramatic conflicts are vividly apparent because the clashes of wills and characters take place onstage, right in front of our eyes. Conflicts can also exist between groups, although conflicts between individuals are more identifiable and therefore more common in plays.

Dramatic plots can be simplified and schematized, but most of them are as com-plicated as life itself. Special complications result from a **double** or **multiple plot**—two or more different but related lines of action. Usually one of these plots is the **main plot,** but the **subplot** can be independently important and sometimes even more interesting. Such a situation occurs in Shakespeare's *A Midsummer Night's Dream,* where the exploits of Bottom and the "mechanicals," which form just one of the four strands of plot, are so funny that they often steal the show in productions of the play.

Structure Is the Play's Pattern of Organization

The way a play is arranged or laid out is its **structure.** With variations, many tradi-tional plays contain elements that constitute a structure of *five stages:* (1) *exposition* or *introduction,* (2) *complication* and *development,* (3) *crisis* or *climax,* (4) *falling action,* and (5) *dénouement, resolution,* or *catastrophe.* In the nineteenth century, the German novelist and critic Gustav Freytag (1816–1895) visualized this pattern as a pyramid (though he used six elements rather than five). In the so-called **Freytag pyramid,** the exposition and complication lead up to a high point of tension—the crisis or climax—followed by the falling action and the catastrophe.

This pyramidal pattern of organization can be observed to greater or lesser degrees throughout many plays. Some plays follow the pattern closely, but often there is uncertainty about when one phase of the structure ends and the next one begins. In addition, words defining some of the stages are variable. Even though students of drama agree about the meaning of the first two stages, the terms for the final three are not used with precision. With these reservations, the Freytag pyramid is valuable in the analysis of dramatic plot structure.

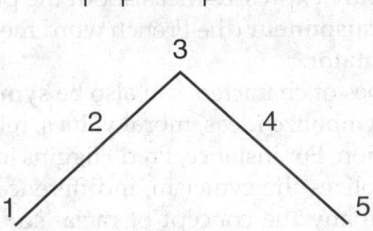

1. Exposition or Introduction
2. Complication and Development
3. Crisis or Climax
4. Falling Action
5. Dénouement, Resolution, or Catastrophe

1. *The **exposition** or **introduction** brings out everything we need to know to understand and follow what is to happen in the play.* In the first part of a drama, the dramatist introduces the play's background, characters, situations, and conflicts. Although exposition is occasionally presented through direct statements to the audience, the better method is to render it dramatically. Both major and minor characters thus perform the task of exposition through dramatic dialogue—describing situations, actions, and plans, and also explaining the traits and motives of other characters. In such a way, Sophocles provides expository material in the prologue to *Oedipus the King* (Chapter 21), featuring Oedipus, the Priest, and Creon. Eugene O'Neill in *Before Breakfast* dramatizes the exposition in the early actions and speeches of the major character, Mrs. Rowland. In *Hamlet*, Horatio's explanations to Barnardo and Marcellus provide vital information about circumstances in the Danish court.

2. *The **complication** and **development** mark the onset of the play's major conflicts.* In this second stage, also called the **rising action,** we see the beginning of difficulties that seem overwhelming and insoluble, as in *Hamlet*, where we learn in the exposition that the death of the king (Hamlet's father) has occurred before the play opens. Complication develops as the characters try to learn answers to some of the following perplexing questions: Was the death a murder? If so, who did it? How was it done? How can the murderer be identified? Is the man suspected of the murder truly guilty? What should be done about the murder? What punishment should there be? In *A Midsummer Night's Dream*, less serious complications result from the development of issues like these: Can young lovers overcome parental opposition? Can a bumbling group of amateur actors successfully perform a play before the highest social group in the nation? Can a squabble among supernatural beings be brought to a peaceful conclusion? In addition, Hwang's *Trying to Find Chinatown* examines complications that arise when Ronnie does not understand why Benjamin considers himself to be Asian American.

3. *The crisis or climax is the culmination of the play's conflicts and complications—the intense moments of decision.* The uncertainty and anxiety of the complication lead to the third stage, the **crisis** ("turning point") or **climax** ("high point"). In this third stage, all the converging circumstances compel the hero or heroine to recognize what needs to be done to resolve the play's major conflict. Another way of considering the crisis or climax is to define it as that point in the play when uncertainty ends and inevitability begins, as when Hamlet vows vengeance after drawing conclusions about the king's reaction to the player scene.

4. *The falling action—a time of avoidance and delay—forms the downward slope of the pyramid, as complicating elements defer the play's conclusion.* In *Hamlet*, for example, a number of scenes make up the falling action: Hamlet's decision not to kill Claudius at prayer, Hamlet's departure for England, the gravedigger scene and the conflicts at Ophelia's grave, and the murderous conspiracy of Claudius and Laertes. In *Oedipus the King*, Oedipus continues to seek confirming evidence about the death of his father, although by the end of Episode 3— the climax—he has all the information he needs to determine that he himself is the murderer.

5. The dénouement is the end, the logical outcome of what has gone before. In the **dénouement** ("unraveling") or **resolution** ("untying"), also called the **catastrophe** ("overturning"), all tragic protagonists undergo suffering or death, all mysteries are explained, all conflicts are resolved, all mistakes are corrected, all dastardly schemes are defeated, all long-lost children are identified, all obstacles to love are overcome, all deserving characters are rewarded, and the play ends. In short, the function of the dénouement is to end complications and conflicts, not to create new ones. It is important to observe that the word *catastrophe* for the final dramatic stage should not necessarily be construed in the sense of a calamity, even though most tragic catastrophes are calamitous. It is probably best, however, to use the words *dénouement* and *resolution* as general descriptions of a play's final stage and to reserve *catastrophe* for tragedies.

Of great significance is that the various points of the pyramid define an abstract model that is applicable to most plays—tragedy, comedy, and tragicomedy alike. Since the time of Shakespeare, however, most dramatists writing in English have been concerned less with dramatic form than with dramatic effect. As a result, many plays in English do not perfectly follow the pattern charted in the Freytag pyramid. You should, therefore, be prepared for plays that conceal or delay essential parts of the exposition; create a number of separate crises and climaxes; confine the climax, falling action, and dénouement into a short space at the play's end; or modify the formal pattern in other significant ways.

Point of View Focuses on a Play's Major Character (or Characters) and Ideas

In fiction, **point of view** refers to the narrative *voice* of the story, the speaker or guiding intelligence through which the characters and actions are presented (see Chapter 2). In drama, the term refers generally to a play's **perspective** or focus— the ways in which dramatists direct attention to the play's characters and their concerns. In the theater, dramatists govern our responses visually by putting major characters on stage and keeping them there. That these characters are always speaking and moving before our eyes makes us devote our attention to them, become involved with them, and see things pretty much as they see things. For example, once the opening speeches of *Hamlet* are over, the play focuses directly on Hamlet and never wavers, even after he lies dead on the stage in the last act. In O'Neill's *Before Breakfast,* the entire play is a monologue spoken by Mrs. Rowland, and we therefore see things from her perspective even though we recognize her limitations and shortcomings.

The dramatist can also keep characters and issues in our minds by causing other characters to speak about them. Thus most of the speeches in Glaspell's *Trifles* are designed to shape our understanding of what Minnie Wright did to her husband on the lonely Wright farm, and why she did it. Because everyone is always talking about Minnie and her boorish but recently murdered husband, the play makes this perspective inescapable.

Tone or Atmosphere Creates Mood and Attitude

Playwrights have unique ways of conveying **tone** or **atmosphere** beyond those techniques used by poets and fiction writers (see Chapter 6). Some of these are vocal ranges, stage gestures (such as rolling one's eyes, throwing up one's hands, staring at another character, holding one's forehead in despair, jumping for joy, making side remarks, and staggering in grief). Even silence, intensive stares, and shifting glances can be effective means for creating moods and controlling attitudes.

Whereas the voices and actions of actors establish mood on the stage, we do not have these guides in reading. There are written guides, however, to dramatic tone: Sometimes a playwright uses stage directions as an indication of tone, as Ibsen does in *A Dollhouse,* directing the inflections of a speaker's voice with the stage direction that she is shaking her head when speaking. Similarly, Hughes suggests the mood of one of his characters in *Mulatto,* with the direction that he "runs" to his mother and hugs her "teasingly."

When such directions are absent—and usually they are—we need to take the diction, tempo, imagery, and context as clues to the tone of specific speeches and whole plays. In the opening scene of *Hamlet,* among the guards, Shakespeare uses short and rapidly delivered sentences to create a mood of fearfulness, anxiety, and apprehensiveness. This opening passage anticipates the Ghost's forthcoming charge of murder against Claudius, and it also prepares us for the ominous events to come in the rest of the play.

One of the most common methods playwrights employ to control the tone of the play is **dramatic irony.** This type of **situational** (as opposed to **verbal**) **irony** refers to circumstances in which characters have only a partial, incorrect, or misguided understanding of what is happening, while both readers and other characters understand the situation completely. Readers hence become concerned about the characters and hope that they will develop understanding quickly enough to avoid the problems bedeviling them and the threats endangering them. The classic example of dramatic irony occurs in Sophocles's *Oedipus the King:* As Oedipus condemns the murderer of his father, he also condemns himself, though unwittingly.

Like many other modern theaters, these theaters feature a **thrust stage** or **apron stage** (like the **platform stage** used in the time of Shakespeare), which enlarges the proscenium stage with an acting area projecting into the audience by twenty or more feet. It is on this apron that a good deal of the acting occurs. Closely related to the apron stage is **theater-in-the-round,** a stage open on all sides like a boxing ring, surrounded by the audience. Productions for both types of stages are especially lively because the actors usually enter and leave through the same doorways and aisles used by the audience.

Sets (Scenery) Create the Play's Location and Appearance

Most productions use **sets** (derived from the phrase "set scenes," i.e., fixed scenes) or **scenery** to establish the action in place and time, to underscore the ideas of the director, and to determine the level of reality of the production. Sets are constructed and decorated to indicate a specific place (a living room, a kitchen, a throne room, a forest, a graveyard) or a detached and indeterminate place with a specific atmosphere (an open plain, a vanished past, a nightmarish future). When we first see the stage at the beginning of a performance, it is the scenery that we see, bringing the play to life through walls, windows, stairways, furniture, furnishings, and painted locations. The setting directions for Hwang's *Trying to Find Chinatown* simply state, "A street corner on the Lower East Side, New York City. The Present." One could imagine this being a very bare production with a street sign and some city scenery, or perhaps just a street sign with the proper clothing to indicate the present time.

In most proscenium stages, the sets establish a permanent location or **scene** resembling a framed picture. All characters enter this setting, and they leave once they have achieved their immediate purpose. Such a fixed scene is established in *Oedipus the King,* which is set entirely in front of the royal palace of ancient Thebes, and in *Before Breakfast,* set in the dreary kitchen of a New York apartment. Generally, one-act plays rely on a single setting and a short imagined time of action. Many full-length plays also confine the action to a single setting despite the longer imagined time during which the action takes place.

Because sets are usually elaborate and costly, many producers use single fixed-scene sets that are flexible and easily changed. Some productions employ a single, neutral set throughout the play and then mark scene changes with the physical introduction of movable **properties** (or **props**)—chairs, tables, beds, flower vases, hospital curtain-enclosures, trees, shovels, skulls, and so on. The use of props to mark separate scenes is a necessity in modern productions of plays that require constant scene changes, like *Hamlet.* Interestingly, many productions make scene changes an integral part of the drama by having costumed stagehands, or even the actors themselves, carry props on and off the stage. In a 1995 New York production of *Hamlet,* for example, Hamlet himself (performed by Ralph Fiennes) carried in the chairs needed for the spectators of the player scene.

The constant changing of scenery is sometimes avoided by the use of a **unit set**—a series of platforms, rooms, stairs, and exits that form the locations for all the play's actions. The movement of the characters from place to place within the unit set marks the shifting scenes and changing topics.

Like characters, the setting can be realistic or nonrealistic. A **realistic setting,** sometimes called a **naturalistic setting,** requires extensive construction and properties, for the object is to create as lifelike a stage as possible. In O'Neill's *Before Breakfast,* for example, the setting is a realistic copy of a tacky early-twentieth-century apartment kitchen. By contrast, a **nonrealistic setting** is nonrepresentational and often symbolic. Sometimes a realistic play can be made suggestive and expressive through the use of a nonrealistic setting. Martin's *Beauty* (this chapter), for example, emphasizes the fundamental bareness of the scene by the indication of a "minimalist" setting.

Lighting Creates Clarity, Emphasis, and Mood

In ancient and medieval times, plays were performed in daylight, and hence no artificial illumination was required. With the advent of indoor theaters and evening performances, **lighting** became a necessity. At first, artificial lighting was provided by lanterns, candelabras, sconces, and torches (yes, some theaters burned down), and indirect lighting was achieved by reflectors and valances—all of which were used with great ingenuity and effect. Later, gaslight and limelight lamps replaced the earlier open flames.

The evolution of theater lighting reached its climax with the development of electric lights in the nineteenth century. Today, dramatic performances are enhanced by virtually all the technical features of our electronic age—including specialized lamps, color filters, spotlights, dimmers, and simulated fires. This dazzling technology, which employs hundreds or even thousands of lights of varying intensity in unlimited combination, is used to highlight individual characters, to isolate and emphasize various parts of the stage, to establish times, and generally to shape the moods of individual scenes. Lighting can also divide the stage or a unit set into different acting areas simply through the illumination of one section and the darkening of the rest. The result is that lighting has become an integral element of set design, especially when the dramatist uses a **scrim** (a curtain that becomes transparent when illuminated from behind), which permits great variety in the portrayal of scenes and great rapidity in scene changes. In our day it is a rare stage indeed that does not contain an elaborate, computerized, and complicated (and expensive) lighting system.

Costumes and Makeup Establish the Nature and Appearance of the Actors

Actors make plays vivid by wearing **costumes** and using **makeup,** which help the audience understand a play's time period together with the occupations, mental outlooks, and socioeconomic conditions of the characters. Costumes, which include not only dress but also items such as jewelry, good-luck charms, swords, firearms, and canes, can be used realistically (farm women in plain clothes, a salesman in a business suit, a king in rich robes, a fashionable woman with fine jewelry) or symbolically (a depressed character wearing black). Makeup usually enhances an actor's facial features, just as it can fix the illusion of youth or age or emphasize a character's joy or sorrow.

The Audience Responds to the Performance and Helps to Shape It

To be complete, plays require an interaction of actors and **audience.** Drama enacts fictional or historical events as if they were happening in the present, and members of the audience—whether spectators or readers—are direct witnesses to the dramatic action from start to finish. The audience most definitely has a creative impact on theatrical performances. Although audiences are made up of people who otherwise do not know each other, they have a common bond of interest in the play. Therefore, even though they are isolated by the darkness of the theater in which they sit, they respond communally. Their reactions (e.g., laughter, gasps, applause) provide instant feedback to the actors and thus continually influence the delivery and pace of the performance. For this reason, drama *in the theater* is the most immediate and accessible of the literary arts. There is no intermediary between the audience and the stage action—no narrator, as in prose fiction, and no speaker, as in poetry.

Drama from Ancient Times to Our Own:
Tragedy, Comedy, and Additional Forms

Today, people interested in drama have more options than at any other time in human history. There is professional live theater in many major cities, and touring theatrical troupes reach areas with smaller populations. Many cities and towns have amateur community theaters, and so do many schools and churches. Movie theaters and multiplexes are flourishing. Television has brought film versions of plays to the home screen, together with innumerable situation comedies ("**sitcoms**"), continuous narrative dramas (including **soap operas**), made-for-TV films, documentary dramas ("**docudramas**"), short skits on comedy shows, and many other types. All these different genres ultimately spring from the drama that was developed twenty-six hundred years ago in Athens, the leading ancient Greek city-state. Although subsequent centuries have produced many variations, the types the Athenians created are still as important today as they were then. They are tragedy and comedy.[1]

Tragedy and Comedy Originated in Ancient Greece

During the sixth century BCE, drama first arose from choral presentations the Athenians held during religious festivals celebrating Dionysus, the god of wine, conviviality, sexual vitality, ecstasy, fertility, and freedom. The choruses were made up of young men who sang or chanted lengthy songs that the Athenians called **dithyrambs;** the choruses also performed interpretive dance movements during the presentations. The dithyrambs were not dramatizations but rather recitations, which changed to being dramatic when a member of the chorus was designated to step forward and impersonate a particular hero through the process of **acting.** Soon, additional men from the choruses took acting roles, and the focus of the performances shifted from the choral group to individual actors. Greek **tragedy**

---

[1] Fuller discussions of tragedy and comedy are presented in Chapters 21 and 22.

as we know it had come into being. It was this pattern of drama that during the fifth century BCE produced a golden age of tragedy. Most of the tragedies have been lost, and only a small but very significant number of plays by the three greatest Athenian dramatists—Aeschylus, Sophocles, and Euripides—have survived.

Not long after the emergence of tragedy, **comedy** became an additional feature of the festivals. Because the ancient Athenians encouraged free speech, at least for males, the comedy writers created a boisterous, lewd, and freely critical type of burlesque comedy that later critics called **Old Comedy.** The eleven surviving plays of the comic dramatist Aristophanes represent this tradition. In the fourth century BCE, after Athenian power and freedom had declined because of the debilitating Peloponnesian War at the end of the fifth century BCE, this type of comedy was replaced by **Middle Comedy,** a more social, discreet, and international drama, and then by **New Comedy,** a type of play featuring the development of situation, plot, and character. The best-known writer of New Comedy was Menander, whose plays for centuries were thought to be totally lost. In the past hundred years, however, a number of fragments of his work have been discovered, including one play in its entirety.

Both of these Greek dramatic types have proved long lasting. The introduction of subject matter about loss in the earliest tragedies has led to today's common understanding that tragedy dramatizes an individual's fall from a secure and elevated position to social or personal defeat. Likewise, what we usually consider typical comedies are directly linked to the pattern of ancient New Comedy: plays that dramatize the regeneration of individuals who begin in insecurity and end with their overcoming troubles and anticipating happiness.

Tragedy and Comedy Were of Less Significance in Ancient Rome

The two Athenian dramatic forms were adopted by the Romans during the periods of the Republic (before 29 BCE) and the Empire (after 29 BCE). Although Republican Rome produced writers of note who created comedies (Plautus, c. 254–184 BCE, and Terence, c. 195 or 185–159 BCE), the only significant playwright of imperial times was the tragedian Seneca (4 BCE–65 CE), who wrote "closet dramas"—that is, plays designed to be read in private, household rooms, but not performed in public.

Ancient Drama Faded along with the Breakup of the Western Roman Empire

As the Roman Empire in Western Europe disintegrated in the fifth century CE, many of its institutions, including the theater, disintegrated with it. In the next five centuries, often called the "Dark Ages," Europe fell into feudalism, characterized by political decentralization and social fragmentation. The intellectuals of the period—most of them clergy—were creating Christian theology and establishing the growing church while abandoning the memories and records of the past, of which drama was a major element. As far as we know, there were no public theaters, no patrons able or willing to support public performances, no popular audiences with the money to pay for admission, no official permission by secular and religious authorities to perform plays, and no practicing dramatists—in short, there was no organized theater. It is hard to believe, however, that the human need for stories and fantasies did not remain. Tales and songs were unquestionably passed on from parents to children and community to community throughout these otherwise gloomy centuries.

Medieval Drama Developed as a Part of Church Services

When drama emerged hundreds of years after the fall of Rome, it had little to do with the Greek and Roman dramatic tradition, because it was a creation of the Christian church. It was at some point in the tenth century—approximately when the medieval period or Middle Ages were emerging from the Dark Ages—that the clergy started to realize the potentiality of dramatic presentations within the mass. It was then that the **trope**—a short dramatic interlude performed in conjunction with the mass, either with or without musical accompaniment—developed in the churches. Tropes were not considered as separate dramas, however, but became an integral part of regular services.

The earliest tropes were written for Easter rituals. The prototype of the Easter trope, which is included here, represented the discovery of the empty tomb as evidence of Christ's resurrection. This is the *Visitatio Sepulchri*, or *The Visit to the Sepulcher*, often known as the *Quem Quaeritis* ("Whom are you seeking?") *trope*. This is considered the first European drama, from which all later medieval, renaissance, and modern dramas have developed. Authored by persons who are unknown and forever unknowable, the trope was written to be delivered in Latin and was chanted not for the people but for cloistered monks and priests. It was enacted many times both on the continent and the British Isles, and in later centuries it became a regular feature of Easter worship. It has survived in a variety of forms in medieval manuscripts. Some versions contain detailed directions about performance, and some are cast in a question-and-answer format.

Although the *Quem Quaeritis trope* was part of a ritual, it clearly involved impersonation—and therefore drama—to the degree that priests and monks represented the persons and scenes contained in the gospel accounts of the resurrection. The heart of the trope is that the Angel at the tomb announces the resurrection to the three Marys, who then leave to proclaim the news.

ANONYMOUS

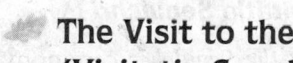

The Visit to the Sepulcher
(Visitatio Sepulchri) (tenth century CE)

[CAST OF CHARACTERS]

[The Angel at the Tomb]
[Mary the Mother of James the Younger and Joses]
[Mary Magdalene]
[Mary of Bethany, the Sister of Martha and Lazarus°]

°Although gospel accounts are in accord about the first two Marys, there is no agreement about the third woman, who is named *Salome* by Mark and *Joanna* by Luke. Neither of the gospel accounts of the Resurrection indicates that Mary of Bethany was the third Mary. Nevertheless, medieval tradition had it that there was a third Mary, and that she was Mary the sister of Lazarus and Martha, most likely on the authority of John 12:7, where Jesus implies that this Mary will be one of those to anoint his dead body.

[*Scene: The Sepulcher in which Christ was entombed after the Crucifixion. The* ANGEL, *dressed in white and holding a palm leaf, enters and sits beside a location curtained off to represent the tomb. Behind the curtain is a table or other surface representing a burial slab on which there is a linen sheet (i.e., the burial shroud supplied by Joseph of Aramathea). The three* MARYS *enter, carrying vessels [thuribles] as though they are intending to anoint Christ's body with aromatic oils and spices. At first they do not see the tomb, and they wander about until they do. Then they stop in front of the* ANGEL.]

ANGEL: Whom are you seeking in this Sepulcher, O followers of Christ?

THE THREE HOLY WOMEN: [*Speaking together.*] Jesus of Nazareth, who was crucified, O heavenly one.

ANGEL: [*Pulling back the curtain to show the empty tomb.*] He is not here. He has been resurrected, as was predicted. Go forth, tell everyone that he is risen. Spread the news!

THE THREE HOLY WOMEN: [*Kneeling and singing.*] Alleluia! Today Christ the Lord, the Son of God, the Mighty Lion, has been resurrected! Thanks be to God! Tell it to all the world!

5 ANGEL: Come and see the place where the Lord was laid.

[*THE THREE HOLY WOMEN examine the empty tomb and, with the* ANGEL, *display the burial shroud.*]

ANGEL: Alleluia! Alleluia! Hurry, tell the disciples that the Lord has risen! Alleluia! Alleluia! [*He exits, singing alleluias.*]

THE THREE HOLY WOMEN: [*Rejoicing, and singing in unison.*] The Lord, who hung on the tree for us, has risen from the grave! Alleluia!

[*They exit, joyfully repeating these lines.*]

QUESTIONS

1. What dramatic characteristics, as opposed to the obvious theology, do you find in this brief play?
2. Describe the play's dramatic actions. What sorts of movements would have been carried out? How extensive might have been the use of properties?
3. How do you imagine this play would have affected people attending the service in which it was performed?

Comparable Dramatic Ceremonies Followed the *Visitatio Sepulchri*

During the eleventh and twelfth centuries, the *Visit to the Sepulcher* ceremony became more elaborate, with additional characters and actions, such as the race by Peter and John to the tomb and Mary Magdalen's recognition of the risen Christ after having first confused him for a gardener. Some of the ceremonies, which were eventually performed before congregations, became extensive enough to require a lengthy performance. Historians of drama observe that this Easter ceremony was *dramatic liturgy* rather than *liturgical drama*, but any congregations present would likely have ignored this distinction. Instead they would have welcomed the ceremony as something totally new, dramatic, vital, and exciting.

In addition to the Easter pageantry, the church also developed special Christmas ceremonies, such as those for the Three Wise Men, the Shepherds, the scene at the stable, the ranting Herod, and the Slaughter of the Innocents (Innocents Day was and still is December 28). These ceremonies were observed as regular parts of Easter and Christmas rituals for hundreds of years after their beginnings in the tenth century.

A New Kind of Drama, the Corpus Christi Play, Grew Independently of the Church

Growing out of the religious dramatic tradition, a full-blown religious and civic drama developed in the fourteenth century. This was the Corpus Christi (i.e., "Body of Christ") play, which evolved just as the drama of ancient Athens had developed out of religious festivals for the god Dionysus in the sixth century BCE.[2] The major expression of the new religious drama came during the celebration of Corpus Christi Day, a celebration of the doctrine of transubstantiation (i.e., during mass, Eucharistic bread and wine are believed to become miraculously transformed into the real body and blood of Christ). The Corpus Christi feast is observed on the first Thursday after Trinity Sunday, which itself is the first Sunday after Pentecost.

Corpus Christi Day regularly featured local processions devoted to the worship of the Eucharist, and in this way it brought religious celebration into the streets and before the public. Because the feast occurred at the end of the liturgical year, it coincided with the beginning of good weather. The winter and spring rains abated, daylight hours lengthened, short trips from country villages to nearby towns became possible, and people could spend an entire day outside and still be comfortable.

The goal of the new plays was to create a complete **cycle,** dramatizing the biblical accounts of world history from the Creation to Judgment Day. The plays were produced by local craft guilds, the members of whom were master tradesmen. Hence the plays were also known as *mysteries,* or *mystery plays.* Naturally, the guild masters wanted to boost the prestige of their towns and their own wealth and power. They therefore welcomed the customers and patrons who thronged to these annual religious celebrations. Although there were as yet no professional acting companies like the one that Shakespeare was to join in the late sixteenth century, the annual staging of the Corpus Christi plays required many participants. The planning by the local guilds was therefore complex and challenging; the result was an engaging and inspiring drama.

As the Corpus Christi observations or celebrations grew in importance, the plays became a highlight of town life in the early summer. By the fifteenth century as many as forty towns had their own cycles. Some were large and elaborate; some—probably those performed in the smaller towns—were modest. Often the performances took place not only on Corpus Christi Thursday but also on Friday and Saturday, thus creating an extensive religious and secular celebration. Although the texts of most of these plays have been lost, cycles from four towns have been preserved. These cycles, named after the towns that presented them, contain more than 150 plays, or "pageants."

See pages 973 and 1022–1027.

English Replaced Latin as the Language of the Corpus Christi Plays

A major influence on the Corpus Christi drama—with profound implications for later drama—was the increasing importance of the English language at this time. During the two centuries following the Norman Conquest in 1066, the ruling and intellectual languages of England had been French and Latin. By the fourteenth century, however, things were changing: English had been enriched with close to 10,000 French words (a huge number of which we still retain) and was reasserting its role as the major language of England. More and more, the governing classes were committed to England—having a centuries-long tradition there—and used English as the language of intellectual and political discourse. Native writers began looking with increased favor on English as a literary language. A new literature in English—including drama—was ripe for development.

Other Religious Dramas Originated after the Corpus Christi Plays

In the course of time, additional types of religious dramas were developed. One of these was the **miracle play,** a devotional dramatization of the lives of saints. In addition, the **morality play** was developed as a genre instructing the faithful in the proper way to lead a devotional life. The most famous of these, in about 1500, was *Everyman,* which even today retains a good deal of interest and power.

In the Renaissance, Ancient and Medieval Traditions Fused to Create a New Secular Drama

In the sixteenth century, drama became liberated from these religious foundations and began rendering the twists and turns of more secular human conflicts. It was also at this time that the drama of ancient Greece and Rome was rediscovered. Therefore, the performing tradition growing out of the medieval church was combined with the surviving ancient tragedies and comedies to create an entirely new drama that quickly reached its highest point in the plays of Shakespeare. In this way, tragedy and comedy, the forms originated by the Athenians, had a revival during the Renaissance in Europe.[3]

New Types of Drama Have Developed Since the Renaissance

Renaissance drama was by no means a copy of ancient forms, however, even though a number of sixteenth- and seventeenth-century playwrights, including Shakespeare, reworked many of the ancient plays. The plays of Renaissance England, and later the plays of the United States, offer mixtures of tragedy and comedy. For example, some of Shakespeare's comedies treat disturbing and potentially destructive topics, just as many of his tragedies include scenes that are farcical,

---

The Renaissance revival of drama also transformed the theater into a business. Earlier drama had been a product of the church and religious life, but during the Renaissance, actors and theater people found that they could make a living in the theater. Although at first there was little money in acting and in writing plays, some of the theater managers were able to do quite well. Shakespeare himself was a theater manager as well as a dramatist and minor actor. He earned enough from his shares in the Globe Theatre to retire in 1611 and leave London to spend his remaining days in his native Stratford-upon-Avon.

witty, and ironic. When the patterns and emotions are truly mixed, the play is called a **tragicomedy,** a term first used by the Roman playwright Plautus. In many ways tragicomedy is the dominant form of twentieth-century drama.

Additional types of drama that evolved from tragedy and comedy include farce, melodrama, and social drama. The major purpose of **farce,** which was also a strong element in the Athenian Old Comedy, is to make audiences laugh. Typically, it is crammed full of extravagant dialogue, stage business, and slapstick, with exaggerated emotions and rapid extremes of action. The "mechanicals" in Shakespeare's *A Midsummer Night's Dream* offer us good examples of farcical action and speech.

Resembling tragedy but stepping back from tragic outcomes is **melodrama,** a form in which most situations and characters are so exaggerated that they seem ridiculous. In its pure form, melodrama brings characters to the brink of ruin but saves them through the superhuman resources of a hero who always arrives just in time to pay the mortgage, save the business, and rescue the heroine, while the grumbling villain flees the stage muttering "Curses, foiled again," or words, believe it or not, to this effect.

The nineteenth century saw the creation of a form of topical drama known as **social drama** (sometimes called **problem play**), a type that still exists as serious drama today. This type of play explores social problems and the individual's place in society. The plays can be tragic, comic, or mixed. Examples of social drama are Ibsen's *A Dollhouse* and Hughes's *Mulatto.*

Despite all these terms and types, keep in mind that classification is not the goal of reading or seeing plays. It is less important to identify the melodramatic elements in O'Neill's *Before Breakfast* than it is to understand and share the experiences and ideas that the play offers.

VISUALIZING PLAYS
Imagining Dramatic Scenes and Actions

As we have noted, drama relies heavily on actors and directors to bring it to life. You might therefore ask why we bother to read plays without seeing them performed. The most obvious answer is that we may never get the chance actually to *see* a professional or amateur performance of a particular play. But we also read plays to familiarize ourselves with important literature. Plays are not simply maps to theatrical production; they are a significant and valuable part of our literary heritage. Dramas like Sophocles's *Oedipus the Kin* and Shakespeare's *Hamlet* have become cultural touchstones. Finally, we read plays in order to have the time to study and understand them. Only through reading do we have the opportunity to look at the parts that make up the whole and to determine how they fit together to create a moving and meaningful experience.

Reading a play, as opposed to attending a performance, carries both advantages and disadvantages. The major disadvantage is that we lack the immediacy of live theater. We do not see a majestic palace or a run-down living room, the rich robes of a king or the pathetic rags of a beggar, a vital and smiling young person or a tired and tearful old person. We do not hear the lovers flirting, the servants complaining, the soldiers boasting, the opponents threatening, the conspirators plotting; nor do we hear fanfares of trumpets or the sounds of a wedding ceremony or a funeral procession.

The primary advantage of reading is that we can consider each element in the play at length, and we can "stage" the play in our imagination and do our best to visualize it. Here are some major things for you to consider: In the theater, the action proceeds at the director's pace. You have no opportunity to turn back to an interesting scene or to reconsider an important speech. In addition, a performance always represents someone else's interpretation. The director and the actors have made choices that emphasize certain avenues of exploration, and thereby they have cut off others. Reading a play allows us to avoid these drawbacks—provided that we read attentively and with understanding. We can read at our own tempo, turn back and reread a particular speech or scene, or explore those implications or ideas that strike us as interesting.

Nevertheless, of the three types of imaginative literature, drama is most particularly suited for your visual imagination. Aids in visualization are readily available to help you in your study. At the present time there are many versions of plays that have been acted and recorded on tape and DVD, or streamed on the Internet via services like YouTube and Netflix. You may look at such commercial versions to stimulate your imagination and give you almost a director's view of how a play might be presented onstage. There are professional interpretations of *Oedipus the King*, *A Dollhouse*, and *Fences* that you might consult. In addition, there are a great many versions of *Hamlet* on DVD. Looking at selected scenes from any of these performances will give you a sense of the choices made by various directors, and therefore you can achieve a heightened awareness of how you yourself might want the plays to look, and to sound.

As a specimen scene, we might consider Shakespeare's *Hamlet* 1.5, in which Hamlet sees and hears the Ghost for the first time as the Ghost describes his murder at the hand of Claudius—his brother and Hamlet's uncle. In addition, the Ghost charges Hamlet to avenge the murder. This scene is most crucial, and it might be called Hamlet's principal information scene, for it deeply affects his understanding and also his objectives during the play. When he first appears, he is sad and depressed and is wearing black for mourning, as a result of his father's death and the quick remarriage of his mother and Claudius. But after the scene with the Ghost, who provides seemingly reliable testimony that Claudius is a murderer, Hamlet becomes a person consumed with the intention of gaining revenge. So the scene is pivotal, and you, or any reader, would want the scene to seem authentic and believable.

It's useful to begin thinking about any play by considering how you would set a scene up if you were in charge. How do you think you yourself might demonstrate the scene's importance? How would you make the scenery look? How complete should everything in the scene be made to appear? That is, should the Ghost be totally visible, or should he perhaps be somewhat obscured, or should he be seen through a haze, in order to emphasize his ghostliness? What sorts of costumes would you use? How would you make the Elsinore walls and battlements seem like a place where significant truth is to be expressed? How would you show Hamlet's agitation when he first sees the Ghost? How would you show the ways in which Hamlet's encounter with the Ghost affects him? After the encounter, when Hamlet's companions rejoin him, how should he behave?

How would you demonstrate his comments about the Ghost's voice under the stage? What do his words show about his mental state, and how should the actor in the role of Hamlet deliver these words?

For brief illustration here about how the Ghost's scene may be visualized, we might refer to seven different DVD versions of the scene in productions featuring Kenneth Branagh, Ethan Hawke, Derek Jacobi, Kevin Kline, Laurence Olivier, Campbell Scott, and David Tennant.[4] Perhaps the most traditional setting of our scene is in the Olivier version of 1948, in black and white, that shows many stone walls and stairs, in which a good deal of smoke and fog obscure the scene and also surrounds the Ghost when the camera is focused on him. Smoke and fog also surround the Ghost in the Tennant version, with the smoke curling around the Ghost as though he has just emerged from the fires of Hell. When this Ghost disappears, only a cloud of smoke or fog remains to show his last location. The Jacobi version, in color, uses a staging that is similar to this. Fog is also present in the Campbell Scott color version, in which the confrontation of Hamlet and the Ghost takes place on an ocean shore, with a mild surf, rather than high on the parapets of Elsinore. When Hamlet tells his companions that the Ghost can tunnel under the earth very rapidly, the Scott version realistically confirms this action, for the Ghost's hands actually appear at various places coming out of the beach sand, most startlingly when the hand clasps the sword on which all the men have sworn silence. A comparable and also more elaborate treatment is the Branagh version, where the scene is no longer on the battlements but in a snowy woods and underbrush, and the presence of the Ghost makes the entire earth seem to boil and smoke. The eyes of the Branagh Ghost are penetrating and mysteriously nonhuman, and when Hamlet asks his companions to swear, the Ghost's assenting command literally fractures the earth, a shaking and disturbance that also characterize the David Tennant version. The Ethan Hawke version is different from these because the action takes place within Hamlet's room in a New York apartment. When we first see the Ghost (acted by Sam Shepard), he is outside, on a terrace, appearing to be an ordinary businessman and looking out at the city. It is then that Hamlet lets him in through the door to his computer room. There is nothing ghostly here, as in the other versions, but all seems ordinary, and the room actually seems rather cluttered. Things are so ordinary, in fact, that the TV set in the room is on, and is showing a picture. Is the state of this messy computer room meant to suggest anything about Hamlet's mind? Comparably, the Ghost scene in the Tennant version shows an interior, but a dark one, as though everything has been happening on what seems to be a darkened and deserted dance floor.

William Shakespeare's Hamlet: A Kenneth Branagh Film, dir. Kenneth Branagh, perf. Kenneth Branagh, Julie Christie, Billy Crystal, and Derek Jacobi. Castle Rock Entertainment, 1996, 2007.

Hamlet, dir. and adapt. Michael Almerayda, perf. Ethan Hawke. Buena Vista Home Entertainment, 2000.

Hamlet, perf. Derek Jacobi. Ambrose Video Publishing, BBX & Time-Life Films, 1980.

William Shakespeare's Hamlet, dir. Kevin Kline and Kirk Browning, perf. Kevin Kline. Educational Broadcasting Corp, 1990.

Laurence Olivier's Hamlet, dir. Laurence Olivier, perf. Laurence Olivier. Two Cities Film Ltd., 1948, Criterion Collection 82, 2000.

Hamlet, dir. and adapt. Campbell Scott and Eric Simonson, perf. Campbell Scott. Artisan Entertainment, 2000.

Hamlet, dir. Gregory Dean, perf. David Tennant, Patrick Stewart, Penny Downie, Mariah Gale. BBC Wales, 2009, 2010.

A scene from Sir Laurence Olivier's *Hamlet:* The costuming of Olivier's *Hamlet*, shown above, is traditionally Shakespearean.

The point here is that you can boost your own imaginative reconstruction of the scene, and any other scene in any other play, by considering what others have done. The key is your own reading and thinking. What were other viewers trying to do and to show? How might you want to do things differently? What other effects might be achieved? You will need to figure out what stage effects might be needed. What sorts of lighting would best bring out the scene? What would be the significance of spotlighting, if you were to use it? Think. What scenes might best be done in close-up? What sorts of stage movement might there be? A particularly tension-filled moment is created in the Jacobi version of the Ghost scene, for example, when Hamlet falls dangerously backward from a high stairway, seemingly heading toward severe injury, but his companions catch him and save him. What does that production gain by this action, which is not called for in the text of the play? Another question you might deal with concerns how the characters interact with each other, as when Hamlet, after returning from his encounter with the Ghost, tells his friends that "There's ne'er a villain dwelling in all Denmark / But he's an arrant knave" (1.5.124–25). Should Horatio's response be spoken seriously, or comically? Other questions you can raise might concern whether some of the action, from *Hamlet* or any other play, should be cut for production.

You might also think about questions of costuming. One might expect to see a *Hamlet* production done in clothing that was customary at the time of Shakespeare, as in the Olivier and Jacobi versions. You might ask about the effect

A scene from Ethan Hawke's *Hamlet*: As seen in this production still, late twentieth-century costumes were used in Hawke's version of the play.

of more recent costumes, as in the Branagh and Scott versions, or ordinary late twentieth-century everyday garb, as in the Hawke and Tennant versions. And you should also consider the modes of speech, and their effect on your imaginary production. The Olivier Ghost, for example, speaks as we might expect a ghost to speak, in deep tones, slowly. In the Branagh version, the Ghost's speech is accompanied by noisy wind of seemingly hurricane velocity. This is not so in the Jacobi version, in which this Ghost, who is angry about having been murdered, speaks rapidly and forcefully about the circumstances of his death. He is not happy, and he clearly wants Hamlet to be disturbed also. The Ghost in the Tennant version is shrill and loud—perhaps the loudest of all the Ghosts in these versions. The Ghost in the Hawke version is quietly conversational, in keeping with the interior in which the action takes place, and before he leaves he embraces Hamlet, his son, even if he is a Ghost and therefore, supposedly, nonsubstantial at the time of the action. Indeed, this ghost looks very substantial and very realistic.

In a word, try to use the advantages of reading and study, together with your own imagination. You have the time and freedom to read carefully, reflect deeply, and follow your thoughts. Think. Rely on whatever experiences you can gain from theatrical productions, movies, and recorded productions to enhance your reading. Stage the play as fully as you can in the theater of your mind. Become the director, producer, set designer, lighting technician, and costume designer, and pretend that you control all the actors. Build whatever mental presentations you like, dress your actors as you see fit, and move the characters across the stage of your mind. Enjoy.

Plays for Study

Susan Glaspell . . . . Trifles, 982

David Henry Hwang . . . . Trying to Find Chinatown, 994

Jane Martin . . . . Beauty, 1000

Eugene O'Neill . . . . Before Breakfast, 1005

SUSAN GLASPELL (1882–1948)

Susan Glaspell, a writer of both plays and fiction, was a native of Iowa. She was educated at Drake University and the University of Chicago. In her thirties she moved to the Northeast and became interested in theater. Along with her husband, George Cook, she was a founder and director of the Provincetown Players of Cape Cod in 1914. The organization encouraged lesser-known young dramatists and was often experimental, but nevertheless it became successful enough to justify the opening of a second theater in New York. The first offerings of the theater were many one-act plays, featuring the earlier works of Glaspell herself, Eugene O'Neill, Edna Ferber, Edmund Wilson, and Edna St. Vincent Millay.

Glaspell wrote or coauthored over ten plays for the Provincetown Players, including Suppressed Desires (1914), Close the Book (1917), Women's Honor (1918), Tickless Time (1918), Bernice (1919, her first full-length play), The Inheritors (1921), and The Verge (1921). After 1922, however, she gave up the theater and turned almost exclusively to fiction. The exception was Alison's House (1930), a play loosely based on the life and family of Emily Dickinson, for which she won a Pulitzer Prize.

Glaspell deals with diverse topics in her drama, including misunderstood parentage, the effects of psychoanalysis, rejection of the machine age, the function and importance of honor, the tensions between political conservatives and liberals, and the onset of psychosis. Running through much of her work are strongly feminist ideas, based on a critique of the power— personal, social, and political—that men possess and that women are denied. Usually, Glaspell focuses on the negative and destructive effects that male–female relationships have on women, but she also stresses the ways in which women cope with their circumstances. To maintain character integrity and to preserve their domestic strength, they are forced into roles that are characterized not by direct but by indirect action.

Trifles, Glaspell's best-known drama, displays these characteristics. She wrote it in ten days for the Provincetown Players, who produced the play in 1916. Its inspiration was a murder trial she had covered while working as a reporter for a Des Moines newspaper before moving to the Northeast. In 1917 she refashioned the material for the short story "A Jury of Her Peers," with which *Trifles* can be compared (see p. 202). Although Glaspell preserves a considerable amount of dramatic dialogue in the story, the additions and changes she makes are indicative of the differences between drama and fiction.

Trifles concerns a murder investigation, but the play is not a mystery. Soon after the characters enter and go about their business, the two women characters begin to uncover the circumstances that reveal the killer and the nature of the crime. Once the facts are established, however, the action focuses on the significant details of motive. Indeed, the heart of the play consists of the contrasting ways in which the men and the women attempt to uncover and understand the motive. The men—the county attorney and the sheriff, accompanied by Hale—look for signs of violent rage, and they move onstage and offstage throughout the house in their search. The women—Mrs. Hale and Mrs. Peters—stay onstage and draw their conclusions from the ordinary, everyday details of a farm woman's kitchen. It is finally the women, not the men, who realize the true power that comes from understanding. Their realization—as well as their strength—leads them to their final decisions about how to judge the killer and treat the evidence.

The language that Glaspell gives to her characters is in keeping with the plain and simple lives the characters lead: simple, specific, and unadorned. Of the two groups, the women are more direct in the expression of their ideas. Once they realize the gravity of the situation they are exploring, however, they become indirect, but only because they fear to speak the words that describe the truths they have discovered. By contrast, the men usually talk convivially and smugly about the crime and their own roles in life, patronizingly among themselves about the women, and almost scornfully to the women about womanly concerns.

Trifles (1916)

CAST OF CHARACTERS

George Henderson, county attorney
Henry Peters, sheriff
Lewis Hale, a neighboring farmer
Mrs. Peters
Mrs. Hale

SCENE: *The kitchen in the now abandoned farmhouse of JOHN WRIGHT, a gloomy kitchen, and left without having been put in order—unwashed pans under the sink, a loaf of bread outside the breadbox, a dish-towel on the table—other signs of incompleted work. At the rear the outer door opens and the SHERIFF comes in followed by the COUNTY ATTORNEY and HALE. The SHERIFF and HALE are men in middle life, the COUNTY ATTORNEY is a young man; all are much bundled up and go at once to the stove. They are followed by the two women—the SHERIFF's wife first; she is a slight wiry woman, a thin nervous face. MRS. HALE is larger and would ordinarily be called more comfortable looking, but she is disturbed now and looks fearfully about as she enters. The women have come in slowly, and stand close together near the door.*

COUNTY ATTORNEY: [*Rubbing his hands.*] This feels good. Come up to the fire, ladies.

MRS. PETERS: [*After taking a step forward.*] I'm not—cold.

SHERIFF: [*Unbuttoning his overcoat and stepping away from the stove as if to mark the beginning of official business.*] Now, Mr. Hale, before we move things about, you explain to Mr. Henderson just what you saw when you came here yesterday morning.

COUNTY ATTORNEY: By the way, has anything been moved? Are things just as you left them yesterday?

SHERIFF: [*Looking about.*] It's just the same. When it dropped below zero last night I thought I'd better send Frank out this morning to make a fire for us—no use getting pneumonia with a big case on, but I told him not to touch anything except the stove—and you know Frank.

COUNTY ATTORNEY: Somebody should have been left here yesterday.

SHERIFF: Oh—yesterday. When I had to send Frank to Morris Center for that man who went crazy—I want you to know I had my hands full yesterday. I knew you could get back from Omaha by today and as long as I went over everything here myself—

COUNTY ATTORNEY: Well, Mr. Hale, tell just what happened when you came here yesterday morning.

5

The five principal actors arrive in the cold and bleak kitchen of the Wright farm at the beginning of Glaspell's *Trifles* in the original 1916 production, featuring Marjorie Vonnegut, Elinor M. Cox, John Kind, Arthur Hohl, and T. W. Gibson.

HALE: Harry and I had started to town with a load of potatoes. We came along the road from my place and as I got here I said, "I'm going to see if I can't get John Wright to go in with me on a party telephone." I spoke to Wright about it once before and he put me off, saying folks talked too much anyway, and all he asked was peace and quiet—I guess you know about how much he talked himself; but I thought maybe if I went to the house and talked about it before his wife, though I said to Harry that I didn't know as what his wife wanted made much difference to John—

10   **COUNTY ATTORNEY:** Let's talk about that later, Mr. Hale. I do want to talk about that, but tell now just what happened when you got to the house.

HALE: I didn't hear or see anything; I knocked at the door, and still it was all quiet inside. I knew they must be up, it was past eight o'clock. So I knocked again, and I thought I heard somebody say, "Come in." I wasn't sure, I'm not sure yet, but I opened the door—this door [*Indicating the door by which the two women are still standing.*] and there in that rocker—[*Pointing to it.*] sat Mrs. Wright.

[*They all look at the rocker.*]

COUNTY ATTORNEY: What—was she doing?

HALE: She was rockin' back and forth. She had her apron in her hand and was kind of— pleating it.

COUNTY ATTORNEY: And how did she—look?

15   **HALE:** Well, she looked queer.

COUNTY ATTORNEY: How do you mean—queer?

HALE: Well, as if she didn't know what she was going to do next. And kind of done up.

COUNTY ATTORNEY: How did she seem to feel about your coming?

HALE: Why, I don't think she minded—one way or other. She didn't pay much attention. I said, "How do, Mrs. Wright, it's cold, ain't it?" And she said, "Is it?"—and went on kind of pleating at her apron. Well, I was surprised; she didn't ask me to come up to the stove, or to set down, but just sat there, not even looking at me, so I said, "I want to see John." And then she—laughed. I guess you would call it a laugh. I thought of Harry and the team outside, so I said a little sharp: "Can't I see John?" "No," she says, kind o' dull like. "Ain't he home?" says I. "Yes," says she, "he's home." "Then why can't I see him?" I asked her, out of patience. "'Cause he's dead," says she. "*Dead*?" says I. She just nodded her head, not getting a bit excited, but rockin' back and forth. "Why—where is he?" says I, not knowing what to say. She just pointed upstairs—like that. [*Himself pointing to the room above.*] I got up, with the idea of going up there. I walked from there to here—then I says, "Why, what did he die of?" "He died of a rope round his neck," says she, and just went on pleatin' at her apron. Well, I went out and called Harry. I thought I might—need help. We went upstairs and there he was lyin'—

COUNTY ATTORNEY: I think I'd rather have you go into that upstairs, where you can point   20
    it all out. Just go on now with the rest of the story.

HALE: Well, my first thought was to get that rope off. It looked . . . [*Stops, his face twitches.*]
    . . . but Harry, he went up to him, and he said, "No, he's dead all right, and we'd bet-
    ter not touch anything." So we went back downstairs. She was still sitting that same
    way. "Has anybody been notified?" I asked. "No," says she, unconcerned. "Who did
    this, Mrs. Wright?" said Harry. He said it businesslike—and she stopped pleatin' of
    her apron. "I don't know," she says. "You don't *know*?" says Harry. "No," says she.
    "Weren't you sleepin' in the bed with him?" says Harry. "Yes," says she, "but I was
    on the inside." "Somebody slipped a rope round his neck and strangled him and
    you didn't wake up?" says Harry. "I didn't wake up," she said after him. We must
    'a looked as if we didn't see how that could be, for after a minute she said, "I sleep
    sound." Harry was going to ask her more questions but I said maybe we ought to let
    her tell her story first to the coroner, or the sheriff, so Harry went fast as he could to
    Rivers' place, where there's a telephone.

COUNTY ATTORNEY: And what did Mrs. Wright do when she knew that you had gone for
    the coroner?

HALE: She moved from that chair to this one over here [*Pointing to a small chair in the corner.*]
    and just sat there with her hands held together and looking down. I got a feeling that I
    ought to make some conversation, so I said I had come in to see if John wanted to put
    in a telephone, and at that she started to laugh, and then she stopped and looked at
    me—scared. [*The COUNTY ATTORNEY, who has had his notebook out, makes a note.*] I dunno,
    maybe it wasn't scared. I wouldn't like to say it was. Soon Harry got back, and then
    Dr. Lloyd came, and you, Mr. Peters, and so I guess that's all I know that you don't.

COUNTY ATTORNEY: [*Looking around.*] I guess we'll go upstairs first—and then out to the
    barn and around there. [*To the SHERIFF.*] You're convinced that there was nothing
    important here—nothing that would point to any motive.

SHERIFF: Nothing here but kitchen things.   25

[*The COUNTY ATTORNEY, after again looking around the kitchen, opens the door of a cupboard closet. He gets up on a chair and looks on a shelf. Pulls his hand away, sticky.*]

COUNTY ATTORNEY: Here's a nice mess.

[*The women draw nearer.*]

MRS. PETERS: [*To the other woman.*] Oh, her fruit; it did freeze. [*To the LAWYER.*] She
    worried about that when it turned so cold. She said the fire'd go out and her jars
    would break.

SHERIFF: Well, can you beat the women! Held for murder and worryin' about her preserves.

COUNTY ATTORNEY: I guess before we're through she may have something more serious than preserves to worry about.

30 **HALE:** Well, women are used to worrying over trifles.

[*The two women move a little closer together.*]

COUNTY ATTORNEY: [*With the gallantry of a young politician.*] And yet, for all their worries, what would we do without the ladies? [*The women do not unbend. He goes to the sink, takes a dipperful of water from the pail and pouring it into a basin, washes his hands. Starts to wipe them on the roller towel, turns it for a cleaner place.*] Dirty towels! [*Kicks his foot against the pans under the sink.*] Not much of a housekeeper, would you say, ladies?

MRS. HALE: [*Stiffly.*] There's a great deal of work to be done on a farm.

COUNTY ATTORNEY: To be sure. And yet [*With a little bow to her.*] I know there are some Dickson county farmhouses which do not have such roller towels.

[*He gives it a pull to expose its full length again.*]

MRS. HALE: Those towels get dirty awful quick. Men's hands aren't always as clean as they might be.

35 **COUNTY ATTORNEY:** Ah, loyal to your sex, I see. But you and Mrs. Wright were neighbors. I suppose you were friends, too.

MRS. HALE: [*Shaking her head.*] I've not seen much of her of late years. I've not been in this house—it's more than a year.

COUNTY ATTORNEY: And why was that? You didn't like her?

MRS. HALE: I liked her all well enough. Farmers' wives have their hands full, Mr. Henderson. And then—

COUNTY ATTORNEY: Yes—?

40 **MRS. HALE:** [*Looking about.*] It never seemed a very cheerful place.

COUNTY ATTORNEY: No—it's not cheerful. I shouldn't say she had the homemaking instinct.

MRS. HALE: Well. I don't know as Wright had, either.

COUNTY ATTORNEY: You mean that they didn't get on very well?

MRS. HALE: No, I don't mean anything. But I don't think a place'd be any cheerfuller for John Wright's being in it.

45 **COUNTY ATTORNEY:** I'd like to talk more of that a little later. I want to get the lay of things upstairs now.

[*He goes to the left, where three steps lead to a stair door.*]

SHERIFF: I suppose anything Mrs. Peters does'll be all right. She was to take in some clothes for her, you know, and a few little things. We left in such a hurry yesterday.

COUNTY ATTORNEY: Yes, but I would like to see what you take, Mrs. Peters, and keep an eye out for anything that might be of use to us.

MRS. PETERS: Yes, Mr. Henderson.

[*The women listen to the men's steps on the stairs, then look about the kitchen.*]

MRS. HALE: I'd hate to have men coming into my kitchen, snooping around and criticizing.

[*She arranges the pans under the sink which the LAWYER had shoved out of place.*]

50 **MRS. PETERS:** Of course it's no more than their duty.

The men are watching as Mr. Hale (Gregory Aldrich) gets in trouble with his wife, Mrs. Hale (June Thiele), in a 2004 student production of *Trifles,* directed by Rachel Blackwell, at the University of Alaska, Fairbanks.

MRS. HALE: Duty's all right, but I guess that deputy sheriff that came out to make the fire might have got a little of this on. [*Gives the roller towel a pull.*] Wish I'd thought of that sooner. Seems mean to talk about her for not having things slicked up when she had to come away in such a hurry.

MRS. PETERS: [*Who had gone to a small table in the left rear corner of the room, and lifted one end of a towel that covers a pan.*] She had bread set.

[*Stands still.*]

MRS. HALE: [*Eyes fixed on a loaf of bread beside the breadbox, which is on a low shelf at the other side of the room. Moves slowly toward it.*] She was going to put this in there. [*Picks up loaf, then abruptly drops it. In a manner of returning to familiar things.*] It's a shame about her fruit. I wonder if it's all gone. [*Gets up on the chair and looks.*] I think there's some here that's all right, Mrs. Peters. Yes—here; [*Holding it toward the window.*] this is cherries, too. [*Looking again.*] I declare I believe that's the only one. [*Gets down, bottle in her hand. Goes to the sink and wipes it off on the outside.*] She'll feel awful bad after all her hard work in the hot weather. I remember the afternoon I put up my cherries last summer.

[*She puts the bottle on the big kitchen table, center of the room. With a sigh, is about to sit down in the rocking-chair. Before she is seated realizes what chair it is; with a slow look at it, steps back. The chair which she has touched rocks back and forth.*]

Mrs. Peters: Well, I must get those things from the front room closet. [*She goes to the door at the right, but after looking into the other room, steps back.*] You coming with me, Mrs. Hale? You could help me carry them.

[*They go in the other room; reappear, Mrs. Peters carrying a dress and skirt, Mrs. Hale following with a pair of shoes.*]

55   **Mrs. Peters:** My, it's cold in there.

[*She puts the clothes on the big table and hurries to the stove.*]

Mrs. Hale: [*Examining the skirt.*] Wright was close. I think maybe that's why she kept so much to herself. She didn't even belong to the Ladies Aid. I suppose she felt she couldn't do her part, and then you don't enjoy things when you feel shabby. She used to wear pretty clothes and be lively, when she was Minnie Foster, one of the town girls singing in the choir. But that—oh, that was thirty years ago. This all you was to take in?

Mrs. Peters: She said she wanted an apron. Funny thing to want, for there isn't much to get you dirty in jail, goodness knows. But I suppose just to make her feel more natural. She said they was in the top drawer in this cupboard. Yes, here. And then her little shawl that always hung behind the door. [*Opens stair door and looks.*] Yes, here it is.

[*Quickly shuts door leading upstairs.*]

Mrs. Hale: [*Abruptly moving toward her.*] Mrs. Peters?
Mrs. Peters: Yes, Mrs. Hale?
60   **Mrs. Hale:** Do you think she did it?
Mrs. Peters: [*In a frightened voice.*] Oh, I don't know.
Mrs. Hale: Well, I don't think she did. Asking for an apron and her little shawl. Worrying about her fruit.
Mrs. Peters: [*Starts to speak, glances up, where footsteps are heard in the room above. In a low voice.*] Mr. Peters says it looks bad for her. Mr. Henderson is awful sarcastic in a speech and he'll make fun of her sayin' she didn't wake up.
Mrs. Hale: Well, I guess John Wright didn't wake when they was slipping that rope under his neck.
65   **Mrs. Peters:** No, it's strange. It must have been done awful crafty and still. They say it was such a—funny way to kill a man, rigging it all up like that.
Mrs. Hale: That's just what Mr. Hale said. There was a gun in the house. He says that's what he can't understand.
Mrs. Peters: Mr. Henderson said coming out that what was needed for the case was a motive; something to show anger, or—sudden feeling.
Mrs. Hale: [*Who is standing by the table.*] Well, I don't see any signs of anger around here. [*She puts her hand on the dish towel which lies on the table, stands looking down at table, one half of which is clean, the other half messy.*] It's wiped to here. [*Makes a move as if to finish work, then turns and looks at loaf of bread outside the breadbox. Drops towel. In that voice of coming back to familiar things.*] Wonder how they are finding things upstairs. I hope she had it a little more redd-up° up there. You know, it seems kind of *sneaking*. Locking her up in town and then coming out here and trying to get her own house to turn against her!
Mrs. Peters: But Mrs. Hale, the law is the law.

°68 *redd-up:* neat, arranged in order.

MRS. HALE: I s'pose 'tis. [*Unbuttoning her coat.*] Better loosen up your things,   70
MRS. PETERS: You won't feel them when you go out.

[MRS. PETERS *takes off her fur tippet,° goes to hang it on hook at back of room, stands looking at the under part of the small corner table.*]

MRS. PETERS: She was piecing a quilt.

[*She brings the large sewing basket and they look at the bright pieces.*]

MRS. HALE: It's log cabin pattern. Pretty, isn't it? I wonder if she was goin' to quilt it or just knot it?

[*Footsteps have been heard coming down the stairs. The* SHERIFF *enters followed by* HALE *and the* COUNTY ATTORNEY.]

SHERIFF: They wonder if she was going to quilt it or just knot it!

[*The men laugh; the women look abashed.*]

COUNTY ATTORNEY: [*Rubbing his hands over the stove.*] Frank's fire didn't do much up   75
there, did it? Well, let's go out to the barn and get that cleared up.

[*The men go outside.*]

MRS. HALE: [*Resentfully.*] I don't know as there's anything so strange, our takin' up our time with little things while we're waiting for them to get the evidence. [*She sits down at the big table smoothing out a block with decision.*] I don't see as it's anything to laugh about.
MRS. PETERS: [*Apologetically.*] Of course they've got awful important things on their minds.

[*Pulls up a chair and joins* MRS. HALE *at the table.*]

MRS. HALE: [*Examining another block.*] Mrs. Peters, look at this one. Here, this is the one she was working on, and look at the sewing! All the rest of it has been so nice and even. And look at this! It's all over the place! Why, it looks as if she didn't know what she was about!

[*After she has said this they look at each other, then start to glance back at the door. After an instant* MRS. HALE *has pulled at a knot and ripped the sewing.*]

MRS. PETERS: Oh, what are you doing, Mrs. Hale?
MRS. HALE: [*Mildly.*] Just pulling out a stitch or two that's not sewed very good. [*Threading a needle.*] Bad sewing always made me fidgety.   80
MRS. PETERS: [*Nervously.*] I don't think we ought to touch things.
MRS. HALE: I'll just finish up this end. [*Suddenly stopping and leaning forward.*] Mrs. Peters?
MRS. PETERS: Yes, Mrs. Hale?
MRS. HALE: What do you suppose she was so nervous about?
MRS. PETERS: Oh—I don't know. I don't know as she was nervous. I sometimes sew aw-   85
ful queer when I'm just tired. [MRS. HALE *starts to say something, looks at* MRS. PETERS, *then goes on sewing.*] Well I must get these things wrapped up. They may be through sooner than we think. [*Putting apron and other things together.*] I wonder where I can find a piece of paper, and string.

°71 S.D. *tippet:* scarflike garment of fur or wool for the neck and shoulders.

MRS. HALE: In that cupboard, maybe.

MRS. PETERS: [*Looking in cupboard.*] Why, here's a bird-cage. [*Holds it up.*] Did she have a bird, Mrs. Hale?

MRS. HALE: Why, I don't know whether she did or not—I've not been here for so long. There was a man around last year selling canaries cheap, but I don't know as she took one; maybe she did. She used to sing real pretty herself.

MRS. PETERS: [*Glancing around.*] Seems funny to think of a bird here. But she must have had one, or why would she have a cage? I wonder what happened to it?

90 **MRS. HALE:** I s'pose maybe the cat got it.

MRS. PETERS: No, she didn't have a cat. She's got that feeling some people have about cats—being afraid of them. My cat got in her room and she was real upset and asked me to take it out.

MRS. HALE: My sister Bessie was like that. Queer, ain't it?

MRS. PETERS: [*Examining the cage.*] Why, look at this door. It's broke. One hinge is pulled apart.

MRS. HALE: [*Looking too.*] Looks as if someone must have been rough with it.

95 **MRS. PETERS:** Why, yes.

[*She brings the cage forward and puts it on the table.*]

MRS. HALE: I wish if they're going to find any evidence they'd be about it. I don't like this place.

MRS. PETERS: But I'm awful glad you came with me, Mrs. Hale. It would be lonesome for me sitting here alone.

MRS. HALE: It would, wouldn't it? [*Dropping her sewing.*] But I tell you what I do wish, Mrs. Peters. I wish I had come over sometimes when she was here. I—[*Looking around the room.*]—wish I had.

MRS. PETERS: But of course you were awful busy, Mrs. Hale—your house and your children.

100 **MRS. HALE:** I could've come. I stayed away because it weren't cheerful—and that's why I ought to have come. I—I've never liked this place. Maybe because it's down in a hollow and you don't see the road. I dunno what it is, but it's a lonesome place and always was. I wish I had come over to see Minnie Foster sometimes. I can see now—

[*Shakes her head.*]

MRS. PETERS: Well, you mustn't reproach yourself, Mrs. Hale. Somehow we just don't see how it is with other folks until—something comes up.

MRS. HALE: Not having children makes less work—but it makes a quiet house, and Wright out to work all day, and no company when he did come in. Did you know John Wright, Mrs. Peters?

MRS. PETERS: Not to know him; I've seen him in town. They say he was a good man.

MRS. HALE: Yes—good; he didn't drink, and kept his word as well as most, I guess, and paid his debts. But he was a hard man, Mrs. Peters. Just to pass the time of day with him—[*Shivers.*] Like a raw wind that gets to the bone. [*Pauses, her eye falling on the cage.*] I should think she would 'a wanted a bird. But what do you suppose went with it?

105 **MRS. PETERS:** I don't know, unless it got sick and died.

[*She reaches over and swings the broken door, swings it again, both women watch it.*]

MRS. HALE: You weren't raised round here, were you? [*MRS. PETERS shakes her head.*] You didn't know—her?

Mrs. Peters: Not till they brought her yesterday.

Mrs. Hale: She—come to think of it, she was kind of like a bird herself—real sweet and pretty, but kind of timid and—fluttery. How—she—did—change. [*Silence; then as if struck by a happy thought and relieved to get back to everyday things.*] Tell you what, Mrs. Peters, why don't you take the quilt in with you? It might take up her mind.

Mrs. Peters: Why, I think that's a real nice idea, Mrs. Hale. There couldn't possibly be any objection to it, could there? Now, just what would I take? I wonder if her patches are in here—and her things.

[*They look in the sewing basket.*]

Mrs. Hale: Here's some red. I expect this has got sewing things in it. [*Brings out a fancy box.*] What a pretty box. Looks like something somebody would give you. Maybe her scissors are in here. [*Opens box. Suddenly puts her hand to her nose.*] Why—[Mrs. Peters *bends nearer, then turns her face away.*] There's something wrapped up in this piece of silk.   110

Mrs. Peters: Why, this isn't her scissors.

Mrs. Hale: [*Lifting the silk.*] Oh, Mrs. Peters—it's—

[Mrs. Peters *bends closer.*]

Mrs. Peters: It's the bird.

Mrs. Hale: [*Jumping up.*] But, Mrs. Peters—look at it! Its neck! Look at its neck! It's all—other side *to.*

Mrs. Peters: Somebody—wrung—its—neck.   115

[*Their eyes meet. A look of growing comprehension, of horror. Steps are heard outside.* Mrs. Hale *slips box under quilt pieces, and sinks into her chair. Enter* Sheriff *and* County Attorney. Mrs. Peters *rises.*]

County Attorney: [*As one turning from serious things to little pleasantries.*] Well, ladies, have you decided whether she was going to quilt it or knot it?

Mrs. Peters: We think she was going to—knot it.

County Attorney: Well, that's interesting, I'm sure. [*Seeing the bird-cage.*] Has the bird flown?

Mrs. Hale: [*Putting more quilt pieces over the box.*] We think the—cat got it.

County Attorney: [*Preoccupied.*] Is there a cat?   120

[Mrs. Hale *glances in a quick covert way at* Mrs. Peters.]

Mrs. Peters: Well, not *now.* They're superstitious, you know. They leave.

County Attorney: [*To* Sheriff Peters, *continuing an interrupted conversation.*] No sign at all of anyone having come from the outside. Their own rope. Now let's go up again and go over it piece by piece. [*They start upstairs.*] It would have to have been someone who knew just the—

[Mrs. Peters *sits down. The two women sit there not looking at one another, but as if peering into something and at the same time holding back. When they talk now it is in the manner of feeling their way over strange ground, as if afraid of what they are saying, but as if they cannot help saying it.*]

Mrs. Hale: She liked the bird. She was going to bury it in that pretty box.

MRS. PETERS: [*In a whisper.*] When I was a girl—my kitten—there was a boy took a hatchet, and before my eyes—and before I could get there—[*Covers her face an instant.*] If they hadn't held me back I would have—[*Catches herself, looks upstairs where steps are heard, falters weakly.*]—hurt him.

125 **MRS. HALE:** [*With a slow look around her.*] I wonder how it would seem never to have had any children around. [*Pause.*] No, Wright wouldn't like the bird—a thing that sang. She used to sing. He killed that, too.

MRS. PETERS: [*Moving uneasily.*] We don't know who killed the bird.

MRS. HALE: I knew John Wright.

MRS. PETERS: It was an awful thing was done in this house that night, Mrs. Hale. Killing a man while he slept, slipping a rope around his neck that choked the life out of him.

MRS. HALE: His neck. Choked the life out of him.

[*Her hand goes out and rests on the bird-cage.*]

130 **MRS. PETERS:** [*With rising voice.*] We don't know who killed him. We don't know.

MRS. HALE: [*Her own feeling not interrupted.*] If there'd been years and years of nothing, then a bird to sing to you, it would be awful—still, after the bird was still.

MRS. PETERS: [*Something within her speaking.*] I know what stillness is. When we homesteaded in Dakota, and my first baby died—after he was two years old, and me with no other then—

MRS. HALE: [*Moving.*] How soon do you suppose they'll be through, looking for the evidence?

MRS. PETERS: I know what stillness is. [*Pulling herself back.*] The law has got to punish crime, Mrs. Hale.

135 **MRS. HALE:** [*Not as if answering that.*] I *wish* you'd seen Minnie Foster when she wore a white dress with blue ribbons and stood up there in the choir and sang. [*A look around the room.*] Oh, I wish I'd come over here once in a while! That was a crime! That was a crime! Who's going to punish that?

MRS. PETERS: [*Looking upstairs.*] We mustn't—take on.

MRS. HALE: I might have known she needed help! I know how things can be—for women. I tell you, it's queer, Mrs. Peters. We live close together and we live far apart. We all go through the same things—it's all just a different kind of the same thing. [*Brushes her eyes, noticing the bottle of fruit, reaches out for it.*] If I was you I wouldn't tell her her fruit was gone. Tell her it *ain't*. Tell her it's all right. Take this in to prove it to her. She—she may never know whether it was broke or not.

MRS. PETERS: [*Takes the bottle, looks about for something to wrap it in; takes petticoat from the clothes brought from the other room, very nervously begins winding this around the bottle. In a false voice.*] My, it's a good thing the men couldn't hear us. Wouldn't they just laugh! Getting all stirred up over a little thing like a—dead canary. As if that could have anything to do with—with—wouldn't they *laugh*!

[*The men are heard coming down stairs.*]

MRS. HALE: [*Under her breath.*] Maybe they would—maybe they wouldn't.

140 **COUNTY ATTORNEY:** No, Peters, it's all perfectly clear except a reason for doing it. But you know juries when it comes to women. If there was some definite thing. Something to show—something to make a story about—a thing that would connect up with this strange way of doing it—

[*The women's eyes meet for an instant. Enter HALE from outer door.*]

HALE: Well, I've got the team° around. Pretty cold out there.

COUNTY ATTORNEY: I'm going to stay here a while by myself. [*To the SHERIFF.*] You can send Frank out for me, can't you? I want to go over everything. I'm not satisfied that we can't do better.

SHERIFF: Do you want to see what Mrs. Peters is going to take in?

[*The COUNTY ATTORNEY goes to the table, picks up the apron, laughs.*]

COUNTY ATTORNEY: Oh, I guess they're not very dangerous things the ladies have picked out. [*Moves a few things about, disturbing the quilt pieces which cover the box. Steps back.*] No, Mrs. Peters doesn't need supervising. For that matter, a sheriff's wife is married to the law. Ever think of it that way, Mrs. Peters?

MRS. PETERS: Not—just that way.   145

SHERIFF: [*Chuckling.*] Married to the law. [*Moves toward the other room.*] I just want you to come in here a minute, George. We ought to take a look at these windows.

COUNTY ATTORNEY: [*Scoffingly.*] Oh, windows!

SHERIFF: We'll be right out, Mr. Hale.

[*HALE goes outside. The SHERIFF follows the COUNTY ATTORNEY into the other room. Then MRS. HALE rises, hands tight together, looking intensely at MRS. PETERS, whose eyes make a slow turn, finally meeting MRS. HALE's. A moment MRS. HALE holds her, then her own eyes point the way to where the box is concealed. Suddenly MRS. PETERS throws back quilt pieces and tries to put the box in the bag she is wearing. It is too big. She opens box, starts to take bird out, cannot touch it, goes to pieces, stands there helpless. Sound of a knob turning in the other room. MRS. HALE snatches the box and puts it in the pocket of her big coat. Enter COUNTY ATTORNEY and SHERIFF.*]

COUNTY ATTORNEY: [*Facetiously.*] Well, Henry, at least we found out that she was not going to quilt it. She was going to—what is it you call it, ladies?

MRS. HALE: [*Her hand against her pocket.*] We call it—knot it, Mr. Henderson.   150

CURTAIN

°141 *team*: team of horses.

QUESTIONS

1. How does the first entrance of the characters establish a distinction between the men and women in the play? What is suggested by the different reactions of the men and women to the frozen preserves?

2. What does Mr. Hale report to the County Attorney in his extended narrative? How observant is he? How accurate?

3. What is needed for a strong legal case against Minnie? What does the Sheriff conclude about the kitchen? What do his conclusions tell you about the men?

4. What are the women's conclusions about the bad sewing? What does Mrs. Hale do about it? At this point, what might she be thinking about the murder?

5. Of what importance are Mrs. Hale's descriptions (a) of Minnie as a young woman and (b) of the Wrights' marriage?

6. What do the women deduce from the broken birdcage and the dead bird? How are these symbolic, and what do they symbolize?

7. How did Minnie Wright murder her husband? What hints lead you to this solution? What information permits the women to make the right inferences about the crime and the method of strangulation?

8. What does Mrs. Hale do with the "trifles" of evidence? Why? How is her reaction to the evidence different from that of Mrs. Peters? What conflict develops between these women? How is it resolved?

9. Why does Mrs. Hale feel guilty about her relationship with Minnie Wright? To what degree does her guilt shape her decisions and actions?

GENERAL QUESTIONS

1. To what does the title of this play refer? How does this irony of the word *trifles* help shape the play's meaning?

2. What are the men like? Are they round characters or flat? How observant are they? What is their attitude toward their jobs? Toward their own importance? Toward the women and "kitchen things"?

3. What is Mrs. Hale like? How observant is she? What is her attitude toward the men and their work, and toward herself?

4. Some critics argue that Minnie is the play's most important character, even though she never appears onstage. Do you agree? Why do you think Glaspell did not make Minnie a speaking character?

5. How is symbolism employed to establish and underscore the play's meaning? Consider especially the birdcage, the dead bird, and the repeated assertion that Mrs. Wright was going to "knot" (tie) rather than "quilt" (sew) the quilt.

DAVID HENRY HWANG (b. 1957)

Born in Los Angeles, David Henry Hwang received a bachelor's degree from Stanford University and later attended the Yale School of Drama. He has had an immensely prolific and successful career in the theater. His first play FOB *(1980) depicts the conflicts between established Asian Americans and recent Asian immigrants. Several successful plays followed, including* The Dance and the Railroad *(1981) and* Family Devotions *(1981). In 1988 his* M. Butterfly, *a play loosely based on Giacomo Puccini's opera, premiered on Broadway. In addition to winning the Drama Desk Award and the Outer Critics Circle Award for best play, it won the Tony Award for Best Play, making Hwang the first Asian American to win this award. Hwang's post-*M. Butterfly *work comprises librettos, including* Aida *with music by Elton John and collaborations with the composer Philip Glass, and television scripts, including* Blind Alleys *(with Frederic Kimball) and* Golden Gate. *Hwang's recent play* Chinglish *won the Joseph Jefferson Award and premiered on Broadway in 2011.*

In Trying to Find Chinatown *Hwang displays his keen ear for realistic dialogue and his knowledge of the inner conflicts that arise from cultural differences. Ronnie and Benjamin, the two characters, resonate so strongly because their anxieties and dreams reflect the American experience.*

Trying to Find Chinatown (1996)

CHARACTERS

Benjamin Caucasian male, early twenties
Ronnie Asian American male, mid-twenties

Time And Place: A street corner on the Lower East Side, New York City. The present.

Note On Music: Obviously, it would be foolish to require that the actor portraying RONNIE *perform the specified violin music live. The score of this play can be played on tape over the house speakers, and the actor can feign playing the violin using a bow treated with soap. However, in order to effect a convincing illusion, it is desirable that the actor possess some familiarity with the violin or another stringed instrument.*

Darkness. Over the house speakers, sound fades in: Hendrix-like virtuoso rock 'n' roll riffs—heavy feedback, distortion, phase shifting, wah-wah—amplified over a tiny Fender pug-nose.

Lights fade up to reveal that the music's being played over a solid-body electric violin by RONNIE, *a Chinese-American male in his mid-twenties; he is dressed in retro-'60s clothing and has a few requisite '90s body mutilations. He's playing on a sidewalk for money, his violin case open before him; change and a few stray bills have been left by previous passersby.*

BENJAMIN *enters; he's in his early twenties, blond, blue-eyed, a Midwestern tourist in the big city. He holds a scrap of paper in his hands, scanning street signs for an address. He pauses before* RONNIE, *listens for a while. With a truly bravura run,* RONNIE *concludes the number and falls to his knees, gasping.* BENJAMIN *applauds.*

BENJAMIN: Good. That was really great. [*Pause*] I didn't . . . I mean, a fiddle . . . I mean, I'd   1
heard them at square dances, on country stations and all, but I never . . . wow, this
must really be New York City!

[BENJAMIN *applauds, starts to walk on. Still on his knees,* RONNIE *clears his throat loudly.*]

Oh, I . . . you're not just doing this for your health right?

[BENJAMIN *reaches in his pocket, pulls out a couple of coins.* RONNIE *clears his throat again.*]

Look, I'm not a millionaire, I'm just . . .

[BENJAMIN *pulls out his wallet, removes a dollar bill.* RONNIE *nods his head and gestures toward the violin case as he takes out a pack of cigarettes, lights one.*]

RONNIE: And don't call it a "fiddle," OK?
BENJAMIN: Oh. Well, I didn't mean to —   5
RONNIE: You sound like a wuss. A hick. A dipshit.
BENJAMIN: It just slipped out. I didn't really—
RONNIE: If this was a fiddle, I'd be sitting here with a cob pipe, stomping my cowboy
boots and kicking up hay. Then I'd go home and fuck my cousin.
BENJAMIN: Oh! Well, I don't really think —
RONNIE: Do you see a cob pipe? Am I fucking my cousin?   10
BENJAMIN: Well, no, not at the moment, but—
RONNIE: All right. Then this is a violin, now you give me your money, and I ignore the
insult. Herein endeth the lesson.

[*Pause.*]

BENJAMIN: Look, a dollar's more than I've ever given to a . . . to someone asking for
money.
RONNIE: Yeah, well, this is New York. Welcome to the cost of living.
BENJAMIN: What I mean is, maybe in exchange, you could help me— ?   15
RONNIE: Jesus Christ! Do you see a sign around my neck reading "Big Apple Fucking
Tourist Bureau"?
BENJAMIN: I'm just looking for an address, I don't think it's far from here, maybe you could . . . ?

[BENJAMIN *holds out his scrap of paper,* RONNIE *snatches it away.*]

RONNIE: You're lucky I'm such a goddamn softy. [*He looks at the paper*] Oh, fuck you. Just
suck my dick, you and the cousin you rode in on.

BENJAMIN: I don't get it! What are you— ?

20 RONNIE: Eat me. You know exactly what I—

BENJAMIN: I'm just asking for a little—

RONNIE: "13 Doyers Street"? Like you don't know where that is?

BENJAMIN: Of course I don't know! That's why I'm asking—

RONNIE: C'mon, you trailer-park refugee. You don't know that's Chinatown?

25 BENJAMIN: Sure I know that's Chinatown.

RONNIE: I know you know that's Chinatown.

BENJAMIN: So? That doesn't mean I know where Chinatown—

RONNIE: So why is it that you picked *me*, of all the street musicians in the city—to point
you in the direction of Chinatown? Lemme guess—is it the earring? No, I don't think
so. The Hendrix riffs? Guess again, you fucking moron.

BENJAMIN: Now, wait a minute. I see what you're—

30 RONNIE: What are you gonna ask me next? Where you can find the best dim sum in the
city? Whether I can direct you to a genuine opium den? Or do I happen to know
how you can meet Miss Saigon for a night of nookie-nookie followed by a good old-
fashioned ritual suicide? Now, get your white ass off my sidewalk. One dollar doesn't
even begin to make up for all this aggravation. Why don't you go back home and race
bullfrogs, or whatever it is you do for—?

BENJAMIN: Brother, I can absolutely relate to your anger. Righteous rage, I suppose, would
be a more appropriate term. To be marginalized, as we are, by a white racist patriarchy,
to the point where the accomplishments of our people are obliterated from the history
books, this is cultural genocide of the first order, leading to the fact that you must do
battle with all of Euro-America's emasculating and brutal stereotypes of Asians—the
opium den, the sexual objectification of the Asian female, the exoticized image of a
tourist's Chinatown which ignores the exploitation of workers, the failure to unionize,
the high rate of mental illness and tuberculosis—against these, each day, you rage, no,
not as a victim, but as a survivor, yes, brother, a glorious warrior survivor!

[*Silence.*]

RONNIE: Say what?

BENJAMIN: So, I hope you can see that my request is not—

RONNIE: Wait, wait.

35 BENJAMIN: —motivated by the sorts of racist assumptions—

RONNIE: But, but where . . . how did you learn all that?

BENJAMIN: All what?

RONNIE: All that—you know—oppression stuff—tuberculosis . . .

BENJAMIN: It's statistically irrefutable. TB occurs in the community at a rate—

40 RONNIE: Where did *you* learn it?

BENJAMIN: I took Asian-American studies. In college.

RONNIE: Where did you go to college?

BENJAMIN: University of Wisconsin. Madison.

RONNIE: Madison, Wisconsin?

45 BENJAMIN: That's not where the bridges are, by the way.

RONNIE: Huh? Oh, right . . .

BENJAMIN: You wouldn't believe the number of people who—

RONNIE: They have Asian-American studies in Madison, Wisconsin? Since when?

BENJAMIN: Since the last Third World Unity hunger strike. [*Pause*] Why do you look so surprised? We're down.

RONNIE: I dunno. It just never occurred to me, the idea of Asian students in the Midwest 50 going on a hunger strike.

BENJAMIN: Well, a lot of them had midterms that week, so they fasted in shifts. [*Pause*] The administration never figured it out. The Asian students put that "They all look alike" stereotype to good use.

RONNIE: OK, so they got Asian-American studies. That still doesn't explain—

BENJAMIN: What?

RONNIE: Well . . . what *you* were doing taking it?

BENJAMIN: Just like everyone else. I wanted to explore my roots. And, you know, the 55 history of oppression which is my legacy. After a lifetime of assimilation, I wanted to find out who I really am.

[*Pause.*]

RONNIE: And did you?

BENJAMIN: Sure, I learned to take pride in my ancestors who built the railroads, my Popo who would make me a hot bowl of jok with thousand-day-old eggs when the white kids chased me home yelling, "Gook! Chink! Slant-eyes!"

RONNIE: OK, OK, that's enough!

BENJAMIN: Painful to listen to, isn't it?

RONNIE: I don't know what kind of bullshit ethnic studies program they're running over 60 in Wuss-consin, but did they bother to teach you that in order to find your Asian "roots," it's a good idea to first be Asian?

[*Pause.*]

BENJAMIN: Are you speaking metaphorically?

RONNIE: No! Literally! Look at your skin!

BENJAMIN: You know, it's very stereotypical to think that all Asian skin tones conform to a single hue.

RONNIE: You're white! Is this some kind of redneck joke or something? Am I the first person in the world to tell you this?

BENJAMIN: Oh! Oh! Oh! 65

RONNIE: I know real Asians are scarce in the Midwest, but . . . Jesus!

BENJAMIN: No, of course, I . . . I see where your misunderstanding arises.

RONNIE: Yeah. It's called, "You white."

BENJAMIN: It's just that—in my hometown of Tribune, Kansas, and then at school—see, everyone knows me—so this sort of thing never comes up. [*He offers his hand*] Benjamin Wong. I forget that a society wedded to racial constructs constantly forces me to explain my very existence.

RONNIE: Ronnie Chang. Otherwise known as "The Bow Man." 70

BENJAMIN: You see, I was adopted by Chinese-American parents at birth. So, clearly, I'm an Asian-American—

RONNIE: Even though you're blond and blue-eyed.

BENJAMIN: Well, you can't judge my race by my genetic heritage alone.

RONNIE: If genes don't determine race, what does?

BENJAMIN: Perhaps you'd prefer that I continue in denial, masquerading as a white man? 75

RONNIE: You can't just wake up and say, "Gee, I *feel* black today."

BENJAMIN: Brother, I'm just trying to find what you've already got.

RONNIE: What do I got?

BENJAMIN: A home. With your people. Picketing with the laundry workers. Taking refuge from the daily slights against your masculinity in the noble image of Gwan Gung.

80 **RONNIE:** Gwan who?

BENJAMIN: C'mon—the Chinese god of warriors and—what do you take me for? There're altars to him up all over the community.

RONNIE: I dunno what community you're talking about, but it's sure as hell not mine.

[*Pause.*]

BENJAMIN: What do you mean?

RONNIE: I mean, if you wanna call Chinatown *your* community, OK, knock yourself out, learn to use chopsticks, big deal. Go ahead, try and find your "roots" in some dim sum parlor with headless ducks hanging in the window. Those places don't tell you a thing about who *I* am.

85 **BENJAMIN:** Oh, I get it.

RONNIE: You get what?

BENJAMIN: You're one of those self-hating, *assimilated* Chinese-Americans, aren't you?

RONNIE: Oh, Jesus.

BENJAMIN: You probably call yourself "Oriental," huh? Look, maybe I can help you. I have some books I can–

90 **RONNIE:** Hey, I read all those Asian identity books when you were still slathering on industrial-strength sunblock. [*Pause*] Sure, I'm Chinese. But folks like you act like that means something. Like, all of a sudden, you know who I am. You think identity's that simple? That you can wrap it all up in a neat package and say, "I have ethnicity, therefore I am"? All you fucking ethnic fundamentalists. Always settling for easy answers. You say you're looking for identity, but you can't begin to face the real mysteries of the search. So instead, you go skin-deep, and call it a day. [*Pause. He turns away from* BENJAMIN *and starts to play his violin—slow and bluesy.*]

BENJAMIN: So what are you? "Just a human being"? That's like saying you *have* no identity. If you asked me to describe my dog, I'd say more than, "He's just a dog."

RONNIE: What—you think if I deny the importance of my race, I'm nobody? There're worlds out there, worlds you haven't even begun to understand. Open your eyes. Hear with your ears.

[RONNIE *holds his violin at chest level, but does not attempt to play during the following monologue. As he speaks, rock and jazz violin tracks fade in and out over the house speakers, bringing to life the styles of music he describes.*]

I concede—it was called a fiddle long ago—but that was even before the birth of jazz. When the hollering in the fields, the rank injustice of human bondage, the struggle of God's children against the plagues of the devil's white man, when all these boiled up into that bittersweet brew, called by later generations, the blues. That's when fiddlers like Son Sims held their chin rests at their chests, and sawed away like the hillbillies still do today. And with the coming of ragtime appeared the pioneer Stuff Smith, who sang as he stroked the catgut, with his raspy, Louis Armstrong-voice—gruff and sweet like the timbre of horsehair riding south below the fingerboard—and who finally sailed for Europe to find ears that would hear. Europe—where Stephane Grappelli initiated a magical French violin, to be passed from generation to generation—first he, to Jean-Luc Ponty, then Ponty to Didier Lockwood. Listening to Grappelli play "A Nightingale Sang in Berkeley Square" is to understand not only the song of birds, but also how they learn to fly, fall in love on the wing, and finally falter one day, to wait for darkness beneath a London street lamp. And Ponty—he showed how the modern violin man can accompany the shadow of his own lead lines, which cascade, one over another, into some nether world beyond the range of human hearing. Joe Venuti. Noel Pointer. Sven Asmussen. Even the Kronos Quartet, with their arrangement of "Purple Haze." Now, tell me, could any legacy be more rich more crowded with mythology and heroes to inspire pride? What can I say if the banging of a gong or the clinking of a pickax on the Transcontinental Railroad fails to move me even as much as one note, played through a violin MIDI controller by Michael Urbaniak? [*He puts his violin to his chin, begins to play a jazz composition of his own invention*] Does it have to sound like Chinese opera before people like you decide I know who I am?

[BENJAMIN *stands for a long moment, listening to* RONNIE *play. Then, he drops his dollar into the case, turns and exits right.* RONNIE *continues to play a long moment. Then* BENJAMIN *enters downstage left, illuminated in his own spotlight. He sits on the floor of the stage, his feet dangling off the lip. As he speaks,* RONNIE *continues playing his tune, which becomes underscoring for* BENJAMIN'S *monologue. As the music continues, does it slowly begin to reflect the influence of Chinese music?*]

BENJAMIN: When I finally found Doyers Street, I scanned the buildings for Number 13. Walking down an alley where the scent of freshly steamed char siu bao lingered in the air, I felt immediately that I had entered a world where all things were finally familiar. [*Pause*] An old woman bumped me with her shopping bag—screaming to her friend in Cantonese, though they walked no more than a few inches apart. Another man—shouting to a vendor in Sze-Yup. A youth, in white undershirt, perhaps a recent newcomer, bargaining with a grocer in Hokkien. I walked through this ocean of dialects, breathing in the richness with deep gulps, exhilarated by the energy this symphony brought to my step. And when I finally saw the number 13, I nearly wept at my good fortune. An old tenement, paint peeling, inside walls no doubt thick with a century of grease and broken dreams—and yet, to me, a temple—the house where my father was born. I suddenly saw it all: Gung Gung, coming home from his sixteen-hour days pressing shirts he could never afford to own, bringing with him candies for my father, each sweet wrapped in the hope of a better life. When my father left the ghetto, he swore he would never return. But he had, this day, in the thoughts and memories of his son, just six months after his death. And as I sat on the stoop, I pulled a hua-mio from my pocket, sucked on it, and felt his spirit returning. To this place where his ghost, and the dutiful hearts of all his descendants, would always call home. [*He listens for a long moment*] And I felt an ache in my heart for all those lost souls, denied this most important of revelations: to know who they truly are.

[BENJAMIN *sucks his salted plum and listens to the sounds around him.* RONNIE *continues to play. The two remain oblivious of one another. Lights fade slowly to black.*]

End of play

QUESTIONS

1. Does the encounter between Ronnie and Benjamin seem realistic? Do you think two people their age and of their time would speak as they do?
2. Do you think Ronnie's cursing is understandable? Why is he so angry at Benjamin?

3. What do you think Ronnie means when he says to Benjamin, "There're worlds out there, worlds you haven't even begun to understand."

4. What is Benjamin looking for in Chinatown? What does this say about how he feels about his own identity?

GENERAL QUESTIONS

1. Do you think it is important for people to know their identity? Who has a better under-standing of his own identity, Ronnie or Benjamin? Benjamin refers to people who don't "know who they truly are" as "lost souls." What do you think he means by this?

2. Ronnie does not want to be identified solely by his ethnicity. Why not? What is the importance of knowing cultures other than your own?

JANE MARTIN (b. ?)

"Jane Martin" is a dramatist about whom nothing is known publicly. A common conclusion is that she is a resident of Kentucky, because many of her plays were first produced at the ATL–Actors Theatre of Louisville. Some biographers have concluded that the name "Jane Martin" is a pseud-onym of Jon Jory, who up until 2000 was the artistic director at the Actors Theatre. The fact is, however, that nobody is telling. What is clear is that an extremely talented and original drama-tist using the name "Jane Martin" has been writing plays and getting them produced since 1981, when her first play, Talking With, *was first performed at the Actors Theatre, and then achieved both national and international acclaim. Martin's plays have also gone beyond Louisville. For example, the play* Keely and Du—*about the difficulties associated with abortion—was first performed in Philadelphia and was a finalist for a Pulitzer Prize in 1994. It also received the Best New Play designation of the American Theater Critics Association for that year. In addition, Martin's* Good Boys *was produced at the Tyrone Guthrie Theater in Minneapolis in 2002, and her* Sez She *was also performed in Minneapolis, in 2006, at the Illusion Theatre.*

In *Beauty,* Martin has created a brief play—a scene, really—between two young women. Each woman is excellent in her own way, but the two also envy each other for reasons that they themselves have perhaps not previously realized. Such a subject could potentially lead to a fairly extensive dramatic examination of internal feelings. But the major situation of the play's narrative pushes the sub-ject in a different direction—toward the farcical happening with which the play concludes. In the meantime, Martin's dialogue creates humor and a good deal of interest. Bethany and Carla, though similar in many ways, are different, but the overriding event of the play brings about something of a reconciliation of motives, and also leads to the play's final speeches embodying the preposterous and farci-cal conclusion.

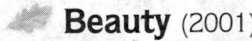 Beauty (2001)

CHARACTERS

Carla
Bethany

Scene: An apartment. Minimalist set. A young woman, CARLA, *on the phone.*

CARLA: In love with me? You're in love with me? Could you describe yourself again? Uh-huh. Uh-huh. And you spoke to me? [*A knock, at the door.*] Listen, I always hate to interrupt a marriage proposal, but . . . could you possibly hold that thought?

[*Puts phone down and goes to door. BETHANY, the same age as CARLA, and a friend, is there. She carries the sort of mid-eastern lamp we know from ALADDIN.*]

BETHANY: Thank God you were home. I mean, you're not going to believe this!
CARLA: Somebody on the phone. [*Goes back to it.*]
BETHANY: I mean, I just had a beach urge, so I told them at work my uncle was dying . . .
CARLA: [*Motions to BETHANY for quiet.*] And you were the one in the leather jacket with the   5
tattoo? What was the tattoo? [*CARLA again asks BETHANY, who is gesturing wildly that she should hang up, to cool it.*] Look, a screaming eagle from shoulder to shoulder, maybe. There were a lot of people in the bar.
BETHANY: [*Gesturing and mouthing.*] I have to get back to work.
CARLA: [*On phone.*] See, the thing is, I'm probably not going to marry someone I can't remember . . . particularly when I don't drink. Sorry. Sorry. Sorry. [*She hangs up.*] Madness.
BETHANY: So I ran out to the beach . . .
CARLA: This was some guy I never met who apparently offered me a beer . . .
BETHANY: . . . low tide and this . . . [*The lamp.*] . . . was just sitting there, lying there . . .   10
CARLA: . . . and he tracks me down . . .
BETHANY: . . . on the beach, and I lift this lid thing . . .
CARLA: . . . and seriously proposes marriage.
BETHANY: . . . and a genie comes out.
CARLA: I mean, that's twice in a . . . what?   15
BETHANY: A genie comes out of this thing.
CARLA: A genie?
BETHANY: I'm not kidding, the whole Disney kind of thing, swirling smoke, and then this twenty-foot-high, see-through guy in like an Arabian outfit.
CARLA: Very funny.
BETHANY: Yes, funny, but twenty feet high! I look up and down the beach, I'm alone. I   20
don't have my pepper spray or my hand alarm. You know me, when I'm petrified I joke. I say his voice is too high for Robin Williams, and he says he's a castrati. Naturally. Who else would I meet?
CARLA: What's a castrati?
BETHANY: You know . . .

[*The appropriate gesture.*]

CARLA: Bethany, dear one, I have three modeling calls. I am meeting Ralph Lauren!°
BETHANY: Okay, good. Ralph Lauren. Look, I am not kidding!
CARLA: You're not kidding what?!   25
BETHANY: There is a genie in this thingamajig.
CARLA: Uh-huh. I'll be back around eight.
BETHANY: And he offered me *wishes!*
CARLA: Is this some elaborate practical joke because it's my birthday?
BETHANY: No, happy birthday, but I'm like crazed because I'm on this deserted beach   30

°23 Ralph Lauren (b. 1939) is the principal owner of the Ralph Lauren fashion and design empire, and an acknowledged leader of American fashion.

with a twenty-foot-high, see-through genie, so like sarcastically . . . you know how I
need a new car . . . I said fine, gimme 25,000 dollars . . .

CARLA: On the beach with the genie?

BETHANY: Yeah, right, exactly, and it rains down out of the sky.

CARLA: Oh sure.

BETHANY: [*Pulling a wad out of her purse.*] Count it, those are thousands. 1 lost one in the surf.

[*CARLA sees the top bill. Looks at BETHANY, who nods encouragement. CARLA thumbs through them.*]

35 **CARLA:** These look real.

BETHANY: Yeah.

CARLA: And they rained down out of the sky?

BETHANY: Yeah.

CARLA: You've been really strange lately, are you dealing?

40 **BETHANY:** Dealing what? I've even given up chocolate.

CARLA: Let me see the genie.

BETHANY: Wait, wait.

CARLA: Bethany, I don't have time to screw around. Let me see the genie or let me go on
my appointments.

BETHANY: Wait! So I pick up the money . . . see, there's sand on the money . . . and I'm like
nuts so I say, you know, "Okay, look, ummm, big guy, my uncle is in the hospital" . . .
because as you know when I said to the people at work my uncle was dying, I was on
one level telling the truth although it had nothing to do with the beach, but he was in
Intensive Care after the accident, and that's on my mind, so I say, okay, Genie, heal my
uncle . . . which is like impossible given he was hit by two trucks, and the genie says,
"Yes, Master" . . . like they're supposed to say, and he goes into this like kind of whirlwind, kicking up sand and stuff, and I'm like, "Oh my God!" and the air clears, and he
bows, you know, and says, "It is done, Master," and I say, "Okay, whatever-you-are,
I'm calling on my cell phone," and I get it out and I get this doctor who is like dumb-
struck who says my uncle came to, walked out of Intensive Care, and left the hospital!
I'm not kidding, Carla.

45 **CARLA:** On your mother's grave?

BETHANY: On my mother's grave.

[*They look at each other.*]

CARLA: Let me see the genie.

BETHANY: No, no, look, that's the whole thing. . . I was just, like, reacting, you know,
responding, and that's already two wishes . . . although I'm really pleased about my
uncle, the $25,000 thing, I could have asked for $10 million, and there is only one wish
left.

CARLA: So ask for $10 million.

50 **BETHANY:** I don't think so. I don't think so. I mean, I gotta focus in here. Do you have a
sparkling water?

CARLA: No. Bethany, I'm missing Ralph Lauren now. Very possibly my one chance to go
from catalogue model to the very, very big time, so, if you are joking, stop joking.

BETHANY: Not joking. See, see, the thing is, I know what I want. In my guts. Yes. Underneath my entire bitch of a life is this unspoken, ferocious, all-consuming urge . . .

CARLA: [*Trying to get her to move this along.*] Ferocious, all-consuming urge . . .

BETHANY: I want to be like you.

55 **CARLA:** Me?

BETHANY: Yes.

CARLA: Half the time you don't even like me.

BETHANY: Jealous. The ogre of jealousy.

CARLA: You're the one with the $40,000 job straight out of school. You're the one who has published short stories. I'm the one hanging on by her fingernails in modeling. The one who has creeps calling her on the phone. The one who had to have a nose job.

BETHANY: I want to be beautiful.   60

CARLA: You are beautiful.

BETHANY: Carla, I'm not beautiful.

CARLA: You have charm. You have personality. You know perfectly well you're pretty.

BETHANY: "Pretty," see, that's it. Pretty is the minor leagues of beautiful. Pretty is what people discover about you after they know you. Beautiful is what knocks them out across the room. *Pretty,* you get called a couple of times a year; *beautiful* is 24 hours a day.

CARLA: Yeah? So?   65

BETHANY: So?! We're talking *beauty* here. Don't say "So?" Beauty is the real deal. You are the center of any moment of your life. People stare. Men flock. I've seen you get offered discounts on makeup for no reason. Parents treat beautiful children better. Studies show your income goes up. You can have sex anytime you want it. Men have to know me. That takes up to a year. I'm continually horny.

CARLA: Bethany, I don't even like sex. I can't have a conversation without men coming on to me. I have no privacy. I get hassled on the street. They start pressuring me from the beginning. Half the time, it never occurs to them to start with a conversation. Smart guys like you. You've had three long-term relationships, and you're only twenty-three. I haven't had one. The good guys, the smart guys are scared to death of me. I'm surrounded by male bimbos who think a preposition is when you go to school away from home. I have no woman friends except you. I don't even want to talk about this!

BETHANY: I knew you'd say something like this. See, you're "in the club" so you can say this. It's the way beauty functions as an elite. You're trying to keep it all for yourself.

CARLA: I'm trying to tell you it's no picnic.

BETHANY: But it's what everybody wants. It's the nasty secret at large in the world.   70
It's the unspoken tidal desire in every room and on every street. It's the unspoken, the soundless whisper . . . millions upon millions of people longing hopelessly and forever to stop being whatever they are and be beautiful, but the difference between those ardent multitudes and me is that I have a goddamn genie and one more wish!

CARLA: Well, it's not what I want. This is me, Carla. I have never read a whole book. Page 6, I can't remember page 4. The last thing I read was "The Complete Idiot's Guide to WordPerfect." I leave dinner parties right after the dessert because I'm out of conversation. You know the dumb blond joke about on the application where it says, "Sign here," she put Sagittarius? I've done that. Only beautiful guys approach me, and that's because they want to borrow my eye shadow. I barely exist outside a mirror! You don't want to *be me.*

BETHANY: None of you tell the truth. That's why you have no friends. We can all see you're just trying to make us feel better because we aren't in your league. This only proves to me it should be my third wish. Money can only buy things. Beauty makes you the center of the universe.

[BETHANY *picks up the lamp.*]

CARLA: Don't do it. Bethany, don't wish it! I am telling you you'll regret it.

[BETHANY *lifts the lid. There is a tremendous crash, and the lights go out. Then they flicker and come back up, revealing* BETHANY *and* CARLA *on the floor where they have been thrown by the explosion. We don't realize it at first, but they have exchanged places.*]

CARLA/BETHANY: Oh God.°

75 BETHANY/CARLA: Oh God.

CARLA/BETHANY: Am I bleeding? Am I dying?

BETHANY/CARLA: I'm so dizzy. You're not bleeding.

CARLA/BETHANY: Neither are you.

BETHANY/CARLA: I feel so weird.

80 CARLA/BETHANY: Me too. I feel . . . [*Looking at her hands.*] Oh, my God, I'm wearing your jewelry. I'm wearing your nail polish.

BETHANY/CARLA: I know I'm over here, but I can see myself over there.

CARLA/BETHANY: I'm wearing your dress. I have your legs!!

BETHANY/CARLA: These aren't my shoes. I can't meet Ralph Lauren wearing these shoes!

CARLA/BETHANY: I wanted to be beautiful, but I didn't want to be you.

85 BETHANY/CARLA: Thanks a lot!!

CARLA/BETHANY: I've got to go. I want to pick someone out and get laid.

BETHANY/CARLA: You can't just walk out of here in my body!

CARLA/BETHANY: Wait a minute. Wait a minute. What's eleven eighteenths of 1,726?

BETHANY/CARLA: Why?

90 CARLA/BETHANY: I'm a public accountant. I want to know if you have my brain.

BETHANY/CARLA: One hundred thirty-two and a half.°

CARLA/BETHANY: You have my brain.

BETHANY/CARLA: What shade of Rubenstein lipstick does Cindy Crawford wear with teal blue?

CARLA/BETHANY: Raging Storm.

95 BETHANY/CARLA: You have my brain. You poor bastard.

CARLA/BETHANY: I don't care. Don't you see?

BETHANY/CARLA: See what?

CARLA/BETHANY: We both have the one thing, the one and only thing everybody wants.

BETHANY/CARLA: What is that?

100 CARLA/BETHANY: It's better than beauty for me; it's better than brains for you.

BETHANY/CARLA: What? What?!

CARLA/BETHANY: Different problems.

BLACKOUT

°74 In these last speeches, the original character is indicated by the second speech prefix. Thus, "Carla/Bethany" actually refers to Bethany, who after the transformation now looks like Carla. Similarly, the prefix "Bethany/Carla" is Carla, who is now looking like Bethany. °91 The correct answer is actually 1,054.777. . . .

QUESTIONS

1. Describe the differences in character between Bethany and Carla. What is Bethany's occupation? What is Carla's? How does the dialogue reveal that both women actually envy each other? Why do they have these feelings?

2. In the first fourteen speeches, Bethany and Carla seem to be speaking as though they have not heard each other. What happens to bring Carla to attention, and thus to begin the actual dialogue between them?

3. What has happened to Bethany on the beach? Is this incident serious or comic? What has happened to the first two of her three "wishes"? Why is it important to the structure of the play that two of the three wishes have been used?

GENERAL QUESTIONS

1. What truly important personal issues are actually raised in the dialogue between Carla and Bethany? How are Bethany's issues raised in her comparison of being beautiful or being pretty? How do Bethany's thoughts lead her to her final wish? In what way does the title *Beauty* embody the play's major ideas?

2. It is likely that Carla/Bethany's concluding speech would make an audience laugh. To what degree, however, might the observation about "the one and only thing everybody wants" be considered seriously? Is it true that people really want "different problems"?

EUGENE O'NEILL (1888–1953)

Eugene O'Neill is one of America's great playwrights. He wrote more than forty plays and won three Pulitzer Prizes. He is still the only U.S. dramatist to have received the Nobel Prize for literature (in 1936).

O'Neill was born in New York, the son of a well-known actor, and was educated sporadically as his parents traveled from city to city on theatrical tours. Eventually he studied at Princeton, but he left to go to work, first in a mail-order house and then in Honduras, where he engaged in prospecting. He then began a brief career as a seaman, traveling on both sides of the Atlantic. He contracted tuberculosis in about 1912, and while in a sanitarium he began to write plays. Upon release he studied playwriting at Harvard, but by 1916 he had left to try his luck as a playwright with the Provincetown Players, the same company that Susan Glaspell helped found and where she began her writing career. It was in 1916, the same year that Glaspell wrote Trifles, *that the Provincetown Players produced O'Neill's first drama,* Bound East for Cardiff.

O'Neill maintained a close connection with the Provincetown Players for several years, providing them with ten one-act plays between 1916 and 1920. Among these were Thirst *(1916),* Before Breakfast *(1916),* Fog *(1917),* The Long Voyage Home *(1917),* Ile *(1917), and* The Rope *(1917). His later (and longer) works include* The Emperor Jones *(1920),* Anna Christie *(1921),* Desire Under the Elms *(1924),* Strange Interlude *(1928),* Mourning Becomes Electra *(1931), and* The Iceman Cometh *(1946). O'Neill also wrote an autobiographical play,* Long Day's Journey into Night *(1936), that at his request was withheld until after his death. Staged on Broadway in 1956, it received the Pulitzer Prize in drama (O'Neill's third Pulitzer); it was later made into a film starring Katharine Hepburn.*

Before Breakfast, though one of O'Neill's earliest plays, shows his characteristic control of point of view, conflict, character, and setting. The play was first staged in December 1916, by the Provincetown Players in New York City's Greenwich Village (where Christopher Street, the address of the Rowlands' apartment, is located). The play contains little action, and yet it is charged with conflict. The plot is simple and straightforward—a wife onstage berates her offstage husband for twenty minutes. The conflict between them is long-standing and bitter, and it is resolved in the play's horrifying conclusion.

Above all, *Before Breakfast* illustrates O'Neill's skillful control over dramatic point of view. By giving Mrs. Rowland every word spoken on the stage, O'Neill causes the audience to understand everything as it is filtered through her mind. Indeed, the play is a bravura piece for a gifted actress. Because Mrs. Rowland dominates the stage so completely, it is tempting to see her character as one of constantly nagging spitefulness. It is to O'Neill's credit, however, that she is not without basic strength, and that her bitterness is not without cause. Alfred, the unseen and unheard offstage husband, has contributed to their estranged relationship.

Of particular note in indicating the impasse that the characters have reached are O'Neill's extensive stage directions describing the setting. We learn that the Rowlands' flat is in Greenwich Village, the traditional New York home of artists, poets, and actors. On the one hand, therefore, the flat suggests Alfred's artistic aspirations, but on the other, the poverty of the surroundings indicates the sad truth that such dreams cannot be sustained unless someone pays the rent.

The language of Mrs. Rowland, the only speaking character in the play, indicates both her lack of education and her intense dissatisfaction. Phrases such as "I got," "like I was," "liable" for "likely," and "sewing my fingers off" suggest that her knowledge of language has not been derived from education and study. Her speech also suggests the social gulf that originally separated her from Alfred, a gulf that they tried to bridge in their marriage but which now has opened up irretrievably. A number of other phrases embody the taunts that Mrs. Rowland directs at Alfred ("pawn, pawn, pawn," "like a man," "a fine life," "in trouble," etc.).

Before Breakfast (1916)

CHARACTERS

Mrs. Rowland, the wife
Mr. Alfred Rowland, the husband [who remains unseen, offstage]

SCENE. *A small room serving both as kitchen and dining room in a flat on Christopher Street, New York City. In the rear, to the right, a door leading to the outer hallway. On the left of the doorway, a sink, and a two-burner gas stove. Over the stove, and extending to the left wall, a wooden closet for dishes, etc. On the left, two windows looking out on a fire escape where several potted plants are dying of neglect. Before the windows, a table covered with oilcloth. Two cane-bottomed chairs are placed by the table. Another stands against the wall to the right of door in rear. In the right wall, rear, a doorway leading into a bedroom. Farther forward, different articles of a man's and a woman's clothing are hung on pegs. A clothes line is strung from the left corner, rear, to the right wall, forward.*

It is about eight thirty in the morning of a fine, sunshiny day in the early fall.

Mrs. Rowland enters from the bedroom, yawning, her hands still busy putting the finishing touches on a slovenly toilet by sticking hairpins into her hair, which is bunched up in a drab-colored mass on top of her round head. She is of medium height and inclined to a shapeless stoutness, accentuated by her formless blue dress, shabby and worn. Her face is characterless, with small regular features and eyes of a nondescript blue. There is a pinched expression about her eyes and nose and her weak, spiteful mouth. She is in her early twenties but looks much older.

She comes to the middle of the room and yawns, stretching her arms to their full length. Her drowsy eyes stare about the room with the irritated look of one to whom a long sleep has not been a long rest. She goes wearily to the clothes hanging on the right and takes an apron from a hook. She ties it about her waist, giving vent to an exasperated "damn" when the knot fails to obey her clumsy fingers. Finally gets it tied and goes slowly to the gas stove and lights one burner. She fills the coffee pot at the sink and sets it over the flame. Then slumps down into a chair by the table and puts a hand over her forehead as if she were suffering from headache. Suddenly her face brightens as though she had remembered something, and she casts a quick glance at the dish closet; then looks sharply at the bedroom door and listens intently for a moment or so.

MRS. ROWLAND: [*In a low voice.*] Alfred! Alfred! [*There is no answer from the next room and she continues suspiciously in a louder tone.*] You needn't pretend you're asleep. [*There is no reply to this from the bedroom, and, reassured, she gets up from her chair and tiptoes cautiously to the dish closet. She slowly opens one door, taking great care to make no noise, and slides out, from their hiding place behind the dishes, a bottle of Gordon gin and a glass. In doing so she disturbs the top dish, which rattles a little. At this sound she starts guiltily and looks with sulky defiance at the doorway to the next room.*]

[*Her voice trembling.*] Alfred!

[*After a pause, during which she listens for any sound, she takes the glass and pours out a large drink and gulps it down; then hastily returns the bottle and glass to their hiding place. She closes the closet door with the same care as she had opened it, and, heaving a great sigh of relief, sinks down into her chair again. The large dose of alcohol she has taken has an almost immediate effect. Her features become more animated, she seems to gather energy, and she looks at the bedroom door with a hard, vindictive smile on her lips. Her eyes glance quickly about the room and are fixed on a man's coat and vest which hang from a hook at right. She moves stealthily over to the open doorway and stands there, out of sight of anyone inside, listening for any movement.*]

[*Calling in a half-whisper.*] Alfred!

[*Again there is no reply. With a swift movement she takes the coat and vest from the hook and returns with them to her chair. She sits down and takes the various articles out of each pocket but quickly puts them back again. At last, in the inside pocket of the vest, she finds a letter.*]

[*Looking at the handwriting—slowly to herself.*] Hmm! I knew it.

[*She opens the letter and reads it. At first her expression is one of hatred and rage, but as she goes on to the end it changes to one of triumphant malignity. She remains in deep thought for a moment, staring before her, the letter in her hands, a cruel smile on her lips. Then she puts the letter back in

Mrs. Rowland (Lona Leigh) attends to the coffee in the 2001 Provincetown Playhouse, New York City, production of *Before Breakfast,* directed by Stephen Kennedy Murphy, lighting by Matthew E. Adelson, and sets by Roger Hanna.

the pocket of the vest, and still careful not to awaken the sleeper, hangs the clothes up again on the same hook, and goes to the bedroom door and looks in.]

5   *[In a loud, shrill voice.]* Alfred! *[Still louder.]* Alfred! *[There is a muffled, yawning groan from the next room.]* Don't you think it's about time you got up? Do you want to stay in bed all day? *[Turning around and coming back to her chair.]* Not that I've got any doubts about your being lazy enough to stay in bed forever. *[She sits down and looks out of the window, irritably.]* Goodness knows what time it is. We haven't even got any way of telling the time since you pawned your watch like a fool. The last valuable thing we had, and you knew it. It's been nothing but pawn, pawn, pawn, with you—anything to put off getting a job, anything to get out of going to work like a man.

[She taps the floor with her foot nervously, biting her lips.]

[After a short pause.] Alfred! Get up, do you hear me? I want to make that bed before I go out. I'm sick of having this place in a continual muss on your account. *[With a certain vindictive satisfaction.]* Not that we'll be here long unless you manage to get some money some place. Heaven knows I do my part—and more—going out to sew every day while you play the gentleman and loaf around bar rooms with that good-for-nothing lot of artists from the Square.°

[A short pause during which she plays nervously with a cup and saucer on the table.]

And where are you going to get money, I'd like to know? The rent's due this week and you know what the landlord is. He won't let us stay a minute over our time. You say you *can't* get a job. That's a lie and you know it. You never even look for one. All you do is moon around all day writing silly poetry and stories that no one will buy—and no wonder they won't. I notice I can always get a position, such as it is; and it's only that which keeps us from starving to death.

[Gets up and goes over to the stove—looks into the coffee pot to see if the water is boiling; then comes back and sits down again.]

You'll have to get money to-day some place. I can't do it all, and I won't do it all. You've got to come to your senses. You've got to beg, borrow, or steal it somewheres. *[With a contemptuous laugh.]* But where, I'd like to know? You're too proud to beg, and you've borrowed the limit, and you haven't the nerve to steal.

[After a pause—getting up angrily.] Aren't you up yet, for heaven's sake? It's just like you to go to sleep again, or pretend to. *[She goes to the bedroom door and looks in.]* Oh, you are up. Well, it's about time. You needn't look at me like that. Your airs don't fool me a bit any more. I know you too well—better than you think I do—you and your goings-on. *[Turning away from the door—meaningly.]* I know a lot of things, my dear. Never mind what I know, now. I'll tell you before I go, you needn't worry. *[She comes to the middle of the room and stands there, frowning.]*

10   *[Irritably.]* Hmm! I suppose I might as well get breakfast ready—not that there's anything much to get. *[Questioningly.]* Unless you have some money? *[She pauses for an answer from the next room which does not come.]* Foolish question! *[She gives a short, hard laugh.]* I ought to know you better than that by this time. When you left here in such a huff last night I knew what would happen. You can't be trusted for a second. A nice condition you

---

°6 *Square:* Washington Square, at the center of Greenwich Village in New York.

came home in! The fight we had was only an excuse for you to make a beast of yourself. What was the use pawning your watch if all you wanted with the money was to waste it in buying drink?

[*Goes over to the dish closet and takes out plates, cups, etc., while she is talking.*]

Hurry up! It don't take long to get breakfast these days, thanks to you. All we got this morning is bread and butter and coffee; and you wouldn't even have that if it wasn't for me sewing my fingers off. [*She slams the loaf of bread on the table with a bang.*]

The bread's stale. I hope you'll like it. *You* don't deserve any better, but I don't see why *I* should suffer.

[*Going over to the stove.*] The coffee'll be ready in a minute, and you needn't expect me to wait for you.

[*Suddenly with great anger.*] What on earth are you doing all this time? [*She goes over to the door and looks in.*] Well, you're *almost* dressed at any rate. I expected to find you back in bed. That'd be just like you. How awful you look this morning! For heaven's sake, shave! You're disgusting! You look like a tramp. No wonder no one will give you a job. I don't blame them—when you don't even look halfway decent. [*She goes to the stove.*] There's plenty of hot water right here. You've got no excuse. [*Gets a bowl and pours some of the water from the coffee pot into it.*] Here.

[*He reaches his hand into the room for it. It is a sensitive hand with slender fingers. It trembles and some of the water spills on the floor.*]

[*Tauntingly.*] Look at your hand tremble! You'd better give up drinking. You can't   15
stand it. It's just your kind that get the D.T.'s. That would be the last straw! [*Looking down at the floor.*] Look at the mess you've made of this floor—cigarette butts and ashes all over the place. Why can't you put them on a plate? No, you wouldn't be considerate enough to do that. You never think of me. You don't have to sweep the room and that's all you care about.

[*Takes the broom and commences to sweep viciously, raising a cloud of dust. From the inner room comes the sound of a razor being stropped.*]°

[*Sweeping.*] Hurry up! It must be nearly time for me to go. If I'm late I'm liable to lose my position, and then I couldn't support you any longer. [*As an afterthought she adds sarcastically.*] And then you'd have to go to work or something dreadful like that. [*Sweeping under the table.*] What I want to know is whether you're going to look for a job today or not. You know your family won't help us any more. They've had enough of you, too. [*After a moment's silent sweeping.*] I'm about sick of all this life. I've a good notion to go home, if I wasn't too proud to let them know what a failure you've been—you, the millionaire Rowland's only son, the Harvard graduate, the poet, the catch of the town—Huh! [*With bitterness.*] There wouldn't be many of them now envy my catch if they knew the truth. What has our marriage been, I'd like to know? Even before your *millionaire* father died owing everyone in the world money, you certainly never wasted any of your time on your wife. I suppose you thought I'd ought to be glad you were *honorable* enough to marry me—after getting me into trouble. You were ashamed of me with your fine friends because my father's only a grocer, that's what you were. At least he's honest, which is more than any one could say about yours. [*She is sweeping steadily toward the door. Leans on her broom for a moment.*]

°15 S.D. *stropped:* Alfred is using a leather strap to sharpen a straight razor, the kind barbers still use, with a very sharp steel blade that is hinged to a handle.

You hoped every one'd think you'd been forced to marry me, and pity you, didn't you? You didn't hesitate much about telling me you loved me, and making me believe your lies, before it happened, did you? You made me think you didn't want your father to buy me off as he tried to do. I know better now. I haven't lived with you all this time for nothing. [*Somberly.*] It's lucky the poor thing was born dead, after all. What a father you'd have been!

[*Is silent, brooding moodily for a moment—then she continues with a sort of savage joy.*]

But I'm not the only one who's got you to thank for being unhappy. There's one other, at least, and *she* can't hope to marry you now. [*She puts her head into the next room.*] How about Helen? [*She starts back from the doorway, half frightened.*]

Don't look at me that way! Yes, I read her letter. What about it? I got a right to. I'm your wife. And I know all there is to know, so don't lie. You needn't stare at me so. You can't bully me with your superior airs any longer. Only for me you'd be going without breakfast this very morning. [*She sets the broom back in the corner—whiningly.*] You never did have any gratitude for what I've done. [*She comes to the stove and puts the coffee into the pot.*] The coffee's ready. I'm not going to wait for you. [*She sits down in her chair again.*]

20   [*After a pause—puts her hand to her head—fretfully.*] My head aches so this morning. It's a shame I've got to go to work in a stuffy room all day in my condition. And I wouldn't if you were half a man. By rights I ought to be lying on my back instead of you. You know how sick I've been this last year; and yet you object when I take a little something to keep up my spirits. You even didn't want me to take that tonic I got at the drug store. [*With a hard laugh.*] I know you'd be glad to have me dead and out of your way; then you'd be free to run after all these silly girls that think you're such a wonderful, misunderstood person—this Helen and the others. [*There is a sharp exclamation of pain from the next room.*]

[*With satisfaction.*] There! I knew you'd cut yourself. It'll be a lesson to you. You know you oughtn't to be running around nights drinking with your nerves in such an awful shape. [*She goes to the door and looks in.*]

What makes you so pale? What are you staring at yourself in the mirror that way for? For goodness sake, wipe that blood off your face! [*With a shudder.*] It's horrible. [*In relieved tones.*] There, that's better. I never could stand the sight of blood. [*She shrinks back from the door a little.*] You better give up trying and go to a barber shop. Your hand shakes dreadfully. Why do you stare at me like that? [*She turns away from the door.*] Are you still mad at me about that letter? [*Defiantly.*] Well, I had a right to read it. I'm your wife. [*She comes to the chair and sits down again. After a pause.*]

I knew all the time you were running around with someone. Your lame excuses about spending the time at the library didn't fool me. Who is this Helen, anyway? One of those artists? Or does she write poetry, too? Her letter sounds that way. I'll bet she told you your things were the best ever, and you believed her, like a fool. Is she young and pretty? I was young and pretty, too, when you fooled me with your fine, poetic talk; but life with you would soon wear anyone down. What I've been through!

[*Goes over and takes the coffee off the stove.*] Breakfast is ready. [*With a contemptuous glance.*] Breakfast! [*Pours out a cup of coffee for herself and puts the pot on the table.*] Your coffee'll be cold. What are you doing—still shaving, for heaven's sake? You'd better give it up. One of these mornings you'll give yourself a serious cut. [*She cuts off bread and butters it. During the following speeches she eats and sips her coffee.*]

25   I'll have to run as soon as I've finished eating. One of us has got to work. [*Angrily.*] Are you going to look for a job today or aren't you? I should think some of your fine

friends would help you, if they really think you're so much. But I guess they just like to hear you talk. [*Sits in silence for a moment.*]

I'm sorry for this Helen, whoever she is. Haven't you got any feelings for other people? What will her family say? I see she mentions them in her letter. What is she going to do—have the child—or go to one of those doctors? That's a nice thing, I must say. Where can she get the money? Is she rich? [*She waits for some answer to this volley of questions.*]

Hmm! You won't tell me anything about her, will you? Much I care. Come to think of it, I'm not so sorry for her after all. She knew what she was doing. She isn't any schoolgirl, like I was, from the looks of her letter. Does she know you're married? Of course, she must. All your friends know about your unhappy marriage. I know they pity you, but they don't know my side of it. They'd talk different if they did.

[*Too busy eating to go on for a second or so.*]

This Helen must be a fine one, if she knew you were married. What does she expect, then? That I'll divorce you and let her marry you? Does she think I'm crazy enough for that—after all you've made me go through? I guess not! And you can't get a divorce from me and you know it. No one can say *I've* ever done anything wrong. [*Drinks the last of her cup of coffee.*]

She deserves to suffer, that's all I can say. I'll tell you what I think; I think your Helen is no better than a common street-walker, that's what I think. [*There is a stifled groan of pain from the next room.*]

Did you cut yourself again? Serves you right. [*Gets up and takes off her apron.*] Well, I've got to run along. [*Peevishly.*] This is a fine life for me to be leading! I won't stand for your loafing any longer. [*Something catches her ear and she pauses and listens intently.*] There! You've overturned the water all over everything. Don't say you haven't. I can hear it dripping on the floor. [*A vague expression of fear comes over her face.*] Alfred! Why don't you answer me? 30

[*She moves slowly toward the room. There is the noise of a chair being overturned and something crashes heavily to the floor. She stands, trembling with fright.*]

Alfred! Alfred! Answer me! What is it you knocked over? Are you still drunk? [*Unable to stand the tension a second longer she rushes to the door of the bedroom.*]
Alfred!

[*She stands in the doorway looking down at the floor of the inner room, transfixed with horror. Then she shrieks wildly and runs to the other door, unlocks it and frenziedly pulls it open, and runs shrieking madly into the outer hallway.*]

[*The curtain falls.*]

QUESTIONS

1. What does the setting tell you about the Rowlands?
2. How is Mrs. Rowland described in the opening stage directions? How does O'Neill use adjectives to shape your initial response to her? How does the rest of the play sustain or alter this image?
3. How does Mrs. Rowland speak to Alfred? What does she complain about? What does she accuse Alfred of being and doing?
4. What happened during Mrs. Rowland's premarital affair with Alfred? Why didn't she let Alfred's father "buy her off"?

5. Where is the play's crisis? Which character comes to a crisis? What leads you to conclude that the character and play have reached a crisis?

6. Mrs. Rowland precipitates the climax by discussing Alfred's affair. What do we learn about Helen? What pushes Alfred over the edge?

GENERAL QUESTIONS

1. How does the setting define the characters, their relationship, and their life? What details of setting are most significant?

2. Is Mrs. Rowland flat or round? Static or dynamic? Individualized or stereotyped? Why has she been given no first name?

3. Why is Alfred Rowland kept off stage (except for his hand) and given no dialogue? How does this affect the play?

4. Alfred is presented from his wife's point of view. How accurate is this portrait? To what degree does Alfred justify his wife's accusations?

5. Why does O'Neill present the history of Alfred's family and his relationship with Mrs. Rowland out of chronological order? What is the effect of this method of presentation?

WRITING ABOUT THE ELEMENTS OF DRAMA

Although some aspects of drama, such as lighting and stage movement, are purely theatrical, drama shares a number of elements with fiction and poetry. The planning and the writing processes for essays about drama are therefore similar to those used for essays on the other genres. As you plan, select a play and an appropriate element or series of elements.

Once you select the play, choose a focus, which will be your central idea. For example, you might argue that a character is flat, static, nonrealistic, or symbolic of good or evil. Or, to assert relationships among elements, you might claim that a play's meaning is shaped and emphasized through setting or through conflict.

Topics for Discovering Ideas

PLOT, ACTION, CONFLICT. (See also Chapter 1.) In planning an essay on plot or structure, demonstrate how actions and conflicts unfold. In addition, link this concern to other dramatic elements, such as tone or theme. In general, this topic breaks down into three areas—conflict, plot, and structure. For conflict, determine what the conflicts are, which one is central, and how it is resolved. What kind of conflict is it? Does it suggest any general behavioral patterns? For plot, determine the separate stages of development. What is the climax? The dénouement? How are they anticipated or foreshadowed? In examining plot structures and patterns, determine whether the play has a subplot or second plot. If so, how is it related to the main plot? Is a significant pattern of action repeated? If so, what is the effect? To what extent do these parallel or repetitive patterns influence theme and meaning? How do they control your responses?

CHARACTERS. (See also Chapter 3.) Focus on a significant figure and formulate a central idea about his or her personality, function, or meaning. Is the character round or flat? Static or dynamic? Individualized or stereotyped? Realistic or nonrealistic? Symbolic? How is the character described in the stage directions? By other characters? By himself or herself? What does he or she do, think, say? What is the character's attitude toward the environment? The action? Other characters? Himself or herself? To what extent does he or she articulate and/or embody key ideas in the play?

POINT OF VIEW AND PERSPECTIVE. (See also Chapter 2.) In many plays, such as *Hamlet* (Chapter 21) and *Before Breakfast*, the playwright presents the action from the perspective of an individual character. The audience therefore sees things as this character sees the same things, influences them, and is influenced by them. When you deal with such a technique, consider how the perspective affects the play's structure and meaning. Why is this point of view useful or striking? What does it suggest about character? Theme? To what extent does your reaction to the play correspond with or diverge from this perspective?

Another feature of perspective is that characters may speak directly to the audience, in a *soliloquy*, or indirectly, in a *monologue*. In dealing with these perspectives, consider whether you sympathize with the character doing the speaking. What information does the character convey? What is he or she trying to prove? What is the tone of the speech? What do these devices contribute to your response? Generally, what does the perspective contribute to your understanding of the play?

SETTING, SETS, AND PROPS. (See also Chapter 4.) Normally, you will not write about setting and properties in isolation; such an essay would simply produce a detailed description of the setting(s) and objects. Instead, a discussion of setting in drama should be linked to another element, such as character, mood, or meaning. Such an essay will demonstrate the ways in which setting(s) and objects help establish the play's time, place, characters, lifestyle, values, or ideas.

When dealing with a single setting, pay close attention to the opening stage directions and any other directions or dialogue that describe the environment or objects. In plays with multiple settings, you will normally select one or two for examination. Ask yourself whether the setting is realistic or nonrealistic and to what extent it may be symbolic. What details and objects are specified? What do these tell you about the time, the place, and the characters and their way of life and values? To what extent does the setting contribute to the play's tone, atmosphere, impact, and meaning?

STYLE, DICTION, AND IMAGERY. (See also Chapters 6, 12, and 13.) As with setting, try to connect the devices of language to some other element, such as tone, character, or meaning. Investigate the play's levels of diction and types of dialect, jargon, slang, or clichés. To what extent do these techniques define the characters and support or undercut their ideas? What connotative words or phrases are repeated? Which are spoken at particularly significant moments? What striking or consistent threads of imagery, metaphor, tone, or meaning do you find? How do all these aspects of language shape your reaction?

TONE AND ATMOSPHERE. (See also Chapters 6, 13, and 15.) Try to deal with *how* the tone is established and *what* impact it has on the play's meaning. Seek those devices the playwright employs to control your attitudes toward individual characters, situations, and outcomes. Look for clues in stage directions, diction, imagery, rhetorical devices, tempo, and context. Is tone articulated directly? Or indirectly, through irony? Also try to establish the presence of dramatic irony: To what extent do you (as a reader or spectator) know more than many of the onstage characters?

SYMBOLISM AND ALLEGORY. (See also Chapters 7 and 17.) Try to determine the characters, objects, settings, situations, actions, words or phrases, and/or costumes that seem to be symbolic. What do they symbolize, and how do you know that they are symbolic? Are they universal or contextual? Is the symbolism extensive and consistent enough to form an allegorical system? If so, what are the two levels of meaning addressed by the allegory? To what extent does the symbolism or allegory shape the play's meaning and your responses to it?

THEME. (See also Chapter 8.) The questions and areas of concern listed above should help you in discussing theme. Try to connect theme with various other aspects of the play, such as character, conflict, action, setting, language, or symbolism. What key ideas does the play explore, and what aspects of the play convey these ideas most emphatically? In dealing with each topic and question, isolate the elements and devices that have the strongest impact on meaning.

Strategies for Organizing Ideas

For an essay on drama, you might choose from a number of strategies. In discussing the crimes of Claudius in Shakespeare's *Hamlet*, you might choose (1) the testimony of the Ghost to Hamlet, (2) Claudius's reaction to the players' scene, (3) his speech as he is praying, and (4) his poisoning of the cup, showing how these actions convincingly establish his villainy. For such essays, you might devote separate paragraphs to each element, or you might use two or more paragraphs for each element as you develop your ideas further.

Similar strategies can be found for every possible type of essay on drama. In dealing with the character of Willie in Miller's *Death of a Salesman*, for example, you could analyze the difference between Willie's view of things and reality by examining his interactions with a number of the play's characters, like Biff, Charley, and Bernard. Each of these characters could be featured in a separate paragraph about how and why his version of reality is so different from Willy's. Similarly, in writing about language in plays like Anton Chekhov's *The Bear* (Chapter 22), you might establish how the particular play connects qualities of speech to revelations about topics such as character and idea. Thus, Smirnov's constant use of exclamations, shouts, and profanity, at least until shortly before the play's end, establish his irascibility.

REFERRING TO PLAYS AND PARTS OF PLAYS

Italicize the titles of plays as you would do for book titles. In referring to commonly discussed works of literature, some instructors may prefer that you assume that your reader may have a text different from yours. Therefore, you will need to provide the information necessary for finding the exact location, regardless of the edition of the text that you use.

In the body of your essay: For a play with act, scene, and line numbers, refer to *Act* (Arabic numeral), *scene* (Arabic numeral), and *line* number (Arabic numeral), separated by commas. If you are including the reference in the prose of your essay, for clarity, spell out these words: *Hamlet accuses his mother of offenses against his father in Act 3, scene 4, line 9,* or *Claudius defends his own status as king in Act 4, scene 5, lines 120–23.*

In direct quotations including block quotations (set apart from your own writing): If you are using a parenthetical reference to cite your quotation, write the Arabic numbers in parentheses following the quotation, as in (*3.1.33*). Use periods to separate these numbers: *Hamlet's famous soliloquy makes use of vivid martial imagery in its early lines when it states that "The slings and arrows of outrageous fortune, / Or to take arms against a sea of troubles," (3.1.59–60).* This citation reveals that in any edition of *Hamlet*, the reader could find this line in Act 3, scene 1, lines 59–60. The sample paper at the end of Chapter 21 illustrates this type of citation.

For stage directions, prefaces, scene directions, and casts of characters: If you are referring to or quoting from the preface, cast of characters section (sometimes called Dramatis Personae), stage directions, or scene directions, you should clarify in your *prose* what material you are referring to or quoting from: *"The scene directions for Act 1 of Ibsen's* A Dollhouse *describe the comfortable home of the Helmer family (1489)";* or *In the section marked "Action" beginning Act 1 of* Mulatto, *Hughes states that Colonel Norwood's living room is 'long outdated' (1352). "In the 'Cast of Characters' list of* Mulatto, *Hughes indicates that Colonel Norwood is a 'commanding' person"* (1352). Note that in these examples, the parenthetical citations have referred readers to the page where the material appears in this anthology; many instructors will prefer this style of reference, especially for prose plays or lesser known plays. The reader can then be assumed to use the works cited list to find the exact edition you are using. The important thing about referring to parts of plays is that you be clear and exact. The guidance offered here will cover most situations, but complications and exceptions will occur. When they do, always ask your instructor what to do and what systems of reference to use.

Illustrative Student Essay

Although underlined sentences are not recommended by MLA style, they are used in this illustrative essay as teaching tools to emphasize the central idea, thesis sentence, and topic sentences.

Cooper 1

Cameron Cooper

Professor Ortiz

English 129

6 April 2014

Eugene O'Neill's Use of Negative Descriptions and Stage Directions
in *Before Breakfast*° as a Means of Revealing Character

[1]   In the one-act *Before Breakfast*, O'Neill dramatizes the suicidal crisis and climax of a worsening husband-wife relationship. The story of the marriage is clear. Mrs. Rowland, when still a young girl, was naive and opportunistic. She seduced and then married Alfred Rowland, who she thought was the heir of his father's millions. Her resulting pregnancy ended in stillbirth. As if this were not enough, Alfred's father died not a millionaire, but a pauper. <u>During the years of these disappointments, Mrs. Rowland has lost whatever pleasantness she once possessed and has descended into a state of personal neglect, alcoholism, and selfishness.</u>* To bring out these traits early in the play, O'Neill <u>relies on negative descriptions and stage directions.</u>†

[2]   <u>The descriptions of Mrs. Rowland's personal neglect emphasize her loss of self-esteem.</u> The directions indicate that she has allowed her figure to become "a shapeless stoutness," and that she has piled her hair into a "drab-colored mass." This neglect of her physical person is capped off, according to O'Neill's description, by her blue dress, which is "shabby and worn" and "formless" (1006). Clearly, the shabbiness and excessive wear may result from poverty and thus show little about her character, but the formlessness of the dress indicates a characteristic lack of concern about appearance, also shown

---

°**This play appears on pages 1006–11.**
*Central idea.
†Thesis sentence.

Cooper 2

by her stoutness and her hair. This slovenliness shows how she wants to appear in public, because she is dressed and ready to go to work for the day. O'Neill's negative descriptions thus define her lack of self-respect.

Similarly uncomplimentary, O'Neill's directions about her sneakiness reveal   [3] her dependence on alcohol. A serious sign of distress, even though it might also be funny onstage, is the direction indicating that she takes out a bottle of gin that she keeps hidden in a "dish closet" (1007). With this stage direction O'Neill symbolizes the weakest trait of the secret drinker, which he also shows in the direction that Mrs. Rowland brightens up once she has taken a stiff jolt of gin:

> The large dose of alcohol she has taken has an almost immediate
> effect. Her features become more animated, she seems to gather
> energy, and she looks at the bedroom with a hard, vindictive smile on
> her lips. (1007)

It is safe to assume that these stage directions, on the morning of the play's action, would also have applied to her behavior on many previous mornings. In short, O'Neill is telling us that Mrs. Rowland is a secret alcoholic.

The furtiveness of her drinking also shows up in her search of Alfred's   [4] clothing, which also shows her selfishness and bitterness. When she methodically empties his pockets and uncovers the letter that we soon learn is from his mistress, the stage directions show that she unhesitatingly reads the letter. Then O'Neill directs the actress to form "a cruel smile on her lips" as she thinks about what to do with this new information (1007). As with the drinking, we see Mrs. Rowland rifling through Alfred's things only this once, but the action suggests that this secretive prying is a regular feature of her life. However, it is her discovery on *this* morning—before breakfast—that is the key to the action, because her extensive monologue against her husband, which constitutes most of the play, allows her to vent all her hatred by reproaching him about his lack of work, his neglect of her, the time he spends with friends, and his love affair.

While O'Neill uses these stage directions and descriptions to convey   [5] Mrs. Rowland's unpleasantness, he provides balance in her speeches and additional actions. He makes her a master of harangue, but there is nothing either in the directions or in her speeches to indicate that she wants to drive

Cooper 3

Alfred to suicide. Indeed, her horror at his suicide is genuine—just as it concludes the play with an incredible shock. In addition, on the positive side, her speeches show that despite her alcoholism and anger she is actually functioning in the outside world—as a seamstress—and that it is she who provides the meager money on which the couple is living (1008). In addition, she is working despite the fact that she has been feeling ill for a period of time (1010). She also has enough concern for Alfred to bring him hot water for shaving (1009).

[6]   It is clear that O'Neill wants us to conclude that if Mrs. Rowland were a supportive person, Alfred might not be the nervous alcoholic who cuts his throat in the bathroom. However, the play does not make clear that he ever could have been better, even with the maximum support of a perfect wife. Certainly, Mrs. Rowland is not supportive. The stage directions and speeches show that she is limited by her weakness and bitterness. With such defects of character, she has unquestionably never given Alfred any support at all, and probably never could. Everything that O'Neill shows us about her indicates that she is petty and selfish, and that she originally married Alfred expecting to receive and not to give.

[7]   As things stand at the beginning of the play, then, Alfred is at the brink of despair, and Mrs. Rowland's bitter and reproachful speeches drive him to self-destruction. Despite all the malice that O'Neill attributes to her character through the stage descriptions and directions, however, it is not possible to say that she is the sole cause of Alfred's suicide. O'Neill shows that Mrs. Rowland is an unpleasant, spiteful, and messy whiner, but it is not possible to reach any further conclusions.

Cooper 4

Work Cited

O'Neill, Eugene. *Before Breakfast. Literature: An Introduction to Reading and Writing, Compact Edition.* Ed. Edgar V. Roberts and Robert Zweig. 6th ed. New York: Pearson, 2015. 1006–11. Print.

Commentary on the Essay

This essay shows how dramatic conventions can be considered in reference to the analysis of character. Although the essay refers briefly to Mrs. Rowland's speeches, it stresses those descriptions and directions that O'Neill designs specifically for the actress performing the role. The essay thus indicates one way to discuss a play, as distinguished from a story or poem.

The introductory paragraph contains enough of the story about Mrs. Rowland and her husband to help the reader make sense of the subsequent material about the stage directions and descriptions. Throughout the essay, paragraph transitions are effected by words such as *similarly, also, while*, and *then*.

Paragraph 2, the first of the body, deals with O'Neill's stage directions concerning Mrs. Rowland's slovenly appearance and personal care. Paragraphs 3 and 4 are concerned with directions about her behavior—first her excessive drinking and then her search of Alfred's clothing. Paragraph 5 briefly attempts to consider how O'Neill uses Mrs. Rowland's speeches and other actions to balance the totally negative portrait he builds up through the negative stage directions.

Paragraphs 6 and 7 close the essay. Paragraph 6 considers how the stage directions lead no further than the conclusion that the Rowland' marriage is a terrible one. Paragraph 7 continues the argument of paragraph 6, with the additional thought that O'Neill's stage directions do not justify concluding that Mrs. Rowland's spiteful character is the cause of her husband's suicide.

USING SOURCES EFFECTIVELY

PARAPHRASING TO MAKE SURE READERS UNDERSTAND THE WORK

Good paraphrasing of a character's words and actions ensures readers have a solid understanding of what has actually happened in a literary work, especially when reading a printed play where the dialogue is not accompanied by the dramatic action and the actor's interpretations, as it would be in a live production. Eugene O'Neill's short play, *Before Breakfast*, presents Cameron Cooper with some interesting challenges for his essay. Because no one but Mrs. Rowland speaks throughout the entire play, he must make sure his audience clearly understands the action of the play so he can then offer his analysis of the playwright's technical use of negative descriptions and stage directions.

In paragraph 6, Cooper's first draft quoted directly from the play, but the words alone did not help him sufficiently demonstrate his critical point.

> O'Neill shows us that Alfred's suicide surprises his wife from the stage directions: "[She stands in the doorway looking down at the floor of the inner room, transfixed with horror.]" (942). •——

This passage shows Mrs. Rowland's shock, but it is not clear what has happened to her husband.

This quotation shows what Mrs. Rowland does for work, but it is not really useful or necessary by itself in furthering the essay's main idea.

> While she seemed very angry at Alfred, she was continuing to support him by working as a seamstress, and she tells him: "Heaven knows I do my part—and more—going out to sew every day while you play the gentleman . . . ." (939)

In revising this passage, Cooper understands that these quotations only indicate what the character says, so he must "fill in the blanks" with his paraphrase so her actions and their significance are apparent.

By paraphrasing effectively, Cooper fleshes out the "facts" of the story beyond the mere dialogue and provides a fuller narrative so he can examine the playwright's technique.

> He makes her a master of harangue but there is nothing either in the directions or in her speeches to indicate that she wants to drive Alfred to suicide. Indeed, her horror at his suicide is genuine—just as it concludes the play with an incredible shock. In addition, on the positive side, her speeches show that despite her alcoholism and anger, she is actually functioning in the outside world—as a seamstress—and that it is she who provides the meager money on which couple is living (939).

Cooper makes clearer the action of the play that can be sometimes hidden behind Mrs. Rowland one-sided monologue, and he uses this clearer rendition to help his readers more fully understand the dramatic action and to better support his thesis. (For more information on Paraphrasing, see page 511.)

Writing Topics About the Elements of Drama

Writing Paragraphs

1. Write a paragraph explaining the conclusion of O'Neill's *Before Breakfast*. In light of the preceding monologue of Mrs. Rowland, how can you explain her reactions to what she sees in the adjoining room?

2. Write a paragraph in which you point out how Martin establishes the opening of *Beauty*. In short, how does she avoid making explanations but instead dramatizes the situation?

Writing Essays

1. O'Neill's *Before Breakfast* is set in an apartment in Greenwich Village in Lower Manhattan around 1916. It was performed in Greenwich Village in December 1916. Write an essay that deals with the following questions.

   a. What do you make of this convergence of settings—artistic and realistic?
   b. What do you think O'Neill assumed about his original audience's reaction to the setting?

2. Write an essay on either of the following topics. Before you begin writing, you might read Chapter 25, on Critical Approaches, for suggestions on how to proceed.

   a. The viewpoint of the men in *Trifles*.
   b. A feminist analysis of Mrs. Rowland in *Before Breakfast*.

3. On the basis of the plays included in this chapter, write an essay dealing with the characteristics of the dramatic form. Consider topics such as dialogue, monologue, soliloquy, action, vocal ranges, staging, comparative lengths of plays, pauses in speech, stage directions, laughter, seriousness, and the means by which the dramatists engage the audience in characters and situations.

Creative Writing Assignment

1. Write a short dialogue between two characters of your own choice. They may be either young or old, and may be speaking about personal, political, financial, artistic, or other issues or problems. They may be focusing on themselves, or they may be discussing someone else, and there may be a need for at least one of the characters to make an important choice or follow a previously established plan. What is important is to have the two characters engage in a mutual discussion that reaches a conclusion of some sort. After this exercise, write a brief analysis of the writing problems you encountered in your dramatic presentation and how you tried to solve these problems.

Library Assignment

1. Using the catalogue in your library or online resources, look up the category *Drama—Criticism*, or *Drama—History and Criticism*, whatever title your sources use. You will find a number of categories, such as the relationship of drama to (a) elements, (b) history, (c) origin, (d) philosophy, (e) production, (f) religion, (g) stagecraft, and (h) themes. Develop a short bibliography on one of these topics and take out two or three of the relevant books. Describe them briefly, and explain—and criticize if possible—the principal ideas in one of the chapters.

Chapter 21
The Tragic Vision: Affirmation Through Loss

AFTER STUDYING THIS MATERIAL, YOU SHOULD BE ABLE TO DO THE FOLLOWING:

- Describe the history of tragedy from its origin in ancient Greece
- Define the elements and plan of tragedy as explained by Aristotle
- Illustrate ironic elements in tragedy, especially dramatic irony
- Discuss the ancient Greek theaters, choruses, and actors
- Describe Renaissance drama and the theater of Shakespeare
- Analyze types of tragedies from different historical periods

Tragedy is drama in which a major character undergoes a loss but also achieves illumination or a new perspective. It is considered the most elevated literary form because it concentrates affirmatively on the religious and cosmic implications of its major character's misfortunes. In ancient Greece, it originated as a key element in Athenian religious festivals during the decades before Athens became a major military, economic, and cultural power during the fifth century BCE.

Tragedy, however, was not religious in a sectarian sense. It did not dramatize religious doctrines and did not present a consistent religious view. To the Athenians, religion connected the past with the present and with the gods, and through this connection it served to enrich individuals, society, and the state.

Originally, tragedy in Athens was associated with the worship of Dionysus, who was one of the twelve principal gods, and who, it was thought, transformed human personality, freed people from care and grief, ensured their fertility, and provided them with joy. To elevate this god in the eyes of his fellow Athenians, the Athenian tyrant Peisistratus (ruled 560–527 BCE) added the worship of Dionysus to the regular religious festivals that the Athenians held in honor of their gods.[1]

Ancient religion is difficult for us to comprehend fully because of our completely different religious traditions and the passage of 2,500 years of history. In its origins, Greek religion was local in nature—a by-product of the geographic isolation of the various Greek city-states. Collective worship of a single god within centrally located religious buildings—like the churches, temples, and mosques we know today—did not then exist. Instead, the Greeks believed in many gods with varying powers and interests who could travel invisibly and at will from place to place within their dominions. Consequently the Greeks erected many separate local shrines and sanctuaries, which were considered holy to particular gods and where people might place offerings and say prayers. (See Acts, 17:24, for a reference to such shrines in the Ancient Near East.) Throughout the Greek world there were apparently more than 300 shrines dedicated to Asclepius, the God of Healing and Medicine, where worshipers could pray individually for their ailments to be cured. In important city-states like Athens and Corinth, large temples were dedicated to gods, such as Zeus, Athena, and Apollo, whom leading citizens especially revered. Even then, the temples were not

The Origins of Tragedy

From the standpoint of drama, the most significant of these Dionysian festivals were the **Lenaia**—a short celebration held in January (the Greek month *Gamelion*)–and the **City Dionysia** (or **Great Dionysia**)—a weeklong event in March-April (*Elaphebolion*, the month of stags). In the sixth century BCE, ceremonies held during the festival of the City Dionysia began to include tragedy, although not in the form that has been transmitted to us. The philosopher and critic Aristotle (384–322 BCE), writing almost two hundred years after these events, claimed that the first tragedies developed from a choral ode called a **dithyramb**—an ode or song that was sung or chanted and also danced by large choruses of men at the festivals.[2] According to Aristotle, the first tragedies were choral improvisations originating with "the authors of the Dithyramb" (*Poetics* IV.12, p. 19).

The Stories of Tragedy Were Drawn from Tales of Prehistoric Times

From Aristotle's claim, we can conclude that tragedy soon took on the characteristics and conventions that elevated it. For subject matter, writers turned to well-known stories or myths or legends about the heroes and demigods of the prehistoric period between the vanished age of bronze and the living age of iron. These myths described individual adventures and achievements, including epic explorations and battles that had taken place principally during the time of the Trojan War. Like the stories that we know from the Bible, the Greek myths illustrated divine-human relationships and also served as examples or models of heroic behavior. With few exceptions, these myths became the fixed subject matter of tragedy. Indeed, Aristotle called them the "received legends" that by his time in the fourth century BCE had become the "usual subjects of tragedy" (*Poetics* IX.8, p. 37).

The mythical heroes—many of whom were objects of cult worship—were kings, queens, princes, and princesses. They engaged in conflicts; they suffered; and, often, they died. Although they were great and noble, they were nevertheless human, and a common critical judgment is that they were dominated by **hubris** or **hybris** (arrogant pride, insolence, contemptuous violence), which was manifested in destructive actions such as deceit, subterfuge, lying, betrayal, revenge, cruelty, murder, suicide, patricide, infanticide, and self-mutilation. By truthfully demonstrating the faults of these heroes along with their greatness, the writers of tragedy also invoked philosophical and religious issues that provided meaning and value in the face of misfortune and suffering.

---

designed for mass worship, but rather were considered resident sanctuaries for the gods themselves. Therefore, the major space in the temples was a holy-of-holies reserved only for the god. To make public this essentially private worship, the Greek city-states held religious festivals such as the Athenian celebrations of Dionysus and Athena.

S. H. Butcher, *Aristotle's Theory of Poetry and Fine Art*, 4th ed. (New York: Dover, 1951) 19 (VI.12). All parenthetical references to Aristotle are from this edition, but see also Stephen Halliwell, *The Poetics of Aristotle: Translation and Commentary* (Chapel Hill: U of North Carolina P, 1987). The origin of the word *dithyramb* is obscure. Some ancient etymologists claimed that the word was derived from the legendary "double birth" of Dionysus. This derivation is based on the idea that dithyramb is a compound (*dis*, "two," and *thyra*, "door") referring to the myth that Zeus removed Dionysus from the womb of his mother, Semele, and then placed the fetus within his thigh. When Zeus removed Dionysus, the god had "come through the door" of birth twice. This derivation, however, has been disputed.

The Word "Tragedy" Underwent an Elevation in Meaning

One of the genuine puzzles about tragedy is the word itself, which combines the Greek words *tragos* ("goat") and *oide* ("ode" or "song")—a "goat ode" or "goat song." This meaning raises the question of how so unlikely a word is linked to the tragic form. One often-repeated answer is that the word was first applied to choral ceremonials performed at the ritual sacrifice of a goat. Another is that the word described a choral competition in which a goat was the prize.

A more persuasive recent answer is that the word **tragedy** stemmed from the word *tragoidoi*, or "billy goat singers," which was applied negatively to the young men (*ephebes*) in the choruses.[3] The ephebes were military trainees between the ages of eighteen and twenty, and, probably, those trainees who were best at close-order drill were selected for their ability as chorus members to carry out precision dance movements. Because of their youth, however, they were still likened to young goats.[4] Indeed, tragedy was originally not called *tragodia* (tragedy) at all, but rather *tragoidoi*, as though the chorus members were more important than the speeches they recited. This explanation is consistent with the improvisatory origins of tragedy as explained by Aristotle. In the decades following its beginnings, the genre grew in importance, quality, and stature, and the word *tragedy* underwent the accompanying elevation that it still possesses.

Tragedy Evolved from a Choral Form to a Dramatic Form

Because the surviving Athenian plays are dominated by acting parts, modern readers sometimes conclude that the chorus parts annoyingly interrupt the main action. It may be surprising to recognize that in the beginning there were no individual actors at all, only choruses. The introduction of actors—and their eventual domination—was one of the improvisations that Aristotle associates with the evolution of tragedy. We can surmise that during a festival performance of a now unknown choral ode, the chorus leader stepped forward to deliver lines introducing and linking the choral speeches. Because of this special function, the new speaker—called a **hypocrites** (hip-POCK-rih-TAYSS), which became the word for actor—was soon separated and distinguished from the chorus.

The next essential step was impersonation, or the assuming of a dramatic role. The *hypocrites* would represent a hero, and the chorus would represent groups such as townspeople, worshipers, youths, or elders. With the commencement of such role-playing, genuine drama had begun. According to tradition, the first *hypocrites* or actor—and therefore the acknowledged founder of the acting profession—was the writer and choral leader Thespis, in about 536–533 BCE, during the reign of Peisistratus.

For this argument, see John J. Winkler, "The Ephebes' Song: *Tragodia* and *Polis*," in John J. Winkler and Froma I. Zeitlin, eds., *Nothing to Do with Dionysos? Athenian Drama in Its Social Context* (Princeton: Princeton UP, 1990) 20–62. For a discussion of the military nature of the ancient Greek city-state, see Paul Rahe, "The Martial Republics of Classical Greece," *The Wilson Quarterly*, vol. 17, no. 1 (Winter 1993): 58–70.

There is nothing unusual about this comparison. In English a common everyday word for a child is *kid*, which is the standard word (along with *kit*) for a young goat and also other young animals.

🍂 THE ORIGIN OF TRAGEDY IN BRIEF

In the sixth century BCE, **tragedy** originated in Athens at the time of the City Dionysia, one of the major religious festivals held to celebrate Dionysus, a liberating god and one of the twelve major gods of the city. As a genre, tragedy first featured improvisations on a type of choral ode called a *dithyramb*. It then evolved, as Aristotle says, "by slow degrees" (*Poetics* IV.12, p. 19), developing new elements as they seemed appropriate and necessary.

One of the vital new elements was an emphasis on the misfortune or death of a major character.* This emphasis resulted not from a preconceived theoretical design, however, but rather from the reality of suffering in the lives of the heroic subjects. As writers of tragedy developed the cosmic and religious implications of such adversity, performances offered philosophic, religious, moral, and civic benefits, and therefore, presumably, simply attending the performance of a tragedy came to be regarded as the fulfillment of a religious obligation.

Because tragedy was originally linked to the choral dithyrambs, it is important to stress that *tragedy began as a dramatic form for choruses, not for actors*. Even after actors became dominant in the plays, the chorus was important enough for Aristotle to state that "the chorus should be regarded as one of the actors" (XVIII.7, p. 69).

---

*Although the tragic protagonist often dies at the play's end, the extant Athenian tragedies do not follow this pattern rigidly. It is true that the major figures suffer, and sometimes they die, but often they escape punishment entirely, and they may even receive divine pardon.

The Ancient Athenian Competitions in Tragedy

Once Thespis set the pattern of action involving actor and chorus, the writing of tragedies as a competition within the Dionysian festivals became institutionalized.

The Tragic Dramatists Competed for the Honor of Having Their Plays Performed

Early each summer, a number of dramatists vied for the honor of having their plays performed at the next City Dionysia, to be held the following spring. They prepared three tragedies (a **trilogy**)[5] together with a **satyr play** (a boisterous burlesque) and submitted the four works to the Eponymous Archon, one of the city's two principal magistrates and the man for whom the year was named. The three best submissions were approved, or "given a chorus," for performance at the festival. On the last day of the festival, after the performances were over, the Archon awarded a prize to the tragic playwright voted best for that year. There was also a prize for the best writer of a comedy. The winner's prize was not money, but rather a crown of ivy and the glory of triumph.

In the earliest dramas, the trilogies shared a common subject, as may be seen in the *Oresteia* of Aeschylus, which is a cycle of three plays on the subject of the royal house of Agamemnon. But by the time of Sophocles and Euripides, connected trilogies were no longer required. Sophocles' *Oedipus the King* and *Oedipus at Colonus*, for example, were submitted at widely different times.

The Three Greatest Athenian Tragic Playwrights Were Aeschylus, Sophocles, and Euripides

To gain the honor of victory during the centuries of the competitions, many writers of tragedy composed and submitted many plays. The total number must have been exceedingly large, certainly in the high hundreds and likely in the thousands. Most of these have long since vanished because there were no more than a few copies of each play, all handwritten on perishable papyrus scrolls, and because there was no systematic and secure way of preserving the copies.

A small number of works by three tragic playwrights, however, have survived. These dramatists are **Aeschylus** (525–456 BCE), who added a second actor; **Sophocles** (c. 496–406 BCE), who added a third actor, created scene design, and enlarged the chorus from twelve to fifteen; and **Euripides** (c. 484–406 BCE). These three playwrights did not win prizes every time they entered the competitions, but a consensus grew that they were the best, and by the middle of the fourth century BCE, their works were recognized as classics. Although tragedies seem to have been originally intended for only one performance—at the festival for which they competed—an exception was made for these three dramatists, whose tragedies were then performed repeatedly both in Athens and elsewhere in the Greek-speaking world.

The combined output of the three classic playwrights was slightly more than three hundred plays, of which three-fourths were tragedies and one-fourth were satyr plays. For as many as 800 years after the end of the fifth century BCE, these plays, together with many other Greek tragedies, satyr plays, and comedies, were available to readers who could afford to buy copies or to pay scribes to copy them.[6] However, with the increasing dominance of Christianity, the plays fell into neglect because they were considered pagan and also because vellum or parchment, which made up the pages of the books (*codexes* or *codices*) that replaced papyrus scrolls, was enormously expensive and was reserved for Christian works. Most of the unique and priceless copies of Athenian plays were subsequently forgotten, burned, or thrown out with the garbage.

Thirty-Three Tragedies by the Three Great Athenian Tragedians Have Survived to the Present Day

The Greek dramatic tradition might have vanished entirely had it not been for the efforts of Byzantine scholars during the ninth century CE, when Constantinople became the center of a revival of interest in classical Greek language and literature. A primary characteristic of this revival was the copying and preservation of important texts—including those of the major Greek writers. We may conclude that the scholars and scribes copied as many of the plays as they could locate, and that they tried to shelter their copies in the supposedly secure monastery libraries.

In the third century BCE, a complete hand-copied set of Greek plays was apparently deposited in the Egyptian Royal Library that formed a part of the Ptolemaic museum and palace of Alexandria, but at some point all the holdings were lost, thrown away, or destroyed, just as the palace and museum were destroyed. In modern Alexandria, the location of the ancient library is not exactly known. Current underwater explorations in the harbor of Alexandria may yet result, however, in increased knowledge about the location of the library. See Luciano Canfora, *The Vanished Library: A Wonder of the Ancient World* (Berkeley: U of California P, 1990).

However, security was impossible to maintain during those centuries. Fire, neglect, time, political destabilization, and pillage (such as the sack of Constantinople by Christian Crusaders in 1204) took an enormous toll on the Byzantine manuscript collections. Even so, seven tragedies by Aeschylus, seven by Sophocles, and ten by Euripides somehow were saved from destruction.[7] Additionally, in the fourteenth century, a scholar named Demetrius Triclinius made a lucky find of scrolls containing nine more plays by Euripides (part of what was once a complete set), bringing the total of Euripidean plays to nineteen. Therefore, of all the hundreds upon hundreds of plays written by all the Greek tragic playwrights, only thirty-three still survive intact. These plays make up the complete Greek tragedy as we know it.[8]

There is, however, just a little more: Many ancient writers often quoted brief passages from plays that were not otherwise preserved, and these portions therefore still exist. Moreover, many collectors living in ancient Egypt owned copies of the plays, and not everything from these collections was lost. In recent centuries, papyrus and vellum fragments—some quite extensive—have been recovered by archaeologists from such unlikely locations as ancient Egyptian rubbish dumps, tombs, and the linings of coffins.[9]

Aristotle and the Nature of Tragedy

Because Aristotle's *Poetics* (*Peri Poietikes*), the first section of his major critical work, survives substantially intact from antiquity, he is in effect the Western world's first critic and aesthetician. From him, later critics derived the various "**rules**" of tragic composition. He also wrote a second part of the *Poetics* concerning comedy. This second work is lost, but enough fragments and summaries survive to permit a partial hypothetical reconstruction.[10] Aristotle also considered aspects of literature in parts of other philosophical works, principally the *Ethics* and the *Politics*. In addition he, along with his students, assembled a catalog of Greek tragedy from its beginnings to his own time (the *Didaskaliae*), even though much of this catalog did not survive antiquity. He was therefore able to base his criticism on virtually

---

Many standard reference works contain the assertion that these twenty-four plays were selected by an unnamed Byzantine schoolmaster for use in the Byzantine schools and that this anthology was widely adopted and exclusively used thereafter. This claim would explain why the anthologized plays were preserved while unanthologized plays were lost. L. D. Reynolds and N. G. Wilson, in their authoritative *Scribes and Scholars: A Guide to the Transmission of Greek and Latin Literature*, 3rd ed. (Oxford UP, 1991), question this hypothesis. They point out that there is no historical record that such an anthology was ever made, that modern scholars are in truth ignorant "of the origin of the selection," and that therefore "it is perhaps best to abandon the idea that a conscious act of selection by an individual was a primary factor in determining the survival of texts" (p. 54).

The survival of Greek drama was under constant threat until the first printed editions were published at the beginning of the sixteenth century.

There are some interesting leads that may yet yield additional copies of ancient texts. The finds from the excavations at Oxyrrhynchus, in Egypt, have been stored in boxes at the University of Oxford. Because they have been considered unreadable, they have lain neglected for more than a hundred years. The recent use of special ultraviolet light, however, has now made it possible for the first time to read and record the texts of the documents. It is possible that copies of ancient plays may be among the finds. In addition, a private library at the Villa of the Papyri in Herculaneum, in Italy, has been unrecoverable ever since 79 CE, when it was buried beneath the pyroclastic flow from Vesuvius during the disastrous eruption that covered Pompeii and Herculaneum. Recent efforts have suggested that diligent archaeological work might yet produce copies of ancient manuscripts, possibly including copies of Greek plays. All this is yet for the future.

See Richard Janko, trans., *Aristotle, Poetics I with the Tractatus Coislinianus, A Hypothetical Reconstruction of Poetics II, the Fragments of the On Poets* (Indianapolis: Hackett, 1987) 47–55.

the entire body of Greek tragedy, including written copies of many plays, since lost, that he had probably never seen performed. No one before or after Aristotle has had more firsthand knowledge of Greek tragedy. His criticism is therefore especially valuable because it rests not only on his acute powers of observation but also on his unique and encyclopedic knowledge.

As we have seen, Aristotle states that tragedy grew out of improvisations related to dithyrambic choral odes. He adds that once tragedy reached its "natural" or ideal form it stopped evolving (*Poetics* IV.12, p. 19). His observations are designed to explain the ideal characteristics of tragedy. Throughout the *Poetics* he stresses concepts of exactitude, proportion, appropriateness, and control. His famous definition of tragedy is in accord with these concepts. In the sixth chapter of the *Poetics*, he states that tragedy is "an imitation of an action that is serious, complete, and of a certain magnitude; in language embellished with each kind of artistic ornament, the several kinds being found in separate parts of the play; in the form of action, not of narrative; through pity and fear effecting the proper purgation of these emotions" (VI.2, p. 23).

To Aristotle, the Key to Tragedy Is the Concept of Catharsis

The last part of this definition—that purgation or **catharsis** is the end or goal of tragedy—crystallizes the earlier parts. In Aristotle's view, tragedy arouses the powerful emotions of pity and fear (*eleos* and *phobos*), and, through the experience of the drama, brings about a "proper purgation" or purification of these emotions. Originally, the word *catharsis* was a medical term, and therefore many interpreters argue that tragedy produces a therapeutic effect through an actual purging or "vomiting" of emotions—a sympathetic release of feelings that produces emotional relief and encourages psychological health. In other words, tragedy heals.

A complementary and more compelling view is that tragic catharsis has a larger public and moral purpose. In this sense, Aristotle's description of tragedy is an implicit argument defending literature itself against the strong disapproval of his teacher, Plato.[11] Both master and pupil accepted the premise that human beings behave thoughtlessly and stupidly as a result of uncontrolled emotion. While in the grip of deep feelings, people cannot be virtuous and can do no good for others because they make bad decisions that produce bad personal, social, political, military, and moral results. Consequently, if individual temperance and public justice are to prevail, there is a universal need to moderate and regulate the emotions. Because Plato states that the emotionalism of literature is untrue, undignified, and unreasonable, he denies that literature can address this need.

But in the *Poetics* and in relevant parts of other works, Aristotle asserts that tragedy does indeed address the need, and does so through the process of catharsis. By arousing our dominant feelings of pity and fear, tragedy trains our emotions and *habituates* us to measure, shape, channel, and control our passions. Through catharsis, we develop a condition of poise and balance among

---

See Janko, especially pp. xvi–xx, and Butcher's discussion on pp. 245–51 of *Aristotle's Theory of Poetry and Fine Art*.

emotional forces, and we achieve this balanced state harmlessly because the artistic context of tragedy gives us immunity from the personal damage that our deepest passions might produce in our actual lives. It is the habitual compassion for the plights of others that makes us part of our civic and national communities and that ultimately develops our greater humanity. Tragedy therefore is vital in the growth of personal and collective virtue, for people who regularly experience the emotional catharsis or regulation of tragedy will be led to measure and direct their loves and their hates, to pledge their loyalties sensibly, and to make balanced decisions and take balanced actions, both for themselves and for the public.

It is important to stress the Aristotelian idea that catharsis is also brought about by other literary genres, especially comedy and epic, and, in addition, by music. In other words, artistic works have in common that they cleanse or purify the emotions. It is through the continuous and renewed shaping and regulating of feelings—catharsis—that tragedy, like literature and art broadly, encourages and develops ethical sensibility, and therefore on philosophical, religious, and political grounds it is defensible and necessary.

The Tragic Plot Is Structured to Arouse and Shape Emotions

In the light of the concept of catharsis, Aristotle's description of the formal aspects and characteristics of tragedy can be seen as an outline of the ways in which these characteristics first arouse the emotions and then shape them.

THE TRAGIC PLOT REQUIRES THE REPRESENTATION OF A SINGLE MAJOR ACTION. Aristotle concedes that tragedy is not true in the sense that history is true. He therefore stresses that a tragic plot, or **muthos,** is not an exact imitation or duplication of life, but rather a **representation** or *mimesis.* The concept of representation acknowledges both the moral role of the writer and the artistic freedom needed to create works conducive to proper responses. A tragic plot therefore consists of a self-contained and concentrated single action. Anything outside this action, such as unrelated incidents in the life of the major character, is not to be contained in the play. The action of *Oedipus the King,* for example, is focused on Oedipus's determination as king of Thebes to free his city from the pestilence that is destroying it. Although other aspects of his life are introduced in the play's dialogue because they are relevant to the action, they are reported rather than dramatized. Only those incidents integral to the action are included in the play.

TRAGIC RESPONSES ARE BROUGHT TO A HEAD THROUGH REVERSAL, RECOGNITION, AND SUFFERING. Aristotle's discussion of the three major elements of tragic plot is particularly significant. The elements all appear near the conclusion of a tragic play because they are the probable and inevitable results of the early elements of exposition and complication. First is the "**reversal** of the situation" (**peripeteia**) from apparent good to bad, or a "change [usually also a surprise] by which the action veers round to its opposite," as in *Oedipus the King,* where the outcome is the reverse of what Oedipus intends and expects (XI.1, p. 41).

Even if the outcome is unhappy—especially if it is unhappy—it is "the right ending" (XIII.6, p. 47) because it is the most tragic; that is, it evokes the greatest degree of pity and fear.

Second is "a change from ignorance to knowledge, producing love or hate between the persons destined by the poet for good or bad fortune." Aristotle calls this change *anagnorisis* or **recognition** (XI.2, p. 41). In the best and most powerful tragedies, according to him, the reversal and the recognition occur together and create surprise. Aristotle considers recognition to be the discovery of the true identity and involvement of persons, the establishment of guilt or innocence, and the revelation of previously unknown details, for "it is upon such situations that the issues of good or bad fortune will depend" (XI.4, p. 41). One might add that recognition is of major importance because ideally, upon discovering the truth, the protagonist acknowledges errors and accepts responsibility. In *Oedipus the King*, Oedipus finally recognizes his own guilt even though during most of the play he has been trying to escape it. He then becomes the agent of his own punishment. Because such recognition illustrates that human beings have the strength to preserve their integrity even in adversity, it is one of the elements making tragedy the highest of all literary forms.

Aristotle describes the third part of plot as a "**scene of suffering**" (pathos) that he defines as "a destructive or painful action, such as death on the stage, bodily agony, wounds, and the like" (XI.6, p. 43). He stresses that the destructive or painful action, including death, should be caused by "those who are near or dear to one another" (XIV.4, pp. 49–50). That is, violence should occur within a royal household or family rather than against a hostile foe. Because the trust, love, and protectiveness that one hopes for in a family is replaced by treachery, hate, and mayhem, the suffering of the tragic protagonist is one of the major ways in which tragedy arouses fear and pity.

Additional Aristotelian Tragic Requirements Are Seriousness, Completeness, and Magnitude

The first part of Aristotle's definition, asserting that a tragedy is "serious, complete, and of a certain magnitude," can be seen as a vital aspect of his analysis of how tragedy shapes responses. The term **seriousness**, meaning elevated or significant, concerns the play's tone and level of life, in contrast with the boisterousness and ribaldry of Athenian comedies. While comedy represents human character as less serious than it is, tragedy shows it as more serious (II.4, p. 13). Seriousness is also a consequence of the political and cosmological dimensions of the issues in which the heroic characters are engaged. By **completeness**, we understand that a tragedy must be shaped and perfected into a logical and finished whole. The beginning, the middle, and the ending must be so perfectly placed that changing or removing any part would spoil the work's integrity (VII.2–3, p. 31). By stating that a tragedy should be of a "certain" or proportional **magnitude**, Aristotle refers to a balance of length and subject matter. The play should be short enough to "be easily embraced by the memory" and long enough to "admit of a change . . . from good fortune to bad" (VII.5–7, p. 33). In other words, everything is artistically balanced; nothing superfluous is included, and nothing essential is omitted.

For Aristotle, Appropriate Diction and Song Are Necessary in Tragedy

For modern readers, Aristotle's description of tragic structure is more easily understood than his discussion of tragic language. His statement about tragic poetry—that it is the "mere metrical arrangement of the words" (VI.4, p. 25)—is clear as far as it goes, for the plays themselves show that the tragic playwrights used poetic forms deliberately and exactly. As for **song** (*melos*), Aristotle's claim that it is "a term whose sense everyone understands" (VI.4, p. 25) is not illuminating. What is therefore significant about his discussion of verse and song is his statement that the "several kinds of artistic ornament are to be found in separate parts of the play" (VI.2, p. 23). That is, where verse is appropriate, the tragic playwrights include poetry as a means of elevating the drama; where music and song are appropriate, they include these to increase beauty and intensify the drama. As with the other aspects of tragedy, therefore, the most fitting standards of judgment are placement, balance, and appropriateness.

The Tragedy's Hero Is the Focus of Sympathetic Tragic Emotions

Aristotle's description of the tragic protagonist or hero, though not included in his definition of tragedy, is integral to the concept of catharsis and therefore to his description of tragedy. As with the other parts of his analysis, he demonstrates the exact effects and limits of the topic—the perfected balance of form necessary to bring about proper tragic responses. To this end, he states that we, as normally imperfect human beings, are able to sympathize with a "highly renowned and prosperous" protagonist because that protagonist is also imperfect—a person who exists between extremes, just "like ourselves" (XIII.2, p. 45). The misfortunes of this noble protagonist are caused not by "vice" or "depravity" but rather by "some great error or frailty" (XIII.4, p. 47). Aristotle's word for such shortcomings is *hamartia,* which is often translated as **tragic flaw,** and it is this flaw that makes the protagonist human—neither a saint nor a villain. If the protagonist were a saint (one who is "eminently good and just"), his or her suffering would be undeserved and unfair, and our pity would be overwhelmed by indignation and anger—not a proper tragic reaction. Nor could we pity a villain enduring adversity and pain, for we would judge the suffering to be deserved, and our primary response would then be satisfaction—also not a proper reaction. Therefore, an ideal tragedy is fine-tuned to control our emotions exactly, producing horror and fear because the suffering protagonist is a person like ourselves, and pity because the suffering far exceeds what the protagonist deserves.

☞ ARISTOTLE'S VIEW OF TRAGEDY IN BRIEF

Aristotle's definition of tragedy hinges on his idea that tragedy, as a dramatic form, is designed to evoke powerful emotions and thereby, through catharsis, to serve a salutary political, moral, and ethical purpose. The tragic incidents and plot must be artistically constructed to produce the "essential tragic effect" (VI.12, p. 27). Therefore Aristotle stresses that plot and incidents, arranged for this effect, form the end or goal—the "chief thing of all"—of tragedy (VI.10, p. 27).

Irony in Tragedy

Implicit in the excessiveness of tragic suffering is the idea that the universe is mysterious and often unfair and that unseen but powerful forces—fate, fortune, circumstances, and the gods—directly intervene in human life. Ancient Athenian belief was that the gods give rewards or punishments to suit their own purposes, which mortals cannot bring about, prevent, or understand. For example, in *Prometheus Bound* (attributed to Aeschylus), the god Hephaestus binds Prometheus to a rock in the Scythian Mountains as punishment for having given fire and technology to humankind. (A good deed produces suffering.) Conversely, in *Medea*, Euripides shows that the god Apollo permits Medea to escape after killing her own children. (A criminal deed produces reward.)

Situational and Cosmic Irony Are Essential in Tragedy

These examples illustrate the pervasiveness of **situational irony** and **cosmic irony** in tragedy. Characters find themselves in unforeseeable difficulties that are caused by others or that they themselves inadvertently cause. When they try to resolve these difficulties responsibly and nobly, their actions do not produce the desired results— this is consistent with Aristotle's idea of reversal—and usually things come out badly. For example, Oedipus brings suffering on himself just when he succeeds— and *because* he succeeds—in rescuing his city. Whether on the personal or cosmic level, therefore, there is no escape—no way to evade responsibility, and no way to change the unalterable laws that thrust human beings into such situations.

Situational irony and cosmic irony are not confined to ancient tragedies. Shakespeare's tragic hero Hamlet speaks about the "divinity that shapes our ends," thus expressing the unpredictability of hopes, plans, and achievements, and also the wisdom of resignation. In *Death of a Salesman* (this chapter), Miller's hero, Willy Loman, is gripped not so much by divine power as by time—the agent of destruction being the inexorable force of economic circumstances.

The Tragic Dilemma Confronts the Problem of Free Will Versus Fate

These ironies are connected to what is called the **tragic dilemma**—a situation that forces the tragic protagonist to make a difficult choice. The tragic dilemma has also been called a "lose-lose" situation. Thus, Oedipus cannot shirk his duty as king of Thebes because that would be ruinous. He therefore tries to eliminate his city's affliction, but that course is also ruinous. In other words, the choices posed in a tragic dilemma seemingly permit freedom of will, but the consequences of any choice demonstrate the inescapable fact that powerful forces, perhaps even fate or inevitability, baffle even the most reasonable and noble intentions. As Shakespeare's Hamlet states, "O cursèd spite, / That ever I was born to set it right" (1.5.188–89).

Dramatic Irony Focuses Attention on the Tragic Limitations of Human Vision and Knowledge

It is from a perspective of something like divinity that we as readers or spectators perceive the action of tragedies. We are like the gods because we always know more than the characters. Such dramatic irony permits us, for example, to know what Oedipus does not know: In defensive rage he killed his real father, and he himself is therefore his city's bane. Similar dramatic irony can be found in *Hamlet*, for we realize that Claudius murdered Hamlet's father while Hamlet himself has only unsubstantiated accusations of this truth. The underlying basis of **dramatic irony** in real life is of course that no one can know the future, and few if any can anticipate accident, illness, and all the social, economic, political, and military adversity that may invade and destroy our ways of life.

The Ancient Athenian Audience and Theater

Athenian audiences of the fifth century BCE, predominantly free men but also a small number of women, took their theater seriously. Indeed, as young men many citizens had taken active parts in the parades and choruses. Admission was charged for those able to pay, but subsidies allowed poorer people to attend as well. Rich Athenians, as a duty (*liturgeia*) to the state, underwrote the costs of the productions—except for three professional actors who were paid by the government. Each wealthy man, for his contribution, was known as a *choragos*, or choral sponsor. To gain public recognition, the choragos sometimes performed as the leader of the chorus.

Ancient Athenian Theater Originated in the Marketplace, or *Agora*

In the beginning, tragic performances were given specially designated space in the Athenian *agora*, or marketplace. In the center of the performing area was an altar dedicated to Dionysus, around which the choruses danced and chanted. Apparently, wooden risers must have been set up for the spectators around the performers.

Ancient Greek Plays Were Performed in the Athenian Theater of Dionysus

By the early fifth century BCE, a half-circular outdoor theater or amphitheater (a *theatron* was a "place for seeing") was constructed at the base of the southern hill of the Acropolis in the area sacred to Dionysus. All later performances of Athenian tragedies were held at this **Theater of Dionysus,** which held as many as fourteen thousand people (the comic dramatist Aristophanes estimated that thirteen thousand were in attendance at one of his plays). In the earliest days of the theater, most spectators sat on the sloping ground, but eventually wooden and then stone benches were constructed in the rising semicircle, with more elegant seating for dignitaries in front. Although the theater was outdoors, the acoustics were sufficiently good to permit audiences to hear both the chorus and the actors, provided that the audience remained reasonably quiet during performances.

THE ORCHESTRA WAS THE FOCAL POINT OF BOTH SIGHT AND SOUND. Centered at the base of the hill—the focus of attention—was a round area modeled on the space that had been used in the agora. This was the *orchestra* (or-KESS-tra) or "dancing place," which was about sixty-five feet in diameter. Here, each chorus sang its odes and performed its dance movements to the rhythm of a double-piped flute (*aulos*), an instrument that was also used to mark the step in military drill. In the center was a permanent altar.

THE SKENE WAS A VERSATILE BUILDING USED FOR BOTH ACTION AND ENTRANCES. Behind the *orchestra* was a building for actors, costumes, and props called the *skene* (*SKAY-nay*, "tent"), from which is derived our modern word *scene*. Originally a tent or hut, the *skene* was later made of wood and decorated to provide backdrops for the various plays. Some theater historians argue that the stage itself was a wooden platform (**proskenion** [*pro-SKAY-nee-on*], the origin of the modern *proscenium*) in front of the *skene* to elevate the actors and set them off from the chorus. At the center of the *skene*, a double door for entrances and exits opened out to the stage and the *orchestra*. Through this door a large platform (**ekkyklyma** [eck-KEEK-lee-mah]) could be rolled out to show interior scenes. There was no curtain.

The roof of the *skene* was sometimes used as a place of action (as in Aeschylus's *Agamemnon*). A **mechane** (*may-KAH-nay*), or crane, was also located there so that actors playing gods could be swung up, down, and around as a mark of divine power. It was this crane that inspired the comic dramatist Menander to coin the phrase **theos apo mechanes**, or, in Latin, **deus ex machina** ("a god out of the machine"), terms that refer to an artificial and/or illogical action or device introduced at a play's end to bring otherwise impossible conflicts to a satisfactory solution.

THE ACTORS PERFORMED IN ALL STAGE AND ORCHESTRA AREAS, AND THE CHORUS PERFORMED IN THE ORCHESTRA. The performing space for the actors was mainly in front of the *skene*. The space for the chorus was the entire *orchestra*. The chorus entered the *orchestra*—and left it at the end of the play—along the aisles between the retaining wall of the hillside seats and the front of the *skene*. Each of these lateral walkways was known as a **parados** ("way in"), the name also given to the chorus's entry scene. The actors often used the *skene* for entrances and exits, but they were also free to use either of the walkways.

The ancient theater at Epidaurus, Greece.

View of a modern production of Sophocles's *Oedipus at Colonus* at the Theater of Epidaurus. Note the size of the orchestra, the formation and gestures of the chorus (fifteen members, in masks, together with the choral leader), the central altar, the reconstructed *skene*, and the single actor on the proscenium.

THE THEATER WAS REPAIRED AND RESTORED A NUMBER OF TIMES IN ANTIQUITY. In the centuries after it was built, the Theater of Dionysus was remodeled and restored a number of times. Aeschylus's trilogy the *Oresteia* was performed in 458 BCE, for example, not long after a renovation. The ruins that can be seen on the south slope of the Acropolis today are not those of the theater known by Sophocles but rather those of a Roman restoration. A better sense of how the theater might have looked during the time of Sophocles can be gained from the Theater of Epidaurus, which during antiquity was considered one of the best Greek theaters and today remains in excellent condition.

Ancient Greek Tragic Actors and Their Costumes

The task of the three competing playwrights who had been "given a chorus" by the Archon to stage their works during the **City Dionysia** (and later during the **Lenaia**) was to plan, choreograph, and direct the productions, usually with the aid of professionals. By performance time, the dramatists would already have spent many weeks preparing the three assigned actors and fifteen choristers. They also would have directed rehearsals for a small number of auxiliary chorus members and other silent extras taking roles such as servants and soldiers.

Costumes Distinguished the Actors from the Chorus

All these participants needed costumes. The chorus members were lightly clad, for ease of movement, and were apparently barefoot. The main actors wore the identifying costumes of tragedy—namely, sleeved robes, boots, and masks. Their robes were heavily decorated and embroidered. Their calf-high leather boots, called *kothornoi* or, in English, **buskins,** were like the elegant boots worn by the patron god Dionysus in painting and statuary. During the following centuries, the buskins became elevator shoes that made the tragic actors taller, in keeping with their heroic stature.

Masks Worn by Chorus and Actors Helped the Audience Recognize and Distinguish the Characters

A vital aspect of costuming was the use of conventionalized plaster and linen masks, which were designed to identify and delineate characters. These were of particular help for those in the audience who sat at increasing distances away and up from the orchestra and stage, and who therefore would have had trouble seeing facial expressions. As many as twenty-eight different kinds of masks were in use for the tragic productions. Each mask portrayed a distinct facial type and expression (e.g., king, queen, young woman or man, old woman or man, servant, shepherd). The choristers wore identical masks for their group roles. Apparently the masks covered the entire head, except for openings for seeing, breathing, and speaking. They included a high headdress and, when necessary, a beard.

The masks, along with costume changes, gave the actors great versatility. Each actor could assume a number of different roles simply by entering the *skene*, changing mask and costume, and reentering as a new character. Thus, in *Oedipus the King* a single actor could represent the seer Tiresias and later reappear as the Messenger. The masks even made it possible for two actors, or even all three, to perform as the same character in separate parts of the play if the need arose.

Performance and the Formal Organization of Greek Tragedy

On performance days, the competing playwrights staged their plays from morning to afternoon, first the tragedies, then the satyr plays (and after these, comedies by other writers). Because plays were performed with a minimum of scenery and props, dramatists used dialogue to establish times and locations. Each tragedy was performed in the order of the formally designated sections that modern editors have marked in the printed texts. It is therefore possible to describe the production of a play in terms of these structural divisions.

The First Part Was the Prologue, the Play's Exposition

There was considerable variety in the performance of the **prologue.** Sometimes it was given by a single actor, speaking as either a mortal or a god. In *Oedipus the King*, Sophocles used all three actors for the prologue (Oedipus, the Priest, and Creon), speaking to themselves and also to the chorus, which would have been acting as the Theban populace.

The Second Part Was the Parados, the Entry of the Chorus into the Orchestra

The entrance of the chorus into the orchestra was the *parados*. Once in the orchestra, the chorus remained there until the play's end. Because they were required to project their voices to spectators in the top seats, they both sang and chanted their lines. They also moved rhythmically in a number of stanzaic *strophes* (turns), *antistrophes* (counterturns), and *epodes* (units following the songs). These dance movements, regulated by the rhythm of the *aulos* or flute as in a military drill, were done in straight-line formations of five or three, but we do not know whether the chorus stopped or continued moving when delivering their lines. After the *parados*, the choristers would necessarily have knelt or sat at attention, in this way focusing on the activities of the actors and, when necessary, responding as a group.

THE PLAY'S PRINCIPAL ACTION CONSISTED OF FOUR EPEISODIA AND STASIMA. With the chorus as a model audience, the drama itself was developed in four full sections or acting units. The major part of each section was the ***epeisodia***, or **episode.** Each episode featured the actors, who presented both action and speech, including swift one-line interchanges known as ***stichomuthia***, or **stichomythy.**

When the episode ended, the actors withdrew.[12] The following second part of the acting section was called a ***stasimon*** (plural ***stasima***), performed by the chorus in the *orchestra*. Like the *parados*, the *stasima* required dance movements, along with the chanting and singing of strophes, antistrophes, and epodes. The topics concerned the play's developing action, although over time the *stasima* became more general and therefore less integral to the play.

The Play Concluded with the *Exodos*

When the last of the four episode-*stasimon* sections had been completed, the *exodos* (literally, "a way out"), or the final section, commenced. It contained the resolution of the drama, the exit of the actors, and the last pronouncements, dance movements, and exit of the chorus.

The Role of the Chorus Was Diminished as Greek Tragedy Evolved

We know little about tragic structure at the very beginning of the form, but Athenian tragedies of the fifth century BCE followed the pattern just described. Aeschylus, whose works are the earliest surviving Athenian tragedies, lengthened the episodes, thus emphasizing the actors and diminishing "the importance of the Chorus" (*Poetics* IV.13, p. 19). Sophocles made the chorus even less important. Euripides, Sophocles's younger contemporary, concentrated on the episodes, making the chorus almost incidental. In later centuries, dramatists dropped the choral sections completely, establishing the pattern for the five-act structure adopted by Roman dramatists and later by Renaissance dramatists.

For example, at the end of the first episode of *Oedipus the King*, Oedipus goes into the *skene*—the palace—while a servant leads Tiresias off along the *parados*, thus indicating that he is leaving Thebes entirely.

Plays for Study

Sophocles. . . . . Oedipus the King, 1038

William Shakespeare. . . . . Hamlet, 1079

Arthur Miller . . . . Death of a Salesman, 1182

SOPHOCLES (c. 496–406 BCE)

Sophocles was born between 500 and 494 BCE into an affluent Athenian family. He began acting and singing early, and he served as a choral leader in the celebrations for the defeat of the Persians at Marathon in 480 BCE. In 468 he won highest festival honors for the first play he submitted for competition, Triptolemos. *He wrote at least 120 plays, approximately ninety of them tragedies, and he won the prize a record twenty-four times. He was also an active citizen. He was twice elected general of his tribe, and he served as a priest in the cult of Asclepius, the god of healing. Because of his dramatic and public achievements, he was venerated during his lifetime, and after his death in 406–405 BCE, a cult was established in his honor.*

When *Oedipus the King* was first performed between 430 and 425 BCE, most of the audience would have known the general outlines of the story inasmuch as it was one of the "received legends" of tragedy: the antagonism of the gods Hephaestus and Hera toward Cadmus of Thebes (of whom Oedipus was a descendant); the prophecy that the Theban king Laius would be killed by his own son; the exposure of the newly born Oedipus on a mountainside; his rescue by a well-meaning shepherd; his youth spent as the adopted son of King Polybus and Queen Merope of Corinth; his trip to Delphi to learn his origins; his impetuous murder of Laius (a stranger to him); his solution of the Sphinx's riddle; his ascension as king of Thebes and his marriage to Queen Jocasta, his mother; his reign as king; the plague that afflicted Thebes; his attempts at restoration; and Jocasta's suicide when the truth of Oedipus's past is revealed.

Although these details were commonly known, there was disagreement about the outcome of Oedipus's life. One version told that he remarried, had four children with his new wife, reigned long and successfully, died in battle, and was finally worshiped as a hero. Sophocles, however, dramatizes a version—either borrowed or of his own creation—that tells of Oedipus's self-imposed punishment.

As we have said, Aristotle prized *Oedipus the King* so highly that he used it to illustrate many of his principles of tragedy. Of particular interest is that the play embodies the so-called three **unities**, which are implicit in the *Poetics* although Aristotle does not dwell on them. Sophocles creates *unity of place* by using the front of the royal palace of Thebes as the location for the entire action. He creates *unity of action* by dramatizing only those activities leading to Oedipus's recognition of the true scourge of the city. Finally, he creates *unity of time* because the stage or action time coincides with real-life time. In fact, the play's time is considerably shorter than the "single revolution of the sun" (*sic*) that Aristotle recommends as the proper period for a complete tragic action (V.4, p. 23). Above all, *Oedipus the King* meets Aristotle's requirements for one of the very best plays because of the skill with which Sophocles makes Oedipus's recognition of his guilt coincide exactly with the disastrous reversal of his fortunes (XI.2, p. 41).

Oedipus the King (430– 425 BCE)

Translated by Thomas Gould

CHARACTERS

Oedipus,° the King of Thebes
Priest of Zeus, Leader of the Suppliants
Creon, Oedipus's Brother-in-law
Chorus, a Group of Theban Elders
Choragos, Spokesman of the Chorus
Tiresias, a blind Seer or Prophet
Jocasta, the Queen of Thebes
Messenger, from Corinth, once a Shepherd
Herdsman, once a Servant of Laius
Second Messenger, a Servant of Oedipus

MUTES

Suppliants, Thebans seeking Oedipus's help
Attendants, for the Royal Family
Servants, to lead Tiresias and Oedipus
Antigone, Daughter of Oedipus and Jocasta
Ismene, Daughter of Oedipus and Jocasta

[*The action takes place during the day in front of the royal palace in Thebes. There are two altars (left and right) on the Proscenium and several steps leading down to the Orchestra. As the play opens, Thebans of various ages who have come to beg* OEDIPUS *for help are sitting on these steps and in part of the Orchestra. These suppliants are holding branches of laurel or olive which have strips of wool° wrapped around them.* OEDIPUS *enters from the palace (the central door of the Skene).*]

PROLOGUE

OEDIPUS: My children, ancient Cadmus'° newest care,
        why have you hurried to those seats, your boughs
        wound with the emblems of the suppliant?
        The city is weighed down with fragrant smoke,
        with hymns to the Healer° and the cries of mourners.   5
        I thought it wrong, my sons, to hear your words
        through emissaries, and have come out myself,
        I, Oedipus, a name that all men know.

°*Oedipus:* The name means "swollen foot." It refers to the mutilation of Oedipus's feet by his father, Laius, before the infant was sent to Mount Cithaeron to be put to death by exposure. °S.D. *wool:* Branches wrapped with wool are traditional symbols of prayer or supplication. °1 *Cadmus:* Oedipus's great-great-grandfather (although he does not know this) and the founder of Thebes. °5 *Healer:* Apollo, god of prophecy, light, healing, justice, purification, and destruction.

[OEDIPUS *addresses the* PRIEST.]

Old man—for it is fitting that you speak
10   for all—what is your mood as you entreat me,
      fear or trust? You may be confident
      that I'll do anything. How hard of heart
      if an appeal like this did not rouse my pity!
PRIEST: You, Oedipus, who hold the power here,
15   you see our several ages, we who sit
      before your altars—some not strong enough
      to take long flight, some heavy in old age,
      the priests, as I of Zeus,° and from our youths
      a chosen band. The rest sit with their windings
20   in the markets, at the twin shrines of Pallas,°
      and the prophetic embers of Isménos.°
      Our city, as you see yourself, is tossed
      too much, and can no longer lift its head
      above the troughs of billows red with death.
25   It dies in the fruitful flowers of the soil,
      it dies in its pastured herds, and in its women's
      barren pangs. And the fire-bearing god°
      has swooped upon the city, hateful plague,
      and he has left the house of Cadmus empty.
30   Black Hades° is made rich with moans and weeping.
      Not judging you an equal of the gods,
      do I and the children sit here at your hearth,
      but as the first of men, in troubled times
      and in encounters with divinities.
35   You came to Cadmus' city and unbound
      the tax we had to pay to the harsh singer,°
      did it without a helpful word from us,
      with no instruction; with a god's assistance
      you raised up our life, so we believe.
40   Again now Oedipus, our greatest power,
      we plead with you, as suppliants, all of us,
      to find us strength, whether from a god's response,
      or learned in some way from another man.
      I know that the experienced among men
45   give counsels that will prosper best of all.
      Noblest of men, lift up our land again!

°18 *Zeus:* father and king of the gods. °20 *Pallas:* Athena, goddess of wisdom, arts, crafts, and war. °21 *Isménos:* a reference to the temple of Apollo near the river Ismenos in Thebes. Prophecies were made here by "reading" the ashes of the altar fires. °27 *fire-bearing god:* contagious fever viewed as a god. °30 *Black Hades:* refers to both the underworld, where the spirits of the dead go, and the god of the underworld. °36 *harsh singer:* the Sphinx, a monster with a woman's head, a lion's body, and wings. The "tax" that Oedipus freed Thebes from was the destruction of all the young men who failed to solve the Sphinx's riddle and were subsequently devoured. The Sphinx always asked the same riddle: "What goes on four legs in the morning, two legs at noon, and three legs in the evening, and yet is weakest when supported by the largest number of feet?" Oedipus discovered the correct answer—man, who crawls in infancy, walks in his prime, and uses a stick in old age—and thus ended the Sphinx's reign of terror. The Sphinx destroyed herself when Oedipus answered the riddle. Oedipus's reward for freeing Thebes of the Sphinx was the throne and the hand of the recently widowed Jocasta.

Think also of yourself; since now the land
calls you its Savior for your zeal of old,
oh let us never look back at your rule
as men helped up only to fall again!   50
Do not stumble! Put our land on firm feet!
The bird of omen was auspicious then,
when you brought that luck; be that same man again!
The power is yours; if you will rule our country,
rule over men, not in an empty land.   55
A towered city or a ship is nothing
if desolate and no man lives within.

OEDIPUS: Pitiable children, oh I know, I know
the yearnings that have brought you. Yes, I know
that you are sick. And yet, though you are sick,   60
there is not one of you so sick as I.
For your affliction comes to each alone,
for him and no one else, but my soul mourns
for me and for you, too, and for the city.
You do not waken me as from a sleep,   65
for I have wept, bitterly and long,
tried many paths in the wanderings of thought,
and the single cure I found by careful search
I've acted on: I sent Menoeceus' son,
Creon, brother of my wife, to the Pythian   70
halls of Phoebus,° so that I might learn
what I must do or say to save this city.
Already, when I think what day this is,
I wonder anxiously what he is doing.
Too long, more than is right, he's been away.   75
But when he comes, then I shall be a traitor
if I do not do all that the god reveals.

PRIEST: Welcome words! But look, those men have signaled
that it is Creon who is now approaching!

OEDIPUS: Lord Apollo! May he bring Savior Luck,   80
a Luck as brilliant as his eyes are now!

PRIEST: His news is happy, it appears. He comes,
forehead crowned with thickly berried laurel.°

OEDIPUS: We'll know, for he is near enough to hear us.

[*Enter* CREON *along one of the Parados.*]

Lord, brother in marriage, son of Menoeceus!   85
What is the god's pronouncement that you bring?

CREON: It's good. For even troubles, if they chance
to turn out well, I always count as lucky.

OEDIPUS: But what was the response? You seem to say
I'm not to fear—but not to take heart either.   90

CREON: If you will hear me with these men present,
I'm ready to report—or go inside.

°70–71 *Pythian . . . Phoebus:* the temple of Phoebus Apollo's oracle or prophet at Delphi. °83 *laurel:* Creon is wearing a garland of laurel leaves, sacred to Apollo.

[CREON *moves up the steps toward the palace.*]

OEDIPUS: Speak out to all! The grief that burdens me
  concerns these men more than it does my life.

95 **CREON:** Then I shall tell you what I heard from the god.
  The task Lord Phoebus sets for us is clear:
  drive out pollution sheltered in our land,
  and do not shelter what is incurable.

OEDIPUS: What is our trouble? How shall we cleanse ourselves?

100 **CREON:** We must banish or murder to free ourselves
  from a murder that blows storms through the city.

OEDIPUS: What man's bad luck does he accuse in this?

CREON: My Lord, a king named Laius ruled our land
  before you came to steer the city straight.

105 **OEDIPUS:** I know. So I was told—I never saw him.

CREON: Since he was murdered, you must raise your hand
  against the men who killed him with their hands.

OEDIPUS: Where are they now? And how can we ever find
  the track of ancient guilt now hard to read?

110 **CREON:** In our own land, he said. What we pursue,
  that can be caught; but not what we neglect.

OEDIPUS: Was Laius home, or in the countryside—
  or was he murdered in some foreign land?

CREON: He left to see a sacred rite, he said;

115 He left, but never came home from his journey.

OEDIPUS: Did none of his party see it and report—
  someone we might profitably question?

CREON: They were all killed but one, who fled in fear,
  and he could tell us only one clear fact.

120 **OEDIPUS:** What fact? One thing could lead us on to more
  if we could get a small start on our hope.

CREON: He said that bandits chanced on them and killed him—
  with the force of many hands, not one alone.

OEDIPUS: How could a bandit dare so great an act—

125 unless this was a plot paid off from here!

CREON: We thought of that, but when Laius was killed,
  we had no one to help us in our troubles.

OEDIPUS: It was your very kingship that was killed!
  What kind of trouble blocked you from a search?

130 **CREON:** The subtle-singing Sphinx asked us to turn
  from the obscure to what lay at our feet.

OEDIPUS: Then I shall begin again and make it plain.
  It was quite worthy of Phoebus, and worthy of you,
  to turn our thoughts back to the murdered man,

135 and right that you should see me join the battle
  for justice to our land and to the god.
  Not on behalf of any distant kinships,
  it's for myself I will dispel this stain.
  Whoever murdered him may also wish

140 to punish me—and with the selfsame hand.
  In helping him I also serve myself.
  Now quickly, children: up from the altar steps,

and raise the branches of the suppliant!
Let someone go and summon Cadmus' people:
say I'll do anything.   145

[*Exit an* ATTENDANT *along one of the Parados.*]

Our luck will prosper
if the god is with us, or we have already fallen.
PRIEST: Rise, my children; that for which we came,
he has himself proclaimed he will accomplish.
May Phoebus, who announced this, also come
as Savior and reliever from the plague.   150

[*Exit* OEDIPUS *and* CREON *into the Palace. The* PRIEST *and the* SUPPLIANTS *exit left and right along the Parados. After a brief pause, the* CHORUS *(including the* CHORAGOS*) enters the Orchestra from the Parados.*]

PARADOS

Strophe° 1
CHORUS: Voice from Zeus,° sweetly spoken, what are you
that have arrived from golden
Pytho° to our shining
Thebes? I am on the rack, terror
        shakes my soul.   155
Delian Healer,° summoned by "iē!"
I await in holy dread what obligation, something new
or something back once more with the revolving years,
        you'll bring about for me.
Oh tell me, child of golden Hope,   160
            deathless Response!

Antistrophe 1
I appeal to you first, daughter of Zeus,
        deathless Athena,
        and to your sister who protects this land,
        Artemis,° whose famous throne is the whole circle   165
of the marketplace,
and Phoebus, who shoots from afar: iō!
Three-fold defenders against death, appear!
If ever in the past, to stop blind ruin
        sent against the city,   170
you banished utterly the fires of suffering,
        come now again!

Strophe 2
Ah! Ah! Unnumbered are the miseries
I bear. The plague claims all

°151 *Strophe:* Strophe and antistrophe (line 162) are stanzaic units referring to movements, countermovements, and gestures that the Chorus performed while singing or chanting in the orchestra. See p. 1037. °151 *Voice from Zeus:* a reference to Apollo's prophecy. Zeus taught Apollo how to prophesy. °153 *Pytho:* Delphi. °156 *Delian Healer:* Apollo. °165 *Artemis:* goddess of virginity, childbirth, and hunting.

175 our comrades. Nor has thought found yet a spear
by which a man shall be protected. What our glorious
earth gives birth to does not grow. Without a birth
from cries of labor
    do the women rise.
180 One person after another
    you may see, like flying birds,
faster than indomitable fire, sped
to the shore of the god that is the sunset.°

Antistrophe 2
And with their deaths unnumbered dies the city.
185 Her children lie unpitied on the ground,
spreading death, unmourned.
Meanwhile young wives, and gray-haired mothers with them,
on the shores of the altars, from this side and that,
suppliants from mournful trouble,
190   cry out their grief.
A hymn to the Healer shines,
the flute a mourner's voice.
Against which, golden goddess, daughter of Zeus,
    send lovely Strength.

Strophe 3
195 Cause raging Ares°—who,
    armed now with no shield of bronze,
burns me, coming on amid loud cries—
to turn his back and run from my land,
with a fair wind behind, to the great
200   hall of Amphitritē,°
or to the anchorage that welcomes no one,
Thrace's troubled sea!
If night lets something get away at last,
    it comes by day.
205 Fire-bearing god . . .
    you who dispense the might of lightning,
Zeus! Father! Destroy him with your thunderbolt!

[*Enter* OEDIPUS *from the palace.*]

Antistrophe 3
Lycēan Lord!° From your looped
    bowstring, twisted gold,
210 I wish indomitable missiles might be scattered
and stand forward, our protectors; also fire-bearing
radiance of Artemis, with which
    she darts across the Lycian mountains.

°183 *god . . . sunset:* Hades, god of the underworld. °195 *Ares:* god of war and destruction. °200 *Amphitritē:* the Atlantic Ocean. °208 *Lycēan Lord:* Apollo.

I call the god whose head is bound in gold,
with whom this country shares its name,
Bacchus,° wine-flushed, summoned by "euoi!,"   215
     Maenads' comrade,
to approach ablaze
     with gleaming . . . . . .
pine, opposed to that god-hated god.   220

EPISODE 1

OEDIPUS: I hear your prayer. Submit to what I say
and to the labors that the plague demands
and you'll get help and a relief from evils.
I'll make the proclamation, though a stranger
to the report and to the deed. Alone,   225
had I no key, I would soon lose the track.
Since it was only later that I joined you,
to all the sons of Cadmus I say this:
whoever has clear knowledge of the man
who murdered Laius, son of Labdacus,   230
I command him to reveal it all to me—
nor fear if, to remove the charge, he must
accuse himself: his fate will not be cruel—
he will depart unstumbling into exile.
But if you know another, or a stranger,   235
to be the one whose hand is guilty, speak:
I shall reward you and remember you.
But if you keep your peace because of fear,
and shield yourself or kin from my command,
hear you what I shall do in that event: 240
I charge all in this land where I have throne
and power, shut out that man—no matter who—
both from your shelter and all spoken words,
nor in your prayers or sacrifices make
him partner, not allot him lustral° water.   245
All men shall drive him from their homes: for he
is the pollution that the god-sent Pythian
response has only now revealed to me.
In this way I ally myself in war
with the divinity and the deceased.°   250
And this curse, too, against the one who did it,
whether alone in secrecy, or with others:
may he wear out his life unblest and evil!
I pray this, too: if he is at my hearth
and in my home, and I have knowledge of him,   255
may the curse pronounced on others come to me.
All this I lay to you to execute,
for my sake, for the god's, and for this land
now ruined, barren, abandoned by the gods.

°216 *Bacchus:* Dionysus, god of wine. °245 *lustral:* purifying. °250 *the deceased:* Laius.

260   Even if no god had driven you to it,
       you ought not to have left this stain uncleansed,
       the murdered man a nobleman, a king!
       You should have looked! But now, since, as it happens,
       It's I who have the power that he had once,
265   and have his bed, and a wife who shares our seed,
       and common bond had we had common children
       (had not his hope of offspring had bad luck—
       but as it happened, luck lunged at his head);
       because of this, as if for my own father,
270   I'll fight for him, I'll leave no means untried,
       to catch the one who did it with his hand,
       for the son of Labdacus, of Polydôrus,
       of Cadmus before him, and of Agênor.°
       This prayer against all those who disobey:
275   the gods send out no harvest from their soil,
       nor children from their wives. Oh, let them die
       victims of this plague, or of something worse.
       Yet for the rest of us, people of Cadmus,
       we the obedient, may Justice, our ally,
280   and all the gods, be always on our side!
CHORAGOS: I speak because I feel the grip of your curse:
       the killer is not *I*. Nor can I point
       to him. The one who set us to this search,
       Phoebus, should also name the guilty man.
285 **OEDIPUS:** Quite right, but to compel unwilling gods—
       no man has ever had that kind of power.
CHORAGOS: May I suggest to you a second way?
OEDIPUS: A second or a third—pass over nothing!
CHORAGOS: I know of no one who sees more of what
290   Lord Phoebus sees than Lord Tiresias.
       My Lord, one might learn brilliantly from him.
OEDIPUS: Nor is this something I have been slow to do.
       At Creon's word I sent an escort—twice now!
       I am astonished that he has not come.
295 **CHORAGOS:** The old account is useless. It told us nothing.
OEDIPUS: But tell it to me. I'll scrutinize all stories.
CHORAGOS: He is said to have been killed by travelers.
OEDIPUS: I have heard, but the one who did it no one sees.
CHORAGOS: If there is any fear in him at all,
300   he won't stay here once he has heard that curse.
OEDIPUS: He won't fear words: he had no fear when he did it.

[*Enter* TIRESIAS *from the right, led by a* SERVANT *and two of Oedipus's* ATTENDANTS.]

CHORAGOS: Look there! There is the man who will convict him!
       It's the god's prophet they are leading here.
       one gifted with the truth as no one else.
305 **OEDIPUS:** Tiresias, master of all omens—
       public and secret, in the sky and on the earth—

°272–73 *son . . . Agênor:* refers to Laius by citing his genealogy.

your mind, if not your eyes, sees how the city
lives with a plague, against which Thebes can find
no Saviour or protector, Lord, but you.
For Phoebus, as the attendants surely told you,   310
returned this answer to us: liberation
from the disease would never come unless
we learned without a doubt who murdered Laius—
put them to death, or sent them into exile.
Do not begrudge us what you may learn from birds   315
or any other prophet's path you know!
Care for yourself, the city, care for me,
care for the whole pollution of the dead!
We're in your hands. To do all that he can
to help another is man's noblest labor.   320

TIRESIAS: How terrible to understand and get
no profit from the knowledge! I knew this,
but I forgot, or I had never come.

OEDIPUS: What's this? You've come with very little zeal.

TIRESIAS: Let me go home! If you will listen to me,   325
You will endure your troubles better—and I mine.

OEDIPUS: A strange request, not very kind to the land
that cared for you—to hold back this oracle!

TIRESIAS: I see your understanding comes to you
inopportunely. So that won't happen to me . . .   330

OEDIPUS: Oh, by the gods, if you understand about this,
don't turn away! We're on our knees to you.

TIRESIAS: None of you understands! I'll never bring
my grief to light—will not speak of yours.

OEDIPUS: You know and won't declare it! Is your purpose   335
to betray us and to destroy this land?

TIRESIAS: I will grieve neither of us. Stop this futile
cross-examination. I'll tell you nothing!

OEDIPUS: Nothing? You vile traitor! You could provoke
a stone to anger! You still refuse to tell?   340
Can nothing soften you, nothing convince you?

TIRESIAS: You blamed anger in me—you haven't seen.
Can nothing soften you, nothing convince you?

OEDIPUS: Who wouldn't fill with anger, listening
to words like yours which now disgrace this city?   345

TIRESIAS: It will come, even if my silence hides it.

OEDIPUS: If it will come, then why won't you declare it?

TIRESIAS: I'd rather say no more. Now if you wish,
respond to that with all your fiercest anger!

OEDIPUS: Now I am angry enough to come right out   350
with this conjecture: you, I think, helped plot
the deed; you did it—even if your hand
cannot have struck the blow. If you could see,
I should have said the deed was yours alone.

TIRESIAS: Is that right! Then I charge you to abide   355
by the decree you have announced: from this day
say no word to either these or me,
for you are the vile polluter of this land!

OEDIPUS: Aren't you appalled to let a charge like that
360   come bounding forth? How will you get away?
TIRESIAS: You cannot catch me. I have the strength of truth.
OEDIPUS: Who taught you this? Not your prophetic craft!
TIRESIAS: You did. You made me say it. I didn't want to.
OEDIPUS: Say what? Repeat it so I'll understand.
365   **TIRESIAS:** I made no sense? Or are you trying me?
OEDIPUS: No sense I understood. Say it again!
TIRESIAS: I say you are the murderer you seek.
OEDIPUS: Again that horror! You'll wish you hadn't said that.
TIRESIAS: Shall I say more, and raise your anger higher?
370   **OEDIPUS:** Anything you like! Your words are powerless.
TIRESIAS: You live, unknowing, with those nearest to you
         in the greatest shame. You do not see the evil.
OEDIPUS: You won't go on like that and never pay!
TIRESIAS: I can if there is any strength in truth.
375   **OEDIPUS:** In truth, but not in you! You have no strength,
         blind in your ears, your reason, and your eyes.
TIRESIAS: Unhappy man! Those jeers you hurl at me
         before long all these men will hurl at you.
OEDIPUS: You are the child of endless night; it's not
380   for me or anyone who sees to hurt you.
TIRESIAS: It's not my fate to be struck down by you.
         Apollo is enough. That's his concern.
OEDIPUS: Are these inventions Creon's or your own?
TIRESIAS: No, your affliction is yourself, not Creon.
385   **OEDIPUS:** Oh success!—in wealth, kingship, artistry,
         in any life that wins much admiration—
         the envious ill will stored up for you!
         to get at my command, a gift I did not
         seek, which the city put into my hands,
390   my loyal Creon, colleague from the start,
         longs to sneak up in secret and dethrone me.
         So he's suborned this fortuneteller—schemer!
         deceitful beggar-priest!—who has good eyes
         for gains alone, though in his craft he's blind.
395   Where were your prophet's powers ever proved?
         Why, when the dog who chanted verse° was here,
         did you not speak and liberate this city?
         Her riddle wasn't for a man chancing by
         to interpret; prophetic art was needed,
400   but you had none, it seems—learned from birds
         or from a god. I came along, yes I,
         Oedipus the ignorant, and stopped her—
         by using thought, not augury from birds.
         And it is I whom you may wish to banish,
405   so you'll be close to the Creontian throne.
         You—and the plot's concocter—will drive out
         pollution to your grief; you look quite old
         or you would be the victim of that plot!

°396 *dog . . . verse:* the Sphinx.

CHORAGOS: It seems to us that this man's words were said
    in anger, Oedipus, and yours as well.   410
    Insight, not angry words, is what we need,
    the best solution to the god's response.
TIRESIAS: You are the king, and yet I am your equal
    in my right to speak. In that I too am Lord,
    for I belong to Loxias,° not you.   415
    I am not Creon's man. He's nothing to me.
    Hear this, since you have thrown my blindness at me:
    Your eyes can't see the evil to which you've come,
    nor where you live, nor who is in your house.
    Do you know your parents? Now knowing, you are   420
    their enemy, in the underworld and here.
    A mother's and a father's double-lashing
    terrible-footed curse will soon drive you out.
    Now you can see, then you will stare into darkness.
    What place will not be harbor to your cry,   425
    or what Cithaeron° not reverberate
    when you have heard the bride-song in your palace
    to which you sailed? Fair wind to evil harbor!
    Nor do you see how many other woes
    will level you to yourself and to your children.   430
    So, at my message, and at Creon, too,
    splatter muck! There will never be a man
    ground into wretchedness as you will be.
OEDIPUS: Am I to listen to such things from him!
    May you be damned! Get out of here at once!   435
    Go! Leave my palace! Turn around and go!

[*TIRESIAS begins to move away from* OEDIPUS.]

TIRESIAS: I wouldn't have come had you not sent for me.
OEDIPUS: I did not know you'd talk stupidity,
    or I wouldn't have rushed to bring you to my house.
TIRESIAS: Stupid I seem to you, yet to your parents   440
    who gave you natural birth I seemed quite shrewd.
OEDIPUS: Who? Wait! Who is the one who gave me birth?
TIRESIAS: This day will give you birth,° and ruin too.
OEDIPUS: What murky, riddling things you always say!
TIRESIAS: Don't you surpass us all at finding out?   445
OEDIPUS: You sneer at what you'll find has brought me greatness.
TIRESIAS: And that's the very luck that ruined you.
OEDIPUS: I wouldn't care, just so I saved the city.
TIRESIAS: In that case I shall go. Boy, lead the way!
OEDIPUS: Yes, let him lead you off. Here, underfoot,   450
    you irk me. Gone, you'll cause no further pain.
TIRESIAS: I'll go when I have said what I was sent for.
    Your face won't scare me. You can't ruin me.

°415 *Loxias:* Apollo. °426 *Cithaeron:* reference to the mountain on which Oedipus was to be exposed as an infant.
°443 *give you birth:* that is, identify your parents.

I say to you, the man whom you have looked for
455 as you pronounced your curses, your decrees
on the bloody death of Laius—he is here!
A seeming stranger, he shall be shown to be
a Theban born, though he'll take no delight
in that solution. Blind, who once could see,
460 a beggar who was rich, through foreign lands
he'll go and point before him with a stick.
To his beloved children, he'll be shown
a father who is also brother; to the one
who bore him, son and husband; to his father,
465 his seed-fellow and killer. Go in
and think this out; and if you find I've lied,
say then I have no prophet's understanding!

[*Exit* TIRESIAS, *led by a* SERVANT. OEDIPUS *exits into the palace with his* ATTENDANTS.]

STASIMON 1

Strophe 1

CHORUS: Who is the man of whom the inspired
           rock of Delphi° said
470   he has committed the unspeakable
           with blood-stained hands?
       Time for him to ply a foot
       mightier than those of the horses
           of the storm in his escape;
475   upon him mounts and plunges the weaponed
       son of Zeus,° with fire and thunderbolts,
       and in his train the dreaded goddesses
       of Death, who never miss.

Antistrophe 1

       The message has just blazed,
480   gleaming from the snows
       of Mount Parnassus: we must track
           everywhere the unseen man.
       He wanders, hidden by wild
       forests, up through caves
485   and rocks, like a bull,
       anxious, with an anxious foot, forlorn.
       He puts away from him the mantic° words come from earth's
       navel,° at its center, yet these live
       forever and still hover round him.

Strophe 2

490   Terribly he troubles me,
           the skilled interpreter of birds!°

°469 *rock of Delphi*: Apollo's oracle at Delphi. °476 *son of Zeus*: Apollo. °487 *mantic*: prophetic. °487–88 *earth's navel*: Delphi. °491 *interpreter of birds*: Tiresias. The Chorus is troubled by his accusations.

I can't assent, nor speak against him.
  Both paths are closed to me.
I hover on the wings of doubt,
  not seeing what is here nor what's to come.   495
What quarrel started in the house of Labdacus°
or in the house of Polybus,°
  either ever in the past
  or now, I never
heard, so that . . . with this fact for my touchstone   500
I could attack the public
  fame of Oedipus, by the side of the Labdaceans
an ally, against the dark assassination.

Antistrophe 2

No, Zeus and Apollo
  understand and know things   505
mortal; but that another man
  can do more as a prophet than I can—
for that there is no certain test,
  though, skill to skill,
one man might overtake another.   510
No, never, not until
  I see the charges proved,
when someone blames him shall I nod assent.
For once, as we all saw, the winged maiden° came
against him: he was seen then to be skilled,   515
  proved, by that touchstone, dear to the people. So,
never will my mind convict him of the evil.

EPISODE 2

[*Enter* CREON *from the right door of the skene and speaks to the* CHORUS.]

CREON: Citizens, I hear that a fearful charge
  is made against me by King Oedipus!
  I had to come. If, in this crisis,   520
  he thinks that he has suffered injury
  from anything that I have said or done,
  I have no appetite for a long life—
  bearing a blame like that! It's no slight blow,
  the punishment I'd take from what he said: 525
  it's the ultimate hurt to be called traitor
  by the city, by you, by my own people!
CHORAGOS: The thing that forced that accusation out
  could have been anger, not the power of thought.
CREON: But who persuaded him that thoughts of mine   530
  had led the prophet into telling lies?
CHORAGOS: I do not know the thought behind his words.

°496 *house of Labdacus:* the line of Laius. °497 *Polybus:* Oedipus's foster father. °514 *winged maiden:* the Sphinx.

CREON: But did he look straight at you? Was his mind right
    when he said that I was guilty of this charge?
535 CHORAGOS: I have no eyes to see what rulers do.
    But here he comes himself out of the house.

[*Enter* OEDIPUS *from the palace.*]

OEDIPUS: What? You here? And can you really have
    the face and daring to approach my house
    when you're exposed as its master's murderer
540   and caught, too, as the robber of my kingship?
    Did you see cowardice in me, by the gods,
    or foolishness, when you began this plot?
    Did you suppose that I would not detect
    your stealthy moves, or that I'd not fight back?
545   It's your attempt that's folly, isn't it—
    tracking without followers or connections,
    kingship which is caught with wealth and numbers?
CREON: Now wait! Give me as long to answer back!
    Judge me for yourself when you have heard me!
550 OEDIPUS: You're eloquent, but I'd be slow to learn
    from you, now that I've seen your malice toward me.
CREON: That I deny. Hear what I have to say.
OEDIPUS: Don't you deny it! You are the traitor here!
CREON: If you consider mindless willfulness
555   a prized possession, you are not thinking sense.
OEDIPUS: If you think you can wrong a relative
    and get off free, you are not thinking sense.
CREON: Perfectly just, I won't say no. And yet
    what is this injury you say I did you?
560 OEDIPUS: Did you persuade me, yes or no, to send
    someone to bring that solemn prophet here?
CREON: And I still hold to the advice I gave.
OEDIPUS: How many years ago did your King Laius . . .
CREON: Laius! Do what? Now I don't understand.
565 OEDIPUS: Vanish—victim of a murderous violence?
CREON: That is a long count back into the past.
OEDIPUS: Well, was this seer then practicing his art?
CREON: Yes, skilled and honored just as he is today.
OEDIPUS: Did he, back then, ever refer to me?
570 CREON: He did not do so in my presence ever.
OEDIPUS: You did inquire into the murder then.
CREON: We had to, surely, though we discovered nothing.
OEDIPUS: But the "skilled" one did not say this then? Why not?
CREON: I never talk when I am ignorant.
575 OEDIPUS: But you're not ignorant of your own part.
CREON: What do you mean? I'll tell you if I know.
OEDIPUS: Just this: if he had not conferred with you
    he'd not have told about my murdering Laius.
CREON: If he said that, you are the one who knows.
580   But now it's fair that you should answer me.
OEDIPUS: Ask on! You won't convict me as the killer.

CREON: Well then, answer. My sister is your wife?
OEDIPUS: Now there's a statement that I can't deny.
CREON: You two have equal power in this country?
OEDIPUS: She gets from me whatever she desires.   585
CREON: And I'm a third? The three of us are equals?
OEDIPUS: That's where you're treacherous to your kinship!
CREON: But think about this rationally, as I do.
    First look at this: do you think anyone
    prefers the anxieties of being king   590
    to untroubled sleep—if he has equal power?
    I'm not the kind of man who falls in love
    with kingship. I am content with a king's power.
    And so would any man who's wise and prudent.
    I get all things from you, with no distress;   595
    as king I would have onerous duties, too.
    How could the kingship bring me more delight
    than this untroubled power and influence?
    I'm not misguided yet to such a point
    that profitable honors aren't enough.   600
    As it is, all wish me well and all salute;
    those begging you for something have me summoned,
    for their success depends on that alone.
    Why should I lose all this to become king?
    A prudent mind is never traitorous.   605
    Treason's a thought I'm not enamored of;
    nor could I join a man who acted so.
    In proof of this, first go yourself to Pytho°
    and ask if I brought back the true response.
    Then, if you find I plotted with that portent   610
    reader,° don't have me put to death by your vote
    only—I'll vote myself for my conviction.
    Don't let an unsupported thought convict me!
    It's not right mindlessly to take the bad
    for good or to suppose the good are traitors.   615
    Rejecting a relation who is loyal
    is like rejecting life, our greatest love.
    In time you'll know securely without stumbling,
    for time alone can prove a just man just,
    though you can know a bad man in a day.   620
CHORAGOS: Well said, to one who's anxious not to fall.
    Swift thinkers, Lord, are never safe from stumbling.
OEDIPUS: But when a swift and secret plotter moves
    against me, I must make swift counterplot.
    If I lie quiet and await his move,   625
    he'll have achieved his aims and I'll have missed.
CREON: You surely cannot mean you want me exiled!
OEDIPUS: Not exiled, no. Your death is what I want!
CREON: If you would first define what envy is . . .
OEDIPUS: Are you still stubborn! Still disobedient?   630

°608 *Pytho:* Delphi. °610–11 *portent reader:* Apollo's oracle or prophet.

CREON: I see you cannot think!

OEDIPUS: For me I can.

CREON: You should for me as well!

OEDIPUS: But you're a traitor!

CREON: What if you're wrong?

OEDIPUS: Authority must be maintained.

CREON: Not if the ruler's evil.

OEDIPUS: Hear that, Thebes!

635   CREON: It is my city too, not yours alone!

CHORAGOS: Please don't, my Lords! Ah, just in time, I see
        Jocasta there, coming from the palace.
        With her help you must settle your quarrel.

[*Enter* JOCASTA *from the Palace.*]

JOCASTA: Wretched men! What has provoked this ill-
640   advised dispute? Have you no sense of shame,
        with Thebes so sick, to stir up private troubles?
        Now go inside! And Creon, you go home!
        Don't make a general anguish out of nothing!

CREON: My sister, Oedipus your husband here
645   sees fit to do one of two hideous things:
        to have me banished from the land—or killed!

OEDIPUS: That's right: I caught him, Lady, plotting harm
        against my person—with a malignant science.

CREON: May my life fail, may I die cursed, if I
650   did any of the things you said I did!

JOCASTA: Believe his words, for the god's sake, Oedipus,
        in deference above all to his oath
        to the gods. Also for me, and for these men!

KOMMOS°

Strophe 1

CHORUS: Consent, with will and mind,
655   my king, I beg of you!

OEDIPUS: What do you wish me to surrender?

CHORUS: Show deference to him who was not feeble in time past
        and is now great in the power of his oath!

OEDIPUS: Do you know what you're asking?

CHORUS: Yes.

OEDIPUS: Tell me then.

660   CHORUS: Never to cast into dishonored guilt, with an unproved
        assumption, a kinsman who has bound himself by curse.

OEDIPUS: Now you must understand, when you ask this,
        you ask my death or banishment from the land.

Strophe 2

CHORUS: No, by the god who is the foremost of all gods,
665   the Sun! No! Godless,
                friendless, whatever death is worst of all,

°654 *Kommos:* a dirge or lament sung by the Chorus and one or more of the chief characters.

let that be my destruction, if this
    thought ever moved me!
But my ill-fated soul
    this dying land   670
wears out—the more if to these older troubles
she adds new troubles from the two of you!
OEDIPUS: Then let him go, though it must mean my death,
    or else disgrace and exile from the land.
My pity is moved by your words, not by his—   675
he'll only have my hate, wherever he goes.
CREON: You're sullen as you yield; you'll be depressed
    when you've passed through this anger. Natures like yours
are hardest on themselves. That's as it should be.
OEDIPUS: Then won't you go and let me be?
CREON: I'll go.   680
Though you're unreasonable, they know I'm righteous.

                                                          [Exit CREON.]

Antistrophe 1

CHORUS: Why are you waiting, Lady?
    Conduct him back into the palace!
JOCASTA: I will, when I have heard what chanced.
CHORUS: Conjectures—words alone, and nothing based on thought.   685
    But even an injustice can devour a man.
JOCASTA: Did the words come from both sides?
CHORUS: Yes.
JOCASTA: What was said?
CHORUS: To me it seems enough! enough! the land already troubled,
    that this should rest where it has stopped.   690
OEDIPUS: See what you've come to in your honest thought,
    in seeking to relax and blunt my heart?

Antistrophe 2

CHORUS: I have not said this only once, my Lord.
    That I had lost my sanity,
        without a path in thinking—   695
be sure this would be clear
        if I put you away
who, when my cherished land
        wandered crazed
with suffering, brought her back on course.   700
Now, too, be a lucky helmsman!
JOCASTA: Please, for the god's sake, Lord, explain to me
    the reason why you have conceived this wrath?
OEDIPUS: I honor you, not them,° and I'll explain
    to you how Creon has conspired against me.   705
JOCASTA: All right, if that will explain how the quarrel started.
OEDIPUS: He says I am the murderer of Laius!

°704 *them:* the Chorus.

JOCASTA: Did he claim knowledge or that someone told him?
OEDIPUS: Here's what he did: he sent that vicious seer
710   so he could keep his own mouth innocent.
JOCASTA: Ah then, absolve yourself of what he charges!
Listen to this and you'll agree, no mortal
is ever given skill in prophecy.
I'll prove this quickly with one incident.
715   It was foretold to Laius—I shall not say
by Phoebus himself, but by his ministers—
that when his fate arrived he would be killed
by a son who would be born to him and me.
And yet, so it is told, foreign robbers
720   murdered him, at a place where three roads meet.
As for the child I bore him, not three days passed
before he yoked the ball-joints of its feet,°
then cast it, by others' hands, on a trackless mountain.
That time Apollo did not make our child
725   a patricide, or bring about what Laius
feared, that he be killed by his own son.
That's how prophetic words determined things!
Forget them. The things a god must track
he will himself painlessly reveal.
730   **OEDIPUS:** Just now, as I was listening to you, Lady,
what a profound distraction seized my mind!
JOCASTA: What made you turn around so anxiously?
OEDIPUS: I thought you said that Laius was attacked
and butchered at a place where three roads meet.
735   **JOCASTA:** That is the story, and it is told so still.
OEDIPUS: Where is the place where this was done to him?
JOCASTA: The land's called Phocis, where a two-forked road
comes in from Delphi and from Daulia.
OEDIPUS: And how much time has passed since these events?
740   **JOCASTA:** Just prior to your presentation here
as king this news was published to the city.
OEDIPUS: Oh, Zeus, what have you willed to do to me?
JOCASTA: Oedipus, what makes your heart so heavy?
OEDIPUS: No, tell me first of Laius' appearance,
745   what peak of youthful vigor he had reached.
JOCASTA: A tall man, showing his first growth of white.
He had a figure not unlike your own.
OEDIPUS: Alas! It seems that in my ignorance
I laid those fearful curses on myself.
750   **JOCASTA:** What is it, Lord? I flinch to see your face.
OEDIPUS: I'm dreadfully afraid the prophet sees.
But I'll know better with one more detail.
JOCASTA: I'm frightened too. But ask: I'll answer you.
OEDIPUS: Was his retinue small, or did he travel
755   with a great troop, as would befit a prince?
JOCASTA: There were just five in all, one a herald.
There was a carriage, too, bearing Laius.

°722 *ball-joints of its feet:* the ankles.

OEDIPUS: Alas! Now I see it! But who was it,
　　Lady, who told you what you know about this?
JOCASTA: A servant who alone was saved unharmed.　　　　　　760
OEDIPUS: By chance, could he be now in the palace?
JOCASTA: No, he is not. When he returned and saw
　　you had the power of the murdered Laius,
　　he touched my hand and begged me formally
　　to send him to the fields and to the pastures,　　　　　765
　　so he'd be out of sight, far from the city.
　　I did. Although a slave, he well deserved
　　to win this favor, and indeed far more.
OEDIPUS: Let's have him called back in immediately.
JOCASTA: That can be done, but why do you desire it?　　　770
OEDIPUS: I fear, Lady, I have already said
　　too much. That's why I wish to see him now.
JOCASTA: Then he shall come; but it is right somehow
　　that I, too, Lord, should know what troubles you.
OEDIPUS: I've gone so deep into the things I feared　　　775
　　I'll tell you everything. Who has a right
　　greater than yours, while I cross through this chance?
　　Polybus of Corinth was my father,
　　my mother was the Dorian Meropē.
　　I was first citizen, until this chance　　　　　　780
　　attacked me—striking enough, to be sure,
　　but not worth all the gravity I gave it.
　　This: at a feast a man who'd drunk too much
　　denied, at the wine, I was my father's son.
　　I was depressed and all that day I barely　　　　785
　　held it in. Next day I put the question
　　to my mother and father. They were enraged
　　at the man who'd let this fiction fly at me.
　　I was much cheered by them. And yet it kept
　　grinding into me. His words kept coming back.　　　790
　　Without my mother's or my father's knowledge
　　I went to Pytho. But Phoebus sent me away
　　dishonoring my demand. Instead, other
　　wretched horrors he flashed forth in speech.
　　He said that I would be my mother's lover,　　　795
　　show offspring to mankind they could not look at,
　　and be his murderer whose seed I am.°
　　When I heard this, and ever since, I gauged
　　the way to Corinth by the stars alone,
　　running to a place where I would never see　　　　800
　　the disgrace in the oracle's words come true.
　　But I soon came to the exact location
　　where, as you tell of it, the king was killed.
　　Lady, here is the truth. As I went on,
　　when I was just approaching those three roads,　　　805
　　a herald and a man like him you spoke of

°797 *be . . . am:* that is, murder my father.

came on, riding a carriage drawn by colts.
Both the man out front and the old man himself°
tried violently to force me off the road.

810 The driver, when he tried to push me off,
I struck in anger. The old man saw this, watched
me approach, then leaned out and lunged down
with twin prongs° at the middle of my head!
He got more than he gave. Abruptly—struck

815 once by the staff in this my hand—he tumbled
out, head first, from the middle of the carriage.
And then I killed them all. But if there is
a kinship between Laius and this stranger,
who is more wretched than the man you see?

820 Who was there born more hated by the gods?
For neither citizen nor foreigner
may take me in his home or speak to me.
No, they must drive me off. And it is I
who have pronounced these curses on myself!

825 I stain the dead man's bed with these my hands,
by which he died. Is not my nature vile?
Unclean?—if I am banished and even
in exile I may not see my own parents,
or set foot in my homeland, or else be yoked

830 in marriage to my mother, and kill my father,
Polybus, who raised me and gave me birth?
If someone judged a cruel divinity
did this to me, would he not speak the truth?
You pure and awful gods, may I not ever

835 see that day, may I be swept away
from men before I see so great and so
calamitous a stain fixed on my person!
CHORAGOS: These things seem fearful to us, Lord, and yet,
until you hear it from the witness, keep hope!

840 **OEDIPUS:** That is the single hope that's left to me,
to wait for him, that herdsman—until he comes.
JOCASTA: When he appears, what are you eager for?
OEDIPUS: Just this: if his account agrees with yours
then I shall have escaped this misery.

845 **JOCASTA:** But what was it that struck you in my story?
OEDIPUS: You said he spoke of robbers as the ones
who killed him. Now: if he continues still
to speak of many, then I could not have killed him.
One man and many men just do not jibe.

850 But if he says one belted man, the doubt
is gone. The balance tips toward me. I did it.
JOCASTA: No! He told it as I told you. Be certain.
He can't reject that and reverse himself.
The city heard these things, not I alone.

°808 *old man himself:* Laius. °812–13 *lunged . . . prongs:* Laius strikes Oedipus with a two-pronged horse goad
or whip.

But even if he swerves from what he said,   855
he'll never show that Laius' murder, Lord,
occurred just as predicted. For Loxias
expressly said my son was doomed to kill him.
The boy—poor boy—he never had a chance
to cut him down, for he was cut down first.   860
Never again, just for some oracle
will I shoot frightened glances right and left.
OEDIPUS: That's full of sense. Nonetheless, send a man
to bring that farm hand here. Will you do it?
JOCASTA: I'll send one right away. But let's go in.   865
Would I do anything against your wishes?

[*Exit* OEDIPUS *and* JOCASTA *through the central door into the palace.*]

STASIMON 2

Strophe 1

CHORUS: May there accompany me
      the fate to keep a reverential purity in what I say,
   in all I do, for which the laws have been set forth
   and walk on high, born to traverse the brightest,   870
      highest upper air; Olympus° only
      is their father, nor was it
      mortal nature
      that fathered them, and never will
      oblivion lull them into sleep;   875
      the god in them is great and never ages.

Antistrophe 1

   The will to violate, seed of the tyrant,
   if it has drunk mindlessly of wealth and power,
   without a sense of time or true advantage,
      mounts to a peak, then   880
   plunges to an abrupt . . . destiny,
      where the useful foot
      is of no use. But the kind
   of struggling that is good for the city
   I ask the god never to abolish.   885
   The god is my protector: never will I give that up.

Strophe 2

   But if a man proceeds disdainfully
         in deeds of hand or word
   and has no fear of Justice
         or reverence for shrines of the divinities   890
   (may a bad fate catch him
         for his luckless wantonness!),
   if he'll not gain what he gains with justice
   and deny himself what is unholy,
   or if he clings, in foolishness, to the untouchable   895

°871 *Olympus:* Mount Olympus, home of the gods, treated as a god.

(what man, finally, in such an action, will have strength
enough to fend off passion's arrows from his soul?),
if, I say, this kind of
      deed is held in honor—
900   why should I join the sacred dance?

Antistrophe 2

No longer shall I visit and revere
      Earth's navel the untouchable,
nor visit Abae's° temple,
      or Olympia,°
905   if the prophecies are not matched by events
      for all the world to point to.
No, you who hold the power, if you are rightly called
Zeus the king of all, let this matter not escape you
and your ever-deathless rule,
910   for the prophecies to Laius fade . . .
and men already disregard them;
nor is Apollo anywhere
      glorified with honors.
Religion slips away.

EPISODE 3

[*Enter* JOCASTA *from the palace carrying a branch wound with wool and a jar of incense. She is attended by two women.*]

915   **JOCASTA:** Lords of the realm, the thought has come to me
      to visit shrines of the divinities
      with suppliant's branch in hand and fragrant smoke.
      For Oedipus excites his soul too much
      with alarms of all kinds. He will not judge
920   the present by the past, like a man of sense.
      He's at the mercy of all terror-mongers.

[*JOCASTA approaches the altar on the right and kneels.*]

      Since I can do no good by counseling,
      Apollo the Lycēan!—you are the closest—
      I come a suppliant, with these my vows,
925   for a cleansing that will not pollute him.
      For when we see him shaken we are all
      afraid, like people looking at their helmsman.

[*Enter a* MESSENGER *along one of the Parados. He sees* JOCASTA *at the altar and then addresses the*
CHORUS.]

      MESSENGER: I would be pleased if you would help me, stranger.
      Where is the palace of King Oedipus?
930   Or tell me where he is himself, if you know.

°903 *Abae:* a town in Phocis where there was another oracle of Apollo. °904 *Olympia:* site of the oracle of Zeus.

CHORUS: This is his house, stranger. He is within.
   This is his wife and mother of his children.
MESSENGER: May she and her family find prosperity,
   if, as you say, her marriage is fulfilled.
JOCASTA: You also, stranger, for you deserve as much   935
   for your gracious words. But tell me why you've come.
   What do you wish? Or what have you to tell us?
MESSENGER: Good news, my Lady, both for your house and
   husband.
JOCASTA: What is your news? And who has sent you to us?   940
MESSENGER: I come from Corinth. When you have heard my
   news
   you will rejoice, I'm sure—and grieve perhaps.
JOCASTA: What is it? How can it have this double power?
MESSENGER: They will establish him their king, so say   945
   the people of the land of Isthmia.°
JOCASTA: But is old Polybus not still in power?
MESSENGER: He's not, for death has clasped him in the tomb.
JOCASTA: What's this? Has Oedipus' father died?
MESSENGER: If I have lied then I deserve to die.   950
JOCASTA: Attendant! Go quickly to your master,
   and tell him this.

                    [*Exit an* ATTENDANT *into the palace.*]

            Oracles of the gods!
   Where are you now? The man whom Oedipus
   fled long ago, for fear that he should kill him—
   he's been destroyed by chance and not by him!   955

[*Enter* OEDIPUS *from the palace.*]

OEDIPUS: Darling Jocasta, my beloved wife,
   Why have you called me from the palace?
JOCASTA: First hear what this man has to say. Then see
   what the god's grave oracle has come to now!
OEDIPUS: Where is he from? What is this news he brings me?   960
JOCASTA: From Corinth. He brings news about your father:
   that Polybus is no more! that he is dead!
OEDIPUS: What's this, old man? I want to hear you say it.
MESSENGER: If this is what must first be clarified,
   please be assured that he is dead and gone.   965
OEDIPUS: By treachery or by the touch of sickness?
MESSENGER: Light pressures tip agèd frames into their sleep.
OEDIPUS: You mean the poor man died of some disease.
MESSENGER: And of the length of years that he had tallied.
OEDIPUS: Aha! Then why should we look to Pytho's vapors,°   970
   or to the birds that scream above our heads?°
   If we could really take those things for guides,
   I would have killed my father. But he's dead!

°946 *land of Isthmia:* Corinth, which is on an isthmus. °970 *Pytho's vapors:* the prophecies of the oracle at Delphi.
°971 *birds . . . heads:* the prophecies derived from interpreting the flights of birds.

He is beneath the earth, and here am I,
975 who never touched a spear. Unless he died
of longing for me and I "killed" him that way!
No, in this case, Polybus, by dying, took
the worthless oracle to Hades with him.

JOCASTA: And wasn't I telling you that just now?

980 OEDIPUS: You were indeed. I was misled by fear.

JOCASTA: You should not care about this anymore.

OEDIPUS: I must care. I must stay clear of my mother's bed.

JOCASTA: What's there for man to fear? The realm of chance
prevails. True foresight isn't possible.
985 His life is best who lives without a plan.
This marriage with your mother—don't fear it.
How many times have men in dreams, too, slept
with their own mothers! Those who believe such things
mean nothing endure their lives most easily.

990 OEDIPUS: A fine, bold speech, and you are right, perhaps,
except that my mother is still living,
so I must fear her, however well you argue.

JOCASTA: And yet your father's tomb is a great eye.

OEDIPUS: Illuminating, yes. But I still fear the living.

995 MESSENGER: Who is the woman who inspires this fear?

OEDIPUS: Meropē, Polybus' wife, old man.

MESSENGER: And what is there about her that alarms you?

OEDIPUS: An oracle, god-sent and fearful, stranger.

MESSENGER: Is it permitted that another know?

1000 OEDIPUS: It is. Loxias once said to me
I must have intercourse with my own mother
and take my father's blood with these my hands.
So I have long lived far away from Corinth.
This has indeed brought much good luck, and yet,
1005 to see one's parents' eyes is happiest.

MESSENGER: Was it for this that you have lived in exile?

OEDIPUS: So I'd not be my father's killer, sir.

MESSENGER: Had I not better free you from this fear,
my Lord? That's why I came—to do you service.

1010 OEDIPUS: Indeed, what a reward you'd get for that!

MESSENGER: Indeed, this is the main point of my trip,
to be rewarded when you get back home.

OEDIPUS: I'll never rejoin the givers of my seed!°

MESSENGER: My son, clearly you don't know what you're doing.

1015 OEDIPUS: But how is that, old man? For the gods' sake, tell me!

MESSENGER: If it's because of them you won't go home.

OEDIPUS: I fear that Phoebus will have told the truth.

MESSENGER: Pollution from the ones who gave you seed?

OEDIPUS: That is the thing, old man, I always fear.

1020 MESSENGER: Your fear is groundless. Understand that.

OEDIPUS: Groundless? Not if I was born their son.

MESSENGER: But Polybus is not related to you.

OEDIPUS: Do you mean Polybus was not my father?

°1013 *givers of my seed:* that is, my parents. Oedipus still thinks Meropē and Polybus are his parents.

Messenger: No more than I. We're both the same to you.
Oedipus: Same? One who begot me and one who didn't?   1025
Messenger: He didn't beget you any more than I did.
Oedipus: But then, why did he say I was his son?
Messenger: He got you as a gift from my own hands.
Oedipus: He loved me so, though from another's hands?
Messenger: His former childlessness persuaded him.   1030
Oedipus: But had you bought me, or begotten me?
Messenger: Found you. In the forest hallows of Cithaeron.
Oedipus: What were you doing traveling in that region?
Messenger: I was in charge of flocks which grazed those mountains.
Oedipus: A wanderer who worked the flocks for hire?   1035
Messenger: Ah, but that day. I was your savior, son.
Oedipus: From what? What was my trouble when you took me?
Messenger: The ball-joints of your feet might testify.
Oedipus: What's that? What makes you name that ancient trouble?
Messenger: Your feet were pierced and I am your rescuer.   1040
Oedipus: A fearful rebuke those tokens left for me!
Messenger: That was the chance that names you who you are.
Oedipus: By the gods, did my mother or my father do this?
Messenger: That I don't know. He might who gave you to me.
Oedipus: From someone else? You didn't chance on me?   1045
Messenger: Another shepherd handed you to me.
Oedipus: Who was he? Do you know? Will you explain!
Messenger: They called him one of the men of—was it Laius?
Oedipus: The one who once was king here long ago?
Messenger: That is the one! The man was shepherd to him.   1050
Oedipus: And is he still alive so I can see him?
Messenger: But you who live here ought to know that best.
Oedipus: Does any one of you now present know
    about the shepherd whom this man has named?
    Have you seen him in town or in the fields? Speak out!   1055
    The time has come for the discovery!
Choragos: The man he speaks of, I believe, is the same
    as the field hand you have already asked to see.
    But it's Jocasta who would know this best.
Oedipus: Lady, do you remember the man we just   1060
    now sent for—is that the man he speaks of?
Jocasta: What? The man he spoke of? Pay no attention!
    His words are not worth thinking about. It's nothing.
Oedipus: With clues like this within my grasp, give up?
    Fail to solve the mystery of my birth?   1065
Jocasta: For the love of the gods, and if you love your life,
    give up this search! My sickness is enough.
Oedipus: Come! Though my mothers for three generations
    were in slavery, you'd not be lowborn!
Jocasta: No, listen to me! Please! Don't do this thing!   1070
Oedipus: I will not listen; I will search out the truth.
Jocasta: My thinking is for you—it would be best.
Oedipus: This "best" of yours is starting to annoy me.
Jocasta: Doomed man! Never find out who you are!

1075   **OEDIPUS:** Will someone go and bring that shepherd here?
         Leave her to glory in her wealthy birth!
JOCASTA: Man of misery! No other name
         shall I address you by, ever again.

[*Exit JOCASTA into the palace after a long pause.*]

CHORAGOS: Why has your lady left, Oedipus,
1080   hurled by a savage grief? I am afraid
         disaster will come bursting from this silence.
OEDIPUS: Let it burst forth! However low this seed
         of mine may be, yet I desire to see it.
         She, perhaps—she has a woman's pride—
1085   is mortified by my base origins.
         But I who count myself the child of Chance,
         the giver of good, shall never know dishonor.
         She is my mother,° and the months my brothers
         who first marked out my lowness, then my greatness.
1090   I shall not prove untrue to such a nature
         by giving up the search for my own birth.

STASIMON 3

Strophe
CHORUS: If I have mantic power
         and excellence in thought,
         by Olympus,
1095   you shall not, Cithaeron, at tomorrow's
         full moon,
         fail to hear us celebrate you as the countryman
         of Oedipus, his nurse and mother,
         or fail to be the subject of our dance,
1100   since you have given pleasure
         to our king.
Phoebus, whom we summon by "iē!,"
may this be pleasing to you!

Antistrophe
         Who was your mother, son?
1105   which of the long-lived nymphs
         after lying with Pan,°
            the mountain roaming . . . Or was it a bride
         of Loxias?°
         For dear to him are all the upland pastures.
1110   Or was it Mount Cyllēnē's lord,°
         or the Bacchic god,°
            dweller of the mountain peaks,
         who received you as a joyous find
         from one of the nymphs of Helicon,
1115   the favorite sharers of his sport?

°1088 *She . . . mother:* Chance is my mother. °1106 *Pan:* god of shepherds and woodlands, half man and half goat.
°1108 *Loxias:* Apollo. °1110 *Mount Cyllēnē's lord:* Hermes, messenger of the gods. °1111 *Bacchic god:* Dionysus.

EPISODE 4

OEDIPUS: If someone like myself, who never met him,
    may calculate—elders, I think I see
    the very herdsman we've been waiting for.
    His many years would fit that man's age,
    and those who bring him on, if I am right,   1120
    are my own men. And yet, in real knowledge,
    you can outstrip me, surely: you've seen him.

[*Enter the old* HERDSMAN *escorted by two of Oedipus's* ATTENDANTS. *At first, the* HERDSMAN *will not look at* OEDIPUS.]

CHORAGOS: I know him, yes, a man of the house of Laius,
    a trusty herdsman if he ever had one.
OEDIPUS: I ask you first, the stranger come from Corinth: 1125
    is this the man you spoke of?
MESSENGER: That's he you see.
OEDIPUS: Then you, old man. First look at me! Now answer:
    did you belong to Laius' household once?
HERDSMAN: I did. Not a purchased slave but raised in the palace.
OEDIPUS: How have you spent your life? What is your work?   1130
HERDSMAN: Most of my life now I have tended sheep.
OEDIPUS: Where is the usual place you stay with them?
HERDSMAN: On Mount Cithaeron. Or in that district.
OEDIPUS: Do you recall observing this man there?
HERDSMAN: Doing what? Which is the man you mean?   1135
OEDIPUS: This man right here. Have you had dealings with him?
HERDSMAN: I can't say right away. I don't remember.
MESSENGER: No wonder, master. I'll bring clear memory
    to his ignorance. I'm absolutely sure
    he can recall it, the district was Cithaeron,   1140
    he with a double flock, and I, with one,
    lived close to him, for three entire seasons,
    six months long, from spring right to Arcturus.°
    Then for the winter I'd drive mine to my fold,
    and he'd drive his to Laius' pen again.   1145
    Did any of the things I say take place?
HERDSMAN: You speak the truth, though it's from long ago.
MESSENGER: Do you remember giving me, back then,
    a boy I was to care for as my own?
HERDSMAN: What are you saying? Why do you ask me that?   1150
MESSENGER: There, sir, is the man who was that boy!
HERDSMAN: Damn you! Shut your mouth! Keep your silence!
OEDIPUS: Stop! Don't you rebuke his words.
    Your words ask for rebuke far more than his.
HERDSMAN: But what have I done wrong, most royal master?   1155

°1143 *from spring right to Arcturus:* that is, from spring to early fall, when the summer star Arcturus (in the constellation Boôtes) was no longer visible in the early evening sky. It did not rise at night again until early in the following spring.

OEDIPUS: Not telling of the boy of whom he asked.

HERDSMAN: He's ignorant and blundering toward ruin.

OEDIPUS: Tell it willingly—or under torture.

HERDSMAN: Oh god! Don't—I am old—don't torture me!

1160 OEDIPUS: Here! Someone put his hands behind his back!

HERDSMAN: But why? What else would you find out, poor man?

OEDIPUS: Did you give him the child he asks about?

HERDSMAN: I did. I wish that I had died that day!

OEDIPUS: You'll come to that if you don't speak the truth.

1165 HERDSMAN: It's if I speak that I shall be destroyed.

OEDIPUS: I think this fellow struggles for delay.

HERDSMAN: No, no! I said already that I gave him.

OEDIPUS: From your own home, or got from someone else?

HERDSMAN: Not from my own. I got him from another.

1170 OEDIPUS: Which of these citizens? What sort of house?

HERDSMAN: Don't—by the gods!—don't, master, ask me more!

OEDIPUS: It means your death if I must ask again.

HERDSMAN: One of the children of the house of Laius.

OEDIPUS: A slave—or born into the family?

1175 HERDSMAN: I have come to the dreaded thing, and I shall say it.

OEDIPUS: And I to hearing it, but hear I must.

HERDSMAN: He was reported to have been—his son.
     Your lady in the house could tell you best.

OEDIPUS: Because she gave him to you?

HERDSMAN: Yes, my lord.

OEDIPUS: What was her purpose?

1180 HERDSMAN: I was to kill the boy.

OEDIPUS: The child she bore?

HERDSMAN: She dreaded prophecies.

OEDIPUS: What were they?

HERDSMAN: The word was that he'd kill his parents.

OEDIPUS: Then why did you give him up to this old man?

HERDSMAN: In pity, master—so he would take him home,

1185   to another land. But what he did was save him
    for this supreme disaster. If you are the one
    he speaks of—know your evil birth and fate!

OEDIPUS: Ah! All of it was destined to be true!
    Oh light, now may I look my last upon you,

1190   shown monstrous in my birth, in marriage monstrous,
    a murderer monstrous in those I killed.

                               [*Exit* OEDIPUS, *running into the palace.*]

STASIMON 4

Strophe 1

CHORUS: Oh generations of mortal men,
    while you are living, I will
        appraise your lives at zero!

1195   What man

comes closer to seizing lasting blessedness
than merely to seize its semblance,
and after living in this semblance, to plunge?
With your example before us,
with your destiny, yours,   1200
    suffering Oedipus, no mortal
can I judge fortunate.

Antistrophe 1

For he,° outranging everybody,
shot his arrow° and became the lord
    of wide prosperity and blessedness,   1205
oh Zeus, after destroying
the virgin with the crooked talons,°
singer of oracles; and against death,
in my land, he arose a tower of defense.
From which time you were called my king   1210
and granted privileges supreme—in mighty
Thebes the ruling lord.

Strophe 2

But now—whose story is more sorrowful than yours?
Who is more intimate with fierce calamities,
with labors, now that your life is altered?   1215
Alas, my Oedipus, whom all men know:
one great harbor.°—
one alone sufficed for you,
as son and father,
when you tumbled,° plowman° of the woman's chamber.   1220
How, how could your paternal
    furrows, wretched man,
endure you silently so long.

Antistrophe 2

Time, all-seeing, surprised you living an unwilled life
and sits from of old in judgment on the marriage, not a marriage, 1225
where the begetter is the begot as well.
Ah, son of Laius . . . ,
would that—oh, would that
I had never seen you!
I wail, my scream climbing beyond itself   1230
from my whole power of voice. To say it straight:
    from you I got new breath—
but I also lulled my eye to sleep.°

°1203 *he:* Oedipus. °1204 *shot his arrow:* took his chances; made a guess at the Sphinx's riddle. °1207 *virgin . . . talons:* the Sphinx. °1217 *one great harbor:* metaphorical allusion to Jocasta's body. °1220 *tumbled:* were born and had sex. *plowman:* Plowing is used here as a sexual metaphor. °1233 *I . . . sleep:* I failed to see the corruption you brought.

EXODOS

[Enter the SECOND MESSENGER *from the palace.]*

SECOND MESSENGER: You who are first among the citizens,
what deeds you are about to hear and see!
What grief you'll carry, if, true to your birth,
you still respect the house of Labdacus!
Neither the Ister nor the Phasis river
could purify this house, such suffering
does it conceal, or soon must bring to light—
willed this time, not unwilled. Griefs hurt worst
which we perceive to be self-chosen ones.
CHORAGOS: They were sufficient, the things we knew before,
to make us grieve. What can you add to those?
SECOND MESSENGER: The thing that's quickest said and quickest heard:
our own, our royal one, Jocasta's dead.
CHORAGOS: Unhappy queen! What was responsible?
SECOND MESSENGER: Herself. The bitterest of these events
is not for you, you were not there to see,
but yet, exactly as I can recall it,
you'll hear what happened to that wretched lady.
She came in anger through the outer hall,
and then she ran straight to her marriage bed,
tearing her hair with the fingers of both hands.
Then, slamming shut the doors when she was in,
she called to Laius, dead so many years,
remembering the ancient seed which caused
his death, leaving the mother to the son
to breed again an ill-born progeny.
She mourned the bed where she, alas, bred double—
husband by husband, children by her child.
From this point on I don't know how she died,
for Oedipus then burst in with a cry,
and did not let us watch her final evil.
Our eyes were fixed on him. Wildly he ran
to each of us, asking for his spear
and for his wife—no wife: where he might find
the double mother-field, his and his children's.
He raved, and some divinity then showed him—
for none of us did so who stood close by.
With a dreadful shout—as if some guide were leading—
he lunged through the double doors; he bent the hollow
bolts from the sockets, burst into the room,
and there we saw her, hanging from above,
entangled in some twisted hanging strands.
He saw, was stricken, and with a wild roar
ripped down the dangling noose. When she, poor woman,
lay on the ground, there came a fearful sight:
he snatched the pins of worked gold from her dress,
with which her clothes were fastened: these he raised
and struck into the ball-joints of his eyes.°

Line numbers in left margin: 1235, 1240, 1245, 1250, 1255, 1260, 1265, 1270, 1275, 1280

°1281 *ball-joints of his eyes:* his eyeballs. Oedipus blinds himself in both eyes at the same time.

He shouted that they would no longer see
the evils he had suffered or had done,
see in the dark those he should not have seen,
and know no more those he once sought to know.   1285
While chanting this, not once but many times
he raised his hand and struck into his eyes.
Blood from his wounded eyes poured down his chin,
not freed in moistening drops, but all at once
a stormy rain of black blood burst like hail.   1290
These evils, coupling them, making them one,
have broken loose upon both man and wife.
The old prosperity that they had once
was true prosperity, and yet today,
mourning, ruin, death, disgrace, and every   1295
evil you could name—not one is absent.
CHORAGOS: Has he allowed himself some peace from all this grief?
SECOND MESSENGER: He shouts that someone slide the bolts and show
to all the Cadmeians the patricide,
his mother's—I can't say it, it's unholy—   1300
so he can cast himself out of the land,
not stay and curse his house by his own curse.
He lacks the strength, though, and he needs a guide,
for his is a sickness that's too great to bear.
Now you yourself will see: the bolts of the doors   1305
are opening. You are about to see
a vision even one who hates must pity.

[Enter the blinded OEDIPUS *from the palace, led in by a household* SERVANT.]

CHORAGOS: This suffering sends terror through men's eyes,
terrible beyond any suffering
my eyes have touched. Oh man of pain,   1310
what madness reached you? Which god from far off,
surpassing in range his longest spring,
        struck hard against your god-abandoned fate?
Oh man of pain,
I cannot look upon you— though there's so much   1315
I would ask you, so much to hear,
so much that holds my eyes—
        so awesome the convulsions you send through me.
OEDIPUS: Ah! Ah! I am a man of misery.
Where am I carried? Pity me! Where   1320
is my voice scattered abroad on wings?
        Divinity, where has your lunge transported me?
CHORAGOS: To something horrible, not to be heard or seen.

KOMMOS

Strophe 1
OEDIPUS: Oh, my cloud
of darkness, abominable, unspeakable as it attacks me,   1325
not to be turned away, brought by an evil wind!
Alas!

Again alas! Both enter me at once:
the sting of the prongs,° the memory of evils!

1330   CHORUS: I do not marvel that in these afflictions
you carry double griefs and double evils.

Antistrophe 1

OEDIPUS: Ah, friend,
so you at least are there, resolute servant!
Still with a heart to care for me, the blind man.

1335   Oh! Oh!
I know that you are there. I recognize
even inside my darkness, that voice of yours.
CHORUS: Doer of horror, how did you bear to quench
your vision? What divinity raised your hand?

Strophe 2

1340   OEDIPUS: It was Apollo there, Apollo, friends,
who brought my sorrows, vile sorrows to their perfection,
these evils that were done to me.
But the one who struck them with his hand,
that one was none but I, in wretchedness.

1345   For why was I to see
when nothing I could see would bring me joy?
CHORUS: Yes, that is how it was.
OEDIPUS: What could I see, indeed,
or what enjoy—what greeting

1350   is there I could hear with pleasure, friends?
Conduct me out of the land
as quickly as you can!
Conduct me out, my friends,
the man utterly ruined,

1355   supremely cursed,
the man who is by gods
the most detested of all men!
CHORUS: Wretched in disaster and in knowledge:
oh, I could wish you'd never come to know!

Antistrophe 2

1360   OEDIPUS: May he be destroyed, whoever freed the savage shackles
from my feet when I'd been sent to the wild pasture,
whoever rescued me from murder
and became my savior—
a bitter gift:

1365   if I had died then,
I'd not have been such grief to self and kin.
CHORUS: I also would have had it so.
OEDIPUS: I'd not have returned to be my father's
murderer; I'd not be called by men

1370   my mother's bridegroom.

°1329 *prongs*: refers to both the whip that Laius used and the two gold pins Oedipus used to blind himself.

Now I'm without a god,
    child of a polluted parent,
fellow progenitor with him
    who gave me birth in misery.
If there's an evil that   1375
    surpasses evils, that
has fallen to the lot of Oedipus.

CHORAGOS: How can I say that you have counseled well?
Better not to be than live a blind man.

OEDIPUS: That this was not the best thing I could do—   1380
don't tell me that, or advise me any more!
Should I descend to Hades and endure
to see my father with these eyes? Or see
my poor unhappy mother? For I have done,
to both of these, things too great for hanging.   1385
Or is the sight of children to be yearned for,
to see new shoots that sprouted as these did?
Never, never with these eyes of mine!
Nor city, nor tower, nor holy images
of the divinities! For I, all-wretched,   1390
most nobly raised—as no one else in Thebes—
deprived myself of these when I ordained
that all expel the impious one—god-shown
to be polluted, and the dead king's son!°
Once I exposed this great stain upon me,   1395
could I have looked on these with steady eyes?
No! No! And if there were a way to block
the source of hearing in my ears, I'd gladly
have locked up my pitiable body,
so I'd be blind and deaf. Evils shut out—   1400
that way my mind could live in sweetness.
Alas, Cithaeron,° why did you receive me?
Or when you had me, not killed me instantly?
I'd not have had to show my birth to mankind.
Polybus, Corinth, halls—ancestral,   1405
they told me—how beautiful was your ward,
a scar that held back festering disease!
Evil my nature, evil my origin.
You, three roads, and you, secret ravine,
you oak grove, narrow place of those three paths   1410
that drank my blood° from these my hands, from him
who fathered me, do you remember still
the things I did to you? When I'd come here,
what I then did once more? Oh marriages! Marriages!
You gave us life and when you'd planted us   1415
you sent the same seed up, and then revealed
fathers, brothers, sons, and kinsman's blood,

°1392–94 *I . . . son:* Oedipus refers to his own curse against the murderer as well as his sins of patricide and incest.
°1402 *Cithaeron:* the mountain on which the infant Oedipus was exposed. °1411 *my blood:* i.e., the blood of my father, Laius, and therefore my family's blood.

and brides, and wives, and mothers, all the most
atrocious things that happen to mankind!
1420   One should not name what never should have been.
Somewhere out there, then, quickly, by the gods,
cover me up, or murder me, or throw me
to the ocean where you will never see me more!

[*Oedipus moves toward the Chorus and they back away from him.*]

Come! Don't shrink to touch this wretched man!
1425   Believe me, do not be frightened! I alone
· of all mankind can carry these afflictions.

[*Enter Creon from the palace with Attendants.*]

Choragos: Tell Creon what you wish for. Just when we need him
he's here. He can act, he can advise you.
He's now the land's sole guardian in your place.
1430   **Oedipus:** Ah! Are there words that I can speak to him?
What ground for trust can I present? It's proved
that I was false to him in everything.
Creon: I have not come to mock you, Oedipus,
nor to reproach you for your former falseness.
1435   You men, if you have no respect for sons
of mortals, let your awe for the all-feeding
flames of lordly Hēlius° prevent
your showing unconcealed so great a stain,
abhorred by earth and sacred rain and light.
1440   Escort him quickly back into the house!
If blood kin only see and hear their own
afflictions, we'll have no impious defilement.
Oedipus: By the gods, you've freed me from one terrible fear,
so nobly meeting my unworthiness:
1445   grant me something—not for me; for you!
Creon: What do you want that you should beg me so?
Oedipus: To drive me from the land at once, to a place
where there will be no man to speak to me!
Creon: I would have done just that—had I not wished
1450   to ask first of the god what I should do.
Oedipus: His answer was revealed in full—that I,
the patricide, unholy, be destroyed.
Creon: He said that, but our need is so extreme,
it's best to have sure knowledge what must be done.
1455   **Oedipus:** You'll ask about a wretched man like me?
Creon: Is it not time you put your trust in the god?
Oedipus: But I bid you as well, and shall entreat you.
Give her who is within what burial
you will—you'll give your own her proper rites;
1460   but me—do not condemn my fathers' land
to have me dwelling here while I'm alive,

°1437 *Hēlius:* the sun.

but let me live on mountains—on Cithaeron
famed as mine, for my mother and my father,
while they yet lived, made it my destined tomb,
and I'll be killed by those who wished my ruin!   1465
And yet I know: no sickness will destroy me,
nothing will: I'd never have been saved
when left to die unless for some dread evil.
Then let my fate continue where it will!
As for my children, Creon, take no pains   1470
for my sons—they're men and they will never lack
the means to live, wherever they may be—
but my two wretched, pitiable girls,
who never ate but at my table, never
were without me—everything that I   1475
would touch, they'd always have a share of it—
please care for them! Above all, let me touch
them with my hands and weep aloud my woes!
Please, my Lord!
Please, noble heart! Touching with my hands,   1480
I'd think I held them as when I could see.

[*Enter* ANTIGONE *and* ISMENE *from the palace with* ATTENDANTS.]

What's this?
Oh gods! Do I hear, somewhere, my two dear ones
sobbing? Has Creon really pitied me
and sent to me my dearest ones, my children?   1485
Is that it?
CREON: Yes, I prepared this for you, for I knew
you'd feel this joy, as you have always done.
OEDIPUS: Good fortune, then, and, for your care, be guarded
far better by divinity than I was!   1490
Where are you, children? Come to me! Come here
to these my hands, hands of your brother, hands
of him who gave you seed, hands that made
these once bright eyes to see now in this fashion.

[*OEDIPUS embraces his daughters.*]

He, children, seeing nothing, knowing nothing,   1495
he fathered you where his own seed was plowed.
I weep for you as well, though I can't see you,
imagining your bitter life to come,
the life you will be forced by men to live.
What gatherings of townsmen will you join,   1500
what festivals, without returning home
in tears instead of watching holy rites?
And when you've reached the time for marrying,
where, children, is the man who'll run the risk
of taking on himself the infamy   1505
that will wound you as it did my parents?
What evil is not here? Your father killed

his father, plowed the one who gave him birth,
and from the place where he was sown, from there
1510   he got you, from the place he too was born.
These are the wounds: then who will marry you?
No man, my children. No, it's clear that you
must wither in dry barrenness, unmarried.

[*OEDIPUS addresses* CREON.]

Son of Menoeceus! You are the only father
1515   left to them—we two who gave them seed
are both destroyed: watch that they don't become
poor, wanderers, unmarried—they are your kin.
Let not my ruin be their ruin, too!
No, pity them! You see how young they are,
1520   bereft of everyone, except for you.
Consent, kind heart, and touch me with your hand!

[*CREON grasps* OEDIPUS'S *right hand.*]

You, children, if you had reached an age of sense,
I would have counseled much. Now, pray you may live
always where it's allowed, finding a life
1525   better than his was, who gave you seed.
CREON: Stop this now. Quiet your weeping. Move away, into the house.
OEDIPUS: Bitter words, but I obey them.
CREON: There's an end to all things.
OEDIPUS: I have first this request.
CREON: I will hear it.
OEDIPUS: Banish me from my homeland.
CREON: You must ask that of the god.
OEDIPUS: But I am the gods' most hated man!
1530   **CREON:**   Then you will soon get what you want.
OEDIPUS: Do you consent?
CREON: I never promise when, as now, I'm ignorant.
OEDIPUS: Then lead me in.
CREON: Come. But let your hold fall from your children.
OEDIPUS: Do not take them from me, ever!
CREON: Do not wish to keep all of the
power. You had power, but that power did not follow you through life.

[*OEDIPUS'S daughters are taken from him and led into the palace by* ATTENDANTS. *OEDIPUS is led into the palace by a* SERVANT. CREON *and the other* ATTENDANTS *follow. Only the* CHORUS *remains.*]

1535   **CHORUS:** People of Thebes, my country, see: here is that Oedipus—
he who "knew" the famous riddle, and attained the highest power,
whom all citizens admired, even envying his luck!
See the billows of wild troubles which he has entered now!
Here is the truth of each man's life: we must wait, and see his end,
1540   scrutinize his dying day, and refuse to call him happy
till he has crossed the border of his life without pain.

[*Exit the* CHORUS *along each of the Parados.*]

QUESTIONS

1. *Prologue and Parados.* What is the situation in Thebes as the play begins? Why does Oedipus want to discover the murderer of Laius?
2. *Episode 1 and Stasimon 1.* When Tiresias refuses to speak, how is the reaction of Oedipus characteristic of him? What other examples of this behavior can you find?
3. When Tiresias does speak, he speaks the truth. Why doesn't Oedipus accept the story that Tiresias tells?
4. *Episode 2 and Stasimon 2.* Of what does Oedipus accuse Creon, and how does Creon defend himself? Is Creon convincing? Why or why not?
5. What does Jocasta have to say about oracles and prophecy? Why do you think she expresses this attitude? How do her views differ from those of the Chorus?
6. When does Oedipus begin to think that he himself is the murderer? What details lead him to this conclusion?
7. *Episode 3 and Stasimon 3.* Why does the news from the Messenger from Corinth at first seem good? How is the situation reversed?
8. *Episode 4 and Stasimon 4.* What do you make of the coincidences that the same Herdsman (a) saved the infant Oedipus from death, (b) was the lone survivor of the attack on Laius and also the sole witness to the attack, and (c) will provide testimony that will destroy Oedipus?
9. What moral does the Chorus express about the life and downfall of Oedipus?

GENERAL QUESTIONS

1. In *Oedipus the King,* the peripeteia, anagnorisis, and catastrophe all occur at the same moment. When is this moment? Who is most severely affected by it?
2. Sophocles describes Oedipus's life piecemeal, out of chronological order. Put the details into chronological order, and consider how you might dramatize them. Why does Sophocles's ordering of events make for an effective play? Be sure to emphasize some of the coincidences in the life and career of Oedipus.
3. What is the major conflict in the play? What other conflicts does Sophocles bring out? How is the complexity of the conflicts brought out by Sophocles?
4. In the light of your understanding of tragedy and the tragic hero, describe *Oedipus the King* as a tragedy.
5. Describe Sophocles's use of dramatic irony in the play.
6. Describe the functions of the Chorus and the Choragos. Explain the relationship of the choral odes to the play's actions.

Renaissance Drama and Shakespeare's Theater

In the early years of the English Renaissance, there was a flourishing native tradition of theater that had developed first within the church and then with the cooperation of the church.[13] The bridge from religious drama to the drama of the Renaissance was created in a number of ways. Of great importance was the growth of traveling dramatic professional companies, who performed their plays in local

---

For an account of the medieval dramatic tradition, see Chapter 20, pp. 973–76.

inn yards—square or quadrangular spaces surrounded by the rooms of the inn. In addition, plays were performed at court, in the great rooms of aristocratic houses, in the law courts, and at universities.

Aside from this well-established performing tradition, the immediate influence on the creation of a new drama was the development of a taste for dramatic topics drawn from nonreligious sources. The earliest of such plays in the sixteenth century was the so-called **Tudor interlude,** named after the monarchs of the Tudor family who ruled England from 1485 to 1603. *Interlude* is a misnomer, for the plays were often quite long. The interludes, supported by the nobility, were tragedies, comedies, or historical plays that were performed by both professional actors and students. They sometimes featured abstract and allegorical characters and provided opportunities for both music and farcical action.

After the middle of the sixteenth century, the revival of ancient drama and culture became increasingly prominent. The dominating influence was the Roman dramatist Seneca (4 BCE–65 CE), eight of whose tragedies, derived from Greek tragedy, had survived from antiquity. A vital quality of the Senecan tragedies was that they were violent and bloody, and thus they gave a classical precedent for the revenge and murder that were to be featured in much Elizabethan drama. Seneca became important not so much because he had written great works but rather because he had written in Latin. He could therefore be readily understood by a generation of new dramatists who had been schooled in Roman history, culture, language, and literature.

Shakespeare Became a Theatrical Entrepreneur as Well as a Writer

The first group of these Elizabethan playwrights included Christopher Marlowe, Thomas Kyd, Robert Greene, George Peele, Thomas Lodge, and John Lyly. These were the men whose plays William Shakespeare watched and acted in when he first arrived in London from Stratford-upon-Avon in the late 1580s. By 1594 he had joined the Lord Chamberlain's Men, the most popular of the London acting companies. He rose swiftly as both an actor and dramatist, and by 1599 he had become an active partner with the company (called the "King's Men" after the accession of James I in 1603) in a venture to construct a new theater, the Globe, within a stone's throw of the earlier theater, the Rose. It was for exclusive production at the Globe that Shakespeare wrote some of his greatest plays (including *Hamlet*) from 1599 to 1608, when the company began playing alternately at the outdoor Globe and the indoor Blackfriars (formerly a part of a monastery that had been adapted for theatrical presentations).

The Globe Was a Small but Versatile Theater That Strongly Influenced the Nature of Shakespeare's Plays

Compared with the massive Greek outdoor amphitheaters, the Globe was small. Some theater historians have calculated that it could have held an audience of as many as two to three thousand, although this estimate seems excessive, for half that number would have been extremely large. Moreover, we need not suppose that the theater was always filled to squeezing room only.

THE GLOBE WAS A "RING"-TYPE THEATER OPEN TO THE SKY.   Recent archaeological excavations of the site of the Globe, together with a complete reconstruction based on the knowledge newly gained, show that it was a twenty-sided building. For practical purposes it was round—as it is shown in a contemporary drawing—and its outer diameter was approximately a hundred feet. From above, it would have resembled a ring, or, as Shakespeare called the type in *Henry V*, a "wooden O." Its central yard was open to the sky, a detail that it had appropriated from the confined areas of the inns. The **platform stage,** covered by a roof, was built thirty feet into the yard at the building's south side. Because of the uncertainty and ca-priciousness of English weather, the acting season extended from spring through fall. During the wettest and coldest months, the theater was not used.

THE GLOBE PROVIDED A NUMBER OF ACTING AREAS.   This thrust stage was close to five feet high—probably lower in front (*downstage*) and higher in back (*upstage*). Actors could move anywhere on this stage to speak their lines. On the second level above the stage was a gallery for spectators, musicians, and actors (as in the bal-cony scene in Shakespeare's *Romeo and Juliet*). Actors might enter this gallery to de-liver lines, and then they might also descend from there to the main stage. The area below the stage was called the *hell*. At center stage there was a trapdoor to the hell that was used for the entrances and exits of devils, monsters, and ghosts such as the Ghost of Hamlet's father. Downstage, holding up the protective roof, there were two columns. The ceiling of this roof, called the *heavens*, was decorated with color-ful paintings. A hut on the roof itself contained machinery for lowering and raising actors who took the roles of fairies, witches, and gods. Behind the upstage area, which could be curtained off for interior scenes, there was a small and cramped *tiring house* and storage area where actors changed their costumes and waited for their cues. Two or three doors opened outward from the tiring house to the stage.

THERE WERE THREE LOCATIONS FOR THE AUDIENCE.   The admission price permit-ted spectators into the ground area. Those who remained there stood during the entire performance and crowded as close as they could to the stage. These people, who were patronizingly called the *groundlings*, often endured rain and cold in ad-dition to the discomfort of their need to stand. For additional charges, spectators could get out of bad weather by sitting in one of the three seating levels within the roofed galleries (part of the "O"). Those who could afford it paid still another charge for seats directly on the stage—a custom that continued in English theaters until the time of David Garrick in the eighteenth century.

THE GLOBE, LIKE OTHER ELIZABETHAN THEATERS, MANDATED ITS OWN PRODUCTION AND STAGE CONVENTIONS.   Just as in the Athenian theater, there was no artificial lighting, and performances therefore took place in the afternoon. The plays were performed rapidly, without intermissions or indications of act and scene changes except for occasional rhymed couplets. With no curtain and no scenery, the exits and entrances of the actors indicated shifts in scene. This type of scene division produced swift changes in time and place and made for great fluidity and fast pacing.

   The conditions of performance and the physical shape of the theater resulted in a number of theatrical conventions. The two columns supporting the stage roof, for example, were versatile. Sometimes they represented trees or the sides of buildings, and conventionally they were used as places of concealment and for eavesdropping. Time, place, and circumstances of weather were established through dialogue, as in the opening scene of *Hamlet* when Horatio speaks of "the morn, in russet mantle clad" (line 165), or in *As You Like It*, when Rosalind says, "This is the forest of Arden" (2.4.15).

The Globe's relatively small size and its thrust stage made for intimate performances. There was little separation of audience and actors, unlike the *orchestra* in Greek theaters that widened the distance between actors and spectators, or with the proscenium and curtain of many modern theaters. The groundlings surrounding the thrust stage at a typical Elizabethan performance were extremely close to the actors at all times. The close proximity of the groundlings and of those spectators who had paid to sit on the stage itself encouraged much interaction between actors and audience. This closeness led to two unique stage conventions. One of these, the **aside,** permitted a character to make brief remarks directly to the audience or to another character without the rest of the characters' hearing the words. In the other, the **soliloquy,** a character alone onstage described his or her thoughts or plans directly to the audience. For example, when Hamlet delivers his second soliloquy, he criticizes his emotional detachment from his father's murder and explains how he plans to test Claudius's guilt (2.2.524–80). Under such circumstances, members of the Elizabethan audience almost literally became additional members of the cast.

THE ACTORS FOLLOWED ESTABLISHED CONVENTIONS IN GESTURE AND COSTUME.

The actors in Shakespeare's day were legally bound to the company of which they were members. Without the protection of the company, they were considered "rogues and vagabonds." In England the actors were male, with adolescent boys performing the women's roles because women were excluded from the stage. The actors used no masks. Instead, they developed expressions and gestures that would seem to us, today, excessively stylized. The acting mannerisms sometimes seemed excessive to Shakespeare, too, as is indicated by Hamlet's instructions to the traveling actors. He tells them not to "saw the air too much with your hand" and not to "tear a passion to tatters, to very rags" (3.2.4–9).

The actors wore elaborate costumes to demonstrate the nature and status of the characters. Thus kings always wore robes and crowns, and they carried orbs and scepters. A fool (a type of comic and ironic commentator) wore a multicolored or *motley* costume, and clowns and "mechanicals" wore the common clothing of the humble classes, as with the "hempen homespuns" of *A Midsummer Night's Dream* (Chapter 22). Ragged clothing indicated a reduction in circumstances, as in *King Lear*, and Ophelia's description of Hamlet's disordered clothing in the second act of *Hamlet* indicates the prince's disturbed mental condition (2.1.74–82). Whenever characters took on a disguise, as in *As You Like It*, this disguise was impenetrable to the other characters.

The New Globe Theatre Has Been Built Near the Site of Shakespeare's Globe

Shakespeare's Globe burned in 1613. The rebuilt Globe that replaced it was torn down by the Puritans under Oliver Cromwell in 1644, on the grounds that drama encouraged vice and free thought. From then on the location was variously occupied by tenements, breweries, other buildings, and a road. In the late 1980s, however, archaeological excavations took place at the sites of both the Globe and the nearby Rose Theater, and the subsequent discoveries provided exciting new information about theaters and theatergoing in Shakespeare's day. In addition, recent excavations have revealed the foundations of an earlier London theater that was known simply as "The Theater." A reconstruction of the Globe is now complete—not at the original location but close by. The original site could not be used because it was preempted by a protected building and a vital street leading to Southwark Bridge. Theatergoers in London are now able to attend performances of Shakespeare's plays in this new theater under conditions almost identical to those that Shakespeare's audiences and acting company knew, including, for the "groundlings," rain, wind, cold, and the discomfort of standing.[14]

WILLIAM SHAKESPEARE (1564–1616)

Shakespeare was born in 1564 in Stratford-upon-Avon, in western England. He attended the Stratford grammar school; he married Anne Hathaway in 1582, and he and his wife had three children. He left his family and moved to London some time between 1585 and 1592. During this period he became a professional actor, and he also began writing plays and poems. Because the London theaters were closed during the plague years 1592–1594, he apparently worked at other jobs, about which we know nothing. By 1595, however, he was recognized as a major writer of comedies and tragedies. He soon be-
came a member of the Lord Chamberlain's Men, the leading theatrical company, and, as we have seen, he became a shareholder in the new Globe Theatre in 1599. Fortunately, he realized good returns from the business venture and also from his plays, and he became moderately wealthy. He stopped writing for the stage in 1611, having written a total of thirty-seven plays, of which eleven were tragedies. He also collaborated in writing a few other plays. During his retirement he lived in his native Stratford. He died in 1616 and is buried next to the altar of Stratford's Trinity Church, beneath a bust and an inscribed gravestone.

When the Lord Chamberlain's Men first staged *Hamlet* in 1602 at the Globe, it was not the first time the story had been dramatized on the London stage. There is evidence that a play based on the Hamlet story, now lost, had been performed before 1589. Therefore, at least some of the theatergoers might have known the story.

Even if none of them knew the story, however, they would have known the tradition of **revenge tragedy.** The Elizabethans had been introduced to the drama of vengeance through the English translations of Seneca's tragedies during the 1570s and early 1580s. Another important precedent was Thomas Kyd's *Spanish Tragedy* (c. 1587), the first English play in the revenge tradition, which featured a hero who commits suicide. The major conventions of the genre were a ghost who calls for vengeance and a revenger who pretends to be insane at least part of the time. Above all, the tradition required that the revenger would also die, no matter how good a person or how just his cause.

Although Elizabethan audiences were prepared for *Hamlet* by the revenge formula, they could have anticipated neither a protagonist of Hamlet's likeableness and complexity nor a play of such profundity. The earlier revengers were flat characters with a single fixation on righting wrongs through personal vengeance. Hamlet, however, is acutely aware of the political and moral corruption

See J. R. Mulryne and Margaret Shewring, eds., *Shakespeare's Globe Rebuilt* (Cambridge: Cambridge UP, 1997). Further information about the Globe Theatre may be found at the Shakespeare Globe Center, USA, www .sgc.umd.edu.

of the Danish court, and he reflects on the fallen state of humanity. Experiencing despair and guilt, he even contemplates suicide. He learns from his experiences and meditations, discovering that he must look beyond reason and philosophy for ways of coping with the world. He also develops patience and learns to trust in Providence, the "divinity that shapes our ends" (5.2.10).

The play itself demonstrates the far-reaching effects of evil, which branches inexorably outward from Claudius's initial act of murder. The evil ensnares innocent and guilty alike. Hamlet, the avenger, becomes the direct and indirect cause of deaths, and as a result, he in turn also becomes an object of revenge. By the play's end, all the major and two of the minor characters are dead: Polonius, Ophelia, Rosencrantz, Guildenstern, Gertrude, Claudius, Laertes, and, finally, Hamlet himself. The play's crowning irony is that Hamlet does not complete his vengeance because of the murder of his father, King Hamlet, as he originally sets out to do. Rather, he kills Claudius immediately upon learning that the king has murdered Gertrude, his mother.

In the centuries since Shakespeare wrote *Hamlet*, the play has remained among the most popular, most moving, and most effective plays in the world. It has been translated into scores of languages. Major actors from Shakespeare's day to ours—including Richard Burbage as the first Hamlet, and John Barrymore, Kenneth Branagh, Ralph Fiennes, Mel Gibson, Ethan Hawke, Derek Jacobi, Kevin Kline, Laurence Olivier, and Nicol Williamson—have starred in the role. Beyond the play's stage popularity, *Hamlet* has become one of the central documents of Western civilization. Somehow, most people know about Hamlet and are familiar with passages like "To be or not to be," "The play's the thing," and "The undiscovered country, from whose bourn / No traveler returns" even if they have never read the play or seen a live or filmed performance.

The Tragedy of Hamlet, Prince of Denmark (c. 1602)

Edited by Alice Griffin*

CHARACTERS

    Claudius, King of Denmark
    Hamlet, Son to the former, and nephew to the present King
    Polonius, Lord Chamberlain
    Horatio, Friend to Hamlet
    Laertes, Son to Polonius
    Valtemand
    Cornelius
    Rosencrantz } Courtiers
    Guildenstern
    Osric
    A Gentleman

Professor Griffin's text for *Hamlet* was the Second Quarto (edition) published in 1604, with modifications based on the First Folio, published in 1623. Stage directions in those editions are printed here without brackets; added stage directions are printed within brackets. We have edited Griffin's notes for this text.

A Priest
Marcellus ⎤
Barnardo ⎦ Officers
Francisco, a Soldier
Reynaldo, Servant to Polonius
Players
Two Clowns, gravediggers
Fortinbras, Prince of Norway
A Norwegian Captain
English Ambassadors
Gertrude, Queen of Denmark, mother to Hamlet
Ophelia, Daughter to Polonius
Ghost of Hamlet's Father
Lords, Ladies, Officers, Soldiers, Sailors, Messengers, Attendants

[*Scene: Elsinore*]

ACT 1

Scene 1. [A platform on the battlements of the castle]

Enter BARNARDO *and* FRANCISCO, *two Sentinels.*

BARNARDO: Who's there?
FRANCISCO: Nay, answer me. Stand and unfold° yourself.
BARNARDO: Long live the king.
FRANCISCO: Barnardo?
BARNARDO: He.   5
FRANCISCO: You come most carefully upon your hour.
BARNARDO: 'Tis now struck twelve, get thee to bed Francisco.
FRANCISCO: For this relief much thanks, 'tis bitter cold, And I am sick at heart.
BARNARDO: Have you had quiet guard?
FRANCISCO: Not a mouse stirring.
BARNARDO: Well, good night: 10
    If you do meet Horatio and Marcellus,
    The rivals° of my watch, bid them make haste.

Enter HORATIO *and* MARCELLUS.

FRANCISCO: I think I hear them. Stand ho, who is there?
HORATIO: Friends to this ground.
MARCELLUS: And liegemen° to the Dane
FRANCISCO: Give you good night.
MARCELLUS: O, farewell honest soldier,   15
    Who hath relieved you?
FRANCISCO: Barnardo hath my place;
    Give you good night.   *Exit* FRANCISCO.
MARCELLUS: Holla, Barnardo!
BARNARDO: Say,
    What, is Horatio there?
HORATIO: A piece of him.

°2 *unfold:* reveal. °12 *rivals:* partners. °14 *liegemen:* subjects. *Dane:* King of Denmark.

BARNARDO: Welcome Horatio, welcome good Marcellus.

20 **HORATIO:** What, has this thing appeared again tonight?

BARNARDO: I have seen nothing.

MARCELLUS: Horatio says 'tis but our fantasy,°
    And will not let belief take hold of him,
    Touching this dreaded sight twice seen of us,
25   Therefore I have entreated him along
    With us to watch the minutes of this night,
    That if again this apparition come,
    He may approve° our eyes and speak to it.

HORATIO: Tush, tush, 'twill not appear.

BARNARDO: Sit down awhile,
30   And let us once again assail your ears,
    That are so fortified against our story,
    What we have two nights seen.

HORATIO: Well, sit we down,
    And let us hear Barnardo speak of this.

BARNARDO: Last night of all,
35   When yon same star that's westward from the pole°
    Had made his course t'illume that part of heaven
    Where now it burns, Marcellus and myself,
    The bell then beating one—

Enter GHOST.

MARCELLUS: Peace, break thee off, look where it comes again.

40 **BARNARDO:** In the same figure like the king that's dead.

MARCELLUS: Thou art a scholar, speak to it Horatio.

BARNARDO: Looks a' not like the king? mark it Horatio.

HORATIO: Most like, it harrows me with fear and wonder.

BARNARDO: It would be spoke to.

MARCELLUS: Question it Horatio.

45 **HORATIO:** What art thou that usurp'st° this time of night,
    Together with that fair and warlike form,
    In which the majesty of buried Denmark°
    Did sometimes° march? by heaven I charge thee speak.

MARCELLUS: It is offended.

BARNARDO: See, it stalks away.

50 **HORATIO:** Stay, speak, speak, I charge thee speak.   *Exit GHOST*

MARCELLUS: 'Tis gone and will not answer.

BARNARDO: How now Horatio, you tremble and look pale,
    Is not this something more than fantasy?
    What think you on't?

55 **HORATIO:** Before my God I might not this believe,
    Without the sensible and true avouch°
    Of mine own eyes.

MARCELLUS: Is it not like the king?

°22 *fantasy:* imagination. °28 *approve:* prove reliable. °35 *pole:* North Star. °45 *usurp'st:* wrongfully occupy (both the time and the shape of the dead king). °47 *buried Denmark:* the buried King of Denmark. °48 *sometimes:* formerly. °56 *sensible . . . avouch:* assurance of the truth of the senses.

HORATIO: As thou art to thyself.
    Such was the very armour he had on,
    When he the ambitious Norway° combated: 60
    So frowned he once, when in an angry parle°
    He smote the sledded Polacks° on the ice.
    'Tis strange.
MARCELLUS: Thus twice before, and jump° at this dead hour,
    With martial stalk hath he gone by our watch.   65
HORATIO: In what particular thought to work, I know not,
    But in the gross and scope° of mine opinion,
    This bodes some strange eruption to our state.
MARCELLUS: Good now sit down, and tell me he that knows,
    Why this same strict and most observant watch   70
    So nightly toils the subject° of the land,
    And why such daily cast of brazen cannon
    And foreign mart,° for implements of war,
    Why such impress° of shipwrights, whose sore° task
    Does not divide the Sunday from the week,   75
    What might be toward° that this sweaty haste
    Doth make the night joint-labourer with the day,
    Who is't that can inform me?
HORATIO: That can I.
    At least the whisper goes so; our last king,
    Whose image even but now appeared to us,   80
    Was as you know by Fortinbras of Norway,
    Thereto pricked on by a most emulate° pride,
    Dared to the combat; in which our valiant Hamlet
    (For so this side of our known world esteemed him)
    Did slay this Fortinbras, who by a sealed compact,°   85
    Well ratified by law and heraldry,°
    Did forfeit (with his life) all those his lands
    Which he stood seized° of, to the conqueror:
    Against the which a moiety competent°
    Was gagèd° by our King, which had returned   90
    To the inheritance of Fortinbras,
    Had he been vanquisher; as by the same co-mart,°
    And carriage of the article designed,°
    His fell to Hamlet; now sir, young Fortinbras,
    Of unimprovèd mettle° hot and full,   95
    Hath in the skirts° of Norway here and there
    Sharked up° a list of lawless resolutes°
    For food and diet to some enterprise
    That hath a stomach° in't, which is no other,
    As it doth well appear unto our state,   100

°60 *Norway:* King of Norway. °61 *parle:* parley, verbal battle. °62 *sledded Polacks:* Polish soldiers on sleds. °64 *jump:* just. °67 *gross and scope:* general view. °71 *toils the subject:* makes the subjects toil. °73 *mart:* trade. °74 *impress:* conscription. *sore:* difficult. °76 *toward:* forthcoming. °82 *emulate:* rivaling. °85 *compact:* treaty. °86 *law and heraldry:* heraldic law regulating combats. °89 *moiety competent:* equal amount. °90 *gagèd:* pledged. °92 *co-mart:* joint bargain. °93 *carriage . . . designed:* intent of the treaty drawn up. °95 *unimproved mettle:* untested (1) metal (2) spirit. °96 *skirts:* outskirts. °97 *Sharked up:* gathered up indiscriminately (as a shark preys). *lawless resolutes:* determined outlaws. °88 *seized:* possessed. °99 *stomach:* show of courage.

> But to recover of us by strong hand
> And terms compulsatory, those foresaid lands
> So by his father lost; and this I take it,
> Is the main motive of our preparations,
> 105 The source of this our watch, and the chief head°
> Of this post-haste and romage° in the land.
>
> **BARNARDO:** I think it be no other, but e'en so;
> Well may it sort° that this portentous figure
> Comes armèd through our watch so like the king
> 110 That was and is the question of these wars.
>
> **HORATIO:** A mote it is to trouble the mind's eye:
> In the most high and palmy° state of Rome,
> A little ere the mightiest Julius fell,
> The graves stood tenantless, and the sheeted dead
> 115 Did squeak and gibber in the Roman Streets,
> As stars with trains of fire,° and dews of blood,
> Disasters° in the sun; and the moist star,°
> Upon whose influence Neptune's empire stands,
> Was sick almost to doomsday with eclipse.
> 120 And even the like precurse° of feared events,
> As harbingers preceding still° the fates
> And prologue to the omen° coming on,
> Have heaven and earth together demonstrated
> Unto our climatures° and countrymen.

Enter GHOST.

> 125 But soft, behold, lo where it comes again.
> I'll cross° it though it blast me: *Spreads his arms.*
>   stay illusion,
> If thou hast any sound or use of voice,
> Speak to me.
> If there be any good thing to be done
> 130 That may to thee do ease, and grace° to me,
> Speak to me.
> If thou art privy° to thy country's fate
> Which happily° foreknowing may avoid,
> O speak:
> 135 Or if thou hast uphoarded in thy life
> Extorted treasure in the womb of earth,
> For which they say you spirits oft walk in death,

The cock crows.

> Speak of it, stay and speak. Stop it Marcellus.

°105 *head:* fountainhead. °106 *romage:* bustle (rummage). °108 *sort:* turn out. °112 *palmy:* triumphant. °116 *stars . . . fire:* meteors. °117 *Disasters:* unfavorable portents. *moist star:* moon. °120 *precurse:* portent. °121 *still:* always. °122 *omen:* disaster. °124 *climatures:* regions. °126 *cross:* (1) cross its path (2) spread my arms to make a cross of my body (to ward against evil). °130 *grace:* (1) honor (2) blessedness. °132 *art privy:* know secretly of. °133 *happily:* perhaps.

MARCELLUS: Shall I strike it with my partisan?°
HORATIO: Do, if it will not stand
BARNARDO: 'Tis here.   140
HORATIO: 'Tis here.
MARCELLUS: 'Tis gone.   *Exit* GHOST.
    We do it wrong being so majestical,
    To offer it the show of violence,
    For it is as the air, invulnerable,
    And our vain blows malicious mockery.°   145
BARNARDO: It was about to speak when the cock crew.°
HORATIO: And then it started like a guilty thing,
    Upon a fearful summons; I have heard,
    The cock that is the trumpet to the morn,
    Doth with his lofty and shrill-sounding throat   150
    Awake the god of day, and at his warning
    Whether in sea or fire, in earth or air,°
    Th'extravagant and erring° spirit hies°
    To his confine, and of the truth herein
    This present object made probation.°   155
MARCELLUS: It faded on the crowing of the cock.
    Some say that ever 'gainst° that season comes
    Wherein our Saviour's birth is celebrated
    This bird of dawning singeth all night long,
    And then they say no spirit dare stir abroad,   160
    The nights are wholesome,° then no planets strike,°
    No fairy takes,° nor witch hath power to charm,
    So hallowed, and so gracious is that time.
HORATIO: So have I heard and do in part believe it.
    But look, the morn in russet° mantle clad   165
    Walks o'er the dew of yon high eastward hill:
    Break we our watch up and by my advice
    Let us impart what we have seen tonight
    Unto young Hamlet, for upon my life
    This spirit dumb to us, will speak to him: 170
    Do you consent we shall acquaint him with it,
    As needful in our loves,° fitting our duty?
MARCELLUS: Let's do't I pray, and I this morning know
    Where we shall find him most convenient.   *Exeunt.*°

Scene 2. [A room of state in the castle]

Flourish.° *Enter* CLAUDIUS *King of Denmark,* GERTRUDE *the Queen,* [*members of the*] *Council: as*
POLONIUS; *and his son* LAERTES, HAMLET, [VALTEMAND *and* CORNELIUS] *cum aliis.*°

KING: Though yet of Hamlet our dear brother's death

°139 *partisan:* spear. °145 *malicious mockery:* mockery because they only imitate harm. °146 *cock crew:* traditional signal for ghosts to return to their confines. °152 *sea . . . air:* the four elements (inhabited by spirits, each
indigenous to a particular element). °153 *extravagant and erring:* going beyond its bounds (vagrant) and wandering.
hies: hastens. °155 *made probation:* gave proof. °157 *'gainst:* just before. °161 *wholesome:* healthy (night air was
considered unhealthy). *strike:* exert evil influence. °162 *takes:* bewitches. °165 *russet:* reddish. °172 *needful . . .
loves:* urged by our friendship. °174 S.D. *Exeunt:* all exit. S.D. *Flourish:* fanfare or trumpets. *cum aliis:* with others.

The memory be green, and that it us befitted
To bear our hearts in grief, and our whole kingdom
To be contracted in one brow of woe,
5   Yet so far hath discretion fought with nature,°
That we° with wisest sorrow think on him
Together with remembrance of ourselves:°
Therefore our sometime° sister,° now our queen,
Th'imperial jointress° to this warlike state,
10 Have we as 'twere with a defeated joy,
With an auspicious, and a dropping eye,°
With mirth in funeral, and with dirge in marriage,
In equal scale weighing delight and dole,
Taken to wife: nor have we herein barred
15 Your better wisdoms,° which have freely gone
With this affair along—for all, our thanks.
Now follows that you know, young Fortinbras,
Holding a weak supposal of our worth°
Or thinking by our late dear brother's death
20 Our state to be disjoint and out of frame,°
Colleaguèd° with this dream of his advantage,°
He hath not failed to pester us with message
Importing the surrender of those lands
Lost by his father, with all bands° of law,
25 To our most valiant brother—so much for him:
Now for ourself, and for this time of meeting,
Thus much the business is. We have here writ
To Norway, uncle of young Fortinbras—
Who impotent and bed-rid scarcely hears
30 Of this his nephew's purpose—to suppress
His further gait° herein, in that the levies,
The lists, and full proportions are all made
Out of his subject;° and we here dispatch
You good Cornelius, and you Valtemand,
35 For bearers of this greeting to old Norway,
Giving to you no further personal power
To business with the king, more than the scope
Of these delated° articles allow:
Farewell, and let your haste commend your duty.°
40 **CORNELIUS, VALTEMAND:** In that, and all things, will we show our duty.
KING: We doubt it nothing, heartily farewell.

Exeunt VALTEMAND and CORNELIUS.

And now Laertes what's the news with you?

°5 *nature:* natural impulse (of grief). °6 *we:* royal plural. The King speaks not only for himself, but for his entire government. °7 *remembrance of ourselves:* reminder of our duties. °8 *sometime:* former. *sister:* sister-in-law. °9 *jointress:* widow who inherits the estate. °11 *auspicious . . . eye:* one eye happy, the other tearful. °14–15 *barred . . . wisdoms:* failed to seek and abide by your good advice. °18 *weak . . . worth:* low opinion of my ability in office. °20 *out of frame:* tottering. °21 *Colleaguèd:* supported. *advantage:* superiority. °24 *bands:* bonds. °31 *gait:* progress. °31–33 *levies . . . subject:* Taxes, conscriptions, and supplies are all obtained from his subjects. °38 *delated:* prescribed; defined. °39 *haste . . . duty:* prompt departure signify your respect.

You told us to some suit, what is't Laertes?
You cannot speak of reason to the Dane
And lose your voice;° what wouldst thou beg, Laertes,   45
That shall not be my offer, not thy asking?°
The head is not more native° to the heart,
The hand more instrumental to the mouth,
Than is the throne of Denmark to thy father.
What wouldst thou have, Laertes?

LAERTES: My dread lord,   50
Your leave and favour° to return to France,
From whence, though willingly I came to Denmark
To show my duty in your coronation,
Yet now I must confess, that duty done,
My thoughts and wishes bend again toward France,   55
And bow them to your gracious leave and pardon.°

KING: Have you your father's leave? What says Polonius?

POLONIUS: He hath my lord wrung from me my slow leave
By laboursome petition, and at last
Upon his will I sealed my hard consent.°   60
I do beseech you give him leave to go.

KING: Take thy fair hour Laertes, time be thine,
And thy best graces spend it at thy will.
But now my cousin° Hamlet, and my son—

HAMLET: [*Aside.*] A little more than kin,° and less than kind.°   65

KING: How is it that the clouds still hang on you?

HAMLET: Not so my lord, I am too much in the sun.°

QUEEN: Good Hamlet cast thy nighted colour° off
And let thine eye look like a friend on Denmark,°
Do not for ever with thy vailèd° lids   70
Seek for thy noble father in the dust,
Thou know'st 'tis common, all that lives must die,
Passing through nature to eternity.

HAMLET: Ay madam, it is common.°

QUEEN: If it be,
Why seems it so particular with thee?   75

HAMLET: Seems, madam? nay it is, I know not "seems."
'Tis not alone my inky cloak, good mother,
Nor customary suits of solemn black,
Nor windy suspiration of forced breath,
No, nor the fruitful river in the eye,°   80
Nor the dejected haviour° of the visage,

°45 *lose your voice:* speak in vain. °46 *offer . . . asking:* grant even before requested. °47 *native:* related. °51 *leave and favour:* kind permission. °56 *pardon:* allowance. °60 *Upon . . . consent:* (1) At his request, I gave my grudging consent. (2) On the soft sealing wax of his (legal) will, I stamped my approval. °64 *cousin:* kinsman (used for relatives outside the immediate family). °65 *more than kin:* too much of a kinsman, being both uncle and stepfather. *less than kind:* (1) unkind because of being a kin (proverbial) and taking the throne from the former king's son (2) unnatural (as it was considered incest to marry the wife of one's dead brother). °67 *in the sun:* (1) in presence of the king (often associated metaphorically with the sun) (2) proverbial: "out of heaven's blessing into the warm sun" (3) of a "son." °68 *nighted colour:* black. °69 *Denmark:* the King of Denmark. °70 *vailèd:* downcast. °74 *common:* (1) general (2) vulgar. °79–80 *windy . . . eye:* (hyperbole used to describe exaggerated sighs and tears). °81 *haviour:* behavior.

Together with all forms, moods, shapes of grief,
That can denote me truly: these indeed seem,
For they are actions that a man might play,°
But I have that within which passes show,
These but the trappings and the suits of woe.°

KING: 'Tis sweet and commendable in your nature Hamlet,
To give these mourning duties to your father:
But you must know your father lost a father,
That father lost, lost his, and the survivor bound
In filial obligation for some term
To do obsequious sorrow:° but to persever
In obstinate condolement,° is a course
Of impious stubbornness, 'tis unmanly grief,
It shows a will most incorrect to heaven,
A heart unfortified, a mind impatient,
An understanding simple and unschooled:
For what we know must be, and is as common
As any the most vulgar thing to sense,°
Why should we in our peevish opposition
Take it to heart? Fie, 'tis a fault to heaven,
A fault against the dead, a fault to nature,
To reason most absurd, whose common theme
Is death of fathers, and who still° hath cried
From the first corse,° till he that died today,
"This must be so." We pray you throw to earth
This unprevailing° woe, and think of us
As of a father, for let the world take note
You are the most immediate° to our throne,
And with no less nobility of love
Than that which dearest father bears his son,
Do I impart toward you. For your intent
In going back to school in Wittenberg,
It is most retrograde° to our desire,
And we beseech you, bend you° to remain
Here in the cheer and comfort of our eye,
Our chiefest courtier, cousin, and our son.

QUEEN: Let not thy mother lose her prayers Hamlet,
I pray thee stay with us, go not to Wittenberg.

HAMLET: I shall in all my best obey you madam.

KING: Why 'tis a loving and a fair reply,
Be as ourself in Denmark. Madam come,
This gentle and unforced accord of Hamlet
Sits smiling to my heart, in grace whereof,
No jocund health that Denmark drinks today,
But the great cannon to the clouds shall tell,

---

84 *play*: act. °86 *trappings . . . woe*: outward, superficial costumes of mourning. °92 *do obsequious sorrow*: express sorrow befitting obsequies or funerals. °93 *condolement*: grief. °99 *As any . . . sense*: as the most ordinary thing the senses can perceive. °104 *still*: always. °105 *corse*: corpse (of Abel, also, ironically, the first fratricide). °107 *unprevailing*: useless. °109 *most immediate*: next in succession (though Danish kings were elected by the council, an Elizabethan audience might feel that Hamlet, not Claudius, should be king). °114 *retrograde*: movement (of planets) in a reverse direction. °115 *beseech . . . you*: hope you will be inclined.

And the king's rouse° the heaven shall bruit° again,
Re-speaking earthly thunder; come away.

Flourish: Exeunt all but HAMLET.

HAMLET: O that this too too sullied° flesh would melt,
Thaw and resolve itself into a dew,   130
Or that the Everlasting had not fixed
His canon° 'gainst self-slaughter. O God, God,
How weary, stale, flat, and unprofitable
Seem to me all the uses of this world!
Fie on't, ah fie, 'tis an unweeded garden   135
That grows to seed, things rank° and gross in nature
Possess it merely.° That it should come to this,
But two months dead, nay not so much, not two,
So excellent a king, that was to this
Hyperion° to a satyr,° so loving to my mother,   140
That he might not beteem° the winds of heaven
Visit her face too roughly—heaven and earth,
Must I remember? why, she would hang on him
As if increase of appetite had grown
By what it fed on,° and yet within a month—   145
Let me not think on't: Frailty, thy name is woman—
A little month or ere those shoes were old
With which she followed my poor father's body
Like Niobe° all tears, why she, even she—
O God, a beast that wants° discourse of reason   150
Would have mourned longer—married with my uncle,
My father's brother, but no more like my father
Than I to Hercules: within a month,
Ere yet the salt of most unrighteous° tears
Had left the flushing° in her gallèd° eyes,   155
She married. O most wicked speed, to post°
With such dexterity to incestuous° sheets:
It is not, nor it cannot come to good,
But break my heart, for I must hold my tongue.

Enter HORATIO, MARCELLUS *and* BARNARDO.

HORATIO: Hail to your lordship.
HAMLET: I am glad to see you well;   160
Horatio, or I do forget my self.
HORATIO: The same my lord, and your poor servant ever.
HAMLET: Sir my good friend, I'll change° that name with you:
And what make you from Wittenberg, Horatio?
Marcellus.   165

°127 *rouse*: toast that empties the wine cup. *bruit*: sound. °129 *sullied*: tainted. °132 *canon*: divine edict. °136 *rank*:
(1) luxuriant, excessive (2) bad-smelling. °137 *merely*: entirely. °140 *Hyperion*: god of the sun. *satyr*: part-goat,
part-man woodland deity (noted for lust). °141 *beteem*: allow. °144–145 *As if . . . on*: as if the more she fed, the
more her appetite increased. °149 *Niobe*: who boasted of her children before Leto and was punished by their
destruction; Zeus changed the weeping mother to a stone dropping continual tears. °150 *wants*: lacks. °154 *unrigh-
teous*: because untrue. °155 *flushing*: redness. *gallèd*: rubbed sore. °156 *post*: rush. °157 *incestuous*: the church
forbade marriage to one's brother's widow. °163 *change*: exchange (and be called your friend).

MARCELLUS: My good lord.

HAMLET: I am very glad to see you: good even, sir.
But what in faith make you from Wittenberg?

HORATIO: A truant disposition, good my lord.

170 **HAMLET:** I would not hear your enemy say so,
Nor shall you do mine ear that violence
To make it truster of your own report
Against yourself. I know you are no truant,
But what is your affair in Elsinore?

175 We'll teach you to drink deep ere you depart.

HORATIO: My Lord, I came to see your father's funeral.

HAMLET: I prithee do not mock me, fellow student,
I think it was to see my mother's wedding.

HORATIO: Indeed my lord it followed hard upon.

180 **HAMLET:** Thrift, thrift, Horatio, the funeral baked meats°
Did coldly° furnish forth the marriage tables.
Would I had met my dearest° foe in heaven
Or ever I had seen that day Horatio.
My father, methinks I see my father.

HORATIO: Where my lord?

185 **HAMLET:**   In my mind's eye Horatio.

HORATIO: I saw him once, a' was a goodly° king.

HAMLET: A' was a man, take him for all in all,
I shall not look upon his like again.

HORATIO: My lord, I think I saw him yesternight.

190 **HAMLET:** Saw? Who?

HORATIO: My lord, the king your father.

HAMLET: The king my father?

HORATIO: Season your admiration° for a while
With an attent ear till I may deliver
Upon the witness of these gentlemen
This marvel to you.

195 **HAMLET:**   For God's love let me hear!

HORATIO: Two nights together had these gentlemen,
Marcellus and Barnardo, on their watch
In the dead waste and middle of the night,
Been thus encountered. A figure like your father

200 Armed at point exactly, cap-a-pe,°
Appears before them, and with solemn march,
Goes slow and stately by them; thrice he walked
By their oppressed° and fear-surprisèd eyes
Within his truncheon's° length, whilst they distilled°

205 Almost to jelly with the act of fear,
Stand dumb and speak not to him; this to me
In dreadful secrecy° impart they did,
And I with them the third night kept the watch,
Where as they had delivered, both in time,

°180 *funeral baked meats:* food prepared for the funeral. °181 *coldly:* when cold. °182 *dearest:* direst. °186 *goodly:* handsome. °192 *Season your admiration:* control your wonder. °200 *at point . . . cap-a-pe:* in every detail, head to foot. °203 *oppressed:* overcome by horror. °204 *truncheon:* staff (of office). *distilled:* dissolved. °207 *in dreadful secrecy:* as a dread secret.

Form of the thing, each word made true and good,   210
The apparition comes: I knew your father,
These hands are not more like.
HAMLET: But where was this?
MARCELLUS: My lord upon the platform where we watch.
HAMLET: Did you not speak to it?
HORATIO: My lord I did,
But answer made it none, yet once methought   215
It lifted up it° head, and did address
Itself to motion° like as it would speak:
But even then the morning cock crew loud,
And at the sound it shrunk in haste away
And vanished from our sight.
HAMLET: 'Tis very strange.   220
HORATIO: As I do live my honoured lord 'tis true,
And we did think it writ down in our duty
To let you know of it.
HAMLET: Indeed indeed sirs, but this troubles me.
Hold you the watch tonight?
ALL: We do my lord.   225
HAMLET: Armed say you?
ALL: Armed my lord.
HAMLET: From top to toe?
ALL: My lord from head to foot.
HAMLET: Then saw you not his face.
HORATIO: O yes my lord, he wore his beaver° up.   230
HAMLET: What, looked he frowningly?
HORATIO: A countenance more in sorrow than in anger.
HAMLET: Pale, or red?
HORATIO: Nay, very pale.
HAMLET: And fixed his eyes upon you?
HORATIO: Most constantly.
HAMLET: I would I had been there.   235
HORATIO: It would have much amazed you.
HAMLET: Very like, very like, stayed it long?
HORATIO: While one with moderate haste might tell° a hundred.
MARCELLUS, BARNARDO: Longer, longer.
HORATIO: Not when I saw't.
HAMLET: His beard was grizzled,° no?   240
HORATIO: It was as I have seen it in his life,
A sable silvered.°
HAMLET: I will watch tonight;
Perchance 'twill walk again.
HORATIO: I warr'nt it will.
HAMLET: If it assume my noble father's person,
I'll speak to it though hell itself should gape   245
And bid me hold my peace;° I pray you all
If you have hitherto concealed this sight

°216 *it*: its. °216–17 *address . . . motion*: start to move. °230 *beaver*: visor. °238 *tell*: count. °240 *grizzled*: gray. °242 *A sable silvered*: black flecked with gray. °245–46 *though hell . . . peace*: despite the risk of hell (for speaking to a demon) warning me to be silent.

> Let it be tenable° in your silence still,
> And whatsoever else shall hap tonight,
> 250   Give it an understanding but no tongue.
> I will requite your loves, so fare you well:
> Upon the platform 'twixt eleven and twelve
> I'll visit you.
> **ALL:**   Our duty to your honour.
> **HAMLET:** Your loves, as mine to you:° farewell.   *Exeunt. [HAMLET remains.]*
> 255   My father's spirit (in arms) all is not well,
> I doubt° some foul play, would the night were come;
> Till then sit still my soul. Foul deeds will rise,
> Though all the earth o'erwhelm them to men's eyes.   *Exit.*

Scene 3. [Polonius's chambers]

Enter LAERTES and OPHELIA his sister.

> **LAERTES:** My necessaries are embarked, farewell,
> And sister, as the winds give benefit
> And convoy° is assistant, do not sleep
> But let me hear from you.
> **OPHELIA:**   Do you doubt that?
> 5   **LAERTES:** For Hamlet, and the trifling of his favour,
> Hold it a fashion, and a toy in blood,°
> A violet in the youth of primy nature,°
> Forward,° not permanent, sweet, not lasting,
> The perfume and suppliance of° a minute,
> No more.
> **OPHELIA:**   No more but so?
> 10   **LAERTES:**   Think it no more.
> For nature crescent° does not grow alone
> In thews and bulk,° but as this temple waxes°
> The inward service of the mind and soul
> Grows wide withal.° Perhaps he loves you now,
> 15   And now no soil nor cautel° doth besmirch
> The virtue of his will:° but you must fear,
> His greatness weighed,° his will is not his own,
> For he himself is subject to his birth:
> He may not as unvalued persons° do,
> 20   Carve° for himself, for on his choice depends
> The sanctity and health of this whole state,
> And therefore must his choice be circumscribed
> Unto the voice and yielding° of that body

°248 *tenable*: held, kept. °254 *Your loves . . . you*: offer your friendship (rather than duty) in exchange for mine. °256 *doubt*: fear. °3 *convoy*: conveyance. °6 *toy in blood*: whim of the passions. °7 *youth of primy nature*: early spring. °8 Forward: premature. °9 *suppliance of*: supplying diversion for. °11 *nature crescent*: man as he grows. °12 *thews and bulk*: sinews and body. *temple waxes*: body grows (1 Cor. 6:19). °14 *withal*: at the same time. °15 *cautel*: deceit. °16 *will*: desire. °17 *weighed*: considered. °19 *unvalued persons*: common people. °20 *Carve*: choose (as does the one who carves the food). °23 *voice and yielding*: approving vote.

Whereof he is the head. Then if he says he loves you,
It fits your wisdom so far to believe it   25
As he in his particular act and place
May give his saying deed,° which is no further
Than the main voice of Denmark goes withal.
Then weigh what loss your honour may sustain
If with too credent° ear you list° his songs,   30
Or lose your heart, or your chaste treasure open
To his unmast'red importunity.°
Fear it Ophelia, fear it my dear sister,
And keep you in the rear of your affection,
Out of the shot and danger of desire.   35
The chariest° maid is prodigal enough
If she unmask her beauty to the moon.
Virtue itself 'scapes not calumnious strokes.
The canker galls the infants° of the spring
Too oft before their buttons° be disclosed,   40
And in the morn and liquid dew of youth
Contagious blastments° are most imminent.
Be wary then, best safety lies in fear,
Youth to itself rebels,° though none else near.
OPHELIA: I shall the effect° of this good lesson keep   45
As watchman to my heart: but good my brother,
Do not as some ungracious° pastors do,
Show me the steep and thorny way to heaven,
Whiles like a puffed and reckless libertine
Himself the primrose path of dalliance treads,   50
And recks not his own rede.°

Enter POLONIUS.

LAERTES: O fear me not,°
I stay too long, but here my father comes:
A double blessing is a double grace,
Occasion smiles upon a second leave.°
POLONIUS: Yet here Laertes? aboard, aboard for shame,   55
The wind sits in the shoulder of your sail,
And you are stayed for: there, my blessing with thee,
And these few precepts in thy memory
Look thou character.° Give thy thoughts no tongue,
Nor any unproportioned thought his act: 60

°26–27 *in his . . . deed:* limited by personal responsibilities and rank, may perform what he promises. °30 *credent:* credulous. *list:* listen to. °31–32 *your chaste . . . importunity:* lose your virginity to his uncontrolled persistence. °36 *chariest:* most cautious. °39 *canker . . . infants:* cankerworm or caterpillar harms the young plants. °40 *buttons:* buds. °42 *blastments:* blights. °44 *to itself rebels:* lusts by nature. °45 *effect:* moral. °47 *ungracious:* lacking God's grace. °51 *recks . . . rede:* does not follow his own advice. *fear me not:* Don't worry about me. °54 *Occasion . . . leave:* opportunity favors a second leave-taking. °59 *character:* write, impress, imprint.

Be thou familiar, but by no means vulgar;°
Those friends thou hast, and their adoption tried,°
Grapple them unto thy soul with hoops of steel,
But do not dull° thy palm with entertainment
65 Of each new-hatched unfledged° comrade. Beware
Of entrance to a quarrel, but being in,
Bear't that th'opposèd may beware of thee.
Give every man thy ear, but few thy voice:
Take each man's censure,° but reserve thy judgment.
70 Costly thy habit° as thy purse can buy,
But not expressed in fancy,° rich, not gaudy,
For the apparel oft proclaims the man,
And they in France of the best rank and station,
Are of a most select and generous chief° in that:
75 Neither a borrower nor a lender be,
For loan oft loses both itself and friend,
And borrowing dulls the edge of husbandry;°
This above all, to thine own self be true
And it must follow as the night the day,
80 Thou canst not then be false to any man.
Farewell, my blessing season° this in thee.

LAERTES: Most humbly do I take my leave my lord.

POLONIUS: The time invites you, go, your servants tend.°

LAERTES: Farewell Ophelia, and remember well
What I have said to you.

85 **OPHELIA:**   'Tis in my memory locked,
And you yourself shall keep the key of it.

LAERTES: Farewell.   *Exit* LAERTES.

POLONIUS: What is't Ophelia he hath said to you?

OPHELIA: So please you, something touching the Lord Hamlet.

90 **POLONIUS:** Marry,° well bethought:
'Tis told me he hath very oft of late
Given private time to you, and you yourself
Have of your audience been most free and bounteous.
If it be so, as so 'tis put on me,
95 And that in way of caution, I must tell you,
You do not understand yourself so clearly
As it behooves my daughter, and your honour.
What is between you? give me up the truth.

OPHELIA: He hath my lord of late made many tenders°
100 Of his affection to me.

POLONIUS: Affection, puh, you speak like a green girl
Unsifted° in such perilous circumstance.
Do you believe his tenders as you call them?

OPHELIA: I do not know my lord what I should think.

°61 *vulgar:* indiscriminately friendly. °62 *adoption tried:* loyalty proved. °64 *dull:* get calluses on. °65 *new-hatched unfledged:* new and untested. °69 *censure:* opinion. °70 *habit:* clothing. °71 *expressed in fancy:* so fantastic as to be ridiculous. °74 *select . . . chief:* judicious and noble eminence. °77 *husbandry:* thrift. °81 *season:* bring to maturity. °83 *tend:* attend, wait. °90 *Marry:* a mild oath, from "By the Virgin Mary." °99 *tenders:* offers (see lines 106–9). °102 *Unsifted:* untested.

POLONIUS: Marry, I will teach you; think yourself a baby   105
       That you have ta'en these tenders° for true pay
       Which are not sterling.° Tender yourself more dearly,°
       Or (not to crack the wind of the poor phrase,
       Running it thus°) you'll tender me a fool.°
OPHELIA: My lord he hath importuned me with love   110
       In honourable fashion.
POLONIUS: Ay, fashion you may call it, go to, go to.
OPHELIA: And hath given countenance° to his speech, my lord,
       With almost all the holy vows of heaven.
POLONIUS: Ay, springes° to catch woodcocks.° I do know   115
       When the blood burns, how prodigal the soul
       Lends the tongue vows: these blazes daughter,
       Giving more light than heat, extinct in both,
       Even in their promise, as it is a-making,°
       You must not take for fire. From this time   120
       Be something scanter of your maiden presence,
       Set your entreatments at a higher rate
       Than a command to parle;° for Lord Hamlet,
       Believe so much in him that he is young,
       And with a larger tether may he walk   125
       Than may be given you: in few° Ophelia,
       Do not believe his vows, for they are brokers°
       Not of that dye which their investments° show,
       But mere implorators° of unholy suits,
       Breathing° like sanctified and pious bonds,°   130
       The better to beguile. This is for all,
       I would not in plain terms from this time forth
       Have you so slander any moment leisure
       As to give words or talk with the Lord Hamlet.
       Look to't I charge you, come your ways.°   135
OPHELIA: I shall obey, my lord.   [*Exeunt.*]

Scene 4. [The platform on the battlements]

Enter HAMLET, HORATIO and MARCELLUS.

HAMLET: The air bites shrewdly,° it is very cold.
HORATIO: It is a nipping and an eager° air.
HAMLET: What hour now?
HORATIO: I think it lacks of twelve.
MARCELLUS: No, it is struck.   5

°106 *tenders:* offers (of money). °107 *sterling:* genuine (currency). *Tender . . . dearly:* hold yourself at a higher value. °108–09 *crack . . . thus:* make the phrase lose its breath. °109 *tender . . . fool:* (1) make me look foolish (2) present me with a baby. °113 *countenance:* confirmation. °115 *springes:* snares. *woodcocks:* snipelike birds (believed to be stupid and therefore easily trapped). °118–19 *extinct . . . a-making:* losing both appearance, because of brevity, and substance, because of broken promises. °122–23 *Set . . . parle:* Don't rush to negotiate a surrender as soon as the besieger asks for a discussion of terms. °126 *few:* short. °127 *brokers:* (1) business agents (2) procurers. °128 *investments:* (1) business ventures (2) clothing. °129 *implorators:* solicitors. °130 *Breathing:* speaking softly. *bonds:* pledges. °135 *come your ways:* come along. °1 *shrewdly:* fiercely. °2 *eager:* sharp.

HORATIO: Indeed? I heard it not: it then draws near the season°
Wherein the spirit held his wont to walk.

A flourish of trumpets, and two pieces [of ordnance] go off.

What does this mean my lord?
HAMLET: The king doth wake° tonight and takes his rouse,°
10   Keeps wassail° and the swagg'ring up-spring° reels:
And as he drains his draughts of Rhenish° down,
The kettle-drum and trumpet thus bray out
The triumph of his pledge.°
HORATIO: Is it a custom?
HAMLET: Ay marry is't,
15   But to my mind, though I am native here
And to the manner born,° it is a custom
More honoured in the breach than the observance.°
This heavy-headed revel east and west
Makes us traduced and taxed of° other nations:
20   They clepe° us drunkards, and with swinish phrase
Soil our addition,° and indeed it takes
From our achievements, though performed at height,°
The pith and marrow of our attribute.°
So oft it chances in particular men,
25   That for some vicious mole of nature° in them,
As in their birth, wherein they are not guilty
(Since nature cannot choose his origin),
By the o'ergrowth of some complexion,°
Oft breaking down the pales° and forts of reason,
30   Or by some habit, that too much o'er-leavens°
The form of plausive° manners—that these men,
Carrying I say the stamp of one defect,
Being nature's livery,° or fortune's star,°
His virtues else be they as pure as grace,
35   As infinite as man may undergo,
Shall in the general censure° take corruption
From that particular fault: the dram of evil
Doth all the noble substance often doubt,
To his own scandal.°

Enter GHOST.

°6 *season:* time, period. °9 *wake:* stay awake. *rouse:* drinks that empty the cup. °10 *Keeps wassail:* holds drinking bouts. *up-spring:* a vigorous German dance. °11 *Rhenish:* Rhine wine. °13 *triumph . . . pledge:* victory of emptying the cup with one draught. °16 *to . . . born:* accustomed to the practice since birth. °17 *More . . . observance:* better to break than to observe. °19 *traduced and taxed of:* defamed and taken to task by. °20 *clepe:* call. °20–21 *with swinish . . . addition:* blemish our reputation by comparing us to swine. °22 *at height:* to the maximum. °23 *attribute:* reputation. °25 *mole of nature:* natural blemish. °28 *o'er growth . . . complexion:* overbalance of one of the body's four humors or fluids believed to determine temperament. °29 *pales:* defensive enclosures. °30 *too much o'er-leavens:* excessively modifies (like too much leaven in bread). °31 *plausive:* pleasing. °33 *nature's livery:* marked by nature. *fortune's star:* destined by chance. °36 *general censure:* public opinion. °37–39 *the dram . . . scandal:* the minute quantity of evil often casts doubt upon his noble nature, to his shame.

HORATIO: Look my lord, it comes.
HAMLET: Angels and ministers of grace defend us: 40
    Be thou a spirit of health, or goblin damned,°
    Bring with thee airs from heaven, or blasts from hell,
    Be thy intents wicked, or charitable,
    Thou com'st in such a questionable° shape,
    That I will speak to thee. I'll call thee Hamlet,   45
    King, father, royal Dane. O answer me,
    Let me not burst in ignorance, but tell
    Why thy canonized° bones hearsèd° in death
    Have burst their cerements?° why the sepulchre,
    Wherein we saw thee quietly interred   50
    Hath oped his ponderous and marble jaws,
    To cast thee up again? What may this mean
    That thou, dead corse, again in complete steel
    Revisits thus the glimpses of the moon,
    Making night hideous, and we fools of nature°   55
    So horridly to shake our disposition
    With thoughts beyond the reaches of our souls,
    Say why is this? wherefore? what should we do?   *GHOST beckons HAMLET.*
HORATIO: It beckons you to go away with it,
    As if it some impartment did desire°   60
    To you alone.
MARCELLUS: Look with what courteous action
    It waves you to a more removèd ground,
    But do not go with it.
HORATIO: No, by no means.
HAMLET: It will not speak, then I will follow it.
HORATIO: Do not my lord.
HAMLET: Why what should be the fear?   65
    I do not set my life at a pin's fee,°
    And for my soul, what can it do to that
    Being a thing immortal as itself;
    It waves me forth again, I'll follow it.
HORATIO: What if it tempt you toward the flood my lord,   70
    Or to the dreadful summit of the cliff
    That beetles o'er° his base into the sea,
    And there assume some other horrible form
    Which might deprive your sovereignty of reason,°
    And draw you into madness? think of it,   75
    The very place puts toys of desperation,°
    Without more motive, into every brain
    That looks so many fathoms to the sea
    And hears it roar beneath.

°41 *spirit . . . damned:* true ghost or demon from hell. °44 *questionable:* question-raising. °48 *canonized:* buried in accordance with church edict. *hearsèd:* entombed. °49 *cerements:* waxed cloth wrappings. °55 *fools of nature:* mocked by our natural limitations when faced with the supernatural. °60 *some . . . desire:* desired to impart something. °66 *fee:* value. °72 *beetles o'er:* overhangs. °74 *deprive . . . reason:* dethrone your reason from its sovereignty. °76 *toys of desperation:* desperate whims.

HAMLET:	It waves me still:

80   Go on, I'll follow thee.

MARCELLUS: You shall not go my lord.

HAMLET:	Hold off your hands.

HORATIO: Be ruled, you shall not go.

HAMLET:	My fate cries out,

    And makes each petty artire° in this body

    As hardy as the Nemean lion's° nerve;°

85   Still am I called, unhand me gentlemen,

    By heaven I'll make a ghost of him that lets° me:

    I say away; go on, I'll follow thee.   *Exeunt GHOST and HAMLET.*

HORATIO: He waxes desperate° with imagination.

MARCELLUS: Let's follow, 'tis not fit thus to obey him.

90 **HORATIO:** Have after—to what issue will this come?

MARCELLUS: Something is rotten in the state of Denmark.

HORATIO: Heaven will direct it.

MARCELLUS:	Nay, let's follow him.	*Exeunt.*

Scene 5. [Another part of the platform]

Enter GHOST and HAMLET.

HAMLET: Whither wilt thou lead me? Speak, I'll go no further.

GHOST: Mark me.

HAMLET:	I will.

GHOST:	My hour is almost come

    When I to sulphurous and tormenting flames

    Must render up myself.

HAMLET:	Alas poor ghost.

5 **GHOST:** Pity me not, but lend thy serious hearing

    To what I shall unfold.

HAMLET: Speak, I am bound° to hear.

GHOST: So art thou to revenge, when thou shalt hear.

HAMLET: What?

GHOST:	I am thy father's spirit,

10   Doomed for a certain term to walk the night,

    And for the day confined to fast in fires,

    Till the foul crimes done in my days of nature°

    Are burnt and purged away: but that I am forbid

    To tell the secrets of my prison-house,

15   I could a tale unfold whose lightest word

    Would harrow up thy soul, freeze thy young blood,

    Make thy two eyes like stars start from their spheres,°

    Thy knotted and combinèd locks to part,

    And each particular hair to stand an° end,

20   Like quills upon the fretful porpentine:°

°83 *artire*: ligament. °84 *Nemean lion*: killed by Hercules as one of his twelve labors. *nerve*: sinew. °86 *lets*: prevents. °88 *waxes desperate*: grows frantic. °12 *crimes . . . nature*: sins committed during my life on earth. °17 *spheres*: (1) orbits (according to Ptolemy, each planet was confined to a sphere revolving around the earth) (2) sockets. °6 *bound*: obliged by duty. °19 *an*: on. °20 *fretful porpentine*: angry porcupine.

But this eternal blazon° must not be
To ears of flesh and blood; list, list, O list:
If thou didst ever thy dear father love—
HAMLET: O God!
GHOST: Revenge his foul and most unnatural murder.   25
HAMLET: Murder?
GHOST: Murder most foul, as in the best it is,
But this most foul, strange and unnatural.
HAMLET: Haste me to know't, that I with wings as swift
    As meditation or the thoughts of love,   30
    May sweep to my revenge.
GHOST: I find thee apt,°
    And duller shouldst thou be than the fat° weed
    That rots itself in ease on Lethe wharf,°
    Wouldst thou not stir in this; now Hamlet hear,   35
    'Tis given out, that sleeping in my orchard,°
    A serpent stung me, so the whole ear of Denmark
    Is by a forgèd process° of my death
    Rankly abused:° but know thou noble youth,
    The serpent that did sting thy father's life   40
    Now wears his crown.
HAMLET: O my prophetic soul!
    My uncle?
GHOST: Ay, that incestuous, that adulterate° beast,
    With witchcraft of his wit, with traitorous gifts,
    O wicked wit and gifts, that have the power   45
    So to seduce; won to his shameful lust
    The will of my most seeming-virtuous queen;
    O Hamlet, what a falling-off was there,
    From me whose love was of that dignity
    That it went hand in hand, even with the vow   50
    I made to her in marriage, and to decline
    Upon° a wretch whose natural gifts were poor
    To° those of mine;
    But virtue, as it never will be moved,
    Though lewdness court it in a shape of heaven,°   55
    So lust, though to a radiant angle linked,
    Will sate itself in a celestial bed
    And prey on garbage.
    But soft, methinks I scent the morning air,
    Brief let me be; sleeping within my orchard,   60
    My custom always of the afternoon,
    Upon my secure° hour thy uncle stole
    With juice of cursèd hebona° in a vial,
    And in the porches of my ears did pour
    The leperous° distilment, whose effect   65

°21 *eternal blazon*: revelation about eternity. °32 *apt*: ready. °33 *fat*: slimy. °34 *Lethe wharf*: the banks of Lethe
(river in Hades from which spirits drank to forget their past lives). °36 *orchard*: garden. °38 *process*: account.
°39 *abused*: deceived. °43 *adulterate*: adulterous. °51–52 *decline Upon*: descend to. °53 *To*: compared to. °55 *shape of
heaven*: angelic appearance. °62 *secure*: unsuspecting. °63 *hebona*: poisonous sap of the ebony or henbane.
°65 *leperous*: leprosy-causing.

Holds such an enmity with blood of man,
That swift as quicksilver it courses through
The natural gates and alleys of the body,
And with a sudden vigour it doth posset°
70　And curd, like eager° droppings into milk,
The thin and wholesome° blood; so did it mine,
And a most instant tetter° barked about°
Most lazar°-like with vile and loathsome crust
All my smooth body.
75　Thus was I sleeping by a brother's hand,
Of life, of crown, of queen at once dispatched,
Cut off even in the blossoms of my sin,
Unhouseled, disappointed, unaneled,°
No reck'ning° made, but sent to my account°
80　With all my imperfections on my head;
O horrible, O horrible, most horrible!
If thou hast nature in thee bear it not,
Let not the royal bed of Denmark be
A couch for luxury° and damnèd incest.
85　But howsoever thou pursues this act,
Taint not thy mind, nor let thy soul contrive
Against thy mother aught,° leave her to heaven,
And to those thorns that in her bosom lodge
To prick and sting her. Fare thee well at once,
90　The glow-worm shows the matin° to be near
And 'gins to pale this uneffectual fire:°
Adieu, adieu, adieu, remember me.　　　　　　　　　　　　　　　*Exit.*

HAMLET:　O all you host of heaven! O earth! what else?
And shall I couple° hell? O fie! Hold, hold my heart,
95　And you my sinews, grow not instant old,
But bear me stiffly up; remember thee?
Ay thou poor ghost, while memory holds a seat
In this distracted globe.° Remember thee?
Yea, from the table° of my memory
100　I'll wipe away all trivial fond° records,
All saws of books,° all forms, all pressures° past
That youth and observation copied there,
And thy commandment all alone shall live
Within the book and volume of my brain,
105　Unmixed with baser matter, yes by heaven:
O most pernicious woman!
O villain, villain, smiling damnèd villain!
My tables,° meet° it is I set it down

°69 *posset:* curdle.　°70 *eager:* sour.　°71 *wholesome:* healthy.　°72 *tetter:* skin eruption. *barked about:* covered (like bark on a tree).　°73 *lazar:* leper.　°78 *Unhouseled . . . unaneled:* without final sacrament, unprepared (without confession) and lacking extreme unction (anointing).　°79 *reck'ning:* (1) accounting (2) payment of my bill (3) confession and absolution. *account:* judgment.　°84 *luxury:* lust.　°87 *aught:* anything.　°90 *matin:* dawn.　°91 *'gins . . . fire:* his light becomes ineffective, made pale by day.　°94 *couple:* engage in a contest against.　°98 *distracted globe:* (his head).　°99 *table:* tablet, "table-book."　°100 *fond:* foolish.　°101 *saws of books:* maxims (sayings) copied from books. *forms, all pressures:* ideas, impressions, meditations, etc.　°108 *tables:* tablet; notepad. *meet:* fitting.

That one may smile, and smile, and be a villain,
At least I am sure it may be so in Denmark.   110
So uncle, there you are: now to my word,°
It is 'Adieu, adieu, remember me.'
I have sworn't.

Enter HORATIO *and* MARCELLUS.

HORATIO: My lord, my lord!
MARCELLUS: Lord Hamlet!
HORATIO: Heaven secure° him.
HAMLET: So be it.   115
MARCELLUS: Illo, ho, ho, my lord!
HAMLET: Hillo, ho, ho, boy, come° bird, come.
MARCELLUS: How is't my noble lord?
HORATIO: What news my lord?
HAMLET: O, wonderful!
HORATIO: Good my lord, tell it.
HAMLET: No, you will reveal it.   120
HORATIO: Not I my lord, by heaven.
MARCELLUS: Nor I my lord.
HAMLET: How say you then, would heart of man once think it?
    But you'll be secret?
BOTH: Ay, by heaven, my lord.
HAMLET: There's ne'er a villain dwelling in all Denmark
    But he's an arrant° knave.   125
HORATIO: There needs no ghost my lord, come from the grave
    To tell us this.
HAMLET: Why right, you are in the right,
    And so without more circumstance° at all
    I hold it fit that we shake hands and part,
    You, as your business and desire shall point you,   130
    For every man hath business and desire
    Such as it is, and for my own poor part,
    Look you, I will go pray.
HORATIO: These are but wild and whirling words my lord.
HAMLET: I am sorry they offend you, heartily,   135
    Yes faith, heartily.
HORATIO: There's no offence my lord.
HAMLET: Yes by Saint Patrick, but there is Horatio,
    And much offence too: touching this vision here,
    It is an honest° ghost, that let me tell you:
    For your desire to know what is between us,   140
    O'ermaster't as you may. And now good friends,
    As you are friends, scholars, and soldiers,
    Give me one poor request.
HORATIO: What is't, my lord? we will.

°111 *word*: motto (to guide my actions). °114 *secure*: protect. °117 *Hillo . . . come*: falconer's cry with which
Hamlet replies to their calls. °125 *arrant*: thoroughgoing. °128 *circumstance*: ceremony. °139 *honest*: true (not
a devil in disguise).

145	**HAMLET:** Never make known what you have seen tonight.
	BOTH: My lord we will not.
	HAMLET: Nay, but swear't.
	HORATIO: In faith
	My lord, not I.
	MARCELLUS: Nor I my lord, in faith.
	HAMLET: Upon my sword.
	MARCELLUS: We have sworn my lord already.
	HAMLET: Indeed, upon my sword,° indeed.

150   **GHOST:** Swear.   GHOST *cries under the stage.*
       HAMLET: Ha, ha, boy, say'st thou so, art thou there, truepenny°?
             Come on, you hear this fellow in the cellarage,
             Consent to swear.
       HORATIO: Propose the oath my lord.
       HAMLET: Never to speak of this that you have seen.
155   Swear by my sword.
       GHOST: [*Beneath.*] Swear.
       HAMLET: Hic et ubique?° then we'll shift our ground:
             Come hither gentlemen,
             And lay your hands again upon my sword,
160   Swear by my sword
             Never to speak of this that you have heard.
       GHOST: [*Beneath.*] Swear by his sword.
       HAMLET: Well said old mole, canst work i'th' earth so fast?
             A worthy pioner°—once more remove;° good friends.
165   **HORATIO:** O day and night, but this is wondrous strange.
       HAMLET: And therefore as a stranger give it welcome.
             There are more things in heaven and earth Horatio,
             Than are dreamt of in your philosophy.
             But come,
170   Here as before, never so help you mercy,
             How strange or odd some'er I bear myself,
             (As I perchance hereafter shall think meet
             To put an antic disposition on°)
             That you at such times seeing me, never shall
175   With arms encumbered° thus, or this head-shake,
             Or by pronouncing of some doubtful phrase,
             As "Well, well, we know," or "We could an if we would,"
             Or "If we list° to speak," or "There be and if they might,"
             Or such ambiguous giving out, to note
180   That you know aught of me; this do swear,
             So grace and mercy at your need help you.
       GHOST: [*Beneath.*] Swear. [*They swear.*]
       HAMLET: Rest, rest, perturbed spirit: so gentlemen,
             With all my love I do commend me to you,°
185   And what so poor a man as Hamlet is,
             May do t'express his love and friending to you

°149 *sword:* the cross-shaped hilt. °151 *truepenny:* old pal. °157 *Hic et ubique:* here and everywhere. °164 *pioner:* digger (army trencher). *remove:* move elsewhere. °173 *put . . . on:* assume a mad or grotesque behavior. °175 *encumbered:* folded. °178 *list:* please. °184 *commend . . . you:* put myself in your hands.

God willing shall not lack: let us go in together,
And still° your fingers on your lips I pray.
The time is out of joint: O cursèd spite,
That ever I was born to set it right.   190
Nay come, let's go together.   *Exeunt.*

ACT 2

Scene 1. [Polonius's chambers]

Enter old POLONIUS *with his man* REYNALDO.

POLONIUS: Give him this money, and these notes Reynaldo.
REYNALDO: I will my lord.
POLONIUS: You shall do marvellous° wisely, good Reynaldo,
       Before you visit him, to make inquire
       Of his behaviour.
REYNALDO: My lord, I did intend it.   5
POLONIUS: Marry, well said, very well said; look you sir,
       Inquire me first what Danskers° are in Paris,
       And how, and who, what means, and where they keep,°
       What company, at what expense, and finding
       By this encompassment° and drift of question   10
       That they do know my son, come you more nearer
       Than your particular demands° will touch it,
       Take you as 'twere some distant knowledge of him,
       As thus, "I know his father, and his friends,
       And in part him"—do you mark this, Reynaldo?   15
REYNALDO: Ay, very well my lord.
POLONIUS: "And in part him, but," you may say, "not well,
       But if't be he I mean, he's very wild,
       Addicted so and so;" and there put on him
       What forgeries° you please, marry none so rank°   20
       As may dishonour him, take heed of that,
       But sir, such wanton, wild, and usual slips,
       As are companions noted and most known
       To youth and liberty.
REYNALDO: As gaming my lord.
POLONIUS: Ay, or drinking, fencing, swearing,   25
       Quarrelling, drabbing°—you may go so far.
REYNALDO: My lord, that would dishonour him.
POLONIUS: Faith no, as you may season it in the charge.°
       You must not put another scandal on him,
       That he is open to incontinency,°   30
       That's not my meaning, but breathe his faults so quaintly°
       That they may seem the taints of° liberty,
       The flash and outbreak of a fiery mind,

°188 *still:* always. °3 *marvellous:* wonderfully. °7 *Danskers:* Danes. °8 *keep:* lodge. °10 *encompassment:* roundabout
way. °12 *particular demands:* specific questions. °20 *forgeries:* inventions. *rank:* excessive. °26 *drabbing:* whoring.
°28 *season . . . charge:* temper the charge as you make it. °30 *incontinency:* uncontrolled lechery. °31 *quaintly:*
delicately. °32 *taints of:* blemishes due to.

A savageness in unreclaimèd blood,°
Of general assault.°

35 REYNALDO: But my good lord—
POLONIUS: Wherefore° should you do this?
REYNALDO: Ay my lord,
I would know that.
POLONIUS: Marry sir, here's my drift,
And I believe it is a fetch of warrant:°
40 You laying these slight sullies on my son,
As 'twere a thing a little soiled i'th' working,°
Mark you, your party in converse, him you would sound,
Having ever seen° in the prenominate crimes°
The youth you breathe of guilty, be assured
45 He closes with you in this consequence,°
"Good sir," or so, or "friend," or "gentleman,"
According to the phrase, or the addition°
Of man and country.
REYNALDO: Very good my lord.
POLONIUS: And then sir, does a'° this, a' does, what was I
50 about to say?
By the mass I was about to say something,
Where did I leave?
REYNALDO: At "closes in the consequence,"
At "friend, or so, and gentleman."
POLONIUS: At "closes in the consequence," ay marry,
55 He closes thus, "I know the gentleman,
I saw him yesterday, or th'other day,
Or then, or then, with such or such, and as you say,
There was a' gaming, there o'ertook in's rouse,°
There falling out at tennis," or perchance
60 "I saw him enter such a house of sale,"
Videlicet,° a brothel, or so forth. See you now,
Your bait of falsehood takes this carp of truth,
And thus do we of wisdom, and of reach,°
With windlasses,° and with assays of bias,°
65 By indirections find directions out:
So by my former lecture and advice
Shall you my son; you have me, have you not?
REYNALDO: My lord I have.
POLONIUS: God bye ye, fare ye well.
REYNALDO: Good my lord.
70 POLONIUS: Observe his inclination in yourself.°
REYNALDO: I shall my lord.
POLONIUS: And let him ply° his music.
REYNALDO: Well my lord.

°34 *unreclaimèd blood:* unbridled passion. °35 *general assault:* attacking all (young men). °36 *Wherefore:* why.
°39 *fetch of warrant:* trick guaranteed to succeed. °41 *working:* handling. °43 *Having ever seen:* if he has ever seen.
prenominate crimes: aforenamed sins. °45 *closes . . . consequence:* comes to terms with you as follows. °47 *addition:*
title, form of address. °49 *a':* he. °58 *o'ertook in's rouse:* overcome by drunkenness. °61 *Videlicet:* namely. °63 *reach:*
far-reaching knowledge. °64 *windlasses:* roundabout approaches. *assays of bias:* indirect attempts. °70 *in yourself:*
personally. °72 *ply:* practice.

POLONIUS: Farewell.

Exit REYNALDO.

Enter OPHELIA.

How now Ophelia, what's the matter?
OPHELIA: O my lord, my lord, I have been so affrighted.
POLONIUS: With what, i'th'name of God?   75
OPHELIA: My lord, as I was sewing in my closet,°
    Lord Hamlet with his doublet all unbraced,°
    No hat upon his head, his stockings fouled,
    Ungart'red, and down-gyvèd° to his ankle,
    Pale as his shirt, his knees knocking each other,   80
    And with a look so piteous in purport°
    As if he had been loosèd out of hell
    To speak of horrors, he comes before me.
POLONIUS: Mad for thy love?
OPHELIA: My lord I do not know,
    But truly I do fear it.
POLONIUS: What said he?   85
OPHELIA: He took me by the wrist, and held me hard,
    Then goes he to the length of all his arm,°
    And with his other hand thus o'er his brow,
    He falls to such perusal of my face
    As° a' would draw it; long stayed he so,   90
    At last, a little shaking of mine arm,
    And thrice his head thus waving up and down,
    He raised a sigh so piteous and profound
    As it did seem to shatter all his bulk,°
    And end his being; that done, he lets me go,   95
    And with his head over his shoulder turned
    He seemed to find his way without his eyes,
    For out adoors he went without their helps,
    And to the last bended their light on me.
POLONIUS: Come, go with me, I will go seek the king,   100
    This is the very ecstasy° of love,
    Whose violent property fordoes itself,°
    And leads the will to desperate undertakings
    As oft as any passion under heaven
    That does afflict our natures: I am sorry.   105
    What, have you given him any hard words of late?
OPHELIA: No my good lord, but as you did command
    I did repel his letters, and denied
    His access to me.
POLONIUS: That hath made him mad.
    I am sorry that with better heed and judgment
    I had not quoted° him. I feared he did but trifle   110

°76 *closet:* private room. °77 *doublet all unbraced:* jacket all unfastened. °79 *down-gyvèd:* down around his ankles
(like prisoners' fetters or gyves). °81 *purport:* expression. °87 *goes . . . arm:* holds me at arm's length. °90 *As:* as if.
°94 *bulk:* body. °101 *ecstasy:* madness. °102 *Whose . . . itself:* that, by its violent nature, destroys the lover.
°111 *quoted:* observed.

And meant to wrack° thee, but beshrew my jealousy.°
By heaven it is as proper to our age
To cast beyond ourselves in our opinions,°
115   As it is common for the younger sort
To lack discretion; come, go we to the king,
This must be known, which being kept close, might move
More grief to hide, than hate to utter love.°   [*Exeunt.*]

Scene 2. [A room in the castle]

Flourish. Enter KING *and* QUEEN, ROSENCRANTZ *and* GUILDENSTERN, *cum aliis.*

KING: Welcome dear Rosencrantz and Guildenstern.
Moreover° that we much did long to see you,
The need we have to use you did provoke
Our hasty sending. Something have you heard
5   Of Hamlet's transformation—so call it.
Sith° nor th'exterior nor the inward man
Resembles that it was. What it should be,
More than his father's death, that thus hath put him
So much from th'understanding of himself,
10   I cannot dream of: I entreat you both,
That being of so young days° brought up with him,
And sith so neighboured to his youth and haviour,
That you vouchsafe your rest° here in our court
Some little time, so by your companies
15   To draw him on to pleasures, and to gather
So much as from occasion you may glean,
Whether aught to us unknown afflicts him thus,
That opened° lies within our remedy.
QUEEN: Good gentlemen, he hath much talked of you,
20   And sure I am, two men there are not living
To whom he more adheres. If it will please you
To show us so much gentry° and good will,
As to expend your time with us awhile,
For the supply and profit of our hope,
25   Your visitation shall receive such thanks
As fits a king's remembrance.
ROSENCRANTZ: Both your majesties
Might by the sovereign power you have of us,
Put your dread pleasures more into command
Than to entreaty.
GUILDENSTERN: But we both obey,
30   And here give up ourselves in the full bent,°
To lay our service freely at your feet
To be commanded.

°112 *wrack:* ruin. *beshrew my jealousy:* curse my suspicion. °113–14 *proper . . . opinions:* natural for old people to read more into something than is actually there. °117–18 *being kept . . . love:* if kept secret, might cause more grief than if we risked the king's displeasure. °2 *Moreover:* in addition to the fact. °6 *Sith:* since. °11 *of . . . days:* from your early days. °13 *vouchsafe your rest:* agree to stay. °18 *opened:* discovered. °22 *gentry:* courtesy. °30 *in the full bent:* to the utmost (in archery, bending the bow).

KING: Thanks Rosencrantz, and gentle Guildenstern.
QUEEN: Thanks Guildenstern, and gentle Rosencrantz.
And I beseech you instantly to visit   35
My too much changèd son. Go some of you
And bring these gentlemen where Hamlet is.
GUILDENSTERN: Heavens make our presence and our practices°
Pleasant and helpful to him.
QUEEN: Ay, amen.

                          Exeunt ROSENCRANTZ and GUILDENSTERN.

Enter POLONIUS.

POLONIUS: Th'ambassadors from Norway my good lord,   40
Are joyfully returned.
KING: Thou still° hast been the father of good news.
POLONIUS: Have I, my lord? Assure you, my good liege,
I hold my duty as I hold my soul,
Both to my God and to my gracious king;   45
And I do think, or else this brain of mine
Hunts not the trail of policy° so sure
As it hath used to do, that I have found
The very cause of Hamlet's lunacy.
KING: O speak of that, that do I long to hear.   50
POLONIUS: Give first admittance to th'ambassadors,
My news shall be the fruit° to that great feast.
KING: Thyself do grace to them, and bring them in.   [*Exit POLONIUS.*]
He tells me my dear Gertrude, he hath found
The head and source of all your son's distemper.   55
QUEEN: I doubt° it is no other but the main,
His father's death and our o'erhasty marriage.
KING: Well, we shall sift him.

Enter POLONIUS, VALTEMAND, and CORNELIUS.

                          Welcome, my good friends.
Say Valtemand, what from our brother Norway?
VALTEMAND: Most fair return of greetings and desires;   60
Upon our first,° he sent out to suppress
His nephew's levies, which to him appeared
To be a preparation 'gainst the Polack,
But better looked into, he truly found
It was against your highness, whereat grieved   65
That so his sickness, age, and impotence
Was falsely borne in hand,° sends out arrests
On Fortinbras, which he in brief obeys,
Receives rebuke from Norway, and in fine,°
Makes vow before his uncle never more   70

°38 *practices:* (1) actions (2) plots. °42 *still:* always. °47 *policy:* (1) politics (2) plots. °52 *fruit:* dessert. °56 *doubt:* suspect. °61 *first:* first presentation. °67 *borne in hand:* deceived. °69 *fine:* finishing.

To give th'assay° of arms against your majesty:
Whereon old Norway, overcome with joy,
Gives him threescore thousand crowns in annual fee,
And his commission to employ those soldiers
75 So levied (as before) against the Polack,
With an entreaty herein further shown,
That it might please you to give quiet pass°
Through your dominions for this enterprise,
On such regards of safety and allowance
As therein are set down.

80 KING: It likes° us well,   [*Giving a paper.*]
And at our more considered time° we'll read,
Answer, and think upon this business:
Meantime, we thank you for your well-took labour,
Go to your rest, at night we'll feast together.
Most welcome home.   *Exeunt* AMBASSADORS.

85 POLONIUS: This business is well ended.
My liege and madam, to expostulate°
What majesty should be, what duty is,
Why day is day, night night, and time is time.
Were nothing but to waste night, day, and time.
90 Therefore since brevity is the soul of wit,°
And tediousness the limbs and outward flourishes,°
I will be brief. Your noble son is mad:
Mad call I it, for to define true madness,
What is't but to be nothing else but mad?
But let that go.
95 QUEEN: More matter, with less art.
POLONIUS: Madam, I swear I use no art at all:
That he is mad 'tis true: 'tis true, 'tis pity,
And pity 'tis 'tis true: a foolish figure,°
But farewell it, for I will use no art.
100 Mad let us grant him then, and now remains
That we find out the cause of this effect,
Or rather say, the cause of this defect,
For this effect defective comes by cause:
Thus it remains, and the remainder thus.
105 Perpend.°
I have a daughter, have while she is mine,
Who in her duty and obedience, mark,
Hath given me this, now gather and surmise.
[*Reads.*] "To the celestial, and my soul's idol, the most
110 beautified° Ophelia,"—
That's an ill phrase, a vile phrase, "beautified" is a vile
phrase, but you shall hear. Thus: [*Reads.*]
       "In her excellent white bosom, these," &c.—
QUEEN: Came this from Hamlet to her?

°71 *assay:* test.   °77 *pass:* passage.   °80 *likes:* pleases.   °81 *at . . . time:* when time is available for consideration.
°86 *expostulate:* discuss.   °90 *wit:* understanding.   °91 *tediousness . . . flourishes:* embellishments and flourishes cause
tedium.   °98 *figure:* rhetorical figure.   °105 *Perpend:* consider.   °110 *beautified:* beautiful.

POLONIUS: Good madam stay awhile, I will be faithful.   [*Reads.*] 115
     "Doubt thou the stars are fire,
        Doubt that the sun doth move,°
     Doubt° truth to be a liar,
        But never doubt I love.
     O dear Ophelia, I am ill at these numbers, I have not 120
     art to reckon° my groans, but that I love thee best, O
     most best, believe it. Adieu.
        Thine evermore, most dear lady, whilst
     this machine° is to° him, Hamlet."
     This in obedience hath my daughter shown me, 125
     And more above hath his solicitings,
     As they fell out by time, by means, and place,
     All given to mine ear.
KING: But how hath she
     Received his love?
POLONIUS: What do you think of me?
KING: As of a man faithful and honourable. 130
POLONIUS: I would fain prove so. But what might you think
     When I had seen this hot love on the wing,
     As I perceived it (I must tell you that)
     Before my daughter told me, what might you,
     Or my dear majesty your queen here think, 135
     If I had played the desk or table-book,°
     Or given my heart a winking° mute and dumb,
     Or looked upon this love with idle° sight,
     What might you think? No, I went round to work,
     And my young mistress this I did bespeak, 140
     "Lord Hamlet is a prince out of thy star,°
     This must not be:" and then I prescripts° gave her
     That she should lock herself from his resort,°
     Admit no messengers, receive no tokens:
     Which done, she took the fruits of my advice, 145
     And he repellèd, a short tale to make,
     Fell into a sadness, then into a fast,
     Thence to a watch,° thence into a weakness,
     Thence to a lightness,° and by this declension,
     Into the madness wherein now he raves, 150
     And all we mourn for.
KING: Do you think 'tis this?
QUEEN: It may be, very like.
POLONIUS: Hath there been such a time, I would fain know that,
     That I have positively said "'Tis so,"
     When it proved otherwise?
KING: Not that I know. 155
POLONIUS: Take this, from this, if this be otherwise;

°117 *move:* as it was believed to do, around the earth. °118 *Doubt:* suspect. °121 *reckon:* express in meter. °124 *machine:* body. *to:* attached to. °136 *played . . . book:* kept it concealed as in a desk or personal notebook. °137 *given . . . winking:* had my heart shut its eyes to the matter. °138 *idle:* unseeing. °141 *out . . . star:* out of your sphere (above you in station). °142 *prescripts:* orders. °143 *resort:* company. °148 *watch:* sleeplessness. °149 *lightness:* lightheadedness.

[*Points to his head and shoulder.*]

> If circumstances lead me, I will find
> Where truth is hid, though it were hid indeed
> Within the center.

KING: How may we try° it further?

160 POLONIUS: You know sometimes he walks four hours together
> Here in the lobby.

QUEEN: So he does indeed.

POLONIUS: At such a time, I'll loose° my daughter to him.
> Be you and I behind an arras° then,
> Mark the encounter: if he love her not,
165 And be not from his reason fall'n thereon,
> Let me be no assistant for a state,°
> But keep a farm and carters.

KING: We will try it.

Enter HAMLET *reading on a book.*

QUEEN: But look where sadly the poor wretch comes reading.

POLONIUS: Away, I do beseech you both away,
170 I'll board him presently,° O give me leave.   *Exeunt* KING *and* QUEEN.
> How does my good Lord Hamlet?

HAMLET: Well, God-a-mercy.

POLONIUS: Do you know me, my lord?

HAMLET: Excellent well, you are a fishmonger.°

175 POLONIUS: Not I my lord.

HAMLET: Then I would you were so honest a man.

POLONIUS: Honest, my lord?

HAMLET: Ay sir, to be honest as this world goes, is to be one
> man picked out of ten thousand.

180 POLONIUS: That's very true, my lord.

HAMLET: For if the sun breed maggots° in a dead dog, being a good
> kissing carrion°—have you a daughter?

POLONIUS: I have my lord.

HAMLET: Let her not walk i'th'sun:° conception° is a blessing, but as
185 your daughter may conceive, friend look to 't.

POLONIUS: [*Aside.*] How say you by that? Still harping on my daughter,
> yet he knew me not at first, a' said I was a fishmonger.
> A' is far gone, far gone, and truly in my youth, I suffered
> much extremity for love, very near this. I'll speak to him
190 again. What do you read my lord?

HAMLET: Words, words, words.

POLONIUS: What is the matter my lord?

HAMLET: Between who?

°159 *try:* test. °162 *loose:* (1) release (2) turn loose. °163 *arras:* hanging tapestry. °166 *assistant . . . state:* state official. °170 *board him presently:* approach him immediately. °174 *fishmonger:* (1) fish dealer (2) pimp. °181 *breed maggots:* in the belief that the rays of the sun caused maggots to breed in dead flesh. °182 *kissing carrion:* piece of flesh for kissing. °184 *Let . . . sun:* (1) proverbial: "out of God's blessing, into the warm sun" (2) because the sun is a breeder (3) don't let her go near me (with a pun on "sun" and "son"). *conception:* (1) understanding (2) pregnancy.

POLONIUS: I mean the matter° that you read, my lord.

HAMLET: Slanders sir; for the satirical rogue says here, that old men   195
have grey beards, that their faces are wrinkled, their eyes
purging thick amber and plum-tree gum,° and that they
have a plentiful lack of wit, together with most weak
hams. All which sir, though I most powerfully and
potently believe, yet I hold it not honesty° to have it thus set   200
down, for yourself sir shall grow old as I am: if like a crab
you could go backward.

POLONIUS: [*Aside.*] Though this be madness, yet there is method
in't.
Will you walk out of the air° my lord?   205

HAMLET: Into my grave.

POLONIUS: [*Aside.*] Indeed that's out of the air; how pregnant°
sometimes his replies are, a happiness° that often
madness hits on, which reason and sanity could not so
prosperously° be delivered of. I will leave him, and   210
suddenly contrive the means of meeting between him
and my daughter. My honourable lord, I will most
humbly take leave of you.

HAMLET: You cannot sir take from me anything that I will more
willingly part withal: except my life, except my life,   215
except my life.

POLONIUS: Fare you well my lord.

HAMLET: These tedious old fools.

Enter ROSENCRANTZ *and* GUILDENSTERN.

POLONIUS: You go to seek the Lord Hamlet, there he is.

ROSENCRANTZ: [*To Polonius.*] God save you sir.   [*Exit* POLONIUS.]   220

GUILDENSTERN: My honoured lord.

ROSENCRANTZ: My most dear lord.

HAMLET: My excellent good friends, how dost thou Guildenstern?
Ah Rosencrantz, good lads, how do you both?

ROSENCRANTZ: As the indifferent° children of the earth.   225

GUILDENSTERN: Happy, in that we are not over-happy:
On Fortune's cap we are not the very button.°

HAMLET: Nor the soles of her shoe?

ROSENCRANTZ: Neither my lord.

HAMLET: Then you live about her waist, or in the middle of her   230
favours?

GUILDENSTERN: Faith, her privates° we.

HAMLET: In the secret parts of Fortune? O most true, she is a
strumpet.° What news?

ROSENCRANTZ: None my lord, but that the world's grown honest.   235

°194 *matter*: (1) content (Polonius's meaning) (2) cause of a quarrel (Hamlet's interpretation). °197 *purging . . .
gum*: exuding a viscous yellowish discharge. °200 *honesty*: decency. °205 *out . . . air*: in the belief that fresh air
was bad for the sick). °207 *pregnant*: full of meaning. °208 *happiness*: aptness. °210 *prosperously*: successfully.
°225 *indifferent*: ordinary. °227 *On Fortune's . . . button*: we are not at the height of our fortunes.   °232 *privates*:
(1) intimate friend (2) private parts. °234 *strumpet*: inconstant woman, giving favor to many.

HAMLET: Then is doomsday near: but your news is not true. Let me
    question more in particular: what have you my good
    friends, deserved at the hands of Fortune, that she sends
    you to prison hither?

240 **GUILDENSTERN:** Prison, my lord?

HAMLET: Denmark's a prison.

ROSENCRANTZ: Then is the world one.

HAMLET: A goodly one, in which there are many confines, wards,°
    and dungeons; Denmark being one o'th'worst.

245 **ROSENCRANTZ:** We think not so my lord.

HAMLET: Why then 'tis none to you; for there is nothing either good
    or bad, but thinking makes it so: to me it is a prison.

ROSENCRANTZ: Why then your ambition makes it one: 'tis too narrow for
    your mind.

250 **HAMLET:** O God, I could be bounded in a nutshell, and count
    myself a king of infinite space; were it not that I have bad
    dreams.

GUILDENSTERN: Which dreams indeed are ambition: for the very substance
    of the ambitious, is merely the shadow of a dream.

255 **HAMLET:** A dream itself is but a shadow.

ROSENCRANTZ: Truly, and I hold ambition of so airy and light a quality,
    that it is but a shadow's shadow.

HAMLET: Then are our beggars bodies, and our monarchs and
    outstretched heroes the beggars' shadows:° shall we to th'

260   court? for by my fay,° I cannot reason.

BOTH: We'll wait upon° you.

HAMLET: No such matter. I will not sort° you with the rest of my
    servants: for to speak to you like an honest man, I am most
    dreadfully attended. But in the beaten way of friendship,

265   what make you at Elsinore?

ROSENCRANTZ: To visit you my lord, no other occasion.

HAMLET: Beggar that I am, I am even poor in thanks, but I thank
    you, and sure dear friends, my thanks are too dear a
    halfpenny:° were you not sent for? is it your own inclining?

270   is it a free° visitation? come, come, deal justly with me,
    come, come, nay speak.

GUILDENSTERN: What should we say my lord?

HAMLET: Anything but to th'purpose: you were sent for, and there
    is a kind of confession in your looks, which your modesties

275   have not craft enough to colour: I know the good king and
    queen have sent for you.

ROSENCRANTZ: To what end my lord?

HAMLET: That you must teach me: but let me conjure° you, by the
    rights of our fellowship, by the consonancy of our youth,°

280   by the obligation of our ever-preserved love, and by what

---

243 *wards:* cells. °258–59 *Then are . . . shadows:* then beggars are the true substance and ambitious kings and heroes the elongated shadows of beggars' bodies (for only a real substance can cast a shadow). °260 *fay:* faith. °261 *wait upon:* attend. °262 *sort:* class. °268–69 *too dear a halfpenny:* worth not even a halfpenny (as I have no influence). °270 *free:* voluntary. °278 *conjure:* appeal to. °279 *consonancy . . . youth:* agreement in our ages.

more dear a better proposer can charge you withal,° be
even and direct with me whether you were sent for or no.

ROSENCRANTZ: [*Aside to GUILDENSTERN.*] What say you?

HAMLET: Nay then, I have an eye of° you: If you love me,
hold not off.   285

GUILDENSTERN: My lord, we were sent for.

HAMLET: I will tell you why, so shall my anticipation prevent° your
discovery,° and your secrecy to the king and queen moult
no feather.° I have of late, but wherefore I know not, lost all
my mirth, forgone all custom of exercises: and indeed it   290
goes so heavily with my disposition, that this goodly
frame the earth, seems to me a sterile promontory, this
most excellent canopy the air, look you, this brave°
o'erhanging firmament, this majestical roof fretted° with
golden fire,° why it appeareth nothing to me but a foul and   295
pestilent congregation of vapours.° What a piece of work is
a man! How noble in reason, how infinite in faculties,° in
form and moving, how express° and admirable in action,
how like an angel in apprehension, how like a god: the
beauty of the world; the paragon of animals; and yet to   300
me, what is this quintessence of dust? Man delights not
me, no, nor woman neither, though by your smiling, you
seem to say so.

ROSENCRANTZ: My lord, there was no such stuff in my thoughts.

HAMLET: Why did ye laugh then, when I said man delights not me?   305

ROSENCRANTZ: To think, my lord, if you delight not in man, what lenten
entertainment° the players shall receive from you: we coted°
them on the way, and hither are they coming to offer you
service.

HAMLET: He that plays the king shall be welcome, his majesty shall   310
have tribute of me, the adventurous knight° shall use his
foil and target,° the lover shall not sigh gratis,° the humorous
man° shall end his part in peace,° the clown shall make
those laugh whose lungs are tickle o'th'sere,° and the lady
shall say her mind freely: or the blank verse shall halt° for't.   315
What players are they?

ROSENCRANTZ: Even those you were wont to take such delight in, the
tragedians of the city.

HAMLET: How chances it they travel? Their residence° both in
reputation and profit was better both ways.   320

ROSENCRANTZ: I think their inhibition comes by the means of the late innovation.°

°281 *withal:* with. °284 *of:* on. °287 *prevent:* forestall. °288 *discovery:* disclosure. °288–89 *moult no feather:* change
in no way. °293 *brave:* splendid. °294 *fretted:* ornamented with fretwork. °295 *golden fire:* stars. °296 *pestilent . . .
vapours:* clouds were believed to carry contagion. °297 *faculties:* physical powers. °298 *express:* well framed.
°306–7 *lenten entertainment:* meager treatment. °307 *coted:* passed. °311 *adventurous knight:* knight errant (a
popular stage character). °312 *foil and target:* sword blunted for stage fighting, and small shield. °312 *gratis:* without
applause. °312–13 *humorous man:* eccentric character with a dominant trait, caused by an excess of one of the
four humors, or bodily fluids. °313 *in peace:* without interruption. °314 *tickle o'th'sere:* attuned to respond to
laughter, as the finely adjusted gunlock responds to the touch of the trigger (fr. hunting). °315 *halt:* limp (if she
adds her own opinions and spoils the meter). °319 *residence:* i.e., in a city theatre. °321 *inhibition . . . innovation:*
i.e., they were forced out of town by a more popular theatrical fashion. The following speeches allude to the "War
of the Theatres" (1601–1602) between the child and adult acting companies.

HAMLET: Do they hold the same estimation they did when I was in
  the city; are they so followed?

ROSENCRANTZ: No indeed are they not.

325 **HAMLET:** How comes it? Do they grow rusty?

ROSENCRANTZ: Nay, their endeavour keeps in the wonted pace; but there
  is sir an aery° of children, like eyases,° that cry out on the
  top of question,° and are most tyrannically° clapped for't:
  these are now the fashion, and so berattle° the common
330   stages° (so they call them) that many wearing rapiers° are
  afraid of goose-quills,° and dare scarce come thither.

HAMLET: What, are they children? Who maintains 'em? How are
  they escoted?° Will they pursue the quality no longer than
  they can sing?° Will they not say afterwards if they should
335   grow themselves to common players (as it is most like, if
  their means are not better) their writers do them wrong, to
  make them exclaim against their own succession?°

ROSENCRANTZ: Faith, there has been much to-do on both sides: and the
  nation holds it no sin to tarre° them to controversy. There
340   was for a while, no money bid for argument,° unless the
  poet and the player went to cuffs in the question.°

HAMLET: Is't possible?

GUILDENSTERN: O there has been much throwing about of brains.

HAMLET: Do the boys carry it away?°

345 **ROSENCRANTZ:** Ay, that they do my lord, Hercules and his load too.°

HAMLET: It is not very strange, for my uncle is king of Denmark,
  and those that would make mows° at him while my father
  lived, give twenty, forty, fifty, a hundred ducats apiece
  for his picture in little.° 'Sblood,° there is something in this
350   more than natural, if philosophy° could find it out.

               A flourish for the PLAYERS.

GUILDENSTERN: There are the players.

HAMLET: Gentlemen, you are welcome to Elsinore: your hands,
  come then, th'appurtenance° of welcome is fashion and
  ceremony; let me comply with you in this garb,° lest my
355   extent° to the players, which I tell you must show fairly
  outwards, should more appear like entertainment than
  yours.° You are welcome: but my uncle-father, and aunt-mother,
  are deceived.

°327 *aery:* nest. *eyases:* young hawks. °327–28 *that cry . . . question:* whose shrill voices can be heard above all others.
°328 *tyrannically:* strongly. °329 *berattle:* berate. °329–30 *common stages:* public playhouses (the children's companies performed in private theatres). °330 *wearing rapiers:* worn by gentlemen. °331 *goose-quills:* pens (of
satirical dramatists who wrote for the children). °333 *escoted:* supported. °333–34 *pursue . . . sing:* continue acting only until their voices change. °337 *succession:* inheritance. °339 *tarre:* provoke. °340 *bid for argument:* paid
for the plot of a proposed play. °341 *went . . . question:* came to blows on the subject. °344 *carry it away:* carry off
the prize. °345 *Hercules . . . too:* Shakespeare's own company at the Globe Theatre, whose sign was Hercules
carrying the globe of the world. °347 *mows:* mouths, grimaces. °349 *little:* a miniature. *'Sblood:* by God's blood.
°350 *philosophy:* science. °353 *appurtenance:* accessory. °354 *comply . . . garb:* observe the formalities with you in
this style. °355 *extent:* i.e., of welcome. °356–57 *should . . . yours:* should appear more hospitable than yours.

GUILDENSTERN: In what my dear lord?

HAMLET: I am but mad north-north-west; when the wind is southerly,   360
I know a hawk from a handsaw.°

Enter POLONIUS.

POLONIUS: Well be with you, gentlemen.

HAMLET: Hark you Guildenstern, and you too, at each ear a hearer:
that great baby you see there is not yet out of his swaddling
clouts.°   365

ROSENCRANTZ: Happily° he is the second time come to them, for they say
an old man is twice a child.

HAMLET: I will prophesy, he comes to tell me of the players, mark
it.—You say right sir, a Monday morning, 'twas then
indeed.   370

POLONIUS: My lord, I have news to tell you.

HAMLET: My lord, I have news to tell you. When Roscius° was an
actor in Rome—

POLONIUS: The actors are come hither, my lord

HAMLET: Buz, buz.°   375

POLONIUS: Upon my honour.

HAMLET: Then came each actor on his ass—

POLONIUS: The best actors in the world, either for tragedy, comedy,
history, pastoral, pastoral-comical, historical-pastoral,
tragical-historical, tragical-comical-historical-pastoral,   380
scene individable,° or poem unlimited.° Seneca cannot be
too heavy, nor Plautus° too light for the law of writ, and the
liberty:° these are the only men.

HAMLET: O Jephthah,° judge of Israel, what a treasure hadst thou!

POLONIUS: What a treasure had he, my lord?   385

HAMLET: Why
  "One fair daughter and no more,
    The which he loved passing° well."

POLONIUS: [*Aside.*] Still on my daughter

HAMLET: Am I not i'th' right, old Jephthah?   390

POLONIUS: If you call me Jephthah my lord, I have a daughter that I
love passing well.

HAMLET: Nay, that follows not.

POLONIUS: What follows then, my lord?

HAMLET: Why   395
  "As by lot, God wot,"
and then you know
  "It came to pass, as most like° it was:"
the first row° of the pious chanson will show you more, for
look where my abridgement° comes.   400

°367 *I know . . . handsaw:* I can tell the difference between two things that are unlike ("hawk" = [1] bird of prey
[2] mattock, pickaxe; "handsaw" = [1] hernshaw or heron bird [2] small saw). °364–65 *swaddling clouts:* strips of
cloth binding a newborn baby. °366 *Happily:* perhaps. °372 *Roscius:* famous Roman actor. °375 *Buz, buz:* contemptuous. °381 *scene individable:* play observing the unities (time, place, action). *poem unlimited:* play ignoring
the unities. °381–82 *Seneca, Plautus:* Roman writers of tragedy and comedy, respectively. °382–83 *law . . . liberty:*
"rules" regarding the unities and those exercising freedom from the unities. °384 *Jephthah:* who was forced to
sacrifice his only daughter because of a rash promise (Judges 11:29–39). °388 *passing:* surpassingly. °398 *like:* likely.
°399 *row:* stanza. °400 *abridgement:* the players who will cut short my song.

Enter four or five PLAYERS.

You are welcome masters, welcome all. I am glad to see
thee well: welcome, good friends. O my old friend, why
thy face is valanced° since I saw thee last, com'st thou to
beard me in Denmark? What, my young lady° and
405   mistress? by'r lady, your ladyship is nearer to heaven than
when I saw you last, by the altitude of a chopine.° Pray
God your voice, like a piece of uncurrent° gold, be not
cracked within the ring.° Masters, you are all welcome:
we'll e'en to't like French falconers, fly at any thing we see:°
410   we'll have a speech straight. Come give us a taste of your
quality: come, a passionate speech.
1. PLAYER: What speech, my good lord?
HAMLET: I heard thee speak me a speech once, but it was never
acted, or if it was, not above once, for the play I remember
415   pleased not the million, 'twas caviary to the general,° but it
was (as I received it, and others, whose judgments in such
matters cried in the top of mine°) an excellent play, well
digested in the scenes, set down with as much modesty as
cunning.° I remember one said there were no sallets.° In the
420   lines, to make the matter savoury, nor no matter in the
phrase that might indict the author of° affection, but called
it an honest method, as wholesome as sweet, and by very
much more handsome than fine:° one speech in't I chiefly
loved, 'twas Aeneas' tale to Dido, and thereabout of it
425   especially where he speaks of Priam's slaughter.° If it live in
your memory begin at this line, let me see, let me see:
    "The rugged Pyrrhus,° like th'Hyrcanian beast'°—
'tis not so: it begins with Pyrrhus—
    "The rugged Pyrrhus, he whose sable° arms,
430 Black as his purpose, did the night resemble
When he lay couched in th'ominous horse,°
Hath now this dread and black complexion smeared
With heraldy more dismal: head to foot
Now is he total gules,° horridly tricked°
435 With blood of fathers, mothers, daughters, sons,
Baked and impasted° with the parching° streets,
That lend a tyrannous and damnèd light
To their lord's murder. Roasted in wrath and fire,

°403 *valanced:* fringed with a beard. °404 *lady:* boy playing women's role. °406 *chopine:* thick-soled shoe.
°407 *uncurrent:* not legal tender. °408 *ring:* (1) ring enclosing the design on a gold coin (to crack it within the ring
[to steal the gold] made it "uncurrent") (2) sound. °409 *fly . . . see:* undertake any difficulty. °415 *caviary . . .
general:* like caviar, too rich for the general public. °417 *cried . . . mine:* spoke with more authority than mine.
°418–19 *modesty as cunning:* moderation as skill. °421 *indict . . . of:* charge . . . with. °423
handsome than fine: dignified than finely wrought. °425 *Priam's slaughter:* the murder of the King of Troy (as told
in the *Aeneid*). °427 *Pyrrhus:* son of Achilles. *Hyrcanian beast:* tiger noted for fierceness. °429 *sable:* black.
°431 *horse:* the hollow wooden horse used by the Greeks to enter Troy. °434 *gules:* red. *horridly tricked:* horribly
decorated. °436 *impasted:* coagulated. *parching:* because the city was on fire.

And thus o'er-sizèd° with coagulate gore,
With eyes like carbuncles,° the hellish Pyrrhus   440
Old grandsire Priam seeks;"
So proceed you.

POLONIUS: 'Fore God, my lord, well spoken, with good accent and
good discretion.°

1. PLAYER: "Anon he finds him,   445
Striking too short at Greeks, his antique° sword,
Rebellious to his arm, lies where it falls,
Repugnant to command,° unequal matched,
Pyrrhus at Priam drives, in rage strikes wide,
But with the whiff and wind of his fell° sword,   450
Th'unnerved father falls: then senseless Ilium,°
Seeming to feel this blow, with flaming top
Stoops to his base; and with a hideous crash
Takes prisoner Pyrrhus' ear. For lo, his sword
Which was declining on the milky head   455
Of reverend Priam, seemed i'th'air to stick;
So as a painted° tyrant Pyrrhus stood,
And like a neutral to his will and matter,°
Did nothing:
But as we often see, against° some storm,   460
A silence in the heavens, the rack° stand still,
The bold winds speechless, and the orb° below
As hush as death, anon the dreadful thunder
Doth rend the region, so after Pyrrhus' pause,
A rousèd vengeance sets him new awork,   465
And never did the Cyclops'° hammers fall
On Mars's armour, forged for proof eterne,°
With less remorse than Pyrrhus' bleeding sword
Now falls on Priam.
Out, out, thou strumpet Fortune: all you gods,   470
In general synod° take away her power,
Break all the spokes and fellies from her wheel,°
And bowl the round nave° down the hill of heaven
As low as to the fiends."°

POLONIUS: This is too long.   475

HAMLET: It shall to the barber's with your beard; prithee say on: he's
for a jig, or a tale of bawdry, or he sleeps. Say on, come to
Hecuba.

1. PLAYER: "But who, ah woe, had seen the mobled° queen—"

HAMLET: "The mobled queen"?   480

POLONIUS: That's good, "mobled queen" is good.

°439 *o'er-sizèd:* covered over. °440 *carbuncles:* red gems. °444 *discretion:* interpretation. °446 *antique:* ancient.
°448 *Repugnant to command:* refusing to obey its commander. °450 *fell:* savage. °451 *senseless Ilium:* unfeeling Troy.
°457 *painted:* pictured. °458 *like . . . matter:* unmoved by either his purpose or its achievement. °460 *against:* before.
°461 *rack:* clouds. °462 *orb:* earth. °466 *Cyclops:* workmen of Vulcan, armorer of the gods. °467 *for proof eterne:*
to be eternally invincible. °471 *synod:* assembly. °472 *fellies . . . wheel:* curved pieces of the rim of the wheel that
fortune turns, representing a man's fortunes. °473 *nave:* hub. °474 *fiends:* i.e., of hell. °479 *mobled:* muffled in a scarf.

1. PLAYER: "Run barefoot up and down, threat'ning the flames
    With bissom rheum,° a clout° upon that head
    Where late the diadem stood, and for a robe,
485   About her lank and all o'er-teemèd° loins,
    A blanket in the alarm of fear caught up—
    Who this had seen, with tongue in venom steeped,
    'Gainst Fortune's state° would treason have pronounced;
    But if the gods themselves did see her then,
490   When she saw Pyrrhus make malicious sport
    In mincing with his sword her husband's limbs,
    The instant burst of clamour that she made,
    Unless things mortal move them not at all,
    Would have made milch° the burning eyes of heaven,
495   And passion in the gods."
POLONIUS: Look where° he has not turned° his colour, and has tears in's
    eyes, prithee no more.
HAMLET: 'Tis well, I'll have thee speak out the rest of this soon.
    Good my lord, will you see the players well bestowed,° do
500   you hear, let them be well used, for they are the abstract°
    and brief chronicles° of the time; after your death you were
    better have a bad epitaph than their ill report while you
    live.
POLONIUS: My lord, I will use them according to their desert.°
505 **HAMLET:** God's bodkin° man, much better. Use every man after° his
    desert, and who shall 'scape whipping? Use them after
    you own honour and dignity: the less they deserve, the
    more merit is in your bounty. Take them in.
POLONIUS: Come sirs.
                           Exeunt POLONIUS and PLAYERS.
510 **HAMLET:** Follow him friends, we'll hear a play tomorrow; [*Stops the*
    FIRST PLAYER.] dost thou hear me, old friend, can you play
    The Murder of Gonzago?
1. PLAYER: Ay my lord.
HAMLET: We'll ha't tomorrow night. You could for a need° study a
515   speech of some dozen or sixteen lines, which I would set
    down and insert in't, could you not?
1. PLAYER: Ay my lord.
HAMLET: Very well, follow that lord, and look you mock him not.

                                        [*Exit FIRST PLAYER.*]

    [*To ROSENCRANTZ and GUILDENSTERN.*] My good friends, I'll
520   leave you till night, you are welcome to Elsinore.
ROSENCRANTZ: Good my lord.

                     [*Exeunt ROSENCRANTZ and GUILDENSTERN.*]

°483 *bissom rheum:* binding tears. *clout:* cloth. °485 *o'er-teemèd:* worn out by excessive childbearing. °488 *state:* reign. °494 *milch:* milky, moist. °496 *where:* whether. *turned:* changed. °499 *bestowed:* lodged. °500 *abstract:* summary (noun). °501 *brief chronicles:* history in brief. °504 *desert:* merit. °505 *God's bodkin:* God's little body, the communion wafer (an oath). *after:* according to. °514 *for a need:* if necessary.

HAMLET: Ay so, God bye to you.—Now I am alone.
O what a rogue and peasant slave am I.
Is it not monstrous that this player here,
But in a fiction, in a dream of passion,°   525
Could force his soul so to his own conceit°
That from her working all his visage wanned,°
Tears in his eyes, distraction in his aspect,
A broken voice, and his whole function° suiting
With forms° to his conceit; and all for nothing,   530
For Hecuba!
What's Hecuba to him, or he to Hecuba,
That he should weep for her? what would he do,
Had he the motive and the cue for passion
That I have? he would drown the stage with tears,   535
And cleave the general ear° with horrid speech,
Make mad the guilty and appal the free,°
Confound° the ignorant, and amaze indeed
The very faculties of eyes and ears; yet I,
A dull and muddy-mettled° rascal, peak°   540
Like John-a-dreams,° unpregnant of° my cause,
And can say nothing; no, not for a king,
Upon whose property and most dear life,
A damned defeat was made: am I a coward?
Who calls me villain, breaks my pate° across,   545
Plucks off my beard° and blows it in my face,
Tweaks me by the nose, gives me the lie i'th'throat
As deep as to the lungs,° who does me this?
Ha, 'swounds,° I should take it; for it cannot be
But I am pigeon-livered,° and lack gall   550
To make oppression bitter, or ere this
I should ha' fatted all the region kites°
With this slave's offal: bloody, bawdy villain,
Remorseless, treacherous, lecherous, kindless° villain!
O vengeance!   555
Why what an ass am I, this is most brave,°
That I, the son of a dear father murdered,
Prompted to my revenge by heaven and hell,
Must like a whore unpack my heart with words,
And fall a-cursing like a very drab,°   560
A scullion,° fie upon't, foh.
About, my brains; hum, I have heard,
That guilty creatures sitting at a play,
Have by the very cunning of the scene
Been struck so to the soul, that presently°   565

°525 *dream of passion:* portrayal of emotion. °526 *conceit:* imagination. °527 *wanned:* grew pale. °529 *function:* bearing. °530 *With forms:* in appearance. °536 *general ear:* ears of all in the audience. °537 *free:* innocent. °538 *Confound:* confuse. °540 *muddy-mettled:* dull-spirited. *peak:* pine, mope. °541 *John-a-dreams:* a daydreaming fellow. *unpregnant of:* unstirred by. °545 *pate:* head. °546 *Plucks . . . beard:* a way of giving insult. °547–48 *gives . . . lungs:* insults me by calling me a liar of the worst kind (the lungs being deeper than the throat). °549 *'swounds:* God's wounds. °550 *pigeon-livered:* meek and uncouraging. °552 *region kites:* vultures of the upper air. °554 *kindless:* unnatural. °556 *brave:* fine. °560 *drab:* whore. °561 *scullion:* kitchen wench. °565 *presently:* immediately.

They have proclaimed their malefactions:
For murder, though it have no tongue, will speak
With most miraculous organ: I'll have these players
Play something like the murder of my father

570   Before mine uncle, I'll observe his looks,
I'll tent° him to the quick, if a' do blench°
I know my course. The spirit that I have seen
May be a devil, and the devil hath power
T'assume a pleasing shape, yea, and perhaps

575   Out of my weakness, and my melancholy,
As he is very potent with such spirits,
Abuses me to damn me; I'll have grounds
More relative than this: the play's the thing
Wherein I'll catch the conscience of the king.   *Exit.*

ACT 3

Scene 1. [A room in the castle]

Enter KING, QUEEN, POLONIUS, OPHELIA, ROSENCRANTZ, GUILDENSTERN, LORDS.

KING: And can you by no drift of conference°
Get from him why he puts on this confusion,°
Grating so harshly all his days of quiet
With turbulent and dangerous lunacy?

5   **ROSENCRANTZ:** He does confess he feels himself distracted,
But from what cause, a' will by no means speak.

GUILDENSTERN: Nor do we find him forward to be sounded,°
But with a crafty madness keeps aloof
When we would bring him on to some confession
Of his true state.

10   **QUEEN:**   Did he receive you well?

ROSENCRANTZ: Most like a gentleman.

GUILDENSTERN: But with much forcing of his disposition.°

ROSENCRANTZ: Niggard of question,° but of our demands
Most free in his reply.

QUEEN: Did you assay° him

15   To any pastime?

ROSENCRANTZ: Madam, it so fell out that certain players
We o'er-raught° on the way: of these we told him,
And there did seem in him a kind of joy
To hear of it: they are here about the court,

20   And as I think, they have already order
This night to play before him.

POLONIUS: 'Tis most true,
And he beseeched me to entreat your majesties
To hear and see the matter.°

°571 *tent*: probe. *blench*: An "askance and strange . . ." look (Sonnet 110, line 6). 1 *drift of conference*: turn of conversation. °2 *puts . . . confusion*: seems so distracted ("puts on" indicates the king's private suspicion that Hamlet is playing mad). °7 *forward . . . sounded*: disposed to be sounded out. °12 *forcing . . . disposition*: forcing himself to be so. °13 *Niggard of question*: unwilling to talk. °14 *assay*: tempt. °17 *o'er-raught*: overtook. °24 *matter*: i.e., of the play.

KING: With all my heart, and it doth much content me   25
    To hear him so inclined.
    Good gentlemen, give him a further edge,°
    And drive his purpose into these delights.
ROSENCRANTZ: We shall my lord.   [*Exeunt* ROSENCRANTZ *and* GUILDENSTERN.]
KING: Sweet Gertrude, leave us too,
    For we have closely° sent for Hamlet hither,   30
    That he, as 'twere by accident, may here
    Affront° Ophelia;
    Her father and myself, lawful espials,°
    Will so bestow° ourselves, that seeing unseen,
    We may of their encounter frankly° judge,   35
    And gather by him as he is behaved,
    If't be th'affliction of his love or no
    That thus he suffers for.
QUEEN: I shall obey you.
    And for your part Ophelia, I do wish
    That your good beauties be the happy cause   40
    Of Hamlet's wildness, so shall I hope your virtues
    Will bring him to his wonted° way again,
    To both your honours.
OPHELIA: Madam, I wish it may.   [*Exit* QUEEN.]
POLONIUS: Ophelia, walk you here—Gracious,° so please you,
    We will bestow ourselves—read on this book,°   45
    That show of such an exercise° may colour°
    Your loneliness; we are oft to blame in this,
    'Tis too much proved,° that with devotion's visage
    And pious action, we do sugar o'er
    The devil himself.
KING: [*Aside.*] O 'tis too true,°   50
    How smart a lash that speech doth give my conscience.
    The harlot's cheek, beautied with plast'ring art,
    Is not more ugly to° the thing that helps it,
    Than is my deed to my most painted word:°
    O heavy burden!   55
POLONIUS: I hear him coming, let's withdraw my lord.

                                    Exeunt.

Enter HAMLET.
HAMLET: To be, or not to be, that is the question,
    Whether 'tis nobler in the mind° to suffer
    The slings and arrows of outrageous fortune,
    Or to take arms against a sea of troubles,   60

°27 *give . . . edge:* encourage his keen interest. °30 *closely:* secretly. °32 *Affront:* meet face to face with. °33 *espials:* spies. °34, 45 *bestow:* place. °35 *frankly:* freely. °42 *wonted:* customary. °44 *Gracious:* i.e., Your Grace. °45 *book:* (of prayer). °46 *exercise:* religious exercise. *colour:* make plausible. °48 *'Tis . . . proved:* it is all too apparent. °50 *'tis too true:* the king's first indication that he is guilty. °53 *to:* compared to. °52–54 *harlot's cheek . . . word:* just as the harlot's cheek is even uglier by contrast to the makeup that tries to beautify it, so my deed is uglier by contrast to the hypocritical words under which I hide it. °58 *nobler in the mind:* best, according to "sovereign" reason.

And by opposing, end them: to die, to sleep,
No more; and by a sleep, to say we end
The heart-ache, and the thousand natural shocks
That flesh is heir to; 'tis a consummation
65   Devoutly to be wished. To die, to sleep,
To sleep, perchance to dream, ay there's the rub,°
For in that sleep of death what dreams may come
When we have shuffled off this mortal coil°
Must give us pause—there's the respect°
70   That makes calamity of so long life:°
For who would bear the whips and scorns of time,
Th'oppressor's wrong, the proud man's contumely,°
The pangs of disprized love, the law's delay,°
The insolence of office,° and the spurns
75   That patient merit of th'unworthy takes,
When he himself might his quietus° make
With a bare bodkin;° who would fardels° bear,
To grunt and sweat under a weary life,
But that the dread of something after death,
80   The undiscovered° country, from whose bourn°
No traveler returns, puzzles the will,
And makes us rather bear those ills we have,
Than fly to others that we know not of.
Thus conscience does make cowards of us all,
85   And thus the native hue° of resolution
Is sicklied o'er with the pale cast of thought,
And enterprises of great pitch° and moment,°
With this regard° their currents turn awry,°
And lose the name of action. Soft you now,
90   The fair Ophelia—Nymph, in thy orisons°
Be all my sins remembered.
OPHELIA: Good my lord,
How does your honour for this many a day.°
HAMLET: I humbly thank you: well, well, well.
OPHELIA: My lord, I have remembrances of yours
95   That I have longèd long to re-deliver,
I pray you now receive them.
HAMLET: No, not I,
I never gave you aught.
OPHELIA: My honoured lord, you know right well you did,
And with them words of so sweet breath° composed
100   As made the things more rich: their perfume lost,
Take these again, for to the noble mind

°66 *rub:* obstacle. °68 *mortal coil:* (1) turmoil of mortal life (2) coil of flesh encircling the body. °69 *respect:* consideration. °70 *makes calamity of so long life:* makes living long a calamity. °72 *contumely:* contempt. °73 *law's delay:* longevity of lawsuits. °74 *office:* officials. °76 *quietus:* settlement of his debt.   °77 *bare bodkin:* mere dagger. *fardels:* burdens. °78 *undiscovered:* unknown, unexplored. *bourn:* boundary. °85 *native hue:* natural complexion. °87 *pitch:* height, excellence. *moment:* importance. °88 *regard:* consideration. *their currents turn awry:* change their course. °90 *orisons:* prayers (referring to her prayer book). °92 *this . . . day:* all these days. °99 *breath:* speech.

Rich gifts wax° poor when givers prove unkind.
There my lord.
HAMLET: Ha, ha, are you honest°?
OPHELIA: My lord.   105
HAMLET: Are you fair°?
OPHELIA: What means your lordship?
HAMLET: That if you be honest and fair, your honesty should admit
no discourse to your beauty.°
OPHELIA: Could beauty my lord, have better commerce than with   110
honesty?
HAMLET: Ay truly, for the power of beauty will sooner transform
honesty° from what it is to a bawd,° than the force of
honesty can translate beauty into his likeness. This was
sometime° a paradox, but now the time gives it proof. I did   115
love you once.
OPHELIA: Indeed my lord, you made me believe so.
HAMLET: You should not have believed me, for virtue cannot so
inoculate our old stock, but we shall relish of it.° I loved you not.
OPHELIA: I was the more deceived.   120
HAMLET: Get thee to a nunnery,° why wouldst thou be a breeder of
sinners? I am myself indifferent honest,° but yet I could
accuse me of such things, that it were better my mother
had not borne me: I am very proud, revengeful, ambitious,
with more offences at my beck,° than I have thoughts   125
to put them in, imagination to give them shape, or time to
act them in: what should such fellows as I do, crawling
between earth and heaven? we are arrant° knaves all,
believe none of us, go thy ways to a nunnery. Where's
your father?   130
OPHELIA: At home my lord.
HAMLET: Let the doors be shut upon him, that he may play the fool
nowhere but in's own house. Farewell.
OPHELIA: O help him, you sweet heavens.
HAMLET: If thou dost marry, I'll give thee this plague° for thy dowry: 135
be thou as chaste as ice, as pure as snow, thou shalt not
escape calumny; get thee to a nunnery, go, farewell. Or if
thou wilt needs marry, marry a fool, for wise men know
well enough what monsters° you make of them: to a nunnery
go, and quickly too, farewell.   140
OPHELIA: O heavenly powers, restore him.
HAMLET: I have heard of your paintings too, well enough. God hath
given you one face, and you make yourselves another: you

°102 *wax:* grow. °104 *honest:* (1) chaste (2) truthful. °106 *fair:* (1) beautiful (2) honorable. °108–09 *admit . . . beauty:* (1) not allow communication with your beauty (2) not allow your beauty to be used as a trap (Hamlet may have overheard the Polonius-Claudius plot or spotted their movement behind the arras). °113 *honesty:* chastity. *bawd:* procurer, pimp. °115 *sometime:* once. °119 *inoculate . . . it:* change our sinful nature (as a tree is grafted to improve it) but we will keep our old taste (as will the fruit of the grafted tree). °121 *nunnery:* (1) cloister (2) slang for "brothel" (cf. "bawd" above). °122 *indifferent honest:* reasonably virtuous. °125 *beck:* beckoning. °128 *arrant:* absolute. °135 *plague:* curse. °139 *monsters:* horned cuckolds (men whose wives were unfaithful).

145

jig,° you amble, and you lisp,° you nick-name God's
creatures, and make your wantonness your ignorance,° go to,
I'll no more on't, it hath made me mad. I say we will have
no moe° marriage. Those that are married already, all but
one shall live, the rest shall keep as they are: to a nunnery,
go.   *Exit* HAMLET.

150

OPHELIA: O what a noble mind is here o'erthrown!
The courtier's, soldier's, scholar's, eye, tongue, sword,
Th'expectancy and rose° of the fair state,
The glass° of fashion, and the mould of form,°
Th'observed of all observers, quite quite down,

155

And I of ladies most deject and wretched,
That sucked the honey of his music vows,
Now see that noble and most sovereign° reason
Like sweet bells jangled, out of tune and harsh,
That unmatched form and feature° of blown° youth

160

Blasted with ecstasy,° O woe is me,
T'have seen what I have seen, see what I see.

Enter KING *and* POLONIUS.

KING: Love? his affections° do not that way tend,
Nor what he spake, though it lacked form a little,
Was not like madness. There's something in his soul

165

O'er which his melancholy sits on brood,
And I do doubt,° the hatch and the disclose°
Will be some danger; which for to prevent,
I have in quick determination
Thus set it down: he shall with speed to England,

170

For the demand of our neglected° tribute:
Haply° the seas, and countries different,
With variable° objects, shall expel
This something°-settled matter in his heart,
Whereon his brains still beating puts him thus

175

From fashion of himself.° What think you on't?

POLONIUS: It shall do well. But yet do I believe
The origin and commencement of his grief
Sprung from neglected° love. How now Ophelia?
You need not tell us what Lord Hamlet said,

180

We heard it all. My lord, do as you please,
But if you hold it fit, after the play,
Let his queen-mother all alone entreat him
To show his grief, let her be round° with him,
And I'll be placed (so please you) in the ear

°144 *jig:* walk in a mincing way. *lisp:* put on affected speech. °145 *make your . . . ignorance:* excuse your caprices
as being due to ignorance. °147 *moe:* more. °152 *expectancy and rose:* fair hope. °153 *glass:* mirror. *mould of form:*
model of manners. °157 *sovereign:* because it should rule. °159 *feature:* external appearance. *blown:* flowering.
°160 *Blasted with ecstasy:* blighted by madness. °162 *affections:* emotions, afflictions. °165–66 *on brood . . . hatch
. . . disclose:* metaphor of a hen sitting on eggs. °166 *doubt:* fear. °170 *neglected:* being unpai. °171 *Haply:* perhaps.
°172 *variable:* varied. °173 *something:* somewhat-. °175 *fashion of himself:* his usual self. °178 *neglected:* unrequited.
°183 *round:* direct.

Of° all their conference. If she find° him not,   185
To England send him: or confine him where
Your wisdom best shall think.
KING: It shall be so,
Madness in great ones must not unwatched go.   *EXEUNT.*

Scene 2. [A hall in the castle]

Enter HAMLET and three of the PLAYERS.

HAMLET: Speak the speech° I pray you as I pronounced it to you,
trippingly on the tongue, but if you mouth it° as many of
your players do, I had as lief the town-crier spoke my
lines. Nor do not saw the air too much with your hand
thus, but use all gently, for in the very torrent, tempest,   5
and as I may say, whirlwind of your passion, you must
acquire and beget° a temperance that may give it smoothness.
O it offends me to the soul, to hear a robustious°
periwig-pated° fellow tear a passion to tatters, to very rags,
to split the ears of the groundlings,° who for the most part   10
are capable of° nothing but inexplicable dumb shows° and
noise: I would have such a fellow whipped for o'erdoing
Termagant.° It out-herods Herod,° pray you avoid it.
1. PLAYER: I warrant you honour.
HAMLET: Be not too tame neither, but let your own discretion be   15
your tutor, suit the action to the word, the word to the
action, with this special observance, that you o'erstep not
the modesty° of nature: for any thing so o'erdone, is from°
the purpose of playing, whose end both at the first, and
now, was and is, to hold as 'twere the mirror up to nature,   20
to show virtue her own feature, scorn° her own image, and
the very age and body of the time his form and pressure.°
Now this overdone, or come tardy off,° though it make the
unskilful° laugh, cannot but make the judicious grieve, the
censure of the which one,° must in your allowance°   25
o'erweigh a whole theatre of others. O there be players
that I have seen play, and heard others praise, and that
highly (not to speak it profanely) that neither having
th'accent of Christians, nor the gait of Christian, pagan,
nor man, have so strutted and bellowed, that I have   30
thought some of nature's journeymen° had made men, and
not made them well, they imitated humanity so
abominably.

°184–85 *in the ear Of:* so as to overhear. °186 *find:* find out. °1 *the speech:* i.e., that Hamlet has inserted. °2 *mouth it:* deliver it slowly and overdramatically. °7 *acquire and beget:* achieve for yourself and instill in other actors. °8 *robustious:* boisterous. °9 *periwig-pated:* wig-wearing. °10 *groundlings:* audience who paid least and stood on the ground floor. °11 *capable of:* able to understand. *dumb shows:* pantomimed synopses of the action to follow. °13 *Termagant:* violent, ranting character in the guild or mystery plays. *out-herods Herod:* outdoes even Herod, King of Judea, who commanded the slaughter of the Innocents and who was a ranting tyrant in the Corpus Christi plays. See p. 975. °18 *modesty:* moderation. *from:* away from. °21 *scorn:* that which should be scorned. °22 *age . . . pressure:* shape of the times in its accurate impression. °23 *come tardy off:* understated, underdone. °24 *unskilful:* unsophisticated. °25 *one:* the judicious. *allowance:* estimation. °31 *journeymen:* artisans working for others and not yet masters of their trades.

1. PLAYER: I hope we have reformed that indifferently° with us, sir.

35 **HAMLET:** O reform it altogether, and let those that play your clowns
speak no more than is set down for them,° for there be of
them that will themselves laugh, to set on some quantity
of barren° spectators to laugh too, though in the meantime,
some necessary question° of the play be then to be considered:

40 that's villainous, and shows a most pitiful ambition
in the fool that uses it. Go make you ready.   *Exeunt PLAYERS.*

Enter POLONIUS, ROSENCRANTZ, and GUILDENSTERN.

How now my lord, will the king hear this piece of work?
POLONIUS: And the queen too, and that presently.
HAMLET: Bid the players make haste.   *Exit POLONIUS.*

45 Will you two help to hasten them?
ROSENCRANTZ: Ay my lord.   *Exeunt they two.*
HAMLET: What ho, Horatio!

Enter HORATIO.

HORATIO: Here sweet lord, at your service.
HAMLET: Horatio, thou art e'en as just° a man

50 As e'er my conversation coped withal.°
HORATIO: O my dear lord.
HAMLET: Nay, do not think I flatter,
For what advancement may I hope from thee,
That no revenue hast but thy good spirits
To feed and clothe thee? Why should the poor be flattered?

55 No, let the candied° tongue lick° absurd pomp,
And crook the pregnant° hinges of the knee
Where thrift may follow fawning.° Dost thou hear,
Since my dear soul was mistress of her choice,
And could of men distinguish her election,°

60 Sh'hath sealed° thee for herself, for thou hast been
As one in suff'ring all that suffers nothing,
A man that Fortune's buffets° and rewards
Hast ta'en with equal thanks; and blest are those
Whose blood° and judgment are so well co-mingled,

65 That they are not a pipe for Fortune's finger
To sound what stop° she please.° Give me that man
That is not passion's slave, and I will wear him
In my heart's core, ay in my heart of heart,
As I do thee. Something too much of this.

70 There is a play tonight before the king,
One scene of it comes near the circumstance

°34 *indifferently:* reasonably well. °36 *speak no more . . . them:* stick to their lines. 38 *barren:* witless. °39 *question:*
dialogue. °49 *just:* well balanced. °50 *coped withal:* had to do with. °55–57 *candied . . . fawning:* metaphor of a
dog licking and fawning for candy. °55 *candied:* flattering. *lick:* pay court to. °56 *pregnant:* quick in motion.
°56–57 *crook . . . fawning:* obsequiously kneel when personal profit may ensue. °59 *election:* choice. °60 *sealed:* confirmed.
°62 *buffets:* blows. °64 *blood:* passions. °66 *sound . . . please:* play whatever tune she likes. *stop:* finger hole in wind
instrument for varying the sound.

Which I have told thee of my father's death.
I prithee when thou seest that act afoot,
Even with the very comment° of thy soul
Observe my uncle: if his occulted° guilt   75
Do not itself unkennel° in one speech,
It is a damnèd ghost° that we have seen,
And my imaginations are as foul
As Vulcan's stithy,° give him heedful note,
For I mine eyes will rivet to his face,   80
And after we will both our judgments join
In censure of his seeming.°
HORATIO: Well my lord,
If a' steal aught the whilst this play is playing,
And 'scape detecting, I will pay° the theft.   *Sound a flourish.*
HAMLET: They are coming to the play. I must be idle,°   85
Get you a place.

*Enter trumpets and kettledrums, KING, QUEEN, POLONIUS, OPHELIA, ROSENCRANTZ, GUILDENSTERN,
and other LORDS attendant, with his GUARD carrying torches. Danish March.*

KING: How fares° our cousin Hamlet?
HAMLET: Excellent i'faith, of the chameleon's dish: I eat the air,°
promise-crammed, you cannot feed capons so.°
KING: I have nothing with° this answer Hamlet, these words are   90
not mine.°
HAMLET: No, nor mine now. [*To POLONIUS.*] My lord, you played
once i'th'university you say?
POLONIUS: That did I my lord, and was accounted a good actor.
HAMLET: What did you enact?   95
POLONIUS: I did enact Julius Caesar, I was killed i'th'Capitol, Brutus
killed me.
HAMLET: It was a brute part of him to kill so capital a calf there. Be
the players ready?
ROSENCRANTZ: Ay my lord, they stay upon your patience.°   100
QUEEN: Come hither my dear Hamlet, sit by me.
HAMLET: No, good mother, here's metal more attractive.°
POLONIUS: [*To the KING.*] O ho, do you mark that?
HAMLET: Lady, shall I lie in your lap?
OPHELIA: No my lord.   105
HAMLET: I mean, my head upon your lap?
OPHELIA: Ay my lord.
HAMLET: Do you think I meant country° matters?

°74 *very comment:* acutest observation. °75 *occulted:* hidden. °76 *unkennel:* force from hiding. °77 *damnèd ghost:*
devil (not the ghost of my father). °79 *Vulcan's stithy:* the forge of the blacksmith of the gods. °82 *censure . . .
seeming:* (1) judgment of his appearance (2) disapproval of his pretending. °84 *pay:* i.e., for. °85 *be idle:* act mad.
°87 *fares:* does, but Hamlet takes it to mean "eats" or "dines." °88 *eat the air:* the chameleon supposedly ate air,
but Hamlet also puns on "heir." °89 *you cannot . . . so:* (1) even a capon cannot feed on air and your promises (2)
like a capon stuffed with food before being killed, I am stuffed (fed up) with your promises. °90 *nothing with:*
nothing to do with. °91 *not mine:* not in answer to my question. °100 *stay . . . patience:* await your permission.
°102 *metal more attractive:* (1) iron more magnetic (2) stuff ("mettle") more beautiful. °108 *country:* rustic, sexual
(with a pun on a slang word for the female sexual organ).

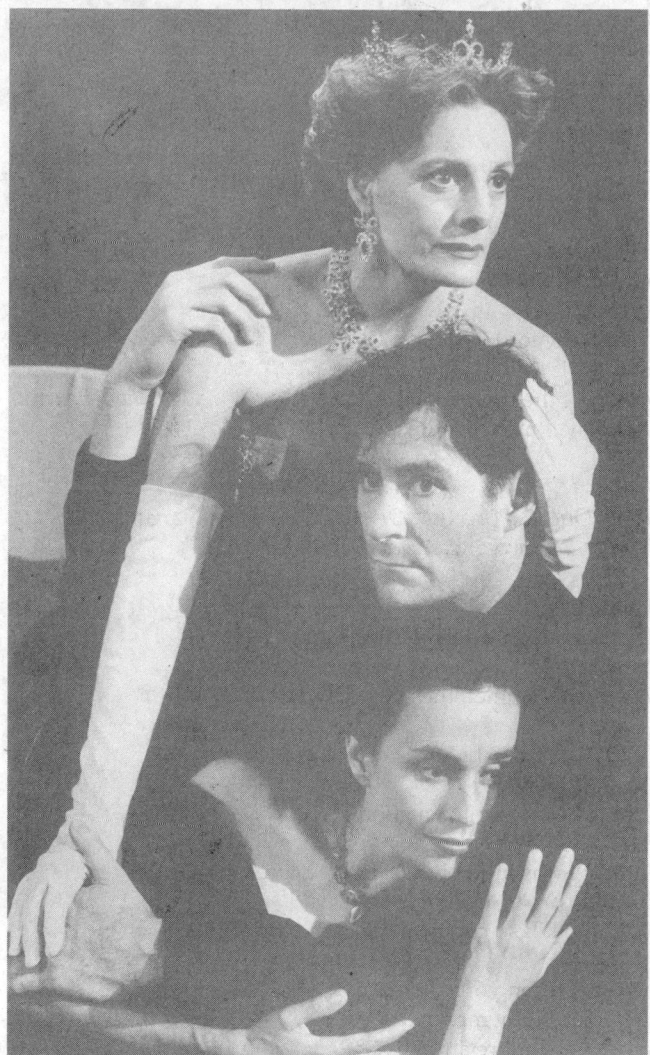

Hamlet (played by Kevin Kline), Queen Gertrude (played by Dana Ivy), and Ophelia (played by Diane Venora) in the New York Shakespeare Festival production of *Hamlet* (1990), directed by Mr. Kline for the Public Broadcasting System.

OPHELIA:	I think nothing my lord.
110 **HAMLET:**	That's a fair thought to lie between maids' legs.
OPHELIA:	What is, my lord?
HAMLET:	Nothing.
OPHELIA:	You are merry my lord.
HAMLET:	Who, I?
115 **OPHELIA:**	Ay my lord.
HAMLET:	O God, your only jig-maker: what should a man do but be merry, for look you how cheerfully my mother looks, and my father died within's two hours.
OPHELIA:	Nay, 'tis twice two months my lord.
120 **HAMLET:**	So long? Nay then let the devil wear black, for I'll have a suit of sables,° O heavens, die two months ago, and not

---

°121 *sables:* (1) rich fur (2) black mourning garb.

forgotten yet? Then there's hope a great man's memory
may outlive his life half a year, but by'r lady° a' must build
churches then, or else shall a' suffer not thinking on,° with
the hobby-horse,° whose epitaph is "For O, for O, the   125
hobby-horse is forgot."

The trumpets sound. Dumb Show° follows. Enter a King and a Queen, very lovingly, the Queen
embracing him, and he her. She kneels and makes show of protestation unto him. He takes her up,
and declines his head upon her neck. He lies him down upon a bank of flowers; she seeing him asleep
leaves him: anon comes in another man, takes off his crown, kisses it, pours poison in the sleeper's
ears, and leaves him: the Queen returns, finds the King dead, and makes passionate action. The poi-
soner with some three or four mutes° comes in again, seeming to condole with her. The dead body is
carried away. The poisoner wooes the Queen with gifts: she seems harsh and unwilling awhile, but
in the end accepts his love.

                                                              Exeunt.

OPHELIA: What means this, my lord?
HAMLET: Marry, this is miching mallecho,° it means mischief.
OPHELIA: Belike this show imports the argument° of the play.

Enter PROLOGUE.

HAMLET: We shall know by this fellow: the players cannot keep   130
     counsel,° they'll tell all.
OPHELIA: Will a' tell us what this show meant?
HAMLET: Ay, or any show that you will show him. Be not you ashamed to show, he'll not
     shame to tell you what it means.
OPHELIA: You are naught,° you are naught, I'll mark the play.   135
PROLOGUE: For us and for our tragedy,
     Here stooping to your clemency,
     We beg your hearing patiently.   [*Exit.*]
HAMLET: Is this a prologue, or the posy° of a ring?
OPHELIA: 'Tis brief, my lord.   140
HAMLET: As woman's love.

Enter PLAYER KING *and* QUEEN.

PLAYER KING: Full thirty times hath Phoebus' cart° gone round
     Neptune's salt wash,° and Tellus' orbèd ground,°
     And thirty dozen moons with borrowed sheen
     About the world have times twelve thirties been,   145
     Since love our hearts, and Hymen° did our hands
     Unite commutual,° in most sacred bands.
PLAYER QUEEN: So many journeys may the sun and moon
     Make us again count o'er ere love be done,

°123 *by'r lady*: by Our Lady (the Virgin Mary). °124 *not thinking on*: being forgotten. °125 *hobby-horse*: (1) character in the May games (2) slang for "prostitute." °126 S.D.: *Dumb Show*: pantomimed synopsis of the action to
follow. °126 S.D.: *mutes*: actors without speaking parts. °128 *miching mallecho*: skulking mischief. °129 *imports the*
argument: signifies the plot. °131 *counsel*: a secret. °135 *naught*: naughty, lewd. °139 *posy*: motto (engraved in a ring).
°142 *Phoebus' cart*: chariot of the sun. °143 *wash*: sea. *Tellus . . . ground*: the earth (Tellus was a Roman earth goddess).
°146 *Hymen*: Roman god of marriage. °147 *commutual*: mutually.

150   But woe is me, you are so sick of late,
       So far from cheer, and from your former state,
       That I distrust you:° yet though I distrust,
       Discomfort you, my lord, it nothing must.
       For women fear too much, even as they love,
155   And women's fear and love hold quantity,°
       In neither aught, or in extremity:°
       Now what my love is, proof° hath made you know,
       And as my love is sized, my fear is so.
       Where love is great, the littlest doubts are fear,
160   Where little fears grow great, great love grows there.
PLAYER KING: Faith, I must leave thee love, and shortly too,
       My operant° powers their functions leave° to do,
       And thou shalt live in this fair world behind,
       Honoured, beloved, and haply° one as kind
165   For husband shalt thou—.
PLAYER QUEEN: O confound the rest:
       Such love must needs be treason in my breast.
       In second husband let me be accurst,
       None wed the second, but who killed the first.
HAMLET: [*Aside.*] That's wormwood,° wormwood.
170 **PLAYER QUEEN:** The instances° that second marriage move°
       Are base respects of thrift,° but none of love.
       A second time I kill my husband dead,
       When second husband kisses me in bed.
PLAYER KING: I do believe you think what now you speak,
175   But what we do determine, oft we break:
       Purpose is but the slave to memory
       Of violent birth but poor validity.°
       Which now like fruit unripe sticks on the tree,
       But fall unshaken when they mellow be.
180   Most necessary 'tis that we forget
       To pay ourselves what to ourselves is debt.°
       What to ourselves in passion we propose,
       The passion ending, doth the purpose lose.
       The violence of either grief or joy
185   Their own enactures° with themselves destroy:
       Where joy most revels, grief doth most lament;
       Grief joys, joy grieves, on slender accident.
       This world is not for aye,° nor 'tis not strange
       That even our loves should with our fortunes change:
190   For 'tis a question left us yet to prove,
       Whether love lead fortune, or else fortune love.°
       The great man down, you mark his favourite flies,
       The poor advanced, makes friends of enemies:

°152 *distrust you:* am worried about you. °155 *quantity:* proportion. °156 *In neither . . . extremity:* their love and fear are either absent or excessive. °157 *proof:* experience. °162 *operant:* vital. *leave:* cease. °164 *haply:* perhaps. °169 *wormwood:* bitter (like the herb). °170 *instances:* causes. *move:* motivate. °171 *respects of thrift:* consideration of profit. °177 *validity:* strength. °180–81 *Most ... debt:* we are easy creditors to ourselves and forget our former promises (debts). °185 *enactures:* fulfillments. °188 *aye:* ever. °191 *fortune love:* fortune lead love.

And hitherto doth love on fortune tend,
For who not needs, shall never lack a friend,   195
And who in want a hollow friend doth try,
Directly seasons him° his enemy.
But orderly to end where I begun,
Our wills and fates do so contrary run,
That our devices still° are overthrown,   200
Our thoughts are ours, their ends none of our own.
So think thou wilt no second husband wed,
But die thy thoughts when thy first lord is dead.
PLAYER QUEEN: Nor earth to me give food, nor heaven light,
Sport and repose lock from me day and night,   205
To desperation turn my trust and hope,
An anchor's° cheer in prison be my scope,
Each opposite that blanks° the face of joy,
Meet what I would have well, and it destroy,
Both here and hence° pursue me lasting strife,   210
If once a widow, ever I be wife.
HAMLET: If she should break it now.
PLAYER KING: 'Tis deeply sworn: sweet, leave me here awhile,
My spirits grow dull, and fain° I would beguile
The tedious day with sleep.   *Sleeps.*   215
PLAYER QUEEN: Sleep rock thy brain.
And never come mischance between us twain.   *Exit.*
HAMLET: Madam, how like you this play?
QUEEN: The lady doth protest too much methinks.
HAMLET: O but she'll keep her word.
KING: Have you heard the argument?° Is there no offence in't? 220
HAMLET: No, no, they do but jest, poison in jest, no offence
i'th'world.
KING: What do you call the play?
HAMLET: The Mouse-trap. Marry, how? Tropically:° this play is the
image of a murder done in Vienna: Gonzago is the duke's   225
name, his wife Baptista, you shall see anon, 'tis a knavish
piece of work, but what of that? Your majesty, and we
that have free° souls, it touches us not: let the galled jade
winch,° our withers are unwrung.°

Enter LUCIANUS.

This is one Lucianus, nephew to the king.   230
OPHELIA: You are as good as a chorus,° my lord.
HAMLET: I could interpret between you and your love, if I could see
the puppets dallying.
OPHELIA: You are keen my lord, you are keen.°

°197 *seasons him:* causes him to become. °200 *devices still:* plans always. °207 *anchor's:* hermit's. °208 *opposite that blanks:* contrary event that pales. °210 *here and hence:* in this world and the next. °214 *fain:* gladly. °220 *argument:* plot. °224 *Tropically:* figuratively. °228 *free:* innocent. °228–29 *galled jade winch:* chafed old horse wince (from its sores). °231 *chorus:* actor who introduced the action. °229 *withers are unwrung:* (1) shoulders are unchafed (2) consciences are clear. °234 *keen:* (1) sharp (Ophelia's meaning) (2) sexually excited (Hamlet's interpretation).

235   **HAMLET:** It would cost you a groaning to take off mine edge.

OPHELIA: Still better and worse.°

HAMLET: So you mistake° your husbands. Begin, murderer. Pox,°
leave thy damnable faces° and begin. Come, the croaking
raven doth bellow for revenge.

240   **LUCIANUS:** Thoughts black, hands apt, drugs fit, and time agreeing,
Confederate season, else no creature seeing,°
Thou mixture rank, of midnight weeds collected,
With Hecate's° ban° thrice blasted, thrice infected,
Thy natural magic, and dire property,

245   On wholesome° life usurps immediately.   *Pours the poison in his ears.*

HAMLET: A' poisons him i'th'garden for's estate, his name's Gonzago,
the story is extant, and written in very choice
Italian, you shall see anon how the murderer gets the love
of Gonzago's wife.

250   **OPHELIA:** The king rises.

HAMLET: What, frighted with false fire°?

QUEEN: How fares my lord?

POLONIUS: Give o'er the play.

KING: Give me some light. Away!   *Exeunt all but HAMLET and HORATIO.*

255   **ALL:** Lights, lights, lights!

HAMLET: Why, let the stricken deer go weep,
The hart ungallèd° play,°
For some must watch while some must sleep,
Thus runs the world away.

260   Would not this° sir, and a forest of feathers,° if the rest of my
fortunes turn Turk with° me, with two Provincial roses° on
my razed° shoes, get me a fellowship° in a cry° of players?

HORATIO: Half a share.°

HAMLET: A whole one, I.

265   For thou dost know, O Damon° dear,
This realm dismantled was
Of Jove° himself, and now reigns here
A very very—pajock.°

HORATIO: You might have rhymed.°

270   **HAMLET:** O good Horatio, I'll take the ghost's word for a thousand
pound. Didst perceive?

HORATIO: Very well my lord.

HAMLET: Upon the talk of the poisoning?

HORATIO: I did very well note him.

Enter ROSENCRANTZ and GUILDENSTERN.

°236 *better and worse:* better wit but a worse meaning, with a pun on "better" and "bitter." °237 *mistake:* mis-take.
Pox: a plague on it. °238 *faces:* exaggerated facial expressions. °241 *Confederate . . . seeing:* no one seeing me
except time, my confederate. °243 *Hecate:* goddess of witchcraft. *ban:* evil spell. °245 *wholesome:* healthy. °251 *false
fire:* discharge of blanks (not gunpowder). °256–57 *deer . . . play:* the belief that a wounded deer wept, abandoned by the others. °257 *ungallèd:* unhurt. °260 *this:* i.e., sample (of my theatrical talent). *feathers:* plumes
(worn by actors). °261 *turn Turk with:* cruelly turn against. *Provincial roses:* rosettes named for Provins, France.
°262 *razed:* slashed, decorated with cutouts. *fellowship:* partnership. *cry:* pack, troupe. °263 *share:* divisions of
profits among members of a theatrical production company. °265 *Damon:* legendary ideal friend to Pythias.
°267 *Jove:* Hamlet's father. °268 *pajock:* peacock (associated with lechery). °269 *rhymed:* used "ass" instead of
"pajock."

HAMLET: Ah ha, come, some music. Come, the recorders.°   275
For if the king like not the comedy,
Why then belike he likes it not, perdy.°
Come, some music.

GUILDENSTERN: Good my lord, vouchsafe me a word with you.

HAMLET: Sir, a whole history.   280

GUILDENSTERN: The king, sir—

HAMLET: Ay sir, what of him?

GUILDENSTERN: Is in his retirement, marvellous distempered.

HAMLET: With drink sir?

GUILDENSTERN: No my lord, with choler.°   285

HAMLET: Your wisdom should show itself more richer to signify
this to the doctor: for, for me to put him to his purgation,°
would perhaps plunge him into more choler.

GUILDENSTERN: Good my lord, put your discourse into some frame,° and
start not so wildly from my affair.   290

HAMLET: I am tame sir, pronounce.

GUILDENSTERN: The queen your mother, in most great affliction of spirit,
hath sent me to you.

HAMLET: You are welcome.

GUILDENSTERN: Nay good my lord, this courtesy is not of the right breed.°   295
If it shall please you to make me a wholesome° answer, I
will do your mother's commandment: if not, your pardon°
and my return shall be the end of my business.

HAMLET: Sir I cannot.

ROSENCRANTZ: What, my lord?   300

HAMLET: Make you a wholesome answer: my wit's diseased. But
sir, such answer as I can make, you shall command, or
rather as you say, my mother: therefore no more, but to
the matter. My mother you say.

ROSENCRANTZ: Then thus she says, your behaviour hath struck her into   305
amazement and admiration.°

HAMLET: O wonderful son that can so 'stonish a mother. But is there
no sequel at the heels of this mother's admiration? Impart.

ROSENCRANTZ: She desires to speak with you in her closet°
ere you go to bed.   310

HAMLET: We shall obey, were she ten times our mother. Have you
any further trade with us?

ROSENCRANTZ: My lord, you once did love me.

HAMLET: And do still, by these pickers and stealers.°

ROSENCRANTZ: Good my lord, what is your cause of distemper? You do   315
surely bar the door upon your own liberty, if you deny
your griefs to your friend.°

HAMLET: Sir, I lack advancement.

ROSENCRANTZ: How can that be, when you have the voice° of the king
himself for your succession in Denmark?   320

°275 *recorders:* soft-toned woodwind instruments, similar to flutes. °277 *perdy:* by God (*pardieu*). °285 *choler:* anger.
°287 *purgation:* (1) purging of excessive bile (2) judicial investigations (3) purgatory. °289 *frame:* order.
°295 *breed:* (1) species (2) manners. °296 *wholesome:* reasonable. °297 *pardon:* permission to depart. °306 *admiration:* wonder. °309 *closet:* private room, bedroom. °314 *pickers and stealers:* hands (from the prayer, "Keep my hands from picking and stealing"). °316–17 *deny . . . friend:* refuse to let your friend know the cause of your suffering.
°319 *voice:* vote.

HAMLET: Ay sir, but 'while the grass grows'°—the proverb is
    something musty.°

Enter the PLAYERS *with recorders.*

    O the recorders, let me see one. To withdraw° with you,
    why do you go about to recover the wind of me,° as if you
325   would drive me into a toil°?
GUILDENSTERN: O my lord, if my duty be too bold, my love is too
    unmannerly.°
HAMLET: I do not well understand that. Will you play
    upon this pipe°?
330 GUILDENSTERN: My lord I cannot.
HAMLET: I pray you.
GUILDENSTERN: Believe me. I cannot.
HAMLET: I do beseech you.
GUILDENSTERN: I know no touch of it° my lord.
335 HAMLET: It is as easy as lying; govern these ventages° with your
    fingers and thumb, give it breath with your mouth, and it
    will discourse most eloquent music. Look you, these are
    the stops.
GUILDENSTERN: But these cannot I command to any utt'rance of harmony,
340   I have not the skill.
HAMLET: Why look you now how unworthy a thing you make of
    me: you would play upon me, you would seem to know
    my stops, you would pluck out the heart of my mystery,
    you would sound me from my lowest note to the top of my
345   compass;° and there is much music, excellent voice in this
    little organ,° yet cannot you make it speak. 'Sblood, do you
    think I am easier to be played on than a pipe? Call me what
    instrument you will, though you can fret° me, you cannot
    play upon me.

Enter POLONIUS.

350   God bless you sir.
POLONIUS: My lord, the queen would speak with you, and presently.
HAMLET: Do you see yonder cloud that's almost in shape of a camel?
POLONIUS: By th'mass and 'tis, like a camel indeed.
HAMLET: Methinks it is like a weasel.
355 POLONIUS: It is backed like a weasel.
HAMLET: Or like a whale?
POLONIUS: Very like a whale.
HAMLET: Then I will come to my mother by and by.°
    [*Aside.*] They fool me to the top of my bent.°
360   I will come by and by.

°322 *while . . . grows:* the proverb ends: "the horse starves." °323 *something musty:* somewhat too old and trite
(to finish). °324 *withdraw:* speak privately. °324 *recover . . . me:* drive me toward the wind, as with a prey, to
avoid its scenting the hunter. °325 *toil:* snare. °326–27 *is too unmannerly:* makes me forget my good manners.
°329 *pipe:* recorder. °334 *know . . . it:* have no skill at fingering it. °335 *ventages:* holes, stops. °345 *compass:* range.
°346 *organ:* musical instrument. °348 *fret:* (1) irritate (2) play an instrument that has "frets" or bars to guide the
fingering. °358 *by and by:* very soon. °359 *fool me . . . bent:* force me to play the fool to my utmost.

POLONIUS: I will say so.   *Exit.*
HAMLET: "By and by" is easily said.
          Leave me, friends.   [*Exeunt all but HAMLET.*]
          'Tis now the very witching time of night.
          When churchyards yawn,° and hell itself breathes out   365
          Contagion° to this world: now could I drink hot blood,
          And do such bitter business as the day
          Would quake to look on: soft, now to my mother—
          O heart, lose not thy nature,° let not ever
          The soul of Nero° enter this firm bosom,   370
          Let me be cruel, not unnatural.
          I will speak daggers to her, but use none:
          My tongue and soul in this be hypocrites,°
          How in my words somever she be shent,°
          To give them seals,° never my soul consent.   *Exit.*   375

Scene 3. [A room in the castle]

Enter KING, ROSENCRANTZ, and GUILDENSTERN.

KING: I like him not, nor stands it safe with us
          To let his madness range. Therefore prepare you,
          I your commission will forthwith dispatch,°
          And he to England shall along with you:
          The terms of our estate° may not endure   5
          Hazard so near's° as doth hourly grow
          Out of his brows.°
GUILDENSTERN: We will ourselves provide:°
          Most holy and religious fear it is
          To keep those many many bodies safe
          That live and feed upon your majesty.   10
ROSENCRANTZ: The single and peculiar° life is bound
          With all the strength and armour of the mind
          To keep itself from noyance,° but much more
          That spirit, upon whose weal° depends and rests
          The lives of many; the cess° of majesty   15
          Dies not alone, but like a gulf° doth draw
          What's near it, with it. O'tis a massy wheel
          Fixed on the summit of the highest mount,
          To whose huge spokes, ten thousand lesser things
          Are mortised° and adjoined, which when it falls,   20
          Each small annexment, petty consequence,
          Attends° the boist'rous ruin. Never alone
          Did the king sigh, but with a general groan.

°365 *churchyards yawn:* graves open. °366 *Contagion:* (1) evil (2) diseases. °369 *nature:* natural affection. °370 *Nero:* (who killed his mother). °373 *My tongue . . . hypocrites:* I will speak cruelly but intend no harm. °374 *shent:* chastized. °375 *give them seals:* confirm them with action (as a legal "deed" is confirmed with a "seal"). °3 *forthwith dispatch:* immediately have prepared. °5 *terms . . . estate:* circumstances of my royal office. °6 *near's:* near us. °7 *brows:* effronteries. *provide:* prepare. °11 *peculiar:* individual. °13 *noyance:* harm. °14 *weal:* well-being. °15 *cess:* cessation, death. °16 *gulf:* whirlpool. °20 *mortised:* securely fitted. °22 *Attends:* accompanies.

KING: Arm° you I pray you, to this speedy voyage,
25   For we will fetters put about this fear,
        Which now goes too free-footed.
ROSENCRANTZ: We will haste us.

[*Exeunt* ROSENCRANTZ *and* GUILDENSTERN.]

Enter POLONIUS.

POLONIUS: My lord, he's going to his mother's closet:
        Behind the arras I'll convey myself
        To hear the process.° I'll warrant she'll tax him home,
30   And as you said, and wisely was it said,
        'Tis meet° that some more audience than a mother,
        Since nature makes them partial, should o'erhear
        The speech of vantage,° fare you well my liege,°
        I'll call upon you ere you go to bed,
        And tell you what I know.
35 **KING:**   Thanks, dear my lord.   [*Exit* POLONIUS.]
        O my offence is rank, it smells to heaven,
        It hath the primal eldest curse° upon't,
        A brother's murder. Pray can I not,
        Though inclination be as sharp as will.°
40   My stronger guilt defeats my strong intent,
        And like a man to double business bound,
        I stand in pause where I shall first begin,
        And both neglect; what if this cursèd hand
        Were thicker than itself with brother's blood,
45   Is there not rain enough in the sweet heavens
        To wash it white as snow? Whereto serves mercy
        But to confront the visage of offence?°
        And what's in prayer but this two-fold force,
        To be forestallèd° ere we come to fall,
50   Or pardoned being down? Then I'll look up,
        My fault is past. But O what form of prayer
        Can serve my turn? "Forgive me my foul murder":
        That cannot be, since I am still possessed
        Of those effects° for which I did the murder:
55   My crown, mine own ambition, and my queen.
        May one be pardoned and retain th'offence?
        In the corrupted currents of this world,
        Offence's gilded hand may shove by justice,
        And oft 'tis seen the wicked prize itself
60   Buys out the law;° but 'tis not so above,
        There is no shuffling,° there the action lies

°24 *Arm:* prepare. °29 *the process:* what proceeds. °31 *meet:* fitting. °33 *of vantage:* from an advantageous position. *liege:* lord. °37 *primal . . . curse:* curse of Cain. °39 *inclination . . . will:* my desire to pray is as strong as my determination to do so. °47 *confront . . . offence:* plead in man's behalf against sin (at the Last Judgment). °49 *forestallèd:* prevented. °54 *effects:* results. °59–60 *wicked . . . law:* fruits of the crime bribe the judge. °61 *shuffling:* evasion.

In his true nature,° and we ourselves compelled
Even to the teeth and forehead of our faults°
To give in evidence. What then? What rests?°
Try what repentance can. What can it not?   65
Yet what can it, when one can not repent?
O wretched state? O bosom black as death!
O limèd soul, that struggling to be free,
Art more engaged;° help, angels, make assay:°
Bow stubborn knees, and heart with strings of steel,   70
Be soft as sinews of the new-born babe,
All may be well.   [*He kneels.*]

Enter HAMLET.

HAMLET: Now might I do it pat,° now a' is a-praying,
    And now I'll do't, [*Draws his sword.*] and so a' goes to heaven,
    And so am I revenged: that would be scanned:°   75
    A villain kills my father, and for that,
    I his sole son, do this same villain send
    To heaven.
    Why, this is hire and salary, not revenge.
    A' took my father grossly,° full of bread,°   80
    With all his crimes° broad blown,° as flush° as May,
    And how his audit° stands who knows save heaven,
    But in our circumstance and course of thought,
    'Tis heavy° with him: and am I then revenged
    To take him in the purging of his soul,   85
    when he is fit and seasoned° for his passage?
    No.   [*Sheuthes his sword.*]
    Up sword, and know thou a more horrid hent,°
    When he is drunk asleep, or in his rage,
    Or in th'incestuous pleasure of his bed,   90
    At game, a-swearing, or about some act
    That has no relish° of salvation in't,
    Then trip him that his heels may kick at heaven,
    And that his soul may be as damned and black
    As hell whereto it goes; my mother stays,   95
    This physic° but prolongs thy sickly days   *Exit.*
KING: [*Rises.*] My words fly up, my thoughts remain below,
    Words without thoughts never to heaven go.   *Exit.*

°61–62 *action . . . nature:* (1) deed is seen in its true nature (2) legal action is sustained according to the truth.
°63 *to the teeth . . . faults:* meeting our sins face to face. °64 *rests:* remains. °68–69 *limèd . . . engaged:* like a bird
caught in lime (a sticky substance spread on twigs as a snare), the soul in its struggle to clear itself only becomes
more entangled. °69 *make assay:* I'll make an attempt. °73 *pat:* opportunely. °75 *would be scanned:* needs closer
examination. °80 *grossly:* unpurified (by final rites). *bread:* self-indulgence. °81 *crimes:* sins. *broad blown:* in full
flower. *flush:* lusty. °82 *audit:* account. °84 *heavy:* grievous. °86 *seasoned:* ready (prepared). °88 *horrid hent:* horrible opportunity ("hint") for seizure ("hent") by me. °92 *relish:* taste. °96 *physic:* (1) medicine (2) purgation of
your soul by prayer.

Scene 4. [The Queen's closet]

Enter QUEEN *and* POLONIUS.

POLONIUS: A' will come straight, look you lay home° to him,
    Tell him his pranks have been too broad° to bear with,
    And that your grace hath screened and stood between
    Much heat° and him. I'll silence me° even here:
5   Pray you be round with him.
HAMLET: [*Within.*] Mother, mother, mother.
QUEEN: I'll war'nt you,
    Fear me not. Withdraw, I hear him coming.   [*POLONIUS hides behind the arras.*]

Enter HAMLET.

HAMLET: Now mother, what's the matter?
QUEEN: Hamlet, thou hast thy father much offended.
10 HAMLET: Mother, you have my father much offended.
QUEEN: Come, come, you answer with an idle° tongue.
HAMLET: Go, go, you question with a wicked tongue.
QUEEN: Why, how now Hamlet?
HAMLET: What's the matter now?
QUEEN: Have you forgot me?
HAMLET: No by the rood,° not so,
15   You are the queen, your husband's brother's wife,
    And would it were not so, you are my mother.
QUEEN: Nay, then I'll set those to you that can speak.°
HAMLET: Come, come, and sit you down, you shall not budge,
    You go not till I set you up a glass°
20   Where you may see the inmost part of you.
QUEEN: What wilt thou do? Thou wilt not murder me?
    Help, help, ho!
POLONIUS: [*Behind the arras.*] What ho! help, help, help!
HAMLET: How now, a rat? dead for a ducat,° dead.   *Kills* POLONIUS [*through the arras.*]

25 POLONIUS: O I am slain!
QUEEN: O me, what hast thou done?
HAMLET: Nay I know not,
    Is it the king?
QUEEN: O what a rash and bloody deed is this!
HAMLET: A bloody deed, almost as bad, good mother,
30   As kill a king, and marry with his brother.
QUEEN: As kill a king?
HAMLET: Ay lady, it was my word.
    [*To* POLONIUS.] Thou wretched, rash, intruding fool, farewell,
    I took thee for thy better,° take thy fortune,
35   Thou find'st to be too busy is some danger.

°1 *lay home:* thrust home; speak sharply. °2 *broad:* unrestrained. °4 *heat:* anger. *silence me:* hide in silence. °11 *idle:* foolish. °14 *rood:* cross. °17 *speak:* i.e., to you as you should be spoken to. °19 *glass:* looking glass. °24 *for a ducat:* I wager a ducat (an Italian gold coin). °34 *thy better:* the king.

[*To the* QUEEN.] Leave wringing of your hands, peace, sit you down,
And let me wring your heart, for so I shall
If it be made of penetrable stuff,
If damnèd custom° have not brazed° it so,
That it be proof° and bulwark against sense.°   40

QUEEN: What have I done, that thou dar'st wag thy tongue
In noise so rude against me?

HAMLET: Such an act
That blurs the grace and blush of modesty,
Calls virtue hypocrite, takes off the rose°
From the fair forehead of an innocent love   45
And sets a blister there,° makes marriage vows
As false as dicers' oaths, O such a deed,
As from the body of contraction° plucks
The very soul and sweet religion makes
A rhapsody° of words; heaven's face does glow,°   50
Yea this solidity and compound mass°
With heated visage, as against the doom,°
Is thought-sick at the act.

QUEEN: Ay me, what act,
That roars so loud, and thunders in the index°?

HAMLET: Look here upon this picture, and on this,   55
The counterfeit presentment° of two brothers:
See what a grace was seated on this brow,
Hyperion's° curls, the front° of Jove himself,
An eye like Mars, to threaten and command,
A station° like the herald Mercury,   60
New-lighted on a heaven-kissing hill,
A combination and a form indeed,
Where every god did seem to set his seal
To give the world assurance of a man.
This was your husband. Look you now what follows.   65
Here is your husband, like a mildewed ear,°
Blasting° his wholesome brother. Have you eyes?
Could you on this fair mountain leave to feed,°
And batten° on this moor? Ha! Have you eyes?
You cannot call it love, for at your age   70
The hey-day in the blood° is tame, it's humble,
And waits upon the judgment, and what judgment
Would step from this to this? Sense° sure you have
Else could you not have motion,° but sure that sense
Is apoplexed,° for madness would not err,   75
Nor sense to ecstasy was ne'er so thralled°

<hr>

°39 *custom:* habit. *brazed:* brass-plated (brazened). °40 *proof:* armor. *sense:* sensibility. °44 *rose:* (symbol of perfection and innocence). °46 *blister there:* whores were punished by being branded on the forehead. °48 *body of contraction:* marriage contract. °50 *rhapsody:* (meaningless) mixture. *glow:* blush. °51 *solidity . . . mass:* solid earth, compounded of the four elements. °52 *against the doom:* expecting Judgment Day. °54 *index:* (1) table of contents (2) prologue. °56 *counterfeit presentment:* painted likeness. °58 *Hyperion:* Greek sun god. *front:* forehead. °60 *station:* bearing. °66 *ear:* i.e., of grain. °67 *Blasting:* blighting. °68 *leave to feed:* leave off feeding. °69 *batten:* gorge yourself. °70 *hey-day in the blood:* youthful passion. °73 *Sense:* perception by the senses. °74 *motion:* impulse. °75 *apoplexed:* paralyzed. °76 *sense . . . thralled:* sensibility was never so enslaved by madness.

But it reserved some quantity of choice
To serve in such a difference.° What devil was't
That thus hath cozened you at hoodman-blind?°
80   Eyes without feeling, feeling without sight,
Ears without hands or eyes, smelling sans all,°
Or but a sickly part of one true sense
Could not so mope:° O shame, where is thy blush?
Rebellious hell,
85   If thou canst mutine° in a matron's bones,
To flaming youth let virtue be as wax
And melt in her own fire. Proclaim no shame
When the compulsive° ardour gives the charge,°
Since frost itself as actively doth burn,
And reason panders will.°
90 **QUEEN:**   O Hamlet, speak no more,
Thou turn'st my eyes into my very soul,
And there I see such black and grainèd° spots
As will not leave their tinct.°
HAMLET: Nay, but to live
In the rank sweat of an enseamèd° bed,
95   Stewed in corruption, honeying, and making love
Over the nasty sty.
QUEEN: O speak to me no more,
These words like daggers enter in mine ears,
No more, sweet Hamlet.
HAMLET: A murderer and a villain,
100   A slave that is not twentieth part the tithe°
Of your precedent lord, a vice° of kings,
A cutpurse° of the empire and the rule,
That from a shelf the precious diadem stole
And put it in his pocket.
QUEEN: No more.
105 **HAMLET:** A king of shreds and patches—

Enter the GHOST *in his night-gown.°*

Save me and hover o'er me with your wings,
You heavenly guards. What would your gracious figure?
QUEEN: Alas, he's mad.
HAMLET: Do you not come your tardy son to chide,
110   That lapsed in time and passion° lets go by
Th'important acting of your dread command?
O say!
GHOST: Do not forget: this visitation
Is but to whet thy almost blunted purpose.

°78 *in . . . difference:* where the difference was so great. °79 *cozened . . . blind:* cheated you at blindman's bluff. °81 *sans all:* without the other senses. °83 *so mope:* be so dull. °85 *mutine:* rebel, mutiny. °88 *compulsive:* compelling. *gives the charge:* attacks. °90 *panders will:* pimps for lust. °92 *grainèd:* dyed in grain, unfading. °93 *leave their tinct:* lose their color. °94 *enseamèd:* greasy. °100 *tithe:* one-tenth part.°101 *vice:* buffoon (like the character of Vice in the morality plays). °102 *cutpurse:* pickpocket. °S.D.: *night-gown:* dressing gown.°110 *lapsed . . . passion:* having let time elapse and passion cool.

But look, amazement on thy mother sits,   115
O step between her and her fighting soul,
Conceit° in weakest bodies strongest works,
Speak to her Hamlet.
HAMLET: How is it with you lady?
QUEEN: Alas, how is't with you,
      That you do bend your eye on vacancy,°   120
      And with th'incorporal° air do hold discourse?
      Forth at your eyes your spirits° wildly peep,
      And as the sleeping soldiers in th'alarm,
      Your bedded° hairs, like life in excrements,°
      Start up and stand an° end. O gentle son,   125
      Upon the heat and flame of thy distemper
      sprinkle cool patience. Whereon do you look?
HAMLET: On him, on him, look you how pale he glares,
      His form and cause conjoined, preaching to stones,
      Would make them capable.° Do not look upon me,   130
      Lest with this piteous action you convert
      My stern effects,° then what I have to do
      Will want° true colour,° tears perchance for blood.
QUEEN: To whom do you speak this?
HAMLET: Do you see nothing there?
QUEEN: Nothing at all, yet all that is I see.   135
HAMLET: Nor did you nothing hear?
QUEEN: No, nothing but ourselves.
HAMLET: Why look you there, look how it steals away,
      My father in his habit as he lived,°
      Look where he goes, even now out at the portal.   [*Exit* GHOST.]
QUEEN: This is the very coinage of your brain,   140
      This bodiless creation ecstasy
      Is very cunning in.°
HAMLET: Ecstasy?
      My pulse as yours doth temperately keep time,
      And makes as healthful music. It is not madness
      That I have uttered; bring me to the test   145
      And I the matter will re-word, which madness
      Would gambol° from. Mother, for love of grace,
      Lay not that flattering unction° to your soul,
      That not your trespass but my madness speaks,
      It will but skin and film the ulcerous place,   150
      Whiles rank corruption mining° all within,
      Infects unseen. Confess yourself to heaven,
      Repent what's past, avoid what is to come,
      And do not spread the compost° on the weeds

°117 *Conceit:* imagination. °120 *vacancy:* she cannot see the ghost. °121 *incorporal:* bodiless. °122 *spirits:* vital forces. °124 *bedded:* lying flat. *excrements:* outgrowths (of the body). °125 *an:* on. °130 *capable:* i.e., of feeling pity. °131–32 *convert . . . effects:* transform my outward signs of sternness. °133 *want:* lack. *colour:* (1) complexion (2) motivation. °138 *habit . . . lived:* clothing he wore when alive. °141– 42 *bodiless . . . cunning in:* madness (ecstasy) is very skillful in causing an affected person to hallucinate. °147 *gambol:* leap. °148 *unction:* salve. °151 *mining:* undermining. °154 *compost:* manure.

155   To make them ranker. Forgive me this my virtue,°
       For in the fatness° of these pursy° times
       Virtue itself of vice must pardon beg,
       Yea curb and woo° for leave to do him° good.
       QUEEN: O Hamlet, thou hast cleft my heart in twain.
160   **HAMLET:** O throw away the worser part of it,
       And live the purer with the other half.
       Good night, but go not to my uncle's bed,
       Assume° a virtue if you have it not.
       That monster custom, who all sense doth eat
165   Of habits evil,° is angel yet in this,
       That to the use° of actions fair and good,
       He likewise gives a frock or livery
       That aptly° is put on. Refrain tonight,
       And that shall lend a kind of easiness
170   To the next abstinence, the next more easy:
       For use° almost can change the stamp° of nature,
       And either . . . the° devil, or throw him out
       With wondrous potency: once more good night,
       And when you are desirous to be blessed,
175   I'll blessing beg of you. For this same lord,°
       I do repent; but heaven hath pleased it so
       To punish me with this, and this with me,
       That I must be their scourge and minister.°
       I will bestow° him and will answer well°
180   The death I gave him; so again good night.
       I must be cruel only to be kind;
       This bad begins, and worse remains behind.°
       One word more, good lady.
       QUEEN: What shall I do?
185   **HAMLET:** Not this by no means that I bid you do:
       Let the bloat° king tempt you again to bed,
       Pinch wanton on your cheek, call you his mouse,
       And let him for a pair of reechy° kisses,
       Or paddling in your neck with his damned fingers,
190   Make you to ravel° all this matter out
       That I essentially am not in madness,
       But mad in craft. 'Twere good you let him know,
       For who that's but a queen, fair, sober, wise,
       Would from a paddock, from a bat, a gib,°
195   Such dear concernings hide? who would do so?
       No, in despite of sense and secrecy,
       Unpeg the basket on the house's top,

°155 *virtue:* sermon on virtue. °156 *fatness:* grossness. *pursy:* flabby. °158 *curb and woo:* bow and plead. *him:* vice. °163 *Assume:* put on the guise of. °164–65 *all sense . . . evil:* confuses the sense of right and wrong in a habitué. °166 *use:* habit. °168 *aptly:* readily. °171 *use:* habit. *stamp:* form. °172 *either . . . the:* word omitted, for which "tame," "curl," "lodge," and "quell" have been suggested. °175 *lord:* Polonius. °178 *their . . . minister:* heaven's punishment and agent of retribution.   °179 *bestow:* stow away. *answer well:* assume full responsibility for. °182 *bad . . . behind:* is a bad beginning to a worse end to come. °186 *bloat:* bloated with dissipation. °188 *reechy:* filthy. °190 *ravel:* unravel. °194 *paddock, bat, gib:* toad, bat, tomcat ("familiars" or demons in animal shape that attend on witches).

Let the birds fly, and like the famous ape,
To try conclusions° in the basket creep,
And break your own neck down.°   200
QUEEN: Be thou assured, if words be made of breath,
    And breath of life, I have no life to breathe
    What thou hast said to me.
HAMLET: I must to England, you know that.
QUEEN: Alack,
    I had forgot: 'tis so concluded on.   205
HAMLET: There's letters sealed, and my two school-fellows,
    Whom I will trust as I will adders fanged,
    They bear the mandate, they must sweep my way
    And marshal me to knavery:° let it work,
    For 'tis the sport to have the enginer°   210
    Hoist with his own petar,° and't shall go hard
    But I will delve one yard below their mines,
    And blow them at the moon: O 'tis most sweet
    When in one line two crafts directly meet.°
    This man shall set me packing,°   215
    I'll lug the guts into the neighbour room;
    Mother good night indeed. This counsellor
    Is now most still, most secret, and most grave,
    Who was in life a foolish prating knave.
    Come sir, to draw toward an end with you.   220
    Good night mother.   *Exit* HAMLET *tugging in* POLONIUS.

ACT 4

Scene 1. [A room in the castle]

Enter KING *and* QUEEN *with* ROSENCRANTZ *and* GUILDENSTERN.

KING: There's matter in these sighs, these profound heaves,
    You must translate, 'tis fit we understand them.
    Where is your son?
QUEEN: Bestow this place on us° a little while.

                                            Exeunt ROSENCRANTZ *and* GUILDENSTERN.

    Ah mine own lord, what have I seen tonight!   5
KING: What, Gertrude? How does Hamlet?
QUEEN: Mad as the sea and wind when both contend
    Which is the mightier, in his lawless fit,
    Behind the arras hearing something stir,

°197–200 *Unpeg . . . down:* the story refers to an ape that climbs to the top of a house and opens a basket of birds; when the birds fly away, the ape crawls into the basket, tries to fly, and breaks his neck. The point is that if she gives away Hamlet's secret, she harms herself. °199 *try conclusions:* experiment. °208–09 *sweep . . . knavery:* like the marshal who went before a royal procession, clearing the way, so Rosencrantz and Guildenstern clear Hamlet's path to some unknown evil. °210 *enginer:* maker of war engines. °211 *Hoist . . . petar:* blown up by his own bomb. °214 *in one . . . meet:* the digger of the mine and the digger of the countermine meet halfway in their tunnels. °215 *packing:* (1) i.e., my bags (2) rushing away (3) plotting. °4 *Bestow . . . us:* leave us.

10   Whips out his rapier, cries "A rat, a rat,"
                   And in this brainish apprehension° kills
                   The unseen good old man.
KING: O heavy deed!
                   It had been so with us° had we been there:
                   His liberty is full of threats to all,
15   To you yourself, to us, to every one.
                   Alas, how shall this bloody deed be answered?
                   It will be laid to us,° whose providence°
                   Should have kept short,° restrained, and out of haunt°
                   This mad young man; but so much was our love,
20   We would not understand what was most fit,
                   But like the owner of a foul disease,
                   To keep it from divulging,° let it feed
                   Even on the pith of life: where is he gone?
QUEEN: To draw apart the body he hath killed,
25   O'er whom his very madness, like some ore
                   Among a mineral of metals base,°
                   Shows itself pure: a' weeps for what is done.
KING: O Gertrude, come away:
                   The sun no sooner shall the mountains touch,
30   But we will ship him hence and this vile deed
                   We must with all our majesty and skill
                   Both countenance° and excuse. Ho Guildenstern!

Enter ROSENCRANTZ and GUILDENSTERN.

                   Friends both, go join you with some further aid;
                   Hamlet in madness hath Polonius slain,
35   And from his mother's closet hath he dragged him.
                   Go seek him out, speak fair, and bring the body
                   Into the chapel; I pray you haste in this.   *[Exeunt GENTLEMEN.]*
                   Come Gertrude, we'll call up our wisest friends,
                   And let them know both what we mean to do
40   And what's untimely done: [so haply slander,]
                   Whose whisper o'er the world's diameter,
                   As level° as the cannon to his blank°
                   Transports his° poisoned shot, may miss our name,
                   And hit the woundless° air. O come away,
45   My soul is full of discord and dismay.   *Exeunt.*

Scene 2. [Another room in the castle]

Enter HAMLET.

HAMLET: Safely stowed.
GENTLEMEN WITHIN: Hamlet, Lord Hamlet!

°11 *brainish apprehension:* insane delusion. °13 *us:* me (royal plural). °17 *laid to us:* blamed on me. *providence:* foresight. °18 *short:* tethered by a short leash. *out of haunt:* away from others. °22 *divulging:* being divulged. °25–26 *ore . . . base:* pure ore (such as gold) in a mine of base metal. °32 *countenance:* defend. °42 *As level:* with a straight aim. *blank:* white bull's-eye at the target's center. °43 *his:* slander's. °44 *woundless:* invulnerable.

HAMLET: But soft, what noise, who calls on Hamlet?
    O here they come.

Enter ROSENCRANTZ and GUILDENSTERN.

ROSENCRANTZ: What have you done my lord with the dead body?   5
HAMLET: Compounded it with dust whereto 'tis kin.
ROSENCRANTZ: Tell us where 'tis that we may take it thence,
    And bear it to the chapel.
HAMLET: Do not believe it.
ROSENCRANTZ: Believe what?   10
HAMLET: That I can keep your counsel° and not mine own.° Besides,
    to be demanded of° a sponge, what replication° should be
    made by the son of a king?
ROSENCRANTZ: Take you me for a sponge, my lord?
HAMLET: Ay sir, that soaks up the king's countenance,° his rewards,   15
    his authorities. But such officers do the king best service in
    the end; he keeps them like an apple in the corner of his
    jaw, first mouthed to be last swallowed: when he needs
    what you have gleaned, it is but squeezing you, and
    sponge, you shall be dry again.   20
ROSENCRANTZ: I understand you not my lord.
HAMLET: I am glad of it: a knavish speech sleeps in° a foolish ear.
ROSENCRANTZ: My lord, you must tell us where the body is, and go with
    us to the king.
HAMLET: The body is with the king, but the king° is not with the   25
    body. The king is a thing—
GUILDENSTERN: A thing my lord?
HAMLET: Of nothing, bring me to him. Hide fox, and all after.°   *Exeunt.*

Scene 3. [Another room in the castle]

Enter KING and two or three.

KING: I have sent to seek him, and to find the body:
    How dangerous is it that this man goes loose,
    Yet must not we put the strong law on him,
    He's loved of the distracted multitude,°
    Who like not in° their judgment, but their eyes,   5
    And where 'tis so, th'offender's scourge° is weighed
    But never the offence: to bear all° smooth and even,
    This sudden sending him away must seem
    Deliberate pause° diseases desperate grown,
    By desperate appliance° are relieved,   10
    Or not at all.

°11 *counsel:* (1) advice (2) secret. *keep . . . own:* follow your advice and not keep my own secret. °12 *demanded of:* questioned by. *replication:* reply to a charge. °15 *countenance:* favor. °22 *sleeps in:* means nothing to. °25 *king . . . king:* Hamlet's father . . . Claudius. °28 *Hide fox . . . after:* cry in a children's game, like hide-and-seek. °4 *distracted multitude:* confused mob. °5 *in:* according to. °6 *scourge:* punishment. °7 *bear all:* carry out everything. °9 *Deliberate pause:* considered delay. °10 *appliance:* remedy.

Enter ROSENCRANTZ *and all the rest.*

How now, what hath befallen?

ROSENCRANTZ: Where the dead body is bestowed my lord,
 We cannot get from him.

KING: But where is he?

ROSENCRANTZ: Without, my lord, guarded,° to know your pleasure.

KING: Bring him before us.

15 ROSENCRANTZ: Ho, bring in the lord.

Enter HAMLET *(guarded) and* GUILDENSTERN.

KING: Now Hamlet, where's Polonius?

HAMLET: At supper.

KING: At supper? where?

HAMLET: Not where he eats, but where a' is eaten: a certain
20 convocation of politic° worms are e'en° at him. Your worm is your
 only emperor for diet, we fat all creatures else to fat us,
 and we fat ourselves for maggots. Your fat king and your
 lean beggar is but variable service,° two dishes but to one
 table, that's the end.

25 KING: Alas, alas.

HAMLET: A man may fish with the worm that hath eat of a king, and
 eat of the fish that hath fed of that worm.

KING: What dost thou mean by this?

HAMLET: Nothing but to show you how a king may go a progress°
30 through the guts of a beggar.

KING: Where is Polonius?

HAMLET: In heaven, send thither to see. If your messenger find him
 not there, seek him i'th'other place yourself: but if indeed
 you find him not within this month, you shall nose him as
35 you go up the stairs into the lobby.

KING: [*To* ATTENDANTS.] Go seek him there.

HAMLET: A' will stay till you come.   [*Exeunt.*]

KING: Hamlet, this deed, for thine especial safety—
 Which we do tender,° as we dearly grieve
40 For that which thou hast done—must send thee hence
 With fiery quickness. Therefore prepare thyself,
 The bark is ready, and the wind at help,°
 Th'associates tend,° and every thing is bent
 For England.

HAMLET: For England.

KING: Ay, Hamlet.

HAMLET: Good.

45 KING: So is it if thou knew'st our purposes.

HAMLET: I see a cherub° that sees them: but come, for England.
 Farewell dear mother.

°14 *guarded:* Hamlet is under guard until he boards the ship. °20 *politic:* (1) statesmanlike (2) crafty. *e'en:* even now. °23 *variable service:* different types of food. °29 *go a progress:* make a splendid royal journey from one part of the country to another. °39 *tender:* cherish. °42 *at help:* helpful. °43 *tend:* wait. °46 *cherub:* considered the watchmen of heaven.

KING: Thy loving father, Hamlet.
HAMLET: My mother: father and mother is man and wife, man and
    wife is one flesh, and so my mother: come, for England.   *Exit.* 50
KING: [*To* ROSENCRANTZ *and* GUILDENSTERN.]
    Follow him at foot,° tempt him with speed aboard,
    Delay it not, I'll have him hence tonight.
    Away, for every thing is sealed and done
    That else leans on° th'affair, pray you make haste.   [*Exeunt.*]
    And England,° if my love thou hold'st at aught—   55
    As my great power thereof may give thee sense,
    Since yet thy cicatrice° looks raw and red
    After the Danish sword, and thy free awe
    Pays homage° to us—thou mayst not coldly set°
    Our sovereign process,° which imports at full   60
    By letters congruing° to that effect,
    The present° death of Hamlet. Do it England,
    For like the hectic° in my blood he rages,
    And thou must cure me; till I know 'tis done,
    Howe'er my haps,° my joys were ne'er begun.   *Exit.* 65

Scene 4. [A plain in Denmark]

Enter FORTINBRAS *with his army over the stage.*

FORTINBRAS: Go captain, from me greet the Danish king,
    Tell him that by his license, Fortinbras
    Craves the conveyance of° a promised march
    Over his kingdom. You know the rendezvous:
    If that his majesty would aught with us,   5
    We shall express our duty in his eye,°
    And let him know so.
CAPTAIN: I will do't, my lord.
FORTINBRAS: Go softly° on.   *Exit.*

Enter HAMLET, ROSENCRANTZ, [GUILDENSTERN,] *etc.*

HAMLET: Good sir whose powers° are these?
CAPTAIN: They are of Norway sir.
HAMLET: How purposed sir I pray you?   10
CAPTAIN: Against some part of Poland.
HAMLET: Who commands them sir?
CAPTAIN: The nephew to old Norway, Fortinbras.
HAMLET: Goes it against the main° of Poland sir,   15
    Or for some frontier?
CAPTAIN: Truly to speak, and with no addition,
    We go to gain a little patch of ground

°51 *at foot:* at his heels. 54 *leans on:* relates to. °55 *England:* King of England. *my love . . . aught:* you place any
value on my favor. °57 *cicatrice:* scar. °58–59 *free . . . homage:* awe which you, though free, still show by paying
homage. °59 *coldly set:* lightly estimate. °60 *process:* command. °61 *congruing:* agreeing. °62 *present:* immediate.
°63 *hectic:* fever. °65 *haps:* fortunes. °3 *conveyance of:* escort for. °6 *in his eye:* face to face. °8 *softly:* slowly. °9 *powers:*
troops. °15 *main:* body.

That hath in it no profit but the name.°
20   To pay five ducats, five, I would not farm it;
         Nor will it yield to Norway or the Pole
         A ranker° rate, should it be sold in fee.°
HAMLET: Why then the Polack never will defend it.
CAPTAIN: Yes, it is already garrisoned.
25 HAMLET: Two thousand souls, and twenty thousand ducats
         Will not debate the question of° this straw:°
         This is th'imposthume of much wealth and peace,°
         That inward breaks, and shows no cause without
         Why the man dies. I humbly thank you sir.
CAPTAIN: God bye you sir.   [*Exit.*]
30 ROSENCRANTZ: Will't please you go my lord?
HAMLET: I'll be with you straight, go a little before.

                                          [*Exeunt all but* HAMLET.]

         How all occasions do inform against me,
         And spur my dull revenge. What is a man
         If his chief good and market° of his time
35   Be but to sleep and feed? a beast, no more:
         Sure he that made us with such large discourse,°
         Looking before and after,° gave us not
         That capability and god-like reason
         To fust° in us unused. Now whether it be
40   Bestial oblivion,° or some craven° scruple
         Of thinking too precisely on th'event°—
         A thought which quartered hath but one part wisdom,
         And ever three parts coward—I do not know
         Why yet I live to say "This thing's to do,"
45   Sith I have cause, and will, and strength, and means
         To do't; examples gross° as earth exhort me:
         Witness this army of such mass and charge,°
         Led by a delicate and tender° prince,
         Whose spirit with divine ambition puffed,
50   Makes mouths° at the invisible event,°
         Exposing what is mortal, and unsure,
         To all that fortune, death, and danger dare,
         Even for an egg-shell. Rightly to be great,
         Is not to stir without great argument,
55   But greatly to find quarrel in a straw
         When honour's at the stake.° How stand I then
         That have a father killed, a mother stained,

°19 *name:* glory. °22 *ranker:* higher (as annual interest on the total). *in fee:* outright. °26 *debate . . . of:* settle the dispute over. *straw:* triviality. °27 *imposthume . . . peace:* swelling discontent (inner abscess) resulting from too much wealth and peace. °34 *market:* profit. °36 *discourse:* power of reasoning. °37 *Looking . . . after:* seeing causes and effects. °40 *Bestial oblivion:* forgetfulness, as a beast forgets its parents. *craven:* cowardly. °41 *event:* outcome. °46 *gross:* obvious. °47 *charge:* expense. °48 *delicate and tender:* gentle and young. °50 *mouths:* faces. *event:* outcome. °53–56 *Rightly . . . stake:* the truly great do not fight without just cause ("argument"), but it is nobly ("greatly") done to fight even for a trifle if honor is at stake.

Excitements° of my reason, and my blood,
And let all sleep, while to my shame I see
The imminent death of twenty thousand men,   60
That for a fantasy and trick° of fame
Go to their graves like beds, fight for a plot
Whereon the numbers cannot try the cause,°
Which is not tomb enough and continent°
To hide the slain. O from this time forth,   65
My thoughts be bloody, or be nothing worth.   *Exit.*

Scene 5. [A room in the castle]

Enter QUEEN, HORATIO *and a* GENTLEMAN.

QUEEN: I will not speak with her.
GENTLEMAN: She is importunate, indeed distract,°
Her mood will needs be° pitied.
QUEEN: What would she have?
GENTLEMAN: She speaks much of her father, says she hears
There's tricks i'th'world, and hems,° and beats her heart,   5
Spurns enviously at straws,° speaks things in doubt°
That carry but half sense: her speech is nothing,
Yet the unshapèd use of it doth move
The hearers to collection;° they aim° at it,
And botch° the words up fit to their own thoughts,   10
Which as her winks, and nods, and gestures yield them,
Indeed would make one think there might be thought,
Though nothing sure, yet much unhappily.
HORATIO: 'Twere good she were spoken with, for she may strew
Dangerous conjectures in ill-breeding minds.   15
QUEEN: Let her come in.   *Exit* GENTLEMAN.
[*Aside.*] To my sick soul, as sin's true nature is;°
Each toy° seems prologue to some great amiss,°
So full of artless jealousy° is guilt,
It spills itself, in fearing to be spilt.   20

Enter OPHELIA, *distracted.°*

OPHELIA: Where is the beauteous majesty of Denmark?
QUEEN: How now Ophelia?
OPHELIA: [*Sings.*] How should I your true love know
                    From another one?
                    By his cockle hat and staff,°   25
                    And his sandal shoon.°

°58 *Excitements:* incentives. °61 *fantasy and trick:* illusion and trifle. °63 *Whereon . . . cause:* too small to accommodate all the troops fighting for it. °64 *continent:* container. °2 *distract:* insane. °3 *will needs be:* needs to be. °5 *hems:* coughs. °6 *Spurns . . . straws:* reacts maliciously to trifles. *in doubt:* ambiguous. °9 *collection:* inference. *aim:* guess. °10 *botch:* patch. °17 *as sin's . . . is:* as is natural for the guilty. °18 *toy:* trifle. *amiss:* disaster. °19 *artless jealousy:* uncontrollable suspicion. °20 S.D.: *distracted:* insane. °25 *cockle hat and staff:* marks of the pilgrim, the cockle shell symbolizing his journey to the shrine of St. James; the pilgrim was a common metaphor for the lover. °26 *shoon:* shoes.

QUEEN: Alas sweet lady, what imports this song?
OPHELIA: Say you? nay, pray you mark.
    [*Sings.*] He is dead and gone, lady,
30   He is dead and gone,
            At his head a grass-green turf,
            At his heels a stone.
     O ho.
QUEEN: Nay but Ophelia—
OPHELIA: Pray you mark.
35   [*Sings.*] White his shroud as the mountain snow—

Enter KING.

QUEEN: Alas, look here my lord.
OPHELIA: [*Sings.*] Larded° all with sweet flowers,
     Which bewept to the ground did not go,
         With true-love showers.
40 KING: How do you, pretty lady?
OPHELIA: Well, God 'ild° you. They say the owl was a baker's
     daughter.° Lord, we know what we are, but know not what
     we may be. God be at your table.°
KING: Conceit° upon her father.
45 OPHELIA: Pray you let's have no words of this, but when they ask
     you what it means, say you this:
     [*Sings.*] Tomorrow is Saint Valentine's day,
         All in the morning betime,°
         And I a maid at your window
50   To be your Valentine.
     Then up he rose, and donned his clo'es,
         And dupped° the chamber door,
     Let in the maid, that out a maid,
         Never departed more.
55 KING: Pretty Ophelia.
OPHELIA: Indeed, la, without an oath I'll make an end on't.
     [*Sings.*] By Gis° and by Saint Charity,
         Alack and fie for shame,
     Young men will do't, if they come to't,
60   By Cock° they are to blame.
     Quoth she, Before you tumbled me,
         You promised me to wed.
     He answers. So would I ha' done, by yonder sun,
         An° thou hadst not come to my bed.
65 KING: How long hath she been thus?
OPHELIA: I hope all will be well. We must be patient, but I cannot
     choose but weep to think they would lay him i'th' cold
     ground. My brother shall know of it, and so I thank you

°37 *Larded:* trimmed. °41 *God 'ild:* God yield (reward). °41–42 *owl . . . daughter:* in a medieval legend, a baker's daughter was turned into an owl because she gave Jesus short weight on a loaf of bread. °43 *God . . . table:* a blessing at dinner. °44 *Conceit:* thinking. °48 *betime:* early (because the first woman a man saw on Valentine's Day would be his true love). °52 *dupped:* opened. °57 *Gis:* contraction of "Jesus." °60 *Cock:* vulgarization of "God" in oaths. °64 *An:* if.

for your good counsel. Come, my coach: good night
ladies, good night. Sweet ladies, good night, good night.   [*Exit* OPHELIA.]   70
KING: Follow her close, give her good watch I pray you.   [*Exit* HORATIO.]
   O this is the poison of deep grief, it springs
   All from her father's death, and now behold:
   O Gertrude, Gertrude,
   When sorrows come, they come not single spies,   75
   But in battalions: first her father slain,
   Next, your son gone, and he most violent author
   Of his own just remove, the people muddied,°
   Thick and unwholesome in their thoughts and whispers
   For good Polonius' death: and we have done but greenly°   80
   In hugger-mugger° to inter him: poor Ophelia
   Divided from herself and her fair judgment,
   Without the which we are pictures or mere beasts,
   Last, and as much containing° as all these,
   Her brother is in secret come from France,   85
   Feeds on his wonder,° keeps himself in clouds,°
   And wants not buzzers° to infect his ear
   With pestilent speeches of his father's death,
   Wherein necessity, of matter beggared,
   Will nothing stick our person to arraign°   90
   In ear and ear:° O my dear Gertrude, this
   Like to a murdering-piece° in many places
   Gives me superfluous death.   *A noise within.*
QUEEN: Alack, what noise is this?
KING: Attend!   *Enter a* MESSENGER.
   Where are my Switzers.° Let them guard the door.   95
   What is the matter?
MESSENGER: Save yourself, my lord.
   The ocean, overpeering of his list,°
   Eats not the flats° with more impiteous haste
   Than young Laertes in a riotous head°
   O'erbears your officers: the rabble call him lord,   100
   And as the world were now but to begin,
   Antiquity forgot, custom not known,
   The ratifiers and props of every word,
   They cry "Choose we, Laertes shall be king!"
   Caps, hands, and tongues applaud it to the clouds,   105
   "Laertes shall be king, Laertes king!"   *A noise within.*
QUEEN: How cheerfully on the false trail they cry.
   O this is counter,° you false Danish dogs.
KING: The doors are broke.

Enter LAERTES *with others.*

°78 *muddied:* stirred up. °80 *done but greenly:* acted like amateurs. °81 *hugger-mugger:* secret haste. °84 *contain-*
ing: i.e., cause for sorrow. °86 *Feeds . . . wonder:* sustains himself by wondering about his father's death. *clouds:*
gloom, obscurity. °87 *wants not buzzers:* lacks not whispering gossips. °89–90 *Wherein . . . arraign:* in which the
tellers, lacking facts, will not hesitate to accuse me. °91 *In ear and ear:* whispering from one ear to another.
°92 *murdering-piece:* small cannon shooting shrapnel, to inflict numerous wounds. °95 *Switzers:* Swiss guards.
°97 *overpeering . . . list:* rising above its usual limits. °98 *flats:* lowlands. °99 *head:* armed force. °108 *counter:* following the scent backward.

110 **LAERTES:** Where is this king? Sirs, stand you all without.°
DANES: No, let's come in.
LAERTES: I pray you give me leave.°
DANES: We will, we will.   [*They retire.*]
LAERTES: I thank you, keep the door. O thou vile king,
     Give me my father.
QUEEN: Calmly, good Laertes.
115 **LAERTES:** That drop of blood that's calm proclaims me bastard,
     Cries cuckold° to my father, brands° the harlot
     Even here between the chaste unsmirchèd brows
     Of my true mother.
KING: What is the cause Laertes,
     That thy rebellion looks so giant-like?
120   Let him go Gertrude, do not fear° our person,
     There's such divinity° doth hedge a king,
     That treason can but peep to° what it would,
     Acts little of his° will. Tell me Laertes,
     Why thou art this incensed. Let him go Gertrude.
125   Speak man.
LAERTES: Where is my father?
KING: Dead.
QUEEN: But not by him.
KING: Let him demand his fill.
LAERTES: How came he dead? I'll not be juggled with.
     To hell allegiance, vows to the blackest devil,
130   Conscience and grace, to the profoundest pit.
     I dare damnation: to this point I stand,
     That both the worlds I give to negligence,°
     Let come what comes, only I'll be revenged
     Most thoroughly for my father.
KING: Who shall stay you?
135 **LAERTES:** My will, not all the world's:°
     And for my means, I'll husband° them so well,
     They shall go far with little.
KING: Good Laertes,
     If you desire to know the certainty
     Of your dear father, is't writ in your revenge
140   That swoopstake,° you will draw both friend and foe,
     Winner and loser?
LAERTES: None but his enemies.
KING: Will you know them then?
LAERTES: To his good friends thus wide I'll ope my arms,
     And like the kind life-rend'ring pelican,°
     Repast them with my blood.
145 **KING:**   Why now you speak

°110 *without:* outside. °111 *leave:* i.e., to enter alone. °116 *cuckold:* betrayed husband. *brands:* so harlots were punished. °120 *fear:* i.e., for. °121 *divinity:* divine protection. °122 *peep to:* strain to see. °123 *his:* treason's. °132 *both . . . negligence:* I care nothing for this world or the next. °135 *world's:* i.e., will. °136 *husband:* economize. °140 *swoopstake:* sweeping in all the stakes in a game, both of winner and loser. °144 *pelican:* the mother pelican was believed to nourish her young with blood pecked from her own breast.

Like a good child, and a true gentleman.
That I am guiltless of your father's death,
And am most sensibly° in grief for it,
It shall as level° to your judgment 'pear
As day does to your eye.   150

[*A noise within.*]

[*Crowd shouts.*] Let her come in.
LAERTES: How now, what noise is that?

Enter OPHELIA.

O heat, dry up my brains, tears seven time salt,
Burn out the sense and virtue° of mine eye!
By heaven, thy madness shall be paid with weight,°   155
Till our scale turn the beam,° O rose of May,
Dear maid, kind sister, sweet Ophelia:
O heavens, is't possible a young maid's wits
Should be as mortal as an old man's life?
Nature is fine in love, and where 'tis fine,   160
It sends some previous instance of itself
after the thing it loves.°
OPHELIA: [*Sings.*] They bore him barefaced on the bier,
              Hey non nonny, nonny, hey nonny:
              And in his grave rained many a tear—   165
      Fare you well my dove.
LAERTES: Hadst thou thy wits, and didst persuade revenge,
    It could not move thus.
OPHELIA: You must sing "adown adown," and you call him adown-a.
    O how the wheel becomes it.° It is the false steward that   170
        stole his master's daughter.
LAERTES: This nothing's more than matter.°
OPHELIA: There's rosemary,° that's for remembrance, pray you love
    remember: and there is pansies, that's for thoughts.
LAERTES: A document° in madness, thoughts and remembrance   175
    fitted.°
OPHELIA: There's fennel for you, and columbines.° There's rue° for
    you, and here's some for me, we may call it herb of grace°
    o'Sundays: O, you must wear your rue with a difference.°
    There's daisy,° I would give you some violets,° but they   180

°148 *sensibly:* feelingly. °149 *level:* plain. °154 *sense and virtue:* feeling and power. °155 *with weight:* with equal weight. °156 *turn the beam:* outweigh the other side. °160–62 *Nature . . . loves:* filial love that is so refined and pure sends some precious token (her wits) after the beloved dead. °170 *wheel becomes it:* refrain ("adown") suits the subject (Polonius's fall). °172 *This . . . matter:* This nothing is more eloquent than same speech. °173 *There's rosemary:* given to Laertes; she may be distributing imaginary or real flowers. °175 *document:* lesson. °175–76 *thoughts . . . fitted:* thoughts of revenge matched with remembrance of Polonius. °177 *fennel . . . columbines:* given to the king, symbolizing flattery and ingratitude. *rue:* given to the queen, symbolizing sorrow or repentance. °178 *herb of grace:* because it symbolizes repentance. °179 *with a difference:* for a different reason (Ophelia's is for sorrow and the queen's for repentance). °180 *daisy:* symbolizing dissembling. *violets:* symbolizing faithfulness.

withered all when my father died: they say a' made a good
     end;
          [*Sings.*] For bonny sweet Robin is all my joy.
LAERTES: Thought and affliction, passion, hell itself,
185   She turns to favour and to prettiness.
OPHELIA: [*Sings.*] And will a' not come again,
                    And will a' not come again?
                    No, no, he is dead,
                    Go to thy death-bed,
190   He never will come again.
                    His beard was as white as snow,
                    All flaxen was his poll,°
                    He is gone, he is gone,
                    And we cast away moan,
195   God ha' mercy on his soul.
          And of all Christian souls, I pray God. God bye you.

                                             Exit OPHELIA.

LAERTES: Do you see this, O God?
KING: Laertes, I must commune with your grief,
          Or you deny me right: go but apart,
200   Make choice of whom your wisest friends you will,
          And they shall hear and judge 'twixt you and me;
          If by direct or by collateral° hand
          They find us touched,° we will our kingdom give,
          Our crown, our life, and all that we call ours
205   To you in satisfaction; but if not,
          Be you content to lend your patience to us,
          And we shall jointly labour with your soul
          To give it due content.
LAERTES: Let this be so.
          His means of death, his obscure funeral,
210   No trophy,° sword, nor hatchment° o'er his bones,
          No noble rite, nor formal ostentation,°
          Cry° to be heard as 'twere from heaven to earth,
          That I must call't in question.
KING: So you shall,
          And where th'offence is, let the great axe fall.
215   I pray you go with me.   [*Exeunt.*]

Scene 6. [Another room in the castle]

Enter HORATIO *and others.*

HORATIO: What are they that would speak with me?
GENTLEMAN: Seafaring men sir, they say they have letters for you.

°192 *flaxen . . . poll:* white was his head. °202 *collateral:* indirect. °203 *touched:* tainted with guilt. °210 *trophy:* memorial. *hatchment:* tablet displaying coat of arms.   °211 *ostentation:* ceremony. °212 *Cry:* cry out.

HORATIO: Let them come in.   [*Exit* ATTENDANT.]
    I do not know from what part of the world
    I should be greeted, if not from Lord Hamlet.   5

Enter SAILORS.

SAILOR: God bless you sir.
HORATIO: Let him bless thee too.
SAILOR: A'shall sir, an't please him. There's a letter for you sir, it
    came from th'ambassador that was bound for England, if
    your name be Horatio, as I am let to know it is.   10
HORATIO: [*Reads the letter.*] "Horatio, when thou shalt have
    overlooked° this, give these fellows some means to the king,
    they have letters for him. Ere we were two days old at sea,
    a pirate of very warlike appointment° gave us chase.
    Finding ourselves too slow of sail, we put on a compelled   15
    valour, and in the grapple° I boarded them. On the instant
    they got clear of our ship, so I alone became their prisoner.
    They have dealt with me like thieves of mercy,° but they
    knew what they did. I am to do a good turn for them. Let
    the king have the letters I have sent, and repair° thou to me   20
    with as much speed as thou wouldst fly death. I have
    words to speak in thine ear will make thee dumb, yet are
    they much too light for the bore° of the matter. These good
    fellows will bring thee where I am. Rosencrantz and
    Guildenstern hold their course for England. Of them I   25
    have much to tell thee. Farewell.
            He that thou knowest thine, Hamlet."
    Come, I will give you way° for these your letters,
    And do't the speedier that you may direct me
    To him from whom you brought them.   *Exeunt.*   30

Scene 7. [Another room in the castle]

Enter KING *and* LAERTES.

KING: Now must your conscience my acquittance seal,°
    And you must put me in your heart for friend,
    Sith you have heard and with a knowing ear,
    That he which hath your noble father slain
    Pursued my life.
LAERTES: It well appears: but tell me   5
    Why you proceeded not against these feats
    So crimeful and so capital in nature,
    As by your safety, greatness, wisdom, all things else,
    You mainly were stirred up.°
KING: O for two special reasons,
    Which may to you perhaps seem much unsinewed,°   10

°12 *overlooked:* read over. °14 *appointment:* equipment. °16 *in the grapple:* when the pirate ship hooked onto ours.
°18 *of mercy:* merciful. °20 *repair:* come. °23 *bore:* size, caliber. °28 *way:* access (to the king). °1 *my acquittance seal:* confirm my acquittal. °9 *mainly . . . up:* were strongly urged. °10 *much unsinewed:* very weak.

But yet to me they're strong. The queen his mother
Lives almost by his looks, and for myself,
My virtue or my plague, be it either which,
She's so conjunctive° to my life and soul,
15   That as the star moves not but in his sphere,°
I could not but by her. The other motive,
Why to a public count° I might not go,
Is the great love the general gender° bear him,
Who dipping all his faults in their affection,
20   Would like the spring that turneth wood to stone,°
Convert his gyves to graces,° so that my arrows,
Too slightly timbered° for so loud a wind,
Would have reverted to my bow again,
And not where I had aimed them.
25 **LAERTES:** And so have I a noble father lost,
A sister driven into desperate terms,°
Whose worth, if praises may go back° again,
Stood challenger on mount of all the age
For her perfections.° But my revenge will come.
30 **KING:** Break not your sleeps for that, you must not think
That we are made of stuff so flat and dull,
That we can let our beard be shook with danger,
And think it pastime. You shortly shall hear more,
I loved your father, and we love ourself,
35   And that I hope will teach you to imagine—

Enter a MESSENGER *with letters.*

How now. What news?
MESSENGER: Letters my lord, from Hamlet.
These to your majesty, this to the queen.
KING: From Hamlet? Who brought them?
MESSENGER: Sailors my lord they say, I saw them not:
40   They were given me by Claudio, he received them
Of him that brought them.
KING: Laertes you shall hear them:
Leave us.   [*Exit* MESSENGER.]
[*Reads*] "High and mighty, you shall know I am set naked° on
your kingdom. Tomorrow shall I beg leave to see your kingly
45   eyes, when I shall, first asking your pardon° thereunto,
recount the occasion of my sudden and more strange return.
                                                  Hamlet."
What should this mean? Are all the rest come back?
Or is it some abuse,° and no such thing?
LAERTES: Know you the hand?

°14 *conjunctive:* closely allied.°15 *in his sphere:* referring to the Ptolemaic belief that each planet, fixed in its own sphere, revolved around the earth. °17 *count:* accounting. °18 *general gender:* common people. °20 *the spring . . . stone:* the baths of King's Newnham in Warwickshire were described as being able to turn wood into stone because of their high concentrations of lime. °21 *Convert . . . graces:* regard his fetters (had he been imprisoned) as honors. °22 *slightly timbered:* light-shafted. °26 *desperate terms:* madness. °27 *go back:* i.e., before her madness. °28–29 *challenger . . . perfections:* like a challenger on horseback, ready to defend against the world her claim to perfection. °43 *naked:* without resources. °45 *pardon:* permission. °49 *abuse:* deception.

KING: 'Tis Hamlet's character.° "Naked,"   50
    And in a postscript here he says "alone."
    Can you devise me?°
LAERTES: I am lost in it my lord, but let him come,
    It warms the very sickness in my heart
    That I shall live and tell him to his teeth,   55
    "Thus didest thou."
KING: If it be so Laertes—
    As how should it be so? how otherwise?—
    Will you be ruled by me?
LAERTES: Ay my lord,
    So you will not o'errule me to a peace.
KING: To thine own peace: if he be now returned,   60
    As checking at° his voyage, and that he means
    No more to undertake it, I will work him
    To an exploit, now ripe in my device,°
    Under the which he shall not choose but fall:
    And for his death no wind of blame shall breathe,   65
    But even his mother shall uncharge the practice,°
    And call it accident.
LAERTES: My lord, I will be ruled,
    The rather if you could devise it so
    That I might be the organ.°
KING: It falls right.
    You have been talked of since your travel much,   70
    And that in Hamlet's hearing, for a quality
    Wherein they say you shine: your sum of parts°
    Did not together pluck such envy from him
    As did that one, and that in my regard
    Of the unworthiest siege.°
LAERTES: What part is that my lord?   75
KING: A very riband° in the cap of youth,
    Yet needful too, for youth no less becomes°
    The light and careless livery° that it wears,
    Than settled age his sables° and his weeds°
    Importing health and graveness; two months since,°   80
    Here was a gentleman of Normandy—
    I have seen myself, and served against the French,
    And they can° well on horseback—but this gallant
    Had witchcraft in't, he grew unto his seat,
    And to such wondrous doing brought his horse,   85
    As had he been incorpsed and demi-natured°
    With the brave beast. So far he topped my thought,
    That I in forgery of° shapes and tricks
    Come short of what he did.

°50 *character:* handwriting. °52 *devise me:* explain it. °61 *checking at:* altering the course of (when the falcon forsakes one quarry for another). °63 *ripe in my device:* already planned by me. °66 *uncharge the practice:* acquit the plot (of treachery). °69 *organ:* instrument. °72 *your sum of parts:* all your accomplishments. °75 *siege:* rank. °76 *riband:* decoration. °77 *becomes:* befits. °78 *livery:* clothing (denoting rank or occupation). °79 *sables:* fur-trimmed gowns. *weeds:* garments. °80 *since:* ago. °83 *can:* can do. °86 *incorpsed . . . natured:* made into one body, sharing half its nature. °88 *in forgery of:* imagining.

	LAERTES:	A Norman was't?
90	KING:	A Norman.

LAERTES: Upon my life, Lamord.°

KING: The very same.

LAERTES: I know him well, he is the brooch° indeed
        And gem of all the nation.

KING: He made confession° of you,
95   And gave you such a masterly report
        For art and exercise in your defence,
        And for your rapier most especial,
        That he cried out 'twould be a sight indeed
        If one could match you; the scrimers° of their nation
100   He swore had neither motion, guard, nor eye,
        If you opposed them; sir this report of his
        Did Hamlet so envenom° with his envy,
        That he could nothing do but wish and beg
        Your sudden coming o'er to play with him.
        Now out of this—

105 LAERTES: What out of this, my lord?

KING: Laertes, was your father dear to you?
        Or are you like the painting of a sorrow,
        A face without a heart?

LAERTES: Why ask you this?

KING: Not that I think you did not love your father.
110   But that I know love is begun by time,
        And that I see in passages of proof,°
        Time qualifies° the spark and fire of it:
        There lives within the very flame of love
        A kind of wick or snuff that will abate it,°
115   And nothing is at a like goodness still,°
        For goodness growing to a plurisy,°
        Dies in his own too-much. That we would do
        We should do when we would: for this "would"° changes,
        And hath abatements and delays as many
120   As there are tongues, are hands, are accidents,
        And then this "should"° is like a spendthrift sigh,
        That hurts by easing,° but to the quick° of th'ulcer:
        Hamlet comes back, what would you undertake
        To show yourself in deed your father's son
        More than in words?

125 LAERTES: To cut his throat i'th'church.

KING: No place indeed should murder sanctuarize,°
        Revenge should have no bounds: but good Laertes,
        Will you do this, keep close within your chamber:
        Hamlet returned shall know you are come home,

°91 *Lamord:* a name meaning "death" (la mort in French). °92 *brooch:* ornament. °94 *confession:* report. °99 *scrimers:* fencers. °102 *envenom:* poison. °111 *passages of proof:* examples drawn from experience. °112 *qualifies:* weakens. °114 *snuff . . . it:* charred end of the wick that will diminish the flame. °115 *still:* always. °116 *plurisy:* excess. °118 *"would":* will to act. °121 *"should":* reminder of one's duty. °121–22 *spendthrift . . . easing:* A sigh which, though giving temporary relief, wastes life, as each sigh draws a drop of blood away from the heart (a common Elizabethan belief). °122 quick: most sensitive spot. °126 *murder sanctuarize:* give sanctuary to murder.

We'll put on° those shall praise your excellence,   130
And set a double varnish on the fame
The Frenchman gave you, bring you in fine° together,
And wager on your heads; he being remiss,°
Most generous, and free from all contriving,
Will not peruse the foils, so that with ease,   135
Or with a little shuffling, you may choose
A sword unbated,° and in a pass of practice°
Requite him for your father.

LAERTES: I will do't,
And for the purpose, I'll anoint my sword.
I bought an unction° of a mountebank°   140
So mortal,° that but dip a knife in it,
Where it draws blood, no cataplasm° so rare,
Collected from all simples° that have virtue°
Under the moon,° can save the thing from death
That is but scratched withal: I'll touch my point   145
With this contagion, that if I gall° him slightly,
It may be death.

KING: Let's further think of this,
Weigh what convenience both of time and means
May fit us to our shape;° if this should fail,
And that our drift° look through° our bad performance,   150
'Twere better not assayed; therefore this project
Should have a back or second that might hold
If this did blast in proof.° Soft, let me see,
We'll make a solemn wager on your cunnings°—
I ha't: 155
When in your motion you are hot and dry,
As make your bouts more violent to that end,
And that he calls for drink, I'll have prepared him
A chalice for the nonce,° whereon but sipping,
If he by chance escape your venomed stuck,°   160
Our purpose may hold there; but stay, what noise?

Enter QUEEN.

How, sweet queen?
QUEEN: One woe doth tread upon another's heel,
So fast they follow; your sister's drowned, Laertes.
LAERTES: Drowned! O where?   165
QUEEN: There is a willow grows aslant a brook,
That shows his hoar° leaves in the glassy stream,
There with fantastic garlands did she make

°130 *put on:* incite. °132 *in fine:* finally. °133 *remiss:* easy-going. °137 *unbated:* not blunted (the edges and points were blunted for fencing). *pass of practice:* (1) match for exercise (2) treacherous thrust. °140 *unction:* ointment. *mountebank:* quack doctor, medicine man. °141 *mortal:* deadly. °142 *cataplasm:* poultice. °143 *simples:* herbs. *virtue:* power (of healing). °144 *Under the moon:* (when herbs were supposed to be collected to be most effective). °146 *gall:* scratch. °149 *shape:* plan. °150 *drift:* aim. *look through:* be exposed by. °153 *blast in proof:* fail when tested (as a bursting cannon). °154 *cunnings:* skills. °159 *nonce:* occasion. °160 *stuck:* thrust. °167 *hoar:* gray (on the underside).

Of crow-flowers,° nettles, daisies, and long purples,°
170   That liberal° shepherds give a grosser name,
But our cold° maids do dead men's fingers call them.
There on the pendent boughs her coronet weeds°
Clamb'ring to hang, an envious sliver° broke,
When down her weedy trophies and herself
175   Fell in the weeping brook: her clothes spread wide,
And mermaid-like awhile they bore her up,
Which time she chanted snatches of old tunes,
As one incapable of° her own distress,
Or like a creature native and induced
180   Unto° that element: but long it could not be
Till that her garments, heavy with their drink,
Pulled the poor wretch from her melodious lay
To muddy death.
LAERTES: Alas, then she is drowned?
QUEEN: Drowned, drowned.
185   **LAERTES:** Too much of water hast thou, poor Ophelia,
And therefore I forbid my tears; but yet
It is our trick, nature her custom holds,
Let shame say what it will; when these° are gone,
The woman will be out.° Adieu my lord,
190   I have a speech o'fire that fain would blaze,
But that this folly douts it.°   *Exit.*
KING: Let's follow, Gertrude,
How much I had to do to calm his rage;
Now fear I this will give it start again,
Therefore let's follow.   *Exeunt.*

ACT 5

Scene 1. [A churchyard]

Enter two CLOWNS°

1. **CLOWN:** Is she to be buried in Christian burial,° when she wilfully seeks her own
    salvation?°
2. **CLOWN:** I tell thee she is, therefore make her grave straight.° The
    crowner hath sat on her,° and finds it Christian burial.
5   1. **CLOWN:** How can that be, unless she drowned herself in her own
    defence?°
2. **CLOWN:** Why, 'tis found so.
1. **CLOWN:** It must be "se offendendo,"° it cannot be else: for here lies
    the point: if I drown myself wittingly, it argues an act,

---

°169 *crow-flowers:* buttercups. *long purples:* spike-like early orchid. °170 *liberal:* libertine. °171 *cold:* chaste.
°172 *coronet weeds:* garland of weeds. °173 *envious sliver:* malicious branch. °178 *incapable of:* unable to understand. °179–80 *induced Unto:* endowed by nature to exist in. °188 *these:* i.e., tears. °189 *woman . . . out:* womanly
habits will be out of me. °191 *folly douts it:* tears put it out. °S.D.: *clowns:* rustics. °1 *Christian burial:* consecrated ground within a churchyard (where suicides were not allowed burial). °2 *salvation:* i.e., "damnation."
The gravediggers make a number of such "mistakes," later termed "malapropisms." °3 *straight:* straightaway, at
once. °4 *crowner . . . her:* coroner has ruled on her case. °5–6 *her own defence:* as self-defense justifies homicide,
so may it justify suicide. °8 *"se offendendo":* he means "se defendendo," in self-defense.

and an act hath three branches, it is to act, to do, and to   10
perform; argal,° she drowned herself wittingly.

2. CLOWN: Nay, but hear you, Goodman Delver.

1. CLOWN: Give me leave: here lies the water, good. Here stands the
man, good. If the man go to this water and drown himself,
it is, will he nill he,° he goes, mark you that. But if the   15
water come to him, and drown him, he drowns not
himself. Argal, he that is not guilty of his own death, shortens not his own
life.

2. CLOWN: But is this law?

1. CLOWN: Ay marry is't, crowner's quest° law.   20

2. CLOWN: Will you ha' the truth on't? If this had not been a
gentlewoman, she would have been buried out o'Christian
burial.

1. CLOWN: Why there thou say'st, and the more pity that great folk
should have countenance° in this world to drown or hang   25
themselves more than their even-Christen.° Come, my
spade; there is no ancient gentlemen but gardeners,
ditchers and grave-makers; they hold up Adam's profession.

2. CLOWN: Was he a gentleman?

1. CLOWN: A' was the first that ever bore arms.°   30

2. CLOWN: Why, he had none.

1. CLOWN: What, art a heathen? How dost thou understand the
Scripture? The Scripture says Adam digged; could he dig
without arms? I'll put another question to thee; if thou
answerest me not to the purpose, confess thyself—   35

2. CLOWN: Go to.

1. CLOWN: What is he that builds stronger than either the mason, the
shipwright, or the carpenter?

2. CLOWN: The gallows-maker, for that frame outlives a thousand
tenants.   40

1. CLOWN: I like thy wit well in good faith, the gallows does well, but
how does it well? It does well to those that do ill. Now
thou dost ill to say the gallows is built stronger than the
church. Argal, the gallows may do well to thee.° To't
again, come.   45

2. CLOWN: "Who builds stronger than a mason, a shipwright, or a
carpenter?"

1. CLOWN: Ay, tell me that, and unyoke.°

2. CLOWN: Marry, now I can tell.

1. CLOWN: To't.   50

2. CLOWN: Mass,° I cannot tell.

1. CLOWN: Cudgel thy brains no more about it, for your dull ass will
not mend his pace with beating, and when you are asked
this question next, say "a grave-maker:" the houses he
makes last till doomsday. Go get thee to Yaughan,° and   55
fetch me a stoup° of liquor.   [*Exit* 2. CLOWN.]

Enter HAMLET *and* HORATIO *afar off.*

°11 *argal:* corruption of "ergo" = therefore. °15 *will he nill he:* will he or will he not (willy nilly). °20 *quest:*
inquest. °25 *countenance:* privilege. °26 *even-Christen:* fellow Christian. °30 *arms:* with a pun on "coat of arms."
°44 *to thee:* i.e., by hanging you. °48 *unyoke:* unharness (your wits, after this exertion). °51 *Mass:* by the mass.
°55 *Yaughan:* probably a local innkeeper. °56 *stoup:* stein, drinking mug.

1. CLOWN: [*Sings.*] In youth when I did love, did love,
                    Methought it was very sweet,
                To contract oh the time for a° my behove,°
60   O methought there a was nothing a meet.°
HAMLET: Has this fellow no feeling of his business, that a'sings in
    grave-making?
HORATIO: Custom hath made it in him a property of easiness.°
HAMLET: 'Tis e'en so, the hand of little employment hath the
65   daintier sense.°
1. CLOWN: [*Sings.*] But age with his stealing steps
                    Hath clawed me in his clutch,
                And hath shipped me intil° the land,
                As if I had never been such.

[*Throws up a skull.*]

70 HAMLET: That skull had a tongue in it, and could sing once: how the
            knave jowls° it to the ground, as if'twere Cain's jaw-bone,°
            that did the first murder. This might be the pate of a
            politician, which this ass now o'erreaches;° one that
            would circumvent° God, might it not?
75 HORATIO: It might my lord.
    HAMLET: Or of a courtier, which could say "Good morrow sweet
            lord, how dost thou good lord?" This might be my lord
            such-a-one, that praised my lord such-a-one's horse, when
            a'meant to beg it, might it not?
80 HORATIO: It might my lord.
    HAMLET: Why e'en so, and now my Lady Worm's, chopless,° and
            knocked about the mazzard° with a sexton's spade; here's
            fine revolution an° we had the trick° to see't. Did these
            bones cost no more the breeding, but to play at loggets°
85   with them? Mine ache to think on't.

1. CLOWN: [*Sings.*] A pick-axe and a spade, a spade,
                    For and a shrouding sheet,
                O a pit of clay for to be made
                For such a guest is meet.°   [*Throws up another skull.*]
90 HAMLET: There's another: why may not that be the skull of a
            lawyer? Where be his quiddities° now, his quillets,° his
            cases, his tenures,° and his tricks? Why does he suffer this
            rude knave now to knock him about the sconce° with a
            dirty shovel, and will not tell him of his action of battery?
95   Hum, this fellow might be in's time a great buyer of land,
            with his statutes,° his recognizances,° his fines,° his double

---

°59 *oh, a:* (he grunts as he works). *behove:* benefit. °60 *meet:* suitable. °63 *Custom . . . easiness:* being accustomed
to it has made him indifferent. °65 *daintier sense:* finer sensibility (being uncalloused). °68 *intil:* into. °71 *jowls:*
casts (with obvious pun). *Cain's jaw-bone:* the jawbone of an ass with which Cain murdered Abel. °73 *o'erreaches:*
(1) reaches over (2) gets the better of. °74 *would circumvent:* tried to outwit. °81 *chopless:* lacking the lower jaw.
°82 *mazzard:* head. °83 *an:* if. *trick:* knack. °84 *loggets:* game in which small pieces of wood were thrown at fixed
stakes.°89 *meet:* fitting. °91 *quiddities:* subtle definition. *quillets:* minute distinctions. °92 *tenures:* property holdings. °93 *sconce:* head. °96 *statutes:* mortgages. *recognizances:* promissory bonds. °96–97 *fines, recoveries:* legal
processes for transferring real estate.

vouchers,° his recoveries:° is this the fine° of his fines, and
the recovery° of his recoveries, to have his fine pate full of
fine dirt? Will his vouchers vouch him no more of his
purchases, and double ones too, than the length and   100
breadth of a pair of indentures?° The very conveyances° of
his lands will scarcely lie in this box,° and must th'inheritor°
himself have no more, ha?

HORATIO: Not a jot more my lord.

HAMLET: Is not parchment made of sheep-skins?   105

HORATIO: Ay my lord, and of calves'-skins too.

HAMLET: They are sheep and calves which seek out assurance° in
    that. I will speak to this fellow. Whose grave's this, sirrah?

1. CLOWN: Mine sir:
    [*Sings.*] O a pit of clay for to be made   110
           For such a guest is meet.

HAMLET: I think it be thine indeed, for thou liest in't.

1. CLOWN: You lie out on't° sir, and therefore 'tis not yours; for my
    part I do not lie in't, and yet it is mine.

HAMLET: Thou dost lie in't, to be in't and say it is thine: 'tis for the   115
    dead, not for the quick,° therefore thou liest.

1. CLOWN: 'Tis a quick lie sir, 'twill away again from me to you.

HAMLET: What man dost thou dig it for?

1. CLOWN: For no man sir.

HAMLET: What woman then?   120

1. CLOWN: For none neither.

HAMLET: Who is to be buried in't?

1. CLOWN: One that was a woman sir, but rest her soul she's dead.

HAMLET: How absolute° the knave is, we must speak by the card,° or
    equivocation° will undo us. By the lord, Horatio, this   125
    three years I have took note of it, the age is grown so
    picked,° that the toe of the peasant comes so near the heel of
    the courtier, he galls his kibe.° How long hast thou been
    grave-maker?

1. CLOWN: Of all the days i'th'year I came to't that day that our last   130
    king Hamlet overcame Fortinbras.

HAMLET: How long is that since?

1. CLOWN: Cannot you tell that? Every fool can tell that. It was the very
    day that young Hamlet was born: he that is mad and
    sent into England.   135

HAMLET: Ay marry, why was he sent into England?

1. CLOWN: Why because a' was mad: a' shall recover his wits there, or
    if a' do not, 'tis no great matter there.

HAMLET: Why?

1. CLOWN: 'Twill not be seen in him there, there the men are as mad   140
    as he.

°97 *vouchers:* persons who vouched for a title to real estate. *fine:* end. °98 *recovery:* attainment. °100–01 *length
. . . indentures:* contracts in duplicate, which spread out, would just cover his grave. °101 *conveyances:* deeds.
°102 *box:* the grave. *inheritor:* owner. °107 *assurance:* (1) security (2) transfer of land. °113 *on:* of. °116 *quick:*
living. °124 *absolute:* precise. *by the card:* exactly to the point (card on which compass points are marked).
°125 *equivocation:* ambiguity. °127 *picked:* fastidious ("picky"). °128 *galls his kibe:* chafes the sore on the courtier's
heel.

Hamlet (Mel Gibson) contemplates the power of death while looking at the skull of the king's jester, Yorick, in the 1990 film production of *Hamlet*, directed by Franco Zeffirelli.

HAMLET: How came he mad?

1. CLOWN: Very strangely they say.

HAMLET: How strangely?

145 **1. CLOWN:** Faith, e'en with losing his wits.

HAMLET: Upon what ground?

1. CLOWN: Why here in Denmark: I have been sexton here man and
boy thirty years.

HAMLET: How long will a man lie i'th'earth ere he rot?

150 **1. CLOWN:** Faith, if a' be not rotten before a' die, as we have many
pocky° corses nowadays that will scarce hold the laying in,
a' will last you some eight year, or nine year. A tanner will
last you nine year.

HAMLET: Why he more than another?

155 **1. CLOWN:** Why sir, his hide is so tanned with his trade, that a' will
keep out water a great while; and your water is a sore°
decayer of your whoreson dead body. Here's a skull now:
this skull hath lain you i'th'earth three-and-twenty years.

HAMLET: Whose was it?

160 **1. CLOWN:** A whoreson mad fellow's it was, whose do you think it
was?

HAMLET: Nay, I know not.

1. CLOWN: A pestilence on him for a mad rogue, a' poured a flagon of
Rhenish° on my head once; this same skull sir, was sir,

165 Yorick's skull, the king's jester.

°151 *pocky*: rotten (with venereal disease). °156 *sore*: grievous. °164 *Rhenish*: Rhine wine.

HAMLET: This?

1. CLOWN: E'en that.

HAMLET: Let me see. [*Takes the skull.*] Alas poor Yorick, I knew him
    Horatio, a fellow of infinite jest, of most excellent fancy,°
    he hath borne me on his back a thousand times: and now   170
    how abhorred in my imagination it is: my gorge rises at it.
    Here hung those lips that I have kissed I know not how
    oft. Where be your gibes now? your gambols, your songs,
    your flashes of merriment, that were wont to set the table
    on a roar?° not one now to mock your own grinning? quite   175
    chop-fallen?° Now get you to my lady's chamber, and tell
    her, let her paint an inch thick, to this favour° she must
    come. Make her laugh at that. Prithee Horatio, tell me one
    thing.

HORATIO: What's that, my lord?   180

HAMLET: Dost thou think Alexander looked o' this fashion
    i'th'earth?

HORATIO: E'en so.

HAMLET: And smelt so? Pah!   [*Puts down the skull.*]

HORATIO: E'en so my lord.   185

HAMLET: To what base uses we may return, Horatio. Why may not
    imagination trace the noble dust of Alexander, til a'find it
    stopping a bung-hole?°

HORATIO: 'Twere to consider too curiously,° to consider so.

HAMLET: No faith, not a jot, but to follow him thither with modesty°   190
    enough, and likelihood to lead it; as thus: Alexander died,
    Alexander was buried, Alexander returneth to dust, the
    dust is earth, of earth we make loam,° and why of that loam
    whereto he was converted, might they not stop a
    beer-barrel?   195
        Imperious Caesar, dead and turned to clay,
        Might stop a hole to keep the wind away.
        O that that earth which kept the world in awe,
        Should patch a wall t'expel the winter's flaw.°
    But soft, but soft awhile, here comes the king,   200
    The queen, the courtiers.

Enter KING, QUEEN, LAERTES, [*Doctor of Divinity*]*, and a coffin, with Lords attendant.*

                    Who is this they follow?
    And with such maimèd° rites? This doth betoken
    The corse they follow did with desp'rate hand
    Fordo it° own life; 'twas of some estate.°
    Couch° we awhile, and mark.   [*They retire.*]

HAMLET: That is Laertes,   205
    A very noble youth: mark.

LAERTES: What ceremony else?

°169 *fancy:* imagination. °175 *on a roar:* roaring with laughter. °176 *chop-fallen:* (1) lacking a lower jaw (2)
dejected, "down in the mouth." °177 *favour:* appearance. °188 *bung-hole:* hole in a cask. °189 *curiously:* minutely.
°190 *modesty:* moderation. °193 *loam:* a clay mixture used as plaster. °199 *flaw:* windy gusts. °202 *maimèd:* abbreviated.
°204 *Fordo it:* destroy its. *estate:* social rank. °205 *Couch:* hide.

DOCTOR: Her obsequies have been as far enlarged
        As we have warranty: her death was doubtful,°
210   And but that great command o'ersways the order,
        She should in ground unsanctified have lodged
        Til the last trumpet: for charitable prayers,
        Shards,° flints and pebbles should be thrown on her:
        Yet here she is allowed her virgin crants,°
215   Her maiden strewments,° and the bringing home
        Of° bell and burial.
LAERTES: Must there no more be done?
DOCTOR: No more be done:
        We should profane the service of the dead,
        To sing sage requiem°° and such rest to her
        As to peace-parted souls.
220 **LAERTES:**   Lay her i'th'earth,
        And from her fair and unpolluted flesh
        May violets spring: I tell thee churlish priest,
        A minist'ring angel shall my sister be,
        When thou liest howling.
HAMLET: What, the fair Ophelia?
225 **QUEEN:** [*Scattering flowers.*] Sweets to the sweet, farewell.
        I hoped thou shouldst have been my Hamlet's wife:
        I thought thy bride-bed to have decked, sweet maid,
        And not have strewed thy grave.
LAERTES: O treble woe
        Fall ten times treble on that cursèd head
230   Whose wicked deed thy most ingenious sense°
        Deprived thee of. Hold off the earth awhile,
        Till I have caught her once more in mine arms;   *Leaps in the grave.*
        Now pile your dust upon the quick° and dead,
        Till of this flat a mountain you have made
235   T'o'ertop old Pelion,° or the skyish head
        Of blue Olympus.
HAMLET: [*Comes forward.*] What is he whose grief
        Bears such an emphasis? whose phrase of sorrow
        Conjures the wand'ring stars,° and makes them stand
240   Like wonder-wounded hearers? This is I,
        Hamlet the Dane.   *HAMLET leaps in after LAERTES.*
LAERTES: [*Grapples with him.*] The devil take thy soul.
HAMLET: Thou pray'st not well,
        I prithee take thy fingers from my throat,
245   For though I am not splenitive° and rash,
        Yet have I in me something dangerous,
        Which let thy wiseness fear; hold off thy hand.
KING: Pluck them asunder.
QUEEN: Hamlet, Hamlet!

°209 *doubtful:* suspicious. °213 *Shards:* bits of broken pottery. °214 *crants:* garland. °215 *strewments:* flowers strewn on the grave. °215–16 *bringing home Of:* laying to rest with. °219 *sage requiem:* solemn dirge. °230 *sense:* mind. °233 *quick:* live. °235 *Pelion:* mountain (on which the Titans placed Mt. Ossa, to scale Mt. Olympus and reach the gods). °239 *Conjures . . . stars:* casts a spell over the planets. °245 *splenitive:* quick-tempered (anger was thought to originate in the spleen).

ALL: Gentlemen!
HORATIO: Good my lord, be quiet.

[*ATTENDANTS part them, and they come out of the grave.*]

HAMLET: Why, I will fight with him upon this theme   250
    Until my eyelids will no longer wag.
QUEEN: O my son, what theme?
HAMLET: I loved Ophelia, forty thousand brothers
    Could not with all their quantity of love
    Make up my sum. What wilt thou do for her?   255
KING: O he is mad, Laertes.
QUEEN: For love of God, forbear° him.
HAMLET: 'Swounds,° show me what thou't do:
    Woo't° weep? woo't fight? woo't fast? woo't tear thyself?
    Woo't drink up eisel?° eat a crocodile?°   260
    I'll do't. Dost thou come here to whine?
    To outface me with leaping in her grave?
    Be buried quick with her, and so will I.
    And if thou prate of mountains, let them throw
    Millions of acres on us, till our ground,   265
    Singeing his pate against the burning zone,°
    Make Ossa° like a wart. Nay, an thou'lt mouth,
    I'll rant as well as thou.
QUEEN: This is mere° madness,
    And thus awhile the fit will work on him:
    Anon as patient as the female dove   270
    When that her golden couplets° are disclosed,
    His silence will sit drooping.
HAMLET: Hear you sir,
    What is the reason that you use me thus?
    I loved you ever; but it is no matter.
    Let Hercules himself do what he may,   275
    The cat will mew, and dog will have his day.   *Exit HAMLET.*
KING: I pray thee good Horatio, wait upon him.   [*HORATIO follows.*]
    [*Aside to Laertes.*] Strengthen your patience in our last night's speech,
    We'll put the matter to the present push°—
    Good Gertrude, set some watch over your son—   280
    This grave shall have a living monument.°
    An hour of quiet shortly shall we see,
    Till then, in patience our proceeding be.   *Exeunt.*

Scene 2. [A hall in the castle]

Enter HAMLET and HORATIO.

HAMLET: So much for this sir, now shall you see the other;
    You do remember all the circumstance.

257 *forbear*: be patient with. °258 *'Swounds*: corruption of "God's wounds." °259 *Woo't*: wilt thou. °260 *eisel*: vinegar (thought to reduce anger and encourage melancholy). *crocodile*: associated with hypocritical tears. °266 *burning zone*: sun's sphere. °267 *Ossa*: see note to line 235. °268 *mere*: absolute. °271 *golden couplets*: fuzzy yellow twin fledglings. °279 *present push*: immediate test. °281 *living monument*: (1) lasting tombstone (2) living sacrifice (Hamlet) to memorialize it.

HORATIO: Remember it my lord!

HAMLET: Sir, in my heart there was a kind of fighting

5   That would not let me sleep; methought I lay

Worse than the mutines in the bilboes.° Rashly—

And praised be rashness for it: let us know,

Our indiscretion sometimes serves us well

When our deep plots do pall,° and that should learn us

10   There's a divinity that shapes our ends,

Rough-hew them how we will—

HORATIO: That is most certain.

HAMLET: Up from my cabin,

My sea-gown° scarfed about me, in the dark

Groped I to find out them, had my desire,

15   Fingered° their packet, and in fine° withdrew

To mine own room again, making so bold,

My fears forgetting manners, to unseal

Their grand commission; where I found, Horatio—

Ah royal knavery—an exact command,

20   Larded° with many several sorts of reasons,

Importing Denmark's health, and England's too,

With ho, such bugs and goblins in my life,°

That on the supervise,° no leisure bated,°

No, not to stay° the grinding of the axe,

My head should be struck off.

25 **HORATIO:**   Is't possible?

HAMLET: Here's the commission, read it at more leisure.

But wilt thou hear now how I did proceed?

HORATIO: I beseech you.

HAMLET: Being thus be-netted round with villainies,

30   Ere I could make a prologue to my brains,

They had begun the play.° I sat me down,

Devised a new commission, wrote it fair°—

I once did hold it, as our statists° do,

A baseness° to write fair, and laboured much

35   How to forget that learning, but sir now

It did me yeoman's° service: wilt thou know

Th'effect of what I wrote?

HORATIO: Ay, good my lord.

HAMLET: An earnest conjuration° from the king,

As England was his faithful tributary,

40   As love between them like the palm might flourish,

As peace should still her wheaten garland wear

And stand a comma° 'tween their amities,

°6 *mutines . . . bilboes:* mutineers in shackles. °9 *pall:* fail. °13 *sea-gown:* short-sleeved knee-length gown worn by seamen. °15 *Fingered:* got my fingers on. *in fine:* to finish. °20 *Larded:* embellished. °22 *bugs . . . life:* imaginary evils attributed to me, like imaginary goblins ("bugs") meant to frighten children. °23 *supervise:* looking over (the commission). *leisure bated:* delay excepted. °24 *stay:* await. °30–31 *Ere . . . play:* Before I could outline the action in my mind, my brains started to play their part. °32 *wrote it fair:* wrote a finished (neat) copy, a "fair copy." °33 *statists:* statesmen. °34 *baseness:* mark of humble status. °36 *yeoman's:* (in the sense of "faithful"). °38 *conjuration:* entreaty (he parodies the rhetoric of such documents). °42 *comma:* connection.

And many such like "as'es"° of great charge,°
That on the view and know of these contents,
Without debatement further, more or less,   45
He should those bearers put to sudden death,
Not shriving° time allowed.

HORATIO: How was this sealed?

HAMLET: Why even in that was heaven ordinant,°
I had my father's signet° in my purse,
Which was the model° of that Danish seal: 50
Folded the writ up in the form of th'other,
Subscribed° it, gave't th'impression,° placed it safely,
The changeling° never known: now the next day
Was our sea-fight, and what to this was sequent
Thou knowest already.   55

HORATIO: So Guildenstern and Rosencrantz go to't.

HAMLET: Why man, they did make love to this employment,°
They are not near my conscience, their defeat
Does by their own insinuation° grow:
'Tis dangerous when the baser nature comes   60
Between the pass° and fell° incensed points
Of mighty opposites.

HORATIO: Why, what a king is this!

HAMLET: Does it not, think thee, stand me now upon°—
He that hath killed my king, and whored my mother,
Popped in between th'election° and my hopes,   65
Thrown out his angle° for my proper° life,
And with such cozenage°—is't not perfect conscience
To quit° him with this arm? And isn't not to be damned,
To let this canker of our nature° come
In further evil?   70

HORATIO: It must be shortly known to him from England
What is the issue of the business there.

HAMLET: It will be short, the interim is mine,
And a man's life's no more than to say "One."°
But I am very sorry good Horatio,   75
That to Laertes I forgot myself;
For by the image of my cause, I see
The portraiture of his;° I'll court his favours:
But sure the bravery° of his grief did put me
Into a towering passion.

HORATIO: Peace, who comes here?   80

Enter young OSRIC.

°43 *as'es:* (1) the "as" clauses in the commission (2) asses. *charge:* (1) weight (in the clauses) (2) burdens (on the asses). °47 *shriving:* confession and absolution. °48 *was heaven ordinant:* it was divinely ordained. °49 *signet:* seal. °50 *model:* replica. °52 *Subscribed:* signed. *impression:* i.e., of the seal. °53 *changeling:* substitute (baby imp left when an infant was spirited away). °57 *did . . . employment:* asked for it. °59 *insinuation:* intrusion. °61 *pass:* thrust. *fell:* fierce. °63 *stand . . . upon:* become incumbent upon me now. °65 *election:* (the Danish king was so chosen). °66 *angle:* fishing hook. *proper:* very own. °67 *cozenage:* deception. °68 *quit:* repay, requite. °69 *canker of our nature:* cancer of humanity. °74 *to say "One":* to score one hit in fencing. °77–78 *by the image . . . his:* in the depiction of my situation, I see the reflection of his. °79 *bravery:* ostentation.

OSRIC: Your lordship is right welcome back to Denmark.

HAMLET: I humbly thank you sir. [*Aside to Horatio.*] Dost know this
　　　water-fly?

HORATIO: No my good lord.

85 HAMLET: Thy state is the more gracious,° for 'tis a vice to know him:
　　　he hath much land, and fertile: let a beast be lord of beasts,
　　　and his crib shall stand at the king's mess;° 'tis a chough,°
　　　but as I say, spacious in the possession of dirt.

OSRIC: Sweet lord, if you lordship were at leisure, I should
90　　　impart a thing to you from his majesty.

HAMLET: I will receive it sir, with all diligence of spirit; put your
　　　bonnet° to his right use, 'tis for the head.

OSRIC: I thank your lordship, it is very hot.

HAMLET: No, believe me 'tis very cold, the wind is northerly.

95 OSRIC: It is indifferent° cold my lord indeed.

HAMLET: But yet methinks it is very sultry and hot for my
　　　complexion.°

OSRIC: Exceedingly, my lord, it is very sultry, as 'twere, I cannot
　　　tell how: but my lord, his majesty bade me signify to you
100　　　that a' has laid a great wager on your head. Sir, this is the
　　　matter—

HAMLET: [*Moves him to put on his hat.*] I beseech you remember—

OSRIC: Nay good my lord, for mine ease,° in good faith. Sir, here
　　　is newly come to court Laertes, believe me, an absolute
105　　　gentleman, full of most excellent differences,° of very soft
　　　society, and great showing: indeed to speak feelingly of
　　　him, he is the card° or calendar of gentry: for you shall find
　　　in him the continent of what part a gentleman would see.°

HAMLET: Sir, his definement° suffers no perdition° in you, though I
110　　　know to divide him inventorially would dozy°
　　　th'arithmetic of memory, and yet but yaw neither, in
　　　respect of his quick sail,° but in the verity of extolment,° I
　　　take him to be a soul of great article,° and his infusion° of
　　　such dearth and rareness, as to make true diction of him,
115　　　his semblable° is his mirror, and who else would trace° him,
　　　his umbrage,° nothing more.°

OSRIC: Your lordship speaks most infallibly of him.

HAMLET: The concernancy° sir? why do we wrap the gentleman in
　　　our more rawer breath?°

120 OSRIC: Sir?

°85 *gracious:* favorable. °86–87 *let a beast . . . mess:* An ass who owns enough property can eat with the king.
°87 *chough:* chattering bird, jackdaw. °92 *bonnet:* hat. °95 *indifferent:* reasonably. °97 *complexion:* temperament.
°103 *for mine ease:* for my own comfort. °105 *differences:* accomplishments. °107 *card:* shipman's compass card.
°108 *continent . . . see:* continuing the marine metaphor (1) geographical continent (2) all the qualities a gentleman would look for. °109–16 *Sir . . . more:* Hamlet outdoes Osric in affected speech. °109 *definement:* description. *perdition:* loss. °110 *dozy:* dizzy. °111–12 *yaw . . . sail:* (1) moving in an unsteady course (as another boat
would do, trying to catch up with Laertes's "quick sail") (2) staggering to one trying to list his accomplishments.
°112 *in . . . extolment:* to praise him truthfully. °113 *article:* scope. *infusion:* essence. °114–16 *as to make . . . more:*
to describe him truly I would have to employ his mirror to depict his only equal—himself, and who would follow
him is only a shadow. °115 *semblable:* equal. *trace:* (1) describe (2) follow. °116 *umbrage:* shadow. °118 *concer-
nancy:* relevance. °119 *rawer breath:* crude speech.

HORATIO: Is't not possible to understand in another tongue?° You
    will do't sir, really.
HAMLET: What imports the nomination° of this gentleman?
OSRIC: Of Laertes?
HORATIO: His purse is empty already, all's golden words are spent.   125
HAMLET: Of him, sir.
OSRIC: I know you are not ignorant—
HAMLET: I would you did sir, yet in faith if you did, it would not
    much approve me.° Well, sir.
OSRIC: You are not ignorant of what excellence Laertes is—   130
HAMLET: I dare not confess that, lest I should compare with him in
    excellence, but to know a man well were to know himself.°
OSRIC: I mean sir for his weapon, but in the imputation° laid on
    him by them in his meed,° he's unfellowed.°
HAMLET: What's his weapon?   135
OSRIC: Rapier and dagger.
HAMLET: That's two of his weapons—but well.
OSRIC: The king sir, hath wagered with him six Barbary horses,
    against which he has impawned,° as I take it, six French
    rapiers and poniards,° with their assigns,° as girdle, hangers,°   140
    and so. Three of the carriages° in faith very dear to
    fancy,° very responsive to the hilts, most delicate carriages,
    and of very liberal conceit.°
HAMLET: What call you the carriages?
HORATIO: I knew you must be edified by the margent° ere you had   145
    done.
OSRIC: The carriages sir, are the hangers.
HAMLET: The phrase would be more germane to the matter, if we
    could carry a cannon by our sides: I would it might be
    hangers till then, but on: six Barbary horses against six   150
    French swords, their assigns, and three liberal-conceited
    carriages—that's the French bet against the Danish. Why
    is this all "impawned" as you call it?
OSRIC: The king sir, hath laid sir, that in a dozen passes between
    yourself and him, he shall not exceed you three hits;° he   155
    hath laid on twelve for nine, and it would come to
    immediate trial, if your lordship would vouchsafe the
    answer.°
HAMLET: How if I answer no?
OSRIC: I mean my lord, the opposition of your person in trial.   160
HAMLET: Sir, I will walk here in the hall; if it please his majesty, it is
    the breathing time° of day with me; let the foils be brought,
    the gentleman willing, and the king hold his purpose, I

°121 *Is't not . . . tongue:* Cannot Osric understand his own way of speaking when used by another? °123 *nomination:* naming. °128–29 *if you did . . . me:* If you found me to be "not ignorant," it would prove little (as you are no judge of ignorance). °132 *to know . . . himself:* to know a man well, one must first know oneself. °133 *imputation:* repute. °134 *meed:* worth. *unfellowed:* unequaled. °139 *impawned:* staked. °140 *poniards:* daggers. *assigns:* accessories. *girdle, hangers:* belt, straps attached thereto, from which swords were hung. °141 *carriages:* hangers. °141–42 *dear to fancy:* rare in design. °143 *liberal conceit:* elaborate conception. °145 *margent:* marginal note. °154–55 *laid . . . three hits:* wagered that in twelve bouts Laertes must win three more than Hamlet. °158 *answer:* acceptance of the challenge (Hamlet interprets as "reply"). °162 *breathing time:* exercise period.

165   will win for him an I can, if not, I will gain nothing but my
shame and the odd hits.

OSRIC: Shall I re-deliver you° e'en so?

HAMLET: To this effect sir, after what flourish your nature will.°

OSRIC: I commend° my duty to your lordship.   [*Exit* OSRIC.]

HAMLET: Yours, yours.

170   He does well to commend it himself, there are no tongues
else for's turn.°

HORATIO: This lapwing° runs away with the shell on his head.

HAMLET: A' did comply° sir, with his dug° before a' sucked it: thus
has he—and many more of the same bevy that I know the

175   drossy° age dotes on—only got the tune of the time, and
out of an habit of encounter,° a kind of yeasty collection,°
which carries them through and through the most fond
and winnowed° opinions; and do but blow them to their
trial, and bubbles are out.°

Enter a LORD.

180   LORD: My lord, his majesty commended him to you by young
Osric, who brings back to him that you attend him in
the hall. He sends to know if your pleasure hold to play
with Laertes, or that you will take longer time.

HAMLET: I am constant to my purposes, they follow the king's

185   pleasure, if his fitness speaks,° mine is ready: now or
whensoever, provided I be so able as now.

LORD: The king, and queen, and all are coming down.

HAMLET: In happy time.

LORD: The queen desires you to use some gentle entertainment°

190   to Laertes, before you fall to play.

HAMLET: She well instructs me.   [*Exit* LORD.]

HORATIO: You will lose this wager, my lord.

HAMLET: I do not think so, since we went into France, I have been in
continual practice, I shall win at the odds; but thou

195   wouldst not think how ill all's here about my heart: but it
is no matter.

HORATIO: Nay good my lord—

HAMLET: It is but a foolery, but it is such a kind of gaingiving° as
would perhaps trouble a woman.

200   HORATIO: If your mind dislike any thing, obey it. I will forestall their
repair° hither, and say you are not fit.

HAMLET: Not a whit, we defy augury;° there is a special providence
in the fall of a sparrow.° If it be now, 'tis not to come:

°166 *re-deliver you:* take back your answer. °167 *after . . . will:* embellished as you wish. °168 *commend:* offer (Hamlet interprets as "praise"). °170–71 *no tongues . . . turn:* no others who would. °172 *lapwing:* reported to be so precocious that it ran as soon as hatched. °173 *comply:* observe the formalities of courtesy. *dug:* mother's breast. °175 *drossy:* frivolous. °176 *habit of encounter:* habitual association (with others as frivolous). *yeasty collection:* frothy assortment of phrases. °177–78 *fond and winnowed:* trivial and considered. °178–79 *blow . . . out:* blow on them to test them and they are gone. °185 *his fitness speaks:* it agrees with his convenience. °189 *gentle entertainment:* friendly treatment. °198 *gaingiving:* misgiving. °201 *repair:* coming. °202 *augury:* omens. °202–03 *special . . . sparrow:* "Are not two sparrows sold for a farthing? and one of them shall not fall on the ground without your Father": Matthew 10:29.

if it be not to come, it will be now; if it be not now,
yet it will come—the readiness is all. Since no man has   205
aught of what he leaves, what is't to leave betimes?° let
be.

A table prepared. Trumpets, Drums, and officers with cushions. Enter KING, QUEEN, and all the
state, [OSRIC], foils, daggers, and LAERTES.

KING: Come Hamlet, come and take this hand from me.
    [*Puts Laertes' hand into Hamlet's.*]
HAMLET: Give me your pardon sir, I have done you wrong,
    But pardon't as you are a gentleman.   210
    This presence knows, and you must needs have heard,
    How I am punished with a sore distraction.°
    What I have done
    That might your nature, honour, and exception°
    Roughly awake, I here proclaim was madness: 215
    Was't Hamlet wronged Laertes? never Hamlet.
    If Hamlet from himself be ta'en away,
    And when he's not himself, does wrong Laertes,
    Then Hamlet does it not, Hamlet denies it:
    Who does it then? his madness. If't be so,   220
    Hamlet is of the faction that is wronged,
    His madness is poor Hamlet's enemy.
    Sir, in this audience,
    Let my disclaiming from a purposed evil,
    Free me so far in your most generous thoughts,   225
    That I have shot my arrow o'er the house
    And hurt my brother.°
LAERTES: I am satisfied in nature,
    Whose motive in this case should stir me most
    To my revenge, but in my terms of honour
    I stand aloof, and will no reconcilement,   230
    Till by some elder masters of known honour
    I have a voice and precedent° of peace
    To keep my name ungored:° but till that time,
    I do receive your offered love, like love,
    And will not wrong it.
HAMLET: I embrace it freely,   235
    And will this brother's wager frankly° play.
    Give us the foils: come on.
LAERTES: Come, one for me.
HAMLET: I'll be your foil° Laertes, in mine ignorance
    Your skill shall like a star i'th' darkest night
    Stick fiery off° indeed.
LAERTES: You mock me sir.   240

°206 *betimes:* early (before one's time). °212 *sore distraction:* grievous madness. °214 *exception:* disapproval.
°226–27 *That I have . . . brother:* that it was accidental. °232 *voice and precedent:* opinion based on precedent.
°233 *name ungored:* reputation uninjured. Laertes says that he cannot accept Hamlet's apology formally until
he is assured that his acceptance will not harm his honor or damage his reputation. °236 *frankly:* freely.
°238 *foil:* (1) the blunted sword with which they fence (2) leaf of metal set under a jewel to make it shine more
brilliantly. °240 *Stick fiery off:* show in shining contrast.

HAMLET: No, by this hand.

KING: Give them the foils young Osric. Cousin° Hamlet,
    You know the wager.

HAMLET: Very well my lord.
    Your grace has laid the odds o'th'weaker side.

245   **KING:** I do not fear it, I have seen you both,
    But since he is bettered,° we have therefore odds.

LAERTES: This is too heavy: let me see another.°

HAMLET: This likes° me well, these foils have all a° length?

OSRIC: Ay my good lord.   *Prepare to play.*

250   **KING:** Set me the stoups° of wine upon that table:
    If Hamlet give the first or second hit,
    Or quit in answer of° the third exchange,
    Let all the battlements their ordnance fire.
    The king shall drink to Hamlet's better breath,

255   And in the cup an union° shall he throw,
    Richer than that which four successive kings
    In Denmark's crown have worn: give me the cups,
    And let the kettle° to the trumpet speak,
    The trumpet to the cannoneer without,

260   The cannons to the heavens, the heaven to earth,
    "Now the king drinks to Hamlet." Come begin.
    And you the judges bear a wary eye.   *Trumpets the while.*

HAMLET: Come on sir.

LAERTES: Come my lord.   *They play.*

HAMLET: One.

LAERTES: No.

HAMLET: Judgment.

OSRIC: A hit, a very palpable hit.

Flourish. Drum, trumpets and shot. A piece° goes off.

LAERTES: Well, again.

265   **KING:** Stay, give me drink. Hamlet, this pearl is thine.
    Here's to thy health: give him the cup.

HAMLET: I'll play this bout first, set it by a while.
    Come.   *[They play.]*
         Another hit. What say you?

LAERTES: A touch, a touch, I do confess't.

270   **KING:** Our son shall win.

QUEEN: He's fat° and scant of breath.
    Here Hamlet, take my napkin,° rub thy brows.
    The queen carouses° to thy fortune, Hamlet.   *[She takes HAMLET'S cup.]*

HAMLET: Good madam.

KING: Gertrude, do not drink.

QUEEN: I will my lord, I pray you pardon me.

275   **KING:** *[Aside.]* It is the poisoned cup, it is too late.

HAMLET: I dare not drink yet madam: by and by.

°242 *Cousin:* kinsman. °246 *bettered:* either (1) judged to be better or (2) better trained. °247 *another:* the unbated and poisoned sword. °248 *likes:* pleases all. *a:* all the same. °250 *stoups:* goblets. °252 *quit in answer of:* score a draw in. °255 *union:* large pearl. °258 *kettle:* kettledrum. °264 S.D.: *piece:* i.e., a cannon. °270 *fat:* sweating (sweat was thought to be melted body fat). °271 *napkin:* handkerchief. °272 *carouses:* drinks.

QUEEN: Come, let me wipe thy face.

LAERTES: [*To the King.*] My lord, I'll hit him now.

KING: I do not think't.

LAERTES: [*Aside.*] And yet 'tis almost 'gainst my conscience.

HAMLET: Come for the third Laertes, you do but dally,   280
   I pray you pass° with your best violence,
   I am afeard you make a wanton of me.°

LAERTES: Say you so? Come on.   *Play.*

OSRIC: Nothing neither way.   [*They break off.*]

LAERTES: Have at you now.°   [*Wounds HAMLET.*]

                    In scuffling they change rapiers.

KING: Part them, they are incensed.   285

HAMLET: Nay, come again.   [*The QUEEN falls.*]

                                              [*HAMLET wounds LAERTES.*]

OSRIC: Look to the queen there, ho!

HORATIO: They bleed on both sides. How is it, my lord?

OSRIC: How is't, Laertes?

LAERTES: Why as a woodcock° to my own springe,° Osric,
   I am justly killed with mine own treachery.   290

HAMLET: How does the queen?

KING: She sounds° to see them bleed.

QUEEN: No, no, the drink, the drink, O my dear Hamlet,
   The drink, the drink, I am poisoned.   [*Dies.*]

HAMLET: O villainy! ho! let the door be locked,
   Treachery, seek it out!   295

LAERTES: It is here Hamlet. Hamlet, thou art slain,
   No medicine in the world can do thee good,
   In thee there is not half an hour of life,
   The treacherous instrument is in thy hand,
   Unbated° and envenomed. The foul practice°   300
   Hath turned itself on me, lo, here I lie
   Never to rise again: thy mother's poisoned:
   I can no more: the king, the king's to blame.

HAMLET: The point envenomed too:
   Then venom, to thy work.   *Hurts the KING.*   305

ALL: Treason! treason!

KING: O yet defend me friends, I am but hurt.°

HAMLET: Here, thou incestuous, murderous, damnèd Dane,
   Drink off this potion: is thy union here?
   Follow my mother.   *KING dies.*

LAERTES: He is justly served,   310
   It is a poison tempered° by himself:
   Exchange forgiveness with me, noble Hamlet,
   Mine and my father's death come not upon thee,°
   Nor thine on me.   *Dies.*

°281 *pass:* thrust. °282 *make a wanton of me:* are indulging me like a spoiled child. °285 *Have . . . now:* the bout is over when Laertes attacks Hamlet and catches him off guard.   °289 *woodcock:* snipe-like bird (believed to be foolish and therefore easily trapped). *springe:* trap. °291 *sounds:* swoons. °300 *Unbated:* not blunted. *practice:* plot. °307 *but hurt:* only wounded. °311 *tempered:* mixed. °313 *come . . . thee:* are not to be blamed on you.

315   **HAMLET:** Heaven make thee free° of it, I follow thee.
        I am dead, Horatio; wretched queen, adieu.
        You that look pale, and tremble at this chance,
        That are but mutes,° or audience to this act,
        Had I but time, as this fell sergeant° Death
320   Is strict in his arrest, O I could tell you—
        But let it be; Horatio, I am dead,
        Thou livest, report me and my cause aright
        To the unsatisfied.°
    HORATIO: Never believe it;
325   I am more an antique Roman° than a Dane:
        Here's yet some liquor left.
    HAMLET: As thou'rt a man,
        Give me the cup, let go, by heaven I'll ha't.
        O God, Horatio, what a wounded name,
        Things standing thus unknown, shall live behind me.
330   If thou didst ever hold me in thy heart,
        Absènt thee from felicity awhile,
        And in this harsh world draw thy breath in pain
        To tell my story.   *A march afar off, and shot within.*
                What warlike noise is this?
    OSRIC: Young Fortinbras with conquest come from Poland,
335   To th'ambassadors of England gives
        This warlike volley.
    HAMLET: O I die Horatio,
        The potent poison quite o'er-crows° my spirit,
        I cannot live to hear the news from England,
        But I do prophesy th'election° lights
340   On Fortinbras, he has my dying voice,°
        So tell him, with th'occurrents more and less°
        Which have solicited°—the rest is silence.   *Dies.*
    HORATIO: Now cracks a noble heart: good night sweet prince,
        And flights of angels sing thee to thy rest.
345   Why does the drum come hither?

Enter FORTINBRAS and English Ambassadors, with drum, colours, and attendants.

    FORTINBRAS: Where is this sight?
    HORATIO: What is it you would see?
        If aught of woe, or wonder, cease your search.
    FORTINBRAS: This quarry cries on havoc.° O proud death,
        What feast is toward° in thine eternal cell,
350   That thou so many princes at a shot
        So bloodily hast struck?
    AMBASSADOR: The sight is dismal,
        And our affairs from England come too late;

°315 *free:* guiltless. °318 *mutes:* actors without speaking parts. °319 *fell sergeant:* cruel sheriff's officer. °323 *unsatis-fied:* uninformed. °325 *antique Roman:* ancient Roman (who considered suicide honorable). °337 *o'er-crows:* overpowers, conquers. °339 *election:* for king of Denmark. °340 *voice:* vote. °341 *occurrents more and less:* events great and small. °342 *solicited:* incited me. °348 *quarry . . . havoc:* heap of dead bodies proclaims slaughter done here. °349 *toward:* in preparation.

The ears° are senseless that should give us hearing,
To tell him his commandment is fulfilled,
That Rosencrantz and Guildenstern are dead: 355
Where should we have our thanks?
HORATIO: Not from his mouth,
Had it th'ability of life to thank you;
He never gave commandment for their death;
But since so jump° upon this bloody question,
You from the Polack wars, and you from England   360
Are here arrived, give order that these bodies
High on a stage be placèd to the view,
And let me speak to th'yet unknowing world
How these things came about; so shall you hear
Of carnal, bloody and unnatural acts,   365
Of accidental judgments, casual° slaughters,
Of deaths put on° by cunning and forced cause,°
And in this upshot, purposes mistook,
Fall'n on th'inventors' heads:° all this can I
Truly deliver.
FORTINBRAS: Let us haste to hear it,   370
And call the noblest to the audience.
For me, with sorrow I embrace my fortune;
I have some rights of memory° in this kingdom,
Which now to claim my vantage° doth invite me.
HORATIO: Of that I shall have also cause to speak,   375
And from his mouth whose voice will draw on more:°
But let this same° be presently performed,
Even while men's minds are wild,° lest more mischance
On° plots and errors happen.
FORTINBRAS: Let four captains
Bear Hamlet like a soldier to the stage,   380
For he was likely, had he been put on,°
To have proved most royal; and for his passage,°
The soldiers' music and the rite of war
Speak loudly for him:
Take up the bodies, such a sight as this,   385
Becomes the field, but here shows much amiss.
Go bid the soldiers shoot.

Exeunt marching: after the which a peal of ordnance are shot off.

°353 *ears:* of Claudius. °359 *jump:* opportunely. °366 *casual:* unpremeditated. °367 *put on:* prompted by. *forced cause:* being forced to act in self-defense. °368–369 *purposes . . . heads:* plots gone wrong and destroying their inventors. °373 *of memory:* remembered. °374 *vantage:* advantageous position. °376 *draw on more:* influence more (votes). °377 *this same:* this telling of the story. °378 *wild:* upset. °379 *On:* on top of. °381 *put on:* i.e., put on the throne. °382 *passage:* i.e., to the next world.

QUESTIONS

1. *Act 1.* How do you learn in the first scene that something is wrong in Denmark?
2. In scene 2, how does Claudius appear? Does he seem rational? Good? A good administrator? A competent ruler? A loving husband and uncle?
3. What does Hamlet reveal about his own mental and psychological state in his first soliloquy?
4. Why do both Laertes and Polonius caution Ophelia about Hamlet's interest in her?
5. What does the Ghost tell Hamlet to do and not to do? Why does Hamlet believe he needs independent proof about the validity of the Ghost?
6. *Act 2.* Who is Polonius? What is his analysis of Hamlet's "madness"? What do his speeches show us about him?
7. Describe Hamlet's self-accusation in the "O What a Rogue" soliloquy (2.2.524–80). To what degree is his accusation justified?
8. *Act 3.* How do you react to Hamlet's treatment of Ophelia in Act 3, scene 1? What evidence suggests that he knows he is being watched by Claudius and Polonius?
9. What does Hamlet think of Claudius's reaction to "The Murder of Gonzago"? Why does Claudius not react to the dumb-show before the play-within-a-play?
10. Why does Hamlet not kill Claudius when the King is at prayer?
11. Describe Hamlet's treatment of Gertrude during their confrontation in her private room. Is Hamlet justified in his treatment? Why does the Ghost appear here?
12. *Act 4.* How are Laertes's wishes for revenge like Hamlet's wishes for revenge?
13. How does Claudius plan to use Laertes's desire for vengeance against Hamlet? To what extent does Laertes allow himself to be used?
14. *Act 5.* Comic relief is a humorous episode designed to ease tension. How does the scene of the gravediggers qualify as comic relief? Why is comic relief appropriate at this point of the play? How does the scene broaden the play's themes?
15. Describe the lessons that Hamlet tells Horatio he has learned about life. How does this understanding show that Hamlet has changed? Why is it ironic?
16. How is Gertrude killed? Hamlet? Laertes? Claudius? Why does Hamlet insist that Horatio not commit suicide?

GENERAL QUESTIONS

1. Describe Claudius. Is he purely evil, or is he merely a flawed human being? Could the play also be called "The Tragedy of Claudius, King of Denmark"?
2. Characterize Horatio. Why does Hamlet trust and admire him? How is he different from Rosencrantz and Guildenstern? Are these characters round or flat? How can one justify Hamlet's arrangement for the deaths of Rosencrantz and Guildenstern?
3. *Hamlet* is full of conflicts that oppose people to other people, to society, and to themselves. List all the conflicts you can find in the play. Decide which of these is the central conflict, and explain your choice.
4. What is the crisis of *Hamlet*? When does it occur? Whom does it affect? What is the catastrophe? The resolution?
5. In Act 4, Claudius notes that "sorrows come . . . in battalions." By the end of the play these sorrows include the deaths of all the major characters except Horatio. To what degree can Claudius be held responsible for all the sorrows of the play? Which sorrows may be particularly traced to Hamlet?

6. How does Shakespeare demonstrate that *Hamlet* is a tragedy of the state as well as the individual? Is the condition of Denmark better or worse at the end of the play than at the beginning?

Tragedy from Shakespeare to Arthur Miller

Shakespeare's tragedies feature people of elevated station, such as kings, princes, dukes, and generals. When he creates characters of a lower status, he often treats them as comic, as we see in the gravediggers in *Hamlet* and the "hempen homespuns" in *A Midsummer Night's Dream*. This traditional distinction was based on the common assumption of the time that social order rested on the lives and trials of the elite and powerful. The magnitude of the deeds— and errors—of royalty was a primary element giving tragedy its larger dimensions. Yet it was to people of the lesser orders that the future belonged. They were to become the beneficiaries of belief in the dignity not just of the few, but of the many.

As long as monarchy and despotism remained the principal political systems in Europe, however, most writers of tragedy continued to draw their subject matter from activities of the noble persons. But one can see anticipations of things to come. In the eighteenth century, an interesting experiment in tragedy—and also therefore a play looking toward the future—was *The London Merchant* (1731) by George Lillo (1693–1739), which forsook socially superior characters altogether and instead dramatized the "history" of a young boy, the worker's apprentice George Barnwell, who makes an error that leads to theft, murder, arrest, and finally the gallows. Lillo's aim was primarily moral and exemplary—the play was just as much a sermon as a drama. The impact of *The London Merchant* was not that the human spirit is elevated through adversity or that human beings should stand in awe before the tragic potential of their acts; rather it was that audiences should avoid mistakes such as those made by Lillo's unfortunate protagonist. It was clear that writers of tragedy would ultimately need to face the problem of reconciling the treatment of ordinary people with the tragic ideal of human dignity and nobility.

In the late eighteenth century, a number of political revolutions began that continued into and throughout much of the twentieth. Most of these depended on the theory, or hope, that human beings are perfectible, but the political beliefs of modern democracy did not add to the tradition of tragedy until the mid-twentieth century with the emergence of the talent of Arthur Miller (1915– 2005). Miller's tragic plays are drawn from the modern world as we know it. His characters are common people—those who live in modern cities, and who walk, drive, or take the bus to work; those who go to modern schools, succeed or fail there, and then go on to make their ordinary livings. These are the people we know and see every day, those whose lives and tragedies are the stuff of Miller's greatest play, *Death of a Salesman*, first performed in February 1949. Miller's major character is indeed one of the workers, a salesman, and also a family man—Willy Loman.

Death of a Salesman: Tragedy, Symbolism, and Broken Dreams

In writing a tragedy about Willy's struggle and failure, Miller effectively redefines the nature of tragedy in modern times. In a *New York Times* essay published shortly after the Broadway opening, Miller argues that "the common man is as apt a subject for tragedy in its highest sense as kings were."[15] He asserts that tragedy springs from the individual's quest for a proper place in the world and from his or her readiness "to lay down . . . life, if need be, to secure . . . [a] sense of personal dignity." Willy is ordinary, the "low man." He is self-deluded, deceitful, unfaithful, and weak; he denies the truth when he is confronted with it. But Miller links Willy's defects with his quest for dignity: "the flaw or crack in the character is really . . . his inherent unwillingness to remain passive in the face of what he conceives to be a challenge to his dignity, his image of his rightful status." It is with great justice that Linda, Willy's wife, asserts to her sons that attention must be paid to so significant a person. In this sense, Miller meets the challenge of creating a modern character worthy of tragic elevation.

Miller's first title of the play was *The Inside of His Head*, and his initial visualization, "conceived half in laughter," was that of "an enormous face the height of the proscenium arch which would appear and then open up, and we would see the inside of a man's head."[16] Ironically, Miller saw the inside of Willy's head as "a mass of contradictions" that are embodied within the play as a function of two types of time and action: real and remembered. Willy's memory is always with him, shaping the way he reacts to the present. Sometimes past events even occur along with present action, as in Act 1 when Willy speaks with his dead brother, whom he is remembering at the same time that he is involved in a card game.

Like the acting of past events, the setting of *Death of a Salesman* is realistic but also symbolic. The play demonstrates the degree to which Miller relies on developments in the physical theater that took place between Shakespeare's day and our own. He adapts both the concepts of the picture-frame proscenium stage and the apron stage. The Loman house—set on the stage—is a framework with three rooms (or acting areas). The forestage and apron are used for all scenes away from the house and for memory scenes. The house is hemmed in by apartment houses and lit with an "angry glow of orange"—suggesting that Willy's present existence is urbanized and claustrophobic. When memory takes over, the apartment houses disappear (a technique of lighting), and the orange glow gives way to pastoral colors and the shadows of leaves—the setting for dreams about past times and receding hopes.

Death of a Salesman is very much about dreams, illusions, and self-deception. Willy's central illusion—is it his tragic flaw?—is the American dream of economic success gained by the merchandising of the self. The dream of being "well liked" is embodied in a series of smaller dreams (illusions, lies) that Willy has tried to instill in his sons. But reality destroys these dreams. Willy's expectation of a New York City job and a salary, for example, is wrecked by his disastrous encounter with his younger but unsympathetic boss. Only Linda escapes the tyranny of dreams. She

---

"Tragedy and the Common Man," *New York Times*, February 27, 1949, sec. 2, p. 1.
Arthur Miller, "Introduction to the Collected Plays," *Arthur Miller's Collected Plays* (New York: Viking, 1957) 23.

Stage set for *Death of a Salesman.*

serves and supports Willy completely, but she remains firmly planted in the real world of house payments, insurance premiums, and support for Willy.

At the end of the play, we are left with a number of questions about the degree to which Willy recognizes and understands the illusory nature of his dreams and his self-image. He does recognize that he has run out of lies, and that he has nothing left to sell. He also understands—according to Miller—his alienation from true values.

> Had Willy been unaware of his separation from values that endure he would have died contentedly while polishing his car. . . . But he was agonized by his awareness of being in a false position, so constantly haunted by the hollowness of all he had placed his faith in, so aware, in short, that he must somehow be filled with his spirit or fly apart, that he staked his life on the ultimate assertion.[17]

Yet even then, Willy is still gripped by delusion. He imagines that his insurance money will make Biff "magnificent," and he dreams that his funeral will be massive. Ironically, Biff has already abandoned the business world, and only five people come to the funeral. Miller's view of Willy's ambiguous life is perhaps expressed by Willy's two sons in the *Requiem* scene. Biff states that Willy's dreams, like his life, were illusory: "He had all the wrong dreams. All, all wrong" (*Requiem*, speech 16). Willy's other son, ironically named Happy, provides an alternative judgment about Willy: "[Willy] had a good dream. It's the only dream you can have—to come out number-one man" (*Requiem*, speech 25).

Miller, pp. 34–35.

ARTHUR MILLER (1915–2005)

*Arthur Aster Miller was born in New York in 1915 and educated at the
University of Michigan, where he won a prize for a play he had written
as an undergraduate. After graduation he wrote with the Federal Theater Project (part of President Roosevelt's New Deal). When that project lost funding, he wrote radio plays, a novel, and, during World War
II, an account of military training. His first play,* The Man Who Had
All the Luck, *met little success on Broadway in 1944. After the war he
quickly catapulted into fame as a dramatist with* All My Sons *(1947);*
Death of a Salesman *(1949);* An Enemy of the People *(1951, an
adaptation of Ibsen's play);* The Crucible *(1953); and* A View from the Bridge *(1955). Many of
these combine his interests in family relationships and sociopolitical issues. For instance,* All My
Sons *explores the character of Joe Keller, an industrialist and war profiteer who had allowed faulty
engines to be installed in U.S. military aircraft during World War II. The play investigates Keller's
guilt and his emerging realization that the airmen who died because of his defective engines were
"all" his sons. Another of Miller's most important plays,* The Crucible, *reflects the suspicions and
unfounded accusations rampant in the McCarthy era early in the 1950s.*

Miller's later work includes the screenplay The Misfits *(1961), the last film in which
Marilyn Monroe, who was then his wife, starred; and the plays* After the Fall *(1964),* Incident
at Vichy *(1964, made into a film in 1973 and done as a radio play in 2002),* The Price *(1968),*
Fame *(1970),* The Reason Why *(1972),* The Creation of the World and Other Business
(1972), The Archbishop's Ceiling *(1976),* The American Clock *(1980),* Playing for Time
(1985), I Can't Remember Anything *(1987),* Clara *(1987), a filmscript titled* Everybody
Wins *(1990),* The Ride Down Mount Morgan *(1991, London),* Broken Glass *(1994),* Some
Kind of Love Story *(1998), and* Resurrection Blues *(2002, Minneapolis). In 1996* The
Crucible *was revised and presented as a successful film, directed by Nicholas Hytner, with
Daniel Day-Lewis, Winona Ryder, and Paul Scofield.*

Death of a Salesman (1949)

CHARACTERS

Willy Loman

Linda, his wife

Biff ⎱
          ⎰ his sons
Happy ⎰

Uncle Ben

Charley

Bernard

The Woman

Howard Wagner

Jenny

Stanley

Miss Forsythe

Letta

The action takes place in WILLY LOMAN'S *house and yard and in various places he visits in the New
York and Boston of today.*

ACT 1

*A melody is heard, played upon a flute. It is small and fine, telling of grass and trees and the horizon.
The curtain rises.*

Before us is the Salesman's house. We are aware of towering, angular shapes behind it, surrounding it on all sides. Only the blue light of the sky falls upon the house and forestage; the surrounding area shows an angry glow of orange. As more light appears, we see a solid vault of apartment houses around the small, fragile-seeming home. An air of the dream clings to the place, a dream rising out of reality. The kitchen at center seems actual enough, for there is a kitchen table with three chairs, and a refrigerator. But no other fixtures are seen. At the back of the kitchen there is a draped entrance, which leads to the living-room. To the right of the kitchen, on a level raised two feet, is a bedroom furnished only with a brass bedstead and a straight chair. On a shelf over the bed a silver athletic trophy stands. A window opens onto the apartment house at the side.

Behind the kitchen, on a level raised six and a half feet, is the boys' bedroom, at present barely visible. Two beds are dimly seen, and at the back of the room a dormer window. (This bedroom is above the unseen living-room.) At the left a stairway curves up to it from the kitchen.

The entire setting is wholly or, in some places, partially transparent. The roof-line of the house is one-dimensional; under and over it we see the apartment buildings. Before the house lies an apron, curving beyond the forestage into the orchestra. This forward area serves as the back yard as well as the locale of all Willy's imaginings and of his city scenes. Whenever the action is in the present the actors observe the imaginary wall-lines, entering the house only through its door at the left. But in the scenes of the past these boundaries are broken, and characters enter or leave a room by stepping "through" a wall onto the forestage.

[From the right, WILLY LOMAN, the Salesman, enters, carrying two large sample cases. The flute plays on. He hears but is not aware of it. He is past sixty years of age, dressed quietly. Even as he crosses the stage to the doorway of the house, his exhaustion is apparent. He unlocks the door, comes into the kitchen, and thankfully lets his burden down, feeling the soreness of his palms. A word-sigh escapes his lips—it might be "Oh, boy, oh, boy." He closes the door, then carries his cases out into the living-room, through the draped kitchen doorway.]

[LINDA, his wife, has stirred in her bed at the right. She gets out and puts on a robe, listening. Most often jovial, she has developed an iron repression of her exceptions to WILLY's behavior—she more than loves him, she admires him, as though his mercurial nature, his temper, his massive dreams and little cruelties, served her only as sharp reminders of the turbulent longings within him, longings which she shares but lacks the temperament to utter and follow to their end.]

LINDA: *[hearing WILLY outside the bedroom, calls with some trepidation]* Willy!

WILLY: It's all right. I came back.

LINDA: Why? What happened? *[slight pause]* Did something happen, Willy?

WILLY: No, nothing happened.

LINDA: You didn't smash the car, did you?

WILLY: *[with casual irritation]* I said nothing happened. Didn't you hear me?   5

LINDA: Don't you feel well?

WILLY: I'm tired to the death. *[The flute has faded away. He sits on the bed beside her, a little numb.]* I couldn't make it. I just couldn't make it, Linda.

LINDA: *[very carefully, delicately]* Where were you all day? You look terrible.

WILLY: I got as far as a little above Yonkers.° I stopped for a cup of coffee. Maybe it was   10
    the coffee.

LINDA: What?

WILLY: *[after a pause]* I suddenly couldn't drive any more. The car kept going off onto the
    shoulder, y'know?

°10 *Yonkers:* Yonkers is immediately north of New York City, touching the city limits of the Bronx. Because Willy lives in Brooklyn, to the south, he got no more than thirty or thirty-five miles from home.

LINDA: [*helpfully*] Oh. Maybe it was the steering again. I don't think Angelo knows the Studebaker.

WILLY: No, it's me, it's me. Suddenly I realize I'm goin' sixty miles an hour and I don't remember the last five minutes. I'm—I can't seem to—keep my mind to it.

15 LINDA: Maybe it's your glasses. You never went for your new glasses.

WILLY: No, I see everything. I came back ten miles an hour. It took me nearly four hours from Yonkers.

LINDA: [*resigned*] Well, you'll just have to take a rest, Willy, you can't continue this way.

WILLY: I just got back from Florida.

LINDA: But you didn't rest your mind. Your mind is overactive, and the mind is what counts, dear.

20 WILLY: I'll start out in the morning. Maybe I'll feel better in the morning. [*She is taking off his shoes.*] These goddam arch supports are killing me.

LINDA: Take an aspirin. Should I get you an aspirin? It'll soothe you.

WILLY: [*with wonder*] I was driving along, you understand? And I was fine. I was even observing the scenery. You can imagine, me looking at scenery, on the road every week of my life. But it's so beautiful up there, Linda, the trees are so thick, and the sun is warm. I opened the windshield and just let the warm air bathe over me. And then all of a sudden I'm goin' off the road! I'm tellin' ya, I absolutely forgot I was driving. If I'd've gone the other way over the white line I might've killed somebody. So I went on again—and five minutes later I'm dreamin' again, and I nearly—[*He presses two fingers against his eyes.*] I have such thoughts, I have such strange thoughts.

LINDA: Willy, dear. Talk to them again. There's no reason why you can't work in New York.

WILLY: They don't need me in New York. I'm the New England man. I'm vital in New England.

25 LINDA: But you're sixty years old. They can't expect you to keep traveling every week.

WILLY: I'll have to send a wire to Portland. I'm supposed to see Brown and Morrison tomorrow morning at ten o'clock to show the line. Goddammit, I could sell them! [*He starts putting on his jacket.*]

LINDA: [*taking the jacket from him*] Why don't you go down to the place tomorrow and tell Howard you've simply got to work in New York? You're too accommodating, dear.

WILLY: If old man Wagner was alive I'd a been in charge of New York now! That man was a prince, he was a masterful man. But that boy of his, that Howard, he don't appreciate. When I went north the first time, the Wagner Company didn't know where New England was!

LINDA: Why don't you tell those things to Howard, dear?

30 WILLY: [*encouraged*] I will, I definitely will. Is there any cheese?

LINDA: I'll make you a sandwich.

WILLY: No, go to sleep. I'll take some milk. I'll be up right away. The boys in?

LINDA: They're sleeping. Happy took Biff on a date tonight.

WILLY: [*interested*] That so?

35 LINDA: It was so nice to see them shaving together, one behind the other, in the bathroom. And going out together. You notice? The whole house smells of shaving lotion.

WILLY: Figure it out. Work a lifetime to pay off a house. You finally own it, and there's nobody to live in it.

LINDA: Well, dear, life is a casting off. It's always that way.

WILLY: No, no, some people—some people accomplish something. Did Biff say anything after I went this morning?

LINDA: You shouldn't have criticized him, Willy, especially after he just got off the train. You mustn't lose your temper with him.

40 WILLY: When the hell did I lose my temper? I simply asked him if he was making any money. Is that a criticism?

LINDA: But, dear, how could he make any money?

WILLY: [*worried and angered*] There's such an undercurrent in him. He became a moody man. Did he apologize when I left this morning?

LINDA: He was crestfallen, Willy. You know how he admires you. I think if he finds himself, then you'll both be happier and not fight any more.

WILLY: How can he find himself on a farm? Is that a life? A farmhand? In the beginning, when he was young, I thought, well, a young man, it's good for him to tramp around, take a lot of different jobs. But it's more than ten years now and he has yet to make thirty-five dollars a week!

LINDA: He's finding himself, Willy.   45

WILLY: Not finding yourself at the age of thirty-four is a disgrace!

LINDA: Shh!

WILLY: The trouble is he's lazy, goddammit!

LINDA: Willy, please!

WILLY: Biff is a lazy bum!   50

LINDA: They're sleeping. Get something to eat. Go on down.

WILLY: Why did he come home? I would like to know what brought him home.

LINDA: I don't know. I think he's still lost, Willy. I think he's very lost.

WILLY: Biff Loman is lost. In the greatest country in the world a young man with such— personal attractiveness, gets lost. And such a hard worker. There's one thing about Biff—he's not lazy.

LINDA: Never.   55

WILLY: [*with pity and resolve*] I'll see him in the morning; I'll have a nice talk with him. I'll get him a job selling. He could be big in no time. My God! Remember how they used to follow him around in high school? When he smiled at one of them their faces lit up. When he walked down the street . . . [*He loses himself in reminiscences.*]

LINDA: [*trying to bring him out of it*] Willy, dear, I got a new kind of American-type cheese today. It's whipped.

WILLY: Why do you get American when I like Swiss?

LINDA: I just thought you'd like a change—

WILLY: I don't want a change! I want Swiss cheese. Why am I always being contradicted?   60

LINDA: [*with a covering laugh*] I thought it would be a surprise.

WILLY: Why don't you open a window in here, for God's sake?

LINDA: [*with infinite patience*] They're all open dear.

WILLY: The way they boxed us in here. Bricks and windows, windows and bricks.

LINDA: We should've bought the land next door.   65

WILLY: The street is lined with cars. There's not a breath of fresh air in the neighborhood. The grass don't grow any more, you can't raise a carrot in the back yard. They should've had a law against apartment houses. Remember those two beautiful elm trees out there? When I and Biff hung the swing between them?

LINDA: Yeah, like being a million miles from the city.

WILLY: They should've arrested the builder for cutting those down. They massacred the neighborhood. [*lost*] More and more I think of those days, Linda. This time of year it was lilac and wisteria. And then the peonies would come out, and the daffodils. What fragrance in this room!

LINDA: Well, after all, people had to move somewhere.

WILLY: No, there's more people now.   70

LINDA: I don't think there's more people. I think—

WILLY: There's more people! That's what's ruining this country! Population is getting out of control. The competition is maddening! Smell the stink from that apartment house! And another one on the other side . . . How can they whip cheese?

[*On WILLY's last line, BIFF and HAPPY raise themselves up in their beds, listening.*]

LINDA: Go down, try it. And be quiet.

WILLY: [*turning to Linda, guiltily*] You're not worried about me, are you, sweetheart?

75 **BIFF:** What's the matter?

HAPPY: Listen!

LINDA: You've got too much on the ball to worry about.

WILLY: You're my foundation and my support, Linda.

LINDA: Just try to relax, dear. You make mountains out of molehills.

80 **WILLY:** I won't fight with him any more. If he wants to go back to Texas, let him go.

LINDA: He'll find his way.

WILLY: Sure. Certain men just don't get started till later in life. Like Thomas Edison, I
think. Or B. F. Goodrich.° One of them was deaf. [*He starts for the bedroom doorway.*] I'll
put my money on Biff.

LINDA: And Willy —if it's warm Sunday we'll drive in the country. And we'll open the
windshield, and take lunch.

WILLY: No, the windshields don't open on the new cars.

85 **LINDA:** But you opened it today.

WILLY: Me? I didn't. [*He stops.*] Now isn't that peculiar! Isn't that a remarkable—[*He
breaks off in amazement and fright as the flute is heard distantly.*]

LINDA: What, darling?

WILLY: That is the most remarkable thing.

LINDA: What, dear?

90 **WILLY:** I was thinking of the Chevvy. [*slight pause*] Nineteen twenty-eight . . . when I had that
red Chevvy—[*Breaks off.*] That funny? I coulda sworn I was driving that Chevvy today.

LINDA: Well, that's nothing. Something must've reminded you.

WILLY: Remarkable. Ts. Remember those days? The way Biff used to simonize that car?
The dealer refused to believe there was eighty thousand miles on it. [*He shakes his
head.*] Heh! [*to* LINDA] Close your eyes, I'll be right up. [*He walks out of the bedroom.*]

HAPPY: [*to* BIFF] Jesus, maybe he smashed up the car again!

LINDA: [*calling after* WILLY] Be careful on the stairs, dear! The cheese is on the middle shelf!
[*She turns, goes over to the bed, takes his jacket, and goes out of the bedroom.*]

[*Light has risen on the boys' room. Unseen,* WILLY *is heard talking to himself, "Eighty thousand miles,"
and a little laugh.* BIFF *gets out of bed, comes downstage a bit, and stands attentively.* BIFF *is two years
older than his brother* HAPPY, *well built, but in these days bears a worn air and seems less self-assured.
He has succeeded less, and his dreams are stronger and less acceptable than* HAPPY'S. HAPPY *is tall,
powerfully made. Sexuality is like a visible color on him, or a scent that many women have discovered.
He, like his brother, is lost, but in a different way, for he has never allowed himself to turn his face toward defeat and is thus more confused and hard-skinned, although seemingly more content.*]

95 **HAPPY:** [*getting out of bed*] He's going to get his license taken away if he keeps that up. I'm
getting nervous about him, y'know, Biff?

BIFF: His eyes are going.

HAPPY: No, I've driven with him. He sees all right. He just doesn't keep his mind on it. I
drove into the city with him last week. He stops at a green light and then it turns red
and he goes. [*He laughs.*]

BIFF: Maybe he's color-blind.

HAPPY: Pop? Why he's got the finest eye for color in the business. You know that.

°82 *Thomas Edison, B. F. Goodrich:* Thomas A. Edison (1847–1931) was an American inventor who developed
the electric light and the phonograph. Benjamin Franklin Goodrich (1841–88) founded the B. F. Goodrich Rubber and Tire Company. It was Edison who suffered from deafness.

BIFF: [*sitting down on his bed*] I'm going to sleep. 100

HAPPY: You're not still sour on Dad, are you, Biff?

BIFF: He's all right, I guess.

WILLY: [*underneath them, in the living-room*] Yes, sir, eighty thousand miles—eighty-two thousand!

BIFF: You smoking?

HAPPY: [*holding out a pack of cigarettes*] Want one? 105

BIFF: [*taking a cigarette*] I can never sleep when I smell it.

WILLY: What a simonizing job, heh!

HAPPY: [*with deep sentiment*] Funny, Biff y'know? Us sleeping in here again? The old beds. [*He pats his bed affectionately.*] All the talk that went across those two beds, huh? Our whole lives.

BIFF: Yeah. Lotta dreams and plans.

HAPPY: [*with a deep and masculine laugh*] About five hundred women would like to know 110 what was said in this room.

[*They share a soft laugh.*]

BIFF: Remember that big Betsy something—what the hell was her name—over on Bush-wick Avenue?

HAPPY: [*combing his hair*] With the collie dog!

BIFF: That's the one. I got you in there, remember?

HAPPY: Yeah, that was my first time—I think. Boy, there was a pig! [*They laugh, almost crudely.*] You taught me everything I know about women. Don't forget that.

BIFF: I bet you forgot how bashful you used to be. Especially with girls. 115

HAPPY: Oh, I still am, Biff.

BIFF: Oh, go on.

HAPPY: I just control it, that's all. I think I got less bashful and you got more so. What happened, Biff? Where's the old humor, the old confidence? [*He shakes BIFF's knee. BIFF gets up and moves restlessly about the room.*] What's the matter?

BIFF: Why does Dad mock me all the time?

HAPPY: He's not mocking you, he— 120

BIFF: Everything I say there's a twist of mockery on his face. I can't get near him.

HAPPY: He just wants you to make good, that's all. I wanted to talk to you about Dad for a long time, Biff. Something's—happening to him. He—talks to himself.

BIFF: I noticed that this morning. But he always mumbled.

HAPPY: But not so noticeable. It got so embarrassing I sent him to Florida. And you know something? Most of the time he's talking to you.

BIFF: What's he say about me? 125

HAPPY: I can't make it out.

BIFF: What's he say about me?

HAPPY: I think the fact that you're not settled, that you're still kind of up in the air . . .

BIFF: There's one or two other things depressing him, Happy.

HAPPY: What do you mean? 130

BIFF: Never mind. Just don't lay it all to me.

HAPPY: But I think if you just got started—I mean—is there any future for you out there?

BIFF: I tell ya, Hap, I don't know what the future is. I don't know—what I'm supposed to want.

HAPPY: What do you mean?

BIFF: Well, I spent six or seven years after high school trying to work myself up. Shipping 135 clerk, salesman, business of one kind or another. And it's a measly manner of existence.

To get on that subway on the hot mornings in summer. To devote your whole life to keeping stock, or making phone calls, or selling or buying. To suffer fifty weeks of the year for the sake of a two-week vacation, when all you really desire is to be outdoors, with your shirt off. And always to have to get ahead of the next fella. And still—that's how you build a future.

HAPPY: Well, you really enjoy it on a farm? Are you content out there?

BIFF: [*with rising agitation*] Hap, I've had twenty or thirty different kinds of jobs since I left home before the war, and it always turns out the same. I just realized it lately. In Nebraska when I herded cattle, and the Dakotas, and Arizona, and now in Texas. It's why I came home now, I guess, because I realized it. This farm I work on, it's spring there now, see? And they've got about fifteen new colts. There's nothing more inspiring or— beautiful than the sight of a mare and a new colt. And it's cool there now, see? Texas is cool now, and it's spring. And whenever spring comes to where I am, I suddenly get the feeling, my God, I'm not gettin' anywhere! What the hell am I doing, playing around with horses, twenty-eight dollars a week! I'm thirty-four years old, I oughta be makin' my future. That's when I come running home. And now, I get here, and I don't know what to do with myself. [*after a pause*] I've always made a point of not wasting my life, and everytime I come back here I know that all I've done is to waste my life.

HAPPY: You're a poet, you know that, Biff? You're a—you're an idealist!

BIFF: No, I'm mixed up very bad. Maybe I oughta get married. Maybe I oughta get stuck into something. Maybe that's my trouble. I'm like a boy. I'm not married, I'm not in business, I just—I'm like a boy. Are you content, Hap? You're a success, aren't you? Are you content?

140   HAPPY: Hell, no!

BIFF: Why? You're making money, aren't you?

HAPPY: [*moving about with energy, expressiveness*] All I can do now is wait for the merchandise manager to die. And suppose I get to be merchandise manager? He's a good friend of mine, and he just built a terrific estate on Long Island. And he lived there about two months and sold it, and now he's building another one. He can't enjoy it once it's finished. And I know that's just what I would do. I don't know what the hell I'm workin' for. Sometimes I sit in my apartment—all alone. And I think of the rent I'm paying. And it's crazy. But then, it's what I always wanted. My own apartment, a car, and plenty of women. And still, goddammit, I'm lonely.

BIFF: [*with enthusiasm*] Listen, why don't you come out West with me?

HAPPY: You and I, heh?

145   BIFF: Sure, maybe we could buy a ranch. Raise cattle, use our muscles. Men built like we are should be working out in the open.

HAPPY: [*avidly*] The Loman Brothers, heh?

BIFF: [*with vast affection*] Sure, we'd be known all over the counties!

HAPPY: [*enthralled*] That's what I dream about, Biff. Sometimes I want to just rip my clothes off in the middle of the store and outbox that goddam merchandise manager. I mean I can outbox, outrun, and outlift anybody in that store, and I have to take orders from those common, petty sons-of-bitches till I can't stand it any more.

BIFF: I'm tellin' you, kid, if you were with me I'd be happy out there.

150   HAPPY: [*enthused*] See, Biff, everybody around me is so false that I'm constantly lowering my ideals . . .

BIFF: Baby, together we'd stand up for one another, we'd have someone to trust.

HAPPY: If I were around you—

BIFF: Hap, the trouble is we weren't brought up to grub for money. I don't know how to do it.

HAPPY: Neither can I!

155   BIFF: Then let's go!

HAPPY: The only thing is—what can you make out there?

BIFF: But look at your friend. Builds an estate and then hasn't the peace of mind to live in it.

HAPPY: Yeah, but when he walks into the store the waves part in front of him. That's fifty-two thousand dollars a year coming through the revolving door, and I got more in my pinky finger than he's got in his head.

BIFF: Yeah, but you just said—

HAPPY: I gotta show some of those pompous, self-important executives over there that   160
Hap Loman can make the grade. I want to walk into the store the way he walks in. Then I'll go with you, Biff. We'll be together yet, I swear. But take those two we had tonight. Now weren't they gorgeous creatures?

BIFF: Yeah, yeah, most gorgeous I've had in years.

HAPPY: I get that any time I want, Biff. Whenever I feel disgusted. The only trouble is, it gets like bowling or something. I just keep knockin' them over and it doesn't mean anything. You still run around a lot?

BIFF: Naa. I'd like to find a girl—steady, somebody with substance.

HAPPY: That's what I long for.

BIFF: Go on! You'd never come home.   165

HAPPY: I would! Somebody with character, with resistance! Like Mom, y'know? You're gonna call me a bastard when I tell you this. That girl Charlotte I was with tonight is engaged to be married in five weeks. [*He tries on his new hat.*]

BIFF: No kiddin'!

HAPPY: Sure, the guy's in line for the vice-presidency of the store. I don't know what gets into me, maybe I just have an overdeveloped sense of competition or something, but I went and ruined her, and furthermore I can't get rid of her. And he's the third executive I've done that to. Isn't that a crummy characteristic? And to top it all, I go to their weddings! [*Indignantly, but laughing*] Like I'm not supposed to take bribes. Manufacturers offer me a hundred-dollar bill now and then to throw an order their way. You know how honest I am, but it's like this girl, see. I hate myself for it. Because I don't want the girl, and, still, I take it and—I love it!

BIFF: Let's go to sleep.

HAPPY: I guess we didn't settle anything, heh?   170

BIFF: I just got one idea that I think I'm going to try.

HAPPY: What's that?

BIFF: Remember Bill Oliver?

HAPPY: Sure, Oliver is very big now. You want to work for him again?

BIFF: No, but when I quit he said something to me. He put his arm on my shoulder and   175
he said, "Biff, if you ever need anything, come to me."

HAPPY: I remember that. That sounds good.

BIFF: I think I'll go to see him. If I could get ten thousand or even seven or eight thousand dollars I could buy a beautiful ranch.

HAPPY: I bet he'd back you. 'Cause he thought highly of you, Biff. I mean, they all do. You're well liked, Biff. That's why I say to come back here, and we both have the apartment. And I'm tellin' you, Biff, any babe you want . . .

BIFF: No, with a ranch I could do the work I like and still be something. I just wonder though. I wonder if Oliver still thinks I stole that carton of basketballs.

HAPPY: Oh, he probably forgot that long ago. It's almost ten years. You're too sensitive.   180
Anyway, he didn't really fire you.

BIFF: Well, I think he was going to. I think that's why I quit. I was never sure whether he knew or not. I know he thought the world of me, though. I was the only one he'd let lock up the place.

WILLY: [*below*] You gonna wash the engine, Biff?

HAPPY: *Shh!*

[*BIFF looks at HAPPY, who is gazing down, listening. WILLY is mumbling in the parlor.*]

HAPPY: You hear that?

[*They listen. WILLY laughs warmly.*]

185   **BIFF:** [*growing angry*] Doesn't he know Mom can hear that?
WILLY: Don't get your sweater dirty, Biff!

[*A look of pain crosses BIFF's face.*]

HAPPY: Isn't that terrible! Don't leave again, will you? You'll find a job here. You gotta
stick around. I don't know what to do about him, it's getting embarrassing.
WILLY: What a simonizing job!
BIFF: Mom's hearing that!
190   **WILLY:** No kiddin', Biff, you got a date? Wonderful!
HAPPY: Go on to sleep. But talk to him in the morning, will you?
BIFF: [*reluctantly getting into bed*] With her in the house. Brother!
HAPPY: [*getting into bed*] I wish you'd have a good talk with him.

[*The light on their room begins to fade.*]

BIFF: [*to himself in bed*] That selfish, stupid . . .
195   **HAPPY:** Sh . . . Sleep, Biff.

[*Their light is out. Well before they have finished speaking, WILLY's form is dimly seen below in the
darkened kitchen. He opens the refrigerator, searches in there, and takes out a bottle of milk. The
apartment houses are fading out, and the entire house and surroundings become covered with leaves.
Music insinuates itself as the leaves appear.*]

WILLY: Just wanna be careful with those girls, Biff, that's all. Don't make any promises. No promises of any kind. Because a girl, y'know, they always believe what
you tell 'em, and you're very young, Biff, you're too young to be talking seriously
to girls.

[*Light rises on the kitchen. WILLY, talking, shuts the refrigerator door and comes downstage to the
kitchen table. He pours milk into a glass. He is totally immersed in himself, smiling faintly.*]

WILLY: Too young entirely, Biff. You want to watch your schooling first. Then when
you're all set, there'll be plenty of girls for a boy like you. [*He smiles broadly at a
kitchen chair.*] That so? The girls pay for you? [*He laughs.*] Boy, you must really be
makin' a hit.

[*WILLY is gradually addressing—physically—a point offstage, speaking through the wall of the
kitchen, and his voice has been rising in volume to that of a normal conversation.*]

WILLY: I been wondering why you polish the car so careful. Ha! Don't leave the hubcaps,
boys. Get the chamois to the hubcaps. Happy, use newspaper on the windows, it's
the easiest thing. Show him how to do it, Biff! You see, Happy? Pad it up, use it like
a pad. That's it, that's it, good work. You're doin' all right, Hap. [*He pauses, then nods
in approbation for a few seconds, then looks upward.*] Biff, first thing we gotta do when we

get time is clip that big branch over the house. Afraid it's gonna fall in a storm and hit the roof. Tell you what. We get a rope and sling her around, and then we climb up there with a couple of saws and take her down. Soon as you finish the car, boys, I wanna see ya. I got a surprise for you, boys.

Biff: [*offstage*] Whatta ya got, Dad?

Willy: No, you finish first. Never leave a job till you're finished—remember that. [*looking   200 toward the "big trees"*] Biff, up in Albany I saw a beautiful hammock. I think I'll buy it next trip, and we'll hang it right between those two elms. Wouldn't that be something? Just swingin' there under those branches. Boy, that would be . . .

[*Young Biff and Young Happy appear from the direction Willy was addressing. Happy carries rags and a pail of water. Biff, wearing a sweater with a block "S," carries a football.*]

Biff: [*pointing in the direction of the car offstage*] How's that, Pop, professional?

Willy: Terrific. Terrific job, boys. Good work, Biff.

Happy: Where's the surprise, Pop?

Willy: In the back seat of the car.

Happy: Boy! [*He runs off.*]   205

Biff: What is it, Dad? Tell me, what'd you buy?

Willy: [*laughing, cuffs him*] Never mind, something I want you to have.

Biff: [*turns and starts off*] What is it, Hap?

Happy: [*offstage*] It's a punching bag!

Biff: Oh, Pop!   210

Willy: It's got Gene Tunney's° signature on it!

[*Happy runs onstage with a punching bag.*]

Biff: Gee, how'd you know we wanted a punching bag?

Willy: Well, it's the finest thing for the timing.

Happy: [*lies down on his back and pedals with his feet*] I'm losing weight, you notice, Pop?

Willy: [*to Happy*] Jumping rope is good too.   215

Biff: Did you see the new football I got?

Willy: [*examining the ball*] Where'd you get a new ball?

Biff: The coach told me to practice my passing.

Willy: That so? And he gave you the ball, heh?

Biff: Well, I borrowed it from the locker room. [*He laughs confidentially.*]   220

Willy: [*laughing with him at the theft*] I want you to return that.

Happy: I told you he wouldn't like it!

Biff: [*angrily*] Well, I'm bringing it back!

Willy: [*stopping the incipient argument, to Happy*] Sure, he's gotta practice with a regulation ball, doesn't he? [*to Biff*] Coach'll probably congratulate you on your initiative!

Biff: Oh, he keeps congratulating my initiative all the time, Pop.   225

Willy: That's because he likes you. If somebody else took that ball there'd be an uproar. So what's the report, boys, what's the report?

Biff: Where'd you go this time, Dad? Gee we were lonesome for you.

Willy: [*pleased, puts an arm around each boy and they come down to the apron*] Lonesome, heh?

Biff: Missed you every minute.

°211 *Gene Tunney:* James Joseph Tunney (1898–1978), a boxer who won the heavyweight championship from Jack Dempsey in 1926 and retired undefeated in 1928.

230   **WILLY:** Don't say? Tell you a secret, boys. Don't breathe it to a soul. Someday I'll have my own business, and I'll never have to leave home any more.

   HAPPY: Like Uncle Charley, heh?

   WILLY: Bigger than Uncle Charley! Because Charley is not—liked. He's liked, but he's not—well liked.

   BIFF: Where'd you go this time, Dad?

   WILLY: Well, I got on the road, and I went north to Providence. Met the Mayor.

235   **BIFF:** The Mayor of Providence!

   WILLY: He was sitting in the hotel lobby.

   BIFF: What'd he say?

   WILLY: He said, "Morning!" And I said, "You got a fine city here, Mayor." And then he had coffee with me. And then I went to Waterbury. Waterbury is a fine city. Big clock city, the famous Waterbury clock. Sold a nice bill there. And then Boston—Boston is the cradle of the Revolution. A fine city. And a couple of other towns in Mass., and on to Portland and Bangor and straight home!

   BIFF: Gee, I'd love to go with you sometime, Dad.

240   **WILLY:** Soon as summer comes.

   HAPPY: Promise?

   WILLY: You and Hap and I, and I'll show you all the towns. America is full of beautiful towns and fine, upstanding people. And they know me, boys, they know me up and down New England. The finest people. And when I bring you fellas up, there'll be open sesame for all of us, 'cause one thing, boys: I have friends. I can park my car in any street in New England, and the cops protect it like their own. This summer, heh?

   BIFF AND HAPPY: [*together*] Yeah! You bet!

   WILLY: We'll take our bathing suits.

245   **HAPPY:** We'll carry your bags, Pop!

   WILLY: Oh, won't that be something! Me comin' into the Boston stores with you boys carryin' my bags. What a sensation!

[*BIFF is prancing around, practicing passing the ball.*]

   WILLY: You nervous, Biff, about the game?

   BIFF: Not if you're gonna be there.

   WILLY: What do they say about you in school, now that they made you captain?

250   **HAPPY:** There's a crowd of girls behind him everytime the classes change.

   BIFF: [*taking WILLY's hand*] This Saturday, Pop, this Saturday—just for you, I'm going to break through for a touchdown.

   HAPPY: You're supposed to pass.

   BIFF: I'm takin' one play for Pop. You watch me, Pop, and when I take off my helmet, that means I'm breakin' out. Then you watch me crash through that line!

   WILLY: [*kisses BIFF*] Oh, wait'll I tell this in Boston!

[*BERNARD enters in knickers. He is younger than BIFF, earnest and loyal, a worried boy.*]

255   **BERNARD:** Biff, where are you? You're supposed to study with me today.

   WILLY: Hey, looka Bernard. What're you lookin' so anemic about, Bernard?

   BERNARD: He's gotta study, Uncle Willy. He's got Regents° next week.

   HAPPY: [*tauntingly, spinning BERNARD around*] Let's box, Bernard!

°257 *Regents:* a statewide high school proficiency examination administered in New York.

BERNARD: Biff! [*He gets away from* HAPPY.] Listen, Biff, I heard Mr. Birnbaum say that if you don't start studyin' math he's gonna flunk you, and you won't graduate. I heard him!

WILLY: You better study with him, Biff. Go ahead now.   260

BERNARD: I heard him!

BIFF: Oh, Pop, you didn't see my sneakers! [*He holds up a foot for* WILLY *to look at.*]

WILLY: Hey, that's a beautiful job of printing!

BERNARD: [*wiping his glasses*] Just because he printed University of Virginia on his sneakers doesn't mean they've got to graduate him, Uncle Willy!

WILLY: [*angrily*] What're you talking about? With scholarships to three universities they're gonna flunk him?   265

BERNARD: But I heard Mr. Birnbaum say—

WILLY: Don't be a pest, Bernard! [*to his boys*] What an anemic!

BERNARD: Okay, I'm waiting for you in my house, Biff.

[BERNARD *goes off. The* LOMANS *laugh.*]

WILLY: Bernard is not well liked, is he?

BIFF: He's liked, but he's not well liked.   270

HAPPY: That's right, Pop.

WILLY: That's just what I mean. Bernard can get the best marks in school, y'understand, but when he gets out in the business world, y'understand, you are going to be five times ahead of him. That's why I thank Almighty God you're both built like Adonises. Because the man who makes an appearance in the business world, the man who creates personal interest, is the man who gets ahead. Be liked and you will never want. You take me, for instance. I never have to wait in line to see a buyer. "Willy Loman is here!" That's all they have to know, and I go right through.

BIFF: Did you knock them dead, Pop?

WILLY: Knocked 'em cold in Providence, slaughtered 'em in Boston.

HAPPY: [*on his back, pedaling again*] I'm losing weight, you notice, Pop?   275

[LINDA *enters, as of old, a ribbon in her hair, carrying a basket of washing.*]

LINDA: [*with youthful energy*] Hello, dear!

WILLY: Sweetheart!

LINDA: How'd the Chevvy run?

WILLY: Chevrolet, Linda, is the greatest car ever built. [*to the boys*] Since when do you let your mother carry wash up the stairs?

BIFF: Grab hold there, boy!   280

HAPPY: Where to, Mom?

LINDA: Hang them up on the line. And you better go down to your friends, Biff. The cellar is full of boys. They don't know what to do with themselves.

BIFF: Ah, when Pop comes home they can wait!

WILLY: [*laughs appreciatively*] You better go down and tell them what to do, Biff.

BIFF: I think I'll have them sweep out the furnace room.   285

WILLY: Good work, Biff.

BIFF: [*goes through wall-line of kitchen to doorway at back and calls down*] Fellas! Everybody sweep out the furnace room! I'll be right down!

VOICES: All right! Okay, Biff.

BIFF: George and Sam and Frank, come out back! We're hangin' up the wash! Come on, Hap, on the double! [*He and* HAPPY *carry out the basket.*]

LINDA: The way they obey him!   290

WILLY: Well, that's training, the training. I'm tellin' you, I was sellin' thousands and thousands, but I had to come home.

LINDA: Oh, the whole block'll be at that game. Did you sell anything?

WILLY: I did five hundred gross in Providence and seven hundred gross in Boston.

LINDA: No! Wait a minute, I've got a pencil. [*She pulls pencil and paper out of her apron pocket.*] That makes your commission . . . Two hundred—my God! Two hundred and twelve dollars!

295 **WILLY:** Well, I didn't figure it yet, but . . .

LINDA: How much did you do?

WILLY: Well, I—I did—about a hundred and eighty gross in Providence. Well, no—it came to—roughly two hundred gross on the whole trip.

LINDA: [*without hesitation*] Two hundred gross. That's . . . [*She figures.*]

WILLY: The trouble was that three of the stores were half closed for inventory in Boston. Otherwise I woulda broke records.

300 **LINDA:** Well, it makes seventy dollars and some pennies. That's very good.

WILLY: What do we owe?

LINDA: Well, on the first there's sixteen dollars on the refrigerator—

WILLY: Why sixteen?

LINDA: Well, the fan belt broke, so it was a dollar eighty.

305 **WILLY:** But it's brand new.

LINDA: Well, the man said that's the way it is. Till they work themselves in, y'know.

[*They move through the wall-line into the kitchen.*]

WILLY: I hope we didn't get stuck on that machine.

LINDA: They got the biggest ads of any of them!

WILLY: I know, it's a fine machine. What else?

310 **LINDA:** Well, there's nine-sixty for the washing machine. And for the vacuum cleaner there's three and a half due on the fifteenth. Then the roof, you got twenty-one dollars remaining.

WILLY: It don't leak, does it?

LINDA: No, they did a wonderful job. Then you owe Frank for the carburetor.

WILLY: I'm not going to pay that man! That goddam Chevrolet, they ought to prohibit the manufacture of that car!

LINDA: Well, you owe him three and a half. And odds and ends, comes to around a hundred and twenty dollars by the fifteenth.

315 **WILLY:** A hundred and twenty dollars! My God, if business don't pick up I don't know what I'm gonna do!

LINDA: Well, next week you'll do better.

WILLY: Oh, I'll knock 'em dead next week. I'll go to Hartford. I'm very well liked in Hartford. You know, the trouble is, Linda, people don't seem to take to me.

[*They move onto the forestage.*]

LINDA: Oh, don't be foolish.

WILLY: I know it when I walk in. They seem to laugh at me.

320 **LINDA:** Why? Why would they laugh at you? Don't talk that way, Willy.

[*WILLY moves to the edge of the stage. LINDA goes into the kitchen and starts to darn stockings.*]

WILLY: I don't know the reason for it, but they just pass me by. I'm not noticed.

LINDA: But you're doing wonderful, dear. You're making seventy to a hundred dollars a week.

WILLY: But I gotta be at it ten, twelve hours a day. Other men—I don't know—they do it easier. I don't know why—I can't stop myself—I talk too much. A man oughta come in with a few words. One thing about Charley. He's a man of few words, and they respect him.

LINDA: You don't talk too much, you're just lively.

WILLY: [*smiling*] Well, I figure, what the hell, life is short, a couple of jokes. [*to himself*] I joke too much! [*The smile goes.*] 325

LINDA: Why? You're—

WILLY: I'm fat. I'm very—foolish to look at, Linda. I didn't tell you, but Christmas time I happened to be calling on F. H. Stewarts, and a salesman I know, as I was going in to see the buyer I heard him say something about—walrus. And I—I cracked him right across the face. I won't take that. I simply will not take that. But they do laugh at me. I know that.

LINDA: Darling . . .

WILLY: I gotta overcome it. I know I gotta overcome it. I'm not dressing to advantage, maybe.

LINDA: Willy, darling, you're the handsomest man in the world— 330

WILLY: Oh, no, Linda.

LINDA: To me you are. [*slight pause*] The handsomest.

[*From the darkness is heard the laughter of a woman. WILLY doesn't turn to it, but it continues through LINDA's lines.*]

LINDA: And the boys, Willy. Few men are idolized by their children the way you are.

[*Music is heard as behind a scrim, to the left of the house, THE WOMAN, dimly seen, is dressing.*]

WILLY: [*with great feeling*] You're the best there is, Linda, you're a pal, you know that? On the road—on the road I want to grab you sometimes and just kiss the life outa you.

[*The laughter is loud now, and he moves into a brightening area at the left, where THE WOMAN has come from behind the scrim and is standing, putting on her hat, looking into a "mirror" and laughing.*]

WILLY: Cause I get so lonely—especially when business is bad and there's nobody to talk 335
to. I get the feeling that I'll never sell anything again, that I won't make a living for you, or a business, a business for the boys. [*He talks through THE WOMAN's subsiding laughter; THE WOMAN primps at the "mirror."*] There's so much I want to make for—

THE WOMAN: Me? You didn't make me, Willy. I picked you.

WILLY: [*pleased*] You picked me?

THE WOMAN: [*who is quite proper-looking, WILLY's age*] I did. I've been sitting at that desk watching all the salesmen go by, day in, day out. But you've got such a sense of humor, and we do have such a good time together, don't we?

WILLY: Sure, sure. [*He takes her in his arms.*] Why do you have to go now?

THE WOMAN: It's two o'clock . . . 340

WILLY: No, come on in! [*He pulls her.*]

THE WOMAN: . . . my sisters'll be scandalized. When'll you be back?

WILLY: Oh, two weeks about. Will you come up again?

THE WOMAN: Sure thing. You do make me laugh. It's good for me. [*She squeezes his arm, kisses him.*] And I think you're a wonderful man.

WILLY: You picked me, heh? 345

THE WOMAN: Sure. Because you're so sweet. And such a kidder.

WILLY: Well, I'll see you next time I'm in Boston.

THE WOMAN: I'll put you right through to the buyers.

WILLY: [*slapping her bottom*] Right. Well, bottoms up!

350 **THE WOMAN:** [*slaps him gently and laughs*] You just kill me, Willy. [*He suddenly grabs her and kisses her roughly.*] You kill me. And thanks for the stockings. I love a lot of stockings. Well, good night.

WILLY: Good night. And keep your pores open!

THE WOMAN: Oh, Willy!

[*THE WOMAN bursts out laughing, and LINDA's laughter blends in. THE WOMAN disappears into the dark. Now the area at the kitchen table brightens. LINDA is sitting where she was at the kitchen table, but now is mending a pair of her silk stockings.*]

LINDA: You are, Willy. The handsomest man. You've got no reason to feel that—

WILLY: [*coming out of THE WOMAN's dimming area and going over to LINDA*] I'll make it all up to you, Linda, I'll—

355 **LINDA:** There's nothing to make up, dear. You're doing fine, better than—

WILLY: [*noticing her mending*] What's that?

LINDA: Just mending my stockings. They're so expensive—

WILLY: [*angrily, taking them from her*] I won't have you mending stockings in this house! Now throw them out!

[*LINDA puts the stockings in her pocket.*]

BERNARD: [*entering on the run*] Where is he? If he doesn't study!

360 **WILLY:** [*moving to the forestage, with great agitation*] You'll give him the answers!

BERNARD: I do, but I can't on a Regents! That's state exam! They're liable to arrest me!

WILLY: Where is he? I'll whip him, I'll whip him!

LINDA: And he'd better give back that football, Willy, it's not nice.

WILLY: Biff! Where is he? Why is he taking everything?

365 **LINDA:** He's too rough with the girls, Willy. All the mothers are afraid of him!

WILLY: I'll whip him!

BERNARD: He's driving the car without a license!

[*THE WOMAN's laugh is heard.*]

WILLY: Shut up!

LINDA: All the mothers—

370 **WILLY:** Shut up!

BERNARD: [*backing quietly away and out*] Mr. Birnbaum says he's stuck up.

WILLY: Get outa here!

BERNARD: If he doesn't buckle down he'll flunk math! [*He goes off.*]

LINDA: He's right, Willy, you've gotta—

375 **WILLY:** [*exploding at her*] There's nothing the matter with him! You want him to be a worm like Bernard? He's got spirit, personality . . .

[*As he speaks, LINDA, almost in tears, exits into the living-room. WILLY is alone in the kitchen, wilting and staring. The leaves are gone. It is night again, and the apartment houses look down from behind.*]

WILLY: Loaded with it. Loaded! What is he stealing? He's giving it back, isn't he? Why is he stealing? What did I tell him? I never in my life told him anything but decent things.

[*HAPPY in pajamas has come down the stairs; WILLY suddenly becomes aware of HAPPY's presence.*]

HAPPY: Let's go now, come on.

WILLY: [*sitting down at the kitchen table*] Huh! Why did she have to wax the floors herself? Everytime she waxes the floors she keels over. She knows that!

HAPPY: Shh! Take it easy. What brought you back tonight?

WILLY: I got an awful scare. Nearly hit a kid in Yonkers. God! Why didn't I go to Alaska   380 with my brother Ben that time! Ben! That man was a genius, that man was success incarnate! What a mistake! He begged me to go.

HAPPY: Well, there's no use in—

WILLY: You guys! There was a man started with the clothes on his back and ended up with diamond mines!

HAPPY: Boy, someday I'd like to know how he did it.

WILLY: What's the mystery? The man knew what he wanted and went out and got it! Walked into a jungle, and comes out, the age of twenty-one, and he's rich! The world is an oyster, but you don't crack it open on a mattress!

HAPPY: Pop, I told you I'm gonna retire you for life.   385

WILLY: You'll retire me for life on seventy goddam dollars a week? And your women and your car and your apartment, and you'll retire me for life! Christ's sake, I couldn't get past Yonkers today! Where are you guys, where are you? The woods are burning! I can't drive a car!

[*CHARLEY has appeared in the doorway. He is a large man, slow of speech, laconic, immovable. In all he says, despite what he says, there is pity, and now, trepidation. He has a robe over pajamas, slippers on his feet. He enters the kitchen.*]

CHARLEY: Everything all right?

HAPPY: Yeah, Charley, everything's . . .

WILLY: What's the matter?

CHARLEY: I heard some noise. I thought something happened. Can't we do something about the walls? You sneeze in here, and in my house hats blow off.   390

HAPPY: Let's go to bed, Dad. Come on.

[*CHARLEY signals to HAPPY to go.*]

WILLY: You go ahead, I'm not tired at the moment.

HAPPY: [*to WILLY*] Take it easy, huh? [*He exits.*]

WILLY: What're you doin' up?

CHARLEY: [*sitting down at the kitchen table opposite WILLY*] Couldn't sleep good. I had a heartburn.   395

WILLY: Well, you don't know how to eat.

CHARLEY: I eat with my mouth.

WILLY: No, you're ignorant. You gotta know about vitamins and things like that.

CHARLEY: Come on, let's shoot. Tire you out a little.

WILLY: [*hesitantly*] All right. You got cards?   400

CHARLEY: [*taking a deck from his pocket*] Yeah, I got them. Someplace. What is it with those vitamins?

WILLY: [*dealing*] They build up your bones. Chemistry.

CHARLEY: Yeah, but there's no bones in a heartburn.

WILLY: What are you talkin' about? Do you know the first thing about it?

CHARLEY: Don't get insulted.   405

WILLY: Don't talk about something you don't know anything about.

[*They are playing. Pause.*]

CHARLEY: What're you doin' home?

WILLY: A little trouble with the car.

CHARLEY: Oh, [*pause*] I'd like to take a trip to California.

410 WILLY: Don't say.

CHARLEY: You want a job?

WILLY: I got a job, I told you that. [*after a slight pause*] What the hell are you offering me a job for?

CHARLEY: Don't get insulted.

WILLY: Don't insult me.

415 CHARLEY: I don't see no sense in it. You don't have to go on this way.

WILLY: I got a good job. [*slight pause*] What do you keep comin' in for?

CHARLEY: You want me to go?

WILLY: [*after a pause, withering*] I can't understand it. He's going back to Texas again. What the hell is that?

CHARLEY: Let him go.

420 WILLY: I got nothin' to give him, Charley, I'm clean, I'm clean.

CHARLEY: He won't starve. None a them starve. Forget about him.

WILLY: Then what have I got to remember?

CHARLEY: You take it too hard. To hell with it. When a deposit bottle is broken you don't get your nickel back.

WILLY: That's easy enough for you to say.

425 CHARLEY: That ain't easy for me to say.

WILLY: Did you see the ceiling I put up in the living-room?

CHARLEY: Yeah, that's a piece of work. To put up a ceiling is a mystery to me. How do you do it?

WILLY: What's the difference?

CHARLEY: Well, talk about it.

430 WILLY: You gonna put up a ceiling?

CHARLEY: How could I put up a ceiling?

WILLY: Then what the hell are you bothering me for?

CHARLEY: You're insulted again.

WILLY: A man who can't handle tools is not a man. You're disgusting.

435 CHARLEY: Don't call me disgusting, Willy.

[UNCLE BEN, *carrying a valise and an umbrella, enters the forestage from around the right corner of the house. He is a stolid man, in his sixties, with a mustache and an authoritative air. He is utterly certain of his destiny, and there is an aura of far places about him. He enters exactly as* WILLY *speaks.*]

WILLY: I'm getting awfully tired, Ben.

[BEN'S *music is heard.* BEN *looks around at everything.*]

CHARLEY: Good, keep playing; you'll sleep better. Did you call me Ben?

[BEN *looks at his watch.*]

WILLY: That's funny. For a second there you reminded me of my brother Ben.

BEN: I only have a few minutes. [*He strolls, inspecting the place.* WILLY *and* CHARLEY *continue playing.*]

440 CHARLEY: You never heard from him again, heh? Since that time?

WILLY: Didn't Linda tell you? Couple of weeks ago we got a letter from his wife in Africa. He died.

CHARLEY: That so.

BEN: [*chuckling*] So this is Brooklyn, eh?

CHARLEY: Maybe you're in for some of his money.

WILLY: Naa, he had seven sons. There's just one opportunity I had with that man ...   445
BEN: I must make a train, William. There are several properties I'm looking at in Alaska.
WILLY: Sure, sure! If I'd gone with him to Alaska that time, everything would've been totally different.
CHARLEY: Go on, you'd froze to death up there.
WILLY: What're you talking about?
BEN: Opportunity is tremendous in Alaska, William. Surprised you're not up there.   450
WILLY: Sure, tremendous.
CHARLEY: Heh?
WILLY: There was the only man I ever met who knew the answers.
CHARLEY: Who?
BEN: How are you all?   455
WILLY: [taking a pot, smiling] Fine, fine.
CHARLEY: Pretty sharp tonight.
BEN: Is Mother living with you?
WILLY: No, she died a long time ago.
CHARLEY: Who?   460
BEN: That's too bad. Fine specimen of a lady, Mother.
WILLY: [to CHARLEY] Heh?
BEN: I'd hoped to see the old girl.
CHARLEY: Who died?
BEN: Heard anything from Father, have you?   465
WILLY: [unnerved] What do you mean, who died?
CHARLEY: [taking a pot] What're you talkin' about?
BEN: [looking at his watch] William, it's half-past eight!
WILLY: [As though to dispel his confusion he angrily stops CHARLEY's hand.] That's my build!
CHARLEY: I put the ace—   470
WILLY: If you don't know how to play the game I'm not gonna throw my money away on you!
CHARLEY: [rising] It was my ace, for God's sake!
WILLY: I'm through, I'm through!
BEN: When did Mother die?
WILLY: Long ago. Since the beginning you never knew how to play cards.   475
CHARLEY: [picks up the cards and goes to the door] All right! Next time I'll bring a deck with five aces.
WILLY: I don't play that kind of game!
CHARLEY: [turning to him] You ought to be ashamed of yourself!
WILLY: Yeah?
CHARLEY: Yeah! [He goes out.]   480
WILLY: [slamming the door after him] Ignoramus!
BEN: [as WILLY comes toward him through the wall-line of the kitchen] So you're William.
WILLY: [shaking BEN's hand] Ben! I've been waiting for you so long! What's the answer? How did you do it?
BEN: Oh, there's a story in that.

[LINDA enters the forestage, as of old, carrying the wash basket.]

LINDA: Is this Ben?   485
BEN: [gallantly] How do you do, my dear.
LINDA: Where've you been all these years? Willy's always wondered why you—
WILLY: [pulling BEN away from her impatiently] Where is Dad? Didn't you follow him? How did you get started?

BEN: Well, I don't know how much you remember.

490 **WILLY:** Well, I was just a baby, of course, only three or four years old—

BEN: Three years and eleven months.

WILLY: What a memory, Ben!

BEN: I have many enterprises, William, and I have never kept books.

WILLY: I remember I was sitting under the wagon in—was it Nebraska?

495 **BEN:** It was South Dakota, and I gave you a bunch of wild flowers.

WILLY: I remember you walking away down some open road.

BEN: [*laughing*] I was going to find Father in Alaska.

WILLY: Where is he?

BEN: At that age I had a very faulty view of geography, William. I discovered after a few days that I was heading due south, so instead of Alaska, I ended up in Africa.

500 **LINDA:** Africa!

WILLY: The Gold Coast!

BEN: Principally diamond mines.

LINDA: Diamond mines!

BEN: Yes, my dear. But I've only a few minutes—

505 **WILLY:** No! Boys! Boys! [*YOUNG BIFF and HAPPY appear.*] Listen to this. This is your Uncle Ben, a great man! Tell my boys, Ben!

BEN: Why, boys, when I was seventeen I walked into the jungle, and when I was twenty-one I walked out. [*He laughs.*] And by God I was rich.

WILLY: [*to the boys*] You see what I been talking about? The greatest things can happen!

BEN: [*glancing at his watch*] I have an appointment in Ketchikan Tuesday week.

WILLY: No, Ben. Please tell about Dad. I want my boys to hear. I want them to know the kind of stock they spring from. All I remember is a man with a big beard, and I was in Mamma's lap, sitting around a fire, and some kind of high music.

510 **BEN:** His flute. He played the flute.

WILLY: Sure, the flute, that's right!

[*New music is heard, a high, rollicking tune.*]

BEN: Father was a very great and a very wild-hearted man. We would start in Boston, and he'd toss the whole family into the wagon, and then he'd drive the team right across the country; through Ohio, and Indiana, Michigan, Illinois, and all the Western states. And we'd stop in the towns and sell the flutes that he'd made on the way. Great inventor, Father. With one gadget he made more in a week than a man like you could make in a lifetime.

WILLY: That's just the way I'm bringing them up, Ben—rugged, well liked, all-around.

BEN: Yeah? [*to BIFF*] Hit that, boy—hard as you can. [*He pounds his stomach.*]

515 **BIFF:** Oh, no, sir!

BEN: [*taking boxing stance*] Come on, get to me! [*He laughs.*]

BIFF: Okay! [*He cocks his fists and starts in.*]

WILLY: Go to it, Biff! Go ahead, show him!

LINDA: [*to WILLY*] Why must he fight, dear?

520 **BEN:** [*sparring with BIFF*] Good boy! Good boy!

WILLY: How's that, Ben, heh?

HAPPY: Give him the left, Biff!

LINDA: Why are you fighting?

BEN: Good boy! [*suddenly comes in, trips BIFF, and stands over him, the point of his umbrella poised over BIFF's eye.*]

525 **LINDA:** Look out, Biff!

BIFF: Gee!

BEN: [*patting BIFF's knee*] Never fight fair with a stranger, boy. You'll never get out of the jungle that way. [*taking LINDA's hand and bowing*] It was an honor and a pleasure to meet you, Linda.

LINDA: [*withdrawing her hand coldly, frightened*] Have a nice—trip.

BEN: [*to WILLY*] And good luck with your—what do you do?

WILLY: Selling.   530

BEN: Yes. Well . . . [*He raises his hand in farewell to all.*]

WILLY: No, Ben, I don't want you to think . . . [*He takes BEN's arm to show him.*] It's Brooklyn, I know, but we hunt too.

BEN: Really, now.

WILLY: Oh, sure, there's snakes and rabbits and—that's why I moved out here. Why, Biff can fell any one of these trees in no time! Boys! Go right over to where they're building the apartment house and get some sand. We're gonna rebuild the entire front stoop right now! Watch this, Ben!

BIFF: Yes, sir! On the double, Hap!

HAPPY: [*as he and BIFF run off*] I lost weight, Pop, you notice? [*CHARLEY enters in knickers,*   535
even before the boys are gone.]

CHARLEY: Listen, if they steal any more from that building the watchman'll put the cops on them!

LINDA: [*to WILLY*] Don't let Biff . . .

[*BEN laughs lustily.*]

WILLY: You shoulda seen the lumber they brought home last week. At least a dozen six-by-tens worth all kinds a money.

CHARLEY: Listen, if that watchman—   540

WILLY: I gave them hell, understand. But I got a couple of fearless characters there.

CHARLEY: Willy, the jails are full of fearless characters.

BEN: [*clapping WILLY on the back, with a laugh at CHARLEY*] And the stock exchange, friend!

WILLY: [*joining in BEN's laughter*] Where are the rest of your pants?

CHARLEY: My wife bought them.   545

WILLY: Now all you need is a golf club and you can go upstairs and go to sleep. [*to Ben*] Great athlete! Between him and his son Bernard they can't hammer a nail!

BERNARD: [*rushing in*] The watchman's chasing Biff!

WILLY: [*angrily*] Shut up! He's not stealing anything!

LINDA: [*alarmed, hurrying off left*] Where is he? Biff, dear! [*She exits.*]

WILLY: [*moving toward the left, away from BEN*] There's nothing wrong. What's the matter   550
with you?

BEN: Nervy boy. Good!

WILLY: [*laughing*] Oh, nerves of iron, that Biff!

CHARLEY: Don't know what it is. My New England man comes back and he's bleedin', they murdered him up there.

WILLY: It's contacts, Charley, I got important contacts!

CHARLEY: [*sarcastically*] Glad to hear it, Willy. Come in later, we'll shoot a little casino. I'll   555
take some of your Portland money. [*He laughs at WILLY and exits.*]

WILLY: [*turning to BEN*] Business is bad, it's murderous. But not for me, of course.

BEN: I'll stop by on my way back to Africa.

WILLY: [*longingly.*] Can't you stay a few days? You're just what I need, Ben, because I—I have a fine position here, but I—well, Dad left when I was such a baby and I never had a chance to talk to him and I still feel—kind of temporary about myself.

BEN: I'll be late for my train.

[*They are at opposite ends of the stage.*]

560   WILLY: Ben, my boys—can't we talk? They'd go into the jaws of hell for me, see, but I—
    BEN: William, you're being first-rate with your boys. Outstanding, manly chaps!
    WILLY: [*hanging on to his words*] Oh, Ben, that's good to hear! Because sometimes I'm
        afraid that I'm not teaching them the right kind of—Ben, how should I teach them?
    BEN: [*giving great weight to each word, and with a certain vicious audacity*] William, when I
        walked into the jungle, I was seventeen. When I walked out I was twenty-one. And,
        by God, I was rich! [*He goes off into darkness around the right corner of the house.*]
    WILLY: . . . was rich! That's just the spirit I want to imbue them with! To walk into a
        jungle! I was right! I was right! I was right!

[*BEN is gone, but WILLY is still speaking to him as LINDA, in her nightgown and robe, enters the
kitchen, glances around for WILLY, then goes to the door of the house, looks out and sees him. Comes
down to his left. He looks at her.*]

565   LINDA: Willy, dear? Willy?
    WILLY: I was right!
    LINDA: Did you have some cheese? [*He can't answer.*] It's very late, darling. Come to bed,
        heh?
    WILLY: [*looking straight up*] Gotta break your neck to see a star in this yard.
    LINDA: You coming in?
570   WILLY: Whatever happened to that diamond watch fob? Remember? When Ben came
        from Africa that time? Didn't he give me a watch fob with a diamond in it?
    LINDA: You pawned it, dear. Twelve, thirteen years ago. For Biff's radio correspondence
        course.
    WILLY: Gee, that was a beautiful thing. I'll take a walk.
    LINDA: But you're in your slippers.
    WILLY: [*starting to go around the house at the left*] I was right! I was! [*Half to LINDA, as he goes,
        shaking his head*] What a man! There was a man worth talking to. I was right!
575   LINDA: [*calling after WILLY*] But in your slippers, Willy!

[*WILLY is almost gone when BIFF, in his pajamas, comes down the stairs and enters the kitchen.*]

    BIFF: What is he doing out there?
    LINDA: Sh!
    BIFF: God Almighty, Mom, how long has he been doing this?
    LINDA: Don't, he'll hear you.
580   BIFF: What the hell is the matter with him?
    LINDA: It'll pass by morning.
    BIFF: Shouldn't we do anything?
    LINDA: Oh, my dear, you should do a lot of things, but there's nothing to do, so go to
        sleep.

[*HAPPY comes down the stairs and sits on the steps.*]

    HAPPY: I never heard him so loud, Mom.
585   LINDA: Well, come around more often; you'll hear him. [*She sits down at the table and mends
        the lining of WILLY'S jacket.*]
    BIFF: Why didn't you ever write me about this, Mom?
    LINDA: How would I write to you? For over three months you had no address.

BIFF: I was on the move. But you know I thought of you all the time. You know that, don't you, pal?

LINDA: I know, dear, I know. But he likes to have a letter. Just to know that there's still a possibility for better things.

BIFF: He's not like this all the time, is he?   590

LINDA: It's when you come home he's always the worst.

BIFF: When I come home?

LINDA: When you write you're coming, he's all smiles, and talks about the future, and— he's just wonderful. And then the closer you seem to come, the more shaky he gets, and then, by the time you get here, he's arguing, and he seems angry at you. I think it's just that maybe he can't bring himself to—to open up to you. Why are you so hateful to each other? Why is that?

BIFF: [*evasively*] I'm not hateful, Mom.

LINDA: But you no sooner come in the door than you're fighting!   595

BIFF: I don't know why. I mean to change. I'm tryin', Mom, you understand?

LINDA: Are you home to stay now?

BIFF: I don't know. I want to look around, see what's doin'.

LINDA: Biff, you can't look around all your life, can you?

BIFF: I just can't take hold, Mom. I can't take hold of some kind of a life.   600

LINDA: Biff, a man is not a bird, to come and go with the springtime.

BIFF: Your hair . . . [*He touches her hair.*] Your hair got so gray.

LINDA: Oh, it's been gray since you were in high school. I just stopped dyeing it, that's all.

BIFF: Dye it again, will ya? I don't want my pal looking old. [*He smiles.*]

LINDA: You're such a boy! You think you can go away for a year and . . . You've got to get it into your head now that one day you'll knock on this door and there'll be strange people here—   605

BIFF: What are you talking about? You're not even sixty, Mom.

LINDA: But what about your father?

BIFF: [*lamely*] Well, I meant him, too.

HAPPY: He admires Pop.

LINDA: Biff, dear, if you don't have any feeling for him, then you can't have any feeling for me.   610

BIFF: Sure I can, Mom.

LINDA: No. You can't just come to see me, because I love him. [*with a threat, but only a threat, of tears*] He's the dearest man in the world to me, and I won't have anyone making him feel unwanted and low and blue. You've got to make up your mind now, darling, there's no leeway any more. Either he's your father and you pay him that respect, or else you're not to come here. I know he's not easy to get along with— nobody knows that better than me—but . . .

WILLY: [*from the left, with a laugh*] Hey, hey, Biffo!

BIFF: [*starting to go out after WILLY*] What the hell is the matter with him? [*HAPPY stops him.*]

LINDA: Don't—don't go near him!   615

BIFF: Stop making excuses for him! He always, always wiped the floor with you. Never had an ounce of respect for you.

HAPPY: He's always had respect for—

BIFF: What the hell do you know about it?

HAPPY: [*surlily*] Just don't call him crazy!

BIFF: He's got no character—Charley wouldn't do this. Not in his own house—spewing out that vomit from his mind.   620

HAPPY: Charley never had to cope with what he's got to.

BIFF: People are worse off than Willy Loman. Believe me, I've seen them!

LINDA: Then make Charley your father, Biff. You can't do that, can you? I don't say he's a great man. Willy Loman never made a lot of money. His name was never in the paper. He's not the finest character that ever lived. But he's a human being, and a terrible thing is happening to him. So attention must be paid. He's not to be allowed to fall into his grave like an old dog. Attention, attention must be finally paid to such a person. You called him crazy—

BIFF: I didn't mean—

625 **LINDA:** No, a lot of people think he's lost his—balance. But you don't have to be very smart to know what his trouble is. The man is exhausted.

HAPPY: Sure!

LINDA: A small man can be just as exhausted as a great man. He works for a company thirty-six years this March, opens up unheard-of territories to their trademark, and now in his old age they take his salary away.

HAPPY: [*indignantly*] I didn't know that, Mom.

LINDA: You never asked, my dear! Now that you get your spending money someplace else you don't trouble your mind with him.

630 **HAPPY:** But I gave you money last—

LINDA: Christmas time, fifty dollars! To fix the hot water it cost ninety-seven fifty! For five weeks he's been on straight commission,° like a beginner, an unknown!

BIFF: Those ungrateful bastards!

LINDA: Are they any worse than his sons? When he brought them business, when he was young, they were glad to see him. But now his old friends, the old buyers that loved him so and always found some order to hand him in a pinch—they're all dead, retired. He used to be able to make six, seven calls a day in Boston. Now he takes his valises out of the car and puts them back and takes them out again and he's exhausted. Instead of walking he talks now. He drives seven hundred miles, and when he gets there no one knows him any more, no one welcomes him. And what goes through a man's mind, driving seven hundred miles home without having earned a cent? Why shouldn't he talk to himself? Why? When he has to go to Charley and borrow fifty dollars a week and pretend to me that it's his pay? How long can that go on? How long? You see what I'm sitting here and waiting for? And you tell me he has no character? The man who never worked a day but for your benefit? When does he get the medal for that? Is this his reward—to turn around at the age of sixty-three and find his sons, who he loved better than his life, one a philandering bum—

HAPPY: Mom!

635 **LINDA:** That's all you are, my baby! [*To* BIFF] And you! What happened to the love you had for him? You were such pals! How you used to talk to him on the phone every night! How lonely he was till he could come home to you!

BIFF: All right, Mom. I'll live here in my room, and I'll get a job. I'll keep away from him, that's all.

LINDA: No, Biff. You can't stay here and fight all the time.

BIFF: He threw me out of this house, remember that.

LINDA: Why did he do that? I never knew why.

640 **BIFF:** Because I know he's a fake and he doesn't like anybody around who knows!

LINDA: Why a fake? In what way? What do you mean?

BIFF: Just don't lay it all at my feet. It's between me and him—that's all I have to say. I'll chip in from now on. He'll settle for half my pay check. He'll be all right. I'm going to bed. [*He starts for the stairs.*]

°631 *straight commission:* refers to the fact that Willy is receiving no salary, only a commission (percentage) on the sales he makes.

LINDA: He won't be all right.

BIFF: [*turning on the stairs, furiously*] I hate this city and I'll stay here. Now what do you want?

LINDA: He's dying, Biff.   645

[*HAPPY turns quickly to her, shocked.*]

BIFF: [*after a pause*] Why is he dying?

LINDA: He's been trying to kill himself.

BIFF: [*with great horror*] How?

LINDA: I live from day to day.

BIFF: What're you talking about?   650

LINDA: Remember I wrote you that he smashed up the car again? In February?

BIFF: Well?

LINDA: The insurance inspector came. He said that they have evidence. That all these accidents in the last year—weren't—weren't—accidents.

HAPPY: How can they tell that? That's a lie.

LINDA: It seems there's a woman . . . [*She takes a breath as*]   655

BIFF: [*sharply but contained*] What woman?

LINDA: [*simultaneously*] . . . and this woman . . .

LINDA: What?

BIFF: Nothing. Go ahead.

LINDA: What did you say?   660

BIFF: Nothing. I just said what woman?

HAPPY: What about her?

LINDA: Well, it seems she was walking down the road and saw his car. She says that he wasn't driving fast at all, and that he didn't skid. She says he came to that little bridge, and then deliberately smashed into the railing, and it was only the shallowness of the water that saved him.

BIFF: Oh, no, he probably just fell asleep again.

LINDA: I don't think he fell asleep.   665

BIFF: Why not?

LINDA: Last month . . . [*with great difficulty*] Oh, boys, it's so hard to say a thing like this! He's just a big stupid man to you, but I tell you there's more good in him than in many other people. [*She chokes, wipes her eyes.*] I was looking for a fuse. The lights blew out, and I went down the cellar. And behind the fuse box—it happened to fall out—was a length of rubber pipe—just short.

HAPPY: No kidding?

LINDA: There's a little attachment on the end of it. I knew right away. And sure enough, on the bottom of the water heater there's a new little nipple on the gas pipe.

HAPPY: [*angrily*] That—jerk.   670

BIFF: Did you have it taken off?

LINDA: I'm—I'm ashamed to. How can I mention it to him? Every day I go down and take away that little rubber pipe. But, when he comes home, I put it back where it was. How can I insult him that way? I don't know what to do. I live from day to day, boys. I tell you, I know every thought in his mind. It sounds so old-fashioned and silly, but I tell you he put his whole life into you and you've turned your backs on him. [*She is bent over in the chair, weeping, her face in her hands.*] Biff, I swear to God! Biff, his life is in your hands!

HAPPY: [*to BIFF*] How do you like that damned fool!

BIFF: [*kissing her*] All right, pal, all right. It's all settled now. I've been remiss. I know that, Mom. But now I'll stay, and I swear to you, I'll apply myself. [*kneeling in front of her, in* *a fever of self-reproach*] It's just—you see, Mom, I don't fit in business. Not that I won't try. I'll try, and I'll make good.

675   **HAPPY:** Sure you will. The trouble with you in business was you never tried to please people.

BIFF: I know, I—

HAPPY: Like when you worked for Harrison's. Bob Harrison said you were tops, and then you go and do some damn fool thing like whistling whole songs in the elevator like a comedian.

BIFF: [*against* HAPPY] So what? I like to whistle sometimes.

HAPPY: You don't raise a guy to a responsible job who whistles in the elevator!

680   **LINDA:** Well, don't argue about it now.

HAPPY: Like when you'd go off and swim in the middle of the day instead of taking the line around.

BIFF: [*his resentment rising*] Well, don't you run off? You take off sometimes, don't you? On a nice summer day?

HAPPY: Yeah, but I cover myself!

LINDA: Boys!

685   **HAPPY:** If I'm going to take a fade the boss can call any number where I'm supposed to be and they'll swear to him that I just left. I'll tell you something that I hate to say, Biff, but in the business world some of them think you're crazy.

BIFF: [*angered*] Screw the business world!

HAPPY: All right, screw it! Great, but cover yourself!

LINDA: Hap, Hap!

BIFF: I don't care what they think! They've laughed at Dad for years, and you know why? Because we don't belong in this nuthouse of a city! We should be mixing cement on some open plain, or—or carpenters. A carpenter is allowed to whistle!

[WILLY *walks in from the entrance of the house, at left.*]

690   **WILLY:** Even your grandfather was better than a carpenter. [*Pause. They watch him.*] You never grew up. Bernard does not whistle in the elevator, I assure you.

BIFF: [*as though to laugh* WILLY *out of it*] Yeah, but you do, Pop.

WILLY: I never in my life whistled in an elevator! And who in the business world thinks I'm crazy?

BIFF: I didn't mean it like that, Pop. Now don't make a whole thing out of it, will ya?

WILLY: Go back to the West! Be a carpenter, a cowboy, enjoy yourself!

695   **LINDA:** Willy, he was just saying—

WILLY: I heard what he said!

HAPPY: [*trying to quiet* WILLY] Hey, Pop, come on now . . .

WILLY: [*continuing over* HAPPY'S *line*] They laugh at me, heh? Go to Filene's, go to the Hub, go to Slattery's,° Boston. Call out the name Willy Loman and see what happens! Big shot!

BIFF: All right, Pop.

700   **WILLY:** Big!

BIFF: All right!

WILLY: Why do you always insult me?

BIFF: I didn't say a word! [*to* LINDA] Did I say a word?

LINDA: He didn't say anything, Willy.

705   **WILLY:** [*going to the doorway of the living room*] All right, good night, good night.

LINDA: Willy, dear, he just decided . . .

°698 *Filene's, the Hub, Slattery's:* department stores in New England.

WILLY: [*to* BIFF] If you get tired hanging around tomorrow, paint the ceiling I put up in the living-room.

BIFF: I'm leaving early tomorrow.

HAPPY: He's going to see Bill Oliver, Pop.

WILLY: [*interestedly*] Oliver? For what?   710

BIFF: [*with reserve, but trying, trying*] He always said he'd stake me. I'd like to go into business, so maybe I can take him up on it.

LINDA: Isn't that wonderful?

WILLY: Don't interrupt. What's wonderful about it? There's fifty men in the City of New York who'd stake him. [*to* BIFF] Sporting goods?

BIFF: I guess so. I know something about it and—

WILLY: He knows something about it! You know sporting goods better than Spalding, for   715
God's sake! How much is he giving you?

BIFF: I don't know. I didn't even see him yet, but—

WILLY: Then what're you talkin' about?

BIFF: [*getting angry*] Well, all I said was I'm gonna see him, that's all!

WILLY: [*turning away*] Ah, you're counting your chickens again.

BIFF: [*starting left for the stairs*] Oh, Jesus, I'm going to sleep!   720

WILLY: [*calling after him*] Don't curse in this house!

BIFF: [*turning*] Since when did you get so clean?

HAPPY: [*trying to stop them*] Wait a . . .

WILLY: Don't use that language to me! I won't have it!

HAPPY: [*grabbing* BIFF, *shouts*] Wait a minute! I got an idea. I got a feasible idea. Come here,   725
Biff, let's talk this over now, let's talk some sense here. When I was down in Florida
last time, I thought of a great idea to sell sporting goods. It just came back to me. You
and I, Biff—we have a line, the Loman Line. We train a couple of weeks, and put on a
couple of exhibitions, see?

WILLY: That's an idea!

HAPPY: Wait! We form two basketball teams, see? Two waterpolo teams. We play each
other. It's a million dollars' worth of publicity. Two brothers, see? The Loman Brothers. Displays in the Royal Palms—all the hotels. And banners over the ring and the
basketball court: "Loman Brothers." Baby, we could sell sporting goods!

WILLY: That is a one-million-dollar idea!

LINDA: Marvelous!

BIFF: I'm in great shape as far as that's concerned.   730

HAPPY: And the beauty of it is, Biff, it wouldn't be like a business. We'd be out playin'
ball again . . .

BIFF: [*enthused*] Yeah, that's . . .

WILLY: Million-dollar . . .

HAPPY: And you wouldn't get fed up with it, Biff. It'd be the family again. There'd be the
old honor, and comradeship, and if you wanted to go off for a swim or somethin'—
well, you'd do it! Without some smart cooky gettin' up ahead of you!

WILLY: Lick the world! You guys together could absolutely lick the civilized world.   735

BIFF: I'll see Oliver tomorrow. Hap, if we could work that out . . .

LINDA: Maybe things are beginning to—

WILLY: [*wildly enthused, to* LINDA] Stop interrupting! [*to* BIFF] But don't wear sport jacket
and slacks when you see Oliver.

BIFF: No, I'll—

WILLY: A business suit, and talk as little as possible, and don't crack any jokes.   740

BIFF: He did like me. Always liked me.

LINDA: He loved you!

WILLY: [*to* LINDA] Will you stop! [*to* BIFF] Walk in very serious. You are not applying for a boy's job. Money is to pass. Be quiet, fine, and serious. Everybody likes a kidder, but nobody lends him money.

HAPPY: I'll try to get some myself, Biff. I'm sure I can.

745 **WILLY:** I see great things for you kids. I think your troubles are over. But remember, start big and you'll end big. Ask for fifteen. How much you gonna ask for?

BIFF: Gee, I don't know—

WILLY: And don't say "Gee." "Gee" is a boy's word. A man walking in for fifteen thousand dollars does not say "Gee!"

BIFF: Ten, I think, would be top though.

WILLY: Don't be so modest. You always started too low. Walk in with a big laugh. Don't look worried. Start off with a couple of your good stories to lighten things up. It's not what you say, it's how you say it—because personality always wins the day.

750 **LINDA:** Oliver always thought the highest of him—

WILLY: Will you let me talk?

BIFF: Don't yell at her, Pop, will ya?

WILLY: [*angrily*] I was talking, wasn't I?

BIFF: I don't like you yelling at her all the time, and I'm tellin' you, that's all.

755 **WILLY:** What're you, takin' over this house?

LINDA: Willy—

WILLY: [*turning on her*] Don't take his side all the time, godammit!

BIFF: [*furiously*] Stop yelling at her!

WILLY: [*suddenly pulling on his cheek, beaten down, guilt ridden*] Give my best to Bill Oliver—he may remember me.

[*He exits through the living-room doorway.*]

760 **LINDA:** [*her voice subdued*] What'd you have to start that for? [BIFF *turns away.*] You see how sweet he was as soon as you talked hopefully? [*She goes over to* BIFF.] Come up and say good night to him. Don't let him go to bed that way.

HAPPY: Come on, Biff, let's buck him up.

LINDA: Please, dear. Just say good night. It takes so little to make him happy. Come. [*She goes through the living-room doorway, calling upstairs from within the living-room.*] Your pajamas are hanging in the bathroom, Willy!

HAPPY: [*looking toward where* LINDA *went out*] What a woman! They broke the mold when they made her. You know that, Biff?

BIFF: He's off salary. My God, working on commission!

765 **HAPPY:** Well, let's face it: he's no hot-shot selling man. Except that sometimes, you have to admit, he's a sweet personality.

BIFF: [*deciding*] Lend me ten bucks, will ya? I want to buy some new ties.

HAPPY: I'll take you to a place I know. Beautiful stuff. Wear one of my striped shirts tomorrow.

BIFF: She got gray. Mom got awful old. Gee, I'm gonna go in to Oliver tomorrow and knock him for a—

HAPPY: Come on up. Tell that to Dad. Let's give him a whirl. Come on.

770 **BIFF:** [*steamed up*] You know, with ten thousand bucks, boy!

HAPPY: [*as they go into the living-room*] That's the talk, Biff, that's the first time I've heard the old confidence out of you! [*from within the living-room, fading off*] You're gonna live with me, kid, and any babe you want just say the word . . . [*The last lines are hardly heard. They are mounting the stairs to their parents' bedroom.*]

LINDA: [*entering her bedroom and addressing* WILLY, *who is in the bathroom. She is straightening the bed for him.*] Can you do anything about the shower? It drips.

WILLY: [*from the bathroom*] All of a sudden everything falls to pieces! Goddam plumbing, oughta be sued, those people. I hardly finished putting it in and the thing . . . [*His words rumble off.*]

LINDA: I'm just wondering if Oliver will remember him. You think he might?

WILLY: [*coming out of the bathroom in his pajamas*] Remember him? What's the matter with you, you crazy? If he'd've stayed with Oliver he'd be on top by now! Wait'll Oliver gets a look at him. You don't know the average caliber any more. The average young man today—[*He is getting into bed*]—is got a caliber of zero. Greatest thing in the world for him was to bum around.   775

[*BIFF and HAPPY enter the bedroom. Slight pause.*]

WILLY: [*stops short, looking at BIFF*] Glad to hear it, boy.

HAPPY: He wanted to say good night to you, sport.

WILLY: [*to BIFF*] Yeah. Knock him dead, boy. What'd you want to tell me?

BIFF: Just take it easy, Pop. Good night. [*He turns to go.*]

WILLY: [*unable to resist*] And if anything falls off the desk while you're talking to him— like a package or something—don't you pick it up. They have office boys for that.   780

LINDA: I'll make a big breakfast—

WILLY: Will you let me finish? [*to BIFF*] Tell him you were in the business in the West. Not farm work.

BIFF: All right, Dad.

LINDA: I think everything—

WILLY: [*going right through her speech*] And don't undersell yourself. No less than fifteen thousand dollars.   785

BIFF: [*unable to bear him*] Okay. Good night, Mom. [*He starts moving.*]

WILLY: Because you got a greatness in you, Biff, remember that. You got all kinds a greatness . . . [*He lies back, exhausted.*]

[*BIFF walks out.*]

LINDA: [*calling after BIFF*] Sleep well, darling!

HAPPY: I'm gonna get married, Mom. I wanted to tell you.

LINDA: Go to sleep, dear.   790

HAPPY: [*going*] I just wanted to tell you.

WILLY: Keep up the good work. [*HAPPY exits.*] God . . . remember that Ebbets Field° game? The championship of the city?

LINDA: Just rest. Should I sing to you?

WILLY: Yeah. Sing to me. [*LINDA hums a soft lullaby.*] When that team came out—he was the tallest, remember?

LINDA: Oh, yes. And in gold.   795

[*BIFF enters the darkened kitchen, takes a cigarette, and leaves the house. He comes downstage into a golden pool of light. He smokes, staring at the night.*]

WILLY: Like a young god. Hercules—something like that. And the sun, the sun all around him. Remember how he waved to me? Right up from the field, with the representatives of three colleges standing by? And the buyers I brought, and the cheers when he

---

°792 *Ebbets Field:* the baseball stadium of the Brooklyn Dodgers before they moved to Los Angeles in 1958. Biff had played there in a city championship football game. See 2.210 (p. 1218).

came out—Loman, Loman, Loman! God Almighty, he'll be great yet. A star like that, magnificent, can never really fade away!

[*The light on* WILLY *is fading. The gas heater begins to glow through the kitchen wall, near the stairs, a blue flame beneath red coils.*]

LINDA: [*timidly*] Willy dear, what has he got against you?
WILLY: I'm so tired. Don't talk any more.

[BIFF *slowly returns to the kitchen. He stops, stares toward the heater.*]

LINDA: Will you ask Howard to let you work in New York?
800 WILLY: First thing in the morning. Everything'll be all right.

[BIFF *reaches behind the heater and draws out a length of rubber tubing. He is horrified and turns his head toward* WILLY'S *room, still dimly lit, from which the strains of* LINDA'S *desperate but monotonous humming rise.*]

WILLY: [*staring through the window into the moonlight*] Gee, look at the moon moving between the buildings!

[BIFF *wraps the tubing around his hand and quickly goes up the stairs.*]

ACT 2

[*Music is heard, gay and bright. The curtain rises as the music fades away.* WILLY, *in shirt sleeves, is sitting at the kitchen table, sipping coffee, his hat in his lap.* LINDA *is filling his cup when she can.*]

WILLY: Wonderful coffee. Meal in itself.
LINDA: Can I make you some eggs?
WILLY: No. Take a breath.
LINDA: You look so rested, dear.
5 WILLY: I slept like a dead one. First time in months. Imagine, sleeping till ten on a Tuesday morning. Boys left nice and early, heh?
LINDA: They were out of here by eight o'clock.
WILLY: Good work!
LINDA: It was so thrilling to see them leaving together. I can't get over the shaving lotion in this house!
WILLY: [*smiling*] Mmm—
10 LINDA: Biff was very changed this morning. His whole attitude seemed to be hopeful. He couldn't wait to get downtown to see Oliver.
WILLY: He's heading for a change. There's no question, there simply are certain men that take longer to get—solidified. How did he dress?
LINDA: His blue suit. He's so handsome in that suit. He could be a—anything in that suit!

[WILLY *gets up from the table.* LINDA *holds his jacket for him.*]

WILLY: There's no question, no question at all. Gee, on the way home tonight I'd like to buy some seeds.
LINDA: [*laughing*] That'd be wonderful. But not enough sun gets back there. Nothing'll grow any more.

WILLY: You wait, kid, before it's all over we're gonna get a little place out in the country,   15
and I'll raise some vegetables, a couple of chickens . . .

LINDA: You'll do it yet, dear.

[*WILLY walks out of his jacket, LINDA follows him.*]

WILLY: And they'll get married, and come for a weekend. I'd build a little guest house.
'Cause I got so many fine tools, all I'd need would be a little lumber and some peace
of mind.

LINDA: [*joyfully*] I sewed the lining . . .

WILLY: I could build two guest houses, so they'd both come. Did he decide how much
he's going to ask Oliver for?

LINDA: [*getting him into the jacket*] He didn't mention it, but I imagine ten or fifteen   20
thousand. You going to talk to Howard today?

WILLY: Yeah. I'll put it to him straight and simple. He'll just have to take me off the road.

LINDA: And Willy, don't forget to ask for a little advance, because we've got the insurance
premium. It's the grace period now.

WILLY: That's a hundred . . . ?

LINDA: A hundred and eight, sixty-eight. Because we're a little short again.

WILLY: Why are we short?   25

LINDA: Well, you had the motor job on the car . . .

WILLY: That goddam Studebaker!

LINDA: And you got one more payment on the refrigerator . . .

WILLY: But it just broke again!

LINDA: Well, it's old, dear.   30

WILLY: I told you we should've bought a well-advertised machine. Charley bought a
General Electric and it's twenty years old and it's still good, that son-of-a-bitch.

LINDA: But, Willy—

WILLY: Whoever heard of a Hastings refrigerator? Once in my life I would like to own
something outright before it's broken! I'm always in a race with the junkyard! I just
finished paying for the car and it's on its last legs. The refrigerator consumes belts like
a goddam maniac. They time those things. They time them so when you finally paid
for them, they're used up.

LINDA: [*buttoning up his jacket as he unbuttons it*] All told, about two hundred dollars
would carry us, dear. But that includes the last payment on the mortgage. After this
payment, Willy, the house belongs to us.

WILLY: It's twenty-five years!   35

LINDA: Biff was nine years old when we bought it.

WILLY: Well, that's a great thing. To weather a twenty-five year mortgage is—

LINDA: It's an accomplishment.

WILLY: All the cement, the lumber, the reconstruction I put in this house! There ain't a
crack to be found in it any more.

LINDA: Well, it served its purpose.   40

WILLY: What purpose? Some stranger'll come along, move in, and that's that. If only Biff
would take this house, and raise a family . . . [*He starts to go.*] Good-by, I'm late.

LINDA: [*suddenly remembering*] Oh, I forgot! You're supposed to meet them for dinner.

WILLY: Me?

LINDA: At Frank's Chop House on Forty-eighth near Sixth Avenue.

WILLY: Is that so! How about you?   45

LINDA: No, just the three of you. They're gonna blow you to a big meal!

WILLY: Don't say! Who thought of that?

LINDA: Biff came to me this morning, Willy, and he said, "Tell Dad, we want to blow him to a big meal." Be there six o'clock. You and your two boys are going to have dinner.

WILLY: Gee whiz! That's really somethin'. I'm gonna knock Howard for a loop, kid. I'll get an advance, and I'll come home with a New York job. Goddammit, now I'm gonna do it!

50 **LINDA:** Oh, that's the spirit, Willy!

WILLY: I will never get behind a wheel the rest of my life!

LINDA: It's changing, Willy, I can feel it changing!

WILLY: Beyond a question. G'by, I'm late. [*He starts to go again.*]

LINDA: [*calling after him as she runs to the kitchen table for a handkerchief*] You got your glasses?

55 **WILLY:** [*feels for them, then comes back in*] Yeah, yeah, got my glasses.

LINDA: [*giving him the handkerchief*] And a handkerchief.

WILLY: Yeah, handkerchief.

LINDA: And your saccharine?

WILLY: Yeah, my saccharine.

60 **LINDA:** Be careful on the subway stairs.

[*She kisses him, and a silk stocking is seen hanging from her hand. WILLY notices it.*]

WILLY: Will you stop mending stockings? At least while I'm in the house. It gets me nervous. I can't tell you. Please.

[*LINDA hides the stocking in her hand as she follows WILLY across the forestage in front of the house.*]

LINDA: Remember, Frank's Chop House.

WILLY: [*passing the apron*] Maybe beets would grow out there.

LINDA: [*laughing*] But you tried so many times.

65 **WILLY:** Yeah. Well, don't work hard today. [*He disappears around the right corner of the house.*]

LINDA: Be careful!

[*As Willy vanishes, LINDA waves to him. Suddenly the phone rings. She runs across the stage and into the kitchen and lifts it.*]

LINDA: Hello? Oh, Biff! I'm so glad you called, I just . . . Yes, sure, I just told him. Yes, he'll be there for dinner at six o'clock, I didn't forget. Listen, I was just dying to tell you. You know that little rubber pipe I told you about? That he connected to the gas heater? I finally decided to go down the cellar this morning and take it away and destroy it. But it's gone! Imagine? He took it away himself, it isn't there! [*She listens.*] When? Oh, then you took it. Oh—nothing, it's just that I'd hoped he'd taken it away himself. Oh, I'm not worried, darling, because this morning he left in such high spirits, it was like the old days! I'm not afraid any more. Did Mr. Oliver see you? . . . Well, you wait there then. And make a nice impression on him, darling. Just don't perspire too much before you see him. And have a nice time with Dad. He may have big news too . . . That's right, a New York job. And be sweet to him tonight, dear. Be loving to him. Because he's only a little boat looking for a harbor. [*She is trembling with sorrow and joy.*] Oh, that's wonderful, Biff, you'll save his life. Thanks, darling. Just put your arm around him when he comes into the restaurant. Give him a smile. That's the boy . . . Good-by, dear . . . You got your comb? . . . That's fine. Good-by, Biff dear.

[*In the middle of her speech,* HOWARD WAGNER, *thirty-six, wheels in a small typewriter table on which is a wire-recording machine and proceeds to plug it in. This is on the left forestage. Light slowly fades on* LINDA *as it rises on* HOWARD. HOWARD *is intent on threading the machine and only glances over his shoulder as* WILLY *appears.*]

WILLY: Pst! Pst!
HOWARD: Hello, Willy, come in.
WILLY: Like to have a little talk with you, Howard.   70
HOWARD: Sorry to keep you waiting. I'll be with you in a minute.
WILLY: What's that, Howard?
HOWARD: Didn't you ever see one of these? Wire recorder.
WILLY: Oh. Can we talk a minute?
HOWARD: Records things. Just got delivery yesterday. Been driving me crazy, the most   75
   terrific machine I ever saw in my life. I was up all night with it.
WILLY: What do you do with it?
HOWARD: I bought it for dictation, but you can do anything with it. Listen to this. I had
   it home last night. Listen to what I picked up. The first one is my daughter. Get this.
   [*He flicks the switch and "Roll out the Barrel" is heard being whistled.*] Listen to that kid
   whistle.
WILLY: That is lifelike, isn't it?
HOWARD: Seven years old. Get that tone.
WILLY: Ts, ts. Like to ask a little favor if you . . .   80

[*The whistling breaks off, and the voice of* HOWARD'S DAUGHTER *is heard.*]

HIS DAUGHTER: "Now you, Daddy."
HOWARD: She's crazy for me! [*Again the same song is whistled.*] That's me! Ha! [*He winks.*]
WILLY: You're very good!

[*The whistling breaks off again. The machine runs silent for a moment.*]

HOWARD: Sh! Get this now, this is my son.
HIS SON: "The capital of Alabama is Montgomery; the capital of Arizona is Phoenix; the   85
   capital of Arkansas is Little Rock; the capital of California is Sacramento . . ." [*and on,
   and on*]
HOWARD: [*holding up five fingers*] Five years old, Willy!
WILLY: He'll make an announcer some day!
HIS SON: [*continuing*] "The capital . . ."
HOWARD: Get that—alphabetical order! [*The machine breaks off suddenly.*] Wait a minute.
   The maid kicked the plug out.
WILLY: It certainly is a—   90
HOWARD: Sh, for God's sake!
HIS SON: "It's nine o'clock, Bulova watch time. So I have to go to sleep."
WILLY: That really is—
HOWARD: Wait a minute! The next is my wife.

[*They wait.*]

HOWARD'S VOICE: "Go on, say something." [*pause*] "Well, you gonna talk?"   95
HIS WIFE: "I can't think of anything."
HOWARD'S VOICE: "Well, talk—it's turning."

His Wife: [*shyly, beaten*] "Hello." [*Silence*] "Oh, Howard, I can't talk into this . . ."

Howard: [*snapping the machine off*] That was my wife.

100 **Willy:** That is a wonderful machine. Can we—

Howard: I tell you, Willy, I'm gonna take my camera, and my bandsaw, and all my hobbies, and out they go. This is the most fascinating relaxation I ever found.

Willy: I think I'll get one myself.

Howard: Sure, they're only a hundred and a half. You can't do without it. Supposing you wanna hear Jack Benny,° see? But you can't be at home at that hour. So you tell the maid to turn the radio on when Jack Benny comes on, and this automatically goes on with the radio . . .

Willy: And when you come home you . . .

105 **Howard:** You can come home twelve o'clock, one o'clock, any time you like, and you get yourself a Coke and sit yourself down, throw the switch, and there's Jack Benny's program in the middle of the night!

Willy: I'm definitely going to get one. Because lots of time I'm on the road, and I think to myself, what I must be missing on the radio!

Howard: Don't you have a radio in the car?

Willy: Well, yeah, but who ever thinks of turning it on?

Howard: Say, aren't you supposed to be in Boston?

110 **Willy:** That's what I want to talk to you about, Howard. You got a minute?

[*He draws a chair in from the wing.*]

Howard: What happened? What're you doing here?

Willy: Well . . .

Howard: You didn't crack up again, did you?

Willy: Oh, no. No . . .

115 **Howard:** Geez, you had me worried there for a minute. What's the trouble?

Willy: Well, tell you the truth, Howard, I've come to the decision that I'd rather not travel any more.

Howard: Not travel! Well, what'll you do?

Willy: Remember, Christmas time, when you had the party here? You said you'd try to think of some spot for me here in town.

Howard: With us?

120 **Willy:** Well, sure.

Howard: Oh, yeah, yeah. I remember. Well, I couldn't think of anything for you, Willy.

Willy: I tell ya, Howard. The kids are all grown up, y'know. I don't need much any more. If I could take home—well, sixty-five dollars a week, I could swing it.

Howard: Yeah, but Willy, see I—

Willy: I tell ya why, Howard. Speaking frankly and between the two of us, y'know—I'm just a little tired.

125 **Howard:** Oh, I could understand that, Willy. But you're a road man, Willy, and we do a road business. We've only got a half-dozen salesmen on the floor here.

Willy: God knows, Howard, I never asked a favor of any man. But I was with the firm when your father used to carry you up here in his arms.

Howard: I know that, Willy, but—

Willy: Your father came to me the day you were born and asked me what I thought of the name of Howard, may he rest in peace.

°103 *Jack Benny:* (1894–1974), vaudeville, radio, television, and movie comedian.

HOWARD: I appreciate that, Willy, but there just is no spot here for you. If I had a spot I'd slam you right in, but I just don't have a single solitary spot.

[*He looks for his lighter.* WILLY *has picked it up and gives it to him. Pause.*]

WILLY: [*with increasing anger*] Howard, all I need to set my table is fifty dollars a week.   130
HOWARD: But where am I going to put you, kid?
WILLY: Look, it isn't a question of whether I can sell merchandise, is it?
HOWARD: No, but it's a business, kid, and everybody's gotta pull his own weight.
WILLY: [*desperately*] Just let me tell you a story, Howard—
HOWARD: 'Cause you gotta admit, business is business.   135
WILLY: [*angrily*] Business is definitely business, but just listen for a minute. You don't understand this. When I was a boy—eighteen, nineteen—I was already on the road. And there was a question in my mind as to whether selling had a future for me. Because in those days I had a yearning to go to Alaska. See, there were three gold strikes in one month in Alaska, and I felt like going out. Just for the ride, you might say.
HOWARD: [*barely interested*] Don't say.
WILLY: Oh, yeah, my father lived many years in Alaska. He was an adventurous man. We've got quite a little streak of self-reliance in our family. I thought I'd go out with my older brother and try to locate him, and maybe settle in the North with the old man. And I was almost decided to go, when I met a salesman in the Parker House.° His name was Dave Singleman. And he was eighty-four years old, and he'd drummed merchandise in thirty-one states. And old Dave, he'd go up to his room, y'understand, put on his green velvet slippers—I'll never forget—and pick up his phone and call the buyers, and without ever leaving his room, at the age of eighty-four, he made his living. And when I saw that, I realized that selling was the greatest career a man could want. 'Cause what could be more satisfying than to be able to go, at the age of eighty-four, into twenty or thirty different cities, and pick up a phone, and be remembered and loved and helped by so many different people? Do you know? when he died—and by the way he died the death of a salesman, in his green velvet slippers in the smoker of the New York, New Haven and Hartford, going into Boston—when he died, hundreds of salesmen and buyers were at his funeral. Things were sad on a lotta trains for months after that. [*He stands up.* HOWARD *has not looked at him.*] In those days there was personality in it, Howard. There was respect, and comradeship, and gratitude in it. Today, it's all cut and dried, and there's no chance for bringing friendship to bear—or personality. You see what I mean? They don't know me any more.
HOWARD: [*moving away, to the right*] That's just the thing, Willy.
WILLY: If I had forty dollars a week—that's all I'd need. Forty dollars, Howard.   140
HOWARD: Kid, I can't take blood from a stone, I—
WILLY: [*desperation is on him now*] Howard, the year Al Smith° was nominated, your father came to me and—
HOWARD: [*starting to go off*] I've got to see some people, kid.
WILLY: [*stopping him*] I'm talking about your father! There were promises made across this desk! You mustn't tell me you've got people to see—I put thirty-four years into this firm, Howard, and now I can't pay my insurance! You can't eat the orange and throw the peel away—a man is not a piece of fruit! [*after a pause*] Now pay attention. Your father—in 1928 I had a big year. I averaged a hundred and seventy dollars a week in commissions.

°138 *Parker House*: a hotel in Boston. °142 *Al Smith*: Alfred E. Smith was governor of New York State (1919–21, 1923–29) and the Democratic presidential candidate defeated by Herbert Hoover in 1928.

145   **HOWARD:** [*impatiently*] Now, Willy, you never averaged—

      WILLY: [*banging his hand on the desk*] I averaged a hundred and seventy dollars a week in the year of 1928! And your father came to me—or rather, I was in the office here—it was right over this desk—and he put his hand on my shoulder—

      HOWARD: [*getting up*] You'll have to excuse me, Willy, I gotta see some people. Pull yourself together. [*going out*] I'll be back in a little while.

[*On* HOWARD'S *exit, the light on his chair grows very bright and strange.*]

      WILLY: Pull myself together! What the hell did I say to him? My God, I was yelling at him! How could I! [WILLY *breaks off, staring at the light, which occupies the chair, animating it. He approaches this chair, standing across the desk from it.*] Frank, Frank, don't you remember what you told me that time? How you put your hand on my shoulder, and Frank . . . [*He leans on the desk and as he speaks the dead man's name he accidentally switches on the recorder, and instantly*]

      HOWARD'S SON: ". . . of New York is Albany. The capital of Ohio is Cincinnati, the capital of Rhode Island is . . ." [*The recitation continues.*]

150   **WILLY:** [*leaping away with fright, shouting*] Ha! Howard! Howard! Howard!

      HOWARD: [*rushing in*] What happened?

      WILLY: [*pointing at the machine, which continues nasally, childishly, with the capital cities*] Shut it off! Shut it off!

      HOWARD: [*pulling the plug out*] Look, Willy . . .

      WILLY: [*pressing his hands to his eyes*] I gotta get myself some coffee. I'll get some coffee . . .

[WILLY *starts to walk out.* HOWARD *stops him.*]

155   **HOWARD:** [*rolling up the cord*] Willy, look . . .

      WILLY: I'll go to Boston.

      HOWARD: Willy, you can't go to Boston for us.

      WILLY: Why can't I go?

      HOWARD: I don't want you to represent us. I've been meaning to tell you for a long time now.

160   **WILLY:** Howard, are you firing me?

      HOWARD: I think you need a good long rest, Willy.

      WILLY: Howard—

      HOWARD: And when you feel better, come back, and we'll see if we can work something out.

      WILLY: But I gotta earn money, Howard. I'm in no position to—

165   **HOWARD:** Where are your sons? Why don't your sons give you a hand?

      WILLY: They're working on a very big deal.

      HOWARD: This is no time for false pride, Willy. You go to your sons and you tell them that you're tired. You've got two great boys, haven't you?

      WILLY: Oh, no question, no question, but in the meantime . . .

      HOWARD: Then that's that, heh?

170   **WILLY:** All right, I'll go to Boston tomorrow.

      HOWARD: No, no.

      WILLY: I can't throw myself on my sons. I'm not a cripple!

      HOWARD: Look, kid, I'm busy this morning.

      WILLY: [*grasping* HOWARD'S *arm*] Howard, you've got to let me go to Boston!

175   **HOWARD:** [*hard, keeping himself under control*] I've got a line of people to see this morning. Sit down, take five minutes, and pull yourself together, and then go home, will ya? I need the office, Willy. [*He starts to go, turns, remembering the recorder, starts to push off the table holding the recorder.*] Oh, yeah. Whenever you can this week, stop by and

drop off the samples. You'll feel better, Willy, and then come back and we'll talk. Pull yourself together, kid, there's people outside.

[HOWARD *exits, pushing the table off left.* WILLY *stares into space, exhausted. Now the music is heard—*BEN's *music—first distantly, then closer. As* WILLY *speaks,* BEN *enters from the right. He carries valise and umbrella.*]

WILLY: Oh, Ben, how did you do it? What is the answer? Did you wind up the Alaska deal already?

BEN: Doesn't take much time if you know what you're doing. Just a short business trip. Boarding ship in an hour. Wanted to say good-by.

WILLY: Ben, I've got to talk to you.

BEN: [*glancing at his watch*] Haven't much time, William.

WILLY: [*crossing the apron to* BEN] Ben, nothing's working out. I don't know what to do.　　180

BEN: Now, look here, William. I've bought timberland in Alaska and I need a man to look after things for me.

WILLY: God, timberland! Me and my boys in those grand outdoors!

BEN: You've a new continent at your doorstep, William. Get out of these cities, they're full of talk and time payments and courts of law. Screw on your fists and you can fight for a fortune up there.

WILLY: Yes, yes! Linda, Linda!

[LINDA *enters as of old, with the wash.*]

LINDA: Oh, you're back?　　185

BEN: I haven't much time.

WILLY: No, wait! Linda, he's got a proposition for me in Alaska.

LINDA: But you've got—[*to* BEN] He's got a beautiful job here.

WILLY: But in Alaska, kid, I could—

LINDA: You're doing well enough, Willy!

BEN: [*to* LINDA] Enough for what, my dear?　　190

LINDA: [*frightened of* BEN *and angry at him*] Don't say those things to him! Enough to be happy right here, right now. [*to* WILLY, *while* BEN *laughs*] Why must everybody conquer the world? You're well liked, and the boys love you, and someday—[*to* BEN]—why old man Wagner told him just the other day that if he keeps it up he'll be a member of the firm, didn't he, Willy?

WILLY: Sure, sure. I am building something with this firm, Ben, and if a man is building something he must be on the right track, mustn't he?

BEN: What are you building? Lay your hand on it. Where is it?

WILLY: [*hesitantly*] That's true, Linda, there's nothing.

LINDA: Why? [*to* BEN] There's a man eighty-four years old—　　195

WILLY: That's right, Ben, that's right. When I look at that man I say, what is there to worry about?

BEN: Bah!

WILLY: It's true, Ben. All he has to do is go into any city, pick up the phone, and he's making his living and you know why?

BEN: [*picking up his valise*] I've got to go.　　200

WILLY: [*holding* BEN *back*] Look at this boy!

[BIFF, *in his high school sweater, enters carrying suitcase.* HAPPY *carries* BIFF's *shoulder guards, gold helmet, and football pants.*]

WILLY: Without a penny to his name, three great universities are begging for him, and from there the sky's the limit, because it's not what you do, Ben. It's who you know and the smile on your face! It's contacts, Ben, contacts! The whole wealth of Alaska passes over the lunch table at the Commodore Hotel,° and that's the wonder, the wonder of this country, that a man can end with diamonds here on the basis of being liked! [*He turns to* BIFF.] And that's why when you get out on that field today it's important. Because thousands of people will be rooting for you and loving you. [*to* BEN, *who has again begun to leave*] And Ben! when he walks into a business office his name will sound out like a bell and all the doors will open to him! I've seen it, Ben, I've seen it a thousand times! You can't feel it with your hand like timber, but it's there!

BEN: Good-by, William.

WILLY: Ben, am I right? Don't you think I'm right? I value your advice.

205   BEN: There's a new continent at your doorstep, William. You could walk out rich. Rich! [*He is gone.*]

WILLY: We'll do it here, Ben! You hear me? We're gonna do it here!

[YOUNG BERNARD *rushes in. The gay music of the Boys is heard.*]

BERNARD: Oh, gee, I was afraid you left already!

WILLY: Why? What time is it?

BERNARD: It's half-past one!

210   WILLY: Well, come on, everybody! Ebbets Field next stop! Where's the pennants? [*He rushes through the wall-line of the kitchen and out into the dining-room.*]

LINDA: [*to* BIFF] Did you pack fresh underwear?

BIFF: [*who has been limbering up*] I want to go!

BERNARD: Biff, I'm carrying your helmet, ain't I?

HAPPY: No, I'm carrying the helmet.

215   BERNARD: Oh, Biff, you promised me.

HAPPY: I'm carrying the helmet.

BERNARD: How am I going to get in the locker room?

LINDA: Let him carry the shoulder guards. [*She puts her coat and hat on in the kitchen.*]

BERNARD: Can I, Biff? 'Cause I told everybody I'm going to be in the locker room.

220   HAPPY: In Ebbets Field it's the clubhouse.

BERNARD: I meant the clubhouse. Biff!

HAPPY: Biff!

BIFF: [*grandly, after a slight pause.*] Let him carry the shoulder guards.

HAPPY: [*as he gives* BERNARD *the shoulder guards*] Stay close to us now.

[WILLY *rushes in with the pennants.*]

225   WILLY: [*handing them out*] Everybody wave when Biff comes out on the field. [HAPPY *and* BERNARD *run off.*] You set now, boy?

[*The music has died away.*]

BIFF: Ready to go, Pop. Every muscle is ready.

WILLY: [*at the edge of the apron*] You realize what this means?

BIFF: That's right, Pop.

WILLY: [*feeling* BIFF's *muscles*] You're comin' home this afternoon captain of the All-Scholastic Championship Team of the City of New York.

°202 *Commodore Hotel:* a large hotel in New York City.

BIFF: I got it, Pop. And remember, pal, when I take off my helmet, that touchdown is for   230
you.

WILLY: Let's go! [*He is starting out, with his arm around* BIFF, *when* CHARLEY *enters, as of old,
in knickers.*] I got no room for you, Charley.

CHARLEY: Room? For what?

WILLY: In the car.

CHARLEY: You goin' for a ride? I wanted to shoot some casino.

WILLY: [*furiously*] Casino! [*incredulously*] Don't you realize what today is?   235

LINDA: Oh, he knows, Willy. He's just kidding you.

WILLY: That's nothing to kid about!

CHARLEY: No, Linda, what's goin' on?

LINDA: He's playing in Ebbets Field.

CHARLEY: Baseball in this weather?   240

WILLY: Don't talk to him. Come on, come on! [*He is pushing them out.*]

CHARLEY: Wait a minute, didn't you hear the news?

WILLY: What?

CHARLEY: Don't you listen to the radio? Ebbets Field just blew up.

WILLY: You go to hell! [CHARLEY *laughs. Pushing them out.*] Come on, come on! We're   245
late.

CHARLEY: [*as they go*] Knock a homer, Biff, knock a homer!

WILLY: [*the last to leave, turning to* CHARLEY] I don't think that was funny, Charley. This is
the greatest day of his life.

CHARLEY: Willy, when are you going to grow up?

WILLY: Yeah, heh? When this game is over, Charley, you'll be laughing out the other side
of your face. They'll be calling him another Red Grange.° Twenty-five thousand a
year.

CHARLEY: [*kidding*] Is that so?

WILLY: Yeah, that's so.   250

CHARLEY: Well, then, I'm sorry, Willy. But tell me something.

WILLY: What?

CHARLEY: Who is Red Grange?

WILLY: Put up your hands. Goddam you, put up your hands!   255

[CHARLEY, *chuckling, shakes his head and walks away, around the left corner of the stage.* WILLY *follows him. The music rises to a mocking frenzy.*]

WILLY: Who the hell do you think you are, better than everybody else? You don't know
everything, you big, ignorant, stupid . . . Put up your hands!

[*Light rises, on the right side of the forestage, on a small table in the reception room of* CHARLEY's
office. Traffic sounds are heard. BERNARD, *now mature, sits whistling to himself. A pair of tennis
rackets and an overnight bag are on the floor beside him.*]

WILLY: [*offstage*] What are you walking away for? Don't walk away! If you're going to say
something say it to my face! I know you laugh at me behind my back. You'll laugh
out of the other side of your goddam face after this game. Touchdown! Touchdown!
Eighty thousand people! Touchdown. Right between the goal posts.

[BERNARD *is a quiet, earnest, but self-assured young man.* WILLY's *voice is coming from right upstage now.* BERNARD *lowers his feet off the table and listens.* JENNY, *his father's secretary, enters.*]

°249 *Red Grange:* Harold Edward Grange (1903–91), all-America halfback (1923–25) at the University of
Illinois.

JENNY: [*distressed*] Say, Bernard, will you go out in the hall?

BERNARD: What is that noise? Who is it?

260 **JENNY:** Mr. Loman. He just got off the elevator.

BERNARD: [*getting up*] Who's he arguing with?

JENNY: Nobody. There's nobody with him. I can't deal with him any more, and your father gets all upset everytime he comes. I've got a lot of typing to do, and your father's waiting to sign it. Will you see him?

WILLY: [*entering*] Touchdown! Touch—[*He sees* JENNY.] Jenny, Jenny, good to see you. How're ya? Workin'? Or still honest?

JENNY: Fine. How've you been feeling?

265 **WILLY:** Not much any more, Jenny. Ha, ha! [*He is surprised to see the rackets.*]

BERNARD: Hello, Uncle Willy.

WILLY: [*almost shocked*] Bernard! Well, look who's here! [*He comes quickly, guiltily, to* BERNARD *and warmly shakes his hand.*]

BERNARD: How are you? Good to see you.

WILLY: What are you doing here?

270 **BERNARD:** Oh, just stopped off to see Pop. Get off my feet till my train leaves. I'm going to Washington in a few minutes.

WILLY: Is he in?

BERNARD: Yes, he's in his office with the accountants. Sit down.

WILLY: [*sitting down*] What're you going to do in Washington?

BERNARD: Oh, just a case I've got there, Willy.

275 **WILLY:** That so? [*Indicating the rackets*] You going to play tennis there?

BERNARD: I'm staying with a friend who's got a court.

WILLY: Don't say. His own tennis court. Must be fine people, I bet.

BERNARD: They are, very nice. Dad tells me Biff's in town.

WILLY: [*with a big smile*] Yeah, Biff's in. Working on a very big deal, Bernard.

280 **BERNARD:** What's Biff doing?

WILLY: Well, he's been doing very big things in the West. But he decided to establish himself here. Very big. We're having dinner. Did I hear your wife had a boy?

BERNARD: That's right. Our second.

WILLY: Two boys! What do you know!

BERNARD: What kind of a deal has Biff got?

285 **WILLY:** Well, Bill Oliver—very big sporting-goods man—he wants Biff very badly. Called him in from the West. Long distance, carte blanche, special deliveries. Your friends have their own private tennis court?

BERNARD: You still with the old firm, Willy?

WILLY: [*after a pause*] I'm—I'm overjoyed to see how you made the grade, Bernard, overjoyed. It's an encouraging thing to see a young man really—really—Looks very good for Biff—very—[*He breaks off, then*] Bernard—[*He is so full of emotion, he breaks off again.*]

BERNARD: What is it, Willy?

WILLY: [*small and alone*] What—what's the secret?

290 **BERNARD:** What secret?

WILLY: How—how did you? Why didn't he ever catch on?

BERNARD: I wouldn't know that, Willy.

WILLY: [*confidentially, desperately*] You were his friend, his boyhood friend. There's something I don't understand about it. His life ended after that Ebbets Field game. From the age of seventeen nothing good ever happened to him.

BERNARD: He never trained himself for anything.

295 **WILLY:** But he did, he did. After high school he took so many correspondence courses. Radio mechanics; television; God knows what, and never made the slightest mark.

BERNARD: [*taking off his glasses*] Willy, do you want to talk candidly?

WILLY: [*rising, faces BERNARD*] I regard you as a very brilliant man, Bernard. I value your advice.

BERNARD: Oh, the hell with the advice, Willy. I couldn't advise you. There's just one thing I've always wanted to ask you. When he was supposed to graduate, and the math teacher flunked him—

WILLY: Oh, that son-of-a-bitch ruined his life.

BERNARD: Yeah, but, Willy, all he had to do was go to summer school and make up that   300
subject.

WILLY: That's right, that's right.

BERNARD: Did you tell him not to go to summer school?

WILLY: Me? I begged him to go. I ordered him to go!

BERNARD: Then why wouldn't he go?

WILLY: Why? Why! Bernard, that question has been trailing me like a ghost for the last   305
fifteen years. He flunked the subject, and laid down and died like a hammer hit him!

BERNARD: Take it easy, kid.

WILLY: Let me talk to you—I got nobody to talk to. Bernard, Bernard, was it my fault?
Y'see? It keeps going around in my mind, maybe I did something to him. I got nothing to give him.

BERNARD: Don't take it so hard.

WILLY: Why did he lay down? What is the story there? You were his friend!

BERNARD: Willy, I remember, it was June, and our grades came out. And he'd flunked   310
math.

WILLY: That son-of-a-bitch!

BERNARD: No, it wasn't right then. Biff just got very angry, I remember, and he was ready
to enroll in summer school.

WILLY: [*surprised*] He was?

BERNARD: He wasn't beaten by it at all. But then, Willy, he disappeared from the block
for almost a month. And I got the idea that he'd gone up to New England to see you.
Did he have a talk with you then?

[*WILLY stares in silence.*]

BERNARD: Willy?   315

WILLY: [*with a strong edge of resentment in his voice*] Yeah, he came to Boston. What about it?

BERNARD: Well, just that when he came back—I'll never forget this, it always mystifies
me. Because I'd thought so well of Biff, even though he'd always taken advantage
of me. I loved him, Willy, y'know? And he came back after that month and took his
sneakers—remember the sneakers with "University of Virginia" printed on them? He
was so proud of those, wore them every day. And he took them down in the cellar,
and burned them up in the furnace. We had a fist fight. It lasted at least half an hour.
Just the two of us, punching each other down the cellar, and crying right through it.
I've often thought of how strange it was that I knew he'd given up his life. What happened in Boston, Willy?

[*WILLY looks at him as at an intruder.*]

BERNARD: I just bring it up because you asked me.

WILLY: [*angrily*] Nothing. What do you mean, "What happened?" What's that got to do
with anything?

BERNARD: Well, don't get sore.   320

WILLY: What are you trying to do, blame it on me? If a boy lays down is that my fault?
BERNARD: Now, Willy, don't get—
WILLY: Well, don't—don't talk to me that way! What does that mean, "What happened?"

[*CHARLEY enters. He is in his vest, and he carries a bottle of bourbon.*]

CHARLEY: Hey, you're going to miss that train. [*He waves the bottle.*]
325   BERNARD: Yeah, I'm going. [*He takes the bottle.*] Thanks, Pop. [*He picks up his rackets and bag.*]
         Good-by, Willy, and don't worry about it. You know, "If at first you don't succeed . . ."
      WILLY: Yes, I believe in that.
      BERNARD: But sometimes, Willy, it's better for a man just to walk away.
      WILLY: Walk away?
      BERNARD: That's right.
330   WILLY: But if you can't walk away?
      BERNARD: [*after a slight pause*] I guess that's when it's tough. [*extending his hand*] Good-by, Willy.
      WILLY: [*shaking BERNARD's hand*] Good-by, boy.
      CHARLEY: [*an arm on BERNARD's shoulder*] How do you like this kid? Gonna argue a case in
         front of the Supreme Court.
      BERNARD: [*protesting*] Pop!
335   WILLY: [*genuinely shocked, pained, and happy*] No! The Supreme Court!
      BERNARD: I gotta run. 'By, Dad!
      CHARLEY: Knock 'em dead, Bernard!

[*BERNARD goes off.*]

WILLY: [*as CHARLEY takes out his wallet*] The Supreme Court! And he didn't even mention it!
      CHARLEY: [*counting out money on the desk*] He doesn't have to—he's gonna do it.
340   WILLY: And you never told him what to do, did you? You never took any interest in him.
      CHARLEY: My salvation is that I never took any interest in anything. There's some
         money—fifty dollars. I got an accountant inside.
      WILLY: Charley, look . . . [*with difficulty*] I got my insurance to pay. If you can manage
         it—I need a hundred and ten dollars.

[*CHARLEY doesn't reply for a moment; merely stops moving.*]

WILLY: I'd draw it from my bank but Linda would know, and I . . .
      CHARLEY: Sit down, Willy.
345   WILLY: [*moving toward the chair*] I'm keeping an account of everything, remember. I'll pay
         every penny back. [*He sits.*]
      CHARLEY: Now listen to me, Willy . . .
      WILLY: I want you to know I appreciate . . .
      CHARLEY: [*sitting down on the table*] Willy, what're you doin'? What the hell is goin' on in
         your head?
      WILLY: Why? I'm simply . . .
350   CHARLEY: I offered you a job. You can make fifty dollars a week. And I won't send you
         on the road.
      WILLY: I've got a job.
      CHARLEY: Without pay? What kind of job is a job without pay? [*He rises.*] Now, look, kid,
         enough is enough. I'm no genius but I know when I'm being insulted.
      WILLY: Insulted!
      CHARLEY: Why don't you want to work for me?
355   WILLY: What's the matter with you? I've got a job.

CHARLEY: Then what're you walkin' in here every week for?

WILLY: [*getting up*] Well, if you don't want me to walk in here—

CHARLEY: I am offering you a job.

WILLY: I don't want your goddam job!

CHARLEY: When the hell are you going to grow up?   360

WILLY: [*furiously*] You big ignoramus, if you say that to me again I'll rap you one! I don't care how big you are! [*He's ready to fight.*]

[*Pause.*]

CHARLEY: [*kindly, going to him*] How much do you need, Willy?

WILLY: Charley, I'm strapped. I'm strapped. I don't know what to do. I was just fired.

CHARLEY: Howard fired you?

WILLY: That snotnose. Imagine that? I named him. I named him Howard.   365

CHARLEY: Willy, when're you gonna realize that them things don't mean anything? You named him Howard, but you can't sell that. The only thing you got in this world is what you can sell. And the funny thing is that you're a salesman, and you don't know that.

WILLY: I've tried to think otherwise, I guess. I always felt that if a man was impressive, and well liked, that nothing—

CHARLEY: Why must everybody like you? Who liked J. P. Morgan?° Was he impressive? In a Turkish bath he'd look like a butcher. But with his pockets on he was very well liked. Now listen, Willy, I know you don't like me, and nobody can say I'm in love with you, but I'll give you a job because—just for the hell of it, put it that way. Now what do you say?

WILLY: I   I just can't work for you, Charley.

CHARLEY: What're you, jealous of me?   370

WILLY: I can't work for you, that's all, don't ask me why.

CHARLEY: [*angered, takes out more bills*] You been jealous of me all your life, you damned fool! Here, pay your insurance. [*He puts the money in* WILLY's *hand.*]

WILLY: I'm keeping strict accounts.

CHARLEY: I've got some work to do. Take care of yourself. And pay your insurance.

WILLY: [*moving to the right*] Funny, y'know? After all the highways, and the trains, and   375
the appointments, and the years, you end up worth more dead than alive.

CHARLEY: Willy, nobody's worth nothin' dead. [*after a slight pause*] Did you hear what I said?

[WILLY *stands still, dreaming.*]

CHARLEY: Willy!

WILLY: Apologize to Bernard for me when you see him. I didn't mean to argue with him. He's a fine boy. They're all fine boys, and they'll end up big—all of them. Someday they'll all play tennis together. Wish me luck, Charley. He saw Bill Oliver today.

CHARLEY: Good luck.

WILLY: [*on the verge of tears*] Charley, you're the only friend I got. Isn't that a remarkable   380
thing? [*He goes out.*]

CHARLEY: Jesus!

°368 *J. P. Morgan:* John Pierpont Morgan (1837–1913) was the founder of U.S. Steel and the head of a gigantic family fortune that was enlarged by his son, John Pierpont Morgan (1867–1943). Charley is probably referring to the son.

[CHARLEY *stares after him a moment and follows. All light blacks out. Suddenly raucous music is heard, and a red glow rises behind the screen at right.* STANLEY, *a young waiter, appears, carrying a table, followed by* HAPPY, *who is carrying two chairs.*]

STANLEY: [*putting the table down*] That's all right, Mr. Loman. I can handle it myself. [*He turns and takes the chairs from* HAPPY *and places them at the table.*]

HAPPY: [*glancing around.*] Oh, this is better.

STANLEY: Sure, in the front there you're in the middle of all kinds a noise. Whenever you got a party, Mr. Loman, you just tell me and I'll put you back here. Y' know, there's a lotta people they don't like it private, because when they go out they like to see a lotta action around them because they're sick and tired to stay in the house by theirself. But I know you, you ain't from Hackensack.° You know what I mean?

385 HAPPY: [*sitting down*] So how's it coming, Stanley?

STANLEY: Ah, it's a dog's life. I only wish during the war they'd a took me in the Army. I coulda been dead by now.

HAPPY: My brother's back, Stanley.

STANLEY: Oh, he come back, heh? From the Far West.

HAPPY: Yeah, big cattle man, my brother, so treat him right. And my father's coming too.

390 STANLEY: Oh, your father too!

HAPPY: You got a couple of nice lobsters?

STANLEY: Hundred per cent, big.

HAPPY: I want them with claws.

STANLEY: Don't worry. I don't give you no mice. [HAPPY *laughs.*] How about some wine? It'll put a head on the meal.

395 HAPPY: No. You remember, Stanley, that recipe I brought you from overseas? With the champagne in it?

STANLEY: Oh, yeah, sure. I still got it tacked up yet in the kitchen. But that'll have to cost a buck apiece anyways.

HAPPY: That's all right.

STANLEY: What'd you, hit a number or somethin'?

HAPPY: No, it's a little celebration. My brother is—I think he pulled off a big deal today. I think we're going into business together.

400 STANLEY: Great! That's the best for you. Because a family business, you know what I mean?—that's the best.

HAPPY: That's what I think.

STANLEY: 'Cause what's the difference? Somebody steals? It's in the family. Know what I mean? [*sotto voce*]° Like this bartender here. The boss is goin' crazy what kinda leak he's got in the cash register. You put it in but it don't come out.

HAPPY: [*raising his head*] Sh!

STANLEY: What?

405 HAPPY: You notice I wasn't lookin' right or left, was I?

STANLEY: No.

HAPPY: And my eyes are closed.

STANLEY: So what's the—?

HAPPY: Strudel's comin'.

410 STANLEY: [*catching on, looks around*] Ah, no, there's no—

[*He breaks off as a furred, lavishly dressed* GIRL *enters and sits at the next table. Both follow her with their eyes.*]

°384 *Hackensack:* a city in northeastern New Jersey; Stanley uses the name as a reference to unsophisticated visitors to New York City. °402 *sotto voce:* spoken in an undertone or "stage" whisper.

Stanley: Geez, how'd ya know?

Happy: I got radar or something. [*staring directly at her profile*] Oooooooo . . . Stanley.

Stanley: I think that's for you, Mr. Loman.

Happy: Look at that mouth. Oh God. And the binoculars.

Stanley: Geez, you got a life, Mr. Loman.   415

Happy: Wait on her.

Stanley: [*going to the* Girl's *table*] Would you like a menu, ma'am?

Girl: I'm expecting someone, but I'd like a—

Happy: Why don't you bring her—excuse me, miss, do you mind? I sell champagne, and I'd like you to try my brand. Bring her a champagne, Stanley.

Girl: That's awfully nice of you.   420

Happy: Don't mention it. It's all company money. [*He laughs.*]

Girl: That's a charming product to be selling, isn't it?

Happy: Oh, gets to be like everything else. Selling is selling, y'know.

Girl: I suppose.

Happy: You don't happen to sell, do you?   425

Girl: No, I don't sell.

Happy: Would you object to a compliment from a stranger? You ought to be on a magazine cover.

Girl: [*looking at him a little archly*] I have been.

[*Stanley comes in with a glass of champagne.*]

Happy: What'd I say before, Stanley? You see? She's a cover girl.

Stanley: Oh, I could see, I could see.   430

Happy: [*to the* Girl] What magazine?

Girl: Oh, a lot of them. [*She takes the drink.*] Thank you.

Happy: You know what they say in France, don't you? "Champagne is the drink of the complexion"—Hya, Biff!

[*Biff has entered and sits with* Happy.]

Biff: Hello, kid. Sorry I'm late.

Happy: I just got here. Uh, Miss —?   435

Girl: Forsythe.

Happy: Miss Forsythe, this is my brother.

Biff: Is Dad here?

Happy: His name is Biff. You might've heard of him. Great football player.

Girl: Really? What team?   440

Happy: Are you familiar with football?

Girl: No. I'm afraid I'm not.

Happy: Biff is quarterback with the New York Giants.

Girl: Well, that is nice, isn't it? [*She drinks.*]

Happy: Good health.   445

Girl: I'm happy to meet you.

Happy: That's my name. Hap. It's really Harold, but at West Point they called me Happy.

Girl: [*now really impressed*] Oh, I see. How do you do? [*She turns her profile.*]

Biff: Isn't Dad coming?

Happy: You want her?   450

Biff: Oh, I could never make that.

HAPPY: I remember the time that idea would never come into your head. Where's the old confidence, Biff?

BIFF: I just saw Oliver—

HAPPY: Wait a minute. I've got to see that old confidence again. Do you want her? She's on call.

455   **BIFF:** Oh, no. [*He turns to look at the* GIRL.]

HAPPY: I'm telling you. Watch this. [*turning to the* GIRL] Honey? [*She turns to him.*] Are you busy?

GIRL: Well, I am . . . but I could make a phone call.

HAPPY: Do that, will you, honey? And see if you can get a friend. We'll be here for a while. Biff is one of the greatest football players in the country.

GIRL: [*standing up*] Well, I'm certainly happy to meet you.

460   **HAPPY:** Come back soon.

GIRL: I'll try.

HAPPY: Don't try, honey, try hard.

[*The* GIRL *exits.* STANLEY *follows, shaking his head in bewildered admiration.*]

HAPPY: Isn't that a shame now? A beautiful girl like that? That's why I can't get married. There's not a good woman in a thousand. New York is loaded with them, kid!

BIFF: Hap, look—

465   **HAPPY:** I told you she was on call!

BIFF: [*strangely unnerved*] Cut it out, will ya? I want to say something to you.

HAPPY: Did you see Oliver?

BIFF: I saw him all right. Now look, I want to tell Dad a couple of things and I want you to help me.

HAPPY: What? Is he going to back you?

470   **BIFF:** Are you crazy? You're out of your goddam head, you know that?

HAPPY: Why? What happened?

BIFF: [*breathlessly*] I did a terrible thing today, Hap. It's been the strangest day I ever went through. I'm all numb, I swear.

HAPPY: You mean he wouldn't see you?

BIFF: Well, I waited six hours for him, see? All day. Kept sending my name in. Even tried to date his secretary so she'd get me to him, but no soap.

475   **HAPPY:** Because you're not showin' the old confidence, Biff. He remembered you, didn't he?

BIFF: [*stopping* HAPPY *with a gesture*] Finally, about five o'clock, he comes out. Didn't remember who I was or anything. I felt like such an idiot, Hap.

HAPPY: Did you tell him my Florida idea?

BIFF: He walked away. I saw him for one minute. I got so mad I could've torn the walls down! How the hell did I ever get the idea I was a salesman there? I even believed myself that I'd been a salesman for him! And then he gave me one look and—I realized what a ridiculous lie my whole life has been! We've been talking in a dream for fifteen years. I was a shipping clerk.

HAPPY: What'd you do?

480   **BIFF:** [*with great tension and wonder*] Well, he left, see. And the secretary went out. I was all alone in the waiting-room. I don't know what came over me, Hap. The next thing I know I'm in his office—paneled walls, everything. I can't explain it. I—Hap, I took his fountain pen.

HAPPY: Geez, did he catch you?

BIFF: I ran out. I ran down all eleven flights. I ran and ran and ran.

HAPPY: That was an awful dumb—what'd you do that for?

BIFF: [*agonized*] I don't know, I just—wanted to take something. I don't know. You gotta help me, Hap, I'm gonna tell Pop.

HAPPY: You crazy? What for?   485

BIFF: Hap, he's got to understand that I'm not the man somebody lends that kind of money to. He thinks I've been spiting him all these years and it's eating him up.

HAPPY: That's just it. You tell him something nice.

BIFF: I can't.

HAPPY: Say you got a lunch date with Oliver tomorrow.

BIFF: So what do I do tomorrow?   490

HAPPY: You leave the house tomorrow and come back at night and say Oliver is thinking it over. And he thinks it over for a couple of weeks, and gradually it fades away and nobody's the worse.

BIFF: But it'll go on forever!

HAPPY: Dad is never so happy as when he's looking forward to something!

[*WILLY enters.*]

HAPPY: Hello, scout!

WILLY: Gee, I haven't been here in years!   495

[*STANLEY has followed WILLY in and sets a chair for him. STANLEY starts off but HAPPY stops him.*]

HAPPY: Stanley!

[*STANLEY stands by, waiting for an order.*]

BIFF: [*going to WILLY with guilt, as to an invalid*] Sit down, Pop. You want a drink?

WILLY: Sure, I don't mind.

BIFF: Let's get a load on.

WILLY: You look worried.   500

BIFF: N-no. [*to STANLEY*] Scotch all around. Make it doubles.

STANLEY: Doubles, right. [*He goes.*]

WILLY: You had a couple already, didn't you?

BIFF: Just a couple, yeah.

WILLY: Well, what happened, boy? [*nodding affirmatively, with a smile*] Everything go all   505
right?

BIFF: [*takes a breath, then reaches out and grasps WILLY's hand*] Pal . . . [*He is smiling bravely, and WILLY is smiling too.*] I had an experience today.

HAPPY: Terrific, Pop.

WILLY: That so? What happened?

BIFF: [*high, slightly alcoholic, above the earth*] I'm going to tell you everything from first to last. It's been a strange day. [*Silence. He looks around, composes himself as best he can, but his breath keeps breaking the rhythm of his voice.*] I had to wait quite a while for him, and—

WILLY: Oliver?   510

BIFF: Yeah, Oliver. All day, as a matter of cold fact. And a lot of—instances—facts, Pop, facts about my life came back to me. Who was it, Pop? Who ever said I was a salesman with Oliver?

WILLY: Well, you were.

BIFF: No, Dad, I was a shipping clerk.

WILLY: But you were practically—

515 **BIFF:** [*with determination*] Dad, I don't know who said it first, but I was never a salesman for Bill Oliver.

WILLY: What're you talking about?

BIFF: Let's hold on to the facts tonight, Pop. We're not going to get anywhere bullin' around. I was a shipping clerk.

WILLY: [*angrily*] All right, now listen to me—

BIFF: Why don't you let me finish?

520 **WILLY:** I'm not interested in stories about the past or any crap of that kind because the woods are burning, boys, you understand? There's a big blaze going on all around. I was fired today.

BIFF: [*shocked*] How could you be?

WILLY: I was fired, and I'm looking for a little good news to tell your mother, because the woman has waited and the woman has suffered. The gist of it is that I haven't got a story left in my head, Biff. So don't give me a lecture about facts and aspects. I am not interested. Now what've you got to say to me?

[*STANLEY enters with three drinks. They wait until he leaves.*]

WILLY: Did you see Oliver?

BIFF: Jesus, Dad!

525 **WILLY:** You mean you didn't go up there?

HAPPY: Sure he went up there.

BIFF: I did. I—saw him. How could they fire you?

WILLY: [*on the edge of his chair*] What kind of a welcome did he give you?

BIFF: He won't even let you work on commission?

530 **WILLY:** I'm out! [*driving*] So tell me, he gave you a warm welcome?

HAPPY: Sure Pop, sure!

BIFF: [*driven*] Well, it was kind of—

WILLY: I was wondering if he'd remember you. [*to HAPPY*] Imagine, man doesn't see him for ten, twelve years and gives him that kind of a welcome!

HAPPY: Damn right!

535 **BIFF:** [*trying to return to the offensive*] Pop, look—

WILLY: You know why he remembered you, don't you? Because you impressed him in those days.

BIFF: Let's talk quietly and get this down to the facts, huh?

WILLY: [*as though BIFF had been interrupting*] Well, what happened? It's great news, Biff. Did he take you into his office or'd you talk in the waiting-room?

BIFF: Well, he came in, see, and—

540 **WILLY:** [*with a big smile*] What'd he say? Betcha he threw his arm around you.

BIFF: Well, he kinda—

WILLY: He's a fine man. [*to HAPPY*] Very hard man to see, y'know.

HAPPY: [*agreeing*] Oh, I know.

WILLY: [*to BIFF*] Is that where you had the drinks?

545 **BIFF:** Yeah, he gave me a couple of—no, no!

HAPPY: [*cutting in*] He told him my Florida idea.

WILLY: Don't interrupt. [*to BIFF*] How'd he react to the Florida idea?

BIFF: Dad, will you give me a minute to explain?

WILLY: I've been waiting for you to explain since I sat down here! What happened? He took you into his office and what?

550 **BIFF:** Well—I talked. And—and he listened, see.

WILLY: Famous for the way he listens, y'know. What was his answer?
BIFF: His answer was—[*He breaks off, suddenly angry.*] Dad, you're not letting me tell you
     what I want to tell you!
WILLY: [*accusing, angered*] You didn't see him, did you?
BIFF: I did see him!
WILLY: What'd you insult him or something? You insulted him, didn't you?   555
BIFF: Listen, will you let me out of it, will you just let me out of it!
HAPPY: What the hell!
WILLY: Tell me what happened!
BIFF: [*to* HAPPY] I can't talk to him!

[*A single trumpet note jars the ear. The light of green leaves stains the house, which holds the air of night and a dream.* YOUNG BERNARD *enters and knocks on the door of the house.*]

YOUNG BERNARD: [*frantically*] Mrs. Loman, Mrs. Loman!   560
HAPPY: Tell him what happened!
BIFF: [*to* HAPPY] Shut up and leave me alone!
WILLY: No, no! You had to go and flunk math!
BIFF: What math? What're you talking about?
YOUNG BERNARD: Mrs. Loman, Mrs. Loman!   565

[LINDA *appears in the house, as of old.*]

WILLY: [*wildly*] Math, math, math!
BIFF: Take it easy, Pop!
YOUNG BERNARD: Mrs. Loman!
WILLY: [*furiously*] If you hadn't flunked you'd've been set by now!
BIFF: Now, look, I'm gonna tell you what happened, and you're going to listen to me.   570
YOUNG BERNARD: Mrs. Loman!
BIFF: I waited six hours—
HAPPY: What the hell are you saying?
BIFF: I kept sending in my name but he wouldn't see me. So finally he . . .

[*He continues unheard as light fades low on the restaurant.*]

YOUNG BERNARD: Biff flunked math!   575
LINDA: No!
YOUNG BERNARD: Birnbaum flunked him! They won't graduate him!
LINDA: But they have to. He's gotta go to the university. Where is he? Biff! Biff!
YOUNG BERNARD: No, he left. He went to Grand Central.
LINDA: Grand—You mean he went to Boston!   580
YOUNG BERNARD: Is Uncle Willy in Boston?
LINDA: Oh, maybe Willy can talk to the teacher. Oh, the poor, poor boy!

[*Light on house area snaps out.*]

BIFF: [*at the table, now audible, holding up a gold fountain pen*] . . . so I'm washed up with
     Oliver, you understand? Are you listening to me?
WILLY: [*at a loss*] Yeah, sure. If you hadn't flunked—
BIFF: Flunked what? What're you talking about?   585
WILLY: Don't blame everything on me! I didn't flunk math—you did! What pen?

HAPPY: That was awful dumb, Biff, a pen like that is worth—

WILLY: [*seeing the pen for the first time*] You took Oliver's pen?

BIFF: [*weakening*] Dad, I just explained it to you.

590 **WILLY:** You stole Bill Oliver's fountain pen!

BIFF: I didn't exactly steal it! That's just what I've been explaining to you!

HAPPY: He had it in his hand and just then Oliver walked in, so he got nervous and stuck it in his pocket!

WILLY: My God, Biff!

BIFF: I never intended to do it, Dad!

595 **OPERATOR'S VOICE:** Standish Arms, good evening!

WILLY: [*shouting*] I'm not in my room!

BIFF: [*frightened*] Dad, what's the matter? [*He and* HAPPY *stand up.*]

OPERATOR: Ringing Mr. Loman for you!

WILLY: I'm not there, stop it!

600 **BIFF:** [*horrified, gets down on one knee before* WILLY] Dad, I'll make good, I'll make good. [WILLY *tries to get to his feet.* BIFF *holds him down.*] Sit down now.

WILLY: No, you're no good, you're no good for anything.

BIFF: I am, Dad, I'll find something else, you understand? Now don't worry about anything. [*He holds up* WILLY'S *face.*] Talk to me, Dad.

OPERATOR: Mr. Loman does not answer. Shall I page him?

WILLY: [*attempting to stand, as though to rush and silence the Operator*] No, no, no!

605 **HAPPY:** He'll strike something, Pop.

WILLY: No, no . . .

BIFF: [*desperately, standing over* WILLY] Pop, listen! Listen to me! I'm telling you something good. Oliver talked to his partner about the Florida idea. you listening? He—he talked to his partner, and he came to me . . . I'm going to be all right, you hear? Dad, listen to me, he said it was just a question of the amount!

WILLY: Then you . . . got it?

HAPPY: He's gonna be terrific, Pop!

610 **WILLY:** [*trying to stand*] Then you got it, haven't you? You got it! You got it!

BIFF: [*agonized, holds* WILLY *down*] No, no. Look, Pop. I'm supposed to have lunch with them tomorrow. I'm just telling you this so you'll know that I can still make an impression, Pop. And I'll make good somewhere, but I can't go tomorrow, see?

WILLY: Why not? You simply—

BIFF: But the pen, Pop!

WILLY: You give it to him and tell him it was an oversight!

615 **HAPPY:** Sure, have lunch tomorrow!

BIFF: I can't say that—

WILLY: You were doing a crossword puzzle and accidentally used his pen!

BIFF: Listen, kid, I took those balls years ago, now I walk in with his fountain pen? That clinches it, don't you see? I can't face him like that! I'll try elsewhere.

PAGE'S VOICE: Paging Mr. Loman!

620 **WILLY:** Don't you want to be anything?

BIFF: Pop, how can I go back?

WILLY: You don't want to be anything, is that what's behind it?

BIFF: [*now angry at* WILLY *for not crediting his sympathy*] Don't take it that way! You think it was easy walking into that office after what I'd done to him? A team of horses couldn't have dragged me back to Bill Oliver!

WILLY: Then why'd you go?

625 **BIFF:** Why did I go? Why did I go? Look at you! Look at what's become of you!

[*Off left,* THE WOMAN *laughs.*]

WILLY: Biff, you're going to go to that lunch tomorrow, or—
BIFF: I can't go. I've got no appointment!
HAPPY: Biff, for . . . !
WILLY: Are you spiting me?
BIFF: Don't take it that way! Goddammit!   630
WILLY: [*strikes* BIFF *and falters away from the table*] You rotten little louse! Are you spiting me?
THE WOMAN: Someone's at the door, Willy!
BIFF: I'm no good, can't you see what I am?
HAPPY: [*separating them*] Hey, you're in a restaurant! Now cut it out, both of you! [*The girls enter.*] Hello, girls, sit down.

[THE WOMAN *laughs, off left.*]

MISS FORSYTHE: I guess we might as well. This is Letta.   635
THE WOMAN: Willy, are you going to wake up?
BIFF: [*ignoring* WILLY] How're ya, miss, sit down. What do you drink?
MISS FORSYTHE: Letta might not be able to stay long.
LETTA: I gotta get up very early tomorrow. I got jury duty. I'm so excited! Were you fellows ever on a jury?
BIFF: No, but I been in front of them! [*The girls laugh.*] This is my father.   640
LETTA: Isn't he cute? Sit down with us, Pop.
HAPPY: Sit him down, Biff!
BIFF: [*going to him*] Come on, slugger, drink us under the table. To hell with it! Come on, sit down, pal.

[*On* BIFF'*s last insistence,* WILLY *is about to sit.*]

THE WOMAN: [*now urgently*] Willy, are you going to answer the door!

[THE WOMAN'*s call pulls* WILLY *back. He starts right, befuddled.*]

BIFF: Hey, where are you going?   645
WILLY: Open the door.
BIFF: The door?
WILLY: The washroom . . . the door . . . where's the door?
BIFF: [*leading* WILLY *to the left*] Just go straight down.

[WILLY *moves left.*]

THE WOMAN: Willy, Willy, are you going to get up, get up, get up, get up?   650

[WILLY *exits left.*]

LETTA: I think it's sweet you bring your daddy along.
MISS FORSYTHE: Oh, he isn't really your father!
BIFF: [*at left, turning to her resentfully*] Miss Forsythe, you've just seen a prince walk by. A fine, troubled prince. A hard-working, unappreciated prince. A pal, you understand? A good companion. Always for his boys.
LETTA: That's so sweet.
HAPPY: Well, girls, what's the program? We're wasting time. Come on, Biff. Gather   655
round. Where would you like to go?
BIFF: Why don't you do something for him?

HAPPY: Me!

BIFF: Don't you give a damn for him, Hap?

HAPPY: What're you talking about? I'm the one who—

BIFF: I sense it, you don't give a good goddam about him. [*He takes the rolled-up hose from his pocket and puts it on the table in front of HAPPY.*] Look what I found in the cellar, for
660   Christ's sake. How can you bear to let it go on?

HAPPY: Me? Who goes away? Who runs off and—

BIFF: Yeah, but he doesn't mean anything to you. You could help him—I can't! Don't you understand what I'm talking about? He's going to kill himself, don't you know that?

HAPPY: Don't I know it! Me!

BIFF: Hap, help him! Jesus . . . help him . . . Help me, help me, I can't bear to look at his face! [*Ready to weep, he hurries out, up right.*]

665   **HAPPY:** [*staring after him*] Where are you going?

MISS FORSYTHE: What's he so mad about?

HAPPY: Come on, girls, we'll catch up with him.

MISS FORSYTHE: [*as HAPPY pushes her out*] Say, I don't like that temper of his!

HAPPY: He's just a little overstrung, he'll be all right!

670   **WILLY:** [*off left, as THE WOMAN laughs*] Don't answer! Don't answer!

LETTA: Don't you want to tell your father—

HAPPY: No, that's not my father. He's just a guy. Come on, we'll catch Biff, and, honey, we're going to paint this town! Stanley, where's the check! Hey, Stanley!

[*They exit. STANLEY looks toward left.*]

STANLEY: [*calling to HAPPY indignantly*] Mr. Loman! Mr. Loman!

[*STANLEY picks up a chair and follows them off. Knocking is heard off left. THE WOMAN enters, laughing. WILLY follows her. She is in a black slip; he is buttoning his shirt. Raw, sensuous music accompanies their speech.*]

WILLY: Will you stop laughing? Will you stop?

675   **THE WOMAN:** Aren't you going to answer the door? He'll wake the whole hotel.

WILLY: I'm not expecting anybody.

THE WOMAN: Whyn't you have another drink, honey, and stop being so damn self-centered?

WILLY: I'm so lonely.

THE WOMAN: You know you ruined me, Willy? From now on, whenever you come to the office, I'll see that you go right through to the buyers. No waiting at my desk any more, Willy. You ruined me.

680   **WILLY:** That's nice of you to say that.

THE WOMAN: Gee, you are self-centered! Why so sad? You are the saddest, self-centeredest soul I ever did see-saw. [*She laughs. He kisses her.*] Come on inside, drummer boy. It's silly to be dressing in the middle of the night. [*As knocking is heard.*] Aren't you going to answer the door?

WILLY: They're knocking on the wrong door.

THE WOMAN: But I felt the knocking! And he heard us talking in here. Maybe the hotel's on fire!

WILLY: [*his terror rising*] It's a mistake.

685   **THE WOMAN:** Then tell him to go away!

WILLY: There's nobody there.

THE WOMAN: It's getting on my nerves, Willy. There's somebody standing out there and it's getting on my nerves!

WILLY: [*pushing her away from him*] All right, stay in the bathroom here, and don't come out. I think there's a law in Massachusetts about it, so don't come out. It may be that new room clerk. He looked very mean. So don't come out. It's a mistake, there's no fire.

[*The knocking is heard again. He takes a few steps away from her, and she vanishes into the wing. The light follows him, and now he is facing YOUNG BIFF, who carries a suitcase. BIFF steps toward him. The music is gone.*]

BIFF: Why didn't you answer?
WILLY: Biff! What are you doing in Boston?   690
BIFF: Why didn't you answer? I've been knocking for five minutes, I called you on the phone—
WILLY: I just heard you. I was in the bathroom and had the door shut. Did anything happen home?
BIFF: Dad—I let you down.
WILLY: What do you mean?
BIFF: Dad . . .   695
WILLY: Biffo, what's this about? [*putting his arm around BIFF*] Come on, let's go downstairs and get you a malted.
BIFF: Dad, I flunked math.
WILLY: Not for the term?
BIFF: The term. I haven't got enough credits to graduate.
WILLY: You mean to say Bernard wouldn't give you the answers?   700
BIFF: He did, he tried, but I only got a sixty-one.
WILLY: And they wouldn't give you four points?
BIFF: Birnbaum refused absolutely. I begged him, Pop, but he won't give me those points. You gotta talk to him before they close the school. Because if he saw the kind of man you are, and you just talked to him in your way, I'm sure he'd come through for me. The class came right before practice, see, and I didn't go enough. Would you talk to him? He'd like you, Pop. You know the way you could talk.
WILLY: You're on. We'll drive right back.
BIFF: Oh, Dad, good work! I'm sure he'll change it for you!   705
WILLY: Go downstairs and tell the clerk I'm checkin' out. Go right down.
BIFF: Yes, sir! See, the reason he hates me, Pop—one day he was late for class so I got up at the blackboard and imitated him. I crossed my eyes and talked with a lithp.
WILLY: [*laughing*] You did? The kids like it?
BIFF: They nearly died laughing!
WILLY: Yeah? What'd you do?   710
BIFF: The thquare root of thixthy twee is . . . [*WILLY bursts out laughing; BIFF joins him.*] And in the middle of it he walked in!

[*WILLY laughs and THE WOMAN joins in offstage.*]

WILLY: [*without hesitation*] Hurry downstairs and—
BIFF: Somebody in there?
WILLY: No, that was next door.

[*THE WOMAN laughs offstage.*]

BIFF: Somebody got in your bathroom!   715
WILLY: No, it's the next room, there's a party—

THE WOMAN: [*enters, laughing. She lisps this.*] Can I come in? There's something in the bathtub, Willy, and it's moving!

[WILLY *looks at* BIFF, *who is staring open-mouthed and horrified at* THE WOMAN.]

WILLY: Ah—you better go back to your room. They must be finished painting by now. They're painting her room so I let her take a shower here. Go back, go back . . . [*He pushes her.*]

THE WOMAN: [*resisting*] But I've got to get dressed, Willy, I can't—

720   **WILLY:** Get out of here! Go back, go back . . . [*suddenly striving for the ordinary*] This is Miss Francis, Biff, she's a buyer. They're painting her room. Go back, Miss Francis, go back . . .

THE WOMAN: But my clothes, I can't go out naked in the hall!

WILLY: [*pushing her offstage*] Get outa here! Go back, go back!

[BIFF *slowly sits down on his suitcase as the argument continues offstage.*]

THE WOMAN: Where's my stockings? You promised me stockings, Willy!

WILLY: I have no stockings here!

725   **THE WOMAN:** You had two boxes of size nine sheers for me, and I want them!

WILLY: Here, for God's sake, will you get outa here!

THE WOMAN: [*enters holding a box of stockings*] I just hope there's nobody in the hall. That's all I hope. [*To* BIFF] Are you football or baseball?

BIFF: Football.

THE WOMAN: [*angry, humiliated*] That's me too. G'night. [*She snatches her clothes from* WILLY, *and walks out.*]

730   **WILLY:** [*after a pause*] Well, better get going. I want to get to the school first thing in the morning. Get my suits out of the closet. I'll get my valise. [BIFF *doesn't move.*] What's the matter? [BIFF *remains motionless, tears falling.*] She's a buyer. Buys for J. H. Simmons. She lives down the hall—they're painting. You don't imagine—[*He breaks off. After a pause*] Now listen, pal, she's just a buyer. She sees merchandise in her room and they have to keep it looking just so . . . [*Pause. Assuming command*] All right, get my suits. [BIFF *doesn't move.*] Now stop crying and do as I say. I gave you an order. Biff, I gave you an order! Is that what you do when I give you an order? How dare you cry! [*putting his arm around* BIFF] Now look, Biff, when you grow up you'll understand about these things. You mustn't—you mustn't overemphasize a thing like this. I'll see Birnbaum first thing in the morning.

BIFF: Never mind.

WILLY: [*getting down beside* BIFF] Never mind! He's going to give you those points. I'll see to it.

BIFF: He wouldn't listen to you.

WILLY: He certainly will listen to me. You need those points for the U. of Virginia.

735   **BIFF:** I'm not going there.

WILLY: Heh? If I can't get him to change that mark you'll make it up in summer school. You've got all summer to—

BIFF: [*his weeping breaking from him*] Dad . . .

WILLY: [*infected by it*] Oh, my boy . . .

BIFF: Dad . . .

740   **WILLY:** She's nothing to me, Biff. I was lonely, I was terribly lonely.

BIFF: You—you gave her Mama's stockings! [*His tears break through and he rises to go.*]

WILLY: [*grabbing for* BIFF] I gave you an order!

BIFF: Don't touch me, you—liar!

WILLY: Apologize for that!

BIFF: You fake! You phony little fake! [*Overcome, he turns quickly and weeping fully goes out*   745
    with his suitcase. WILLY is left on the floor on his knees.]
WILLY: I gave you an order! Biff, come back here or I'll beat you! Come back here! I'll whip you!

[*STANLEY comes quickly in from the right and stands in front of WILLY.*]

WILLY: [*shouts at STANLEY*] I gave you an order . . .
STANLEY: Hey, let's pick it up, pick it up, Mr. Loman. [*He helps WILLY to his feet.*] Your
    boys left with the chippies. They said they'll see you home.

[*A SECOND WAITER watches some distance away.*]

WILLY: But we were supposed to have dinner together.

[*Music is heard, WILLY's theme.*]

STANLEY: Can you make it?   750
WILLY: I'll—sure, I can make it. [*Suddenly concerned about his clothes*] Do I—I look all right?
STANLEY: Sure, you look all right. [*He flicks a speck off WILLY's lapel.*]
WILLY: Here—here's a dollar.
STANLEY: Oh, your son paid me. It's all right.
WILLY: [*putting it in STANLEY's hand*] No, take it. You're a good boy.   755
STANLEY: Oh, no, you don't have to . . .
WILLY: Here—here's some more, I don't need it any more. [*After a slight pause.*] Tell me—
    is there a seed store in the neighborhood?
STANLEY: Seeds? You mean like to plant?

[*As WILLY turns, STANLEY slips the money back into his jacket pocket.*]

WILLY: Yes. Carrots, peas . . .
STANLEY: Well, there's hardware stores on Sixth Avenue, but it may be too late now.   760
WILLY: [*anxiously*] Oh, I'd better hurry. I've got to get some seeds. [*He starts off to the*
    right.] I've got to get some seeds, right away. Nothing's planted. I don't have a thing
    in the ground.

[*WILLY hurries out as the light goes down. STANLEY moves over to the right after him, watches him
off. The other waiter has been staring at WILLY.*]

STANLEY: [*to the WAITER*] Well, whatta you looking at?

[*The WAITER picks up the chairs and moves off right. STANLEY takes the table and follows him. The light
fades on this area. There is a long pause, the sound of the flute coming over. The light gradually rises on
the kitchen, which is empty. HAPPY appears at the door of the house, followed by BIFF. HAPPY is carrying
a large bunch of long-stemmed roses. He enters the kitchen, looks around for LINDA. Not seeing her, he
turns to BIFF, who is just outside the house door, and makes a gesture with his hands, indicating "Not
here, I guess." He looks into the living-room and freezes. Inside, LINDA, unseen, is seated, WILLY's coat on
her lap. She rises ominously and quietly and moves toward HAPPY, who backs up into the kitchen, afraid.*]

HAPPY: Hey, what're you doing up? [*LINDA says nothing but moves toward him implacably.*]
    Where's Pop? [*He keeps backing to the right, and now LINDA is in full view in the doorway
    to the living-room.*] Is he sleeping?

LINDA: Where were you?

765   HAPPY: [*trying to laugh it off*] We met two girls, Mom, very fine types. Here, we brought
you some flowers. [*offering them to her*] Put them in your room, Ma.

[*She knocks them to the floor at BIFF's feet. He has now come inside and closed the door behind him.
She stares at BIFF, silent.*]

HAPPY: Now what'd you do that for? Mom, I want you to have some flowers—

LINDA: [*cutting HAPPY off, violently to BIFF*] Don't you care whether he lives or dies?

HAPPY: [*going to the stairs*] Come upstairs, Biff.

BIFF: [*with a flare of disgust, to HAPPY*] Go away from me! [*to LINDA*] What do you mean,
lives or dies? Nobody's dying around here, pal.

770   LINDA: Get out of my sight! Get out of here!

BIFF: I wanna see the boss.

LINDA: You're not going near him!

BIFF: Where is he? [*He moves into the living-room and LINDA follows.*]

LINDA: [*shouting after BIFF*] You invite him for dinner. He looks forward to it all day—[*BIFF
appears in his parents' bedroom, looks around, and exits.*]—and then you desert him there.
There's no stranger you'd do that to!

775   HAPPY: Why? He had a swell time with us. Listen, when I—[*LINDA comes back into the
kitchen.*]—desert him I hope I don't outlive the day!

LINDA: Get out of here!

HAPPY: Now look, Mom . . .

LINDA: Did you have to go to women tonight? You and your lousy rotten whores!

[*BIFF re-enters the kitchen.*]

HAPPY: Mom, all we did was follow Biff around trying to cheer him up! [*to BIFF*] Boy,
what a night you gave me!

780   LINDA: Get out of here, both of you, and don't come back! I don't want you tormenting
him any more. Go on now, get your things together! [*to BIFF*] You can sleep in his
apartment. [*She starts to pick up the flowers and stops herself.*] Pick up this stuff, I'm not
your maid any more. Pick it up, you bum, you!

[*HAPPY turns his back to her in refusal. BIFF slowly moves over and gets down on his knees, picking
up the flowers.*]

LINDA: You're a pair of animals! Not one, not another living soul would have had the
cruelty to walk out on that man in a restaurant!

BIFF: [*not looking at her*] Is that what he said?

LINDA: He didn't have to say anything. He was so humiliated he nearly limped when he
came in.

HAPPY: But, Mom, he had a great time with us—

785   BIFF: [*cutting him off violently*] Shut up!

[*Without another word, HAPPY goes upstairs.*]

LINDA: You! You didn't even go in to see if he was all right!

BIFF: [*still on the floor in front of LINDA, the flowers in his hand; with self-loathing*] No. Didn't.
Didn't do a damned thing. How do you like that, heh? Left him babbling in a toilet.

LINDA: You louse. You . . .

BIFF: Now you hit it on the nose! [*He gets up, throws the flowers in the wastebasket.*] The scum of the earth, and you're looking at him!

LINDA: Get out of here!   790

BIFF: I gotta talk to the boss, Mom. Where is he?

LINDA: You're not going near him. Get out of his house!

BIFF: [*with absolute assurance, determination*] No. We're gonna have an abrupt conversation, him and me.

LINDA: You're not talking to him!

[*Hammering is heard from outside the house, off right. BIFF turns toward the noise.*]

LINDA: [*suddenly pleading*] Will you please leave him alone?   795

BIFF: What's he doing out there?

LINDA: He's planting the garden!

BIFF: [*quietly*] Now? Oh, my God!

[*BIFF moves outside, LINDA following. The light dies down on them and comes up on the center of the apron as WILLY walks into it. He is carrying a flashlight, a hoe, and a handful of seed packets. He raps the top of the hoe sharply to fix it firmly, and then moves to the left, measuring off the distance with his foot. He holds the flashlight to look at the seed packets, reading off the instructions. He is in the blue of night.*]

WILLY: Carrots . . . quarter-inch apart. Rows . . . one-foot rows. [*He measures it off.*] One foot. [*He puts down a package and measures off.*] Beets. [*He puts down another package and measures again.*] Lettuce. [*He reads the package, puts it down.*] One foot—[*He breaks off as BEN appears at the right and moves slowly down to him.*] What a proposition, ts, ts. Terrific, terrific. 'Cause she's suffered, Ben, the woman has suffered. You understand me? A man can't go out the way he came in, Ben, a man has got to add up to something. You can't, you can't—[*BEN moves toward him as though to interrupt.*] You gotta consider, now. Don't answer so quick. Remember, it's a guaranteed twenty-thousand-dollar proposition. Now look, Ben, I want you to go through the ins and outs of this thing with me. I've got nobody to talk to, Ben, and the woman has suffered, you hear me?

BEN: [*standing still, considering*] What's the proposition?   800

WILLY: It's twenty thousand dollars on the barrelhead. Guaranteed, gilt-edged, you understand?

BEN: You don't want to make a fool of yourself. They might not honor the policy.

WILLY: How can they dare refuse? Didn't I work like a coolie to meet every premium on the nose? And now they don't pay off? Impossible!

BEN: It's called a cowardly thing, William.

WILLY: Why? Does it take more guts to stand here the rest of my life ringing up a zero?   805

BEN: [*yielding*] That's a point, William. [*He moves, thinking, turns.*] And twenty thousand—that *is* something one can feel with the hand, it is there.

WILLY: [*now assured, with rising power*] Oh, Ben, that's the whole beauty of it! I see it like a diamond, shining in the dark, hard and rough, that I can pick up and touch in my hand. Not like—like an appointment! This would not be another damned-fool appointment, Ben, and it changes all the aspects. Because he thinks I'm nothing, see, and so he spites me. But the funeral—[*straightening up*] Ben, that funeral will be massive! They'll come from Maine, Massachusetts, Vermont, New Hampshire! All the old-timers with the strange license plates—that boy will be thunder-struck. Ben, because he never realized—I am known! Rhode Island, New York, New Jersey—I am known, Ben, and he'll see it with his eyes once and for all. He'll see what I am, Ben! He's in for a shock, that boy!

BEN: [*coming down to the edge of the garden*] He'll call you a coward.

WILLY: [*suddenly fearful*] No, that would be terrible.

810 **BEN:** Yes. And a damned fool.

WILLY: No, no, he mustn't, I won't have that! [*He is broken and desperate.*]

BEN: He'll hate you, William.

[*The gay music of the Boys is heard.*]

WILLY: Oh, Ben, how do we get back to all the great times? Used to be so full of light, and comradeship, the sleigh-riding in winter, and the ruddiness on his cheeks. And always some kind of good news coming up, always something nice coming up ahead. And never even let me carry the valises in the house, and simonizing, simonizing that little red car! Why, why can't I give him something and not have him hate me?

BEN: Let me think about it. [*He glances at his watch.*] I still have a little time. Remarkable proposition, but you've got to be sure you're not making a fool of yourself.

[*BEN drifts upstage and goes out of sight. BIFF comes down from the left.*]

815 **WILLY:** [*suddenly conscious of BIFF, turns and looks up at him, then begins picking up the packages of seeds in confusion*] Where the hell is that seed? [*Indignantly*] You can't see nothing out here! They boxed in the whole goddam neighborhood!

BIFF: There are people all around here. Don't you realize that?

WILLY: I'm busy. Don't bother me.

BIFF: [*taking the hoe from WILLY*] I'm saying good-by to you, Pop. [*WILLY looks at him, silent, unable to move.*] I'm not coming back any more.

WILLY: You're not going to see Oliver tomorrow?

820 **BIFF:** I've got no appointment, Dad.

WILLY: He put his arm around you, and you've got no appointment?

BIFF: Pop, get this now, will you? Everytime I've left it's been a fight that sent me out of here. Today I realized something about myself and I tried to explain it to you and I—I think I'm just not smart enough to make any sense out of it for you. To hell with whose fault it is or anything like that. [*He takes WILLY's arm.*] Let's just wrap it up, heh? Come on in, we'll tell Mom. [*He gently tries to pull WILLY to left.*]

WILLY: [*frozen, immobile, with guilt in his voice*] No, I don't want to see her.

BIFF: Come on! [*He pulls again, and WILLY tries to pull away.*]

825 **WILLY:** [*highly nervous*] No, no, I don't want to see her.

BIFF: [*tries to look into WILLY's face, as if to find the answer there*] Why don't you want to see her?

WILLY: [*more harshly now*] Don't bother me, will you?

BIFF: What do you mean, you don't want to see her? You don't want them calling you yellow, do you? This isn't your fault; it's me, I'm a bum. Now come inside! [*WILLY strains to get away.*] Did you hear what I said to you?

[*WILLY pulls away and quickly goes by himself into the house. BIFF follows.*]

LINDA: [*to WILLY*] Did you plant, dear?

830 **BIFF:** [*at the door, to LINDA*] All right, we had it out. I'm going and I'm not writing any more.

LINDA: [*going to WILLY in the kitchen*] I think that's the best way, dear. 'Cause there's no use drawing it out, you'll just never get along.

[*WILLY doesn't respond.*]

BIFF: People ask where I am and what I'm doing, you don't know, and you don't care. That way it'll be off your mind and you can start brightening up again. All right? That clears it, doesn't it? [*WILLY is silent, and BIFF goes to him.*] You gonna wish me luck, scout? [*He extends his hand.*] What do you say?

LINDA: Shake his hand, Willy.

WILLY: [*turning to her, seething with hurt*] There's no necessity to mention the pen at all, y'know.

BIFF: [*gently*] I've got no appointment, Dad.   835

WILLY: [*erupting fiercely*] He put his arm around . . .

BIFF: Dad, you're never going to see what I am, so what's the use of arguing? If I strike oil I'll send you a check. Meantime forget I'm alive.

WILLY: [*to LINDA*] Spite, see?

BIFF: Shake hands, Dad.

WILLY: Not my hand.   840

BIFF: I was hoping not to go this way.

WILLY: Well, this is the way you're going. Good-by.

[*BIFF looks at him a moment, then turns sharply and goes to the stairs.*]

WILLY: [*stops him with*] May you rot in hell if you leave this house!

BIFF: [*turning*] Exactly what is it that you want from me?

WILLY: I want you to know, on the train, in the mountains, in the valleys, wherever you   845
go, that you cut down your life for spite!

BIFF: No, no.

WILLY: Spite, spite, is the word of your undoing! And when you're down and out, remember what did it. When you're rotting somewhere beside the railroad tracks, remember, and don't you dare blame it on me!

BIFF: I'm not blaming it on you!

WILLY: I won't take the rap for this, you hear?

[*HAPPY comes down the stairs and stands on the bottom step, watching.*]

BIFF: That's just what I'm telling you!   850

WILLY: [*sinking into a chair at the table, with full accusation*] You're trying to put a knife in me—don't think I don't know what you're doing!

BIFF: All right, phony! Then let's lay it on the line. [*He whips the rubber tube out of his pocket and puts it on the table.*]

HAPPY: You crazy—

LINDA: Biff! [*She moves to grab the hose, but BIFF holds it down with his hand.*]

BIFF: Leave it here! Don't move it!   855

WILLY: [*not looking at it*] What is that?

BIFF: You know goddam well what that is.

WILLY: [*caged, wanting to escape*] I never saw that.

BIFF: You saw it. The mice didn't bring it into the cellar! What is this supposed to do, make a hero out of you? This supposed to make me sorry for you?

WILLY: Never heard of it.   860

BIFF: There'll be no pity for you, you hear it? No pity!

WILLY: [*to LINDA*] You hear the spite!

BIFF: No, you're going to hear the truth—what you are and what I am!

LINDA: Stop it!

WILLY: Spite!   865

HAPPY: [*coming down toward* BIFF] You cut it now!

BIFF: [*to* HAPPY] The man don't know who we are! The man is gonna know! [*to* WILLY] We never told the truth for ten minutes in this house!

HAPPY: We always told the truth!

BIFF: [*turning on him*] You big blow, are you the assistant buyer? You're one of the two assistants to the assistant, aren't you?

870 **HAPPY:** Well, I'm practically—

BIFF: You're practically full of it! We all are! And I'm through with it. [*to* WILLY] Now hear this, Willy, this is me.

WILLY: I know you!

BIFF: You know why I had no address for three months? I stole a suit in Kansas City and I was in jail. [*to* LINDA, *who is sobbing*] Stop crying. I'm through with it.

[LINDA *turns from them, her hands covering her face.*]

WILLY: I suppose that's my fault!

875 **BIFF:** I stole myself out of every good job since high school!

WILLY: And whose fault is that?

BIFF: And I never got anywhere because you blew me so full of hot air I could never stand taking orders from anybody! That's whose fault it is!

WILLY: I hear that!

LINDA: Don't, Biff!

880 **BIFF:** It's goddam time you heard that! I had to be boss big shot in two weeks, and I'm through with it!

WILLY: Then hang yourself! For spite, hang yourself!

BIFF: No! Nobody's hanging himself, Willy! I ran down eleven flights with a pen in my hand today. And suddenly I stopped, you hear me? And in the middle of that office building, do you hear this? I stopped in the middle of that building and I saw—the sky. I saw the things that I love in this world. The work and the food and time to sit and smoke. And I looked at the pen and said to myself, what the hell am I grabbing this for? Why am I trying to become what I don't want to be? What am I doing in an office, making a contemptuous, begging fool of myself, when all I want is out there, waiting for me the minute I say I know who I am! Why can't I say that, Willy?

[*He tries to make* WILLY *face him, but* WILLY *pulls away and moves to the left.*]

WILLY: [*with hatred, threateningly.*] The door of your life is wide open!

BIFF: Pop! I'm a dime a dozen, and so are you!

885 **WILLY:** [*turning on him now in an uncontrolled outburst*] I am not a dime a dozen! I am Willy Loman, and you are Biff Loman!

[BIFF *starts for* WILLY, *but is blocked by* HAPPY. *In his fury,* BIFF *seems on the verge of attacking his father.*]

BIFF: I am not a leader of men, Willy, and neither are you. You were never anything but a hard-working drummer who landed in the ash can like all the rest of them! I'm one dollar an hour, Willy! I tried seven states and couldn't raise it. A buck an hour! Do you gather my meaning? I'm not bringing home any prizes any more, and you're going to stop waiting for me to bring them home!

WILLY: [*directly to* BIFF] You vengeful, spiteful mutt!

Linda Loman (Mildred Dunnock) and Happy (Cameron Mitchell) restrain Biff (Arthur Kennedy) as he reproaches his father Willy (Lee J. Cobb) in the Morosco Theatre, New York City, original production of *Death of a Salesman,* staged by Elia Kazan.

[BIFF *breaks from* HAPPY. WILLY, *in fright, starts up the stairs.* BIFF *grabs him.*]

BIFF: [*at the peak of his fury*] Pop I'm nothing! I'm nothing, Pop. Can't you understand that? There's no spite in it any more. I'm just what I am, that's all.

[BIFF's *fury has spent itself, and he breaks down, sobbing, holding on to* WILLY, *who dumbly fumbles for* BIFF's *face.*]

WILLY: [*astonished*] What're you doing? What're you doing? [*to* LINDA] Why is he crying?

BIFF: [*crying, broken*] Will you let me go, for Christ's sake? Will you take that phony dream and burn it before something happens? [*Struggling to contain himself, he pulls away and moves to the stairs.*] I'll go in the morning. Put him—put him to bed. [*Exhausted,* BIFF *moves up the stairs to his room.*]

890

WILLY: [*after a long pause, astonished, elevated*] Isn't that—isn't that remarkable? Biff—he likes me!

LINDA: He loves you, Willy!

HAPPY: [*deeply moved*] Always did, Pop.

WILLY: Oh, Biff! [*staring wildly*] He cried! Cried to me. [*He is choking with his love, and now cries out his promise.*] That boy—that boy is going to be magnificent!

[BEN *appears in the light just outside the kitchen.*]

895   **BEN:** Yes, outstanding, with twenty thousand behind him.

LINDA: [*sensing the racing of his mind, fearfully, carefully*] Now come to bed, Willy. It's all settled now.

WILLY: [*finding it difficult not to rush out of the house*] Yes, we'll sleep. Come on. Go to sleep, Hap.

BEN: And it does take a great kind of a man to crack the jungle.

[*In accents of dread,* BEN's *idyllic music starts up.*]

HAPPY: [*his arm around* LINDA] I'm getting married, Pop, don't forget it. I'm changing everything. I'm gonna run that department before the year is up. You'll see, Mom. [*He kisses her.*]

900   **BEN:** The jungle is dark but full of diamonds, Willy.

[WILLY *turns, moves, listening to* BEN.]

LINDA: Be good. You're both good boys, just act that way, that's all.

HAPPY: 'Night, Pop. [*He goes upstairs.*]

LINDA: [*to* WILLY] Come, dear.

BEN: [*with greater force*] One must go in to fetch a diamond out.

905   **WILLY:** [*to* LINDA, *as he moves slowly along the edge of the kitchen, toward the door*] I just want to get settled down, Linda. Let me sit alone for a little.

LINDA: [*almost uttering her fear*] I want you upstairs.

WILLY: [*taking her in his arms*] In a few minutes, Linda. I couldn't sleep right now. Go on, you look awful tired. [*He kisses her.*]

BEN: Not like an appointment at all. A diamond is rough and hard to the touch.

WILLY: Go on now. I'll be right up.

910   **LINDA:** I think this is the only way, Willy.

WILLY: Sure, it's the best thing.

BEN: Best thing!

WILLY: The only way. Everything is gonna be—go on, kid, get to bed. You look so tired.

LINDA: Come right up.

915   **WILLY:** Two minutes.

[LINDA *goes into the living-room, then reappears in her bedroom.* WILLY *moves just outside the kitchen door.*]

WILLY: Loves me. [*wonderingly*] Always loved me. Isn't that a remarkable thing? Ben, he'll worship me for it!

BEN: [*with promise*] It's dark there, but full of diamonds.

WILLY: Can you imagine that magnificence with twenty thousand dollars in his pocket?

LINDA: [*calling from her room*] Willy! Come up!

920   **WILLY:** [*calling into the kitchen*] Yes! Yes. Coming! It's very smart, you realize that, don't you, sweetheart? Even Ben sees it. I gotta go, baby. 'By! 'By! [*going over to* BEN, *almost dancing*] Imagine? When the mail comes he'll be ahead of Bernard again!

BEN: A perfect proposition all around.

WILLY: Did you see how he cried to me? Oh, if I could kiss him, Ben!

BEN: Time, William, time!

WILLY: Oh, Ben, I always knew one way or another we were gonna make it, Biff and I!

925   **BEN:** [*looking at his watch*] The boat. We'll be late. [*He moves slowly off into the darkness.*]

WILLY: [*elegiacally, turning to the house*] Now when you kick off, boy, I want a seventy-yard boot, and get right down the field under the ball, and when you hit, hit low and hit hard, because it's important, boy. [*He swings around and faces the audience.*] There's all kinds of important people in the stands, and the first thing you know . . . [*suddenly realizing he is alone*] Ben! Ben, where do I . . . ? [*He makes a sudden movement of search.*] Ben, how do I . . . ?

LINDA: [*calling*] Willy, you coming up?

WILLY: [*uttering a gasp of fear, whirling about as if to quiet her*] Sh! [*He turns around as if to find his way; sounds, faces, voices, seem to be swarming in upon him and he flicks at them, crying*] Sh! Sh! [*Suddenly music, faint and high, stops him. It rises in intensity, almost to an unbearable scream. He goes up and down on his toes, and rushes off around the house.*] Shhh!

LINDA: Willy?

[*There is no answer. LINDA waits. BIFF gets up off his bed. He is still in his clothes. HAPPY sits up. BIFF stands listening.*]

LINDA: [*with real fear*] Willy, answer me! Willy!   930

[*There is the sound of a car starting and moving away at full speed.*]

LINDA: No!

BIFF: [*rushing down the stairs*] Pop!

[*As the car speeds off, the music crashes down in a frenzy of sound, which becomes the soft pulsation of a single cello string. BIFF slowly returns to his bedroom. He and HAPPY gravely don their jackets. LINDA slowly walks out of her room. The music has developed into a dead march. The leaves of day are appearing over everything. CHARLEY and BERNARD, somberly dressed, appear and knock on the kitchen door. BIFF and HAPPY slowly descend the stairs to the kitchen as CHARLEY and BERNARD enter. All stop a moment when LINDA, in clothes of mourning, bearing a little bunch of roses, comes through the draped doorway into the kitchen. She goes to CHARLEY and takes his arm. Now all move toward the audience, through the wall-line of the kitchen. At the limit of the apron, LINDA lays down the flowers, kneels, and sits back on her heels. All stare down at the grave.*]

REQUIEM

CHARLEY: It's getting dark, Linda.

[*LINDA doesn't react. She stares at the grave.*]

BIFF: How about it, Mom? Better get some rest, heh? They'll be closing the gate soon.

[*LINDA makes no move. Pause.*]

HAPPY: [*deeply angered*] He had no right to do that. There was no necessity for it. We would've helped him.

CHARLEY: [*grunting*] Hmmm.

BIFF: Come along, Mom.   5

LINDA: Why didn't anybody come?

CHARLEY: It was a very nice funeral.

LINDA: But where are all the people he knew? Maybe they blame him.

CHARLEY: Naa. It's a rough world, Linda. They wouldn't blame him.

10   **LINDA:** I can't understand it. At this time especially. First time in thirty-five years we were just about free and clear. He only needed a little salary. He was even finished with the dentist.

CHARLEY: No man only needs a little salary.

LINDA: I can't understand it.

BIFF: There were a lot of nice days. When he'd come home from a trip; or on Sundays, making the stoop; finishing the cellar; putting on the new porch; when he built the extra bathroom; and put up the garage. You know something, Charley, there's more of him in that front stoop than in all the sales he ever made.

CHARLEY: Yeah. He was a happy man with a batch of cement.

15   **LINDA:** He was so wonderful with his hands.

BIFF: He had all the wrong dreams. All, all, wrong.

HAPPY: [*almost ready to fight BIFF*] Don't say that!

BIFF: He never knew who he was.

CHARLEY: [*stopping HAPPY's movement and reply. To BIFF*] Nobody dast blame this man. You don't understand. Willy was a salesman. And for a salesman, there is no rock bottom to the life. He don't put a bolt to a nut, he don't tell you the law or give you medicine. He's a man way out there in the blue, riding on a smile and a shoeshine. And when they start not smiling back—that's an earthquake. And then you get yourself a couple of spots on your hat, and you're finished. Nobody dast blame this man. A salesman is got to dream, boy. It comes with the territory.

20   **BIFF:** Charley, the man didn't know who he was.

HAPPY: [*infuriated*] Don't say that!

BIFF: Why don't you come with me, Happy?

HAPPY: I'm not licked that easily. I'm staying right in this city, and I'm gonna beat this racket! [*He looks at BIFF, his chin set.*] The Loman Brothers!

BIFF: I know who I am, kid.

25   **HAPPY:** All right, boy. I'm gonna show you and everybody else that Willy Loman did not die in vain. He had a good dream. It's the only dream you can have—to come out number-one man. He fought it out here, and this is where I'm gonna win it for him.

BIFF: [*with a hopeless glance at HAPPY, bends toward his mother*] Let's go, Mom.

LINDA: I'll be with you in a minute. Go on, Charley. [*He hesitates.*] I want to, just for a minute. I never had a chance to say good-by.

[*CHARLEY moves away, followed by HAPPY. BIFF remains a slight distance up and left of LINDA. She sits there, summoning herself. The flute begins, not far away, playing behind her speech.*]

LINDA: Forgive me, dear. I can't cry. I don't know what it is, but I can't cry. I don't understand it. Why did you ever do that? Help me, Willy, I can't cry. It seems to me that you're just on another trip. I keep expecting you. Willy, dear, I can't cry. Why did you do it? I search and search and I search, and I can't understand it, Willy. I made the last payment on the house today. Today, dear. And there'll be nobody home. [*A sob rises in her throat.*] We're free and clear. [*sobbing more fully, released*] We're free. [*BIFF comes slowly toward her.*] We're free . . . We're free . . .

[*BIFF lifts her to her feet and moves out up right with her in his arms. LINDA sobs quietly. BERNARD and CHARLEY come together and follow them, followed by HAPPY. Only the music of the flute is left on the darkening stage as over the house the hard towers of the apartment buildings rise into sharp focus, and the curtain falls.*]

QUESTIONS

ACT 1

1. What do you learn about Willy from the first stage direction?

2. What instances of stealing are in the play? Why do Biff and Happy steal? Where did they learn about stealing? How is stealing related to salesmanship?

3. In Act 1 Willy claims that "I never in my life told him [Biff] anything but decent things." Is this assertion true? What does it show you about Willy?

ACT 2 AND REQUIEM

4. What does Willy's difficulty with machines—especially his car, the refrigerator, and Howard's tape recorder—suggest about him? To what extent are these machines symbolic?

5. When Willy sees Bernard in Charley's office, he asks, "What—what's the secret?" What secret is he asking about? Does such a secret exist?

6. In Act 2 Willy buys seeds and tries to plant a garden at night. Why is Willy so disturbed that "nothing's planted" and "I don't have a thing in the ground"? What do this garden and having "things in the ground" mean to Willy?

7. In Act 2, speech 867, Biff claims that "we never told the truth for ten minutes in this house!" What does he mean? To what extent is he right?

8. Linda's last line in the play—"We're free . . . We're free"—seems to refer to the house mortgage. In what other ways, however, might you take it?

GENERAL QUESTIONS

1. How does Miller use lighting, the set, blocking, and music to differentiate between action in the present and "memory" action?

2. The stage directions are full of information that cannot be played. In describing Happy, for example, Miller notes that "sexuality is like a color on him." What is the function of such stage directions?

3. How is Willy's suicide foreshadowed throughout the play? To what extent does this foreshadowing create tension?

4. Which characters are "real" and which are "hallucinations" that spring from Willy's memory? What are the major differences between these two groups?

5. Which characters are symbolic and what do they symbolize?

6. Describe the character of Willy Loman. What are his good qualities? In what ways does he have heroic stature? What are his bad qualities? To what extent is his "fall" the result of his flaws, and to what extent is it caused by circumstances beyond his control?

7. How is the relationship between Charley and Bernard different from the one between Willy and his sons? Why is this difference important?

8. Discuss Linda's character and role. In what ways is she supportive of Willy? In what ways does she encourage his deceptions and self-delusions?

9. What sort of person is Happy? What has he inherited from Willy? How is he a debasement of Willy? To what degree is he successful or happy?

10. Willy claims that success in business is based not on "what you do" but on "who you know and the smile on your face! It's contacts . . . a man can end up with diamonds on the basis of being well liked." How does the play support or reject this assertion?

11. Most of Willy's memories—Ben's visit, Boston, the football game—are from 1928. Why does Willy's memory return to 1928? Why is the contrast between 1928 and the present significant for Willy and for the play as a whole?

WRITING ABOUT TRAGEDY

As you plan and write an essay about tragedy, keep in mind all the elements of drama. A full discussion of traditional approaches to these elements—plot, character, point of view, setting, language, tone, symbol, and theme—is found in Chapter 20. Review this material before you begin your essay.

Although the basic elements remain consistent in tragedy, the form requires a few special considerations. In planning to write about plot and conflict, you might explore the crisis or climax—that point at which the downfall becomes inevitable. Similarly, you might consider the degree to which the conflicts shape or accelerate the tragic action. With character, pay special attention to the tragic protagonist and the major antagonists: What is the connection between the protagonist's strengths and weaknesses? To what extent does the protagonist bring about or cooperate with his or her own destruction? What key characteristics and behavior patterns ensure both the protagonist's heroic stature and fall? In dealing with tone, consider the degree to which the play is ironic. Do you know more about what is going on than the protagonist? Than most of the characters? If so, how does your knowledge affect your understanding of the play?

Along with these considerations, all the traditional elements of drama can provide fruitful essays about tragic drama. Here, however, we introduce an additional way of writing about literature: an examination of a problem. This approach can be employed to write about prose fiction, poetry, or any type of dramatic literature. Our discussion will naturally focus on tragedy—specifically *Hamlet*—and the plays in which problem solving can generate effective essays about tragic drama.

An Essay About a Problem

A **problem** is any question put before you that you cannot answer easily and correctly. The question "Who is the major character in *Hamlet*?" is not a problem, because the obvious answer is Hamlet. Let us, however, ask another question: "Why is it *correct* to say that Hamlet is the major character?" This question is not as easy as the first, and for this reason it creates a problem. It requires that we think about our answer, even though we do not need to search very far. Hamlet is the title character. He is involved in most of the actions of the play. He is so much the center of our liking and concern that his death causes sadness and regret. To "solve" this problem has required a set of responses, all of which provide answers to the question "Why?"

More complex, however, and more typical of most problems, are questions like these: "Why does Hamlet talk of suicide in his first soliloquy?" "Why does he treat Ophelia so coarsely in the 'nunnery' scene?" "Why does he delay in avenging his father's death?" "Why does he so immediately and uncritically accept Laertes's challenge to the concluding duel?" Essays on a problem are normally concerned with such questions because they require a good deal of thought, together with a number of interpretations knitted together into an entire essay. More broadly, dealing with problems is one of the major tasks of the intellectual, scientific, social, and political disciplines. Being able to advance and then explain solutions is therefore one of the most important techniques that you can acquire.

Strategies for Organizing Ideas

Your first purpose is to convince readers that your solution is a good one. This you do by making sound conclusions from supporting evidence. In nonscientific subjects like literature, you rarely find absolute proofs, so your conclusions will not be *proved* in the way you prove triangles congruent in geometry. But your organization, your use of facts from the text, your interpretations, and your application of general or specific knowledge should all make your conclusions convincing. Thus your basic strategy is *persuasion.*

1. *Demonstrate that conditions for a solution are fulfilled.* This type of development is the most basic in writing—namely, illustration. You first explain that certain conditions need to exist for your solution to be plausible. Your central idea—really a brief answer to the question—is that the conditions do indeed exist. Your development is to show how the conditions can be found in the work.

    Suppose that you are writing on the problem of why Hamlet delays revenge against Claudius. Suppose also that you make the point that Hamlet delays because he is never sure that Claudius is guilty. This is your "solution" to the problem. In your essay you support your answer by challenging the credibility of the information Hamlet receives about the crime (i.e., the two visits from the Ghost and Claudius's distress at the play within the play). Once you have "attacked" these sources of data on the grounds that they are unreliable, you have succeeded because your solution is consistent with the details of the play.

2. *Analyze words in the phrasing of the problem.* Your object in this approach is to clarify important words in the statement of the problem and then to decide how applicable they are. This kind of attention to words, in fact, might give you enough material for all or part of your essay. Thus, an essay on the problem of Hamlet's delay might focus in part on a treatment of the word *delay:* What, really, does *delay* mean? For Hamlet, is there a difference between delay that is reasonable and delay that is unreasonable? Does Hamlet delay unreasonably? Is his delay the result of a psychological fault? Would speedy revenge be more or less reasonable than the delay? By the time you have answered such pointed questions, you will also have sufficient material for your full essay.

3. *Refer to literary conventions or expectations.* With this strategy, the argument is to establish that the problem can be solved by reference to the literary mode or conventions of a work, or to the limitations of the work itself. In other words, what appears to be a problem is really no more than a normal characteristic. A problem about the artificiality of

the choruses in *Oedipus the King*, might be resolved by reference to the fact that choruses were a normal feature of Greek drama. In a similar manner, the knowledge that delay is a convention of all revenge tragedy might provide a key to the problem of Hamlet's apparent procrastination.

4. *Argue against possible objections.* With this strategy, you raise your own objections and then argue against them. Called **procatalepsis** or **anticipation,** this approach helps you sharpen your arguments, because *anticipating* and dealing with objections forces you to make analyses and use facts that you might otherwise overlook. Although procatalepsis can be used point by point throughout your essay, you may find it most useful at the end.

The situation to imagine is that someone is raising objections to your solution to the problem. It is then your task to show that the objections (1) are not accurate or valid, (2) are not strong or convincing, or (3) are based on unusual rather than usual conditions (on an exception and not the rule). Here are some examples of these approaches.

1. *The objection is not accurate or valid.* You reject this objection by showing that either the interpretation or the conclusions are wrong and also by emphasizing that the evidence supports your solution.

   Although Hamlet's delay is reasonable, the claim might be made that his duty is to kill Claudius in revenge immediately after the Ghost's accusations. This claim is not persuasive because it assumes that Hamlet knows everything the audience knows. The audience accepts the Ghost's word that Claudius is guilty, but Hamlet has no certain reason to believe the Ghost. Would it not seem insane for Hamlet to kill Claudius, who reigns legally, and then to claim he did it because of the Ghost's words? The argument for speedy revenge is not good because it is based on an incorrect view of Hamlet's situation.

2. *The objection is not strong or convincing.* You *concede* that the objection has some truth or validity, but you then try to show that it is weak and that your own solution is stronger.

   One might claim that Claudius's distress at the play within the play is evidence for his guilt and that therefore Hamlet should carry out his revenge right away. This argument has merit, and Hamlet's speech after Claudius has fled the scene ("I'll take the Ghost's word for a thousand pound") shows that the "conscience of the king" has been caught. But the king's guilty behavior is not a strong cause for killing him. Hamlet could justifiably ask for an investigation of his father's death on these grounds, but he could not justify a revenge killing. Claudius could not be convicted in any court on the testimony that he was disturbed at seeing *The Murder of Gonzago*. Even after the play within the play, the reasons for delay are stronger than for action.

3. *The objection depends on unusual rather than usual conditions.* You reject the objection on the grounds that it could be valid only if normal conditions were suspended. The objection depends on an exception, not a rule.

> The case for quick action is simple: Hamlet should kill Claudius right after seeing the Ghost (1.3) or else after seeing the King's reaction to the stage murder of Gonzago (3.2) or else after seeing the Ghost again (3.4). Redress under these circumstances, goes the argument, must be both personal and extralegal. This argument wrongly assumes that due process does not exist in the Denmark of Hamlet and Claudius. Nothing in the play indicates that the Danes, even though they carouse a bit, do not value legality and the rules of evidence. Thus Hamlet cannot rush out to kill Claudius because he knows that the king has not had anything close to due process. The argument for quick action is poor because it rests on an exception being made from civilized law.

Remember that writing an essay on a problem requires you to argue a position: Either there is a solution or there is not. To develop your position requires that you show the steps to your conclusion. Your general thematic form is thus (1) to describe the conditions that need to be met for the solution you propose, and then (2) to demonstrate that these conditions exist. If you assert that there is no solution, then your form would be the same for the first part, but your second part—the development—would show that these conditions have *not* been met.

In developing your response, use one or more of the strategies described in this chapter. These are, again, (1) to demonstrate that conditions for a solution are fulfilled, (2) to analyze the words in the phrasing of the problem, (3) to refer to literary conventions or expectations, and (4) to argue against possible objections. You might combine these. Thus, if we assume that your argument is that Hamlet's delay is reasonable, you might first consider the word *delay* (strategy 2). Then you might use strategy 1 to explain the reasons for Hamlet's delay. Finally, to answer objections to your argument, you might show that Hamlet acts promptly when he believes he is justified (strategy 4). Whatever your topic, the important thing is to use the method or methods that best help you make a good argument for your solution.

In your conclusion, try to affirm the validity of your solution in view of the supporting evidence. You might do this by reemphasizing your strongest points, or you might simply present a brief summary. Or you might think of your argument as still continuing and thus use the strategy of procatalepsis or anticipation to raise and answer possible objections to your solution, as in the last paragraph of the following illustrative essay.

Illustrative Student Essay

Although underlined sentences are not recommended by MLA style, they are used in this illustrative essay as teaching tools to emphasize the central idea, thesis sentence, and topic sentences.

Rezik 1

Antonio Rezik

Professor Tomaiuolo

English 312

1 November 2014

The Problem of Hamlet's Apparent Delay°

[1]   Many readers and spectators of Shakespeare's *Hamlet* have been puzzled by the prince's apparent failure to kill Claudius quickly. Early in the play, the Ghost calls on his son to "Revenge his foul and most unnatural murder" (1.5.25). Hamlet, however, delays his vengeance until the end of the play. The problem results from why does he not act sooner. <u>The answer is that there is no unjustified delay and that in fact Hamlet acts as quickly as possible.</u>* <u>This becomes evident when we examine the conventions of revenge tragedy, the actual "call to revenge," and the steps that Hamlet takes to achieve vengeance.</u>†

[2]   <u>Revenge tragedy obviously requires that vengeance be delayed until the closing moments of the play.</u> Given this limitation, Shakespeare must justify the wide gap of time between the call to revenge in Act 1 and the killing of Claudius in Act 5. We find such justification in the unreliability of the Ghost's initial accusation, Hamlet's need for additional evidence, and the events that occur after this evidence is obtained.

[3]   The Ghost's accusations and demands are straightforward: he accuses his brother of murdering him and he calls on his son for vengeance. <u>Shakespeare is careful, however, to establish that this testimony is doubtful.</u> Horatio questions the Ghost's truthfulness and motives, and he warns Hamlet that the spirit might "assume some other horrible form / Which might deprive your

°**This play appears on pages 1080–1177.**
*Central idea.
†Thesis sentence.

sovereignty of reason, / And draw you into madness" (1.4.73–75). Hamlet
himself expresses doubt about the Ghost (2.2.573–79):

> The spirit that I have seen
>
> May be a devil, and the devil hath power
>
> T'assume a pleasing shape, yea, and perhaps
>
> Out of my weakness, and my melancholy,
>
> As he is very potent with such spirits,
>
> Abuses me to damn me; I'll have grounds
>
> More relative than this.

The prince thus cannot act on the unsupported word of the Ghost; he needs
more evidence.

[4] There is no delay at this point in the play, because Hamlet quickly begins
developing a plan of action. Immediately after speaking with the Ghost,
he decides to cover himself under an "antic disposition" while he gathers
information. He swears his companions to silence and warns them not to react
knowingly if he should seem to behave strangely or insanely (1.5.169–79).
His idea is that this pose will make him less a subject of suspicion and will
therefore make others less careful.

[5] Once Hamlet has begun his plan, he takes advantage of every opportunity
to carry out his vengeance. When the players come to Elsinore, he adroitly
plans to test Claudius by making him publicly view a play, *The Murder of
Gonzago*, which shows a murder just like Claudius's murder of Hamlet's
father. Hamlet states that Claudius's appearance will give him the clue he
needs to confirm the Ghost's information (2.2.571–73).

> I'll observe his looks,
>
> I'll tent him to the quick, if a' do blench
>
> I know my course.

Once the king breaks up the performance in great agitation, which Hamlet
correctly interprets as an admission of guilt, Hamlet declares confidence
in the Ghost ("I'll take the ghost's word for a thousand pound" [3.2.271–
72]). Moreover, he is psychologically ready to act against the king, for

Rezik 3

he asserts that he could "drink hot blood, / And do such bitter business as the day / Would quake to look on" (3.2.367–69). Without doubt, Hamlet is only a prayer away from stabbing Claudius, for when he sees the king kneeling, his opportunity has merged with his desire and also with his promise to the Ghost. He tells the audience, "Now might I do it pat, now a' is a-praying, / And now I'll do't" (3.3.73–74).

[6]   But he does not "do't," and for this reason he is open to the accusation that he cannot act. Again, however, Shakespeare carefully justifies this hesitation. The prince does not want to send Claudius's soul to heaven by killing him at prayer. This reason is not simply an excuse for delay. Rather, Hamlet wants his revenge to match Claudius's treacherous murder of the previous King Hamlet, who died without the chance to pray and repent (3.3.88–95):

> Up sword, and know thou a more horrid hent,
>
> When he is drunk asleep, or in his rage,
>
> Or in th'incestuous pleasure of his bed,
>
> At game, a-swearing, or about some act
>
> That has no relish of salvation in't,
>
> Then trip him that his heels may kick at heaven,
>
> And that his soul may be as damned and black
>
> As hell whereto it goes.

This deferral is in keeping with the code of personal blood vengeance, whereby the revenge must match or exceed the original crime. There is no question of Hamlet's incapacity to act, because his putting up his sword is reasonable and justifiable.

[7]   From this point on, Hamlet acts or reacts to every situation as the opportunity presents itself. After he kills Polonius, Claudius initiates a counterplot to send Hamlet off to England and execution. Clearly, Hamlet's chances to kill the king are thus reduced to zero. It is not until Act 5 that Hamlet gets back to Denmark, after having decisively thwarted Claudius's murderous instructions by turning them against Rosencrantz and Guildenstern. He makes it clear to Horatio, however, that he will take

Rezik 4

the earliest opportunity, and that "the readiness is all" (5.2.205). Once the rigged fencing match is under way, the opportunity finally comes. Claudius, Hamlet learns, has not only killed his father but has poisoned his mother, and he himself is about to die from Laertes's poisoned sword. Upon such certain information, Hamlet immediately kills Claudius. When the revenge is complete, the Ghost, who began the cry for vengeance, is nowhere to be heard or seen, and four bodies lie on the stage.

Thus, we see that the issue of Hamlet's delay—and the vengeance [8] does take four acts to carry out—is really not a problem. The prince acts in accordance with the code of revenge as quickly as circumstances permit. Although the text of the play supports this solution, critics might still argue that procrastination is an issue because Hamlet twice accuses himself of delay. This objection does not take into consideration that Hamlet's perception of time and action is distorted by his eagerness for vengeance. From Hamlet's subjective point of view, any break in activity is delay. From our objective viewpoint, however, delay is not a true problem.

Rezik 5

Work Cited

Shakespeare, William. *The Tragedy of Hamlet, Prince of Denmark. Litera-ture: An Introduction to Reading and Writing, Compact Edition.* Ed. Edgar V. Roberts and Robert Zweig. 6th ed. New York: Pearson, 2015. 1080–1177. Print.

Commentary on the Essay

The structure of the essay illustrates strategy 1 (p. 1247). Paragraph 2, however, makes brief use of strategy 3 in its reference to the conventions of revenge tragedy. In both paragraphs 6 and 8, the argument is carried on by use of *procatalepsis,* or strategy 4, whereby a counterargument is raised and then answered.

USING SOURCES EFFECTIVELY

QUOTING TEXTS TO ILLUSTRATE YOUR KEY POINT

When writing about drama, quoting the actual language of the text often provides the strongest and most focused evidence of your main idea. However, where poetry and fiction may sometimes be suitably illustrated with just a word or a key phrase from the primary work, drama may lend itself to quoting longer passages to capture the essence of the scene. While paraphrasing and summarizing some of a play's action may be necessary to provide adequate context for readers, quoting the work's exact language often advances the argument most strongly.

For example, in paragraph 3, Antonio Rezik uses somewhat lengthy quotations from Acts 1 and 2 to forcefully drive home his thesis, that Hamlet delays his revenge thoughtfully and purposely:

> The Ghost's accusations and demands are straightforward: he accuses his brother of murdering him and he calls on his son for vengeance. Shakespeare is careful, however, to establish that this testimony is doubtful. Horatio questions the Ghost's truthfulness and motives, and he warns Hamlet that the spirit might "assume some other horrible form / Which might deprive your sovereignty of reason, / And draw you into madness" (1.4.73–75). Hamlet himself expresses doubt about the ghost:

Hamlet is often criticized for being "indecisive," but using this quote shows that even his trusted friend advises him to proceed slowly.

> > The spirit that I have seen
> >
> > May be a devil, and the devil hath power
> >
> > T'assume a pleasing shape, yea, and perhaps
> >
> > Out of my weakness, and my melancholy,
> >
> > As he is very potent with such spirits,
> >
> > Abuses me to damn me; I'll have grounds
> >
> > More relative than this. (2.2.573–79)

By quoting Hamlet's entire statement, Rezik provides convincing proof for his thesis.

> The prince thus cannot act on the unsupported word of the Ghost; he needs more evidence.

The author makes the rhetorical decision to offer well-chosen textual proof that Hamlet proceeds carefully and rationally before avenging his father's death. Hamlet considers how misleading this apparition may be, and he vows to go slowly and gather more confirming evidence. The quoted passage both focuses the readers on Rezik's main point and gives his argument authority.

Later in the essay (paragraph 7), Rezik presents a powerful statement from the text to signal the end of Hamlet's delaying tactics, using a short but famous phrase often cited as proof that Hamlet is *not* ready:

> He makes clear to Horatio, however, that he will take the earliest opportunity, and that "readiness is all" (5.2.205).

A long passage is not needed here. The three-word statement serves to show pointedly that Hamlet has now gathered his facts and is determined to act.

The essayist's use of a longer passage from the work to provide clear evidence of Hamlet's thought process and then a short one to demonstrate his willingness to move ahead without further delay effectively supports the author's thesis, "solving" the "problem of the play." (For more information on quotation, see pages 53–57.)

The introductory paragraph raises the problem of Hamlet's apparent delay and offers a brief statement of the solution (the central idea). This plan is developed in paragraphs 2–7 in exactly the same order in which the issues are raised in the introduction. Paragraph 2 deals with the meaning and requirements of revenge, and paragraph 3 takes up the issue of the Ghost's reliability. Paragraphs 4 and 5 deal with Hamlet's attempts to corroborate the Ghost's accusations, and paragraphs 6 and 7 consider the subsequent action. Note that each paragraph in the argument grows naturally out of the one that precedes it, just as all the paragraphs are linked to the introductory paragraph.

The concluding paragraph asserts that the original problem is solved; the paragraph then summarizes the steps of the solution. It also continues the argument by raising and then dealing with a possible objection.

Writing Topics About Tragedy

Writing Paragraphs

1. In a paragraph develop an argument for one of these assertions referring to Sophocles's *Oedipus the King*.
   a. Oedipus's fall is the result of fate, predestination, and the gods, and it would happen no matter what kind of person he is.
   b. Oedipus's fall is the result only of his character and has nothing to do with fate or the gods.

Writing Essays

1. Much has been made of the contrast in *Oedipus the King* between vision and blindness. Write an essay that considers this contrast as it is related to the character of Oedipus. How are blindness and seeing reversed, with regard to his understanding about the curse on the city, his attempts to ferret out the guilty ones, his awakening perceptions of his own responsibility and guilt, and his self-blinding? How can Tiresias be compared and contrasted with Oedipus?

2. Write an essay considering the degree to which Gertrude and Ophelia in *Hamlet* justify Hamlet's assertion "Frailty, thy name is woman" (1.2.146). Questions you might take into account concern the status of these women, their power to exert their own individuality and to make their own decisions, Gertrude as a royal queen and Ophelia as an aristocratic daughter, their capacity to undergo the pain of bereavement, Hamlet's own feelings about the death of his father, and so on.

3. Hamlet, Laertes, and Fortinbras are young men whose fathers have been killed and who set out to avenge these deaths. Their courses of action, however, are different. In an essay, consider these three as typical or archetypal sons. What characteristics do they share? What, in turn, makes them individual and distinct? Compare and contrast how each character deals with his father's death. Which approach seems most reasonable to you? Most emotional? Most effective? For additional directions in handling comparison and contrast, consult Chapter 26.

4. Considering *Oedipus the King*, *Hamlet*, and *Death of a Salesman*, write an essay defining and explaining tragedy. Include references to the nature of the tragic protagonists, the situations they face, their solutions to their problems, their responses to the consequences of their actions, and their worthiness of character. Be sure to compare and contrast the actions and speeches of the characters in the plays as evidence.

Creative Writing Assignment

1. Write a monologue for a character in which he or she reveals a tragic flaw. Your character may be talking about a situation that needs action or a plot to avenge an action taken against him or her. Try to deal with the issue of what constitutes a "flaw." It might be a shortcoming of understanding about the issue or difficulty the character faces. Or it might also be a result of insufficient knowledge that the character might be ignoring. To write such a monologue, you may refer to details and happenings that need reference, while at the same time these details do not need complete explanation.

Library Assignment

1. Use your library or the Internet to locate materials on tragedy. Some general topics might include *ancient and modern tragedy*, *definitions*, *emotions*, *heroes*, *passions*, *problems*, and *questions*. You might also wish to locate specific books on Aristotle and tragedy or on *Oedipus the King* or *Hamlet*.

Chapter 22
The Comic Vision: Restoring the Balance

AFTER STUDYING THIS MATERIAL, YOU SHOULD BE ABLE TO DO THE FOLLOWING:

- Understand the growth of comedy in ancient Greece and Rome
- Discuss the patterns, characters, and language of comedy
- Explain types of comedy, including high comedy and low comedy
- Critique the theatrical and literary elements of comedies

Comedy is the fraternal twin of tragedy. As a form it was first created in the ancient Greek world, like tragedy, and the two forms bear many family resemblances.[1] Comedy is often filled with tragic potential, and tragedy sometimes is built on a story that is potentially comic. Indeed, tragedy can be seen as an abortive or incomplete comedy in which affairs take a negative turn, and comedy can be considered a tragedy in which the truth is discovered (or covered up), the hero saves the day, the villain is overcome, the hero and heroine are united, and equilibrium and balance are restored. The major differences are that tragedy moves toward despair or death, whereas comedy moves toward success, happiness, and marriage. Tragic diction is elevated and heroic. Comic diction can be elevated too, but often it is common or colloquial, and although it is frequently witty, it is also sometimes witless and bawdy. The primary difference is that the mask of tragedy despairs, grieves, and weeps, whereas the mask of comedy rejoices, smiles, and laughs.

The Origins of Comedy

In the *Poetics*, Aristotle states that he knows less about the origin of Athenian comedy than of tragedy because comedy "was not at first treated seriously" (V.2, p. 21).[2] He does say, however, that comedy developed as an improvisatory form (IV.12, p. 19) just as tragedy did. Most comic improvisations were an outgrowth of "phallic songs," which were bacchanalian processions that took place during the **Lenaia,** the Athenian religious festival held in January–February each year during *Gamelion,* the month of weddings, just following the winter solstice.

For a more detailed discussion of how drama developed within the ancient Athenian religious festivals, see Chapter 21, pages 1023–1027.

S. H. Butcher, *Aristotle's Theory of Poetry and Fine Art,* 4th ed. (New York: Dover, 1951) 21 (V.2). All parenthetical references to Aristotle are from this edition.

The word *comedy* is consistent with this explanation, for as "a *komos* song" its Greek meaning is "a song of revels" or "a song sung by merrymakers." The revels, like the tragedies, were religious in ways that the Greeks considered meaningful but that seem secular to us today. During parades or processions at the Lenaia, the merrymakers expressed their joy boisterously, traded bawdy and obscene remarks with spectators, lampooned public persons, wore ceremonial phalluses, and dressed in paunchy costumes suggesting feasting, fatness, fertility, friskiness, frolic, and fun. We may conclude that these *komos* processions were supported officially in the belief and hope that human ceremonies would encourage divine favor and bring about prosperity and happiness. As the form developing out of such processions, comedy began with many of these characteristics and has retained them to the present day. If one may generalize about subsequent comedies—even those that are cold sober rather than boisterous—it is clear that love, marriage, and ritualized celebrations of a happy future are usually major concerns.

The Athenians Held Competitions for Comedy, Just as for Tragedy

Tragedy originated in Athens, but the same does not appear to be true of comedy. Rather, comedy coexisted in the areas surrounding Greece called *Magna Graecia* ("Greater Greece"). Aristotle himself admitted that it was "late" when comic performances were separated from the phallic songs (V.2, p. 21); that is, comedy followed tragedy by many years. The earliest certain date for the existence of Athenian comedy is 486 BCE, when a writer named Chionides won a state-sponsored comedy competition. Although the earliest comedies apparently consisted of little more than loosely connected lampoons, they were regarded highly enough to justify regular competitions. Comedies were scheduled on each day of the festivals, following the tragedies and satyr plays.

According to Aristotle, the first writer to transform comedy by creating a thematic plot development was Crates, who won the first of his three prizes in about the mid-fifth century BCE (V.3, p. 21). It was at this time that comedies became popular enough to justify an additional state comedy competition, which was instituted in about 440 BCE. For the remainder of the century, writers of comedy as well as tragedy tried to win prizes for their new plays at both the Lenaia and the City Dionysia.

The Earliest Greek Comedy Is Called Old Comedy

The comedies of the fifth century BCE, called **Old Comedy** or **Old Attic Comedy** by later historians, followed intricate structural patterns and displayed complex poetic conventions. Nevertheless, they bore the marks of their origins in the bacchanalian *komos* processions. The actors (three or four men) and the members of the chorus (twenty-four men), each dressed in a distortingly padded costume, wore a character-defining mask, and displayed a ceremonial phallus. The role of the chorus usually dictated the comedy's title (e.g., *The Frogs*, *The Wasps*). Customarily, the plot was fantastic and impossible, and the dialogue was farcical and bawdy. In the tradition of satires and tirades associated with the phallic songs and with early comedy, the comic dramatists freely lashed public persons (usually but not always without legal reprisal).

Although the most successful comedy writer of the fifth century BCE was Magnes (fl. 475–450 BCE), who won perhaps as many as eleven times, the only writer whose works survive is Aristophanes (c. 450–385 BCE), who won four times. His plays constitute our principal firsthand knowledge of Greek Old Comedy. He wrote at least thirty-two comedies. Fortunately, eleven have survived, along with fragments of some of his other plays. His plots and actions are outrageous, his characters are funny, and his language is satirical, bawdy, and biting.

Middle Comedy Became Prominent After Aristophanes

Aristophanes lived into the next period of Greek comedy, called **Middle Comedy.** His plays *Ecclesiazusae* (*The Women at the Assembly*, c. 392 BCE) and *Plutus* (*Plutus, the God of Riches*, 388 BCE) ushered in Middle Comedy. All the Middle Comedy plays by other authors are lost, although there are many extant fragments. Middle Comedy eliminated some of the complex patterns of Old Comedy and treated more broadly international and less narrowly Athenian topics. Political criticism was abandoned, and character types such as the braggart soldier were introduced. The role of the chorus was diminished or eliminated (as with tragedy), and the exaggerated costumes were eliminated.

New Comedy, a Type of Romantic Comedy, Flourished After Middle Comedy

By the end of the fourth century BCE, Middle Comedy was supplanted by **New Comedy.** The most important of the New Comedy dramatists was Menander (342–292 BCE), who was heralded in ancient times as the greatest comic writer of them all. Everyone knows quotations from Menander, such as "I call a fig a fig, a spade a spade," "The gods first make mad those they intend to destroy," and "He who fights and runs away lives to fight another day." St. Paul quotes him in 1 Corinthians 15:33 ("Be not deceived: evil communications corrupt good manners."), but after the fifth century CE, copies of Menander's plays were no longer available and for the next fourteen centuries they were presumed totally lost. In the last hundred years, however, many Menandrian manuscripts have been discovered, mostly in the sands of Egypt. We now have Menander's *Dyscolus* (*The Grouch*) in its entirety, and near-complete versions of some of his other comedies, together with numerous fragments and passages.[3] In total, the titles of close to one hundred of his plays are known. His comedies, which are romantic rather than satirical, employ such stock characters as young lovers, stubborn fathers, clever slaves, and long-separated relatives.

Roman Comedy Was Composed Largely in the Third and Second Centuries BCE

After Menander, Greek power in the Mediterranean waned and was replaced by the might of Rome. In the third century BCE, Roman comedy began and flourished,

---

See David R. Slavitt and Palmer Bovie, eds., *Menander: The Grouch, Desperately Seeking Justice, Closely Cropped Locks, The Girl from Samos, The Shield* (Philadelphia: U of Pennsylvania P, 1998).

largely through the translation and adaptation of Greek New Comedies. The significant Roman writers were Plautus (c. 254–184 BCE), with twenty surviving comedies, and Terence (c. 186–159 BCE), whose six comedies have all survived from antiquity. Briefly, the comedies of Plautus are brisk, and those of Terence are more restrained. The central issue in most of the Roman comedies is the overcoming of a **blocking agent,** or obstruction to true love, which could be almost anyone or anything—a rival lover, an angry father, a family feud, an old law, a previously arranged marriage, or differences in social class. The pattern of action, traditionally called the **plot of intrigue** or **intrigue plot,** stems from the stratagems that young lovers undertake to overcome the blocking agent, so that the outcome frequently heralds the victory of youth over age and the passing of control from one generation to the next.

Comedy from Roman Times to the Renaissance

By the time the Roman Empire was established in 29 BCE, the writing of comedy had largely disappeared because pantomime entertainments and public spectacles such as chariot races and gladiatorial combat had preempted Roman dramatic creativity. Comedy thus accompanied tragedy into fifteen hundred years of obscurity—a period when the Roman Empire rose and fell, the Dark Ages descended, and the medieval period emerged. Although many comic and farcical scenes were included in the mystery cycles of late medieval times,[4] comedy as a form was not established again until the Renaissance.

Once reintroduced, comedy grew rapidly. By 1500 the six plays of Terence had been revived and were achieving wide recognition, followed by the twenty surviving plays of Plautus. When English dramatists began writing comedies, they followed Roman conventions. The English plays of the mid-sixteenth century contained five acts and observed the unities of time, place, and action, thus justifying the claim that they were "regular" (i.e., following the generally accepted regulations or "rules"). Character types from the Roman comedies, such as the intriguing couple, the fussing father, and the bragging soldier, initially predominated. Soon, more specifically English types appeared, anticipating the roisterers of Shakespeare's *Henry IV* plays and the "hempen homespuns" of *A Midsummer Night's Dream*. By the end of the sixteenth century, when Shakespeare had completed many of his comedies, English comedy was in full bloom. It has often been observed that this comedy was Latin in structure but English in character.

When the sixteenth century began, the chief obstacle to a wide public assimilation of drama had been the absence of institutionalized theaters. London authorities, maintaining that attending plays was a sinful public nuisance that took citizens away from work and responsibility, banned theaters within the city itself. Builders therefore had to construct theaters outside the London city limits. For example, the Rose and the Globe, where Shakespeare saw his plays produced from the mid-1590s to 1611, were built in Southwark across the Thames. We should realize that many people in Shakespeare's audiences got to the theater by walking over London Bridge or by being ferried across the river, and that they returned home the same way.

For a description of the medieval mystery or Corpus Christi plays, see Chapter 20, pages 974–76.

The Patterns, Characters, and Language of Comedy

Dictionaries sometimes give *funny* as a synonym for *comic,* but the two terms are not identical. Words like *funny, amusing, comical,* or *humorous* define our emotional conditioning to incidents, and our reactions always depend on context. We usually think it is funny or comical to see an actor in a slapstick routine falling down, being hit in the face with a cream pie, or being struck with a paddle. We laugh because we know that everything is staged and that no real harm is being done. But if we leave the theater and see some of the same things occurring on the streets, we are horrified to recognize that someone is enduring real harm and real pain. Street violence occurs randomly, with no apparent purpose, and there is nothing funny or comic about it. But onstage all actions occur as part of a governing pattern or plan leading to a satisfying outcome. It is the context that makes the difference.

Comedy Implies a Complete Narrative Pattern of Humorous Action

Comedy as a genre involves patterns of humorous or comic situations and actions that make up a complete and coherent story. Often the situations are simply ordinary; sometimes they are fantastic; sometimes they are even bizarre. But they are always resolvable and correctible (unless we are dealing with the special genre of **problem comedy** [see Chapter 24]). The patterns grow out of character and situation, and they reach a resolution in a logical or at least an understandable pattern of development. In considering comic patterns, we perceive most dialogue and activity—even serious problems and dangerous situations—as amusing, entertaining, and usually instructive.

COMEDY DRAMATIZES A PATTERN OF EDUCATION AND CHANGE. In many comedies the principal characters benefit from learning about themselves and their commitments, about living well and loving deeply, about getting along with the people around them, and about finding their place in the world. This "education," which they receive in the play, enables them to improve, and the process of their learning reaches its height in crucial moments of illumination and change. The characters realize their past errors, are ready to amend them, and also are human and humble enough to ask forgiveness, which, according to the comic pattern, is promptly granted. In many comedies, particularly those that touch on significant social and political problems, the audience is also educated, and the play's implication is that improvement should occur in the world just as it has occurred on the stage.

COMIC PROBLEMS FLOURISH AMID CHAOS AND POTENTIAL DISASTER. Before the moments of change leading to the comic conclusion, however, comedy must introduce many of the problems and complications that could, in real life, lead not to happiness but to unhappiness and even to calamity. These problems can be personal, social, political, economic, or military; in short, they may enter every arena of human affairs. A man wants to find a place in the world and to gain his fortune, and he also wants to find love. A woman wants to find love also, but must be reserved and somewhat aloof when meeting suitors. A number of people want to succeed in a business venture. A politician is accused of corruption and thus needs help in exonerating himself. A man and woman in love become angry or disenchanted because others tell them lies about each other. Another man and woman need to overcome family hostility so that they may successfully begin their lives together with the approval of everyone around them. Still another man and woman, upon meeting for the first time, become so angry they threaten to do away with each other. Failure, though it is to be always overcome in comedy, is never far distant; it lurks over the horizon, around corners, in business rooms, in malicious telephone calls, and on the Internet, waiting to emerge and scatter uncertainty, indecisiveness, and distress.

All such situations, which might possibly lead to ruin, are the stuff of comedy. The worse things seem, and the more apparently chaotic, the better. In a good comic complication, the problems are constantly being fueled by misunderstanding, mistaken identity, misdirection, misinformed speech, errors in judgment, faults in intelligence, excessive or unreasonable behavior, and coincidences that stretch credulity. In "Pops" by Edwin Sanchez, Tomas is the only character that we hear, yet we are able to imagine a great deal about how the father feels about his relationship with his son.

THE COMIC CLIMAX IS THE PEAK OF CONFUSION.   Such complications lead ultimately to the comic **climax,** which is the moment or moments in the play when everything reaches the peak of confusion and when no good solution seems in sight. Misunderstanding is dominant, pressure is at a high point, and choices must be made even though solutions seem impossible. The **catastrophe**—the changing or turning point—is frequently launched by a sudden revelation in which a new fact, a misunderstood event, or a previously hidden identity is explained to characters and audience at the same time, and then things undergo a turnaround and start rushing toward improvement.

THE COMIC DÉNOUEMENT RESTORES SANITY AND CALM.   In most comedies, the events of the **dénouement** resolve initial difficulties and allow for the comic resolution, which dramatizes how things are set right at every level of action. Errors are explained, personal lives are straightened out, people at odds with each other are reconciled, promises are made for the future, new families are formed through marriage, and a stable social order is reestablished.

Comic Characters Are More Limited Than Characters in Tragedy

Comic characters are relatively limited because they are almost necessarily representative and common rather than individual and heroic. Characters with breadth or individuality are therefore not typical of comedy. Instead, comedy gives us stock characters who represent classes, types, and generations. In Shakespeare's *A Midsummer Night's Dream* many of the characters are representative and stock figures. Egeus is a conventionally indignant and unreasonable father, and Hermia and Lysander are typical young lovers (along with Helena and Demetrius). In *Post-its (Notes on a Marriage)* by Paul Dooley and Winnie Holzman, the two characters remain limited throughout the action of the play which represents an entire marriage.

Comic Language Is a Vital Vehicle of Humor

As in other types of literature, comic dramatists use language to delineate character, to establish tone and mood, and to express ideas and feelings. In comedy, however, language is also one of the most important vehicles for humor. Some comedies are characterized by elegant and witty language, others by puns and bawdy jokes.

Characters in comedy tend either to be masters of language or to be mastered by it. Those who are skillful with language can use a witty phrase to satirize their foes and friends alike. Those who are unskilled with language, like Bottom in *A Midsummer Night's Dream*, bungle their speeches because they misuse words and stumble into inadvertent puns. Both types of characters are amusing; we smile a knowing smile with the wits and laugh aloud at the would-be wits and the bunglers. In *Post-its (Notes on a Marriage)* the couple communicates by short notes and never go beyond a superficial understanding of their problems. Each character excels at being inarticulate.

Types of Comedy

Differences in comic style, content, and intent that have evolved over the centuries make it possible to divide comedy into various types. The broadest of these divisions, based on both style and content, separates comic literature into *high comedy* and *low comedy*.

High Comedy Develops Mainly from Character

Ideally, **high comedy** (a term coined by George Meredith in 1877 in *The Idea of Comedy*) is witty, graceful, and sophisticated. The problems and complications are more closely related to character than to situation, even though, admittedly, they develop out of situations. The appeal of high comedy is to the intellect, for the comic resolution must come about because the characters learn enough to accept adjustments and changes in their lives. A simple change of situation alone will not do for high comedy. The types of high comedy are these:

1. *Romantic comedy focuses on problems of youthful love.* One of the major kinds of high comedy is **romantic comedy,** which views action and character from the standpoint of earnest young lovers like Hermia and Lysander in *A Midsummer Night's Dream*. Ultimately derived from Roman comedy, a romantic comedy is built on a plot of intrigue featuring lovers who try to overcome opposition (as, for example, Egeus) to achieve a successful union. The aim of such plays is amusement and entertainment rather than ridicule and reform. Although vice and folly may be exposed in romantic comedy, especially the follies of the antagonists blocking the young lovers, the dominant impulse is toleration and amused indulgence.

2. *Comedy of manners tests the strength of social customs and assumptions.* Related to romantic comedy is the **comedy of manners,** an important type from the seventeenth century to our own times. The comedy of manners examines and satirizes attitudes and customs in the light of high intellectual and moral

standards. The dialogue is witty and sophisticated, and characters are often measured according to their linguistic and intellectual powers. The love plots are serious and real, even though they share with romantic comedy the need to create intrigues to overcome opposition and impediments. The realism and seriousness in some of the manners comedies written in Restoration England (1660–1700) are so significant that one might consider them not only as plays of manners but also as plays of social and personal problems.

3. *Satiric comedy, like all satire, ridicules vices and follies.* Midway between high and low comedy is **satiric comedy,** which is based in a comic attack on foolishness and/or viciousness. The playwright of satiric comedy assumes the perspective of a rational and moderate observer measuring human life against a moderate norm that is represented by high and serious characters. Members of the audience are invited to share this viewpoint as they, along with the dramatist, heap scorn upon the vicious and laugh loudly at the eccentric and the foolish.

Low Comedy Dwells Amid the Silly and the Bumbling

In **low comedy,** emphasis is on funny remarks and outrageous circumstances. Complications develop from situation and plot rather than from character. Plays of this type are by definition full of physical humor and stage business—a character rounds his forefinger and thumb to imitate a hole in a wall, through which other characters speak; an irascible man constantly breaks furniture; a character masquerading as a doctor takes the pulse of a father to determine his daughter's medical condition; characters who have just declared their love are visited by people to whom they formerly swore love.

The quintessential type of low comedy is **farce,** which is derived from the Latin word *farsus,* meaning "stuffed." Henry Fielding, in the prologue to his 1730 (and 1734) play *The Author's Farce,* points out that the aim of farce "is but to make you laugh." Farces are mainly outlandish physical comedies overflowing with silly characters, unlikely happenings, wild clowning, improbable pratfalls, extravagant language, and bawdy jokes.

Another type of farce is the ***commedia dell'arte,*** a prototypical comic drama that developed among traveling companies in Italy and France in the sixteenth and seventeenth centuries. The broadly humorous characters of *commedia dell'arte* recurred from play to play with consistent names and characteristics. The action usually involved a plot of intrigue. The lovers were the permanently youthful and glowing *Inamorato* and *Inamorata,* who were aided by Inamorata's clever servant, the *soubrette,* to overcome *Pantaloon,* the foolish and presuming old man. The servant characters were *Harlequin* (who was invisible) and *Columbine* (his sweetheart, also invisible), who were joined in highjinks by *Pierrot* (a clown lover) and *Scaramouche* (the soldier). Other stock characters, most of whom were derived from Greek New Comedy by way of Roman comedy, have in turn become constant features of much subsequent comedy.

With characters of low comedy, of course, there is much tomfoolery and improvisation—the major qualities of the extreme form of farce, **slapstick,** which is named after the double paddles ("slap sticks") that made loud cracking noises when actors in the *commedia dell'arte* used them for striking each other. Slapstick depends heavily on exaggerated actions, poses, and facial expressions. In slapstick there is constant onstage business with objects such as paddles, pies, pails, paint, paste, or toilet paper, along with wild and silly actions such as squirming, hiding, stumbling, tripping, tumbling, falling, and flopping.

Other Kinds of Comedy Emphasize Complexity and Absurdity

Other types of modern and contemporary comedy include **ironic comedy, realistic comedy,** and **comedy of the absurd.** All of these shun the happy endings of traditional comedy. Often the blocking agents are successful, the protagonists are defeated, and the initial problem—either a realistic or an absurdist dilemma—remains unresolved. Such comedies, which began to appear in the late nineteenth century, illustrate the complexities and absurdities of modern life and the funny but futile efforts that people make when coming to grips with existence.

Many types of traditional comedies still flourish. Romantic comedies, comedies of manners, and farces can be found on innumerable stages and movie screens. They revolve about a central situation that might be quite ordinary. (Will Herman get along with a visiting business associate? Will Sue be accepted by schoolmates at her new school? Will Jim get a date for the prom?) Such situations find their ways into the huge numbers of **sitcoms (situation comedies)** that occupy considerable space on prime-time television programming.

In view of the variety of comedy, it is most important to recognize that comedy is rarely a pure and discrete form. High comedies might include crude physical humor, especially with characters who do not appear to be very likeable. Low comedies can sometimes contain wit and elegance. Satiric comedies might deal with successful young lovers. Romantic comedies can mock the vices and follies of weird and eccentric characters. Farce and slapstick can contain satire on social values and conventions.

Plays for Study

William Shakespeare . . . . A Midsummer Night's Dream, 1265
Anton Chekhov . . . . The Bear, A Joke in One Act, 1322
Paul Dooley and Winnie Holzman . . . Post-its (Notes on a Marriage), 1331
Edwin Sánchez . . . . Pops, 1335

WILLIAM SHAKESPEARE (1564–1616)

For a brief biography and portrait, see Chapter 21, page 1079.

A Midsummer Night's Dream was written early in Shakespeare's career, in 1594 or 1595.[5] It is a romantic comedy dramatizing the idea that "the course of true love never did run smooth." This central line of action, which owes much to Roman

See Chapter 21, pages 1075–79, for a description of Shakespeare's theater and career as a dramatist.

comedy, involves blocked love, a journey of circumvention and education that takes the lovers from the world of laws and problems into an imaginary world of chaos and transformations, and an ultimate victory back in the world of daylight and order.

The subject of *A Midsummer Night's Dream* is love. Shakespeare skillfully interweaves this topic in the play's four separate plots, four groups of characters, and four styles of language. Each plot explores the nature of love, the madness of irrational love, and the harmony needed for regenerative love.

In the *overplot*—the action that establishes the time for the play—the relationship is between the rulers, Theseus and Hippolyta, who have undergone a change from irrational war to rational peace. As such, they represent the dynastic continuity of the state, the order of the daylight world of Athens, and the rigor of law. These characters are the rulers, and they speak predominantly in blank verse (unrhymed iambic pentameter; see Glossary.

The two connected *middle love plots* concern the adventures of the four lovers and the actions of Oberon and Titania. The four lovers, embodying the most passionate and insistent phase of love, are from the upper class, and they speak mainly in rhymed couplets. During their long night of illusion in the woods, conjured by Oberon and his servant, Puck, their adventures drive them toward rationality, and they recognize and accept the need for faithfulness and constancy. The parallel middle plot involves the conflict between Oberon and Titania, the king and queen of the fairies, because of their mutually exclusive wishes to control a "changeling" child. Oberon is "jealous" and wants the child as an attendant, but Titania wants to keep him in her service because his mother had been Titania's attendant, friend, and confidante. With great power over Titania, Oberon humbles her, and she then reacknowledges his superiority—the proper attitude of a wife, according to Elizabethan males. Oberon and Titania, of course, are supernatural forces. Although they and the other fairies speak in both blank verse and rhymed couplets, the fairies are the only singing characters and also the only characters to speak in iambic tetrameter.

The examination of love in the subplot occurs partly in Titania's relationship with Bottom—the most hilarious instance of love's madness in the play—and partly in the play-within-a-play about Pyramus and Thisby. This play, filled with "very tragical mirth," echoes the central plot of *A Midsummer Night's Dream* and demonstrates, again, the pitfalls and unpredictability of love. It also emphasizes the happy and harmonious marriages and rapprochements that occur in both the overplot and the middle plots.

While *A Midsummer Night's Dream* is chiefly about love, it is equally concerned with the complicated relationship of perception, imagination, passion, art, and illusion. In Act 5 Theseus asserts that "The lunatic, the lover, and the poet" are alike because they all try to make reality conform with their own imaginations and desires (5.1.7–22). It would seem that chaos is therefore a normal human state, but, as Hippolyta concludes in response to Theseus, order and certainty somehow prevail, "howsoever" extraordinary and almost miraculous this result may seem (lines 23–27). The movement of the play is governed by these ideas that, along with the brilliant language and comic actions, are directly attributable to the genius of Shakespeare.

🍂 A Midsummer Night's Dream (1600; c. 1594)

Edited by Alice Griffin*

THE NAMES OF THE ACTORS

Theseus, *Duke of Athens*
Egeus, *father of Hermia*
Lysander, *beloved of Hermia*
Demetrius, *in love with Hermia, favoured by Egeus*
Philostrate, *Master of the Revels to Theseus*
Peter Quince, *a carpenter (Prologue)***
Nick Bottom, *a weaver (Pyramus)***
Francis Flute, *a bellows-mender (Thisby)***
Tom Snout, *a tinker (Wall)***
Snug, *a joiner (Lion)***
Robin Starveling, *a tailor (Moonshine)***
Hippolyta, *Queen of the Amazons, betrothed to Theseus*
Hermia, *daughter of Egeus, in love with Lysander*
Helena, *in love with Demetrius*
Oberon, *King of the Fairies*
Titania, *Queen of the Fairies*
Puck, *or Robin Goodfellow*
Peaseblossom⎫
Cobweb   ⎬ *Fairies*
Moth   ⎪
Mustardseed⎭

Other Fairies attending Oberon and Titania. Attendants on Theseus and Hippolyta.

SCENE. *Athens, and a wood nearby*

ACT 1

[Scene 1. Athens. The palace of Theseus]

Enter THESEUS, HIPPOLYTA,° [PHILOSTRATE,] *with others.*

THESEUS: Now fair Hippolyta, our nuptial hour
  Draws on apace: four happy days bring in
  Another moon: but O, methinks how slow
  This old moon wanes! she lingers° my desires,
  Like to a stepdame or a dowager,°   5
  Long withering out° a young man's revenue.
HIPPOLYTA: Four days will quickly steep themselves in night:
  Four nights will quickly dream away the time:

Professor Griffin's text for *A Midsummer Night's Dream* is the First Quarto (edition) published in 1600, with modifications based on the Quarto edition of 1619 and the First Folio, published in 1623. Stage directions in those editions are printed here without brackets; added stage directions are printed within brackets. We have edited Griffin's notes for this text. **Characters who play in the interlude.
°S.D.: *Theseus, Hippolyta:* In Greek legend, Theseus captured the Amazon Queen Hippolyta and brought her to Athens where they were married. °4 *lingers:* delays the fulfillment of. °5 *dowager:* a widow supported by her dead husband's heirs. °6 *withering out:* (1) depleting (2) growing withered.

And then the moon, like to a silver bow
10   New-bent in heaven, shall behold the night
Of our solemnities.
THESEUS: Go Philostrate,
Stir up the Athenian youth to merriments,
Awake the pert° and nimble spirit of mirth,
15   The pale companion° is not for our pomp.   [*Exit* PHILOSTRATE.]
Hippolyta, I wooed thee with my sword,
And won thy love doing thee injuries;
But I will wed thee in another key,
With pomp, with triumph,° and with revelling.

Enter EGEUS *and his daughter* HERMIA, LYSANDER *and* DEMETRIUS.

20   **EGEUS:** Happy be Theseus, our renownèd duke.
THESEUS: Thanks good Egeus:° what's the news with thee?
EGEUS: Full of vexation come I, with complaint
Against my child, my daughter Hermia.
Stand forth Demetrius. My noble lord,
25   This man hath my consent to marry her.
Stand forth Lysander. And my gracious duke,
This man hath bewitched the bosom of my child.
Thou, thou Lysander, thou hast given her rhymes,
And interchanged love tokens with my child:
30   Thou hast by moonlight at her window sung,
With feigning voice, verses of feigning° love,
And stol'n the impression of her fantasy°
With bracelets of thy hair, rings, gauds,° conceits,°
Knacks,° trifles, nosegays, sweetmeats—messengers
35   Of strong prevailment in unhardened youth.
With cunning hast thou filched my daughter's heart,
Turned her obedience, which is due to me,
To stubborn harshness. And my gracious duke,
Be it so° she will not here before your grace
40   Consent to marry with Demetrius,
I beg the ancient privilege of Athens:
As she is mine, I may dispose of her:
Which shall be, either to this gentleman,
Or to her death, according to our law
45   Immediately° provided in that case.
THESEUS: What say you, Hermia? Be advised, fair maid.
To you your father should be as a god:
One that composed your beauties: yea and one
To whom you are but as a form in wax
50   By him imprinted, and within his power

°13 *pert:* lively. °15 *companion:* fellow (contemptuous). °19 *triumph:* public festival. °21 *Egeus:* trisyllabi.
°31 *feigning:* (1) deceptive (2) desirous ("faining"). °32 *stol'n . . . fantasy:* stealthily imprinted your image upon
her fancy. °33 *gauds:* trinkets. °*conceits:* either (a) love poetry, or (b) love tokens. °34 *Knacks:* knick-knacks.
°39 *Be it so:* if it be that. °45 *Immediately:* precisely.

    To leave the figure, or disfigure it:
    Demetrius is a worthy gentleman.
HERMIA: So is Lysander.
THESEUS: In himself he is:
    But in this kind, wanting your father's voice,°
    The other must be held the worthier.   55
HERMIA: I would my father looked but with my eyes.
THESEUS: Rather your eyes must with his judgment look.
HERMIA: I do entreat your grace to pardon me.
    I know not by what power I am made bold,
    Nor how it may concern my modesty,   60
    In such a presence, here to plead my thoughts:
    But I beseech your grace that I may know
    The worst that may befall me in this case,
    If I refuse to wed Demetrius.
THESEUS: Either to die the death, or to abjure   65
    For ever the society of men.
    Therefore fair Hermia, question your desires,
    Know of your youth,° examine well your blood,°
    Whether, if you yield not to your father's choice,
    You can endure the livery° of a nun,   70
    For aye° to be in shady cloister mewed,°
    To live a barren sister all your life,
    Chanting faint hymns to the cold fruitless moon.°
    Thrice blessèd they that master so their blood,
    To undergo such maiden pilgrimage: 75
    But earthlier happy° is the rose distilled,°
    Than that which, withering on the virgin thorn,
    Grows, lives, and dies, in single blessedness.
HERMIA: So will I grow, so live, so die my lord,
    Ere I will yield my virgin patent° up   80
    Unto his lordship, whose unwishèd yoke
    My soul consents not to give sovereignty.
THESEUS: Take time to pause, and by the next moon,
    The sealing day betwixt my love and me,
    For everlasting bond of fellowship,   85
    Upon that day either prepare to die
    For disobedience to your father's will,
    Or else to wed Demetrius, as he would,
    Or on Diana's altar to protest°
    For aye, austerity and single life.   90
DEMETRIUS: Relent, sweet Hermia, and Lysander, yield
    Thy crazèd° title to my certain right.
LYSANDER: You have her father's love, Demetrius:
    Let me have Hermia's: do you marry him.

°54 *in . . . voice:* in this respect, lacking your father's approval. °68 *Know . . . youth:* ask yourself as a young person. °*blood:* passions. °70 *livery:* habit. °71 *aye:* ever. °*mewed:* shut up. °73 *moon:* the moon goddess Diana represented unmarried chastity. °76 *earthlier happy:* more happy on earth. °*distilled:* i.e., into perfume (thus its essence is passed on, as to a child). °80 *patent:* privilege. °89 *protest:* vow. °92 *crazèd:* flawed.

95 **EGEUS:** Scornful Lysander, true, he hath my love:
  And what is mine, my love shall render him.
  And she is mine, and all my right of her
  I do estate° unto Demetrius.
 LYSANDER: I am, my lord, as well derived° as he,
100   As well possessed;° my love is more than his:
  My fortunes every way as fairly ranked
  (If not with vantage) as° Demetrius':
  And, which is more than all these boasts can be,
  I am beloved of beauteous Hermia.
105   Why should not I then prosecute my right?
  Demetrius, I'll avouch it to his head,°
  Made love to Nedar's daughter, Helena,
  And won her soul: and she, sweet lady, dotes,
  Devoutly dotes, dotes in idolatry,
110   Upon this spotted° and inconstant man.
 THESEUS: I must confess that I have heard so much,
  And with Demetrius thought to have spoke thereof:
  But being over-full of self-affairs,
  My mind did lose it. But Demetrius come,
115   And come Egeus, you shall go with me:
  I have some private schooling for you both.
  For you fair Hermia, look you arm yourself,
  To fit your fancies to your father's will;
  Or else the law of Athens yields you up
120   (Which by no means we may extenuate)
  To death or to a vow of single life.
  Come my Hippolyta, what cheer my love?
  Demetrius and Egeus, go along:
  I must employ you in some business
125   Against° our nuptial, and confer with you
  Of something nearly° that concerns yourselves.
 EGEUS: With duty and desire we follow you.

       Exeunt.° Manent° LYSANDER and HERMIA.

 LYSANDER: How now my love? Why is your cheek so pale?
  How chance the roses there do fade so fast?
130 **HERMIA:** Belike° for want of rain, which I could well
  Beteem° them from the tempest of my eyes.
 LYSANDER: Ay me, for aught that I could ever read,
  Could ever hear by tale or history,
  The course of true love never did run smooth;
135   But either it was different in blood—
 HERMIA: O cross! too high° to be enthralled to low.°
 LYSANDER: Or else misgraffed° in respect of years—

°98 *estate:* transfer. °99 *well derived:* well born. °100 *well possessed:* wealthy. °102 *with vantage, as:* better, than. °106 *avouch . . . head:* prove it to his face. °110 *spotted:* stained. °125 *Against:* in preparation for. °126 *nearly:* closely. °127 S.D.: *Exeunt:* they exit. °*Manent:* they remain. °130 *Belike:* likely. °131 *Beteem:* (1) pour out on (2) allow. °136 *high:* highborn. °*enthralled to low:* made a slave to one of low birth. °137 *misgraffed:* badly joined.

HERMIA: O spite! too old to be engaged to young.
LYSANDER: Or else it stood upon the choice of friends—
HERMIA: O hell! to choose love by another's eyes.   140
LYSANDER: Or if there were a sympathy in choice,
    War, death, or sickness did lay siege to it;
    Making it momentany° as a sound,
    Swift as a shadow, short as any dream,
    Brief as the lightning in the collied° night,   145
    That, in a spleen,° unfolds both heaven and earth;
    And ere a man hath power to say "Behold,"
    The jaws of darkness do devour it up:
    So quick bright things come to confusion.
HERMIA: If then true lovers have been ever crossed,°   150
    It stands as an edict in destiny:
    Then let us teach our trial patience,°
    Because it is a customary cross,
    As due to love as thoughts and dreams and sighs,
    Wishes and tears; poor Fancy's° followers.   155
LYSANDER: A good persuasion: therefore hear me, Hermia:
    I have a widow aunt, a dowager,
    Of great revenue, and she hath no child:
    From Athens is her house remote seven leagues,
    And she respects° me as her only son: 160
    There gentle Hermia, may I marry thee,
    And to that place the sharp Athenian law
    Cannot pursue us. If thou lov'st me then,
    Steal forth thy father's house tomorrow night:
    And in the wood, a league without the town,   165
    Where I did meet thee once with Helena
    To do observance to a morn of May,°
    There will I stay° for thee.
HERMIA: My good Lysander,
    I swear to thee, by Cupid's strongest bow,
    By his best arrow, with the golden head,°   170
    By the simplicity of Venus' doves,
    By that which knitteth souls and prospers loves,
    And by that fire which burned the Carthage queen,
    When the false Troyan° under sail was seen,
    By all the vows that ever men have broke,   175
    (In number more than ever women spoke)
    In that same place thou hast appointed me,
    Tomorrow truly will I meet with thee.
LYSANDER: Keep promise love: look, here comes Helena.

Enter HELENA.

°143 *momentany:* momentary. °145 *collied:* black as coal. °146 *in a spleen:* impulsively, in a sudden outburst. °150 *ever crossed:* evermore thwarted. °152 *teach . . . patience:* teach ourselves to be patient. °155 *Fancy:* love (sometimes infatuation). °160 *respects:* regards. °167 *do . . . May:* celebrate May Day. °168 *stay:* wait. °170 *golden head:* The arrow with the gold head causes love. °173–74 *Carthage queen . . . false Troyan:* Dido, who burned herself to death on a funeral pyre when Trojan Aeneas deserted her.

180   HERMIA: God speed fair Helena: whither away?
      HELENA: Call you me fair? That fair again unsay.
          Demetrius loves your fair:° O happy fair!
          Your eyes are lodestars,° and your tongue's sweet air°
          More tuneable than lark to shepherd's ear,
185   When wheat is green, when hawthorn buds appear.
          Sickness is catching: O were favour° so,
          Yours would I catch, fair Hermia, ere I go,
          My ear should catch your voice,° my eye your eye,°
          My tongue should catch your tongue's sweet melody.
190   Were the world mine, Demetrius being bated,°
          The rest I'd give to be to you translated.°
          O teach me how you look, and with what art
          You sway the motion of Demetrius' heart.
      HERMIA: I frown upon him; yet he loves me still.
195   HELENA: O that your frowns would teach my smiles such skill.
      HERMIA: I give him curses; yet he gives me love.
      HELENA: O that my prayers could such affection move.
      HERMIA: The more I hate, the more he follows me.
      HELENA: The more I love, the more he hateth me.
200   HERMIA: His folly, Helena, is no fault of mine.
      HELENA: None but your beauty; would that fault were mine.
      HERMIA: Take comfort: he no more shall see my face:
          Lysander and myself will fly this place.
          Before the time I did Lysander see,
205   Seemed Athens as a paradise to me:
          O then, what graces in my love do dwell,
          That he hath turned a heaven unto a hell!
      LYSANDER: Helen, to you our minds we will unfold:
          Tomorrow night, when Phoebe° doth behold
210   Her silver visage in the wat'ry glass,°
          Decking with liquid pearl the bladed grass
          (A time that lovers' flights doth still° conceal)
          Through Athens gates have we devised to steal.
      HERMIA: And in the wood, where often you and I
215   Upon faint primrose beds were wont to lie,
          Emptying our bosoms of their counsel° sweet,
          There my Lysander and myself shall meet,
          And thence from Athens turn away our eyes,
          To see new friends and stranger companies.°
220   Farewell, sweet playfellow: pray thou for us:
          And good luck grant thee thy Demetrius.
          Keep word Lysander: we must starve our sight
          From lovers' food,° till morrow deep midnight.

°182 *your fair:* i.e., beauty. °183 *lodestars:* guiding stars. °*air:* music. °186 *favour:* appearance. °188 *My ear . . . voice:* my ear should catch the tone of your voice. °*my eye your eye:* my eye should catch the way you glance. °190 *bated:* subtracted, excepted. °191 *translated:* transformed. °209 *Phoebe:* Diana, the moon. °210 *wat'ry glass:* mirror of the water. °212 *still:* always. °216 *counsel:* secrets. °219 *stranger companies:* the companionship of strangers. °223 *lovers' food:* the sight of the loved one.

LYSANDER: I will my Hermia.   *Exit HERMIA.*
                Helena adieu:
    As you on him, Demetrius dote on you.°   *Exit LYSANDER.*   225
HELENA: How happy some, o'er other some, can be!
    Through Athens I am thought as fair as she.
    But what of that? Demetrius thinks not so:
    He will not know what all but he do know.
    And as he errs, doting on Hermia's eyes,   230
    So I, admiring of his qualities.
    Things base and vile, holding no quantity.°
    Love can transpose to form and dignity.
    Love looks not with the eyes, but with the mind:
    And therefore is winged Cupid painted blind.   235
    Nor hath Love's mind of any judgment taste:
    Wings, and no eyes, figure° unheedy haste.
    And therefore is Love said to be a child:
    Because in choice he is so oft beguiled.
    As waggish boys in game themselves forswear: 240
    So the boy Love is perjured everywhere.
    For ere Demetrius looked on Hermia's eyne,°
    He hailed down oaths that he was only mine.
    And when this hail some heat from Hermia felt,
    So he dissolved, and show'rs of oaths did melt.   245
    I will go tell him of fair Hermia's flight:
    Then to the wood will he tomorrow night
    Pursue her: and for this intelligence,°
    If I have thanks, it is a dear expense.°
    But herein mean I to enrich my pain,   250
    To have his sight° thither and back again.   *Exit.*

[Scene 2. Quince's house]

*Enter QUINCE the Carpenter; and SNUG the Joiner; and BOTTOM the Weaver; and FLUTE the Bellows-
mender; and SNOUT the Tinker; and STARVELING the Tailor.°*

QUINCE: Is all our company here?
BOTTOM: You were the best to call them generally,° man by man,
    according to the scrip.
QUINCE: Here is the scroll of every man's name which is thought
    fit, through all Athens, to play in our interlude° before   5
    the duke and the duchess, on his wedding-day at night.
BOTTOM: First good Peter Quince, say what the play treats on,
    then read the names of the actors: and so grow to a point.

°225 *As . . . you:* As you dote on Demetrius, so may Demetrius also dote on you. °232 *holding no quantity:* out of
proportion. °237 *figure:* symbolize. °242 *eyne:* eyes. °248 *intelligence:* information. °249 *dear expense:* costly outlay
(on Demetrius's part). °250–51 *But . . . sight:* but I will be rewarded just by the sight of him. S.D.: the low
characters' names describe their work: *Quince:* quoins, wooden wedges used in building. *Snug:* fitting snugly, suiting a joiner of furniture. *Bottom:* bobbin or core on which yarn is wound. *Flute:* mender of fluted church organs
and bellows. *Snout:* spout (of the kettles he mends). °*Starveling:* tailors being traditionally thin. °2 *generally:*
Bottom often uses the wrong word; here he means the opposite: "severally, one by one." °5 *interlude:* short play.

QUINCE: Marry,° our play is "The most lamentable comedy, and
10   most cruel death of Pyramus and Thisby."
BOTTOM: A very good piece of work I assure you, and a merry. Now
    good Peter Quince, call forth your actors by the scroll.
    Masters, spread yourselves.
QUINCE: Answer as I call you. Nick Bottom the weaver?
15 **BOTTOM:** Ready: name what part I am for, and proceed.
QUINCE: You, Nick Bottom, are set down for Pyramus.
BOTTOM: What is Pyramus? A lover, or a tyrant?
QUINCE: A lover that kills himself, most gallant, for love.
BOTTOM: That will ask some tears in the true performing of it. If I
20   do it, let the audience look to their eyes: I will move
    storms: I will condole° in some measure. To the rest—
    yet my chief humour° is for a tyrant. I could play Ercles°
    rarely, or a part to tear a cat in, to make all split.°
        The raging rocks
25   And shivering shocks,
        Shall break the locks
          Of prison gates,
        And Phibbus' car°
        Shall shine from far,
30   And make and mar
          The foolish Fates.
    This was lofty. Now name the rest of the players. This is
    Ercles' vein, a tyrant's vein: a lover is more condoling.
QUINCE: Francis Flute, the bellows-mender?
35 **FLUTE:** Here Peter Quince.
QUINCE: Flute, you must take Thisby on you.
FLUTE: What is Thisby? A wand'ring knight?
QUINCE: It is the lady that Pyramus must love.
FLUTE: Nay faith, let not me play a woman: I have a beard
40   coming.
QUINCE: That's all one:° you shall play it in a mask, and you may
    speak as small° as you will.
BOTTOM: And° I may hide my face, let me play Thisby too: I'll speak
    in a monstrous little voice; "Thisne, Thisne," "Ah
45   Pyramus, my lover dear, thy Thisby dear, and lady
    dear."
QUINCE: No, no, you must play Pyramus: and Flute, you Thisby.
BOTTOM: Well, proceed.
QUINCE: Robin Starveling, the tailor?
50 **STARVELING:** Here Peter Quince.
QUINCE: Robin Starveling, you must play Thisby's mother. Tom
    Snout, the tinker?
SNOUT: Here Peter Quince.
QUINCE: You, Pyramus' father; myself, Thisby's father; Snug the
55   joiner, you the lion's part: and I hope here is a play
    fitted.°

°9 *Marry:* indeed (mild oath, corruption of "by the Virgin Mary"). °21 *condole:* lament. °22 *humour:* inclination.
°*Ercles:* Hercules (typified by ranting). °23 *tear . . . split:* terms for ranting and raving on the stage. °28 *Phibbus'*
car: Phoebus Apollo's chariot. °41 *That's all one:* never mind. °42 *small:* softly. °43 *And:* if. °56 *fitted:* cast.

Snug: Have you the lion's part written? Pray you, if it be, give
it me: for I am slow of study.

Quince: You may do it extempore: for it is nothing but roaring.

Bottom: Let me play the lion too. I will roar, that° I will do any   60
man's heart good to hear me. I will roar, that I will make
the duke say "Let him roar again: let him roar again."

Quince: And you should do it too terribly, you would fright the
duchess and the ladies, that they would shriek: and
that were enough to hang us all.   65

All: That would hang us, every mother's son.

Bottom: I grant you, friends, if you should fright the ladies out of
their wits, they would have no more discretion but to
hang us: but I will aggravate° my voice so, that I will roar
you as gently as any sucking dove: I will roar you and   70
'twere° any nightingale.

Quince: You can play no part but Pyramus: for Pyramus is a
sweet-faced man; a proper° man as one shall see in a
summer's day; a most lovely gentleman-like man: therefore
you must needs play Pyramus.   75

Bottom: Well: I will undertake it. What beard were I best to play
it in?

Quince: Why, what you will.

Bottom: I will discharge it in either your straw-colour beard, your
orange-tawny beard, your purple-in-grain° beard, or your   80
French-crown-colour° beard, your perfit yellow.

Quince: Some of your French crowns° have no hair at all; and
then you will play barefaced. But masters here are your
parts, and I am to entreat you, request you, and desire
you, to con° them by tomorrow night: and meet me in the   85
palace wood, a mile without the town, by moonlight;
there will we rehearse: for if we meet in the city, we
shall be dogged with company, and our devices° known.
In the meantime, I will draw a bill of properties,° such
as our play wants. I pray you fail me not.   90

Bottom: We will meet, and there we may rehearse most obscenely°
and courageously. Take pain, be perfit: adieu.

Quince: At the duke's oak we meet.

Bottom: Enough: hold, or cut bow-strings.°   *Exeunt.*

ACT 2

[Scene 1. A wood near Athens]

Enter a Fairy *at one door, and* Robin Goodfellow *[*Puck*] at another.*

Puck: How now spirit, whither wander you?

°60 *that:* so that. °69 *aggravate:* he means "moderate." °70–71 *and 'twere:* as if it were. °73 *proper:* handsome.
°80 *purple-in-grain:* dyed permanently purple. °81 *French-crown-colour:* golden, like French crowns (gold coins).
°82 *French crowns:* bald heads believed to be caused by syphilis, the "French" disease. °85 *con:* learn by heart.
°88 *devices:* plans. °89 *bill of properties:* list of stage props. °91 *obscenely:* he may mean "fittingly" or "obscurely."
°94 *hold, or cut bow-strings:* meaning uncertain, but equivalent to "fish, or cut bait."

FAIRY: Over hill, over dale,
    Thorough bush, thorough brier,
    Over park, over pale,°
5   Thorough flood, thorough fire:
    I do wander everywhere,
    Swifter than the moon's sphere:
    And I serve the Fairy Queen,
    To dew° her orbs° upon the green.
10   The cowslips° tall her pensioners° be,
    In their gold coats, spots you see:
    Those be rubies, fairy favours.°
    In those freckles live their savours.°
    I must go seek some dewdrops here,
15   And hang a pearl in every cowslip's ear.
    Farewell thou lob° of spirits: I'll be gone,
    Our queen and all her elves come here anon.
PUCK: The king doth keep his revels here tonight.
    Take heed the queen come not within his sight.
20   For Oberon is passing fell° and wrath,
    Because that she, as her attendant, hath
    A lovely boy, stol'n from an Indian king:
    She never had so sweet a changeling.°
    And jealous Oberon would have the child
25   Knight of his train, to trace° the forests wild.
    But she, perforce,° withholds the lovèd boy,
    Crowns him with flowers, and makes him all her joy.
    And now, they never meet in grove or green,
    By fountain clear, or spangled starlight sheen,
30   But they do square,° that all their elves for fear
    Creep into acorn cups, and hide them there.
FAIRY: Either I mistake your shape and making quite,
    Or else you are that shrewd and knavish sprite
    Called Robin Goodfellow. Are not you he
35   That frights the maidens of the villagery,
    Skim milk,° and sometimes labour in the quern,°
    And bootless° make the breathless housewife churn,
    And sometime make the drink to bear no barm,°
    Mislead night-wanderers, laughing at their harm?
40   Those that Hobgoblin call you, and sweet Puck,
    You do their work, and they shall have good luck.
    Are not you he?
PUCK: Thou speakest aright;
    I am that merry wanderer of the night.
    I jest to Oberon, and make him smile,
45   When I a fat and bean-fed horse beguile,

°4 *pale*: enclosure. °9 *dew*: bedew. °*orbs*: fairy rings (circles of high grass). °10 *cowslips*: primroses. °*pensioners*: royal bodyguards. °12 *favours*: gifts. °13 *savours*: perfumes. °16 *lob*: lout, lubber. °20 *passing fell*: surpassingly fierce. °23 *changeling*: creature exchanged by fairies for a stolen baby (among the fairies, the stolen child). °25 *trace*: traverse. °26 *perforce*: by force. °30 *square*: quarrel. °36 *Skim milk*: steals the cream off the milk. °*quern*: hand-mill for grinding grain. °37 *bootless*: without result. °38 *barm*: foamy head (therefore the drink was flat).

Neighing in likeness of a filly foal;
And sometime lurk I in a gossip's° bowl,
In very likeness of a roasted crab,°
And when she drinks, against her lips I bob,
And on her withered dewlap° pour the ale.   50
The wisest aunt, telling the saddest tale,
Sometime for three-foot stool mistaketh me:
Then slip I from her bum, down topples she,
And "tailor"° cries, and falls into a cough;
And then the whole quire° hold their hips and laugh,   55
And waxen° in their mirth, and neeze,° and swear
A merrier hour was never wasted° there.
But room° fairy: here comes Oberon.
FAIRY: And here, my mistress. Would that he were gone.

Enter [OBERON] the King of Fairies, at one door with his TRAIN, and the QUEEN [TITANIA], at another, with hers.

OBERON: Ill met by moonlight, proud Titania.   60
QUEEN: What, jealous Oberon? Fairy, skip hence.
I have forsworn his bed and company.
OBERON: Tarry, rash wanton.° Am not I thy lord?
QUEEN: Then I must be thy lady; but I know
When thou hast stol'n away from fairyland,   65
And in the shape of Corin° sat all day,
Playing on pipes of corn,° and versing love
To amorous Phillida.° Why art thou here
Come from the farthest steep of India?
But that, forsooth, the bouncing Amazon,°   70
Your buskined° mistress and your warrior love,
To Theseus must be wedded; and you come,
To give their bed joy and prosperity.
OBERON: How canst thou thus, for shame, Titania,
Glance at my credit with° Hippolyta,   75
Knowing I know thy love to Theseus?
Didst thou not lead him through the glimmering night,
From Perigenia, whom he ravishèd?
And make him with fair Aegles break his faith,
With Ariadne, and Antiopa?°   80
QUEEN: These are the forgeries of jealousy:
And never, since the middle summer's spring,°
Met we on hill, in dale, forest, or mead,
By pavèd° fountain, or by rushy brook,

°47 *gossip's:* old woman's. °48 *crab:* crabapple (often put into ale). °50 *dewlap:* loose skin hanging about the throat. °54 *"tailor":* variously explained: perhaps the squatting position of the tailor, or "tailard"—one with a tail. °55 *quire:* choir, group. °56 *waxen:* increase. °*neeze:* sneeze. °57 *wasted:* spent. °58 *room:* make room. °63 *Tarry, rash wanton:* wait, headstrong one. °66–68 *Corin,* °*Phillida:* traditional names in pastoral literature for a shepherd and his loved one, respectively. °67 *corn:* wheat straws. °70 *Amazon:* Hippolyta. °71 *buskined:* wearing boots. °75 *Glance . . . credit with:* hint at my favors from. °78–80 *Perigenia . . . Antiopa:* women that Theseus supposedly loved and deserted. °82 *middle . . . spring:* beginning of midsummer. °84 *pavèd:* with a pebbly bottom.

85   Or in the beachèd margent° of the sea,
        To dance our ringlets to the whistling wind,
        But with thy brawls° thou hast disturbed our sport.
        Therefore° the winds, piping to us in vain,
        As in revenge, have sucked up from the sea
90   Contagious° fogs: which falling in the land,
        Hath every pelting° river made so proud,
        That they have overborne their continents.°
        The ox hath therefore stretched his yoke in vain,
        The ploughman lost his sweat, and the green corn°
95   Hath rotted, ere his youth attained a beard:°
        The fold° stands empty in the drownèd field,
        And crows are fatted with the murrion° flock.
        The nine men's morris° is filled up with mud;
100   And the quaint mazes° in the wanton green,°
        For lack of tread, are undistinguishable.
        The human mortals want° their winter here,
        No night is now with hymn or carol blest;
        Therefore the moon, the governess of floods,
        Pale in her anger, washes all the air,
105   That rheumatic diseases do abound.
        And thorough this distemperature,° we see
        The seasons alter: hoary-headed frosts
        Fall in the fresh lap of the crimson rose,
        And on old Hiems'° thin and icy crown,
110   An odorous chaplet° of sweet summer buds
        Is, as in mockery, set. The spring, the summer,
        The childing° autumn, angry winter change
        Their wonted liveries:° and the mazèd° world,
        By their increase, now knows not which is which:
115   And this same progeny of evils comes
        From our debate, from our dissension:
        We are their parents and original.
        OBERON: Do you amend it then: it lies in you.
        Why should Titania cross her Oberon?
120   I do but beg a little changeling boy,
        To be my henchman.°
        QUEEN: Set your heart at rest.
        The fairy land buys not the child of me.
        His mother was a vot'ress° of my order:
        And in the spicèd Indian air, by night,
125   Full often hath she gossiped by my side.

°85 *margent:* margin, shore. °87 *brawls:* A brawl was a group dance—*branle* in French—obviously accompanied by noisy shouting and clapping. °88–117 *Therefore . . . original:* the disturbance in nature reflects the discord between Oberon and Titania. °90 *Contagious:* spreading pestilence. °91 *pelting:* paltry. °92 *overborne their continents:* overflown the banks that contain them. °94 *corn:* grain. °95 *beard:* the tassels on ripened grain. °96 *fold:* enclosure for livestock. °97 *murrion:* dead from murrain, a cattle disease. °98 *nine men's morris:* game played on squares cut in the grass on which stones or disks are moved. °99 *quaint mazes:* intricate paths. °*wanton green:* luxuriant grass. °101 *want:* lack. °106 *distemperature:* upset in nature. °109 *Hiems:* god of winter. °110 *odorous chaplet:* sweet-smelling wreath. °112 *childing:* fruitful. °113 *wonted liveries:* accustomed dress. °*mazèd:* amazed. °121 *henchman:* attendant. °123 *vot'ress:* vowed and devoted follower.

And sat with me on Neptune's yellow sands,
Marking th' embarkèd traders° on the flood:
When we have laughed to see the sails conceive,
And grow big-bellied with the wanton° wind:
Which she, with pretty and with swimming gait,   130
Following (her womb then rich with my young squire)
Would imitate, and sail upon the land,
To fetch me trifles, and return again,
As from a voyage, rich with merchandise.
But she, being mortal, of that boy did die,   135
And for her sake, do I rear up her boy:
And for her sake, I will not part with him.
OBERON: How long within this wood intend you stay?
QUEEN: Perchance till after Theseus' wedding day.
If you will patiently dance in our round,°   140
And see our moonlight revels, go with us:
If not, shun me, and I will spare° your haunts.
OBERON: Give me that boy, and I will go with thee.
QUEEN: Not for thy fairy kingdom. Fairies away
We shall chide downright, if I longer stay.   145

Exeunt [TITANIA and her TRAIN.]

OBERON: Well, go thy way. Thou shalt not from this grove,
Till I torment thee for this injury.
My gentle Puck come hither: thou remem̄b'rest,
Since° once I sat upon a promontory,
And heard a mermaid, on a dolphin's back,   150
Uttering such dulcet and harmonious breath,
That the rude° sea grew civil° at her song,
And certain stars shot madly from their spheres,
To hear the sea-maid's music.
PUCK: I remember.
OBERON: That very time, I saw (but thou couldst not)   155
Flying between the cold moon and the earth,
Cupid, all armed: a certain aim he took
At a fair Vestal,° thronèd by the west,
And loosed his love-shaft smartly from his bow,
As it should pierce a hundred thousand hearts: 160
But I might see young Cupid's fiery shaft
Quenched in the chaste beams of the wat'ry moon:
And the imperial vot'ress° passèd on,
In maiden meditation, fancy-free.°
Yet marked I where the bolt° of Cupid fell.   165
It fell upon a little western flower;
Before, milk-white; now purple with love's wound,

°127 *traders:* merchant ships. °129 *wanton:* sportive. °140 *round:* round dance. °142 *spare:* shun. °149 *Since:* when. °152 *rude:* rough. °*civil:* calm. °158 *Vestal:* virgin, probable reference to Queen Elizabeth. °163 *imperial vot'ress:* royal devotee (Queen Elizabeth) of Diana. °164 *fancy-free:* free from love. °165 *bolt:* arrow.

And maidens call it love-in-idleness.°
Fetch me that flow'r: the herb I showed thee once.
170   The juice of it, on sleeping eyelids laid,
Will make or man or woman madly dote
Upon the next live creature that it sees.
Fetch me this herb, and be thou here again
Ere the leviathan° can swim a league.

175   **PUCK:** I'll put a girdle round about the earth,
In forty minutes.   [*Exit.*]

OBERON: Having once this juice,
I'll watch Titania when she is asleep,
And drop the liquor of it in her eyes:
180   The next thing then she waking looks upon,
(Be it on lion, bear, or wolf, or bull,
On meddling monkey, or on busy° ape)
She shall pursue it, with the soul of love.
And ere I take this charm from off her sight
185   (As I can take it with another herb)
I'll make her render up her page to me.
But who comes here? I am invisible,
And I will overhear their conference.

Enter DEMETRIUS, HELENA *following him.*

DEMETRIUS: I love thee not: therefore pursue me not.
190   Where is Lysander and fair Hermia?
The one I'll slay: the other slayeth me.
Thou told'st me they were stol'n unto this wood:
And here am I, and wood° within this wood:
Because I cannot meet my Hermia.
195   Hence, get thee gone, and follow me no more.

HELENA: You draw me, you hard-hearted adamant:°
But yet you draw not iron, for my heart
Is true as steel. Leave you your power to draw,
And I shall have no power to follow you.

200   **DEMETRIUS:** Do I entice you? Do I speak you fair?°
Or rather do I not in plainest truth
Tell you I do not, nor I cannot love you?

HELENA: And even for that, do I love you the more:
I am your spaniel: and Demetrius,
205   The more you beat me, I will fawn on you.
Use me but as your spaniel: spurn me, strike me,
Neglect me, lose me: only give me leave,
Unworthy as I am, to follow you.
What worser place can I beg in your love
210   (And yet a place of high respect with me)
Than to be usèd as you use your dog.

°168 *love-in-idleness:* pansy. °174 *leviathan:* whale. °182 *busy:* mischievous. °193 *wood:* crazy. °196 *adamant:* (1) magnet (2) impenetrably hard lodestone. °200 *speak you fair:* speak to you in a kindly way.

DEMETRIUS: Tempt not too much the hatred of my spirit,
For I am sick, when I do look on thee.
HELENA: And I am sick, when I look not on you.
DEMETRIUS: You do impeach° your modesty too much,   215
To leave the city and commit yourself
Into the hands of one that loves you not,
To trust the opportunity of night,
And the ill counsel of a desert° place,
With the rich worth of your virginity.   220
HELENA: Your virtue is my privilege:° For that°
It is not night, when I do see your face,
Therefore I think I am not in the night.
Nor doth this wood lack worlds of company,
For you, in my respect,° are all the world.   225
Then how can it be said I am alone,
When all the world is here to look on me?
DEMETRIUS: I'll run from thee and hide me in the brakes,°
And leave thee to the mercy of wild beasts.
HELENA: The wildest hath not such a heart as you.   230
Run when you will: the story shall be changed;
Apollo flies, and Daphne° holds the chase:
The dove pursues the griffin:° the mild hind°
Makes speed to catch the tiger. Bootless° speed,
When cowardice pursues, and valour flies.   235
DEMETRIUS: I will not stay° thy questions. Let me go:
Or if thou follow me, do not believe
But I shall do thee mischief in the wood.   [*Exit* DEMETRIUS.]
HELENA: Ay, in the temple, in the town, the field,
You do me mischief. Fie Demetrius,   240
Your wrongs do set a scandal on my sex:
We cannot fight for love, as men may do:
We should be wooed, and were not made to woo.
I'll follow thee and make a heaven of hell,
To die upon the hand I love so well.   *Exit.*   245
OBERON: Fare thee well nymph. Ere he do leave this grove,
Thou shalt fly him, and he shall seek thy love.

Enter PUCK.

Hast thou the flower there? Welcome wanderer.
PUCK: Ay, there it is.
OBERON: I pray thee give it me.
I know a bank where the wild thyme blows,   250
Where oxlips and the nodding violet grows,
Quite over-canopied with luscious woodbine,
With sweet musk-roses, and with eglantine:

°215 *impeach:* discredit. °219 *desert:* deserted. °221 *Your . . . privilege:* your attraction is my excuse (for coming).
°*for that:* because. °225 *respect:* regard. °228 *brakes:* thickets. °232 *Apollo . . . Daphne:* in Ovid, Apollo pursues
Daphne, who turns into a laurel tree. °233 *griffin:* legendary beast with the head of an eagle and the body of a lion.
°*hind:* doe. °234 *Bootless:* useless. °236 *stay:* wait for.

There sleeps Titania, sometime of the night,
255   Lulled in these flowers, with dances and delight:
And there the snake throws° her enamelled skin,
Weed° wide enough to wrap a fairy in.
And with the juice of this, I'll streak her eyes,
And make her full of hateful fantasies.
260   Take thou some of it, and seek through this grove:
A sweet Athenian lady is in love
With a disdainful youth: anoint his eyes.
But do it when the next thing he espies
May be the lady. Thou shalt know the man
265   By the Athenian garments he hath on.
Effect it with some care, that he may prove
More fond° on her, than she upon her love:
And look thou meet me ere the first cock crow.
PUCK: Fear not my lord: your servant shall do so.   *Exeunt.*

[Scene 2. Another part of the wood]

Enter TITANIA *Queen of Fairies with her train.*

QUEEN: Come, now a roundel° and a fairy song:
Then, for the third part of a minute, hence—
Some to kill cankers in the musk-rose buds,
Some war with reremice° for their leathren wings,
5   To make my small elves coats, and some keep back
The clamorous owl, that nightly hoots and wonders
At our quaint° spirits. Sing me now asleep:
Then to your offices,° and let me rest.

Fairies sing.

FIRST FAIRY: You spotted snakes with double° tongue,
10   Thorny hedgehogs be not seen,
Newts and blind-worms,° do no wrong,
Come not near our Fairy Queen.
CHORUS [*dancing.*]: Philomele,° with melody,
Sing in our sweet lullaby,
15   Lulla, lulla, lullaby, lulla, lulla, lullaby.
Never harm,
Nor spell, nor charm,
Come our lovely lady nigh.
So good night, with lullaby.
20   FIRST FAIRY: Weaving spiders come not here:
Hence you long-legged spinners, hence:
Beetles black approach not near:
Worm nor snail do no offence.
CHORUS [*dancing.*]: Philomele, with melody, &c.   *She sleeps.*

°256 *throws:* casts off. °257 *weed:* garment. °267 *fond:* doting, madly in love. °1 *roundel:* dance in a ring.
°4 *reremice:* bats. °7 *quaint:* dainty. °8 *offices:* duties. °9 *double:* forked. °11 *blind-worms:* legless lizards. °13 *Philomele:*
the nightingale.

SECOND FAIRY: Hence away: now all is well: 25
   One aloof stand sentinel.   [*Exeunt fairies.*]

Enter OBERON [and applies the flower juice to TITANIA's eyelids.]

OBERON: What thou seest, when thou dost wake,
   Do it for thy true love take:
   Love and languish for his sake.
   Be it ounce,° or cat, or bear,   30
   Pard,° or boar with bristled hair,
   In thy eye that shall appear,
   When thou wak'st, it is thy dear:
   Wake when some vile thing is near.   [*Exit.*]

Enter LYSANDER and HERMIA.

LYSANDER: Fair love, you faint with wand'ring in the wood: 35
   And to speak troth° I have forgot our way.
   We'll rest us Hermia, if you think it good,
   And tarry for the comfort of the day.
HERMIA: Be't so Lysander: find you out a bed:
   For I upon this bank will rest my head.   40
LYSANDER: One turf shall serve as pillow for us both,
   One heart, one bed, two bosoms, and one troth.°
HERMIA: Nay good Lysander: for my sake, my dear,
   Lie further off yet; do not lie so near.
LYSANDER: O take the sense, sweet, of my innocence.°   45
   Love takes the meaning in love's conference.°
   I mean that my heart unto yours is knit,
   So that but one heart we can make of it:
   Two bosoms interchainèd with an oath,
   So then two bosoms and a single troth.   50
   Then by your side no bed-room me deny:
   For lying so, Hermia, I do not lie.
HERMIA: Lysander riddles very prettily.
   Now much beshrew° my manners and my pride,
   If Hermia meant to say Lysander lied.   55
   But gentle friend, for love and courtesy,
   Lie further off, in human modesty:
   Such separation as may well be said
   Becomes a virtuous bachelor and a maid,
   So far be distant, and good night sweet friend: 60
   Thy love ne'er alter till thy sweet life end.
LYSANDER: Amen, amen, to that fair prayer say I,
   And then end life, when I end loyalty.
   Here is my bed: sleep give thee all his rest.

°30 *ounce:* lynx. °31 *Pard:* leopard. °36 *troth:* truth. °42 *troth:* true love. °45 *take . . . innocence:* understand the innocence of my remark. °46 *Love . . . conference:* Love enables lovers to understand each other when they converse. °54 *beshrew:* curse.

65   **HERMIA:** With half that wish, the wisher's eyes be pressed.°   *They sleep.*

Enter PUCK.

    PUCK: Through the forest have I gone,
        But Athenian found I none,
        On whose eyes I might approve°
        This flower's force in stirring love.
70   Night and silence. Who is here?
        Weeds° of Athens he doth wear:
        This is he (my master said)
        Despisèd the Athenian maid:
        And here the maiden, sleeping sound,
75   On the dank and dirty ground.
        Pretty soul, she durst not lie
        Near this lack-love, this kill-courtesy.
        Churl, upon thy eyes I throw
        All the power this charm doth owe.°
80   When thou wak'st, let love forbid
        Sleep his seat on thy eyelid.°
        So awake when I am gone:
        For I must now to Oberon.   *Exit.*

Enter DEMETRIUS and HELENA running.

    HELENA: Stay, thou kill me, sweet Demetrius.
85   **DEMETRIUS:** I charge thee hence, and do not haunt me thus.
    HELENA: O, wilt thou darkling° leave me? Do not so.
    DEMETRIUS: Stay on thy peril: I alone will go.   *Exit DEMETRIUS.*
    HELENA: O, I am out of breath in this fond° chase:
        The more my prayer, the lesser is my grace.°
90   Happy is Hermia, wheresoe'er she lies:
        For she hath blessèd and attractive eyes.
        How came her eyes so bright? Not with salt tears:
        If so, my eyes are oft'ner washed than hers.
        No, no: I am as ugly as a bear:
95   For beasts that meet me run away for fear.
        Therefore no marvel, though Demetrius
        Do as a monster, fly my presence thus.
        What wicked and dissembling glass° of mine,
        Made me compare with Hermia's sphery eyne!°
100   But who is here? Lysander, on the ground?
        Dead, or asleep? I see no blood, no wound.
        Lysander, if you live, good sir awake.
    LYSANDER: [*Wakes.*] And run through fire, I will for thy sweet sake.
        Transparent° Helena, nature shows art,
105   That through thy bosom, makes me see thy heart.

°65 *pressed:* i.e., by sleep. °68 *approve:* test. °71 *Weeds:* garments. °79 *owe:* own. °80–81 *forbid . . . eyelid:* make you sleepless (with love). °86 *darkling:* in the dark. °88 *fond:* foolishly doting. °89 *my grace:* favor shown to me. °98 *glass:* looking glass. °99 *sphery eyne:* starry eyes. °104 *Transparent:* radiant.

Where is Demetrius? O how fit a word
Is that vile name to perish on my sword!
HELENA: Do not say so, Lysander, say not so.
What though he love your Hermia? Lord, what though?
Yet Hermia still loves you: then be content.   110
LYSANDER: Content with Hermia? No: I do repent
The tedious minutes I with her have spent.
Not Hermia, but Helena I love.
Who will not change a raven for a dove?
The will of man is by his reason swayed:°   115
And reason says you are the worthier maid.
Things growing are not ripe until their season:
So I, being young, till now ripe° not to reason.
And touching now the point° of human skill,°
Reason becomes the marshal to my will,   120
And leads me to your eyes; where I o'erlook
Love's stories, written in love's richest book.
HELENA: Wherefore° was I to this keen mockery born?
When at your hands did I deserve this scorn?
Is't not enough, is't not enough, young man,   125
That I did never, no, nor never can,
Deserve a sweet look from Demetrius' eye,
But you must flout° my insufficiency?
Good troth you do me wrong, good sooth you do,
In such disdainful manner me to woo.   130
But fare you well: perforce I must confess,
I thought you lord of more true gentleness.°
O, that a lady, of one man refused,
Should of another, therefore be abused!   *Exit.*
LYSANDER: She sees not Hermia. Hermia, sleep thou there,   135
And never mayst thou come Lysander near.
For, as a surfeit of the sweetest things
The deepest loathing to the stomach brings:
Or as the heresies that men do leave,
Are hated most of those they did deceive: 140
So thou, my surfeit and my heresy,
Of all be hated; but the most, of me:
And all my powers, address your love and might,
To honour Helen, and to be her knight.   *Exit.*
HERMIA: [*Wakes.*] Help me Lysander, help me: do thy best   145
To pluck this crawling serpent from my breast.
Ay me, for pity. What a dream was here?
Lysander, look how I do quake with fear.
Methought a serpent eat my heart away,
And you sat smiling at his cruel prey.°   150
Lysander: what, removed? Lysander, lord!
What, out of hearing, gone? No sound, no word?
Alack, where are you? Speak, and if you hear:

°115 *swayed:* ruled. °118 *ripe:* mature. °119 *point:* peak. °*skill:* knowledge. °123 *Wherefore:* why. °128 *flout:* mock.
°132 *lord . . . gentleness:* more of a gentleman. °150 *prey:* preying.

Speak, of° all loves. I swoon almost with fear.
155   No? Then I well perceive you are not nigh:
Either death, or you, I'll find immediately.   *Exit.*

ACT 3

[Scene 1. The wood]

Enter the CLOWNS [QUINCE, SNUG, BOTTOM, FLUTE, SNOUT, *and* STARVELING.]

BOTTOM: Are we all met?
QUINCE: Pat, pat: and here's a marvellous convenient place for
    our rehearsal. This green plot shall be our stage, this
    hawthorn brake° our tiring-house,° and we will do it in
5   action, as we will do it before the duke.
BOTTOM: Peter Quince?
QUINCE: What sayest thou, bully° Bottom?
BOTTOM: There are things in this Comedy of Pyramus and Thisby
    that will never please. First, Pyramus must draw a sword
10   to kill himself; which the ladies cannot abide. How
    answer you that?
SNOUT: By'r lakin,° a parlous° fear.
STARVELING: I believe we must leave the killing out, when all is done.
BOTTOM: Not a whit: I have a device to make all well. Write me
15   a prologue, and let the prologue seem to say, we will
    do no harm with our swords, and that Pyramus is not
    killed indeed: and for the more better assurance, tell
    them that I Pyramus am not Pyramus, but Bottom the
    weaver: this will put them out of fear.
20   QUINCE: Well, we will have such a prologue, and it shall be
    written in eight and six.°
BOTTOM: No, make it two more: let it be written in eight and
    eight.
SNOUT: Will not the ladies be afeared of the lion?
25   STARVELING: I fear it, I promise you.
BOTTOM: Masters, you ought to consider with yourselves, to bring
    in (God shield us) a lion among ladies, is a most dreadful
    thing. For there is not a more fearful wild fowl than
    your lion living: and we ought to look to't.
30   SNOUT: Therefore another prologue must tell he is not a lion.
BOTTOM: Nay, you must name his name, and half his face must be
    seen through the lion's neck, and he himself must speak
    through, saying thus, or to the same defect:° "Ladies,"
    or "Fair ladies—I would wish you," or "I would request
35   you," or "I would entreat you, not to fear,
    not to tremble: my life for yours. If you think I come
    hither as a lion, it were pity of my life. No, I am no

°154 *of:* for the sake of. °4 *brake:* thicket. °*tiring-house:* dressing room. °7 *bully:* "old pal." °12 *By'r lakin:* mild oath, "by Our Lady." °*parlous:* awful, perilous. °21 *eight and six:* alternate lines of eight and six syllables (the ballad meter). °33 *defect:* he means "effect."

such thing: I am a man as other men are." And there
indeed let him name his name, and tell them plainly he
is Snug the joiner.   40

QUINCE: Well, it shall be so, but there is two hard things: that is,
to bring the moonlight into a chamber: for you know,
Pyramus and Thisby meet by moonlight.

SNOUT: Doth the moon shine that night we play our play?

BOTTOM: A calendar, a calendar: look in the almanac: find out   45
moonshine, find out moonshine.

QUINCE: Yes, it doth shine that night.

BOTTOM: Why then may you leave a casement of the great
chamber window, where we play, open; and the moon may
shine in at the casement.   50

QUINCE: Ay, or else one must come in with a bush of thorns° and
a lantern, and say he comes to disfigure,° or to present,
the person of Moonshine. Then, there is another thing;
we must have a wall in the great chamber: for Pyramus
and Thisby, says the story, did talk through the chink   55
of a wall.

SNOUT: You can never bring in a wall. What say you, Bottom?

BOTTOM: Some man or other must present wall: and let him have
some plaster, or some loam, or some rough-cast° about
him, to signify wall; and let him hold his fingers thus: 60
and through that cranny, shall Pyramus and Thisby whisper.

QUINCE: If that may be, then all is well. Come, sit down every
mother's son, and rehearse your parts. Pyramus, you
begin: when you have spoken your speech, enter into that
brake, and so every one according to his cue.   65

Enter PUCK.

PUCK: What hempen homespuns° have we swagg'ring here,
So near the cradle of the Fairy Queen?
What, a play toward?° I'll be an auditor,
An actor too perhaps, if I see cause.

QUINCE: Speak Pyramus. Thisby stand forth.   70

PYRAMUS: Thisby, the flowers of odious savours sweet—

QUINCE: "Odorous, odorous."

PYRAMUS: —odours savours sweet,
So hath thy breath, my dearest Thisby dear.
But hark, a voice: stay thou but here awhile,   75
And by and by I will to thee appear.   *Exit* PYRAMUS.
                                                                 [*Exit*.]

PUCK: A stranger Pyramus than e'er played here.

THISBY: Must I speak now?

QUINCE: Ay marry must you. For you must understand he goes
but to see a noise that he heard, and is to come again.   80

°51 *bush of thorns:* bundle of firewood (the man in the moon was supposed to have been placed there as a punishment
for gathering wood on Sundays). °52 *disfigure:* he means "figure," symbolize. °59 *rough-cast:* coarse plaster of lime
and gravel. °66 *hempen homespuns:* wearers of clothing spun at home from hemp. °68 *toward:* in preparation.

THISBY: Most radiant Pyramus, most lily-white of hue,
    Of colour like the red rose, on triumphant brier,
    Most brisky juvenal,° and eke most lovely Jew,°
    As true as truest horse, that yet would never tire,
85   I'll meet thee Pyramus, at Ninny's tomb.
QUINCE: "Ninus' tomb,"° man: why, you must not speak that yet.
    That you answer to Pyramus. You speak all your part
    at once, cues and all. Pyramus, enter; your cue is past:
    it is "never tire."
90 **THISBY:** O—As true as truest horse, that yet would never tire.

Enter PYRAMUS with the ass-head [followed by PUCK].

PYRAMUS: If I were fair, Thisby, I were only thine.
QUINCE: O monstrous! O strange! We are haunted. Pray masters,
    fly masters. Help!   *The clowns all exeunt.*
PUCK: I'll follow you: I'll lead you about a round,°
95   Through bog, through bush, through brake, through brier.
    Sometime a horse I'll be, sometime a hound,
      A hog, a headless bear, sometime a fire,
    And neigh, and bark, and grunt, and roar, and burn,
    Like horse, hound, hog, bear, fire, at every turn.   *Exit.*
100 **BOTTOM:** Why do they run away? This is a knavery of them to
    make me afeared.

Enter SNOUT.

SNOUT: O Bottom, thou art changed. What do I see on thee?
BOTTOM: What do you see? You see an ass-head of your own, do
    you?   *[Exit SNOUT.]*

Enter QUINCE.

105 **QUINCE:** Bless thee Bottom, bless thee. Thou art translated.°   *Exit.*
BOTTOM: I see their knavery. This is to make an ass of me, to
    fright me if they could: but I will not stir from this
    place, do what they can. I will walk up and down here,
    and will sing that they shall hear I am not afraid.
110   *[Sings.]*   The woose° cock, so black of hue,
                With orange tawny bill,
                The throstle,° with his note so true,
                The wren, with little quill.°
TITANIA: What angel wakes me from my flow'ry bed?
115 **BOTTOM:** *[Sings.]* The finch, the sparrow, and the lark,
                The plain-song° cuckoo gray:
                Whose note full many a man doth mark,
                And dares not answer, nay.

°83 *brisky juvenal:* lively youth. °*Jew:* diminutive of either "juvenal" or "jewel." °86 *Ninus' tomb:* (tomb of the founder of Nineveh, and meeting place of the lovers in Ovid's version of the Pyramus story).   °94 *about a round:* in circles, like a round dance (round about). °105 *translated:* transformed. °110 *woose:* ousel, blackbird. °112 *throstle:* thrush. °113 *quill:* piping note. °116 *plain-song:* sounding a simple unvaried note.

For indeed, who would set his wit to° so foolish a bird?
Who would give a bird the lie,° though he cry "cuckoo"°   120
never so?°

TITANIA: I pray thee, gentle mortal, sing again.
Mine ear is much enamoured of thy note:
So is mine eye enthrallèd to thy shape
And thy fair virtue's force (perforce°) doth move me,   125
On the first view to say, to swear, I love thee.

BOTTOM: Methinks mistress, you should have little reason for
that. And yet, to say the truth, reason and love keep
little company together now-a-days. The more the pity,
That some honest neighbours will not make them friends.   130
Nay, I can gleek° upon occasion.

TITANIA: Thou art as wise as thou art beautiful.

BOTTOM: Not so neither: but if I had wit enough to get out of
this wood, I have enough to serve mine own turn.

TITANIA: Out of this wood do not desire to go: 135
Thou shalt remain here, whether thou wilt or no.
I am a spirit of no common rate:°
The summer still doth tend upon my state,°
And I do love thee: therefore go with me.
I'll give thee fairies to attend on thee: 140
And they shall fetch thee jewels from the deep,
And sing, while thou on pressèd flowers dost sleep:
And I will purge thy mortal grossness so,
That thou shalt like an airy spirit go.
Peaseblossom, Cobweb, Moth,° and Mustardseed!   145

Enter four FAIRIES.

PEASEBLOSSOM: Ready.
COBWEB: And I.
MOTH: And I.
MUSTARDSEED: And I.
ALL: Where shall we go?

TITANIA: Be kind and courteous to this gentleman,
Hop in his walks and gambol in° his eyes,
Feed him with apricocks° and dewberries,°   150
With purple grapes, green figs, and mulberries.
The honey-bags steal from the humblebees,°
And for night-tapers, crop° their waxen thighs,
And light them at the fiery glow-worm's eyes,
To have my love to bed and to arise: 155
And pluck the wings from painted butterflies,
To fan the moonbeams from his sleeping eyes.
Nod to him elves, and do him courtesies.

°119 *set . . . to:* match his wit against. °120 *Who . . . lie:* who could call a bird a liar. °*"cuckoo"*: which sounded
like "cuckoo" = a deceived husband. °121 *never so:* i.e., often. °125 *perforce:* by force. °131 *gleek:* joke satirically.
°137 *rate:* rank, value. °138 *still . . . state:* always serves as an attendant in my royal train. °145 *Moth:* mote
(so pronounced), tiny speck. °149 *gambol in:* caper before. °150 *apricocks:* apricots. °*dewberries:* blackberries.
°152 *humblebees:* bumblebees. °153 *crop:* clip.

PEASEBLOSSOM: Hail, mortal.

160   **COBWEB:** Hail.

MOTH: Hail.

MUSTARDSEED: Hail.

BOTTOM: I cry your worships mercy,° heartily: I beseech your
worship's name.

165   **COBWEB:** Cobweb.

BOTTOM: I shall desire you of more acquaintance, good Master
Cobweb: if I cut my finger,° I shall make bold with you.
Your name, honest gentleman?

PEASEBLOSSOM: Peaseblossom.

170   **BOTTOM:** I pray you commend me° to Mistress Squash,° your mother,
and to Master Peascod,° your father. Good Master Peaseblossom,
I shall desire you of more acquaintance, too.
Your name I beseech you sir?

MUSTARDSEED: Mustardseed.

175   **BOTTOM:** Good Master Mustardseed, I know your patience well.
That same cowardly giant-like ox beef hath devoured
many a gentleman of your house. I promise you, your
kindred hath made my eyes water ere now. I desire you
of more acquaintance, good Master Mustardseed.

180   **TITANIA:** Come wait upon him: lead him to my bower.
The moon methinks looks with a wat'ry eye:
And when she weeps, weeps every little flower,
Lamenting some enforcèd° chastity.
Tie up my lover's tongue, bring him silently.   *Exeunt.*

[Scene 2. Another part of the wood]

Enter [OBERON,] *King of Fairies, solus.*°

OBERON: I wonder if Titania be awaked;
Then what it was that next came in her eye,
Which she must dote on in extremity.

Enter PUCK.

Here comes my messenger. How now, mad spirit?
5   What night-rule° now about this haunted grove?

PUCK: My mistress with a monster is in love.
Near to her close and consecrated bower,
While she was in her dull° and sleeping hour,
A crew of patches,° rude mechanicals,°
10   That work for bread upon Athenian stalls,°
Were met together to rehearse a play,
Intended for great Theseus' nuptial day:
The shallowest thickskin of that barren sort,°

°163 *I . . . mercy:* I respectfully beg your pardons. °167 *cut my finger:* cobwebs were used to stop bleeding.
°170 *commend me:* offer my respects. °*Squash:* unripe peapod. °171 *Peascod:* ripe peapod. °183 *enforcèd:* violated.
°S.D. *solus:* alone. °5 *night-rule:* diversion ("misrule") in the night. °8 *dull:* drowsy. °9 *patches:* fools. °*mechanicals:*
workers. °10 *stalls:* shops. °13 *barren sort:* stupid crew.

Who Pyramus presented in their sport,
Forsook his scene and entered in a brake: 15
When I did him at this advantage take,
An ass's nole° I fixèd on his head.
Anon° his Thisby must be answerèd,
And forth my mimic° comes. When they him spy,
As wild geese, that the creeping fowler° eye,   20
Or russet-pated choughs,° many in sort,°
Rising and cawing at the gun's report,
Sever themselves and madly sweep the sky,
So at his sight away his fellows fly:
And at our stamp, here o'er and o'er one falls: 25
He murder cries, and help from Athens calls.
Their sense thus weak, lost with their fears thus strong,
Made senseless things begin to do them wrong.
For briers and thorns at their apparel snatch:
Some° sleeves, some hats; from yielders, all things catch°   30
I led them on in this distracted° fear,
And left sweet Pyramus translated there:
When in that moment (so it came to pass)
Titania waked, and straightway loved an ass.
OBERON: This falls out better than I could devise.   35
But has thou yet latched° the Athenian's eyes
With the love-juice, as I did bid thee do?
PUCK: I took him sleeping (that is finished too)
And the Athenian woman by his side;
That when he waked, of force° she must be eyed.   40

Enter DEMETRIUS *and* HERMIA.

OBERON: Stand close:° this is the same Athenian.
PUCK: This is the woman: but not this the man.
DEMETRIUS: O why rebuke you him that loves you so?
Lay breath so bitter on your bitter foe.
HERMIA: Now I but chide: but I should use thee worse,   45
For thou, I fear, hast given me cause to curse.
If thou hast slain Lysander in his sleep,
Being o'er shoes in blood, plunge in the deep,
And kill me too.
The sun was not so true unto the day,   50
As he to me. Would he have stolen away
From sleeping Hermia? I'll believe as soon
This whole° earth may be bored,° and that the moon
May through the center creep, and so displease
Her brother's noontide with th' Antipodes.°   55
It cannot be but thou hast murdered him.
So should a murderer look; so dead,° so grim.

°17 *nole:* head, noodle. °18 *Anon:* presently. °19 *mimic:* actor. °20 *fowler:* hunter of fowl. °21 *russet-pated choughs:* grey-headed jackdaws. °*sort:* a flock. °30 *Some:* i.e., snatch. °*from yielders . . . catch:* everything joins in to harm the weak.   °31 *distracted:* maddened. °36 *latched:* moistened. °40 *of force:* by necessity. °41 *close:* hidden. °53 *whole:* solid. °*be bored:* have a hole bored through it. °55 *Her brother's . . . Antipodes:* the noon of her brother sun, by appearing among the Antipodes (the people on the other side of the earth). °57 *dead:* deadly.

DEMETRIUS: So should the murdered look, and so should I,
    Pierced through the heart with your stern cruelty.
60   Yet you, the murderer, look as bright, as clear
    As yonder Venus in her glimmering sphere.°
HERMIA: What's this to my Lysander? Where is he?
    Ah good Demetrius, wilt thou give him me?
DEMETRIUS: I had rather give his carcass to my hounds.
65 **HERMIA:** Out dog, out cur! Thou driv'st me past the bounds
    Of maiden's patience. Hast thou slain him then?
    Henceforth be never numbered among men.
    O, once tell true: tell true, even for my sake:
    Durst thou have looked upon him, being awake?
70   And hast thou killed him sleeping? O brave touch!°
    Could not a worm,° an adder, do so much?
    An adder did it: for with doubler tongue°
    Than thine, thou serpent, never adder stung.
DEMETRIUS: You spend your passion on a misprised mood°
75   I am not guilty of Lysander's blood:
    Nor is he dead, for aught that I can tell.
HERMIA: I pray thee, tell me then that he is well.
DEMETRIUS: And if I could, what should I get therefore?
HERMIA: A privilege never to see me more:
80   And from thy hated presence part I so:
    See me no more, whether he be dead or no.   *Exit.*
DEMETRIUS: There is no following her in this fierce vein.
    Here therefore for a while I will remain.
    So sorrow's heaviness doth heavier grow
85   For debt that bankrout sleep doth sorrow owe:°
    Which now in some slight measure it will pay,
    If for his tender° here I make some stay.°   *Lies down.*
OBERON: What hast thou done? Thou hast mistaken quite,
    And laid the love-juice on some true-love's sight.
90   Of thy misprision° must perforce° ensue
    Some true love turned, and not a false turned true.
PUCK: Then fate o'errules, that one man holding troth,
    A million fail, confounding° oath on oath.°
OBERON: About the wood, go swifter than the wind,
95   And Helena of Athens look thou find.
    All fancy-sick° she is, and pale of cheer,°
    With sighs of love, that costs the fresh blood dear.
    By some illusion see thou bring her here:
    I'll charm his eyes against she do appear.°
100 **PUCK:** I go, I go, look how I go.
    Swifter than arrow from the Tartar's bow.°   *Exit.*

°61 *sphere:* in the Ptolemaic system, each planet moved in its own sphere around the earth.   °70 *brave touch:* splendid stroke (ironic). °71 *worm:* snake. °72 *doubler tongue:* (1) tongue more forked (2) more deceitful speech. °74 *on . . . mood:* in mistaken anger. °85 *For debt . . . owe:* because sleep cannot pay the debt of repose he owes the man who is kept awake by sorrow. °87 *tender:* offer. °*stay:* pause. °90 *misprision:* mistake. °*perforce:* of necessity. °93 *confounding:* destroying. °*oath on oath:* one oath after another. °96 *fancy-sick:* lovesick. °*cheer:* face. °99 *against . . . appear:* in preparation for her appearance. °101 *Tartar's bow:* the Tartars, who used powerful Oriental bows, were famed as archers.

OBERON: Flower of this purple dye,
Hit with Cupid's archery,
Sink in apple of his eye:
When his love he doth espy,   105
Let her shine as gloriously
As the Venus of the sky.
When thou wak'st, if she be by,
Beg of her for remedy.

Enter PUCK.

PUCK: Captain of our fairy band,   110
Helena is here at hand,
And the youth, mistook by me,
Pleading for a lover's fee.°
Shall we their fond pageant° see?
Lord, what fools these mortals be!   115
OBERON: Stand aside. The noise they make
Will cause Demetrius to awake.
PUCK: Then will two at once woo one:
That must needs be sport alone.°
And those things do best please me   120
That befall prepost'rously.

Enter LYSANDER *and* HELENA.

LYSANDER: Why should you think that I should woo in scorn?
Scorn and derision never come in tears.
Look when I vow, I weep: and vows so born,
In their nativity all truth appears.°   125
How can these things in me seem scorn to you,
Bearing the badge° of faith to prove them true?
HELENA: You do advance your cunning more and more.
When truth kills truth,° O devilish-holy fray!
These vows are Hermia's. Will you give her o'er?   130
Weigh oath with oath, and you will nothing weigh.
Your vows to her and me, put in two scales,
Will even weigh: and both as light as tales.
LYSANDER: I had no judgment, when to her I swore.
HELENA: Nor none, in my mind, now you give her o'er.   135
LYSANDER: Demetrius loves her: and he loves not you.
DEMETRIUS: [*Awakes.*] O Helen, goddess, nymph, perfect, divine,
To what, my love, shall I compare thine eyne!
Crystal is muddy. O, how ripe in show,
Thy lips, those kissing cherries, tempting grow!   140
That pure congealèd white, high Taurus'° snow,
Fanned with the eastern wind, turns to a crow,

°113 *fee:* reward. °114 *fond pageant:* foolish spectacle. °119 *alone:* unique. °124–25 *vows . . . appears:* vows born in weeping must be true ones. °127 *badge:* (1) outward signs (2) family crest. °129 *truth kills truth:* Former true love is killed by vows of present true love. °141 *Taurus:* mountain range in Asia Minor.

When thou hold'st up thy hand. O let me kiss
This princess of pure white,° this seal of bliss.

145 **HELENA:** O spite! O hell! I see you all are bent
To set against me, for your merriment.
If you were civil,° and knew courtesy,
You would not do me thus much injury.
Can you not hate me, as I know you do,
150 But you must join in souls° to mock me too?
If you were men, as men you are in show,
You would not use a gentle lady so;
To vow, and swear, and superpraise my parts,°
When I am sure you hate me with your hearts.
155 You both are rivals, and love Hermia:
And now both rivals, to mock Helena.
A trim° exploit, a manly enterprise,
To conjure tears up in a poor maid's eyes
With your derision. None of noble sort
160 Would so offend a virgin, and extort°
A poor soul's patience, all to make you sport.

LYSANDER: You are unkind, Demetrius: be not so.
For you love Hermia: this you know I know.
And here, with all good will, with all my heart,
165 In Hermia's love I yield you up my part:
And yours of Helena to be bequeath,
Whom I do love, and will do to my death.

HELENA: Never did mockers waste more idle breath.

DEMETRIUS: Lysander, keep thy Hermia: I will none,°
170 If e'er I loved her, all that love is gone.
My heart to her but as guest-wise sojourned:°
And now to Helen is it home returned,
There to remain.

LYSANDER: Helen, it is not so.

DEMETRIUS: Disparage not the faith thou dost not know,
175 Lest to thy peril thou aby it dear.°
Look where thy love comes: yonder is thy dear.

Enter HERMIA.

HERMIA: Dark night, that from the eye his function takes,
The ear more quick of apprehension makes.
Wherein it doth impair the seeing sense,
180 It pays the hearing double recompense.
Thou art not by mine eye, Lysander, found:
Mine ear, I thank it, brought me to thy sound.
But why unkindly didst thou leave me so?

LYSANDER: Why should he stay, whom love doth press to go?

185 **HERMIA:** What love could press Lysander from my side?

°144 *princess . . . white:* sovereign example of whiteness (her hand). °147 *civil:* well behaved. °150 *join in souls:* agree in spirit. °153 *parts:* qualities. °157 *trim:* fine (ironic). °160 *extort:* wring. °169 *none:* have none of her. °171 *to her . . . sojourned:* visited her only as a guest. °175 *aby it dear:* buy it at a high price.

LYSANDER: Lysander's love, that would not let him bide—
    Fair Helena: who more engilds the night
    Than all your fiery oes and eyes of light.°
    Why seek'st thou me? Could not this make thee know,
    The hate I bare thee made me leave thee so?   190
HERMIA: You speak not as you think: it cannot be.
HELENA: Lo: She is one of this confederacy.
    Now I perceive they have conjoined all three,
    To fashion this false sport in spite of° me.
    Injurious° Hermia, most ungrateful maid,   195
    Have you conspired, have you with these contrived
    To bait° me with this foul derision?
    Is all the counsel° that we two have shared,
    The sisters' vows, the hours that we have spent,
    When we have chid the hasty-footed time   200
    For parting us; O, is all forgot?
    All schooldays' friendship, childhood innocence?
    We Hermia, like two artificial° gods,
    Have with our needles created both one flower,
    Both on one sampler,° sitting on one cushion,   205
    Both warbling of one song, both in one key;
    As if our hands, our sides, voices, and minds
    Had been incorporate.° So we grew together,
    Like to a double cherry, seeming parted,
    But yet an union in partition,   210
    Two lovely berries moulded on one stem:
    So with two seeming bodies, but one heart,
    Two of the first, like coats in heraldry,
    Due but to one, and crownèd with one crest.°
    And will you rent° our ancient love asunder,   215
    To join with men in scorning your poor friend?
    It is not friendly, 'tis not maidenly.
    Our sex, as well as I, may chide you for it;
    Though I alone do feel the injury.
HERMIA: I am amazèd at your passionate words: 220
    I scorn you not. It seems that you scorn me.
HELENA: Have you not set Lysander, as in scorn,
    To follow me, and praise my eyes and face?
    And made your other love, Demetrius
    (Who even but now did spurn° me with his foot)   225
    To call me goddess, nymph, divine, and rare,
    Precious, celestial? Wherefore speaks he this
    To her he hates? And wherefore doth Lysander
    Deny your love, so rich within his soul,
    And tender° me (forsooth) affection,   230
    But by your setting on, by your consent?

°188 oes . . . light: stars. °194 in spite of: to spite. °195 Injurious: insulting. °197 bait: attack. °198 counsel: secrets. °203 artificial: skilled in art. °205 sampler: work of embroidery. °208 incorporate: in one body. °213–14 Two . . . crest: (the two bodies being) like double coats of arms joined under one crest (with one heart). °215 rent: rend, tear. °225 spurn: kick. °230 tender: offer.

What though I be not so in grace° as you,
So hung upon with love, so fortunate,
But miserable most, to love unloved?
235   This you should pity, rather than despise.
HERMIA: I understand not what you mean by this.
HELENA: Ay, do. Persèver, counterfeit sad° looks:
Make mouths upon° me when I turn my back:
Wink each at other, hold the sweet jest up.
240   This sport well carried, shall be chronicled.°
If you have any pity, grace, or manners,
You would not make me such an argument.°
But fare ye well: 'tis partly my own fault:
Which death or absence soon shall remedy.
245   **LYSANDER:** Stay, gentle Helena: hear my excuse,
My love, my life, my soul, fair Helena.
HELENA: O excellent!
HERMIA: Sweet, do not scorn her so.
DEMETRIUS: If she cannot entreat,° I can compel.
LYSANDER: Thou canst compel no more than she entreat.
250   Thy threats have no more strength than her weak prayers.
Helen, I love thee, by my life I do:
I swear by that which I will lose for thee.
To prove° him false that says I love thee not.
DEMETRIUS: I say I love thee more than he can do.
255   **LYSANDER:** If thou say so, withdraw, and prove° it too.
DEMETRIUS: Quick, come.
HERMIA: Lysander, whereto tends all this?
LYSANDER: Away, you Ethiope.°
DEMETRIUS: No, no, sir,
Seem to break loose: take on as you would follow;
But yet come not.° You are a tame man, go.
260   **LYSANDER:** Hang off,° thou cat, thou burr: vile thing, let loose;
Or I will shake thee from me like a serpent.
HERMIA: Why are you grown so rude? What change is this,
Sweet love?
LYSANDER: Thy love? Out, tawny Tartar, out;
265   Out, loathèd med'cine: O hated potion, hence!
HERMIA: Do you not jest?
HELENA: Yes sooth: and so do you.
LYSANDER: Demetrius, I will keep my word° with thee.
DEMETRIUS: I would I had your bond.° For I perceive
A weak bond holds you. I'll not trust your word.
270   **LYSANDER:** What? Should I hurt her, strike her, kill her dead?
Although I hate her, I'll not harm her so.
HERMIA: What? Can you do me greater harm than hate?
Hate me, wherefore?° O me, what news,° my love?

°232 *in grace:* favored. °237 *sad:* serious. °238 *mouths upon:* faces at. °240 *chronicled:* written down in the history books. °242 *argument:* subject (of your mockery). °248 *entreat:* sway you by entreaty. °253, 255 *prove:* i.e., by a duel. °257 *Ethiope:* because she is a brunette. °258–59 *Seem . . . not:* You only seem to break loose from Hermia and pretend to follow me to a duel, but you actually hold back. °260 *Hang off:* let go. °267 *keep my word:* i.e., to duel. °268 *bond:* written agreement. °273 *wherefore:* why. °*what news:* what's the matter.

Am not I Hermia? Are not you Lysander?
I am as fair now, as I was erewhile.°   275
Since night, you loved me; yet since night, you left me.
Why then, you left me—O, the gods forbid—
In earnest, shall I say?
LYSANDER: Ay, by my life:
And never did desire to see thee more.
Therefore be out of hope, of question, of doubt: 280
Be certain: nothing truer: 'tis no jest
That I do hate thee, and love Helena.
HERMIA: O me, you juggler,° you canker blossom,°
You thief of love: what, have you come by night,
And stol'n my love's heart from him?
HELENA: Fine, i' faith.   285
Have you no modesty, no maiden shame,
No touch of bashfulness? What, will you tear
Impatient answers from my gentle tongue?
Fie, fie, you counterfeit, you puppet,° you.
HERMIA: Puppet? Why so—ay, that way goes the game.   290
Now I perceive that she hath made compare
Between our statures, she hath urged her height,
And with her personage, her tall personage,
Her height (forsooth) she hath prevailed with him.
And are you grown so high in his esteem.   295
Because I am so dwarfish and so low?
How low am I, thou painted maypole? Speak:
How low am I? I am not yet so low,
But that my nails can reach unto thine eyes.
HELENA: I pray you, though you mock me, gentlemen,   300
Let her not hurt me. I was never curst:°
I have no gift at all in shrewishness:
I am a right maid for my cowardice:°
Let her not strike me. You perhaps may think,
Because she is something lower than myself,   305
That I can match her.
HERMIA: Lower? Hark again.
HELENA: Good Hermia, do not be so bitter with me,
I evermore did love you Hermia.
Did ever keep your counsels, never wronged you;
Save that in love unto Demetrius,   310
I told him of your stealth unto this wood.
He followed you: for love I followed him.
But he hath chid me hence, and threatened me
To strike me, spurn me, nay to kill me too;
And now, so° you will let me quiet go,   315
To Athens will I bear my folly back,
And follow you no further. Let me go.
You see how simple and how fond° I am.

°275 *erewhile*: a short while ago. °283 *juggler*: deceiver. °*canker blossom*: worm that causes canker in blossoms.
°289 *puppet*: Hermia is short and Helena tall. °301 *curst*: bad-tempered. °303 *right . . . cowardice*: true woman
in being cowardly. °315 *so*: if. °318 *fond*: foolish.

HERMIA: Why, get you gone. Who is't that hinders you?

320 HELENA: A foolish heart, that I leave here behind.

HERMIA: What, with Lysander?

HELENA: With Demetrius.

LYSANDER: Be not afraid: she shall not harm thee Helena.

DEMETRIUS: No sir: she shall not, though you take her part.

HELENA: O when she's angry, she is keen and shrewd.°

325   She was a vixen when she went to school:

         And though she be but little, she is fierce.

HERMIA: "Little" again? Nothing but "low" and "little"?

         Why will you suffer her to flout° me thus?

         Let me come to her.

LYSANDER: Get you gone, you dwarf;

330   You minimus,° of hind'ring knot-grass° made;

         You bead, you acorn.

DEMETRIUS: You are too officious

         In her behalf that scorns your services.

         Let her alone: speak not of Helena,

         Take not her part. For if thou dost intend°

335   Never so little show of love to her,

         Thou shalt aby it.°

LYSANDER: Now she holds me not:

         Now follow, if thou dar'st, to try whose right,

         Of thine or mine, is most in Helena.°

DEMETRIUS: Follow? Nay, I'll go with thee, cheek by jowl.

Exeunt LYSANDER *and* DEMETRIUS.

340 HERMIA: You, mistress, all this coil is long of° you.

         Nay, go not back.

HELENA: I will not trust you, I,

         Nor longer stay in your curst company

         Your hands than mine are quicker for a fray:

         My legs are longer though, to run away.   [*Exit.*]

345 HERMIA: I am amazed,° and know not what to say.   *Exit.*

OBERON: This is thy negligence: still thou mistak'st,

         Or else commit'st thy knaveries wilfully.

PUCK: Believe me, king of shadows, I mistook.

         Did not you tell me I should know the man

350   By the Athenian garments he had on?

         And so far blameless proves my enterprise,

         That I have 'nointed an Athenian's eyes:

         And so far am I glad it so did sort,°

         As this their jangling I esteem a sport.

355 OBERON: Thou seest these lovers seek a place to fight;

         Hie therefore Robin, overcast the night,

         The starry welkin° cover thou anon

°324 *keen and shrewd:* sharp and malicious. °328 *flout:* mock. °330 *minimus:* smallest of creatures. °*knot-grass:* weed believed to stunt the growth if eaten. °334 *intend:* extend. °336 *aby it:* buy it dearly. °337–38 *try . . . Helena:* prove by fighting which of us has most right to Helena. °340 *coil is long of:* turmoil is because of. °345 *amazed:* confused. °353 *sort:* turn out. °357 *welkin:* sky.

With drooping fog as black as Acheron,°
And lead these testy° rivals so astray,
As° one come not within another's way.   360
Like to Lysander sometime frame thy tongue:
Then stir Demetrius up with bitter wrong:°
And sometime rail thou like Demetrius:
And from each other look thou lead them thus;
Till o'er their brows death-counterfeiting sleep   365
With leaden legs and batty wings doth creep:
Then crush this herb into Lysander's eye;
Whose liquor hath this virtuous° property,
To take from thence all error with his might,
And make his eyeballs roll with wonted° sight.   370
When they next wake, all this derision°
Shall seem a dream, and fruitless vision,
And back to Athens shall the lovers wend,
With league whose date° till death shall never end.
Whiles I in this affair do thee employ,   375
I'll to my queen and beg her Indian boy:
And then I will her charmèd eye release
From monster's view, and all things shall be peace.
PUCK: My fairy lord, this must be done with haste,
For night's swift dragons cut the clouds full fast: 380
And yonder shines Aurora's harbinger,°
At whose approach, ghosts wand'ring here and there,
Troop home to churchyards: damnèd spirits all,
That in crossways° and floods° have burial,
Already to their wormy beds are gone: 385
For fear lest day should look their shames upon,
They wilfully themselves exile from light,
And must for aye consort° with black-browed night.
OBERON: But we are spirits of another sort.
I with the morning's love have oft made sport,°   390
And like a forester, the groves may tread
Even till the eastern gate all fiery red,
Opening on Neptune, with fair blessèd beams,
Turns into yellow gold his salt green streams.
But notwithstanding, haste, make no delay: 395
We may effect this business yet ere day.   [*Exit.*]
PUCK: Up and down, up and down,
    I will lead them up and down.
    I am feared in field and town.
    Goblin, lead them up and down.   400
    Here comes one.

°358 *Acheron:* one of the four rivers in the underworld. °359 *testy:* irritable. °360 *As:* so that. °362 *wrong:* insult.
°368 *virtuous:* potent. °370 *wonted:* (previously) accustomed. °371 *derision:* laughable interlude. °374 *date:* term.
°381 *Aurora's harbinger:* the morning star heralding Aurora, the dawn. °384 *crossways:* cross-roads, where suicides were buried. °*floods:* those who drowned. °388 *aye consort:* ever associate. °390 *morning's . . . sport:* hunted
with Cephalus (beloved of Aurora and himself devoted to his wife Procris, whom he killed by accident; "sport"
also = "amorous dalliance," and "love" = Aurora's love for Oberon).

Enter LYSANDER.

LYSANDER: Where art thou, proud Demetrius? Speak thou now.
PUCK: Here villain, drawn° and ready. Where art thou?
LYSANDER: I will be with thee straight.
PUCK: Follow me then
     To plainer° ground.   [*Exit* LYSANDER.]

Enter DEMETRIUS.

405 DEMETRIUS: Lysander, speak again.
     Thou runaway, thou coward, art thou fled?
     Speak: in some bush? Where dost thou hide thy head?
PUCK: Thou coward, art thou bragging to the stars,
     Telling the bushes that thou look'st for wars,
410 And wilt not come? Come recreant,° come thou child,
     I'll whip thee with a rod. He is defiled
     That draws a sword on thee.
DEMETRIUS: Yea, art thou there?
PUCK: Follow my voice: we'll try no manhood° here.   *Exeunt.*

[*Enter* LYSANDER.]

LYSANDER: He goes before me and still dares me on:
415 When I come where he calls, then he is gone
     The villain is much lighter-heeled than I;
     I followed fast: but faster he did fly,
     That fallen am I in dark uneven way,
     And here will rest me. [*Lie down.*] Come thou gentle day,
420 For if but once thou show me thy grey light.
     I'll find Demetrius and revenge this spite.   [*Sleeps.*]

Enter PUCK *and* DEMETRIUS.

PUCK: Ho, ho, ho! Coward, why com'st thou not?
DEMETRIUS: Abide° me, if thou dar'st, for well I wot°
     Thou run'st before me, shifting every place,
425 And dar'st not stand, nor look me in the face.
     Where art thou now?
PUCK: Come hither: I am here.
DEMETRIUS: Nay then thou mock'st me. Thou shalt buy this dear,°
     If ever I thy face by daylight see.
     Now go thy way. Faintness constraineth me
430 To measure out my length on this cold bed.
     By day's approach look to be visited.   [*Lies down and sleeps.*]

Enter HELENA.

°403 *drawn:* with sword drawn. °405 *plainer:* more level. °410 *recreant:* oath-breaker, coward. °413 *try no manhood:* test no valor. °423 *Abide:* wait for. °*wot:* know. °427 *buy this dear:* pay dearly for this.

HELENA: O weary night, O long and tedious night,
    Abate° thy hours; shine comforts° from the east,
    That I may back to Athens by daylight,
    From these that my poor company detest: 435
    And sleep, that sometimes shuts up sorrow's eye.
    Steal me awhile from mine own company.   *Sleeps.*
PUCK: Yet but three? Come one more,
    Two of both kinds makes up four.
    Here she comes, curst° and sad.   440
    Cupid is a knavish lad,
    Thus to make poor females mad.

Enter HERMIA.

HERMIA: Never so weary, never so in woe,
      Bedabbled with the dew, and torn with briers:
        I can no further crawl, no further go: 445
         My legs can keep no pace with my desires.
        Here will I rest me till the break of day.
        Heavens shield Lysander, if they mean a fray.   *[Lies down and sleeps.]*
PUCK: On the ground,
    Sleep sound: 450
    I'll apply
    To your eye,
  Gentle lover, remedy.   *[Squeezes the love-juice on* LYSANDER'S *eyelids.]*
    When thou wak'st,
    Thou tak'st   455
    True delight
    In the sight
  Of thy former lady's eye:
  And the country proverb known,
  That every man should take his own,   460
  In your waking shall be shown.
    Jack shall have Jill:
    Naught shall go ill:
  The man shall have his mare again, and all shall be well.
                       [Exit PUCK. *The lovers remain asleep on stage.]*

ACT 4

[Scene 1. The Wood]

Enter [TITANIA] QUEEN OF FAIRIES, *and* [BOTTOM] THE CLOWN, *and* FAIRIES, *and the* KING
[OBERON] *behind them* [*unseen*].

TITANIA: Come sit thee down upon this flow'ry bed,
      While I thy amiable° cheeks do coy,°
      And stick musk-roses in thy sleek smooth head,
      And kiss thy fair large ears, my gentle joy.

°433 *Abate:* shorten. °*shine comforts:* may strength and power shine. °440 *curst:* cross. °2 *amiable:* lovely. °*coy:* caress.

Titania, Queen of the Fairies (Juliet Mills) is entranced by the ass-eared Bottom (Paul Hardwick) in the Royal Shakespeare Company production of *A Midsummer Night's Dream* (1959–62) at the Aldwych Theatre, London—director, Peter Hall.

5   **BOTTOM:** Where's Peaseblossom?

   PEASEBLOSSOM: Ready.

   BOTTOM: Scratch my head, Peaseblossom. Where's Mounsieur
      Cobweb?

   COBWEB: Ready.

10   **BOTTOM:** Mounsieur Cobweb, good mounsieur, get you your
      weapons in your hand, and kill me a red-hipped
      humblebee on the top of a thistle: and good mounsieur,
      bring me the honey-bag. Do not fret yourself too much in
      the action, mounsieur: and good mounsieur have a care the

15   honey-bag break not, I would be loath to have you
      overflowen with a honey bag, signior. Where's Mounsieur
      Mustardseed?

   MUSTARDSEED: Ready.

   BOTTOM: Give me your neaf,° Mounsieur Mustardseed. Pray you

20   leave your curtsy,° good mounsieur.

   MUSTARDSEED: What's your will?

   BOTTOM: Nothing, good mounsieur, but to help Cavalery° Cobweb
      to scratch. I must to the barber's mounsieur, for
      methinks I am marvellous hairy about the face. And I am

25   such a tender ass, if my hair do but tickle me, I must
      scratch.

   TITANIA: What, will thou hear some music, my sweet love?

°19 *neaf*: fist. °20 *leave your curtsy*: either (1) stop bowing, or (2) replace your hat. °22 *Cavalery*: he means "cavalier."

BOTTOM: I have a reasonable good ear in music. Let's have the tongs°
and the bones.°
TITANIA: Or say, sweet love, what thou desirest to eat.   30
BOTTOM: Truly, a peck of provender. I could munch your good
dry oats. Methinks I have a great desire to a bottle° of hay.
Good hay, sweet hay, hath no fellow.
TITANIA: I have a venturous fairy that shall seek
The squirrel's hoard, and fetch thee new nuts.   35
BOTTOM: I had rather have a handful or two of dried pease. But
I pray you, let none of your people stir me: I have an
exposition of° sleep come upon me.
TITANIA: Sleep thou, and I will wind thee in my arms.
Fairies, be gone, and be all ways° away.   [*Exeunt* FAIRIES.]   40
So doth the woodbine the sweet honeysuckle
Gently entwist: the female ivy so
Enrings the barky fingers of the elm.
O how I love thee! how I dote on thee!   [*They sleep.*]

Enter ROBIN GOODFELLOW [PUCK].

OBERON: [*Advances.*] Welcome good Robin. Seest thou this sweet sight?   45
Her dotage now I do begin to pity.
For meeting her of late behind the wood,
Seeking sweet favours° for this hateful fool,
I did upbraid her and fall out with her.
For she his hairy temples then had rounded   50
With coronet of fresh and fragrant flowers
And that same dew which sometime° on the buds
Was wont to° swell like round and orient° pearls,
Stood now within the pretty flowerets' eyes,
Like tears that did their own disgrace bewail.   55
When I had at my pleasure taunted her,
And she in mild terms begged my patience,
I then did ask of her her changeling child:
Which straight she gave me, and her fairy sent
To bear him to my bower in fairy land.   60
And now I have the boy, I will undo
This hateful imperfection of her eyes.
And gentle Puck, take this transformèd scalp
From off the head of this Athenian swain;
That he awaking when the other do,   65
May all to Athens back again repair,°
And think no more of this night's accidents,°
But as the fierce vexation of a dream.
But first I will release the Fairy Queen.

°28 *tongs:* crude music made by striking tongs with a piece of metal. °29 *bones:* pieces of bone held between the
fingers and clapped together rhythmically. °32 *bottle:* bundle. °38 *exposition of:* he means "disposition to."
°40 *all ways:* in every direction. °48 *favours:* bouquets as love tokens. °52 *sometime:* formerly. °53 *Was wont to:*
used to. °*orient:* where the most beautiful pearls came from. °66 *repair:* return. °67 *accidents:* incidents.

70   Be as thou wast wont to be:
         See, as thou wast wont to see.
         Dian's bud o'er Cupid's flower°
         Hath such force and blessèd power.
         Now my Titania, wake you, my sweet queen.
75 **TITANIA:** My Oberon, what visions have I seen!
         Methought I was enamoured of an ass.
   OBERON: There lies your love.
   TITANIA: How came these things to pass?
         O, how mine eyes do loathe his visage now!
   OBERON: Silence awhile Robin, take off this head:
80   Titania, music call, and strike more dead
         Than common sleep of all these five the sense.°
   TITANIA: Music, ho music! such as charmeth sleep.
   PUCK: Now, when thou wak'st, with thine own fools' eyes peep.
   OBERON: Sound music: *Music still.°*
                  Come my queen, take hands with me,
85   And rock the ground whereon these sleepers be.   *[Dance.]*
         Now thou and I are new in amity,
         And will tomorrow midnight solemnly
         Dance in Duke Theseus' house triumphantly,°
         And bless it to all fair prosperity.
90   There shall the pairs of faithful lovers be
         Wedded, with Theseus, all in jollity.
   PUCK: Fairy King, attend and mark:
         I do hear the morning lark.
   OBERON: Then my queen, in silence sad,°
95   Trip we after the night's shade:
         We the globe can compass soon,
         Swifter than the wand'ring moon.
   TITANIA: Come my lord, and in our flight,
         Tell me how it came this night,
100   That I sleeping here was found,
         With these mortals on the ground.   *Exeunt.*

Wind° horns. Enter THESEUS, HIPPOLYTA, EGEUS *and all his train.*

   THESEUS: Go one of you, find out the forester:
         For now our observation° is performed.
         And since we have the vaward° of the day,
105   My love shall hear the music of my hounds.
         Uncouple° in the western valley, let them go:
         Dispatch I say, and find the forester.   *[Exit an* ATTENDANT.*]*
         We will, fair queen, up to the mountain's top,
         And mark the musical confusion
110   Of hounds and echo in conjunction.

°72 *Dian's bud . . . flower:* Diana's bud counteracts the effects of love-in-idleness, the pansy. °80–81 *strike . . .
sense:* Make these five (the lovers and Bottom) sleep more soundly. °84 S.D. *still:* continuously. °88 *triumphantly:* in celebration. °94 *sad:* serious. °101 S.D. *wind:* blow, sound. °103 *observation:* observance of the
May Day rites. °104 *vaward:* vanguard, earliest part. °106 *Uncouple:* unleash (the dogs).

HIPPOLYTA: I was with Hercules and Cadmus° once,
    When in a wood of Crete they bayed the bear,°
    With hounds of Sparta;° never did I hear
    Such gallant chiding. For besides the groves,
    The skies, the fountains, every region near   115
    Seemed all one mutual cry. I never heard
    So musical a discord, such sweet thunder.
THESEUS: My hounds are bred out of the Spartan kind:
    So flewed, so sanded;° and their heads are hung
    With ears that sweep away the morning dew,   120
    Crook-kneed, and dewlapped° like Thessalian bulls;
    Slow in pursuit; but matched in mouth like bells,
    Each under each.° A cry° more tuneable
    Was never holloa'd to, nor cheered with horn,
    In Crete, in Sparta, nor in Thessaly.   125
    Judge when you hear. But soft.° What nymphs are these?
EGEUS: My lord, this is my daughter here asleep,
    And this Lysander, this Demetrius is,
    This Helena, old Nedar's Helena.
    I wonder of their being here together.   130
THESEUS: No doubt they rose up early to observe
    The rite of May: and hearing our intent,
    Came here in grace° of our solemnity.
    But speak Egeus, is not this the day
    That Hermia should give answer of her choice?   135
EGEUS: It is, my lord.
THESEUS: Go bid the huntsmen wake them with their horns.

Shout within: wind horns. They all start up.

    Good morrow, friends. Saint Valentine is past.
    Begin these wood-birds but to couple now?°
LYSANDER: Pardon, my lord.   *[They kneel.]*
THESEUS: I pray you all, stand up.   140
    I know you two are rival enemies.
    How comes this gentle concord in the world,
    That hatred is so far from jealousy,°
    To sleep by hate° and fear no enmity?
LYSANDER: My lord, I shall reply amazedly,   145
    Half sleep, half waking. But as yet, I swear,
    I cannot truly say how I came here.
    But as I think—for truly would I speak,
    And now I do bethink me, so it is—
    I came with Hermia hither. Our intent   150

°111 *Cadmus:* mythical builder of Thebes. °112 *bayed the bear:* brought the bear to bay, to its last stand.
°113 *hounds of Sparta:* a breed famous for their swiftness and quick scent. °119 *flewed, so sanded:* with hanging
cheeks, so sand-colored. °121 *dewlapped:* with skin hanging from the chin. °122–23 *matched . . . each:* with each
voice matched for harmony with the next in pitch, like bells in a chime. °123 *cry:* pack of dogs. °126 *soft:* wait.
°133 *grace:* honor. °138–39 *Saint . . . now:* birds traditionally chose their mates on St. Valentine's Day.
°143 *jealousy:* suspicion. °144 *hate:* one it hates.

Was to be gone from Athens, where we might,
Without° the peril of the Athenian law—

EGEUS: Enough, enough, my lord: you have enough.
I beg the law, the law upon his head:
155   They would have stol'n away, they would, Demetrius,
Thereby to have defeated you and me:
You of your wife, and me of my consent:
Of my consent that she should be your wife.

DEMETRIUS: My lord, fair Helen told me of their stealth,
160   Of this their purpose hither, to this wood,
And I in fury hither followed them;
Fair Helena in fancy° following me.
But my good lord, I wot not by what power
(But by some power it is) my love to Hermia,
165   Melted as the snow, seems to me now
As the remembrance of an idle gaud,°
Which in my childhood I did dote upon:
And all the faith, the virtue of my heart,
The object and the pleasure of mine eye,
170   Is only Helena. To her, my lord,
Was I betrothed ere I saw Hermia:
But like a sickness,° did I loathe this food.
But as in health, come° to my natural taste,
Now I do wish it, love it, long for it.
175   And will for evermore be true to it.

THESEUS: Fair lovers, you are fortunately met.
Of this discourse we more will hear anon.
Egeus, I will overbear your will:
For in the temple, by and by,° with us,
180   These couples shall eternally be knit.
And for the morning now is something worn,°
Our purposed hunting shall be set aside.
Away with us to Athens. Three and three,
We'll hold a feast in great solemnity.
185   Come Hippolyta.

Exeunt DUKE [HIPPOLYTA, EGEUS] and LORDS.

DEMETRIUS: These things seem small and undistinguishable,
Like far-off mountains turned into clouds.

HERMIA: Methinks I see these things with parted° eye,
When everything seems double.

HELENA: So methinks:
190   And I have found Demetrius, like a jewel,
Mine own, and not mine own.°

°152 *Without:* beyond. °162 *in fancy:* out of doting love. °166 *idle gaud:* trifling toy. °172 *sickness:* sick person. °173 *come:* i.e., back. °179 *by and by:* immediately. °181 *something worn:* somewhat worn on. °188 *parted:* divided (each eye seeing a separate image). °190–91 *like . . . own:* like a person who finds a jewel: the finder is the owner, but insecurely so.

DEMETRIUS: Are you sure
    That we are awake? It seems to me,
    That yet we sleep, we dream. Do not you think
    The duke was here, and bid us follow him?
HERMIA: Yea, and my father.
HELENA: And Hippolyta.   195
LYSANDER: And he did bid us follow to the temple.
DEMETRIUS: Why then, we are awake: let's follow him,
    And by the way let us recount our dreams.   *Exeunt lovers.*
BOTTOM: [*Wakes.*] When my cue comes, call me, and I will answer.
    My next is "Most fair Pyramus." Hey ho. Peter Quince?   200
    Flute the bellows-mender? Snout the tinker? Starveling?
    God's my life! Stol'n hence, and left me asleep? I have
    had a most rare vision. I have had a dream, past the wit
    of man to say what dream it was. Man is but an ass, if he
    go about° to expound this dream. Methought I was—   205
    there is no man can tell what. Methought I was, and
    methought I had—but man is but a patched fool,° if he
    will offer to say what methought I had. The eye of man
    hath not heard, the ear of man hath not seen, man's hand is
    not able to taste, his tongue to conceive, nor his   210
    heart to report, what my dream was. I will get Peter
    Quince to write a ballad of this dream: it shall be called
    Bottom's Dream; because it hath no bottom: and I
    will sing it in the latter end of our play, before the duke.
    Peradventure, to make it the more gracious, I shall sing   215
    it at her° death.   *Exit.*

[Scene 2. Athens, Quince's house]

Enter QUINCE, FLUTE, SNOUT, and STARVELING.

QUINCE: Have you sent to Bottom's house? Is he come home yet?
STARVELING: He cannot be heard of. Out of doubt he is transported.°
FLUTE: If he come not, then the play is marred. It goes not forward,
    doth it?
QUINCE: It is not possible. You have not a man in all Athens able   5
    to discharge° Pyramus but he.
FLUTE: No, he hath simply the best wit of any handicraft man in Athens.
QUINCE: Yea, and the best person too, and he is a very paramour
    for a sweet voice.
FLUTE: You must say "paragon." A paramour is (God bless us)   10
    a thing of naught.°

Enter SNUG THE JOINER.

SNUG: Masters, the duke is coming from the temple, and there
    is two or three lords and ladies more married. If our
    sport had gone forward, we had all been made men.°

°205 *go about:* attempt. °207 *patched fool:* fool dressed in motley. °216 *her:* Thisby's. °2 *transported:* carried away
(by spirits). °6 *discharge:* portray. °11 *of naught:* wicked, naughty. °14 *made men:* men made rich.

15   **FLUTE:** O sweet bully Bottom. Thus hath he lost sixpence a day°
        during his life: he could not have 'scaped sixpence a day.
        And the duke had not given him sixpence a day for playing
        Pyramus, I'll be hanged. He would have deserved it.
        Sixpence a day in Pyramus, or nothing.

Enter BOTTOM.

20   **BOTTOM:** Where are these lads? Where are these hearts?
     QUINCE: Bottom! O most courageous° day! O most happy hour!
     BOTTOM: Masters, I am to discourse wonders: but ask me not what.
        For if I tell you, I am not true Athenian. I will tell you
        everything, right as it fell out.
25   **QUINCE:** Let us hear, sweet Bottom.
     BOTTOM: Not a word of me. All that I will tell you is, that the
        duke hath dined. Get your apparel together, good
        strings to your beards, new ribbands to your pumps, meet
        presently° at the palace, every man look o'er his part: for
30   the short and the long is, our play is preferred.° In any
        case, let Thisby have clean linen: and let not him that
        plays the lion pare his nails, for they shall hang out for
        the lion's claws. And most dear actors, eat no onions nor
        garlic, for we are to utter sweet breath: and I do not
35   doubt but to hear them say it is a sweet comedy. No more
        words: away, go away.   *Exeunt.*

ACT 5

[Scene 1. The palace of Theseus]

Enter THESEUS, HIPPOLYTA, *and* PHILOSTRATE, *and his* LORDS.

   HIPPOLYTA: 'Tis strange, my Theseus, that these lovers speak of.
   THESEUS: More strange than true. I never may believe
        These antick° fables, nor these fairy toys.°
        Lovers and madmen have such seething brains,
5   Such shaping fantasies,° that apprehend
        More than cool reason ever comprehends.
        The lunatic, the lover, and the poet,
        Are of imagination all compact.°
        One sees more devils than vast hell can hold:
10   That is the madman. The lover, all as frantic,
        Sees Helen's beauty in a brow of Egypt.°
        The poet's eye, in a fine frenzy rolling,
        Doth glance from heaven to earth, from earth to heaven.
        And as imagination bodies forth
15   The forms of things unknown, the poet's pen
        Turns them to shapes, and gives to airy nothing,
        A local habitation and a name.

°15 *sixpence a day:* i.e., as a pension. °21 *courageous:* he may mean "auspicious." °29 *presently:* immediately.
°30 *preferred:* recommended (for presentation). °3 *antick:* fantastic. °*fairy toys:* trivial fairy stories. °5 *fantasies:*
imaginations. °8 *of . . . compact:* totally composed of imagination. °11 *a brow of Egypt:* the swarthy face of a gypsy
(believed to come from Egypt).

Such tricks hath strong imagination,
That if it would but apprehend some joy,
It comprehends° some bringer of that joy.   20
Or in the night, imagining some fear,
How easy is a bush supposed a bear.
HIPPOLYTA: But all the story of the night told over,
And all their minds transfigured so together,
More witnesseth than fancy's images,°   25
And grows to something of great constancy:°
But howsoever, strange and admirable.°

Enter LOVERS: LYSANDER, DEMETRIUS, HERMIA, *and* HELENA.

THESEUS: Here come the lovers, full of joy and mirth.
Joy, gentle friends, joy and fresh days of love
Accompany your hearts.
LYSANDER: More° than to us   30
Wait in your royal walks, your board, your bed.
THESEUS: Come now, what masques,° what dances shall we have,
To wear away this long age of three hours
Between our after-supper° and bed-time?
Where is our usual manager of mirth?   35
What revels are in hand? Is there no play,
To ease the anguish of a torturing hour?
Call Philostrate.
PHILOSTRATE: Here, mighty Theseus.
THESEUS: Say, what abridgment° have you for this evening?
What masque,° what music? How shall we beguile   40
The lazy time, if not with some delight?
PHILOSTRATE: There is a brief° how many sports are ripe.°
Make choice of which your highness will see first.

[*Gives a paper.*]

THESEUS: "The battle with the Centaurs, to be sung
By an Athenian eunuch to the harp."   45
We'll none of that. That have I told my love
In glory of my kinsman Hercules.
"The riot of the tipsy Bacchanals,
Tearing the Thracian singer in their rage."°
That is an old device: and it was played   50
When I from Thebes came last a conqueror.
"The thrice three Muses mourning for the death
Of Learning, late deceased in beggary."
That is some satire keen and critical,

°20 *comprehends:* includes. °25 *More . . . images:* testifies that it is more than just imagination. °26 *constancy:* certainty. °27 *admirable:* to be wondered at. °30 *More:* even more (joy and love). °32, 40 *masques:* lavish courtly entertainments combining song and dance. °34 *after-supper:* late supper. °39 *abridgment:* either (1) diversion to make the hours seem shorter, or (2) short entertainment. °40 *masque:* a light musical or non-musical drama, usually allegorical or mythological in subject, with many dances and pantomime actions. Often the actors wore masks. °42 *brief:* list. °*ripe:* ready. °48–49 *riot . . . rage:* The singer Orpheus of Thrace was torn limb from limb by the Maenads, frenzied female priests of Bacchus.

55   Not sorting with° a nuptial ceremony.
          "A tedious brief scene of young Pyramus
          And his love Thisby; very tragical mirth."
          Merry and tragical? Tedious and brief?
          That is hot ice and wondrous strange snow.
60   How shall we find the concord of this discord?
     PHILOSTRATE: A play there is, my lord, some ten words long,
          Which is as brief as I have known a play:
          But by ten words, my lord, it is too long,
          Which makes it tedious: for in all the play
65   There is not one word apt, one player fitted.°
          And tragical, my noble lord, it is:
          For Pyramus therein doth kill himself.
          Which when I saw rehearsed, I must confess,
          Made mine eyes water; but more merry tears
70   The passion of loud laughter never shed.
     THESEUS: What are they that do play it?
     PHILOSTRATE: Hard-handed men, that work in Athens here,
          Which never laboured in their minds till now:
          And now have toiled their unbreathed° memories
75   With this same play, against° your nuptial.
     THESEUS: And we will hear it.
     PHILOSTRATE: No, my noble lord,
          It is not for you. I have heard it over,
          And it is nothing, nothing in the world;
          Unless you can find sport in their intents,
80   Extremely stretched and conned° with cruel pain.
          To do your service.
     THESEUS: I will hear that play.
          For never anything can be amiss,
          When simpleness and duty tender° it.
          Go bring them in, and take your places, ladies.   *[Exit* PHILOSTRATE.]
85   **HIPPOLYTA:** I love not to see wretchedness o'ercharged,°
          And duty in his service perishing.
     THESEUS: Why, gentle sweet, you shall see no such thing.
     HIPPOLYTA: He says they can do nothing in this kind.°
     THESEUS: The kinder we, to give them thanks for nothing.
90   Our sport shall be to take what they mistake.
          And what poor duty cannot do, noble respect
          Takes it in might, not merit.°
          Where I have come, great clerks° have purposèd
          To greet me with premeditated welcomes;
95   Where I have seen them shiver and look pale,
          Make periods in the midst of sentences,
          Throttle° their practised accent in their fears,
          And in conclusion dumbly have broke off,

°55 *sorting with:* befitting. °65 *fitted:* (well) cast. °74 *unbreathed:* unpracticed, unexercised. °75 *against:* in preparation for. °80 *stretched and conned:* strained and memorized. °83 *tender:* offer. °85 *wretchedness o'ercharged:* poor
fellows taxing themselves too much. °88 *in this kind:* of this sort. °91–92 *noble . . . merit:* a noble nature considers
the sincerity of effort rather than the skill of execution. °93 *clerks:* scholars. °97 *Throttle:* choke on.

Not paying me a welcome. Trust me, sweet,
Out of this silence yet I picked a welcome: 100
And in the modesty of fearful duty°
I read as much as from the rattling tongue
Of saucy and audacious eloquence.
Love, therefore, and tongue-tied simplicity,
In° least, speak most, to my capacity.° 105

[*Enter* PHILOSTRATE.]

PHILOSTRATE: So please your grace, the Prologue is addressed.°
THESEUS: Let him approach.

Flourish trumpets. Enter the PROLOGUE [QUINCE].

PROLOGUE: If we offend, it is with our good will.
    That you should think, we come not to offend,
    But with good will. To show our simple skill, 110
    That is the true beginning of our end.
    Consider then, we come but in despite.°
    We do not come, as minding to content you,
    Our true intent is. All for your delight,
    We are not here. That you should here repent you, 115
    The actors are at hand: and by their show,
    You shall know all, that you are like to know.°
THESEUS: This fellow doth not stand upon points.°
LYSANDER: He hath rid his prologue like a rough colt: he knows
    not the stop.° A good moral my lord: it is not enough 120
    to speak; but to speak true.
HIPPOLYTA: Indeed he hath played on his prologue like a child on a
    recorder:° a sound, but not in government.°
THESEUS: His speech was like a tangled chain: nothing impaired, but
    all disordered. Who is next? 125

Enter PYRAMUS *and* THISBY, WALL, MOONSHINE, *and* LION.

PROLOGUE: Gentles, perchance you wonder at this show,
        But wonder on, till truth make all things plain.
    This man is Pyramus, if you would know:
    This beauteous lady, Thisby is certain.
    This man, with lime and rough-cast,° doth present 130
        Wall, that vile wall which did these lovers sunder:
    And through Wall's chink, poor souls, they are content
        To whisper. At the which, let no man wonder.
    This man, with lantern, dog, and bush of thorn,
        Presenteth Moonshine. For if you will know, 135

°101 *fearful duty:* subjects whose devotions gave them stage fright. °105 *In:* i.e., saying. °*capacity:* way of thinking.
°106 *addressed:* ready. °108–17 *If . . . know:* Quince's blunders in punctuation exactly reverse the meaning.
°112 *despite:* malice. °118 *stand upon points:* (1) pay attention to punctuation (2) bother about the niceties (of
expression). °120 *stop:* (1) halt, or (2) period. °123 *recorder:* flutelike wind instrument. °*in government:* well managed.
°130 *rough-cast:* rough plaster made of lime and gravel.

By moonshine did these lovers think no scorn
  To meet at Ninus' tomb, there, there to woo:
This grisly beast (which Lion hight° by name)
The trusty Thisby, coming first by night,
140   Did scare away, or rather did affright:
And as she fled, her mantle she did fall:°
  Which Lion vile with bloody mouth did stain.
Anon comes Pyramus, sweet youth and tall,°
  And finds his trusty Thisby's mantle slain:
145   Whereat, with blade, with bloody blameful blade,
  He bravely broached° his boiling bloody breast.
And Thisby, tarrying in mulberry shade,
  His dagger drew, and died. For all the rest,
Let Lion, Moonshine, Wall, and lovers twain.
150   At large° discourse, while here they do remain.

THESEUS: I wonder if the lion be to speak.

DEMETRIUS: No wonder, my lord: one lion may, when many asses do.

       Exeunt [PROLOGUE, PYRAMUS,] LION, THISBY, MOONSHINE.

WALL: In this same interlude° it doth befall
That I, one Snout by name, present a wall:
155   And such a wall, as I would have you think,
That had in it a crannied hole or chink:
Through which the lovers, Pyramus and Thisby,
Did whisper often, very secretly.
This loam, this rough-cast, and this stone doth show
160   That I am that same wall: the truth is so.
And this the cranny is, right and sinister,°
Through which the fearful lovers are to whisper.

THESEUS: Would you desire lime and hair to speak better?

DEMETRIUS: It is the wittiest° partition° that ever I heard discourse,
165   my lord.

Enter PYRAMUS.

THESEUS: Pyramus draws near the wall: silence.

PYRAMUS: O grim-looked night, O night with hue so black,
    O night, which ever art when day is not:
  O night, O night, alack, alack, alack,
170   I fear my Thisby's promise is forgot.
And thou O wall, O sweet, O lovely wall,
    That stand'st between her father's ground and mine,
Thou wall, O wall, O sweet and lovely wall,
  Show me thy chink, to blink through with mine eyne.°

              [WALL *holds up his fingers.*]

°138 *hight:* is called. °141 *fall:* let fall. °143 *tall:* brave. °146 *broached:* opened (Shakespeare parodies the overuse of alliteration in the earlier bombastic Elizabethan plays). °150 *At large:* in full. °153 *interlude:* short play. °161 *right and sinister:* from right to left (he probably uses the fingers of his right and left hands to form the cranny). °164 *wittiest:* most intelligent. °*partition:* (1) wall (2) section of a learned book or speech. °174 *eyne:* eyes.

     Thanks, courteous wall. Jove shield thee well for this.   175
        But what see I? No Thisby do I see.
     O wicked wall, through whom I see no bliss,
        Cursed be thy stones for thus deceiving me.
THESEUS: The wall methinks being sensible,° should curse again.°
PYRAMUS: No in truth sir, he should not. "Deceiving me" is   180
    Thisby's cue: she is to enter now, and I am to spy her
    through the wall. You shall see it will fall pat° as I told you:
    yonder she comes.

Enter THISBY.

THISBY: O wall, full often hast thou heard my moans,
     For parting my fair Pyramus and me.   185
     My cherry lips have often kissed thy stones;
        Thy stones with lime and hair knit up in thee.
PYRAMUS: I see a voice: now will I to the chink,
        To spy and I can hear my Thisby's face.
        Thisby?   190
THISBY: My love thou art, my love I think.
PYRAMUS: Think what thou wilt, I am thy lover's grace:
     And, like Limander,° am I trusty still.
THISBY: And I like Helen,° till the Fates me kill.
PYRAMUS: Not Shafalus to Procrus,° was so true.   195
THISBY: As Shafalus to Procrus, I to you.
PYRAMUS: O kiss me through the hole of this vile wall.
THISBY: I kiss the wall's hole, not your lips at all.
PYRAMUS: Wilt thou at Ninny's° tomb meet me straightway?
THISBY: Tide° life, tide death, I come without delay.   200

                          [*Exeunt* PYRAMUS *and* THISBY.]

WALL: Thus have I, Wall, my part dischargèd so;
     And being done, thus Wall away doth go.   *Exit.*
THESEUS: Now is the mural° down between the two neighbours.
DEMETRIUS: No remedy my lord, when walls are so wilful to hear
    without warning.°   205
HIPPOLYTA: This is the silliest stuff that ever I heard.
THESEUS: The best in this kind are but shadows,° and the worst are
    no worse, if imagination amend them.
HIPPOLYTA: It must be your imagination then, and not theirs.
THESEUS: If we imagine no worse of them than they of themselves,   210
    they may pass for excellent men. Here come two noble
    beasts in, a man and a lion.

Enter LION *and* MOONSHINE.

°179 *sensible:* capable of feelings and perception. °*again:* back. °182 *pat:* exactly. °193 *Limander:* he means "Leander." °194 *Helen:* he means "Hero." °195 *Shafalus to Procrus:* he means "Cephalus" and "Procris." °199 *Ninny:* fool (he means "Ninus"). °200 *Tide:* come, betide. °203 *mural:* wall. °205 *without warning:* either (a) without warning the parents, or (b) unexpectedly. °207 *in . . . shadows:* of this sort are only plays (or only actors).

LION: You ladies, you, whose gentle hearts do fear
    The smallest monstrous mouse that creeps on floor,
215   May now perchance both quake and tremble here.
    When lion rough in wildest rage doth roar.
    Then know that I, as Snug the joiner am
    A lion fell,° nor else no lion's dam:°
    For if I should as lion come in strife
220   Into this place, 'twere pity on my life.
THESEUS: A very gentle beast, and of a good conscience.
DEMETRIUS: The very best at a beast,° my lord, that e'er I saw.
LYSANDER: This lion is a very fox for his valour.
THESEUS: True: and a goose for his discretion.
225 DEMETRIUS: Not so my lord: for his valour cannot carry his discretion,
    and the fox carries the goose.
THESEUS: His discretion, I am sure, cannot carry his valour: for the
    goose carries not the fox. It is well: leave it to his discretion,
    and let us listen to the moon.
230 MOONSHINE: This lanthorn° doth the hornèd moon present—
DEMETRIUS: He should have worn the horns on his head.°
THESEUS: He is no crescent, and his horns are invisible within the
    circumference.
MOONSHINE: This lanthorn doth the hornèd moon present;
235   Myself, the man i' th' moon do seem to be.
THESEUS: This is the greatest error of all the rest; the man should
    be put into the lanthorn. How is it else the man i' th' moon?
DEMETRIUS: He dares not come there for the candle; for you see, it
240   is already in snuff.°
HIPPOLYTA: I am aweary of this moon. Would he would change.
THESEUS: It appears, by his small light of discretion, that he is in
    the wane: but yet in courtesy, in all reason, we must stay°
    the time.
245 LYSANDER: Proceed, Moon.
MOONSHINE: All that I have to say, is to tell you that the lanthorn is
    the moon, I the man i' th' moon, this thornbush my
    thornbush, and this dog my dog.
DEMETRIUS: Why, all these should be in the lanthorn: for all these are
250   in the moon. But silence: here comes Thisby.

Enter THISBY.

THISBY: This is old Ninny's tomb. Where is my love?
LION: Oh!   *The* LION *roars.* THISBY *runs off.*
DEMETRIUS: Well roared, Lion.
THESEUS: Well run, Thisby.
255 HIPPOLYTA: Well shone, Moon. Truly, the moon shines with a good
    grace.

[*The* LION *shakes* THISBY's *mantle.*]

°218 *fell:* fierce. °*nor . . . dam:* and not a lioness. °222 *best, beast:* pronounced similarly. °230 *lanthorn:* lantern (once made of horn). °230–31 *hornèd . . . head:* referring to the cuckold or deceived husband, who supposedly grew horns. °240 *in snuff:* (1) in need of snuffing (having a long, burnt-out wick or snuff) (2) in a temper. °243 *stay:* await.

THESEUS: Well moused,° Lion.

DEMETRIUS: And then came Pyramus.

Enter PYRAMUS. [*Exit* LION.]

LYSANDER: And so the lion vanished.

PYRAMUS: Sweet moon, I thank thee for thy sunny beams,   260
  I thank thee, moon, for shining now so bright.
 For by thy gracious, golden, glittering gleams,
  I trust to take of truest Thisby sight.
 But stay: O spite!
 But mark, poor knight,   265
 What dreadful dole° is here?
  Eyes, do you see!
  How can it be!
 O dainty duck, O dear!
  Thy mantle good,   270
  What, stained with blood?
 Approach, ye Furies° fell:
  O Fates!° come, come:
  Cut thread and thrum.°
 Quail,° crush, conclude, and quell.°   275

THESEUS: This passion, and the death of a dear friend, would go
 near to make a man look sad.

HIPPOLYTA: Beshrew° my heart, but I pity the man.

PYRAMUS: O wherefore Nature, didst thou lions frame?   280
  Since lion vile hath here deflowered my dear.
 Which is—no, no—which was the fairest dame
  That lived, that loved, that liked, that looked with cheer.
  Come tears, confound:
   Out sword, and wound
  The pap° of Pyramus: 285
   Ay, that left pap,
   Where heart doth hop. [*Stabs himself.*]
  Thus die, I, thus, thus, thus.
   Now am I dead,
   Now am I fled,   290
  My soul is in the sky.
  Tongue lose thy light,
   Moon° take thy flight,   [*Exit* MOONSHINE.]
  Now die, die, die, die, die.   [*Dies.*]

DEMETRIUS: No die,° but an ace° for him. For he is but one.   295

LYSANDER: Less than an ace, man. For he is dead, he is nothing.

THESEUS: With the help of a surgeon, he might yet recover, and
 prove an ass.

°257 *moused:* shaken, as a cat shakes a mouse. °266 *dole:* grief. °272 *Furies:* classical spirits of the underworld who avenged murder. °273 *Fates:* three sisters who spun the thread of human destiny, which at will was cut with a shears. °274 *thrum:* fringelike end of the warp in weaving. °275 *Quail:* subdue. °*quell:* kill. °278 *Beshrew:* curse (meant lightly). °285 *pap:* breast. °292–93 *Tongue . . . Moon:* He reverses the two subjects. °295 *die:* singular of "dice." °*ace:* a throw of one at dice.

HIPPOLYTA: How chance Moonshine is gone before Thisby comes
300   back and finds her lover?

Enter THISBY.

THESEUS: She will find him by starlight. Here she comes, and her
        passion ends the play.
HIPPOLYTA: Methinks she should not use a long one for such a
        Pyramus: I hope she will be brief.
305   **DEMETRIUS:** A mote will turn the balance, which Pyramus, which
        Thisby, is the better: he for a man, God warr'nt° us;
        she for a woman, God bless us.
LYSANDER: She hath spied him already with those sweet eyes.
DEMETRIUS: And thus she means,° videlicet°—
310   **THISBY:** Asleep my love?
                    What, dead, my dove?
        O Pyramus, arise,
            Speak, speak. Quite dumb?
            Dead, dead? A tomb
315   Must cover thy sweet eyes.
            These lily lips,
            This cherry nose,
        These yellow cowslip° cheeks,
            Are gone, are gone:
320   Lovers, make moan:
        His eyes were green as leeks.
            O Sisters Three,°
            Come, come to me,
        With hands as pale as milk,
325   Lay them in gore,
            Since you have shore
        With shears his thread of silk.
            Tongue, not a word:
            Come trusty sword,
330   Come blade, my breast imbrue°   [*Stabs herself.*]
            And farewell friends:
            Thus Thisby ends:
            Adieu, adieu, adieu.   [*Dies.*]
THESEUS: Moonshine and Lion are left to bury the dead.
335   **DEMETRIUS:** Ay, and Wall too.
BOTTOM: [*Starts up.*] No, I assure you, the wall is down that parted
        their fathers. Will it please you to see the Epilogue, or
        to hear a Bergomask° dance between two of our company?
THESEUS: No epilogue, I pray you; for your play needs no excuse.
340   Never excuse: for when the players are all dead, there
        need none to be blamed. Marry, if he that writ it had
        played Pyramus and hanged himself in Thisby's garter,

---

°306 *warr'nt:* warrant, protect. °309 *means:* laments. °*videlicet:* namely. °318 *cowslip:* yellow primrose. °322 *Sisters Three:* the Fates. °330 *imbrue:* stain with gore. °338 *Bergomask:* exaggerated country dance.

it would have been a fine tragedy: and so it is truly, and
very notably discharged. But come, your Bergomask:
let your Epilogue alone.   [*A dance.*] 345
The iron tongue° of midnight hath told° twelve.
Lovers, to bed, 'tis almost fairy time.°
I fear we shall outsleep the coming morn,
As much as we this night have overwatched.
This palpable gross° play hath well beguiled   350
The heavy gait of night. Sweet friends, to bed.
A fortnight hold we this solemnity,
In nightly revels, and new jollity.   *Exeunt.*

Enter PUCK [*with a broom*].

PUCK: Now the hungry lion roars,
        And the wolf behowls the moon;   355
    Whilst the heavy° ploughman snores,
        All with weary task fordone.°
    Now the wasted brands° do glow,
    Whilst the screech-owl, screeching loud,
        Puts the wretch that lies in woe°   360
    In remembrance of a shroud.
        Now it is the time of night,
    That the graves, all gaping wide,
        Every one lets forth his sprite,°
    In the church-way paths to glide.   365
        And we fairies, that do run
    By the triple Hecate's° team,°
        From the presence of the sun,
    Following darkness like a dream,
    Now are frolic:° not a mouse   370
    Shall disturb this hallowed house.
    I am sent with broom before,
    To sweep the dust° behind° the door.

Enter KING *and* QUEEN OF FAIRIES, *with all their train.*

OBERON: Through the house give glimmering light,
        By the dead and drowsy fire,   375
    Every elf and fairy sprite,
        Hop as light as bird from brier,
    And this ditty after me,
        Sing, and dance it trippingly.
TITANIA: First rehearse your song by rote,   380
        To each word a warbling note.

°346 *iron tongue:* i.e., of the bell. °*told:* counted, tolled. °347 *fairy time:* from midnight to daybreak. °350 *palpable gross:* obvious and crude. °356 *heavy:* sleepy. °357 *fordone:* worn out, "done in." °358 *wasted brands:* burnt logs. °360 *wretch . . . woe:* sick person. °364 *sprite:* spirit, ghost. °367 *triple Hecate:* the moon goddess, identified as Cynthia in heaven, Diana on earth, and Hecate in hell. °*team:* dragons that pull the chariot of the night moon. °370 *frolic:* frolicsome. °373 *To sweep the dust:* Puck often helped with household chores. °*behind:* from behind.

Hand in hand, with fairy grace,
Will we sing and bless this place.   [*Song and dance.*]

OBERON: Now, until the break of day,
385   Through this house each fairy stray.
To the best bride-bed will we,
Which by us shall blessèd be:
And the issue° there create,°
Ever shall be fortunate:
390   So shall all the couples three
Ever true in loving be:
And the blots of Nature's hand°
Shall not in their issue stand.
Never mole, harelip, nor scar,
395   Nor mark prodigious,° such as are
Despisèd in nativity,
Shall upon their children be.
With this field-dew consecrate.
Every fairy take his gait,°
400   And each several° chamber bless,
Through this palace, with sweet peace;
And the owner of its blest,
Ever shall in safety rest.
Trip away: make no stay:
405   Meet me all by break of day.   *Exeunt* [*all but* PUCK].

PUCK: If we shadows have offended,
Think but this, and all is mended,
That you have but slumbered here,
While these visions did appear.
410   And this weak and idle° theme,
No more yielding but° a dream,
Gentles, do not reprehend.
If you pardon, we will mend.°
And as I am an honest Puck,
415   If we have unearnèd luck,
Now to scape the serpent's tongue,°
We will make amends, ere long:
Else the Puck a liar call.
So, good night unto you all.
420   Give me your hands,° if we be friends;
And Robin shall restore amends.°   [*Exit.*]

°388 *issue:* children. °*create:* created. °392 *blots . . . hand:* birth defects. °395 *mark prodigious:* unnatural birthmark. °399 *take his gait:* proceed. °400 *several:* separate. °410 *idle:* foolish. °411 *No . . . but:* yielding nothing more than. °413 *mend:* improve. °416 *serpent's tongue:* hissing of the audience. °420 *hands:* applause. °421 *restore amends:* do better in the future.

QUESTIONS

ACT 1

1. Describe the relationship between Theseus and Hippolyta. What does each of them represent? How does Shakespeare show us that they have different attitudes toward their marriage?

2. Characterize Hermia and Lysander. What blocks their relationship? How do they plan to circumvent these obstructions?

3. What are Helena's feelings about herself? About Hermia? About Demetrius? How might you account for her self-image?

4. Why have the mechanicals gathered at Quince's house? How does Shakespeare show us that Bottom is eager, ill-educated, energetic, and funny?

ACT 2

5. What is Puck's job? What do you find out about his personality, habits, and pastimes in his first conversation?

6. Why are Titania and Oberon fighting with each other, and what are the specific consequences of their conflict?

7. What does Oberon plan to do to Titania? Why? What is "love-in-idleness"? What power does it have? What does it symbolize?

8. Why are Demetrius and Helena in the woods? What does Oberon decide to do to them? What error occurs? What happens to Lysander when Helena awakens him?

ACT 3

9. How and why does Puck change Bottom? How is this transformation appropriate? What happens when Bottom awakens Titania? Why?

10. What does Oberon decide to do when he realizes that Puck has made a mistake? What is Puck's attitude toward the confusion he has created?

11. What happens when Helena awakens Demetrius? How does this situation reverse the one that began the play? Explain Helena's reaction to the behavior of Demetrius and Lysander.

12. What real dangers (tragic potential) do the lovers face in Act 3? How do Oberon and Puck deal with these dangers? What is their plan? How successful is it?

ACT 4

13. Why does Oberon cure Titania of her infatuation with Bottom? How does the relationship between Oberon and Titania change? How is this change symbolized? Why is it significant?

14. How are the relationships among the four lovers straightened out? How does each explain his or her feelings? What does Theseus decide about the couples? Why is this significant?

ACT 5

15. What momentous event occurs offstage and is briefly reported in Act 5?

16. Describe Pyramus and Thisby. What blocks their relationship? How do they plan to circumvent these obstructions? What happens to them?

17. What is the significance of the fairy masque (a combination of poetry, music, dance, and drama) that ends the play?

18. What does Puck's epilogue suggest about you as a reader or spectator? How does it reinforce the connections among dreaming, imagination, illusion, and drama?

GENERAL QUESTIONS

1. To what extent are the characters in this play conventional and representative types? What is the effect of Shakespeare's style of characterization?

2. Are any of the characters symbolic? If so, what do they symbolize? How does such symbolism reinforce the themes of the play?

3. How does Shakespeare employ language, imagery, and poetic form to define the characters in this play and differentiate among the various groups of characters?

4. To what extent do the two settings—city and woods—structure the play? Where does exposition occur? Complication and catastrophe? The comic resolution? How complete is the resolution? Why is the round-trip journey from one setting to the other necessary for the lovers? The rulers? The "hempen homespuns"?

5. What are the similarities or parallels in plot and theme between *A Midsummer Night's Dream* and "Pyramus and Thisby"? To what degree are they versions of the same play with different endings? Why do you think Shakespeare included the play-within-the-play in *A Midsummer Night's Dream?*

6. In the first soliloquy of the play, Helena discusses love. What kind of love is she talking about? What are its qualities and characteristics? How far do the relationships in the play bear out her ideas about love?

7. How well do the mechanicals understand the nature of dramatic illusion? What sorts of production problems concern them? How do they solve these?

8. What ideas about drama and the ways in which audiences respond to it does *A Midsummer Night's Dream* explore?

9. Compare the play-within-a-play in *A Midsummer Night's Dream* to the one in Act 3 of *Hamlet.* How are the internal plays and situations similar? Different? What parallels do you see in the connections between each play-within-a-play and the larger play in which each occurs?

Comedy Since Shakespeare

The subject of comedy in the centuries from Shakespeare to the present is vast. In all the major European countries, and also (later) in the United States, there were many comic dramatists. Some of them were successful in their time but are neglected today, such as Eugène Scribe in France. Some, such as Anton Chekhov in Russia, are known not only for their comedy but also for other works (such as Chekhov's many stories).

In England in the seventeenth century, dramatists such as William Wycherley (1640–1716) and William Congreve (1670–1729) created a sophisticated type of drama in the comedy-of-manners tradition that is termed "Restoration comedy" because it developed after King Charles II was reestablished on the English throne in 1660. The Restoration comedies combined and contrasted elegant and boisterous manners, and they often dealt with serious social and sexual problems. In the first part of the eighteenth century, dramatists created "sentimental" drama. Sentimental comedies showed individuals who verge on behavioral excesses but who eventually conform to morality because their goodness of heart overcomes their personal interests, feelings, and self-indulgence—hence the term "sentimental."

The first half of the eighteenth century saw the popularity of other forms such as the musical play and the burlesque play. The musical play was first known as **ballad opera;** later it was called **comic opera;** today it is called **musical comedy,** or simply a **musical.** The characteristic of a musical play is the combination of spoken dialogue and brief songs. The first such play was *The Beggar's Opera* (1728) by John Gay (1685–1732). *The Beggar's Opera* was also a burlesque that satirized the Italian operas so popular in the early eighteenth century. Henry Fielding (1707–54), best known for his later novels, wrote at least nine ballad operas in the mode of *The Beggar's Opera,* and he also wrote the best of English **burlesques,** *Tom Thumb* (1730, 1731). Also unique in Fielding's comic writing were a number of five-act plays dealing with serious social situations. Comic operas reached their high point in the nineteenth century with the Savoy Operas of William Gilbert (1836–1911) and Arthur Sullivan (1842–1900). The Gilbert and Sullivan operas, such as *H.M.S. Pinafore* (1878), *The Mikado* (1885), and *The Pirates of Penzance* (1879) are regularly performed today by both professionals and amateurs. In the United States during the twentieth century, the musical comedy form became a major force, as with the plays of Richard Rodgers (1902–1979) and Oscar Hammerstein II (1895–1960), and Alan Jay Lerner (1918–1986) and Frederick Loewe (1901–1988).

At the turn of the nineteenth century the major comic dramatists in addition to Chekhov were Oscar Wilde (1854–1900) and George Bernard Shaw (1856–1950), all of whose plays are still regularly revived and well attended. The twentieth century marked the appearance of numbers of important comic dramatists, including many, like Eugene O'Neill, who are better known for more serious plays. A number of writers divided their time between theater and film, such as George Kaufman (1889–1961), whose *The Man Who Came to Dinner* (1939) was successful both onstage and on the screen. For a time, Kaufman also wrote film scripts for some of the early film comedies of the Marx Brothers. Many other comic playwrights experimented with comedy. Such a writer is Arthur Kopit (b. 1937), whose *Oh Dad, Poor Dad, Mamma's Hung You in the Closet and I'm Feelin' So Sad* (1961) created a great stir when it was first performed. Of particular note is the development of the "theater of the absurd." Some significant plays in this tradition are *Waiting for Godot* (1953) by Samuel Beckett (1906–1989), *Rhinocéros* (1960) by Jean Genet (1910–1986), and *The Homecoming* (1960) by Harold Pinter (1930–2008), which was revived on the New York stage in 2007.

The technology of the twentieth century has had a great influence on the development of comedy. When radio became prominent in the 1930s, a number of short radio comic dramas developed that were broadcast regionally and nationally on a daily basis, such as "Vic and Sade," written by Paul Rhymer, and "Ma Perkins," by Robert Andrews, Orvin Tovrov, and others, both of which were heard by millions who sat regularly during the day beside their radios. With the advent of television in the 1950s there was a virtual explosion of so-called soap operas, or "soaps," and situation comedies, or "sitcoms," in the tradition of the earlier radio shows. Some of the more prominent sitcoms among the many have been *I Love Lucy, The Jackie*

Gleason Show, Frasier, Friends, Seinfeld, and *The Office.* Although the shorter radio comedies were performed daily during the height of the radio years in the 1930s and 1940s, the longer television sitcoms, because of greater and more elaborate production requirements, have generally been presented weekly.

Comedy today is characterized by great variety. All the types described earlier (see pp. 1263–65) are regularly being presented. Serious plays may contain comic and farcical elements. Farcical and comic plays may introduce serious sequences and also may contain strong elements of satire. Satirical plays may contain songs to complement the onstage action and also to divert and entertain. Writers at the beginning of the twenty-first century clearly were continuing to combine the various comic forms that were brought into prominence by Shakespeare and the comic dramatists in the centuries that followed him.

ANTON CHEKHOV (1860–1904)

Anton Chekhov was born in Taganrog in southern Russia in 1860, the son of a merchant and grandson of a serf. He entered medical school in Moscow in 1879, graduating in 1884. While a student he was also obligated to help support his family, and he turned to writing stories, jokes, and potboilers for pay under a variety of pen names, one of which was "The Doctor Without Patients." The Bear *belongs to the end of this early period, ten years before Chekhov's association with the Moscow Art Theater at the end of the century.*

Chekhov tended to downplay The Bear, *referring to it as a "joke" and a "vaudeville"— both words suggesting a farcical work with little form or substance. Nevertheless the play was greatly acclaimed and financially successful, to the author's amazement and delight. Three months after its first performance in 1888, he likened* The Bear *to a "milk cow" ("cash cow") because, to his happiness, it earned him a steady income.*

The Bear is a farce, a dramatic form designed preeminently to evoke laughter, and it therefore contains extravagant language and boisterous and sudden action. But there is also an underlying seriousness that sustains the humor. In their way, both Smirnov and Mrs. Popov have been failures; they could conceivably sink into lives of depression and futility, and both are walking a very fine line as the play begins. Chekhov makes clear that Mrs. Popov is filled with resentment at her unfaithful and now dead husband, and also that she is chafing under her self-imposed resolution to lead a life of mourning and self-denial in his memory. Smirnov is having difficulty with creditors, and he admits that his relationships with the many women he has known have ended unhappily. He is therefore both cynical and angry.

The climax of the play is the improbable and preposterous challenge to a duel that Smirnov offers Mrs. Popov, resolved by the equally preposterous outcome. Despite the improbabilities of the play, however, the actions are not impossible because they manifest the true internal needs of the main characters. Chekhov's friend Leo Tolstoy (1828–1910), who criticized some of Chekhov's late plays, laughed heartily at *The Bear*, and countless audiences and readers since then have joined him in laughter.

The Bear, A Joke in One Act (1900)

CAST OF CHARACTERS

Mrs. Popov, *a widow of seven months, Mrs. Popov is small and pretty, with dimples. She is a landowner. At the start of the play, she is pining away in memory of her dead husband.*

Grigory Stepanovich Smirnov, *easily angered and loud, Smirnov is older. He is a landowner, too, and a man of substance.*

Luka, *Mrs. Popov's footman [a servant whose main tasks were to wait table and attend the carriages, in addition to general duties]. He is old enough to feel secure in telling Mrs. Popov what he thinks.*

Gardener, Coachman, Workmen, *who enter at the end.*

SCENE. *The drawing room of* MRS. POPOV's *country home.*

[MRS. POPOV, *in deep mourning, does not remove her eyes from a photograph.*]

LUKA: It isn't right, madam . . . you're only destroying yourself. . . . The chambermaid and the cook have gone off berry picking; every living being is rejoicing; even the cat knows how to be content, walking around the yard catching birds, and you sit in your room all day as if it were a convent, and you don't take pleasure in anything. Yes, really! Almost a year has passed since you've gone out of the house!

MRS. POPOV: And I shall never go out. . . . What for? My life is already ended. He lies in his grave; I have buried myself in these four walls . . . we are both dead.

LUKA: There you go again! Your husband is dead, that's as it was meant to be, it's the will of God, may he rest in peace. . . . You've done your mourning and that will do. You can't go on weeping and mourning forever. My wife died when her time came, too. . . . Well? I grieved, I wept for a month, and that was enough for her; the old lady wasn't worth a second more. [*Sighs.*] You've forgotten all your neighbors. You don't go anywhere or accept any calls. We live, so to speak, like spiders. We never see the light. The mice have eaten my uniform. It isn't as if there weren't any nice neighbors—the district is full of them . . . there's a regiment stationed at Riblov, such officers—they're like candy—you'll never get your fill of them! And in the barracks, never a Friday goes by without a dance; and, if you please, the military band plays music every day. . . . Yes, madam, my dear lady: you're young, beautiful, in the full bloom of youth—if only you took a little pleasure in life . . . beauty doesn't last forever, you know! In ten years' time, you'll be wanting to wave your fanny in front of the officers—and it will be too late.

MRS. POPOV: [*Determined.*] I must ask you never to talk to me like that! You know that when Mr. Popov died, life lost all its salt for me. It may seem to you that I am alive, but that's only conjecture! I vowed to wear mourning to my grave and not to see the light of day. . . . Do you hear me? May his departed spirit see how much I love him. . . . Yes, I know, it's no mystery to you that he was often mean to me, cruel . . . and even unfaithful, but I shall remain true to the grave and show him I know how to love. There, beyond the grave, he will see me as I was before his death. . . .

LUKA: Instead of talking like that, you should be taking a walk in the garden or have Toby or Giant harnessed and go visit some of the neighbors. . . .

MRS. POPOV: Ai! [*She weeps.*]

LUKA: Madam! Dear lady! What's the matter with you! Christ be with you!

MRS. POPOV: Oh, how he loved Toby! He always used to ride on him to visit the Korchagins or the Vlasovs. How wonderfully he rode! How graceful he was when he pulled at the reins with all his strength! Do you remember? Toby, Toby! Tell them to give him an extra bag of oats today.

5

LUKA: Yes, madam.

[*Sound of loud ringing.*]

10   MRS. POPOV: [*Shudders.*] Who's that? Tell them I'm not at home!

LUKA: Of course, madam. [*He exits.*]

MRS. POPOV: [*Alone. Looks at the photograph.*] You will see, Nikolai, how much I can love and forgive . . . my love will die only when I do, when my poor heart stops beating. [*Laughing through her tears.*] Have you no shame? I'm a good girl, a virtuous little wife. I've locked myself in and I'll be true to you to the grave, and you . . . aren't you ashamed, you chubby cheeks? You deceived me, you made scenes, for weeks on end you left me alone. . . .

LUKA: [*Enters, alarmed.*] Madam, somebody is asking for you. He wants to see you. . . .

MRS. POPOV: But didn't you tell them that since the death of my husband, I don't see anybody?

15   LUKA: I did, but he didn't want to listen; he spoke about some very important business.

MRS. POPOV: I am *not at home!*

LUKA: That's what I told him . . . but . . . the devil . . . he cursed and pushed past me right into the room . . . he's in the dining room right now.

MRS. POPOV: [*Losing her temper.*] Very well, let him come in . . . such manners! [*LUKA goes out.*] How difficult these people are! What does he want from me? Why should he disturb my peace? [*Sighs.*] But it's obvious I'll have to go live in a convent. . . . [*Thoughtfully.*] Yes, a convent. . . .

SMIRNOV: [*Enters while speaking to LUKA.*] You idiot, you talk too much. . . . Ass! [*Sees MRS. POPOV and changes to dignified speech.*] Madam, may I introduce myself: retired lieutenant of the artillery and landowner, Grigory Stepanovich Smirnov! I feel the necessity of troubling you about a highly important matter. . . .

20   MRS. POPOV: [*Refusing her hand.*] What do you want?

SMIRNOV: Your late husband, whom I had the pleasure of knowing, has remained in my debt for two twelve-hundred-ruble notes. Since I must pay the interest at the agricultural bank tomorrow, I have come to ask you, madam, to pay me the money today.

MRS. POPOV: One thousand two hundred. . . . And why was my husband in debt to you?

SMIRNOV: He used to buy oats from me.

MRS. POPOV: [*Sighing, to LUKA.*] So, Luka, don't you forget to tell them to give Toby an extra bag of oats.

[*LUKA goes out.*]

[**To SMIRNOV:**] If Nikolai, my husband, was in debt to you, then it goes without saying that I'll pay; but please excuse me today. I haven't any spare cash. The day after tomorrow, my steward will be back from town and I will give him instructions to pay you what is owed; until then I cannot comply with your wishes. . . . Besides, today is the anniversary—exactly seven months ago my husband died, and I'm in such a mood that I'm not quite disposed to occupy myself with money matters.

25   SMIRNOV: And I'm in such a mood that if I don't pay the interest tomorrow, I'll be owing so much that my troubles will drown me. They'll take away my estate!

MRS. POPOV: You'll receive your money the day after tomorrow.

SMIRNOV: I don't want the money the day after tomorrow. I want it today.

MRS. POPOV: You must excuse me. I can't pay you today.

SMIRNOV: And I can't wait until after tomorrow.

30   MRS. POPOV: What can I do, if I don't have it now?

SMIRNOV: You mean to say you can't pay?

MRS. POPOV: I can't pay. . . .

SMIRNOV: Hm! Is that your last word?

MRS. POPOV: That is my last word.

SMIRNOV: Positively the last?   35

MRS. POPOV: Positively.

SMIRNOV: Thank you very much. We'll make a note of that. [*Shrugs his shoulders.*] And people want me to be calm and collected! Just now, on the way here, I met a tax officer and he asked me: why are you always so angry, Grigory Stepanovich? Goodness' sake, how can I be anything but angry? I need money desperately. . . . I rode out yesterday early in the morning, at daybreak, and went to see all my debtors; and if only one of them had paid his debt . . . I was dog-tired, spent the night God knows where—a Jewish tavern beside a barrel of vodka. . . . Finally I got here, fifty miles from home, hoping to be paid, and you treat me to a "mood." How can I help being angry?

MRS. POPOV: It seems to me that I clearly said: My steward will return from the country and then you will be paid.

SMIRNOV: I didn't come to your steward, but to you! What the hell, if you'll pardon the expression, would I do with your steward?

MRS. POPOV: Excuse me, my dear sir, I am not accustomed to such profane expressions nor to such a tone. I'm not listening to you any more. [*Goes out quickly.*]   40

SMIRNOV: [*Alone.*] Well, how do you like that? "A mood." . . . "Husband died seven months ago"! Must I pay the interest or mustn't I? I ask you: Must I pay, or must I not? So, your husband's dead, and you're in a mood and all that finicky stuff . . . and your steward's away somewhere; may he drop dead. What do you want me to do? Do you think I can fly away from my creditors in a balloon or something? Or should I run and bash my head against the wall? I go to Gruzdev—and he's not at home; Yaroshevich is hiding, with Kuritsin it's a quarrel to the death and I almost throw him out the window; Mazutov has diarrhea, and this one is in a "mood." Not one of these swine wants to pay me! And all because I'm too nice to them! I'm a sniveling idiot, I'm spineless, I'm an old lady! I'm too delicate with them! So, just you wait! You'll find out what I'm like! I won't let you play around with me, you devils! I'll stay and stick it out until she pays. Rrr! . . . How furious I am today, how furious! I'm shaking inside from rage and I can hardly catch my breath. . . . Damn it! My God, I even feel sick! [*He shouts.*] Hey, you!

LUKA: [*Enters.*] What do you want?

SMIRNOV: Give me some beer or some water! [*LUKA exits.*] What logic is there in this! A man needs money desperately, it's like a noose around his neck—and she won't pay because, you see, she's not disposed to occupy herself with money matters! . . . That's the logic of a woman! That's why I never did like and do not like to talk to women. I'd rather sit on a keg of gunpowder than talk to a woman. Brr! . . . I even have goose pimples, this broad has put me in such a rage! All I have to do is see one of those spoiled bitches from a distance, and I get so angry it gives me a cramp in the leg. I just want to shout for help.

LUKA: [*Entering with water.*] Madam is sick and won't see anyone.

SMIRNOV: Get out! [*LUKA goes.*] Sick and won't see anyone! No need to see me . . . I'll stay   45
and sit here until you give me the money. You can stay sick for a week, and I'll stay for a week . . . if you're sick for a year, I'll stay a year. . . . I'll get my own back, dear lady! You can't impress me with your widow's weeds and your dimpled cheeks . . . we know all about those dimples! [*Shouts through the window.*] Semyon, unharness the horses! We're not going away quite yet! I'm staying here! Tell them in the stable to give the horses some oats! You brute, you let the horse on the left side get all tangled up in the reins again! [*Teasing.*] "Never mind" . . . I'll give you a never mind! [*Goes away from the window.*] Shit! The heat is unbearable and nobody pays up. I slept badly last night and on top of everything else this broad in mourning is "in a mood" . . . my head aches. . . . [*Drinks, and grimaces.*] Shit! This is water! What I need is a drink! [*Shouts.*] Hey, you!

LUKA: [*Enters.*] What is it?

SMIRNOV: Give me a glass of vodka. [*LUKA goes out.*] Oaf! [*Sits down and examines himself.*] Nobody would say I was looking well! Dusty all over, boots dirty, unwashed, unkempt, straw on my waistcoat. . . . The dear lady probably took me for a robber. [*Yawns.*] It's not very polite to present myself in a drawing room looking like this; oh well, who cares? . . . I'm not here as a visitor but as a creditor, and there's no official costume for creditors. . . .

LUKA: [*Enters with vodka.*] You're taking liberties, my good man. . . .

SMIRNOV: [*Angrily.*] What?

50 **LUKA:** I . . . nothing . . . I only . . .

SMIRNOV: Who are you talking to? Shut up!

LUKA: [*Aside.*] The devil sent this leech. An ill wind brought him. . . . [*LUKA goes out.*]

SMIRNOV: Oh how furious I am! I'm so mad I could crush the whole world into a powder! I even feel faint! [*Shouts.*] Hey, you!

MRS. POPOV: [*Enters, eyes downcast.*] My dear sir, in my solitude, I have long ago grown unaccustomed to the masculine voice and I cannot bear shouting. I must request you not to disturb my peace and quiet!

55 **SMIRNOV:** Pay me my money and I'll go.

MRS. POPOV: I told you in plain language: I haven't any spare cash now; wait until the day after tomorrow.

SMIRNOV: And I also told you respectfully, in plain language: I don't need the money the day after tomorrow, but today. If you don't pay me today, then tomorrow I'll have to hang myself.

MRS. POPOV: But what can I do if I don't have the money? You're so strange!

SMIRNOV: Then you won't pay me now? No?

60 **MRS. POPOV:** I can't. . . .

SMIRNOV: In that case, I can stay here and wait until you pay. . . . [*Sits down.*] You'll pay the day after tomorrow? Excellent! In that case I'll stay here until the day after tomorrow. I'll sit here all that time . . . [*Jumps up.*] I ask you: Have I got to pay the interest tomorrow, or not? Or do you think I'm joking?

MRS. POPOV: My dear sir, I ask you not to shout! This isn't a stable!

SMIRNOV: I wasn't asking you about a stable but about this: Do I have to pay the interest tomorrow or not?

MRS. POPOV: You don't know how to behave in the company of a lady!

65 **SMIRNOV:** No, I don't know how to behave in the company of a lady!

MRS. POPOV: No, you don't! You are an ill-bred, rude man! Respectable people don't talk to a woman like that!

SMIRNOV: Ach, it's astonishing! How would you like me to talk to you? In French, perhaps? [*Lisps in anger.*] *Madame, je vous prie*° . . . how happy I am that you're not paying me the money. . . . Ah, pardon, I've made you uneasy! Such lovely weather we're having today! And you look so becoming in your mourning dress. [*Bows and scrapes.*]

MRS. POPOV: That's rude and not very clever!

SMIRNOV: [*Teasing.*] Rude and not very clever! I don't know how to behave in the company of ladies. Madam, in my time I've seen far more women than you've seen sparrows. Three times I've fought duels over women; I've jilted twelve women, nine have jilted me! Yes! There was a time when I played the fool; I became sentimental over women, used honeyed words, fawned on them, bowed and scraped. . . . I loved, suffered, sighed at the moon; I became limp, melted, shivered . . . I loved passionately, madly, every which way, devil take me, I chattered away like a magpie about

---

°67 *Madame, je vous prie*: I beg you, Madam.

the emancipation of women, ran through half my fortune as a result of my tender feelings; but now, if you will excuse me, I'm on to your ways! I've had enough! Dark eyes, passionate eyes, ruby lips, dimpled cheeks; the moon, whispers, bated breath—for all that I wouldn't give a good goddamn. Present company excepted, of course, but all women, young and old alike, are affected clowns, gossips, hateful, consummate liars to the marrow of their bones, vain, trivial, ruthless, outrageously illogical, and as far as this is concerned [*taps on his forehead*], well, excuse my frankness, any sparrow could give pointers to a philosopher in petticoats! Look at one of those romantic creatures: muslin, ethereal demigoddess, a thousand raptures, and you look into her soul—a common crocodile! [*Grips the back of a chair; the chair cracks and breaks.*] But the most revolting part of it all is that this crocodile imagines that she has, above everything, her own privilege, a monopoly on tender feelings. The hell with it—you can hang me upside down by that nail if a woman is capable of loving anything besides a lapdog. All she can do when she's in love is slobber! While the man suffers and sacrifices, all her love is expressed in playing with her skirt and trying to lead him around firmly by the nose. You have the misfortune of being a woman, you know yourself what the nature of a woman is like. Tell me honestly: Have you ever in your life seen a woman who is sincere, faithful, and constant? You never have! Only old and ugly ladies are faithful and constant! You're more liable to meet a horned cat or a white woodcock than a faithful woman!

MRS. POPOV: Pardon me, but in your opinion, who is faithful and constant in love? The   70
   man?

SMIRNOV: Yes, the man!

MRS. POPOV: The man! [*Malicious laugh.*] Men are faithful and constant in love! That's news! [*Heatedly.*] What right have you to say that? Men are faithful and constant! For that matter, as far as I know, of all the men I have known and now know, my late husband was the best. . . . I loved him passionately, with all my being, as only a young intellectual woman can love; I gave him my youth, my happiness, my life, my fortune; he was my life's breath; I worshiped him as if I were a heathen, and . . . and, what good did it do—this best of men himself deceived me shamelessly at every step of the way. After his death, I found his desk full of love letters; and when he was alive—it's terrible to remember—he used to leave me alone for weeks at a time, and before my eyes he flirted with other women and deceived me. He squandered my money, made a mockery of my feelings . . . and, in spite of all that, I loved him and was true to him . . . and besides, now that he is dead, I am still faithful and constant. I have shut myself up in these four walls forever and I won't remove these widow's weeds until my dying day. . . .

SMIRNOV: [*Laughs contemptuously.*] Widow's weeds . . . I don't know what you take me for! As if I didn't know why you wear that black outfit and bury yourself in these four walls! Well, well! It's no secret, so romantic! When some fool of a poet passes by this country house, he'll look up at your window and think: "Here lives the mysterious Tamara, who, for the love of her husband, buried herself in these four walls." We know these tricks!

MRS. POPOV: [*Flaring.*] What? How dare you say that to me?

SMIRNOV: You may have buried yourself alive, but you haven't forgotten to powder   75
   yourself!

MRS. POPOV: How dare you use such expressions with me?

SMIRNOV: Please don't shout. I'm not your steward! You must allow me to call a spade a spade. I'm not a woman and I'm used to saying what's on my mind! Don't you shout at me!

MRS. POPOV: I'm not shouting, you are! Please leave me in peace!

SMIRNOV: Pay me my money and I'll go.

80 **MRS. POPOV:** I won't give you any money!

SMIRNOV: Yes, you will.

MRS. POPOV: To spite you, I won't pay you anything. You can leave me in peace!

SMIRNOV: I don't have the pleasure of being either your husband or your fiancé, so please don't make scenes! [*Sits down.*] I don't like it.

MRS. POPOV: [*Choking with rage.*] You're sitting down?

85 **SMIRNOV:** Yes, I am.

MRS. POPOV: I ask you to get out!

SMIRNOV: Give me my money . . . [*Aside.*] Oh, I'm so furious! Furious!

MRS. POPOV: I don't want to talk to impudent people! Get out of here! [*Pause.*] You're not going? No?

SMIRNOV: No.

90 **MRS. POPOV:** No?

SMIRNOV: No!

MRS. POPOV: We'll see about that. [*Rings.*]

[*LUKA enters.*]

Luka, show the gentleman out!

LUKA: [*Goes up to SMIRNOV.*] Sir, will you please leave, as you have been asked. You mustn't . . .

SMIRNOV: [*Jumping up.*] Shut up! Who do you think you're talking to? I'll make mince-meat out of you!

95 **LUKA:** [*His hand to his heart.*] Oh my God! Saints above! [*Falls into chair.*] Oh, I feel ill! I can't catch my breath!

MRS. POPOV: Where's Dasha? Dasha! [*She shouts.*] Dasha! Pelagea! Dasha! [*She rings.*]

LUKA: Oh! They've all gone berry picking . . . there's nobody at home . . . I'm ill! Water!

MRS. POPOV: Will you please get out!

SMIRNOV: Will you please be more polite?

100 **MRS. POPOV:** [*Clenches her fist and stamps her feet.*] You're nothing but a crude bear! A brute! A monster!

SMIRNOV: What? What did you say?

MRS. POPOV: I said that you were a bear, a monster!

SMIRNOV: [*Advancing toward her.*] Excuse me, but what right do you have to insult me?

MRS. POPOV: Yes, I am insulting you . . . so what? Do you think I'm afraid of you?

105 **SMIRNOV:** And do you think just because you're one of those romantic creations, that you have the right to insult me with impunity? Yes? I challenge you!

LUKA: Lord in Heaven! Saints above! . . . Water!

SMIRNOV: Pistols!

MRS. POPOV: Do you think just because you have big fists and you can bellow like a bull, that I'm afraid of you? You're such a bully!

SMIRNOV: I challenge you! I'm not going to let anybody insult me, and I don't care if you are a woman, a delicate creature!

110 **MRS. POPOV:** [*Trying to get a word in edgewise.*] Bear! Bear! Bear!

SMIRNOV: It's about time we got rid of the prejudice that only men must pay for their insults! Devil take it, if women want to be equal, they should behave as equals! Let's fight!

MRS. POPOV: You want to fight! By all means!

SMIRNOV: This minute!

MRS. POPOV: This minute! My husband had some pistols . . . I'll go and get them right away. [*Goes out hurriedly and then returns.*] What pleasure I'll have putting a bullet through that thick head of yours! The hell with you! [*She goes out.*]

SMIRNOV: I'll shoot her down like a chicken! I'm not a little boy or a sentimental puppy. I   115
don't care if she is delicate and fragile.

LUKA: Kind sir! Holy father! [*Kneels.*] Have pity on a poor old man and go away from
here! You've frightened her to death and now you're going to shoot her?

SMIRNOV: [*Not listening to him.*] If she fights, then it means she believes in equality of
rights and emancipation of women. Here the sexes are equal! I'll shoot her like a
chicken! But what a woman! [*Imitates her.*] "The hell with you! . . . I'll put a bullet
through that thick head of yours! . . ." What a woman! How she blushed, her eyes
shone . . . she accepted my challenge! To tell the truth, it was the first time in my life
I've seen a woman like that. . . .

LUKA: Dear sir, please go away! I'll pray to God on your behalf as long as I live!

SMIRNOV: That's a woman for you! A woman like that I can understand! A real woman!
Not a sour-faced nincompoop but fiery, gunpowder! Fireworks! I'm even sorry to
have to kill her!

LUKA: [*Weeps.*] Dear sir . . . go away!   120

SMIRNOV: I positively like her! Positively! Even though she has dimpled cheeks, I like her! I'm
almost ready to forget about the debt. . . . My fury has diminished. Wonderful woman!

MRS. POPOV: [*Enters with pistols.*] Here they are, the pistols. Before we fight, you must
show me how to fire. . . . I've never had a pistol in my hands before. . . .

LUKA: Oh dear Lord, for pity's sake. . . . I'll go and find the gardener and the coachman. . . .
What did we do to deserve such trouble? [*Exit.*]

SMIRNOV: [*Examining the pistols.*] You see, there are several sorts of pistols . . . there are
special dueling pistols, the Mortimer with primers. Then there are Smith and Wesson
revolvers, triple action with extractors . . . excellent pistols! . . . they cost a minimum
of ninety rubles a pair. . . . You must hold the revolver like this . . . [*Aside.*] What eyes,
what eyes! A woman to set you on fire!

MRS. POPOV: Like this?   125

SMIRNOV: Yes, like this . . . then you cock the pistol . . . take aim . . . put your head back a
little . . . stretch your arm out all the way . . . that's right . . . then with this finger press on
this little piece of goods . . . and that's all there is to do . . . but the most important thing
is not to get excited and aim without hurrying . . . try to keep your arm from shaking.

MRS. POPOV: Good . . . it's not comfortable to shoot indoors. Let's go into the garden.

SMIRNOV: Let's go. But I'm giving you advance notice that I'm going to fire into the air.

MRS. POPOV: That's the last straw! Why?

SMIRNOV: Why? . . . Why . . . because it's my business, that's why.   130

MRS. POPOV: Are you afraid? Yes? Aahhh! No, sir. You're not going to get out of it that
easily! Be so good as to follow me! I will not rest until I've put a hole through your
forehead . . . that forehead I hate so much! Are you afraid?

SMIRNOV: Yes, I'm afraid.

MRS. POPOV: You're lying! Why don't you want to fight?

SMIRNOV: Because . . . because you . . . because I like you.

MRS. POPOV: [*Laughs angrily.*] He likes me! He dares say that he likes me! [*Points to the*   135
door.] Out!

SMIRNOV: [*Loads the revolver in silence, takes cap and goes; at the door, stops for half a minute
while they look at each other in silence; then he approaches Mrs. Popov hesitantly.*] Listen. . . .
Are you still angry? I'm extremely irritated, but, do you understand me, how can I
express it . . . the fact is, that, you see, strictly speaking . . . [*He shouts.*] Is it my fault,
really, for liking you? [*Grabs the back of a chair, which cracks and breaks.*] Why the hell
do you have such fragile furniture! I like you! Do you understand? I . . . I'm almost in
love with you!

MRS. POPOV: Get away from me—I hate you!

SMIRNOV: God, what a woman! I've never in my life seen anything like her! I'm lost! I'm done for! I'm caught like a mouse in a trap!

MRS. POPOV: Stand back or I'll shoot!

140   **SMIRNOV:** Shoot! You could never understand what happiness it would be to die under the gaze of those wonderful eyes, to be shot by a revolver which was held by those little velvet hands. . . . I've gone out of my mind! Think about it and decide right away, because if I leave here, then we'll never see each other again! Decide . . . I'm a nobleman, a respectable gentleman, of good family. I have an income of ten thousand a year. . . . I can put a bullet through a coin tossed in the air . . . I have some fine horses. . . . Will you be my wife?

MRS. POPOV: [*Indignantly brandishes her revolver.*] Let's fight! I challenge you!

SMIRNOV: I'm out of my mind . . . I don't understand anything . . . [*Shouts.*] Hey, you, water!

MRS. POPOV: [*Shouts.*] Let's fight!

SMIRNOV: I've gone out of my mind. I'm in love like a boy, like an idiot! [*He grabs her hand, she screams with pain.*] I love you! [*Kneels.*] I love you as I've never loved before! I've jilted twelve women, nine women have jilted me, but I've never loved one of them as I love you. . . . I'm weak, I'm a limp rag. . . . I'm on my knees like a fool, offering you my hand. . . . Shame, shame! I haven't been in love for five years, I vowed I wouldn't; and suddenly I'm in love, like a fish out of water. I'm offering my hand in marriage. Yes or no? You don't want to? You don't need to! [*Gets up and quickly goes to the door.*]

145   **MRS. POPOV:** Wait!

SMIRNOV: [*Stops.*] Well?

MRS. POPOV: Nothing . . . you can go . . . go away . . . wait. . . . No, get out, get out! I hate you! But—don't go! Oh, if you only knew how furious I am, how angry! [*Throws revolver on table.*] My fingers are swollen from that nasty thing. . . . [*Tears her handkerchief furiously.*] What are you waiting for? Get out!

SMIRNOV: Farewell!

MRS. POPOV: Yes, yes, go away! [*Shouts.*] Where are you going? Stop. . . . Oh, go away! Oh, how furious I am! Don't come near me! Don't come near me!

150   **SMIRNOV:** [*Approaching her.*] How angry I am with myself! I'm in love like a student. I've been on my knees. . . . It gives me the shivers. [*Rudely.*] I love you! A lot of good it will do me to fall in love with you! Tomorrow I've got to pay the interest, begin the mowing of the hay. [*Puts his arm around her waist.*] I'll never forgive myself for this. . . .

MRS. POPOV: Get away from me! Get your hands away! I . . . hate you! I . . . challenge you!

[*Prolonged kiss, LUKA enters with an ax, the GARDENER with a rake, the COACHMAN with a pitchfork, and WORKMEN with cudgels.*]

LUKA: [*Catches sight of the pair kissing.*] Lord in heaven! [*Pause.*]

MRS. POPOV: [*Lowering her eyes.*] Luka, tell them in the stable not to give Toby any oats today.

                         CURTAIN

QUESTIONS

1. What was Mrs. Popov's life like with her late husband? What did she learn about him after his death? How has this knowledge affected her?

2. Who is Smirnov? What is he like, and how do you know? Why does he say what he does about women?

3. Why is Luka important? How do his responses highlight the emotions developing between Smirnov and Mrs. Popov?

4. What causes Mrs. Popov to call Smirnov a bear, a brute, a monster? What is his immediate response?

5. Why is Toby significant? How does he symbolize the shifting emotions of Mrs. Popov?

GENERAL QUESTIONS

1. Where did you laugh in the play? Analyze those moments and try to determine the causes of your laughter.

2. From this play, what conclusions can you draw about farce as a dramatic form? Consider the breaking chairs, the shouting, the challenge, the attitude of Smirnov about being shot, the shifting of feelings, etc.

3. How does Chekhov's presentation of the characters of Smirnov and Mrs. Popov make their reversal of feelings seem normal and logical, although sudden, unexpected, and surprising?

4. What are the major ideas or themes in *The Bear*? Consider vows made by the living to the dead, the difficulty of keeping resolutions, the nature of powerful emotions, the need to maintain conventions and expectations, and so on.

PAUL DOOLEY (b. 1928) and WINNIE HOLZMAN (b. 1954)

Born in West Virginia, Paul Dooley has at various times written a comic strip and worked as a stand-up comedian, a magician, and a clown. He is, however, primarily known as an actor. He has had a prolific career in the movies, including roles in The Out-of-Towners *(1970),* Death Wish *(1974),* A Wedding *(1978),* Breaking Away *(1979),* Popeye *(1980),* Sixteen Candles *(1984),* The Player *(1992),* Waiting for Guffman *(1997),* Runaway Bride *(1999),* Madison *(2005), and* Hairspray *(2007). His television credits include* Angels in the Endzone *(1996) and* Scrubs *(2009). He is married to Winnie Holzman.*

Born in New York City, Winnie Holzman studied at Princeton University and received a master's degree from New York University. She wrote the book for the Broadway musical Wicked *(2003), for which she won the Drama Desk Award for Outstanding Book of a Musical and was nominated for a Tony Award. Her television credits include* The Wonder Years *(1990),* Thirtysomething *(1990–1991), and* Huge *(2010). She is married to Paul Dooley.*

Post-its is an updated version of A. R. Gurney's Love Letters, *which debuted in 1989 off-Broadway. In it a couple is reading notes and letters that they have written to each other over many years. Dooley and Holzman's play explores a couple's relationship over a long period of time in the highly condensed language of brief notes. One could imagine a new play based on the previous two featuring a couple communicating through texting via their smartphones.*

Post-its (Notes on a Marriage) (1998)

[*There is a chair with a small table and a glass of water on either side of the stage, à la A.R. Gurney's* Love Letters. *The* ACTOR *and* ACTRESS *enter simultaneously from either wing, dressed simply. Each grasps a handful of Post-its as if it were a script. They sit, modestly acknowledging each other and the audience. Each takes out a pair of reading glasses, puts them on. The* ACTOR *lifts his first Post-it to begin . . . and reads. Every line is read from a Post-it.*]

ACTOR: Had an early meeting, couldn't bear to wake you. Close front door hard or it won't lock. PS: Last night was incredible.

ACTRESS: Helped myself to breakfast. You need milk. PS: Next time, wake me.

ACTOR: Hey, sleepyhead. Tried to wake you. Not easy. Left you some coffee, hope you like it black.

ACTRESS: Thought I should spend at least one night this week at my place. Picked up some milk; you don't have to pay me back.

ACTOR: Off to work, extra set of keys on hall table.

ACTRESS: Darling: Went jogging with Lila. If you go out, we need milk. Wow. I can't believe we're a "we"!

ACTOR: Hon: If you have time, could you pick up my shirts? Ticket on hall table. Thanks. PS: Milk.

ACTRESS: Shirts are in your closet. Your mother called. She seemed surprised to hear my voice. You obviously never mentioned me. [*Icy.*] Your shirts come to fourteen-fifty.

ACTOR: Gone to florist. Back soon. Hope you liked the chocolates.

ACTRESS: Darling, don't go in the den.

ACTOR: Sweetheart, I understand how much it means to you, but at this stage of our relationship I'm just not ready . . . to have a dog.

ACTRESS: [*After a beat.*] We need Milk-Bones. [*Next Post-it.*] Your mother called; call her. [*Next Post-it.*] Did you call your mother? [*Next Post-it.*] Went to lunch with your mother. Back soon.

ACTOR: Your new best friend my mother called. Call her.

ACTRESS: We need milk. Also, your mom mentioned how much you hate Eugene. I don't think Eugene's so bad. You should hear *my* middle name. Thank God *my* mother's dead!

ACTOR: Please do not mention the name Eugene to me ever again. Thank you.

ACTRESS: Shopping list: Pistachio ice cream. Sardines. Those tiny little cheeses that come in that cute little net bag. . . . They're so adorable, they make me cry.

ACTOR: Darling: I understand how much it means to you, but at this stage of our relationship I'm just not ready—

ACTRESS: We need Pampers. And baby wipes. And we need to get married.

ACTOR: Meet me City Hall, six sharp. You bring old and borrowed; I'll do new and blue. Mom will stay with Eugenia.

ACTRESS: Note to self: Find breast pump.

ACTOR: Take cold shower.

ACTRESS: Lose forty pounds.

ACTOR: Redirect sex drive into career. [*Next Post-it.*] Home late. Don't wait up.

ACTRESS: Hey, stranger, if you're not too busy, could you call Eugenia tonight, around bedtime? Just to see if she recognizes your voice?

ACTOR: Hon: Sorry about your birthday. PS: I got the raise!

ACTRESS: To the new vice president in charge of marketing. We need milk. Please advise.

ACTOR: Hon: I think we're out of milk. [*Next Post-it.*] Still no milk!

ACTRESS: If you want it so bad, get it yourself. The milk train doesn't stop here anymore.

ACTOR: If you can't even mange to get to the store—get some household help!

ACTRESS: [*Icy.*] Have gone to bed. Dinner is in fridge. If there is something in particular you wish for dinner tomorrow night, please leave note to that effect, and I will have Ursula or Carla or *Jose*, if it's *heavy*, pick it up. [*Beat.*] I can't take this anymore! We barely— [*Turns Post-it over.*] —communicate! There's got to be more to this marriage than a few hastily scribbled words on a small square of pastel paper! [*Beat.*] By the way, we're out of Post-its.

ACTOR: You think I *want* to spend every night at the office? You have absolutely no concept of how a business is run.

ACTRESS: To Whom It May Concern: Regarding your Post-it of June the tenth, allow me to clarify my position—up yours. Eugenia and I will be at your mother's. PS: *You* need milk.

[*The* ACTOR *glances over at the* ACTRESS, *she sips her water, coolly avoids his gaze. Finally . . .*]

ACTOR: Call her at my mother's. [*Next Post-it.*] Must call her. [*Next Post-it.*] Reminder: Take out garbage. Call her. [*Next Post-it.*] People to call: Her.

[*The* ACTOR *looks over again at the* ACTRESS. *She continues to ignore him.*]

ACTOR: Shopping list: Small loaf bread. Half pint milk. Soup for one. [*Next Post-it.*] Scotch for one. [*Next Post-it.*] Inflatable doll. [*Next Post-it.*] Scotch for two.

[*The* ACTRESS *looks at him. He catches her eye. Caught, she hastily looks away.*]

ACTOR: Things to tell her. That I'm sorry. That I miss her. That all I want—all I ever wanted—is for her to be happy.

[*The* ACTRESS *turns to him, touched by this. Then . . . takes the next Post-it. Reads.*]

ACTRESS: We need milk.
ACTOR: Dearest—have gone down to the end of the driveway to get the paper. Back soon.
ACTRESS: Honey, that therapist called back. He can see you Monday.
ACTOR: Sweetie, your therapist says your Tuesday is now Friday.
ACTRESS: What a session! Dr. K. believes that part of me is locked in unconscious competition with you, and envious of your masculine role. By the way, we need cucumbers, sausages, and a really big zucchini.
ACTOR: At last—a breakthrough today with Dr. G. It all became crystal clear. My mother. My father. *His* mother. You. *Your* mother. [*Turns Post-it over, continues.*] I see our entire marriage in a new light! I must free myself from the past so we can truly have a future. This changes everything.
ACTRESS: Hon: A Diet Coke exploded all over that note you left. Hope it wasn't important.

[*He stares at her. Oblivious to his reaction, she reads the next Post-it.*]

Took Eugenia to Brownies. Back soon.
ACTOR: Took Eugenia to kickboxing. Back soon.
ACTRESS: Took Eugenia to therapy. Could be a while.
ACTOR: Someone named Olaf called. Needs your résumé. What résumé?
ACTRESS: I landed the job! I start Monday! [*Next Post-it.*] Last minute meeting. I'll try to call. [*Next Post-it.*] I'll be working late, don't wait up. [*Next Post-it.*] I'm glad you waited. Last night was incredible.
ACTOR: Drove Eugenia to DMV. Hope she doesn't drive me home.
ACTRESS: Eugenia called. Loves college. Mentioned someone named Tyrone. Doesn't miss us at all.
ACTOR: Pick up travel brochures.
ACTRESS: Eugenia called. When can we meet Tyrone?
ACTOR: Schedule trip to campus when we get back.
ACTRESS: Sweetheart: Travel agent called. Cruise is confirmed! The honeymoon we never had! A time for us to leave all this behind and enjoy ten glorious days of total togetherness.

[*A long, silent beat. Very long. Very silent. They both look straight ahead. Finally he lifts the next Post-it.*]

ACTOR: [*With great relief.*] *God,* it's good to be home! [*Next Post-it.*] Dinner Wednesday with Eugenia and what's-his-name.

ACTRESS: Tyrone called—it's a boy. Kareem Eugene.

ACTOR: Eugenia called. Loves being a mom.

ACTRESS: Off to throw pots! Back soon! [*Next Post-it.*] Don't forget—we're bird-watching Thursday! [*Next Post-it.*] What night is good for square dancing?

ACTOR: Any night you want—we're free! Nothing to tie us down.

ACTOR: Eugenia called. Could we take Kareem for the weekend?

ACTRESS: Tyrone called. Could we take Kareem for spring break?

ACTOR: Kareem called. Could he spend the summer with us? Again. [*Next Post-it.*] Took Kareem to DMV.

ACTRESS: Honey—last night was incredible. I couldn't believe how long it went on. You've *got* to do something about your snoring.

ACTOR: Shopping list: Bengay. Dentucreme. Viagra.

ACTRESS: Wrinkles Away. I-Can't-Believe-It's-Support-Hose. Estrogen in a Drum.

ACTOR: We need milk of magnesia.

ACTRESS: Call Medicare.

ACTOR: You left your keys in the door again.

ACTRESS: Do you have my keys?

ACTOR: I can't find my glasses.

ACTRESS: Have you seen my cane?

ACTOR: How can I see your cane if I can't find my glasses?

ACTRESS: Gone for walk.

ACTOR: Where are you? Next time you go out, leave me a note!

ACTRESS: Sweetheart—dinner in oven. Taking nap. Love ya.

[*There's a pause as lights slowly fade on the* ACTRESS. *Then . . .*]

ACTOR: Call Emily. Also cousin Ruthie. Send note to Father McKay and everyone who sent flowers. [*Beat.*] The service was lovely. Everybody said so. [*Beat.*] I was looking through your things for that locket you said Eugenia should have. I could hardly believe what I found. You'd saved every Post-it I ever wrote you. I wish I'd saved yours. I could be reading them now. [*Beat.*] Back soon. Going to the store. We need milk.

QUESTIONS

1. Why do you think the two characters are simply called "actor" and "actress"? How would you describe their relationship?

2. What kinds of problems are revealed about the relationship between the two characters in the play? Do they resolve those problems?

3. What is the relationship like between the two characters and their daughter?

4. What results from the characters not speaking in complete sentences? What do you think the playwright is saying about marriage by the way the characters communicate?

GENERAL QUESTIONS

1. One could argue that if a play were written today with the same theme as *Post-its* it might be about a couple communicating by texting. What are the advantages or disadvantages of communicating with friends or family in this way?

2. Do you think most people change drastically over the course of a marriage or stay the same? If they change, in what ways does this happen?

3. In what ways might the view of marriage in *Post-its* be considered positive or negative?

EDWIN SÁNCHEZ (b.1955)

*Born in Puerto Rico and raised in New York, Edwin Sánchez gradu-
ated from the Yale School of Drama in 1994. He initially pursued
an acting career but eventually turned to writing drama. His plays
include* Clean *(1995), which was nominated by the American Theater Critics as best new play;* Unmerciful Good Fortune *(1996),
which won the AT&T Onstage New Play Award;* Barefoot Boy
with Shoes On *(1999), which was performed in Russia; and* Pops
(1997), which was published in Laugh Lines: Short Comic Plays
*(1997). Sánchez has won numerous awards including the 1995
Berrilla Kerr Foundation Award, the 1994 Princess Grace Playwriting Award, and the 1993
Eugene O'Neill Scholarship. He is a member of the Dramatists Guild.*

    In Pops *Sánchez displays his ear for realistic speech, the problems of immigrant life, and
the emotional bonds between family members. Tomás, the sixteen-year-old character of* Pops*,
embodies many of the conflicts involved in the clash of different cultures.*

POPS (2003)

[*The theme to* I Love Lucy *plays in the background. The volume comes up then disappears.* TOMÁS,
sixteen, stands center stage.]

TOMÁS: Can I just say, I hated Lucy. I used to have to watch it all the time with my Pops.
He would call her La Colora, the Redhead. He thought she was so funny. He'd come
home late at night from work, sneak me out of bed, and we'd watch *I Love Lucy*
reruns. Now, that was kinda cute when I was a kid, but the older I got, the more tired
it got, you know what I'm saying? When my father wanted to be funny he'd walk
around the house saying [*Thick Desi accent.*], "Lucy, 'splain." My father's English was
pretty bad as it is. "Lucy, 'splain." Funnee, Pops. Laugh riot. Parents should never be
allowed to try to be funny. So one night he drags me out of bed again, and I'm so not
in the mood, I don't even remember why, and we're sitting there watching Lucy and
my father is laughing as loud as Ricky would. You know, almost like he's pronounc-
ing "Ha-ha-ha." And I couldn't take it anymore and I snapped, "Man, why do you
think that's still so funny? You've only seen it, like, a hundred times." My father
got real quiet after that and I felt terrible. So I started laughing really hard, trying to
make it up to him, you know. But he didn't dare laugh anymore. I think my father
thought I was smarter than him, so if I told him he shouldn't laugh, then he shouldn't
laugh. He went to bed early that night. He was a busboy and he had a breakfast
shift the next day at the restaurant where he worked. Windows on the World at the
World Trade Center. He didn't come home the next day. Or ever. I had to go with my
mother to all these agencies to translate for her, but no one could help us. "He was
a busboy, not a citizen." I tried to explain it to my mother in Spanish, but she would
just look at them and say, "Please, 'splain." And people would roll their eyes, or try to
be nice or get impatient and try to get us out of whatever office we were in. "Busboy,
not a citizen." We had the wake in our apartment. We didn't have a body, of course,
just a picture of my Pops. He was smiling in it. All our relatives and neighbors were
there, and the priest came by. I stood in a corner, facing away from his picture. From
the laugh I had silenced. I could see my mother on the sofa, crying quietly, people
trying to comfort her. I turned then and walked up to my father's picture, and outta
nowhere, it started. [*In perfect Lucy.*] "Are you tired, run-down, listless? Do you poop
out at parties?" The room fell to a dead hush. [*Lucy-like.*] "The answer to all your
problems are in this biddle lottle." [*Quickly corrects himself as Lucy did.*] "Little bottle!"

My cousins started to scream with laughter, my uncle looked like he wanted to kill me, and my mother just stared at me. But I couldn't stop. I was by Lucy possessed. I started doing all her bits, I was, like, "Lucy's Greatest Hits." Lucy trapped in the icebox, Lucy as a showgirl with a heavy headdress, Lucy in the chocolate factory. Pretty soon everybody is laughing so loud you can barely hear me. The priest calls out "Do Lucy in the wine vat!" Like now I'm getting requests? I look at my mother and she is laughing so hard tears are flowing down her cheeks. And when I finally break, when I can't take it anymore, I cry like Lucy did when Ricky caught her doing something she shouldn't have. [*Lucy-like.*] "Wah!!!!!!!" [*Changing to real pain. Silence.*] My mother now has to work two jobs, she wanted us to stay in the U.S. because that's what my father wanted. The busboy, not the citizen. He never got a plaque and no one mentions him or nothing, so I like to think that every time there's an *I Love Lucy* rerun on, it's a tribute to my father. And baby, that Colora, she is on twenty-four hours a day.

[*Theme to* I Love Lucy *returns.*]

QUESTIONS

1. What is the relationship between Tomás and his father? Does the relationship change from before and after his father leaves for work?

2. What does Tomás find annoying about his father in the beginning of the play? Why does Tomás change his mind about whether *I Love Lucy* is funny or not?

3. Why do you think Tomás's father leaves and never returns to his family?

4. Why do you think Tomás's father wanted his family to stay in the United States?

5. What is the main theme of *Pops?* In reference to the theme, is Tomás's behavior at the wake appropriate?

GENERAL QUESTIONS

1. What do you think are the main reasons why immigrants come to the United States? Why do you think Tomás's father came?

2. What circumstances might make us reconsider our relationship to a family member?

WRITING ABOUT COMEDY

For an essay about comedy, you can choose any of the topics discussed in this chapter, such as *plot, conflict, character, point of view, setting, style, tone, symbolism,* or *theme.* You might choose one of these, or two or more; for example, how language and action define character, how character and symbol convey meaning, or how setting may influence comic structure.

Planning and prewriting strategies for each of these conventional elements are discussed at some length in Chapter 20 (pp. 1012–15) and in other chapters on prose fiction and poetry. As you develop your essay on comedy, you will find it helpful to look at these suggestions.

For the most part, planning and writing about specific features of comedy are much like addressing the same topics in other forms of drama, short stories, and poetry. However, a few areas of consideration—such as plot, character, and language—are especially significant in comic drama and can be handled in a distinctive fashion.

Questions for Discovering Ideas

PLOT, CONFLICT, STRUCTURE. What problems, adversities, or abnormal situations are in place at the comedy's opening? How is this initial situation complicated? Do the complications spring mainly from character or from situation? If from character, what aspects of behavior or personality create the problems? If from situation, what dilemmas or troubles plague the characters? What kinds of complications dominate—misunderstandings, disagreements, mistakes in identity, situational problems, or emotional entanglements? How important is coincidence?

What problems and complications occur early? Who is the comic protagonist (or protagonists) and what is the protagonist's goal (money, success, marriage, land, freedom)? How is the protagonist blocked (fathers, rivals, laws, customs, his or her own personality)? How threatening is the obstruction? What plans are hatched to overcome the blocking agents? Are the plans sensible or silly? Who initiates and executes the plans? To what extent do plans succeed (or fail)—because of chance and good luck or because of skillful planning and manipulation?

Describe the conflicts. Which conflict is central, and whom do the conflicts involve? Do they result from personality clashes or from situations? To what degree are they related to blocking activities? How does the action reach the crisis, and which characters are involved? What choices, decisions, plans, or conclusions become necessary? What events or revelations (of character, emotion, background) produce the catastrophe, and how do these affect characters, circumstances, and relationships?

In the comic resolution, to what extent are loose ends tied up and lives straightened out? Is reasonable order restored and regeneration assured or implied? Is the resolution satisfying? Disturbing? Does it leave you happy or thoughtful, or both? Are you amused by farce, pleased by romance, or disturbed by satire? If there is to be a marriage, whom will it bring together? What will the marriage settle, or whom will it divide? Most importantly, how can you account for your responses to the resolution and the play as a whole? How do they reflect the general aims of comedy?

CHARACTER. Which characters are realistic, conventional, round, flat, changing, standing still? Who is the protagonist or lover, the antagonist or blocking agent? Which characters seem excessive, eccentric, or irrational? What is the nature of their excesses? To what extent do the excesses define the characters? How do you respond to the excessive or exaggerated characters? Does the comedy provide a "cure" for the excesses? In other words, do the characters learn and change? If so, why and how? If not, why not?

From what classes are the characters derived? What class characteristics do you find? Who are the stock or stereotyped characters, and what is their significance to the protagonist? How does the playwright bring the characters to life? Who is the choric figure or *raisonneur*, if there is one? Who is the confidant? Which character can be considered a foil (or foils)?

LANGUAGE. Does the language consist of witty turns of phrase, confusions, puns, misunderstandings, or a mixture? Which characters are masters of language and which are mastered by it? Do characters use the same type of language and level of diction consistently? To what extent does language expose a character's self-interest or hypocrisy? If the language is witty and sparkling, what devices make it work effectively? If it is garbled and filled with misunderstandings, what types of errors does the playwright put into the characters' mouths? How does the language shape your response to characters, to ideas, and to the play as a whole?

Strategies for Organizing Ideas

To develop a central idea, isolate the feature you wish to explore and consider how it affects the shape and impact of the play. For *A Midsummer Night's Dream*, for example, you might focus on Puck's character and function. You might also develop a link between Puck's conventional role as a tricky servant with his love of mischief and the chaos he creates. Remember that it is difficult to develop essays from sentences like "Puck is a comic character" or "*The Bear* should be considered as a joke, as Chekhov himself called it." A more focused assertion that also reveals your thematic development is necessary, such as "Puck, modeled on the tricky servant of Roman comedy, causes most of the play's confusion," or "*The Bear* achieves humor through the exaggerated attitudes and speeches of Smirnov and Mrs. Popov."

Organize your essay by grouping related types of details together (such as observations about characters, actions, direct statements, and specific words), and choose your own order of presentation. In writing about Puck as a tricky servant and creator of chaos, for example, you might present only one kind of detail—such as direct statements—and introduce these not in their order in the play but rather as they contribute to your analysis of Puck's character.

More often than not, your supporting details will represent a variety of types of evidence—dramatic dialogue and action, individual soliloquies, special properties (such as a love potion or a disguise), or the failure or development of various plans. For example, you might support an assertion about Puck by referring to his reputation, actions, and attitudes as though each of these is equally important. Other possible strategies are to demonstrate how the topics are related according to cause and effect, to build the topics from the least to the most significant, and to trace how a common idea or image provides unity. Whatever your method of development, be sure to validate your arguments with supporting details.

A summary of key points will make your conclusion useful and effective. In addition, you can show how your conclusions in the body of the essay bear upon larger aspects of the play's meaning.

Illustrative Student Essay

Although underlined sentences are not recommended by MLA style, they are used in this illustrative essay as teaching tools to emphasize the central idea, thesis sentence, and topic sentences.

Walls 1

Suzanne Walls

Professor Tompkins

English 210

14 January 2014

Setting as Symbol and Comic Structure in Shakespeare's

A Midsummer Night's Dream°

A Midsummer Night's Dream might be considered light and incon-   [1]

sequential. The changes of mind undergone by the two sets of lovers, the

placing of an ass's head on one of the characters, the presence of unrealistic

fairies, the acting of a silly sketch—all seem very far out. But the play is more

serious than that. It dramatizes the accidental and arbitrary origins of love,

even though it considers this serious subject in the good-natured medium of

comedy.* To bring out both message and merriment, Shakespeare uses two

settings—the city of Athens and the nearby forest. The play's comic structure

is governed by the movements between the order and the chaos that these two

locations represent.†

At the play's beginning, Athens is presented as a haven of daylight,   [2]

order, and law. In this setting, Duke Theseus has absolute authority, fathers

are always right, and the law permits Egeus to "dispose" of Hermia "either to

this gentleman [Demetrius], / Or to her death" (1.1.43–44). The city is also the

place for the exposition and the beginning of complications. Here, we meet

the various groups of characters (except the fairies) and learn about the initial

problem—namely, that the relationship between Hermia and Lysander is

°This play appears on pages 1267–1318.
*Central idea.
†Thesis sentence.

Walls 2

blocked by a raging father, a rival suitor, and an old law. In order to flee and then to overcome these obstructions, Lysander asks Hermia to meet him in the woods. Her agreement begins a journey from Athens to the forest that ultimately includes everyone in the play—the four lovers, Egeus, the city rulers, and the "mechanicals."

[3]   The play's second location, the woods outside Athens, is the kingdom of Oberon and Titania, the king and queen of the fairies. It is a world of moonlight, chaos, madness, and dreams, a world that symbolizes the power of imagination and passion. The disorder in this world has many sources, including Oberon's jealousy, Titania's infatuation, and Puck's delight in mischief. When the lovers and the mechanicals enter this setting, they also become disordered and chaotic.

[4]   The woods are the setting for complication, crisis, and catastrophe. Confusion dominates the action here. Puck disrupts the mechanicals' rehearsal and transforms Bottom into a monster with the head of a jackass. In addition, the passions of the lovers are rearranged several times by Oberon and Puck through the magic of "love-in-idleness," a flower that symbolizes the irrational and overwhelming power of love. Although the first two adjustments of the lovers' feelings are done to help them in their plights, each has the effect of raising the levels of complication and disorder. Puck gleefully observes that his actions are the cause of the play's confusions (3.2.120–21):

> those things do best please me
> That befall prepost'rously.

Puck is right; his first application of love-in-idleness causes Lysander to fall wildly in love with Helena, and his second does the same to Demetrius.

[5]   The crisis and dénouement of the main plot also occur in the woods. A crisis occurs when the two lovers challenge each other and the women attack each other. At this point, complication and idiocy are at a peak, and the fairies must develop a plan to resolve the threats. Puck therefore misleads the lovers into ending their potential duel, and he adjusts their emotions one more time. The dénouement—the revelation of the newly restored emotions—occurs the

Walls 3

next morning at the edge of the woods, in the presence of Egeus, Theseus, and
Hippolyta. Thus, it ends the confusing relationships occurring in the forest
and begins the regularity of relationships in the more orderly world of city and
society.

Resolution—the marriages and the mechanicals' production of *Pyramus*   [6]
and Thisby—occurs in the first setting, the city, which represents law and
order. But the journey to the second setting has had a significant effect on the
urban world both for Theseus and for the lovers. The law has been softened
and Egeus has been overruled; the young lovers have been allowed to marry
as they like, and their lives have been set right. In the end, this second setting
has also become the dream world of night and the supernatural, and the fairy
dance and blessings closing the play only emphasize the harmony and the
regenerative implications of the comic resolutions.

Setting, symbolism, and comic pattern thus combine in *A Midsummer*   [7]
Night's Dream to produce an intricately plotted structure. Each element
reinforces the others, bringing the play toward completion although time
after time there seems to be no way out. The marvel of the play is that
the two settings represent, realistically, two opposed states of being, and,
dramatically, two distinct stages of comic structure. The journey *out of* Athens,
into the woods, and then *back to* the city is also a journey *from* exposition and
adversity, *through* complication, crisis, and catastrophe, and then *forward to*
comic resolution.

Walls 4

Work Cited

Shakespeare, William. *A Midsummer Night's Dream. Literature: An Introduction to Reading and Writing, Compact Edition.* Ed. Edgar V. Roberts
and Robert Zweig. 6th ed. New York: Pearson, 2015. 1267–1318. Print.

Commentary on the Essay

This essay deals with three elements of *A Midsummer Night's Dream*: setting, symbols, and comic structure. It demonstrates the way a number of different topics can be combined in a single essay. Consequently, the essay is organized to reflect the journey from the city to the woods and then back to the city.

The body of the essay takes up the settings, their symbolic meaning, and the relationship between setting and structure. Paragraph 2 deals with Athens both as a world of law and order and as the setting for exposition and the beginnings of complication. The supporting details include circumstance, actions, and dialogue.

Paragraphs 3–5 deal with the middle of the journey and of the play. Paragraph 3 discusses the symbolic implications of the forest setting, and paragraphs 4 and 5 take up the connection between the setting and comic structure, specifically, complication, crisis, and dénouement. Again, the supporting details in these paragraphs are a mixture of actions, circumstances, and direct quotations.

Paragraph 6 deals briefly with the return to the city, linking this setting with the play's comic resolution. The concluding paragraph returns to the idea of how *A Midsummer Night's Dream* connects setting, symbol, and comic pattern.

Writing Topics About Comedy

Writing Paragraphs

1. Choose one comic character from *A Midsummer Night's Dream*, *Beauty*, or *The Bear*. In a paragraph describe how this character functions in the play to bring about the final comic outcome of the play. You might consider how the character interacts with other characters or what part he or she plays in bringing about an action that furthers the plot.

Writing Essays

1. Treat the lovers in *A Midsummer Night's Dream* as types or archetypes (see Chapter 25). In an essay consider the following questions. What is their situation? What problems block the fulfillment of their love? How serious are these problems? What actions and ruses do they plan to make things right? How are the pairs of lovers in the two plays similar? Different?

2. Write an essay describing Shakespeare's comic technique in *A Midsummer Night's Dream*. Consider these questions: Is the basic situation serious? How does Shakespeare keep it comic? How does the boisterousness of the low characters influence your perceptions of the lovers and the courtly characters? Would the play be as interesting without Bottom and his crowd or without the fairies and their involvement? How does the comic outcome depend on the boisterousness and colorfulness provided by the players and the fairies? For research on Shakespeare as a comic dramatist, you might wish to consult Henry B. Charlton's classic study *Shakespeare's Comedies* (rpt. 1972) and/or a more recent book by Michael Mangan, *A Preface to Shakespeare's Comedies* (1996).

3. *The Bear* is one of Chekhov's most popular comedies. Read another Chekhov play (for example, *The Cherry Orchard, The Seagull, Three Sisters,* or *Uncle Vanya*) and compare it to *The Bear* (characters with characters, dialogue with dialogue, situations with situations, and so on). As you make your comparison, attempt to explain the continued popularity of *The Bear*.

Creative Writing Assignment

1. Write a comic scene of your own between two people. Your scene might feature two people who are angry with each other, as in *The Bear*, or who are friends, as in *Beauty*, or acquaintances, as in *Trifles* (Chapter 20). You might also try a dialogue between one person under a spell and another person in normal touch with reality, as in *A Midsummer Night's Dream*. After you finish your scene, write a short essay explaining the principles on which you've written your scene, such as the reasons for your choice of material, your use of jokes (if any), straightforward dialogue, anger, outrage, amused responses, and so on. Try to enjoy doing this.

Library Assignment

1. Write an essay about the nature of comedy, using *A Midsummer Night's Dream, Beauty,* or *The Bear* as material. Deal with issues such as the following: How can comic material be defined? Does the happy outcome of a serious action qualify a play as a comedy, or should no action be serious? When is a comedy no longer comic but tragic? Are jokes necessary? Is farcical action necessary? Where are the edges between comedy and farce, and absurdity, on the one hand, and comedy and tragedy on the other? For a research component for this topic, you might wish to introduce materials from books by Wylie Sypher (1956, rpt. 1982, an edition of two classic essays on comedy), G. S. Amur (1963), Robert Corrigan (1965), Robert B. Heilman (1978), T. G. A. Nelson (1990), Athene Seyler (1990), Frances Teague (1994), and Janet Suzman (1995).

Chapter 23
Visions of Dramatic Reality and Nonreality: Varying the Idea of Drama as Imitation

AFTER STUDYING THIS MATERIAL, YOU SHOULD BE ABLE TO DO THE FOLLOWING:

- Explain the development of realistic and nonrealistic drama
- Define the elements of realistic and nonrealistic drama
- Appraise the conventional aspects of dramatic structure in realistic and nonrealistic plays

A major dimension of drama is the relationship to reality that dramatists seek to create. From Aristotle's description of the origin of tragedy, we may conclude that drama was originally considered to be an "imitation of an action"; that is, each play represents a significant and discrete series of actions that make up a complete story in the lives of the major characters. The drama focuses only on those actions and speeches that are integral to the story, and the outcome of the action is the logically necessary consequence of the conflicts and issues raised in the play. To achieve such concentration, dramatists introduce restrictions and nonrealistic conventions that aid the presentation of the story. Thus there can be no absolutely realistic drama in the sense of the straightforward duplication of life. Rather, the issue is how far drama goes either toward or away from reality.

Realism and Nonrealism in Drama

The most important difference between realistic and nonrealistic drama concerns the play's relationships to the audience, the theater, and the world at large. In **realistic drama,** the playwright seeks to create an *illusion* of reality—*verisimilitude*. The situations, problems, characters, dialogue, and other elements are all those that might genuinely exist in the real world. The play presents a self-contained action in a world that professes to imitate reality. Ideally, the illusion of reality is never compromised; the actors never drop out of character; the audience is never addressed; and the play never acknowledges that it is a play.

In **nonrealistic drama,** even the pretense to achieve realism is abandoned, and the goal instead is to present essential features of character and society through techniques that *do not* try to mirror life. Nonrealistic drama employs whatever conventions the playwright finds useful. It can be full of devices that break through the illusion on the stage (or the page) and scream out that the play is a play—a work of art, a stylized imitation of something remotely connected to life.

Nonrealistic Drama Has Prevailed During Most of Dramatic History

From ancient Greek tragedy through Victorian melodrama, plays were artificial and conventionalized. The conventions of drama changed from age to age—choruses and masks in Greek tragedy, soliloquies and blank verse in Elizabethan plays, rhymed couplets in French and much English neoclassical drama. Although these conventions were nonrealistic, audiences and readers accepted them as normal features of dramatic presentation. The enduring eloquence and power of the nonrealistic tradition can be found in plays like Sophocles's *Oedipus the King* Shakespeare's *Hamlet,* and Miller's *Death of a Salesman* (all in Chapter 21).

By the nineteenth century, artificial and romantic drama dominated the stage. These plays featured lavish sets, gorgeous costumes, flamboyant acting, conventionalized plots, and happy endings. The characters were exaggerated and idealized—heroes saving the day, heroines swooning at every opportunity, and villains twirling their mustaches and leering at the audience as they plotted to steal the hero's sweetheart and swindle him out of his money.

Realistic Drama Developed in Opposition to Unrealistic Drama

In reaction to the unrealistic tradition, and as a likely development coincidental with democratic theories of society and government, a number of nineteenth-century dramatists created plays that presented realistic characters in realistic situations and that explored the real problems of contemporary society. The rebellion began slowly, and most of these writers were Europeans; among them Émile Zola (French), Henrik Ibsen (Norwegian), Maxim Gorki (Russian), and George Bernard Shaw (Irish-English). American realists, who came to this tradition somewhat later than the Europeans, included Eugene O'Neill, Langston Hughes, and Susan Glaspell (pp. 1005, 1349, 982).

DRAMATIC REALISM ATTEMPTS TO EXPLORE PEOPLE'S LIVES. In keeping with the goal of verisimilitude, realistic plays eliminate traditional but artificial dramatic conventions that do not occur in daily life, such as disguises, overheard conversations, asides, soliloquies, and verse. At its best, realistic drama is a close examination of character in conflict. The plots are straightforward and progress chronologically. The characters look, speak, and act as much as possible like real people. The settings are middle-class living rooms, the country houses of the wealthy, the squalid slums of the poor. Usually the plays explore ideas about the nature of humanity in conflict with social customs and prejudices.

REALISTIC THEATRICAL PRODUCTIONS EMPHASIZE LIFELIKE SETTINGS. The new realism called for equally new and realistic methods of production and action. Most theaters of the nineteenth century featured a darkened auditorium, a proscenium arch separating the audience from the players, and a picture-frame stage. The spectators watched the play as though the fourth wall of a room had been removed. The illusion was that the audience was eavesdropping on private conversations and events.

The settings and stage directions for realistic drama became as detailed and lifelike as possible. When the curtain went up, the audience saw a completely furnished room or office, much like the ones in which they themselves lived or worked. Ibsen's description of the setting for Act 1 of *A Dollhouse* (1879) (Chapter 24), for example, calls for the duplication of Norwegian middle-class living and dining rooms of the late nineteenth century, complete with a piano, a coffee table, arm-chairs, a ceramic tile heating stove, easy chairs, a rocking-chair, and a bookcase. Lighting and costumes were equally realistic. Lighting was designed to duplicate the natural light at a particular time of day or the lamps burning in a room at night. Similarly, the lavish and beautiful costumes of nineteenth-century melodrama gave way to detailed realism in dress and makeup on the stage.

REALISTIC DRAMA REQUIRES ACTORS TO DUPLICATE THE SPEECH AND MANNERISMS OF LIVING PEOPLE. The most radical and permanent change caused by the new realism was in acting styles. In the Victorian theater, actors stood in one place, assumed a conventional stance, and declaimed their lines. In realistic drama the acting became more natural and intimate. Actors began to combine movement with dialogue and to play "within the scene" to each other rather than to the spectators.

These changes were due, in large measure, to Konstantin Stanislavsky (1863–1938), one of the founders of the Moscow Art Theater (1898) and the inventor of what we now term *method acting*. Stanislavsky argued that actors had to build characterizations on a lifelong study of inner truths and motivation. He taught actors to search inwardly, within the depths of their own imaginations, for the feelings, motivations, and behavior of the characters they portray.

A New Nonrealistic Drama Was Created in Opposition to Realism

No sooner had realism taken over the stage than a new nonrealistic drama began to emerge as a reaction against realism. Many playwrights in Europe and the United States decided that realism had gone too far and that the quest for minutely real-istic details had sacrificed the essence of drama—character and universal truth. Playwrights began to explore every avenue of antirealistic drama.

A CONSEQUENCE OF NONREALISTIC DRAMA WAS EXPERIMENTAL STAGING. At the same time, new types of stages and theaters began to appear. The **thrust stage,** a feature of Elizabethan theaters, was reintroduced. It projected into the audience, thus helping to destroy the fourth-wall principle of realistic drama. The **arena stage,** or **theater-in-the-round,** was developed, which also called for new concepts in drama and production.[1]

Playwrights like Luigi Pirandello (Italian, 1867–1936) and Bertolt Brecht (German, 1898–1956) wrote plays that required only minimal sets or no sets at all. In this same tradition, many works, like those of Edward Albee (b. 1928), call for little more than suggestive sets that can be brought on stage by no more than a few stage hands. To a degree, both Miller's *Death of a Salesman* (Chapter 21) and Williams's *The Glass Menagerie* share in this tradition. Miller presents us with three rooms for his characters, together with a thrust stage in

---

See pages 968–69 for an additional discussion of stages.

which dream sequences take place, while Williams utilizes projected images and claims that his scenes are "not realistic." Such characteristics remind us constantly that we are reading or watching a play—an illusion and an imitation—rather than real life.

Elements of Realistic and Nonrealistic Drama

THE TWO KINDS OF DRAMA IMPLY GREAT DIFFERENCES IN THEIR PRESENTATION OF NARRATIVE. Because realistic plays, like life, unfold chronologically, the *story* (as opposed to the *play*) is usually nearing conclusion when the stage action begins. In Glaspell's *Trifles* (Chapter 20), for example, the story comprises incidents from Minnie Wright's youth, her marital difficulties, and her reaction against her husband. All this, however, is presented in conversation; it all occurred *before* the play begins. Such events from the past have a profound impact on the present action in realistic drama, but the play itself presents only the last part of the story.

In nonrealistic drama, the structure of the plot is more fluid. Action shifts easily from the present to the past with little or no transition. Flashbacks are mixed with present action, and the entire play dramatizes the past through a present perspective. In Williams's *The Glass Menagerie*, recollected past action is revealed through the present memories of the narrator. Similarly, the action in Miller's *Death of a Salesman* constantly shifts between the present and memories of the past.

DRAMATIC CHARACTERS ARE SHAPED ACCORDING TO WHETHER THEY ARE CONCEIVED REALISTICALLY OR NONREALISTICALLY. The characters in realistic drama are as much as possible like living people. They can be representative, symbolic, or even stock characters, but they must sound and act like normal human beings, with backgrounds, emotions, motivations, and last names as well as first names. There must be reasons for their actions, words, conflicts, and relationships. Most important, they must be consistent. Their responses, decisions, and characteristics must be the same as in real life. Such fidelity to life is apparent in realistic plays like Glaspell's *Trifles* and Hughes's *Mulatto*.

In modern nonrealistic drama, the characters can be nameless figures who have no background or motivation and who drop in and out of character, or who assume a number of different functions at different times, according to the dramatist's need. Tom is such a character in Williams's *The Glass Menagerie*. At various times he is a character in the action, a narrator who provides background and commentary, and a stage manager. As a character, he interacts with Laura and Amanda; as a narrator, he speaks directly to the audience; as a stage manager, he occasionally cues the technicians offstage about music and lighting.

These distinctions do not mean that realistic characters are always round and nonrealistic ones always flat. The way in which a playwright develops characters, realistically or nonrealistically, does not control the degree to which they are developed. Thus, true-to-life characters like Mr. Hale in *Trifles* or Jim O'Connor in *The Glass Menagerie* are flat. By the same token, nonrealistic characters, like Tom in *The Glass Menagerie* or Willy Loman in *Death of a Salesman*, have enough depth and scope to be considered fully round.

LANGUAGE IS A SIGN OF THE DEGREES OF REALITY OR NONREALITY. In a realistic play, the language accurately represents the diction appropriate to the class or group of people portrayed. There is no poetry, no radical shift in style, and no direct address to the reader or speaker. In *Mulatto*, for instance, Cora and her uneducated children consistently use the vernacular speech patterns of African Americans living in the South during the 1930s. Similarly, the characters in Glaspell's *Trifles* sound like Midwestern farmers and small-town residents.

Such verisimilitude is not required in nonrealistic drama. Playwrights employ any linguistic devices that suit their needs. Some characters therefore speak in verse, clichés, or even nonsense sounds. Others have two or three separate speeds of presentation, as Tom does in *The Glass Menagerie*. Dramatists are free to introduce songs or hymns into the play, and some characters speak directly to the audience. Often the characters talk as though they are in a dream, or are living through their memories, or are so preoccupied with their concerns that the other characters are incidental to them.

THE STAGE ITSELF IS A GRAPHIC GUIDE TO THE LEVEL OF REALITY. Such differences in plot, characterization, and language are matched by differences in production techniques. Whereas the staging of a realistic drama must be true to life, as in *A Dollhouse*, nonrealistic drama is usually staged with few or no realistic effects. While the sets are based in reality, they are primarily symbolic and expressive of mood, employing lighting and a semitransparent painted cloth (called a **scrim**) to create the simultaneous effect of multiple places or times. Carefully controlled lighting indicates flashbacks, changes in mood, and shifts of location, and spotlights illuminate and emphasize objects and characters in ways that never happen in reality. In addition, the dramatist of a nonrealistic play is free to introduce music, special sound effects, words or images projected onto a wall or screen, action that flows off the stage into the auditorium, and speeches made directly to the spectators or the reader. All these and other devices break the illusion of reality and demand that we consider the play as an artistic construction. Such nonrealistic dramatic effects are described in the stage directions for both *Death of a Salesman* and *The Glass Menagerie*.

In this way, nonrealistic drama moved progressively farther away from realism throughout the latter half of the twentieth century. With the development of flexible theaters, in which the seats in certain locations are removed, with acting areas being set up throughout the house, the action of plays has moved offstage and into the space once occupied by the audience.

Paradoxically, as such drama becomes more nonrealistic, the theater itself, as a place for acting and performing, becomes the dominant reality. In the 1960s and 1970s, acting companies like the Living Theater in New York experimented with plays that began onstage, moved into the audience, and ended on the streets outside. Such productions represent the edge of drama. In the mid-1980s, the Old Vic Company in London produced *The Creation*—a series of medieval mystery plays—in which the actors mingled among the spectators, separating only when their parts were called for. Whenever new scenes were introduced, the standing spectators were (literally) swept aside to provide space, so that acting areas were being shaped by the shifting audience. A production that remained popular into this century was *Tony 'n' Tina's Wedding* (1988), which represented the staging of a wedding and reception (in two different locations, one a church and the other a restaurant).[2] Because performers and audience were to interact, particularly at the reception, many members of the audience took on impromptu acting and speaking roles. Every performance was therefore spontaneous and unique. An argument might be made that such one-time performances represent superrealism, but in fact they blur the distinction between drama and the real world to the point where art almost ceases to be art, and all action everywhere—both real life and stage life—seems entirely to be performance.

Most Plays Offer a Blend of Realism and Nonrealism

To this point we have been speaking as though realistic and nonrealistic drama were always at opposite extremes, but most plays are not purely realistic or nonrealistic. Rather, the terms represent the opposite ends of a continuum, and most plays fall somewhere between the extremes. Glaspell's *Trifles*, Wilson's *Fences*, Hughes's *Mulatto*, and Ibsen's *A Dollhouse*, for example, are highly realistic, yet each modifies its realism through symbolism and selective emphasis. Conversely, the staging of *The Glass Menagerie*, being "a memory play," is nonrealistic in many respects, yet it is based on easily recognized characterizations of people in a strained family relationship. Williams's *The Glass Menagerie* falls near the middle of the continuum; it combines realistic language and characterization with nonrealistic settings, lighting, and structure.

Plays for Study

Langston Hughes . . . . Mulatto, 1349
Edward Bok Lee . . . . .El Santo Americano, 1374
Tennessee Williams . . . . The Glass Menagerie, 1378
August Wilson. . . . . Fences, 1427

LANGSTON HUGHES (1902–1967)

For a discussion of Langston Hughes's early life and career, and his work in poetry, see pages 849–52.

In 1931, just before he reached the age of thirty, and while he was still beginning his writing career, Hughes traveled to Russia. He spent a year there and worked on a Soviet film about racial relations in the United States. When he returned he was filled with ideas, and his writing continued in the direction of exposing racism and inequality in America. A major result was his first collection of stories, The Ways of White Folks, *which came out in 1934. This was a book in which he fictionalizes his disaffection with the condition of African Americans both in the South and in the North. One of these stories was "Father and Son," a version of the material that he turned into his two-act play* Mulatto. *Produced at the Vanderbilt Theater in New York in October 1935, the play had a run of 373 performances—the record at that time for a Broadway play by an African American dramatist.*

Tony 'n' Tina's *Wedding* ran in New York for close to seventeen years and became so firmly fixed that it created its own website at www.tonylovestina.com, a practice now common with many long-running plays. The play was performed in eleven other American cities and also in Europe, Asia, and Australia, with as many as a hundred different performing sites worldwide.

Hughes and the African American Theater After 1920

During these years, the growing African American theater was dominated by two major themes, the first being the customs and problems of Southern blacks. The most pressing problem was the cruelty and injustice of lynching. Angelina Weld Grimke's *Rachael* (1920) and James Miller's *Never No More* (1932) openly condemned the practice. Dennis Donaghue's *Legal Murder* (1934) was an attack on the false conviction for rape of nine young black men from Scottsboro, Alabama, a topic that Hughes also treated in his early drama *Scottsboro Limited: Four Poems and a Play in Verse* (1932). The second major theme concerned the adjustments that blacks needed to make after they left the South and migrated to cities in the North. Frank Wilson's *Meek Mose* was perhaps the most optimistic of these plays, in which dispossessed blacks discover oil on their new property. More typical were Garland Anderson's *Appearances* (1925), about how a black bellhop overcomes false charges of rape, and Wallace Thurman's *Harlem* (1929), about the difficulties of a black family living in Chicago. This theme also dominates Lorraine Hansberry's *A Raisin in the Sun*, the now-classic drama that marked the coming of age of post–World War II African American playwrights.

Hughes's Career as a Dramatist

Although Hughes is not thought of principally as a dramatist, he wrote plays throughout his career. In addition to the plays already mentioned, he wrote *Little Ham* (1936) and *Soul Gone Home* (1937), a short fantasy play. As the first production for the radical Suitcase Theater, which he founded after returning as a correspondent from the Spanish Civil War, he wrote *Don't You Want to Be Free* (1938). He collaborated with Arna Bontemps in *When the Jack Hollers* (1936) and with Zora Neale Hurston in *Mule Bone* (reissued in 1991). In 1948 he wrote the lyrics for the Kurt Weill and Elmer Rice musical *Street Scene*, perhaps the best known of the plays in which he was involved. In 1951 he produced a libretto, *Just Around the Corner*, and in 1957 he wrote *Simply Heavenly*, a blues-musical play featuring the character Jesse Semple, whom he had created as a character in his weekly columns for the *Chicago Defender*. Although *Simply Heavenly* (which is a musical version of an earlier play, *Semple Takes a Wife*) concludes optimistically, one can find within it the serious theme of frustration resulting from the difficulties that African Americans experience in seeking identity and recognition. Semple says, at one point:

> I'm broke, busted, and disgusted. And just spent mighty near my last nickel for a paper—and there ain't no news in it about colored folks. Unless we commit murder, robbery or rape, or are being chased by a mob, do we get on the front page, or hardly on the back. (I.5)

Hughes's interests in the last decades of his life were in the musical theater, particularly the introduction of gospel-related music and jazz. Three of his major efforts were *Black Nativity* (1961), *The Gospel Glory* (1962), and *Jericho-Jim Crow* (1964). His output as a dramatist was indeed great, even if it may be overshadowed by his preeminence as a poet and writer of fiction.

Mulatto and the Reality of the Southern Black Experience

Hughes's *Mulatto* deals with life in the South during the 1930s, a time when the system of white control over blacks was absolute and uncompromisingly harsh and brutal. Hughes's first conception of the play—a troubled relationship between father and son—is a perennial one. Colonel Tom Norwood and Robert Lewis, his mulatto son, recognize their relationship but also hate and reject each other. In *Mulatto* the realistic cause of conflict is the "color line"—the symbolic line that people of different races must cross in order to accept each other as human beings. Acceptance is an ideal goal, just as the color line is an insurmountable obstacle in the society that the play depicts. The lack of ability or will to cross the line governs the pattern of action and also the violent outcome. Colonel Norwood has lived in the same house with Cora Lewis for many years, and they do well together as long as he is not confronted with the issue of his paternity or challenged about his control over the plantation. There is no way he can recognize the four "yard blacks" on his plantation as his legitimate children, however, unless he is willing to forsake his identity as a white.

There are many other marks of dramatic realism, particularly the exploitation of black women (described in Act 1, speech 61), the front entrance of the Norwood house, Robert's complaints about Miss Gray, and his speeding with the Ford. All of his so-called uppity actions would not be unacceptable to white society if Robert were white, but because he is black they indicate a state of revolt. In addition, Robert's identity as half white, half black—he is called "yellow" by Colonel Tom—leaves him in an anomalous position, for he is not "white" enough to be equal or "black" enough to be subservient. The reality of his situation leads him to hate both whites and blacks alike, and the sudden eruption of his seething anger leads to his violence.

Mulatto reflects the reality of language in the South of the 1930s. Hughes's blacks, except for Robert and Sallie, use southern black vernacular (called "darky talk" by Hughes). The introduction of such speech in literature was controversial at the time. Many black intellectuals who had also been a part of the Harlem Renaissance believed that dialect should be shunned, on the principle that it reinforced negative African American stereotypes. However, Hughes believed using the vernacular was correct because it was truthful and realistic, enabling writers to demonstrate that blacks are not stereotypes, that they face human problems just like everyone else, and that they succeed and fail just like everyone else. Moreover, there were precedents for the realistic use of dialect that had been set by Mark Twain in *Tom Sawyer* and *Huckleberry Finn*, both of which are acknowledged classics of American literature.

Mulatto is one of Hughes's most important plays. In 1950 he refashioned it as a libretto, titled *The Barrier*, which was set to music by the composer Jan Meyerowitz. In addition, the play was translated into Spanish and published in South America in 1954.

Mulatto (1935)

CHARACTERS

Colonel Thomas Norwood, Plantation owner, a still vigorous man of about sixty, nervous, refined, quick-tempered, and commanding; a widower who is the father of four living mulatto children by his Negro housekeeper.

Cora Lewis, A brown woman in her forties who has kept the house and been the mistress of Colonel Norwood for some thirty years.

William Lewis, The oldest son of Cora Lewis and the Colonel; a fat, easy-going, soft looking mulatto of twenty-eight; married.

Sallie Lewis, The seventeen-year-old daughter, very light with sandy hair and freckles, who could pass for white.

Robert Lewis [Bert], Eighteen, the youngest boy; strong and well-built; a light mulatto with ivory-yellow skin and proud thin features like his father's; as tall as the Colonel, with the same gray-blue eyes, but with curly black hair instead of brown; of a fiery, impetuous temper—immature and willful—resenting his blood and the circumstances of his birth.

Fred Higgins, A close friend of Colonel Norwood; a county politician; fat and elderly, conventionally Southern.

Sam, An old Negro retainer, a personal servant of the Colonel.

Billy, The small son of William Lewis; a chubby brown kid about five.

Talbot, The overseer.

Mose, An elderly Negro, chauffeur for Mr. Higgins.

A Storekeeper

An Undertaker

Undertaker's Helper, Voice offstage only.

The Mob

ACT 1

TIME. *An afternoon in early fall.*

SETTING. *The same.*

ACTION. *The living room of the Big House on a plantation in Georgia. Rear center of the room, a vestibule with double doors leading to the porch; at each side of the doors, a large window with lace curtains and green shades; at left a broad flight of stairs leading to the second floor; near the stairs, downstage, a doorway leading to the dining room and kitchen; opposite at right of stage, a door to the library. The room is furnished in the long outdated horsehair and walnut style of the nineties; a crystal chandelier, a large old-fashioned rug, a marble-topped table, upholstered chairs. At the right there is a small cabinet. It is a very clean, but somewhat shabby and rather depressing room, dominated by a large oil painting of NORWOOD's wife of his youth on the center wall. The windows are raised. The afternoon sunlight streams in.*

ACTION. *As the curtain rises, the stage is empty. The door at the right opens and COLONEL NORWOOD enters, crossing the stage toward the stairs, his watch in his hand. Looking up, he shouts:*

NORWOOD: Cora! Oh Cora!

CORA: [*Heard above*] Yes, sir, Colonel Tom.

NORWOOD: I want to know if that child of yours means to leave here this afternoon?

CORA: [*At head of steps now*] Yes, sir, she's goin' directly. I's gettin' her ready now, packin' up an' all. 'Course, she wants to tell you goodbye 'fore she leaves.

5   NORWOOD: Well, send her down here. Who's going to drive her to the railroad? The train leaves at three—and it's after two now. You ought to know you can't drive ten miles in no time.

CORA: [*Above*] Her brother's gonna drive her. Bert. He ought to be back here most any time now with the Ford.

NORWOOD: [*Stopping on his way back to the library*] Ought to be back here? Where's he gone?

CORA: [*Coming downstairs nervously*] Why, he driv in town 'fore noon, Colonel Tom. Said he were lookin' for some tubes or somethin' 'nother by de mornin' mail for de radio he's been riggin' up out in de shed.

NORWOOD: Who gave him permission to be driving off in the middle of the morning? I bought that Ford to be used when I gave orders for it to be used, not . . .

CORA: Yes, sir, Colonel Tom, but . . .   10

NORWOOD: But what? [*Pausing. Then deliberately*] Cora, if you want that hardheaded yellow son of yours to get along around here, he'd better listen to me. He's no more than any other black buck on this plantation—due to work like the rest of 'em. I don't take such a performance from nobody under me—driving off in the middle of the day to town, after I've told him to bend his back in that cotton. How's Talbot going to keep the rest of those darkies working right if that boy's allowed to set that kind of an example? Just because Bert's your son, and I've been damn fool enough to send him off to school for five or six years, he thinks he has a right to privileges, acting as if he owned this place since he's been back here this summer.

CORA: But, Colonel Tom . . .

NORWOOD: Yes, I know what you're going to say. I don't give a damn about him! There's no nigger-child of mine, yours, ours—no darkie—going to disobey me. I put him in that field to work, and he'll stay on this plantation till I get ready to let him go. I'll tell Talbot to use the whip on him, too, if he needs it. If it hadn't been that he's yours, he'd-a had a taste of it the other day. Talbot's a damn good overseer, and no saucy, lazy Nigras stay on this plantation and get away with it. [*To* CORA] Go on back upstairs and see about getting Sallie out of here. Another word from you and I won't send your [*Sarcastically*] pretty little half-white daughter anywhere, either. Schools for darkies! Huh! If you take that boy of yours for an example, they do 'em more harm than good. He's learned nothing in college but impudence, and he'll stay here on this place and work for me awhile before he gets back to any more schools. [*He starts across the room.*]

CORA: Yes, sir, Colonel Tom. [*Hesitating*] But he's just young, sir. And he was mighty broke up when you said last week he couldn't go back to de campus. [COLONEL NORWOOD *turns and looks at* CORA *commandingly. Understanding, she murmurs*] Yes, sir. [*She starts upstairs, but turns back.*] Can't I run and fix you a cool drink, Colonel Tom?

NORWOOD: No, damn you! Sam'll do it.   15

CORA: [*Sweetly*] Go set down in de cool, then, Colonel. 'Taint good for you to be goin' on this way in de heat. I'll talk to Robert maself soon's he comes in. He don't mean nothing—just smart and young and kinder careless, Colonel Tom, like ma mother said you used to be when you was eighteen.

NORWOOD: Get on upstairs, Cora. Do I have to speak again? Get on! [*He pulls the cord of the servants' bell.*]

CORA: [*On the steps*] Does you still be in the mind to tell Sallie good-bye?

NORWOOD: Send her down here as I told you. [*Impatiently*] Where's Sam? Send him here first. [*Fuming*] Looks like he takes his time to answer that bell. You colored folks are running the house to suit yourself nowadays.

CORA: [*Coming downstairs again and going toward the door under the steps*] I'll get Sam for you.   20

[CORA *exits left.* NORWOOD *paces nervously across the floor. Goes to the window and looks out down the road. Takes a cigar from his pocket, sits in a chair with it unlighted, scowling. Rises, goes toward servants' bell and rings it again violently as* SAM *enters, out of breath.*]

NORWOOD: What the hell kind of a tortoise race is this? I suppose you were out in the sun somewhere sleeping?

SAM: No, sah, Colonel Norwood. Just tryin' to get Miss Sallie's valises down to de yard so's we can put 'em in de Ford, sah.

NORWOOD: [*Out of patience*] Huh! Darkies waiting on darkies! I can't get service in my own house. Very well. [*Loudly*] Bring me some whiskey and soda, and ice in a glass. Is that damn Frigidaire working right? Or is Livonia still too thickheaded to know how to run it? Any ice cubes in the thing?

SAM: Yes, sah, Colonel, yes, sah. [*Backing toward door left*] 'Scuse me, please sah, but [*As NORWOOD turns toward library*] Cora say for me to ask you is it all right to bring that big old trunk what you give Sallie down by de front steps. We ain't been able to tote it down them narrer little back steps, sah. Cora, say, can we bring it down de front way through here?

25 **NORWOOD:** No other way? [*SAM shakes his head*] Then pack it on through the back, quick. Don't let me catch you carrying any of Sallie's baggage out of that front door here. You-all'll be wanting to go in and out the front way next. [*Turning away, complaining to himself*] Darkies have been getting mighty fresh in this part of the country since the war. The damn Germans should've . . . [*To SAM*] Don't take that trunk out that front door.

SAM: [*Evilly, in a cunning voice*] I's seen Robert usin' de front door—when you ain't here, and he comes up from de cabin to see his mammy. [*SALLIE, the daughter, appears at the top of the stairs, but hesitates about coming down.*]

NORWOOD: Oh, you have, have you? Let me catch him and I'll break his young neck for him. [*Yelling at SAM*] Didn't I tell you some whiskey and soda an hour ago?

[*SAM exits left. SALLIE comes shyly down the stairs and approaches her father. She is dressed in a little country-style coat-suit ready for traveling. Her features are Negroid, although her skin is very fair. COLONEL NORWOOD gazes down at her without saying a word as she comes meekly toward him, half-frightened.*]

SALLIE: I just wanted to tell you goodbye, Colonel Norwood, and thank you for letting me go back to school another year, and for letting me work here in the house all summer where mama is. [*NORWOOD says nothing. The girl continues in a strained voice as if making a speech*] You mighty nice to us colored folks certainly, and mama says you the best white man in Georgia. [*Still NORWOOD says nothing. The girl continues.*] You been mighty nice to your—I mean to us colored children, letting my sister and me go off to school. The principal says I'm doing pretty well and next year I can go to Normal and learn to be a teacher. [*Raising her eyes*] You reckon I can, Colonel Tom?

NORWOOD: Stand up straight and let me see how you look. [*Backing away*] Hum-m-m! Getting kinder grown, ain't you? Do they teach you in that school to have good manners, and not be afraid of work, *and to respect white folks?*

30 **SALLIE:** Yes, sir, I been taking up cooking and sewing, too.

NORWOOD: Well, that's good. As I recall it, that school turned your sister out a right smart cook. Cora tells me she's got a good job in some big hotel in Chicago. I'm thinking about you going on up North there with her in a year or two. You're getting too old to be around here, and too womanish. [*He puts his hands on her arms as if feeling her flesh.*]

SALLIE: [*Drawing back slightly*] But I want to live down here with mama. I want to teach school in that there empty school house by the Cross Roads what hasn't had a teacher for five years.

[*SAM has been standing with the door cracked, overhearing the conversation. He enters with the drink and places it on the table, right. NORWOOD sits down, leaving the girl standing, as SAM pours out a drink.*]

NORWOOD: Don't get that into your head, now. There's been no teacher there for years—and there won't be any teacher there, either. Cotton teaches these pickaninnies enough around here. Some of 'em's too smart as it is. The only reason I did have a teacher there once was to get you young ones o' Cora's educated. I gave you all a chance and I hope you appreciate it. [*He takes a long drink.*] Don't know why I did it. No other white man in these parts ever did it, as I know of. [*To SAM*] Get out of here! [*SAM exits left.*] Guess I couldn't stand to see Cora's kids working around here dumb as the rest of these no-good darkies—need a dozen of 'em to chop one row of cotton, or to keep a house clean. Or maybe I didn't want Talbot eyeing you gals. [*Taking another drink*] Anyhow, I'm glad you and Bertha turned out right well. Yes, hum-m-m! [*Straightening up*] You know I tried to do something for those brothers of yours, too, but William's stupid as an ox—good for work, though—and that Robert's just an impudent, hardheaded, yellow young fool. I'm gonna break his damn neck for him if he don't watch out. Or else put Talbot on him.

SALLIE: [*Suddenly frightened*] Please, sir, don't put the overseer on Bert, Colonel Tom. He was the smartest boy at school, Bert was. On the football team, too. Please, sir, Colonel Tom. Let brother work here in the house, or somewhere else where Talbot can't mistreat him. He ain't used . . .

NORWOOD: [*Rising*] Telling me what to do, heh? [*Staring at her sternly*] I'll use the back of   35
my hand across your face if you don't hush. [*He takes another drink. The noise of a Ford is heard outside.*] That's Bert now, I reckon. He's to take you to the railroad line, and while you're riding with him, you better put some sense into his head. And tell him I want to see him as soon as he gets back here. [*CORA enters left with a bundle and an umbrella. SAM and WILLIAM come downstairs with a big square trunk, and exit hurriedly, left.*]

SALLIE: Yes, sir, I'll tell him.

CORA: Colonel Tom, Sallie ain't got much time now. [*To the girl*] Come on, chile. Bert's here. Yo' big brother and Sam and Livonia and everybody's all waiting at de back door to say goodbye. And your baggage is being packed in. [*Noise of another car is heard outside.*] Who else is that there coming up de drive? [*CORA looks out the window.*] Mr. Higgins' car, Colonel Tom. Reckon he's coming to see you . . . Hurry up out o' this front room, Sallie. Here, take these things of your'n [*Hands her the bundle and parasol*] while I opens de door for Mr. Higgins. [*In a whisper*] Hurry up, chile! Get out! [*NORWOOD turns toward the front door as CORA goes to open it.*]

SALLIE: [*Shyly to her father*] Goodbye, Colonel Tom.

NORWOOD: [*His eyes on the front door, scarcely noticing the departing SALLIE, he motions.*] Yes, yes goodbye! Get on now! [*CORA opens the front door as her daughter exits left.*] Well, well! Howdy do, Fred. Come in, come in! [*CORA holds the outer door of the vestibule wide as FRED HIGGINS enters with rheumatic dignity, supported on the arm of his chauffeur, MOSE, a very black Negro in a slouchy uniform. CORA closes the door and exits left hurriedly, following SALLIE.*]

NORWOOD: [*Smiling*] How's the rheumatiz today? Women or licker or heat must've made   40
it worse—from the looks of your speed!

HIGGINS: [*Testily, sitting down puffing and blowing in a big chair*] I'm in no mood for fooling, Tom, not now. [*To MOSE*] All right. [*The CHAUFFEUR exits front. HIGGINS continues angrily.*] Norwood, that damned yellow nigger buck of yours that drives that new Ford tried his best just now to push my car off the road, then got in front of me and blew dust in my face for the last mile coming down to your gate, trying to beat me in here—which he did. Such a deliberate piece of impudence I don't know if I've ever seen out of a nigger before in all the sixty years I've lived in this country. [*The noise of the Ford is heard going out the drive, and the cries of the NEGROES shouting farewells to SALLIE. HIGGINS listens indignantly.*] What kind of crazy coons have you got on your place, anyhow? Sounds like a black Baptist picnic to me. [*Pointing to the window with his cane*] Tom, listen to that.

NORWOOD: [*Flushing*] I apologize to you, Fred, for each and every one of my darkies. [*SAM enters with more ice and another glass.*] Permit me to offer you a drink. I realize I've got to tighten down here.

HIGGINS: Mose tells me that was Cora's boy in that Ford—and that young black fool is what I was coming here to talk to you about today. That boy! He's not gonna be around here long—not the way he's acting. The white folks in town'll see to that. Knowing he's one of your yard niggers, Norwood, I thought I ought to come and tell you. The white folks at the Junction aren't intending to put up with him much longer. And I don't know what good the jail would do him once he got in there.

NORWOOD: [*Tensely*] What do you mean, Fred—jail? Don't I always take care of the folks on my plantation without any help from the Junction's police force? Talbot can do more with an unruly black buck than your marshal.

45   **HIGGINS:** Warn't lookin' at it that way, Tom. I was thinking how weak the doors to that jail is. They've broke 'em down and lynched four niggers to my memory since it's been built. After what happened this morning, you better keep that yellow young fool out o' town from now on. It might not be safe for him around there—today, or no other time.

NORWOOD: What the hell? [*Perturbed*] He went in just now to take his sister to the depot. Damn it, I hope no ruffians'll break up my new Ford. What was it, Fred, about this morning?

HIGGINS: You haven't heard? Why, it's all over town already. He sassed out Miss Gray in the post office over a box of radio tubes that come by mail.

NORWOOD: He did, heh?

HIGGINS: Seems like the stuff was sent C.O.D. and got here all smashed up, so he wouldn't take it. Paid his money first before he saw the box was broke. Then wanted the money order back. Seems like the post office can't give money orders back—rule against it. Your nigger started to argue, and the girl at the window—Miss Gray—got scared and yelled for some of the mail clerks. They threw Bert out of the office, that's all. But that's enough. Lucky nothing more didn't happen. [*Indignantly*] That Bert needs a damn good beating—talking back to a white woman—and I'd like to give it to him myself, the way he kicked the dust up in my eyes all the way down the road coming out here. He was mad, I reckon. That's one yellow buck don't know his place, Tom, and it's your fault he don't—sending 'em off to be educated.

50   **NORWOOD:** Well, by God, I'll show him. I wish I'd have known it before he left here just now.

HIGGINS: Well, he's sure got mighty aggravating ways for a buck his color to have. Drives down the main street and don't stop for nobody, white or black. Comes in my store and if he ain't waited on as quick as the white folks are, he walks out and tells the clerk his money's as good as a white man's any day. Said last week standing out on my store front that he wasn't *all* nigger no how; said his name was Norwood—not Lewis, like the rest of his family—and part of your plantation here would be his when you passed out—and all that kind of stuff, boasting to the walleyed coons listening to him.

NORWOOD: [*Astounded*] Well, I'll be damned!

HIGGINS: Now, Tom, you know that don't go 'round these parts 'o Georgia, nor nowhere else in the South. A darkie's got to keep in his place down here. Ruinous to other niggers hearing that talk, too. All this postwar propaganda on the radio about freedom and democracy—why the niggers think it's meant for them! And that Eleanor Roosevelt,° she ought to been muzzled. She's driving our niggers crazy—your boy included! Crazy! Talking about civil rights. Ain't been no race trouble in our country for three years—

°53 *Eleanor Roosevelt:* Eleanor Roosevelt (1884–1962), the wife of President Franklin D. Roosevelt, was an outspoken champion of minority causes.

since the Deekin's lynching—but I'm telling you, Norwood, you better see that that buck of yours goes away from here. I'm speaking on the quiet, but I can see ahead. And what happened this morning about them radio tubes wasn't none too good.

NORWOOD: [*Beside himself with rage*] A black ape! I—I . . .

HIGGINS: You been too decent to your darkies, Norwood. That's what's the matter with   55
you. And then the whole country suffers from a lot of impudent bucks who take lessons from your crowd. Folks been kicking about that, too. Guess you know it. Maybe that's the reason you didn't get that nomination for committeeman a few years back.

NORWOOD: Maybe 'tis, Higgins. [*Rising and pacing the room*] God damn niggers! [*Furiously*] Everything turns on niggers, niggers, niggers! No wonder Yankees call this the Black Belt! [*He pours a large drink of whiskey.*]

HIGGINS: [*Soothingly*] Well, let's change the subject. Hand me my glass, there, too.

NORWOOD: Pardon me, Fred. [*He puts ice in his friend's glass and passes him the bottle.*]

HIGGINS: Tom, you get excited too easy for warm weather. . . . Don't ever show black folks they got you going, though. I think sometimes that's where you make your mistake. Keep calm, keep calm—and then you command. Best plantation manager I ever had never raised his voice to a nigger—and they were scared to death of him.

NORWOOD: Have a smoke. [*Pushes cigars toward HIGGINS*]   60

HIGGINS: You ought've married again, Tom—brought a white woman out here on this damn place o' yours. A woman could help you run things. Women have soft ways, but they can keep things humming. Nothing but blacks in the house—a man gets soft like niggers are inside. [*Puffing at cigar*] And living with a colored woman! Of course, I know we all have 'em—I didn't know you could make use of a white girl till I was past twenty. Thought too much o' white women for that—but I've given many a yellow gal a baby in my time. [*Long puff at cigar*] But for a man's own house you need a wife, not a black woman.

NORWOOD: Reckon you're right, Fred, but it's too late to marry again now. [*Shrugging his shoulders*] Let's get off of darkies and women for awhile. How's crops? [*Sitting down*] How's politics going?

HIGGINS: Well, I guess you know the Republicans is trying to stir up trouble for us in Washington. I wish the South had more men like Bilbo and Rankin° there. But, say, by the way, Lawyer Hotchkiss wants to see us both about that budget money next week. He's got some real Canadian stuff at his office, in his filing case, too—brought back from his vacation last summer. Taste better'n this old mountain juice we get around here. Not meaning to insult your drinks, Tom, but just remarking. I serve the same as you myself, label and all.

NORWOOD: [*Laughing*] I'll have you know, sir, that this is prewar licker, sir!

HIGGINS: Hum-m-m! Well, it's got me feelin' better'n I did when I come in here—what-   65
ever it is. [*Puffs at his cigar*] Say, how's your cotton this year?

NORWOOD: Doin' right well, specially down in the south field. Why not drive out that road when you leave and take a look at it? I'll ride down with you. I want to see Talbot, anyhow.

HIGGINS: Well, let's be starting. I got to be back at the Junction by four o'clock. Promised to let that boy of mine have the car to drive over to Thomasville for a dance tonight.

NORWOOD: One more shot before we go. [*He pours out drinks.*] The young ones must have their fling, I reckon. When you and I grew up down here it used to be a carriage and the best pair of black horses when you took the ladies out—now it's an automobile. That's a good lookin' new car of yours, too.

°63 *Bilbo, Rankin:* Theodore Bilbo (1877–1947), senator from Mississippi from 1935 to 1947, and John Eliot Rankin (1882–1960), Mississippi representative to the House from 1921 to 1953, were both noted advocates of white supremacy.

HIGGINS: Right nice.

70 **NORWOOD:** Been thinking about getting a new one myself, but money's been kinder tight this year, and conditions are none too good yet, either. Reckon that's why everybody's so restless. [*He walks toward stairs calling.*] Cora! Oh, Cora! . . . If I didn't have a few thousand put away, I'd feel the pinch myself. [*As CORA appears on the stairs.*] Bring me my glasses up there by the side of my bed. . . . Better whistle for Mose, hadn't I, Higgins? He's probably 'round back with some of his women. [*Winking*] You know I got some nice black women in this yard.

HIGGINS: Oh, no, not Mose. I got my servants trained to stay in their places—right where I want 'em—while they're working for me. Just open the door and tell him to come in here and help me out. [*NORWOOD goes to the door and calls the CHAUFFEUR. MOSE enters and assists his master out to the car. CORA appears with the glasses, goes to the vestibule and gets the COLONEL's hat and cane which she hands him.*]

NORWOOD: [*To CORA*] I want to see that boy o' yours soon as I get back. That won't be long, either. And tell him to put up that Ford of mine and don't touch it again.

CORA: Yes, sir, I'll have him waiting here. [*In a whisper*] It's hot weather, Colonel Tom. Too much of this licker makes your heart upset. It ain't good for you, you know. [*NORWOOD pays her no attention as he exits toward the car. The noise of the departing motor is heard. CORA begins to tidy up the room. She takes a glass from a side table. She picks up a doily that was beneath the glass and looks at it long and lovingly. Suddenly she goes to the door left and calls toward the kitchen.*] William, you William! Com'ere, I want to show you something. Make haste, son. [*As CORA goes back toward the table, her eldest son, WILLIAM, enters carrying a five-year-old boy.*] Look here at this purty doily yo' sister made this summer while she been here. She done learned all about sewing and making purty things at school. Ain't it nice, son?

WILLIAM: Sho' is. Sallie takes after you, I reckon. She's a smart little crittur, ma. [*Sighs*] De Lawd knows, I was dumb at school. [*To his child*] Get down, Billy, you's too heavy. [*He puts the boy on the floor.*] This here sewin's really fine.

75 **BILLY:** [*Running toward the big upholstered chair and jumping up and down on the spring seat*] Gityap! I's a mule driver. Haw! Gee!

CORA: You Billy, get out of that chair 'fore I skins you alive. Get on into de kitchen, sah.

BILLY: I'm playin' horsie, grandma. [*Jumps up in the chair*] Horsie! Horsie!

CORA: Get! That's de Colonel's favorite chair. If he knows any little darkie's been jumpin' on it, he raise sand. Get on, now.

BILLY: Ole Colonel's ma grandpa, ain't he? Ain' he ma white grandpa?

80 **WILLIAM:** [*Snatching the child out of the chair*] Boy, I'm gonna fan your hide if you don't hush!

CORA: Shs-ss-s! You Billy, hush yo' mouth! Chile, where you hear that? [*To her son*] Some o' you all been talking too much in front o' this chile. [*To the boy*] Honey, go on in de kitchen till yo' daddy come. Get a cookie from 'Vonia and set down on de back porch. [*Little BILLY exits left.*]

WILLIAM: Ma, you know it 'twarn't me told him. Bert's the one been goin' all over de plantation since he come back from Atlanta remindin' folks right out we's Colonel Norwood's chilluns.

CORA: [*Catching her breath*] Huh!

WILLIAM: He comes down to my shack tellin' Billy and Marybell they got a white man for grandpa. He's gonna get my chilluns in trouble sho'—like he got himself in trouble when Colonel Tom whipped him.

85 **CORA:** Ten or 'leven years ago, warn't it?

WILLIAM: And Bert's *sho'* in trouble now. Can't go back to that college like he could-a if he'd-a had any sense. You can't fool with white folks—an de Colonel ain't never really liked Bert since that there first time he beat him, either.

CORA: No, he ain't. Leastwise, he ain't understood him. [*Musing sadly in a low voice*] Time Bert was 'bout seven, warn't it? Just a little bigger'n yo' Billy.

WILLIAM: Yes.

CORA: Went runnin' up to Colonel Tom out in de horse stables when de Colonel was showin' off his horses—I 'members so well—to fine white company from town. Lawd, that boy's always been foolish! He went runnin' up and grabbed a-holt de Colonel and yelled right in front o' de white folks' faces, "O, papa, Cora say de dinner's ready, papa!" Ain't never called him papa before, and I don't know where he got it from. And Colonel Tom knocked him right backwards under de horse's feet.

WILLIAM: And when de company were gone, he beat that boy unmerciful.   90

CORA: I thought sho' he were gonna kill ma chile that day. And he were mad at me, too, for months. Said I was teaching you chilluns who they pappy were. Up till then Bert had been his favorite little colored child 'round here.

WILLIAM: Sho' had.

CORA: But he never like him no more. That's why he sent him off to school so soon to stay, winter and summer, all these years. I had to beg and plead to have him home this summer—but I's sorry now I ever got that boy back here again.

WILLIAM: He's sho' growed more like de Colonel all de time, ain't he? Bert thinks he's a real white man hisself now. Look at de first thing he did when he come home, he ain't seen de Colonel in six years—and Bert sticks out his hand fo' to shake hands with him!

CORA: Lawd! That chile!   95

WILLIAM: Just like white folks! And de Colonel turns his back and walks off. Can't blame him. He ain't used to such doings from colored folks. God knows what's got into Bert since he come back. He's acting like a fool—just like he was a boss man round here. Won't even say "Yes, sir" and "No, sir" no more to de white folks. Talbot asked him warn't he gonna work in de field this mornin'. Bert say "No!" and turn and walk away. White man so mad, I could see him nearly foam at de mouth. If he warn't yo' chile, ma, he'd been knocked in de head fo' now.

CORA: You's right.

WILLIAM: And you can't talk to him. I tried to tell him something the other day, but he just laughed at me, and said we's all just scared niggers on this plantation. Says he ain't no nigger, no how. He's a Norwood. He's half-white, and he's gonna act like it. [*In amazement at his brother's daring*] And this is Georgia, too!

CORA: I's scared to death for de boy, William. I don't know what to do. De Colonel says he won't send him off to school no mo'. Says he's mo' sassy and impudent now than any nigger he ever seed. Bert never has been like you was, and de girls, quiet and sensible like you knowed you had to be. [*She sits down.*] De Colonel say he's gonna make Bert stay here now and work on this plantation like de rest of his niggers. He's gonna show him what color he is. Like that time when he beat him for callin' him "papa." He say he's gwine to teach him his place and make de boy know where he belongs. Seems like me or you can't show him. Colonel Tom has to take him in hand, or these white folks'll kill him around here and then—oh, My God!

WILLIAM: A nigger's just got to know his place in de South, that's all, ain't he, ma?   100

CORA: Yes, son. That's all, I reckon.

WILLIAM: And ma brother's one damn fool nigger. Don't seems like he knows nothin'. He's gonna ruin us all round here. Makin' it bad for everybody.

CORA: Oh, Lawd, have mercy! [*Beginning to cry*] I don't know what to do. De way he's acting up can't go on. Way he's acting to de Colonel can't last. Somethin's gonna happen to ma chile. I had a bad dream last night, too, and I looked out and seed de moon all red with blood. I seed a path o' living blood across this house, I tell you, in my sleep. Oh, Lawd, have mercy! [*Sobbing*] Oh, Lawd, help me in ma troubles. [*The noise of the* *returning Ford is heard outside.* CORA *looks up, rises, and goes to the window.*] There's de chile now, William. Run out to de back door and tell him I wants to see him. Bring him in here where Sam and Livonia and de rest of 'em won't hear ever'thing we's sayin'. I got to talk to ma boy. He's ma baby boy, and he don't know de way.

[*Exit* WILLIAM *through the door left.* CORA *is wiping her eyes and pulling herself together when the front door is flung open with a bang and* ROBERT *enters.*]

ROBERT: [*Running to his mother and hugging her teasingly*] Hello, ma! Your daughter got off, and I've come back to keep you company in the parlor! Bring out the cookies and lemonade. *Mister* Norwood's here!

105   **CORA:** [*Beginning to sob anew*] Take yo' hands off me, boy! Why don't you mind? Why don't you mind me?

ROBERT: [*Suddenly serious, backing away*] Why, mamma, what's the matter? Did I scare you? Your eyes are all wet! Has somebody been telling you 'bout this morning?

CORA: [*Not heeding his words*] Why don't you mind me, son? Ain't I told you and told you not to come in that front door, never? [*Suddenly angry*] Will somebody have to beat it into you? What's got wrong with you when you was away at that school? What am I gonna do?

ROBERT: [*Carelessly*] Oh, I knew that the Colonel wasn't here. I passed him and old man Higgins on the road down by the south patch. He wouldn't even look at me when I waved at him. [*Half playfully*] Anyhow, isn't this my old man's house? Ain't I his son and heir? [*Grandly, strutting around*] Am I not Mr. Norwood, Junior?

CORA: [*Utterly serious*] I believe you goin' crazy, Bert. I believes you wants to get us all killed or run away or something awful like that. I believes . . . [WILLIAM *enters left.*]

110   **WILLIAM:** Where's Bert? He ain't come round back—[*Seeing his brother in the room*] How'd you get in here?

ROBERT: [*Grinning*] Houses have front doors.

WILLIAM: Oh, usin' de front door like de white folks, heh? You gwine do that once too much.

ROBERT: Yes, like de white folks. What's a front door for, you rabbit-hearted coon?

WILLIAM: Rabbit-hearted coon's better'n a dead coon any day.

115   **ROBERT:** I wouldn't say so. Besides you and me's only half-coons, anyhow, big boy. And I'm gonna act like my white half, not my black half. Get me, kid?

WILLIAM: Well, you ain't gonna act like it long here in de middle o' Georgy. And you ain't gonna act like it when de Colonel's around, either.

ROBERT: Oh, no? My stay down here'll be short and sweet, boy, short and sweet. The old man won't send me away to college no more—so you think I'm gonna stick around and work in the fields? Like fun! I might stay here awhile and teach some o' you dark-ies to think like men, maybe—till it gets too much for the old Colonel—but no more bowing down to white folks for me—not Robert Norwood.

CORA: Hush, son!

ROBERT: Certainly not right on my own old man's plantation—Georgia or no Georgia.

120   **WILLIAM:** [*Scornfully*] I hears you.

ROBERT: You can do it if you want to, but I'm ashamed of you. I've been away from here six years. [*Boasting*] I've learned something, seen people in Atlanta, and Richmond, and Washington where the football team went—real colored people who don't have to take off their hats to white folks or let 'em go to bed with their sisters—like that young Higgins boy, asking me what night Sallie was comin' to town. A damn cracker! [*To* CORA] 'Scuse me, ma. [*Continuing*] Back here in these woods maybe Sam and Livonia and you and mama and everybody's got their places fixed for 'em, but not me. [*Seriously*] Nobody's gonna fix a place for me. I'm old man Norwood's son. Nobody fixed a place for him. [*Playfully again*] Look at me. I'm a 'fay boy. [*Pretends* *to shake his hair back*] See these gray eyes? I got the right to everything everybody else has. [*Punching his brother in the belly*] Don't talk to me, old slavery-time Uncle Tom.

WILLIAM: [*Resentfully*] I ain't playin', boy. [*Pushes younger brother back with some force*] I ain't playin' a-tall.

CORA: All right, chilluns, stop. Stop! And William, you take Billy and go on home. 'Vonia's got to get supper and she don't like no young-uns under her feet in de kitchen. I wants to talk to Bert in here now 'fore Colonel Tom gets back. [*Exit* WILLIAM *left.* CORA *continues to* BERT.] Sit down, child, right here a minute and listen.

ROBERT: [*Sitting down*] All right, ma.

CORA: Hard as I's worked and begged and humbled maself to get de Colonel to keep you   125
chilluns in school, you comes home wid yo' head full o' stubbornness and yo' mouth full o' sass for me an' de white folks an' everybody. You know can't no colored boy here talk like you's been doin' to no white folks, let alone to de Colonel and that old devil of a Talbot. They ain't gonna stand fo' yo' sass. Not only you, but I 'spects we's all gwine to pay fo' it, every colored soul on this place. I was scared to death today fo' yo' sister, Sallie, scared de Colonel warn't gwine to let her go back to school, neither, 'count o' yo' doins, but he did, thank Gawd—and then you come near makin' her miss de train. Did she have time to get her ticket and all?

ROBERT: Sure! Had to drive like sin to get there with her, though. I didn't mean to be late getting back here for her, ma, but I had a little run-in about them radio tubes in town.

CORA: [*Worried*] What's that?

ROBERT: The tubes was smashed when I got 'em, and I had already made out my money order, so the woman in the post office wouldn't give the three dollars back to me. All I did was explain to her that we could send the tubes back—but she got hot because there were two or three white folks waiting behind me to get stamps, I guess. So she yells at me to move on and not give her any of my "educated nigger talk." So I said, "I'm going to finish showing you these tubes before I move on"—and then she screamed and called the mail clerk working in the back, and told him to throw me out. [*Boasting*] He didn't do it by himself, though. Had to call all the white loafers out in the square to get me through that door.

CORA: [*Fearfully*] Lawd have mercy!

ROBERT: Guess if I hadn't-a had the Ford then, they'd've beat me half-to-death, but when   130
I saw how many crackers there was, I jumped in the car and beat it on away.

CORA: Thank God for that!

ROBERT: Not even a football man [*Half-boasting*] like me could tackle the whole junction. 'Bout a dozen colored guys standing around, too, and not one of 'em would help me—the dumb jiggaboos! They been telling me ever since I been here, [*Imitating darky talk*] "You can't argue wid whut folks, man. You better stay out o' this Junction. You must ain't got no sense, nigger! You's a fool" . . . Maybe I am a fool, ma—but I didn't want to come back here nohow.

CORA: I's sorry I sent for you.

ROBERT: Besides you, there ain't nobody in this country but a lot of evil white folks and cowardly niggers. [*Earnestly*] I'm no nigger, anyhow, am I, ma? I'm half-white. The Colonel's my father—the richest man in the county—and I'm not going to take a lot of stuff from nobody if I do have to stay here, not from the old man either. He thinks I ought to be out there in the sun working, with Talbot standing over me like I belonged in the chain gang. Well, he's got another thought coming! [*Stubbornly*] I'm a Norwood—not a field-hand nigger.

CORA: You means you ain't workin' no mo'?   135

ROBERT: [*Flaring*] No, I'm not going to work in the fields. What did he send me away to school for—just to come back here and be his servant, or pick his hills of cotton?

CORA: He sent you away to de school because *I* asked him and begged him, and got down on my knees to him, that's why. [*Quietly*] And now I just wants to make you see some sense, if you can. I knows, honey, you reads in de books and de papers, and you knows a lot more'n I do. But, chile, you's in Georgy—and I don't see how it is you don't know where you's at. This ain't up North—and even up yonder where we hears it's so fine, yo' sister has to pass for white to get along good.

ROBERT: [*Bitterly*] I know it.

CORA: She ain't workin' in no hotel kitchen like de Colonel thinks. She's in a office type-writing. And Sallie's studyin' de typewriter, too, at de school, but yo' pappy don't know it. I knows we ain't s'posed to study nothin' but cookin' and hard workin' here in Georgy. That's all I ever done, or knowed about. I been workin' on this very place all ma life—even 'fore I come to live in this Big House. When de Colonel's wife died, I come here, and borned you chilluns. And de Colonel's been real good to me in his way. Let you all sleep in this house with me when you was little, and sent you all off to school when you growed up. Ain't no white man in this county done that with his cullud chilluns before, far as I can know. But you—Robert, be awful, awful careful! When de Colonel comes back, in a few minutes, he wants to talk to you. Talk right to him, boy. Talk like you was colored, 'cause you ain't white.

140 **ROBERT:** [*Angrily*] And I'm not black either. Look at me, mama. [*Rising and throwing up his arms*] Don't I look like my father? Ain't I as light as he is? Ain't my eyes gray like his eyes are? [*The noise of a car is heard outside.*] Ain't this our house?

CORA: That's him now. [*Agitated*] Hurry, chile, and let's get out of this room. Come on through yonder to the kitchen. [*She starts toward the door left.*] And I'll tell him you're here.

ROBERT: I don't want to run into the kitchen. Isn't this our house? [*As CORA crosses hurriedly left, ROBERT goes toward the front door.*] The Ford is parked out in front, anyway.

CORA: [*At the door left to the rear of the house*] Robert! Robert! [*As ROBERT nears the front door, COLONEL NORWOOD enters, almost runs into the boy, stops at the threshold and stares unbelievingly at his son. CORA backs up against the door left.*]

NORWOOD: Get out of here! [*He points toward the door to rear of the house where CORA is standing.*]

145 **ROBERT:** [*Half-smiling*] Didn't you want to talk to me?

NORWOOD: Get out of here!

ROBERT: Not that way. [*THE COLONEL raises his cane to strike the boy. CORA screams. BERT draws himself up to his full height, taller than the old man and looking very much like him, pale and proud. The man and the boy face each other. NORWOOD does not strike.*]

NORWOOD: [*In a hoarse whisper*] Get out of here. [*His hand is trembling as he points.*]

CORA: Robert! Come on, son, come on! Oh, my God, come on. [*Opening the door left*]

150 **ROBERT:** Not that way, ma. [*ROBERT walks proudly out the front door. NORWOOD, in an impotent rage, crosses the room to a small cabinet right, opens it nervously with a key from his pocket, takes out a pistol, and starts toward the front door. CORA overtakes him, seizes his arm, stops him.*]

CORA: He's our son, Tom. [*She sinks slowly to her knees, holding his body.*] Remember, he's our son.

Curtain

ACT 2

Scene 1

TIME. *After supper. Sunset.*

SETTING. *The same.*

ACTION. *As the curtain rises, the stage is empty. Through the windows the late afternoon sun makes two bright paths toward the footlights. SAM, carrying a tray bearing a whiskey bottle and a bowl of ice, enters left and crosses toward the library. He stoops at the door right, listens a moment, knocks, then opens the door and goes in. In a moment* SAM *returns. As he leaves the library, he is heard reply-ing to a request of* NORWOOD's.

SAM: Yes, sah, Colonel! Sho' will, sah! Right away, sah! Yes, sah, I'll tell him. [*He closes the door and crosses the stage muttering to himself.*] Six o'clock. Most nigh that now. Better tell Cora to get that boy right in here. Can't nobody else do notin' with that fool Bert but Cora. [*He exits left. Can be heard calling*] Cora! You, Cora . . .

[*Again the stage is empty. Off stage, outside, the bark of a dog is heard, the sound of Negroes singing down the road, the cry of a child. The breeze moves the shadows of leaves and tree limbs across the sunlit paths from the windows. The door left opens and* CORA *enters, followed by* ROBERT.]

CORA: [*Softly to* ROBERT *behind her in the dining room*] It's all right, son. He ain't come out yet, but it's nearly six, and that's when he said he wanted you, but I was afraid maybe you was gonna be late. I sent for you to come up here to de house and eat supper with me in de kitchen. Where'd you eat yo' vittuals at, chile?

ROBERT: Down at Willie's house, ma. After the old man tried to hit me you still want me to hang around and eat up here?

CORA: I wanted you to be here on time, honey, that's all. [*She is very nervous.*] I kinder likes to have you eat with me sometimes, too, but you ain't et up here more'n once this summer. But this evenin' I just wanted you to be here when de Colonel sent word for you, 'cause we's done had enough trouble today.

ROBERT: He's not here on time, himself, is he?   5

CORA: He's in de library. Sam couldn't get him to eat no supper tonight, and I ain't seen him a-tall.

ROBERT: Maybe he wants to see me in the library, then.

CORA: You know he don't 'low no colored folks in there 'mongst his books and things 'cept Sam. Some o' his white friends goes in there, but none o' us.

ROBERT: Maybe he wants to see *me* in there, though.

CORA: Can't you never talk sense, Robert? This ain't no time for foolin' and jokin.' Nearly   10
thirty years in this house and I ain't never been in there myself, not once, 'mongst de Colonel's papers. [*The clock strikes six.*] Stand over yonder and wait till he comes out. I's gwine on upstairs now, so's he can talk to you. And don't aggravate him no mo' fo' God's sake. Agree to whatever he say. I's scared fo' you, chile, de way you been actin', and de fool tricks you done today, and de trouble about de post office besides. Don't aggravate him. Fo' yo' sake, honey, 'cause I loves you—and fo' all de po' colored folks on this place what has such a hard time when his humors get on him— agree to whatever he say, will you Bert?

ROBERT: All right, ma. [*Voice rising*] But he better not start to hit me again.

CORA: Shs-ss-s! He'll hear you. He's right in there.

ROBERT: [*Sullenly*] This was the day I ought to have started back to school—like my sister. I stayed my summer out here, didn't I? Why didn't he keep his promise to me? You said if I came home I could go back to college again.

CORA: Shs-ss-s! He'll be here now. Don't say nothin,' chile, I's done all I could.

ROBERT: All right, ma.   15

CORA: [*Approaching the stairs*] I'll be in ma room, honey, where I can hear you when you goes out. I'll come down to de back door and see you 'fore you goes back to de shack. Don't aggravate him, chile.

[*She ascends the stairs. The boy sits down sullenly, left, and stares at the door opposite from which his father must enter. The clock strikes the quarter after six. The shadows of the window curtains have lengthened on the carpet. The sunshine has deepened to a pale orange, and the light paths grow less distinct across the floor. The boy sits up straight in his chair. He looks at the library door. It opens.* NORWOOD *enters. He is bent and pale. He looks across the room and sees the boy. Suddenly he straightens up. The old commanding look comes into his face. He strides directly across the room toward his son. The boy, half afraid, half defiant, yet sure of himself, rises. Now that* ROBERT *is standing, the white man turns, goes back to a chair near the table, right, and seats himself. He takes out a cigar, cuts off the end and lights it, and in a voice of mixed condescension and contempt, he speaks to his son.* ROBERT *remains standing near the chair.*]

NORWOOD: I don't want to have to beat you another time as I did when you were a child. The next time I might not be able to control myself. I might kill you if I touched you again. I been runnin' this plantation for thirty-five years, and I never had to beat a Nigra as old as you are. I never had to beat one of Cora's children either—but you. The rest of 'em had sense 'nough to keep out of my sight, and to speak to me like they should . . . I don't have any trouble with my colored folks. Never have trouble. They do what I say, or what Mr. Talbot says, and that's all there is to it, I give 'em a chance. If they turn in their crops they get paid. If they're workin' for wages, they get paid. If they want to spend their money on licker, or buy an old car, or fix up their cabins, they can. Do what they choose long as they know their places and it don't hinder their work. And to Cora's young ones I give all the chances any colored folks ever had in these parts. More'n many a white child's had. I sent you all off to school. Let Bertha go on up North when she got grown and educated. Intend to let Sallie do the same. Gave your brother William that house he's living in when he got married, pay him for his work, help him out if he needs it. None of my darkies suffer. Sent you to college. Would have kept on, would have sent you back today, but I don't intend to pay for no darky, or white boy either if I had one, that acts the way you've been acting. And certainly for no black fool. Now I want to know what's wrong with you? I don't usually talk about what I'm going to do with anybody on this place. It's my habit to tell people *what to do*, not to discuss it with 'em. But I want to know what's the matter with you—whether you're crazy or not. In that case, you'll have to be locked up. And if you aren't, you'll have to change your ways a damn sight or it won't be safe for you here, and you know it—venting your impudence on white women, parking the car in front of my door, driving like mad through the Junction, and going, everywhere, just as you please. Now, I'm going to let you talk to me, but I want you to talk right.

ROBERT: [*Still standing*] What do you mean, "talk right"?

NORWOOD: I mean talk like a nigger should to a white man.

20 ROBERT: Oh! But I'm not a nigger, Colonel Tom. I'm your son.

NORWOOD: [*Testily*] You're Cora's boy.

ROBERT: Women don't have children by themselves.

NORWOOD: Nigger women don't know the fathers. You're a bastard.

[ROBERT *clenches his fist.* NORWOOD *turns toward the drawer where the pistol is, takes it out, and lays it on the table. The wind blows the lace curtains at the windows, and sweeps the shadows of falling leaves across the paths of sunlight on the floor.*]

ROBERT: I've heard that before. I've heard it from Negroes, and I've heard it from white folks. Now I hear it from you. [*Slowly*] You're talking about my mother.

25 NORWOOD: I'm talking about Cora, yes. Her children are bastards.

ROBERT: [*Quickly*] And you're their father. [*Angrily*] How come I look like you, if you're not my father?

NORWOOD: Don't shout at me, boy. I can hear you. [*Half-smiling*] How come your skin is yellow and your elbows rusty? How come they threw you out of the post office today for talking to a white woman? How come you're the crazy young buck you are?

ROBERT: They had no right to throw me out. I asked for my money back when I saw the broken tubes. Just as you had no right to raise that cane today when I was standing at the door of this house where *you* live, while *I* have to sleep in a shack down the road with the field hands. [*Slowly*] But my mother sleeps with you.

NORWOOD: You don't like it?

ROBERT: No, I don't like it.   30

NORWOOD: What can you do about it?

ROBERT: [*After a pause*] I'd like to kill all the white men in the world.

NORWOOD: [*Starting*] Niggers like you are hung to trees.

ROBERT: I'm not a nigger.

NORWOOD: You don't like your own race? [*ROBERT is silent.*] Yet you don't like white folks   35
either?

ROBERT: [*Defiantly*] You think I ought to?

NORWOOD: You evidently don't like me.

ROBERT: [*Boyishly*] I used to like you, when I first knew you were my father, when I was a little kid, before that time you beat me under the feet of your horses. [*Slowly*] I liked you until then.

NORWOOD: [*A little pleased*] So you did, heh? [*Fingering his pistol*] A pickaninny calling me "papa." I should've broken your young neck for that first time. I should've broken your head for you today, too—since I didn't then.

ROBERT: [*Laughing scornfully*] You should've broken my head?   40

NORWOOD: Should've gotten rid of you before this. But you was Cora's child. I tried to help you. [*Aggrieved*] I treated you decent, schooled you. Paid for it. But tonight you'll get the hell off this place and stay off. Get the hell out of this county. [*Suddenly furious*] Get out of this state. Don't let me lay eyes on you again. Get out of here now. Talbot and the storekeeper are coming up here this evening to talk cotton with me. I'll tell Talbot to *see* that you go. That's all. [*NORWOOD motions toward the door, left.*] Tell Sam to come in here when you go out. Tell him to make a light here.

ROBERT: [*Impudently*] Ring for Sam—I'm not going through the kitchen. [*He starts toward the front door.*] I'm not your servant. You're not going to tell me what to do. You're not going to have Talbot run me off the place like a field hand you don't want to use any more.

NORWOOD: [*Springing between his son and the front door, pistol in hand*] You black bastard! [*ROBERT goes toward him calmly, grasps his father's arm and twists it until the gun falls to the floor. The older man bends backward in startled fury and pain.*] Don't you dare put your . . .

ROBERT: [*Laughing*] Why don't you shoot, papa? [*Louder*] Why don't you shoot?

NORWOOD: [*Gasping as he struggles, fighting back*] . . . black . . . hands . . . on . . . you . . .   45

ROBERT: [*Hysterically, as he takes his father by the throat*] Why don't you shoot, papa? [*NORWOOD's hands claw the air helplessly. ROBERT chokes the struggling white man until his body grows limp*] Why don't you shoot! [*Laughing*] Why don't you shoot? Huh? Why?

[*CORA appears at the top of the stairs, hearing the commotion. She screams.*]

CORA: Oh, my God! [*She rushes down. ROBERT drops the body of his father at her feet in a path of flame from the setting sun. CORA starts and stares in horror.*]

ROBERT: [*Wildly*] Why didn't he shoot, mama? He didn't want *me* to live. Why didn't he shoot? [*Laughing*] He was the boss. Telling me what to do. Why didn't he shoot, then? He was the white man.

CORA: [*Falling on the body*] Colonel Tom! Colonel Tom! Tom! Tom! [*Gazes across the corpse at her son*] He's yo' father, Bert.

ROBERT: He's dead. The white man's dead. My father's dead. [*Laughing*] I'm living.   50

CORA: Tom! Tom! Tom!

ROBERT: Niggers are living. He's dead. [*Picks up the pistol*] This is what he wanted to kill me with, but he's dead. I can use it now. Use it on all the white men in the world, because they'll be coming looking for me now. [*Stuffs the pistol into his shirt*] They'll want me now.

CORA: [*Rising and running toward her boy*] Quick, chile, out that way, [*Pointing toward the front door*] so they won't see you in de kitchen. Make for de swamp, honey. Cross de fields fo' de swamp. Go de crick way. In runnin' water, dogs can't smell no tracks. Hurry, chile!

ROBERT: Yes, mama. I can go out the front way now, easy. But if I see they gonna get me before I can reach the swamp, I'm coming back here, mama, and [*Proudly*] let them take me out of my father's house—if they can. [*Pats the gun under his shirt*] They're not going to string me up to some roadside tree for the crackers to laugh at.

55 **CORA:** [*Moaning aloud*] Oh, O-o-o! Hurry! Hurry, chile!

ROBERT: I'm going, ma. [*He opens the door. The sunset streams in like a river of blood.*]

CORA: Run, chile!

ROBERT: Not out of my father's house. [*He exits slowly, tall and straight against the sun.*]

CORA: Fo' God's sake, hurry, chile! [*Glancing down the road*] Lawd have mercy! There's Talbot and de storekeeper in de drive. They sees my boy! [*Moaning*] They sees ma boy. [*Relieved*] But thank God, they's passin' him! [*CORA backs up against the wall in the vestibule. She stands as if petrified as TALBOT and the STOREKEEPER enter.*]

60 **TALBOT:** Hello, Cora. What's the matter with you? Where's that damn fool boy o' your'n goin', coming out the front door like he owned the house? What's the matter with you, woman? Can't you talk? Can't you talk? Where's Norwood? Let's have some light in this dark place. [*He reaches behind the door and turns on the lights. CORA remains backed up against the wall, looking out into the twilight, watching ROBERT as he goes across the field.*] Good God, Jim! Look at this! [*The two white men stop in horror before the sight of NORWOOD's body on the floor.*]

STOREKEEPER: He's blue in the face. [*Bends over the body*] That nigger we saw walking out the door! [*Rising excitedly*] That nigger bastard of Cora's . . . [*Stooping over the body again*] Why the Colonel's dead!

TALBOT: That nigger! [*Rushes toward the door*] He's running toward the swamp now . . . We'll get him . . . Telephone town—there, in the library. Telephone the sheriff. Get men, white men, after that nigger.

[*The STOREKEEPER rushes into the library. He can be heard talking excitedly on the phone.*]

STOREKEEPER: Sheriff! Sheriff! Is this the sheriff? I'm calling from Norwood's plantation. That nigger, Bert, has just killed Norwood—and run, headed for the swamp. Notify the gas station at the crossroads! Tell the boys at the sawmill to head him off at the creek. Warn everybody to be on the lookout. Call your deputies! Yes! Spread a dragnet. Get out the dogs. Meanwhile we'll start after him. [*He slams the phone down and comes back into the room.*] Cora, where's Norwood's car? In the barn? [*CORA does not answer.*]

TALBOT: Talk, you black bitch!

[*She remains silent. TALBOT runs, yelling and talking, out into the yard, followed by the STOREKEEPER. Sounds of excited shouting outside, and the roar of a motor rushing down the drive. In the sky the twilight deepens into early night. CORA stands looking into the darkness.*]

65 **CORA:** My boy can't get to de swamp now. They's telephoned the white folks down that way. So he'll come back home now. Maybe he'll turn into de crick and follow de branch home directly. [*Protectively*] But they shan't get him. I'll make a place for to hide him. I'll make a place upstairs down under de floor, under ma bed. In a minute ma boy'll be runnin' from de white folks with their hounds and their ropes and their

guns and everything they uses to kill po' colored folks with. [*Distressed*] Ma boy'll be out there runnin'. [*Turning to the body on the floor*] Colonel Tom, you hear me? Our boy, out there runnin'. [*Fiercely*] *You* said he was ma boy—*ma* bastard boy. I heard you . . . but he's yours too . . . but yonder in de dark runnin'—runnin' from yo' people, from white people. [*Pleadingly*] Why don't you get up and stop 'em? He's *your* boy. His eyes is gray—like your eyes. He's tall like you's tall. He's proud like you's proud. And he's runnin'—runnin' from po' white trash what ain't worth de little finger o' nobody what's got your blood in 'em, Tom. [*Demandingly*] Why don't you get up from there and stop 'em, Colonel Tom? What's that you say? He ain't your chile? He's ma bastard chile? My yellow bastard chile? [*Proudly*] Yes, he's mine. But don't call him that. Don't you touch him. Don't you put your white hands on him. You's beat him enough, and cussed him enough. Don't you touch him now. He is *ma* boy and no white folks gonna touch him now. That's finished. I'm gonna make a place for him upstairs under ma bed. [*Backs away from the body toward the stairs*] He's ma chile. Don't you come in ma bedroom while he's up there. Don't you come to my bed no mo'. I calls you to help me now, and you just lays there. I calls you for to wake up, and you just lays there. Whenever you called me, in de night, I woke up. When you called for me to love, I always reached out ma arms fo' you. I borned you five chilluns and now one of 'em is out yonder in de dark runnin' from yo' people. Our youngest boy out yonder in de dark runnin'. [*Accusingly*] He's runnin' from you, too. You said he warn't your'n—he's just Cora's po' little yellow bastard. But he *is* your'n, Colonel Tom. [*Sadly*] And he's runnin' from you. You are out yonder in de dark, [*Points toward the door*] runnin' our chile, with de hounds and de gun in yo' hand, and Talbot's followin' 'hind you with a rope to hang Robert with. [*Confidently*] I been sleepin' with you too long, Colonel Tom, not to know that this ain't you layin' down there with yo' eyes shut on de floor. You can't fool me—you ain't never been so still like this before—you's out yonder runnin' ma boy through de fields in de dark, runnin' ma poor little helpless Bert through de fields in de dark to lynch him. . . . Damn you, Colonel Norwood! [*Backing slowly up the stairs, staring at the rigid body below her*] Damn you, Thomas Norwood! God damn you!

Curtain

Scene 2

TIME. *One hour later. Night.*

SETTING. *The same.*

ACTION. *As the curtain rises, the* UNDERTAKER *is talking to* SAM *at the outer door. All through this act the approaching cries of the man hunt are heard.*

UNDERTAKER: Reckon there won't be no orders to bring his corpse back out here, Sam. None of us ain't seen Talbot or Mr. Higgins, but I'm sure they'll be having the funeral in town. The coroner told us to bring the body into the Junction. Ain't nothin' but niggers left out here now.

SAM: [*Very frightened*] Yes, sah! Yes, sah! You's right, sah! Nothin' but us niggers, sah!

UNDERTAKER: The Colonel didn't have no relatives far as you know, did he, Sam?

SAM: No, sah. Ain't had none. No, sah! You's right, sah!

UNDERTAKER: Well, you got everything o' his locked up around here, ain't you? Too bad there ain't no white folks about to look after the Colonel's stuff, but every white man that's able to walk's out with the posse. They'll have that young nigger swingin' before ten.

SAM: [*Trembling*] Yes, sah, yes, sah! I 'spects so. Yes, sah!

UNDERTAKER: Say, where's that woman the Colonel's been living with—where's that black housekeeper, Cora, that murderin's bastard's mother?

SAM: She here, sah! She's up in her room.

UNDERTAKER: [*Curiously*] I'd like to see how she looks. Get her down here. Say, how about a little drink before we start that ride back to town, for me and my partner out there with the body?

10   **SAM:** Cora got de keys to all de licker, sah!

UNDERTAKER: Well, get her down here then, double quick! [*SAM goes up the stairs. The UNDERTAKER leans in the front doorway talking to his partner outside in the wagon*] Bad business, a white man having saucy nigger children on his hands, and his black woman living in his own house.

VOICE OUTSIDE: Damn right, Charlie.

UNDERTAKER: Norwood didn't have a gang o' yellow gals, though, like Higgins and some o' these other big bugs. Just this one bitch far's I know, livin' with him damn near like a wife. Didn't even have much company out here. And they tell me ain't been a white woman stayed here overnight since his wife died when I was a baby. [*SAM's shuffle is heard on the stairs.*] Here comes a drink, I reckon, boy. You needn't get down off the ambulance. I'll have Sam bring it out there to you. [*SAM descends followed by CORA who comes down the stairs. She says nothing. The UNDERTAKER looks up grinning at CORA.*] Well, so you're the Cora that's got these educated nigger children? Hum-m! Well, I guess you'll see one of 'em swinging full of bullet holes when you wake up in the morning. They'll probably hang him to that tree down here by the Colonel's gate—'cause they tell me he strutted right out the front gate past that tree after the murder. Or maybe they'll burn him. How'd you like to see him swinging there roasted in the morning when you wake up, girlie?

CORA: [*Calmly*] Is that all you wanted to say to me?

15   **UNDERTAKER:** Don't get smart! Maybe you think there's nobody to boss you now. We gonna have a little drink before we go. Get out a bottle of rye.

CORA: I takes ma orders from Colonel Norwood, sir.

UNDERTAKER: Well, you'll take no more orders from him. He's dead out there in my wagon—so get along and get the bottle.

CORA: He's out yonder with de mob, not in your wagon.

UNDERTAKER: I tell you he's in my wagon!

20   **CORA:** He's out there with de mob.

UNDERTAKER: God damn! [*To his partner outside*] I believe this black woman's gone crazy in here. [*To CORA*] Get the keys out for that licker, and be quick about it! [*CORA does not move. SAM looks from one to the other, frightened.*]

VOICE OUTSIDE: Aw, to hell with the licker, Charlie. Come on, let's start back to town. We want to get in on some of that excitement, too. They should've found that nigger by now—and I want to see 'em drag him out here.

UNDERTAKER: All right, Jim. [*To CORA and SAM*] Don't you all go to bed until you see that bonfire. You niggers are getting besides yourselves around Polk County. We'll burn a few more of you if you don't be careful. [*He exits, and the noise of the dead-wagon going down the road is heard.*]

SAM: Oh, Lawd, hab mercy on me! I prays, Lawd hab mercy! O, ma Lawd, ma Lawd, ma Lawd! Cora, is you a fool? *Is you a fool?* Why didn't you give de mens de licker, riled as these white folks is? In ma old age is I gonna be burnt by de crackers? Lawd, is I sinned? Lawd, what has I done? [*Suddenly stops moaning and becomes schemingly calm*] I don't have to stay here tonight, does I? I done locked up de Colonel's library, and he can't be wantin' nothin'. No, ma Lawd, he won't want nothin' now. He's with Jesus— or with de devil, one. [*To CORA*] I's gwine on away from here. Sam's gwine in town to his chilluns' house, and I ain't gwine by no road either. I gwine through de holler where I don't have to pass no white folks.

CORA: Yes, Samuel, you go on. De Colonel can get his own drinks when he comes back tonight.   25

SAM: [*Bucking his eyes in astonishment at* CORA] Lawd God Jesus!

[*He bolts out of the room as fast as his old legs will carry him.* CORA *comes down stairs, looks for a long moment out into the darkness, then closes the front door and draws the blinds. She looks down at the spot where the* COLONEL'S *body lay.*]

CORA: All de colored folks are runnin' from you tonight. Po' Colonel Tom, you too old now to be out with de mob. You got no business goin', but you had to go, I reckon. I 'members that time they hung Luke Jordon, you sent yo' dogs out to hunt him. The next day you killed all de dogs. You were kinder softhearted. Said you didn't like that kind of sport. Told me in bed one night you could hear them dogs howlin' in yo' sleep. But de time they burnt de courthouse when that po' little cullud boy was locked up in it cause they said he hugged a white girl, you was with 'em again. Said you had to go help 'em. Now you's out chasin' ma boy. [*As she stands at the window, she sees a passing figure.*] There goes yo' other woman, Colonel Tom, Livonia is runnin' from you too, now. She would've wanted you last night. Been wantin' you again ever since she got old and fat and you stopped layin' with her and put her in the kitchen to cook. Don't think I don't know, Colonel Tom. Don't think I don't remember them nights when you used to sleep in that cabin down by de spring. I knew 'Vonia was there with you. I ain't no fool, Colonel Tom. But she ain't bore you no chilluns. I'm de one that bore 'em. [*Musing*] White mens, and colored womens, and little bastard chilluns—that's de old way of de South—but it's ending now. Three of your yellow brothers yo' father had by Aunt Sallie Deal—what had to come and do your laundry to make her livin'—you got colored relatives scattered all over this county. Them de ways o' de South—mixtries, mixtries. [WILLIAM *enters left, silently, as his mother talks. She is sitting in a chair now. Without looking up*] Is that you, William?

WILLIAM: Yes, ma, it's me.

CORA: Is you runnin' from him, too?

WILLIAM: [*Hesitatingly*] Well, ma, you see . . . don't you think kinder . . . well, I reckon   30
I ought to take Libby and ma babies on down to de church house with Reverend Martin and them, or else get 'long to town if I can hitch up them mules. They's scared to be out here, my wife and her ma. All de folks done gone from de houses down yonder by de branch, and you can hear de hounds a bayin' off yonder by de swamp, and cars is tearin' up that road, and de white folks is yellin' and hollerin' and carryin' on somethin' terrible over toward de brook. I done told Robert 'bout his foolishness. They's gonna hang him sure. Don't you think you better be comin' with us, ma. That is, do you want to? 'Course we can go by ourselves, and maybe you wants to stay here and take care o' de big house. I don't want to leave you, ma, but I . . . I . . .

CORA: Yo' brother'll be back, son, then I won't be by myself.

WILLIAM: [*Bewildered by his mother's sureness*] I thought Bert went . . . I thought he run . . . I thought . . .

CORA: No, honey. He went, but they ain't gonna get him out there. I sees him comin' back here now, to be with me. I's gwine to guard him 'till he can get away.

WILLIAM: Then de white folks'll come here, too.

CORA: Yes, de Colonel'll come back here sure. [*The deep baying of the hounds is heard at a*   35
distance through the night.] Colonel Tom will come after his son.

WILLIAM: My God, ma! Come with us to town.

CORA: Go on, William, go on! Don't wait for them to get back. You never was much like neither one o' them—neither de Colonel or Bert—you's mo' like de field hands. Too much o' ma blood in you, I guess. You never liked Bert much, neither, and you always was afraid of de Colonel. Go on, son, and hide yo' wife and her ma and your chilluns. Ain't nothin' gonna hurt you. You never did go against nobody. Neither did I, till tonight. Tried to live right and not hurt a soul, white or colored. [*Addressing space*] I tried to live right, Lord. [*Angrily*] Tried to live right, Lord. [*Throws out her arms resentfully as if to say, "and this is what you give me."*] What's de matter, Lawd, you ain't with me?

[*The hounds are heard howling again.*]

WILLIAM: I'm gone, ma. [*He exits fearfully as his mother talks.*]
CORA: [*Bending over the spot on the floor where the* COLONEL *has lain. She calls.*] Colonel Tom! Colonel Tom! Colonel Tom! Look! Bertha and Sallie and William and Bert, all your chilluns, runnin' from you, and you layin' on de floor there, dead! [*Pointing*] Out yonder with the mob, dead. And when you come home, upstairs in my bed on top of my body, dead. [*Goes to the window, returns, sits down, and begins to speak as if remembering a far-off dream.*] Colonel Thomas Norwood! I'm just poor Cora Lewis, Colonel Norwood. Little black Cora Lewis, Colonel Norwood. I'm just fifteen years old. Thirty years ago, you put your hands on me to feel my breasts, and you say, "You a pretty little piece of flesh, ain't you? Black and sweet, ain't you?" And I lift up ma face, and you pull me to you, and we laid down under the trees that night, and I wonder if your wife'll know when you go back up the road into the big house. And I wonder if my mama'll know it, when I go back to our cabin. Mama said she

Colonel Thomas Norwood (played here by James Kirkwood) enjoyed a complicated and predatory long-term relationship with his housekeeper and mistress, Cora Lewis (played by Mercedes Gilbert), pictured here in the long-running original production of *Mulatto* at the Vanderbilt Theater in New York, October, 1935.

nursed you when you was a baby, just like she nursed me. And I loved you in the dark, down there under that tree by de gate, afraid of you and proud of you, feelin' your gray eyes lookin' at me in de dark. Then I cried and cried and told ma mother about it, but she didn't take it hard like I thought she'd take it. She said fine white mens like de young Colonel always took good care o' their colored womens. She said it was better than marryin' some black field hand and workin' all your life in de cotton and cane. Better even than havin' a job like ma had, takin' care o' de white chilluns. Takin' care o' you, Colonel Tom. [*As* CORA *speaks the sound of the approaching mob gradually grows louder and louder. Auto horns, the howling of dogs, the far-off shouts of men, full of malignant force and power, increase in volume.*] And I was happy because I liked you, 'cause you was tall and proud, 'cause you said I was sweet to you and called me purty. And when yo' wife died—de Mrs. Norwood [*Scornfully*] that never bore you any chilluns, the pale beautiful Mrs. Norwood that was like a slender pine tree in de winter frost . . . I knowed you wanted me. I was full with child by you then—William, it was—our first boy. And ma mammy said, go up there and keep de house for Colonel Tom, sweep de floors and make de beds, and by and by, you won't have to sweep de floors and make no beds. And what ma mammy said was right. It all come true. Sam and Rusus and 'Vonia and Lucy did de waitin' on you and me, and de washin' and de cleanin' and de cookin'. And all I did was a little sewin' now and then, and a little preservin' in de summer and a little makin' of pies and sweet cakes and things you like to eat on Christmas. And de years went by. And I was always ready for you when you come to me in de night. And we had them chilluns, your chilluns and mine, Tom Norwood, all of 'em! William, born dark like me, dumb like me, and then Baby John what died; then Bertha, white and smart like you; and then Bert with your eyes and your ways and your temper, and mighty nigh your color; then Sallie, nearly white, too, and smart, and purty. But Bert was yo' chile! He was always yo' child . . . Good-looking, and kind, and headstrong, and strange, and stubborn, and proud like you, and de one I could love most 'cause he needed de most lovin'. And he wanted to call you "papa," and I tried to teach him no, but he did it anyhow and [*Sternly*] you beat him, Colonel Thomas Norwood. And he growed up with de beatin' in his heart and your eyes in his head, and your ways, and your pride. And this summer he looked like you that time I first knowed you down by de road under them trees, young and fiery and proud. There was no touchin' Bert, just like there was no touchin' you. I could only love him, like I loved you. I could only love him. But I couldn't talk to him, because he hated you. He had your ways—and you beat him! After you beat that chile, then you died, Colonel Norwood. You died here in this house, and you been living dead a long time. You lived dead. [*Her voice rises above the nearing sounds of the mob.*] And when I said this evenin', "Get up! Why don't you help me?" You'd done been dead a long time—a long time before you laid down on this floor, here, with the breath choked out o' you—and Bert standin' over you living, living, living. That's why you hated him. And you want to kill him. Always, you wanted to kill him. Out there with de hounds and de torches and de cars and de guns, you want to kill ma boy. But you won't kill him! He's comin' home first. He's comin' home to me. He's comin' home! [*Outside the noise is tremendous now, the lights of autos flash on the window curtains, there are shouts and cries.* CORA *sits, tense, in the middle of the room.*] He's comin' home!

A MAN'S VOICE: [*Outside*] He's somewhere on this lot.

ANOTHER VOICE: Don't shoot, men. We want to get him alive.

VOICE: Close in on him. He must be in them bushes by the house.

FIRST VOICE: Porch! Porch! Porch! There he is yonder—running to the door!

40

[*Suddenly shots are heard. The door bursts open and* ROBERT *enters, firing back into the darkness. The shots are returned by the mob, breaking the windows. Flares, lights, voices, curses, screams.*]

VOICES: Nigger! Nigger! Nigger! Get the nigger!

[CORA *rushes toward the door and bolts it after her son's entrance.*]

45   **CORA:** [*Leaning against the door*] I was waiting for you, honey. Yo' hiding place is all ready, upstairs, under ma bed, under de floor. I sawed a place there fo' you. They can't find you there. Hurry—before yo' father comes.

ROBERT: [*Panting*] No time to hide, ma. They're at the door now. They'll be coming up the back way, too. [*Sounds of knocking and the breaking of glass*] They'll be coming in the windows. They'll be coming in everywhere. And only one bullet left, ma. It's for me.

CORA: Yes, it's fo' you, chile. Save it. Go upstairs in mama's room. Lay on ma bed and rest.

ROBERT: [*Going slowly toward the stairs with the pistol in his hand*] Goodnight, ma. I'm awful tired of running, ma. They been chasing me for hours.

CORA: Goodnight, son.

[CORA *follows him to the foot of the steps. The door begins to give at the forcing of the mob. As* ROBERT *disappears above, it bursts open. A great crowd of white men pour into the room with guns, ropes, clubs, flashlights, and knives.* CORA *turns on the stairs, facing them quietly.* TALBOT, *the leader of the mob, stops.*]

50   **TALBOT:** Be careful, men. He's armed. [*To* CORA] Where is that yellow bastard of yours—upstairs?

CORA: Yes, he's going to sleep. Be quiet, you all. Wait. [*She bars the way with outspread arms.*]

TALBOT: [*Harshly*] Wait, hell! Come on, boys, let's go. [*A single shot is heard upstairs.*] What's that?

CORA: [*Calmly*] My boy . . . is gone . . . to sleep!

[TALBOT *and some of the men rush up the stairway,* CORA *makes a final gesture of love toward the room above. Yelling and shouting, through all the doors and windows, a great crowd pours into the room. The roar of the mob fills the house, the whole night, the whole world. Suddenly* TALBOT *returns at the top of the steps and a hush falls over the crowd.*]

TALBOT: Too late, men. We're just a little too late.

[*A sigh of disappointment rises from the mob.* TALBOT *comes down the stairs, walks up to* CORA *and slaps her once across the face. She does not move. It is as though no human hand can touch her again.*]

Curtain

QUESTIONS

Act 1

1. Throughout the act—and the play—why are the children of Colonel Norwood and Cora referred to as just Cora's children?
2. Why does the Colonel deny permission for Sallie's bags to be carried through the front door?
3. Throughout the act, what do we learn about Robert's attitudes toward his circumstances on the plantation? What do the Colonel and Higgins say about his attitude? Once Robert appears, what does he himself say about his situation?

4. What does the Colonel say about Sallie's ambition to reopen a nearby school? What does he advise her to do instead?

5. Who is Talbot? What does he represent? Why does he not appear until late in the second act?

6. What does Higgins report about how Robert has behaved in town? What does he tell Colonel Norwood to do about it?

7. As expressed in speech 61, what is Higgins's attitude toward black women? What does this attitude disclose about his character?

8. Describe the effect on both Robert and Colonel Norwood of the childhood incident when Robert called the Colonel "papa."

9. What has the Colonel decided to do about Robert? What are Cora's fears not only for Robert but for others?

Act 2, Scene 1

10. What are the issues in the confrontation between Robert and Colonel Norwood?

11. What is Robert's dilemma (speech 35)? What has the Colonel now determined to do about Robert?

12. What is Robert's response to the Colonel's display of the gun, and his threat to use it?

13. What do Talbot and the storekeeper do once they learn that Colonel Norwood is dead? What chance does Robert have to escape?

14. Why does Cora speak so extensively over the Colonel's body?

Act 2, Scene 2

15. Why are the undertaker and his companion introduced at this point? What are they like?

16. According to Cora (speech 27), what was the nature of the old "ways" of the South?

17. What is the purpose of Cora's second extensive monologue (speech 39)?

18. What finally happens to Robert? Why does Talbot slap Cora at the end?

GENERAL QUESTIONS

1. Describe *Mulatto* as a realistic play. Why is it important that the play contain many details about the plantation and the customs of the country?

2. What is the symbolism of the front door? The incident at the post office in town? Driving the Ford fast?

3. Describe Colonel Norwood. What characteristics of a Southern plantation owner does he exhibit? What is shown about him by his having sent Robert and his sisters away to school? What does Cora say about him before and after he is dead?

4. Describe the character of Robert. What are his dominant traits? How politic is he in dealing with his circumstances? To what extent does he bring about his own destruction?

5. Describe Cora. What has her life been like? To what degree has she sacrificed her individuality to stay with Colonel Norwood? How does she try to protect her children? In her two major lengthy speeches, what seems to be happening to her?

6. In light of the historical time when the play was written and produced, could there have been any other outcome?

EDWARD BOK LEE (b. 1974)

Edward Bok Lee is an energetic and eclectic writer, who in the first decade of the twenty-first century has earned considerable recognition and praise. His work has been performed on stages across Asia and North America, including the Tyrone Guthrie Theater in Minneapolis, where he developed El Santo Americano. *His many awards and honors include the American Book Award for Poetry in 2012 for his collection* Whorled, *the PEN Open Book Award in 2006, and the Minnesota Book Award in 2012. He studied in Korea as well as in Kazakhstan and at the University of North Dakota and the University of Minnesota. He received an MFA from Brown University. He currently teaches Writing at Metropolitan State University.*

El Santo Americano (2001)

CHARACTERS

Clay, a man
Evalana, his wife

TIME. Present
PLACE. The desert at night.

CLAY [*driving at night, 80 mph*]: that's because in Mexico it's normal to wear a mask. almost everybody does. silk and satin and form-fitting lycra. it makes the whole body more aerodynamic. you ought see them flying around, doing triple flips in mid-air. they got these long flowing capes like colorful wings sprouting from their shoulders. they don't talk much, though. not the great ones. the silence is mysterious. it adds a kind of weight to them when they climb into the ring. get a guy with that much gold and glitter on him here and you know he'd have to talk shit. in Mexico they just wrestle. the masks come from thousands and thousands of years ago. fiestas. ancient rituals. slip one over your head and you could become a tiger or donkey, a bat or giant lizard. a corn spirit dancing under the clouds for rain. those were your gods if you lived back then. you'll like it there in Mexico. don't you think you'll like it there? Jesse?

[*EVALANA, brooding, eventually looks in the backseat then faces front again.*]

CLAY: he asleep back there?
   a growing boy needs his sleep.
   yes he does.
   you hungry?
EVALANA: don't talk to me.
CLAY: hard to fall asleep on an empty stomach.
EVALANA: i can't sleep.
CLAY: you ain't tried to.

[*She checks her outburst, then looks in the backseat again, perhaps adjusting their son's blanket, then faces front. they drive on for a time.*]

CLAY [*looking in rearview mirror*]: hey there Jesse.
   you have a nice nap?
   we'll be there come morning, so you just sit back.

how you like that comic book i got you?
Jesse?
what's the matter, boy? you not feeling well?
Jesse?
EVALANA: sometimes he sleeps with his eyes open.
CLAY: like you.
EVALANA: i do not sleep with my eyes open.
CLAY: how do you know?
EVALANA: i know.
CLAY: how?
EVALANA: 'cause someone would have said something. including you.
CLAY: people do all kinds of things they're not aware of.
    my daddy used to wander through the house all night, buck naked,
    up and down the stairs. opening and closing windows.
    carrying only his briefcase chockfull of all the vending machine products he sold.
    combs. candy. chicken bouillon.
    my momma warned if we woke him up he'd have a heart attack.
    so we just let him sleepwalk.
    he didn't know.
EVALANA: maybe somebody should have told him.
CLAY: he didn't want to know.

[*They drive on.*]

EVALANA: you talk in your sleep.
    you snore.
    you drool.
    and you fart. all night.

[*They drive on awhile.*]

CLAY: i love you, Ev.
EVALANA: jesus, Clay. listen to yourself.
    your whole life you been faking it.
    fake husband. fake father.
    fake man. that's what they ought to call you:
    Fake Man.

[CLAY *drives on for a little while longer through the night, then pulls the car to a stop on the side of the road and gets out. he walks a good ways away from the car, holding a flashlight in one hand and a gun in the other—not aimed at her, but clearly present, under the starlight.* EVALANA *hesitates, then gets out, the flashlight's beam now on her.*]

CLAY [*directs flashlight beam to a place in the brush*]: there's a bush over there.

[EVALANA, *hesitant at first, then grabs her purse and crosses past* CLAY.]

EVALANA [*off*]: i won't run!
i promise!

[CLAY *thinks, then lowers flashlight beam and switches it off. dim moonlight. sounds of desert at night.*]

CLAY: you should have seen me last week, Ev!

Darton, he cut me a break! he didn't have to, but he did 'cause i been loyal to him all these years! you remember when we used to work at the turkey plant together! the smell on my hands when i'd come home and try to kiss you . . .

the match was against the eleventh-ranked contender! brand new guy, from Montreal! Kid Canuck they call him! long blonde hair, tan, all bulked up in white trunks with a red maple leaf you know where! some rich producer's nephew or something! he was scheduled to wrestle the Sheik in the opening match, but the old guy had a hernia while they was warming up, so Darton, he give me a break and put me on the bill against Kid Canuck at the last minute!

we didn't have time to choreograph much action! i think he was kind of nervous! two minutes in he starts grabbing my hair! hard! for real! trying to get the audience more into it! he wasn't telegraphing his head butts neither! soon enough my nose was a cherry caught under a dumptruck! the blood all over sure got the crowd into it boy! up till then they was pretty quiet, waiting for the main headliners to come out!

raking my eyes, slapping my face. i told him to ease up, it don't work like that here, but he wasn't listening. dancing around. cursing at me in French. winding his right arm up, then smacking me hard with the left until both my ears are firebells going off.

now i can take just about anything. you know me. i've been pile-drived, figure-foured, and suplexed into losses by the best of them. but on this particular night, something happened. and one pop i took in the mouth shot my adrenaline way up, my blood running all over hell now like carbolic acid, and him twisting my arm for real, not giving a flying fuck about my bad elbow, my bad back, or my five-year-old son, who don't even like to watch wrestling no more 'cause he's ashamed, 'cause his friends call his daddy a loser, and he don't know what to say or believe in, and the next thing i knew i had that pretty boy son of a bitch Kid Canuck down hard on the mat in a scorpion leg lock!!

they had to haul him off on a stretcher!

i was a little dazed yet, and the crowd, they didn't know what to think!

then the referee threw my arm up under the hot lights and before i knew it all the noise in the arena was more like cheering! it was a chemical thing! at first some people in the upper bleachers stood up! and then all of them did! everywhere! stomping, and starting to chant my name! and not 'cause they hated the other guy! they didn't! they was cheering 'cause i beat the guy fair and square! he gave up out of pain, right there in the middle of the ring! i had him wrenched in that scorpion leg lock a good two minutes screaming like a baby, like a cut pig, like a man in real pain! and they knew it!

you can't fake that! they'd seen so much phony bullshit through the years, and they could tell this match was different! and they appreciated that! they appreciated being shown the truth, just once in their sorry-ass lives!

Darton threw a wet towel at my face in the locker room.

i went out on a limb for you! he says. six months of planning and promotion! tens of thousands of dollars! t-shirts! coffee mugs! now who the hell's gonna believe Kid Canuck is a contender for the federation championship when he lost his debut match to you!!

i told him i was sorry, and after a while he put his hand on my shoulder. asked me what i'd been thinking there in the ring. tell me the truth, he says. so i can go home and feel at least a little bad about firing your dumb ass.

and i wanted to say that i did it for you.

for my wife, Evalana, who i never gave nothing to believe in.

and i did it for my boy, Jesse, who only ever got to see his daddy get beat time and again. i wanted to tell him i did it 'cause my wife and child was out there in the audience. not living in some other town. i wanted to say you was both out there watching over me. 'cause where else would you be?

Ev? Evalana!

[CLAY *switches on the flashlight and directs its beam onto the "bush" in the desert.* EVALANA *has run off. he directs the flashlight all around, searching in vain.*]

shit.

[CLAY *turns off the flashlight and sits down on a stone. in the moonlight, he pulls out from his pocket a colorful Mexican wrestler's mask and slips it over his head. he sits there in the darkness alone for a moment. he then, as a little boy might, twirls the gun on his finger, and pretends what it'd be like to shoot himself in the head. he tries it from a couple different angles, in strange fun. eventually he places the gun in his mouth, holds it there for a second or two with his hand, then lets go. it remains stuck there in his mouth from here on out. eventually, out of the darkness of the desert,* EVALANA *reappears.*]

EVALANA: once, when i was about Jesse's age, we took a trip to California. Disneyland. we drove all the way cross country in Daddy's Ford Falcon. Ma said it was the honeymoon she never got. a lot of the highway had just been tarred, and you could feel it. i thought we was gonna sail on forever into the future. it was somewhere in Arizona that Daddy woke us all up so we could see this great big dam at night. we stood there looking down at the bright lights and roaring darkness. Ma moved off to one side and stared down, a thousand feet.
i knew she wanted to jump.
then suddenly, she pointed at something. look, Ev, she said. a rainbow!
Shane and Darlene came running over, climbing up on the guard-rail but they couldn't see nothing. neither could Daddy.
a few hours later, somewhere outside of Flagstaff i told them i saw that rainbow too. it wasn't just Ma who saw it. i saw it too. Shane and Darlene were asleep now. Ma didn't say nothing. we drove on deeper into the night. then Daddy looked at me. i could see his eyes in the rear view mirror. hovering there in the blackness. "there's no such thing as a rainbow at night," he said. "not a real rainbow anyway."
the next day at dusk we camped on high ground. from where i stood looking down, you could see all the layers of sediment carved in the side of the mountains they cleared away for the highways a long time ago. red, black, brown, white, and sometimes almost blue, like a human vein in the side of a mountain, running parallel to the horizon. i stood there a long time, watching all the layers of earthen rainbows darkening all around me. then slowly, i noticed something. in the far distance, a cluster of fallen stars. only, it wasn't a cluster of stars, but a town. far off the highway, down there in the middle of nowhere. you wouldn't even notice it by day. but at night you could see something. twinkling. i imagined i'd been born in that town, and that that was where we was all heading back to. not Disneyland. but that town shining with tiny stars that weren't really stars, surrounded by rainbows that weren't really rainbows. but erosion. as far as the eye could see. for thousands and thousands of years. both real and imaginary. like that town down there in the valley at night. just barely shimmering. like . . . Eden.

[*We hear the sound of their car start and drive off into the night.* CLAY *in mask with gun still in mouth and* EVALANA *slowly turn to watch the vehicle go, converging closer together as they walk and watch.* "JESSE" *has driven off into the night. once the sound of the car has faded into the distance,* CLAY *in mask with gun in mouth and* EVALANA *slowly turn to one another. after a moment,* EVALANA *reaches up and removes the gun from* CLAY's *mouth and slowly points it at him.*]

Fade to black.]

QUESTIONS

1. Why does Evalana say that she will not run when Clay stops the car for the break?

2. When Clay describes the wrestling match he has won, why does he assert that the crowd of spectators at the event appreciated the honesty and genuineness of his victory?

3. Toward the end of the play, what does Clay conclude about the reality of the desert town in the far distance, as contrasted with the unreality of a place like Disneyland? How does the play comment on the difference between what's "phony" and what's "the truth"?

4. What happens to the car at the end of the play? How realistic is this, considering that it is likely Jesse (a five-year-old) is doing the driving while the parents are being stranded at the side of the road?

5. What, at the play's end, do you think that Evalana will do with the gun that she takes from Clay's mouth and is now beginning to point at Clay? Why? What do these concluding details tell you about the family relationships that have been developing throughout the play?

TENNESSEE WILLIAMS (1911–1983)

Tennessee Williams (1911–1983) grew up in Mississippi and Missouri, and many of his plays reflect the attitudes and customs that he encountered in his early years. Until he was eight, his family lived in genteel poverty, mostly in Columbus, Mississippi. In 1919 the family moved to a lower-class neighborhood in St. Louis. Williams, who was sickly and bookish, tried to escape from poverty and family conflicts by writing and going to the movies. One of his few companions during those years was his shy and withdrawn sister, Rose.

He entered the University of Missouri in 1931, but the Depression and family poverty forced him to drop out and go to work in a shoe warehouse. After two years of this work, he suffered a nervous collapse, but he finally finished college at the University of Iowa. He then began wandering the country, doing odd jobs and also writing. His first full-length play, Battle of Angels, *was produced in 1940 but was unsuccessful. He continued to write, however, and was able to get* The Glass Menagerie *staged in 1945. The critical and popular success of this play marked the beginning of many good years in the theater. Along with Arthur Miller, during the 1940s and 1950s Williams dominated the American stage, going on to write many one-act plays and more than fifteen full-length dramas (many of which became successful films), including* A Streetcar Named Desire *(1947, Pulitzer Prize),* The Rose Tattoo *(1951),* Cat on a Hot Tin Roof *(1955, Pulitzer Prize),* Suddenly Last Summer *(1958), and* The Night of the Iguana *(1961).*

The Glass Menagerie, written in 1944 and produced with favorable reviews in Chicago and New York in 1945, is a largely autobiographical play that explores the family dynamics, delusions, and personalities of the Wingfields. Williams originally developed his ideas for the play in a short story called "Portrait of a Girl in Glass" and then in a screenplay for Metro-Goldwyn-Mayer titled *The Gentleman Caller*. In these treatments as well as in *The Glass Menagerie*, Laura Wingfield is modeled after his sister, Rose Williams. The least competent member of the family, she is crippled by her own insecurity and her mother's expectations. At every opportunity, Laura withdraws into a world of glass figurines and old phonograph records left by her father when he abandoned the family. Amanda Wingfield is patterned after Williams's mother. She valiantly tries to hold the family together and provide for Laura's future, but her perspectives are skewed by her romanticized memories of a gracious Southern past of plantations, formal dances, and "gentleman callers." Tom, a figure based on the playwright himself, is desperate to escape the trap of his impoverished family. He seeks to emulate the long-missing father and move out of the drab Wingfield apartment into adventure and experience.

The play offers a fascinating mixture of realistic and nonrealistic dramatic techniques. The realistic elements are the characters (excluding Tom when he narrates) and the language. This is especially true of Amanda's language, in which Williams skillfully recreates the diction and cadences characteristic of the Deep South. As he points out in his production notes and stage directions, the play's structure and staging are nonrealistic. Williams employs various devices nonrealistically—including the narrator, music, lighting, and screen projections—to underscore the emotions of his characters and to explore ideas about family and personality.

One of Williams's most effective nonrealistic techniques in *The Glass Menagerie* is its structure as "a memory play," and therefore its illustration of how a first-person narrator can be used in a drama. The characters and the action are not real and they do not exist in the present. Rather, they represent Tom's memories and feelings about events that occurred approximately five years earlier, when America was in the grip of the Great Depression, when the Spanish Civil War had resulted in the imposition of a fascist dictatorship in Spain, and when World War II was beginning in Europe. As the narrator, Tom exists at the time of the action (1944), but the events he introduces are occurring in about 1939. When Tom becomes a character in the Wingfield household, he is the Tom of this earlier period, quite distinct from his identity as the present narrator. Thus, the action in the apartment is not strictly a realistic recreation of life. Instead, even though the actions and characters seem realistic, they are exaggerated and reshaped as Tom remembers them and regrets them.

 ## The Glass Menagerie (1945)

THE CHARACTERS

Amanda Wingfield *(the mother)*
 A little woman of great but confused vitality clinging frantically to another time and place. Her characterization must be carefully created, not copied from type. She is not paranoiac, but her life is paranoia. There is much to admire in Amanda, and as much to love and pity as there is to laugh at. Certainly she has endurance and a kind of heroism, and though her foolishness makes her unwittingly cruel at times, there is tenderness in her slight person.

Laura Wingfield *(her daughter)*
 Amanda, having failed to establish contact with reality, continues to live vitally in her illusions, but Laura's situation is even graver. A childhood illness has left her crippled, one leg slightly shorter than the other, and held in a brace. This defect need not be more than suggested on the stage. Stemming from this, Laura's separation increases till she is like a piece of her own glass collection, too exquisitely fragile to move from the shelf.

Tom Wingfield *(her son)*
 And the narrator of the play. A poet with a job in a warehouse. His nature is not remorseless, but to escape from a trap he has to act without pity.

Jim O'Connor *(the gentleman caller)*
 A nice, ordinary, young man.

PRODUCTION NOTES°

Being a "memory play," *The Glass Menagerie* can be presented with unusual freedom of convention. Because of its considerably delicate or tenuous material, atmospheric touches and subtleties of direction play a particularly important part. Expressionism and all other unconventional techniques in drama have only one valid aim, and that is a closer approach to truth. When a play employs unconventional techniques, it is not, or certainly shouldn't be, trying to escape its responsibility of dealing with reality, or interpreting experience, but is actually or should be attempting to find a closer approach, a more penetrating and vivid expression of things as they are. The straight realistic play with its genuine Frigidaire and authentic ice-cubes, its characters who speak exactly as its audience speaks, corresponds to the academic landscape and has the same virtue of a photographic likeness. Everyone should know nowadays the unimportance of the photographic in art: that truth, life, or reality is an organic thing which the poetic imagination can represent or suggest, in essence, only through transformation, through changing into other forms than those which were merely present in appearance.

These remarks are not meant as a preface only to this particular play. They have to do with a conception of a new, plastic theatre which must take the place of the exhausted theatre of realistic conventions if the theatre is to resume vitality as a part of our culture.

THE SCREEN DEVICE: There is *only one important difference between the original and the acting version of the play* and that is the *omission* in the latter of the device that I tentatively included in my *original* script. This device was the use of a screen on which were projected magic-lantern slides bearing images or titles. I do not regret the omission of this device from the original Broadway production. The extraordinary power of Miss Taylor's° performance made it suitable to have the utmost simplicity in the physical production. But I think it may be interesting to some readers to see how this device was conceived. So I am putting it into the published manuscript. These images and legends, projected from behind, were cast on a section of wall between the front-room and dining-room areas, which should be indistinguishable from the rest when not in use.

The purpose of this will probably be apparent. It is to give accent to certain values in each scene. Each scene contains a particular point (or several) which is structurally the most important. In an episodic play, such as this, the basic structure or narrative line may be obscured from the audience; the effect may seem fragmentary rather than architectural. This may not be the fault of the play so much as a lack of attention in the audience. The legend or image upon the screen will strengthen the effect of what is merely allusion in the writing and allow the primary point to be made more simply and lightly than if the entire responsibility were on the spoken lines. Aside from this structural value, I think the screen will have a definite emotional appeal, less definable but just as important. An imaginative producer or director may invent many other uses for this device than those indicated in the present script. In fact the possibilities of the device seem much larger to me than the instance of this play can possibly utilize.

THE MUSIC: Another extra-literary accent in this play is provided by the use of music. A single recurring tune, "The Glass Menagerie,"° is used to give emotional emphasis to suitable passages. This tune is like circus music, not when you are on the grounds or in the immediate vicinity of the parade, but when you are at some distance and very likely thinking of something else. It seems under those circumstances to continue almost interminably and it weaves in and out of your preoccupied consciousness; then it is the lightest, most delicate

---

°The production notes are by Williams and are part of the play. °P.N. *Miss Taylor's:* The role of Amanda was first played by the American actress Laurette Taylor (1884–1946). °P.N. *"The Glass Menagerie":* Original music, including this recurrent theme, was composed for the play by Paul Bowles.

music in the world and perhaps the saddest. It expresses the surface vivacity of life with the underlying strain of immutable and inexpressible sorrow. When you look at a piece of delicately spun glass you think of two things: how beautiful it is and how easily it can be broken. Both of those ideas should be woven into the recurring tune, which dips in and out of the play as if it were carried on a wind that changes. It serves as a thread of connection and allusion between the narrator with his separate point in time and space and the subject of his story. Between each episode it returns as reference to the emotion, nostalgia, which is the first condition of the play. It is primarily Laura's music and therefore comes out most clearly when the play focuses upon her and the lovely fragility of glass which is her image.

THE LIGHTING: The lighting in the play is not realistic. In keeping with the atmosphere of memory, the stage is dim. Shafts of light are focused on selected areas or actors, sometimes in contradistinction to what is the apparent center. For instance, in the quarrel scene between Tom and Amanda, in which Laura has no active part, the clearest pool of light is on her figure. This is also true of the supper scene, when her silent figure on the sofa should remain the visual center. The light upon Laura should be distinct from the others, having a peculiar pristine clarity such as light used in early religious portraits of female saints or madonnas. A certain correspondence to light in religious paintings, such as El Greco's,° where the figures are radiant in atmosphere that is relatively dusky, could be effectively used throughout the play. (It will also permit a more effective use of the screen.) A free, imaginative use of light can be of enormous value in giving a mobile, plastic quality to plays of a more or less static nature.

Tennessee Williams

SCENE 1

The Wingfield apartment is in the rear of the building, one of those vast hive-like conglomerations of cellular living-units that flower as warty growths in overcrowded urban centers of lower middle-class population and are symptomatic of the impulse of this largest and fundamentally enslaved section of American society to avoid fluidity and differentiation and to exist and function as one interfused mass of automatism.

The apartment faces an alley and is entered by a fire escape, a structure whose name is a touch of accidental poetic truth, for all of these huge buildings are always burning with the slow and implacable fires of human desperation. The fire escape is part of what we see—that is, the landing of it and steps descending from it.

The scene is memory and is therefore nonrealistic. Memory takes a lot of poetic license. It omits some details; others are exaggerated, according to the emotional value of the articles it touches, for memory is seated predominantly in the heart. The interior is therefore rather dim and poetic.

At the rise of the curtain, the audience is faced with the dark, grim rear wall of the Wingfield tenement. This building is flanked on both sides by dark, narrow alleys which run into murky canyons of tangled clotheslines, garbage cans, and the sinister latticework of neighboring fire escapes. It is up and down these side alleys that exterior entrances and exits are made during the play. At the end of Tom's opening commentary, the dark tenement wall slowly becomes transparent° and reveals the interior of the ground-floor Wingfield apartment.

Nearest the audience is the living room, which also serves as a sleeping room for LAURA, *the sofa unfolding to make her bed. Just beyond, separated from the living room by a wide arch or second proscenium with transparent faded portieres° (or second curtain), is the dining room. In an old-*

°P.N. *El Greco:* Greek painter (c. 1548–1614) who lived in Spain; typical paintings by El Greco have elongated and distorted figures and extremely vivid foreground lighting set against a murky background. °S.D. *transparent:* The wall is painted on a scrim, a transparent curtain that is opaque when lit from the front and transparent when lit from behind. °S.D. *portieres:* curtains hung in a doorway; in production, these may also be painted on a scrim.

fashioned whatnot° in the living room are seen scores of transparent glass animals. A blown-up photograph of the father hangs on the wall of the living room, to the left of the archway. It is the face of a very handsome young man in a doughboy's° First World War cap. He is gallantly smiling, ineluctably smiling, as if to say "I will be smiling forever."

Also hanging on the wall, near the photograph, are a typewriter keyboard chart and a Gregg shorthand diagram. An upright typewriter on a small table stands beneath the charts.

The audience hears and sees the opening scene in the dining room through both the transparent fourth wall of the building and the transparent gauze portieres of the dining-room arch. It is during this revealing scene that the fourth wall slowly ascends, out of sight. This transparent exterior wall is not brought down again until the very end of the play, during Tom's final speech.

The narrator is an undisguised convention of the play. He takes whatever license with dramatic convention is convenient to his purposes.

Tom enters, dressed as a merchant sailor, and strolls across to the fire escape. There he stops and lights a cigarette. He addresses the audience.

Tom: Yes, I have tricks in my pocket, I have things up my sleeve. But I am the opposite of a stage magician. He gives you illusion that has the appearance of truth. I give you truth in the pleasant disguise of illusion.

To begin with, I turn back time. I reverse it to that quaint period, the thirties, when the huge middle class of America was matriculating in a school for the blind. Their eyes had failed them, or they had failed their eyes, and so they were having their fingers pressed forcibly down on the fiery Braille alphabet of a dissolving economy.

In Spain there was revolution. Here there was only shouting and confusion. In Spain there was Guernica.° Here there were disturbances of labor, sometimes pretty violent, in otherwise peaceful cities such as Chicago, Cleveland, Saint Louis. . . . This is the social background of the play.

[Music begins to play.]

The play is memory. Being a memory play, it is dimly lighted, it is sentimental, it is not realistic. In memory everything seems to happen to music. That explains the fiddle in the wings.

I am the narrator of the play, and also a character in it. The other characters are my mother, Amanda, my sister, Laura, and a gentleman caller who appears in the final scenes. He is the most realistic character in the play, being an emissary from a world of reality that we were somehow set apart from. But since I have a poet's weakness for symbols, I am using this character also as a symbol; he is the long-delayed but always expected something that we live for.

There is a fifth character in the play who doesn't appear except in this larger-than-life-size photograph over the mantel. This is our father who left us a long time ago. He was a telephone man who fell in love with long distances; he gave up his job with the telephone company and skipped the light fantastic out of town. . . .

The last we heard of him was a picture postcard from Mazatlan, on the Pacific coast of Mexico, containing a message of two words: "Hello—Goodbye!" and no address.

I think the rest of the play will explain itself. . . .

[Amanda's voice becomes audible through the portieres.]

°S.D. *whatnot*: a small set of shelves for ornaments. *doughboy*: popular name for an American infantryman during World War I. 1.3 *Guernica*: a Basque town that was destroyed in 1937 by German planes fighting on General Franco's side during the Spanish Civil War. The huge mural *Guernica*, painted by Pablo Picasso, depicts the horror of that bombardment.

[*Legend on screen: "Où sont les neiges."°*]

[TOM *divides the portieres and enters the dining room.* AMANDA *and* LAURA *are seated at a drop-leaf table. Eating is indicated by gestures without food or utensils.* AMANDA *faces the audience.* TOM *and* LAURA *are seated profile. The interior has lit up softly and through the scrim we see* AMANDA *and* LAURA *seated at the table.*]

AMANDA: [*calling*] Tom?

TOM: Yes, Mother.

AMANDA: We can't say grace until you come to the table!

TOM: Coming, Mother. [*He bows slightly and withdraws, reappearing a few moments later in his*   5
    place at the table.]

AMANDA: [*to her son*] Honey, don't push with your fingers. If you have to push with some-
    thing, the thing to push with is a crust of bread. And chew—chew! Animals have
    secretions in their stomachs which enable them to digest food without mastication,
    but human beings are supposed to chew their food before they swallow it down. Eat
    food leisurely, son, and really enjoy it. A well-cooked meal has lots of delicate flavors
    that have to be held in the mouth for appreciation. So chew your food and give your
    salivary glands a chance to function!

[TOM *deliberately lays his imaginary fork down and pushes his chair back from the table.*]

TOM: I haven't enjoyed one bite of this dinner because of your constant directions on how
    to eat it. It's you that make me rush through meals with your hawklike attention to
    every bite I take. Sickening—spoils my appetite—all this discussion of—animals'
    secretion—salivary glands—mastication!

AMANDA: [*lightly*] Temperament like a Metropolitan star.°

[TOM *rises and walks toward the living room.*]

    You're not excused from the table.

TOM: I'm getting a cigarette.

AMANDA: You smoke too much.   10

[LAURA *rises.*]

LAURA: I'll bring in the blanc mange.°

[TOM *remains standing with his cigarette by the portieres.*]

AMANDA: [*rising*] No, sister, no, sister°—you be the lady this time and I'll be the darky.

LAURA: I'm already up.

AMANDA: Resume your seat, little sister—I want you to stay fresh and pretty—for gentle-
    men callers!

LAURA: [*sitting down*] I'm not expecting any gentlemen callers.   15

AMANDA: [*crossing out to the kitchenette, airily*] Sometimes they come when they are least
    expected! Why, I remember one Sunday afternoon in Blue Mountain°—

°1.8 S.D. *"Où sont les neiges."*: "Where are the snows (of yesteryear)," refrain from "The Ballade of Dead Ladies" by the French poet François Villon (c. 1431–1463). °8 *Metropolitan star:* the Metropolitan Opera in New York City; opera stars are traditionally considered to be highly temperamental. °11 *blanc mange:* a bland molded pudding or custard. °12 *sister:* In the American South of Amanda's youth, the oldest daughter in a family was frequently called "sister" by her parents and siblings. °16 *Blue Mountain:* an imaginary town in northwest Mississippi modeled after Clarksville, where Williams spent much of his youth. Blue Mountain (Clarksville) is at the northern edge of the Mississippi Delta, a large fertile plain that supports numerous plantations. This is the recollected world of Amanda's youth—plantations, wealth, black servants, and gentlemen callers who were the sons of cotton planters.

[*She enters the kitchenette.*]

Tom: I know what's coming!
Laura: Yes. But let her tell it.
Tom: Again?
20   **Laura:** She loves to tell it.

[*Amanda returns with a bowl of dessert.*]

Amanda: One Sunday afternoon in Blue Mountain—your mother received—*seventeen!*—
   gentlemen callers! Why, sometimes there weren't chairs enough to accommodate them
   all. We had to send the nigger over to bring in folding chairs from the parish house.
Tom: [*remaining at the portieres*] How did you entertain those gentlemen callers?
Amanda: I understood the art of conversation!
Tom: I bet you could talk.
25   **Amanda:** Girls in those days knew how to talk, I can tell you.
Tom: Yes?

[*Image on screen: Amanda as a girl on a porch, greeting callers.*]

Amanda: They knew how to entertain their gentlemen callers. It wasn't enough for a girl
   to be possessed of a pretty face and a graceful figure—although I wasn't slighted in
   either respect. She also needed to have a nimble wit and a tongue to meet all occasions.
Tom: What did you talk about?
Amanda: Things of importance going on in the world! Never anything coarse or common
   or vulgar.

[*She addresses Tom as though he were seated in the vacant chair at the table though he remains by
the portieres. He plays this scene as though reading from a script.°*]

My callers were gentleman—all! Among my callers were some of the most prominent
young planters of the Mississippi Delta—planters and sons of planters!

[*Tom motions for music and a spot of light on Amanda. Her eyes lift, her face glows, her voice becomes rich and elegiac.*]

[*Screen legend: "Où sont les neiges d'antan?"°*]

There was young Champ Laughlin who later became vice-president of the
Delta Planters Bank. Hadley Stevenson who was drowned in Moon Lake and left
his widow one hundred and fifty thousand in Government bonds. There were the
Cutrere brothers, Wesley and Bates. Bates was one of my bright particular beaux! He
got in a quarrel with that wild Wainwright boy. They shot it out on the floor of Moon
Lake Casino. Bates was shot through the stomach. Died in the ambulance on his way
to Memphis. His widow was also well provided-for, came into eight or ten thousand
acres, that's all. She married him on the rebound—never loved her—carried my picture on him the night he died! And there was that boy that every girl in the Delta had
set her cap for! That beautiful, brilliant young Fitzhugh boy from Greene County!
30   **Tom:** What did he leave his widow?
Amanda: He never married! Gracious, you talk as though all of my old admirers had
   turned up their toes to the daisies!

°29.1 S.D. *script:* Here Tom becomes both a character in the play and the stage manager. °29.2 S.D. *"Où sont les
neiges d'antan?":* Where are the snows of yesteryear? See the note on page 1383.

TOM: Isn't this the first you've mentioned that still survives?

AMANDA: That Fitzhugh boy went North and made a fortune—came to be known as the Wolf of Wall Street! He had the Midas touch,° whatever he touched turned to gold! And I could have been Mrs. Duncan J. Fitzhugh, mind you! But—I picked your *father!*

LAURA: [*rising*] Mother, let me clear the table.

AMANDA: No, dear, you go in front and study your typewriter chart. Or practice your shorthand a little. Stay fresh and pretty!—It's almost time for our gentlemen callers to start arriving. [*She flounces girlishly toward the kitchenette.*] How many do you suppose we're going to entertain this afternoon?

[*TOM throws down the paper and jumps up with a groan.*]

LAURA: [*alone in the dining room*] I don't believe we're going to receive any, Mother.

AMANDA: [*reappearing airily*] What? No one?—not one? You must be joking!

[*LAURA nervously echoes her laugh. She slips in a fugitive manner through the half-open portieres and draws them gently behind her. A shaft of very clear light is thrown on her face against the faded tapestry of the curtains. Faintly the music of "The Glass Menagerie" is heard as she continues lightly:*]

Not one gentleman caller? It can't be true! There must be a flood, there must have been a tornado!

LAURA: It isn't a flood, it's not a tornado, Mother. I'm just not popular like you were in Blue Mountain. . . .

[*TOM utters another groan. LAURA glances at him with a faint, apologetic smile. Her voice catches a little:*]

Mother's afraid I'm going to be an old maid.

[*The scene dims out with the "Glass Menagerie" music.*]

SCENE 2

On the dark stage the screen is lighted with the image of blue roses. Gradually LAURA's figure becomes apparent and the screen goes out. The music subsides.

LAURA is seated in the delicate ivory chair at the small clawfoot table. She wears a dress of soft violet material for a kimono—her hair is tied back from her forehead with a ribbon. She is washing and polishing her collection of glass. AMANDA appears on the fire escape steps. At the sound of her ascent, LAURA catches her breath, thrusts the bowl of ornaments away, and seats herself stiffly before the diagram of the typewriter keyboard as though it held her spellbound. Something has happened to AMANDA. It is written in her face as she climbs to the landing: a look that is grim and hopeless and a little absurd. She has on one of those cheap or imitation velvety-looking cloth coats with imitation fur collar. Her hat is five or six years old, one of those dreadful cloche hats that were worn in the late Twenties, and she is clutching an enormous black patent-leather pocketbook with nickel clasps and initials. This is her full-dress outfit, the one she usually wears to the D.A.R.° Before entering she looks through the door. She purses her lips, opens her eyes very wide, rolls them upward and shakes her head. Then she slowly lets herself in the door. Seeing her mother's expression, LAURA touches her lips with a nervous gesture.

LAURA: Hello, Mother, I was—[*She makes a nervous gesture toward the chart on the wall.* AMANDA *leans against the shut door and stares at* LAURA *with a martyred look.*]

°33 *Midas touch:* In Greek mythology, King Midas was given the power to turn everything he touched into gold.
°S.D. *D.A.R.:* Daughters of the American Revolution, a patriotic women's organization (founded in 1890) open only to women whose ancestors aided the American Revolution.

AMANDA: Deception? Deception? [*She slowly removes her hat and gloves, continuing the sweet suffering stare. She lets the hat and gloves fall on the floor—a bit of acting.*]

LAURA: [*shakily*] How was the D.A.R. meeting?

[*AMANDA slowly opens her purse and removes a dainty white handkerchief which she shakes out delicately and delicately touches to her lips and nostrils.*]

Didn't you go to the D.A.R. meeting, Mother?

AMANDA: [*faintly, almost inaudibly*]—No.—No. [*then more forcibly:*] I did not have the strength—to go to the D.A.R. In fact, I did not have the courage! I wanted to find a hole in the ground and hide myself in it forever! [*She crosses slowly to the wall and removes the diagram of the typewriter keyboard. She holds it in front of her for a second, staring at it sweetly and sorrowfully— then bites her lips and tears it in two pieces.*]

5   **LAURA:** [*faintly*] Why did you do that, Mother?

[*AMANDA repeats the same procedure with the chart of the Gregg Alphabet.*]

Why are you—

AMANDA: Why? Why? How old are you, Laura?

LAURA: Mother, you know my age.

AMANDA: I thought you were an adult; it seems that I was mistaken. [*She crosses slowly to the sofa and sinks down and stares at LAURA.*]

LAURA: Please don't stare at me, Mother.

[*AMANDA closes her eyes and lowers her head. There is a ten-second pause.*]

10   **AMANDA:** What are we going to do, what is going to become of us, what is the future?

[*There is another pause.*]

LAURA: Has something happened, Mother?

[*AMANDA draws a long breath, takes out the handkerchief again, goes through the dabbing process.*]

Mother, has—something happened?

AMANDA: I'll be all right in a minute, I'm just bewildered—[*She hesitates.*]—by life. . . .

LAURA: Mother, I wish that you would tell me what's happened!

AMANDA: As you know, I was supposed to be inducted into my office at the D.A.R. this afternoon.

[*Screen image: A swarm of typewriters.*]

But I stopped off at Rubicam's Business College to speak to your teachers about your having a cold and ask them what progress they thought you were making down there.

15   **LAURA:** Oh. . . .

AMANDA: I went to the typing instructor and introduced myself as your mother. She didn't know who you were.

"Wingfield," she said, "We don't have any such student enrolled at the school!"

I assured her she did, that you had been going to classes since early in January.

"I wonder," she said, "if you could be talking about that terribly shy little girl who dropped out of school after only a few days' attendance?"

"No," I said, "Laura, my daughter, has been going to school every day for the past six weeks!"

"Excuse me," she said. She took the attendance book out and there was your name, unmistakably printed, and all the dates you were absent until they decided that you had dropped out of school.

I still said, "No, there must have been some mistake! There must have been some mix-up in the records!"

And she said, "No—I remember her perfectly now. Her hands shook so that she couldn't hit the right keys! The first time we gave a speed test, she broke down completely—was sick at the stomach and almost had to be carried into the wash room! After that morning she never showed up any more. We phoned the house but never got any answer"—While I was working at Famous-Barr,° I suppose, demonstrating those—

[*She indicates a brassiere with her hands.*]

Oh! I felt so weak I could barely keep on my feet! I had to sit down while they got me a glass of water! Fifty dollars' tuition, all of our plans—my hopes and ambitions for you—just gone up the spout, just gone up the spout like that.

[*LAURA draws a long breath and gets awkwardly to her feet. She crosses to the Victrola and winds it up.°*]

What are you doing?

LAURA: Oh! [*She releases the handle and returns to her seat.*]

AMANDA: Laura, where have you been going when you've gone out pretending that you were going to business college?

LAURA: I've just been going out walking.

AMANDA: That's not true.

LAURA: It is. I just went walking.   20

AMANDA: Walking? Walking? In winter? Deliberately courting pneumonia in that light coat? Where did you walk to, Laura?

LAURA: All sorts of places—mostly in the park.

AMANDA: Even after you'd started catching that cold?

LAURA: It was the lesser of two evils, Mother.   25

[*Screen image: Winter scene in a park.*]

I couldn't go back there. I—threw up—on the floor!

AMANDA: From half past seven till after five every day you mean to tell me you walked around the park, because you wanted to make me think that you were still going to Rubicam's Business College?

LAURA: It wasn't as bad as it sounds. I went inside places to get warmed up.

AMANDA: Inside where?

LAURA: I went in the art museum and the bird houses at the Zoo. I visited the penguins every day! Sometimes I did without lunch and went to the movies. Lately I've been spending most of my afternoons in the Jewel Box, that big glass house where they raise the tropical flowers.

AMANDA: You did all this to deceive me, just for deception? [*LAURA looks down.*] Why?   30

LAURA: Mother, when you're disappointed, you get that awful suffering look on your face, like the picture of Jesus' mother in the museum!

AMANDA: Hush!

LAURA: I couldn't face it.

[*There is a pause. A whisper of strings is heard. Legend on screen: "The Crust of Humility."*]

°16.8 *Famous-Barr*: a department store in St. Louis. °16.11 S.D. *winds it up*: Laura is using a spring-powered (rather than electric) phonograph that has to be rewound frequently.

AMANDA: [*hopelessly fingering the huge pocketbook*] So what are we going to do the rest of our lives? Stay home and watch the parades go by? Amuse ourselves with the glass menagerie, darling? Eternally play those worn-out phonograph records your father left as a painful reminder of him? We won't have a business career—we've given that up because it gave us nervous indigestion! [*She laughs wearily.*] What is there left but dependency all our lives? I know so well what becomes of unmarried women who aren't prepared to occupy a position. I've seen such pitiful cases in the South— barely tolerated spinsters living upon the grudging patronage of sister's husband or brother's wife!—stuck away in some little mousetrap of a room—encouraged by one in-law to visit another—little birdlike women without any nest—eating the crust of humility all their life!

Is that the future that we've mapped out for ourselves? I swear it's the only alternative I can think of! [*She pauses.*] It isn't a very pleasant alternative, is it? [*She pauses again.*] Of course—some girls *do marry.*

[*LAURA twists her hands nervously.*]

Haven't you ever liked some boy?

35   **LAURA:** Yes. I liked one once. [*She rises.*] I came across his picture a while ago.
AMANDA: [*with some interest*] He gave you his picture?
LAURA: No, it's in the yearbook.
AMANDA: [*disappointed*] Oh—a high school boy.

[*Screen image: JIM as the high school hero bearing a silver cup.*]

LAURA: Yes. His name was Jim. [*She lifts the heavy annual from the claw-foot table.*] Here he is in *The Pirates of Penzance.*°
40   **AMANDA:** [*absently*] The what?
LAURA: The operetta the senior class put on. He had a wonderful voice and we sat across the aisle from each other Mondays, Wednesdays and Fridays in the Aud. Here he is with the silver cup for debating! See his grin?
AMANDA: [*absently*] He must have had a jolly disposition.
LAURA: He used to call me—Blue Roses.

[*Screen image: Blue roses.*]

AMANDA: Why did he call you such a name as that?
45   **LAURA:** When I had that attack of pleurosis—he asked me what was the matter when I came back. I said pleurosis—he thought that I said Blue Roses! So that's what he always called me after that. Whenever he saw me, he'd holler, "Hello, Blue Roses!" I didn't care for the girl that he went out with. Emily Meisenbach. Emily was the best-dressed girl at Soldan. She never struck me, though, as being sincere. . . . It says in the Personal Section—they're engaged. That's—six years ago! They must be married by now.
AMANDA: Girls that aren't cut out for business careers usually wind up married to some nice man. [*She gets up with a spark of revival.*] Sister, that's what you'll do!

[*LAURA utters a startled, doubtful laugh. She reaches quickly for a piece of glass.*]

°39 *The Pirates of Penzance:* a comic light opera (1879) by W. S. Gilbert and Arthur Sullivan.

LAURA: But, Mother—
AMANDA: Yes? [*She goes over to the photograph.*]
LAURA: [*in a tone of frightened apology*] I'm—crippled!
AMANDA: Nonsense! Laura, I've told you never, never to use that word.
Why, you're not crippled, you just have a little defect—hardly noticeable, even!
When people have some slight disadvantage like that, they cultivate other things to
make up for it—develop charm—and vivacity—and—*charm*! That's all you have to do!
[*She turns again to the photograph.*] One thing your father had *plenty of*—was *charm*!

[*The scene fades out with music.*]

SCENE 3

[*Legend on screen: "After the fiasco—"*

TOM *speaks from the fire escape landing.*]

TOM: After the fiasco at Rubicam's Business College, the idea of getting a gentleman caller
for Laura began to play a more and more important part in Mother's calculations. It
became an obsession. Like some archetype of the universal unconscious, the image of
the gentleman caller haunted our small apartment. . . .

[*Screen image: A young man at the door of a house with flowers.*]

An evening at home rarely passed without some allusion to this image, this specter,
this hope. . . . Even when he wasn't mentioned, his presence hung in Mother's preoccupied look and in my sister's frightened, apologetic manner—hung like a sentence
passed upon the Wingfields!
    Mother was a woman of action as well as words. She began to take logical steps
in the planned direction. Late that winter and in the early spring—realizing that extra
money would be needed to properly feather the nest and plume the bird—she conducted
a vigorous campaign on the telephone, roping in subscribers to one of those magazines
for matrons called *The Homemaker's Companion,* the type of journal that features the
serialized sublimations of ladies of letters who think in terms of delicate cuplike breasts,
slim, tapering waists, rich, creamy thighs, eyes like wood smoke in autumn, fingers that
soothe and caress like strains of music, bodies as powerful as Etruscan sculpture.

[*Screen image: The cover of a glamor magazine.*

AMANDA *enters with the telephone on a long extension cord. She is spotlighted in the dim stage.*]

AMANDA: Ida Scott? This is Amanda Wingfield! We missed you at the D.A.R. last
Monday! I said to myself: She's probably suffering with that sinus condition! How is
that sinus condition?
Horrors! Heaven have mercy!—You're a Christian martyr, yes, that's what you are, a
Christian martyr!
    Well, I just now happened to notice that your subscription to the *Companion's*
about to expire! Yes, it expires with the next issue, honey!—just when that wonderful
new serial by Bessie Mae Hopper is getting off to such an exciting start. Oh, honey,
it's something that you can't miss! You remember how *Gone with the Wind*° took

---

°2.3 *Gone with the Wind:* An immensely popular novel (1936) by Margaret Mitchell (1900–1949), set in the
South before, during, and after the Civil War. Scarlett O'Hara was the heroine.

everybody by storm? You simply couldn't go out if you hadn't read it. All every-
body *talked* was Scarlett O'Hara. Well, this is a book that critics already compare to
Gone with the Wind. It's the *Gone with the Wind* of the post-World-War generation!—
What?—Burning?—Oh, honey, don't let them burn, go take a look in the oven and
I'll hold the wire! Heavens—I think she's hung up!

[*The scene dims out.*]

[*Legend on screen: "You think I'm in love with Continental Shoemakers?"*]

[*Before the lights come up again, the violent voices of* TOM *and* AMANDA *are heard. They are quarreling behind the portieres. In front of them stands* LAURA *with clenched hands and panicky expression. A clear pool of light is on her figure throughout this scene.*]

TOM: What in Christ's name am I—
AMANDA: [*shrilly*] Don't you use that—
5   TOM: —supposed to do!
AMANDA: —expression! Not in my—
TOM: Ohhh!
AMANDA: —presence! Have you gone out of your senses?
TOM: I have, that's true, *driven* out!
10 AMANDA: What is the matter with you, you—big—BIG—IDIOT!
TOM: Look!—I've got *no thing*, no single thing—
AMANDA: Lower your voice!
TOM: —in my life here that I can call my OWN! Everything is—
AMANDA: Stop that shouting!
15 TOM: Yesterday you confiscated my books! You had the nerve to—
AMANDA: I took that horrible novel back to the library—yes! That hideous book by that
    insane Mr. Lawrence.°

[TOM *laughs wildly.*]

    I cannot control the output of diseased minds or people who cater to them—

[TOM *laughs still more wildly.*]

    BUT I WON'T ALLOW SUCH FILTH BROUGHT INTO MY HOUSE! No, no, no, no, no!
TOM: House, house! Who pays rent on it, who makes a slave of himself to—
AMANDA: [*fairly screeching*] Don't you DARE to—
TOM: No, no, I mustn't say things! I've got to just—
20 AMANDA: Let me tell you—
TOM: I don't want to hear any more!

[*He tears the portieres open. The dining-room area is lit with turgid smoky red glow. Now we see*
AMANDA; *her hair is in metal curlers and she is wearing a very old bathrobe, much too large for
her slight figure, a relic of the faithless Mr. Wingfield. The upright typewriter now stands on the
drop-leaf table, along with a wild disarray of manuscripts. The quarrel was probably precipitated by*
AMANDA's *interruption of* TOM's *creative labor. A chair lies overthrown on the floor. Their gesticu-
lating shadows are cast on the ceiling by the fiery glow.*]

°16 *Mr. Lawrence:* D. H. Lawrence (1885–1930), English poet and fiction writer, popularly known as an advocate of passion and sexuality. See "The Horse Dealer's Daughter," p. 392.

AMANDA: You *will* hear more, you—
TOM: No, I won't hear more, I'm going out!
AMANDA: You come right back in—
TOM: Out, out, out! Because I'm—   25
AMANDA: Come back here, Tom Wingfield! I'm not through talking to you!
TOM: Oh, go—
LAURA: [*desperately*]—Tom!
AMANDA: You're going to listen, and no more insolence from you! I'm at the end of my
    patience!

[*He comes back toward her.*]

TOM: What do you think I'm at? Aren't I supposed to have any patience to reach the end   30
    of, Mother? I know, I know. It seems unimportant to you, what I'm *doing*—what I
    want to do—having a little *difference* between them! You don't think that—
AMANDA: I think you've been doing things that you're ashamed of. That's why you act
    like this. I don't believe that you go every night to the movies. Nobody goes to the
    movies night after night. Nobody in their right minds goes to the movies as often as
    you pretend to. People don't go to the movies at nearly midnight, and movies don't
    let out at two A.M. Come in stumbling. Muttering to yourself like a maniac! You get
    three hours' sleep and then go to work. Oh, I can picture the way you're doing down
    there. Moping, doping, because you're in no condition.
TOM: [*wildly*] No, I'm in no condition!
AMANDA: What right have you got to jeopardize your job? Jeopardize the security of us
    all? How do you think we'd manage if you were—
TOM: Listen! You think I'm crazy about the *warehouse*? [*He bends fiercely toward her slight
    figure.*] You think I'm in love with the Continental Shoemakers? You think I want to
    spend fifty-five *years* down there in that—*celotex interior!* with—*fluorescent—tubes!*
    Look! I'd rather somebody picked up a crowbar and battered out my brains—than
    go back mornings! I *go!* Every time you come in yelling that God damn *"Rise and
    Shine!" "Rise and Shine!"* I say to myself, "How *lucky dead* people are!" But I get up.
    I *go!* For sixty-five dollars a month I give up all that I dream of doing and being
    ever! And you say self—*self's* all I ever think of. Why, listen, if self is what I thought
    of, Mother, I'd be where he is—GONE! [*He points to his father's picture.*] As far as the
    system of transportation reaches! [*He starts past her. She grabs his arm.*] Don't grab at
    me, Mother!
AMANDA: Where are you going?   35
TOM: I'm going to the *movies!*
AMANDA: I don't believe that lie!

[*TOM crouches toward her, overtowering her tiny figure. She backs away, gasping.*]

TOM: I'm going to opium dens! Yes, opium dens, dens of vice and criminals' hangouts,
    Mother. I've joined the Hogan Gang,° I'm a hired assassin, I carry a tommy gun in a
    violin case! I run a string of cat houses in the Valley! They call me Killer, Killer Wing-
    field, I'm leading a double life, a simple, honest warehouse worker by day, by night a
    dynamic *czar* of the *underworld, Mother.* I go to gambling casinos, I spin away fortunes

---

°38 *Hogan Gang:* one of the major criminal organizations in St. Louis in the 1920s and 1930s.

on the roulette table! I wear a patch over one eye and a false mustache, sometimes I put on green whiskers. On those occasions they call me—*El Diablo!*° Oh, I could tell you many things to make you sleepless! My enemies plan to dynamite this place. They're going to blow us all sky-high some night! I'll be glad, very happy, and so will you! You'll go up, up on a broomstick, over Blue Mountain with seventeen gentlemen callers! You ugly—babbling old—*witch*. . . .

[*He goes through a series of violent, clumsy movements, seizing his overcoat, lunging to the door, pulling it fiercely open. The women watch him, aghast. His arm catches in the sleeve of the coat as he struggles to pull it on. For a moment he is pinioned by the bulky garment. With an outraged groan he tears the coat off again, splitting the shoulder of it, and hurls it across the room. It strikes against the shelf of* LAURA'S *glass collection, and there is a tinkle of shattering glass.* LAURA *cries out as if wounded.*

Music.

Screen legend: "The Glass Menagerie."]

LAURA: [*shrilly*] My glass!—menagerie. . . . [*She covers her face and turns away.*]

[*But* AMANDA *is still stunned and stupefied by the "ugly witch" so that she barely notices this occurrence. Now she recovers her speech.*]

40   **AMANDA:** [*in an awful voice*] I won't speak to you—until you apologize!

[*She crosses through the portieres and draws them together behind her.* TOM *is left with* LAURA. LAURA *clings weakly to the mantel with her face averted.* TOM *stares at her stupidly for a moment. Then he crosses to the shelf. He drops awkwardly on his knees to collect the fallen glass, glancing at* LAURA *as if he would speak but couldn't.*

"The Glass Menagerie" music steals in as the scene dims out.]

SCENE 4

The interior of the apartment is dark. There is a faint light in the alley. A deep-voiced bell in a church is tolling the hour of five.

   TOM *appears at the top of the alley. After each solemn boom of the bell in the tower, he shakes a little noisemaker or rattle as if to express the tiny spasm of man in contrast to the sustained power and dignity of the Almighty. This and the unsteadiness of his advance make it evident that he has been drinking. As he climbs the few steps to the fire escape landing light steals up inside.* LAURA *appears in the front room in a nightdress. She notices that* TOM'S *bed is empty.* TOM *fishes in his pockets for his door key, removing a motley assortment of articles in the search, including a shower of movie ticket stubs and an empty bottle. At last he finds the key, but just as he is about to insert it, it slips from his fingers. He strikes a match and crouches below the door.*

TOM: [*bitterly*] One crack—and it falls through!

[LAURA *opens the door.*]

LAURA: Tom! Tom, what are you doing?
TOM: Looking for a door key.
LAURA: Where have you been all this time?
5   **TOM:** I have been to the movies.

°38 *El Diablo:* the devil.

LAURA: All this time at the movies?

TOM: There was a very long program. There was a Garbo° picture and a Mickey Mouse and a travelogue and a newsreel and a preview of coming attractions. And there was an organ solo and a collection for the Milk Fund—simultaneously—which ended up in a terrible fight between a fat lady and an usher!

LAURA: [*innocently*] Did you have to stay through everything?

TOM: Of course! And, oh I forgot! There was a big stage show! The headliner on this stage show was Malvolio° the Magician. He performed wonderful tricks, many of them, such as pouring water back and forth between pitchers. First it turned to wine and then it turned to beer and then it turned to whisky. I know it was whisky it finally turned into because he needed somebody to come up out of the audience to help him, and I came up—both shows! It was Kentucky Straight Bourbon. A very generous fellow, he gave souvenirs. [*He pulls from his back pocket a shimmering rainbow-colored scarf.*] He gave me this. This is his magic scarf. You can have it, Laura. You wave it over a canary cage and you get a bowl of goldfish. You wave it over the goldfish bowl and they fly away canaries. . . . But the wonderfullest trick of all was the coffin trick. We nailed him into a coffin and he got out of the coffin without removing one nail. [*He has come inside.*] There is a trick that would come in handy for me—get me out of this two-by-four situation! [*He flops onto the bed and starts removing his shoes.*]

LAURA: Tom—shhh!   10

TOM: What're you shushing me for?

LAURA: You'll wake up Mother.

TOM: Goody, goody! Pay 'er back for all those "Rise an' Shines." [*He lies down, groaning.*] You know it don't take much intelligence to get yourself into a nailed-up coffin, Laura. But who in hell ever got himself out of one without removing one nail?

[*As if in answer, the father's grinning photograph lights up. The scene dims out.*]

[*Immediately following, the church bell is heard striking six. At the sixth stroke the alarm clock goes off in* AMANDA's *room, and after a few moments we hear her calling: "Rise and Shine! Rise and Shine! Laura, go tell your brother to rise and shine!"*]

TOM: [*sitting up slowly*] I'll rise—but I won't shine.

[*The light increases.*]

AMANDA: Laura, tell your brother his coffee is ready.   15

[LAURA *slips into the front room.*]

LAURA: Tom!—It's nearly seven. Don't make Mother nervous.

[*He stares at her stupidly.*]

[*Beseechingly.*] Tom, speak to Mother this morning. Make up with her, apologize, speak to her!

TOM: She won't to me. It's her that started not speaking.

LAURA: If you just say you're sorry she'll start speaking.

TOM: Her not speaking—is that such a tragedy?

LAURA: Please—please!   20

°7 *Garbo:* Greta Garbo (1905–1990), Swedish star of American silent and early sound films. °9 *Malvolio:* the name, borrowed from a puritanical character in Shakespeare's *Twelfth Night*, means "malevolence" or "ill-will."

AMANDA: [*calling from the kitchenette*] Laura, are you going to do what I asked you to do, or do I have to get dressed and go out myself?

LAURA: Going, going—soon as I get on my coat!

[*She pulls on a shapeless felt hat with a nervous, jerky movement, pleadingly glancing at* TOM. *She rushes awkwardly for her coat. The coat is one of* AMANDA's, *inaccurately made-over, the sleeves too short for* LAURA.]

Butter and what else?

AMANDA: [*entering from the kitchenette*] Just butter. Tell them to charge it.

LAURA: Mother, they make such faces when I do that.

25   AMANDA: Sticks and stones can break our bones, but the expression on Mr. Garfinkel's face won't harm us! Tell your brother his coffee is getting cold.

LAURA: [*at the door*] Do what I asked you, will you, will you, Tom?

[*He looks sullenly away.*]

AMANDA: Laura, go now or just don't go at all!

LAURA: [*rushing out*] Going—going!

[*A second later she cries out.* TOM *springs up and crosses to the door.* TOM *opens the door.*]

TOM: Laura?

30   LAURA: I'm all right. I slipped, but I'm all right.

AMANDA: [*peering anxiously after her*] If anyone breaks a leg on those fire-escape steps, the landlord ought to be sued for every cent he possesses! [*She shuts the door. Now she remembers she isn't speaking to* TOM *and returns to the other room.*]

[*As* TOM *comes listlessly for his coffee, she turns her back to him and stands rigidly facing the window on the gloomy gray vault of the areaway. Its light on her face with its aged but childish features is cruelly sharp, satirical as a Daumier print.*°

The music of "Ave Maria"° is heard softly.

TOM *glances sheepishly but sullenly at her averted figure and slumps at the table. The coffee is scalding hot; he sips it and gasps and spits it back in the cup. At his gasp,* AMANDA *catches her breath and half turns. Then she catches herself and turns back to the window.* TOM *blows on his coffee, glancing sidewise at his mother. She clears her throat.* TOM *clears his. He starts to rise, sinks back down again, scratches his head, clears his throat again.* AMANDA *coughs.* TOM *raises his cup in both hands to blow on it, his eyes staring over the rim of it at his mother for several moments. Then he slowly sets the cup down and awkwardly and hesitantly rises from the chair.*]

TOM: [*hoarsely*] Mother. I—I apologize, Mother.

[AMANDA *draws a quick, shuddering breath. Her face works grotesquely. She breaks into childlike tears.*]

I'm sorry for what I said, for everything that I said, I didn't mean it.

AMANDA: [*sobbingly*] My devotion has made me a witch and so I make myself hateful to my children!

TOM: *No*, you don't.

°31.2 S.D. *Daumier print:* Honoré Daumier (1808–1879), French painter and engraver whose prints frequently satirized his society. °31.3 S.D. *"Ave Maria":* a Roman Catholic prayer to the Virgin Mary; the musical setting called for here is by Franz Schubert (1797–1828).

AMANDA: I worry so much, don't sleep, it makes me nervous!   35
TOM: [*gently*] I understand that.
AMANDA: I've had to put up a solitary battle all these years. But you're my right-hand
    bower!° Don't fall down, don't fail!
TOM: [*gently*] I try, Mother.
AMANDA: [*with great enthusiasm*] Try and you will succeed! [*The notion makes her breathless.*]
    Why, you—you're just full of natural endowments! Both of my children—they're
    unusual children! Don't you think I know it? I'm so—*proud!* Happy and—feel I've—
    so much to be thankful for but—promise me one thing, son!
TOM: What, Mother?   40
AMANDA: Promise, son, you'll—never be a drunkard!
TOM: [*turns to her grinning*] I will never be a drunkard, Mother.
AMANDA: That's what frightened me so, that you'd be drinking! Eat a bowl of Purina!
TOM: Just coffee, Mother.
AMANDA: Shredded wheat biscuit?   45
TOM: No. No, Mother, just coffee.
AMANDA: You can't put in a day's work on an empty stomach. You've got ten minutes—
    don't gulp! Drinking too-hot liquids makes cancer of the stomach. . . . Put cream in.
TOM: No, thank you.
AMANDA: To cool it.
TOM: No! No, thank you, I want it black.   50
AMANDA: I know, but it's not good for you. We have to do all that we can to build ourselves
    up. In these trying times we live in, all that we have to cling to is—each other. . . .
    That's why it's so important to—Tom, I—I sent out your sister so I could discuss
    something with you. If you hadn't spoken I would have spoken to you. [*She sits
    down.*]
TOM: [*gently*] What is it, Mother, that you want to discuss?
AMANDA: *Laura!*

[*TOM puts his cup down slowly.*]

[*Legend on screen "Laura." Music: "The Glass Menagerie."*]

TOM: —Oh.—Laura . . .
AMANDA: [*touching his sleeve*] You know how Laura is. So quiet but—still water runs deep!   55
    She notices things and I think she—broods about them.

[*TOM looks up.*]

    A few days ago I came in and she was crying.
TOM: What about?
AMANDA: You.
TOM: Me?
AMANDA: She has an idea that you're not happy here.
TOM: What gave her that idea?   60
AMANDA: What gives her any idea? However, you do act strangely.—I'm not criticizing,
    understand *that!* I know your ambitions do not lie in the warehouse, that like every-
    body in the whole wide world—you've had to—make sacrifices, but—Tom—Tom—
    life's not easy, it calls for—Spartan endurance! There's so many things in my heart
    that I cannot describe to you! I've never told you but I—*loved* your father. . . .
TOM: [*gently*] I know that, Mother.

°37 *right-hand bower*, or *rightbower*: the Jack of trump in the card game *500*, the second-highest card (below the joker).

AMANDA: And you—when I see you taking after his ways! Staying out late—and—well, you *had* been drinking the night you were in that—terrifying condition! Laura says that you hate the apartment and that you go out nights to get away from it! Is that true, Tom?

TOM: No. You say there's so much in your heart that you can't describe to me. That's true of me, too. There's so much in my heart that I can't describe to *you*! So let's respect each other's—

65   **AMANDA:** But, why—*why*, Tom—are you always so *restless*? Where do you *go* to, nights?

TOM: I—go to the movies.

AMANDA: Why do you go to the movies so much, Tom?

TOM: I go to the movies because—I like adventure. Adventure is something I don't have much of at work, so I go to the movies.

AMANDA: But, Tom, you go to the movies *entirely* too *much*!

70   **TOM:** I like a lot of adventure.

[*AMANDA looks baffled, then hurt. As the familiar inquisition resumes, TOM becomes hard and impatient again. AMANDA slips back into her querulous attitude toward him.*

Image on screen: A sailing vessel with Jolly Roger.°]

AMANDA: Most young men find adventure in their careers.

TOM: Then most young men are not employed in a warehouse.

AMANDA: The world is full of young men employed in warehouses and offices and factories.

TOM: Do all of them find adventure in their careers?

75   **AMANDA:** They do or they do without it! Not everybody has a craze for adventure.

TOM: Man is by instinct a lover, a hunter, a fighter, and none of those instincts are given much play at the warehouse!

AMANDA: Man is by instinct! Don't quote instinct to me! Instinct is something that people have got away from! It belongs to animals! Christian adults don't want it!

TOM: What do Christian adults want, then, Mother?

AMANDA: Superior things! Things of the mind and the spirit! Only animals have to satisfy instincts! Surely your aims are somewhat higher than theirs! Than monkeys—pigs—

80   **TOM:** I reckon they're not.

AMANDA: You're joking. However, that isn't what I wanted to discuss.

TOM: [*rising*] I haven't much time.

AMANDA: [*pushing his shoulders*] Sit down.

TOM: You want me to punch in red° at the warehouse, Mother?

85   **AMANDA:** You have five minutes. I want to talk about Laura.

[*Screen legend: "Plans and Provisions."*]

TOM: All right! What about Laura?

AMANDA: We have to be making some plans and provisions for her. She's older than you, two years, and nothing has happened. She just drifts along doing nothing. It frightens me terribly how she just drifts along.

TOM: I guess she's the type that people call home girls.

AMANDA: There's no such type, and if there is, it's a pity! That is unless the home is hers, with a husband!

90   **TOM:** What?

°70.2 S.D. *Jolly Roger*: the traditional flag of a pirate ship—a skull and crossbones on a field of black. °84 *punch in red*: arrive late for work; the time clock stamps late arrival times in red on the time card.

AMANDA: Oh, I can see the handwriting on the wall as plain as I see the nose in front of my face! It's terrifying! More and more you remind me of your father! He was out all hours without explanation!—Then *left! Goodbye!* And me with the bag to hold. I saw that letter you got from the Merchant Marine. I know what you're dreaming of. I'm not standing here blindfolded. [*She pauses.*] Very well, then. Then do it! But not till there's somebody to take your place.

TOM: What do you mean?

AMANDA: I mean that as soon as Laura has got somebody to take care of her, married, a home of her own, independent—why, then you'll be free to go wherever you please, on land, on sea, whichever way the wind blows you! But until that time you've got to look out for your sister. I don't say me because I'm old and don't matter! I say for your sister because she's young and dependent.

I put her in business college—a dismal failure! Frightened her so it made her sick at the stomach. I took her over to the Young People's League at the church. Another fiasco. She spoke to nobody, nobody spoke to her. Now all she does is fool with those pieces of glass and play those worn-out records. What kind of a life is that for a girl to lead?

TOM: What can I do about it?

AMANDA: Overcome selfishness! Self, self, self is all that you ever think of!   95

[TOM *springs up and crosses to get his coat. It is ugly and bulky. He pulls on a cap with earmuffs.*]

Where is your muffler? Put your wool muffler on!

[*He snatches it angrily from the closet, tosses it around his neck and pulls both ends tight.*]

Tom! I haven't said what I had in mind to ask you.

TOM: I'm too late to—

AMANDA: [*catching his arm—very importunately; then shyly*] Down at the warehouse, aren't there some—nice young men?

TOM: No!

AMANDA: There *must* be—*some* . . .

TOM: Mother—[*He gestures.*]   100

AMANDA: Find out one that's clean-living—doesn't drink and ask him out for sister!

TOM: What?

AMANDA: For *sister!* To *meet!* Get *acquainted!*

TOM: [*stamping to the door*] Oh, my go-osh!

AMANDA: Will you? [*He opens the door. She says, imploringly:*] Will you?   105

[*He starts down the fire escape.*]

Will you? Will you, dear?

TOM: [*calling back*] Yes!

[AMANDA *closes the door hesitantly and with a troubled but faintly hopeful expression.*

Screen image: The cover of a glamor magazine.

The spotlight picks up AMANDA *on the phone.*]

AMANDA: Ella Cartwright? This is Amanda Wingfield! How are you honey? How is that kidney condition? [*There is a five-second pause.*] Horrors! [*There is another pause.*]

You're a Christian martyr, yes, honey, that's what you are, a Christian martyr! Well, I just now happened to notice in my little red book that your subscription to the *Companion* has just run out! I knew that you wouldn't want to miss out on the wonderful serial starting in this new issue. It's by Bessie Mae Hopper, the first thing she's written since *Honeymoon for Three*. Wasn't that a strange and interesting story? Well, this one is even lovelier, I believe. It has a sophisticated, society background. It's all about the horsey set on Long Island!

[*The light fades out.*]

SCENE 5

[*Legend on the screen: "Annunciation."*]

Music is heard as the light slowly comes on.

It is early dusk of a spring evening. Supper has just been finished in the Wingfield apartment. AMANDA *and* LAURA, *in light-colored dresses, are removing dishes from the table in the dining room, which is shadowy, their movements formalized almost as a dance or ritual, their moving forms as pale and silent as moths.* TOM, *in white shirt and trousers, rises from the table and crosses toward the fire escape.*]

AMANDA: [*as he passes her*] Son, will you do me a favor?
TOM: What?
AMANDA: Comb your hair! You look so pretty when your hair is combed!

[TOM *slouches on the sofa with the evening paper. Its enormous headline reads: "Franco Triumphs."°*]

There is only one respect in which I would like you to emulate your father.
TOM: What respect is that?
5   AMANDA: The care he always took of his appearance. He never allowed himself to look untidy.

[*He throws down the paper and crosses to the fire escape.*]

Where are you going?
TOM: I'm going out to smoke.
AMANDA: You smoke too much. A pack a day at fifteen cents a pack. How much would that amount to in a month? Thirty times fifteen is how much, Tom? Figure it out and you will be astounded at what you could save. Enough to give you a night-school course in accounting at Washington U.!° Just think what a wonderful thing that would be for you, son!

[TOM *is unmoved by the thought.*]

TOM: I'd rather smoke. [*He steps out on the landing, letting the screen door slam.*]
AMANDA: [*sharply*] I know! That's the tragedy of it. . . . [*Alone, she turns to look at her husband's picture.*]

[*Dance music: "The World Is Waiting for the Sunrise!"°*]

10   TOM: [*to the audience*] Across the alley from us was the Paradise Dance Hall. On evenings in spring the windows and doors were open and the music came outdoors. Sometimes the lights were turned out except for a large glass sphere that hung from the ceiling. It would turn slowly about and filter the dusk with delicate rainbow colors. Then the orchestra played a waltz or a tango, something that had a slow and sensuous rhythm. Couples would come outside, to the relative privacy of the alley.

°3.1 S.D. *"Franco Triumphs"*: Francisco Franco (1892–1975), dictator of Spain from 1939 until his death, was the general of the victorious Falangist armies in the Spanish Civil War (1936–1939). °7 *Washington U*: Washington University, a highly competitive liberal arts school in St. Louis. °9.1 S.D. *"The World . . . Sunrise"*: popular song, copyright 1919, written by Eugene Lockhart and Ernest Seitz.

You could see them kissing behind ash pits and telephone poles. This was the compensation for lives that passed like mine, without any change or adventure. Adventure and change were imminent in this year. They were waiting around the corner for all these kids. Suspended in the mist over Berchtesgaden, caught in the folds of Chamberlain's umbrella. In Spain there was Guernica!° But here there was only hot swing music and liquor, dance halls, bars, and movies, and sex that hung in the gloom like a chandelier and flooded the world with brief, deceptive rainbows. . . . All the world was waiting for bombardments!

[*AMANDA turns from the picture and comes outside.*]

AMANDA: [*sighing*] A fire escape landing's a poor excuse for a porch. [*She spreads a newspaper on a step and sits down, gracefully and demurely as if she were settling into a swing on a Mississippi veranda.*] What are you looking at?

TOM: The moon.

AMANDA: Is there a moon this evening?

TOM: It's rising over Garfinkel's Delicatessen.

AMANDA: So it is! A little silver slipper of a moon. Have you made a wish on it yet?   15

TOM: Um-hum.

AMANDA: What did you wish for?

TOM: That's a secret.

AMANDA: A secret, huh? Well, I won't tell mine either. I will be just as mysterious as you.

TOM: I bet I can guess what yours is.   20

AMANDA: Is my head so transparent?

TOM: You're not a sphinx.°

AMANDA: No, I don't have secrets. I'll tell you what I wished for on the moon. Success and happiness for my precious children! I wish for that whenever there's a moon, and when there isn't a moon, I wish for it, too.

TOM: I thought perhaps you wished for a gentleman caller.

AMANDA: Why do you say that?   25

TOM: Don't you remember asking me to fetch one?

AMANDA: I remember suggesting that it would be nice for your sister if you brought home some nice young man from the warehouse. I think that I've made that suggestion more than once.

TOM: Yes, you have made it repeatedly.

AMANDA: Well?

TOM: We are going to have one.   30

AMANDA: What?

TOM: A gentleman caller!

[*The annunciation is celebrated with music.*

AMANDA rises.

Image on screen: A caller with a bouquet.]

°10 *Berchtesgaden . . . Guernica:* The three names mentioned are all foreshadowings of World War II. Berchtesgaden, a resort in the Bavarian Alps, was Adolf Hitler's favorite residence. Neville Chamberlain was the British prime minister who signed the Munich Pact with Hitler in 1938, allowing Nazi Germany to occupy parts of Czechoslovakia. Chamberlain, who always carried an umbrella, declared that he had ensured "peace in our time." The bombardment of Guernica during the Spanish Civil War made the name of the town synonymous with the horrors of war, and especially the killing of civilian women and children. (See page 1382, note to 1.3.) °22 *sphinx:* a mythological monster with the head of a woman and body of a lion, famous for her riddles.

AMANDA: You mean you have asked some nice young man to come over?

TOM: Yep. I've asked him to dinner.

35 **AMANDA:** You really did?

TOM: I did!

AMANDA: You did, and did he—*accept?*

TOM: He did!

AMANDA: Well, well—well, well! That's—lovely!

40 **TOM:** I thought that you would be pleased.

AMANDA: It's definite then?

TOM: Very definite.

AMANDA: Soon?

TOM: Very soon.

45 **AMANDA:** For heaven's sake, stop putting on and tell me some things, will you?

TOM: What things do you want me to tell you?

AMANDA: *Naturally* I would like to know when he's *coming!*

TOM: He's coming tomorrow.

AMANDA: *Tomorrow?*

50 **TOM:** Yep. Tomorrow.

AMANDA: But, Tom!

TOM: Yes, Mother?

AMANDA: Tomorrow gives me no time!

TOM: Time for what?

55 **AMANDA:** Preparations! Why didn't you phone me at once, as soon as you asked him, the minute that he accepted? Then, don't you see, I could have been getting ready!

TOM: You don't have to make any fuss.

AMANDA: Oh, Tom, Tom, Tom, of course I have to make a fuss! I want things nice, not sloppy! Not thrown together. I'll certainly have to do some fast thinking, won't I?

TOM: I don't see why you have to think at all.

AMANDA: You just don't know. We can't have a gentleman caller in a pigsty! All my wedding silver has to be polished, the monogrammed table linen ought to be laundered! The windows have to be washed and fresh curtains put up. And how about clothes? We have to *wear* something, don't we?

60 **TOM:** Mother, this boy is no one to make a fuss over!

AMANDA: Do you realize he's the first young man we've introduced to your sister? It's terrible, disgraceful that poor little sister has never received a single gentleman caller! Tom, come inside! [*She opens the screen door.*]

TOM: What for?

AMANDA: I want to ask you some things.

TOM: If you're going to make such a fuss, I'll call it off, I'll tell him not to come!

65 **AMANDA:** You certainly won't do anything of the kind. Nothing offends people worse than broken engagements. It simply means I'll have to work like a Turk! We won't be brilliant, but we will pass inspection. Come on inside.

[*TOM follows her inside, groaning.*]

Sit down.

TOM: Any particular place you would like me to sit?

AMANDA: Thank heavens I've got that new sofa! I'm also making payments on a floor lamp I'll have sent out! And put the chintz covers on, they'll brighten things up! Of course I'd hoped to have these walls re-papered. . . . What is the young man's name?

Tom: His name is O'Connor.

Amanda: That, of course, means fish°—tomorrow is Friday! I'll have that salmon loaf—with Durkee's dressing! What does he do? He works at the warehouse?

Tom: Of course! How else would I—   70

Amanda: Tom, he—doesn't drink?

Tom: Why do you ask me that?

Amanda: Your father *did!*

Tom: Don't get started on that!

Amanda: He *does* drink, then?   75

Tom: Not that I know of!

Amanda: Make sure, be certain! The last thing I want for my daughter's a boy who drinks!

Tom: Aren't you being a little bit premature? Mr. O'Connor has not yet appeared on the scene!

Amanda: But will tomorrow. To meet your sister, and what do I know about his character? Nothing! Old maids are better off than wives of drunkards!

Tom: Oh, my God!   80

Amanda: Be still!

Tom: [*leaning forward to whisper*] Lots of fellows meet girls whom they don't marry!

Amanda: Oh, talk sensibly, Tom—and don't be sarcastic! [*She has gotten a hairbrush.*]

Tom: What are you doing?

Amanda: I'm brushing that cowlick down! [*She attacks his hair with the brush.*] What is this   85
young man's position at the warehouse?

Tom: [*submitting grimly to the brush and the interrogation*] This young man's position is that of a shipping clerk, Mother.

Amanda: Sounds to me like a fairly responsible job, the sort of job *you* would be in if you just had more *get-up.* What is his salary? Have you any idea?

Tom: I would judge it to be approximately eighty-five dollars a month.

Amanda: Well—not princely, but—

Tom: Twenty more than I make.   90

Amanda: Yes, how well I know! But for a family man, eighty-five dollars a month is not much more than you can just get by on. . . .

Tom: Yes, but Mr. O'Connor is not a family man.

Amanda: He might be, mightn't he? Some time in the future?

Tom: I see. Plans and provisions.

Amanda: You are the only young man that I know of who ignores the fact that the future   95
becomes the present, the present the past, and the past turns into everlasting regret if you don't plan for it!

Tom: I will think that over and see what I can make of it.

Amanda: Don't be supercilious with your mother! Tell me some more about this—what do you call him?

Tom: James D. O'Connor. The D. is for Delaney.

Amanda: Irish on *both* sides! *Gracious!* And he doesn't drink?

Tom: Shall I call him up and ask him right this minute?   100

Amanda: The only way to find out about those things is to make discreet inquiries at the proper moment. When I was a girl in Blue Mountain and it was suspected that a young man drank, the girl whose attentions he had been receiving, if any girl *was,* would sometimes speak to the minister of his church, or rather her father would if her

---

°69 *fish:* Amanda assumes that O'Connor is Catholic. Until the 1960s, Roman Catholics were required by the church to abstain from meat on Fridays.

father was living, and sort of feel him out on the young man's character. That is the way such things are discreetly handled to keep a young woman from making a tragic mistake!

Tom: Then how did you happen to make a tragic mistake?

Amanda: That innocent look of your father's had everyone fooled! He *smiled*—the world was *enchanted!* No girl can do worse than put herself at the mercy of a handsome appearance! I hope that Mr. O'Connor is not too good-looking.

Tom: No, he's not too good-looking. He's covered with freckles and hasn't too much of a nose.

105 **Amanda:** He's not right-down homely, though?

Tom: Not right-down homely. Just medium homely, I'd say.

Amanda: Character's what to look for in a man.

Tom: That's what I've always said, Mother.

Amanda: You've never said anything of the kind and I suspect you would never give it a thought.

110 **Tom:** Don't be so suspicious of me.

Amanda: At least I hope he's the type that's up and coming.

Tom: I think he really goes in for self-improvement.

Amanda: What reason have you to think so?

Tom: He goes to night school.

115 **Amanda:** [*beaming*] Splendid! What does he do, I mean study?

Tom: Radio engineering and public speaking!

Amanda: Then he has visions of being advanced in the world! Any young man who studies public speaking is aiming to have an executive job some day! And radio engineering? A thing for the future! Both of these facts are very illuminating. Those are the
sort of things that a mother should know concerning any young man who comes to
call on her daughter. Seriously or—not.

Tom: One little warning. He doesn't know about Laura. I didn't let on that we had dark
ulterior motives. I just said, why don't you come and have dinner with us? He said
okay and that was the whole conversation.

Amanda: I bet it was! You're eloquent as an oyster. However, he'll know about Laura
when he gets here. When he sees how lovely and sweet and pretty she is, he'll thank
his lucky stars he was asked to dinner.

120 **Tom:** Mother, you mustn't expect too much of Laura.

Amanda: What do you mean?

Tom: Laura seems all those things to you and me because she's ours and we love her. We
don't even notice she's crippled any more.

Amanda: Don't say crippled! You know that I never allow that word to be used!

Tom: But face facts, Mother. She is and—that's not all—

125 **Amanda:** What do you mean "not all"?

Tom: Laura is very different from other girls.

Amanda: I think the difference is all to her advantage.

Tom: Not quite all—in the eyes of others—strangers—she's terribly shy and lives in a
world of her own and those things make her seem a little peculiar to people outside
the house.

Amanda: Don't say peculiar.

130 **Tom:** Face the facts. She is.

[*The dance hall music changes to a tango that has a minor and somewhat ominous tone.*]

Amanda: In what way is she peculiar—may I ask?

TOM: [*gently*] She lives in a world of her own—a world of little glass ornaments, Mother. . . .

[*He gets up.* AMANDA *remains holding the brush, looking at him, troubled.*]

> She plays old phonograph records and—that's about all—[*He glances at himself in the mirror and crosses to the door.*]

AMANDA: [*sharply*] Where are you going?   135

TOM: I'm going to the movies. [*He goes out the screen door.*]

AMANDA: Not to the movies, every night to the movies! [*She follows quickly to the screen door.*] I don't believe you always go to the movies!

[*He is gone.* AMANDA *looks worriedly after him for a moment. Then vitality and optimism return and she turns from the door, crossing to the portieres.*]

> Laura! Laura!

[LAURA *answers from the kitchenette.*]

LAURA: Yes, Mother.

AMANDA: Let those dishes go and come in front!

[LAURA *appears with a dish towel.* AMANDA *speaks to her gaily.*]

> Laura, come here and make a wish on the moon!

[*Screen image: The Moon.*]

LAURA: [*entering*] Moon—moon?

AMANDA: A little silver slipper of a moon. Look over your left shoulder, Laura, and make a wish!

[LAURA *looks faintly puzzled as if called out of sleep.* AMANDA *seizes her shoulders and turns her at an angle by the door.*]

> Now! Now, darling, *wish!*

LAURA: What shall I wish for, Mother?   140

AMANDA: [*her voice trembling and her eyes suddenly filling with tears*] Happiness! Good fortune!

[*The sound of the violin rises and the stage dims out.*]

SCENE 6

[*The light comes up on the fire escape landing.* TOM *is leaning against the grill, smoking. Screen image: The high school hero.*]

TOM: And so the following evening I brought Jim home to dinner. I had known Jim slightly in high school. In high school Jim was a hero. He had tremendous Irish good nature and vitality with the scrubbed and polished look of white chinaware. He seemed to move in a continual spotlight. He was a star in basketball, captain of the debating club, president of the senior class and the glee club and he sang the male lead in the annual light operas. He was always running or bounding, never just walking. He seemed always at the point of defeating the law of gravity. He was shooting with such velocity through his adolescence that you would logically expect him to arrive at nothing short of the White House by the time he was thirty. But Jim apparently ran into more inter-ference after his graduation from Soldan. His speed had definitely slowed. Six years after he left high school he was holding a job that wasn't much better than mine.

[*Screen image: The Clerk.*]

He was the only one at the warehouse with whom I was on friendly terms. I was valuable to him as someone who could remember his former glory, who had seen him win basketball games and the silver cup in debating. He knew of my secret practice of retiring to a cabinet of the washroom to work on poems when business was slack in the warehouse. He called me Shakespeare. And while the other boys in the warehouse regarded me with suspicious hostility, Jim took a humorous attitude toward me. Gradually his attitude affected the others, their hostility wore off and they also began to smile at me as people smile at an oddly fashioned dog who trots across their path at some distance.

I knew that Jim and Laura had known each other at Soldan, and I had heard Laura speak admiringly of his voice. I didn't know if Jim remembered her or not. In high school Laura had been as unobtrusive as Jim had been astonishing. If he did remember Laura, it was not as my sister, for when I asked him to dinner, he grinned and said, "You know, Shakespeare, I never thought of you as having folks!" He was about to discover that I did. . . .

[*Legend on screen: "The accent of a coming foot."*]

[*The light dims out on* TOM *and comes up in the Wingfield living room—a delicate lemony light. It is about five on a Friday evening of late spring which comes "scattering poems in the sky."*

AMANDA *has worked like a Turk in preparation for the gentleman caller. The results are astonishing. The new floor lamp with its rose silk shade is in place, a colored paper lantern conceals the broken light fixture in the ceiling, new billowing white curtains are at the windows, chintz covers are on the chairs and sofa, a pair of new sofa pillows make their initial appearance. Open boxes and tissue paper are scattered on the floor.*

LAURA *stands in the middle of the room with lifted arms while* AMANDA *crouches before her, adjusting the hem of a new dress, devout and ritualistic. The dress is colored and designed by memory. The arrangement of* LAURA'S *hair is changed; it is softer and more becoming. A fragile, unearthly prettiness has come out in* LAURA: *she is like a piece of translucent glass touched by light, given a momentary radiance, not actual, not lasting.*]

AMANDA: [*impatiently*] Why are you trembling?
LAURA: Mother, you've made me so nervous!
AMANDA: How have I made you nervous?
5 LAURA: By all this fuss! You make it seem so important!
AMANDA: I don't understand you, Laura. You couldn't be satisfied with just sitting home, and yet whenever I try to arrange something for you, you seem to resist it. [*She gets up.*] Now take a look at yourself. No, wait! Wait just a moment—I have an idea!
LAURA: What is it now?

[AMANDA *produces two powder puffs which she wraps in handkerchiefs and stuffs in* LAURA'S *bosom.*]

LAURA: Mother, what are you doing?
AMANDA: They call them "Gay Deceivers"!
10 LAURA: I won't wear them!
AMANDA: You will!
LAURA: Why should I?
AMANDA: Because, to be painfully honest, your chest is flat.
LAURA: You make it seem like we were setting a trap.
15 AMANDA: All pretty girls are a trap, a pretty trap, and men expect them to be.

[*Legend on screen: "A pretty trap."*]

Now look at yourself, young lady. This is the prettiest you will ever be! [*She stands back to admire* LAURA.] I've got to fix myself now! You're going to be surprised by your mother's appearance!

[AMANDA *crosses through the portieres, humming gaily.* LAURA *moves slowly to the long mirror and stares solemnly at herself. A wind blows the white curtains inward in a slow, graceful motion and with a faint, sorrowful sighing.*]

AMANDA: [*from somewhere behind the portieres*] It isn't dark enough yet.

[LAURA *turns slowly before the mirror with a troubled look.*]

Legend on screen: "This is my sister: Celebrate her with strings!" Music plays.]

AMANDA: [*laughing, still not visible*] I'm going to show you something. I'm going to make a spectacular appearance!

LAURA: What is it, Mother?

AMANDA: Possess your soul in patience—you will see! Something I've resurrected from that old trunk! Styles haven't changed so terribly much after all. . . . [*She parts the portieres.*] Now just look at your mother! [*She wears a girlish frock of yellowed voile with a blue silk sash. She carries a bunch of jonquils—the legend of her youth is nearly revived. Now she speaks feverishly:*] This is the dress in which I led the cotillion. Won the cake-walk twice at Sunset Hill, wore one Spring to the Governor's Ball in Jackson!° See how I sashayed around the ballroom, Laura? [*She raises her skirt and does a mincing step around the room.*] I wore it on Sundays for my gentlemen callers! I had it on the day I met your father. . . . I had malaria fever all that Spring. The change of climate from East Tennessee to the Delta—weakened resistance. I had a little temperature all the time—not enough to be serious—just enough to make me restless and giddy! Invitations poured in—parties all over the Delta! "Stay in bed," said Mother, "you have a fever!"—but I just wouldn't. I took quinine° but kept on going, going! Evenings, dances! Afternoons, long, long rides! Picnics—lovely! So lovely, that country in May—all lacy with dogwood, literally flooded with jonquils! That was the spring I had the craze for jonquils. Jonquils became an absolute obsession. Mother said, "Honey, there's no more room for jonquils." And still I kept on bringing in more jonquils. Whenever, wherever I saw them, I'd say, "Stop! Stop! I see jonquils!" I made the young men help me gather the jonquils! It was a joke, Amanda and her jonquils. Finally there were no more vases to hold them, every available space was filled with jonquils. No vases to hold them? All right, I'll hold them myself! And then I—[*She stops in front of the picture. Music plays.*] met your father! Malaria fever and jonquils and then—this—boy. . . . [*She switches on the rose-colored lamp.*] I hope they get here before it starts to rain. [*She crosses the room and places the jonquils in a bowl on the table.*] I gave your brother a little extra change so he and Mr. O'Connor could take the service car home.

LAURA: [*with an altered look*] What did you say his name was?   20

AMANDA: O'Connor.

LAURA: What is his first name?

AMANDA: I don't remember. Oh, yes, I do. It was—Jim.

[LAURA *sways slightly and catches hold of a chair.*]

Legend on screen: "Not Jim!"]

°19 *Jackson:* capital of Mississippi. Amanda refers to the social events of her youth. A cotillion is a formal ball, often given for debutantes. The cakewalk is a strutting dance step. *quinine:* long used as a standard drug to control malaria.

LAURA: [*faintly*] Not—Jim!

25   **AMANDA:** Yes, that was it, it was Jim! I've never known a Jim that wasn't nice!

[*The music becomes ominous.*]

LAURA: Are you sure his name is Jim O'Connor?

AMANDA: Yes. Why?

LAURA: Is he the one that Tom used to know in high school?

AMANDA: He didn't say so. I think he just got to know him at the warehouse.

30   **LAURA:** There was a Jim O'Connor we both knew in high school—[*Then, with effort.*] If that
is the one that Tom is bringing to dinner—you'll have to excuse me, I won't come to
the table.

AMANDA: What sort of nonsense is this?

LAURA: You asked me once if I'd ever liked a boy. Don't you remember I showed you this
boy's picture?

AMANDA: You mean the boy you showed me in the yearbook?

LAURA: Yes, that boy.

35   **AMANDA:** Laura, Laura, were you in love with that boy?

LAURA: I don't know, Mother. All I know is I couldn't sit at the table if it was him!

AMANDA: It won't be him! It isn't the least bit likely. But whether it is or not, you will come
to the table. You will not be excused.

LAURA: I'll have to be, Mother.

AMANDA: I don't intend to humor your silliness, Laura. I've had too much from you and
your brother, both! So just sit down and compose yourself till they come. Tom has
forgotten his key so you'll have to let them in, when they arrive.

40   **LAURA:** [*panicky*] Oh, Mother—*you* answer the door!

AMANDA: [*lightly*] I'll be in the kitchen—busy!

LAURA: Oh, Mother, please answer the door, don't make me do it!

AMANDA: [*crossing into the kitchenette*] I've got to fix the dressing for the salmon. Fuss,
fuss—silliness!—over a gentleman caller!

[*The door swings shut, LAURA is left alone.*

Legend on screen: "Terror!"

*She utters a low moan and turns off the lamp—sits stiffly on the edge of the sofa, knotting her fingers
together.*

Legend on screen: "The Opening of a Door!"

TOM *and* JIM *appear on the fire escape steps and climb to the landing. Hearing their approach,* LAURA
rises with a panicky gesture. She retreats to the portieres. The doorbell rings. LAURA *catches her
breath and touches her throat. Low drums sound.*]

AMANDA: [*calling*] Laura, sweetheart! The door!

[LAURA *stares at it without moving.*]

45   **JIM:** I think we just beat the rain.

TOM: Uh-huh. [*He rings again, nervously.* JIM *whistles and fishes for a cigarette.*]

AMANDA: [*very, very gaily*] Laura, that is your brother and Mr. O'Connor! Will you let them
in, darling?

[LAURA *crosses toward the kitchenette door.*]

LAURA: [*breathlessly*] Mother—you go to the door!

[AMANDA *steps out of the kitchenette and stares furiously at* LAURA. *She points imperiously at the door.*]

LAURA: Please, please!

AMANDA: [*in a fierce whisper*] What is the matter with you, you silly thing?   50

LAURA: [*desperately*] Please, you answer it, *please!*

AMANDA: I told you I wasn't going to humor you, Laura. Why have you chosen this moment to lose your mind?

LAURA: Please, please, please, you go!

AMANDA: You'll have to go to the door because I can't.

LAURA: [*despairingly*] I can't either!   55

AMANDA: Why?

LAURA: I'm *sick!*

AMANDA: I'm sick, too—of your nonsense! Why can't you and your brother be normal people? Fantastic whims and behavior!

[TOM *gives a long ring.*]

Preposterous goings on! Can you give me one reason—[*She calls out lyrically.*] Coming! Just one second!—why you should be afraid to open a door? Now you answer it, Laura!

LAURA: Oh, oh, oh . . . [*She returns through the portieres, darts to the Victrola, winds it frantically and turns it on.*]

AMANDA: Laura Wingfield, you march right to that door!   60

LAURA: *Yes—yes, Mother!*

[*A faraway, scratchy rendition of "Dardanella"° softens the air and gives her strength to move through it. She slips to the door and draws it cautiously open.* TOM *enters with the caller,* JIM O'CONNOR.]

TOM: Laura, this is Jim. Jim, this is my sister, Laura.

JIM: [*stepping inside*] I didn't know that Shakespeare had a sister!

LAURA: [*retreating, stiff and trembling, from the door*] How—how do you do?

JIM: [*heartily, extending his hand*] Okay!   65

[LAURA *touches it hesitantly with hers.*]

JIM: Your hand's *cold*, Laura!

LAURA: Yes, well—I've been playing the Victrola. . . .

JIM: Must have been playing classical music on it! You ought to play a little hot swing music to warm you up!

LAURA: Excuse me—I haven't finished playing the Victrola. . . . [*She turns awkwardly and hurries into the front room. She pauses a second by the Victrola. Then she catches her breath and darts through the portieres like a frightened deer.*]

JIM: [*grinning*] What was the matter?   70

TOM: Oh—with Laura? Laura is—terribly shy.

JIM: Shy, huh? It's unusual to meet a shy girl nowadays. I don't believe you ever mentioned you had a sister.

TOM: Well, now you know. I have one. Here is the *Post Dispatch.*° You want a piece of it?

JIM: Uh-huh.

TOM: What piece? The comics?   75

°61 S.D. *"Dardanella"*: a popular song and dance tune, copyright 1914, by Fred Fisher, Felix Bernard, and Johnny S. Black. °73 *Post Dispatch*: the *St. Louis Post Dispatch*, a newspaper.

Jim: Sports! [*He glances at it.*] Ole Dizzy Dean° is on his bad behavior.

Tom: [*uninterested*] Yeah? [*He lights a cigarette and goes over to the fire-escape door.*]

Jim: Where are you going?

Tom: I'm going out on the terrace.

80 **Jim:** [*going after him*] You know, Shakespeare—I'm going to sell you a bill of goods!

Tom: What goods?

Jim: A course I'm taking.

Tom: Huh?

Jim: In public speaking! You and me, we're not the warehouse type.

85 **Tom:** Thanks—that's good news. But what has public speaking got to do with it?

Jim: It fits you for—executive positions!

Tom: Awww.

Jim: I tell you it's done a helluva lot for me.

[*Image on screen: Executive at his desk.*]

Tom: In what respect?

90 **Jim:** In every! Ask yourself what is the difference between you an' me and men in the office down front? Brains?—No!—Ability?—No! Then what? Just one little thing—

Tom: What is that one little thing?

Jim: Primarily it amounts to—social poise! Being able to square up to people and hold your own on any social level!

Amanda: [*from the kitchenette*] Tom?

Tom: Yes, Mother?

95 **Amanda:** Is that you and Mr. O'Connor?

Tom: Yes, Mother.

Amanda: Well, you just make yourselves comfortable in there.

Tom: Yes, Mother.

Amanda: Ask Mr. O'Connor if he would like to wash his hands.

100 **Jim:** Aw, no —no—thank you—I took care of that at the warehouse. Tom—

Tom: Yes?

Jim: Mr. Mendoza was speaking to me about you.

Tom: Favorably?

Jim: What do you think?

105 **Tom:** Well—

Jim: You're going to be out of a job if you don't wake up.

Tom: I am waking up—

Jim: You show no signs.

Tom: The signs are interior.

[*Image on screen: The sailing vessel with the Jolly Roger again.*]

110 **Tom:** I'm planning to change. [*He leans over the fire escape rail, speaking with quiet exhilaration. The incandescent marquees and signs of the first-run movie houses light his face from across the alley. He looks like a voyager.*] I'm right at the point of committing myself to a future that doesn't include the warehouse and Mr. Mendoza or even a night-school course in public speaking.

Jim: What are you gassing about?

Tom: I'm tired of the movies.

°76 *Dizzy Dean:* Jerome Herman (or Jay Hanna) Dean (1911–1974), outstanding pitcher with the St. Louis Cardinals during the 1930s, and later a radio announcer.

JIM: Movies!

TOM: Yes, movies! Look at them—[*a wave toward the marvels of Grand Avenue*] All of those glamorous people—having adventures—hogging it all, gobbling the whole thing up! You know what happens? People go to the *movies* instead of *moving!* Hollywood characters are supposed to have all the adventures for everybody in America, while everybody in America sits in a dark room and watches them have them! Yes, until there's a war. That's when adventure becomes available to the masses! *Everyone's* dish, not only Gable's!° Then the people in the dark room come out of the dark room to have some adventures themselves—goody, goody! It's our turn now, to go to the South Sea Island—to make a safari—to be exotic, far-off! But I'm not patient. I don't want to wait till then. I'm tired of the *movies* and I am *about* to *move!*

JIM: [*incredulously*] Move?   115

TOM: Yes.

JIM: When?

TOM: Soon!

JIM: Where? Where?

[*The music seems to answer the question, while* TOM *thinks it over. He searches in his pockets.*]

TOM: I'm starting to boil inside. I know I seem dreamy, but inside—well, I'm boiling!   120
Whenever I pick up a shoe, I shudder a little thinking how short life is and what I am doing! Whatever that means, I know it doesn't mean shoes—except as something to wear on a traveler's feet! [*He finds what he has been searching for in his pockets and holds out a paper to* JIM.] Look—

JIM: What?

TOM: I'm a member.

JIM: [*reading*] The Union of Merchant Seamen.

TOM: I paid my dues this month, instead of the light bill.

JIM: You will regret it when they turn off the lights.   125

TOM: I won't be here.

JIM: How about your mother?

TOM: I'm like my father. The bastard son of a bastard! Did you notice how he's grinning in his picture in there? And he's been absent going on sixteen years!

JIM: You're just talking, you drip. How does your mother feel about it?

TOM: Shhh! Here comes Mother! Mother is not acquainted with my plans!   130

AMANDA: [*coming through the portieres*] Where are you all?

TOM: On the terrace, Mother.

[*They start inside. She advances to them.* TOM *is distinctly shocked at her appearance. Even* JIM *blinks a little. He is making his first contact with the girlish Southern vivacity and in spite of the night-school course in public speaking is somewhat thrown off the beam by the unexpected outlay of social charm. Certain responses are attempted by* JIM *but are swept aside by* AMANDA'S *gay laughter and chatter.* TOM *is embarrassed but after the first shock* JIM *reacts very warmly. He grins and chuckles, is altogether won over.*

Image on screen: AMANDA *as a girl.*]

AMANDA: [*coyly smiling, shaking her girlish ringlets*] Well, well, well, so this is Mr. O'Connor. Introductions entirely unnecessary. I've heard so much about you from my boy. I finally

---

°114 *Gable:* Clark Gable (1901–1960), popular American screen actor and matinee idol from the 1930s until his death.

Amanda (Jessica Tandy) tries to charm the Gentleman Caller (John Heard) on behalf of her indifferent daughter Laura (Amanda Plummer) in the Eugene O'Neill Theater production of *The Glass Menagerie,* directed by John Dexter (1983–1984).

said to him, Tom—good gracious!—why don't you bring this paragon to supper? I'd like to meet this nice young man at the warehouse!—instead of just hearing him sing your praises so much! I don't know why my son is so stand-offish—that's not Southern behavior!

Let's sit down and—I think we could stand a little more air in here! Tom, leave the door open. I felt a nice fresh breeze a moment ago. Where has it gone to? Mmm, so warm already! And not quite summer, even. We're going to burn up when summer really gets started. However, we're having—we're having a very light supper. I think light things are better fo' this time of year. The same as light clothes are. Light clothes an' light food are what warm weather calls fo'. You know our blood gets so thick during th' winter—it takes a while fo' us to *adjust* ourselves!—when the season changes. . . . It's come so quick this year. I wasn't prepared. All of sudden—heavens! Already summer! I ran to the trunk an' pulled out this light dress—terribly old! Historical almost! But feels so good—so good an' co-ol, y'know. . . .

Tom: Mother—

Amanda: Yes, honey?   135

Tom: How about—supper?

Amanda: Honey, you go ask Sister if supper is ready! You know that Sister is in full charge of supper! Tell her you hungry boys are waiting for it. [*To* Jim.] Have you met Laura?

Jim: She—

Amanda: Let you in? Oh, good, you've met already! It's rare for a girl as sweet an' pretty as Laura to be domestic! But Laura is, thank heavens, not only pretty but also very domestic. I'm not at all. I never was a bit. I never could make a thing but angel-food cake. Well, in the South we had so many servants. Gone, gone, gone. All vestige of gracious living! Gone completely! I wasn't prepared for what the future brought me. All of my gentlemen callers were sons of planters and so of course I assumed that I would be married to one and raise my family on a large piece of land with plenty of servants. But man proposes—and woman accepts the proposal! to vary that old, old saying a little but—I married no planter! I married a man who worked for the telephone company! That gallantly smiling gentleman over there! [*She points to the picture.*] A telephone man who—fell in love with long-distance! Now he travels and I don't even know where! But what am I going on for about my—tribulations? Tell me yours—I hope you don't have any! Tom?

Tom: [*returning*] Yes, Mother?   140

Amanda: Is supper nearly ready?

Tom: It looks to me like supper is on the table.

Amanda: Let me look—[*She rises prettily and looks through the portieres.*] Oh lovely! But where is Sister?

Tom: Laura is not feeling well and she says that she thinks she'd better not come to the table.

Amanda: What? Nonsense! Laura? Oh, Laura!   145

Laura: [*from the kitchenette, faintly*] Yes, Mother.

Amanda: You really must come to the table. We won't be seated until you come to the table! Come in, Mr. O'Connor. You sit over there and I'll . . . Laura? Laura Wingfield! You're keeping us waiting, honey! We can't say grace until you come to the table!

[*The kitchenette door is pushed weakly open and* Laura *comes in. She is obviously quite faint, her lips trembling, her eyes wide and staring. She moves unsteadily toward the table.*]

Screen legend: "Terror!"

Outside a summer storm is coming on abruptly. The white curtains billow inward at the windows and there is a sorrowful murmur from the deep blue dusk.

Laura *suddenly stumbles; she catches at a chair with a faint moan.*]

Tom: Laura!

Amanda: Laura!

[*There is a clap of thunder.*

Screen legend: "Ah!"]

[*despairingly*] Why, Laura, you are ill, darling! Tom, help your sister into the living room, dear! Sit in the living room, Laura—rest on the sofa. Well! [*To* Jim *as* Tom *helps his sister to the sofa in the living room.*] Standing over the hot stove made her ill! I told her that it was just too warm this evening, but—

[*Tom comes back to the table.*]

Is Laura all right now?

150   **TOM:** Yes.

AMANDA: What is that? Rain? A nice cool rain has come up! [*She gives* JIM *a frightened look.*] I think we may—have grace—now . . . [TOM *looks at her stupidly.*] Tom, honey—you say grace!

TOM: Oh . . . "For these and all thy mercies—"

[*They bow their heads,* AMANDA *stealing a nervous glance at* JIM. *In the living room* LAURA, *stretched on the sofa, clenches her hand to her lips, to hold back a shuddering sob.*]

God's Holy Name be praised—

[*The scene dims out.*]

SCENE 7

[*It is half an hour later. Dinner is just being finished in the dining room,* LAURA *is still huddled upon the sofa, her feet drawn under her, her head resting on a pale blue pillow, her eyes wide and mysteriously watchful. The new floor lamp with its shade of rose-colored silk gives a soft, becoming light to her face, bringing out the fragile, unearthly prettiness which usually escapes attention. From outside there is a steady murmur of rain, but it is slackening and soon stops; the air outside becomes pale and luminous as the moon breaks through the clouds. A moment after the curtain rises, the lights in both rooms flicker and go out.*]

JIM: Hey, there, Mr. Light Bulb!

[AMANDA *laughs nervously.*

Legend on screen: "Suspension of a public service."]

AMANDA: Where was Moses when the lights went out? Ha-ha. Do you know the answer to that one, Mr. O'Connor?

JIM: No, Ma'am, what's the answer?

AMANDA: In the dark!

[JIM *laughs appreciatively.*]

Everybody sit still. I'll light the candles. Isn't it lucky we have them on the table? Where's a match? Which of you gentlemen can provide a match?

5   **JIM:** Here.

AMANDA: Thank you, Sir.

JIM: Not at all, Ma'am!

AMANDA: [*as she lights the candles*] I guess the fuse has burnt out. Mr. O'Connor, can you tell a burnt-out fuse? I know I can't and Tom is a total loss when it comes to mechanics. [*They rise from the table and go into the kitchenette, from where their voices are heard.*] Oh, be careful you don't bump into something. We don't want our gentleman caller to break his neck. Now wouldn't that be a fine howdy-do?

JIM: Ha-ha! Where is the fuse-box?

10   **AMANDA:** Right here next to the stove. Can you see anything?

JIM: Just a minute.

AMANDA: Isn't electricity a mysterious thing? Wasn't it Benjamin Franklin who tied a key to a kite? We live in such a mysterious universe, don't we? Some people say that science clears up all the mysteries for us. In my opinion it only creates more! Have you found it yet?

JIM: No, Ma'am. All these fuses look okay to me.

AMANDA: Tom!

15   **TOM:** Yes, Mother?

AMANDA: That light bill I gave you several days ago. That one I told you we got the notices about?

[*Legend on screen: "Ha!"*]

TOM: Oh—yeah.

AMANDA: You didn't neglect to pay it by any chance?

TOM: Why, I—

AMANDA: Didn't! I might have known it!   20

JIM: Shakespeare probably wrote a poem on that light bill, Mrs. Wingfield.

AMANDA: I might have known better than to trust him with it! There's such a high price for negligence in this world!

JIM: Maybe the poem will win a ten-dollar prize.

AMANDA: We'll just have to spend the remainder of the evening in the nineteenth century, before Mr. Edison made the Mazda lamp!°

JIM: Candlelight is my favorite kind of light.   25

AMANDA: That shows you're romantic! But that's no excuse for Tom. Well, we got through dinner. Very considerate of them to let us get through dinner before they plunged us into everlasting darkness, wasn't it, Mr. O'Connor?

JIM: Ha-ha!

AMANDA: Tom, as a penalty for your carelessness you can help me with the dishes.

JIM: Let me give you a hand.

AMANDA: Indeed you will not!   30

JIM: I ought to be good for something.

AMANDA: Good for something? [*Her tone is rhapsodic.*] *You?* Why, Mr. O'Connor, nobody, *nobody's* given me this much entertainment in years—as you have!

JIM: Aw, now, Mrs. Wingfield!

AMANDA: I'm not exaggerating, not one bit! But Sister is all by her lonesome. You go keep her company in the parlor! I'll give you this lovely old candelabrum that used to be on the altar at the Church of the Heavenly Rest. It was melted a little out of shape when the church burnt down. Lightning struck it one spring. Gypsy Jones was holding a revival at the time and he intimated that the church was destroyed because the Episcopalians gave card parties.

JIM: Ha-ha.   35

AMANDA: And how about you coaxing Sister to drink a little wine? I think it would be good for her! Can you carry both at once?

JIM: Sure. I'm Superman!

AMANDA: Now, Thomas, get into this apron!

[*JIM comes into the dining room, carrying the candelabrum, its candles lighted, in one hand and a glass of wine in the other. The door of the kitchenette swings closed on AMANDA's gay laughter; the flickering light approaches the portieres. LAURA sits up nervously as JIM enters. She can hardly speak from the almost intolerable strain of being alone with a stranger.*

Screen legend: "I don't suppose you remember me at all!"

At first, before JIM's warmth overcomes her paralyzing shyness, LAURA's voice is thin and breathless, as though she had just run up a steep flight of stairs. JIM's attitude is gently humorous. While the incident is apparently unimportant, it is to LAURA the climax of her secret life.]

JIM: Hello there, Laura.

°24 *Mazda lamp:* Thomas A. Edison (1847–1931) developed the first practical incandescent lamp in 1879.

40   **Laura:** [*faintly*] Hello.

[*She clears her throat.*]

Jim: How are you feeling now? Better?
Laura: Yes. Yes, thank you.
Jim: This is for you. A little dandelion wine. [*He extends the glass toward her with extravagant gallantry.*]
45   **Laura:** Thank you.
Jim: Drink it—but don't get drunk!

[*He laughs heartily.* Laura *takes the glass uncertainly; she laughs shyly.*]

Where shall I set the candles?
Laura: Oh—oh, anywhere . . .
Jim: How about here on the floor? Any objections?
Laura: No.
Jim: I'll spread a newspaper under to catch the drippings. I like to sit on the floor. Mind if I do?
50   **Laura:** Oh, no.
Jim: Give me a pillow?
Laura: What?
Jim: A pillow!
Laura: Oh . . . [*She hands him one quickly.*]
55   **Jim:** How about you? Don't you like to sit on the floor?
Laura: Oh—yes.
Jim: Why don't you, then?
Laura: I—will.
Jim: Take a pillow!

[Laura *does. She sits on the floor on the other side of the candelabrum.* Jim *crosses his legs and smiles engagingly at her.*]

I can't hardly see you sitting way over there.
60   **Laura:** I can—see you.
Jim: I know, but that's not fair, I'm in the limelight.

[Laura *moves her pillow closer.*]

Good! Now I can see you! Comfortable?
Laura: Yes.
Jim: So am I. Comfortable as a cow! Will you have some gum?
Laura: No, thank you.
65   **Jim:** I think that I will indulge, with your permission. [*He musingly unwraps a stick of gum and holds it up.*] Think of the fortune made by the guy that invented the first piece of chewing gum. Amazing, huh? The Wrigley Building° is one of the sights of Chicago—I saw it when I went up to the Century of Progress.° Did you take in the Century of Progress?
Laura: No, I didn't.
Jim: Well, it was quite a wonderful exposition. What impressed me most was the Hall of Science. Gives you an idea of what the future will be in America, even more wonderful than the present time is! [*There is a pause.* Jim *smiles at her.*] Your brother tells me you're shy. Is that right—Laura?

°65 *Wrigley Building:* Finished in 1924, this was one of the first skyscrapers in the United States. *Century of Progress:* a world's fair held in Chicago (1933–1934) to celebrate the city's centennial.

LAURA: I—don't know.

JIM: I judge you to be an old-fashioned type of girl. Well, I think that's a pretty good type to be. Hope you don't think I'm being too personal—do you?

LAURA: [*Hastily, out of embarrassment*] I believe I *will* take a piece of gum, if you—don't   70
mind. [*clearing her throat*] Mr. O'Connor, have you—kept up with your singing?

JIM: Singing? Me?

LAURA: Yes. I remember what a beautiful voice you had.

JIM: When did you hear me sing?

[LAURA *does not answer, and in the long pause which follows a man's voice is heard singing offstage.*]

VOICE:
> O blow, ye winds, heigh-ho,
> A-roving I will go!
> I'm off to my love
> With a boxing glove—
> Ten thousand miles away!°

JIM: You say you've heard me sing?   75

LAURA: Oh, yes! Yes, very often . . . I—don't suppose—you remember me—at all?

JIM: [*smiling doubtfully*] You know I have an idea I've seen you before. I had that idea soon as you opened the door. It seemed almost like I was about to remember your name. But the name that I started to call you—wasn't a name! And so I stopped myself before I said it.

LAURA: Wasn't it—Blue Roses?

JIM: [*springing up, grinning*] Blue Roses! My gosh, yes—Blue Roses! That's what I had on my tongue when you opened the door! Isn't it funny what tricks your memory plays? I didn't connect you with high school somehow or other. But that's where it was; it was high school. I didn't even know you were Shakespeare's sister! Gosh, I'm sorry.

LAURA: I didn't expect you to. You—barely knew me!   80

JIM: But we did have a speaking acquaintance, huh?

LAURA: Yes, we—spoke to each other.

JIM: When did you recognize me?

LAURA: Oh, right away!

JIM: Soon as I came in the door?   85

LAURA: When I heard your name I thought it was probably you. I knew that Tom used to know you a little in high school. So when you came in the door—well, then I was—sure.

JIM: Why didn't you *say* something, then?

LAURA: [*breathlessly*] I didn't know what to say, I was—too surprised!

JIM: For goodness' sakes! You know, this sure is funny!

LAURA: Yes! Yes, isn't it, though . . .   90

JIM: Didn't we have a class in something together?

LAURA: Yes, we did.

JIM: What class was that?

LAURA: It was—singing—chorus!

JIM: Aw!   95

LAURA: I sat across the aisle from you in the Aud.

JIM: Aw!

°74 *O blow . . .* : This is a simplified version of the refrain of "A Capital Ship" (1885), a song that Charles E. Carryl (1841–1920) wrote for the music of the early-nineteenth-century Irish sea shanty "Ten Thousand Miles Away."

Laura: Mondays, Wednesdays, and Fridays.

Jim: Now I remember—you always came in late.

100 **Laura:** Yes, it was so hard for me, getting upstairs. I had that brace on my leg—it clumped so loud!

Jim: I never heard any clumping.

Laura: [*wincing at the recollection*] To me it sounded like—thunder!

Jim: Well, well, well, I never even noticed.

Laura: And everybody was seated before I came in. I had to walk in front of all those people. My seat was in the back row. I had to go clumping all the way up the aisle with everyone watching!

105 **Jim:** You shouldn't have been self-conscious.

Laura: I know, but I was. It was always such a relief when the singing started.

Jim: Aw, yes, I've placed you now! I used to call you Blue Roses. How was it that I got started calling you that?

Laura: I was out of school a little while with pleurosis. When I came back you asked me what was the matter. I said I had pleurosis—you thought that I said *Blue Roses*. That's what you always called me after that!

Jim: I hope you didn't mind.

110 **Laura:** Oh, no—I liked it. You see, I wasn't acquainted with many—people. . . .

Jim: As I remember you sort of stuck by yourself.

Laura: I—I—never have had much luck at—making friends.

Jim: I don't see why you wouldn't.

Laura: Well, I—started out badly.

115 **Jim:** You mean being—

Laura: Yes, it sort of—stood between me—

Jim: You shouldn't have let it!

Laura: I know, but it did, and—

Jim: You were shy with people!

120 **Laura:** I tried not to be but never could—

Jim: Overcome it?

Laura: No, I—I never could!

Jim: I guess being shy is something you have to work out of kind of gradually.

Laura: [*sorrowfully*] Yes—I guess it—

Jim: Takes time!

125 **Laura:** Yes—

Jim: People are not so dreadful when you know them. That's what you have to remember! And everybody has problems, not just you, but practically everybody has got some problems. You think of yourself as having the only problems, as being the only one who is disappointed. But just look around you and you will see lots of people as disappointed as you are. For instance, I hoped when I was going to high school that I would be further along at this time, six years later, than I am now. You remember that wonderful write-up I had in *The Torch?*

Laura: Yes! [*She rises and crosses to the table.*]

Jim: It said I was bound to succeed in anything I went into!

[*Laura returns with the high school yearbook.*]

Holy Jeez! *The Torch!*

[*He accepts it reverently. They smile across the book with mutual wonder. Laura crouches beside him and they begin to turn the pages. Laura's shyness is dissolving in his warmth.*]

130 **Laura:** Here you are in *The Pirates of Penzance!*

JIM: [*wistfully*] I sang the baritone lead in that operetta.

LAURA: [*raptly*] So—*beautifully!*

JIM: [*protesting*] Aw—

LAURA: Yes, yes—beautifully—beautifully!

JIM: You heard me?   135

LAURA: All three times!

JIM: No!

LAURA: Yes!

JIM: All three performances?

LAURA: [*looking down*] Yes.   140

JIM: Why?

LAURA: I—wanted to ask you to—autograph my program. [*She takes the program from the back of the yearbook and shows it to him.*]

JIM: Why didn't you ask me to?

LAURA: You were always surrounded by your own friends so much that I never had a chance to.

JIM: You should have just—   145

LAURA: Well, I—thought you might think I was—

JIM: Thought I might think you was—what?

LAURA: Oh—

JIM: [*with reflective relish*] I was beleaguered by females in those days.

LAURA: You were terribly popular!   150

JIM: Yeah—

LAURA: You had such a—friendly way—

JIM: I was spoiled in high school.

LAURA: Everybody—liked you!

JIM: Including you?   155

LAURA: I—yes, I—did, too—[*She gently closes the book in her lap.*]

JIM: Well, well, well! Give me that program, Laura.

[*She hands it to him. He signs it with a flourish.*]

There you are—better late than never!

LAURA: Oh, I—what a—surprise!

JIM: My signature isn't worth very much right now. But some day- -maybe—it will increase in value! Being disappointed is one thing and being discouraged is something else. I am disappointed but I am not discouraged. I'm twenty-three years old. How old are you?

LAURA: I'll be twenty-four in June.   160

JIM: That's not old age!

LAURA: No, but—

JIM: You finished high school?

LAURA: [*with difficulty*] I didn't go back.

JIM: You mean you dropped out?   165

LAURA: I made bad grades in my final examinations. [*She rises and replaces the book and the program on the table. Her voice is strained.*] How is—Emily Meisenbach getting along?

JIM: Oh, that kraut-head!

LAURA: Why do you call her that?

JIM: That's what she was.

LAURA: You're not still—going with her?   170

JIM: I never see her.

LAURA: It was in the "Personal" section that you were—engaged!

Jim: I know, but I wasn't impressed by that—propaganda!

Laura: It wasn't—the truth?

175 Jim: Only in Emily's optimistic opinion!

Laura: Oh—

[*Legend: "What have you done since high school?"*

Jim *lights a cigarette and leans indolently back on his elbows smiling at* Laura *with a warmth and charm which lights her inwardly with altar candles. She remains by the table, picks up a piece from the glass menagerie collection, and turns it in her hands to cover her tumult.*]

Jim: [*after several reflective puffs on his cigarette*] What have you done since high school?

[*She seems not to hear him.*]

Huh?

[Laura *looks up.*]

I said what have you done since high school, Laura?

Laura: Nothing much.

Jim: You must have been doing something these six long years.

180 Laura: Yes.

Jim: Well, then, such as what?

Laura: I took a business course at business college—

Jim: How did that work out?

Laura: Well, not very—well—I had to drop out, it gave me—indigestion—

[Jim *laughs gently.*]

185 Jim: What are you doing now?

Laura: I don't do anything—much. Oh, please don't think I sit around doing nothing! My glass collection takes up a good deal of time. Glass is something you have to take good care of.

Jim: What did you say—about glass?

Laura: Collection I said—I have one—[*She clears her throat and turns away again, acutely shy.*]

Jim: [*abruptly*] You know what I judge to be the trouble with you? Inferiority complex! Know what that is? That's what they call it when someone low-rates himself! I understand it because I had it too. Although my case was not so aggravated as yours seems to be. I had it until I took up public speaking, developed my voice, and learned that I had an aptitude for science. Before that time I never thought of myself as being outstanding in any way whatsoever! Now I've never made a regular study of it, but I have a friend who says I can analyze people better than doctors that make a profession of it. I don't claim that to be necessarily true, but I can sure guess a person's psychology. Laura! [*He takes out his gum.*] Excuse me, Laura. I always take it out when the flavor is gone. I'll use this scrap of paper to wrap it in. I know how it is to get it stuck on a shoe. [*He wraps the gum in paper and puts it in his pocket.*] Yep—that's what I judge to be your principal trouble. A lack of confidence in yourself as a person. You don't have the proper amount of faith in yourself. I'm basing that fact on a number of your remarks and also on certain observations I've made. For instance that clumping you thought was so awful in high school. You say that you even dreaded to walk into class. You see what you did? You dropped out of school, you gave up an education because of a clump, which as far as I know was practically nonexistent! A little physical defect is what you have. Hardly noticeable even! Magnified thousands of times by imagination! You know what my strong advice to you is? Think of yourself as *superior* in some way!

LAURA: In what way would I think?   190

JIM: Why, man alive, Laura! Just look about you a little. What do you see? A world full of common people! All of 'em born and all of 'em going to die! Which of them has one-tenth of your good points! Or mine! Or anyone else's, as far as that goes—gosh! Everybody excels in some one thing. Some in many! [*He unconsciously glances at himself in the mirror.*] All you've got to do is discover in *what!* Take me, for instance. [*He adjusts his tie at the mirror.*] My interest happens to lie in electro-dynamics. I'm taking a course in radio engineering at night school, Laura, on top of a fairly responsible job at the warehouse. I'm taking that course and studying public speaking.

LAURA: Ohhhh.

JIM: Because I believe in the future of television! [*turning his back to her*] I wish to be ready to go up right along with it. Therefore I'm planning to get in on the ground floor. In fact I've already made the right connections and all that remains is for the industry itself to get under way! Full steam—[*His eyes are starry.*] Knowledge—Zzzzzp! Money— Zzzzzp!—Power! That's the cycle democracy is built on!

[*His attitude is convincingly dynamic.* LAURA *stares at him, even her shyness eclipsed in her absolute wonder. He suddenly grins.*]

I guess you think I think a lot of myself!

LAURA: No—o-o-o, I—

JIM: Now how about you? Isn't there something you take more interest in than anything   195
else?

LAURA: Well, I do—as I said—have my—glass collection—

[*A peal of girlish laughter rings from the kitchenette.*]

JIM: I'm not right sure I know what you're talking about. What kind of glass is it?

LAURA: Little articles of it, they're ornaments mostly! Most of them are little animals made out of glass, the tiniest little animals in the world. Mother calls them a glass menag- erie! Here's an example of one, if you'd like to see it! This one is one of the oldest. It's nearly thirteen.

[*Music: "The Glass Menagerie." He stretches out his hand.*]

Oh, be careful—if you breathe, it breaks!

JIM: I'd better not take it. I'm pretty clumsy with things.

LAURA: Go, on, I trust you with him! [*She places the piece in his palm.*] There now—you're   200
holding him gently! Hold him over the light, he loves the light! You see how the light shines through him?

JIM: It sure does shine!

LAURA: I shouldn't be partial, but he is my favorite one.

JIM: What kind of a thing is this one supposed to be?

LAURA: Haven't you noticed the single horn on his forehead?

JIM: A unicorn, huh?   205

LAURA: Mmmm-hmmm!

JIM: Unicorns—aren't they extinct in the modern world?

LAURA: I know!

JIM: Poor little fellow, he must feel sort of lonesome.

LAURA: [*smiling*] Well, if he does, he doesn't complain about it. He stays on a shelf with   210
some horses that don't have horns and all of them seem to get along nicely together.

JIM: How do you know?

LAURA: [*lightly*] I haven't heard any arguments among them!

Jim: [*grinning*] No arguments, huh? Well, that's a pretty good sign! Where shall I set him?

Laura: Put him on the table. They all like a change of scenery once in a while!

215 **Jim:** Well, well, well, well—[*He places the glass piece on the table, then raises his arms and stretches.*] Look how big my shadow is when I stretch!

Laura: Oh, oh, yes—it stretches across the ceiling!

Jim: [*crossing to the door*] I think it's stopped raining. [*He opens the fire-escape door and the background music changes to a dance tune.*] Where does the music come from?

Laura: From the Paradise Dance Hall across the alley.

Jim: How about cutting the rug a little, Miss Wingfield?

220 **Laura:** Oh, I—

Jim: Or is your program filled up? Let me have a look at it. [*He grasps an imaginary card.*] Why, every dance is taken! I'll just have to scratch some out.

[*Waltz music: "La Golondrina"°*]

Ahh, a waltz! [*He executes some sweeping turns by himself, then holds his arms toward* Laura.]

Laura: [*breathlessly*] I—can't dance.

Jim: There you go, that inferiority stuff!

Laura: I've never danced in my life!

225 **Jim:** Come on, try!

Laura: Oh, but I'd step on you!

Jim: I'm not made out of glass.

Laura: How—how—how do we start?

Jim: Just leave it to me. You hold your arms out a little.

230 **Laura:** Like this?

Jim: [*taking her in his arms*] A little bit higher. Right. Now don't tighten up, that's the main thing about it—relax.

Laura: [*laughing breathlessly*] It's hard not to.

Jim: Okay.

Laura: I'm afraid you can't budge me.

235 **Jim:** What do you bet I can't? [*He swings her into motion.*]

Laura: Goodness, yes, you can!

Jim: Let yourself go, now, Laura, just let yourself go.

Laura: I'm—

Jim: Come on!

240 **Laura:** —trying!

Jim: Not so stiff—easy does it!

Laura: I know but I'm—

Jim: Loosen th' backbone! There now, that's a lot better.

Laura: Am I?

245 **Jim:** Lots, lots better! [*He moves her about the room in a clumsy waltz.*]

Laura: Oh, my!

Jim: Ha-ha!

Laura: Oh, my goodness!

Jim: Ha-ha-ha!

[*They suddenly bump into the table, and the glass piece on it falls to the floor.* Jim *stops the dance.*]

°221.1 S.D. *"La Golondrina"*: a popular Mexican song (1883) written by Narciso Serradel Sevilla (1843–1910). It is not a waltz.

What did we hit?   250
LAURA: Table.
JIM: Did something fall off it? I think—
LAURA: Yes.
JIM: I hope that it wasn't the little glass horse with the horn!
LAURA: Yes. [*She stoops to pick it up.*]   255
JIM: Aw, aw, aw. Is it broken?
LAURA: Now it is just like all the other horses.
JIM: It's lost its—
LAURA: Horn! It doesn't matter. Maybe it's a blessing in disguise.
JIM: You'll never forgive me. I bet that that was your favorite piece of glass.
LAURA: I don't have favorites much. It's no tragedy, Freckles. Glass breaks so easily. No   260
   matter how careful you are. The traffic jars the shelves and things fall off them.
JIM: Still I'm awfully sorry that I was the cause.
LAURA: [*smiling*] I'll just imagine he had an operation. The horn was removed to make
   him feel less—freakish!

[*They both laugh.*]

   Now he will feel more at home with the other horses, the ones that don't have horns. . . .
JIM: Ha-ha, that's very funny! [*Suddenly he is serious.*] I'm glad to see that you have a sense
   of humor. You know—you're—well—very different! Surprisingly different from
   anyone else I know! [*His voice becomes soft and hesitant with a genuine feeling.*] Do you
   mind me telling you that?

[*LAURA is abashed beyond speech.*]

   I mean it in a nice way—

[*LAURA nods shyly, looking away.*]

   You make me feel sort of—I don't know how to put it! I'm usually pretty good at
   expressing things, but—this is something that I don't know how to say!

[*LAURA touches her throat and clears it—turns the broken unicorn in her hands. His voice becomes
softer.*]

   Has anyone ever told you that you were pretty?

[*There is a pause, and the music rises slightly. LAURA looks up slowly, with wonder, and shakes her
head.*]

   Well, you are! In a very different way from anyone else. And all the nicer because
   of the difference, too.

[*His voice becomes low and husky. LAURA turns away, nearly faint with the novelty of her emotions.*]

   I wish that you were my sister. I'd teach you to have some confidence in yourself.
   The different people are not like other people, but being different is nothing to be
   ashamed of. Because other people are not such wonderful people. They're one hundred times one thousand. You're one times one! They walk all over the earth. You just
   stay here. They're common as—weeds, but—you—well, you're—*Blue Roses!*

[*Image on screen: Blue Roses. The music changes.*]

LAURA: But blue is wrong for—roses. . . .
JIM: It's right for you! You're—pretty!   265

LAURA: In what respect am I pretty?

JIM: In all respects—believe me! Your eyes—your hair—are pretty! Your hands are pretty! [*He catches hold of her hand.*] You think I'm making this up because I'm invited to dinner and have to be nice. Oh, I could do that! I could put on an act for you, Laura, and say lots of things without being very sincere. But this time I am. I'm talking to you sincerely. I happened to notice you had this inferiority complex that keeps you from feeling comfortable with people. Somebody needs to build your confidence up and make you proud instead of shy and turning away and—blushing. Somebody—ought to—*kiss* you, Laura!

[*His hand slips slowly up her arm to her shoulder as the music swells tumultuously. He suddenly turns about and kisses her on the lips. When he releases her, LAURA sinks on the sofa with a bright, dazed look. JIM backs away and fishes in his pocket for a cigarette.*

Legend on screen: "A souvenir."]

   Stumblejohn!

[*He lights the cigarette, avoiding her look. There is a peal of girlish laughter from AMANDA in the kitchenette. LAURA slowly raises and opens her hand. It still contains the little broken glass animal. She looks at it with a tender, bewildered expression.*]

   Stumblejohn! I shouldn't have done that—that was way off the beam. You don't smoke, do you?

[*She looks up, smiling, not hearing the question. He sits beside her rather gingerly. She looks at him speechlessly—waiting. He coughs decorously and moves a little further aside as he considers the situation and senses her feelings, dimly, with perturbation. He speaks gently.*]

   Would you—care for a mint?

[*She doesn't seem to hear him but her look grows brighter even.*]

   Peppermint? Life Saver? My pocket's a regular drugstore—wherever I go. . . . [*He pops a mint in his mouth. Then he gulps and decides to make a clean breast of it. He speaks slowly and gingerly.*] Laura, you know, if I had a sister like you, I'd do the same thing as Tom. I'd bring out fellows and—introduce her to them. The right type of boys—of a type to—appreciate her. Only—well—he made a mistake about me. Maybe I've got no call to be saying this. That may not have been the idea in having me over. But what if it was? There's nothing wrong about that. The only trouble is that in my case—I'm not in a situation to—do the right thing. I can't take down your number and say I'll phone. I can't call up next week and—ask for a date. I thought I had better explain the situation in case you—misunderstood it and—I hurt your feelings. . . .

[*There is a pause. Slowly, very slowly, LAURA's look changes, her eyes returning slowly from his to the glass figure in her palm. AMANDA utters another gay laugh in the kitchenette.*]

LAURA: [*faintly*] You—won't—call again?

JIM: No, Laura, I can't. [*He rises from the sofa.*] As I was just explaining, I've—got strings on me, Laura, I've—been going steady! I go out all the time with a girl named Betty. She's a home-girl like you, and Catholic, and Irish, and in a great many ways we—get along fine. I met her last summer on a moonlight boat trip up the river to Alton,° on the *Majestic*. Well—right away from the start it was—love!

°269 *Alton*: a city in Illinois about twenty miles north of St. Louis on the Mississippi River.

[*Legend: Love!*]

LAURA sways slightly forward and grips the arm of the sofa. He fails to notice, now enrapt in his own comfortable being.]

Being in love has made a new man of me!

[*Leaning stiffly forward, clutching the arm of the sofa, LAURA struggles visibly with her storm. But JIM is oblivious; she is a long way off.*]

The power of love is really pretty tremendous! Love is something that—changes the whole world, Laura!

[*The storm abates a little and LAURA leans back. He notices her again.*]

It happened that Betty's aunt took sick, she got a wire and had to go to Centralia.° So Tom—when he asked me to dinner—I naturally just accepted the invitation, not knowing that you—that he—that I—[*He stops awkwardly.*] Huh—I'm a stumblejohn!

[*He flops back on the sofa. The holy candles on the altar of LAURA's face have been snuffed out. There is a look of almost infinite desolation. JIM glances at her uneasily.*]

I wish that you would—say something.

[*She bites her lip which was trembling and then bravely smiles. She opens her hand again on the broken glass figure. Then she gently takes his hand and raises it level with her own. She carefully places the unicorn in the palm of his hand, then pushes his fingers closed upon it.*]

What are you—doing that for? You want me to have him? Laura?

[*She nods.*]

What for?

LAURA: A—souvenir. . . .   270

[*She rises unsteadily and crouches beside the Victrola to wind it up.*]

Legend on screen: "Things have a way of turning out so badly!" Or image: "Gentleman caller waving goodbye—gaily."

At this moment AMANDA rushes brightly back into the living room. She bears a pitcher of fruit punch in an old-fashioned cut-glass pitcher, and a plate of macaroons. The plate has a gold border and poppies painted on it.]

AMANDA: Well, well, well! Isn't the air delightful after the shower? I've made you children a little liquid refreshment. [*She turns gaily to JIM.*] Jim, do you know that song about lemonade?

> "Lemonade, lemonade
> Made in the shade and stirred with a spade—
> Good enough for any old maid!"

JIM: [*uneasily*] Ha-ha! No—I never heard it.

AMANDA: Why, Laura! You look so serious!

JIM: We were having a serious conversation.

AMANDA: Good! Now you're better acquainted!   275

JIM: [*uncertainly*] Ha-ha! Yes.

°269.4 *Centralia*: a city in Illinois about sixty miles east of St. Louis.

AMANDA: You modern young people are much more serious-minded than my generation. I was so gay as a girl!

JIM: You haven't changed, Mrs. Wingfield.

AMANDA: Tonight I'm rejuvenated! The gaiety of the occasion, Mr. O'Connor! [*She tosses her head with a peal of laughter, spilling some lemonade.*] Oooo! I'm baptizing myself!

280   JIM: Here—let me—

AMANDA: [*setting the pitcher down*] There now. I discovered we had some maraschino cherries. I dumped them in, juice and all!

JIM: You shouldn't have gone to that trouble, Mrs. Wingfield.

AMANDA: Trouble, trouble? Why, it was loads of fun! Didn't you hear me cutting up in the kitchen? I bet your ears were burning! I told Tom how outdone with him I was for keeping you to himself so long a time! He should have brought you over much, much sooner! Well, now that you've found your way, I want you to be a very frequent caller! Not just occasional but all the time. Oh, we're going to have a lot of gay times together! I see them coming! Mmm, just breathe that air! So fresh, and the moon's so pretty! I'll skip back out—I know where my place is when young folks are having a—serious conversation!

JIM: Oh, don't go out, Mrs. Wingfield. The fact of the matter is I've got to be going.

285   AMANDA: Going, now? You're joking! Why, it's only the shank of the evening,° Mr. O'Connor!

JIM: Well, you know how it is.

AMANDA: You mean you're a young workingman and have to keep workingmen's hours. We'll let you off early tonight. But only on the condition that next time you stay later. What's the best night for you? Isn't Saturday night the best night for you workingmen?

JIM: I have a couple of time-clocks to punch, Mrs. Wingfield. One at morning, another one at night!

AMANDA: My, but you *are* ambitious! You work at night, too?

290   JIM: No, Ma'am, not work but—Betty!

[*He crosses deliberately to pick up his hat. The band at the Paradise Dance Hall goes into a tender waltz.*]

AMANDA: Betty? Betty? Who's—Betty!

[*There is an ominous cracking sound in the sky.*]

JIM: Oh, just a girl. The girl I go steady with!

[*He smiles charmingly. The sky falls.*

Legend: "The Sky Falls."]

AMANDA: [*a long-drawn exhalation*] Ohhh . . . Is it a serious romance, Mr. O'Connor?

JIM: We're going to be married the second Sunday in June.

295   AMANDA: Ohhh—how nice! Tom didn't mention that you were engaged to be married.

JIM: The cat's not out of the bag at the warehouse yet. You know how they are. They call you Romeo and stuff like that. [*He stops at the oval mirror to put on his hat. He carefully shapes the brim and the crown to give a discreetly dashing effect.*] It's been a wonderful evening, Mrs. Wingfield. I guess this is what they mean by Southern hospitality.

AMANDA: It really wasn't anything at all.

°285 *shank of the evening:* still early, the best part of the evening.

JIM: I hope it don't seem like I'm rushing off. But I promised Betty I'd pick her up at the Wabash depot, an' by the time I get my jalopy down there her train'll be in. Some women are pretty upset if you keep 'em waiting.

AMANDA: Yes, I know—the tyranny of women! [*She extends her hand.*] Goodbye, Mr. O'Connor. I wish you luck—and happiness—and success! All three of them, and so does Laura! Don't you, Laura?

LAURA: Yes!   300

JIM: [*taking LAURA's hand*] Goodbye, Laura. I'm certainly going to treasure that souvenir. And don't you forget the good advice I gave you. [*He raises his voice to a cheery shout.*] So long, Shakespeare! Thanks again, ladies. Good night!

[*He grins and ducks jauntily out. Still bravely grimacing, AMANDA closes the door on the gentleman caller. Then she turns back to the room with a puzzled expression. She and LAURA don't dare to face each other. LAURA crouches beside the Victrola to wind it.*]

AMANDA: [*faintly*] Things have a way of turning out so badly. I don't believe that I would play the Victrola. Well, well—well! Our gentleman caller was engaged to be married? [*She raises her voice.*] Tom!

TOM: [*from the kitchenette*] Yes, Mother?

AMANDA: Come in here a minute. I want to tell you something awfully funny.

TOM: [*entering with a macaroon and a glass of the lemonade*] Has the gentleman caller gotten   305
away already?

AMANDA: The gentleman caller has made an early departure. What a wonderful joke you played on us!

TOM: How do you mean?

AMANDA: You didn't mention that he was engaged to be married.

TOM: Jim? Engaged?

AMANDA: That's what he just informed us.   310

TOM: I'll be jiggered! I didn't know about that.

AMANDA: That seems very peculiar.

TOM: What's peculiar about it?

AMANDA: Didn't you call him your best friend down at the warehouse?

TOM: He is, but how did I know?   315

AMANDA: It seems extremely peculiar that you wouldn't know your best friend was going to be married!

TOM: The warehouse is where I work, not where I know things about people!

AMANDA: You don't know things anywhere! You live in a dream; you manufacture illusions!

[*He crosses to the door.*]

Where are you going?

TOM: I'm going to the movies.

AMANDA: That's right, now that you've had us make such fools of ourselves. The effort,   320
the preparations, all the expense! The new floor lamp, the rug, the clothes for Laura! All for what? To entertain some other girl's fiancé! Go to the movies, go! Don't think about us, a mother deserted, an unmarried sister who's crippled and has no job! Don't let anything interfere with your selfish pleasure! Just go, go, go—to the movies!

TOM: All right, I will! The more you shout about my selfishness to me the quicker I'll go, and I won't go to the movies!

AMANDA: Go, then! Go to the moon—you selfish dreamer!

[TOM *smashes his glass on the floor. He plunges out on the fire escape, slamming the door.* LAURA *screams in fright. The dance-hall music becomes louder.* TOM *stands on the fire escape, gripping the rail. The moon breaks through the storm clouds, illuminating his face.*

Legend on screen: "And so goodbye . . ."

TOM's *closing speech is timed with what is happening inside the house. We see, as though through soundproof glass, that* AMANDA *appears to be making a comforting speech to* LAURA, *who is huddled upon the sofa. Now that we cannot hear the mother's speech, her silliness is gone and she has dignity and tragic beauty.* LAURA's *hair hides her face until, at the end of the speech, she lifts her head to smile at her mother.* AMANDA's *gestures are slow and graceful, almost dancelike, as she comforts her daughter. At the end of her speech she glances a moment at the father's picture—then withdraws through the portieres. At the close of* TOM's *speech,* LAURA *blows out the candles, ending the play.*]

TOM: I didn't go to the moon, I went much further—for time is the longest distance between
two places. Not long after that I was fired for writing a poem on the lid of a shoe box.
I left Saint Louis. I descended the steps of this fire escape for a last time and followed,
from then on, in my father's footsteps, attempting to find in motion what was lost in
space. I traveled around a great deal. The cities swept about me like dead leaves, leaves
that were brightly colored but torn away from the branches. I would have stopped, but
I was pursued by something. It always came upon me unawares, taking me altogether
by surprise. Perhaps it was a familiar bit of music. Perhaps it was only a piece of transparent glass. Perhaps I am walking along a street at night, in some strange city, before
I have found companions. I pass the lighted window of a shop where perfume is sold.
The window is filled with pieces of colored glass, tiny transparent bottles in delicate
colors, like bits of a shattered rainbow. Then all at once my sister touches my shoulder.
I turn around and look into her eyes. Oh, Laura, Laura, I tried to leave you behind me,
but I am more faithful than I intended to be! I reach for a cigarette, I cross the street, I run
into the movies or a bar, I buy a drink, I speak to the nearest stranger—anything that
can blow your candles out!

[LAURA *bends over the candles.*]

For nowadays the world is lit by lightning! Blow out your candles, Laura—and
so good bye. . . .

[*She blows the candles out.*]

QUESTIONS

1. What does the setting described in the opening stage direction tell you about the Wingfields? Consider especially the adjectives and the symbolism of the alley and the fire
escape.
2. Who is the "fifth character" in the play, and how is his presence established? In what
ways is Tom a parallel to this character?
3. What does Amanda reveal about her past in scene 1? How does Williams reveal that
Amanda often dwells in the past?
4. What happened to Laura at Rubicam's Business College? How can you account for her
behavior? What plan of Amanda's did she upset?
5. What new plan for Laura's future does Amanda begin to develop in scene 2? Why is
the plan impracticable? Why is the image of Jim introduced here?

6. Summarize the argument between Tom and Amanda in scene 3. What does Amanda assert about Tom? What does he claim about his life? Why is Laura spotlighted throughout the argument?

7. What sort of agreement does Amanda try to reach with Tom about Laura in scene 4?

8. How do Amanda and Laura react to the news of a gentleman caller? Describe Laura's feelings toward Jim during the conversation and the dancing in scene 7. Describe how he changes after the kiss.

9. Explain the symbolism of the unicorn (both whole and broken). Why does Laura give it to Jim as a souvenir?

10. What is Tom's situation at the end? To what degree has he achieved his dreams of escape and adventure?

11. Describe Amanda's and Laura's concluding situations. Why does Laura blow out the candles? What is the future for these women?

GENERAL QUESTIONS

1. Explain the most striking nonrealistic aspects of the play. What do these contribute to the play's meaning and impact? Which aspect is the most effective? Why?

2. Which characters in the play change significantly? To what extent do the characters succeed or fail? How do they try to escape the realities they face?

3. Consider Tom as character and narrator. Explain why his language changes as he shifts between narrator and character. What does the character dream about and strive for? What does the narrator learn about these dreams and strivings?

4. Explain why Laura cannot deal with reality. What does her glass menagerie symbolize?

5. Williams says that there is much to admire, pity, and laugh at in Amanda. What aspects of her character are admirable? Pitiable? Laughable? Which reaction is dominant for you at the close of the play? Why?

6. Tom calls Jim the play's "most realistic character." In what ways is Jim realistic? How are his dreams and goals more (or less) realistic than Tom's?

7. At the opening, Tom (as narrator) mentions the "social background," and he remarks on it throughout. Discuss how this background relates to the play, especially the events occurring in Europe.

8. Discuss the play's religious allusion and imagery, especially Malvolio the Magician, the "Ave Maria," the "Annunciation," the Paradise Dance Hall, and Laura's candles. How do these references affect the play's level of reality?

AUGUST WILSON (1945–2005)

To judge from the poverty of his birth and early days, one might never have supposed that August Wilson would eventually become one of America's most celebrated dramatists. His birth name was Frederick August Kittel, the fourth of six children. His father was an immigrant German, a baker, who never spent much time with the family, and by the time Wilson was five his father and mother had separated. Wilson's mother, Daisy Wilson, was an African American, and did housecleaning. It was she who taught August how to read when he was only four. When Wilson's father died, in 1965, Wilson changed his name to "August Wilson" to honor his mother. Daisy had remarried and, with her new husband and her family, had moved to a more prestigious neighborhood than the "hill district" where the

family had previously resided. In the new school system, Wilson, the only African American student, experienced great hostility, both from fellow students and also from some of the teachers. He wrote a research paper about Napoleon, and his instructor accused him of plagiarizing it. Because of such disparagement, Wilson left school, though still in ninth grade, and began a program of self-education at a branch of Pittsburgh's Carnegie Library. He educated himself so well that eventually the library granted him a degree. It was just one of the special degrees he received, for he would later be granted two dozen honorary doctorates.

Wilson's young adulthood was also not auspicious, but he was slowly moving in the direction of becoming a writer. Three years before America became fully engaged in the Vietnam conflict, he signed up for a three-year hitch in the army, but somehow he was able to secure a discharge after a year, and he then began doing odd jobs for his subsistence. He bought a typewriter in 1965, and declared that he was a poet. At the age of 23, he co-founded the Black Horizon on the Hill Theater in Pittsburgh, and began haltingly to write a few plays, which were not distinguished or very successful. He moved to Minneapolis/St. Paul, and stayed there for a number of years. Later he moved to Seattle, his final home, where he became one of the founders of the Seattle Repertory Theater. When living in Minnesota, he had begun working for the Minnesota Science Museum, and was given the duty of dramatizing Native American folk tales for visiting children. It was this rather journeyman task that confirmed his decision to pursue his career in drama.

It is apparent that at some point during his years of movement from place to place, he developed the ambitious idea that would inform his major dramatic output during his lifetime career as dramatist. He planned a full cycle of ten plays, to be called "The Pittsburgh Cycle," in which he would explore the lives and times of African Americans during the twentieth century. His aim was to dramatize the "comedy and tragedy" of blacks who were the descendants of the slaves who had been granted freedom at the time of the Civil War. Each of the plays was to deal with life during one of the decades, though Wilson did not write them in the chronological order of their topic matter. The settings of all but one of the plays is the Pittsburgh "hill district"—the location where his family had lived during the early years of his life. The ten plays are the following: Gem of the Ocean *(1900–1910), written 2003;* Joe Turner's Come and Gone *(1910–1920), written 1986;* Ma Rainey's Black Bottom *(1920–1930), written 1984;* The Piano Lesson *(1930–1940), written 1987, Pulitzer Prize;* Seven Guitars *(1940–1950), written 1995;* Fences *(1957, 1965), written 1985, Pulitzer Prize;* Two Trains Running *(1960–1970), written 1990;* Jitney *(1970–1980), written 1982;* King Hedley, II *(1980-1990), written 1999;* Radio Golf *(1990–2000), written 2005.*

Although Wilson's first forty years were both an artistic and financial struggle, his later life was characterized by great recognition and praise. Fences, *one of his best-known plays, was acclaimed for the 1987 production on Broadway, directed by Lloyd Richards and starring James Earl Jones. It won a Pulitzer Prize for Drama, and was additionally distinguished with a Tony Award. For Wilson, it was also financially rewarding. His play* The Piano Lesson *received a Pulitzer Prize in 1990, along with the New York Drama Critics' Circle Award. In Wilson's final years of life, prizes and honorary degrees almost cascaded upon him. When he succumbed to cancer in 2005, he was recognized as one of America's leading dramatists.*

The Background of *Fences*

Fences, written in the mid-1980s, is about a period in the 1950s during the growth of the Civil Rights movement under Dr. Martin Luther King Jr., but before the advent of the Black Power movement of the 1960s. Although there was progress in the 1950s, the country was nevertheless still racist. It is important to recognize that major league baseball, after World War II, was becoming integrated, though slowly. The "Old Negro Leagues" had produced Black players with great ability, but with little public support and recognition. In the late 1940s, changes had begun to take place. Jackie Robinson became the first African American to have become a player in the National League, and Monte Irvin led the way in the American League. By the mid-1950s, there were stalwart players like Minnie Minoso (b. 1922), Ernie Banks (b. 1931), and Elston Howard (1929–1980). The last Negro League player to move to the Big Leagues was Hank Aaron, who became almost a regular yearly member of the All-Star National League teams. He went on to set the professional record of 755 home runs, which stood unchallenged until June 2007.

In short, encouraging things were happening, and that is the backdrop of the world of baseball that is so much a part of the life and outlook of Troy Maxson (i.e., "maximum son"), August Wilson's protagonist in *Fences*. It is clear that Troy was a player who could hit the ball over fences, but it is also clear that circumstances prevented him from doing so through an entire baseball career. Wilson creates Troy as being too old to benefit from the integration of professional baseball, and also of American society, that was taking place at the time. Troy had spent the prime part of his youth in prison, and it was there that he was able to develop his baseball talents. The result is that with all his ability, he had become too old to be one of those to break baseball's "color line." This despite the fact that Satchel Paige had joined the Cleveland Indians in 1948, at the age of 42, almost exactly the same age that Wilson visualizes for Troy. Paige pitched for four major league teams, and did not finally retire until he was 59. Troy believes that he could have done just as well, and, as he says, "If you could play . . . then they ought to have let you play." Instead of excelling at hitting balls over the fence, however, he is in the process of retreat, and he is deeply unhappy about being no more than a garbage collector. The fence he builds around his house during the play is symbolically a fence of his own suspicion, anger, and cynicism, preventing him from glorying in the world where he might have conquered.

All this is important in considering the character of Troy. He is a special example of those whose lives were demonstrably marred by discrimination in the twentieth century. (Let us remember that *Fences* is a part of Wilson's chronicle of Black life during the ten decades from 1900 to 2000.) Wilson is careful to show that discrimination hurt Troy's family life during his boyhood. He was particularly afflicted by his father, who was "just as evil as he could be," as Troy tells his son Lyons. In 1.4 Troy describes the events of his leaving home at the age of 14. He had been raised on a cotton farm in the South, and his life was the "stoop labor" of endless cotton picking and cotton baling. Troy's father's attack on him underlies his hostility toward the dreams of his own son, Cory ("heart"), about going into professional football. Despite his negative attitude about Cory's hopes, however, Troy has moved beyond the narrow brutality of his own father. In 2.4, the most agitated and also the most moving scene in the play, Troy has the opportunity to swing a baseball bat at Cory, and thus he has the absolute power over Cory that his own father had exerted over him. But Troy turns away from violence, in a scene that recalls the famous "duel averted" scene in the popular eighteenth-century play *The Conscious Lovers* (1722), by Sir Richard Steele (1672–1729). Although Troy gives up his destructive power, however, he permanently alienates himself from his son.

Named after the ancient mythical city described by Homer, Troy is not only the major character of *Fences*, but he is also one of the major characters to have been created by a twentieth-century dramatist. He is a character of immense power, a leader, but by no means is he perfect. He is a drinker, he is unfaithful, and he is a man of contradictions. As he strays, he tries to justify his straying, but he is not convincing. He does not understand love, but he does understand duty, and that is his compensating strength. He somewhat resembles the biblical patriarch Jacob, who wrestles with God (Genesis 32:24–32). Troy's perception is that he has wrestled with Death. A major theme in his story is that Death will inevitably win, but that he, Troy, is confident in himself, and defiant. He announces, as though Death is listening, "I be ready for you . . . but I ain't gonna be easy" (2.4.97). Although he is imperfect, he has great inner strength, and he is, above all, memorable.

Fences (1985)

for Lloyd Richards,° *who adds to whatever be touches*
When the sins of our fathers visit us
We do not have to play host.
We can banish them with forgiveness
As God, in His Largeness and Laws.
—August Wilson

CAST OF CHARACTERS

Troy Maxson, [fifty-three years old; a powerful man; now a garbage collector, though formerly a ballplayer and home-run hitter in the old "Negro leagues"]
Jim Bono, Troy's friend [of "thirty odd years"; acts as a conscience for Troy]
Rose, Troy's wife [of eighteen years]
Lyons, Troy's oldest son by a previous marriage
Gabriel, Troy's brother [severely injured in World War II]
Cory, Troy and Rose's son [ready to graduate from high school; an aspiring athlete]
Raynell, Troy's daughter [with Alberta; Raynell is seven in Act 2, Scene 5]

SETTING

The setting is the yard which fronts the only entrance to the Maxson household, an ancient two-story brick house set back off a small alley in a big-city neighborhood. The entrance to the house is gained by two or three steps leading to a wooden porch badly in need of paint.

A relatively recent addition to the house and running its full width, the porch lacks congruence. It is a sturdy porch with a flat roof. One or two chairs of dubious value sit at one end where the kitchen window opens onto the porch. An old-fashioned icebox stands silent guard at the opposite end.

The yard is a small dirt yard, partially fenced, except for the last scene, with a wooden saw horse, a pile of lumber, and other fence-building equipment set off to the side. Opposite is a tree from which hangs a ball made of rags. A baseball bat leans against the tree. Two oil drums serve as garbage receptacles and sit near the house at right to complete the setting.

THE PLAY

Near the turn of the century, the destitute of Europe sprang on the city with tenacious claws and an honest and solid dream. The city devoured them. They swelled its belly until it burst into a thousand furnaces and sewing machines, a thousand butcher shops and bakers' ovens, a thousand churches and hospitals and funeral parlors and moneylenders.

°*Lloyd Richards:* Richards (1919–2006) is perhaps best known for having directed Lorraine Hansberry's *A Raisin in the Sun* in 1959, making him the first African American to direct a play on Broadway. Richards was a staunch friend and supportive colleague of Wilson, and eventually he directed six Broadway productions of Wilson plays, including *Fences* in 1987.

The city grew. It nourished itself and offered each man a partnership limited only by his talent, his guile and his willingness and capacity for hard work. For the immigrants of Europe, a dream dared and won true.

The descendants of African slaves were offered no such welcome or participation. They came from places called the Carolinas and the Virginias, Georgia, Alabama, Mississippi, and Tennessee. They came strong, eager, searching. The city rejected them and they fled and settled along the riverbanks and under bridges in shallow, ramshackle houses made of sticks and tarpaper. They collected rags and wood. They sold the use of their muscles and their bodies. They cleaned houses and washed clothes, they shined shoes, and in quiet desperation and vengeful pride, they stole, and lived in pursuit of their own dream. That they could breathe free, finally, and stand to meet life with the force of dignity and whatever eloquence the heart could call upon.

By 1957, the hard-won victories of the European immigrants had solidified the industrial might of America. War had been confronted and won with new energies that used loyalty and patriotism as its fuel. Life was rich, full, and flourishing. The Milwaukee Braves won the World Series, and the hot winds of change that would make the sixties a turbulent, racing, dangerous, and provocative decade had not yet begun to blow full.

ACT 1

Scene 1

It is 1957. TROY *and* BONO *enter the yard, engaged in conversation.* TROY *is fifty-three years old, a large man with thick, heavy hands; it is this largeness that he strives to fill out and make an accommodation with. Together with his blackness, his largeness informs his sensibilities and the choices he has made in his life.*

Of the two men, BONO *is obviously the follower. His commitment to their friendship of thirty-odd years is rooted in his admiration of* TROY's *honesty, capacity for hard work, and his strength, which* BONO *seeks to emulate.*

It is Friday night, payday, and the one night of the week the two men engage in a ritual of talk and drink. TROY *is usually the most talkative and at times he can be crude and almost vulgar, though he is capable of rising to profound heights of expression. The men carry lunch buckets and wear or carry burlap aprons and are dressed in clothes suitable to their jobs as garbage collectors.*

BONO: Troy, you ought to stop that lying!

TROY: I ain't lying! The nigger had a watermelon this big. [*He indicates with his hands.*] Talking about . . . "What watermelon, Mr. Rand?" I liked to fell out! "What watermelon, Mr. Rand?" . . . And it sitting there big as life.

BONO: What did Mr. Rand say?

TROY: Ain't said nothing. Figure if the nigger too dumb to know he carrying a watermelon, he wasn't gonna get much sense out of him. Trying to hide that great big old watermelon under his coat. Afraid to let the white man see him carry it home.

BONO: I'm like you . . . I ain't got no time for them kind of people.   5

TROY: Now what he look like getting mad cause he see the man from the union talking to Mr. Rand?

BONO: He come to me talking about . . . "Maxson gonna get us fired." I told him to get away from me with that. He walked away from me calling you a troublemaker. What Mr. Rand say?

TROY: Ain't said nothing. He told me to go down the Commissioner's office next Friday. They called me down there to see them.

BONO: Well, as long as you got your complaint filed, they can't fire you. That's what one of them white fellows tell me.

10   **TROY:** I ain't worried about them firing me. They gonna fire me cause I asked a question? That's all I did. I went to Mr. Rand and asked him, "Why? Why you got the white mens driving and the colored lifting?" Told him, "What's the matter, don't I count? You think only white fellows got sense enough to drive a truck. That ain't no paper job! Hell, anybody can drive a truck. How come you got all whites driving and the colored lifting?" He told me "take it to the union." Well, hell, that's what I done! Now they wanna come up with this pack of lies.

BONO: I told Brownie if the man come and ask him any questions . . . just tell the truth! It ain't nothing but something they done trumped up on you cause you filed a complaint on them.

TROY: Brownie don't understand nothing. All I want them to do is change the job description. Give everybody a chance to drive the truck. Brownie can't see that. He ain't got that much sense.

BONO: How you figure he be making out with that gal be up at Taylors' all the time . . . that Alberta gal?

TROY: Same as you and me. Getting just as much as we is. Which is to say nothing.

15   **BONO:** It is, huh? I figure you doing a little better than me . . . and I ain't saying what I'm doing.

TROY: Aw, nigger, look here . . . I know you. If you had got anywhere near that gal, twenty minutes later you be looking to tell somebody. And the first one you gonna tell . . . that you gonna want to brag to . . . is me.

BONO: I ain't saying that, I see where you be eyeing her.

TROY: I eye all the women. I don't miss nothing. Don't never let nobody tell you Troy Maxson don't eye the women.

BONO: You been doing more than eyeing her. You done bought her a drink or two.

20   **TROY:** Hell yeah, I bought her a drink! What that mean? I bought you one, too. What that mean cause I buy her a drink? I'm just being polite.

BONO: It's all right to buy her one drink. That's what you call being polite. But when you wanna be buying two or three . . . that's what you call eyeing her.

TROY: Look here, as long as you known me . . . you ever known me to chase after women?

BONO: Hell yeah! Long as I done known you. You forgetting I knew you when.

TROY: Naw, I'm talking about since I been married to Rose?

25   **BONO:** Oh, not since you been married to Rose. Now, that's the truth, there, I can say that.

TROY: All right then! Case closed.

BONO: I see you be walking up around Alberta's house. You supposed to be at Taylors' and you be walking up around there.

TROY: What you watching where I'm walking for? I ain't watching after you.

BONO: I seen you walking around there more than once.

30   **TROY:** Hell, you liable to see me walking anywhere! That don't mean nothing cause you see me walking around there.

BONO: Where she come from anyway? She just kinda showed up one day.

TROY: Tallahassee. You can look at her and tell she one of them Florida gals. They got some big healthy women down there. Grow them right up out the ground. Got a little bit of Indian in her. Most of them niggers down in Florida got some Indian in them.

BONO: I don't know about that Indian part. But she damn sure big and healthy. Women wear some big stockings. Got them great big old legs and hips as wide as the Mississippi River.

TROY: Legs don't mean nothing. You don't do nothing but push them out of the way. But them hips cushion the ride!

35   **BONO:** Troy, you ain't got no sense.

TROY: It's the truth! Like you riding on Goodyears!

ROSE enters from the house. She is ten years younger than TROY, her devotion to him stems from her recognition of the possibilities of her life without him: a succession of abusive men and their babies, a life of partying and running the streets, the Church, or aloneness with its attendant pain and frustration. She recognizes TROY'S spirit as a fine and illuminating one and she either ignores or forgives his faults, only some of which she recognizes. Though she doesn't drink, her presence is an integral part of the Friday night rituals. She alternates between the porch and the kitchen, where supper preparations are under way.

ROSE: What you all out here getting into?

TROY: What you worried about what we getting into for? This is men talk, woman.

ROSE: What I care what you all talking about? Bono, you gonna stay for supper?

BONO: No, I thank you, Rose. But Lucille say she cooking up a pot of pigfeet.   40

TROY: Pigfeet! Hell, I'm going home with you! Might even stay the night if you got some pigfeet. You got something in there to top them pigfeet, Rose?

ROSE: I'm cooking up some chicken. I got some chicken and collard greens.

TROY: Well, go on back in the house and let me and Bono finish what we was talking about. This is men talk. I got some talk for you later. You know what kind of talk I mean. You go on and powder it up.

ROSE: Troy Maxson, don't you start that now!

TROY: [*puts his arm around her.*] Aw, woman . . . come here. Look here. Bono . . . when I   45
met this woman . . . I got out that place, say, "Hitch up my pony, saddle up my mare . . . there's a woman out there for me somewhere." I looked here. Looked there. Saw Rose and latched on to her. I latched on to her and told her—I'm gonna tell you the truth—I told her, "Baby, I don't wanna marry, I just wanna be your man." Rose told me . . . tell him what you told me, Rose.

ROSE: I told him if he wasn't the marrying kind, then move out the way so the marrying kind could find me.

TROY: That's what she told me. "Nigger, you in my way. You blocking the view! Move out the way so I can find me a husband." I thought it over two or three days. Come back—

ROSE: Ain't no two or three days nothing. You was back the same night.

TROY: Come back, told her . . . "Okay, baby . . . but I'm gonna buy me a banty rooster and put him out there in the backyard . . . and when he see a stranger come, he'll flap his wings and crow. . . ." Look here, Bono, I could watch the front door by myself . . . it was that back door I was worried about.

ROSE: Troy, you ought not talk like that. Troy ain't doing nothing but telling a lie.   50

TROY: Only thing is . . . when we first got married . . . forget the rooster . . . we ain't had no yard!

BONO: I hear you tell it. Me and Lucille was staying down there on Logan Street. Had two rooms with the outhouse in the back. I ain't mind the outhouse none. But when that god-damn wind blow through there in the winter . . . that's what I'm talking about! To this day I wonder why in the hell I ever stayed down there for six long years. But see, I didn't know I could do no better. I thought only white folks had inside toilets and things.

ROSE: There's a lot of people don't know they can do no better than they doing now. That's just something you got to learn. A lot of folks still shop at Bella's.

TROY: Ain't nothing wrong with shopping at Bella's. She got fresh food.

ROSE: I ain't said nothing about if she got fresh food. I'm talking about what she charge.   55
She charge ten cents more than the A&P.

TROY: The A&P ain't never done nothing for me. I spends my money where I'm treated right. I go down to Bella, say, "I need a loaf of bread, I'll pay you Friday." She give it to me. What sense that make when I got money to go and spend it somewhere else and ignore the person who done right by me? That ain't in the Bible.

ROSE: We ain't talking about what's in the Bible. What sense it make to shop there when she overcharge?

TROY: You shop where you want to. I'll do my shopping where the people been good to me.

ROSE: Well, I don't think it's right for her to overcharge. That's all I was saying.

60   **BONO:** Look here . . . I got to get on. Lucille going be raising all kind of hell.

TROY: Where you going, nigger? We ain't finished this pint. Come here, finish this pint.

BONO: Well, hell, I am . . . if you ever turn the bottle loose.

TROY: [*hands him the bottle.*] The only thing I say about the A&P is I'm glad Cory got that job down there. Help him take care of his school clothes and things. Gabe done moved out and things getting tight around here. He got that job. . . . He can start to look out for himself.

ROSE: Cory done went and got recruited by a college football team.

65   **TROY:** I told that boy about that football stuff. The white man ain't gonna let him get no-where with that football. I told him when he first come to me with it. Now you come telling me he done went and got more tied up in it. He ought to go and get recruited in how to fix cars or something where he can make a living.

ROSE: He ain't talking about making no living playing football. It's just something the boys in school do. They gonna send a recruiter by to talk to you. He'll tell you he ain't talking about making no living playing football. It's a honor to be recruited.

TROY: It ain't gonna get him nowhere. Bono'll tell you that.

BONO: If he be like you in the sports . . . he's gonna be all right. Ain't but two men ever played baseball as good as you. That's Babe Ruth and Josh Gibson.° Them's the only two men ever hit more home runs than you.

TROY: What it ever get me? Ain't got a pot to piss in or a window to throw it out of.

70   **ROSE:** Times have changed since you was playing baseball, Troy. That was before the war. Times have changed a lot since then.

TROY: How in hell they done changed?

ROSE: They got lots of colored boys playing ball now. Baseball and football.

BONO: You right about that, Rose. Times have changed, Troy. You just come along too early.

TROY: There ought not never have been no time called too early! Now you take that fellow . . . What's that fellow they had playing right field for the Yankees back then? You know who I'm talking about, Bono. Used to play right field for the Yankees.

75   **ROSE:** Selkirk?°

TROY: Selkirk! That's it! Man batting .269, understand? .269! What kind of sense that make? I was hitting .432 with thirty-seven home runs! Man batting .269 and play-ing right field for the Yankees! I saw Josh Gibson's daughter yesterday. She walking around with raggedy shoes on her feet. Now I bet you Selkirk's daughter ain't walk-ing around with raggedy shoes on the feet! I bet you that!

°68 *Babe Ruth and Josh Gibson:* George Herman Ruth, "Babe" Ruth (1895–1948), had a baseball career that lasted from 1914 to 1935. During this time he set many batting records, including his number of home runs in a season in 1927 (60) and total home runs (714). In 1957, no one had surpassed either of these records, and no one was close. Ruth was one of the first men to be made a member of the Baseball Hall of Fame. His record for a single season lasted until 1961, when Roger Maris hit 61. Joshua Gibson (1911–1947), a catcher, is considered as one of the greatest home run hitters in baseball history, though he never was permitted to play in the major leagues. In seventeen seasons in the Negro Leagues, and in corollary exhibition games, he may have batted as high as .384, and may have hit more than 800 home runs. One of the claims made about him is that he was the only batter to have hit a home run out of Yankee Stadium. He was elected posthumously to Baseball's Hall of Fame in 1972.
°75 *Selkirk:* George Alexander ("Twinkletoes") Selkirk (1908–1987), played for the Yankees for nine seasons from 1934 to 1942. When Babe Ruth retired in 1935, Selkirk became the regular Yankee right fielder. His major league lifetime batting average was .290, and he batted .269 in 1940. He hit a total of 108 home runs during his career, with 576 RBI. After 1942, he left the Yankees to serve in World War II.

ROSE: They got a lot of colored baseball players now. Jackie Robinson was the first. Folks had to wait for Jackie Robinson.°

TROY: I done seen a hundred niggers play baseball better than Jackie Robinson. Hell, I know some teams Jackie Robinson couldn't even make! What you talking about Jackie Robinson. Jackie Robinson wasn't nobody. I'm talking about if you could play ball then they ought to have let you play. Don't care what color you were. Come telling me I come along too early. If you could play . . . then they ought to have let you play.

TROY takes a long drink from the bottle.

ROSE: You gonna drink yourself to death. You don't need to be drinking like that.

TROY: Death ain't nothing. I done seen him. Done wrassled with him. You can't tell me   80
nothing about death. Death ain't nothing but a fastball on the outside corner. And you know what I'll do to that! Lookee here, Bono . . . am I lying? You get one of them fastballs, about waist high, over the outside corner of the plate where you can get the meat of the bat on it . . . and good god! You can kiss it goodbye. Now, am I lying?

BONO: Naw, you telling the truth there. I seen you do it.

TROY: If I'm lying . . . that 450 feet worth of lying! [*Pause.*] That's all death is to me. A fastball on the outside corner.

ROSE: I don't know why you want to get on talking about death.

TROY: Ain't nothing wrong with talking about death. That's part of life. Everybody gonna die. You gonna die, I'm gonna die. Bono's gonna die. Hell, we all gonna die.

ROSE: But you ain't got to talk about it. I don't like to talk about it.   85

TROY: You the one brought it up. Me and Bono was talking about baseball . . . you tell me I'm gonna drink myself to death. Ain't that right, Bono? You know I don't drink this but one night out of the week. That's Friday night. I'm gonna drink just enough to where I can handle it. Then I cuts it loose. I leave it alone. So don't you worry about me drinking myself to death. 'Cause I ain't worried about Death. I done seen him. I done wrestled with him. Look here, Bono . . . I looked up one day and Death was marching straight at me. Like Soldiers on Parade! The Army of Death was marching straight at me. The middle of July, 1941. It got real cold just like it be winter. It seem like Death himself reached out and touched me on the shoulder. He touched me just like I touch you. I got cold as ice and Death standing there grinning at me.

ROSE: Troy, why don't you hush that talk.

TROY: I say . . . what you want, Mr. Death? You be wanting me? You done brought your army to be getting me? I looked him dead in the eye. I wasn't fearing nothing. I was ready to tangle. Just like I'm ready to tangle now. The Bible say be ever vigilant.° That's why I don't get but so drunk. I got to keep watch.

ROSE: Troy was right down there in Mercy Hospital. You remember he had pneumonia? Laying there with a fever talking plumb out of his head.

TROY: Death standing there staring at me . . . carrying that sickle in his hand. Finally he   90
say, "You want bound over for another year?" See, just like that . . . "You want bound over for another year?" I told him, "Bound over hell! Let's settle this now!" It seem like he kinda fell back when I said that, and all the cold went out of me. I reached down and grabbed that sickle and threw it just as far as I could throw it . . . and me and him commenced to wrestling. We wrestled for three days and three nights. I can't say where I found the strength from. Everytime it seemed like he was gonna get the best of me, I'd reach way down deep inside myself and find the strength to do him one better.

°77 *Jackie Robinson:* Robinson (1919–1972) led the way for equality in professional sports when he became the first African American to play major league baseball in 1947. He went on to have a sterling if brief major league career. He was made a member of the Baseball Hall of Fame in 1962. °88 *vigilant:* See I Peter 5:8.

ROSE: Every time Troy tell that story he find different ways to tell it. Different things to make up about it.

TROY: I ain't making up nothing. I'm telling you the facts of what happened. I wrestled with Death for three days and three nights and I'm standing here to tell you about it. [*Pause.*] All right. At the end of the third night we done weakened each other to where we can't hardly move. Death stood up, throwed on his robe . . . had him a white robe with a hood on it. He threwed on that robe and went off to look for his sickle. Say, "I'll be back." Just like that. "I'll be back." I told him, say, "Yeah, but . . . you gonna have to find me!" I wasn't no fool. I wasn't going looking for him. Death ain't nothing to play with. And I know he's gonna get me. I know I got to join his army . . . his camp followers. But as long as I keep my strength and see him coming . . . as long as I keep up my vigilance . . . he's gonna have to fight to get me. I ain't going easy.

BONO: Well, look here, since you got to keep up your vigilance . . . let me have the bottle.

TROY: Aw hell, I shouldn't have told you that part. I should have left out that part.

95 **ROSE:** Troy be talking that stuff and half the time don't even know what he be talking about.

TROY: Bono know me better than that.

BONO: That's right. I know you. I know you got some Uncle Remus° in your blood. You got more stories than the devil got sinners.

TROY: Aw hell, I done seen him too! Done talked with the devil.

ROSE: Troy, don't nobody wanna be hearing all that stuff.

LYONS enters the yard from the street. Thirty-four years old, TROY's son by a previous marriage, he sports a neatly trimmed goatee, sport coat, white shirt, tieless and buttoned at the collar. Though he fancies himself a musician, he is more caught up in the rituals and "idea" of being a musician than in the actual practice of the music. He has come to borrow money from TROY, and while he knows he will be successful, he is uncertain as to what extent his lifestyle will be held up to scrutiny and ridicule.

100 **LYONS:** Hey, Pop.

TROY: What you come "Hey, Popping" me for?

LYONS: How you doing, Rose? [*He kisses her.*] Mr. Bono. How you doing?

BONO: Hey, Lyons . . . how you been?

TROY: He must have been doing all right. I ain't seen him around here last week.

105 **ROSE:** Troy, leave your boy alone. He come by to see you and you wanna start all that nonsense.

TROY: I ain't bothering Lyons. [*Offers him the bottle.*] Here . . . get you a drink. We got an understanding. I know why he come by to see me and he know I know.

LYONS: Come on, Pop . . . I just stopped by to say hi . . . see how you was doing.

TROY: You ain't stopped by yesterday.

ROSE: You gonna stay for supper, Lyons? I got some chicken cooking in the oven.

110 **LYONS:** No, Rose . . . thanks. I was just in the neighborhood and thought I'd stop by for a minute.

TROY: You was in the neighborhood all right, nigger. You telling the truth there. You was in the neighborhood 'cause it's my payday.

LYONS: Well, hell, since you mentioned it . . . let me have ten dollars.

TROY: I'll be damned! I'll die and go to hell and play blackjack with the devil before I give you ten dollars.

BONO: That's what I wanna know about . . . that devil you done seen.

115 **LYONS:** What . . . Pop done seen the devil? You too much, Pops.

°97 *Uncle Remus:* A reference to the Uncle Remus stories (1881) of Joel Chandler Harris.

TROY: Yeah, I done seen him. Talked to him too!

ROSE: You ain't seen no devil. I done told you that man ain't had nothing to do with the devil. Anything you can't understand, you want to call it the devil.

TROY: Look here, Bono . . . I went down to see Hertzberger about some furniture. Got three rooms for two-ninety-eight. That what it say on the radio. "Three rooms . . . two-ninety-eight." Even made up a little song about it. Go down there . . . man tell me I can't get no credit. I'm working every day and can't get no credit. What to do? I got an empty house with some raggedy furniture in it. Cory ain't got no bed. He's sleeping on a pile of rags on the floor. Working every day and can't get no credit. Come back here—Rose'll tell you—madder than hell. Sit down . . . try to figure what I'm gonna do. Come a knock on the door. Ain't been living here but three days. Who know I'm here? Open the door . . . devil standing there bigger than life. White fellow . . . got on good clothes and everything. Standing there with a clipboard in his hand. I ain't had to say nothing. First words come out of his mouth was . . . "I understand you need some furniture and can't get no credit." I liked to fell over. He say, "I'll give you all the credit you want, but you got to pay the interest on it." I told him, "Give me three rooms worth and charge whatever you want." Next day a truck pulled up here and two men unloaded them three rooms. Man what drove the truck give me a book. Say send ten dollars, first of every month to the address in the book and everything will be all right. Say if I miss a payment the devil was coming back and it'll be hell to pay. That was fifteen years ago. To this day . . . the first of the month I send my ten dollars, Rose'll tell you.

ROSE: Troy lying.

TROY: I ain't never seen that man since. Now you tell me who else that could have been but the devil? I ain't sold my soul or nothing like that, you understand. Naw, I wouldn't have truck with the devil about nothing like that. I got my furniture and pays my ten dollars the first of the month just like clockwork.   120

BONO: How long you say you been paying this ten dollars a month?

TROY: Fifteen years!

BONO: Hell, ain't you finished paying for it yet? How much the man done charged you?

TROY: Ah hell, I done paid for it. I done paid for it ten times over! The fact is I'm scared to stop paying it.

ROSE: Troy lying. We got that furniture from Mr. Glickman. He ain't paying no ten dollars a month to nobody.   125

TROY: Aw hell, woman. Bono know I ain't that big a fool.

LYONS: I was just getting ready to say . . . I know where there's a bridge for sale.

TROY: Look here, I'll tell you this . . . it don't matter to me if he was the devil. It don't matter if the devil give credit. Somebody has got to give it.

ROSE: It ought to matter. You going around talking about having truck with the devil. . . . God's the one you gonna have to answer to. He's the one gonna be at the Judgment.

LYONS: Yeah, well, look here, Pop. . . . Let me have that ten dollars. I'll give it back to you. Bonnie got a job working at the hospital.   130

TROY: What I tell you, Bono? The only time I see this nigger is when he wants something. That's the only time I see him.

LYONS: Come on, Pop, Mr. Bono don't want to hear all that. Let me have the ten dollars. I told you Bonnie working.

TROY: What that mean to me? "Bonnie working." I don't care if she working. Go ask her for the ten dollars if she working. Talking about "Bonnie working." Why ain't you working?

LYONS: Aw, Pop, you know I can't find no decent job. Where am I gonna get a job at? You know I can't get no job.

135 TROY: I told you I know some people down there. I can get you on the rubbish if you want to work. I told you that the last time you came by here asking me for something.

LYONS: Naw, Pop . . . thanks. That ain't for me. I don't wanna be carrying nobody's rubbish. I don't wanna be punching nobody's time clock.

TROY: What's the matter, you too good to carry people's rubbish? Where you think that ten dollars you talking about come from? I'm just supposed to haul people's rubbish and give my money to you cause you too lazy to work. You too lazy to work and wanna know why you ain't got what I got.

ROSE: What hospital Bonnie working at? Mercy?

LYONS: She's down at Passavant° working in the laundry.

140 TROY: I ain't got nothing as it is. I give you that ten dollars and I got to eat beans the rest of the week. Naw . . . you ain't getting no ten dollars here.

LYONS: You ain't got to be eating no beans. I don't know why you wanna say that.

TROY: I ain't got no extra money. Gabe done moved over to Miss Pearl's paying her the rent and things done got tight around here. I can't afford to be giving you every payday.

LYONS: I ain't asked you to give me nothing. I asked you to loan me ten dollars. I know you got ten dollars.

TROY: Yeah, I got it. You know why I got it? 'Cause I don't throw my money away out there in the streets. You living the fast life . . . wanna be a musician . . . running around in them clubs and things . . . then, you learn to take care of yourself. You ain't gonna find me going and asking nobody for nothing. I done spent too many years without.

145 LYONS: You and me is two different people, Pop.

TROY: I done learned my mistake and learned to do what's right by it. You still trying to get something for nothing. Life don't owe you nothing. You owe it to yourself. Ask Bono. He'll tell you I'm right.

LYONS: You got your way of dealing with the world . . . I got mine. The only thing that matters to me is the music.

TROY: Yeah, I can see that! It don't matter how you gonna eat . . . where your next dollar is coming from. You telling the truth there.

LYONS: I know I got to eat. But I got to live too. I need something that gonna help me to get out of the bed in the morning. Make me feel like I belong in the world. I don't bother nobody. I just stay with the music cause that's the only way I can find to live in the world. Otherwise there ain't no telling what I might do. Now I don't come criticizing you and how you live. I just come by to ask you for ten dollars. I don't wanna hear all that about how I live.

150 TROY: Boy, your mamma did a hell of a job raising you.

LYONS: You can't change me, Pop. I'm thirty-four years old. If you wanted to change me, you should have been there when I was growing up. I come by to see you . . . ask for ten dollars and you want to talk about how I was raised. You don't know nothing about how I was raised.

ROSE: Let the boy have ten dollars, Troy.

TROY: [To LYONS.] What the hell you looking at me for? I ain't got no ten dollars. You know what I do with my money. [To ROSE.] Give him ten dollars if you want him to have it.

ROSE: I will. Just as soon as you turn it loose.

155 TROY: [handing ROSE the money.] There it is. Seventy-six dollars and forty-two cents. You see this, Bono? Now, I ain't gonna get but six of that back.

°139 *Passavant:* The University of Pittsburgh Medical Center Passavant, in Pittsburgh.

ROSE: You ought to stop telling that lie. Here, Lyons. [*She hands him the money.*]

LYONS: Thanks, Rose. Look . . . I got to run . . . I'll see you later.

TROY: Wait a minute. You gonna say, "Thanks, Rose" and ain't gonna look to see where she got that ten dollars from? See how they do me, Bono?

LYONS: I know she got it from you, Pop. Thanks. I'll give it back to you.

TROY: There he go telling another lie. Time I see that ten dollars . . . he'll be owing me   160
thirty more.

LYONS: See you, Mr. Bono.

BONO: Take care, Lyons!

LYONS: Thanks, Pop. I'll see you again. [*LYONS exits the yard.*]

TROY: I don't know why he don't go and get him a decent job and take care of that woman he got.

BONO: He'll be all right, Troy. The boy is still young.   165

TROY: The *boy* is thirty-four years old.

ROSE: Let's not get off into all that.

BONO: Look here . . . I got to be going. I got to be getting on. Lucille gonna be waiting.

TROY: [*puts his arm around* ROSE.] See this woman, Bono? I love this woman. I love this woman so much it hurts. I love her so much . . . I done run out of ways of loving her. So I got to go back to basics. Don't you come by my house Monday morning talking about time to go to work . . . 'cause I'm still gonna be stroking!

ROSE: Troy! Stop it now!   170

BONO: I ain't paying him no mind, Rose. That ain't nothing but gin-talk. Go on, Troy. I'll see you Monday.

TROY: Don't you come by my house, nigger! I done told you what I'm gonna be doing.

The lights go down to black.

ACT 1

Scene 2

The lights come up on ROSE *hanging up clothes. She hums and sings softly to herself. It is the following morning.*

ROSE: [*sings.*]

Jesus, be a fence all around me every day
Jesus, I want you to protect me as I travel on my way.
Jesus, be a fence all around me every day.
                    [*TROY enters from the house.*]
Jesus, I want you to protect me
As I travel on my way.

[*To* TROY.] Morning. You ready for breakfast? I can fix it soon as I finish hanging up these clothes.

TROY: I got the coffee on. That'll be all right. I'll just drink some of that this morning.

ROSE: That 651 hit yesterday. That's the second time this month. Miss Pearl hit for a dollar. . . . Seem like those that need the least always get lucky. Poor folks can't get nothing.

TROY: Them numbers don't know nobody. I don't know why you fool with them. You and Lyons both.

ROSE: It's something to do.   5

TROY: You ain't doing nothing but throwing your money away.

ROSE: Troy, you know I don't play foolishly. I just play a nickel here and a nickel there.

TROY: That's two nickels you done thrown away.

ROSE: Now I hit sometimes . . . that makes up for it. It always comes in handy when I do hit. I don't hear you complaining then.

10   TROY: I ain't complaining now. I just say it's foolish. Trying to guess out of six hundred ways which way the number gonna come. If I had all the money niggers, these Negroes, throw away on numbers for one week—just one week—I'd be a rich man.

ROSE: Well, you wishing and calling it foolish ain't gonna stop folks from playing numbers. That's one thing for sure. Besides . . . some good things come from playing numbers. Look where Pope done bought him that restaurant off of numbers.

TROY: I can't stand niggers like that. Man ain't had two dimes to rub together. He walking around with his shoes all run over bumming money for cigarettes. All right. Got lucky there and hit the numbers . . .

ROSE: Troy, I know all about it.

TROY: Had good sense, I'll say that for him. He ain't throwed his money away. I seen niggers hit the numbers and go through two thousand dollars in four days. Man bought him that restaurant down there . . . fixed it up real nice . . . and then didn't want nobody to come in it! A Negro go in there and can't get no kind of service. I seen a white fellow come in there and order a bowl of stew. Pope picked all the meat out of the pot for him. Man ain't had nothing but a bowl of meat! Negro come behind him and ain't got nothing but the potatoes and carrots. Talking about what numbers do for people, you picked a wrong example. Ain't done nothing but make a worser fool out of him than he was before.

15   ROSE: Troy, you ought to stop worrying about what happened at work yesterday.

TROY: I ain't worried. Just told me to be down there at the Commissioner's office on Friday. Everybody think they gonna fire me. I ain't worried about them firing me. You ain't got to worry about that. [*Pause.*] Where's Cory? Cory in the house? [*Calls.*] Cory?

ROSE: He gone out.

TROY: Out, huh? He gone out 'cause he know I want him to help me with this fence. I know how he is. That boy scared of work.

GABRIEL enters. He comes halfway down the alley and, hearing TROY's voice, stops.

TROY: [*continues.*] He ain't done a lick of work in his life.

20   ROSE: He had to go to football practice. Coach wanted them to get in a little extra practice before the season start.

TROY: I got his practice . . . running out of here before he get his chores done.

ROSE: Troy, what is wrong with you this morning? Don't nothing set right with you. Go on back in there and go to bed . . . get up on the other side.

TROY: Why something got to be wrong with me? I ain't said nothing wrong with me.

ROSE: You got something to say about everything. First it's the numbers . . . then it's the way the man runs his restaurant . . . then you done got on Cory. What's it gonna be next? Take a look up there and see if the weather suits you . . . or is it gonna be how you gonna put up the fence with the clothes hanging in the yard.

25   TROY: You hit the nail on the head then.

ROSE: I know you like I know the back of my hand. Go on in there and get you some coffee . . . see if that straighten you up. 'Cause you ain't right this morning.

TROY starts into the house and sees GABRIEL. GABRIEL starts singing. TROY's brother, he is seven years younger than TROY. Injured in World War II, he has a metal plate in his head. He carries an old trumpet tied around his waist and believes with every fiber of his being that he is the Archangel Gabriel. He carries a chipped basket with an assortment of discarded fruits and vegetables he has picked up in the strip district and which he attempts to sell.

GABRIEL: [*singing*].

> Yes, ma'am I got plums
> You ask me how I sell them
> Oh ten cents apiece
> Three for a quarter
> Come and buy now
> 'Cause I'm here today
> And tomorrow I'll be gone.

GABRIEL enters.

GABRIEL: Hey, Rose!

ROSE: How you doing Gabe?

GABRIEL: There's Troy . . . Hey, Troy!   30

TROY: Hey, Gabe. [*Exit into kitchen.*]

ROSE: [*to* GABRIEL.] What you got there?

GABRIEL: You know what I got, Rose. I got fruits and vegetables.

ROSE: [*looking in basket.*] Where's all these plums you talking about?

GABRIEL: I ain't got no plums today, Rose. I was just singing that. Have some tomorrow. Put   35
me in a big order for plums. Have enough plums tomorrow for St. Peter and everybody.

TROY reenters from kitchen, crosses to steps.

[*To* ROSE.] Troy's mad at me.

TROY: I ain't mad at you. What I got to be mad at you about? You ain't done nothing to me.

GABRIEL: I just moved over to Miss Pearl's to keep out from in your way. I ain't mean no
harm by it.

TROY: Who said anything about that? I ain't said anything about that.

GABRIEL: You ain't mad at me, is you?

TROY: Naw . . . I ain't mad at you, Gabe. If I was mad at you I'd tell you about it.   40

GABRIEL: Got me two rooms. In the basement. Got my own door too. Wanna see my key?
[*He holds up a key.*] That's my own key! My two rooms!

TROY: Well, that's good, Gabe. You got your own key . . . that's good.

ROSE: You hungry, Gabe? I was just fixing to cook Troy his breakfast.

GABRIEL: I'll take some biscuits. You got some biscuits? Did you know when I was in
heaven . . . every morning me and St. Peter would sit down by the gate and eat some
big fat biscuits? Oh, yeah! We had us a good time. We'd sit there and eat us them
biscuits and then St. Peter would go off to sleep and tell me to wake him up when it's
time to open the gates for the judgment.

ROSE: Well, come on . . . I'll make up a batch of biscuits.   45

ROSE exits into the house.

GABRIEL: Troy . . . St. Peter got your name in the book. I seen it. It say . . . Troy Maxson. I
say . . . I know him! He got the same name like what I got. That's my brother!

TROY: How many times you gonna tell me that, Gabe?

GABRIEL: Ain't got my name in the book. Don't have to have my name. I done died and
went to heaven. He got your name though. One morning St. Peter was looking at his
book . . . marking it up for the judgment . . . and he let me see your name. Got it in
there under M. Got Rose's name . . . I ain't seen it like I seen yours . . . but I know it's
in there. He got a great big book. Got everybody's name what was ever been born.
That's what he told me. But I seen your name. Seen it with my own eyes.

TROY: Go on in the house there. Rose going to fix you something to eat.

50 **GABRIEL:** Oh, I ain't hungry. I done had breakfast with Aunt Jemimah. She come by and cooked me up a whole mess of flapjacks. Remember how we used to eat them flapjacks?

TROY: Go on in the house and get you something to eat now.

GABRIEL: I got to sell my plums. I done sold some tomatoes. Got me two quarters. Wanna see? [*He shows* TROY *his quarters.*] I'm gonna save them and buy me a new horn so St. Peter can hear me when it's time to open the gates. [GABRIEL *stops suddenly. Listens.*] Hear that? That's the hellhounds. I got to chase them out of here. Go on get out of here! Get out!

[GABRIEL *exits singing.*]

Better get ready for the judgment
Better get ready for the judgment
My Lord is coming down

ROSE *enters from the house.*

TROY: He's gone off somewhere.

GABRIEL: [*offstage.*]

Better get ready for the judgment
Better get ready for the judgment morning
Better get ready for the judgment
My God is coming down

55 **ROSE:** He ain't eating right. Miss Pearl say she can't get him to eat nothing.

TROY: What you want me to do about it, Rose? I done did everything I can for the man. I can't make him get well. Man got half his head blown away . . . what you expect?

ROSE: Seem like something ought to be done to help him.

TROY: Man don't bother nobody. He just mixed up from that metal plate he got in his head. Ain't no sense for him to go back into the hospital.

ROSE: Least he be eating right. They can help him take care of himself.

60 **TROY:** Don't nobody wanna be locked up, Rose. What you wanna lock him up for? Man go over there and fight the war . . . messin' around with them Japs, get half his head blow off . . . and they give him a lousy three thousand dollars. And I had to swoop down on that.

ROSE: Is you fixing to go into that again?

TROY: That's the only way I got a roof over my head . . . cause of that metal plate.

ROSE: Ain't no sense you blaming yourself for nothing. Gabe wasn't in no condition to manage that money. You done what was right by him. Can't nobody say you ain't done what was right by him. Look how long you took care of him . . . till he wanted to have his own place and moved over there with Miss Pearl.

TROY: That ain't what I'm saying woman! I'm just stating the facts. If my brother didn't have that metal plate in his head . . . I wouldn't have a pot to piss in or a window to throw it out of. And I'm fifty-three years old. Now see if you can understand that!

TROY *gets up from the porch and starts to exit the yard.*

65 **ROSE:** Where you going off to? You been running out of here every Saturday for weeks. I thought you was gonna work on this fence?

TROY: I'm gonna walk down to Taylors'. Listen to the ball game. I'll be back in a bit. I'll work on it when I get back.

He exits the yard. The lights go to black.

ACT 1

Scene 3

The lights come up on the yard. It is four hours later. ROSE is taking down the clothes from the line. CORY enters carrying his football equipment.

ROSE: Your daddy like to had a fit with you running out of here this morning without doing your chores.

CORY: I told you I had to go to practice.

ROSE: He say you were supposed to help him with this fence.

CORY: He been saying that the last four or five Saturdays, and then he don't never do nothing, but go down to Taylors'. Did you tell him about the recruiter?

ROSE: Yeah, I told him.   5

CORY: What he say?

ROSE: He ain't said nothing too much. You get in there and get started on your chores before he gets back. Go on and scrub down them steps before he gets back here hollering and carrying on.

CORY: I'm hungry. What you got to eat, Mama?

ROSE: Go on and get started on your chores. I got some meat loaf in there. Go on and make you a sandwich . . . and don't leave no mess in there.

CORY exits into the house. ROSE continues to take down the clothes. TROY enters the yard and sneaks up and grabs her from behind.

Troy! Go on, now. You liked to scared me to death. What was the score of the game? Lucille had me on the phone and I couldn't keep up with it.

TROY: What I care about the game? Come here, woman. [*He tries to kiss her.*]   10

ROSE: I thought you went down Taylors' to listen to the game. Go on, Troy! You supposed to be putting up this fence.

TROY: [*attempting to kiss her again.*] I'll put it up when I finish with what is at hand.

ROSE: Go on, Troy. I ain't studying you.

TROY: [*chasing after her.*] I'm studying you . . . fixing to do my homework!

ROSE: Troy, you better leave me alone.   15

TROY: Where's Cory? That boy brought his butt home yet?

ROSE: He's in the house doing his chores.

TROY: [*calling.*] Cory! Get your butt out here, boy!

ROSE exits into the house with the laundry. TROY goes over to the pile of wood, picks up a board, and starts sawing. CORY enters from the house.

TROY: You just now coming in here from leaving this morning?

CORY: Yeah, I had to go to football practice.   20

TROY: Yeah, what?

CORY: Yessir.

TROY: I ain't but two seconds off you noway. The garbage sitting in there overflowing . . . you ain't done none of your chores . . . and you come in here talking about "Yeah."

CORY: I was just getting ready to do my chores now, Pop . . .

TROY: Your first chore is to help me with this fence on Saturday. Everything else come   25 after that. Now get that saw and cut them boards.

CORY takes the saw and begins cutting the boards. TROY continues working. There is a long pause.

CORY: Hey, Pop . . . why don't you buy a TV?

TROY: What I want with a TV? What I want one of them for?

CORY: Everybody got one. Earl, Ba Bra . . . Jesse!

TROY: I ain't asked you who had one. I say what I want with one?

30   **CORY:** So you can watch it. They got lots of things on TV. Baseball games and everything. We could watch the World Series.

TROY: Yeah . . . and how much this TV cost?

CORY: I don't know. They got them on sale for around two hundred dollars.

TROY: Two hundred dollars, huh?

CORY: That ain't that much, Pop.

35   **TROY:** Naw, it's just two hundred dollars. See that roof you got over your head at night? Let me tell you something about that roof. It's been over ten years since that roof was last tarred. See now . . . the snow come this winter and sit up there on that roof like it is . . . and it's gonna seep inside. It's just gonna be a little bit . . . ain't gonna hardly notice it. Then the next thing you know, it's gonna be leaking all over the house. Then the wood rot from all that water and you gonna need a whole new roof. Now, how much you think it cost to get that roof tarred?

CORY: I don't know.

TROY: Two hundred and sixty-four dollars . . . cash money. While you thinking about a TV, I got to be thinking about the roof . . . and whatever else go wrong here. Now if you had two hundred dollars, what would you do . . . fix the roof or buy a TV?

CORY: I'd buy a TV. Then when the roof started to leak . . . when it needed fixing . . . I'd fix it.

TROY: Where you gonna get the money from? You done spent it for a TV. You gonna sit up and watch the water run all over your brand new TV.

40   **CORY:** Aw, Pop. You got money. I know you do.

TROY: Where I got it at, huh?

CORY: You got it in the bank.

TROY: You wanna see my bankbook? You wanna see that seventy-three dollars and twenty-two cents I got sitting up in there?

CORY: You ain't got to pay for it all at one time. You can put a down payment on it and carry it on home with you.

45   **TROY:** Not me. I ain't gonna owe nobody nothing if I can help it. Miss a payment and they come and snatch it right out of your house. Then what you got? Now, soon as I get two hundred dollars clear, then I'll buy a TV. Right now, as soon as I get two hundred and sixty-four dollars, I'm gonna have this roof tarred.

CORY: Aw . . . Pop!

TROY: You go on and get you two hundred dollars and buy one if ya want it. I got better things to do with my money.

CORY: I can't get no two hundred dollars. I ain't never seen two hundred dollars.

TROY: I'll tell you what . . . you get you a hundred dollars and I'll put the other hundred with it.

50   **CORY:** All right, I'm gonna show you.

TROY: You gonna show me how you can cut them boards right now.

CORY *begins to cut the boards. There is a long pause.*

CORY: The Pirates won today. That makes five in a row.

TROY: I ain't thinking about the Pirates. Got an all-white team. Got that boy . . . that Puerto Rican boy . . . Clemente.° Don't even half-play him. That boy could be something if they give him a chance. Play him one day and sit him on the bench the next.

°53 *Clemente:* Roberto Clemente (1934–1972), one of the all-time best right fielders, played 18 seasons for the Pittsburgh Pirates. In 1957 he was still relatively new, and did not play full time, though Cory is correct in claiming that he was getting "lots of chances to play." Clemente eventually got 3,000 hits, and his lifetime average was .317. He was killed in a plane crash in December 1972.

CORY: He gets a lot of chances to play.

TROY: I'm talking about playing regular. Playing every day so you can get your timing. 55
That's what I'm talking about.

CORY: They got some white guys on the team that don't play every day. You can't play everybody at the same time.

TROY: If they got a white fellow sitting on the bench . . . you can bet your last dollar he can't play! That colored guy got to be twice as good before he get on the team. That's why I don't want you to get all tied up in them sports. Man on the team and what it get him? They got colored on the team and don't use them. Same as not having them. All them teams the same.

CORY: The Braves got Hank Aaron and Wes Covington.° Hank Aaron hit two home runs today. That makes forty-three.

TROY: Hank Aaron ain't nobody. That what you supposed to do. That's how you supposed to play the game. Ain't nothing to it. It's just a matter of timing . . . getting the right follow-through. Hell, I can hit forty-three home runs right now!

CORY: Not off no major-league pitching, you couldn't. 60

TROY: We had better pitching in the Negro leagues. I hit seven home runs off of Satchel Paige.° You can't get no better than that!

CORY: Sandy Koufax.° He's leading the league in strikeouts.

TROY: I ain't thinking of no Sandy Koufax.

CORY: You got Warren Spahn and Lew Burdette.° I bet you couldn't hit no home runs off of Warren Spahn.

TROY: I'm through with it now. You go on and cut them boards. [*Pause.*] Your mama tell 65
me you done got recruited by a college football team? Is that right?

CORY: Yeah. Coach Zellman say the recruiter gonna be coming by to talk to you. Get you to sign the permission papers.

TROY: I thought you supposed to be working down there at the A&P. Ain't you suppose to be working down there after school?

CORY: Mr. Stawicki say he gonna hold my job for me until after the football season. Say starting next week I can work weekends.

TROY: I thought we had an understanding about this football stuff? You suppose to keep up with your chores and hold that job down at the A&P. Ain't been around here all day on a Saturday. Ain't none of your chores done . . . and now you telling me you done quit your job.

CORY: I'm going to be working weekends. 70

TROY: You damn right you are! And ain't no need for nobody coming around here to talk to me about signing nothing.

CORY: Hey, Pop . . . you can't do that. He's coming all the way from North Carolina.

°58 *Hank Aaron and Wes Covington:* Both were relatively new players for the Milwaukee Braves in 1957. Aaron (b. 1934) played for the Braves for 18 seasons, and at his retirement in 1976 he was the all-time career home run champion, with 755. Covington's career was not illustrious, lasting only 10 years. °61 *Satchel Paige:* Leroy Robert (Satchel) Paige (1906–1982) was a legendary pitcher in the Negro Leagues for more than 20 years, and he ultimately was inducted into Baseball's Hall of Fame. He joined the Cleveland Indians in 1948 when he was already in his forties. His major league career was consequently not outstanding, though baseball fans were enthusiastic about him whenever he pitched. During the year 1957, Paige was involved in exhibition games. His last game as a pitcher took place in 1966, when he was 60 years old. He has been considered one of the all-time best pitchers. °62 *Sandy Koufax:* Sandy Koufax (b. 1935), was in his third professional year in 1957, with the Brooklyn Dodgers. His best years were yet to come, in the 1960s, after the Dodgers moved to Los Angeles. °64 *Warren Spahn and Lew Burdette:* Both Spahn (1921–2003) and Burdette (1926–2007) were stalwart pitchers for the Milwaukee Braves during the 1950s. Spahn won 21 games in 1957, and won the Cy Young Award. He still holds the record for the greatest number of wins by a left-handed pitcher (363). Burdette won 17 games that year, and won three games in the World Series against the Yankees.

TROY: I don't care where he coming from. The white man ain't gonna let you get nowhere with that football noway. You go on and get your book-learning so you can work yourself up in that A&P or learn how to fix cars or build houses or something, get you a trade. That way you have something can't nobody take away from you. You go on and learn how to put your hands to some good use. Besides hauling people's garbage.

CORY: I get good grades, Pop. That's why the recruiter wants to talk with you. You got to keep up your grades to get recruited. This way I'll be going to college. I'll get a chance . . .

75 **TROY:** First you gonna get your butt down there to the A&P and get your job back.

CORY: Mr. Stawicki done already hired somebody else 'cause I told him I was playing football.

TROY: You a bigger fool than I thought . . . to let somebody take away your job so you can play some football. Where you gonna get your money to take out your girlfriend and whatnot? What kind of foolishness is that to let somebody take away your job?

CORY: I'm still gonna be working weekends.

TROY: Naw . . . naw. You getting your butt out of here and finding you another job.

80 **CORY:** Come on, Pop! I got to practice. I can't work after school and play football too. The team needs me. That's what Coach Zellman say . . .

TROY: I don't care what nobody else say. I'm the boss . . . you understand? I'm the boss around here. I do the only saying what counts.

CORY: Come on, Pop!

TROY: I asked you . . . did you understand?

CORY: Yeah . . .

85 **TROY:** What?!

CORY: Yessir.

TROY: You go on down there to that A&P and see if you can get your job back. If you can't do both . . . then you quit the football team. You've got to take the crookeds with the straights.

CORY: Yessir. [*Pause.*] Can I ask you a question?

TROY: What the hell you wanna ask me? Mr. Stawicki the one you got the questions for.

90 **CORY:** How come you ain't never liked me?

TROY: Liked you? Who the hell say I got to like you? What law is there say I got to like you? Wanna stand up in my face and ask a damn fool-ass question like that. Talking about liking somebody. Come here, boy, when I talk to you.

CORY comes over to where TROY is working. He stands slouched over and TROY shoves him on his shoulder.

Straighten up, goddammit! I asked you a question . . . what law is there say I got to like you?

CORY: None.

TROY: Well, all right then! Don't you eat every day? [*Pause.*] Answer me when I talk to you! Don't you eat every day?

CORY: Yeah.

95 **TROY:** Nigger, as long as you in my house, you put that sir on the end of it when you talk to me.

CORY: Yes . . . sir.

TROY: You eat every day.

CORY: Yessir!

TROY: Got a roof over your head.

100 **CORY:** Yessir!

TROY: Got clothes on your back.

CORY: Yessir.

TROY: Why you think that is?

CORY: 'Cause of you.

TROY: Ah, hell I know it's 'cause of me . . . but why do you think that is?   105

CORY: [*hesitant.*] 'Cause you like me.

TROY: Like you? I go out of here every morning . . . bust my butt . . . putting up with them crackers every day . . . 'cause I like you? You are the biggest fool I ever saw. [*Pause.*] It's my job. It's my responsibility! You understand that? A man got to take care of his family. You live in my house . . . sleep you behind on my bedclothes . . . fill you belly up with my food . . . cause you my son. You my flesh and blood. Not 'cause I like you! 'Cause it's my duty to take care of you. I owe a responsibility to you! Let's get this straight right here . . . before it go along any further . . . I ain't got to like you. Mr. Rand don't give me my money come payday 'cause he likes me. He gives me 'cause he owe me. I done give you everything I had to give you. I gave you your life! Me and your mama worked that out between us. And liking your black ass wasn't part of the bargain. Don't you try and go through life worrying about if somebody like you or not. You best be making sure they doing right by you. You understand what I'm saying boy?

CORY: Yes sir.

TROY: Then get the hell out of my face, and get on down to that A&P.

ROSE has been standing behind the screen door for much of the scene. She enters as CORY exits.

ROSE: Why don't you let the boy go ahead and play football, Troy? Ain't no harm in that.   110
He's just trying to be like you with the sports.

TROY: I don't want him to be like me! I want him to move as far away from my life as he can get. You the only decent thing that ever happened to me. I wish him that. But I don't wish him a thing else from my life. I decided seventeen years ago that boy wasn't getting involved in no sports. Not after what they did to me in the sports.

ROSE: Troy, why don't you admit you was too old to play in the major leagues? For once . . . why don't you admit that?

TROY: What do you mean too old? Don't come telling me I was too old. I just wasn't the right color. Hell, I'm fifty-three years old and can do better than Selkirk's .269 right now!

ROSE: How's was you gonna play ball when you were over forty? Sometimes I can't get no sense out of you.

TROY: I got good sense, woman. I got sense enough not to let my boy get hurt over playing   115
no sports. You been mothering that boy too much. Worried about if people like him.

ROSE: Everything that boy do . . . he do for you. He wants you to say "Good job, son." That's all.

TROY: Rose, I ain't got time for that. He's alive. He's healthy. He's got to make his own way. I made mine. Ain't nobody gonna hold his hand when he get out there in that world.

ROSE: Times have changed from when you was young, Troy. People change. The world's changing around you and you can't even see it.

TROY: [*slow, methodical.*] Woman . . . I do the best I can do. I come in here every Friday. I carry a sack of potatoes and a bucket of lard. You all line up at the door with your hands out. I give you the lint from my pockets. I give you my sweat and my blood. I ain't got no tears. I done spent them. We go upstairs in that room at night . . . and I fall down on you and try to blast a hole into forever. I get up Monday morning . . . find my lunch on the table. I go out. Make my way. Find my strength to carry me through to the next Friday. [*Pause.*] That's all I got, Rose. That's all I got to give. I can't give nothing else.

TROY exits into the house. The lights go down to black.

ACT 1

Scene 4

It is Friday. Two weeks later. CORY *starts out of the house with his football equipment. The phone rings.*

CORY: [*calling.*] I got it! [*He answers the phone and stands in the screen door talking.*] Hello? Hey, Jesse. Naw . . . I was just getting ready to leave now.

ROSE: [*calling.*] Cory!

CORY: I told you, man, them spikes is all tore up. You can use them if you want, but they ain't no good. Earl got some spikes.

ROSE: [*calling.*] Cory!

5   CORY: [*calling to* ROSE.] Mam? I'm talking to Jesse. [*into phone.*] When she say that? [*Pause.*] Aw, you lying, man. I'm gonna tell her you said that.

ROSE: [*calling.*] Cory, don't you go nowhere!

CORY: I got to go to the game, Ma! [*into the phone.*] Yeah, hey, look, I'll talk to you later. Yeah, I'll meet you over Earl's house. Later. Bye, Ma.

CORY *exits the house and starts out the yard.*

ROSE: Cory, where you going off to? You got that stuff all pulled out and thrown all over your room.

CORY: [*in the yard.*] I was looking for my spikes. Jesse wanted to borrow my spikes.

10   ROSE: Get up there and get that cleaned up before your daddy get back in here.

CORY: I got to go to the game! I'll clean it up *when I get back.* [CORY *exits.*]

ROSE: That's all he need to do is see that room all messed up.

ROSE *exits into the house.* TROY *and* BONO *enter the yard.* TROY *is dressed in clothes other than his work clothes.*

BONO: He told him the same thing he told you. Take it to the union.

TROY: Brownie ain't got that much sense. Man wasn't thinking about nothing. He wait until I confront them on it . . . then he wanna come crying seniority. [*calls.*] Hey, Rose!

15   BONO: I wish I could have seen Mr. Rand's face when he told you.

TROY: He couldn't get it out of his mouth! Liked to bit his tongue! When they called me down there to the Commissioner's office . . . he thought they was gonna fire me. Like everybody else.

BONO: I didn't think they was gonna fire you. I thought they was gonna put you on the warning paper.

TROY: Hey, Rose! [*To* BONO.] Yeah, Mr. Rand like to bit his tongue.

TROY *breaks the seal on the bottle, takes a drink, and hands it to* BONO.

BONO: I see you run right down to Taylors' and told that Alberta gal.

20   TROY: [*calling.*] Hey Rose! [*To* BONO.] I told everybody. Hey, Rose! I went down there to cash my check.

ROSE: [*entering from the house.*] Hush all that hollering, man! I know you out here. What they say down there at the Commissioner's office?

TROY: You supposed to come when I call you, woman. Bono'll tell you that. [*To* BONO.] Don't Lucille come when you call her?

ROSE: Man, hush your mouth. I ain't no dog . . . talk about "come when you call me."

TROY: [*puts his arm around* ROSE.] You hear this, Bono? I had me an old dog used to get up-pity like that. You say, "C'mere, Blue!" . . . and he just lay there and look at you. End up getting a stick and chasing him away trying to make him come.

25   ROSE: I ain't studying you and your dog. I remember you used to sing that old song.

James Earl Jones (as Troy Maxson) sitting on a porch surrounded from left to right by Charles Brown (as Lyons), Mary Alice (as Rose), and Ray Aranha (as Jim Bono) in a 1987 stage production of *Fences* directed by Lloyd Richards at the 46th Street Theater in New York City.

TROY: [*he sings.*]
> Hear it ring! Hear it ring!
> I had a dog his name was Blue.

ROSE: Don't nobody wanna hear you sing that old song.
TROY: [*sings*]. You know Blue was mighty true.
ROSE: Used to have Cory running around here singing that song.
BONO: Hell, I remember that song myself.   30
TROY: [*sings.*]
> You know Blue was a good old dog
> Blue treed a possum in a hollow log.

That was my daddy's song. My daddy made up that song.
ROSE: I don't care who made it up. Don't nobody wanna hear you sing it.
TROY: [*makes a song like calling a dog.*] Come here, woman.
ROSE: You come in here carrying on, I reckon they ain't fired you. What they say down there at the Commissioner's office?
TROY: Look here, Rose. . . . Mr. Rand called me into his office today when I got back from   35
talking to them people down there . . . it come from up top . . . he called me in and told me they was making me a driver.
ROSE: Troy, you kidding!
TROY: No I ain't. Ask Bono.
ROSE: Well, that's great, Troy. Now you don't have to hassle them people no more.

LYONS enters from the street.

TROY: Aw hell, I wasn't looking to see you today. I thought you was in jail. Got it all over the front page of the *Courier* about them raiding Sefus's place . . . where you be hanging out with all them thugs.

40 **LYONS:** Hey, Pop . . . that ain't got nothing to do with me. I don't go down there gambling. I go down there to sit in with the band. I ain't got nothing to do with the gambling part. They got some good music down there.

TROY: They got some rogues . . . is what they got.

LYONS: How you been, Mr. Bono? Hi, Rose.

BONO: I see where you playing down at the Crawford Grill tonight.

ROSE: How come you ain't brought Bonnie like I told you? You should have brought Bonnie with you, she ain't been over in a month of Sundays.

45 **LYONS:** I was just in the neighborhood . . . thought I'd stop by.

TROY: Here he come . . .

BONO: Your daddy got a promotion on the rubbish. He's gonna be the first colored driver. Ain't got to do nothing but sit up there and read the paper like them white fellows.

LYONS: Hey, Pop . . . if you knew how to read you'd be all right.

BONO: Naw . . . naw . . . you mean if the nigger knew how to drive he'd be all right. Been fighting with them people about driving and ain't even got a license. Mr. Rand know you ain't got no driver's license?

50 **TROY:** Driving ain't nothing. All you do is point the truck where you want it to go. Driving ain't nothing.

BONO: Do Mr. Rand know you ain't got no driver's license? That's what I'm talking about. I ain't asked if driving was easy. I asked if Mr. Rand know you ain't got no driver's license.

TROY: He ain't got to know. The man ain't got to know my business. Time he find out, I have two or three driver's licenses.

LYONS: [*going into his pocket.*] Say, look here, Pop . . .

TROY: I knew it was coming. Didn't I tell you, Bono? I know what kind of "Look here, Pop" that was. The nigger fixing to ask me for some money. It's Friday night. It's my payday. All them rogues down there on the avenue . . . the ones that ain't in jail . . . and Lyons is hopping in his shoes to get down there with them.

55 **LYONS:** See, Pop . . . if you give somebody else a chance to talk sometimes, you'd see that I was fixing to pay you back your ten dollars like I told you. Here . . . I told you I'd pay you when Bonnie got paid.

TROY: Naw . . . you go ahead and keep that ten dollars. Put it in the bank. The next time you feel like you wanna come by here and ask me for something . . . you go on down there and get that.

LYONS: Here's your ten dollars, Pop. I told you I don't want you to give me nothing. I just wanted to borrow ten dollars.

TROY: Naw . . . you go on and keep that for the next time you want to ask me.

LYONS: Come on, Pop . . . here go your ten dollars.

60 **ROSE:** Why don't you go on and let the boy pay you back, Troy?

LYONS: Here you go, Rose. If you don't take it I'm gonna have to hear about it for the next six months. [*He hands her the money.*]

ROSE: You can hand yours over here too, Troy.

TROY: You see this, Bono. You see how they do me.

BONO: Yeah, Lucille do me the same way.

GABRIEL is heard singing off stage. He enters.

65 **GABRIEL:** Better get ready for the Judgment! Better get ready for . . . Hey! . . . Hey! . . . There's Troy's boy!

LYONS: How are you doing, Uncle Gabe?

GABRIEL: Lyons . . . The King of the Jungle! Rose . . . hey, Rose. Got a flower for you. [*He takes a rose from his pocket.*] Picked it myself. That's the same rose like you is!

ROSE: That's right nice of you, Gabe.

LYONS: What you been doing, Uncle Gabe?

GABRIEL: Oh, I been chasing hellhounds and waiting on the time to tell St. Peter to open   70
the gates.

LYONS: You been chasing hellhounds, huh? Well . . . you doing the right thing, Uncle
Gabe. Somebody got to chase them.

GABRIEL: Oh, yeah . . . I know it. The devil's strong. The devil ain't no pushover. Hellhounds
snipping at everybody's heels. But I got my trumpet waiting on the Judgment time.

LYONS: Waiting on the Battle of Armageddon, huh?

GABRIEL: Ain't gonna be too much of a battle when God get to waving that Judgment
sword. But the people's gonna have a hell of a time trying to get into heaven if them
gates ain't open.

LYONS: [*putting his arm around GABRIEL.*] You hear this, Pop. Uncle Gabe, you all right!   75

GABRIEL: [*laughing with LYONS.*] Lyons! King of the Jungle.

ROSE: You gonna stay for supper, Gabe? Want me to fix you a plate?

GABRIEL: I'll take a sandwich, Rose. Don't want no plate. Just wanna eat with my hands.
I'll take a sandwich.

ROSE: How about you, Lyons? You staying? Got some short ribs cooking.

LYONS: Naw, I won't eat nothing till after we finished playing. [*Pause.*] You ought to come   80
down and listen to me play, Pop.

TROY: I don't like that Chinese music. All that noise.

ROSE: Go on in the house and wash up, Gabe . . . I'll fix you a sandwich.

GABRIEL: [*to LYONS, as he exits.*] Troy's mad at me.

LYONS: What you mad at Uncle Gabe for, Pop?

ROSE: He thinks Troy's mad at him 'cause he moved over to Miss Pearl's.   85

TROY: I ain't mad at the man. He can live where he want to live at.

LYONS: What he move over there for? Miss Pearl don't like nobody.

ROSE: She don't mind him none. She treats him real nice. She just don't allow all that singing.

TROY: She don't mind that rent he be paying . . . That's what she don't mind.

ROSE: Troy, I ain't going through that with you no more. He's over there cause he want to   90
have his own place. He can come and go as he please.

TROY: Hell, he could come and go as he please here. I wasn't stopping him. I ain't put no
rules on him.

ROSE: It ain't the same thing, Troy. And you know it. [*GABRIEL comes to the door.*] Now,
that's the last I wanna hear about that. I don't wanna hear nothing else about Gabe
and Miss Pearl. And next week . . .

GABRIEL: I'm ready for my sandwich, Rose.

ROSE: And next week . . . when that recruiter come from that school . . . I want you to sign
that paper and go on and let Cory play football. Then that'll be the last I have to hear
about that.

TROY: [*to ROSE as she exits in to the house.*] I ain't thinking about Cory nothing.   95

LYONS: What . . . Cory got recruited? What school he going to?

TROY: That boy walking around here smelling his piss . . . thinking he's grown. Thinking
he's gonna do what he want, irrespective of what I say. Look here, Bono . . . I left the
Commissioner's office and went down to the A&P . . . that boy ain't working down
there. He lying to me. Telling me he got his job back . . . telling me he working weekends . . . telling me he working after school . . . . Mr. Stawicki tell me he ain't working
down there at all!

LYONS: Cory just growing up. He's just busting at the seams trying to fill out your shoes.

TROY: I don't care what he's doing. When he get to the point where he wanna disobey me . . . then it's time for him to move on. Bono'll tell you that. I bet he ain't never disobeyed his daddy without paying the consequences.

100   **BONO:** I ain't never had a chance. My daddy came on through . . . but I ain't never knew him to see him . . . or what he had on his mind or where he went. Just moving on through. Searching out the New Land. That's what the old folks used to call it. See a fellow moving around from place to place . . . woman to woman . . . called it searching out the New Land. I can't say if he ever found it. I come along, didn't want no kids. Didn't know if I was gonna be in one place long enough to fix on them right as their daddy. I figured I was going searching too. As it turned out I been hooked up with Lucille near about as long as your daddy been with Rose. Going on sixteen years.

TROY: Sometimes I wish I hadn't known my daddy. He ain't cared nothing about no kids. A kid to him wasn't nothing. All he wanted was for you to learn how to walk so he could start you to working. When it come time for eating . . . he ate first. If there was anything left over, that's what you got. Man would sit down and eat two chickens and give you the wing.

LYONS: You ought to stop that, Pop. Everybody feed their kids. No matter how hard times is . . . everybody care about their kids. Make sure they have something to eat.

TROY: The only thing my daddy cared about was getting them bales of cotton in to Mr. Lubin. That's the only thing that mattered to him. Sometimes I used to wonder why he was living. Wonder why the devil hadn't come and got him. "Get them bales of cotton in to Mr. Lubin" and find out he owe him money . . .

LYONS: He should have just went on and left when he saw he couldn't get nowhere. That's what I would have done.

105   **TROY:** How he gonna leave with eleven kids? And where he gonna go? He ain't knew how to do nothing but farm. No, he was trapped and I think he knew it. But I'll say this for him . . . he felt a responsibility toward us. Maybe he ain't treated us the way I felt he should have . . . but without that responsibility he could have walked off and left us . . . made his own way.

BONO: A lot of them did. Back in those days what you talking about . . . they walk out their front door and just take on down one road or another and keep on walking.

LYONS: There you go! That's what I'm talking about.

BONO: Just keep on walking till you come to something else. Ain't you never heard of nobody having the walking blues? Well, that's what you call it when you just take off like that.

TROY: My daddy ain't had them walking blues! What you talking about? He stayed right there with his family. But he was just as evil as he could be. My mama couldn't stand him. Couldn't stand that evilness. She run off when I was about eight. She sneaked off one night after he had gone to sleep. Told me she was coming back for me. I ain't never seen her no more. All his women run off and left him. He wasn't good for nobody. When my turn come to head out, I was fourteen and got to sniffing around Joe Canewell's daughter. Had us an old mule we called Greyboy. My daddy sent me out to do some plowing and I tied up Greyboy and went to fooling around with Joe Canewell's daughter. We done found us a nice little spot, got real cozy with each other. She about thirteen and we done figured we was grown anyway . . . so we down there enjoying ourselves . . . ain't thinking about nothing. We didn't know Greyboy had got loose and wandered back to the house and my daddy was looking for me. We down there by the creek enjoying ourselves when my daddy come up on us. Surprised us. He had them leather straps off the mule and commenced to whupping me like there was no tomorrow. I jumped up, mad and embarrassed. I was scared of my daddy. When he commenced to whupping on me . . . quite naturally I run to get out of the way. [*Pause.*] Now I thought he was mad 'cause I ain't done my work. But I see where he was chasing me off so he could have the gal for himself. When I see what the matter of it was, I lost all fear of my daddy. Right there is where I become a man . . . at fourteen years of age. [*Pause.*] Now it was my turn to run him off. I picked up them same reins that he had used on me. I picked up them reins and commenced to whupping on him. The gal jumped up and run him off . . . and when my daddy turned to face me, I could see why the devil had never come to get him . . . 'cause he was the devil himself. I don't know what happened. When I woke up, I was laying right there by the creek, and Blue . . . this old dog we had . . . was licking my face. I thought I was blind. I couldn't see nothing. Both my eyes were swollen shut. I laid there and cried. I didn't know what I was gonna do. The only thing I knew was the time had come for me to leave my daddy's house. And right there the world suddenly got big. And it was a long time before I could cut it down to where I could handle it. Part of that cutting down was when I got to the place where I could feel him kicking in my blood and knew that the only thing that separated us was the matter of a few years.

GABRIEL enters from the house with a sandwich.

LYONS: What you got there, Uncle Gabe?   110
GABRIEL: Got me a ham sandwich. Rose gave me a ham sandwich.
TROY: I don't know what happened to him. I done lost touch with everybody except Gabriel. But I hope he's dead. I hope he found some peace.
LYONS: That's a heavy story, Pop. I didn't know you left home when you was fourteen.
TROY: And didn't know nothing. The only part of the world I knew was the forty-two acres of Mr. Lubin's land. That's all I knew about life.
LYONS: Fourteen's kinda young to be out on your own. [*Phone rings.*] I don't even think I   115
was ready to be out on my own at fourteen. I don't know what I would have done.
TROY: I got up from the creek and walked on down to Mobile. I was through with farming. Figured I could do better in the city. So I walked the two hundred miles to Mobile.
LYONS: Wait a minute . . . you ain't walked no two hundred miles, Pop. Ain't nobody gonna walk no two hundred miles. You talking about some walking there.
BONO: That's the only way you got anywhere back in them days.
LYONS: Shhh. Damn if I wouldn't have hitched a ride with someday!
TROY: Who you gonna hitch it with? They ain't had no cars and things like they got now.   120
We talking about 1918.
ROSE: [*entering.*] What you all out here getting into?
TROY: [*to ROSE.*] I'm telling Lyons how good he got it. He don't know nothing about this I'm talking.
ROSE: Lyons, that was Bonnie on the phone. She say you supposed to pick her up.
LYONS: Yeah, okay Rose.
TROY: I walked on down to Mobile and hitched up with some of them fellows that was   125
heading this way. Got up here and found out . . . not only couldn't you get a job . . . you couldn't find no place to live. I thought I was in freedom. Shhh. Colored folks living down there on the river banks in whatever kind of shelter they could find for themselves. Right down there under the Brady Street Bridge. Living in shacks made of sticks and tarpaper. Messed around there and went from bad to worse. Started stealing. First it was food. Then I figured, hell, if I steal money I can buy me some food. Buy me some shoes too! One thing led to another. Met your mama. I was young and anxious to be a man. Met your mama and had you. What I do that for? Now I got to worry about feeding you and her. Got to steal three times as much. Went out one

day looking for somebody to rob . . . that's what I was, a robber. I'll tell you the truth. I'm ashamed of it today. But it's the truth. Went to rob this fellow . . . pulled out my knife . . . and he pulled out a gun. Shot me in the chest. I felt just like somebody had taken a hot branding iron and laid it on me. When he shot me I jumped at him with my knife. They told me I killed him and they put me in the penitentiary and locked me up for fifteen years. That's where I met Bono. That's where I learned how to play baseball. Got out that place and your mama had taken you and went on to make life without me. Fifteen years was a long time for her to wait. But that fifteen years cured me of that robbing stuff. Rose'll tell you. She asked me when I met her if I had gotten all that foolishness out of my system. And I told her, "Baby, it's you and baseball all what count with me." You hear me, Bono? I meant it too. She say, "Which one comes first?" I told her, "Baby, ain't no doubt it's baseball . . . but you stick and get old with me and we'll both outlive this baseball." Am I right, Rose? And it's true.

ROSE: Man, hush your mouth. You ain't said no such thing. Talking about, "Baby you know you'll always be number one with me." That's what you was talking.

TROY: You hear that, Bono. That's why I love her.

BONO: Rose'll keep you straight. You get off the track, she'll straighten you up.

ROSE: Lyons, you better get on up and get Bonnie. She waiting on you.

130 LYONS: [*gets up to go.*] Hey, Pop, why don't you come on down to the Grill and hear me play?

TROY: I ain't going down there. I'm too old to be sitting around in them clubs.

BONO: You got to be good to play down at the Grill.

LYONS: Come on, Pop . . .

TROY: I got to get up in the morning.

135 LYONS: You ain't got to stay long.

TROY: Naw, I'm gonna get my supper and go on to bed.

LYONS: Well, I got to go. I'll see you again.

TROY: Don't you come around my house on my payday.

ROSE: Pick up the phone and let somebody know you coming. And bring Bonnie with you. You know I'm always glad to see her.

140 LYONS: Yeah, I'll do that, Rose. You take care now. See you, Pop. See you, Mr. Bono. See you, Uncle Gabe.

GABRIEL: Lyons! King of the Jungle! [*LYONS exits.*]

TROY: Is supper ready, woman? Me and you got some business to take care of. I'm gonna tear it up too.

ROSE: Troy, I done told you now!

TROY: [*puts his arm around BONO.*] Aw hell, woman . . . this is Bono. Bono like family. I done known this nigger since . . . how long I done know you?

145 BONO: It's been a long time.

TROY: I done know this nigger since Skippy was a pup. Me and him done been through some times.

BONO: You sure right about that.

TROY: Hell, I done know him longer than I known you. And we still standing shoulder to shoulder. Hey look here, Bono . . . a man can't ask for no more than that. [*drinks to him.*] I love you, nigger.

BONO: Hell, I love you too . . . I got to get home see my woman. You got yours in hand. I got to get mine.

BONO starts to exit as CORY enters the yard, dressed in his football uniform. He gives TROY a hard, uncompromising look.

150 CORY: What you do that for, Pop?

He throws his helmet down in the direction of TROY.

ROSE: What's the matter? Cory . . . What's the matter?

CORY: Papa done went up to the school and told Coach Zellman I can't play football no
more. Wouldn't even let me play the game. Told him to tell the recruiter not to come.

ROSE: Troy . . .

TROY: What you Troying me for. Yeah, I did it. And the boy know why I did it.

CORY: Why you wanna do that to me? That was the one chance I had.   155

ROSE: Ain't nothing wrong with Cory playing football, Troy.

TROY: The boy lied to me. I told the nigger if he wanna play football . . . to keep up his
chores and hold down that job at the A&P. That was the conditions. Stopped down
there to see Mr. Stawicki . . .

CORY: I can't work after school during the football season, Pop! I tried to tell you that Mr.
Stawicki's holding my job for me. You don't never want to listen to nobody. And then
you wanna go and do this to me!

TROY: I ain't done nothing to you. You done it to yourself.

CORY: Just cause you didn't have a chance! You just scared I'm gonna be better than you,   160
that's all.

TROY: Come here.

ROSE: Troy . . .

CORY *reluctantly crosses over to* TROY.

TROY: All right! See. You done made a mistake.

CORY: I didn't even do nothing!

TROY: I'm gonna tell you what your mistake was. See . . . you swung at the ball and didn't   165
hit it. That's strike one. See, you in the batter's box now. You swung and you missed.
That's strike one. Don't you strike out!

Lights fade to black.

ACT 2

Scene 1

The following morning. CORY *is at the tree hitting the ball with the bat. He tries to mimic* TROY, *but
his swing is awkward, less sure.* ROSE *enters from the house.*

ROSE: Cory, I want you to help me with this cupboard.

CORY: I ain't quitting the team. I don't care what Poppa say.

ROSE: I'll talk to him when he gets back. He had to go see about your Uncle Gabe. The police done arrested him. Say he was disturbing the peace. He'll be back directly. Come
on in here and help me clean out the top of this cupboard.

CORY *exits into the house.* ROSE *sees* TROY *and* BONO *coming down the alley.*

Troy. . . what they say down there?

TROY: Ain't said nothing. I give them fifty dollars and they let him go. I'll talk to you
about it. Where's Cory?

ROSE: He's in there helping me clean out these cupboards.   5

TROY: Tell him to get his butt out here.

TROY and BONO go over to the pile of wood. BONO picks up the saw and begins sawing.

TROY: [*to BONO.*] All they want is the money. That makes six or seven times I done went down there and got him. See me coming they stick out their hands.

BONO: Yeah. I know what you mean. That's all they care about . . . that money. They don't care about what's right. [*Pause.*] Nigger, why you got to go and get some hard wood? You ain't doing nothing but building a little old fence. Get you some soft pine wood. That's all you need.

TROY: I know what I'm doing. This is outside wood. You put pine wood inside the house. Pine wood is inside wood. This here is outside wood. Now you tell me where the fence is gonna be?

10   **BONO:** You don't need this wood. You can put it up with pine wood and it'll stand as long as you gonna be here looking at it.

TROY: How you know how long I'm gonna be here, nigger? Hell, I might just live forever. Live longer than old man Horsely.

BONO: That's what Magee used to say.

TROY: Magee's a damn fool. Now you tell me who you ever heard of gonna pull their own teeth with a pair of rusty pliers.

BONO: The old folks . . . my granddaddy used to pull his teeth with pliers. They ain't had no dentists for the colored folks back then.

15   **TROY:** Get clean pliers! You understand? Clean pliers! Sterilize them! Besides we ain't living back then. All Magee had to do was walk over to Doc Goldblum's.

BONO: I see where you and that Tallahassee gal . . . that Alberta . . . I see where you all done got tight.

TROY: What you mean "got tight"?

BONO: I see where you be laughing and joking with her all the time.

TROY: I laughs and jokes with all of them, Bono. You know me.

20   **BONO:** That ain't the kind of laughing and joking I'm talking about.

CORY enters from the house.

CORY: How you doing, Mr. Bono?

TROY: Cory? Get that saw from Bono and cut some wood. He talking about the wood's too hard to cut. Stand back there, Jim, and let that young boy show you how it's done.

BONO: He's sure welcome to it. [*CORY takes the saw and begins to cut the wood.*] Whew-e-e! Look at that. Big old strong boy. Look like Joe Louis.° Hell, must be getting old the way I'm watching that boy whip through that wood.

CORY: I don't see why Mama want a fence around the yard noways.

25   **TROY:** Damn if I know either. What the hell she keeping out with it? She ain't got nothing nobody want.

BONO: Some people build fences to keep people out . . . and other people build fences to keep people in. Rose wants to hold on to you all. She loves you.

TROY: Hell, nigger, I don't need nobody to tell me my wife loves me. Cory . . . go on in the house and see if you can find that other saw.

CORY: Where's it at?

TROY: I said find it! Look for it till you find it! [*CORY exits into the house.*] What's that supposed to mean? Wanna keep us in?

°24 *Joe Louis:* Louis (1914–1981), known as the "Brown Bomber," was a dominant black heavyweight who became champion in 1937, and held the championship for 11 years. By 1957 he had long since retired from boxing, and had become a wrestler. He retired from that in 1957 because of an injury. He was proverbial for his power in the ring.

Bono: Troy . . . I done known you seem like damn near my whole life. You and Rose both. I   30
done know both of you all for a long time. I remember when you met Rose. When you
was hitting them baseball out the park. A lot of them old gals was after you then. You
had the pick of the litter. When you picked Rose, I was happy for you. That was the first
time I knew you had any sense. I said . . . My man Troy knows what he's doing . . . I'm
gonna follow this nigger . . . he might take me somewhere. I been following you too. I
done learned a whole heap of things about life watching you. I done learned how to tell
where the shit lies. How to tell it from the alfalfa. You done learned me a lot of things.
You showed me how to not make the same mistakes . . . to take life as it comes along
and keep putting one foot in front of the other. [*Pause.*] Rose a good woman, Troy.

Troy: Hell, nigger, I know she a good woman. I been married to her for eighteen years.
What you got on your mind, Bono?

Bono: I just say she a good woman. Just like I say anything. I ain't got to have nothing on
my mind.

Troy: You just gonna say she a good woman and leave it hanging out there like that?
Why you telling me she a good woman?

Bono: She loves you, Troy. Rose loves you.

Troy: You saying I don't measure up. That's what you trying to say. I don't measure up   35
cause I'm seeing this other gal. I know what you trying to say.

Bono: I know what Rose means to you, Troy. I'm just trying to say I don't want to see you
mess up.

Troy: Yeah, I appreciate that, Bono. If you was messing around on Lucille I'd be telling
you the same thing.

Bono: Well, that's all I got to say. I just say that because I love you both.

Troy: Hell, you know me . . . I wasn't out there looking for nothing. You can't find a
better woman than Rose. I know that. But seems like this woman just stuck onto me
where I can't shake her loose. I done wrestled with it, tried to throw her off me . . . but
she just stuck on tighter. Now she's stuck on for good.

Bono: You's in control . . . that's what you tell me all the time. You responsible for what   40
you do.

Troy: I ain't ducking the responsibility of it. As long as it sets right in my heart . . . then
I'm okay. 'Cause that's all I listen to. It'll tell me right from wrong every time. And I
ain't talking about doing Rose no bad turn. I love Rose. She done carried me a long
ways and I love and respect her for that.

Bono: I know you do. That's why I don't want to see you hurt her. But what you gonna
do when she find out? What you got then? If you try and juggle both of them . . .
sooner or later you gonna drop one of them. That's common sense.

Troy: Yeah, I hear what you saying, Bono. I been trying to figure a way to work it out.

Bono: Work it out right, Troy. I don't want to be getting all up between you and Rose's
business . . . but work it so it come out right.

Troy: Ah hell, I get all up between you and Lucille's business. When you gonna get that   45
woman that refrigerator she been wanting? Don't tell me you ain't got no money
now. I know who your banker is. Mellon don't need that money bad as Lucille want
that refrigerator. I'll tell you that.

Bono: Tell you what I'll do . . . when you finish building this fence for Rose . . . I'll buy
Lucille that refrigerator.

Troy: You done stuck your foot in your mouth now!

Troy grabs up a board and begins to saw. Bono starts to walk out the yard.

Hey, nigger . . . where you going?

BONO: I'm going home. I know you don't expect me to help you now. I'm protecting my money. I wanna see you put that fence up by yourself. That's what I want to see. You'll be here another six months without me.

TROY: Nigger, you ain't right.

50 **BONO:** When it comes to my money . . . I'm right as fireworks on the Fourth of July.

TROY: All right, we gonna see now. You better get out your bankbook.

BONO exits, and TROY continues to work. ROSE enters from the house.

ROSE: What they say down there? What's happening with Gabe?

TROY: I went down there and got him out. Cost me fifty dollars. Say he was disturbing the peace. Judge set up a hearing for him in three weeks. Say to show cause why he shouldn't be recommitted.

ROSE: What was he doing that cause them to arrest him?

55 **TROY:** Some kids was teasing him and he run them off home. Say he was howling and carrying on. Some folks seen him and called the police. That's all it was.

ROSE: Well, what's you say? What'd you tell the judge?

TROY: Told him I'd look after him. It didn't make no sense to recommit the man. He stuck out his big greasy palm and told me to give him fifty dollars and take him on home.

ROSE: Where's he at now? Where'd he go off to?

TROY: He's gone about his business. He don't need nobody to hold his hand.

60 **ROSE:** Well, I don't know. Seem like that would be the best place for him if they did put him into the hospital. I know what you're gonna say. But that's what I think would be best.

TROY: The man done had his life ruined fighting for what? And they wanna take and lock him up. Let him be free. He don't bother nobody.

ROSE: Well, everybody got their own way of looking at it I guess. Come on and get your lunch. I got a bowl of lima beans and some cornbread in the oven. Come and get something to eat. Ain't no sense you fretting over Gabe.

ROSE turns to go into the house.

TROY: Rose . . . got something to tell you.

ROSE: Well, come on . . . wait till I get this food on the table.

65 **TROY:** Rose! [*She stops and turns around.*] I don't know how to say this. [*Pause.*] I can't explain it none. It just sort of grows on you till it gets out of hand. It starts out like a little bush . . . and the next thing you know it's a whole forest.

ROSE: Troy . . . what is you talking about?

TROY: I'm talking, woman, let me talk. I'm trying to find a way to tell you . . . I'm gonna be a daddy. I'm gonna be somebody's daddy.

ROSE: Troy . . . you're not telling me this? You're gonna be . . . what?

TROY: Rose . . . now . . . see . . .

70 **ROSE:** You telling me you gonna be somebody's daddy? You telling your *wife* this?

GABRIEL: [*enters from the street. He carries a rose in his hand.*] Hey, Troy! Hey, Rose!

ROSE: I have to wait eighteen years to hear something like this.

GABRIEL: Hey, Rose . . . I got a flower for you. [*He hands it to her.*] That's a rose. Same rose like you is.

ROSE: Thanks, Gabe.

75 **GABRIEL:** Troy, you ain't mad at me is you? Them bad mens come and put me away. You ain't mad at me is you?

TROY: Naw, Gabe, I ain't mad at you.

ROSE: Eighteen years and you wanna come with this.

GABRIEL: [*takes a quarter out of his pocket.*] See what I got? Got a brand new quarter.

TROY: Rose . . . it's just . . .

ROSE: Ain't nothing you can say, Troy. Ain't no way of explaining that.   80

GABRIEL: Fellow that give me this quarter had a whole mess of them. I'm gonna keep this quarter till it stop shining.

ROSE: Gabe, go on in the house there. I got some watermelon in the Frigidaire. Go on and get you a piece.

GABRIEL: Say, Rose . . . you know I was chasing hellhounds and them bad mens come and get me and take me away. Troy helped me. He come down there and told them they better let me go before he beat them up. Yeah, he did!

ROSE: You go on and get you a piece of watermelon, Gabe. Them bad mens is gone now.

GABRIEL: Okay, Rose . . . gonna get me some watermelon. The kind with the stripes on it.   85

GABRIEL exits into the house.

ROSE: Why, Troy? Why? After all these years to come dragging this in to me now. It don't make no sense at your age. I could have expected this ten or fifteen years ago, but not now.

TROY: Age ain't got nothing to do with it, Rose.

ROSE: I done tried to be everything a wife should be. Everything a wife could be. Been married eighteen years and I got to live to see the day you tell me you been seeing another woman and done fathered a child by her. And you know I ain't never wanted no half nothing in my family. My whole family is half. Everybody got different fathers and mothers . . . my two sisters and my brother. Can't hardly tell who's who. Can't never sit down and talk about Papa and Mama. It's your papa and your mama and my papa and my mama . . .

TROY: Rose . . . stop it now.

ROSE: I ain't never wanted that for none of my children. And now you wanna drag your   90 behind in here and tell me something like this.

TROY: You ought to know. It's time for you to know.

ROSE: Well, I don't want to know, goddamn it!

TROY: I can't just make it go away. It's done now. I can't wish the circumstance of the thing away.

ROSE: And you don't want to either. Maybe you want to wish me and my boy away. Maybe that's what you want? Well, you can't wish us away. I've got eighteen years of my life invested in you. You ought to have stayed upstairs in my bed where you belong.

TROY: Rose . . . now listen to me . . . we can get a handle on this thing. We can talk this   95 out . . . come to an understanding.

ROSE: All of a sudden it's "we." Where was "we" at when you was down there rolling around with some godforsaken woman? "We" should have come to an understanding before you started making a damn fool of yourself. You're a day late and a dollar short when it comes to an understanding with me.

TROY: It's just . . . She gives me a different idea . . . a different understanding about myself. I can step out of this house and get away from the pressures and problems . . . be a different man. I ain't got to wonder how I'm gonna pay the bills or get the roof fixed. I can just be a part of myself that I ain't never been.

ROSE: What I want to know . . . is do you plan to continue seeing her. That's all you can say to me.

TROY: I can sit up in her house and laugh. Do you understand what I'm saying. I can laugh out loud . . . and it feels good. It reaches all the way down to the bottom of my shoes. [*Pause.*] Rose, I can't give that up.

100 **Rose:** Maybe you ought to go on and stay down there with her . . . if she's a better woman than me.

Troy: It ain't about nobody being a better woman or nothing. Rose, you ain't the blame. A man couldn't ask for no woman to be a better wife than you've been. I'm responsible for it. I done locked myself into a pattern trying to take care of you all that I forgot about myself.

Rose: What the hell was I there for? That was my job, not somebody else's.

Troy: Rose, I done tried all my life to live decent . . . to live a clean . . . hard . . . useful life. I tried to be a good husband to you. In every way I knew how. Maybe I come into the world backwards, I don't know. But . . . you born with two strikes on you before you come to the plate. You got to guard it closely . . . always looking for the curve ball on the inside corner. You can't afford to let none get past you. You can't afford a call strike. If you going down . . . you going down swinging. Everything lined up against you. What you gonna do. I fooled them, Rose. I bunted. When I found you and Cory and a halfway decent job . . . I was safe. Couldn't nothing touch me. I wasn't gonna strike out no more. I wasn't going back to the penitentiary. I wasn't gonna lay in the streets with a bottle of wine. I was safe. I had me a family. A job. I wasn't gonna get that last strike. I was on first looking for one of them boys to knock me in. To get me home.

Rose: You should have stayed in my bed, Troy.

105 **Troy:** Then when I saw that gal . . . she firmed up my backbone. And I got to thinking that if I tried . . . I just might be able to steal second. Do you understand after eighteen years I wanted to steal second.

Rose: You should have held me tight. You should have grabbed me and held on.

Troy: I stood on first base for eighteen years and I thought . . . well, goddamn it . . . go on for it!

Rose: We're not talking about baseball! We're talking about you going off to lay in bed with another woman . . . and then bring it home to me. That's what we're talking about. We ain't talking about no baseball.

Troy: Rose, you're not listening to me. I'm trying the best I can to explain it to you. It's not easy for me to admit that I been standing in the same place for eighteen years.

110 **Rose:** I been standing with you! I been right here with you, Troy. I got a life too. I gave eighteen years of my life to stand in the same spot with you. Don't you think I ever wanted other things? Don't you think I had dreams and hopes? What about my life? What about me? Don't you think it ever crossed my mind to want to know other men? That I wanted to lay up somewhere and forget about my responsibilities? That I wanted someone to make me laugh so I could feel good? You not the only one who's got wants and needs. But I held on to you, Troy. I took all my feelings, my wants and needs, my dreams . . . and I buried them inside you. I planted a seed and watched and prayed over it. I planted myself inside you and waited to bloom. And it didn't take me no eighteen years to find out the soil was hard and rocky and it wasn't never gonna bloom. But I held on to you, Troy. I held you tighter. You was my husband. I owed you everything I had. Every part of me I could find to give you. And upstairs in that room . . . with the darkness falling in on me . . . I gave everything I had to try and erase the doubt that you wasn't the finest man in the world. And wherever you was going . . . I wanted to be there with you. 'Cause you was my husband. 'Cause that's the only way I was gonna survive as your wife. You always talking about what you give . . . and what you don't have to give. But you take too. You take . . . and don't even know nobody's giving!

Rose turns to exit into the house; Troy grabs her arm.

Troy: You say I take and don't give!
Rose: Troy! You're hurting me!

TROY: You say I take and don't give!

ROSE: Troy . . . you're hurting my arm! Let go!

TROY: I done give you everything I got. Don't you tell that lie on me.   115

ROSE: Troy!

TROY: Don't you tell that lie on me!

CORY: [*enters from the house.*] Mama!

ROSE: Troy. You're hurting me.

TROY: Don't you tell me about no taking and giving.   120

CORY comes up behind TROY and grabs him. TROY, surprised, is thrown off balance just as CORY throws a glancing blow that catches him on the chest and knocks him down. TROY is stunned, as is CORY.

ROSE: Troy. Troy. No! [*TROY gets to his feet and starts at CORY.*] Troy . . . no. Please! Troy!

ROSE pulls on TROY to hold him back. TROY stops himself.

TROY: [*to CORY.*] All right. That's strike two. You stay away from around me, boy. Don't you strike out. You living with a full count. Don't you strike out.

TROY exits out the yard as the lights go down.

ACT 2

Scene 2

It is six months later, early afternoon. TROY enters from the house and starts to exit the yard. ROSE enters from the house.

ROSE: Troy, I want to talk to you.

TROY: All of a sudden, after all this time, you want to talk to me, huh? You ain't wanted to talk to me for months. You ain't wanted to talk to me last night. You ain't wanted no part of me then. What you wanna talk to me about now?

ROSE: Tomorrow's Friday.

TROY: I know what day tomorrow is. You think I don't know tomorrow's Friday? My whole life I ain't done nothing but look to see Friday coming and you got to tell me it's Friday.

ROSE: I want to know if you're coming home.   5

TROY: I always come home, Rose. You know that. There ain't never been a night I ain't come home.

ROSE: That ain't what I mean . . . and you know it. I want to know if you're coming straight home after work.

TROY: I figure I'd cash my check . . . hang out at Taylors' with the boys . . . maybe play a game of checkers . . .

ROSE: Troy, I can't live like this. I won't live like this. You livin' on borrowed time with me. It's been going on six months now you ain't been coming home.

TROY: I be here every night. Every night of the year. That's 365 days.   10

ROSE: I want you to come home tomorrow after work.

TROY: Rose . . . I don't mess up my pay. You know that now. I take my pay and I give it to you. I don't have no money but what you give me back. I just want to have little time to myself . . . a little time to enjoy life.

ROSE: What about me? When's my time to enjoy life?

TROY: I don't know what to tell you, Rose. I'm doing the best I can.

ROSE: You ain't been home from work but time enough to change your clothes and run out . . . and you wanna call that the best you can do?   15

TROY: I'm going over to the hospital to see Alberta. She went into the hospital this afternoon. Look like she might have the baby early. I won't be gone long.

Rose: Well, you ought to know. They went over to Miss Pearl's and got Gabe today. She said you told them to go ahead and lock him up.

Troy: I ain't said no such thing. Whoever told you that is telling a lie. Pearl ain't doing nothing but telling a big fat lie.

Rose: She ain't had to tell me. I read it on the papers.

20 **Troy:** I ain't told them nothing of the kind.

Rose: I saw it right there on the papers.

Troy: What it say, huh?

Rose: It said you told them to take him.

Troy: Then they screwed that up, just the way they screw up everything. I ain't worried about what they got on the paper.

25 **Rose:** Say the government sent part of his check to the hospital and the other part to you.

Troy: I ain't got nothing to do with that if that's the way it works. I ain't made up the rules about how it work.

Rose: You did Gabe just like you did Cory. You wouldn't sign the paper for Cory . . . but you signed for Gabe. You signed that paper.

The telephone is heard ringing inside the house.

Troy: I told you I ain't signed nothing, woman! The only thing I signed was the release form. Hell, I can't read, I don't know what they had on that paper! I ain't signed nothing about sending Gabe away.

Rose: I said send him to the hospital . . . you said let him be free . . . now you done went down there and signed him to the hospital for half his money. You went back on yourself, Troy. You gonna have to answer for that.

30 **Troy:** See now . . . you been over there talking to Miss Pearl. She done got mad 'cause she ain't getting Gabe's rent money. That's all it is. She's liable to say anything.

Rose: Troy, I seen where you signed the paper.

Troy: You ain't seen nothing I signed. What she doing got papers on my brother anyway? Miss Pearl telling a big fat lie. And I'm gonna tell her about it too! You ain't seen nothing I signed. Say . . . you ain't seen nothing I signed.

Rose exits into the house to answer the telephone. Presently she returns.

Rose: Troy . . . that was the hospital. Alberta had the baby.

Troy: What she have? What is it?

35 **Rose:** It's a girl.

Troy: I better get on down to the hospital to see her.

Rose: Troy . . .

Troy: Rose . . . I got to go see her now. That's only right . . . what's the matter . . . the baby's all right, ain't it?

Rose: Alberta died having the baby.

40 **Troy:** Died . . . you say she's dead? Alberta's dead?

Rose: They said they done all they could. They couldn't do nothing for her.

Troy: The baby? How's the baby?

Rose: They say it's healthy. I wonder who's gonna bury her.

Troy: She had family, Rose. She wasn't living in the world by herself.

45 **Rose:** I know she wasn't living in the world by herself.

Troy: Next thing you gonna want to know if she had any insurance.

Rose: Troy, you ain't got to talk like that.

TROY: That's the first thing that jumped out your mouth. "Who's gonna bury her?" Like I'm fixing to take on that task for myself.

ROSE: I am your wife. Don't push me away.

TROY: I ain't pushing nobody away. Just give me some space. That's all. Just give me some room to breathe.   50

ROSE exits into the house. TROY walks about the yard.

[*with a quiet rage that threatens to consume him.*] All right . . . Mr. Death. See now . . . I'm gonna tell you what I'm gonna do. I'm gonna take and build me a fence around this yard. See? I'm gonna build me a fence around what belongs to me. And then I want you to stay on the other side. See? You stay over there until you're ready for me. Then you come on. Bring your army. Bring your sickel. Bring your wrestling clothes. I ain't gonna fall down on my vigilance this time. You ain't gonna sneak up on me no more. When you ready for me . . . when the top of your list say Troy Maxson . . . that's when you come around here. You come up and knock on the front door. Ain't nobody else got nothing to do with this. This is between you and me. Man to man. You stay on the other side of that fence until you ready for me. Then you come up and knock on the front door. Anytime you want. I'll be ready for you.

The lights go down to black.

ACT 2

Scene 3

The lights come up on the porch. It is late evening three days later. ROSE sits listening to the ball game waiting for TROY. The final out of the game is made and ROSE switches off the radio. TROY enters the yard carrying an infant wrapped in blankets. He stands back from the house and calls.

ROSE enters and stands on the porch. There is a long, awkward silence, the weight of which grows heavier with each passing second.

TROY: Rose . . . I'm standing here with my daughter in my arms. She ain't but a wee bittie little old thing. She don't know nothing about grownups' business. She innocent . . . and she ain't got no mama.

ROSE: What you telling me for, Troy? [*She turns and exits into the house.*]

TROY: Well . . . I guess we'll just sit out here on the porch.

He sits down on the porch. There is an awkward indelicateness about the way he handles the baby. His largeness engulfs and seems to swallow it. He speaks loud enough for ROSE to hear.

A man's got to do what's right for him. I ain't sorry for nothing I done. It felt right in my heart. [*To the baby.*] What you smiling at? Your daddy's a big man. Got these great big old hands. But sometimes he's scared. And right now your daddy's scared cause we sitting out here and ain't got no home. Oh, I been homeless before. I ain't had no little baby with me. But I been homeless. You just be out on the road by your lonesome and you see one of them trains coming and you just kinda go like this . . . [*He sings as a lullaby.*]

Please, Mr. Engineer let a man ride the line
Please, Mr. Engineer let a man ride the line
I ain't got no ticket please let me ride the blinds

ROSE enters from the house. TROY, hearing her steps behind him, stands and faces her.

She's my daughter, Rose. My own flesh and blood. I can't deny her no more than I can deny them boys. [*Pause.*] You and them boys is my family. You and them and this child is all I got in the world. So I guess what I'm saying is . . . I'd appreciate it if you'd help me take care of her.

ROSE: Okay, Troy . . . you're right. I'll take care of your baby for you . . . 'cause . . . like you say . . . she's innocent . . . and you can't visit the sins of the father upon the child. A motherless child has got a hard time. [*She takes the baby from him.*] From right now . . . this child got a mother. But you a womanless man.

ROSE turns and exits into the house with the baby. Lights go down to black.

ACT 2

Scene 4

It is two months later. LYONS enters the street. He knocks on the door and calls.

LYONS: Hey, Rose! [*Pause.*] Rose!

ROSE: [*from inside the house.*] Stop that yelling. You gonna wake up Raynell. I just got her to sleep.

LYONS: I just stopped by to pay Papa this twenty dollars I owe him. Where's Papa at?

ROSE: He should be here in a minute. I'm getting ready to go down to the church. Sit down and wait on him.

5 LYONS: I got to go pick up Bonnie over her mother's house.

ROSE: Well, sit it down there on the table. He'll get it.

LYONS: [*enters the house and sets the money on the table.*] Tell Papa I said thanks. I'll see you again.

ROSE: All right, Lyons. We'll see you.

LYONS starts to exit as CORY enters.

CORY: Hey, Lyons.

10 LYONS: What's happening, Cory? Say man, I'm sorry I missed your graduation. You know I had a gig and couldn't get away. Otherwise, I would have been there, man. So what you doing?

CORY: I'm trying to find a job.

LYONS: Yeah I know how that go, man. It's rough out here. Jobs are scarce.

CORY: Yeah, I know.

LYONS: Look here, I got to run. Talk to Papa . . . he know some people. He'll be able to help get you a job. Talk to him . . . see what he say.

15 CORY: Yeah . . . all right, Lyons.

LYONS: You take care. I'll talk to you soon. We'll find some time to talk.

LYONS exits the yard. CORY wanders over to the tree, picks up the bat, and assumes a batting stance. He studies an imaginary pitcher and swings. Dissatisfied with the result, he tries again. TROY enters. They eye each other for a beat. CORY puts the bat down and exits the yard. TROY starts into the house as ROSE exits with RAYNELL. She is carrying a cake.

TROY: I'm coming in and everybody's going out.

ROSE: I'm taking this cake down to the church for the bake sale. Lyons was by to see you. He stopped by to pay you your twenty dollars. It's laying in there on the table.

Troy: [*going into his pocket.*] Well . . . here go this money.

Rose: Put it in there on the table, Troy. I'll get it.   20

Troy: What time you coming back?

Rose: Ain't no use in you studying me. It don't matter what time I come back.

Troy: I just asked you a question, woman. What's the matter . . . can't I ask you a question?

Rose: Troy, I don't want to go into it. Your dinner's in there on the stove. All you got to do is heat it up. And don't you be eating the rest of them cakes in there. I'm coming back for them. We having a bake sale at the church tomorrow.

Rose exits the yard. Troy sits down on the steps, takes a pint bottle from his pocket, opens it, and drinks. He begins to sing.

Troy:

> Hear it ring! Hear it ring!   25
> Had an old dog his name was Blue
> You know Blue was mighty true
> You know Blue as a good old dog
> Blue trees a possum in a hollow log
> You know from that he was a good old dog

Bono: [*enters the yard.*] Hey, Troy.

Troy: Hey, what's happening, Bono?

Bono: I just thought I'd stop by to see you.

Troy: What you stop by and see me for? You ain't stopped by in a mouth of Sundays. Hell, I must owe you money or something.

Bono: Since you got your promotion I can't keep up with you. Used to see you every day.   30
Now I don't even know what route you working.

Troy: They keep switching me around. Got me out in Greentree now . . . hauling white folks' garbage.

Bono: Greentree, huh? You lucky, at least you ain't got to be lifting them barrels. Damn if they ain't getting heavier. I'm gonna put in my two years and call it quits.

Troy: I'm thinking about retiring myself.

Bono: You got it easy. You can drive for another five years.

Troy: It ain't the same, Bono. It ain't like working the back of the truck. Ain't got nobody   35
to talk to . . . feel like you working by yourself. Naw, I'm thinking about retiring.
How's Lucille?

Bono: She all right. Her arthritis get to acting up on her sometime. Saw Rose on my way in. She going down to the church, huh?

Troy: Yeah, she took up going down there. All them preachers looking for somebody to fatten their pockets. [*Pause.*] Got some gin here.

Bono: Naw, thanks. I just stopped by to say hello.

Troy: Hell, nigger . . . you can take a drink. I ain't never known you to say no to a drink. You ain't got to work tomorrow.

Bono: I just stopped by. I'm fixing to go over to Skinner's. We got us a domino game go-   40
ing over his house every Friday.

Troy: Nigger, you can't play no dominoes. I used to whup you four games out of five.

Bono: Well, that learned me. I'm getting better.

Troy: Yeah? Well, that's all right.

Bono: Look here . . . I got to be getting on. Stop by sometime, huh?

Troy: Yeah, I'll do that, Bono. Lucille told Rose you bought her a new refrigerator.   45

Bono: Yeah, Rose told Lucille you had finally built your fence . . . so I figured we'd call it even.

Troy: I knew you would.

BONO: Yeah . . . okay. I'll be talking to you.

TROY: Yeah, take care, Bono. Good to see you. I'm gonna stop over.

50   **BONO:** Yeah. Okay, Troy. [*BONO exits.*]

TROY: [*drinks from the bottle.*]

> *Old Blue died and I dig his grave*
> *Let him down with a golden chain*
> *Every night when I hear old Blue bark*
> *I know Blue treed a possum in Noah's Ark*
> *Hear it ring! Hear it ring!*

CORY enters the yard. They eye each other for a beat. TROY is sitting in the middle of the steps. CORY walks over.

CORY: I got to get by.

TROY: Say what? What's you say?

CORY: You in my way. I got to get by.

55   **TROY:** You got to get by where? This is my house. Bought and paid for. In full. Took me
fifteen years. And if you wanna go in my house and I'm sitting on the steps . . . you
say excuse me. Like your mama taught you.

CORY: Come on, Pop . . . I got to get by.

CORY starts to maneuver his way past TROY. TROY grabs his leg and shoves him back.

TROY: You just gonna walk over top of me?

CORY: I live here too!

TROY: [*advancing toward him.*] You just gonna walk over top of me in my own house?

60   **CORY:** I ain't scared of you.

TROY: I ain't asked if you was scared of me. I asked you if you was fixing to walk over top
of me in my own house? That's the question. You ain't gonna say excuse me? You just
gonna walk over top of me?

CORY: If you wanna put it like that.

TROY: How else am I gonna put it?

CORY: I was walking by you to go into the house cause you sitting on the steps drunk,
singing to yourself. You can put it like that.

65   **TROY:** Without saying excuse me??? [*CORY doesn't respond.*] I asked you a question. Without saying excuse me???

CORY: I ain't got to say excuse me to you. You don't count around here no more.

TROY: Oh, I see . . . I don't count around here no more. You ain't got to say excuse me to
your daddy. All of a sudden you done got so grown that your daddy don't count
around here no more . . . Around here in his own house and yard that he done paid
for with the sweat of his brow. You done got so grown to where you gonna take over.
You gonna take over my house. Is that right? You gonna wear my pants. You gonna
go in there and stretch out on my bed. You ain't got to say excuse me cause I don't
count around here no more. Is that right?

CORY: That's right. You always talking this dumb stuff. Now, why don't you just get out
my way?

TROY: I guess you got someplace to sleep and something to put in your belly. You got
that, huh? You got that? That's what you need. You got that, huh?

70   **CORY:** You don't know what I got. You ain't got to worry about what I got.

TROY: You right! You one hundred percent right! I done spent the last seventeen years
worrying about what you got. Now it's your turn, see? I'll tell you what to do. You

grown . . . we done established that. You a man. Now, let's see you act like one. Turn your behind around and walk out this yard. And when you get out there in the alley . . . you can forget about this house. See? 'Cause this is my house. You go on and be a man and get your own house. You can forget about this. 'Cause this is mine. You go on and get yours cause I'm through with doing for you.

CORY: You talking about what you did for me . . . what'd you ever give me?

TROY: Them feet and bones! That pumping heart, nigger! I give you more than anybody else is ever gonna give you.

CORY: You ain't never gave me nothing! You ain't never done nothing but hold me back. Afraid I was gonna be better than you. All you ever did was try and make me scared of you. I used to tremble every time you called my name. Every time I heard your footsteps in the house. Wondering all the time . . . what's Papa gonna say if I do this? . . . What's he gonna say if I do that? . . . What's Papa gonna say if I turn on the radio? And mama, too . . . she tries . . . but she's scared of you.

TROY: You leave your mama out of this. She ain't got nothing to do with this.   75

CORY: I don't know how she stand you . . . after what you did to her.

TROY: I told you to leave your mama out of this! [*He advances toward* CORY.]

CORY: What you gonna do . . . give me a whupping? You can't whup me no more. You're too old. You just an old man.

TROY: [*shoves him on his shoulder.*] Nigger! That's what you are. You just another nigger on the street to me!

CORY: You crazy! You know that?   80

TROY: Go on now! You got the devil in you. Get on away from me!

CORY: You just a crazy old man . . . talking about I got the devil in me.

TROY: Yeah, I'm crazy! If you don't get on the other side of that yard . . . I'm gonna show you how crazy I am! Go on . . . get the hell out of my yard.

CORY: It ain't your yard. You took Uncle Gabe's money he got from the army to buy this house and then you put him out.

TROY: [*advances on* CORY.] Get your black ass out of my yard! [*Troy's advance backs* CORY   85
up against the tree. CORY grabs up the bat.]

CORY: I ain't going nowhere! Come on . . . put me out! I ain't scared of you.

TROY: That's my bat!

CORY: Come on!

TROY: Put my bat down!

CORY: Come on, put me out. [*CORY swings at* TROY, *who backs across the yard.*] What's the   90
matter? You so bad . . . put me out! [*TROY advances toward* CORY.]

CORY: [*backing up.*] Come on! Come on!

TROY: You're gonna have to use it! You wanna draw that bat back on me . . . you're gonna have to use it.

CORY: Come on! . . . Come on!

CORY *swings the bat at* TROY *a second time. He misses.* TROY *continues to advance toward him.*

TROY: You're gonna have to kill me! You wanna draw that bat back on me. You're gonna have to kill me.

CORY, *backed up against the tree, can go no farther.* TROY *taunts him. He sticks out his head and offers him a target.*

Come on! Come on!

CORY *is unable to swing the bat.* TROY *grabs it.*

95 **TROY:** Then I'll show you.

CORY and TROY struggle over the bat. The struggle is fierce and fully engaged. TROY ultimately is the stronger and takes the bat from CORY and stands over him ready to swing. He stops himself.

> Go on and get away from around my house.

CORY: [*stung by his defeat, picks himself up, walks slowly out of the yard and up the alley.*] Tell Mama I'll be back for my things.

TROY: They'll be on the other side of that fence. [*CORY exits.*] I can't taste nothing. Helluljah! I can't taste nothing no more. [*TROY assumes a batting posture and begins to taunt Death, the fastball on the outside corner.*] Come on! It's between you and me now! Come on! Anytime you want! Come on! I be ready for you . . . but I ain't gonna be easy.

The lights go down on the scene.

ACT 2

Scene 5

The time is 1965. The lights come up in the yard. It is the morning of TROY's funeral. A funeral plaque with a light hangs beside the door. There is a small garden plot off to the side. There is noise and activity in the house as ROSE, LYONS, and BONO have gathered.

> *The door opens and RAYNELL, seven years old, enters dressed in a flannel nightgown. She crosses to the garden and pokes around with a stick. ROSE calls from the house.*

ROSE: Raynell!

RAYNELL: Mam?

ROSE: What you doing out there?

RAYNELL: Nothing.

5 **ROSE:** [*comes to the door.*] Girl, get in here and get dressed. What you doing?

RAYNELL: Seeing if my garden growed.

ROSE: I told you it ain't gonna grow overnight. You got to wait.

RAYNELL: It don't look like it never gonna grow. Dag!

ROSE: I told you a watched pot never boils. Get in here and get dressed.

10 **RAYNELL:** This ain't even no pot, Mama.

ROSE: You just have to give it a chance. It'll grow. Now you come on and do what I told you. We got to be getting ready. This ain't no morning to be playing around. You hear me?

RAYNELL: Yes, mam.

ROSE exits into the house. RAYNELL continues to poke at her garden with a stick. CORY enters. He is dressed in a Marine corporal's uniform, and carries a duffelbag. His posture is that of a military man, and his speech has a clipped sternness.

CORY: [*to RAYNELL.*] Hi. [*Pause.*] I bet your name is Raynell.

RAYNELL: Uh huh.

15 **CORY:** Is your mama home?

RAYNELL: [*runs up on the porch and calls through the screen door.*] Mama . . . there's some man out here. Mama?

ROSE: [*comes to the door.*] Cory? Lord have mercy! Look here, you all!

ROSE and CORY embrace in a tearful reunion as BONO and LYONS enters from the house dressed in funeral clothes.

Bono: Aw, looka here . . .

Rose: Done got all grown up!

Cory: Don't cry, Mama. What you crying about?   20

Rose: I'm just so glad you made it.

Cory: Hey Lyons. How you doing, Mr. Bono.

Lyons: [*goes to embrace* Cory.] Look at you, man. Look at you. Don't he look good, Rose. Got them Corporal stripes.

Rose: What took you so long?

Cory: You know how the Marines are, Mama. They got to get all their paperwork straight   25
before they let you do anything.

Rose: Well, I'm sure glad you made it. They let Lyons come. Your Uncle Gabe's still in the hospital. They don't know if they gonna let him out or not. I just talked to them a little while ago.

Lyons: A Corporal in the United States Marines.

Bono: Your daddy knew you had it in you. He used to tell me all the time.

Lyons: Don't he look good, Mr. Bono?

Bono: Yeah, he remind me of Troy when I first met him. [*Pause.*] Say, Rose, Lucille's   30
down at the church with the choir. I'm gonna go down and get the pallbearers lined up. I'll be back to get you all.

Rose: Thanks, Jim.

Cory: See you, Mr. Bono.

Lyons: [*with his arm around* Raynell.] Cory . . . look at Raynell. Ain't she precious? She gonna break a whole lot of hearts.

Rose: Raynell, come and say hello to your brother. This is your brother, Cory. You re-   member Cory.

Raynell: No, Mam.

Cory: She don't remember me, Mama.   35

Rose: Well, we talk about you. She heard us talk about you. [*To* Raynell.] This is your brother, Cory. Come on and say hello.

Raynell: Hi.

Cory: Hi. So you're Raynell. Mama told me a lot about you.

Rose: You all come on into the house and let me fix you some breakfast. Keep up your   40
strength.

Cory: I ain't hungry, Mama.

Lyons: You can fix me something, Rose. I'll be in there in a minute.

Rose: Cory, you sure you don't want nothing? I know they ain't feeding you right.

Cory: No, Mama . . . thanks. I don't feel like eating. I'll get something later.

Rose: Raynell . . . get on upstairs and get that dress on like I told you.   45

Rose and Raynell *exit into the house.*

Lyons: So . . . I hear you thinking about getting married.

Cory: Yeah, I done found the right one, Lyons. It's about time.

Lyons: Me and Bonnie been split up about four years now. About the time Papa retired. I guess she just got tired of all them changes I was putting her through. [*Pause.*] I always knew you was gonna make something out yourself. Your head was always in the right direction. So . . . you gonna stay in . . . make it a career . . . put in your twenty years?

Cory: I don't know. I got six already, I think that's enough.

Lyons: Stick with Uncle Sam and retire early. Ain't nothing out here. I guess Rose told   50
you what happened with me. They got me down the workhouse. I thought I was be-ing slick cashing other people's checks.

CORY: How much time you doing?

LYONS: They give me three years. I got that beat now. I ain't got but nine more months. It ain't so bad. You learn to deal with it like anything else. You got to take the crookeds with the straights. That's what Papa used to say. He used to say that when he struck out. I seen him strike out three times in a row . . . and the next time up he hit the ball over the grandstand. Right out there in Homestead Field.° He wasn't satisfied hitting in the seats . . . he want to hit it over everything! After the game he had two hundred people standing around waiting to shake his hand. You got to take the crookeds with the straights. Yeah, Papa was something else.

CORY: You still playing?

LYONS: Cory . . . you know I'm gonna do that. There's some fellows down there we got us a band . . . we gonna try and stay together when we get out . . . but yeah, I'm still playing. It still helps me to get out of bed in the morning. As long as it do that I'm gonna be right there playing and trying to make some sense out of it.

55 **ROSE:** [*calling.*] Lyons, I got these eggs in the pan.

LYONS: Let me go on and get these eggs, man. Get ready to go bury Papa. [*Pause.*] How you doing? You doing all right?

CORY nods. LYONS touches him on the shoulder and they share a moment of silent grief. LYONS exits into the house. CORY wanders about the yard. RAYNELL enters.

RAYNELL: Hi.

CORY: Hi.

RAYNELL: Did you used to sleep in my room?

60 **CORY:** Yeah . . . that used to be my room.

RAYNELL: That's what Papa call it. "Cory's room." It got your football in the closet.

ROSE: [*comes to the door.*] Raynell, get in there and get them good shoes on.

RAYNELL: Mama, can't I wear these? Them other one hurt my feet.

ROSE: Well, they just gonna have to hurt your feet for a while. You ain't said they hurt your feet when you went down to the store and got them.

65 **RAYNELL:** They didn't hurt then. My feet done got bigger.

ROSE: Don't you give me no backtalk now. You get in there and get them shoes on. [*RAYNELL exits into the house.*] Ain't too much changed. He still got that piece of rag tied to that tree. He was out here swinging that bat. I was just ready to go back in the house. He swung that bat and then he just fell over. Seem like he swung it and stood there with this grin on his face . . . and then he just fell over. They carried him on down to the hospital, but I knew there wasn't no need . . . why don't you come on in the house?

CORY: Mama . . . I got something to tell you. I don't know how to tell you this . . . but I've got to tell you . . . I'm not going to Papa's funeral.

ROSE: Boy, hush your month. That's your daddy you talking about. I don't want hear that kind of talk this morning. I done raised you to come to this? You standing there all healthy and grown talking about you ain't going to your daddy's funeral?

CORY: Mama . . . listen . . .

70 **ROSE:** I don't want to hear it, Cory. You just get that thought out of your head.

CORY: I can't drag Papa with me everywhere I go. I've got to say no to him. One time in my life I've got to say no.

°52 *Homestead Field:* i.e., Forbes Field, the home field of the Homestead Grays of the Negro Leagues. The Grays played in the field from 1939 until 1948.

ROSE: Don't nobody have to listen to nothing like that. I know you and your daddy ain't seen eye to eye, but I ain't got to listen to that kind of talk this morning. Whatever was between you and your daddy . . . the time has come to put it aside. Just take it and set it over there on the shelf and forget about it. Disrespecting your daddy ain't gonna make you a man, Cory. You got to find a way to come to that on your own. Not going to your daddy's funeral ain't gonna make you a man.

CORY: The whole time I was growing up . . . living in his house . . . Papa was like a shadow that followed you everywhere. It weighted on you and sunk into your flesh. It would wrap around you and lay there until you couldn't tell which one was you anymore. That shadow digging in your flesh. Trying to crawl in. Trying to live through you. Everywhere I looked, Troy Maxson was staring back at me . . . hiding under the bed . . . in the closet. I'm just saying I've got to find a way to get rid of that shadow, Mama.

ROSE: You just like him. You got him in you good.

CORY: Don't tell me that, Mama.

ROSE: You Troy Maxson all over again.   75

CORY: I don't want to be Troy Maxson. I want to be me.

ROSE: You can't be nobody but who you are, Cory. That shadow wasn't nothing but you growing into yourself. You either got to grow into it or cut it down to fit you. But that's all you got to make life with. That's all you got to measure yourself against that world out there. Your daddy wanted you to be everything he wasn't . . . and at the same time he tried to make you into everything he was. I don't know if he was right or wrong . . . but I do know he meant to do more good than he meant to do harm. He wasn't always right. Sometimes when he touched he bruised. And sometimes when he took me in his arms he cut. When I first met your daddy I thought . . . Here is a man I can lay down with and make a baby. That's the first thing I thought when I seen him. I was thirty years old and had done seen my share of men. But when he walked up to me and said, "I can dance a waltz that'll make you dizzy," I thought, Rose Lee, here is a man that you can open yourself up to and be filled to bursting. Here is a man that can fill all them empty spaces you been tipping around the edges of. One of them empty spaces was being somebody's mother. I married your daddy and settled down to cooking his supper and keeping clean sheets on the bed. When your daddy walked through the house he was so big he filled it up. That was my first mistake. Not to make him leave some room for me. For my part in the matter. But at that time I wanted that. I wanted a house that I could sing in. And that's what your daddy gave me. I didn't know to keep up his strength I had to give up little pieces of mine. I did that. I took on his life as mine and mixed up the pieces so that you couldn't hardly tell which was which anymore. It was my choice. It was my life and I didn't have to live it like that. But that's what life offered me in the way of being a woman and I took it. I grabbed hold of it with both hands. By the time Raynell came into the house, me and your daddy had done lost touch with one another. I didn't want to make my blessing off of nobody's misfortune . . . but I took on to Raynell like she was all them babies I had wanted and never had.

The phone rings.

Like I'd been blessed to relive a part of my life. And if the Lord see fit to keep up my strength . . . I'm gonna do her just like your daddy did you . . . I'm gonna give her the best of what's in me.

RAYNELL: [*entering, still with her old shoes.*] Mama . . . Reverend Tolliver on the phone.

ROSE exits into the house.

Hi.

80   **CORY:** Hi.

RAYNELL: You in the Army or the Marines?

CORY: Marines.

RAYNELL: Papa said it was the Army. Did you know Blue?

CORY: Blue? Who's Blue?

85   **RAYNELL:** Papa's dog what he sing about all the time.

CORY: [*singing.*]

> *Hear it ring! Hear it ring!*
> *I had a dog his name was Blue*
> *You know Blue was mighty true*
> *You know Blue was a good old dog*
> *Blue treed a possum in a hollow log*
> *You know from that he was a good old dog.*
> *Hear it ring! Hear it ring!*

RAYNELL joins in singing.

CORY AND RAYNELL:

> *Blue treed a possum out on a limb*
> *Blue looked at me and I looked at him*
> *Grabbed that possum and put him in a sack*
> *Blue stayed there till I came back*
> *Old Blue's feets was big and round*
> *Never allowed a possum to touch the ground.*
> *Old Blue died and I dug his grave*
> *I dug his grave with a silver spade*
> *Let him down with a golden chain*
> *Any every night I call his name*
> *Go on Blue, you good dog you*
> *Go on Blue, you good dog you.*

RAYNELL:

> *Blue laid down and died like a man*
> *Blue laid down and died . . .*

BOTH:

> *Blue laid down and died like a man*
> *Now he's treeing possums in the Promised Land*
> *I'm gonna tell you this to let you know*
> *Blue's gone where the good dogs go*
> *When I hear old Blue bark*
> *When I hear old Blue bark*
> *Blue treed a possum in Noah's Ark*
> *Blue treed a possum in Noah's Ark.*

90   **ROSE:** [*comes to the screen door.*] Cory, we gonna be ready to go in a minute.

CORY: [*to* RAYNELL.] You go on in the house and change them shoes like Mama told you so we can go to Papa's funeral.

RAYNELL: Okay, I'll be back.

RAYNELL exits into the house. CORY *gets up and crosses over to the tree.* ROSE *stands in the screen door watching him.* GABRIEL *enters from the alley.*

GABRIEL: [*calling.*] Hey, Rose!

Rose: Gabe?

Gabriel: I'm here, Rose. Hey Rose, I'm here!   95

Rose: [*enters from the house.*] Lord . . . Look here, Lyons!

Lyons: See, I told you, Rose . . . I told you they'd let him come.

Cory: How you doing, Uncle Gabe?

Lyons: How you doing, Uncle Gabe?

Gabriel: Hey, Rose. It's time. It's time to tell St. Peter to open the gates. Troy, you ready? You ready, Troy. I'm gonna tell St. Peter to open the gates. You get ready now.   100

Gabriel, with great fanfare, braces himself to blow. The trumpet is without a mouthpiece. He puts the end of it into his mouth and blows with great force, like a man who has been waiting some twenty-odd years for this single moment. No sound comes out of the trumpet. He braces himself and blows again with the same results. A third time he blows. There is a weight of impossible description that falls away and leaves him bare and exposed to a frightful realization. It is a trauma that a sane and normal mind would be unable to withstand. He begins to dance. A slow, strange dance, eerie and life-giving. A dance of atavistic signature and ritual. Lyons attempts to embrace him. Gabriel pushes Lyons away. He begins to howl in what is an attempt at song, or perhaps a song turning back into itself in an attempt at speech. He finishes his dance and the gates of heaven stand open as wide as God's closet. That's the way that go!

[BLACKOUT]

QUESTIONS

Act 1, Scene 1

1. Who is Troy Maxson? Who is Jim Bono? What are they doing as the play opens? What kind of complaint has Troy filed with commissioner? How is this complaint connected with the basic overall thought of the first scene?

2. Why does the discussion between Troy and Bono turn toward how Troy is behaving toward women other than his wife? Why does Troy deny any connections with "that Alberta gal"?

3. Describe Rose. How did Rose and Troy decide to wed? What seem to be their present feelings for each other?

4. Who is Lyons? What has Lyons come to see Troy about? Why does Troy tell the story of his having seen the devil? Whom has he actually seen? How is this story connected to the major themes of the play?

Act 1, Scene 2

5. Why has Rose been playing the numbers?

6. Who is Gabriel? What has happened to him? In what way is he a symbol of Troy, his family, and his race?

Act 1, Scene 3

7. Who is Cory? Whose child is he? What is his relationship to Lyons? What ambition does Cory seem to have? What does Troy want for him instead? (See also the end of 1.3.) What is the reason behind Troy's thought about Cory's athletic ability? Why is there such a conflict between the father and the son? In what way is Rose connected to Troy's discussion of how he regards his role with Cory?

8. What is the purpose of the discussion about the cost of a television set as opposed to the cost of repairing the roof?

9. Why does Troy explain his role about supporting his family? What does this explanation show about Troy? Why do Troy's words likely disappoint Cory?

Act 1, Scene 4

10. Who is Alberta? What is her relationship with Troy? Why is she mentioned so early in this scene?

11. What success has Troy had with his appeal at work? What does Troy say about not having a driver's license? Why does he disparage the act of driving a motor vehicle? What does this discussion show about his character?

12. What is significant about Gabriel's claim that he has been chasing hellhounds?

13. What forced Troy to leave home at the age of 14? What was his attitude toward his own father? What was Troy's story after he left home? How did he learn about baseball? Why does Wilson stress that Troy would have been in his twenties before he was able to develop his baseball skills? What is the implied difference between Troy's baseball career and the careers of white players?

14. Why has Cory not been allowed to play in the football game? What is his reaction to learning that Troy has spoken to his football coach? What does Cory see as a possible outcome of this conflict?

Act 2, Scene 1

15. What is the purpose of the discussion about hard and soft woods at the beginning of this scene? Why does Troy prefer hard wood instead of soft for the outside fence?

16. What has happened to Gabriel? What has Troy done to help Gabriel? What does Troy think of the judge who has been involved in Gabriel's case? In the course of the play, what do we learn about how Troy has acquired the money to pay for the house in which he and his family live? How is this detail important in the relationship between Cory and Troy?

17. Why does Bono believe that he can speak confidentially to Troy about his extramarital affair?

18. Describe the crisis scene between Troy and Rose. How does Troy explain what has happened? How does he explain his involvement with Alberta? What is Rose's response to the situation? How is Troy's attitude toward Cory affected by what happens between him and Rose?

Act 2, Scene 2

19. What are relationships like in the Maxson house, six months after the events in scene 1?

20. What has happened to Gabriel? What has Troy had to do with it?

21. What has happened to Alberta?

22. What is the significance of Troy's speech to "Mr. Death"? How is this speech echoed at the end of the play? Why does Troy, here, resolve to complete the fence that has been under construction for virtually the entire play up to this point?

Act 2, Scene 3

23. What is the major action taking place in this scene?

Act 2, Scene 4

24. What is the significance of the fact that Lyons is paying back Troy the 20 dollars he owes?

25. What is Troy's attitude toward ministers? What changes do you perceive have taken place in Troy's character in the course of the play?

Act 2, Scene 5

26. What has happened in the eight-year interval since scene 4? What is to be the major action of scene 5? What has happened to Cory? To Lyons? Who is Raynell? What is her first response to Cory? What is happening to the family at the play's end?

GENERAL QUESTIONS

1. Explain the importance of big-league baseball in the play. What has been Troy's connection to baseball? In what way is Troy an authority on well-known baseball stars of the 1950s? Who is Josh Gibson? How does Troy come to have known Josh Gibson? In what way is Josh Gibson's career symbolic in the play?

2. Why is this play titled *Fences*? In what way are fences used symbolically by Wilson? What fences pertain to Troy? In what way is Jesus a fence around Rose? Does Jesus separate her from others or make her special? What fences separate Troy and Cory? What fences separate Troy and Lyons? What other meanings of fences can you think of that might apply to this play?

3. What is the significance of Troy's dog "Blue"? Why is Blue regularly mentioned in the course of the play? What is the significance of the duet, about the dog, sung by Cory and Raynell? What does their singing suggest about their attitudes toward Troy?

4. How might *Fences* be considered as a play about the relationship of fathers and sons? What is the importance of Bono's story about his father? What does Troy's account of his experience with his own father tell us about Troy? About his attitude toward his own sons? Describe the relationship between Troy and Lyons. Why does antagonism verging on hatred and outright violence between Troy and Cory develop in 2.4? What is Troy trying to establish? In what way is Troy superior to his own father, when it comes to his relationship with Cory? Why does Cory tell Troy that he is no more than "just an old man"? How does the situation escalate between Troy and Cory? How does it get resolved?

5. Explain the symbolism and meaning of Gabriel's being alone on stage at the play's end. Why is it Gabriel who is the last speaker in the play? What is the meaning of Gabriel's dance? Why does the play end as it does, with the image of Gabriel trying to blow his horn, but with no sound coming out? What is the meaning of the Gate of Heaven as the final vision? In what way is the gate also a fence?

6. What significance should one attach to the names of the play's characters: Troy, Rose, Bono, Cory, Lyons, Raynell, Gabriel? In what ways might the names be considered symbolic?

7. Describe the language, which has been called "Black English," used by the characters in *Fences*. What grammatical "rules" do the characters follow? What rules do they ignore? Is there ever any passage that is rendered obscure by the speech patterns? What difficulties, if any, does this speech offer to a modern reader? What is gained for the play by the use of this type of speech?

8. What is the relationship of the epigraph by Wilson ("As God . . .") to the events of the play?

WRITING ABOUT REALISTIC AND NONREALISTIC DRAMA

Your essay should take into account the traditional elements of drama—plot, character, language, setting, symbol, and theme. Conventional approaches to these elements are discussed in Chapter 20 (pp. 1012–15), and you may want to review this material. As you plan your essay, your overall concern should be to determine the relative degrees of realism or nonrealism with which the elements are presented and developed. Your discoveries here will enable you to describe the ways in which the play establishes its views and ideas about life and the world. In short, how do conventional aspects of dramatic structure, together with the degree of realism or nonrealism, create a perspective that is the unique quality of the play?

Questions for Discovering Ideas

PLOT. Does the play unfold in a chronological order that imitates reality, or does it mix past and present action? Is the action true to life or stylized? Are the conflicts resolved realistically, or does the playwright employ a conventional and perhaps improbable happy (or sad) ending? How does the realistic or nonrealistic development of these aspects affect the play's meaning and impact?

CHARACTER. Are the characters realistic or symbolic, representative, or stereotyped? Are they round or flat? Are they motivated by lifelike considerations, like Amanda in *The Glass Menagerie*, who lives only in the past? Or are they motivated by the play's requirements, like the narrator, who has the artificial role of speaking directly to the audience? Are the characters consistent, or do they drop in and out of character? Are their clothing and makeup (as described in the stage directions) an imitation of real life, or are they theatrical and nonrealistic? Are all the characters developed in the same manner, or are there differences in the degree of realism you find in each? Is one character more or less realistic than any of the others? If so, why? Of what importance is this character to the play as a whole?

LANGUAGE. Look carefully at the diction, style, and patterns of the dialogue. In realistic drama, what is the nature of the speeches? Is the language colloquial, formal, low? Is it appropriate for the characters? Is the dialogue normal or natural, granted the situation? Do the characters speak loudly? Do they whisper? Shout? Why? What pattern or consistency can you discover by studying how the characters speak? Within the confines of realistic drama, what normal or realistic variations occur? (For example, a letter is read aloud; a phone conversation occurs; a character is alone onstage and speaks to characters offstage as in O'Neill's *Before Breakfast* [Chapter 20], or a character speaks to characters who do not hear.) What proportion of the dialogue is ordinary two- or three-way conversation? How much variation occurs, and what kind is it? Why do you think the dramatists have varied the normal dialogue, and how do these variations shape your perception of the play?

In nonrealistic drama, some dialogue will be realistically normal or appear so, but much of it will be shaped by the play's nonrealistic premise. How do you identify nonrealistic speech? Do you find nonrealistic devices such as verse, song, or unnatural and patterned repetition? Does any character seem to be speaking in different voices? If so, why? Which characters seem to ignore other characters and speak instead to the air or to the audience? How extensive is such direct address? Does a single character do most of this talking? If so, what is he or she like? What does the character tell you about himself or herself? About the other characters in the play? The background? Plot? Action? Setting? Staging? How accurate and objective is this character? How does this direct address shape and control your responses?

In sum, how do all aspects of language determine the extent to which the play effectively communicates ideas and emotions to you? As you deal with language, also consider the significance of other aspects of sound indicated in the stage directions, such as sound effects (as in *A Dollhouse* [Chapter 24]) or music (as in *Death of a Salesman* [Chapter 21]).

SETTING. To what degree do the stage directions present the setting as realistic or nonrealistic? Do the directions call for the reproduction of an actual room or place? How much specific detail is included? If less than a fully realistic setting is described, how far does the playwright go in reducing the setting to the bare stage? How much of the physical theater does the playwright indicate that he or she wants you to see or imagine? To what extent do you find symbolic, impressionistic, and nonrealistic devices, such as transparent walls? How do the stage directions describe lighting? Is the lighting used realistically, to recreate natural illumination, or nonrealistically, to spotlight and emphasize specific places, objects, characters, or actions? Most important, how does the setting and its degree of realism (or nonrealism) contribute to the impact and meaning of the play?

SYMBOLISM. Because symbols operate in life as they do in art, there is symbolism both in the realistic plays of Glaspell and Wilson and in the relatively nonrealistic dramas of Miller and Williams. Are symbols introduced through realistic or logical techniques, or do they appear illogically and nonrealistically? You can focus your exploration directly on the symbol and its meaning (the front doorway in *Mulatto*) or the nonrealistic methods through which it is established (the blue roses in *The Glass Menagerie*).

THEME. What are the important concepts in the play, and how are they conveyed? Be sure to give special consideration to significantly realistic or nonrealistic techniques. In considering a realistic play like *Trifles* or *Mulatto*, explore the ways in which realism in character, action, and setting contribute to the play's ideas. Conversely, consider how Williams employs a strikingly nonrealistic device, such as the music or the screen projections, to convey and emphasize the themes of *The Glass Menagerie*.

Strategies for Organizing Ideas

Your central idea should show how realistic or nonrealistic elements affect part or all of the play. Try to connect the topic with its effect. For example, begin with sentences such as these: (1) "Tom as a nonrealistic narrator and realistic character unifies *The Glass Menagerie* and gives the play a coherent and subjective point of view." (2) "In *A Dollhouse*, Krogstad's exposure of Nora's forgery makes Nora realize the weakness of her marriage, and thus it brings the marriage of the Helmers to a breaking point."

The supporting details can be organized in any way that produces a logical and convincing essay. If you are writing about the ways in which nonrealistic devices emphasize meaning in *The Glass Menagerie*, for example, you might organize your essay around the setting, the lighting, and the screen device. When your essay focuses on only one element, you can organize your supporting details to reflect the order in which they occur in the play.

In your conclusion you might raise larger issues than you have already raised, or you might make broader connections not only about your topics but also about the play as a whole. You might also reconsider the significance of the play's general level of realistic or nonrealistic techniques.

Illustrative Student Essay

Although underlined sentences are not recommended by MLA style, they are used in this illustrative essay as teaching tools to emphasize the central idea, thesis sentence, and topic sentences.

Jhaveri 1

Deepunkhar Jhaveri

Professor Gordon

English 121

5 May 2014

Realism and Nonrealism in Tom's Triple Role in *The Glass Menagerie*°

[1]   In *The Glass Menagerie*, Tennessee Williams combines realistic and nonrealistic elements to explore the personalities and conflicts of the Wingfield family. One of his most effective nonrealistic elements in the play is his use of Tom in three different roles.* As a realistic character within the action, a nonrealistic stage manager of the action, and a nonrealistic narrator of the entire play, Tom combines three functions that strongly shape our perceptions.†

°**This play appears on pages 1379–1426.**
*Central idea.
†Thesis sentence.

Jhaveri 2

As a realistic character involved in the recollected action of the play, Tom   [2]
is ensnared by the economic and emotional demands of his family and his job.
In the opening description of the characters, Williams explains Tom's plight:
"to escape from a trap he [Tom] has to act without pity." In addition, Tom
himself dramatically expresses his need to escape from his stifling life at home.
He discusses this need with his mother in scene 3, with Laura in scene 4, and,
above all, with Jim in scene 6. Here, we see that Tom craves not only escape
but also adventure. He tells Jim, "I'm planning a change." And he clearly
expresses his desire to move out of the prison house of the family:

> It's our turn now, to go to the South Sea Island—to make a safari—
> to be exotic, far off! But I'm not patient. I don't want to wait till
> then, I'm tired of the *movies* and I am *about to move*!
> I'm starting to boil inside. I know I seem dreamy, but inside—well,
> I'm boiling! (1409)

These expressions of his need to escape define a major line of the realistic
thought and action in *The Glass Menagerie*.

Tom's realism as a character is undercut by his momentary role as a stage   [3]
manager in scene 1. Here, he speaks with Amanda "as though reading from a
script." In this same scene, "Tom motions for music and a spot of light on
Amanda." Although this device is abandoned, the image of Tom holding an
imaginary script and giving cues to the musicians and the lighting technicians
breaks any possible illusions that the play is imitating real life. The role as
manager emphasizes the fact that *The Glass Menagerie* is a play designed for
the stage and for live actors carrying out conventional stage roles.

Tom's part in shaping and unifying the play is most apparent in his   [4]
nonrealistic function as narrator. In this role, he stands aside from the action
occurring in the Wingfield apartment, and he also speaks directly to us. He
introduces the characters, provides background, and supplies an ongoing
commentary. In addition, he presents his own subjective views and also
personifies the play's theme of escape. As a character out of the past—the one
actually involved in the play's action—he represents a yearning for freedom
and adventure. As the narrator of the present action, he speaks truths that

his character in its past role has not yet learned, and he thus recognizes that escape from the past is impossible. When the play closes, he tells us that he remains trapped (1426), and thus he provides a final perspective on the central theme of escape.

[5]   The second striking aspect of Tom's function as narrator concerns his complete control of the play. Because he is the narrator, the action in *The Glass Menagerie* represents Tom's memories of events, rather than the events themselves. In the first speech of scene 1, he tells us, "The play is memory. Being a memory play, it is dimly lighted, it is sentimental, it is not realistic." Since the events from the past that occur onstage emerge from Tom's memory, it is he who provides an overriding unity and perspective. We perceive everything through his mind and from his point of view. As a nonrealistic narrator, he holds the stage action together and totally controls our responses.

[6]   Williams thus uses Tom in three distinct ways to create unity and perspective. As a realistic character aching to leave the confinement of home, Tom embodies the theme of escape. As a nonrealistic stage manager, he illustrates the artificiality of the dramatic literary form and stresses the legendary nature of the action. As the play's narrator, he imposes a subjective but coherent control over the action and offers thematic resolution. The nonrealistic aspects of his roles mesh perfectly with other devices that Williams employs nonrealistically, especially the slides, music, and lighting.

[7]   Whether realistic or unrealistic, however, *The Glass Menagerie* is about life—its desires, its dreams, its need for independent action, its disappointments, and its poignancy. If Williams did not dramatize these issues, the technique alone would not make a great play. But he does dramatize them, and as a result the freedom of action and character he achieves through the combination of roles for Tom enables him to achieve a remarkable unity of topic, merging past with present and reality with unreality. Williams's use of Tom is a major reason for which *The Glass Menagerie* may be considered a great modern drama.

Jhaveri 4

Work Cited

Williams, Tennessee. *The Glass Menagerie*. *Literature: An Introduction to Reading and Writing, Compact Edition*. Ed. Edgar V. Roberts and Robert Zweig. 6th ed. New York: Pearson Longman, 2015. 1379–1426. Print.

Commentary on the Essay

This essay shows how Williams's manipulation of Tom creates artistic and thematic unity in *The Glass Menagerie*. The primary focus is on character, but a number of distinct topics are taken up in connection with this element because the essay concerns Tom as a character, stage director, and narrator.

The body of the essay (paragraphs 2–5) takes up these three roles in the order listed in the introduction. Notice that this order does not reflect the sequence in which these roles occur in the play. Rather, they are organized to reflect a progression from the most realistic to the most nonrealistic aspects of Tom's three different functions. Thus, paragraph 2 discusses Tom as a realistic character and connects him to one of the play's central themes—entrapment and the desire to escape. Paragraphs 3, 4, and 5 shift to a consideration of Tom first as stage manager and second as narrator. These paragraphs explain the nonrealistic nature of these roles and explore the effects of Tom as the nonrealistic figure.

The concluding two paragraphs (6 and 7) provide a review and summary of the three roles Tom plays and the effects each produces in connection with theme and unity. In addition, they suggest a connection between the nonrealistic aspects of Tom's roles and the play's great power.

Throughout the body, direct quotation of dialogue or action as indicated in the stage directions is employed as supporting evidence. Quotations are used to validate specific points and are documented either within parentheses or in the body of discourse itself.

Writing Topics About Dramatic Reality and Nonreality

Writing Paragraphs

1. The screen device described in Williams's Production Notes (see p. 1380) is omitted from most productions of *The Glass Menagerie*. In a paragraph describe why. Consider the advantages or disadvantages of referring to this device in the printed text. How do the screen images affect your reading?

2. Describe Hughes's symbolism in *Mulatto.* How does the symbolism bring out the black/white differences in the play? Choose a location, object, or action that is symbolic. In a paragraph describe it as a symbol. In what way is the symbol realistic? If it were not realistic, would it be successful as a symbol? Explain.

Writing Essays

1. Compare the families of the Wingfields in *The Glass Menagerie,* Colonel Norwood in *Mulatto,* and the Maxsons in *Fences* (to which you might wish to add the Helmers in *A Dollhouse* [Chapter 24] and the Wrights in *Trifles* [Chapter 20]). In an essay describe what concept of family these plays present. What good and bad effects are produced within the families? Which effect predominates? How realistic are the internal family dissensions? How serious? How essential to the various plots? What is unusual or illogical about the dissensions? How? Why?

2. Compare the set descriptions of *Fences* and *The Glass Menagerie.* In an essay describe what elements of realism or nonrealism are common to both. How? To what apparent purpose, in terms of your perceptions of the characters? What effects would the sets have on the performances of the play, and on audience perceptions of the plays? How? Why?

3. Let us suppose that a fellow student has said to you that even when a play is nonrealistic, it is nevertheless realistic, and, conversely, even when a play is realistic, it is also nonrealistic. When you hear this remark, you decide to consider this apparently contradictory issue with him/her. With reference to *Fences* and *Mulatto,* which can be termed realistic, and to *The Glass Menagerie,* which you may consider nonrealistic, develop an argument essay (see Chapter 26) either for or against the idea first proposed by the fellow student.

Creative Writing Assignment

1. Write two separate versions of a scene of your own. (Some possible topics: a woman confronts her boyfriend upon learning that he has been seeing someone else; a man has an interview with his boss and learns that he is being fired; an army lieutenant tells his platoon that they are about to be attacked; a woman realizes that she is the best salesperson in the firm.) In the first, aim for total reality; in the second, for total unreality. What differences do you think your intentions in each case require of you as a practicing dramatist? What different requirements are made on your dialogue, on your action, on your setting, and on your costuming and suggested makeup for your actors? What elements do you think are the most unrealistic in your unrealistic version, and why do you believe you make them so unrealistic? Does the lack of realism, in your judgment, make your scene either more or less dramatic? Write an introductory essay to your two versions explaining these and other principles of your dramatic composition.

Library Assignment

1. Write a research essay on the concept and practice of literary realism. To begin your research, you might wish to use books like these: Hugh S. Davies, *Realism in the Drama* (Cambridge, Cambridge UP, 1934); John B. Moore, *The Comic and the Realistic in English Drama* (New York: Russell & Russell, 1965); Harold H. Kolb, *The Illusion of Life: American Realism as a Literary Form* (Charlottesville: U of Virginia P, 1969); and Joseph P. Stern, *On Realism* (Boston: Routledge, 1973).

2. Consider any of the plays in this chapter using a feminist approach (see Chapter 25 for a discussion of this topic). In an essay describe what elements of realism or nonrealism are relevant to such a discussion. To aid your essay you might wish to use a study by Patricia R. Schroeder, *The Feminist Possibilities of Dramatic Realism* (Madison: Fairleigh Dickinson UP, 1996).

Chapter 24
Henrik Ibsen and the Realistic Problem Play: *A Dollhouse*

AFTER STUDYING THIS MATERIAL, YOU SHOULD BE ABLE TO DO THE FOLLOWING:

- Describe Ibsen's life and major prose plays
- Identify the realistic issues and problems in Ibsen's *A Dollhouse*
- Explore a variety of critical opinions on Ibsen's *A Dollhouse*

The Norwegian playwright Henrik Johan Ibsen (1828–1906) is the acknowledged originator—the "father"—of modern drama. He deserves this recognition because of his pioneering dramatizations of challenging and sometimes shocking private and public issues. Today there are few restrictions on dramatists except success at the box office. Plays may range freely on almost any subject, such as the drug culture, sexual inclinations, AIDS, the right to commit suicide, the problems of real-estate dealers, the life of a fan dancer, violence, family dissension, homosexuality, the Vietnam War or the Kuwait War or the Afghanistan War or the Iraq War, and the aftereffects of the atrocities of 9/11/01. If one includes film as drama, there is virtually no limit to the topics that dramatists currently explore. It is well to stress that writers for the stage have not always been this free and that Ibsen was in the forefront of the struggle for unbridled dramatic expression. A brief consideration of some of his major dramatic topics shows his originality and daring: the blinding and crippling effects of congenital syphilis, a woman's renunciation of a traditional protective marriage, suicide, the manipulations of people seeking personal benefits, the sacrifices of pursuing truth, the rejection of a child by a parent, and the abandonment of personal happiness in favor of professional interests.

Ibsen's Life and Early Work

From Ibsen's beginnings, there was little to indicate how important he was to become. He was born in Skien (*SHEE-en*), Norway, a small town just seventy miles southwest of the capital, Christiania (now Oslo). Although his parents had been prosperous, they went bankrupt when he was only seven, and in the years that followed the family suffered the miseries of poverty. When Ibsen was fifteen, he was apprenticed to a pharmacist, and he seemed headed for an undistinguished career in this profession even though he hated it. By 1849, however, when he wrote

Catiline, his first play in verse, it was clear that the theater was to be his life. Largely through the efforts of the famous violinist Ole Bull, a new National Theater had been established in Bergen, and Ibsen was appointed its director. He stayed in Bergen for six years and then went to Christiania, where for the next five years he tried to fashion a genuine Norwegian national theater. His attempts proved fruitless, for the theater went bankrupt in 1862. After writing *The Pretenders* in 1864, he secured enough governmental travel money to enable him to leave Norway. For the next twenty-seven years he lived in Germany and Italy in what has been called a self-imposed exile.

Although this first part of Ibsen's theatrical career was devoted to many practical matters—production, management, directing, and finances—he was also constantly writing. His early plays were in verse and were mainly nationalist and romantic, as a few representative titles suggest: *Lady Inger of Oestraat* (1855), *The Feast of Solhaug* (1856), and *Olaf Liljekrans* (1857). In his first ten years in Germany and Italy he finished four plays. The best known of these is *Peer Gynt* (1867), a fantasy play about a historical Norwegian hero, Peer Gynt, who is saved from spiritual emptiness by the love of the devoted heroine Solveig. Today, *Peer Gynt* is best known because of the incidental music written for it by Norway's major composer, Edvard Grieg (1843–1907). Ibsen asked Grieg to compose the music for the initial performances in 1876. Grieg's response was enthusiastic and creative, and the result is still enjoyed by millions today. Ibsen also supplied the poem for which Grieg composed one of his loveliest songs, "A Swan."

Ibsen's Major Prose Plays

During the years when Ibsen was fighting poverty and establishing his career in the theater, Europe was undergoing great political and intellectual changes. Throughout the nineteenth century, Ibsen's home country, Norway, was trying to release itself from the domination of neighboring Sweden and to establish its own territorial and national integrity. In Ibsen's twentieth year, 1848, the February Uprising in Paris resulted in the deposition of the French king and the establishment of a new French republic. This same year also saw the publication of the *Communist Manifesto* of Karl Marx (1818–1883). In 1864, the year Ibsen left Norway, Marx's first socialist International was held in London. In addition, during the time Ibsen lived in Italy and Germany, both countries were going through the tenuous political processes of becoming authentic nation-states. In short, change was everywhere.

Ibsen also was changing and growing as a thinker and dramatist, driven by the idea that a forward and creative drama could bring about deeper and more permanent changes than could be effected by soldiers and politicians. To this end he developed the realistic **problem play**—a theatrical work that posits a major personal, social, professional, or political problem that occasions the play's dramatic conflicts and tensions. Each problem is timely, topical, and realistic, as are Ibsen's characters, places, situations, and outcomes. In this vein, Ibsen wrote the twelve prose problem plays on which his reputation rests: *The Pillars of Society* (1877), *A Dollhouse* (1879), *Ghosts* (1881), *An Enemy of the People* (1882), *The Wild*

Duck (1884), *Rosmersholm* (1886), *The Lady from the Sea* (1888), *Hedda Gabler* (1890), *The Master Builder* (1892), *Little Eyolf* (1894), *John Gabriel Borkman* (1896), and *When We Dead Awaken* (1899). He finished the first eight of these plays while living in Germany and Italy, the last four after returning to Norway in 1891.

In these major plays Ibsen dramatizes human beings breaking free from restrictions and inhibitions and trying to establish their individuality and freedom—freedom of self, inquiry, pursuit of truth, artistic dedication, and, above all, the freedom of love. In attempting to achieve these goals, Ibsen's dramatic characters find internal opposition in self-interest, self-indulgence, and self-denial, and external opposition in the personal and political influences and manipulations of others. Because the plays are designed to be realistic, Ibsen's characters fall short of their goals. At best they achieve a respite in their combat, as in *An Enemy of the People*, or begin a quest in new directions, as in *A Dollhouse*. They always make great sacrifices, sometimes losing life itself, as in *Hedda Gabler* and *John Gabriel Borkman*.

A Dollhouse: Ibsen's Best-Known Problem Play

A Dollhouse (*Et Dukkehjem*, 1879)[1] is representative of Ibsen's realistic problem dramas. Its scenes are realistic, including appropriate furniture, a piano, a Christmas tree, carpeting, and wall engravings. Its characters are in the process of realistically confronting overwhelming personal, marital, and economic problems. Realism extends also to the technique of presentation, particularly the exposition about the root causes of the problems that come to a head in the play itself. As *A Dollhouse* unfolds, we learn that years earlier, Nora Helmer had extended herself beyond her means to save Torvald from a near-fatal illness.

Ibsen's Symbolism in *A Dollhouse*

A Dollhouse is representative of Ibsen's realism, but it is also replete with contextual symbolism, like the major plays that came before and after it. At the end of the late play *John Gabriel Borkman*, for example, the major character freezes to death, an occurrence symbolic of what he had done to himself much earlier by denying love. In reference to *A Dollhouse*, the title itself symbolizes the dependent and dehumanized role of the wife within traditional middle-class marriages. In addition, the entire nation of Norway (cold, legal, male) is contrasted symbolically with Italy (warm, emotional, female). Ironically, the break in the Helmers' marriage is symbolically aligned with events that occur or have occurred in both locations. Other symbols in *A Dollhouse* are the Christmas tree, the children's presents, the death of Dr. Rank, and the mailbox.

Ibsen's title *Et Dukkehjem* literally means the home (*hjem*) of a doll or puppet (*dukke*). *A Doll's House*, the traditional and most common English title of the play, is not an accurate rendering of *dukkehjem*, and, in addition, it is misleading because of some of the connotations of our word *doll*. Recent translators have used *A Doll House* as the title, but this form is not in regular use. Our English word for a toy house for dolls is listed in collegiate dictionaries as *dollhouse*, a one-word compound. *A Dollhouse* is therefore preferable to the other two titles because it accurately renders *Et Dukkehjem*, and it is also the form accepted in current dictionaries.

A Dollhouse as a "Well-Made Play"

The plot and structure of *A Dollhouse* show Ibsen's use of the conventions of the **well-made play** (*la pièce bien faite*), a form developed and popularized in nineteenth-century France by Eugène Scribe (1791–1861) and Victorien Sardou (1831–1908). Ibsen was familiar with well-made plays, having directed many of them himself at Bergen and Christiania. The well-made play follows a rigid and efficient structure in which the drama begins at the story's climax. Usually the plot is built on a secret known by the audience and perhaps one or two of the characters. The well-made play thus begins in suspense and offers a pattern of increasing tension produced through exposition and the timely arrivals of new characters (like Krogstad) and threatening news or props like the disclosure of Nora's earlier financial transactions. In the course of action of the well-made play, the fortunes of the protagonist go from a low point, through a *peripeteia* or reversal (Aristotle's concept), to a high point at which the protagonist confronts and defeats the villain.

Although Ibsen makes use of many of the structural elements of the well-made play, he varies and departs from the pattern to suit his realistic purposes. Thus in *A Dollhouse* his variation is that Nora's confrontation with Krogstad, who is the apparent villain, does not lead to a satisfactory resolution, but rather precipitates the more significant albeit intractable confrontation with her husband. In *A Dollhouse*, just as in many other Ibsen plays, there is not a traditionally well-made victorious outcome; rather there are provisional outcomes—adjustments—in keeping with the realistic concept that as life goes on, problems continue.

The Timeliness and Dramatic Power of *A Dollhouse*

Ibsen's focus on real life issues and problems has given his plays continued timeliness and strength. Thus *A Dollhouse* vividly portrays the totally dependent position of married women in the nineteenth century. Most notably, a woman could not borrow funds legally without a man's cosignature, and Nora had been forced to violate the law to obtain the money to restore her husband's health. The mailbox, to which Torvald has the only key, symbolizes this limitation, and the ultimate disclosure of the box's contents, rather than freeing Nora and Torvald, highlights her dependency. Today's feminism has stressed the issues of female freedom and equality, together with many other issues vital to women, but the need for feminine individuality and independence has not been more originally and forcefully dramatized than in *A Dollhouse*.

Bibliographic Studies

Because of Ibsen's importance, there have been many translations and editions of the plays. The Modern Library Giant edition of Farquharson Sharp's translations of *Eleven Plays by Henrik Ibsen* (introduction by H. L. Mencken) has been a mainstay for many decades. Rolf Fjelde published paperback translations in 1970 and followed these up with *The Complete Major Prose Plays* in 1978 (twelve plays). Michael Meyer's translations (sixteen plays in four paperback volumes, 1986) are of major significance. Other individual and collected plays have been translated by Peter Watts, Una Ellis-Fermor, James McFarlane, Christopher Hampton, Inger Lignell, Nicholas Rudall, William Archer, Christopher Fry, and Kenneth McLeish. These names by no means constitute a complete list. A short edition of Ibsen's poetry has been translated by Michael Feingold (1987).

The major biography of Ibsen is Halvdan Koht, *Life of Ibsen*, translated and edited by Einar Haugen and A. E. Santaniello (New York: Blom, 1971). Significant critical and biographical studies include George Bernard Shaw, *The Quintessence of Ibsenism* (1891; rpt. 1957), the pioneering work of Ibsen criticism; Rolf Fjelde, *Ibsen: A Collection of Critical Essays* (Englewood Cliffs: Prentice Hall, 1965); Michael Meyer, *Henrik Ibsen: The Farewell to Poetry 1864–1882* (London: Hart-Davis, 1971); James Hurt, *Catiline's Dream: An Essay on Ibsen's Plays* (Urbana: U of Illinois P, 1972); Clela Allphin, *Women in the Plays of Henrik Ibsen* (New York: Revisionist, 1975); Harold Clurman, *Ibsen* (New York: Macmillan, 1977); Einar Haugen, *Ibsen's Drama: Author to Audience* (Minneapolis: U of Minnesota P, 1979); David Thomas, *Henrik Ibsen* (London: Macmillan, 1983); Yvonne Shafer, ed., *Approaches to Teaching Ibsen's* A Doll House (New York: MLA, 1985); Charles R. Lyons, ed., *Critical Essays on Henrik Ibsen* (Boston: Hall, 1987); Frederick Marker and Lise-Lone Marker, *Ibsen's Lively Art* (New York: Cambridge UP, 1989); Joan Templeton, "The *Doll House* Backlash: Criticism, Feminism, and Ibsen," *PMLA* 104 (1989): 28–40; Naomi Lebowitz, *Ibsen and the Great World* (Baton Rouge: Louisiana UP, 1990); Errol Durbach, *A Doll's House: Ibsen's Myth of Transformation* (Boston: Twayne, 1991); Brian Johnston, *The Ibsen Cycle: The Design of the Plays from* Pillars of Society *to* When We Dead Awaken (University Park: Pennsylvania State UP, 1992); and James McFarlane, ed., *The Cambridge Companion to Ibsen* (Cambridge: Cambridge UP, 1994).

HENRIK IBSEN (1828–1906)

 ## A Dollhouse (*Et Dukkehjem*) (1879)

Translated by R. Farquharson Sharp

CHARACTERS

Torvald Helmer, a lawyer and bank manager
Nora, his wife
Doctor Rank, the "greatest friend" of the Helmers
Mrs. Christine Linde, Nora's old friend, recently widowed, returning after a ten-year absence
Nils Krogstad, a lawyer and bank clerk
Ivar, Bob, and Emmy, the Helmers' three young children
Anne, their nurse
Helen, a housemaid
A Porter

The action takes place in the HELMER's apartment.

ACT 1

SCENE. A room furnished comfortably and tastefully, but not extravagantly. At the back, a door to the right leads to the entrance hall, another to the left leads to HELMER's study. Between the doors stands a piano. In the middle of the left-hand wall is a door, and beyond it a window. Near the window are a round table, armchairs and a small sofa. In the right-hand wall, at the farther end, another door; and on the same side, nearer the footlights, a stove, two easy chairs and a rocking-chair; between the stove and the door, a small table. Engravings on the walls; a cabinet with china and other small objects; a small book case with well-bound books. The floors are carpeted, and a fire burns in the stove. It is winter.

A bell rings in the hall; shortly afterwards the door is heard to open. Enter NORA, humming a tune and in high spirits. She is in outdoor dress and carries a number of parcels; these she lays on the table to the right. She leaves the outer door open after her, and through it is seen a PORTER who is carrying a Christmas Tree and a basket, which he gives to the MAID who has opened the door.

NORA: Hide the Christmas Tree carefully, Helen. Be sure the children do not see it till this evening, when it is dressed. [*to the PORTER, taking out her purse.*] How much?

PORTER: Sixpence.

NORA: There is a shilling. No, keep the change. [*The PORTER thanks her, and goes out. NORA shuts the door. She is laughing to herself, as she takes off her hat and coat. She takes a packet of macaroons from her pocket and eats one or two; then goes cautiously to her husband's door and listens.*] Yes, he is in.

[*Still humming, she goes to the table on the right.*]

HELMER: [*calls out from his room*] Is that my little lark twittering out there?

NORA: [*busy opening some of the parcels*] Yes, it is!   5

HELMER: Is my little squirrel bustling about?

NORA: Yes!

HELMER: When did my squirrel come home?

NORA: Just now. [*puts the bag of macaroons into her pocket and wipes her mouth*] Come in here, Torvald, and see what I have bought.

HELMER: Don't disturb me. [*A little later, he opens the door and looks into the room, pen in hand.*] Bought, did you say? All these things? Has my little spendthrift been wasting money again?   10

NORA: Yes, but, Torvald, this year we really can let ourselves go a little. This is the first Christmas that we have not needed to economise.

HELMER: Still, you know, we can't spend money recklessly.

NORA: Yes, Torvald, we may be a wee bit more reckless now, mayn't we? Just a tiny wee bit! You are going to have a big salary and earn lots and lots of money.

HELMER: Yes, after the New Year; but then it will be a whole quarter before the salary is due.

NORA: Pooh! we can borrow till then.   15

HELMER: Nora! [*goes up to her and takes her playfully by the ear*] The same little featherhead! Suppose, now, that I borrowed fifty pounds to-day, and you spent it all in the Christmas week, and then on New Year's Eve a slate fell on my head and killed me, and—

NORA: [*putting her hands over his mouth*] Oh! don't say such horrid things.

HELMER: Still, suppose that happened—what then?

NORA: If that were to happen, I don't suppose I should care whether I owed money or not.

HELMER: Yes, but what about the people who had lent it?   20

NORA: They? Who would bother about them? I should not know who they were.

HELMER: That is like a woman! But seriously, Nora, you know what I think about that. No debt, no borrowing. There can be no freedom or beauty about a home life that depends on borrowing and debt. We two have kept bravely on the straight road so far, and we will go on the same way for the short time longer that there need be any struggle.

Nora: [*moving towards the stove*] As you please, Torvald.

Helmer: [*following her*] Come, come, my little skylark must not droop her wings. What is this! Is my little squirrel out of temper? [*taking out his purse*] Nora, what do you think I have got here?

25   **Nora:** [*turning around quickly*] Money!

Helmer: There you are. [*gives her some money*] Do you think I don't know what a lot is wanted for housekeeping at Christmas-time?

Nora: [*counting*] Ten shillings—a pound—two pounds! Thank you, thank you, Torvald; that will keep me going for a long time.

Helmer: Indeed it must.

Nora: Yes, yes, it will. But come here and let me show you what I have bought. And all so cheap! Look, here is a new suit for Ivar, and a sword; and a horse and a trumpet for Bob; and a doll and dolly's bedstead for Emmy—they are very plain, but anyway she will soon break them in pieces. And here are dress-lengths and handkerchiefs for the maids; old Anne ought really to have something better.

30   **Helmer:** And what is in this parcel?

Nora: [*crying out*] No, no! you mustn't see that till this evening.

Helmer: Very well. But now tell me, you extravagant little person, what would you like for yourself?

Nora: For myself? Oh, I am sure I don't want anything.

Helmer: Yes, but you must. Tell me something reasonable that you would particularly like to have.

32   **Nora:** No, I really can't think of anything—unless, Torvald—

Helmer: Well?

Nora: [*playing with his coat buttons, and without raising her eyes to his*] If you really want to give me something, you might—you might—

Helmer: Well, out with it!

Nora: [*speaking quickly*] You might give me money, Torvald. Only just as much as you can afford; and then one of these days I will buy something with it.

40   **Helmer:** But, Nora—

Nora: Oh, do! dear Torvald; please, please do! Then I will wrap it up in beautiful gilt paper and hang it on the Christmas Tree. Wouldn't that be fun?

Helmer: What are little people called that are always wasting money?

Nora: Spendthrifts—I know. Let us do as you suggest, Torvald, and then I shall have time to think what I am most in want of. That is a very sensible plan, isn't it?

Helmer: [*smiling*] Indeed it is—that is to say, if you were really to save out of the money I give you, and then really buy something for yourself. But if you spend it all on the house-keeping and any number of unnecessary things, then I merely have to pay up again.

45   **Nora:** Oh but, Torvald—

Helmer: You can't deny it, my dear little Nora. [*puts his arm round her waist*] It's a sweet little spendthrift, but she uses up a deal of money. One would hardly believe how expensive such little persons are!

Nora: It's a shame to say that. I do really save all I can.

Helmer: [*laughing*] That's very true—all you can. But you can't save anything!

Nora: [*smiling quietly and happily*] You haven't any idea how many expenses we skylarks and squirrels have, Torvald.

50   **Helmer:** You are an odd little soul. Very like your father. You always find some new way of wheedling money out of me, and, as soon as you have got it, it seems to melt

in your hands. You never know where it has gone. Still, one must take you as you are. It is in the blood; for indeed it is true that you can inherit these things, Nora.

NORA: Ah, I wish I had inherited many of papa's qualities.

HELMER: And I would not wish you to be anything but just what you are, my sweet little skylark. But, do you know, it strikes me that you are looking rather—what shall I say—rather uneasy to-day?

NORA: Do I?

HELMER: You do, really. Look straight at me.

NORA: [*looks at him*] Well?   55

HELMER: [*wagging his finger at her*] Hasn't Miss Sweet-Tooth been breaking rules in town to-day?

NORA: No; what makes you think that?

HELMER: Hasn't she paid a visit to the confectioner's?

NORA: No, I assure you, Torvald—

HELMER: Not been nibbling sweets?   60

NORA: No, certainly not.

HELMER: Not even taken a bite at a macaroon or two?

NORA: No, Torvald, I assure you really—

HELMER: There, there, of course I was only joking.

NORA: [*going to the table on the right*] I should not think of going against your wishes.   65

HELMER: No, I am sure of that! besides, you gave me your word—[*going up to her*]. Keep your little Christmas secrets to yourself, my darling. They will all be revealed to-night when the Christmas Tree is lit, no doubt.

NORA: Did you remember to invite Doctor Rank?

HELMER: No. But there is no need; as a matter of course he will come to dinner with us. However, I will ask him when he comes in this morning. I have ordered some good wine. Nora, you can't think how I am looking forward to this evening.

NORA: So am I! And how the children will enjoy themselves, Torvald!

HELMER: It is splendid to feel that one has a perfectly safe appointment, and a big enough   70 income. It's delightful to think of, isn't it?

NORA: It's wonderful!

HELMER: Do you remember last Christmas? For a full three weeks beforehand you shut yourself up every evening till long after midnight, making ornaments for the Christmas Tree and all the other fine things that were to be a surprise to us. It was the dullest three weeks I ever spent!

NORA: I didn't find it dull.

HELMER: [*smiling*] But there was precious little result, Nora.

NORA: Oh, you shouldn't tease me about that again. How could I help the cat's going in   75 and tearing everything to pieces?

HELMER: Of course you couldn't, poor little girl. You had the best of intentions to please us all, and that's the main thing. But it is a good thing that our hard times are over.

NORA: Yes, it is really wonderful.

HELMER: This time I needn't sit here and be dull all alone, and you needn't ruin your dear eyes and your pretty little hands—

NORA: [*clapping her hands*] No, Torvald, I needn't any longer, need I! It's wonderfully lovely to hear you say so! [*taking his arm*] Now I will tell you how I have been thinking we ought to arrange things, Torvald. As soon as Christmas is over—[*A bell rings in the hall.*] There's the bell. [*She tidies the room a little.*] There's someone at the door. What a nuisance!

HELMER: If it is a caller, remember I am not at home.   80

MAID: [*in the doorway*] A lady to see you, ma'am—a stranger.

NORA: Ask her to come in.

MAID: [*to* HELMER] The doctor came at the same time, sir.

HELMER: Did he go straight into my room?

85   **MAID:** Yes sir.

[HELMER *goes into his room. The* MAID *ushers in* MRS. LINDE, *who is in travelling dress, and shuts the door.*]

MRS. LINDE: [*in a dejected and timid voice*] How do you do, Nora?

NORA: [*doubtfully*] How do you do—

MRS. LINDE: You don't recognise me, I suppose.

NORA: No, I don't know—yes, to be sure, I seem to—[*suddenly*] Yes! Christine! Is it really you?

90   **MRS. LINDE:** Yes, it is I.

NORA: Christine! To think of my not recognising you! And yet how could I—[*in a gentle voice*] How you have altered, Christine!

MRS. LINDE: Yes, I have indeed. In nine, ten long years—

NORA: Is it so long since we met? I suppose it is. The last eight years have been a happy time for me, I can tell you. And so now you have come into the town, and have taken this long journey in winter—that was plucky of you.

MRS. LINDE: I arrived by steamer this morning.

95   **NORA:** To have some fun at Christmas-time, of course. How delightful! We will have such fun together! But take off your things. You are not cold, I hope. [*helps her*] Now we will sit down by the stove, and be cosy. No, take this arm-chair; I will sit here in the rocking-chair. [*takes her hands*] Now you look like your old self again; it was only the first moment—You are a little paler, Christine, and perhaps a little thinner.

MRS. LINDE: And much, much older, Nora.

NORA: Perhaps a little older; very, very little; certainly not much. [*stops suddenly and speaks seriously*] What a thoughtless creature I am, chattering away like this. My poor, dear Christine, do forgive me.

MRS. LINDE: What do you mean, Nora?

NORA: [*gently*] Poor Christine, you are a widow.

100   **MRS. LINDE:** Yes; it is three years ago now.

NORA: Yes, I knew; I saw it in the papers. I assure you, Christine, I meant ever so often to write to you at the time, but I always put it off and something always prevented me.

MRS. LINDE: I quite understand, dear.

NORA: It was very bad of me, Christine. Poor thing, how you must have suffered. And he left you nothing?

MRS. LINDE: No.

105   **NORA:** And no children?

MRS. LINDE: No.

NORA: Nothing at all, then?

MRS. LINDE: Not even any sorrow or grief to live upon.

NORA: [*looking incredulously at her*] But, Christine, is that possible?

110   **MRS. LINDE:** [*smiles sadly and strokes her hair*] It sometimes happens, Nora.

NORA: So you are quite alone. How dreadfully sad that must be. I have three lovely children. You can't see them just now, for they are out with their nurse. But now you must tell me all about it.

MRS. LINDE: No, no; I want to hear you.

NORA: No, you must begin. I mustn't be selfish to-day; to-day I must only think of your affairs. But there is one thing I must tell you. Do you know we have just had a great piece of good luck?

MRS. LINDE: No, what is it?

NORA: Just fancy, my husband has been made manager of the Bank!   115

MRS. LINDE: Your husband? What good luck!

NORA: Yes, tremendous! A barrister's profession is such an uncertain thing, especially if
he won't undertake unsavoury cases; and naturally Torvald has never been willing
to do that, and I quite agree with him. You may imagine how pleased we are! He is to
take up his work in the Bank at the New Year, and then he will have a big salary and
lots of commissions. For the future we can live quite differently—we can do just as
we like. I feel so relieved and so happy, Christine! It will be splendid to have heaps of
money and not need to have any anxiety, won't it?

MRS. LINDE: Yes, anyhow I think it would be delightful to have what one needs.

NORA: No, not only what one needs, but heaps and heaps of money.

MRS. LINDE: [*smiling*] Nora, Nora haven't you learnt sense yet? In our schooldays you   120
were a great spendthrift.

NORA: [*laughing*] Yes, that is what Torvald says now. [*wags her finger at her*] But "Nora,
Nora" is not so silly as you think. We have not been in a position for me to waste
money. We have both had to work.

MRS. LINDE: You too?

NORA: Yes; odds and ends, needlework, crochet-work, embroidery, and that kind of
thing. [*dropping her voice*] And other things as well. You know Torvald left his office
when we were married? There was no prospect of promotion there, and he had to try
and earn more than before. But during the first year he overworked himself dreadfully. You see, he had to make money every way he could, and he worked early and
late; but he couldn't stand it, and fell dreadfully ill, and the doctors said it was necessary for him to go south.

MRS. LINDE: You spent a whole year in Italy didn't you?

NORA: Yes. It was no easy matter to get away, I can tell you. It was just as Ivar was born;   125
but naturally we had to go. It was a wonderfully beautiful journey, and it saved Torvald's life. But it cost a tremendous lot of money, Christine.

MRS. LINDE: So I should think.

NORA: It cost about two hundred and fifty pounds. That's a lot, isn't it?

MRS. LINDE: Yes, and in emergencies like that it is lucky to have the money.

NORA: I ought to tell you that we had it from papa.

MRS. LINDE: Oh, I see. It was just about that time that he died, wasn't it?   130

NORA: Yes; and, just think of it, I couldn't go and nurse him. I was expecting little Ivar's birth
every day and I had my poor sick Torvald to look after. My dear, kind father—I never
saw him again, Christine. That was the saddest time I have known since our marriage.

MRS. LINDE: I know how fond you were of him. And then you went off to Italy?

NORA: Yes; you see we had money then, and the doctors insisted on our going, so we
started a month later.

MRS. LINDE: And your husband came back quite well?

NORA: As sound as a bell!   135

MRS. LINDE: But—the doctor?

NORA: What doctor?

MRS. LINDE: I thought your maid said the gentleman who arrived here just as I did was
the doctor?

NORA: Yes, that was Doctor Rank, but he doesn't come here professionally. He is our
greatest friend, and comes in at least once every day. No, Torvald has not had an
hour's illness since then, and our children are strong and healthy and so am I. [*jumps
up and claps her hands*] Christine! Christine! it's good to be alive and happy!—But how
horrid of me; I am talking of nothing but my own affairs. [*sits on a stool near her, and*

rests her arms on her knees] You mustn't be angry with me. Tell me, is it really true that you did not love your husband? Why did you marry him?

140 MRS. LINDE: My mother was alive then, and was bedridden and helpless, and I had to provide for my two younger brothers; so I did not think I was justified in refusing his offer.

NORA: No, perhaps you were quite right. He was rich at that time, then?

MRS. LINDE: I believe he was quite well off. But his business was a precarious one; and, when he died, it all went to pieces and there was nothing left.

NORA: And then?—

MRS. LINDE: Well, I had to turn my hand to anything I could find—first a small shop, then a small school, and so on. The last three years have seemed like one long working-day, with no rest. Now it is at an end, Nora. My poor mother needs me no more, for she is gone; and the boys do not need me either; they have got situations and can shift for themselves.

145 NORA: What a relief you must feel it—

MRS. LINDE: No, indeed; I only feel my life unspeakably empty. No one to live for any more. [*gets up restlessly*] That was why I could not stand the life in my little backwater any longer. I hope it may be easier here to find something which will busy me and occupy my thoughts. If only I could have the good luck to get some regular work— office work of some kind—

NORA: But, Christine, that is so frightfully tiring, and you look tired out now. You had far better go away to some watering-place.

MRS. LINDE: [*walking to the window*] I have no father to give me money for a journey, Nora.

NORA: [*rising*] Oh, don't be angry with me.

150 MRS. LINDE: [*going up to her*] It is you that must not be angry with me, dear. The worst of a position like mine is that it makes one so bitter. No one to work for, and yet obliged to be always on the look-out for chances. One must live, and so one becomes self- ish. When you told me of the happy turn your fortunes have taken—you will hardly believe it—I was delighted not so much on your account as on my own.

NORA: How do you mean?—Oh, I understand. You mean that perhaps Torvald could get you something to do.

MRS. LINDE: Yes, that was what I was thinking of.

NORA: He must, Christine. Just leave it to me; I will broach the subject very cleverly—I will think of something that will please him very much. It will make me so happy to be of some use to you.

MRS. LINDE: How kind you are, Nora, to be so anxious to help me! It is doubly kind in you, for you know so little of the burdens and troubles of life.

155 NORA: I—? I know so little of them?

MRS. LINDE: [*smiling*] My dear! Small household cares and that sort of thing!—You are a child, Nora.

NORA: [*tosses her head and crosses the stage*] You ought not to be so superior.

MRS. LINDE: No?

NORA: You are just like the others. They all think that I am incapable of anything really serious—

160 MRS. LINDE: Come, come—

NORA: —that I have gone through nothing in this world of cares.

MRS. LINDE: But, my dear Nora, you have just told me all your troubles.

NORA: Pooh!—those were trifles. [*lowering her voice*] I have not told you the important thing.

MRS. LINDE: The important thing? What do you mean?

165 NORA: You look down upon me altogether, Christine—but you ought not to. You are proud, aren't you, of having worked so hard and so long for your mother?

MRS. LINDE: Indeed, I don't look down on any one. But it is true that I am both proud and glad to think that I was privileged to make the end of my mother's life almost free from care.

NORA: And you are proud to think of what you have done for your brothers.

MRS. LINDE: I think I have the right to be.

NORA: I think so, too. But now, listen to this; I too have something to be proud of and glad of.

MRS. LINDE: I have no doubt you have. But what do you refer to?   170

NORA: Speak low. Suppose Torvald were to hear! He mustn't on any account—no one in the world must know, Christine, except you.

MRS. LINDE: But what is it?

NORA: Come here [*pulls her down on the sofa beside her*] Now I will show you that I too have something to be proud and glad of. It was I who saved Torvald's life.

MRS. LINDE: "Saved"? How?

NORA: I told you about our trip to Italy. Torvald would never have recovered if he had   175
not gone there—

MRS. LINDE: Yes, but your father gave you the necessary funds.

NORA: [*smiling*] Yes, that is what Torvald and all the others think, but—

MRS. LINDE: But—

NORA: Papa didn't give us a shilling. It was I who procured the money.

MRS. LINDE: You? All that large sum?   180

NORA: Two hundred and fifty pounds. What do you think of that?

MRS. LINDE: But, Nora, how could you possibly do it? Did you win a prize in the Lottery?

NORA: [*contemptuously*] In the Lottery? There would have been no credit in that.

MRS. LINDE: But where did you get it from, then?

NORA: [*humming and smiling with an air of mystery*] Hm, hm! Aha!   185

MRS. LINDE: Because you couldn't have borrowed it.

NORA: Couldn't I? Why not?

MRS. LINDE: No, a wife cannot borrow without her husband's consent.

NORA: [*tossing her head*] Oh, if it is a wife who has any head for business—a wife who has the wit to be a little bit clever—

MRS. LINDE: I don't understand it at all, Nora.   190

NORA: There is no need you should. I never said I had borrowed the money. I may have got it some other way. [*lies back on the sofa*] Perhaps I got it from some other admirer. When anyone is as attractive as I am—

MRS. LINDE: You are a mad creature.

NORA: Now, you know you're full of curiosity, Christine.

MRS. LINDE: Listen to me, Nora dear. Haven't you been a little bit imprudent?

NORA: [*sits up straight*] Is it imprudent to save your husband's life?   195

MRS. LINDE: It seems to me imprudent, without his knowledge, to—

NORA: But it was absolutely necessary that he should not know! My goodness, can't you understand that? It was necessary he should have no idea what a dangerous condition he was in. It was to me that the doctors came and said that his life was in danger, and that the only thing to save him was to live in the south. Do you suppose I didn't try, first of all, to get what I wanted as if it were for myself? I told him how much I should love to travel abroad like other young wives; I tried tears and entreaties with him; I told him that he ought to remember the condition I was in, and that he ought to be kind and indulgent to me; I even hinted that he might raise a loan. That nearly made him angry, Christine. He said I was thoughtless, and that it was his duty as my husband not to indulge me in my whims and caprices—as I believe he called them. Very well I thought, you must be saved—and that was how I came to devise a way out of the difficulty—

MRS. LINDE: And did your husband never get to know from your father that the money had not come from him?

NORA: No, never. Papa died just at that time. I had meant to let him into the secret and beg him never to reveal it. But he was so ill then—alas, there never was any need to tell him.

200 MRS. LINDE: And since then have you never told your secret to your husband?

NORA: Good Heavens, no! How could you think so? A man who has such strong opinions about these things! And besides, how painful and humiliating it would be for Torvald, with his manly independence, to know that he owed me anything! It would upset our mutual relations altogether; our beautiful happy home would no longer be what it is now.

MRS. LINDE: Do you mean never to tell him about it?

NORA: [*meditatively, and with a half smile*] Yes—some day, perhaps, after many years, when I am no longer as nice-looking as I am now. Don't laugh at me! I mean of course, when Torvald is no longer as devoted to me as he is now; when my dancing and dressing-up and reciting have palled on him; then it may be a good thing to have something in reserve—[*breaking off*] What nonsense! That time will never come. Now, what do you think of my great secret, Christine? Do you still think I am of no use? I can tell you, too, that this affair has caused me a lot of worry. It has been by no means easy for me to meet my engagements punctually. I may tell you that there is something that is called, in business, quarterly interest, and another thing called payment in installments, and it is always so dreadfully difficult to manage them. I have had to save a little here and there, where I could, you understand. I have not been able to put aside much from my housekeeping money, for Torvald must have a good table. I couldn't let my children be shabbily dressed; I have felt obliged to use up all he gave me for them, the sweet little darlings!

MRS. LINDE: So it has all had to come out of your own necessaries of life, poor Nora?

205 NORA: Of course. Besides, I was the one responsible for it. Whenever Torvald has given me the money for new dresses and such things, I have never spent more than half of it; I have always bought the simplest and cheapest things. Thank Heaven, any clothes look well on me, and so Torvald has never noticed it. But it was often very hard on me, Christine—because it is delightful to be really well dressed, isn't it?

MRS. LINDE: Quite so.

NORA: Well, then I have found other ways of earning money. Last winter I was lucky enough to get a lot of copying to do; so I locked myself up and sat writing every evening until quite late at night. Many a time I was desperately tired; but all the same it was a tremendous pleasure to sit there working and earning money. It was like being a man.

MRS. LINDE: How much have you been able to pay off in that way?

NORA: I can't tell you exactly. You see, it is very difficult to keep an account of a business matter of that kind. I only know that I have paid every penny that I could scrape together. Many a time I was at my wit's end. [*smiles*] Then I used to sit here and imagine that a rich old gentleman had fallen in love with me—

210 MRS. LINDE: What! Who was it?

NORA: Be quiet!—that he had died; and that when his will was opened it contained, written in big letters, the instruction: "The lovely Mrs. Nora Helmer is to have all I possess paid over to her at once in cash."

MRS. LINDE: But, my dear Nora—who could the man be?

NORA: Good gracious, can't you understand? There was no old gentleman at all; it was only something that I used to sit here and imagine, when I couldn't think of any way of procuring money. But it's all the same now; the tiresome old person can stay where he is, as far as I am concerned; I don't care about him or his will either, for I am free from care now. [*jumps up*] My goodness, it's delightful to think of, Christine! Free from care! To be able to be free from care, quite free from care; to be able to play and romp with the children; to be able to keep the house beautifully and have everything just as Torvald likes it! And, think of it, soon the spring will come and the big blue sky! Perhaps we shall be able to take a little trip—perhaps I shall see the sea again! Oh, it's a wonderful thing to be alive and be happy. [*A bell is heard in the hall.*]

MRS. LINDE: [*rising*] There is the bell; perhaps I had better go.

NORA: No, don't go; no one will come in here; it is sure to be for Torvald.   215

SERVANT: [*at the hall door*] Excuse me, ma'am—there is a gentleman to see the master, and as the doctor is with him—

NORA: Who is it?

KROGSTAD: [*at the door*] It is I, Mrs. Helmer. [*MRS. LINDE starts, trembles, and turns to the window.*]

NORA: [*takes a step towards him, and speaks in a strained, low voice*] You? What is it? What do you want to see my husband about?

KROGSTAD: Bank business—in a way. I have a small post in the Bank, and I hear your   220
husband is to be our chief now—

NORA: Then it is—

KROGSTAD: Nothing but dry business matters, Mrs. Helmer; absolutely nothing else.

NORA: Be so good as to go into the study, then. [*She bows indifferently to him and shuts the door into the hall; then comes back and makes up the fire in the stove.*]

MRS. LINDE: Nora—who was that man?

NORA: A lawyer, of the name of Krogstad.   225

MRS. LINDE: Then it really was he.

NORA: Do you know the man?

MRS. LINDE: I used to—many years ago. At one time he was a solicitor's clerk in our town.

NORA: Yes, he was.

MRS. LINDE: He is greatly altered.   230

NORA: He made a very unhappy marriage.

MRS. LINDE: He is a widower now, isn't he?

NORA: With several children. There now, it is burning up.

[*Shuts the door of the stove and moves the rocking-chair aside.*]

MRS. LINDE: They say he carries on various kinds of business.

NORA: Really! Perhaps he does; I don't know anything about it. But don't let us think of   235
business; it is so tiresome.

DOCTOR RANK: [*comes out of HELMER's study. Before he shuts the door he calls to him.*] No, my dear fellow, I won't disturb you; I would rather go in to your wife for a little while. [*shuts the door and sees MRS. LINDE*] I beg your pardon; I am afraid I am disturbing you too.

NORA: No, not at all. [*introducing him*] Doctor Rank, Mrs. Linde.

RANK: I have often heard Mrs. Linde's name mentioned here. I think I passed you on the stairs when I arrived, Mrs. Linde?

MRS. LINDE: Yes, I go up very slowly; I can't manage stairs well.

RANK: Ah! some slight internal weakness?   240

MRS. LINDE: No, the fact is I have been overworking myself.

RANK: Nothing more than that? Then I suppose you have come to town to amuse yourself with our entertainments?

MRS. LINDE: I have come to look for work.

RANK: Is that a good cure for overwork?

MRS. LINDE: One must live, Doctor Rank.   245

RANK: Yes, the general opinion seems to be that it is necessary.

NORA: Look here, Doctor Rank—you know you want to live.

RANK: Certainly. However wretched I may feel, I want to prolong the agony as long as possible. All my patients are like that. And so are those who are morally diseased; one of them, and a bad case too, is at this very moment with Helmer—

MRS. LINDE: [*sadly*] Ah!

250 NORA: Whom do you mean?

RANK: A lawyer of the name of Krogstad, a fellow you don't know at all. He suffers from a diseased moral character, Mrs. Helmer; but even he began talking of its being highly important that he should live.

NORA: Did he? What did he want to speak to Torvald about?

RANK: I have no idea; I only heard that it was something about the Bank.

NORA: I didn't know this—what's his name—Krogstad had anything to do with the Bank.

255 RANK: Yes, he has some sort of appointment there. [*to* MRS. LINDE] I don't know whether you find also in your part of the world that there are certain people who go zealously snuffing about to smell out moral corruption, and, as soon as they have found some, put the person concerned into some lucrative position where they can keep their eye on him. Healthy natures are left out in the cold.

MRS. LINDE: Still I think the sick are those who most need taking care of.

RANK: [*shrugging his shoulders*] Yes, there you are. That is the sentiment that is turning Society into a sickhouse.

[NORA, *who has been absorbed in her thoughts, breaks out into smothered laughter and claps her hands.*]

RANK: Why do you laugh at that? Have you any notion what Society really is?

NORA: What do I care about tiresome Society? I am laughing at something quite different, something extremely amusing. Tell me, Doctor Rank, are all the people who are employed in the Bank dependent on Torvald now?

260 RANK: Is that what you find so extremely amusing?

NORA: [*smiling and humming*] That's my affair! [*walking about the room*] It's perfectly glorious to think that we have—that Torvald has so much power over so many people. [*takes the packet from her pocket*] Doctor Rank, what do you say to a macaroon?

RANK: What, macaroons? I thought they were forbidden here.

NORA: Yes, but these are some Christine gave me.

MRS. LINDE: What! I?—

265 NORA: Oh, well, don't be alarmed! You couldn't know that Torvald had forbidden them. I must tell you that he is afraid they will spoil my teeth. But, bah!—once in a way— That's so, isn't it, Doctor Rank? By your leave? [*puts a macaroon into his mouth*] You must have one too, Christine. And I shall have one, just a little one—or at most two. [*walking about*] I am tremendously happy. There is just one thing in the world now that I should dearly love to do.

RANK: Well, what is that?

NORA: It's something I should dearly love to say, if Torvald could hear me.

RANK: Well, why can't you say it?

NORA: No, I daren't; it's so shocking.

270 MRS. LINDE: Shocking?

RANK: Well, I should not advise you to say it. Still, with us you might. What is it you would so much like to say if Torvald could hear you?

NORA: I should just love to say—Well, I'm damned!

RANK: Are you mad?

MRS. LINDE: Nora, dear—!

275 RANK: Say it, here he is!

NORA: [*hiding the packet*] Hush! Hush! Hush!

[HELMER *comes out of his room, with his coat over his arm and his hat in his hands.*]

NORA: Well, Torvald dear, have you got rid of him?
HELMER: Yes, he has just gone.
NORA: Let me introduce you—this is Christine, who has come to town.
HELMER: Christine—? Excuse me, but I don't know—
NORA: Mrs. Linde, dear; Christine Linde.   280
HELMER: Of course. A school friend of my wife's, I presume?
MRS. LINDE: Yes, we have known each other since then.
NORA: And just think, she has taken a long journey in order to see you.
HELMER: What do you mean?   285
MRS. LINDE: No, really, I—
NORA: Christine is tremendously clever at book-keeping, and she is frightfully anxious to
    work under some clever man, so as to perfect herself—
HELMER: Very sensible, Mrs. Linde.
NORA: And when she heard you had been appointed manager of the Bank—the news
    was telegraphed, you know—she travelled here as quick as she could. Torvald, I am
    sure you will be able to do something for Christine, for my sake, won't you?
HELMER: Well, it is not altogether impossible. I presume you are a widow, Mrs. Linde?   290
MRS. LINDE: Yes.
HELMER: And have had some experience of book-keeping?
MRS. LINDE: Yes, a fair amount.
HELMER: Ah! well, it's very likely I may be able to find something for you—
NORA: [*clapping her hands*] What did I tell you? What did I tell you?   295
HELMER: You have just come at a fortunate moment, Mrs. Linde.
MRS. LINDE: How am I to thank you?
HELMER: There is no need. [*puts on his coat*] But to-day you must excuse me—
RANK: Wait a minute; I will come with you.

[*Brings his fur coat from the hall and warms it at the fire.*]

NORA: Don't be long away, Torvald dear.   300
HELMER: About an hour, not more.
NORA: Are you going too, Christine?
MRS. LINDE: [*putting on her cloak*] Yes, I must go and look for a room.
HELMER: Oh, well then, we can walk down the street together.
NORA: [*helping her*] What a pity it is we are so short of space here: I am afraid it is impos-   305
    sible for us—
MRS. LINDE: Please don't think of it! Good-bye, Nora dear, and many thanks.
NORA: Good-bye for the present. Of course you will come back this evening. And you
    too, Dr. Rank. What do you say? If you are well enough? Oh, you must be! Wrap
    yourself up well.

[*They go to the door all talking together. Children's voices are heard on the staircase.*]

NORA: There they are. There they are! [*She runs to open the door. The* NURSE *comes in with
    the children.*] Come in! Come in! [*stoops and kisses them*] Oh, you sweet blessings! Look
    at them, Christine! Aren't they darlings?

RANK: Don't let us stand here in the draught.

310 **HELMER:** Come along, Mrs. Linde; the place will only be bearable for a mother now!

[*RANK, HELMER and MRS. LINDE go downstairs. The NURSE comes forward with the children; NORA shuts the hall door.*]

NORA: How fresh and well you look! Such red cheeks!—like apples and roses. [*The children all talk at once while she speaks to them.*] Have you had great fun? That's splendid! What, you pulled both Emmy and Bob along on the sledge?—both at once?—that was good. You are a clever boy, Ivar. Let me take her for a little, Anne. My sweet little baby doll! [*takes the baby from the MAID and dances it up and down*] Yes, yes, mother will dance with Bob too. What! Have you been snowballing? I wish I had been there too! No, no, I will take their things off, Anne; please let me do it, it is such fun. Go in now, you look half frozen. There is some coffee for you on the stove.

[*The NURSE goes into the room on the left. NORA takes off the children's things and throws them about, while they all talk to her at once.*]

NORA: Really! Did a big dog run after you? But it didn't bite you? No, dogs don't bite nice little dolly children. You mustn't look at the parcels, Ivar. What are they? Ah, I dare-say you would like to know. No, no—it's something nasty! Come, let us have a game! What shall we play at? Hide and Seek? Yes, we'll play Hide and Seek. Bob shall hide first. Must I hide? Very well, I'll hide first.

[*She and the children laugh and shout, and romp in and out of the room; at last NORA hides under the table, the children rush in and look for her, but do not see her; they hear her smothered laughter, run to the table, lift up the cloth and find her. Shouts of laughter. She crawls forward and pretends to frighten them. Fresh laughter. Meanwhile there has been a knock at the hall door, but none of them has noticed it. The door is half opened, and KROGSTAD appears. He waits a little; the game goes on.*]

KROGSTAD: Excuse me, Mrs. Helmer.

NORA: [*with a stifled cry, turns round and gets up on to her knees*] Ah! what do you want?

315 **KROGSTAD:** Excuse me, the outer door was ajar; I suppose someone forgot to shut it.

NORA: [*rising*] My husband is out, Mr. Krogstad.

KROGSTAD: I know that.

NORA: What do you want here, then?

KROGSTAD: A word with you.

320 **NORA:** With me?—[*to the children, gently*] Go in to nurse. What? No, the strange man won't do mother any harm. When he has gone we will have another game. [*She takes the children into the room on the left, and shuts the door after them.*] You want to speak to me?

KROGSTAD: Yes, I do.

NORA: To-day? It is not the first of the month yet.

KROGSTAD: No, it is Christmas Eve, and it will depend on yourself what sort of a Christmas you will spend.

NORA: What do you want? To-day it is absolutely impossible for me—

325 **KROGSTAD:** We won't talk about that till later on. This is something different. I presume you can give me a moment?

NORA: Yes—yes, I can—although—

KROGSTAD: Good. I was in Olsen's Restaurant and saw your husband going down the street—

NORA: Yes?

KROGSTAD: With a lady.

NORA: What then? 330

KROGSTAD: May I make so bold as to ask if it was a Mrs. Linde?

NORA: It was.

KROGSTAD: Just arrived in town?

NORA: Yes, to-day.

KROGSTAD: She is a great friend of yours, isn't she? 335

NORA: She is. But I don't see—

KROGSTAD: I knew her too, once upon a time.

NORA: I am aware of that.

KROGSTAD: Are you? So you know all about it; I thought as much. Then I can ask you, without beating about the bush—is Mrs. Linde to have an appointment in the Bank?

NORA: What right have you to question me, Mr. Krogstad?—You, one of my husband's 340 subordinates! But since you ask, you shall know. Yes, Mrs. Linde *is* to have an appointment. And it was I who pleaded her cause, Mr. Krogstad, let me tell you that.

KROGSTAD: I was right in what I thought, then.

NORA: [*walking up and down the stage*] Sometimes one has a tiny little bit of influence, I should hope. Because one is a woman, it does not necessarily follow that—. When anyone is in a subordinate position, Mr. Krogstad, they should really be careful to avoid offending anyone who—who—

KROGSTAD: Who has influence?

NORA: Exactly.

KROGSTAD: [*changing his tone*] Mrs. Helmer, you will be so good as to use your influence 345 on my behalf.

NORA: What? What do you mean?

KROGSTAD: You will be so kind as to see that I am allowed to keep my subordinate position in the Bank.

NORA: What do you mean by that? Who proposes to take your post away from you?

KROGSTAD: Oh, there is no necessity to keep up the pretence of ignorance. I can quite understand that your friend is not very anxious to expose herself to the chance of rubbing shoulders with me; and I quite understand, too, whom I have to thank for being turned out.

NORA: But I assure you— 350

KROGSTAD: Very likely; but, to come to the point, the time has come when I should advise you to use your influence to prevent that.

NORA: But, Mr. Krogstad, I *have* no influence.

KROGSTAD: Haven't you? I thought you said yourself just now—

NORA: Naturally I did not mean you to put that construction on it. I! What should make you think I have any influence of that kind with my husband?

KROGSTAD: Oh, I have known your husband from our student days. I don't suppose he is 355 any more unassailable than other husbands.

NORA: If you speak slightingly of my husband, I shall turn you out of the house.

KROGSTAD: You are bold, Mrs. Helmer.

NORA: I am not afraid of you any longer. As soon as the New Year comes, I shall in a very short time be free of the whole thing.

KROGSTAD: [*controlling himself*] Listen to me, Mrs. Helmer. If necessary, I am prepared to fight for my small post in the Bank as if I were fighting for my life.

NORA: So it seems. 360

KROGSTAD: It is not only for the sake of the money; indeed, that weighs least with me in the matter. There is another reason—well, I may as well tell you. My position is this. I daresay you know, like everybody else, that once, many years ago, I was guilty of an indiscretion.

NORA: I think I have heard something of the kind.

KROGSTAD: The matter never came into court; but every way seemed to be closed to me after that. So I took to the business that you know of. I had to do something; and, honestly, I don't think I've been one of the worst. But now I must cut myself free from all that. My sons are growing up; for their sake I must try and win back as much respect as I can in the town. This post in the Bank was like the first step up for me—and now your husband is going to kick me downstairs again into the mud.

NORA: But you must believe me, Mr. Krogstad; it is not in my power to help you at all.

365   **KROGSTAD:** Then it is because you haven't the will; but I have means to compel you.

NORA: You don't mean that you will tell my husband that I owe you money?

KROGSTAD: Hm!—suppose I were to tell him?

NORA: It would be perfectly infamous of you. [*sobbing*] To think of his learning my secret, which has been my joy and pride, in such an ugly, clumsy way—that he should learn it from you! And it would put me in a horribly disagreeable position—

KROGSTAD: Only disagreeable?

370   **NORA:** [*impetuously*] Well, do it, then!—and it will be the worse for you. My husband will see for himself what a blackguard you are, and you certainly won't keep your post then.

KROGSTAD: I asked you if it was only a disagreeable scene at home that you were afraid of?

NORA: If my husband does get to know of it, of course he will at once pay you what is still owing, and we shall have nothing more to do with you.

KROGSTAD: [*coming a step nearer*] Listen to me, Mrs. Helmer. Either you have a very bad memory or you know very little of business. I shall be obliged to remind you of a few details.

NORA: What do you mean?

375   **KROGSTAD:** When your husband was ill, you came to me to borrow two hundred and fifty pounds.

NORA: I didn't know any one else to go to.

KROGSTAD: I promised to get you that amount—

NORA: Yes, and you did so.

KROGSTAD: I promised to get you that amount, on certain conditions. Your mind was so taken up with your husband's illness, and you were so anxious to get the money for your journey, that you seem to have paid no attention to the conditions of our bargain. Therefore it will not be amiss if I remind you of them. Now, I promised to get the money on the security of a bond which I drew up.

380   **NORA:** Yes, and which I signed.

KROGSTAD: Good. But below your signature there were a few lines constituting your father a surety for the money; those lines your father should have signed.

NORA: Should? He did sign them.

KROGSTAD: I had left the date blank; that is to say your father should himself have inserted the date on which he signed the paper. Do you remember that?

NORA: Yes, I think I remember—

385   **KROGSTAD:** Then I gave you the bond to send by post to your father. Is that not so?

NORA: Yes.

KROGSTAD: And you naturally did so at once, because five or six days afterwards you brought me the bond with your father's signature. And then I gave you the money.

NORA: Well, haven't I been paying it off regularly?

KROGSTAD: Fairly so, yes. But—to come back to the matter in hand—that must have been a very trying time for you, Mrs. Helmer?

390   **NORA:** It was, indeed.

KROGSTAD: Your father was very ill, wasn't he?

NORA: He was very near his end.

KROGSTAD: And died soon afterwards?

NORA: Yes.

KROGSTAD: Tell me, Mrs. Helmer, can you by any chance remember what day your father   395
died?—on what day of the month, I mean.

NORA: Papa died on the 29th of September.

KROGSTAD: That is correct; I have ascertained it for myself. And, as that is so, there is a
discrepancy [*taking a paper from his pocket*] which I cannot account for.

NORA: What discrepancy? I don't know—

KROGSTAD: The discrepancy consists, Mrs. Helmer, in the fact that your father signed this
bond three days after his death.

NORA: What do you mean? I don't understand—   400

KROGSTAD: Your father died on the 29th of September. But, look here; your father has dated
his signature the 2nd of October. It is a discrepancy, isn't it? [*NORA is silent.*] Can you
explain it to me? [*NORA is still silent.*] It is a remarkable thing, too, that the words "2nd of
October," as well as the year, are not written in your father's handwriting but in one that
I think I know. Well, of course it can be explained; your father may have forgotten to date
his signature, and someone else may have dated it haphazard before they knew of his
death. There is no harm in that. It all depends on the signature of the name; and *that* is
genuine, I suppose, Mrs. Helmer? It was your father himself who signed his name here?

NORA: [*after a short pause, throws her head up and looks defiantly at him*] No, it was not. It was
I that wrote papa's name.

KROGSTAD: Are you aware that is a dangerous confession?

NORA: In what way? You shall have your money soon.

KROGSTAD: Let me ask you a question; why did you not send the paper to your father?   405

NORA: It was impossible; papa was so ill. If I had asked him for his signature, I should
have had to tell him what the money was to be used for; and when he was so ill himself I couldn't tell him that my husband's life was in danger—it was impossible.

KROGSTAD: It would have been better for you if you had given up your trip abroad.

NORA: No, that was impossible. That trip was to save my husband's life; I couldn't give
that up.

KROGSTAD: But did it never occur to you that you were committing a fraud on me?

NORA: I couldn't take that into account; I didn't trouble myself about you at all. I couldn't   410
bear you, because you put so many heartless difficulties in my way, although you
knew what a dangerous condition my husband was in.

KROGSTAD: Mrs. Helmer, you evidently do not realise clearly what it is that you have
been guilty of. But I can assure you that my one false step, which lost me all my reputation, was nothing more or nothing worse than what you have done.

NORA: You? Do you ask me to believe that you were brave enough to run a risk to save
your wife's life?

KROGSTAD: The law cares nothing about motives.

NORA: Then it must be a very foolish law.

KROGSTAD: Foolish or not, it is the law by which you will be judged, if I produce this   415
paper in court.

NORA: I don't believe it. Is a daughter not to be allowed to spare her dying father anxiety
and care? Is a wife not to be allowed to save her husband's life? I don't know much
about law; but I am certain that there must be laws permitting such things as that.
Have you no knowledge of such laws—you who are a lawyer? You must be a very
poor lawyer, Mr. Krogstad.

KROGSTAD: Maybe. But matters of business—such business as you and I have had together—do you think I don't understand that? Very well. Do as you please. But let me
tell you this—if I lose my position a second time, you shall lose yours with me.

[*He bows, and goes out through the hall.*]

NORA: [*appears buried in thought for a short time, then tosses her head*] Nonsense! Trying to frighten me like that!—I am not so silly as he thinks. [*begins to busy herself putting the children's things in order*] And yet—? No, it's impossible! I did it for love's sake.

CHILDREN: [*in the doorway on the left*] Mother, the stranger man has gone out through the gate.

420 **NORA:** Yes, dears, I know. But, don't tell anyone about the stranger man. Do you hear? Not even papa.

CHILDREN: No, mother; but will you come and play again?

NORA: No, no—not now.

CHILDREN: But, mother, you promised us.

NORA: Yes, but I can't now. Run away in; I have such a lot to do. Run away in, my sweet little darlings. [*She gets them into the room by degrees and shuts the door on them; then sits down on the sofa, takes up a piece of needlework and sews a few stitches, but soon stops.*] No! [*throws down the work, gets up, goes to the hall door and calls out*] Helen! bring the Tree in. [*goes to the table on the left, opens a drawer, and stops again*] No, no! it is quite impossible!

425 **MAID:** [*coming in with the Tree*] Where shall I put it, ma'am?

NORA: Here, in the middle of the floor.

MAID: Shall I get you anything else?

NORA: No, thank you. I have all I want.

[*Exit MAID.*]

NORA: [*begins dressing the tree*] A candle here—and flowers here—. The horrible man! It's all nonsense—there's nothing wrong. The Tree shall be splendid! I will do everything I can think of to please you, Torvald!—I will sing for you, dance for you—[*HELMER comes in with some papers under his arm.*] Oh! are you back already?

430 **HELMER:** Yes. Has anyone been here?

NORA: Here? No.

HELMER: That is strange. I saw Krogstad going out of the gate.

NORA: Did you? Oh yes, I forgot, Krogstad was here for a moment.

HELMER: Nora, I can see from your manner that he has been here begging you to say a good word for him.

435 **NORA:** Yes.

HELMER: And you were to appear to do it of your own accord; you were to conceal from me the fact of his having been here; didn't he beg that of you too?

NORA: Yes, Torvald, but—

HELMER: Nora, Nora, and you would be a party to that sort of thing? To have any talk with a man like that, and give him any sort of promise? And to tell me a lie into the bargain?

NORA: A lie—?

440 **HELMER:** Didn't you tell me no one had been here? [*shakes his finger at her*] My little song-bird must never do that again. A song-bird must have a clean beak to chirp with—no false notes! [*puts his arm round her waist*] That is so, isn't it? Yes, I am sure it is. [*lets her go*] We will say no more about it. [*sits down by the stove*] How warm and snug it is here!

[*Turns over his papers.*]

NORA: [*after a short pause, during which she busies herself with the Christmas Tree*] Torvald!

HELMER: Yes.

NORA: I am looking forward tremendously to the fancy dress ball at the Stenborgs' the day after to-morrow.

HELMER: And I am tremendously curious to see what you are going to surprise me with.

NORA: It was very silly of me to want to do that.   445

HELMER: What do you mean?

NORA: I can't hit upon anything that will do; everything I think of seems so silly and insignificant.

HELMER: Does my little Nora acknowledge that at last?

NORA: [*standing behind his chair with her arms on the back of it*] Are you very busy, Torvald?

HELMER: Well—   450

NORA: What are all those papers?

HELMER: Bank business.

NORA: Already?

HELMER: I have got authority from the retiring manager to undertake the necessary changes in the staff and in the rearrangement of the work; and I must make use of the Christmas week for that, so as to have everything in order for the new year.

NORA: Then that was why this poor Krogstad—   455

HELMER: Hm!

NORA: [*leans against the back of his chair and strokes his hair*] If you hadn't been so busy I should have asked you a tremendously big favour, Torvald.

HELMER: What is that? Tell me.

NORA: There is no one has such good taste as you. And I do so want to look nice at the fancy-dress ball. Torvald, couldn't you take me in hand and decide what I shall go as, and what sort of a dress I shall wear?

HELMER: Aha! so my obstinate little woman is obliged to get someone to come to her rescue?   460

NORA: Yes, Torvald, I can't get along a bit without your help.

HELMER: Very well, I will think it over, we shall manage to hit upon something.

NORA: That is nice of you. [*Goes to the Christmas Tree. A short pause*] How pretty the red flowers look—. But, tell me, was it really something very bad that this Krogstad was guilty of?

HELMER: He forged someone's name. Have you any idea what that means?

NORA: Isn't it possible that he was driven to do it by necessity?   465

HELMER: Yes; or, as in so many cases, by imprudence. I am not so heartless as to condemn a man altogether because of a single false step of that kind.

NORA: No you wouldn't, would you, Torvald?

HELMER: Many a man has been able to retrieve his character, if he has openly confessed his fault and taken his punishment.

NORA: Punishment—?

HELMER: But Krogstad did nothing of that sort; he got himself out of it by a cunning trick, and that is why he has gone under altogether.   470

NORA: But do you think it would—?

HELMER: Just think how a guilty man like that has to lie and play the hypocrite with everyone, how he has to wear a mask in the presence of those near and dear to him, even before his own wife and children. And about the children—that is the most terrible part of it all, Nora.

NORA: How?

HELMER: Because such an atmosphere of lies infects and poisons the whole life of a home. Each breath the children take in such a house is full of the germs of evil.

NORA: [*coming nearer him*] Are you sure of that?   475

HELMER: My dear, I have often seen it in the course of my life as a lawyer. Almost everyone who has gone to the bad early in life has had a deceitful mother.

NORA: Why do you only say—mother?

HELMER: It seems most commonly to be the mother's influence, though naturally a bad father's would have the same result. Every lawyer is familiar with the fact. This Krogstad, now, has been persistently poisoning his own children with lies and dissimulation; that is why I say he has lost all moral character. [*holds out his hands to her*] That is why my sweet little Nora must promise me not to plead his cause. Give me your hand on it. Come, come, what is this? Give me your hand. There now, that's settled. I assure you it would be quite impossible for me to work with him; I literally feel physically ill when I am in the company of such people.

NORA: [*takes her hand out of his and goes to the opposite side of the Christmas Tree*] How hot it is in here; and I have such a lot to do.

480   **HELMER:** [*getting up and putting his papers in order*] Yes, and I must try and read through some of these before dinner; and I must think about your costume, too. And it is just possible I may have something ready in gold paper to hang up on the Tree. [*Puts his hand on her head*] My precious little singing-bird!

[*He goes into his room and shuts the door after him.*]

NORA: [*after a pause, whispers*] No, no—it isn't true. It's impossible; it must be impossible.

[*The* NURSE *opens the door on the left.*]

NURSE: The little ones are begging so hard to be allowed to come in to mamma.
NORA: No, no, no! Don't let them come in to me! You stay with them, Anne.
NURSE: Very well, ma'am.

[*Shuts the door.*]

482   **NORA:** [*pale with terror*] Deprave my little children? Poison my home? [*a short pause. Then she tosses her head.*] It's not true. It can't possibly be true.

ACT 2

THE SAME SCENE. *The Christmas Tree is in the corner by the piano, stripped of its ornaments and with burnt-down candle-ends on its dishevelled branches.* NORA's *cloak and hat are lying on the sofa. She is alone in the room, walking about uneasily. She stops by the sofa and takes up her cloak.*

NORA: [*drops the cloak*] Someone is coming now! [*goes to the door and listens*] No—it is no one. Of course, no one will come to-day, Christmas Day—nor tomorrow either. But, perhaps—[*opens the door and looks out*] No, nothing in the letter-box; it is quite empty. [*comes forward*] What rubbish! of course he can't be in earnest about it. Such a thing couldn't happen; it is impossible—I have three little children.

[*Enter the* NURSE *from the room on the left, carrying a big cardboard box.*]

NURSE: At last I have found the box with the fancy dress.
NORA: Thanks; put it on the table.
NURSE: [*doing so*] But it is very much in want of mending.
5   **NORA:** I should like to tear it into a hundred thousand pieces.
NURSE: What an idea! It can easily be put in order—just a little patience.
NORA: Yes, I will go and get Mrs. Linde to come and help me with it.
NURSE: What, out again? In this horrible weather? You will catch cold, ma'am, and make yourself ill.

NORA: Well, worse than that might happen. How are the children?

NURSE: The poor little souls are playing with their Christmas presents, but—   10

NORA: Do they ask much for me?

NURSE: You see, they are so accustomed to have their mamma with them.

NORA: Yes, but, nurse, I shall not be able to be so much with them now as I was before.

NURSE: Oh well, young children easily get accustomed to anything.

NORA: Do you think so? Do you think they would forget their mother if she went away   15
altogether?

NURSE: Good heavens!—went away altogether?

NORA: Nurse, I want you to tell me something I have often wondered about—how could
you have the heart to put your own child out among strangers?

NURSE: I was obliged to, if I wanted to be little Nora's nurse.

NORA: Yes, but how could you be willing to do it?

NURSE: What, when I was going to get such a good place by it? A poor girl who has got   20
into trouble should be glad to. Besides, that wicked man didn't do a single thing for
me.

NORA: But I suppose your daughter has quite forgotten you.

NURSE: No, indeed she hasn't. She wrote to me when she was confirmed, and when she
was married.

NORA: [putting her arms round her neck] Dear old Anne, you were a good mother to me
when I was little.

NURSE: Little Nora, poor dear, had no other mother but me.

NORA: And if my little ones had no other mother, I am sure you would—What nonsense   25
I am talking! [opens the box] Go in to them. Now I must—. You will see tomorrow how
charming I shall look.

NURSE: I am sure there will be no one at the ball so charming as you, ma'am.

[Goes into the room on the left.]

NORA: [begins to unpack the box, but soon pushes it away from her] If only I dared go out. If
only no one would come. If only I could be sure nothing would happen here in the
meantime. Stuff and nonsense! No one will come. Only I mustn't think about it. I will
brush my muff. What, lovely gloves! Out of my thoughts, out of my thoughts! One,
two, three, four, five, six—[Screams.] Ah! there is someone coming—

[Makes a movement towards the door, but stands irresolute.]

[Enter MRS. LINDE from the hall, where she has taken off her cloak and hat.]

NORA: Oh, it's you, Christine. There is no one else out there, is there? How good of you to
come!

MRS. LINDE: I heard you were up asking for me.

NORA: Yes, I was passing by. As a matter of fact, it is something you could help me with.   30
Let us sit down here on the sofa. Look here. To-morrow evening there is to be a
fancy-dress ball at the Stenborgs', who live about us; and Torvald wants me to go as a
Neapolitan fisher-girl, and dance the Tarantella that I learnt at Capri.

MRS. LINDE: I see; you are going to keep up the character.

NORA: Yes, Torvald wants me to. Look, here is the dress; Torvald had it made for me
there, but now it is all so torn, and I haven't any idea—

MRS. LINDE: We will easily put that right. It is only some of the trimming come unsewn
here and there. Needle and thread? Now then, that's all we want.

NORA: It *is* nice of you.

35 **MRS. LINDE:** [*sewing*] So you are going to be dressed up to-morrow, Nora. I will tell you what—I shall come in for a moment and see you in your fine feathers. But I have completely forgotten to thank you for a delightful evening yesterday.

NORA: [*gets up, and crosses the stage*] Well I don't think yesterday was as pleasant as usual. You ought to have come to town a little earlier, Christine. Certainly Torvald does understand how to make a house dainty and attractive.

MRS. LINDE: And so do you, it seems to me; you are not your father's daughter for nothing. But tell me, is Doctor Rank always as depressed as he was yesterday?

NORA: No; yesterday it was very noticeable. I must tell you that he suffers from a very dangerous disease. He has consumption of the spine, poor creature. His father was a horrible man who committed all sorts of excesses; and that is why his son was sickly from childhood, do you understand?

MRS. LINDE: [*dropping her sewing*] But, my dearest Nora, how do you know anything about such things?

40 **NORA:** [*walking about*] Pooh! When you have three children, you get visits now and then from—from married women, who know something of medical matters, and they talk about one thing and another.

MRS. LINDE: [*goes on sewing. A short silence*] Does Doctor Rank come here every day?

NORA: Every day regularly. He is Torvald's most intimate friend, and a great friend of mine too. He is just like one of the family.

MRS. LINDE: But tell me this—is he perfectly sincere? I mean, isn't he the kind of man that is very anxious to make himself agreeable?

NORA: Not in the least. What makes you think that?

45 **MRS. LINDE:** When you introduced him to me yesterday, he declared he had often heard my name mentioned in this house; but afterwards I noticed that your husband hadn't the slightest idea who I was. So how could Doctor Rank—?

NORA: That is quite right, Christine. Torvald is so absurdly fond of me that he wants me absolutely to himself, as he says. At first he used to seem almost jealous if I mentioned any of the dear folk at home, so naturally I gave up doing so. But I often talk about such things with Doctor Rank, because he likes hearing about them.

MRS. LINDE: Listen to me, Nora. You are still very like a child in many things, and I am older than you in many ways and have a little more experience. Let me tell you this— you ought to make an end of it with Doctor Rank.

NORA: What ought I to make an end of?

MRS. LINDE: Of two things, I think. Yesterday you talked some nonsense about a rich admirer who was to leave you money—

50 **NORA:** An admirer who doesn't exist, unfortunately! But what then?

MRS. LINDE: Is Doctor Rank a man of means?

NORA: Yes, he is.

MRS. LINDE: And has no one to provide for?

NORA: No, no one; but—

55 **MRS. LINDE:** And comes here every day?

NORA: Yes, I told you so.

MRS. LINDE: But how can this well-bred man be so tactless?

NORA: I don't understand you at all.

MRS. LINDE: Don't prevaricate, Nora. Do you suppose I don't guess who lent you the two hundred and fifty pounds?

60 **NORA:** Are you out of your senses? How can you think of such a thing! A friend of ours, who comes here every day! Do you realise what a horribly painful position that would be?

MRS. LINDE: Then it really isn't he?

NORA: No, certainly not. It would never have entered into my head for a moment. Besides, he had no money to lend then; he came into his money afterwards.

MRS. LINDE: Well, I think that was lucky for you, my dear Nora.

NORA: No, it would never have come into my head to ask Doctor Rank. Although I am
quite sure that if I had asked him—

MRS. LINDE: But of course you won't.   65

NORA: Of course not. I have no reason to think it could possibly be necessary. But I am
quite sure that if I told Doctor Rank—

MRS. LINDE: Behind your husband's back?

NORA: I *must* make an end of it with the other one, and that will be behind his back too. I
must make an end of it with him.

MRS. LINDE: Yes, that is what I told you yesterday, but—

NORA: [*walking up and down*] A man can put a thing like that straight much easier than a   70
woman—

MRS. LINDE: One's husband, yes.

NORA: Nonsense! [*standing still*] When you pay off a debt you get your bond back, don't you?

MRS. LINDE: Yes, as a matter of course.

NORA: And can tear it into a hundred thousand pieces, and burn it up—the nasty dirty paper!

MRS. LINDE: [*looks hard at her, lays down her sewing and gets up slowly*] Nora, you are con-   75
cealing something from me.

NORA: Do I look as if I were?

MRS. LINDE: Something has happened to you since yesterday morning. Nora, what is it?

NORA: [*going nearer to her*] Christine! [*listens*] Hush! There's Torvald come home. Do you
mind going in to the children for the present? Torvald can't bear to see dressmaking
going on. Let Anne help you.

MRS. LINDE: [*gathering some of the things together*] Certainly—but I am not going away
from here till we have had it out with one another.

[*She goes into the room on the left, as* HELMER *comes in from the hall.*]

NORA: [*going up to* HELMER] I have wanted you so much, Torvald dear.   80

HELMER: Was that the dressmaker?

NORA: No, it was Christine; she is helping me to put my dress in order. You will see I
shall look quite smart.

HELMER: Wasn't that a happy thought of mine, now?

NORA: Splendid! But don't you think it is nice of me, too, to do as you wish?

HELMER: Nice?—because you do as your husband wishes? Well, well, you little rogue, I   85
am sure you did not mean it in that way. But I am not going to disturb you; you will
want to be trying on your dress, I expect.

NORA: I suppose you are going to work.

HELMER: Yes. [*shows her a bundle of papers*] Look at that. I have just been into the bank.
[*Turns to go into his room.*]

NORA: Torvald.

HELMER: Yes.

NORA: If your little squirrel were to ask you for something very, very prettily—?   90

HELMER: What then?

NORA: Would you do it?

HELMER: I should like to hear what it is, first.

NORA: Your squirrel would run about and do all her tricks if you would be nice, and do
what she wants.

HELMER: Speak plainly.   95

NORA: Your skylark would chirp about in every room, with her song rising and falling—

HELMER: Well, my skylark does that anyhow.

NORA: I would play the fairy and dance for you in the moonlight, Torvald.

HELMER: Nora—you surely don't mean that request you made of me this morning?

100 **NORA:** [*going near him*] Yes, Torvald, I beg you so earnestly—

HELMER: Have you really the courage to open up that question again?

NORA: Yes, dear, you *must* do as I ask; you *must* let Krogstad keep his post in the Bank.

HELMER: My dear Nora, it is his post that I have arranged Mrs. Linde shall have.

NORA: Yes, you have been awfully kind about that; but you could just as well dismiss some other clerk instead of Krogstad.

105 **HELMER:** This is simply incredible obstinacy! Because you chose to give him a thought-less promise that you would speak for him, I am expected to—

NORA: That isn't the reason, Torvald. It is for your own sake. This fellow writes in the most scurrilous newspapers; you have told me so yourself. He can do you an un-speakable amount of harm. I am frightened to death of him—

HELMER: Ah, I understand; it is recollections of the past that scare you.

NORA: What do you mean?

HELMER: Naturally you are thinking of your father.

110 **NORA:** Yes—yes, of course. Just recall to your mind what these malicious creatures wrote in the papers about papa, and how horribly they slandered him. I believe they would have procured his dismissal if the Department had not sent you over to inquire into it, and if you had not been so kindly disposed and helpful to him.

HELMER: My little Nora, there is an important difference between your father and me. Your father's reputation as a public official was not above suspicion. Mine is, and I hope it will continue to be so, as long as I hold my office.

NORA: You never can tell what mischief these men may contrive. We ought to be so well off, so snug and happy here in our peaceful home, and have no cares—you and I and the children, Torvald! That is why I beg you so earnestly—

HELMER: And it is just by interceding for him that you make it impossible for me to keep him. It is already known at the Bank that I mean to dismiss Krogstad. Is it to get about now that the new manager has changed his mind at his wife's bidding—

NORA: And what if it did?

115 **HELMER:** Of course!—if only this obstinate little person can get her way! Do you suppose I am going to make myself ridiculous before my whole staff, to let people think that I am a man to be swayed by all sorts of outside influence? I should very soon feel the consequences of it, I can tell you! And besides, there is one thing that makes it quite impossible for me to have Krogstad in the Bank as long as I am manager.

NORA: Whatever is that?

HELMER: His moral failings I might perhaps have overlooked, if necessary—

NORA: Yes, you could—couldn't you?

HELMER: And I hear he is a good worker, too. But I knew him when we were boys. It was one of those rash friendships that so often prove an incubus in afterlife. I may as well tell you plainly, we were once on very intimate terms with one another. But this tactless fellow lays no restraint on himself when other people are present. On the contrary, he thinks it gives him the right to adopt a familiar tone with me, and every minute it is "I say, Helmer, old fellow!" and that sort of thing. I assure you it is extremely painful for me. He would make my position in the Bank intolerable.

120 **NORA:** Torvald, I don't believe you mean that.

HELMER: Don't you? Why not?

NORA: Because it is such a narrow-minded way of looking at things.

HELMER: What are you saying? Narrow-minded? Do you think I am narrow-minded?

NORA: No, just the opposite, dear—and it is exactly for that reason.

HELMER: It's the same thing. You say my point of view is narrow-minded, so I must be   125
so too. Narrow-minded! Very well—I must put an end to this. [*goes to the hall-door and
calls*] Helen!

NORA: What are you going to do?

HELMER: [*looking among his papers*] Settle it. [*Enter* MAID.] Look here; take this letter and
go downstairs with it at once. Find a messenger and tell him to deliver it, and be
quick. The address is on it, and here is the money.

MAID: Very well, sir.

[*Exits with the letter.*]

HELMER: [*putting his papers together*] Now then, little Miss Obstinate.

NORA: [*breathlessly*] Torvald—what was that letter?   130

HELMER: Krogstad's dismissal.

NORA: Call her back, Torvald! There is still time. Oh Torvald, call her back! Do it for my
sake—for your own sake—for the children's sake! Do you hear me, Torvald? Call her
back!! You don't know what that letter can bring upon us.

HELMER: It's too late.

NORA: Yes, it's too late.

HELMER: My dear Nora, I can forgive the anxiety you are in, although really it is an insult   135
to me. It is, indeed. Isn't it an insult to think that I should be afraid of a starving quill-
driver's vengeance? But I forgive you nevertheless, because it is such eloquent witness
to your great love for me. [*takes her in his arms*] And that is as it should be, my own
darling Nora. Come what will, you may be sure I shall have both courage and strength
if they be needed. You will see I am man enough to take everything upon myself.

NORA: [*in a horror-stricken voice*] What do you mean by that?

HELMER: Everything, I say—

NORA: [*recovering herself*] You will never have to do that.

HELMER: That's right. Well, we will share it, Nora, as man and wife should. That is how
it shall be. [*caressing her*] Are you content now? There! there!—not these frightened
dove's eyes! The whole thing is only the wildest fancy!—Now, you must go and play
through the Tarantella and practise with your tambourine. I shall go into the inner
office and shut the door, and I shall hear nothing; you can make as much noise as you
please. [*turns back at the door*] And when Rank comes, tell him where he will find me.

[*Nods to her, takes his papers and goes into his room, and shuts the door after him.*]

NORA: [*bewildered with anxiety, stands as if rooted to the spot, and whispers*] He is capable   140
of doing it. He will do it. He will do it in spite of everything.—No, not that! Never,
never! Anything rather than that! Oh, for some help, some way out of it! [*The door-bell
rings.*] Doctor Rank! Anything rather than that—anything, whatever it is!

[*She puts her hands over her face, pulls herself together, goes to the door and opens it.* RANK *is standing without, hanging up his coat. During the following dialogue it begins to grow dark.*]

NORA: Good-day, Doctor Rank. I knew your ring. But you mustn't go in to Torvald now; I
think he is busy with something.

RANK: And you?

NORA: [*brings him in and shuts the door after him*] Oh, you know very well I always have
time for you.

RANK: Thank you. I shall make use of as much of it as I can.

145   **NORA:** What do you mean by that? As much of it as you can?

RANK: Well, does that alarm you?

NORA: It was such a strange way of putting it. Is anything likely to happen?

RANK: Nothing but what I have long been prepared for. But I certainly didn't expect it to happen so soon.

NORA: [*gripping him by the arm*] What have you found out? Doctor Rank, you must tell me.

150   **RANK:** [*sitting down by the stove*] It is all up with me. And it can't be helped.

NORA: [*with a sigh of relief*] Is it about yourself?

RANK: Who else? It is no use lying to one's self. I am the most wretched of all my patients, Mrs. Helmer. Lately I have been taking stock of my internal economy. Bankrupt! Probably within a month I shall lie rotting in the churchyard.

NORA: What an ugly thing to say!

RANK: The thing itself is cursedly ugly, and the worst of it is that I shall have to face so much more that is ugly before that. I shall only make one more examination of myself; when I have done that, I shall know pretty certainly when it will be that the horrors of dissolution will begin. There is something I want to tell you. Helmer's refined nature gives him an unconquerable disgust at everything that is ugly; I won't have him in my sick-room.

155   **NORA:** Oh, but, Doctor Rank—

RANK: I won't have him there. Not on any account. I bar my door to him. As soon as I am quite certain that the worst has come, I shall send you my card with a black cross on it, and then you will know that the loathsome end has begun.

NORA: You are quite absurd to-day. And I wanted you so much to be in a really good humour.

RANK: With death stalking beside me?—To have to pay this penalty for another man's sin! Is there any justice in that? And in every single family, in one way or another, some such inexorable retribution is being exacted—

NORA: [*putting her hands over her ears*] Rubbish! Do talk of something cheerful.

160   **RANK:** Oh, it's a mere laughing matter, the whole thing. My poor innocent spine has to suffer for my father's youthful amusements.

NORA: [*sitting at the table on the left*] I suppose you mean that he was too partial to asparagus and pâté de foie gras, don't you.

RANK: Yes, and to truffles.

NORA: Truffles, yes. And oysters too, I suppose?

RANK: Oysters, of course, that goes without saying.

165   **NORA:** And heaps of port and champagne. It is sad that all these nice things should take their revenge on our bones.

RANK: Especially that they should revenge themselves on the unlucky bones of those who have not had the satisfaction of enjoying them.

NORA: Yes, that's the saddest part of it all.

RANK: [*with a searching look at her*] Hm!—

NORA: [*after a short pause*] Why did you smile?

170   **RANK:** No, it was you that laughed.

NORA: No, it was you that smiled, Doctor Rank!

RANK: [*rising*] You are a greater rascal than I thought.

NORA: I am in a silly mood to-day.

RANK: So it seems.

175   **NORA:** [*putting her hands on his shoulders*] Dear, dear Doctor Rank, death mustn't take you away from Torvald and me.

RANK: It is a loss you would easily recover from. Those who are gone are soon forgotten.

NORA: [*looking at him anxiously*] Do you believe that?

RANK: People form new ties, and then—

NORA: Who will form new ties?

RANK: Both you and Helmer, when I am gone. You yourself are already on the high road   180
to it, I think. What did that Mrs. Linde want here last night?

NORA: Oho!—you don't mean to say you are jealous of poor Christine?

RANK: Yes, I am. She will be my successor in this house. When I am done for, this woman
will—

NORA: Hush! don't speak so loud. She is in that room.

RANK: To-day again. There, you see.

NORA: She has only come to sew my dress for me. Bless my soul, how unreasonable you   185
are! [*sits down on the sofa*] Be nice now, Doctor Rank, and tomorrow you will see how
beautifully I shall dance, and you can imagine I am doing it all for you—and for
Torvald too, of course. [*takes various things out of the box*] Doctor Rank, come and sit
down here, and I will show you something.

RANK: [*sitting down*] What is it?

NORA: Just look at those!

RANK: Silk stockings.

NORA: Flesh-coloured. Aren't they lovely? It is so dark here now, but to-morrow—. No, no,
no! you must only look at the feet. Oh well, you may have leave to look at the legs too.

RANK: Hm!—   190

NORA: Why are you looking so critical? Don't you think they will fit me?

RANK: I have no means of forming an opinion about that.

NORA: [*looks at him for a moment*] For shame! [*hits him lightly on the ear with the stockings*]
That's to punish you. [*folds them up again*]

RANK: And what other nice things am I to be allowed to see?

NORA: Not a single thing more, for being so naughty. [*She looks among the things, humming*   195
to herself.]

RANK: [*after a short silence*] When I am sitting here, talking to you as intimately as this, I cannot
imagine for a moment what would have become of me if I had never come into this house.

NORA: [*smiling*] I believe you do feel thoroughly at home with us.

RANK: [*in a lower voice, looking straight in front of him*] And to be obliged to leave it all—

NORA: Nonsense, you are not going to leave it.

RANK: [*as before*] And not be able to leave behind one the slightest token of one's grati-   200
tude, scarcely even a fleeting regret—nothing but an empty place which the first
comer can fill as well as any other.

NORA: And if I asked you now for a—? No!

RANK: For what?

NORA: For a big proof of your friendship—

RANK: Yes, yes!

NORA: I mean a tremendously big favour—   205

RANK: Would you really make me so happy for once?

NORA: Ah, but you don't know what it is yet.

RANK: No—but tell me.

NORA: I really can't, Doctor Rank. It is something out of all reason; it means advice, and
help, and a favour—

RANK: The bigger a thing it is the better. I can't conceive what it is you mean. Do tell me.   210
Haven't I your confidence?

NORA: More than anyone else. I know you are my truest and best friend, and so I will tell
you what it is. Well, Doctor Rank, it is something you must help me to prevent. You
know how devotedly, how inexpressibly deeply Torvald loves me; he would never
for a moment hesitate to give his life for me.

RANK: [*leaning towards her*] Nora—do you think he is the only one—?

NORA: [*with a slight start*] The only one—?

RANK: The only one who would gladly give his life for your sake.

215 NORA: [*sadly*] Is that it?

RANK: I was determined you should know it before I went away, and there will never be a better opportunity than this. Now you know it, Nora. And now you know, too, that you can trust me as you would trust no one else.

NORA: [*rises, deliberately and quietly*] Let me pass.

RANK: [*makes room for her to pass him, but sits still*] Nora!

NORA: [*at the hall door*] Helen, bring in the lamp. [*goes over to the stove*] Dear Doctor Rank, that was really horrid of you.

220 RANK: To have loved you as much as anyone else does? Was that horrid?

NORA: No, but to go and tell me so. There was really no need—

RANK: What do you mean? Did you know—? [*MAID enters with lamp, puts it down on the table, and goes out.*] Nora—Mrs. Helmer—tell me, had you any idea of this?

NORA: Oh, how do I know whether I had or whether I hadn't? I really can't tell you—To think you could be so clumsy, Doctor Rank! We were getting on so nicely.

RANK: Well, at all events you know now that you can command me, body and soul. So won't you speak out?

225 NORA: [*looking at him*] After what happened?

RANK: I beg you to let me know what it is.

NORA: I can't tell you anything now.

RANK: Yes, yes. You mustn't punish me in that way. Let me have permission to do for you whatever a man may do.

NORA: You can do nothing for me now. Besides, I really don't need any help at all. You will find that the whole thing is merely fancy on my part. It really is so—of course it is! [*sits down in the rocking-chair, and looks at him with a smile*] You are a nice sort of man, Doctor Rank!—don't you feel ashamed of yourself, now the lamp has come?

230 RANK: Not a bit. But perhaps I had better go—for ever?

NORA: No, indeed, you shall not. Of course you must come here just as before. You know very well Torvald can't do without you.

RANK: Yes, but you?

NORA: Oh, I am always tremendously pleased when you come.

RANK: It is just that, that put me on the wrong track. You are a riddle to me. I have often thought that you would almost as soon be in my company as in Helmer's.

235 NORA: Yes—you see there are some people one loves best, and others whom one would almost always rather have as companions.

RANK: Yes, there is something in that.

NORA: When I was at home, of course I loved papa best. But I always thought it tremendous fun if I could steal down into the maid's room, because they never moralised at all, and talked to each other about such entertaining things.

RANK: I see—it is *their* place I have taken.

NORA: [*jumping up and going to him*] Oh, dear, nice Doctor Rank, I never meant that at all. But surely you can understand that being with Torvald is a little like being with papa—

[*Enter MAID from the hall.*]

240 MAID: If you please, ma'am. [*whispers and hands her a card*]

NORA: [*glancing at the card*] Oh! [*puts it in her pocket*]

RANK: Is there anything wrong?

NORA: No, no, not in the least. It is only something—it is my new dress—

RANK: What? Your dress is lying there.

NORA: Oh, yes, that one; but this is another. I ordered it. Torvald mustn't know about it—   245

RANK: Oho! Then that was the great secret.

NORA: Of course. Just go in to him; he is sitting in the inner room. Keep him as long as—

RANK: Make your mind easy; I won't let him escape. [*goes into* HELMER's *room*]

NORA: [*to the* MAID] And he is standing waiting in the kitchen?

MAID: Yes; he came up the back stairs.   250

NORA: But didn't you tell him no one was in?

MAID: Yes, but it was no good.

NORA: He won't go away?

MAID: No; he says he won't until he has seen you, ma'am.

NORA: Well, let him come in—but quietly. Helen, you mustn't say anything about it to   255
anyone. It is a surprise for my husband.

MAID: Yes, ma'am, I quite understand.   [*Exit.*]

NORA: This dreadful thing is going to happen! It will happen in spite of me! No, no, no, it
can't happen—it shan't happen!

[*She bolts the door of* HELMER's *room. The* MAID *opens the hall door for* KROGSTAD *and shuts it after
him. He is wearing a fur coat, high boots and a fur cap.*]

NORA: [*advancing towards him*] Speak low—my husband is at home.

KROGSTAD: No matter about that.

NORA: What do you want of me?   260

KROGSTAD: An explanation of something.

NORA: Make haste then. What is it?

KROGSTAD: You know, I suppose, that I have got my dismissal.

NORA: I couldn't prevent it, Mr. Krogstad. I fought as hard as I could on your side, but it
was no good.

KROGSTAD: Does your husband love you so little, then? He knows that what I can expose   265
you to, and yet he ventures—

NORA: How can you suppose that he has any knowledge of the sort?

KROGSTAD: I didn't suppose so at all. It would not be the least like our dear Torvald
Helmer to show so much courage—

NORA: Mr. Krogstad, a little respect for my husband, please.

KROGSTAD: Certainly—all the respect he deserves. But since you have kept the matter so
carefully to yourself, I make bold to suppose that you have a little clearer idea, than
you had yesterday, of what it actually is that you have done?

NORA: More than you could ever teach me.   270

KROGSTAD: Yes, such a bad lawyer as I am.

NORA: What is it you want of me?

KROGSTAD: Only to see how you were, Mrs. Helmer. I have been thinking about you all
day long. A mere cashier, a quill-driver, a—well, a man like me—even he has a little
of what is called feeling, you know.

NORA: Show it, then; think of my little children.

KROGSTAD: Have you and your husband thought of mine? But never mind about that. I   275
only wanted to tell you that you need not take this matter too seriously. In the first
place there will be no accusation made on my part.

NORA: No, of course not; I was sure of that.

KROGSTAD: The whole thing can be arranged amicably; there is no reason why anyone
should know anything about it. It will remain a secret between us three.

NORA: My husband must never get to know anything about it.

KROGSTAD: How will you be able to prevent it? Am I to understand that you can pay the balance that is owing?

280 **NORA:** No, not just at present.

KROGSTAD: Or perhaps that you have some expedient for raising the money soon?

NORA: No expedient that I mean to make use of.

KROGSTAD: Well, in any case, it would have been of no use to you now. If you stood there with ever so much money in your hand, I would never part with your bond.

NORA: Tell me what purpose you mean to put it to.

285 **KROGSTAD:** I shall only preserve it—keep it in my possession. No one who is not concerned in the matter shall have the slightest hint of it. So that if the thought of it has driven you to any desperate resolution—

NORA: It has.

KROGSTAD: If you had it in your mind to run away from your home—

NORA: I had.

KROGSTAD: Or even something worse—

290 **NORA:** How could you know that?

KROGSTAD: Give up the idea.

NORA: How did you know I had thought of *that*?

KROGSTAD: Most of us think of that at first. I did, too—but I hadn't the courage.

NORA: [*faintly*] No more had I.

295 **KROGSTAD:** [*in a tone of relief*] No, that's it, isn't it—you hadn't the courage either?

NORA: No, I haven't—I haven't.

KROGSTAD: Besides, it would have been a great piece of folly. Once the first storm at home is over—. I have a letter for your husband in my pocket.

NORA: Telling him everything?

KROGSTAD: In as lenient a manner as I possibly could.

300 **NORA:** [*quickly*] He mustn't get the letter. Tear it up. I will find some means of getting money.

KROGSTAD: Excuse me, Mrs. Helmer, but I think I told you just now—

NORA: I am not speaking of what I owe you. Tell me what sum you are asking my husband for, and I will get the money.

KROGSTAD: I am not asking your husband for a penny.

NORA: What do you want, then?

305 **KROGSTAD:** I will tell you. I want to rehabilitate myself, Mrs. Helmer; I want to get on; and in that your husband must help me. For the last year and a half I have not had a hand in anything dishonourable, and all that time I have been struggling in most restricted circumstances. I was content to work my way up step by step. Now I am turned out, and I am not going to be satisfied with merely being taken into favour again. I want to get on, I tell you. I want to get into the Bank again, in a higher position. Your husband must make a place for me—

NORA: That he will never do!

KROGSTAD: He will; I know him; he dare not protest. And as soon as I am in there again with him, then you will see! Within a year I shall be the manager's right hand. It will be Nils Krogstad and not Torvald Helmer who manages the Bank.

NORA: That's a thing you will never see!

KROGSTAD: Do you mean that you will—?

310 **NORA:** I have courage enough for it now.

KROGSTAD: Oh, you can't frighten me. A fine, spoilt lady like you—

NORA: You will see, you will see.

KROGSTAD: Under the ice, perhaps? Down into the cold, coal-black water? And then, in the spring, to float up to the surface, all horrible and unrecognisable, with your hair fallen out—

NORA: You can't frighten me.

KROGSTAD: Nor you me. People don't do such things, Mrs. Helmer. Besides, what use   315
would it be? I should have him completely in my power all the same.

NORA: Afterwards? When I am no longer—

KROGSTAD: Have you forgotten that it is I who have the keeping of your reputation? [*NORA stands speechlessly looking at him.*] Well, now, I have warned you. Do not do anything foolish. When Helmer has had my letter, I shall expect a message from him. And be sure you remember that it is your husband himself who has forced me into such ways as this again. I will never forgive him for that. Good-bye, Mrs. Helmer.

[*Exit through the hall.*]

NORA: [*goes to the hall door, opens it slightly and listens*] He is going. He is not putting the letter in the box. Oh no, no! that's impossible! [*opens the door by degrees*] What is that? He is standing outside. He is not going downstairs. Is he hesitating? Can he—

[*A letter drops into the box; then KROGSTAD's footsteps are heard, till they die away as he goes downstairs. NORA utters a stifled cry and runs across the room to the table by the sofa. A short pause.*]

NORA: In the letter-box. [*steals across to the hall door*] There it lies—Torvald, Torvald, there is no hope for us now!

[*MRS. LINDE comes in from the room on the left, carrying the dress.*]

MRS. LINDE: There, I can't see anything more to mend now. Would you like to try it on—?   320

NORA: [*in a hoarse whisper*] Christine, come here.

MRS. LINDE: [*throwing the dress down on the sofa*] What is the matter with you? You look so agitated!

NORA: Come here. Do you see that letter? There, look—you can see it through the glass in the letter-box.

MRS. LINDE: Yes, I see it.

NORA: That letter is from Krogstad.   325

MRS. LINDE: Nora—it was Krogstad who lent you the money!

NORA: Yes, and now Torvald will know all about it.

MRS. LINDE: Believe me, Nora, that's the best thing for both of you.

NORA: You don't know all. I forged a name.

MRS. LINDE: Good heavens—!   330

NORA: I only want to say this to you, Christine—you must be my witness.

MRS. LINDE: Your witness? What do you mean? What am I to—?

NORA: If I should go out of my mind—and it might easily happen—

MRS. LINDE: Nora!

NORA: Or if anything else should happen to me—anything, for instance, that might   335
prevent my being here—

MRS. LINDE: Nora! Nora! you are quite out of your mind.

NORA: And if it should happen that there were someone who wanted to take all the responsibility, all the blame, you understand—

MRS. LINDE: Yes, yes—but how can you suppose—?

NORA: Then you must be my witness, that it is not true, Christine. I am not out of my mind at all; I am in my right senses now, and I tell you no one else has known anything about it; I, and I alone, did the whole thing. Remember that.

340   **MRS. LINDE:** I will, indeed. But I don't understand all this.

NORA: How should you understand it? A wonderful thing is going to happen.

MRS. LINDE: A wonderful thing?

NORA: Yes, a wonderful thing!—But it is so terrible, Christine; it *mustn't* happen, not for all the world.

MRS. LINDE: I will go at once and see Krogstad.

345   **NORA:** Don't go to him; he will do you some harm.

MRS. LINDE: There was a time when he would gladly do anything for my sake.

NORA: He?

MRS. LINDE: Where does he live?

NORA: How should I know—? Yes [*feeling in her pocket*] here is his card. But the letter, the letter—!

350   **HELMER:** [*calls from his room, knocking at the door*] Nora!

NORA: [*cries out anxiously*] Oh, what's that? What do you want?

HELMER: Don't be so frightened. We are not coming in; you have locked the door. Are you trying on your dress?

NORA: Yes, that's it. I look so nice, Torvald.

MRS. LINDE: [*who has read the card*] I see he lives at the corner here.

355   **NORA:** Yes, but it's no use. It is hopeless. The letter is lying there in the box.

MRS. LINDE: And your husband keeps the key?

NORA: Yes, always.

MRS. LINDE: Krogstad must ask for his letter back unread, he must find some pretence—

NORA: But it is just at this time that Torvald generally—

360   **MRS. LINDE:** You must delay him. Go in to him in the meantime. I will come back as soon as I can.

[*She goes out hurriedly through the hall door.*]

NORA: [*goes to* HELMER'S *door, opens it and peeps in*] Torvald!

HELMER: [*from the inner room*] Well? May I venture at last to come into my own room again? Come along, Rank, now you will see—[*halting in the doorway*] But what is this?

NORA: What is what, dear?

HELMER: Rank led me to expect a splendid transformation.

365   **RANK:** [*in the doorway*] I understood so, but evidently I was mistaken.

NORA: Yes, nobody is to have the chance of admiring me in my dress until tomorrow.

HELMER: But, my dear Nora, you look so worn out. Have you been practising too much?

NORA: No, I have not practised at all.

HELMER: But you will need to—

370   **NORA:** Yes, indeed I shall, Torvald. But I can't get on a bit without you to help me; I have absolutely forgotten the whole thing.

HELMER: Oh, we will soon work it up again.

NORA: Yes, help me, Torvald. Promise that you will! I am so nervous about it—all the people—. You must give yourself up to me entirely this evening. Not the tiniest bit of business—you mustn't even take a pen in your hand. Will you promise, Torvald dear?

HELMER: I promise. This evening I will be wholly and absolutely at your service, you helpless little mortal. Ah, by the way, first of all I will just—

[*Goes towards the hall door.*]

NORA: What are you going to do there?

HELMER: Only see if any letters have come.   375

NORA: No, no! don't do that, Torvald!

HELMER: Why not?

NORA: Torvald, please don't. There is nothing there.

HELMER: Well, let me look. [*Turns to go to the letter-box. NORA, at the piano, plays the first bars of the Tarantella. HELMER stops in the doorway.*] Aha!

NORA: I can't dance to-morrow if I don't practise with you.   380

HELMER: [*going up to her*] Are you really so afraid of it, dear.

NORA: Yes, so dreadfully afraid of it. Let me practise at once; there is time now, before we go to dinner. Sit down and play for me, Torvald dear; criticise me, and correct me as you play.

HELMER: With great pleasure, if you wish me to.

[*Sits down at the piano.*]

NORA: [*takes out of the box a tambourine and a long variegated shawl. She hastily drapes the shawl round her. Then she springs to the front of the stage and calls out.*] Now play for me! I am going to dance!

[*HELMER plays and NORA dances. RANK stands by the piano behind HELMER and looks on.*]

HELMER: [*as he plays*] Slower, slower!   385

NORA: I can't do it any other way.

HELMER: Not so violently, Nora!

NORA: This is the way.

HELMER: [*stops playing*] No, no—that is not a bit right.

NORA: [*laughing and swinging the tambourine*] Didn't I tell you so?   390

RANK: Let me play for her.

HELMER: [*getting up*] Yes, do. I can correct her better then.

[*RANK sits down at the piano and plays. NORA dances more and more wildly. HELMER has taken up a position beside the stove, and during her dance gives her frequent instructions. She does not seem to hear him; her hair comes down and falls over her shoulders; she pays no attention to it, but goes on dancing. Enter MRS. LINDE.*]

MRS. LINDE: [*standing as if spell-bound in the doorway*] Oh!—

NORA: [*as she dances*] Such fun, Christine!

HELMER: My dear darling Nora, you are dancing as if your life depended on it.   395

NORA: So it does.

HELMER: Stop, Rank; this is sheer madness. Stop, I tell you! [*RANK stops playing, and NORA suddenly stands still. HELMER goes up to her.*] I could never have believed it. You have forgotten everything I taught you.

NORA: [*throwing away the tambourine*] There, you see.

HELMER: You will want a lot of coaching.

NORA: Yes, you see how much I need it. You must coach me up to the last minute. Promise me that, Torvald!   400

HELMER: You can depend on me.

NORA: You must not think of anything but me, either to-day or to-morrow; you mustn't open a single letter—not even open the letter-box—

HELMER: Ah, you are still afraid of that fellow—

NORA: Yes, indeed I am.

405   **HELMER:** Nora, I can tell from your looks that there is a letter from him lying there.

NORA: I don't know; I think there is; but you must not read anything of that kind now. Nothing horrid must come between us till this is all over.

RANK: [*whispers to* HELMER] You mustn't contradict her.

HELMER: [*taking her in his arms*] The child shall have her way. But to-morrow night, after you have danced—

NORA: Then you will be free.

[MAID *appears in the doorway to the right.*]

410   **MAID:** Dinner is served, ma'am.

NORA: We will have champagne, Helen.

MAID: Very good, ma'am.

[*Exit.*]

HELMER: Hullo!—are we going to have a banquet?

NORA: Yes, a champagne banquet till the small hours. [*calls out*] And a few macaroons, Helen—lots, just for once!

415   **HELMER:** Come, come, don't be so wild and nervous. Be my own little skylark, as you used.

NORA: Yes, dear, I will. But go in now and you too, Doctor Rank. Christine, you must help me to do up my hair.

RANK: [*whispers to* HELMER *as they go out*] I suppose there is nothing—she is not expecting anything?

HELMER: Far from it, my dear fellow; it is simply nothing more than this childish nervousness I was telling you of.

[*They go into the right-hand room.*]

NORA: Well!

420   **MRS. LINDE:** Gone out of town.

NORA: I could tell from your face.

MRS. LINDE: He is coming home to-morrow evening. I wrote a note for him.

NORA: You should have let it alone; you must prevent nothing. After all, it is splendid to be waiting for a wonderful thing to happen.

MRS. LINDE: What is it that you are waiting for?

425   **NORA:** Oh, you wouldn't understand. Go in to them, I will come in a moment. [MRS. LINDE *goes into the dining-room.* NORA *stands still for a little while, as if to compose herself. Then she looks at her watch.*] Five o'clock. Seven hours till midnight; and then four-and-twenty hours till the next midnight. Then the Tarantella will be over. Twenty-four and seven? Thirty-one hours to live.

HELMER: [*from the doorway on the right*] Where's my little skylark?

NORA: [*going to him with her arms outstretched*] Here she is!

ACT 3

THE SAME SCENE. *The table has been placed in the middle of the stage, with chairs round it. A lamp is burning on the table. The door into the hall stands open. Dance music is heard in the room above.* MRS. LINDE *is sitting at the table idly turning over the leaves of a book; she tries to read, but does not seem able to collect her thoughts. Every now and then she listens intently for a sound at the outer door.*

MRS. LINDE: [*looking at her watch*] Not yet—and the time is nearly up. If only he does not—. [*listens again*] Ah, there he is. [*Goes into the hall and opens the outer door carefully. Light footsteps are heard on the stairs. She whispers.*] Come in. There is no one here.

KROGSTAD: [*in the doorway*] I found a note from you at home. What does this mean?

MRS. LINDE: It is absolutely necessary that I should have a talk with you.

KROGSTAD: Really? And is it absolutely necessary that it should be here?

MRS. LINDE: It is impossible where I live; there is no private entrance to my rooms. Come in; we are quite alone. The maid is asleep, and the Helmers are at the dance upstairs.   5

KROGSTAD: [*coming into the room*] Are the Helmers really at a dance to-night?

MRS. LINDE: Yes, why not?

KROGSTAD: Certainly—why not?

MRS. LINDE: Now, Nils, let us have a talk.

KROGSTAD: Can we two have anything to talk about?   10

MRS. LINDE: We have a great deal to talk about.

KROGSTAD: I shouldn't have thought so.

MRS. LINDE: No, you have never properly understood me.

KROGSTAD: Was there anything else to understand except what was obvious to all the world—a heartless woman jilts a man when a more lucrative chance turns up?

MRS. LINDE: Do you believe I am as absolutely heartless as all that? And do you believe that I did it with a light heart?   15

KROGSTAD: Didn't you?

MRS. LINDE: Nils, did you really think that?

KROGSTAD: If it were as you say, why did you write to me as you did at the time?

MRS. LINDE: I could do nothing else. As I had to break with you, it was my duty also to put an end to all that you felt for me.

KROGSTAD: [*wringing his hands*] So that was it, and all this—only for the sake of money!   20

MRS. LINDE: You must not forget that I had a helpless mother and two little brothers. We couldn't wait for you, Nils; your prospects seemed hopeless then.

KROGSTAD: That may be so, but you had no right to throw me over for any one else's sake.

MRS. LINDE: Indeed I don't know. Many a time did I ask myself if I had the right to do it.

KROGSTAD: [*more gently*] When I lost you, it was as if all the solid ground went from under my feet. Look at me now—I am a shipwrecked man clinging to a bit of wreckage.

MRS. LINDE: But help may be near.   25

KROGSTAD: It *was* near; but then you came and stood in my way.

MRS. LINDE: Unintentionally, Nils. It was only to-day that I learnt it was your place I was going to take in the Bank.

KROGSTAD: I believe you, if you say so. But now that you know it, are you not going to give it up to me?

MRS. LINDE: No, because that would not benefit you in the least.

KROGSTAD: Oh, benefit, benefit—I would have done it whether or no.   30

MRS. LINDE: I have learnt to act prudently. Life, and hard, bitter necessity have taught me that.

KROGSTAD: And life has taught me not to believe in fine speeches.

MRS. LINDE: Then life has taught you something very reasonable. But deeds you must believe in?

KROGSTAD: What do you mean by that?

MRS. LINDE: You said you were like a shipwrecked man clinging to some wreckage.   35

KROGSTAD: I had good reason to say so.

MRS. LINDE: Well, I am like a shipwrecked woman clinging to some wreckage—no one to mourn for, no one to care for.

KROGSTAD: It was your own choice.

MRS. LINDE: There was no other choice—then.

40   KROGSTAD: Well, what now?

MRS. LINDE: Nils, how would it be if we two shipwrecked people could join forces?

KROGSTAD: What are you saying?

MRS. LINDE: Two on the same piece of wreckage would stand a better chance than each on their own.

KROGSTAD: Christine!

45   MRS. LINDE: What do you suppose brought me to town?

KROGSTAD: Do you mean that you gave me a thought?

MRS. LINDE: I could not endure life without work. All my life, as long as I can remember, I have worked, and it has been my greatest and only pleasure. But now I am quite alone in the world—my life is so dreadfully empty and I feel so forsaken. There is not the least pleasure in working for one's self. Nils, give me someone and something to work for.

KROGSTAD: I don't trust that. It is nothing but a woman's overstrained sense of generosity that prompts you to make such an offer of yourself.

MRS. LINDE: Have you ever noticed anything of the sort in me?

50   KROGSTAD: Could you really do it? Tell me—do you know all about my past life?

MRS. LINDE: Yes.

KROGSTAD: And do you know what they think of me here?

MRS. LINDE: You seemed to me to imply that with me you might have been quite another man.

KROGSTAD: I am certain of it.

55   MRS. LINDE: Is it too late now?

KROGSTAD: Christine, are you saying this deliberately? Yes, I am sure you are. I see it in your face. Have you really the courage, then—?

MRS. LINDE: I want to be a mother to someone, and your children need a mother. We two need each other. Nils, I have faith in your real character—I can dare anything together with you.

KROGSTAD: [*grasps her hands*] Thanks, thanks, Christine! Now I shall find a way to clear myself in the eyes of the world. Ah, but I forgot—

MRS. LINDE: [*listening*] Hush! The Tarantella! Go, go!

60   KROGSTAD: Why? What is it?

MRS. LINDE: Do you hear them up there? When that is over, we may expect them back.

KROGSTAD: Yes, yes—I will go. But it is all no use. Of course you are not aware what steps I have taken in the matter of the Helmers.

MRS. LINDE: Yes. I know all about that.

KROGSTAD: And in spite of that have you the courage to—?

65   MRS. LINDE: I understand very well to what lengths a man like you might be driven by despair.

KROGSTAD: If I could only undo what I have done!

MRS. LINDE: You can. Your letter is lying in the letter-box now.

KROGSTAD: Are you sure of that?

MRS. LINDE: Quite sure, but—

70   KROGSTAD: [*with a searching look at her*] Is that what it all means?—that you want to save your friend at any cost? Tell me frankly. Is that it?

MRS. LINDE: Nils, a woman who has once sold herself for another's sake, doesn't do it a second time.

KROGSTAD: I will ask for my letter back.

MRS. LINDE: No, no.

KROGSTAD: Yes, of course I will. I will wait here till Helmer comes; I will tell him he must give me my letter back—that it only concerns my dismissal—that he is not to read it—

MRS. LINDE: No, Nils, you must not recall your letter.   75
KROGSTAD: But, tell me, wasn't it for that very purpose that you asked me to meet you
here?
MRS. LINDE: In my first moment of fright, it was. But twenty-four hours have elapsed
since then, and in that time I have witnessed incredible things in this house. Helmer
must know all about it. This unhappy secret must be disclosed; they must have a
complete understanding between them, which is impossible with all this concealment
and falsehood going on.
KROGSTAD: Very well, if you will take the responsibility. But there is one thing I can do in
any case, and I shall do it at once.
MRS. LINDE: [*listening*] You must be quick and go! The dance is over; we are not safe a
moment longer.
KROGSTAD: I will wait for you below.   80
MRS. LINDE: Yes, do. You must see me back to my door.
KROGSTAD: I have never had such an amazing piece of good fortune in my life.

[*Goes out through the outer door. The door between the room and the hall remains open.*]

MRS. LINDE: [*tidying up the room and laying her hat and cloak ready*] What a difference! what
a difference! Someone to work for and live for—a home to bring comfort into. That
I will do, indeed. I wish they would be quick and come—[*listens*] Ah, there they are
now. I must put on my things.

[*Takes up her hat and cloak. HELMER's and NORA's voices are heard outside; a key is turned, and
HELMER brings NORA almost by force into the hall. She is in an Italian costume with a large black
shawl round her; he is in evening dress and a black domino which is flying open.*]

NORA: [*hanging back in the doorway, and struggling with him*] No, no, no!—don't take me in.
I want to go upstairs again; I don't want to leave so early.
HELMER: But, my dearest Nora—   85
NORA: Please, Torvald dear—please, *please*—only an hour more.
HELMER: Not a single minute, my sweet Nora. You know that was our agreement. Come
along into the room; you are catching cold standing there.

[*He brings her gently into the room, in spite of her resistance.*]

MRS. LINDE: Good evening.
NORA: Christine!
HELMER: You here, so late, Mrs. Linde?   90
MRS. LINDE: Yes, you must excuse me; I was so anxious to see Nora in her dress.
NORA: Have you been sitting here waiting for me?
MRS. LINDE: Yes, unfortunately I came too late, you had already gone upstairs; and I
thought I couldn't go away without having seen you.
HELMER: [*taking off NORA's shawl*] Yes, take a good look at her. I think she is worth look-
ing at. Isn't she charming, Mrs. Linde?
MRS. LINDE: Yes, indeed she is.   95
HELMER: Doesn't she look remarkably pretty? Everyone thought so at the dance. But she
is terribly self-willed, this sweet little person. What are we to do with her? You will
hardly believe that I had almost to bring her away by force.
NORA: Torvald, you will repent not having let me stay, even if it were only for half an
hour.

HELMER: Listen to her, Mrs. Linde! She had danced her Tarantella, and it had been a tremendous success, as it deserved—although possibly the performance was a trifle too realistic—a little more so, I mean, than was strictly compatible with the limitations of art. But never mind about that! The chief thing is, she had made a success—she had made a tremendous success. Do you think I was going to let her remain there after that, and spoil the effect? No indeed! I took my charming little Capri maiden—my capricious little Capri maiden, I should say—on my arm; took one quick turn round the room; a curtsey on either side, and, as they say in novels, the beautiful apparition disappeared. An exit ought always to be effective, Mrs. Linde; but that is what I cannot make Nora understand. Pooh! this room is hot. [*throws his domino on a chair and opens the door of his room*] Hullo! it's all dark in here. Oh, of course—excuse me—.

[*He goes in and lights some candles.*]

NORA: [*in a hurried and breathless whisper*] Well?

100   **MRS. LINDE:** [*in a low voice*] I have had a talk with him.

NORA: Yes, and—

MRS. LINDE: Nora, you must tell your husband all about it.

NORA: [*in an expressionless voice*] I knew it.

MRS. LINDE: You have nothing to be afraid of as far as Krogstad is concerned; but you
      must tell him.

105   **NORA:** I won't tell him.

MRS. LINDE: Then the letter will.

NORA: Thank you, Christine. Now I know what I must do. Hush—!

HELMER: [*coming in again*] Well, Mrs. Linde, have you admired her?

MRS. LINDE: Yes, and now I will say good-night.

110   **HELMER:** What already? Is this yours, this knitting?

MRS. LINDE: [*taking it*] Yes, thank you, I had very nearly forgotten it.

HELMER: So you knit?

MRS. LINDE: Of course.

HELMER: Do you know, you ought to embroider.

115   **MRS. LINDE:** Really? Why?

HELMER: Yes, it's far more becoming. Let me show you. You hold the embroidery thus in
      your left hand, and use the needle with the right—like this—with a long, easy sweep.
      Do you see?

MRS. LINDE: Yes, perhaps—

HELMER: But in the case of knitting—that can never be anything but ungraceful; look
      here—the arms close together, the knitting-needles going up and down—it has a sort
      of Chinese effect—. That was really excellent champagne they gave us.

MRS. LINDE: Well,—good-night, Nora, and don't be self-willed any more.

120   **HELMER:** That's right, Mrs. Linde.

MRS. LINDE: Good-night, Mr. Helmer.

HELMER: [*accompanying her to the door*] Good-night, good-night. I hope you will get home
      all right. I should be very happy to—but you haven't any great distance to go. Good-
      night, good-night. [*She goes out; he shuts the door after her, and comes in again.*] Ah!—at
      last we have got rid of her. She is a frightful bore, that woman.

NORA: Aren't you very tired, Torvald?

HELMER: No, not in the least.

125   **NORA:** Nor sleepy?

HELMER: Not a bit. On the contrary, I feel extraordinarily lively. And you?—you really
      look both tired and sleepy.

NORA: Yes, I am very tired. I want to go to sleep at once.

HELMER: There, you see it was quite right of me not to let you stay there any longer.

NORA: Everything you do is quite right, Torvald.

HELMER: [*kissing her on the forehead*] Now my little skylark is speaking reasonably. Did   130
you notice what good spirits Rank was in this evening?

NORA: Really? Was he? I didn't speak to him at all.

HELMER: And I very little, but I have not for a long time seen him in such good form.
[*looks for a while at her and then goes nearer to her*] It is delightful to be at home by ourselves again, to be all alone with you—you fascinating, charming little darling!

NORA: Don't look at me like that, Torvald.

HELMER: Why shouldn't I look at my dearest treasure?—at all the beauty that is mine, all
my very own?

NORA: [*going to the other side of the table*] You mustn't say things like that to me to-   135
night.

HELMER: [*following her*] You have still got the Tarantella in your blood, I see. And it
makes you more captivating than ever. Listen—the guests are beginning to go now.
[*in a lower voice*] Nora—soon the whole house will be quiet.

NORA: Yes, I hope so.

HELMER: Yes, my own darling Nora. Do you know, when I am out at a party with you
like this, why I speak so little to you, keep away from you, and only send a stolen
glance in your direction now and then?—do you know why I do that? It is because I
make believe to myself that we are secretly in love, and you are my secretly promised
bride, and that no one suspects there is anything between us.

NORA: Yes, yes—I know very well your thoughts are with me all the time.

HELMER: And when we are leaving, and I am putting the shawl over your beautiful   140
young shoulders—on your lovely neck—then I imagine that you are my young bride
and that we have just come from the wedding, and I am bringing you for the first
time into our home—to be alone with you for the first time—quite alone with my shy
little darling! All this evening I have longed for nothing but you. When I watched the
seductive figures of the Tarantella, my blood was on fire; I could endure it no longer,
and that was why I brought you down so early—

NORA: Go away, Torvald! You must let me go. I won't—

HELMER: What's that? You're joking, my little Nora! You won't—you won't? Am I not
your husband—?

[*A knock is heard at the outer door.*]

NORA: [*starting*] Did you hear—?

HELMER: [*going into the hall*] Who is it?

RANK: [*outside*] It is I. May I come in for a moment?   145

HELMER: [*in a fretful whisper*] Oh, what does he want now? [*aloud*] Wait a minute! [*unlocks
the door*] Come, that's kind of you not to pass by our door.

RANK: I thought I heard your voice, and felt as if I should like to look in. [*with a swift glance
round*] Ah, yes!—these dear familiar rooms. You are very happy and cosy in here, you two.

HELMER: It seems to me that you looked after yourself pretty well upstairs too.

RANK: Excellently. Why shouldn't I? Why shouldn't one enjoy everything in this world?—
at any rate as much as one can, and as long as one can. The wine was capital—

HELMER: Especially the champagne.   150

RANK: So you noticed that too? It is almost incredible how much I managed to put away!

NORA: Torvald drank a great deal of champagne tonight, too.

RANK: Did he?

NORA: Yes, and he is always in such good spirits afterwards.

155 RANK: Well, why should one not enjoy a merry evening after a well-spent day?

HELMER: Well spent? I am afraid I can't take credit for that.

RANK: [*clapping him on the back*] But I can, you know!

NORA: Doctor Rank, you must have been occupied with some scientific investigation to-day.

RANK: Exactly.

160 HELMER: Just listen!—little Nora talking about scientific investigations!

NORA: And may I congratulate you on the result?

RANK: Indeed you may.

NORA: Was it favourable, then?

RANK: The best possible, for both doctor and patient—certainty.

165 NORA: [*quickly and searchingly*] Certainty?

RANK: Absolute certainty. So wasn't I entitled to make a merry evening of it after that?

NORA: Yes, you certainly were, Doctor Rank.

HELMER: I think so too, so long as you don't have to pay for it in the morning.

RANK: Oh well, one can't have anything in this life without paying for it.

170 NORA: Doctor Rank—are you fond of fancy-dress balls?

RANK: Yes, if there is a fine lot of pretty costumes.

NORA: Tell me—what shall we two wear at the next?

HELMER: Little featherbrain!—are you thinking of the next already?

RANK: We two? Yes, I can tell you. You shall go as a good fairy—

175 HELMER: Yes, but what do you suggest as an appropriate costume for that?

RANK: Let your wife go dressed just as she is in everyday life.

HELMER: That was really very prettily turned. But can't you tell us what you will be?

RANK: Yes, my dear friend, I have quite made up my mind about that.

HELMER: Well?

180 RANK: At the next fancy dress ball I shall be invisible.

HELMER: That's a good joke!

RANK: There is a big black hat—have you never heard of hats that make you invisible? If you put one on, no one can see you.

HELMER: [*suppressing a smile*] Yes, you are quite right.

RANK: But I am clean forgetting what I came for. Helmer, give me a cigar—one of the dark Havanas.

185 HELMER: With the greatest pleasure. [*offers him his case*]

RANK: [*takes a cigar and cuts off the end*] Thanks.

NORA: [*striking a match*] Let me give you a light.

RANK: Thank you. [*She holds the match for him to light his cigar.*] And now good-bye!

HELMER: Good-bye, good-bye, dear old man!

190 NORA: Sleep well, Doctor Rank.

RANK: Thank you for that wish.

NORA: Wish me the same.

RANK: You? Well, if you want me to: sleep well! And thanks for the light.

[*He nods to them both and goes out.*]

HELMER: [*in a subdued voice*] He has drunk more than he ought.

195 NORA: [*absently*] Maybe. [*HELMER takes a bunch of keys out of his pocket and goes into the hall.*] Torvald! what are you going to do there?

HELMER: Empty the letter-box; it is quite full; there will be no room to put the newspaper in to-morrow morning.

NORA: Are you going to work to-night?

HELMER: You know quite well I'm not. What is this? Some one has been at the lock.

NORA: At the lock—?

HELMER: Yes, someone has. What can it mean? I should never have thought the maid—.   200
Here is a broken hairpin. Nora, it is one of yours.

NORA: [*quickly*] Then it must have been the children—

HELMER: Then you must get them out of those ways. There, at last I have got it open.
[*Takes out the contents of the letter-box, and calls to the kitchen.*] Helen!—Helen, put out
the light over the front door. [*Goes back into the room and shuts the door into the hall.
He holds out his hand full of letters.*] Look at that—look what a heap of them there are.
[*turning them over*] What on earth is that?

NORA: [*at the window*] The letter—No! Torvald, no!

HELMER: Two cards—of Rank's.

NORA: Of Doctor Rank's?   205

HELMER: [*looking at them*] Doctor Rank. They were on the top. He must have put them in
when he went out.

NORA: Is there anything written on them?

HELMER: There is a black cross over the name. Look there—what an uncomfortable idea!
It looks as if he were announcing his own death.

NORA: It is just what he is doing.

HELMER: What? Do you know anything about it? Has he said anything to you?   210

NORA: Yes. He told me that when the cards came it would be his leave-taking from us. He
means to shut himself up and die.

HELMER: My poor old friend. Certainly I knew we should not have him very long with
us. But so soon! And so he hides himself away like a wounded animal.

NORA: If it has to happen, it is best it should be without a word—don't you think so,
Torvald?

HELMER: [*walking up and down*] He had so grown into our lives. I can't think of him as
having gone out of them. He, with his sufferings and his loneliness, was like a cloudy
background to our sunlit happiness. Well, perhaps it is best so. For him, anyway.
[*standing still*] And perhaps for us too, Nora. We two are thrown quite upon each other
now. [*puts his arms round her*] My darling wife, I don't feel as if I could hold you tight
enough. Do you know, Nora, I have often wished that you might be threatened by
some great danger, so that I might risk my life's blood, and everything, for your sake.

NORA: [*disengages herself, and says firmly and decidedly*] Now you must read your letters,   215
Torvald.

HELMER: No, no; not to-night. I want to be with you, my darling wife.

NORA: With the thought of your friend's death—

HELMER: You are right, it has affected us both. Something ugly has come between us—
the thought of the horrors of death. We must try and rid our minds of that. Until
then—we will each go to our own room.

NORA: [*hanging on his neck*] Good-night, Torvald—Good-night!

HELMER: [*kissing her on the forehead.*] Good-night, my little singing-bird. Sleep sound,   220
Nora. Now I will read my letters through.

[*He takes his letters and goes into his room, shutting the door after him.*]

NORA: [*gropes distractedly about, seizes* HELMER's *domino, throws it round her, while she says in
quick, hoarse, spasmodic whispers*] Never to see him again. Never! Never! [*puts her shawl
over her head*] Never to see my children again either—never again. Never! Never!—
Ah! the icy, black water—the unfathomable depths—If only it were over! He has got
it now—now he is reading it. Good-by, Torvald and my children!

[*She is about to rush out through the hall, when* HELMER *opens his door hurriedly and stands with an open letter in his hand.*]

HELMER: Nora!

NORA: Ah!—

HELMER: What is this? Do you know what is in this letter?

225 NORA: Yes, I know. Let me go! Let me get out!

HELMER: [*holding her back*] Where are you going?

NORA: [*trying to get free*] You shan't save me, Torvald!

HELMER: [*reeling*] True? Is this true, that I read here? Horrible! No, no—it is impossible that it can be true.

NORA: It is true. I have loved you above everything else in the world.

230 HELMER: Oh, don't let us have any silly excuses.

NORA: [*taking a step towards him*] Torvald—!

HELMER: Miserable creature—what have you done?

NORA: Let me go. You shall not suffer for my sake. You shall not take it upon yourself.

HELMER: No tragedy airs, please. [*locks the hall door*] Here you shall stay and give me an explanation. Do you understand what you have done? Answer me? Do you understand what you have done?

235 NORA: [*looks steadily at him and says with a growing look of coldness in her face*] Yes, now I am beginning to understand thoroughly.

HELMER: [*walking about the room*] What a horrible awakening! All these eight years—she who was my joy and pride—a hypocrite, a liar—worse, worse—a criminal! The unutterable ugliness of it all! For shame! For shame! [NORA *is silent and looks steadily at him. He stops in front of her.*] I ought to have suspected that something of the sort would happen. I ought to have foreseen it. All your father's want of principle—be silent!— all your father's want of principle has come out in you. No religion, no morality, no sense of duty—. How I am punished for having winked at what he did! I did it for your sake, and this is how you repay me.

NORA: Yes, that's just it.

HELMER: Now you have destroyed all my happiness. You have ruined all my future. It is horrible to think of! I am in the power of an unscrupulous man; he can do what he likes with me, ask anything he likes of me, give me any orders he pleases—I dare not refuse. And I must sink to such miserable depths because of a thoughtless woman!

NORA: When I am out of the way, you will be free.

240 HELMER: No fine speeches, please. Your father had always plenty of those ready, too. What good would it be to me if you were out of the way, as you say? Not the slightest. He can make the affair known everywhere; and if he does, I may be falsely suspected of having been a party to your criminal action. Very likely people will think I was behind it all—that it was I who prompted you! And I have to thank you for all this— you whom I have cherished during the whole of our married life. Do you understand now what it is you have done for me?

NORA: [*coldly and quietly*] Yes.

HELMER: It is so incredible that I can't take it in. But we must come to some understanding. Take off that shawl. Take it off, I tell you. I must try and appease him some way or another. The matter must be hushed up at any cost. And as for you and me, it must appear as if everything between us were just as before—but naturally only in the eyes of the world. You will still remain in my house, that is a matter of course. But I shall not allow you to bring up the children; I dare not trust them to you. To think that I should be obliged to say so to one whom I have loved so dearly, and whom I still—. No, that is all over. From this moment happiness is not the question; all that concerns us is to save the remains, the fragments, the appearance—

[*A ring is heard at the front-door bell.*]

HELMER: [*with a start*] What is that? So late! Can the worst—? Can he—? Hide yourself, Nora. Say you are ill.

[*NORA stands motionless. HELMER goes and unlocks the hall door.*]

MAID: [*half-dressed, comes to the door*] A letter for the mistress.

HELMER: Give it to me. [*takes the letter, and shuts the door*] Yes, it is from him. You shall not   245
have it; I will read it myself.

NORA: Yes, read it.

HELMER: [*standing by the lamp*] I scarcely have the courage to do it. It may mean ruin for both of us. No, I must know. [*tears open the letter, runs his eye over a few lines, looks at a paper enclosed and gives a shout of joy*] Nora! [*She looks at him questioningly.*] Nora!—No, I must read it once again—. Yes, it is true! I am saved! Nora, I am saved!

NORA: And I?

HELMER: You too, of course; we are both saved, both you and I. Look, he sends you your bond back. He says he regrets and repents—that a happy change in his life—never mind what he says! We are saved, Nora! No one can do anything to you. Oh, Nora, Nora!—no, first I must destroy these hateful things. Let me see—. [*takes a look at the bond*] No, no, I won't look at it. The whole thing shall be nothing but a bad dream to me. [*tears up the bond and both letters, throws them all into the stove, and watches them burn*] There—now it doesn't exist any longer. He says that since Christmas Eve you—. These must have been three dreadful days for you, Nora.

NORA: I have fought a hard fight these three days.   250

HELMER: And suffered agonies, and seen no way out but—. No, we won't call any of the horrors to mind. We will only shout with joy, and keep saying "It's all over! It's all over!" Listen to me, Nora. You don't seem to realise that it is all over. What is this?— such a cold, set face! My poor little Nora, I quite understand; you don't feel as if you could believe that I have forgiven you. But it is true, Nora, I swear it; I have forgiven you everything. I know that what you did, you did out of love for me.

NORA: That is true.

HELMER: You have loved me as a wife ought to love her husband. Only you had not sufficient knowledge to judge of the means you used. But do you suppose you are any the less dear to me, because you don't understand how to act on your own responsibility? No, no; only lean on me; I will advise you and direct you. I should not be a man if this womanly helplessness did not just give you a double attractiveness in my eyes. You must not think any more about the hard things I said in my first moment of consternation, when I thought everything was going to overwhelm me. I have forgiven you, Nora; I swear to you I have forgiven you.

NORA: Thank you for your forgiveness.

[*She goes out through the door to the right.*]

HELMER: No, don't go—. [*looks in*] What are you doing in there?   255

NORA: [*from within*] Taking off my fancy dress.

HELMER: [*standing at the open door*] Yes, do. Try and calm yourself, and make your mind easy again, my frightened little singing-bird. Be at rest, and feel secure; I have broad wings to shelter you under. [*walks up and down by the door*] How warm and cosy our home is, Nora. Here is shelter for you; here I will protect you like a hunted dove that I have saved from a hawk's claws. I will bring peace to your poor beating heart. It will come, little by little, Nora, believe me. Tomorrow morning you will look upon it all quite differently; soon everything will be just as it was before. Very soon you won't need me to assure you that I have forgiven you; you will yourself feel the certainty that I have done so. Can you suppose I should ever think of such a thing as repudiating you, or even reproaching you? You have no idea what a true man's heart is like, Nora. There is something so indescribably sweet and satisfying, to a man, in the knowledge that he has forgiven his wife—forgiven her freely, and with all his heart. It seems as if that had made her, as it were, doubly his own; he has given her a new life, so to speak; and she has in a way become both wife and child to him. So you shall be for me after this, my little scared, helpless darling. Have no anxiety about anything, Nora; only be frank and open with me, and I will serve as will and conscience both to you—. What is this? Not gone to bed? Have you changed your things?

NORA: [*in everyday dress*] Yes, Torvald, I have changed my things now.

HELMER: But what for?—so late as this.

260 NORA: I shall not sleep to-night.

HELMER: But, my dear Nora—

NORA: [*looking at her watch*] It is not so very late. Sit down here, Torvald. You and I have much to say to one another.

[*She sits down at one side of the table.*]

HELMER: Nora—what is this?—this cold, set face?

NORA: Sit down. it will take some time; I have a lot to talk over with you.

265 HELMER: [*sits down at the opposite side of the table*] You alarm me, Nora!—and I don't understand you.

NORA: No, that is just it. You don't understand me, and I have never understood you either—before to-night. No, you mustn't interrupt me. You must simply listen to what I say. Torvald, this is a settling of accounts.

HELMER: What do you mean by that?

NORA: [*after a short silence*] Isn't there one thing that strikes you as strange in our sitting here like this?

HELMER: What is that?

270 NORA: We have been married now eight years. Does it not occur to you that this is the first time we two, you and I, husband and wife, have had a serious conversation?

HELMER: What do you mean by serious?

NORA: In all these eight years—longer than that—from the very beginning of our acquaintance, we have never exchanged a word on any serious subject.

HELMER: Was it likely that I would be continually and for ever telling you about worries that you could not help me to bear?

NORA: I am not speaking about business matters. I say that we have never sat down in earnest together to try and get at the bottom of anything.

275 HELMER: But, dearest Nora, would it have been any good to you?

NORA: That is just it; you have never understood me. I have been greatly wronged, Torvald—first by papa and then by you.

HELMER: What! By us two—by us two, who have loved you better than anyone else in the world?

NORA: [*shaking her head*] You have never loved me. You have only thought it pleasant to be in love with me.

HELMER: Nora, what do I hear you saying?

280 NORA: It is perfectly true, Torvald. When I was at home with papa, he told me his opinion about everything, and so I had the same opinions; and if I differed from him I concealed

Torvald Helmer (Sam Waterston) begs Nora (Liv Ullmann) to reconsider her decision to leave home in the Joseph Papp New York Shakespeare Festival production (1995) of *A Dollhouse* (director, Tormod Skagestad).

the fact, because he would not have liked it. He called me his doll-child, and he played with me just as I used to play with my dolls. And when I came to live with you—

HELMER: What sort of an expression is that to use about our marriage?

NORA: [*undisturbed*] I mean that I was simply transferred from papa's hands into yours. You arranged everything according to your own taste, and so I got the same tastes as you—or else I pretended to, I am really not quite sure which—I think sometimes the one and sometimes the other. When I look back on it, it seems to me as if I had been living here like a poor woman—just from hand to mouth. I have existed merely to perform tricks for you, Torvald. But you would have it so. You and papa have committed a great sin against me. It is your fault that I have made nothing of my life.

HELMER: How unreasonable and how ungrateful you are, Nora! Have you not been happy here?

NORA: No, I have never been happy. I thought I was, but it has never really been so.

285 **HELMER:** Not—not happy!

NORA: No, only merry. And you have always been so kind to me. But our home has been nothing but a playroom. I have been your doll-wife, just as at home I was papa's doll-child; and here the children have been my dolls. I thought it great fun when you played with me, just as they thought it great fun when I played with them. That is what our marriage has been, Torvald.

HELMER: There is some truth in what you say—exaggerated and strained as your view of it is. But for the future it shall be different. Playtime shall be over, and lesson-time shall begin.

NORA: Whose lessons? Mine, or the children's?

HELMER: Both yours and the children's, my darling Nora.

290 **NORA:** Alas, Torvald, you are not the man to educate me into being a proper wife for you.

HELMER: And you can say that!

NORA: And I—how am I fitted to bring up the children?

HELMER: Nora!

NORA: Didn't you say so yourself a little while ago—that you dare not trust me to bring them up?

295 **HELMER:** In a moment of anger! Why do you pay any heed to that?

NORA: Indeed, you were perfectly right. I am not fit for the task. There is another task I must undertake first. I must try and educate myself—you are not the man to help me in that. I must do that for myself. And that is why I am going to leave you now.

HELMER: [*springing up*] What do you say?

NORA: I must stand quite alone, if I am to understand myself and everything about me. It is for that reason that I cannot remain with you any longer.

HELMER: Nora! Nora!

300 **NORA:** I am going away from here now, at once. I am sure Christine will take me in for the night—

HELMER: You are out of your mind! I won't allow it! I forbid you!

NORA: It is no use forbidding me anything any longer. I will take with me what belongs to myself. I will take nothing from you, either now or later.

HELMER: What sort of madness is this!

NORA: To-morrow I shall go home—I mean, to my old home. It will be easiest for me to find something to do there.

305 **HELMER:** You blind, foolish woman!

NORA: I must try and get some sense, Torvald.

HELMER: To desert your home, your husband and your children! And you don't consider what people will say!

NORA: I cannot consider that at all. I only know that it is necessary for me.

HELMER: It's shocking. This is how you would neglect your most sacred duties.

310 **NORA:** What do you consider my most sacred duties?

HELMER: Do I need to tell you that? Are they not your duties to your husband and your children?

NORA: I have other duties just as sacred.

HELMER: That you have not. What duties could those be?

NORA: Duties to myself.

315 **HELMER:** Before all else, you are a wife and a mother.

NORA: I don't believe that any longer. I believe that before all else I am a reasonable human being, just as you are—or, at all events, that I must try and become one. I know quite well, Torvald, that most people would think you right, and that views of that kind are to be found in books; but I can no longer content myself with what most people say, or with what is found in books. I must think over things for myself and get to understand them.

HELMER: Can you not understand your place in your own home? Have you not a reliable guide in such matters as that?—have you no religion?

NORA: I am afraid, Torvald, I do not exactly know what religion is.

HELMER: What are you saying?

NORA: I know nothing but what the clergyman said when I went to be confirmed. He told us that religion was this, and that, and the other. When I am away from all this, and am alone, I will look into that matter too. I will see if what the clergyman said is true, or at all events if it is true for me.   320

HELMER: This is unheard of in a girl of your age! But if religion cannot lead you aright, let me try and awaken your conscience. I suppose you have some moral sense? Or— answer me—am I to think you have none?

NORA: I assure you, Torvald, that is not an easy question to answer. I really don't know. The thing perplexes me altogether. I only know that you and I look at it in quite a different light. I am learning, too, that the law is quite another thing from what I supposed; but I find it impossible to convince myself that the law is right. According to it a woman has no right to spare her old dying father, or to save her husband's life. I can't believe that.

HELMER: You talk like a child. You don't understand the conditions of the world in which you live.

NORA: No, I don't. But now I am going to try. I am going to see if I can make out who is right, the world or I.

HELMER: You are ill, Nora; you are delirious; I almost think you are out of your mind.   325

NORA: I have never felt my mind so clear and certain as to-night.

HELMER: And is it with a clear and certain mind that you forsake your husband and your children?

NORA: Yes, it is.

HELMER: Then there is only one possible explanation.

NORA: What is that?   330

HELMER: You do not love me any more.

NORA: No, that is just it.

HELMER: Nora!—and you can say that?

NORA: It gives me great pain, Torvald, for you have always been so kind to me, but I cannot help it. I do not love you any more.

HELMER: [*regaining his composure*] Is that a clear and certain conviction too?   335

NORA: Yes, absolutely clear and certain. That is the reason why I will not stay here any longer.

HELMER: And can you tell me what I have done to forfeit your love?

NORA: Yes, indeed I can. It was to-night, when the wonderful thing did not happen; then I saw you were not the man I had thought you.

HELMER: Explain yourself better—I don't understand you.

NORA: I have waited so patiently for eight years; for, goodness knows, I knew very well that wonderful things don't happen every day. Then this horrible misfortune came upon me; and then I felt quite certain that the wonderful thing was going to happen at last. When Krogstad's letter was lying out there, never for a moment did I imagine that you would consent to accept this man's conditions. I was so absolutely certain that you would say to him: Publish the thing to the whole world. And when that was done—   340

HELMER: Yes, what then?—when I had exposed my wife to shame and disgrace?

NORA: When that was done, I was so absolutely certain, you would come forward and take everything upon yourself, and say: I am the guilty one.

HELMER: Nora—!

NORA: You mean that I would never have accepted such a sacrifice on your part? No, of course not. But what would my assurances have been worth against yours? That was the wonderful thing which I hoped for and feared; and it was to prevent that, that I wanted to kill myself.

345 **HELMER:** I would gladly work night and day for you, Nora—bear sorrow and want for your sake. But no man would sacrifice his honour for the one he loves.

NORA: It is a thing hundreds of thousands of women have done.

HELMER: Oh, you think and talk like a heedless child.

NORA: Maybe. But you neither think nor talk like the man I could bind myself to. As soon as your fear was over—and it was not fear for what threatened me, but for what might happen to you—when the whole thing was past, as far as you were concerned it was exactly as if nothing at all had happened. Exactly as before, I was your little skylark, your doll, which you would in future treat with doubly gentle care, because it was so brittle and fragile. [*getting up*] Torvald—it was then it dawned upon me that for eight years I had been living here with a strange man, and had borne him three children—. Oh, I can't bear to think of it! I could tear myself into little bits!

HELMER: [*sadly*] I see, I see. An abyss has opened between us—there is no denying it. But, Nora, would it not be possible to fill it up?

350 **NORA:** As I am now, I am no wife for you.

HELMER: I have it in me to become a different man.

NORA: Perhaps—if your doll is taken away from you.

HELMER: But to part!—to part from you! No, no, Nora, I can't understand that idea.

NORA: [*going out to the right*] That makes it all the more certain that it must be done.

[*She comes back with her cloak and hat and a small bag which she puts on a chair by the table.*]

355 **HELMER:** Nora, Nora, not now! Wait till to-morrow.

NORA: [*putting on her cloak*] I cannot spend the night in a strange man's room.

HELMER: But can't we live here like brother and sister—?

NORA: [*putting on her hat*] You know very well that would not last long. [*puts the shawl round her*] Good-bye, Torvald. I won't see the little ones. I know they are in better hands than mine. As I am now, I can be of no use to them.

HELMER: But some day, Nora—some day?

360 **NORA:** How can I tell? I have no idea what is going to become of me.

HELMER: But you are my wife, whatever becomes of you.

NORA: Listen, Torvald. I have heard that when a wife deserts her husband's house, as I am doing now, he is legally freed from all obligations towards her. In any case I set you free from all your obligations. You are not to feel yourself bound in the slightest way, any more than I shall. There must be perfect freedom on both sides. See here is your ring back. Give me mine.

HELMER: That too?

NORA: That too.

365 **HELMER:** Here it is.

NORA: That's right. Now it is all over. I have put the keys here. The maids know all about everything in the house—better than I do. To-morrow, after I have left her, Christine will come here and pack up my own things that I brought with me from home. I will have them sent after me.

HELMER: All over! All over!—Nora, shall you never think of me again?

NORA: I know I shall often think of you and the children and this house.

HELMER: May I write to you, Nora?

370 **NORA:** No—never. You must not do that.

HELMER: But at least let me send you—
NORA: Nothing—nothing—
HELMER: Let me help you if you are in want.
NORA: No. I can receive nothing from a stranger.
HELMER: Nora—can I never be anything more than a stranger to you?   375
NORA: [*taking her bag*] Ah, Torvald, the most wonderful thing of all would have to happen.
HELMER: Tell me what that would be!
NORA: Both you and I would have to be so changed that—. Oh, Torvald, I don't believe any longer in wonderful things happening.
HELMER: But I will believe in it. Tell me? So changed that—?
NORA: That our life together would be a real wedlock. Good-bye.   380

[*She goes out through the hall.*]

HELMER: [*sinks down on a chair at the door and buries his face in his hands*] Nora! Nora! [*looks round, and rises*] Empty. She is gone. [*A hope flashes across his mind.*] The most wonderful thing of all—?

[*The sound of a door slamming is heard from below.*]

QUESTIONS

Act 1

1. What does the opening stage direction reveal about the Helmer family? About the time of year?
2. Explain the ways Nora and Torvald behave toward each other.
3. What does Torvald's refusal to consider borrowing and debt tell you about him (speech 22)? Where else in the play are these characteristics important?
4. What have the Helmer finances been like in the past? How is their situation about to change?
5. How are Mrs. Linde and Nora alike? Different? Why is it ironic that Nora helps Christine get a job at the bank? How will this affect Krogstad? Nora?
6. How does Ibsen show that Krogstad is a threat when he first appears?
7. Why should Nora's scene with her children in Act 1 not be cut in production? What does it show about Nora and the household?
8. What is Nora's secret "crime"? What is the explanation and justification for it? At the end of the act, what new problems does she face?

Act 2

9. What is symbolized by the stripped Christmas tree?
10. What is implied about Nora's self-perceptions when she calls herself "your little squirrel" and "your skylark"?
11. After sending Krogstad's dismissal, Torvald tells Nora that "You will see I am man enough to take everything upon myself" (speech 135). How does this speech conform to Nora's hopes? How is it ironic?
12. Why does Nora flirt with Dr. Rank? How and why does he distress her?
13. Why does Nora dance the tarantella so wildly?
14. What is the "wonderful thing" that Nora is waiting for?

Act 3

15. Explain Christine's past rejection of Krogstad. Why will she accept him now? How will their union differ from the Helmers' marriage?
16. What does Christine decide to do about Krogstad's letter? Why?
17. Explain the reactions of Torvald and Nora to the death of Dr. Rank.
18. Describe Torvald's reaction to Krogstad's first letter. How does Nora respond to Torvald? How do you respond to him? Why?
19. Explain what Nora learns about Torvald, herself, her marriage, and her identity as a woman as a result of Torvald's responses. Why does she decide to leave?

GENERAL QUESTIONS

1. Which elements and aspects of *A Dollhouse* are the most realistic and which are the least? Explain.
2. Consider Ibsen's symbolism, with reference to Dr. Rank, the macaroons, the Christmas tree, the presents, the locked mailbox, the dance, Nora's black shawl, her change of clothing in Act 3, and the door slam at the play's close.
3. Is Nora a victim of circumstances or a villain who brings about problems? What is Ibsen's view? What is yours? Why?
4. Describe the "role-playing" in the Helmer marriage. Does any evidence suggest that Nora knows she is playing a role? What degree of self-awareness, if any, characterizes Torvald's role-playing?
5. When Nora asks Torvald to restore Krogstad's job, Torvald refuses on the ground that he should not give in to his wife's pressure (Act 2, speech 113). Later, he claims that their marriage is destroyed, but that they should keep up the appearance of marital stability (Act 3, speech 242). In the light of such statements, describe Torvald's character. What concerns him most about life and marriage?
6. A major theme in the play is that weakness and corruption are passed from generation to generation. Examine this theme in connection with Krogstad and his sons, Nora and her children, Nora and her father, and Dr. Rank.
7. Discuss the ideas about individual growth, marriage, and social convention in the play. How are these ideas developed and related? Which character most closely embodies Ibsen's ideas?
8. Write an essay about any or all of the following questions:
   a. Is *A Dollhouse* a comedy, a tragedy, or something in between?
   b. How do the play's characters change for the better (or worse)?
   c. How negative, or affirmative, is the conclusion? Why?

Edited Selections from Criticism of Ibsen's *A Dollhouse* and Other Plays

The following selected criticism is intended to supply details and ideas for research essays on Ibsen's *A Dollhouse*. For a more detailed bibliography, consult the "Bibliographic Studies" section (pp. 1487–88), which may be augmented with your college library catalogue and the most recent volumes of the *MLA International Bibliography* available in your library's reference section together with online references. The bracketed page numbers in these selections refer to the original pagination of the sources included here. Footnotes, original passages in Norwegian, and unnecessary references have been deleted in these selections.

1. Freedom, Truth, and Society—Rhetoric and Reality[2]

During the night of 9 January 1871, a young Dane lay awake in his hospital bed in Rome writing. He was committing to paper a poem to which he had given the title "To Henrik Ibsen." He had recently received a letter from Ibsen—a letter carrying a powerful appeal to him to put himself at the head of the "revolution of the human spirit" which the age cried out for. In the poem which formed his enthusiastic response, the young Dane—the critic Georg Brandes (1842–1927)—described how all those mendacious and authoritarian forces of the contemporary age would be brought low when "the intellectuals" made their revolt. And he raised the banner of freedom and progress with the words: "Truth and Freedom are one and the same." [68]

Time after time in the years that followed, Ibsen was himself to raise this same revolutionary banner—with truth and freedom as the central watchwords. In later years these concepts could sound both abstract and ambiguous; nevertheless, within their historical context, they served as a battle cry in the struggle against the prevailing situation. "Truth" alone—that truth of the new age such as a Brandes and an Ibsen saw it—could achieve liberation. Without truth there could be no change, no genuine "freedom." This was the ideological basis for that quartet of realistic social plays which Ibsen published in the years between 1877 and 1882: *Pillars of Society, A Doll's House, Ghosts* and *An Enemy of the People.* In both the first and the last of these plays the double-barrelled phrase "truth and freedom" is used as a rallying cry and as a definition of what in the final instance the problematic reality of the day—"society"—lacked. This was the battle-ground on which Ibsen and Brandes found each other and where they could make common cause. However unlike they may have been, one thing they were agreed on: that *they* were conducting the case for progress and the future. They did not stand alone, but they must be counted as the indisputable leaders in the campaign for a modern, radical and realistic literature in the cultural life of Scandinavia of this age. It was these two who most powerfully challenged the values of the existing middle-class society and who formulated the basic rights and liberties of the individual. [69]

In November of the same year in which he wrote his poem to Ibsen, Brandes began a series of public lectures in Copenhagen on the literature of nineteenth-century Europe. These lectures provoked great attention and controversy, precisely because in them Brandes called upon writers to revolt. He did it in the light of an ideology of liberation which he himself linked directly to the ideas of freedom which underlay the French Revolution of 1789.

His main concern, Brandes declared, was not *political* opposition, for political liberty had very largely been assured. What was at stake was "liberty of the spirit," "liberty of thought and of the human condition." The entire range of "social

---

From Bjorn Hemmer, "Ibsen and the Realistic Problem Drama," in James McFarlane, ed., *The Cambridge Companion to Ibsen* (Cambridge: Cambridge UP, 1994).

values" would have to be changed radically by the younger generation before a new and vigorous literature could begin any new growth. But in Brandes's view it was surely the writers themselves who ought to take the lead in this work on behalf of progress.

What Brandes directs his criticism against is a conservative, stagnant society which "under the mask of liberty has all the features of tyranny." His target is Victorian society with its facade of false morality and its manipulation of public opinion. It is this same kind of society that Ibsen turns the searchlight on in his first realistic dramas. The people who live in such a society know the weight of "public opinion" and of all those agencies which keep watch over society's "law and order": the norms, the conventions and the traditions which in essence belong to the past but which continue into the present and there thwart individual liberty in a variety of ways. Not all see this as a problem. Consul Bernick, the bank manager Torvald Helmer and Pastor Manders have all accepted the premises for this kind of bourgeois living and have adapted to society's demands—without any awareness of the cost in human terms. In their own estimation, their task is to confirm the existing social structure—"pillars of society."

[70]   The point that Ibsen and Brandes were making was that this kind of society could not satisfy the natural need of the individual for freedom. It all had to do with power, with status and with the role of the sexes. The repressive attitude of bourgeois society towards everything that threatened its own position of power demonstrated only too clearly how far it had moved from the standpoint of the revolutionary citizens of 1789. The question of political and spiritual liberty had been thrust into the background by what had constantly been the motivating force in the life of the individual: economic freedom. Capital gave a position of power in society; and once those positions had been won, the bourgeois individual had acquired something which had to be defended. In this way, the bourgeois individual became a defender of the status quo and a traitor to his own officially expressed values. Official rhetoric was one thing; the realities on the other hand were something else.

It is this which forms the background to Ibsen's and Brandes's criticism of contemporary society. They found in their age a clear dichotomy between ideology and practice, a contradiction between the official and the private life of the bourgeois individual. Behind the splendour of the Victorian family facade there was to be found a much murkier reality. It was precisely these contradictions, this problematical element, in the bourgeois world that Ibsen made his special field as a realistic commentator on contemporary life. Both Ibsen and Brandes wanted to make the individual the sustaining element in society and thereby dethrone the bourgeois family as the central institution of society. From the perspective of the bourgeois individual the family is a micro-society which mirrors the nature of the macro-society and which is to bear witness to its health. In *Pillars of Society* the scoundrelly Consul Bernick is praised by the young teacher Rørlund for his "exemplary family life"; and the consul's fellow-conspirator, the businessman Rummel, delivers himself of the following pronouncement: "A man's home ought to be like a showcase." But he himself recommends an *arranged* family tableau behind the glass walls.

In the spirit of liberalism, Ibsen lets the individual's status in the family stand as an illustration of his position in the wider society. The power structure within the walls of the domestic home reflects the hierarchical power structures which prevail in the wider world. But those who participate in public life also encounter other repressive forces. Consul Bernick eventually admits that he feels like an isolated tool of an uncomprehending and crippled society, controlled in all his actions.

The main social perspective in Ibsen's first realistic plays coincides with the [71] perspective of Brandes's lecture series on "Main Currents in Nineteenth Century Literature." Here Brandes had presented a well-formulated programme for a new "modern" literature. His challenge to his fellow authors was primarily that they should enter into their own times and make contemporary concrete reality the subject of their writing: "What shows a literature in our own day to be a living thing is the fact of its subjecting problems to debate . . . For a literature to submit nothing to debate is tantamount to its being in the process of losing all significance."

What sort of "problems" he had in mind is illustrated by the examples he immediately adduces: marriage, religion, property rights, the relationships between the sexes, and social conditions. The objectives of his programme seem to have been both social and aesthetic. Brandes's idea was not that literature should become an instrument of abstract debate about prevailing social problems; his intention was to point out that if literature was to have any useful function at all, it had to come to grips with those conditions which invade and determine the concrete existence of the individual. Literature—as he put it—was to deal with "our life," not with "our dreams."

If Ibsen's dramas in the period 1877 to 1882 have come to be designated as realistic *problem* plays, this has to be seen against the background of Brandes's formula-like statement. Some Ibsen scholars prefer the rubric "critical realism"; others again have chosen to apply the term "modern contemporary drama" to the whole series of works after 1877. Each of these different designations nevertheless has a bearing on one or other of the central elements in the kind of literary realism which Ibsen practised: on social problems, on critical perspective and contemporaneity. Indeed this last is often accepted as one of the defining characteristics of realism: "*Il faut être de temps.*"

Within the framework of these dramas, Ibsen concentrates on some phase in [72] the contemporary situation where a latent crisis suddenly becomes visible. In this way he was able to embody contemporary social problems through the medium of an individual's destiny. This is another of realism's main tenets in the matter of individual characterization: the particular is to throw light on the general, and from one's response to a particular individual one should be able to glimpse the socially representative type. This, according to René Wellek, is an almost universal demand in theories of realism. It marks not only a polemical break with romantic characterization, but is also linked to realism's demand for objective reality and to its implicit didactic tendency. "Truth" and "sincerity" are concepts central to Linda Nochlin's account of the realists' own definition of where they stand. It may sound paradoxical to say that the realists combined on the one hand a wish for the objective presentation of reality with a didactic purpose on the other; but the paradox is illusory. A work of realism aspires to convey a moral message of general validity, and this is why the realist has need of the socially representative type. In Ibsen this sometimes leads to a difficult balancing act between over-explicitness and caricatured characterization on the one hand, and on the other an objective evocation of plausible human types, where the author's presence is less evident. Viewed from a later standpoint in time, there are some things—particularly his treatment of selected male characters—that might prompt one to set a question mark against his "realism."

* * *

[73]   In his poetic practice, Ibsen demonstrates time after time that he conceives of truth as something individual and subjective. It is always the minority which is right. This is why he lets Nora go out into the world alone both to find out who she really is and to be able to re-assess values and concepts. Ibsen has her sweep aside any doubts about what the problem is: "I must try to discover who is right, society or me." She admits her husband is right when he says she no longer understands the society they live in. As a dramatist, Ibsen must make it evident to his audience that Nora, as the drama moves towards its close, is truer and freer than before— and that her path is one of general validity. Helmer has mobilized the rhetoric of established society to keep Nora within the framework of the community and of the family. The reaction of the public was—and possibly still is—dependent on whether Nora's (and Ibsen's) use of an alternative rhetoric carries greater weight and conviction.

Nora's situation illustrates the pattern central to Ibsen's realistic problem dramas: the individual in opposition to a hostile society. The structure of the conflict is simple—and nobody can be in any doubt as to where the author's sympathies lie. Collective aberration about which ideals or values are true and which are false means that Ibsen sets in motion a process whereby concepts which are central to the bourgeois world are subject to re-definition. It is a striking feature of, for example, *Ghosts* that the reactionary Manders and the radical Helene Alving both make use of the concept of "the ideal," despite their having totally contradictory views of the meaning of "truth" and of individual "freedom" in life. Ibsen clearly saw that the concepts of established bourgeois society needed a new content—something which he himself drew attention to in a letter to Brandes. In this same letter he writes of the need for "a revolution of the human spirit," and claimed that the 1789 rallying-cry of "Liberty, equality, fraternity" needed filling with new meaning.

[74]   Perhaps the battle-lines between the conservative bourgeoisie and the radical intelligentsia in Scandinavia in this age of Ibsen and Brandes were not as clearly drawn as all this might suggest. The literary history of Northern Europe has very largely been based on the premises of radicalism. The perspective may not entirely falsify history, but it does somewhat oversimplify it. There are distinctly conservative elements to be found in Ibsen's works of social criticism; and he gave clear acknowledgement of the part he played within the society he was attacking: "One never stands totally without some share of responsibility or guilt in the society

to which one belongs." This is why he defines, in one and the same breath, the writing of poetry as the passing of judgement upon one's own self. Some of the phenomena he criticized were things he well knew from his own inner life. Honest introspection—what he was inclined to call "self-anatomy"—had made it clear to him that he too bore the stamp of the Victorian society of the day. Life and learning were not always the same, as he admitted in a speech to Norwegian students in Christiania in 1874. The irony directed at those who histrionically held high the banner of the ideal at no great cost to themselves lost none of its point when applied to himself and to fellow writers.

Nevertheless he stood distanced, an outsider, from the society he was criticizing. Like Brandes, he was marginalized in respect of the collective life of his own people—not least by the concrete fact of his own twenty-seven years in exile. It was a stance which gave Ibsen both a personal freedom as an artist and also the clarifying perspective of distance—something he always claimed as a necessity for himself as a writer.

It is something of a paradox that, in this socially critical phase of his authorship, he was able to create a large and broadly based market among the wider European public for his art. What he had to offer to this bourgeois public was a successive chronicling of their own vices and lies. Granted the setting of his works was Norwegian, but the perspective on Victorian morality was international enough when he allowed it to reveal its defects.

It is not to be wondered at that Ibsen's dramas provoked scandal and outrage. [75] Yet at the same time he won a large following, including many of those whom he had attacked. Even a proportion of "the pillars of society" found it worthwhile to listen to what this author had to say. This could well imply that bourgeois society had not entirely lost its sense of its past and of its own lost ideals. Even bourgeois society was ready to acknowledge that contemporary reality might have its problems—with socially destabilizing phenomena like industrialization, positivism, liberalism, secularization, political polarization and the like. Society in the 1870s was becoming increasingly fluid. Only the most conservative forces wished to defend its "law and order" by neutralizing such "enemies of the people" as Ibsen and Brandes. But strong resistance could be found—and this gave Ibsen an adversary and the stuff of conflict for his dramas. The opposition consisted of all those who wished to withdraw within the circle of their own little community, their small township or their family—there to defend their world against the threat from the new or larger world "out there." Ibsen himself in these years was a resident of this wider and freer European cultural scene. And he wrote about Norwegian provincial life. When for his first realistic problem drama he chose as its setting "a small, Norwegian coastal town," this was clearly connected to its being a milieu he was greatly familiar with from his childhood and early years. As an observant outsider he had lived in a small community of this kind—in Grimstad in the 1840s—and it was here he had first begun his career as a writer. Patterns and tensions—social, economic and psychological—present themselves much more clearly in a small and easily surveyable community of this kind than in a larger and more pluralist society. For a dramatist, a society of this sort could nicely function as a social laboratory.

2. Ibsen's Feminist Characters[3]

[34]   Anyone who claims that Ibsen thought of Nora as a silly, hysterical, or selfish woman is either ignoring or misrepresenting the plain truth, present from the earliest to the most recent biographies, that Ibsen admired, even adored, Nora Helmer. Among all his characters, she was the one he liked best and found most real. While working on *A Doll House*, he announced to Suzannah Ibsen, his wife, "I've just seen Nora. She came right over to me and put her hand on my shoulder." The quick-witted Suzannah replied at once, "What was she wearing?" In a perfectly serious tone, Ibsen answered, "A simple blue woolen dress."

[35]   After *A Doll House* had made him famous, Ibsen was fond of explaining that his heroine's "real" name was "Eleanora" but that she had been called "Nora" from childhood. Bergliot Bjornson Ibsen, the playwright's daughter-in-law, tells the story of how she and her husband, Sigurd, on one of the last occasions on which they saw Ibsen out of bed in the year he died, asked permission to name their newborn daughter "Eleanora." Ibsen was greatly moved. "God bless you, Bergliot," he said to her. He had, in fact, christened his own Nora with a precious gift, for both "Nora" and "Eleanora" were names given to the sister of Ole Schulerud, one of the few close friends of Ibsen's life, who in the early years of grinding poverty believed in Ibsen's genius and tirelessly hawked his first play to bookseller after bookseller, finally spending his small inheritance to pay for its publication.

    Ibsen was inspired to write *A Doll House* by the terrible events in the life of his protégé Laura Petersen Kieler, a Norwegian journalist of whom he was extremely fond. Married to a man with a phobia about debt, she had secretly borrowed money to finance an Italian journey necessary for her husband's recovery from tuberculosis. She worked frantically to reimburse the loan, exhausting herself in turning out hackwork, and when her earnings proved insufficient, in desperation she forged a check. On discovering the crime, her husband demanded a legal separation on the grounds that she was an unfit mother and had her placed in an asylum, where she was put in the insane ward. Throughout the affair, Ibsen, her confidant and adviser, was greatly disturbed; he brooded on the wife, "forced to spill her heart's blood," as he wrote in a letter to her, and on the oblivious husband, allowing his wife to slave away on unworthy jobs, concerned neither about her physical welfare nor her work. Having done all for love, Laura Kieler was treated monstrously for her efforts by a husband obsessed with his standing in the eyes of the world. In Ibsen's working notes for *A Doll House* we find:

> She has committed forgery, and is proud of it; for she has done it out of love for her husband, to save his life. But this husband of hers takes his standpoint, conventionally honorable, on the side of the law, and sees the situation with male eyes.

The conflict between love and law, between heart and head, between feminine and masculine, is the moral center of *A Doll House*. But Ibsen would sharpen life's blurred edges to meet art's demand for plausibility. The heroine would be a housewife, not a writer, and the hackwork not bad novels but copying; her antagonist, the husband, would not be a cruel brute but a kind guardian: rather than put her into

From Joan Templeton, "The *Doll House* Backlash: Criticism, Feminism, and Ibsen." *PMLA* 104 (1989): 28–40.

an asylum, he would merely denounce her as an unfit wife and mother, permitting her to receive bed and board, and then, once his reputation was safe, would offer to forgive her and take her back on the spot. The Helmers, in other words, would be "normal." And this normality would transform a sensational *fait divers* into a devastating picture of the ordinary relations between wife and husband and allow Ibsen to treat what he called, in a letter to Edmund Gosse, "the problems of married life." Moreover, he would reverse the ending: the original Nora, the career journalist, had begged to be taken back; his housewife would sadly, emphatically refuse to stay.

A year after *A Doll House* appeared, when Ibsen was living in Rome, a Scandinavian woman arrived there, who had left her husband and small daughter to run away with her lover. The Norwegian exile community considered her behavior unnatural and asked Ibsen what he thought. "It is not unnatural, only it is unusual" was Ibsen's opinion. The woman made it a point to speak with Ibsen, but to her surprise he treated her offhandedly. "Well, I did the same thing your Nora did," she said, offended. Ibsen replied quietly, "My Nora went alone."

A favorite piece of evidence in the argument that Ibsen was not interested in women's rights is his aversion to John Stuart Mill. It is popular to quote Ibsen's remark to Georg Brandes about Mill's declaration that he owed the best things in his writing to his wife, Harriet Taylor: "'Fancy!' [Ibsen] said smiling, 'if you had to read Hegel or Krause with the thought that you did not know for certain whether it was Mr. or Mrs. Hegel, Mr. or Mrs. Krause you had before you!'" But in fact, Brandes, one of Ibsen's closest associates and probably the critic who understood him best, reports this mot in a discussion of Ibsen's wholehearted support of the women's movement. He notes that Mill's assertion "seemed especially ridiculous to Ibsen, with his marked individualism," and explains that although Ibsen had at first little sympathy for feminism—perhaps, Brandes guesses, because of "irritation at some of the ridiculous forms the movement assumed"—this initial response gave way "to a sympathy all the more enthusiastic" when he saw that it was "one of the great rallying points in the battle of progress." [36]

A well-known, perhaps embarrassing fact about Ibsen, never brought up in discussions disclaiming his interest in women's rights, is that when he made the banquet speech denying that he had consciously worked for the movement, he was primarily interested in young women and annoyed by the elderly feminists who surrounded him. During the seventieth-birthday celebrations, Ibsen constantly exhibited his marked and, as Michael Meyer has it, "rather pathetic longing for young girls." He had already had several romantic friendships, including one that had caused a family scandal and threatened to wreck his marriage. In the light of this fully documented biographical information about the aging playwright, is his intention in *A Doll House* more likely to be revealed by what he said in irritation at a banquet or by what he wrote twenty years earlier in sketching out his play?

> A woman cannot be herself in the society of today, which is exclusively a masculine society, with laws written by men, and with accusers and judges who judge feminine conduct from the masculine standpoint.

A Doll House is not about Everybody's struggle to find him- or herself but, according to its author, about Everywoman's struggle against Everyman.

A Doll House is a natural development of the play Ibsen had just written, the unabashedly feminist *Pillars of Society*; both plays reflect Ibsen's extremely privileged feminist education, which he shared with few other nineteenth-century male authors and which he owed to a trio of extraordinary women: Suzannah Thoresen Ibsen, his wife; Magdalen Thoresen, his colleague at the Norwegian National Theatre in Bergen, who was Suzannah's stepmother and former governess; and Camilla Wergeland Collett, Ibsen's literary colleague, valued friend, and the founder of Norwegian feminism.

Magdalen Thoresen wrote novels and plays and translated the French plays Ibsen put on as a young stage manager at the Bergen theater. She was probably the first "New Woman" he had ever met. She pitied the insolvent young writer, took him under her wing, and brought him home. She had passed her strong feminist principles on to her charge, the outspoken and irrepressible Suzannah, who adored her strong-minded stepmother and whose favorite author was George Sand. The second time Ibsen met Suzannah he asked her to marry him. Hjordis, the fierce shield-maiden of *The Vikings at Helgeland*, the play of their engagement, and Svanhild, the strong-willed heroine of *Love's Comedy*, the play that followed, owe much to Suzannah Thoresen Ibsen. Later, Nora's way of speaking would remind people of Suzannah's.

The third and perhaps most important feminist in Ibsen's life was his friend Camilla Collett, one of the most active feminists in nineteenth-century Europe and founder of the modern Norwegian novel. Fifteen years before Mill's *Subjection of Women*, Collett wrote *Amtmandens Døtre (The Governor's Daughters)*. Faced with the choice of a masculine nom de plume or no name at all on the title page, Collett brought out her novel anonymously in two parts in 1854 and 1855, but she nonetheless became widely known as the author. Its main argument, based on the general feminist claim that women's feelings matter, is that women should have the right to educate themselves and to marry whom they please. In the world of the governor's daughters, it is masculine success that matters. Brought up to be ornaments and mothers, women marry suitable men and devote their lives to their husbands' careers and to their children. The novel, a cause célèbre, made Collett famous overnight.

Collett regularly visited the Ibsens in their years of exile in Germany, and she and Suzannah took every occasion to urge Ibsen to take up the feminist cause. They had long, lively discussions in the years preceding *A Doll House*, when feminism had become a strong movement and the topic of the day in Scandinavia. Collett was in Munich in 1877, when Ibsen was hard at work on *Pillars of Society*, and Ibsen's biographer Koht speculates that Ibsen may have deliberately prodded her to talk about the women's movement in order to get material for his dialogue. In any case, the play undoubtedly owes much to the conversations in the Ibsen household, as well as to the Norwegian suffragette Aasta Hansteen, the most notorious woman in the country. Deliberately provocative, Hansteen took to the platform wearing men's boots and carrying a whip to protect herself against the oppressor. A popular news item during the Ibsens' visit to Norway in 1874, Hansteen became the model for Lona Hessel, the shocking *raisonneuse* of *Pillars of Society*.

[37] The play opens with a striking image of woman's place in the world: eight ladies participating in what has been, since antiquity, the most quintessentially female activity in literature—they are "busy sewing"—as they listen to the town

schoolmaster read aloud from *Woman as the Servant of Society*. Lona Hessel bursts in, and when the ladies ask her how she can aid their "Society for the Morally Disabled," she suggests, "I can air it out." Returning from America, where she is rumored to have sung in saloons (even for money!), lectured, and written a book, Lona is the New Woman with a vengeance who teaches the others the truth. Lona had loved Bernick, but she packed her bags when he rejected her to marry for money. Bernick turns out not to have been much of a loss, however; he has reduced his wife, Betty, to an obedient cipher and made a personal servant of his sister, Martha, a paradigm of the nineteenth-century spinster who devotes her life to a male relative. Martha's story may have had its source in *The Governor's Daughters*. Like Collett's Margarethe, Martha had once loved a young man but, too modest to declare her feelings, suffered in silence. She now lives for her brother, who is insufferable when he speaks of her; she is a "nonentity," he explains, "who'll take on whatever comes along." It is in explaining Martha's exemplary function in life that Bernick speaks the line, "People shouldn't always be thinking of themselves first, especially women." Dina Dorf, Bernick's ward, disregards this happy maxim, and though she agrees to marry, she tells her husband-to-be, "But first I want to work, become something the way you have. I don't want to be a thing that's just taken along." Dina knows beforehand what Nora learns after eight years of marriage: "I have to try to educate myself. . . . I've got to do it alone."

Pillars of Society, little known and played outside Scandinavia and Germany, is one of the most radically feminist works of nineteenth-century literature. Ibsen took the old maid, the butt of society's ridicule, a figure of pity and contempt, and made her a heroine. Rejected as unfit to be a wife, Lona Hessel refuses to sacrifice herself to a surrogate family and escapes to the New World, where she leads an independent, authentic life. As *raisonneuse*, she summarizes his point of view for Bernick and the rest: "This society of yours is a bachelors' club. You don't see women."

It is simply not true, then, that Ibsen was not interested in feminism. It is also not true that "there is no indication that Ibsen was thinking of writing a feminist play when he first began to work seriously on *A Doll House* in the summer of 1879." In the spring of that year, while Ibsen was planning his play, a scandalous incident, easily available in the biographies, took place that proves not only Ibsen's interest in women's rights but his passionate support for the movement. Ibsen had made two proposals to the Scandinavian Club in Rome, where he was living: that the post of librarian be opened to women candidates and that women be allowed to vote in club meetings. In the debate on the proposal, he made a long, occasionally eloquent speech, part of which follows:

> Is there anyone in this gathering who dares assert that our ladies are inferior to us in culture, or intelligence, or knowledge, or artistic talent? I don't think many men would dare suggest that. Then what is it men fear? I hear there is a tradition here that women are cunning intriguers, and that therefore we don't want them. Well, I have encountered a good deal of male intrigue in my time.

Ibsen's first proposal was accepted, the second not, failing by one vote. He left the club in a cold rage. A few days later, he astonished his compatriots by appearing at a gala evening. People thought he was penitent. But he was planning a surprise:

facing the ballroom and its dancing couples, he interrupted the music to make a terrible scene, haranguing the celebrants with a furious tirade. He had tried to bring them progress, he shouted, but their cowardly resistance had refused it. The women were especially contemptible, for it was for them he had tried to fight. A Danish countess fainted and had to be removed, but Ibsen continued, growing more and more violent. Gunnar Heiberg, who was present, later gave this account of the event:

> As his voice thundered it was as though he were clarifying his own thoughts, as his tongue chastised it was as though his spirit were scouring the darkness in search of his present spiritual goal—his poem [*A Doll House*]—as though he were personally bring-ing out his theories, incarnating his characters. And when he was done, he went out into the hall, took his overcoat and walked home.

[38]

In 1884, five years after *A Doll House* had made Ibsen a recognized champion of the feminist cause, he joined with H. E. Berner, president of the Norwegian Women's Rights League, and with his fellow Norwegian writers Bjornson, Lie, and Kielland, in signing a petition to the Storting, the Norwegian par-liament, urging the passage of a bill establishing separate property rights for married women. When he returned the petition to Bjornson, Ibsen wryly commented that the Storting should not be interested in men's opinions: "To consult men in such a matter is like asking wolves if they desire better protec-tion for the sheep." He also spoke of his fears that the current campaign for universal suffrage would come to nothing. The solution, which he despaired of seeing, would be the formation of a "strong, resolute progressive party" that would include in its goals "the statutory improvement of the position of woman."

It is foolish to apply the formalist notion that art is never sullied by argu-ment to Ibsen's middle-period plays, written at a time when he was an outspoken and direct fighter in what he called the "mortal combat between two epochs." Ibsen was fiercely his own man, refusing all his life to be claimed by organiza-tions or campaigns of many sorts, including the Women's Rights League and the movement to remove the mark of Sweden from the Norwegian flag. And he had a deeply conservative streak where manners were concerned (except when he lost his temper), for he was acutely suspicious of show. Temperamentally, Ibsen was a loner. But he was also, as Georg Brandes declared, "a born polemist." While it is true that Ibsen never reduced life to "ideas," it is equally true that he was pas-sionately interested in the events and ideas of his day. He was as deeply anchored in his time as any writer has been before or since. Writing to his German translator a year after the publication of *A Doll House*, Ibsen offered one of the truest self-appraisals a writer has ever made:

> Everything that I have written is intimately connected with what I have lived through, even if I have not lived it myself. Every new work has served me as emancipation and catharsis; for none of us can escape the responsibility and the guilt of the society to which we belong.

3. A Marxist Approach to *A Doll House*[4]

Theatrical production is a process that illuminates the dramatic text, and criticism [76] is the tool that enables theater artists to make the most effective choices. This is the central premise of Drama 102 (Play Analysis), in which we discuss eight or so plays from a variety of critical viewpoints. Although some of the plays lend themselves more readily to a particular kind of analysis (such as a Jungian reading of *The Emperor Jones*), we point out that this affinity should not exclude additional insights that can be gained from a structuralist or feminist reading. We stress that criticism is a preamble to production and that plays are complex and multifaceted. Moreover, we discourage the theatrical sleight of hand that frequently reduces plays to a single metaphor, and we encourage our students to view drama through the lenses of differing approaches.

In teaching *A Doll House* we first examine the text from a traditional point of view stressing historical and biographical considerations. We review Ibsen's commitment to women's rights and his interest in the career of Laura Kieler, who some critics believe was the model for Nora. Indeed, F. L. Lucas has stated that "one cannot fully understand Nora without knowing something of the strange, yet true story of Laura Kieler." By comparing the two women it is possible to watch Ibsen's heroine emerge from the despair and pain that characterized much of Kieler's life.

Still, the historical and biographical approach is limiting, and our next step is to explore the play through another lens. (The metaphor of the "lens" we have found to be particularly effective since it implies that there are no right or wrong interpretations but rather discoveries that can be made by studying a play from more than one vantage point.) The critical method that has stimulated many of our recent students—and that concerns us here—is a Marxist reading of the play. Marxist criticism is a complex topic, and, as the recent work of Fredric Jameson, Henri Arvon, and Raymond Williams exemplifies, critical methodologies vary widely. Moreover, many American students come to Marxist aesthetics with reluctance, conditioned partly by a distrust of all things Russian. Thus we try to emphasize specific issues on which critics agree, and we assign short readings from Terry Eagleton's *Marxism and Literary Criticism* as a point of departure.

It is important, of course, to review Marx's early writings with their humanistic focus and analysis of class structure. Notions of the dialectic and of human alienation are productive ways of introducing students to Marx since alienation seems to be a concept with which they can identify. This approach has the added value of breaking down some initial prejudices toward the subject matter. By stressing the human side of Marx's work, we can reduce student resistance and encourage a more objective view of the social analysis that follows. [77]

We then talk about the text of the play as an objectification of the author's idea, a process that is a creative act but that in dialectical terms is imperfect because it can never completely express Ibsen's vision or totally repress unconscious ideas that shape the text. Drawing on both Terry Eagleton and Louis Althusser (*Lenin and*

From Barry Witham and John Lutterbie, "A Marxist Approach to *A Doll House*," in Yvonne Shafer, ed., *Approaches to Teaching Ibsen's* A Doll House (New York: MLA, 1985).

Philosophy), we define ideology as a false consciousness, a system of beliefs and ideas that functions to disguise the inequities of a class-based society. Using this definition to examine the play, we stress the concept that ideology is shaped by both what is in the text (Torvald's domination of Nora) and by what is "absent" (Nora's relationship with her mother). One of the primary goals of any Marxist analysis is the investigation of ideological content, and the existence of this content allows Marxist critics to argue that all works of art are political. This is a highly controversial point with many students, and the discussions often become heated as we examine its implications.

We then focus on the economic realities of Ibsen's world. *A Doll House* is especially suited to this type of examination because the bank—an obvious and blatant symbol for money—stands at the center of the play. Torvald has just been appointed manager. Mrs. Linde wants to work there, as does Krogstad. And Nora's jubilation at the beginning of the play is directly related to the financial security ensured by Torvald's new job. Moreover, an economic analysis quickly reveals how the consciousness of the characters is shaped and determined by their class and status. Even though Downs has argued that "except for three virtual supernumeraries, all the persons of the play belong to the educated middle class," it is clear that class differences do exist. Torvald stands for the moneyed elite—in this case the bank owners—while Mrs. Linde and Krogstad function as workers struggling to maintain a subsistence income.

[78] A principal tenet of Marxist criticism is that human consciousness is a product of social conditions and that human relationships are often subverted by and through economic considerations. Mrs. Linde has sacrificed a genuine love to provide for her brothers, and Krogstad has committed a crime to support his children. Anne-Marie, the maid, has also been the victim of her economic background. Because she's "a girl who's poor and gotten in trouble," her relationship with her child has been interrupted and virtually destroyed. In each instance the need for money is linked with the ability to exist. But while the characters accept the social realities of their misfortunes, they do not appear to question how their human attitudes have been thoroughly shaped by socioeconomic considerations.

Once students begin to perceive how consciousness is affected by economics, a Marxist reading of Ibsen's play can illuminate a number of areas. Krogstad, for example, becomes less of a traditional villain when we realize that he is fighting for his job at the bank "as if it were life itself." And his realization of the senselessness of their lives is poignantly revealed when he reflects on Mrs. Linde's past, "all this simply for money." Even Dr. Rank speaks about his failing health and imminent death in entirely financial terms. "These past few days I've been auditing my internal accounts. Bankrupt! Within a month I'll probably be laid out and rotting in the churchyard."

All these characters, however, serve as foils for the central struggle between Nora and Torvald and highlight the pilgrimage that Nora makes in the play. At the outset two things are clear: (1) Nora is enslaved by Torvald in economic terms, and (2) she equates personal freedom with the acquisition of wealth. The play begins joyfully not only because it is the holiday season but also because Torvald's promotion to bank manager will ensure "a safe, secure job with a comfortable salary." Nora is happy because she sees the future in wholly economic terms. "Won't it be lovely to have stacks of money and not a care in the world?"

What she learns, however, is that financial enslavement is symptomatic of other forms of enslavement—master–slave, male–female, sexual objectification, all of which characterize her relationship with Torvald—and that money is no guarantee of happiness. At the end of the play she renounces not only her marital vows but also her financial dependence because she has discovered that personal and human freedom are not measured in economic terms.

This discovery also prompts her to reexamine the society of which she is a part and leads us into a consideration of the ideology in the play. In what sense has Nora committed a criminal offense in forging her father's name? Is it indeed just that she should be punished for an altruistic act, one that cost her dearly both in terms of self-denial and the destruction of her family? Ibsen's defense of Nora is clear, of course, and his implicit indictment of a society that encourages this kind of injustice stimulates a discussion of the assumptions that created the law.

One of the striking things about *A Doll House* is how Anne-Marie accepts her alienation from her child as if it were natural, given the circumstances of class and money. It does not occur to her that laws were framed by other people and thus are capable of imperfection and susceptible to change. Nora broke a law that not only tries to stop thievery (the appropriation of capital) by outlawing forgery but also discriminates against anyone deemed a bad risk. Question leads to question as the class investigates why women were bad risks and why they had difficulty finding employment. It becomes obvious that the function of women in this society was not "natural" but artificial, a role created by their relationship to the family and by their subservience to men. In the marketplace they were a labor force expecting subsistence wages and providing an income to supplement that earned by their husbands or fathers. . . . [79]

Viewing the play through the lens of Marxist aesthetics does make one thing clear. Nora's departure had ramifications for her society that went beyond the marriage bed. By studying the play within the context of its socioeconomic structure, we can see how the ideology in the text affects the characters and how they perpetuate the ideology. The conclusion of *A Doll House* was a challenge to the economic superstructures that had controlled and excluded the Noras of the world by manipulating their economic status and, by extension, their conscious estimation of themselves and their place in society.

Chapter 24A
Writing a Research Essay on Drama

AFTER STUDYING THIS MATERIAL, YOU SHOULD BE ABLE TO DO THE FOLLOWING:

- Understand the issues and topics you need to discover in doing your own research
- Develop a plan for organizing an effective research essay
- Construct persuasive analyses of plays, using secondary sources and proper documentation form

At the end of the fiction section of this book, Chapter 10A (p. 500) contains a chapter on the use of research as the basis of an essay of term-paper length on fiction. A shorter essay embodying research is included in Chapter 19A (p. 951). Because the objects and goals of research are general, most of the materials in these research chapters are also essential for research projects in drama. It is therefore necessary to consult these earlier chapters for many relevant ways to engage in detailed research about drama as well as about both fiction and poetry.

Any of the questions and essay assignments on drama described in Chapters 20 to 24 can serve as the basic topic as a guide for you to find helpful research materials. Because of the general nature of research, research essays about drama are not markedly different from the research introduced in writing about fiction and poetry. As a help in such assignments with all the genres, there are extra materials for research in Chapter 9 on the fiction of Poe; in Chapter 18, on the poetry of Dickinson, Frost, Hughes, and Plath; and in Chapter 24, on the drama of Ibsen.

Topics to Discover in Research

Your goal in doing research on drama should always be to discover materials that have a meaningful bearing on the play or plays about which you are writing. As with both fiction and poetry, some things to look for might be these:

- *The period of time when the play was written, together with significant events.* The illustrative research essay on the Ghost in Shakespeare's *Hamlet* that follows below introduces sixteenth-century ideas about the nature of ghosts and the supernatural. If you look at the introduction and notes to Hughes's *Mulatto* (pp. 1352–73), you will see that the play is concerned with details of racism in the American South in the 1930s, and that particular events at that time may have a bearing on our understanding of the play.

- *Social, natural, and/or political circumstances at the time of the poem or poems.* What was the dominant political situation at the time? Who were the sorts of persons in political power? What attitudes were prevalent at the time with regard to the circumstances of nature? The characters in O'Neill's *Before Breakfast* are representative of people living close to the edge in New York's Greenwich Village in the second decade of the twentieth century, with all that this way of life implied.

- *Biographical details about a dramatist.* At what time in his or her life did the dramatist write the play? What kind of work was he or she doing at the time, and which of his or her particular concerns might be relevant to our understanding of the play? Did the dramatist write anything about the play in personal correspondence, if any exists? What was this? Are there any results of interviews with the dramatist that might be introduced to explain the play? What were the dramatist's aims in creating the particular play, to the degree that it is possible to discover these aims?

- *Specific or general thoughts by the dramatist that are relevant to the poem/poems.* Sometimes there might be details about a dramatist's thoughts on the thinking and reading he or she was doing, or on works of art seen, or on religious or philosophical musings. Sometimes these concerns must be inferred. Langston Hughes was deeply concerned about the circumstances of African Americans in the United States, and his *Mulatto* is a deeply felt play dramatizing his concerns.

In planning your essay, you should aim at a normal type of essay for the play you have chosen. Often, you might select an individual character and the importance of that character to the play's action or structure. Or you may wish to describe the character's interests or language. Much of what you may do of course depends on the nature of the play and what you discover about it. The section "Writing About the Elements of Drama" in Chapter 20, beginning on page 1012, will give you ideas for how to select and develop your topic. Of greatest importance, of course, is your integration of research discoveries into the development of your essay. The following illustrative research essay indicates a term-paper-length treatment of the Ghost, a major character in Shakespeare's *Hamlet*. You will observe that the essay treats the character of the Ghost and also goes on to describe other aspects of the Ghost's significance in the play at large.

Illustrative Student Essay Written with the Aid of Research

Although underlined sentences are not recommended by MLA style, they are used in this illustrative essay as teaching tools to emphasize the central idea, thesis sentence, and topic sentences.

The Ghost in *Hamlet*°

Outline

Use 1 inch top margin, 1 inch bottom and side margin; double-space throughout.

I. Introduction

    A. The Importance of the Ghost in *Hamlet*

    B. The Ghost's Influence on the Play's Themes

II. The Ghost's Status as a Spirit

III. The Ghost's Character

IV. The Ghost's Importance in the Structure of the Play

V. The Ghost's Effect

VI. Conclusion

In MLA style, the header has the student's last name and page number.

Kruse 1

Toni Ann Kruse

Professor Rios

English 364

11 May 2014

Put identifying information in upper-left corner, double-space.

Center title one double space below identifying information.

I. Introduction

A. The Importance of the Ghost in *Hamlet*

[1]   Even though the Ghost of Hamlet's father is present in only a few scenes of *Hamlet,* he is a dominating presence.* He appears twice in the first scene, and this entire scene itself is about the meaning of these appearances. He enters again in the fourth scene of Act 1, when he beckons to Hamlet and leads him offstage—in this way providing an early illustration of Hamlet's courage

°This play appears on pages 1080–1177.
*Central idea.

Kruse 2

(Edgar 257). In the fifth scene of Act 1 he speaks for the first time, explaining how his brother Claudius murdered him, and exhorting his son, Hamlet, to kill Claudius in retribution. Because this cry for revenge directly or indirectly causes the rest of the play's action, it is clear, as Marjorie Garber puts it, that "the dead man turned Ghost is more powerful than he was when living" (304). After some words which the Ghost speaks from under the stage, he does not enter again until the fourth scene of Act 3, in the queen's private rooms, when he reveals himself to Hamlet—but not to Gertrude—to reproach the Prince for not yet having killed Claudius. The Ghost is not present at the play's end, but the actions he sets in motion are concluded there, and hence his effect is always dominant.

B. The Ghost's Influence on the Play's Themes

Not only is the Ghost dominant over actions, but he is also directly linked to many of the play's themes. William Kerrigan calls the Ghost a "nightmind" who introduces the mental darkness of evil that pervades the play (42). In addition, the Ghost intensifies the play's "interior suffering" (Paris 85). This suffering is brought out in Hamlet's anguished soliloquies and also in the pain of Ophelia, Laertes, and even Claudius himself. Another theme is shown by the Ghost's commands to Hamlet—those of responsibility, whether personal, political, or conjugal (McFarland 15). Hamlet of course does not rush right out to kill Claudius, despite the Ghost's urgings, and hence the Ghost is indirectly responsible for the theme of hesitation—this great "Sphinx of modern Literature"—which has become one of the weaknesses cited most frequently about Hamlet's character (Jones 22). The Ghost's scary presence also poses questions about the power of superstition, terror, and fear (Campbell 211). Beyond all this, deeply within the psychological realm, the Ghost has been cited as a "confirmation" of the influence of "psychic residues in governing and shaping human life" (McFarland 34), not to mention the significance of the Oedipus complex in the development of Hamlet's character.

Because the Ghost is so important, one hardly needs to justify studying him. His importance can be traced in his spirit nature, his influence on the

[2]

In MLA style, put only page number in parentheses when author is named in the sentence.

In MLA style, put author and page number in parentheses when author is not named in the sentence.

[3]

Kruse 3

play's structure, and his effect on Hamlet and therefore indirectly on all the major characters.†

II. The Ghost's Status as a Spirit

[4]

When citing plays in MLA style, cite the act, scene, and line number.

The Ghost is shown as an apparition of questionable and vague status. When Hamlet first sees the Ghost, he asks whether he sees "a spirit of health, or goblin damned" (1.4.40). Horatio adds that Hamlet is "desperate with imagination" (1.4.87), thus throwing doubt on the Ghost's reality even though the vision is seen by everyone onstage. When speaking with Hamlet, the Ghost is vague about his out-of-earth location, complaining that he is suffering hellish fires but intimating that he will be compelled to do so only until his earthly sins are purged away. Although this description, according to Anthony Holden, indicates that "the Ghost . . . occupies an authentically Catholic version of Purgatory" (28), and Dobson and Wells state that "the Ghost seems to belong to a Catholic theology rather than a Protestant one" (182), Shakespeare's treatment is ambiguous. The Ghost says that he is allowed to walk the earth for a certain time—presumably, in the first act, only at night. But then, in Act 3, scene 4, the Ghost appears in the Queen's private room. Does this visit take place at night or during the day? This inconsistency about where and when the Ghost spends his time may have been deliberate on Shakespeare's part, for showing a ghost straight out of purgatory might have seemed dangerously close to Catholic doctrine. It was apparently safest for writers in the dominant Anglican culture to show the ghost only of a person who was "freshly dead or on the point of death" (O'Meara 15), and also to make the details vague and ambiguous.

[5]

The status and existence of Shakespeare's Ghost therefore reflects uncertainties during the Elizabethan period. Lily Campbell offers a number of ways in which Elizabethans dealt with these uncertainties. First, James VI of Scotland, who at the time *Hamlet* was first performed was soon to be James I of England, wrote about departed spirits and emphasized that the devil himself could choose the shape of loved ones to deceive and corrupt living persons.

---

†Thesis sentence.

Kruse 4

It is this danger that Hamlet specifically describes. Second, as already
mentioned, some Elizabethan religious thinkers held it possible for souls
in purgatory to return to earth for a time and speak to the living. Third,
scientifically oriented thinkers interpreted ghostly appearances as a sign
of madness or deep melancholia (Campbell 121), or what O'Meara calls
"sorrowful imagination" (19). There were apparently a number of "tests"
that might have enabled people to determine the authenticity of ghosts. Most
of these required that the spirit should show goodness of character and give
comfort to the living (Campbell 123).

The Ghost of Hamlet's father both passes and fails these tests. He is not   [6]
totally bad (Campbell 126), but he urges Hamlet to commit murder, something
that no ghost trying to reach heaven would possibly do (McFarland 36).
Although the Ghost describes the pain of a soul in purgatory, he does so to
create fear, not to urge Hamlet to seek salvation. Thus he is more like the devil
than a spirit on the way to redemption (Prosser 133–34; Frye 22). Another
sign suggesting the Ghost's devilishness is that he withholds his appearance
from Gertrude when he shows himself to Hamlet in Act 3, scene 4 (Campbell
124). Hamlet creates his own test of the Ghost by getting the touring actors
to perform *The Murder of Gonzago*. Once he sees the King's disturbance at
the play, Hamlet concludes that the Ghost is real and not just a "figment of
his melancholy imagination" (Harrison 883). Perhaps the best answer to the
conflicting views of the Ghost is given by Lily Campbell, who suggests that the
ambiguity indicates the general uncertainty about ghosts among Shakespeare's
contemporaries (127). In other words, there was no unanimity about the
nature and motivation of ghosts, and Shakespeare's Ghost reflected common
Elizabethan understanding and attitudes.

III. The Ghost's Character

Uncertainty and theology aside, the Ghost is probably Shakespeare's   [7]
rendering of what he thought a ghost would be like. Shakespeare inherited a
tradition of noisy, bloodthirsty ghosts from his sources—what Harold Fisch
calls a "Senecan ghost" (91). There was also a tradition of "hungry ghosts,"

Kruse 5

who were spirits prowling about the earth "searching for the life they were deprived of" (Austin 93). In this tradition, Shakespeare's Ghost is bloodthirsty, although ironically not as bloodthirsty as Hamlet himself becomes during the play (Gottschalk 166). The Ghost is surrounded by awe and horror (DeLuca 147) and is frightening, both to the soldiers at the beginning of the play and also to Hamlet in Act 3, scene 4 (Charney, *Style* 167–68). It seems that horror is the main effect that Shakespeare wanted the Ghost to achieve.

[8] Although the Ghost is bloodthirsty and horrible, he has redeeming qualities (Alexander 30). He is toned down from a ghost in an anonymous and lost earlier play, perhaps a first version of *Hamlet* by Shakespeare himself, which was described by Shakespeare's contemporary Thomas Lodge (1558–1625) (Bloom 383). Lodge talked about "ye ghost which cried so miserally [pitifully, sorrowfully] at ye theator . . . *Hamlet, reuenge*" [sic]. Shakespeare's Ghost also cries out for vengeance, but as a former loving husband he is still concerned for the welfare of Hamlet's mother, Gertrude, directing his son to treat her kindly and help her (Kerrigan 54). Also, as a former king, he voices concern about the reputation and future of Denmark (Gottschalk 165). Paul Gottschalk points to these redeeming qualities to indicate that the Ghost is concerned with "restoration" as well as "retaliation" (166)—a view not shared by Norman Austin, who calls the Ghost "the spirit of ruin" (105).

[9] Indeed, the Ghost has many qualities of a living human being. For example, he is witty, as Maurice Charney observes about the following interchange between the Ghost and Hamlet just at the beginning of the revelation speeches in Act 1, scene 5, lines 6–7:

When citing dialogue between two or more characters, indent the quotation 1 inch (or ten spaces) and type each character's name next to the corresponding dialogue in all caps followed by a period.

> HAMLET. Speak, I am bound to hear.
>
> GHOST. So art thou to revenge, when thou shalt hear.

In other words, even though the Ghost may have come "with . . . airs from heaven, or blasts from hell" (1.4.41), he is still mentally alert enough to make a pun out of Hamlet's word "bound" (Charney, *Style* 118). To this quickness can be added his shrewd ability to judge his son's character. He knows that

Kruse 6

Hamlet may neglect duty, and hence his last words in Act 1, scene 5, are "remember me," and his first words in Act 3, scene 4, are "Do not forget." A. C. Bradley suggests that these speeches indicate Shakespeare's master touch in the development of the Ghost's character (126).

The Ghost also shows other human traits. He strongly feels remorse   **[10]**
about his lifelong crimes and "imperfections" for which his sudden death did not give him time to atone. It is this awareness that has made him bitter and vengeful. Also, he has a sense of appropriateness that extends to what he wears. Thus, at the beginning he appears on the parapets dressed in full armor. This battle uniform is in keeping with the location and also with his vengeful mission (Aldus 54). The armor is intimidating, a means of enforcing the idea that the Ghost in death has become a "spirit of hatred" (Austin 99). By contrast, in the closet scene he wears a dressing gown ["in his habit as he lived," 3.4.135], as though he is prepared for ordinary palace activities of both business and leisure (Charney, *Style* 26).

IV. The Ghost's Importance in the Structure of the Play

Shakespeare's great strength as a dramatist is shown not only in his   **[11]**
giving the Ghost such a round, full character but also in his integrating the Ghost fully within the play's structure. According to Peter Alexander, the Ghost is "indispensable" in the plot as the force that sets things in motion (29). The Ghost is also a director and organizer as well as an informer—a figure who keeps the action moving until there is no stopping it (Aldus 100). A careful study of his speeches shows that he is a manipulator, playing on his son's emotions to make him hurry to kill the king. In addition, the Ghost is persistent, because his return to Hamlet in Act 3, scene 4, to "whet thy almost blunted purpose" (line 111) is the mark of a manager who nervously intervenes when his directions are being neglected or delayed.

The Ghost is also significant in a major structure of the play. During the   **[12]**
imagined period when the events at Elsinore are taking place, Denmark is undergoing a national preparation for war against Norway (Alexander 34). Structurally, the beginning and ending of *Hamlet* are marked by the fear of

Kruse 7

war and the political takeover by "Young Fortinbras" of Norway, who is like Hamlet because King Hamlet, now the Ghost, had killed Old Fortinbras in single combat. Young Fortinbras is therefore as much an avenger as Hamlet (Honan 283), and the cause is King Hamlet, who now as a Ghost pushes Hamlet to vengeance. So strong is the Ghost's anger against Claudius that he insists on revenge even if it means the defeat of his country in the face of impending war. Ironically, the Ghost in death brings about the passing of the political stability he courageously promoted in life.

[13]   An additional major structure also involves the Ghost. Maurice Charney observes that the Ghost is significant in the "symmetrical" poison plots in the play (*Style* 39). The first of these plots, the poisoning of King Hamlet, is described by the Ghost himself in Act 1, scene 5. The poisoning of the player king in Act 3, scene 2, is a reenactment of the first murder, and it occurs in approximately the middle of the action. The final poisonings—of Gertrude, Laertes, Claudius, and finally Hamlet himself (from the poisoned sword of Laertes)—occur in Act 5, scene 2, the play's last scene. These actions have value as symbolic frames that measure the deterioration of the play's major characters.

V. The Ghost's Effect

[14]   Beyond the Ghost's practical and structural importance in the action, he has profound psychological influence, mainly negative, on the characters. Roy Walker describes him as a "prologue" to the "omen" of Hamlet himself, who is the agent of the "dread purpose" of vengeance (220). Because Hamlet is already suffering depression after his father's death, this murderous mission opens the wounds of his vulnerability (Campbell 127–28). Literally, Hamlet must give up everything he has ever learned, even "the movement of existence itself," so that he can carry out the Ghost's commands (McFarland 32–33). In Harold Bloom's words, "everything in the play depends upon Hamlet's response to the Ghost" (387). Because of this malign ghostly influence, Hamlet is gripped by a melancholy that undermines his love for Ophelia, his possible friendship with Laertes, and his relationship with his mother (Kirsch 31; Kott 49). The effects

Kruse 8

are like radiating waves, with the Ghost at the center as a relentless, destructive force. No one escapes.

This overwhelming ghostly force possesses Hamlet once the first   [15]
encounter has occurred. This possession is shown both literally and
figuratively when the Ghost goes under the stage in Act 1, scene 5, and
hears Hamlet's conversation with Horatio and the guards. The Ghost
thus represents "dimensions of reality" beyond what we see on the stage, a
mysterious world "elsewhere" that dominates the very souls of living persons
(Charney, "Asides" 127). As a result of this ever-present force, which as far as
Hamlet is concerned might become visible at any moment, Hamlet is denied
the healing that might normally occur after the death of a parent (Kirsch 26).
The steady pressure to kill Claudius disrupts any movement to mental health
and creates what Kirsch calls a "pathology of depression" (26) that inhibits
Hamlet's actions (Bradley 123), causes his Oedipal preoccupation with
the sexuality of his parents (Kirsch 22), and brings about his desire for the
oblivion of suicide (Kirsch 27).

It is, finally, this power over his son that gives the Ghost the greatest   [16]
influence in the play. Once the Ghost has appeared, Hamlet is not and never
can be the same. He loses the dignity and composure that he has assumed
as his right as a prince of Denmark and as a student in quest of knowledge
(McFarland 38). The Ghost's commands make it impossible for Hamlet
to solve problems through negotiation—the way he would likely have
chosen as prince and student. The commands force him instead into a plan
requiring murder. What could be more normal than hesitation under such
circumstances? Despite all of Hamlet's reflections, however, the web of
vengeance woven by the Ghost finally closes in on all those caught in it, both
the deserving and undeserving. There is no solution but the final one—real
death, which is the literal conclusion of the symbolic death represented by the
Ghost when he first appears on the Elsinore battlements.

VI. Conclusion

The Ghost is real in the play's action and structure. He is seen by the   [17]
characters on the stage, and when he speaks we hear him. He is made round

Kruse 9

and full by Shakespeare, and his motivation is direct and clear, even though the signs of his spirit nature are presented ambiguously. But the Ghost is more. He has been made a ghost by the greed and envy of Claudius, and for this reason he becomes in the play either a conscious or an unwitting agent of the "unseen Fates or forces" of his own doom (Walker 220). What he brings is the horror that lurks within the depths of good, moral people, waiting to overwhelm them and destroy them. Once the horror is released, there is no restraining it, and those who are hurt cannot be rescued. The tragedy is that there is no way to win against these odds.

Kruse 10

Works Cited

Aldus, P. J. *Mousetrap: Structure and Meaning in Hamlet*. Toronto: U of Toronto P, 1977. Print.

Alexander, Peter. *Hamlet: Father and Son*. Oxford: Clarendon, 1955. Print.

Austin, Norman. "Hamlet's Hungry Ghost." *Shenandoah* 37.1 (1987): 78–105. *GoogleBooks*. Web. 4 December 2014.

Bloom, Harold. *Shakespeare: The Invention of the Human*. New York: Riverhead, 1998. Print.

Bradley, A. C. *Shakespearean Tragedy*. 1904. London: Macmillan, 1950. *Project Gutenberg*. Web. 28 June 2014.

Campbell, Lily B. *Shakespeare's Tragic Heroes: Slaves of Passion*. New York: Barnes, 1959. Print.

Charney, Maurice. "Asides, Soliloquies, and Offstage Speech in Hamlet." *Shakespeare and the Sense of Performance: Essays in the Tradition of Performance Criticism in Honor of Bernard Beckerman*. Ed. Marvin and Ruth Thompson. Newark: U of Delaware P, 1989. 116–31. Print.

---. *Style in Hamlet*. Princeton: Princeton UP, 1969. Print.

DeLuca, Diana Macintyre. "The Movements of the Ghost in *Hamlet*." *Shakespeare Quarterly* 24.1 (1973): 147–54. *JSTOR*. Web. 10 May 2014.

In MLA style, the list of sources, called the Works Cited, begins a new page. Double-space throughout.

List sources in alphabetical order.

Kruse 11

Dobson, Michael, and Stanley Wells. *The Oxford Companion to Shakespeare*. Oxford: Oxford UP, 2001. Print.

Edgar, Irving I. *Shakespeare, Medicine, and Psychiatry*. New York: Philosophical Library, 1970. Print.

Fisch, Harold. *Hamlet and the Word*. New York: Ungar, 1971. Print.

Frye, Roland Mushat. *The Renaissance Hamlet: Issues and Responses in 1600*. Princeton: Princeton UP, 1984. Print.

Garber, Marjorie. "Hamlet: Giving Up the Ghost." *William Shakespeare: Hamlet*. Ed. Suzanne L. Wofford. Boston: Bedford, 1994. 297–331. Print.

Gottschalk, Paul. "Hamlet and the Scanning of Revenge." *Shakespeare Quarterly* 24.2 (1973): 155–70. *JSTOR*. Web. 5 May 2014.

Harrison, G. B., ed. *Shakespeare: The Complete Works*. New York: Harcourt, 1948. Print.

Holden, Anthony. *William Shakespeare: The Man Behind the Genius: A Biography*. 1968. Boston: Little, 1999. Print.

Honan, Park. *Shakespeare: A Life*. Oxford: Oxford UP, 1998. Print.

Jones, Ernest. *Hamlet and Oedipus*. 1949. New York: Doubleday, 1954. Print.

Kerrigan, William. *Hamlet's Perfection*. Baltimore: Johns Hopkins UP, 1994. Print.

Kirsch, Arthur. "Hamlet's Grief." *ELH* 48.1 (1981): 17–36. *JSTOR*. Web. 10 May 2014.

Kott, Jan. *Shakespeare, Our Contemporary*. Trans. Boleslaw Taborski. 1967. London: Methuen, 1970. Print.

McFarland, Thomas. *Tragic Meanings in Shakespeare*. New York: Random, 1966. Print.

O'Meara, John. "Hamlet and the Fortunes of Sorrowful Imagination: A Re-examination of the Genesis and Fate of the Ghost." *Cahiers Elisabéthains* 35 (1989): 15–25. Print.

Paris, Jean. *Shakespeare*. Trans. Richard Seaver. New York: Grove, 1960. Print.

Kruse 12

Prosser, Eleanor. *Hamlet and Revenge.* 2nd ed. Stanford: Stanford UP, 1971. Print.

Shakespeare, William. *The Tragedy of Hamlet, Prince of Denmark. Literature: An Introduction to Reading and Writing, Compact Edition.* Ed. Edgar V. Roberts and Robert Zweig. 6th ed. New York: Pearson, 2015. 1080–1177. Print.

Walker, Roy. "*Hamlet*: The Opening Scene." *Shakespeare: Modern Essays in Criticism.* Ed. Leonard F. Dean. New York: Oxford UP, 1961. Print.

Commentary on the Essay

This essay illustrates an assignment requiring twenty-seven sources and about 2,500 words. The sources were located through an examination of library catalogs, the *MLA Bibliography,* library databases, the Internet, and the bibliographies in some of the listed books. They represent the range of materials available in a college library with a selective, but by no means exhaustive, set of holdings. Two of the sources (Austin and O'Meara) were obtained through interlibrary loan.

The writing itself is developed from the sources listed. Originality (see p. 515) is provided by the structure and development of the essay, additional observations not existing in the sources, and transitions. The topic outline is placed appropriately at the beginning—a pattern you can follow unless your instructor asks for a more detailed outline, or, perhaps, for no outline at all.

Because the essay is concerned with only one work—and one subject about that work—it demonstrates approach 1 (p. 501). The essay is eclectic, introducing discussions of ideas, character, style, and structure. These four topics fulfill the goal of covering the ground thoroughly within the confines of the assignment. A shorter research assignment might deal with no more than, say, the Ghost's character, ignoring other topics. A longer essay might deal further with the philosophical and theological meanings of ghosts during the Elizabethan period, or a more detailed study of all the traits of the Ghost's character, and so on.

The central idea of the essay is stressed in paragraph 1, along with an assertion that the Ghost is a major influence in the play, together with a concession that the Ghost is only a minor character in the action. The research for this paragraph is derived primarily from a reading of the play itself. Paragraph 2, continuing the exploration of the central idea, demonstrates that the Ghost figures in the major themes of *Hamlet.* Paragraph 3 is mainly functional, being used as the location of the thesis sentence.

Part II, containing paragraphs 4–6, deals with the Ghost's status as a spirit. Part III, with paragraphs 7–10, is concerned with the Ghost's human rather than spiritual characteristics. Part IV, with paragraphs 11–13, deals with the significance of the Ghost in the major structures that dominate the play. Part V, with three paragraphs, considers the Ghost's negative and overwhelming influence over the major figures of *Hamlet*, the emphasis being the character of Hamlet as the transferring agent of the Ghost's destructive revenge. The concluding paragraph (17) sums up the essay with the final idea of how the Ghost affects the tragic nature of *Hamlet*.

The list of works cited is the basis of all parenthetical references in the essay, in accordance with the *MLA Handbook for Writers of Research Papers*, 7th ed. Using these references, an interested reader can consult the sources for a more detailed development of the ideas in the illustrative essay. The works cited can also serve as a springboard for expanded research.

USING SOURCES EFFECTIVELY

SUMMARIZING SOURCES LENDS AUTHORITY TO YOUR ARGUMENT

Research essays require a thorough investigation of a variety of secondary sources that can shed valuable light on the paper's argument. Here, a clear and well-integrated summary of relevant sources for readers provides background for Toni Ann Kruse's main idea. Further, by presenting a broader context for the thesis, summarizing allows the writer to focus subsequently on a more specific element of the work. In paragraph 2, Kruse uses an efficient overview of a range of critical opinions to serve as a solid foundation for her own essay, "The Ghost in *Hamlet*":

> Not only is the Ghost dominant over actions, but he is also directly linked to many of the play's themes. William Kerrigan calls the Ghost a "nightmind" who introduces the mental darkness of evil that pervades the play (42). In addition, the Ghost intensifies the play's "interior suffering" (Paris 85). This suffering is brought out in Hamlet's anguished soliloquies and also in the pain of Ophelia, Laertes, and even Claudius himself. Another theme is shown by the Ghost's commands to Hamlet—those of responsibility, whether personal, political, or conjugal (McFarland 15). Hamlet of course does not rush right out to kill Claudius, despite the

Ghost's urgings, and hence the Ghost is indirectly responsible for the theme of hesitation—this great "Sphinx of modern Literature"—which has become one of the weaknesses cited most frequently about Hamlet's character (Jones 22). The Ghost's scary presence also poses questions about the power of superstition, terror, and fear (Campbell 211). Beyond all this, deeply within the psychological realm, the Ghost has been cited as a "confirmation" of the influence of "psychic residues in governing and shaping human life" (McFarland 34), not to mention the significance of the Oedipus complex in the development of Hamlet's character.

Because the Ghost is so important, one hardly needs to justify studying him. His importance can be traced in his spirit nature, his influence on the play's structure, and his effect on Hamlet and therefore indirectly on all the major characters.

> After briefly surveying the interpretations of five different critics, Kruse can state her thesis clearly. Its importance has been forcefully established.

The rest of the essay frequently refers to these and other secondary works, but summarizing the main ideas of her sources early helps Kruse show the scholarly context for her own critical approach to the Ghost's role in the play and to prove the value of her interpretation. (For more information on summarizing, see pages 509–516.)

PART V

Special Writing Topics About Literature

Chapter 25
Critical Approaches Important in the Study of Literature

AFTER STUDYING THIS MATERIAL, YOU SHOULD BE ABLE TO DO THE FOLLOWING:

- Understand the range of critical approaches to writing about literature
- Recognize the primary features of different critical approaches to literature
- Implement different critical theories and approaches in evaluating literary works

A number of critical theories or approaches for understanding and interpreting literature are available to critics and students alike.[1] Many of these were developed during the twentieth century to create a discipline of literary studies comparable with disciplines in the natural and social sciences. Literary critics have often borrowed liberally from other disciplines (e.g., history, psychology, politics, anthropology) but have primarily aimed at developing literature as a study in its own right.

At the heart of the various critical approaches are many fundamental questions: What is literature? What does it do? Is its concern primarily to tell stories, to divert attention, to entertain, to communicate ideas, to persuade, and to teach, or is it to describe and interpret reality or to explore and explain emotions—or is it all of these? To what degree is literature an art as opposed to a medium for imparting knowledge? What more does it do than express ideas? How does it get its ideas across? What can it contribute to intellectual, artistic, political, and social thought and history? How is literature used, and how and why is it misused? Is it private? Public? What theoretical and technical expertise may be invoked to enhance literary studies? How valuable was literature in the past, and how valuable is it now? To what degree should literature be in the vanguard of social and political change?

Questions such as these indicate that criticism is concerned not only with reading and interpreting stories, poems, and plays but also with establishing theoretical understanding. Because of such extensive aims, a full explanation and illustration of the approaches would fill the pages of a long book. The following descriptions are therefore intended as no more than brief introductions. Bear in mind that in the hands of skilled critics, the approaches are so subtle, sophisticated, and complex that they are not only critical stances but also philosophies.

Although the various approaches provide widely divergent ways to study literature and literary problems, they reflect major tendencies rather than absolute straitjacketing. Not every approach is appropriate for every work, nor are the approaches always mutually

---

[1] Some of the approaches described in this chapter are presented more simply in Part I (pp. 21–26) as basic study techniques for writing about literary works.

exclusive. Even the most devoted practitioners of the methods do not pursue them rigidly. In addition, some of the approaches are more "user friendly" than others for certain types of discoveries. To a degree at least, most critics therefore take a particular approach but utilize methods that technically belong to one or more of the other approaches. A critic stressing the topical/historical approach, for example, might introduce the close study of a work that is associated with the method of the New Criticism. Similarly, a psychoanalytical critic might include details about archetypes. In short, a great deal of criticism is *pragmatic* or *eclectic* rather than rigid.

Ten approaches will be considered here: (1) *moral/intellectual;* (2) *topical/historical;* (3) *new critical/formalist;* (4) *structuralist;* (5) *feminist/gender studies/queer theory;* (6) *economic determinist/Marxist;* (7) *psychological/psychoanalytic;* (8) *archetypal/ symbolic/mythic;* (9) *deconstructionist;* and (10) *reader-response.*

The object of learning about these approaches, like everything else in this book, is to help you develop your own capacities as a reader and writer. Accordingly, following each of the descriptions is a brief paragraph showing how Hawthorne's story "Young Goodman Brown" (Chapter 7, p. 342) might be considered in the light of the particular approach. The illustrative paragraphs following the discussion of structuralism, for example, show an application of the structuralist approach to Goodman Brown and his story, and so also with the feminist approach, the economic determinist approach, and the others. These paragraphs are followed by additional commentary illustrating the same approaches based on other literary works. Whenever you are doing your own writing about literature, you are free to use the various approaches as part or all of your assignment, if you believe the approach may help you.

Moral/Intellectual

The **moral/intellectual critical approach** is concerned with content, ideas, and values (see also Chapter 8). The approach is as old as literature itself, for literature is a traditional mode of inculcating thought, morality, philosophy, and religion. The concern in moral/intellectual criticism is not only to discover meaning but also to determine whether works of literature are both *true* and *significant*.

To study literature from the moral/intellectual perspective is therefore to determine whether a work conveys a lesson or a message and whether it can help readers lead better lives and improve their understanding of the world. What ideas does the work contain? How strongly does the work bring forth its ideas? What application do the ideas have to the work's characters and situations? How may the ideas be evaluated intellectually? Morally? Discussions based on such questions do not imply that literature is primarily a medium of moral and intellectual exhortation. Ideally, moral/intellectual criticism should differ from sermonizing to the degree that readers should always be left with their own decisions about whether to assimilate the ideas of a work and about whether the ideas—and values—are personally or morally acceptable.

Sophisticated critics have sometimes demeaned the moral/intellectual approach on the grounds that "message hunting" reduces a work's artistic value by treating it like a sermon or political speech, but the approach will be valuable as long as readers expect literature to be applicable to their own lives.

Example: Hawthorne's "Young Goodman Brown"

"Young Goodman Brown" raises the issue of how an institution designed for human eleva-tion, such as the religious system of colonial Salem, can be so ruinous. Does the failure result from the system itself or from the people who misunderstand it? Is what is true of religion as practiced by Brown also true of social and political institutions? Should any religious or political philosophy be given greater significance than goodwill and mutual trust? One of the major virtues of "Young Goodman Brown" is that it provokes questions like these but at the same time provides a number of satisfying answers. A particularly important one is that religious and moral beliefs should not be used to justify the condemnation of others. Another important answer is that attacks made from the refuge of a religion or group, such as Brown's Puritanism, are dangerous because the judge may condemn without thought and without personal responsibility.

Second Example: Stafford's "Traveling Through the Dark," page 944

William Stafford's "Traveling Through the Dark" presents a moral quandary. While the speaker is driving along a narrow road at night, he comes upon the carcass of a doe. Upon investigation, he finds that the doe is pregnant with a live fawn. It is customary to throw dead animals off the side of the road in order to remove the danger of having a swerving car veer off the road. But in the present situation, the speaker "hesitates." The living fawn com-plicates the moral option, for now life must be taken. As the speaker hesitates, he "could hear the wilderness listen" because moral decisions are not only an individual's domain but affect all of us. "I thought hard for us all" the speaker says, but then adds "my only swerving" as if uncertain if it is presumptuous for one person to think for all people. Some-times, however, it is a human being's responsibility to make a decision, and one may argue whether the right one was made in this instance. As if to highlight the human quandary that moral situations put us in, Stafford refers to the car as aiming its headlights, as if the car were conscious. Despite that, it is only human beings who are responsible for moral action. Nature merely "listens," and objects merely "light" the path toward decision. In "Traveling Through the Dark" Stafford, through a simple situation that might confront almost anyone, probes many of the issues raised by moral action.

Readings

Buckley, Vincent. *Poetry and Morality: Studies in the Criticism of Matthew Arnold, T. S. Eliot, and F. R. Leavis.* London: Chatto and Windus, 1959. Print.

Else, Gerald F. *Plato and Aristotle on Poetry.* Chapel Hill: U of North Carolina P, 1986. Print.

Farrell, James T. *Literature and Morality.* New York: Vanguard, 1947. Print.

Foerster, Norman. *American Criticism: A Study in Literary Theory from Poe to the Present.* 1928. New York: Russell and Russell, 1962. Print.

Gardner, John. *On Moral Fiction.* New York: Basic Books, 1978. Print.

McCloskey, Mary A. *Kant's Aesthetic.* Basingstoke: Macmillan, 1987. Print.

Olson, Elder. *Aristotle's Poetics and English Literature.* Chicago: U of Chicago P, 1965. Print.

Sartre, Jean-Paul. *What Is Literature?* New York: Philosophical Library, 1966. Print.

Wallis, R. T. *Neoplatonism.* London: Duckworth, 1995. Print.

Topical/Historical

The **topical/historical critical approach** stresses the relationship of literature to its historical period, and for this reason it has had a long life. Although much literature may be applicable to many places and times, much of it also directly reflects the intellectual and social worlds of the authors. When was the work written? What were the circumstances that produced it? What major issues does it deal with? How does it fit into the author's career? Keats's poem "On First Looking into Chapman's Homer" (p. 641), for example, is his excited response to his reading of one of the major literary works of Western civilization. Hardy's "Channel Firing" (p. 617) is an ironically acerbic response to continued armament and preparation for war in the past, in the present, and in the future.

The topical/historical approach investigates relationships of this sort, including the elucidation of words and concepts that today's readers may not immediately understand. It may also include biographical information about the author or be informed by a sociological study. For instance, knowing that Dudley Randall was writing "Ballad of Birmingham" (p. 749) at the height of the Civil Rights struggle in America adds social significance to his description of a tragic bombing. Obviously, the approach requires the assistance of footnotes, dictionaries, library catalogs, histories, and handbooks.

A common criticism of the topical/historical approach is that in the extreme, it deals with background knowledge rather than with literature itself. It is possible, for example, for a topical/historical critic to describe a writer's life, the period of the writer's work, and the social and intellectual ideas of the time—all without ever considering the meaning, importance, and value of any of that writer's works themselves.

A reaction against such an unconnected use of historical details is the so-called **New Historicism.** This approach justifies the parallel reading of both literary and nonliterary works in order to bring an informed understanding of the context of a literary work. The new historicist assumes that history is not a "fixed" essence but a literary construction. As such, history is a prism through which a society views itself; a work of literature is given resonance by seeing the nonobjective context in which it was produced. This approach justifies the introduction of historical knowledge by integrating it with the understanding of particular texts. Readers of Arnold's "Dover Beach" (p. 887), for example, sometimes find it difficult to follow the meaning of Arnold's statement "The Sea of Faith / Was once, too, at the full." Historical background has a definite role to play here. In Arnold's time there developed a method of treating the Bible as a historical document rather than a divinely inspired revelation. This approach has been called the "Higher Criticism" of the Bible, and to many thoughtful people the Higher Criticism undermined the concept that the Bible was divine, infallible, and inerrant. Therefore Arnold's idea is that the "Sea of Faith" is no longer at full tide but is now rather at an ebb. Because the introduction of such historical material is designed to facilitate the reading of the poem—and also the reading of other literature of the period—the New Historicism represents an integration of knowledge and interpretation. As a principle, New Historicism entails the acquisition of as much historical information as possible because our knowledge of the relationship of literature to its historical period can never be complete. The practitioner of historical criticism must always seek new information on the grounds that it may prove relevant to the understanding of various literary works.

Cultural Study is a more recent approach that justifies the analyses of non-literary materials such as television and radio shows, movies, brochures, and advertisements. By not privileging literature over mass culture, Cultural Studies critics are able to open up new areas of interest. Langston Hughes's poem "Harlem" (p. 856) for example, was written in 1951 about possible resentment of African Americans when faced with constant discrimination. In 1985, August Wilson created his drama *Fences* (p. 1430), in which baseball has been a vital element in the life of the major character, Troy Maxson. Both works—the poem and the play—are made vital because they reflect the treatment of African Americans by the dominant white races in American society. It therefore becomes relevant that in 1947 Jackie Robinson became the first African American ball player to play baseball for a major league team, and that soon after, increasing numbers of black ballplayers were joining major league clubs. Reading newspaper accounts of the problems they faced provides insights into both "Harlem" and *Fences*.

🌿 Example: Hawthorne's "Young Goodman Brown"

"Young Goodman Brown" is an allegorical story by Nathaniel Hawthorne (1804–1864), the major New England writer who probed deeply into the relationship between religion and guilt. His ancestors had been involved in religious persecutions, including the Salem witch trials, and he, living 150 years afterward, wanted to analyze the weaknesses and uncertainties of the sin-dominated religion of the earlier period, a tradition of which he was a resentful heir. Not surprisingly, therefore, the story about "Young Goodman Brown" takes place in Salem during Puritan times, and Hawthorne's implied judgments are those of a severe critic of how the harsh old religion destroyed personal and family relationships. Although the immediate concerns of the story belong to a vanished age, Hawthorne's treatment remains valuable because it remains timely.

🌿 Second Example: Jarrell's "The Death of the Ball Turret Gunner," page 550

Juxtaposing World War II propaganda posters with Randall Jarrell's 1945 poem "The Death of the Ball Turret Gunner," gives special meaning to both. In an American poster of 1943 the words BATTLE OF GERMANY at the top and JOIN THE AIR CREW at the bottom are boldly visible. In the middle is a group of bombers flying in neat formation high above a bombed German city. All that is rising from below is smoke emanating from the site of the bombing. One gets the impression that a bombing run is an orderly operation and that the bombers are high above any danger and immune from it. A British poster of the same year, with the words BACK THEM UP at the bottom, shows a fighter plane in close-up as it drops bombs on a German city. In the background other fighters can be seen in formation, apparently leaving the city after a successful bombing raid. While these posters imply a heroic struggle against an enemy, they only point obliquely to any danger. Jarrell's poem confronts the darker realities of war. The gunner of this poem is not consumed by his heroic duty. He seems to be born into his nightmarish situation, for he says "From my mother's sleep I fell into the State." His height above the action does not suggest safety but rather a remote detachment from the "dream of life." Describing his own death and how he was "washed . . . out of the turret with a hose," the speaker manifests the horrifying impersonality of war. This "dialogue" between World War II posters and Randell Jarrell's poem gives the reader a richer understanding of the many motives and outcomes of an event so dangerous and complex as war.

Readings

During, Simon, ed. *The Cultural Studies Reader*. New York: Routledge, 1993. Print.

Greenblatt, Stephen. *Renaissance Self-Fashioning: From More to Shakespeare*. Chicago: U of Chicago P, 1980. Print.

_____, ed. *Repressing the English Renaissance*. Berkeley: U of California P, 1988. Print.

Hoggart, Richard. *The Uses of Literacy: Changing Patterns in English Mass Culture*. Harmondsworth: Penguin, 1957. Print.

LaCapra, Dominick. *History and Criticism*. Ithaca: Cornell UP, 1985. Print.

Lindenberger, Herbert, ed. *History in Literature: On Value, Genre, Institutions*. New York: Columbia UP, 1990. Print.

McGann, Jerome. *The Beauty of Inflections: Literary Investigations in Historical Method and Theory*. Oxford: Clarendon P, 1985. Print.

_____, ed. *Historical Studies and Literary Criticism*. Madison: U of Wisconsin P, 1985. Print.

Said, Edward W. *Orientalism*. New York: Random House, 1978. Print.

_____. *Culture and Imperialism*. New York: Knopf, 1993. Print.

Thomas, Brook. *The New Historicism and Other Old-Fashioned Topics*. Princeton: Princeton UP, 1991. Print.

New Critical/Formalist

The **new critical/formalist approach** (the **new criticism**) has been a dominant force in modern literary studies. It focuses on literary texts as formal works of art, and for this reason it can be seen as a reaction against the topical/historical approach. The objection raised by new critics is that as topical/historical critics consider literary history, they evade direct contact with actual texts.

The inspiration for the new critical/formalist approach was the French practice of *explication de texte*, a method that emphasizes detailed examination and explanation. (See "Writing an Explication of a Poem," pp. 563–64.) The new criticism is at its most brilliant in the formal analysis of smaller units such as entire poems and short passages. For the analysis of larger structures, the new criticism also utilizes a number of techniques that have been selected as the basis of chapters in this book. Discussions of point of view, tone, plot, character, and structure, for example, are formal ways of looking at literature that are derived from the new criticism.

The aim of the new critical study of literature is to provide readers not only with the means of explaining the content of works (what, specifically, does a work say?) but also with the insights needed for evaluating the artistic quality of individual works and writers (how well is it said?). A major aspect of new critical thought is that content and form—including all ideas, ambiguities, subtleties, and even apparent contradictions—were originally within the conscious or subconscious control of the author. There are no accidents. It does not necessarily follow, however, that today's critic is able to define the author's intentions exactly, for such intentions require knowledge of biographical details that are irretrievably lost. Each literary work therefore takes on its own existence and identity, and the critic's work is to discover a reading or readings that explain the facts of the text. It should be noted that the new critic does not claim infallible interpretations and does not exclude the validity of multiple readings of the same work.

Dissenters from the new criticism have noted a tendency by new critics to ignore relevant knowledge that history and biography can bring to literary studies. In addition, the approach has been subject to the charge that stressing the explication of texts alone fails to deal with literary value and appreciation. In other words, the new critics, in explaining the meaning of literature, sometimes neglect the reasons for which readers find literature stimulating and valuable.

Example: Hawthorne's "Young Goodman Brown"

A major aspect of Hawthorne's "Young Goodman Brown" is that the details are so vague and dreamlike that many readers are uncertain about what is happening. The action is a nighttime walk by the protagonist, Young Goodman Brown, into a deep forest where he encounters a mysterious satanic ritual that leaves him bitter and misanthropic. This much seems clear, but the precise nature of Brown's experience is not clear, nor is the identity of the stranger (father, village elder, devil) who accompanies Brown as he begins his walk. At the story's end Hawthorne's narrator states that the whole episode may have been no more than a dream or nightmare. Yet when morning comes, Brown walks back into town as though returning from an overnight trip, and he recoils in horror from his fellow villagers, including his wife, Faith. Could his attitude result from nothing more than a nightmare? Even at the story's end these uncertainties remain. For this reason one may conclude that Hawthorne deliberately creates the uncertainties to reveal how people like Brown build defensive walls of judgment around themselves. The story thus implies that the real source of Brown's anger is as vague as his nocturnal walk, but he doesn't understand it in this way. Because Brown's vision and judgment are absolute, he rejects everyone around him, even if the cost is a life of bitter suspicion and spiritual isolation.

Example: Robinson's "Richard Cory," page 590

Edwin Arlington Robinson's *Richard Cory* is a tightly structured poem in which all the traditional elements of verse are orchestrated to form a unified and clear meaning. The four quatrains, in iambic pentameter lines, rhyme *abab cdcd efef ghgh*, forming a predictable pattern that boldly frames the ironic ending: "And Richard Cory, one calm summer night, / Went home and put a bullet through his head." The "regal" diction describing Richard Cory, contrasted with the bland circumstances of the townspeople, lets the reader know why Cory was so envied, and the diction also carries the poem forward to its shocking conclusion. The people of the town are walking on the "pavement" and "flutter" at the sight of the neighbor they envy: Richard Cory is "a gentleman from sole to crown, / . . . and imperially slim." Each stanza is modulated by images of Cory himself, or at least as he is perceived by those around him, along with the images of the townspeople themselves. The townspeople, including the speaker who is one of them, are so envious of Cory that they "curse" their own predicament and would rather be in his place. Yet, upon close scrutiny, the reader can see how the images describing Cory are superficial, as if only the "surface" of his personality were enough to judge him. He was "slim" and "rich" and "admirably schooled," but no reference is made to his thoughts, feelings, or aspirations. By the common and unimaginative standards of the speaker, the final irony is surprising, yet by the standards of the reader it is not surprising. As in many works of art, the title of the poem is significant. Did anyone know the "heart" of Richard Cory, the "core" of his existence?

Readings

Brooks, Cleanth. *The Well Wrought Urn: Studies in the Structure of Poetry.* New York: Reynal and Hitchcock, 1947. Print.

Brooks, Cleanth, and Robert Penn Warren. *Understanding Poetry.* 4th ed. New York: Holt, 1938. Print.

Empson, William. *Seven Types of Ambiguity.* London: Chatto and Windus, 1930. Print.

Krieger, Murray. *The New Apologists for Poetry.* Minneapolis: U of Minnesota P, 1986. Print.

Ransom, John Crowe. *The New Criticism.* Norfolk: New Directions, 1941. Print.

Richards, I. A. *Principles of Literary Criticism.* New York: Harcourt Brace, 1924. Print.

Wellek, Rene, and Austin Warren. *Theory of Literature.* New York: Harcourt Brace, 1949. Print.

Wimsatt, William K. *The Verbal Icon: Studies in the Meaning of Poetry.* Lexington: UP of Kentucky, 1954. Print.

Structuralist

The principle of the **stucturalist critical approach** stems from the attempt to find relationships and connections among elements that appear to be separate and unique. Just as physical science reveals unifying universal principles of matter such as gravity and the forces of electromagnetism (and is constantly searching for a "unified field theory"), the structuralist critic attempts to discover the forms unifying all literature. Thus a structuralist description of Maupassant's "The Necklace" (p. 7) stresses that the main character, Mathilde, is an *active* protagonist who undergoes a *test* (or series of tests) and emerges with a victory, though not the kind she had originally hoped for. The same might be said of Mrs. Popov and Smirnov in Chekhov's *The Bear* (p. 1322). If this same kind of structural view is applied to Bierce's "An Occurrence at Owl Creek Bridge" (p. 87), the protagonist is defeated in the test. Generally, the structuralist approach applies such patterns to other works of literature to determine that certain protagonists are active or submissive, that they pass or fail their tests, or that they succeed or fail at other encounters. The key is that many apparently unrelated works reveal many common patterns or contain similar structures with important variations.

The structuralist approach is important because it enables critics to discuss works from widely separate cultures and historical periods. In this respect, critics have followed the leads of modern anthropologists, most notably Claude Lévi-Strauss (1908–1990). Along such lines, critics have undertaken the serious examination of folk and fairy tales. Some of the groundbreaking structuralist criticism, for example, was devoted to the structural analysis of themes, actions, and characters to be found in Russian folktales. The method also bridges popular and serious literature, making little distinction between the two insofar as the description of the structures is concerned. Indeed, structuralism furnishes an ideal approach for comparative literature, and the method also enables critics to consolidate genres such as modern romances, detective tales, soap operas, sitcoms, and film.

Like new criticism, structuralism aims at comprehensiveness of description, and many critics would insist that the two are complementary and not separate. A distinction is that new criticism is at its best in dealing with smaller units of literature, whereas structuralist criticism is best in the analysis of narratives and therefore larger units such as novels, myths, stories, plays, and films. Because structuralism shows how fiction is organized into various typical situations, the approach merges with the *archetypal* approach (see below, p. 1582), and at times it is difficult to find any distinctions between structuralist and archetypal criticism.

Structuralism, however, deals not just with narrative structures but also with structures of any type, wherever they occur. For example, structuralism makes considerable use of linguistics. Modern linguistic scholars have determined that there is a difference between "deep structures" and "surface structures" in language. A structuralist analysis of style, therefore, emphasizes how writers utilize such structures. The structuralist interpretation of language also perceives distinguishing types or "grammars" of language that are recurrent in various types of literature. Suppose, for example, that you encounter opening passages like the following:

1. Once upon a time a young prince fell in love with a young princess. He was in love so deeply that he wanted to declare his love for her, and early one morning he left his castle on his white charger, along with his retainers and servants, riding toward her castle home high in the distant and cloud-topped mountains.

2. Early that morning, Alan found himself thinking about Anne. He had thought that she was being ambiguous when she said she loved him, and his feelings about her were not certain. His further thought left him still unsure.

The words of these two passages create different and distinct frames of reference. One is a fairy tale of the past, the other a modern internalized reflection of feeling. The passages therefore demonstrate how language itself fits into predetermined patterns or structures. Similar uses of language structures can be associated with other types of literature.

Example: Hawthorne's "Young Goodman Brown"

Young Goodman Brown is a hero who is passive, not active. He is a *witness*, a *receiver* rather than a *doer*. His only action—taking his trip in the forest—occurs at the story's beginning. After that point, he no longer acts but instead is acted upon, and his reactions to what he sees around him put his life's beliefs to a test. Of course, many protagonists undergo similar testing (such as rescuing victims and overcoming particularly terrible dragons), and they emerge as heroes or conquerors. Not so with Goodman Brown. He is a responder who allows himself to be victimized by his own perceptions—or misperceptions. Despite all his previous experiences with his wife and with the good people of his village, he generalizes too hastily. He lets the single disillusioning experience of his nightmare govern his entire outlook on others, and thus he fails his test and turns his entire life into darkness.

Second Example: Jackson's "The Lottery," page 139

Shirley Jackson's story "The Lottery" is a powerful indictment of tradition for its own sake. The narrator/resident of a small town explains how a yearly lottery is held to determine who among its citizens is to be stoned. Apparently the purpose of this ritual has generally been forgotten, but the rules governing its execution are known in great detail. The plot is given resonance and predictability by following two structurally determined elements—the basic outline of a tragedy and the outlines of a contest. Like a traditional tragedy the story begins in apparent innocence and happiness and ends in definite calamity. It is a "sunny" day when the lottery is about to begin, "the flowers . . . [are] blossoming profusely," and the town folk are in a jovial mood. The tension builds with the "drawing" from the black box, and the story ends with the stoning and presumed death of the victim. The horror of the story is not to be found in an individual but rather in the collective, slavish acquiescence to a shockingly anachronistic ritual. As in tragedy, the end is the inevitable outcome, for once we know that the people accept the rules of the town lottery, the end is predictable. The townspeople do not know why they must stone someone, but they know that when they partake in the lottery and follow its rules, someone will "win" the contest and meet his or her doom. Understanding the basic elements of tragedy and reading "The Lottery" as a contest or game gives the story a comprehensible and predictable form.

Readings

Barthes, Roland. *Writing Degree Zero.* 1953. New York: Beacon, 1970. Print.

_____. *Critical Essays.* 1964. Evanston: Northwestern UP, 1970. Print.

_____. *Mythologies.* 1957. New York: Hill and Wang, 1972. Print.

Cassirer, Ernst. *Symbol, Myth, and Culture.* New Haven: Yale UP, 1979. Print.

Caws, Peter. *Structuralism: The Art of the Intelligible.* Atlantic Highlands: Humanities, 1988. Print.

Culler, Jonathan. *Structuralist Poetics.* Ithaca: Cornell UP, 1975. Print.

Genette, Gerard. *Narrative Discourse: An Essay in Method.* Ithaca: Cornell UP, 1980. Print.

Greimas, A. J. *Structural Semantics: An Attempt at a Method.* Lincoln: U of Nebraska P, 1984. Print.

Lane, Michael, ed. *Structuralism: A Reader.* London: Cape, 1970. Print.

Macksey, Richard, and Eugenio Donato, eds. *The Structuralism Controversy: The Languages of Criticism and the Sciences of Man.* Baltimore: Johns Hopkins UP, 1970. Print.

Feminist Criticism/Gender Studies/Queer Theory

Feminist criticism/gender studies/queer theory displays divergent interests drawing insights from many disciplines. It is a still evolving and rich field of inquiry. *Feminist criticism* had its genesis in the women's movement of the 1960s, shares many of its concerns, and has applied them to the study of literature. One of the early aims of feminist critics was to question the traditional canon and claim a place in it for neglected women writers. Writers such as Mary Shelley, Elizabeth Gaskell, Christina Rossetti, Kate Chopin, and Charlotte Perkins Gilman—three of whom are represented in this book—have been given great critical attention as a result. Feminist critics also delineate the ways both male and female characters are portrayed in literature, looking at how societal norms about sexual difference are either enforced or subverted, and focusing partly on patriarchal structures and institutions such as marriage. As early as the beginning of the twentieth century, Virginia Woolf questioned whether there was a feminine/masculine divide in writing styles, a contentious subject among feminist critics to this day. Feminist critics are also interested in how interpreting texts differs between the sexes. For instance, in *A Map for Rereading* (1980), the critic Annette Kolodny analyzes how men and women read the same stories differently.

Gender studies, a more recent critical approach, brings attention to gender rather than to sexual differences. Gender studies critics see the masculine/feminine divide as socially constructed and not innate. Drawing partly on the works of the French philosopher Michel Foucault (1926–1984) such as *The History of Sexuality* and *Madness and Civilization*, which explore the way powerful institutions organize our society and way of thinking. Such critics apply Foucault's ideas to understanding patriarchal structures and their representations in literature. Many studies have also built on the insights of psychoanalysis and deconstruction (see below), questioning Freud's male-oriented categories and seeking insights into the way language is constructed and the way it affects our thinking. In the essay *Laugh of the Medusa* (1975), Hélène Cixous applies deconstructionist insights about binary oppositions to a study of discourse about women, showing how it disparages women. Thus, while men's discourse in relation to women's may highlight such separate ways of thinking as logic/inconsistency, it is the traditional patriarchal way of thinking that values male over female experience.

A more recent critical orientation, which came to prominence in the early 1990s, is *queer theory*, which also appropriates many of the insights of deconstruction, particularly its understanding that binary oppositions are relative and that thinking about matters such as sexual orientation is partly ideological and partly social. Many queer theorists see the heterosexual/homosexual divide as less distinct than has commonly been believed. Queer theorists are interested in how homosexuals are portrayed in literature and whether they write or read literature differently from heterosexuals. Queer theory has brought attention to recent literary works, dealing explicitly with lesbian and gay themes, along with attention to sometimes "veiled" references to the same themes in writers whose works make up the standard canon. Much of queer theory is theoretical; one example, applied to reading a particular work, is Jonathan Crewe's essay, "Queering 'The Yellow Wallpaper'? Charlotte Perkins Gilman and the Politics of Form" (*Tulsa Studies in Women's Literature* 14.2 [1995]: 273–93).

Example: Hawthorne's "Young Goodman Brown"

At the beginning of "Young Goodman Brown," Brown's wife, Faith, is seen only peripherally. In the traditional patriarchal spirit of wife-as-adjunct, she tells her new husband of her fears, and then asks him to stay at home and take his journey at some other time.

Hawthorne does not give her the intelligence or dignity, however, to let her explain her concern (or might he not have been interested in what she had to say?) and she therefore remains in the background with her pink hair ribbon as her distinguishing symbol of submissive inferiority. During the mid-forest satanic ritual, she appears again and is given power, but only the power to cause her husband to go astray. Once she is led in as a novice in the practice of demonism, her husband falls right in step. Unfortunately, by following her, Brown can conveniently excuse himself from guilt by claiming that "she" had made him do it, just as Eve, in some traditional views of the fall of humankind, compelled Adam to eat the apple (Genesis 3:16–17). Hawthorne's attention to the male protagonist, in other words, permits him to neglect the independence and integrity of a female protagonist.

Second Example: Chopin's "The Story of an Hour," page 306

"The Story of an Hour" by Kate Chopin is about a woman who is told that her husband has died in a train accident. Rather than feeling devastated by this news as her family and friends expect, she feels strangely free and happy to pursue a life for herself. While the story's plot suggests obvious themes of interest for feminist critics, a closer look at many details reveals how language, institutions, and expected demeanor suppress the natural desires and aspirations of women. The protagonist of the story is referred to as "Mrs. Mallard" while her husband is called by his name, Brently Mallard, which has nothing to do with his marital status. Assuming that because of a heart condition Louise Mallard might not survive the bad news, she is told by her sister indirectly "in broken sentences:" of her husband's fate. At first she reacts predictably by weeping "with sudden, wild abandonment." Soon, however, Louise finds herself resisting a feeling that is finally identified as "freedom." In her last few moments of solitude, she imagines a life devoted only to herself and not to being molded by the will of another. Her resistance indicates the pull of societal norms, while her anticipation of possible liberation is a sign of her true inner self. When, at the end of the story, Louise sees her husband appear, perfectly safe and unharmed, she dies of a heart attack, which is diagnosed by attending doctors as a result "of joy that kills." Since there is no indication that Brently Mallard was anything but a good husband, we may assume that it was freedom from the bonds of marriage itself and the overpowering will of a man that turned a supposedly tragic event into a liberating one. "The Story of an Hour" is a powerful commentary on the institution of marriage as it suppresses the natural desires and pursuits of women.

Readings

Brownstein, Rachel. *Becoming a Heroine: Reading About Women in Novels.* New York: Viking, 1982. Print.

Cameron, Deborah. *Feminism in Linguistic Theory.* London: Macmillan, 1992. Print.

Delany, Sheila. *Writing Women: Women Writers and Women in Literature, Medieval to Modern.* New York: Schocken, 1984. Print.

Gilbert, Sandra M., and Susan Gubar. *The Madwoman in the Attic: The Woman Writer and the Nineteenth-Century Literary Imagination.* New Haven: Yale UP, 1979. Print.

Jacobus, Mary. *Women's Writing and Writing About Women.* New York: Barnes and Noble, 1979. Print.

Kauffman, Linda, ed. *Gender and Theory: Dialogues on Feminist Criticism.* New York: Blackwell, 1985. Print.

Kolodny, Annette. "Some Notes on Defining a 'Feminist Literary Criticism.'" *Critical Inquiry 2* (1975): 75–92. Print.

Lilly, Mark, ed. *Lesbian and Gay Writing.* London: Macmillan, 1990. Print.

Sedgwick, Eve Kosovsky. *Between Men: English Literature and Male Homosocial Desire.* New York: Columbia UP, 1985. Print.

Showalter, Elaine. *A Literature of Their Own: British Women Novelists from Bronte to Lessing.* Princeton: Princeton UP, 1977. Print.

Woods, Greg, *A History of Gay Literature.* New Haven: Yale UP, 1999. Print.

Economic Determinist/Marxist

The concept of cultural and economic determinism—and its corollary, the **economic determinist/Marxist critical approach**—is one of the major political ideas of the nineteenth century. Karl Marx (1818–1883) emphasized that the primary influence on life was economic, and he saw society enmeshed in a continuous conflict between capitalist oppressors and oppressed working people. The literature that emerged from this kind of analysis often features individuals who are coping with the ill effects of economic disadvantage. Sometimes called "proletarian" literature, it focuses on persons of the lower class—the poor and oppressed who spend their lives in endless drudgery and misery, and whose attempts to rise to the top usually result in renewed oppression.

Marx's political ideas were never widely accepted in the United States and have faded still more after the political breakup of the Soviet Union, but the idea of economic determinism (and the related term *Social Darwinism*) is still credible. As a result, much literature can be judged from an economic perspective even though the economic critics may not be Marxian: What is the economic status of the characters? What happens to them as a result of this status? How do they fare against economic and political odds? What other conditions stemming from their class does the writer emphasize (e.g., poor education, poor nutrition, poor health care, inadequate opportunity)? To what extent does the work fail by overlooking the economic, social, and political implications of its material? In what other ways does economic determinism affect the work? How should readers consider the story in today's developed or underdeveloped world? Seemingly, Hawthorne's story "Young Goodman Brown," which we have used for analysis in these discussions, has no major economic implications, but an economic determinist/Marxist critical approach might take the following turns. (See also p. 1547, for a Marxist reading of Ibsen's *A Dollhouse.*)

Example: Hawthorne's "Young Goodman Brown"

"Young Goodman Brown" is a fine story just as it is. It deals with the false values instilled by the skewed acceptance of sin-dominated religion, but it overlooks the economic implications of this situation. One might suspect that the real story in the little world of Goodman Brown's Salem should be about the disruption that an alienated member of society can produce. After Brown's condemnation and distrust of others forces him into his own shell of sick imagination, Hawthorne does not consider how such a disaffected character would injure the economic and public life of the town. Consider this, just for a moment: Why would the people from whom Brown recoils in disgust want to deal with him in business or personal matters? In town meetings, would they want to follow his opinions on crucial issues of public concern and investment? Would his preoccupation with sin and damnation make him anything more than a horror in his domestic life? Would his wife, Faith, be able to discuss household management with him or to ask him about methods of caring for the children? All these questions of course are pointed toward another story—a story that Hawthorne did not write. They also indicate the shortcomings of Hawthorne's approach, because it is clear that the major result of Young Goodman Brown's selfish preoccupation with evil would be a serious disruption of the economic and political affairs of his small community.

Second Example: Bambara's "The Lesson," page 387

Toni Cade Bambara's "The Lesson" explores the economic disparities among people who exist in close proximity in a modern American city. Set in New York, the narrator, Sylvia, a young African American girl, describes a day when she and her friends visit F.A.O. Schwarz, a toy store in Manhattan. They are escorted there by Miss Moore, a recently arrived college-educated woman to the neighborhood who takes it upon herself to help the neighborhood children see a small slice of the real world. At first, Sylvia disparages Miss Moore, saying how "she was always planning these boring ass things for us to do" and describes her physical features in great detail, such as her lack of makeup and "fish-white" feet. The day of the visit to the toy store is an eye-opening experience for the narrator and other children. At the store they see extravagantly expensive items such as a microscope that costs $300 and a "handcrafted sailboat of fiberglass at one thousand one hundred ninety-five dollars." The contrast between their economic situation and the opulence they are exposed to gradually helps the children see an aspect of the real world that they had not been aware of. One of the girls remarks that "'this is not much of a democracy if you ask me. Equal chance to pursue happiness means an equal crack at the dough, don't it?'" This comment is in such stark contrast to the earlier wisecracks of the children that it signals a sudden awareness of the realities of economic differences among people who live so close together. Economic differences are further highlighted by Sylvia's decision to keep what remains of the $5 Miss Moore gave her to pay taxi fare to the toy store. What remains is enough to "'get half a chocolate layer and then go to the Sunset and still have plenty of money for potato chips and ice cream sodas.'" The story ends on Sylvia's defiant tone. "But ain't nobody going to beat me at nuthin." This refers to her friend Sugar running ahead of her, but metaphorically points to the challenge that economic realities will play in her future life.

Readings

Adorno, Theodor. *Prisms: Cultural Criticism and Society.* 1955. London: Neville Spearman, 1967. Print.

Althusser, Louis. *For Marx.* New York: Pantheon, 1969. Print.

Bakhtin, Mikhail. *Between Phenomenology and Marxism.* New York: Cambridge UP, 1995. Print.

Demetz, Peter. *Marx, Engels, and the Poets: Origins of Marxist Literary Criticism.* Chicago: U of Chicago P, 1967. Print.

Dowling, William. *Jameson, Althusser, Marx: An Introduction to the Political Unconscious.* Ithaca: Cornell UP, 1984. Print.

Eagleton, Terry. *Criticism and Ideology: A Study in Marxist Literary Theory.* London: New Left, 1976. Print.

Frow, John. *Marxism and Literary History.* Ithaca: Cornell UP, 1986. Print.

Jameson, Frederic. *Marxism and Form: Twentieth Century Dialectical Theories of Literature.* Princeton: Princeton UP, 1971. Print.

Lukacs, Georg. *Realism in Our Time: Literature and the Class Struggle.* 1957. New York: Harper and Row, 1964. Print.

Marcuse, Herbert. *The Aesthetic Dimension: Toward a Critique of Marxist Aesthetics.* Boston: Beacon, 1978. Print.

Psychological/Psychoanalytic

The scientific study of the mind is a product of psychodynamic theory as established by Sigmund Freud (1856–1939) and of the psychoanalytic method practiced by his followers. Psychoanalysis provided a new key to the understanding of character by claiming that behavior is caused by hidden and unconscious motives. It was greeted as a revelation with far-reaching implications for all intellectual pursuits. Not surprisingly it has had a profound and continuing effect on post-Freudian literature.

In addition, its popularity produced the **psychological/psychoanalytic approach** to criticism.[2] Some critics use the approach to explain fictional characters, as in the landmark interpretation by Freud and Ernest Jones that Shakespeare's Hamlet suffers from an Oedipus complex. Still other critics use it as a way of analyzing authors and the artistic process. For example, John Livingston Lowes's study *The Road to Xanadu* presents a detailed examination of the mind, reading, and neuroses of Coleridge, the author of "Kubla Khan" (p. 612).

Critics using the psychoanalytic approach treat literature somewhat like information about patients in therapy. In the work itself, what are the obvious and hidden motives that cause a character's behavior and speech? How much background (e.g., repressed childhood trauma, adolescent memories) does the author reveal about a character? How purposeful is this information with regard to the character's psychological condition? How much is important in the analysis and understanding of the character?

In the consideration of authors, critics utilizing the psychoanalytic model consider questions like these: What particular life experiences explain characteristic subjects or preoccupations? Was the author's life happy? Miserable? Upsetting? Solitary? Social? Can the death of someone in the author's family be associated with melancholy situations in that author's work? All eleven brothers and sisters of the English poet Thomas Gray, for example, died before reaching adulthood. Gray was the only one of the twelve to survive. In his poetry, Gray often deals with death, and he is therefore considered one of the "Graveyard School" of eighteenth-century poets. A psychoanalytical critic might make much of this connection.

See also Chapter 3, "Characters: The People in Fiction," pages 176–237.

Example: Hawthorne's "Young Goodman Brown"

At the end of "Young Goodman Brown," Hawthorne's major character is no longer capable of normal existence. His nightmare should be read as a symbol of what in reality would have been lifelong mental subjection to the type of puritanical religion that emphasizes sin and guilt. Such preoccupation with sin is no hindrance to psychological health if the preoccupied people are convinced that God forgives them and grants them mercy. In their dealings with others, they remain healthy as long as they believe that other people have the same sincere trust in divine forgiveness. If their own faith is weak and uncertain, however, and if they cannot believe in forgiveness, then they are likely to transfer their own guilt—really a form of personal terror—to others. They remain conscious of their own sins, but they find it easy to claim that others are sinful—even those who are spiritually spotless, and even their own family, who should be dearest to them. When this process of projection or transference occurs, such people have created the rationale of condemning others because of their own guilt. The price that they pay is a life of gloom, a fate that Hawthorne designates for Goodman Brown after his nightmare about demons in human form.

Example: Browning's "My Last Duchess," page 892

"My Last Duchess" by Robert Browning is a dramatic monologue based loosely on the real-life Duke of Ferrara, Alfonso II (1533–1597). In presumably discussing a marriage proposal with an envoy, the duke reveals his jealousy, egocentrism, and greed. The duke points to a painting of his former duchess and notices her happy "countenance," which was easily aroused by strangers. From what we gather from Browning's poem about the malevolent duke, it is plausible that he had his apparently cheerful wife killed. Getting back to the business at hand, the duke escorts the envoy down the stairs, but not before pointing out a painting of Neptune "taming a seahorse." Besides indicating a love of possessions, his reference to the painting and its subject of taming also suggests a consciousness of subjugation and the desire to bend others to his will—certainly a sign of how he will treat the future duchess. While some psychological studies may point to the poet's frame of mind, "My Last Duchess" is a study of how a poem may imply a personality through a speaker's unsuspecting words.

Readings

Bloom, Harold. *The Anxiety of Influence.* New York: Oxford UP, 1975. Print.

Bowie, Malcolm. *Freud, Proust, and Lacan: Theory as Fiction.* New York: Cambridge UP, 1987. Print.

Gilbert, Sandra, and Susan Gubar. *The Madwoman in the Attic.* New Haven: Yale UP, 1979. Print.

Gilman, Sander L., ed. *Introducing Psychoanalytic Theory.* New York: Brunner/Mazel, 1982. Print.

Holland, Norman N. *The Dynamics of Literary Response.* New York: Oxford UP, 1968. Print.

Lacan, Jacques. *Ecrits: A Selection.* New York: Norton, 2004. Print.

Shamdsani, Sonu, and Michael Munchow, eds. *Speculations After Freud: Psychoanalysis, Philosophy, and Culture.* New York: Routledge, 1994. Print.

Skura, Meredith Anne. *The Literary Use of the Psychoanalytic Process*. New Haven: Yale UP, 1981. Print.

Wright, Elizabeth. *Psychoanalytic Criticism: Theory in Practice*. New York and London: Methuen, 1984. Print.

Archetypal/Symbolic/Mythic

The **archetypal/symbolic/mythic critical approach,** derived from the work of the Swiss psychoanalyst Carl Jung (1875–1961), presupposes that human life is built up out of patterns, or *archetypes* ("first molds" or "first patterns") that are similar throughout various cultures and historical times.[3] The approach is similar to the structuralist analysis of literature, because both approaches stress the connections that may be discovered in literature written in different times and in vastly different locations in the world.

In literary evaluation, the archetypal approach is used to support the claim that the very best literature is grounded in archetypal patterns. The archetypal critic therefore looks for archetypes such as God's creation of human beings, the sacrifice of a hero, or the search for paradise. How does an individual story, poem, or play fit into any of the archetypal patterns? What truths does this correlation provide (particularly truths that cross historical, national, and cultural lines)? How closely does the work fit the archetype? What variations can be seen? What meaning or meanings do the connections have?

The most tenuous aspect of archetypal criticism is Jung's assertion that the recurring patterns provide evidence for a "universal human consciousness" that all of us, by virtue of our humanity, still retain in our minds and in our very blood.

Not all critics accept the hypothesis of a universal human consciousness, but they nevertheless consider the approach important for comparisons and contrasts (p. 1589). Many human situations, such as adolescence, dawning love, the search for success, the reconciliation with one's mother and father, and the encroachment of age and death, are similar in structure and can be analyzed as archetypes. For example, the following situations can be seen as a pattern or archetype of initiation: A young man discovers the power of literature and understanding (Keats's "On First Looking into Chapman's Homer," p.641); a man determines the importance of truth and fidelity amidst uncertainty (Arnold's "Dover Beach," p.887); a man and woman fall in love despite their wishes to remain independent (Chekhov's *The Bear*, page 1322); a woman gains strength and integrity because of previously unrealized inner resources (Maupassant's "The Necklace," p.6). The archetypal approach encourages the analysis of variations on the same theme, as in Glaspell's "A Jury of Her Peers" (p. 202) and Faulkner's "A Rose for Emily" (p. 95) when characters choose to ignore the existence of a crime (one sort of initiation) and also, as a result, assert their own individuality and freedom (another sort of initiation).

Symbolism is also considered in Chapters 7 and 17.

Example: Hawthorne's "Young Goodman Brown"

In the sense that Young Goodman Brown undergoes a change from psychological normality to rigidity, the story is a reverse archetype of the initiation ritual. According to the archetype of successful initiation, initiates seek to demonstrate their worthiness to become full-fledged members of society. Telemachus in Homer's *Odyssey*, for example, is a young man who in the course of the epic goes through the initiation rituals of travel, discussion, and battle. But in "Young Goodman Brown" we see initiation in reverse, for just as there is an archetype of successful initiation, Brown's initiation leads him into failure. In the private areas of life on which happiness depends, he falls short. He sees evil in his fellow villagers, condemns his minister, and shrinks even from his own family. His life therefore becomes filled with despair and gloom. His suspicions are those of a Puritan of long ago, but the timeliness of Hawthorne's story is that the archetype of misunderstanding and condemnation has not changed. Today's headlines of misery and war are produced by the same kind of intolerance that is exhibited by Goodman Brown.

Second Example: Frost's "Birches," page 844

Interpreting Frost's poem "Birches" symbolically gives the poem a special depth that it otherwise might not have. On the literal level the poem is about a man who describes birch trees in winter and who states his belief that a lonely boy has perhaps been swinging on them. The poem moves from the third person to the first and we come to realize that the speaker is reminiscing about his own childhood: "So I was once myself a swinger of birches." Many of the rich images of the poem are sexually suggestive. The trunks of the trees are "trailing their leaves on the ground / Like girls on hands and knees that throw their hair / Before them over their heads to dry in the sun." The speaker also describes a boy "riding" the trees "Until he took the stiffness out of them." And while hanging on the tree branches he learned "about not launching out too soon." While these images have clear suggestions about sexuality, the poem ends with the alternate yearning to ride the trees toward heaven and to return back to earth. Reading the poem symbolically thus opens up resonant avenues of interpretation. Expression is given to the dual nature of humankind—physical and spiritual release. By describing the boy swinging on birch trees Frost is expressing the desire for sexual fulfillment and spiritual release from earthly constraints. A rich, evocative poem emerges when "Birches" is read symbolically.

Readings

Barber, C. L. *Shakespeare's Festive Comedy: A Study of Dramatic Form and Its Relation to Social Custom.* Princeton: Princeton UP, 1972. Print.

Bloom, Harold. *Shelley's Mythmaking.* New Haven: Yale UP, 1959. Print.

Bodkin, Maud. *Archetypal Patterns in Poetry.* London: Oxford UP, 1934. Print.

Bush, Douglas. *Mythology and the Renaissance Tradition in English Poetry.* New York: W. W. Norton, 1963. Print.

Chase, Richard. *Quest for Myth.* Baton Rouge: Louisiana State UP, 1949. Print.

Frye, Northrop. *Anatomy of Criticism: Four Essays.* Princeton: Princeton UP, 1957. Print.

Hyman, Stanley Edgar. *The Tangled Bank.* New York: Atheneum, 1962. Print.

Deconstructionist

The **deconstructionist critical approach**—which deconstructionists explain not as an approach but rather as a performance or as a strategy of reading—was developed by the French philosopher Jacques Derrida (1930–2004). In the 1970s and 1980s it became a major mode of criticism by critiquing a Western philosophical tradition known as *logocentrism*—the belief that speech is a direct expression of a speaker's intention, that it has a direct correspondence to reality, and that it is therefore the privileged arbiter of interpretation. By exposing what he saw as the fallacious assumptions of logocentrism, Derrida sought to undermine the basis of stable meanings derivable from language. The implications for reading and therefore for literary studies were far-reaching.

Deconstructionist critics begin literary analysis by assuming the instability of language and the impossibility of arriving at a fixed standard to anchor interpretation. The dictum, in Derrida's *Of Grammatology*, that "There is nothing outside the text" indicates the denial of any authoritative referent outside of words. Texts are always self-contradictory because they can always be reread to undermine an apparently stable interpretation. In part, this is due to how meaning is derived from binary oppositions such as speech/writing, male/female, good/ evil. Each word of the pair obtains its significance by contrast with the other, so that its meaning is relative, not absolute. A female may therefore be defined as lacking male features or a male as lacking female traits. In addition, each set of opposites has been arranged hierarchically; speech, for instance, is considered more immediate and therefore closer to reality than writing and therefore speech is the privileged member of the set speech/writing. These pairings are social constructs and form part of our way of thinking, even if they do not necessarily reflect reality.

Other strategies for undermining the stability of texts are to see how they have "gaps," or missing pieces of information, or words with several meanings and connotations, that therefore "de-center" the meaning of the texts. While a poem may seem to mean one thing when our habitual, formalistic reading strategies are applied to it, it can be shown to have a completely different meaning as well. Additional readings will yield still other meanings. The text is therefore said to "deconstruct" itself as the reading strategies applied to it are merely pointing out contradictory elements that inhere in the nature of language itself.

While formalist critics aim at resolving contradictions and ambiguities to form a unified literary work, deconstructionists aim to find disunity and disruptions in the language of a text. The typical deconstructionist strategy is to start with a standard formalistic reading of a text and then undermine that interpretation in order to yield a new one. The deconstructionist does not deny that interpretations are possible, only that there is no basis for appealing to final, absolute ones. Deconstruction has yielded some new, imaginative readings of canonical literature. Some critics of deconstruction argue that the "initial" formalistic readings of the deconstructionist strategy are the most rewarding and that often deconstructionist interpretations are incoherent.

Example: Hawthorne's "Young Goodman Brown"

There are many uncertainties in the details of "Young Goodman Brown." If one starts with the stranger on the path, one might conclude that he could be Brown's father, because he recognizes Brown immediately and speaks to him jovially. On the other hand, the stranger could be the devil (he is recognized as such by Goody Cloyse) because of his wriggling walking stick. After disappearing, the stranger also takes on the characteristics of an omniscient cult leader and seer, because at the satanic celebration he knows all the secret sins committed by Brown's neighbors and the community of greater New England. Additionally, he might represent a perverted conscience whose aim is to mislead and befuddle people by steering them into the holier-than-thou judgmental attitude that Brown adopts. This method would be truly diabolical—to use religion in order to bring people to their own damnation. That the stranger is an evil force is therefore clear, but the pathways of his evil are not as clear. He seems to work his mission of damnation by reaching the souls of persons like Goodman Brown through means ordinarily attributed to conscience. If the stranger represents a satanic conscience, what are we to suppose that Hawthorne is asserting about what is considered real conscience?

Second Example: Auden's "Musée des Beaux Arts," page 888

"Musée des Beaux Arts" may be read as a poem about an indifferent universe in the face of human suffering. Auden posits the "old master" painters of the Renaissance as depicting this situation correctly: "About suffering they were never wrong." Suffering apparently takes place in the midst of the dull happenings of everyday life, the speaker asserts. The poem ends by focusing on a specific example—Breughel's depiction of the mythic Icarus, who fell into the sea because he flew too close to the sun. No notice is apparently taken by the characters in the painting of the splash made by the falling body as it enters the water. While the poem may be read as being unified around the theme of indifference to suffering, alternate interpretations arise when the poem is deconstructed. The title of the poem indicates the museum where Breughel's painting may be seen. Museums are, in part, repositories of historical events. By referring to a painting in a specific place, Auden lets the reader know that he or she may see a depiction of Icarus's suffering. While the figures in the painting turn away from the fallen Icarus, the observer of the painting—like the reader of the poem—is made conscious of Icarus's story and his suffering. While the dichotomy-event (Icarus falling)/depiction of event (painting and poem of Icarus falling) may suggest a priority to the event itself, it is ironically Auden's poem that encourages us to think of the anguish Icarus must have felt as he fell. In describing the "white legs [of Icarus] disappearing into the green/Water," Auden focuses our attention to suffering and death. "Turns" is a key word in the poem. Auden describes how everyone in the scene "turns away/Quite leisurely from the disaster." Just as something may turn away from an event, the same motion of turning may return us to the same event, in this instance, a contemplation of suffering. While indifference to suffering may be one theme of "Musée des Beaux Arts," deconstructing the poem also shows how it "pulls" in other directions. The language of the poem itself tugs the reader in different directions.

Readings

Abrams, M. H. "The Deconstructive Angel." *Doing Things with Texts*. New York and London: Norton, 1989. Print.

Arac, Jonathan, Wlad Godzich, and Wallace Martin, eds. *The Yale Critics: Deconstruction in America*. Minneapolis: U of Minnesota P, 1983. Print.

De Man, Paul. *Blindness and Insight*. New York: Oxford UP, 1971. Print.

Derrida, Jacques. *Of Grammatology*. 1967. Baltimore: Johns Hopkins UP, 1976. Print.

_____. *Writing and Difference*. 1967. Chicago: U of Chicago P, 1978. Print.

Hartman, Geoffrey. *Saving the Text: Literature/Derrida/Philosophy*. Baltimore: Johns Hopkins UP, 1981 Print.

Miller, J. Hillis. *Fiction and Repetition: Seven English Novels*. Cambridge: Harvard UP, 1982. Print.

_____. *The Linguistic Moment: From Wordsworth to Stevens*. Princeton: Princeton UP, 1985. Print.

_____. *The Ethics of Reading: Kant, de Man, Eliot, Trollope, James, and Benjamin*. New York: Columbia UP, 1987. Print.

Silverman, Hugh J., and Gary E. Aylesworth, eds. *The Textual Sublime: Deconstruction and Its Differences*. Albany: State U of New York P, 1990. Print.

Reader-Response

The **reader-response critical approach** is rooted in *phenomenology*, a branch of philosophy that deals with the understanding of how things appear. The phenomenological idea of knowledge is based on the separation of the reality of our thoughts from the reality of the world. Our quest for truth is to be found not in the external world itself but rather in our mental *perception* and interpretation of externals. All that we human beings can know—actual *knowledge*—is our collective and personal understanding of the world and our conclusions about it.

As a consequence of the phenomenological concept, reader-response theory holds that the reader is a necessary third party in the author-text-reader relationship that constitutes the literary work. The work, in other words, is not fully created until readers make a *transaction* with it by assimilating it and *actualizing* it in the light of their own knowledge and experience. The representative questions of the theory are these: What does this work mean to me, in my present intellectual and moral makeup? How can the work improve my understanding and widen my insights? How can my increasing understanding help me understand the work more deeply? The theory is that the free interchange or transaction that such questions bring about leads toward interest and growth, so that readers can assimilate literary works and accept them as parts of their lives and as parts of the civilization in which they live.

As an initial way of reading, the reader-response method may be personal and anecdotal. In addition, by stressing response rather than interpretation, one of the leading exponents of the method (Stanley Fish) has raised the extreme question about whether texts, by themselves, have objective identity. These aspects have been cited as both a shortcoming and an inconsequentiality of the method.

It is therefore important to stress that the reader-response theory is *open*. It permits beginning readers to bring their own personal reactions to literature, but it also aims to increase their discipline and skill. The more that readers bring to literature through their interests and disciplined studies, the more "competent" and comprehensive their "transactions" will be. It is possible, for example, to explain the structure of a work not according to commonly recognized categories such as exposition and climax but rather according to the personal reactions of representative readers. The contention is that structure, like other avenues of literary study such as tone or the comprehension of figurative language, refers to clearly definable responses that readers experience when reading and transacting with works. By such means, literature is subject not only to outward and objective analysis but also to inward and psychological response.

The reader-response approach thus lends an additional dimension to the critical awareness of literature. If literary works imply that readers should possess special knowledge in fields such as art, politics, science, philosophy, religion, or morality, then competent readers will seek out such knowledge and utilize it in developing their responses. Also, because students experience many similar intellectual and cultural disciplines, it is logical to conclude that responses will tend not to diverge but rather to coalesce; agreements result not from personal but from cultural similarities. The reader-response theory, then, can and should be an avenue toward informed and detailed understanding of literature, but the initial emphasis is the *transaction* that readers make with literary works.

Example: Hawthorne's "Young Goodman Brown"

"Young Goodman Brown" is worrisome because it shows so disturbingly that good intentions may cause harmful results. I think that a person with too high a set of expectations is ripe for disillusionment, just as Goodman Brown is. When people don't measure up to this person's standard of perfection, they can be thrown aside as though they are worthless. They may be good people, but whatever past mistakes they have made make it impossible for the person with high expectations to endure them. Goodman Brown makes the same kind of misjudgment, expecting perfection and turning sour when he learns about flaws. It is not that he is not a good man, because he is shown at the start as a person of belief and stability. He uncritically accepts his nightmare revelation that everyone else is evil, however (including his parents), and he finally distrusts everyone because of this baseless suspicion. He cannot look at his neighbors without avoiding them like an "anathema," and he turns away from his own wife "without a greeting" (p. 349). Brown's problem is that he equates being human with being unworthy. By such a distorted standard of judgment, all of us fail, and that is what makes the story so disturbing.

Second Example: Roethke's "My Papa's Waltz," page 706

"My Papa's Waltz" by Theodore Roethke shows how complicated relationships between father and son may be. While it is the memory of a spirited "waltz" that the speaker, as a child, had with his father, the emotions it evokes are not so easy to pin down. On the one hand, the speaker recalls what might have seemed a happy time, with father and son romping "until the pans / slid from the kitchen shelf" and the boy danced off to bed "Still clinging to your [the father's] shirt." There is, however, a darker side to this memory as suggested by images that border on abuse. The whiskey on the father's breath "Could make a small boy dizzy." Also, the father "scraped a buckle" every time he missed a step of the dance and "beat time" on the boy's head; in addition, the speaker's memory is that his mother was an unhappy witness to this rough play. That her "countenance / Could not unfrown itself" suggests a disapproving uneasiness. The regular stanzas and short lines indicate the symmetry and balance of an orderly dance, but the more disturbing images imply violence. This double-edged emotion points to the complex nature of love and the ambivalent feelings we may have toward a parent. We might wish sometimes that our memories could be resolved into one overwhelming feeling, but "My Papa's Waltz," through its rich imagery, evokes the true nature of most relationships. They aren't easily categorized.

Readings

Altick, Richard. *The English Common Reader: A Social History of the Mass Reading Public 1800–1900.* Chicago: U of Chicago P, 1957. Print.

Bleich, David. *Readings and Feelings: An Introduction to Subjective Criticism.* Urbana: National Council of Teachers of English, 1975. Print.

Booth, Wayne C. *The Rhetoric of Fiction.* 2nd ed. Chicago: U of Chicago P, 1983. Print.

Fish, Stanley. *Is There a Text in This Class? The Authority of Interpretive Communities.* Cambridge: Harvard UP, 1980. Print.

Holland, Norman N. *The Dynamics of Literary Response.* New York: Oxford UP, 1968. Print.

Iser, Wolfgang. *The Implied Reader: Pattern of Communication in Prose Fiction From Bunyan to Beckett.* Baltimore: Johns Hopkins UP, 1974. Print.

Leavis, Q. D. *Fiction and the Reading Public.* London: Chatto and Windus, 1932. Print.

Mailloux, Steven J. *Interpretive Conventions.* Ithaca: Cornell UP, 1982. Print.

Richards, I. A. *Practical Criticism: A Study of Literary Judgment.* New York: Harcourt, Brace, 1935. Print.

Sartre, Jean-Paul. *What Is Literature?* New York: Philosophical Library, 1966. Print.

Suleiman, Susan, and Inge Crosman, eds. *The Reader in the Text: Essays on Audience and Interpretation.* Princeton: Princeton UP, 1980. Print.

Chapter 26
Three Types of Writing About Literature

AFTER STUDYING THIS MATERIAL, YOU SHOULD BE ABLE TO DO THE FOLLOWING:

- Employ comparison-contrast writing strategies to analyze multiple works critically
- Employ reader-response writing strategies to interpret a literary work in light of a reader's personal experiences
- Employ argumentative writing strategies to make a convincing case for your interpretation of a work

1. Comparison-Contrast and Extended Comparison-Contrast

Comparison-contrast analysis and extended comparison-contrast analysis are the acts of putting literary works side by side—juxtaposing them, looking at them together—for a variety of purposes such as description, enhanced understanding, evaluation, and decision making. The technique underlies other important techniques, specifically (1) the analysis of causes and effects, and (2) the scientific method of constant-and-variable analysis. Significant questions may be asked about all these methods: How is *A* both like and unlike *B*? What are the causes of *A*? How does a change in *A* affect *B*? These are all questions that call into play the technique of comparison and contrast.

The educational significance of the technique is to encourage you to make connections—*one of the most important aspects of productive thinking*. As long as things *seem* different and disconnected they in fact *are* different and disconnected. In practice, they are two separate and distinct entities. But when you can demonstrate that they have similarities and connections, then you can make relationships clear. You are in a position both to stress points of likeness and also to emphasize just what makes literary works distinct and unique. For all these reasons, it is vital for you to find similarities and differences through the technique of comparison and contrast. In a very real sense, the language of comparison and contrast is also the language of active and creative thinking.

The immediate goals of a comparison-contrast essay on literary works are to compare and contrast different authors; two or more works by the same author; different drafts of the same work; or characters, incidents, techniques, and ideas in the same work or in a number of separate works. Developing a comparison-contrast analysis enables you to study works in perspective. No matter what works you consider together, the method helps you get at the essence of a work or writer. Similarities are brought out by comparison; differences are brought out by contrast. In other words, you can enhance your understanding of what a thing *is* by using comparison-contrast to determine what it *is not*.

For example, our understanding of Shakespeare's Sonnet 30, "When to the Sessions of Sweet Silent Thought" (Chapter 14, p. 663) can be augmented if we compare it with Denise Levertov's poem "A Time Past" (Chapter 13, p. 621). Both poems treat recollections of past experiences told by a speaker to a listener, and we as readers become, as it were, witnesses to the poems. Both poems refer to persons, dead or absent, with whom the speakers were closely involved. In these respects, the poems are comparable.

In addition to these similarities, there are significant differences. Shakespeare's speaker numbers the dead persons as friends whom he laments generally. Levertov's speaker refers to a number of vanished people, but her major focus is on one person with whom she had been in love, whose sight at one time made her joyful and happy. Levertov's topics are the sorrow of past memory and lost love, the inexorable power of change, and the causes of isolation and regret. Shakespeare refers to dead friends as a way of accounting for present sorrows, but then his speaker turns to the present and asserts that thinking about the "dear friend" being addressed enables him to restore past "losses" and end all "sorrows." In Levertov's poem, there is recognition of both past and present, but no reconciliation. Instead the speaker focuses on the unpleasantness and distastefulness of the changes that time has wrought. Both poems are similarly retrospective, but they differ widely in their conclusions about how the present has been altered by the past.

Guidelines for the Comparison-Contrast Method

The preceding example, although brief, shows how the comparison-contrast method makes it possible to identify leading similarities and distinguishing differences in two works. Frequently you can overcome the difficulties you might encounter in understanding one work by comparing and contrasting it with another work on a comparable subject. A few guidelines will help direct your efforts in writing comparison-contrast essays.

Clarify Your Intention

When planning a comparison-contrast essay, first decide on your goal, for you can use the method in a number of ways. One objective is the equal and mutual illumination of two (or more) works. For example, in an essay comparing Welty's "A Worn Path" (Chapter 5, p. 288) with Hawthorne's "Young Goodman Brown" (Chapter 7, p. 342) you might (1) compare ideas, characters, or methods in these stories equally, without stressing or favoring either; (2) emphasize "Young Goodman Brown," and therefore use "A Worn Path" as material for highlighting Hawthorne's story; (3) illustrate the superiority of one story over another; or (4) emphasize a method or idea that you think is especially noteworthy or appropriate.

A first task, therefore, is to decide what to emphasize. The illustrative essay on pages 1596–99 gives "equal time" to both works being considered, without claiming the superiority of either. Unless you have a different rhetorical goal, this essay provides a suitable example for most comparisons.

Find Common Grounds for Comparison

The second stage in preparing a comparison-contrast essay is to select and articulate a common ground for discussion. It is pointless to compare dissimilar things, because the resulting conclusions will not have much value. Instead, compare like with like: idea with idea, characterization with characterization, setting with setting, point of view with point of view, tone with tone. Nothing much can be learned from a comparison of Frost's view of individuality and Chekhov's view of love, but a comparison of the relationship of individuality with identity and character in Frost and Chekhov suggests common ground, with the promise of significant ideas to be developed through the examination of similarities and differences.

In seeking common ground, you will need to be inventive and creative. For instance, if you compare Maupassant's "The Necklace" (p. 7) and Chekhov's *The Bear* (p. 1322), these two works at first may seem dissimilar. Yet common ground can be discovered, such as the treatment of self-deceit, the effects of chance on human affairs, and the authors' views of women. Although other works may seem even more dissimilar than these, it is usually possible to find a common ground for comparison and contrast. Much of your success in an essay of this type depends on your finding a workable basis—a common denominator—for comparison.

Integrate the Bases of Comparison

Let us assume that you have decided on your rhetorical purpose and on the basis or bases of your comparison. You have done your reading and taken notes, and you have a rough idea of what you want to say. The remaining problem is the treatment of your material.

One method is to make your points first about one work and then about the other. Unfortunately, such a comparison makes your paper seem like two separate lumps. ("Work 1" takes up one half of your paper to make one lump, and "Work 2" takes up the other half to make a second lump.) Also, the method involves repetition because you must repeat many points when you treat the second subject.

Therefore, a better method is to treat the major aspects of your main idea and to refer to the two (or more) works as they support your arguments. Thus you refer constantly to *both* works, sometimes within the same sentence, and remind your reader of the point of your discussion. There are reasons for the superiority of this method: (1) You do not repeat your points needlessly, for you develop them as you raise them. (2) By constantly referring to the two works, you make your points without requiring a reader with a poor memory to reread previous sections.

As a model, here is a paragraph on "Night and the Natural World as a Basis of Comparison in Frost's 'Desert Places' (p. 741) and Arnold's 'Dover Beach' (p. 887)." The virtue of the paragraph is that it uses material from each of the poems simultaneously as the substance for the development of the ideas, as nearly as the time sequence of sentences allows. For illustration, the sentences are numbered.

(1) Both Frost's and Arnold's poems begin by describing in detail the evening landscapes in front of the speakers, which cause them to then contemplate life and mortality. (2) As the night woods fill with snow, Frost makes a connection between the onset of winter and the beginning of death and the desolation of the natural world. (3) With this natural description, Frost also symbolically refers to empty, secret, dead places in the inner spirit—crannies of the soul where bleak winter snowfalls correspond to selfishness and indifference. (4) In stark contrast, Arnold describes an inviting, lovely evening scene on the English coast, with gleaming moonlight on the waves and sweet night air. (5) However, this seemingly pleasant world, which should not be frightening at all, causes the speaker to contemplate how the natural world has remained constant and unchanging through time while all human life is fleeting and fragile. (6) Both poems therefore employ scenes of the natural world at night as focal points for thinking about the meaning of life. (7) Because Arnold's poem is addressed to a lover, the speaker uses his observations of life's transience as an argument for the couple to commit to one another. (8) Frost, on the other hand, turns the snow and the emptiness of the universe inward to show the speaker's inner bleakness, and, by extension, the fearfulness of life. (9) The poems thus use common and similar points of reference for quite different purposes and effects.

This paragraph links Arnold's use of the night setting to that of Frost. Three sentences speak of both authors together; three speak of Frost alone and three of Arnold alone, but all the sentences are unified topically. This interweaving of references indicates that the writer has learned both poems well enough to consider them together, and it also enables the writing to be more pointed and succinct than if the works were separately treated.

You can learn from this example: If you develop your essay by putting your two subjects constantly together, you will write economically and pointedly (not only for essays but also for tests). Beyond that, if you digest the material as successfully as this method indicates, you demonstrate that you are fulfilling a major educational goal—the assimilation and *use* of material. Too often, because you learn things separately (in separate works and courses, at separate times), you tend also to compartmentalize them. Instead, you should always try to relate them, to *synthesize* them. Comparison and contrast help in this process of putting together, of seeing things not as fragments but as parts of wholes.

Avoid the Tennis-Ball Method

As you make your comparison, do not confuse an interlocking method with a "tennis-ball" method, in which you bounce your subject back and forth constantly and repetitively, almost as though you were hitting observations back and forth over a net. The tennis-ball method is shown in the following example from a comparison of the characters Mathilde (Maupassant's "The Necklace") and Mrs. Popov (Chekhov's *The Bear*).

Mathilde is a young married woman; Mrs. Popov is also young but a widow. Mathilde has a limited social life, and she doesn't have more than one friend; Mrs. Popov chooses to lead a life of solitude. Mathilde's daydreams about wealth are responsible for her misfortune, and Mrs. Popov's dedication to the memory of her husband is capable of ruining her life. Mathilde is made unhappy because of her shortcomings, but Mrs. Popov is rescued despite her shortcomings. In Mathilde's case the focus is on adversity not only causing trouble but also strengthening character. Similarly, in Mrs. Popov's case the focus is on a strong person realizing her strength regardless of her conscious decision to weaken herself.

Imagine the effect of an entire essay written in this invariable 1, 2, 1, 2, 1, 2 order. Aside from the inflexible patterning of subjects, the tennis-ball method does not permit much illustrative development. You should not feel so constrained that you cannot take two or more sentences to develop a point about one writer or subject before you include comparative references to another. If you remember to interlock the two subjects of comparison, however, as in the paragraph about Frost and Shakespeare, your method will give you the freedom to develop your topics fully.

The Extended Comparison-Contrast Essay

For a longer essay about a number of works—such as a limited research paper, comprehensive exam questions, and the sort of extended essay required at the end of a semester—comparison-contrast is an essential method. You may wish to compare the works on the basis of elements such as ideas, plot, language, structure, character, metaphor, point of view, or setting. Because of the larger number of works, however, you will need to modify the way in which you employ comparison-contrast. Suppose you are dealing with not just two works but with six, seven, or more. You need first to find a common ground to use as your central, unifying idea, just as you do for a comparison of only two works. Once you establish the common ground, you can classify or group your works on the basis of the similarities and differences they exemplify with regard to the topic. The idea is to get two *groups* for comparison, not just *two works*.

Let us assume that three or four works treat a topic in one way but that two or three do it in another (e.g., either criticism or praise of wealth and trade, the joys or sorrows of love, the enthusiasm of youth, gratitude for life, or the disillusionment of age). In writing about these works, you might treat the topic itself in a straightforward comparison-contrast method but use details from the works within the groupings as the material that you use for illustration and argument.

To make your essay as specific as possible, it is best to stress only a small number of works with each of your subpoints. Once you have established these points, there is no need to go into abundant detail with all the other works you are studying. Instead, you need to make no more than brief references to the other works, for your purpose should be to strengthen your points without creating more and more examples. Once you go to another subpoint, you should then use different works for illustration, so that by the end of your essay, you will have given due attention to each work in your assignment. In this way—by treating many works in small comparative groups—you can keep your essay reasonably brief, for there is no need to go into unproductive detail.

As an example, the illustrative essay on pages 1600–04 shows how this grouping may be done. In the first part of the body of this essay, six works are used comparatively to show how private needs conflict with social and public demands. The next part shows how three works can be compared and contrasted in the ways they treat the topic of public concerns as expressed through law.

CITING REFERENCES IN A LONGER COMPARISON-CONTRAST ESSAY

For the longer comparison-contrast essay, you may find a problem in making references to many different works. Generally you do not need to repeat references. For example, if you refer to Louise of Chopin's "The Story of an Hour" (Chapter 6) or to Minnie Wright of Glaspell's "A Jury of Her Peers" (Chapter 3), you should make the full references only once and then refer later just to the character, story, or author, according to your needs.

When you quote lines or passages or when you cite actions or characters in special ways, you should use parenthetical references, as in the illustrative essay on page 1604. Be guided by the following principle: If you make a specific reference that you think your reader might want to examine in more detail, supply the line or page number. If you refer to minor details that might easily be unnoticed or forgotten, also supply the appropriate number. Your intention should be to include the appropriate locating numbers whenever you are in doubt about references.

WRITING A COMPARISON-CONTRAST ESSAY

In planning your essay, you should first narrow and simplify your topic so that you can handle it conveniently. If your subject is a comparison of two poets (as in the illustrative comparison-contrast essay on Lowell and Owen, p. 1596), choose one or two of each poet's poems on the same or a similar topic, and write your essay about these.

Once you have found an organizing principle, along with the relevant works, begin to refine and to focus the direction of your essay. As you study each work, note common or contrasting elements and use these to form your central idea. At the same time, you can select the most illustrative works and classify them according to your topic, such as war, love, work, faithfulness, or self-analysis.

Strategies for Organizing Ideas

Begin by stating the works, authors, characters, or ideas that you are considering; then show how you have narrowed the topic. Your central idea should briefly highlight the principal grounds of comparison and contrast, such as that both works treat a common topic, exhibit a similar idea, use a similar form, or develop an identical attitude, and also that major or minor differences help make the works unique. You may also assert that one work is superior to the other, if you wish to make this judgment and defend it.

The body of your essay is governed by the works and your basis of comparison (presentations of ideas, depictions of character, uses of setting, qualities of style and tone, uses of poetic form, uses of comparable imagery or symbols, uses of point of view, and so on). For a comparison-contrast treatment on such a basis, your goal should be to shed light on both (or more) of the works you are treating. For example, you might examine stories written in the first-person point of view (see Chapter 2). An essay on this topic might compare the ways in which each author uses point of view to achieve similar or distinct effects, or it might compare poems that employ similar images, symbols, or ironic methods. Sometimes, the process can be as simple as identifying female or male protagonists and comparing the ways in which their characters are developed. Another obvious approach is to compare the *subjects*, as opposed to the *idea*. You might identify works dealing with general subjects such as love, death, youth, race, or war. Such groupings provide a basis for excellent comparisons and contrasts.

As you develop your essay, remember to keep comparison-contrast foremost. That is, your discussions of point of view, figurative language, or whatever should not so much explain these topics *as topics* but rather should explore similarities and differences of the works you are comparing. If your topic is an idea, for example, you need to explain the idea, but just enough to establish points of similarity or difference. As you develop such an essay, you might illustrate your arguments by referring to related uses of elements such as setting, characterization, symbolism, point of view, or metaphor. When you introduce these new subjects, you will be on target as long as you use them in the context of comparison-contrast.

In concluding, you might reflect on other ideas or techniques in the works you have compared, make observations about similar qualities, or summarize briefly the grounds of your comparison. If there is a point you have considered especially important, you might stress that point again in your conclusion. Also, your comparison might have led you to conclude that one work—or group of works—is superior to another. Stressing that point again would make an effective conclusion.

Illustrative Student Essay (Two Works)

Although underlined sentences are not recommended by MLA style, they are used in this illustrative essay as teaching tools to emphasize the central idea, thesis sentence, and topic sentences.

Mane 1

Marcelino Manc

Professor Park

English 123

11 April 2014

The Treatment of Responses to War in Amy Lowell's "Patterns"

and Wilfred Owen's "Anthem for Doomed Youth"°

[1]   Lowell's "Patterns" and Owen's "Anthem for Doomed Youth" are both underlined: powerful and unique condemnations of war.* Owen's short poem speaks broadly and generally about the ugliness of war and also about large groups of sorrowful people. Lowell's longer poem focuses on the personal grief of just one person. In a sense, Lowell's poem begins where Owen's ends, a fact that accounts for both the similarities and the differences between the two works. The antiwar themes can be compared on the basis of their subjects, their lengths, their concreteness, and their use of a common metaphor.†

[2]   "Anthem for Doomed Youth" attacks war more directly than "Patterns." Owen's opening line "What passing-bells for those who die as cattle?" suggests that in war human beings are depersonalized before they are slaughtered, like so much meat, and his observations about the "monstrous" guns and the "shrill, demented" shells unambiguously condemn the horrors of war. By contrast, in "Patterns," warfare is far away, on another continent, intruding only when the messenger delivers the letter stating that the speaker's fiancé has been killed (lines 63–64). A comparable situation governs the last six lines of Owen's poem, quietly describing how those at home respond to the news that their loved ones have died in war. Thus the antiwar focus in "Patterns" is the contrast between the calm, peaceful life of the speaker's garden and the anguish of her responses.

°These poems appear in Chapter 19 and Chapter 13, respectively.
*Central idea.
†Thesis sentence.

Mane 2

In "Anthem for Doomed Youth," the stress is more on the external horrors of war that bring about the need for ceremonies honoring the dead.

Another major difference between the poems is their wide discrepancy   [3]
in length. "Patterns" is an interior monologue or meditation of 107 lines, but it could not be shorter and still be convincing. In the poem the speaker thinks of the past and contemplates her future loneliness. Her final outburst, "Christ! What are patterns for?" could make no sense if she did not explain her situation as extensively as she does. "Anthem for Doomed Youth," however, is brief—a fourteen-line sonnet—because it is more general and less personal than "Patterns." Although Owen's speaker shows great sympathy, he or she views the sorrows of others distantly, unlike Lowell, who goes right into the mind and spirit of the grieving woman. Owen's use, in his last six lines, of phrases such as "tenderness of patient minds" and "drawing down of blinds" is a powerful representation of deep grief. He gives no further details even though thousands of individual stories might be told. In contrast, Lowell tells just one of these stories as she focuses on her solitary speaker's lost hopes and dreams. Thus the contrasting lengths of the poems are determined by each poet's treatment of the topic.

Despite these differences of approach and length, both poems are similarly   [4]
concrete and real. Owen moves from the real scenes and sounds of far-off battlefields to the homes of the many soldiers who have been killed in battle, but Lowell's scene is a single place—the garden of her speaker's estate. The speaker walks on real gravel along garden paths that contain daffodils, squills, a fountain, and a lime tree. She thinks of her clothing and her ribboned shoes, and also of her fiancé's boots, sword hilts, and buttons. The images in Owen's poem are equally real but are not associated with individuals as in "Patterns." Thus Owen's images are those of cattle, bells, rifle shots, shells, bugles, candles, and window blinds. Although both poems reflect reality, Owen's details are more general and public; Lowell's are more specific and intimate.

Along with this concreteness, the poems share a major metaphor: that   [5]
cultural patterns both control and frustrate human wishes and hopes.

Mane 3

In "Patterns," this metaphor is shown in warfare itself (106), which is the pinnacle of organized human patterns of destruction. Further examples of the metaphor are found in details about clothing (particularly the speaker's stiff, confining gown in lines 5, 18, 21, 73, and 101, and also the lover's military boots in lines 46 and 49); the orderly, formal garden paths in which the speaker is walking (1 and 93); her restraint at hearing about her lover's death; and her courtesy, despite her grief, in ordering refreshment for the messenger (69). Within such rigid patterns, her hopes for happiness have vanished, along with the sensuous spontaneity symbolized by her lover's hope to make love with her on a "shady seat" in the garden (85–89). The metaphor of the constricting pattern is also seen in "Anthem for Doomed Youth," except that in this poem, the pattern is the funeral, not love or marriage. Owen's speaker contrasts the calm, peaceful tolling of "passing-bells" (1) to the frightening sounds of war represented by the "monstrous anger of the guns," "the stuttering rifles' rapid rattle," and "the demented choirs of wailing shells" (2–8). Thus, while Lowell uses the metaphor to reveal the irony of hope and desire being destroyed by war, Owen uses it to reveal the irony of war's negation of peaceful ceremonies.

[6]   Though in these ways the poems share topics and some aspects of treatment, they are distinct and individual. "Patterns" includes many references to visible things, whereas "Anthem for Doomed Youth" emphasizes sound (and silence). Both poems conclude on powerfully emotional although different notes. Owen's poem dwells on the pathos and sadness that war brings to many unnamed people, and Lowell's expresses the most intimate thoughts of a woman who is alone in her first agony of grief. Although neither poem attacks the usual platitudes and justifications for war (the needs to mobilize, to sacrifice, to achieve peace through fighting, and so on), the attack is there by implication, for both poems make their appeal by stressing how war destroys the relationships that make life worth living. For this reason, despite their differences, both "Patterns" and "Anthem for Doomed Youth" are parallel anti-war poems, and both are strong expressions of feeling.

Mane 4

Works Cited

Lowell, Amy. "Patterns." *Literature: An Introduction to Reading and Writing, Compact Edition.* Ed. Edgar V. Roberts and Robert Zweig. 6th ed. New York: Pearson, 2015. 921–23. Print.

Owen, Wilfred. "Anthem for Doomed Youth." *Literature: An Introduction to Reading and Writing, Compact Edition.* Ed. Edgar V. Roberts and Robert Zweig. 6th ed. New York: Pearson, 2015. 607. Print.

Commentary on the Essay

This essay shows how approximately equal attention can be given to the two works being studied. Words stressing similarity are *common, share, equally, parallel, both, similar,* and *also*. Contrasts are stressed by *while, whereas, different, dissimilar, contrast, although,* and *except*. Transitions from paragraph to paragraph are not different in this type of essay from those in other essays. Thus, the phrases *despite, along with this,* and *in these ways,* which are used here, could be used anywhere for the same transitional purpose.

The central idea—that the poems mutually condemn war—is brought out in paragraph 1, together with the supporting idea that the poems blend into each other because both show responses to news of battle casualties.

Paragraph 2, the first in the body, discusses how each poem brings out its attack on warfare. Paragraph 3 explains the differing lengths of the poems as a function of differences in perspective. Because Owen's sonnet views war and its effects at a distance, it is brief, but because Lowell's interior monologue views death intimately, she provides more detail and greater length.

Paragraph 4, on the topic of concreteness and reality, shows that the two works can receive equal attention without the bouncing back and forth of the tennis-ball method. Three of the sentences in this paragraph (3, 4, and 6) are devoted exclusively to details in one poem or the other, but sentences 1, 2, 5, and 7 refer to both works, stressing points of broad or specific comparison. The scheme demonstrates that the two works are, in effect, interlocked within the paragraph.

Paragraph 5, the last in the body, considers the similar and dissimilar ways in which the poems treat the common metaphor of cultural patterns.

The conclusion, paragraph 6, summarizes the central idea, and it also stresses the ways in which the poems, although similar, are distinct and unique.

Illustrative Student Essay (Extended Comparison-Contrast)

Although underlined sentences are not recommended by MLA style, they are used in this illustrative essay as teaching tools to emphasize the central idea, thesis sentence, and topic sentences.

Mane 1

Marcelino Mane

Professor Park

English 123

19 May 2014

Literary Treatments of the Conflicts Between Private and Public Life

[1]   The conflict between private or personal life, on the one hand, and public or civic and national life, on the other, is a topic common to many literary works.° Authors show that individuals try to maintain their personal lives and commitments even though they are tested and stressed by public and external forces. Ideally, individuals should have the freedom to follow their own wishes independently of the outside world. It is a fact, however, that living itself causes people to venture into the public world and therefore to encounter conflicts. Getting married, following a profession, observing the natural world, looking at a person's possessions, taking a walk—all these draw people into the public world in which rules, regulations, and laws override private wishes. To greater and lesser degrees, such conflicts are found in Arnold's "Dover Beach," Bierce's "An Occurrence at Owl Creek Bridge," Chekhov's *The Bear*, Glaspell's *Trifles*, Chopin's "The Story of an Hour," Hardy's "Channel Firing," Hawthorne's "Young Goodman Brown," Keats's "Bright Star," and Lowell's "Patterns."* In these works, conflicts are shown between interests of individuals and those of the social, legal, and military public.†

°Central idea.
*These works appear in Chapters 19, 1, 22, 20, 6, 13, 7, 14, 19, respectively.
†Thesis sentence.

Mane 2

One of the major private-public conflicts is created by the way in which [2]
characters respond to social conventions and expectations. In Chekhov's *The
Bear*, for example, Mrs. Popov has given up her personal life to memorialize
her dead husband. She resolves to wear black, to swear eternal fidelity, and
to stay in her house for an entire year. And she does all this to fulfill what she
considers her public role as a grieving widow. Fortunately for her, Smirnov
arrives on the scene and arouses her enough to make her give up this foolish
pose. Not as fortunate is Hawthorne's Goodman Brown in "Young Goodman
Brown." Brown's obligation is much less public and also more philosophical
than Mrs. Popov's because his religiously inspired vision of evil fills him with
lifelong gloom. Although Mrs. Popov is easily moved away from her position
by the prospect of immediate life and vitality, Brown's mindless distrust locks
him into a fear of evil from which not even his faithful wife can shake him. The
two characters therefore go in entirely different directions—Mrs. Popov toward
personal fulfillment and Goodman Brown toward personal destruction.

A major idea in the various works is that philosophical or religious [3]
difficulties such as those of Goodman Brown force a crisis in an individual
life. In Arnold's "Dover Beach" the speaker expresses regret about
uncertainty and the loss of religious faith that symbolically wear away
civilization just like surf beating on the stones of Dover Beach. This
situation might be expected to make a person as dreary and depressed as
Goodman Brown actually is. Arnold's speaker, however, in the lines "Ah,
love, let us be true / To one another," finds power in personal fidelity and
commitment (lines 29–30). In other words, the public world of "human
misery" and the diminishing "Sea of Faith" is beyond control, and
therefore all that is left is personal commitment. This is not to say that
"Young Goodman Brown," as a story, is negative, for Hawthorne implies
that a positive personal life lies in the denial of choices like those made by
Brown and in the acceptance of choices like those made by Mrs. Popov
and Arnold's speaker. It is only fair, however, to observe that Hawthorne
does not state this idea directly.

Mane 3

[4]   To deny or to ignore the public world is a possible option that, under some circumstances, can be chosen. For example, "Dover Beach" reflects a conscious decision to ignore the philosophic and religious uncertainty that the speaker finds in the intellectual and public world. Even more independent of such a public world, Keats's "Bright Star" brings out its ideas as a meditation about a purely personal situation. Keats's speaker, addressing a distant star, considers his need for steadfastness in his relationship with his "fair love." In Chopin's "The Story of an Hour" Louise embodies an interesting variation on the personal matters brought up in these two sonnets. At first, she is crushed by the news coming from the public world that her husband has been killed. Her first vision of herself is that of a grieving, private widow. As she thinks about things, however, she quickly begins to anticipate the liberation and freedom—to become free to explore the public world— that widowhood will give her. Ironically, it is the reappearance of her husband, who moves freely in the public world, that causes her sudden heart failure. What she looked forward to as the possibility of free choice to do what she wants and to go where she wishes has suddenly been withdrawn from her by her renewed status within the publicly sanctioned system of marriage, and it is her recognition of her abrupt loss of this possibility that triggers the end of her life.

[5]   The complexity of the conflicts between private and public life is brought out in the way in which structures secure their power through law and legality. With immense power, the law often acts as an arbitrary form of public judgment that disregards personal needs and circumstances. This idea is brought out on the most personal level in Glaspell's *Trifles,* in which the two major characters, both women, urgently confront the conflict between their personal identification with the accused woman, Minnie, and their public obligation to the law. One of the women, Mrs. Peters, is reminded that she is "married to the law," but she and Mrs. Hale suppress the evidence that they know would condemn Minnie, even though technically—by law, that is—their knowledge is public property. Their way of resolving the conflict is therefore

Mane 4

to reject the public demands made upon them, and to accept their own private
wishes and thoughts about personal behavior.

It is works about warfare that especially highlight how irreconcilable   [6]
the conflicts between personal and public concerns can become. A comic
but nevertheless real instance is dramatized by Hardy in "Channel Firing."
In this poem, set in a church graveyard, the skeleton of "Parson Thirdly"
views "gunnery practice out at sea" (line 10) as evidence that his "forty
year" dedication to serving his church was a waste of time. His conclusion
is that he would have been better off ignoring his public role and instead
sticking "to pipes and beer." Although Thirdly is disillusioned, he has not
been as deeply affected personally by warfare as the speaker of Lowell's
"Patterns." Her fiancé, she learns, has been killed fighting abroad; and his
death leads her to question—and by implication to doubt—the external
"patterns" that have suddenly destroyed her personal plans for life
(line 107). Unlike both these characters, who are deeply affected by the
effects of warfare, Peyton Farquhar, the main character in Bierce's "An
Occurrence at Owl Creek Bridge," is actually killed by his commitment
to a public concern—that of the Southern forces in the Civil War. As in
"Channel Firing" and "Patterns," Farquhar's situation shows how the
public world may exert absolute power over the private.

The works examined here are in general agreement that, under ideal   [7]
conditions, private life should be supreme over public life. They also
demonstrate that in many ways, the public world invades the private
world with a wide range of effects, from making people behave foolishly to
destroying them utterly. Naturally, the tone of the works is shaped by the
degree of seriousness of the conflict. Chekhov's *The Bear* is good-humored
and farcical because the characters overcome the social roles in which
they are cast. More sober are works such as "Dover Beach" and "Young
Goodman Brown," in which characters either are overcome by public
commitments or deliberately turn their backs on them. In the highest
range of seriousness are works such as "Patterns," and "An Occurrence at
Owl Creek Bridge," in which the individual is crushed by irresistible

Mane 5

public forces. <u>The works compared and contrasted here show varied and powerful conflicts between public demands and personal interests.</u>

Mane 6

Work Cited

Selected works. *Literature: An Introduction to Reading and Writing, Compact Edition*. Ed. Edgar V. Roberts and Robert Zweig. 6th ed. New York: Pearson, 2015. Print.

Commentary on the Essay

This essay, combining for discussion all three genres of fiction, poetry, and drama, is visualized as an assignment at the end of a unit of study. The expectation prompting the assignment is that a fairly large number of literary works can be profitably compared on the basis of a unifying subject, idea, or technique. For this essay, the works—five poems, three stories, and two short plays—are compared and contrasted on the common topic of private-public conflicts. It is obviously impossible to discuss all the works in detail in every paragraph. The essay therefore shows how a writer may introduce a large number of works in a straightforward comparison-contrast method without a need for detailed comparison of each work with every other work on each of the major subtopics (social, legal, military).

Thus, the first section, consisting of paragraphs 2–4, treats six of the works. In paragraph 2, however, only two works are discussed, and in paragraph 3 one of these works is carried over for comparison with only one additional work. The fourth paragraph springs out of the second, utilizing one of the works discussed there and then bringing out comparisons with three additional works.

The same technique is used in the rest of the essay: Paragraph 5 introduces only one work; paragraph 6 introduces two additional works; and paragraph 7 introduces three works for comparison and contrast. Each of the ten works is therefore discussed at least once in terms of how it contributes to the major topic. One might note that the essay concentrates on a relatively small number of the works, such as Chekhov's *The Bear* and Hawthorne's "Young Goodman Brown," but that as newer topics are introduced, the essay goes on to works that are more closely connected to these topics.

The technique of extended comparison-contrast used in this way shows how the various works can be defined and distinguished in relation to the common idea. The concluding paragraph summarizes these distinctions by suggesting a continuous line along which each of the works may be placed.

Even so, the treatment of so many texts might easily cause crowding and confusion. The division of the major topic into subtopics, as noted, is a major means of trying to make the essay easy to follow. An additional means is the introduction of transitional words and phrases such as *also, choose,* and *one of the major conflicts.*

An extended comparison-contrast essay cannot present a full treatment of each of the works. The works are unique, and there are many elements that do not yield to the comparison-contrast method. Ideas that are particularly important in Hardy's "Channel Firing," for example, are (1) that human beings need eternal rest and not eternal life, (2) that God is amused by—or indifferent to—human affairs, (3) that religious callings or vocations may be futile, and (4) that war itself is the supreme form of cruelty. All these topics could be treated in another essay, but they do not pertain to the particular goals of this particular illustrative essay. A topic compatible with the general private-public topic is needed, and the connection is readily made (paragraph 6) through the character of Hardy's Parson Thirdly. Because the essay deals with the conflicts brought out by Thirdly's comments, Hardy's poem is linked to all the other works for comparative purposes. So it is with the other works, each of which could also be the subject of analysis from many standpoints other than comparison-contrast. The effect of the comparison of all the works collectively, however, is the enhanced understanding of each of the works separately. To achieve such an understanding and to explain it are the major goals of the extended comparison-contrast method.

Writing Topics for Comparison and Contrast

1. The use of the speaker in Arnold's "Dover Beach" (p. 887) and Hardy's "Channel Firing" (p. 617).
2. The description of fidelity to love in Keats's "Bright Star" (p. 644) to Arnold's "Dover Beach" (p. 887) or Lowell's "Patterns" (p. 921).
3. The view of women in Chekhov's *The Bear* (p. 1322) and Maupassant's "The Necklace" (p. 7) or in Glaspell's *Trifles* (p. 982) and O'Neill's *Before Breakfast* (p. 1005).
4. The use of descriptive scenery in Hawthorne's "Young Goodman Brown" (p. 342) and Lowell's "Patterns" (p. 921) or in Poe's "The Masque of the Red Death" (p. 431) and Bierce's "An Occurrence at Owl Creek Bridge" (p. 87).
5. Symbols of disapproval in Hardy's "Channel Firing" (p. 617) and Frost's "Desert Places" (p. 741).
6. Treatments of religion in "Latin Women Pray" by Ortiz Cofer (p. 589) and "Batter My Heart" by Donne (p. 585).
7. Any of the foregoing topics applied to a number of separate works. Consult the Topical and Thematic Table of Contents at the beginning of the book for additional ideas.

2. Reader-Response: How a Reader's Reactions Lead Toward Interpretation

(See also page 1586.)

Reader-response essays are based on the idea that meaning in a literary work involves the interaction between the words and ideas of a text and a reader's response to them. As such, the reader's frame of mind, background, and assumptions are all important factors in how that reader brings a work of literature to life. While readers may not themselves share many aspects of a particular character—in a play, for instance—there may still be qualities of that play that may have a particular meaning to him or her. For instance, in reading Shakespeare's *Hamlet* (p. 1080) most readers will know little, if anything, about what it was like to be a Danish prince in the late sixteenth century, but they can nevertheless understand what it means to want revenge for a terrible wrong or to understand how hesitation might be an alternative to taking decisive action. How readers react to the different issues in a work might be strongly tied to the times in which they live. For instance, modern readers of Theodore Roethke's "My Papa's Waltz" (p. 706) may view the father's behavior as abusive and may be acutely aware of his alcoholism. However, readers at the time the poem was written (1942) may have been less sensitive and more accepting of the behavior associated with drinking, and therefore might have viewed the father's behavior as rough but not particularly unusual or threatening.

A topic thus arises: Which of the two interpretations is more valid, the one made at the time of Roethke's composition or the "contemporary" one? According to reader-response critics, both interpretations are valid because different readers approach their reading with varying experiences and assumptions. A work of fiction, a poem, or a play may evoke different responses depending on the ideas, feelings, and thoughts of the individual reader, in addition to bringing about differing interpretations of events, actions, and characters. In the illustrative essay on Auden's "Musée des Beaux Arts" (p. 888), the writer contemplates suffering in the modern world and her response to it. The poem "comes to life" for her as a reader because it offers alternative views of how to react to a world in which suffering exists constantly in different forms.

Important Elements of a Reader-Response Essay

A reader-response essay allows you to write about what a story, poem, or play means to you rather than having to "figure out" the "real meaning" behind the work or having to summarize what various critics have said about it. As a reader, you come to a work with experiences and ideas that will help bring the work to life. Your unique personal perspective will help readers of your essay see the work in a new way. This is not to say, however, that your reading of a work can be haphazard or that your interpretations can go in any direction at all. John

Updike's "A & P" (p. 320) may be about growing up or about facing new challenges, but it is certainly not about "going to college" or about "living in a new country." To interpret works in terms of your own reactions to them does not allow you to propose implausible readings that will leave your audience with little confidence that your essay has anything valid or thoughtful to say.

Your interpretation, even though it might reflect your own experience, must always and forever be grounded in the work. You should be able to back up your view about the work with evidence to support the position that you take. As you read, something in the work, such as a poem or a scene in a play, may stand out; it may shock you, surprise you, or make you think about a similar event or events that you or someone you know experienced. These *reactions* may form the basis of your reader-response paper. For instance, after reading Ibsen's *A Dollhouse* (p. 1488), you may have a strong reaction to the way Nora is treated, or you may be surprised at the way she leaves her husband. Your *thesis statement* or *thesis argument* for a reader-response paper about *A Dollhouse* may be "Nora did the right thing by leaving her husband." A reader-response essay about *Hamlet* may have a thesis statement such as "Revenge may seem desirable in thought, but is not favorable at all when one tries to carry it out."

A reader-response essay may also focus on issues that relate to your own history, associations, values, and beliefs. For example, reading Jackson's story "The Lottery" (p. 139) may help you reflect on rituals that you observe (in church or synagogue, or within the family or your circle of friends) but are not sure why, or in which you no longer believe. Your thesis for such an essay may be "Just as Jackson's 'The Lottery' is about a ritual carried out with no one understanding why I also perform family [religious, friendship] rituals without knowing why I am doing so." The body paragraphs of your essay should give your reader a good idea of what happens in the story, poem, or play and should record your own reactions to it. Keep in mind that the purpose of your essay is to illuminate both your knowledge of the story and your explanations of how your experience brings the story to "life."

Illustrative Student Essay (Reader-Response)

Topic: What Issues Does Auden's Poem "Musée Des Beaux Arts" Raise About How You View Suffering in the World?

Although underlined sentences are not recommended by MLA style, they are used in this illustrative essay as teaching tools to emphasize the central idea, thesis sentence, and topic sentences.

Zweig 1

Micol Zweig

Professor Dadawala

English 286

12 May 2014

Opposite Personal Responses to W. H. Auden's

"Musée des Beaux Arts"

[1]   The first stanza of Auden's "Musée des Beaux Arts" raises the theme

of private suffering in general terms, and observes that people's daily

routines incline them to ignore the tragic experiences of others:°

> How, when the aged are reverently, passionately waiting
>
> For the miraculous birth, there always must be
>
> Children who did not specially want it to happen, skating
>
> On a pond at the edge of the wood:
>
> (lines 5–8)

[2]   Auden highlights this point with a reference to Brueghel's painting

"Landscape with the Fall of Icarus" (c. 1858), a famous painting that is

displayed in the Musées Royaux des Beaux-Arts de Belgique in Brussels,

Belgium. Icarus, a Greek mythical figure, flew too close to the sun, and the

wax connecting his "wings" melted and lost their lift. Needless to say, Icarus

fell out of the sky and hurtled back to the planet. As Brueghel painted the

mythical scene, Icarus is falling into the ocean and drowning, and he struggles

for a moment with his bare legs in the air. Auden interprets Brueghel's scene:

°**Central idea.**

Zweig 2

Fig. 1. *Landscape with the Fall of Icarus* by Pieter Brueghel the Elder (c. 1558, Musées Royaux des Beaux-Arts de Belgique, Brussels).

    . . . how everything turns away

    Quite leisurely from the disaster; the ploughman may

    Have heard the splash, the forsaken cry,

                           (14–16)

The poet offers his readers an opposite and double-sided message. [3] He suggests that people are indifferent to the suffering of others, and at the same time he ironically illuminates the immense human importance of the private suffering of just one.* The poem, like the painting, makes the reader wonder what Auden is truly saying about human suffering. Is private suffering the natural order of the world? Is it of utmost importance to acknowledge the suffering of others?

    Auden is correct in observing that the private suffering of one person [4] is usually ignored by other people. Even today, the knowledge of genocide, poverty, and disease does not stop those more fortunate from living their lives. Auden, on the one hand, points out that we human beings suffer

*Thesis sentence.

Zweig 3

from our inability to learn and enrich our own lives with this knowledge, but he also suggests that it is this ignorance that allows us to carry on harmoniously. As he says, the ploughman in the foreground, although he may have heard the splash and the cry, continues to plough. And, along with the dreamy shepherd, ". . . the dogs go on with their doggy life and the torturer's horse / Scratches its innocent behind on a tree" (12–13). As the young boy Icarus plunges to his death in the ocean, "the expensive delicate ship" sails "calmly on" (19, 20). This image is one of calm harmony within the background of a calamitous individual tragedy. In my own life, I find that I must, as a matter of self-preservation, become numb to the constant suffering around me. If I were to show active compassion for every person, like Icarus, who meets disaster, and for the twenty children who die from disease and famine every minute of each day, I would be prevented from handling my own responsibilities. If I stopped for every instance of pain and suffering in the world, I would find it impossible to play an active role in my own life, and also in the ongoing responsibilities of living in society. Auden forces us to realize this sad but true reality about us all.

[5]   It is ironic that Auden would use Icarus as an example to highlight his point about indifference to suffering, since many people understand this story as one of individual affliction, and they can sympathize and can learn from that tragedy. While people can easily ignore the suffering of each individual person, art forces them to look at it. Although life goes on after each single person's suffering, a poem or a painting can highlight a single tragedy, as representative of other tragedies like it, and along this avenue people can allow themselves to feel and show compassion. Sometimes a movie about a sad and lonely person, or a documentary about the hurricane in Haiti or a tsunami in the Far East, will make me, in a controlled way, face the reality that so many people are suffering. Auden's poem is a reminder that however I go about my own life, a very real "world" of suffering exists out there all the time.

Zweig 4

Auden's "Musée des Beaux Arts" points out the fact that we find [6]
it convenient to ignore tragedy, but at the same time he is forcing us
to confront it. His observations about Brueghel's painting serve as
a reminder that art, both in the past and in the future, forces people
to recognize their own ignorance and to face, for a time at least, the
reality of suffering. At first Auden seems to be making a statement
about the ignorance of human beings, but there is an irony in the word
"suffering" (1), for clearly this—the tragedy of Icarus—has lent itself
as a moral tale of caution on the dangers of vanity and over-ambition
to all people, a notion that the "Old Masters" recognized (2). Auden's
poem clearly highlights this issue in my own life.

Zweig 5

Works Cited

Auden, W. H. "Musée des Beaux Arts." *Literature: An Introduction to*
Reading and Writing, Compact Edition. Ed. Edgar V. Roberts and
Robert Zweig. 6th ed. New York: Pearson, 2015. 888. Print.

Pieter Brueghel the Elder. *Landscape with the Fall of Icarus* c. 1558. Musées
Royaux des Beaux-Arts de Belgique, Brussels.

Commentary on the Essay

The introductory paragraph begins by pointing out the main theme of the poem: how suffering is ignored by most people because of their "daily routines." The writer then points out how this theme is exemplified for Auden in the Brueghel painting of Icarus. The writer then posits the main theme of the paper. Auden's poem raises two possibilities about how one is to view suffering: People are indifferent to it as it is depicted in the painting. However, the poem itself focuses on the suffering of one individual.

In the first paragraph the writer indicates that the suffering of others is often ignored in the pursuit of everyday routines. Further, in the second paragraph the writer points out the "irony" that although the poem points to the indifferent attitude toward suffering that people display, the poem focuses our attention on just that. The writer states: "While people can easily ignore the suffering of each individual person, art forces them to look at it." In her own life, viewing a movie or a documentary can bring the suffering of people to her immediate attention.

In the fourth paragraph, the writer notes how this is also true for tragedies such as "genocide, poverty, and disease." The writer then focuses on her own life, stating that is a necessity for "self-preservation." Turning one's attention to tragedies that are happening every day in the world would distract her from carrying on her own "responsibilities."

In the concluding paragraph the writer reiterates the double-edged response that she has to the reality of suffering. Misery and suffering go on all the time, and by necessity they are ignored, but art, including Auden's poem, reminds us of their presence, even if for no more than a brief time. As a reader-response essay the writer gives examples of the poem's meaning to her, and of how it has helped her focus on this fact of life: suffering is ever-present; it must be ignored for one's life to continue, and yet a work of art will not let us forget its presence.

Writing Topics for Reader-Response Essays

1. What Tim O'Brien's "The Things They Carried" (p. 101) tells you about the importance of remembering an important event in your life.

2. Raymond Carver's "Cathedral" (p. 130) and new ways of thinking about physical handicaps.

3. Robert Frost's "Stopping by Woods on a Snowy Evening" (p. 548) and thinking about crossroads and developments in your own life.

4. People we think we know and Edwin Arlington Robinson's "Richard Cory" (p. 590).

5. How you cope with bitterness and disappointment, and your response to Eugene O'Neill's *Before Breakfast* (p. 1005).

6. August Wilson's *Fences* (p. 1427) and unseen barriers you have come up against, and perhaps created, in your own life.

3. Argument: The Use of Persuasive Reasoning

(See also pages 30–34.)

Defining an Argument Essay

When you are having an argument with someone, you are probably trying to convince that person that you have a valid point to make or that your point is superior to another one. When you are writing an argument essay about a work of literature, you are trying to convince your reader that he or she should agree with you. It may be that you have read an interpretation that you do not agree with and are offering an alternate one or that you have interpreted a fictional work, a poem, or a drama in a way for which other interpretations may be offered.

Important Elements of an Argument Essay

As in any argument in which you are attempting to persuade someone, when you write about a literary topic, it is essential to make a *claim* and then to support that claim with *evidence* from the text that shows the *validity* of the claim. Linking claims to evidence are *warrants*—the stated and sometimes unstated assumptions that are part of an argument. For instance, if you claim that the ghost in *Hamlet* cannot be "real," your warrant may be that ghosts do not exist and that a reader should not be expected to accept them as real even in a fictional work.

The claim in your paper should take the form of a clear *thesis statement* that you state in your introductory paragraph. Your evidence should make up your body paragraphs, in which you discuss such items as the plot, the setting, and the persona or characters. For instance, in arguing that John Updike's "A & P" is about a boy's coming of age, it would be important to understand where Sammy is working, how he views the girls that come into the store, how he reacts to the treatment that the girls get, and the consequences of his actions. Relating all these various elements of the story to your major idea of your argument can make for a convincing paper. For example, quoting the last sentence of "A & P" would give strong evidence that Sammy has been transformed by the events at the store and that he recognizes his entry into adulthood. "His [Lengel's] face was dark gray and his back stiff, as if he'd just had an injection of iron, and my stomach kind of fell as I felt how hard the world was going to be to me hereafter" (p. 324). Another important element of the argument essay might be a *counterargument* or *refutation*. This part of your paper defends against an opposing point of view. It is essential when making a counterargument or refutation that you represent the opposing point of view fairly and relate the strongest elements of that argument in order for your own point of view to be as logical and convincing as possible. If another reader were to assert that "A & P" is about a boy's immaturity because of the decision to quit his job, you might point out that this view does not account for Sammy's realization at the end of the story that he is about to enter a more difficult time in his life. Thus, your argument is anticipating objections to your main thesis.

Arrive at a Claim for a Thesis Statement

As you read a story, poem, or dramatic work you are probably thinking of different approaches or interpretations of the work. Very likely, as you read, you are either consciously or subconsciously testing these interpretations. In thinking about what happens in the work, you may finally arrive at some conclusions about an interpretation that you can support argumentatively. Here is a list of observations about Updike's "A & P" that you might make as you read, followed by some tentative claims, which you may wish to state in the form of a thesis statement.

- Sammy seems okay with his job at the beginning of the story.
- Sammy is very interested in observing the girls as they walk through the store. Obviously, he appreciates girls in bathing suits.
- Sammy doesn't like the way Lengel treats the girls.
- Sammy is trying to be a hero by sticking up for the girls.

Claim Made in a Potential Thesis Statement

- "Sammy's action at the end of 'A & P' is immature and shows that he is unwilling to face up to the consequences of becoming an adult."

Alternate Claim Made for an Alternative Thesis Statement

- "Sammy's action at the end of 'A & P' and his reaction to it shows that he is aware of the adult world he is about to enter."

After seeking evidence from the story about either of these two thesis statements you may realize that there is a great deal of evidence for one but not the other. You might wish to make the stronger thesis statement the basis for your argument essay.

Illustrative Student Essay (Argument)

Assignment for an Argument Essay: Does Sammy's action at the end of Updike's "A & P" indicate that he has decided to enter the adult world or is his action a retreat from the responsibilities of adulthood? Write an argument essay indicating what you think Sammy's action means.

Although underlined sentences are not recommended by MLA style, they are used in this illustrative essay as teaching tools to emphasize the central idea, thesis sentence, and topic sentences.

Zweig 1

Micol Zweig

Professor Dadawala

English 286

12 May 2014

Sammy's Decision to Become an Adult

John Updike's "A & P" is told through the narrator Sammy, the young   [1]

grocery checker, as he sees three girls in "nothing but bathing suits" enter

the A & P (320).° Blatantly contrasted with the rest of the customers and

employees, the girls are barely dressed, and are pacing uniquely "against

the grain" through the aisles in their bare feet. Sammy is paying close

attention to their physical attributes as the girls proceed to check out,

when the manager Lengel, intervenes to berate them for their unacceptable

appearance. Feeling that the chastisement is unnecessary, and that it

represents a world he does not want to be a part of, Sammy quits, and

leaves the store with a clear conscience, nervous about what the future has

in store for him. He is now a man who will henceforward live his life, like

the girls, against the grain. This coming-of-age narrative follows Sammy

through his metamorphosis from an average teenager into a principled and

courageous adult. The events of the story represent Sammy's recognition

of the adult world that he is about to enter.*

°Central idea.
*Thesis statement.

[2]   While the story's action takes place in no more than minutes, for Sammy it represents a life-changing experience as he matures and decides what kind of man he wants to be in the world. At first, when the girls enter the store, Sammy is very taken by their physical appearance. His first observations are at first shallow and common, relating to the girls' physical appearance and their interactions with each other: "There was this chunky one . . . [and] there was this one, with one of those chubby berry-faces, the lips all bunched together under her nose, this one, and a tall one, with black hair that hadn't quite frizzed right" (320). As the girls continue through the aisles Sammy's observations become more complex as he notices how the other patrons go about like sheep through the aisles, all the same, crossing items off their lists. All this is in contrast with the girls who seem to be getting more out of life. As he notices the way the other patrons are looking disparagingly at the girls, he feels bad for them and realizes he doesn't want to be part of a micro-society that encourages conformity and commonness. He recognizes the humdrum quality of his life as the girls proceed to check out. The clicks his register makes, "Hello (*bing*) there, you (*gung*) hap-py *pee*-pul (*splat*)" (323), as they form a song in his head, display the scant flexibility required of his imagination at work. After the girls leave, having been embarrassed by the manager, Sammy abruptly quits his job, realizing that like the girls, he wants to explore a life outside the store where he'll have a chance to become a unique individual. Lengel warns that his parents will be upset, like any parents are upset when their child leaves them to become an adult. Sammy, as he removes his apron, knows that he has now entered adulthood and though he is scared, cannot ever go back. He leaves the store, an adult, ready to explore the scary world.

[3]   An argument can be made that the story is not of Sammy's entrance into adulthood, but his denial of it. If the girls are seen as symbols of naïve and innocent childhood who are not ready to function capably in adult society, then Sammy's action to quit and follow them as they leave can be

Zweig 3

seen as his unwillingness to give in to the adult world of responsibility and social order. Perhaps adulthood is the recognition that life is made up of small tasks, which no matter how mundane, help sustain society and family while childhood is the time to rebel and live in the moment. Perhaps Lengel warns Sammy that his parents will be upset because he will disappoint them in having not been able to function and accept the responsibility of adulthood. It could explain the fear and apprehension he feels when he leaves, having made the decision to perpetuate his childish fancies and naïve view of how things should be.

 While the argument can be made that Sammy rejects the adult **[4]** world, this interpretation denies the moral fabric of the story and robs the narrator of his integrity. Sammy is fully aware of the two spheres of life represented by the girls and the other patrons of the A & P. His ability to recognize and observe, so thoughtfully, everything around him and then to make a firm decision with the awareness that it is final, along with an acceptance that life will be harder from then on, is, as Updike tells us, truly what it means to be an adult.

Zweig 4

Work Cited

Updike, John. "A & P." *Literature: An Introduction to Reading and Writing, Compact Edition*. Ed. Edgar V. Roberts and Robert Zweig. 6th ed. New York: Pearson, 2015. 320–24. Print.

Commentary on the Essay

Paragraph 1 summarizes the main action and setting of the story and what happens to make Sammy resign his job. There is a quotation to give some sense of Sammy's thoughts and his manner of speaking. The paragraph ends with a clear thesis statement that claims that the story is about Sammy's awareness of the adult world that he is about to enter.

Paragraph 2 discusses many of the details that will be important in understanding the context of the final decision to quit his job and the progression of Sammy's thinking as events unfold. It discusses Sammy's initial interest in how the girls look and then in seeing that they seem to be enjoying life at a level that contrasts with Sammy's "humdrum" job. The writer points out that even though the events of the story take place over a period of minutes they are steps to Sammy's recognition of the circumstances of his own life. Finally, the writer tries to explain why Lengel points out that Sammy's parents will feel disappointment at his resignation. All the details that the author relates enforce the claim made in the thesis statement.

Paragraph 3 presents a counterargument stating that Sammy's action may represent an alternate interpretation: Sammy behaves in a way that denies his entrance into adulthood. Evidence for this counterclaim is that becoming an adult requires leaving childhood concerns, accepting responsibility, and working at tasks that may be uninteresting or even boring. Walking away from his job represents a turning away from his responsibilities and therefore from adulthood.

In the concluding paragraph the writer rejects the counterargument because it denies the moral argument of the story and the integrity of the character. The essay ends with the reiteration of the main idea.

Writing Topics for Argument

1. The importance of historical setting in understanding Alice Walker's "Everyday Use" (p. 494).

2. The meaning of marriage underlying Kate Chopin's "The Story of an Hour" (p. 306) and the meaning of marriage today.

3. Self-awareness, or the lack of it, in James Joyce's "Araby" (p. 242) and Katherine Mansfield's "Miss Brill" (p. 218).

4. What Randall Jarrell's "The Death of the Ball Turret Gunner" (p. 550) says about the true cost and pain of war.

5. The importance of unique language strategies in understanding E. E. Cummings's message in "next to of course god America i" (p. 584).

6. The relationship between history and art as exemplified in Salvatore Quasímodo's "Auschwitz" (p. 704).

7. The relationship between plot and character in Shakespeare's *Hamlet* (p. 1080).

8. The relevance of the situation of women as shown in Henrik Ibsen's *A Dollhouse* (p. 1488) to the situation of women today.

Chapter 27
Taking Examinations on Literature

AFTER STUDYING THIS MATERIAL, YOU SHOULD BE ABLE TO DO THE FOLLOWING:

- Understand the purpose and common structures of examinations on literature
- Prepare systematically for taking examinations
- Respond to typical examination questions in a focused and effective way

Getting a good grade on a literature examination is largely a result of intelligent and skillful preparation. Preparation means that you (1) study the material assigned, in conjunction with the comments made in class by your instructor and by fellow students in discussion; (2) develop and reinforce your own thoughts; (3) anticipate exam questions by creating and answering your own practice questions; and (4) understand the precise function of the test.

You should also realize that the test is not designed either to trap you or to hold down your grade. The grade you receive is a reflection of your achievement in the course. If your grades are high, congratulations; keep doing what you have been doing. If your grades are low, however, you can improve them through diligent and systematic study. Those students who can easily do satisfactory work might do superior work if they improved their habits of study and preparation. From whatever level you begin, *you can increase your achievement by improving your study methods.*

Your instructor has three major concerns in evaluating your tests (assuming the correct use of English): (1) to assess the extent of your command over the subject material of the course (How good is your retention?); (2) to assess how well you respond to a question or deal with an issue (How well do you separate the important from the unimportant?); and (3) to assess how well you draw conclusions about the material (How well are you educating yourself?).

Answer the Questions That Are Asked

Many elements go into writing good answers on tests, but *responsiveness* is the most important. A major cause of low exam grades is that students *often do not answer the questions asked*. Does that failure seem surprising? The problem is that some students do no more than retell a story or restate an argument, but they do not zero in on the issues in the question. This problem is not uncommon. Therefore, if you are asked, "Why does . . . ?," be sure to emphasize the *why* and use the *does* primarily to exemplify the *why*. If the question is about *organization*, focus on organization.

If the question is about the *interpretation* of an idea, deal with the interpretation of the idea. In short, *always respond directly to the question or instruction*. Answer what is asked. Compare the following two answers to the same question:

Question: How is the setting of Ambrose Bierce's "An Occurrence at Owl Creek Bridge" (Chapter 1, page 87) important in the story's development?

ANSWER A

The setting of Bierce's "An Occurrence at Owl Creek Bridge" is a major element in the story's development. The first scene is on a railroad bridge in northern Alabama, and the action is that a man, Peyton Farquhar, is about to be hanged. He is a southerner who has been surrounded and captured by Union soldiers. They are ready to string him up and they have the guns and power, so he cannot escape. He is so scared that his own watch seems to be slow and loud, like a cannon. He also thinks about how he might escape, once he is hanged, by freeing his hands and throwing off the noose that will soon be choking and killing him. The scene shifts to the week before, at Farquhar's plantation. A Union spy deceives Farquhar, thereby tempting him to try to sabotage the Union efforts to keep the railroad open. Because the spy tells Farquhar about the punishment, the reader assumes that Farquhar had tried to sabotage the bridge, was caught, and now is going to be hanged. The third scene is also at the bridge, but it is about what Farquhar sees and thinks in his own mind: He imagines that he has been hanged and then escapes. He thinks he falls into the creek, frees himself from the ropes, and makes it to shore, and from there he makes the long walk home. His final vision is of his wife coming out of the house to meet him, with everything looking beautiful in the morning sunshine. Then we find out that all this was just in his mind, because we are back on the bridge, from which Farquhar is swinging, hanged, dead, with a broken neck.

ANSWER B

The setting of Bierce's "An Occurrence at Owl Creek Bridge" is a major element in the story's development. The railroad bridge in northern Alabama, from which the doomed Peyton Farquhar will be hanged, is a frame for the story. The bridge, which begins as a real-life bridge in the first scene, becomes the bridge that the dying man imagines in the third. In between there is a brief scene at Farquhar's home, which took place a week before. The setting thus marks the progression of Farquhar's dying vision. He begins to distort and slow down reality—at the real bridge—when he realizes that there is no escape. The first indication of this distortion is that his watch seems to be ticking as slowly as a blacksmith's hammer. Once he is dropped from the bridge to be hanged, his perceptions slow down time so much that he imagines his complete escape before his death: falling into the water, freeing himself, being shot at, getting to shore, walking through a darkening forest, and returning home in beautiful morning sunshine. The final sentence of the story brutally restores the real situation at the railroad bridge and makes clear that Farquhar is hanging from it and is actually dead despite his imaginings. In all respects, therefore, the setting is essential to the story's development.

Answer A begins well and introduces important details of the story's setting, but it does not answer the question because it does not show how the details figure into the story's development. On the other hand, answer B focuses directly on the connection between the locations and the changes in the protagonist's perceptions. Because of this emphasis, B answers the question and is also shorter than A (288 words for A to 219 for B, according to a computerized count); with the focus directly on the issue, there is no need for irrelevant narrative details. Thus, A is unresponsive and unnecessarily long, whereas B is responsive and includes details only if they exemplify the major points.

Systematic Preparation

Your challenge is how best to prepare yourself to have a knowledgeable and ready mind at examination time. If you simply cram facts into your head for the test in the hope that you can adjust to the questions, you will likely flounder. You need a systematic approach.

Read and Reread the Material on Which You Are to Be Examined

Above all, recognize that your preparation should begin as soon as the course begins, not on the night before the exam. Complete each assignment by the date it is due, for you will understand the classroom discussion only if you know the material (see also the guides for study in Part I, pp. 14–26). Then, about a week before the exam, review each assignment, preferably rereading everything completely. If particular passages were read and discussed in class, make a special point of studying the passages and referring to the notes you took at the time of the discussions. With this preparation, your study on the night before the exam will be fruitful because it is the climax of your preparation, *not your entire preparation*.

Construct Your Own Questions: Go on the Attack

To prepare yourself well for an exam, read *actively*, not passively. Read with a goal, and *go on the attack* by anticipating test conditions—creating and answering your own practice questions. Don't waste time, however, in trying to guess the questions you think your instructor might ask. Guessing correctly might happen (and wouldn't you be absolutely delighted if it did?) but do not turn your study into a game of chance. Instead, arrange the subject matter by asking yourself questions that help you get things straight.

How can you construct your own questions? It is not as hard as you might think. Your instructor may have announced certain topics or ideas to be tested on the exam, and you might develop questions from these, or you might apply general questions to the specifics of your assignments, as in the following examples:

1. *Ideas about a character and the interactions of characters* (see also Chapter 3). What is character *A* like? How does *A* grow or change in the work? What does *A* learn or not learn that brings about the conclusion? To what degree does *A* represent a type or an idea? How does character *B* influence *A*? Does a change in character *C* bring about any corresponding change in *A*?

2. *Ideas about technical and structural questions.* These can be broad, covering everything from point of view (Chapter 2) to poetic form (Chapter 16). The best
guide here is to study those technical aspects that have been discussed in class,
for it is unlikely that you will be asked to go beyond the levels considered in
classroom discussion.

3. *Ideas about events or situations.* What relationship does episode *A* have to situation *B*? Does *C*'s thinking about situation *D* have any influence on the outcome
of event *E*?

4. *Ideas about a problem* (see also Chapter 21, pp. 1246–49). Why is character *A* or
situation *X* this way and not that way? Is the conclusion justified by the ideas
and events leading up to it?

Rephrase Your Notes as Questions

Because your classroom notes are the fullest record you have about your instructor's views, one of the best ways to construct questions is to develop them from
these notes. As you select topics and phrase questions, refer to passages from the
texts that were studied by the class and stressed by your instructor. If there is time,
memorize as many important phrases or lines as you can from the assigned works.
Plan to incorporate these into your answers as evidence to support the points you
make. Remember that it is useful to work not only with main ideas from your
notes but also with matters such as character, setting, imagery, symbolism, ideas,
and organization.

Obviously, you cannot make questions from all your notes, and you will
therefore need to select from those that seem most important. As an example, here
is a short note written by a student during a classroom discussion of Shakespeare's
Hamlet: "A study in how private problems get public, how a private assassination
can produce disastrous national and international consequences." You may devise
the following practice questions from this note:

1. Why may *Hamlet* be seen as a play not only about private problems but also
about public ones?

2. Why should the political consequences of Claudius's murder of Hamlet's father be considered disastrous?

The principle here is that good exam questions do not ask just about *what* but
rather get into the issues of *why.* Observe that both questions introduce the word
why in the phrasing of the notes. Either question creates the need for you to study
pointedly, and neither asks you merely to describe events from the play. Question
1 requires you to consider the wider political effects of Hamlet's hostility toward
Claudius, including Hamlet's murder of Polonius and the subsequent madness of
Ophelia. Question 2, with its emphasis on disaster, leads you to consider not only
the ruination of the hopes and lives of those in the play but also the importance
of young Fortinbras and the eventual establishment of Norwegian control over
Denmark after Claudius and Hamlet have died. If you were to spend fifteen or
twenty minutes writing practice answers to these questions, you could be confident in taking an examination on the material, for you could likely adapt, or even

partially duplicate, your study answers to any exam question about the personal and political results of Claudius's murder of his brother.

Make Up Your Own Questions Even When Time Is Short

Whatever your subject, spend as much study time as possible making and answering your own questions. *Writing practice answers is one of the most important things you can do in preparing for your exam.* Remember also to work with your own remarks and the ideas you develop in the notebook or journal entries that you make when doing your regular assignments (see Part I, pp. 13–18). Many of these will give you additional ideas for your own questions, which you can practice along with the questions you develop from your classroom notes.

Obviously, with limited study time, you will not be able to create your own questions and answers indefinitely. Even so, don't neglect asking and answering your own questions. If time is too short for full practice answers, write out the main heads, or topics, of an answer. When the press of time (or the need for sleep) no longer permits you to make even such a brief outline answer, keep thinking of questions and their answers as you go to the exam. *Never read passively or unresponsively.* Always read with a creative, question-and-answer goal. Always keep thinking of *why* in addition to *what.* Consider your study as a preliminary step leading to writing.

The time you spend in this way will be valuable, for as you practice, you will develop control and therefore confidence. Often those who have difficulty with tests, or claim a phobia about them, prepare passively rather than actively. Your instructor's test questions compel responsiveness, organization, thought, and insight. But a passively prepared student is not ready for this challenge and therefore writes answers that are unresponsive and filled with summary. The grade for such a performance is low, and the student's fear of tests is reinforced. The best way to break such long-standing patterns of fear or uncertainty is to study actively and creatively.

Study with a Classmate

Often the thoughts of another person can help you understand the material to be tested. Find a fellow student with whom you can work comfortably but also productively, for both of you together can help each other individually. In view of the need for steady preparation throughout a course, regular discussions about the material are a good idea. You might also make your joint study systematic by setting aside a specific evening or afternoon for work sessions. Many students have said that they encounter problems in taking examinations because they are unfamiliar with the ways in which questions are phrased. Consequently, they waste time in understanding and interpreting the questions before they begin their answers, and sometimes they lose all their time because they misunderstand the questions entirely. If you work with a fellow student, however, and trade questions, you will be gaining experience (and confidence) in dealing with this basic difficulty about exams. Working with someone else can be extremely rewarding, just as it can also be stimulating and instructive. Make the effort, and you'll never regret it.

Two Basic Types of Questions About Literature

Generally, you should keep in mind two types of questions as you prepare for literature exams. The first type is *factual*, or *mainly objective;* and the second is *general, comprehensive, broad*, or *mainly subjective*. Except for multiple-choice questions, very few questions are purely objective in a literature course.

Anticipate the Kinds of Factual Questions That Might Be Asked

MULTIPLE-CHOICE QUESTIONS ASK YOU TO PICK THE MOST ACCURATE AND LIKELY ANSWERS. Multiple-choice questions are almost necessarily factual. Your instructor will most likely use them for short quizzes, usually on days when an assignment is due, to make sure that you are keeping up with the reading. Multiple-choice questions test your knowledge of facts and your ingenuity in perceiving subtleties of phrasing. On literature exams, however, this type of question is rare.

IDENTIFICATION QUESTIONS ASK FOR ACCURACY, EXPLANATION, AND INTERPRETATION. Identification questions are interesting and challenging because they require you both to know details and also to develop thoughts about them. These types of questions are frequently used as a check on the depth and scope of your reading. In fact, an entire exam could be composed of only identification questions, each requiring perhaps five minutes for you to answer. Here are some typical examples of what you might be asked to identify.

1. *A character*. To identify a character, it is necessary to describe briefly the character's position, main activity, and significance. Let us assume that "Prince Prospero" is the character to be identified. Our answer should state that he is the prince (position) who invites a thousand followers to his castle to enjoy themselves while keeping out the plague of the Red Death in Edgar Allan Poe's "The Masque of the Red Death" (main activity). Prospero's egotism and arrogance are the major causes of the action, and he embodies the story's theme that pride is vain and that death is inescapable (significance). Under the category of "significance," of course, you might develop as many ideas as you have time for, but the short example here is a general model for most identification questions.

2. *Incidents or situations*. To identify an incident or a situation (e.g. "A woman mourns the death of her husband") first describe the circumstances and the principal character involved in them (Mrs. Popov's reaction to her widowhood in Chekhov's play *The Bear*). Then describe the importance of this incident or situation in the work. For example, in *The Bear*, Mrs. Popov is mourning the death of her husband, and in the course of the play Chekhov uses her feelings to show amusingly that life and love with real emotion are stronger than allegiance to the dead.

3. *Things, places, and dates*. Your instructor may ask you to identify a hair ribbon (Nathaniel Hawthorne's "Young Goodman Brown") or a beach (Matthew Arnold's "Dover Beach") or the date of Amy Lowell's "Patterns" (1916). For

dates, you may be given a leeway of five or ten years. What is important about a date is not so much exactness as historical and intellectual perspective. The date of Lowell's "Patterns," for example, was the third year of World War I, and the poem consequently reflects a reaction against the protracted and senseless loss of life in war (even though details of the poem itself suggest an eighteenth-century war). To claim "World War I" as the date of the poem would be acceptable as an answer if it happens that you cannot remember the exact date.

4. *Quotations.* You should remember enough of the text to identify a passage taken from it or at least to make an informed guess. Generally, you should (1) locate the quotation, if you remember it, or else describe what you think is the probable location; (2) show the ways in which the quotation is typical of the content and style of the work you have read; and (3) describe the importance of the passage. If you suffer a lapse of memory, write a reasoned and careful explanation of your guess. Even if your guess is not actually correct, the knowledge and cogency of your explanation should give you points.

TECHNICAL AND ANALYTICAL QUESTIONS AND PROBLEMS REQUIRE YOU TO RELATE KNOWLEDGE AND TECHNICAL UNDERSTANDING TO THE ISSUE. In a scale of ascending importance, the third and most difficult type of factual question brings out those matters of writing with which much of this book is concerned: technique and analysis. You might be asked to analyze the *setting, images, point of view*, or *important idea* of a work; you might be asked about the *tone and style* of a story or poem; or you might be asked to *explicate* a poem that may or may not be duplicated for your benefit (if it is not duplicated, woe to students who have not studied their assignments). Questions like these assume that you have technical knowledge, and they also ask you to examine the text within the limitations imposed by the directions.

Obviously, technical questions occur more frequently in advanced courses than in elementary ones, and the questions grow more subtle as the courses become more advanced. Instructors of introductory courses may ask about ideas and problems but will likely not use many of the others unless they state their intentions to do so in advance or unless technical terms have been studied in class.

Questions of this type require fairly long answers, perhaps allowing from fifteen to twenty-five minutes apiece. If you have two or more of these questions, try to space your time sensibly; do not devote eighty percent of your time to one question and leave only twenty percent for the rest.

Understand How Your Responses Will Be Judged and Graded

IDENTIFICATION QUESTIONS PROBE YOUR UNDERSTANDING AND APPLICATION OF FACTS. In all factual questions, your instructor is testing (1) your factual command and (2) your quickness in relating a part to the whole. Thus, suppose you are identifying the incident "A man kills a canary." It is correct to say that Susan Glaspell's play *Trifles* (or her story "A Jury of Her Peers") is the location of the incident, that the murdered farmer John Wright is the killer, and that the canary belonged to his wife, Minnie. Knowledge of these details clearly establishes that you know the facts. But a strong answer must go further. Even in the brief time you have for short answers, you must demonstrate your processes of thought. You should always connect the facts (1) to major causation in the work, (2) to an important idea or ideas, (3) to the development of the work, and (4) for a quotation, to the style. Time is short and you must be selective, but if you can make your answer move from facts to significance, you will always fashion superior responses. Along these lines, let us look at an answer identifying the action from *Trifles*. Because some of the details of the play and the story are slightly different, we will refer only to *Trifles* here:

> The action is from Glaspell's *Trifles*. The man who kills the bird is John Wright, the dead man, and the owner is his wife, Minnie, who, before the story begins, has been jailed on suspicion of murder. The wringing of the little bird's neck is important because it is shown as an indignity and outrage in Minnie Wright's desperate life, and it obviously has made her angry enough to put a rope around Wright's neck to strangle him in his sleep. It is thus the cause not only of the murder but also of the investigation that brings the two lawmen and their wives to the Wright kitchen. In fact, the killing of the bird makes the story possible inasmuch as it is the women who discover the dead bird's remains, and this discovery is the means by which Glaspell highlights them as the major characters of the action. Because the husband's cruelly brutal act shows how bleak the married life of Minnie Wright actually was, it dramatizes the lonely and victimized plight of women in a male-dominated way of life like that on the Wright farm. The discovery also raises the issue of legality and morality, because the women decide to conceal the evidence, therefore protecting Minnie Wright from conviction and punishment.

Any of the points in this answer could be developed as a separate essay, but the paragraph is successful as a short answer because it goes beyond fact to deal with significance. Clearly, such answers are possible at the time of an exam only if you have devoted considerable thought beforehand to the works on which you are tested. The more thinking and practicing you do before an exam, the better your answers will be. Remember this advice as an axiom: *You cannot write superior answers if you do not think extensively before the exam.* By ambitious advance study, you will be able to reduce surprise to a minimum.

LONGER FACTUAL QUESTIONS PROBE YOUR KNOWLEDGE AND YOUR ABILITY TO ORGANIZE YOUR THOUGHTS.   More extended factual questions also require more thoroughly developed organization. Remember that for these questions your skill in writing essays is important because the thought you show in your composition will determine a major share of your instructor's evaluation of your answers. It is therefore best to take several minutes to gather your thoughts before you begin to write. Remember, *a ten-minute planned answer is preferable to a twenty-five-minute unplanned answer.* You do not need to write every possible fact on each particular question. Of greater importance is the use to which you put the facts that you know and the organization and development of your answer. Use a sheet of scratch paper to jot down important facts and your ideas about them in relation to the question. Then put them together, phrase a thesis sentence, and use your facts to exemplify and support your thesis.

It is always necessary to begin your answer pointedly, using key words or phrases from the question or direction if possible, so that your answer will have thematic shape. You should *never* begin an answer with "Because" and then go on from there without referring again to the question. To be most responsive during the short time available for an exam, you should use the question as your guide for your answer. Let us suppose that you have the following question on your test: "How does Glaspell use details in *Trifles* to reveal the character of Minnie Wright?" The most common way to go astray on such a question— and the easiest thing to do also—is to concentrate on Minnie Wright's character rather than on how Glaspell uses detail to bring out her character. The word *how* makes a vast difference in the nature of the final answer, and hence a good method on the exam is to duplicate key phrases in the question to ensure that you make your major points clear. Here is an opening sentence that uses the key words and phrases (italicized here) from the question to organize thought and provide focus.

> Glaspell *uses details* of setting, marital relationships, and personal habits *to reveal the character of Minnie Wright* as a person of great but unfulfilled potential whom anger has finally overcome.

Because this sentence repeats the key phrases from the question and also because it promises to show *how* the details are to be focused on the character, it suggests that the answer to follow will be responsive.

General or Comprehensive Questions Require You to Connect a Number of Works to Broader Matters of Idea and Technique

General or comprehensive questions are particularly important on final examinations, when your instructor is testing your total comprehension of the course material and your thought about it. Considerable time is usually allowed for answering this type of question, which can be phrased in a number of ways.

1. A *direct question* asking about philosophy, underlying attitudes, main ideas, characteristics of style, backgrounds, and so on. Here are some possible questions in this category.

    What use do _____, _____, and _____ make of the topic?

    Define and characterize the short story as a genre of literature, using examples from the stories of _____, _____, and _____ .

    Describe the use of dialogue by _____, _____, and _____.

    Contrast the technique of point of view as used by _____, _____, and _____.

2. A *"comment" question*, often based on an extensive quotation, borrowed from a critic or written by your instructor for the occasion, asking about a broad class of writers, a literary movement, or the like. Your instructor may ask you to

treat this question broadly (taking in many writers) or else to apply the quotation to a specific writer.

3. A *"suppose" question*, such as "What advice might Minnie Wright of Glaspell's *Trifles* give the speakers of Elizabeth Barrett Browning's 'How Do I Love Thee' and Keats's 'Bright Star'?" or "What might the speaker of Lowell's poem 'Patterns' say if she learned that her dead lover was actually a person like Goodman Brown of Hawthorne's 'Young Goodman Brown'?" Although "suppose" questions seem whimsical at first sight, they have a serious design and should prompt original and radical thinking. The first question, for example, might cause a test writer to bring out, from Minnie Wright's perspective, that the love expressed by both speakers overlooks the possibilities of changes in character over a long period. She would likely sympathize with the speaker of "How Do I Love Thee," a woman, but she might also say that the speaker's enthusiasm would need to be augmented by the constant exertion of kindness and mutual understanding. For the speaker of "Bright Star," a man, Mrs. Wright might say that the steadfast love he seeks should be linked to thoughtfulness and constant communication as well as passion.

Although "suppose" questions (and answers) are speculative, the need to respond to them requires a detailed consideration of the works involved, and in this respect the "suppose" question is a salutary means of learning. It is of course difficult to prepare for a "suppose" question, which you can therefore regard as a test not only of your knowledge but also of your adaptability, inventiveness, ingenuity, and power of thought.

Understand How Your Responses to General and Comprehensive Questions Will Be Judged and Graded

When answering broad, general questions, you are dealing with an unstructured situation, and you must not only supply an answer but—equally important—create a *structure* within which your answer can have meaning. You might say that you make up your own specific question out of the original general question. If you were asked to consider the role of women as seen in works by Amy Lowell, Maupassant, and Glaspell, for example, you would structure the question by focusing a number of clearly defined topics. A possible way to begin answering such a question might be this.

> Amy Lowell, Maupassant, and Glaspell present a view of female resilience by demonstrating the inner control, endurance, and power of adaptation of their major characters.

With this sort of focus, you would be able to proceed point-by-point, introducing supporting data as you form your answer.

As a general rule, the best method for answering a comprehensive question is comparison-contrast (see also pps. 1589–1605). The reason is that in dealing with, say, a general question on Lawrence, Chekhov, and Keats, it is too easy to write *three* separate essays rather than *one*. Thus, you should try to create a topic such as "the treatment of real or idealized love" or "the difficulties in male-female relationships" and then develop your answer point by point rather than writer by writer. By creating your answer in this way, you can bring in references to each or all of the writers as they become relevant. If you were to treat each writer separately, your comprehensive answer would lose focus and effectiveness, and it would also be repetitive.

Remember that in judging your response to a general question, your instructor is interested in seeing (1) how effectively you perceive and explain the significant issues in the question, (2) how intelligently and clearly you organize your answer, and (3) how persuasively you link your answer to materials from the work as supporting evidence.

Bear in mind that in answering comprehensive questions, you do not have the freedom or license to write about anything at all, whether it is relevant or not. You must stick to the questions. The freedom you do have, however, is the freedom to create your own organization and development in response to the questions that your instructor has asked you. The underlying idea of the comprehensive, general question is that you possess special knowledge and insights that cannot be discovered by more factual questions. You must therefore demonstrate your power of thinking. You need to formulate your own responses to the material and introduce evidence that reflects your own insights and command of information.

A final thought: Try to enjoy the learning experience that preparing for an exam offers you. You may surprise yourself!

Appendix I

Dramatic Vision on Film: From the Silver Screen to the World of Digital Fantasy

Film is the word most often used for motion pictures, although other common words are *cinema, movies,* and sometimes *pics.* It is a specialized type of drama, utilizing, like drama, the techniques of dialogue, monologue, and action. Also like drama, it employs movement and spectacle. For these reasons, film can be studied for aspects such as character, plot, structure, tone, and symbolism. Unlike drama, however, film embodies many techniques from photography, film chemistry, electronic technology, sound, and editing. Because these techniques are an integral aspect of movies, they require special consideration.

A Thumbnail History of Film

Film arose out of technologies developed in the late nineteenth century. The first of these was the invention of a flexible substance—celluloid—that could accept the chemical emulsions that in the early years of photography could be applied only to glass. Other essential inventions were the motion picture camera and projector, together with a screen coated with silver paint on which the moving pictures could be projected. Once these were in place, and once producers and directors decided to use the medium for full-length dramas, movies as we know them came into existence.

Although the earliest filmmakers thought of motion pictures as private entertainment, they soon recognized that the development of large filmmaking studios, national distribution, and a system of local movie theaters could become extremely lucrative. And that is what happened. The history of film is hence just as much a history of the film business as of the art and development of film dramas and film acting. The enormous potential of the movie business was first realized with the production in 1915 of D. W. Griffith's landmark but still controversial film *Birth of a Nation,* which reaped an enormous profit on a small investment.

The first motion pictures were black and white and were silent. Producers realized that large profits required easily recognized actors with "big names," and so the "star system" made national figures out of actors such as Mary Pickford, Charlie Chaplin, and Rudolph Valentino. In 1928 the first talking picture, *Lights of New York,* was made. Filmed drama—the movie—as we know it today was substantially established in 1934 with the first Technicolor film, *La Cucaracha,* a "short subject," and in 1935 with *Becky Sharp,* a feature film. For a long time afterward, however, most movies continued in black and white, whereas color, which was more expensive to produce, was uncommon. More recently the situation has been reversed, with color now being dominant.

For the greater part of film history, movies depended exclusively on the technology of the motion picture camera, but in recent years this technology has been merged with refined electronic enhancements. Many basic visual images are being augmented by digital visual technicians, who can create virtually entire environments. An inhabited island, for example, can be re-created digitally to seem like a desert island; a costumed man actually sitting on nothing more than a sawhorse can be made to appear as a general leading a company of cavalry; and a jerry-built stairway can be transformed into an elegant staircase for richly robed royalty.

This electronic transformation has brought about a revolution in the ways in which contemporary audiences see movies. The development of videotape, DVD (*digital video disc* or *digital versatile disc*), and digital technology has enabled the private viewing of movies at home in addition to the collective viewing of films exclusively in movie theaters. There are now many movie rental options available in shopping districts and through the mail, and there are DVD film clubs that advertise and sell or rent large selections of movies to members. Movies are normal features of television broadcasts and satellite television, and they can be regularly downloaded through the Internet. The result is that most of the movies that have ever been made are within the reach of anyone with a television screen and the proper playing equipment. Miniaturization has also occurred. People can select film offerings on personal computers, iPods, iPhones, and other electronic devices. In short, there are so many outlets for film that today's students face an embarrassment of riches. Early dramatists dreamed of filling their theaters for a number of consecutive performances, thus reaching perhaps several thousand persons. Film writers today, however, reach millions in first-run movie theaters, and they also gain audiences of additional millions through the electronic equipment in modern homes.

Stage Plays and Film

Although film is a form of drama, there are a number of important differences between film and stage productions. Plays can be produced many times, in many different places, with many different people. In bringing a play to life, the producer and director rely not only on actors but also on artists, scene designers, carpenters, painters, lighting technicians, costume makers, choreographers, music directors, and musicians. For the actual performance of a play, however, the stage itself limits what can be done. In each theater production, the actors, setting, and effects are all physically confined to the stage.

The stage for makers of film, however, is virtually infinite, and the absence of restrictions permits the inclusion of countless details—car chases, underwater adventures, flying geese following an airplane, wartime combat, legislative debates, executive discussions; scenes in living rooms, courtrooms, boxing rings, hotel rooms, football stadiums, and kitchens; and locations in cities and countrysides anywhere—domestic or foreign, modern or ancient. And if a location or setting is not readily available, technicians can dub it in by computer enhancement, as in the various Harry Potter movies that show imaginative settings together with individual actors flying through the air at will—sometimes on broomsticks. Such computerized and digital special effects, in which filmmakers sometimes indulge

🎬 DVD TECHNOLOGY AND FILM STUDY

Of particular importance for today's students of movies is the easy availability of DVDs, many of which are issued with extra features that provide informative background and sidelights for film study—in addition, of course, to the basic film itself. A common "extra" is a film index that permits the viewer to select individual scenes and to replay them at will. Viewers may also find voiceover commentaries by screenwriters, directors, critics, various experts, and principal members of the cast. Additional features for study are selected scenes that were reduced or omitted in the final editing, together with complete alternative "takes" of various scenes. In these respects, many DVDs provide topics and guides for study.

The release of a DVD version of a film may often be considered an event itself in the film's history. The DVD version of Orson Welles's *Citizen Kane* contains a totally remastered edition of the movie, and in addition it features running analyses of the entire movie by both Roger Ebert, a preeminent film critic, and Peter Bogdanovich, a widely recognized film director (Turner Home Video © 2001). The DVD of Terry Gilliam's 1985 film *Brazil* includes instructive interviews about the problems and controversies that preceded and followed the film's release. Of course, not all DVDs are equally elaborate. The reissues of Charlie Chaplin's comedies, for example, contain just the films, such as *City Lights* (one of the American Film Institute's recommendation as a best "romantic" film) and *The Gold Rush*. Even some of the releases of relatively new and successful films do not contain extras.

too liberally, can create dramatic images that were beyond reach for the greatest part of theater, and human, history. In short, the freedom enjoyed by the filmmaker almost limitlessly exceeds the freedom of the play producer. Nothing is left to the audience's imagination.

The two types of dramatic productions—drama and film—are therefore greatly different. Each new production of a play is unlike every other production, because not only the actors but also the appurtenances of the staging are unique. Shakespeare's play *Hamlet*, for example, has been produced innumerable times since Shakespeare's actors at London's Globe Theatre first performed it at the beginning of the seventeenth century, and each subsequent production, including the various filmed versions, has been different from all the rest.[1]

Paradoxically, this same variety cannot easily occur with film. Although the filmmaker has great freedom in producing each individual movie, this freedom also imposes its own limitations. Because of high production costs and also because films reach a mass audience through wide distribution, films are generally released in only one version, perhaps with "remakes" and dubbed versions for foreign audiences. Thus the classic Orson Welles film *Citizen Kane* (1941) is in

---

[1] See Chapter 20, pages 977–81, for a brief discussion of the Ghost scene as presented in seven recent DVD versions of *Hamlet*.

only one form, and although it has been recently restored and re-edited, it remains in this form even though it is frequently shown and seen. Interestingly, no person can ever claim to have seen all the productions of plays like *Hamlet*, but everyone who sees a film like *Citizen Kane* can claim to have seen the one and only version.

The Aesthetics of Film

To the degree that film is confined to a screen, it can be compared visually with the art of the painter and the still photographer. It uses the language of visual art, where one object in a painting can take on special relationships to others as the artist directs the eyes of the observer. A color used in one part can be balanced with the same color, or its complement, in another part. Painters and photographers can introduce certain colors and details as symbols and can suggest allegorical interpretations through the inclusion of mythical figures or universally recognized objects. Particular effects can be achieved with the use of the textures of paint or with control over shutter speed, focus, and various techniques of development. The techniques and effects are extensive.

The filmmaker is able to utilize most of the resources of the still photographer and many of those of the painter and can augment these with special electronic effects. Artistically, the most confining aspect of film is the rectangular screen, but aside from that, film is unrestricted. Based in a dramatic text called a **film script** or **shooting script,** the film uses words and their effects, but it also employs the language of visual art and especially the particular vividness and power of moving pictures. When considering film, then, you should realize that film communicates not only with words but also with various visual techniques. The visual presentation is inseparable from the medium of film itself.

The Techniques of Film

There are many techniques of film, and a full description and documentation of them can be—and has become—extensive.[2] In evaluating film, however, you need to familiarize yourself only with those aspects of technique that have an immediate bearing on your responses and interpretations.

See, for example, David Bleiler, *TLA Film, Video, and DVD Guide 2005: The Discerning Film Lover's Guide;* Roger Ebert, *Roger Ebert's Movie Yearbook 2013* (2012); Roger Ebert, *The Great Movies III* (2011); Louis D. Giannetti, *Understanding Movies,* 12th ed. (2010); Leslie Halliwell, *Halliwell's Film Guide, 2008* (2008); Ephraim Katz, *The Film Encyclopedia,* 7th ed. (2012); Leonard Maltin, *Leonard Maltin's 2014 Movie Guide* (2013); James Monaco, *How to Read a Film: The World of Movies, Media, and Beyond* (2009); Richard Beck Peacock, *The Art of Movie Making: Script to Screen* (2001); John Pym, *Time Out Film Guide 2008,* 16th ed. (2007); Robert Sklar, *A World History of Film* (2003); and David Thomson, *The New Biographical Dictionary of Film,* 5th ed. (2010).

See also the Internet Movie Database for complete data on films of all periods, at www.imdb.com. In 2008, the American Film Institute declared its own recommendations for film history through the issuance of *America's 10 Greatest Films in 10 Classic Genres* (www.afi.com/10top10).

Film Utilizes Special Visual Techniques

THE CAMERA IS THE BASIC TOOL OF FILM. Each film begins with the technique of the camera—buttressed today by electronic effects—which permits great freedom in the presentation of characters and actions. In a film, the visual viewpoint can shift. Thus, a film can begin with a distant shot of the actors—a "long shot"—much like the view of actors onstage. Then the camera can zoom in to show a close-up or zoom out to present a wide and complete panorama. Usually a speaking actor will be the subject of a close-up, but the camera view can also capture other actors' reactions in close-up. You must interpret the effects of close-ups and long shots yourself, but it should be plain that the frequent use of either—or of middle-distance views—is a means by which film directors control viewer perception of characters and situations.

The camera can also move from character to character or from character to object. In this way, film can mark a series of reactions, concentrate your attention on a character's attitude, or comment visually on a character's actions. If a man and woman are in love, for example, the photographic view can shift from the couple to flowers and trees, thus associating their love visually with objects of beauty and growth. Should the flowers be wilted and the trees leafless, however, the visual commentary might be that their love is doomed and hopeless.

The camera also lends itself to the creation of unique effects. A common technique is slow motion, which can be used to emphasize a certain aspect of a person's character. The concentrated focus on a child running happily in a meadow (as in *The Color Purple* [1985] by Steven Spielberg) suggests the joy inherent in such movement. Surprisingly, speed is sometimes indicated by slow motion, which emphasizes strong muscular effort (as in the running scenes in Hugh Hudson's *Chariots of Fire* [1981]).

Many other camera techniques bear on action and character. The focus can be sharp at one point, indistinct at another. Moving a speaking character out of focus can suggest that listeners are bored. Sharp or blurred focus can also show that a character has seen things exactly or inexactly. In action sequences, the camera can be mounted in a moving vehicle to "track" or follow running human beings or horses, speeding bicycles and cars (as in Woody Allen's *Annie Hall* [1977]), or moving sailboats, canoes, speedboats, or rowboats. A camera operator on foot can also be the tracker, or the camera may track ground movement from a helicopter or from the top of a bridge. Movement can also be captured by a rotating focal point that follows a moving object or character. Alternatively, the camera can be fixed while a character or object moves from one side of the frame to the other.

THE IMAGES IN FILM INVOLVE LIGHT, SHADOW, AND COLOR. As in traditional theater, the filmmaker uses light, shadow, and color to reinforce ideas and to create realistic and symbolic effects. Characters in bright light are presumably open and frank, whereas characters in shadow may be hiding something, as in Alan J. Pakula's *All the President's Men* (1976). Flashing or strobe lights might indicate a changeable or sinister character or situation. A scene in sunshine, which brings out colors, and the same scene in rain and clouds or in twilight, all of which mute colors, create different moods. An example of such contrasts is the film *From Hell* (2001), directed by Albert and Allen Hughes, in which virtually the entire action takes place in darkness, and only the final scene is filmed in full light.

Colors, of course, have much the same meaning that they have in any other artistic medium. Blue sky and clear light suggest happiness, while dimly greenish light may indicate something ghoulish. A memorable control of color occurs midway through David O. Selznick's classic film *Gone with the Wind* (1939) when Scarlett O'Hara reflects upon the devastation of her plantation home. She resolves never to be hungry again, and as she speaks she is silhouetted against a darkened orange sky—a background that suggests how totally the way of life she knew as a young woman has been burned away. As in this example, you may expect colors to complement the story of the film. Thus, lovers may wear clothing with the same or complementary colors, whereas people who are not "right" for each other may wear clashing colors.

Action Is the Essence of Film

The strength of film is direct action. Actions of all sorts—running, swimming, driving a car, fighting, embracing and kissing, or even just sitting; chases, trick effects, ambushes—all these and more create a sense of immediate reality, and all are tied (or should be) to narrative development. Scenes of action can run on for several minutes, with little or no accompanying dialogue, to carry on the story or to convey ideas about the interests and abilities of the characters.

Camera Angles and Views of the Heads, Bodies, and Movements of Actors Are Related to a Film's Content

Closely related to the portrayal of action is the way in which film shows the human body (and animal bodies) together with bodily motion and gesture (or body language). The view or perspective that the filmmaker presents is particularly important. A torso shot of a character may stress no more than the content of that character's speech. A close-up shot, however, with the character's head filling the screen, may emphasize motives as well as content. The camera can also distort ordinary expectations of reality. Using wide-angle lenses and close-ups, for example, human subjects can be made to seem bizarre or grotesque, as are the faces in the crowd in Woody Allen's *Stardust Memories* (1980). Sometimes the camera creates other bodily distortions—for example, enlarging the limbs of the forest dweller in Ingmar Bergman's *The Virgin Spring* (1959) or throwing into unnatural prominence a scolding mouth or a suspicious eye. Distortion invites interpretation: The filmmaker may be asserting that certain human beings, even supposedly normal ones, are odd, sinister, intimidating, or psychopathic.

Sound Is Integral to the Presentation and Content of a Film

DIALOGUE AND MUSIC COMPLEMENT FILM DRAMATIZATIONS. The first business of the sound track is the spoken dialogue, which is mixed in editing to be synchronized with the action. There are also many other elements in the sound track. Music, the most important, creates and augments moods. A melody in a major or minor key or in a slow or fast tempo can affect our perception of actions. If a character is thinking deeply, complementary music may be played by muted strings. But if the character is going insane, the music may become discordant and percussive.

Sometimes, music gives a film a special identity. Hudson's *Chariots of Fire* (1981), for example, includes music by Vangelis. Although this music is independently well known, it is always associated with the film. In addition, musical accompaniments can directly render dramatic statement, without dialogue. An example occurs in Welles's *Citizen Kane* (1941). Beginning that portion of the narrative derived from the autobiography of a character who is now dead (the scene first focuses on his statue), the musical sound track by Bernard Herrmann quotes the *Dies Irae* theme from the traditional Mass for the Dead. The instrumentation, however, makes the music funny, and we smile rather than grieve. Incidentally, Herrmann varies the *Dies Irae* theme elsewhere in the film, usually for comic effect.

FILM USES SPECIAL AND OFTEN INGENIOUS SOUND EFFECTS. Special sound effects can also augment a film's action. The sound of a blow can be enhanced electronically to cause an impact similar to the force of the blow itself (as in the boxing scenes from the many *Rocky* films). At times some sounds—such as the noises of wailing people, squeaking or slamming doors, marching feet, or moving vehicles—are electronically filtered to create weird or ghostly effects. Often a character's words echo rapidly and sickeningly to show dismay or anguish.

Editing or Montage

A finished film is a composite, not a continuous work filmed from start to end. The putting together of the film is the process of editing, or **montage** (assemblage, mounting, construction), which at one time involved cutting and gluing, but which now takes place on specially programmed computers. Depending on the flexibility of the film-script, the various scenes of the film are planned before shooting begins, but the major task of montage is accomplished in a studio by editing specialists.

If we again compare film with a stage play, we note that a theatrical production moves continuously, with pauses only for intermissions and scene changes. Your perception of the action is caused by your distance from the stage (perhaps aided by opera glasses or binoculars). Also, even as you move your eyes from one character to another, you still perceive the entire stage. In a film, however, the directors and editors *create* these continuous perceptions for you by piecing together different parts. The editors begin with many "takes" (separately photographed scenes, including many versions of the same scenes). What they select, or "mount," will be the film, and we never see the discarded scenes (unless they appear as special features on a DVD). Thus, it is montage, or editing, that puts everything together.

MONTAGE CREATES NARRATIVE CONTINUITY. The first use of montage, already suggested, is narrative continuity. For example, a climb up a steep cliff can be shown at the bottom, middle, and top (with backward slips and falls to show the danger of the climb and to make viewers catch their breath). All such narrative sequences result from the assembling of individual pieces, each one representing phases of the activity. A classic example of a large number of separate parts forming a narrative unit is the well-known shower murder in Alfred Hitchcock's *Psycho* (1959), where a forty-five-second sequence is made up of seventy-eight different shots (the woman in the shower, the murderer behind the curtain, the attack, the slumping figure, the running water, the dead woman's eye, the bathtub drain, etc.).

MONTAGE PROVIDES EXPLANATION OF CHARACTER AND MOTIVATION. Montage is used in flashbacks to explain ongoing actions or characteristics; or in illustration of a character's thoughts and memories; or in brief examples from the unremembered past of a character suffering from amnesia. It also supplies direct visual explanation of character. A famous example occurs in Welles's *Citizen Kane*. The concluding scene shows overhead views of Kane's vast collection of statuary and mementos. At the very end, the camera focuses on a raging furnace, into which workmen have thrown his boyhood sled that bears the brand name "Rosebud" (we have fleetingly seen Kane playing with the sled as a boy). Because "Rosebud" is Kane's last word, and everyone in the film is trying to decipher its meaning, this final scene reveals that Kane's dying thoughts were of his lost boyhood, before he was taken away from his parents, and that his unhappy life has resulted from early rejection and personal pain. (When we first see him as a boy, he is playing in the snow with his sled.)

MONTAGE FACILITATES DIRECTORIAL COMMENTARY. Montage is also used symbolically as commentary, as in an early sequence in Charlie Chaplin's *Modern Times* (1936) that shows a large group of workers rushing to their factory jobs. Immediately following this scene is a view of a large, milling herd of sheep. By this symbolic montage, Chaplin suggests that the men are being herded and dehumanized by modern industry. Thus, montage and editorial statement go hand in hand.

MONTAGE IS USED IN MANY OTHER WAYS. Montage can also produce other characteristics through camera work, development, and special effects of sound and light. For example, montage editors might reverse an action to emphasize its illogicality or ridiculousness. Editing can also speed up action (which makes even the most serious things funny) or slow things down. It can also blend one scene with another or juxtapose two or more actions in quick succession to show what people are doing while they are separated. The possibilities for creativity and innovation are extensive.

It bears stressing that montage should be thought of as the finishing stage in the readying of the film for presentation. When the photographic and other technical phases of filmmaking are completed, there is often much leftover material—enough to make a movie that would run for many hours and perhaps even days. The movie is definitely not yet ready for distribution.

It is the montage editors who put everything together, sitting at their machines trying, testing, and arranging. They pick and choose to create many separate but connected scenes from the abundance of material at their command. They might begin by selecting a long-shot, and then they might pick out film footage that represents a closer view of the action. A character may begin a gesture as we see him or her from a distance. But by the time the gesture is completed there may be a number of close-up and semi-close-up views of that character. In addition, there may be responses of other characters to the action. Similarly, a group of people may be walking together over the countryside, and at first we see the entire group, maybe of twenty, or forty, or more. And then, through montage, the scene may focus on several characters together. And then one or two individually, and then one of them may stumble, and that in itself creates group reactions. Then the characters may stop to have dinner. Or maybe the group may stop to rest while some of the characters seek their dinner by using fishing equipment or rifles.

In such ways, the number of separate scenes that develop from any particular event can become magnified, modified, and individualized, and the final narrative scene will have been selected and pieced together from many separate views. No movie is ever complete until a considerable amount of montage work has been done on it. And even then what seems to be a final version may still be too long to present as a workable movie, and at that point the montage editors go back to their computers to shorten some scenes and to excise others.

By the time the finished film is presented to the public, it has been through the hands of one or more montage editors who, with the director and others closely involved in the process, have made innumerable artistic decisions about the final version that we see.

WRITING ABOUT FILM

Obviously the first requirement is to see the film, either in a movie theater, on DVD, or streamed to a digital device. No matter how you see it, you should go through it at least twice, taking notes, because your discussion takes on value the more thoroughly you know the material. Include the names of the scriptwriter, director, composer, special effects editor, chief photographer, and major actresses and actors. If particular speeches are worth quoting, remember the general circumstances of the quotation and also, if possible, key words. Take notes on costume and color or (if the film is in black and white) on light and shade. You may need to rely on memory, but if you have a DVD or a device that allows you to pause and rewind, you can easily replay important sections of the film and can verify important details.

Questions for Discovering Ideas

ACTION

- How important is action? Is there much repetition of action, say, in slow motion, or from different angles? Are actors (or animals) viewed closely or distantly? Why?
- What actions are stressed (chases, concealment, gun battles, lovemaking, etc.)? What does the type of action contribute to the film?
- What do close-ups (smiles and laughter, frowns, leers, anxious looks, etc.) show about character and motivation?
- What actions indicate seasonal conditions (e.g., cold by a character's stamping of feet, warmth by the character's removing a coat or shirt)? What connection do these actions have to the film's general ideas?

- Does the action show any changing of mood, say, from sadness to happiness or from indecision to decision?

CINEMATOGRAPHIC TECHNIQUES

- What notable techniques are used (colors, lighting, etc.)? What is their relationship to the film's characterizations and themes?
- What characterizes the use of the camera (tracking, close-ups, distant shots, camera angles, etc.)? How do the camera perspectives reinforce or detract from the film's theme and plot?
- How does the editing (the sequencing of scenes) reinforce or detract from story and theme?
- What scene or scenes best exemplify how the cinematographic techniques interact with the theme, plot, characters, setting, and so on? Why?

ACTING

- How well do the actors adapt to the medium of film? How well do they deliver their lines? How convincing are their performances?
- How well do the actors control their facial expressions and body movement? Are they graceful? Awkward?
- What does their appearance lend to your understanding of their characters?
- Does it seem that the actors are genuinely creating their roles, or are they just reading through the parts?

Strategies for Organizing Ideas

State your central idea and thesis sentence. You should include the background necessary to support points you make in the body of the essay and should also name the major creative and performing persons of the film.

Any of the organizing strategies discussed in this book's previous chapters, such as plot, structure, character, ideas, or setting, are equally valid for an essay on a film, except that you will need to consider them in a visual context. For example, if you choose to discuss the effects of a character on the plot, you need to develop your argument using the evidence of camera techniques, montage, sound effects, and the like.

When discussing film techniques, be sure to have good notes so that your supporting details are accurate. A good method is to concentrate on technique in only a few scenes. If you analyze the effects of montage, for example, you can use a DVD or another digital device to repeat seeing the scene a number of times.

In the conclusion of your essay, you might evaluate the effectiveness of the cinematic form to story and idea. Are all the devices of film used in the best possible way? Is anything overdone? Is anything underplayed? Is the film good, bad, or indifferent up to a point, and then does it change? How? Why?

Writing Topics About Film

Writing Paragraphs

Select a scene of monologue or dialogue in a film of your choice. Write a paragraph about the dramatic (cinematic) speech and language in your selection, and try to deal with issues such as the educational level and way of life of the speakers (based on their diction and their grammar), their interests, their judgments of each other and their attitudes toward each other, their attempts to persuade each other about their ideas or plans, and so on. Because you are writing only a single paragraph, you might in fact find it interesting to concentrate on just one of these issues.

Writing Essays

1. Select a single film technique, such as the use of color, the control of light, or the photographing of action, and write an essay describing how it is used in a film of your choice. For best results, use a DVD for your study. As much as possible, try to explain how the technique is used throughout the film. Determine similar and contrasting features, the relationship of the technique to the development of story and character, and so on.

2. Write an essay explaining how the film techniques of a particular part or section of a film are employed (e.g., camera angles, close-ups or long shots, tracking, on-camera and off-camera speeches, lighting, depth of field). For your essay, you may have to rerun the section a number of times, trying to notice elements for the first time and also reinforcing your first observations.

Creative Writing Assignment

1. Pick out a news story and write your own original film scene based on it, being aware of how your action and dialogue might be adapted to the scene, and how the action and responses might be directed for the actors and camera operators (e.g., "As Character A speaks on such-and-such a topic, his face shows that he is lying"; "the camera zooms slowly in on his face, with a loss of focus"; or "As Character A speaks in response to the topic, the camera focuses on Character B exchanging looks with Character C"). When you are done, write an explanation of how you intend your directions to bring out details about your story and characters.

Library Assignment

1. Consult as many as three of the works by Bleiler, Ebert, Giannetti, Halliwell, Katz, Maltin, Monaco, Peacock, Sklar, and Thomson that are listed in the footnote on page 1633. Write a brief report on the sorts of details that the film critics bring out about the various films they discuss and review. That is, what are the film subjects in which they are interested? How much detail do they bring out about individual films? In their discussions, how completely do they evaluate such matters as the story, the settings, the action, the acting, the topicality of the subject matter, and the originality of the film script? What sorts of things do they praise, and, conversely, what are the sorts of things to which they object?

Appendix II

MLA Recommendations for Documenting Sources

This appendix provides general guidelines for making source citations, and therefore it is intended to augment the section titled "Documenting Your Work" in Chapter 10A. For general information on citation recommendations by the Modern Language Association (MLA), see Joseph Gibaldi, *MLA Handbook for Writers of Research Papers*, 7th ed. (New York: MLA, 2009).

The following examples show the formats you are likely to use most often, both for nonelectronic and electronic references.

(Nonelectronic) Books, Articles, Poems, Letters, Reviews, Recordings, and Programs

Book by One Author

Fitzgerald, F. Scott. *The Great Gatsby*. New York: Scribner, 1925. Print.

Book with No Author Listed

The Pictorial History of the Guitar. New York: Random, 1992. Print.

Book by Two (or Three) Authors

Clemens, Samuel L., and Charles Dudley Warner. *The Gilded Age: A Tale of Today*. Hartford: American, 1874. Print.

Book by Four or More Authors

Guerin, Wilfred L., Earle Labor, Lee Morgan, Jeanne C. Reesman, and John R. Willingham. *A Handbook of Critical Approaches to Literature*. 6th ed. New York: Oxford UP, 2010. Print.

or

Guerin, Wilfred L., et al. *A Handbook of Critical Approaches to Literature*. 6th ed. New York: Oxford UP, 2010. Print.

Two Books by the Same Author

Reynolds, David S. *Beneath the American Renaissance*. Cambridge: Harvard UP, 1988. Print.

———. *Walt Whitman's America: A Cultural Biography*. New York: Knopf, 1995. Print.

Citing a Book

5 Date of Publication

THE

Great Gatsby

BY F. SCOTT FITZGERALD

Then wear the gold hat, if that will move her;
If you can bounce high, bounce for her too,
Till the cry "Lover, gold-hatted, high-bouncing lover,
I must have you!"

—THOMAS PARKE D'INVILLIERS

Prentice Hall
Upper Saddle River, New Jersey 07458

ISBN   0-02-338120-5

Prentice-Hall International (UK) *Limited, London*
Prentice-Hall of Australia Pty. *Limited, Sydney*
Prentice-Hall Canada Inc., *Toronto*
Prentice-Hall Hispanoamericana, S.A., *Mexico*
Prentice-Hall of India Private Limited, *New Delhi*
Prentice-Hall of Japan, Inc., *Tokyo*
Simon & Schuster Asia Pte. Ltd., *Singapore*
Editora Prentice-Hall do Brasil, Ltda., *Rio de Janeiro*

F. SCOTT FITZGERALD

THE GREAT
GATSBY

1 Author

2 Title

3 Place of Publication

4 Publisher

| 1 | 2 | 3 | 4 | 5 |

Fitzgerald, F. Scott. *The Great Gatsby*. Upper Saddle River: Prentice Hall, 1968. Print.

Book with an Editor

Scharnhorst, Gary, ed. *Selected Letters of Bret Harte*. Norman: U of Oklahoma P, 1997. Print.

Book with Two Editors

Dionne, Craig, and Steve Mentz, eds. *Rogues and Early Modern English Culture*. Ann Arbor: U of Michigan P, 2004. Print.

Book with an Author and an Editor

De Quille, Dan. *The Fighting Horse of the Stanislaus*. Ed. Lawrence I. Berkove. Iowa City: U of Iowa P, 1990. Print.

Translated Book

Cervantes Saavedra, Miguel de. *Don Quixote de la Mancha*. Trans. Charles Jarvis. New York: Oxford UP, 1999. Print.

Long Poem Published as a Book

Homer. *The Odyssey*. Trans. Robert Fitzgerald. New York: Vintage, 1990. Print.

Collection of Poetry Published as a Book

Carson, Anne. *Red Doc>*. New York: Knopf, 2013. Print.

Literary Work in an Anthology

Frost, Robert. "Mending Wall." *Literature for Composition: An Introduction to Literature*. Ed. Sylvan Barnet, William Burto, and William Cain. 10th ed. Boston: Pearson, 2014. 222–23. Print.

Introduction, Preface, Foreword, or Afterword in a Book

Pryse, Marjorie. Introduction. *The Country of the Pointed Firs and Other Stories*. By Sarah Orne Jewett. New York: Norton, 1981. v–xix. Print.

Article in a Reference Book

Burt, Stephen. "Twenty-first Century Free Verse." *A New Literary History of America*. Ed. Greil Marcus and Werner Sollors. Cambridge, MA: Belknap Press, 2009. 1030–34. Print.

Article in a Journal

Kruse, Horst. "The Motif of the Flattened Corpse." *Studies in American Humor* 3.4 (1997): 47–53. Print.

Signed Book Review

Lee, Hermione. Rev. of *The Selected Letters of Willa Cather*, by Andrew Jewell and Janis Stout. *New York Review of Books* 50.12 (11 July 2013): 46–49. Print.

Unsigned Book Review

Rev. of *Canons by Consensus: Critical Trends and American Literature Anthologies*, by Joseph Csicsila. *Essays in Arts and Sciences* 24 (2000): 69–74. Print.

Citing a Work in an Anthology

8 The Pages on Which the Work Appears in Anthology

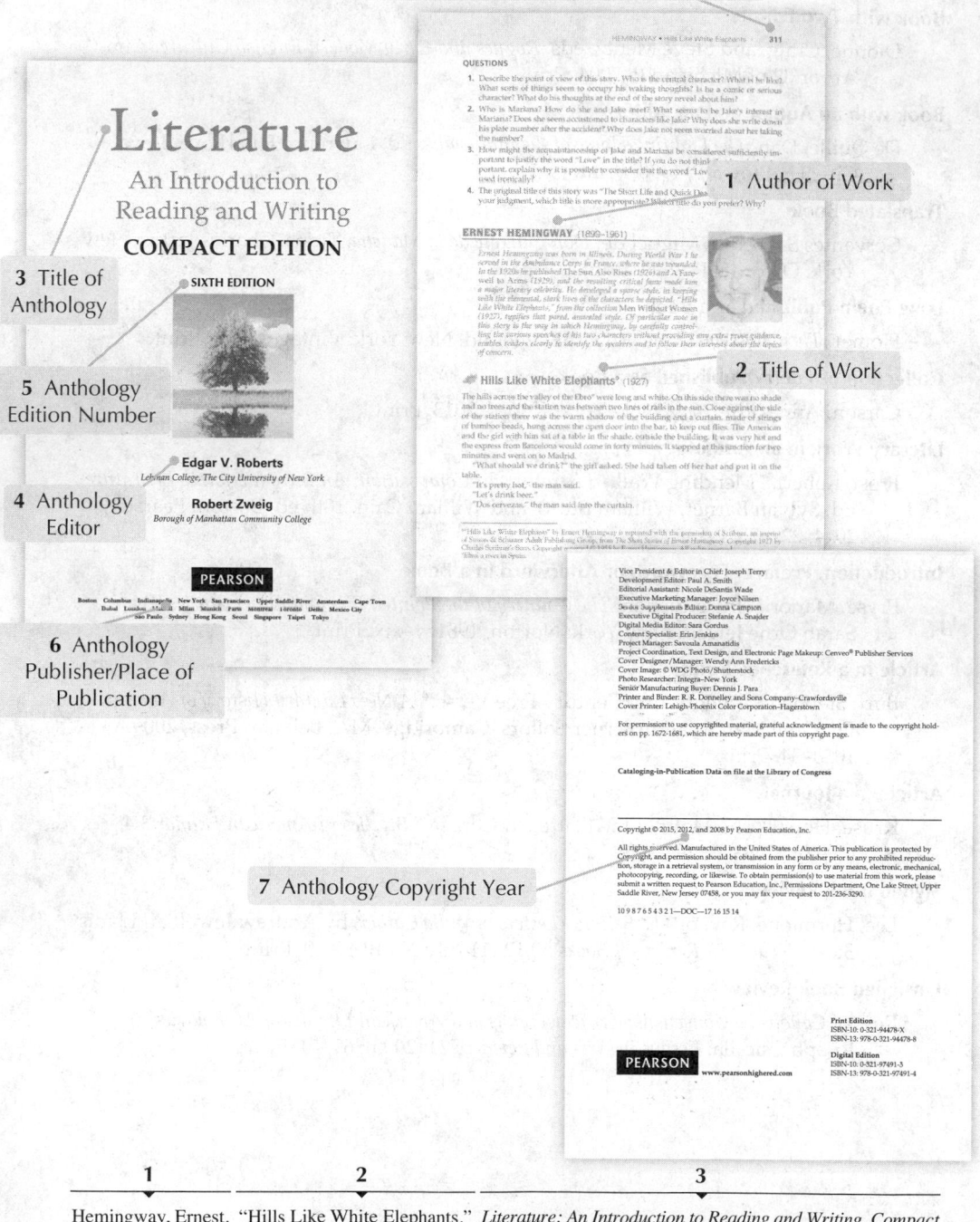

1 Author of Work

3 Title of Anthology

SIXTH EDITION

5 Anthology Edition Number

2 Title of Work

4 Anthology Editor

6 Anthology Publisher/Place of Publication

7 Anthology Copyright Year

1	2	3

Hemingway, Ernest. "Hills Like White Elephants." *Literature: An Introduction to Reading and Writing, Compact*

Edition.   Ed. Edgar V. Roberts and Robert Zweig.   6th ed.   New York: Pearson, 2015.   311–14. Print.

3 cont.	4	5	6	7	8

Citing an Article in a Journal

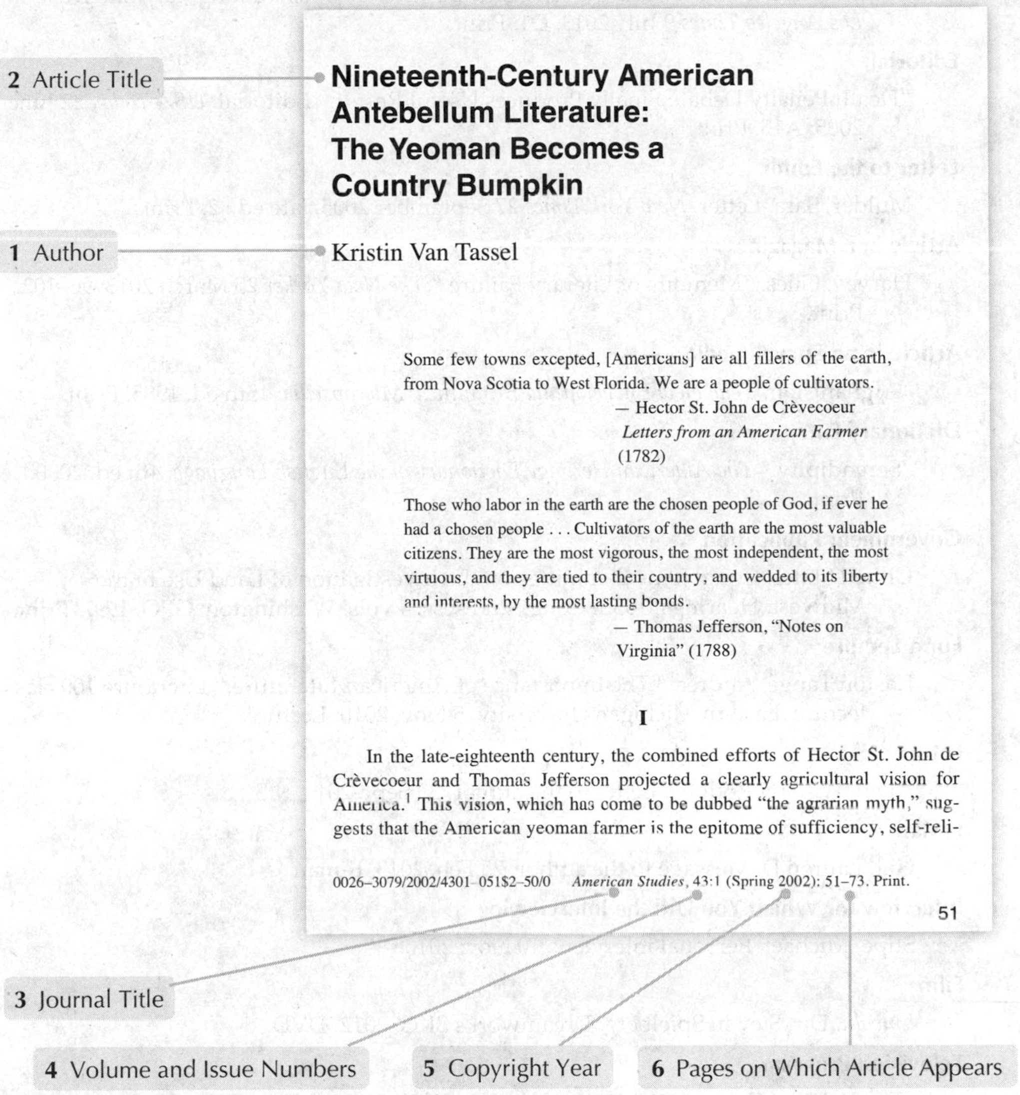

2 Article Title ⎯⎯⎯⎯⎯⎯⎯⎯ • **Nineteenth-Century American Antebellum Literature: The Yeoman Becomes a Country Bumpkin**

1 Author ⎯⎯⎯⎯⎯⎯⎯⎯⎯ • Kristin Van Tassel

Some few towns excepted, [Americans] are all fillers of the earth, from Nova Scotia to West Florida. We are a people of cultivators.
— Hector St. John de Crèvecoeur
Letters from an American Farmer
(1782)

Those who labor in the earth are the chosen people of God, if ever he had a chosen people . . . Cultivators of the earth are the most valuable citizens. They are the most vigorous, the most independent, the most virtuous, and they are tied to their country, and wedded to its liberty and interests, by the most lasting bonds.
— Thomas Jefferson, "Notes on Virginia" (1788)

I

In the late-eighteenth century, the combined efforts of Hector St. John de Crèvecoeur and Thomas Jefferson projected a clearly agricultural vision for America.[1] This vision, which has come to be dubbed "the agrarian myth," suggests that the American yeoman farmer is the epitome of sufficiency, self-reli-

0026–3079/2002/4301–051$2–50/0   *American Studies*, 43:1 (Spring 2002): 51–73. Print.

51

3 Journal Title

4 Volume and Issue Numbers   **5** Copyright Year   **6** Pages on Which Article Appears

Note: A scholarly article in printed form ordinarily provides all necessary information on its first page.

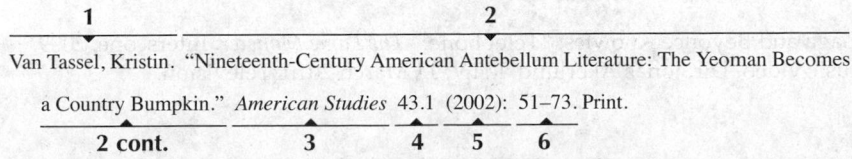

          1   2
Van Tassel, Kristin. "Nineteenth-Century American Antebellum Literature: The Yeoman Becomes

a Country Bumpkin." *American Studies* 43.1 (2002): 51–73. Print.

     2 cont.   **3**   **4**   **5**   **6**

Article in a Newspaper

Chmielewski, Dawn C., and Steven Zeitchik. "Disney's Risk-taking May Bite Dust." *Los Angeles Times* 9 July 2013. D1. Print.

Editorial

"Death Penalty Debate Finally Produces Useful Result." Editorial. *USA Today* 22 June 2005: A15. Print.

Letter to the Editor

Mulder, Sara. Letter. *New York Times* 27 September 2005, late ed.: 2. Print.

Article in a Magazine

Harvey, Giles. "Memoirs of Literary Failure." *The New Yorker* 25 March 2013: 96–102. Print.

Article in an Encyclopedia

"Afghanistan." *The New Encyclopedia Britannica: Micropaedia.* 15th ed. 1985. Print.

Dictionary Entry

"Serendipity." *The American Heritage Dictionary of the English Language.* 4th ed. 2000. Print.

Government Publication

United States. Cong. Joint Committee on the Investigation of Land Use in the Midwest. Hearings. 105th Cong., 2nd sess. 4 vols. Washington: GPO, 1997. Print.

For a Lecture

Kaston Tange, Andrea. "The Importance of American Literature." Literature 100 class lecture. Eastern Michigan University, 5 Nov. 2010. Lecture.

Letter

Allen, William Rodney. Letter to the author. 23 Sept. 2014. MS.

E-Mail

Gill, Lauren D. Message to the author. 25 Feb. 2013. E-mail.

Interview for Which You Did the Interviewing

Stipe, Michael. Personal interview. 10 Nov. 2010.

Film

Lincoln. Dir. Steven Spielberg. Dreamworks SKG. 2012. DVD.

Television Program

"The Rains of Castamere." *Game of Thrones.* HBO. 23 June 2013. Television.

Sound Recording

Timberlake, Justin. *The 20/20 Experience.* RCA Records. 2013. CD.

Song on a Recording

Timberlake, Justin. "Mirrors." *The 20/20 Experience.* RCA Records. 2013. CD.

Music Video

Lady Gaga and Beyoncé Knowles. "Telephone." *The Fame Monster.* Interscope, 2009. Music video. Dir. Jonas Akerlund. MTV. 11 March 2010. Television.

MLA Style Guidelines for Electronic Sources

Many of the guidelines the MLA has authorized for the citation of electronic sources overlap with the MLA recommendations for printed sources, but to avoid ambiguity a number of recommendations bear repetition. Electronic materials are to be documented in basically the same style as printed sources. According to the seventh edition of the *MLA Handbook,* which illustrates virtually all the situations you can ever encounter, the following items need to be included if they are relevant and available.

1. The name of the author, editor, compiler, or translator of the source (if available and relevant), last name first, followed by an abbreviation, such as *ed.,* if appropriate.

2. If there is no author listed in the source, you should list the title first: the title of a poem, short story, article, or similar short work within a scholarly project, database, or periodical (in quotation marks); or the title of a posting to a discussion list or forum (taken from the subject line and enclosed by quotation marks).

3. The title of the larger work, italicized, such as the title of the scholarly project, periodical, or professional or personal site; or, for a professional or personal site with no title, a description such as "Home Page."

4. The name of the editor, compiler, or translator of the larger work (if relevant and if not cited earlier), preceded by (not followed by) any necessary abbreviations, such as *Ed.*

5. Publication information for any printed version of the source, if relevant.

6. The version number of the source (if not part of the title), or, for a journal, the volume number, issue number, or other identifying number. All numbers should be in Arabic numerals, not Roman.

7. The date of publication or posting that you find in your source. Sometimes the original date is no longer available because it has been replaced with an update; if so, cite that. If no date is provided, use the abbreviation "n.d." Dates should be arranged by (a) day of the month, (b) month (the names of longer months may be abbreviated), and (c) year.

8. The name of any institution or organization sponsoring or associated with the website. For a work from a subscription service, the name of the service. For a posting to a discussion list or forum, the name of the list or forum.

9. The number range or total number of pages, paragraphs, or other sections, if they are numbered.

10. The medium of publication, in this case, usually "Web."

11. The date when you consulted the source. If you have looked at the site a number of times, include the most recent date of use.

12. If the site is not easily located through other means, include the electronic address or URL of the source in angle brackets < >. If the URL is too long to fit on one line, the line break should occur after a slash (/) if possible. (Do not introduce hyphenations into the URL as these may be mistaken for actual significant characters in that address.)

Citing an Online Book

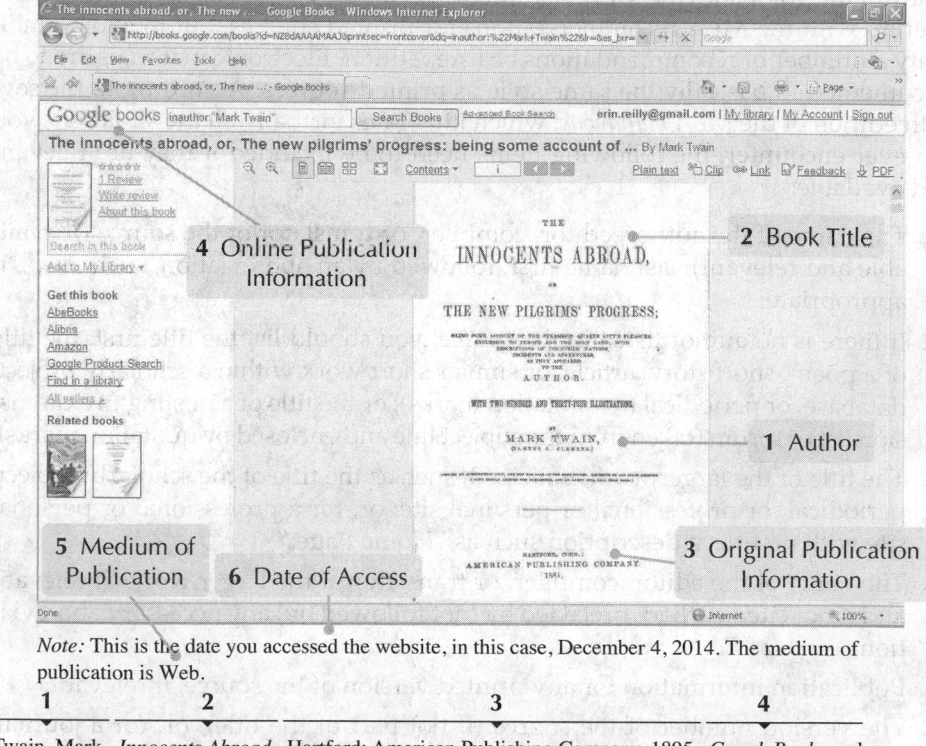

Note: This is the date you accessed the website, in this case, December 4, 2014. The medium of publication is Web.

<u>1</u>   <u>2</u>   <u>3</u>   <u>4</u>

Twain, Mark. *Innocents Abroad*. Hartford: American Publishing Company, 1895. *GoogleBooks*, n.d.

<u>Web. 4 Dec. 2014.</u>
  5   6

Online Book with Print Information

Dickens, Charles. *David Copperfield*. New York: P. F. Collier, 1917. *Bartleby Archive*, 1999. Web. 25 Mar. 2014.

Online Book Without Print Information

Shakespeare, William. *Hamlet*. c. 1601. *Project Gutenberg*. Web. 25 Mar. 2014.

Journal Article on the Web

Hewlett, Beth L., and Christa Ehmann Powers. "How Do You Ground Your Training? Sharing the Principles and Processes of Preparing Educators for Online Writing Instruction." *Kairos* 10.1 (2005): n.p. Web. 10 May 2014.

Newspaper Article on the Web

Faughnder, Ryan. "Film producer crowdfunds documentary about PCH's 'Blood Alley.'" *latimes.com*. Los Angeles Times, 19 August 2013. Web. 27 June 2014.

Journal Article in a Scholarly Database

Yates, Norris W. "The Doubt and Faith of John Updike." *College English* 26.6 (1995): 469–74. *JSTOR*. Web. 12 May 2014.

Citing an Online Newspaper

GuideLIVE

3 Digital Newspaper

Powered by *The Dallas Morning News*

4 Date

THURSDAY, JULY 5, 2007

2 Article Title

1 Author

Selected and with an introduction by Michael Wood

Book review: 'Italo Calvino: Letters, 1941-1985'
By EDWARD NAWOTKA

When the Italian writer Italo Calvino suffered a brain hemorrhage in 1985, the national newspapers ran daily updates on his condition. When he died two weeks later at a hospital in Siena, he was 61 years old and among the most admired post-World War II Italian intellectuals and revered around the world.

"Italy went into mourning, as if a beloved prince had died," Gore Vidal wrote of the funeral.

As author of a volume of Italian folktales — Calvino was called Italy's Grimm — he was read by nearly every child in the country. His novels, such as The Baron in the Trees, The Cloven Viscount, Mr. Palomar and Cosmicomics, were read by nearly every adult with an interest in such things. Everyone else read his political commentary in the newspapers of the day.

The writer to whom he is most frequently compared is the Argentine Jorge Luis Borges, but this applies only so far in that as both writers invented fabulous, wildly imaginative fiction unlike like anything that had come before.

Though Calvino had been writing since just after World War II, when his first novel, in 1947, A Path to the Nest of Spiders, offered a neorealist account of his time in the communist partisans fighting the Nazis, it took until 1974 for American readers to take notice, when Vidal published an appreciative essay in The New York Review of Books. Since then, Calvino's major works have never been out of print in English.

Amazingly, Calvino continues to be published: Earlier this year, Princeton University Press put out a volume of his correspondence, Italo Calvino: Letters, 1941-1985.

Calvino is something of an acquired taste. His novels are complex, puzzling and demanding: He came from a generation of writers who assumed among his readers a level of cultural, scientific, philosophical and historical literacy that isn't nearly as prevalent today. That is not to say that Calvino can't be appreciated by a contemporary reader. Quite the contrary. Calvino's 1979 novel If on a winter's night a traveler opens with the type of bold, declarative statement that echoes today's television characters who talk back to the viewer or, perhaps more appropriately, the typical introductory post on a billion blogs: "You are about to begin reading Italo Calvino's new novel, If on a winter's night a traveler. Relax. Concentrate. Dispel every other thought. Let the world around you fade." The novel itself is composed of 10 first chapters, each in a different literary genre, that never quite come to a climax. Reading it is not so unlike channel surfing or a long, involved session of Web browsing.

Calvino's famous work Invisible Cities comprises a series of 55 portraits of mysterious cities as told to the Tatar emperor Kublai Khan by the Venetian explorer Marco Polo. The city of Zoe, for example, is described as place of "indivisible existence, where every activity that is possible is happening at all times, but creates such a cacophony that all the voices and people become indistinct."

Could you think of a better description of our media-saturated world?

What's most striking about reading this new collection of letters is not necessarily what Calvino says — such collections are primarily published for enthusiasts or academics who come to the book with some prior knowledge of the writer and his work — but the very fact that in today's digital age, we might be the last generation to be treated to such volumes.

Today, everything is quickly lost to the ether of the electronic domain. Letters, when they were written by literary masters, were essays in and of themselves. Email is a pragmatic form and highly disposable (just hit delete); social media, be it Facebook, Twitter or a blog post, merely masquerade as intimate or personal, but how can they be when they are intended for an audience of many (your friends or followers) or even millions?

Letters, on the other hand, have an audience of one; they represent one mind speaking to another. This very notion was not lost on Calvino. In a letter to Vidal to thank him for the New York Review of Books essay, Calvino wrote: "The conclusion of your review contains a statement that seems to me to be important in an absolute way. I don't dare to wonder whether it is true if applied to myself, but it is true as a literary ideal for each of us: the aim that each one of us has to reach has to be that [as Vidal wrote earlier] 'writer and reader become one, or One.' And to encompass both your discourse and mind in a perfect circle, we will say that this One is the Whole."

If reading the work of Calvino does anything — it is very entertaining as well as stimulating — it reminds us that writing is a medium for more than mere commerce, self-promotion or letting our spouse know we'll be picking up the kids at the pool at 5.

Note: This is the date you accessed the website, in this case, August 2, 2013. The medium of publication is Web.

6 Date of Access

5 Medium of Publication

    1   **2**   **3**

Nawotka, Edward. "Book Review: 'Italo Calvino: Letters, 1941–1985'" *The Dallas Morning News*

    27 July 2013. Web. 2 August 2013.

      4   **5**   **6**

Magazine Article on the Web

> Jones, Kenneth. "Bill Gates and Steve Jobs Sing and Dance in New Musical, Nerds, Already a Hit in NYM." *Playbill.com.* 20 September 2005. Web. 25 March 2014.

Artwork on the Web

> Leonardo da Vinci. *Mona Lisa.* Louvre, Paris. n.d. Web. 12 Dec. 2013.

Posting to a Discussion List

> McElhearn, Kirk. "J. S. Bach: Oxford Composer Companion [A review]." Online posting. *Alternative Music,* J. S. Bach. Google Groups, 1 Dec. 2000. Web. 24 April 2014.

Citing a Journal Article from a Database

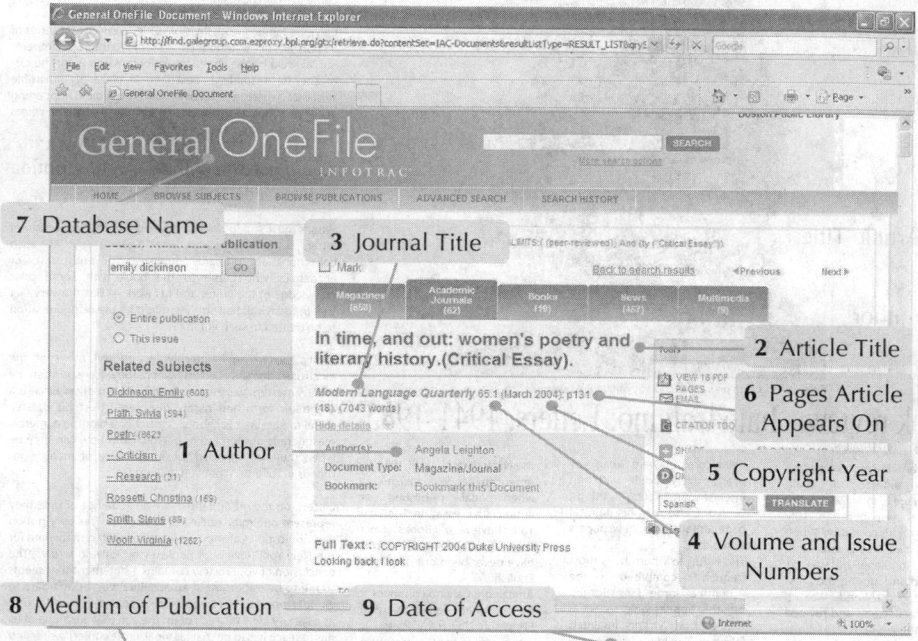

7 Database Name

3 Journal Title

2 Article Title

6 Pages Article Appears On

1 Author

5 Copyright Year

4 Volume and Issue Numbers

8 Medium of Publication

9 Date of Access

Note: This is the date you accessed the website, in this case, December 4, 2014. The medium of publication is Web.

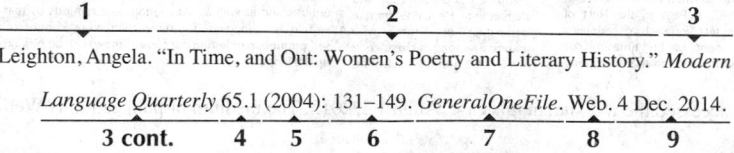

Leighton, Angela. "In Time, and Out: Women's Poetry and Literary History." *Modern Language Quarterly* 65.1 (2004): 131–149. *GeneralOneFile.* Web. 4 Dec. 2014.

Scholarly Project

> *Voice of the Shuttle: Web Site for Humanities Research.* Ed. Alan Liu. U of California Santa Barbara. n.d. Web. 10 April 2014.

Professional Site

>NobelMuseum. The Nobel Foundation, n.d. Web. 25 March 2014.

Personal Site (with URL)

>Barrett, Dan. *The Gentle Giant Home Page.* 19 February 2008. Web. 25 March 2014.
><www.blazemonger.com/GG/index.html>.

Citing a Professional Website

3 Site Sponsor

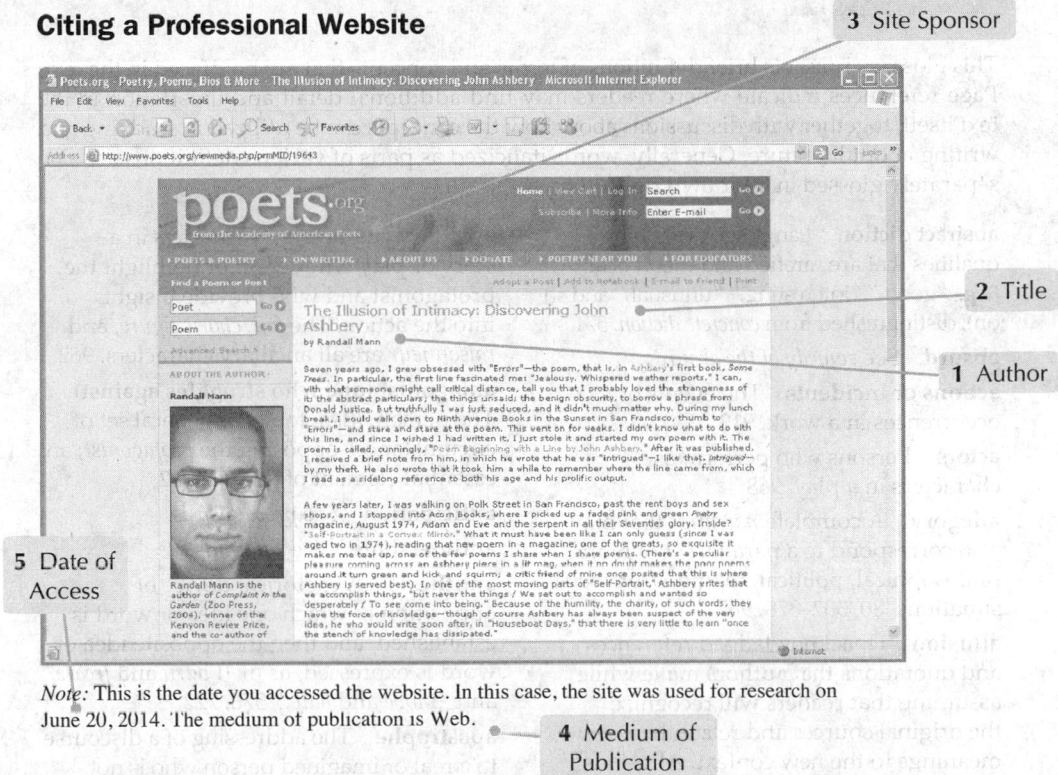

2 Title

1 Author

5 Date of Access

Note: This is the date you accessed the website. In this case, the site was used for research on June 20, 2014. The medium of publication is Web.

4 Medium of Publication

    1   2   3

Mann, Randall. "The Illusion of Intimacy: Discovering John Ashberry." *Academy of American Poets,* 2007.

    Web. 20 June 2014.

    4   5

A Glossary of Important Literary Terms

This glossary presents brief definitions of terms and concepts that are boldfaced in the text. Page references indicate where readers may find additional detail and illustration in the text itself, together with discussions about how the concepts can be utilized in studying and writing about literature. Generally, words italicized as parts of various definitions are also separately glossed in their own right.

abstract diction   Language describing qualities that are rarefied and theoretical (e.g., "good," "interesting," "unusual," and so on); distinguished from *concrete diction*. 571

absurd   See *comedy of the absurd*.

actions or **incidents**   The events or occurrences in a work. 913

actors   Persons who perform as characters in a play. 968

allegory   A complete *narrative* that may also correspond to a parallel set of moral, philosophical, political, religious, or social situations. 80, 332–378, 967

allusion   Unacknowledged references and quotations that authors make while assuming that readers will recognize the original sources and relate their meanings to the new context. Allusions are hence compliments that the author pays to readers for their perceptiveness, knowledge, and awareness. 336, 763–800

anagnorisis or **recognition**   Aristotle's term describing that point in a play, usually the *climax*, when a character experiences recognition and understanding. 1030

analysis   See *commentary*.

analytical sentence outline   A scheme or plan for an essay, arranged according to topics (A, B, C, etc.) and with the topics expressed in sentences. 36

anaphora ("to carry again or repeat")   The repetition of the same word or phrase throughout a work or section of a work. The effect is to lend weight and emphasis. 643

ancillary characters   *Characters* in a story or play who set off or highlight the protagonist and who provide insight into the action. The *foil*, *choric figure*, and *raisonneur* are all ancillary characters. 962

antagonist (one who struggles against)   The person, idea, force, or general set of circumstances opposing the *protagonist*; an essential element of *plot*. 65, 962

anticipation   See *procatalepsis*.

antimetabole   See *chiasmus*.

antithesis   A rhetorical device of opposition in which one idea or word is established, and then the opposite idea or word is expressed, as in "I *burn* and *freeze*" and "I *love* and *hate*." 576, 722

apostrophe   The addressing of a discourse to a real or imagined person who is not present; also, a speech to an abstraction. 643

apron or **thrust stage**   A stage that projects into the auditorium area, thus increasing the space for action; a characteristic feature of Elizabethan theaters and many recent ones. 969

archetypal/symbolic/mythic critical approach   The explanation of literature in terms of archetypal patterns (e.g., God's creation of human beings, the search for paradise, the sacrifice of a hero, the initiation or "test" of a young person). 969

archetype   A character, action, or situation that is a prototype or pattern of human life generally; a situation that occurs over and over again in literature, such as a quest, an initiation, or an attempt to overcome evil. Many *myths* are archetypes. 1582

archon or **eponymous archon**   In ancient Athens, the *eponymous archon*, or *archon eponymous*, was a leading magistrate, after whom the year was named. He made arrangements for the tragedies and comedies to be performed at the yearly festivals in honor of the god Dionysus. 1025

arena stage or **theater-in-the-round**   See *theater-in-the-round*.

argument   The development of a pattern of interpretation or thought with an intent to persuade. In most writing about literature, the persuasive situation is to show the validity of a particular idea or circumstance in a story, poem, or play. More broadly, the term *argument* applies to any situation about which there may be disagreement. Although sometimes argumentative discourse may become disputatious, one should never forget that true arguments should stem from the reasonable interpretation of correct and accurate data. 30–36, 1613–1618

aside   A speech, usually short and often witty or satirical, delivered by a character to the audience or to another character, the convention being that only the intended characters can hear it, along, of course, with the audience. A more extensive speech that is delivered only to the audience when the character is alone on stage is a *soliloquy*. 1078

assertion   A sentence putting an *idea* or *argument* (the subject) into operation (the predicate); necessary for both developing and understanding the idea. 379

atmosphere or **mood**   The emotional aura invoked by a work. 241, 966

audience or **intended reader** or **listener**   (1) The people attending a theatrical production. (2) The intended group of readers for whom a writer writes, such as a group of religious worshippers, or a group of rocket scientists. 971

authorial symbol   See *contextual symbol*.

authorial voice   The *voice* or *persona* used by authors when seemingly speaking for themselves. The use of the term makes it possible to discuss a narration or presentation without assuming that the ideas are necessarily those of the author in his or her own person. See also *speaker*, *point of view*, and *third-person point of view*. 127

ballad or **ballad measure**   A narrative poem, originally a popular form, composed of quatrains in *ballad measure*; that is, a pattern of iambic tetrameter alternating with iambic trimeter and rhyming *x-a-x-a*. 4, 543, 726

ballad opera   An eighteenth-century comic drama, originated by John Gay (1685–1732) in *The Beggar's Opera* (1728), featuring lyrics written for existing and usually well-known tunes, such as "Greensleeves." See also *comic opera*. 1321

beast fable   A narrative, usually short, featuring animals with human characteristics. 336

blank verse   Unrhymed *iambic pentameter*. Most of the poetry in Shakespeare's plays is blank verse, as is the poetry of Milton's *Paradise Lost* and many of Wordsworth's longer poems. 4, 722

blocking   In the performance of a play, the director's plan for the grouping and movement of characters on stage. 968

blocking agent   A person, circumstance, or attitude that obstructs the plans of various characters, such as the parental denial of permission to marry, as in Shakespeare's *A Midsummer Night's Dream*. 1620

box set   In the modern theater, the *realistic setting* of a single room from which the "fourth wall" is missing, so that the stage resembles a picture. 969

brainstorming   The exploration, discovery, and development of details to be assembled for use in a composition. 21–31

burlesque   A form (dramatic, fictional, poetic [and also musical]) designed to create humor through the extreme exaggeration of situations, responses, gestures, and speech. Ridicule is the intention of burlesque, in which nothing is held sacred as long as laughter is achieved. Even the most sedate and holy characters are not spared the exaggeration of burlesque, for no holds are barred creating responses of laughter. 1321

business or **stage business** The gestures, expressions, and general activity (beyond *blocking*) of actors onstage. Usually, business is designed to create laughter. It is often done spontaneously by actors. 968

buskins Elegantly laced boots (*kothorni* or *cothurni*) worn by actors in ancient Greek *tragedy*. Eventually the buskins became elevator shoes to stress the royal status of actors by making them seem especially tall. 1036

cartoon The narrative drawings, with balloon-enclosed speeches, that make up graphic narratives and graphic novels. 67–76

catastrophe The "overturning" of the dramatic *plot*, the fourth stage in the structure immediately following the *climax*; the *dénouement* of a play, in which things are explained and put into place. 965, 1262

catharsis (purgation) Aristotle's concept that *tragedy*, by arousing pity and fear (*eleos* and *phobos*), regularizes and shapes human emotions, and that therefore tragedy, like literature and art generally, is essential in civilized society. 1028

central idea, central argument, or **central statement** (1) The *thesis* or main idea of an essay. (2) The *theme* of a literary work. 30

character An extended verbal representation of a human being, the inner self that determines thought, speech, and behavior. 4, 22, 64, 176–237, 961–963

character, comic Characters who are unrealistic and sometimes exaggerated, representing classes, types, and generations. 1262

chiasmus or **antimetabole** A rhetorical pattern in which words (and also ideas) are repeated in the sequence *abba*, as in "I lead the life I love; I love the life I lead," and "When the issue deteriorates to violence, violence becomes the issue." 576

choragos or **choregus** The sponsor or financial backer of a classical Athenian dramatic production. Often the Athenians honored the choragos by selecting him to serve as the leader (*koryphaios*) of the chorus. 1033

choric figure A character who remains somewhat outside the dramatic *action* and who provides commentary when appropriate. See also *raisonneur*. 962

chorus In ancient Athenian drama, a group of young men—fifteen in tragedies and twenty-four in comedies—who chanted or sang, probably in unison, and who performed dance movements to a flute accompaniment. The chorus was, in effect, a major (and also collective) character in the *drama*. 1024

chronology (the **"logic of time"**) The sequence of events in a work, with emphasis on the complex intertwining of cause and effect. 963

City Dionysia See *Dionysia.*

clerihew A comic and often satiric closed-form poem in four lines, rhyming *abab*, usually on the topic of a famous real or literary person. 727

climax (Greek for "ladder") The high point of *conflict* and tension preceding the *resolution* or *dénouement* of a *story* or *play*; the point of decision, of inevitability and no return. The climax is sometimes equated with the *crisis* in the consideration of dramatic and narrative *structure*. 266, 965

closed-form poetry Poetry written in specific and traditional patterns produced through control of *rhyme*, *meter*, line length, and line groupings. 721–729, 755

close reading The detailed study of a poem or passage, designed to explain characters, motivations, similarities and contrasts of sound, situations, ideas, style, organization, word selections, settings, etc. 563

close-up (film) A camera view of an actor's head and upper body, designed to emphasize the psychological makeup and reactions of the character being portrayed; contrasted with *long shot*. 1634–1635

comedy A literary genre which, like *tragedy*, originated in the *Dionysia* festivals of ancient Athens. Derived from the Greek

Alphabetical List of Authors Included in *Literature*, Sixth Compact Edition

Aesop, ca. 600 BCE
Ai, 1947–2010
Ali, Agha Shahid, 1949–2001
Akhmatova, Anna, 1889–1966
Alexie, Sherman, b. 1966
Alvarez, Julia, b. 1950
Angelou, Maya, b. 1928
Arnold, Matthew, 1822–1888
Arredondo, Ines, 1928–1989
Ashberry, John, b. 1927
Atwood, Margaret, b. 1939
Auden, W. H., 1907–1973
Bambara, Toni Cade, 1939–1995
Baraka, Amira, b. 1934
Baudelaire, Charles, 1821–1867
Berryman, John, 1914–1972
Bierce, Ambrose, 1842–1914?
Bishop, Elizabeth, 1911–1979
Blake, William, 1757–1827
Bogan, Louise, 1897–1970
Borges, Jorge Luis, 1899–1986
Bradstreet, Anne, 1612–1672
Brontë, Emily, 1818–1848
Brooks, Gwendolyn, 1917–2000
Browning, Elizabeth Barrett,
    1806–1864
Browning, Robert, 1812–1889
Burns, Robert, 1759–1796
Bryon, George Gordon
    (Lord), 1788–1824
Carroll, Lewis, 1832–1898
Carruth, Hayden, 1921–2008
Carter, Jimmy, b. 1924
Carver, Raymond, 1939–1989
Chekhov, Anton, 1860–1904
Chin, Marilyn, b. 1955
Chopin, Kate, 1851–1904
Cisneros, Sandra, b. 1954
Clifton, Lucille, b. 1936
Clough, Arthur Hugh,
    1819–1861
Coleman, Anita Scott,
    1890–1960
Coleridge, Samuel Taylor,
    1772–1834
Collins, Billy, b. 1941
Crane, Stephen, 1871–1900
Creeley, Robert, 1926–2005
Cullen, Countee, 1903–1946
Cummings, E. E., 1894–1962
Dickinson, Emily, 1830–1886
Donne, John, 1572–1631
Dooley, Paul, b. 1928
Dove, Rita, b. 1952
Dryden, John, 1631–1700
Dubus, Andre, 1936–1999
Dugan, Alan, 1923–2003
Dunn, Stephen, b. 1939
Dyer, Sir Edward, 1543–1607
Eliot, T. S., 1888–1965
Ellison, Ralph, 1914–1994
Elizabeth I (Elizabeth Tudor,
    Queen Elizabeth I),
    1533–1603
Erdrich, Louise, b. 1954
Espada, Martin, b. 1957

Espaillat, Rihanna, b. 1932
Evans, Mari, b. 1923
Faulkner, William, 1897–1962
Ferlinghetti, Lawrence, b. 1919
Forché, Carolyn, b. 1950
Francis, Robert, 1901–1987
Frost, Robert, 1874–1963
Gaines, Ernest J., b. 1922
García Lorca, Federico,
    1898–1936
Gardner, Isabella, 1915–1981
Gay, John, 1685–1732
Georgakas, Dan, b. 1938
George, Chief Dan, 1899–1981
Gilb, Dagoberto, b. 1950
Gilman, Charlotte Perkins,
    1860–1937
Ginsberg, Allen, 1926–1997
Giovanni, Nikki, b. 1943
Glaspell, Susan, 1882–1948
Graves, Robert, 1895–1985
Griffin, Susan, b. 1943
Halpern, Daniel, b. 1945
Hardy, Thomas, 1840–1928
Harjo, Joy, b. 1951
Harper, Frances E. W., 1825–1911
Hass, Robert, b. 1941
Hawthorne, Nathaniel,
    1804–1864
Hayden, Robert, 1913–1980
H.D. (Hilda Doolittle), 1886–1961
Heaney, Seamus, b. 1939
Hemingway, Ernest, 1899–1961
Henley, William Ernest,
    1849–1903
Herbert, George, 1593–1633
Herrick, Robert, 1591–1674
Heyen, William, b. 1940
Holmes, Janet, 1956
Holzman, Winnie, b. 1954
Hope, A. D., 1907–2000
Hopkins, Gerard Manley,
    1844–1889
Housman, A. E., 1859–1936
Hughes, Langston, 1902–1967
Hurston, Zora Neale, 1891–1960
Hwang, David Henry, b. 1957
Ibsen, Henrik, 1828–1906
Ignatow, David, 1914–1997
Jackson, Shirley, 1919–1965
Jarrell, Randall, 1914–1965
Jeffers, Robinson, 1887–1962
Jonson, Ben, 1573–1637
Joyce, James, 1882–1941
Justice, Donald, 1925–2004
Keats, John, 1795–1821
Kennedy, X. J., b. 1929
Kenyon, Jane, 1947–1990
Kincaid, Jamaica, b. 1949
Kinnell, Galway, b. 1927
Kizer, Carolyn, b. 1925
Koch, Kenneth, 1925–2002
Komunyakaa, Yusef, b. 1947
Lababidi, Yahia, b. 1973
Larkin, Philip, 1922–1985
Lawrence, D. H., 1885–1930

Lee, Edward Bok, 1974
Lee, Li-Young, b. 1957
Levertov, Denise, 1923–1998
Lincoln, Abraham, 1809–1865
Lipschultz, Geri, b. 1951
Lorde, Audre, 1934–1992
Lowell, Amy, 1874–1925
Luke (St. Luke), fl. ca. 90 CE
Lux, Thomas, b. 1946
MacNeice, Louis, 1907–1963
Magnus, Magus, b. 1967
Mansfield, Katherine, 1888–1923
Martin, Jane, b. ????
Marvell, Andrew, 1621–1678
Masefield, John, 1878–1967
Maupassant, Guy de, 1850–1893
McKay, Claude, 1890–1948
Millay, Edna St. Vincent,
    1892–1950
Miller, Arthur, 1915–2005
Milton, John, 1608–1674
Minty, Judith, b. 1937
Momaday, N. Scott, b. 1934
Moore, Marianne, 1887–1972
Mueller, Lisel, b. 1924
Muske-Dukes, Carol, b. 1945
Nash, Ogden, 1902–1971
Nemerov, Howard, 1920–1991
Neruda, Pablo, 1904–1973
Northrup, Jim, b. 1943
Nye, Naomi Shihab, b. 1952
O'Brien, Tim, b. 1946
O'Connor, Flannery, 1925–1964
O'Connor, Frank, 1903–1966
O'Neill, Eugene, 1888–1953
O'Shaughnessy, Arthur,
    1844–1881
Oates, Joyce Carol, b. 1938
Okigbo, Christopher,
    1932–1967
Olds, Sharon, b. 1942
Oliver, Mary, b. 1935
Orozco, Daniel, b. ca.1957
Ortiz Cofer, Judith, b. 1952
Ortiz, Simon, b. 1941
Owen, Wilfred, 1893–1918
Ozick, Cynthia, b. 1928
Packer, ZZ, b. 1973
Parédes, Americo, 1915–1999
Parker, Dorothy, 1893–1967
Pastan, Linda, b. 1932
Paz, Octavio, 1914–1998
Piercy, Marge, b. 1936
Pinsky, Robert, b. 1940
Plath, Sylvia, 1932–1963
Poe, Edgar Allan, 1809–1849
Pope, Alexander, 1688–1744
Porter, Katherine Anne,
    1890–1980
Pound, Ezra, 1885–1972
Quasimodo, Salvatore,
    1901–1968
Randall, Dudley, 1914–2000
Rich, Adrienne, b. 1929
Ríos, Alberto, b. 1952
Rivas, Marguerite, b. 1956

Robinson, Edwin Arlington,
    1869–1935
Roethke, Theodore, 1907–1963
Rukeyser, Muriel, 1913–1980
Ryan, Kay, b. 1945
Salinas, Luis Omar, b. 1937
Sánchez, Edwin, 1955
Sandburg, Carl, 1878–1967
Sassoon, Siegfried, 1886–1967
Savage, Philip Henry, 1868–1899
Scott, Virginia, b. 1938
Serotte, Brenda, b. 1946
Sexton, Anne, 1928–1974
Shakespeare, William,
    1564–1616
Shapiro, Karl, 1913–2000
Shelley, Percy Bysshe,
    1792–1822
Silko, Leslie Marmon, b. 1948
Simic, Charles, b. 1938
Simpson, Louis, 1923–2012
Smith, Stevie, 1902–1971
Snyder, Gary, b. 1930
Song, Cathy, b. 1955
Sophocles, 496–406 BCE
Soto, Gary, b. 1952
Spender, Sir Stephen,
    1909–1995
Stafford, William, 1914–1993
Steinbeck, John, 1902–1968
Stevens, Wallace, 1879–1955
Strand, Mark, b. 1934
Swenson, May, 1919–1989
Tan, Amy, b. 1952
Tate, James, b. 1943
Tennyson, Alfred, Lord,
    1809–1892
Terranova, Elaine, b. 1939
Thomas, Dylan, 1914–1953
Toomer, Jean, 1894–1967
Trethewey, Natasha, b. 1966
Updike, John, 1932–2009
Van Duyn, Mona, 1921–2004
Viorst, Judith, b. 1931
Wakoski, Diane, b. 1937
Walker, Alice, b. 1944
Webb, Phyllis, b. 1927
Welty, Eudora, 1909–2001
Wheatley, Phillis, 1754–1784
Whitman, Walt, 1819–1892
Whur, Cornelius, 1782–1853
Wilbur, Richard, b. 1921
Williams, C. K., b. 1936
Williams, Tennessee,
    1911–1983
Williams, William Carlos,
    1883–1963
Wilson, August, 1945–2005
Wojahn, David, b. 1953
Wordsworth, William,
    1770–1850
Wright, James, 1927–1980
Wyatt, Sir Thomas,
    1503–1542
Yeats, William Butler, 1865–1939
Zimmer, Paul, b. 1934

Corpus Christi play   A type of medieval drama that enacts events from the Bible, such as the killing of Abel by Cain, the domestic problems of Noah, the jealous anger of Herod, and so on. The word is derived from the religious festival of Corpus Christi ("Christ's body"), held in the spring of each year, mainly during the fourteenth century. Also called *mystery plays* because they were performed by individual craft guilds, or *misteries* (so named in honor of the Guild "masters"). See also *cycle*. 975

cosmic irony (irony of fate)   *Situational irony* that reveals a fatalistic or pessimistic view of life. Although individual characters may struggle with great tenacity, their efforts are doomed right from the start (plans cannot be carried out; sickness occurs unexpectedly; friends go back on their words; promises are not kept; meanings are misunderstood; false tales are told; etc.) See *irony*. 1032

costumes   The clothes worn by *actors*, designed to indicate historical periods, social status, economic levels, etc. 970

cothurni   See *buskins*.

couplet   Two lines that may be unified by *rhyme* or, in biblical poetry, by complementary ideas or expressions. 4, 722

crisis   The point of uncertainty and tension in a literary work—the turning point—that results from the *conflicts* and difficulties brought about through the *complications* of the plot. The crisis leads to the *climax*—that is, to the attempts made by the protagonist to resolve the conflict. Sometimes the crisis and the climax are considered as two elements of the same stage of *plot* development. 266, 965

cultural (universal) context   See *topical/ historical context approach.*

cultural or **universal symbol**   A symbol that is recognized and shared as a result of a common political, social, and cultural heritage. See also *contextual symbol*. 79, 333, 764, 967

cycle   (1) A group of closely related works. (2) In medieval religious drama, the complete set of plays performed during the *Corpus Christi* festival, from the creation of the world to the resurrection. As many as forty plays could make up the cycle. During those times, when not many people were able to read, a complete cycle was one of the means by which stories of the Bible were brought to a wider audience. See also *Corpus Christi play*. 976

deconstructionist critical approach   An interpretive literary approach that rejects absolutes but stresses ambiguities and contradictions. 1584

decorum   The convention or expectation that words and subjects should be exactly appropriate—*high* or *formal* words for serious subjects (e.g., *epic poems, tragedy*), and *low* or *informal* words for low subjects (e.g., *limericks, farce*). 575

denotation   The standard, minimal meaning of a word, without implications and connotations. See also *connotation*. 303, 577

dénouement (untying) or **resolution**   The final stage of *plot development*, in which mysteries are explained, characters find their destinies, lovers are united, sanity is restored, and the work is completed. Usually the dénouement is done as speedily as possible, because it occurs after all *conflicts* are ended, and little that is new can then be introduced to hold the interest of readers. 266, 965, 1262

description   The exposition of scenes, actions, attitudes, and feelings. 78

developing character   See *round character*.

device   A *figure of speech*, such as a *metaphor* or a *simile*. See *figure of speech*. 639

deus ex machina ("a god out of the machine"; *theos apo mechanes* in Greek, a phrase attributed to the ancient Greek playwright Menander). In ancient Athenian drama, the entrance of a god to unravel the problems in a *play*. Today, the phrase *deus ex machina* refers to the artificial, convenient, easy, and illogical solution of problems. 1034

dialect   Language characteristics— involving pronunciation, unique words, and vocal rhythms—particular to regions such as New England, the Midwest, or the South, or to separate nations such as Britain and Australia. 523

dialogue   The speeches of two or more characters in a *story*, *play*, or *poem*. 41, 961

diction   Word choice, types of words, and the level of language. 300, 571

diction, formal or **high**   Proper, elevated, elaborate, and often polysyllabic language. 301, 572

diction, informal or **low**   Relaxed, conversational, and familiar language, utilizing contractions and elisions and sometimes employing *slang* and grammatical errors. 301, 572

diction, neutral or **middle**   Correct language characterized by directness and simplicity. 301, 572

dilemma, also **tragic dilemma**   A situation, particularly in tragedy, presenting a character with two choices, either one of which is unacceptable, dangerous, painful, or even lethal. 112, 1032

Dionysia (also **City Dionysia**)   The religious festivals of ancient Athens held to celebrate the god Dionysus. *Tragedy* developed as part of the Great, Dionysia or City Dionysia in March–April, and *comedy* developed as part of a shorter festival, the Lenaia (in February). 1023, 1025, 1035

director   The person in charge of guiding and instructing all persons involved in a dramatic production. 968

discursive poetry   Nonnarrative *poetry* dealing primarily with ideas and personal, social, or political commentary. 4

discursive writing   Distinguished from imaginative writing, discursive writing is concerned with factual presentation and the development of reasonable and logical conclusions. 4

dithyramb   An ancient Athenian poetic form sung by choruses during the earliest *Dionysia*. The first *tragedies* originated as part of the dithyrambs. 971, 1023, 1025

docudrama   A type of dramatic work featuring historical persons and situations, with the intention of bringing past history and politics to life. 971

documentation   Granting recognition to the ideas and words of others, either through textual, parenthetical, or footnote references. 517–522

donnée (French for "given")   The given action or set of assumptions on which a work of literature is based, such as the unpredictability of love, the bleakness and danger of a postwar world, or the inescapability of guilt. See also *postulate* or *premise*. 63

double dactyl   A comic *closed-form* poem in two *quatrains*, written in dactylic dimeter. The second line must be a proper name, and the sixth or seventh a single word. 728

double entendre (French for "double meaning")   Deliberate ambiguity, usually comic, and often sexual. 304

double plot or **multiple plot**   In a play or longer fictional work, the presentation of two or more different but related, connected, and comparable lines of action. 963

double take   A structural device whereby a concluding event or "surprise" brings about a new and more complex understanding of the previous material. 267

drama   An individual play; also plays considered as a group; one of the three major genres of *imaginative literature*. 4, 960–977

dramatic irony   A special kind of *situational irony* in which a character perceives his or her plight in a limited way whereas the audience and one or more of the other characters understand it entirely. 75, 685, 900, 1033

dramatic or **objective point of view**   A *third-person narration* reporting speech and *action* but excluding commentary on the actions and thoughts of the *characters*. 127

dynamic character   A character who tries to assert control by recognition, adjustment, and change. Dynamic changes may be shown in (1) an action or actions, (2) the realization of new strength and therefore the affirmation of previous decisions, (3) the acceptance of new conditions and the need for making changes and improvements, (4) the discovery of unrecognized truths, or (5) the reconciliation of the character with adverse conditions. In a *short story*, there is usually only one dynamic character, whereas in a *novel* there may be many. See *static character*. 181

economic determinist/Marxist critical approach   An interpretive literary approach based on the theories of Karl Marx (1818–1883), stressing that literature is to be judged from the standard of economic and social inequality and oppression. 1578

editing (film)   See *montage*.

ekkyklyma   In ancient Greek theatrical productions, a platform, normally kept inside the **skene**, that could be *rolled out* to show interior scenes. 1034

elegy   A *poem* of lamentation about a death. Often an elegy takes the form of a *pastoral*. 725

enclosing setting   See *framing* or *enclosing setting*.

English (Shakespearean) sonnet   A sonnet form developed by Shakespeare, in *iambic pentameter*, composed of three *quatrains* and a *couplet*, with seven rhymes in the pattern *bab, cdcd, efef, gg*. 724

epic   A long *narrative poem* elevating *character*, *speech*, and *action*. Some of the earliest surviving literary works are epics about the exploits of Gilgamesh, the wrath of Achilles, and the wanderings of Odysseus. 4, 60

epigram   A short and witty *poem*, often in *couplets*, that makes a humorous or satiric point. 4, 727

episode or *episodia*   (1) An acting *scene* or section of Greek tragedy. Divisions separating the episodes were called *stasima*, or sections for the chorus. (2) A self-enclosed portion of a work, such as a section, or a passage of particular narration, dialogue, or location. 1037

epitaph   A short comment or description marking someone's death. Also, a short, witty, and often satiric poem about death. 727

essay   In writing about literature, an essay is a short and tightly organized written composition dealing with a topic such as a character, a major idea, or a particular point of view. Broadly, writing about literature aside, essays also deal with any and all conceivable topics. 26, *passim*

exam, examination   A written or oral test or inquiry designed to discover a person's understanding and capacity to deal with a particular topic or set of topics. 1619–1629

exodos   The final episode in a Greek tragedy, occurring after the last choral ode. 1037

explication   A detailed analysis of a work of literature, often word by word and line by line; a close reading. 541, 563

exposition   The stage of dramatic or narrative structure that introduces all things necessary for the development of the plot. 265, 964

fable   A brief *story* illustrating a moral truth, most often associated with the ancient Greek writer Aesop. See also *beast fable*. 61, 336

falling action   See *catastrophe*.

fantasy   The creation of events that are dreamlike or fantastic, departing from ordinary understanding of *reality* because of apparently illogical *setting*, movement, causality, and *chronology*. Important in *unrealistic* drama and fiction. 63

farce   A word derived from the Latin word *farsus*, meaning "stuffed," farce is an outlandish physical *comedy* overflowing with silly characters, improbable happenings, wild clowning, extravagant language, and bawdy jokes. 977, 1264

feminist critical approach   A critical approach designed to raise consciousness about the importance and unique nature of women in literature. See also *gender studies* and *queer theory*. 24, 1575

fiction   *Narratives* based in the imagination of the author, not in literal, reportorial facts; one of the three major genres of imaginative literature. 60–120

figurative devices   See *figure of speech*.

figurative language   See *figure of speech*.

figure of speech   An organized pattern of comparison that deepens, broadens, extends, illuminates, and emphasizes meaning and also that conforms to particular patterns or forms such as *metaphor*, *simile*, and *parallelism*. 639–77

film   Motion pictures, movies. 1630–1640

film script   The written dramatic text on which a film is based, including directions for movement and expression. 1633

first-person point of view   The use of a first-person *speaker* or *narrator* who tells about things that he or she has seen, done, spoken, heard, thought, and also learned about in other ways. 76, 125, 129, 167

flashback   Also called *selective recollection*. A method of *narration* in which past events are introduced into a present action. 267

flat character   A character, usually minor, who is not individual, but rather useful and structural, static and unchanging; distinguished from *round character*. 181, 962

foil   A character, usually minor, designed to highlight qualities of a major character. 962

form, poetic   The various shapes and organizational modes of poetry. 721–762

formal diction   See *diction, formal* or *high*.

formalist critical approach   See *new critical/formalist critical approach*.

framing or **enclosing setting**   The same features of topic, technique, or setting used at both the beginning and ending of a work so as to "frame" or "enclose" the work. 241

free verse   *Poetry* based on the natural *rhythms* of phrases and normal pauses, not *metrical feet*. See *open-form poetry*. 4, 729

freewriting   See *brainstorming*.

Freytag pyramid   A diagram graphically showing the stages of dramatic *structure*. *Complication* and emotional intensity go upward on the side of the pyramid rising to its peak or point. Once the high point is reached, intensity begins to decrease just as the other side of the pyramid descends to its base. 963

general language   Words referring to broad classes of persons, objects, or phenomena; distinguished from *specific language*. 302, 571

gender studies   A critical approach that brings attention to gender rather than to sexual differences, based on the concept that the masculine/feminine divide is socially constructed and not innate. See also *feminist critical approach* and *queer theory*. 1575

genre   A category of literature, such as *fiction* and *poetry*. Also, a type of work, such as detective fiction, epic poetry, tragedy. 4

Globe Theatre   The outdoor theater built at the end of the sixteenth century just south of the Thames, where many of Shakespeare's plays were originally performed. The Globe was rebuilt in the 1990s to its original appearance, and once again is a flourishing theater close to where it was at the time of Shakespeare. 1076.

graphic narrative or **graphic novel**   A narrative composed of connected artistic or cartoon panels. The essential quality of graphic narrative is the combination of picture and dialogue to convey a story from beginning to end. 67–76

gustatory images   References to impressions of taste. 608

haiku   A verse form derived from Japanese poetry, traditionally containing three lines of 5, 7, and 5 syllables, in that order, and usually treating a topic derived from nature. 4, 727

half rhyme   See *inexact rhyme*.

hamartia   The Greek word for "error or frailty," indicating the tragic flaw that brings about the downfall or suffering of a protagonist. The same Greek word is translated as "sin" in the New Testament. 1031

hero or **heroine**   The major male and female *protagonists* or *protagonists* in a *narrative* or *drama*. The terms are often used to describe leading characters in adventures and romances. 181

heroic couplet   Also called the *neoclassic couplet*. Two successive rhyming lines of *iambic pentameter*, a characteristic of much *poetry* written between 1660 and 1800. Five-stress couplets are often called "heroic" regardless of their topic matter and the period in which they were written. 722

high comedy Elegant *comedies*, characterized by wit and sophistication, in which the complications grow not out of *situation* but rather out of *character*. See also *comedy of manners*. 1263

historical context (also **cultural context** and **intellectual context**) The historical time when a work was written, together with the intellectual and cultural ideas of this period. To study a work of literature in this perspective is to determine the degree to which the work spoke not only to people of its own time but continues to speak to people of the present time (and perhaps to people of all time). 24

historical critical approach See *topical/ historical critical approach*.

hubris or **hybris** ("Insolence, contemptuous violence") The pride and attitudes that lead tragic figures to commit their mistakes or offenses. 1023

humor In literature, those features of a *situation* or expression that provoke laughter and amusement. 305

hymn A hymn is a religious *song*, consisting of one and usually many more replicating rhythmical *stanzas*, designed for religious services. 4

hymnal measure or **hymnal stanza** The hymnal stanza, in iambics, consists of four lines of four stresses or else of four lines of alternating four and three stresses, rhyming *xaxa* or *abab*. See also *ballad measure* and *common measure*. 727

hyperbole See *overstatement*.

hypocrites (pronounced hip-POCK-rih-tayss, meaning "one who plays a part") The ancient Athenian word for *actor*. Our modern word "hypocrite" is derived from this word. 1024

idea or **theme** A concept, thought, opinion, or belief; in literature, a unifying, centralizing conception or *motif*. 19, 25, 65, 379–413

idiom (private or personal language) Usage that produces unique words and phrases within regions, classes, or groups; e.g., standing *on* line or *in* line; carrying a *pail* or a *bucket*; drinking *pop* or *soda*. Also, the habits and structures of particular languages. 573

image or **imagery** References that trigger the mind to fuse together memories of sights (*visual*), sounds (*auditory*), tastes (*gustatory*), smells (*olfactory*), sensations of touch (*tactile*), and perceptions of motion (*kinetic, kinesthetic*). "Image" refers to a single mental creation, "imagery" to images throughout a work or works of a writer or group of writers. Images may be *literal* (descriptive and pictorial) and *metaphorical* (figurative and suggestive). 4, 639–677, 691

imaginative literature *Literature* based in the imagination of the writer; the genres of imaginative literature are *fiction, poetry,* and *drama*. 4, *passim*

imitation The theory that literature is derived from life and is an imaginative duplication of experience; closely connected to *realism* and *verisimilitude*. 240

incidents See *actions*.

incongruity A discrepancy between what is ordinarily or normally expected and what is actually experienced. The resulting gap is often, under the right circumstances, a cause of laughter. 305

informal diction See *diction, informal* or *low*.

intellectual critical approach See *moral/ intellectual critical approach*.

interpretation See *commentary*.

intrigue plot The dramatic rendering of how a young woman and her lover, often aided by a maidservant or *soubrette*, usually foil a *blocking agent* (usually a parent or guardian). 1260

introduction See *exposition*.

invention The process of discovering and determining materials to be included in a composition, whether an *essay* or an imaginative work; a vital phase of planning and developing a composition. 63

ironic comedy A form of comedy in which characters seem to be in the grips of uncontrollable, cosmic forces. The dominant tone is therefore ironic. 1265

irony A major aspect of literary tone, a means of indirection, based on the proposition that even the simplest events in human life may be seen in multiple ways. Irony therefore deals with contradictions and ambiguities—the shadows underlying human existence. It is conveyed through indirection both in situations and in language. *Verbal irony* is language that states the opposite of what is intended. *Dramatic irony* describes the condition of characters who do not know the nature, seriousness, and extent of their circumstances. See also *cosmic irony, situational irony.* 79, 241, 304, 682

irony of fate   See *cosmic irony.*

irony of situation   See *situational irony.*

issue   An assertion or idea to be debated, disputed, or discussed. Sometimes "issue" refers to a problematic or questionable circumstance; sometimes to an idea; and sometimes to something that is going wrong. 67, 380

Italian or **Petrarchan sonnet**   An *iambic pentameter* poem of fourteen lines, divided between the first eight lines (the *octave*) and the last six (the *sestet*). An Italian sonnet uses five rhymes, unlike the *Shakespearean sonnet*, which has seven rhymes. 724

jargon   Language exclusively used by particular groups, such as doctors, lawyers, astronauts, scientists, computer operators, and football players. 574

journal   A notebook or electronic file for recording responses and observations that, for purposes of writing, may be used in the development of *essays.* 13–18

kinesthetic images   Words describing human or animal motion and activity. 608

kinetic images   Words describing general motion. 608

kothorni   See *buskins.*

Lenaia   The ancient Athenian early spring festival for which comedy as a form was first created. 1022, 1038, 1258

lighting   The general word describing the many types, positions, directions, and intensities of artificial lights used in the theater. 970

limerick   A brief poem with preestablished line lengths and rhyming patterns, designed to be comic. More often than not, limericks are risqué. 4, 727

limited point of view, limited third-person point of view, or **limited-omniscient point of view**   A third-person narration in which the actions and thoughts of the protagonist are the primary focus of attention. 77, 124–130

line   The basic unit of length of a poem, appearing as a row of words or sometimes as a single word or even part of a word occupying the space of a line and cohering grammatically through phrases and sentences. Lines in *closed-form poetry* are composed of determinable numbers of *metrical feet*; lines in *open-form poetry* are variable, changing with the poet's subject matter and rhythmical speech patterns. 721

literary research   See *research.*

literature   Written or oral compositions that tell stories, dramatize situations, express emotions, analyze and advocate ideas, and embody ideals. Literature is designed to engage readers emotionally as well as intellectually, with the major genres being *fiction, poetry, drama,* and *nonfiction prose,* and with many separate subforms. 3–5, *passim*

low comedy   Crude, boisterous, and physical *comedies* and *farces,* characterized by sight gags, bawdy jokes, and outrageous situations. 1264

low diction   See *diction, informal* or *low.*

lyric   (1) A short and concentrated poem or song, usually meditative, often personal, and sometimes philosophical. Traditional lyrics follow a fixed stanzaic form, having been originally intended for a musical setting, such as hymns or texts of dramatic arias. The lyrics of many modern poets, however, are comparatively free and unrestricted, and many modern lyrics are designed not for music at all, but rather for silent reading or spoken delivery. (2) The Aristotelian term for the "several kinds of artistic ornament," such as strophes and antistrophes, that are to be used appropriately in a tragedy. 4, 128, 725

magnitude   The third element in Aristotle's definition of *tragedy,* emphasizing that a *play* should be neither too long nor too short, so that artistic balance and proportion can be maintained. 1030

main plot The central and major line of causality and action in a literary work. 963

major mover A major participant in a work's action who either causes things to happen or who is the subject of major events. If the first-person narrator is also a major mover, such as the *protagonist*, that fact gives firsthand authenticity to the narration. 122

makeup The materials, such as cosmetics, wigs, and padding, applied to an actor to change appearance for a specific role, such as a youth, an aged person, or a hunchback. 970

malapropism The comic use of an improperly pronounced word, so that what comes out is a real but also incorrect word. Examples are *odorous* for *odious* (Shakespeare) or *pineapple* for *pinnacle* (Sheridan). The new word must be close enough to the correct word so that the resemblance is immediately recognized, along with the error. See also *pun*. 305.

Marxist critical approach See *economic determinist/Marxist critical approach.*

masks Face coverings worn by ancient Athenian actors to illustrate and define dramatic characters such as youths, warriors, old men, and women. 1036

meaning That which is to be understood in a work; the total combination of ideas, actions, descriptions, and effects. 379–413

melodrama A sentimental dramatic form with an artificially happy ending. 977

melos See *lyric.*

metaphor ("carrying out a change") A *figure of speech* that describes something as though it actually were something else, thereby enhancing understanding and insight. One of the major qualities of poetic language. 78, 639– 670

metaphorical language See *figure of speech.*

metonymy A *figure of speech* in which one thing is used as a substitute for another with which it is closely identified, such as when a speaker says "Dear Hearts" to refer to an audience. 645

middle comedy The Athenian comedies written in the first two-thirds of the fourth century BCE. Middle comedy lessened or eliminated the *chorus* and did away with the exaggerated costumes of the *old comedy*. No complete middle comedies have survived from antiquity. 972, 1259

middle diction See *diction, neutral* or *middle.*

mimesis or **representation** Aristotle's idea that *drama (tragedy)* represents rather than duplicates history. 1029

miracle play A late medieval play dramatizing a miracle or miracles performed by a saint. An outgrowth of the earlier medieval *Corpus Christi play*. 976

monologue (also **monolog**) A long speech spoken by a single character to himself or herself, to the audience, or to an off-stage character. See also *aside, soliloquy*. 961

montage or **editing (film)** The editing or assembling of the various camera "takes," or separately filmed scenes, to make a continuous film. 1636

mood See *atmosphere.*

moral/intellectual critical approach An interpretive literary approach that is concerned primarily with content and values. 1567

morality play A type of medieval and early Renaissance play that dramatizes how to live a pious life. The best-known morality play is the anonymous *Everyman*. 976

motif ("something that moves") Sometimes used in reference to a main *idea* or *theme* in a single work or in many works, such as a *carpe diem* theme, or a comparison of lovers to little worlds. See also *archetype*. 379

motivation The ideas and impulses that propel characters to a particular act or course of action. Motivation is the hallmark quality of a *round character*. 962

multiple plot or **double plot** A development in which two or more stories are both contrasted and woven together, as in Shakespeare's *A Midsummer Night's Dream*. 963

musical comedy A modern prose play integrated with lyrics—and also dances—set to specially composed music. Usually, musical comedies are elaborately and expensively produced. The form is in a line of development from *ballad opera* and *comic opera*. 1321

muthos Aristotle's word for plot, from which our word *myth* is derived. 1029

mystery play See *Corpus Christi play*.

myth, mythology, or **mythos** A *myth* is a story that deals with the relationships of gods to humanity or with battles among heroes in time past. A myth may also be a set of beliefs or assumptions among societies. *Mythology* refers collectively to all the stories and beliefs, either of a single group or number of groups. A system of beliefs and religious or historical doctrines is a *mythos*. 4, 60, 336

mythical reader See *audience*.

mythic critical approach See *archetypal/symbolic/mythic critical approach*.

narration or **narrative fiction** The relating or recounting of a sequence of events or actions. Whereas a narration may be reportorial and historical, *narrative fiction* is primarily creative and imaginative. See also *prose fiction* and *creative nonfiction*. 4, 60, 67

narrative ballad A poem in *ballad measure* telling a story and also containing dramatic speeches. 543

narrator See *speaker*.

naturalistic setting A stage *setting* designed to imitate, as closely as possible, the everyday world, often to the point of emphasizing poverty and dreariness. 970

neutral diction See *diction, neutral* or *middle*.

new comedy Athenian comedy that developed at the end of the fourth century BCE, stressing wit, romanticism, and twists of plot. The most famous of the new comedy writers was Menander (342–292 BCE). His plays were long considered lost, but a small number have luckily come to light in the past hundred years. 972, 1259

new critical/formalist critical approach An interpretive literary approach based on the French practice of *explication de texte* (i.e., the detailed explanation of a text), stressing the form and details of literary works. 1571

new historicism A type of literary criticism that emphasizes the integration of literature, culture, and history. 1569

nonfiction prose A *genre* consisting of essays, articles, and books about real as opposed to fictional occurrences and objects; one of the major *genres* of literature. 4

nonrealistic character An undeveloped and often *symbolic character* without full motivation or individual identity. 962

nonrealistic drama Dreamlike, fantastic, symbolic, and otherwise artificial plays that make no attempt to present an imitation of everyday reality. 1344

nonrealistic setting A staging that is nonrepresentational and often dreamlike and symbolic. 970

novel A long work of prose fiction. 4, 60

objective point of view See *dramatic point of view*.

octave The first eight *lines* of an *Italian sonnet*, unified by topic, rhythm, and *rhyme*. In practice, the first eight lines of any sonnet. 725

ode A stanzaic poem with varying line lengths and often intricate rhyme schemes that contrast it with songs and hymns. 4, 725

Old Comedy or **Old Attic Comedy** The Athenian comedies of the fifth century BCE, featuring song, dance, ribaldry, satire, and invective. The most famous writer of the old comedy is Aristophanes, eleven of whose plays have somehow survived from antiquity. 972, 1258

olfactory imagery *Images* referring to smell. 608

omniscient point of view A *third-person narrative* in which the *speaker* or *narrator*, with no apparent limitations, may describe intentions, actions, reactions, locations, and speeches of any or all of the characters and may also describe their innermost thoughts (when necessary for the development of the *plot*). 77, 127

open-form poetry Poems that avoid traditional structural patterns, such as *rhyme* or *meter*, in favor of other methods of organization. 729, 756

orchestra (a part of a **theater**) (1) In ancient Greek theaters, the *orchestra*, or "dancing place" was the circular area at the base of the amphitheater where the chorus performed. (2) In modern theaters, the word "orchestra" now refers to the ground floor or first floor where the audience sits. Obviously, today's usage refers to a large performing group of musical instrumentalists. 1033

organic unity The interdependence of all elements of a work, including character, actions, speeches, descriptions, thoughts, and observations. The concept of organic unity is attributed to Aristotle. 65

outline See *analytical sentence outline.*

overstatement, hyperbole, or **overreacher** A rhetorical *figure of speech* in which emphasis is achieved through exaggeration. 304, 646

parable A short *allegory* designed to illustrate a religious truth, often associated with Jesus as recorded in the Gospels, primarily Luke. 4, 336

parados (1) Either of the two front aisles leading from the sides to the *orchestra* in ancient Greek amphitheaters, along which the performers could enter or exit. (2) The entry and first lyrical ode of the *chorus* in Greek tragedy, after the *prologue*. 1034

paradox A *figure of speech* embodying a contradiction that is nevertheless true. 643

parallelism A *figure of speech* in which the same grammatical forms are repeated. The last words of our Declaration of Independence, for example, are "our lives, our fortunes, and our sacred honor," with parallel repetition of three nouns, each one modified by the word "our." 576, 722

paranomasia See *pun.*

paraphrase A brief restatement, in one's own words, of all or part of a literary work; a *précis*. 561

pastoral A traditional poetic form with topic material drawn from the usually idealized vocabulary of rural and shepherd life. Famous English pastorals are John Milton's "Lycidas," Matthew

Arnold's "Thyrsis," Alexander Pope's *Pastorals,* and Edmund Spenser's *The Shepheardes Calendar.* 726

pathos The "scene of suffering" in tragedy, which Aristotle defines as "a destructive or painful action, such as death on the stage, bodily agony, wounds, and the like." It is the scene of suffering that is intended to evoke the response of pity (*eleos*) from the audience. 1030

performance An individual production of a play, either for an evening or for an extended period, comprising acting, movement, lighting, sound effects, staging and scenery, ticket sales, and the accommodation of the audience. 967

peripeteia or **reversal** Aristotle's term for a sudden reversal, when the action of a work, particularly a play, veers around quickly to its opposite. 1029

persona See *speaker.*

perspective, dramatic The *point of view* in drama, the way in which the dramatist focuses on major characters and on particular problems. 965

Petrarchan sonnet See *Italian sonnet.*

picture poetry See *visual poetry.*

plagiarism (from a kidnapping, capturing with a net) A writer's use of the language and ideas of another writer or writers without proper acknowledgment. Plagiarism is an exceedingly serious breach of academic honor; some call it intellectual theft, and others call it an academic crime. 511, 519

platform stage A raised stage surrounded by seats for an *arena theater* or *theater-in-the-round.* 969, 1077

plausibility See *probability.*

play See *drama.*

plot The plan or groundwork for a *story* or a *play,* with the *actions* resulting from believable and authentic human responses to a *conflict.* It is causality, conflict, response, opposition, and interaction that make a plot out of a series of *actions.* Aristotle's word for plot is *muthos,* from which the word *myth* was derived. 65, 60–120

plot of intrigue   See *intrigue plot.*

poem, poet, or **poetry**   A variable literary genre that is, foremost, characterized by the rhythmical qualities of language. Whereas poems may be short (including *epigrams* and *haiku* of just a few lines) or long (*epics* of thousands of lines), the essence of poetry is compression, economy, and force, in contrast with the logic and expansiveness of prose. There is no bar to the topics that poets may consider, and poems may range from the personal and lyric to the public and discursive. A *poem* is one poetic work. A *poet* is a person who writes poems. *Poetry* may refer to the poems of one writer, to poems of a number of writers, to all poems generally, or to the aesthetics of poetry considered as an art. 533–570.

point of view   The *speaker, voice, narrator,* or *persona* of a work; the position from which details are perceived and related; a centralizing mind or intelligence; not to be confused with *opinion* or *belief.* 76, 121–175, 540, 965

point-of-view character   The central figure or *protagonist* in a *limited-point-of-view narration,* the character about whom events turn, the focus of attention in the narration. 128

postulate or **premise**   The assumption on which a work of literature is based, such as a level of absolute, literal *reality,* or as a dreamlike, fanciful set of events. See also *donnée.* 63

private or **contextual symbol**   See *contextual symbol.*

probability or **plausibility**   The standard that literature should be concerned with what is likely, common, normal, and usual. 182

problem   A question or issue about the interpretation or understanding of a work. 1246–1253

problem play or **problem comedy**   A type of *play* dealing with a *problem,* whether personal, social, political, environmental, philosophical, or religious. Ibsen's *A Dollhouse* is a problem play, dealing with the role of women in family and society. 977, 1261, 1485

procatalepsis or **anticipation**   A rhetorical strategy whereby the writer raises an objection and then answers it; the goal is to strengthen an argument by dealing with possible objections before a dissenter can raise them. Procatalepsis is thus a writer's way of taking the wind out of an objector's sails. Also called a figure of *presumptuousness* or *presupposal.* 1248

producer   The person in charge of practical matters connected with a stage production, such as securing finances, arranging for theater use, furnishing materials, renting or making costumes and properties, and guaranteeing payments. 968

prologue   In ancient Athenian *tragedy,* the introductory action and speeches before the *parados,* or first entry of the *chorus.* 1036

props or **properties**   The furniture, draperies, and the like used on stage during a play. 969

proscenium, proscenium stage   An arch or frame that delineates a box set and holds the curtain, thus creating the invisible fourth wall through which the audience sees the action of the play. See also *proskenion.* 968

prose fiction   *Imaginative* prose narratives (*short stories* and *novels*) that focus on one or a few *characters* who undergo a change or development as they interact with other characters and deal with their problems. 59–62

prose poem   A short work, laid out to look like prose, but employing the methods of verse, such as rhythm and imagery, for poetic ends. 730–734

proskenion   A raised stage built in front of the *skene* in ancient Greek theaters to separate the *actors* from the *chorus* and to make them more prominent. 1034

protagonist   The central *character* and focus of interest in a *narrative* or *drama.* 65, 181, 962

psychological/psychoanalytic critical approach   An interpretive literary approach stressing how psychology may be used in the explanation of both authors and literary works. 1580

public mythology See *universal mythology*.

pun or ***paranomasia*** Witty wordplay based on the fact that certain words with different meanings have nearly identical or even identical sounds. See also *malapropism*. 645

purgation See *catharsis*.

quatrain (1) A four-line *stanza* or poetic unit. (2) In an *English* or *Shakespearean sonnet*, a group of four *lines* united by *rhyme*. 4, 724

queer theory An interpretive literary approach based on the idea that sexual orientation is partly ideological and partly social. A number of queer theorists see the heterosexual/homosexual divide as less distinct than has traditionally been understood. The application of the theory is the discovery, often previously ignored, that many works contain either obvious or submerged homosexual elements. 1575

quotation In writing about literature, the use of short passages from a designated work in order to illustrate and strengthen an idea by the writer. 53–57

raisonneur A character who remains somewhat detached from the dramatic action and who provides reasoned commentary; a *choric figure*. 963

reader-response critical approach An interpretive literary approach based on the proposition that literary works are not fully created until readers make *transactions* with them by *actualizing* them in the light of their particular knowledge and experience. 1586, 1606–1612

realism or **verisimilitude** The use of true, lifelike, or probable situations and concerns. Also, the theory underlying the depiction of reality in literature. 63, 240

realistic character The accurate *imitation* of individualized men and women. 962

realistic comedy See *ironic comedy*.

realistic drama The dramatic presentation of *action*, thoughts, and

character that are designed to give the illusion of *reality*. 1344

realistic setting A *setting* designed to resemble places that actually exist or that might exist. For example, the setting of Wilson's *Fences* is realistic. 970

recognition See *anagnorisis*.

regular play A play conforming to the traditional *rules* of drama, particularly the *three unities*. Usually a regular play contains five acts (as in the Renaissance up through much of the nineteenth century). More recent regular plays contain three acts, although there is nothing hard and fast about this number. See *rules of drama*. 1038

reliable narrator A *speaker* who has nothing to hide by making misstatements and who is untainted by self-interest. This speaker's *narration* is therefore to be accepted at face value; contrasted with an *unreliable narrator*. 125

repetition See *anaphora*.

representation See *mimesis*.

representative character A *flat character* with the qualities of all other members of a group (clerks, cowboys, detectives, etc.); a *stereotype*. 182

research, literary The systematic use of primary and secondary sources as the basis of studying a literary *problem*. 500–532

resolution See *dénouement*.

response A reader's intellectual and emotional reactions to a literary work. 1586, 1606–1612

Restoration Comedy English *high comedies* written mainly between 1660 and 1700, dealing realistically with personal, social, and sexual issues. 1320

revenge tragedy A popular type of English Renaissance drama, developed by Thomas Kyd, in which a person is called upon (often by a ghost) to avenge the murder of a loved one. Shakespeare's *Hamlet* is in the tradition of revenge tragedy. 1079

reversal See *peripeteia*.

rhetoric The art of persuasive writing; broadly, the art of all effective writing. 576

rising action   The action in a *play* before the climax. See *Freytag pyramid*. 963

romance   (1) Lengthy Spanish and French *stories* of the sixteenth and seventeenth centuries. (2) Modern formulaic *stories* describing the growth of an impulsive, passionate, and powerful love relationship. 4, 52

romantic comedy   Sympathetic *comedy* that presents the adventures of young lovers trying to overcome opposition and achieve a successful union. 1263

round character   A literary character, usually but not necessarily the *protagonist* of a story or play, who is three-dimensional, rounded, authentic, memorable, original, and true to life. A round character is the center of our attention and is both individual and unpredictable. A round character profits from experience and in the course of a story or play undergoes change or development. 180, 962

rules of drama   An important concept of dramatic composition among Renaissance and eighteenth-century critics. They were based on ancient practice and theory, particularly the use of the five-act pyramidal (Freytag) structure and the embodiment of the *three unities* of action, place, and time. Sophocles followed the rules carefully; indeed, the rules were at least partially derived from his example. Shakespeare observed the *unity of action*, but in the interests of *probability* he apparently saw no reason to observe the others. See also *regular play*. 1038

satire   An attack on human follies or vices, as measured positively against a normative religious, moral, or social standard. 685

satiric comedy   A form of *comedy* designed to correct social and individual behavior by ridiculing human vices and follies. 1264

satyr play   A comic and burlesque *play* submitted by the ancient Athenian tragic dramatists along with their groups of three *tragedies*. On each day of tragic performances, the satyr play was performed after the three tragedies. See also *trilogy*. 1025

scene   In a *play*, a part or division (of an act, as in *Hamlet*, or of an entire play, as in *Fences*) in which there is a unity of subject, *setting*, and *actors*. 969

scene of suffering   See *pathos*.

scenery   The artificial environment created onstage to produce the illusion of a specific or generalized place and time. 969

scrim   A stage curtain that becomes transparent when illuminated from upstage, permitting action to take place under various lighting conditions. 970, 1348

second-person point of view   A *narration* in which a second-person listener ("you") is the *protagonist* and the speaker is someone (doctor, parent, rejected lover, etc.) with knowledge that the protagonist does not possess or understand about his or her own actions. Sometimes the "you" of the second person is used popularly and vaguely to signify persons in a general audience, including the speaker. 77, 126, 129, 168

selective recollection   See *flashback*.

sentimental comedy   A type of comedy dramatizing how good nature and morality enable characters to overcome their character flaws, which otherwise seem problematic or even incorrigible. 1321

sequence   The following of one thing upon another in time or chronology. It is the *realistic* or true-to-life basis of the cause-and-effect arrangement necessary in a *plot*. 67

seriousness   The first element in Aristotle's definition of *tragedy*, demonstrating the most elevated and significant aspects of human character. 1030

sestet   (1) A six-line stanza or unit of *poetry*. (2) The last six lines of an *Italian sonnet*. 724

sets   The physical scenery and properties used in a theatrical production. 969

setting   The natural, manufactured, and cultural environment in which characters live and move, including all their possessions, homes, ways of life, and assumptions. 238–264

Shakespearean sonnet   See *English sonnet*.

shaped verse   See *visual poetry*.

short story A compact, concentrated work of *narrative fiction* that may also contain description, dialogue, and commentary. Poe used the term "brief prose tale" before the term "short story" was created, and he emphasized that the form should create a powerful and unified impact. 4, 62

simile A *figure of speech*, using "like" with nouns and "as" with clauses, as in "the trees were bent by the wind *like actors bowing after a performance*." 640

sitcom A serial type of modern television comedy dramatizing the circumstances, assumptions, and actions of a fixed number of characters (hence "situation comedy," or "sitcom"). 971, 1268

situation The given circumstances of a *story*, *poem*, or *play*; a *donnée*. 4

situational irony or **irony of situation** A type of *irony* emphasizing that human beings are enmeshed in forces that greatly exceed their perception, comprehension, and control. 79, 683, 966, 1032

skene ("tent," "hut") In ancient Greek theaters, a building in front of the *orchestra* that contained front and side doors from which actors could make entrances and exits. It served a variety of purposes, including the storage of *costumes* and *props*. The word has given us our modern word *scene*. 1039

slang Informal diction and substandard vocabulary. Some slang is a permanent part of the language (e.g., phrases like "I'll be damned," "That sucks," and our many four-letter words). Other slang is spontaneous, rising within a group (*jargon*) and often then being replaced when new slang emerges. 574

slapstick comedy A type of low *farce* in which the humor depends almost entirely on physical actions and sight gags. 1265

soap opera Also called "soaps," a type of daytime narrative dramatic program, originally created in the 1930s for radio, but which later became popular on television, in which the actions of the various characters take place during not just hours or days, but rather years. The name "soap opera" was given to the drama because many early sponsors were various soap companies. 971

social drama A type of *problem play* that deals with current social issues and the place of individuals in society. 24, 977

soliloquy A speech made by a character, alone on stage, directly to the *audience*, the convention being that the character is revealing his or her inner thoughts, feelings, hopes, and plans. A soliloquy is to be distinguished from an *aside*, which is made to the audience (or confidentially to another character) when other characters are present. 1078

song See *lyric*.

sonnet A poem of fourteen lines (originally designed to be spoken and not sung) in *iambic pentameter*. See *Italian sonnet* and *English sonnet*. 4, 724

speaker The *narrator* of a *story* or *poem*, the *point of view*, often an independent *character* who is completely imagined and consistently maintained by the author. In addition to narrating the essential events of the work (justifying the status of *narrator*), the speaker may also introduce other aspects of his or her knowledge and may express judgments and opinions. Often the character of the speaker is of as much interest in the story as the *actions* or *incidents*. 62, 121, 540

specific language Words referring to objects or conditions that may be perceived, remembered, or imagined; distinguished from *general language*. 571

speeches See *dialogue*.

stage business See *business*.

stage convention See *convention*.

stage directions A playwright's instructions concerning *blocking*, movement, *action*, tone of voice, entrances and exits, *lighting*, *scenery*, and the like. 961

stanza A group of *poetic lines* corresponding to paragraphs in prose; stanzaic *meters* and *rhymes* are usually repeating and systematic. 721

stasimon (plural *stasima*) A *choral ode* separating the *episodes* in Greek tragedies. Because of the word's derivation, it would seem that the chorus remained stationary in the orchestra and watched during the episodes, and then stood before speaking or chanting its designated odes. 1037

static character   A character who undergoes no change; a *flat character*; contrasted with a *dynamic character*. 181, 967

stereotype   A character who is so ordinary and unoriginal that he or she seems to have been cast in a mold; a *representative* character. 182, 962

stichomythy   In ancient Athenian drama, dialogue consisting of one-line speeches designed for rapid interchanges between characters. 1037

stock character   A *flat character* in a standard role with standard *traits,* such as the irate police captain, the bored hotel clerk, the sadistic criminal, etc.; a *stereotype.* 182, 962

story   A *narrative,* usually fictional, and short, centering on a major character, and rendering a complete action. 62

structuralist critical approach   An interpretive literary approach attempting to find relationships and similarities among elements that might originally appear to be separate and discrete. 1573

structure   The arrangement and placement of materials in a work. 65, 265–267, 294–295, 963

style   The manipulation of language; the placement of words in the service of content. 76, 300

subject   The topic that a literary work addresses, such as love, marriage, war, death, and social inequality. 967

subplot   A secondary line of action in a literary work that often comments directly or obliquely on the main plot. See also *multiple plot.* 963

symbol or **symbolism**   A specific word, idea, or object that may stand for ideas, values, persons, or ways of life. 79, 332–378, 763–800, 963, 967

symbolic character   A character whose primary function is symbolic, even though the character also retains normal or *realistic* qualities. 963

symbolic critical approach   See *archetypal/symbolic/mythic critical approach.*

synecdoche   A *figure of speech* in which a part stands for a whole or a whole stands for a part. 963

synesthesia   A *figure of speech* uniting or fusing separate sensations or feelings; the description of one type of perception or thought with words that are appropriate to another. 646

syntax   Word order and sentence structure. An important mark of style is a writer's syntactical patterning (regular patterns and variations), depending on the rhetorical needs of the literary work. 574

tactile imagery   *Images* of touch and responses to touch. 608

tenor (figure of speech)   The ideas conveyed in a *metaphor* or *simile.* See also *vehicle.* 642

tense   Besides embodying reports of actions and circumstances, verbs possess altering forms—tenses—that signify the times when things occur, whether past, present, or future. Perfect and progressive tenses indicate completed or continuing activities. Tense is an important aspect of *point of view* because the notation of time influences the way in which events are perceived and expressed. Narratives are usually told in the past tense, but many recent writers of fiction prefer the present tense for conveying a sense of immediacy. No matter when a sequence of actions is presumed to have taken place, the introduction of *dialogue* changes the action to the present. See *point of view.* 128, 168

tercet or **triplet**   A three-line unit or stanza of *poetry,* usually rhyming aaa, bbb, etc. 723

terza rima   A three-line *stanza* form with the interlocking rhyming pattern aba, bcb, cdc, etc. 724

theater   In ancient Athens, a theater was a "place for seeing." Today it is the name given to the building in which plays and other dramatic productions are performed. It is also a generic name for local or national drama in all its aspects, as in "Tonight we're going to the theater," and "This play is the best of the New York theater this year." 968, 1033

Theater of Dionysus   The ancient Athenian outdoor amphitheater at the base of the Acropolis, where Greek drama began. Today, the remains at the location are not those of the ancient Greek theater but are those of a later Roman-built theater. 1033, 1035

theater-in-the-round   A theater arrangement, often outdoors, in which the audience totally surrounds a *platform* stage, with all actors entering and exiting along the same aisles used by the audience. Also known as an *arena stage*. 669, 1346

theme   (1) The major or central idea of a work. (2) An essay, a short composition developing an interpretation or advancing an argument. (3) The main point or idea that a writer of an essay asserts and illustrates. 66, 379–413, 967

theos apo mechanes   See *deus ex machina*.

thesis sentence or **thesis statement**   An introductory sentence which names the topics and ideas to be developed in the body of an *essay*. 32

third-person point of view   A third-person method of *narration* (*she, he, it, they, them*, etc.), in which the *speaker* or *narrator* is not a part of the story, unlike the involvement of the narrator of a *first-person point of view*. Because the third-person speaker may exhibit great knowledge and understanding, together with other qualities of *character*, he or she is often virtually identified with the author, but this identification is not easily decided. See also *authorial voice, omniscient point of view*. 77, 127, 130, 168

third-person objective point of view   See *dramatic point of view*.

three unities   Traditionally associated with Aristotle's descriptions of drama as expressed in the *Poetics*, the three unities are those of action, place, and time. The unities are a function of *verisimilitude*— the creation of literary works that are as much like reality as possible. Therefore a play should dramatize a single major *action* that takes place in a single place during the approximate time it would take for completion, from beginning to end. During the Renaissance, some critics considered the unities to be essential aspects, or *rules*, of *regular drama*. Later critics considered the unity of action important but minimized the unities of place and time. See also *regular play*. 1038

thrust stage   See *apron stage*.

tiring house   An enclosed area in an Elizabethan theater in which *actors* changed *costumes* and awaited their cues, and in which stage *properties* were kept. The word *tiring* is derived from *attire* (e.g., clothing or costumes). 1077

tone   The techniques and modes of presentation that reveal or create attitudes. 79, 300–331, 678–720, 960

topic sentence   The sentence determining or introducing the subject matter of a paragraph. See also *historical context*. 33

topical/historical critical approach   An interpretive literary approach that stresses the relationship of literature to its historical period. 1569

tragedy   A drama or other literary work that recounts the fall or misfortune of an individual who, while undergoing suffering, deals responsibly with the situations and dilemmas that he or she faces and who thus demonstrates the value of human effort and human existence. 971, 1022–1256

tragic dilemma   See *dilemma*.

tragic flaw   See *hamartia*.

tragicomedy   A literary work—*drama* or *story*—containing a mixture of *tragic* and *comic* elements. 977

trait   A typical mode of behavior; the study of major traits provides a guide to the description of *character*. 177

trilogy   A group of three literary works, usually related or unified. For the ancient Athenian festivals of Dionysus, each competing tragic dramatist submitted a trilogy (three *tragedies*), together with a *satyr play*. 1025

triplet   See *tercet*.

trope   A short dramatic dialogue inserted into the church mass during the early Middle Ages. 973

Tudor Interlude   Tragedies, comedies, or historical plays performed by both professional actors and students during the reigns of Henry VII and Henry VIII (i.e., the first half of the sixteenth century). The Tudor Interludes sometimes featured abstract and allegorical characters and provided opportunities for both music and farcical action. 1076

unchanging character   See *flat character*.

understatement   A *figure of speech* by which details and ideas are deliberately underplayed or undervalued in order to create emphasis—a form of *irony*. 304, 646

unit set   A series of platforms, rooms, stairs, and exits that form the locations for all of a play's actions. A unit set enables scenes to be changed rapidly, without the drawing of a curtain and the placement of new sets. 969

unities   See *three unities*.

universal symbol   See *cultural symbol*.

unreliable narrator   A speaker who through ignorance, self-interest, or lack of capacity may tell lies and distort details. Locating the truth in an unreliable narrator's story requires careful judgment and not inconsiderable skepticism. See also *reliable narrator*. 126

value or **values**   The attachment of worth, significance, and desirability to an *idea* so that the idea is judged not only for its significance as thought but also for its importance as a goal, ideal, or standard. 380

vehicle   The image or reference of figures of speech, such as a *metaphor* or *simile*; it is the vehicle that carries or embodies the *tenor*. See also *tenor*. 642

verbal irony   Language stressing the importance of an idea by stating the opposite of what is meant. Verbal irony may convey humor, but as often as not it also reflects serious criticism and even bitterness and mockery of particular facets of life and the universe. See *irony*. 79, 304, 683, 966

verisimilitude (i.e., **"like truth"**)   A characteristic whereby the *setting*, circumstances, *characters*, *dialogue*, *actions*, and outcomes in a work are designed to seem true, lifelike, real, plausible, and probable. See also *realism*. 63, 182, 240

villanelle   A *closed-form* poem of nineteen lines, composed of five *tercets* and a concluding *quatrain*. The form requires that whole lines be repeated in a specific order and that only two rhyming sounds occur throughout. See also *tercet*. 4, 724

visual imagery   Language describing visible objects and situations. 605

visual poetry   Poetry written so that the lines form a recognizable shape, such as a pair of wings or a geometrical figure. Also called *concrete poetry* or *shaped verse*. 730–735

voice   See *point of view* and *speaker*.

well-made play (*la pièce bien faite*)   A form developed and popularized in nineteenth-century France by Eugène Scribe (1791–1861) and Victorien Sardou (1831–1908). Typically, the well-made play is built on both secrets and the timely arrivals of new characters and complications. The protagonist faces adversity and ultimately overcomes it. Ibsen's *A Dollhouse* exhibits many characteristics of the well-made play. 1487

words   The spoken and written signifiers of thoughts, objects, and actions—the building blocks of language. At the latest count, the editors of the *Oxford English Dictionary* estimate that there are more than a million words in the English language. 300–331

Credits

PHOTOS

Index of Authors, Titles, and First Lines

A & P, 320
A doe stands at the roadside, 764
A dented spider like a show drop white, 842
A narrow Fellow In the Grass, 807
A noiseless patient spider, 790
Abortions will not let you forget, 544
About suffering they were never wrong, 888
Advice to Young Ladies, 911
Acquainted with the Night, 848
Aesop
  The Fox and the Grapes, 337
After Apple-Picking, 843
After great pain, a formal feeling
  comes –, 808
*After Great Pain, a Formal Feeling
  Comes*, 808
After Making Love We Hear Footsteps, 917
Afternoon, 928
Ai
  Conversation, 882
Akhmatova, Anna
  Willow, 883
Alexie, Sherman
  *On the Amtrak from Boston to New York
  City*, 883
Ali, Agha Shahid
  Postcard from Kashmir, 884
All we need is fourteen lines, well, thirteen
  now, 738
Along the garden ways just now, 702
Alvarez, Julia
  Woman's Work, 884
American Poetry, 555
And another regrettable thing about
  death, 947
And I grew up in patterned tranquility, 883
Angelou, Maya
  Still I Rise, 885
Annabel Lee, 930
Anonymous, (Navajo)
  Healing Prayer from the Beautyway Chant, 886

Anonymous
  Sir Patrick Spens, 541
Anonymous
  Spun on High, Dark Clouds, 727
Anonymous
  The Myth of Atalanta, 338
Anonymous
  *The Visit to the Sepulcher (Visitatio
  Sepulchri)*, 973
Answer, The, 913
Antaeus/Anchises, 923
Anthem for Doomed Youth, 607
anyone lived in a pretty how
  town, 895
anyone lived in a pretty how town, 895
*Apology for Using the Word "Heart" in Too
  Many Poems, An*, 582
Araby, 242
Ariel, 867
Arnold, Mathew
  Dover Beach, 887
Arredondo, Inés Camelo
  The Shunammite, 81
Art of Poetry, The, 889
As I sd to my, 583
As virtuous men pass mildly away, 649
Ashbery, John
  The Cathedral Is, 580
At the factory I worked, 942
Atwood Margaret
  Happy Endings, 385
  You fit into me, 888
Auden, W. H.
  Musée des Beaux Arts, 888
  The Unknown Citizen, 687
Aunt Jennifer's tigers prance across a
  screen, 933
Aunt Jennifer's Tigers, 934
Auschwitz, 704
Author to Her Book, The, 890
Auto Wreck, 941

Autumn Begins at Martin's Ferry, Ohio, 710
Autumn Leaves, 772

Back in a yard where ringers groove a
    ditch, 783
Bad Man, 853
Bagel, The, 698
Ballad of Birmingham, 749
Ballad of the Landlord, 853
Bambara, Toni Cade
    The Lesson, 387
Baraka, Amiri
    Legacy, 770
Barn Burning, 462
Batter my heart, three-personed God;
    for You, 585
Battle Royal, 268
Bear, The, 924
Bear, A Joke in One Act, The, 1323
Beat! Beat! Drums!, 948
Beat! beat! drums!—blow! bugles!
    blow!, 948
Baudelaire, Charles
    Exotic Perfume, 580
Beauty, 1000
Beauty of the Trees, The, 905
Because I Could Not Stop for Death, 545
Because I could not stop for Death, 545
Before Breakfast, 1006
Behold her, single in the field, 710
Bent double, like old beggars under
    sacks, 680
Berryman, John
    Dream Song 14, 736
Bierce, Ambrose
    An Occurrence at Owl Creek
    Bridge, 88
Bilingual/Bilingue, 904
Birches, 844
Bishop, Elizabeth
    The Fish, 608
    One Art, 736
    Sestina, 737
Black Cat, The, 435
Black reapers with the sound of steel on
    stones, 753
Blake, William
    The Lamb, 581
    On Another's Sorrow, 688
    The Tyger, 647
Body my house, 945

Bogan, Louise
    Women, 888
Borges, Jorge Luis
    The Art of Poetry, 889
Bradstreet, Anne
    The Author to Her Book, 890
    To My Dear and Loving Husband, 890
Break, Break, Break, 664
Break, break, break, 664
Bright, 701
Bright Star, 644
Bright star! would I were steadfast as thou
    art, 644
Bright with the armpit-dazzle of a
    lioness, 701
Brontë, Emily
    Love and Friendship, 891
    No Coward Soul Is Mine, 771
Brooks, Gwendolyn
    The Mother, 544
    We Real Cool, 891
Brownies, 155
Browning, Elizabeth Barret
    Sonnets from the Portuguese, Number 14:
    If Thou Must Love Me, 611
    Sonnets from the Portuguese: Number 43,
    How Do I Love Thee?, 892
Browning, Robert
    My Last Duchess, 892
Buffalo Bill's, 731
Buffalo Bill's Defunct, 731
Bully, 695
Burns, Robert
    A Red, Red Rose, 648
Bustle in a House, The, 808
By the roots of my hair some god got hold
    of me, 873

Call the roller of big cigars, 945
Can I see another's woe? 688
Canonization, The, 774
Cargoes, 606
Carroll, Lewis
    Jabberwocky, 581
Carruth, Hayden
    An Apology for Using the Word "Heart" in
    Too Many Poems, 582
Carter, Jimmy
    I Wanted to Share My Father's World, 689
Carver, Raymond
    Cathedral, 131

Cask of Amontillado, The, 250

Catch, 547

Cathedral, 131

Cathedral Is, The, 580

Channel Firing, 617

Chekhov, Anton

  The Bear, A Joke in One Act, 1323

Chicago, 936

Chief Dan George

  The Beauty of the Trees, 905

Chin, Marilyn

  Autumn Leaves, 772

Chipmunk chewing the Chippendale, 657

Chopin, Kate

  The Story of an Hour, 307

Chrysanthemums, The, 358

Cinderella, 938

Cinquains for Rocky, 910

Cisneros, Sandra

  Mericans, 93

Clifton, Lucille

  cutting greens, 772

  homage to my hips, 690

Clough, Arthur Hugh

  Say Not the Struggle Nought Availeth, 773

Cofer, Judith Ortiz

  Latin Women Pray, 589

Coleman, Anita Scott

  Unfinished Masterpieces, 339

Coleridge, Samuel Taylor

  Kubla Khan, 612

Collage of Echoes, 777

Collar, The, 778

Collins, Billy

  Days, 894

  The Names, 691

  Schoolsville, 534

  Sonnet, 739

Colonel, The, 734

Colossus, The, 868

Come gather 'round people, 899

Come my Celia, let us prove, 744

Conjoined, 656

Constantly Risking Absurdity, 740

Constantly risking absurdity and
  death, 740

Convergence of the Twain, The, 652

Conversation, 882

Corinna's Going A-Maying, 909

Crane, Stephen

  Do Not Weep, Maiden, for War Is Kind, 895

Creeley, Robert

  I Know a Man, 583

Crib, 591

Cullen, Countee

  Yet Do I Marvel, 692

Cummings, E. E.

  anyone lived in a pretty how town, 895

  Buffalo Bill's Defunct, 731

  if there are any heavens, 896

  next to of course god america i, 584

  she being Brand / -new, 693

curling them around, 772

cutting greens, 772

cut, 862

Daddy, 870

Daffodils (I Wandered Lonely as a Cloud), 595

Dance, The, 754

Day Zimmer Lost Religion, The, 596

Days, 894

Daystar, 897

Dead in There, 854

Death of a Salesman, 1182

Death of the Ball Turret Gunner, The, 550

Death, be not proud, though some have
  callèd thee, 897

Desert Places, 741

Design, 848

Dickinson, Emily

  After Great Pain, a Formal Feeling Comes,
    808

  Because I Could Not Stop for Death, 545

  The Bustle in a House, 808

  "Faith" Is a Fine Invention, 809

  I Cannot Live with You, 809

  I Died for Beauty – but Was Scarce, 810

  I Dwell in Possibility, 810

  I Felt a Funeral in My Brain, 811

  I Heard a Fly Buzz – When I Died, 811

  I Like to See It Lap the Miles, 812

  I'm Nobody! Who Are You?, 812

  I Never Lost as Much but Twice, 812

  I Taste a Liquor Never Brewed, 813

  Much Madness Is Divinest Sense, 813

  My Life Closed Twice Before Its Close, 813

  A Narrow Fellow in the Grass, 807

  *One Need Not Be a Chamber – To Be
    Haunted,* 814

  Safe in Their Alabaster Chambers, 814

  Some Keep the Sabbath Going to Church, 814

  The Soul Selects Her Own Society, 815

Success Is Counted Sweetest, 815
Tell All the Truth but Tell It Slant, 816
There Is No Frigate Like a Book, 816
There's a Certain Slant of Light, 816
Triumph May Be of Several Kinds, 817
Wild Nights – Wild Nights!, 817
Didja ever hear a sound, 926
Dimensions, 709
Disillusionment of Ten O'Clock, 593
Do Not Go Gentle into That Good Night, 752
Do not go gentle into that good night, 752
Do Not Weep, Maiden, for War Is Kind, 895
Do Not Weep, Maiden, for War Is Kind, 895
Do they dream of past lives and unlived
    dreams, 917
Dollhouse (Et Dukkehjem), A, 1488
Dolor, 591
Donne, John
    The Canonization, 774
    Holy Sonnet 10: Death Be Not Proud, 897
    *Holy Sonnet 14: Batter My Heart, Three-
        Personed God*, 585
    A Valediction: Forbidding Mourning, 649
Dooley, Paul and **Holzman, Winnie**
    Post-its (Notes on a Marriage), 1331
Dove, Rita
    Daystar, 897
    The House Slave, 546
Dover Beach, 887
Dream Boogie, 855
Dream On, 629
Dream Song 14, 736
Dream Variations, 855
Dreamers, 937
Dressing for work, 938
Droning a drowsy syncopated tune, 862
Dryden, John
    To the Memory of Mr. Oldham, 739
Dugan, Alan
    Untitled Poem, 651
Dulce et Decorum Est, 680
Dunn, Stephen
    Hawk, 776
Dyer, Sir Edward
    My Mind to Me a Kingdom Is, 898
Dying, 703
Dylan, Bob
    The Times They Are a-Changin', 899

Each one is a gift, no doubt, 894
Eagle, The, 723

Eagle Poem, 549
Earth Tremors Felt in Missouri, 666
Eating Poetry, 593
Edge, 872
El Santo Americano, 1374
Eliot, T. S.
    The Love Song of J. Alfred Prufrock, 900
    Preludes, 613
Ellison, Ralph
    Battle Royal, 268
Emperor of Ice-Cream, The, 945
Epigram from the French, 685
*Epigram, Engraved on the Collar of a Dog
    Which I Gave to His Royal Highness*, 686
Erdrich, Louise
    Indian Boarding School: The Runaways,
        615
Espada, Martín
    Bully, 695
    Latin Night at the Pawnshop, 904
Espaillat, Rhina
    Bilingual/Bilingüe, 904
Evans, Mari
    I Am a Black Woman, 695
Every Day You Play, 625
Every day you play with the light of the
    universe, 625
Everyday Use, 494
Exile, Pursued by a Bear, 657
Exotic Perfume, 580

Face like a chocolate bar, 860
Facing It, 699
Facing West from California's Shores, 667
Facing west from California's shores, 667
"Faith" Is a Fine Invention, 809
"Faith" Is a Fine Invention, 809
Fall of the House of Usher, The, 420
Far from the Vistula, along the northern
    plain, 704
Farewell, too little and too lately
    known, 739
Faulkner, William
    Barn Burning, 462
    A Rose for Emily, 96
Fear No More the Heat o' th' Sun, 707
Fear no more the heat o' th' sun, 707
Fences, 1430
Ferlinghetti, Lawrence
    Constantly Risking Absurdity, 740
Fifteen miles, 936

Final Thing, A, 919

Fire and Ice, 847

First Confession, 315

First-Rate Wife, The, 679

Fish, The (Bishop), 608

Fish, The (Moore), 624

Five years have past; five summers, with
    the length, 557

For Godsake hold your tongue, and let me
    love, 774

For I can snore like a bullhorn, 917

For me, the naked and the nude, 578

Forche, Carolyn
    The Colonel, 734

Fork, 629

Fox and the Grapes, The, 337

Francis, Robert
    Catch, 547

Freud created the ego and the id, 588

From my mother's sleep I fell into the
    State, 550

From the Greek for, 591

Frost, Robert
    Acquainted with the Night, 848
    After Apple-Picking, 843
    Birches, 844
    Desert Places, 741
    Design, 848
    Fire and Ice, 847
    The Gift Outright, 849
    In White (An Early Version of "Design,"
        p. 848), 842
    Mending Wall, 842
    Nothing Gold Can Stay, 847
    "Out, Out—", 846
    The Oven Bird, 847
    The Road Not Taken, 845
    The Silken Tent, 848
    Stopping by Woods on a Snowy
        Evening, 548

Full of Life Now, 949

Full of life now, compact, visible, 949

Gaines, Ernest J.
    The Sky Is Gray, 184

Gardner, Isabella
    Collage of Echoes, 777

Gay, John
    Let Us Take the Road, 645

Georgakis, Dan
    Hiroshima Crewman, 777

Get up! get up for shame! the blooming
    morn, 909

Gift Outright, The, 849

Gilb, Dagoberto
    Love in L.A., 309

Gilman, Charlotte Perkins
    The Yellow Wallpaper, 473

Ginsberg, Allen
    A Supermarket in California, 742

Giovanni, Nikki
    Poetry, 905

Girl, 483

Girl, A, 933

Glancing over my shoulder at the
    past, 534

Glaspell, Susan
    A Jury of Her Peers, 202
    Trifles, 983

Glass Menagerie, The, 1379

Glory be to God for dappled things, 912

Good Man Is Hard to Find, A, 484

Good Morning, daddy!, 855

Graves, Robert
    The Naked and the Nude, 578

Grenade, 747

Griffin, Susan
    Love Should Grow Up Like a Wild Iris in
        the Fields, 616

H. D. (Hilda Doolittle)
    Heat, 618

Had he and I but met, 548

Had we but world enough, and
    time, 784

Halpern, Daniel
    Snapshot of Hué, 906

Hammon and the Beans, The, 403

Hanging Man, The, 873

Happy Endings, 385

Hardy, Thomas
    Channel Firing, 617
    The Convergence of the Twain, 652
    In Time of "The Breaking of
        Nations," 778
    The Man He Killed, 548
    The Ruined Maid, 907
    The Workbox, 683

Harjo, Joy
    Eagle Poem, 549
    Remember, 653

Harlem, 856

Harper, Frances E. W.
  She's Free!, 908
Hass, Robert
  Spring Rain, 908
Hawk, 776
Hawthorne, Nathaniel
  Young Goodman Brown, 342
Hayden, Robert
  Those Winter Sundays, 909
He clasps the crag with crooked
  hands;, 723
He might compare you to a summer's
  day, 789
He was found by the Bureau of Statistics
  to be, 687
Healing Prayer from the Beautyway Chant,
  886
Heaney, Seamus
  Mid-Term Break, 697
Heat, 618
Helen, thy beauty is to me, 626
Hemingway, Ernest
  Hills Like White Elephants, 311
Henley, William Ernest
  When You Are Old, 697
Herbert, George
  The Collar, 778
  The Pulley, 619
  Virtue, 743
Here a Pretty Baby Lies, 537
Here a pretty baby lies, 537
Here lies, to each her parents' ruth, 550
Herrick, Robert
  Corinna's Going A-Maying, 909
  Here a Pretty Baby Lies, 537
Heyen, William
  Mantle, 732
Hills Like White Elephants, 311
Hiroshima Crewman, 777
Hog Butcher for the World, 936
Holmes, Janet
  Cinquains for Rocky, 910
Holy Sonnet 10: Death Be Not Proud, 897
*Holy Sonnet 14: Batter My Heart, Three-
  Personed God*, 585
homage to my hips, 690
Home's the place we head for in our
  sleep, 615
Homes where children live exude a
  pleasant rumpledness, 554

Hope, 536
Hope, A.D.
  Advice to Young Ladies, 911
Hopkins, Gerard Manley
  Pied Beauty, 912
  Spring, 620
Horse Dealer's Daughter, The, 392
House Slave, The, 546
Housman, A. E.
  To an Athlete Dying Young, 585
  When I was one-and-twenty, 913
How do I love thee? Let me count the
  ways, 892
How say that by law we may torture and
  chase, 908
How the days went, 920
Hughes, Langston
  Bad Man, 853
  Ballad of the Landlord, 853
  Dead in There, 854
  Dream Boogie, 855
  Dream Variations, 855
  Harlem, 856
  I, Too, 856
  Let America Be America Again, 857
  Mulatto, 1352
  Negro, 859
  The Negro Speaks of Rivers, 859
  125th Street, 860
  Po' Boy Blues, 860
  Subway Rush Hour, 860
  Theme for English B, 861
  The Weary Blues, 862
Hurston, Zora Neale
  Spunk, 215
Hurt Hawks, 620
Hwang, David Henry
  Trying to Find Chinatown, 994

I Am a Black Woman, 695
I am a black woman, 695
I am a Negro:, 859
I am his Highness' dog at Kew, 686
I am sorry to speak of death again, 753
I am silver and exact. I have no
  preconceptions, 877
I am that last, that, 919
I Cannot Live with You, 809
I cannot live with You, 809
I caught a tremendous fish, 608

I chopped down the house that you had
    been saving to live in next summer, 551
I Died for Beauty – But Was Scarce, 810
I died for Beauty – but was scarce, 810
I do not want a plain box, I want a
    sarcophagus, 876
I doubt not God is good, well-meaning,
    kind, 692
I Dwell in Possibility, 810
I dwell in Possibility –, 810
I Felt a Funeral, in My Brain, 811
I felt a Funeral, in my Brain, 811
I Find No Peace, 669
I find no peace, and all my war is done, 669
I found a dimpled spider fat and white,
    848
I grieve and dare not show my
    discontent, 665
I hated the fact that they had planned me,
    she had taken, 702
I have been one acquainted with the night,
    848
I have done it again, 873
I have eaten, 557
I have known the inexorable sadness of
    pencils, 591
I have no promises to keep, 777
I have seen it, 935
I Hear America Singing, 949
I hear America singing, the varied carols I
    hear:, 949
I Heard a Fly Buzz – When I Died, 811
I heard a Fly buzz – when I died, 811
I Know a Man, 583
I know this happiness, 587
I Like to See It Lap the Miles, 812
I like to see it lap the Miles, 812
I'm a bad, bad man, 853
I'm a riddle in nine syllables, 876
I met a traveller from an antique land, 751
I Never Lost as Much but Twice, 812
I never lost as much but twice, 812
I sat all morning in the college sick bay, 697
I shall never get you put together entirely,
    868
I stopped to pick up the bagel, 698
I struck the board, and cry'd "No more;, 778
I Taste a Liquor Never Brewed, 813
I taste a liquor never brewed, 813
*I Think Continually of Those Who Were Truly
    Great*, 592

I think continually of those who were truly
    great, 592
I, Too, 856
I, too, sing America, 856
I've known rivers, 859
I wake to sleep, and take my waking
    slow, 751
I walk down the garden paths, 921
I walk the purple carpet into your eye, 666
I wandered lonely as a cloud, 595
I want you to know one thing, 658
I Wanted to Share My Father's World, 689
I was born in war, WW Two, 553
I would be wandering in distant fields, 748
I'm Nobody! Who Are You?, 812
I'm Nobody! Who Are You?, 812
Ibsen, Henrik
    A Dollhouse (Et Dukkehjem), 1488
If ever two were one, then surely we, 890
If the moon smiled, she would resemble
    you, 877
if there are any heavens my mother will
    (all by herself) have, 896
if there are any heavens, 896
If thou must love me, let it be for nought, 611
If You Forget Me, 658
Ignatow, David
    The Bagel, 698
In a Farmhouse, 936
In a solitude of the sea, 652
In a Station of the Metro, 627
In Bondage, 748
In Brueghel's great picture, The Kermess,
    754
In China, even the peasants, 708
In the Beginning of the End, 588
In the school auditorium, 694
In the Shreve High football stadium, 711
In the south, sleeping against, 770
In Time of "The Breaking of Nations," 778
*In White (An Early Version of "Design,"
    p. 848)*, 842
In Xanadu did Kubla Khan, 612
Indian Boarding School: The Runaways, 615
Ink runs from the corners of my mouth, 593
Inside Out, 666
It hovers in dark corners, 536
It was many and many a year ago, 930
*It's Only Rock and Roll but I Like It": The Fall
    of Saigon*, 631
Its quick soft silver bell beating, beating, 941

Jabberwocky, 581
Jackson, Shirley
   The Lottery, 139
Jarrell, Randall
   The Death of the Ball Turret Gunner, 550
Jeffers, Robinson
   The Answer, 913
   Hurt Hawks, 620
   The Purse-Seine, 780
Jilting of Granny Weatherall, The, 352
Jonson, Ben
   On My First Daughter, 550
   To Celia, 744
Joyce, James
   Araby, 242
Jury of Her Peers, A, 202
Justice, Donald
   On the Death of Friends in Childhood, 914
   Order in the Streets, 914

Kashmir shrinks into my mailbox, 884
Keats, John
   Bright Star, 644
   La Belle Dame Sans Merci: A Ballad, 781
   Ode on a Grecian Urn, 914
   Ode to a Nightingale, 745
   On First Looking into Chapman's Homer, 641
   To Autumn, 654
Kennedy, X. J.
   Old Men Pitching Horseshoes, 783
Kenyon, Jane
   Let Evening Come, 655
Kincaid, Jamaica
   Girl, 483
Kinnel, Galway
   After Making Love We Hear Footsteps, 917
Kizer, Carolyn
   Night Sounds, 586
Koch, Kenneth
   from Variations on a Theme by William
     Carlos Williams, 551
Komunyakaa, Yusef
   Facing It, 699
   Grenade, 747
Kubla Khan, 612

La Belle Dame Sans Merci: A Ballad, 781
Lababidi, Yahia
   What Do Animals Dream?, 917
Lady Lazarus, 873
Lamb, The, 581

Landlord, landlord, 853
Larkin, Philip
   Talking in Bed, 918
Last Words, 876
Latin Night at the Pawnshop, 904
   Latin Women Pray, 589
Latin women pray, 589
Lawrence, D. H.
   The Horse Dealer's Daughter, 392
Lee, Edward Bok
   El Santo Americano, 1374
Lee, Li-Young
   A Final Thing, 919
Legacy, 770
Lesson, The, 387
Let America Be America Again, 857
Let America Be America again, 857
Let Evening Come, 655
Let me not to the marriage of true minds, 728
Let the light of late afternoon, 655
Let Us Take the Road, 645
Let us take the road, 645
Levertov, Denise
   Of Being, 587
   A Time Past, 621
Life Cycle of Common Man, 925
Life, friends, is boring. We must not say
   so, 736
Lincoln, Abraham
   My Childhood's Home, 700
Lines Composed a Few Miles Above Tintern
   Abbey on Revisiting the Banks of the
   Wye During a Tour, June 13, 1798, 557
Lipschultz, Geri
   In the Beginning of the End, 588
   Slow Dance of the Heart, 277
Little Lamb, who made thee? 581
Living in Sin, 934
London, 668
Look, children, here is the shy, 660
Looking at Each Other, 662
Lorca, Federico García
   Sonnet of the Sweet Complaint, 651
Lord Byron (George Gordon, Lord Byron)
   She Walks in Beauty, 893
Lorde, Audre, 920
   Now that I Am Forever with Child, 920
Lost Sister, 708
Lottery, The, 139
Love and Friendship, 891
Love Calls us to the Things of This World, 949

Love in L.A., 309

Love is like the wild rose-briar, 891

Love Should Grow Up Like a Wild Iris in the Fields, 616

Love should grow up like a wild iris in the fields, 616

The Love Song of J. Alfred Prufrock, 900

Love Symphony, A, 702

Lowell, Amy
　Patterns, 921
　The Taxi, 622

Luke
　The Parable of the Prodigal Son, 350

Lux, Thomas
　The Voice You Hear When You Read Silently, 623

MacNeice, Louis
　Snow, 552

Magnus, Magus
　Antaeus/Anchises, 923
　An Old Soldier Cleans His Rifle for the Last Time, 552

Man He Killed, The, 548

Man to Send Rain Clouds, The, 254

Mansfield, Katherine
　Miss Brill, 219

Mantle, 732

Mantle ran so hard, they said, 732

Marks, 929

Martin, Jane
　Beauty, 1000

Marvell, Andrew
　To His Coy Mistress, 784

Masfield, John
　Cargoes, 606

Masque of the Red Death, The, 431

Maupassant, Guy de
　The Necklace, 7

McKay, Claude
　In Bondage, 748

Mending Wall, 842

Mericans, 93

Metaphors, 876

Mexicans Begin Jogging, 942

Midsummer Night's Dream, A, 1267

Mid-Term Break, 697

Millay, Edna St. Vincent
　Travel, 924
　What Lips My Lips Have Kissed, and Where, and Why, 924

Miller, Arthur
　Death of a Salesman, 1182

Milton by Firelight, 788

Milton! thou should'st be living at this hour, 668

Milton, John
　On His Blindness (When I Consider How My Light Is Spent), 749

Mingled, 860

Minty, Judith
　Conjoined, 656

Mirror, 877

Miss Brill, 219

Momaday, N. Scott
　The Bear, 924

Moment the Two Worlds Meet, The, 927

Moore, Marianne
　The Fish, 624

Mother, The, 544

"Mother dear, may I go downtown, 749

Much have I travell'd in the realms of gold, 641

Much Madness Is Divinest Sense, 813

Much Madness is divinest Sense – 813

Mueller, Lisel
　Hope, 536

Mulatto, 1352

Musée des Beaux Arts, 888

Muske-Dukes, Carol
　Real Estate, 785

My black face fades, 699

My Childhood's Home, 700

My childhood's home I see again, 700

My father liked them separate, one there, 904

My father, who works with stone, 927

My heart aches, and a drowsy numbness pains, 745

My hips are a desk, 929

My husband gives me an A, 929

My Last Duchess, 892

My Life Closed Twice Before Its Close, 813

My life closed twice before its close;, 813

My long two-pointed ladder's sticking through a tree, 843

My Mind to Me a Kingdom Is, 898

My mind to me a kingdom is, 898

My mistress' eyes are nothing like the sun, 628

My Mother's Face, 938

My Papa's Waltz, 706

Myth of Atalanta, The, 338

Naked and the Nude, The, 578
Names, The, 691
Narrow Fellow in the Grass, A, 807
Nash, Ogden
  Exit, Pursued by a Bear, 657
Nature's first green is gold, 847
Necklace, The, 7
Negro, 859
Negro Speaks of Rivers, The, 859
Nemerov, Howard
  Life Cycle of Common Man, 925
Neruda, Pablo
  Every Day You Play, 625
  If You Forget Me, 658
Never let me lose the marvel, 651
Never until the mankind making, 946
next to of course god america i, 584
next to of course god america I, 584
Night Sounds, 586
No Coward Soul Is Mine, 771
No Coward Soul Is Mine, 771
Nobody heard him, the dead man, 942
Noiseless Patient Spider, A, 790
Northrup, Jim
  Ogichidag, 553
  wahbegan, 926
Not marble, nor the gilded monuments, 555
Not Waving but Drowning, 942
Nothing Gold Can Stay, 847
Nothing is so beautiful as Spring, 620
Nothing to be said about it, and everything, 703
Now that I Am Forever with Child, 920
Now the rain is falling, freshly, in the intervals between sunlight, 908
Now winter downs the dying of the year, 790
number one I slouch in bed, 712
Nye, Naomi Shihab
  Where Children Live, 554

"O Hell, what doe mine eyes with grief behold?" 788
"O 'melia, my dear, this does everything crown!, 907
O my Luve's like a red, red rose, 649
O what can ail thee, knight at arms, 781
O wind, rend open the heat, 617
O'Brien, Tim
  The Things They Carried, 101

O'Connor, Flannery
  A Good Man Is Hard to Find, 484
O'Connor, Frank
  First Confession, 315
O'Neill, Eugene
  Before Breakfast, 1006
O'Shaughnessy, Arthur
  A Love Symphony, 702
Oates, Joyce Carol
  Where Are You Going, Where Have You Been?, 145
Occurrence at Owl Creek Bridge, An, 88
Odd, the baby's scabbed face peeking over, 556
Ode on a Grecian Urn, 914
Ode to a Nightingale, 745
Oedipus the King, 1039
Of Being, 587
Ogichidag, 553
Okigbo, Christopher
  Bright, 701
Old Men Pitching Horseshoes, 783
Old Soldier Cleans his Rifle for the Last Time, An, 552
The old wooden steps to the front door, 621
Olds, Sharon
  The Moment the Two Worlds Meet, 927
  The Planned Child, 702
Oliver, Mary
  Showing the Birds, 660
  Wild Geese, 786
On Another's Sorrow, 688
On autumn nights, eyes closed, when, sensuous, 580
On Being Brought from Africa to America, 948
On First Looking into Chapman's Homer, 641
On His Blindness (When I Consider How My Light Is Spent), 749
On Monsieur's Departure, 665
On My First Daughter, 550
On the Amtrak from Boston to New York City, 883
On the Death of Friends in Childhood, 914
Once upon a midnight dreary, while I pondered, weak and weary, 931
One Art, 736
One Need Not Be a Chamber – To Be Haunted, 814
One need not be a chamber – to be Haunted –, 814

1.2.3., 914
125th Street, 860
Only a man harrowing clods, 778
Oranges, 943
Order in the Streets, 914
Orientation, 284
Orozco, Daniel
  Orientation, 284
Ortiz, Simon
  A Story of How a Wall Stands, 927
Our ancestors scraped the ground, 661
Our sardine fishermen work at night in
  the dark of the moon; 780
Out of the East, Beauty has come
  home, 885
Out, Out—, 846
Oven Bird, The, 847
Owen, Wilfred
  Anthem for Doomed Youth, 607
  Dulce et Decorum Est, 680
Ozick, Cynthia
  The Shawl, 246
Ozymandias, 751

Packer, ZZ
  Brownies, 155
Parable of the Prodigal Son, The, 350
Paredes, Américo
  The Hammon and the Beans, 403
Parker, Dorothy
  Afternoon, 928
  Résumé, 929
Pastan, Linda
  Marks, 929
Patterns, 921
Perfection Wasted, 947
Pied Beauty, 912
Piercy, Marge
  The Secretary Chant, 929
  A Work of Artifice, 660
Pilgrimage, 661
Pinsky, Robert
  Dying, 703
Planned Child, The, 702
Plath Sylvia
  Ariel, 867
  The Colossus, 868
  Cut, 869
  Daddy, 870
  Edge, 872
  The Hanging Man, 873

Lady Lazarus, 873
Last Words, 876
Metaphors, 876
Mirror, 877
Song for a Summer's Day, 878
The Rival, 877
Tulips, 878
Po' Boy Blues, 860
Poe, Edgar Allan
  Annabel Lee, 930
  The Black Cat, 435
  The Cask of Amontillado, 250
  The Fall of the House of Usher, 420
  The Masque of the Red Death, 431
  The Raven, 931
  The Tell-Tale Heart, 440
  To Helen, 626
Poetics Against the Angel of Death, 753
Poetry, 905
poetry is motion graceful, 905
Pope, Alexander
  Epigram from the French, 685
  *Epigram, Engraved on the Collar of a Dog
    Which I Gave to His Royal Highness*, 686
Pops, 1335
Porter, Katherine Anne
  The Jilting of Granny Weatherall, 352
Postcard from Kashmir, 884
Post-its (Notes on a Marriage), 1331
Pound, Ezra
  A Girl, 933
  In a Station of the Metro, 627
Preludes, 613
Pulley, The, 619
Purse-Seine, The, 780
The quake last night was nothing
  personal, 666

Quasímodo, Salvatore
  Auschwitz, 704
Question, 945
Quinquireme of Nineveh from distant
  Ophir, 606

Randall, Dudley
  Ballad of Birmingham, 749
Raven, The, 931
Razors pain you, 929
Real Estate, 785
Reapers, 753
Reconciliation, 754

Red, Red Rose, A, 648

Red Wheelbarrow, The, 950

Refusal to Mourn the Death, by Fire, of a
    Child in London, A, 946

Remember, 653

Remember the sky that you were born
    under, 653

Résumé, 929

Revolutionary Petunias, 947

Rich, Adrienne
    Aunt Jennifer's Tigers, 934
    Living in Sin, 934

Richard Cory, 590

Ríos, Albert
    The Vietnam Wall, 935

Rival, The, 877

Rivas, Marguerite
    Pilgrimage, 661

Road Not Taken, The, 845

Robinson, Edwin Arlington
    Richard Cory, 590

Roethke, Theodore
    Dolor, 591
    My Papa's Waltz, 706
    The Waking, 751

Rose for Emily, A, 96

Roughly figured, this man of moderate
    habits, 925

Ruined Maid, The, 907

Rukeyser, Muriel
    Looking at Each Other, 662

Rush Hour, 556

Ryan, Kay
    Crib, 591
    We're Building the Ship as We Sail It, 787

S'io credesse che mia risposta fosse, 900

Safe in Their Alabaster Chambers, 814

Safe in their Alabaster Chambers –, 814

Salinas, Luis Omar
    In a Farmhouse, 936

Sammy Lou of Rue, 947

Sánchez, Edwin
    Pops, 1335

Sandburg, Carl
    Chicago, 936

Sassoon, Siegfried
    Dreamers, 937

Savage, Philip Henry
    Shorter Poem 13, 628

Say Not the Struggle Nought Availeth, 773

Say not the struggle nought availeth, 773

Schoolsville, 534

Scott, Virginia
    Snow, 764

Season of mists and mellow fruitfulness!, 654

Second Coming, The, 792

Secretary Chant, The, 929

See, here's the workbox, little wife, 683

September rain falls on the house, 737

Serotte, Brenda
    My Mother's Face, 938

Sestina, 737

Sexton, Anne
    Cinderella, 938

Shakespeare, William
    Fear No More the Heat o' th' Sun, 707
    A Midsummer Night's Dream, 1267
    Sonnet 18: Shall I Compare Thee to a
        Summer's Day?, 663
    Sonnet 29: When in Disgrace with Fortune
        and Men's Eyes, 941
    Sonnet 30: When to the Sessions of Sweet
        Silent Thought, 663
    Sonnet 55: Not Marble, Nor the Gilded
        Monuments, 555
    Sonnet 116: Let Me Not to the Marriage of
        True Minds, 728
    Sonnet 130: My Mistress' Eyes Are
        Nothing Like the Sun, 628
    The Tragedy of Hamlet, Prince of Denmark,
        1080

Shall I compare thee to a summer's
    day? 663

Shapiro, Karl
    Auto Wreck, 941

Shawl, The, 246

she being Brand / -new, 693

she being Brand -new; and you, 693

She had thought the studio would keep
    itself, 934

She is as in a field a silken tent, 848

She walks in Beauty, 893

She walks in beauty, like the night, 893

She wanted a little room for thinking, 897

Shelley, Percy Bysshe
    Ozymandias, 751

She's Free!, 908

Shorter Poem 13, 628

Showing the Birds, 660

Shunammite, The, 81

Silken Tent, The, 848

Silko, Leslie Marmon
    The Man to Send Rain Clouds, 254

Simic, Charles
Fork, 629
Simpson, Louis
American Poetry, 555
Sir Patrick Spens, 541
Sir, I admit your general rule, 685
Sky Is Gray, The, 184
Slated for demolition, 580
Slow Dance of the Heart, 277
Smith, Stevie
Not Waving but Drowning, 942
Snapshot of Hué, 906
Snow (MacNeice), 552
Snow (Scott), 764
Snow falling and night falling fast, oh,
fast, 741
Snyder, Gary
Milton by Firelight, 788
so much depends upon, 950
Soldiers are citizens of death's grey
land, 937
Solitary Reaper, The, 710
Some Keep the Sabbath Going to Church, 814
Some keep the Sabbath going to
Church –, 814
Some people go their whole lives, 629
Some say the world will end in fire, 847
Sometimes, 854
Something there is that doesn't love a wall,
842
Somewhere in California, 777
Song, Cathy
Lost Sister, 708
Song for a Summer's Day, 878
Sonnet, 739
Sonnet 18: Shall I Compare Thee to a Sum-
mer's Day?, 663
Sonnet 29: When in Disgrace with Fortune
and Men's Eyes, 941
Sonnet 30: When to the Sessions of Sweet
Silent Thought, 663
Sonnet 55: Not Marble, Nor the Gilded
Monuments, 555
Sonnet 116: Let Me Not to the Marriage of
True Minds, 728
Sonnet 130: My Mistress' Eyes Are Nothing
Like the Sun, 628
Sonnet of the Sweet Complaint, 651
Sonnets from the Portuguese, Number 14:
If Thou Must Love Me, 611
Sonnets from the Portuguese: Number 43,
How Do I Love Thee?, 892

Sophocles
Oedipus the King, 1039
Soto, Gary
Mexicans Begin Jogging, 942
Oranges, 943
Soul Selects Her Own Society, The, 815
Speciously individual, 651
Spender, Stephen
I Think Continually of Those Who Were
Truly Great, 592
Spring, 620
Spring Rain, 908
Spun in High, Dark Clouds, 727
Spun in high, dark clouds, 727
Spunk, 215
Stafford, William
Traveling Through the Dark, 944
Stasis in darkness., 867
Steinbeck, John
The Chrysanthemums, 358
Stevens, Wallace
Disillusionment of Ten O'Clock, 593
The Emperor of Ice-Cream, 945
Still I Rise, 885
Stopping by Woods on a Snowy Evening, 548
Story of an Hour, The, 307
Story of How a Wall Stands, A, 927
Strand, Mark
Eating Poetry, 593
Subway Rush Hour, 860
Success Is Counted Sweetest, 815
Success is counted sweetest, 815
Sundays too my father got up early, 909
Supermarket in California, A, 742
Sweet day, so cool, so calm, so bright, 743
Swenson, May
Question, 945
Women, 733

Talking in Bed, 918
Talking in bed ought to be easiest, 918
Tan, Amy
Two Kinds, 222
Tate, James
Dream On, 629
Taxi, The, 622
Tell All the Truth but Tell It Slant, 816
Tell all the truth but tell it slant –, 816
Tell-Tale Heart, The, 440
Tennyson, Alfred, Lord
Break, Break, Break, 664
The Eagle, 723

Terranova, Elaine
  Rush Hour, 556
That night your great guns, unawares, 617
That's my last Duchess painted on the
  wall, 892
That's the moment I always think of—
  when the, 927
the voice you hear when you read
  silently, 623
Theme for English B, 861
The apparition of a salsa band, 904
The apparition of these faces in the
  crowd, 627
The art of losing isn't hard to master; 736
The beauty of the trees, 905
The bonsai tree, 660
The broken pillar of the wing jags from the
  clotted shoulder, 620
The Bustle in a House, 808
The buzz saw snarled and rattled in the
  yard, 846
The dead piled up, thick, fragrant, on the
  fire escape, 772
The eyes open to a cry of pulleys, 949
The first fear, 787
The first horn lifts its arm over the dew-lit
  grass, 546
The first Sunday I missed Mass on
  purpose, 596
The first time I walked, 943
The flash of sunlight from a bit of glass, 628
The Giant of Greek myth was an invincible
  wrestler because when he touched
  the Earth, his mother, his strength
  was renewed., 924
The gutteral stammer of the chopper
  blades, 631
The houses are haunted, 593
The instructor said, 861
The king sits in Dunfermline town, 541
The land was ours before we were the
  land's, 849
The lies I could tell, 594
The moonlight on my bed keeps me
  awake, 586
The onion in my cupboard, a monster,
  actually, 656
The railroad track is miles away, 924
The room was suddenly rich and
  the great bay-window was, 552
The sea is calm tonight, 887
The Soul selects her own Society –, 815

The tulips are too excitable, it is winter
  here, 878
The whiskey on your breath, 706
The white woman across the aisle from me
  says, 883
The winter evening settles down, 613
The woman is perfected, 872
Then what is the answer?—Not to be
  deluded by dreams, 913
There is a singer everyone has heard, 847
There is a world somewhere else that is
  unendurable, 709
There Is No Frigate Like a Book, 816
There is no Frigate like a book, 816
There's a Certain Slant of Light, 816
There's a certain slant of light, 816
these hips are big hips, 690
They are riding bicycles on the other side, 906
The Things They Carried, 101
This brief effusion I indite, 679
This is a pain I mostly hide, 689
This Is Just to Say, 557
This strange thing must have crept, 629
Thomas, Dylan
  Do Not Go Gentle into That Good Night, 752
  *A Refusal to Mourn the Death, by Fire, of a
    Child in London*, 946
Those Winter Sundays, 909
Thou ill-formed offspring of my feeble
  brain, 889
Thou still unravish'd bride of
  quietness, 914
The time you won your town the
  race, 585
Through fen and farmland walking, 878
Time Past, A, 621
Times They Are a-Changin', The, 899
To an Athlete Dying Young, 585
To Autumn, 654
To fling my arms wide, 855
To Celia, 744
To gaze at a river made of time and
  water, 889
To Helen, 626
To His Coy Mistress, 784
To My Dear and Loving Husband, 890
To pray you open your whole self, 549
To the Memory of Mr. Oldham, 739
Toomer, Jean
  Reapers, 753
Tragedy of Hamlet, Prince of Denmark, The, 1080
Travel, 924

Traveling Through the Dark, 944
Traveling through the dark I found a deer, 944
The tree has entered my hands, 933
Trethewey, Natasha
  White Lies, 594
Trifles, 983
Triumph May Be of Several Kinds, 817
Triumph- may be of Several Kinds-, 817
Trying to Find Chinatown, 994
Tudor Elizabeth, Queen Elizabeth I
  On Monsieur's Departure, 665
Tulips, 792
Turning and turning in the widening gyre, 792
'Twas brillig, and the slithy toves, 581
'Twas mercy brought me from my Pagan land, 948
Two boys uncoached are tossing a poem together, 547
Two Hangovers, 712
Two Kinds, 222
Two roads diverged in a yellow wood, 845
Tyger, The, 647
Tyger! Tyger! burning bright, 647

Unfinished Masterpieces, 339
Unknown Citizen, The, 687
Untitled Poem, 651
Updike, John
  A & P, 320
  Perfection Wasted, 947

Valediction: Forbidding Mourning, A, 649
Van Duyn, Mona
  Earth Tremors Felt in Missouri, 666
from *Variations on a Theme by William Carlos Williams*, 551
Vietnam Wall, The, 935
Viorst, Judith
  A Wedding Sonnet for the Next Generation, 789
Virtue, 743
Visit to the Sepulcher, The (Visitatio Sepulchri), 973
Voice You Hear When You Read Silently, The, 623

wade through black jade, 624
wahbegan, 926

Waking, The, 751
Wakoski, Diane
  Inside Out, 666
Walker, Alice
  Everyday Use, 494
  Revolutionary Petunias, 947
Weary Blues, The, 862
We Real Cool, 891
We real cool, 891
We shall not ever meet them bearded in heaven, 914
We smile at each other, 882
We're Building the Ship as We Sail It, 787
Webb, Phyllis
  Poetics Against the Angel of Death, 753
Wedding Sonnet for the Next Generation, A, 789
Welty, Eudora
  A Worn Path, 288
What a needy, desperate thing, 776
What a thrill, 869
What Do Animals Dream?, 917
What does it mean? Lord knows; least of all I, 582
What happens to a dream deferred?, 856
What Lips My Lips Have Kissed, and Where, and Why, 924
What lips my lips have kissed, and where, and why, 924
What passing-bells for these who die as cattle?, 607
What ruse of vision, 924
What thoughts I have of you tonight, Walt Whitman, for, 742
Wheatley, Phillis
  On Being Brought from Africa to America, 948
When God at first made man, 619
When I am old, and comforted, 928
When I consider how my light is spent, 749
When I go away from you, 622
When I Heard the Learn'd Astronomer, 730
When I heard the Learn'd astronomer, 730
When I see birches bend to left and right, 844
When I was home de, 860
When I was one-and-twenty, 913
When I was one-and-twenty, 913

When to the sessions of sweet silent thought, 663

When you are old and grey and full of sleep, 713

When You Are Old (Henley), 697

When You Are Old (Yeats), 713

When you are old, and I am passed away, 697

When, in disgrace with Fortune and men's eyes, 941

Whenever Richard Cory went down town, 590

Where Are You Going, Where Have You Been?, 145

Where Children Live, 554

White Lies, 594

Whitman, Walt
 Beat! Beat! Drums!, 948
 Facing West from California's Shores, 667
 Full of Life Now, 949
 I Hear America Singing, 949
 A Noiseless Patient Spider, 790
 Reconciliation, 754
 When I Heard the Learn'd Astronomer, 730

Who says a woman's work isn't high art?, 884

Whose woods these are I think I know, 548

Whur, Cornelius
 The First-Rate Wife, 679

Wilbur, Richard
 Love Calls us to the Things of This World, 949
 Year's End, 790

Wild Geese, 786

Wild Nights – Wild Nights!, 817

Wild Nights   Wild Nights!, 817

Williams, William Carlos
 The Dance, 754
 This Is Just to Say, 557
 The Red Wheelbarrow, 950

Williams, C. K.
 Dimensions, 709

Williams, Tennessee
 The Glass Menagerie, 1379

Willow, 883

Wilson, August
 Fences, 1430

Wojahn, David

It's Only Rock and Roll but I Like It": The Fall of Saigon, 631

Woman's Work, 884

Women (Bogan), 888

Women (Swenson), 733

Women have no wilderness in them, 888

Women should be pedestals..., 733

Word over all, beautiful as the sky, 754

Wordsworth, William
 Daffodils (I Wandered Lonely as a Cloud), 595
 Lines Composed a Few Miles Above Tintern Abbey on Revisiting the Banks of the Wye During a Tour, June 13, 1798, 557
 London, 668
 The Solitary Reaper, 710

Work of Artifice, A, 660

Workbox, The, 683

Worn Path, A, 288

Wright, James
 Autumn Begins at Martin's Ferry, Ohio, 711
 Two Hangovers, 712

Wyatt, Sir Thomas
 I Find No Peace, 669

Year's End, 790

Yeats, William Butler
 The Second Coming, 792
 When You Are Old, 713

Yellow Wallpaper, The, 473

Yes, we were looking at each other, 662

Yesterday, I lay awake in the palm of the night, 691

Yet Do I Marvel, 692

You always read about it, 938

You do not do, you do not do, 870

You do not have to be good, 786

You fit into me, 888

you fit into me, 888

You may write me down in history, 885

You think you earned this space on earth, 785

You want, 910

Young Goodman Brown, 342

Zimmer, Paul
 The Day Zimmer Lost Religion, 596

Alphabetical List of Authors Included in *Literature*, Sixth Compact Edition

Aesop, ca. 600 BCE
Ai, 1947–2010
Ali, Agha Shahid, 1949–2001
Akhmatova, Anna, 1889–1966
Alexie, Sherman, b. 1966
Alvarez, Julia, b. 1950
Angelou, Maya, b. 1928
Arnold, Matthew, 1822–1888
Arredondo, Ines, 1928–1989
Ashberry, John, b. 1927
Atwood, Margaret, b. 1939
Auden, W. H., 1907–1973
Bambara, Toni Cade, 1939–1995
Baraka, Amira, b. 1934
Baudelaire, Charles, 1821–1867
Berryman, John, 1914–1972
Bierce, Ambrose, 1842–1914?
Bishop, Elizabeth, 1911–1979
Blake, William, 1757–1827
Bogan, Louise, 1897–1970
Borges, Jorge Luis, 1899–1986
Bradstreet, Anne, 1612–1672
Brontë, Emily, 1818–1848
Brooks, Gwendolyn, 1917–2000
Browning, Elizabeth Barrett, 1806–1864
Browning, Robert, 1812–1889
Burns, Robert, 1759–1796
Bryon, George Gordon (Lord), 1788–1824
Carroll, Lewis, 1832–1898
Carruth, Hayden, 1921–2008
Carter, Jimmy, b. 1924
Carver, Raymond, 1939–1989
Chekhov, Anton, 1860–1904
Chin, Marilyn, b. 1955
Chopin, Kate, 1851–1904
Cisneros, Sandra, b. 1954
Clifton, Lucille, b. 1936
Clough, Arthur Hugh, 1819–1861
Coleman, Anita Scott, 1890–1960
Coleridge, Samuel Taylor, 1772–1834
Collins, Billy, b. 1941
Crane, Stephen, 1871–1900
Creeley, Robert, 1926–2005
Cullen, Countee, 1903–1946
Cummings, E. E., 1894–1962
Dickinson, Emily, 1830–1886
Donne, John, 1572–1631
Dooley, Paul, b. 1928
Dove, Rita, b. 1952
Dryden, John, 1631–1700
Dubus, Andre, 1936–1999
Dugan, Alan, 1923–2003
Dunn, Stephen, b. 1939
Dyer, Sir Edward, 1543–1607
Eliot, T. S., 1888–1965
Ellison, Ralph, 1914–1994
Elizabeth I (Elizabeth Tudor, Queen Elizabeth I), 1533–1603
Erdrich, Louise, b. 1954
Espada, Martin, b. 1957

Espaillat, Rhianna, b. 1932
Evans, Mari, b. 1923
Faulkner, William, 1897–1962
Ferlinghetti, Lawrence, b. 1919
Forché, Carolyn, b. 1950
Francis, Robert, 1901–1987
Frost, Robert, 1874–1963
Gaines, Ernest J., b. 1922
García Lorca, Federico, 1898–1936
Gardner, Isabella, 1915–1981
Gay, John, 1685–1732
Georgakas, Dan, b. 1938
George, Chief Dan, 1899–1981
Gilb, Dagoberto, b. 1950
Gilman, Charlotte Perkins, 1860–1937
Ginsberg, Allen, 1926–1997
Giovanni, Nikki, b. 1943
Glaspell, Susan, 1882–1948
Graves, Robert, 1895–1985
Griffin, Susan, b. 1943
Halpern, Daniel, b. 1945
Hardy, Thomas, 1840–1928
Harjo, Joy, b. 1951
Harper, Frances E. W., 1825–1911
Hass, Robert, b. 1941
Hawthorne, Nathaniel, 1804–1864
Hayden, Robert, 1913–1980
H.D. (Hilda Doolittle), 1886–1961
Heaney, Seamus, b. 1939
Hemingway, Ernest, 1899–1961
Henley, William Ernest, 1849–1903
Herbert, George, 1593–1633
Herrick, Robert, 1591–1674
Heyen, William, b. 1940
Holmes, Janet, 1956
Holzman, Winnie, b. 1954
Hope, A. D., 1907–2000
Hopkins, Gerard Manley, 1844–1889
Housman, A. E., 1859–1936
Hughes, Langston, 1902–1967
Hurston, Zora Neale, 1891–1960
Hwang, David Henry, b. 1957
Ibsen, Henrik, 1828–1906
Ignatow, David, 1914–1997
Jackson, Shirley, 1919–1965
Jarrell, Randall, 1914–1965
Jeffers, Robinson, 1887–1962
Jonson, Ben, 1573–1637
Joyce, James, 1882–1941
Justice, Donald, 1925–2004
Keats, John, 1795–1821
Kennedy, X. J., b. 1929
Kenyon, Jane, 1947–1990
Kincaid, Jamaica, b. 1949
Kinnell, Galway, b. 1927
Kizer, Carolyn, b. 1925
Koch, Kenneth, 1925–2002
Komunyakaa, Yusef, b. 1947
Lababidi, Yahia, b. 1973
Larkin, Philip, 1922–1985
Lawrence, D. H., 1885–1930

Lee, Edward Bok, 1974
Lee, Li-Young, b. 1957
Levertov, Denise, 1923–1998
Lincoln, Abraham, 1809–1865
Lipschultz, Geri, b. 1951
Lorde, Audre, 1934–1992
Lowell, Amy, 1874–1925
Luke (St. Luke), fl. ca. 90 CE
Lux, Thomas, b. 1946
MacNeice, Louis, 1907–1963
Magnus, Magus, b. 1967
Mansfield, Katherine, 1888–1923
Martin, Jane, b. ????
Marvell, Andrew, 1621–1678
Masefield, John, 1878–1967
Maupassant, Guy de, 1850–1893
McKay, Claude, 1890–1948
Millay, Edna St. Vincent, 1892–1950
Miller, Arthur, 1915–2005
Milton, John, 1608–1674
Minty, Judith, b. 1937
Momaday, N. Scott, b. 1934
Moore, Marianne, 1887–1972
Mueller, Lisel, b. 1924
Muske-Dukes, Carol, b. 1945
Nash, Ogden, 1902–1971
Nemerov, Howard, 1920–1991
Neruda, Pablo, 1904–1973
Northrup, Jim, b. 1943
Nye, Naomi Shihab, b. 1952
O'Brien, Tim, b. 1946
O'Connor, Flannery, 1925–1964
O'Connor, Frank, 1903–1966
O'Neill, Eugene, 1888–1953
O'Shaughnessy, Arthur, 1844–1881
Oates, Joyce Carol, b. 1938
Okigbo, Christopher, 1932–1967
Olds, Sharon, b. 1942
Oliver, Mary, b. 1935
Orozco, Daniel, b. ca.1957
Ortiz Cofer, Judith, b. 1952
Ortiz, Simon, b. 1941
Owen, Wilfred, 1893–1918
Ozick, Cynthia, b. 1928
Packer, ZZ, b. 1973
Parédes, Americo, 1915–1999
Parker, Dorothy, 1893–1967
Pastan, Linda, b. 1932
Paz, Octavio, 1914–1998
Piercy, Marge, b. 1936
Pinsky, Robert, b. 1940
Plath, Sylvia, 1932–1963
Poe, Edgar Allan, 1809–1849
Pope, Alexander, 1688–1744
Porter, Katherine Anne, 1890–1980
Pound, Ezra, 1885–1972
Quasimodo, Salvatore, 1901–1968
Randall, Dudley, 1914–2000
Rich, Adrienne, b. 1929
Ríos, Alberto, b. 1952
Rivas, Marguerite, b. 1956

Robinson, Edwin Arlington, 1869–1935
Roethke, Theodore, 1907–1963
Rukeyser, Muriel, 1913–1980
Ryan, Kay, b. 1945
Saenz, Benjamin Alire, b. 1954
Salinas, Luis Omar, b. 1937
Sánchez, Edwin, 1955
Sandburg, Carl, 1878–1967
Sassoon, Siegfried, 1886–1967
Scott, Virginia, b. 1938
Serotte, Brenda, b. 1946
Sexton, Anne, 1928–1974
Shakespeare, William, 1564–1616
Shapiro, Karl, 1913–2000
Shelley, Percy Bysshe, 1792–1822
Silko, Leslie Marmon, b. 1948
Simic, Charles, b. 1938
Simpson, Louis, 1923–2012
Smith, Stevie, 1902–1971
Snyder, Gary, b. 1930
Song, Cathy, b. 1955
Sophocles, 496–406 BCE
Soto, Gary, b. 1952
Spender, Sir Stephen, 1909–1995
Stafford, William, 1914–1993
Steinbeck, John, 1902–1968
Stevens, Wallace, 1879–1955
Strand, Mark, b. 1934
Swenson, May, 1919–1989
Tan, Amy, b. 1952
Tate, James, b. 1943
Tennyson, Alfred, Lord, 1809–1892
Terranova, Elaine, b. 1939
Thomas, Dylan, 1914–1953
Toomer, Jean, 1894–1967
Trethewey, Natasha, b. 1966
Updike, John, 1932–2009
Van Duyn, Mona, 1921–2004
Viorst, Judith, b. 1931
Wakoski, Diane, b. 1937
Walker, Alice, b. 1944
Webb, Phyllis, b. 1927
Welty, Eudora, 1909–2001
Wheatley, Phillis, 1754–1784
Whitman, Walt, 1819–1892
Whur, Cornelius, 1782–1853
Wilbur, Richard, b. 1921
Williams, C. K., b. 1936
Williams, Tennessee, 1911–1983
Williams, William Carlos, 1883–1963
Wilson, August, 1945–2005
Wojahn, David, b. 1953
Wordsworth, William, 1770–1850
Wright, James, 1927–1980
Wyatt, Sir Thomas, 1503–1542
Yeats, William Butler, 1865–1939
Zimmer, Paul, b. 1934